Street by Street

KU-266-603

LONDON

2nd edition June 2002

© Automobile Association Developments Limited 2002

Ordnance Survey® This product includes map data licensed from Ordnance Survey® with the permission of the Controller of Her Majesty's Stationery Office. © Crown copyright 2002. All rights reserved. Licence No: 399221.

All rights reserved. No part of this publication may be reproduced, stored in a retrieval system, or transmitted in any form or by any means– electronic, mechanical, photocopying, recording or otherwise – unless the permission of the publisher has been given beforehand.

Published by AA Publishing (a trading name of Automobile Association Developments Limited, whose registered office is Millstream, Maidenhead Road, Windsor, Berkshire SL4 5GD. Registered number 1878835).

The Post Office is a registered trademark of Post Office Ltd. in the UK and other countries.

Schools address data provided by Education Direct.

One-way street data provided by:
Tele Atlas © Tele Atlas N.V.

Mapping produced by the Cartographic Department of The Automobile Association. A01424

A CIP Catalogue record for this book is available from the British Library.

Printed by G. Canale & C. S.P.A., Torino, Italy

The contents of this atlas are believed to be correct at the time of the latest revision. However, the publishers cannot be held responsible for loss occasioned to any person acting or refraining from action as a result of any material in this atlas, nor for any errors, omissions or changes in such material. This does not affect your statutory rights. The publishers would welcome information to correct any errors or omissions and to keep this atlas up to date. Please write to Publishing, The Automobile Association, Fanum House (FH17), Basing View, Basingstoke, Hampshire, RG21 4EA.

Ref: MD038z

Key to map pages — ii-iii

Key to map symbols — iv-1

Enlarged scale pages — 2-33

Street by Street — 34-253

Index – towns & villages — 254-256

Index – streets — 256-351

Index – featured places — 351-373

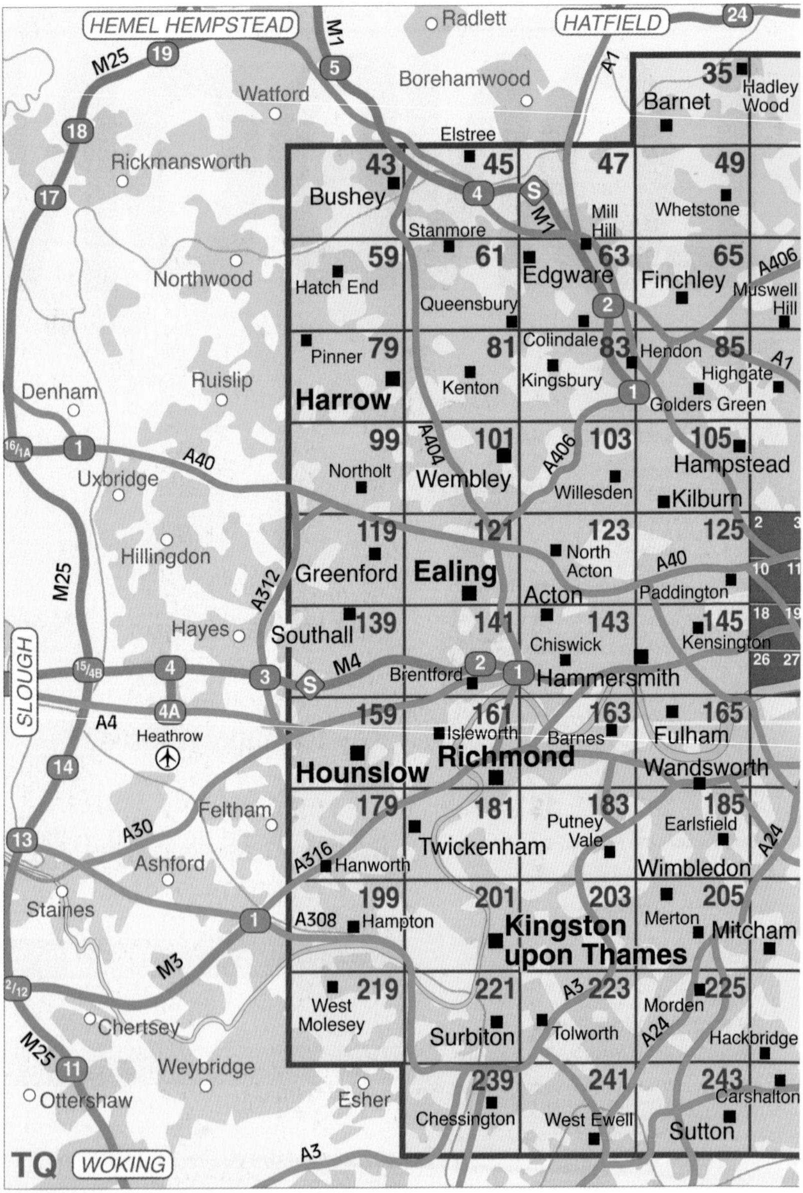

ii

HEMEL HEMPSTEAD   Radlett   HATFIELD   24

M25   19   M1   5   Borehamwood

Watford   Elstree   35   Barnet   Hadley Wood

Rickmansworth   43   45   47   49
18   Bushey   Mill Hill   Whetstone
17   Stanmore   M1

Northwood   59   61   63   65   A406
Hatch End   Queensbury   Edgware   Finchley   Muswell Hill

Denham   Pinner   79   81   Colindale   83   Hendon   85   A1
Ruislip   Harrow   Kenton   Kingsbury   Highgate   Golders Green

Uxbridge   99   101   103   105
16/1A   1   Northolt   Wembley   Willesden   Hampstead   Kilburn

Hillingdon   A40   119   121   123   125   2   3
M25   Greenford   Ealing   North Acton   A40   10   11
A312   Acton   Paddington   18   19

Hayes   139   141   143   145   26   27
SLOUGH   Southall   M4   Chiswick   Kensington
15/4B   4   3   S   Brentford   2   1   Hammersmith

A4   4A   159   161   163   165
14   Heathrow   Isleworth   Barnes   Fulham
Feltham   Hounslow   Richmond   Wandsworth

13   A30   179   181   183   185
Ashford   Hanworth   Twickenham   Putney Vale   Earlsfield   A24
Staines   A316   Wimbledon

199   201   203   205
1   A308   Hampton   Kingston   Merton   Mitcham
M3   upon Thames

219   221   223   225
11   West Molesey   Surbiton   A3   Morden   Hackbridge
Ottershaw   Chertsey   Tolworth   A24
Weybridge

239   241   243
Esher   Chessington   West Ewell   Carshalton
Otterspool   Sutton

TQ   WOKING   A3

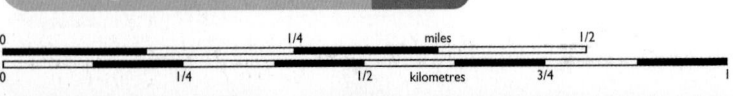

Enlarged scale pages 1:10,000   6.3 inches to 1 mile

0   1/4   miles   1/2
0   1/4   kilometres   1/2   3/4   1

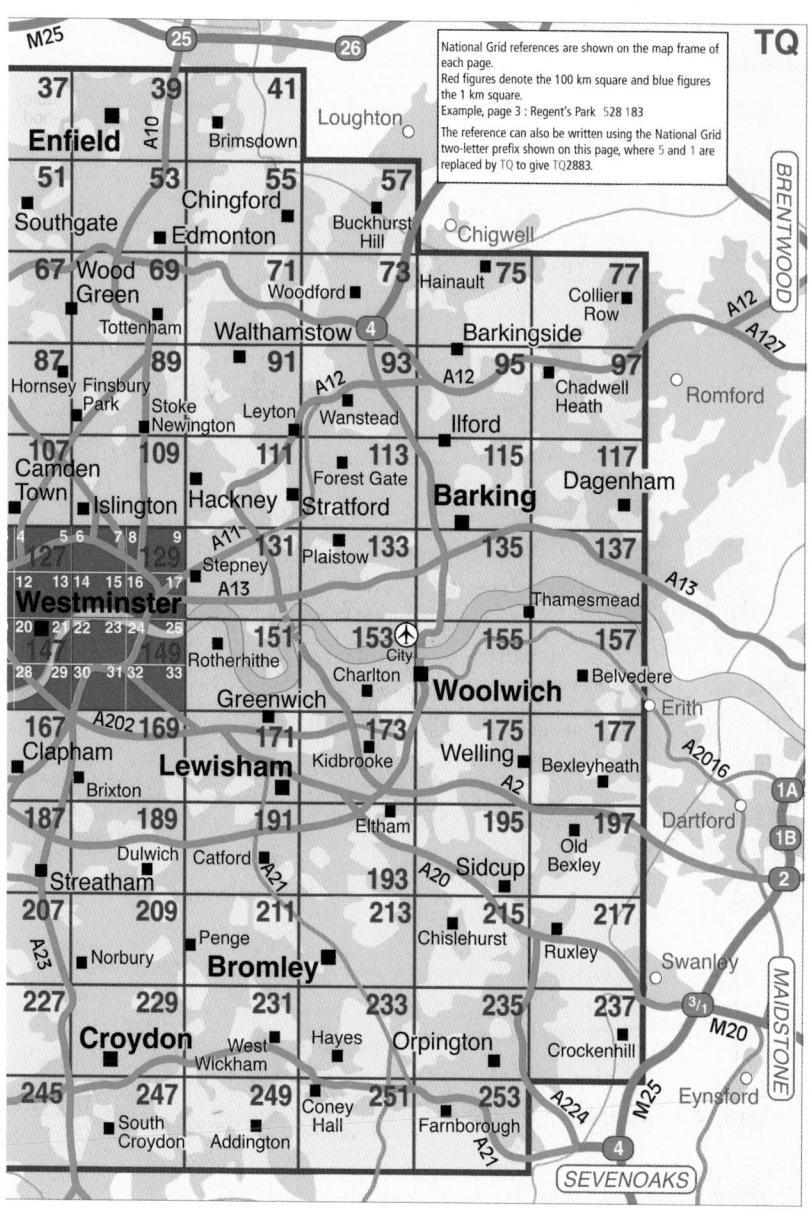

National Grid references are shown on the map frame of each page.
Red figures denote the 100 km square and blue figures the 1 km square.
Example, page 3 : Regent's Park 528 183

The reference can also be written using the National Grid two-letter prefix shown on this page, where 5 and 1 are replaced by TQ to give TQ2883.

3.2 inches to 1 mile   **Scale of main map pages** 1:20,000

iv

Junction 9	Motorway & junction
Services	Motorway service area
	Primary road single/dual carriageway
Services	Primary road service area
	A road single/dual carriageway
	B road single/dual carriageway
	Other road single/dual carriageway
	Minor/private road, access may be restricted
← ←	One-way street
	Pedestrian area
	Track or footpath
	Road under construction
	Road tunnel
AA	AA Service Centre
P	Parking
P+	Park & Ride
	Bus/coach station
	Railway & main railway station
	Railway & minor railway station

	Underground station
	Light railway & station
+++++++++	Preserved private railway
LC	Level crossing
•—•—•	Tramway
----------	Ferry route
....	Airport runway
— · — · — ·	County, administrative boundary
▼▼▼▼▼▼▼	Mounds
93	Page continuation
	River/canal, lake, pier
	Aqueduct, lock, weir
465 ▲ Winter Hill	Peak (with height in metres)
	Beach
	Coniferous woodland
	Broadleaved woodland
	Mixed woodland
	Park

	Cemetery		Theme park
	Built-up area		Abbey, cathedral or priory
	Featured building		Castle
	City wall		Historic house or building
A&E	Hospital with 24-hour A&E department	Wakehurst Place NT	National Trust property
PO	Post Office		Museum or art gallery
	Public library		Roman antiquity
i	Tourist Information Centre		Ancient site, battlefield or monument
	Petrol station Major suppliers only		Industrial interest
†	Church/chapel		Garden
	Public toilets		Arboretum
	Toilet with disabled facilities		Farm or animal centre
PH	Public house AA recommended		Zoological or wildlife collection
	Restaurant AA inspected		Bird collection
	Theatre or performing arts centre		Nature reserve
	Cinema	V	Visitor or heritage centre
	Golf course		Country park
▲	Camping AA inspected		Cave
	Caravan site AA inspected		Windmill
	Camping & caravan site AA inspected		Distillery, brewery or vineyard

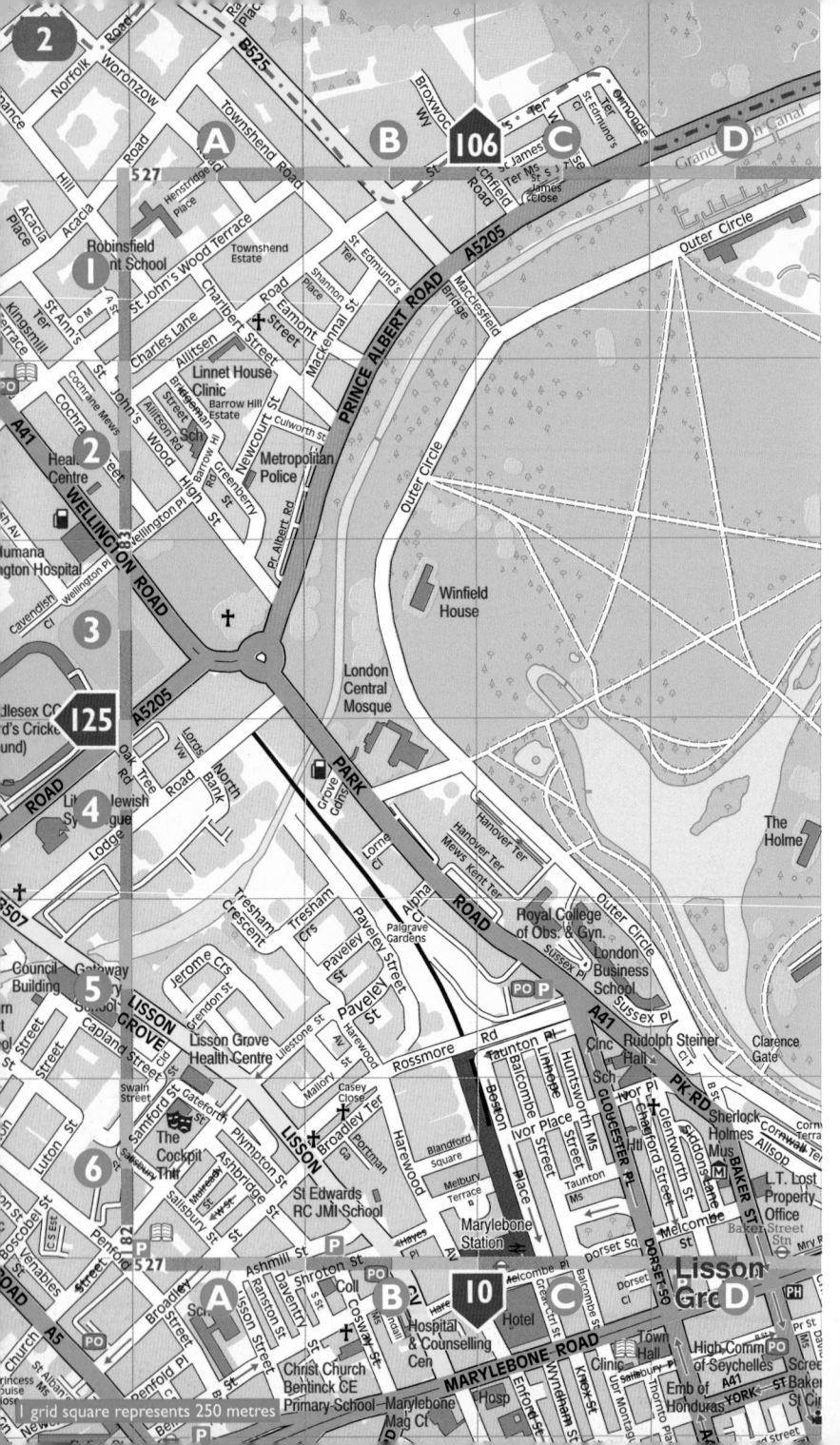

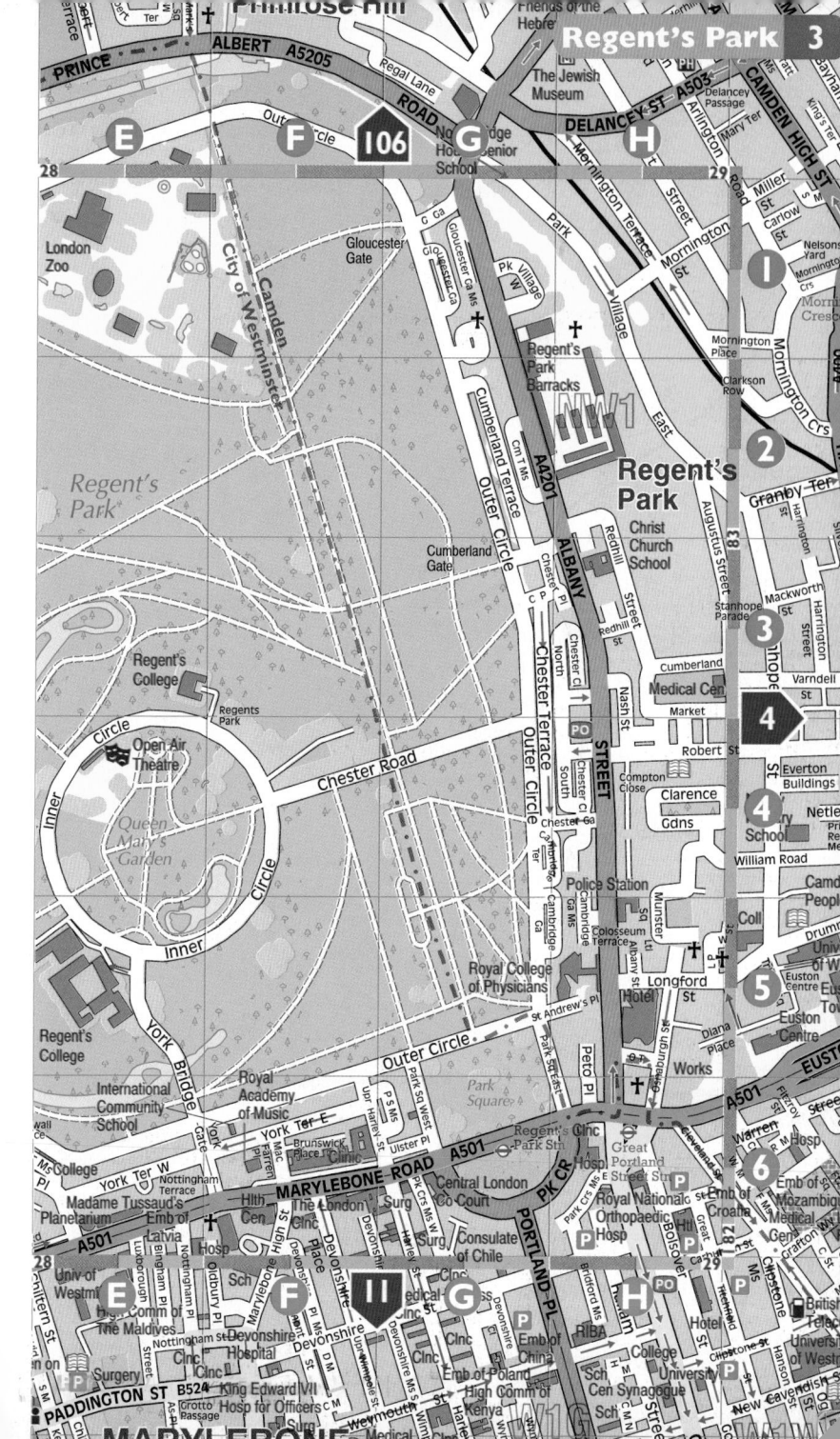

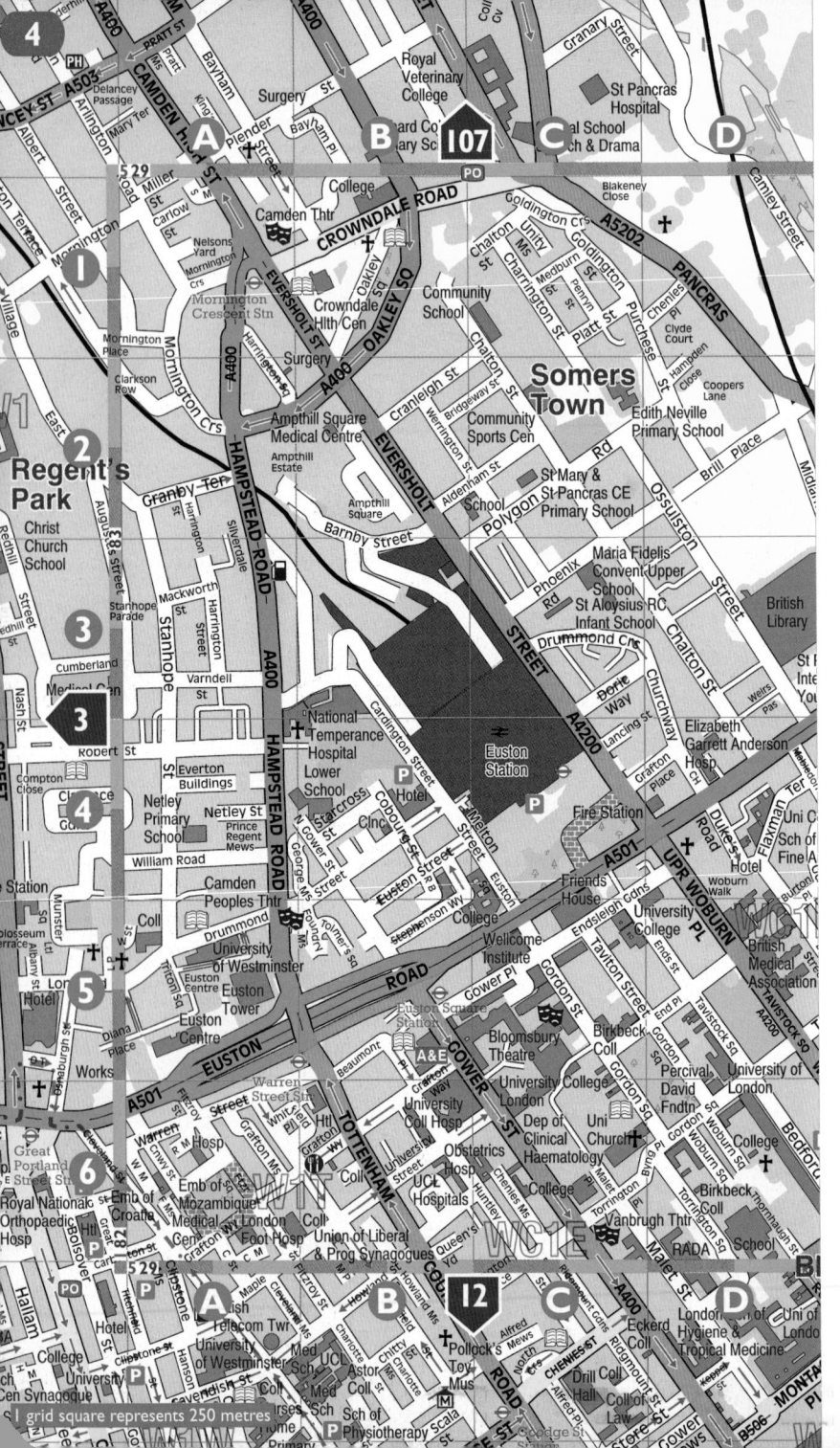

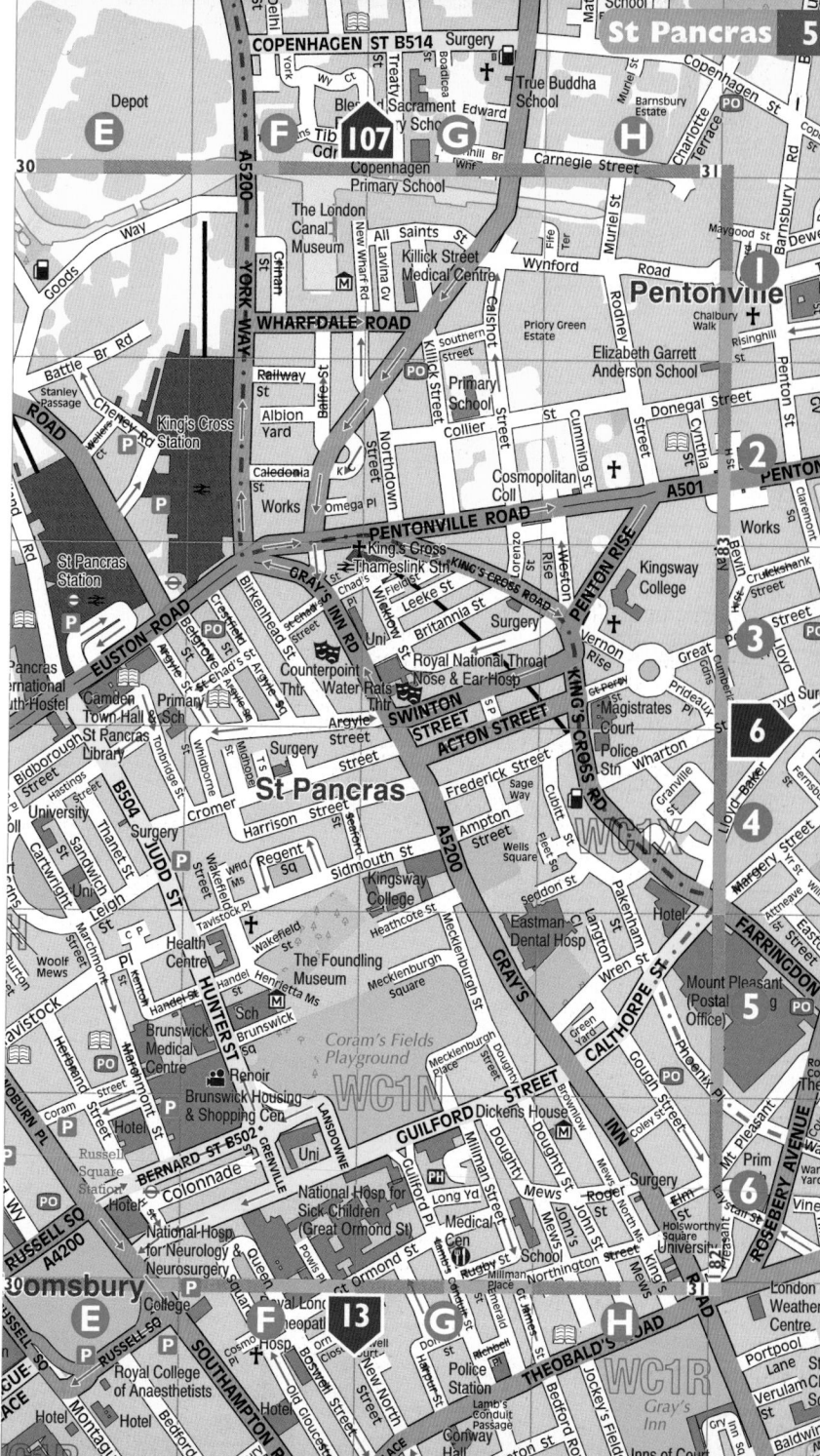

COPENHAGEN ST B514 Surgery

Depot

E F **107** G H

True Buddha School

Bleddyn Sacrament School

Barnsbury Estate

Edward

Carnegie Street

Copenhagen Primary School

York Way
A5200
YORK WAY

The London Canal Museum

All Saints St

Killick Street Medical Centre

Lavina Gv

Fire Ter

Wynford Road

Maygood St
Barnsbury Rd

Dewey Rd

Pentonville

Goods Way

WHARFDALE ROAD

New Wharf Rd

Priory Green Estate

Rodney St

Chalbury Walk

I

Battle Br Rd

Stanley Passage

Cheney Rd
Wellers Ct
Caledonia St
P

Railway St

Albion Yard

King's Cross Station

Balfe St
Northdown Street
Killick Street
Southern Street
Collier St

Elizabeth Garrett Anderson School

Risinghill

Penton St
Penton Gv

Caledonia St

K

Omega Pl

Primary School
Cumming St

Donegal Street

Cynthia St

2 **PENTONVI**

Claremont

ROAD

St Pancras Station
P

PENTONVILLE ROAD

Cosmopolitan Coll

A501

Works

Bevin W
Cruickshank Street

3 PO

Amwell

EUSTON ROAD

GRAY'S INN ROAD

King's Cross Thameslink Stn

St Chad's St

KING'S CROSS ROAD

PENTON RISE

Kingsway College

Street

Lloyd

Cobb Surgery

Pancras International Youth Hostel

Camden Town Hall & Sch
St Pancras Library

Birkenhead St
Belgrove St
Crestfield St
Argyle St
St Chad's St
Argyle St

Counterpoint Thtr
Water Rats Thtr

Leeke St
Uni
Britannia St
Surgery

Royal National Throat Nose & Ear Hosp

Lorenzo
Weston Rise
Vernon Rise
Gt Percy

Magistrates Court
Police Stn

Prideaux

Great Gdns

Street

4

Bidborough Street
Hastings
University

Whidborne
Tonbridge St
Midhope

SWINTON
ACTON STREET
Argyle Street

KING'S CROSS RD

Wharton

Granville

Lloyd Baker Street

Fernsbury

6

Cartwright
Uni

Cromer

St Pancras

Harrison Street

Frederick Street

Sage Way
Cubitt St

Margery Street

Easton
Wilmington

Sandwich St
Leigh St
B504
JUDD ST

Surgery

P

Regent Sq

Sidmouth St

Ampton Street

Wells Square

Fleet
Seddon St

Pakenham

FARRINGDON

4

Woolf Mews

Thanet St

Tavistock Pl

Wakefield
Wfld Ms

Kingsway College

Heathcote St

Mecklenburgh St
Langton

Eastman Dental Hosp

Wren St

Hotel

Cartwright
Marchmont

Burton

Health Centre
C P

Handel St

Wakefield St

The Foundling Museum

Mecklenburgh Square

GRAY'S

Gough Street

Mount Pleasant (Postal Office)

5 g PO

Tavistock

Herbrand
PO

Hunter St
Marchmont St
Handel St
Sch
Brunswick Sq

Coram's Fields Playground

Mecklenburgh Place

Doughty Street

Green Street

WC1N

Doughty

Calthorpe St

Phoenix Pl

Mt Pleasant
Roseb
Court
The A

Bar

Warner

Woburn Pl

Brunswick Medical Centre

Renoir

Brunswick Housing & Shopping Cen

Brownlow St

Hotel

Roger St

Surgery

John's St

Mews

King's Mews

Holsworthy Square
Universi

6

Warner
Yard
Vine

Coram St
P

RUSSELL SQ
A4200

Russell Square Station

Hotels
P

BERNARD ST B502
Colonnade

Lansdowne
Grenville

Uni

GUILFORD STREET

Dickens House

Long Yd

Millman St

Elm St

Prim

ROSEBERY AVENUE

6

Prim

Vine

omsbury

RUSSELL SQ

E

SOUTHAMPTON RD

F

Royal College of Anaesthetists

Royal Lond Hospital Homeopath

13

New North Street

G

National Hosp for Sick Children (Great Ormond St)

National Hosp for Neurology & Neurosurgery

Queen Sq

Gt Ormond St

Guilford Pl

Medical Cen

Powis Pl

Rugby St

Emerald St
Harpur St

Cosmo Pl
Orde
Old Gloucester St
Boswell Street

Montague
Bedford

National Hosp

Royal London

Theobald's
Dombey St
Emerald

Milman St
Northington Street
St James's
Roger St

Lamb's Conduit Passage

Police Station

THEOBALD'S ROAD

H

London Weather Centre

Portpool Lane

St A CE P Sch

Verulam

Montague
Bedford

Conway Hall

Princeton St
New North St

Jockey's Fields

Gray's Inn

WC1R

Baldwin's

Hotel

Hotel

Inns of Court

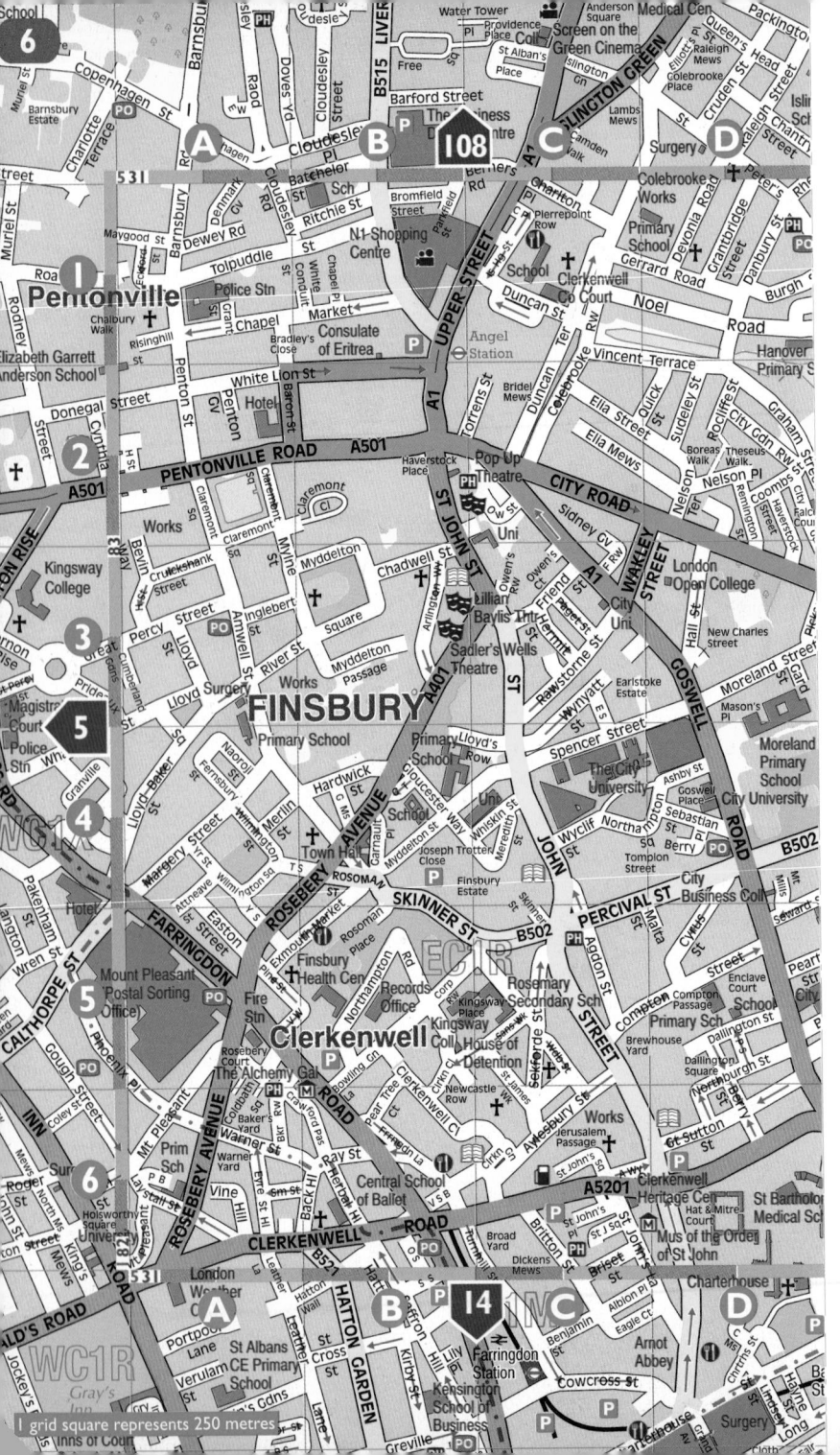

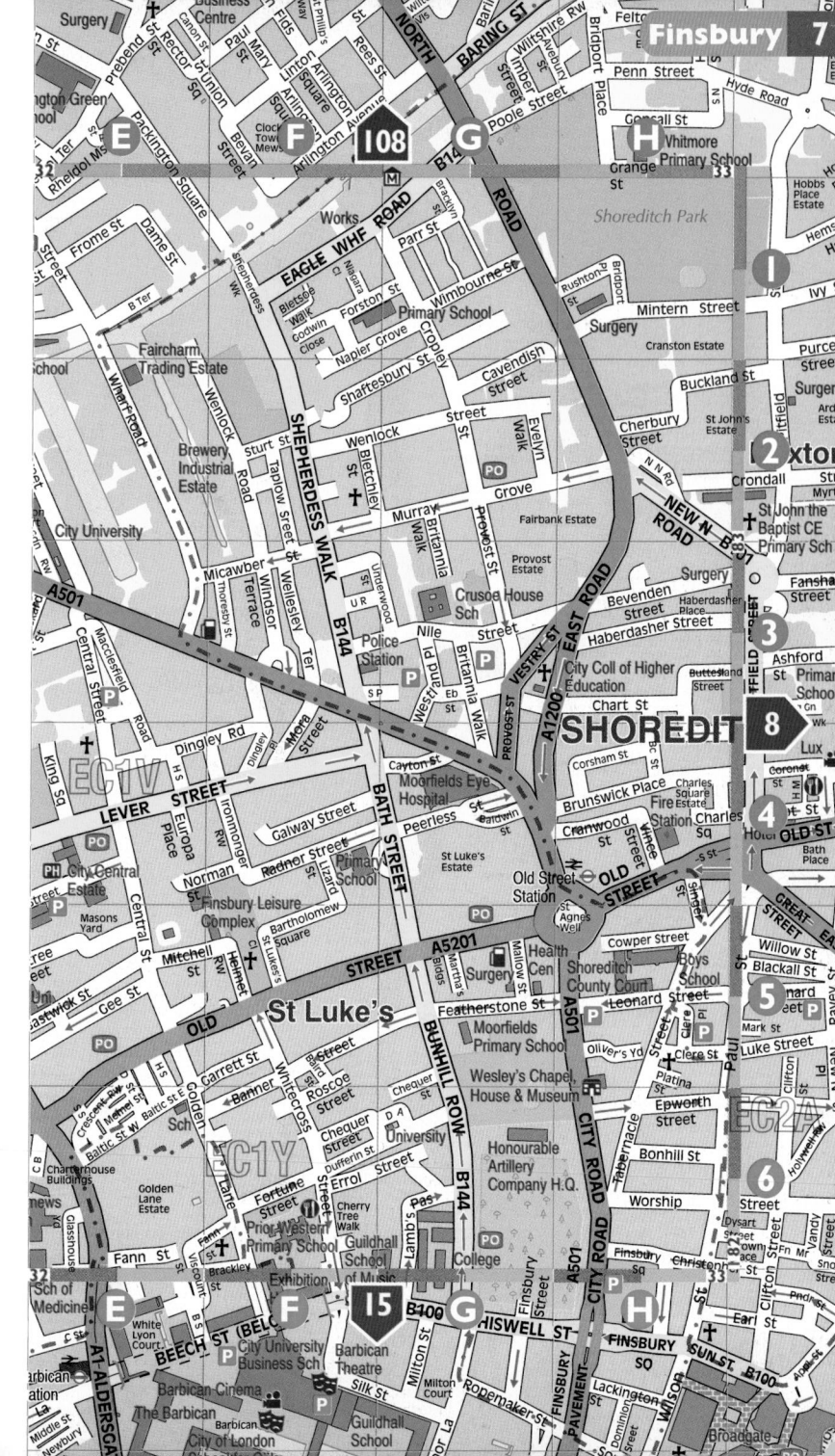

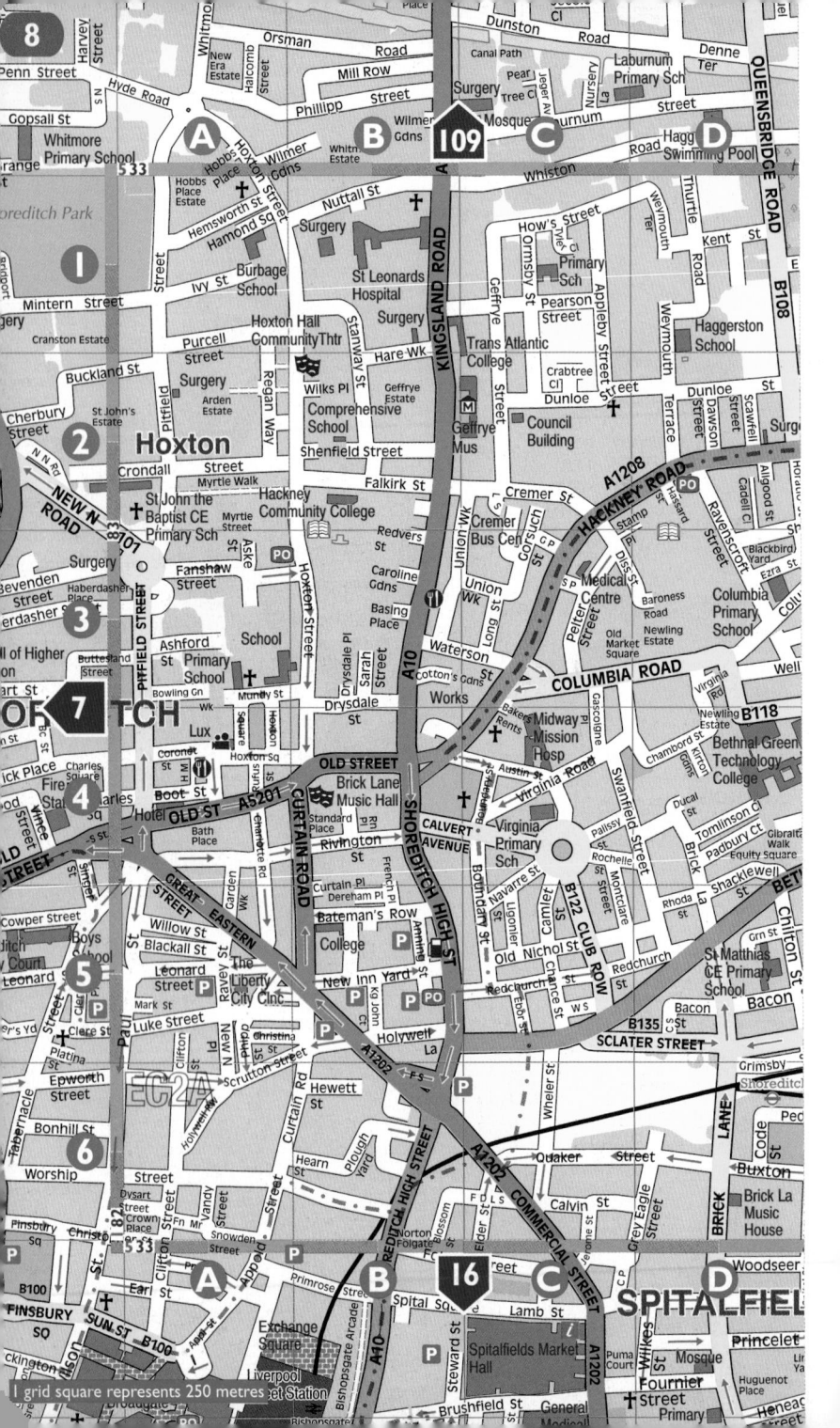

I grid square represents 250 metres

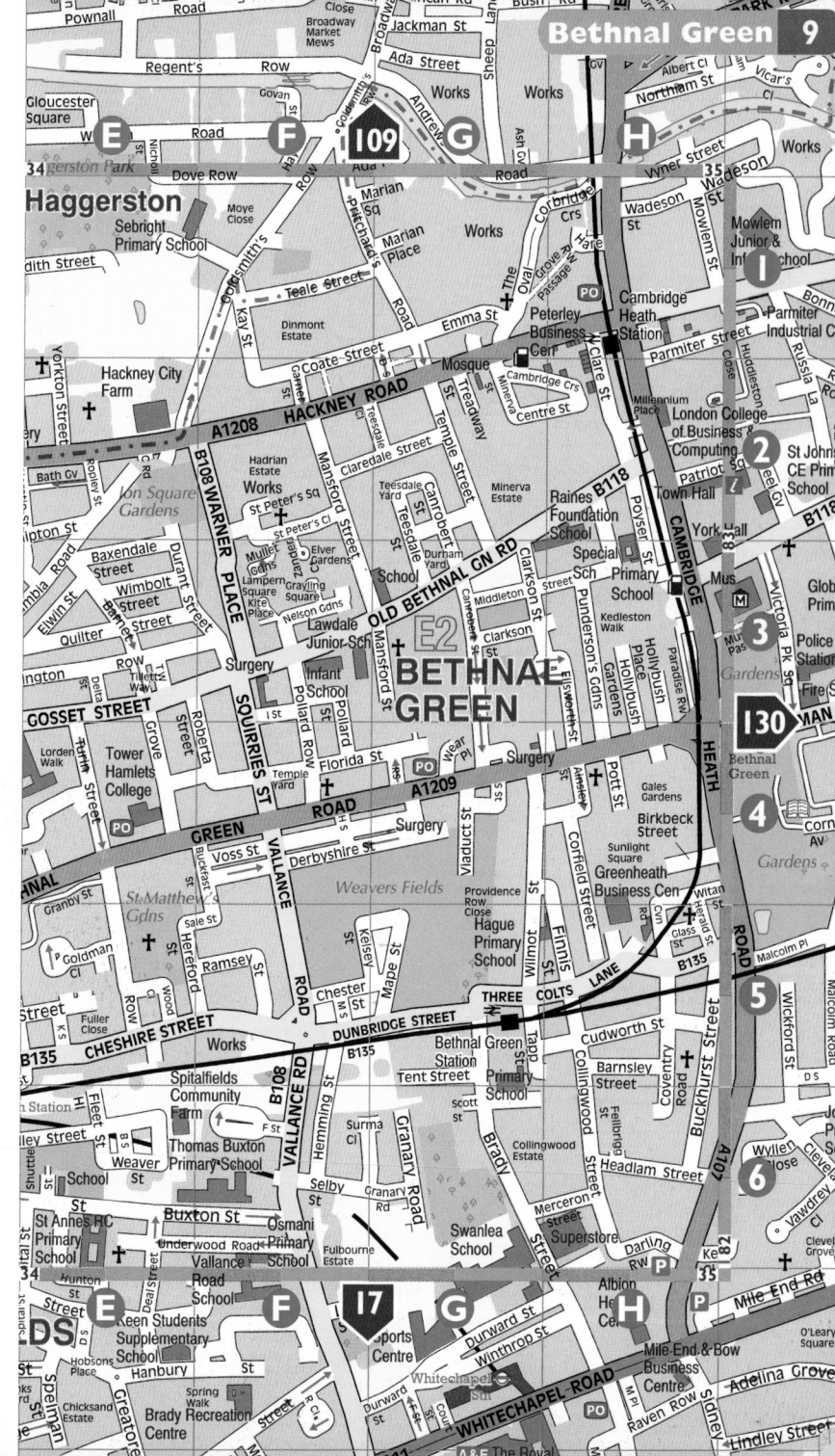

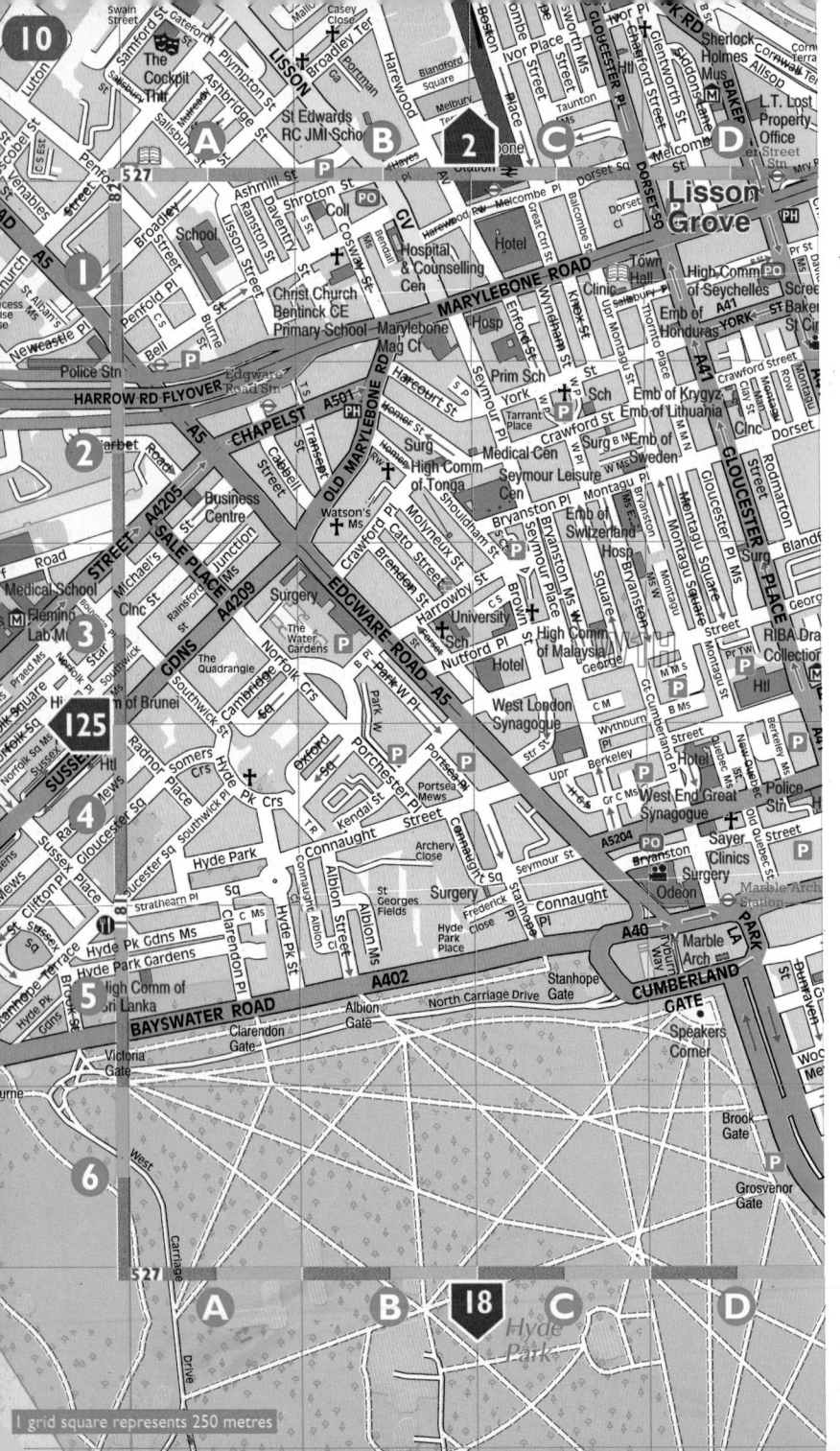

1 grid square represents 250 metres

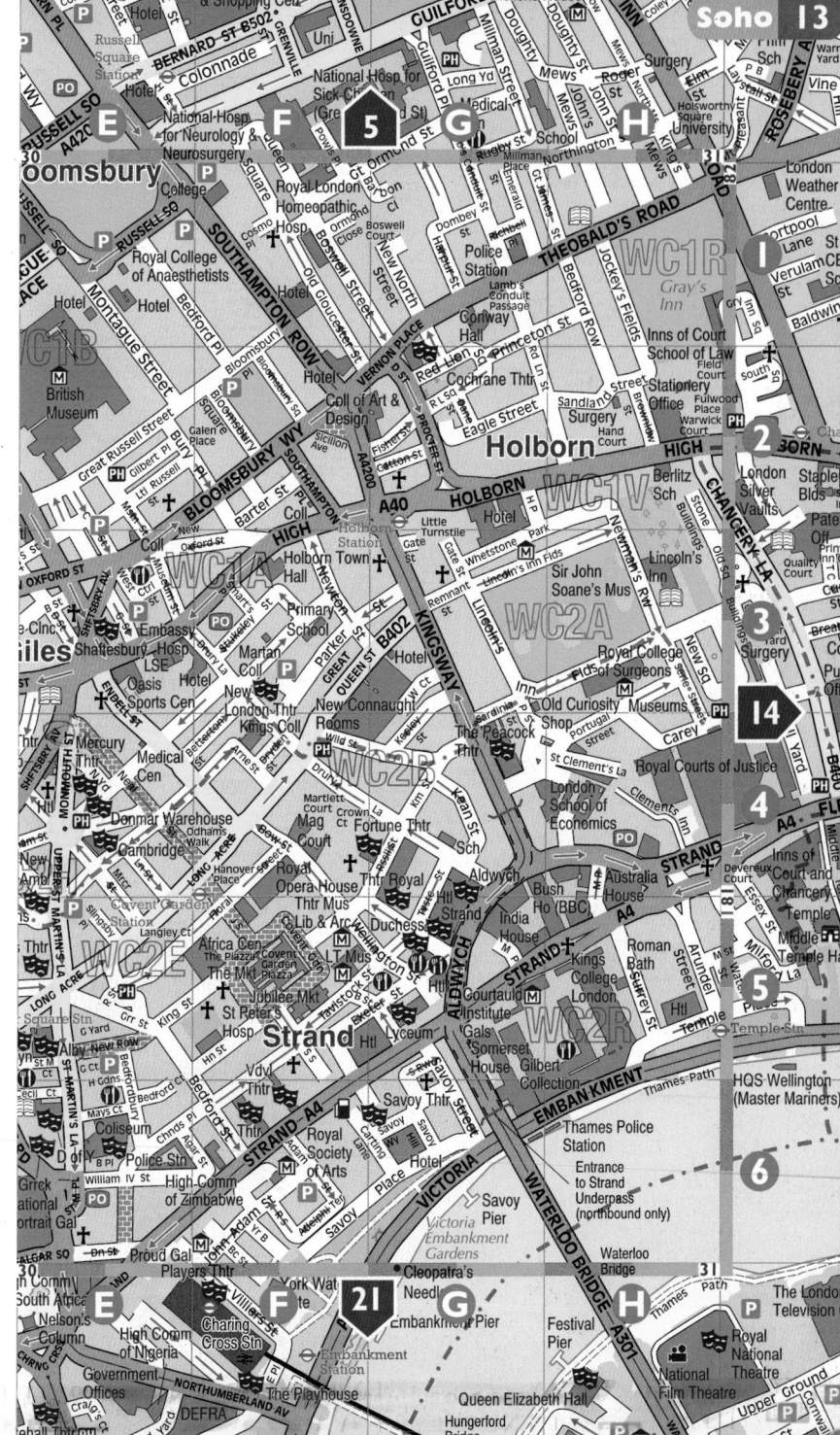

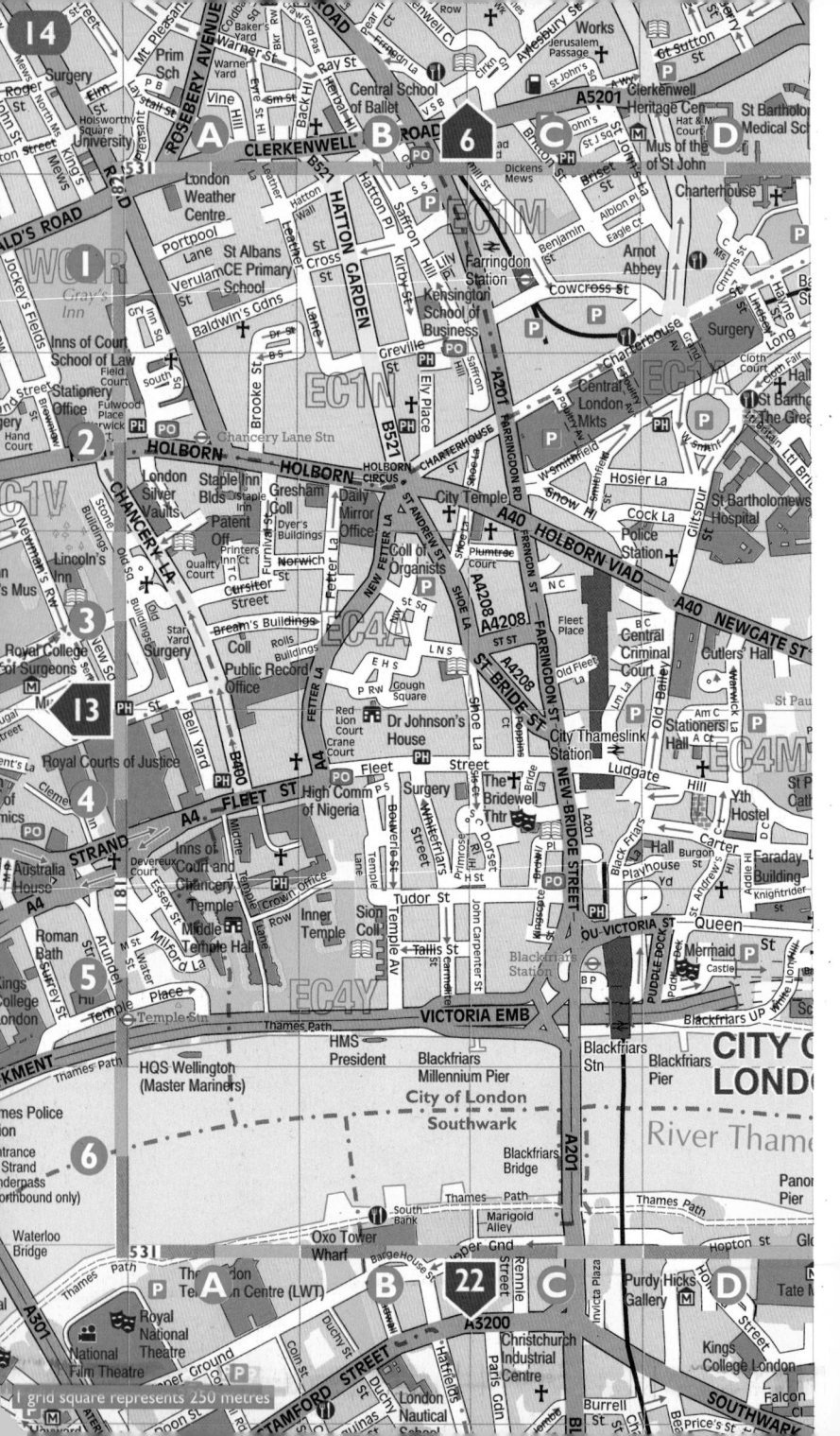

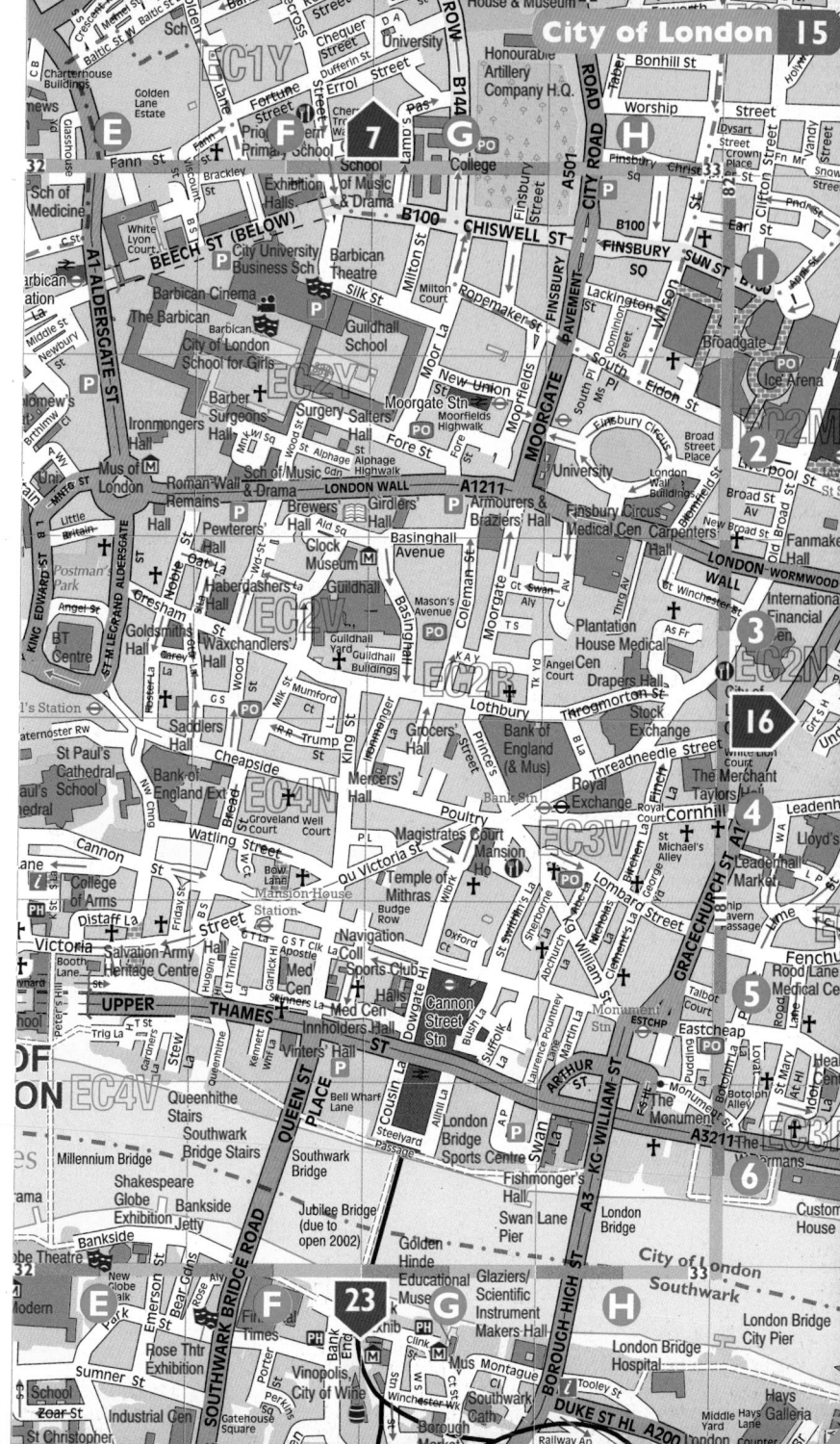

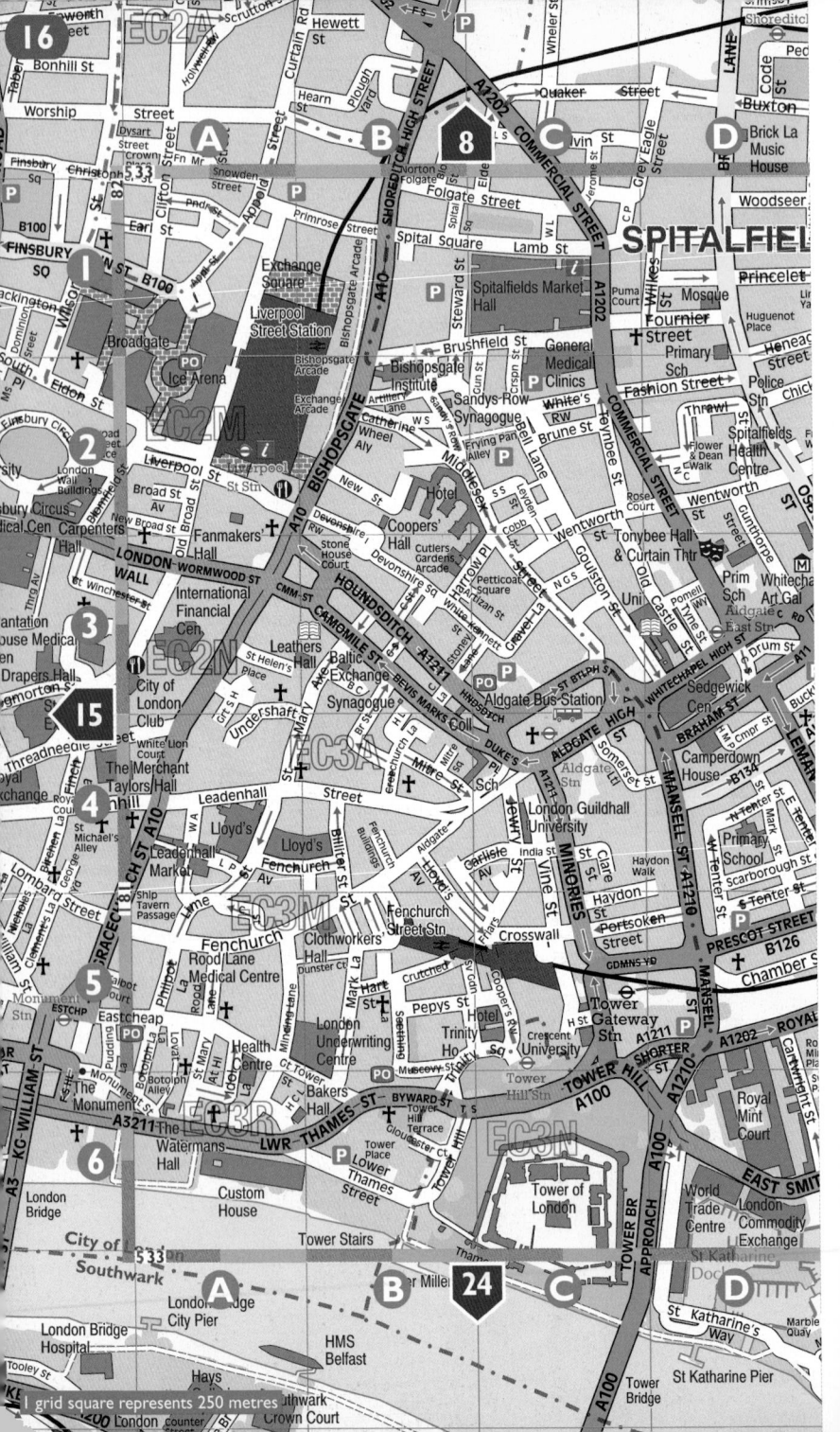

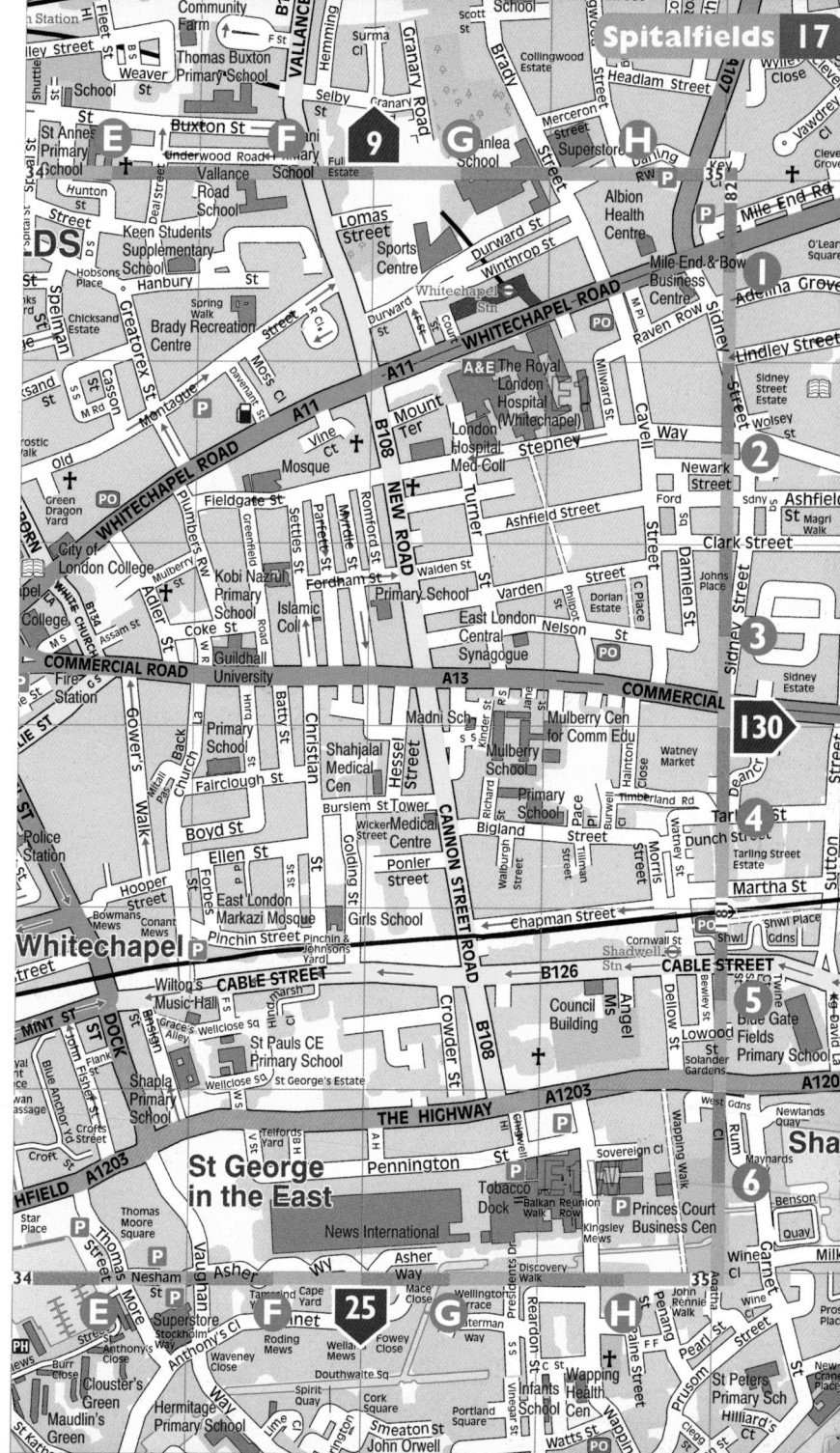

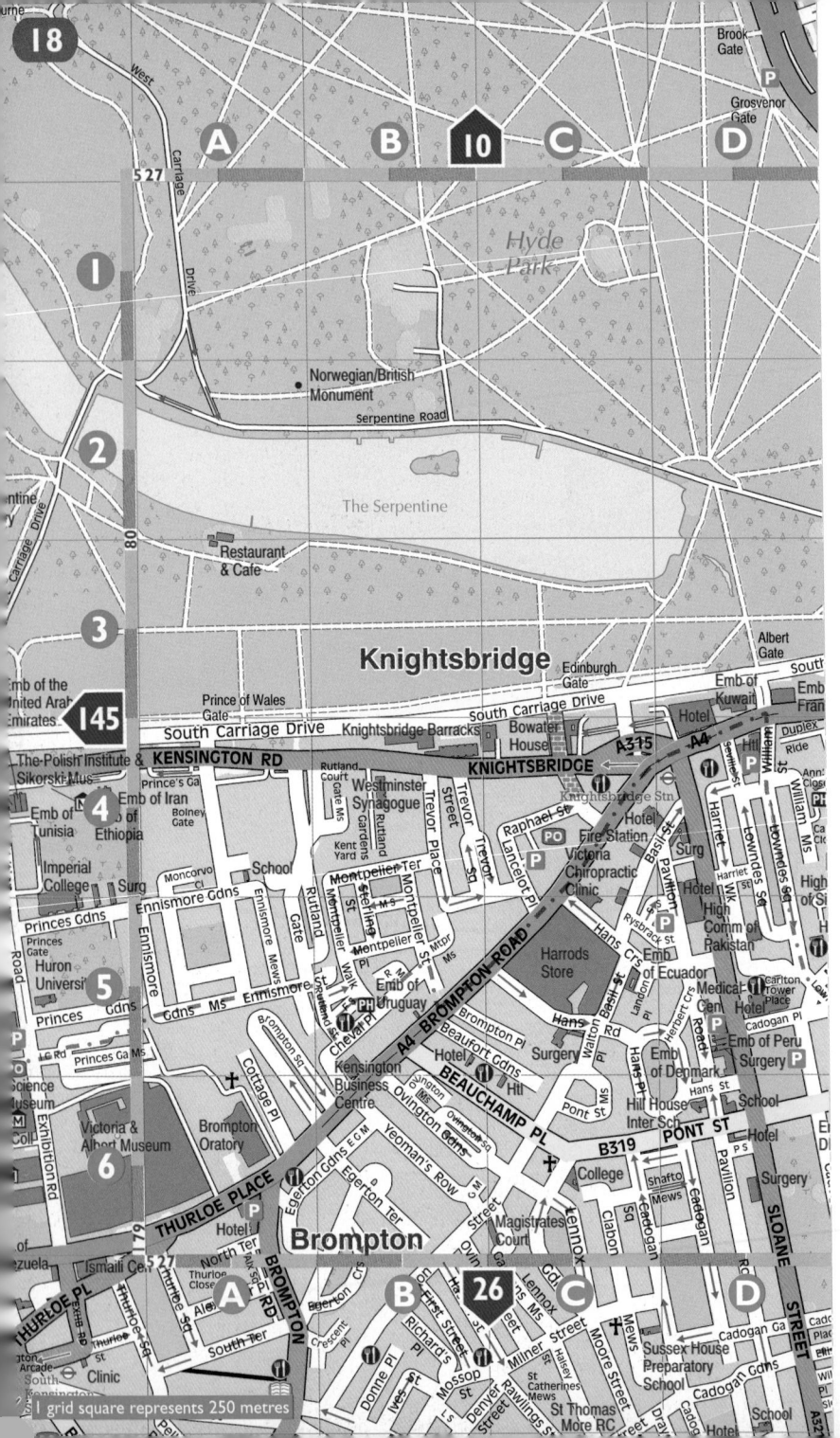

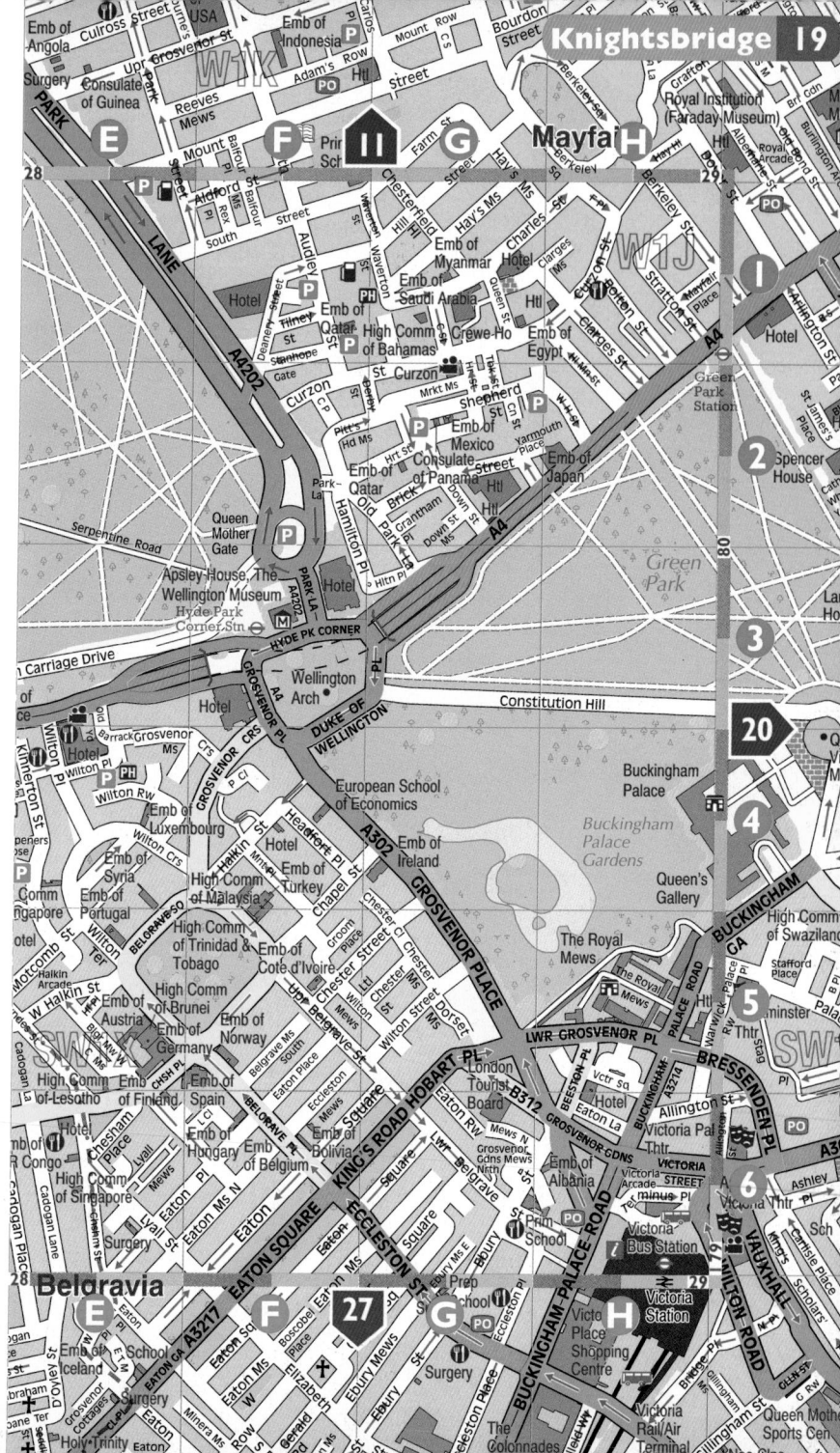

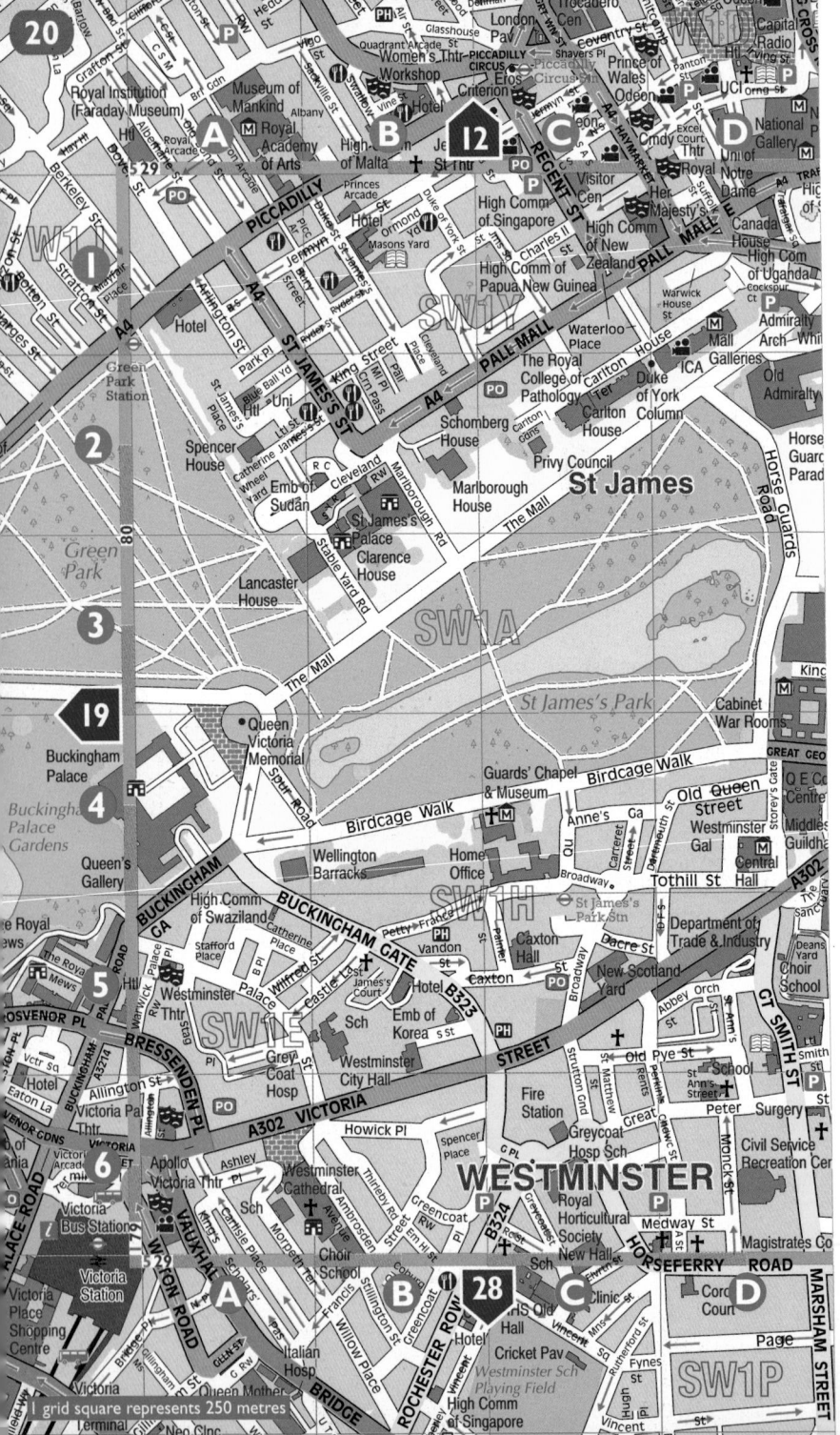

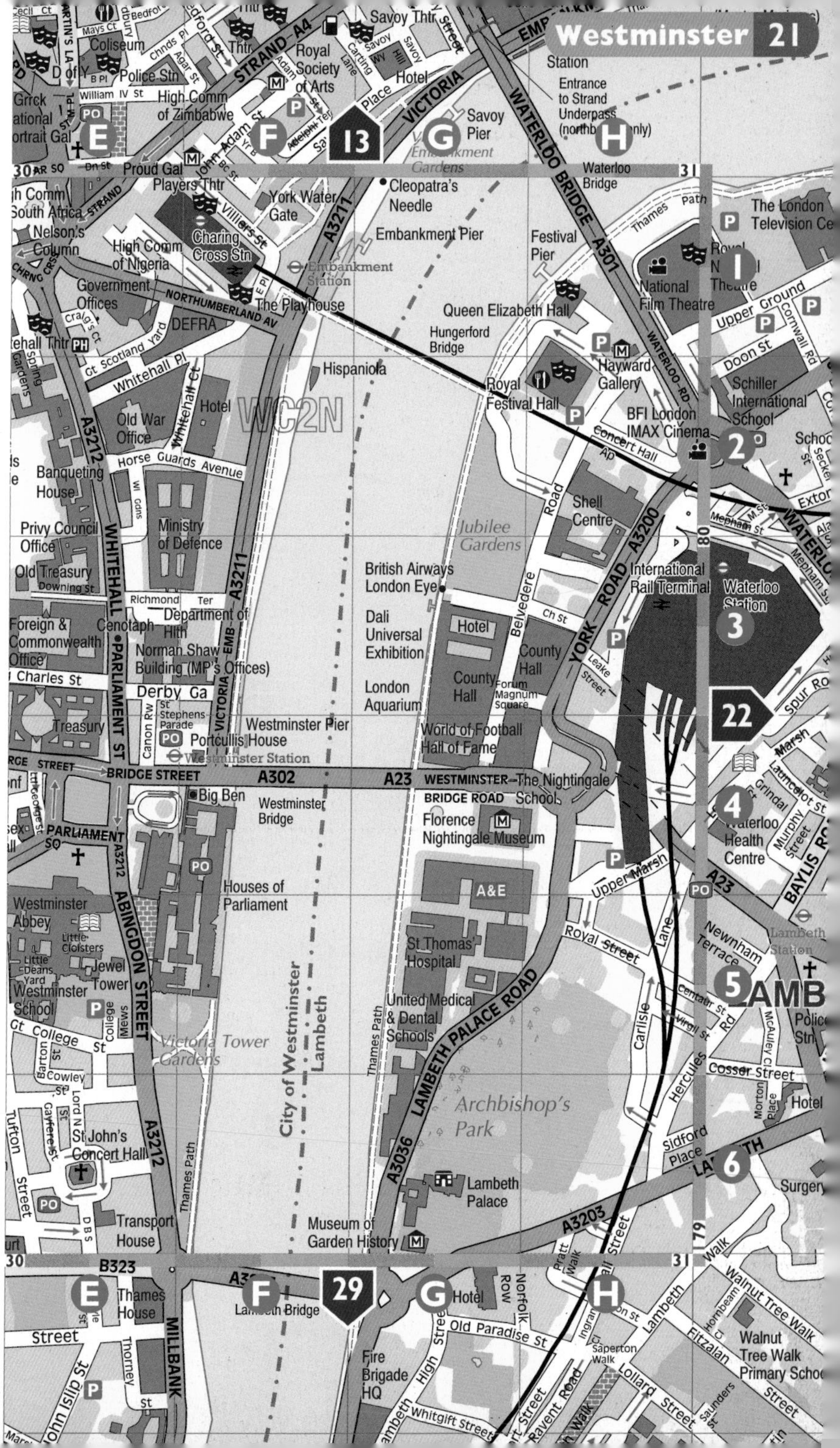
Savoy Thtr
Coliseum
Mays Ct
Chandos Pl
Agar St
Police Stn
William IV St
High Comm of Zimbabwe
STRAND A4
Royal Society of Arts
Savoy Hill
Hotel
Carting Lane
Adam St
Place
VICTORIA
WATERLOO BRIDGE A301
Station
Entrance to Strand Underpass (northbound only)
National Portrait Gal
E
F
G
H
13
Savoy Pier
Embankment Gardens
John Adam St
Proud Gal
Players Thtr
STRAND
Villiers St
York Water Gate
Cleopatra's Needle
Waterloo Bridge
Thames Path
The London Television Centre
High Comm of South Africa
Nelson's Column
High Comm of Nigeria
Charing Cross Stn
A3211
Embankment Pier
Embankment Station
Festival Pier
Royal National Theatre
I
National Film Theatre
Government Offices
NORTHUMBERLAND AV
The Playhouse
Queen Elizabeth Hall
Upper Ground
Cornwall Rd
Craig's Ct
DEFRA
Whitehall Thtr
Gt Scotland Yard
Whitehall Pl
Hungerford Bridge
Hayward Gallery
WATERLOO RD
Doon St
Spring Gardens
Hispaniola
Royal Festival Hall
Schiller International School
Whitehall Ct
Hotel
WC2N
Old War Office
A3212
BFI London IMAX Cinema
Concert Hall Ap
2
School
Horse Guards Avenue
Banqueting House
Wl Gdns
Ministry of Defence
Road
Shell Centre
Jubilee Gardens
A3200
Mepham St
WATERLOO
Exton
Privy Council Office
WHITEHALL
80
Old Treasury
Downing St
British Airways London Eye
Belvedere
International Rail Terminal
Waterloo Station
Richmond Ter
Department of Hlth
Dali Universal Exhibition
Ch St
YORK ROAD
3
Foreign & Commonwealth Office
Cenotaph
Norman Shaw Building (MP's Offices)
Hotel
County Hall
Leake Street
Charles St
PARLIAMENT ST
Derby Ga
VICTORIA EMB
London Aquarium
County Hall
Forum Magnum Square
Spur Rd
Treasury
Canon Rw
St Stephens Parade
Portcullis House
Westminster Pier
World of Football Hall of Fame
22
Westminster Station
GE STREET
BRIDGE STREET
A302
A23
WESTMINSTER
The Nightingale School
Marsh
Lancelot St
Big Ben
Westminster Bridge
BRIDGE ROAD
Florence Nightingale Museum
Grindal
4
Waterloo Health Centre
Murphy Street
BAYLIS RO
PARLIAMENT SQ
A3212
Houses of Parliament
A&E
Upper Marsh
A23
Westminster Abbey
Little Cloisters
ABINGDON STREET
Royal Street
Lane
Newnham Terrace
Lambeth Station
Little Deans Yard
Jewel Tower
St Thomas' Hospital
LAMB
Westminster School
College Mews
City of Westminster
Lambeth
United Medical & Dental Schools
LAMBETH PALACE ROAD
Carlisle
Centaur St
Virgil St
5
Police Stn
Gt College St
Victoria Tower Gardens
Thames Path
Hercules
Cosser Street
McAuley Cl
Barton St
Cowley St
Lord N St
Gayfere St
Archbishop's Park
Morton Place
Hotel
Tufton Street
St John's Concert Hall
A3212
Thames Path
A3036
Sidford Place
LAMBETH
6
Surgery
Lambeth Palace
A3203
Transport House
Museum of Garden History
Pratt Walk
Walk
30
B323
31
29
Thames House
Lambeth Bridge
Hotel
Norfolk Row
Walnut Tree Walk
Street
MILLBANK
Thorney St
High Street
Old Paradise St
Lambeth
Hornbeam Cl
Walnut Tree Walk Primary School
Fire Brigade HQ
Saperton Walk
Fitzalan Street
John Islip St
Whitgift Street
Lollard Street
Saunders St
Street

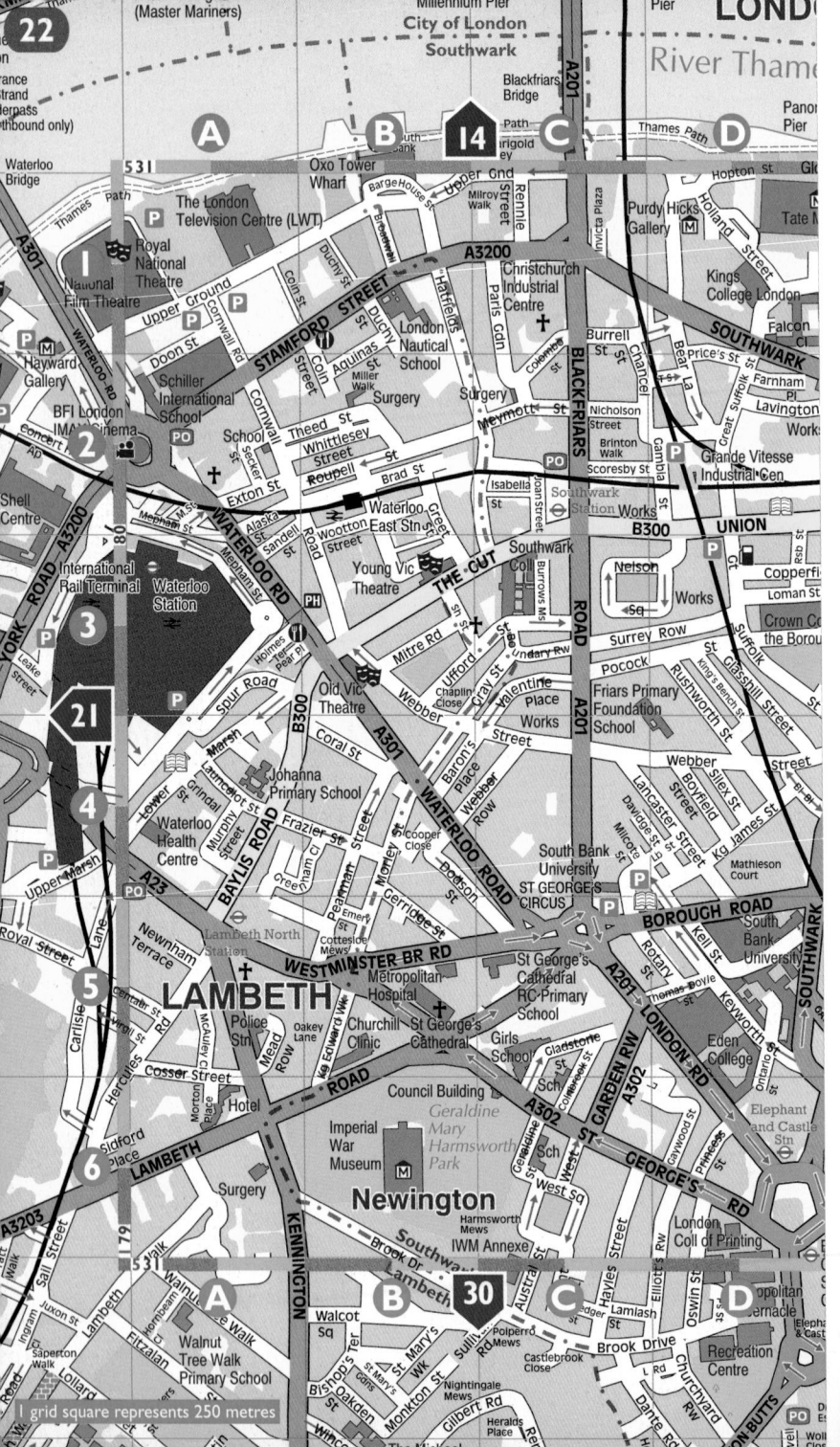

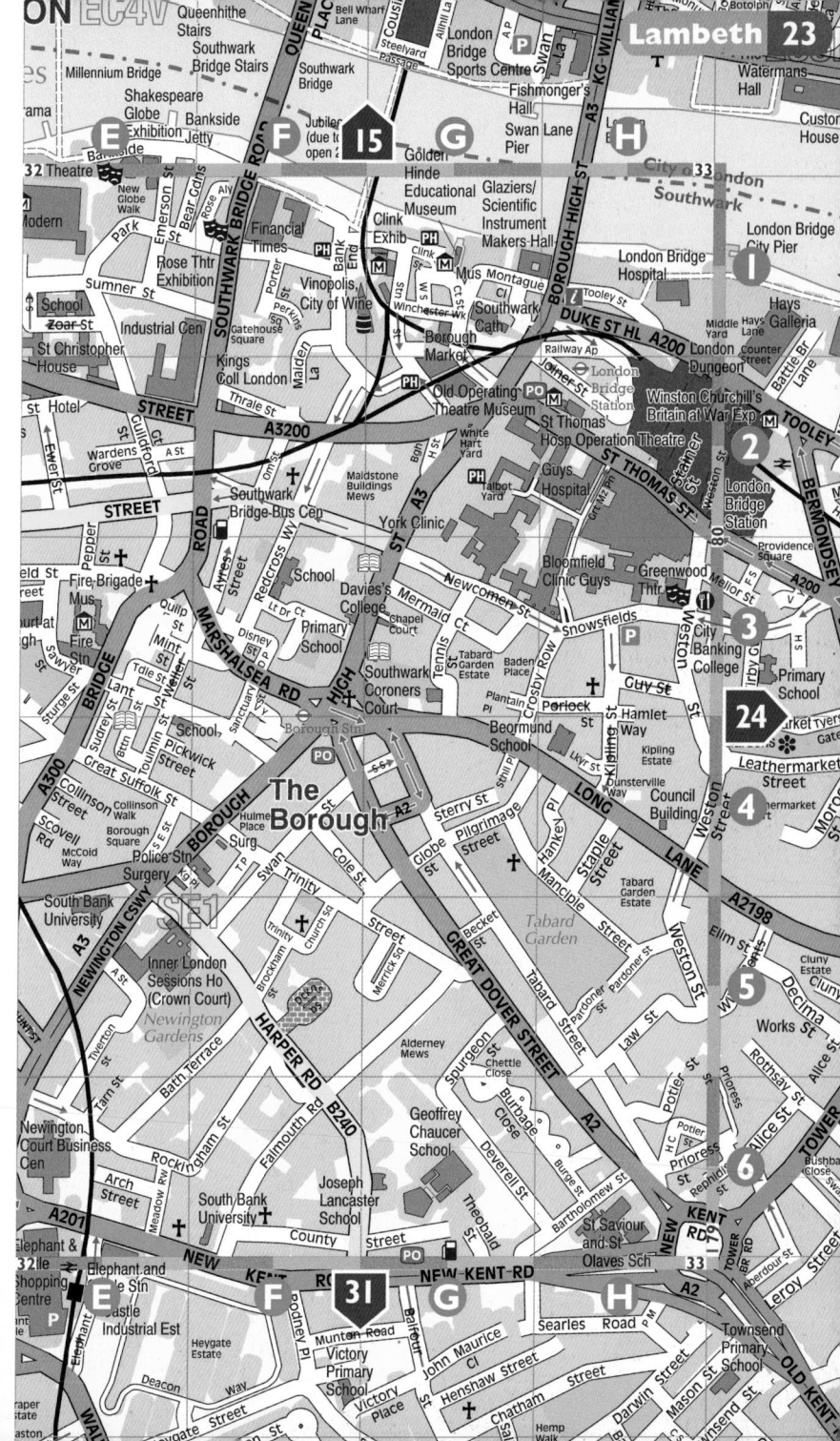

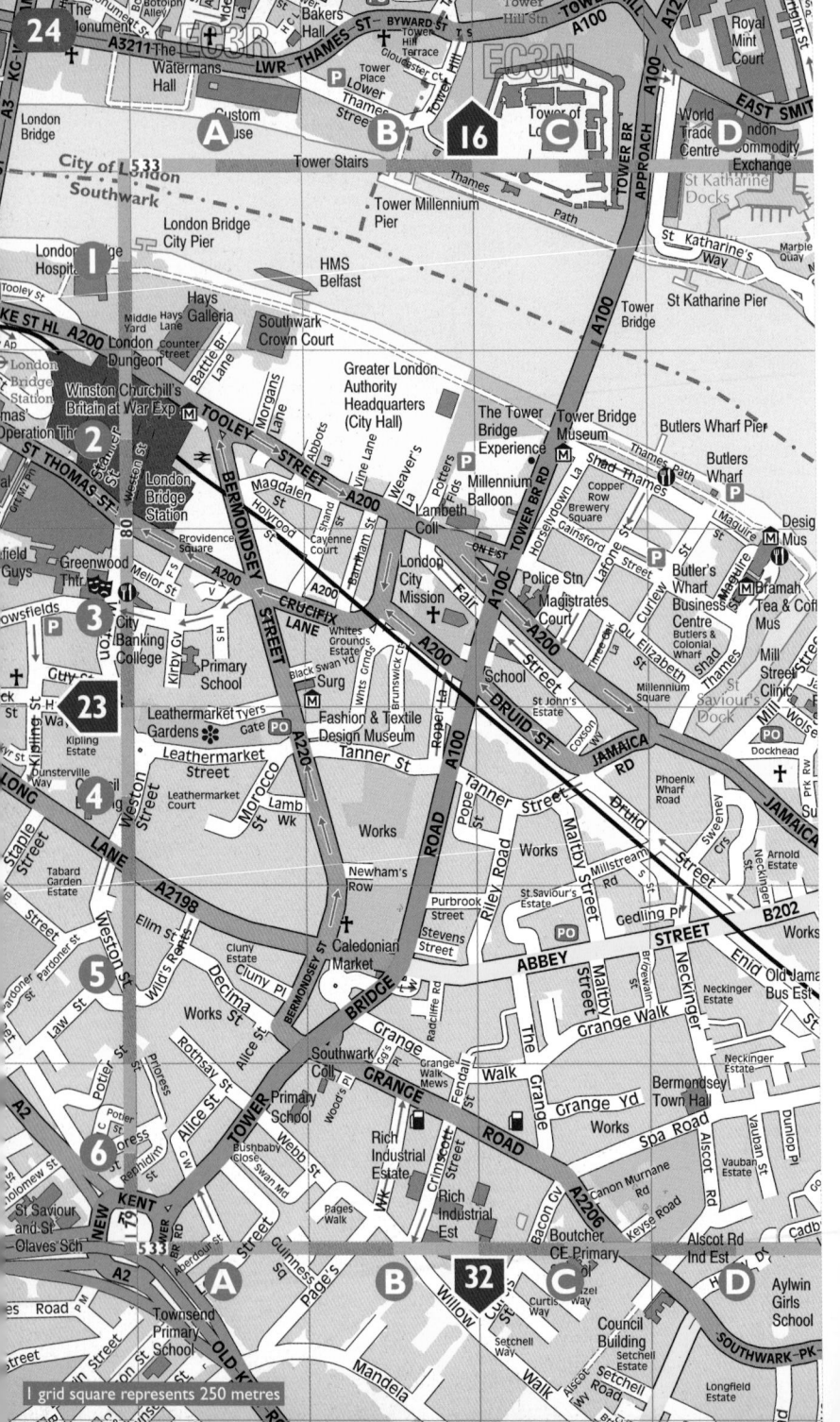

I grid square represents 250 metres

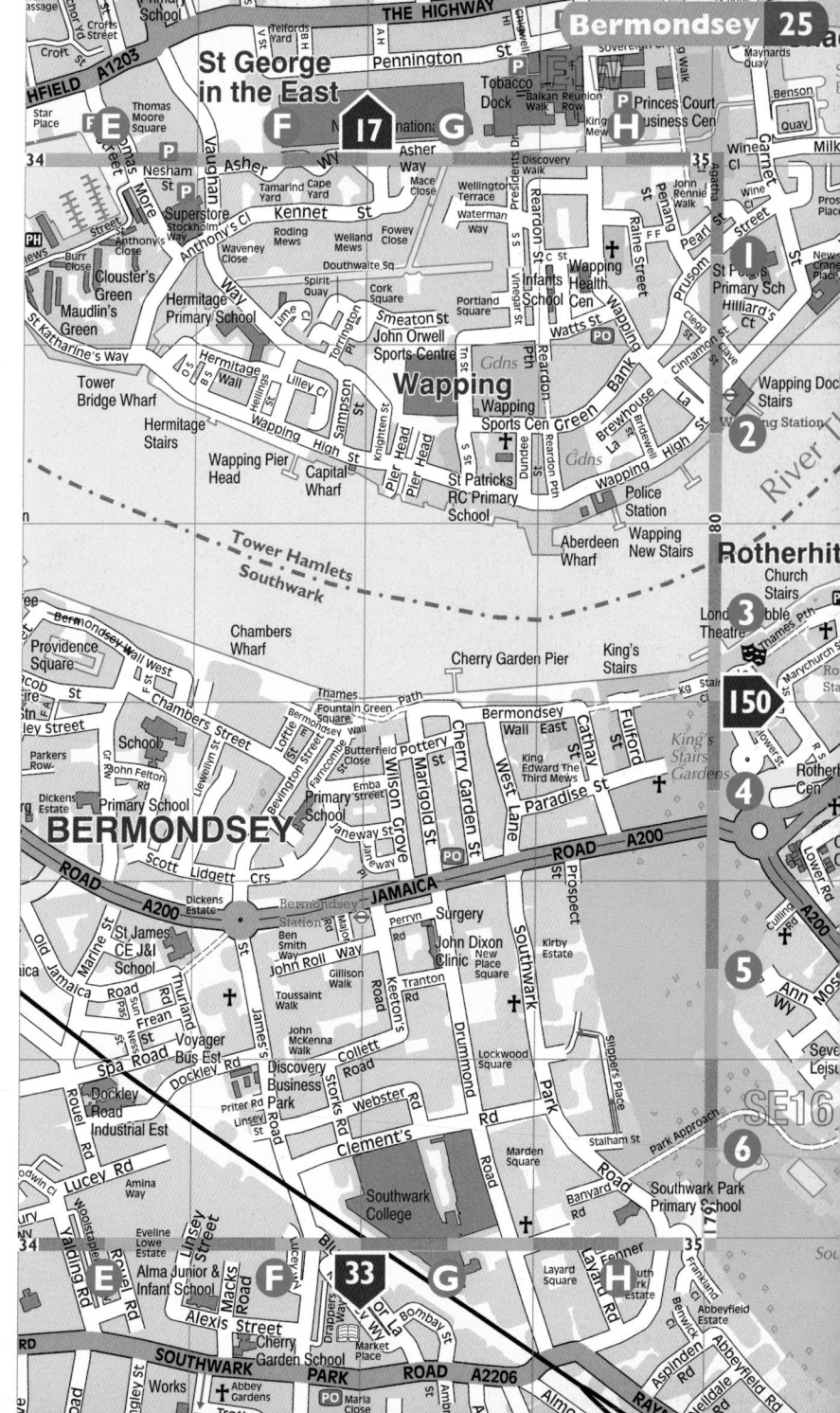

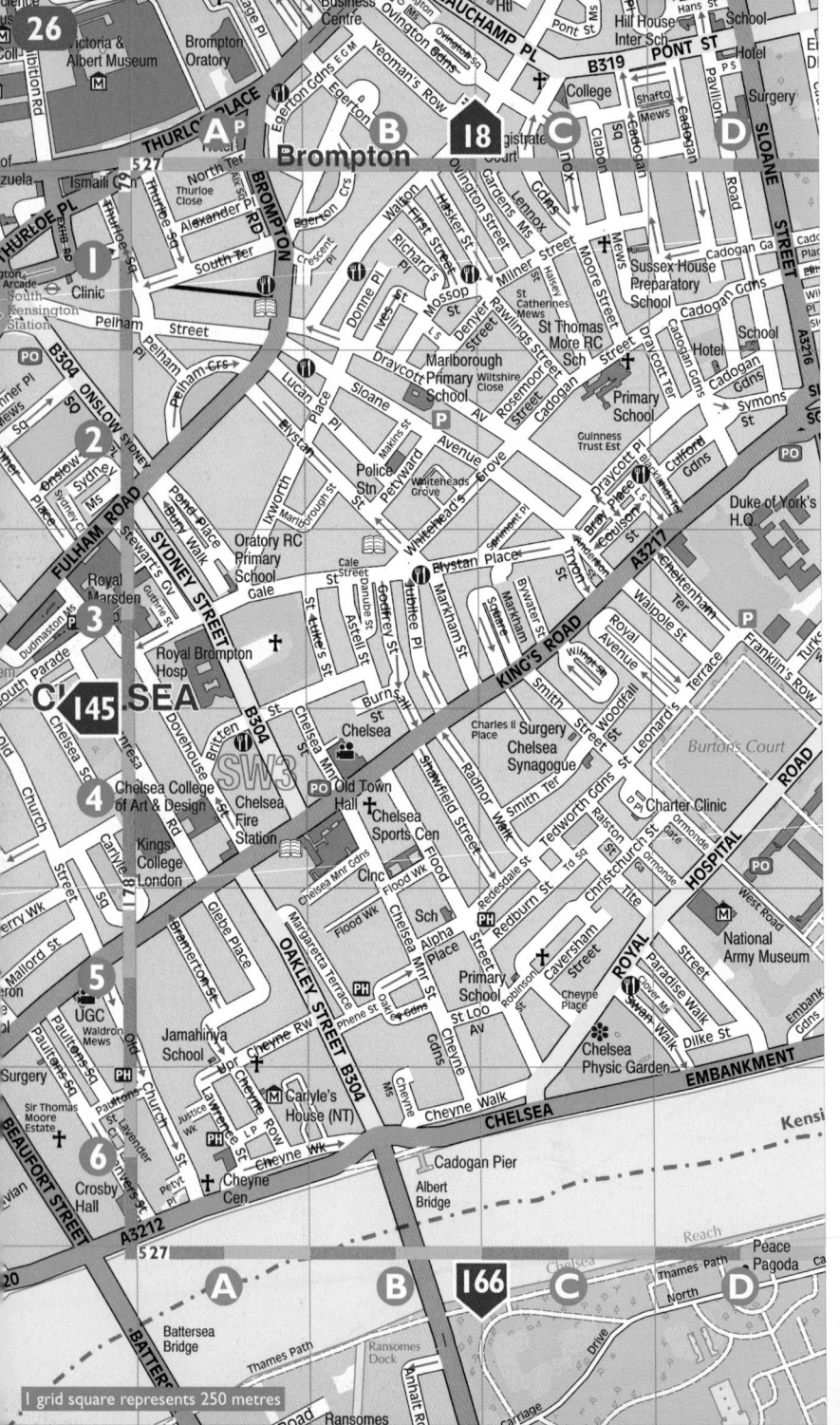

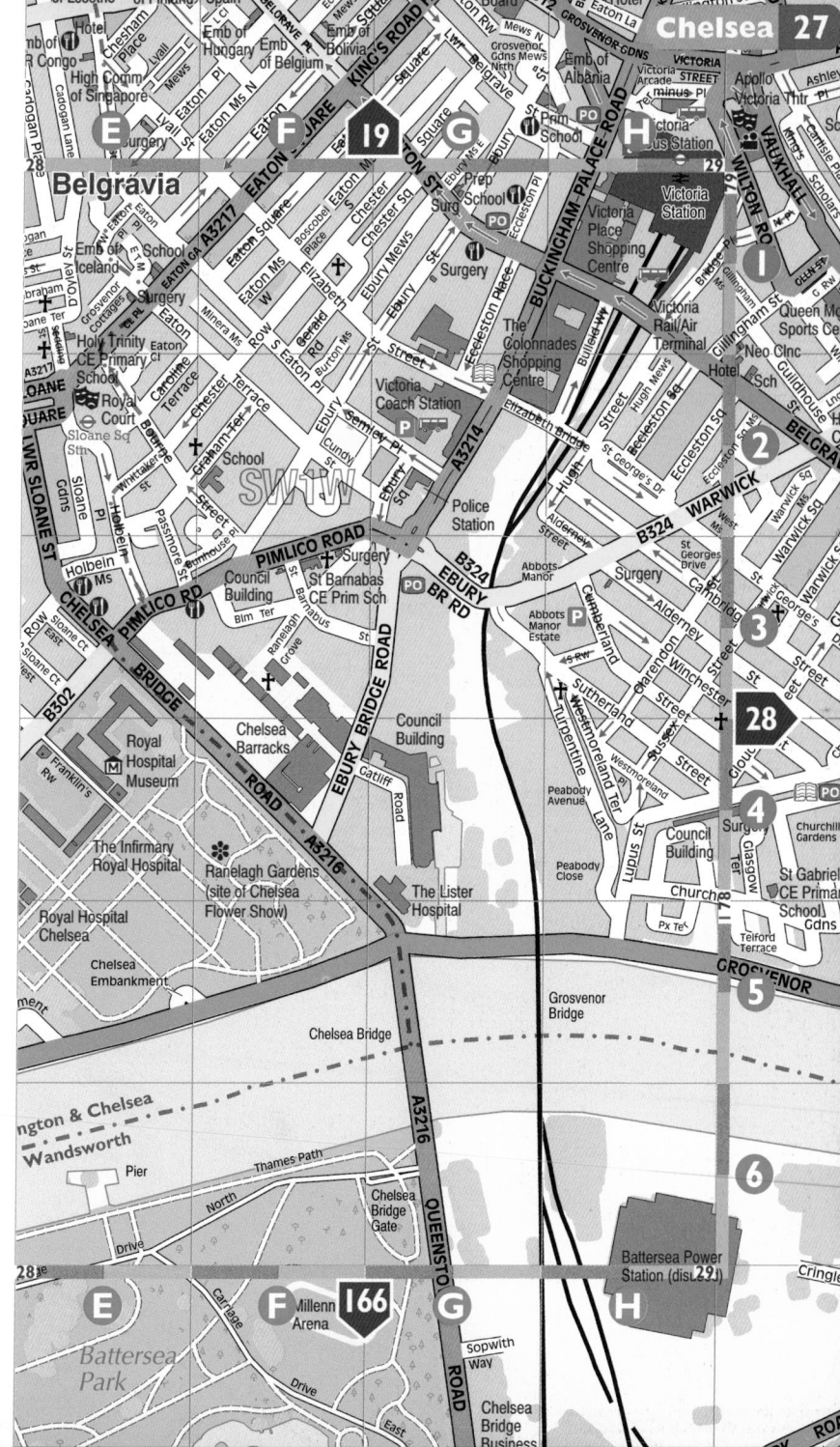

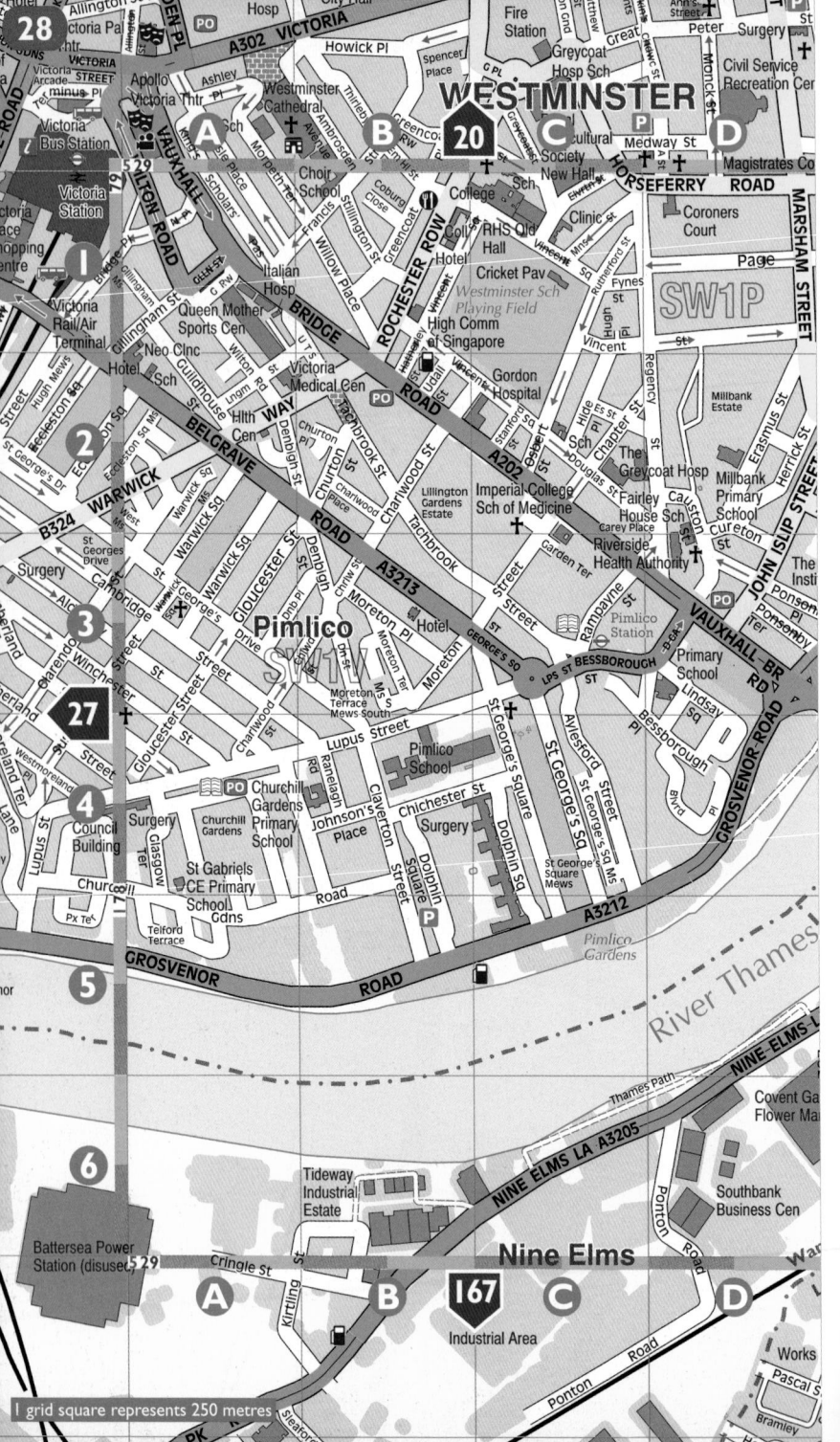

I grid square represents 250 metres

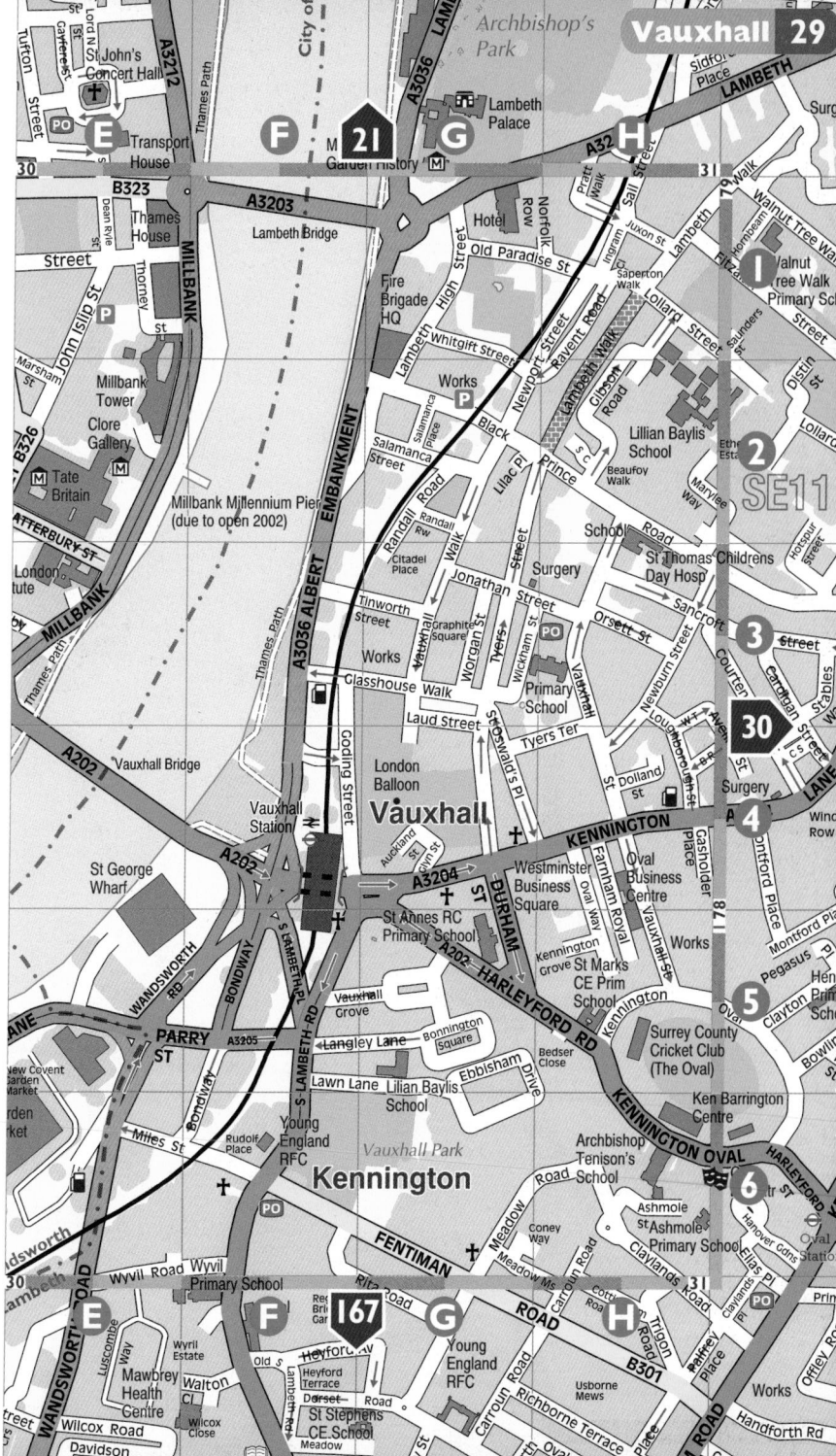

Archbishop's Park

LAMBETH

Surger

City of

A3212

Tufton Street

Lord N St Garden St

John's Concert Hall

Sidford Place

Walnut Tree Walk

PO

E

Transport House

F

21

G

Lambeth Palace

H

A32

Hornbeam

LAMBETH

Walnut Tree Walk

Walnut Tree Walk Primary Sch

Garden History

M

M

Old Paradise St

Juxon st

Saperton Walk

Pratt Walk

Sail Street

Lambeth

I

Street B323

Thames House

A3203

Lambeth Bridge

Hotel

Norfolk Row

Saunders

Distin

Street

Dean Ryle

Thorney

Ingram

Lambeth High Street

Newport Street

Ravent Road

Lambeth Walk

Gibson Road

Street

Lollard St

Lollard Street

30

Fire Brigade HQ

Lillian Baylis School

Street

MILLBANK

P

Marsham

John Islip St

St

Millbank Tower

Clore Gallery

Lambeth Whitgift Street

Works

P

Black

Salamanca Place

Lilac Pl

Prince

Street

S C

Beaufoy Walk

MaryLee Way

Ethe Esta

2

SE11

B326

M

Tate Britain

M

Salamanca Street

Randall Road

Randall Rw

Walk

School

Road

St Thomas Childrens Day Hosp

Hotspur Street

London tute

ATTERBURY ST

Millbank Millennium Pier (due to open 2002)

Citadel Place

Tinworth Street

Jonathan Street

Surgery

Sancroft

3

Street

MILLBANK

Thames Path

A3036 ALBERT EMBANKMENT

Graphite Sq

Vauxhall

Worgan St

Tyers

Street

Wickham

PO

Orsett St

Newburn Street

Courter

Stables

Way

MILLBANK

Works

Glasshouse Walk

Primary School

Vauxhall

30

A202

Vauxhall Bridge

Goding Street

Laud Street

London Balloon

Oswald's Pl

Tyers Ter

St Dolland St

Loughborough St

LANE

Avenue

Surgery

A

Windr Row

Vauxhall Station

Vauxhall

KENNINGTON

4

St George Wharf

Auckland St

Glun St

A3204

DURHAM ST

Westminster Business Square

Farnham Road

Oval Way

Oval Business Centre

Gasholder place

Vauxhall St

Montford Place

Montford Plac

WANDSWORTH RD

BONDWAY

S LAMBETH PL

St Annes RC Primary School

A202 HARLEYFORD RD

Kennington Grove

St Marks CE Prim School

Kennington

Works

Pegasus

Clayton St

Henr Prima Scho

5

LANE

PARRY ST

A3205

Vauxhall Grove

Langley Lane

Bonnington Square

Ebbisham

Drive

Bedser Close

Surrey County Cricket Club (The Oval)

Oval

Bowling

New Covent Garden Market

Lawn Lane

Lilian Baylis School

Ken Barrington Centre

HARLEYFORD

rden rket

BONDWAY

Miles St

Young England RFC

Rudolf Place

Vauxhall Park

Archbishop Tenison's School

Road

KENNINGTON OVAL

6

r St

Oval Station

Wandsworth

PO

Kennington

Road

Ashmole st Ashmole Primary School

Clavlands

Hanover cdns

Elias Pl

PO

Prim

ROAD

FENTIMAN

Coney Way

Meadow Ms

Carroun Road

Cott Roa

Trigon Road

PARK

Works

Handforth Rd

E

F

167

G

ROAD

H

B301

Wyvil Road

Wyvil

Primary School

Heyford Av

Red Bri Car

Ritz Road

Young England RFC

Carroun Road

Richborne Terrace

Usborne Mews

Parkly Place

Offley Ro

Luscombe

Mawbrey Health Centre

Walton Cl

Wilcox Close

Heyford Terrace

Old S

Dorset Road

St Stephens CE School

Meadow

Oval pl

Cre

Wyrll Estate

Wilcox Road

Davidson

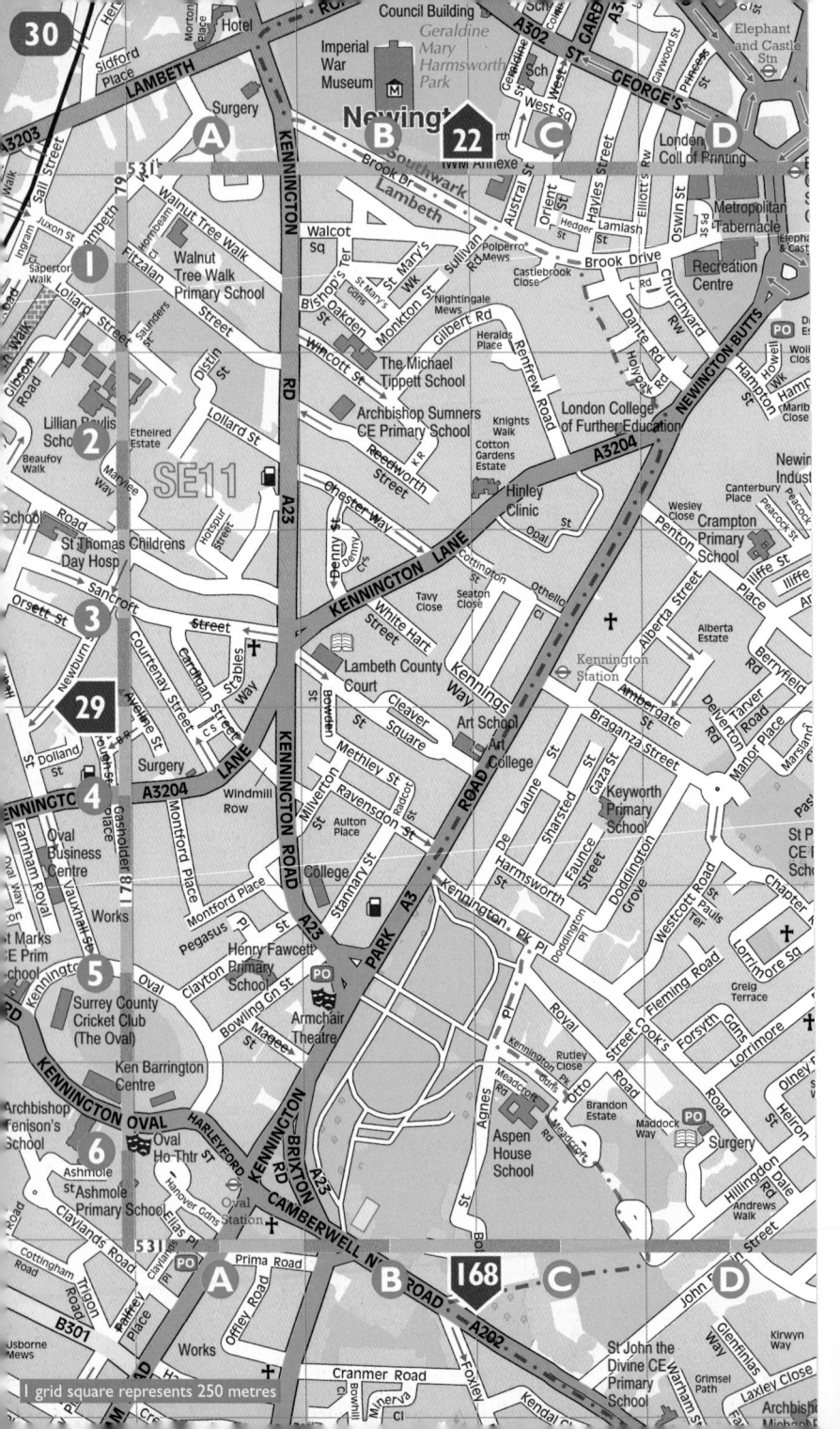

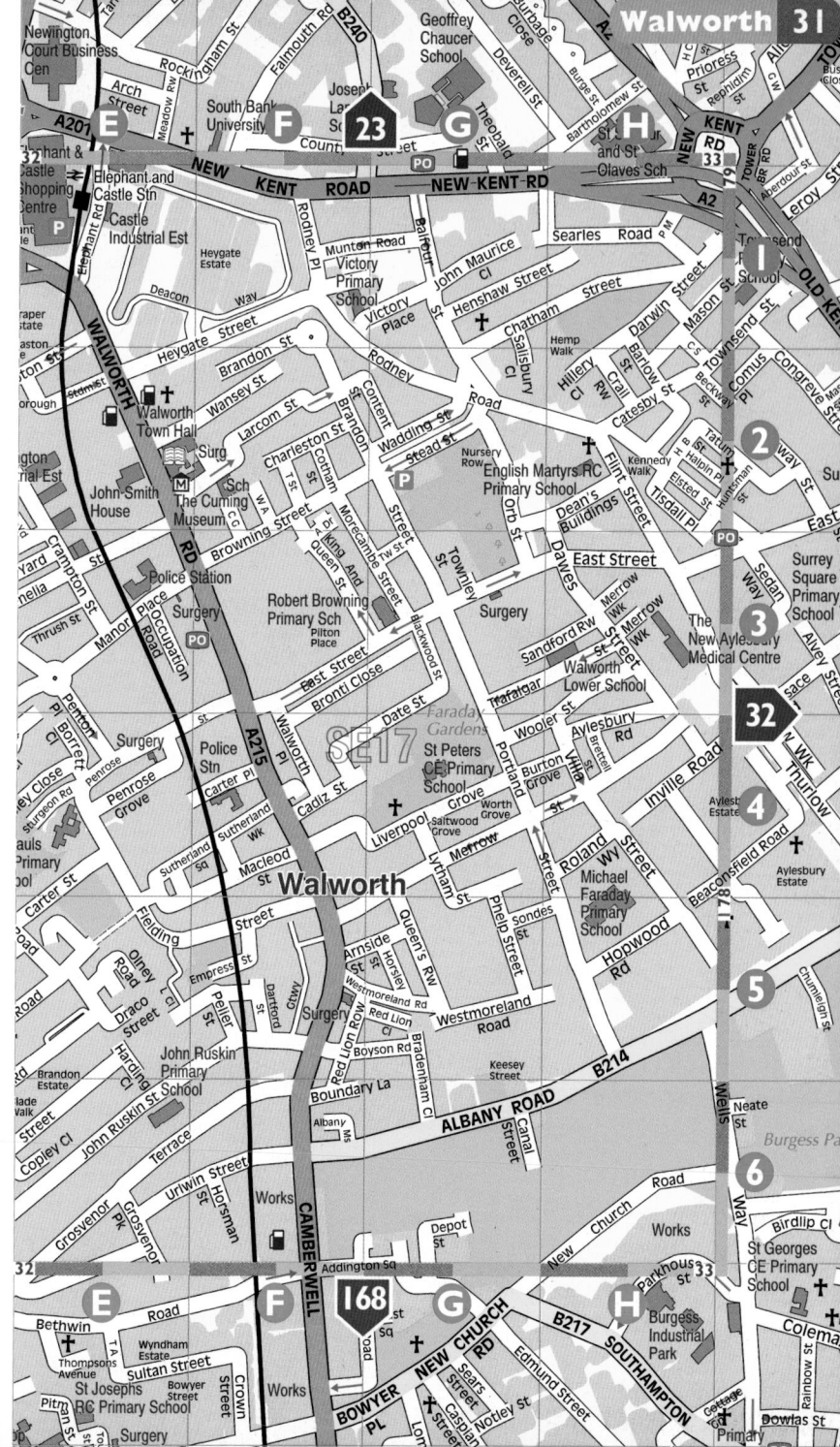

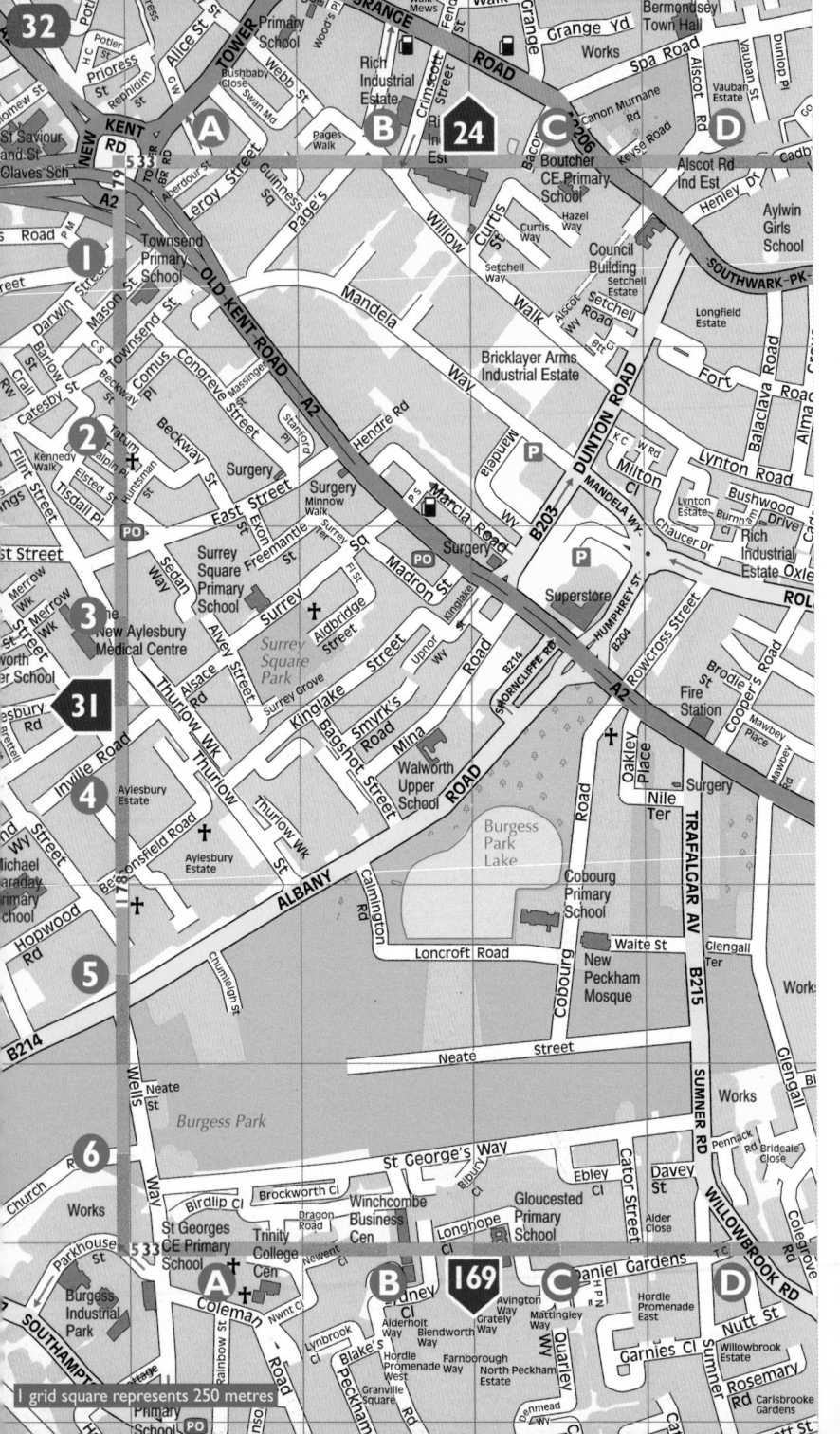

1 grid square represents 250 metres

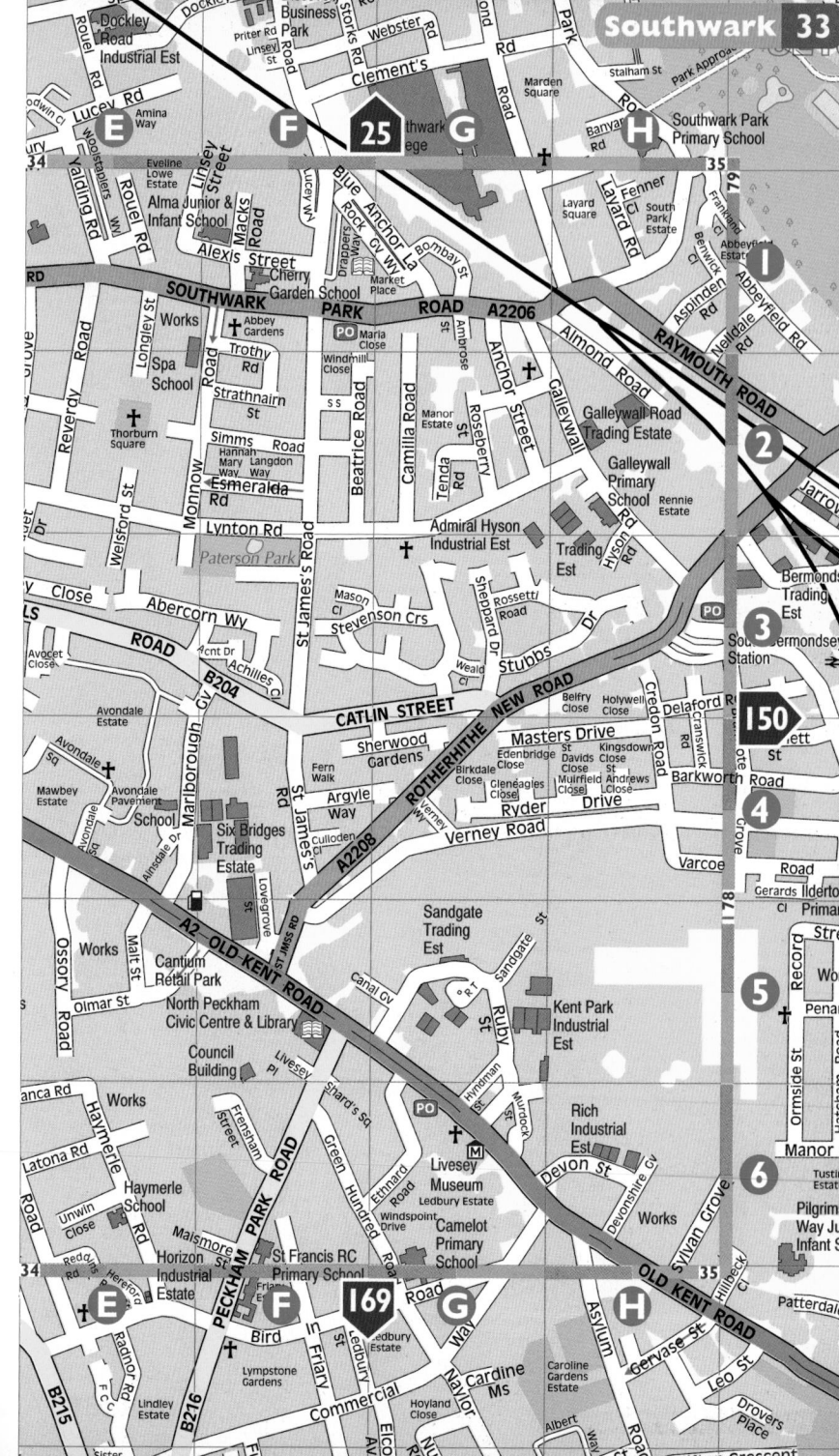

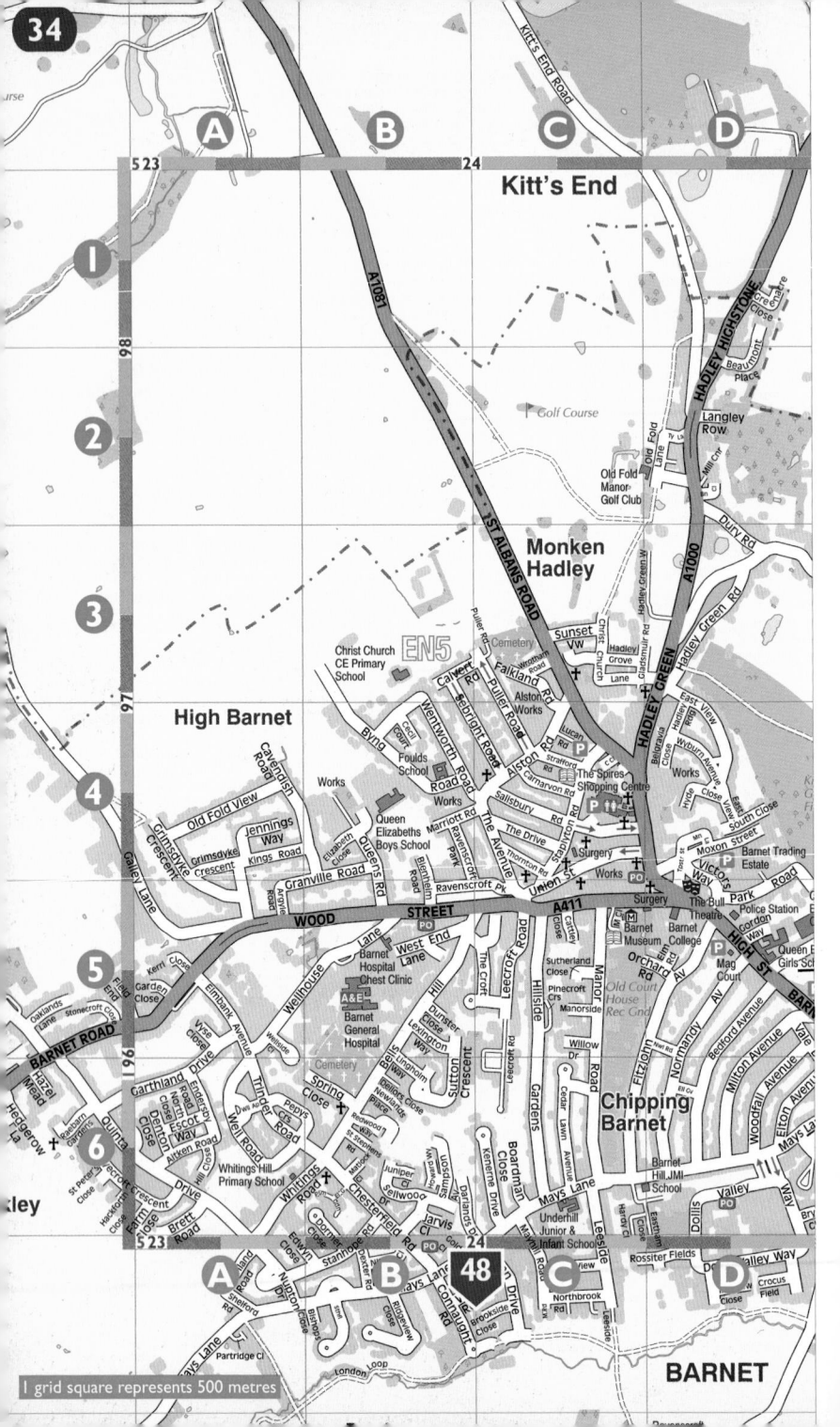

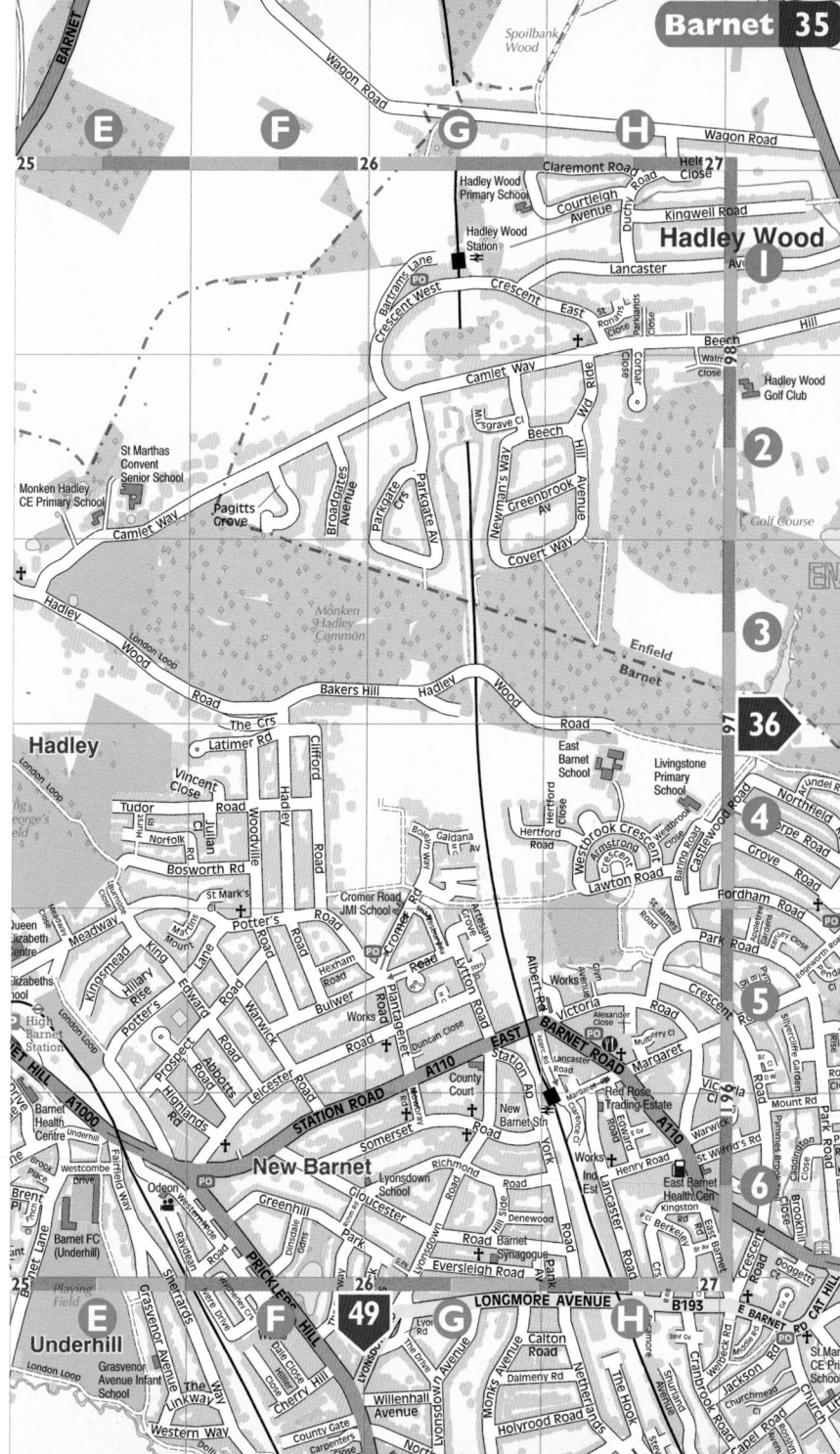

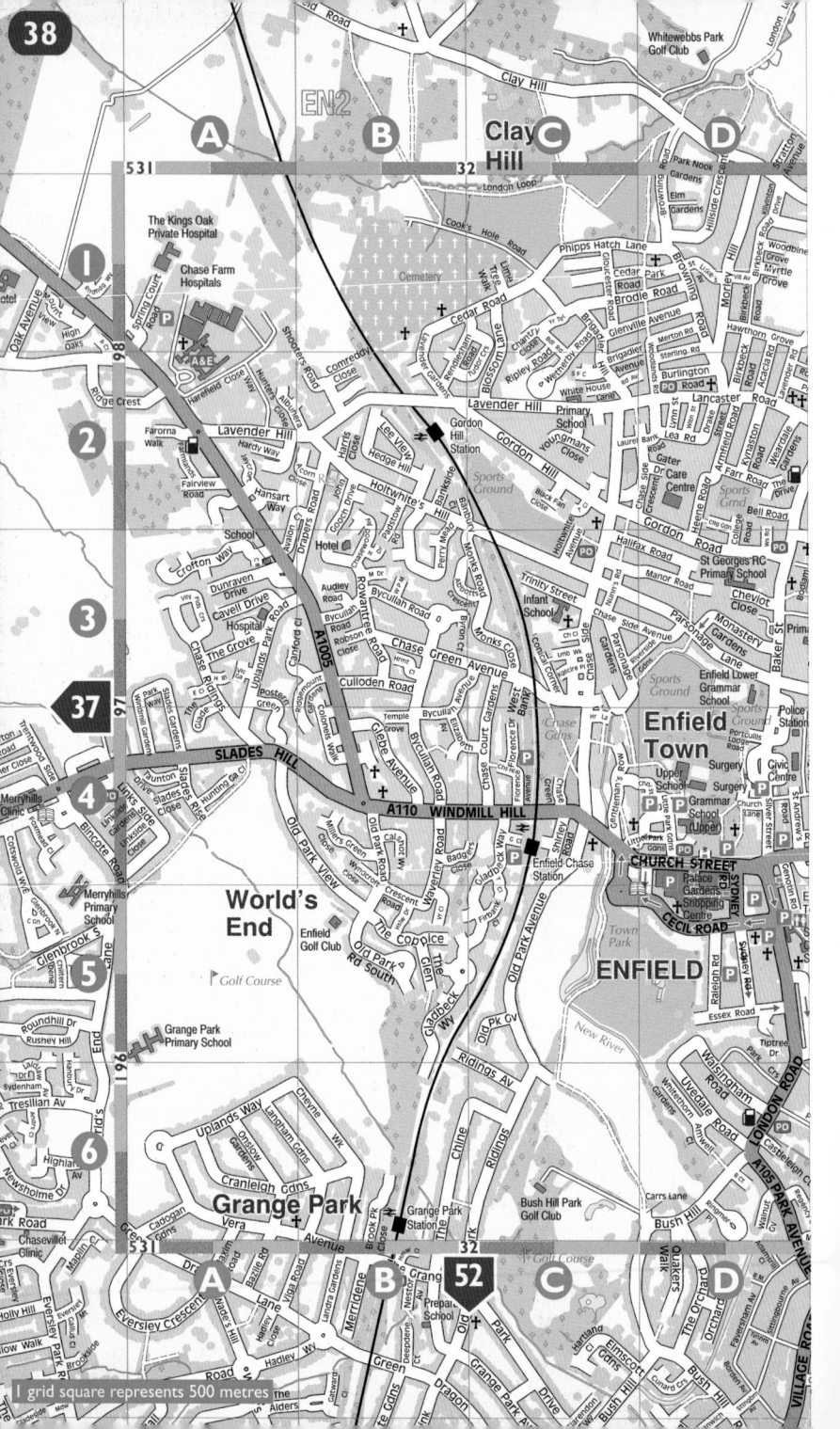

EN2

Clay Hill

A B C D

531 32

Clay Hill

Whitewebbs Park
Golf Club

Clay Hill

London Loop

Cook's Hole Road

The Kings Oak
Private Hospital

Chase Farm
Hospitals

Cemetery

Phipps Hatch Lane

Cedar Road

Glenville Avenue

Blossom Lane

Lavender Hill

Gordon Hill
Station

Gordon Hill

Primary School

Youngmans Close

Gater
Dr Care
Centre

Farr Road

Bell Road

Gordon Road

St Georges RC
Primary School

Halifax Road

Manor Road

Cheviot
Close

Monastery
Gardens

Baker
Lane

Police
Station

Civic
Centre

**Enfield
Town**

Trinity Street
Infant
School

Chase Side Avenue

Parsonage

Sports
Ground

Enfield Lower
Grammar
School

Upper
School

Grammar
School
(Upper)

Church
Street

Lavender Hill

Lee View

Hedge Hill

Holtwhite's

Hotel

Audley
Road

Aycullan Road

Culloden Road

Chase Green Avenue

Temple
Grove

Aycullan Road

Glebe Avenue

West Bank

Chase Court Gardens

Chase
Gdns

37

97

SLADES HILL

A1005

Old Park View

A110 WINDMILL HILL

Sale
Road

Gladbeck Way

Enfield Chase
Station

CHURCH STREET

Palace
Gardens
Shopping
Centre

SYDNEY RD

CECIL ROAD

Crofton Way

Dunraven
Drive

Cavell Drive

Hospital

The Grove

Robson Close

The Glade

**World's
End**

Enfield
Golf Club

Old Park
Rd South

The Coppice

The
Glen

ENFIELD

Town
Park

New River

Merryhills
Primary
School

Glenbrook

Roundhill Dr

Rushey Hill

Grange Park
Primary School

Golf Course

Gladbeck
Wy

Old Pk Gv

Ridings AV

Raleigh Rd

Essex Road

Walsingham
Road

Uvedale
Road

LONDON ROAD

A105 PARK AVENUE

Uplands Way

Langham Gdns

Cherne
Wk

Cranleigh Gdns

Grange Park

Vera

Avenue

Chine

Ridings

Bush Hill Park
Golf Course

Carrs Lane

Bush Hill

Eversley Crescent

Merridene

Grange Park
Station

Green

52

Golf Course

Quakers
Walk

Prepal
School

Grange Park Drive

Old
Park

VILLAGE ROAD

A B C D

531 32

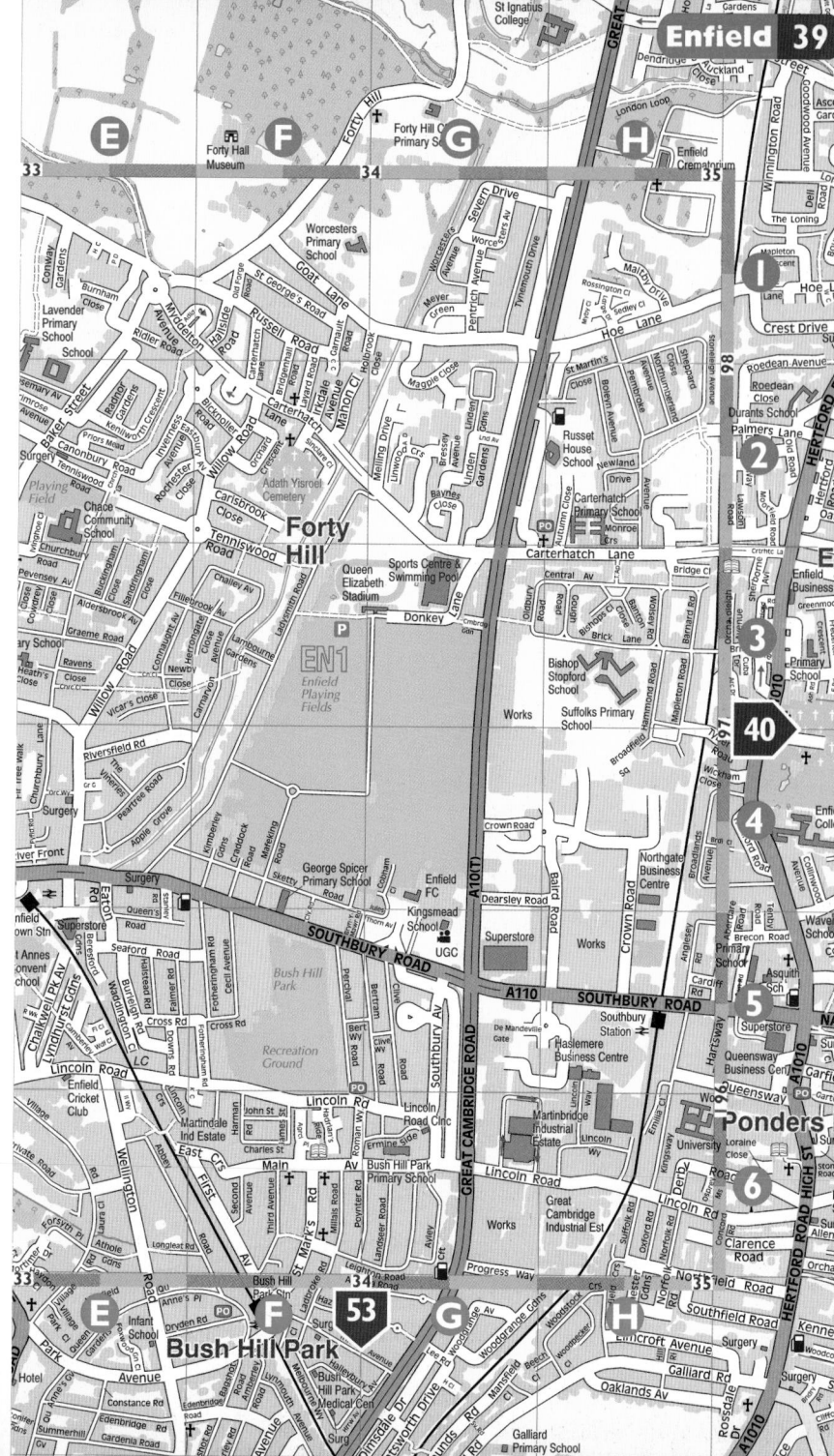

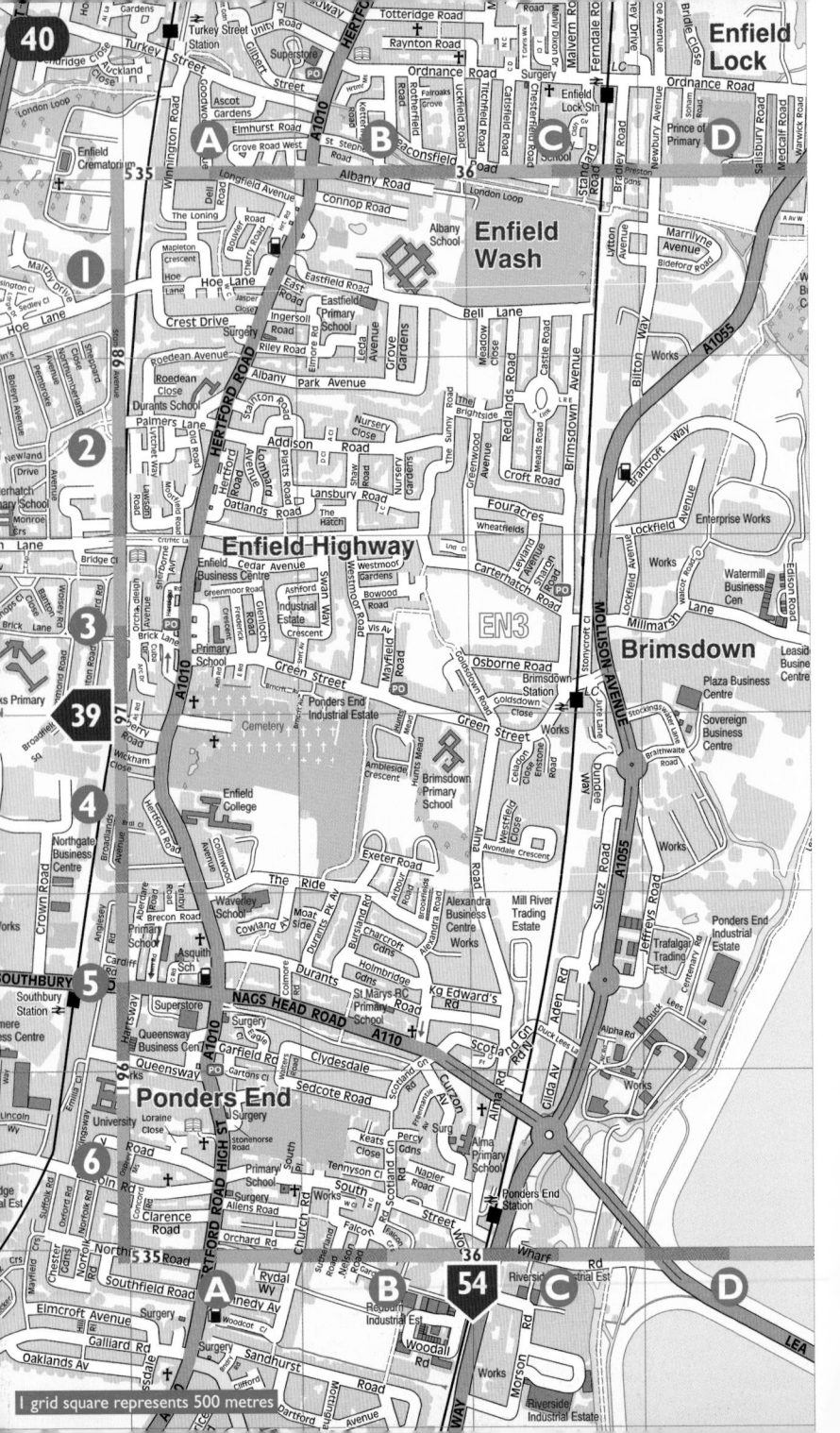

Sewardstone

Gilwell Park

King George's Reservoir

Lee Valley Campsite

Hawkswood School & Centre

Yardley Primary School

Essex County Waltham Forest

SEWARDSTONE ROAD A112

Hawes Lane

Butlers Drive

Godwin Close

London Loop

Daws Hill

Gilwell Lane

Mill Lane

Mott Street

Bury Road

Farm La

Hornbeam Lane

Woodr

Golf

West E Golf Cl

Harston Drive

Meadcroft Crescent

Crompton Pl

Brunswick Rd

London Loop

Essex County

Enfield

Boardman Av

Antlers Hi

Yardley La

Yardley

Sewardstone Road

Gilwell Cl

River Lea or Lee

A112

Hawkwo

55

Hawkdene

Epping Way

Mark Av

Margaret

VALLEY ROAD

Epping Gld

Forest View

Lond op

Golf Course

S

37 38 39

98

97

96

E F G H

I
2
3
4
5
6

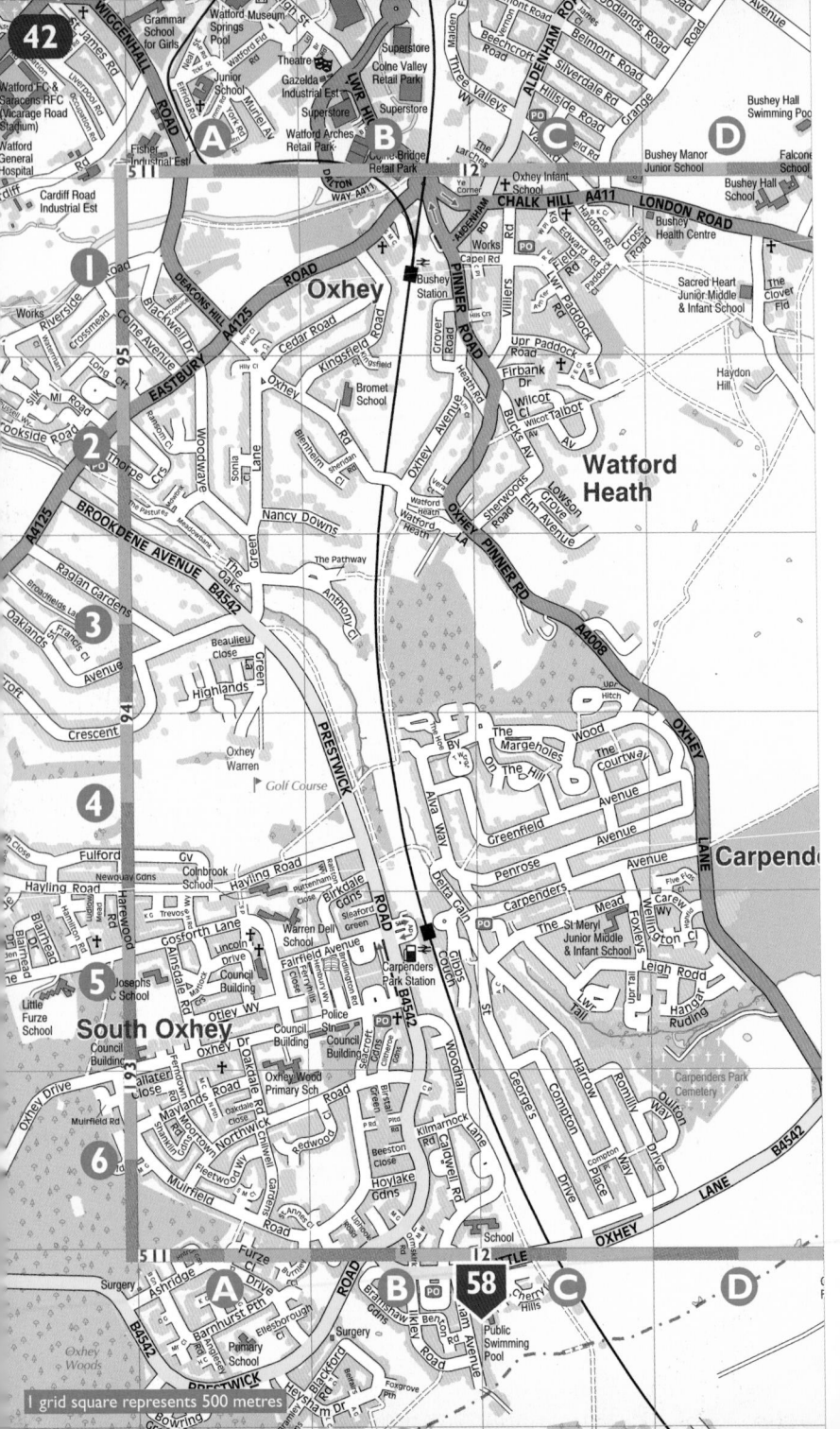

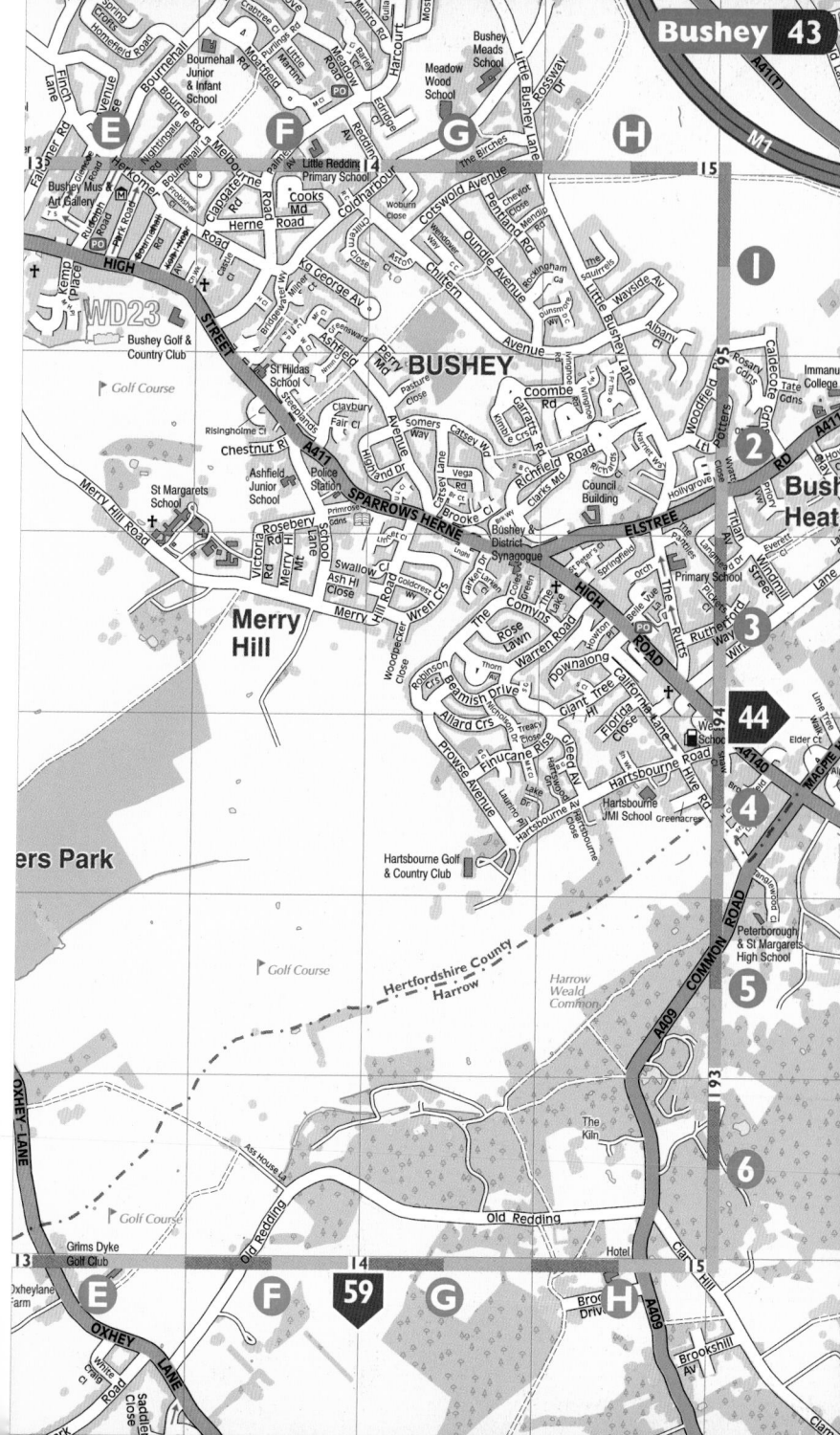

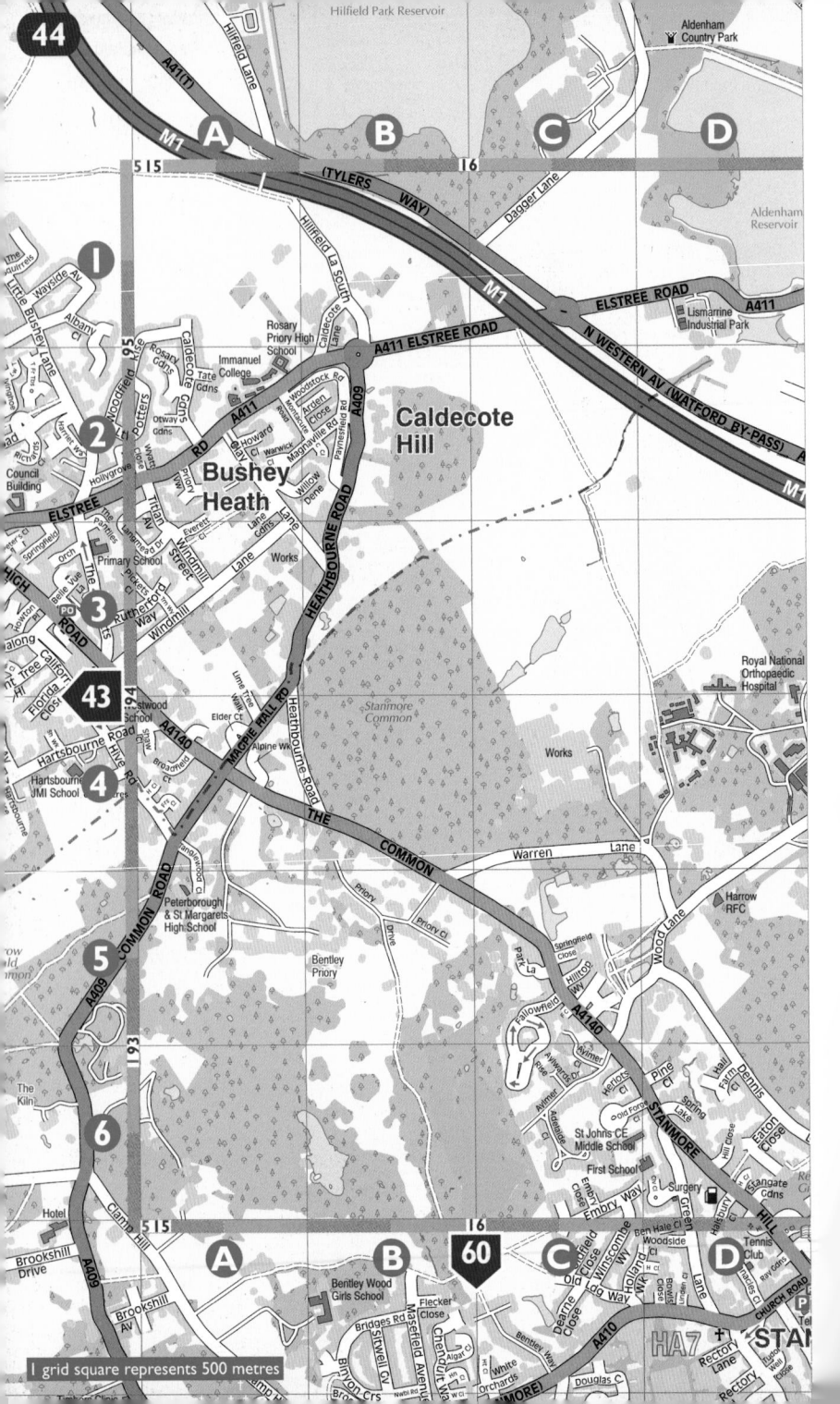

I grid square represents 500 metres

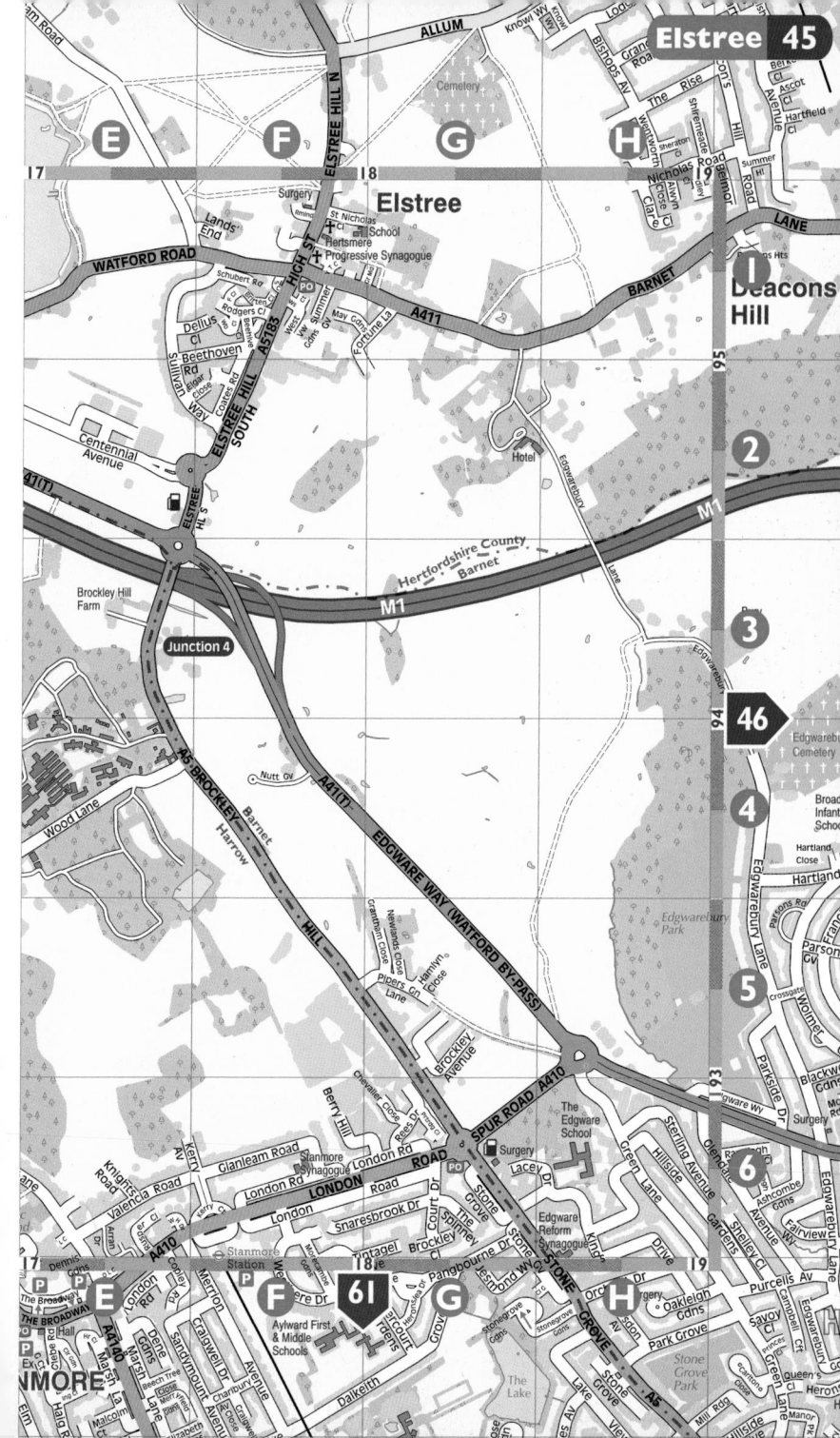

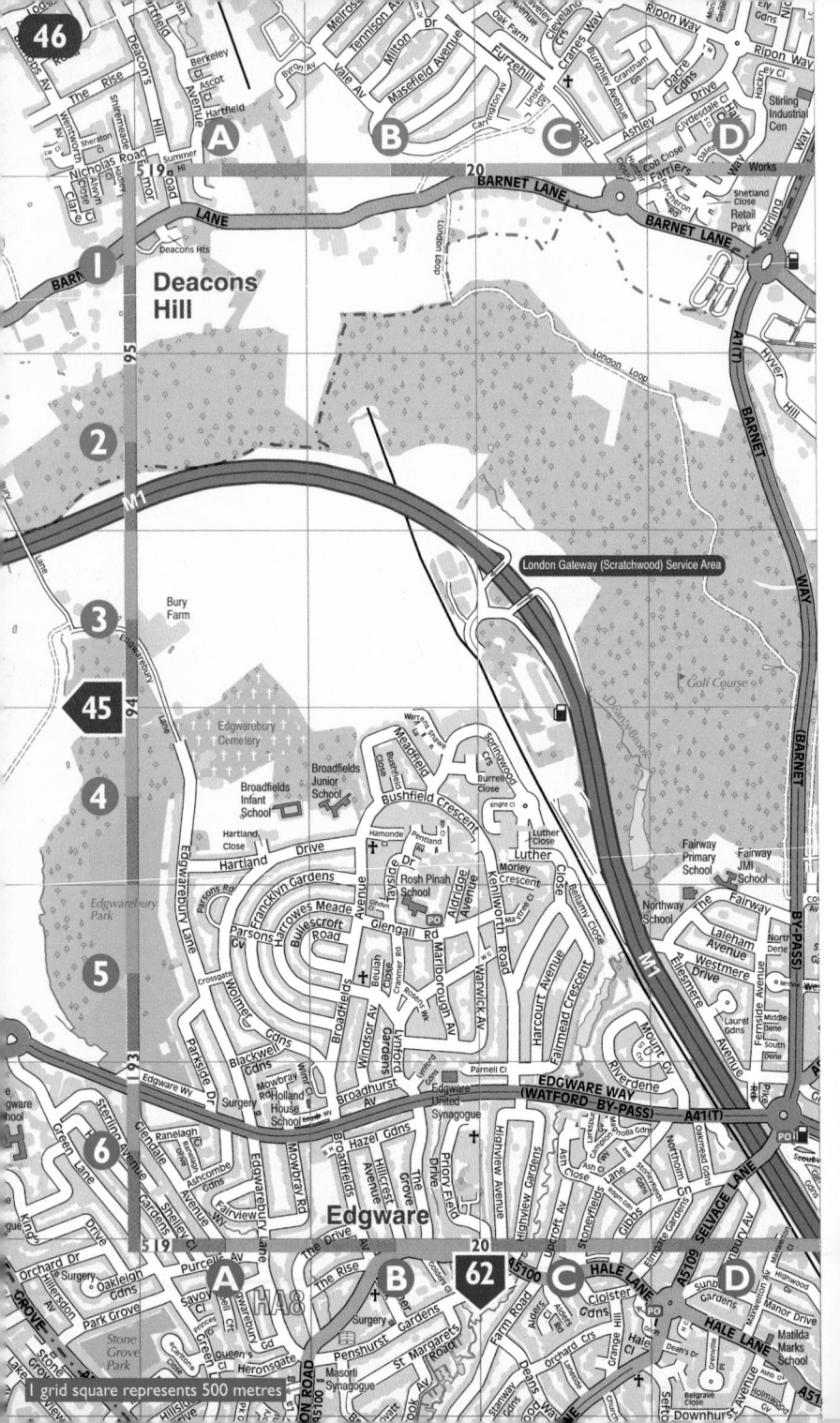

1 grid square represents 500 metres

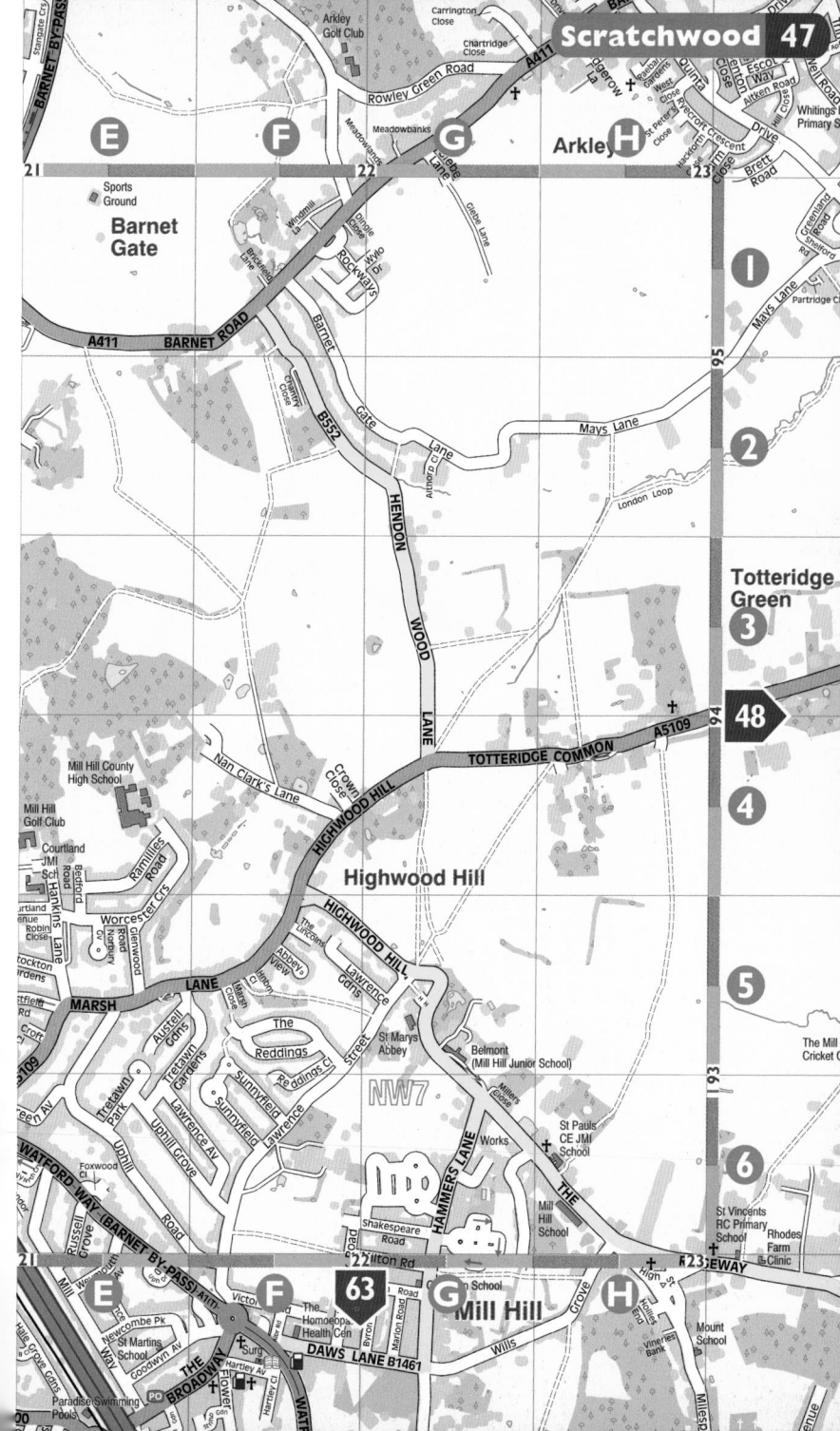

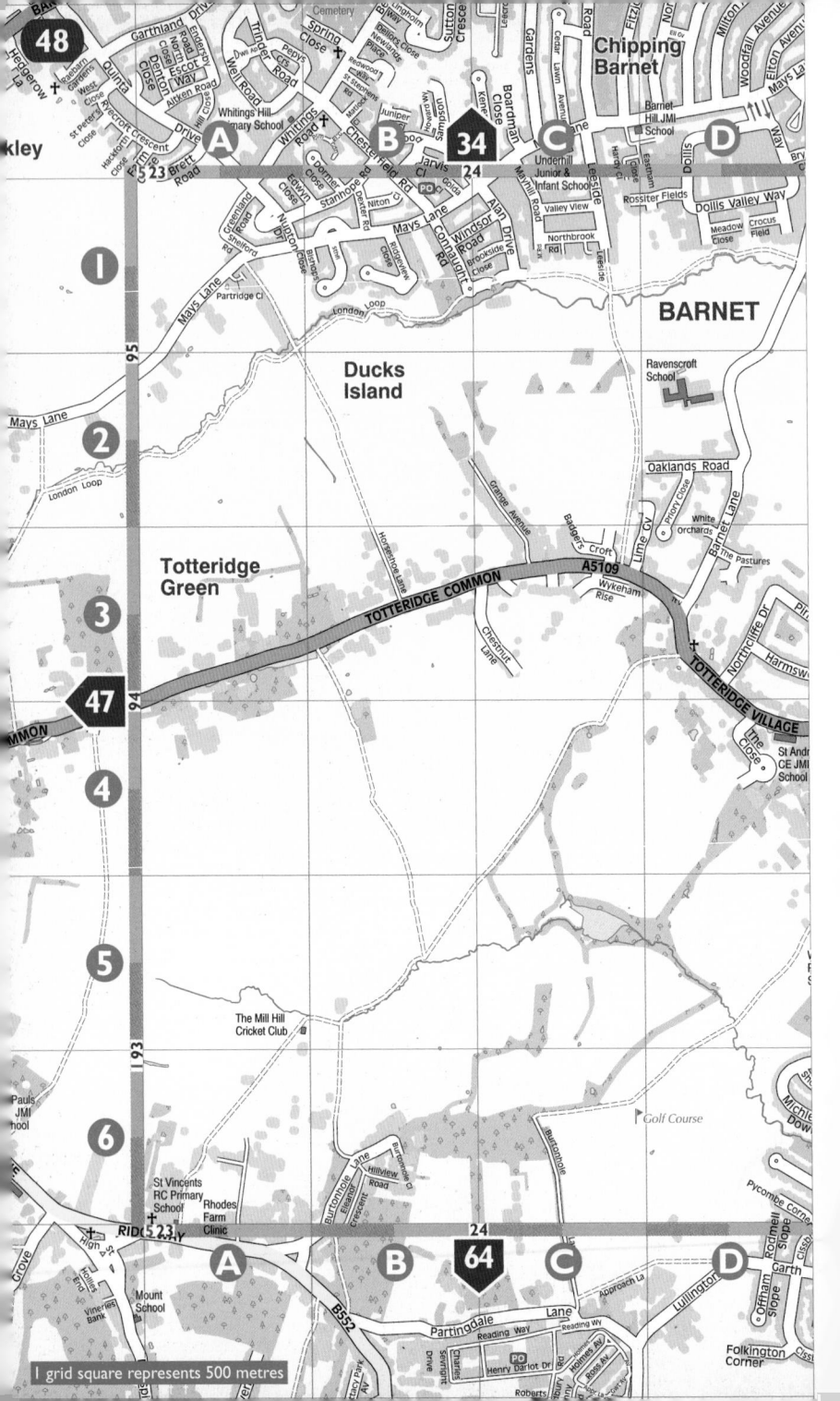

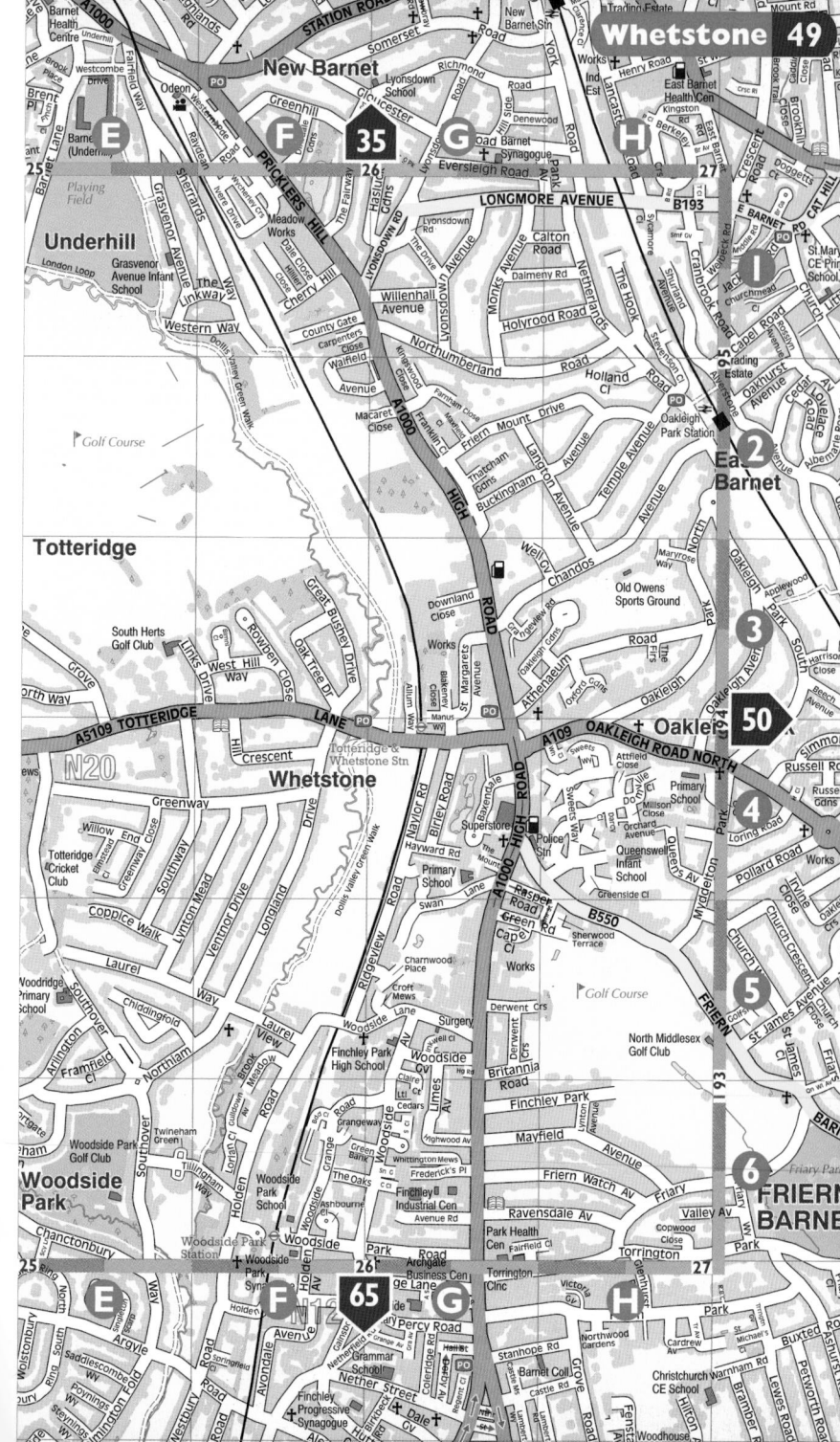

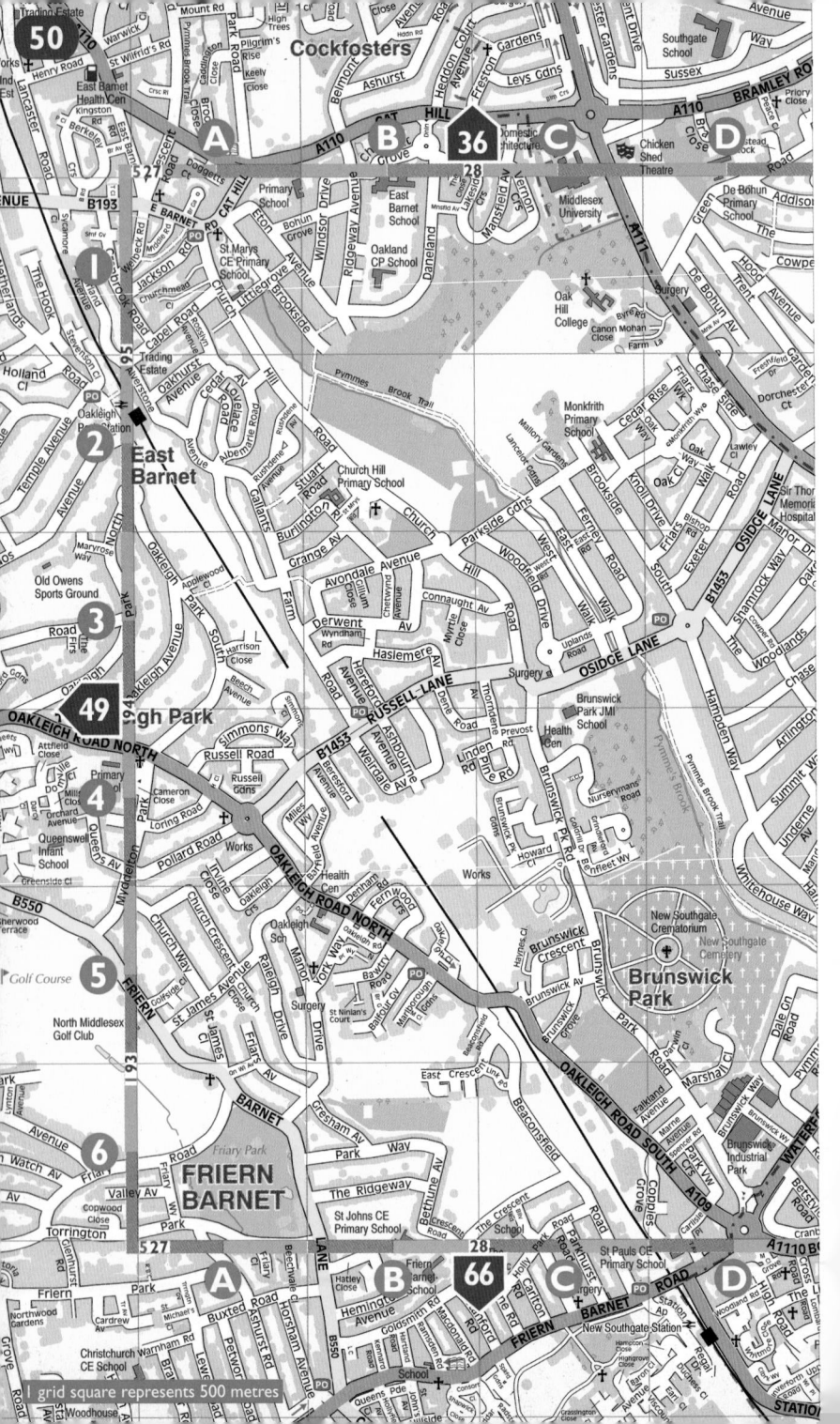

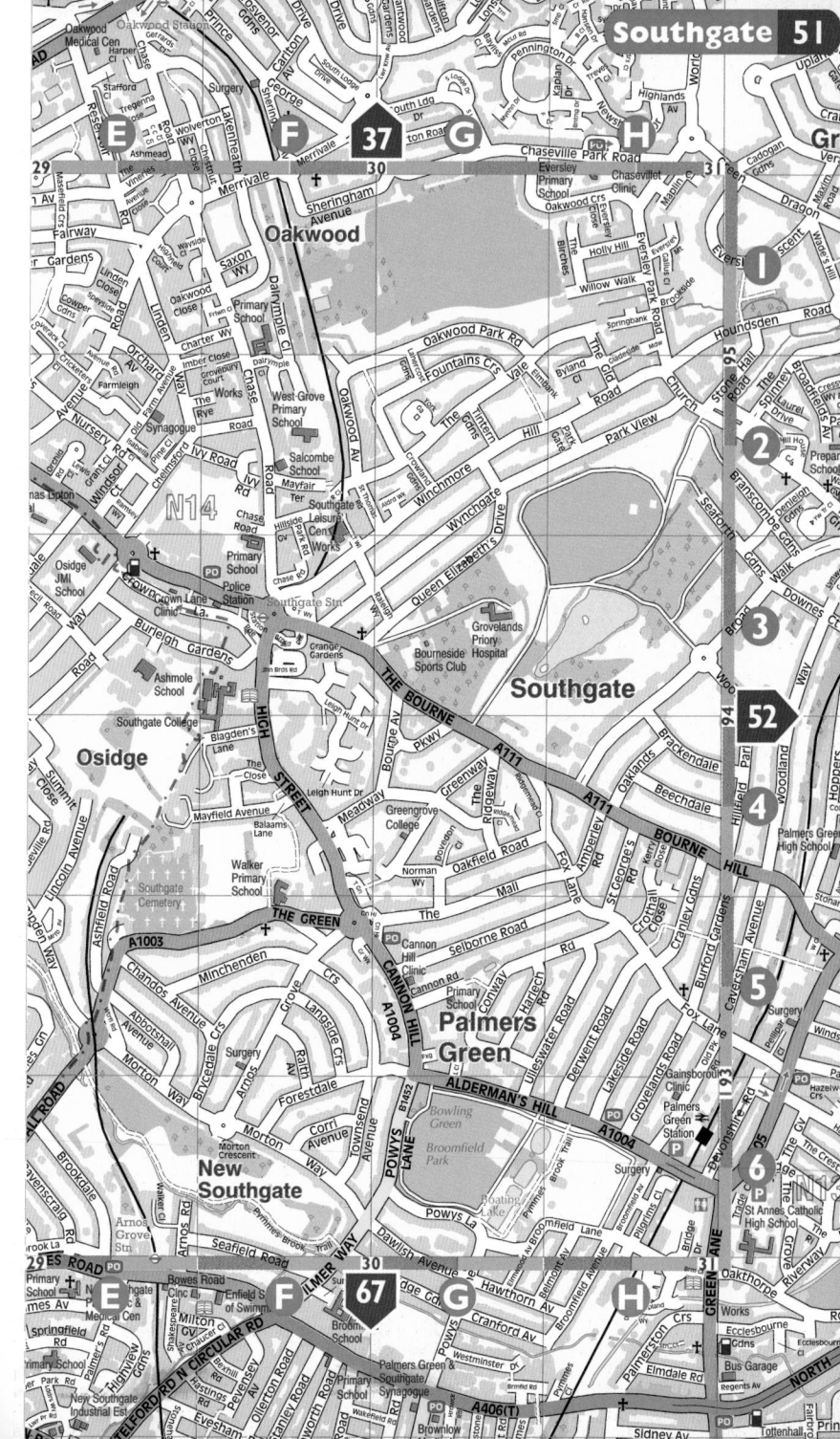

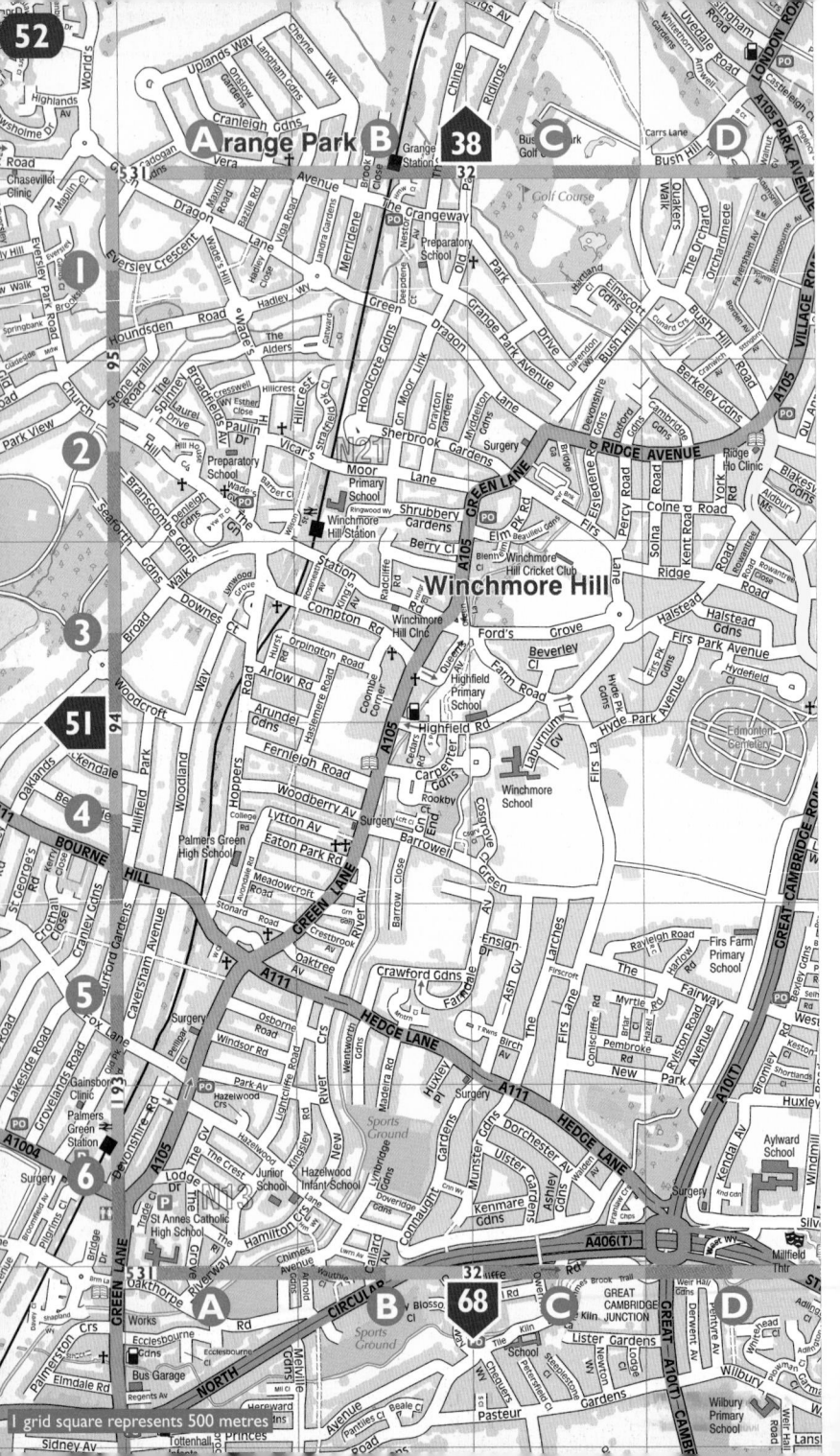

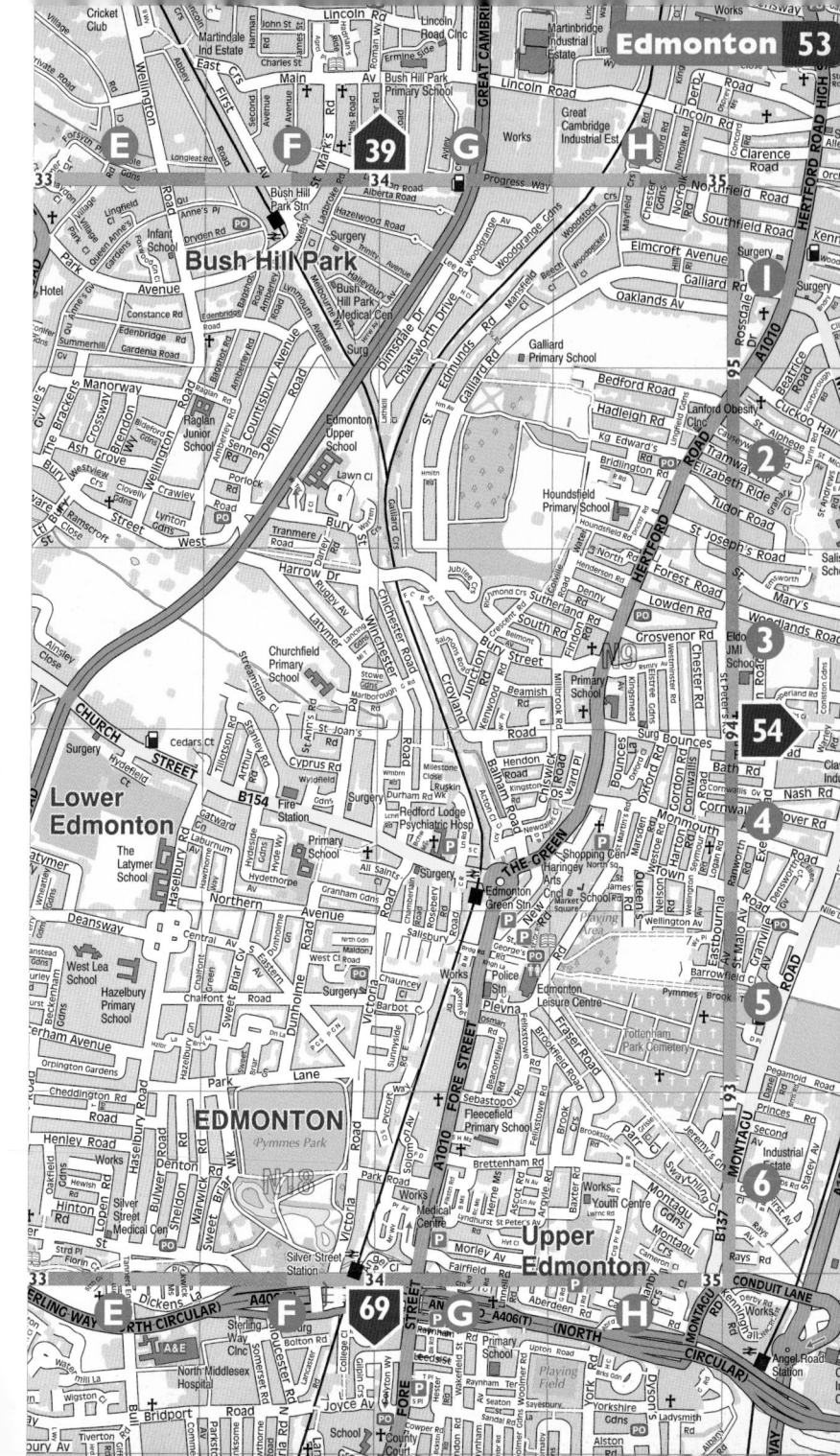

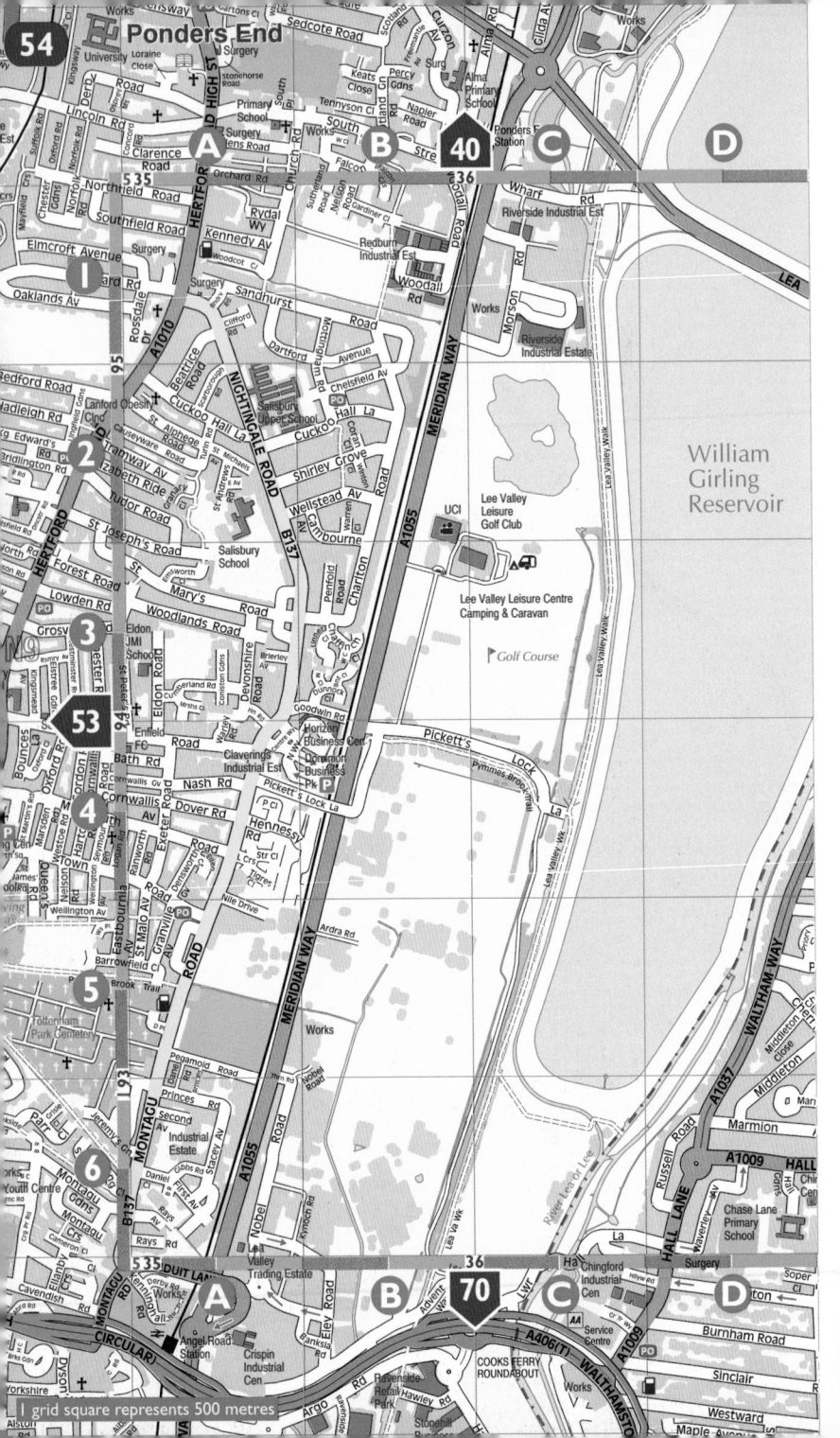

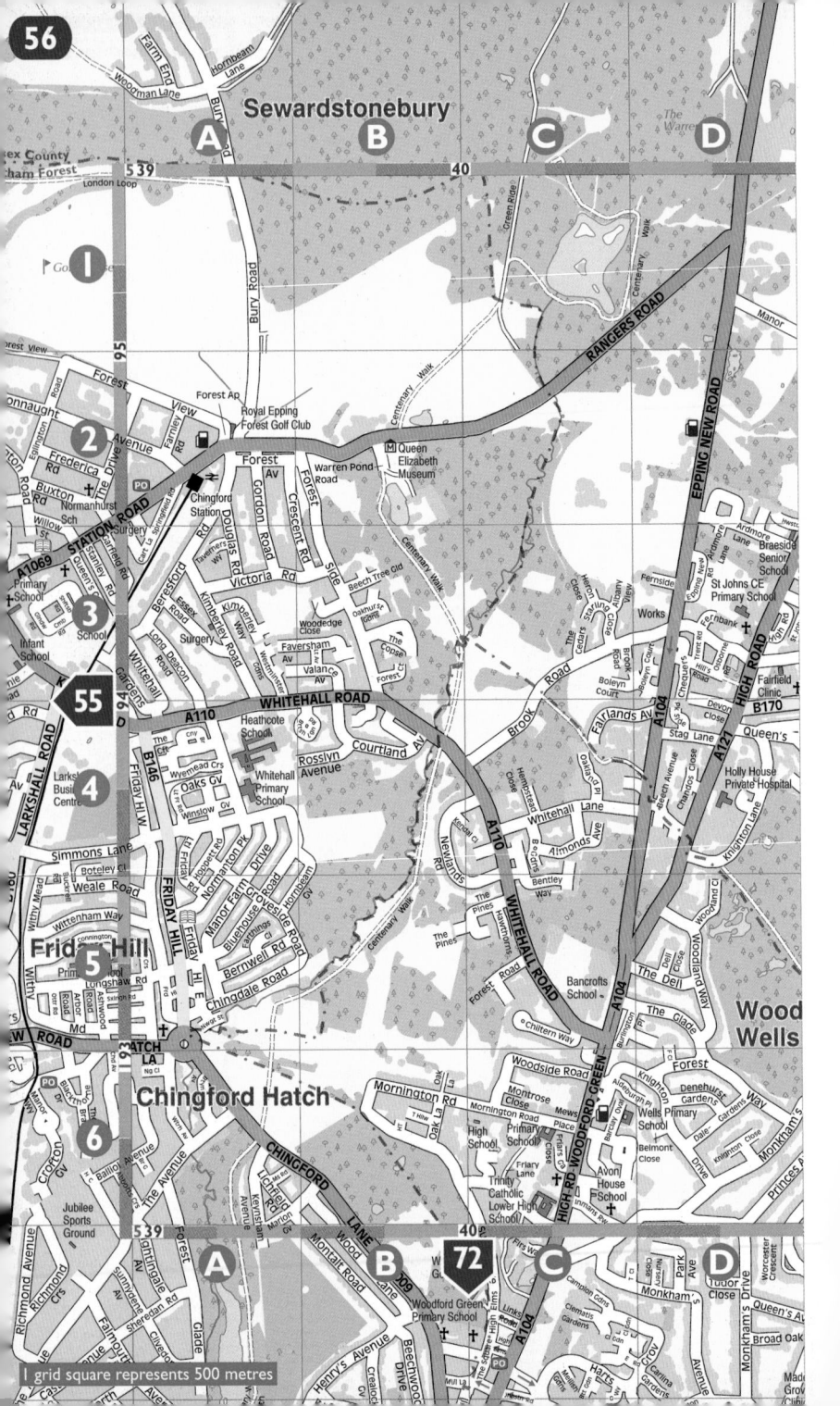

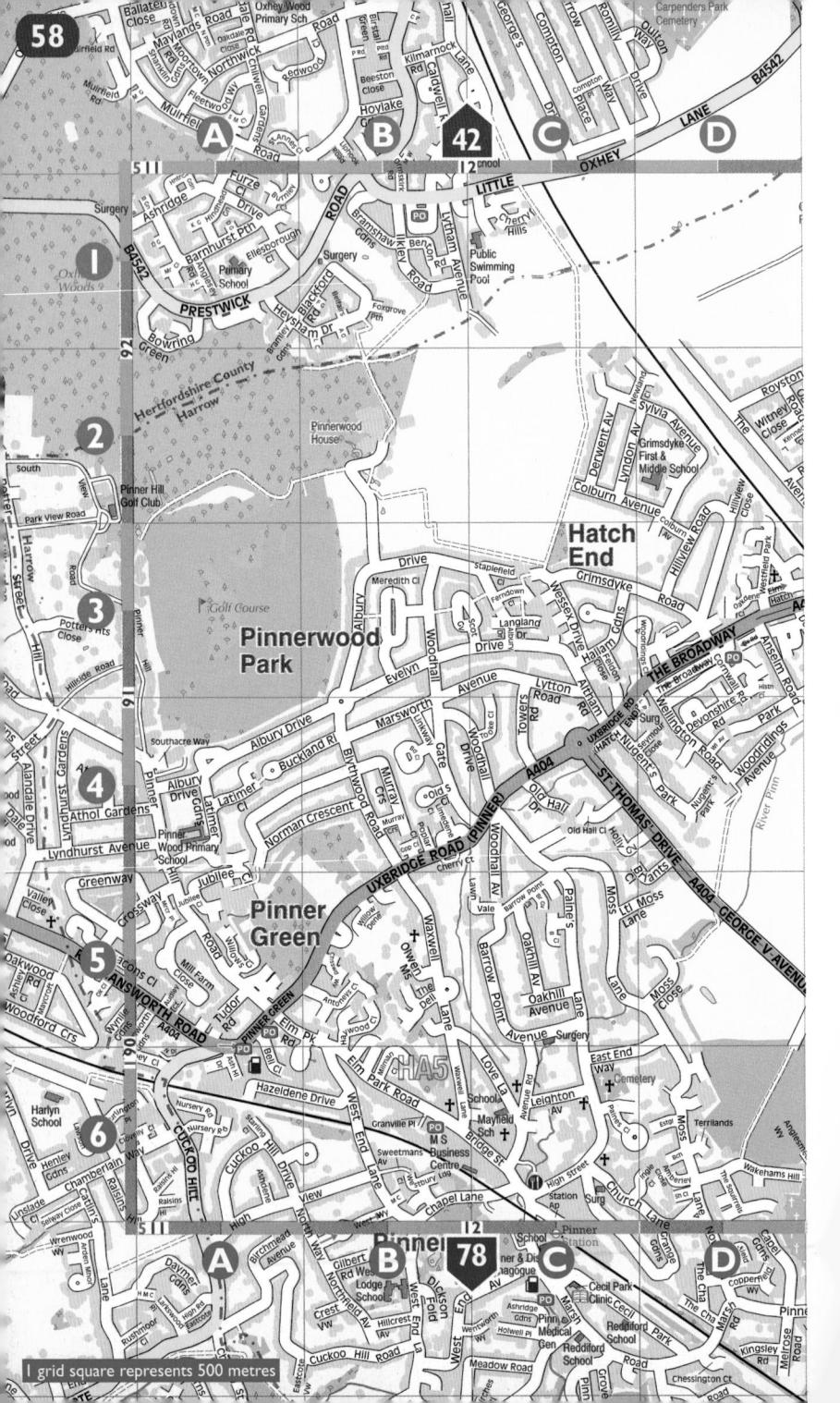

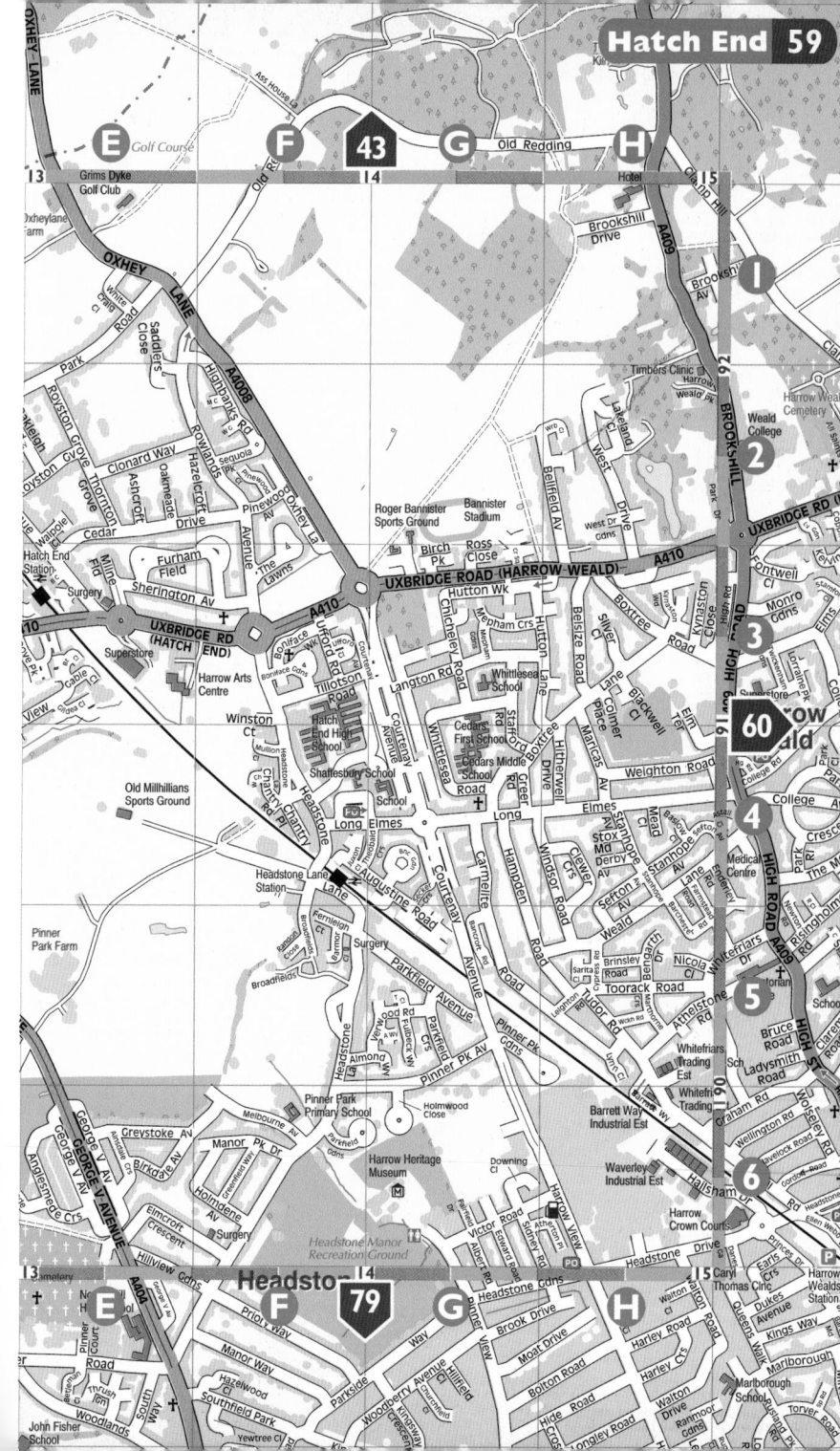

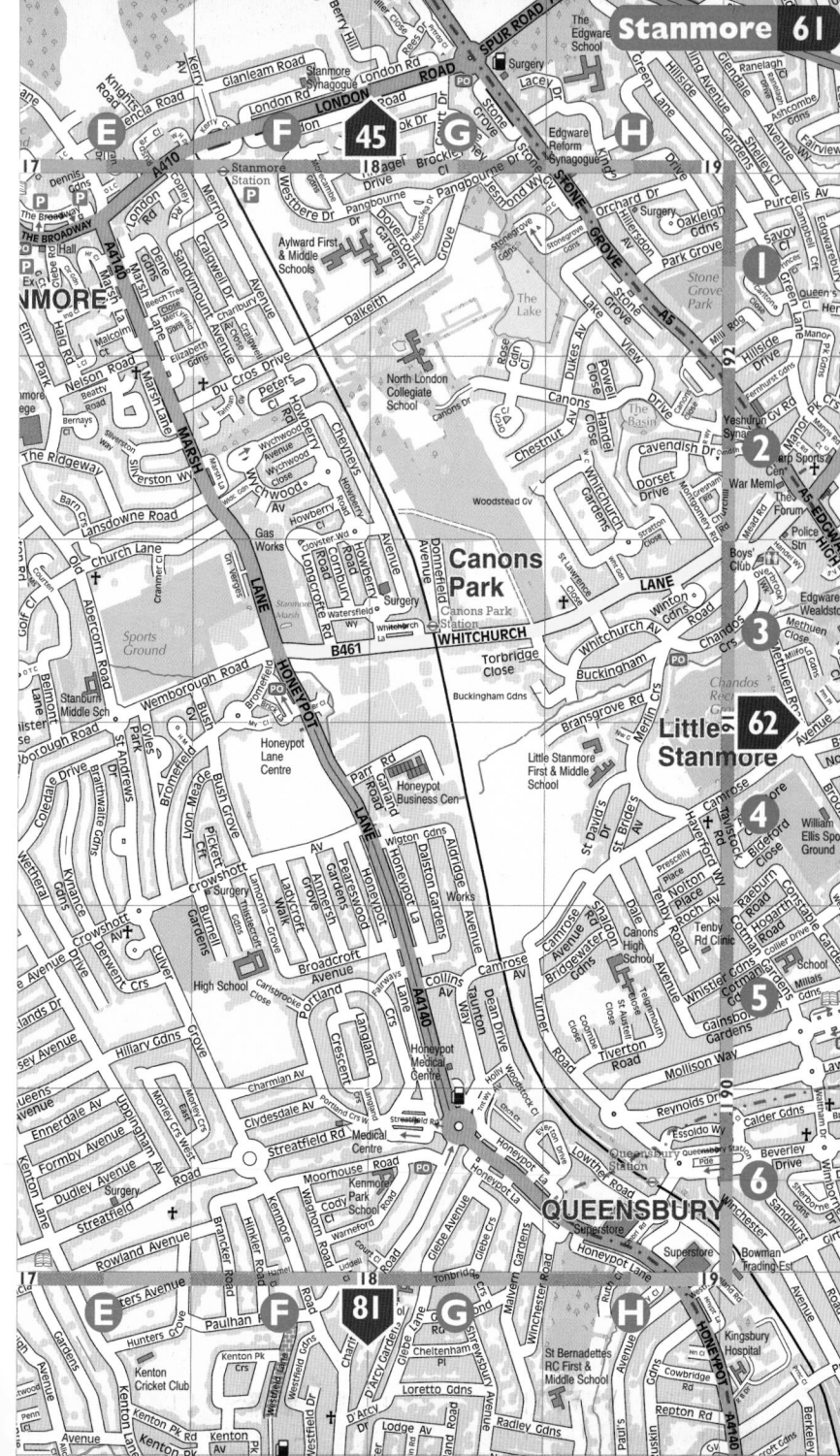

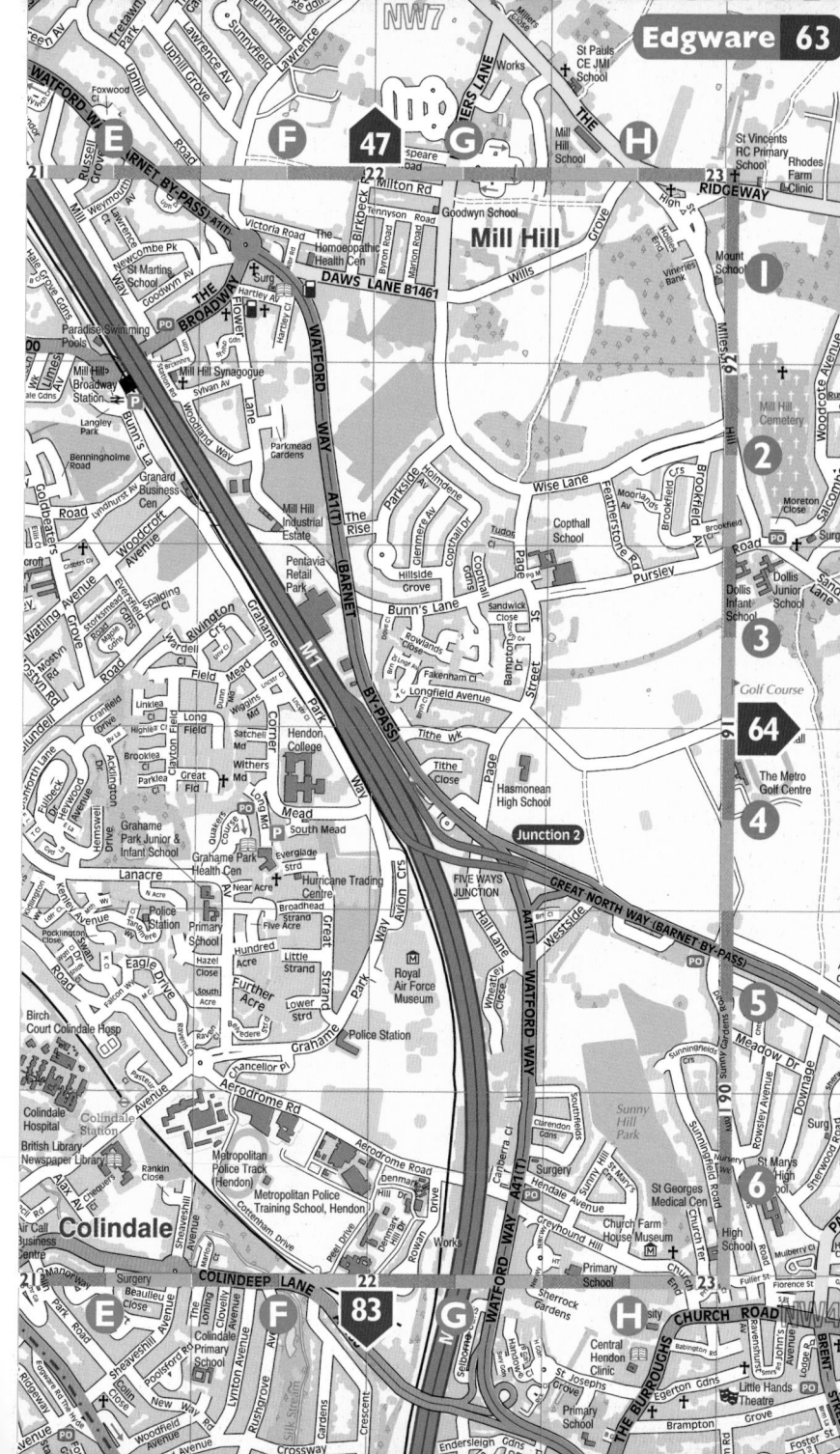

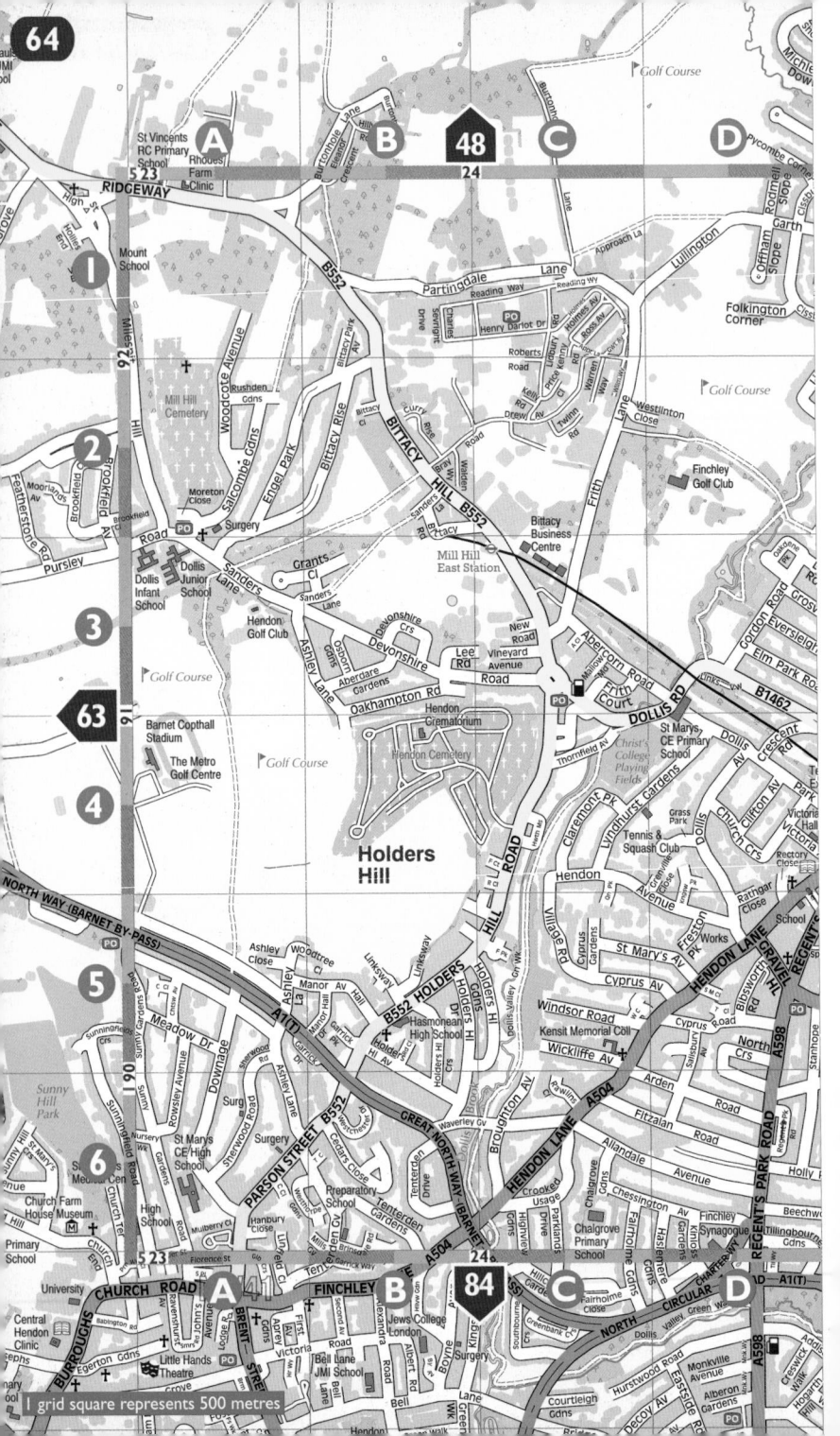

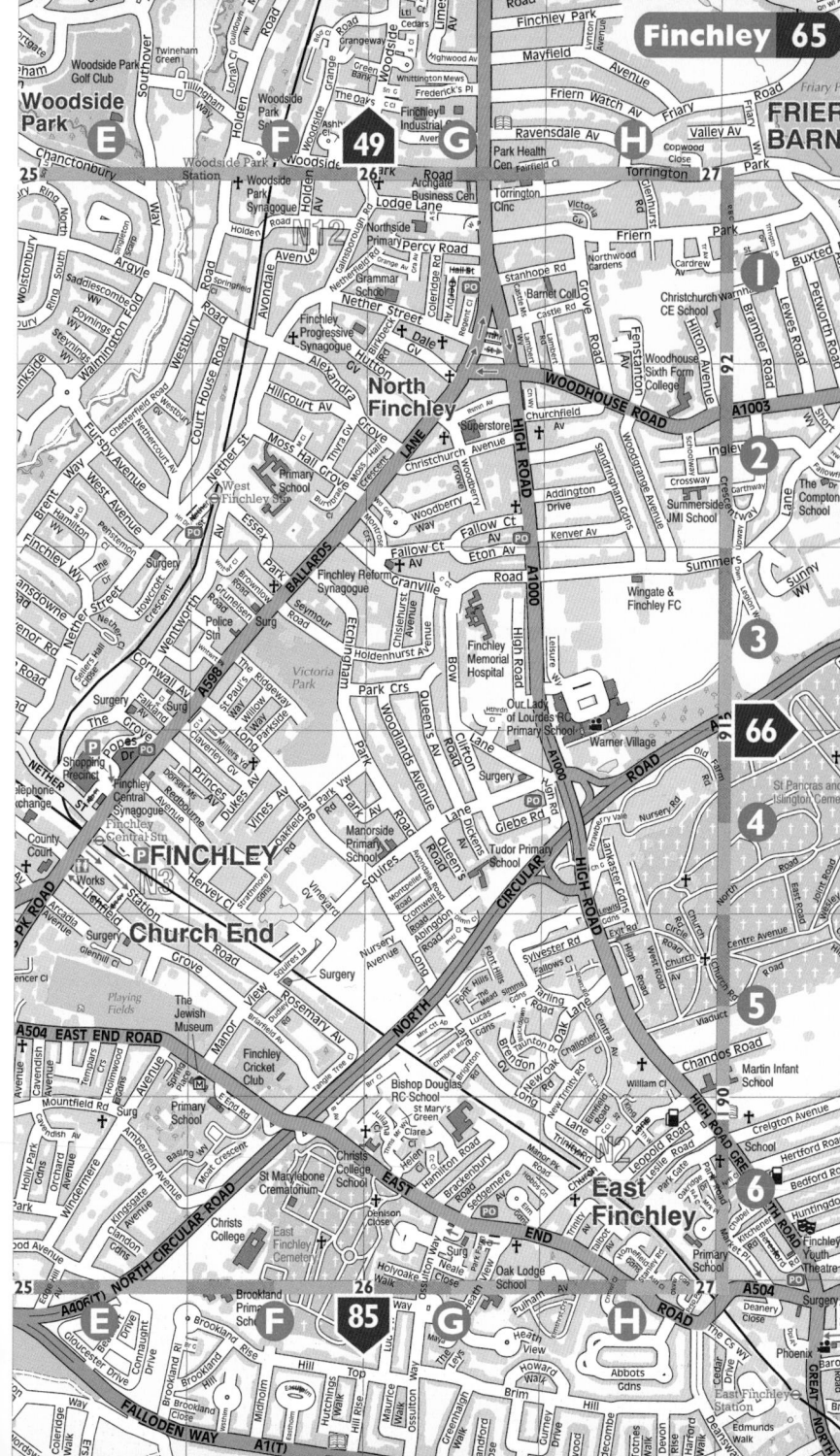

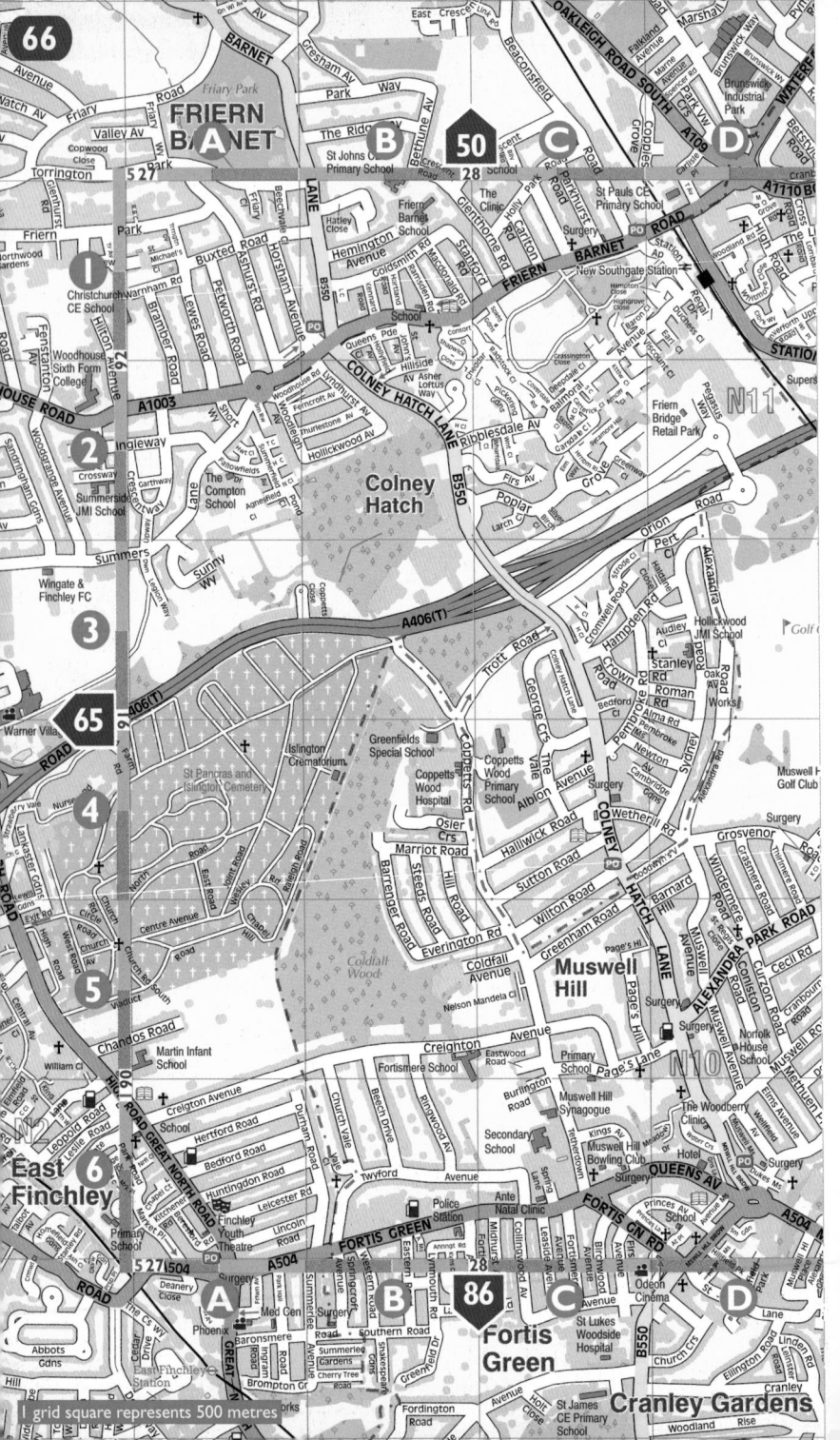

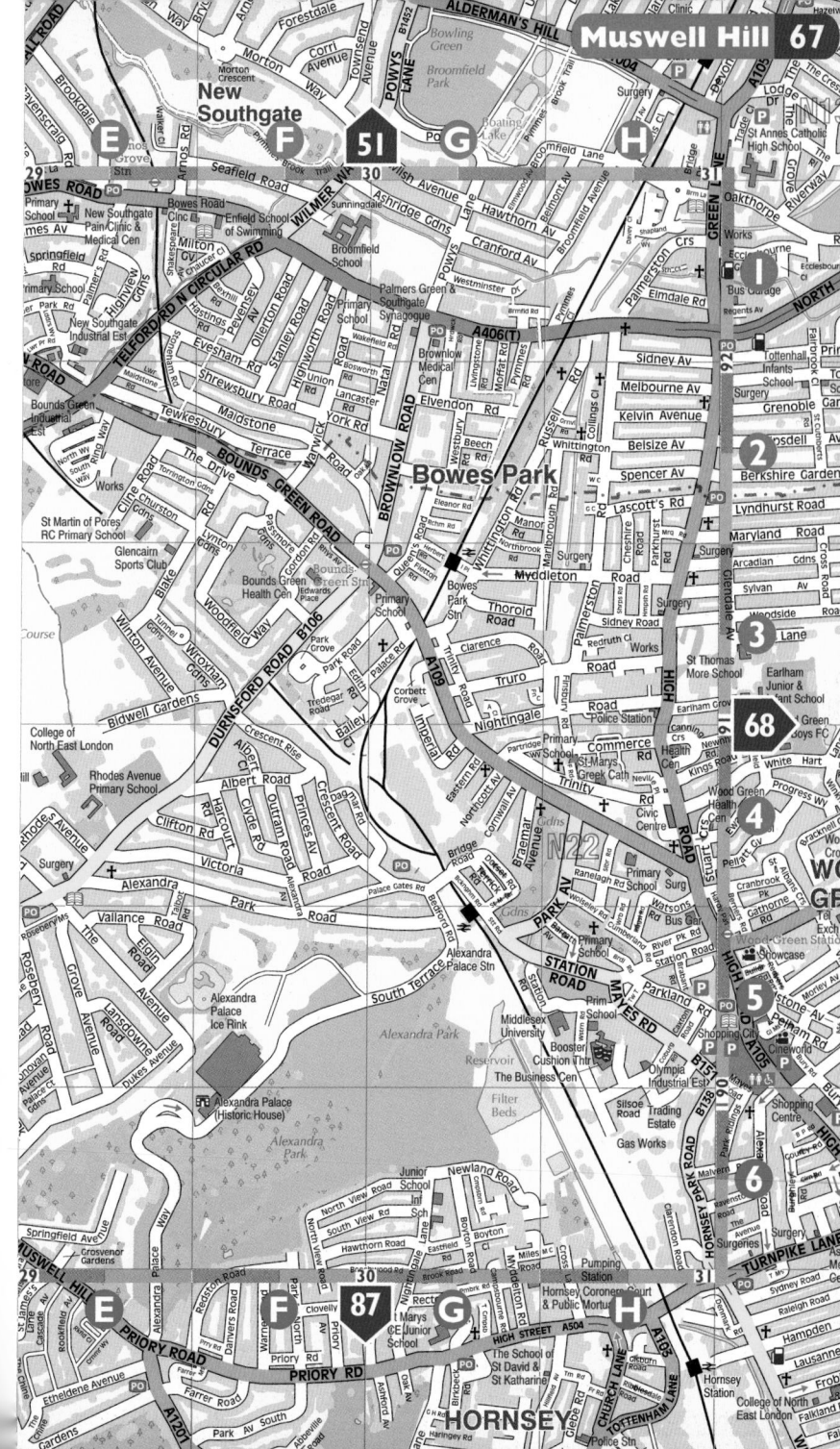

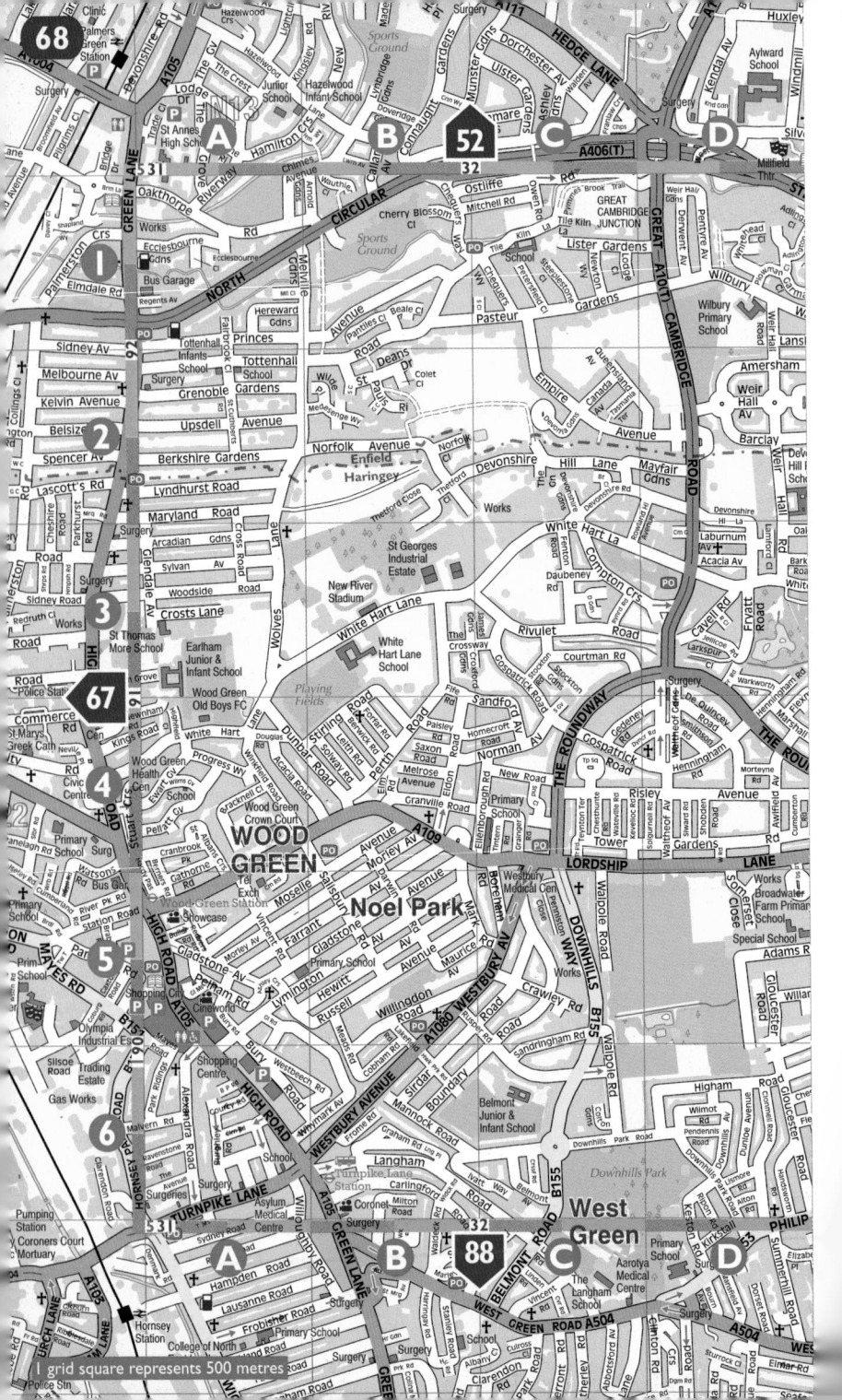

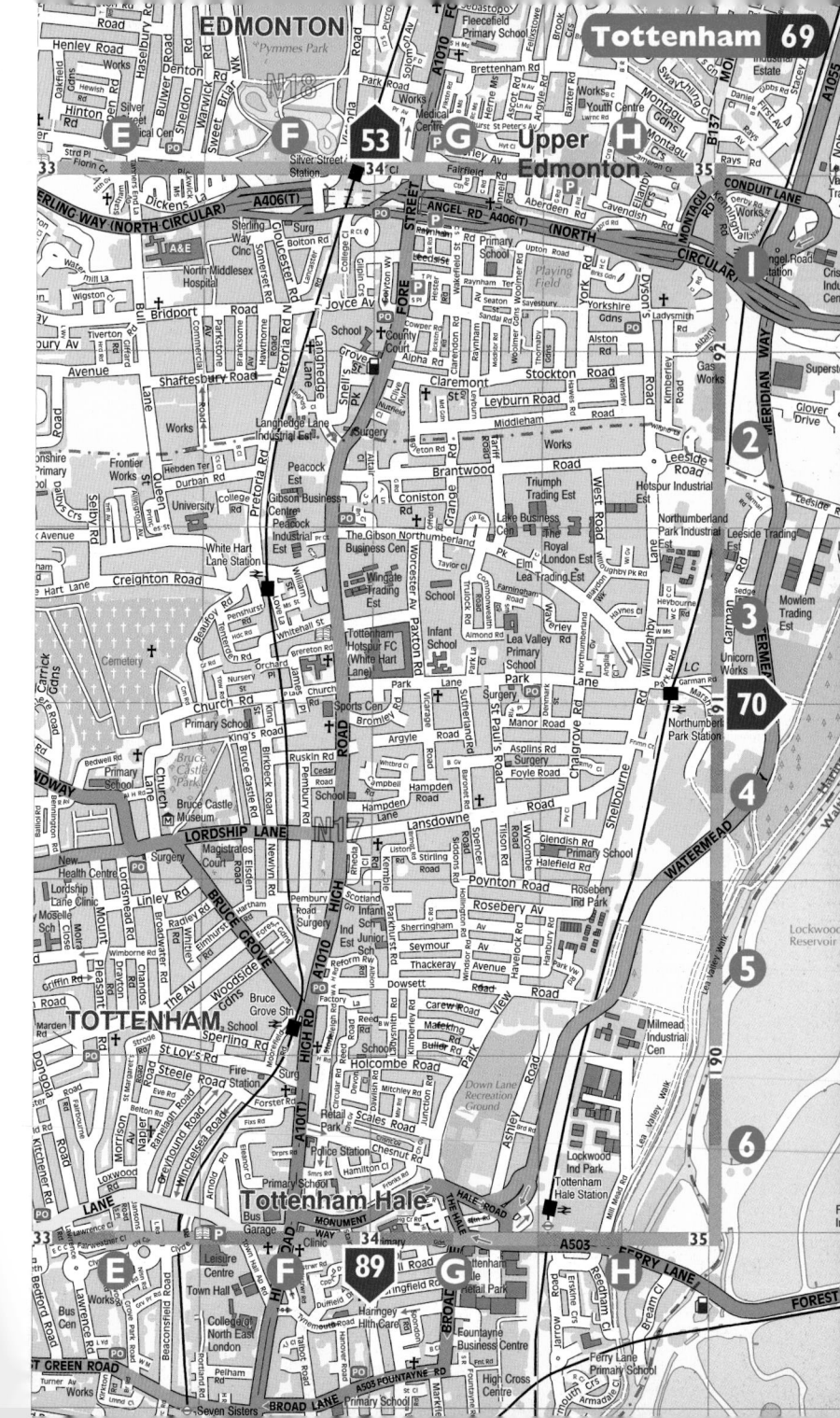

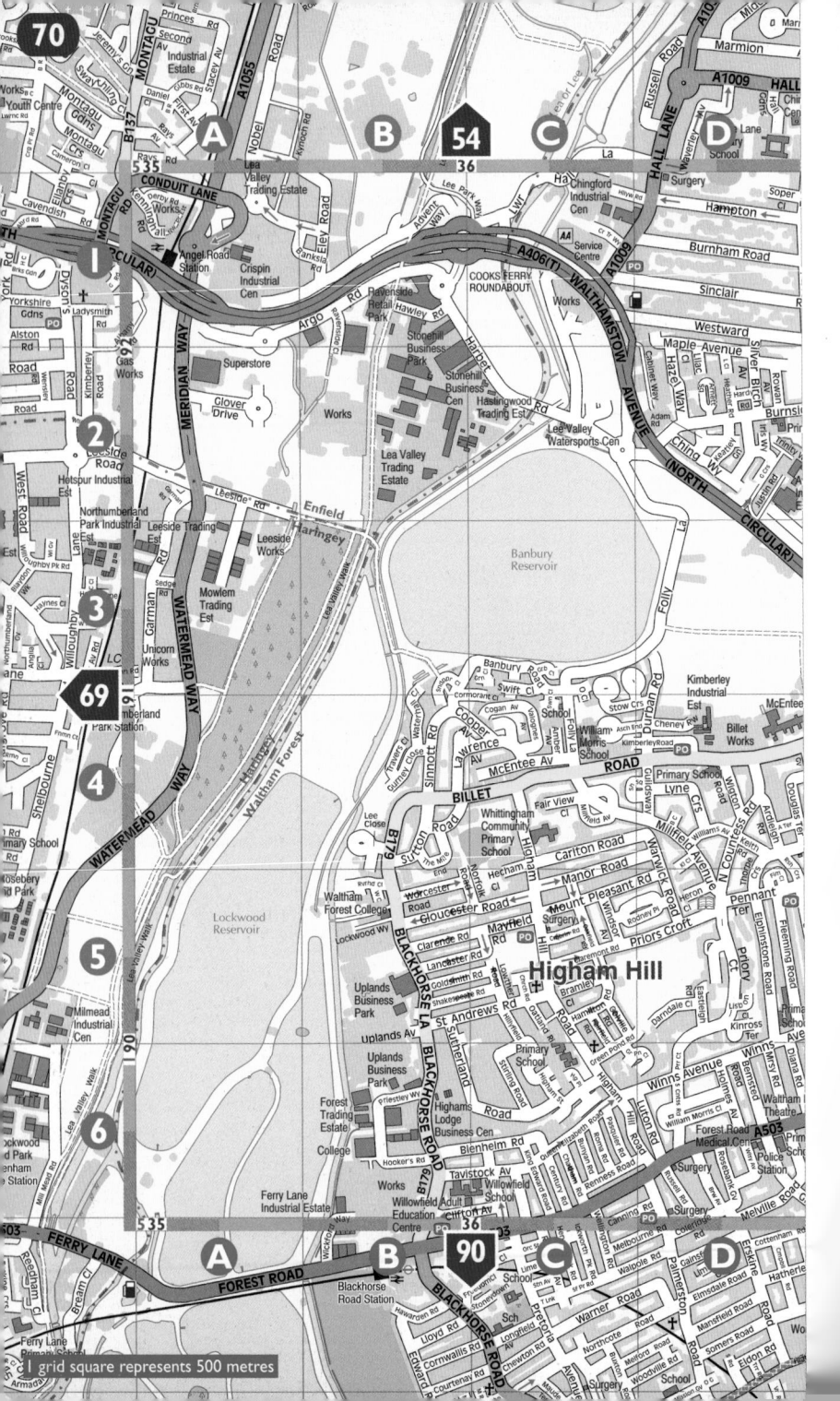

grid square represents 500 metres

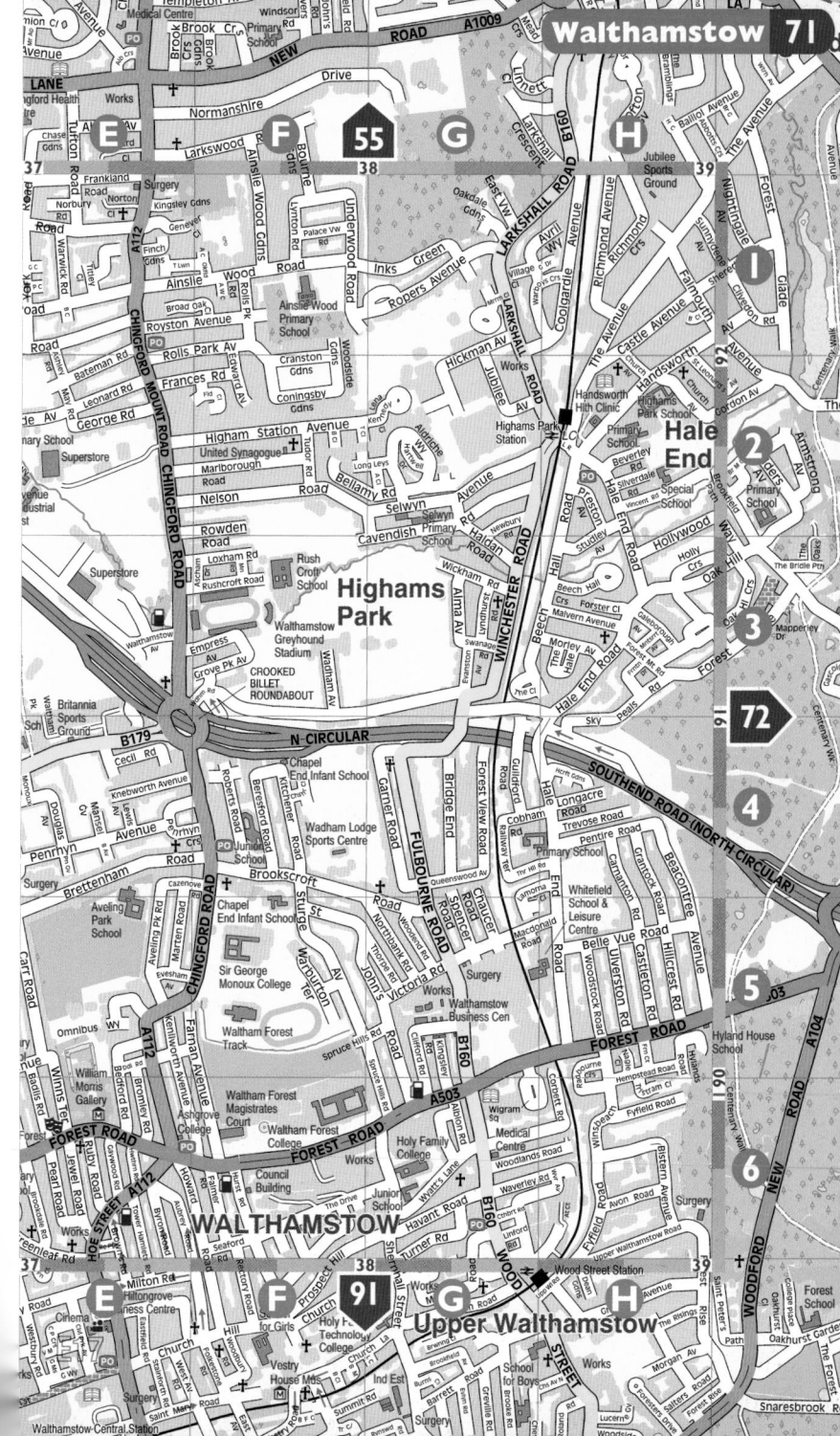

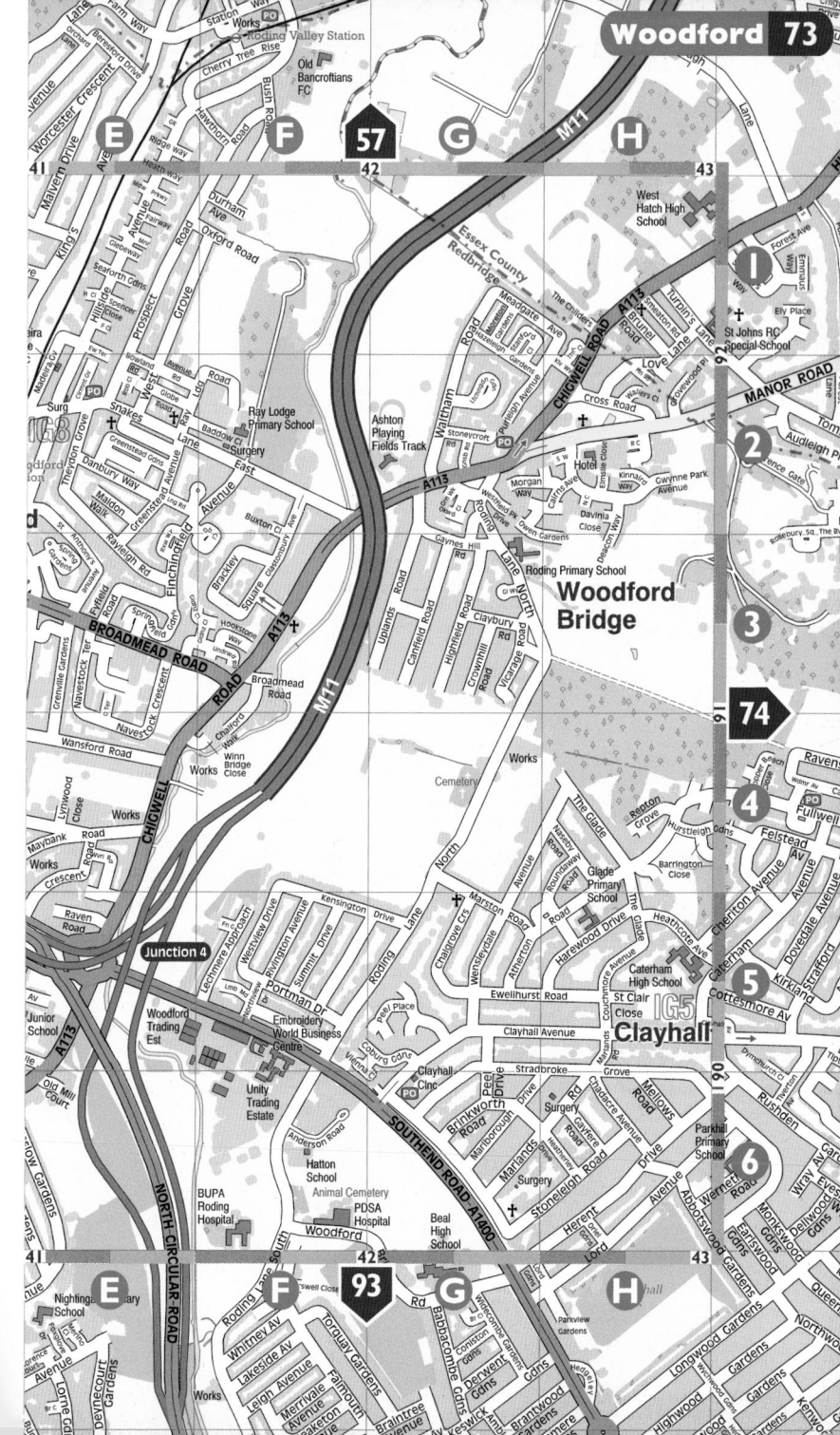

I grid square represents 500 metres

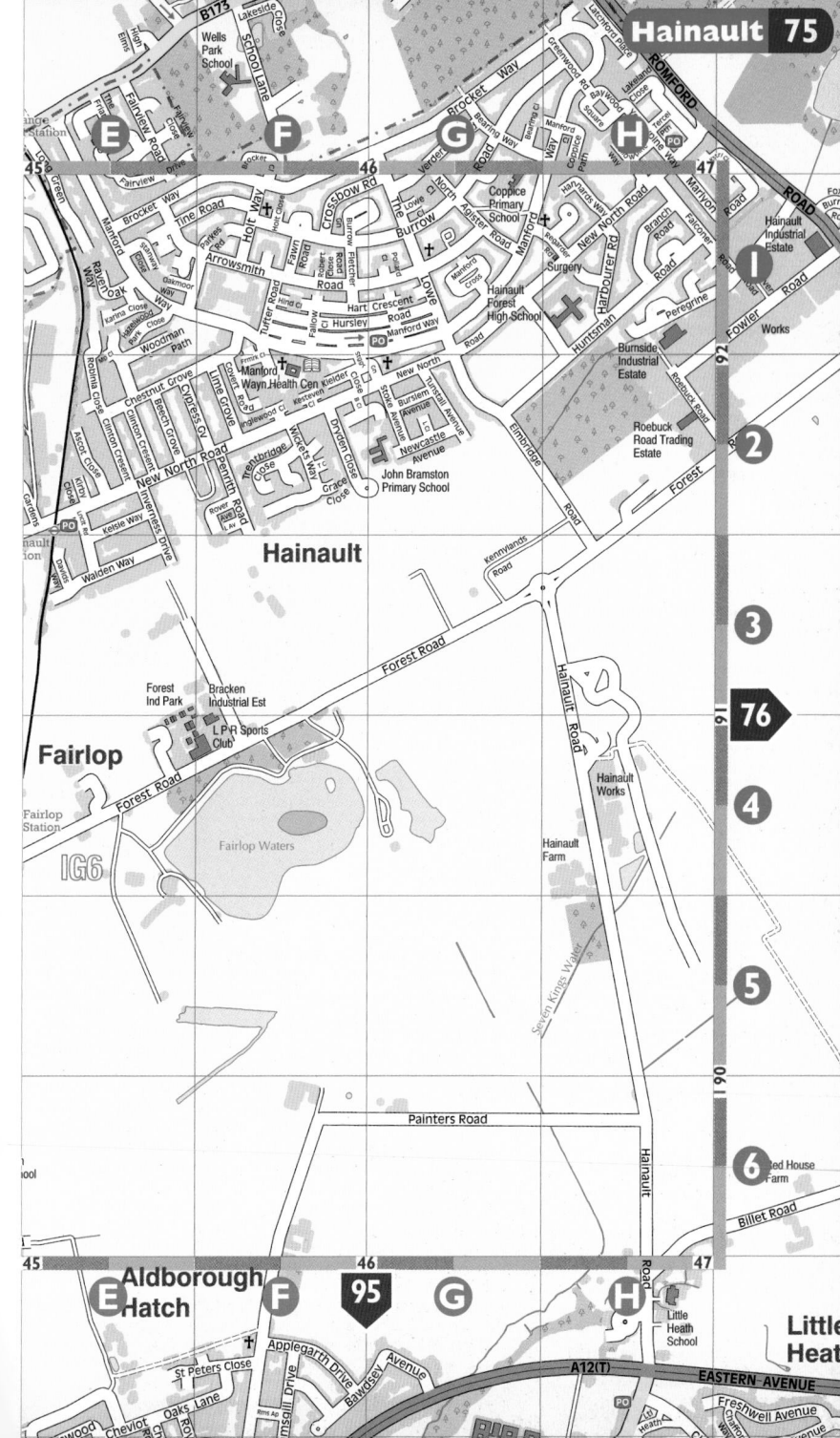

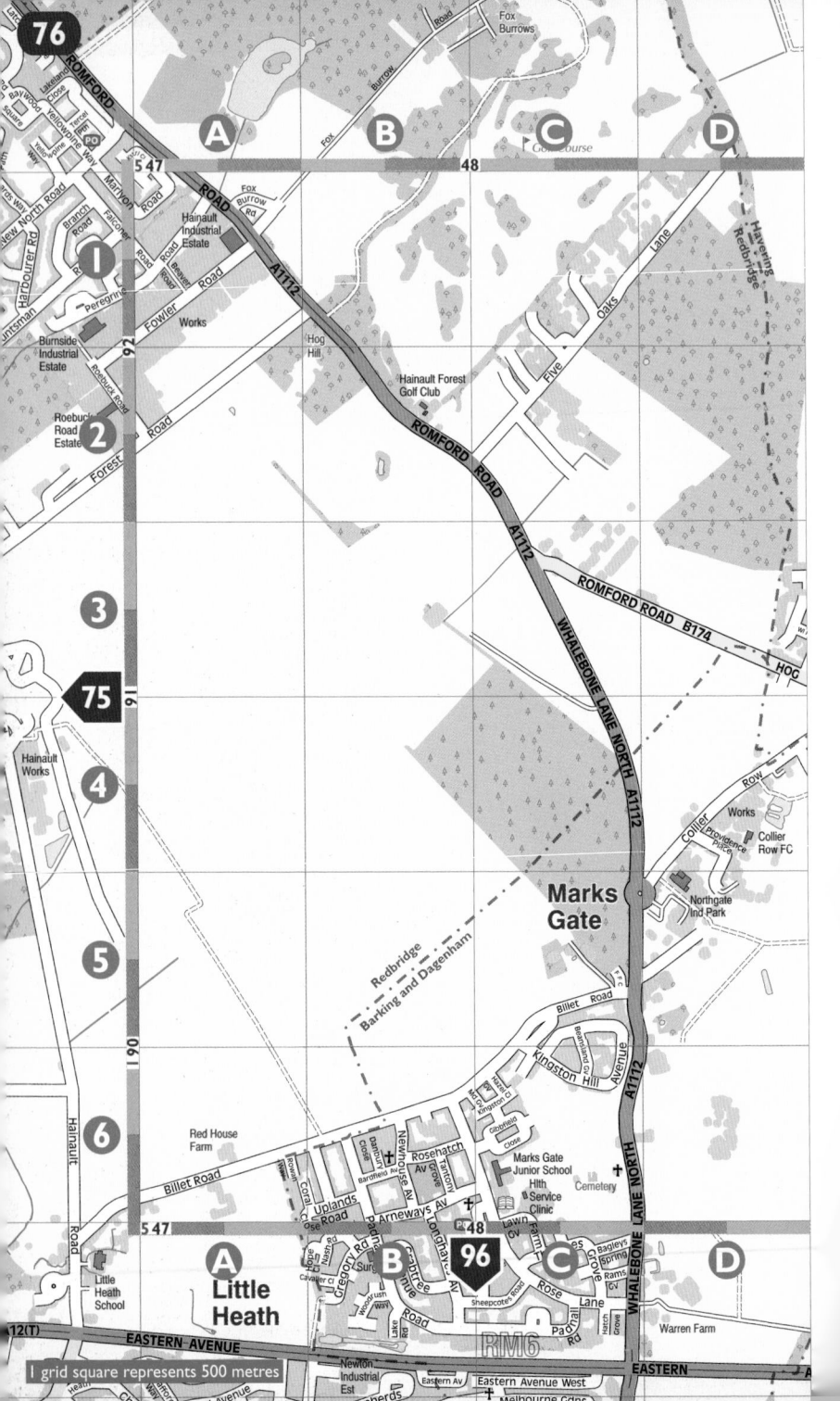

I grid square represents 500 metres

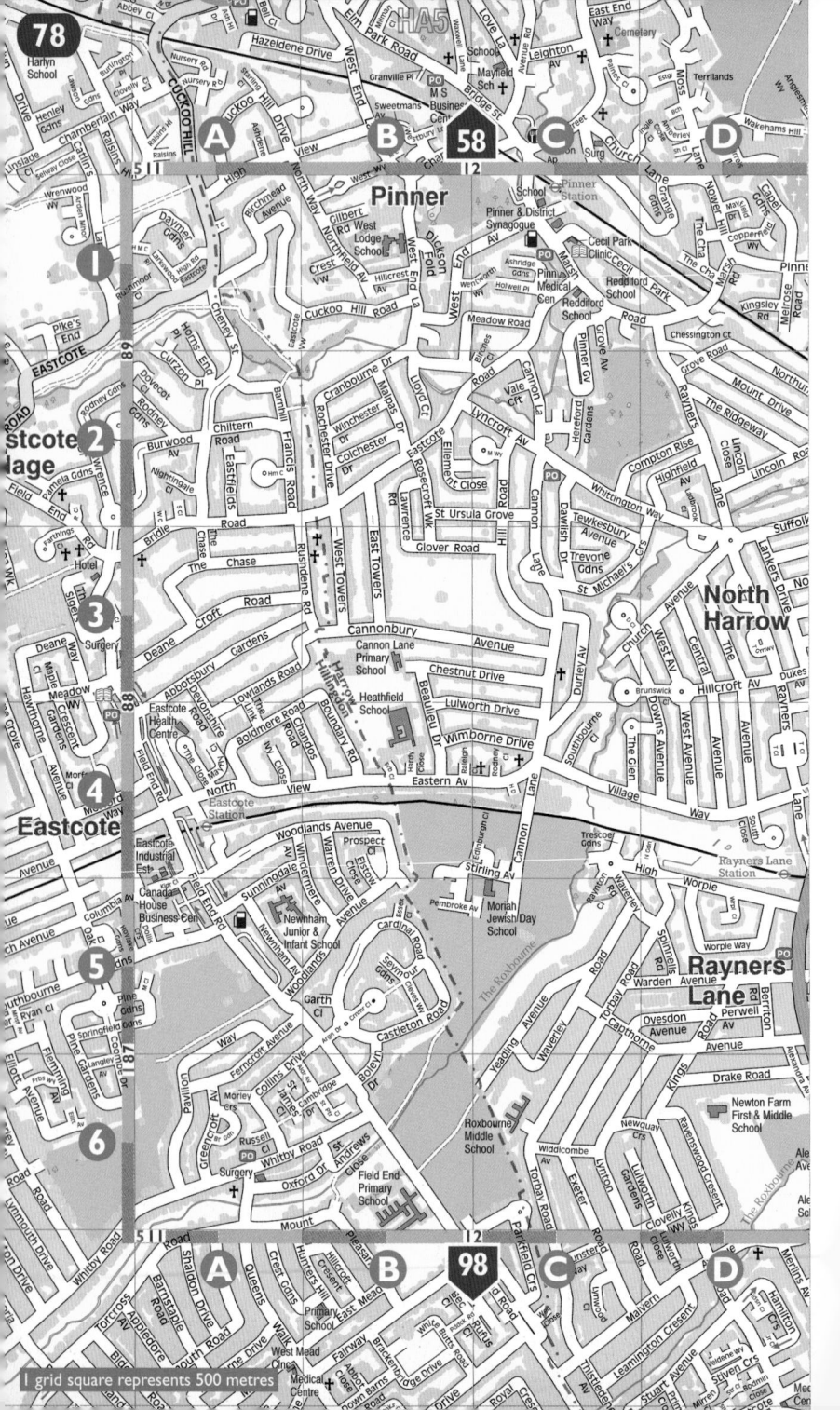

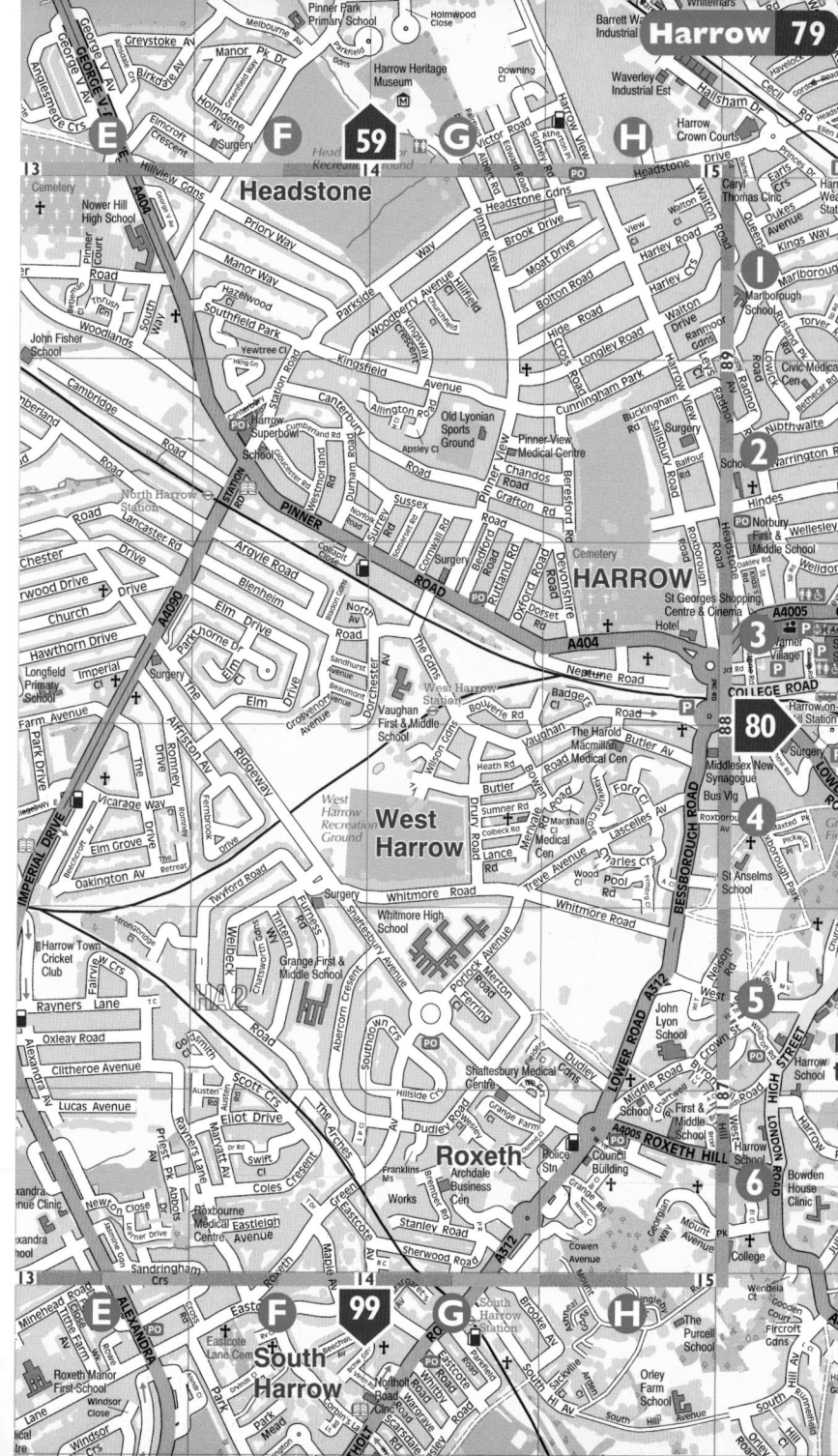

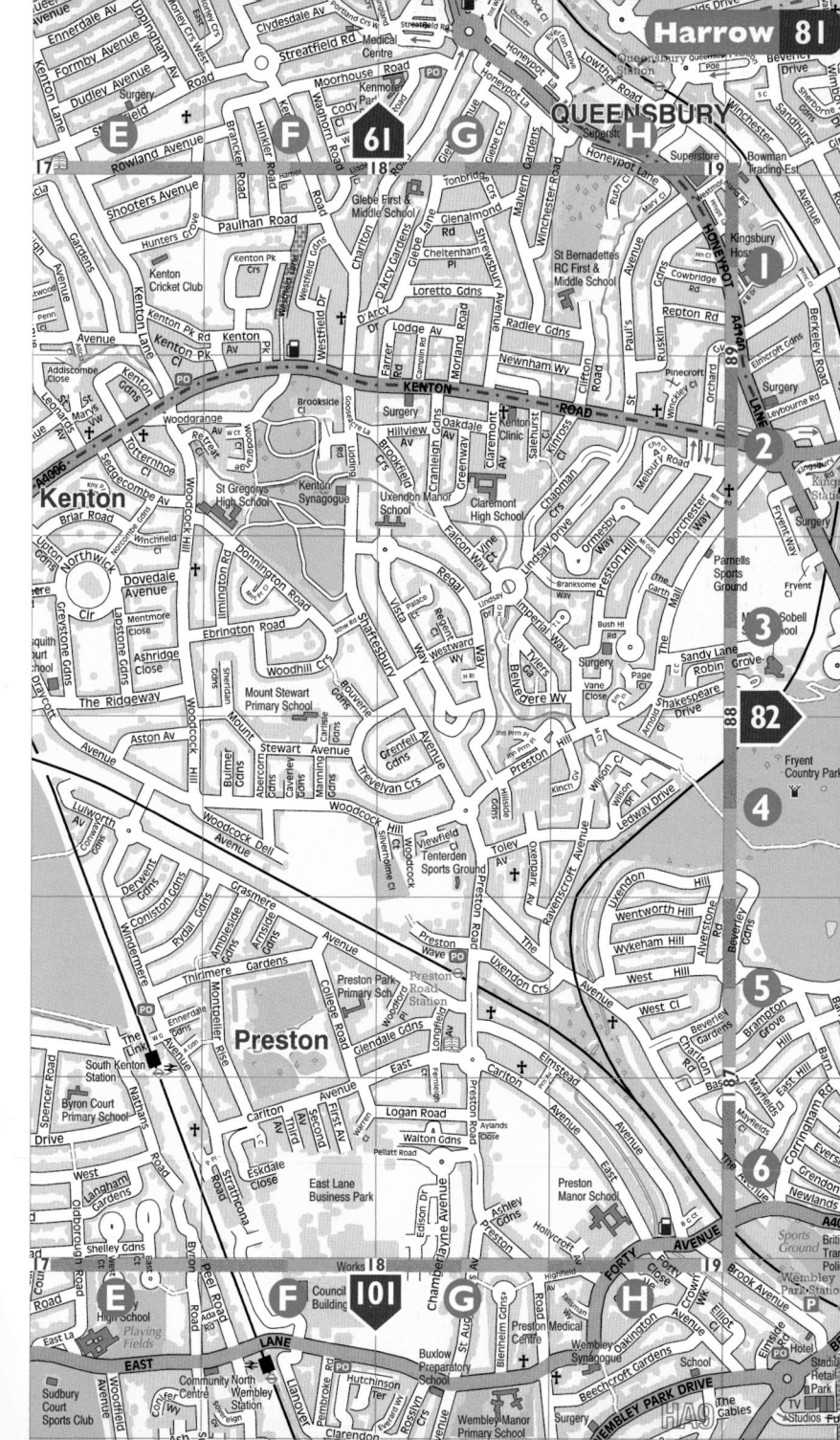

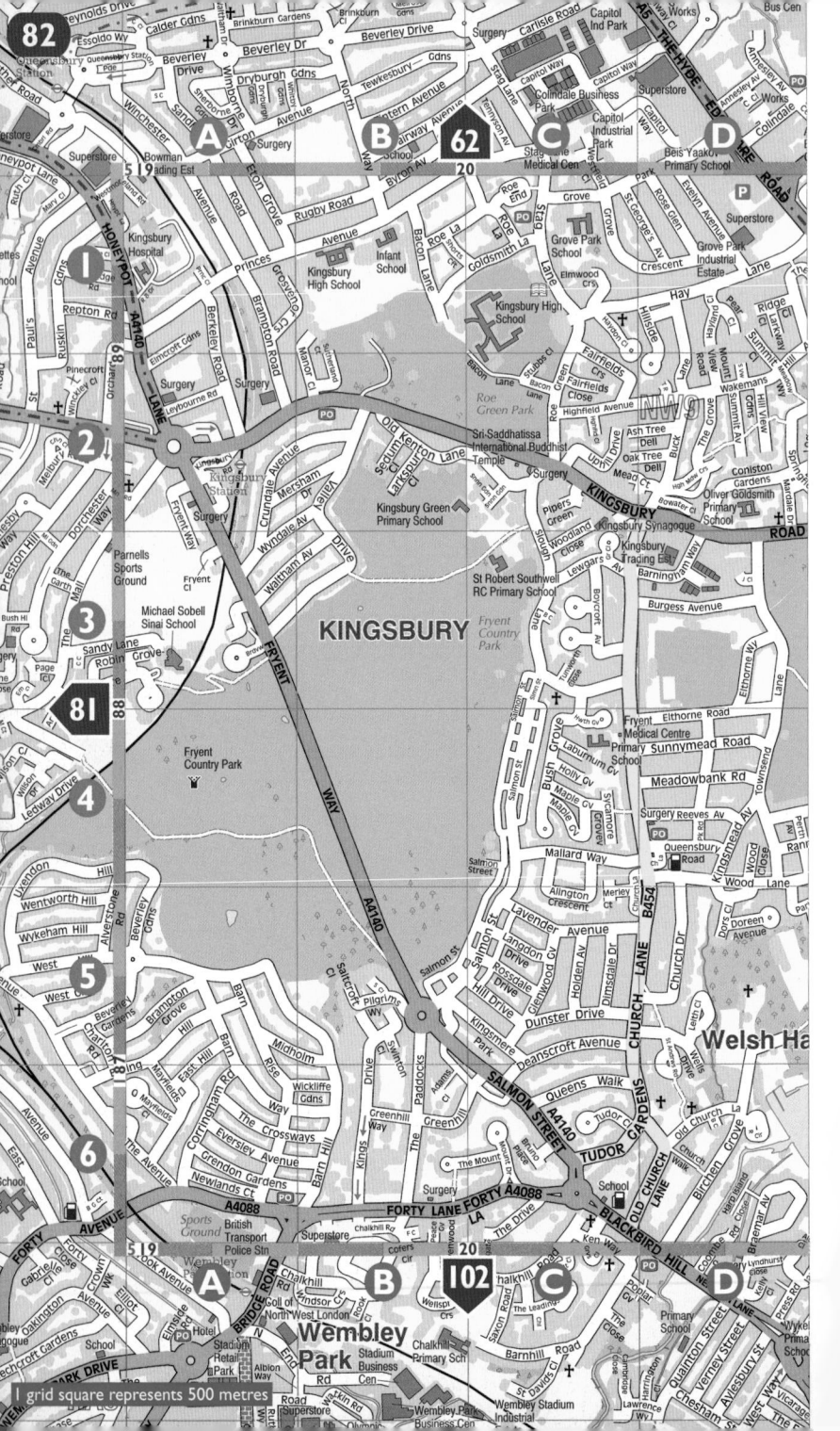

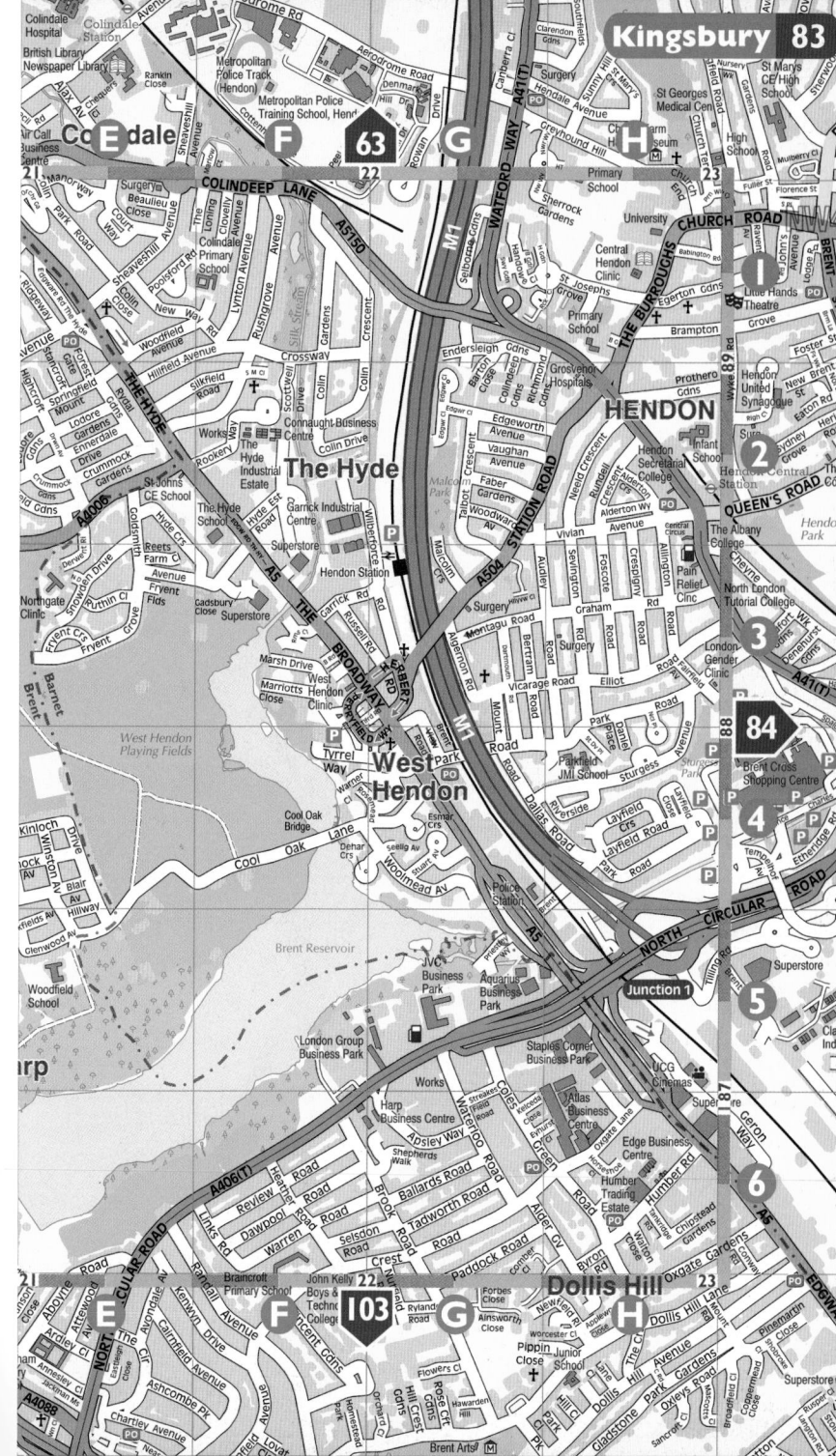

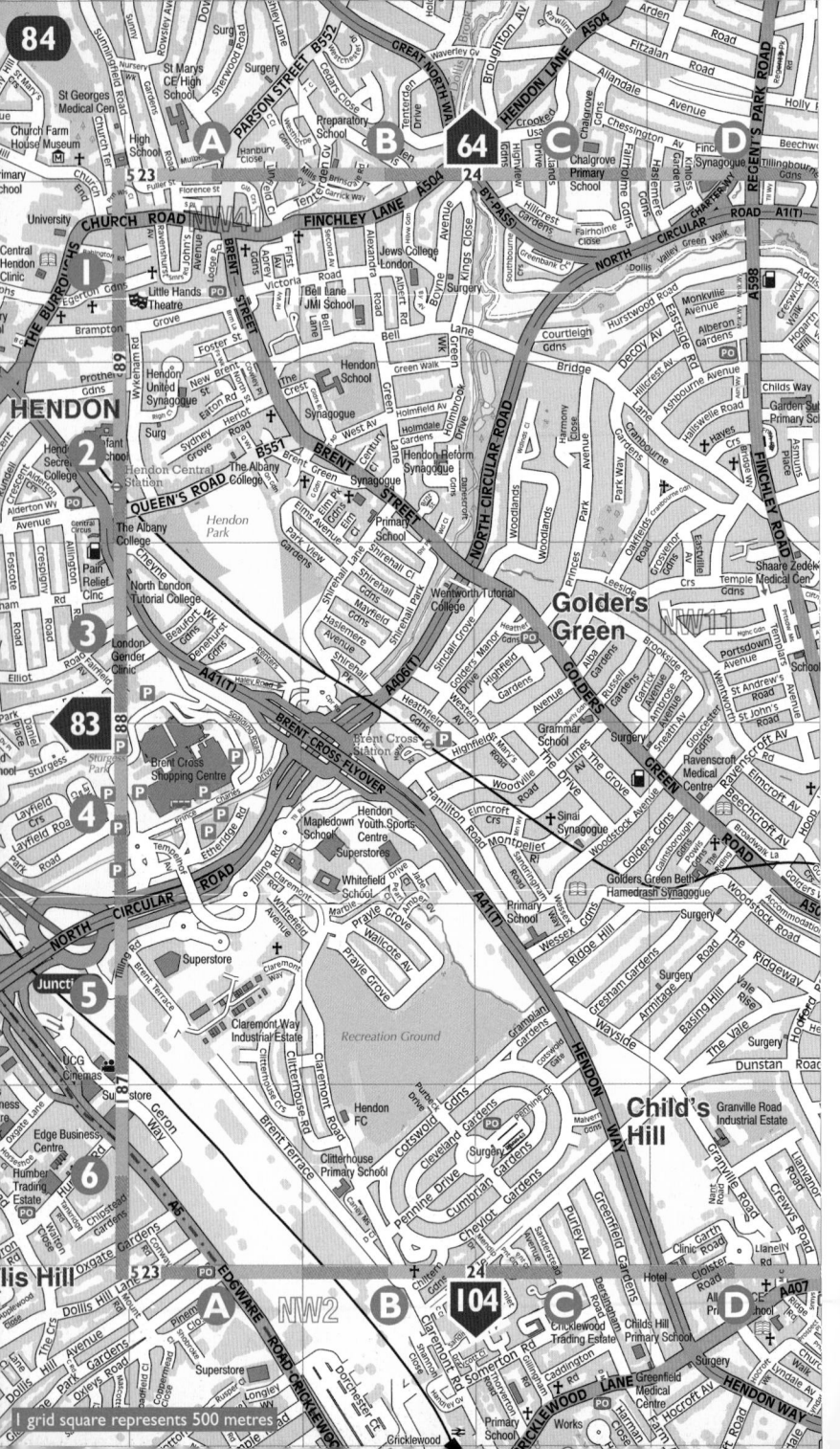

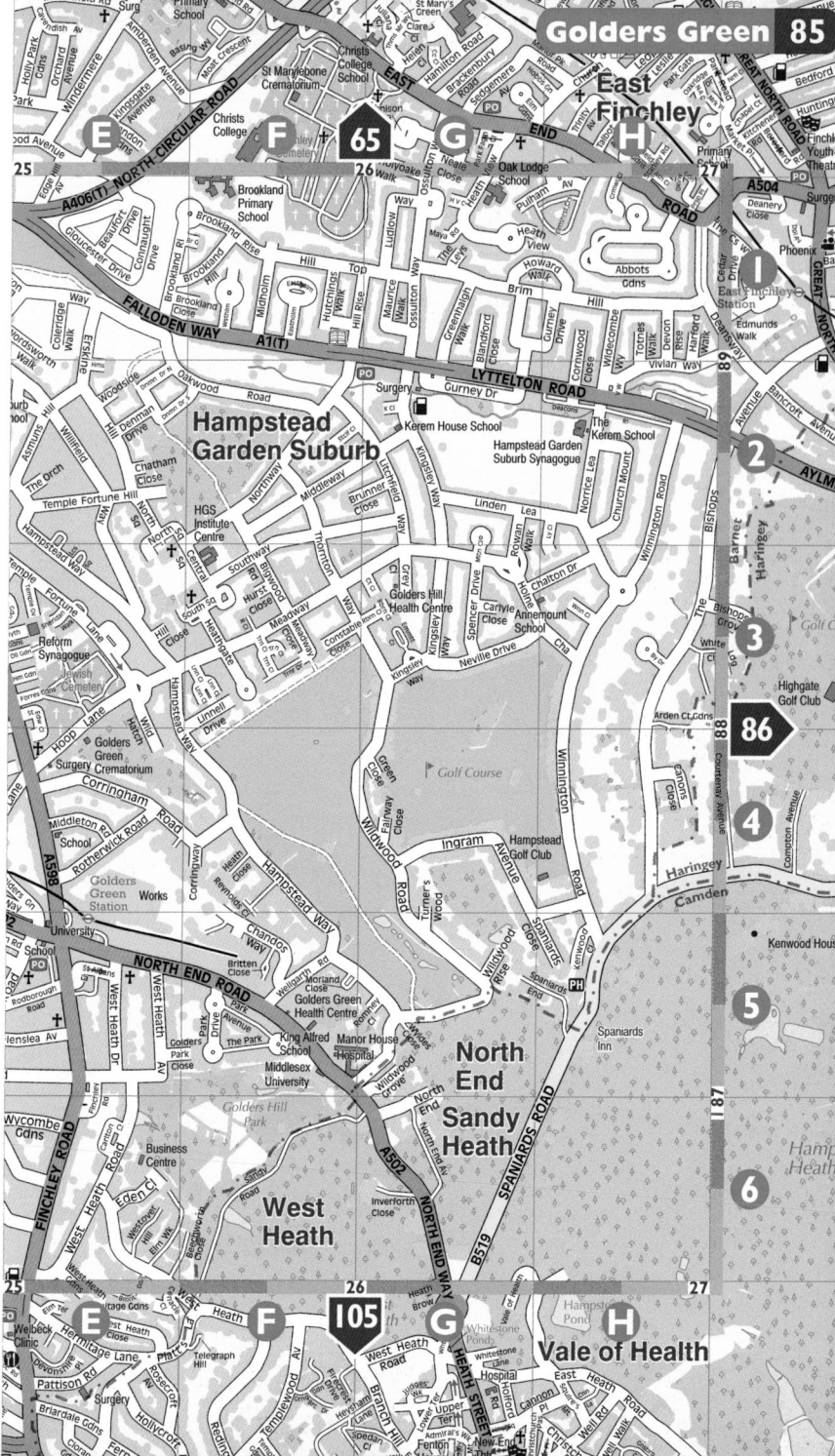

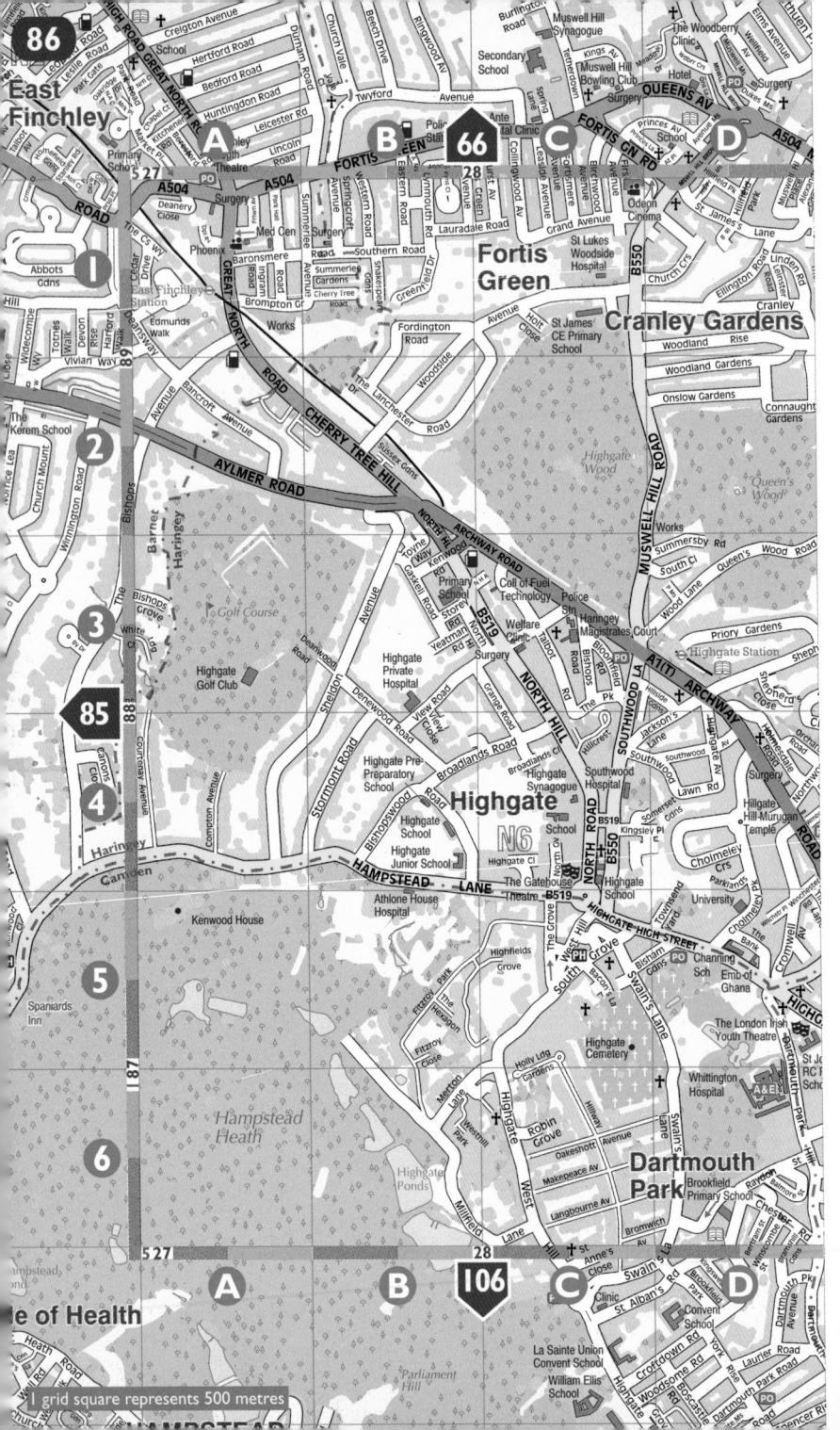

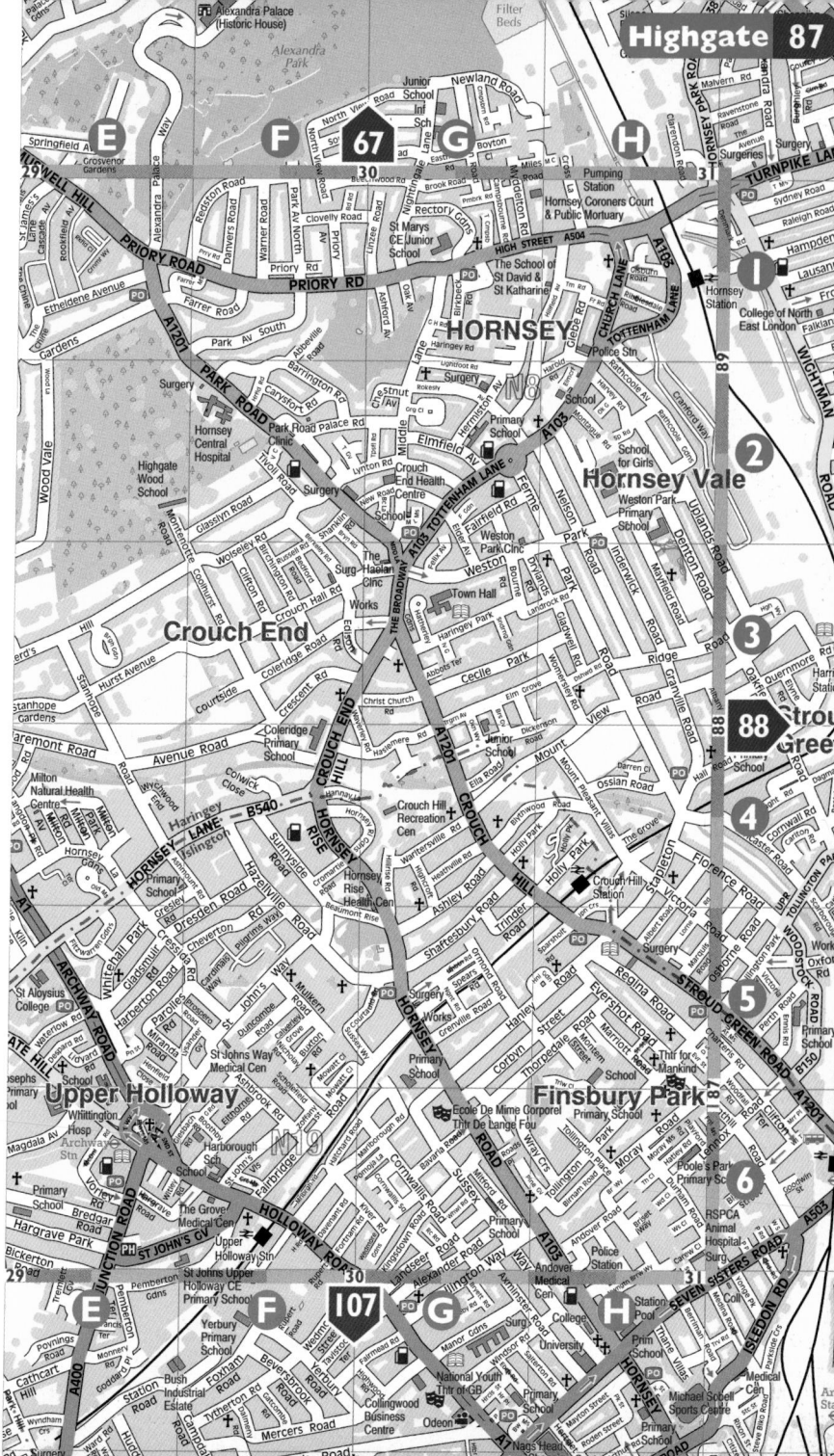

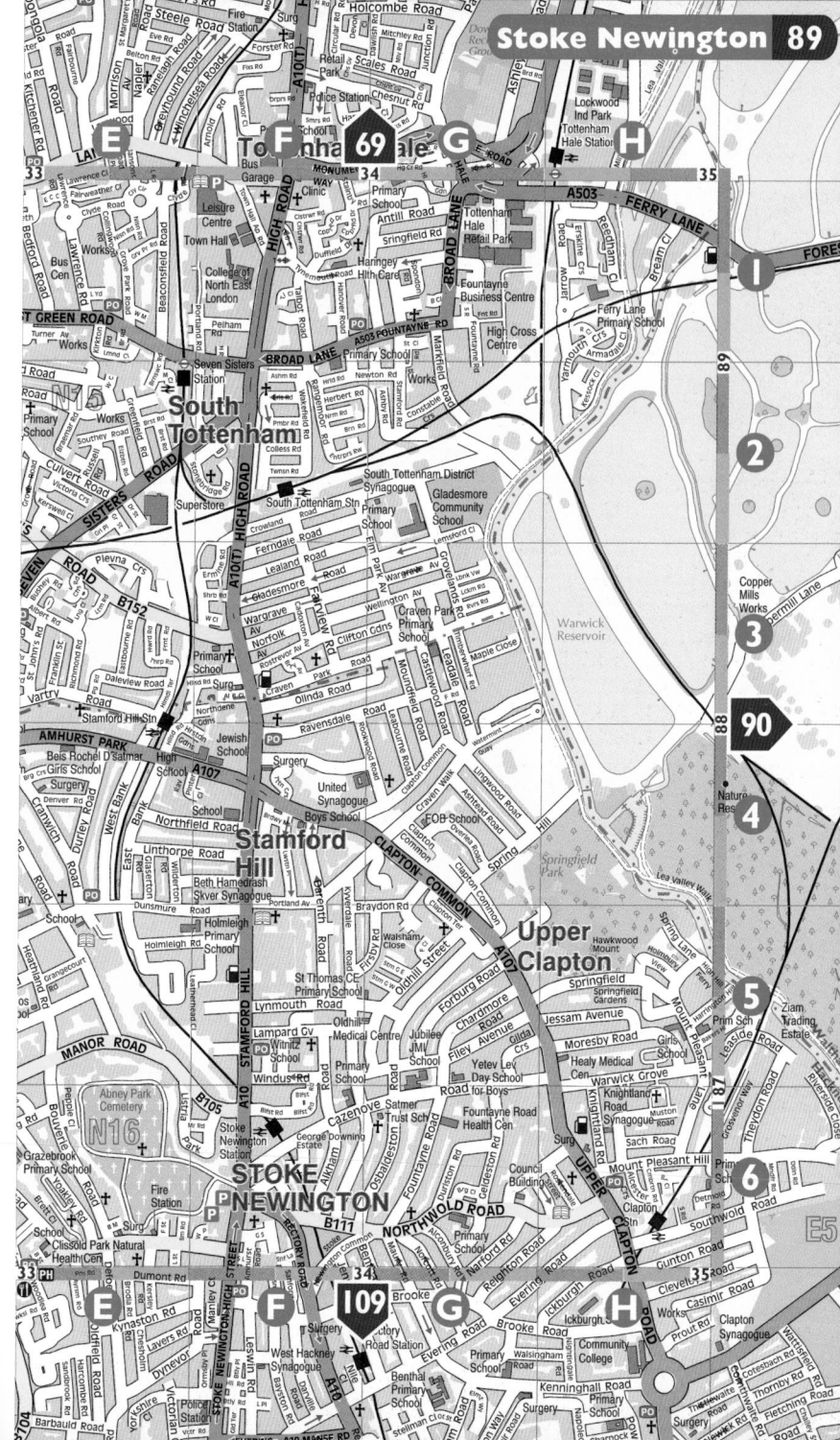

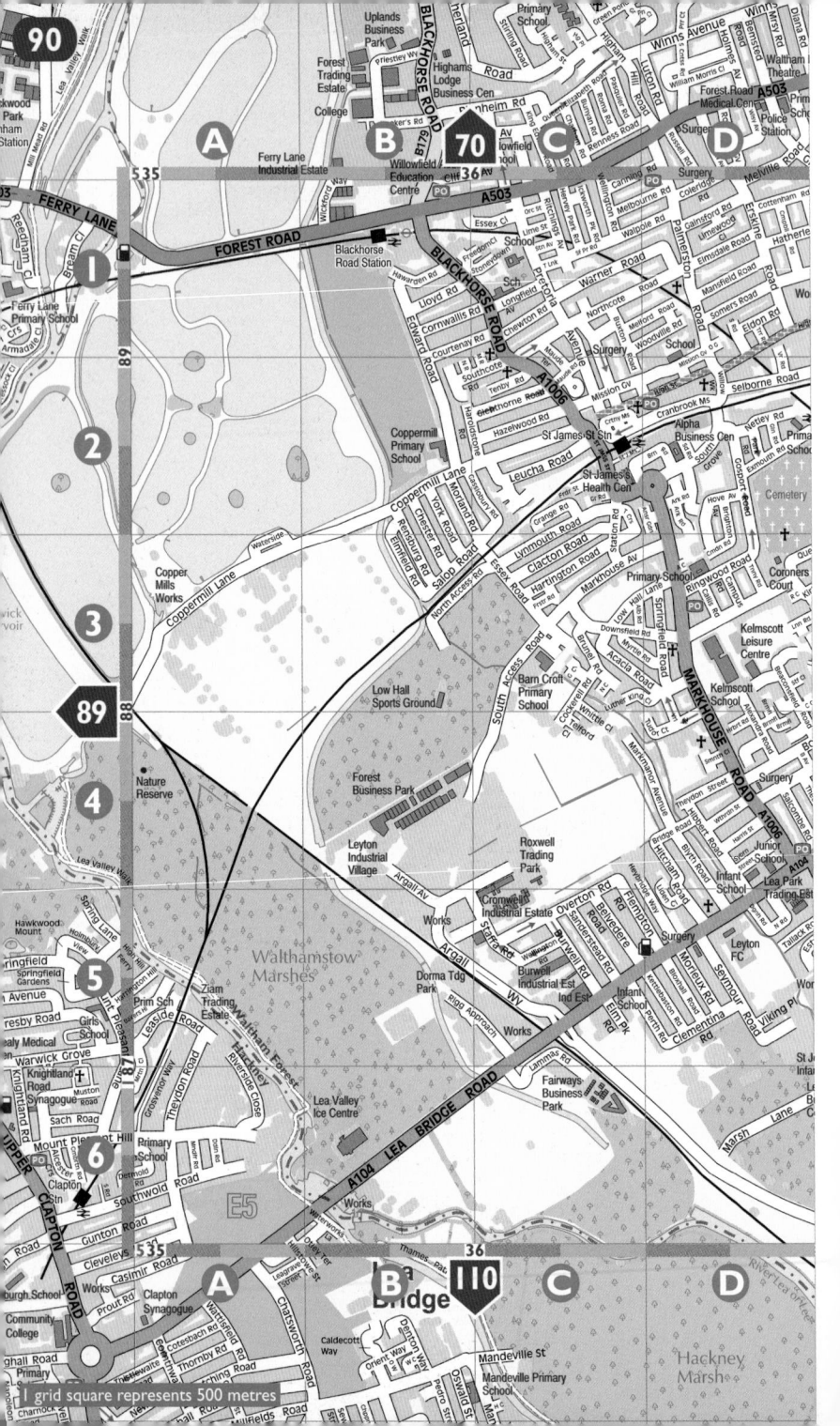

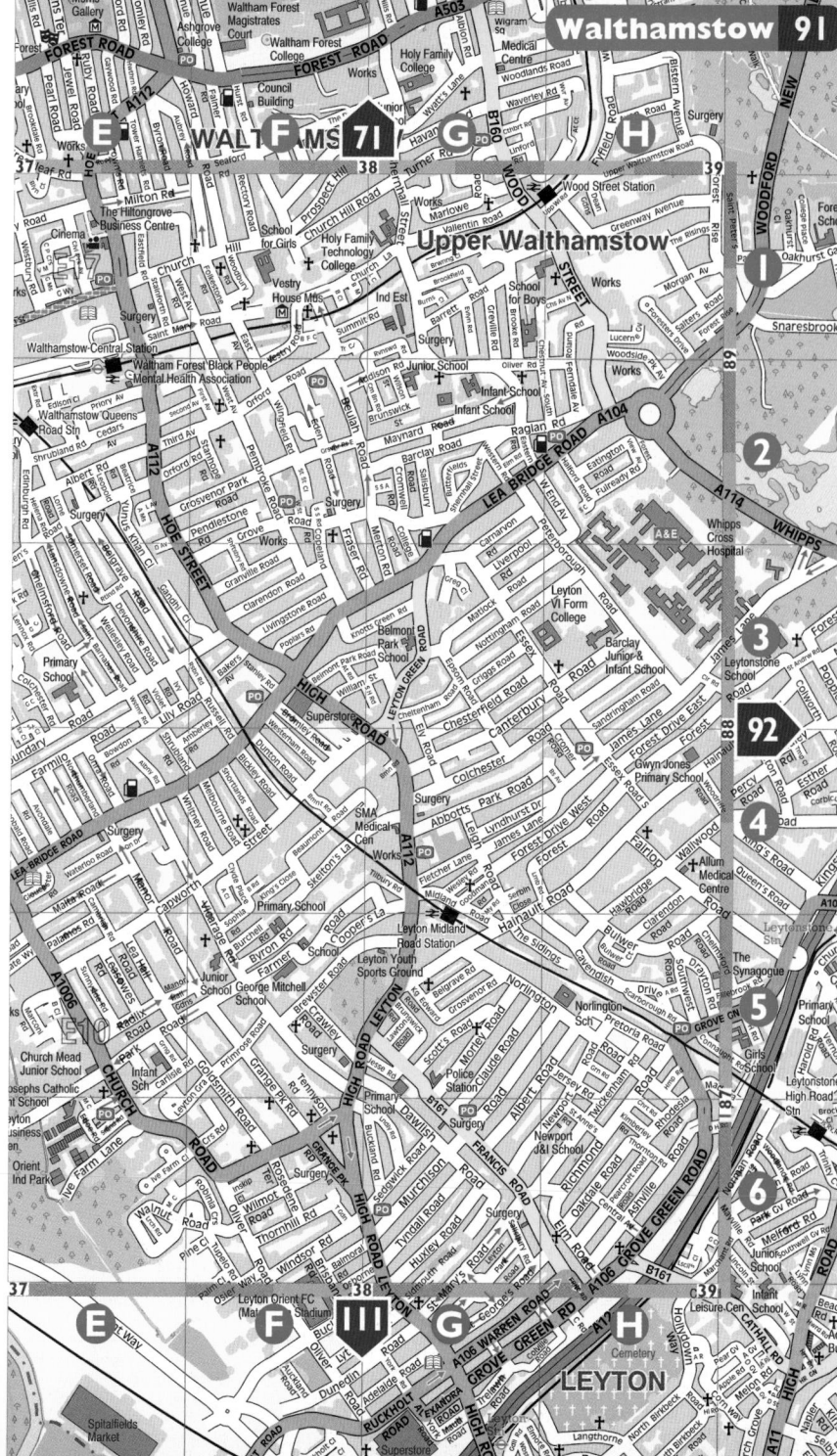

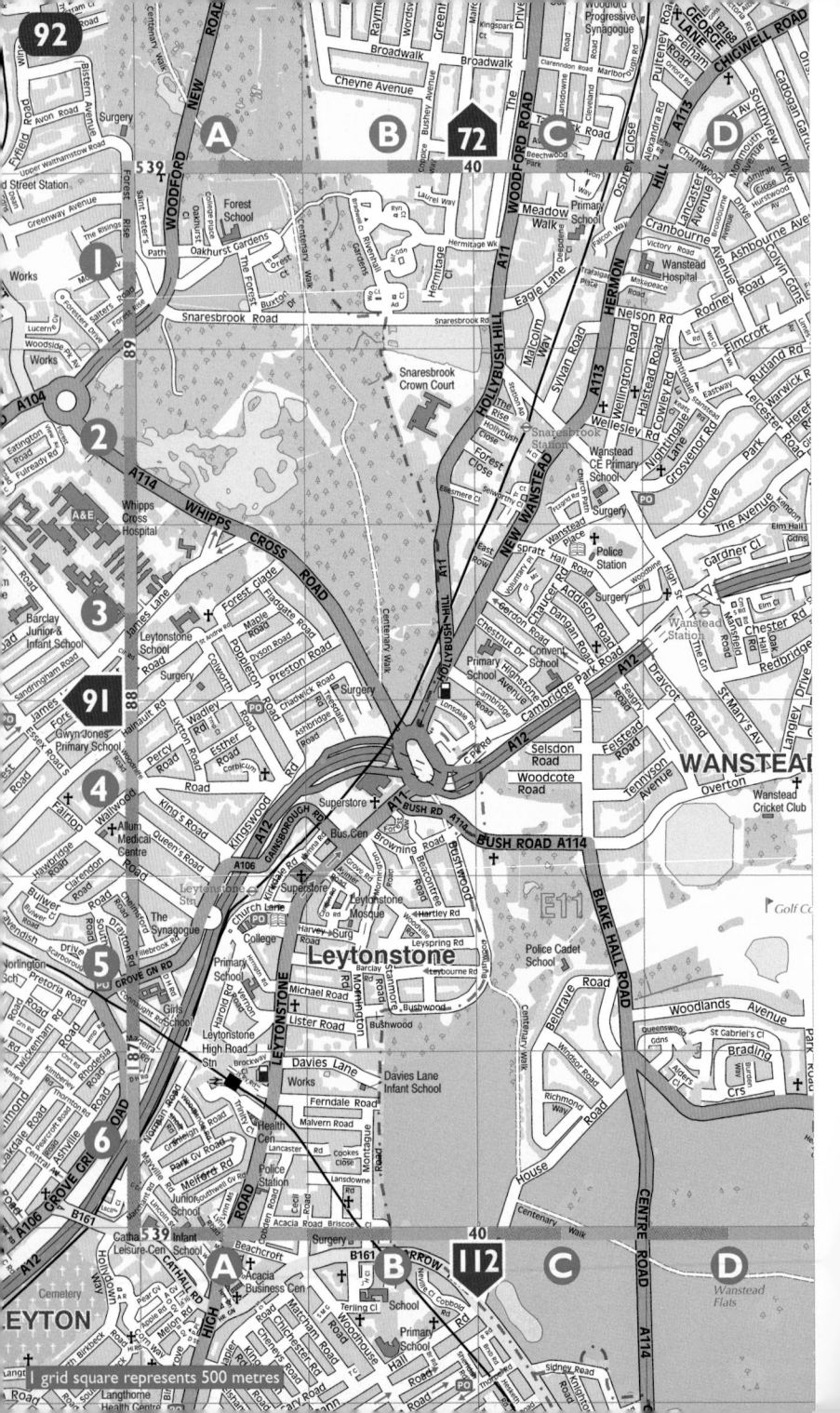

1 grid square represents 500 metres

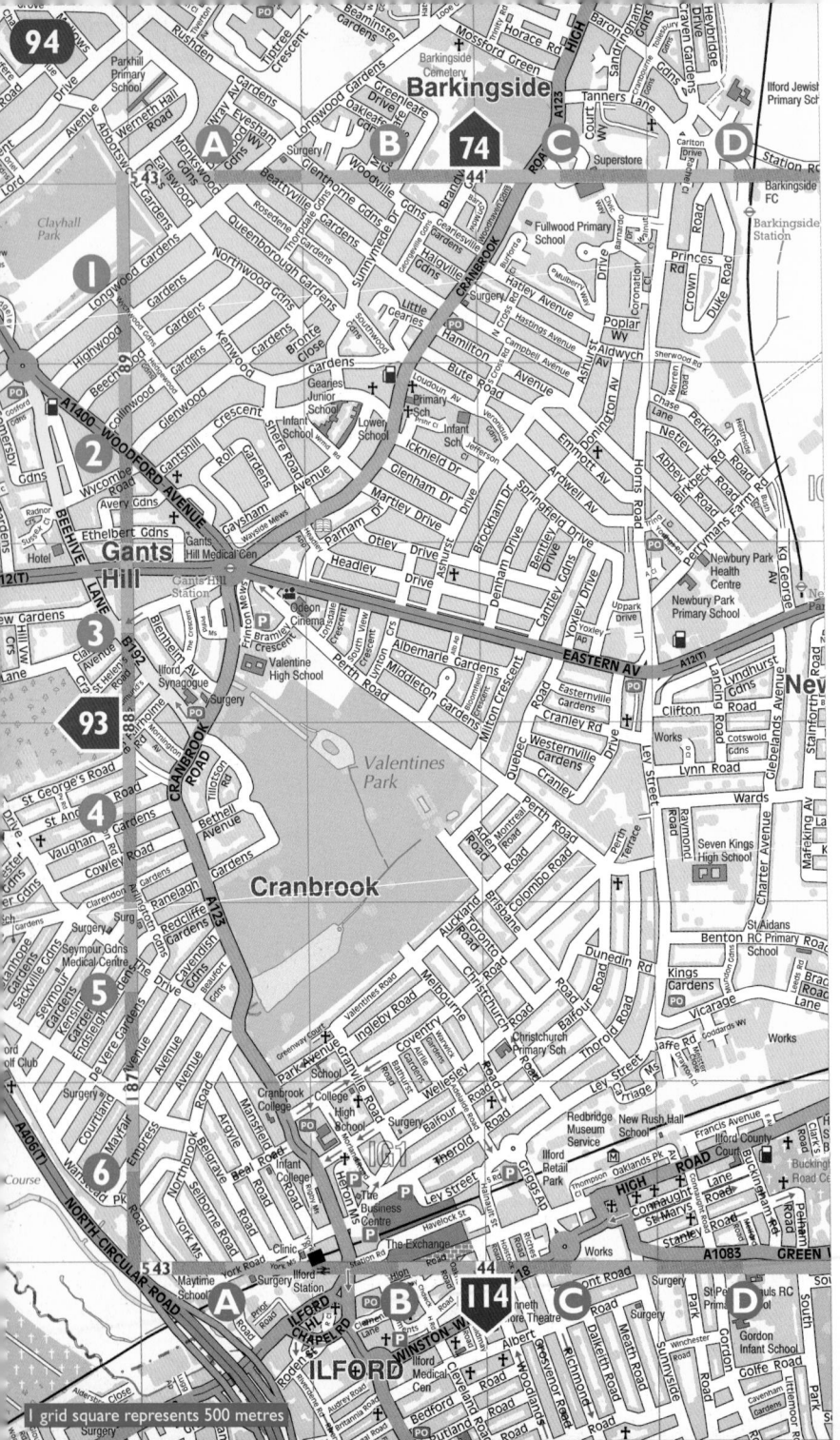

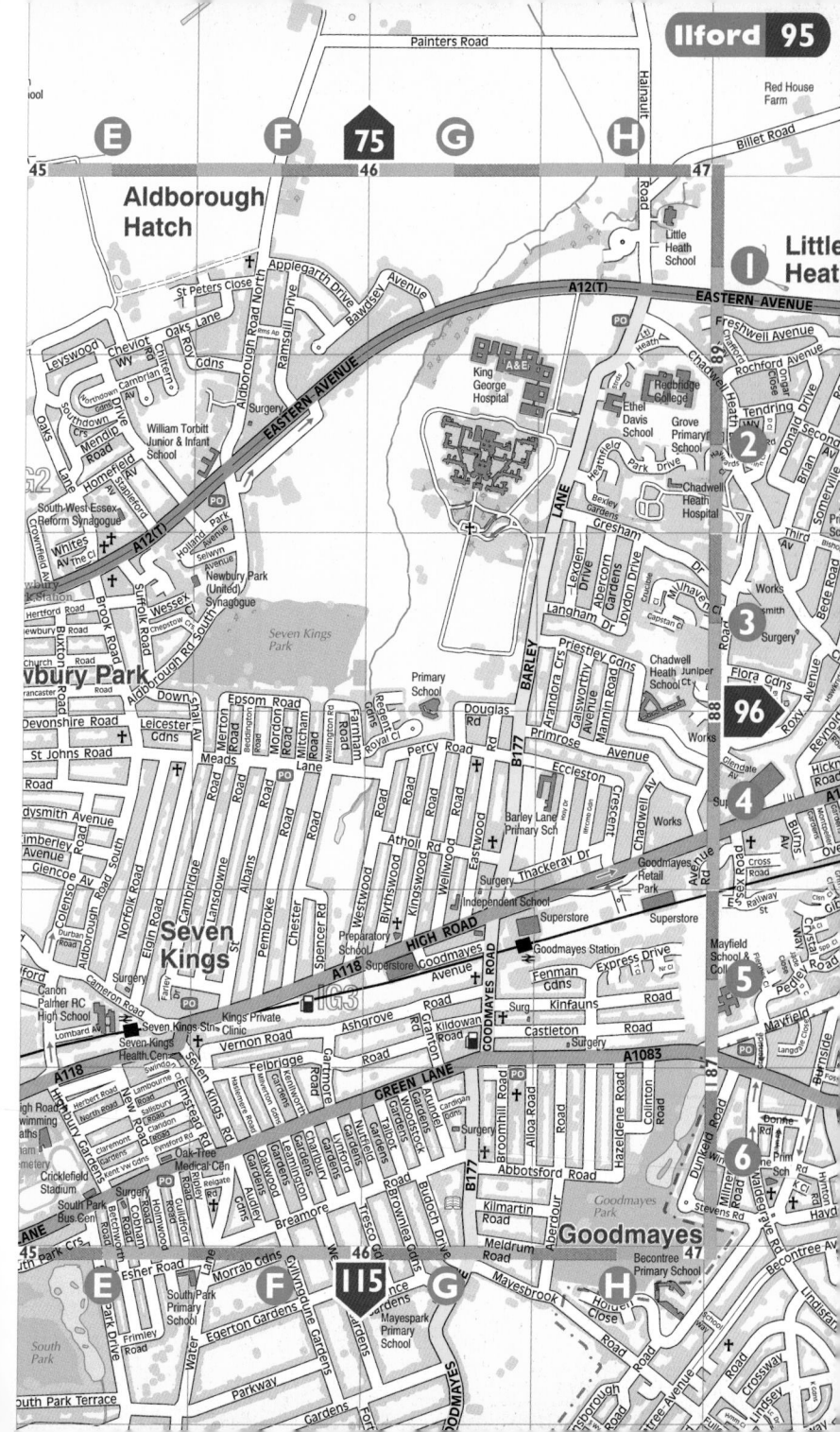

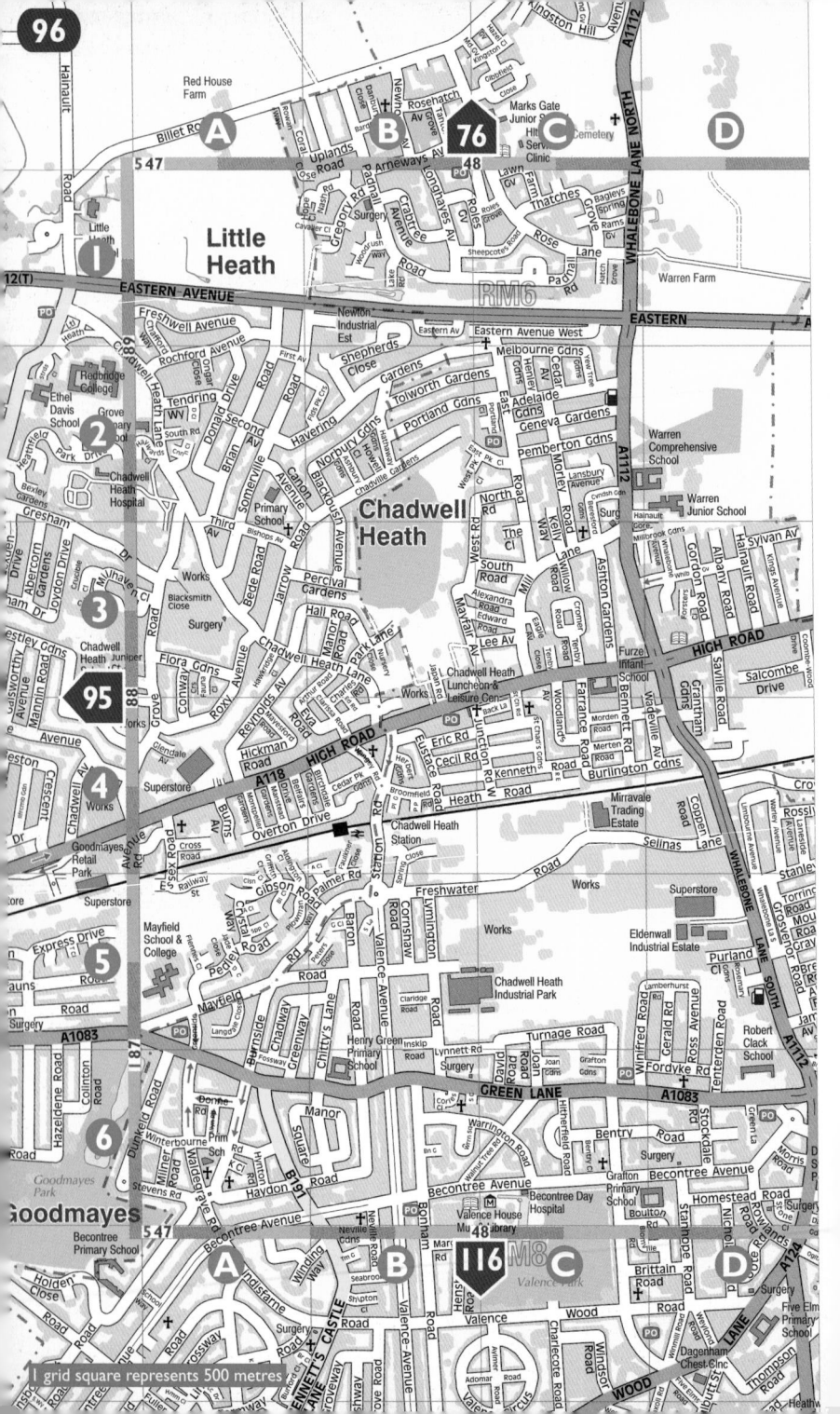

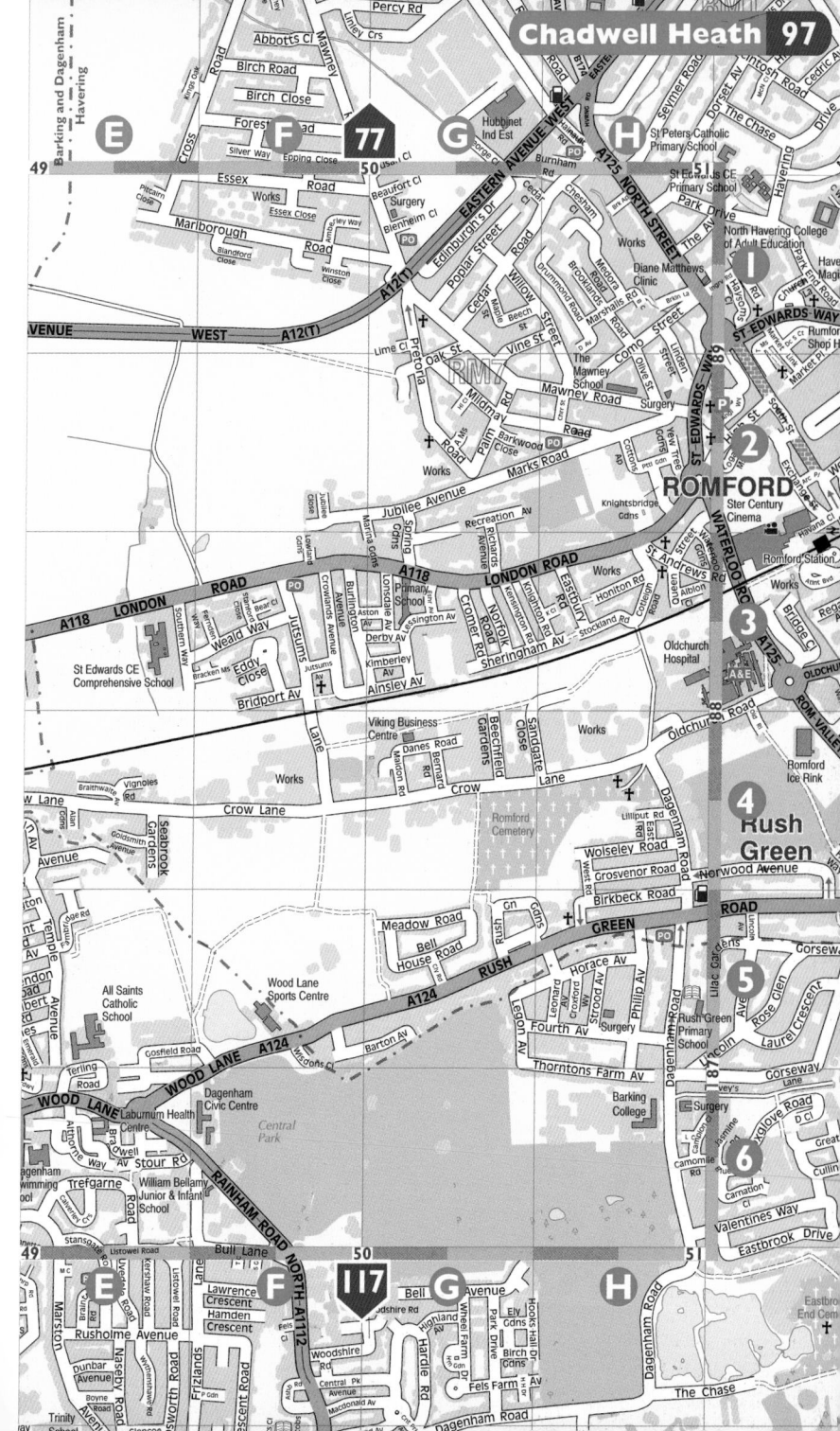

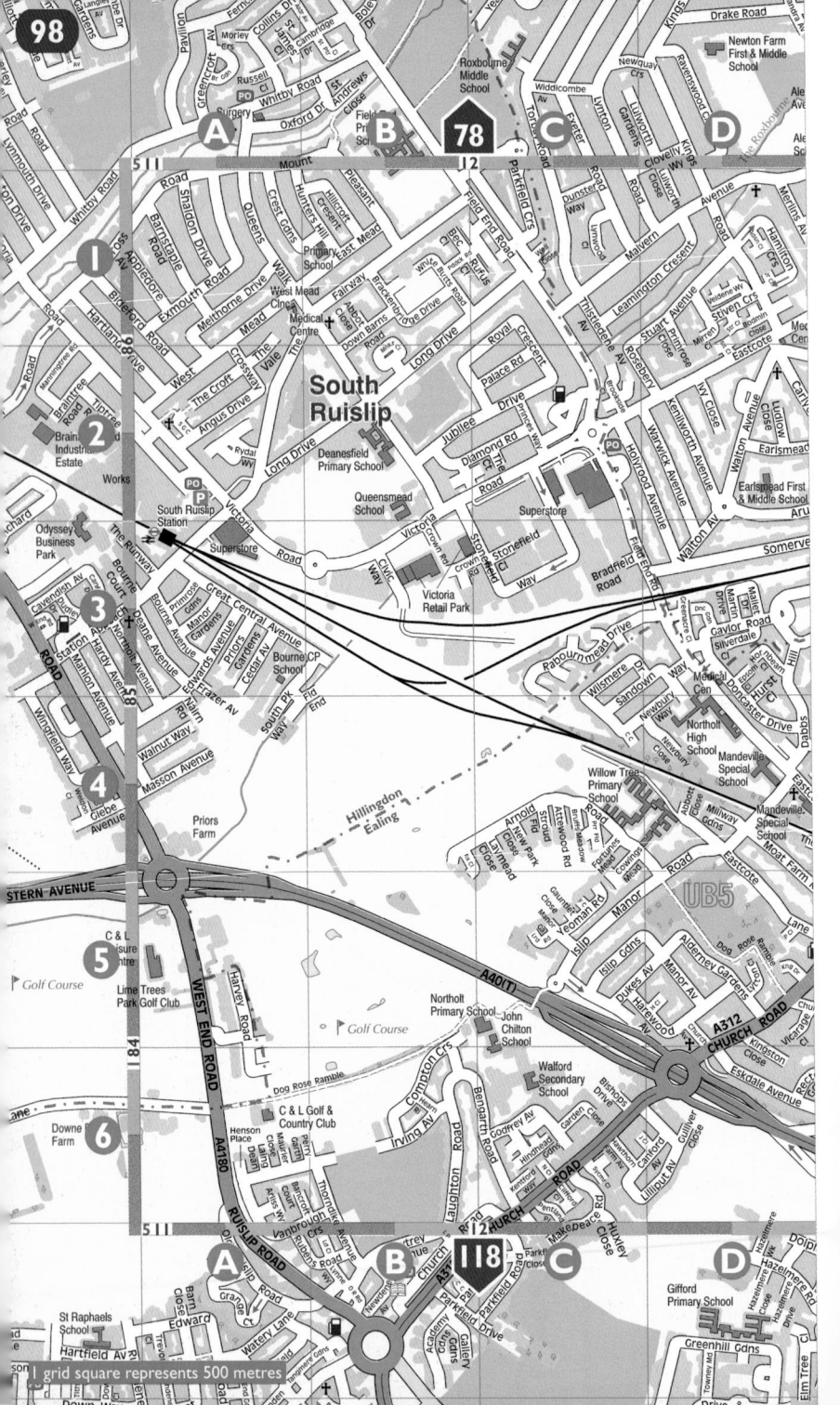

98

South Ruislip

UB5

1 grid square represents 500 metres

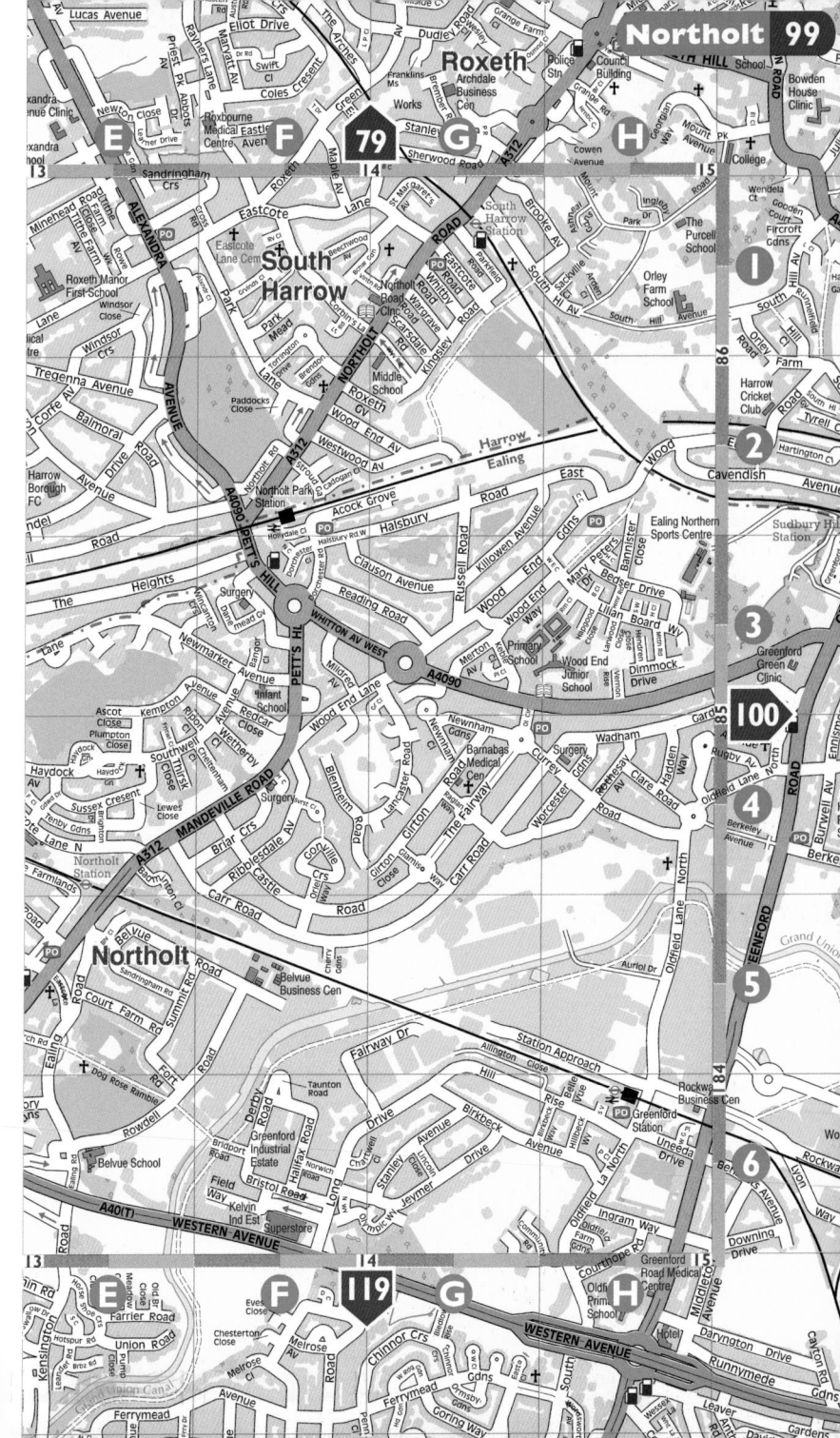

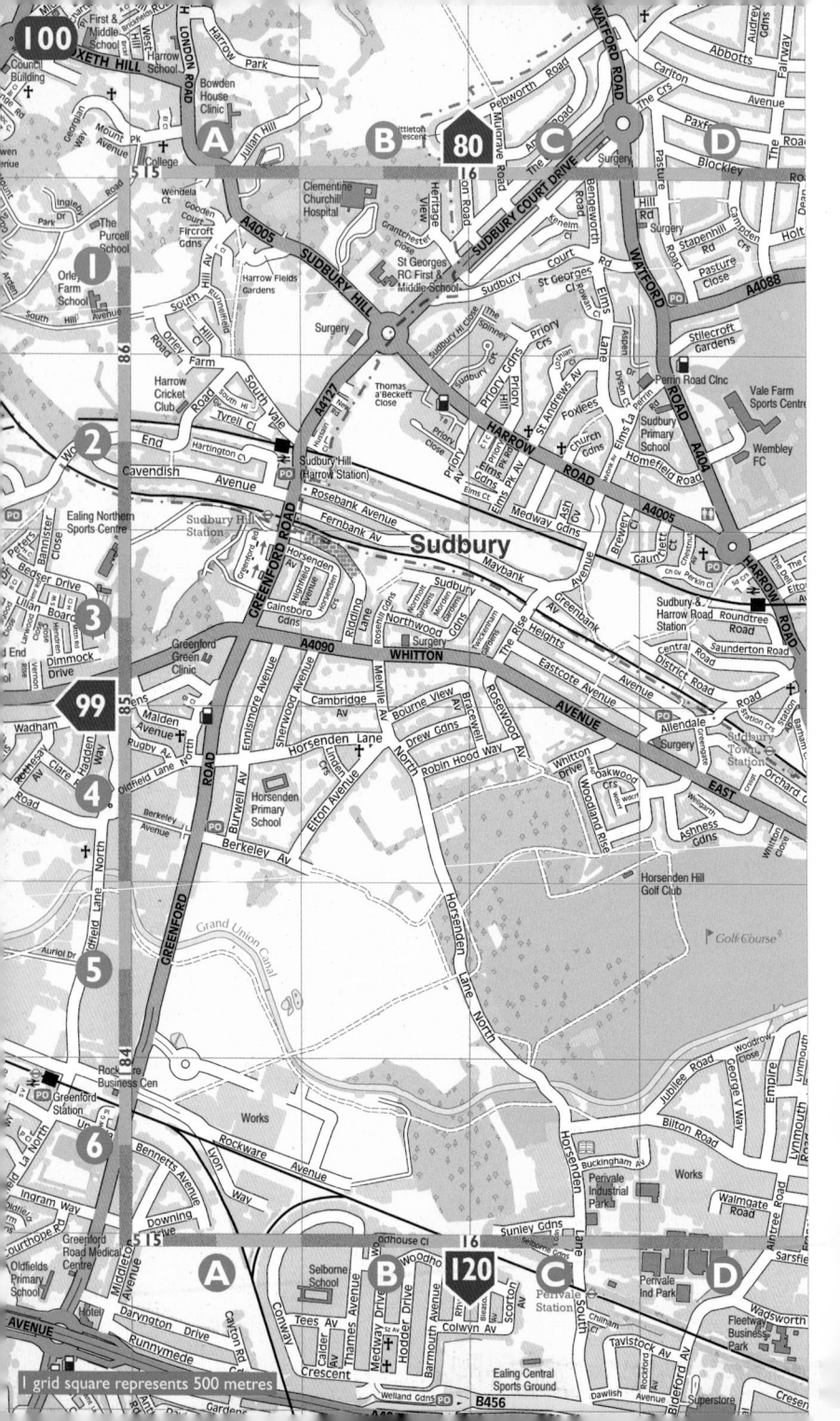

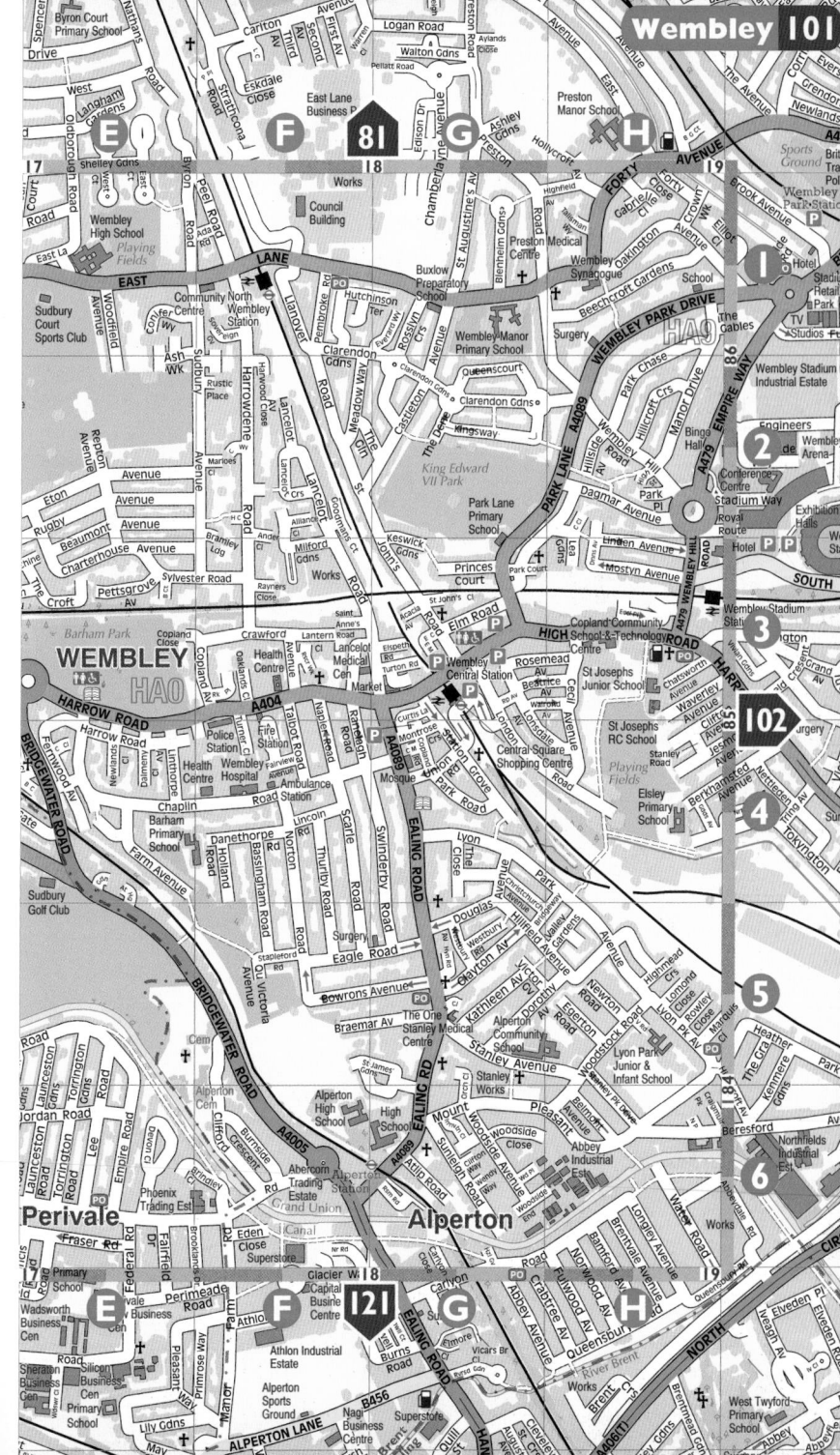

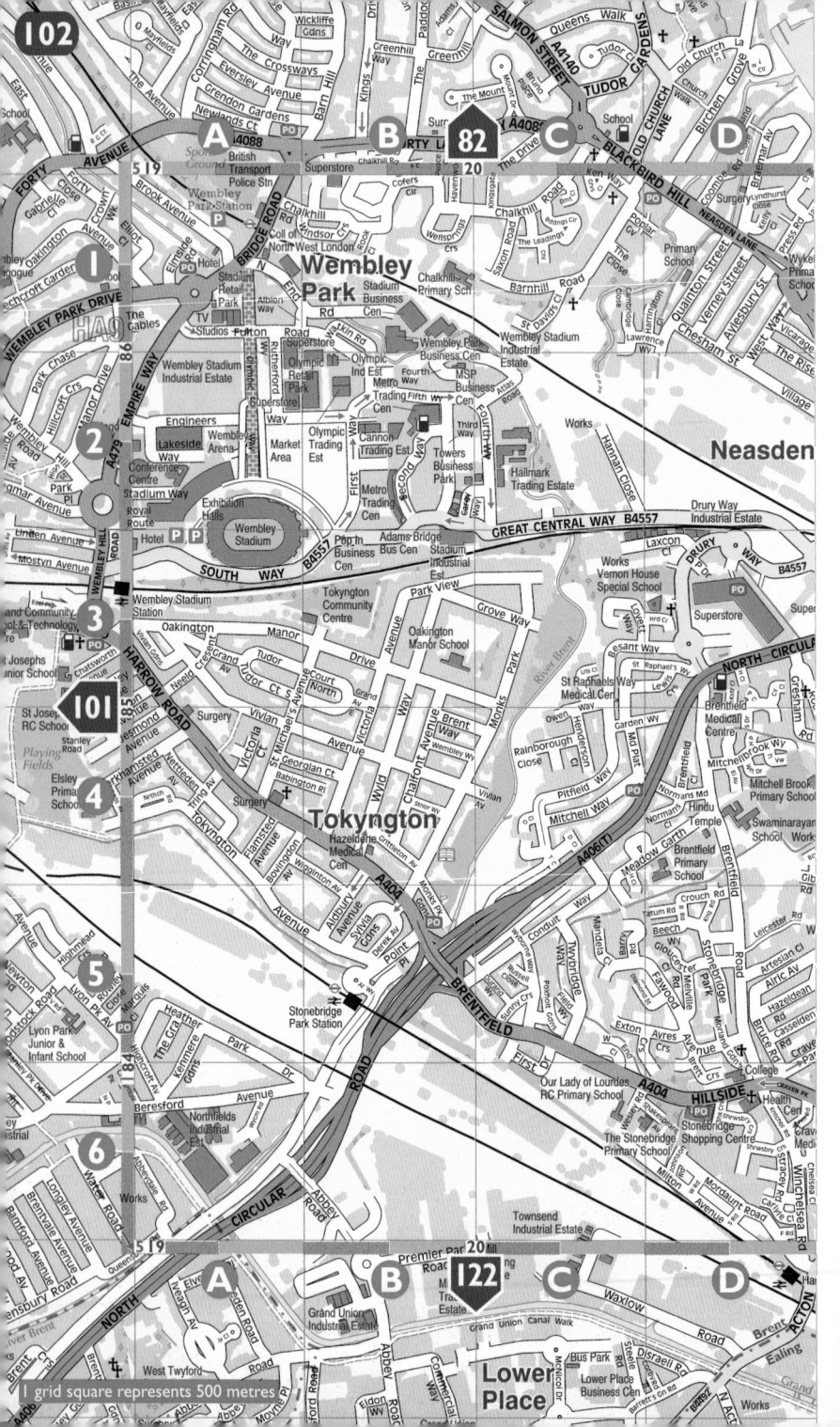

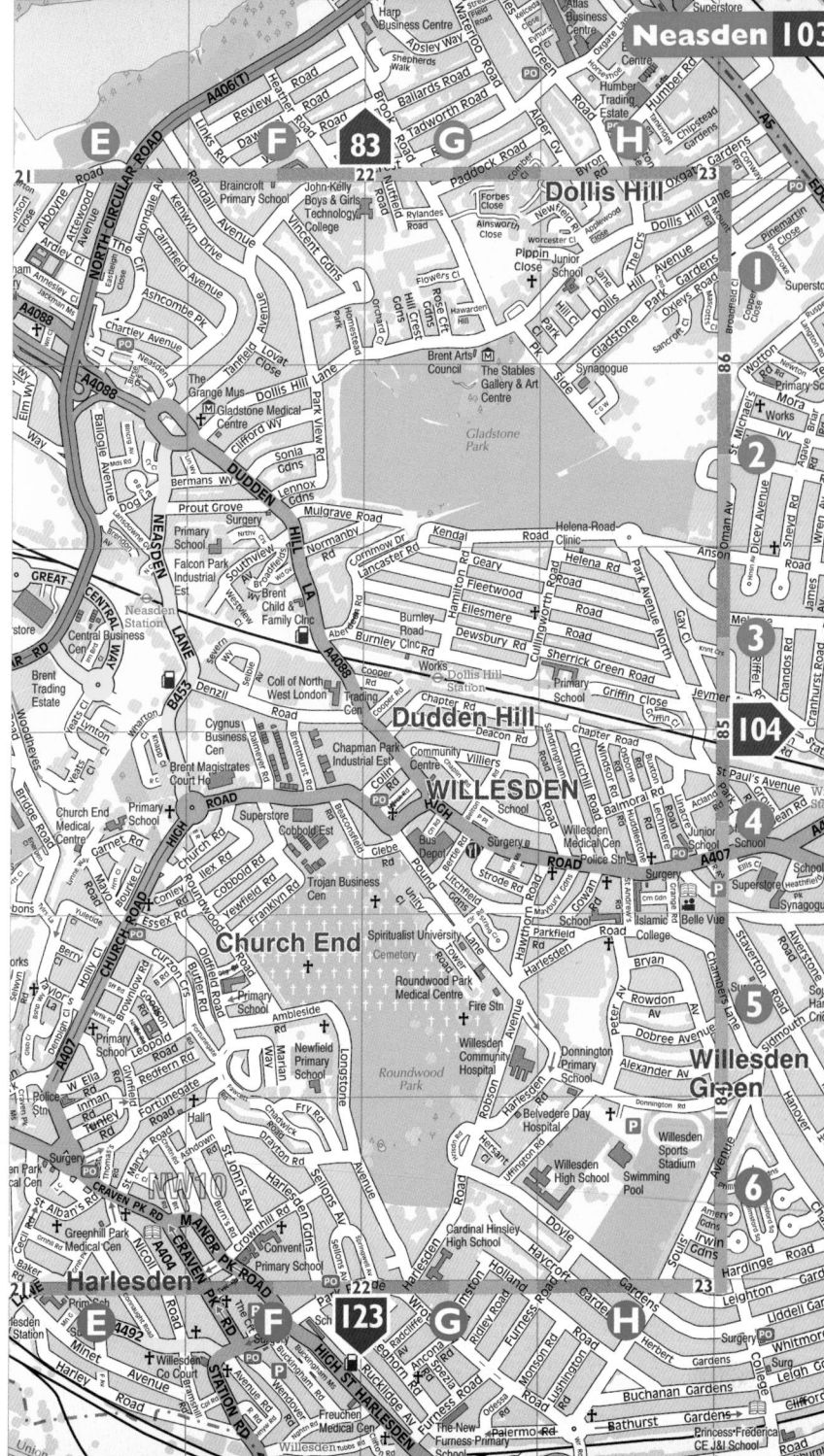

Dollis Hill

Gladstone Park

Dudden Hill

WILLESDEN

Church End

NW10

Harlesden

Willesden Green

Roundwood Park

123

83

104

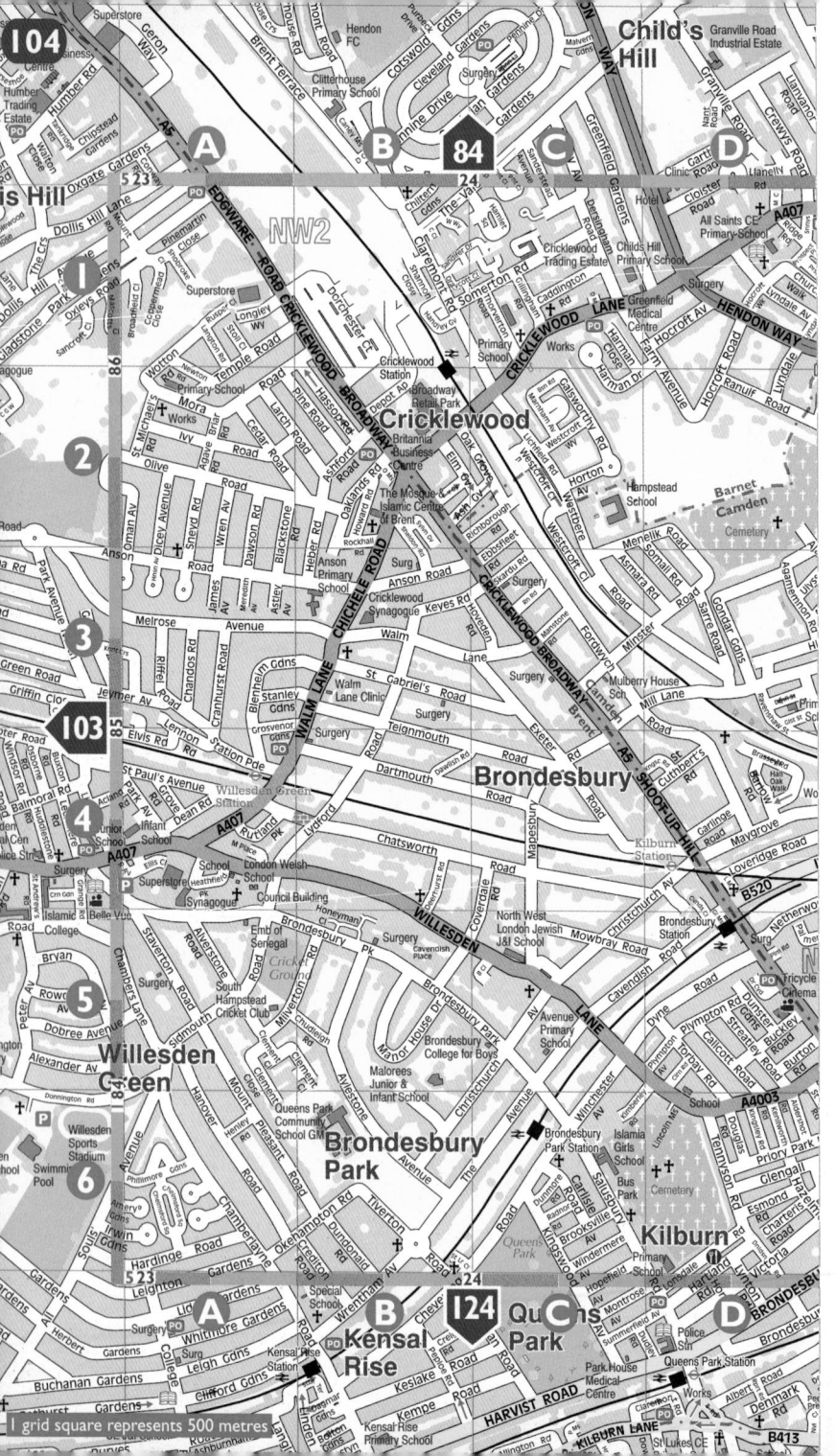

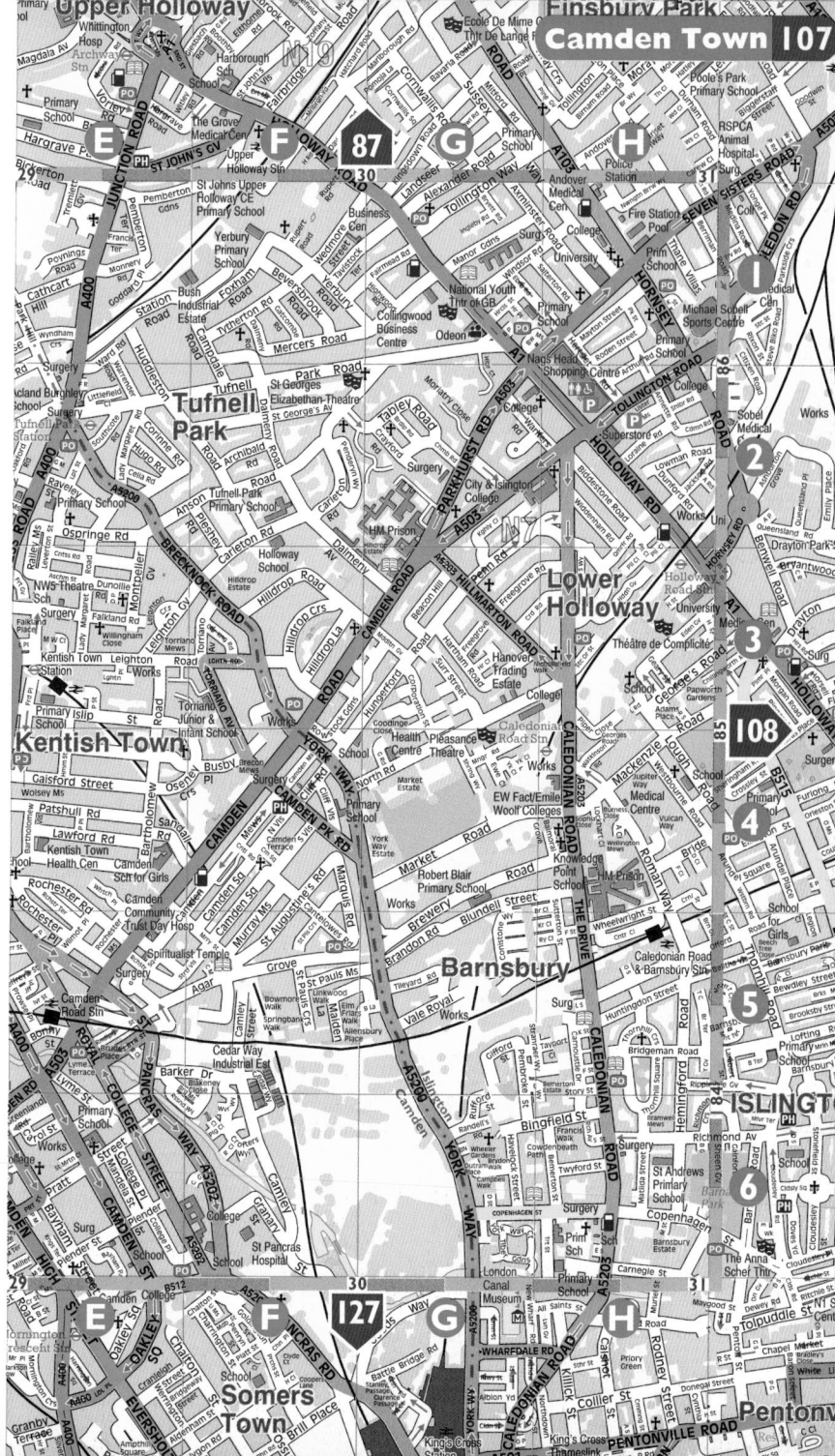

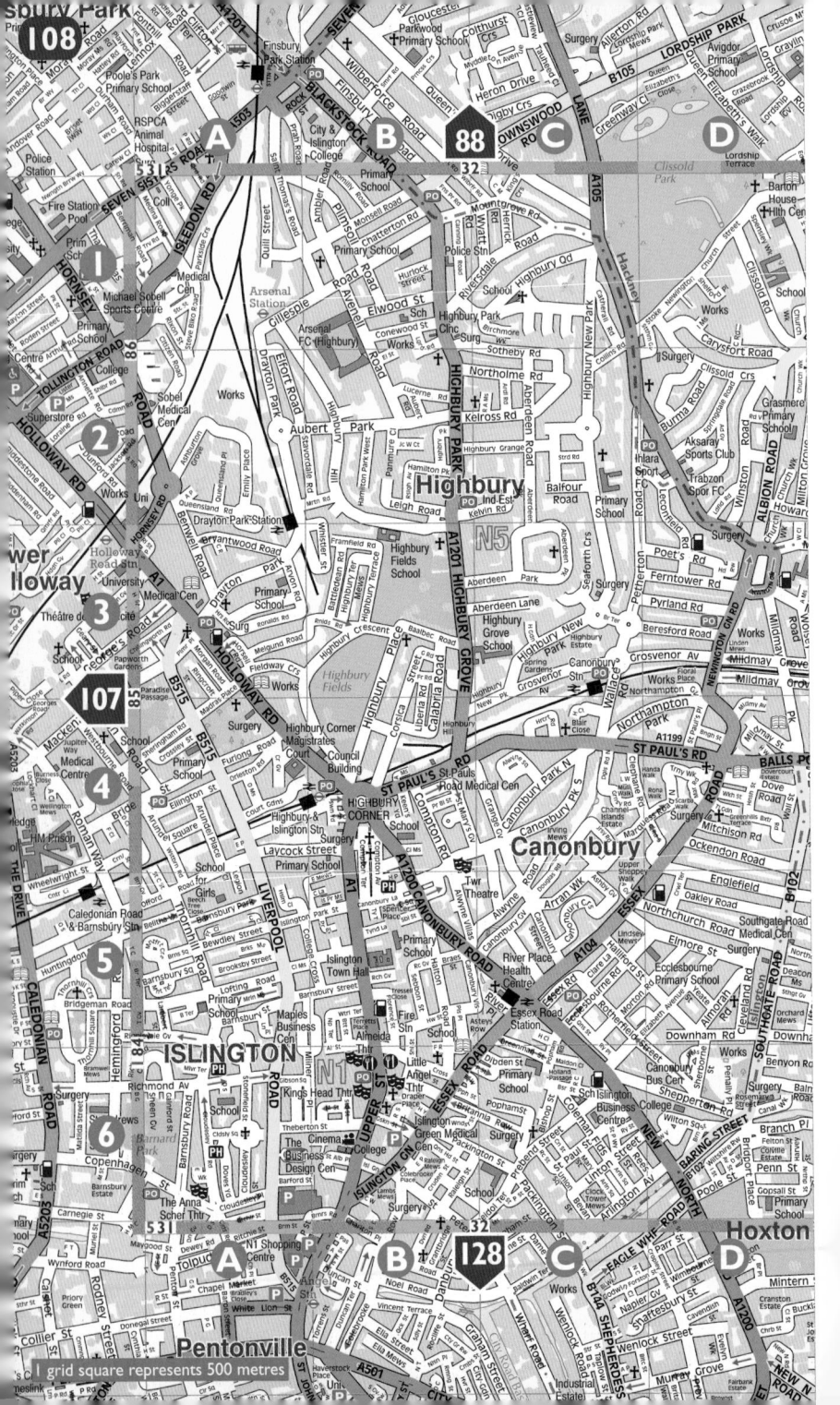

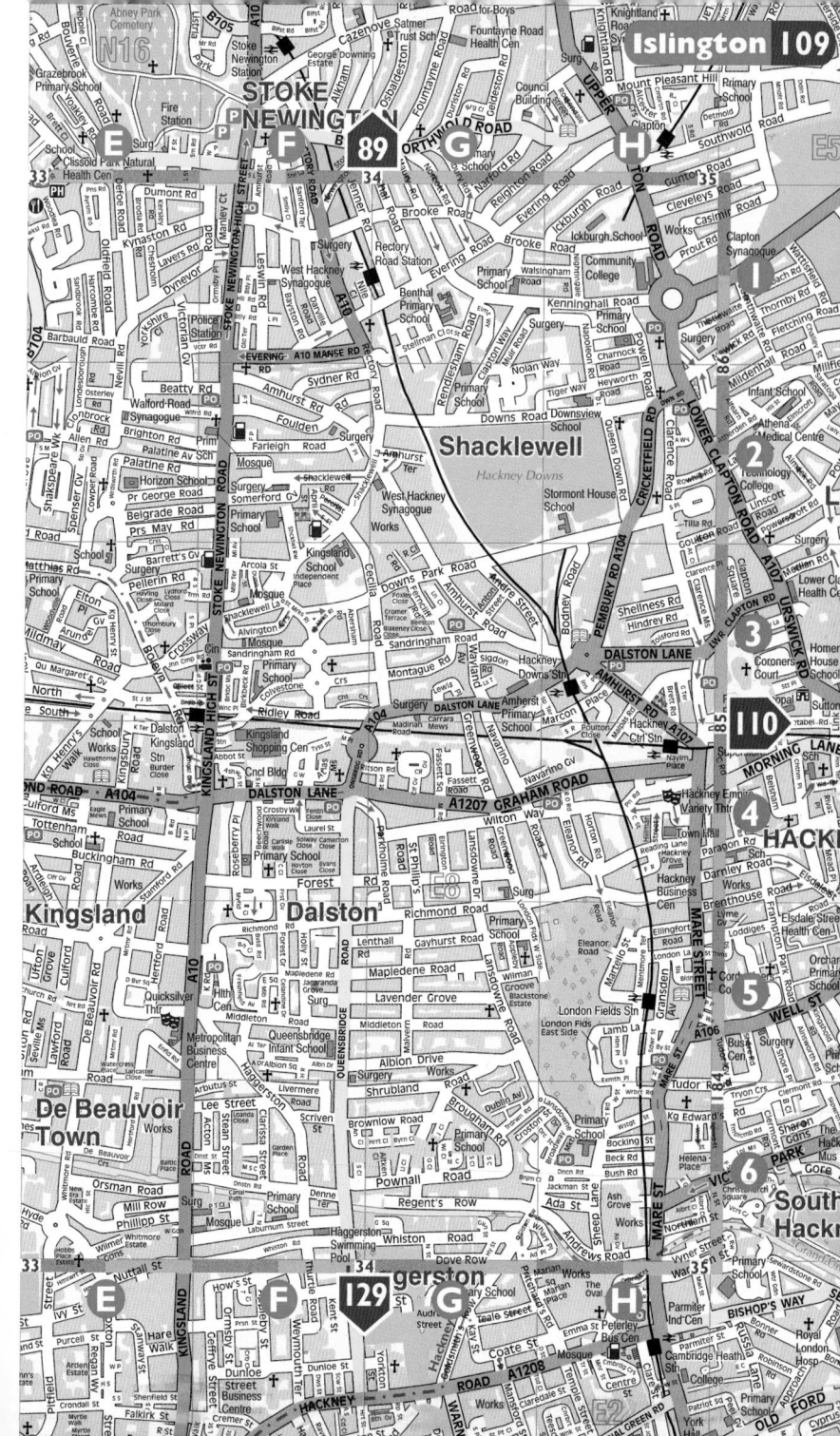

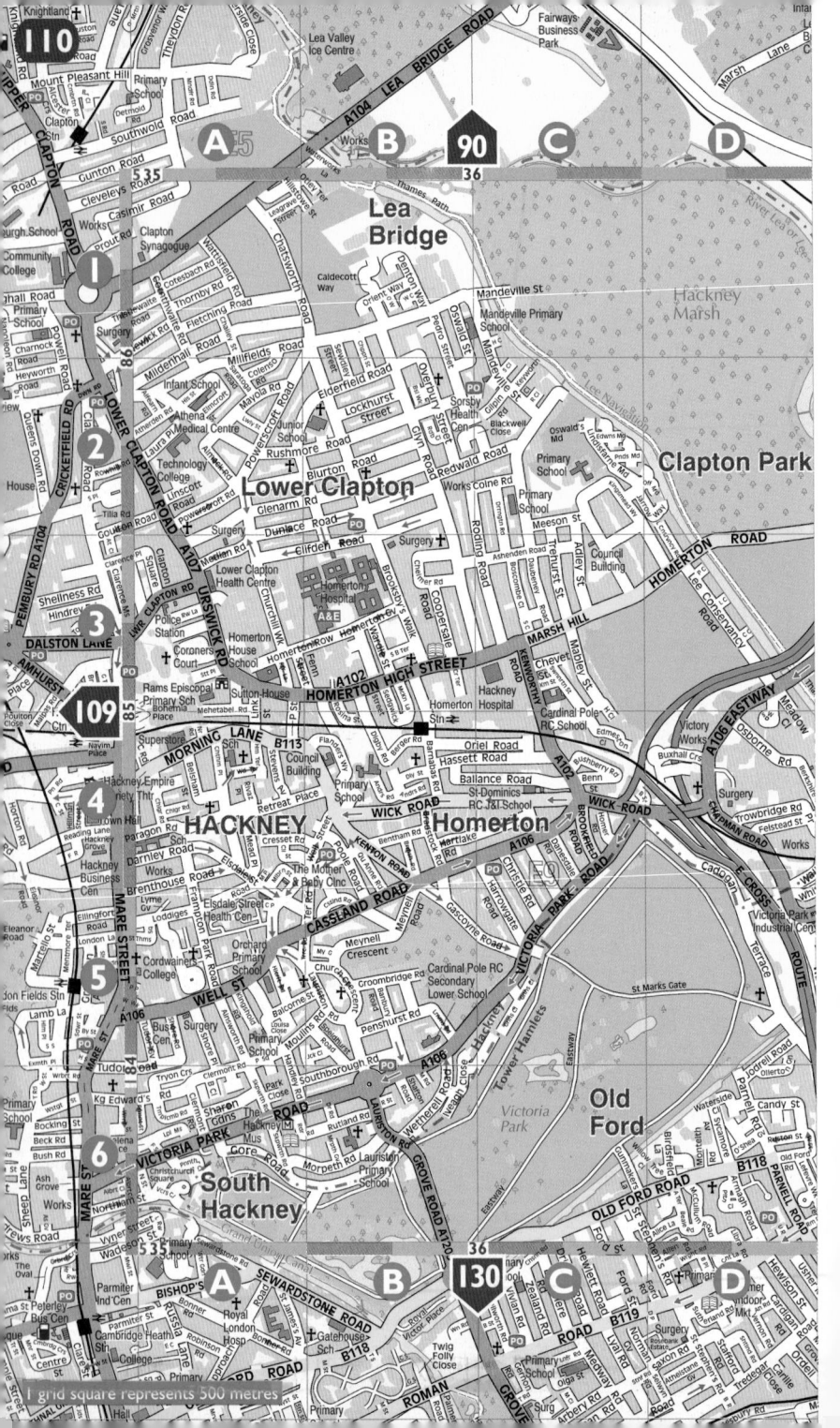

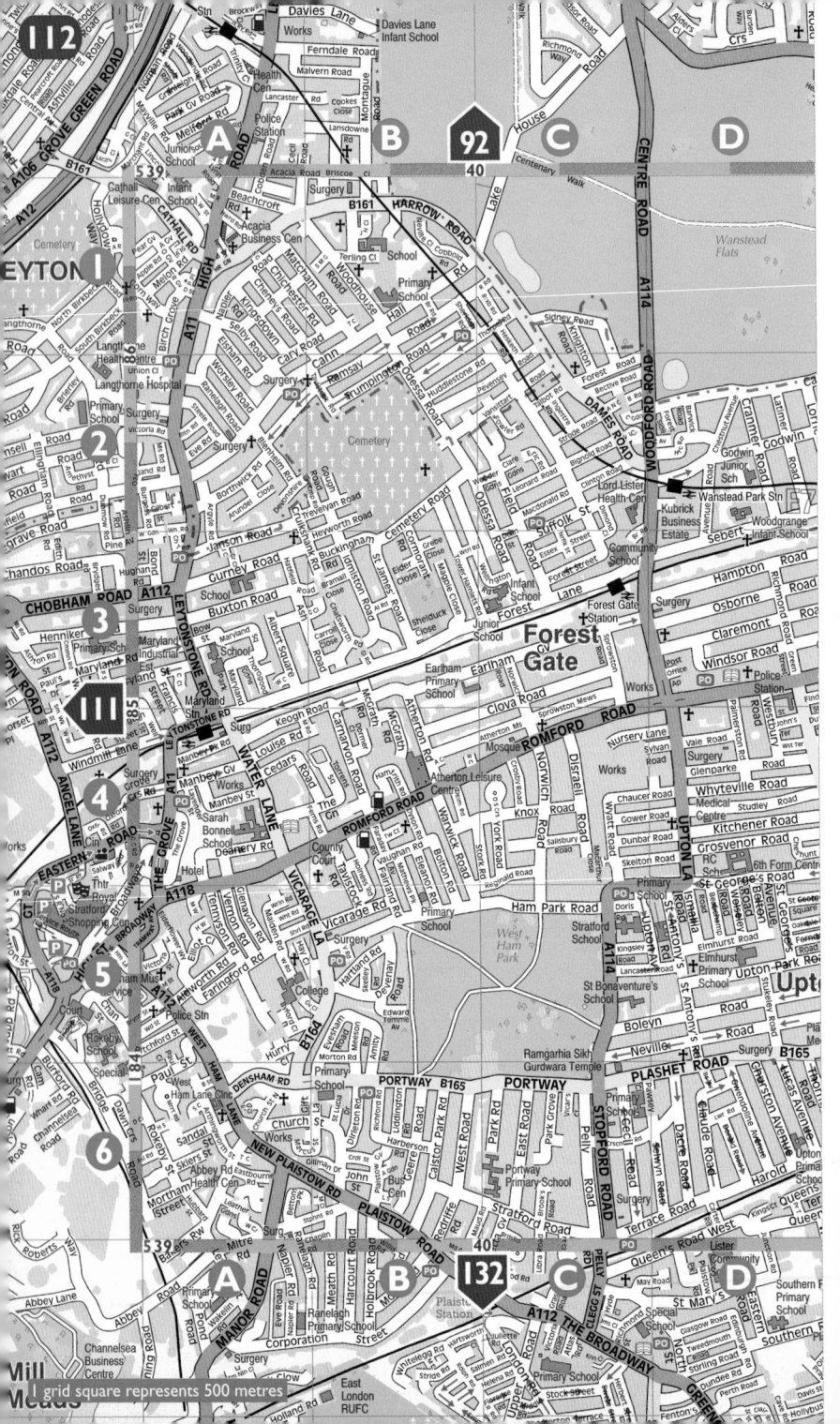

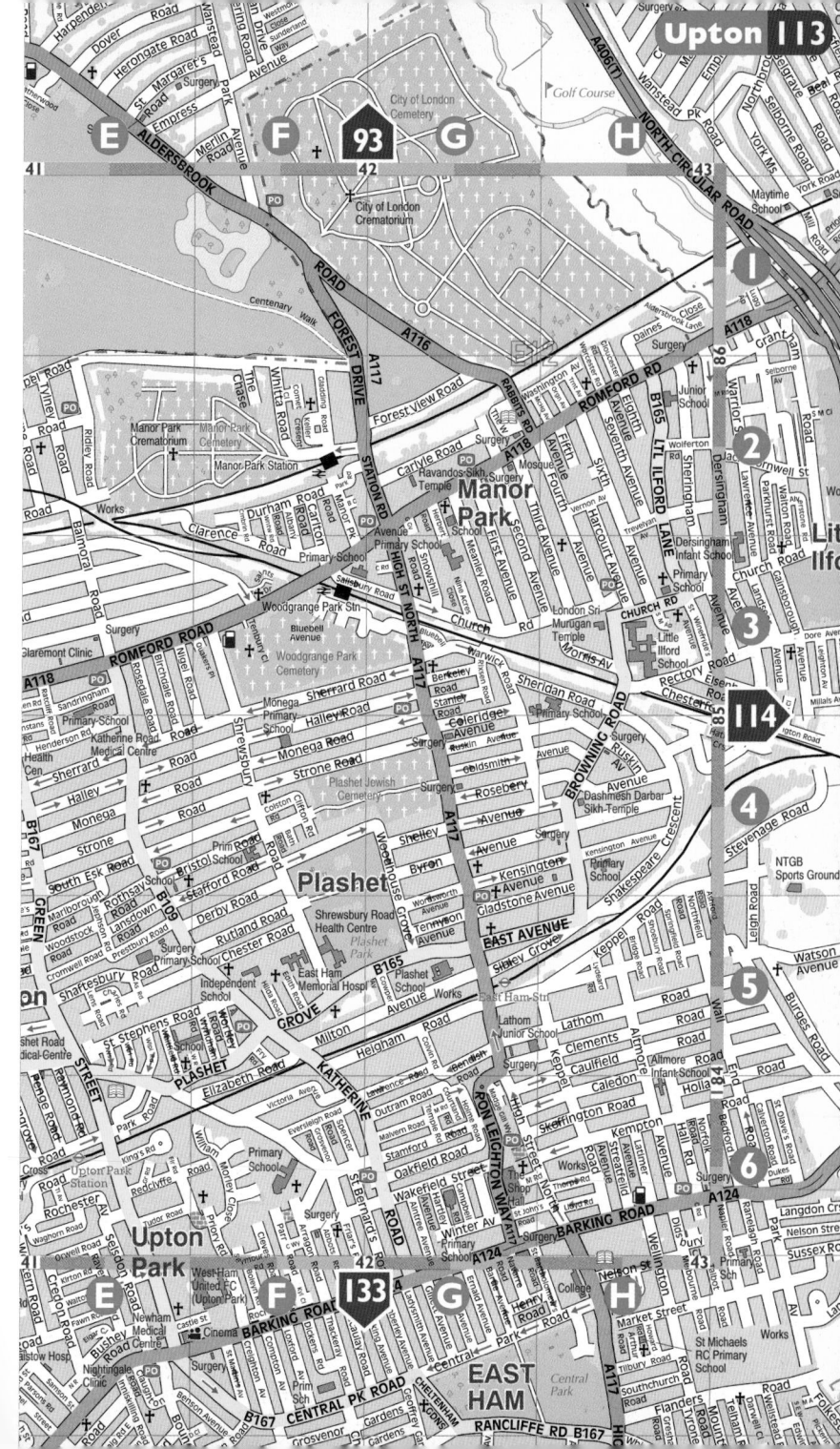

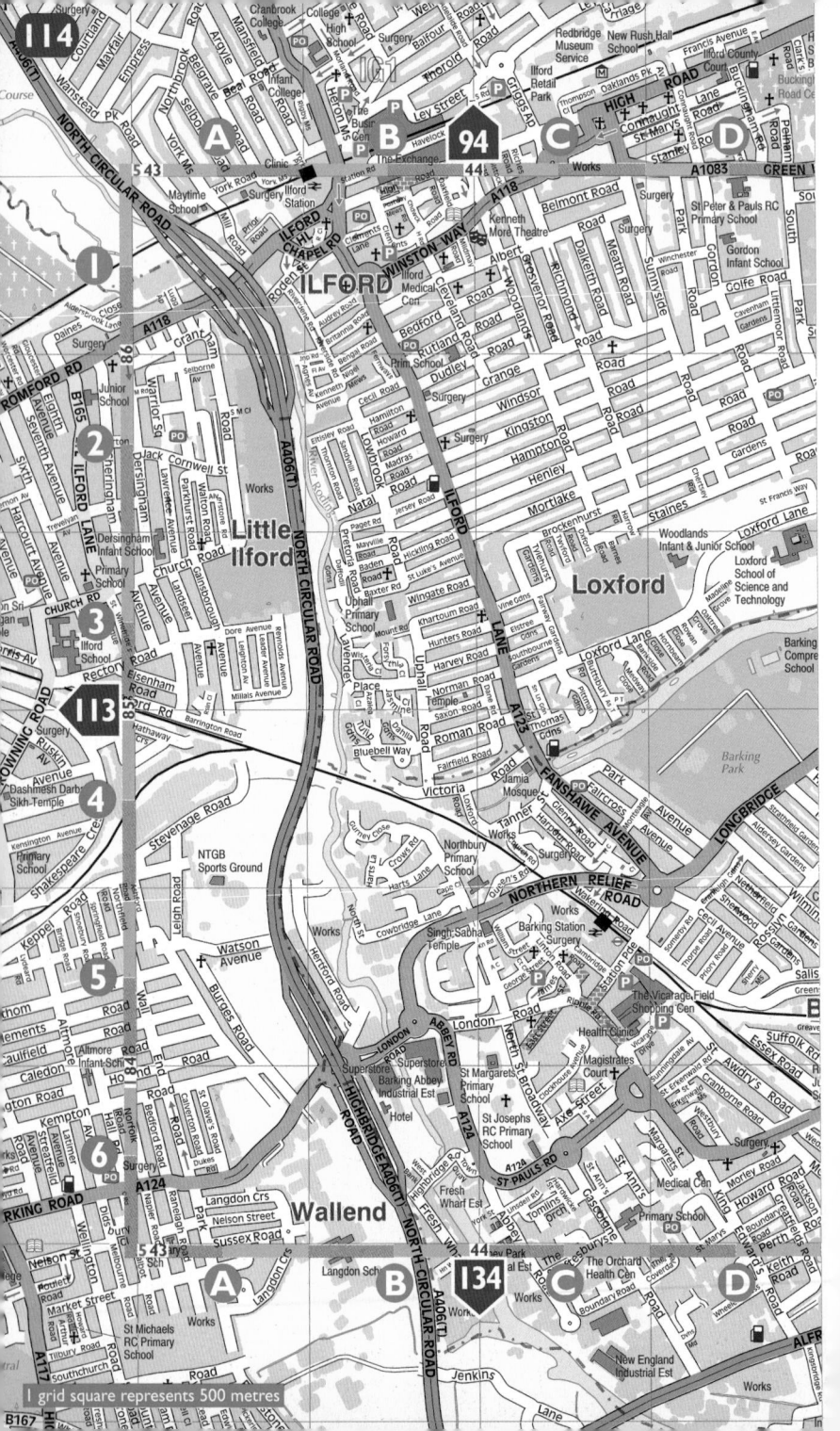

I grid square represents 500 metres

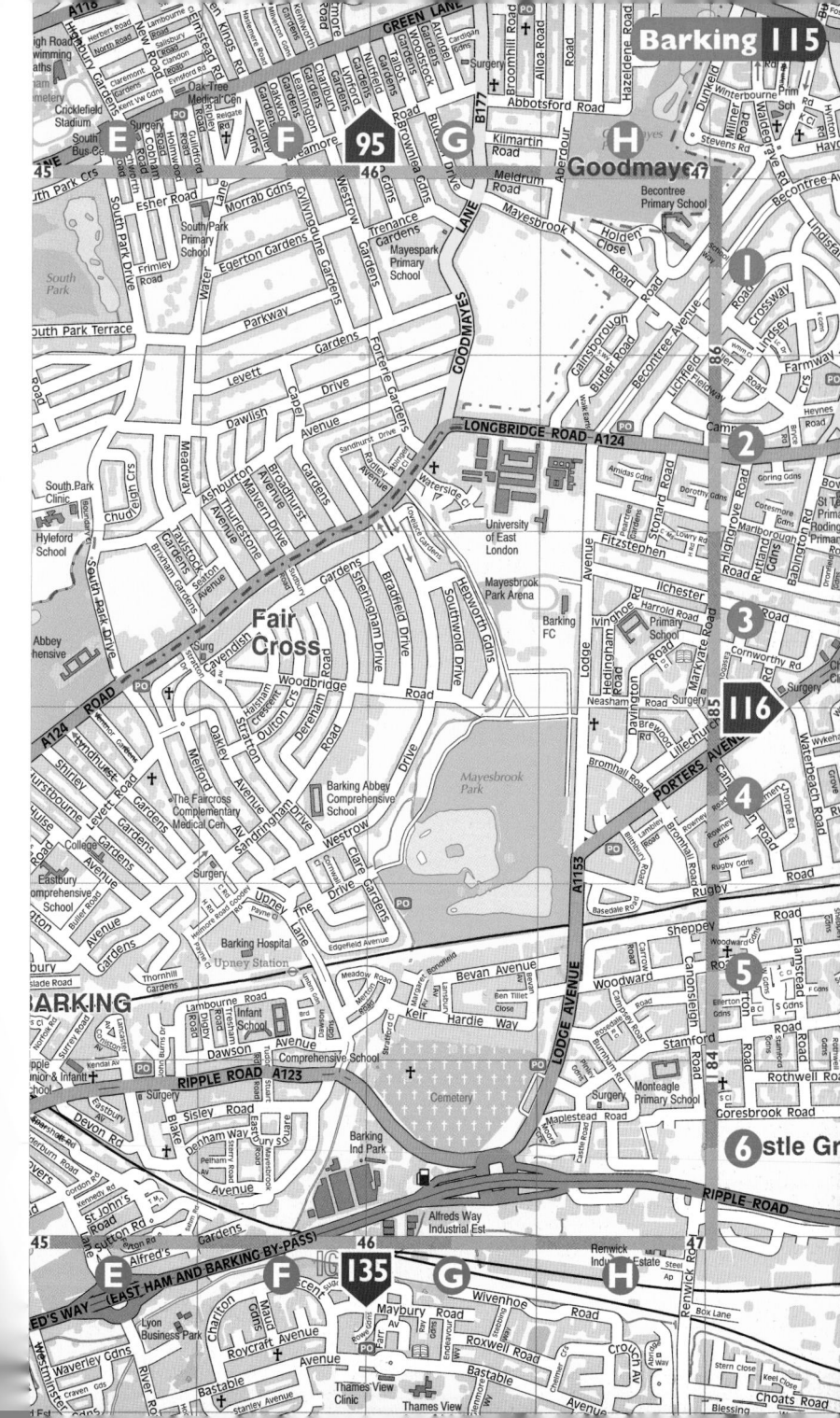

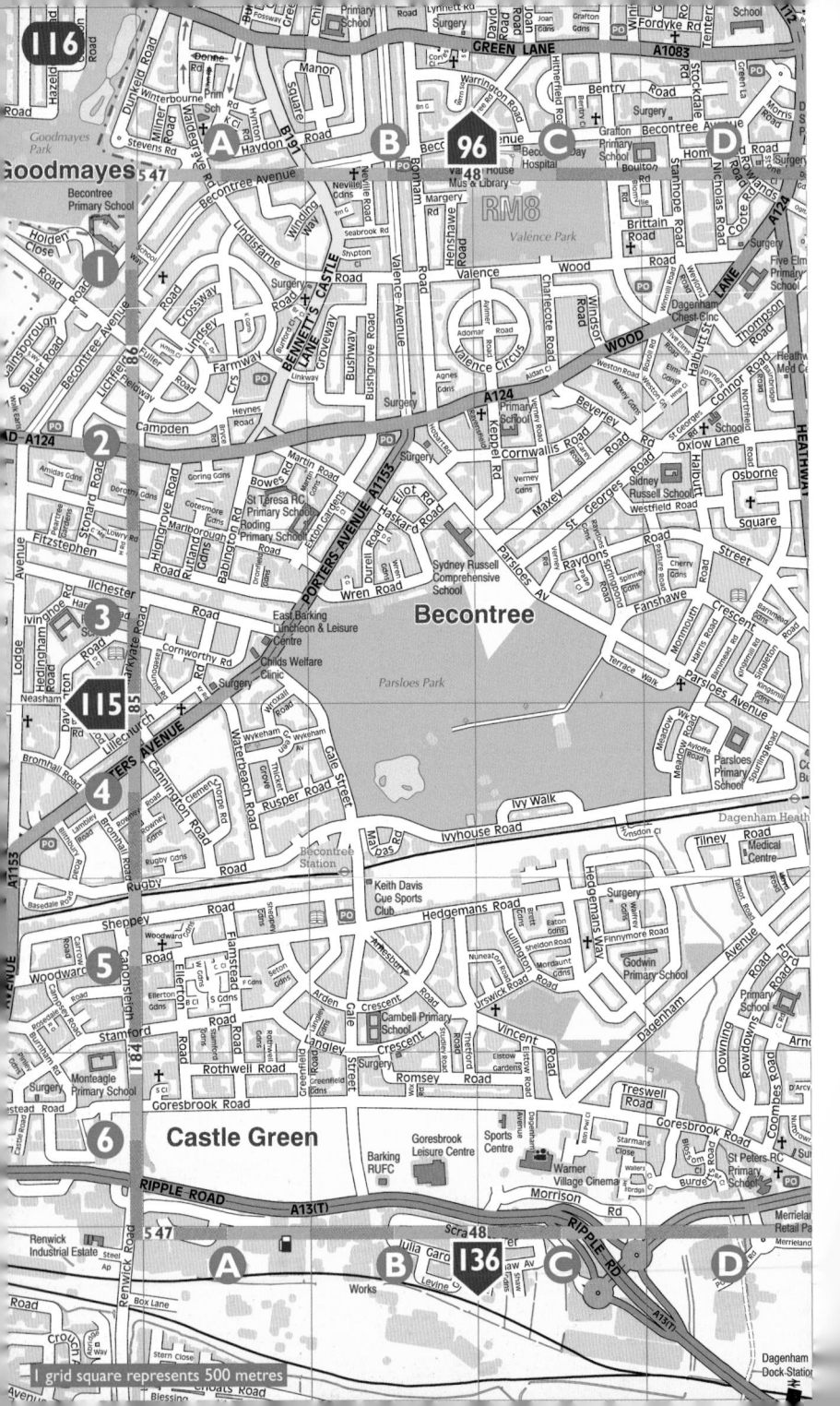

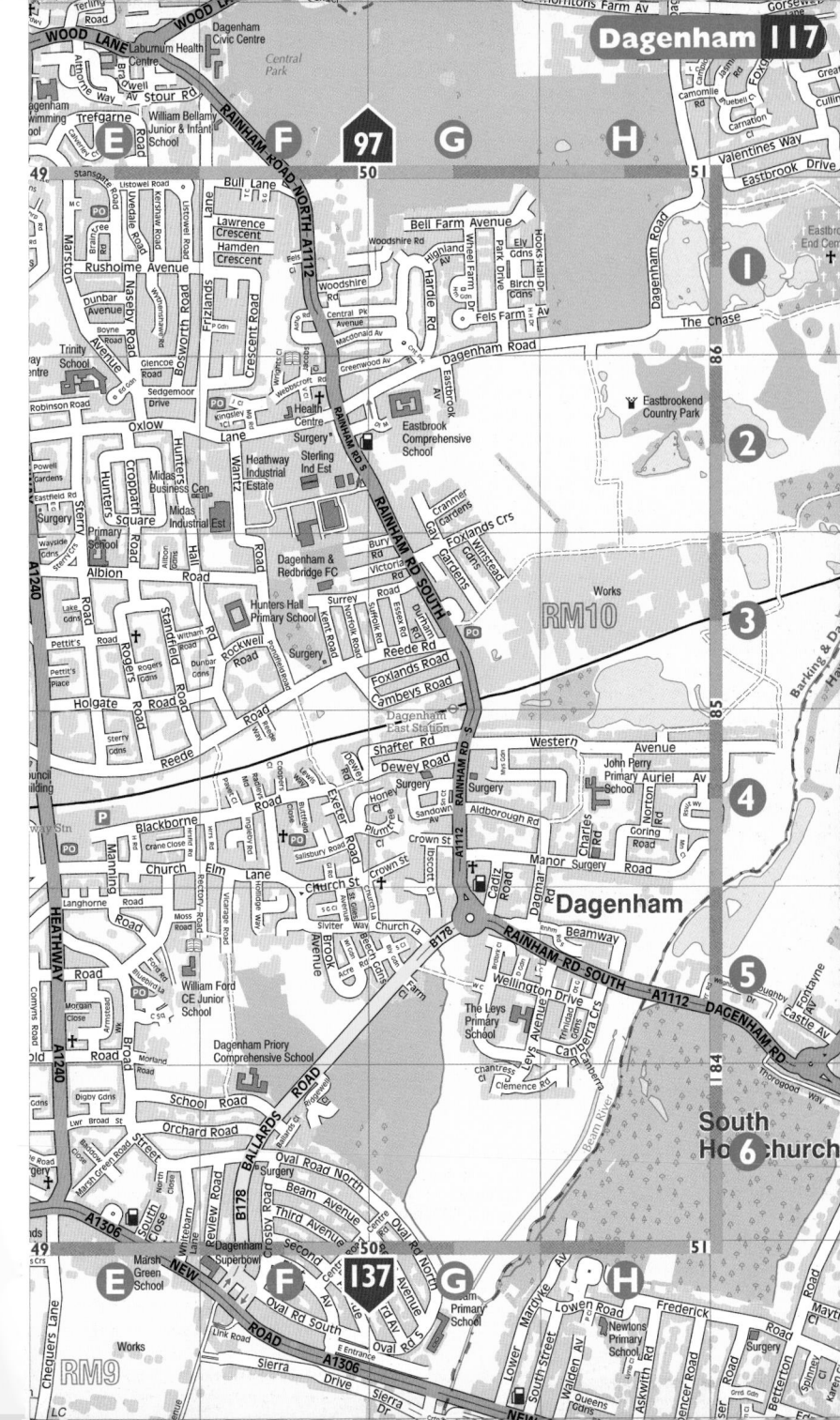

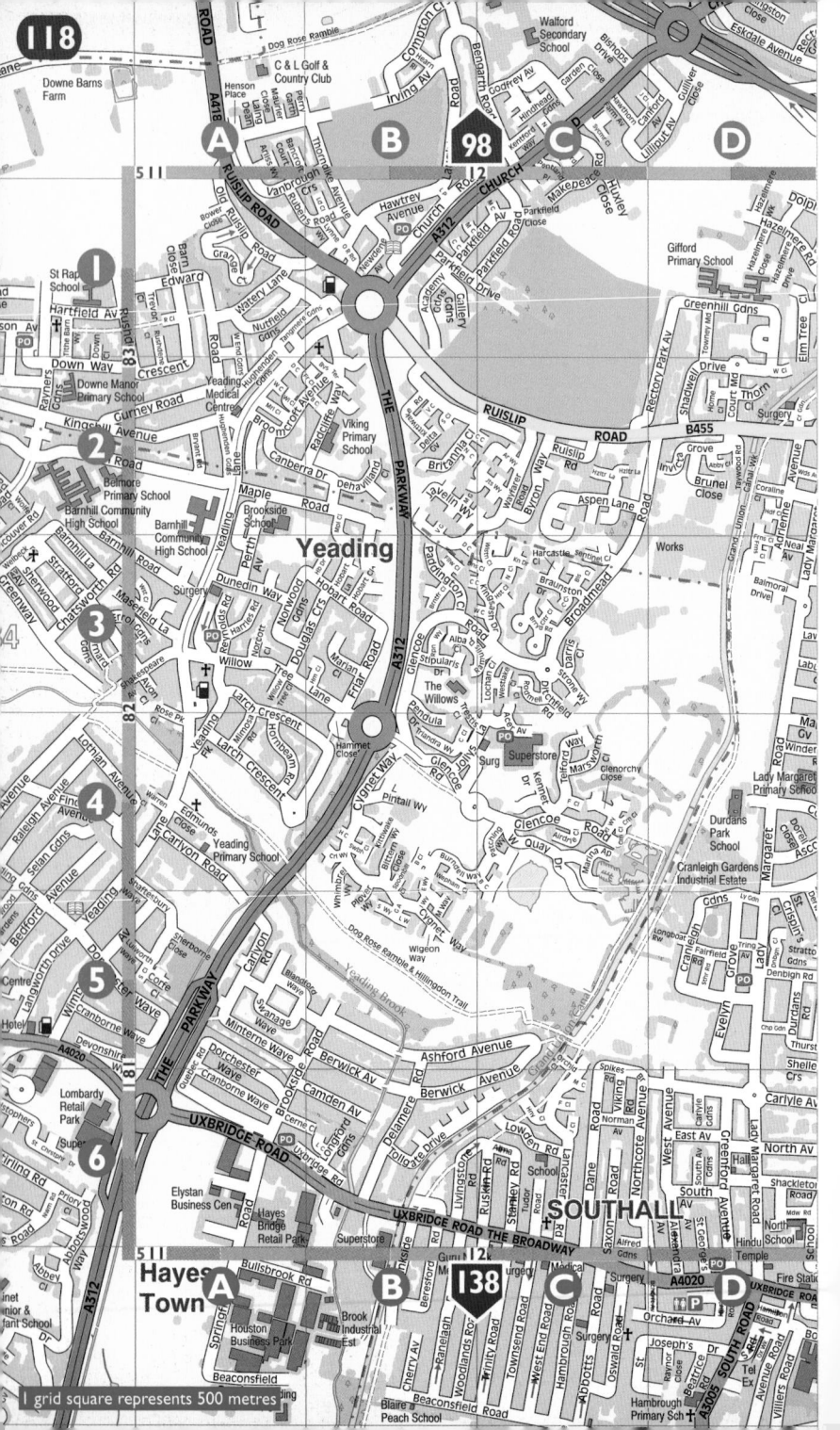

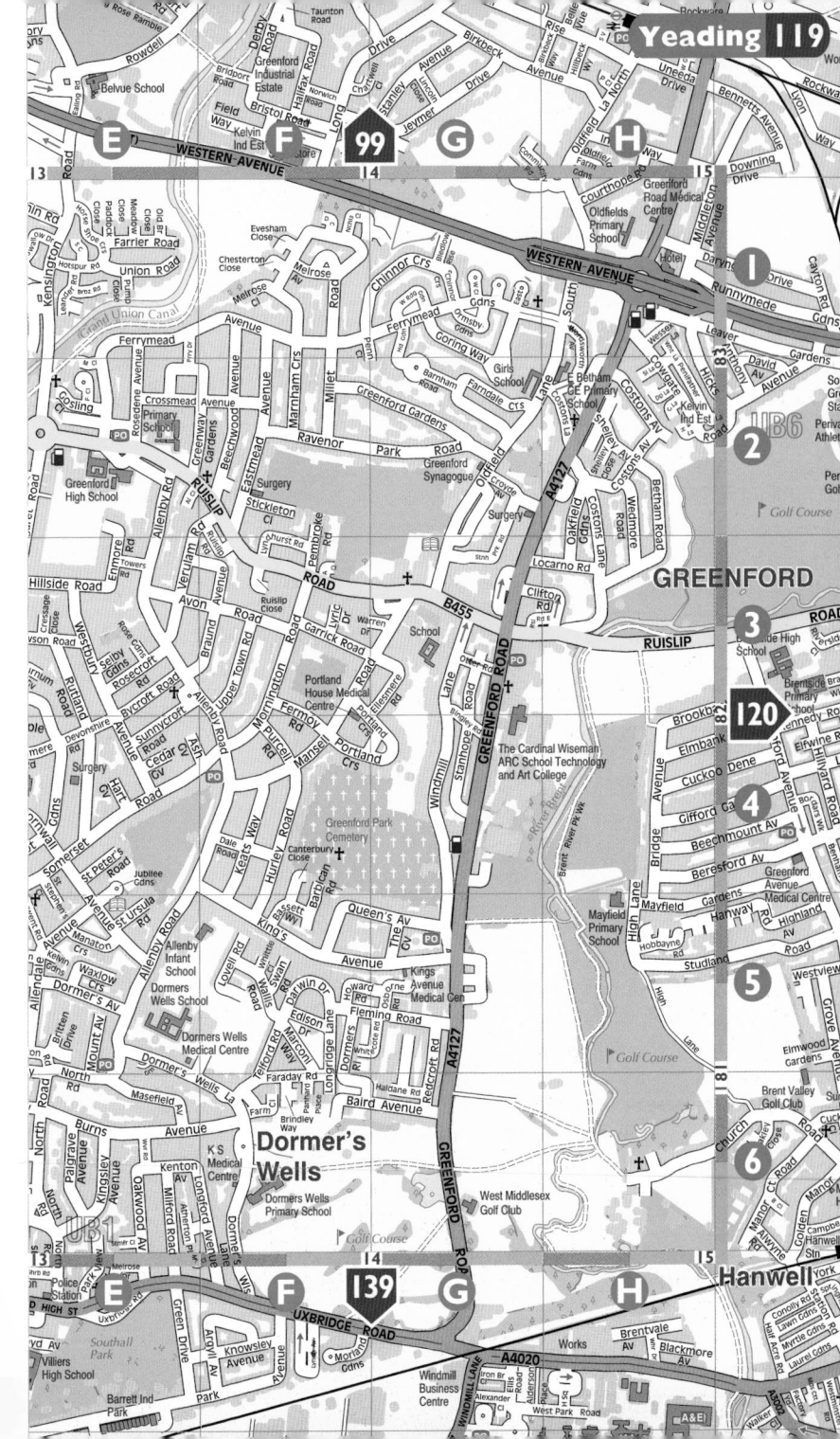

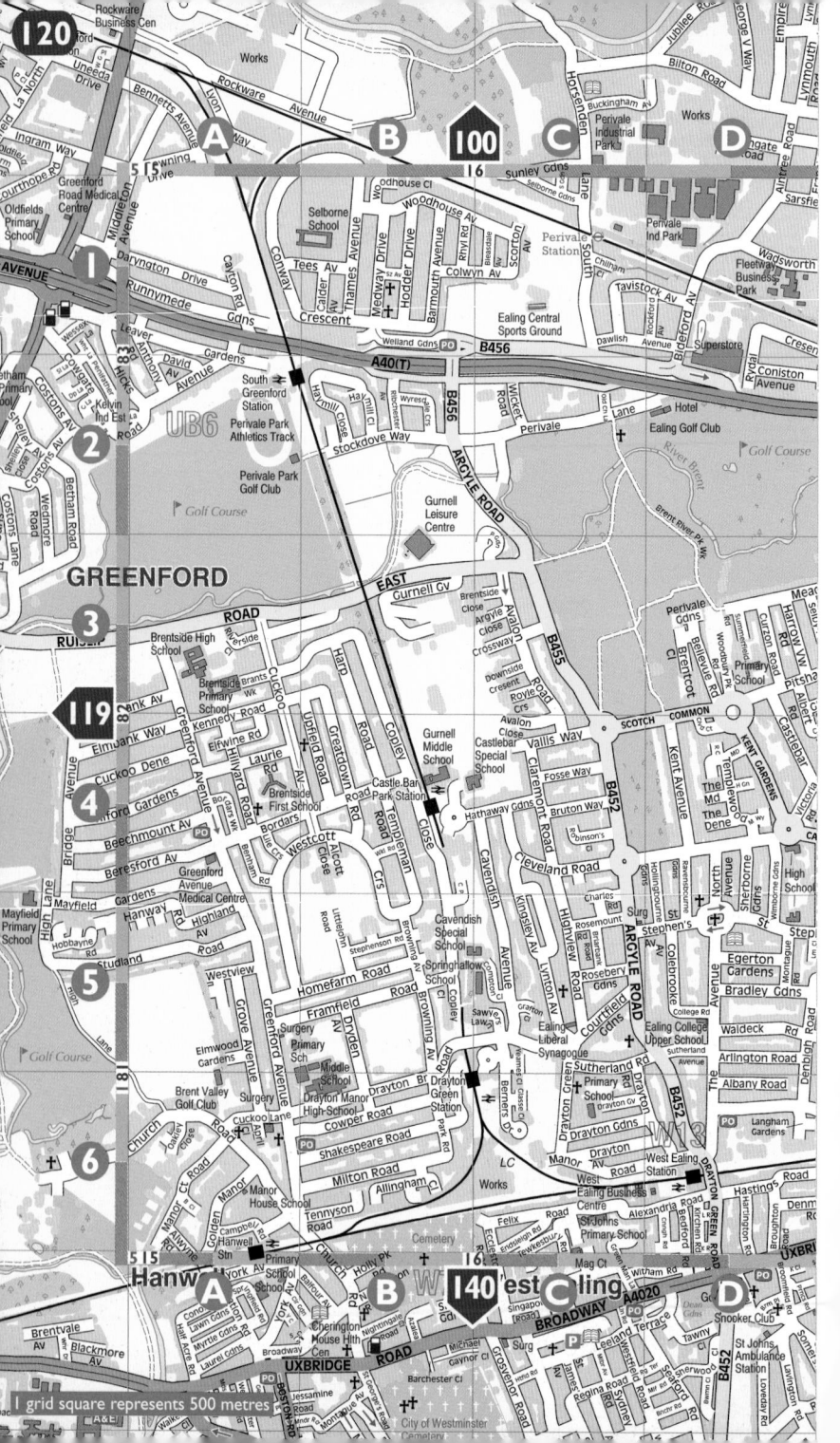

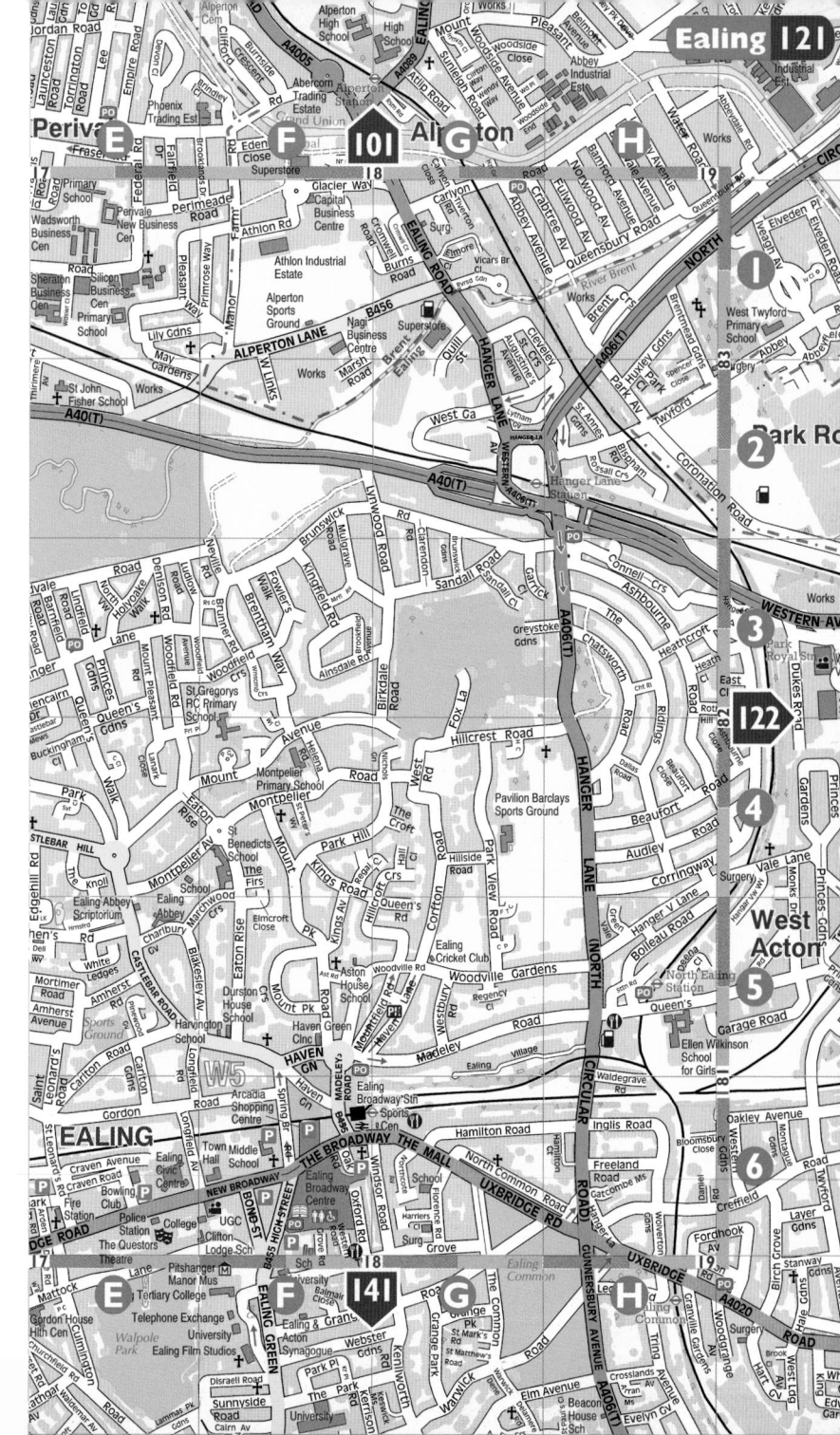

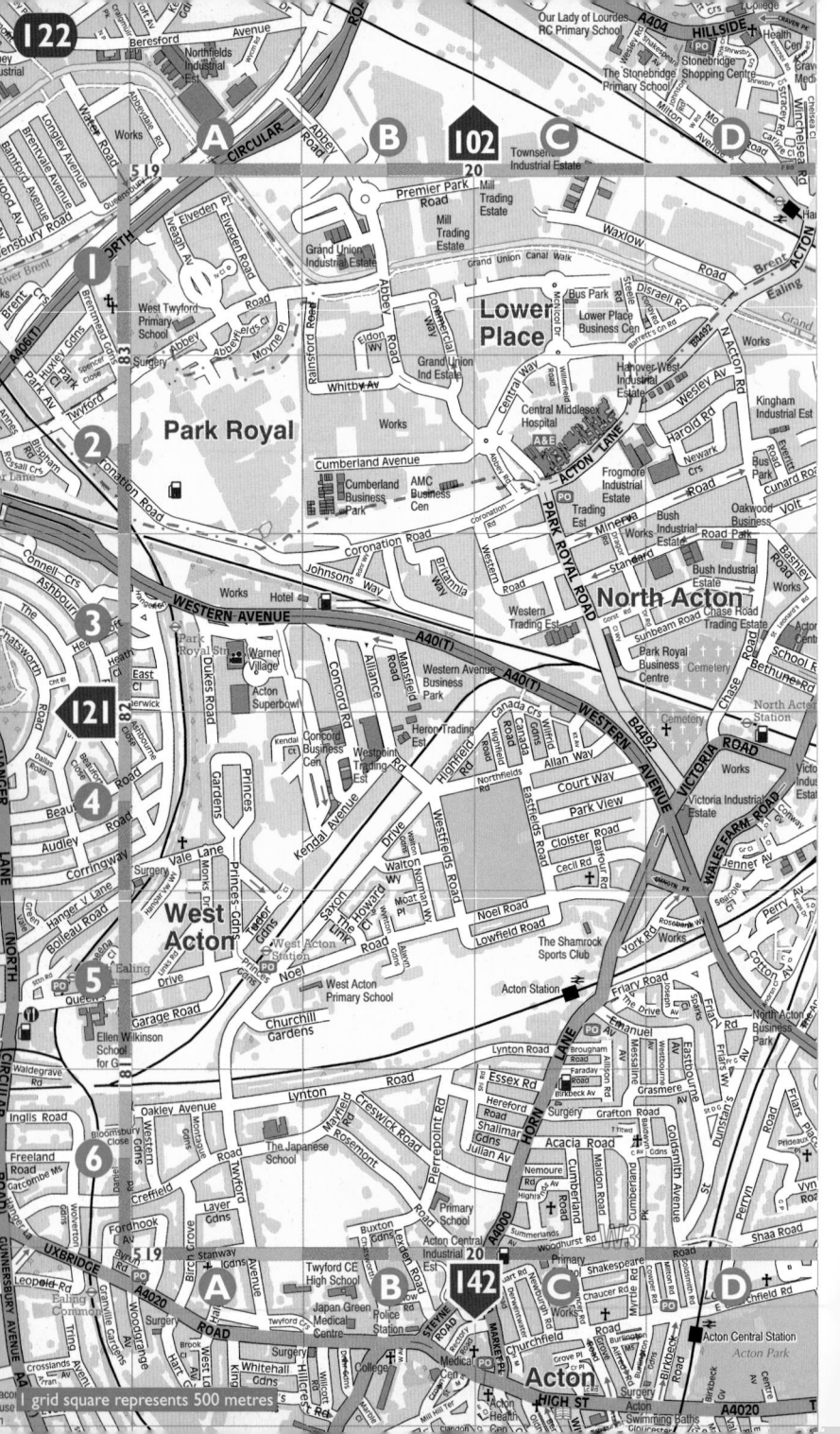

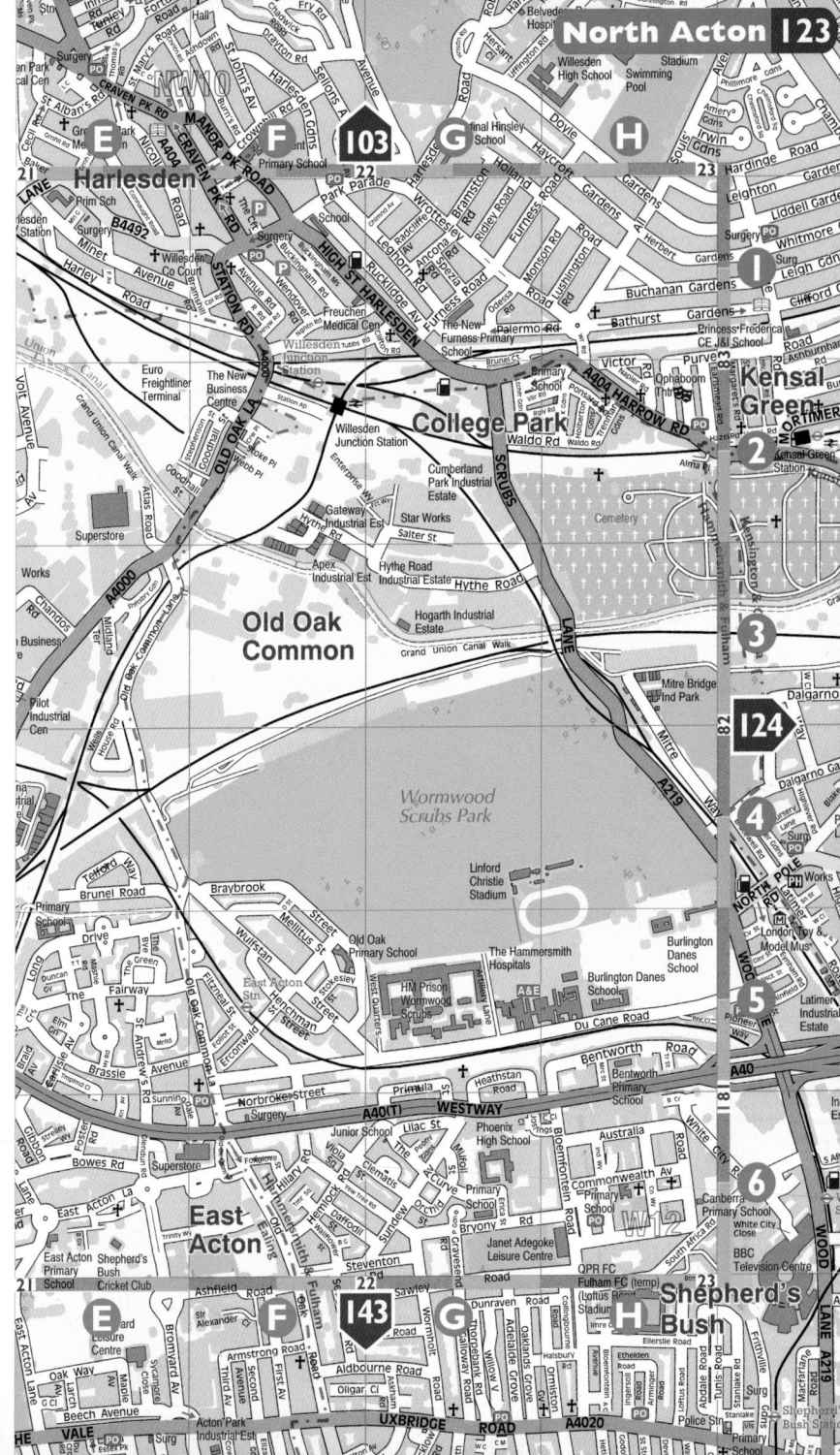

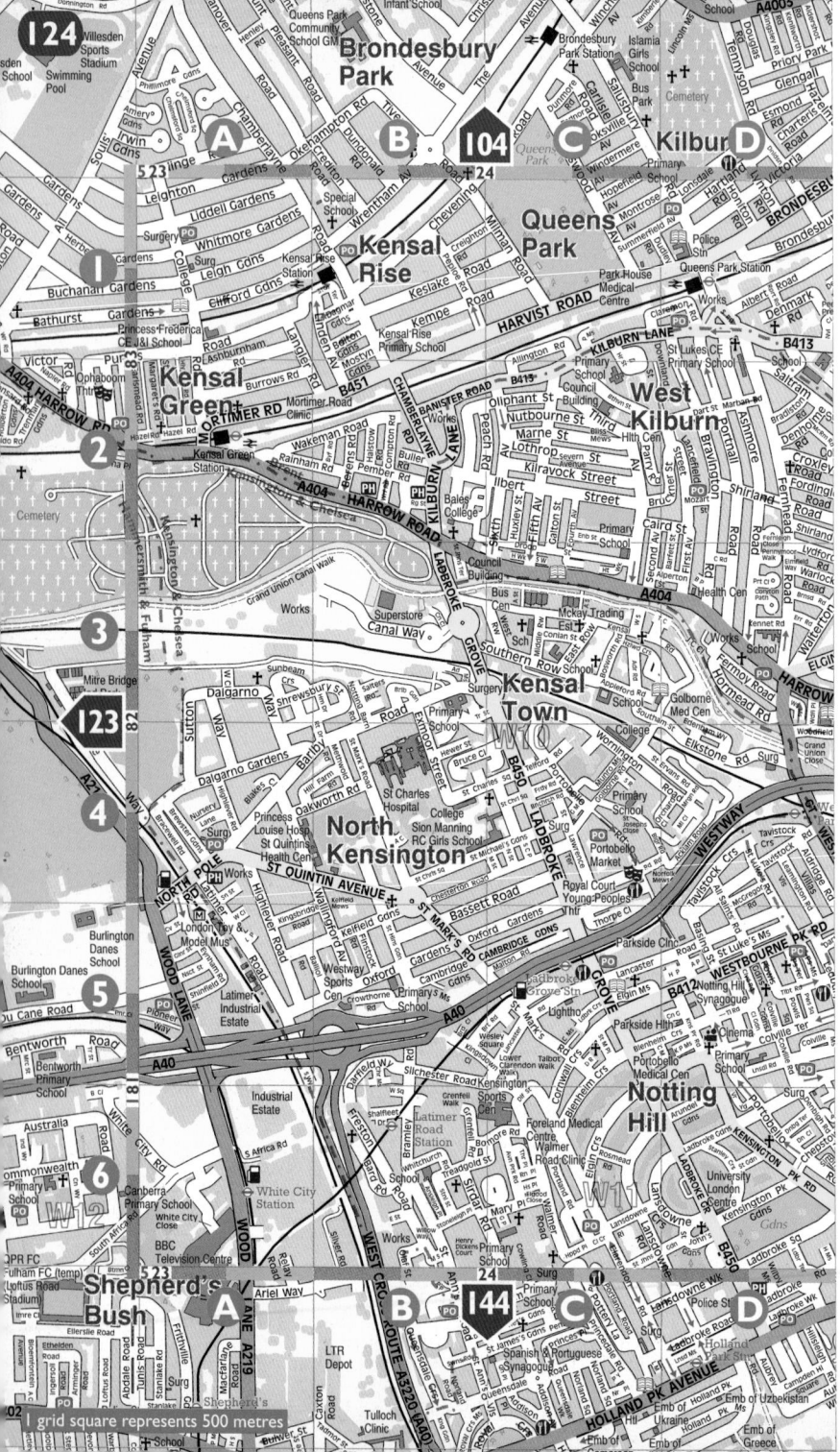

1 grid square represents 500 metres

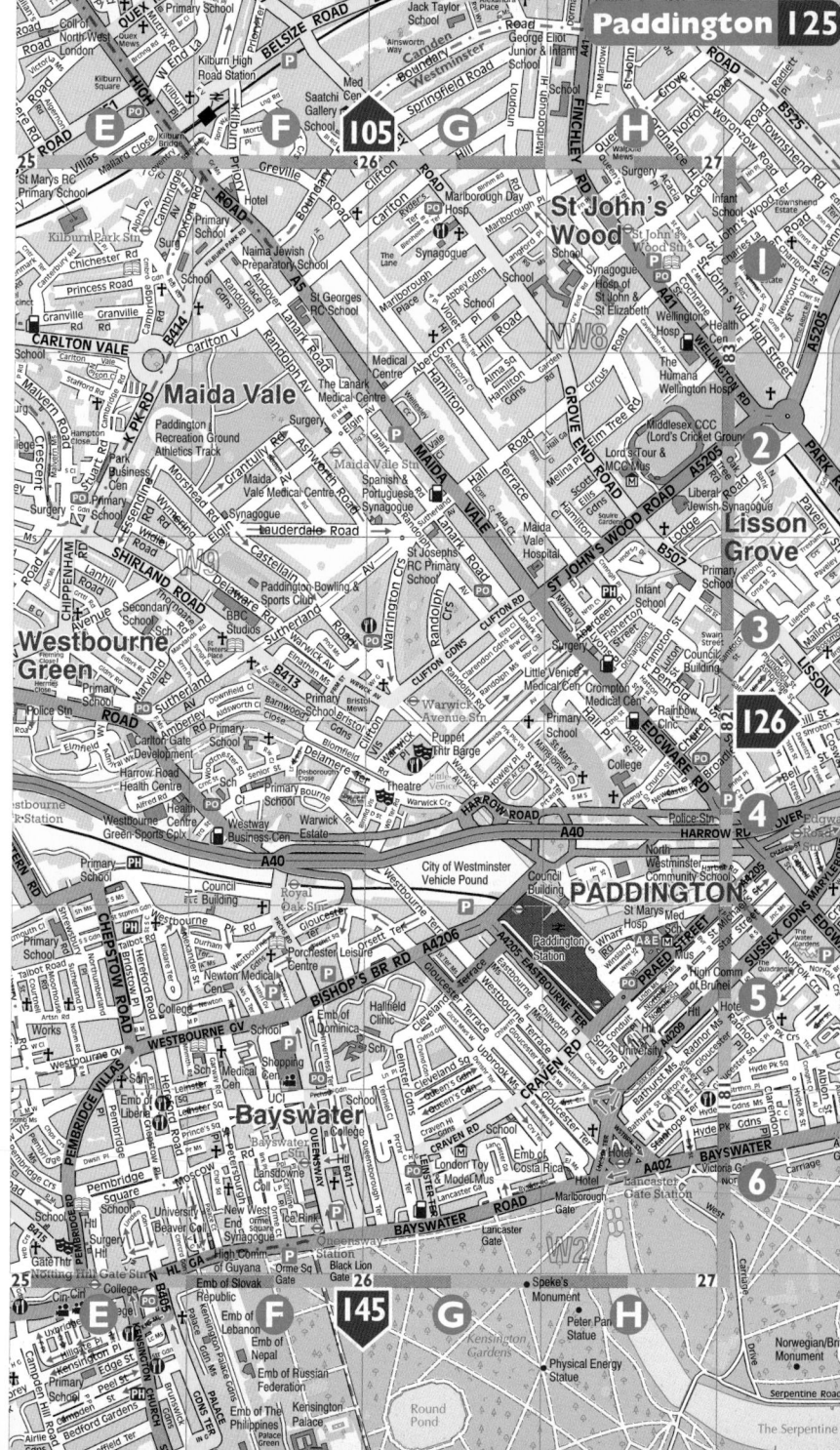

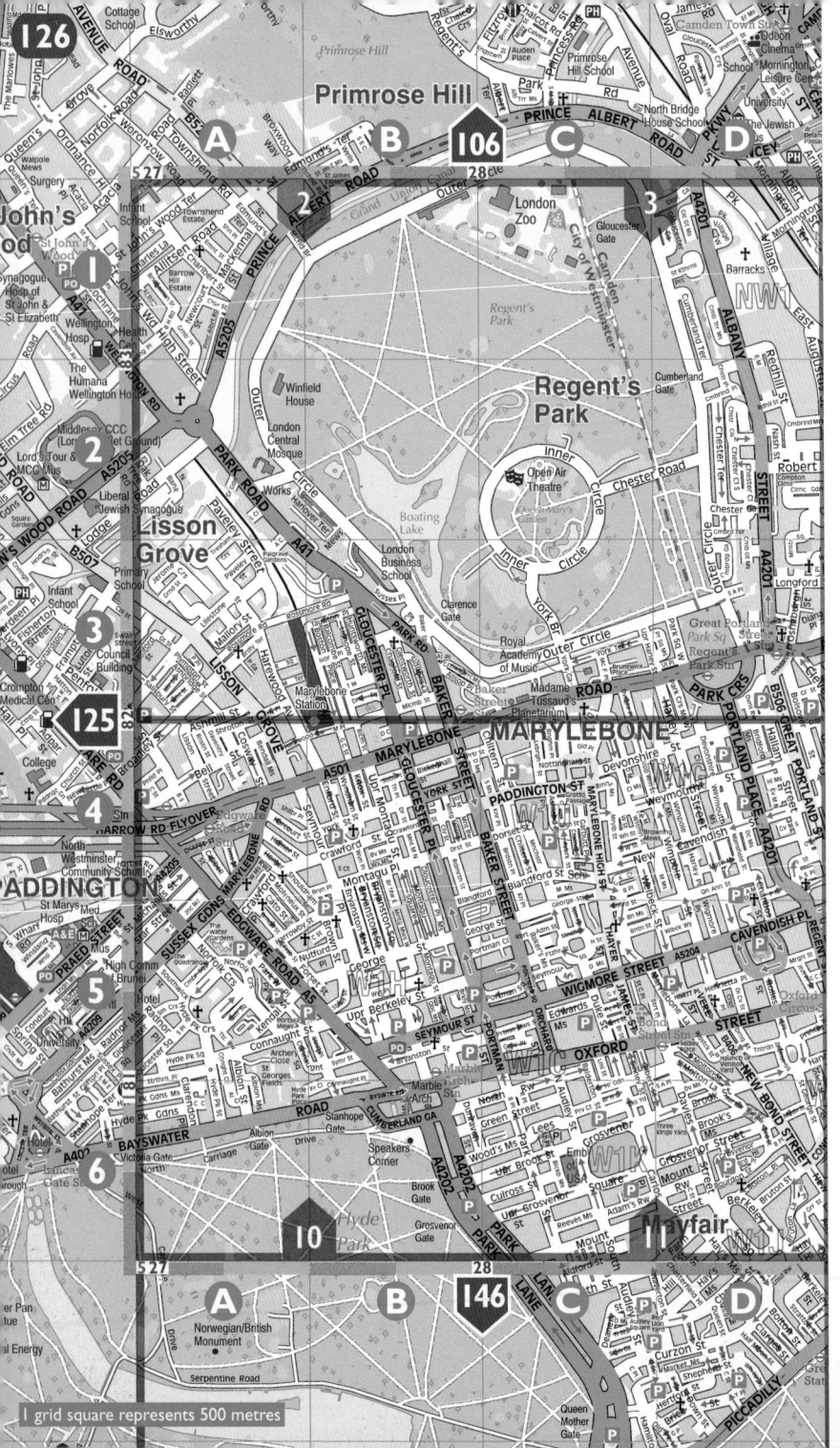

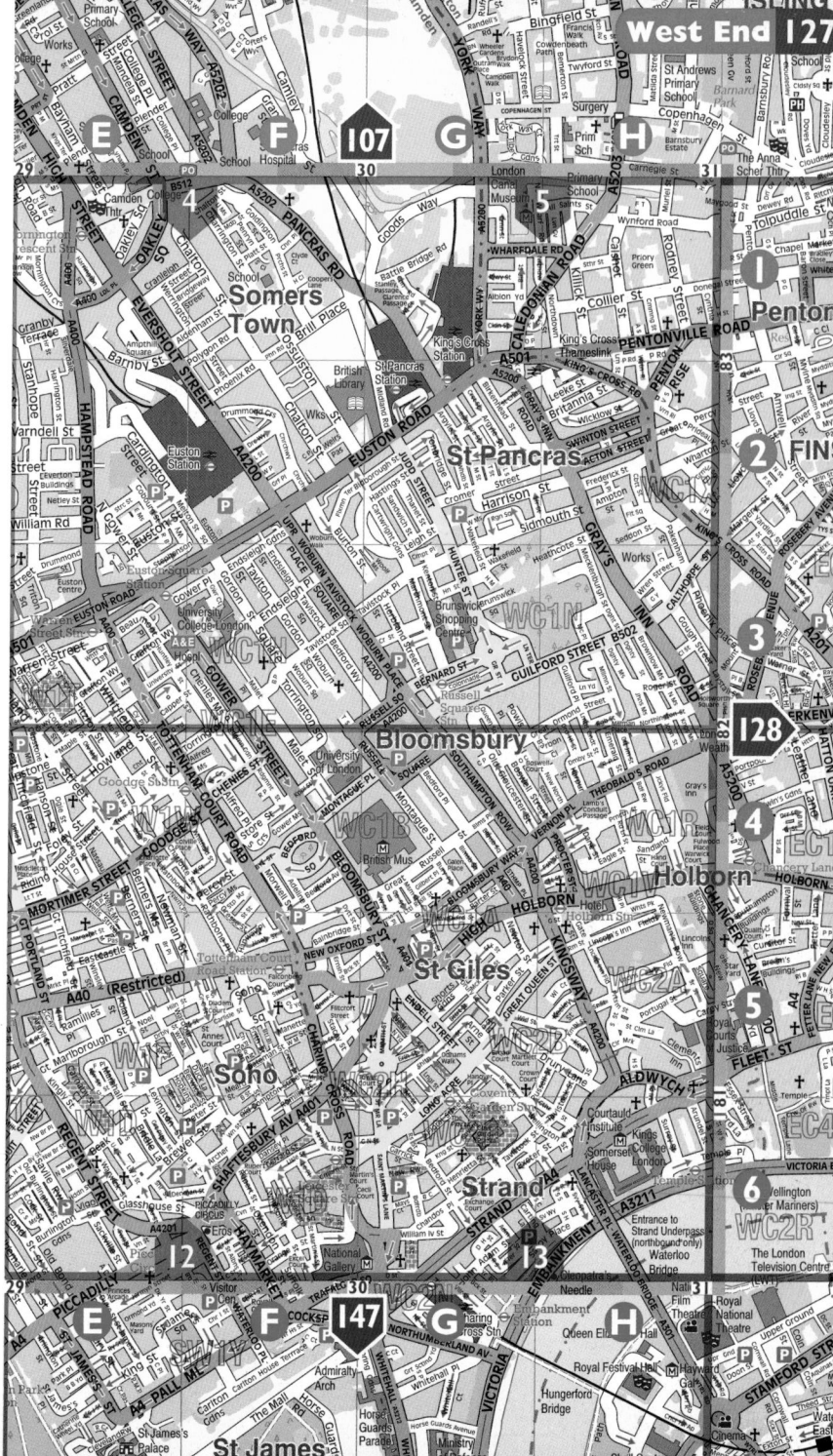

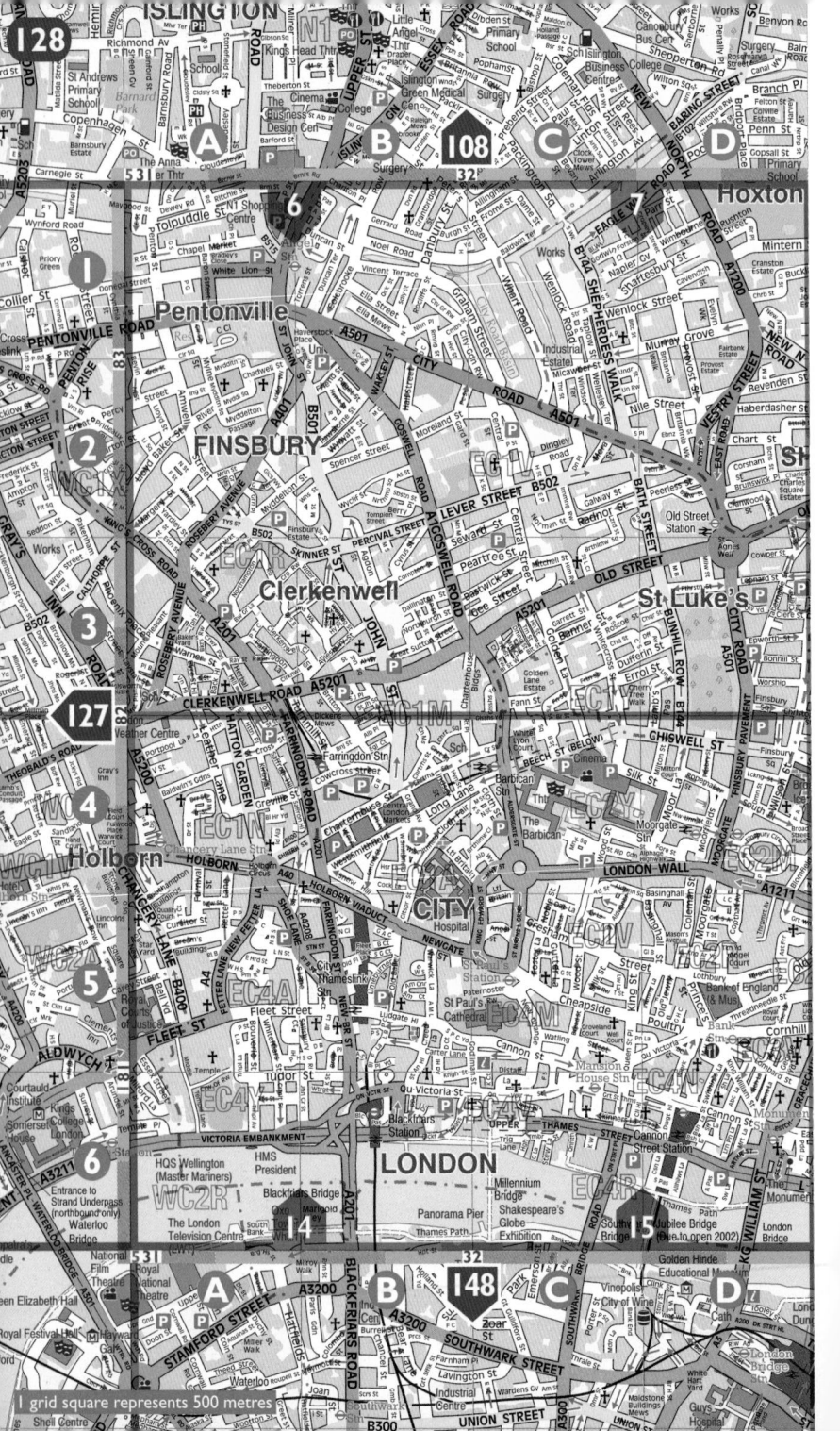

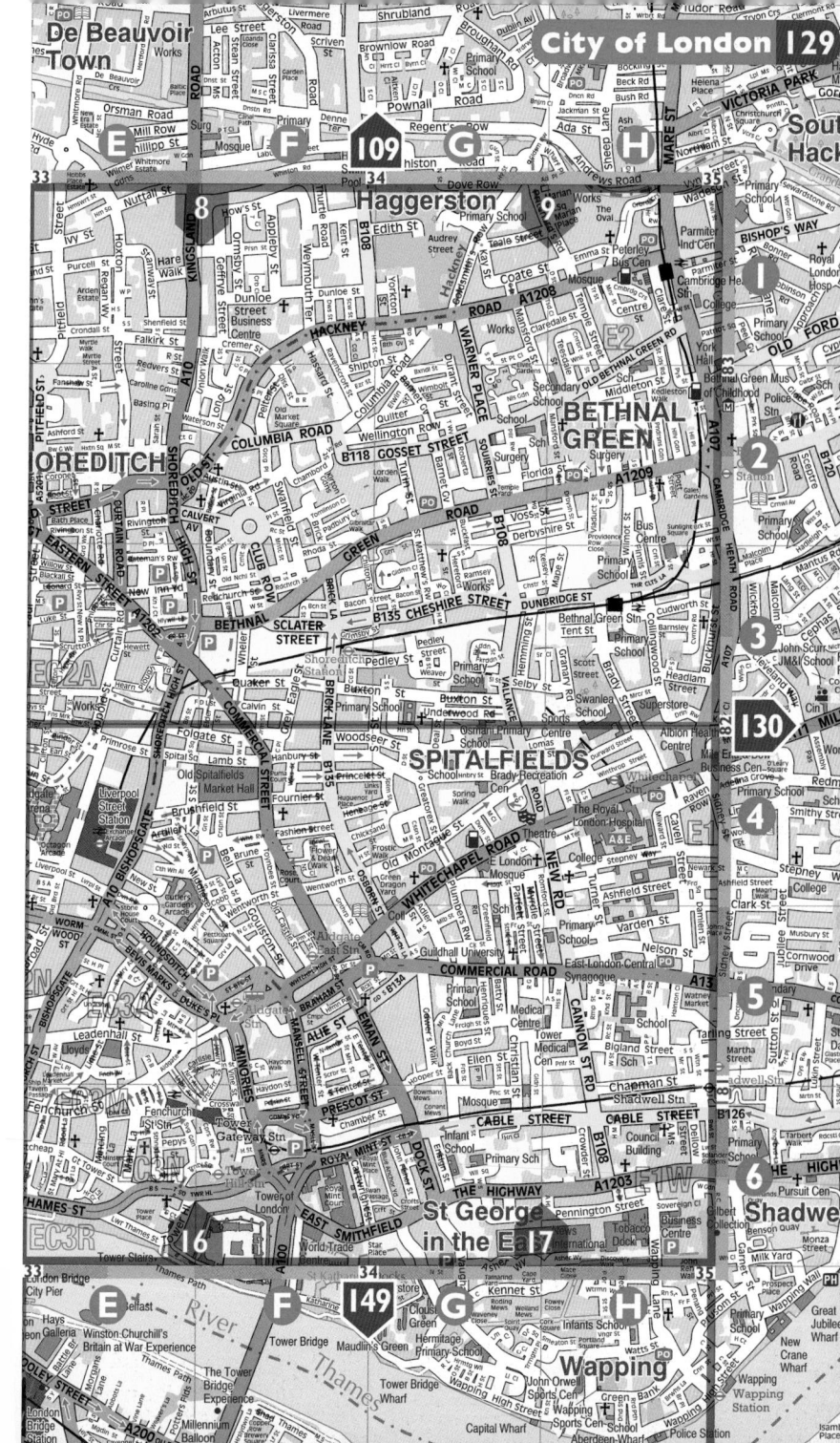

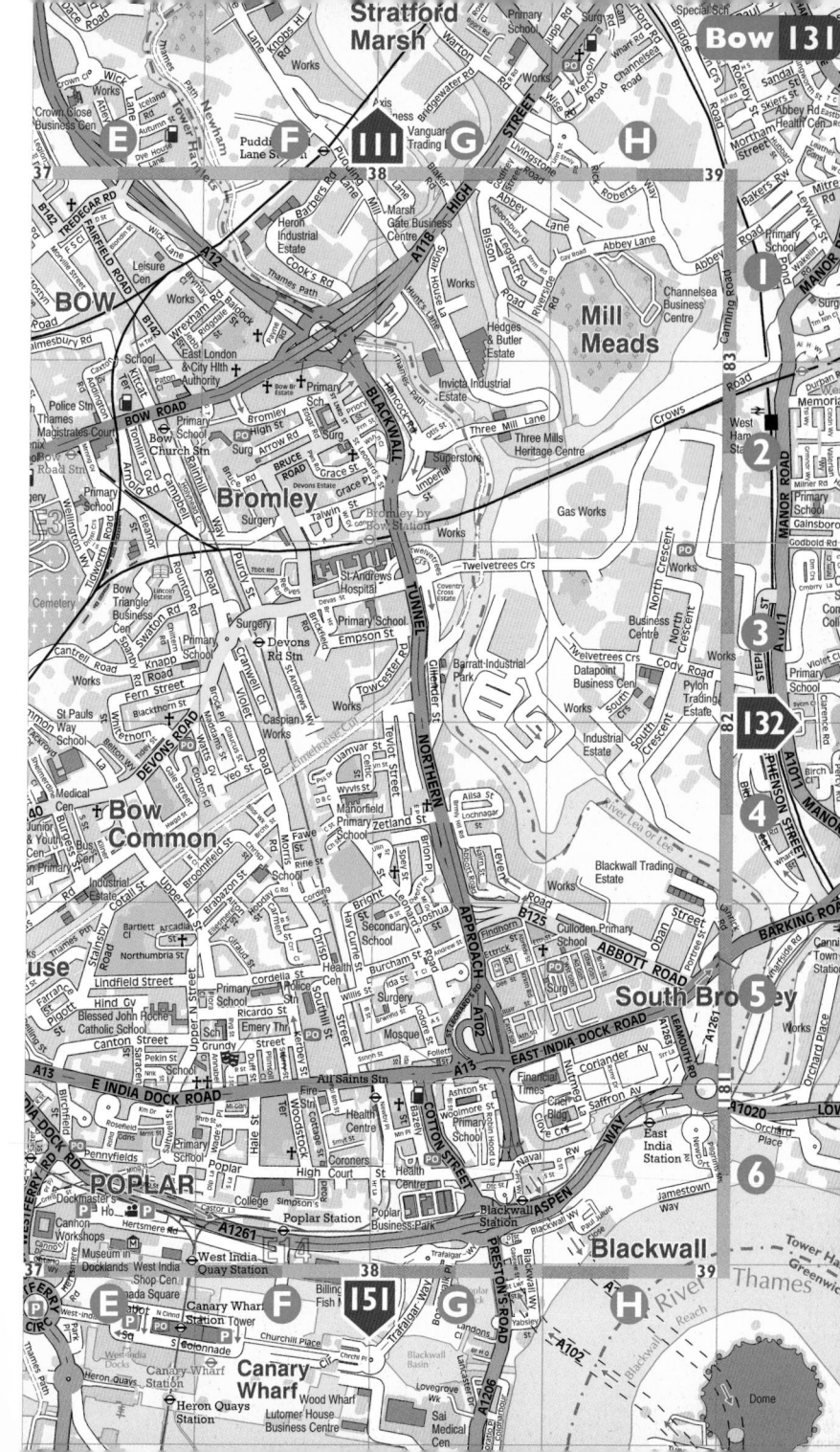

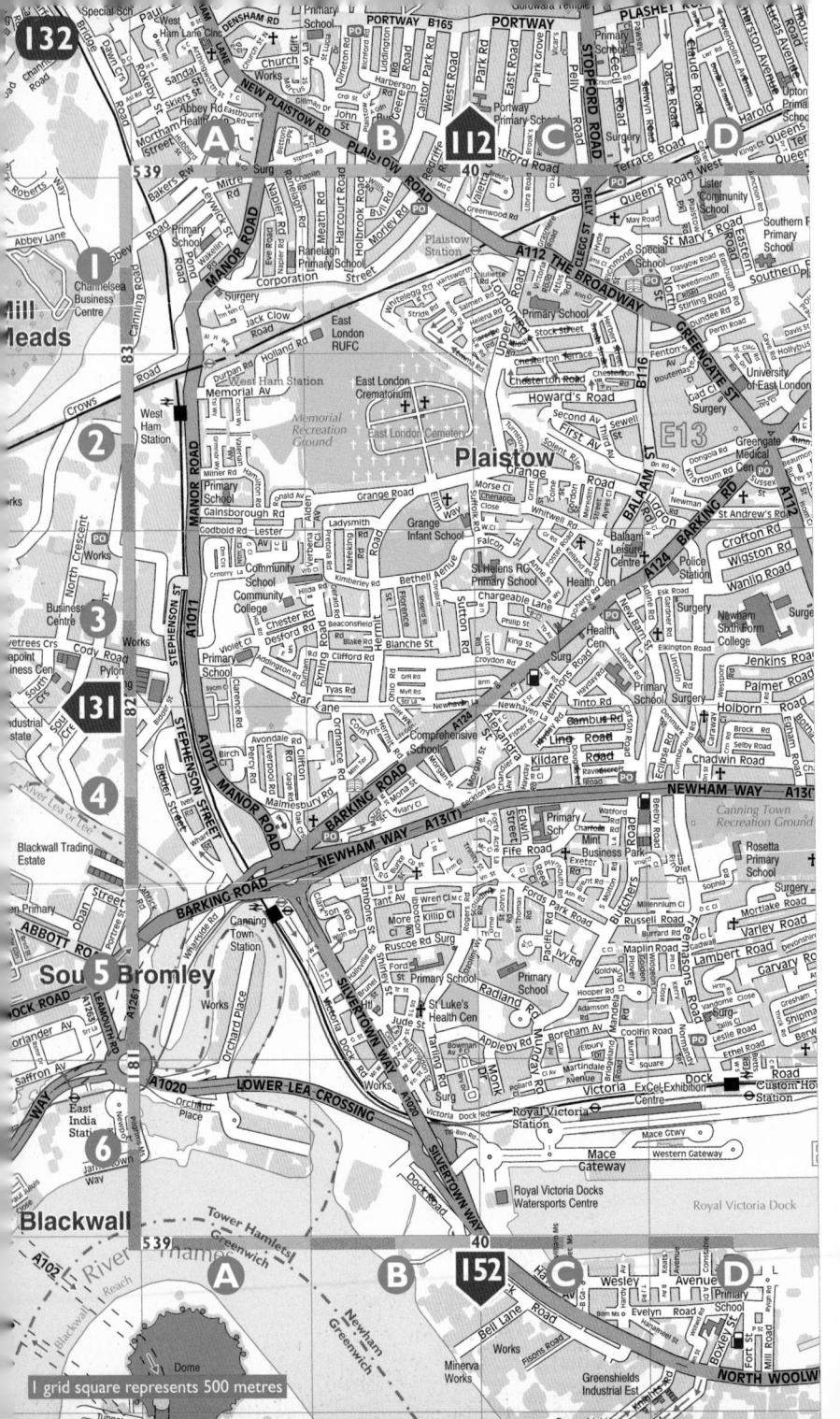

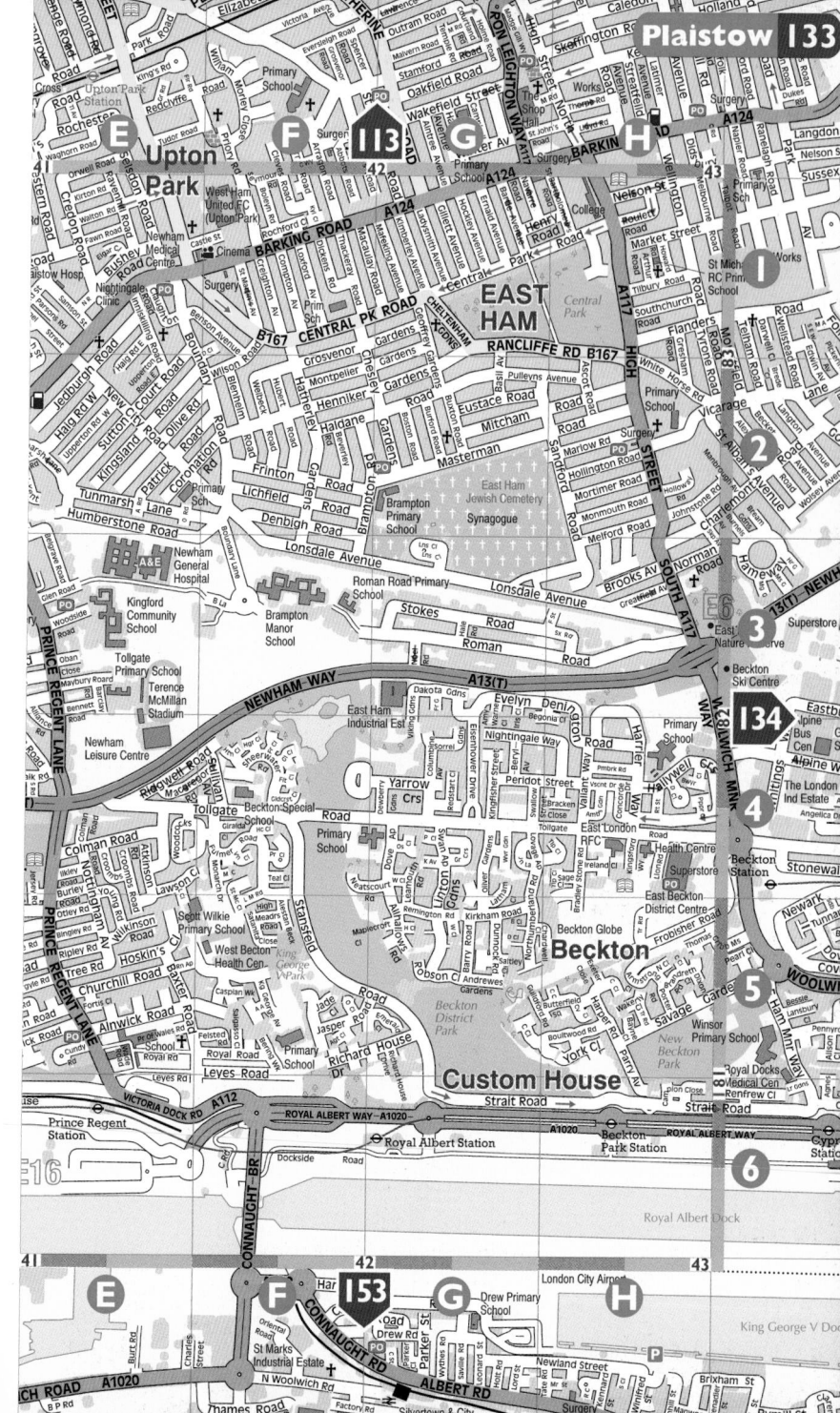

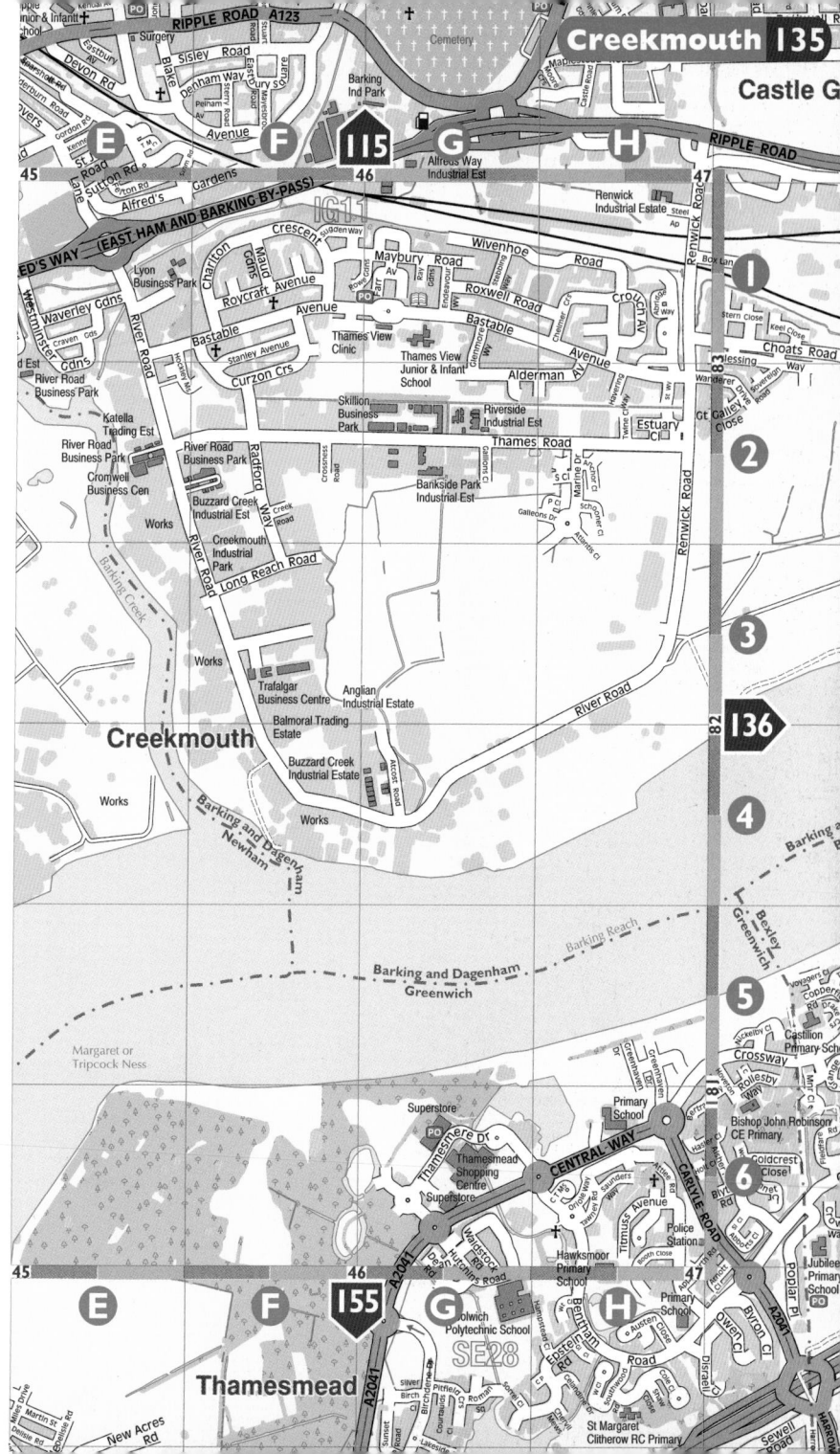

Castle G

Thamesmead

Creekmouth

SE28

136

Castle Green

A RIPPLE ROAD   A13(T)   **B**   **116**   **C**   **D**

Renwick
Industrial Estate

Goresbrook Road

Rothwell Road

Romsey Road

Treswell Road

Goresbrook Road

Barking RUFC

Goresbrook Leisure Centre

Sports Centre

Scrattons Ter

Julia Gardens

Works

1

Box Lane

Stern Close

Keel Close

Choats Road

Gt Galley Close

2 Estuary Cl

3

River Road

135

Choats Road

Hindmans Way

Power Station

Industrial Estate

Chequers Lane

Thunderer

River Thames

4 Barking and Dagenham
Bexley

Cross Ness

Bexley
Greenwich

Barking Reach

5

Riverside Golf Club

Fairway Drive

Castillon Primary School

Crossway

Voyagers Cl
Coppersield Place
Thamesmere

Golf Course

Cherbury Close

Longworth

6 CENTRAL WAY

Primary School

Bishop John Robinson CE Primary

Goldcrest Close

Crossway

Police Station

Blyth Rd

Titmuss Avenue

Walsham

Haldane Road

Jubilee Primary School

A Byron Cl   Owen Cl   **B**   **156**   **C**   **D**

Belvedere

Clitherow RC Primary

A2016

Dagenham Dock Station

Merrielands Retail Pk

St Peters RC Primary

Works

RIPPLE RD   A13(T)

1 grid square represents 500 metres

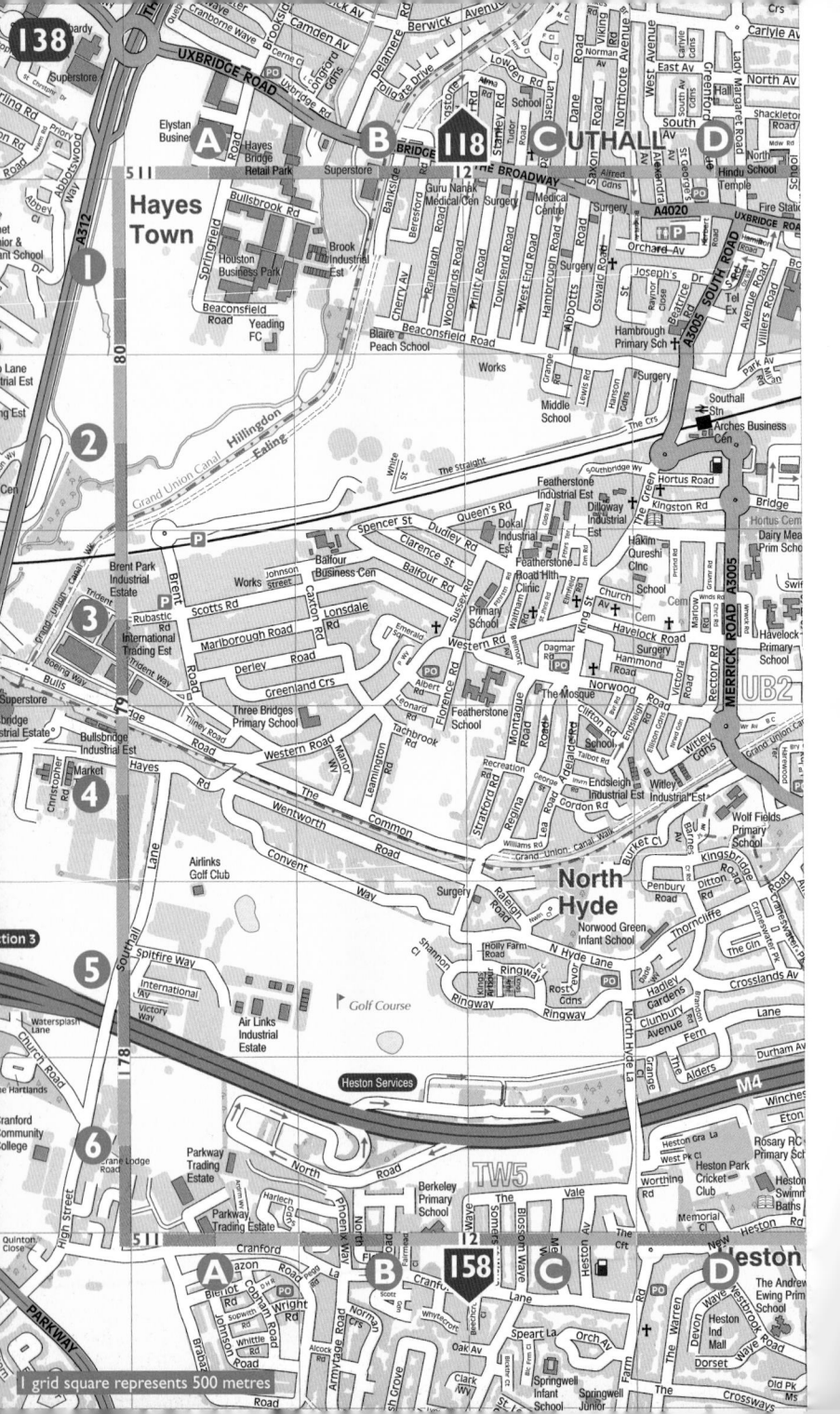

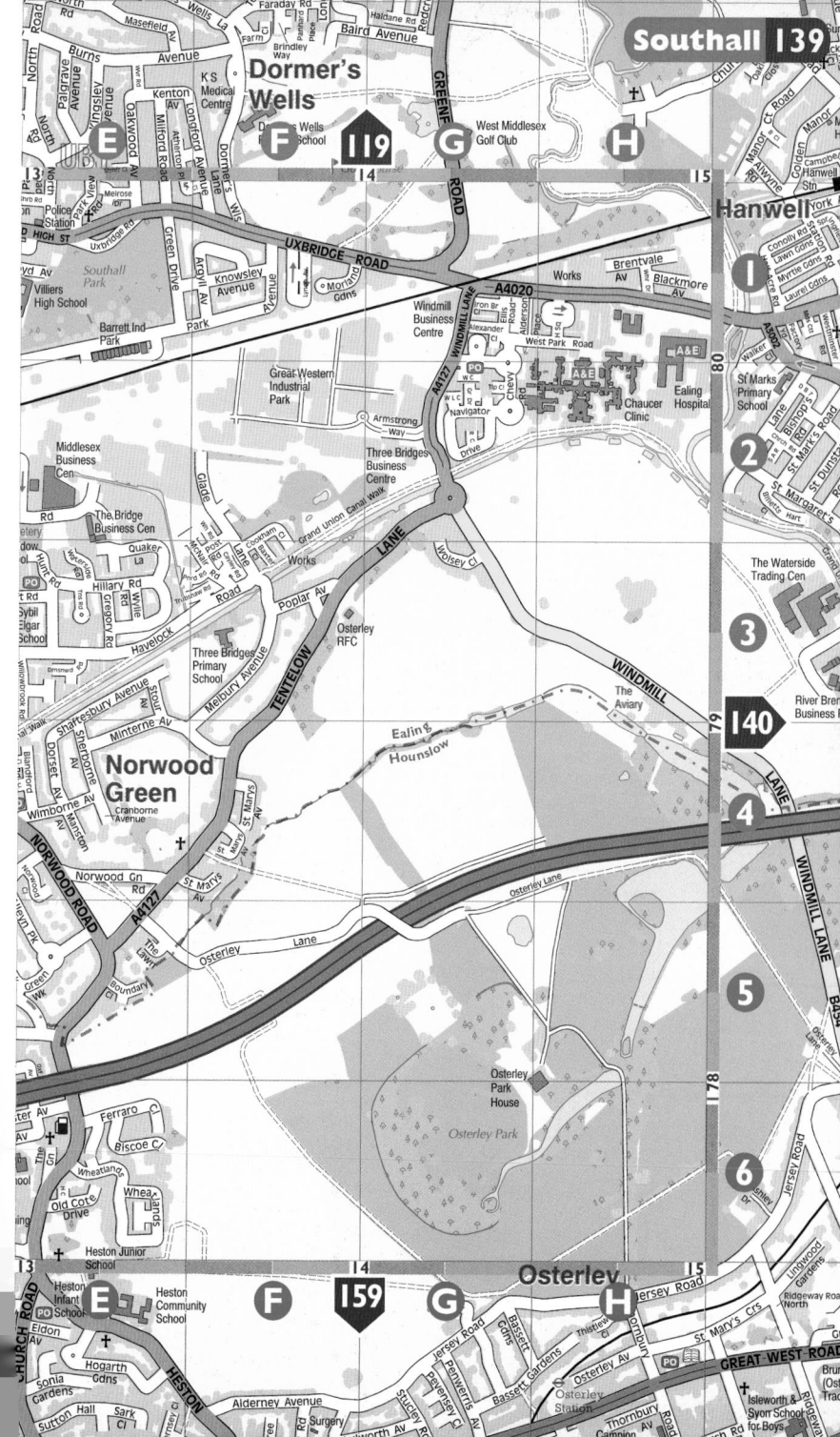

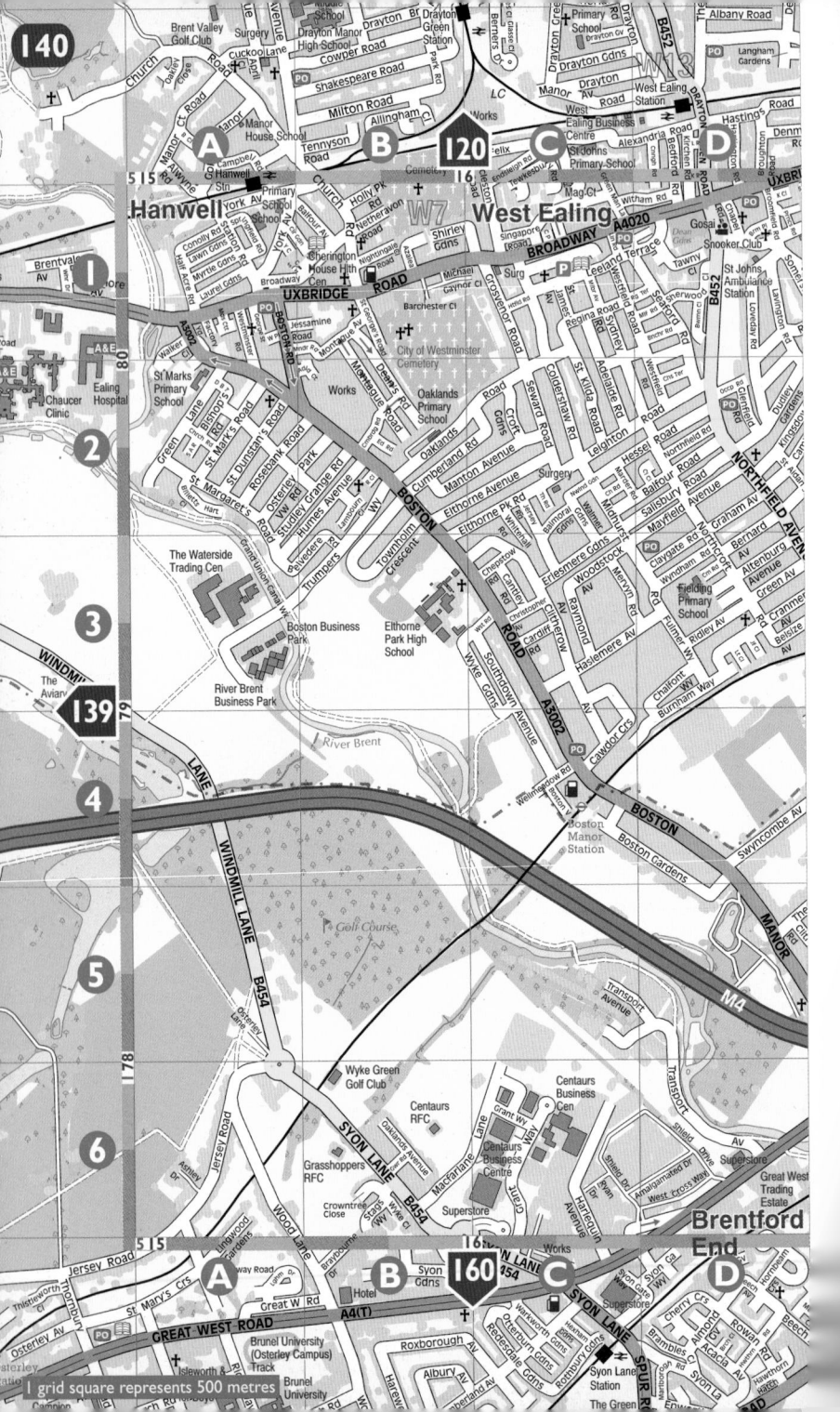

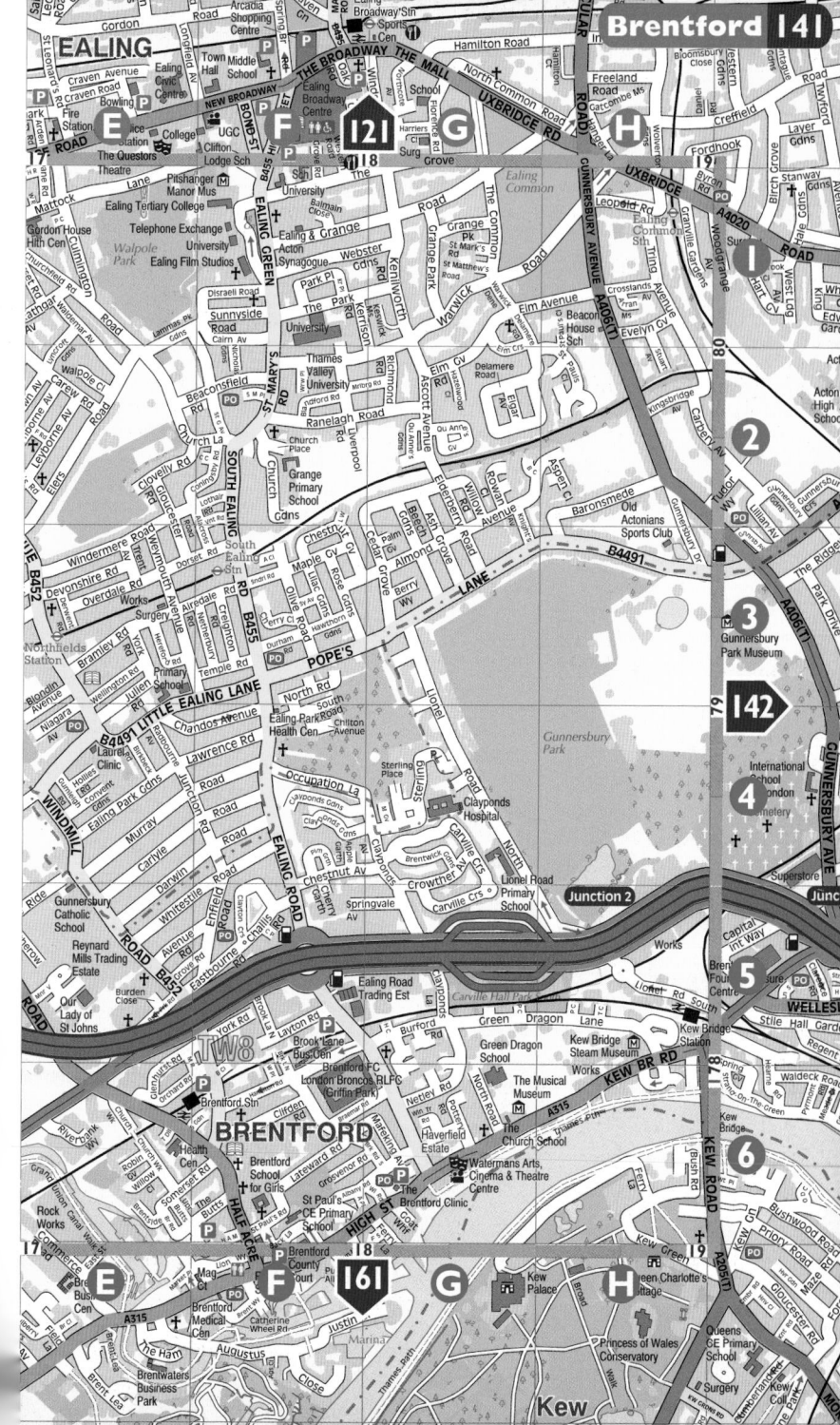

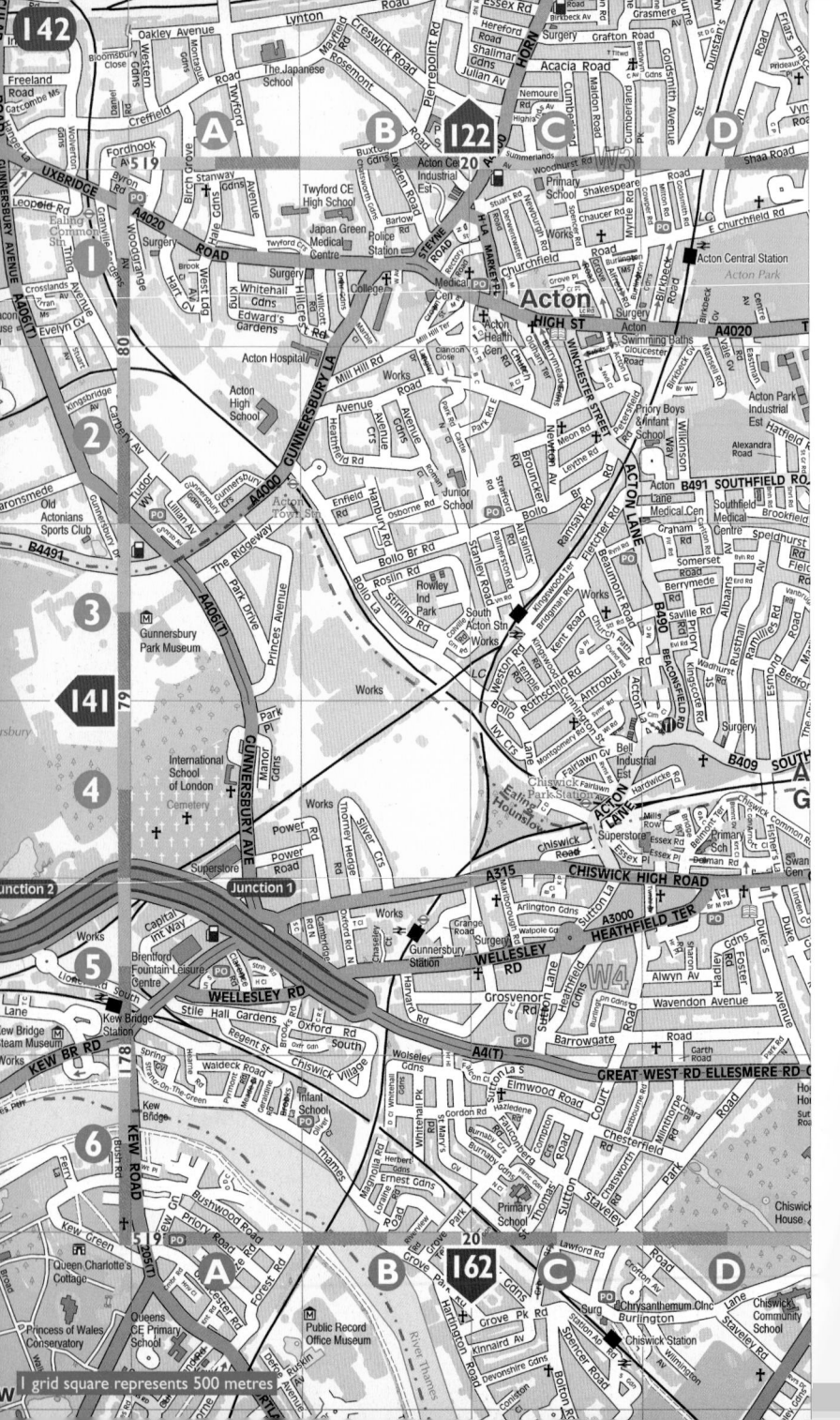

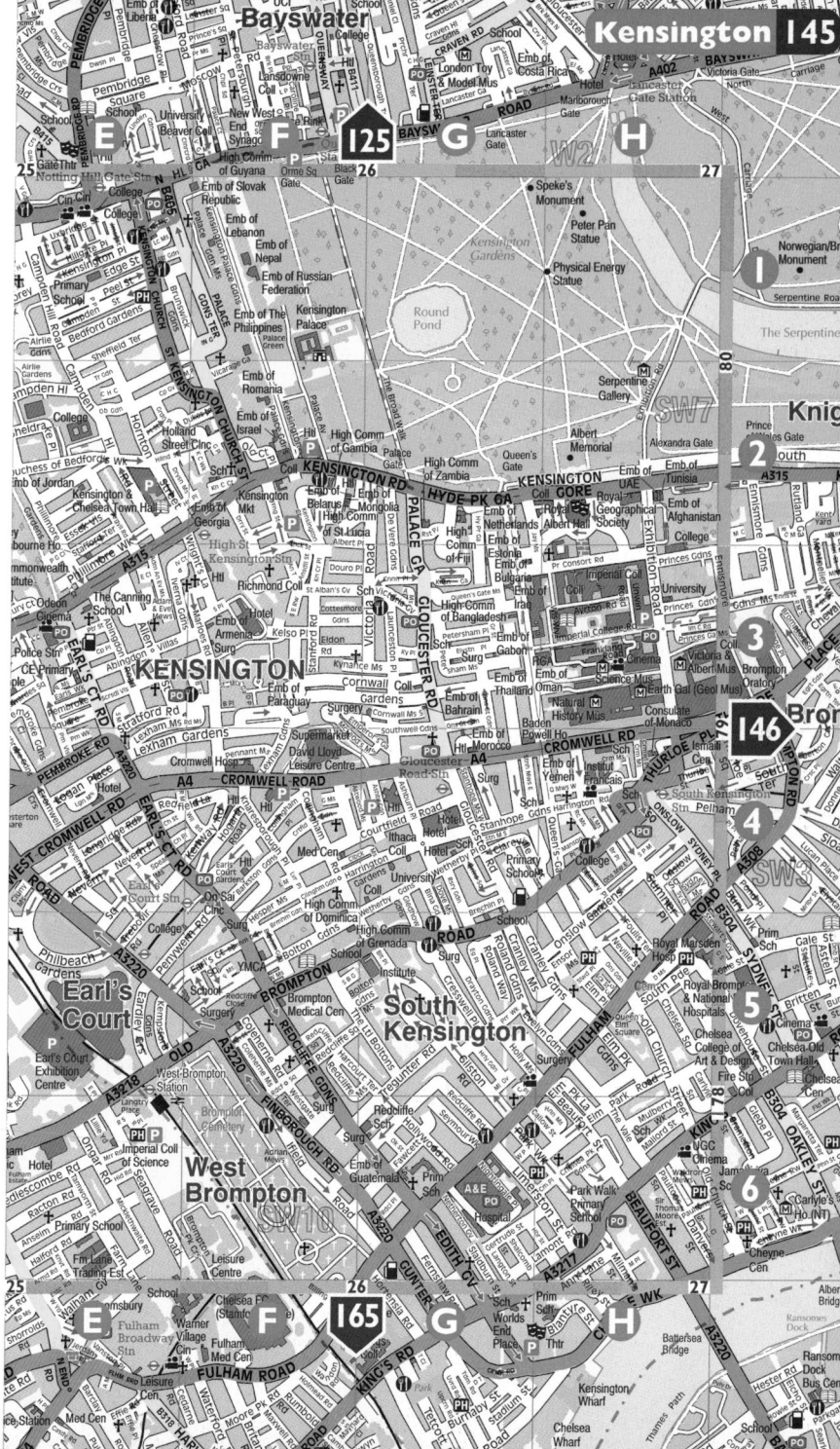

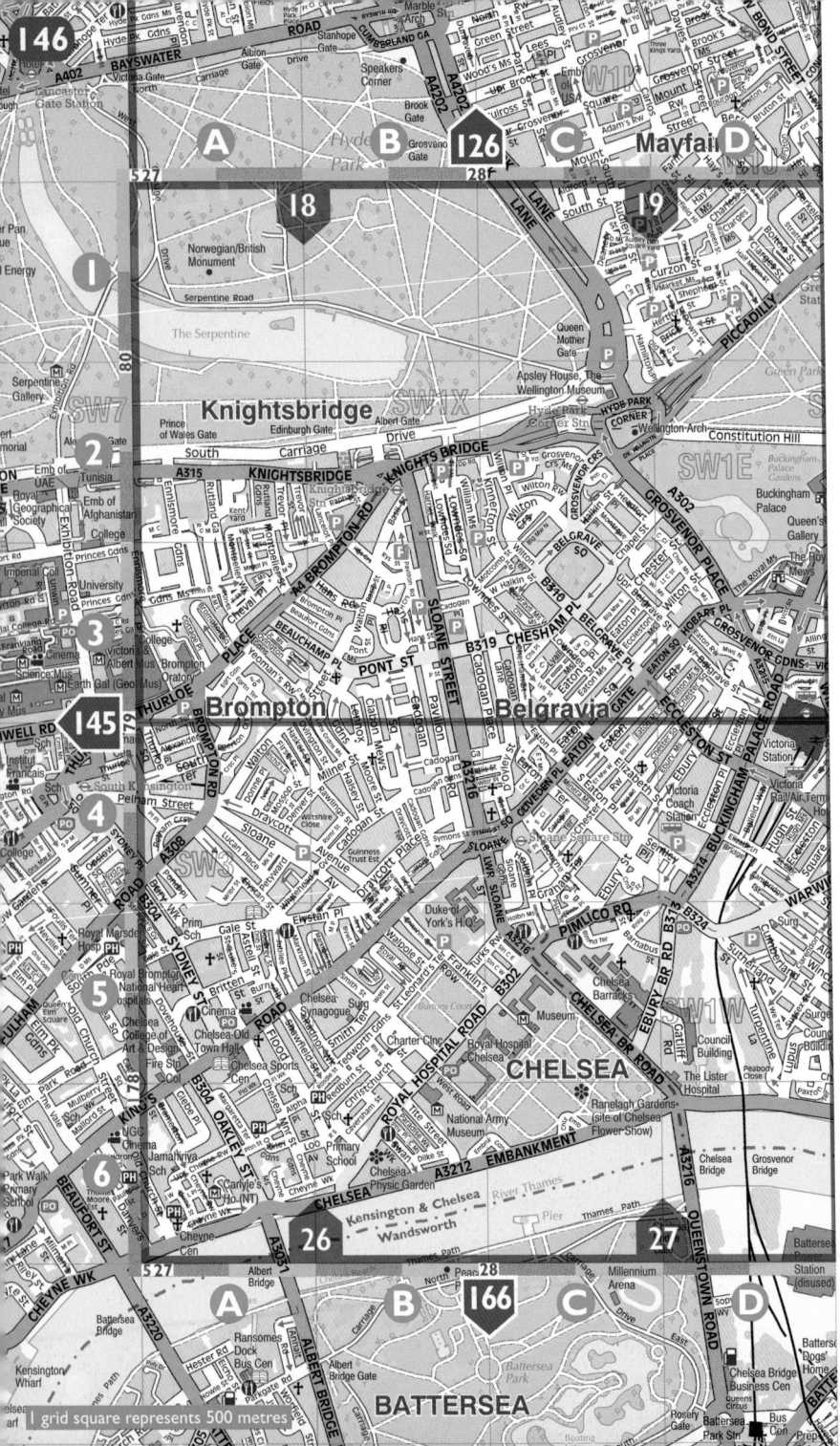

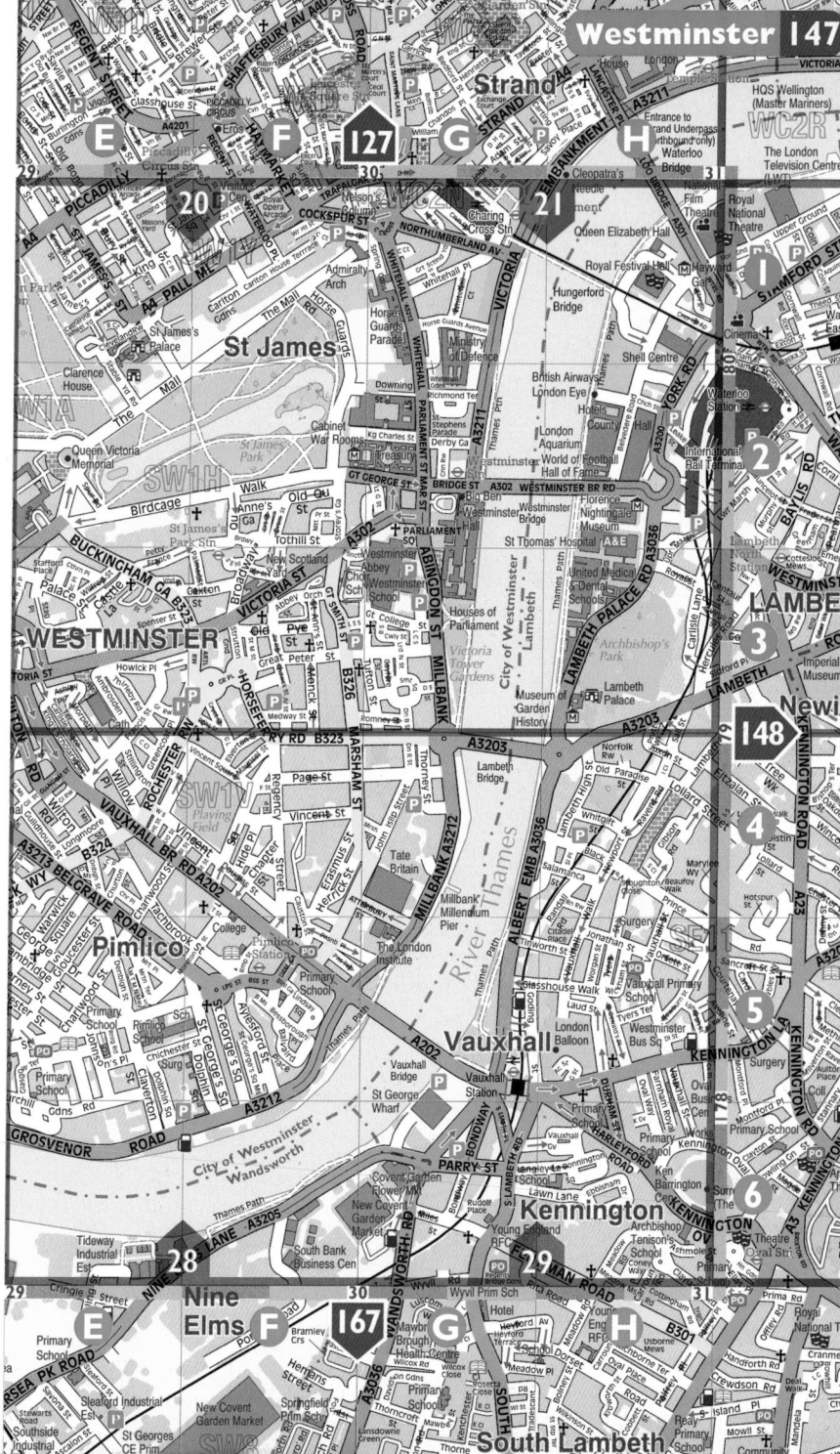

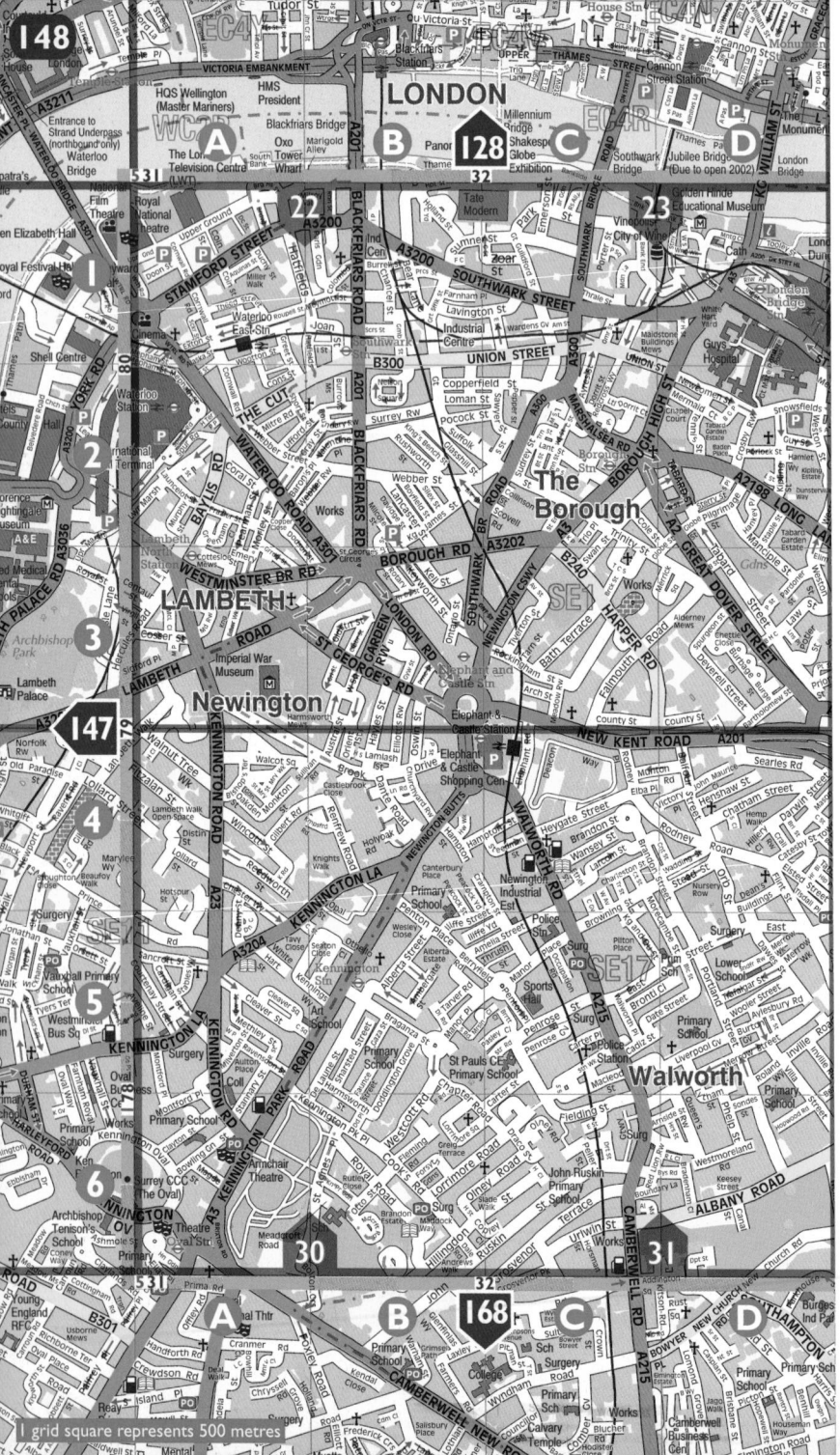

I grid square represents 500 metres

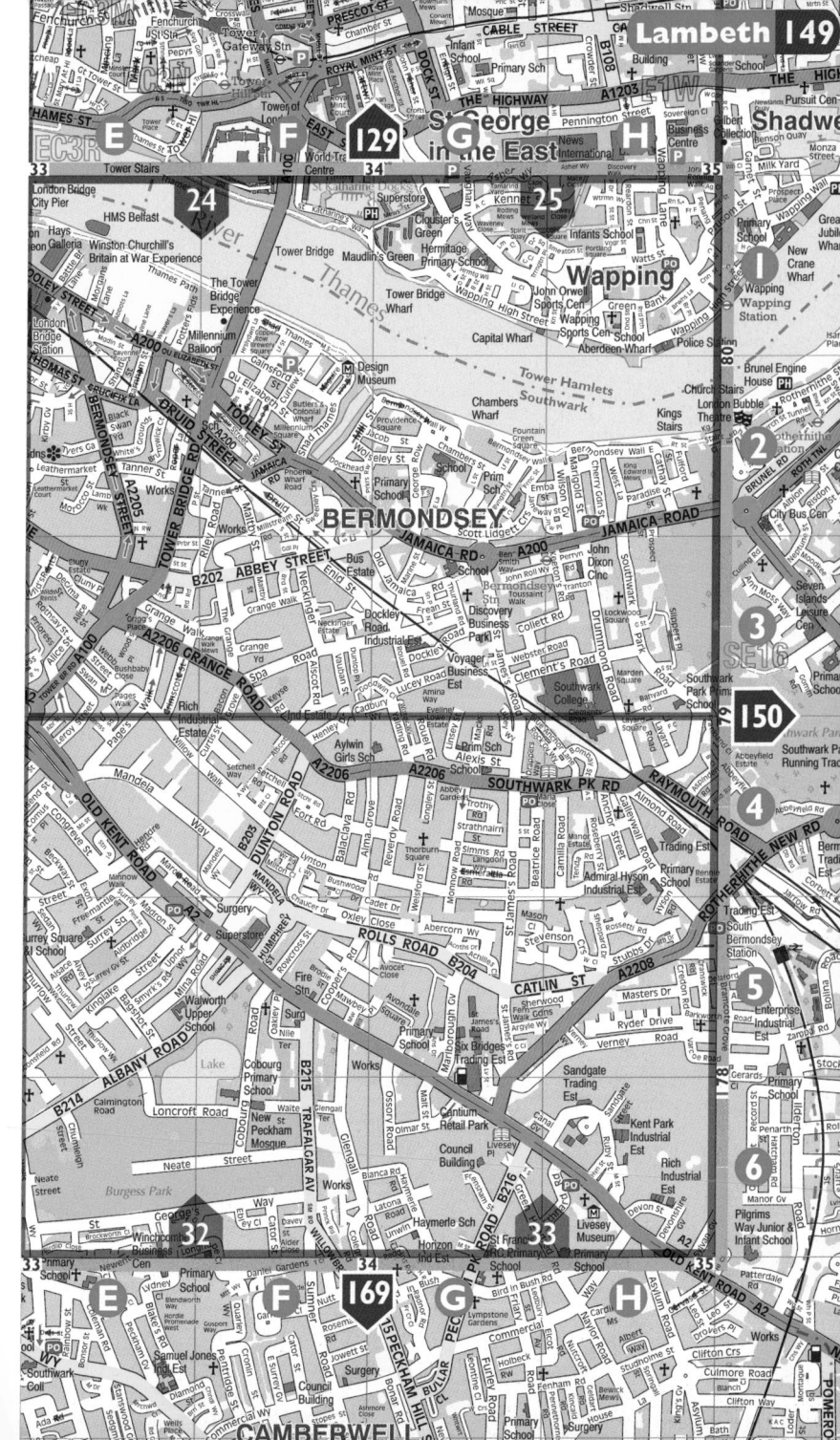

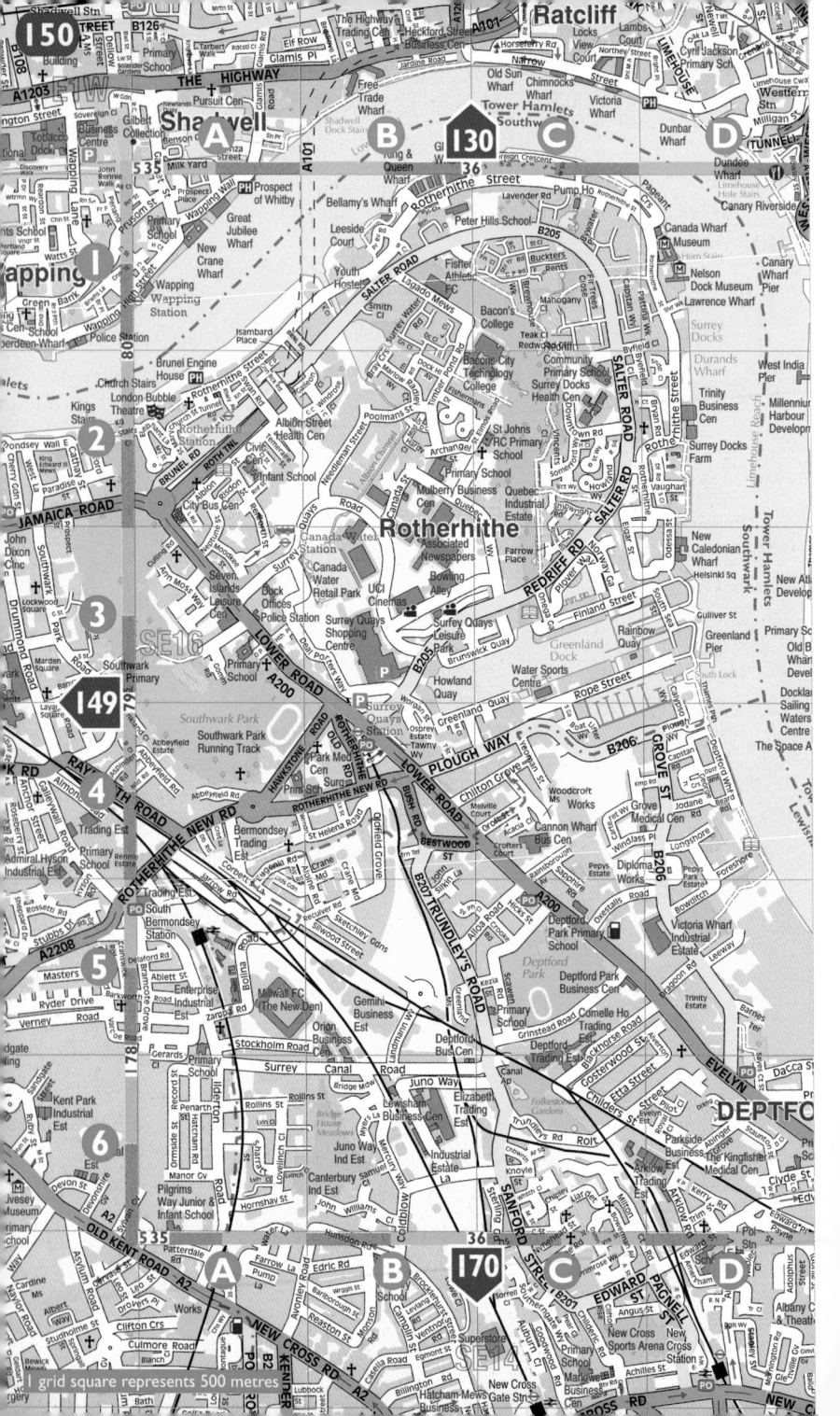
1 grid square represents 500 metres

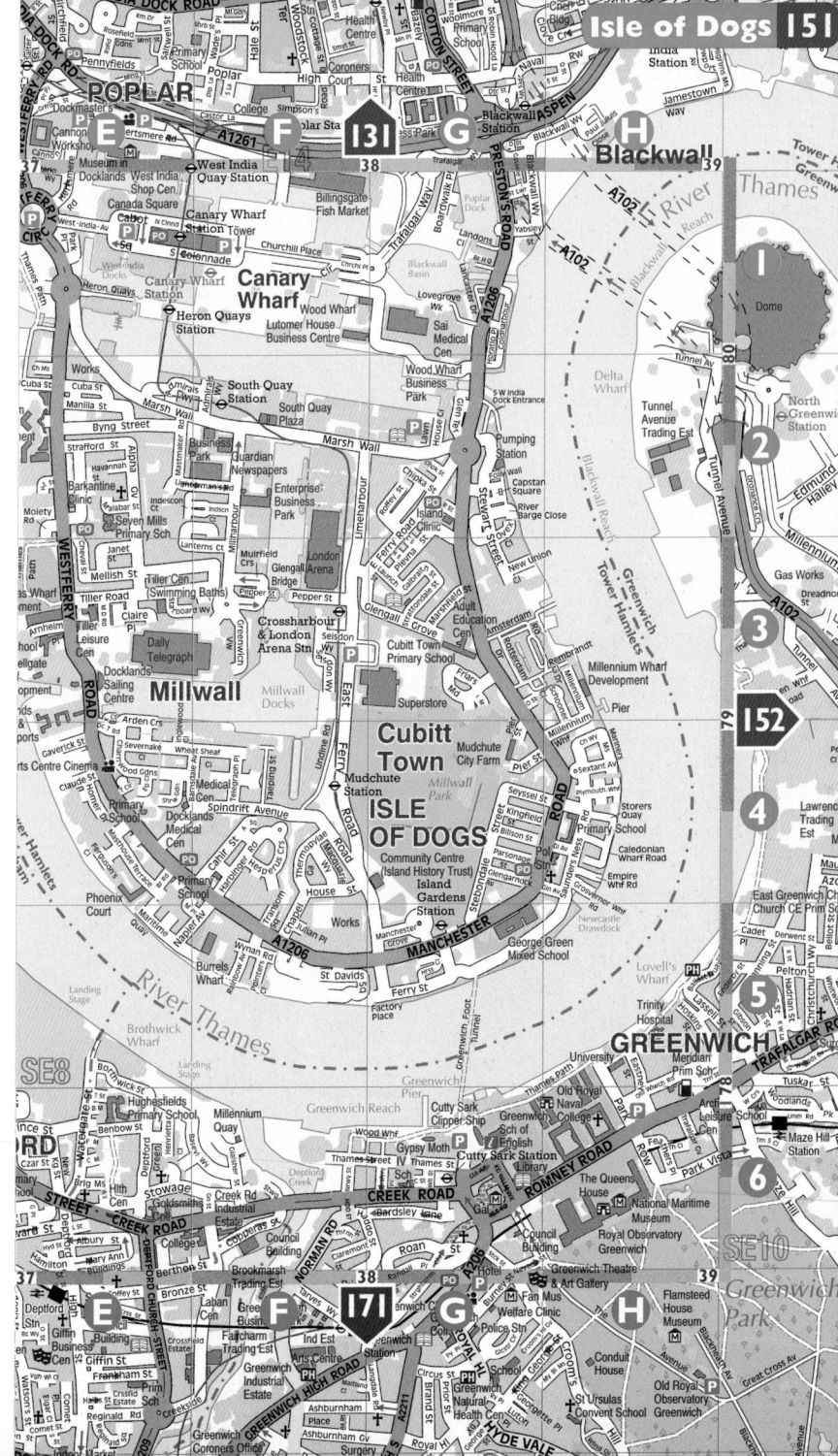

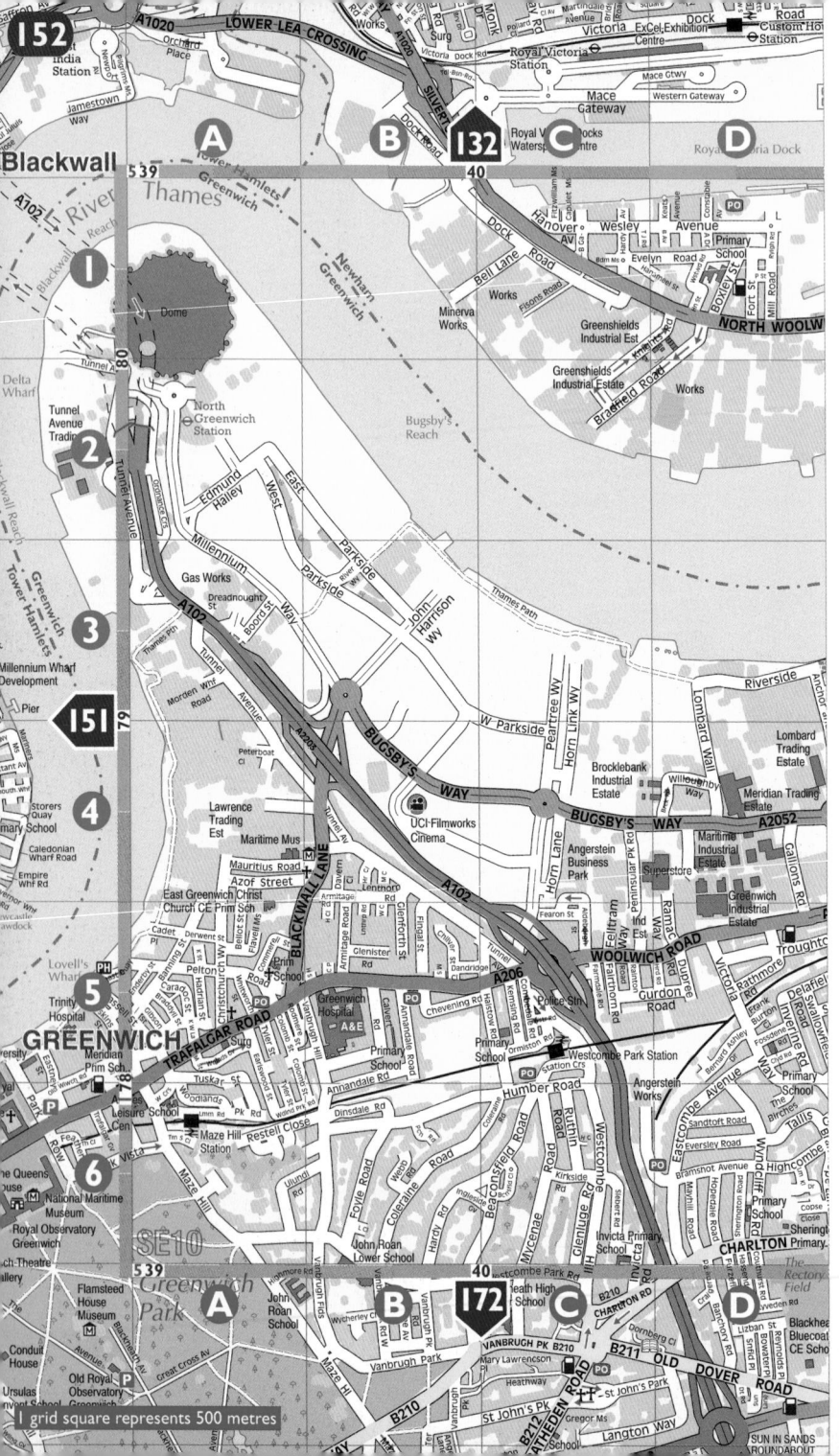

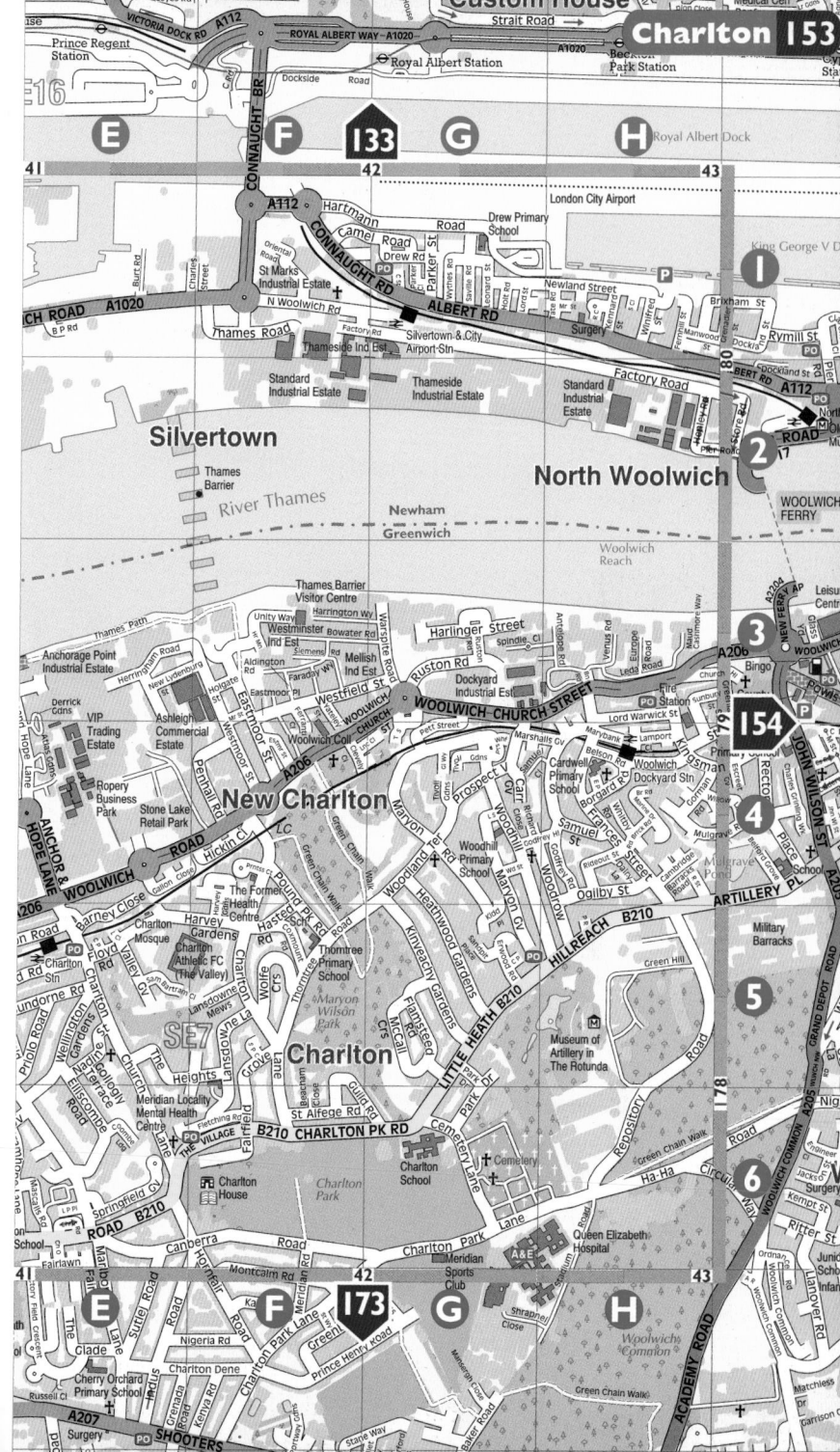

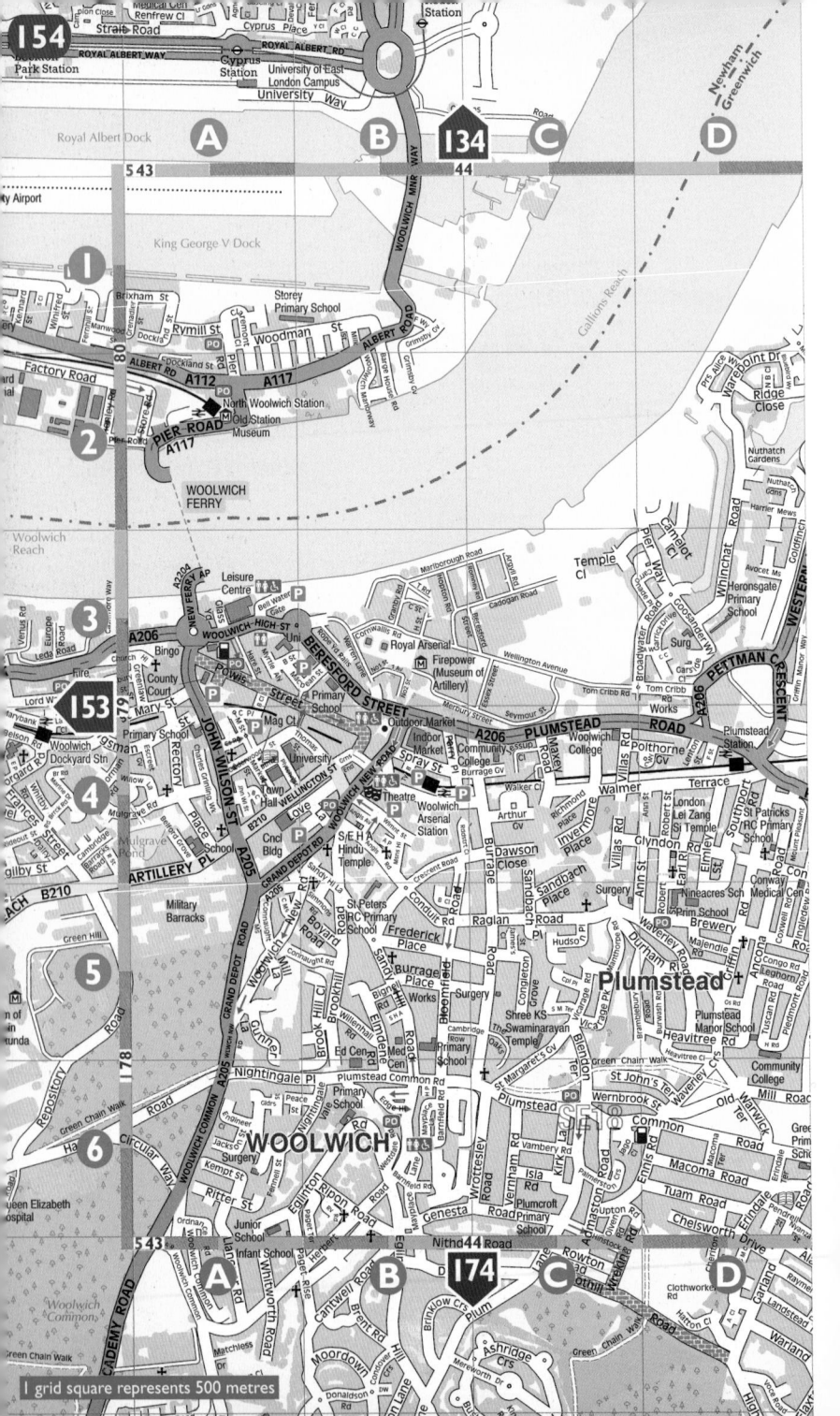

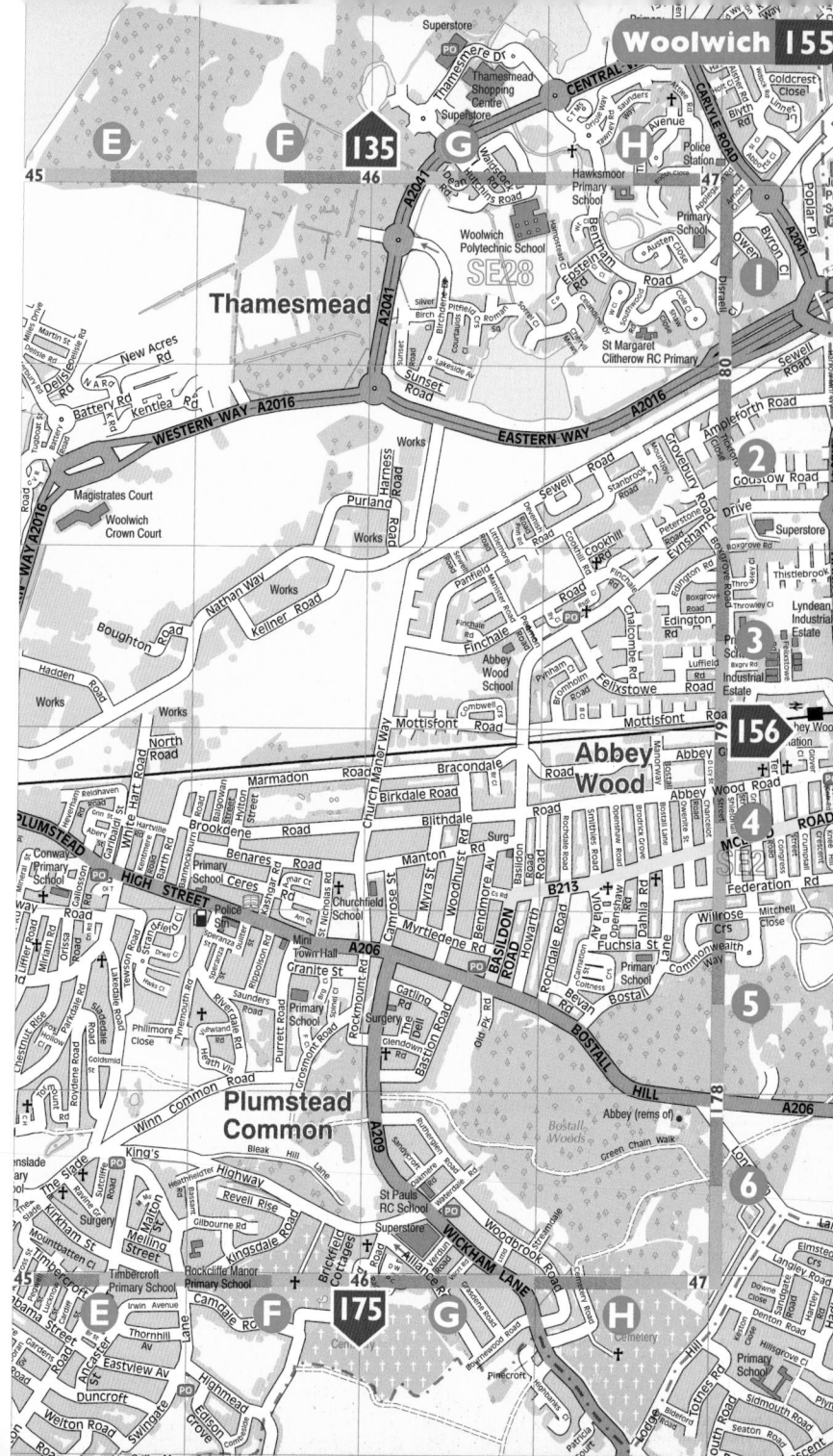

Thamesmead

SE28

Abbey Wood

SE2

Plumstead

Plumstead Common

Bostall Woods

Woolwich Crown Court

Woolwich Polytechnic School

Magistrates Court

Woolwich Crown Court

Shopping Centre

St Margaret Clitherow RC Primary

Abbey Wood School

St Pauls RC School

Rockcliffe Manor Primary School

Lyndean Industrial Estate

Industrial Estate

135

175

156

E   F   G   H   I

45   46   47

WESTERN WAY A2016

EASTERN WAY A2016

PLUMSTEAD HIGH STREET

BOSTALL HILL A206

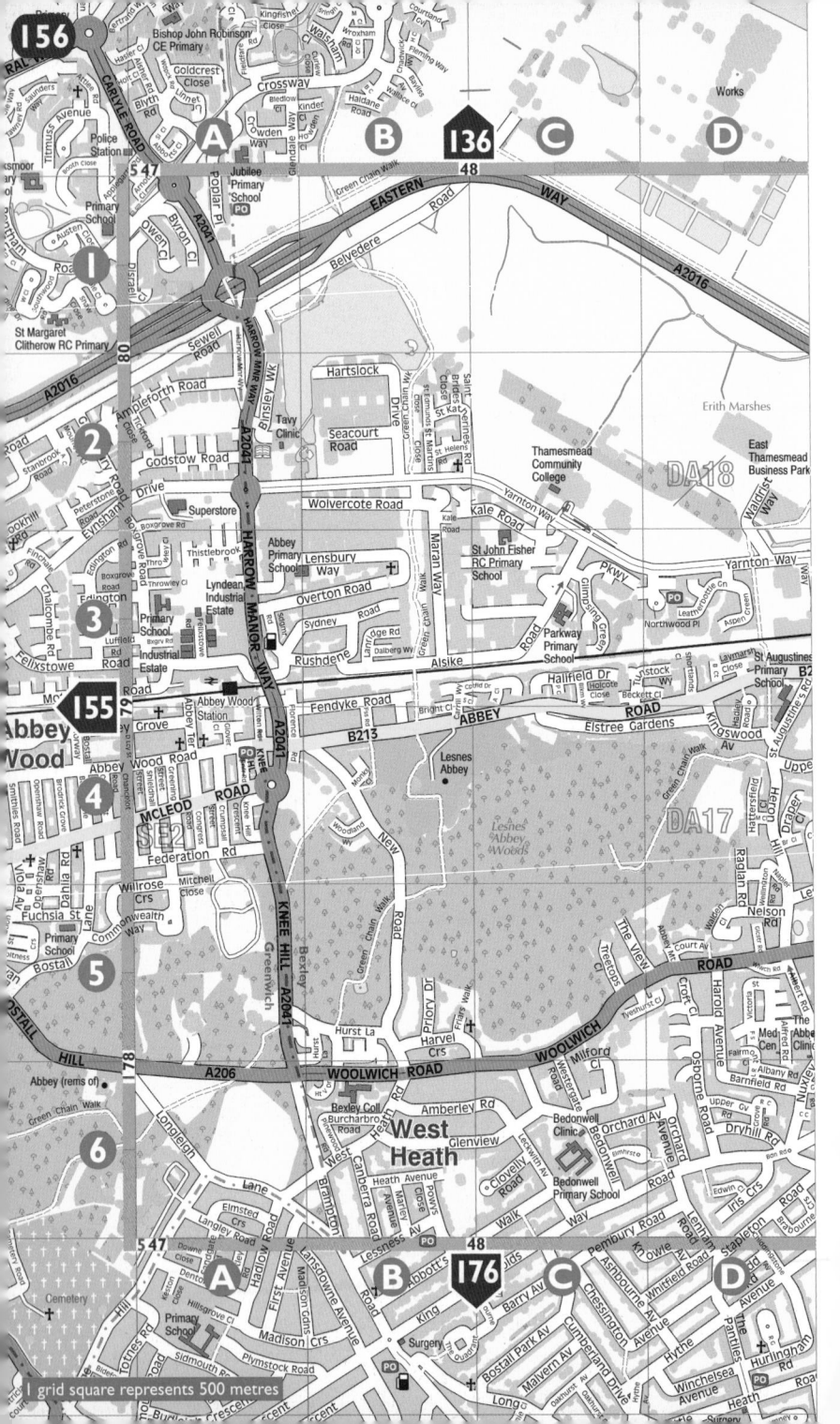

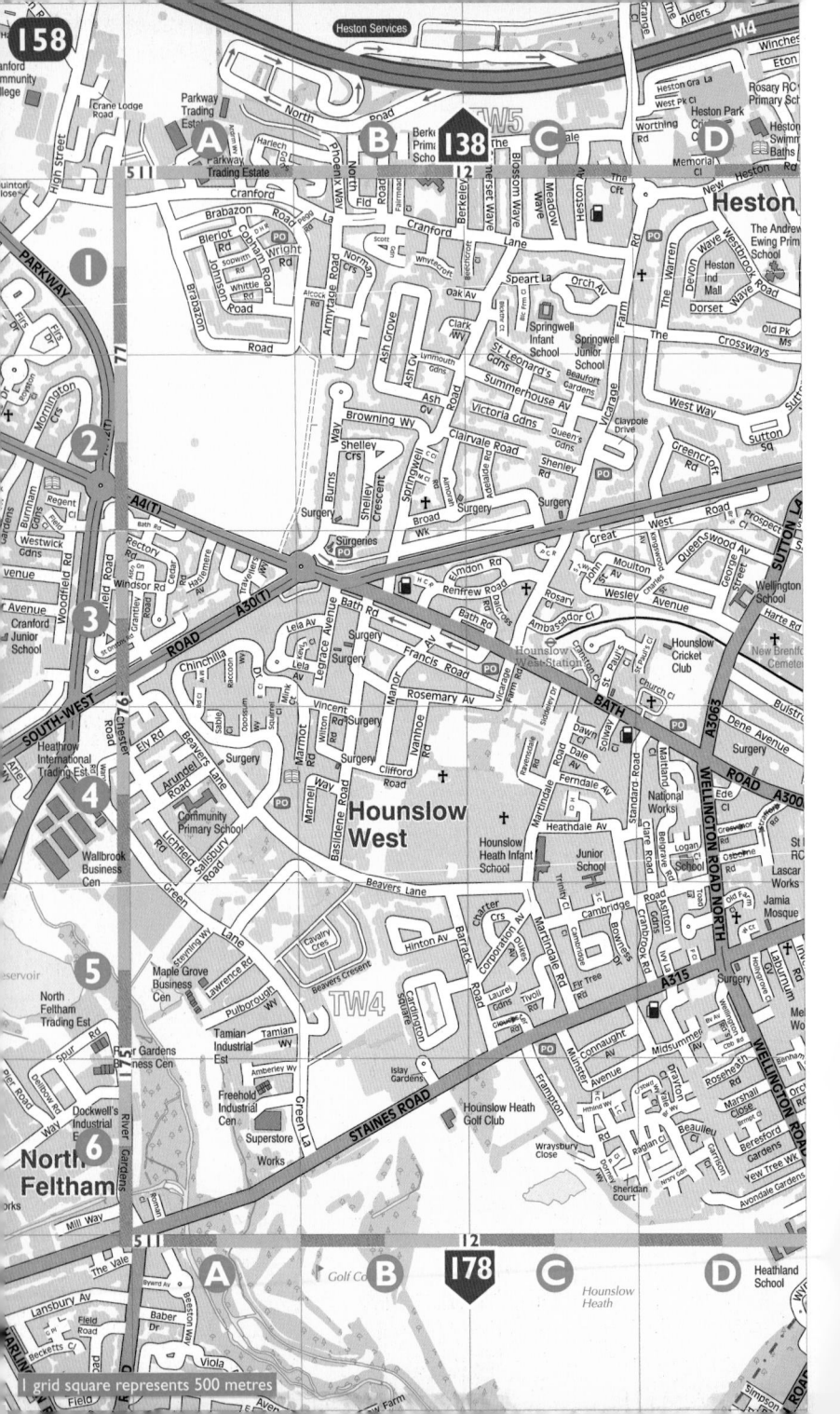

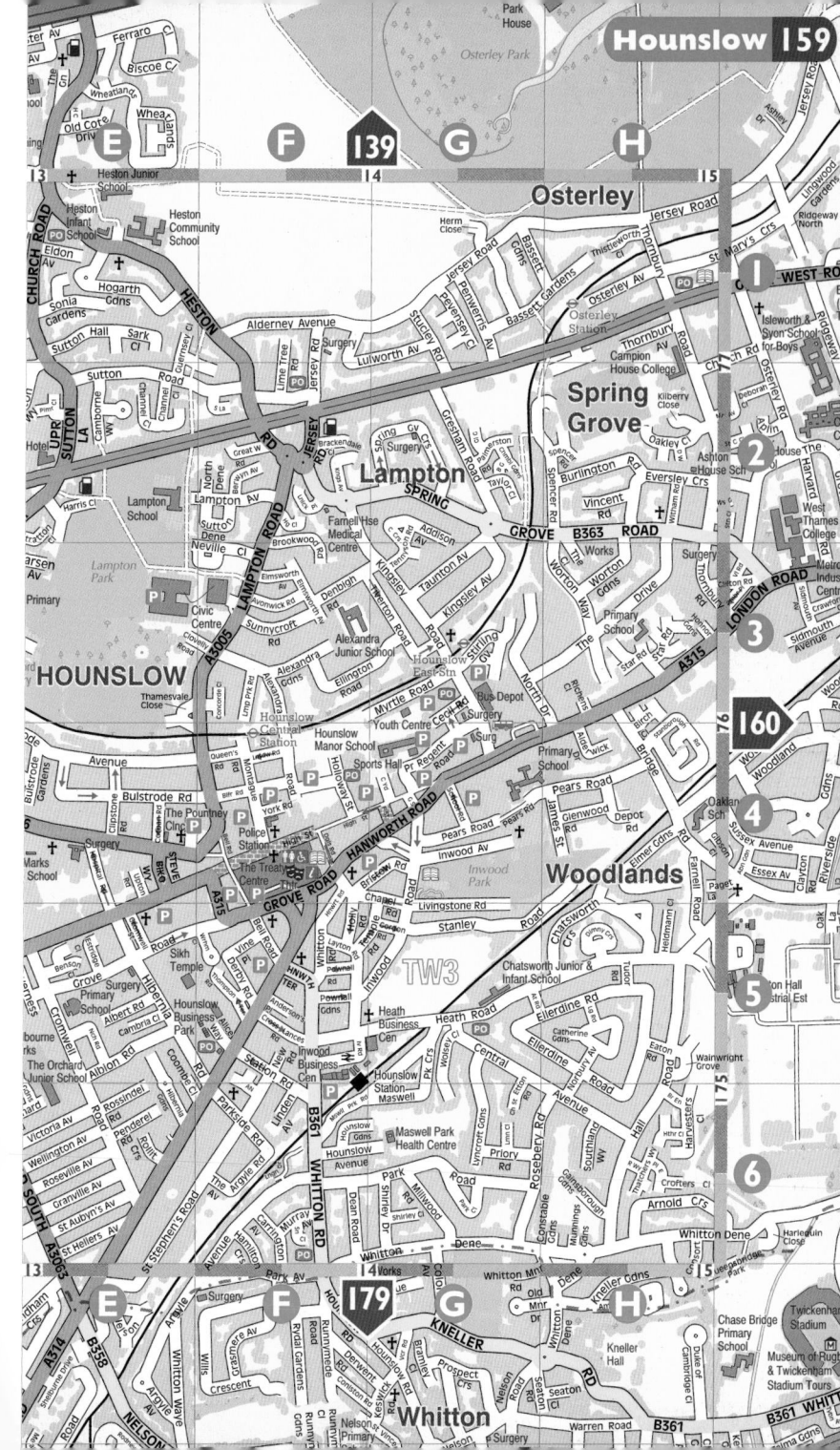

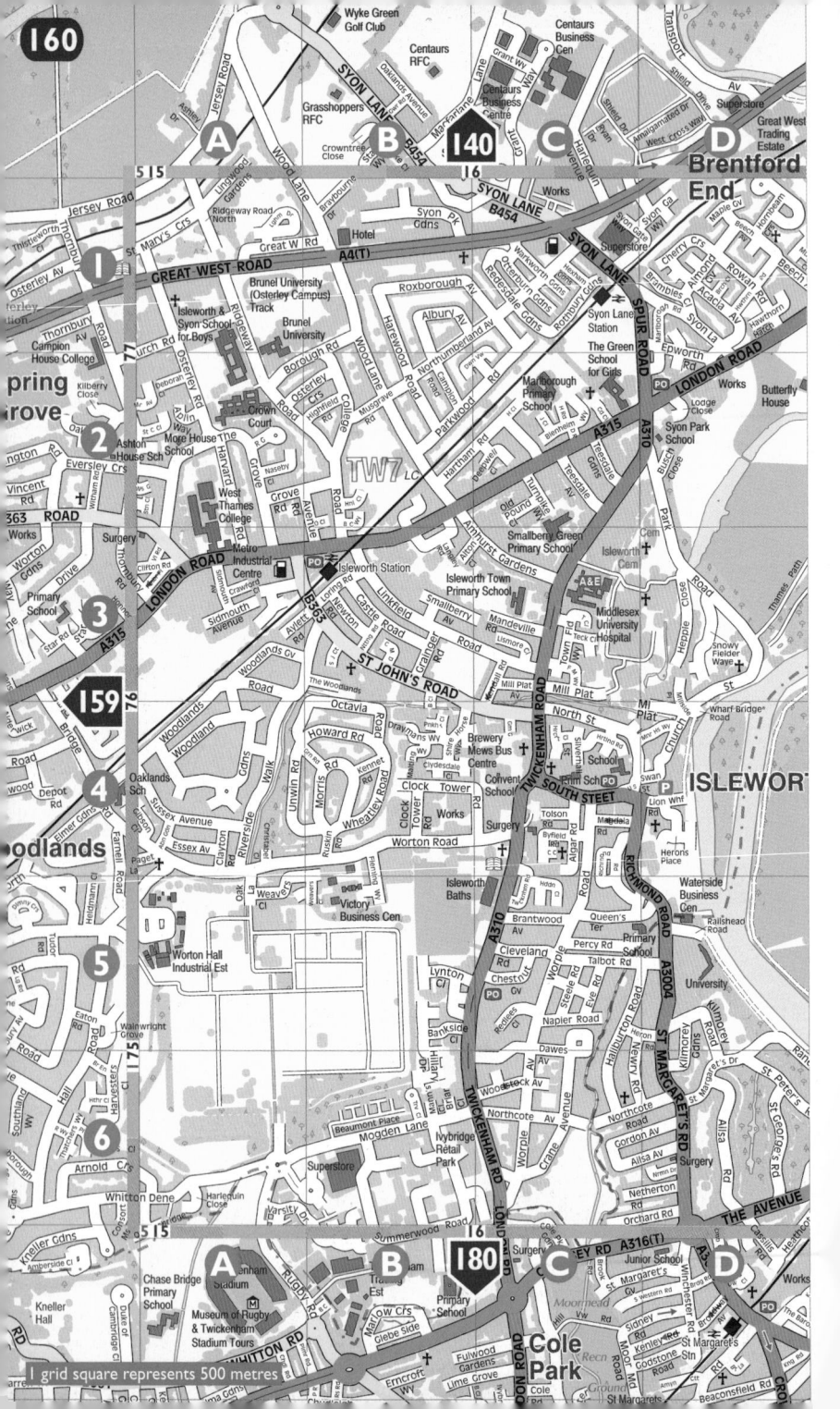

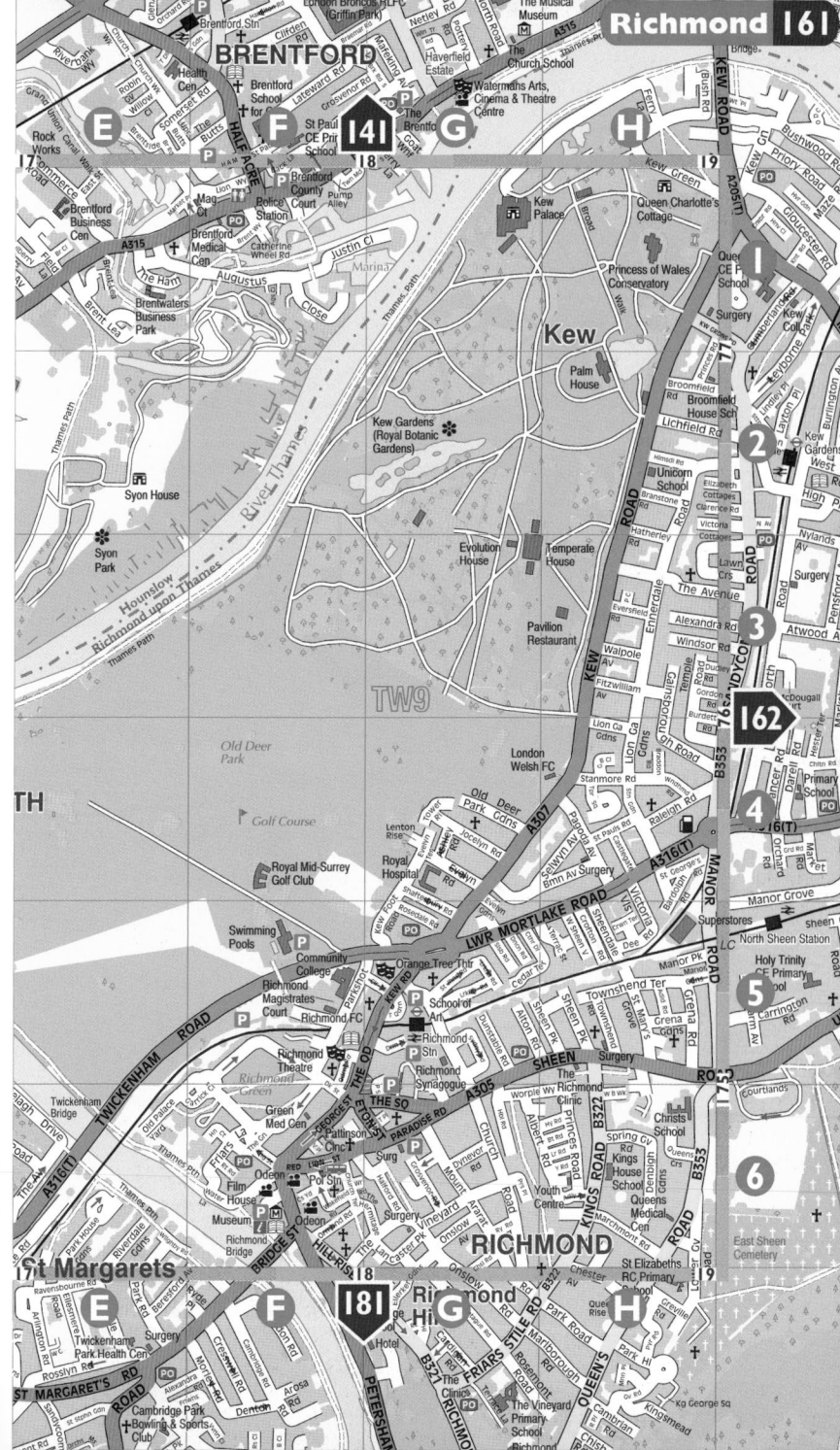

BRENTFORD

London Broncos RLFC
(Griffin Park)

The Musical
Museum

The Church School

Watermans Arts,
Cinema & Theatre
Centre

Kew Palace

Queen Charlotte's
Cottage

Princess of Wales
Conservatory

Kew

Palm
House

Kew Gardens
(Royal Botanic
Gardens)

Evolution
House

Temperate
House

Pavilion
Restaurant

TW9

Old Deer
Park

London
Welsh FC

Golf Course

Royal Mid-Surrey
Golf Club

Royal
Hospital

Richmond upon Thames

Hounslow

River Thames

Syon House

Syon
Park

LWR MORTLAKE ROAD

Superstores

North Sheen Station

Swimming
Pools

Community
College

Orange Tree Thtr

Richmond
Magistrates
Court

Richmond FC

Holy Trinity
CE Primary
School

School of
Art

Richmond
Stn

Richmond
Synagogue

Richmond
Theatre

Green
Med Cen

Orange Tree Thtr

Odeon

Film
House

Museum

Richmond
Bridge

Twickenham
Bridge

RICHMOND

Christs
School

Kings
House
School

Queens
Medical
Cen

St Elizabeths
RC Primary
School

Richmond
Hi

East Sheen
Cemetery

St Margarets

Twickenham
Park Health Cen

Cambridge Park
Bowling & Sports
Club

The Vineyard
Primary
School

Richmond

TWICKENHAM ROAD

PETERSHAM

RICHMOND ROAD

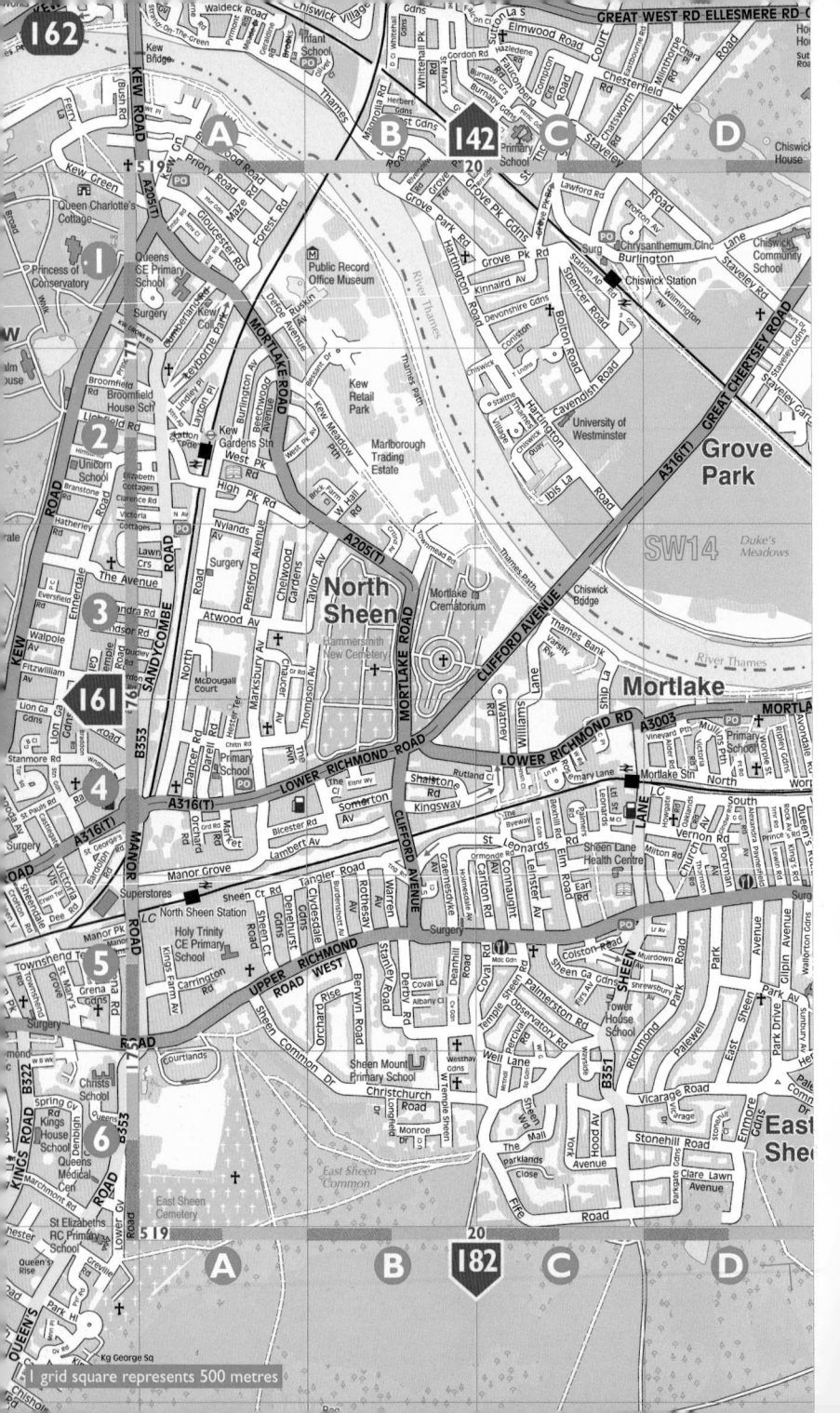

1 grid square represents 500 metres

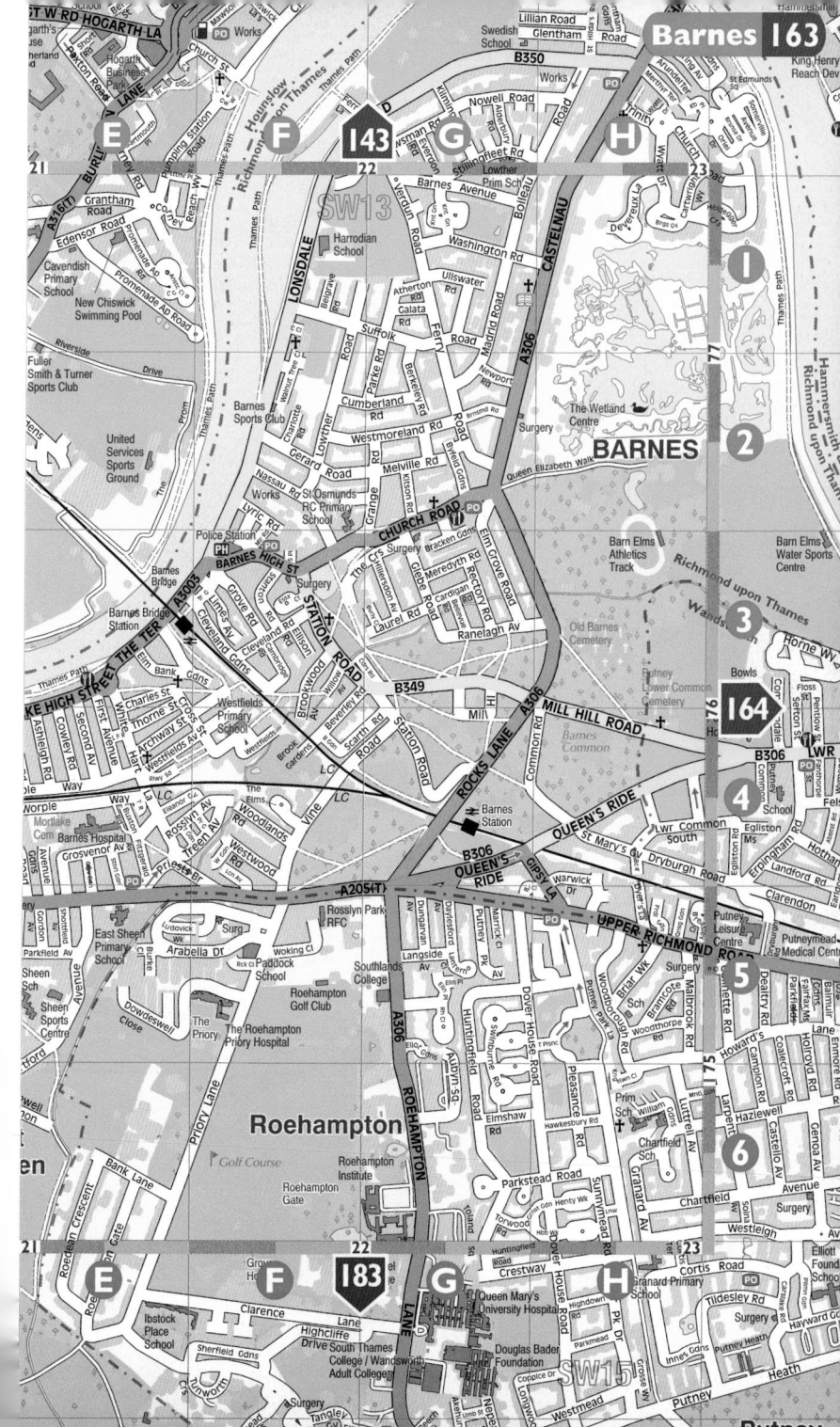

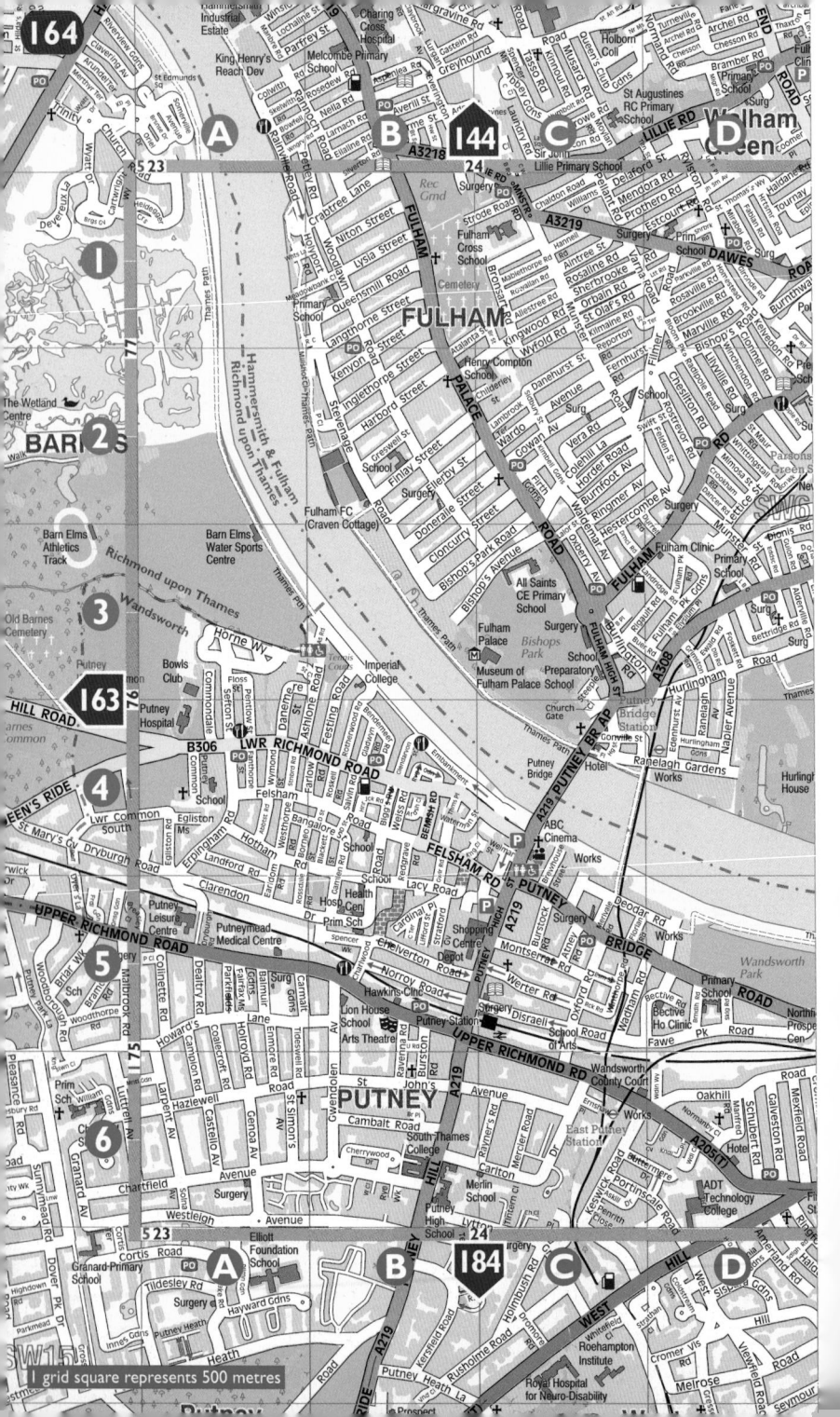

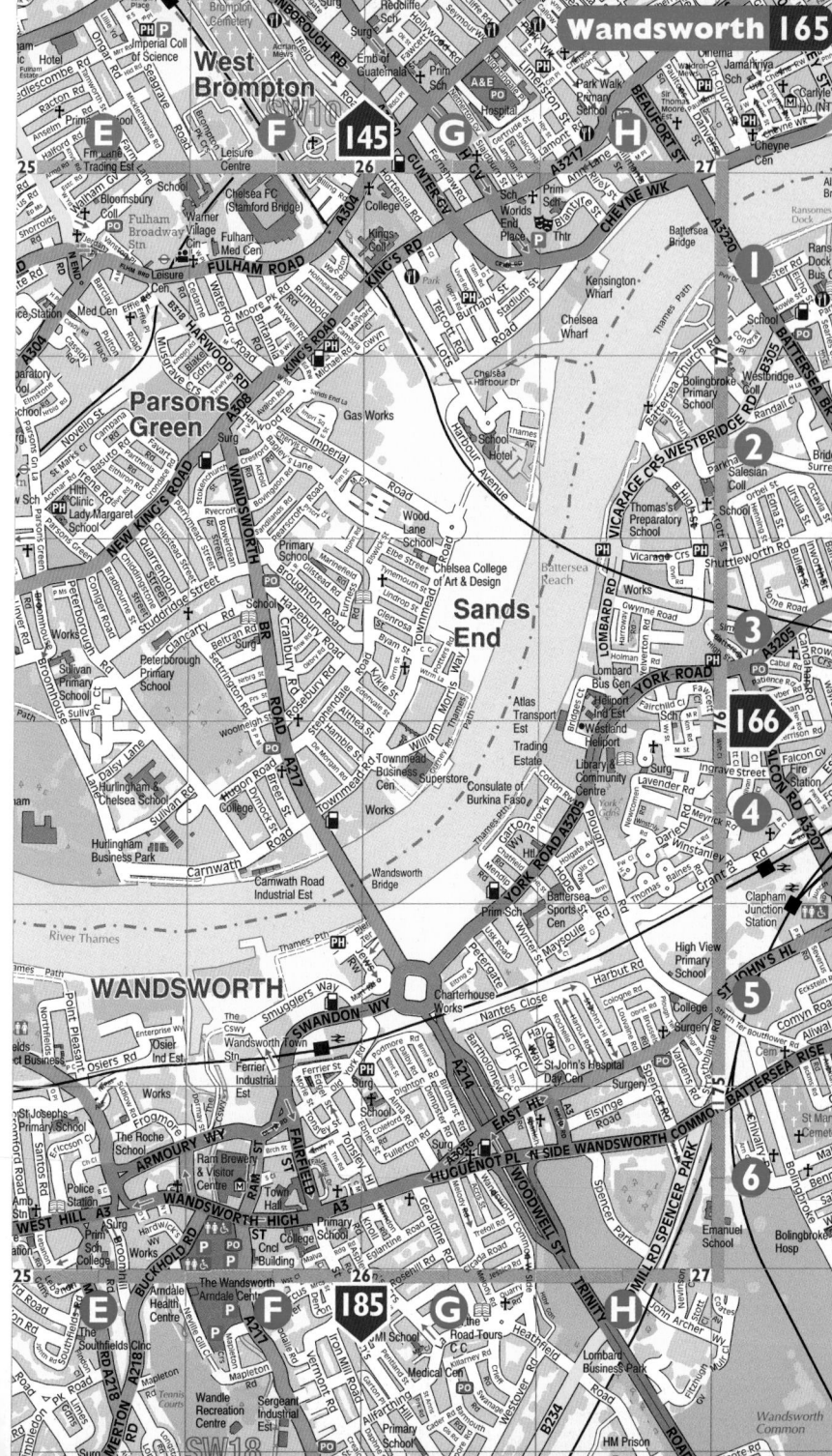

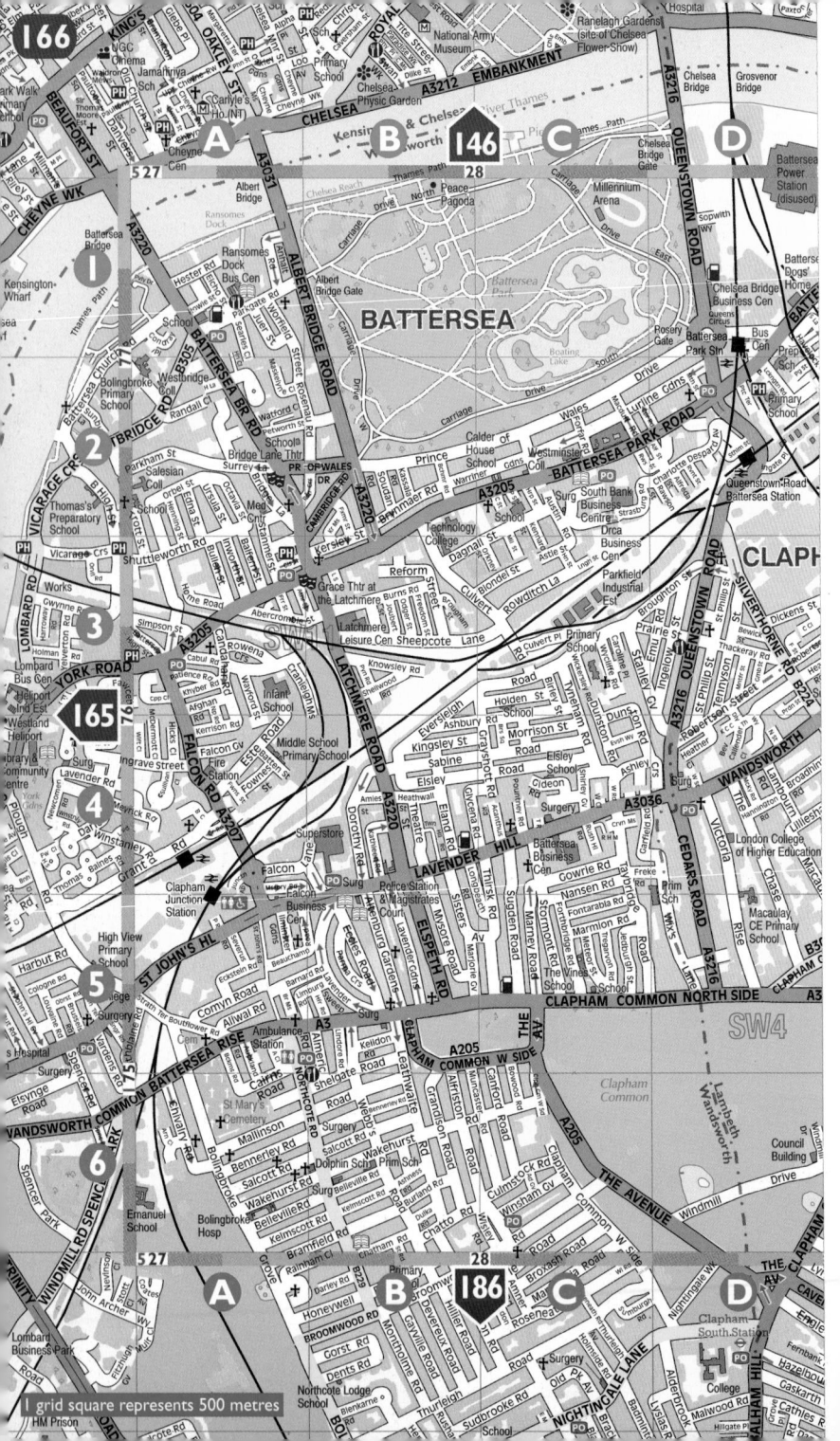

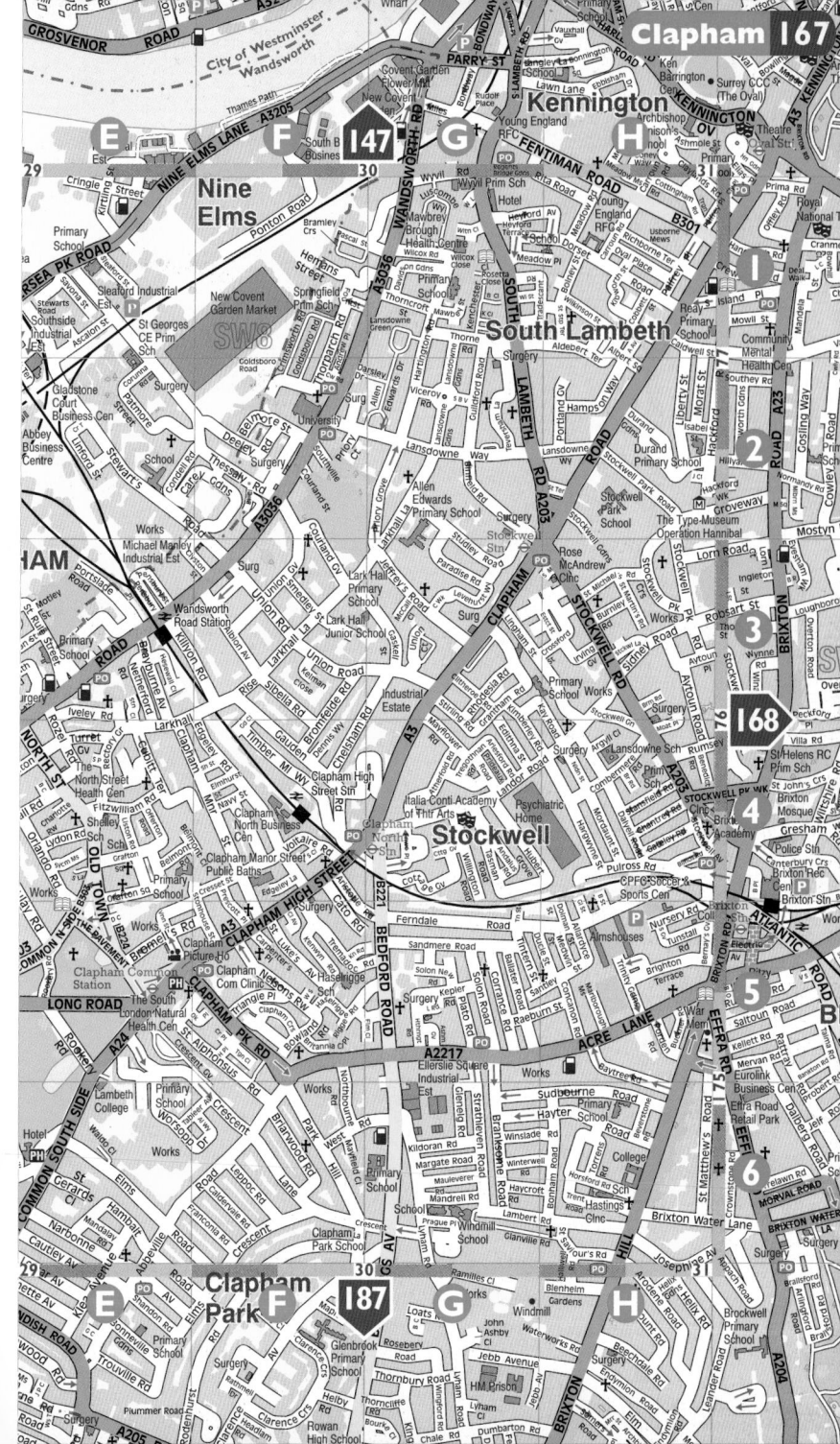

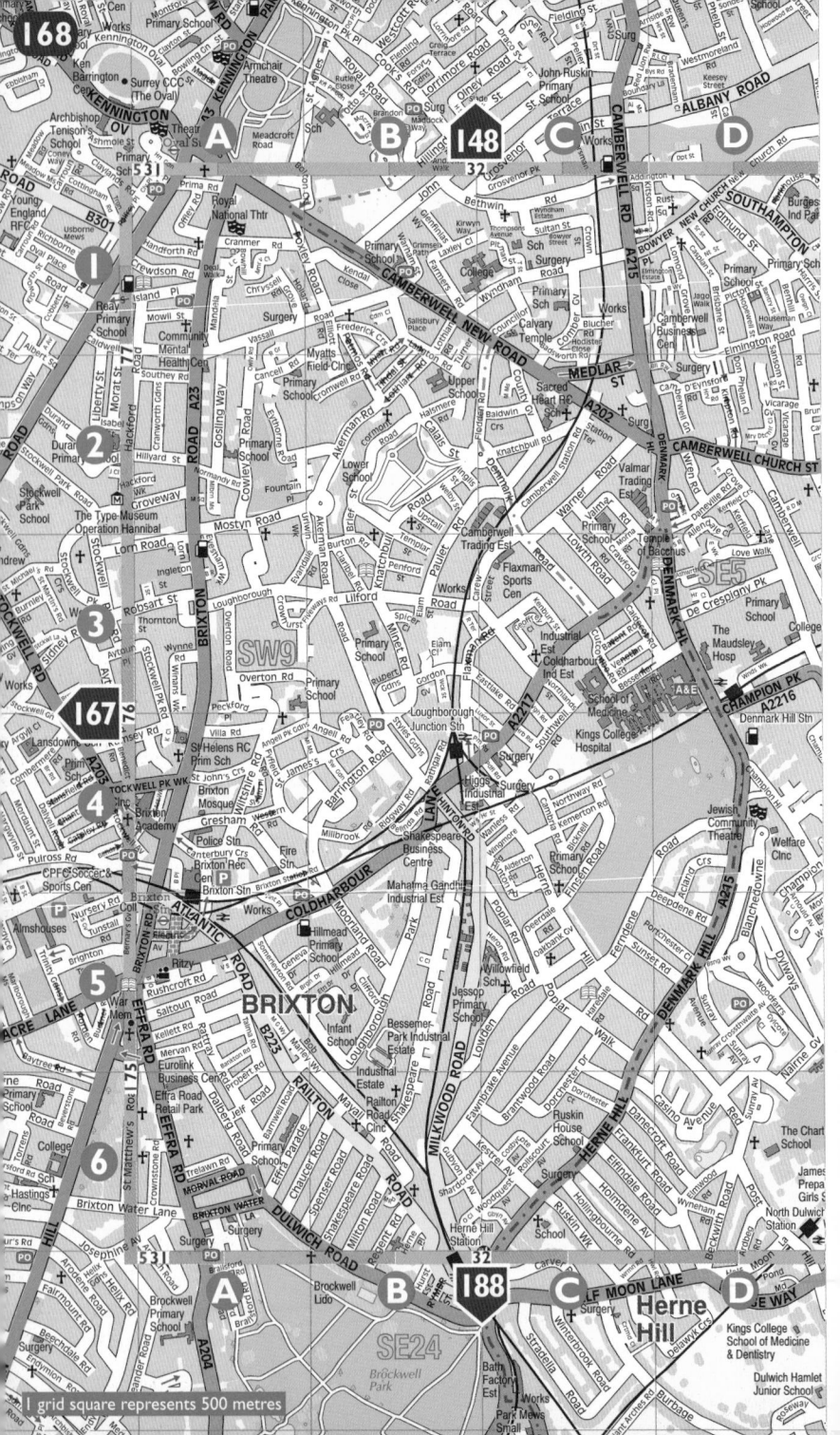

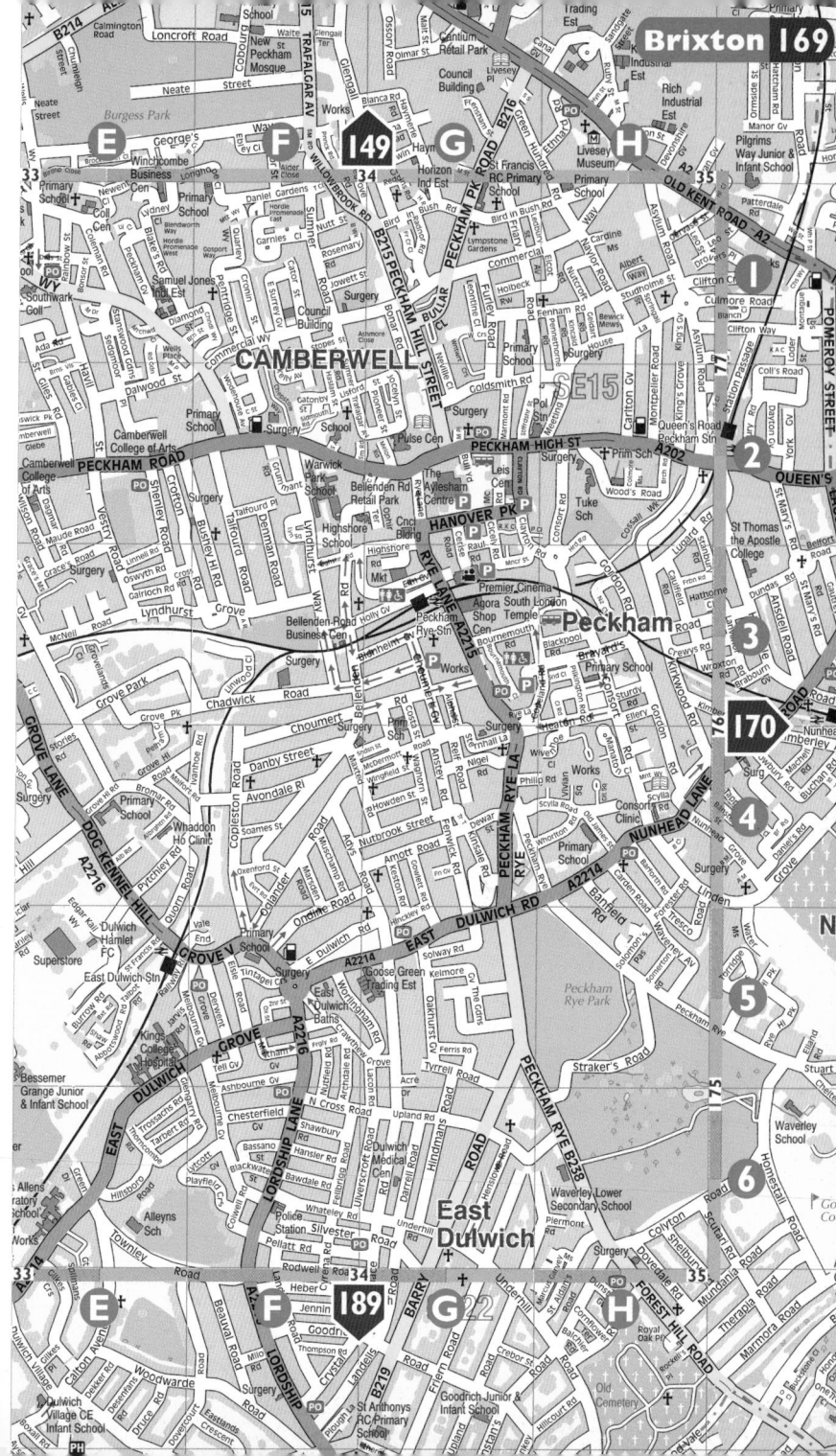

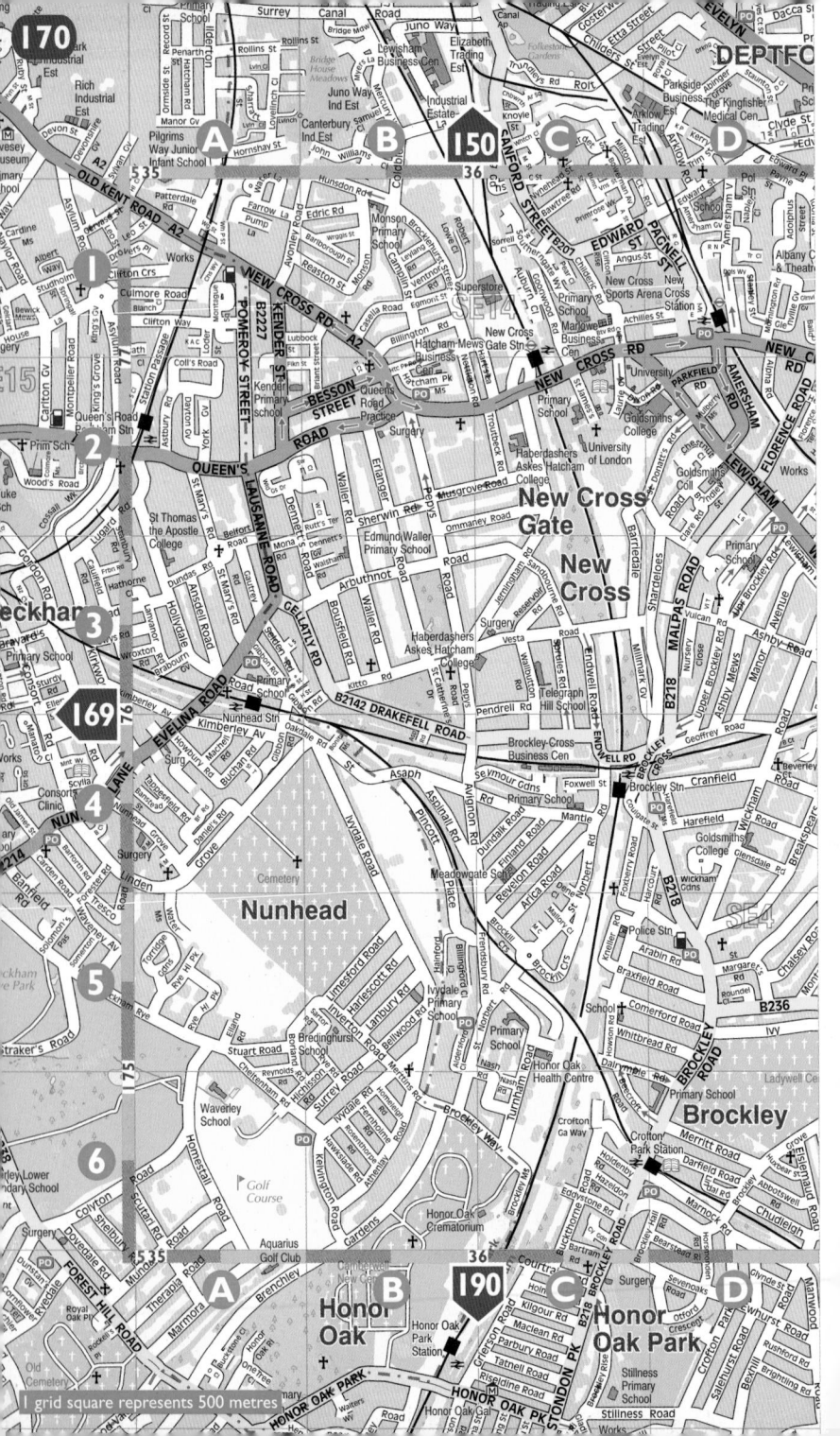

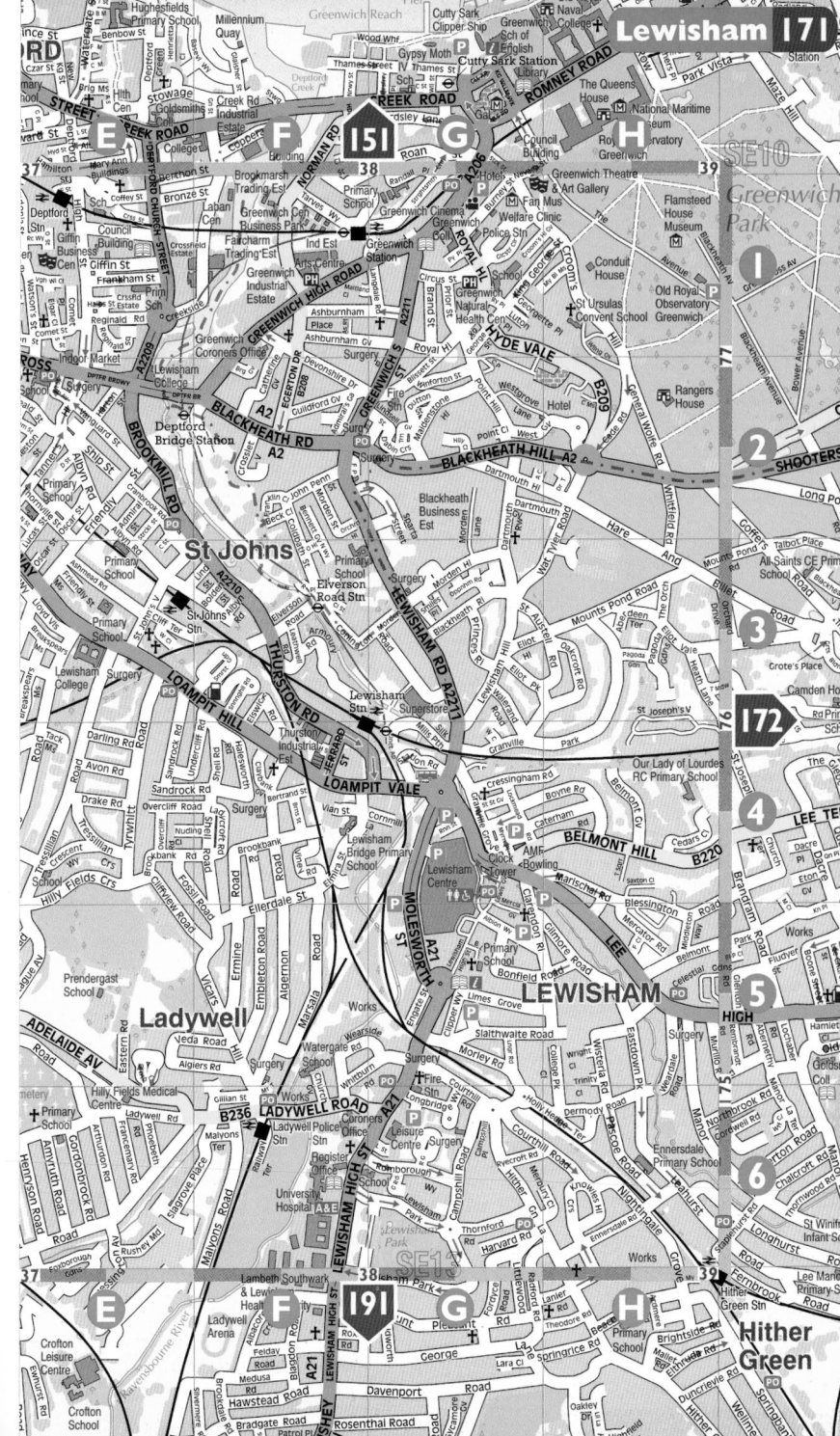

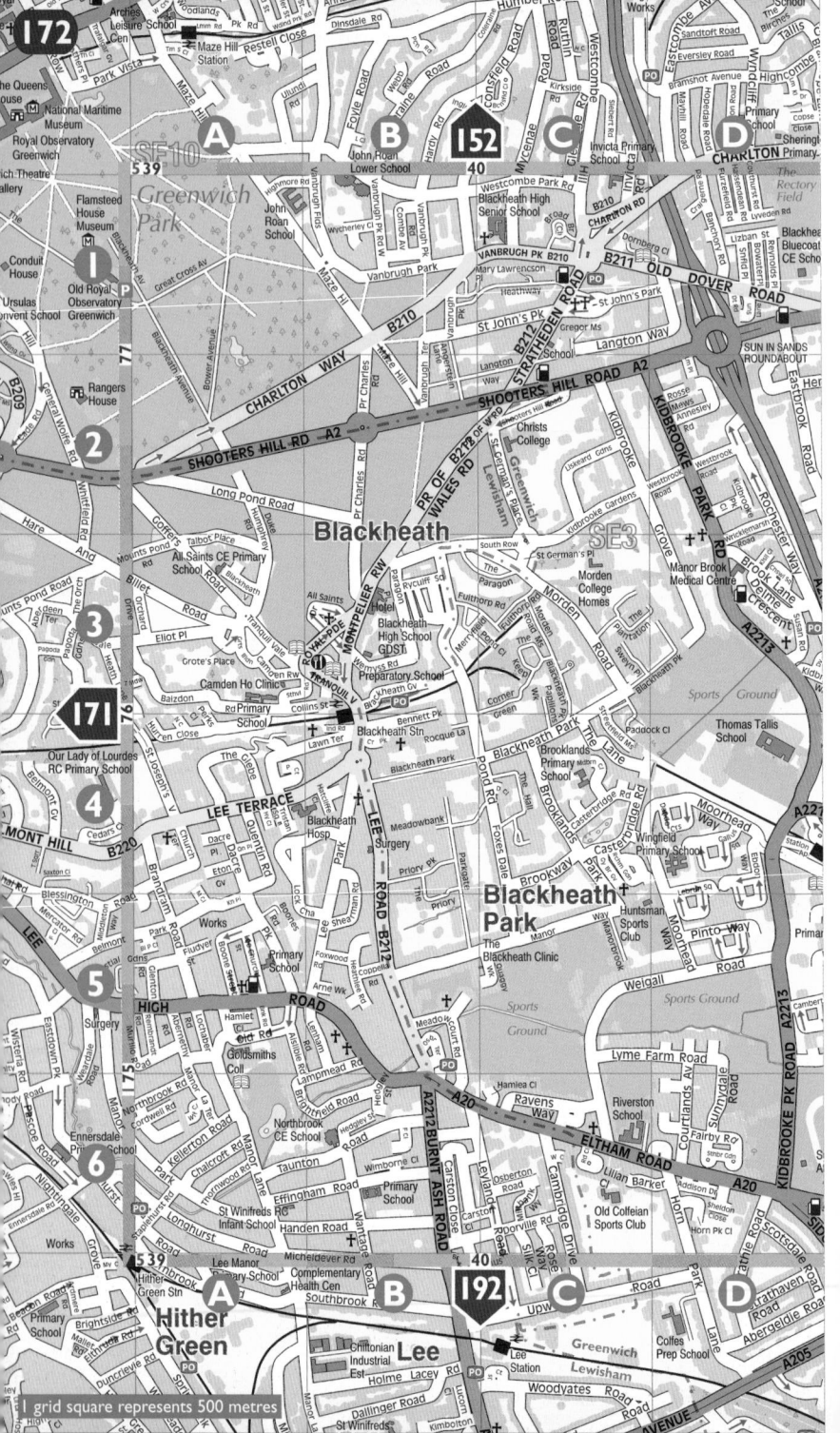

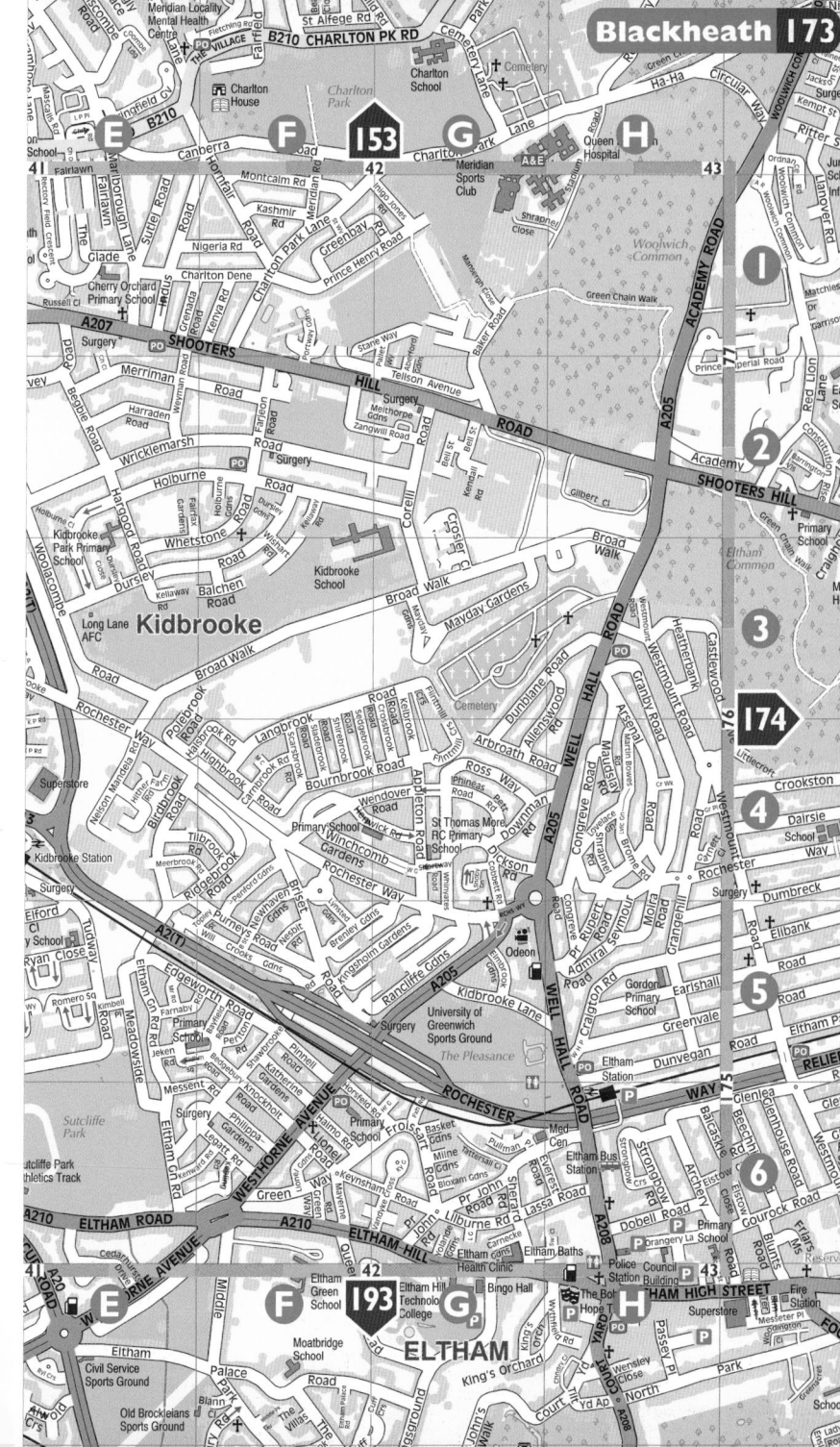

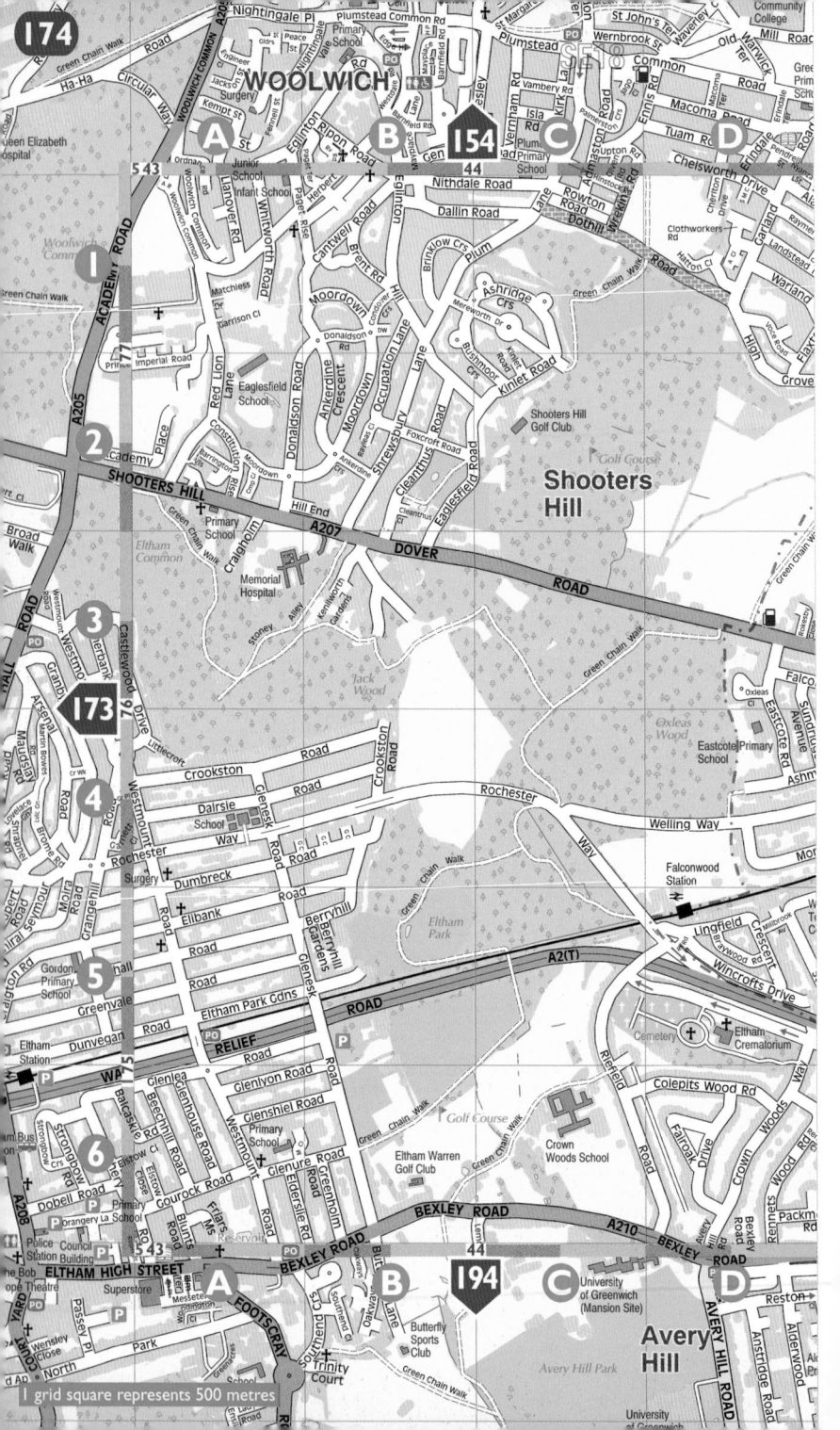

I grid square represents 500 metres

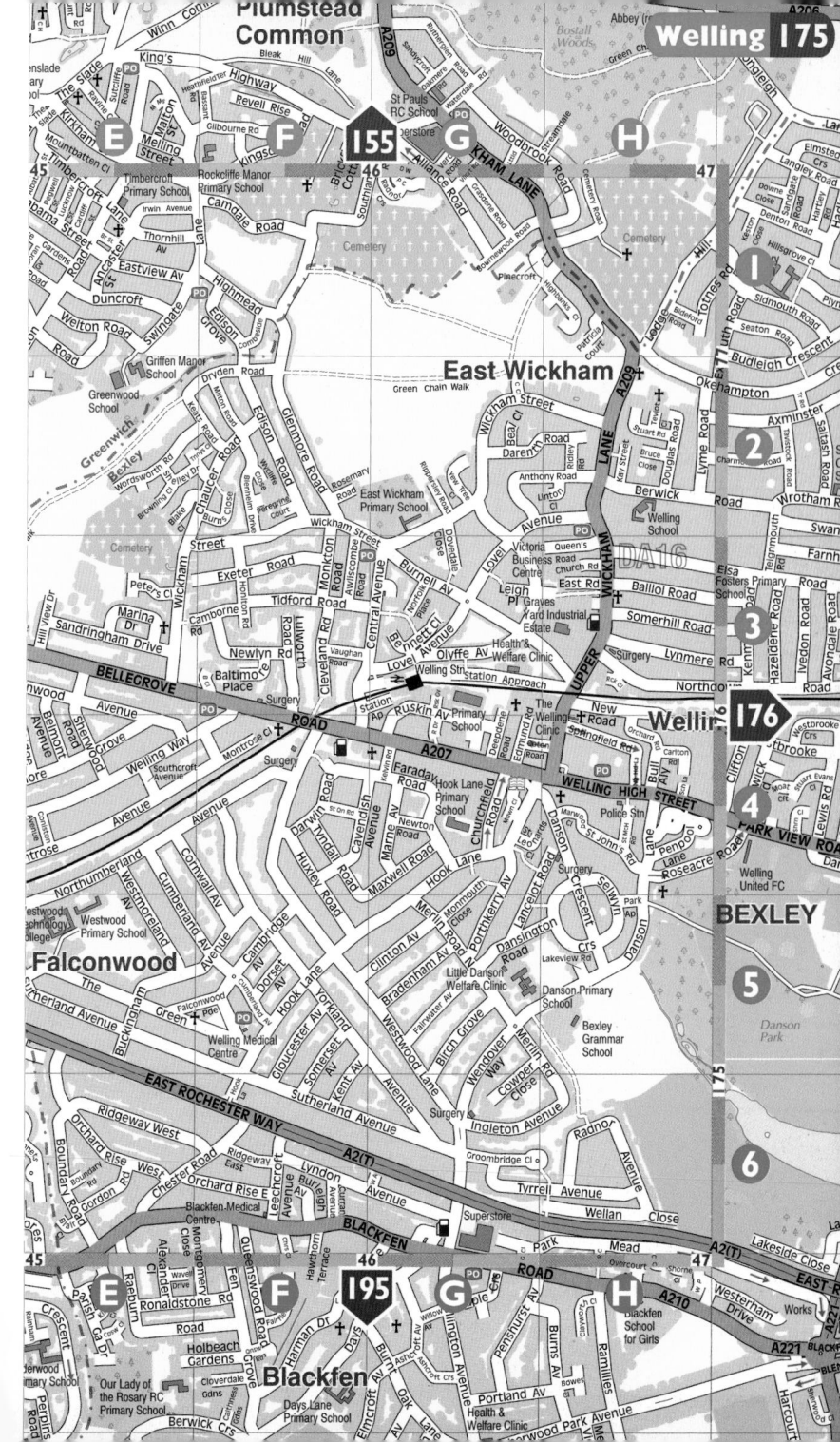

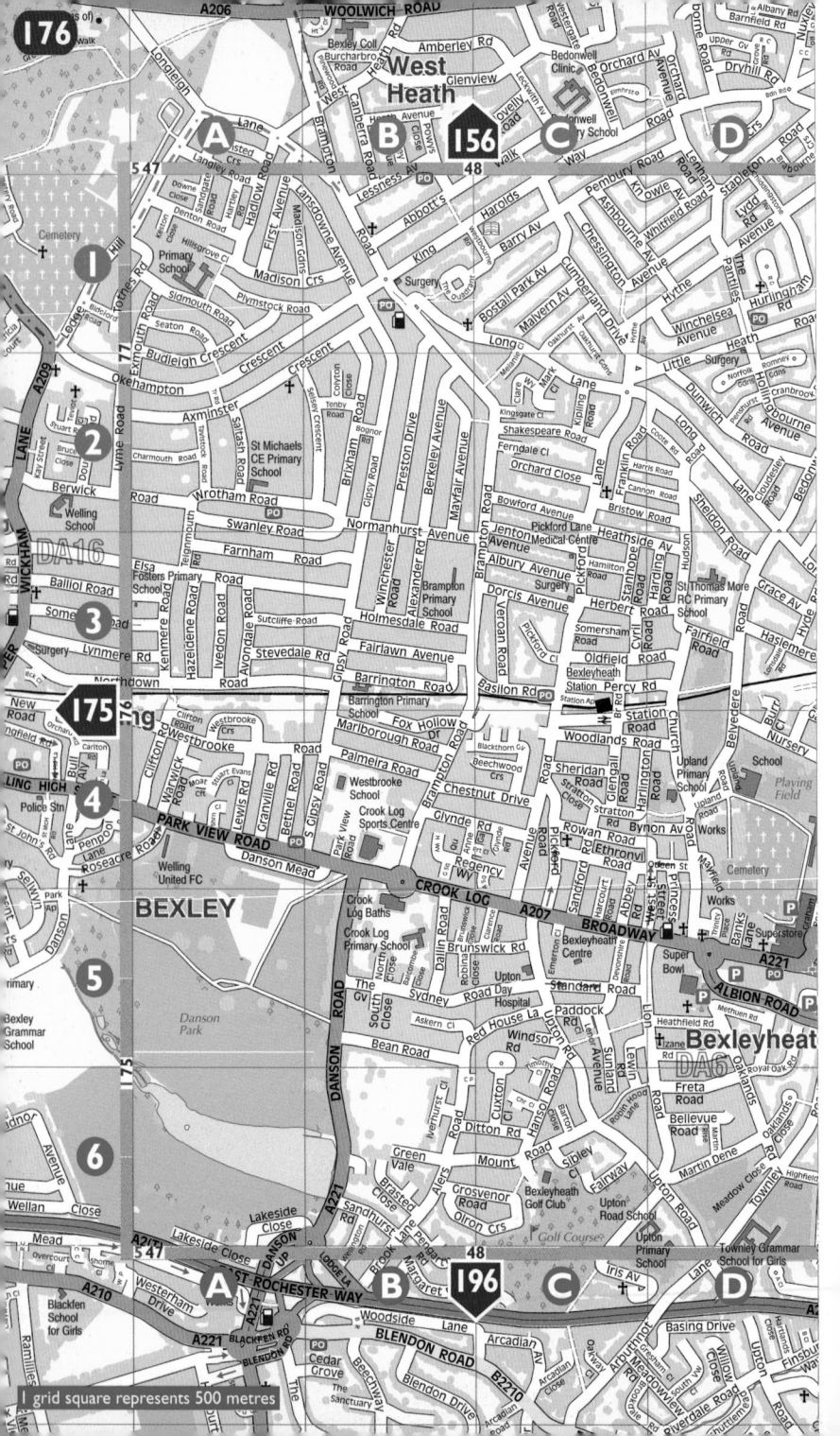

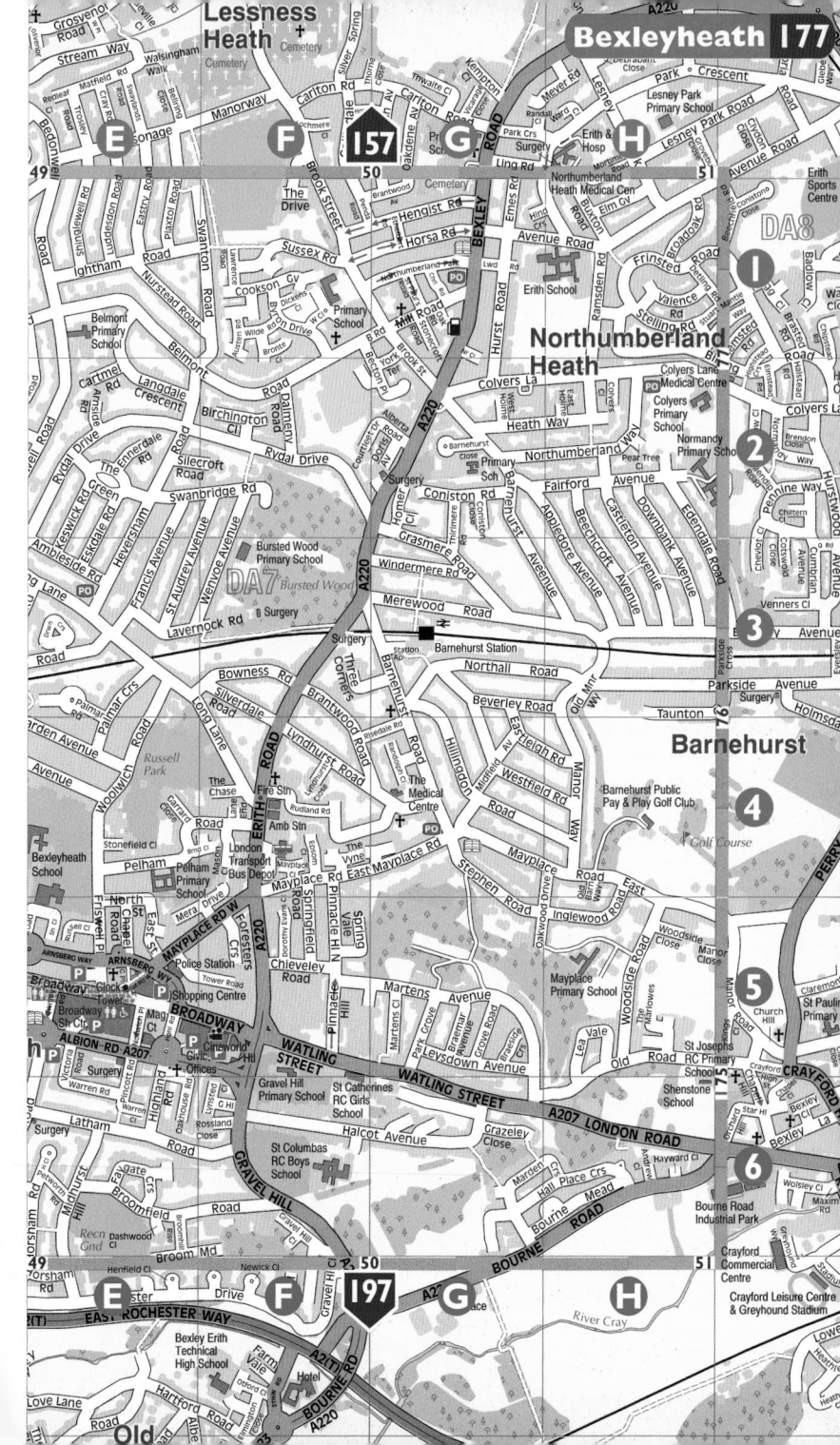

I grid square represents 500 metres

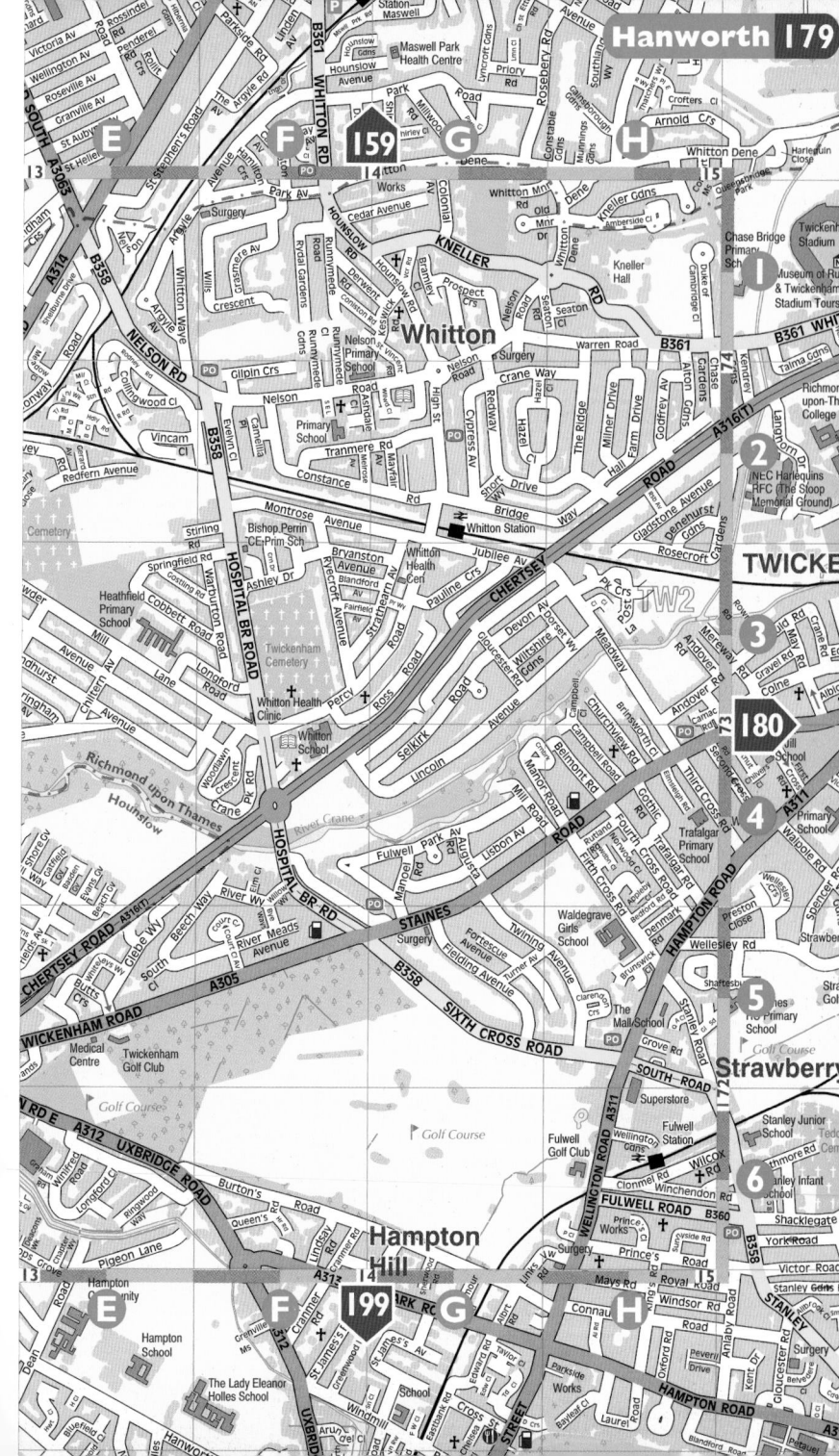

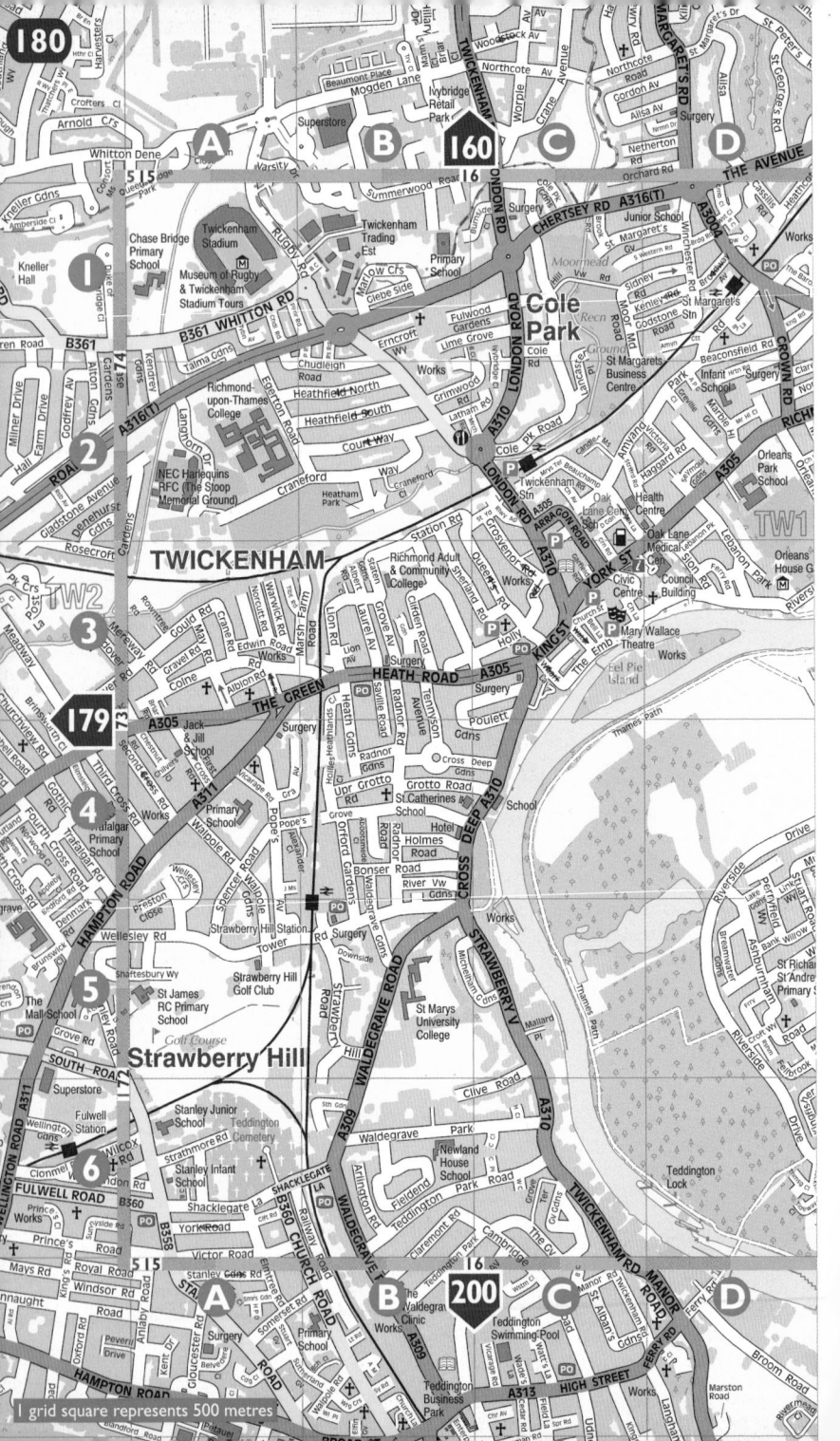

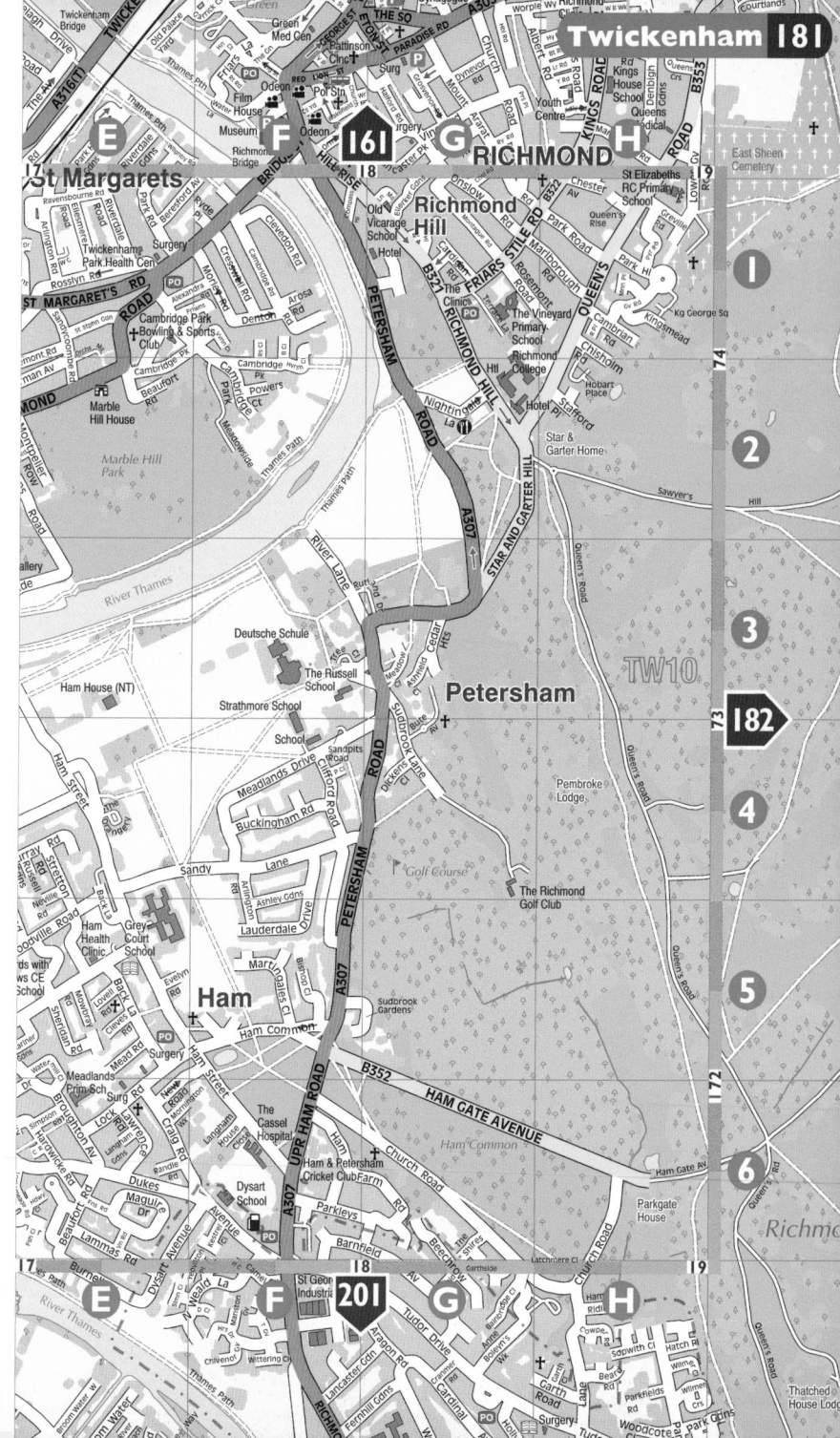

KINGS ROAD
ROAD B353
B351

Courtlands
Christs
School
Kings
House
School
Queens
Medical
Cen
St Elizabeths
RC Primary
School
Queens
Rise
Park Hi
QUEENS
Chisholm
Hobart
Place
Home
broke
Queens Road

Sheen Mount
Primary School
Christchurch
Road
Longfield
Monroe
DF

East Sheen
Common
East Sheen
Cemetery

Well Lane
Sheen W
Mall
The
parklands
Close
York
Wood Av

Westham
gdns
W Temple Sheen
Sheen Gate

Vicarage Road
garage
Stonehill Road

Enmore
Gdns

East
She

Clare L
Aven

162
20
Fife
Road

A   **B**   **C**   **D**

519

74

Kg George Sq
Kingsmead
Cambrian
Rd
1

Bog
Lodge

Sawyer's
Hill
2

TW10
181
73
3

White
Lodge

Richmond
Park

Pen
Ponds

4

5

172

Isabella
Plantation
6
Parkgate
House

Richmond Park

Queens Road

Robinwood
Place

KINGSTON VA

Grasme
Avenue

Ullswater

Church Road

Ham
Ridings

Sapwith Cl   Hatch
wilme
Bear
parkfields wilme
Thatched

A308

Robin H

Kingst
Un

Coombe
Coombe

Robin H
Primary
School

D

519
A   **B**   **C**

20
202

Richmond
Kingston
KINGSTON HILL
Thames
Thames

Coombe Rdge

Coombe Park

Kingston Va

Ladderstile Ride
Coombe Rise
Coombe

1 grid square represents 500 metres

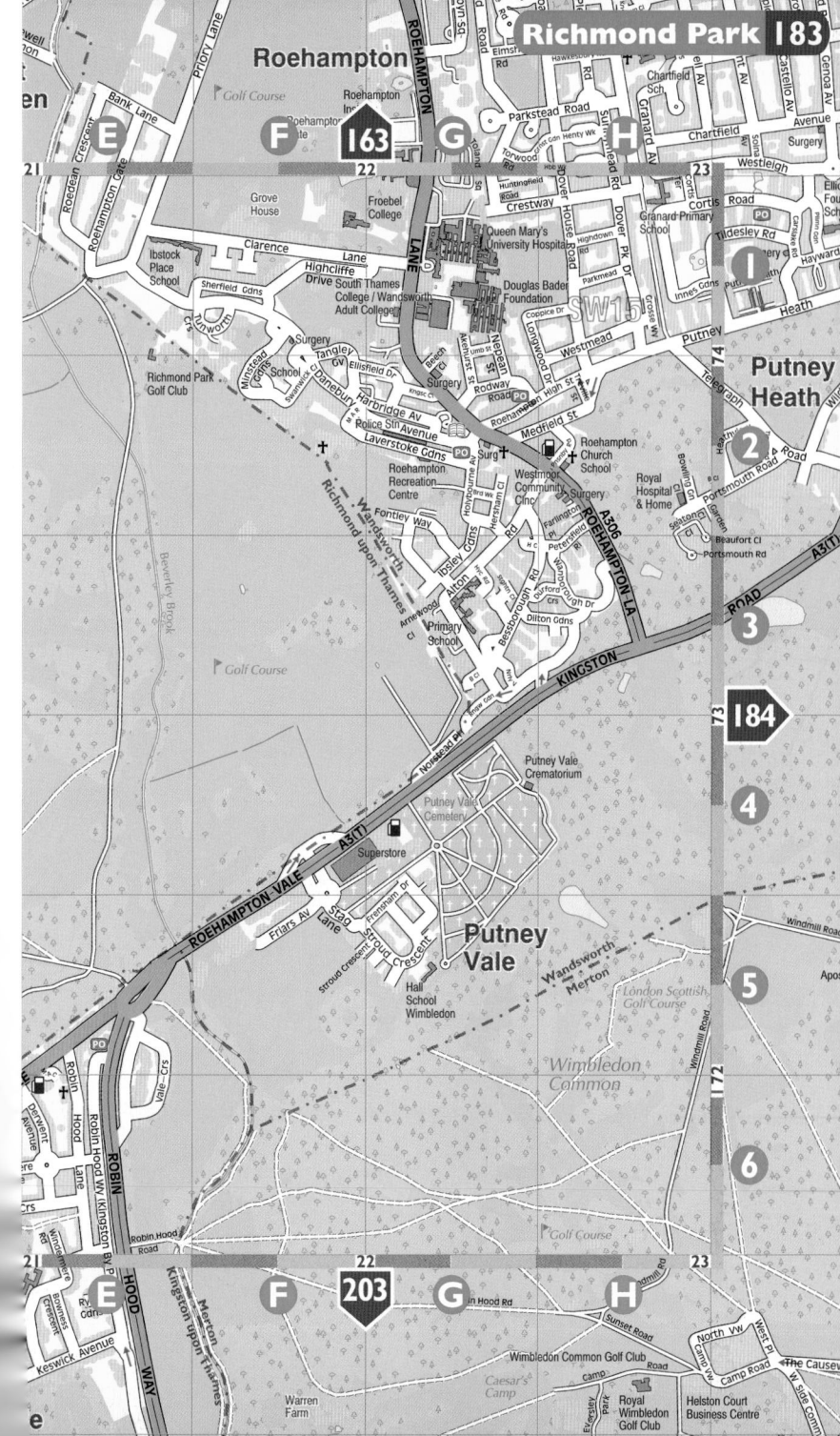

Roehampton

Golf Course

Roehampton Inn

E

Bank Lane

Roehampton Gate

Roedean Crescent

F

Roehampton Gate

Golf Course

163

G

Parkstead Road

Eimshill Rd

Torwood Gdns Henty Wk

Chartfield Sch

Chartfield Av

Castello Av

Genoa Av

H

Chartfield Av

Surgery

Westleigh Av

Elliot Four Scho

Grove House

Froebel College

Clarence Lane

Highcliffe Drive South Thames College / Wandsworth Adult College

Ibstock Place School

Sherfield Gdns

Tilworth

Richmond Park Golf Club

Munstead Gdns

Surgery

School

Stonebun

Tangley

Ellisfield Dr

Swinburne

Beech Av

Queen Mary's University Hospital

Douglas Bader Foundation

Coppice Dr

Highdown Rd

Parkmead

SW15

Crestway

Huntingfield Road

Dover House Road

Dover Pk Dr

Westmead

Longwood

Crosse W

Putney

Cortis Road

Granard Primary School

Inner Gdns

Tidesley Rd

Hayward G

Carisvel Rd

I

Heath

Putney Heath

Telegraph Rd

2

Wildcr

Harbridge Av

Laverstoke Gdns

Richmond Park Golf Club

Police Stn Avenue

GV

School

Clanebun

Surgery

Surg

PO

Rodway

Roehampton High St

Medfield St

PO

Roehampton Church School

Royal Hospital & Home

Beaufort Cl

Portsmouth Rd

Portsmouth Rd

Beverley Brook

Wandsworth Richmond upon Thames

Fontley Way

Roehampton Recreation Centre

Ibsley Gdns

Howsman

Alton

Arnewood Cl

Westmoor Community Clinic

Surgery

Farlington

Petersfield

Beckborough Rd

Wayford Cr

Wanborough Dr

Dilton Gdns

Sefton Gdns

A306

ROEHAMPTON LA

A3(T)

3

Golf Course

Primary School

KINGSTON

ROAD

73

184

Putney Vale Crematorium

4

Putney Vale Cemetery

ROEHAMPTON VALE

A3(T)

Superstore

Stag Lane

Friars Av

Frimpton Dr

Stroud Crescent

Stroud Crescent

Hall School Wimbledon

Putney Vale

Wandsworth Merton

London Scottish Golf Course

Windmill Road

5

Aposte

PO

Derwent Avenue

Robin Hood

Robin Hood Way (Kingston By P)

ROBIN HOOD WAY

Vale Crs

Robin Hood Lane

Wimbledon upon Thames

Kingston upon Thames

Windmill Road

Wimbledon Common

72

6

Robin Hood Road

Golf Course

RY Gdns

Keswick Avenue

E

HOOD

Bewshers Crescent

Merton upon Thames

Kingston upon Thames

Warren Farm

F

203

Merton upon Thames

G

n Hood Rd

Caesar's Camp

Evesway

Park

Royal Wimbledon Golf Club

Windmill Rd

H

Sunset Road

Wimbledon Common Golf Club

Road

camp

camp

Road

Helston Court Business Centre

North Vw

West Pl

Camp Vw

Camp Road

W. Side Comm

The Causew

21 / 22 / 23

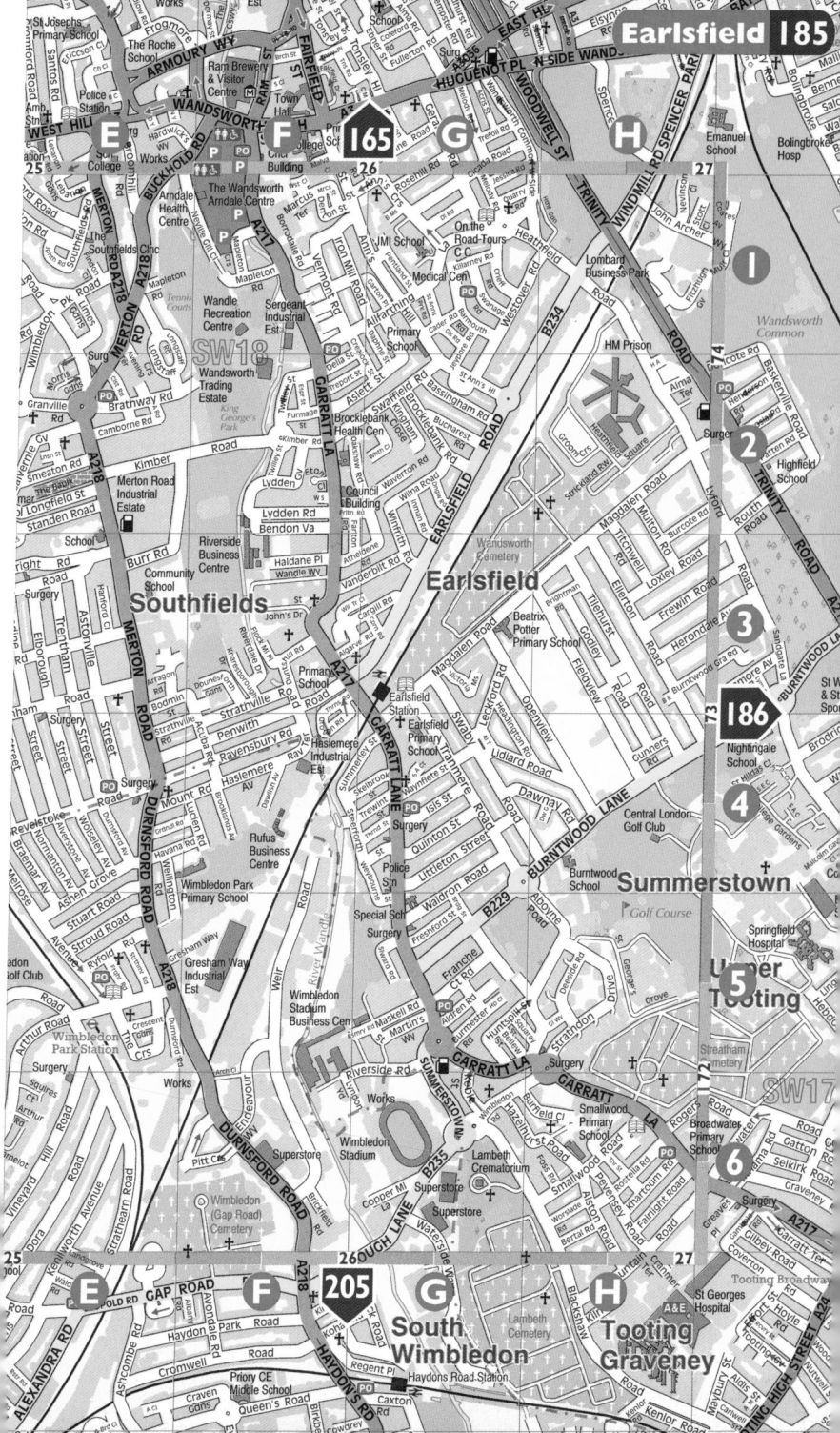

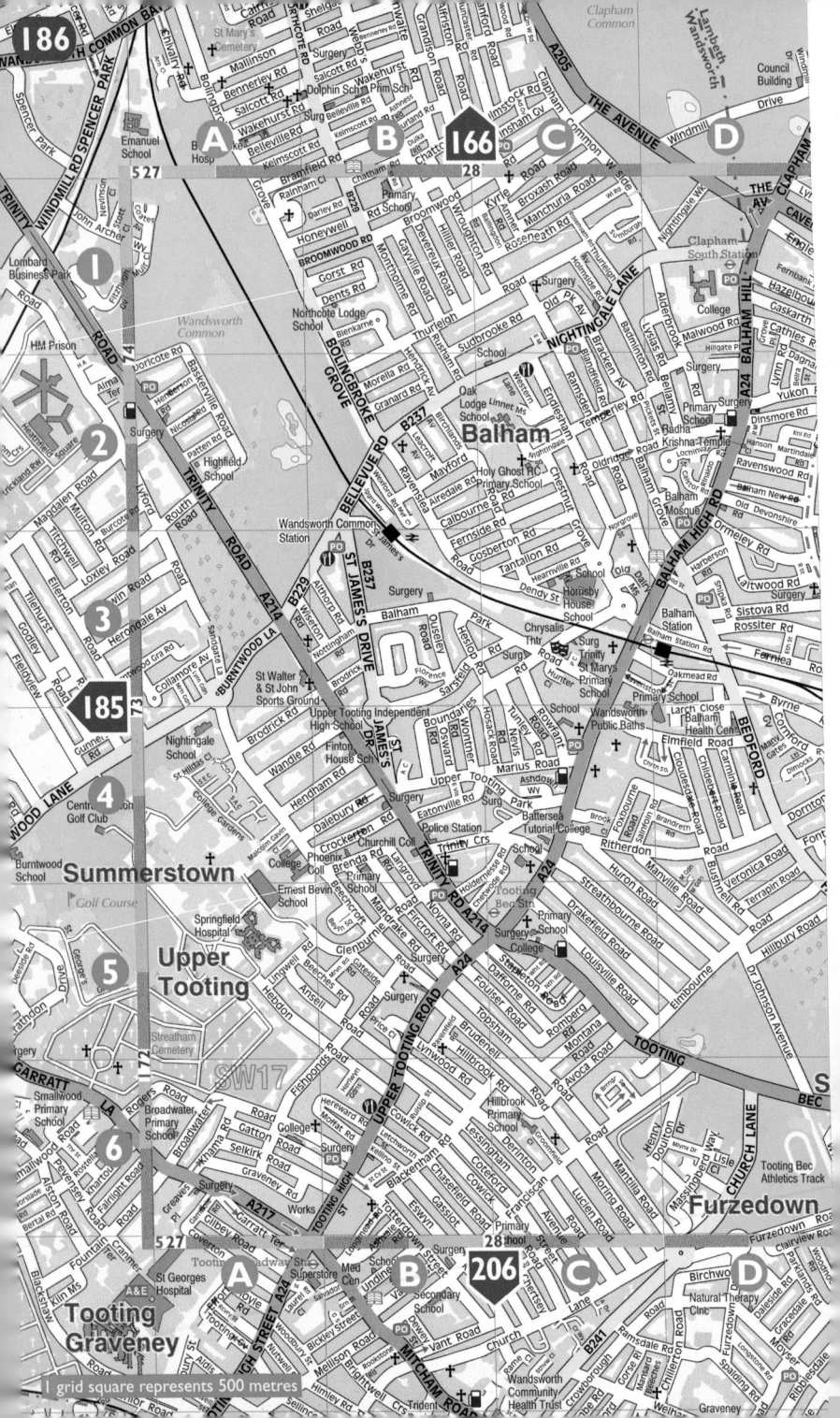

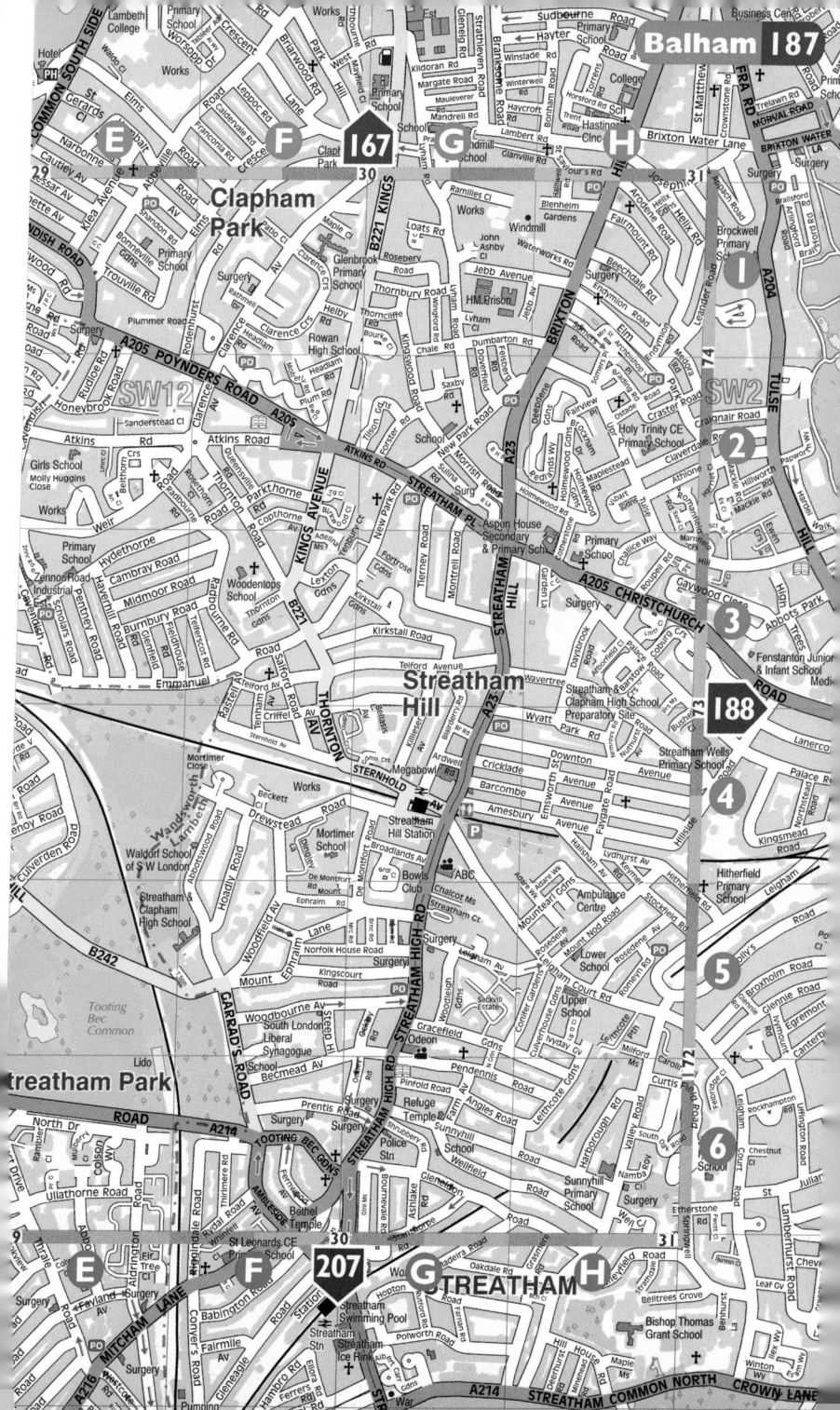

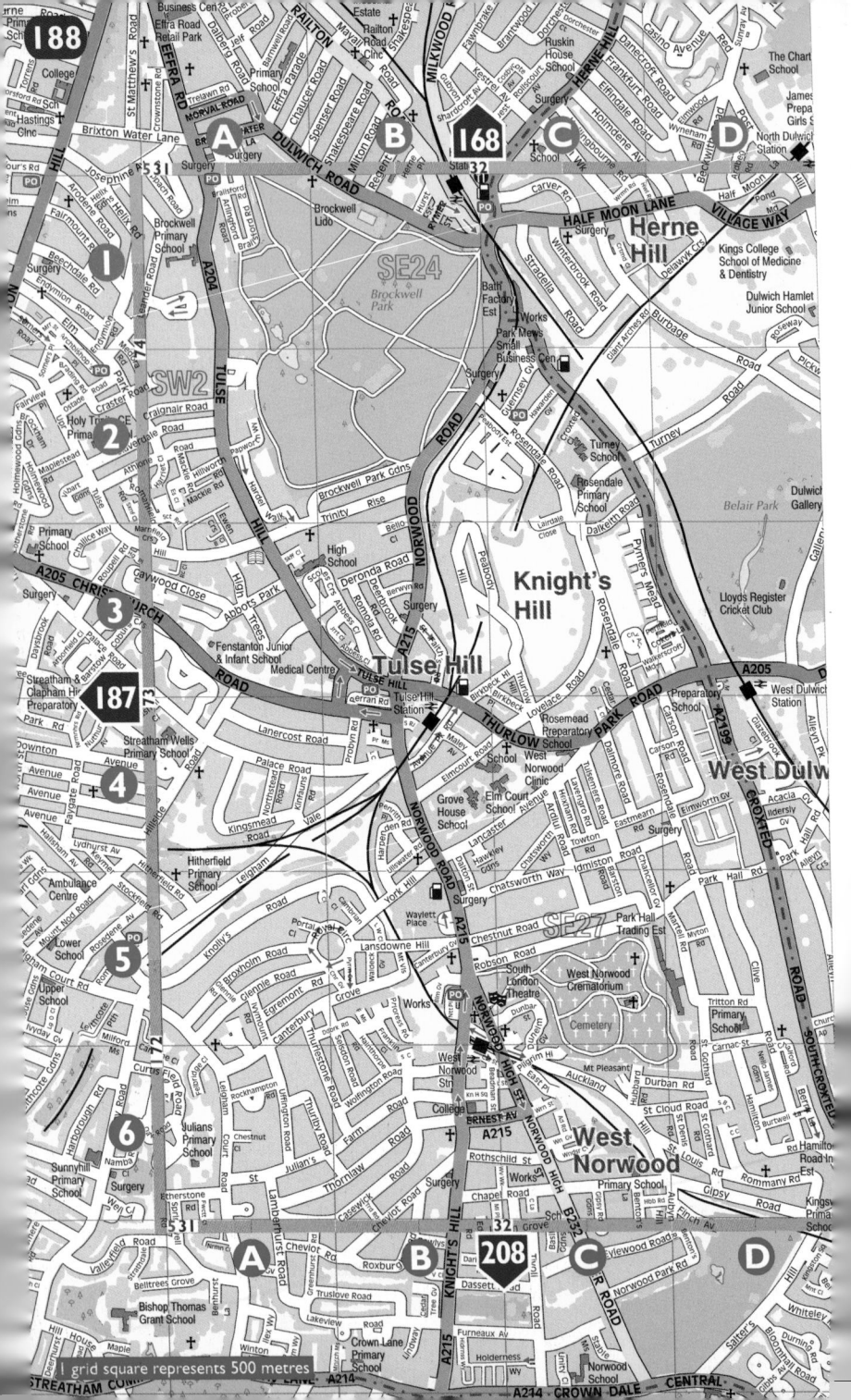

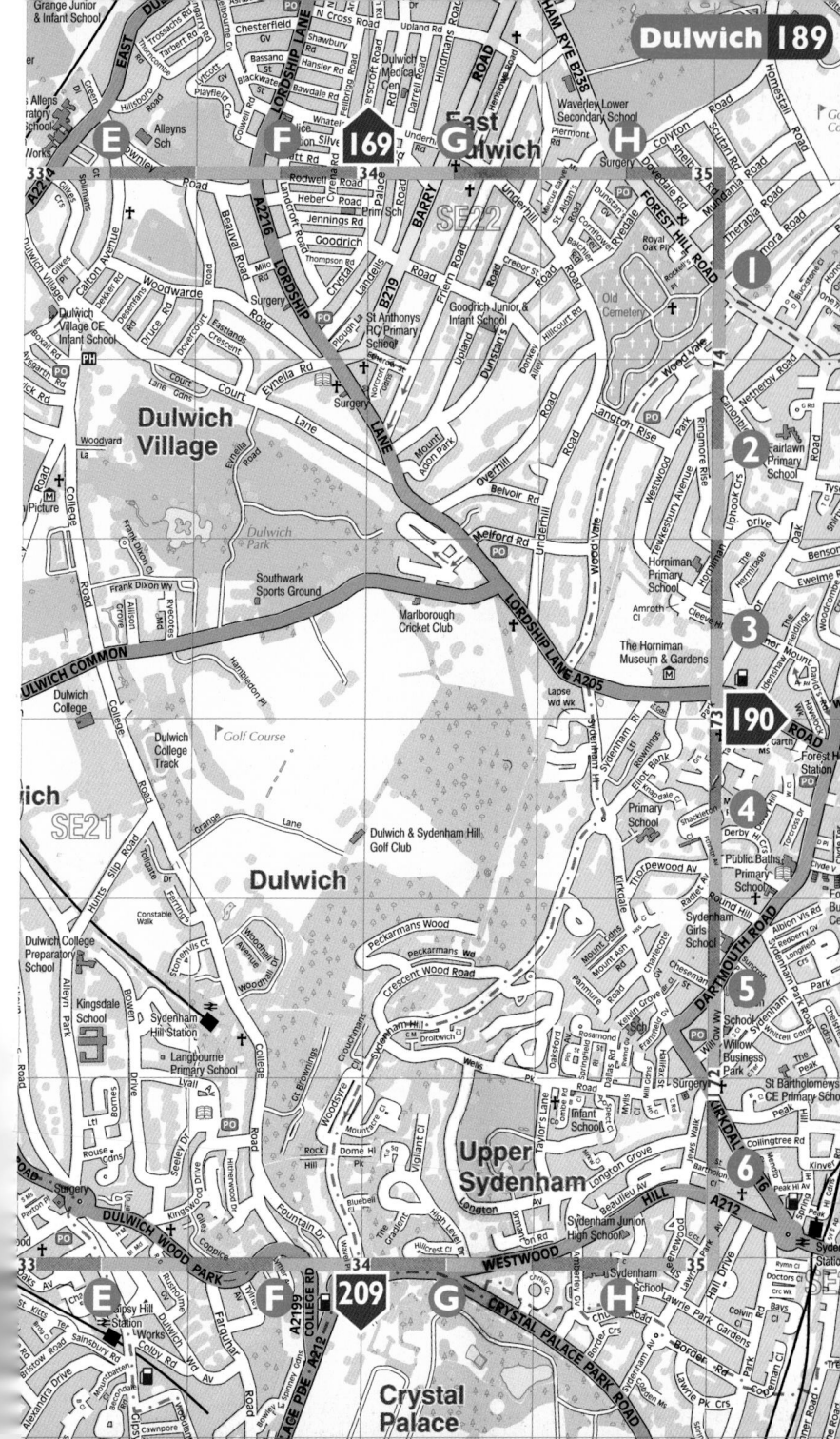

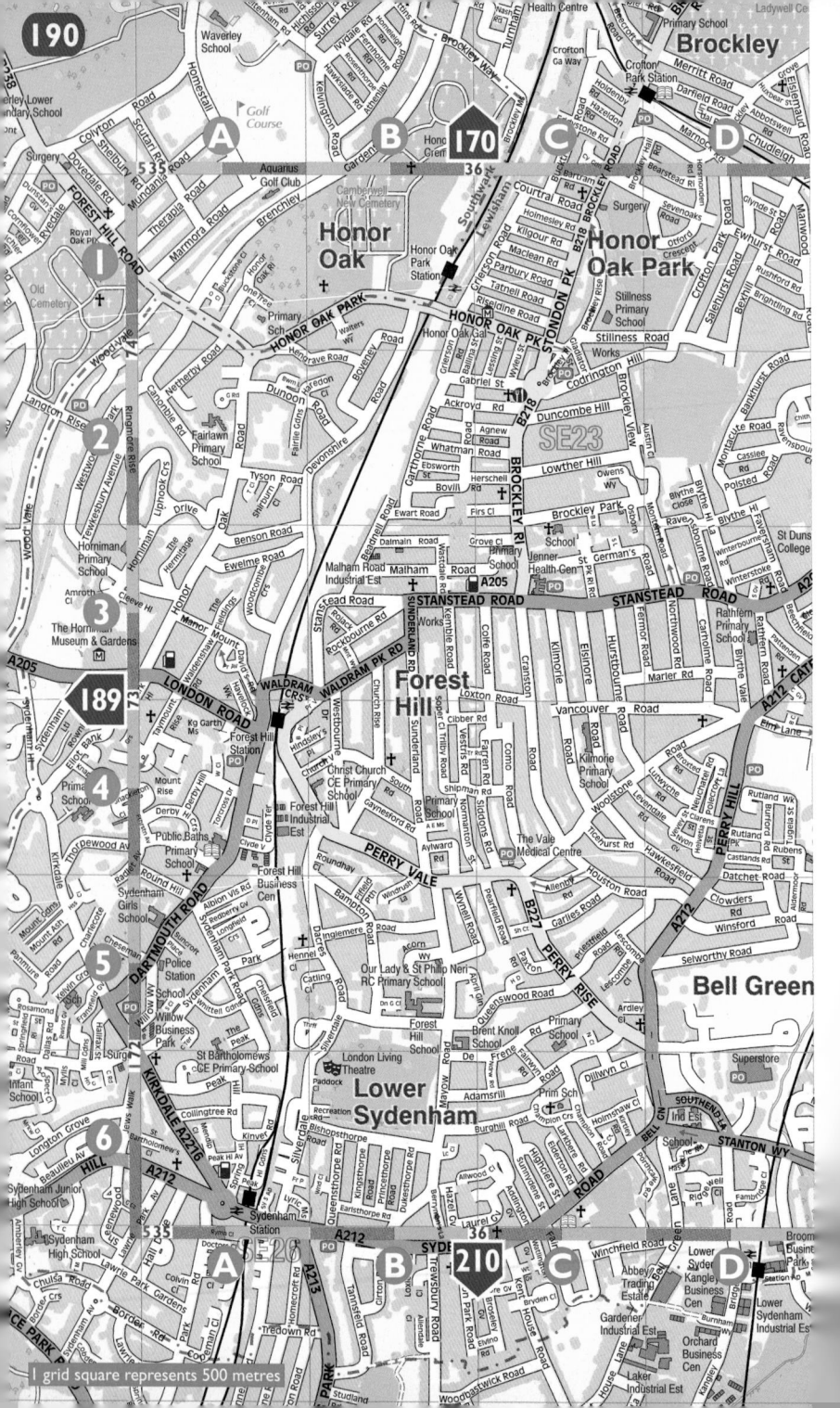

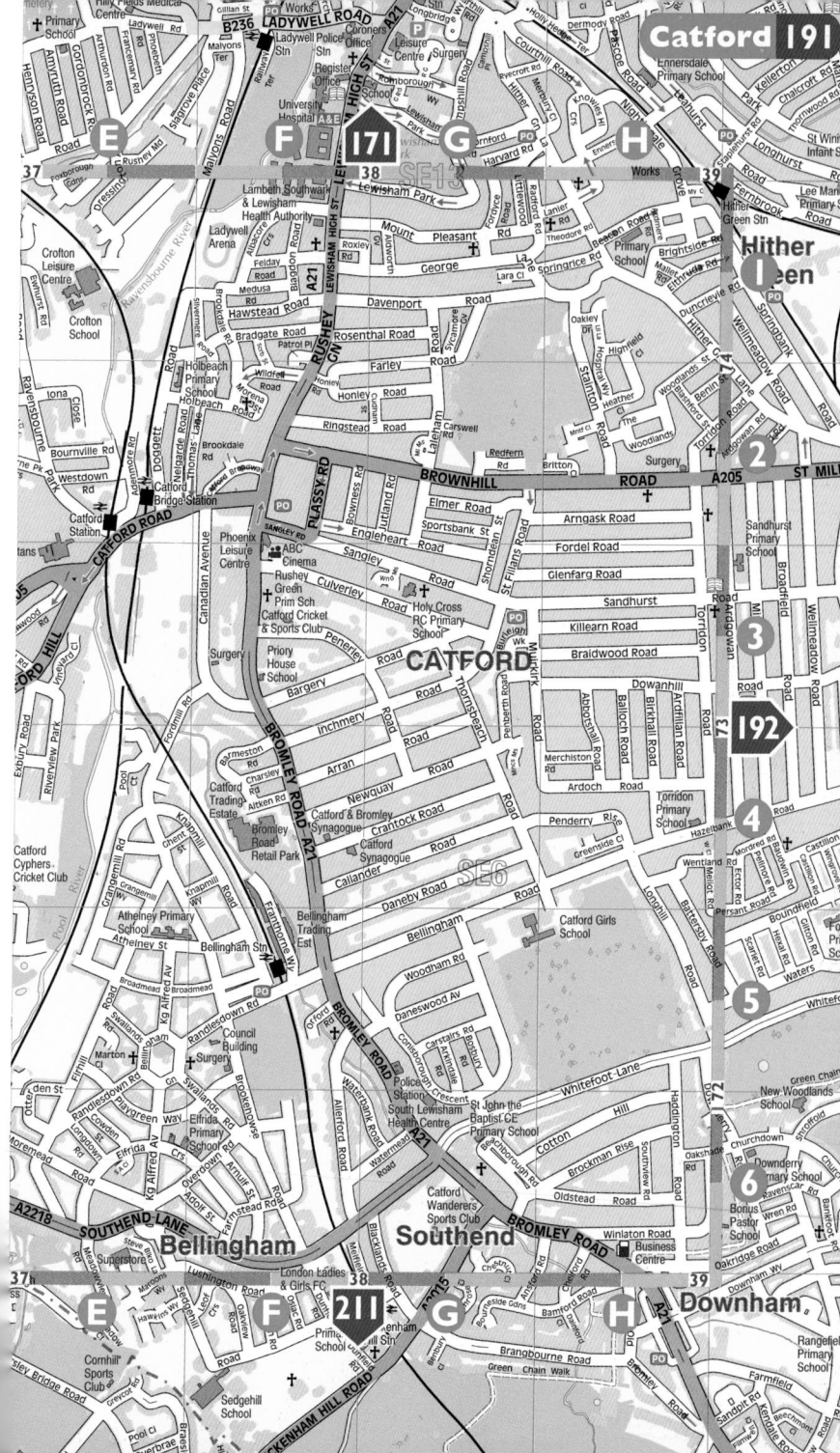

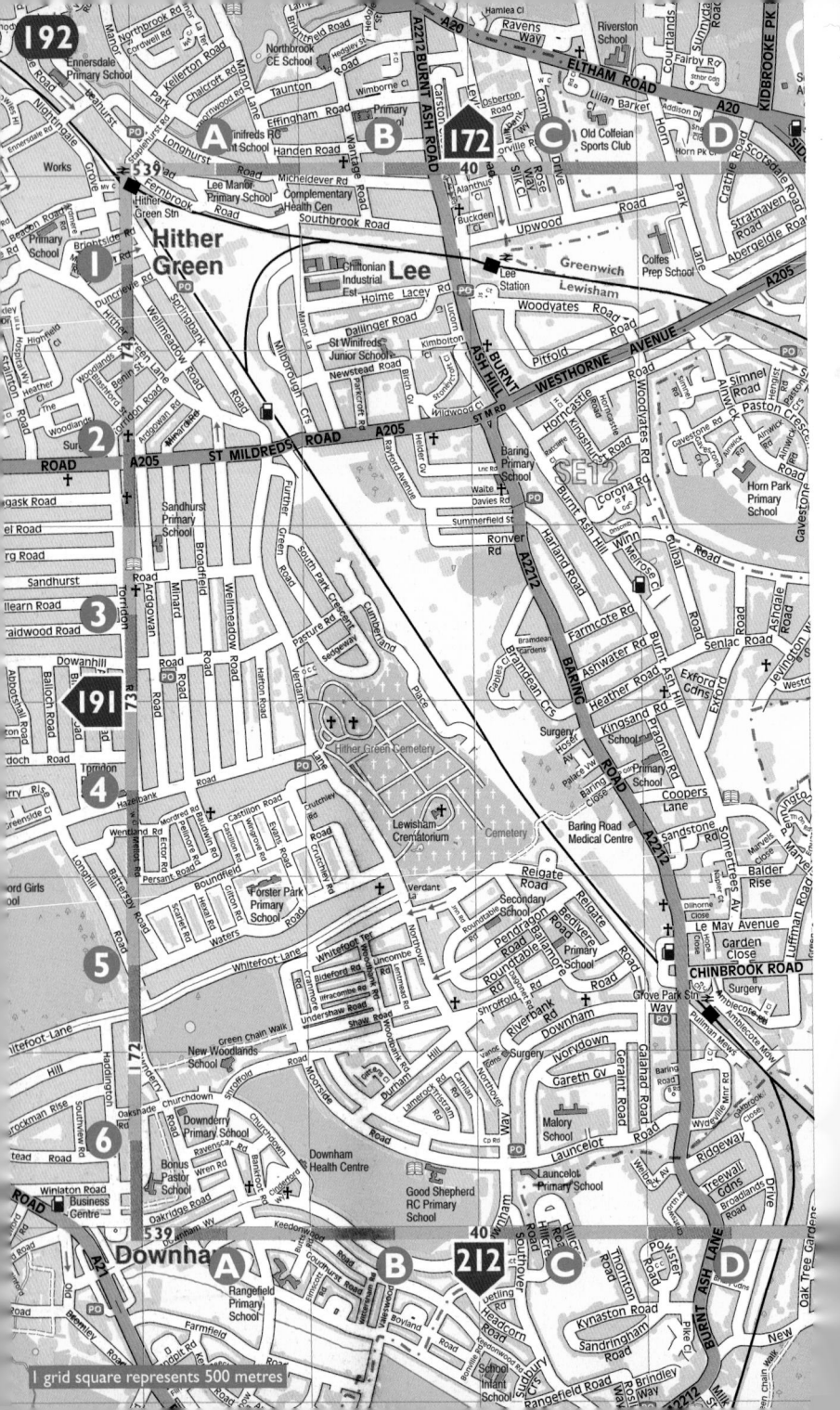

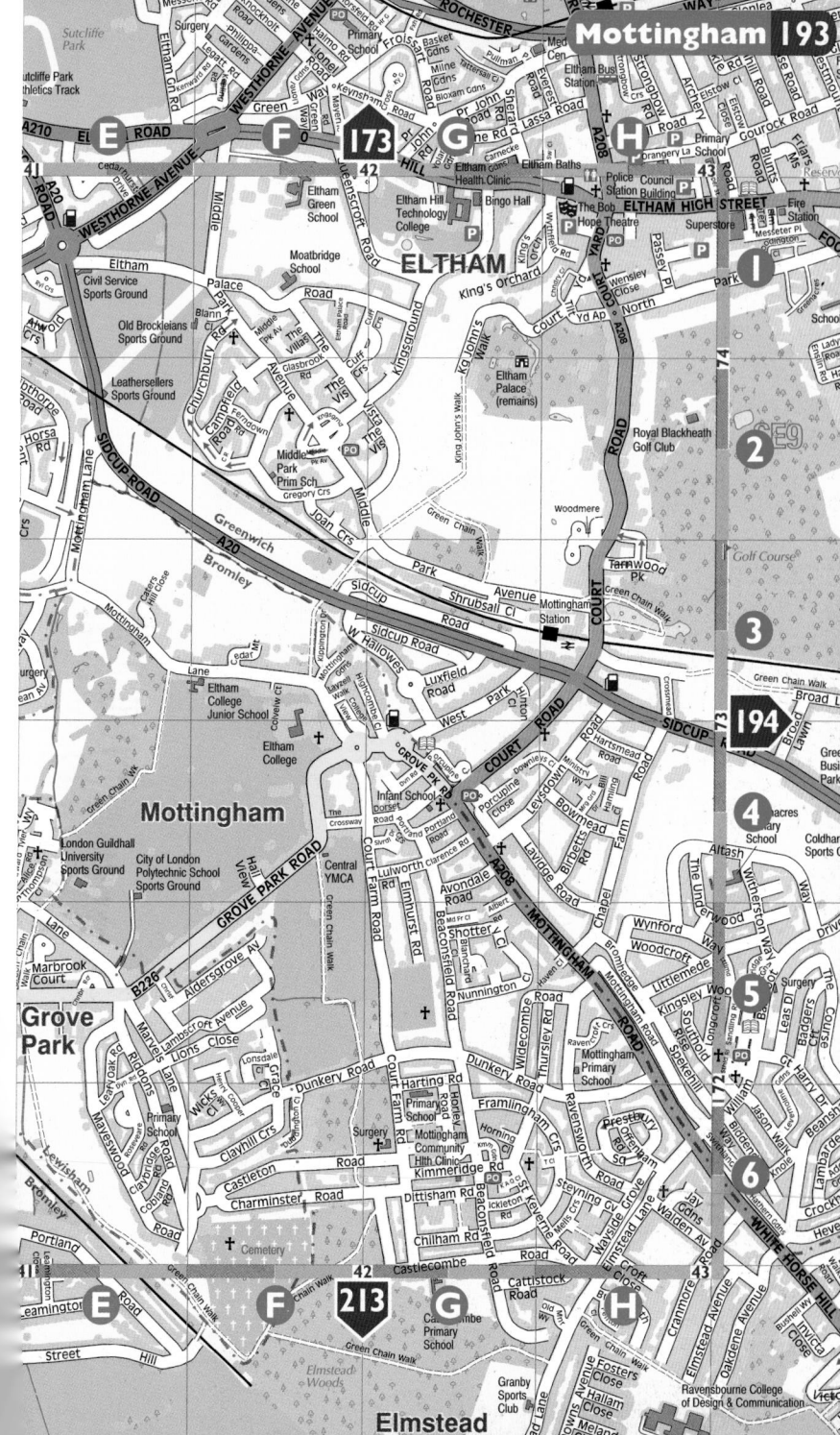

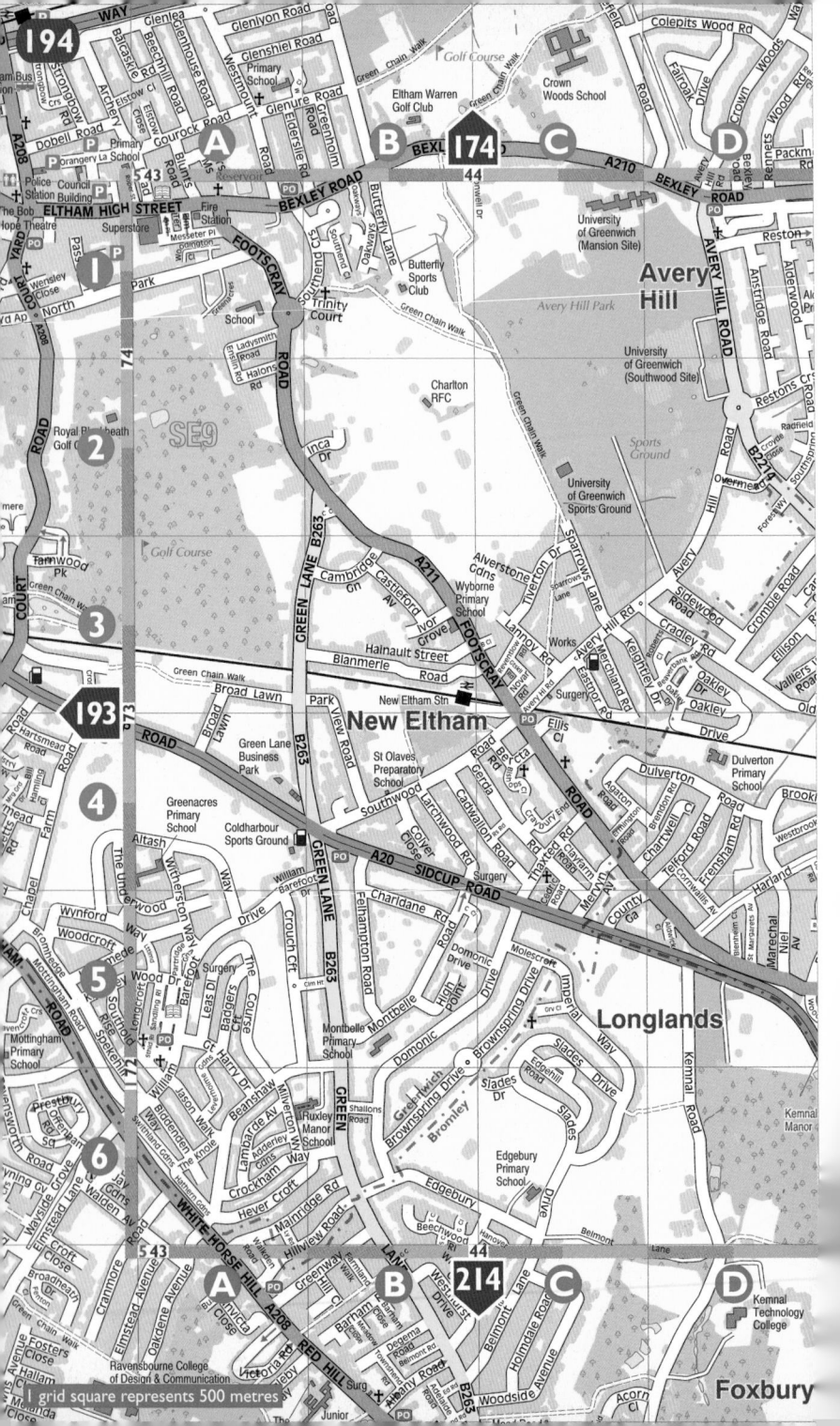

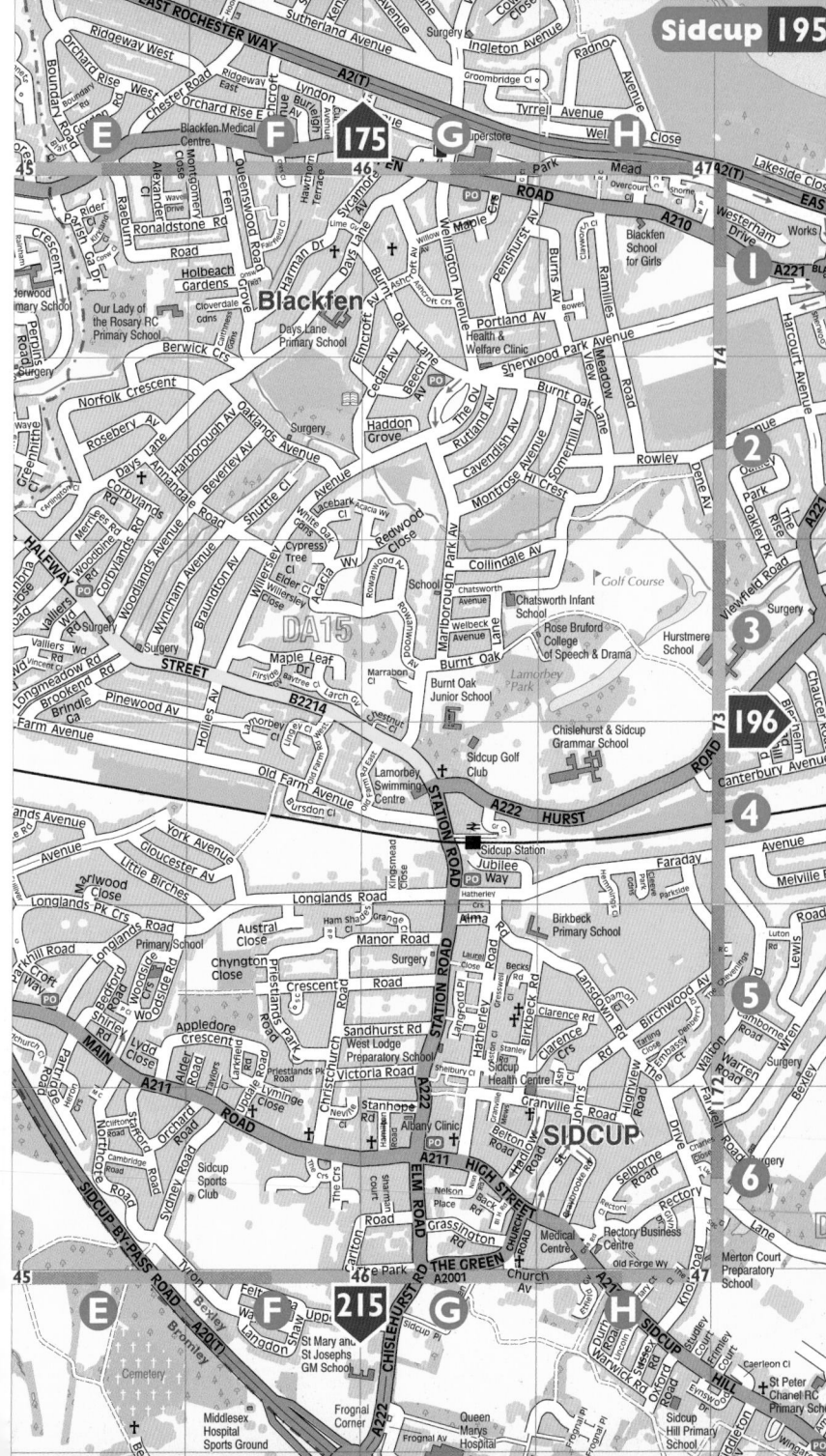

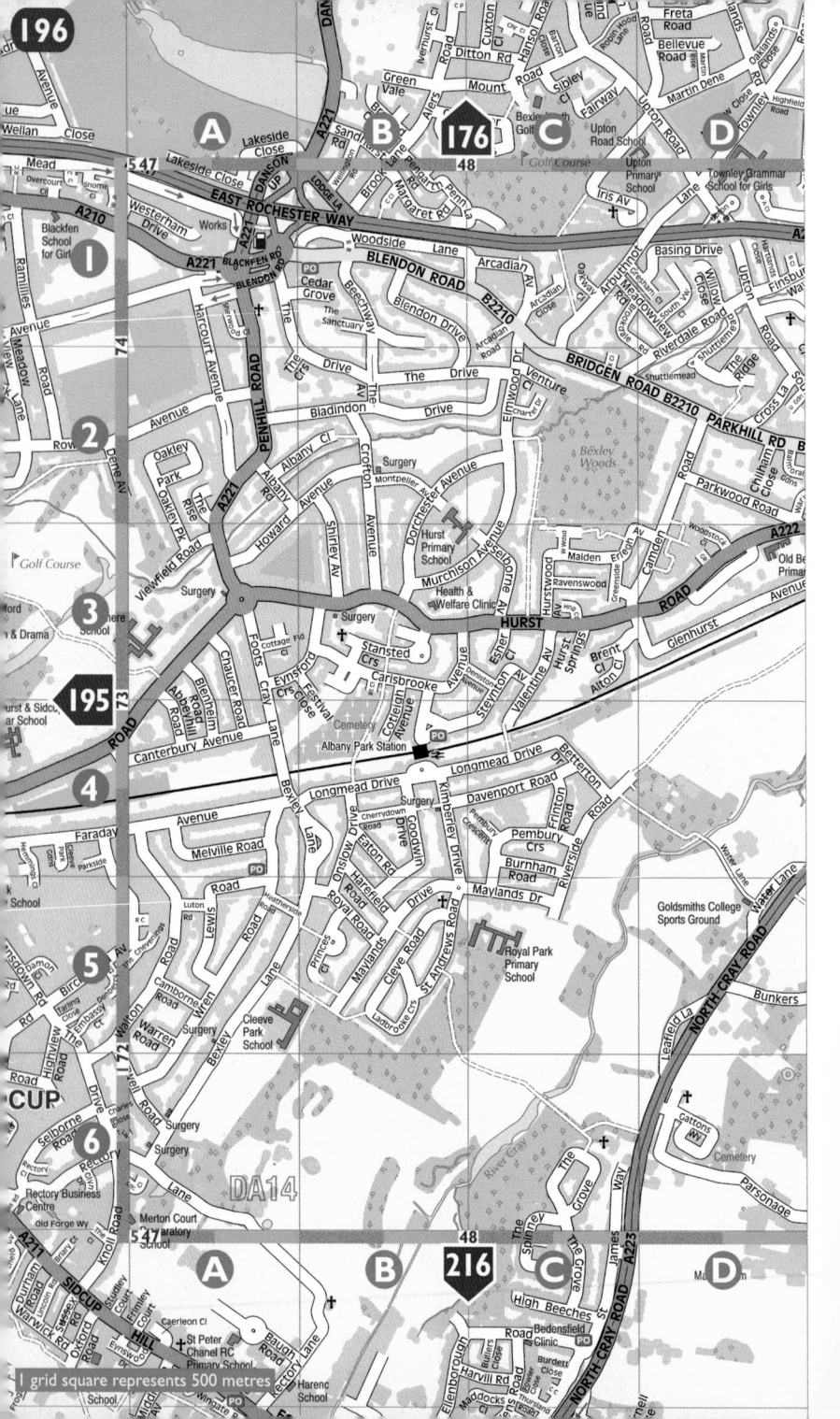

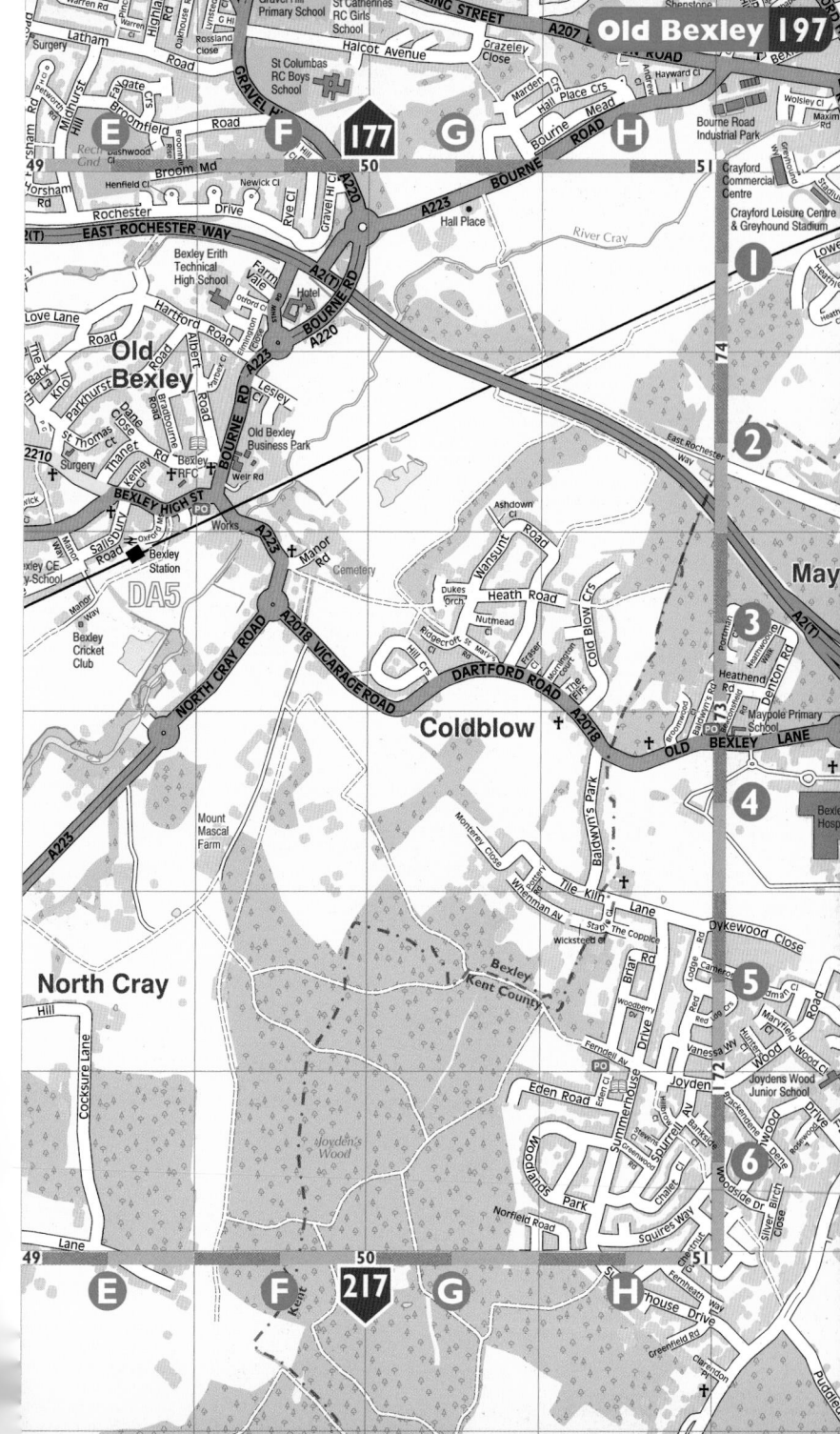

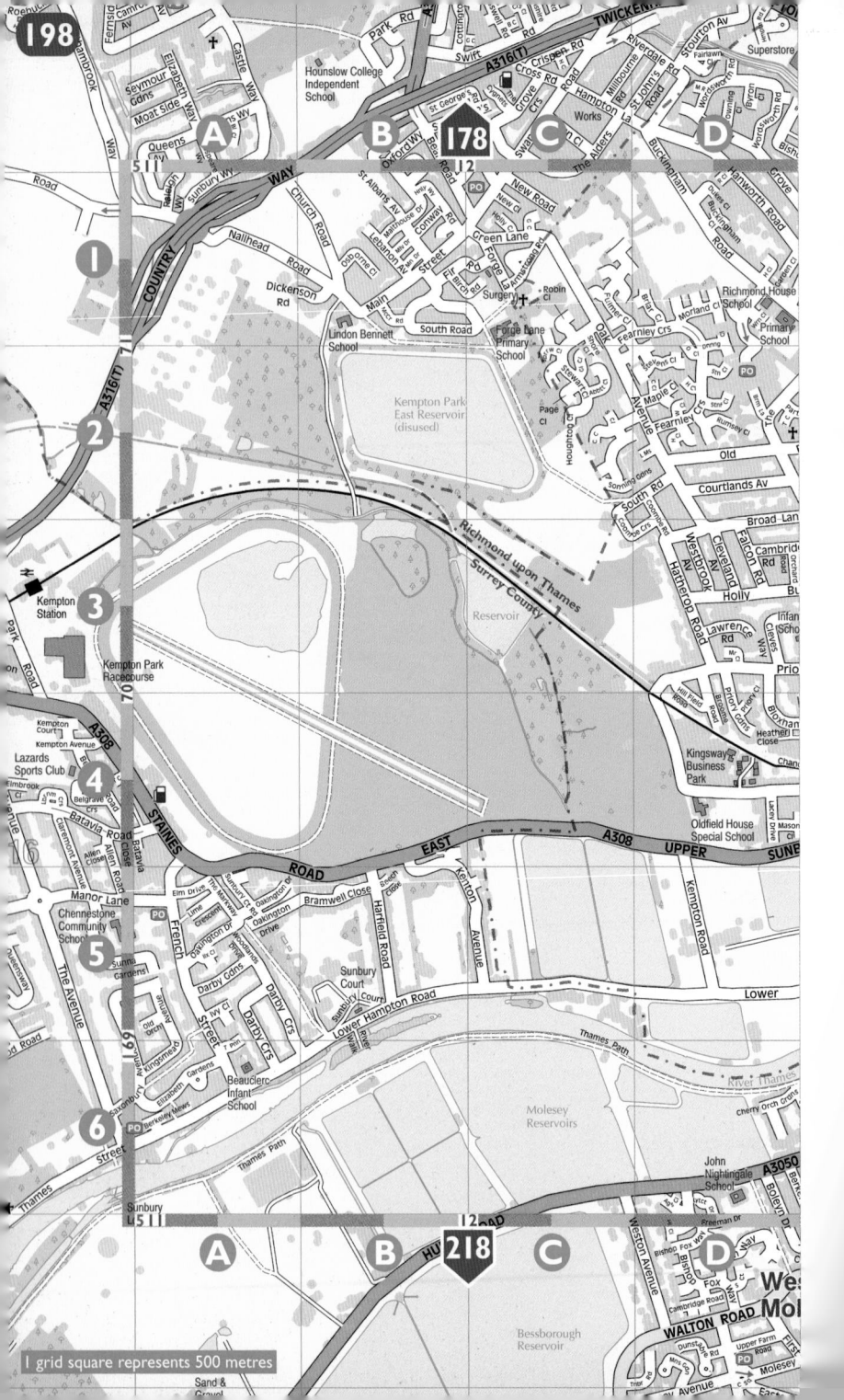

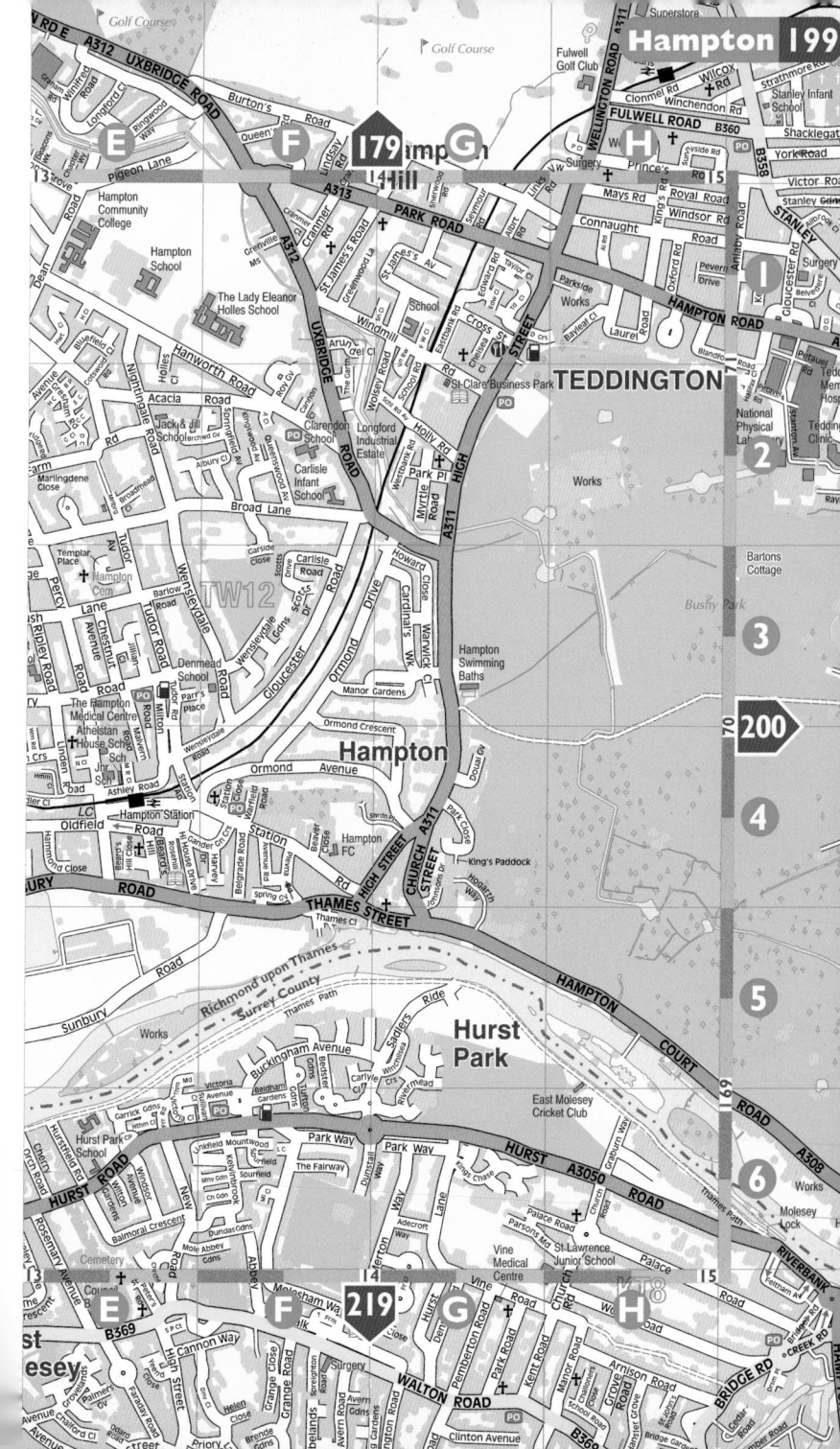

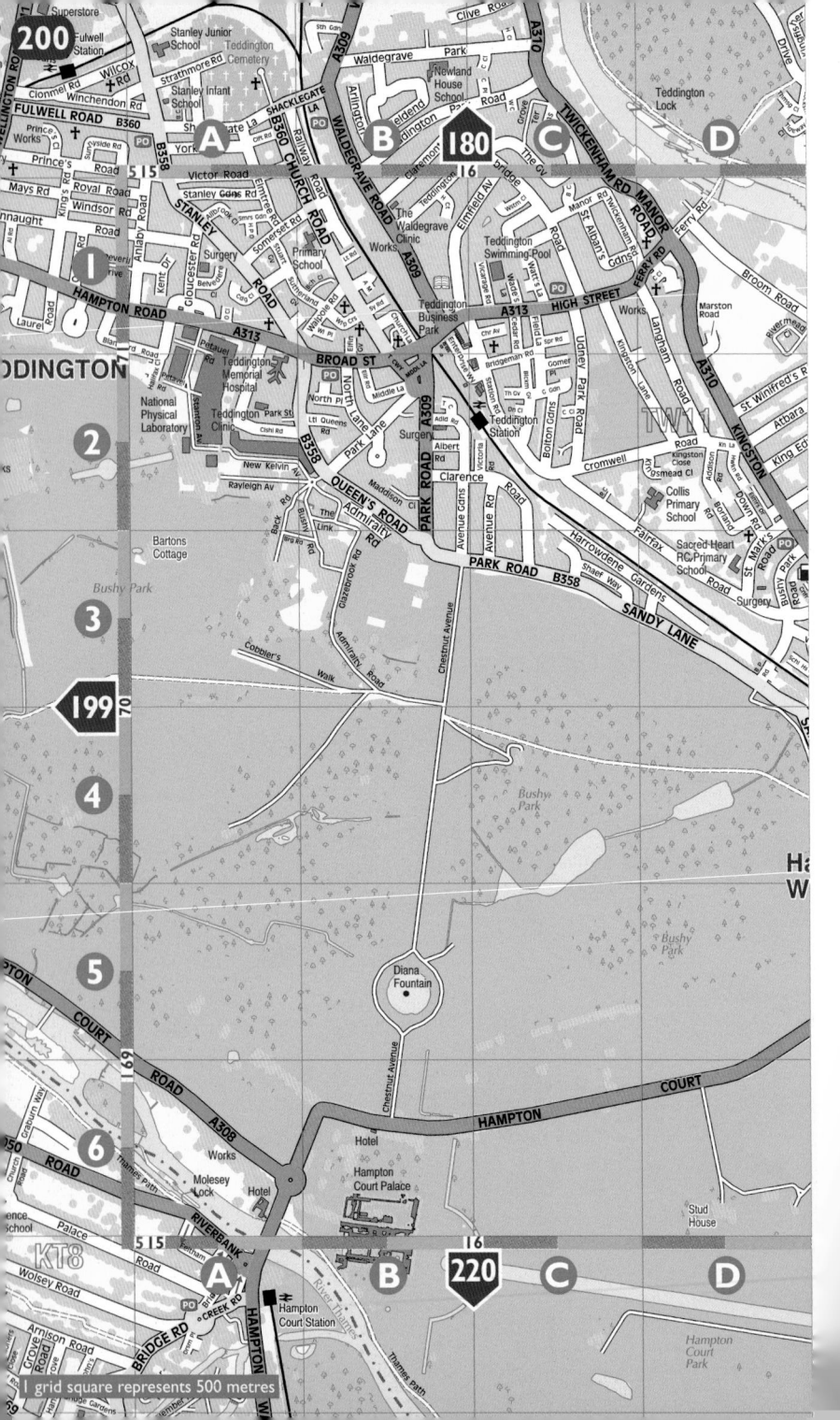

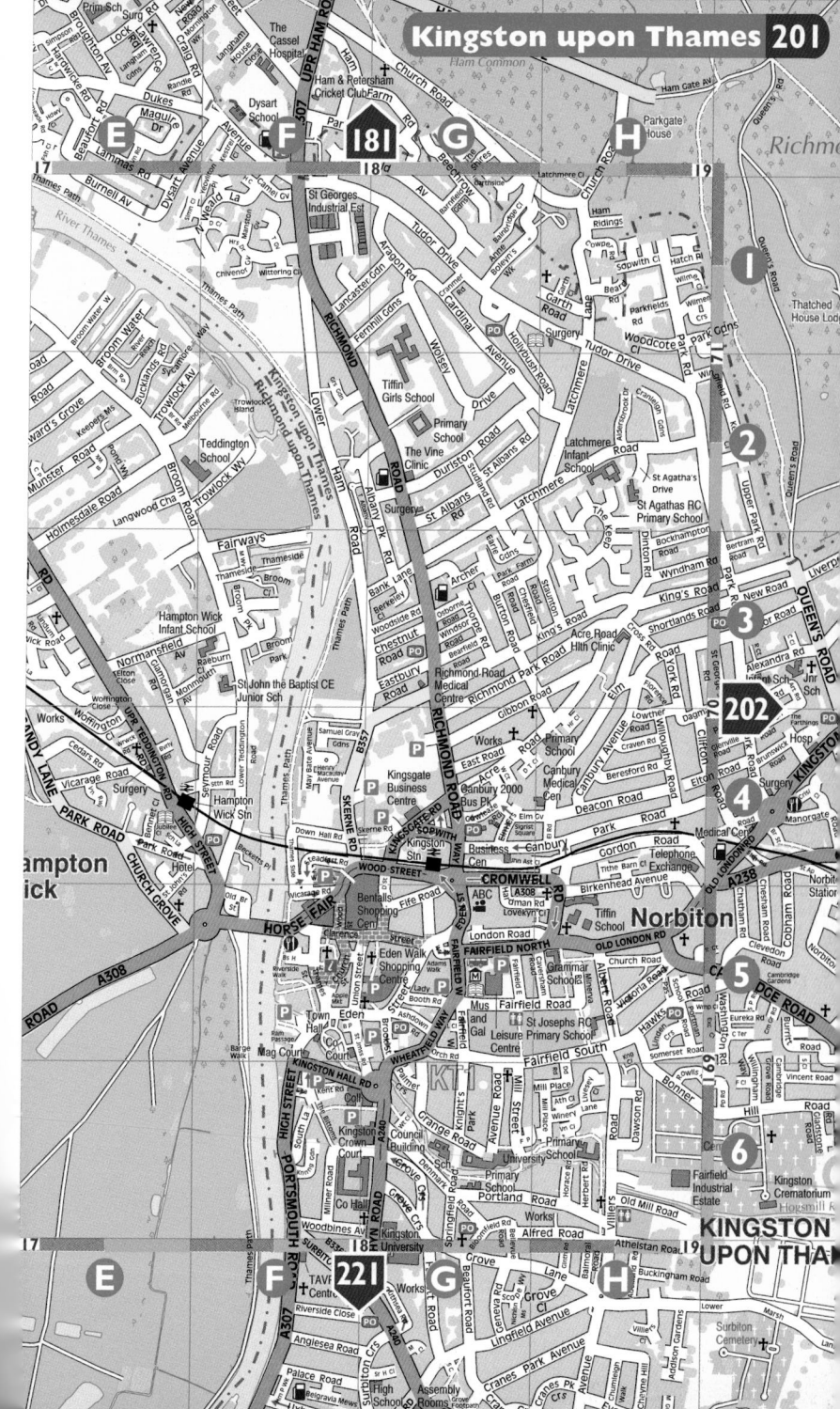

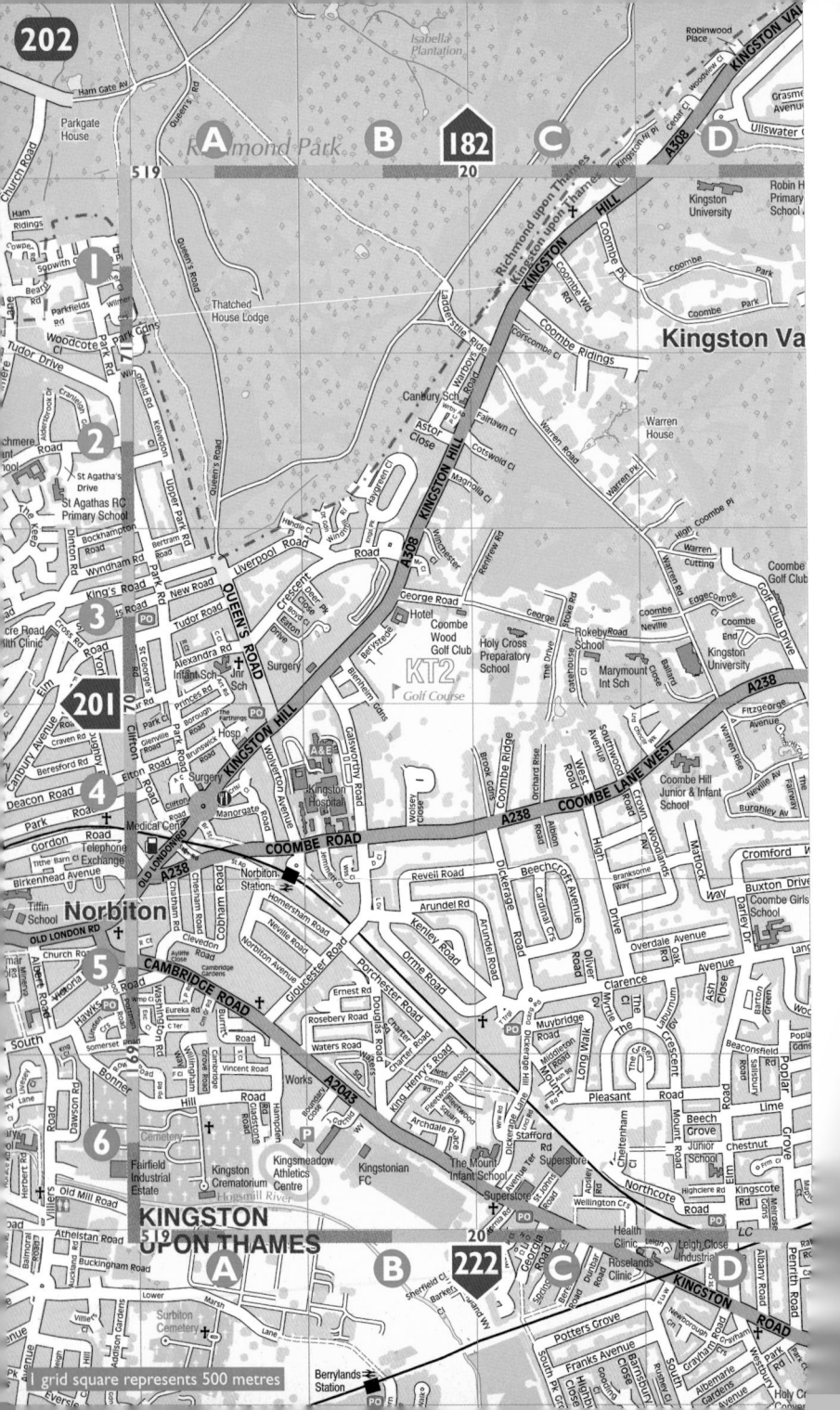

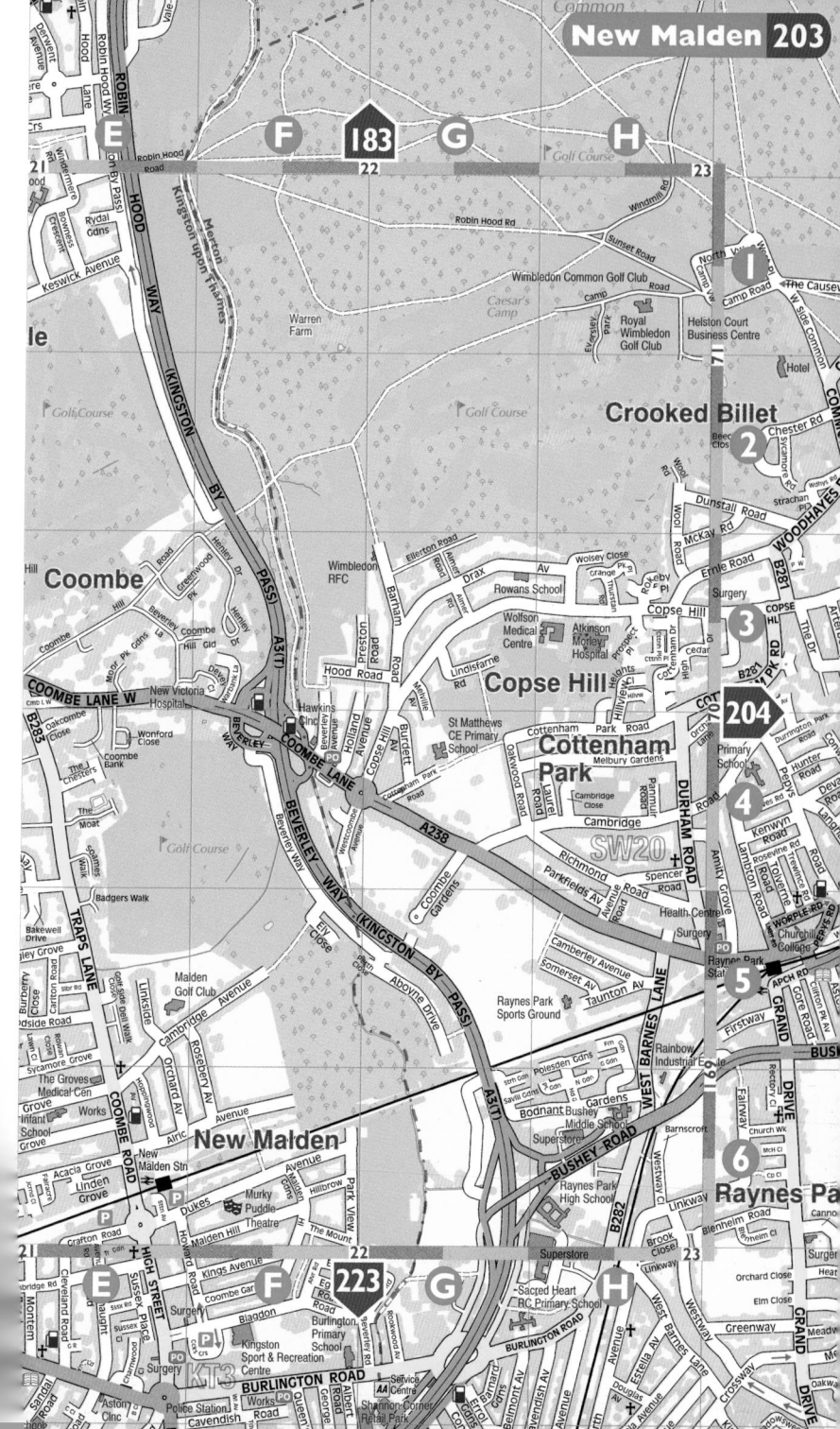

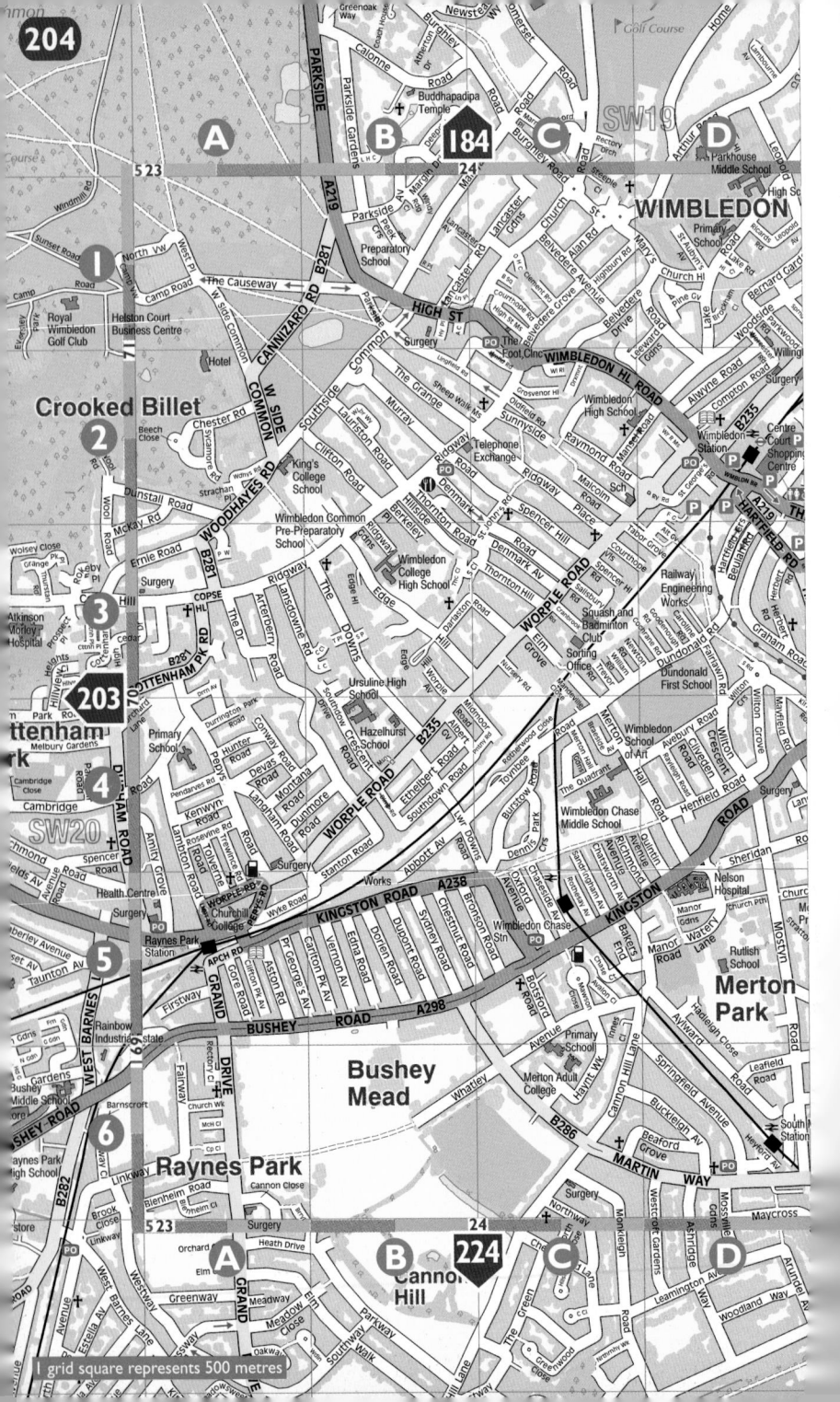

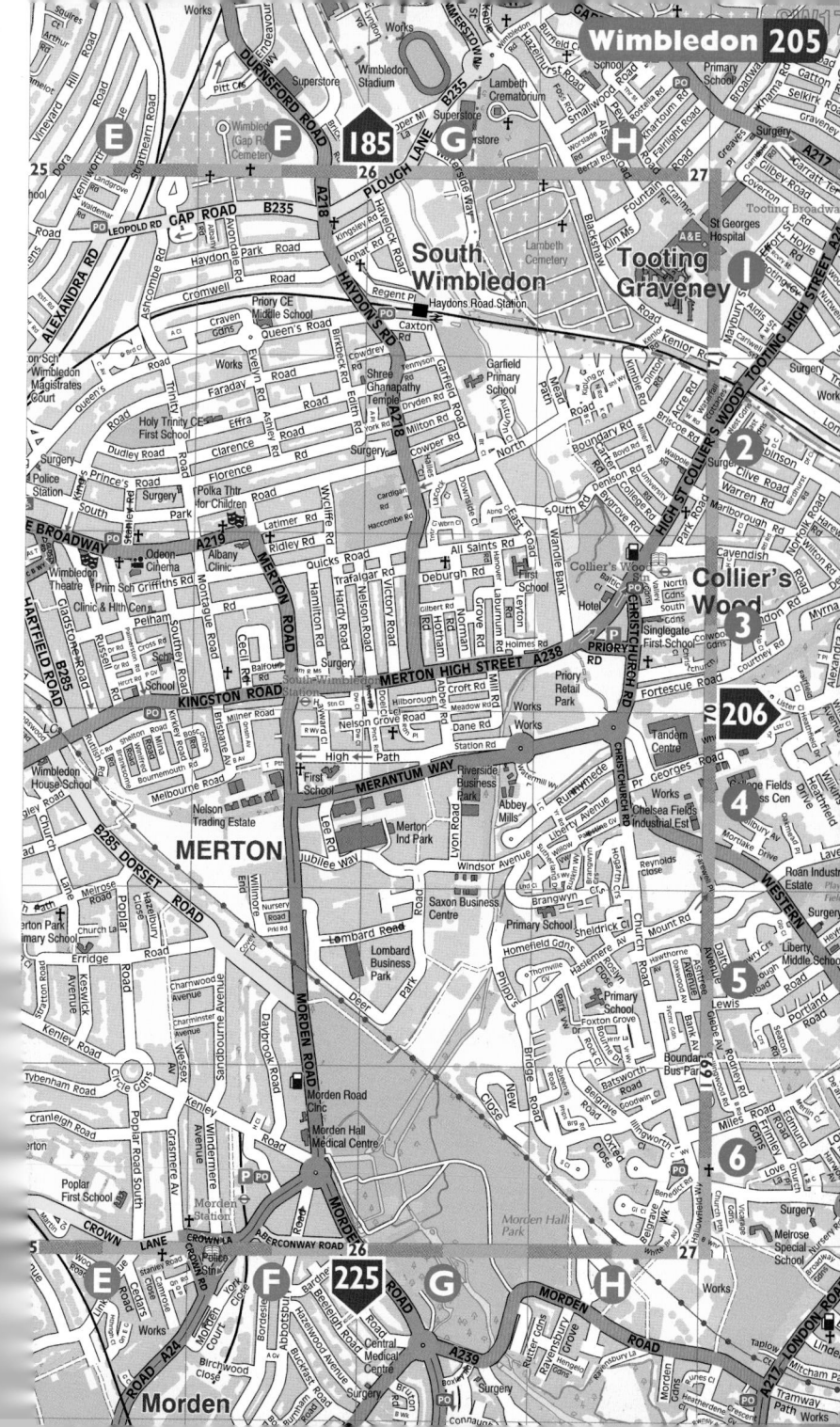

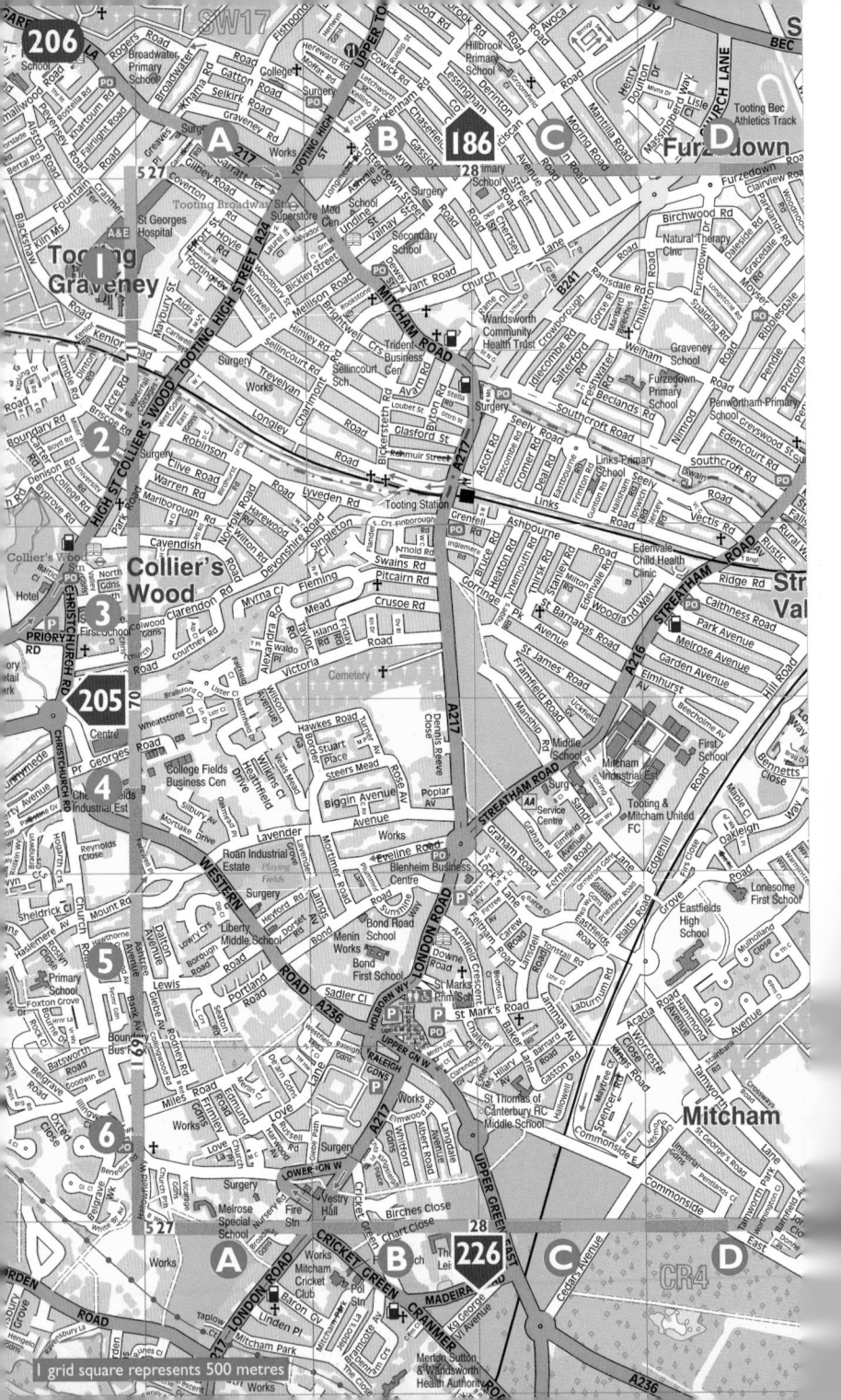

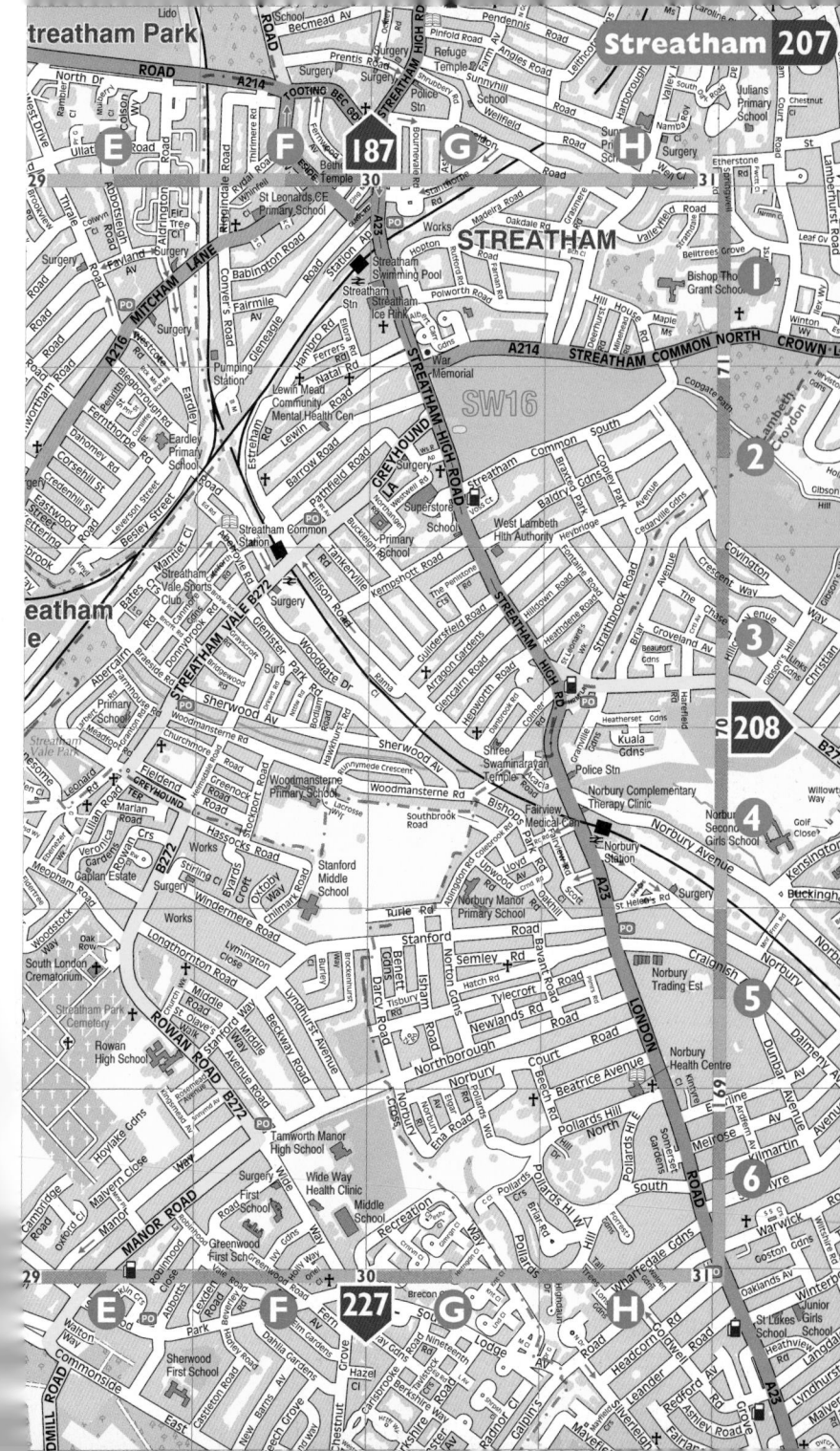

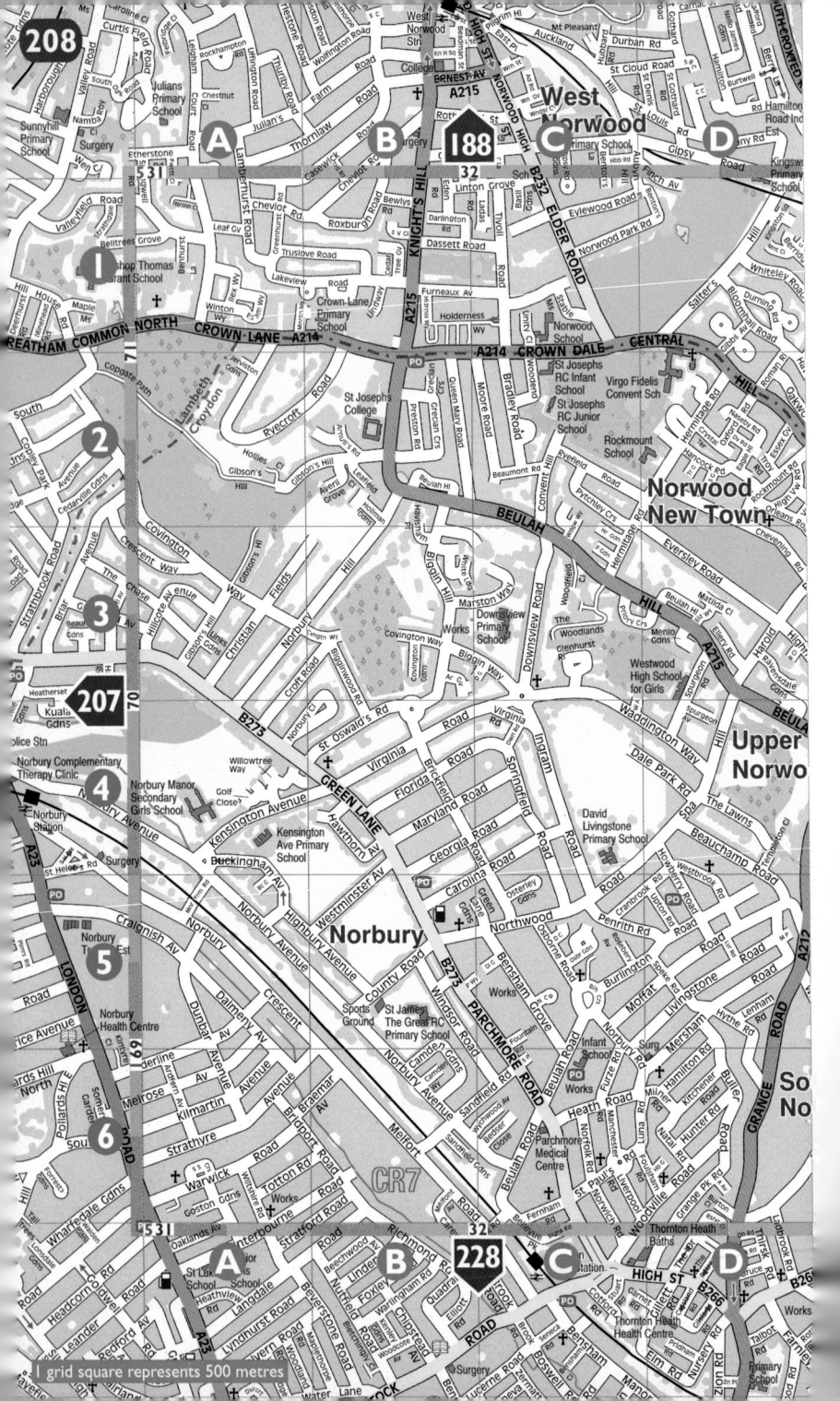

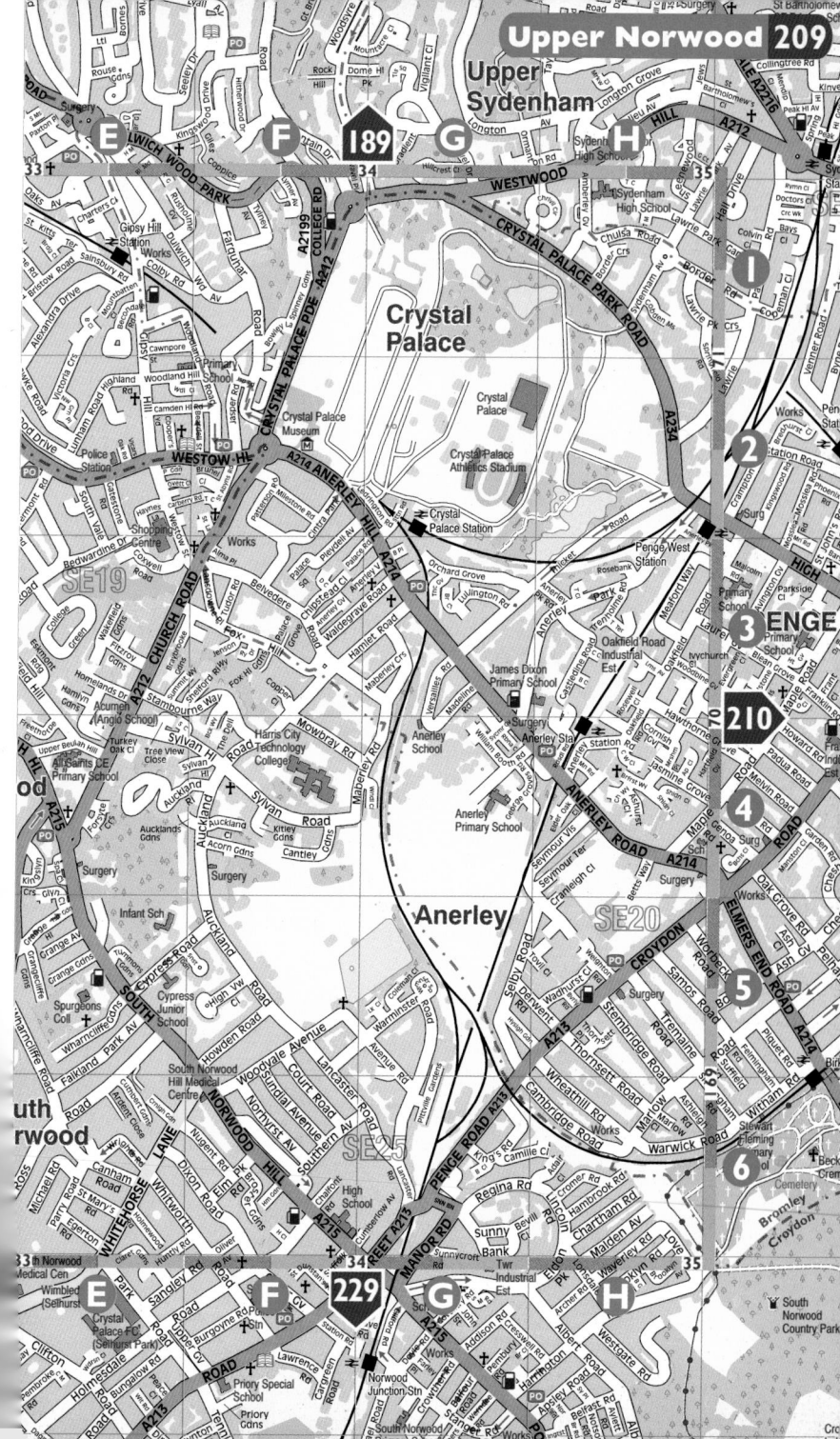

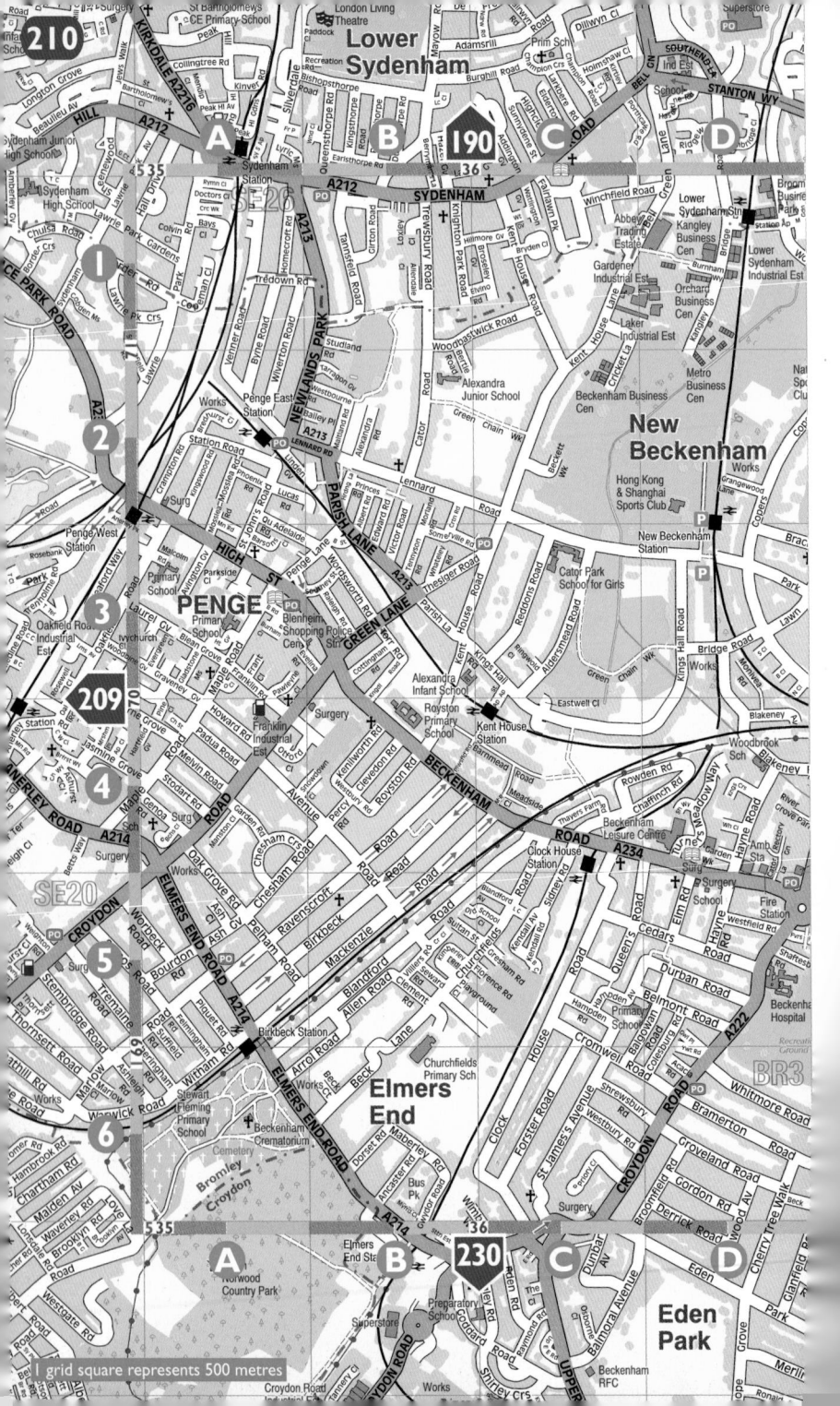

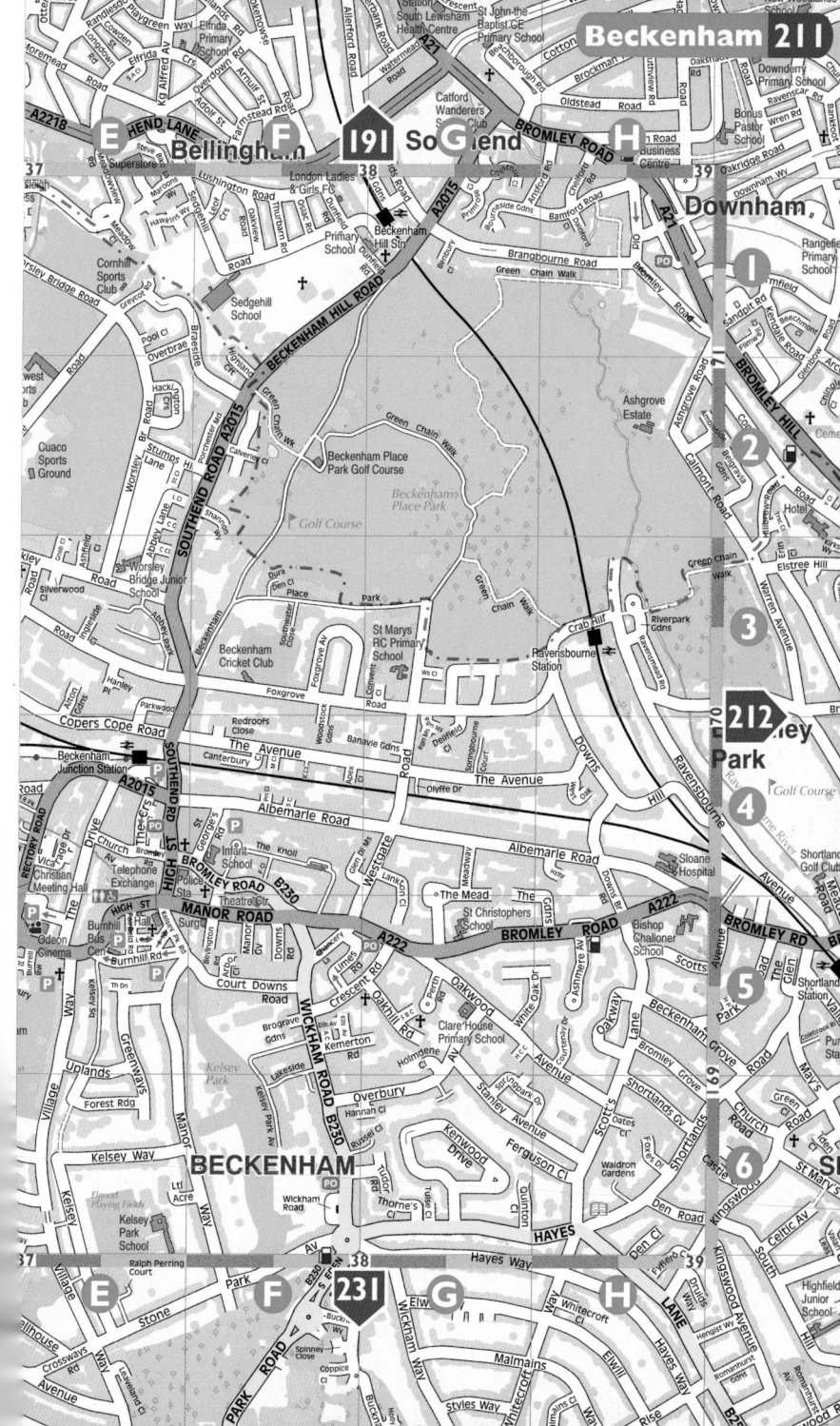

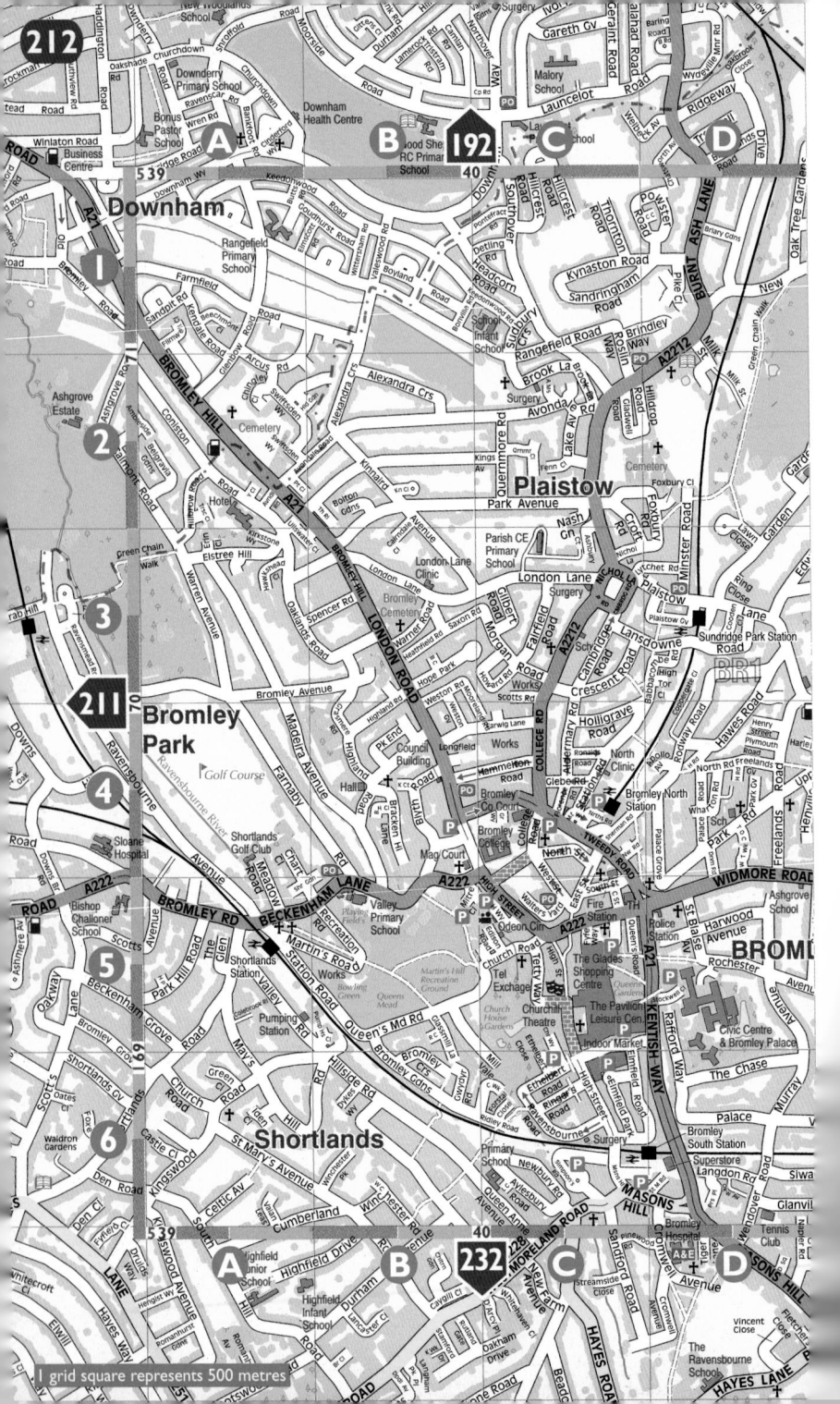

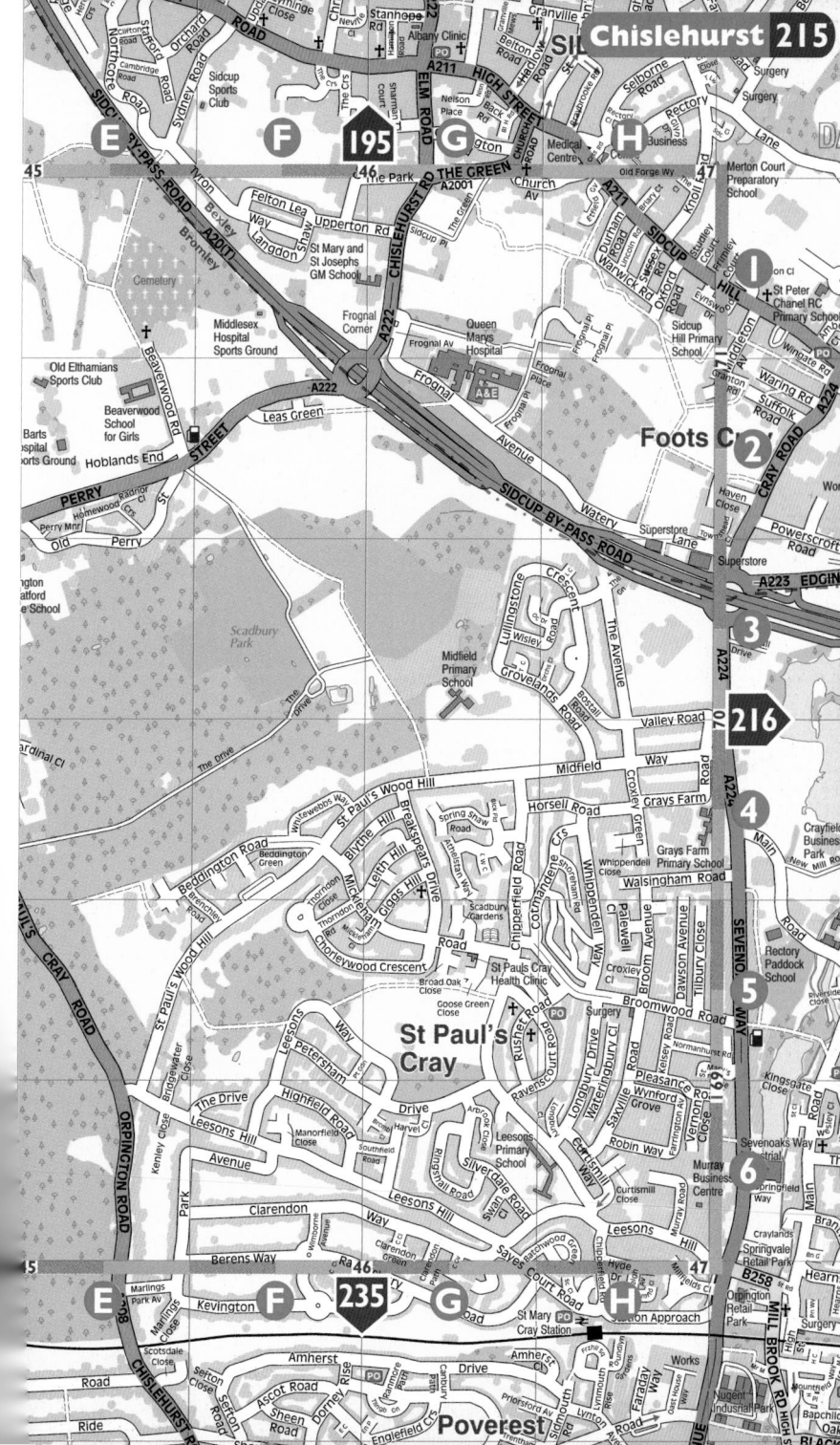

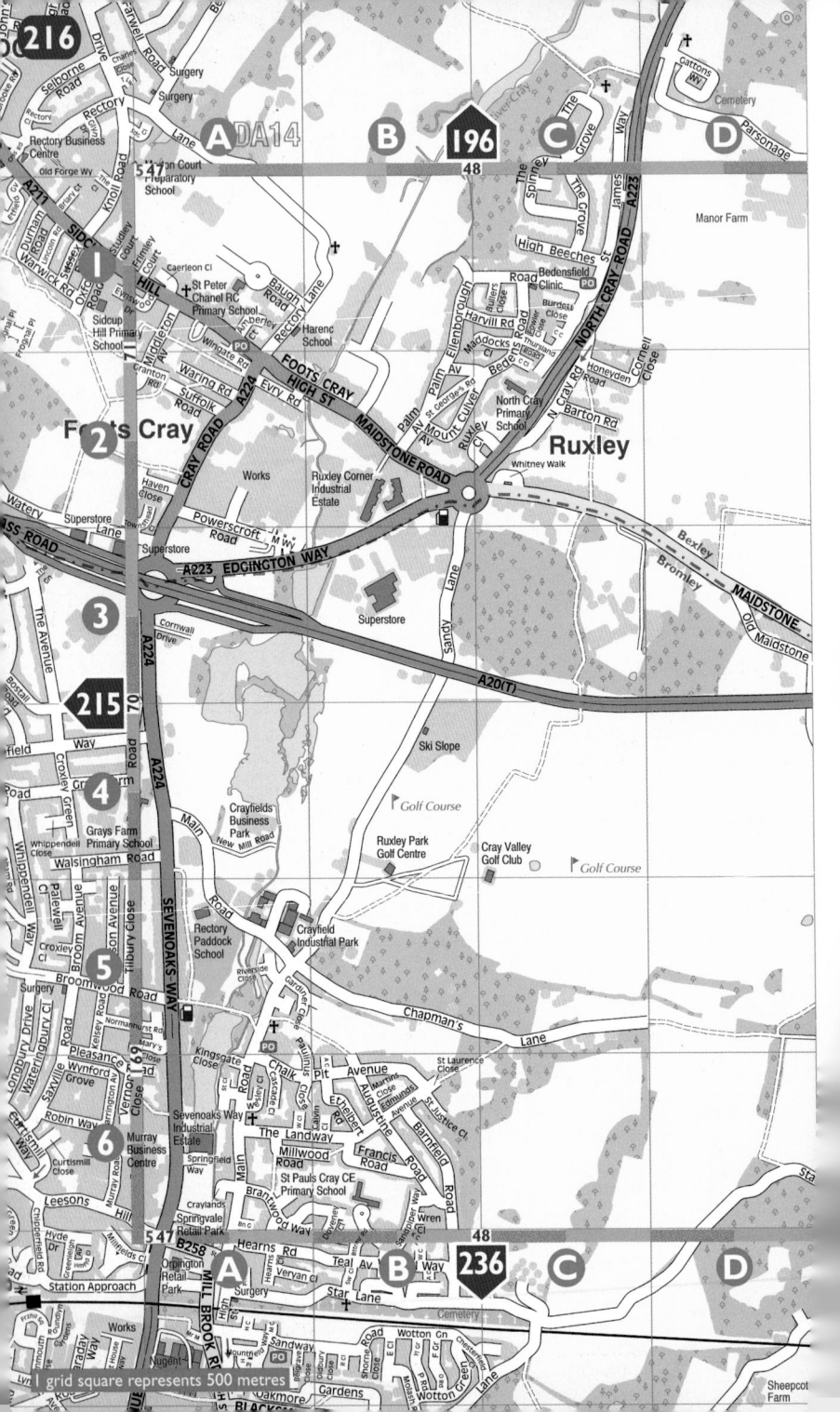

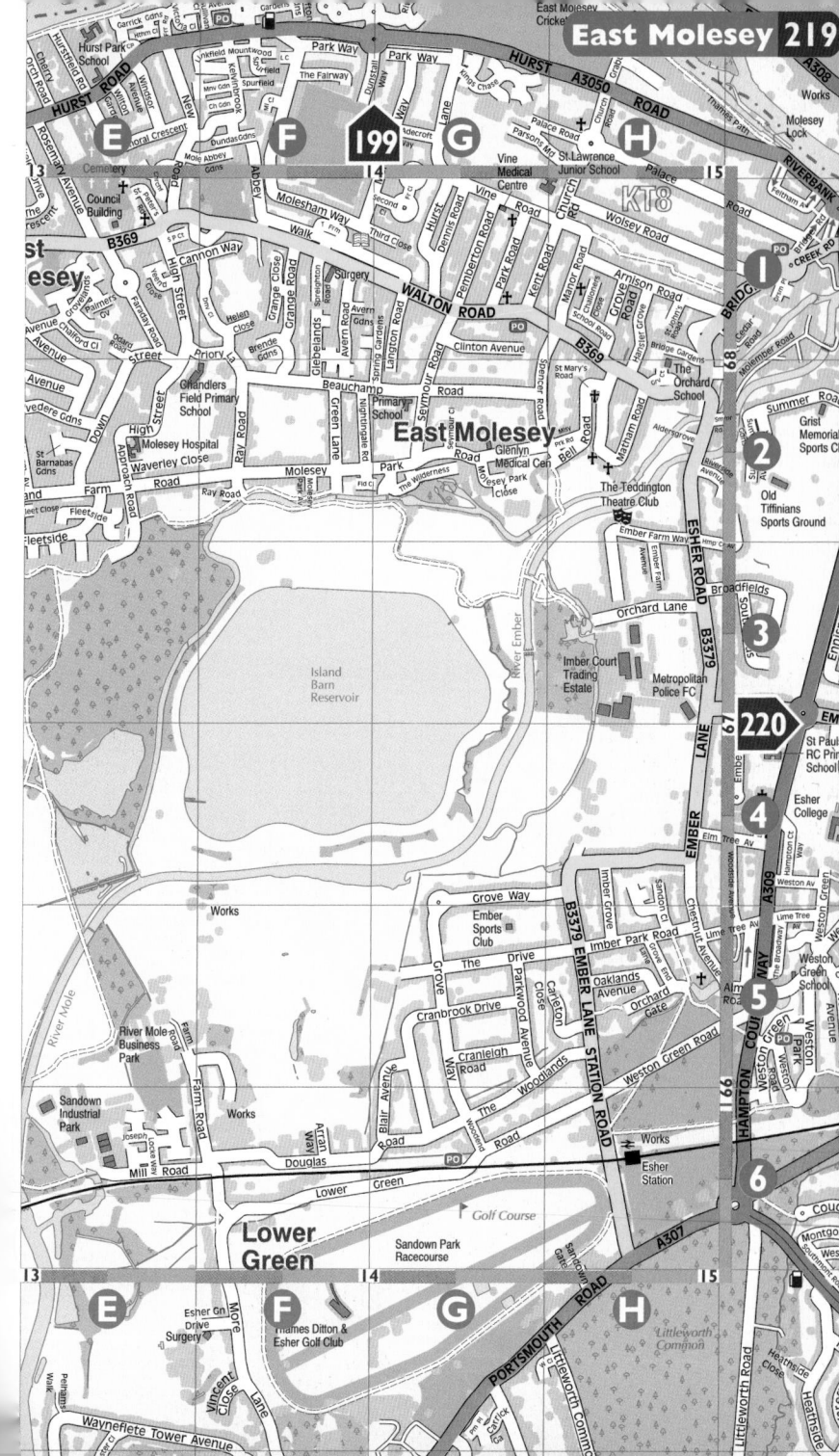

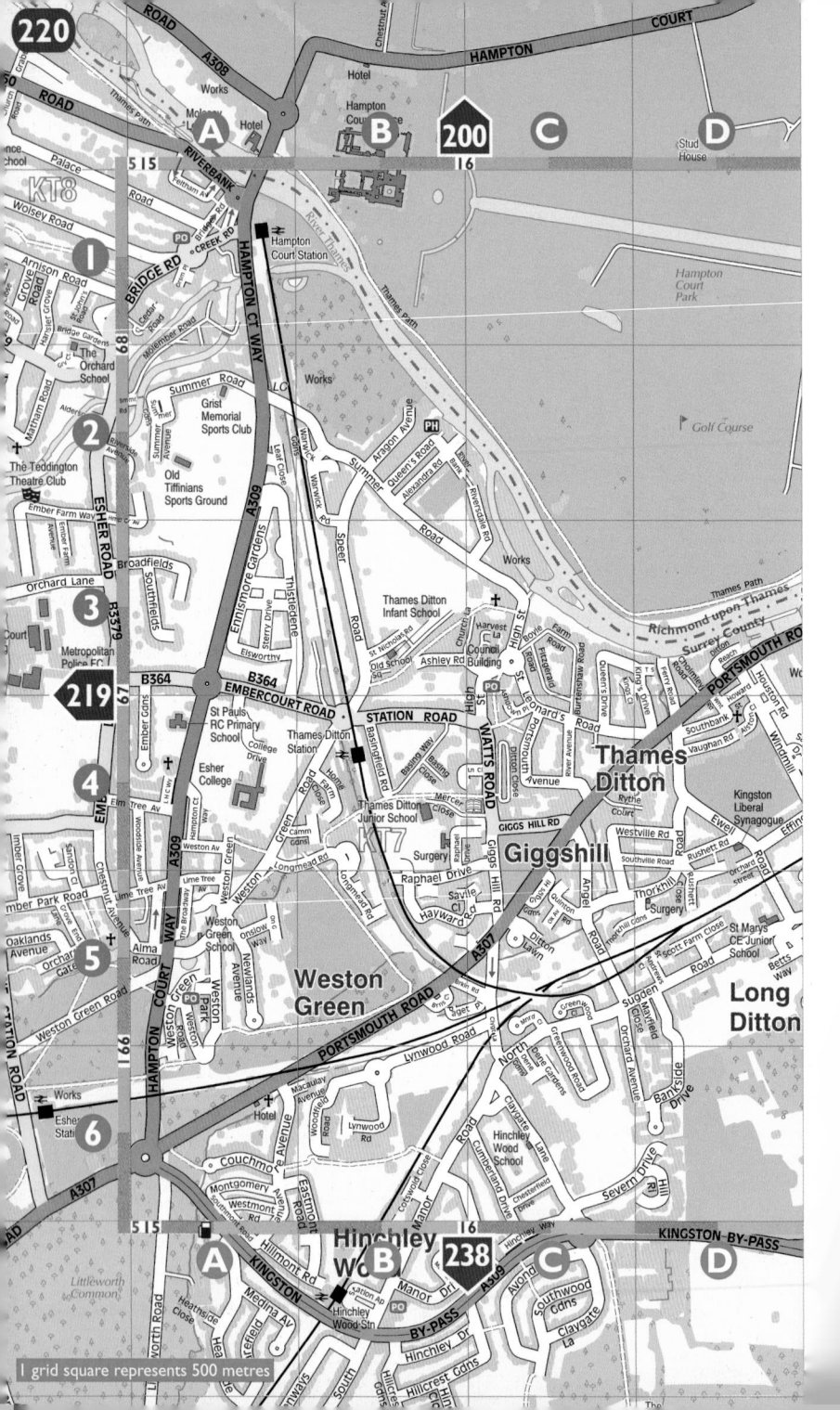

220

ROAD
A308
ROAD
HAMPTON   COURT

HAMPTON   COURT

Works
Thames Path
Molesey
Hotel
RIVERBANK   **A**   Hotel   Hampton   **B**   **200**   **C**   **D**   Stud
                                                                    Court   16   House
515   Feltham Av
KT8   BRIDGE RD   CREEK RD
Wolsey Road   Road
Arnison Road   **1**   Hampton Court Station   Hampton
Grove   Court
Harriet Grove   Bridge Gardens   Molember Road   Thames Path   Park
Matham Road
The Orchard   Alder   Summer Road   Works
School   Grist
ESHER ROAD   **2**   Summer   Memorial   Aragon Avenue   PH
The Teddington   Avenue   Sports Club   Queen's Road   Golf Course
Theatre Club   Old Tiffinians   Warwick   Alexandra Rd   Riverside Rd
Ember Farm Way   Sports Ground   Rd   Summer   Road
Ember Farm Ave   Road   Works
Broadfields   Thistledene   Speer   Aragon Avenue
Orchard Lane   **3**   Southfields   Elsworthy   Road   Thames Ditton   Richmond upon Thames
B5379   Ennismore Gardens   Sterry Drive   St Nicholas Rd   Infant School   Surrey County
Court   Metropolitan   B364   Old School   Ashley Rd   Church St   Thames Path
219   Police FC   EMBERCOURT ROAD   STATION ROAD   Council   High St   Boyle   Portsmouth Rd
Ember Gdns   St Pauls   Building   St Leonard's Road   Ferry Rd   PORTSMOUTH RD
EWE   RC Primary   Thames Ditton   Basingfield Rd   Queen's Drive   King's Rd
4   School   Station   Watts Road   ditton Close   Southbank   Vaughan Rd
Elm Tree Av   Esher   College   Basing Way   Mercer   Thames   Kingston
Sandown Ct   College   drive   Home   Basing   Close   Avenue   Ditton   Liberal
Woodside Avenue   Hampton Ct   Farm   Thames Ditton   Giggs Hill Rd   Synagogue
Imber Grove   Rd   Green   Junior School   KT7   Giggshill   Rushett Rd   Ewell
Oaklands   **5**   Alma   Weston   Camm   Surgery   Angel   Westville Rd   Thorkhill   Orchard
Avenue   Road   Green   Gdns   Longmead Rd   Raphael Drive   Road   Southville Road   Road   street
Orchard   HAMPTON COURT WAY   School   Newlands   Savile   Surgery
Gate   The Broadway   Weston   Weston   Lime Tree   Hayward   Ditton   St Marys
STATION ROAD   A309   Avenue   Green Road   Longmead Rd   Scott Farm Close   CE Junior
Weston   Lynwood Road   North   Hinchley   School
Weston   PORTSMOUTH ROAD   Macaulay   Road   Greenwood Gdns   Orchard   Betts
Green   Avenue   Clayeste Lane   Avenue   way
Works   Hotel   Woodstock   Lynwood   Hinchley   Sugden Road   **Long**
6   Esher   Rd   Wood   Mayfield   Bankside   **Ditton**
Stn   Couchmore   School   Chesterfield   Severn Drive   Drive
A307   Montgomery   Eastmont   Cumberland Drive
Westmont   Road   Hinchley Dr
515   **Hinchley**   16   KINGSTON - BY - PASS   **D**
STATION ROAD   **A**   **B**   **238**   A309   **C**
Littleworth   KINGSTON   Wo   Manor   Avond   Southwood
Common   Hillmont   Hinchley   BY-PASS   Gdns
Medina Av   Wood Stn   Hinchley   Claygate
Heathside   PO   Hinchley Dr   La
Close   North   South   Hillcrest Gdns

I grid square represents 500 metres

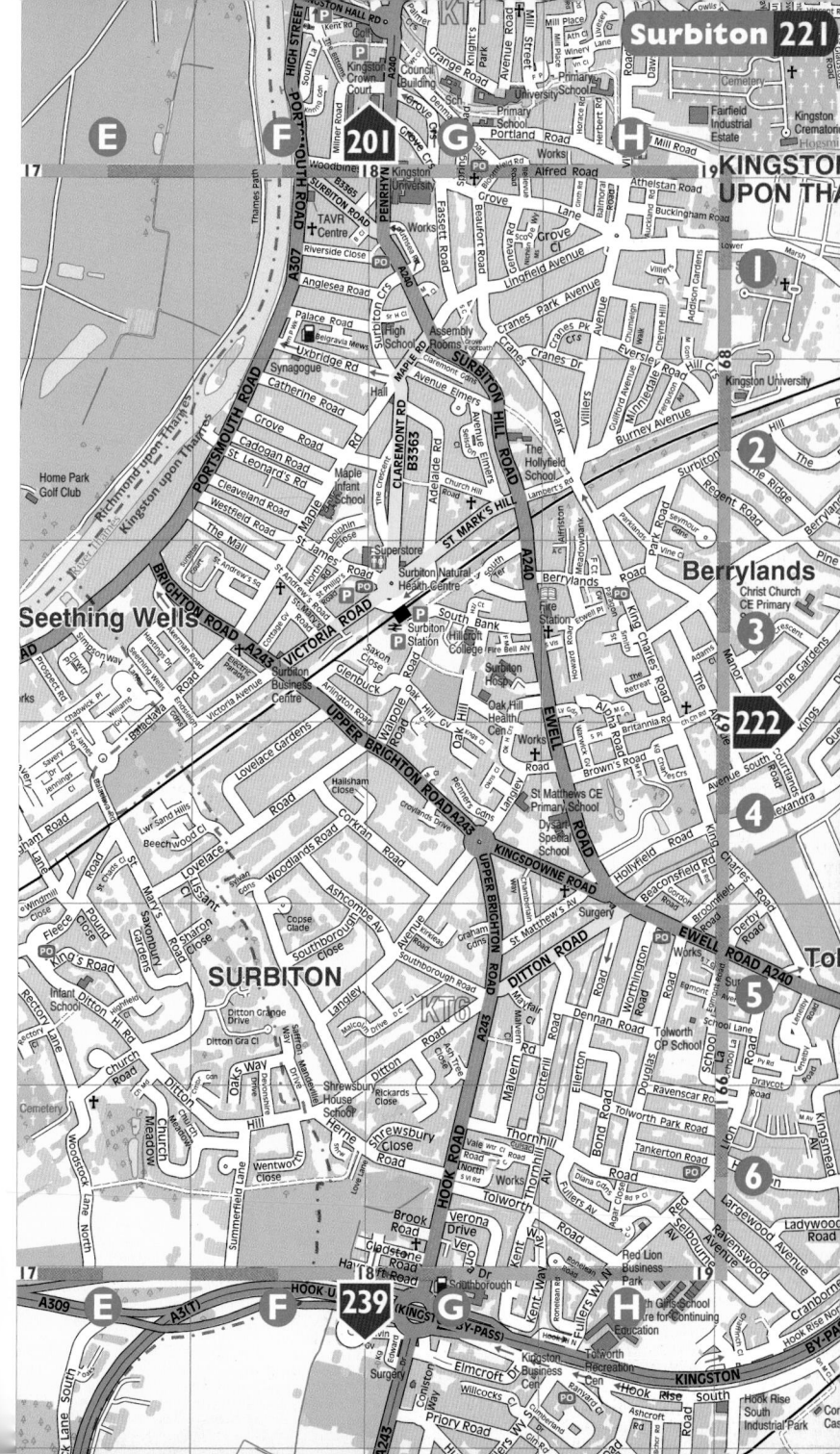

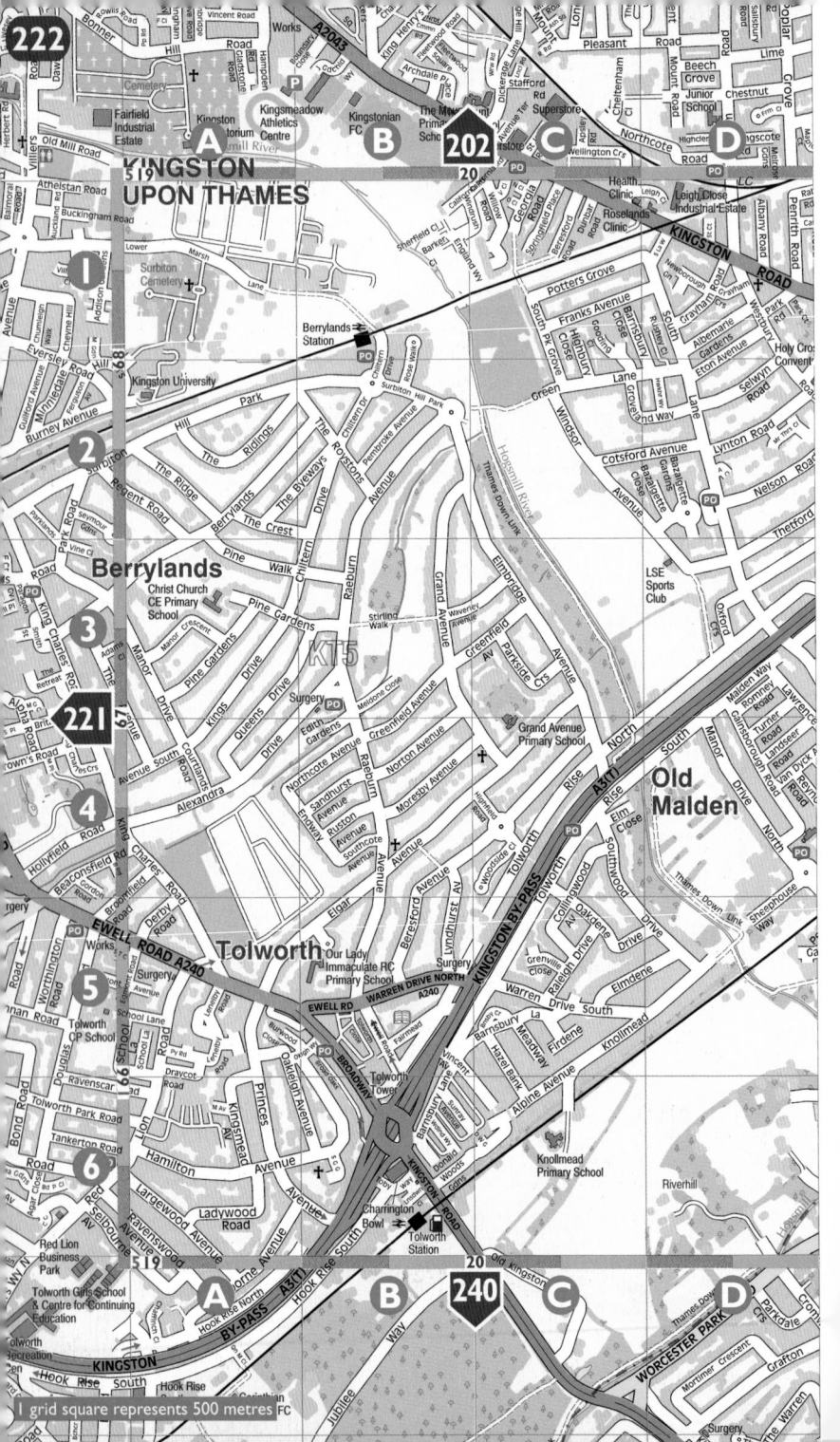

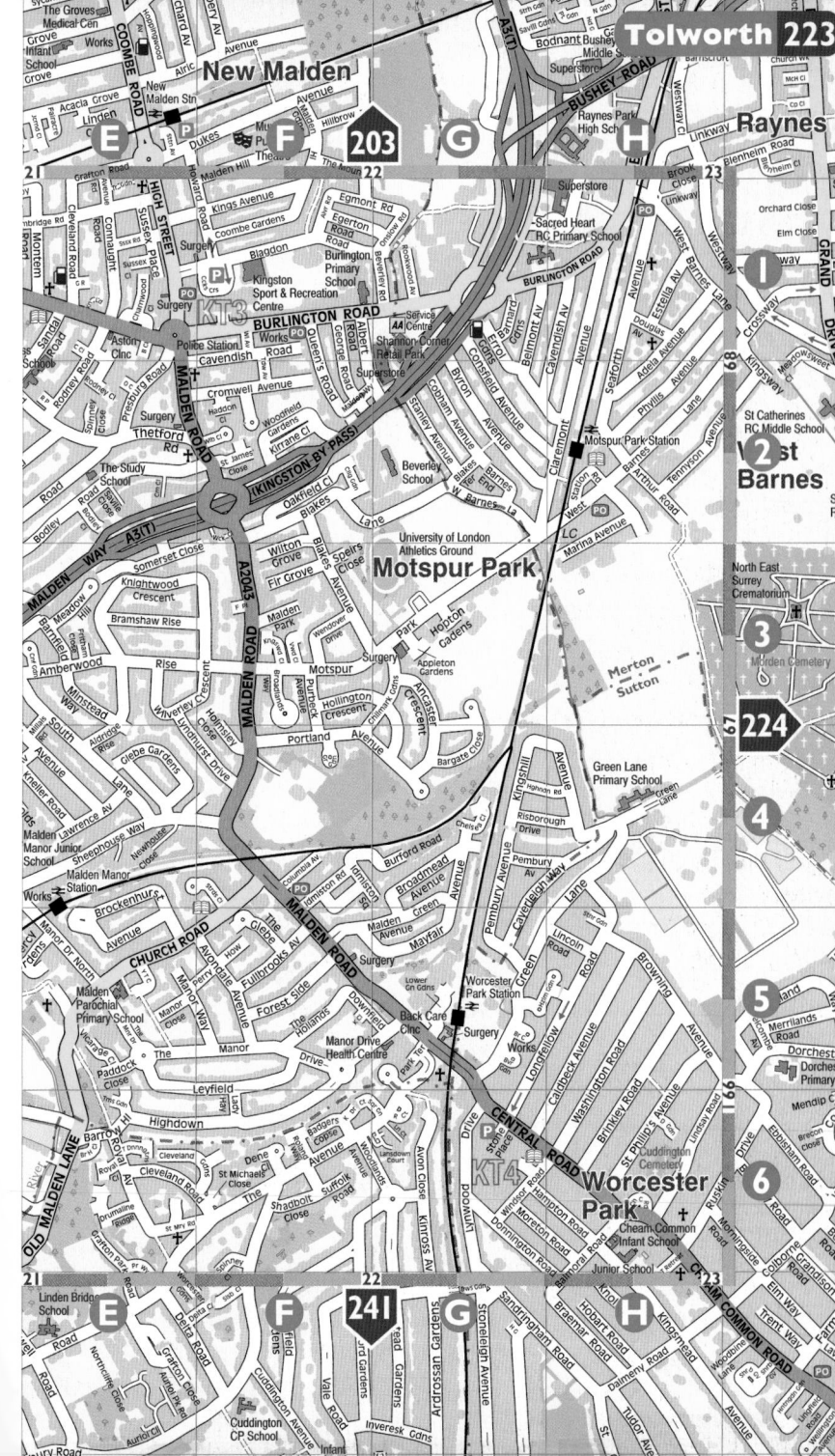

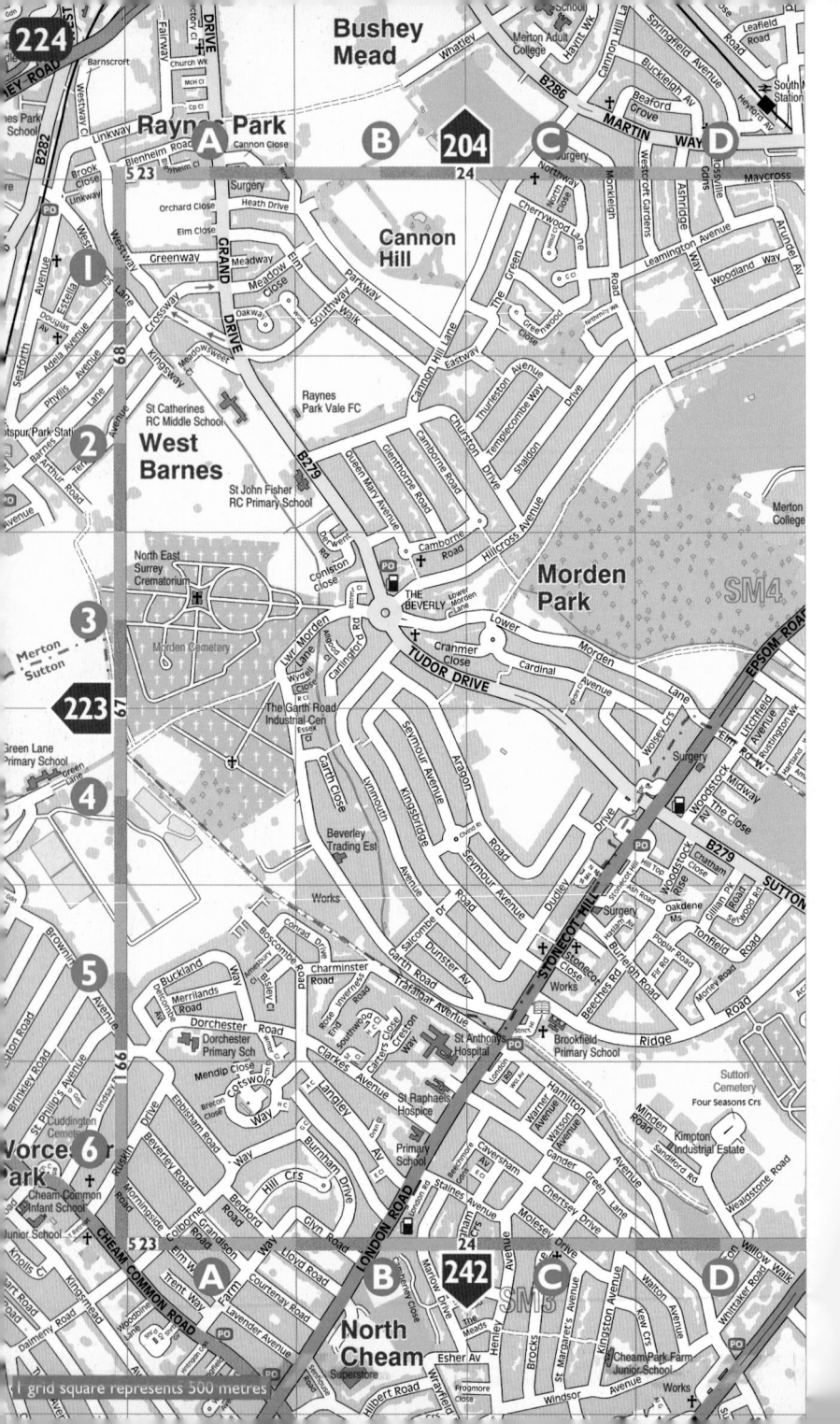

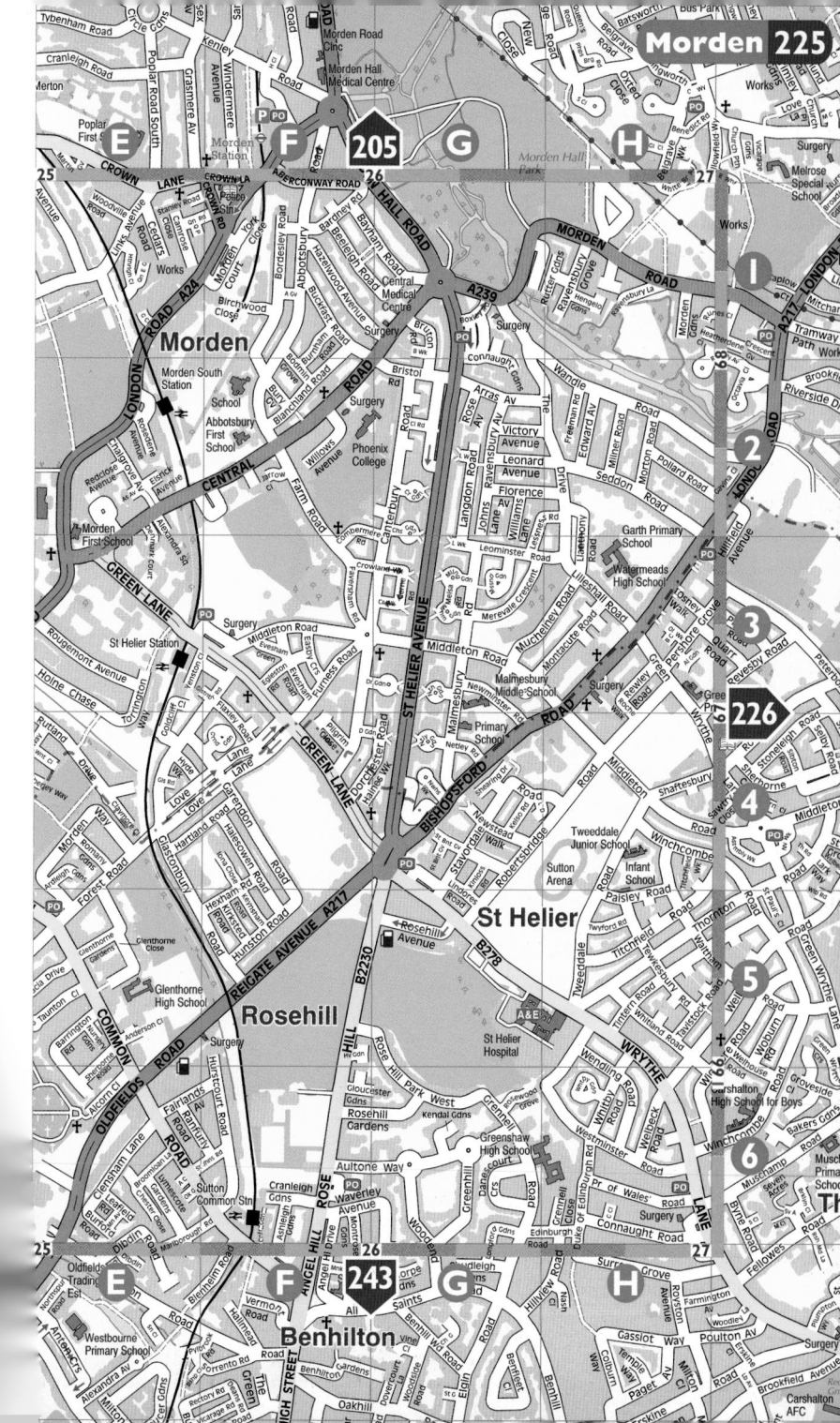

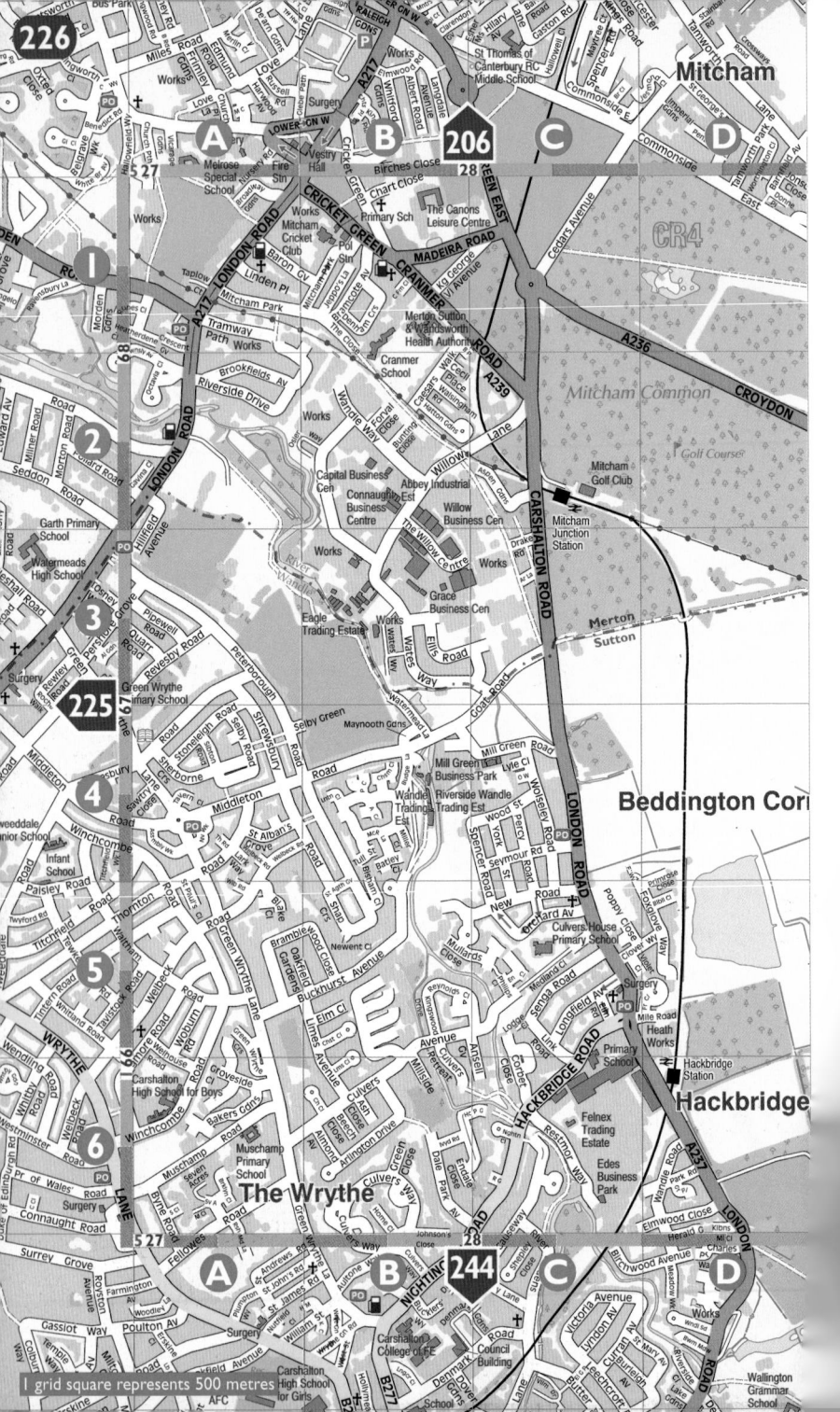

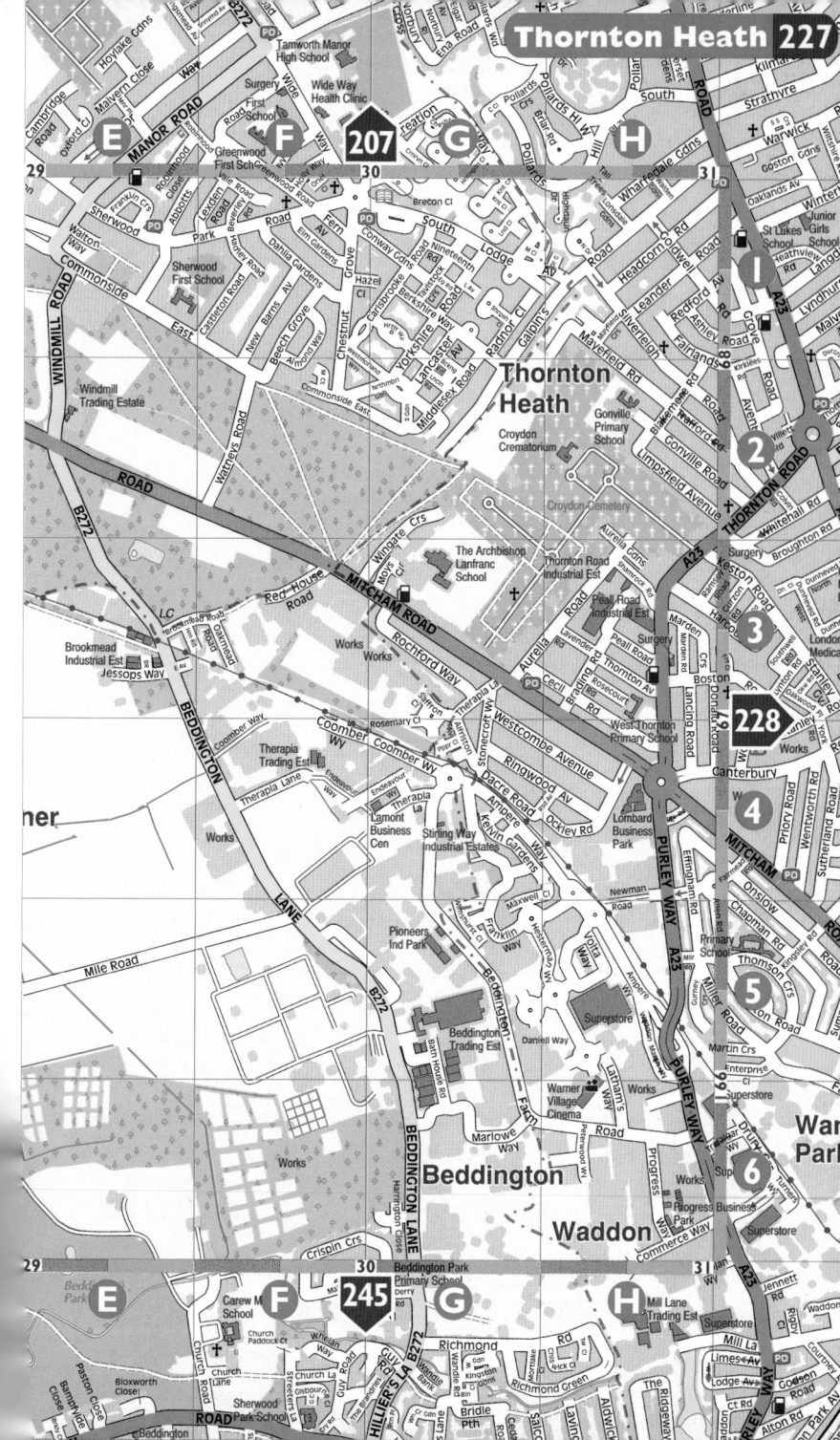

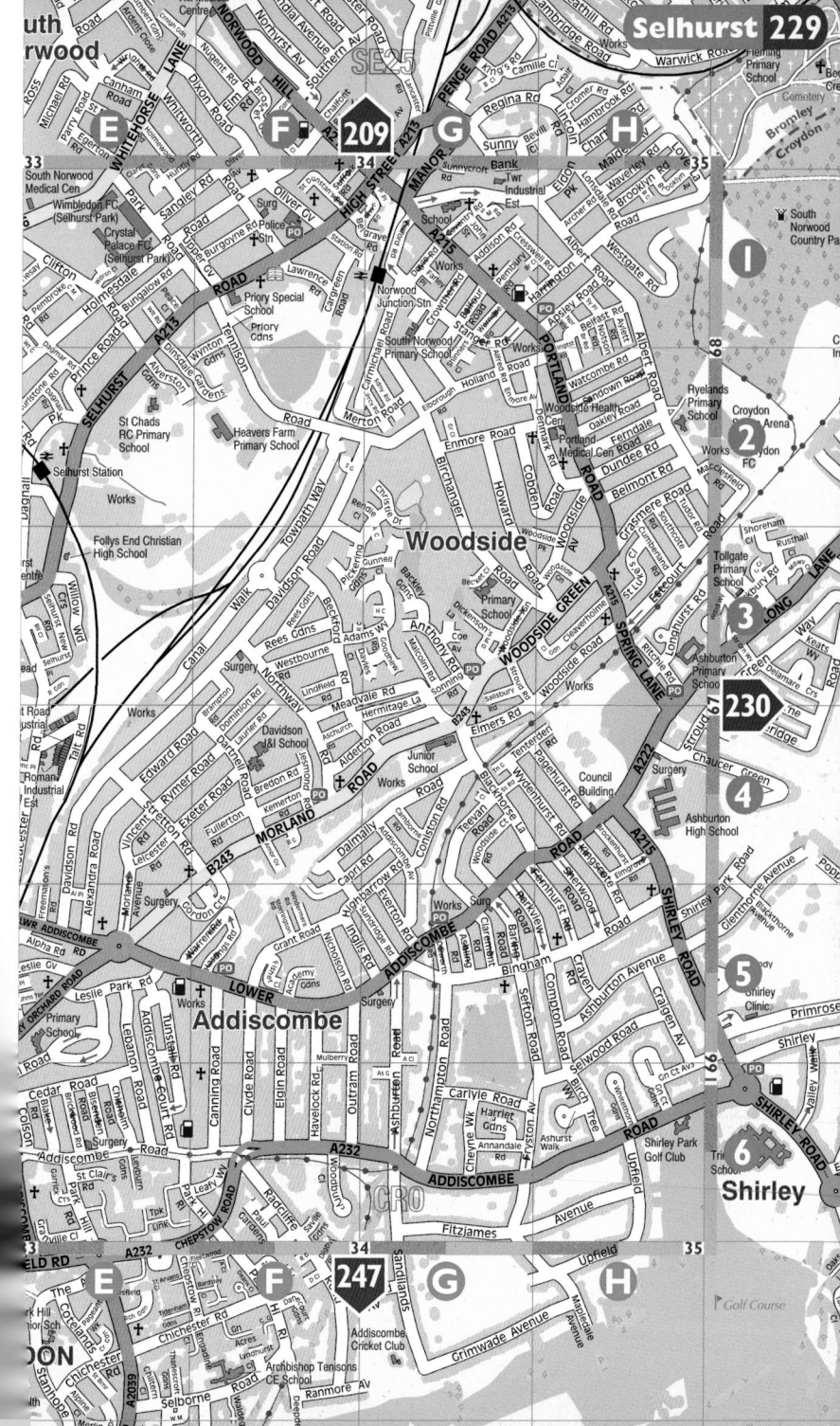

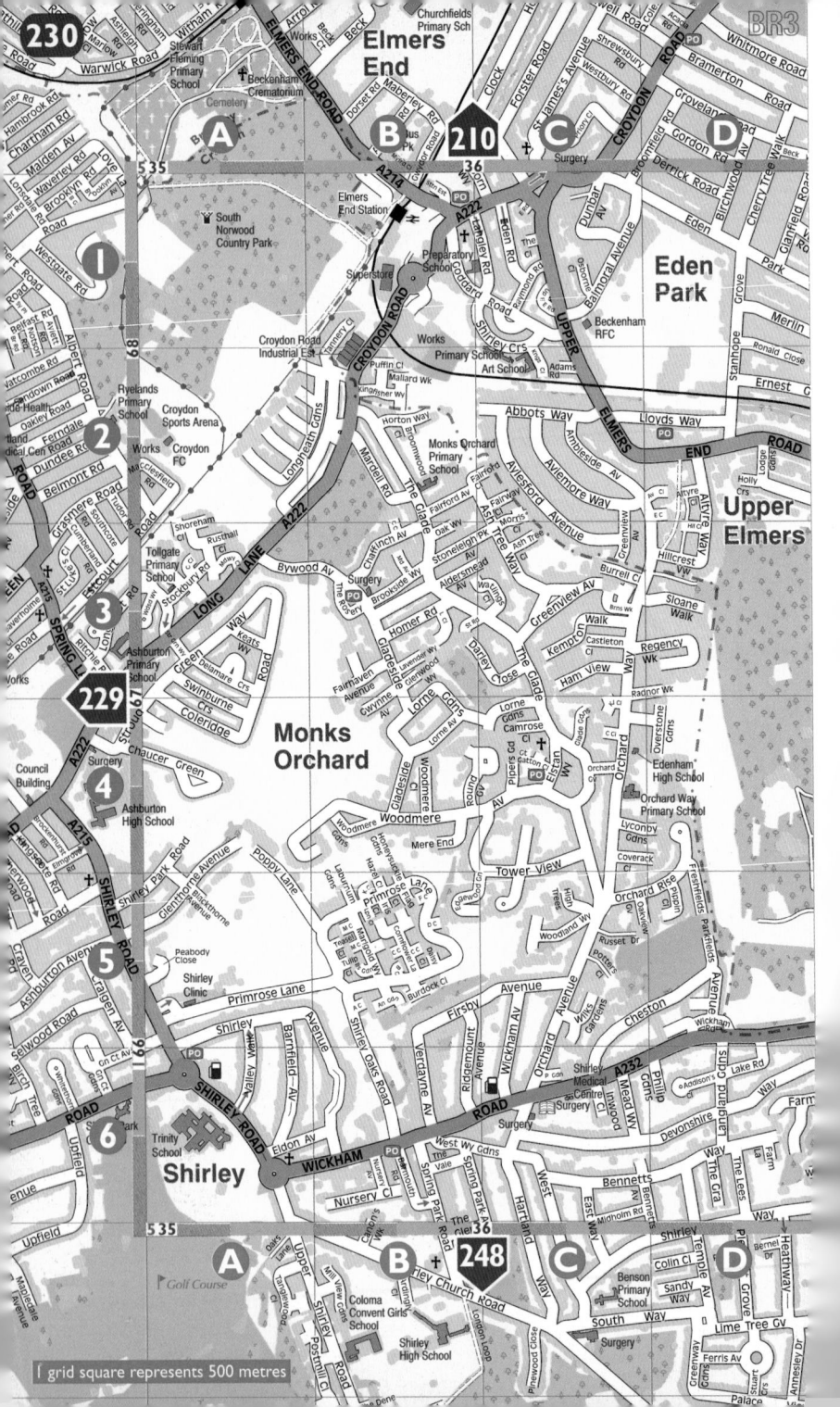

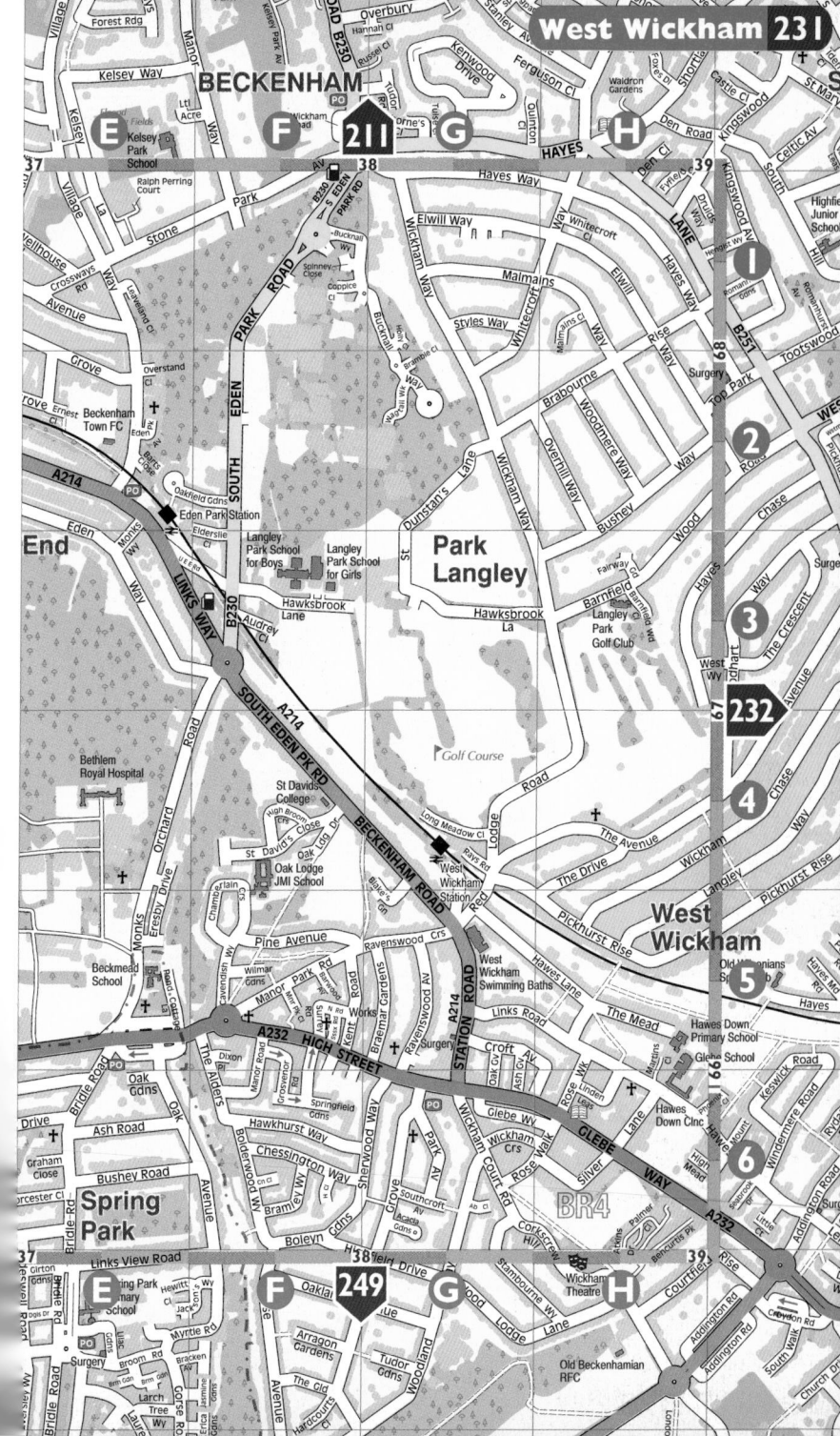

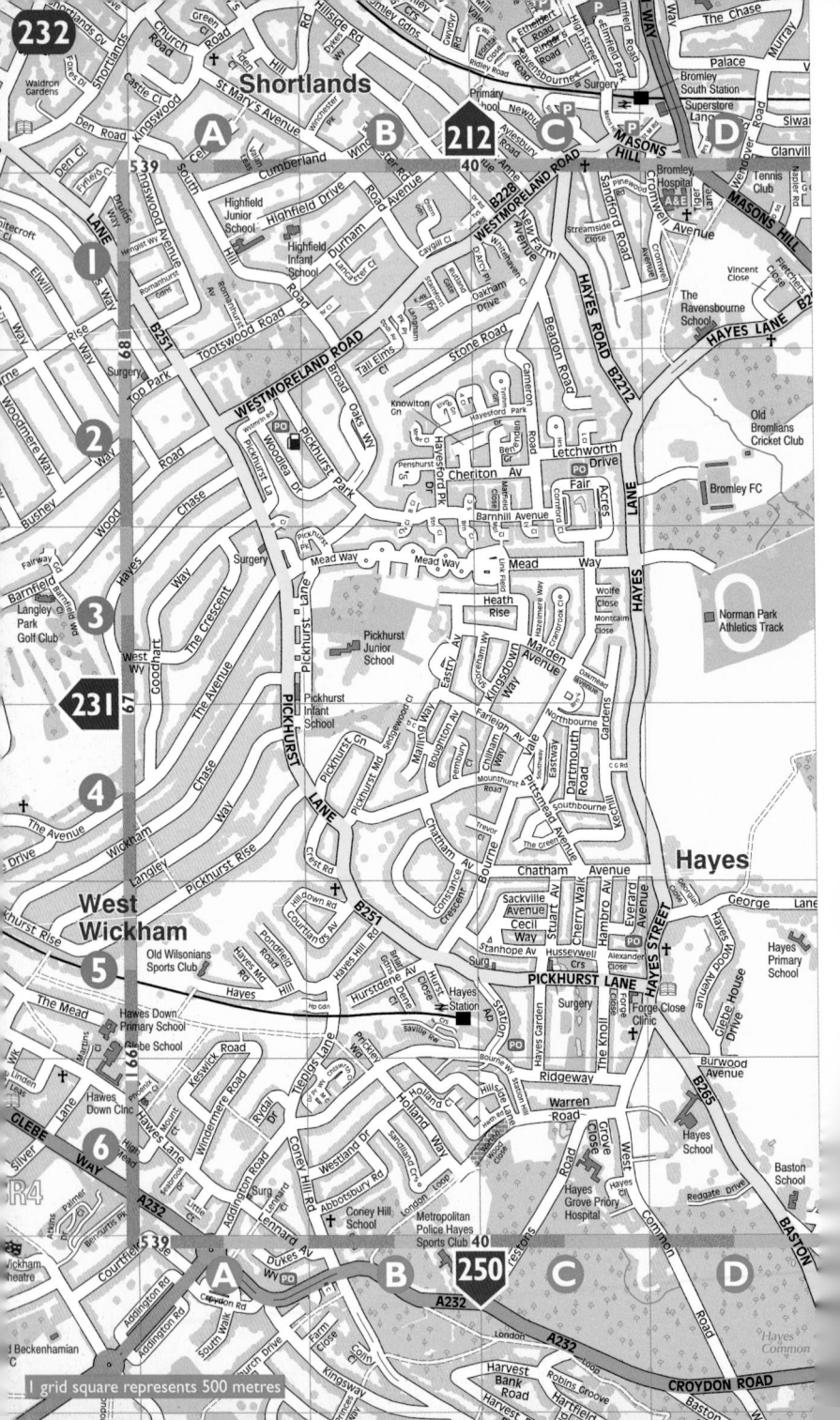

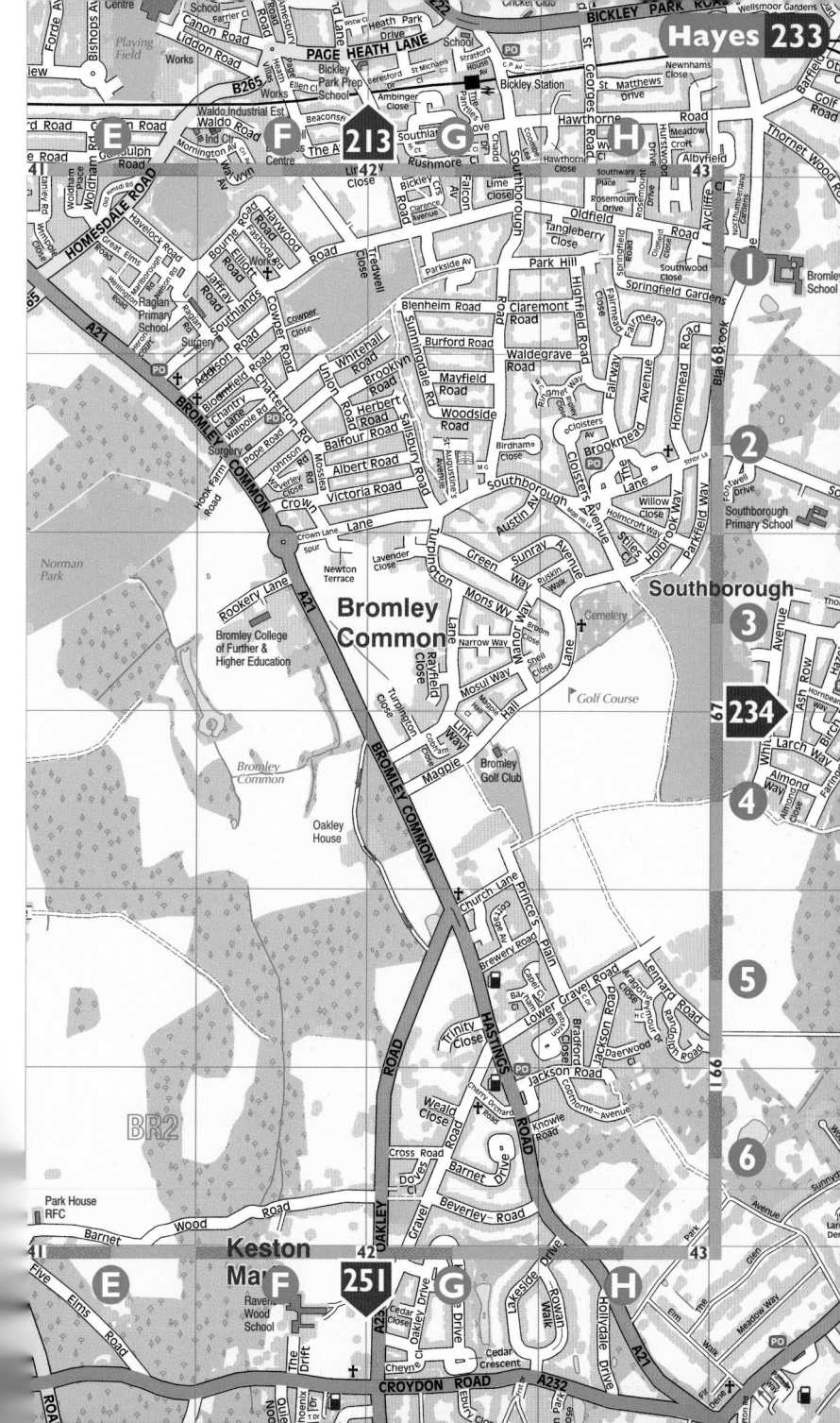

I grid square represents 500 metres

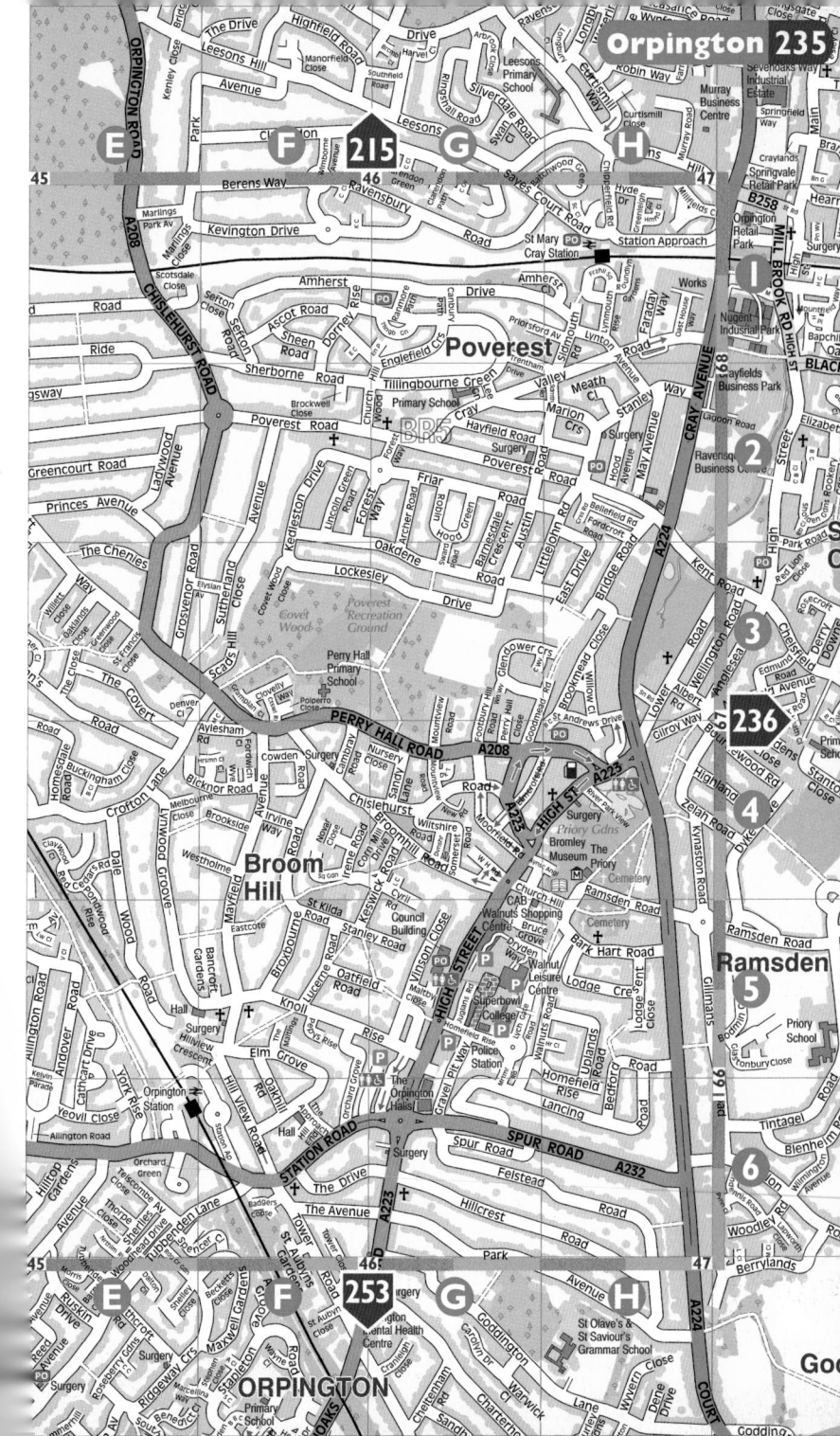

Hockenden

217

Crockenhill

E F G H I

Bourne Wood

Sheepcote Lane

Lane

B258

Crouch Farm

Crockenhill Primary School

CRAY ROAD B258

MAIN RD

Bransell Close

Tylers Green Road

Darns Hill

Old Chapel Road

Tudor Court

Church Road

Newports

Harvest Way

Woodmount

Highcroft

Daltons Road

Lone Barn

Gorse Road

Crown Wood

Bromley Kent County

Furness Swanley FC

Cross Road

Stones Cross

Green Ct Road

GREEN COURT ROAD

Seven Acres

PO

Cemetery

Cemetery

Eynsford Road

Gosenhill Farm

Swanley School

Council Building

St Marys CE Primary School

Swanley Station

Ladds Way

Azalea Drive

OLDSEL ROAD

Approach Road

Pinks

Cranle

Charnock Court

BARTHOL

Super

Police Station

Nightingale

Hart Road

Lime Road

Lilac Gardens

Hewett Place

Lynden Way

Laburnum Av

Cherry Avenue

Rowan Road

Motello Close

Lavender Av

Sermon Drive

Vale Road

Croft

A20(T)

B258

E F G H

Esher Station

A307

HAMPTON

Couchmo
gomery
Westmont Rd
Eastmont Road
Avenue
Hotel
Macaulay Avenue
Lynwood Rd
Lynwood Rd

220
16

Hinchley Wood School

Severn Drive

A B 220 16 C D

KINGSTON
Hillmont Rd
South
Road
Greenways
Medina Av
Hatfield
Heathside Close
Heathside

Hinchley Wood Stn
Manor Drive
BY-PASS
Hinchley Dr
Hillcrest Gdns
Hillcrest Gdns
Hinchley Close
Hinchley

KINGSTON BY-PASS

A309
Avondale Av
Southwood Gdns
Claygate La

The Waffrons

515

65

Littleworth Road

Littleworth Common

Penates
Littleworth La
Littleworth Av
Littlemead

Manor
Oaken Lane

Telegraph Lane

Golf Course

Surbiton Golf Club

Woodstock Lane South

2

Littleworth Road

3

KT10

Raleigh Dr
Hare
Rythe
Cavendish
Simmil Rd
Rd
Drive
H Gdn
Loseberry Rd
Station Rd

The Avenue
Oaken Lane
Meadow
Judge Walk
Woodbourne Drive
Oaken Dr
The Roundway
Applegarth
Crediton
Langbourne Way
Old Claygate Lane
Red Lane
Lower Wd Rd

3

Hare
Loseberry Farm
Milbourne Lodge School

4

Claygate Station
PO
The Pde

Derwent Cl
Oaken Lane
Torrington Rd
Cedar Walk
Surgery
St Leonard's Rd
Elm
Emlyn
Merrilyn Cl
Rosehill
Hermitage C
Oakhill
Trystings Close
Trystings Close
Mount Vw Rd
Berkeley Gardens
Bridle Rd
Lower

A3(T)

Claygate

Loseberry Rd
Albany Crs
Athlone
Firs Cl
Folly Ms
Dalmore Avenue
Blakeden
Church Rd
The
Common
Glenavon Cl
Glenavon Cl
Kinside
Forge Dr
Stevens
Hill View Road
Ruxley Crs

5

Gordon Road
Claremont Rd
Foley
Beaconsfield Road
Claygate Ldg
Qu Anne Dr
Foley
Road
Elizabeth Rd
Claygate Primary School
Vale Croft
Cornwall Av
Dee
Farm
Rd
CSWY
Common Lane
Ruxley Rdg

163

Road
Vale
Coverts
Foxwarren
Holroyd Road
Glebelands
Grandsails

6

515
A3(T)
16

A B A3(T) B C D

1 grid square represents 500 metres

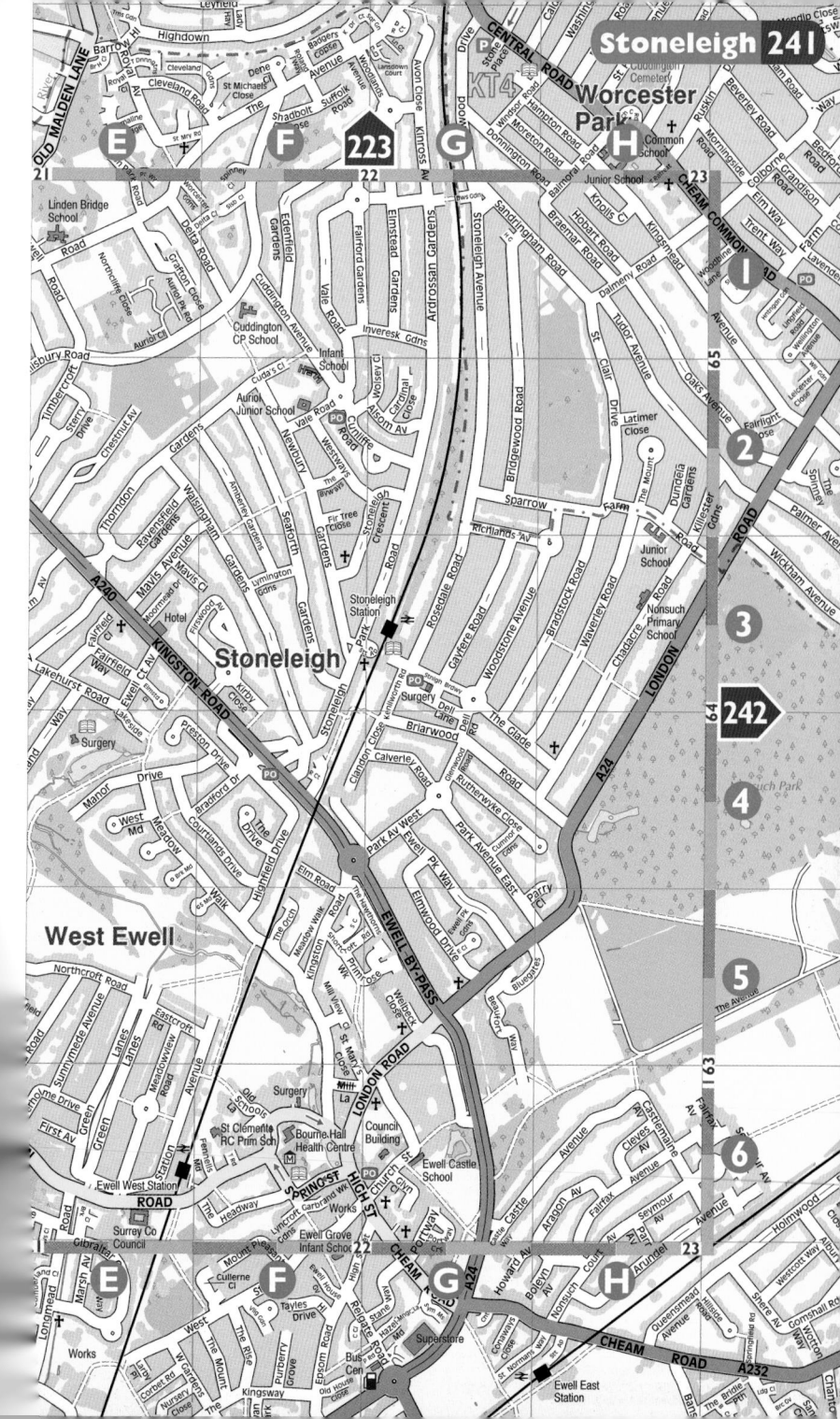

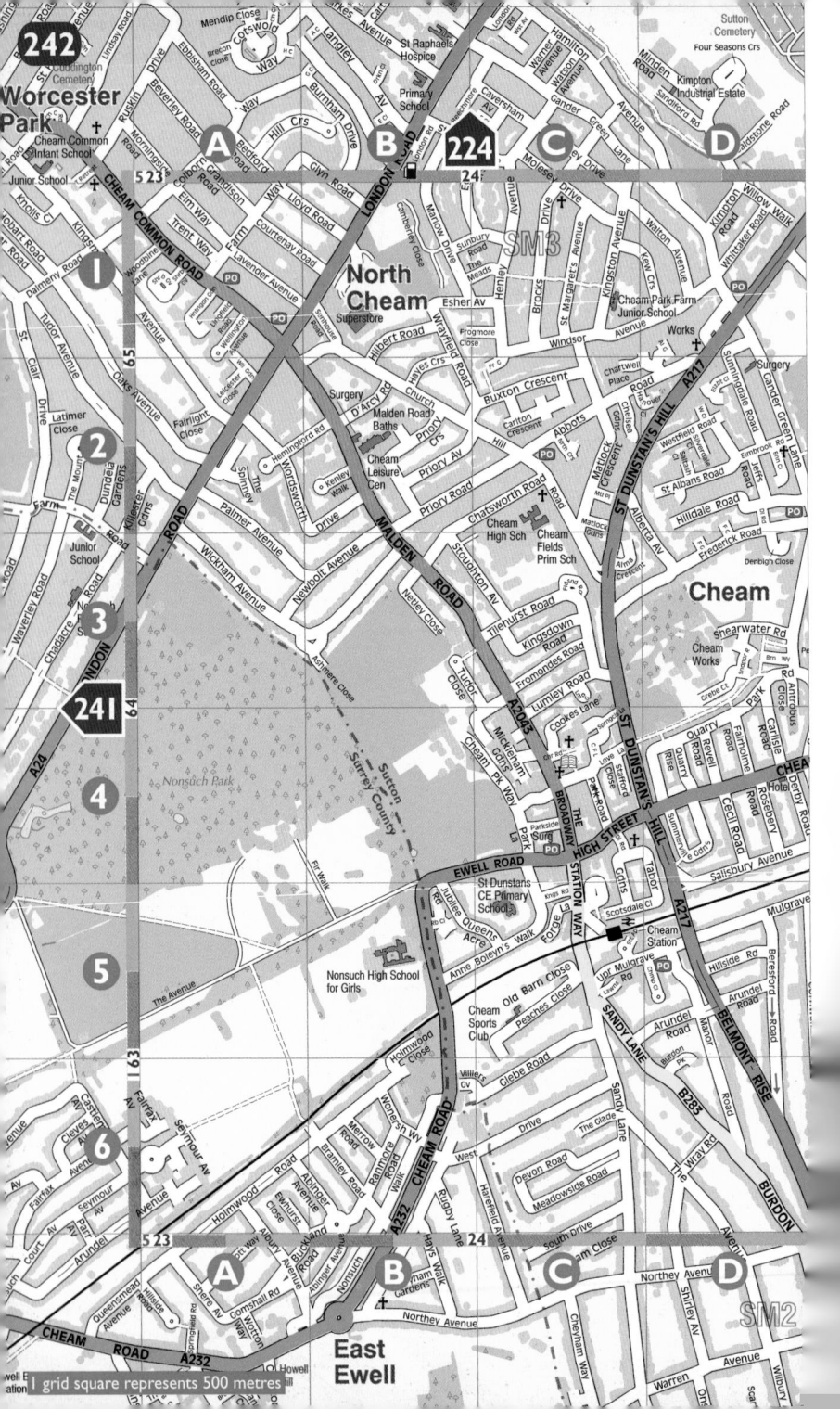

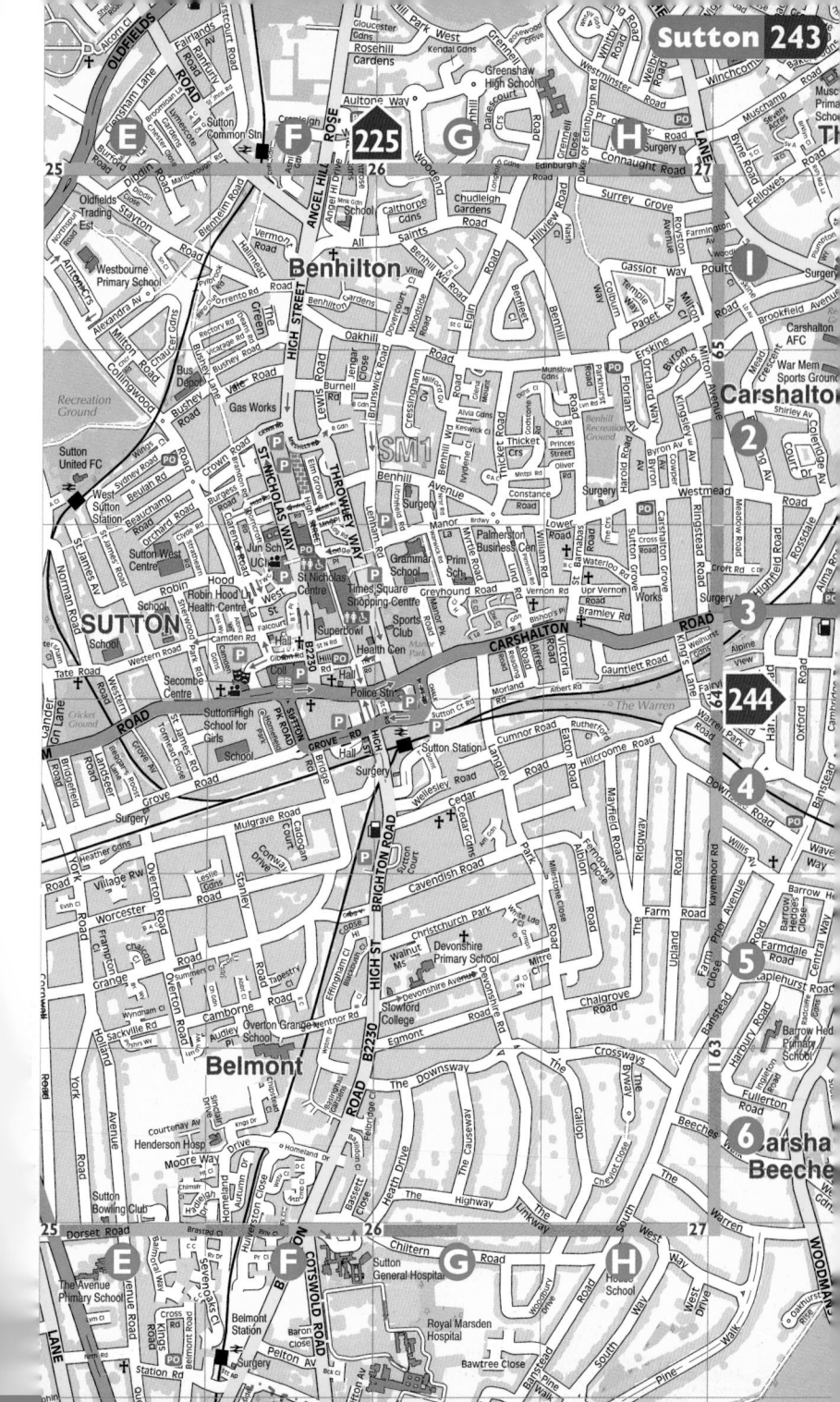

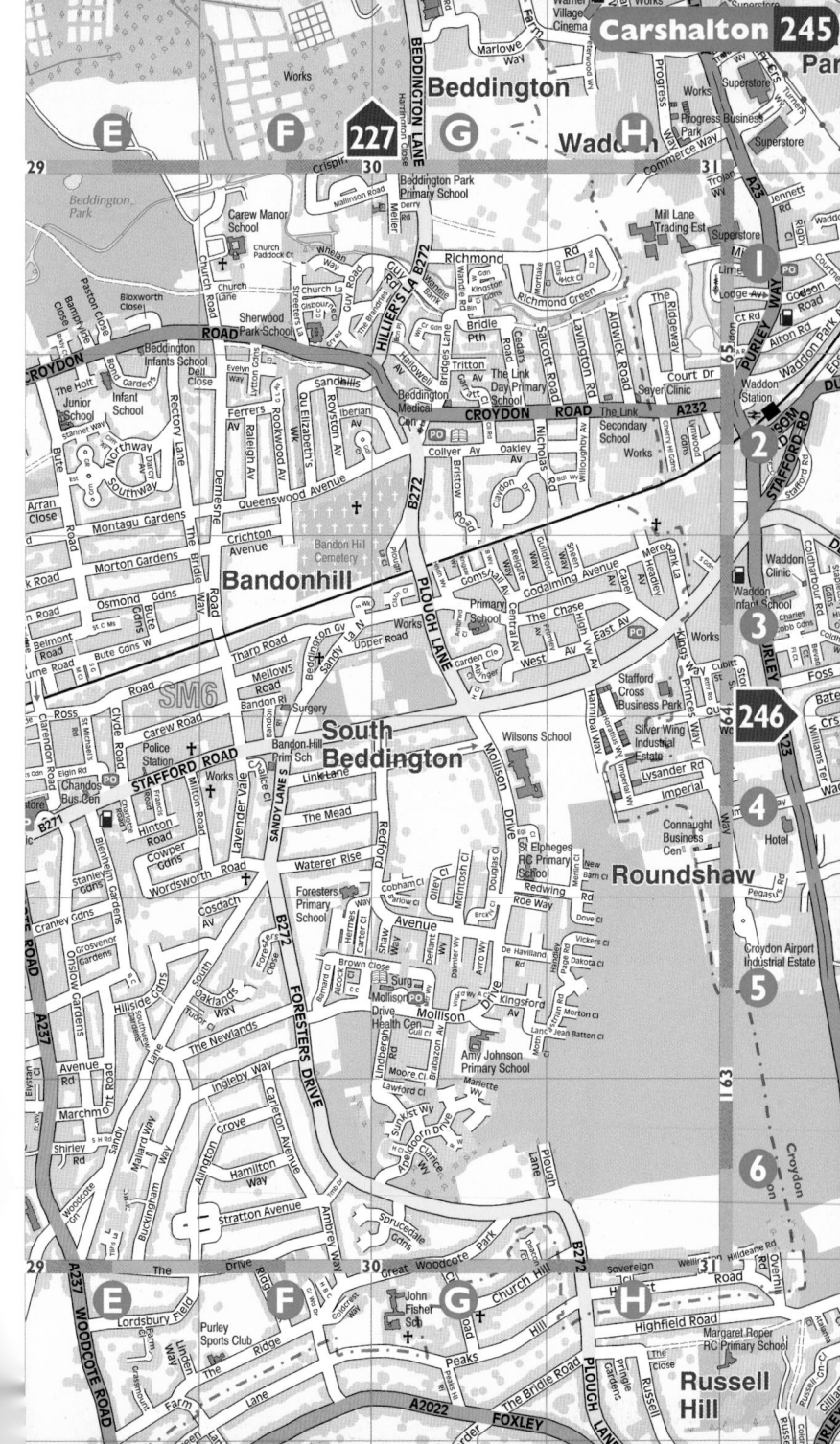

Park

227

246

Beddington

Waddon

Carew Manor School

Beddington Park Primary School

Richmond

Richmond Green

CROYDON

ROAD

A232

The Link Day Primary School

The Link Secondary School

Bandonhill

Bandon Hill Cemetery

Godalming Avenue

The Chase

South Beddington

SM6

Wilsons School

Stafford Cross Business Park

Silver Wing Industrial Estate

Roundshaw

Police Station

STAFFORD ROAD

Foresters Primary School

Connaught Business Cent

St Elpheges RC Primary School

Amy Johnson Primary School

Croydon Airport Industrial Estate

Hotel

Imperial

John Fisher Sch

Purley Sports Club

Highfield Rd

Margaret Reper RC Primary School

Russell Hill

A2022 **FOXLEY**

E **F** **G** **H**

29 **30** **31**

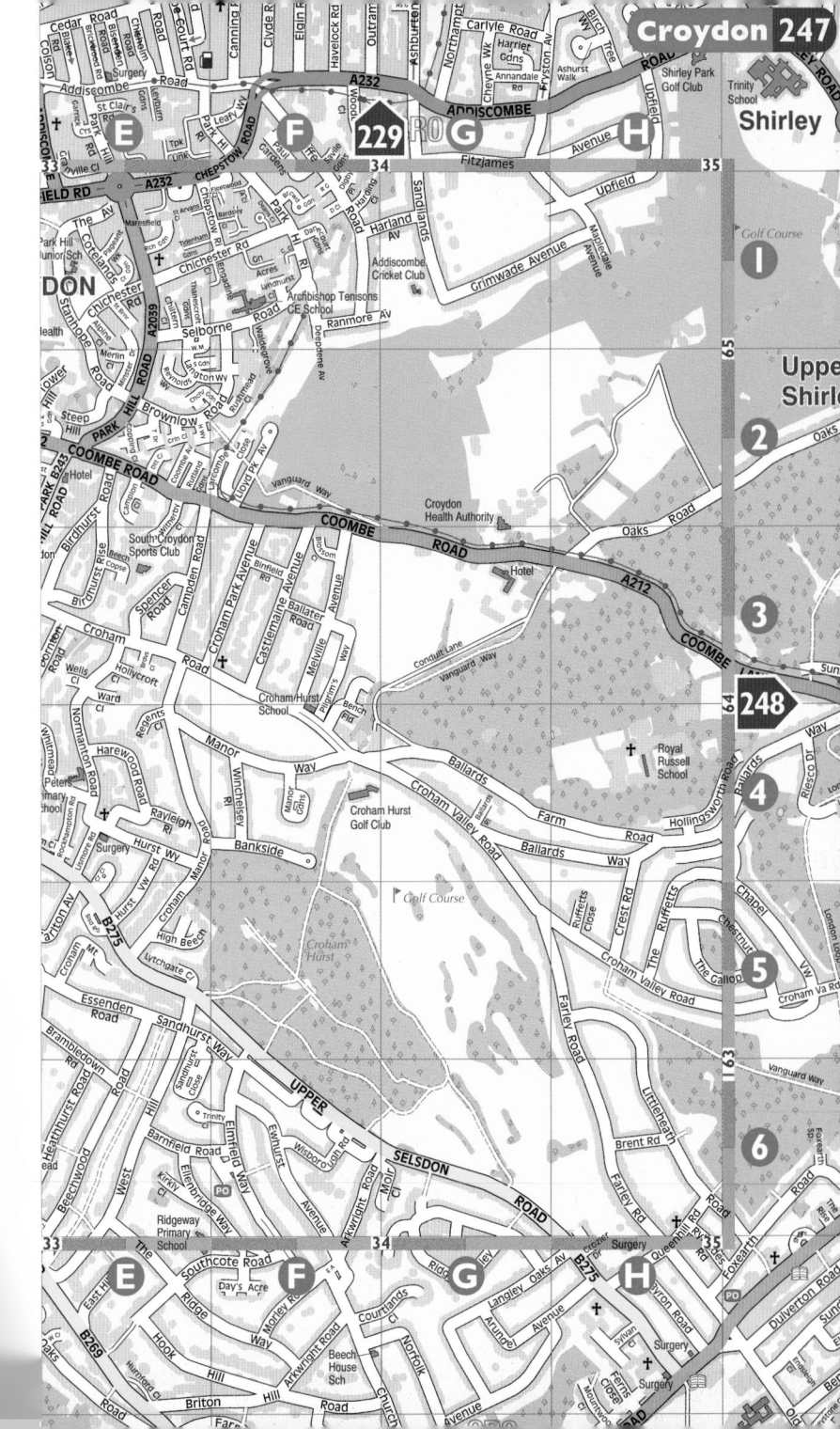

1 grid square represents 500 metres

250
Hawes
Down Clinic

GLEBE
WAY

Silver

R4

A232

539

A

Wickham
theatre

Beckenhamian
C

1

London

St John
Catholic
College

2

Coney
Hall

3

249

64

Bromley
Croydon

4

Gn

5

New
Addington

63

6

539

Vulcan Way

A

Vulcan
Business
Cen

Works

Aragon
Close

GLEBE WAY

A232

Windermere Road

Rycliff Dr

Holland Way

Ridgeway

Warren
Road

B365

Avenue

B

Coney Hall
School

232

Metropo
Police Hayes
Sports Club

40

West

Grove
Close

Hayes
School

C

Baston
School

Baston
Road

D

Redgat

Preston's

Hayes
Grove Priory
Hospital

Common
Road

Baston

A232

London

A232
Loop

CROYDON ROAD

Hayes
Common

Harvest
Bank
Road

Harvest Bank
Road

Robins Grove

Hartfield Crescent

Lawrence Rd

Gates

Baston Manor Road

West
Common

1

Church Drive

Kingsway

Layhams Road

Sylvan Way

Hawthorn Dr

Chestnut Avenue

Birch Tree Avenue

Cherry Tree
Wk

Lime Tree Walk

Monarch
Cl

Queensway

Green

Baston
Manor

Rouse Farm

Layhams Road

Fox

North Pole Lane

Nash Lane

Nash

Layhams Road

Layhams
Farm

40

A
Addington
Business Centre

B

C

D

I grid square represents 500 metres

252

234

251

Crofton

Clareville Road

A232

Oakwood Road

Crofton Avenue

Foxfield Road

The Ridge

Newstead

Tile Farm Road

Newstead Wood School for Girls

Winterborne Avenue

Avebury Road

Willersley

Rusland Avenue

Broughton Road

Orange Road

Torver Way

CROFTON ROAD

Poplar Avenue

Fairbank Av

Birch Road

Jasmine Close

Hazel grove

Sunnydale

Wood Way

Meadow Way

Park Road

The Walk

Hollydale Drive

A21

A65

Mada Road

Pondfield Road

Mere

Mystery Way

Windermere

Grasmere Gardens

Larch Dene

Willow Walk

Starts Close

The Dene

Bromley Hospitals

Crofton Road

PO

Pine Glade

Park Road

Beech Dell

Ninhams Wood

The Birches

Wellbrook Road

Hilda Vale Road

FARNBOROUGH COMMON

Vale Drive

Winton Road

Bassetts Way

Hill

Starts Hill Road

Starts Av

Red Oak Close

Lovibonds

Darrick Wood Swimming Pool

Partridge Drive

Masefield View

Locksbottom

Stables End

Darrick Wood

Norman Close

Broadwater Gardens

Lyndhurst Close

Acorn Way

Pinecrest Gdns

James Road

Isabella Drive

Myer

Arlington Close

Hale Close

Cherrycroft

Rise

Gardens

Darrick Wood Primary School

Beechcroft Road

Melrose

FARNBOROUGH WAY A21

Palmerston

Peel Close

Glebe House

Gladstone Road

PO

Cinden

Oleander Cl

Durrant

Hilborough Way

FARNBOROUGH HILL

B2158

HIGH STREET

Ladycroft Way

Green

Farnborough

Pleasant View

Tye Lane

Church Road

Farnborough Primary School

251

64

The Larches

Shire Lane

Lower Hook Farm

Shire Lane

North End Farm

High Elms Country Park

High Elms Golf Club

Farthing Street

I 63

North End Lane

orange Court Lane

High Elms Road

Golf Course

Road

Hill

Rookery

The Rookery

Standard

Mill Lane

Gorringes

Cuckoo Wood

I grid square represents 500 metres

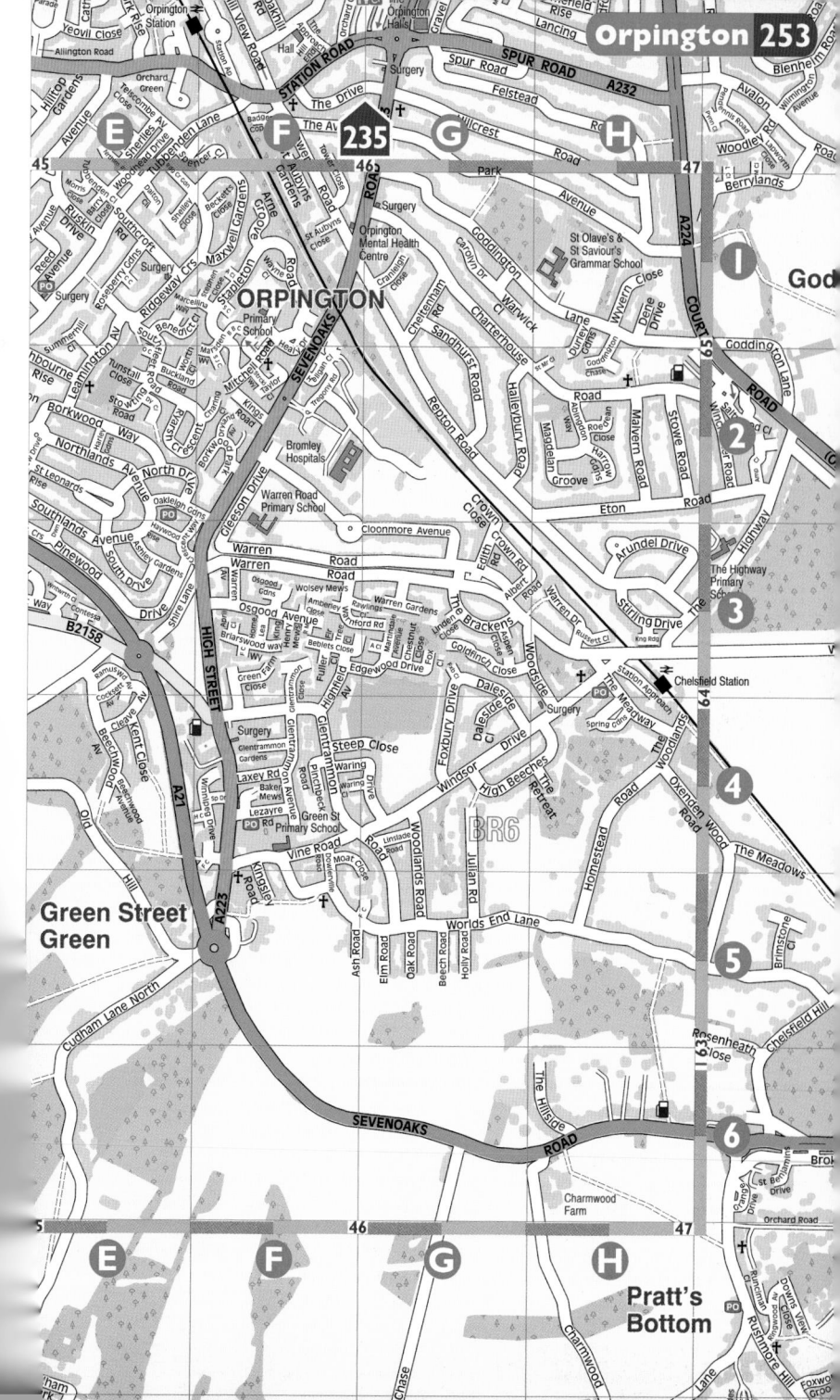

Abbey Wood 155 H4
Acton 142 C1
Acton Green 142 D4
Addington 249 E4
Addiscombe 229 F5
Aldborough Hatch 95 E1
Aldersbrook 93 E5
Alperton 101 G6
Anerley 209 G5
Avery Hill 194 C1
Balham 186 B2
Bandonhill 245 F3
Barking 114 D5
Barkingside 74 B6
Barnehurst 177 H4
Barnes 163 H2
Barnet 48 D1
Barnet Gate 47 E1
Barnsbury 107 G5
Barwell 239 E5
Battersea 166 B1
Bayswater 125 F6
Beckenham 211 F6
Beckton 133 H5
Becontree 116 B3
Beddington 227 G6
Beddington Corner 226 C4
Bedford Park 143 F3
Belgravia 27 E1
Bell Green 190 D5
Bellingham 191 E6
Belmont 60 C5
Belmont 243 E6
Belvedere 157 F5
Benhilton 243 F1
Bermondsey 25 E4
Berrylands 221 H3
Bethnal Green 9 G3
Bexley 176 A5
Bexleyheath 176 D5
Bickley 213 G5
Blackfen 195 F1
Blackheath 172 B3
Blackheath Park 172 C5
Blackwall 131 H6
Bloomsbury 12 D1
The Borough 23 F4
Bow 131 E1
Bow Common 131 E4
Bowes Park 67 G2
Brentford 141 F6
Brentford End 140 D6
Brimsdown 40 C3
Brixton 168 A5
Broad Green 228 B4
Brockley 170 D6
Bromley 131 F2
Bromley 212 D5
Bromley Common 233 F3
Bromley Park 212 A4
Brompton 18 A6
Brondesbury 104 C4
Brondesbury Park 104 B6
Brook Green 144 A3
Broom Hill 235 F4
Brunswick Park 50 C5
Buckhurst Hill 57 E5
Burnt Oak 62 D3
Bushey 43 G2
Bushey Heath 44 A2
Bushey Mead 204 B6
Bush Hill Park 53 E1
Caldecote Hill 44 B2
Camberwell 169 F2
Camden Town 106 C5
Canary Wharf 151 F1
Cannon Hill 224 B1
Canonbury 108 C4
Canons Park 61 G3
Carpenders Park 42 D4
Carshalton 244 A2
Carshalton Beeches 244 A6
Carshalton on
   the Hill 244 B6
Castle Green 116 A6
Catford 191 G5
Chadwell Heath 96 B2
Charlton 153 F5
Cheam 242 D3
Chessington 239 G4
Child's Hill 84 C6
Chingford 55 G4
Chingford Green 55 H3
Chingford Hatch 56 A6

Chipping Barnet 34 C6
Chislehurst 214 C3
Chislehurst West 214 A2
Chiswick 143 F4
Church End 65 E5
Church End 103 F5
City of London 14 D5
Clapham 166 B3
Clapham Park 187 F1
Clapton Park 110 D2
Claygate 238 B4
Clayhall 73 H5
Clerkenwell 6 A5
Cockfosters 36 A6
Coldblow 197 G4
Cole Park 180 C1
Colindale 63 E6
College Park 123 G2
Collier Row 77 G4
Collier's Wood 205 H3
Colney Hatch 66 B2
Coney Hall 250 A2
Coombe 203 E3
Copse Hill 203 G3
Cottenham Park 203 H4
Cranbrook 94 A4
Cranley Gardens 86 C1
Creekmouth 135 E4
Cricklewood 104 B2
Crockenhill 237 H4
Crofton 234 D6
Crooked Billet 203 H2
Crouch End 87 E3
Croydon 246 D1
Crystal Palace 209 G1
Cubitt Town 151 G4
Custom House 133 G6
Dagenham 117 H5
Dalston 109 F5
Dartmouth Park 86 C6
Deacons Hill 46 A1
De Beauvoir Town 109 E6
Deptford 150 D6
Derry Downs 236 B3
Dollis Hill 103 H1
Dormer's Wells 119 F6
Downham 211 H1
Ducks Island 48 B2
Dudden Hill 103 G3
Dulwich 189 F4
Dulwich Village 189 E2
Ealing 121 E6
Earl's Court 145 E5
Earlsfield 185 G3
East Acton 123 E6
East Barnet 49 H2
East Dulwich 169 G6
East Finchley 65 H6
East Ham 133 G1
East Molesey 219 G2
East Sheen 162 D6
East Wickham 175 G2
Eden Park 230 D1
Edgware 46 B6
Edmonton 53 E6
Elmers End 210 B6
Elmstead 213 G1
Elstree 45 G1
Eltham 193 G1
Enfield 38 C5
Enfield Highway 40 A3
Enfield Town 38 D4
Enfield Wash 40 C1
Fair Cross 115 F3
Fairlop 75 E4
Falconwood 175 E5
Farnborough 252 B3
Field Common 218 D4
Finchley 65 E4
Finsbury 6 A3
Finsbury Park 87 H6
Foots Cray 215 H2
Forestdale 248 C6
Forest Gate 112 C3
Forest Hill 190 B3
Fortis Green 86 C1
Forty Hill 39 F2
Foxbury 214 D1
Friday Hill 55 H5
Friern Barnet 50 A6
Fulham 164 B1
Fullwell Cross 74 D4
Furzedown 186 D6
Gants Hill 93 H3

Giggshill 220 C4
Gilwell Park 41 G4
Globe Town 130 B2
Golders Green 84 C3
Goodmayes 95 H6
Gospel Oak 106 C3
Grange Hill 74 D2
Grange Park 38 A6
Greenford 119 H3
Greenhill 80 B2
Green Street Green 253 E5
Greenwich 151 H5
Grove Park 162 D2
Grove Park 193 E5
Hackbridge 226 D6
Hackney 110 A4
Hackney Wick 111 E4
Hadley 35 E4
Hadley Wood 35 H1
Haggerston 8 D1
Hainault 75 F3
Hale End 71 H2
Ham 181 F5
Hammersmith 143 H4
Hampstead 105 H2
Hampstead Garden
   Suburb 85 F2
Hampton 199 F4
Hampton Hill 179 G6
Hampton Wick 200 D4
Hanwell 140 A1
Hanworth 178 B5
Harlesden 123 E1
Harringay 88 A2
Harrow 79 H3
Harrow on the Hill 80 A5
Harrow Weald 60 A3
Hatch End 58 C3
Hayes 232 D4
Hayes Town 138 A1
Headstone 79 F1
Hendon 83 H2
Herne Hill 188 C1
Heston 158 D1
Higham Hill 70 C5
Highams Park 71 F3
High Barnet 34 A4
Highbury 108 B3
Highgate 86 B4
Highwood Hill 47 F4
Hinchley Wood 238 B1
Hither Green 192 A1
Hockenden 217 F6
Holborn 13 G2
Holders Hill 64 B4
Homerton 110 B4
Honor Oak 190 B1
Honor Oak Park 190 C1
Hook 239 G3
Hornsey 87 G1
Hornsey Vale 87 H2
Hounslow 159 E3
Hounslow West 158 B4
Hoxton 8 A2
Hurst Park 199 G5
The Hyde 83 F2
Ilford 114 A1
Isle of Dogs 151 G4
Isleworth 160 D4
Islington 108 A6
Kennington 29 F6
Kensal Green 124 A2
Kensal Rise 124 B1
Kensal Town 124 C3
Kensington 145 E3
Kentish Town 107 E4
Kenton 81 E2
Keston 251 F2
Keston Mark 251 F1
Kevingtown 236 D3
Kew 161 H1
Kidbrooke 173 E3
Kilburn 104 C6
Kingsbury 82 B3
Kingsland 109 E5
Kingston upon Thames 201 H6
Kingston Vale 202 D1
Kitt's End 34 C1
Knightsbridge 18 B3
Knight's Hill 188 C3
Ladywell 171 E5
Lambeth 22 A5
Lampton 159 F2
Lea Bridge 110 B1

Lee 192 B1
Lessness Heath 157 F6
Lewisham 171 G5
Leyton 111 H1
Leytonstone 92 B5
Limehouse 130 C5
Lisson Grove 10 D1
Little Heath 96 A1
Little Ilford 114 A3
Little Stanmore 61 H4
Locksbottom 252 B1
Long Ditton 220 D5
Longlands 194 C5
Lower Clapton 110 A2
Lower Edmonton 53 E4
Lower Green 219 F6
Lower Holloway 107 H3
Lower Place 122 C1
Lower Sydenham 190 B6
Loxford 114 C3
Maida Vale 125 E2
Maitland Park 106 B4
Manor Park 113 G2
Marks Gate 76 C5
Marylebone 11 E2
Mayfair 11 G6
Merry Hill 43 F3
Merton 205 E4
Merton Park 204 D5
Mile End 130 C3
Mill Hill 63 G1
Mill Meads 131 H1
Millwall 151 E3
Mitcham 206 D6
Monken Hadley 34 C3
Monks Orchard 230 A4
Morden 225 E1
Morden Park 224 C3
Mortlake 162 C3
Motspur Park 223 G3
Mottingham 193 E4
Muswell Hill 66 C5
Nash 250 D4
Neasden 102 D2
New Addington 249 H5
New Barnet 35 F6
New Beckenham 210 C2
Newbury Park 94 D3
New Charlton 153 F4
New Cross 170 A4
New Cross Gate 170 C2
New Eltham 194 B4
Newington 22 B6
New Malden 203 F6
New Southgate 51 E6
Nine Elms 167 F1
Noel Park 68 B5
Norbiton 201 H5
Norbury 208 B5
North Acton 122 C5
North Cheam 242 B1
North Cray 197 E5
North End 85 C5
North Finchley 65 G2
North Harrow 78 D3
North Hyde 138 C5
North Kensington 124 B4
Northolt 99 E5
North Sheen 162 B3
Northumberland
   Heath 177 G1
North Wembley 80 D5
North Woolwich 153 G2
Norwood Green 139 E4
Norwood New Town 208 D2
Notting Hill 124 C6
Nunhead 170 A3
Oakleigh Park 49 H4
Oakwood 51 F1
Old Bexley 197 E2
Old Ford 110 C6
Old Malden 222 D4
Old Oak Common 123 F3
Orpington 253 F1
Osidge 51 E4
Osterley 159 G1
Oxhey 42 B1
Paddington 125 H4
Palmers Green 51 G5
Park Langley 231 G3
Park Royal 122 A2
Parsons Green 165 E2
Peckham 169 H3
Penge 210 A3

Pentonville 5 H1	St Paul's Cray 215 G5	Stratford New Town 111 G4
Perivale 101 E6	Sands End 165 G3	Strawberry Hill 179 H5
Petersham 181 G3	Sandy Heath 85 G6	Streatham 207 G1
Petts Wood 234 D1	Seething Wells 220 D3	Streatham Hill 187 G3
Pimlico 28 A3	Selhurst 228 B2	Streatham Park 186 D6
Pinner 78 B1	Seven Kings 95 E5	Streatham Vale 206 D3
Pinner Green 58 A5	Sewardstone 41 H3	Stroud Green 88 A3
Pinnerwood Park 58 A3	Shacklewell 109 G2	Sudbury 100 B3
Plaistow 132 B2	Shadwell 130 A6	Summerstown 185 H4
Plaistow 212 C2	Shepherd's Bush 143 H1	Sundridge 213 E2
Plashet 113 F4	Shirley 230 A6	Surbiton 221 F5
Plumstead 154 C5	Shooters Hill 174 C2	Sutton 243 E3
Plumstead Common 155 F6	Shoreditch 7 H4	Teddington 199 H2
Ponders End 40 A6	Shortlands 212 A6	Temple Mills 111 F3
Poplar 131 E6	Sidcup 195 H6	Thames Ditton 220 C4
Poverest 235 G1	Silvertown 153 E2	Thamesmead 155 F1
Preston 81 F5	Soho 12 C4	Thornton Heath 227 G2
Primrose Hill 106 B6	Somers Town 4 C2	Tokyngton 102 B4
Puddledock 217 H2	Southall 118 C6	Tolworth 222 A5
Putney 164 B6	South Beddington 245 F4	Tooting Graveney 205 H1
Putney Heath 184 A2	Southborough 233 H3	Tottenham 69 E5
Putney Vale 183 G5	South Bromley 131 H5	Tottenham Hale 69 F6
Queensbury 61 G6	South Croydon 246 C4	Totteridge 49 E3
Queens Park 124 C1	Southend 191 G6	Totteridge Green 48 A3
Ramsden 236 A5	Southfields 185 E3	Tufnell Park 107 E2
Ratcliff 130 C6	Southgate 51 G3	Tulse Hill 188 B3
Rayners Lane 78 D5	South Hackney 110 A6	Twickenham 180 A3
Raynes Park 204 A6	South Hampstead 105 G5	Underhill 49 E1
Redbridge 93 E2	South Harrow 99 F1	Upper Clapton 89 G5
Regent's Park 3 H2	South Hornchurch 117 H6	Upper Edmonton 53 G6
Richmond 161 G6	South Kensington 145 G5	Upper Elmers End 230 D2
Richmond Hill 181 G1	South Lambeth 167 G1	Upper Holloway 87 E6
Roehampton 163 F6	South Norwood 208 D6	Upper Norwood 208 D4
Romford 97 H2	South Ruislip 98 B2	Upper Shirley 248 A2
Rosehill 225 F5	South Tottenham 89 E2	Upper Sydenham 189 G6
Rotherhithe 150 B3	South Wimbledon 205 G1	Upper Tooting 186 A5
Roundshaw 245 H4	South Woodford 72 C5	Upper Walthamstow 91 G1
Roxeth 79 G6	Spitalfields 16 C1	Upton 112 D5
Ruxley 216 C2	Spring Grove 159 H2	Upton Park 113 E6
Rydens 218 A6	Spring Park 231 E6	Vale of Health 105 H1
St George in the East 17 F6	Stamford Hill 89 F4	Vauxhall 29 G4
St Giles 12 D3	Stanmore 60 D1	Waddon 227 H6
St Helier 225 G5	Stepney 130 A4	Walham Green 144 D6
St James 20 C2	Stockwell 167 G4	Wallend 114 A6
St Johns 171 E3	Stoke Newington 89 F6	Wallington 244 D3
St John's Wood 125 H1	Stonehill Green 217 G2	Walthamstow 71 E6
St Luke's 7 F5	Stoneleigh 241 F3	Walworth 31 F4
St Margarets 181 E1	Strand 13 F5	Wandle Park 228 A6
St Mary Cray 236 A2	Stratford 111 G5	Wandsworth 165 E5
St Pancras 5 F4	Stratford Marsh 111 F6	Wanstead 92 D4
Wapping 25 G2		
Watford Heath 42 C2		
Wealdstone 60 C6		
Welling 175 H4		
Welsh Harp 82 D5		
Wembley 101 E3		
Wembley Park 102 A1		
West Acton 122 A5		
West Barnes 224 A2		
Westbourne Green 125 E3		
West Brompton 145 F6		
West Dulwich 188 D4		
West Ealing 140 C1		
West Ewell 241 E5		
West Green 68 C6		
West Hampstead 105 E3		
West Harrow 79 G4		
West Heath 85 F6		
West Heath 156 B6		
West Hendon 83 G4		
West Hill 184 C2		
West Kensington 144 B5		
West Kilburn 124 C2		
Westminster 20 B6		
West Molesey 218 D1		
West Norwood 188 C6		
Weston Green 220 A5		
West Wickham 231 H5		
Whetstone 49 F4		
Whitechapel 16 D5		
Whitton 179 G1		
Widmore 213 F5		
Willesden 103 G4		
Willesden Green 103 H5		
Wimbledon 204 C1		
Winchmore Hill 52 B3		
Woodford 72 D2		
Woodford Bridge 73 H3		
Woodford Green 72 C3		
Woodford Wells 56 D5		
Wood Green 68 A4		
Woodlands 159 H4		
Woodside 229 G3		
Woodside Park 49 E6		
Woolwich 154 A6		
Worcester Park 223 H6		
World's End 38 A5		
The Wrythe 226 A6		
Yeading 118 A3		

USING THE STREET INDEX

Street names are listed alphabetically. Each street name is followed by its postal town or area locality, the Postcode District, the page number, and the reference to the square in which the name is found.

Standard index entries are shown as follows:

Aaron Hill Rd *EHAM* E6   **134** A4

Street names and selected addresses not shown on the map due to scale restrictions are shown in the index with an asterisk:

Abbeville Ms *CLAP* * SW4 ....**167** F6

GENERAL ABBREVIATIONS

ACC	ACCESS	COT	COTTAGE	FLDS	FIELDS	INF	INFIRMARY
ALY	ALLEY	COTS	COTTAGES	FLS	FALLS	INFO	INFORMATION
AP	APPROACH	CP	CAPE	FLTS	FLATS	INT	INTERCHANGE
AR	ARCADE	CPS	COPSE	FM	FARM	IS	ISLAND
ASS	ASSOCIATION	CR	CREEK	FT	FORT	JCT	JUNCTION
AV	AVENUE	CREM	CREMATORIUM	FWY	FREEWAY	JTY	JETTY
BCH	BEACH	CRS	CRESCENT	FY	FERRY	KG	KING
BLDS	BUILDINGS	CSWY	CAUSEWAY	GA	GATE	KNL	KNOLL
BND	BEND	CT	COURT	GAL	GALLERY	L	LAKE
BNK	BANK	CTRL	CENTRAL	GDN	GARDEN	LA	LANE
BR	BRIDGE	CTS	COURTS	GDNS	GARDENS	LDG	LODGE
BRK	BROOK	CTYD	COURTYARD	GLD	GLADE	LGT	LIGHT
BTM	BOTTOM	CUTT	CUTTINGS	GLN	GLEN	LK	LOCK
BUS	BUSINESS	CV	COVE	GN	GREEN	LKS	LAKES
BVD	BOULEVARD	CYN	CANYON	GND	GROUND	LNDG	LANDING
BY	BYPASS	DEPT	DEPARTMENT	GRA	GRANGE	LTL	LITTLE
CATH	CATHEDRAL	DL	DALE	GRG	GARAGE	LWR	LOWER
CEM	CEMETERY	DM	DAM	GT	GREAT	MAG	MAGISTRATE
CEN	CENTRE	DR	DRIVE	GTWY	GATEWAY	MAN	MANSIONS
CFT	CROFT	DRO	DROVE	GV	GROVE	MD	MEAD
CH	CHURCH	DRY	DRIVEWAY	HGR	HIGHER	MDW	MEADOWS
CHA	CHASE	DWGS	DWELLINGS	HL	HILL	MEM	MEMORIAL
CHYD	CHURCHYARD	E	EAST	HLS	HILLS	MKT	MARKET
CIR	CIRCLE	EMB	EMBANKMENT	HO	HOUSE	MKTS	MARKETS
CIRC	CIRCUS	EMBY	EMBASSY	HOL	HOLLOW	ML	MALL
CL	CLOSE	ESP	ESPLANADE	HOSP	HOSPITAL	ML	MILL
CLFS	CLIFFS	EST	ESTATE	HRB	HARBOUR	MNR	MANOR
CMP	CAMP	EX	EXCHANGE	HTH	HEATH	MS	MEWS
CNR	CORNER	EXPY	EXPRESSWAY	HTS	HEIGHTS	MSN	MISSION
CO	COUNTY	EXT	EXTENSION	HVN	HAVEN	MT	MOUNT
COLL	COLLEGE	F/O	FLYOVER	HWY	HIGHWAY	MTN	MOUNTAIN
COM	COMMON	FC	FOOTBALL CLUB	IMP	IMPERIAL	MTS	MOUNTAINS
COMM	COMMISSION	FK	FORK	IN	INLET	MUS	MUSEUM
CON	CONVENT	FLD	FIELD	IND EST	INDUSTRIAL ESTATE	MWY	MOTORWAY

N....NORTH	PRIM....PRIMARY	SE....SOUTH EAST	TRL....TRAIL
NE....NORTH EAST	PROM....PROMENADE	SER....SERVICE AREA	TWR....TOWER
NW....NORTH WEST	PRS....PRINCESS	SH....SHORE	U/P....UNDERPASS
O/P....OVERPASS	PRT....PORT	SHOP....SHOPPING	UNI....UNIVERSITY
OFF....OFFICE	PT....POINT	SKWY....SKYWAY	UPR....UPPER
ORCH....ORCHARD	PTH....PATH	SMT....SUMMIT	V....VALE
OV....OVAL	PZ....PIAZZA	SOC....SOCIETY	VA....VALLEY
PAL....PALACE	QD....QUADRANT	SP....SPUR	VIAD....VIADUCT
PAS....PASSAGE	QU....QUEEN	SPR....SPRING	VIL....VILLA
PAV....PAVILION	QY....QUAY	SQ....SQUARE	VIS....VISTA
PDE....PARADE	R....RIVER	ST....STREET	VLS....VILLAGE
PH....PUBLIC HOUSE	RBT....ROUNDABOUT	STN....STATION	VLLS....VILLAS
PK....PARK	RD....ROAD	STR....STREAM	VW....VIEW
PKWY....PARKWAY	RDG....RIDGE	STRD....STRAND	W....WEST
PL....PLACE	REP....REPUBLIC	SW....SOUTH WEST	WD....WOOD
PLN....PLAIN	RES....RESERVOIR	TDG....TRADING	WHF....WHARF
PLNS....PLAINS	RFC....RUGBY FOOTBALL CLUB	TER....TERRACE	WK....WALK
PLZ....PLAZA	RI....RISE	THWY....THROUGHWAY	WKS....WALKS
POL....POLICE STATION	RP....RAMP	TNL....TUNNEL	WLS....WELLS
PR....PRINCE	RW....ROW	TOLL....TOLLWAY	WY....WAY
PREC....PRECINCT	S....SOUTH	TPK....TURNPIKE	YD....YARD
PREP....PREPARATORY	SCH....SCHOOL	TR....TRACK	YHA....YOUTH HOSTEL

POSTCODE TOWNS AND AREA ABBREVIATIONS

ABR/ST....Abridge/Stapleford Abbotts	DEPT....Deptford	KTN/HRWW/WS....Kenton/Harrow Weald/Wealdstone	SNWD....South Norwood
ABYW....Abbey Wood	DUL....Dulwich	KTTN....Kentish Town	SOHO/CST....Soho/Carnaby Street
ACT....Acton	E/WMO/HCT....East & West Molesey/Hampton Court	KUT....Kingston upon Thames	SOHO/SHAV....Soho/Shaftesbury Avenue
ALP/SUD....Alperton/Sudbury	EA....Ealing	KUTN/CMB....Kingston upon Thames north/Coombe	SRTFD....Stratford
ARCH....Archway	EBAR....East Barnet	LBTH....Lambeth	STAN....Stanmore
BAL....Balham	EBED/NFELT....East Bedfont/North Feltham	LEE/GVPK....Lee/Grove Park	STBT....St Bart's
BANK....Bank	ECT....Earl's Court	LEW....Lewisham	STHGT/OAK....Southgate/Oakwood
BAR....Barnet	ED....Edmonton	LEY....Leyton	STHL....Southall
BARB....Barbican	EDGW....Edgware	LINN....Lincoln's Inn	STHWK....Southwark
BARK....Barking	EDUL....East Dulwich	LOTH....Lothbury	STJS....St James's
BARK/HLT....Barkingside/Hainault	EFNCH....East Finchley	LOU....Loughton	STJSPK....St James's Park
BARN....Barnes	EHAM....East Ham	LSQ/SEVD....Leicester Square/Seven Dials	STJWD....St John's Wood
BAY/PAD....Bayswater/Paddington	ELTH/MOT....Eltham/Mottingham	LVPST....Liverpool Street	STLK....St Luke's
BCTR....Becontree	EMB....Embankment	MANHO....Mansion House	STMC/STPC....St Mary Cray/St Paul's Cray
BECK....Beckenham	EN....Enfield	MBLAR....Marble Arch	STNW/STAM....Stoke Newington/Stamford Hill
BELMT....Belmont	ENC/FH....Enfield Chase/Forty Hill	MHST....Marylebone High Street	STP....St Paul's
BELV....Belvedere	ERITH....Erith	MLHL....Mill Hill	STPAN....St Pancras
BERM/RHTH....Bermondsey/Rotherhithe	ERITHM....Erith Marshes	MNPK....Manor Park	STRHM/NOR....Streatham/Norbury
BETH....Bethnal Green	ESH/CLAY....Esher/Claygate	MON....Monument	SUN....Sunbury
BFN/LL....Blackfen/Longlands	EW....Ewell	MORT/ESHN....Mortlake/East Sheen	SURB....Surbiton
BGVA....Belgravia	FARR....Farringdon	MRDN....Morden	SUT....Sutton
BKHH....Buckhurst Hill	FBAR/BDGN....Friern Barnet/Bounds Green	MTCM....Mitcham	SWFD....South Woodford
BKHTH/KID....Blackheath/Kidbrooke	FELT....Feltham	MUSWH....Muswell Hill	SWLY....Swanley
BLKFR....Blackfriars	FENCHST....Fenchurch Street	MV/WKIL....Maida Vale/West Kilburn	SYD....Sydenham
BMLY....Bromley	FITZ....Fitzrovia	MYFR/PICC....Mayfair/Piccadilly	THDT....Thames Ditton
BMSBY....Bloomsbury	FLST/FETLN....Fleet Street/Fetter Lane	MYFR/PKLN....Mayfair/Park Lane	THHTH....Thornton Heath
BORE....Borehamwood	FNCH....Finchley	NFNCH/WDSPK....North Finchley/Woodside Park	THMD....Thamesmead
BOW....Bow	FSBYE....Finsbury east	NKENS....North Kensington	TOOT....Tooting
BROCKY....Brockley	FSBYPK....Finsbury Park	NOXST/BSQ....New Oxford Street/Bloomsbury Square	TOTM....Tottenham
BRXN/ST....Brixton north/Stockwell	FSBYW....Finsbury west	NRWD....Norwood	TPL/STR....Temple/Strand
BRXS/STRHM....Brixton south/Streatham Hill	FSTGT....Forest Gate	NTGHL....Notting Hill	TRDG/WHET....Totteridge/Whetstone
BRYLDS....Berrylands	FSTH....Forest Hill	NTHLT....Northolt	TWK....Twickenham
BTFD....Brentford	FUL/PGN....Fulham/Parsons Green	NWCR....New Cross	TWRH....Tower Hill
BTSEA....Battersea	GDMY/SEVK....Goodmayes/Seven Kings	NWDGN....Norwood Green	UED....Upper Edmonton
BUSH....Bushy	GFD/PVL....Greenford/Perivale	NWMAL....New Malden	VX/NE....Vauxhall/Nine Elms
BXLY....Bexley	GINN....Gray's Inn	OBST....Old Broad Street	WAB....Waltham Abbey
BXLYHN....Bexleyheath north	GLDGN....Golders Green	ORP....Orpington	WALTH....Walthamstow
BXLYHS....Bexleyheath south	GNTH/NBYPK....Gants Hill/Newbury Park	OXHEY....Oxhey	WALW....Walworth
CAMTN....Camden Town	GNWCH....Greenwich	OXSTW....Oxford Street west	WAN....Wanstead
CAN/RD....Canning Town/Royal Docks	GSTN....Garston	PECK....Peckham	WAND/EARL....Wandsworth/Earlsfield
CANST....Cannon Street station	GTPST....Great Portland Street	PEND....Ponders End	WAP....Wapping
CAR....Carshalton	GWRST....Gower Street	PGE/AN....Penge/Anerley	WAT....Watford
CAT....Catford	HACK....Hackney	PIM....Pimlico	WATN....Watford North
CAVSQ/HST....Cavendish Square/Harley Street	HAMP....Hampstead	PIN....Pinner	WATW....Watford West
CDALE/KGS....Colindale/Kingsbury	HAYES....Hayes	PLMGR....Palmers Green	WBLY....Wembley
CEND/HSY/T....Crouch End/Hornsey/Turnpike Lane	HBRY....Highbury	PLSTW....Plaistow	WBPTN....West Brompton
CHARL....Charlton	HCIRC....Holborn Circus	POP/IOD....Poplar/Isle of Dogs	WCHMH....Winchmore Hill
CHCR....Charing Cross	HDN....Hendon	PUR/KEN....Purley/Kenley	WCHPL....Whitechapel
CHDH....Chadwell Heath	HDTCH....Houndsditch	PUT/ROE....Putney/Roehampton	WDGN....Wood Green
CHEAM....Cheam	HEST....Heston	RAIN....Rainham (Gt Lon)	WEA....West Ealing
CHEL....Chelsea	HGT....Highgate	RCH/KEW....Richmond/Kew	WELL....Welling
CHIG....Chigwell	HHOL....High Holborn	RCHPK/HAM....Richmond Park/Ham	WEST....Westminster
CHING....Chingford	HMSMTH....Hammersmith	RDART....Rural Dartford	WESTW....Westminster west
CHSGTN....Chessington	HNHL....Herne Hill	REDBR....Redbridge	WFD....Woodford
CHST....Chislehurst	HNWL....Hanwell	REGST....Regent Street	WHALL....Whitehall
CHSWK....Chiswick	HOL/ALD....Holborn/Aldwych	ROM....Romford	WHTN....Whitton
CITYW....City of London west	HOLWY....Holloway	ROMW/RG....Romford west/Rush Green	WIM/MER....Wimbledon/Merton
CLAP....Clapham	HOM....Homerton	RSLP....Ruislip	WKENS....West Kensington
CLAY....Clayhall	HOR/WEW....Horton/West Ewell	RSQ....Russell Square	WLGTN....Wallington
CLKNW....Clerkenwell	HPTN....Hampton	RYLN/HDSTN....Rayners Lane/Headstone	WLSDN....Willesden
CLPT....Clapton	HRW....Harrow	RYNPK....Raynes Park	WNWD....West Norwood
CMBW....Camberwell	HSLW....Hounslow	SCUP....Sidcup	WOOL/PLUM....Woolwich/Plumstead
CONDST....Conduit Street	HSLWW....Hounslow west	SDTCH....Shoreditch	WOT/HER....Walton-on-Thames/Hersham
COVGDN....Covent Garden	HYS/HAR....Hayes/Harlington	SEVS/STOTM....Seven Sisters/South Tottenham	WPK....Worcester Park
CRICK....Cricklewood	IL....Ilford	SHB....Shepherd's Bush	WWKM....West Wickham
CROY/NA....Croydon/New Addington	IS....Islington	SKENS....South Kensington	YEAD....Yeading
CRW....Collier Row	ISLW....Isleworth		
DAGE....Dagenham east	KENS....Kensington		
DAGW....Dagenham west	KIL/WHAMP....Kilburn/West Hampstead		
DART....Dartford	KTBR....Knightsbridge		

1 - Abb

Index - streets

1

1 Av WOOL/PLUM SE18 ....154 B3

A

Aaron Hill Rd EHAM E6 ....134 A4
Abbess Cl BRXS/STRHM SW2 ....188 B3
Abbeville Ms CLAP * SW4 ....167 F6
Abbeville Rd CEND/HSY/T N8 ....87 F1
  CLAP SW4 ....187 E1
Abbey Av ALP/SUD HA0 ....121 G1
Abbey Crs BELV DA17 ....157 E4
Abbeydale Rd ALP/SUD HA0 ....101 H6
Abbey Dr TOOT SW17 ....206 C1
Abbeyfield Est
  BERM/RHTH SE16 ....33 H1
  BERM/RHTH SE16 ....150 A4
Abbeyfield Rd
  BERM/RHTH SE16 ....150 A4
Abbeyfields Cl WLSDN NW10 ....122 A3
Abbey Gdns BERM/RHTH SE16 ....33 F1
  HMSMTH W6 ....
  STJWD NW8 ....125 C1
Abbey Gv ABYW SE2 ....155 H4
Abbeyhill Rd BFN/LL DA15 ....196 A6
Abbey La BECK BR3 ....211 E5
  SRTFD E15 ....131 C1
Abbey Ms WALTH E17 ....91 E2
Abbey Mt BELV DA17 ....156 D5

Abbey Orchard St WEST SW1P 20 D5
Abbey Pk BECK BR3 ....211 E3
Abbey Rd BARK IG11 ....114 B5
  BELV DA17 ....156 B4
  BXLYHS DA6 ....176 C5
  CROY/NA CRO 211 E3
  EN EN1 ....39 E6
  GNTH/NBYPK IG2 ....94 D2
  KIL/WHAMP NW6 ....105 F6
  SRTFD E15 ....131 H1
  WIM/MER SW19 ....205 G3
  WLSDN NW10 ....102 B6
Abbey St PLSTW E13 ....132 C3
  STHWK SE1 ....24 C5
Abbey Ter ABYW SE2 ....156 A3
Abbey Vw MLHL NW7 ....47 F5
Abbey Wk E/WMO/HCT KT8 ....199 F6
Abbey Wood Rd ABYW SE2 ....155 H4

Abbot Cl RSLP HA4 ....98 B1
Abbotsbury Cl SRTFD E15 ....131 C1
  WKENS * W14 ....119 G2
Abbotsbury Gdns PIN HA5 ....78 A3
Abbotsbury Ms PECK SE15 ....170 A4
Abbotsbury Rd MRDN SM4 ....225 F1
  WKENS W14 ....144 C2
  WWKM BR4 ....232 B6
Abbots Cl STMC/STPC BR5 ....234 C5
Abbots Dr RYLN/HDSTN HA2 ....79 E6
Abbotsford Av
  SEVS/STOTM N15 ....88 C1
Abbotsford Gdns WFD IG8 ....52 C3
Abbotsford Rd GDMY/SEVK IG3 ....95 G6
Abbots Gdns EFNCH N2 ....85 H1
Abbots Gn CROY/NA CRO 248 B4
Abbotshade Rd
  BERM/RHTH * SE16 ....150 B1

Abbotshall Rd STHGT/OAK N14 ....51 E5
Abbotsall Rd CAT SE6 ...191 H3
Abbots La STHWK SE1 ...24 B2
Abbotsleigh Cl BELMT SM2 ...245 F5
Abbotsleigh Rd STRHM/NOR SW16 ...187 G6
Abbots Mnr PIM SW1V ...27 G3
Abbots Manor Est PIM SW1V ...27 G3
Abbotsmede Cl TWK TW1 ...180 B4
Abbots Pk BRXS/STRHM SW2 ...188 A3
Abbot's Pl KIL/WHAMP NW6 ...105 F6
Abbots Rd CHEAM SM3 ...242 C2
EDGW HA8 ...62 D3
EHAM E6 ...113 F6
Abbots Ter CEND/HSY/T N8 ...87 G3
Abbotstone Rd PUT/ROE SW15 ...164 A4
Abbots St HACK E8 ...109 F4
Abbots Wk KENS * W8 ...145 F3
Abbots Wy BECK BR3 ...230 C2
Abbotswell Rd BROCKY SE4 ...170 D6
Abbotswood Cl BELV DA17 ...156 C5
Abbotswood Gdns CLAY IG5 ...73 H6
Abbotswood Rd EDUL SE22 ...169 G5
STRHM/NOR SW16 ...187 F5
Abbott Av RYNPK SW20 ...204 B5
Abbott Cl HPTN TW12 ...161 G1
NTHLT UB5 ...84 A1
Abbott Rd POP/IOD E14 ...131 G4
Abbotts Cl IS * N1 ...108 C5
ROMW/RG RM7 ...77 F6
THMD SE28 ...128 A6
Abbotts Crs CHING E4 ...55 H6
ENC/FH EN2 ...38 B3
Abbotts Md RCHPK/HAM * TW10 ...181 E6
Abbotts Park Rd LEY E10 ...90 A6
Abbotts Rd BAR EN5 ...35 F5
MTCM CR4 ...227 E1
STHL UB1 ...138 C1
Abbott's Wk BXLYHN DA7 ...176 B1
Abbs Cross Gdns HCH RM12 ...75 H5
Abdale Rd SHB W12 ...143 H1
Aberavon Rd BOW E3 ...130 C2
Abercairn Rd STRHM/NOR SW16 ...207 E3
Aberconway Rd MRDN SM4 ...205 F3
Abercorn Cl MLHL NW7 ...46 C4
STJWD NW8 ...125 G2
Abercorn Crs RYLN/HDSTN HA2 ...79 F5
Abercorn Gdns CHDH RM6 ...95 H5
KTN/HRWW/WS HA3 ...81 F4
Abercorn Pl STJWD NW8 ...125 G2
Abercorn Rd MLHL NW7 ...46 C4
STAN HA7 ...61 E5
Abercorn Wy STHWK SE1 ...39 C2
Abercrombie Dr EN EN1 ...39 C2
Abercrombie St BTSEA SW11 ...166 A3
Abercrombie St WWKM BR4 ...231 G6
Aberdare Gdns KIL/WHAMP NW6 ...105 F5
MLHL NW7 ...64 B3
Aberdare Rd PEND EN3 ...40 A5
Aberdeen Cottages STAN * HA7 ...61 E3
Aberdeen La HBRY N5 ...108 H2
Aberdeen Pde UED * N18 ...69 H1
Aberdeen Pl STJWD NW8 ...125 H1
Aberdeen Rd CROY/NA CR0 ...246 C2
HBRY N5 ...108 C2
KTN/HRWW/W HA3 ...80 C5
UED N18 ...69 C1
WLSDN NW10 ...103 F3
Aberdeen Ter BKHTH/KID SE3 ...171 H3
Aberdour Rd BETH E2 ...115 H1
Aberdour St STHWK SE1 ...32 A1
Aberfeldy St POP/IOD E14 ...131 C5
Aberford Gdns WOOL/PLUM SE18 ...173 C2
Aberfoyle Rd STNW/STAM * N16 ...89 F6
Aboyne Dr RYNPK SW20 ...203 C5
Aboyne Rd TOOT SW17 ...185 H5
WLSDN NW10 ...103 E1
Abridge Gdns CRW RM5 ...77 E2
Abridge Wy BARK IG11 ...135 H1
Abyssinia Cl BTSEA SW11 ...166 A5
Acacia Av ALP/SUD HA0 ...101 H5
BTFD TW8 ...160 D1
TOTM N17 ...68 D3
Acacia Cl DEPT SE8 ...150 C4
KTN/HRWW/W HA3 ...60 A2
STMC/STPC BR5 ...234 C2
Acacia Dr CHEAM SM3 ...224 D5
Acacia Gdns STJWD * NW8 ...125 H1
WWKM BR4 ...231 G6
Acacia Gv DUL SE21 ...188 D4
NWMAL KT3 ...203 E6
Acacia Pl STJWD NW8 ...125 H1
Acacia Rd ACT W3 ...122 C6
BECK BR3 ...236 D2
ENC/FH EN2 ...38 C2
HPTN TW12 ...199 E2
MTCM CR4 ...199 E2
STJWD NW8 ...125 H1
STRHM/NOR SW16 ...187 H1
WALTH E17 ...90 C3
WAN E11 ...92 A6

WDGN N22 ...68 A4
The Acacias EBAR * EN4 ...35 H6
Acacia Wy BFN/LL DA15 ...195 F2
Academy Gdns CROY/NA CR0 ...229 F5
NTHLT UB5 ...83 C1
Academy Pl WOOL/PLUM SE18 ...173 H2
Academy Rd WOOL/PLUM SE18 ...173 H1
Acanthus Dr STHWK SE1 ...33 C5
Acanthus Rd BTSEA SW11 ...166 C4
Accommodation Rd GLDGN NW11 ...84 D4
Ace Pde CHSGTN * KT9 ...239 C1
Acer Av YEAD UB4 ...118 C3
Acfold Rd FUL/PGN SW6 ...165 F2
Achilles Cl STHWK SE1 ...33 F5
Achilles Rd KIL/WHAMP NW6 ...88 E4
Achilles St NWCR SE14 ...170 C1
Acklam Rd NKENS W10 ...124 D4
Acklington Dr CDALE/KGS NW9 ...63 E4
Ackmar Rd FUL/PGN SW6 ...165 E2
Ackroyd Dr BOW E3 ...130 A4
Ackroyd Rd FSTH SE23 ...190 B2
Acland Cl WOOL/PLUM SE18 ...174 D1
Acland Crs CMBW SE5 ...168 D5
Acland Rd CRICK NW2 ...103 H4
Acock Gv NTHLT UB5 ...99 F2
Acol Rd KIL/WHAMP NW6 ...105 E5
Acorn Cl CHING E4 ...71 F1
CHST BR7 ...214 C4
ENC/FH EN2 ...38 A2
HPTN TW12 ...199 F2
STAN HA7 ...60 D3
Acorn Gdns ACT W3 ...122 D4
NRWD SE19 ...209 F4
Acorn Pde PECK * SE15 ...169 H1
Acorn Wy FSTH SE23 ...190 B5
ORP BR6 ...252 B2
Acre Dr EDUL SE22 ...169 H3
Acre La BRXS/STRHM SW2 ...167 H5
CAR SM5 ...244 C2
Acre Rd DAGE RM10 ...117 E1
KUTN/CMB KT2 ...201 C4
WIM/MER SW19 ...205 H2
Acris St WAND/EARL SW18 ...165 G6
Acton Cl ED N9 ...53 C4
Acton Hl Ms ACT * W3 ...142 B1
Acton Ms HACK E8 ...109 F6
Acton St FSBYW WC1X ...5 H4
Acuba Rd WAND/EARL SW18 ...185 F4
Ada Ct MV/WKIL W9 ...2 C3
Ada Gdns POP/IOD E14 ...131 H5
SRTFD E15 ...112 B6
Adair Cl SNWD SE25 ...209 H6
Adair Rd NKENS W10 ...124 C3
Adam & Eve Ms KENS W8 ...145 E3
Adam Rd CHING E4 ...70 D2
Adams Cl BRYLDS KT5 ...221 H5
NFNCH/WDSP N12 ...65 E3
WBLY HA0 ...68 B4
Adams Ms WDGN * N22 ...67 H3
Adamson Rd CAN/RD E16 ...132 C5
HAMP NW3 ...106 H4
Adams Pl HOLWY N7 ...107 H5
Adamsrill Rd SYD SE26 ...190 B6
Adams Rd BECK BR3 ...230 C2
TOTM N17 ...68 B6
Adam St CHCR WC2N ...11 G6
Adams Wy CROY/NA CR0 ...214 A6
Adams Wk KUT KT1 ...201 C5
Adam St FUL/PGN * SW6 ...165 F2
Adam Wk FUL/PGN * SW6 ...164 A1
Ada Pl BETH E2 ...109 G6
Ada St HACK E8 ...109 H6
Adderley Gdns ELTH/MOT SE9 ...194 A6
Adderley Gv BTSEA SW11 ...166 C6
Adderley Rd KTN/HRWW/W HA3 ...60 B4
Adderley St POP/IOD E14 ...131 G5
Addington Rd NFNCH/WDSP N12 ...65 H2
Addington Gv SYD SE26 ...190 C6
Addington Rd BOW E3 ...131 E2
CAN/RD E16 ...132 A3
CROY/NA CR0 ...228 A5
FSBYPK N4 ...88 A4
SAND/SEL CR2 ...211 H6
WWKM BR4 ...249 G2
Addington Sq CMBW SE5 ...168 C1
Addington Village Rd CROY/NA CR0 ...248 D4
Addis Cl PEND EN3 ...40 B2
Addiscombe Av CROY/NA CR0 ...229 C4
Addiscombe Cl KTN/HRWW/W HA3 ...81 C2
Addiscombe Court Rd CROY/NA CR0 ...229 E5
Addiscombe Gv CROY/NA CR0 ...228 D6
Addiscombe Rd CROY/NA CR0 ...229 E5
Addison Av HSLW TW3 ...159 G2
STHGT/OAK N14 ...50 D1
Addison Cl NTGHL W11 ...144 A1
STMC/STPC BR5 ...234 C5
Addison Crs WKENS W14 ...144 C3
Addison Dr LEE/GVPK SE12 ...172 D6
Addison Gdns BRYLDS KT5 ...221 H1
WKENS W14 ...143 H3
Addison Gv CHSWK W4 ...118 B3
Addison Pl NTGHL W11 ...144 C1
Addison Rd BARK/HLT IG6 ...74 C4
HAYES BR2 ...233 F2
NTGHL W11 ...144 C1
PEND EN3 ...40 A2
SNWD SE25 ...229 G1
TEDD TW11 ...180 C2
WALTH E17 ...91 F2
WAN E11 ...92 C3
Addison's Cl CROY/NA CR0 ...230 A1
Addison Wy GLDGN NW11 ...84 D1
HYS/HAR UB3 ...94 D4
NTHWD HA6 ...40 D6
Addle Hill BLKFR EC4V ...14 D5
Addle St CITYW * EC2V ...15 F3
Adecroft Wy E/WMO/HCT KT8 ...199 H2
Adela Av NWMAL KT3 ...218 H2
Adelaide Av BROCKY SE4 ...171 E5
Adelaide Cl EN EN1 ...39 E1
STAN HA7 ...44 C6
Adelaide Ct HNWL W7 ...140 B2

Adelaide Gdns CHDH RM6 ...96 C2
Adelaide Gv SHB W12 ...143 G1
Adelaide Rd CHST BR7 ...214 B1
HAMP NW3 ...106 D5
HEST TW5 ...158 C2
IL IG1 ...90 C1
LEY E10 ...111 C1
NWDGN UB2 ...138 C4
RCH/KEW TW9 ...161 H5
SURB KT6 ...221 G2
TEDD TW11 ...200 B2
WAND/EARL SW18 ...165 E6
WEA W13 ...142 C2
Adelaide St CHCR * WC2N ...13 G6
Adelaide Ter BTFD * TW8 ...141 F5
Adela St NKENS W10 ...124 C3
Adelina Gv WCHPL E1 ...130 A4
Adelina Ms BAL SW12 ...187 F3
Adeline Pl RSQ WC1B ...12 D2
Adeliza Cl BARK IG11 ...114 C5
Adelphi Ter CHCR WC2N ...13 F6
Adeney Cl HMSMTH W6 ...144 B6
Aden Gv STNW/STAM N16 ...87 H5
Adenmore Rd CAT SE6 ...191 E2
Aden Rd IL IG1 ...90 B4
PEND EN3 ...41 C5
Adie Rd HMSMTH W6 ...144 A3
Adine Rd PLSTW E13 ...132 C3
Adler St WCHPL E1 ...17 E3
Adley St CLPT E5 ...110 C3
Adlington Cl UED N18 ...68 A2
Admaston Rd WOOL/PLUM SE18 ...174 C1
Admiral Cl STMC/STPC BR5 ...236 B1
Admiral Ms NKENS W10 ...124 B3
Admirals Cl SWFD E18 ...92 D1
Admiral Seymour Rd ELTH/MOT SE9 ...173 H5
Admiral's Ga GNWCH SE10 ...171 F2
Admiral Sq WBPTN * SW10 ...165 E2
Admiral St DEPT SE8 ...151 E2
Admiral's Wk HAMP NW3 ...107 H1
Admirals Wy POP/IOD E14 ...151 F2
Admiralty Rd TEDD TW11 ...200 B2
Admiral Wk MV/WKIL W9 ...125 E4
Adolf St CAT SE6 ...191 E6
Adolphus Rd FSBYPK N4 ...88 B5
Adolphus St DEPT SE8 ...170 D1
Adomar Rd BCTR RM8 ...116 B1
Adpar St BAY/PAD W2 ...125 H4
Adrian Ms WBPTN SW10 ...165 F4
Adrienne Av STHL UB1 ...118 D3
Advance Rd WNWD SE27 ...188 D6
Advent Wy UED N18 ...70 B1
Adys Lawn CRICK * NW2 ...103 H4
Adys Rd PECK SE15 ...169 F4
Aerodrome Rd CDALE/KGS NW9 ...63 F3
Aerodrome Wy HEST TW5 ...136 A4
Affleck St IS * N1 ...5 H2
Afghan Rd BTSEA SW11 ...166 A3
Aftab Ter WCHPL * E1 ...9 G1
Agamemnon Rd KIL/WHAMP NW6 ...104 D3
Agar Cl SURB KT6 ...221 H6
Agar Gv CAMTN NW1 ...107 F5
Agate Cl CAN/RD E16 ...134 A3
Agate Rd HMSMTH W6 ...144 A3
Agatha Cl WAP E1W ...146 C2
Agaton Rd ELTH/MOT SE9 ...194 C4
Agave Rd CRICK NW2 ...104 A2
Agdon St FSBYE EC1V ...6 B5
Agincourt Rd HAMP NW3 ...106 B2
Agister Rd CHIG IG7 ...75 C1
Agnes Av IL IG1 ...114 A2
Agnes Cl EHAM E6 ...136 A6
Agnesfield Cl NFNCH/WDSP N12 ...66 A2
Agnes Gdns BCTR RM8 ...91 C4
Agnes Riley Gdns CLAP * SW4 ...187 E2
Agnes Rd ACT W3 ...143 F2
Agnes St POP/IOD E14 ...130 D5
Agnew Rd FSTH SE23 ...190 C2
Agricola Pl EN EN1 ...39 F6
Aidan Cl DAGW RM9 ...116 C2
Ailsa Av TWK TW1 ...160 B5
Ailsa Rd TWK TW1 ...160 D6
Ailsa St POP/IOD E14 ...131 C4
Ainger Ms HAMP NW3 ...106 B5
Ainger Rd HAMP NW3 ...106 B5
Ainsdale Cl ORP BR6 ...234 D5
Ainsdale Crs PIN HA5 ...59 H6
Ainsdale Dr STHWK SE1 ...33 H4
Ainsdale Rd EA W5 ...101 H2
OXHEY WD19 ...42 A5
Ainsley Av ROMW/RG RM7 ...75 C3
Ainsley Cl ED N9 ...53 E5
Ainslie Wood Crs CHING E4 ...71 H1
Ainslie Wood Gdns CHING E4 ...71 H1
Ainslie Wood Rd CHING E4 ...71 E1
Ainsty St BERM/RHTH * SE16 ...150 A2
Ainsworth Cl CMBW * SE5 ...169 F1
CRICK NW2 ...82 C5
Ainsworth Rd CROY/NA CR0 ...228 B5
HOM E9 ...110 D6
Ainsworth Wy STJWD NW8 ...105 H6
Aintree Av EHAM E6 ...113 G6
Aintree Crs BARK/HLT IG6 ...74 C1
Aintree Est FUL/PGN * SW6 ...165 C1
Aintree Rd GFD/PVL UB6 ...100 D1
Aintree St FUL/PGN SW6 ...165 C1
Airdrie Cl IS * N1 ...107 H5
YEAD UB4 ...118 C4
Airedale Av CHSWK W4 ...118 C4
Airedale Av South CHSWK * W4 ...143 F3
Airedale Rd BAL SW12 ...186 D3
EA W5 ...141 E3
Airlie Gdns IL IG1 ...90 C1
KENS W8 ...145 E1
Air St REGST W1B ...12 B6
Aisgill Av ECT SW5 ...144 D5
Aisher Rd THMD SE28 ...116 D6
Aislibie Rd LEW SE13 ...172 A5
Aiten Pl HMSMTH W6 ...143 H3
Aitken Cl HACK E8 ...109 G6
MTCM CR4 ...226 B6
Aitken Rd BAR EN5 ...31 H2
CAT SE6 ...191 F4
Aitman Dr CHSWK * W4 ...142 A5
Ajax Av CDALE/KGS NW9 ...63 G6
Ajax Rd KIL/WHAMP NW6 ...104 D2

Akabusi Cl SNWD SE25 ...229 H3
Akehurst St PUT/ROE SW15 ...183 G1
Akenside Rd HAMP NW3 ...105 H3
Akerman Rd CMBW SE5 ...168 B2
SURB KT6 ...220 D1
Alabama St WOOL/PLUM SE18 ...174 D1
Alacross Rd EA W5 ...141 E2
Alan Dr BAR EN5 ...48 C1
Alan Gdns ROMW/RG RM7 ...97 F4
Alan Hocken Wy SRTFD E15 ...132 A1
Alan Rd WIM/MER SW19 ...204 C1
Alanthus Cl LEE/GVPK SE12 ...192 B1
Alaska St STHWK SE1 ...17 H4
Alba Cl YEAD UB4 ...118 B3
Albacore Crs LEW SE13 ...191 F1
Alba Gdns GLDGN NW11 ...84 C3
Albany MYFR/PICC W1J ...10 A6
Albany Cl BUSH WD23 ...43 H1
BXLY DA5 ...196 A2
MORT/ESHN SW14 ...162 B5
WALTH E17 ...88 B1
Albany Cottages HNWL * W7 ...140 A1
Albany Ctyd MYFR/PICC * W1J ...10 A6
Albany Crs EDGW HA8 ...62 A3
ESH/CLAY KT10 ...238 A4
Albany Ms IS * N1 ...108 H1
KUTN/CMB * KT2 ...201 F2
SUT SM1 ...243 F3
WALW SE17 ...31 F6
Albany Pde BTFD * TW8 ...141 G6
Albany Pk PEND * EN3 ...40 A3
Albany Park Av PEND EN3 ...40 A2
Albany Park Rd KUTN/CMB KT2 ...201 F2
Albany Pl BTFD TW8 ...141 H6
HOLWY N7 ...108 A2
Albany Rd BELV DA17 ...156 D6
BTFD TW8 ...141 G6
BXLY DA5 ...196 A2
CHDH RM6 ...96 D3
CHST BR7 ...214 B1
EA W5 ...120 D5
FSBYPK N4 ...87 H4
MNPK E12 ...113 F2
NWMAL KT3 ...222 D1
UED N18 ...69 H1
WALTH E17 ...89 F2
WEA W13 ...90 D3
WIM/MER SW19 ...205 F1
Albany Rw EFNCH * N2 ...66 B3
Albany St CAMTN NW1 ...3 H5
Albany Ter RCHPK/HAM * TW10 ...161 H6
The Albany KUTN/CMB KT2 ...201 F2
Albany Vw BKHH IG9 ...56 C3
Albatross St WOOL/PLUM SE18 ...175 E1
Albemarle Ap GNTH/NBYPK IG2 ...94 B3
Albemarle Av WHTN TW2 ...172 D3
Albemarle Gdns GNTH/NBYPK IG2 ...94 B3
NWMAL KT3 ...222 D1
Albemarle Pk BECK * BR3 ...211 F4
STAN * HA7 ...61 E1
Albemarle Rd BECK BR3 ...211 F4
EBAR EN4 ...50 A2
Albemarle St CONDST W1S ...12 A6
Albemarle Wy FARR EC1M ...6 C6
Alberon Gdns GLDGN NW11 ...64 D5
Alberta Av SUT SM1 ...242 C2
Alberta Est WALW SE17 ...30 D3
Alberta Rd BXLYHN DA7 ...157 F1
EN EN1 ...53 F1
Alberta St WALW SE17 ...30 D3
VX/NE SW8 ...167 H1
Albert Av CHING E4 ...55 E6
BTSEA SW5 ...166 B1
Albert Bridge Ga BTSEA SW11 ...166 B1
Albert Carr Gdns STRHM/NOR SW16 ...207 G1
Albert Cl HOM E9 ...109 H6
WDGN N22 ...67 F4
Albert Cottages WCHPL * E1 ...17 E1
Albert Crs CHING E4 ...55 E6
Albert Dr WIM/MER SW19 ...184 C4
Albert Emb LBTH SE11 ...29 F1
Albert Gdns WCHPL E1 ...130 B5
Albert Ga KTBR SW1X ...18 D3
Albert Gv RYNPK * SW20 ...204 B4
Albert Ms BROCKY * SE4 ...170 D5
FSBYPK * N4 ...87 H5
KENS W8 ...145 F2
POP/IOD * E14 ...130 C6
Albert Pl FNCH N3 ...145 F2
KENS W8 ...145 F2
Albert Rd BCTR RM8 ...96 D5
BELMT SM2 ...243 H5
BELV DA17 ...156 D5
BKHH IG9 ...39 F4
EA W5 ...97 F3
EHAM E6 ...113 H2
ELTH/MOT SE9 ...193 G5
FSBYPK N4 ...87 F6
FBAR/BDGN N11 ...65 F2
HDN NW4 ...64 B1
HPTN TW12 ...199 G1
HSLW TW3 ...159 E5
IL IG1 ...90 C6
KIL/WHAMP NW6 ...124 D1
KUT KT1 ...201 H5
MLHL NW7 ...45 H1
MTCM CR4 ...206 D6
NWDGN UB2 ...138 B3
ORP BR6 ...253 G5
PGE/AN SE20 ...210 B6
RYLN/HDSTN HA2 ...59 H6
SEVS/STOTM N15 ...89 E3
SNWD SE25 ...225 G3
STMC/STPC BR5 ...235 H2
SWFD E18 ...92 D6
TEDD TW11 ...200 B2
TOTM N17 ...50 B6
WALTH E17 ...91 F1
WAN E11 ...92 C1
WDGN N22 ...67 F4
Albert Sq SRTFD E15 ...112 A3
VX/NE SW8 ...167 H1

Albert St CAMTN NW1 106 D6
NFNCH/WDSP N12 65 G1
Albert Ter CAMTN NW1 106 C6
EA * W5 120 D3
WLSDN * NW10 102 D6
Albert Terrace Ms CAMTN NW1 106 C6
Albert Wy PECK SE15 169 H1
Albion Av MUSWH N10 66 C4
VX/NE SW8 167 F3
Albion Cl BAY/PAD W2 10 B5
ROMW/RG RM7 97 H3
Albion Dr HACK E8 109 F5
Albion Est BERM/RHTH * SE16 150 A2
Albion Gdns HMSMTH W6 143 H4
Albion Ga BAY/PAD W2 10 B5
Albion Gv STNW/STAM N16 109 E2
Albion Ms BAY/PAD W2 10 B4
Albion Pl FARR EC1M 14 C1
HMSMTH W6 143 H4
SNWD * SE25 209 G6
Albion Rd BELMT SM2 243 H4
BXLYHS DA6 176 D5
DAGE RM10 117 E3
HSLW TW3 159 F5
KUTN/CMB KT2 202 C4
STNW/STAM N16 108 D3
TOTM N17 69 F5
WALTH E17 71 G6
WHTN TW2 180 A3
Albion Sq HACK E8 109 F5
Albion St BAY/PAD W2 10 B4
BERM/RHTH SE16 150 A2
CROY/NA CR0 228 B5
Albion Ter CHING * E4 41 F5
HACK E8 109 F5
Albion Villas Rd FSTH SE23 190 A5
Albion Wy LEW SE13 171 G5
STBT EC1A 15 E2
WBLY HA9 102 A1
Albion Yd IS N1 5 F2
Albrighton Rd CMBW SE5 169 E4
Albuhera Cl ENC/FH EN2 38 A2
Albury Av BELMT SM2 242 A6
BXLYHN DA7 176 C3
ISLW TW7 160 B1
Albury Cl HOR/WEW KT19 240 B6
HPTN TW12 199 E2
Albury Dr PIN HA5 58 A4
Albury Ms MNPK E12 93 F5
Albury Rd CHSGTN KT9 239 G3
Albury St DEPT SE8 151 E6
Albyfield BMLY BR1 213 H6
Albyn Rd DEPT SE8 171 E2
Alcester Crs CLPT E5 89 H6
Alcester Rd WLGTN SM6 244 D2
Alcock Cl WLGTN SM6 245 F5
Alcock Rd HEST TW5 158 B1
Alconbury Rd CLPT E5 89 G6
Alcorn Cl CHEAM SM3 225 E6
Alcott Cl HNWL W7 120 B4
Aldborough Rd DAGE RM10 117 G4
Aldborough Rd North
GNTH/NBYPK IG2 95 F2
Aldborough Rd South
GDMY/SEVK IG3 95 E5
Aldbourne Rd ACT W3 143 F1
Aldbridge St WALW SE17 32 B3
Aldburgh Ms MHST W1U 11 F3
Aldbury Av WBLY HA9 102 B5
Aldbury Ms WCHMH N21 52 D2
Aldebert Ter VX/NE SW8 167 H1
Aldeburgh Pl WFD IG8 56 C6
Aldeburgh St GNWCH SE10 152 C5
Alden Av SRTFD E15 132 B2
Aldenham Rd OXHEY WD19 42 B1
Aldenham St CAMTN NW1 4 B2
Alden Md PIN * HA5 59 E3
Aldensley Rd HMSMTH W6 143 H3
Alderbrook Rd BAL SW12 186 D1
Alderbury Rd BARN SW13 143 G6
Alder Cl PECK SE15 32 C6
Alder Gv CRICK NW2 83 G6
Alderholt Wy PECK * SE15 169 E1
Alderman Av BARK IG11 135 G2
Aldermanbury CITYW * EC2V 15 F3
Aldermanbury Sq CITYW EC2V 15 F2
Alderman Judge Ml KUT * KT1 201 G5
Alderman's Hl PLMGR N13 51 G6
Aldermary Rd BMLY BR1 212 C4
Aldermoor Rd CAT SE6 190 D5
Alderney Av HEST TW5 159 F1
Alderney Gdns NTHLT UB5 98 D5
Alderney Ms STHWK SE1 23 G5
Alderney Rd WCHPL E1 130 B3
Alderney St PIM SW1V 27 H3
Alder Rd MORT/ESHN SW14 162 D4
SCUP DA14 195 E5
Alders Av WFD IG8 72 A2
Aldersbrook Av EN EN1 39 E3
Aldersbrook Dr KUTN/CMB KT2 201 H2
Aldersbrook La MNPK E12 113 H1
Aldersbrook Rd MNPK E12 93 E6
Alders Cl EA W5 141 F3
EDGW HA8 62 C1
WAN E11 92 D6
Aldersey Gdns BARK IG11 114 D4
Aldersford Cl BROCKY SE4 170 B5
Aldersgate St STBT EC1A 15 E3
Aldersgrove E/WMO/HCT KT8 219 H2
Aldersgrove Av
LEE/GVPK SE12 193 E5
Aldershot Rd
KIL/WHAMP NW6 104 D6
Aldershot Ter
WOOL/PLUM * SE18 174 A1
Aldersmead Av
CROY/NA CR0 230 B3
Aldersmead Rd BECK BR3 210 C3
Alderson Pl STHL UB1 139 G1
Alderson St NKENS W10 124 C3
Alders Rd EDGW HA8 62 C1
The Alders FELT TW13 198 C1
NWDGN UB2 138 D6
STRHM/NOR * SW16 187 E6
WCHMH N21 52 A1
WWKM BR4 231 F5
Alderton Cl WLSDN NW10 82 D6
Alderton Crs HDN NW4 83 H2
Alderton Rd CROY/NA CR0 229 F4
HNHL SE24 168 C4
Alderton Wy HDN NW4 83 H2
Alderville Rd FUL/PGN SW6 164 D3
Alder Wy SWLY BR8 217 H5
Alderwick Dr HSLW TW3 159 H4
Alderwood Rd ELTH/MOT SE9 194 D1
Aldford St MYFR/PKLN W1K 19 E1
Aldgate FENCHST EC3M 16 B4
Aldgate Barrs WCHPL * E1 16 D3
Aldgate High St TWRH EC3N 16 C4
Aldine St SHB W12 144 A2
Aldington Cl CHDH RM6 96 A4
Aldington Rd
WOOL/PLUM SE18 153 F3
Aldis Ms TOOT SW17 206 A1
Aldis St TOOT SW17 206 A1
Aldred Rd KIL/WHAMP NW6 105 E3
Aldren Rd TOOT SW17 185 G5
Aldrich Crs CROY/NA CR0 249 G6
Aldriche Wy CHING E4 71 G2
Aldrich Gdns CHEAM SM3 242 D1
Aldrich Ter WAND/EARL SW18 185 G4
Aldridge Av EDGW HA8 46 B5
PEND EN3 41 E1
RSLP HA4 78 A6
STAN HA7 61 G4
Aldridge Ri NWMAL KT3 223 E4
Aldridge Road Vls
NTGHL W11 124 D4
Aldridge Wk STHGT/OAK N14 51 G2
Aldrington Rd
STRHM/NOR SW16 207 E1
Aldsworth Cl MV/WKIL W9 125 F3
Aldwick Cl CHST BR7 194 D5
Aldwick Rd CROY/NA CR0 245 H1
Aldworth Gv LEW SE13 191 G1
Aldworth Rd SRTFD E15 112 A5
Aldwych TPL/STR WC2R 13 G5
Aldwych Av BARK/HLT IG6 94 C1
Alers Rd BXLYHS DA6 176 B6
Alesia Cl WDGN N22 67 G3
Alestan Beck Rd CAN/RD E16 133 F5
Alexander Av WLSDN NW10 103 H5
Alexander Cl BFN/LL DA15 175 E6
EBAR EN4 35 H5
HAYES BR2 232 C5
STHL UB1 139 G1
WHTN TW2 180 A4
Alexander Evans Ms
FSTH SE23 190 B4
Alexander Ms BAY/PAD W2 125 F5
Alexander Pl SKENS SW7 26 A1
Alexander Rd ARCH N19 107 G1
CHST BR7 214 B2
WELL DA16 176 B3
Alexander Sq CHEL SW3 26 A1
Alexander St BAY/PAD W2 125 E5
Alexander Ter ABYW * SE2 155 H5
Alexandra Av BTSEA * SW11 166 C2
RYLN/HDSTN HA2 78 D5
STHL UB1 118 D6
SUT SM1 243 E1
WDGN N22 67 F4
Alexandra Cl RYLN/HDSTN HA2 99 E1
Alexandra Cottages
NWCR * SE14 170 D2
Alexandra Crs BMLY BR1 212 B2
Alexandra Dr BRYLDS KT5 222 A4
NRWD SE19 209 E1
Alexandra Gdns CAR SM5 244 C6
HSLW TW3 159 F3
MUSWH N10 86 D1
Alexandra Ga SKENS SW7 145 H2
Alexandra Gv FSBYPK N4 88 B5
NFNCH/WDSP N12 65 F1
Alexandra Ms EFNCH N2 66 B6
Alexandra Palace Wy
CEND/HSY/T N8 87 E1
Alexandra Pde
RYLN/HDSTN * HA2 99 F2
Alexandra Park Rd
MUSWH N10 66 D5
WDGN N22 67 E4
Alexandra Pl CROY/NA CR0 229 E5
SNWD SE25 228 D2
STJWD NW8 105 G6
Alexandra Rd BTFD * TW8 141 F6
CEND/HSY/T N8 68 A6
CHDH RM6 96 B3
CHSWK W4 142 D2
CROY/NA CR0 229 E5
ED * N9 53 H2
EHAM E6 134 A2
HDN NW4 84 B1
HSLW TW3 159 F3
KUTN/CMB KT2 202 A3
MORT/ESHN SW14 162 D4
MUSWH N10 66 D3
PEND EN3 40 B5
RCH/KEW TW9 161 H3
SEVS/STOTM N15 88 D2
STJWD NW8 105 G5
SWFD E18 72 D6
SYD SE26 210 B2
THDIT KT7 220 B2
TWK TW1 181 E1
WALTH E17 90 D3
WIM/MER SW19 206 A3
Alexandra Sq MRDN SM4 225 E2
Alexandra St CAN/RD E16 132 C4
NWCR SE14 170 C1
Alexandria Rd WEA W13 120 C6
Alexis St BERM/RHTH SE16 33 E1
Alfearn Rd CLPT E5 110 A2
Alford Gn CROY/NA CR0 249 H4
Alford Pl IS * N1 7 F2
Alford Rd ERITH DA8 157 G5
Alfoxton Av SEVS/STOTM N15 88 B1
Alfreda St BTSEA SW11 166 D2
Alfred Cl CHSWK W4 142 D4
Alfred Gdns STHL UB1 118 C6
Alfred Ms FITZ W1T 12 C1
Alfred Pl FITZ W1T 12 C1
Alfred Rd ACT W3 142 C1
BAY/PAD W2 125 E4
BELV DA17 156 D5
BKHH IG9 57 F4
FELT TW13 178 A4
FSTGT E7 112 B3
KUT KT1 201 G6
SNWD SE25 229 G2
SUT SM1 243 G3
Alfred's Gdns BARK IG11 135 E1
Alfred St BOW E3 130 D2
Alfred's Way
(East Ham & Barking By-Pass)
BARK IG11 134 D1
Alfred Vls WALTH * E17 91 G1
Alfreton Cl WIM/MER SW19 184 B5
Alfriston BRYLDS KT5 221 H3
Alfriston Av CROY/NA CR0 227 G4
RYLN/HDSTN HA2 79 E3
Alfriston Cl BRYLDS KT5 221 H3
Alfriston Rd BTSEA SW11 166 B6
Algar Cl STAN HA7 60 B1
Algar Rd ISLW TW7 160 C4
Algarve Rd WAND/EARL SW18 185 F3
Algernon Rd HDN NW4 83 G3
KIL/WHAMP NW6 105 E6
LEW SE13 171 F5
Algiers Rd LEW SE13 171 E5
Alguin Ct STAN * HA7 61 E2
Alibon Gdns DAGE RM10 117 E3
Alice La BOW E3 110 D6
Alice Ms TEDD TW11 200 B1
Alice St STHWK SE1 24 A6
Alice Thompson Cl
LEE/GVPK SE12 193 E4
Alice Walker Cl HNHL * SE24 168 B5
Alice Wy HSLW TW3 159 F5
Alicia Av KTN/HRWW/W HA3 80 D1
Alicia Cl KTN/HRWW/W HA3 81 E1
Alicia Gdns KTN/HRWW/W HA3 80 D1
Alie St WCHPL E1 16 D4
Alington Crs CDALE/KGS NW9 82 C5
Alington Gv WLGTN SM6 245 F6
Alison Cl CROY/NA CR0 230 B5
EHAM E6 134 A5
Aliwal Ms BTSEA * SW11 166 A5
Aliwal Rd BTSEA SW11 166 A5
Alkerden Rd CHSWK W4 143 E5
Alkham Rd STNW/STAM N16 89 F6
Allan Barclay Cl
STNW/STAM N16 89 F3
Allan Cl NWMAL KT3 222 D2
Allandale Av FNCH N3 64 C6
Allan Wy ACT W3 122 C4
Allard Cl STMC/STPC BR5 236 A4
Allard Crs BUSH WD23 43 G4
Allardyce St CLAP SW4 167 H5
Allbrook Cl TEDD TW11 200 A1
Allcroft Rd KTTN NW5 106 C3
Allenby Av SAND/SEL CR2 246 C6
Allenby Cl GFD/PVL UB6 119 E2
Allenby Rd FSTH SE23 190 C5
GFD/PVL UB6 119 E5
Allen Cl MTCM CR4 206 D4
Allendale Av STHL UB1 119 E5
Allendale Cl CMBW SE5 168 D3
SYD SE26 210 B1
Allendale Rd GFD/PVL UB6 100 D4
Allen Edwards Dr VX/NE SW8 167 G2
Allen Rd BECK BR3 210 B5
BOW E3 130 D1
CROY/NA CR0 227 H4
STNW/STAM N16 109 E2
Allensbury Pl HOLWY N7 107 F5
Allens Rd PEND EN3 40 A6
Allen St KENS W8 145 E3
Allenswood Rd ELTH/MOT SE9 173 G4
Allerford Rd CAT SE6 191 F6
Allerton Rd STNW/STAM N16 88 C6
Allestree Rd FUL/PGN SW6 164 C1
Alleyn Crs DUL SE21 188 D4
Alleyndale Rd BCTR RM8 96 A6
Alleyn Pk DUL SE21 188 D4
NWDGN UB2 138 D5
Alleyn Rd DUL SE21 188 D5
Allfarthing La
WAND/EARL SW18 185 G1
Allgood Cl MRDN SM4 224 B3
Allgood St BETH E2 8 D2
Allhallows La CANST EC4R 15 G6
Allhallows Rd EHAM E6 133 G5
All Hallows Rd TOTM N17 69 E4
Alliance Cl ALP/SUD HA0 101 F2
Alliance Rd ACT W3 122 B3
PLSTW E13 133 E3
WOOL/PLUM SE18 155 G6
Allied Wy ACT * W3 143 E2
Allingham Cl HNWL W7 120 B6
Allington Av TOTM N17 69 E2
Allington Cl GFD/PVL UB6 99 G5
WIM/MER SW19 204 B1
Allington Rd HDN NW4 83 H2
NKENS W10 124 C2
ORP BR6 235 E5
RYLN/HDSTN HA2 79 G2
Allington St WESTW SW1E 19 H6
Allison Cl GNWCH SE10 171 G2
Allison Gv DUL SE21 189 E3
Allison Rd ACT W3 122 C5
CEND/HSY/T N8 88 A2
Allitsen Rd STJWD NW8 2 A2
Allitson Rd STJWD NW8 2 A2
Allnutt Wy CLAP SW4 167 F6
Alloa Rd DEPT SE8 150 B5
GDMY/SEVK IG3 95 H6
Allonby Gdns WBLY HA9 81 E5
Alloway Rd BOW E3 130 C2
Allport Ms WCHPL * E1 130 A4
All Saints' Cl ED N9 53 F4
All Saints Dr BKHTH/KID SE3 172 B3
All Saints Ms
KTN/HRWW/W HA3 60 A2
All Saints Pas
WAND/EARL * SW18 165 E6
All Saints' Rd ACT W3 142 C2
NTGHL W11 124 D4
SUT SM1 243 F1
WIM/MER SW19 205 G3
All Saints St IS N1 5 G1
Allsop Pl CAMTN NW1 2 D6
All Souls' Av WLSDN NW10 123 H1
All Souls' Pl REGST W1B 11 H2
Allum Wy TRDG/WHET N20 49 G3
Allwood Cl SYD SE26 190 B6
Alma Av CHING E4 71 G3
Almack Rd CLPT E5 110 A2
Alma Cl MUSWH * N10 66 D4
Alma Ct RYLN/HDSTN * HA2 79 H6
Alma Crs SUT SM1 242 C3
Alma Gv STHWK SE1 32 D2
Alma Pl NRWD SE19 209 F3
THHTH CR7 228 A2
WLSDN NW10 123 H2
Alma Rd CAR SM5 244 A3
ESH/CLAY KT10 220 A5
MUSWH N10 66 C3
PEND EN3 40 C6
SCUP DA14 195 G5
STHL UB1 118 C6
STMC/STPC BR5 236 B6
WAND/EARL SW18 165 G6
Alma Rw KTN/HRWW/W * HA3 59 H4
Alma Sq STJWD NW8 125 G2
Alma St KTTN NW5 106 D4
SRTFD E15 111 H4
Alma Ter BOW E3 110 D6
KENS * W8 145 E3
WAND/EARL SW18 185 H2
Almeida St IS N1 108 B6
Almeric Rd BTSEA SW11 166 B5
Almer Rd RYNPK SW20 203 G3
Almington St FSBYPK * N4 87 G5
Almond Av CAR SM5 226 B6
EA W5 141 G3
Almond Cl HAYES BR2 234 A4
Almond Dr SWLY BR8 217 H6
Almond Gv BTFD TW8 160 D1
Almond Rd BERM/RHTH SE16 33 H1
TOTM N17 69 G3
Almonds Av BKHH IG9 56 C4
Almond Wy HAYES BR2 234 A4
MTCM CR4 227 F2
RYLN/HDSTN HA2 59 F5
Almorah Rd HEST TW5 158 B2
IS N1 108 D5
Almshouse La CHSGTN KT9 239 E6
Alnwick Gv MRDN SM4 225 F1
Alnwick Rd CAN/RD E16 133 E5
LEE/GVPK SE12 192 D2
Alperton La ALP/SUD HA0 121 F2
Alperton St NKENS W10 124 C3
Alphabet Gdns CAR SM5 225 H3
Alpha Cl CAMTN NW1 2 B5
Alpha Gv POP/IOD E14 151 E2
Alpha Pl CHEL SW3 26 B5
KIL/WHAMP NW6 125 E1
MRDN * SM4 224 B4
Alpha Rd BRYLDS KT5 221 H3
CHING E4 55 E5
CROY/NA CR0 229 E5
HPTN TW12 199 H1
NWCR SE14 170 D2
PEND EN3 40 C5
UED N18 69 G2
Alpha St PECK SE15 169 G3
Alphea Cl WIM/MER SW19 206 A3
Alpine Av BRYLDS KT5 222 C6
Alpine Cl CROY/NA CR0 247 E1
Alpine Copse BMLY BR1 214 A5
Alpine Gv HOM * E9 110 A5
Alpine Rd BERM/RHTH SE16 150 A4
Alpine Vw SUT SM1 244 A3
Alpine Wk BUSH WD23 44 A4
Alpine Wy EHAM E6 134 A4
Alric Av NWMAL KT3 203 E6
WLSDN NW10 102 D5
Alroy Rd FSBYPK N4 88 A4
Alsace Rd WALW SE17 32 A3
Alscot Rd BERM/RHTH SE16 24 D6
Alscot Wy STHWK SE1 32 C1
Alsike Rd BELV DA17 156 B3
Alsom Av HOR/WEW KT19 241 F2
Alston Cl THDIT KT7 220 D4
Alston Rd BAR EN5 34 C4
TOOT SW17 185 H6
UED N18 69 H1
Altair Cl UED N18 69 F2
Altash Wy ELTH/MOT SE9 193 H4
Altenburg Av WEA W13 140 D3
Altenburg Gdns BTSEA SW11 166 B5
Alt Gv WIM/MER SW19 204 D3
Altham Ct RYLN/HDSTN * HA2 59 F4
Altham Rd PIN HA5 58 C3
Althea St FUL/PGN SW6 165 F3
Althorne Gdns SWFD E18 92 B1
Althorne Wy DAGE RM10 97 E6
Althorp Cl TRDG/WHET N20 47 G2
Althorpe Rd HRW * HA1 79 G2
Althorp Rd TOOT SW17 186 B3
Altmore Av EHAM E6 113 H5
Alton Av STAN HA7 60 B3
Alton Cl BXLY DA5 196 C3
ISLW TW7 160 B3
Alton Gdns BECK BR3 211 E3
WHTN TW2 179 H2
Alton Rd CROY/NA CR0 246 A1
PUT/ROE SW15 183 G3
RCH/KEW TW9 161 G5
TOTM N17 68 D6
Alton St POP/IOD E14 131 F4
Altyre Cl BECK BR3 230 D2
Altyre Rd CROY/NA CR0 228 D6
Altyre Wy BECK BR3 230 D2
Alvanley Gdns
KIL/WHAMP NW6 105 F3
Alva Wy OXHEY WD19 42 B4
Alverstone Av EBAR EN4 49 H2
WAND/EARL SW18 185 E4
Alverstone Gdns
ELTH/MOT SE9 194 B3
Alverstone Rd CRICK NW2 104 A5
MNPK E12 114 A2
NWMAL KT3 223 F1
WBLY HA9 81 H5
Alverston Gdns SNWD SE25 229 E2
Alverton St DEPT SE8 150 D5
Alveston Av KTN/HRWW/W HA3 60 D6
Alvey St WALW SE17 32 A3
Alvia Gdns SUT SM1 243 G2
Alvington Crs HACK E8 109 F3
Alway Av HOR/WEW KT19 240 C3
Alwold Crs LEE/GVPK SE12 193 E1
Alwyn Av CHSWK W4 142 D5
Alwyn Cl BORE WD6 45 H1
CROY/NA CR0 249 F5
Alwyne La IS * N1 108 B5
Alwyne Pl IS * N1 108 C4
Alwyne Rd HNWL W7 120 A6
IS N1 108 C5
WIM/MER SW19 204 D2
Alwyne Sq IS N1 108 C4
Alwyne Vls IS N1 108 B5

Alwyn Gdns ACT W3.....122 B5
Alyn Bank CEND/HSY/T* N8.....87 F3
Alyth Gdns GLDGN NW11.....84 D3
Amalgamated Dr BTFD TW8.....140 C6
Amanda Cl CHIG IG7.....74 D2
Amanda Ms ROMW/RG RM7.....77 F2
Amar Ct WOOL/PLUM SE18.....155 F4
Amardeep Ct
 WOOL/PLUM SE18.....155 F5
Amazon St WCHPL* E1.....17 G4
Ambassador Cl HSLW TW3.....108 B6
Ambassador Gdns EHAM E6.....133 H4
Ambassador Sq POP/IOD E14.....151 E4
Amber Av WALTH E17.....70 C4
Amber Cl CRICK NW2.....84 B5
Amberley Cl ORP BR6.....253 F5
 PIN HA5.....58 D6
Amberley Gdns
 HOR/WEW KT19.....241 F2
 SYD SE26.....189 H6
Amberley Rd ABYW SE2.....156 B6
 BKHH IG9.....57 E3
 EN EN1.....53 F1
 LEY E10.....91 E4
 MV/WKIL W9.....125 E4
 PLMGR N13.....41 H4
Amberley Wy HSLWW TW4.....158 A6
 MRDN SM4.....224 D4
 ROMW/RG RM7.....97 F1
Amberside Cl ISLW TW7.....119 H1
Amber St SRTFD* E15.....111 H4
Amberwood Cl WLGTN SM6.....245 G3
Amberwood Ri NWMAL KT3.....223 E3
Amblecote Cl LEE/GVPK SE12.....192 D5
Amblecote Meadow
 LEE/GVPK SE12.....192 D5
Amblecote Rd LEE/GVPK SE12.....192 D5
Ambleside BMLY BR1.....211 H2
Ambleside Av BECK BR3.....250 C2
 STRHM/NOR SW16.....187 F6
 WOT/HER KT12.....218 A5
Ambleside Cl LEY E10.....91 F4
Ambleside Crs PEND EN3.....40 B4
Ambleside Gdns BELMT SM2.....258 A4
 REDBR IG4.....93 G1
 WBLY HA9.....81 F5
Ambleside Rd BXLYHN DA7.....177 G3
 WLSDN NW10.....105 F5
Ambrey Wy WLGTN SM6.....245 F6
Ambrook Rd BELV DA17.....157 H2
Ambrosden Av WEST SW1P.....20 B6
Ambrose Av GLDGN NW11.....84 C3
Ambrose Cl ORP BR6.....253 F1
Ambrose St BERM/RHTH SE16.....35 G1
Amelia St WALW SE17.....30 D3
Amen Cnr STP EC4M.....14 D4
Amen Ct STP EC4M.....14 D4
America Sq TWRH* EC3N.....16 C5
America St STHWK SE1.....21 F2
Amerland Rd
 WAND/EARL SW18.....184 D1
Amersham Av UED N18.....68 D2
Amersham Gv NWCR SE14.....170 D1
Amersham Rd CROY/NA CRO.....228 C3
 NWCR SE14.....170 D1
Amersham V NWCR SE14.....170 D1
Amery Gdns WLSDN NW10.....103 H6
Amery Rd HRW HA1.....80 C6
Amesbury Av
 BRXS/STRHM SW2.....187 G4
Amesbury Cl WPK KT4.....224 A5
Amesbury Dr CHING E4.....25 F4
Amesbury Rd BMLY BR1.....213 F6
 DAGW RM9.....116 B5
 FELT TW13.....178 D4

WOOL/PLUM SE18.....154 D5
Andace Park Gdns BMLY* BR1.....213 E4
Andalus Rd BRXN/ST SW9.....167 G4
Ander Cl ALP/SUD HA0.....101 F2
Anderson Cl ACT W3.....122 D5
 CHEAM SM3.....225 E5
 WCHMH N21.....37 H6
Anderson Rd HOM E9.....110 B4
 WFD IG8.....57 H5
Anderson's Pl HSLW TW3.....159 F5
Anderson Sq IS* N1.....108 B6
Anderson St CHEL SW3.....26 C5
Anderson Wy BELV DA17.....157 F2
Andover Av CAN/RD E16.....133 F5
Andover Cl CFD/PVL UB6.....119 F3
Andover Pl KIL/WHAMP NW6.....125 F1
Andover Rd HOLWY N7.....67 F6
 ORP BR6.....235 G5
 WHTN TW2.....179 H3
Andover Ter HMSMTH* W6.....143 H4
Andre St HACK E8.....109 G3
Andrew Borde St
 LSO/SEVD* WC2H.....12 D3
Andrew Cl BARK/HLT IG6.....74 D6
 DART DA1.....177 H6
Andrewes Gdns EHAM E6.....133 G5
Andrew Pl VX/NE SW8.....167 F2
Andrews Cl BKHH IG9.....57 E4
 HRW HA1.....60 D1
 STMC/STPC BR5.....216 B6
 WPK KT4.....224 B6
Andrews Rd HACK E8.....109 H6
Andrew St POP/IOD E14.....131 G5
Andrews Wk WALW SE17.....30 D6
Andwell Cl ABYW SE2.....155 H2
Anerley Gv NRWD SE19.....209 F3
Anerley Hill NRWD SE19.....209 F3
Anerley Pk PGE/AN SE20.....209 H3
Anerley Park Rd PGE/AN SE20.....209 H3
Anerley Rd NRWD SE19.....209 G3
 PGE/AN SE20.....209 H4
Anerley Station Rd
 PGE/AN SE20.....209 H4
Anerley V NRWD SE19.....209 F5
Anfield Cl BAL SW12.....188 C1
Angel Cl UED N18.....42 A3
Angel Corner Pde UED* N18.....69 G1
Angel Ct LOTH EC2R.....15 H3
Angelfield HSLW TW3.....159 G1
Angel Hill Dr SUT SM1.....243 F1
Angel Hill Dr SUT SM1.....243 F1
Angelica Dr EHAM E6.....134 A4
Angelica Gdns CROY/NA CRO.....230 B5
Angel La SRTFD E15.....111 H4
Angel Park Gdns
 BRXN/ST SW9.....168 A4
Angel Ms WCHPL E1.....17 H5
Angel Pas CANST EC4R.....15 G6
Angel Rd HRW HA1.....80 A3
 THDIT KT7.....220 C5
Angel Rd (North Circular)
 UED N18.....69 G1
Angel Sq FSBYE* EC1V.....6 C2
Angel St STBT EC1A.....15 E3
Angel Wk HMSMTH W6.....144 H4
Angerstein La BKHTH/KID SE3.....172 F1
Anglers La KTTN NW5.....106 D4
Anglers Reach SURB* KT6.....222 F1
Anglesea Av WOOL/PLUM SE18.....154 H4
Anglesea Rd KUT/HW KT1.....221 F1
 WOOL/PLUM SE18.....154 B4
Anglesey Court Rd CAR SM5.....244 C5
Anglesey Gdns CAR SM5.....244 C6
Anglesey Rd OXHEY WD19.....58 A1
 PEND EN3.....54 C5
Anglesmede Crs PIN HA5.....59 H6
Anglesmede Wy PIN HA5.....58 D6
Angles Rd STRHM/NOR SW16.....187 G6
Anglia Rd BOW E3.....130 D1
Anglo Rd BOW E3.....130 D1
Angrave Ct HACK* E8.....109 G5
Angrave Pas HACK* E8.....109 H6
Angus Dr RSLP HA4.....99 G2
Angus Gdns CDALE/KGS NW9.....62 D4
Angus Rd PLSTW E13.....133 E2
Angus St NWCR SE14.....170 C1
Anhalt Rd BTSEA SW11.....166 A1
Ankerdine Crs
 WOOL/PLUM SE18.....174 D2
Anlaby Rd TEDD TW11.....200 A3
Anley Rd HMSMTH W6.....144 A1
Anmersh Gv STAN HA7.....61 F4
Annabel Cl POP/IOD E14.....131 F5
Anna Cl HACK E8.....109 F6
Annandale Rd BFN/LL DA15.....195 E1
 CHSWK W4.....143 E4
 CROY/NA CRO.....229 G6
 GNWCH SE10.....152 B5
Anna Neagle Cl FSTGT* E7.....112 C1
Annan Wy ROM RM1.....77 H4
Anne Boleyn's Wk BELMT SM2.....242 B5
 KUTN/CMB KT2.....201 E1
Anne Case Ms NWMAL* KT3.....202 D6
Annesley Av CDALE/KGS NW9.....45 G4
Annesley Cl WLSDN NW10.....103 E1
Annesley Dr CROY/NA CRO.....248 D1
Annesley Rd BKHTH/KID SE3.....172 E2
Anne St PLSTW E13.....132 C5
Annett Cl SHB/HRWW/W HA3.....44 C6
Annette Rd HOLWY N7.....67 H2
Anne Wy BARK/HLT IG6.....74 C2
Annexe Market WCHPL* E1.....16 C1
Annie Besant Cl BOW* E3.....110 D6
Anning St SDTCH EC2A.....7 H5
Annington Rd EFNCH N2.....66 A1
Annis Rd HOM* E9.....110 C4
Ann La WBPTN SW10.....165 H1
Ann Moss Wy
 BERM/RHTH SE16.....150 A3
Ann's Cl KTBR SW1X.....18 D3
Ann St WOOL/PLUM SE18.....154 D4
Annsworthy Av THHTH CR7.....208 D6
Ansar Gdns WALTH E17.....90 C2
Ansdell Rd PECK SE15.....170 A3
Ansdell St KENS W8.....145 F3
Ansdell Ter KENS W8.....145 F3
Ansell Gv CAR SM5.....226 B5

Ansell Rd TOOT SW17.....186 A5
Anselm Cl CROY/NA CRO.....247 F1
Anselm Rd FUL/PGN SW6.....145 E6
 PIN HA5.....59 H5
Ansford Rd BMLY BR1.....211 G5
Ansleigh Pl NTGHL W11.....124 B6
Anson Rd CRICK NW2.....77 F5
 HOLWY N7.....107 E2
Anstey Rd PECK SE15.....169 G4
Anstice Cl CHSWK W4.....158 A1
Anstridge Rd ELTH/MOT SE9.....194 D1
Antelope Rd
 WOOL/PLUM SE18.....153 H3
Anthony Cl OXHEY WD19.....42 B3
Anthony Rd CFD/PVL UB6.....120 A1
 SNWD SE25.....229 G3
 WELL DA16.....175 G2
Anthony's Ct WAP E1W.....25 E1
Anthony St WCHPL* E1.....17 H3
Antill Rd BOW E3.....130 C2
 SEVS/STOTM N15.....89 G1
Antill Ter WCHPL E1.....17 H5
Antlers Hi CHING E4.....41 F6
Anton Crs SUT SM1.....243 E1
Antoneys Cl PIN HA5.....58 B5
Anton St HACK E8.....109 G3
Antrim Rd HAMP NW3.....106 H4
Antrobus Cl SUT SM1.....242 D5
Antrobus Rd CHSWK W4.....142 C4
Anvil Cl STRHM/NOR SW16.....207 E3
Apeldoorn Dr WLGTN SM6.....259 F5
Apex Cl BECK BR3.....211 F4
Apex Pde MLHL* NW7.....46 D6
Aplin Wy ISLW TW7.....160 A2
Apollo Av BMLY BR1.....212 D4
Apollo Pl WAN E11.....112 A1
 WBPTN* SW10.....165 H1
Apollo Wy WOOL/PLUM SE18.....154 D3
Apothecary St BLKFR* EC4V.....14 C4
Appach Rd BRXS/STRHM SW2.....186 B1
Apple Blossom Ct VX/NE* SW8.....167 F1
Appleby Cl CHING E4.....71 G2
 SEVS/STOTM N15.....89 G4
 WHTN TW2.....179 H4
Appleby Rd CAN/RD E16.....132 C5
 HACK E8.....109 G5
Appleby St BETH E2.....7 H1
Appledore Av BXLYHN DA7.....177 G2
Appledore Cl EDGW HA8.....62 A4
 HAYES BR2.....232 B2
 TOOT SW17.....186 B4
Appledore Crs BFN/LL DA15.....195 E5
Appleford Rd NKNS W10.....124 C3
Apple Garth BTFD TW8.....141 F4
Applegarth ESH/CLAY KT10.....238 B2
Applegarth Dr
 GNTH/NBYPK IG2.....95 F1
Applegarth Rd THMD SE28.....115 H1
 WKENS* W14.....144 B3
Apple Gv CHSGTN KT9.....239 G2
 EN EN1.....39 G4
Apple Ldg ALP/SUD* HA0.....101 E1
Apple Orch SBFY BR8.....237 F1
Apple Rd WAN E11.....112 A1
Appleton Gdns NWMAL KT3.....222 E5
Appleton Rd ELTH/MOT SE9.....173 G4
Appletree Cl PGE/AN SE20.....209 H4
Appletree Gdns EBAR EN4.....36 A5
Apple Tree Yd STJS* SW1Y.....10 A6
Applewood Cl CRICK NW2.....50 A4
Appold St SDTCH EC2A.....15 G1
Apprentice Wy CLPT E5.....109 H2
Approach La MLHL NW7.....64 C1
Approach Rd BAR EN5.....35 G5
 BETH E2.....130 C1
 E/WMO/HCT KT8.....219 G2
 RYNPK SW20.....221 E1
The Approach ACT W3.....122 D5
 EN EN1.....53 G1
 HDN NW4.....64 B2
 ORP BR6.....235 F6
Aprey Gdns HDN NW4.....64 A1
April Cl HNWL W7.....121 E1
 ORP BR6.....253 F3
April Gln FSTH SE23.....190 B5
April St STNW/STAM N16.....109 F2
Apsley Cl HRW HA1.....60 C2
Apsley Rd NWMAL KT3.....202 A5
 SNWD SE25.....229 H3
Aquarius TWK* TW1.....180 D3
Aquila St STJWD* NW8.....125 H1
Aquinas St STHWK SE1.....14 A6
Arabella Dr PUT/ROE SW15.....163 E5
Arabia Cl CHING E4.....26 A1
Arabin Rd BROCKY SE4.....171 G3
Aragon Av EW KT17.....257 F6
 THDIT KT7.....220 B2
Aragon Cl ENC/FH EN2.....23 E3
 HAYES BR2.....251 H5
 LOU IG10.....57 G1
Aragon Dr BARK/HLT IG6.....74 C2
 RSLP HA4.....79 G1
Aragon Rd KUTN/CMB KT2.....201 G1
 MRDN SM4.....224 D1
Arandora Crs CHDH RM6.....95 H4
Arbery Rd BOW E3.....130 C2
Arbor Cl BECK BR3.....211 F5
Arborfield Cl
 BRXS/STRHM SW2.....186 B1
Arbor Rd CHING E4.....55 H1
Arbroath Gn OXHEY WD19.....42 D3
Arbroath Rd ELTH/MOT SE9.....173 G4
Arbrook La ESH/CLAY KT10.....238 B2
Arbuthnot La BXLY DA5.....176 A5
Arbuthnot Rd NWCR SE14.....170 C1
Arbutus St HACK E8.....109 F6
Arcade Chambers
 ELTH/MOT* SE9.....194 A1
Arcade Pde CHSGTN* KT9.....169 B5
The Arcade ELTH/MOT* SE9.....194 A1
 LVPST* EC2M.....15 H2
 WALTH* E17.....91 E1
Arcadia Av FNCH N3.....47 E5
Arcadia Cl CAR SM5.....244 C2
Arcadian Av BXLY DA5.....196 C1

Arcadian Cl BXLY DA5.....196 C1
Arcadian Gdns WDGN N22.....68 A3
Arcadian Rd BXLY DA5.....196 C2
Arcadia St POP/IOD E14.....131 E5
Archangel St
 BERM/RHTH SE16.....150 B2
Archbishop's Pl
 BRXS/STRHM SW2.....187 H1
Archdale Ct SHB W12.....143 H1
Archdale Pl NWMAL KT3.....202 B6
Archdale Rd EDUL SE22.....169 F3
Archel Rd WKENS W14.....144 D6
Archer Cl KUTN/CMB KT2.....201 G3
Archer Rd SNWD SE25.....229 H1
 STMC/STPC BR5.....235 G3
Archers Dr PEND EN3.....40 A3
Archery Cl BAY/PAD W2.....8 C4
 KTN/HRWW/W HA3.....60 B6
Archery Rd ELTH/MOT SE9.....173 H6
The Arches CHCR* WC2N.....21 F1
 RYLN/HDSTN HA2.....79 F6
Archibald Ms MYFR/PICC W1J.....11 H1
Archibald Rd HOLWY N7.....107 F2
Arch St STHWK SE1.....23 E6
Archway Cl ARCH* N19.....87 E6
 NKNS W10.....124 B4
 WIM/MER SW19.....185 F6
 WLGTN* SM6.....245 G1
Archway Rd ARCH N19.....87 E5
 HGT N6.....66 B2
Archway St BARN SW13.....165 E4
Arcola St HACK E8.....109 F3
Arctic St KTTN NW5.....106 D3
Arcus Rd BMLY BR1.....212 A1
Ardbeg Rd HNHL SE24.....188 D1
Arden Cl BUSH WD23.....44 B2
 HRW HA1.....99 H1
Arden Court Gdns EFNCH N2.....65 H5
Arden Crs DAGW RM9.....116 B5
 POP/IOD E14.....151 E4
Arden Est IS N1.....7 G2
Arden Gv ORP BR6.....252 B2
Arden Rd FNCH N3.....46 B3
 WEA W13.....121 E6
Ardent Cl SNWD SE25.....209 E6
Ardfern Av STRHM/NOR SW16.....208 A6
Ardfillan Rd CAT SE6.....192 A1
Ardgowan Rd CAT SE6.....192 A2
Ardilaun Rd HBRY N5.....108 C2
Ardingly Cl CROY/NA CRO.....248 B1
Ardleigh Gdns CHEAM SM3.....225 E5
Ardleigh Rd IS N1.....109 E4
 WALTH E17.....70 D4
Ardleigh Ter WALTH E17.....70 D4
Ardley Cl FSTH SE23.....190 C1
 WLSDN NW10.....103 C5
Ardlui Rd WNWD SE27.....188 C4
Ardmay Gdns SURB* KT6.....221 G2
Ardmere Rd LEW SE13.....191 H1
Ardmore La BKHH IG9.....56 D5
Ardmore Pl BKHH* IG9.....56 D5
Ardoch Rd CAT SE6.....191 H4
Ardra Rd ED N9.....54 B5
Ardrossan Gdns WPK KT4.....224 C2
Ardshiel Cl PUT/ROE SW15.....164 B4
Ardwell Av BARK/HLT IG6.....94 C2
Ardwell Rd BRXS/STRHM SW2.....187 G4
Ardwick Rd CRICK NW2.....105 F2
Arena Est FSBYPK* N4.....88 B3
Argall Av LEY E10.....90 A4
Argall Wy LEY E10.....90 B5
Argenta Wy WLSDN NW10.....102 B5
Argent Ct SURB* KT6.....222 A6
Argon Ms FUL/PGN SW6.....165 E1
Argon Rd UED N18.....70 B1
Argus Cl ROMW/RG RM7.....77 F2
Argus Wy NTHLT UB5.....118 C2
Argyle Av HSLW TW3.....179 E1
Argyle Cl WEA W13.....103 G4
Argyle Cnr WEA* W13.....120 C6
Argyle Pl HMSMTH W6.....143 H4
Argyle Rd BAR EN5.....34 A5
 CAN/RD E16.....132 D5
 GFD/PVL UB6.....119 F6
 HSLW TW3.....159 F5
 IL IG1.....96 A6
 NFNCH/WDSP N12.....65 E1
 RYLN/HDSTN HA2.....79 F3
 SRTFD E15.....112 A2
 TOTM N17.....50 A5
 UED N18.....56 G6
 WCHPL E1.....130 E3
Argyle Sq STPAN WC1H.....5 F3
Argyle St CAMTN NW1.....5 E4
Argyle Wk STPAN* WC1H.....5 F4
Argyle Wy STHWK SE1.....33 F4
Argyll Av STHL UB1.....116 B1
Argyll Ct BRXS/STRHM SW2.....167 H4
Argyll Gdns EDGW HA8.....62 B5
Argyll Mansions
 WOOL/PLUM SE18.....154 C5
Argyll Rd KENS W8.....145 E2
Argyll St REGST W1B.....12 A4
Arica Rd BROCKY SE4.....171 C2
Ariel Rd KIL/WHAMP NW6.....144 A1
Ariel Wy SHB W12.....144 A1
Aristotle Rd CLAP SW4.....167 F4
Arkindale Rd CAT SE6.....191 G5
Arkley Crs WALTH* E17.....90 D2
Arkley Rd WALTH E17.....90 D2
Arklow Rd NWCR SE14.....152 A5
Arkwright Rd HAMP NW3.....105 H2
Arlesford Rd BRXN/ST SW9.....167 G4
Arlington NFNCH/WDSP N12.....49 E5
Arlington Cl BFN/LL DA15.....195 E2
 LEW* SE13.....171 H6
 SUT SM1.....225 E6
 TWK* TW1.....161 H5
Arlington Ct CAR SM5.....226 B6
Arlington Gdns CHSWK W4.....142 C5
 IL IG1.....93 H4

Attneave St FSBYW WC1X............6 A5
Atwell Rd PECK * SE15.............169 G3
Atwood Av RCH/KEW TW9 ....162 A3
Atwood Rd HMSMTH W6 ....143 H4
Aubert Pk HBRY N5..................108 A2
Aubert Rd HBRY N5.................108 B2
Aubrey Pl STJWD NW8 ....125 C1
Aubrey Rd CEND/HSY/T * N8.....87 G2
  KENS W8 ....144 D1
  WALTH E17 ....71 E6
Aubrey Wk KENS W8...............144 D1
Auburn Cl NWCR SE14............170 C1
Aubyn Hl WNWD SE27 ....188 C6
Aubyn Sq PUT/ROE SW15 ....165 G5
Auckland Cl NRWD SE19 ....209 F4
Auckland Hl WNWD SE27 ....188 C6
Auckland Ri NRWD SE19 ....209 E4
Auckland Rd BTSEA SW11 ....166 A5
  IL IG1..............................94 B5
  KUT KT1.............................221 H1
  LEY E10..............................111 F1
  NRWD SE19 ....209 F4
Aucklands Gdns NRWD SE19 ....209 E4
Auckland St LBTH SE11............29 G4
Aucuba Vls WELL * DA16.........175 H4
Audax CDALE/KGS *
Auden Pl CAMTN NW1.............106 C6
  CHEAM * SM3......................242 A2
Audleigh Pl CHIG IG7...............74 A2
Audley Cl MUSWH N10............66 D3
Audley Ct PIN HA5...................58 A5
  SWFD E18...........................52 D2
Audley Dr CAN/RD E16...........152 D1
Audley Gdns GDMY/SEVK IC5....95 F6
Audley Pl BELMT SM2.............243 F5
Audley Rd EA W5....................121 H4
  ENC/FH EN2.........................38 B3
  HDN NW4............................83 G3
  RCHPK/HAM TW10 ....161 H6
Audley Sq MYFR/PKLN * W1K....19 F1
Audrey Cl BECK BR3...............211 F3
Audrey Gdns ALP/SUD HA0......80 D6
Audrey Rd IL IG1....................114 B1
Audrey St BETH * E2..................9 E1
Audric Cl KUTN/CMB KT2.......202 A4
Augurs La PLSTW E13.............132 D2
Augusta Cl E/WMO/HCT KT8 ...198 D6
Augusta Rd WHTN TW2 ....179 G4
Augustine Rd HMSMTH W6......143 F1
  KTN/HRWW/W HA3................59 F4
  STMC/STPC BR5...................216 B6
Augustus Cl BTFD TW8...........161 F1
  SHB W12............................143 H3
Augustus Rd WIM/MER SW19..184 C3
Augustus St CAMTN NW1...........3 H2
Aultone Wy CAR SM5..............244 B1
  SUT SM1............................225 F6
Aulton Pl LBTH SE11.................30 B4
Aurelia Gdns THHTH CR7.........227 H2
Aurelia Rd CROY/NA CR0........227 G3
Auriel Av DAGE RM10.............117 H4
Auriga Ms IS N1....................108 B1
Auriol Cl HOR/WEW KT19........241 E1
Auriol Dr GFD/PVL UB6............99 H5
Auriol Park Rd WPK KT4..........211 E1
Auriol Rd WKENS W14.............144 C4
Austell Gdns MLHL NW7...........47 E5
Austen Cl THMD SE28.............155 H1
Austen Rd ERITH DA8.............177 F1
  RYLN/HDSTN HA2...................79 F6
Austin Av HAYES BR2.............233 G3
Austin Cl CAT SE6..................190 C2
Austin Friars OBST EC2N..........15 H3
Austin Friars Sq OBST * EC2N...15 H3
  STMC/STPC BR5...................235 G3
Austin St BETH E2......................8 A3
Australia Cl BFN/LL DA15.......195 F5
Australia Rd SHB W12............123 H6
Austral St LBTH SE11................30 C1
Austyn Gdns BRYLDS * KT5.....225 H1
Autumn Cl EN EN1....................39 H3
  WIM/MER SW19....................205 G2
Autumn Dr BELMT SM2............243 F6
Autumn St BOW E3.................111 E6
Avalon Cl ENC/FH EN2.............38 A3
  ORP BR6.............................236 B6
  RYNPK SW20......................204 C4
  WEA W13............................120 C3
Avard Gdns ORP BR6..............236 C2
Avarn Rd TOOT SW17.............206 B2
Avebury Pk SURB * KT6..........222 E1
Avebury Rd ORP BR6..............252 D1
  WAN E11.............................91 H5
  WIM/MER SW19...................204 D4
Avebury St IS N1....................108 D6
Aveline St LBTH SE11...............39 H3
Aveling Park Rd WALTH E17......71 E5
Avelon Rd CRW RM5................57 H2
Avenell Rd FSBYPK N4.............108 B1
Avenning Rd WAND/EARL SW18..183 E1
Avenning Ter WAND/EARL SW18..185 E1
Avenue Cl STHGT/OAK N14.......51 E1
  TEDD TW11.........................200 B3
  WCHMH * N21.......................52 D2
Avenue Crs ACT W3................142 B2
Avenue Elmers SURB KT6.......222 G1
Avenue Gdns ACT W3.............142 B2
  MORT/ESHN SW14................163 A4
  TEDD TW11.........................200 B3
Avenue Ms MUSWH N10..........66 D3
Avenue Pde WCHMH * N21......52 D2
Avenue Park Rd WNWD SE27...188 B4
Avenue Rd ACT W3.................142 B2
  BTFD TW8...........................141 E5
  BXLYHS DA6........................176 C1
  ERITH DA8..........................177 C1
  FSTGT E7............................112 D3
  GDMY/SEVK IG3...................95 H4
  HOT N6...............................66 B4
  HPTN TW12.........................199 F4
  ISLW TW7............................160 A2
  KUT KT1.............................201 G6
  NFNCH/WDSP N12................49 G6
  NWMAL KT3........................204 B2
  PGE/AN SE20.......................210 B4
  PIN HA5...............................58 C6
  RYNPK SW20.......................205 H5
  SEVS/STOTM N15.................68 D2
  SNWD SE25.........................209 C5

STHGT/OAK N14 ....51 E1
STHL UB1.............................138 D1
STRHM/NOR SW16..................207 F5
TEDD TW11..........................200 C5
WFD IG8.................................75 E2
WLGTN SM6.........................245 E5
WLSDN NW10 ....125 F1
Avenue South BRYLDS KT5......225 G1
Avenue Ter NWMAL KT3..........202 C6
  OXHEY WD19........................42 C1
The Avenue BAR EN5..............33 H5
  BECK BR3...........................211 F4
  BELMT SM2.........................242 D6
  BMLY BR1............................213 F6
  BRYLDS SW15......................221 H5
  BTSEA SW11........................166 A3
  BXLY DA5............................196 B2
  CAR SM5.............................244 C5
  CEND/HSY/T N8....................68 A6
  CHING E4..............................51 H4
  CHSWK W4..........................143 E5
  CROY/NA CR0......................247 E1
  ESH/CLAY KT10...................238 A4
  EW KT17.............................242 A5
  FBAR/BDGN N11..................268 D6
  GNWCH SE10.......................171 H1
  HPTN TW12..........................198 D2
  HSLW TW3...........................159 F6
  KIL/WHAMP NW6..................104 B6
  KTN/HRWW/W HA3.................80 B4
  LOU IG10..............................57 C1
  MUSWH N10.........................65 F6
  ORP BR6.............................235 F6
  PIN HA5................................58 D2
  PIN HA5................................78 D5
  RCH/KEW TW9.....................161 H5
  RNK RM1.............................97 H1
  STMC/STPC BR5..................215 H5
  TOTM N17..............................69 E5
  WAN E11..............................92 D3
  WBLY HA9.............................80 A4
  WEA W13............................120 D6
  WPK KT4.............................225 F6
  WWKM BR4.........................231 H4
Averil Gv STRHM/NOR SW16...208 B2
Averill St HMSMTH W6...........148 B6
Avern Gdns E/WMO/HCT KT8..219 F1
Avernons Rd PLSTW E13........132 C4
Avern Rd E/WMO/HCT * KT8...219 F1
  E/WMO/HCT KT8
Avery Farm Rw BGVA * SW1W..27 C2
Avery Gdns GNTH/NBYPK IG2...93 H2
Avery Hill Rd ELTH/MOT SE9...194 C5
Avery Rw MYFR/PKLN W1K.....113 E4
Aviary Cl CAN/RD E16.............132 B4
Aviemore Cl BECK BR3..........230 D2
Aviemore Wy BECK BR3..........230 C2
Avignon Rd BROCKY SE4.......171 G1
Avington Gv PGE/AN SE20......210 A3
Avington Wy PECK * SE15......169 F1
Avion Crs CDALE/KGS NW9.......63 C5
Avis Sq WCHPL E1..................130 E5
Avoca Rd TOOT SW17...........186 A6
Avocet Cl STHWK SE1..............33 E3
Avocet Ms THMD SE28...........154 D5
Avon Cl CUT SM1...................223 C6
  WPK KT4............................223 G6
  YEAD UB4...........................118 A3
Avon Ct PIN * HA5...................59 E3
Avondale Av CRICK NW2..........103 E1
  EBAR EN4.............................33 H6
  ESH/CLAY KT10...................238 C1
  NFNCH/WDSP N12.................65 F1
  WPK KT4.............................223 F5
Avondale Cl LOU IG10..............57 H2
Avondale Ct WFD IG8................57 H1
Avondale Crs PEND EN5...........40 C4
  REDBR IG4............................93 F2
Avondale Dr LOU IG10..............57 H1
Avondale St STHWK SE1..........33 E3
Avondale Gdns HSLWW TW4....158 D6
Avondale Ms BMLY BR1..........212 C2
Avondale Park Gdns
  NTCHL * W11........................124 C6
Avondale Park Rd NTCHL W11..124 C6
Avondale Pavement
  STHWK SE1...........................33 E4
Avondale Ri PECK SE15..........169 F4
Avondale Rd BMLY BR1..........212 A2
  CAN/RD E16.........................132 A4
  ELTH/MOT SE9.....................193 C4
  FNCH N3...............................47 G4
  KTN/HRWW/W HA3.................60 B6
  MORT/ESHN SW14................162 D4
  PLMGR N13...........................51 H2
  SAND/SEL CR2.....................246 C6
  SEVS/STOTM N15..................88 B2
  WALTH E17............................91 E4
  WELL DA16..........................176 A3
  WIM/MER SW19....................185 G5
Avondale Sq STHWK SE1...........33 E4
Avonley Rd NWCR SE14..........170 A1
Avonmore Gdns WKENS * W14..144 D4
Avonmore Rd WKENS W14.......144 C4
Avonmouth St STHWK SE1........23 E5
Avon Rd BROCKY SE4.............171 E4
  GFD/PVL UB6.......................118 C2
  WALTH E17............................72 C1
Avonstowe Cl ORP BR6...........252 C1
Avon Wy SWFD E18..................72 C6
Avonwick Rd HSLW TW3.........159 F1
Avril Wy CHING E4....................71 C1
Avro Wy WLGTN SM6.............245 G5
Awfield Av TOTM N17................68 A1
Awliscombe Rd WELL DA16.....175 F3
Axeholm Av EDGW HA8............62 A4
Axe St BARK IG11...................114 C6
Axholme Av EDGW HA8............62 A4
Axminster Crs WELL DA16......176 A2
Axminster Rd HOLWY N7..........85 E6
Axtaine Rd STMC/STPC BR5....236 B4
Aybrook St MHST W1U.............11 E2
Aycliff Ct KUT * KT1................202 A5
Aycliffe Cl BMLY BR1..............233 E1
Aycliffe Rd SHB W12..............143 F1
Aylands Cl WBLY HA9...............81 G6
Aylesbury Cl FSTGT E7...........112 B4
Aylesbury Est WALW SE17.......32 A4
Aylesbury Rd HAYES BR2.......212 C6
  WALW SE17...........................31 H4

Aylesbury St CLKNW EC1R.........6 C6
  WLSDN NW10.......................102 C1
Aylesford Av BECK BR3...........230 C2
Aylesford St PIM SW1V.............28 C4
Aylesham Cl MLHL NW7............45 E5
Aylesham Rd ORP BR6...........235 C6
Aylestone Av KIL/WHAMP NW6..106 A5
Aylett Rd ISLW TW7................160 A5
  SNWD SE25.........................210 A4
Ayley Cft EN EN1.....................39 G6
Ayliffe Cl KUT KT1..................202 A5
Aylmer Cl STAN HA7.................44 A5
Aylmer Dr STAN HA7.................44 C6
Aylmer Pde EFNCH * N2............86 B2
Aylmer Rd BCTR RM8.............116 C1
  EFNCH N2............................86 B2
  SHB W12.............................143 E2
  WAN E11...............................92 B4
Ayloffe Rd DAGW RM9.............118 B5
Aylton Est BERM/RHTH * SE16..150 A2
Aylward Rd FSTH SE23............190 D4
  RYNPK SW20........................205 F1
Aylwards Ri STAN HA7..............44 C6
Aylward St WCHPL * E1..........131 F5
Aymhoe Rd HMSMTH W6.........143 F4
Aynscombe Angle ORP BR6....235 C4
Ayres Cl PLSTW E13...............132 C2
Ayres Crs WLSDN NW10.........102 B5
Ayres St STHWK SE1.................23 F3
Ayrsome Rd STNW/STAM N16..109 E1
Ayrton Rd SKENS SW7.............145 H3
Aysgarth Rd DUL SE21............188 D1
Aytoun Pl BRXN/ST SW9..........167 H3
Aytoun Rd BRXN/ST SW9.........167 H3
Azalea Cl HNWL W7.................140 B1
  IL IG1................................114 B3
Azalea Ct WDGT * IG8.................72 A3
Azalea Dr SWLY BR8...............237 H1
Azania Ms KTTN NW5.............106 D3
Azenby Rd PECK SE15............169 F4
Azof St GNWCH SE10..............152 A4

B

Baalbec Rd HBRY N5...............108 B3
Babbacombe Cl CHSGTN KT9...239 F3
Babbacombe Gdns REDBR IG4..93 G3
Babbacombe Rd BMLY BR1.....212 D4
Baber Bridge Pde
  EBED/NFELT * TW14............178 B1
Baber Dr EBED/NFELT TW14...178 A1
Babington Ri WBLY HA9...........80 A4
Babington Rd BCTR RM8.........116 A3
  HDN NW4..............................83 H1
Babmaes St STJS SW1Y............11 C6
Bache's St IS N1.......................7 G4
Back Church La WCHPL E1.......13 G4
Back La BTFD TW8.................161 F1
  BXLY DA5...........................197 E2
  CEND/HSY/T N8.....................87 C2
  CHDH RM6............................96 C6
  EDGW HA8............................62 C4
  HAMP NW3.............................85 F2
  RCHPK/HAM TW10................181 G4
Backley Gdns SNWD SE25......229 G3
Back Rd SCUP DA14...............195 G4
  TEDD TW11..........................200 A3
Bacon Gv STHWK SE1.............19 H5
Bacon La CDALE/KGS NW9.......82 E1
  EDGW HA8............................62 A4
Bacon Link CRW RM5...............77 F2
Bacon's La HGT N6...................86 A5
Bacon St BETH E2.....................8 A3
Bacton St BETH E2..................130 A2
Baddow Cl DAGE RM10..........117 E6
  WFD IG8...............................57 H3
Baden Pl STHWK SE1...............23 G3
Baden Powell Cl DAGW RM9...136 C6
  SURB KT6...........................221 H6
Baden Rd CEND/HSY/T N8........87 F1
  IL IG1..................................114 B3
Badger Cl HSLWW TW4...........158 A4
Badgers Cl ENC/FH EN2...........38 B4
  HARH * HA1.........................79 C2
Badgers Copse ORP BR6........235 F6
  WPK KT4............................223 F6
Badgers Ct ELTH/MOT SE9.....194 A1
  TRDG/WHET N20....................48 D2
Badgers Wk NWMAL KT3........203 E5
Badlis Rd WALTH E17................71 E5
Badminton Cl HRW * HA1..........60 D4
  NTHLT UB5............................95 H4
Badminton Ms CAN/RD E16.....152 C2
Badminton Rd BAL SW12........186 C1
Badsworth Rd CMBW SE5.......168 C3
Bagley's La FUL/PGN SW6......148 B2
Bagleys Spring CHDH RM6........96 C1
Bagshot Ct WOOL/PLUM * SE18..174 A2
Bagshot Rd EN EN1...................53 F1
Bagshot St WALW SE17............32 B4
Baildon St DEPT SE8...............170 D1
Bailey Cl FSTGT E7...................67 H3
Bailey Cottages WDGN N22......67 E3
Bailey Pl SYD SE26.................210 A6
Bainbridge Cl KUTN/CMB KT2.201 G1
Bainbridge Rd DAGW RM9......116 D2
Bainbridge St NOXST/BSQ WC1A..12 D3
Baird Av STHL UB1.................120 B6
Baird Cl BUSH WD23.................43 F1
  CDALE/KGS NW9....................62 D3
  LEY E10................................91 E5
Baird Gdns NRWD SE19...........189 G3
Baird Memorial Cottages
  STHGT/OAK * N14..................51 F4
Baird Rd EN EN1.......................39 H4
Baird St STLK EC1Y....................7 F5
Baizdon Rd BKHTH/KID SE3....172 A3
Baker La MTCM CR4...............206 D1
Baker Ms ORP BR6..................253 F1
Baker Rd WLSDN NW10..........105 G6
  WOOL/PLUM SE18................173 G2
Bakers Av WALTH E17...............91 F3
Bakers End RYNPK SW20........205 D5
Bakers Gdns CAR SM5............226 A6

Bakers Hl BAR EN5...................35 E5
  CLPT E5...............................89 H5
Baker's Ms MHST W1U.............11 E3
Bakers Rents BETH E2................8 A4
Baker's Rw CLKNW EC1R...........6 A6
  SRTFD E15...........................132 A1
Baker St CAMTN NW1................2 D6
  EN EN1.................................36 B6
Bakery Cl BRXN/ST * SW9......167 H1
Bakewell Dr NWMAL KT3........203 E5
Balaams La STHGT/OAK N14.....51 F4
Balaam St PLSTW E13............132 C2
Balaclava Rd STHWK SE1..........32 D2
  SURB KT6...........................221 E4
Bala Gn CDALE/KGS * NW9......83 E3
Balcaskie Rd ELTH/MOT SE9...173 H6
Balchen Rd BKHTH/KID SE3....173 F3
Balchier Rd EDUL SE22...........189 H1
Balcombe Cl BXLYHS DA6.......176 B5
Balcombe St CAMTN NW1...........2 D6
Balcome St HOM E9.................110 A5
Balder Ri LEE/GVPK SE12........192 D4
Balderton St MYFR/PKLN W1K...11 F4
Baldock St BOW E3..................131 F1
Baldry Gdns
  STRHM/NOR SW16................207 G2
Baldwins Crs CMBW SE5.........168 C2
Baldwin Gdns HSLW TW3........159 G2
Baldwin's Gdns FSBYW WC1X...14 A1
Baldwin St FSBYE EC1V.............7 G4
Baldwin Ter IS N1.......................6 C2
Baldwins Av ACT W3...............122 C6
Baldwyn's Pk BXLY DA5..........197 H4
Baldwyn's Rd BXLY DA5..........197 H4
Bales Ter ED * N9......................53 F5
Balfern Gv CHSWK W4............144 A5
Balfern St BTSEA SW11...........166 A3
Balfe St IS N1............................5 F2
Balfour Av HNWL W7...............140 B1
Balfour Cv TRDG/WHET N20....33 G5
Balfour Ms BD N9......................53 G5
  MYFR/PKLN W1K...................19 F1
Balfour Pl MYFR/PKLN * W1K...11 F6
Balfour Rd ACT W3..................122 C1
  CAR SM5.............................244 B5
  HAYES BR2.........................233 F2
  HBRY N5.............................108 C2
  HRW HA1..............................79 H2
  HSLW TW3..........................159 F4
  IL IG1.................................94 B6
  NWDGN UB2.........................118 C3
  SNWD SE25.........................229 G1
  WEA W13............................140 B2
  WIM/MER SW19....................205 F3
Balfour St STHWK SE1...............31 G1
Balgonie Rd CHING E4...............55 H3
Balgowan Cl NWMAL KT3........223 E1
Balgowan Rd BECK BR3..........210 C6
Balgowan St
  WOOL/PLUM SE18................155 F4
Balham Gv BAL SW12.............186 C3
Balham High Rd BAL SW12.....186 D5
Balham Hill BAL SW12............186 D3
Balham New Rd BAL SW12......186 D2
Balham Park Rd TOOT SW17...186 B4
Balham Rd ED N9.......................53 C4
Balham Station Rd BAL SW12..186 D3
Balkan Wk WAP E1W.................17 C6
Balladier Wk POP/IOD E14........131 F4
Balladoran Rd BMLY BR1........192 C5
Ballamore Rd BMLY BR1.........192 D5
Ballance Rd HOM E9................110 B4
Ballantine St
  WAND/EARL SW18................184 D2
Ballard Cl KUTN/CMB KT2......202 D3
Ballards Cl DAGE RM10...........118 F6
Ballards Farm Rd
  SAND/SEL CR2.....................247 G4
Ballards La FNCH N3.................65 E1
Ballards Ri SAND/SEL CR2......247 G4
  DAGE RM10.........................118 F6
Ballards Rd CRICK NW2............83 A6
  DAGE RM10.........................118 F6
Ballast Quay GNWCH SE10......151 H5
Ballater Rd CLAP SW4.............167 G5
  SAND/SEL CR2.....................247 F3
Ballina St FSTH SE23..............191 E5
Ballingdon Rd BTSEA SW11.....186 C1
Balliol Av CHING E4...................55 H6
Balliol Rd NKENS W10.............124 A5
  TOTM N17............................68 A2
  WELL DA16..........................175 H3
Balloch Rd CAT SE6................191 H5
Ballogie Av WLSDN NW10.......103 E2
Ballow Cl CMBW * SE5............168 D1
Ball's Pond Pl IS * N1.............108 D4
Balls Pond Rd IS N1................108 D4
Balmain Cl EA W5....................141 F1
Balmer Rd BOW E3..................130 D1
Balmes Rd IS N1.....................108 D4
Balmoral Av BECK BR3...........230 C1
Balmoral Crs E/WMO/HCT KT8..198 B6
Balmoral Gdns BXLY DA5........196 D2
  HNWL W7............................140 C3
Balmoral Ms SHB W12............143 G3
Balmoral Rd CRICK NW2.........103 H4
  FSTGT E7............................113 F2
  KUT KT1..............................221 H1
  LEY E10.................................91 F1
  RYLN/HDSTN HA2..................94 A1
  WPK KT4..............................241 H1
Balmore Crs EBAR EN4.............36 C6
Balmore St KTTN NW5..............86 B3
Balmuir Gdns PUT/ROE SW15..164 A3
Balnacraig Av WLSDN NW10...103 G2
Baltic Cl WIM/MER SW19.........205 H3
Baltic Pl IS N1........................109 E6
Baltic St East STLK EC1Y............7 E6
Baltic St West FARR EC1M..........7 E6
Baltimore Pl WELL DA16..........175 F3
Balvaird Pl PIM SW1V...............31 E6
Balvernie Gv
  WAND/EARL SW18................184 D2
Bamborough Gdns SHG W12...144 A2
Bamford Av ALP/SUD HA0........102 A1
Bamford Rd BARK IG11............96 B5
  BMLY BR1............................191 F4
Bamford Wy CRW RM5..............57 E1
Bampfylde Cl WLGTN SM6.......245 E1

Bampton Dr *MLHL* NW7 ....63 G8
Bampton Rd *FSTH* SE23 ....190 B5
Banavie Gdns *BECK* BR5 ......211 F4
Banbury Cl *ENC/FH* EN2 ....38 B2
Banbury Ct *BELMT* * SM2 .....243 E5
  COVGDN * WC2E 13 E5
Banbury Rd *HOM* E9 ....110 B5
  WALTH E17 ....70 C3
Banbury St *BTSEA* * SW11....166 A8
Banchory Rd *BKHTH/KID* SE3....172 D1
Bancroft Av *ENFNCH* N2 ....86 A2
Bancroft Ct *NTHLT* UB5 ....98 A6
Bancroft Gdns
  KTN/HRWW/W HA3 ....59 G4
  ORP BR6 ....235 F5
Bancroft Rd
  KTN/HRWW/W HA3 ....59 G4
  WCHPL E1 ....130 B2
Bandon Ri *WLGTN* SM6 ....245 F4
Banfield Rd *PECK* SE15 ....169 H4
Bangalore St *PUT/ROE* SW15...164 A4
Bangor Cl *NTHLT* UB5 ....78 D3
Banim St *HMSMTH* W6 ....118 H3
Banister Rd *WLSDN* NW10 ...124 B2
Bank Av *MTCM* CR4 ....205 H5
Bank Buildings *CHING* * E4......51 J5
Bank End *STHWK* SE1 ....23 F1
Bankfoot Rd *BMLY* BR1 ....192 A6
Bankhurst Rd *CAT* SE6 ....190 D2
Bank La *KUTN/CMB* KT2 ....200 J1
  PUT/ROE SW15 ....165 E6
Banksia Rd *UED* N18 ....70 A1
Bankside *ENC/FH* EN2 ....38 B2
  SAND/SEL CR2 ....247 F4
  STHL UB1 ....138 B1
  STHWK SE1 ....15 E6
Bankside Cl *CAR* SM5 ....244 A3
  ISLW TW7 ....160 D5
  RDART DA2 ....197 H6
Bankside Rd *IL* IG1 ....114 C3
Banks La *BXLYHS* DA6 ....176 D5
The Bank *HGT* N6 ....86 D5
Bankton Rd *BRXS/STRHM* SW2...168 A5
Bankwell Rd *LEW* SE13 ....172 A5
Bank Willow
  RCHPK/HAM TW10 ....180 D5
Banner St *STLK* EC1Y 7 F6
Banning St *GNWCH* SE10 ....152 A5
Bannister Cl *BRXS/STRHM* SW2....188 A3
  NTHLT UB5 ....99 H3
Bannister Gdns
  STMC/STPC BR5 ....216 A6
Bannockburn Rd
  WOOL/PLUM SE18 ....155 E4
Banstead Gdns *ED* N9 ....52 D5
Banstead Rd *BELMT* SM2 .....243 H5
  CAR SM5 ....244 A4
Banstead St *PECK* SE15 ......170 A4
Banstead Wy *WLGTN* SM6 ...245 G3
Banstock Rd *EDGW* HA8 ....42 D5
Banting Dr *WCHMH* N21 ....37 H6
Banton Cl *EN* E11 ....39 F4
Bantry St *CMBW* SE5 ....168 D1
Banwell Rd *BXLY* DA5 ....196 B1
Banyard Rd *BERM/RHTH* SE16...79 H6
Bapchild Pl *STMC/STPC* BR5...236 A1
Baptist Gdns *HAMP* NW3 .....106 A4
Barandon Wk *NTGHL* * W11....124 B6
Barbauld Rd *STNW/STAM* N16...109 E1
Barbara Cl *CHIG* IG7 ....52 A2
Barbers Rd *SRTFD* E15 ....131 F1
Barbican Barb *BARB* EC2Y 12 C1
Barbican Rd *GFD/PVL* UB6 ...119 F5
Barb Ms *HMSMTH* W6 ....144 A3
Barbon Cl *BMSBY* WC1N 11 F1
Barbot Cl *ED* N9 ....53 F5
Barchard St *WAND/EARL* SW18...165 F6
Barchester Cl *HNWL* W7 ....140 B1
Barchester Rd
  KTN/HRWW/W HA3 ....59 H4
Barchester St *POP/IOD* E14...131 F4
Barclay Cl *FUL/PGN* * SW6 ...165 E1
  PLSTW E13 ....133 E3
  UED N18 ....68 D2
  WALTH E17 ....91 H2
  WAT E11 ....92 B5
Barcombe Av
  BRXS/STRHM SW2............187 G4
Barcombe Cl *CHST* BR7 ....215 G6
Barden St *WOOL/PLUM* SE18...115 K6
Bardfield Av *CHDH* RM6 ....76 B6
Bardney Rd *MRDN* SM4 ....225 F1
Bardolph Av *CROY/NA* CR0 ...268 A4
Bardolph Rd *HOLWY* N7 ....107 G2
  RCH/KEW TW9 ....161 H5
Bard Rd *NKENS* W10 ....124 B6
Bardsey Pl *WCHPL* E1 ....108 C4
Bardsey Wk *IS* * N1 ....108 C4
Bardsley Cl *CROY/NA* CR0 ....247 F1
Bardsley La *GNWCH* SE10 ....151 F6
Barfett St *NKENS* W10 ....130 D3
Barfield Av *TRDG/WHET* N20...50 B4
Barfield Rd *BMLY* BR1 ....214 A6
  WAN * E11 ....92 B5
Barford Cl *HDN* NW4 ....63 G5
Barford St *IS* N1 ....108 A6
Barforth Rd *PECK* SE15 ....169 H4
Barfreston Wy *PGE/AN* SE20....209 H4
Bargate Cl *NWMAL* KT3 ....223 G4
  WOOL/PLUM SE18 ....155 F5
Barge House Rd *CAN/RD* E16...154 B2
Barge House St *STHWK* SE1....22 B1
Bargery Rd *CAT* SE6 ....191 F3
Barge Wk *KUT* KT1 ....201 F5
Bargrove Cl *PGE/AN* SE20 ...209 G3
Bargrove Crs *CAT* SE6 ....190 D4
Barham Cl *ALP/SUD* HA0 ......100 E4
  CHST BR7 ....214 B1
  HAYES BR2 ....233 G5
  ROMW/RG RM7 ....77 F5
  RYNPK SW20 ....203 G3
Barham Ri *LEE/GVPK* SE12 ...192 C4
Baring Rd *BMLY* BR1 ....192 D6

  CROY/NA CR0 ....229 G5
  EBAR EN4 ....35 H4
Baring St *IS* N1 ....108 D6
Barker Cl *KUT* KT1 ....222 E4
Barker Dr *CAMTN* NW1 ....107 E5
Barkham Rd *TOTM* N17 ....67 J6
Bark Hart Rd *ORP* BR6 ....235 H5
Barking Rd *EHAM* E6 ....115 H6
  POP/IOD E14 ....132 A5
Bark Pl *BAY/PAD* W2 ....125 F6
Barkston Gdns *ECT* SW5 ......14 B5
Barkwood Cl *ROMW/RG* RM7...97 G2
Barkworth Rd
  BERM/RHTH SE16 ....111 J4
Barlborough St *NWCR* SE14...170 B1
Barlby Gdns *NKENS* W10 .....124 B3
Barlby Rd *NKENS* W10 ....124 A4
Barley La *GDMY/SEVK* IG3 .....95 E2
Barley Mow Pas *CHSWK* W4....142 D5
Barlow Cl *WLGTN* SM6 ....245 G4
Barlow Pl *MYFR/PICC* W1J 11 H6
Barlow Rd *ACT* W3 ....118 A6
  CRICK NW2 ....104 D4
  HPTN TW12 ....199 E3
Barlow St *WALW* SE17 ....31 H1
Barlow Wy *DAGW* RM9 ....137 H5
Barmeston Rd *CAT* SE6 ....191 F4
Barmor Cl *RYLN/HDSTN* HA2...59 F5
Barmouth Av *GFD/PVL* UB6...120 B1
Barmouth Rd *CROY/NA* CR0...250 B1
  WAND/EARL SW18 ....185 C1
Barnabas Rd *HOM* E9 ....111 F4
Barnaby Cl *RYLN/HDSTN* HA2...79 C6
Barnaby Pl *SKENS* SW7 ....165 H8
Barnard Cl *CHST* BR7 ....214 D4
  WLGTN SM6 ....245 F5
Barnard Gdns *NWMAL* KT3...223 C1
Barnard Hi *MUSWH* N10 ....66 D5
Barnard Ms *BTSEA* SW11 .....166 A5
Barnardo Dr *BARK/HLT* IG6 .....94 C1
Barnardo Gdns *WCHPL* * E1...130 B5
Barnardo St *WCHPL* E1 ....130 B5
Barnard St *BTSEA* SW11 ......166 A5
  EN EN1 ....39 H3
  MTCM CR4 ....206 C6
Barnards Pl *SAND/SEL* CR2...246 B6
Barnby St *CAMTN* NW1 ....4 B4
  SRTFD E15 ....112 A6
Barn Cl *KTTN* * NW5 ....107 F3
  NTHLT UB5 ....95 G1
Barn Crs *STAN* HA7 ....61 J2
Barnehurst Av *BXLYHN* DA7...177 G2
Barnehurst Cl *ERITH* DA8 .....177 G2
Barnehurst Rd *BXLYHN* DA7...177 G2
Barnes Av *BARN* SW13 ....165 G1
  NWDGN UB2 ....138 D4
Barnes Br *CHSWK* W4 ....163 E3
Barnes Cl *MNPK* E12 ....113 F2
Barnesdale Crs
  STMC/STPC BR5 ....235 G5
Barnes End *NWMAL* KT3 ......223 G2
Barnes High St *BARN* SW13 ...163 F3
Barnes Rd *IL* IG1 ....114 C3
  UED N18 ....54 A6
Barnes St *POP/IOD* E14 ....130 C5
Barnes Ter *DEPT* SE8 ....150 D5
Barnet Dr *HAYES* BR2 ....233 G6
Barnet Gate La *BAR* EN5 ....24 F1
Barnet Gv *BETH* E2 ....96 E2
Barnet Hl *BAR* EN5 ....34 D5
Barnet La *BORE* WD6 ....45 H1
  TRDG/WHET N20 ....48 D5
Barnet Rd *MLHL* NW7 ....46 D2
Barnetts Ct *RYLN/HDSTN* * HA2...99 F1
Barnett St *WCHPL* * E1 ....17 C3
Barnet Wy (Barnet By-Pass)
  MLHL NW7 ....46 D2
Barnet Wood Rd *HAYES* * BR2...250 D1
Barney Cl *CHARL* SE7 ....153 E5
Barn Fld *HAMP* * NW3 ....106 B3
Barnfield *NWMAL* KT3 ....223 E3
Barnfield Av *CROY/NA* CR0...249 J2
  KUTN/CMB KT2 ....181 F6
  MTCM CR4 ....206 C3
Barnfield Cl *SWLY* BR8 ....218 E5
Barnfield Gdns *KUTN/CMB* KT2...201 G1
  WOOL/PLUM * SE18 ....115 G6
Barnfield Rd *BELV* DA17 ....156 D6
  EA W5 ....121 E3
  EDGW HA8 ....44 E5
  SAND/SEL CR2 ....247 E6
  STMC/STPC BR5 ....216 B6
  WOOL/PLUM SE18 ....115 H6
Barnfield Wood Cl *BECK* BR3...231 H3
Barnfield Wood Rd *BECK* BR3...231 H3
Barnham Rd *GFD/PVL* UB6...119 G2
Barnham St *STHWK* SE1 ....24 B3
Barnhill *PIN* HA5 ....78 A2
Barn Hl *WBLY* HA9 ....80 D2
Barnhill Av *HAYES* BR2 ....232 C2
Barnhill Rd *WBLY* HA9 ....102 E1
Barnhurst Pth *OXHEY* WD19...33 H1
Barningham
  CDALE/KGS NW9 ....82 C5
Barnlea Cl *FELT* TW13 ....158 D1
Barnmead Gdns *DAGW* RM9...116 D5
Barnmead Rd *BECK* BR3 ......151 F4
  DAGW RM9 ....116 D5
Barn Ri *WBLY* HA9 ....80 D2
Barnsbury Cl *NWMAL* KT3 ....222 C1
Barnsbury Crs *BRYLDS* KT5...222 B6
Barnsbury Est *IS* * N1 ....107 H6
Barnsbury Gv *HOLWY* N7 .....107 H5
Barnsbury La *BRYLDS* KT5 ...222 B6
Barnsbury Pk *IS* N1 ....108 A5
Barnsbury Rd *IS* N1 ....5 K1
Barnsbury Sq *IS* N1 ....108 A5
Barnsbury St *IS* N1 ....108 A5
Barnsbury Ter *IS* N1 ....108 A5
Barnscroft *RYNPK* SW20 ......203 H6
Barnsdale Av *POP/IOD* E14 ...151 F4
Barnsdale Rd *MV/WKIL* W9 ...124 D3
Barnsley St *WCHPL* E1 ....9 J5
Barnstaple La *LEW* SE13 ......171 C5
Barnstaple Rd *RSLP* HA4 ....98 A1
Barn St *STNW/STAM* N16 ....99 B6
Barn Wy *WBLY* HA9 ....80 A5
Barnwell Rd *BRXS/STRHM* SW2...138 A6
Barnwood Cl *MV/WKIL* W9 ...125 H3
Baron Cl *FBAR/BDGN* N11 ......66 C1

Baroness Rd *BETH* E2 ....8 D5
Baronet Gv *TOTM* N17 ....69 G4
Baronet Rd *TOTM* N17 ....69 G4
Baron Gdns *BARK/HLT* IG6 .....74 C6
Baron Gv *MTCM* CR4 ....226 A1
Baron Rd *BCTR* RM8 ....96 B5
Baron CI *IS* * N1 ....6 A1
Baron's Court Rd *HMSMTH* W6...144 C5
  WKENS * W14 ....144 C5
Baronsfield Rd *TWK* * TW1 ....180 D1
Barons Ga *EBAR* EN4 ....50 A1
Barons Keep *WKENS* * W14 ...144 C5
Barons Md *HRW* HA1 ....80 A1
Baronsmead Rd *BARN* SW13...163 G2
Baronsmede *EA* W5 ....141 H2
Baronsmere Rd *EFNCH* N2 .....86 A1
Baron's Pl *STHWK* SE1 ....22 B4
The Barons *TWK* TW1 ....180 D1
Baron St *IS* N1 ....6 A2
Baron's Wk *CROY/NA* CR0 ....230 C3
Barque Ms *DEPT* SE8 ....151 E6
Barrack Rd *HSLWW* TW4 ......158 B5
Barratt Av *WDGN* N22 ....67 H5
Barratt Wy *KTN/HRWW/W* HA3...60 D3
Barrenger Rd *MUSWH* N10 .....66 A4
Barrett Rd *WALTH* E17 ....91 G1
Barrett's Green Rd
  WLSDN NW10 ....122 C1
Barrett's Ov *STNW/STAM* N16...109 E3
Barrett St *MBLAR* W1H 11 F4
Barrhill Rd *BRXS/STRHM* SW2...187 G4
Barriedale *NWCR* SE14 ....170 C2
Barrier Point Rd *CAN/RD* E16...153 E1
Barringer Sq *TOOT* SW17 ......186 C6
Barrington Cl *CLAY* IG5 ....73 H4
  KTTN NW5 ....106 C3
Barrington Rd *BRXN/ST* SW9...168 B4
  CEND/HSY/T N8 ....87 F2
  CHEAM SM3 ....225 E5
  MNPK E12 ....114 A4
  WELL DA16 ....136 B3
Barrington Vis
  WOOL/PLUM SE18 ....174 A2
Barrington Wk *NRWD* * SE19...209 E2
Barrow Av *CAR* SM5 ....243 J6
Barrow Cl *WCHMH* N21 ....52 B5
Barrowdene Cl *PIN* HA5 ....58 C5
Barrowell Gn *WCHMH* N21 .....52 B4
Barrowfield Cl *ED* N9 ....53 H5
Barrowgate Rd *CHSWK* W4 ...142 C5
Barrow Hedges Cl *CAR* SM5...244 A5
Barrow Hedges Wy *CAR* SM5...244 A5
Barrow Hill *WPK* KT4 ....223 E6
Barrow Hill Cl *WPK* KT4 ....223 E6
Barrow Hill Rd *STJWD* NW8 .....2 A2
Barrow Point Av *PIN* HA5 ....58 C5
Barrow Point La *PIN* HA5 ....58 C5
Barrow Rd *CROY/NA* CR0 .....246 A3
  STRHM/NOR SW16 ....207 F2
Barrs Rd *WLSDN* NW10 ....102 D5
Barrett Rd *BXLYHN* DA7 ....176 C5
  SEVS/STOTM N15 ....89 F3
Barry Cl *ORP* BR6 ....253 E1
Barry Pde *EDUL* * SE22 ....169 G5
Barry Rd *EDUL* SE22 ....169 E1
  EHAM E6 ....135 G5
  WLSDN NW10 ....102 C5
Barset Rd *PECK* SE15 ....170 A4
Barsons Cl *PGE/AN* SE20 .....210 A5
Barston Rd *WNWD* SE27 ......188 D3
Barstow Crs *BRXS/STRHM* SW2...187 H5
Barter St *NOXST/BSQ* WC1A...13 F2
Bartett Cl *POP/IOD* E14 ....131 E5
Barth Rd *WOOL/PLUM* SE18...115 K3
Bartholomew Cl *DBST* EC2N...15 H4
Bartholomew La *KTTN* NW5...107 E4
Bartholomew Sq *FSBYE* EC1Y...7 F5
Bartholomew Vis *KTTN* NW5...23 H6
Bartholomew Vis *KTTN* NW5...107 E4
Bartle Av *EHAM* E6 ....133 C1
Bartle Rd *NTGHL* W11 ....124 B5
Bartlett Cl *POP/IOD* E14 ....131 E5
Bartlett Ct *FLST/FETLN* * EC4A...14 B3
Bartlett St *SAND/SEL* SE2 .....246 D3
Bartlow Gdns *CRW* RM5 ....57 E1
Barton Av * RAIN* RM13 ....137 H3
Barton Cl *BXLYHS* DA6 ....176 C5
  HDN NW4 ....63 G2
Barton Gn *NWMAL* KT3 ....202 D5
  PLSTW E13 ....115 E6
Barton Mdw *BARK/HLT* IG6 .....94 B1
Barton Rd *SCUP* DA14 ....216 C2
  WKENS W14 ....144 C5
The Bartons *BORE* * WD6 ....44 A5
Barton St *WEST* SW1P 21 E6
Bartram Rd *BROCKY* SE4 ......170 C6
Bartrams La *EBAR* EN4 ....35 G1
Bartrip St *HOM* E9 ....111 H5
Barts Cl *BECK* BR3 ....231 E2
Barwark Cl *WOOL/PLUM* SE18...154 A4
Barwell Ct *CHSGTN* * KT9 ......239 E5
Barwick Rd *FSTGT* E7 ....112 D1
Barwood Av *WWKM* BR4 ......231 F5
Basden Gv *FELT* TW13 ....179 K4
Basedale Rd *DAGW* RM9 .....115 H5
Baseing Cl *EHAM* E6 ....136 A3
Basevi Wy *DEPT* SE8 ....151 E6
Bashley Rd *WLSDN* NW10 ....122 D3
Basil Av *EHAM* E6 ....133 G2
Basildene Rd *HSLWW* TW4 ...158 A5
Basildon Av *CLAY* IG5 ....54 A4
Basildon Cl *BELMT* SM2 ....243 F6
Basildon Rd *ABYW* SE2 ....155 G4
Basil Gdns *CROY/NA* CR0 .....198 D7
  WNWD SE27 ....208 C1
Basilon Rd *BXLYHN* DA7 ......176 C3
Basil St *CHEL* SW3 ....18 D4
Basin Ap *POP/IOD* E14 ....130 C5
Basing Cl *THDIT* KT7 ....220 B6
Basingdon Wy *CMBW* SE5 ...168 D5
Basing Dr *BXLY* DA5 ....196 D1
Basingfield Rd *THDIT* KT7 .....220 B6
Basinghall Av *CITYW* EC2V 15 G3
Basinghall St *CITYW* EC2V 15 G3
Basing Hill *GLDGN* NW11 ....84 D5
  WBLY HA9 ....81 H6
Basing Pl *BETH* E2 ....8 B5

Basing St *NTGHL* W11 ....124 D5
Basing Wy *FNCH* N3 ....65 E6
  THDIT KT7 ....220 B6
Basire St *IS* N1 ....108 C6
Baskerville Gdns *WLSDN* NW10...103 E3
Baskerville Rd
  WAND/EARL SW18 ....186 A2
Basket Gdns *ELTH/MOT* SE9...173 G6
Baslow Cl *KTN/HRWW/W* HA3...59 H4
Baslow Wk *CLPT* E5 ....110 B2
Basnett Rd *BTSEA* * SW11 ....166 A1
Bassano St *EDUL* SE22 ....169 F6
Bassant Rd *WOOL/PLUM* SE18...155 K6
Bassein Park Rd *SHB* W12 .....143 F2
Bassett Cl *BELMT* SM2 ....243 E6
Bassett Gdns *ISLW* TW7 ....159 G5
Bassett Rd *NKENS* W10 ....124 B5
Bassetts Cl *ORP* BR6 ....253 B2
Bassett St *KTTN* NW5 ....106 C4
Bassetts Wy *ORP* BR6 ....252 B2
Bassingham Rd *ALP/SUD* HA0...101 H4
  WAND/EARL SW18 ....185 G2
Basswood Cl *PECK* SE15 ......169 H4
Bastable Av *BARK* IG11 ....116 E1
Baston Rd *HAYES* BR2 ....232 D6
Batavia Rd *NWCR* SE14 ....170 C1
Batchelor St *IS* N1 ....6 B1
Batchwood Gn
  STMC/STPC BR5 ....235 G1
Bateman Cl *BARK* IG11 ....114 C4
Bateman Rd *CHING* * E4 ....71 E2
Bateman's Crs *CHSWK* * W4...142 D4
Bateman's Rw *SDTCH* EC2A 8 B5
Bates Crs *CROY/NA* CR0 ....246 A3
  STRHM/NOR SW16 ....207 E3
Bate St *POP/IOD* E14 ....130 B6
Bath Cl *PECK* SE15 ....169 H6
Bathgate Rd *WIM/MER* SW19...184 B5
Bath Gv *BETH* E2 ....8 E2
Bath House Rd *CROY/NA* CR0...227 G5
Bath Pas *KUT* KT1 ....223 E4
Bath Pl *IS* N1 ....8 B2
Bath Rd *CHSWK* W4 ....143 E4
  ED N9 ....53 E1
  FSTGT E7 ....113 H4
Baths Ap *FUL/PGN* * SW6 .....164 D1
Bath St *FSBYE* EC1V 7 F4
Bath Ter *STHWK* SE1 ....23 F4
Bathurst Av *WIM/MER* SW19...205 H4
Bathurst Gdns *WLSDN* NW10...123 H1
Bathurst Ms *BAY/PAD* W2 .....125 H6
Bathurst Rd *IL* IG1 ....94 B5
Bathurst St *BAY/PAD* W2 ......125 H6
Batley Cl *MTCM* CR4 ....226 B4
Batley Pl *STNW/STAM* N16 ...109 F1
Batley Rd *STNW/STAM* N16 ...109 F1
  EN EN1 ....24 C1
Batman Cl *SHB* W12 ....118 E1
Batoum Gdns *HMSMTH* W6...144 A3
Batson St *SHB* W12 ....143 G2
Batsworth Rd *MTCM* CR4 .....205 H6
Batten Cottages
  POP/IOD * E14 ....130 C4
Batten St *BTSEA* SW11 ....166 A1
Battenberg Wk *SNWD* SE25...191 H4
Battersea Br *BTSEA* SW11 ....165 H1
Battersea Bridge Rd
  BTSEA SW11 ....165 H1
Battersea Church Rd
  BTSEA SW11 ....165 H2
Battersea High St *BTSEA* SW11...165 H2
Battersea Park Rd
  BTSEA SW11 ....166 C2
  BTSEA SW11 ....166 A1
Battersea Ri *BTSEA* SW11 ....166 A1
Battersea Sq *BTSEA* * SW11 ...166 A1
Battery Rd *THMD* SE28 ....115 J2
Battishill St *IS* N1 ....108 B5
Battle Bridge La *STHWK* SE1...19 H2
Battle Bridge Rd *CAMTN* NW1...5 E2
Battle Cl *WIM/MER* SW19 .....205 G2
Battledean Rd *HBRY* N5 ....108 B3
Battle Rd *ERITH* DA8 ....157 G4
Batty St *WCHPL* E1 ....17 J3
Baudwin Rd *CAT* SE6 ....192 A4
Baugh Rd *SCUP* DA14 ....216 A1
The Bauk *WAND/EARL* SW18...185 E1
Bavant Rd *STRHM/NOR* SW16...207 E5
Bavaria Rd *ARCH* N19 ....87 E6
Bavent Rd *CMBW* SE5 ....168 D4
Bawdale Rd *EDUL* SE22 ....169 G3
Bawdsey Av *GNTH/NBYPK* IG2...95 F1
Bawtree Rd *NWCR* SE14 ....151 C5
Bawtry Rd *TRDG/WHET* N20...50 C1
Baxendale *TRDG/WHET* N20...49 G3
Baxendale St *BETH* E2 ....8 B4
Baxter Cl *NWDGN* UB2 ....139 F3
Baxter Rd *CAN/RD* E16 ....116 B6
  IL IG1 ....114 B3
  UED N18 ....55 H2
Bay Ct *EA* * W5 ....141 J3
Baycroft Cl *PIN* * HA5 ....58 G6
Bayfield Rd *ELTH/MOT* SE9...173 F5
Bayford Ms *HACK* * E8 ....106 E5
Bayford Rd *WLSDN* NW10 ....124 B1
Bayford St *HACK* E8 ....108 H1
Bayham Pl *CAMTN* NW1 ....4 B1
Bayham Rd *CHSWK* W4 ....142 D3
  MRDN SM4 ....225 F1
Bayleaf Cl *HPTN* TW12 ....199 H1
Bayley St *FITZ* W1T 12 C2
Bayley St *RSTHWK* SE1 ....23 J2
Bayliss Av *THMD* SE28 ....115 K6
Bayliss Cl *STHGT/OAK* N14 .....37 G5
Baynes Cl *EN* EN1 ....24 D3
Baynes St *CAMTN* NW1 ....107 E5
Baynes Ms *HAMP* NW3 ....105 H4
Baynham Cl *CAMTN* NW1 ....4 D5
Baynham Rd *BXLY* DA5 ....196 D5
  MRDN SM4 ....225 F1
Baynham Cl *BXLY* DA5 ....196 D4
Bays Cl *SYD* SE26 ....210 A1
Bayston Rd *STNW/STAM* N16...109 F1
Bayswater Rd *BAY/PAD* W2 ...125 J5
Baythorne St *BOW* E3 ....130 D4

Baytree Cl BFN/LL DA15 ....195 F3
BMLY BR1 ....213 F4
Baytree Rd BRXS/STRHM SW2...167 H5
Bazalgette Cl NWMAL KT3 ....222 D2
Bazalgette Gdns NWMAL KT3 ...222 D2
Bazely St POP/IOD E14 ....131 G6
Bazile Rd WCHMH N21 ....52 A1
Beacham Cl CHARL SE7 ....153 F6
Beachborough Rd BMLY BR1 ...191 G6
Beachcroft Rd WAN E11 ....112 A1
Beach Gv FELT TW13 ....179 E5
Beachy Rd BOW E3 ....111 E5
Beacon Hi HOLWY N7 ....107 G3
Beacon Pl CROY/NA CRO 245 G1
Beacon Rd LEW SE13 ....191 H1
Beaconsfield Cl
  BKHTH/KID SE3 ....152 C6
  CHSWK W4 ....142 C5
Beaconsfield Cottages
  TRDG/WHET * N20 ....49 E5
Beaconsfield Rd
  BKHTH/KID SE3 ....152 C6
  BMLY BR1 ....213 F6
  BRYLDS KT5 ....221 H4
  CAN/RD E16 ....132 B5
  CHSWK W4 ....142 D3
  CROY/NA CRO 228 D3
  EA W5 ....141 E2
  ELTH/MOT SE9 ....193 G5
  ESH/CLAY KT10 ....238 A5
  HYS/HAR UB3 ....138 A1
  LEY * E10 ....111 G1
  NWMAL KT3 ....202 D5
  SEVS/STOTM N15 ....89 E1
  TRDG/WHET N20 ....50 B5
  TWK TW1 ....180 D2
  WALTH E17 ....90 D3
  WALW SE17 ....31 H5
  WLSDN NW10 ....103 H1
Beaconsfield Terrace Rd
  WKENS W14 ....144 C3
Beaconsfield Wk
  FUL/PGN SW6 ....164 D2
Beacontree Av WALTH E17 ....71 H4
Beacontree Rd WAN E11 ....92 B4
Beadlow Cl MRDN SM4 ....225 H3
Beadman Pl WNWD SE27 ....188 B6
Beadman St WNWD SE27 ....188 B6
Beadnell Rd FSTH SE23 ....190 B3
Beadon Rd HAYES BR2 ....232 C1
  HMSMTH W6 ....144 A4
Beaford Gv RYNPK SW20 ....204 C6
Beagles Cl STMC/STPC BR5...236 A4
Beak St REGST W1B 12 A5
Beal Cl WELL DA16 ....175 G2
Beale Cl PLMGR N13 ....68 B1
Beale Pl BOW E3 ....130 D1
Beale Rd BOW E3 ....110 D6
Beal Rd IL IG1 ....46 A6
Beam Av DAGE RM10 ....117 H5
Beaminster Gdns BARK/HLT IG6...74 B6
Beamish Dr BUSH WD23 ....43 C3
Beamish Rd ED N9 ....42 D4
  STMC/STPC BR5 ....236 A4
Beamway DAGE RM10 ....117 H5
Beanacre Cl HOM E9 ....113 H4
Beanshaw ELTH/MOT SE9 ....194 A6
Beansland Gv CHDH RM6 ....76 C5
Bear Cl ROMW/RG RM7 ....75 F3
Beardell St NRWD SE19 ....209 F2
Beardow Gv STHGT/OAK * N14 ..51 E1
Beard Rd RCHPK/HAM TW10 ...201 H1
Beardsfield PLSTW E13 ....112 C6
Beard's Hi HPTN TW12 ....199 E3
Beards Hill Cl HPTN TW12 ....199 E4
Beardsley Wy ACT W3 ....142 D2
Bearfield Rd KUTN/CMB KT2 ...201 G3
Bear Gdns STHWK SE1 ....23 E1
Bear La STHWK SE1 ....22 D1
Bear Rd FELT TW13 ....178 B6
Bearstead Ri BROCKY SE4 ....170 D6
Bearsted Ter BECK * BR3 ....211 E4
Bear St LSQ/SEVD WC2H 12 C5
Beatrice Av STRHM/NOR SW16..207 H6
  WBLY HA9 ....101 G3
Beatrice Cl PIN HA5 ....58 D1
Beatrice Gdns NTHLT * UB5 ....83 H3
Beatrice Pl KENS W8 ....145 E3
Beatrice Rd ED N9 ....54 A2
  FSBYPK N4 ....88 A4
  RCHPK/HAM TW10 ....161 H6
  STHL UB1 ....138 D1
  STHWK SE1 ....33 F2
  WALTH E17 ....91 E2
Beattock Ri MUSWH N10 ....86 D1
Beatty Rd STAN HA7 ....61 E2
  STNW/STAM N16 ....109 E2
Beatty St CAMTN * NW1 ....4 A1
Beattyville Gdns CLAY IG5 ....72 A6
Beauchamp Pl CHEL SW3 ....15 F4
Beauchamp Rd BTSEA SW11 ..166 A5
  E/WMO/HCT KT8 ....219 F2
  FSTGT E7 ....112 D5
  SUT SM1 ....243 E3
  THHTH CR7 ....208 D4
  TWK TW1 ....180 C2
Beauchamp Ter
  PUT/ROE SW15 ....163 H4
Beauclerc Rd HMSMTH W6 ....143 H3
Beaufort EHAM E6 ....154 A4
Beaufort Av KTN/HRWW/WS HA3...80 C1
Beaufort Cl CHING E4 ....71 H1
  EA W5 ....121 H4
  PUT/ROE SW15 ....184 A3
  ROMW/RG RM7 ....97 G1
Beaufort Ct GLDGN NW11 ....85 E1
Beaufort Gdns CHEL SW3 ....15 F4
  HDN NW4 ....84 A3
  HEST TW5 ....158 C2
  IL IG1 ....90 A5
  STRHM/NOR SW16 ....207 H3
Beaufort Rd EA W5 ....121 H4
  KUT KT1 ....221 G1
  RCHPK/HAM TW10 ....160 B6
  TWK TW1 ....181 E2
Beaufort St CHEL SW3 ....145 H6
Beaufort Wy EW KT17 ....241 G5
Beaufoy Rd TOTM N17 ....69 H1
Beaufoy Wk LBTH SE11 ....29 H2

Beaulieu Av CAN/RD E16 ....152 D1
  SYD SE26 ....189 H6
Beaulieu Cl CDALE/KGS NW9 ....83 E1
  HSLWW TW4 ....158 D6
  MTCM CR4 ....206 C4
  OXHEY WD19 ....41 F3
  TWK TW1 ....181 F1
Beaulieu Dr PIN HA5 ....78 B3
Beaulieu Gdns WCHMH N21 ....52 C2
Beaulieu Pl CHSWK W4 ....142 C3
Beaumaris Gn
  CDALE/KGS * NW9 ....83 G3
Beaumont Av ALP/SUD HA0 ..101 E3
  RCH/KEW TW9 ....161 H4
  RYLN/HDSTN HA2 ....79 F3
  WKENS W14 ....144 B5
Beaumont Cl KUTN/CMB * KT2 ..202 A3
Beaumont Ct ALP/SUD HA0 ...101 E3
Beaumont Crs WKENS W14 ...144 D5
Beaumont Gdns HAMP NW3 ...105 E1
Beaumont Gv WCHPL E1 ....130 E3
Beaumont Ms MHST * W1U ...11 F1
  PIN * HA5 ....58 C6
Beaumont Pl BAR EN5 ....34 D2
  FITZ W1T 12 A1
  ISLW TW7 ....160 B6
Beaumont Ri ARCH N19 ....87 F5
Beaumont Rd CHSWK W4 ...142 C3
  LEY E10 ....91 F4
  NRWD SE19 ....208 C2
  PLSTW E13 ....132 D2
  STMC/STPC BR5 ....234 D3
  WIM/MER SW19 ....184 C2
Beaumont Sq WCHPL E1 ....130 B4
Beaumont St MHST W1U 11 F1
Beaumont Ter LEW * SE13 ...192 A2
Beaumont Wk HAMP NW3 ...106 B5
Beauvais Ter NTHLT UB5 ....118 B2
Beauval Rd EDUL SE22 ....189 F1
Beaverbank Rd ELTH/MOT SE9..194 D3
Beaver Cl HPTN TW12 ....199 F4
  PGE/AN * SE20 ....209 G3
Beaver Rd BARK/HLT IG6 ....76 A1
Beavers Crs HSLWW TW4 ...158 B5
Beavers La HSLWW TW4 ...158 A4
Beaverwood Rd CHST BR7 ...215 E1
Beavor La HMSMTH W6 ....143 G4
Bebbington Rd
  WOOL/PLUM * SE18 ....155 E4
Beblets Cl ORP BR6 ....253 F5
Beccles St POP/IOD E14 ....130 D5
Bec Cl RSLP HA4 ....98 B1
Beck Cl LEW SE13 ....171 F2
Beck St BECK BR3 ....210 B6
Beckenham Gdns ED N9 ....53 C5
Beckenham Gv HAYES BR2 ...211 H5
Beckenham Hill Rd BECK BR3...211 F2
Beckenham La HAYES BR2 ...212 A5
Beckenham Place Pk
  BECK BR3 ....211 F3
Beckenham Rd BECK BR3 ...210 B4
  WWKM BR4 ....251 F4
Becket Av EHAM E6 ....134 A2
Becket Cl SNWD SE25 ....229 G3
  WIM/MER * SW19 ....205 F4
Becket Fold HRW * HA1 ....80 B2
Becket Rd UED N18 ....54 A6
Becket St STHWK SE1 ....35 G5
Beckett Cl BELV DA17 ....156 C3
  STRHM/NOR SW16 ....187 F4
  WLSDN NW10 ....82 A5
Becketts Cl ORP BR6 ....253 F1
Becketts Pl KUT KT1 ....201 F4
Beckett Wk BECK BR3 ....210 C2
Beckford Cl WKENS W14 ...144 D4
Beckford Dr STMC/STPC BR5...234 C1
Beckford Pl WALW * SE17 ....31 H4
Beckford Rd CROY/NA CRO ...229 F3
Beck La BECK BR3 ....210 B6
Becklow Rd SHB W12 ....143 G2
Beck River Pk BECK BR3 ....210 C6
Becks Rd SCUP DA14 ....195 G5
Beck Rd HACK E8 ....109 H6
Beckton Rd CAN/RD E16 ....132 B4
Beck Wy BECK BR3 ....210 D6
Beckway Rd
  STRHM/NOR SW16 ....207 F5
Beckway St WALW SE17 ....31 H2
Beckwith Rd HNHL SE24 ....188 D1
Beclands Rd TOOT SW17 ....206 C2
Becmead Av
  KTN/HRWW/WS HA3 ....80 D2
  STRHM/NOR SW16 ....187 H6
Becondale Rd NRWD SE19 ....209 E1
Becontree Av BCTR RM8 ....96 B6
Bective Rd FSTGT E7 ....112 C2
  PUT/ROE SW15 ....165 H3
Becton Pl ERITH DA8 ....177 F1
Bedale Rd ENC/FH EN2 ....38 C1
Bedale St STHWK * SE1 ....23 G2
Bedfardford Farm Rd
  CROY/NA CRO 227 G5
Beddington Gdns CAR SM5 ..244 C4
Beddington Gn
  STMC/STPC BR5 ....215 H4
Beddington La CROY/NA CRO..245 F3
Beddington La CROY/NA CRO..227 G6
  MTCM CR4 ....227 E3
Beddington Rd GDMY/SEVK IG3..95 H1
  STMC/STPC BR5 ....215 F6
Beddington Ter
  CROY/NA CRO 227 H4
Bede Cl PIN HA5 ....59 G6
Bedens Rd SCUP DA14 ....216 C2
Bede Rd CHDH RM6 ....96 A3
Bedfont Cl MTCM CR4 ....206 C5
Bedfont La EBAR EN5 ....34 D6
Bedfordbury CHCR WC2N 11 E5
Bedford Cl CHSWK W4 ....143 E6
  MUSWH N10 ....65 H4
Bedford Cnr CHSWK * W4 ...118 A5
Bedford Ct CHCR WC2N 11 E6
Bedford Gdns KENS W8 ....145 E1
Bedford Hill BAL SW12 ....186 D4
  BAL SW12 ....186 D4
Bedford Ms FNCH * N3 ....65 E1
Bedford Pk CROY/NA CRO ...228 D5
Bedford Pas FUL/PGN * SW6 ..145 H6
Bedford Rd BFN/LL DA15 ....195 G5
  CEND/HSY/T N8 ....67 F3
  CHSWK W4 ....142 D3

CLAP SW4 ....167 G5
  ED N9 ....53 H2
  EFNCH N2 ....66 A6
  EHAM E6 ....114 A6
  MNPK * E12 ....79 G3
  IL IG1 ....114 D1
  MLHL NW7 ....47 E4
  ORP BR6 ....235 H6
  SEVS/STOTM N15 ....88 D1
  SWFD E18 ....72 C5
  WALTH E17 ....71 E5
  WDGN N22 ....67 G4
  WEA W13 ....139 G1
  WHTN TW2 ....179 H5
  WPK KT4 ....224 A6
Bedford Rw FSBYW WC1X 11 H1
Bedford Sq RSQ WC1B 12 D2
Bedford St COVGDN WC2E 13 C5
Bedford Wy STPAN WC1H 4 D6
Bedgebury Gdns
  WIM/MER SW19 ....184 C4
Bedgebury Rd ELTH/MOT SE9..173 F5
Bedivere Rd BMLY BR1 ....192 C5
Bedlow Wy CROY/NA CRO ...245 H2
Bedonwell Rd BELV DA17 ....156 D6
Bedser Cl LBTH SE11 ....29 H5
  THHTH CR7 ....208 D6
Bedser Dr NTHLT UB5 ....81 H3
Bedster Gdns E/WMO/HCT KT8..199 F5
Bedwardine Rd NRWD SE19 ..209 E3
Bedwell Rd BELV DA17 ....157 F2
  TOTM N17 ....69 E4
Beeby Rd CAN/RD E16 ....134 B4
Beech Av ACT W3 ....143 E1
  BFN/LL DA15 ....195 G2
  BKHH IG9 ....56 D4
  BTFD TW8 ....160 D1
  TRDG/WHET N20 ....50 A3
Beech Cl CAR SM5 ....226 B6
  DEPT SE8 ....150 D6
  ED N9 ....53 G2
  PUT/ROE SW15 ....183 G2
  RYNPK SW20 ....204 A2
  SUN TW16 ....198 B5
Beech Copse BMLY BR1 ....213 H2
  SAND/SEL CR2 ....247 E5
Beech Ct ELTH/MOT * SE9 ....193 G1
  SAND/SEL CR2 ....236 A1
  IL IG1 ....72 B4
Beechcroft CHST BR7 ....214 A3
Beechcroft Av BXLYHN DA7 ...177 H2
  GLDGN NW11 ....84 D4
  NWMAL KT3 ....202 C4
  RYLN/HDSTN HA2 ....79 E4
  STHL UB1 ....138 D1
Beechcroft Cl HEST TW5 ....158 C1
  ORP BR6 ....252 D2
  STRHM/NOR SW16 ....207 H1
Beechcroft Gdns WBLY HA9 ..101 H1
Beechcroft Rd CHSGTN KT9 ..239 H2
  MORT/ESHN * SW14 ....161 H1
  ORP BR6 ....252 D2
  SWFD E18 ....72 D5
  TOOT SW17 ....186 B5
Beechdale WCHMH N21 ....51 H4
Beechdale Rd
  BRXS/STRHM SW2 ....187 H1
Beech Dell HAYES BR2 ....251 H2
Beech Dr EFNCH N2 ....66 A6
Beechen Cliff Wy ISLW TW7 ..160 B2
Beechengrove PIN HA5 ....58 D6
The Beeches Av CAR SM5 ....244 A4
Beeches Cl PGE/AN SE20 ....210 A4
  TOOT SW17 ....186 A5
Beeches Rd CHEAM SM3 ....224 C5
  TOOT SW17 ....186 A5
Beeches Wk CAR SM5 ....243 H6
Beechfield Gdns
  ROMW/RG RM7 ....97 G4
Beechfield Rd BMLY BR1 ....213 E5
  CAT SE6 ....190 D3
  FSBYPK N4 ....69 E4
Beech Gdns DAGE RM10 ....117 F5
  EA W5 ....141 G2
Beech Gv BARK/HLT IG6 ....57 H5
  MTCM CR4 ....227 F2
  NWMAL KT3 ....202 C6
Beech Hall Crs CHING E4 ....70 C1
Beech Hall Rd CHING E4 ....70 C1
Beech Hi EBAR EN4 ....35 G2
Beech HI Av EBAR EN4 ....35 G1
Beechhill Rd ELTH/MOT SE9 ..174 A6
Beech House Rd CROY/NA CRO..246 D1
Beech Lawns
  NFNCH/WDSP * N12 ....65 H1
Beechmont Cl BMLY BR1 ....192 B3
Beechmore Gdns CHEAM SM3..224 B6
Beechmore Rd BTSEA SW11 ..166 B3
Beechmount Av HNWL W7 ...119 H4
Beecholme Av MTCM CR4 ...206 D4
Beecholme Est CLPT * E5 ....110 A1
Beech Rd FBAR/BDGN N11 ....49 F2
  ORP BR6 ....253 F5
  STRHM/NOR SW16 ....207 G6
  WELL DA16 ....156 A3
Beechrow KUTN/CMB KT2 ....201 F1
Beech St BARB EC2Y 15 E1
  ROMW/RG RM7 ....75 F1
Beech St (Below) BARB EC2Y ...15 E1
Beech Tree Cl IS N1 ....108 A5
  STAN HA7 ....61 H1
Beech Tree Gld CHING E4 ....56 D3
Beech Tree Pl SUT SM1 ....243 F3
Beechvale Cl NFNCH/WDSP N12..66 A1
Beech Wk MLHL NW7 ....62 D1
Beechway BXLY DA5 ....196 D5
Beech Wy FELT TW13 ....179 G5
  WLSDN NW10 ....102 D1
Beechwood Av FNCH N3 ....64 D6
  GFD/PVL UB6 ....119 F2
  ORP BR6 ....253 E6
  RCH/KEW TW9 ....162 A2
  RYLN/HDSTN HA2 ....79 H1
  THHTH CR7 ....228 B1
Beechwood Cl EFNCH * N2 ....86 B1
  MLHL NW7 ....63 F1
  SURB KT6 ....221 E6
Beechwood Crs BXLYHN DA7 ..176 D2
Beechwood Dr HAYES BR2 ...251 H2
  WFD IG8 ....72 D1
Beechwood Gdns CLAY IG5 ....93 H2
  RYLN/HDSTN HA2 ....99 F1

Beechwood Gv ACT W3 ....123 G6
Beechwood Ms ED N9 ....53 G4
Beechwood Pk SWFD E18 ....72 C6
Beechwood Rd
  CEND/HSY/T N8 ....87 F1
  HACK E8 ....109 E4
  SAND/SEL CR2 ....247 E5
Beechworth Cl HAMP NW3 ....85 F6
Beecroft Rd BROCKY SE4 ....170 C5
Beehive Cl BORE WD6 ....45 F1
  HACK E8 ....109 F4
Beehive La REDBR IG4 ....93 H2
Beehive Pl BRXN/ST SW9 ....168 A4
Beeken Dene ORP BR6 ....252 C2
Beeleigh Rd MRDN SM4 ....225 F1
Beeston Cl HACK E8 ....109 G3
  OXHEY WD19 ....41 G6
Beeston Pl BGVA SW1W 19 H6
Beeston Rd EBAR EN4 ....49 H1
Beeston Wy EBED/NFELT TW14..178 A1
Beethoven Rd BORE WD6 ....45 E2
Beethoven St NKENS W10 ....124 C2
Beeton Cl PIN HA5 ....59 G5
Begbie Rd BKHTH/KID SE3 ....175 E2
Beggar's Roost La SUT SM1 ...243 E4
Begonia Cl EHAM E6 ....133 G4
Begonia Pl HPTN TW12 ....199 F2
Beira St BAL SW12 ....186 D2
Bekesbourne St
  POP/IOD * E14 ....130 C5
Belcroft Cl BMLY BR1 ....212 B5
Beldham Gdns
  E/WMO/HCT KT8 ....199 G6
Belfairs Dr CHDH RM6 ....58 D1
Belfairs Gn OXHEY WD19 ....58 B1
Belfast Rd SNWD SE25 ....229 H1
  STNW/STAM N16 ....89 F6
Belfield Rd HOR/WEW KT19 ..240 B6
Belfont Wk HOLWY N7 ....108 ...
Belford Gv WOOL/PLUM SE18 ..154 A4
Belfort Rd PECK SE15 ....169 H2
Belfry Cl BERM/RHTH * SE16 ....33 H5
Belgrade Rd HPTN TW12 ....199 E2
  STNW/STAM N16 ....109 E2
Belgrave Cl ACT W3 ....142 C2
  MLHL NW7 ....62 D1
  STHGT/OAK N14 ....37 E6
  WOT/HER KT12 ....236 C3
Belgrave Ct POP/IOD * E14 ...105 H5
  STJWD NW8 ....105 F6
Belgrave Gdns STHGT/OAK N14..37 E6
  STJWD NW8 ....105 F6
Belgrave Ms South KTBR SW1X..19 F5
Belgrave Ms West KTBR SW1X..19 E5
Belgrave Pl KTBR SW1X 19 E5
Belgrave Rd BARN SW13 ....146 C6
  HSLWW TW4 ....158 D4
  IL IG1 ....72 B6
  MTCM CR4 ....205 H6
  PIM SW1V 32 A1
  PLSTW E13 ....113 F3
  SNWD SE25 ....229 F1
  SUN TW16 ....198 D1
  WALTH E17 ....69 H3
  WAN E11 ....71 H6
Belgrave Sq KTBR SW1X 19 E5
Belgrave St WCHPL E1 ....131 F4
Belgrave Wk MTCM CR4 ....205 H6
Belgrave Yd BGVA * SW1W ...19 H6
Belgravia Cl BAR EN5 ....34 A3
Belgravia Gdns BMLY BR1 ....212 A2
Belgravia Ms KUT KT1 ....221 F1
Belgrove St CAMTN NW1 ....5 E3
Belinda Rd BRXN/ST SW9 ....168 B4
Belitha Vls IS N1 ....108 A5
Bellamy Cl ECT SW5 ....144 B5
  EDGW HA8 ....46 C5
Bellamy Dr STAN HA7 ....60 D4
Bellamy Rd CHING E4 ....71 F2
  ENC/FH * EN2 ....23 D3
Bellamy St BAL SW12 ....186 D2
Bel La FELT TW13 ....178 C5
Bellasis Av BRXS/STRHM SW2..187 G2
Bell Cl PIN HA5 ....59 G6
Bell Dr WAND/EARL SW18 ....184 A1
Bellefield Rd STMC/STPC BR5 ..235 H2
Bellefields Rd BRXN/ST SW9 ..167 H3
Bellegrove Cl WELL DA16 ....175 F2
Bellegrove Rd WELL DA16 ....175 F2
Bellenden Rd PECK SE15 ....169 F3
Belle Staines Pleasaunce
  CHING E4 ....55 E4
Belleville Rd BTSEA SW11 ....166 A6
Belle Vue GFD/PVL UB6 ....99 H6
Belle Vue La BUSH WD23 ....45 G3
Bellevue Pk THHTH CR7 ....208 C6
Bellevue Pl WCHPL * E1 ....77 G2
  WALTH E17 ....71 F1
Bellevue Rd BARN SW13 ....146 D4
  BXLYHN DA6 ....176 D6
  FBAR/BDGN N11 ....50 B1
  KUT KT1 ....201 G6
  TOOT SW17 ....186 D2
  WEA W13 ....120 D3
Bellew St TOOT SW17 ....185 G5
Bell Farm Av DAGE RM10 ....97 E2
Bellfield CROY/NA CRO 248 D6
Bellfield Av KTN/HRWW/WS HA3..42 C1
Bell Gdns LEY * E10 ....91 H1
  STMC/STPC BR5 ....236 A2
Bellgate Ms KTTN NW5 ....86 B6
Bell Gn SYD SE26 ....190 D5
Bell Green La SYD SE26 ....210 D1
Bell House Rd ROMW/RG RM7..95 G5
Bellina Ms KTTN * NW5 ....86 C5
Bellingham Gn CAT SE6 ....190 D5
Bellingham Rd CAT SE6 ....191 E3
Bell La CAN/RD E16 ....152 C1
  HDN NW4 ....64 B1
  PEND EN3 ....25 G3
  TWK TW1 ....180 C3
  WBLY * HA9 ....81 H3
  WCHPL E1 ....13 H3
Bell Meadow NRWD SE19 ....189 F6
Bello Cl BRXS/STRHM SW2 ...187 H2
Bellot St GNWCH SE10 ....152 A5
Bell Pde HSLW * TW3 ....159 G2
  WWKM * BR4 ....235 E1
Belring Cl BELV DA17 ....157 E6
Bell Rd E/WMO/HCT KT8 ....219 H1
  ENC/FH EN2 ....38 D2
  HSLW TW3 ....159 F4

WELL DA16 ....175 H1
Bidwell Gdns *FBAR/BDGN* N11 ...67 J2
Bidwell St *PECK* * SE15 ....169 H2
Biggerstaff Rd *SRTFD* E15 ...111 G6
Biggerstaff St *FSBYPK* N4 ...54 A1
Biggin Av *MTCM* CR4 ....206 B4
Biggin Wy *NRWD* SE19 ....208 B3
Bigginwood Rd
STRHM/NOR SW16 ....208 B3
Bigg's Rw *PUT/ROE* SW15 ......164 B4
Bigland St *WCHPL* E1 ....17 G4
Bignell Rd *WOOL/PLUM* SE18 ...154 G5
Bignold Rd *FSTGT* E7 ....112 C2
Bigwood Rd *GLDGN* NW11 ....85 F3
Billet Rd *CHDH* RM6 ....76 A6
WALTH E17 ....70 B4
Billets Hart Cl *HNWL* W7 ......140 A2
Bill Hamling Cl *ELTH/MOT* SE9 ...193 H4
Billingford Cl *BROCKY* SE4 ......170 B5
Billing Pl *WBPTN* * SW10 ......165 F1
Billing Rd *WBPTN* SW10 ......165 F1
Billings Cl *DAGW* RM9 ....116 A5
Billing St *WBPTN* * SW10 ......165 F1
Billington Rd *NWCR* SE14 ......170 D1
Billiter Sq *FENCHST* * EC3M ...16 B4
Billiter St *FENCHST* EC3M 16 B4
Billockby Cl *CHSGTN* KT9 ......239 H4
Bilson Sq *POP/IOD* E14 ......151 G4
Bilton Rd *GFD/PVL* UB6 ......100 D6
Bilton Wy *PEND* EN3 ....40 D2
Bina Gdns *ECT* SW5 ....145 G4
Bincote Rd *ENC/FH* EN2 ....37 H4
Binden Rd *SHB* W12 ....161 H3
Binfield Rd *SAND/SEL* CR2 ......247 F3
VX/NE SW8 ....167 G2
Bingfield St *IS* N1 ....107 G6
Bingfield St *IS* * N1 ....107 G6
Bingham Cl *IS* * N1 ....108 B5
Bingham Pl *MHST* W1U 3 E6
Bingham Rd *CROY/NA* CRO 229 G5
Bingham St *IS* N1 ....109 F4
Bingley Rd *CAN/RD* E16 ......133 E5
GFD/PVL UB6 ....119 G3
Binney St *MYFR/PKLN* W1K 11 F5
Binns Rd *CHSWK* W4 ....145 F5
Binsey Wk *ABYW* SE2 ....156 A2
Binstead Cl *VEAD* UB4 ....118 C4
Binyon Crs *STAN* HA7 ....60 B1
Birbetts Rd *ELTH/MOT* SE9 ......193 H4
Birchanger Rd *SNWD* SE25 ......229 G2
Birch Av *PLMGR* N13 ....52 C5
Birch Cl *BKHH* IC9 ....57 F5
BTFD TW8 ....160 D1
CAN/RD E16 ....132 A4
HSLW TW3 ....159 H4
ROMW/RG RM7 ....77 F6
TEDD TW11 ....200 C1
Birchdale Gdns *CHDH* RM6 ......96 B4
Birchdale Rd *FSTGT* E7 ......113 E5
Birchdene Dr *THMD* SE28 ......155 G1
Birchen Cl *CDALE/KGS* NW9 ....82 D6
Birchen Gv *CDALE/KGS* NW9 ....82 D6
Birchen La *BANK* EC3V 15 H4
Birches Cl *MTCM* CR4 ....206 D6
PIN HA5 ....78 C2
The Birches *CHARL* SE7 ......152 D6
CMBW * SE5 ....169 E4
HSLWW * TW4 ....178 D2
ORP BR6 ....242 A2
STHGT/OAK N14 ....51 H1
Birchfield St *POP/IOD* E14 ......131 E6
Birch Gdns *DAGE* RM10 ......117 C1
Birch Gv *ACT* W3 ....142 A1
LEE/GVPK SE12 ....192 B2
WAN E11 ....112 A1
WELL DA16 ....176 B1
Birch HI *CROY/NA* CRO 248 B3
Birchington Cl *BXLYHN* DA7 ......177 F2
Birchington Rd *BRYLDS* KT5 ......221 H4
CEND/HSY/T N8 ....87 E3
KIL/WHAMP NW6 ....105 E6
Birchlands Av *BAL* SW12 ......186 B2
Birch Md *HAYES* BR2 ....234 A6
Birchmead Av *PIN* HA5 ....78 A1
Birchmore Wk *HBRY* N5 ......108 C1
Birch Pk *KTN/HRWW/W* HA3 ...59 G3
Birch Rd *FELT* TW13 ....198 B1
ROMW/RG RM7 ....77 F6
Birch Rw *HAYES* BR2 ....234 A4
Birch Tree Av *WWKM* BR4 ......250 B5
Birch Tree Wy *CROY/NA* CRO ...229 H6
Birch Wk *MTCM* CR4 ....206 D4
Birchwood Av *BECK* BR3 ......230 D1
CAR SM5 ....244 C6
MUSWH N10 ....66 C6
SCUP DA14 ....195 H5
Birchwood Cl *MRDN* SM4 ......225 F1
Birchwood Ct *EDGW* HA8 ......62 C5
Birchwood Dr *HAMP* NW3 ....105 E1
Birchwood Gv *HPTN* TW12 ......199 E2
Birchwood Rd *RDART* DA2 ......217 G3
STMC/STPC BR5 ....234 D1
TOOT SW17 ....206 D1
Birchwood Ter *SWLY* * BR8 ......217 G4
Birdbrook Cl *DAGE* RM10 ......117 C1
Birdbrook Rd *BKHTH/KID* SE3 ...173 E4
Birdcage Wk *STJSPK* SW1H 30 B4
Birdham Cl *BMLY* BR1 ......233 G2
Birdhurst Av *SAND/SEL* CR2 ...246 D2
Birdhurst Gdns *SAND/SEL* CR2 ...246 D2
Birdhurst Ri *SAND/SEL* CR2 ......247 E3
Birdhurst Rd *SAND/SEL* CR2 ......247 E3
WAND/EARL SW18 ....165 G5
WIM/MER SW19 ....206 A2
Bird in Bush Rd *PECK* SE15 ......169 G1
Bird-in-Hand La *BMLY* BR1 ......184 C5
Bird-in-Hand Pas *FSTH* * SE23 ...190 A4
Birdlip Cl *PECK* SE15 ....152 A6
Birds Farm Av *ROMW/RG* RM7 ...75 F4
Birdsfield La *BOW* E3 ....111 H6
Bird St *MHST* W1U 9 F4
Bird Wk *WHTN* TW2 ....178 D3
Birdwood Cl *TEDD* TW11 ......180 A6
Birkbeck Av *ACT* W3 ....122 C6
GFD/PVL UB6 ....96 C6
Birkbeck Gv *ACT* W3 ....142 D1
Birkbeck Hl *DUL* SE21 ....188 B4
Birkbeck Ms *ACT* * W3 ....122 D6
HACK E8 ....109 F3

Birkbeck Pl *DUL* SE21 ....188 B3
Birkbeck Rd *ACT* W3 ....142 D1
BECK BR3 ....210 B5
CEND/HSY/T N8 ....87 C1
EA W5 ....144 E1
ENC/FH EN2 ....38 D1
GNTH/NBYPK IG2 ....94 D2
HACK E8 ....109 F3
MLHL NW7 ....65 F1
NFNCH/WDSP N12 ....65 G1
ROMW/RG RM7 ....97 H5
SCUP DA14 ....195 G5
WALTH E17 ....69 F4
WIM/MER SW19 ....205 F1
Birkbeck St *BETH* E2 ....9 H4
Birkbeck Wy *GFD/PVL* UB6 ......96 H6
Birkdale Av *PIN* HA5 ....59 E6
Birkdale Cl *BERMH/RHTH* SE16 ...35 G4
ORP BR6 ....234 D4
Birkdale Gdns *CROY/NA* CRO ...248 B2
OXHEY WD19 ....42 B1
Birkdale Rd *ABYW* SE2 ....155 G4
EA W5 ....121 G3
Birkenhead Av *KUTN/CMB* KT2 ...201 H5
Birkenhead St *IS* N1 ....5 F3
Birkhall Rd *CAT* SE6 ....191 H5
Birkwood Cl *BAL* SW12 ......187 F2
Birley Rd *TRDG/WHET* N20 ......49 G4
Birley St *BTSEA* SW11 ....166 C3
Birling Rd *ERITH* DA8 ....177 H1
Birnam Rd *HOLWY* N7 ....84 H6
Birse Crs *WLSDN* NW10 ......103 E2
Birstal Gn *OXHEY* WD19 ....42 B6
Birstall Rd *SEVS/STOTM* N15 ...89 E2
Biscay Rd *HMSMTH* W6 ......149 B5
Biscoe Cl *HEST* TW5 ....139 E6
Biscoe Wy *LEW* * SE13 ......171 H5
Bisenden Rd *CROY/NA* CRO 229 E6
Bisham Cl *MTCM* CR4 ....226 B4
Bisham Gdns *HGT* N6 ....86 C5
Bishop Butt Cl *ORP* BR6 ......253 F1
Bishop Ct *RCHPK/HAM* TW10 ...181 F5
Bishop Fox Wy
E/WMO/HCT KT8 ....218 D3
Bishop Ken Rd
KTN/HRWW/W HA3 ....60 D5
Bishop King's Rd *WKENS* W14 ...144 C4
WKENS * W14 ....144 C4
Bishop Rd *STHGT/OAK* N14 ......50 D2
Bishops Av *BMLY* BR1 ....213 E6
CHDH RM6 ....96 B4
FUL/PGN SW6 ....168 B3
PLSTW E13 ....112 D6
The Bishops Av *EFNCH* N2 ......85 H3
Bishop's Bridge Rd
BAY/PAD W2 ....125 F5
Bishops Cl *BAR* EN5 ....48 B1
CHSWK W4 ....142 C5
ELTH/MOT SE9 ....194 C4
EN EN1 ....59 H5
SUT SM1 ....243 E1
WALTH E17 ....91 F1
Bishop's Ct *STP* EC4M 14 C3
Bishops Dr *NTHLT* UB5 ....98 C6
Bishopsford Rd *MRDN* SM4 ......225 G4
Bishopsgate *LVPST* EC2M 16 A2
Bishopsgate Ar *LVPST* EC2M 16 A2
Bishops Gn *BMLY* * BR1 ......213 E4
Bishops Gv *EFNCH* N2 ....85 H5
HPTN TW12 ....179 H4
Bishop's Hall *KUT* KT1 ....201 F5
Bishops Md *CMBW* * SE5 ......168 C1
Bishop's Park Rd
FUL/PGN SW6 ....164 B3
STRHM/NOR SW16 ....207 G4
Bishop's Rd *SUT* SM1 ....243 C5
Bishop's Rd *CROY/NA* CRO 228 B4
FUL/PGN SW6 ....86 C3
HGT N6 ....140 J2
HNWL W7 ....140 J2
Bishop's Ter *LBTH* SE11 ....30 B1
LBTH * SE11 ....30 B1
Bishopstone Rd *SYD* SE26 ......190 A6
Bishops Ter *LBTH* SE11 ....30 B1
Bishops Wk *CHST* BR7 ....214 C4
CROY/NA CRO 248 D3
Bishop's Wy *BETH* E2 ....130 A1
Bishopswood Rd *HGT* N6 ....86 B4
Bishop Wy *WLSDN* NW10 ......103 E5
Bisley Cl *WPK* KT4 ....224 A5
Bispham Rd *WLSDN* NW10 ......100 B3
Bisson Rd *SRTFD* E15 ....131 C1
Bisterne Av *WALTH* E17 ....71 H6
Bittacy Cl *MLHL* NW7 ....64 B2
Bittacy Hl *MLHL* NW7 ....64 B2
Bittacy Park Av *MLHL* NW7 ......64 B2
Bittacy Ri *MLHL* NW7 ....64 A2
Bittacy Rd *MLHL* NW7 ....64 B2
Bittern Cl *HYS/HAR* UB3 ......94 D4
Bittern Pl *WDGN* * N22 ....67 H5
Bittern St *STHWK* SE1 ....23 E4
Bittoms Ct *KUT* * KT1 ....201 F6
The Bittoms *KUT* KT1 ....201 F6
Bixley Cl *NWDGN* UB2 ......138 D4
Blackall St *SDTCH* EC2A 6 D6
Blackberry Farm Cl *HEST* TW5 ...158 C1
Blackberry Fld
STMC/STPC BR5 ....215 G4
Blackbird Hl *CDALE/KGS* NW9 ...82 C6
Blackbird Yd *BETH* E2 ....8 B4
Blackborne Rd *DAGE* RM10 ......98 C5
Black Boy La *SEVS/STOTM* N15 ...88 C2
Blackbrook La *HAYES* BR2 ......234 A2
Blackburne's Ms
MYFR/PKLN W1K 11 E5
Blackburn Rd
KIL/WHAMP NW6 ....105 F4
Blackbush Av *CHDH* RM6 ....96 B2
Blackbush Cl *BELMT* SM2 ......243 F5
Blackdown Cl *EFNCH* N2 ....65 G5
Blackdown Ter
WOOL/PLUM * SE18 ....173 H2
Blackenham Rd *TOOT* SW17 ......186 B6
Blackett St *PUT/ROE* SW15 ......164 D4
Black Fan Cl *ENC/FH* EN2 ......38 C2
Blackfen Pde *BFN/LL* * DA15 ......195 G1
Blackfen Rd *BFN/LL* DA15 ......175 F6
Blackford Cl *SAND/SEL* CR2 ......246 B6
Blackford Rd *OXHEY* WD19 ......58 B1
Blackfriars Br *EMB* EC4Y 14 C5
Black Friars La *BLKFR* EC4V 14 C4
Blackfriars Pas *BLKFR* EC4V 14 C5
Blackfriars Rd *STHWK* SE1 ......22 C1

Blackfriars U/P *BLKFR* EC4V 14 D5
Blackheath Av *CNWCH* SE10 ......171 H1
Blackheath Gv *BKHTH/KID* SE3 ...172 B3
Blackheath HI *GNWCH* SE10 ......171 G2
Blackheath Pk *BKHTH/KID* SE3 ...172 B4
Blackheath Ri *LEW* SE13 ......171 G3
Blackheath Rd *GNWCH* SE10 ......171 F2
Blackheath V *BKHTH/KID* SE3 ...172 A3
Black Horse Ct *STHWK* * SE1 ......33 H6
Blackhorse La *CROY/NA* CRO 229 G4
WALTH E17 ....69 F2
Blackhorse Rd *DEPT* SE8 ......150 C6
Black Horse Rd *ELTH/MOT* SE9 ...193 G6
Blackhorse Rd *WALTH* E17 ....90 B1
Blacklands Rd *CAT* SE6 ....191 G6
Blacklands Ter *CHEL* SW3 ....26 C2
Black Lion La *BAY/PAD* W2 ......125 F6
Black Lion La *HMSMTH* W6 ......143 G4
Blackmans Yd *BETH* * E2 ....8 D5
Blackmore Av *STHL* UB1 ......139 J1
Blackmore Rd *BKHH* IG9 ......57 J2
Blackmore's Gv *TEDD* TW11 ...200 C2
Blackness Cottages
HAYES * BR2 ....251 F6
Blackness La *HAYES* BR2 ......251 F6
Blackpool Rd *PECK* SE15 ......169 H5
Black Prince Rd *LBTH* SE11 ......29 J2
Blackshaw Rd *TOOT* SW17 ......205 H1
Blacksmith Cl *CHDH* RM6 ......96 A1
Blacksmiths La
STMC/STPC BR5 ....236 A3
Black's Rd *HMSMTH* W6 ......144 A5
Blackstock Rd *FSBYPK* N4 ......88 B6
Blackstone Rd *CRICK* NW2 ......104 A3
Black Swan Yd *STHWK* SE1 ......24 A3
Blackthorn Ct *HEST* TW5 ......158 C1
Blackthorn Gv *BXLYHN* DA7 ......176 C4
Blackthorn St *BOW* E3 ....131 E3
Blacktree Ms *BRXN/ST* * SW9 ...168 B2
Blackwall Tunnel Northern Ap
BOW E3 ....131 F2
Blackwall Wy *POP/IOD* E14 ......131 G6
Blackwater Cl *RAIN* RM13 ......137 H4
Blackwater St *EDUL* SE22 ......169 F6
Blackwell Cl *CLPT* E5 ....91 G2
KTN/HRWW/W HA3 ....59 H3
Blackwell Gdns *EDGW* HA8 ......44 C5
Blackwood St *WALW* SE17 ......31 G5
Bladindon Dr *BXLY* DA5 ......196 B2
Bladon Gdns *RYLN/HDSTN* HA2 ...79 F3
Blagden's La *STHGT/OAK* N14 ...51 F4
Blagdon Rd *LEW* SE13 ....191 F1
NWMAL KT3 ....223 F1
Blagdon Wk *TEDD* TW11 ......201 C2
Blagrove Rd *NKENS* W10 ......124 C4
Blair Av *CDALE/KGS* NW9 ....83 E4
ESH/CLAY KT10 ....204 B1
Blair Cl *BFN/LL* DA15 ....175 E6
IS N1 ....108 C4
Blairderry Rd
BRXS/STRHM SW2 ....187 G4
Blair St *POP/IOD* E14 ....131 G5
Blake Av *BARK* IG11 ....115 E6
Blake Cl *CAR* SM5 ....226 A5
NKENS W10 ....124 A4
WELL DA16 ....175 J1
Blakeden Dr *ESH/CLAY* KT10 ...238 B5
Blake Gdns *FUL/PGN* SW6 ......165 E2
Blakehall Rd *CAR* SM5 ....244 A1
Blake Hall Rd *WAN* E11 ......92 D5
Blakemore Rd
STRHM/NOR SW16 ....187 G3
THHTH CR7 ....227 H2
Blakeney Av *BECK* BR3 ......210 D4
Blakeney Cl *CAMTN* NW1 ....4 C1
EA W5 ....44 B2
TRDG/WHET N20 ....49 G3
Blakeney Rd *BECK* BR3 ......210 D4
Blaker Ct *CHARL* * SE7 ......173 E1
Blakes Av *NWMAL* KT3 ......222 B5
Blake Rd *CAN/RD* E16 ......132 B5
CROY/NA CRO 229 F6
FBAR/BDGN N11 ....67 E3
MTCM CR4 ....206 A6
Blakes La *NWMAL* KT3 ......223 P2
Blakesley Av *EA* W5 ......121 H4
Blake's Rd *PECK* SE15 ......169 E1
PECK * SE15 ....169 E1
Blakes Ter *NWMAL* KT3 ......223 G2
Blakeswood Rd *WCHMH* N21 ...52 D2
Blakewood Cl *FELT* TW13 ......178 A6
Blanchard Cl *ELTH/MOT* SE9 ...193 G5
Blanchard Gv *WAB* EN9 ....41 P1
Blanchard Wy *HACK* * E8 ......109 J2
Blanch Cl *PECK* SE15 ....170 A1
Blanchedowne *CMBW* SE5 ......168 D5
Blanche St *CAN/RD* E16 ......131 B3
Blanchland Rd *MRDN* SM4 ......225 F2
Blandfield Rd *BAL* SW12 ......186 C5
Blandford Av *BECK* BR3 ......186 C5
WHTN TW2 ....179 G1
Blandford Cl *CROY/NA* CRO 245 G1
EFNCH N2 ....85 G4
ROMW/RG RM7 ....97 F1
Blandford Crs *CHING* E4 ....44 A6
Blandford Rd *BECK* BR3 ......210 B5
CHSWK W4 ....143 G6
EA W5 ....141 G2
NWDGN UB2 ....137 C5
TEDD TW11 ....199 H1
Blandford Sq *CAMTN* NW1 ......8 B1
Blandford St *MHST* W1U 10 C3
Blandford Waye *YEAD* UB4 ......118 A5
Bland St *ELTH/MOT* SE9 ......175 F6
Blaney Crs *EHAM* E6 ....134 B2
Blanmerle Rd *ELTH/MOT* SE9 ...194 B1
Blann Cl *ELTH/MOT* SE9 ......193 J1
Blantyre St *WBPTN* SW10 ......145 H1
Blantyre Wk *WBPTN* * SW10 ...165 H1
Blashford St *LEW* SE13 ......192 A3
Blawith Rd *HRW* HA1 ....80 A1
Blaydon Cl *TOTM* * N17 ......69 H6
Blaydon Wk *TOTM* N17 ......69 H6
Bleak Hill La *WOOL/PLUM* SE18 ...155 F6

Blean Gv *PGE/AN* SE20 ......210 A3
Bleasdale Av *GFD/PVL* UB6 ......120 C1
Blechynden St *NKENS* * W10 ...124 B6
Bledlow Cl *THMD* SE28 ......136 A6
Bledlow Ri *GFD/PVL* UB6 ......119 C1
Bleeding Heart Yd
HCIRC EC1N 14 B2
Blegborough Rd
STRHM/NOR SW16 ....207 G2
Blendon Dr *BXLY* DA5 ......196 B5
Blendon Ter *WOOL/PLUM* SE18 ...154 C5
Blendworth Wy *PECK* SE15 ......169 E1
Blenheim *CDALE/KGS* NW9 ......63 G5
Blenheim Av *GNTH/NBYPK* IG2 ...94 A3
Blenheim Cl *GFD/PVL* UB6 ......119 H1
OXHEY WD19 ....42 A2
ROMW/RG RM7 ....97 H1
RYNPK SW20 ....204 A6
WCHMH N21 ....52 C3
WLGTN SM6 ....245 E5
Blenheim Ct *BFN/LL* DA15 ......194 D5
WFD IG8 ....72 D3
Blenheim Crs *NTGHL* W11 ......124 C5
SAND/SEL CR2 ....246 C5
Blenheim Dr *WELL* DA16 ......175 F2
Blenheim Gdns
BRXS/STRHM SW2 ....187 H1
CRICK NW2 ....104 A3
KUTN/CMB KT2 ....202 B5
WBLY HA9 ....80 A1
WLGTN SM6 ....245 E4
Blenheim Gv *PECK* SE15 ......169 F3
SAND/SEL CR2 ....246 C6
Blenheim Pk Rd
SAND/SEL CR2 ....246 C6
Blenheim Pas *STJWD* NW8 ......2 A1
Blenheim Ri *SEVS/STOTM* * N15 ...89 F1
Blenheim Rd *BAR* EN5 ....34 B4
CHING E4 ....44 A5
CHSWK W4 ....143 E3
EHAM E6 ....133 F2
FSTGT E7 ....112 A2
HRW HA1 ....60 A6
MNPK E12 ....77 H6
NTHLT UB5 ....80 A4
ORP BR6 ....236 A6
PGE/AN SE20 ....210 A3
RYLN/HDSTN HA2 ....79 F3
RYNPK SW20 ....221 G3
STJWD NW8 ....2 A1
SUT SM1 ....243 E1
WALTH E17 ....70 B6
Blenheim St *MYFR/PKLN* W1K ...11 G2
Blenheim Ter *STJWD* NW8 ......2 A1
Blenheim Wy *ISLW* TW7 ......160 C2
Blenkarne Rd *BTSEA* SW11 ...186 B1
Bleriot Rd *HEST* TW5 ....158 A1
Blessbury Rd *EDGW* HA8 ......62 C4
Blessington Rd *LEW* SE13 ......171 H5
Blessing Wy *BARK* IG11 ......136 A1
Bletchingley Cl *THHTH* CR7 ......228 B1
Bletchley St *IS* N1 ....7 E1
Bletsoe Wk *IS* N1 ....7 F1
Blincoe Cl *WIM/MER* SW19 ...184 B4
Blissett St *GNWCH* SE10 ......171 G2
Bliss Ms *NKENS* W10 ....124 C2
Blisworth Cl *YEAD* UB4 ......118 C3
Blithbury Rd *DAGW* RM9 ......115 H4
Blithdale Rd *ABYW* SE2 ......155 J3
Blithfield St *KENS* W8 ......145 F3
Blockley Rd *ALP/SUD* HA0 ......80 B6
Bloemfontein Av *SHB* W12 ......143 H1
Bloemfontein Rd *SHB* W12 ...123 H6
Blomfield Rd *MV/WKIL* W9 ...125 F4
Blomfield St *LVPST* EC2M 15 H2
Blomfield Vls *BAY/PAD* W2 ...125 F4
Blomville Rd *BCTR* RM8 ....96 C6
Blondel St *BTSEA* SW11 ......165 E4
Blondin Av *EA* W5 ....141 E4
Blondin St *BOW* E3 ....131 E1
Bloomfield Crs
GNTH/NBYPK IG2 ....94 B3
Bloomfield Pl *MYFR/PKLN* W1K ...11 F4
Bloomfield Rd *HAYES* BR2 ......233 F2
HGT N6 ....86 C3
KUT KT1 ....201 G4
WOOL/PLUM SE18 ....154 B5
Bloomfield Ter *BGVA* SW1W 27 F3
Bloom Gv *WNWD* SE27 ......188 B5
Bloomhall Rd *NRWD* SE19 ......208 D1
Bloom Park Rd *FUL/PGN* SW6 ...164 D1
Bloomsbury Cl *EA* W5 ......121 H6
Bloomsbury Pl
NOXST/BSQ WC1A 13 F2
Bloomsbury Sq
NOXST/BSQ WC1A 13 F2
Bloomsbury St *RSQ* WC1B 12 D2
Bloomsbury Wy
NOXST/BSQ WC1A 13 F2
Blore Ct *VX/NE* SW8 ....167 F2
Blossom Cl *DAGW* RM9 ......116 D6
EA W5 ....141 G2
Blossom La *ENC/FH* EN2 ....38 C2
Blossom St *WCHPL* E1 ....16 D1
Blossom Waye *HEST* TW5 ......138 C6
Bloxam Gdns *ELTH/MOT* SE9 ...173 G6
Bloxhall Rd *LEY* E10 ....90 D5
Bloxham Crs *HPTN* TW12 ......198 D4
Bloxworth Cl *WLGTN* SM6 ......245 D1
Blucher Rd *CMBW* SE5 ......168 C1
Blue Anchor La
BERM/RHTH SE16 ....33 F1
Blue Anchor Yd *WCHPL* E1 ......17 E5
Blue Ball Yd *WHALL* SW1A 10 A2
Bluebell Av *FSTGT* E7 ....113 H3
Bluebell Cl *HOM* E9 ....110 A6
MTCM CR4 ....226 D5
SYD SE26 ....189 H6
Bluebell Wy *IL* IG1 ....114 B4
Blueberry Cl *WFD* IG8 ......72 D2
Bluebird La *DAGE* RM10 ......117 E5
Bluebird Wy *THMD* SE28 ......154 D2
Bluefield Cl *HPTN* TW12 ......199 C5
Bluegates *EW* KT17 ....241 G5
Bluehouse Rd *CHING* E4 ......56 B3
Blue Riband Est
CROY/NA * CRO 228 B6
Blundell Rd *EDGW* HA8 ......63 E3
Blundell St *HOLWY* N7 ......107 G5
Blunden Cl *BCTR* RM8 ....96 A5

Blunt Rd CROY/NA CR0 246 D3
Blunts Rd ELTH/MOT SE9 174 A6
Blurton Rd CLPT E5 110 B2
Blyth Cl TWK TW1 180 B1
Blythe Cl FSTH SE23 190 D2
Blythe Hill FSTH SE23 190 D2
 STMC/STPC BR5 215 F4
Blythe Hill La FSTH SE23 190 D2
Blythe Hill Pl FSTH * SE23 190 C2
Blythe Ms WKENS * W14 144 B3
Blythe Rd WKENS W14 144 B3
Blythe V FSTH SE23 190 D3
Blyth Rd BMLY BR1 212 B4
 THMD SE28 136 A6
 WALTH E17 90 D4
Blyth's Whf POP/IOD * E14 130 C6
Blythswood Rd GDMY/SEVK IG3 95 G5
Blythwood Rd FSBYPK N4 87 C4
Boadicea St IS * N1 107 H6
Boardman Av CHING E4 41 F6
Boardman Cl BAR EN5 34 C6
Boardwalk Pl POP/IOD E14 151 G1
Boathouse Wk PECK SE15 169 F1
Boat Lifter Wy
 BERM/RHTH SE16 150 C4
Bob Anker Cl PLSTW E13 112 D2
Bobbin Cl CLAP SW4 167 E4
Bob Marley Wy HNHL SE24 168 A5
Bockhampton Rd
 KUTN/CMB KT2 201 H3
Bocking St HACK E8 109 H6
Boddicott Cl WIM/MER SW19 184 C4
Bodiam Cl EN EN1 38 D3
Bodiam Rd STRHM/NOR SW16 207 F4
Bodley Cl NWMAL KT3 223 E2
Bodley Rd NWMAL KT3 223 E5
Bodmin Cl RYLN/HDSTN HA2 98 D1
Bodmin Gv MRDN SM4 236 A5
Bodmin St WAND/EARL SW18 185 E3
Bodnant Gdns RYNPK SW20 203 G6
Bodney Rd CLPT E5 109 H3
Bognor Gdns OXHEY * WD19 58 A1
Bognor Rd WELL DA16 176 B2
Bohemia Pl HACK E8 110 A4
Bohun Gv EBAR EN4 50 A1
Boileau Rd BARN SW13 131 H6
 EA W5 121 H5
Bolden St DEPT SE8 171 F3
Boldero Pl STJWD * NW8 2 A6
Bolderwood Wy WWKM BR4 231 F6
Boldmere Rd PIN HA5 78 A4
Boleyn Av EN EN1 39 H2
Boleyn Ct BKHH IG9 56 C3
 WALTH E17 91 E1
Boleyn Dr E/WMO/HCT KT8 198 D6
 RSLP HA4 78 B6
Boleyn Gdns DAGE RM10 117 C5
 WWKM BR4 231 F6
Boleyn Rd EHAM E6 231 F6
 FSTGT E7 112 C5
 STNW/STAM N16 109 E3
Boleyn Wy BAR EN5 35 G4
 BARK/HLT IG6 72 C1
Bolina Rd BERM/RHTH SE16 150 A5
Bolingbroke Gv BTSEA SW11 166 A6
Bolingbroke Rd WKENS W14 144 B3
Bolingbroke Wk BTSEA * SW11 165 H1
Bollo Bridge Rd ACT W3 143 B3
Bollo La ACT W3 142 B3
Bolney Ga SKENS SW7 18 A4
Bolney St VX/NE SW8 167 H1
Bolsover St GTPST W1W 3 K6
Bolstead Rd MTCM CR4 206 D4
Bolster Gv WDGN * N22 67 F4
Bolt Ct FLST/FETLN * EC4A 14 B4
Bolton Cl CHSGTN KT9 239 F4
Bolton Crs CMBW SE5 30 B6
Bolton Gdns BMLY BR1 212 B2
 ECT SW5 145 F5
 TEDD TW11 200 C2
 WLSDN NW10 124 B1
Bolton Gardens Ms
 WBPTN SW10 145 F5
Bolton Rd CHSGTN KT9 239 F4
 CHSWK W4 162 C1
 FSTGT E7 112 B4
 HRW HA1 79 G1
 KIL/WHAMP NW6 101 F6
 UED N18 42 (hmm)
 WLSDN NW10 103 G6

Bonsor St CMBW SE5 169 F1
Bonville Gdns HDN NW4 85 C1
Bonville Rd BMLY BR1 212 B1
Booker Rd UED N18 69 C1
Boones Rd LEW SE13 172 A5
Boone St LEW SE13 172 A5
Booth Cl SCNWCH SE10 152 A3
Boothby Rd ARCH N19 87 F6
Booth Cl THMD SE28 135 H6
Booth La BLKFR EC4V 15 H5
Booth Rd CDALE/KGS NW9 62 D4
 CROY/NA * CR0 228 B6
Boot Pde EDGW * HA8 62 A2
Boot St IS N1 7 H5
Borden Av WCHMH N21 52 D1
Border Crs SYD SE26 209 H1
Border Gdns CROY/NA CR0 249 F2
Border Ga MTCM CR4 206 A4
Border Rd SYD SE26 209 H1
Bordesley Rd MRDN * SM4 225 F1
 MRDN SM4 225 F1
Bordon Wk PUT/ROE SW15 183 G2
Boreas Wk IS * N1 6 D2
Boreham Av CAN/RD E16 132 C5
Boreham Rd WDGN N22 68 C4
Borgard Rd WOOL/PLUM SE18 153 H4
Borkwood Pk ORP BR6 253 E2
Borkwood Wy ORP BR6 253 E2
Borland Rd PECK SE15 170 A5
 TEDD TW11 200 C1
Borneo St PUT/ROE SW15 164 A4
Borough High St STHWK SE1 23 C2
Borough Hill CROY/NA CR0 246 B6
Borough Rd ISLW TW7 160 A2
 KUTN/CMB KT2 202 A4
 MTCM CR4 206 A5
 STHWK SE1 22 C5
Borough Sq STHWK SE1 23 E4
Borrett Cl WALW SE17 31 E4
Borrodaile Rd
 WAND/EARL SW18 185 F1
Borrowdale Av
 KTN/HRWW/W HA3 60 C5
Borrowdale Cl REDBR IG4 93 G1
Borthwick Ms SRTFD * E15 81 E5
Borthwick Rd CDALE/KGS NW9 63 F3
 SRTFD E15 112 A2
Borthwick St DEPT SE8 151 E5
Borwick Av WALTH E17 70 C6
Bosbury Rd CAT SE6 191 G5
Boscastle Rd KTTN NW5 106 D1
Boscobel Pl BGVA SW1W 27 F1
Boscobel St STJWD * NW8 2 C5
Boscombe Av LEY E10 71 H4
Boscombe Cl CLPT E5 110 C5
Boscombe Rd SHB W12 143 G2
 TOOT SW17 206 D2
 WIM/MER SW19 205 E4
 WPK KT4 224 A4
Bosgrove CHING E4 55 G3
Boss St STHWK * SE1 24 C3
Bostall Heath ABYW * SE2 156 A5
Bostall La ABYW SE2 155 H4
Bostall Manorway ABYW SE2 155 H4
Bostall Park Av BXLYHN DA7 176 C1
Bostall Rd STMC/STPC BR5 215 H5
Boston Gdns BTFD TW8 140 C4
 CHSWK W4 140 C4
Boston Manor Rd BTFD TW8 140 C4
Boston Pde HNWL * W7 140 A2
Boston Park Rd BTFD TW8 141 E5
Boston Pl CAMTN NW1 2 E6
Boston Rd CROY/NA CR0 227 H3
 EDGW HA8 44 D3
 EHAM E6 133 G2
 HNWL W7 140 A1
Bostonthorpe Rd HNWL * W7 140 A2
Boston V HNWL W7 140 A2
Boswell Ct BMSBY WC1N 15 (hmm)
Boswell Rd THHTH CR7 228 C2
Boswell St BMSBY WC1N 13 H1
Bosworth Cl WALTH E17 70 D4
Bosworth Rd BAR EN5 21 E4
 DAGE RM10 117 E2
 FBAR/BDGN N11 67 F2
 NKENS W10 100 C3
Botany Bay La CHST BR7 214 C5
Botany Cl EBAR EN4 34 C6
Boteley Cl CHING E4 55 H4
Botha Rd PLSTW E13 132 D4
Bothwell Cl CAN/RD E16 132 C4
Bothwell St HMSMTH * W6 144 B6
Botolph Aly MON EC3R 16 H6
Botolph La MON EC3R 16 H6
Botsford Rd RYNPK SW20 204 C5
Bott's Ms BAY/PAD W2 125 E5
Boucher Cl TEDD TW11 200 B1
Boughton Av HAYES BR2 232 B4
Boughton Rd THMD SE28 155 E3
Boulcott St WCHPL E1 105 E5
The Boulevard WFD IG8 74 A3
Boulogne Rd CROY/NA CR0 228 C3
Boulton Rd BCTR RM8 92 A6
Boultwood Rd EHAM E6 133 H5
Bounces La ED N9 53 H4
Bounces Rd ED N9 53 H4
Boundaries Rd BAL SW12 188 A5
 FELT TW13 158 A1
Boundary Av WALTH E17 90 A1
Boundary Cl BARK IG11 115 E2
 GDMY/SEVK IG3 115 F3
 KUT KT1 202 A6
 NWDGN UB2 139 E5
Boundary La PLSTW E13 131 H2
 WALW SE17 31 F6
Boundary Ms STJWD NW8 105 H6
Boundary Rd BARK IG11 134 C1
 BFN/LL DA15 177 F3
 ED N9 54 B5
 PIN HA5 78 A1
 PLSTW E13 95 G6
 STJWD NW8 105 H6
 WALTH E17 105 G1
 WALW SE17 31 H6
Boundary Rw STHWK SE1 22 C3
Boundary St BETH E2 8 C4
Boundary Wy CROY/NA CR0 249 E3
Boundfield Rd CAT SE6 192 A5
Bounds Green Rd
 FBAR/BDGN N11 67 F2
 WDGN N22 67 G3
Bourchier St SOHO/CST W1F 12 C5
Bourdon Pl MYFR/PKLN W1K 11 H5
Bourdon Rd PGE/AN SE20 210 A5
Bourdon St MYFR/PKLN W1K 11 G6
Bourke Cl CLAP SW4 187 G1
 WLSDN NW10 81 E4
Bourlet Cl FITZ W1T 12 A2
Bourn Av EBAR EN4 35 H6
 SEVS/STOTM N15 88 D1
Bournbrook Rd
 BKHTH/KID SE3 173 F4
Bourne Av RSLP HA4 98 A3
 STHGT/OAK N14 51 G4
Bourne Dr MTCM CR4 205 H5
Bourne Est HCIRC * EC1N 14 A1
Bourne Gdns CHING E4 55 F6
Bourne Hill PLMGR * N13 51 H4
Bourne Mead BXLY DA5 177 G6
Bournemouth Cl PECK SE15 169 G3
Bournemouth Rd PECK SE15 169 G3
 WIM/MER SW19 205 E4
Bourne Pde BXLY * DA5 197 F2
Bourne Rd BXLY DA5 197 F2
 CEND/HSY/T N8 87 G3
 FSTGT E7 213 F1
 HAYES BR2 213 F1
Bourneside Crs STHGT/OAK N14 34 D3
Bourneside Gdns CAT SE6 211 G1
Bourne St BGVA SW1W 27 F2
 CROY/NA CR0 228 B6
Bourne Ter BAY/PAD W2 101 G5
The Bourne STHGT/OAK N14 51 G3
Bourne V HAYES BR2 232 C4
Bournevale Rd
 STRHM/NOR SW16 187 G6
Bourne Vw GFD/PVL UB6 100 B4
Bourne Wy HAYES BR2 232 C6
 HOR/WEW KT19 240 C2
 SUT SM1 242 D3
Bournewood Rd
 STMC/STPC BR5 235 H4
 WOOL/PLUM SE18 175 G1
Bournville Rd CAT SE6 191 G6
Bournwell Cl EBAR EN4 36 B4
Bousfield Rd NWCR SE14 170 B5
Boutflower Rd BTSEA SW11 166 A5
Boutique Hall LEW * SE13 171 G5
Bouverie Gdns
 KTN/HRWW/W HA3 61 F5
Bouverie Ms STNW/STAM N16 89 E6
Bouverie Pl BAY/PAD W2 9 G3
Bouverie Rd HRW HA1 79 C5
 STNW/STAM N16 89 E6
Bouverie St EMB EC4Y 14 B4
Bouvier Rd PEND EN3 40 A1
Boveney Rd FSTH SE23 190 B2
Bovill Rd FSTH SE23 190 B2
Bovingdon Av WBLY HA9 102 A4
Bovingdon La CDALE/KGS NW9 63 E4
Bovingdon Rd FUL/PGN SW6 166 A1
Bowater Cl BRXS/STRHM SW2 167 H2
 CDALE/KGS NW9 63 E2
Bowater Pl BKHTH/KID SE3 172 D1
Bowater Rd WOOL/PLUM SE18 135 F1
Bow Bridge Est BOW E3 131 H2
Bow Churchyard STP * EC4M 15 F4
Bow Common La BOW E3 130 D3
Bowden St LBTH SE11 30 B5
Bowditch DEPT SE8 150 D5
Bowdon Rd LEY E10 91 E4
Bowen Dr DUL SE21 189 E5
Bowen Rd HRW HA1 79 C6
Bowen St POP/IOD E14 131 F5
Bowens Wd CROY/NA * CR0 248 D6
Bower Av GNWCH SE10 172 A2
Bower Cl CRW RM5 77 H5
 NTHLT UB5 118 A1
Bowerdean St FUL/PGN SW6 165 F2
Bowerman Av NWCR SE14 150 C6
Bower St WCHPL * E1 105 E5
Bowes Cl BFN/LL DA15 177 H1
Bowes Rd ACT W3 123 G6
 BCTR RM8 116 A2
 FBAR/BDGN N11 66 D1
Bowes Rd (North Circular)
 PLMGR N13 67 G1
Bowfell Rd HMSMTH W6 144 A4
Bowford Av BXLYHN DA7 157 F6
Bowhill Cl BRXN/ST SW9 168 A1
Bowie Cl CLAP SW4 187 F2
Bowland Rd CLAP SW4 167 F3
 WFD IG8 73 E2
Bowland Yd KTBR * SW1X 15 (hmm)
Bow La FNCH N3 65 G3
 STP EC4M 15 F4
Bowley Cl NRWD SE19 209 F1
Bowley La SYD SE26 209 F1
Bowling Green Cl
 PUT/ROE SW15 183 H2
Bowling Green La CLKNW EC1R 6 B6
Bowling Green Pl STHWK * SE1 23 C2
Bowling Green Rw
 WOOL/PLUM SE18 153 H4
Bowling Green St LBTH SE11 30 A5
Bowling Green Wk IS N1 8 A3
Bow Locks BOW * E3 131 G3
Bowman Av CAN/RD E16 132 B5
Bowman Ms
 WAND/EARL SW18 184 D3
Bowmans Cl WEA W13 140 D1
Bowmans Lea FSTH SE23 190 A2
Bowman's Meadow
 WLGTN SM6 244 B6
Bowman's Ms HOLWY N7 107 G1

WCHPL E1 17 E5
Bowman's Pl HOLWY N7 107 G1
Bowmead ELTH/MOT SE9 193 H4
Bowmore Wk CAMTN NW1 107 F5
Bowness Cl HACK * E8 109 F4
Bowness Crs PUT/ROE SW15 203 E1
Bowness Dr HSLWW TW4 158 C5
Bowness Rd BXLYHN DA7 177 F3
 CAT SE6 191 F2
Boxall Rd DUL SE21 189 E1
Boxelder Cl EDGW * HA8 62 C1
Boxgrove Rd ABYW SE2 116 C5
Box La BARK IG11 135 H1
Boxley Rd MRDN SM4 225 G1
Boxley St CAN/RD E16 152 D1
Boxmoor Rd CRW RM5 77 G1
 KTN/HRWW/W HA3 61 H1
Boxoll Rd DAGW RM9 116 D2
Boxted Cl BKHH IG9 57 H5
Boxtree La KTN/HRWW/W HA3 42 C3
Boxtree Rd KTN/HRWW/W HA3 42 C3
Boxworth Gv IS N1 107 H6
Boyard Rd WOOL/PLUM SE18 154 B5
Boyce Wy PLSTW E13 132 C3
Boycroft Av CDALE/KGS NW9 82 C3
Boyd Av STHL UB1 138 D1
Boyd Cl KUTN/CMB KT2 202 A3
Boydell Ct STJWD NW8 105 H5
Boyd Rd WIM/MER SW19 205 H2
Boyd St WCHPL E1 17 E4
Boyfield St STHWK SE1 22 D4
Boyland Rd BMLY BR1 212 B1
Boyle Av STAN HA7 60 C2
Boyle Farm Rd THDIT KT7 220 C3
Boyne Av HDN NW4 64 B1
Boyne Rd DAGE RM10 117 E1
 LEW SE13 171 H4
Boyne Terrace Ms
 NTGHL * W11 144 D1
Boyson Rd WALW SE17 31 F5
Boyton Cl CEND/HSY/T N8 67 G6
 WCHPL E1 130 B3
Boyton Rd CEND/HSY/T N8 67 G6
Brabant Rd WDGN N22 67 H5
Brabazon Av WLGTN SM6 245 G6
Brabazon Rd HEST TW5 135 J2
 NTHLT UB5 119 E1
Brabazon St POP/IOD E14 131 F5
Brabourne Cl NRWD SE19 209 E1
Brabourne Crs BXLYHN DA7 157 G6
Brabourne Hts MLHL NW7 31 G5
Brabourne Ri BECK BR3 211 H2
Brabourn Gv PECK SE15 170 A3
Bracewell Av GFD/PVL UB6 100 B3
Bracewell Rd NKENS W10 124 A4
Bracewood Gdns
 CROY/NA CR0 247 F1
Bracey Ms FSBYPK * N4 87 G2
Bracey St FSBYPK N4 87 (hmm)
 CROY/NA CR0 249 (hmm)
Brackenbridge Dr RSLP HA4 98 B1
Brackenbury Gdns
 HMSMTH W6 143 H3
Brackenbury Rd EFNCH N2 65 H6
 HMSMTH W6 143 H3
Bracken Cl EHAM E6 133 H4
 HSLWW TW4 179 E2
Brackendale WCHMH N21 51 H4
Brackendale Cl HEST TW5 159 F2
Bracken Dr CHIG IG7 74 B2
Bracken End ISLW TW7 159 H6
Bracken Gdns BARN SW13 163 G3 (hmm)
Brackenhill RSLP * HA4 98 C2
Bracken Hill Cl BMLY BR1 212 B1
Bracken Hill La BMLY BR1 212 B1
The Brackens ROMW/RG RM7 97 E3
 ORP BR6 253 G3
The Bracken CHING E4 55 G6 (hmm)
Brackley Cl WLGTN SM6 245 G5
Brackley Rd BECK BR3 143 (hmm)
 CHSWK W4 143 E4
Brackley Sq WFD IG8 73 (hmm)
Brackley St BARB EC2Y 15 F1
Brackley Ter CHSWK W4 143 E5
Bracklyn St IS N1 7 (hmm)
Bracknell Cl WDGN N22 68 A4
Bracknell Gdns HAMP NW3 105 F3
Bracknell Ga HAMP NW3 105 F3
Bracondale Rd ABYW SE2 155 G4
Bradbourne Rd BXLY DA5 177 G6
Bradbourne St FUL/PGN SW6 165 G3
Bradbury Cl NWDGN UB2 136 D3
Bradbury Ms STNW/STAM N16 106 A1
Bradbury St STNW/STAM N16 106 A1
Braddock Cl ISLW TW7 160 B4
Braddon Ct BAR * EN5 34 C4
Braddon Rd RCH/KEW TW9 161 H4
Braddyll St GNWCH SE10 151 H3
Bradenham Av WELL DA16 176 C5
Bradenham Cl WALW SE17 31 G5
Bradenham Rd
 KTN/HRWW/W HA3 61 E1
Braden St MV/WKIL W9 101 G3
Bradfield Dr BARK IG11 115 G3
Bradfield Rd CAN/RD E16 152 C2
 RSLP HA4 98 D3
Bradford Cl HAYES BR2 250 (hmm)
 SYD SE26 189 H6
 UED N18 42 (hmm)
Bradford Dr HOR/WEW KT19 241 F4
Bradford Rd ACT W3 143 F1
 IL IG1 72 D6
Bradgate Rd CAT SE6 191 F1
Brading Crs WAN E11 90 D1
Brading Rd BRXS/STRHM SW2 187 (hmm)
 CROY/NA CR0 227 H5
Brading Ter SHB W12 143 G3
Bradiston Rd MV/WKIL W9 100 (hmm)
Bradley Cl HOLWY N7 107 (hmm)
Bradley Gdns WEA W13 120 D5
Bradley Rd NRWD SE19 208 C2
 PEND EN3 40 C1

WDGN N22..................67 H5
Bradley's Cl IS N1..................6 A1
Bradley Stone Rd EHAM E6...133 H5
Bradman Av EDGW * HA8.....62 C3
Bradmead VX/NE * SW8.....166 D2
Bradmore Park Rd
HMSMTH W6..................143 H3
Bradshaw Cl WIM/MER SW19..205 E2
Bradshaw Cottages
POP/IOD * E14..................130 C5
Bradshaws Cl SNWD SE25....209 G6
Bradstock Rd EW KT17.....241 H5
HOM E9..................110 B4
Brad St STHWK SE1..................22 B2
Bradwell Av DAGE RM10.....97 G6
Bradwell Cl SWFD E18.....92 B1
Bradwell Ms UED N18.....53 C6
Bradwell Rd BKHH IG9.....53 G6
Bradymead EHAM E6.....134 A5
Brady St WCHPL E1.....9 G6
Braemar Av ALP/SUD HA0....101 F5
BXLYHN DA7..................177 G5
THHTH CR7..................208 B6
WDGN N22..................67 G4
WIM/MER SW19..................185 J4
WLSDN NW10..................102 D1
Braemar Gdns BFN/LL DA15..194 D5
CDALE/KGS NW9..................62 D4
WWKM BR4..................231 G5
Braemar Rd BTFD TW8.....141 F6
PLSTW E13..................132 C3
SEVS/STOTM N15..................89 E2
WPK KT4..................241 H1
Braeside BECK BR3.....211 E1
Braeside Av WIM/MER SW19..204 C4
Braeside Cl PIN HA5.....59 E5
Braeside Crs BXLYHN DA7....177 G5
Braeside Rd STRHM/NOR SW16..207 E3
Braes St IS N1.....108 B5
Braesyde Cl BELV DA17.....156 D4
Brafferton Rd CROY/NA CR0..246 C2
Braganza St WALW SE17.....30 C4
Bragg Rd TEDD TW11.....200 A3
Braham St WCHPL E1.....16 D4
Braid Av ACT W3.....123 E5
Braid Cl FELT TW13.....170 H4
Braidwood Rd CAT SE6.....191 H3
Brailsford Cl WIM/MER SW19..206 A3
Brailsford Rd
BRXS/STRHM SW2..................188 A1
Braintree Av REDBR IG4.....93 G2
Braintree Rd DAGE RM10.....117 E1
Braintree St BETH * E2.....130 A2
Brair Bank CAR SM5.....244 C6
Braithwaite Av ROMW/RG RM7..37 F4
Braithwaite Gdns STAN HA7..61 E4
Braithwaite Rd PEND EN3.....40 D3
Bramall Cl FELT * E7.....112 B5
Bramber Rd FUL/PGN SW6....144 D6
NFNCH/WDSP N12..................47 G3
Bramble Acres Cl BELMT SM2..243 E5
Bramble Banks CAR SM5.....244 C6
Bramblebury Rd
WOOL/PLUM SE18..................154 D5
Bramble Cl BECK BR3.....231 G2
CROY/NA CR0..................249 E2
SEVS/STOTM N15..................89 C1
STAN HA7..................61 G1
Bramble Cft ERITH DA8.....157 G4
Brambledown Cl HAYES BR2..232 A3
Brambledown Rd CAR SM5....244 C6
SAND/SEL CR2..................247 E5
Bramble Gdns SHB W12.....123 F6
Bramble La HPTN TW12.....198 D2
Brambles Cl BTFD TW8.....123 G6
The Brambles CHIG IG7.....74 C2
SUT * SM1..................225 H6
WIM/MER * SW19..................204 D1
Bramblewood Cl CAR SM5....226 A5
The Bramblings CHING E4.....55 H6
Bramcote Av MTCM CR4.....226 B1
Bramcote Gv
BERM/RHTH SE16..................150 A5
Bramcote Rd PUT/ROE SW15..163 H5
Bramdean Crs LEE/GVPK SE12..192 C3
Bramdean Gdns
LEE/GVPK SE12..................192 C3
Bramerton Rd BECK BR3.....210 D6
Bramerton St CHEL SW3.....26 A5
Bramfield Rd BTSEA SW11....186 A1
Bramford Rd
WAND/EARL SW18..................165 G5
Bramham Gdns CHSGTN * KT9..239 F3
ECT SW5..................145 F5
Bramhope La CHARL SE7.....152 C6
Bramlands Cl BTSEA SW11....166 A4
Bramley Cl ORP BR6.....254 B5
SAND/SEL CR2..................246 B3
STHGT/OAK N14..................36 D6
WALTH E17..................51 H4
TWK TW1..................179 C1
Bramley Crs GNTH/NBYPK IG2..94 A3
VX/NE SW8..................167 F1
Bramley Gdns OXHEY WD19..58 A2
Bramley Hi SAND/SEL CR2....246 C3
Bramley Hyrst SAND/SEL * CR2..246 C3
Bramley Lge ALP/SUD HA0....101 F2
Bramley Rd BELMT SM2.....242 B6
EA W5..................143 H2
NKENS W10..................124 B6
STHGT/OAK N14..................34 B5
SUT SM1..................243 H4
Bramley Wy HSLWW TW4.....154 D6
WWKM BR4..................231 F6
Brampton Cl CLPT E5.....89 H6
Brampton Gv HDN NW4.....83 H1
KTN/HRWW/W HA3..................80 C1
WBLY HA9..................62 C6
Brampton La HDN NW4.....82 A3
Brampton Park Rd WDGN N22..68 A2
Brampton Rd BXLYHN DA7....176 B6
CDALE/KGS NW9..................62 D5
CROY/NA CR0..................229 F4
EHAM E6..................133 F3
FSBYPK N4..................88 C2
Bramshaw Gdns OXHEY WD19..58 B1
Bramshaw Ri NWMAL KT3.....223 E3
Bramshaw Rd HOM E9.....110 B4
Bramshill Gdns KTTN NW5....106 D1
Bramshill Rd WLSDN NW10....121 E1
Bramshot Av CHARL SE7.....152 D6

Bramston Cl BARK/HLT IG6.....75 F2
Bramston Rd WLSDN NW10....123 G1
Bramwell Cl SUN TW16.....198 B5
Bramwell Ms IS N1.....107 H6
Brancaster Dr MLHL NW7.....45 J4
Brancaster Rd GNTH/NBYPK IG2..94 D3
STRHM/NOR SW16..................187 D5
Brancepeth Gdns BKHH IG9..56 C4
Branch Hi HAMP NW3.....85 G1
Branch Pl IS N1.....108 D6
Branch Rd BARK/HLT IG6.....75 H1
POP/IOD E14..................130 C5
Branch St CMBW SE5.....169 E1
Brancker Rd
KTN/HRWW/W HA3..................61 F6
Brancroft Wy PEND EN3.....40 C2
Brand Cl FSBYPK N4.....88 B5
Brandlehow Rd
PUT/ROE SW15..................164 D5
Brandon Est WALW SE17.....30 C6
WALW SE17..................31 E5
Brandon Ms BARB * EC2Y.....15 G1
Brandon Rd HOLWY N7.....107 G5
NWDGN UB2..................138 D5
SUT SM1..................243 G2
WALTH * E17..................51 F4
Brandon St WALW SE17.....31 F2
Brandram Ms LEW * SE13....172 A5
Brandram Rd LEW SE13.....172 A4
Brandreth Ct HRW * HA1.....80 B3
Brandreth Rd EHAM E6.....133 H5
TOOT SW17..................186 D4
The Brandries WLGTN SM6....245 F1
Brand St GNWCH SE10.....172 F1
Brandville Gdns BARK/HLT IG6..94 B1
Brandy Wy BELMT SM2.....243 E5
Brangbourne Rd BMLY BR1....211 C1
Brangton Rd LBTH SE11.....29 H4
Brangwyn Crs WIM/MER SW19..205 H5
Branksea St FUL/PGN SW6....164 C1
Branksome Av UED N18.....69 F2
Branksome Cl WOT/HER KT12..218 B6
Branksome Rd
BRXS/STRHM SW2..................167 G6
WIM/MER SW19..................205 E4
Branksome Wy
KTN/HRWW/W HA3..................81 H3
NWMAL KT3..................202 C5
Bransby Rd CHSGTN KT9.....239 G5
Branscombe Gdns WCHMH N21..52 A2
Branscombe St LEW SE13....171 F4
Bransdale Cl KIL/WHAMP NW6..105 E6
Bransell Cl SWLY BR8.....235 J2
Branston Crs STMC/STPC BR5..254 D5
Branstone Rd RCH/KEW TW9..161 H2
Brants Wk HNWL W7.....120 A3
Brantwood Av ERITH DA8.....177 C1
ISLW TW7..................160 C5
Brantwood Cl WALTH * E17....71 H1
Brantwood Gdns ENC/FH EN2..37 C5
REDBR IG4..................93 C2
Brantwood Rd BXLYHN DA7....177 F2
HNHL SE24..................168 C6
SAND/SEL CR2..................246 C6
TOTM N17..................69 C2
Brantwood Wy
STMC/STPC BR5..................216 A6
Brasenose Dr BARN SW13.....144 A6
Brasher Cl NTHLT UB5.....99 H3
Brassey Rd KIL/WHAMP NW6..104 D4
Brassey Sq BTSEA SW11.....166 C4
Brassie Av ACT W3.....123 E5
Brasted Cl BXLYHS DA6.....176 B2
SYD SE26..................190 A6
Brathway Rd
WAND/EARL SW18..................185 G2
Bratley St WCHPL E1.....9 G6
Braund Av GFD/PVL UB6.....119 F3
Braundton Av BFN/LL DA15....195 F1
Braunston Dr YEAD UB4.....118 C3
Bravington Pl MV/WKIL W9....124 D2
Bravington Rd MV/WKIL W9..124 D2
Braxfield Rd BROCKY SE4.....170 C5
Braxted Pk STRHM/NOR SW16..207 H2
Brayard's Rd PECK SE15.....169 H3
Braybourne Dr ISLW TW7.....160 B1
Braybrooke Gdns NRWD SE19..206 J3
Braybrook St SHB W12.....123 F4
Brayburne Av VX/NE SW8.....167 G1
Braycourt Av WOT/HER KT12..218 A4
Bray Crs BERM/RHTH SE16....150 B2
Braydon Rd STNW/STAM N16..68 C6
Bray Dr CAN/RD E16.....132 B6
Brayfield Ter IS N1.....108 A5
Brayford Sq WCHPL * E1.....105 E5
Bray Pl CHEL SW3.....26 C5
Bray Rd MLHL NW7.....64 B2
Brayton Gdns ENC/FH EN2.....37 F5
Braywood Rd ELTH/MOT SE9..174 D3
Breach La DAGW RM9.....137 E2
Bread St STP EC4M.....16 C4
Breakspears Dr
STMC/STPC BR5..................215 C4
Breakspears Ms BROCKY SE4..171 F1
Breakspears Rd BROCKY SE4..170 D4
Bream Cl WALTH E17.....89 H1
Bream Gdns EHAM E6.....134 A2
Breamore Cl PUT/ROE SW15..183 G3
Breamore Rd GDMY/SEVK IG3..96 F6
Bream's Buildings LINN WC2A..14 A4
Bream St BOW E3.....111 E5
Breamwater Gdns
RCHPK/HAM TW10..................180 D5
Brearley Cl EDGW HA8.....62 C3
Breasley Cl PUT/ROE SW15..163 H5
Breasy Pl HDN * NW4.....83 H1
Brechin Pl SKENS SW7.....14 D7
Brecknock Rd ARCH N19.....107 C1
Brecknock Road Est ARCH * N19..107 F3
Brecon Cl MTCM CR4.....227 H3
WPK KT4..................224 A6
Brecon Gn CDALE/KGS * NW9..63 E3
Brecon Rd HMSMTH W6.....143 G6
PEND EN3..................40 E5
Brede Cl EHAM E6.....134 A2
Bredgar Rd ARCH N19.....87 C1
Bredhurst Cl PGE/AN SE20....190 D3
Bredon Rd CROY/NA CR0.....229 F4
Breer St FUL/PGN SW6.....165 F4

Breezer's HI WAP E1W.....17 F6
Brember Rd RYLN/HDSTN HA2..79 C6
Bremer Ms WALTH E17.....91 F1
Bremner Rd SKENS * SW7....145 G3
Brenchley Cl CHST BR7.....214 A4
HAYES BR2..................232 B2
Brenchley Gdns FSTH SE23....190 A1
Brenda Rd TOOT SW17.....186 B4
Brende Gdns E/WMO/HCT KT8..219 F1
Brendon SCUP * DA14.....195 H6
Brendon Av WLSDN NW10....103 E2
Brendon Gdns
RYLN/HDSTN HA2..................79 F2
Brendon Gv EFNCH N2.....65 G5
Brendon Rd BCTR RM8.....96 D5
CHST BR7..................194 D4
Brendon St MBLAR W1H.....10 B3
Brendon Vls WCHMH * N21....52 C3
Brendon Wy EN EN1.....53 E2
Brenley Cl MTCM CR4.....228 A1
Brenley Gdns ELTH/MOT SE9..175 F5
Brent Cl BXLY DA5.....196 C5
Brentcot Cl WEA W13.....120 D3
Brent Cross Cl HDN NW4.....83 J1
Brent Cross F/O HDN NW4....84 A3
Brentfield WLSDN NW10.....102 B5
Brentfield Cl WLSDN * NW10..84 B6
Brentfield Gdns CRICK * NW2..84 B4
Brentfield Rd WLSDN NW10..102 A4
Brentford Cl YEAD UB4.....118 B3
Brent Gn HDN NW4.....84 A2
Brentham Wy WEA W13.....121 F3
Brenthouse Rd HACK E8.....109 H5
Brenthurst Rd WLSDN NW10..103 F4
Brent Lea BTFD TW8.....161 E1
Brentmead Cl HNWL W7.....120 A6
Brentmead Gdns
WLSDN NW10..................121 H1
Brenton St POP/IOD E14.....130 C5
Brent Park Rd CDALE/KGS NW9..83 G5
Brent Rd BAR EN5.....35 C6
Brent River Park Wk
WEA W13..................120 D2
Brent Rd BTFD TW8.....141 E6
CAN/RD E16..................132 C5
NWDGN UB2..................138 A3
SAND/SEL CR2..................247 H6
WOOL/PLUM SE18..................174 B1
Brentside BTFD TW8.....141 E6
Brentside Cl WEA W13.....120 D3
Brent St HDN NW4.....84 B2
Brent Ter CRICK NW2.....84 A1
Brentvale Av ALP/SUD HA0....101 H6
STHL UB1..................139 H1
Brent View Rd
CDALE/KGS NW9..................83 C5
Brent Wy BTFD TW8.....161 F1
NFNCH/WDSP N12..................47 G1
WBLY HA9..................102 B3
Brentwick Gdns BTFD TW8....141 G4
Brentwood Cl ELTH/MOT SE9..194 C3
Brereton Rd TOTM N17.....50 B3
Bressenden Pl WESTW SW1E..19 H5
Bressey Av EN EN1.....39 C2
Bressey Gv SWFD E18.....72 B5
Brett Cl NTHLT UB5.....95 H2
STNW/STAM N16..................88 E6
Brett Crs WLSDN NW10.....102 D5
Brettell St WALW SE17.....19 E7
Brettenham Av WALTH E17....51 H5
Brettenham Rd UED N18.....53 C6
WALTH E17..................51 H5
Brett Gdns DAGW RM9.....116 B3
Brett Pk HACK E8.....109 H3
Brett Rd BAR EN5.....34 A6
HACK E8..................109 H3
Brett Vls ACT * W3.....122 D4
Brewer Rd EN EN1.....53 J4
Brewery Cl ALP/SUD HA0.....102 D3
Brewery Rd HAYES BR2.....233 C5
HOLWY N7..................107 G1
WOOL/PLUM SE18..................154 D5
Brewery Sq STHWK SE1.....24 C2
Brewhouse La WAP E1W.....25 H2
Brewhouse Rd
WOOL/PLUM SE18..................154 D5
Brewhouse St PUT/ROE SW15..164 C5
Brewhouse Wk
BERM/RHTH SE16..................150 C1
Brewhouse Yd FSBYE EC1V....5 H6
Brewood Rd BCTR RM8.....115 H4
Brewster Gdns NKENS W10....124 A4
Brewster Rd LEY E10.....91 F5
Brian Rd CHDH RM6.....96 A1
Briants Cl PIN HA5.....58 C4
Briant St NWCR SE14.....170 B2
Briar Av STRHM/NOR SW16....207 H3
Briarbank Rd WEA W13.....120 C5
Briar Cl BKHH IG9.....57 F4
HPTN TW12..................179 G2
ISLW TW7..................160 A6
PLMGR N13..................35 J5
Briar Crs NTHLT UB5.....99 H1
Briardale Gdns HAMP NW3....84 D1
Briarfield Av EFNCH N2.....65 G5
Briar Gdns HAYES BR2.....232 B5
Briar La CAR SM5.....244 C6
CROY/NA CR0..................249 F2
Briar Rd BXLY DA5.....196 A2
CRICK NW2..................104 A2
KTN/HRWW/W HA3..................81 G2
STRHM/NOR SW16..................206 J3
WHTN TW2..................180 A3
Briarswood Wy ORP BR6.....253 F3
Briar Wk EDGW HA8.....62 C3
PUT/ROE SW15..................163 G5
WEA * W13..................120 C3
Briarwood Cl CDALE/KGS NW9..83 G5
Briarwood Dr NTHWD HA6....57 H4
Briarwood Rd CLAP SW4.....167 H4
EW KT17..................241 H4
Briary Cl EDGW HA8.....62 C4
Briary Gdns BMLY BR1.....212 B1
Briary La ED N9.....53 E2
Brickbarn Cl WBPTN * SW10..15 H9
Brick Ct EMB * EC4Y.....14 A4
Brick Farm Cl RCH/KEW TW9..162 B2

Brickfield Cl BTFD TW8.....161 E1
Brickfield Cottages
WOOL/PLUM SE18..................175 F1
Brickfield Farm Gdns ORP BR6..252 C2
Brickfield La BAR EN5.....47 F1
Brickfield Rd BOW E3.....131 F3
THHTH CR7..................208 B4
WIM/MER SW19..................166 C5
Brickfields RYLN/HDSTN HA2..79 H6
Brickfield Vls SUT * SM1.....244 A1
Brick Kiln Cl BUSH WD23.....42 C1
Brick La BETH E2.....9 H1
EN EN1..................39 H5
PEND EN3..................40 A3
STAN HA7..................61 F3
Brick St MYFR/PICC W1J.....19 C2
Brickwood Cl SYD SE26.....189 H5
Brickwood Rd CROY/NA CR0..229 G6
Brideale Cl PECK SE15.....32 D6
Bride Ct BLKFR * EC4V.....14 C4
Bride La EMB EC4V.....14 C4
Bridel Ms FSBYE EC1V.....6 C2
Bride St HOLWY N7.....107 H4
Bridewell Pl BLKFR EC4V.....14 C4
WAP E1W..................25 H2
Bridford Ms REGST W1B.....11 H1
Bridge Av HMSMTH W6.....143 H4
HNWL W7..................119 H4
Bridge Cl EN EN1.....39 H5
NKENS W10..................124 B5
Bridge Dr PLMGR N13.....51 H6
Bridge End WALTH E17.....71 G4
Bridgefield Rd SUT SM1.....243 E4
Bridge Gdns E/WMO/HCT KT8..219 H1
Bridge Ga WCHMH * N21.....52 C2
Bridgehouse EN EN1.....39 G6
Bridge House Quay
POP/IOD E14..................151 G3
Bridgeland Rd CAN/RD E16..132 C6
Bridge La BTSEA SW11.....166 A2
GLDGN NW11..................64 C2
Bridgeman Rd IS N1.....107 H5
TEDD TW11..................200 C2
Bridgeman St ST/WD NW8.....2 C2
Bridge Mdw NWCR SE14.....150 B6
Bridgenhall Rd EN EN1.....39 F2
Bridgen Rd BXLY DA5.....196 C2
Bridge Pde
STRHM/NOR * SW16..................207 G1
WCHMH * N21..................52 C2
Bridge Pl CROY/NA CR0.....228 D5
PIM SW1V..................27 H1
Bridgeport Pl WAP * E1W.....25 H1
Bridge Rd BECK BR3.....210 D3
BELMT SM2..................243 F4
BXLYHN DA7..................176 C4
CHSGTN KT9..................239 K5
E/WMO/HCT KT8..................220 A1
ED N9..................53 G6
EHAM E6..................113 H5
HSLW TW3..................159 H4
LEY E10..................90 A6
NWDGN UB2..................138 D2
SRTFD E15..................111 H6
STMC/STPC BR5..................255 H5
TWK TW1..................180 C1
WDGN N22..................67 G4
WLGTN SM6..................244 D5
Bridge Rw CROY/NA * CR0....228 D5
Bridges La CROY/NA CR0.....245 G2
Bridges Rd STAN HA7.....43 D4
PIN HA5..................58 B6
Bridge St CHSWK W4.....142 A4
TWK TW1..................181 F1
WEST SW1P..................21 H3
Bridge Ter LEW * SE13.....171 H5
SRTFD E15..................111 H5
The Bridge EA * W5.....141 H1
KTN/HRWW/W HA3..................61 G5
Bridgeview HMSMTH W6.....144 A5
Bridge Vls WIM/MER * SW19..205 E1
Bridgewater Cl CHST BR7....215 E6
Bridgewater Gdns EDGW HA8..61 K1
Bridgewater Rd ALP/SUD HA0..100 D4
SRTFD E15..................111 G6
Bridgewater Sq BARB * EC2Y..15 E1
Bridgewater St BARB EC2Y....15 E1
Bridgewater Wy BUSH WD23..43 F1
Bridgeway ALP/SUD HA0.....101 G5
BARK IG11..................115 F5
Bridge Wy GLDGN NW11.....84 B2
WHTN TW2..................179 G2
Bridgewood Cl PGE/AN SE20..209 H3
Bridgewood Rd
STRHM/NOR SW16..................207 F3
WPK KT4..................241 G2
Bridgford St WAND/EARL SW18..185 G5
Bridle Cl HOR/WEW KT19.....142 D5
KUT/HW * KT1..................221 F1
Bridle La SOHO/CST W1F.....12 B5
TWK TW1..................180 D1
Bridle Pth CROY/NA CR0.....245 G2
The Bridle Pth WFD IG8.....72 A3
Bridle Rd CROY/NA CR0.....249 E2
ESH/CLAY KT10..................238 D4
PIN HA5..................58 D5
Bridle Wy CROY/NA CR0.....249 C2
ORP BR6..................252 C2
The Bridle Wy WLGTN SM6..245 E2
Bridlington Rd ED N9.....42 D6
OXHEY WD19..................27 H2
Bridport Av ROMW/RG RM7..97 F3
Bridport Pl IS N1.....7 F1
Bridport Rd NTHLT UB5.....78 A6
THHTH CR7..................208 A6
UED N18..................69 E1
Bridstow Pl BAY/PAD W2.....125 E5
Brief St CMBW SE5.....168 D5
Brierley CROY/NA CR0.....250 A6
Brierley Av ED N9.....54 A1
Brierley Cl SNWD SE25.....197 H5
Brierley Rd BAL SW12.....187 F4
LEY E10..................89 H4
Brier Lea COUL/CHIP CN5....111 H1
Brierly Gdns BETH * E2.....130 A1
Brigade Cl RYLN/HDSTN HA2..79 H6

Brigade St BKHTH/KID * SE3 172 B3
Brigadier Av ENC/FH EN2 38 C2
Brigadier Hl ENC/FH EN2 38 C1
Briggeford Cl CLPT E5 89 G6
Briggs Cl MTCM CR4 206 D4
Bright Cl BELV DA17 156 B4
Brightfield Rd LEW SE13 172 A6
Brightling Rd BROCKY SE4 190 D1
Brightlingsea Pl POP/IOD E14 130 D6
Brightman Rd
 WAND/EARL SW18 185 H5
Brighton Av WALTH E17 90 D2
Brighton Dr NTHLT UB5 99 E4
Brighton Rd BELMT SM2 243 G5
 EFNCH N2 65 G5
 EHAM E6 134 A2
 SAND/SEL CR2 246 C6
 STNW/STAM N16 109 E2
 SURB KT6 221 E5
Brighton Ter BRXN/ST SW9 167 H5
Brightside Rd LEW SE13 191 H1
The Brightside PEND EN3 40 B2
Brightside St POP/IOD E14 131 F5
Brightwell Cl CROY/NA CR0 228 A5
Brightwell Crs TOOT SW17 206 B1
Brig Ms DEPT SE8 151 E6
Brigstock Rd BELV DA17 157 F4
 THHTH CR7 228 B2
Brill Pl CAMTN NW1 4 D2
Brim Hl EFNCH N2 85 G1
Brimpsfield Cl ABYW SE2 155 H3
Brimsdown Av PEND EN3 40 C3
Brindle Ga BFN/LL DA15 195 E3
Brindley Cl BXLYHN DA7 177 E4
 GFD/PVL UB6 101 E6
Brindley St NWCR SE14 170 D2
Brindley Wy BMLY BR1 212 C1
 STHL UB1 119 F6
Brindwood Rd CHING E4 55 E5
Brinkburn Cl ABYW SE2 155 H5
 EDGW HA8 62 B6
Brinkburn Gdns EDGW HA8 62 A6
Brinkley Rd WPK KT4 223 H6
Brinklow Crs
 WOOL/PLUM SE18 174 B1
Brinkworth Rd CLAY IG5 73 G6
Brinkworth Wy HOM * E9 110 D4
Brinsdale Rd KTN/HRWW/W HA3 61 H1
Brinsley St WCHPL * E1 17 H4
Brinsworth Cl WHTN TW2 179 H3
Brinton Wk STHWK SE1 22 C2
Brion Pl POP/IOD E14 131 G4
Brisbane Av WIM/MER SW19 205 F4
Brisbane Rd IL IG1 94 C4
 LEY E10 91 F6
Brisbane St CMBW SE5 168 D7
Briscoe Cl WAN E11 92 B6
Briscoe Rd WIM/MER SW19 205 H2
Briset Rd ELTH/MOT SE9 173 F4
Briset St FARR EC1M 14 C1
Briset Wy HOLWY N7 87 H6
Bristol Gdns MV/WKIL W9 125 F3
Bristol Ms MV/WKIL W9 125 F3
Bristol Park Rd WALTH * E17 90 C1
Bristol Rd FSTGT E7 99 F6
 GFD/PVL UB6 99 F6
 MRDN SM4 225 G2
Briston Gv CEND/HSY/T N8 87 G3
Bristow Rd BXLYHN DA7 176 C2
 CROY/NA CR0 245 G2
 HSLW TW3 159 F4
 NRWD SE19 209 E1
Britannia Cl CLAP SW4 167 F5
 NTHLT UB5 118 B2
Britannia Ga CAN/RD E16 152 C1
Britannia Rd BRYLDS KT5 221 H4
 FUL/PGN SW6 165 F1
 IL IG1 78 B5
 NFNCH/WDSP N12 49 G5
 POP/IOD E14 151 E4
Britannia Rw IS N1 108 B6
Britannia St FSBYW WC1X 5 G3
Britannia Wk IS N1 7 E3
Britannia Wy FUL/PGN SW6 165 F1
 WLSDN NW10 122 B3
British Est BOW E3 130 A2
British Gv CHSWK W4 143 F5
British Grove Pas CHSWK * W4 143 F5
British Legion Rd CHING E4 56 B4
British St BOW E3 130 C2
Brittain Rd BCTR RM8 80 A6
Britten Cl BORE WD6 45 F1
 GLDGN NW11 85 F5
Brittenden Pde ORP * BR6 253 F4
Britten Dr STHL UB1 119 E5
Britten St CHEL SW3 26 A4
Britton Cl CAT SE6 191 H2
Britton St FARR EC1M 6 C6
Brixham Gdns GDMY/SEVK IG3 115 E3
Brixham Rd WELL DA16 176 B2
Brixham St CAN/RD E16 153 H1
Brixton Hill Pl
 BRXS/STRHM SW2 187 H1
Brixton Hill Pl BRXS/STRHM SW2 187 G2
Brixton Ov BRXN/ST SW9 168 A5
Brixton Rd LBTH SE11 30 A6
Brixton Station Rd
 BRXN/ST SW9 168 A4
Brixton Water La
 BRXS/STRHM SW2 167 H6
Broadbent St
 MYFR/PKLN * W1K 11 G5
Broad Bridge Cl
 BKHTH/KID SE3 172 C1
Broad Common Est
 STNW/STAM * N16 89 G5
Broadcoombe SAND/SEL CR2 248 B5
Broad Ct COVGDN * WC2E 13 H4
Broadcroft Av STAN HA7 44 A4
Broadcroft Rd STMC/STPC BR5 234 D4
Broadeaves Cl SAND/SEL CR2 247 E3
Broadfield Cl CRICK NW2 104 A1
Broadfield Ct BUSH WD23 44 A4
Broadfield La CAMTN NW1 107 G5
Broadfield Pde EDGW * HA8 46 B5
Broadfield Rd CAT SE6 192 A3
Broadfields E/WMO/HCT KT8 189 F5
 PIN HA5 59 F5
Broadfields Av EDGW HA8 46 B6
 WCHMH N21 52 A2

Broadfield Hts EDGW HA8 46 B6
Broadfield Sq EN EN1 59 H4
Broadfield Wy WLSDN NW10 103 H3
Broadfield Wy BKHH IG9 57 G5
Broadgates Av EBAR EN4 35 F2
Broadgates Rd
 WAND/EARL SW18 185 H3
Broad Green Av CROY/NA CR0 228 B4
Broadhead Strd
 CDALE/KGS NW9 63 F5
Broadheath Dr CHST BR7 213 H1
Broadhinton Rd CLAP SW4 166 D4
Broadhurst Av EDGW HA8 46 B6
 GDMY/SEVK IG3 115 F2
Broadhurst Cl
 KIL/WHAMP NW6 105 C4
Broadhurst Gdns RSLP HA4 78 A2
 KIL/WHAMP NW6 105 C4
Broadlands FELT TW13 178 D5
Broadlands Av PEND EN3 167 G4
 STRHM/NOR SW16 187 G4
Broadlands Cl HGT N6 86 C4
 STRHM/NOR SW16 187 G4
Broadlands Rd BMLY BR1 192 B6
 HGT N6 86 C4
Broadlands Wy NWMAL KT3 223 F5
Broad La CEND/HSY/T N8 67 E4
 HPTN TW12 199 H4
 SEVS/STOTM N15 68 C2
Broad Lawn ELTH/MOT SE9 194 A3
Broadlawns Ct
Broadley St BAY/PAD W2 125 H4
 STJWD NW8 10 A1
Broadley Ter CAMTN NW1 2 C6
Broadmead Av WPK KT4 207 H5
Broadmead Cl HPTN TW12 199 G1
 PIN * HA5 58 C2
Broadmead Rd WFD IG8 58 C2
 YEAD UB4 118 C5
Broad Oak WFD IG8 72 D1
Broad Oak Cl CHING E4 71 E1
 STMC/STPC BR5 215 G5
Broad Oaks SURB KT6 222 B5
Broad Oaks Wy HAYES BR2 232 B2
Broadstone Pl MHST W1U 11 G2
Broad St DAGE RM10 111 C5
 TEDD TW11 200 B2
Broad Street Av LVPST EC2M 16 A2
Broad Street Pl LVPST EC2M 15 H2
Broadview RYLN/HDSTN * HA2 79 F2
 STRHM/NOR SW16 207 F3
Broad Wk BKHTH/KID SE3 173 E5
 HEST TW5 158 B1
 RCH/KEW TW9 161 H1
 WCHMH N21 38 D6
Broadwalk La GLDGN NW11 64 D4
The Broad Wk KENS W8 145 G2
Broadwall STHWK SE1 22 B1
Broadwater Gdns ORP BR6 252 B2
Broadwater Rd TOOT SW17 186 A6
 WOOL/PLUM SE18 154 D3
Broadway BARK IG11 114 C6
 BXLYHS DA6 176 C3
 HNWL W7 140 A1
 SRTFD E15 111 H5
 STJSPK SW1H 20 C5
 SUT SM1 243 G2
Broadway Av CROY/NA CR0 228 D2
 TWK TW1 160 D1
Broadway Cl WFD IG8 72 D1
Broadway Ct WIM/MER * SW19 206 D1
Broadway Gdns MTCM CR4 194 D1
Broadway Market HACK E8 109 H6
Broadway Market Ms
 HACK * E8 109 H6
Broadway Ms STNW/STAM N16 89 F4
Broadway Pde CHING * E4 71 H2
 RYLN/HDSTN * HA2 79 F2
The Broadway ACT * W3 142 A2
 BCTR RM8 96 D6
 CDALE/KGS NW9 83 F5
 CEND/HSY/T N8 87 G3
 CHEAM SM3 242 C6
 EA W5 121 F6
 FBAR/BDGN * N11 48 B1
 KTN/HRWW/W HA3 60 A5
 MLHL NW7 45 H1
 PIN HA5 58 D3
 PLSTW E13 132 C1
 RYLN/HDSTN * HA2 79 H6
 STAN HA7 43 G6
 THDIT KT7 220 A5
 WFD IG8 72 D1
 WIM/MER SW19 204 D2
Broadwell Pde
 KIL/WHAMP * NW6 105 F1
Broadwick St SOHO/CST W1F 12 B4
Broadwood Ter WKENS * W14 144 D4
Broad Wy FARR EC1M 6 C6
Brocas Cl HAMP NW3 106 A5
Brockdene Dr HAYES BR2 251 F2
Brockdish Av BARK IG11 115 F3
Brockenhurst
 E/WMO/HCT KT8 218 D2
Brockenhurst Av WPK KT4 223 E5
Brockenhurst Gdns IL IG1 96 B5
 MLHL NW7 45 G1
Brockenhurst Ms IS N1 7 E1
Brockenhurst Rd
 CROY/NA CR0 229 H4
Brockenhurst Wy
 STRHM/NOR SW16 207 H2
Brocket Wy CHIG IG7 75 F1
Brockham Cl WIM/MER SW19 204 D1
Brockham Crs CROY/NA CR0 249 H5
Brockham Dr
 BRXS/STRHM SW2 187 H2
 GNTH/NBYPK IG2 96 A3
Brockham St STHWK SE1 23 E4
Brockhurst Cl STAN HA7 60 B2
Brockill Crs BROCKY SE4 190 B1
Brocklebank Rd CHARL SE7 152 B4
 WAND/EARL SW18 185 G2
Brocklehurst St NWCR SE14 170 B1

Brocklesby Rd SNWD SE25 229 H1
Brockley Av EDGW HA8 45 G5
Brockley Cl STAN HA7 45 G6
Brockley Crs STAN HA7 45 G6
Brockley Cross BROCKY SE4 170 C4
Brockley Gv BROCKY SE4 170 D6
Brockley Hall Rd BROCKY SE4 190 C1
Brockley Hl STAN HA7 45 G4
Brockley Ms BROCKY SE4 190 C1
Brockley Pk FSTH SE23 190 C2
Brockley Ri FSTH SE23 171 F6
Brockleyside STAN HA7 45 H4
Brockley Vw FSTH SE23 190 C2
Brockley Vw FSTH SE23 190 C2
Brockman Ri BMLY BR1 191 H6
Brock Pl BOW E3 131 F3
Brock Rd PLSTW E13 132 D4
Brocks Dr CHEAM SM3 242 C1
Brockshot Cl BTFD TW8 141 F6
Brock St PECK * SE15 170 A4
Brockway Cl WAN E11 92 A6
Brockwell Cl STMC/STPC BR5 235 F2
Brockwell Park Gdns
 HNHL SE24 188 B2
Brockworth Cl PECK SE15 32 A6
Brodia Rd STNW/STAM N16 109 E1
Brodie Rd CHING E4 51 G4
 ENC/FH EN2 29 H1
Brodie St STHWK SE1 32 D3
Brodlove La WAP E1W 150 B1
Brodrick Gv ABYW SE2 155 H4
Brodrick Rd TOOT SW17 186 B3
Brograve Gdns BECK BR3 211 F5
Brokesley St BOW E3 130 D3
Broke Wk HACK * E8 109 G6
Bromar Rd CMBW SE5 169 E4
Bromborough Gn OXHEY WD19 58 A1
Bromefield STAN HA7 61 G4
Bromehead St WCHPL E1 130 A5
Bromell's Rd CLAP SW4 167 F4
Brome Rd ELTH/MOT SE9 173 H4
Bromfelde Rd CLAP SW4 167 F4
Bromfield St IS N1 5 H2
Bromhall Rd DAGW RM9 115 H4
Bromhedge ELTH/MOT SE9 193 H5
Bromholm Rd ABYW SE2 155 H1
Bromley Av BMLY BR1 212 A3
Bromley Common HAYES BR2 233 C4
Bromley Crs HAYES BR2 212 B6
Bromley Gdns HAYES BR2 212 B5
Bromley Gv HAYES BR2 211 H5
Bromley Hall Rd POP/IOD E14 131 C4
Bromley High St BOW E3 131 H2
Bromley La CHST BR7 214 C3
Bromley Rd BECK BR3 191 F4
 CAT SE6 191 F4
 CHST BR7 214 B4
 LEY E10 91 F4
 TOTM N17 69 F4
Bromley St WCHPL E1 130 B4
Brompton Ar KTBR * SW1X 16 C1
Brompton Cl HSLW TW4 158 D6
Brompton Cottages
 WBPTN * SW10 145 G6
Brompton Gv EFNCH N2 86 A1
Brompton Park Crs
 FUL/PGN SW6 145 F6
Brompton Pl CHEL SW3 16 B5
Brompton Rd CHEL SW3 26 A1
Brompton Sq CHEL SW3 16 A5
Brompton Ter
 WOOL/PLUM * SE18 174 A2
Bromwich Av HGT N6 86 C6
Bromyard Av ACT W3 143 E1
Brondesbury Ms NW6 105 C5
Brondesbury Pk CRICK NW2 104 D1
Brondesbury Rd
 KIL/WHAMP NW6 124 D1
Brondesbury Vls
 KIL/WHAMP NW6 124 D1
Bronhill Ter TOTM * N17 69 G4
Bronsart Rd FUL/PGN SW6 164 C1
Bronson Rd RYNPK SW20 206 B3
Bronte Cl ERITH DA8 177 F1
 FSTGT * E7 112 C2
 GNTH/NBYPK IG2 94 A1
Bronti Cl WALW SE17 18 C5
Bronze Age Wy BELV DA17 157 G3
Bronze St DEPT SE8 171 E1
Brook Av DAGE RM10 117 F5
 EDGW HA8 62 D2
 WBLY HA9 102 A1
Brookbank Av HNWL W7 119 H4
Brookbank Rd LEW SE13 172 A1
Brook Cl ACT W3 143 A1
 HOR/WEW KT19 242 A5
 RYNPK SW20 223 H1
 TOOT SW17 186 C4
Brook Crs CHING E4 71 H2
 ED N9 53 E6
Brookdale FBAR/BDGN N11 34 B6
Brookdale Rd BXLY DA5 177 F6
 CAT SE6 191 F2
 WALTH E17 91 F1
Brookdene Rd
 WOOL/PLUM SE18 155 E4
Brook Dr RYLN/HDSTN HA2 79 G1
 STHWK SE1 22 B6
Brooke Av RYLN/HDSTN HA2 78 C6
Brooke Cl BUSH WD23 43 G2
Brookehowse Rd CAT SE6 191 F5
Brookend Rd BFN/LL DA15 195 E3
Brooke Rd CLPT E5 109 H1
 WALTH E17 91 H2
Brooke's Market HCIRC * EC1N 14 A1
Brooke St HCIRC EC1N 14 A2
Brooke Wy BUSH WD23 43 G2
Brookfield Av EA W5 121 F3
 MLHL NW7 45 H2
 SUT SM1 243 H1
 WALTH E17 91 G1
Brookfield Cl MLHL NW7 45 H2
Brookfield Crs
 KTN/HRWW/W HA3 61 G2
 MLHL NW7 45 H2
Brookfield Gdns
 ESH/CLAY KT10 238 B4

Brookfield Pk KTTN NW5 106 D1
Brookfield Pth CHING E4 71 H2
Brookfield Rd CHSWK W4 142 D2
 ED N9 54 C4
 HOM E9 110 C4
Brookfields PEND N15 40 B5
Brookfields Av MTCM CR4 226 A2
Brook Gdns BARN SW13 146 B5
 CHING E4 56 A4
 KUTN/CMB KT2 202 C4
Brook Ga BAY/PAD W2 10 C6
Brook Gn HMSMTH W6 148 A3
Brookhill Cl EBAR EN4 36 A6
Brook Hill Cl WOOL/PLUM SE18 154 B5
Brookhill Rd WOOL/PLUM SE18 154 B6
Brookhouse Gdns CHING E4 56 A6
Brooking Rd FSTGT E7 112 C3
Brookland Cl GLDGN NW11 85 E1
Brookland Garth GLDGN NW11 85 E1
Brookland Hi GLDGN NW11 85 E1
Brookland Ri GLDGN NW11 85 E1
Brooklands Ap ROMW/RG RM7 97 H1
Brooklands Av BFN/LL DA15 194 D4
 WAND/EARL SW18 185 H4
Brooklands Cl ROMW/RG RM7 97 H1
Brooklands Ct
 KIL/WHAMP * NW6 104 D5
 WCHMH N21 38 D6
Brooklands Dr GFD/PVL UB6 99 H1
Brooklands La ROMW/RG RM7 97 H1
Brooklands Pk BKHTH/KID SE3 172 C4
Brooklands Rd ROMW/RG RM7 97 H1
 THDIT KT7 220 B5
The Brooklands ISLW * TW7 159 H2
Brook La BKHTH/KID SE3 172 D3
 BMLY BR1 196 B1
 BXLY DA5 177 E6
Brook La North BTFD TW8 141 F5
Brooklea Cl CDALE/KGS NW9 63 E4
Brooklyn Av SNWD SE25 229 H1
Brooklyn Cl CAR SM5 226 A6
Brooklyn Gv SNWD SE25 229 H1
Brooklyn Rd HAYES BR2 233 F2
 SNWD SE25 229 H1
Brook Ms North BAY/PAD W2 241 E4
Brookmead MTCM CR4 227 E3
Brookmead Av HAYES BR2 233 H2
Brookmead Cl ORP BR6 235 H3
Brook Meadow
 NFNCH/WDSP N12 49 E2
Brook Meadow Cl WFD IG8 72 A2
Brookmead Rd CROY/NA CR0 227 E3
Brook Ms North BAY/PAD W2 241 E4
Brookmill Rd DEPT SE8 172 E2
Brook Park Cl WCHMH N21 52 B1
Brook Pl BAR EN5 26 D5
Brook Rd BKHH IG9 56 C1
 CEND/HSY/T N8 83 E3
 CRICK NW2 83 G6
 GNTH/NBYPK IG2 95 E3
 SWLY BR8 217 H6
 THHTH CR7 228 C1
 TWK TW1 160 C1
Brooks Av EHAM E6 131 H4
Brooksbank St HOM * E9 110 B4
Brooksby Ms IS N1 108 A5
Brooksby St IS N1 108 A5
Brookscroft CROY/NA * CR0 248 D6
Brookscroft Rd WALTH E17 71 H4
Brookshill KTN/HRWW/W HA3 60 B1
Brookshill Av
 KTN/HRWW/W HA3 59 H1
Brookshill Dr
 KTN/HRWW/W HA3 59 H1
Brookside BARK/HLT IG6 72 C3
 CAR SM5 226 A4
 EBAR EN4 50 A1
 ORP BR6 235 F4
 WCHMH N21 81 F2
Brookside Cl BAR EN5 98 B1
 KTN/HRWW/W HA3 81 F2
 RSLP HA4 77 H4
Brookside Crs WPK KT4 223 G5
Brookside Rd ED N9 230 B3
 GLDGN NW11 64 C4
 UED N18 53 H6
 YEAD UB4 95 H5
Brookside South EBAR EN4 47 H2
Brookside Wy CROY/NA CR0 230 B3
Brooks La CHSWK W4 142 A6
Brook's Ms MYFR/PKLN W1K 11 H4
Brooks Rd CHSWK W4 142 A6
 PLSTW E13 112 C6
Brook St BAY/PAD W2 10 B5
 BELV DA17 157 F5
 ERITH DA8 157 F5
 KUT KT1 201 G5
 MYFR/PKLN W1K 11 H1
Brooksville Av
 KIL/WHAMP NW6 104 C6
Brookview Rd
 STRHM/NOR SW16 207 E1
Brookville Rd FUL/PGN SW6 164 D1
Brook Wy CHIG IG7 54 C3
Brook Water La HDN * NW4 64 B2
Brookwood Av BARN SW13 163 H4
Brookwood Cl HAYES BR2 232 B1
Brookwood Rd HSLW TW3 159 F1
 WAND/EARL SW18 184 C1
Brom Av STMC/STPC BR5 215 H5
Broom Cl HAYES BR2 251 E3
 TEDD TW11 201 F2
Broomcroft Av NTHLT UB5 118 A2
Broome Rd HPTN TW12 198 D4
Broome Wy CMBW SE5 168 D1
Broomfield WALTH E17 90 B4
Broomfield Av LOU IG10 57 H1
 PLMGR N13 51 H6
Broomfield Cl CRW RM5 77 H2
Broomfield Cottages
 WEA * W13 140 D1
Broomfield La PLMGR N13 67 H1
Broomfield Rd BECK BR3 230 C1
 BRYLDS KT5 221 H5
 BXLYHS DA6 177 E6

CDHH RM6 ....96 B4
PLMGR N13 ....67 C1
RCH/KEW TW9 ....161 H2
TEDD TW11 ....201 E2
WEA W13 ....140 D1
Broomfield Rd POP/IOD E14 ....131 E4
Broom Gdns CROY/NA CR0 ....249 E1
Broomgrove Gdns EDGW HA8 ....62 A4
Broomgrove Rd BRXN/ST SW9 ....107 H3
Broomhill Rd SAND/SEL CR2 ....246 D6
Broomhill Rd BXLYHS DA6 ....177 E6
Broomhill Rd GDMY/SEVK IG3 ....95 G6
ORP BR6 ....235 G4
WAND/EARL SW18 ....165 E6
WFD IG8 ....72 C2
Broomhouse La FUL/PGN SW6 ....165 E3
Broomhouse Rd FUL/PGN SW6 ....165 E3
Broomloan La SUT SM1 ....225 E6
Broom Lock TEDD TW11 ....201 E1
Broom Md BXLYHS DA6 ....197 E1
Broom Pk KUT KT1 ....201 F5
Broom Rd CROY/NA CR0 ....249 E1
TEDD TW11 ....200 D1
Broomsleigh St
  KIL/WHAMP * NW6 ....105 E3
Broom Water TEDD TW11 ....201 E1
Broom Water West
  TEDD TW11 ....201 E1
Broomwood Cl BXLY DA5 ....197 H4
CROY/NA CR0 ....230 B2
Broomwood Rd BTSEA SW11 ....186 B1
STMC/STPC BR5 ....215 H5
Broseley Gv SYD SE26 ....210 C1
Broster Gdns SNWD SE25 ....209 F6
Brougham Rd ACT W3 ....122 C5
HACK E8 ....109 G6
Brougham St BTSEA SW11 ....166 B3
Brough Cl KUTN/CMB * KT2 ....201 F1
VX/NE SW8 ....167 G1
Broughton Av FNCH N3 ....66 A4
RCHPK/HAM TW10 ....181 E6
Broughton Dr HNHL SE24 ....168 A5
Broughton Gdns HGT N6 ....87 E3
Broughton Rd FUL/PGN SW6 ....165 F3
ORP BR6 ....234 D6
THHTH CR7 ....228 A3
WEA W13 ....120 D6
Broughton Road Ap
  FUL/PGN * SW6 ....165 F3
Broughton St VX/NE SW8 ....166 C3
Brouncker Rd ACT W3 ....142 C2
Brow Cl STMC/STPC BR5 ....236 B4
Brow Crs STMC/STPC BR5 ....236 A5
Browells La FELT TW13 ....178 A4
Brownacre St WLGTN SM6 ....210 B6
Brownfield St POP/IOD E14 ....131 G5
Brown Hart Gdns
  MYFR/PKLN W1K 11 E5
Brownhill Rd CAT SE6 ....191 G2
Browning Av HNWL W7 ....120 B5
SUT SM1 ....244 A2
WPK KT4 ....223 H5
Browning Cl HPTN TW12 ....178 D6
MV/WKIL W9 ....101 G3
WALTH E17 ....91 G1
WELL DA16 ....135 H2
Browning Rd ENC/FH EN2 ....12 D1
MNPK E12 ....113 H4
WAN E11 ....92 B4
Browning St WALW SE17 ....31 F5
Browning Wy HEST TW5 ....158 B2
Brownlea Gdns GDMY/SEVK IG3 ....95 G6
Brownlow Ms FSBYW WC1X 5 H5
Brownlow Rd CROY/NA CR0 ....247 G2
FBAR/BDGN N11 ....48 C1
FNCH N3 ....65 G5
FSTGT E7 ....112 C2
HACK E8 ....109 F6
WEA * W13 ....140 C1
WLSDN NW10 ....103 E5
Brownlow St GINN WC1R 13 H2
Brownspring Dr
  ELTH/MOT SE9 ....194 B5
Brown's Bd BRYLDS KT5 ....221 H4
WALTH E17 ....71 E6
Brown St MBLAR W1H 10 C3
Brownswell Rd FNCH N2 ....65 H5
Brownswood Rd FSBYPK N4 ....88 C6
Broxash Rd BTSEA SW11 ....186 C1
Broxbourne Av WAN E11 ....92 D1
Broxbourne House BOW E3 ....131 F3
Broxbourne Rd FSTGT E7 ....94 D1
ORP BR6 ....235 F5
Broxholm Rd WNWD SE27 ....188 A5
Broxted Rd FSTH SE23 ....190 D4
Broxwood Wy STJWD NW8 ....106 A6
Bruce Castle Rd TOTM N17 ....50 B4
Bruce Cl NKENS W10 ....124 B4
WELL DA16 ....135 B6
Bruce Dr SAND/SEL CR2 ....248 B6
Bruce Gdns TRDG/WHET N20 ....50 D5
Bruce Gv ORP BR6 ....235 G5
TOTM N17 .... 69 C5
Bruce Rd BAR * EN5 ....54 C4
BOW E3 ....131 F2
KTN/HRWW/W HA3 ....60 B1
MTCM CR4 ....206 C3
SNWD SE25 ....228 D1
WLSDN NW10 ....102 D5
Bruckner St NKENS W10 ....124 C2
Brudenell Rd TOOT SW17 ....186 B5
Bruffs Meadow NTHLT UB5 ....98 C4
Bruges Pl CAMTN NW1 ....7 G5
Brumfield Rd HOR/WEW KT19 ....240 C5
Brunel Cl NRWD SE19 ....209 F2
NTHLT UB5 ....118 D2
Brunel Ct WLSDN NW10 ....123 G2
Brunel Est BAY/PAD * W2 ....125 E4
Brunel Rd ACT W3 ....123 E4
BERM/RHTH SE16 ....150 A2
WALTH E17 ....90 D2
WFD IG8 ....73 H1
Brunel St CAN/RD E16 ....132 B5
Brunel Wk HSLWW TW4 ....179 E2
Brunel Wy WCHPL E1 ....13 K4
Brune St WCHPL E1 ....13 K2
Brunner Cl GLDGN NW11 ....65 F2
Brunner Rd EA W5 ....121 F3
WALTH E17 ....90 D2
Bruno Pl WBLY HA9 ....82 C6
Brunswick Av FBAR/BDGN N11 ....50 C5

Brunswick Cl BXLYHS DA6 ....176 B5
  PIN HA5 ....78 C3
  THDIT KT7 ....220 B5
  WHTN TW2 ....179 H5
  WOT/HER KT12 ....218 A6
Brunswick Ct STHWK SE1 ....19 H4
Brunswick Crs FBAR/BDGN N11 ....50 C5
Brunswick Gdns BARK/HLT IG6 ....74 C3
  EA W5 ....105 G1
  KENS W8 ....145 E1
Brunswick Gv FBAR/BDGN N11 ....50 C5
  STRHM/NOR SW16 ....207 F2
Brunswick Ms MBLAR W1H 10 D1
  STRHM/NOR SW16 ....207 F2
Brunswick Park Gdns
  FBAR/BDGN N11 ....50 C4
Brunswick Pl
  CAMTN NW1 ....3 E4
  IS N1 ....7 H4
  NRWD SE19 ....209 G3
Brunswick Quay
  BERM/RHTH SE16 ....150 B3
Brunswick Rd BXLYHS DA6 ....176 B5
  EA W5 ....121 F3
  KUTN/CMB KT2 ....202 A4
  LEY E10 ....76 A6
  SEVS/STOTM N15 ....89 E1
  SUT SM1 ....243 F2
  WAB EN9 ....41 E1
Brunswick Sq BMSBY WC1N 5 F5
Brunswick St WALTH E17 ....91 G2
Brunswick Vs CMBW SE5 ....131 H2
Brunswick Wy FBAR/BDGN N11 ....50 C6
Brunton Pl POP/IOD E14 ....130 C5
Brushfield St WCHPL E1 ....16 B1
Brussels Rd BTSEA SW11 ....165 H5
Bruton Cl CHST BR7 ....213 H5
Bruton La MYFR/PICC W1J 11 H6
Bruton Pl MYFR/PKLN W1K 11 H6
Bruton Rd MRDN SM4 ....225 C1
Bruton St MYFR/PICC W1J 11 H6
Bruton Wy WEA W13 ....120 C4
Bryan Av WLSDN NW10 ....103 H5
Bryan Rd BERM/RHTH SE16 ....150 D2
Bryanston Av WHTN TW2 ....179 F3
Bryanston Cl NWDGN UB2 ....138 D4
Brynstone Rd
  CEND/HSY/T N8 ....87 F2
Bryanston Ms East
  MBLAR W1H 10 C2
Bryanston Ms West
  MBLAR W1H 10 C2
Bryanston Pl MBLAR W1H 10 C2
Bryanston Sq MBLAR W1H 10 C3
Bryanston St MBLAR W1H 10 C4
Bryant Cl BAR EN5 ....34 D6
Bryant Rd NTHLT UB5 ....118 A2
Bryant St SRTFD E15 ....111 H5
Bryantwood Rd HOLWY N7 ....108 A3
Brycedale Crs STHGT/OAK N14 ....35 H1
Bryce Rd BCTR RM8 ....116 A2
Bryden Cl SYD SE26 ....210 C1
Brydges Pl CHCR WC2N 13 E6
Brydges Rd SRTFD E15 ....111 H3
Brydon Wk IS N1 ....107 G6
Bryett Rd HOLWY N7 ....107 G1
Brymay Cl BOW E3 ....131 E1
Brymmaer Rd BTSEA SW11 ....166 B2
Bryn-y-Mawr Rd EN EN1 ....39 F5
Bryony Rd SHB W12 ....123 G6
Buchanan Cl WCHMH N21 ....37 H6
Buchanan Gdns WLSDN NW10 ....123 H1
Buchan Rd PECK SE15 ....151 K4
Bucharest Rd
  WAND/EARL SW18 ....185 G2
Buckden Cl LEE/GVPK SE12 ....192 B1
Buckfast Rd MRDN SM4 ....225 F1
Buckfast St BETH E2 ....92 D2
Buckhold Rd
  WAND/EARL SW18 ....185 E1
Buckhurst Av CAR SM5 ....226 A5
Buckhurst St WCHPL E1 ....92 D6
Buckhurst Wy BKHH IG9 ....57 F5
Buckingham Av
  E/WMO/HCT KT8 ....199 F5
  CFD/PVL UB6 ....100 C6
  THHTH CR7 ....208 A4
  TRDG/WHET N20 ....33 G1
  WELL DA16 ....175 E5
Buckingham Cl EA W5 ....121 E4
  EN EN1 ....39 E3
  HPTN TW12 ....198 D1
  STMC/STPC BR5 ....235 E4
Buckingham Ct BELMT * SM2 ....243 E6
Buckingham Dr CHST BR7 ....214 B1
Buckingham Gdns STAN HA7 ....61 C3
  THHTH CR7 ....208 A1
Buckingham Ga WESTW SW1E 20 A5
Buckingham La FSTH SE23 ....190 C2
Buckingham Ms WESTW * SW1E 20 A5
  WLSDN NW10 ....123 F1
Buckingham Palace Rd
  PIM SW1V 27 G1
Buckingham Pde STAN * HA7 ....61 E1
Buckingham Pl WESTW SW1E 20 A5
Buckingham Rd EDGW HA8 ....61 H3
  FELT TW13 ....178 D6
  FSTGT E7 ....112 B3
  HRW HA1 ....60 D1
  IL IG1 ....94 D6
  IS N1 ....109 E6
  KUT KT1 ....191 H1
  LEY E10 ....76 A3
  MTCM CR4 ....227 G2
  RCHPK/HAM TW10 ....181 F4
  SWFD E18 ....72 B4
  WAN E11 ....92 D1
  WDGN N22 ....50 D1
  WLSDN NW10 ....123 F1
Buckingham St CHCR WC2N 13 F6
Buckingham Wy WLGTN SM6 ....245 E6
Buckland Crs HAMP NW3 ....105 H5
Buckland Ri PIN HA5 ....58 A4
Buckland Rd CHSGTN KT9 ....239 H5
  LEY E10 ....76 A6
Bucklands OXHEY * WD19 ....41 F6
Bucklands Rd TEDD TW11 ....201 E2
Buckland St IS N1 ....7 F2
Bucklands Whf KUT * KT1 ....201 F5
Bucklands Wk MRDN SM4 ....225 C1

Buckland Wy WPK KT4 ....224 A5
Buck La CDALE/KGS NW9 ....82 D2
Buckleigh Av RYNPK SW20 ....204 A6
Buckleigh Rd
  STRHM/NOR SW16 ....207 F2
Buckleigh Wy NRWD SE19 ....209 F1
Bucklersbury MANHO * EC4N 15 G4
Bucklers' Wy CAR SM5 ....244 B1
Buckle St WCHPL E1 ....16 D3
Buckley Rd KIL/WHAMP NW6 ....104 D5
Buckmaster Rd BTSEA SW11 ....166 A5
Bucknall St NOXST/BSQ WC1A 13 E3
Bucknall Wy BECK BR3 ....211 G1
Buckner Rd BRXS/STRHM SW2 ....167 H5
Buckrell Rd CHING E4 ....55 H4
Bucks Av OXHEY WD19 ....42 C2
Buckstone Cl FSTH SE23 ....190 A1
Buckstone Rd UED N18 ....50 C1
  WLSDN NW10 ....106 D6
Buckters Rents
  BERM/RHTH SE16 ....150 C1
Buckthorne Rd BROCKY SE4 ....190 C1
Budd Cl NFNCH/WDSPK N12 ....49 F6
Buddings Cir WBLY HA9 ....102 C1
Budge La MTCM CR4 ....244 C1
Budge Rd CEND/HSY/T N8 ....15 G5
Budleigh Crs WELL DA16 ....136 D6
Budoch Dr GDMY/SEVK IG3 ....95 G6
Buer Rd FUL/PGN SW6 ....165 H4
Bugsby's Wy GNWCH SE10 ....152 B4
Bulganak Rd THHTH CR7 ....228 C1
Bulinca St WEST * SW1P 29 E2
Bullace Rw CMBW SE5 ....168 D2
Bull Aly WELL DA16 ....136 C2
Bullar Cl PECK SE15 ....169 G1
Bullard Rd TEDD * TW11 ....200 B2
Bullards Pl BETH E2 ....130 B2
Bullbanks Rd BELV DA17 ....157 G4
Bulleid Wy PIM SW1V 27 H2
Bullen St BTSEA SW11 ....166 A3
Buller Rd BARK IG11 ....115 E5
  THHTH CR7 ....208 D6
  TOTM N17 ....50 D4
  WDGN N22 ....68 A5
  WLSDN NW10 ....124 B2
Bullers Cl SCUP DA14 ....186 C3
Bullers Wood Dr CHST BR7 ....213 G4
Bullescroft Rd EDGW HA8 ....46 A5
Bullivant St POP/IOD E14 ....131 G6
Bull La CHST BR7 ....214 D3
  DAGE RM10 ....117 F1
  UED N18 ....49 H1
Bull Rd SRTFD E15 ....131 F1
Bullrush Cl CROY/NA CR0 ....229 E3
Bullrush Cl CAR SM5 ....225 H6
Bullsbrook Rd HYS/HAR UB3 ....114 A1
Bull Yd PECK SE15 ....169 G2
Bulmer Gdns
  KTN/HRWW/W HA3 ....79 E1
Bulstrode Av HSLW TW3 ....158 D4
Bulstrode Gdns HSLW TW3 ....159 E3
Bulstrode Pl MHST W1U 11 F2
Bulstrode Rd HSLW TW3 ....159 E3
Bulstrode St MHST W1U 11 F3
Bulwer Court Rd WAN E11 ....91 H5
Bulwer Gdns BAR EN5 ....35 G5
Bulwer Rd BAR EN5 ....53 E6
  UED N18 ....53 E6
  WAN E11 ....91 H5
Bulwer St SHB W12 ....144 A1
Bunces La WFD IG8 ....72 B3
Bungalow Rd SNWD SE25 ....229 E1
The Bungalows
  RYLN/HDSTN * HA2 ....98 D1
  STRHM/NOR SW16 ....206 D3
Bunhill Rw STLK EC1Y 7 F6
Bunhouse Pl BGVA SW1W 27 F3
Bunkers Hl SCUP DA14 ....196 D5
Bunning Wy HOLWY * N7 ....107 G5
Bunns La MLHL NW7 ....45 E1
Bunsen St BOW E3 ....130 C1
Bunting Cl ED N9 ....54 B3
  MTCM CR4 ....226 B2
Bunton St WOOL/PLUM SE18 ....154 A3
Bunyan Rd WALTH E17 ....70 C6
Burbage Cl STHWK SE1 ....35 G1
Burbage Rd HNHL SE24 ....188 D1
Burberry Cl NWMAL KT3 ....203 E5
Burbridge Wy TOTM N17 ....69 G5
Burcham St POP/IOD E14 ....131 F5
Burcharbro Rd ABYW SE2 ....156 B6
Burchell Ct BUSH WD23 ....91 F5
Burchell Rd LEY E10 ....91 G5
  PECK SE15 ....169 H2
Burchwall Cl CRW RM5 ....56 D1
Burcote Rd WAND/EARL SW18 ....185 H3
Burcott Rd PUR/KEN CR8 ....141 E6
Burdenshott Av
  RCHPK/HAM TW10 ....162 B5
Burden Wy WAN E11 ....92 D6
Burder Cl IS N1 ....109 E4
Burder Rd IS N1 ....109 E3
Burdett Av RYNPK SW20 ....203 G4
Burdett Cl HNWL * W7 ....140 B1
  SCUP DA14 ....216 C1
Burdett Rd BOW E3 ....130 D5
  CROY/NA CR0 ....228 D3
  RCH/KEW TW9 ....161 H3
Burdock Cl CROY/NA CR0 ....198 A5
Burdock Rd TOTM N17 ....69 G6
Burdon La BELMT SM2 ....242 D6
Burfield Cl TOOT SW17 ....187 F3
Burford Cl BARK/HLT IG6 ....116 A1
  DAGE RM9 ....79 E6
  HNWL W7 ....141 E5
Burford Gdns PLMGR N13 ....51 G5
Burford Rd BMLY BR1 ....213 F2
  BTFD TW8 ....141 G5
  CAT SE6 ....190 D5
  EHAM E6 ....133 G2
  SRTFD E15 ....111 H5
  SUT SM1 ....225 H4
  WPK KT4 ....223 G4
Burford Wk FUL/PGN * SW6 ....165 F1
Burford Wy CROY/NA CR0 ....239 F5
Burges Gv BARN SW13 ....163 H1
Burges Rd EHAM E6 ....114 A5
Burgess Av CDALE/KGS NW9 ....62 D3
Burgess Cl FELT TW13 ....178 C3
Burgess Hl CRICK NW2 ....105 E2

Burgess Rd SRTFD E15 ....112 A2
  SUT SM1 ....243 F2
Burgess St POP/IOD E14 ....131 E4
Burge St STHWK SE1 ....23 H6
Burghill Rd SYD SE26 ....190 B6
Burghley Av NWMAL KT3 ....202 D4
Burghley Hall Cl
  WIM/MER * SW19 ....184 C3
Burghley Pl MTCM CR4 ....206 A3
Burghley Rd CEND/HSY/T N8 ....68 A6
  KTTN NW5 ....106 D2
  WAN * E11 ....92 A5
  WIM/MER SW19 ....166 B6
Burgh St IS N1 ....6 D1
Burgon St BLKFR EC4V 14 D4
Burgos Cl CROY/NA CR0 ....246 A4
Burgos Gv GNWCH SE10 ....172 D5
Burgoyne Rd BRXN/ST SW9 ....167 H4
  FSBYPK N4 ....88 B3
  SNWD SE25 ....229 F1
Burham Cl PGE/AN SE20 ....210 A3
Burhill Gv PIN HA5 ....58 C5
Burke Cl PUT/ROE SW15 ....163 E5
Burke St CAN/RD E16 ....132 B4
Burket Cl NWDGN UB2 ....138 C4
Burland Rd BTSEA SW11 ....166 D4
  CRW RM5 ....77 G2
Burleigh Av BFN/LL DA15 ....175 F6
  WLGTN SM6 ....210 A6
Burleigh Gdns STHGT/OAK N14 ....51 E3
Burleigh Pde STHGT/OAK * N14 ....51 F3
Burleigh Pl PUT/ROE SW15 ....164 B6
Burleigh Rd CHEAM SM3 ....224 C5
  EN EN1 ....39 C5
Burleigh St COVGDN WC2E 13 F5
Burleigh Wk ENC/FH EN2 ....38 D4
Burley Cl CHING E4 ....71 E1
  STRHM/NOR SW16 ....207 F5
Burley Rd CAN/RD E16 ....133 E5
Burlington Ar CONDST W1S 12 A6
Burlington Av RCH/KEW TW9 ....162 A1
  ROMW/RG RM7 ....97 F3
Burlington Cl EBAR EN4 ....50 A3
  FUL/PGN SW6 ....165 C3
  MV/WKIL W9 ....125 E3
  ORP BR6 ....234 B6
Burlington Gdns ACT W3 ....142 C5
  CHDH RM6 ....96 C4
  CHSWK W4 ....142 C5
  CONDST W1S 12 A6
  FUL/PGN SW6 ....165 G3
Burlington La CHSWK W4 ....142 C1
Burlington Pde CRICK * NW2 ....104 B1
Burlington Pl FUL/PGN SW6 ....164 C3
  WFD IG8 ....56 C5
Burlington Ri EBAR EN4 ....50 A3
Burlington Rd CHSWK * W4 ....142 C5
  ENC/FH EN2 ....38 C2
  FUL/PGN SW6 ....164 C3
  ISLW TW7 ....159 H2
  MUSWH N10 ....66 A2
  NWMAL KT3 ....225 F1
  THHTH CR7 ....208 D5
  TOTM N17 ....69 G4
Burma Rd STNW/STAM N16 ....108 D2
Burma Ter NRWD * SE19 ....209 E1
Burmester Rd TOOT SW17 ....185 G5
Burnaby Crs CHSWK W4 ....142 B6
Burnaby Gdns CHSWK W4 ....142 B6
Burnaby St WBPTN SW10 ....165 G1
Burnbrae Cl FNCH N3 ....65 F2
Burnbury Rd BAL SW12 ....187 G1
Burncroft Av PEND EN3 ....24 A5
Burndell Wy YEAD UB4 ....118 B4
Burnell Av RCHPK/HAM TW10 ....180 D1
  WELL DA16 ....175 G3
Burnell Gdns STAN * HA7 ....43 H5
Burnell Rd SUT SM1 ....243 F2
Burnell Wk STHWK * SE1 ....32 D3
Burnels Av EHAM E6 ....134 A2
Burness Cl HOLWY N7 ....107 H4
Burne St CAMTN NW1 ....10 A1
Burney Av BRYLDS KT5 ....221 H2
Burney St GNWCH SE10 ....151 C2
Burnfoot Av FUL/PGN SW6 ....164 C2
Burnham Cl ENC/FH EN2 ....39 E1
  KTN/HRWW/W HA3 ....80 C1
  MLHL NW7 ....45 C3
  STHWK SE1 ....32 D2
Burnham Crs WAN E11 ....93 E1
Burnham Dr WPK KT4 ....225 E6
Burnham Gdns CROY/NA CR0 ....229 F4
  HSLWW TW4 ....134 A6
  HYS/HAR UB3 ....133 G1
Burnham Rd CHING E4 ....71 G2
  DAGW RM9 ....115 G6
  MRDN SM4 ....225 F2
  ROMW/RG RM7 ....77 C2
  SCUP DA14 ....196 D4
Burnham St BETH E2 ....92 D2
  KUTN/CMB KT2 ....202 A4
Burnham Wy SYD SE26 ....191 H5
Burnhill Rd BECK BR3 ....211 E5
Burnley Rd BRXN/ST SW9 ....167 H3
  WLSDN NW10 ....86 A4
Burnsall St CHEL SW3 ....96 C5
  STHL UB1 ....119 E6
Burns Cl TOOT SW17 ....205 H2
  WALTH E17 ....71 G1
  WELL DA16 ....175 F2
Burnside Av CHING E4 ....71 G2
Burnside Cl BAR EN5 ....35 E4
  BERM/RHTH SE16 ....150 D1
  TWK TW1 ....160 C5
Burnside Crs ALP/SUD HA0 ....101 F6
Burnside Rd BCTR RM8 ....96 D5
Burns Rd ALP/SUD HA0 ....102 A4
  BTSEA SW11 ....166 B3
  WEA * W13 ....140 C3
  WLSDN NW10 ....105 H6
Burns Wy HEST TW5 ....158 D2
Burnt Ash HI LEE/GVPK SE12 ....192 B1
Burnt Ash La BMLY BR1 ....212 D1
Burnt Ash Rd LEE/GVPK SE12 ....192 B1
Burntwheate Rd FUL/PGN SW6 ....165 F3
Burnt Oak Broadway EDGW HA8 ....62 B3
Burnt Oak Flds EDGW HA8 ....62 C2
Burnt Oak La BFN/LL DA15 ....195 G4

Burntwood Cl
WAND/EARL SW18.........................185 H3
Burntwood Grange Rd
WAND/EARL SW18.........................185 H3
Buross St *WCHPL* E1..........................17 H5
Burpham Cl *YEAD* UB4.......................118 B4
Burrage Gv *WOOL/PLUM* SE18.........154 B4
Burrage Pl *WOOL/PLUM* SE18..........154 B5
Burrage Rd *WOOL/PLUM* SE18.........154 C4
Burrard Rd *CAN/RD* E16...................132 C5
KIL/WHAMP NW6............................105 E3
Burr Cl *BXLYHN* DA7.........................176 D4
WAP E1W..25 E1
Burrell Cl *CROY/NA* CR0.................230 C5
EDGW HA8...86 B4
Burrell Rw *BECK* BR3.......................211 E5
Burrell St *STHWK* SE1........................22 C1
Burrfield Dr *STMC/STPC* BR5.........236 D4
Burritt Rd *KUT* T1.............................202 A5
Burroughs Cottages
POP/IOD E14..................................130 C4
Burroughs Gdns *HDN* NW4...............83 H1
The Burroughs *HDN* NW4.................83 H1
Burrow Gn *CHIG* IG7..........................75 E1
Burrow Rd *CHIC* IG7...........................75 G1
CMBW SE5.......................................169 E5
Burrows Ms *STHWK* SE1....................22 C5
Burrows Rd *WLSDN* NW10...............124 A2
Burr Rd *WAND/EARL* SW18.............185 G3
Bursar St *STHWK* SE1........................24 A2
Burslem Cl *BAL* DA15......................195 F4
Bursland Rd *PEND* EN3.......................40 B5
Burslem Av *BARK/HLT* IG6.................75 G2
Burslem St *WCHPL* E1........................17 F4
Burstock Rd *PUT/ROE* SW15...........164 C5
Burston Rd *PUT/ROE* SW15...........164 B6
Burstow Rd *RYNPK* SW20.................204 C4
Burtenshaw Rd *THDIT* KT7...............220 C4
Burtley Cl *FSBYPK* N4........................85 E5
Burton Bank *IS* N1...........................108 D5
Burton Cl *CHSGTN* KT9....................239 F5
THHTH CR7.....................................208 D6
Burton Gdns *HEST* TW5....................158 D2
Burton Gv *WALW* SE17........................31 G4
Burtonhole Cl *MLHL* NW7..................48 B6
Burtonhole La *MLHL* NW7..................64 B1
NFNCH/WDSP N12...........................48 C6
Burton La *BRXN/ST* SW9.................168 A3
BRXN/ST SW9.................................147 F2
Burton Pl *STPAN* WC1H.......................4 D5
Burton Rd *BRXN/ST* SW9.................168 A3
KIL/WHAMP NW6............................100 C6
KUTN/CMB KT2..............................201 G3
SWFD E18..72 D6
Burtons Ct *SRTFD* E15.....................111 H5
Burton's Rd *HPTN* TW12..................179 H6
Burton St *STPAN* WC1H........................4 D5
Burt Rd *CAN/RD* E16........................153 E1
Burtwell La *WNWD* SE27.................188 D6
Burwash Cl *STMC/STPC* BR5.........236 A2
Burwash Rd *WOOL/PLUM* SE18.....154 D5
Burwell Av *GFD/PVL* UB6..................100 A4
Burwell Cl *WCHPL* E1..........................17 H4
Burwell Rd *LEY* E10............................90 C5
Burwood Av *HAYES* BR2..................232 D6
PIN HA5...78 A2
Burwood Cl *SURB* KT6.....................222 A5
Burwood Pl *BAY/PAD* W2..................10 B3
Bury Cl *BERM/RHTH* SE16..............150 B1
Bury Ct *HDTCH* EC3A.........................16 B3
Bury Gv *MRDN* SM4.........................225 F2
Bury Pl *NOXST/BSQ* WC1A...............13 E2
Bury Rd *CHING* E4..............................41 H5
DAGE RM10.....................................117 G3
WDGN N22..68 A5
Bury St *ED* N9....................................53 G3
HDTCH EC3A.....................................16 B3
STJS SW1Y..20 A1
Bury St West *ED* N9............................53 E2
Busby Pl *KTTN* NW5.........................107 F4
Busch Cl *ISLW* TW7..........................160 D2
Bushaby Cl *STHWK* SE1.....................24 A6
Bushberry Rd *HOM* E9......................110 C4
Bush Cl *GNTH/NBYPK* IG2..................94 D2
Bush Cottages
WAND/EARL SW18........................165 G6
Bushell Cl *BRXS/STRHM* SW2..........187 H4
Bushell Gn *BUSH* WD23......................43 H4
Bushell St *WAP* E1W..........................25 F2
Bushell Wy *CHST* BR7.......................214 A1
Bushey Av *STMC/STPC* BR5...........234 D4
SWFD E18..72 B6
Bushey Cl *CHING* E4...........................55 G5
Bushey Hill Rd *CMBW* SE5..............169 F2
Bushey La *SUT* SM1..........................243 E1
Bushey Lees *BFN/LL* * DA15............195 F1
Bushey Rd *CROY/NA* CR0................231 E6
PLSTW E13......................................133 E1
RYNPK SW20..................................204 A5
SEVS/STOTM N15.............................89 E5
SUT SM1..243 E2
Bushey Wy *BECK* BR3.......................211 H5
Bushfield Cl *EDGW* HA8.....................46 B4
Bushfield Crs *EDGW* HA8...................46 B4
Bush Gv *CDALE/KGS* NW9.................82 C4
STAN HA7..43 J4
Bushgrove Rd *BCTR* RM8..................91 K2
Bush Hill *WCHMH* N21.......................52 C2
Bush Hill Rd *KTN/HRWW/W* HA3......81 H3
WCHMH N21.....................................52 D1
Bush La *CANST* EC4R..........................15 G5
Bushmead Cl
SEVS/STOTM * N15..........................89 F1
Bushmoor Crs
WOOL/PLUM SE18........................174 A1
Bushnell Rd *TOOT* SW17.................186 D4
Bush Rd *BERM/RHTH* SE16............150 D4
BKHH IG9..57 F6
HACK E8...109 H6
RCH/KEW TW9...............................141 H6
Bushway *BCTR* RM8...........................91 K2
Bushwood *WAN* E11...........................92 B4
Bushwood Rd *RCH/KEW* TW9..........142 A4
Bushy Park Gdns *HPTN* TW12.........179 H1
Bushy Park Rd *TEDD* TW11.............200 D3
Bushy Rd *TEDD* TW11.......................200 A2

Butcher Rw *POP/IOD* E14..................130 B5
Butchers Rd *CAN/RD* E16................132 C5
Bute Av *RCHPK/HAM* TW10.............181 G4
Bute Gdns *HMSMTH* W6..................119 G4
RCHPK/HAM * TW10.......................181 G3
WLGTN SM6....................................245 E3
Bute Gdns West *WLGTN* SM6..........245 E3
Bute Rd *BARK/HLT* IG6......................94 B2
CROY/NA CR0.................................228 A5
WLGTN SM6....................................245 E3
Bute St *SKENS* * SW7......................145 H4
Bute Wk *IS* N1.................................108 D4
Butler Av *HRW* HA1...........................79 H4
Butler Rd *BCTR* RM8.........................115 H2
HRW HA1..79 H4
WLSDN NW10...................................81 H5
Butlers & Colonial Whf
STHWK SE1.......................................24 D3
Butlers Dr *CHING* E4..........................41 G1
Butler St *BETH* * E2.........................130 A2
Butterfield Cl *BERM/RHTH* SE16.......25 F4
TOTM N17..67 J2
TWK TW1...180 B1
Butterfields *WALTH* E17.....................57 J4
Butterfield Sq *EHAM* E6..................135 H5
Butterfly La *ELTH/MOT* SE9............194 B1
Butterfly Wk *CMBW* * SE5...............168 D2
Butterly Wk *WLGTN* SM6.................245 J1
Butteridges Cl *DAGW* RM9..............116 D6
Buttermere Cl *MRDN* SM4...............224 B5
STHWK SE1.......................................32 C1
Buttermere Dr *PUT/ROE* SW15.......164 A1
Buttermere Rd *STMC/STPC* BR5.....236 B1
Buttermere Wk *HACK* * E8..............109 F4
Butterwick *HMSMTH* W6..................144 A4
Buttesworth Gdns *WFD* IG8..............72 C2
Buttesland St *IS* N1..............................7 F4
Buttfield Cl *DAGE* RM10...................117 F4
Buttmarsh Cl
WOOL/PLUM SE18........................154 B5
Buttsbury Rd *IL* IG1.........................114 C3
Butts Crs *FELT* TW13........................179 E5
Butts Rd *BMLY* BR1..........................212 A1
The Butts *BTFD* TW8.........................141 F6
Buxhall Crs *HOM* E9.........................110 D4
Buxted Rd *EDUL* SE22.....................169 E5
HACK E8...109 F5
NFNCH/WDSP N12............................66 A1
Buxton Cl *WFD* IG8.............................75 F2
Buxton Crs *CHEAM* SM5..................242 C2
Buxton Dr *NWMAL* KT3....................202 D5
WAN E11..92 A1
Buxton Gdns *ACT* W3.......................122 B6
Buxton Pth *OXHEY* * WD19................42 A5
Buxton Rd *ARCH* N19..........................87 F5
CHING E4..55 H4
CRICK NW2..81 G3
EHAM E6..133 G2
ERITH DA8.......................................177 H1
GNTH/NBYPK IG2..............................95 E3
MORT/ESHN SW14...........................145 J5
SRTFD E15.......................................112 A5
THHTH CR7......................................228 B2
WALTH E17..90 C1
Buxton St *WCHPL* E1..........................13 K6
Byam St *FUL/PGN* SW6....................166 B1
Byards Cft *STRHM/NOR* SW16........207 F4
Bychurch End *TEDD* * TW11............200 B1
Bycroft Rd *STHL* UB1........................96 B3
Bycroft St *PGE/AN* SE20..................210 B3
Byculla Av *ENC/FH* EN2......................38 B4
Byculla Rd *ENC/FH* EN2......................38 B5
Byefield Cl *BERM/RHTH* SE16.........150 C1
Byelands Cl *BERM/RHTH* SE16.......150 B1
The Eye *ACT* W3..............................125 E5
Bye Ways *WHTN* TW2........................179 F5
The Byeways *BRYLDS* KT5................222 A2
The Bye Wy *KTN/HRWW/W* HA3........60 A4
The Byeway
MORT/ESHN SW14........................162 C4
Byfeld Gdns *BARN* SW13.................163 G2
Byfield Cl *BERM/RHTH* SE16...........150 C2
Byfield Rd *ISLW* TW7........................160 C4
Byford Cl *SRTFD* E15........................112 D6
Bygrove Rd *WIM/MER* SW19............205 H2
Bygrove St *POP/IOD* E14..................131 F5
Byland Cl *ABYW* SE2........................155 H3
WCHMH N21......................................51 H2
Byne Rd *CAR* SM5.............................226 A6
SYD SE26...181 K2
Bynes Rd *SAND/SEL* CR2.................246 D5
Byng Pl *GWRST* WC1E.........................4 C6
Byng Rd *BAR* EN5................................34 B4
Byng St *POP/IOD* E14........................151 E2
Bynon Av *BXLYHN* DA7....................176 C4
Byre Rd *STHGT/OAK* N14...................50 C1
Byrne Rd *BAL* SW12.........................186 D3
Byron Av *CDALE/KGS* NW9................88 B2
MNPK E12...113 G4
NWMAL KT3....................................220 D2
SUT SM1..243 H2
WHTN TW4......................................158 C2
Byron Av East *SUT* SM1...................243 H2
Byron Cl *HACK* E8............................109 G6
HPTN TW12.....................................162 A6
PGE/AN * SE20...............................209 H6
THMD SE28.....................................138 D4
WOT/HER KT12...............................218 C5
Byron Ct *ENC/FH* EN2.........................38 B5
Byron Dr *EFNCH* N2............................85 H3
ERITH DA8.......................................177 F5
Byron Gdns *SUT* SM1.......................243 H2
Byron Hill Rd *RYLN/HDSTN* HA2......78 C5
Byron Ms *HAMP* NW3........................106 A3
Byron Rd *ACT* W3............................117 K5
ALP/SUD HA0....................................61 J6
CRICK NW2..81 J6
HRW HA1..61 E6
KTN/HRWW/W HA3...........................61 G1
LEY E10...91 H5
MLHL NW7..45 H1
WALTH E17..71 H1
Byron St *POP/IOD* E14......................131 G5
Byron Ter *ED* * N9..............................30 A4
Byron Wy *NTHLT* UB5......................117 J2
Bysouth Cl *IL* IG5................................54 A5
By the Wd *OXHEY* WD19.....................42 B4
Bythorn St *BRXN/ST* SW9................167 H4
Byton Rd *TOOT* SW17.......................206 B2
Byward Av *EBED/NFELT* TW14.........178 A1

Byward St *MON* EC3R..........................16 B6
Bywater Pl *BERM/RHTH* SE16.........150 C1
Bywater St *CHEL* SW3.........................26 C5
The Byways *HOR/WEW* KT19.............241 F2
The Byway *BELMT* SM2.....................243 H6
Bywell Pl *GTPST* * W1W......................12 A2
Bywood Av *CROY/NA* CR0................230 A3

C

Cabbell St *CAMTN* NW1......................10 A2
Cabinet Wy *CHING* E4..........................70 D2
Cables Cl *CHICH* SE10......................171 G2
Cables Ct *BELV* DA17........................157 G3
Cable St *WCHPL* E1.............................17 H5
Cable Trade Pk *CHARL* * SE7..........152 C5
Cabot Sq *POP/IOD* E14.....................151 E1
Cabot Wy *EHAM* E6...........................113 J6
Cabul Rd *BTSEA* SW11......................140 D4
Cactus Cl *CMBW* * SE5.....................169 E5
Cadbury Cl *ISLW* TW7......................160 C2
Cadbury Wy *BERM/RHTH* SE16........24 D6
Caddington Cl *EBAR* EN4....................34 A6
Caddington Rd *CRICK* NW2................64 A1
Caddis Cl *STAN* * HA7..........................60 B5
Cadell Cl *BETH* E2................................8 D2
Cade Rd *GNWCH* SE10......................171 H2
Cader Rd *WAND/EARL* SW18..........185 G1
Cadet Dr *STHWK* SE1..........................50 A5
Cadet Pl *GNWCH* SE10......................151 A5
Cadiz Rd *DAGE* RM10.......................117 G5
Cadiz St *WALW* SE17............................31 F4
Cadman Cl *BRXN/ST* SW9.................168 B1
Cadmer Cl *NWMAL* KT3...................223 E1
Cadogan Cl *HOM* * E9.......................110 D6
RYLN/HDSTN HA2..............................99 F2
TEDD TW11.....................................200 A1
Cadogan Ct *BELMT* SM2..................243 F4
Cadogan Gdns *CHEL* SW3..................26 D1
FNCH * N3...47 F5
SWFD E18..72 D6
WCHMH N21......................................38 A6
Cadogan Ga *KTBR* SW1X....................26 D1
Cadogan La *KTBR* SW1X......................16 E6
Cadogan Pl *KTBR* SW1X......................18 D6
Cadogan Rd *SURB* KT6.....................210 C2
WOOL/PLUM SE18...........................154 C3
Cadogan Sq *KTBR* SW1X....................18 D6
Cadogan St *CHEL* SW3........................26 C2
Cadogan Ter *HOM* E9.........................111 G3
Cadoxton Av *SEVS/STOTM* N15.........89 F5
Cadwallon Rd *ELTH/MOT* SE9..........194 D4
Caedmon Rd *HOLWY* N7....................107 H2
Caerleon Cl *ESH/CLAY* KT10...........238 D5
SCUP DA14.......................................196 C2
Caernarvon Cl *MTCM* CR4................207 G6
Caernarvon Dr *CLAY* IG5....................54 A4
Caesars Wk *MTCM* CR4....................226 B2
Cahill St *STLK* * EC1Y........................12 E1
Cahir St *POP/IOD* E14.......................151 F4
Caird St *NKENS* W10.........................100 C2
Cairn Av *EA* W5................................141 F1
Cairndale Cl *BMLY* BR1.....................212 B5
Cairnfield Av *CRICK* NW2..................81 E1
Cairns Av *WFD* IG8..............................73 H2
Cairns Rd *BTSEA* SW11....................166 A1
Cairn Wy *STAN* HA7............................60 B2
Cairo New Rd *CROY/NA* CR0...........228 B6
Cairo Rd *WALTH* E17...........................57 J3
Caistor Park Rd *SRTFD* E15.............112 B6
Caistor Rd *BAL* SW12........................186 D2
Caithness Gdns *BFN/LL* DA15...........195 F1
Caithness Rd *HMSMTH* W6..............144 B3
MTCM CR4.......................................188 B3
Calabria Rd *HBRY* N5........................108 B4
Calais St *CMBW* SE5.........................168 B2
Calbourne Rd *BAL* SW12..................186 D2
Caldbeck Av *WPK* KT4.......................223 H6
Caldecote Gdns *BUSH* WD23.............44 A1
Caldecote La *BUSH* WD23...................44 D1
Caldecot Rd *CMBW* SE5...................168 C3
Caldecott Wy *CLPT* E5......................110 B1
Calder Av *GFD/PVL* UB6...................120 D1
Calder Gdns *EDGW* HA8.....................62 A6
Calderon Rd *WAN* E11.......................111 G2
Calder Rd *MRDN* SM4......................225 G2
Caldervale Rd *CLAP* SW4.................167 F6
Caldew Ct
WOOL/PLUM SE18........................154 A4
Caldicote Gn *CDALE/KGS* * NW9........83 E3
Caldwell Rd *OXHEY* WD19..................42 B6
Caldwell St *BRXN/ST* SW9................167 H1
Caldy Rd *BELV* DA17.........................157 F3
Caldy Wk *IS* * N1...............................108 C4
Caledonian Cl *GDMY/SEVK* * IG3......95 H5
Caledonian Rd *HOLWY* N7..................107 H2
Caledonian Wharf Rd
POP/IOD E14..................................151 H4
Caledonia St *IS* N1...............................5 F2
Caledon Rd *EHAM* E6.......................113 H6
WLGTN SM6....................................244 C2
Cale St *CHEL* SW3...............................26 B5
Calidore Cl *BRXS/STRHM* * SW2.....187 H1
California La *BUSH* WD23....................43 H3
California Rd *NWMAL* KT3................219 H1
Callaby Ter *IS* * N1...........................108 D4
Callaghan Cottages
WCHPL * E1....................................130 A4
Callander Rd *CAT* SE6......................191 F4
The Callanders *BUSH* * WD23...........44 A3
Callard Av *PLMGR* N13........................49 H1
Callcott Rd *KIL/WHAMP* NW6...........108 D1
Callcott St *KENS* W8..........................145 E1
Callingham Cl *POP/IOD* E14............130 D4
Callis Rd *WALTH* E17..........................90 C5
Callow St *CHEL* SW3.........................145 G6
Calmington Rd *CMBW* SE5.................32 B4
Calmont Rd *BMLY* BR1.....................183 E3
Calne Av *CLAY* IG5..............................74 B4
Calonne Rd *WIM/MER* SW19...........184 B6
Calshot Rd *HTHAIR*
Calshot St *IS* N1...................................5 G1
Calshot Wy *ENC/FH* EN2.....................38 D4
HTHAIR TW6
Calthorpe Gdns *EDGW* HA8..............61 K1
SUT SM1..243 G1
Calthorpe St *FSBYW* WC1X.................5 H5
Calton Av *DUL* SE21..........................169 E1
Calton Rd *BAR* EN5.............................49 G1
Calverley Cl *BECK* BR3....................211 F2

Calverley Crs *DAGE* RM10..................97 E6
Calverley Gv *ARCH* N19......................87 F5
Calverley Rd *EW* KT17......................241 G6
Camberley Av *EN* EN1.........................53 E5
Camberley Cl *CHEAM* SM3..................3 E3
RYNPK SW20.....................................205 H5
Camberley Cl *CHEAM* SM3................242 B1
Cambert Wy *ELTH/MOT* SE9............172 D5
Camberwell Church St
CMBW SE5......................................168 D2
Camberwell Glebe *CMBW* SE5.........168 D2
Camberwell Gn *CMBW* SE5..............168 D2
Camberwell Gv *CMBW* SE5..............168 D2
Camberwell New Rd
CMBW SE5......................................168 B1
Camberwell Rd *CMBW* SE5................31 H6
Camberwell Station Rd
CMBW SE5......................................168 C2
Camborne Rd *CROY/NA* CR0............197 G5
Camborne Av *WEA* W13....................140 D2
Camborne Rd *BELMT* SM2...............243 E5
CROY/NA CR0.................................229 G4
MRDN SM4......................................224 B2
SCUP DA14.....................................196 A5
WAND/EARL SW18.........................185 E2
WELL DA16.....................................175 E3
Camborne Wy *HEST* TW5................159 G2
Cambourne Av *ED* N9..........................34 B2
Cambourne Ms *NTGHL* W11.............124 C5
Cambray Rd *BAL* SW12.....................187 E3
ORP BR6..217 E6
Cambria Cl *BFN/LL* DA15.................194 D3
HSLW TW5.......................................159 F5
Cambrian Av *GNTH/NBYPK* IG2........95 E2
Cambrian Cl *WNWD* SE27................188 B5
Cambrian Gn *CDALE/KGS* * NW9......83 E2
Cambrian Rd *LEY* E10...........................91 E4
RCHPK/HAM TW10.........................181 H1
Cambria Rd *CMBW* SE5....................168 C5
Cambria St *FUL/PGN* SW6................165 F1
Cambridge Av *GFD/PVL* UB6............100 B3
KIL/WHAMP NW6............................125 E1
NWMAL KT3....................................203 E5
WELL DA16.....................................175 F5
Cambridge Barracks Rd
WOOL/PLUM SE18........................153 H4
Cambridge Cl *HSLW* TW4.................158 C5
RYNPK SW20.....................................68 A4
WDGN * N22.....................................102 C1
WLSDN NW10...................................81 G1
Cambridge Crs *BETH* E2......................5 J2
TEDD * TW11...................................200 C1
Cambridge Dr *LEE/GVPK* SE12........172 C6
RSLP HA4..78 A6
Cambridge Gdns *EN* EN1....................30 D3
KIL/WHAMP NW6............................125 E1
KIL/WHAMP NW6............................125 E1
KUT KT1..202 A5
MUSWH N10......................................66 B6
TOTM N17..68 D3
WCHMH N21......................................52 D2
Cambridge Ga *CAMTN* NW1...............3 J4
Cambridge Ga Ms *CAMTN* NW1.........3 H4
Cambridge Gn *ELTH/MOT* SE9.........194 B3
Cambridge Gv *HMSMTH* W6............143 H4
PGE/AN * SE20................................209 H4
Cambridge Grove Rd *KUT* KT1..........202 A5
Cambridge Heath Rd *BETH* E2............9 H2
Cambridge Pde *EN* * EN1...................30 C1
Cambridge Pk *TWK* TW1...................181 J1
WAN E11..92 C3
Cambridge Park Rd *WAN* E11.............92 B4
Cambridge Pas *HOM* E9....................110 A5
Cambridge Pl *KENS* * W8..................145 E2
Cambridge Rd *BARK* IG11.................114 C5
BARN SW13.....................................163 E2
BMLY BR1..166 B2
BTSEA SW11...................................244 A4
CAR SM5..141 J5
E/WMO/HCT KT8.............................181 E3
GDMY/SEVK IG3................................95 E4
HNWL W7...140 B2
HPTN TW12.....................................158 D2
HSLW TW4.......................................158 C3
KIL/WHAMP NW6............................125 E1
KUT KT1..202 A5
MTCM CR4.......................................207 G6
NWMAL KT3....................................203 E3
PGE/AN SE20..................................209 K3
RCH/KEW TW9...............................162 A1
RYLN/HDSTN HA2............................78 A4
RYNPK SW20..................................203 H4
SCUP DA14.....................................195 H6
SNWD SE25.....................................209 G6
STHL * UB1.....................................115 J3
TEDD TW11.....................................174 F1
TWK TW1...181 H1
WAN E11..92 C3
Cambridge Rd North
CHSWK W4...142 B5
Cambridge Rd South
CHSWK W4...142 B5
Cambridge Rw
WOOL/PLUM SE18........................154 B5
Cambridge Sq *BAY/PAD* W2..............10 A3
Cambridge St *PIM* SW1V..................29 H6
Cambridge Ter *CAMTN* NW1................3 J3
ED * N9...53 F2
Cambridge Terrace Ms
CAMTN * NW1.................................140 B2
Cambridge Yd *HNWL* * W7...............140 B2
Cambus Cl *YEAD* UB4.......................118 C4
Cambus Rd *CAN/RD* E16..................132 C4
Camdale Rd *WOOL/PLUM* SE18.......175 K4
Camden Av *FELT* TW13....................158 B1
YEAD UB4...118 A6

Camden Av FELT TW13 ....178 A4
YEAD UB4..........................118 A6
Camden Cl CHST BR7 ....214 C4
Camden Gdns CAMTN * NW1 ..106 D5
SUT SM1............................243 F3
THHTH CR7 ....208 B6
Camden Gv CHST BR7 ....214 C4
Camden High St CAMTN NW1 ..106 D6
Camden Hill Rd NRWD SE19 ....209 E2
Camden Ms CAMTN NW1 ....107 E5
Camden Park Rd CAMTN NW1 ..107 F4
CHST BR7 ....213 H5
Camden Pas IS N1 ....6 C1
Camden Rd BXLY DA5..............196 B5
CAMTN NW1 ....106 D6
CAR SM5............................244 B2
SUT SM1............................243 F3
WALTH E17 ....90 D3
WAN E11 ....92 D3
Camden Rd Permanent Wy
CAMTN * NW1......................107 F6
Camden Rw BKHTH/KID SE3 ....172 A3
PIN * HA5...........................58 A6
Camden Sq CAMTN NW1 ....107 F5
Camden St CAMTN NW1 ....106 D6
Camden Ter CAMTN NW1 ....107 F4
Camden Wk IS N1 ....108 B6
Camden Wy CHST BR7 ....213 H5
THHTH CR7 ....208 B6
Cameford Wk NTCHL * W11 ....124 C5
Camel Gv KUTN/CMB KT2 ......201 F1
Camellia Pl WHTN TW2 ....179 F2
Camelot Cl ABYW SE19 ....154 D2
WOOL/PLUM SE18 ....154 D2
Camel Rd CAN/RD E16 ....153 F1
Camera Pl WBPTN SW10 ....145 H5
TRDG/WHET N20 ....50 A4
UED N18 ....53 H6
Cameron Cl BXLY DA5..............197 H5
UED N18 ....53 H6
Cameron Pl WCHPL E1 ....17 H5
Cameron Rd CAT * SE6 ....190 D4
CROY/NA CR0 ....223 H5
GDMY/SEVK IG3 ....65 E5
HAYES BR2.........................232 C2
Cameron Ter LEE/GVPK * SE12 ..192 D5
Camerton Cl HACK E8 ....109 F4
Camilla Rd BERM/RHTH SE16 ....35 G2
Camille Cl SNWD SE25 ....209 G6
Camlan Rd BMLY BR1 ....192 B6
Camlet St BETH E2..................8 E3
Camlet Wy EBAR EN4 ....35 E3
Camley St CAMTN NW1 ....107 F6
Camm Gdns KUT * KT1 ....201 H5
THDIT KT7 ....220 A4
Camomile Av MTCM CR4 ....206 B4
Camomile St LVPST EC2M 13 H3
Camomile Rd ROMW/RG RM7 ....97 H6
Campana Rd FUL/PGN SW6 ......165 J3
Campbell Av BARK/HLT IG6 ......54 C1
Campbell Cl
STRHM/NOR * SW16 ....207 F1
WHTN TW2 ....179 H3
WOOL/PLUM SE18 ....174 A3
Campbell Cottages
MTCM * CR4 ....206 C5
Campbell Cft EDGW HA8..........62 A1
Campbell Gordon Wy
CRICK NW2 ....103 H2
Campbell Rd BOW E3 ....131 G2
CROY/NA CR0 ....196 A4
EHAM E6............................113 G4
FSTGT E7...........................112 A3
HNWL W7 ....97 G6
TOTM N17 ....69 F4
WALTH E17 ....90 D1
Campbell Wk IS N1 ....179 H4
Campdale Rd ARCH N19 ....107 H6
Campden Crs ALP/SUD * HA0 ..100 D1
DAGE RM8 ....111 H2
Campden Gv KENS W8 ....145 E2
Campden Hill KENS * W8 ....145 E2
Campden Hill Pl KENS * W8 ......144 D1
Campden Hill Rd KENS W8 ......144 D1
Campden Hill Sq KENS W8 ......144 D1
Campden House Cl KENS W8 ....145 E2
Campden House Ter
KENS * W8 ....145 E1
Campden Rd SAND/SEL CR2 ....247 E3
Campden St KENS W8 ....145 E1
Campden Ter CHSWK * W4 ......145 E2
Campen Cl WIM/MER SW19 ......184 C4
Campernell Rd WORTH SE27 ....188 D4
Campfield Rd ELTH/MOT SE9 ....195 F2
Campion Cl EHAM E6 ....113 H6
KTN/HRWW/W HA3 ....81 H5
ROMW/RG RM7 ....97 H6
SAND/SEL CR2 ....247 G2
Campion Cl ALP/SUD * HA0 ....100 C1
Campion Gdns WFD IG8 ....72 C1
Campion Pl THMD SE28 ....155 H1
Campion Rd ISLW TW7 ....160 B2
PUT/ROE SW15 ....164 A5
Campion Wy EDGW HA8..........46 C4
Camplin Rd KTN/HRWW/W HA3 ..81 G2
Camplin St NWCR SE14 ....170 D1
Camp Rd WIM/MER SW19 ....203 H1
Campsbourne Pde
CEND/HSY/T N8 ....67 C1
Campsbourne Rd
CEND/HSY/T N8 ....67 C1
The Campsbourne
CEND/HSY/T N8 ....87 C1
Campsey Rd DAGW RM9 ....115 H5
Campshill Pl LEW SE13 ....171 U6
Campshill Rd LEW SE13 ....171 U6
Campus Rd WALTH E17 ....90 D3
Cam Rd SRTFD E15..................111 H6
Camrose Av EDGW HA8............62 A4
ERITH DA8 ....157 F6
STAY HA7...........................43 C4
Camrose Cl CROY/NA CR0 ......230 C4
MRDN SM4.........................225 H3
Camrose St ABYW SE2............155 G5
Canada Av UED N18 ....68 C2
Canada Crs ACT W3 ....122 C4
Canada Park Pde EDGW * HA8 ..62 B4
Canada Rd ACT W3 ....122 C4

Canada St BERM/RHTH SE16 ....150 B2
Canada Wy SHB W12..............123 H6
Canadian Av CAT SE6..............191 F5
Canal Ap DEPT SE8..................150 C6
Canal Cl NKENS W10 ....124 B3
WCHPL E1..........................130 C3
Canal Gv PECK SE15 ....33 J5
Canal Pth HACK E8 ....7 G1
Canal Rd CMBW SE5 ....51 G4
Canal Wk CROY/NA CR0 ....229 E3
IS N1................................108 D6
WLSDN * NW10 ....102 C3
Canal Wy NKENS W10 ....124 B3
Canal Whf GFD/PVL * UB6 ......100 C6
Canberra Cl DAGE RM10 ....117 H5
HDN NW4...........................63 G6
Canberra Crs DAGE RM10 ....117 H5
Canberra Dr NTHLT UB5 ....118 A2
Canberra Rd ABYW SE2............154 D6
CHARL SE7.........................153 G6
EHAM E6............................113 H6
Canbury Av KUTN/CMB KT2 ....201 H4
Canbury Ms SYD SE26 ....189 G5
Canbury Park Rd
KUTN/CMB KT2 ....201 G2
Canbury Pth STMC/STPC BR5 ..235 G1
Cancell Rd BRXN/ST SW9 ....168 A2
Canberra Dr NTHLT UB5 ....118 B2
Candahar Rd BTSEA SW11 ......166 A3
Candler Ms TWK TW1 ....88 D7
Candler St SEVS/STOTM * N15 ..88 D3
Candy St BOW E3 ....110 D6
Caney Ms CRICK NW2..............84 B6
Canfield Gdns
KIL/WHAMP NW6 ....105 F5
Canfield Pl HAMP NW6 ....105 G4
Canfield Rd WFD IG8 ....73 C3
Canford Cl NTHLT UB5 ....98 C6
Canford Cl ENC/FH EN2 ....23 H2
Canford Gdns NWMAL KT3 ......223 E3
Canford Pl TEDD TW11 ....201 E2
Canford Rd BTSEA SW11 ....166 C5
Canham Rd CHSWK W4 ....143 A2
SNWD SE25 ....209 H6
Canmore Gdns
STRHM/NOR SW16 ....207 F3
Cann Hall Rd FSTGT E7 ....112 B2
Canning Crs WDGN N22 ....49 F4
Canning Cross CMBW SE5 ......169 E3
Canning Pl KENS W8 ....145 G3
Canning Place Ms KENS * W8 ..145 G3
Canning Rd CROY/NA CR0 ......229 C6
FSBYPK N4 ....108 B1
KTN/HRWW/W HA3 ....60 A6
SRTFD E15.........................132 A1
WALTH E17 ....90 C1
Cannington Rd DAGW RM9 ......116 A6
Cannizaro Rd WIM/MER SW19 ..204 A2
Cannonbury Av PIN HA5............78 B3
Cannon Cl HPTN TW12............199 F3
RYNPK SW20......................204 A4
Cannon Dr POP/IOD E14..........131 E6
Cannon Hl KIL/WHAMP NW6 ....105 F3
STHGT/OAK N14 ....51 F5
Cannon Hill La MRDN SM4 ......224 B5
Cannon La HAMP NW3 ....105 H1
PIN HA5.............................78 A6
Cannon Mohan Cl EBAR EN4 ....50 C1
Cannonbury Crs IS N1 ....108 C5
Canonbury Gv IS N1 ....108 C5
Canonbury La IS N1 ....108 B5
Canonbury Pk North IS N1 ......108 C4
Canonbury Pk South IS N1 ......108 C4
Canonbury Rd ENC/FH EN2 ......39 E2
IS N1................................108 B4
Canonbury Sq IS N1 ....108 B5
Canonbury Vis IS N1 ....108 B5
Canon Murnane Rd STHWK SE1 ..24 B8
Canon Rw BMLY BR1 ....213 E6
Canon Rd WHALL SW1A 21 E4
Canons Cl EDGW HA8..............61 H2
Carfax Rd CLAP SW4 ....85 H4
Canons Cottages EDGW * HA8 ..61 H2
Canons Dr EDGW HA8..............61 H2
Canonsleigh Rd DAGW RM9 ....116 C6
Canon St IS N1 ....108 C6
Canon's Wk CROY/NA CR0 ......248 B1
Canrobert St BETH E2 ....9 C2
Canterbury Av BFN/LL DA15 ....196 A4
IL IG1................................93 C4
Canterbury Cl BECK BR3..........211 F4
CMBW SE5 ....50 B6
EHAM E6............................113 H6
GFD/PVL UB6 ....118 H4
Canterbury Gv WNWD SE27 ....188 A5
Canterbury Pl WALW SE17 ......30 D2
Canterbury Rd CROY/NA CR0 ..227 H4
FELT TW13 ....178 C4
HRW HA1............................79 F2
KIL/WHAMP NW6 ....125 E1
LEY E10 ....91 G4
MRDN SM4.........................225 G5
RYLN/HDSTN HA2 ....79 F2
Canterbury Ter
KIL/WHAMP NW6 ....125 E1
Cantley Gdns GNTH/NBYPK IG2 ..94 D3
NRWD SE19 ....209 H4
Cantley Rd HNWL W7 ....141 F2
Canton St POP/IOD E14 ....131 E5
Cantrell Rd BOW E3 ....131 E3
Cantwell Rd WOOL/PLUM SE18 ..174 B1
Canvey St STHWK SE1 ....23 G1
Cape Cl BARK IG11 ....114 B5
Capel Av WLGTN SM6..............245 H3
Capel Cl HAYES BR2................233 G5

TRDG/WHET N20 ....49 C5
Capel Gdns GDMY/SEVK IG3 ..115 F2
PIN HA5.............................78 B1
Capel Rd EBAR EN4 ....50 A1
FSTGT E7...........................112 D2
OXHEY WD19 ....42 B1
Capel St KTBR SW1X 18 B4
KTBR * SW1X 19 E4
Capern Rd WAND/EARL SW18 ..185 C5
Cape Rd SEVS/STOTM N15 ......69 G6
Capital Interchange Wy
CHSWK W4 ....142 A5
Capitol Wy CDALE/KGS NW9 ....62 D6
Capland St STJWD NW8 ....2 A3
Caple Pde WLSDN * NW10 ......100 J1
Caple Rd WLSDN NW10 ....119 H1
Caprea Cl YEAD UB4 ....118 B4
Capri Rd CROY/NA CR0 ....229 F6
Capstan Cl CHDH RM6..............65 H5
Capstan Ride ENC/FH EN2 ......23 A3
Capstan Rd DEPT SE8 ....150 D4
Capstan Sq POP/IOD E14 ....133 E2
Capstan Wy BERM/RHTH SE16 ..150 C1
Capstone Rd BMLY BR1 ....192 C6
Capthorne Av RYLN/HDSTN HA2 ..78 C5
Capuchin Cl STAN * HA7 ....60 D2
Capulet Ms CAN/RD E16 ....151 C1
Capworth St LEY E10..............91 J6
Caradoc Evans Cl
FBAR/BDGN * N11 ....66 D1
Caradoc St GNWCH SE10 ....151 A5
Caradon Cl WAN * E11 ....92 A5
Caradon Wy SEVS/STOTM * N15 ..88 D1
Caravel Ms DEPT * SE8 ....151 E6
Caraway Cl PLSTW E13............132 D4
Caraway Pl WLGTN * SM6 ......244 D1
Carberry Rd NRWD SE19 ....209 G2
Carbery Av ACT W3 ....141 H2
Carbis Cl CHING E4 ....55 H5
Carbis Rd POP/IOD E14 ....130 D5
Carburton St GTPST W1W 11 J1
Cardale St POP/IOD E14 ....151 C3
Carden Rd PECK SE15 ....169 H4
Cardiff Rd HNWL W7 ....140 A2
PEND EN3 ....39 H5
Cardiff St WOOL/PLUM SE18 ..175 A3
Cardigan Gdns GDMY/SEVK IG3 ..95 G6
Cardigan Rd BOW E3 ....130 D1
RCHPK/HAM TW10 ....189 H1
WIM/MER SW19 ....205 G2
Cardigan St LBTH SE11 ....30 A3
Cardigan Wk IS * N1................108 C5
Cardinal Av KUTN/CMB KT2 ....201 C1
MRDN SM4.........................224 C3
Cardinal Bourne St
STHWK * SE1 ....23 H6
Cardinal Cl CHST BR7 ....214 D4
EDGW HA8 ....62 A4
MRDN SM4.........................224 C3
WPK KT4............................241 C2
Cardinal Crs NWMAL KT3 ....203 C5
Cardinal Dr BARK/HLT IG6 ......54 C2
WOT/HER KT12 ....188 B5
Cardinal Pl PUT/ROE SW15 ....146 B5
Cardinal Rd RSLP HA4..............78 B5
Cardinal's Wk HPTN TW12 ......199 C3
Cardinal Wy
KTN/HRWW/W HA3 ....81 F5
Cardine Ms PECK SE15............169 H1
Cardington Sq HSLWW TW4 ....188 A6
Cardington St CAMTN NW1 ......4 D3
Cardozo Rd HOLWY N7 ....84 D4
Cardrew Av NFNCH/WDSP N12 ..65 H1
Cardross St HMSMTH W6 ....118 D1
Cardwell Rd HOLWY * N7 ....84 D1
Cardwell Ter HOLWY * N7 ......84 D1
Carew Cl HOLWY N7 ....84 D1
Carew Rd ASHF TW15 ....177 U6
MTCM CR4 ....195 A1
THHTH CR7 ....208 C6
WEA W13 ....141 J2
WLGTN SM6.......................245 H4
Carew St CMBW SE5 ....168 C3
Carew Wy OXHEY WD19 ....41 H2
Carey Gdns VX/NE SW8............167 J2
Carey La CITYW EC2V 12 C4
Carey Pl WEST SW1P 28 C2
Carey Rd DAGW RM9 ....116 C2
Carey St LINN WC2A 11 H4
Carey Wy WBLY HA9 ....102 B2
Carfax Pl CLAP SW4 ....85 H4
The Carfax SYD * SE26............190 H1
Carfree Cl IS N1 ....108 A5
Cargill Rd WAND/EARL SW18 ..185 G3
Cargreen Rd SNWD SE25 ....229 F1
Carholme Rd FSTH SE23 ....190 D3
Carisbrook Cl EN EN1 ....36 C1
Carisbrooke Av BXLY DA5........196 B3
Carisbrooke Cl HEST TW5 ......188 C1
Carisbrooke Ct NTHLT * UB5 ..118 D3
Carisbrooke Gdns PECK * SE15 ..169 F1
Carisbrooke Rd HAYES * BR2 ..233 E1
MTCM CR4 ....227 J1
WALTH E17 ....90 C1
Carleton Av WLGTN SM6..........245 F6
Carleton Gdns ARCH * N19 ......107 J3
Carleton Rd HOLWY N7 ....84 D2
Carleton Vis KTTN * NW5 ....107 F3
Carlile Cl BOW E3 ....130 D1
Carlina Gdns WFD IG8 ....72 D1
Carlingford Rd HAMP NW3 ......84 D6
MRDN SM4.........................224 B3
SEVS/STOTM N15 ....68 C5
Carlisle Av ACT W3 ....125 C5
TWRH EC3N.........................14 B4
Carlisle Cl KUTN/CMB KT2 ......202 A4
PIN HA5.............................78 B3
Carlisle Gdns IL IG1................91 H2
KTN/HRWW/W HA3 ....81 H3
Carlisle La STHWK SE1 ....18 A5
Carlisle Ms CDALE/KGS NW9 ..62 D6
FSBYPK N4..........................67 G5
HPTN TW12 ....199 F3
KIL/WHAMP NW6 ....104 C6
LEY E10 ....91 E5

SUT SM1............................242 D4
Carlisle St SOHO/CST W1F 12 C4
Carlisle Wk HACK E8 ....109 F4
Carlisle Wy TOOT SW17 ....206 C1
Carlos Pl MYFR/PKLN W1K 11 F1
Carlow St CAMTN NW1 ....4 A1
Carlton Av EBED/NFELT TW14 ..178 A1
KTN/HRWW/W HA3 ....81 J3
SAND/SEL CR2....................246 D5
STHGT/OAK N14 ....37 F6
Carlton Av East WBLY HA9 ......81 H6
Carlton Av West ALP/SUD HA0 ..80 D6
Carlton Cl CHSGTN KT9 ....239 F4
EDGW HA8 ....62 A1
HAMP NW3 ....85 E6
Carlton Crs CHEAM SM3 ....261 H3
Carlton Dene SE * KT17 ....241 H5
PUT/ROE SW15 ....164 B6
Carlton Gdns EA W5 ....121 E5
EA W5...............................121 E5
ERITH DA8 ....157 F6
FBAR/BDGN N11..................88 A4
FSBYPK N4..........................67 H5
MNPK E12 ....113 F2
MORT/ESHN SW14 ....162 C4
NWMAL KT3.......................203 E5
SAND/SEL CR2....................245 F1
SCUP DA14 ....215 F1
WALTH E17 ....70 C4
WAN E11............................92 B5
WELL DA16 ....175 H4
Carlton Gn SCUP * DA14 ....195 F6
Carlton Gv PECK SE15............169 H2
Carlton Hl STJWD NW8............2 A1
Carlton House Ter STJS SW1Y ..20 C2
Carlton Ms KIL/WHAMP * NW6 ..105 E3
Carlton Pde WBLY * HA9 ....81 J5
Carlton Park Av RYNPK SW20 ..204 D3
Carlton Rd CHSWK W4 ....121 A6
EA W5...............................121 E6
ERITH DA8 ....157 F6
FBAR/BDGN N11..................88 A4
FSBYPK N4..........................67 H5
MNPK E12 ....113 F2
MORT/ESHN SW14 ....162 C4
NWMAL KT3.......................203 E5
SAND/SEL CR2....................245 F1
SCUP DA14 ....215 F1
WALTH E17 ....70 C4
WAN E11............................92 B5
WELL DA16 ....175 H4
Carlton Sq WCHPL * E1 ....130 B3
Carlton St STJS SW1Y 12 C6
Carlton Ter SYD SE26..............190 A5
UED * N18..........................68 C1
WAN * E11 ....92 D2
Carlton Tower Pl KTBR SW1X....18 D7
Carlton V KIL/WHAMP NW6 ....125 E2
Carlwell St TOOT SW17 ....206 D1
Carlyle Av BMLY BR1 ....213 F6
STHL UB1 ....118 D6
Carlyle Cl E/WMO/HCT KT8 ....199 F5
EFNCH N2..........................65 H3
WLSDN NW10 ....102 D6
Carlyle Gdns STHL UB1 ....118 D6
Carlyle Pl PUT/ROE SW15 ......165 G2
Carlyle Rd CROY/NA CR0 ....229 G6
EA W5...............................141 E4
MNPK E12 ....113 G2
THMD SE28 ....135 H6
Carlyle Sq CHEL SW3 ....145 H5
Carlyon Av RYLN/HDSTN HA2 ..98 D2
Carlyon Cl ALP/SUD HA0 ....101 C6
Carlyon Rd ALP/SUD HA0 ....121 C1
YEAD UB4...........................118 A4
Carlys Cl BECK BR3................210 B1
Carmalt Gdns PUT/ROE SW15 ..164 A5
Carmel Ct KENS * W8..............145 F2
Carmelite Rd
KTN/HRWW/W HA3 ....59 G4
Carmelite St EMB EC4Y 14 B5
Carmen St POP/IOD E14 ....131 F5
Carmichael Cl BTSEA * SW11 ..165 H4
Carmichael Rd SNWD SE25 ....229 C2
Carminia Rd TOOT SW17 ....186 D4
Carnaby St REGST W1B 12 A5
Carnac St WNWD SE27............188 D6
Carnanton Rd WALTH E17 ......71 H4
Carnarvon Av EN EN1 ....39 F5
LEY E10 ....91 G3
SRTFD E15.........................113 C6
SWFD E18 ....72 B4
Carnation St ABYW SE2............155 H6
Carnbrook Rd BKHTH/KID SE3 ..173 F4
Carnecke Gdns ELTH/MOT SE9 ..173 H2
Carnegie Cl SURB KT6..............241 G6
WAB EN9............................41 F1
Carnegie Pl WIM/MER SW19 ..184 A3
Carnegie St IS N1 ....5 J1
Carnforth Cl HOR/WEW KT19 ..240 B4
Carnforth Rd
STRHM/NOR SW16 ....207 F3
Carnoustie Dr IS N1 ....107 H4
Carnwath Rd FUL/PGN SW6 ..166 A6
Carolina Cl SRTFD E15............112 A3
Carolina Rd THHTH CR7 ....208 B5
Caroline Cl CROY/NA CR0 ......247 E2
STRHM/NOR SW16 ....188 A4
WDGN N22 ....49 F6
Caroline Gdns BETH E2 ....8 D4
PECK * SE15 ....169 H1
Caroline Pl BAY/PAD W2 ....14 C3
OXHEY WD19 ....27 G6
VX/NE SW8 ....166 C3
Caroline Pl WIM/MER SW19 ....204 D3
Caroline Rd WIM/MER SW19 ..185 H5
Caroline St WCHPL E1 ....130 D5
Caroline Ter BGVA SW1W 16 D7
Caroline Wk HMSMTH W6 ......168 A1
Carol St CAMTN NW1 ....107 E6
Carpenders Av OXHEY WD19 ..42 C5
Carpenter Gdns WCHMH N21 ..52 B4
Carpenters Ms HOLWY * N7 ....107 F3
Carpenter's Pl CLAP SW4 ....169 J3
Carpenters Rd SRTFD E15 ......111 F5
Carpenter St MYFR/PKLN W1K ..11 G6
Carrara Ms HACK E8 ....109 G3
Carr Gv CW WOOL/PLUM SE18 ..153 C4
Carriage Dr North BTSEA SW11 ..166 B1
Carriage Dr South BTSEA SW11 ..166 B3
Carriage Dr West BTSEA SW11 ..166 B1
Carrick Cl ISLW TW7 ....160 C4
Carrick Dr BARK/HLT IG6 ....54 C4
Carrick Gdns TOTM N17 ....49 J6
Carrick Ms DEPT SE8 ....151 E5
Carrill Wy BELV DA17 ....156 D4
Carrington Av HSLW TW3 ......159 F6
Carrington Cl CROY/NA CR0 ..230 C4

Carrington Gdns FSTGT E7 ....112 C2
Carrington Rd
  RCHPK/HAM TW10 ....162 A5
Carrington Sq
  KTN/HRWW/W HA3 ....59 C3
Carrington St MYFR/PICC W1J ...19 G2
Carrol Cl KTTN NW5 ....106 D2
Carroll Cl SRTFD E15 ....112 B3
Carronade Pl
  WOOL/PLUM SE18 ....154 D3
Carron Cl POP/IOD E14 ....151 F5
Carroun Rd VX/NE SW8 ....167 H1
Carroway La GFD/PVL UB6 ....119 H2
Carrow Rd DAGW RM9 ....115 H5
Carr Rd NTHLT UB5 ....99 F5
  WALTH E17 ....70 D5
Carrs La WCHMH N21 ....38 D6
Carr St POP/IOD E14 ....130 C4
Carshalton Cv SUT SM1 ....243 H2
Carshalton Park Rd CAR SM5 ......244 B4
Carshalton Pl CAR SM5 ....244 C2
Carshalton Rd MTCM CR4 ....226 C2
  SUT SM1 ....243 G5
Carslake Rd PUT/ROE SW15 ....184 A1
Carson Rd CAN/RD E16 ....132 C4
  DUL SE21 ....188 C4
  EHAM E6 ....36 B5
Carstairs Rd CAT SE6 ....191 G5
Carston Cl LEE/GVPK SE12 ....172 B6
Carswell Cl REDBR IG4 ....93 F1
Carswell Rd CAT SE6 ....191 G2
Carter Cl CRW RM5 ....77 F3
  WLGTN SM6 ....245 F5
Carteret St STJSPK SW1H 20 C4
Carteret Wy DEPT SE8 ....150 C4
Carterhatch La EN EN1 ....39 F2
  EN EN1 ....39 F2
  PEND EN3 ....40 A3
Carterhatch Rd PEND EN3 ....40 C1
Carter La BLKFR EC4V 14 D4
Carter Pl WALW SE17 ....31 F4
Carter Rd PLSTW E13 ....112 D6
  WIM/MER SW19 ....205 H2
Carters Cl KTTN * NW5 ....107 F4
  WPK KT4 ....224 B6
Carters Hill Cl ELTH/MOT SE9 ....193 E3
Carter St WALW SE17 ....31 E5
Carter's Yd
  WAND/EARL * SW18 ....165 G6
Carthew Rd HMSMTH W6 ....143 H3
Carthew Vis HMSMTH W6 ....143 H3
Carthusian St FARR EC1M 15 E1
Cartier La TPL/STR WC2R 6 C5
Cart La CHING E4 ....56 A3
Cartmel Cl TOTM N17 ....69 H5
Cartmel Ct NTHLT UB5 ....80 B4
Cartmel Gdns MRDN SM4 ....225 G2
Cartmel Rd BXLYHN DA7 ....177 E2
Cartwright Gdns STPAN WC1H 4 E4
Cartwright St TWRH EC3N 16 D5
Cartwright Wy BARN SW13 ....125 H1
Carver Rd HNHL SE24 ....188 C1
Carville Crs BTFD TW8 ....141 G4
Cary Rd WAN E11 ....112 A2
Carysfort Rd CEND/HSY/T N8 .....66 C1
  STNW/STAM N16 ....108 D1
Cascade Av MUSWH N10 ....87 E1
Cascade Cl STMC/STPC BR5 ....216 A6
Cascade Rd BKHH IG9 ....57 F4
Cascade Rd NWCR SE14 ....170 B1
Casewick Rd WNWD SE27 ....208 B3
Casey Cl CAMTN NW1 ....2 B6
Casimir Rd CLPT E5 ....109 H1
Casino Av HNHL SE24 ....169 G6
Caspian St CMBW SE5 ....168 D1
Caspian Wk CAN/RD E16 ....133 F5
Cassandra Cl NTHLT UB5 ....80 D3
Casseldon Rd WLSDN NW10 ....102 D5
Cassidy Rd FUL/PGN SW6 ....165 J1
Cassilda Rd ABYW SE2 ....155 G4
Cassils Rd TWK TW1 ....180 D1
Cassiobury Rd WALTH E17 ....69 F3
Cassland Rd HOM E9 ....110 B5
  THHTH CR7 ....228 D1
Cassilee Rd CAT SE6 ....190 D2
Casson St WCHPL E1 ....17 E2
Castellain Rd MV/WKIL W9 ....125 F3
Castellane Cl STAN HA7 ....60 B3
Castello Av PUT/ROE SW15 ....164 A6
Castellane BARN SW13 ....163 H1
Casterbridge Rd
  BKHTH/KID SE3 ....172 C4
Casterton St HACK EB 109 H4
Castile Rd WOOL/PLUM SE18 .....154 A4
Castillon Rd CAT SE6 ....192 A4
Castlands Rd CAT SE6 ....190 D4
Castle Av CHING E4 ....71 H2
  EW KT17 ....260 A1
Castlebar Hl WEA W13 ....120 D4
Castlebar Ms EA W5 ....120 D4
Castlebar Pk EA W5 ....120 D4
Castlebar Rd WEA W13 ....121 E5
Castle Baynard St BLKFR EC4V ...14 D5
Castlebrook Cl LBTH SE11 ....30 C1
Castle Cl ACT W3 ....142 B2
  BUSH WD23 ....8 B3
  HAYES BR2 ....211 H6
  WIM/MER SW19 ....184 B5
Castlecombe Dr
  WIM/MER SW19 ....184 B2
Castlecombe Rd
  ELTH/MOT SE9 ....213 G1
  SYD SE26 ....190 C6
Castledine Rd PGE/AN SE20 ......209 H3
Castle Dr REDBR IG4 ....93 G3
Castleford Av ELTH/MOT SE9 .....194 B3
Castleford Cl UED N18 ....69 F2
Castleford Rd CRW/KEW TW9 .....161 H4
Castlehaven Rd CAMTN NW1 ......106 D5
Castle Hill Av CROY/NA CRO 249 F6
Castle Hill Pde WEA * W13 ....120 D6
Castle La WESTW SW1E 20 A5
Castleleigh Ct ENC/FH EN2 ....38 D6
Castlemaine Av EW KT17 ....241 H6
  SAND/SEL CR2 ....247 F3
Castle Md CMBW * SE5 ....146 D6
Castle Ms CAMTN NW1 ....106 D5
  NFNCH/WDSP N12 ....65 C1
Castle Pde EW * KT17 ....241 G5
Castle Pl CAMTN NW1 ....106 D4

Castlereagh St MBLAR W1H 10 C3
Castle Rd CAMTN NW1 ....106 D4
  DAGW RM9 ....115 H6
  ISLW TW7 ....160 B3
  NFNCH/WDSP N12 ....65 C1
  NTHLT UB5 ....80 D4
  NWDGN * UB2 ....138 D3
  PEND EN3 ....40 C2
Castle Rw CHSWK * W4 ....142 D5
Castle St EHAM E6 ....95 E4
  KUT * KT1 ....201 C5
Castleton Av BXLYHN DA7 ....177 H2
  WBLY HA9 ....101 G2
Castleton Cl CROY/NA CRO 230 C5
Castleton Rd GDMY/SEVK IC5 ....95 C5
  LEE/GVPK SE12 ....195 F6
  MTCM CR4 ....227 F1
  RSLP HA4 ....77 H6
  WALTH E17 ....71 H5
Castletown Rd WKENS W14 ......144 C5
Castleview Cl FSBYPK N4 ....88 C5
Castle View Gdns IL IG1 ....93 G3
Castle Vis CRICK * NW2 ....103 G4
Castle Wk SUN * TW16 ....198 A6
Castle Wy FELT TW13 ....178 A6
  WIM/MER SW19 ....184 B5
Castlewood Dr ELTH/MOT SE9 ...173 H3
Castlewood Rd EBAR EN4 ....35 H4
  SEVS/STOTM N15 ....89 C3
Castle Yd HGT N6 ....86 C4
  RCHPK/HAM TW10 ....161 H6
  STHWK * SE1 ....22 D7
Castor La POP/IOD E14 ....131 F6
Caterham Av CLAY IG5 ....74 A5
Caterham Rd LEW SE13 ....171 G4
Catesby St WALW SE17 ....51 J6
Catford Broadway CAT SE6 ....191 F2
Catford Hl CAT SE6 ....190 D3
Catford Island CAT * SE6 ....191 F2
Catford Rd CAT SE6 ....191 E3
Cathall Rd WAN E11 ....91 H6
Cathay St BERM/RHTH SE16 .....25 H4
Cathcart Dr ORP BR6 ....235 E6
Cathcart Hl KTTN NW5 ....107 W10
Cathcart Rd WBPTN * SW10 .....145 F6
Cathcart St KTTN NW5 ....106 D4
Cathedral St STHWK SE1 ....23 C1
Catherald Rd HBRY N5 ....108 C1
Catherine Ct STHGT/OAK N14 ...37 D6
Catherine Dr RCH/KEW TW9 .....161 G5
Catherine Gdns HSLW TW3 ......159 H5
Catherine Griffiths Ct
  CLKNW * EC1R 6 B5
Catherine Gv GNWCH SE10 ......171 F2
Catherine Pl WESTW SW1E 20 A5
Catherine Rd SURB KT6 ....221 F2
Catherine St HOL/ALD * WC2B ...11 G5
Catherine Vis RYNPK * SW20 ....203 H3
Catherine Wheel Aly
  LVPST EC2M 16 B2
Catherine Wheel Rd BTFD TW8 ..161 F1
Catherine Wheel Yd
  WHALL SW1A 20 A2
Cat Hl EBAR EN4 ....36 B6
Cathles Rd BAL SW12 ....186 D1
Cathnor Rd WPLT W12 ....143 H2
Catling Cl FSTH SE23 ....190 A5
Catlin St BERM/RHTH SE16 ......33 F4
Cator La BECK BR3 ....210 D5
Cato Rd CLAP SW4 ....147 H3
Cator Rd CAR SM5 ....244 B3
  SYD SE26 ....210 B2
Cator St PECK SE15 ....32 C6
Cato St MBLAR W1H 10 B2
Catsey La BUSH WD23 ....43 G2
Catsey Wd BUSH WD23 ....43 G2
Catterick Cl FBAR/BDGN N11 ....66 C2
Cattistock Rd ELTH/MOT SE9 ....213 C1
Cattley Cl BAR EN5 ....34 C5
Catton St RSQ WC1B 11 G3
Cauldwell Ter
  WAND/EARL * SW18 ....185 H1
Cauffield Rd EHAM E6 ....113 H5
  PECK SE15 ....169 H3
The Causeway BELMT SM2 ....243 G6
  CAR SM5 ....244 C1
  CHSGTN KT9 ....239 G2
  EFNCH N2 ....65 H1
  ESH/CLAY KT10 ....285 B1
  TEDD TW11 ....180 B2
  WAND/EARL SW18 ....165 H6
  WIM/MER SW19 ....204 A1
Causewayere Rd ED N9 ....43 G4
Causton Cottages
  POP/IOD * E14 ....130 C4
Causton Rd HGT * N6 ....66 B5
Causton Sq DAGE RM10 ....117 E5
Causton St WEST SW1P 28 D2
Cautley Av CLAP SW4 ....167 E6
Cavalier Cl CHDH RM6 ....96 A1
Cavalry Crs HSLWW TW4 ....158 B5
Cavalry Gdns PUT/ROE SW15 ....164 A6
Cavan Pl PIN * HA5 ....58 D4
Cavaye Pl WBPTN SW10 ....145 G5
Cavell Dr ENC/FH EN2 ....38 A3
Cavell Rd CEND/HSY/T N8 ....68 B2
Cavell St WCHPL E1 ....111 H4
Cavendish Av ERITH/ERL DA15 ..195 G2
  ERITH DA8 ....157 G6
  FNCH N3 ....65 E6
  NTHLT UB5 ....98 A3
  NWMAL KT3 ....225 H1
  STJWD NW8 ....125 H1
  WELL DA16 ....176 A4
  WFD IG8 ....72 D5
Cavendish Cl KIL/WHAMP NW6 ..104 D4
  STJWD * NW8 ....125 H2
Cavendish Dr ESH/CLAY KT10 ...238 A3
  WAN E11 ....91 H1
Cavendish Gdns BARK IG11 .....115 F3
  CHDH RM6 ....96 C2
  CLAP * SW4 ....187 E1
  IL IG1 ....94 B5
Cavendish Ms North
  REGST W1B 11 H1
Cavendish Ms South
  GTPST * W1W 11 H2
Cavendish Pde CLAP * SW4 .....167 E5
  HSLWW * TW4 ....158 C3

Cavendish Pl KIL/WHAMP NW6 ..104 B5
  MHST W1U 11 G3
Cavendish Rd BAR EN5 ....34 A4
  BELMT SM2 ....245 G5
  CHING E4 ....71 F3
  CHSWK W4 ....162 C2
  CLAP SW4 ....186 D1
  CROY/NA CRO 228 B5
  FSBYPK N4 ....67 G5
  KIL/WHAMP NW6 ....104 C5
  NWMAL KT3 ....223 F2
  UED N18 ....44 C1
  WIM/MER SW19 ....206 A3
Cavendish Sq CAVSQ/HST * W1C .11 G5
Cavendish St IS N1 ....7 F2
Cavendish Ter FELT * TW13 .....130 D2
Cavendish Wy WWKM BR4 ....231 F5
Cavenham Gdns IL IG1 ....114 D1
Caverleigh Wy WPK KT4 ....225 G5
Caverley Gdns
  KTN/HRWW/W HA3 ....81 F4
Cave Rd PLSTW E13 ....132 D1
  RCHPK/HAM TW10 ....181 E6
Caversham Av CHEAM SM3 ......224 C6
  PLMGR N13 ....52 A5
Caversham Rd KTTN * NW5 .....107 E4
  KUT KT1 ....201 H5
  SEVS/STOTM N15 ....88 C1
Caversham St CHEL SW3 ....26 C5
Caverswall St SHB W12 ....124 A5
Cawdor Crs HNWL W7 ....140 C4
Cawnpore St NRWD SE19 ....209 E1
Caxton Gv BOW E3 ....131 E2
Caxton Ms BTFD * TW8 ....161 F1
Caxton Rd NWDGN UB2 ....138 B3
  SHB W12 ....144 B1
  WDGN N22 ....67 H5
  WIM/MER SW19 ....205 G1
The Caxtons CMBW * SE5 ....168 B1
Caxton St STJSPK SW1H 20 B5
Caxton St North CAN/RD E16 ...132 B5
Cayenne Ct STHWK SE1 ....24 B3
Caygill Cl HAYES BR2 ....215 H1
Cayley Rd NWDGN UB2 ....139 F3
Cayton Rd GFD/PVL UB6 ....120 A1
Cayton St FSBYE EC1V 7 G4
Cazenove Rd STNW/STAM N16 ...89 F6
  WALTH E17 ....51 H5
Cearns Ho EHAM * E6 ....95 H5
Cecil Av BARK IG11 ....114 D5
  EN EN1 ....39 F5
  WBLY HA9 ....80 B3
Cecil Cl CHSGTN KT9 ....239 F2
  EA * W5 ....121 F4
Cecil Ct BAR EN5 ....34 B4
  LSQ/SEVD WC2H 12 D6
Cecile Pk CEND/HSY/T N8 ....67 G5
Cecilia Cl EFNCH N2 ....65 G6
Cecilia Rd HACK E8 ....109 F3
Cecil Pk PIN HA5 ....78 C1
Cecil Rd ACT W3 ....123 H2
  CDALE/KGS NW9 ....62 D6
  CHDH RM6 ....96 B4
  CROY/NA CRO 196 C4
  ENC/FH EN2 ....38 D5
  HSLW TW3 ....159 G4
  IL IG1 ....114 B2
  KTN/HRWW/W HA3 ....60 A6
  MUSWH N10 ....66 B6
  PLSTW E13 ....112 C6
  SUT SM1 ....242 D4
  WALTH E17 ....51 J6
  WAN E11 ....92 A6
  WIM/MER SW19 ....205 F3
  WLSDN NW10 ....103 E6
Cecil Wy HAYES BR2 ....215 H6
Cedar Av BFN/LL DA15 ....195 G2
  CHDH RM6 ....96 C2
  EBAR EN4 ....50 A2
  PEND EN3 ....40 A3
  RSLP HA4 ....98 B2
  WHTN TW2 ....179 F1
Cedar Cl BKHH IG9 ....57 F4
  CAR SM5 ....244 B4
  DUL SE21 ....188 C3
  HAYES BR2 ....251 G1
  KUTN/CMB KT2 ....182 D6
  ROMW/RG RM7 ....75 H1
  SWLY BR8 ....217 G5
Cedar Copse BMLY BR1 ....213 H5
Cedar Ct CHARL * SE7 ....153 E6
  ELTH/MOT * SE9 ....193 G1
  WIM/MER SW19 ....184 B5
Cedar Crs HAYES BR2 ....251 G1
Cedarcroft Rd CHSGTN KT9 .....239 H2
Cedar Dr EFNCH N2 ....86 A1
  PIN HA5 ....42 B3
Cedar Gdns BELMT SM2 ....243 G4
Cedar Gv BXLY DA5 ....196 B3
  EA W5 ....141 F3
  STHL UB1 ....116 B6
Cedar Hts RCHPK/HAM TW10 ....181 G5
Cedarhurst BMLY * BR1 ....212 A3
Cedarhurst Dr ELTH/MOT SE9 ...173 E6
Cedar Lawn Av BAR EN5 ....34 C5
Cedar Mt ELTH/MOT SE9 ....193 F5
Cedarne Rd FUL/PGN SW6 ......146 E1
Cedar Park Gdns CHDH RM6 ....96 B4
Cedar Park Rd ENC/FH EN2 .....23 H1
Cedar Pl CHARL SE7 ....153 E5
  STHGT/OAK N14 ....50 C2
Cedar Rd BELMT SM2 ....243 G4
  BMLY BR1 ....184 A5
  CRICK NW2 ....104 A2
  CROY/NA CRO 229 B6
  E/WMO/HCT KT8 ....220 A1
  ENC/FH EN2 ....38 B1
  HEST TW5 ....135 G1
  OXHEY WD19 ....42 H1
  ROMW/RG RM7 ....97 G1
  TEDD TW11 ....200 C1
  TOTM N17 ....68 B4
Cedars Av MTCM CR4 ....226 C1
  WALTH E17 ....91 E2
Cedars Cl HDN NW4 ....64 B2
  LEW SE13 ....171 H4
Cedars Cottages
  PUT/ROE * SW15 ....183 G1
Cedars Ct ED N9 ....53 E4
Cedars Ms CLAP * SW4 ....166 D5

Cedars Rd BARN SW13 ....163 F3
  BECK BR3 ....210 C5
  CLAP SW4 ....166 D4
  CROY/NA CRO 245 G1
  E/WMO/HCT KT8 ....201 E4
  MRDN SM4 ....225 J4
  SRTFD E15 ....112 A4
  WCHMH N21 ....52 B4
The Cedars BKHH IG9 ....57 F3
  HOM * E9 ....110 B5
  SRTFD * E15 ....112 B6
  TEDD TW11 ....200 B2
Cedar Ter RCH/KEW TW9 ....161 G5
Cedar Tree Gv WNWD SE27 .....208 B1
Cedarville Gdns
  STRHM/NOR SW16 ....207 H2
Cedar Wk ESH/CLAY KT10 ......238 B4
Cedar Wy CAMTN NW1 ....5 J1
Cedric Rd ELTH/MOT SE9 ....194 C5
Celadon Cl PEND EN3 ....40 C4
Celandine Cl POP/IOD * E14 ....131 E4
Celandine Dr HACK E8 ....109 F5
  THMD SE28 ....115 H1
Celandine Wy SRTFD E15 ....132 A2
Celbridge Ms BAY/PAD * W2 ...125 F5
Celestial Gdns LEW SE13 ....171 H5
Celia Rd ARCH N19 ....107 E2
Celtic Av HAYES BR2 ....212 A6
Celtic St POP/IOD E14 ....131 F4
Cemetery La CHARL SE7 ....153 G6
Cemetery Rd ABYW SE2 ....156 B6
  FSTGT E7 ....112 B3
  TOTM N17 ....69 B3
Cenacle Cl HAMP NW3 ....105 E1
Centaur Ct BTFD * TW8 ....141 G5
Centaur St STHWK SE1 ....21 H5
Centenary Rd PEND EN3 ....40 D5
Centenary Wk LOU IC10 ....15 H6
  WAN E11 ....92 C5
  WFD IG8 ....72 A2
Centennial Av BORE WD6 ....45 E2
Centennial Pk BORE * WD6 .....45 E2
Central Av E/WMO/HCT KT8 ....218 D2
  ED N9 ....53 E5
  EFNCH N2 ....65 H1
  EN EN1 ....39 H3
  HSLW TW3 ....159 G5
  PIN HA5 ....59 H6
  WAN E11 ....91 H1
  WELL DA16 ....175 G3
  WLGTN SM6 ....245 E4
Central Buildings EA * W5 ......121 F6
Central Circ HDN NW4 ....83 H2
Central Hl NRWD SE19 ....208 C1
Central Pde ACT * W3 ....142 A2
  E/WMO/HCT KT8 ....218 D1
  GFD/PVL * UB6 ....120 C2
  HRW HA1 ....80 B2
  PEND * EN3 ....40 A3
  PGE/AN * SE20 ....210 B3
  SCUP * DA14 ....195 G5
  STRHM/NOR SW16 ....187 G6
  SURB * KT6 ....219 F4
  WALTH * E17 ....91 E1
Central Park Est HSLWW * TW4 ..158 B5
Central Park Rd EHAM E6 ......133 C1
Central Pl SNWD * SE25 ....229 G1
Central Rd ALP/SUD HA0 ....100 C6
  MRDN SM4 ....225 F2
  WPK KT4 ....225 G5
Central Sq E/WMO/HCT KT8 ....218 D1
  GLDGN NW11 ....85 E3
Central St FSBYE EC1V 7 F4
Central Ter BECK * BR3 ....210 B6
Central Wy CAR SM5 ....244 A5
  FELT TW14 ....135 H6
  WLSDN NW10 ....121 G2
Centre Av ACT W3 ....142 D1
  EFNCH N2 ....65 H3
Centre Common Rd CHST BR7 ..214 C3
Centre Rd DAGE RM10 ....117 G6
  WAN E11 ....92 C6
Centre St BETH E2 ....92 G2
Centre Wy ED N9 ....54 A4
Centric Cl CAMTN * NW1 ....106 D6
Centurian Wy ERITH DA18 ......156 D3
Centurion Cl HOLWY N7 ....107 H5
Centurion Ct WLGTN * SM6 ....226 D6
Centurion La BOW E3 ....111 J1
Century Cl HDN NW4 ....64 B2
Century Ms CLPT * E5 ....110 A2
Century Rd WALTH E17 ....70 C6
Century Yd FSTH * SE23 ....190 H1
Cephas Av WCHPL E1 ....93 E3
Cephas St WCHPL E1 ....130 E1
Ceres Rd WOOL/PLUM SE18 ....155 F4
Cerise Rd PECK SE15 ....169 G2
Cerne Cl YEAD UB4 ....98 D4
Cerne Rd MRDN SM4 ....226 C3
Cervantes Ct BAY/PAD * W2 ....125 F5
Chadacre Av CLAY IG5 ....73 A6
Chadacre Rd EW KT17 ....241 A4
Chadbourn St POP/IOD E14 ....131 H4
Chadd Dr BMLY BR1 ....213 A5
Chadville Gdns CHDH RM6 .....96 B2
Chadway BCTR RM8 ....96 A6
Chadwell Av CHDH RM6 ....96 H4
Chadwell Heath La CHDH RM6 ..95 H1
Chadwell St CLKNW EC1R 6 B3
Chadwick Av CHING E4 ....57 H1
  WCHMH * N21 ....37 H6
  WIM/MER SW19 ....205 G1
Chadwick Cl TEDD TW11 ....200 C2
Chadwick Pl SURB KT6 ....221 E4
Chadwick Rd CMBW SE5 ....168 D5
  IL IG1 ....114 B1
  WLSDN NW10 ....103 F6
Chadwick St WEST SW1P 20 B6
Chadwick Wy THMD SE28 ......136 B6
Chadwin Rd PLSTW E13 ....132 D4
Chaffinch Av CROY/NA CRO 230 B2
Chaffinch Cl CROY/NA CRO 230 B2
  ED N9 ....54 B3
  SURB KT6 ....245 H2
Chaffinch Rd BECK BR3 ....210 C4
Chafford Wy CHDH RM6 ....96 B4
Chagford St CAMTN NW1 ....2 E7
Chailey Av EN EN1 ....39 F3
Chailey Cl HEST TW5 ....158 B2
Chailey St CLPT E5 ....110 A1

Chalbury Wk IS N1.....5 H1
Chalcombe Rd ABYW SE2.....155 H3
Chalcot Cl BELMT SM2.....243 C5
Chalcot Crs CAMTN NW1.....106 B6
Chalcot Gdns HAMP NW3.....106 B4
Chalcot Ms STRHM/NOR SW16.....187 C4
Chalcot Rd BAMW NW1.....106 C6
Chalcot Sq CAMTN NW1.....106 C5
Chalcott Gdns SURB * KT6.....221 E5
Chalcroft Rd LEW SE13.....192 A4
Chaldon Rd FUL/PGN SW6.....164 C1
Chale Rd BRXS/STRHM SW2.....187 C1
Chalet Est MLHL * NW7.....47 G6
Chalfont Av WBLY HA9.....102 B4
Chalfont Gn ED N9.....53 E5
Chalfont Rd ED N9.....53 E5
 SNWD SE25.....29 F6
Chalfont Wk PIN * HA5.....58 A5
Chalfont Wy WEA W13.....140 D3
Chalford Cl E/WMO/HCT KT8.....219 C1
Chalford Rd DUL SE21.....188 D6
Chalford Wk WFD IG8.....73 C5
Chalgrove Av MRDN SM4.....225 E2
Chalgrove Crs CLAY IG5.....73 G5
Chalgrove Gdns FNCH N3.....64 C6
Chalgrove Rd BELMT SM2.....243 C5
 HOM E9.....110 A4
 TOTM N17.....69 H4
Chalice Cl WLGTN SM6.....245 F4
Chalkenden Cl PGE/AN SE20.....209 H3
Chalk Farm Pde HAMP * NW3.....106 C5
Chalk Hl OXHEY WD19.....42 C1
Chalk Hill Rd HMSMTH W6.....144 B4
Chalklands WBLY HA9.....102 D4
Chalk La EBAR EN4.....36 B4
Chalkley Cl MTCM CR4.....206 D3
Chalk Pit Av STMC/STPC BR5.....216 A6
Chalk Pit Rd SUT SM1.....243 G3
Chalk Rd PLSTW E15.....132 D4
Chalkstone Cl WELL DA16.....175 G2
Chalkwell Park Av EN EN1.....39 E5
Chalky La CHSGTN KT9.....259 F6
Challenge Cl WLSDN NW10.....103 E6
Challice Wy BRXS/STRHM SW2.....187 H3
Challin St PGE/AN SE20.....210 A4
Challis Rd BTFD TW8.....141 F5
Challoner Cl EFNCH N2.....65 H5
Challoner Crs WKENS * W14.....144 C5
Challoners Cl E/WMO/HCT KT8.....219 H1
Challoner St WKENS W14.....144 D5
Chalsey Rd BROCKY SE4.....144 C3
Chalton Dr EFNCH N2.....85 G3
Chalton St CAMTN NW1.....4 C1

Chamberlain Cl
 WOOL/PLUM SE18.....154 D3
Chamberlain Cottages
 CMBW * SE5.....168 D2
Chamberlain Crs WWKM BR4.....231 F5
Chamberlain La PIN HA5.....58 D4
Chamberlain Pl WALTH * E17.....70 C6
Chamberlain Rd ED N9.....53 C5
 EFNCH N2.....65 G5
 WEA W13.....161 G2
Chamberlain St HAMP * NW1.....106 B5
Chamberlain Wy SURB KT6.....221 G4
Chamberlayne Rd
 WLSDN NW10.....104 A6
Chamberlens Garages
 HMSMTH * W6.....143 H4
Chambers Gdns EFNCH N2.....65 H4
Chambers La WLSDN NW10.....103 H5
Chambers Rd HOLWY N7.....93 G2
Chambers St BERM/RHTH SE16.....25 H3
Chamber St WCHPL E1.....16 D5
Chambord St BETH E2.....8 D4
Champa Cl SYD SE26.....190 C6
Champion Gv CMBW SE5.....168 D4
Champion Pk CMBW SE5.....168 D4
Champion Pk CMBW SE5.....168 D4
Champion Rd SYD SE26.....190 C6
Champness Cl WNWD SE27.....188 D6
Champness Rd BARK IG11.....115 F5
Champneys OXHEY * WD19.....42 C4
Champneys Cl BELMT SM2.....242 B6
Chancellor Gdns
 SAND/SEL CR2.....246 B6
Chancellor Gv DUL SE21.....188 C4
Chancellor Pl CDALE/KGS NW9.....63 F5
Chancellors Rd HMSMTH W6.....144 B3
Chancellors St HMSMTH W6.....144 A3
Chancellors Whf
 HMSMTH * W6.....144 A5
Chancelot Rd ABYW SE2.....155 H4
Chancel St STHWK SE1.....22 C1
Chancery La BECK BR3.....211 F1
 LINN WC2A.....13 H2
Chance St BETH E2.....8 C5
Chanctonbury Cl
 ELTH/MOT SE9.....194 B5
Chanctonbury Gdns
 BELMT SM2.....243 F5
Chanctonbury Wy
 NFNCH/WDSP N12.....49 E6
Chandler Av CAN/RD E16.....132 C4
Chandler Cl HPTN TW12.....198 D4
Chandlers Ct
 LEE/GVPK * SE12.....192 D4
Chandler Dr ERITH DA8.....157 H4
Chandlers Ms POP/IOD E14.....151 E2
Chandler St WAP E1W.....25 H1
Chandler Wy PECK SE15.....169 F1
Chandos Av EA W5.....161 E4
 STHGT/OAK N14.....51 E5
 TRDG/WHET N20.....49 H3
 WALTH * E17.....71 E5
Chandos Cl BKHH IG9.....55 G5
Chandos Crs EDGW HA8.....61 H3
Chandos Pl CHCR WC2N.....13 E6
Chandos Rd CRICK NW2.....104 A3
 EFNCH N2.....65 H5
 HRW HA1.....78 A4
 PIN HA5.....78 A4
 SRTFD E15.....111 H3
 TOTM N17.....69 H5
 WLSDN NW10.....123 E4
Chandos St CAVSQ/HST W1G.....11 H2
Chandos Wy GLDGN NW11.....85 F5
Channel Cl HEST TW5.....159 G2

Channel Islands Est IS N1.....108 C4
Channelsea Rd SRTFD E15.....111 H6
Chantress Cl DAGE RM10.....117 C6
Chantrey Cl SCUP DA14.....216 C1
Chantrey Rd BRXN/ST SW9.....167 H4
Chantry Cl CINC/FH EN2.....38 C1
 KTN/HRWW/W HA3.....81 H2
 MLHL NW7.....47 F2
 MV/WKIL * W9.....124 D3
Chantry La HAYES BR2.....233 F2
Chantry Pl RYLN/HDSTN HA2.....59 H4
Chantry Rd CHSGTN KT9.....239 H3
 KTN/HRWW/W HA3.....59 H4
Chantry Sq KENS * W8.....145 F3
Chantry St IS * N1.....108 B6
The Chantry CHING * E4.....55 G3
Chantry Wy MTCM CR4.....205 H6
Chant Sq SRTFD * E15.....111 H5
Chant St SRTFD E15.....111 H5
Chapel Cl EFNCH N2.....65 H5
 STHWK SE1.....23 G3
Chapel Farm Rd
 ELTH/MOT SE9.....193 H5
Chapel Hl EFNCH N2.....66 A5
Chapel House St POP/IOD E14.....151 F3
Chapel La PIN HA5.....58 B6
Chapel Market IS N1.....5 H1
Chapel Pl CAVSQ/HST W1G.....10 A4
 IS N1.....6 B1
 TOTM N17.....69 C3
Chapel Rd BXLYHN DA7.....177 F1
 HSLW TW3.....159 F4
 IL IG1.....114 A1
 TWK TW1.....180 D2
 WEA W13.....144 D4
 WNWD SE27.....188 B6
Chapel Side BAY/PAD W2.....125 F6
Chapel St BAY/PAD W2.....10 A2
 ENC/FH EN2.....38 C2
 KTBR SW1X.....19 F5
Chapel Vw SAND/SEL CR2.....232 D6
Chaplemount Rd WFD * IG8.....73 H2
Chaplin Cl ALP/SUD * HA0.....101 F4
 STHWK SE1.....22 C3
Chaplin Rd ALP/SUD HA0.....101 E4
 CRICK NW2.....103 D4
 SRTFD E15.....132 A1
 TOTM * N17.....69 G3
Chapman Crs
 KTN/HRWW/W HA3.....81 C2
Chapman Rd BELV DA17.....157 E5
 CROY/NA CR0.....208 C5
 HOM E9.....110 D4
Chapmans Gn WDGN * N22.....68 A4
Chapman's La STMC/STPC BR5.....216 B5
 SWLY BR8.....217 E5
Chapman Sq WIM/MER SW19.....184 B4
Chapman St WCHPL E1.....17 C5
Chapman Ter WDGN * N22.....68 A4
Chapter Rd CRICK NW2.....103 C3
 WALW SE17.....30 D4
Chapter St WEST SW1P.....28 C2
Chapter Wy HPTN TW12.....179 E6
Chara Pl CHSWK W4.....142 D6
Charcroft Gdns PEND EN3.....40 A5
Chardin Rd CHSWK * W4.....143 E4
Chardmore Rd STNW/STAM N16.....89 G5
Chardwell Cl EHAM E6.....135 C5
Charecroft Wy WKENS W14.....144 C6
Charford Rd CAN/RD E16.....132 C4
Chargeable La PLSTW E13.....132 C3
Chargeable St CAN/RD E16.....132 B3
Charing Cl ORP BR6.....255 F2
Charing Cross CHCR WC2N.....20 D1
Charing Cross Rd
 LSQ/SEVD WC2H.....12 D5
Charlbert St STJWD NW8.....2 C2
Charlbury Av STAN HA7.....63 H1
Charlbury Gdns GDMY/SEVK IG3.....95 F6
Charlbury Gv EA W5.....121 E5
Charldane Rd ELTH/MOT SE9.....194 B5
Charlecote Gv SYD SE26.....189 H5
Charlecote Rd DCTR RM8.....116 C1
Charlemont Rd EHAM E6.....133 H2
Charles Babbage Cl
 CHSGTN KT9.....239 E5
Charles Barry Cl CLAP * SW4.....167 E4
Charles Cl SCUP DA14.....195 H6
Charles Cobb Gdns
 CROY/NA CR0.....246 A3
Charles Coveney Rd
 PECK * SE15.....169 F2
Charles Crs HRW * HA1.....79 H4
 HRW HA1.....79 H4
Charles Dickens Ter
 PGE/AN * SE20.....210 A3
Charlesfield LEE/GVPK SE12.....193 C5
Charles Flemwell Ms
 CAN/RD * E16.....152 C1
Charles Grinling Wk
 WOOL/PLUM SE18.....154 A4
Charles la PI CHEL SW3.....26 D4
Charles II St STJS SW1Y.....12 C2
Charles La STJWD NW8.....2 C1
Charles Pl CAMTN * NW1.....4 B4
Charles Rd CHDH RM6.....96 B4
 DAGE RM10.....117 E5
 FSTGT E7.....113 E5
 WEA W13.....120 C5
 WIM/MER SW19.....205 H4
Charles Sevright Dr MLHL NW7.....64 B1
Charles Sq IS N1.....7 F4
Charles Square Est IS N1.....7 F4
Charles St BARN SW13.....163 E4
 CAN/RD E16.....153 C1
 CROY/NA CR0.....246 C1
 EN EN1.....39 F6
 HSLW TW3.....158 D3
 MYFR/PICC W1J.....19 H1
Charleston St WALW SE17.....31 F2
Charleville Circ SYD SE26.....209 G1
Charleville Rd WKENS W14.....144 C5
Charleville Rd ERITH DA8.....177 G1
Charlmont Rd TOOT SW17.....206 A2
Charlotte Cl BXLYHS DA6.....177 F4
Charlotte Despard Av
 BTSEA * SW11.....166 D2
Charlotte Gdns CRW RM5.....56 D2
Charlotte Ms FITZ W1T.....11 B1
 NKENS W10.....124 B5
Charlotte Pde FSTH * SE23.....190 C4

Charlotte Park Av BMLY BR1.....213 G6
Charlotte Pl FITZ W1T.....12 B2
Charlotte Rd BARN SW13.....163 F2
 IS N1.....8 A4
 WLGTN SM6.....245 G4
Charlotte Row CLAP SW4.....165 H1
Charlotte St FITZ W1T.....12 B1
Charlotte Ter IS * N1.....107 H6
Charlow Cl FUL/PGN SW6.....165 C3
Charlton Church La CHARL SE7.....135 H1
Charlton Dene CHARL SE7.....175 E1
Charlton King's Rd KTTN NW5.....107 F3
Charlton La CHARL SE7.....175 H1
Charlton Park La CHARL SE7.....175 F1
Charlton Park Rd CHARL SE7.....155 F6
Charlton Pl IS N1.....172 C1
 ED N9.....54 B3
 KTN/HRWW/W HA3.....81 F1
 WBLY HA9.....81 H5
 WLSDN NW10.....103 E6
Charlton Wy BKHTH/KID SE3.....172 A2
Charlwood CROY/NA CR0.....248 D6
Charlwood Cl
 KTN/HRWW/W HA3.....60 A2
Charlwood Rd PUT/ROE SW15.....164 B5
Charlwood Rd PUT/ROE SW15.....28 B3
Charlwood Ter PUT/ROE SW15.....164 B5
Charman Av STAN HA7.....61 F6
Charminster Av
 WIM/MER SW19.....205 E5
Charminster Rd
 LEE/GVPK SE12.....193 F6
 WPK KT4.....224 D5
Charmouth Rd WELL DA16.....176 A2
Charnock Rd CLPT E5.....109 H1
Charnwood Av
 WIM/MER SW19.....205 E5
Charnwood Cl NWMAL KT3.....223 E1
Charnwood Dr SWFD E18.....72 D6
Charnwood Gdns
 POP/IOD E14.....151 E4
Charnwood Pl TRDG/WHET N20.....49 G5
Charnwood Rd SNWD SE25.....228 D2
Charnwood St CLPT * E5.....89 C6
Charrington Rd CROY/NA CR0.....228 B6
Charrington St CAMTN NW1.....4 C1
Charsley Rd CAT SE6.....191 F5
Chart Cl CROY/NA CR0.....230 A3
 HAYES BR2.....212 A4
 MTCM CR4.....226 B1
Charter Av GNTH/NBYPK IG2.....94 D5
Charter Crs HSLWW TW4.....158 C5
Charter Dr BXLY DA5.....196 C2
Charterhouse Av ALP/SUD HA0.....101 E3
Charterhouse Bldgs FARR EC1M.....7 E6
Charterhouse Ms FARR EC1M.....14 D1
Charterhouse Rd HACK E8.....109 G3
 ORP BR6.....217 F1
Charterhouse St HCIRC EC1N.....14 B3
The Charterhouse FARR * EC1M.....6 D6
Charteris Rd FSBYPK N4.....67 F6
 KIL/WHAMP NW6.....107 H4
 WFD IG8.....72 D2
The Charter Rd KUT KT1.....202 B6
Charters Cl NRWD SE19.....189 E5
Charter Sq KUT KT1.....202 D6
Charter Wy GLDGN NW11.....84 D1
 STHGT/OAK N14.....51 E1
Chartfield Av PUT/ROE SW15.....163 H6
Chartfield Sq PUT/ROE SW15.....164 A6
Chartham Gv WNWD SE27.....188 H5
Chartham Rd SNWD SE25.....209 H6
Chart Hills Cl THMD SE28.....116 C6
Chartley Av CRICK NW2.....103 E1
 STAN HA7.....60 B2
Chartwell Cl CHST BR7.....214 D6
 CROY/NA CR0.....228 D5
 GFD/PVL UB6.....96 D1
Chartwell Dr ORP BR6.....252 C3
Chartwell Pl CHEAM SM3.....242 C2
 RYLN/HDSTN HA2.....78 D5
Chartwell Wy PGE/AN SE20.....209 H4
Charwood STRHM/NOR * SW16.....188 A6
Chase Ct RYNPK SW20.....204 C5
Chase Court Gdns ENC/FH EN2.....38 B3
Chase Cross Rd CRW RM5.....57 C3
Chasefield Rd TOOT SW17.....186 B6
Chase Gdns CHING E4.....55 E6
 WHTN TW2.....179 H1
Chase Gn ENC/FH EN2.....38 C4
Chase Green Av ENC/FH EN2.....38 C4
Chase Hl ENC/FH EN2.....38 C4
Chase La BARK/HLT IG6.....94 D2
Chaseley Ct CHSWK W4.....142 B5
Chaseley St POP/IOD * E14.....151 E5
Chasemore Cl MTCM CR4.....226 B4
Chasemore Gdns
 CROY/NA CR0.....246 A3
Chase Ridings ENC/FH EN2.....38 A3
Chase Rd ACT W3.....122 D5
 STHGT/OAK N14.....38 D1
Chase Side ENC/FH EN2.....38 C3
 STHGT/OAK N14.....50 C1
Chase Side Av ENC/FH EN2.....38 C3
 RYNPK SW20.....204 C4
Chase Side Crs ENC/FH EN2.....302 D2
The Chase BMLY BR1.....212 D6
 BXLYHN DA7.....177 F4
 CLAP SW4.....166 D2
 CROY/NA CR0.....245 C1
 EDGW HA8.....62 B4
 LOU IG10.....42 D1
 MNPK E12.....113 F2
 PIN HA5.....76 B3
 STAN HA7.....60 B3
 STRHM/NOR SW16.....188 A6
 WLGTN SM6.....245 G5

Chatfield Rd BTSEA SW11.....165 G4
 CROY/NA CR0.....228 B5
Chatham Av HAYES BR2.....232 B4
Chatham Cl CHEAM SM3.....224 D4
 GLDGN NW11.....85 E2
Chatham Pl HOM E14.....110 A4
Chatham Rd BTSEA SW11.....186 B1
 KUTN/CMB KT2.....202 A5
 SWFD E18.....72 B5
 WALTH * E17.....70 C6
Chatham St WALW SE17.....31 H1
 WOOL/PLUM SE18.....154 B3
Chatsfield Pl EA W5.....121 G5
Chatsworth Av BFN/LL DA15.....195 G3
 BMLY BR1.....212 D1
 HDN NW4.....46 A4
 RYNPK SW20.....204 C4
 WBLY HA9.....101 H3
Chatsworth Cl CHSWK * W4.....142 C6
 HDN NW4.....46 A4
 WWKM BR4.....232 B6
Chatsworth Crs HSLW TW3.....159 H5
Chatsworth Dr EN EN1.....53 G2
Chatsworth Est CLPT * E5.....91 G2
Chatsworth Gdns ACT W3.....122 B6
 NWMAL * KT3.....223 F2
 RYLN/HDSTN HA2.....59 H5
Chatsworth Pl MTCM CR4.....206 B6
 TEDD TW11.....180 C5
Chatsworth Ri EA W5.....121 H3
Chatsworth Rd CHEAM SM3.....242 B2
 CHSWK W4.....141 H5
 CLPT E5.....110 A1
 CRICK NW2.....104 B4
 CROY/NA CR0.....246 D2
 EA W5.....121 H3
 FSTGT E7.....112 B5
Chatterton Ms FSBYPK * N4.....108 B1
Chatterton Rd FSBYPK N4.....108 B1
 HAYES BR2.....232 C3
Chatto Rd BTSEA SW11.....166 B6
Chaucer Av RCH/KEW TW9.....162 A3
Chaucer Cl FBAR/BDGN N11.....67 C1
Chaucer Ct NWMAL * KT3.....52 D2
Chaucer Gdns SUT SM1.....243 E2
Chaucer Gn CROY/NA CR0.....229 H4
Chaucer Rd ACT W3.....142 C1
 BFN/LL DA15.....196 C4
 FSTGT E7.....112 C4
 SUT SM1.....71 G4
 WALTH E17.....71 G4
 WAN E11.....92 C3
 WELL DA16.....175 F2
Chauncey Cl ED N9.....53 C5
Chaundrye Cl ELTH/MOT SE9.....193 H1
Chauntler Rd CAN/RD E16.....132 D6
Cheam Common Rd WPK KT4.....225 H6
Cheam Man CHEAM * SM3.....242 A4
Cheam Rd BELMT SM2.....242 B6
 SUT SM1.....242 C4
Cheam St PECK * SE15.....169 H4
Cheapside CITYW EC2V.....15 F4
 EFNCH * N2.....66 B5
 PLMGR N13.....52 C6
 WDGN * N22.....68 C4
Cheddar Cl FBAR/BDGN N11.....66 A5
Cheddington Rd UED N18.....53 E6
Chedworth Cl CAN/RD E16.....132 D6
Cheeseman Cl HPTN TW12.....179 G6
Cheesemans Ter WKENS * W14.....144 D5
Chelford Rd BMLY BR1.....211 H1
Chelmer Crs BARK IG11.....135 H1
Chelmer Rd HOM E9.....110 B3
Chelmsford Av CRW RM5.....57 E3
Chelmsford Cl BELMT SM2.....243 E6
 EHAM E6.....133 H5
 HMSMTH W6.....144 B6
Chelmsford Gdns IL IG1.....75 H5
Chelmsford Rd STHGT/OAK N14.....51 E2
 SWFD E18.....72 B4
 WALTH E17.....91 E3
Chelmsford Sq WLSDN NW10.....104 A6
Chelsea Br CHEL SW3.....27 E5
Chelsea Bridge Ga BTSEA SW11.....27 C4
Chelsea Bridge Rd BGVA SW1W.....27 E3
Chelsea Cl HPTN TW12.....199 G2
 WLSDN NW10.....81 G6
 WPK KT4.....223 G4
Chelsea Crs CRICK * NW2.....104 D4
Chelsea Crs CHEL SW3.....27 E5
Chelsea Gdns CHEAM SM3.....242 C2
Chelsea Harbour Dr
 WBPTN SW10.....165 G2
Chelsea Manor Gdns CHEL SW3.....26 G5
Chelsea Manor St CHEL SW3.....26 B5
Chelsea Park Gdns
 FUL/PGN * SW6.....145 H5
Chelsea Sq CHEL SW3.....145 H5
Chelsea Village
 FUL/PGN * SW6.....165 F1
Chelsfield Av ED N9.....54 D1
Chelsfield Gdns SYD SE26.....190 D3
Chelsfield La STMC/STPC BR5.....256 B4
Chelsfield Rd STMC/STPC BR5.....236 A3
Chelsham Rd CLAP SW4.....167 H4
 SAND/SEL CR2.....246 D5
Chelsworth Dr
 WOOL/PLUM SE18.....154 D6
Cheltenham Av TWK TW1.....180 C2
Cheltenham Cl NTHLT UB5.....96 A6
 NWMAL * KT3.....202 C6
Cheltenham Gdns EHAM E6.....133 C1
 LOU IG10.....57 C1
Cheltenham Pl ACT W3.....142 C2
 KTN/HRWW/W HA3.....91 G3
Cheltenham Rd LEY E10.....90 A5
 ORP BR6.....253 C1
 PECK SE15.....169 H4
Cheltenham Ter CHEL SW3.....26 D5
Chelverton Rd PUT/ROE SW15.....164 B5
Chelwood Cl CHING E4.....45 E3
Chelwood Gdns RCH/KEW TW9.....162 A3
Chelwood Rd CLPT * E5.....132 D2
Chenduit Wy STAN HA7.....60 D1
Cheney Rd CAMTN NW1.....5 E2
Cheney Rw WALTH E17.....70 D4
Cheneys Rd WAN E11.....112 A1
Cheney St PIN HA5.....77 A1
Chenies Ms GWRST WC1E.....4 C6
Chenies Pl CAMTN NW1.....4 D1

Chenies St FITZ W1T 12 C1
The Chenies ORP BR6 235 E3
Cheniston Gdns KENS * W8 145 F3
Chepstow Cl PUT/ROE SW15 164 C6
Chepstow Cnr BAY/PAD * W2 125 E5
Chepstow Crs GDMY/SEVK IG3 95 E3
NTGHL W11 125 E6
Chepstow Gdns STHL UB1 118 D5
Chepstow Pl BAY/PAD W2 125 E6
Chepstow Ri CROY/NA CR0 247 E1
Chepstow Rd BAY/PAD W2 125 E5
CROY/NA CR0 247 E1
HNWL W7 140 C3
Chepstow Vls NTGHL W11 124 D6
Chequers BKHH * IG9 56 D3
BKHH IG9 56 D3
Chequers Cl CDALE/KGS NW9 63 E6
STMC/STPC BR5 235 F1
Chequers La DAGW RM9 136 D3
Chequers Pde PLMGR * N13 68 H3
The Chequers PIN * HA5 58 B6
Chequer St STLK EC1Y 7 F6
Chequers Wy PLMGR N13 68 C1
Cherbury Cl THMD SE28 136 B5
Cherbury St IS N1 7 H2
Cherimoya Gdns
E/WMO/HCT KT8 199 F6
Cherington Rd HNWL * W7 140 B1
Cheriton Av CLAY IG5 74 A5
HAYES BR2 232 B2
Cheriton Cl EA W5 121 E4
EBAR EN4 36 B4
Cheriton Ct WOT/HER KT12 218 A5
Cheriton Dr WOOL/PLUM SE18 174 D1
Cheriton Sq TOOT SW17 186 C4
Cherry Av STHL UB1 138 B1
SWLY BR8 217 H6
Cherry Blossom Cl PLMGR N13 68 B1
Cherry Cl BRXS/STRHM * SW2 188 A2
CAR SM5 226 B6
EA W5 141 F3
MRDN SM4 224 C1
Cherrycot Ri ORP BR6 252 C2
Cherry Ct PIN HA5 58 B5
Cherry Crs BTFD TW8 160 D1
Cherry Croft Gdns PIN * HA5 58 D3
Cherrydown Av CHING E4 54 D5
Cherrydown Cl CHING E4 54 D5
Cherrydown Rd SCUP DA14 196 B4
Cherrydown Wk
ROMW/RG RM7 77 F5
Cherry Gdns DAGW RM9 116 D3
NTHLT UB5 99 F5
Cherry Garden St
BERM/RHTH SE16 25 G4
Cherry Garth BTFD TW8 141 F5
Cherry Hl BAR EN5 49 F1
KTN/HRWW/W HA3 60 A2
Cherry Hill Gdns CROY/NA CR0 245 H2
Cherry Hills OXHEY WD19 58 C1
Cherrylands Cl
CDALE/KGS * NW9 82 C6
Cherry Orch CHARL SE7 153 E6
Cherry Orchard Cl
STMC/STPC BR5 236 A2
Cherry Orchard Gdns
CROY/NA CR0 228 D5
E/WMO/HCT KT8 198 D6
Cherry Orchard Rd
CROY/NA CR0 228 D5
E/WMO/HCT KT8 199 E6
HAYES BR2 233 G6
Cherry Rd PEND EN3 40 A1
Cherry St ROMW/RG RM7 97 H2
Cherry Tree Cl ALP/SUD HA0 100 C2
Cherry Tree Ct CHARL * SE7 153 E6
Cherry Tree Dr
STRHM/NOR * SW16 187 G5
Cherry Tree Hl EFNCH N2 86 A2
Cherry Tree Ri BKHH IG9 57 F6
Cherry Tree Rd EFNCH N2 86 B1
SRTFD E15 112 A3
Cherry Tree Wk BECK BR3 230 D1
STLK EC1Y 7 F6
WWKM BR4 250 B2
Cherry Tree Wy STAN HA7 60 D2
Cherry Wk HAYES BR2 232 C5
Cherry Wy HOR/WEW KT19 240 D4
Cherrywood Cl BOW E3 130 C2
KUTN/CMB KT2 202 A3
Cherrywood Dr
PUT/ROE SW15 164 B6
Cherrywood La MRDN SM4 224 C1
Chertsey Dr CHEAM SM3 224 C6
Chertsey Rd IL IG1 114 D2
TWK TW1 180 C1
WAN E11 91 H6
WHTN TW2 179 G3
Chertsey St TOOT SW17 206 C1
Chervil Ms THMD SE28 155 H1
Cherwell Ct HOR/WEW KT19 240 C2
Cheryls Cl FUL/PGN SW6 165 F2
Cheseman St SYD SE26 189 H5
Chesfield Rd KUTN/CMB KT2 201 G3
Chesham Av HAYES BR2 234 B3
Chesham Cl KTBR * SW1X 19 E6
ROMW/RG RM7 97 H1
Chesham Crs PGE/AN SE20 210 A4
Chesham Ms KTBR SW1X 19 E5
Chesham Pl KTBR SW1X 19 E5
Chesham Rd KUTN/CMB KT2 202 A4
PGE/AN SE20 210 A5
Chesham St KTBR SW1X 19 E6
WLSDN NW10 102 D1
Chesham Ter WEA W13 140 D2
Cheshire Cl MTCM CR4 207 G6
WALTH E17 71 F4
Cheshire Gdns CHSGTN KT9 239 F4
Cheshire Rd WDGN N22 67 H3
Cheshire St BETH E2 9 E5
Chesholm Rd STNW/STAM N16 109 E1
Cheshunt Rd BELV DA17 157 E5
FSTGT E7 112 D4
Chesilton Rd FUL/PGN SW6 164 D2
Chesley Gdns EHAM E6 133 F1
Chesney Crs CROY/NA CR0 249 G5
Chesney St BTSEA SW11 166 C2
Chesnut Av North WALTH E17 91 H1
Chesnut Gv TOTM N17 69 G6
Chesnut Rd TOTM N17 69 G6
Chesnut Rw FNCH * N3 65 E3
Chessington Av BXLYHN DA7 176 C1
FNCH N3 64 C6
Chessington Cl
HOR/WEW KT19 240 C4
Chessington Ct PIN HA5 78 D1
Chessington Hall Gdns
CHSGTN KT9 239 F5
Chessington Hill Pk
CHSGTN KT9 240 A4
Chessington Pde CHSGTN * KT9 239 F3
Chessington Rd CHSGTN KT9 240 A4
Chessington Wy WWKM BR4 231 F6
Chesson Rd WKENS W14 144 D6
Chesswood Wy PIN HA5 58 B5
Chester Av RCHPK/HAM TW10 181 H1
WHTN TW2 178 D3
Chester Cl BARN * SW13 163 H4
KTBR SW1X 19 F4
SUT SM1 225 E6
Chester Cl North CAMTN NW1 3 H3
Chester Cl South CAMTN NW1 3 H4
Chester Crs HACK E8 109 F3
Chester Dr RYLN/HDSTN HA2 79 E3
Chesterfield Cl
STMC/STPC BR5 236 B1
Chesterfield Dr ESH/CLAY KT10 220 C6
Chesterfield Gdns FSBYPK N4 88 B2
GNWCH * SE10 171 H1
MYFR/PICC * W1J 19 G1
Chesterfield Gv EDUL SE22 169 F6
Chesterfield Hl MYFR/PICC W1J 11 G6
Chesterfield Rd BAR EN5 34 B6
CHSWK W4 142 C6
FNCH N3 65 E2
HOR/WEW KT19 240 D5
LEY E10 91 G4
Chesterfield St MYFR/PICC W1J 19 G1
Chesterfield Wy PECK SE15 170 A1
Chesterford Gdns HAMP NW3 105 F2
Chesterford Rd MNPK E12 113 H3
Chester Gdns ED N9 53 H1
MRDN SM4 225 G2
WEA * W13 120 D5
Chester Ga CAMTN NW1 3 G4
Chester Ms KTBR SW1X 19 G5
Chester Pl CAMTN NW1 3 G3
Chester Rd BFN/LL DA15 175 E6
CAMTN NW1 3 F4
CAN/RD E16 132 A3
ED N9 53 H3
FSTGT E7 113 F5
GDMY/SEVK IG3 95 F5
KTTN NW5 86 D6
TOTM N17 68 D6
WALTH E17 90 B2
WAN E11 92 D3
WIM/MER SW19 204 A2
Chester Rw BGVA SW1W 27 E2
Chester Sq BGVA SW1W 27 F1
Chester Square Ms
BGVA * SW1W 19 G6
The Chesters NWMAL KT3 203 F4
Chester St BETH E2 9 F5
BETH * E2 109 G6
KTBR SW1X 19 F5
Chester Ter CAMTN NW1 3 G3
Chesterton Cl GFD/PVL UB6 119 F1
WAND/EARL SW18 165 E6
Chesterton Ct EA * W5 121 F5
Chesterton Rd PLSTW E13 132 C2
Chesterton Sq WKENS W14 144 D4
Chesterton Ter KUT KT1 202 A5
PLSTW E13 132 C2
Chester Wy LBTH SE11 30 B2
Chesthunte Rd TOTM N17 68 C4
Chestnut Aly FUL/PGN * SW6 144 D6
Chestnut Av ALP/SUD HA0 100 D3
BKHH IG9 57 F5
BTFD TW8 141 F5
CEND/HSY/T N8 87 G2
E/WMO/HCT KT8 200 B6
EDGW HA8 61 G2
ESH/CLAY KT10 219 H4
FSTGT E7 112 D2
HOR/WEW KT19 241 E2
HPTN TW12 199 E3
MORT/ESHN * SW14 162 D4
TEDD TW11 200 B3
WWKM BR4 250 A3
Chestnut Av South WALTH E17 91 G1
Chestnut Cl BFN/LL DA15 195 G3
BKHH IG9 57 F5
CAR SM5 226 B5
CAT SE6 191 G6
NWCR SE14 170 D2
ORP BR6 253 G3
STHGT/OAK N14 37 E6
STRHM/NOR SW16 188 A6
Chestnut Cottages
TRDG/WHET * N20 48 C3
Chestnut Dr BXLYHN DA7 176 B4
KTN/HRWW/W HA3 60 B3
PIN HA5 78 B3
WAN E11 92 C3
Chestnut Gv ALP/SUD HA0 100 D3
BAL SW12 186 C2
BARK/HLT IG6 75 E2
EA W5 141 F3
EBAR EN4 36 B6
ISLW TW7 160 C5
MTCM CR4 227 F2
NWMAL KT3 202 D6
RDART DA2 217 H1
SAND/SEL CR2 247 H5
Chestnut La TRDG/WHET N20 48 C3
Chestnut Mnr WLGTN SM6 244 D2
Chestnut Ri BUSH WD23 43 F2
WOOL/PLUM SE18 155 E5
Chestnut Rd KUTN/CMB KT2 201 G3
RYNPK SW20 204 B5
WHTN TW2 180 A4
WNWD SE27 188 B5
The Chestnuts BECK * BR3 210 B6
PIN * HA5 58 D3
Chestnut Ter SUT * SM1 243 F2
Cheston Av CROY/NA CR0 230 C5
Chettle Cl STHWK SE1 23 G5
Chetwode Rd TOOT SW17 186 B5
Chetwynd Av EBAR EN4 50 B3
Chetwynd Rd KTTN NW5 106 D2
Chetwynd Vls KTTN * NW5 106 D2
Chevalier Cl STAN HA7 45 F5
Cheval Pl SKENS SW7 18 B5
Cheval St POP/IOD E14 151 E3
Cheveney Wk HAYES BR2 212 C6
Chevening Rd GNWCH SE10 152 B5
KIL/WHAMP NW6 124 B1
NRWD SE19 208 D3
The Chevenings SCUP DA14 195 H5
Cheverton Rd ARCH N19 87 F5
Chevet St HOM E9 110 C3
Chevington CRICK * NW2 104 D4
Cheviot Cl BELMT SM2 243 H6
BUSH WD23 43 G1
ENC/FH EN2 38 D3
Cheviot Gdns GLDGN NW11 84 B6
Cheviot Rd WNWD SE27 208 B1
Cheviot Wy GNTH/NBYPK IG2 95 E2
Chevron Cl CAN/RD E16 132 C5
Chevy Rd STHL UB1 139 G2
Chewton Rd WALTH E17 90 C1
Cheyne Av SWFD E18 72 B6
WHTN TW2 178 D3
Cheyne Cl HAYES BR2 251 G1
Cheyne Gdns CHEL SW3 26 B5
Cheyne Hl BRYLDS KT5 221 H1
Cheyne Ms CHEL SW3 26 B6
Cheyne Pth WEA W13 120 B4
Cheyne Pl CHEL SW3 26 C5
Cheyne Rw CHEL SW3 26 A6
Cheyne Wk CROY/NA CR0 229 G6
HDN NW4 84 A3
WCHMH N21 38 A6
Cheyneys Av EDGW HA8 61 F2
Chichele Gdns CROY/NA CR0 247 E2
Chichele Rd CRICK NW2 104 B3
Chicheley Rd
KTN/HRWW/W HA3 59 G3
Chicheley St STHWK SE1 21 H3
Chichester Cl BKHTH/KID SE3 173 E1
EHAM E6 133 G5
HPTN TW12 198 D2
Chichester Ct EW * KT17 241 F6
STAN HA7 61 G6
Chichester Gdns IL IG1 93 G4
Chichester Rd BAY/PAD * W2 125 F4
CROY/NA CR0 247 E1
ED N9 53 F3
KIL/WHAMP NW6 125 E1
WAN E11 112 A1
Chichester St PIM SW1V 28 B4
Chichester Wy
EBED/NFELT TW14 178 A2
POP/IOD E14 151 H4
Chicksand Est WCHPL E1 17 E1
Chicksand St WCHPL E1 16 D2
Chiddingfold NFNCH/WDSP N12 49 E5
Chiddingstone Av BXLYHN DA7 156 D6
Chiddingstone St
FUL/PGN SW6 165 E3
Chieveley Pde BXLYHN * DA7 177 F4
Chieveley Rd BXLYHN DA7 177 F5
Chignell Pl WEA W13 140 C1
Chigwell Hl WAP E1W 17 G6
Chigwell Rd SWFD E18 72 D6
Childebert Rd TOOT SW17 186 D4
Childeric Rd NWCR SE14 170 C1
Childerley St FUL/PGN SW6 164 C2
Childers St DEPT SE8 150 C6
The Childers WFD IG8 73 H1
Childs La NRWD * SE19 209 E2
Child's Pl ECT * SW5 145 E4
ECT SW5 145 E4
Child's St ECT * SW5 145 E4
ECT SW5 145 E4
Child's Wk ECT * SW5 145 E4
Childs Wy GLDGN NW11 84 D2
Chilham Cl BXLY DA5 196 D2
GFD/PVL UB6 120 C1
Chilham Rd ELTH/MOT SE9 193 G6
Chilham Wy HAYES BR2 232 C4
Chillerton Rd TOOT SW17 206 C1
Chillingworth Gdns TWK * TW1 180 B4
Chilmark Gdns NWMAL KT3 223 F3
Chilmark Rd
STRHM/NOR SW16 207 F5
Chiltern Av BUSH WD23 43 G1
WHTN TW2 179 E3
Chiltern Cl BUSH WD23 43 F1
CROY/NA CR0 247 E1
WPK KT4 224 A6
Chiltern Dene ENC/FH EN2 37 H5
Chiltern Dr BRYLDS KT5 222 B2
Chiltern Gdns CRICK NW2 104 B1
HAYES BR2 232 B1
Chiltern Rd BOW E3 131 E3
GNTH/NBYPK IG2 95 E1
PIN HA5 78 A2
The Chilterns BELMT * SM2 243 F6
Chiltern St MHST W1U 11 E1
Chiltern Wy WFD IG8 56 C5
Chilthorne Cl CAT SE6 190 D2
Chilton Av EA W5 141 F4
Chilton Gv DEPT SE8 150 B4
Chilton Rd EDGW HA8 62 A2
RCH/KEW TW9 162 A4
Chilton St BETH E2 8 D5
Chilvers Cl WHTN TW2 180 A4
Chilver St GNWCH SE10 152 B5
Chilwell Gdns OXHEY WD19 42 A6
Chilworth Gdns SUT SM1 243 G1
Chilworth Ms BAY/PAD W2 125 G5
Chilworth St BAY/PAD W2 125 G5
Chimes Av PLMGR N13 52 A6
Chinbrook Crs LEE/GVPK SE12 192 D5
Chinbrook Rd LEE/GVPK SE12 193 E5
Chinchilla Dr HSLWW TW4 158 A3
The Chine ALP/SUD HA0 100 D3
MUSWH N10 86 D1
WCHMH N21 52 B1
Chingdale Rd CHING E4 56 A5
Chingford Av CHING E4 55 F5
Chingford La WFD IG8 56 A6
Chingford Mount Rd CHING E4 71 E1
Chingford Rd CHING E4 71 E2
WALTH E17 71 F5
Chingley Cl BMLY BR1 212 A2
Ching Wy WALTH E17 70 D2
Chinnery Cl EN EN1 39 F1
Chinnor Crs GFD/PVL UB6 119 G1
Chipka St POP/IOD E14 151 G2
Chipley St NWCR SE14 150 C6
Chippendale St CLPT E5 110 B1
Chippenham Gdns
KIL/WHAMP NW6 125 E2
Chippenham Ms
MV/WKIL * W9 125 E3
Chippenham Rd MV/WKIL W9 125 E3
Chipperfield Rd
STMC/STPC BR5 215 G5
Chipping Cl BAR EN5 34 C4
Chipstead Av THHTH CR7 228 B1
Chipstead Cl BELMT SM2 243 F6
NRWD SE19 209 F3
Chipstead Gdns CRICK NW2 83 H6
Chipstead St FUL/PGN SW6 165 E2
Chirk Cl YEAD UB4 118 C3
Chisenhale Rd BOW E3 130 C1
Chisholm Rd CROY/NA CR0 229 E6
RCHPK/HAM TW10 181 H1
Chislehurst Av FNCH N3 65 G3
Chislehurst High St CHST BR7 214 B2
Chislehurst Rd BMLY BR1 213 G5
ORP BR6 235 G4
RCHPK/HAM TW10 181 G1
SCUP DA14 215 G1
STMC/STPC BR5 235 E1
Chislet Cl BECK BR3 211 E3
Chisley Rd SEVS/STOTM N15 89 E3
Chiswell Sq BKHTH/KID SE3 172 D3
Chiswell St STLK EC1Y 15 G1
Chiswick Br MORT/ESHN SW14 162 C3
Chiswick Cl CROY/NA CR0 245 H1
Chiswick Common Rd
CHSWK W4 142 D4
Chiswick High Rd CHSWK W4 142 C4
Chiswick House Grounds
CHSWK * W4 142 D6
Chiswick La CHSWK W4 143 E5
Chiswick La South CHSWK W4 143 F6
Chiswick Ml CHSWK W4 143 F6
Chiswick Pk CHSWK * W4 142 C3
Chiswick Pier CHSWK * W4 163 F1
Chiswick Quay CHSWK W4 162 C2
Chiswick Rd CHSWK W4 142 C4
ED N9 53 G4
Chiswick Sq CHSWK W4 143 E6
Chiswick Staithe CHSWK W4 162 B2
Chiswick Village CHSWK W4 142 A6
Chitty's La BCTR RM8 96 B6
Chitty St FITZ W1T 12 B1
Chivalry Rd BTSEA SW11 166 A6
Chivenor Gv KUTN/CMB KT2 201 F1
Chivers Rd CHING E4 55 F5
Choats Rd BARK IG11 136 A1
Chobham Gdns
WIM/MER SW19 184 B4
Chobham Rd SRTFD E15 111 H3
Cholmeley Cl HGT * N6 86 D4
Cholmeley Crs HGT N6 86 D4
Cholmeley Pk HGT N6 86 D5
Cholmley Gdns
KIL/WHAMP NW6 105 E3
Cholmley Rd THDIT KT7 220 D3
Cholmley Ter THDIT * KT7 220 D4
Cholmley Vls THDIT * KT7 220 D4
Cholmondeley Av
WLSDN NW10 123 G1
Chopwell Cl SRTFD * E15 111 H5
Chorleywood Crs
STMC/STPC BR5 215 F5
Choumert Gv PECK SE15 169 G3
Choumert Rd PECK SE15 169 F4
Chow Sq HACK * E8 109 F3
Chrisp St POP/IOD E14 131 F4
Christabel Cl ISLW TW7 160 A4
Christchurch Av ALP/SUD HA0 101 G4
Christ Church Av ERITH DA8 157 H6
Christchurch Av
KIL/WHAMP NW6 104 B6
KTN/HRWW/W HA3 80 C1
NFNCH/WDSP N12 65 G2
TEDD TW11 200 C1
Christchurch Cl ENC/FH EN2 38 C3
NFNCH/WDSP * N12 65 H3
WIM/MER SW19 205 H3
Christchurch Gdns
KTN/HRWW/W HA3 80 C1
Christchurch Hl HAMP NW3 105 H1
Christ Church La BAR EN5 34 C3
Christchurch Ldg EBAR * EN4 36 B5
Christchurch Pk BELMT SM2 243 G5
Christchurch Pas HAMP NW3 105 H1
Christ Church Rd BECK * BR3 211 E5
BRYLDS KT5 221 H4
CEND/HSY/T N8 87 G3
Christchurch Rd BFN/LL DA15 195 F6
BRXS/STRHM SW2 187 H3
IL IG1 94 B5
MORT/ESHN SW14 162 B6
WIM/MER SW19 205 H4
Christchurch Sq HOM E9 110 A6
Christchurch St CHEL SW3 26 C5
Christchurch Ter CHEL * SW3 26 C5
Christchurch Wy GNWCH SE10 152 A5
Christian Flds
STRHM/NOR SW16 208 A3
Christian St WCHPL E1 17 F3
Christie Dr SNWD SE25 229 G2
Christie Rd HOM E9 110 C4
Christina Sq FSBYPK N4 88 B5
Christina St SDTCH EC2A 8 A5
Christopher Av HNWL W7 140 C3
Christopher Cl BFN/LL DA15 175 F6
Christopher Gdns DAGW RM9 116 B3
Christopher Pl CAMTN * NW1 4 D3
Christophers Ms NTGHL * W11 144 C1
Christopher St SDTCH EC2A 7 H6
Chryssell Rd BRXN/ST SW9 168 A1
Chubworthy St NWCR SE14 150 C6
Chudleigh Crs GDMY/SEVK IG3 115 E2
Chudleigh Gdns SUT SM1 243 G1
Chudleigh Rd BROCKY SE4 170 D6
KIL/WHAMP NW6 104 A5
WHTN TW2 180 A1
Chudleigh St WCHPL E1 130 B5
Chulsa Rd SYD SE26 209 H1
Chumleigh St CMBW SE5 32 A5
Chumleigh Wk BRYLDS KT5 221 H1
Church Ap DUL SE21 188 D5
Church Av BECK BR3 211 E4
CAMTN NW1 106 D4
CHING E4 71 H2

EFNCH N2 ....65 H5
MORT/ESHN SW14 ....162 D5
NTHLT UB5 ....98 D5
NWDGN UB2 ....138 C3
PIN HA5 ....78 C3
SCUP DA14 ....215 G1
Churchbury Cl EN EN1 ....39 E3
Churchbury La EN EN1 ....39 E2
Churchbury Rd ELTH/MOT SE9 ....193 F2
   EN EN1 ....39 E3
Church Cl EDGW HA8 ....62 C1
   HSLW TW3 ....158 D3
   KENS * W8 ....145 F2
   TRDG/WHET N20 ....50 A5
Church Crs FNCH N3 ....64 D4
   HOM E9 ....110 D5
   MUSWH N10 ....86 D1
   TRDG/WHET N20 ....50 A5
Churchcroft Cl BAL * SW12 ....186 C2
Churchdown BMLY BR1 ....164 A6
Church Dr CDALE/KGS NW9 ....82 D5
   RYLN/HDSTN HA2 ....79 E3
   WWKM BR4 ....250 A1
Church Elm La DAGE RM10 ....117 E4
Church End HDN NW4 ....63 H6
   WALTH * E17 ....91 F1
Church Farm EBAR * EN4 ....50 B2
Church Farm La CHEAM SM3 ....242 C4
Churchfield Av
   NFNCH/WDSP N12 ....65 G2
Churchfield Cl RYLN/HDSTN HA2 ....79 G1
Churchfield Rd ACT W3 ....142 C1
   WEA W13 ....140 A2
   WELL DA16 ....175 G4
Churchfields E/WMO/HCT KT8 ....199 E6
   GNWCH SE10 ....151 G6
   SWFD E18 ....72 D1
Churchfields Av FELT TW13 ....178 D5
Churchfields Rd BECK BR3 ....210 B5
Churchfield Wy
   NFNCH/WDSP N12 ....65 G2
Church Gdns ALP/SUD HA0 ....100 C2
   EA W5 ....141 F2
Church Garth ARCH * N19 ....87 F6
Church Ga FUL/PGN SW6 ....164 C4
Church Gn BRXN/ST * SW9 ....168 A3
Church Gv KUT1 KT1 ....201 E4
   SYD SE26 ....171 F5
Church Hl CAR SM5 ....244 B5
   HRW HA1 ....80 A5
   ORP BR6 ....235 G4
   WALTH E17 ....91 E1
   WCHMH N21 ....51 A2
   WIM/MER SW19 ....204 D1
   WOOL/PLUM SE18 ....155 H3
Church Hill Rd CHEAM SM3 ....242 B2
   EBAR EN4 ....50 B2
   SURB KT6 ....221 G2
   WALTH E17 ....91 F1
Church Hill Wd
   STMC/STPC BR5 ....235 F2
Church Hyde
   WOOL/PLUM SE18 ....155 A3
Churchill Av KTN/HRWW/W HA3 ....80 D5
Churchill Gdns ACT W3 ....122 A5
   PIM SW1V 28 A4
Churchill Gardens Rd PIM SW1V 27 H4
Churchill Pl POP/IOD E14 ....151 F1
Churchill Rd CAN/RD E16 ....133 E5
   CRICK NW2 ....103 H4
   EDGW HA8 ....61 H2
   KTTN NW5 ....106 D2
   SAND/SEL CR2 ....246 C6
Churchill Ter CHING E4 ....54 A4
Churchill Wk HOM E9 ....110 A3
Churchill Wy BMLY BR1 ....121 G2
Church La CEND/HSY/T N8 ....87 H1
   CHSGTN KT9 ....239 H4
   CHST BR7 ....214 C4
   DAGE RM10 ....117 F4
   ED N9 ....53 G4
   EFNCH N2 ....65 H6
   ENC/FH EN2 ....38 D4
   HAYES BR2 ....233 C6
   KTN/HRWW/W HA3 ....60 B4
   PIN HA5 ....58 D4
   TEDD TW11 ....200 B3
   THDIT KT7 ....220 B3
   TOOT SW17 ....206 B1
   TOTM N17 ....69 E4
   TWK TW1 ....180 C3
   WALTH E17 ....91 G1
   WAN E11 ....92 A5
   WEA W13 ....141 E2
   WIM/MER SW19 ....205 F1
   WLGTN SM6 ....245 F1

GNTH/NBYPK IG2 ....95 E3
HAYES BR2 ....212 A6
HAYES BR2 ....251 F5
HDN NW4 ....63 H2
HEST TW5 ....159 E1
HNWL W7 ....120 B6
HOR/WEW KT19 ....240 D5
ISLW TW7 ....159 H2
KUT KT1 ....201 H5
LEY E10 ....91 E5
MNPK E12 ....113 H3
MTCM CR4 ....195 E4
NRWD SE19 ....209 E3
NTHLT UB5 ....98 D5
NTHLT UB5 ....118 D1
NWDGN UB2 ....138 D1
ORP BR6 ....252 C5
PEND EN3 ....54 A1
RCHPK/HAM TW10 ....161 G6
RCHPK/HAM TW10 ....181 G6
SCUP DA14 ....195 G6
STAN HA7 ....60 D1
SURB KT6 ....221 E5
SWLY BR8 ....237 H5
TEDD TW11 ....180 A6
TOTM N17 ....69 F3
WALTH E17 ....70 C5
WELL DA16 ....175 H3
WIM/MER SW19 ....184 C6
WIM/MER SW19 ....204 C1
WLGTN SM6 ....245 E1
WLSDN NW10 ....99 H6
WPK KT4 ....225 E5
Church Rd South EFNCH N2 ....65 H5
Church Rw CHST BR7 ....214 C4
   FUL/PGN * SW6 ....165 F1
   HAMP NW3 ....83 G2
   WAND/EARL * SW18 ....165 G6
Church Row Ms CHST BR7 ....214 C5
Church St BAY/PAD W2 ....125 H4
   CHSWK W4 ....143 G6
   CROY/NA CR0 ....246 D1
   DAGE RM10 ....117 F5
   ED N9 ....53 E3
   ENC/FH EN2 ....24 E4
   EW KT17 ....241 G6
   HPTN TW12 ....199 G4
   HSLW TW3 ....159 G6
   ISLW TW7 ....160 C4
   KUT KT1 ....201 F5
   SRTFD E15 ....112 A6
   TWK TW1 ....180 C3
Church Street Est
   STJWD * NW8 ....125 H4
Church St North SRTFD E15 ....112 A6
Church Ter FUL/PGN * SW6 ....165 F3
   HDN NW4 ....63 H6
   LEW SE13 ....133 F2
   RCHPK/HAM TW10 ....161 F6
Church V EFNCH N2 ....66 B6
   FSTH SE23 ....190 A4
Churchview Rd WHTN TW2 ....179 H5
Church Wk BTFD TW8 ....141 H1
   BUSH WD23 ....43 E1
   CDALE/KGS NW9 ....82 D6
   CRICK NW2 ....84 A4
   RYNPK SW20 ....204 A6
   STNW/STAM N16 ....108 C3
   STNW/STAM N16 ....108 D3
   THDIT NW16 ....207 E5
Churchway CAMTN NW1 ....4 D4
Church Wy TRDG/WHET N20 ....50 A5
Churchyard Rw LBTH SE11 ....30 D1
Churston Av PLSTW E13 ....112 D6
Churston Cl
   BRXS/STRHM * SW2 ....188 B3
Churston Dr MRDN SM4 ....224 H2
Churston Gdns FBAR/BDGN N11 ....67 A2
Churston Pl CHSWK * W4 ....142 B6
   PIM SW1V 28 B2
Churton St PIM SW1V 28 B2
Chyngton Cl BFN/LL DA15 ....195 F5
Cibber Rd FSTH SE23 ....190 B4
Cicada Rd WAND/EARL SW18 ....185 G1
Cicely Rd PECK SE15 ....169 G2
Cinderford Wy BMLY BR1 ....192 A6
Cinema Pde EDGW * HA8 ....62 A2
Cinnamon Cl CROY/NA * CR0 ....227 G4
Cinnamon St WAP E1W 25 H2
Cintra Pk NRWD SE19 ....209 F3
Circle Gdns WIM/MER SW19 ....205 E6
Circle Rd WOOL/PLUM SE18 ....155 H1
The Circle CRICK NW2 ....103 E1
   MLHL NW7 ....45 E3
The Circuits PIN HA5 ....78 A1
Circular Rd TOTM N17 ....69 F6
Circular Wy WOOL/PLUM SE18 ....153 H6
Circus Ms MBLAR * W1H 10 C7
Circus Pl LVRST * EC2M 13 H2
Circus Rd STJWD NW8 ....125 H2
Circus St GNWCH SE10 ....171 G1
Cirencester St BAY/PAD W2 ....125 F4
Cissbury Ring North
   NFNCH/WDSP N12 ....64 D1
Cissbury Ring South
   NFNCH/WDSP N12 ....64 D1
Cissbury Rd SEVS/STOTM N15 ....68 D2
Citadel Pl LBTH SE11 ....29 G3
Citizen Rd HOLWY N7 ....108 A1
Citron Ter PECK * SE15 ....169 H4
City Barracks SHB * W12 ....144 A1
City Gdn EDGW HA8 ....62 A2
City Garden Rw IS N1 ....6 C2
City Rd FSBYE EC1V 6 C2
   STLK EC1Y * 7
Civic Wy BARK/HLT IG6 ....94 C1
   RSLP HA4 ....98 B3
Clabon Ms KTBR SW1X 18 C6
Clack St BERM/RHTH SE16 ....150 A2
Clacton Rd TOTM * N17 ....70 C1
   WALTH E17 ....89 G1
Claire Ct NFNCH/WDSP N12 ....49 G5
Claire Gdns STAN HA7 ....61 H1
Claire Pl POP/IOD E14 ....151 E3
Clairvale Rd HEST TW5 ....158 B2
Clairview Rd TOOT SW16 ....206 D1
Clairville Gdns HNWL W7 ....140 A1
Clamp Hi KTN/HRWW/W HA3 ....45 H6
Clancarty Rd FUL/PGN SW6 ....165 E3
Clandon Cl ACT W3 ....142 B2

EW KT17 ....241 F4
Clandon Gdns FNCH N3 ....65 E6
Clandon Rd GDMY/SEVK IG3 ....95 E6
Clandon St DEPT SE8 ....171 E3
Clandon Ter RYNPK * SW20 ....204 B5
Clanricarde Gdns BAY/PAD W2 ....125 H6
Clapgate Rd BUSH WD23 ....43 F1
Clapham Common North Side
   CLAP SW4 ....166 D5
Clapham Common South Side
   BTSEA SW11 ....166 C6
Clapham Common West Side
   BTSEA SW11 ....166 C6
Clapham Court Ter CLAP * SW4 ....167 G6
Clapham Crs CLAP SW4 ....167 F5
Clapham High St CLAP SW4 ....167 G6
Clapham Manor St CLAP SW4 ....167 E4
Clapham Park Est CLAP * SW4 ....187 F2
Clapham Park Rd CLAP SW4 ....167 F4
Clapham Park Ter CLAP * SW4 ....167 G5
Clapham Rd BRXN/ST SW9 ....167 G5
Clapham Rd South IS N1 ....108 D4
Claps Gate La EHAM E6 ....116 D4
Clapton Common CLPT E5 ....99 G4
Clapton Sq CLPT E5 ....110 A5
Clapton Ter STNW/STAM N16 ....89 H4
Clapton Wy CLPT E5 ....109 G2
Clare Cl BORE WD6 ....45 H1
   NFNCH N2 ....64 H1
Clare Cnr ELTH/MOT SE9 ....194 B2
Claredale St BETH E2 ....9 F2
Clare Gdns BARK IG11 ....115 F3
   FSTGT E7 ....112 C2
   NTGHL * W11 ....124 C5
Clare La IS N1 ....108 C5
Clare Lawn Av
   MORT/ESHN SW14 ....162 D6
Clare Ms FUL/PGN * SW6 ....165 F1
Claremont Av
   KTN/HRWW/W HA3 ....81 G2
   NWMAL KT3 ....223 H2
Claremont Cl
   BRXS/STRHM SW2 ....187 H3
   CLPT E5 ....154 A1
   IS N1 ....6 A2
   ORP BR6 ....252 A2
Claremont Gdns
   GDMY/SEVK IG3 ....95 C6
   SURB KT6 ....221 C1
Claremont Gv CHSWK W4 ....163 E1
   WFD IG8 ....75 F2
Claremont Pk FNCH N3 ....64 B6
Claremont Rd BMLY BR1 ....233 C1
   CRICK NW2 ....84 A4
   CROY/NA CR0 ....229 G5
   EA W5 ....121 H4
   ESH/CLAY KT10 ....238 A5
   FSTGT E7 ....112 C5
   HGT N6 ....86 D4
   KTN/HRWW/W HA3 ....60 A5
   MV/WKIL W9 ....100 C5
   SURB KT6 ....221 G2
   TEDD TW11 ....200 B3
   TWK TW1 ....180 D2
   WALTH E17 ....71 G4
   WAN E11 ....111 H1
   WEA W13 ....120 C4
Claremont Sq IS N1 ....6 A2
Claremont St GNWCH SE10 ....151 F6
   UED N18 ....69 G2
Claremont Ter THDIT * KT7 ....220 D4
Claremont Vls CMBW * SE5 ....168 D1
   KUT * KT1 ....201 H5
Claremont Wy CRICK NW2 ....84 A5
Clarence Av CLAP SW4 ....187 F2
   HAYES BR2 ....233 C1
   IL IG1 ....90 A5
   NWMAL KT3 ....202 C5
Clarence Cl BUSH WD23 ....44 B2
   EBAR EN4 ....35 H6
Clarence Ct MLHL * NW7 ....63 F1
Clarence Crs CLAP SW4 ....187 F3
   SCUP DA14 ....195 H5
Clarence Gdns CAMTN NW1 ....3 H4
Clarence Ga CAMTN NW1 ....2 D5
Clarence La PUT/ROE SW15 ....183 F1
Clarence Ms CLPT * E5 ....109 H4
Clarence Pas CAMTN * NW1 ....5 E2
Clarence Pl CLPT E5 ....109 H4
Clarence Rd BMLY BR1 ....176 C5
   BXLYHS DA6 ....176 C5
   CAN/RD E16 ....132 A3
   CEND/HSY/T N8 ....67 E3
   CLPT E5 ....109 H2
   CROY/NA CR0 ....228 D4
   ELTH/MOT SE9 ....193 G4
   FSTGT E7 ....115 G2
   KIL/WHAMP NW6 ....104 D5
   PEND EN3 ....25 F1
   RCH/KEW TW9 ....161 H2
   SCUP DA14 ....195 H5
   SEVS/STOTM N15 ....89 G1
   SUT SM1 ....243 F2
   TEDD TW11 ....200 B2
   WALTH E17 ....70 B5
   WDGN N22 ....67 H4
   WIM/MER SW19 ....205 F2
   WLGTN SM6 ....244 D3
Clarence St KUT KT1 ....201 F5
   NWDGN UB2 ....138 B3
   RCH/KEW TW9 ....159 ...
Clarence Ter CAMTN NW1 ....3 E5
   HSLW TW3 ....159 F5
Clarence Vis KUT * KT1 ....201 H5
Clarence Wk CLAP SW4 ....167 H1
Clarendon Cl BAY/PAD * W2 ....10 A5
   STMC/STPC BR5 ....215 G6
Clarendon Crs WHTN TW2 ....179 G5
Clarendon Cross NTGHL W11 ....124 C6
Clarendon Dr PUT/ROE SW15 ....164 A5
Clarendon Gdns HDN NW4 ....45 G5
   IL IG1 ....95 ...
   MV/WKIL W9 ....125 G3
   WBLY HA9 ....101 G2
Clarendon Ga BAY/PAD W2 ....10 A5
Clarendon Gn STMC/STPC BR5 ....235 G1
Clarendon Gv MTCM CR4 ....194 D1
Clarendon Gv MTCM CR4 ....206 B6
   STMC/STPC BR5 ....235 G1

EW KT17 ....241 F4
Clarendon Ms BAY/PAD W2 ....10 A5
Clarendon Pth STMC/STPC BR5 ....235 G1
   RDART DA2 ....217 H1
Clarendon Ri LEW SE13 ....171 G4
Clarendon Rd CEND/HSY/T N8 ....67 H6
   CROY/NA CR0 ....228 B6
   EA W5 ....121 G2
   HRW HA1 ....80 A3
   LEY E10 ....91 F3
   NTGHL W11 ....124 C6
   SEVS/STOTM N15 ....89 H3
   SWFD E18 ....72 C6
   UED N18 ....69 G2
   WDGN * N22 ....67 H5
   WLGTN SM6 ....245 E3
Clarendon St PIM SW1V 27 H1
Clarendon Ter MV/WKIL W9 ....125 G3
Clarendon Wy CHST BR7 ....215 H1
   WCHMH N21 ....52 C2
Clarens St CAT SE6 ....190 D4
Clare Pde NTHLT * UB5 ....99 H4
Clare Rd HSLWW TW4 ....155 H4
   NTHLT UB5 ....99 H4
   NWCR SE14 ....170 D3
   WAN E11 ....91 H3
   WLSDN NW10 ....91 H6
Clare St BETH E2 ....9 H1
Claret Gdns SNWD SE25 ....229 E1
Clareville Gv SKENS * SW7 ....145 G4
Clareville Grove Ms
   SKENS * SW7 ....145 G4
Clareville Rd STMC/STPC BR5 ....234 C6
Clareville St SKENS * SW7 ....145 G4
Clare Wy BXLYHN DA7 ....176 C2
Clarges Ms MYFR/PICC W1J 19 G1
Clarges St MYFR/PICC W1J 19 H1
Claribel Rd BRXN/ST SW9 ....168 B3
Claridge Rd BCTR RM8 ....96 B5
Clarissa Rd CHDH RM6 ....73 H4
Clarissa St HACK E8 ....109 E6
Clarkes Av WPK KT4 ....224 B5
Clarkes Ms CAVSQ/HST W1G 11 F1
Clarks Md BUSH WD23 ....43 G2
Clarkson Rd CAN/RD E16 ....132 B5
Clarkson Rw CAMTN NW1 ....3 H2
Clarkson St BETH E2 ....9 G3
Clark's Rd IL IG1 ....90 D1
Clark St WCHPL E1 ....17 H3
Clark Wy HEST TW5 ....158 B1
Claude Rd LEY E10 ....90 ...
   PECK SE15 ....169 H3
   PLSTW E13 ....112 D6
Claude St POP/IOD E14 ....151 E4
Claudia Pl WIM/MER SW19 ....184 C3
Claughton Rd PLSTW E13 ....113 F1
Clauson Av NTHLT UB5 ....99 F3
Clavell St GNWCH SE10 ....151 G6
Claverdale Rd
   BRXS/STRHM SW2 ....187 G2
Clavering Av BARN SW13 ....143 H6
Clavering Cl TWK TW1 ....180 C6
Clavering Rd MNPK E12 ....95 F5
Claverley Gv FNCH N3 ....65 E1
Claverley Vls FNCH N3 ....65 F1
Claverton St PIM SW1V 28 B4
Clave St E1W 150 A1
Claxton Gv HMSMTH W6 ....144 A4
Clay Av MTCM CR4 ....206 D5
Claybank Gv LEW SE13 ....171 F4
Claybridge Rd LEE/GVPK SE12 ....193 E6
Claybrook Rd HMSMTH W6 ....144 B6
Claybury BUSH WD23 ....44 B2
Claybury Rd WFD IG8 ....74 C4
Claydon Dr CROY/NA CR0 ....245 G2
Claydown Ms
   WOOL/PLUM SE18 ....154 A5
Clayfarm Rd ELTH/MOT SE9 ....194 C4
Claygate Crs CROY/NA CR0 ....249 G4
Claygate La THDIT KT7 ....220 C5
   THDIT KT7 ....220 C5
Claygate Lodge Cl
   ESH/CLAY KT10 ....238 A5
Claygate Rd WEA W13 ....140 D3
Clayhall Av CLAY IG5 ....73 H5
Clayhill Crs LEE/GVPK SE12 ....192 D4
Claylands Pl BRXN/ST SW9 ....168 A1
Claylands Rd VX/NE SW8 ....29 H6
Clay La BUSH WD23 ....44 A2
Claymore Cl MRDN SM4 ....225 E4
Claypole Dr HEST TW5 ....158 C2
Claypole Rd SRTFD * E15 ....131 G1
Clayponds Av BTFD TW8 ....141 G4
Clayponds Gdns BTFD TW8 ....141 F4
Clayponds La BTFD TW8 ....141 G5
Clayside CHIG IG7 ....74 D2
Clays La SRTFD E15 ....111 F3
Clays Lane Cl SRTFD E15 ....111 F3
Clay St MHST W1U 10 D2
Clayton Av ALP/SUD HA0 ....105 H1
Clayton Cl EHAM E6 ....133 H5
Clayton Crs BTFD TW8 ....141 E5
Clayton Fld CDALE/KGS NW9 ....63 E4
Clayton Ms GNWCH SE10 ....171 H2
Clayton Rd CHSGTN KT9 ....239 E2
   ISLW TW7 ....160 A1
   PECK SE15 ....169 G2
   ROMW/RG RM7 ....75 E4
Clayton St LBTH SE11 ....30 A5
Clayton Ter YEAD * UB4 ....118 D4
Claytonville Ter BELV * DA17 ....157 G2
Clay Wood Cl ORP BR6 ....235 E4
Cleanthus Cl WOOL/PLUM SE18 ....174 D3
Cleanthus Rd
   WOOL/PLUM SE18 ....174 B2
Clearbrook Wy WCHPL E1 ....130 A5
Clearwater Pl SURB KT6 ....221 E3
Clearwater Ter WKENS W14 ....144 D2
Clearwell Dr MV/WKIL W9 ....125 F3
Cleave Av ORP BR6 ....253 E4
Cleaveland Rd SURB KT6 ....221 F2
Cleaverholme Cl SNWD SE25 ....229 G5
Cleaver Sq LBTH SE11 ....30 B3
Cleaver St LBTH SE11 ....30 B3
Cleeve Hl FSTH SE23 ....189 H1
Cleeve Park Gdns SCUP DA14 ....195 H1
Cleeve Wy PUT/ROE SW15 ....183 F1
Clegg St PLSTW E13 ....132 C2
   WAP E1W 25 H1

Clematis Cottages *SHB* W12 .....123 C6
Clematis Gdns *WFD* IG8 ....72 C1
Clematis St *SUT* SM1 ....123 F6
Clem Attlee Pde
  FUL/PGN SW6 ....144 D6
Clemence Rd *DAGE* RM10 ....117 G6
Clemence St *POP/IOD* E14 ....130 D4
Clement Av *CLAP* SW4 ....167 F5
Clement Cl *CHSWK* W4 ....142 D4
  WLSDN NW10 ....104 A5
Clementhorpe Rd *DAGW* RM9 ...116 A4
Clementina Rd *LEY* E10 ....80 C6
Clementine Cl *WEA* W13 ....140 D2
Clement Rd *BECK* BR3 ....210 B5
  WIM/MER SW19 ....204 C1
Clements Av *CAN/RD* E16 ....132 C6
Clements Inn *LINN* WC2A 13 H4
Clements La *IL* IG1 ....114 B1
  MANHO EC4N 15 H5
Clements Pl *BTFD* TW8 ....141 F5
Clement's Rd *BERM/RHTH* SE16 .... 113 H6
  IL IG1 ....114 B1
Clendon Wy *WOOL/PLUM* SE18 ...154 D4
Clennam St *STHWK* SE1 ....23 F5
Clensham La *SUT* SM1 ....225 E6
Clenston Ms *MBLAR* W1H 10 C3
Clephane Rd *IS* N1 ....108 C4
Clere Pl *SDTCH* EC2A 7 H5
Clere St *SDTCH* EC2A 7 H5
Clerkenwell Cl *CLKNW* EC1R 6 B6
Clerkenwell Gn *CLKNW* EC1R 6 C6
Clerkenwell Rd *CLKNW* EC1R 6 A6
Clermont Rd *HOM* E9 ....110 A6
Clevedon Rd *KUT* KT1 ....202 A5
  PGE/AN SE20 ....210 B4
  TWK TW1 ....181 F1
Cleveland Av *CHSWK* W4 ....143 H4
  HPTN TW12 ....198 D3
Cleveland Gdns *BARN* SW13 ....163 F3
  BAY/PAD W2 ....125 G5
  CRICK NW2 ....64 A6
  FSBYPK N4 ....88 C2
  WPK KT4 ....223 E6
Cleveland Gv *WCHPL* E1 ....130 A3
Cleveland Ms *FITZ* W1T 12 A1
Cleveland Park Av *WALTH* E17 ....91 E1
Cleveland Park Crs *WALTH* E17 ......91 E1
Cleveland Pl *ST JS* SW1Y 20 B1
Cleveland Ri *RRDN* SM4 ....224 B4
Cleveland Rd *BARN* SW13 ....163 F3
  CHSWK W4 ....142 C3
  ED N9 ....53 H2
  IL IG1 ....114 B1
  IS N1 ....109 G4
  ISLW TW7 ....160 C5
  NWMAL KT3 ....223 E1
  SWFD E18 ....72 C6
  WAN E11 ....94 A3
  WELL DA16 ....175 F3
  WPK KT4 ....223 E6
Cleveland Rw *WHALL* SW1A 20 B2
Cleveland Sq *BAY/PAD* W2 ....125 G6
Cleveland St *CAMTN* NW1 ....5 H6
Cleveland Ter *BAY/PAD* W2 ....125 G5
Cleveland Wy *WCHPL* E1 ....130 A3
Cleveley Crs *EA* W5 ....121 G1
Cleveleys Rd *CLPT* E5 ....109 H1
Cleverly Cl *CHARL* SE7 ....153 F4
Cleverly Est *SHB* * W12 ....143 G1
Cleve Rd *KIL/WHAMP* NW6 ....6 C5
  SCUP DA14 ....196 B5
Cleves Av *EW* KT17 ....241 H6
Cleves Cl *LOU* IG10 ....57 C1
Cleves Gdns *EHAM* E6 ....113 H6
  RCHPK/HAM TW10 ....181 E5
Cleves Wk *BARK/HLT* IG6 ....74 C3
Cleves Wy *HPTN* TW12 ....198 D3
  RSLP HA4 ....78 B5
Clewer Crs *KTN/HRWW/W* HA3 .....59 H4
Clichfen Rd *BTFD* TW8 ....141 F6
  CLPT E5 ....110 A3
Cliff End *NTHLT* UB5 ....98 C6
Clifford Av *BRXN/ST* SW9 ....168 B5
Clifford Gdns *WLSDN* NW10 ....104 A4
Clifford Rd *ALP/SUD* HA0 ....101 F6
  BAR EN5 ....35 F4
  CAN/RD E16 ....132 B3
  ED N9 ....36 A1
  HSLWW TW4 ....158 B4
  RCHPK/HAM TW10 ....181 F4
  SNWD SE25 ....229 G1
  WALTH E17 ....71 G5

WBPTN * SW10 ....145 G6
Clifton Ri *NWCR* SE14 ....170 C1
Clifton Rd *CAN/RD* E16 ....132 A4
  CEND/HSY/T N8 ....87 F3
  EN EN1 ....36 C2
  FSTGT E7 ....113 H4
  GFD/PVL UB6 ....119 G3
  GNTH/NBYPK IG2 ....94 D3
  ISLW TW7 ....160 A3
  KTN/HRWW/W HA3 ....81 H2
  KUTN/CMB KT2 ....201 H4
  MV/WKIL W9 ....125 G3
  NWDGN UB2 ....138 D4
  SCUP DA14 ....195 E6
  SNWD SE25 ....229 E1
  TEDD TW11 ....180 A6
  WDGN N22 ....48 D4
  WELL DA16 ....176 A4
  WIM/MER SW19 ....244 D3
  WLGTN SM6 ....244 D3
  WLSDN NW10 ....123 G1
Clifton St *SDTCH* EC2A 8 A6
Clifton Ter *FSBYPK* N4 ....88 A1
Clifton Vs *MV/WKIL* W9 ....125 F4
Clifton Wy *ALP/SUD* HA0 ....101 G6
  PECK SE15 ....170 A1
Cline Rd *FBAR/BDGN* N11 ....67 E2
Clink St *STHWK* SE1 ....23 C1
Clinton Av *E/WMO/HCT* KT8 ......199 C1
  WELL DA16 ....175 H3
Clinton Crs *BARK/HLT* IG6 ....75 E2
Clinton Rd *BOW* E3 ....130 C2
  FSTGT E7 ....112 C2
  SEVS/STOTM N15 ....88 D1
Clinton Ter *DEPT* * SE8 ....151 E6
  SUT * SM1 ....243 G2
Clipper Cl *BERM/RHTH* SE16 ....150 B2
Clipper Wy *LEW* SE13 ....171 G5
Clippesly Cl *CHSGTN* * KT9 ....239 H4
Clipstone Ms *CTPST* W1W 11 H1
Clipstone Rd *HSLW* TW3 ....159 E4
Clipstone St *GTPST* W1W 11 H1
Clissold Crs *STNW/STAM* N16 ......108 D2
Clissold Rd *STNW/STAM* N16 ......108 D1
Clitheroe Av *RYLN/HDSTN* HA2 .....59 H5
Clitheroe Gdns *OXHEY* WD19 ......42 B5
Clitheroe Rd *BRXN/ST* SW9 ....167 G3
  CRW RM5 ....56 D2
Clitherow Av *HNWL* W7 ....140 C3
Clitherow Rd *BTFD* TW8 ....140 C5
Clitterhouse Crs *CRICK* NW2 ....64 A5
Clitterhouse Rd *CRICK* NW2 ....64 A5
Clive Av *UED* N18 ....50 C2
Cliveden Cl *NFNCH/WDSP* N12 .....47 F1
Cliveden Pl *BGVA* SW1W 27 E1
Cliveden Rd *WIM/MER* SW19 ......204 D4
Clivedon Ct *WEA* W13 ....120 D4
Clivedon Rd *CHING* E4 ....72 A1
Clive Rd *BELV* DA17 ....157 F4
  DUL SE21 ....188 C5
  EN EN1 ....39 G5
  TWK TW1 ....180 B6
  WIM/MER SW19 ....206 A2
Clive Wy *EN* EN1 ....39 G5
Cloak La *BLKFR* EC4V 15 F5
Clockhouse Av *BARK* IG11 ....114 C6
Clockhouse Cl *WIM/MER* SW19 ...184 A5
Clockhouse La *CRW* RM5 ....77 G5
Clock House Pde *PLMGR* * N13 .....68 A1
Clockhouse Pl *PUT/ROE* SW15 ....164 C6
Clock House Rd *BECK* BR3 ....210 C6
Clock Pde *EN* * EN1 ....36 A6
Clock Tower Ms *IS* N1 ....108 D5
  THMD SE28 ....135 H6
Clock Tower Pl *HOLWY* * N7 ....107 G4
Clock Tower Rd *ISLW* TW7 ....160 B4
Cloister Cl *TEDD* TW11 ....200 D1
Cloister Gdns *EDGW* HA8 ....62 C1
  SNWD SE25 ....229 H5
Cloister Rd *ACT* W3 ....122 C4
  CRICK NW2 ....64 C6
Cloisters Av *HAYES* BR2 ....233 H2
Clonard Wy *PIN* HA5 ....59 E2
Clonbrock Rd *STNW/STAM* N16 ...108 E2
Cloncurry St *FUL/PGN* SW6 ....164 B3
Clonmel Cl *RYLN/HDSTN* HA2 ....79 H5
Clonmell Rd *TOTM* N17 ....68 A4
Clonmel Rd *FUL/PGN* SW6 ....144 A1
  TEDD TW11 ....179 H6
Clonmore St
  WAND/EARL SW18 ....184 D3
Cloonmore Av *ORP* BR6 ....253 F3
Clorane Gdns *HAMP* NW3 ....70 D2
The Close *ALP/SUD* HA0 ....101 C4
  BECK BR3 ....230 C1
  BUSH * WD23 ....43 E1
  BXLY DA5 ....197 E1
  CAR SM5 ....244 A6
  CHDH RM6 ....96 C3
  CHEAM SM3 ....224 C6
  EBAR EN4 ....51 E1
  ED N9 ....50 B5
  GNTH/NBYPK IG2 ....90 E5
  ISLW TW7 ....159 H5
  MTCM CR4 ....226 B1
  NWMAL KT3 ....202 C5
  PIN HA5 ....78 A4
  PIN HA5 ....77 H5
  RCH/KEW TW9 ....137 H3
  SCUP DA14 ....215 H1
  SNWD * SE25 ....229 G3
  STHGT/OAK N14 ....51 F4
  STMC/STPC BR5 ....235 E5
  SURB KT6 ....221 G4
  TRDG/WHET N20 ....48 D4
  WBLY HA9 ....82 A5
Cloth Ct *STBT* EC1A 14 C2
Cloth Fair *STBT* EC1A 14 C2
Clothier St *HDTCH* * EC3A 16 B3
Cloth St *STBT* * EC1A 15 E1
Clothworkers Rd
  WOOL/PLUM SE18 ....174 D1
Cloudesdale Rd *TOOT* SW17 ......186 D4
Cloudesley Pl *IS* N1 ....108 A6
Cloudesley Rd *BXLYHN* DA7 ....137 F6
  IS N1 ....108 A6
Cloudesley Sq *IS* N1 ....108 A6
Cloudesley St *IS* N1 ....108 A6
Clouston Cl *WLGTN* SM6 ....245 E4
Clova Rd *FSTGT* E7 ....96 C4

Clove Crs *POP/IOD* E14 ....131 G6
Clovelly Av *CDALE/KGS* NW9 ....83 F1
Clovelly Gdns *EN* EN1 ....53 E2
  ROMW/RG RM7 ....77 F4
Clovelly Rd *BXLYHN* DA7 ....156 C6
  CEND/HSY/T N8 ....87 F1
  CHSWK * W4 ....142 D2
  HSLW TW3 ....159 F1
  WEA W13 ....141 E2
Clovelly Wy *ORP* BR6 ....235 F3
  RYLN/HDSTN HA2 ....98 D1
  WCHPL E1 ....130 A5
Clover Cl *WAN* * E11 ....94 H1
Cloverdale Gdns *BFN/LL* DA15 ....195 F1
The Clover Fld *BUSH* WD23 ....42 D1
Clover Ms *CHEL* SW3 ....36 D5
Clover Wy *MTCM* CR4 ....226 C5
Clove St *PLSTW* E13 ....132 C5
Clowders Rd *CAT* SE6 ....190 D5
Clowser Cl *SUT* SM1 ....243 G3
Cloyster Wd *EDGW* HA8 ....61 F3
Club Gardens Rd *HAYES* BR2 ......232 C4
Club Rw *BETH* E2 ....8 C5
Clunbury Av *NWDGN* UB2 ....138 D5
Cluny Est *STHWK* SE1 ....145 A3
Cluny Ms *ECT* SW5 ....145 A6
Cluny Pl *STHWK* SE1 ....24 A5
Clutton St *POP/IOD* E14 ....131 F4
Clydach Rd *EN* EN1 ....36 F5
Clyde Circ *SEVS/STOTM* N15 ....89 E1
Clyde Ct *CAMTN* NW1 ....4 D1
Clyde Flats *FUL/PGN* * SW6 ....164 D1
Clyde Pl *LEY* E10 ....74 A3
Clyde Rd *CROY/NA* CR0 ....229 F6
  SEVS/STOTM N15 ....89 E1
  SUT SM1 ....243 E3
  WDGN N22 ....67 F4
  WLGTN SM6 ....245 E3
Clydesdale *PEND* EN3 ....40 B5
Clydesdale Av
  KTN/HRWW/W HA3 ....61 F6
Clydesdale Cl *ISLW* TW7 ....160 B4
Clydesdale Gdns
  RCHPK/HAM TW10 ....162 B5
Clydesdale Rd *NTGHL* W11 ....124 D5
Clydesdale St *DEPT* SE8 ....151 H1
Clyde Ter *FSTH* SE23 ....190 A4
Clyde V *FSTH* SE23 ....190 A4
Clyston St *VX/NE* SW8 ....167 E3
Coach & Horses Yd
  CONDST W1S 12 A5
Coach House La *HBRY* * N5 ....108 B2
  WIM/MER SW19 ....184 B6
Coach House Ms *NWCR* * SE14 ...170 B2
Coach House Yd
  HAMP * NW3 ....165 F5
Coaldale Wk *DUL* * SE21 ....164 A5
Coalecroft Rd *PUT/ROE* SW15 ....164 A5
Coates Av *WAND/EARL* SW18 .....186 A1
Coates Hill Rd *BMLY* BR1 ....214 A5
Coates Rd *BORE* WD6 ....45 F2
Coate St *BETH* E2 ....9 F7
Cobbett Rd *ELTH/MOT* SE9 ....173 C4
  WHTN TW2 ....179 E3
Cobbetts Av *REDBR* IG4 ....93 F2
Cobbett St *VX/NE* SW8 ....167 H1
Cobble La *IS* N1 ....108 B5
Cobble Ms *FSBYPK* N4 ....88 C2
Cobbler's Wk *TEDD* TW11 ....200 A3
Cobblestone Pl *CROY/NA* CR0 ....228 C3
Cobbold Ms *SHB* * W12 ....143 F2
Cobbold Rd *SHB* W12 ....112 B1
  WAN E11 ....94 A4
  WLSDN NW10 ....81 H4
Cobb's Rd *HSLWW* TW4 ....158 D5
Cobb St *WCHPL* E1 ....16 C2
Cobden Ms *SYD* SE26 ....209 H1
Cobden Rd *ORP* BR6 ....252 D2
  SNWD SE25 ....229 G2
  WAN E11 ....112 A1
Cobham Av *NWMAL* KT3 ....223 C1
Cobham Cl *BFN/LL* DA15 ....195 H1
  BTSEA * SW11 ....186 A1
  EDGW HA8 ....62 B5
  EN EN1 ....36 D4
  HAYES BR2 ....233 G4
  WLGTN SM6 ....245 G4
Cobham Ms *CAMTN* NW1 ....107 F5
Cobham Pl *BXLYHS* DA6 ....176 B6
Cobham Rd *GDMY/SEVK* IG3 ......91 H6
  HEST TW5 ....158 A1
  KUT KT1 ....202 A5
  WALTH E17 ....91 G1
  WDGN N22 ....68 B6
Cobland Rd *LEE/GVPK* SE12 ......193 G6
Coborn Rd *BOW* E3 ....130 D2
Coborn St *BOW* E3 ....130 D2
Cobourg Dr *CAMTN* NW1 ....8 D2
Cobourg St *CAMTN* NW1 ....4 B4
Coburg Cl *WEST* SW1P 28 C4
Coburg Crs *BRXS/STRHM* SW2 ...187 H3
Coburg Dwellings *WCHPL* * E1 ...130 A6
Coburg Gdns *CLAY* IG5 ....71 F3
Coburg Rd *WDGN* N22 ....67 H5
Cochrane Ms *ST JWD* NW8 ....125 H1
Cochrane Rd *WIM/MER* SW19 ....205 H1
Cochrane St *ST JWD* NW8 ....125 H1
Cockcrow Hl *SURB* * KT6 ....221 F5
Cockerell Rd *WALTH* E17 ....90 C4
Cockfosters Pde *EBAR* * EN4 ....34 B5
Cockfosters Rd *EBAR* EN4 ....36 B1
Cock La *STBT* EC1A 14 C2
Cockmannings La
  STMC/STPC BR5 ....236 B5
Cockmannings Rd
  STMC/STPC BR5 ....236 B4
Cocks Crs *NWMAL* KT3 ....223 F1
Cocksett Av *ORP* BR6 ....253 E4
Cockspur Ct *STJS* SW1Y 20 D1
Cockspur St *STJS* * SW1Y 20 D1
Cocksure La *SCUP* DA14 ....197 E6
Code St *WCHPL* E1 ....9 J7
Codling Cl *WAP* * E1W 150 A3
Codrington Hl *FSTH* SE23 ....191 G3
Codrington Ms *NTGHL* W11 ....124 C5
Codrington Wy *KTN/HRWW/W* HA3 ...61 H6
Cody Rd *CAN/RD* E16 ....131 H3
Coe Av *SNWD* SE25 ....229 G3
Cofers Cir *WBLY* HA9 ....82 D1
Coffey St *DEPT* SE8 ....171 E1

Cogan Av *WALTH* E17 ....70 C4
Coin St *STHWK* SE1 ....22 A1
Coity Rd *KTTN* NW5 ....106 C4
Cokers La *DUL* SE21 ....188 C3
Coke St *WCHPL* E1 ....17 J4
Colbeck Ms *SKENS* SW7 ....145 F4
Colbeck Rd *HRW* HA1 ....79 C4
Colberg Pl *STNW/STAM* * N16 .....68 F4
Colborne Wy *WPK* KT4 ....242 A1
Colburn Av *PIN* HA5 ....58 C2
Colburn Wy *SUT* SM1 ....243 H1
Colby Rd *NRWD* SE19 ....209 E1
Colchester Dr *PIN* HA5 ....78 B2
Colchester Rd *EDGW* HA8 ....62 C3
  WALTH E17 ....91 E3
Colchester St *WCHPL* * E1 ....16 D5
Coldbath Sq *CLKNW* * EC1R 6 A5
Coldbath St *LEW* SE13 ....171 F2
Cold Blow Crs *BXLY* DA5 ....197 H5
Coldblow La *NWCR* SE14 ....170 B1
Coldershaw Rd *HNWL* W7 ....140 C2
Coldfall Av *MUSWH* N10 ....66 B5
Coldharbour *POP/IOD* E14 ....151 G1
Coldharbour Crest
  ELTH/MOT * SE9 ....175 A1
Coldharbour La *BRXN/ST* SW9 ...168 A5
  BUSH WD23 ....43 F1
Coldharbour Pl *CMBW* SE5 ....168 C3
Coldharbour Rd *CROY/NA* CR0 ...246 A3
Coldharbour Wy *CROY/NA* CR0 ...246 A3
Coldstream Gdns
  WAND/EARL SW18 ....184 D1
Colebeck Ms *IS* N1 ....108 B4
Colebert Av *WCHPL* E1 ....130 A3
Colebrooke Av *WEA* W13 ....120 D5
Colebrooke Dr *WAN* E11 ....92 D4
Colebrooke Pl *IS* N1 ....108 B6
Colebrooke Rw *IS* N1 ....6 C2
Colebrook Ri *HAYES* BR2 ....212 A5
Colebrook Rd
  STRHM/NOR SW16 ....207 G4
Colebrook Wy
  FBAR/BDGN N11 ....66 D1
Coleby Pth *CMBW* * SE5 ....168 D1
Cole Cl *THMD* SE28 ....155 H1
Coledale Dr *STAN* * HA7 ....61 G4
Coleford Rd *WAND/EARL* SW18 ..146 C6
Colegrave Rd *SRTFD* E15 ....88 B6
Colegrove Rd *PECK* SE15 ....32 D6
Coleherne Ms *WBPTN* SW10 ......145 F5
Coleherne Rd *WBPTN* SW10 ......145 F5
Colehill Gdns *FUL/PGN* SW6 ......164 C2
Colehill La *FUL/PGN* SW6 ....164 C2
Coleman Cl *SNWD* SE25 ....209 C5
Coleman Fids *IS* N1 ....108 C6
Coleman Rd *BELV* DA17 ....157 E3
  CMBW SE5 ....169 E1
Colemans Heath
  ELTH/MOT SE9 ....194 A5
Coleman St *LOTH* EC2R 15 C3
Colenso Rd *CLPT* E5 ....110 A2
  GNTH/NBYPK IG2 ....95 E5
Cole Park Gdns *TWK* TW1 ....180 C1
Cole Park Rd *TWK* TW1 ....180 C2
Colepits Wood Rd
  ELTH/MOT SE9 ....174 D6
Coleraine Rd *BKHTH/KID* SE3 ....152 B6
  CEND/HSY/T N8 ....66 A6
Coleridge Av *MNPK* E12 ....113 G4
  SUT SM1 ....244 A2
Coleridge Gdns
  KIL/WHAMP NW6 ....105 G5
Coleridge Rd *CEND/HSY/T* N8 .....230 A4
  CROY/NA CR0 ....230 A4
  FSBYPK N4 ....88 A6
  NFNCH/WDSP N12 ....47 G1
  WALTH E17 ....90 C1
Coleridge Sq *WEA* * W13 ....120 C5
Coleridge Wy *GLDGN* NW11 ....85 E1
Coleridge Wy *ORP* BR6 ....235 G3
Cole Rd *TWK* TW1 ....180 C1
Colesburg Rd *BECK* BR3 ....210 D6
Coles Crs *RYLN/HDSTN* HA2 ....59 A4
Coles Gn *BUSH* WD23 ....43 G5
Coles Green Rd *CRICK* NW2 ....83 G5
Coleshill Rd *TEDD* TW11 ....200 A2
Colestown St *BTSEA* SW11 ....166 A3
Cole St *STHWK* SE1 ....23 F4
Colet Cl *PLMGR* N13 ....69 H2
Colet Gdns *WKENS* W14 ....144 B5
Colette Ct *SYD* * SE26 ....191 F6
Coife & Hatcliffe Glebe
  LEW * SE13 ....171 H6
Coife Rd *FSTH* SE23 ....190 C3
Colina Ms *SEVS/STOTM* N15 ....88 B1
Colina Rd *CEND/HSY/T* N8 ....87 E3
Colin Cl *CDALE/KGS* NW9 ....63 C1
  CROY/NA CR0 ....248 D1
  WWKM BR4 ....248 D1
Colin Crs *CDALE/KGS* NW9 ....83 F2
Colindale Av *CDALE/KGS* NW9 .....62 D6
Colindeep Gdns *HDN* NW4 ....83 G2
Colindeep La *CDALE/KGS* NW9 ....83 F1
Colin Dr *CDALE/KGS* NW9 ....83 G2
Colinette Rd *PUT/ROE* SW15 .....164 A5
Colin Park Rd *CDALE/KGS* NW9 ...63 E6
Colin Rd *WLSDN* NW10 ....105 G4
Colinton Rd *BCTR* RM8 ....95 H6
Coliston Rd *WAND/EARL* SW18 ...185 J2
Collamore Av
  WAND/EARL SW18 ....186 A3
Collapit Cl *RYLN/HDSTN* HA2 ....79 F3
Collard Pl *CAMTN* NW1 ....106 C5
College Ap *GNWCH* SE10 ....151 G6
College Ct *KTN/HRWW/W* HA3 ......60 C1
  UED N18 ....179 H3
  WHTN TW2 ....179 H3
College Cl *EA* * W5 ....121 H5
College Crs *KIL/WHAMP* NW6 .....105 G4
College Cross *IS* N1 ....109 A5
College Dr *THDIT* KT7 ....220 A4
College East *WCHPL* * E1 ....16 D2
College Gdns *CHING* E4 ....37 H2
  ENC/FH EN2 ....23 F2
  NWMAL KT3 ....223 F2
  REDBR IG4 ....71 H3
  TOOT SW17 ....186 A4
  UED N18 ....69 F1

College Gn NRWD SE19 ....209 E3
College Gv CAMTN NW1 ....107 F6
College Hl CANST * EC4R 15 F5
College Hill Rd
   KTN/HRWW/W HA3 ....60 A3
College Ms IS N1 ....108 A5
   WEST SW1P 21 E5
College Pde KIL/WHAMP * NW6 ..104 C6
College Park Cl LEW SE13 ....171 H5
College Pl CAMTN NW1 ....107 E6
   WALTH E17 ....32 A1
   WBPTN * SW10 ....165 G1
College Rd BMLY BR1 ....212 C4
   CROY/NA CR0 ....228 D6
   DUL SE21 ....189 E2
   ENC/FH EN2 ....38 D3
   HRW HA1 ....60 A3
   ISLW TW7 ....160 B2
   KTN/HRWW/W HA3 ....60 A4
   LEY E10 ....91 G2
   NRWD SE19 ....209 F1
   TOTM N17 ....69 F2
   WBLY HA9 ....81 F5
   WCHMN N21 ....52 A4
   WEA W13 ....120 D5
   WIM/MER SW19 ....205 H2
   WLSDN NW10 ....124 A1
College St CANST * EC4R 15 F5
College Ter FNCH N3 ....64 D4
College Vw ELTH/MOT SE9 ....193 F3
College Yd KIL/WHAMP * NW6 ....104 C6
   KTTN * NW5 ....106 D5
Collent St HOM E9 ....110 A4
Colless Rd SEVS/STOTM N15 ....89 F2
Collett Rd BERM/RHTH SE16 ....25 F6
Collier Cl EHAM E6 ....154 B6
   HOR/WEW KT19 ....240 A4
Collier Dr EDGW HA8 ....62 A5
Collier Row La CRW RM5 ....77 F4
Collier Row Rd CRW RM5 ....77 E4
   ROMW/RC RM7 ....76 D4
Collier St IS N1 ....5 G2
Colliers Water La THHTH CR7 ....228 A2
Colliers Wd HAYES BR2 ....251 F5
Collindale Av BFN/LL DA15 ....155 G3
   CDALE/KGS NW9 ....63 E6
   ERITH DA8 ....157 F6
Collingbourne Rd SHB W12 ....143 H1
Collingham Gdns ECT SW5 ....145 E4
Collingham Pl ECT SW5 ....145 E4
Collingham Rd ECT SW5 ....145 F4
Collings Cl WDGN N22 ....67 H2
Collington St GNWCH * SE10 ......115 H5
Collingtree Rd SYD SE26 ....190 H4
Collingwood Av BRYLDS KT5 ......222 C5
   MUSWH N10 ....66 C6
Collingwood Cl HSLWW TW4 ......179 E2
Collingwood Cl PCE/AN SE20 .....209 H4
Collingwood Est WCHPL E1 ....9 H3
Collingwood St MTCM CR4 ....206 A5
   SEVS/STOTM N15 ....89 E1
   SUT SM1 ....243 E2
Collingwood St WCHPL E1 ....9 H5
Collins Av STAN HA7 ....61 G5
Collins Dr RSLP HA4 ....78 A6
Collins Rd St STHWK SE1 ....23 E4
Collinson Wk STHWK SE1 ....23 E4
Collins Rd HBRY N5 ....108 C2
Collins St BKHTH/KID SE3 ....172 A3
Collinwood Av PEND EN3 ....40 A4
Collinwood Gdns
   GNTH/NBYPK IG2 ....93 H2
Coll's Rd PECK SE15 ....170 A2
Collyer Av CROY/NA CR0 ....245 G2
Collyer Pl PECK SE15 ....169 G2
Collyer Rd CROY/NA CR0 ....245 G2
Colman Pde EN * EN1 ....39 E4
Colman Rd CAN/RD E16 ....133 E4
Colmar Cl WCHPL E1 ....130 E3
Colmer Pl KTN/HRWW/W HA3 ....34 B5
Colmer Rd STRHM/NOR SW16 ....207 H5
Colmore Ms PECK SE15 ....169 H2
Colmore Rd PEND EN3 ....40 A5
Colnbrook St STHWK SE1 ....22 C6
Colne Ct HOR/WEW KT19 ....240 C2
Colne Rd CLPT E5 ....110 B2
   WCHMH N21 ....52 D2
   WHTN TW2 ....180 A3
Colne St PLSTW E13 ....132 C2
Colney Hatch La
   FBAR/BDGN N11 ....48 B2
Cologne Rd BTSEA SW11 ....165 H3
Colombo Rd IL IG1 ....94 C5
Colombo St STHWK SE1 ....22 C2
Colonels Wk ENC/FH EN2 ....38 B3
Colonial Av WHTN TW2 ....179 G1
Colonial Dr CHSWK W4 ....142 C4
Colonnade BMSBY WC1N 5 E6
The Colonnade DEPT * SE8 ....150 D4
Colosseum Ter CAMTN NW1 ....3 H5
Colson Rd CROY/NA CR0 ....228 D6
Colson Wy STRHM/NOR SW16 ...187 E6
Colsterworth Rd
   SEVS/STOTM N15 ....89 F1
Colston Av CAR SM5 ....244 A2
Colston Rd FSTGT E7 ....113 F4
   MORT/ESHN SW14 ....162 C5
Colthurst Crs FSBYPK N4 ....85 B6
Coltness Crs ABYW SE2 ....155 H5
Colton Gdns TOTM N17 ....68 C6
Colton Rd HRW HA1 ....60 A2
Columbas Dr HAMP * NW3 ....85 H5
Columbia Av EDGW HA8 ....62 B4
   WPK KT4 ....225 F4
Columbia Rd BETH E2 ....8 C3
   PLSTW * E13 ....132 B3
Columbia Whf PEND * EN3 ....40 C6
Columbine Av EHAM E6 ....133 G4
   SAND/SEL CR2 ....246 B5
Columbine Wy LEW * SE13 ....171 G3
Colvestone Crs HACK E8 ....109 F3
Colview Ct ELTH/MOT SE9 ....193 F4
Colville Est IS N1 ....7 H1
Colville Gdns NTGHL W11 ....124 D5
Colville Houses NTGHL * W11 .....124 D5
Colville Ms NTGHL W11 ....124 D5
Colville Pl FITZ W1T 12 B2
Colville Rd ACT W3 ....142 B3
   ED N9 ....53 H5
   NTGHL W11 ....124 D5

WALTH E17 ....70 C5
WAN E11 ....111 G1
Colville Sq NTGHL * W11 ....124 D5
Colville Square Ms
   NTGHL * W11 ....124 D5
Colville Ter NTGHL W11 ....124 D5
Colvin Cl SYD SE26 ....210 A1
Colvin Gdns BARK/HLT IG6 ....74 C3
   CHING E4 ....55 G5
   SWFD E18 ....92 D1
Colvin Rd EHAM E6 ....113 G5
   THHTH CR7 ....188 A2
Colwall Gdns WFD IG8 ....72 C1
Colwell Rd EDUL SE22 ....169 F6
Colwick Cl HGT N6 ....87 F4
Colwith Rd HMSMTH W6 ....144 A6
Colwood Gdns
   WIM/MER SW19 ....205 H3
Colworth Gv WALW SE17 ....31 F2
Colworth Rd CROY/NA CR0 ....229 G5
   WAN E11 ....92 A3
Colwyn Av GFD/PVL UB6 ....120 B1
Colwyn Cl STRHM/NOR SW16 .....207 E1
Colwyn Crs HSLW TW3 ....135 G2
Colwyn Gn CDALE/KGS * NW9 ....83 E3
Colwyn Rd CRICK NW2 ....103 H1
Colyer Cl ELTH/MOT SE9 ....194 B4
Colyers Cl ERITH DA8 ....177 H2
Colyers La ERITH DA8 ....177 G2
Colyton Cl ALP/SUD HA0 ....101 E4
   WELL DA16 ....176 B2
Colyton Rd EDUL SE22 ....169 H6
Colyton Wy UED N18 ....69 C1
Combe Av BKHTH/KID SE3 ....172 B1
Combedale Rd GNWCH SE10 ....152 C5
Comber Cl CRICK NW2 ....103 C1
Comber Gv CMBW SE5 ....168 C5
Combermere Rd BRXN/ST SW9 ...167 H4
   MRDN SM4 ....225 F3
Comberton Rd CLPT E5 ....89 H6
Combeside WOOL/PLUM SE18 ....175 H1
Combes Rd DAGW RM9 ....116 D5
Combwell Crs ABYW SE2 ....155 C5
Comely Bank Rd WALTH E17 ....91 G2
Comeragh Ms WKENS * W14 ....144 C5
Comeragh Rd WKENS W14 ....144 C5
Comerford Rd BROCKY SE4 ....170 C5
Comet Cl MNPK E12 ....113 F2
Comet Pl DEPT SE8 ....171 E1
Comet St DEPT SE8 ....171 E1
Commerce Rd BTFD TW8 ....141 E6
   WDGN N22 ....67 H4
Commerce Wy CROY/NA CR0 ......245 H1
Commercial Rd UED N18 ....69 E1
   WCHPL E1 ....16 D3
Commercial St WCHPL E1 ....8 D6
Commercial Wy WLSDN NW10 ....122 B1
Commerell Pl GNWCH SE10 ....152 B5
Commerell St GNWCH SE10 ....152 A5
Commodore Pde
   STRHM/NOR * SW16 ....207 H3
Commodore St WCHPL E1 ....130 B4
Commondale PUT/ROE SW15 ......164 A3
Common La ESH/CLAY KT10 ....220 A5
Common Rd BARN SW13 ....163 C4
   ESH/CLAY KT10 ....238 C4
   STAN HA7 ....43 H5
Commonside HAYES BR2 ....233 F6
Commonside East MTCM CR4 .....206 C6
   MTCM CR4 ....227 E1
The Common EA W5 ....141 G1
Common Side EPSOM KT18 ....240 B6
   WIDGN N22 ....138 B4
   STAN HA7 ....44 B4
Commonwealth Av SHB W12 ....123 H6
Commonwealth Rd TOTM N17 ....69 C3
Commonwealth Wy ABYW SE2 ....155 H5
Community Rd GFD/PVL UB6 ....99 C6
   SRTFD E15 ....111 H3
Como Rd FSTH SE23 ....190 C4
Como St ROMW/RC RM7 ....75 H2
Compass Hl RCHPK/HAM TW10 ...181 F1
Compayne Gdns
   KIL/WHAMP NW6 ....105 F5
Compton Av EHAM E6 ....133 F1
   HGT N6 ....65 H6
   IS N1 ....108 B4
Compton Cl CAMTN NW1 ....3 H4
   CRICK NW2 ....104 B1
   EDGW HA8 ....62 B4
   WEA W13 ....120 C5
Compton Crs CHSGTN KT9 ....239 G4
   CHSWK W4 ....142 C6
   NTHLT UB5 ....96 A4
   TOTM N17 ....68 C2
Compton Pas FSBYE EC1V 6 D5
Compton Pl OXHEY WD19 ....42 C6
   STPAN WC1H 5 E5
Compton Ri PIN HA5 ....78 C2
Compton Rd CROY/NA CR0 ....229 H5
   IS N1 ....108 B4
   NWMAL SM4 ....52 B3
   WIM/MER SW19 ....177 E6
   WLSDN NW10 ....124 B2
Compton St FSBYE EC1V 6 D5
Compton Ter IS N1 ....108 B4
Comreddy Cl ENC/FH EN2 ....38 B2
Comus Pl WALW SE17 ....32 A2
Comyn Rd BTSEA SW11 ....166 A5
Comyns Cl CAN/RD E16 ....133 A4
Comyns Rd DAGW RM9 ....117 C5
The Comyns BUSH WD23 ....43 C3
Conant Ms WCHPL E1 ....17 E5
Concanon Rd
   BRXS/STRHM * SW2 ....167 H5
Concert Hall Ap STHWK SE1 ....21 H2
Concord Cl NTHLT UB5 ....118 B2
Concorde Cl HSLW TW3 ....159 F3
Concorde Dr EHAM E6 ....133 H4
Concord Rd ACT W3 ....99 F4
   PEND EN3 ....40 A6
Condell Rd VX/NE SW8 ....141 C6
Conder St POP/IOD E14 ....130 C5
Condover Crs
   WOOL/PLUM SE18 ....174 D1
Condray Pl BTSEA SW11 ....144 D6
Conduit Av GNWCH * SE10 ....151 C6
Conduit Ct COVGDN * WC2E 13 C5
Conduit La SAND/SEL CR2 ....247 G5
   UED N18 ....70 A1

Conduit Ms BAY/PAD W2 ....125 H5
Conduit Pl BAY/PAD W2 ....125 H5
Conduit Rd WOOL/PLUM SE18 ....154 B5
Conduit St CONDST W1S 14 A5
Conduit Wy WLSDN NW10 ....102 C5
Conewood St HBRY N5 ....108 B1
Coney Acre DUL SE21 ....188 C3
Coney Burrows CHING E4 ....56 A4
Coney Hall Pde WWKM * BR4 ......250 A1
Coney Hill Rd WWKM BR4 ....232 A6
Coney Wy VX/NE SW8 ....29 C6
Conference Cl CHING E4 ....55 C4
Conference Rd ABYW SE2 ....156 A4
Congleton Gv
   WOOL/PLUM SE18 ....154 C5
Congo Rd WOOL/PLUM SE18 ......154 B5
Congress Rd ABYW SE2 ....156 A3
Congreve Rd ELTH/MOT SE9 ....173 H4
Congreve St WALW SE17 ....32 A2
Conical Cnr ENC/FH EN2 ....38 C5
Conifer Av CRW RM5 ....77 F1
Conifer Cl ORP BR6 ....252 D2
Conifer Gdns EN EN1 ....52 D1
   STRHM/NOR SW16 ....187 H5
   SUT SM1 ....225 F6
Conifers Cl TEDD TW11 ....200 D3
Conifer Wy ALP/SUD HA0 ....101 E1
   SWLY BR8 ....217 G4
Coniger Rd FUL/PCN SW6 ....165 E3
Coningham Ms SHB W12 ....143 G1
Coningham Rd SHB W12 ....143 H3
Coningsby Cottages EA W5 ....141 F2
Coningsby Gdns CHING E4 ....54 A5
Coningsby Rd EA W5 ....141 F2
   FSBYPK N4 ....88 B4
   SAND/SEL CR2 ....246 C6
Conington Rd LEW SE13 ....171 F3
Conisbee Ct STHGT/OAK N14 ....38 D6
Conisborough Crs CAT SE6 ....191 G5
Coniscliffe Cl CHST BR7 ....214 A4
Coniscliffe Rd PLMGR N13 ....52 C5
Coniston Av BARK IG11 ....115 G5
   GFD/PVL UB6 ....120 D2
   WELL DA16 ....175 E4
Coniston Cl BARN SW13 ....146 C6
   BXLYHN DA7 ....177 G2
   MRDN SM4 ....224 B3
Coniston Ct CAB * SW8 ....82 A2
Coniston Wy HOLWY N7 ....107 G5
Coniston Gdns BELMT * SM2 ......243 H4
   CDALE/KGS NW9 ....82 D2
   ED N9 ....54 A3
   REDBR IG4 ....93 G1
   WBLY HA9 ....81 E5
Coniston Rd BMLY BR1 ....212 A2
   BXLYHN DA7 ....177 G2
   CROY/NA CR0 ....226 A6
   MUSWH N10 ....66 A5
   TOTM N17 ....50 C6
   WHTN TW2 ....179 F1
Coniston Wy CHSGTN KT9 ....239 C1
Conlan St NKENS W10 ....124 C3
Conley Rd WLSDN NW10 ....105 E4
Conley St GNWCH * SE10 ....152 A5
Connaught Av CHING E4 ....55 H2
   EBAR EN4 ....39 F4
   EN EN1 ....39 E3
   HSLWW TW4 ....158 C4
   MORT/ESHN SW14 ....162 C4
Connaught Br CAN/RD E16 ....153 F1
Connaught Cl BAY/PAD W2 ....10 A4
   EN EN1 ....30 E3
   LEY * E10 ....90 C6
   SUT SM1 ....225 H6
Connaught Dr GLDGN NW11 ....45 G4
Connaught Gdns MRDN SM4 ....225 C2
   MUSWH N10 ....86 D2
   PLMGR N13 ....52 C5
Connaught La IL IG1 ....94 D5
Connaught Ms FUL/PCN * SW6 ...164 C2
   HAMP * NW3 ....106 A3
   WOOL/PLUM SE18 ....154 A5
Connaught Pl BAY/PAD W2 ....10 A4
Connaught Rd BAR EN5 ....48 B1
   CAN/RD E16 ....133 F6
   CHING * E4 ....56 A2
   FSBYPK N4 ....88 A4
   HRW HA1 ....61 E1
   IL IG1 ....94 D6
   KTN/HRWW/W HA3 ....60 B4
   NWMAL KT3 ....223 E1
   RCHPK/HAM * TW10 ....161 H6
   SUT SM1 ....225 H6
   WALTH * E17 ....91 E2
   WAN E11 ....91 C6
   WEA W13 ....120 D6
   WLSDN NW10 ....123 E1
   WOOL/PLUM SE18 ....154 A5
Connaught Sq BAY/PAD W2 ....10 A4
Connaught St BAY/PAD W2 ....10 A4
Connaught Wy PLMGR N13 ....52 B6
Connell Crs EA W5 ....121 H5
Connemara Cl BORE * WD6 ....25 E2
Connington Crs CHING E4 ....55 H5
Connor Cl CHING E4 ....60 D1
Connor Cl WAN E11 ....91 E3
Connor Ct BARK/HLT IG6 ....74 C4
Connor Rd DAGW RM9 ....116 D2
Connor St HOM * E9 ....111 E6
Conolly Rd HNWL W7 ....140 A1
Conrad Dr WPK KT4 ....224 A5
Consfield Av NWMAL KT3 ....223 G1
Consort Cl FBAR/BDGN N11 ....66 B1
Consort Ms ISLW TW7 ....179 H1
Consort Rd PECK SE15 ....169 H3
Cons St STHWK * SE1 ....22 B5
Constable Av CAN/RD E16 ....153 C1
Constable Cl GLDGN NW11 ....65 F3
Constable Crs SEVS/STOTM N15 ...89 G2
Constable Gdns EDGW HA8 ....62 A4
   ISLW * TW7 ....159 H6
Constable Ms BCTR RM8 ....115 H5
Constable Wk DUL SE21 ....189 E5
Constance Crs HAYES BR2 ....232 B5
Constance Rd CROY/NA CR0 ....228 B4
   EN EN1 ....30 A5
   SUT SM1 ....243 G2
   WHTN TW2 ....179 F2
Constance St CAN/RD E16 ....153 G1
Constantine Rd HAMP NW3 ....105 F2
Constitution Hl WHALL SW1A 16 D3
Constitution Ri
   WOOL/PLUM SE18 ....174 A2

Content St WALW SE17 ....31 E1
Contessa Cl ORP BR6 ....253 E3
Convent Cl BECK BR3 ....211 G3
Convent Gdns EA W5 ....141 E4
   NTGHL W11 ....124 D5
Convent Hl NRWD SE19 ....208 C2
Convent Wy NWDGN UB2 ....138 A4
Conway Cl RAIN RM13 ....99 H6
   STAN HA7 ....43 G4
Conway Crs CHDH RM6 ....96 A4
   GFD/PVL UB6 ....120 A1
Conway Dr BELMT SM2 ....243 F4
Conway Gdns ENC/FH EN2 ....39 E1
   MTCM CR4 ....227 F1
   WBLY HA9 ....81 E4
Conway Gv ACT W3 ....122 D4
Conway Ms FITZ W1T 12 A1
Conway Rd CRICK NW2 ....84 A6
   FELT TW13 ....198 B1
   HSLWW TW4 ....178 D2
   RYNPK SW20 ....202 A1
   SEVS/STOTM N15 ....88 C2
   STHGT/OAK N14 ....51 G5
   WOOL/PLUM SE18 ....154 D4
Conway St FITZ W1T 11 H1
Conybeare HAMP * NW3 ....106 A5
Cooden Cl BMLY BR1 ....212 D3
Cookes Cl WAN E11 ....92 B6
Cookes La CHEAM SM3 ....242 C4
Cookham Cl NWDGN UB2 ....139 F3
Cookham Dene Cl CHST BR7 ....214 D4
Cookham Rd SWLY BR8 ....217 E4
Cookhill Rd ABYW SE2 ....155 H2
Cook's Cl CRW RM5 ....77 G4
Cook's Ferry Rbt UED N18 ....70 C1
Cook's Hole Rd ENC/FH EN2 ....38 B1
Cooks Md BUSH WD23 ....43 F1
Cookson Gv ERITH DA8 ....177 F1
Cook's Rd SRTFD E15 ....131 F1
   WALW SE17 ....67 G6
Coolfin Rd CAN/RD E16 ....132 C5
Coolgardie Av CHING E4 ....71 H1
Coolhurst Rd CEND/HSY/T N8 ....87 F3
Cool Oak Br CDALE/KGS NW9 ....83 F4
Cool Oak La CDALE/KGS NW9 ....83 F4
Coomassie Rd MV/WKIL W9 ....124 D3
Coombe Av CROY/NA CR0 ....247 E2
Coombe Bank NWMAL KT3 ....208 A4
Coombe Cl EDGW HA8 ....61 H5
Coombe Ct WBLY HA9 ....159 E5
Coombe Cnr WCHMH N21 ....52 B3
Coombe Dr KUTN/CMB KT2 ....202 D3
Coombefield Ct NWMAL KT3 ....223 E2
Coombe Gdns NWMAL KT3 ....223 F1
   RYNPK SW20 ....203 G5
Coombe Hill Gld
   KUTN/CMB KT2 ....203 E3
Coombe Hill Rd
   KUTN/CMB KT2 ....203 E3
Coombe House Cha
   NWMAL KT3 ....202 D4
Coombehurst Cl EBAR EN4 ....36 B3
Coombe La CROY/NA CR0 ....247 H5
   RYNPK SW20 ....203 G4
Coombe La West
   KUTN/CMB KT2 ....202 C4
Coombe Lea CHARL SE7 ....153 F6
Coombe Neville
   KUTN/CMB KT2 ....202 C5
Coombe Pk KUTN/CMB KT2 ....202 C1
Coombe Ridings
   KUTN/CMB KT2 ....202 C1
Coombe Ri KUTN/CMB KT2 ....202 C4
Coombe Rd BUSH WD23 ....43 G2
   CHSWK W4 ....143 E5
   CROY/NA CR0 ....246 C2
   HPTN TW12 ....198 D2
   KUTN/CMB KT2 ....203 E3
   NWMAL KT3 ....203 B6
   SAND/SEL CR2 ....247 E2
   SYD SE26 ....189 A6
   WDGN N22 ....49 H5
   WLSDN NW10 ....102 D1
Coomber Wy CROY/NA CR0 ....227 F4
Coombes Rd DAGW RM9 ....118 D6
Coombe Vis
   WAND/EARL * SW18 ....185 G2
Coombe-Wood Dr CHDH RM6 ....96 D3
Coombe Wood Rd
   KUTN/CMB KT2 ....202 C1
Coombs St IS N1 ....6 D3
Coomer Ms FUL/PCN * SW6 ....144 D6
Coomer Pl FUL/PCN SW6 ....144 D6
Cooperage Cl TOTM N17 ....50 C2
Cooper Av WALTH E17 ....70 B4
Cooper Cl STHWK SE1 ....18 A3
Cooper Crs CAR SM5 ....244 B1
Cooper Rd CRICK NW2 ....103 G3
   CROY/NA CR0 ....246 A3
   HDN NW4 ....64 B3
Coopersale Rd HOM E9 ....91 F1
Coopers Cl DAGE RM10 ....117 F4
   WCHPL E1 ....13 D4
   LEE/GVPK SE12 ....192 D4
   LEY * E10 ....91 F5
Coopers La CAMTN NW1 ....5 E2
Cooper's Rd STHWK SE1 ....19 F3
Cooper's Rw TWRH EC3N 16 H6
Cooper St CAN/RD E16 ....132 D5
Cooper's Yd NRWD SE19 ....209 E2
Coote Rd BCTR RM8 ....98 B1
   BXLYHN DA7 ....176 D2
Copeland Rd LEY E10 ....91 E2
   PECK SE15 ....169 H1
Copeman Cl SYD SE26 ....210 A1
Copenhagen Pl POP/IOD E14 ....130 D5
Copenhagen St IS N1 ....107 H6
Cope Pl KENS W8 ....145 E3
Copers Cope Rd BECK BR3 ....210 D3
Cope St BERM/RHTH SE16 ....150 B4
Copford Wk IS * N1 ....7 C6
Copgate Pth
   STRHM/NOR SW16 ....207 H2
Copland Av ALP/SUD HA0 ....101 F3
Copland Cl ALP/SUD HA0 ....80 C6
Copland Ms ALP/SUD HA0 ....101 C4

Copland Rd ALP/SUD HA0....101 G4
Copleston Rd PECK SE15 ...169 F4
Copley Cl CMBW SE5 ....31 E6
HNWL * W7 ....120 A3
Copley Dene BMLY BR1 ......213 H4
Copley Pk STRHM/NOR SW16 ...207 H2
Copley Rd STAN HA7 ....61 E1
Coppard Gdns CHSGTN KT9 ...239 E4
Coppelia Rd BKHTH/KID SE3 ...172 B5
Coppelia Rd BCTR RM8 ....96 D4
Copperas St DEPT SE8 ....151 F6
Copper Beech Cl CLAY IG5 ......74 A4
STMC/STPC BR5 ....236 A2
Copper Cl HNWD SE19 ....209 F3
Copperfield CHIG IG7 ....74 D2
Copperfield Dr
   SEVS/STOTM N15 ....89 F1
Copperfield Rd BOW E3 ....130 C3
   THMD SE28 ....136 A5
Copperfield St STHWK SE1 .....22 D3
Copperfield Wy CHST BR7 ......214 C2
   PIN HA5 ....78 D1
Coppergate Ter BMLY BR1 .....212 D4
Coppermead Cl CRICK NW2 ...104 A1
Copper Mill Dr ISLW TW7 ....160 B3
Copper Mill La TOOT SW17 .....185 G6
Coppermill La WALTH E17 ....66 A5
Copper Rw STHWK SE1 ....24 C2
Coppice Cl BECK BR3 ....251 F1
   KTN/HRWW/W HA3 ....60 B2
   RYNPK SW20 ....204 A6
Coppice Dr PUT/ROE SW15 ....183 G1
The Coppice BAR * EN5 ....49 F1
   BXLY DA5 ....197 H5
   ENC/FH EN2 ....29 H2
   OXHEY WD19 ....42 A1
Coppice Wk TRDG/WHET N20 ...49 E5
Coppice Wy SWFD E18 ....52 A5
Coppies Gv FBAR/BDGN N11 ....50 D6
Coppice Cl CROY/NA CRO 247 G2
The Coppins KTN/HRWW/W HA3 ...60 A2
Coppock Cl BTSEA SW11 ....166 A3
Coppsfield E/WMO/HCT KT8 ...199 E6
Copse Av WWKM BR4 ....249 F1
Copse Cl CHARL SE7 ....152 D6
Copse Gld SIDE KT6 ....221 F5
Copse Hl BELMT SM2 ....243 F5
   RYNPK SW20 ....203 G4
The Copse CHING E4 ....64 B1
   EFNCH * N2 ....66 B6
Copse Vw SAND/SEL CR2 ......248 C6
Copsewood Cl BFN/LL DA15 ...195 G1
Copsewood Rd BELV DA17 ....156 B3
Copthall Av LOTH EC2R 15 H3
Copthall Dr MLHL NW7 ....63 G3
Copthall Gdns MLHL NW7 ....63 G3
   TWK * TW1 ....180 C2
Copthorne Av BAL SW12 ....187 F2
   BARK/HLT IG6 ....74 B2
   HAYES BR2 ....233 H6
Coptic St NOXST/BSQ WC1A ...13 E2
Copton Cl BOW E3 ....131 E4
Copwood Cl NFNCH/WDSP N12 ...49 H4
Coral Cl CHDH RM6 ....76 A6
Coraline Cl STHL UB1 ....118 D2
Coral St STHWK SE1 ....22 B4
Coram St STPAN WC1H 5 E6
Coran Cl ED N9 ....54 B2
Corban Rd HSLW TW3 ....159 E4
Corbar Cl EBAR EN4 ....35 H1
Corbet Cl MTCM CR4 ....226 C5
Corbet Ct BANK EC3V * 16 D5
Corbett Gv FBAR/BDGN N11 ....67 G3
Corbett Rd WALTH E17 ....52 F1
   WAN E11 ....53 E5
Corbett's La BERM/RHTH SE16 ...150 A4
Corbicum WAN E11 ....52 A2
Corbin's La RYLN/HDSTN HA2 ...99 F1
Corbridge Crs BETH E2 ....9 C1
Corby Crs ENC/FH EN2 ....27 G5
Corbylands Rd BFN/LL DA15 ...195 E2
Corbycroft Rd FSBYPK N4 ....67 G5
Corby Rd WLSDN NW10 ....122 C1
Cordelia Cl HNHL SE24 ....168 B5
Cordelia Rd POP/IOD E14 ......131 F5
Cording St POP/IOD E14 ....131 F4
Cordova Rd BOW E3 ....130 C2
Cordwell Rd LEW SE13 ....171 H6
Corelli Rd BKHTH/KID SE3 .....173 G2
Corfe Av RYLN/HDSTN HA2 .....99 F2
Corfe Cl YEAD UB4 ....118 A5
Corfield Rd WCHMH N21 ....37 H6
Corfield St BETH E2 ....90 D2
Corfton Rd EA W5 ....121 G5
Coriander Av POP/IOD E14 .....131 H5
Cories Cl BCTR RM8 ....80 A6
Corinium Cl WBLY HA9 ....101 H2
Corinne Rd ARCH N19 ....107 E2
Corinthian Manorway
   ERITH DA8 ....157 H4
Corinthian Rd ERITH DA8 ....157 H4
Cork St Ms CONDST W1S 12 A6
Corkscrew HI WWKM BR4 ......251 G1
Cork Sq WAP E1W 25 G1
Cork St CONDST W1S 12 A6
Cork Tree Wy CHING E4 ....70 C1
Corlett St CAMTN NW1 ....10 A1
Cormont Rd CMBW SE5 ....168 B2
Cormorant Cl WALTH E17 ....70 A4
Cormorant Rd FSTGT E7 ....112 B3
Cornbury Rd EDGW HA8 ....61 F3
Cornelia St HOLWY N7 ....107 H4
Cornell Cl SCUP DA14 ....216 C2
Cornell Wy CRW RM5 ....77 F1
Corner Fielde
   BRXS/STRHM * SW2 ....187 H3
Corner Gn BKHTH/KID SE3 .....172 C3
Corner Md CDALE/KGS NW9 ....45 F3
The Corner EA * W5 ....141 G1
Corney Reach Wy CHSWK W4 ...146 A5
Corney Rd CHSWK W4 ....146 A5
Cornflower La CROY/NA CRO ...230 B5
Cornflower Ter EDUL SE22 .....169 H1
Comford Cl HAYES BR2 ....232 C1
Cornford Gv BAL SW12 ....186 D4
Cornhill BANK EC3V 15 H4
Cornish Gv PGE/AN SE20 ......209 H4
Corn Mill Dr ORP BR6 ....235 F4

Cornmill La LEW SE13 ....171 F4
Cornmow Dr WLSDN NW10 ...103 F3
Cornshaw Rd BCTR RM8 ....96 B5
Cornthwaite Rd CLPT E5 ....110 A1
Cornwall Av BETH E2 ....130 A2
   ESH/CLAY KT10 ....238 D5
   FNCH N3 ....65 E5
   STHL UB1 ....118 D4
   WDGN N22 ....67 G4
   WELL DA16 ....175 E4
Cornwall Cl BARK IG11 ....115 F4
Cornwall Crs NTGHL W11 ......124 C5
Cornwall Dr STMC/STPC BR5 ...216 A3
Cornwall Gdns SKENS SW7 ....145 G3
   SNWD * SE25 ....229 F1
   WLSDN NW10 ....103 H4
Cornwall Gardens Wk
   SKENS * SW7 ....145 F3
Cornwall Gv CHSWK W4 ....143 E5
Cornwallis Av BFN/LL DA15 ....194 D4
Cornwallis Gv ED N9 ....53 H4
Cornwallis Rd ARCH N19 ....87 C6
   DAGW RM9 ....116 C2
   ED N9 ....53 H4
   WALTH E17 ....90 B1
   WOOL/PLUM SE18 ....154 B5
Cornwallis Sq ARCH N19 ....87 G6
Cornwallis Wk ELTH/MOT SE9 ...173 H4
Cornwall Ms South SKENS SW7 ...145 G3
Cornwall Ms West
   SKENS * SW7 ....145 F3
Cornwall Rd BELMT SM2 ....242 D5
   CROY/NA CRO 228 B6
   FSBYPK N4 ....67 G6
   HRW HA1 ....79 C3
   PIN HA5 ....58 D3
   SEVS/STOTM N15 ....88 D2
   STHWK SE1 ....22 A2
   TWK TW1 ....180 C2
   UED N18 ....69 G1
Cornwall St WCHPL E1 ....17 H5
Cornwall Ter CAMTN NW1 ....2 D6
Cornwall Terrace Ms
   CAMTN NW1 ....2 D6
Corn Wy WAN E11 ....111 H1
Cornwood Cl EFNCH N2 ....85 H4
Cornwood Dr WCHPL E1 ....130 A5
Cornworthy Rd BCTR RM8 ....96 A3
Corona Rd LEE/GVPK SE12 ....192 C1
Coronation Cl BARK/HLT IG6 ...54 C1
   BXLY DA5 ....196 B1
Coronation Rd PLSTW E13 .....133 E2
   WLSDN NW10 ....121 H2
Coronation Vls
   WLSDN * NW10 ....122 B3
Coronet Pde ALP/SUD * HA0 ...101 G4
Coronet St IS N1 ....9 H4
Corporation Av HSLWW TW4 ...158 C5
Corporation Rw CLKNW EC1R ...6 B5
Corporation St HOLWY N7 .....107 G3
   SRTFD E15 ....132 A1
Corrance Rd
   BRXS/STRHM SW2 ....167 G5
Corri Av STHGT/OAK N14 ....51 F6
Corrib Dr SUT SM1 ....244 A3
Corrigan Cl HDN NW4 ....64 A6
Corringham Rd GLDGN NW11 ...85 E4
   WBLY HA9 ....82 B4
Corringway EA W5 ....121 H4
   GLDGN NW11 ....65 F4
Corris Gn CDALE/KGS * NW9 ...83 E3
Corscombe Ct KUTN/CMB KT2 ...202 C1
Corsehill St STRHM/NOR SW16 ...207 E2
Corsham St IS N1 ....6 D5
Corsica St HBRY N5 ....108 B4
Cortayne Rd FUL/PGN * SW6 ...166 C4
Cortina Dr DAGW RM9 ....137 G2
Cortis Rd PUT/ROE SW15 ......183 H1
Cortis Ter PUT/ROE SW15 .....183 H1
Corunna Rd VX/NE SW8 ....167 G2
Corunna Ter VX/NE SW8 ....167 G2
Coryton Pth MV/WKIL W9 ......124 D3
Cosbycote Av HNHL SE24 ....168 C6
Cosdach Av WLGTN SM6 ....245 E6
Cosedge Crs CROY/NA CRO ...246 A3
Cosgrove Cl WCHMH N21 ....52 C4
   YEAD UB4 ....118 B3
Cosmo Pl RSQ WC1B 13 F1
Cosmur Cl SHB W12 ....143 F3
Cossall Wk PECK SE15 ....169 H2
Cosser St STHWK SE1 ....22 B4
Costa St PECK SE15 ....169 G3
Costons Av GFD/PVL UB6 ......119 E2
Costons La GFD/PVL UB6 ......119 E2
Cosway St CAMTN NW1 ....10 B1
Cotall St POP/IOD E14 ....131 E5
Coteford St TOOT SW17 ....186 D1
Cotelands CROY/NA CRO 247 E1
Cotesbach Rd CLPT E5 ....110 A1
Cotesmore Gdns BCTR RM8 ...116 A2
Cotford Rd THHTH CR7 ....228 C1
Cotham St WALW SE17 ....31 F2
Cotherstone HOR/WEW KT19 ...242 D6
Cotherstone Rd
   BRXS/STRHM SW2 ....187 H3
Cotleigh Av BXLY DA5 ....196 B4
Cotleigh Rd KIL/WHAMP NW6 ...105 E5
   ROMW/RG RM7 ....75 E3
Cotman Cl EFNCH N2 ....85 G3
Cotmandene Crs
   STMC/STPC BR5 ....215 H5
Cotman Gdns EDGW HA8 ....62 A1
Cotman Rd WELL DA16 ....175 G4
Cotsford Av NWMAL KT3 ....221 C2
Cotswold Av BUSH WD23 ....43 G1
Cotswold Cl ESH/CLAY KT10 ...221 C6
   KUTN/CMB KT2 ....202 C2
Cotswold Gdns CRICK NW2 .....84 B6
   GNTH/NBYPK IG2 ....72 C3
Cotswold Ga CRICK NW2 ....84 B6
Cotswold Gn ENC/FH EN2 ....37 H5
Cotswold Rd HPTN TW12 ......199 E2
Cotswold St WNWD SE27 .....188 B6
Cotswold Wy ENC/FH EN2 ....27 H5
   WPK KT4 ....224 A6
Cottage Av HAYES BR2 ....233 G5
Cottage Field Cl SCUP DA14 ...196 A5
Cottage Gn CMBW SE5 ....168 D3
Cottage Gv BRXN/ST SW9 .....167 G4

SURB KT6 ....221 F3
Cottage Pl SKENS SW7 ....18 A5
Cottage Rd HOR/WEW KT19 ...240 D5
The Cottages EDGW * HA8 ....62 B3
Cottage St POP/IOD E14 ....131 F6
Cottenham Dr CDALE/KGS NW9 ...63 F6
   RYNPK SW20 ....203 H5
Cottenham Park Rd
   RYNPK SW20 ....203 G4
Cottenham Rd WALTH E17 ....90 D1
Cotterill Rd SURB KT6 ....221 H6
Cottesbrook St NWCR SE14 ...170 C1
Cottesloe Ms STHWK SE1 ....22 B5
Cottesmore Av CLAY IG5 ....73 H5
Cottesmore Gdns KENS W8 ....145 F3
Cottimore La WOT/HER * KT12 ...218 A5
Cottingham Rd PGE/AN SE20 ...210 B5
   VX/NE SW8 ....167 H1
Cottington Cl LBTH SE11 ....30 B6
Cottington St LBTH SE11 ....30 B5
Cotton Av ACT W3 ....122 D5
Cotton Cl DAGW RM9 ....116 A5
Cotton Gardens Est LBTH SE11 ...30 C2
Cottongrass Cl CROY/NA CRO ...230 B5
Cotton Hl BMLY BR1 ....191 H6
Cotton Rw BTSEA SW11 ....165 G4
Cottons Ap ROMW/RG RM7 .....97 H2
Cotton's Gdns BETH E2 ....8 B3
Cotton St POP/IOD E14 ....131 C6
Couchmore Av CLAY IG5 ....73 H5
   ESH/CLAY KT10 ....220 A6
Coulgate St BROCKY SE4 ....171 C2
Coulson Cl BCTR RM8 ....96 A5
Coulson St CHEL SW3 ....26 C3
Coulter Cl YEAD UB4 ....118 C3
Coulter Rd HMSMTH W6 ....143 H3
Councillor St CMBW SE5 ....18 A1
Countess Rd KTTN NW5 ....107 E3
Countisbury Av EN EN1 ....53 F2
Country Wy FELT TW13 ....196 A1
County Ga CHST BR7 ....214 C5
   TRDG/WHET N20 ....49 F1
County Gv CMBW SE5 ....168 C2
County Pde BTFD * TW8 ....161 F1
County Rd EHAM E6 ....134 B4
   THHTH CR7 ....208 B5
County St STHWK SE1 ....23 F6
Coupland Pl WOOL/PLUM SE18 ...154 A5
Courcy Rd CEND/HSY/T N8 ......48 A6
Courier Rd DAGW RM9 ....137 G3
Courland Gv VX/NE SW8 ....167 H4
Courland St VX/NE SW8 ....167 F2
The Courier EL
ELTH/MOT SE9 ....194 A5
Courtauld Rd ARCH N19 ....87 F5
Courtaulds Cl THMD SE28 ....155 C1
Court Av BELV DA17 ....156 D5
Court Cl KTN/HRWW/W HA3 ....44 C4
   HAMP * NW3 ....105 H5
   KTN/HRWW/W HA3 ....61 F6
   WLGTN SM6 ....262 D2
Court Close Av FELT TW13 .....179 F5
Court Crs CHSGTN KT9 ....239 F4
Court Downs Rd BECK BR3 .....211 F5
Court Dr CROY/NA CRO 245 H2
   STAN HA7 ....44 A1
   SUT SM1 ....244 A2
Courtenay Av BELMT SM2 ......243 E6
   HGT N6 ....85 H4
   KTN/HRWW/W HA3 ....59 F3
Courtenay Ms WALTH E17 ....90 C2
Courtenay Rd PGE/AN SE20 ...210 B3
   WALTH E17 ....90 B2
   WBLY * HA9 ....81 H1
   WPK KT4 ....242 A1
Courtenay Sq LBTH SE11 ....30 A4
Courtenay St LBTH SE11 ....29 H3
Courten Ms STAN HA7 ....61 E3
Court Farm Av
   HOR/WEW KT19 ....240 D3
Court Farm Rd ELTH/MOT SE9 ...193 F4
   NTHLT UB5 ....96 B6
Courtfield Av HRW * HA1 ....80 D2
Courtfield Crs HRW HA1 ....80 B2
Courtfield Gdns ECT SW5 ....145 F4
   WEA W13 ....120 C5
Courtfield Ms SKENS * SW7 ...145 F4
Courtfield Ri WWKM BR4 ....249 H1
Courtfield Rd SKENS SW7 ......145 C4
Court Gdns HOLWY N7 ....93 H5
Courthill Rd LEW SE13 ....171 G5
Courthope Rd GFD/PVL UB6 ...119 H1
   HAMP NW3 ....106 D2
   WIM/MER SW19 ....204 C1
Courthouse Vis WIM/MER SW19 ...204 C3
Court House Rd FNCH N3 ....65 E3
Courtland Av CHING E4 ....56 B4
   IL IG1 ....95 H6
   MLHL NW7 ....30 H6
   STRHM/NOR SW16 ....207 H3
Courtland Gv THMD SE28 ......138 B6
Courtland Rd EHAM E6 ....113 G6
Courtlands RCHPK/HAM TW10 ...162 H4
Courtlands Av HAYES BR2 .....232 A5
   HPTN TW12 ....198 D2
   LEE/GVPK SE12 ....174 D6
   RCH/KEW TW9 ....145 G3
   WIM/MER SW19 ....162 B5
Courtlands Dr HOR/WEW KT19 ...247 A4
Court Ld BRYLDS KT5 ....222 A4
Court Lane Gdns DUL SE21 ....189 F2
Courtleet Dr BXLYHN DA7 ......177 F2
Courtleigh Av EBAR EN4 ....35 H1
Courtleigh Gdns GLDGN NW11 ...84 C1
Courtman Rd TOTM N17 ....49 F3
Court Md NTHLT UB5 ....95 H2
Courtmead Cl HNHL SE24 .....188 C1
Courtnell St BAY/PAD W2 ......125 E5
Courtney Cl NRWD SE19 ....209 E6
Courtney Crs CAR SM5 ....248 B5
Courtney Rd CROY/NA CRO ...246 B1
   HOLWY N7 ....108 A3
   WIM/MER SW19 ....206 A3
Courtney Ter BRDCKY SE4 ......190 C1
Court Rd ELTH/MOT SE9 ....193 H5
   NWDGN UB2 ....138 D4
   SNWD SE25 ....209 F5
Court Rd (Orpington By-Pass)
   ORP BR6 ....253 H1

Courtside CEND/HSY/T N8 ....87 F3
   SYD * SE26 ....190 A5
The Courts STRHM/NOR SW16 ...207 G3
Court St BMLY BR1 ....212 C5
   WCHPL E1 ....92 D4
The Court MUSWH * N10 ....87 E1
   RSLP HA4 ....98 C2
Court Wy ACT * N6 ....122 C4
   BARK/HLT IG6 ....74 C6
   CDALE/KGS NW9 ....83 E1
   WHTN TW2 ....180 B2
The Courtway OXHEY WD19 ....42 C4
Court Yd ELTH/MOT SE9 ....193 C1
The Courtyard IS N1 ....107 H5
Cousin La CANST EC4R 16 C1
Couthurst Rd BKHTH/KID SE3 ...152 D6
Coutts Av CHSGTN KT9 ....239 G5
Coutts Crs KTTN * NW5 ....106 C1
Coval Gdns MORT/ESHN SW14 ...162 A3
Coval La MORT/ESHN SW14 ...162 B5
Coval Rd MORT/ESHN SW14 ...162 C5
Covelees Wall EHAM E6 ....134 A5
Covent Gdn COVGDN WC2E 13 F5
Covent Garden Plazza
   COVGDN WC2E 13 F5
Coventry Cl EHAM E6 ....133 H5
   KIL/WHAMP NW6 ....125 E1
Coventry Cross Est BOW E3 ...131 G3
Coventry Rd BETH E2 ....94 B5
   IL IG1 ....94 B5
   SNWD SE25 ....209 G3
   WCHPL E1 ....9 H6
Coventry St MYFR/PICC W1J ...12 C1
Coverack Cl CROY/NA CRO 230 C4
   STHGT/OAK N14 ....51 E1
Coverdale Gdns CROY/NA CRO ...247 F1
Coverdale Rd FBAR/BDGN N11 ...66 C2
   KIL/WHAMP NW6 ....104 C5
   SHB W12 ....143 H1
The Coverdales BARK IG11 ....134 D1
Coverley Cl WCHPL * E1 ....127 F1
Coverton Rd TOOT SW17 ....186 A6
Covert Rd BARK/HLT IG6 ....75 F2
Coverts Rd ESH/CLAY KT10 ...238 B5
The Covert NRWD * SE19 ......209 F3
   ORP BR6 ....235 E3
Covert Wy EBAR EN4 ....35 C5
Covet Wood Cl
   STMC/STPC BR5 ....235 F3
Covey Cl WIM/MER SW19 ......205 H5
Covington Gdns
   STRHM/NOR SW16 ....208 B3
Covington Wy
   STRHM/NOR SW16 ....208 A2
Cowbridge La BARK IG11 ......114 B5
Cowbridge Rd
   KTN/HRWW/W HA3 ....81 H1
Cowcross St FARR EC1M 14 C1
Cowdenbeath Pth IS N1 ....107 C6
Cowden Rd ORP BR6 ....235 F4
Cowden St CAT SE6 ....191 E6
Cowdrey Cl EN EN1 ....24 B4
Cowdrey Rd WIM/MER SW19 ...205 G1
Cowen Av RYLN/HDSTN HA2 ....79 H6
Cowgate Rd GFD/PVL UB6 ....119 H2
Cowings Md NTHLT UB5 ....98 C5
Cowland Av PEND EN3 ....40 A5
Cow La BUSH * WD23 ....43 E1
Cow Leaze EHAM E6 ....134 A5
Cowleaze Rd KUTN/CMB KT2 ...201 C4
Cowley Cl SAND/SEL CR2 ......248 A6
Cowley La WAN * E11 ....112 A1
Cowley Pl HDN NW4 ....64 A2
Cowley Rd ACT W3 ....143 F1
   BRXN/ST SW9 ....168 A2
   IL IG1 ....93 H4
   MORT/ESHN SW14 ....163 E4
   WAN E11 ....90 D2
Cowley St WEST SW1P 21 G5
Cowling Cl NTGHL W11 ....124 C6
Cowper Av EHAM E6 ....113 C5
   SUT SM1 ....245 H1
Cowper Cl HAYES BR2 ....233 F1
   WELL DA16 ....175 C6
Cowper Rd ACT W3 ....142 D1
   BELV DA17 ....157 H4
   HAYES BR2 ....233 F1
   HNWL W7 ....120 A6
   RCHPK/HAM TW10 ....201 H1
   STHGT/OAK N14 ....50 B1
   STNW/STAM N16 ....109 E2
   UED N18 ....50 D3
   WIM/MER SW19 ....205 G2
Cowper St FSBYE EC1V 6 D6
Cowper Ter NKENS * W10 ....124 B4
Cowslip Rd SWFD E18 ....73 E6
Cowthorpe Rd VX/NE SW8 .....167 F2
Coxe Pl KTN/HRWW/W HA3 .....80 C1
Cox La CHSGTN KT9 ....240 B3
   HOR/WEW KT19 ....240 B3
Coxmount Rd CHARL SE7 ......152 C5
Coxson Wy STHWK SE1 ....24 A4
Coxwell Rd NRWD SE19 ....209 E3
   WOOL/PLUM SE18 ....154 D5
Crabbs Croft Cl ORP * BR6 .....252 C3
Crabb Hl BECK BR3 ....211 H3
Crabtree Av ALP/SUD HA0 .....117 H1
   CHDH RM6 ....96 B1
Crabtree Cl BETH E2 ....8 B1
Crabtree La FUL/PGN SW6 .....164 B1
Crabtree Manorway North
   BELV DA17 ....157 G2
Crabtree Manorway South
   BELV DA17 ....157 G2
Craddock Rd EN EN1 ....24 C4
Craddock St CAMTN * NW1 ....106 C4
Cradley Rd ELTH/MOT SE9 .....194 D5
Cragie Lea MUSWH * N10 ....66 B6
Craigen Av CROY/NA CRO 229 H5
Craigerne Rd BKHTH/KID SE3 ...152 B6
Craig Gdns SWFD E18 ....72 B5
Craigholm WOOL/PLUM SE18 ...174 A3
Craigmuir Pk ALP/SUD HA0 ...118 A2
Craignair Rd BRXS/STRHM SW2 ...187 H2
Craignish Av
   STRHM/NOR SW16 ....207 H5
Craig Park Rd UED N18 ....53 H6

Craig Rd RCHPK/HAM TW10 .....181 E6
Craig's Ct WHALL SW1A 21 E1
Craigton Rd ELTH/MOT SE9 .....175 H5
Craigweil Cl STAN HA7 .....61 F1
Craigweil Dr STAN HA7 .....61 F1
Crail Rw WALW SE17 .....31 H2
Cramer St MHST W1U 11 F2
Crammond Cl HMSMTH W6 .....144 C6
Crampton Rd PGE/AN SE20 .....201 A2
Cranberry Cl WALW SE17 .....31 E5
Cranberry Cl HITHL UB5 .....118 D1
Cranberry La CAN/RD E16 .....132 A3
Cranborne Av NWDGN UB2 .....139 E4
   SURB KT6 .....240 A1
Cranborne Rd BARK IG11 .....114 D6
Cranbourne Waye YEAD UB4 .....148 C6
Cranbourne Av WAN E11 .....92 D1
Cranbourne Cl
   STRHM/NOR SW16 .....207 G6
Cranbourne Dr PIN HA5 .....78 B2
Cranbourne Gdns BARK/HLT IG6...74 C6
   GLDGN NW11 .....64 D2
Cranbourne Rd MNPK E12 .....115 C3
   MUSWH N10 .....60 B1
   SRTFD E15 .....111 G2
Cranbrook Cl SLGS/SEVD WC2H ...12 D5
Cranbrook Cl HAYES BR2 .....232 C5
Cranbrook Dr ESH/CLAY KT10 ...219 G5
   WHTN TW2 .....160 C6
Cranbrook La FBAR/BDGN N11 ...50 D6
Cranbrook Ms WALTH E17 .....90 D2
Cranbrook Pk WDGN N22 .....68 A4
Cranbrook Ri IL IG1 .....93 H3
Cranbrook Rd BARK/HLT IG6 .....96 D1
   BXLYHN DA7 .....170 D2
   CHSWK W4 .....145 E5
   DEPT SE8 .....171 E2
   EBAR EN4 .....49 H1
   HSLWW TW4 .....158 D5
   IL IG1 .....94 A4
   THHTH CR7 .....208 C3
   WIM/MER SW19 .....204 C3
Cranbrook St BETH E2 .....130 B1
Cranbury Rd FUL/PGN SW6 .....165 F3
Crane Av ACT W3 .....122 C6
   ISLW TW7 .....160 C6
Cranebank Ms TWK * TW1 .....160 C6
Cranebrook WHTN TW2 .....179 G4
Crane Cl DAGE RM10 .....117 E4
Crane Ct FLST/FETLN EC4A 14 B4
   MORT/ESHN * SW14.....162 D5
Crane Ct WHTN TW2 .....180 B2
Craneford Wy WHTN TW2 .....180 A2
Crane Gv HOLWY N7 .....108 A4
Crane Md BERM/RHTH SE16 .....150 B4
Crane Park Rd WHTN TW2 .....179 G3
Crane Rd WHTN TW2 .....180 A3
Cranesbill Cl CDALE/KGS NW9 ...62 E4
Cranes Dr BRYLDS KT5 .....221 G1
Cranes Pk BRYLDS KT5 .....221 G1
Cranes Park Av SURB KT6 .....221 F1
Cranes Park Crs BRYLDS KT5 ...221 H1
Crane St PECK SE15 .....149 F2
Craneswater Pk NWDGN UB2 ...138 D5
Crane Wy WHTN TW2 .....179 G2
Cranfield Dr CDALE/KGS NW9 ...63 E3
Cranfield Rd BROCKY SE4 .....170 D4
Cranfield Rd East CAR SM5 .....244 C6
Cranfield Rd West CAR * SM5 ...244 B6
Cranford Av PLMGR N13 .....67 G1
Cranford Cl RYNPK * SW20 .....203 H6
Cranford Cottages WAP * E1W ..130 B6
Cranford La HEST TW5 .....158 B1
Cranford St WAP E1W 130 B6
Cranford Wy CEND/HSY/T N8 .....87 H2
Cranhurst Rd CRICK NW2 .....104 A3
Cranleigh Cl BXLY * DA5 .....197 F1
   ORP BR6 .....253 C1
   PGE/AN SE20 .....209 H5
Cranleigh Gdns BARK IG11 .....114 D5
   KTN/HRWW/W HA3 .....61 H1
   KUTN/CMB KT2 .....201 H2
   LOU IG10 .....57 H1
   SNWD SE25 .....209 E6
   STHL UB1 .....118 D5
   SUT SM1 .....225 F6
   WCHMH N21 .....38 A6
Cranleigh Ms BTSEA SW11 .....166 A3
Cranleigh Rd ESH/CLAY KT10 ...219 G5
   SEVS/STOTM N15 .....88 B2
   WIM/MER SW19 .....205 E6
Cranleigh St CAMTN NW1 .....4 B2
Cranley Dr GNTH/NBYPK IG2 .....94 H6
Cranley Gdns MUSWH N10 .....86 D1
   PLMGR N13 .....51 H5
   SKENS SW7 .....145 G5
   WLGTN SM6 .....245 E5
Cranley Ms BTSEA SW11 .....145 G5
Cranley Pl SKENS SW7 .....145 H4
Cranley Rd GNTH/NBYPK IG2 ...94 C3
   PLSTW E13 .....132 D4
Cranley Ter HDN * NW4 .....46 B5
Cranmer Av WEA W13 .....140 D3
Cranmer Cl MRDN SM4 .....224 B5
   RSLP HA4 .....78 B5
   STAN HA7 .....61 G1
Cranmer Ct HPTN TW12 .....199 F1
Cranmer Farm Cl MTCM CR4 ....226 E1
Cranmer Gdns DAGE RM10 .....117 G2
Cranmer Rd BRXN/ST SW9 .....168 A1
   CROY/NA CRO 246 B1
   EDGW HA8 .....46 B5
   FSTGT E7 .....112 D2
   HPTN TW12 .....199 F1
   KUTN/CMB KT2 .....201 C1
   MTCM CR4 .....226 B1
Cranmer Ter TOOT SW17 .....205 H1
The Crescent ACT W3 .....125 E5
Cranmore Av ISLW TW7 .....159 F4
Cranmore Rd BMLY BR1 .....192 A5
   CHST BR7 .....191 G5
Cranmore Wy MUSWH N10 .....87 E1
Cranston Cl HSLW TW3 .....158 C3
Cranston Est IS N1 .....7 E3
Cranston Gdns CHING E4 .....71 F2
Cranston Rd FSTH SE23 .....190 C3
Cranswick Rd BERM/RHTH SE16...150 A5
Crantock Rd CAT SE6 .....191 G4
Cranwell Cl BOW E3 .....131 F3
Cranwich Av WCHMH N21 .....36 H3
Cranwich Rd STNW/STAM N16 ...89 E4
Cranwood St FSBYE EC1V 7 E5
Cranworth Crs CHING E4 .....55 H3

Cranworth Gdns BRXN/ST SW9...168 A2
Craster Rd BRXS/STRHM SW2 ..187 H2
Crathie Rd LEE/GVPK SE12 .....192 D1
Craven Av WEA W13 .....121 E6
Craven Cl CLPT * E5 .....89 A6
Craven Gdns BARK IG11 .....135 E1
   BARK/HLT IG6 .....74 D5
   CRW RM5 .....77 E1
   WIM/MER SW19 .....185 G5
Craven Hill Gdns BAY/PAD W2 ...125 G6
Craven Ms BTSEA * SW11 .....166 C4
Craven Pk WLSDN NW10 .....102 D5
Craven Park Ms WLSDN NW10...103 E5
Craven Park Rd
   STNW/STAM N16 .....89 F3
   WLSDN NW10 .....103 E6
Craven Pas CHCR * WC2N 21 J1
   CROY/NA CRO 229 H5
   KUTN/CMB KT2 .....201 H4
   WEA W13 .....121 E6
   WLSDN NW10 .....102 D6
Craven St CHCR * WC2N 21 J1
Craven Ter BAY/PAD W2 .....125 G6
Crawford Av ALP/SUD HA0 .....101 F3
Crawford Cl ISLW TW7 .....144 A2
Crawford Gdns GFD/PVL UB6 ...118 D2
   PLMGR N13 .....52 B5
Crawford Pas CLKNW EC1R 6 A6
Crawford Pl BAY/PAD W2 .....10 B3
Crawford Rd CMBW SE5 .....168 C3
Crawford St MBLAR W1H 10 C2
Crawley Rd EN EN1 .....53 E2
   LEY E10 .....91 F5
   WDGN N22 .....68 D1
Crawthew Gv EDUL SE22 .....169 F5
Cray Av STMC/STPC BR5 .....235 H2
Craybrooke Rd SCUP DA14 .....195 H6
Craybury End ELTH/MOT SE9 ....194 C2
Crayford Rd HOLWY N7 .....107 G2
Crayke Hi CHSGTN KT9 .....239 C5
Craylands STMC/STPC BR5 .....216 A6
Crayleigh Ter SCUP * DA14 .....216 A2
Cray Rd BELV DA17 .....157 E6
   SCUP DA14 .....216 A2
   SWLY BR8 .....237 G3
Crays Pde STMC/STPC * BR5 ....216 A5
Cray Valley Rd STMC/STPC BR5...235 G2
Crealock Gv WFD IG8 .....72 B1
Crealock St WAND/EARL SW18...185 F1
Crebor St EDUL SE22 .....189 C1
Credenhall Dr HAYES BR2 .....233 H5
Credenhill St
   STRHM/NOR SW16 .....207 E2
Crediton Hi KIL/WHAMP NW6 ...106 A4
Crediton Rd WLSDN NW10 .....104 B6
Crediton Wy ESH/CLAY KT10 ...238 C3
Credon Rd BERM/RHTH SE16.....33 H5
   PLSTW E13 .....133 C1
Creechurch La HDTCH EC3A 16 H4
Creechurch Pl HDTCH * EC3A.....16 B4
Creed La BLKFR EC4V 14 D4
Creek Cottages
   E/WMO/HCT * KT8 .....220 A1
Creek Rd BARK IG11 .....135 F2
   DEPT SE8 .....151 E6
   E/WMO/HCT KT8 .....220 A1
Creekside DEPT SE8 .....151 F5
Creeland Gv CAT SE6 .....190 D5
Creffield Rd ACT W3 .....122 A6
Creighton Av EFNCH N2 .....66 B5
   EHAM E6 .....115 J1
Creighton Cl SHB W12 .....125 H6
Creighton Rd EA W5 .....143 H1
   KIL/WHAMP NW6 .....124 B1
   TOTM N17 .....50 A5
Creighton Av EFNCH N2 .....66 A6
Cremer St BETH E2 .....8 C2
Cremorne Est WBPTN * SW10 ..145 H6
Cremorne Gdns
   HOR/WEW KT19 .....240 D6
Cremorne Rd WBPTN SW10 .....165 G1
Crescent TWRH EC3N 16 C5
Crescent Dr STMC/STPC BR5 ...234 C3
Crescent East EBAR EN4 .....35 C1
Crescent Gdns SWLY BR8 .....217 C5
   WIM/MER SW19 .....185 E5
Crescent Gv CLAP SW4 .....167 G3
   MTCM CR4 .....226 D3
Crescent La CLAP SW4 .....167 F4
Crescent Pl CHEL SW3 .....26 A1
Crescent Ri EBAR EN4 .....36 A6
   FNCH * N3 .....46 D4
   WDGN N22 .....67 C1
Crescent Rd BECK BR3 .....211 F5
   BFN/LL DA15 .....195 F5
   BMLY BR1 .....210 D2
   CEND/HSY/T N8 .....87 F3
   CHING E4 .....56 A2
   DAGE RM10 .....117 F2
   EBAR EN4 .....36 A6
   ED N9 .....53 C3
   ENC/FH EN2 .....38 B5
   FBAR/BDGN N11 .....50 B6
   FNCH N3 .....46 D4
   KUTN/CMB KT2 .....202 A3
   LEY E10 .....91 F6
   PLSTW E13 .....112 C6
   RYNPK SW20 .....204 B4
   SEVS/STOTM * N15 .....68 B6
   SWFD E18 .....73 E4
   WDGN N22 .....67 H4
   WOOL/PLUM SE18 .....154 B5
Crescent Rw STLK EC1Y 7 E6
Crescent St IS * N1 .....107 H5
The Crescent ACT W3 .....125 E5
   ALP/SUD HA0 .....80 D6
   BAR EN5 .....33 E3
   BARN SW13 .....163 E3
   BECK BR3 .....211 E4
   BXLY DA5 .....196 A2
   CRICK NW2 .....63 H3
   E/WMO/HCT KT8 .....218 D1
   FBAR/BDGN N11 .....50 B6
   GNTH/NBYPK IG2 .....96 A3
   LOU IG10 .....57 H1
   NWDGN UB2 .....138 C2
   NWMAL KT3 .....202 C5
   RYLN/HDSTN HA2 .....79 G5
   SCUP DA14 .....195 H4
   SNWD SE25 .....228 D3

SURB KT6 .....221 G2
SUT SM1 .....243 H5
WALTH E17 .....90 C2
WIM/MER SW19 .....185 G5
WWKM BR4 .....255 E3
Crescent Vw LOU IG10 .....57 F1
   ORP BR6 .....255 B5
   STRHM/NOR SW16 .....207 H3
Crescentway HFNCH/WDSP N12...66 A2
Crescent West EBAR EN4 .....35 C1
Crescent Wood Rd DUL SE21...189 G5
Cresford Rd FUL/PGN SW6 .....165 F2
Crespigny Rd HDN NW4 .....83 H1
Cressage Cl STHL UB1 .....119 E3
Cresset Rd HOM E9 .....110 A4
Cresset St CLAP SW4 .....167 F4
Cressfield Cl KTTN NW5 .....106 C5
Cressida Rd ARCH N19 .....84 C3
Cressingham Gv SUT SM1 .....243 G2
Cressingham Rd EDGW HA8 ......62 D5
   LEW SE13 .....171 G4
Cressington Cl
   STNW/STAM N16 .....109 E3
Cresswell Pk BKHTH/KID SE3 ...172 B4
Cresswell Pl WBPTN SW10 .....145 E5
Cresswell Rd FELT TW13 .....178 C5
   SNWD SE25 .....229 C1
   TWK * TW1 .....181 F1
Cresswell Wy WCHMH N21 .....52 H2
Cressy Ct HMSMTH W6 .....145 H3
Cressy Houses WCHPL * E1 .....130 A4
Cressy Pl WCHPL E1 .....130 A4
Cressy Rd HAMP NW3 .....106 B2
Cresswell Ter TWK * TW1 .....159 F4
Crestbrooke Av PLMGR N13 .....52 B5
Crestfield St CAMTN NW1 .....5 F3
Crest Gdns RSLP HA4 .....98 A1
Creston Wy WPK KT4 .....224 D5
Crest Rd CRICK NW2 .....83 C6
   SAND/SEL CR2 .....247 H5
The Crest BRYLDS KT5 .....222 A2
   HDN NW4 .....84 A2
   NFNCH/WDSP * N12 .....47 H5
   PLMGR N13 .....51 G5
Crest Vw PIN HA5 .....78 B3
Crest View Dr STMC/STPC BR5 ...234 A2
Crestway PUT/ROE SW15 .....183 H4
Crestwood Wy HSLWW TW4 ...158 D6
Creswick Ct ACT W3 .....122 B6
Creswick Rd ACT W3 .....122 B6
Creswick Wk BOW * E3 .....111 H2
Crewdson Rd BRXN/ST SW9 ...167 H1
Crewe Pl WLSDN NW10 .....119 H1
Crews St POP/IOD * E14 .....151 E4
Crewys Rd CRICK NW2 .....84 C6
   PECK SE15 .....169 H3
Crichton Av WLGTN SM6 .....245 F5
Crichton Rd CAR SM5 .....244 B5
Crichton St VX/NE * SW8 .....167 E3
Cricketers Arms Rd
   ENC/FH * EN2 .....38 C3
Cricketers Cl CHSGTN KT9 .....239 F3
   STHGT/OAK N14 .....51 E2
Cricketers Ms WD SE26 .....210 A1
Cricketfield Rd CLPT E5 .....110 D2
Cricket Gn MTCM CR4 .....206 D1
Cricket Ground Rd CHST BR7...214 B4
Cricket La BECK BR3 .....210 C2
Cricket Rw EFNCH * N2 .....65 H6
Cricklade Av BRXS/STRHM SW2...187 G4
Cricklewood Broadway
   CRICK NW2 .....104 A1
Cricklewood La CRICK NW2 .....104 A2
Cridland St SRTFD E15 .....112 B6
Crieff Rd WAND/EARL SW18 ...185 C1
Criffel Av BRXS/STRHM SW2 ...187 F4
Crimscott St STHWK SE1 .....24 B6
Crinan St IS N1 .....5 F2
Cringle St VX/NE SW8 .....167 E1
Cripplegate St BARB * EC2Y 15 E1
Crispen Rd FELT TW13 .....178 C6
Crispian Cl WLSDN NW10 .....100 C3
Crispin Crs WLGTN SM6 .....245 F1
Crispin Rd EDGW HA8 .....62 C5
Crispin St WCHPL E1 .....16 D1
Crisp Rd HMSMTH W6 .....144 A5
Cristowe Rd FUL/PGN * SW6 ...164 D3
Criterion Ms ARCH N19 .....87 D6
Cricketers Ms
   WAND/EARL SW18 .....165 C6
Crockenhill HSLW TW3 .....159 F1
Crockenhill Rd STMC/STPC BR5...236 B6
Crockerton Rd TOOT SW17 .....186 B4
Crocus Cl CROY/NA CRO 230 B5
Crocus Fld BAR EN5 .....48 C1
Croft Av WWKM BR4 .....231 G5
Croft Cl BELV DA17 .....156 D5
   CHST BR7 .....213 H1
   MLHL NW7 .....48 H5
Croft Ct BMLY BR1 .....212 C2
   PEND EN3 .....40 A1
   STRHM/NOR SW16 .....208 A3
   SUT SM1 .....243 H5
   WIM/MER SW19 .....205 G3
Crofts Rd HRW HA1 .....80 C5

Crofts St WCHPL E1 .....17 E5
Croft St DEPT SE8 .....150 C4
   WCHPL E1 .....17 E5
The Croft ALP/SUD HA0 .....101 E3
   BAR EN5 .....32 C3
   EDGW HA8 .....62 B4
   EA W5 .....121 G4
   HEST TW5 .....158 C1
   RSLP HA4 .....98 A2
   SWLY BR8 .....217 G6
   WLSDN NW10 .....123 F1
Croft Wy BFN/LL DA15 .....195 E5
   RCHPK/HAM TW10 .....181 C6
Crogsland Rd CAMTN NW1 .....106 C5
Croham Cl SAND/SEL CR2 .....247 E4
Croham Manor Rd
   SAND/SEL CR2 .....247 E5
Croham Mt SAND/SEL CR2 .....247 E5
Croham Park Av
   SAND/SEL CR2 .....247 F3
Croham Rd SAND/SEL CR2 .....246 D3
Croham Valley Rd S
   AND/SEL CR2 .....247 G4
Croindene Rd
   STRHM/NOR SW16 .....207 G4
Cromartie Rd ARCH N19 .....84 F4
Cromarty Vls BAY/PAD * W2 ...125 G6
Crombie Cl REDBR IG4 .....93 H2
Crombie Ms BTSEA * SW11 .....166 A5
Crombie Rd BFN/LL DA15 .....194 D5
Cromer Hyde MRDN * SM4 .....225 F2
Cromer Rd BAR EN5 .....33 G5
   CHDH RM6 .....96 C3
   LEY E10 .....91 H1
   ROMW/RG RM7 .....75 G2
   SNWD SE25 .....209 H6
   TOOT SW17 .....206 C2
   TOTM N17 .....69 G5
Cromer St STPAN WC1H 5 F4
Cromer Ter HACK E8 .....109 G3
Cromer Villas Rd
   WAND/EARL SW18 .....184 D1
Cromford Cl ORP BR6 .....253 H1
Cromford Rd PUT/ROE SW15 ..164 D6
Cromford Wy NWMAL KT3 .....202 D4
Cromix Ct CHST BR7 .....214 B5
Crompton Pl WAB EN9 .....41 E1
Crompton St BAY/PAD * W2 ...125 H3
Cromwell Av HAYES BR2 .....216 B6
   HCT N6 .....86 B5
   HMSMTH W6 .....143 H5
   NWMAL KT3 .....225 H5
Cromwell Cl CHSWK * W4 .....143 B5
   EFNCH N2 .....65 H1
Cromwell Ct ALP/SUD HA0 .....121 C1
Cromwell Crs ECT SW5 .....145 E4
Cromwell Gv HMSMTH W6 .....144 A3
Cromwell Ms SKENS SW7 .....145 H4
Cromwell Pde ALP/SUD * HA0...121 C1
Cromwell Pl ACT W3 .....142 C1
   HCT * N6 .....86 B5
   MORT/ESHN SW14 .....162 C4
   SKENS SW7 .....145 H4
Cromwell Rd ALP/SUD HA0 .....121 F1
   BECK BR3 .....210 C5
   BRXN/ST SW9 .....168 B2
   CROY/NA CRO 228 C4
   ECT SW5 .....145 E4
   FNCH N3 .....47 F1
   FSTGT E7 .....113 C5
   HSLW TW3 .....159 E5
   KUTN/CMB KT2 .....201 C6
   MUSWH N10 .....66 C3
   SKENS SW7 .....145 H4
   TEDD TW11 .....192 A1
   WALTH E17 .....91 G2
   WIM/MER SW19 .....205 E1
   WPK KT4 .....240 D1
Cromwell St HSLW TW3 .....159 E5
Cromwell Ter HSLW * TW3 .....159 E5
Crondace Rd FUL/PGN SW6 .....165 E2
Crondall St IS N1 .....7 H2
Cronin St PECK SE15 .....169 F1
Crooked Billet Rbt CHING E4 .....71 F3
Crooked Usage FNCH N3 .....46 C6
Crooke Rd DEPT SE8 .....150 C5
Crookham Rd FUL/PGN SW6 ...164 D2
Crook Log BXLYHN DA7 .....168 D1
Crookston Rd ELTH/MOT SE9 ...174 B4
Croombs Rd CAN/RD E16 .....133 G4
Croom's Hi GNWCH SE10 .....171 G1
Croom's Hill Gv GNWCH SE10...171 G1
Cropley St IS N1 .....7 G1
Croppath Rd DAGE RM10 .....117 G2
Cropthorne Ct MV/WKIL W9 ...125 G2
Crosby Cl FELT TW13 .....178 A4
Crosby Rd DAGE RM10 .....137 F1
   FSTGT E7 .....112 C4
Crosby Rw STHWK SE1 .....23 G5
Crosby Wk HACK E8 .....109 F4
Crosier Cl WOOL/PLUM SE18 ..173 G2
Crossbow Fld CHIG IG7 .....75 F1
Cross Deep TWK TW1 .....180 A5
Cross Deep Gdns TWK TW1 ...180 A4
Crossfield Est DEPT SE8 .....171 E1
Crossfield Rd HAMP NW3 .....105 G4
   TOTM N17 .....69 F3
Crossfield St DEPT SE8 .....172 C1
Crossford St BRXN/ST SW9 .....167 H1
Crossgate EDGW HA8 .....46 C4
   GFD/PVL UB6 .....100 D4
Cross Keys Cl MHST W1U 11 F2
Cross Lances Rd HSLW TW3 .....159 E3
Crossland Rd THHTH CR7 .....228 B3
Crosslands Av EA W5 .....141 H1
   NWDGN UB2 .....138 C5
Crosslands Pde NWDGN * UB2...138 C5
Crosslands Rd HOR/WEW KT19...138 D4
Cross Lanes Cl BXLY DA5 .....196 D2
   CEND/HSY/T N8 .....66 A3
Crosslet St WALW SE17 .....19 F7
Crosslet V GNWCH SE10 .....171 F2
Crossmead ELTH/MOT SE9 .....174 D1
Crossmead Av GFD/PVL UB6 ...118 A2
Crossness Rd BARK IG11 .....135 C3
Cross Rd BUSH WD23 .....42 C1
   CHDH RM6 .....96 A4

CMBW SE5 ...169 E3
CROY/NA CRO ...228 D5
EN EN1 ...39 E5
FBAR/BDGN N11 ...66 D1
FELT TW15 ...178 C6
HAYES BR2 ...233 G6
HRW HA1 ...79 H1
KTN/HRWW/W HA3 ...60 C5
KUTN/CMB KT2 ...201 H5
ROMW/RG RM7 ...77 E6
RYLN/HDSTN HA2 ...99 E1
SCUP DA14 ...195 H6
STMC/STPC BR5 ...235 H2
SUT SM1 ...243 H3
WDGN N22 ...68 A2
WFD IG8 ...39 G1
WIM/MER SW19 ...205 E3
Cross St BARN SW13 ...163 E3
HPTN TW12 ...199 G1
IS N1 ...108 B6
UED N18 ...50 C4
Crossthwaite Av HNHL SE24 ...168 D5
Crosswall TWRH EC3N ...16 C5
Crossway BCTR RM8 ...116 A1
CDALE/KGS NW9 ...61 E1
EN EN1 ...53 E2
NFNCH/WDSP N12 ...65 H2
NWMAL KT3 ...224 A1
RSLP HA4 ...A2
STMC/STPC BR5 ...234 D1
STNW/STAM N16 ...109 E3
THMD SE28 ...136 A5
WEA W13 ...120 C3
Crossway Pde WDGN * N22 ...68 A2
Crossways BAL SM4 ...243 H6
SAND/SEL CR2 ...248 D5
Crossways Rd BECK BR3 ...231 E1
MTCM CR4 ...206 D6
Crossways Ter CLPT * E5 ...110 A2
The Crossways BRYLDS * KT5 ...222 B5
HEST TW5 ...158 D1
WBLY HA9 ...82 A6
The Cross Wy
KTN/HRWW/W HA3 ...60 A5
The Crossway ELTH/MOT SE9 ...193 F4
UED N18 ...50 C4
Croston St HACK E8 ...109 C6
Crosts La WDGN N22 ...68 A3
Crothall Cl PLMGR N13 ...51 H5
Crouch Av BARK IG11 ...116 A1
Crouch Cl BECK BR3 ...211 E2
Crouch Cft ELTH/MOT SE9 ...194 A5
Crouch End Hi ARCH N19 ...87 F4
Crouch Hall Rd CEND/HSY/T N8 ...87 F3
Crouch Hi ARCH N19 ...87 F2
Crouchmans Cl DUL SE21 ...189 F5
Crouch Rd WLSDN NW10 ...102 D5
Crowborough Pth
OXHEY WD19 ...42 B6
Crowborough Rd TOOT SW17 ...206 C1
Crowden Wy THMD SE28 ...136 A6
Crowder St WCHPL E1 ...104 C6
Crowfoot Cl HOM E9 ...110 D3
Crowhurst Cl BRXN/ST SW9 ...168 A3
Crowhurst Wy
STMC/STPC BR5 ...236 A2
Crowland Gdns STHGT/OAK N14...51 G2
Crowland Rd SEVS/STOTM N15...89 F2
THHTH * CR7 ...228 D2
Crowlands Av ROMW/RG RM7...97 F3
Crowland Ter IS N1 ...109 H4
Crowland Wk MRDN SM4 ...225 F5
Crow La ROMW/RG RM7 ...96 D4
ROMW/RG RM7 ...97 G4
Crowley Crs CROY/NA CRO ...246 A3
Crowline Wk IS * N1 ...108 C4
Crownarc Av KUT * KT1 ...201 F5
Crownbourne Ct SUT * SM1 ...243 F2
Crown Buildings CHING * E4 ...61 H5
Crown Cl BOW E3 ...111 E6
KIL/WHAMP NW6 ...105 F4
MLHL NW7 ...47 F4
ORP BR6 ...253 G2
WOT/HER KT12 ...172 A6
Crown Ct HOL/ALD WC2B ...13 F4
Crown Di NRWD SE19 ...208 C2
Crowndale Rd CAMTN NW1 ...4 B1
Crownfield Av GNTH/NBYPK IG2 ...95 E2
Crownfield Rd SRTFD E15 ...111 H3
Crown Hi CROY/NA * CRO ...228 C6
Crownhill Rd WFD IG8 ...75 G3
WLSDN NW10 ...81 H5
Crown La CHST BR7 ...214 C4
HAYES BR2 ...233 F2
STHGT/OAK N14 ...51 E3
STRHM/NOR SW16 ...208 A1
WIM/MER SW19 ...205 G6
Crown Lane Gdns
WNWD * SE27 ...208 A1
Crown La Sp HAYES BR2 ...233 F3
Crown Office Rw EMB EC4Y ...14 A5
Crown Pde MRDN * SM4 ...225 F1
STHGT/OAK N14 ...51 E3
Crown Pas STJS SW1Y ...20 B2
Crown Pl KTTN NW5 ...106 D4
SDTCH EC2A ...8 A6
Crown Rd BARK/HLT IG6 ...94 D1
EN EN1 ...39 G4
MUSWH N10 ...48 B6
NWMAL KT3 ...202 C4
ORP BR6 ...253 G3
RSLP HA4 ...98 B3
SUT SM1 ...243 F2
TWK TW1 ...180 D1
WIM/MER SW19 ...225 F1
Crownstone Rd
BRXS/STRHM SW2 ...168 A6
Crown St ACT W3 ...142 B1
CMBW SE5 ...168 C1
DAGE RM10 ...117 G4
RYLN/HDSTN HA2 ...78 C1
Crown Ter CRICK * NW2 ...104 B2
RCH/KEW TW9 ...161 H5
STHGT/OAK * N14 ...51 E3
Crownthorne Cl ISLW TW7 ...142 G2
Crown Vis ACT * W3 ...117 G4
Crown Wk WBLY HA9 ...101 H1
Crown Woods Wy
ELTH/MOT SE9 ...174 D6
Crown Yd HSLW TW5 ...159 G4
Crowshott Av STAN HA7 ...61 E5

Crows Rd BARK IG11 ...114 B4
SRTFD E15 ...131 H2
Crowther Av BTFD TW8 ...141 G5
Crowther Rd SNWD SE25 ...229 G1
Crowthorne Dr
WAND/EARL SW18 ...184 D2
Crowthorne Rd NKENS W10 ...124 B5
Croxden Cl EDGW HA8 ...62 A6
Croxden Wk MRDN SM4 ...225 G5
Croxford Gdns WDGN N22 ...68 B3
Croxford Wy ROMW/RG RM7 ...97 H5
Croxley Cl STMC/STPC BR5 ...215 H6
Croxley Gn STMC/STPC BR5 ...215 H4
Croxley Rd MV/WKIL W9 ...100 D2
Croxted Cl DUL SE21 ...188 C2
Croxted Rd DUL SE21 ...188 D4
Croyde Av GFD/PVL UB6 ...119 H2
Croyde Cl ELTH/MOT SE9 ...194 D2
The Croydon F/O
CROY/NA CRO ...246 B2
The Croydon F/O
CROY/NA CRO/NA CRO ...228 B5
Croydon Rd BECK BR3 ...210 C1
CROY/NA CRO ...230 B2
CROY/NA CRO ...245 G2
MTCM CR4 ...244 A2
PGE/AN SE20 ...209 H5
PLSTW E13 ...132 C3
WLGTN SM6 ...244 D2
WLGTN SM6 ...245 E1
WWKM BR4 ...250 A1
Croyland Rd ED N9 ...53 G3
Croylands Dr SURB KT6 ...221 C4
Crozier Ter HOM E9 ...110 B3
Crucible Cl CHDH RM6 ...95 H5
Crucifix La STHWK SE1 ...108 B6
Cruden St IS N1 ...108 B6
Cruikshank St FSBYW WC1X ...6 A3
Cruikshank Rd SRTFD E15 ...112 A2
Crummock Gdns
CDALE/KGS NW9 ...83 G2
Crumpsall St ABYW SE2 ...156 A4
Crundale Av CDALE/KGS NW9 ...82 A3
Crunden Rd SAND/SEL CR2 ...246 D6
Crusader Gdns CROY/NA CRO ...247 E1
Crusoe Ms STNW/STAM N16 ...88 D6
Crusoe Rd ERITH DA8 ...151 H5
MTCM CR4 ...206 B3
Crutched Friars TWRH EC3N ...16 C4
Crutchley Rd CAT SE6 ...192 H4
Crystal Palace NRWD * SE19 ...209 G3
Crystal Palace Pde NRWD SE19 ...209 F2
Crystal Palace Park Rd
NRWD SE19 ...209 G1
Crystal Palace Rd EDUL SE22 ...189 F1
Crystal Palace St NRWD SE19 ...208 C2
Crystal Wy BCTR RM8 ...96 A5
HRW HA1 ...80 B2
Cuba St POP/IOD E14 ...151 E2
Cubitt Sq STHL * UB1 ...139 G1
Cubitt St CROY/NA CRO ...245 H5
FSBYW WC1X ...5 H4
Cubitt Ter CLAP SW4 ...167 G4
Cuckoo Av HNWL W7 ...120 A3
Cuckoo Dene HNWL W7 ...119 H4
Cuckoo Hall La ED N9 ...54 A2
Cuckoo Hi PIN HA5 ...58 A6
Cuckoo Hill Dr PIN HA5 ...58 A6
Cuckoo Hill Rd PIN HA5 ...78 B1
Cuckoo La HNWL W7 ...120 A6
Cuda's Cl HOR/WEW KT19 ...246 A1
Cuddington Av WPK KT4 ...241 H1
Cudham St CAT SE6 ...191 G2
Cudworth St WCHPL E1 ...104 D3
Cuff Crs ELTH/MOT SE9 ...193 F4
Culford Gdns CHEL SW3 ...26 D2
Culford Gv IS N1 ...109 E4
Culgaith Gdns ENC/FH EN2 ...37 C5
Cullen Wy WLSDN NW10 ...122 C3
Culling Rd BERM/RHTH SE16 ...150 A3
Cullington Ct
KTN/HRWW/W HA3 ...80 C1
Cullingworth Rd WLSDN NW10 ...103 F3
Culloden Cl STHWK SE1 ...53 F4
Culloden Rd ENC/FH EN2 ...38 B3
Culloden St POP/IOD E14 ...135 C1
Cullum St FENCHST EC3M ...16 A5
Culmington Pde WEA * W13 ...121 G2
Culmington Rd SAND/SEL CR2 ...246 C5
WEA W13 ...141 G1
Culmore Rd PECK SE15 ...169 H1
Culmstock Rd BTSEA SW11 ...166 C6
Culpepper Cl CHIG IG7 ...74 B2
Culross Cl SEVS/STOTM N15 ...88 C1
Culross St MYFR/PKLN W1K ...11 E6
Culsac Rd SURB KT6 ...222 A5
Culverden Rd BAL SW12 ...187 E5
ECGWT SE SW11 ...41 H3
Culverhouse Gdns
STRHM/NOR SW16 ...187 H6
Culverlands Cl STAN HA7 ...44 A4
Culverley Rd CAT SE6 ...191 F3
Culvers Av CAR SM5 ...226 B6
Culvers Retreat CAR SM5 ...226 C6
Culverstone Cl HAYES BR2 ...232 B5
Culvers Wy CAR SM5 ...226 B6
Culvert Pl BTSEA SW11 ...166 C3
Culvert Rd BTSEA SW11 ...166 B3
SEVS/STOTM N15 ...89 E2
Culworth St STJWD NW8 ...2 A2
Cumberland Av WELL DA16 ...175 F5
WLSDN NW10 ...122 B2
Cumberland Cl BARK/HLT * IG6 ...74 C4
HACK E8 ...109 F4
RYNPK SW20 ...206 B6
TWK TW1 ...180 D1
Cumberland Dr BXLYHN DA7 ...176 C1
CHSGTN KT9 ...239 G1
ESH/CLAY KT10 ...220 C6
Cumberland Gdns FSBYW WC1X ...5 H3
HDN * NW4 ...64 B5
Cumberland Ga BAY/PAD W2 ...9 C4
Cumberland Market
CAMTN NW1 ...3 H3
Cumberland Pk ACT W3 ...122 C6
Cumberland Pl CAMTN NW1 ...3 C3
CAT SE6 ...192 B3
Cumberland Rd ACT W3 ...122 C6

BARN SW13 ...163 F2
ED N9 ...54 A3
HAYES BR2 ...232 A1
HNWL W7 ...140 A2
HRW HA1 ...79 F2
KTN/HRWW/W HA3 ...61 H6
MNPK E12 ...113 F2
PLSTW E13 ...131 C3
RCH/KEW TW9 ...162 A2
SNWD SE25 ...229 H3
WALTH E17 ...70 C5
Cumberland St PIM SW1V ...27 H5
Cumberland Ter CAMTN NW1...3 G2
PGE/AN * SE20 ...209 H3
Cumberland Terrace Ms
CAMTN NW1 ...3 G2
Cumberlow Av SNWD SE25 ...209 G6
Cumberton Rd TOTM N17 ...68 D4
Cumbrae Gdns SURB KT6 ...221 F6
Cumbrian Gdns CRICK NW2 ...84 B6
Cumming St IS N1 ...5 G3
Cumnor Cl BRXN/ST * SW9 ...167 H5
Cumnor Gdns EW KT17 ...241 G4
Cumnor Rd BELMT SM2 ...243 G4
Cunard Crs WCHMH N21 ...52 D1
Cunard Rd WLSDN NW10 ...122 D2
Cundy Rd CAN/RD E16 ...133 E5
Cundy St BGVA SW1W ...27 G3
Cunliffe Rd HOR/WEW KT19 ...241 F2
Cunliffe St STRHM/NOR SW16 ...207 E2
Cunningham Cl CHDH RM6 ...96 A2
WWKM BR4 ...231 F6
Cunningham Pk HRW HA1 ...79 H2
Cunningham Pl STJWD NW8 ...125 H3
Cunningham Rd
SEVS/STOTM N15 ...89 G1
Cunnington St CHSWK W4 ...142 C3
Cupar Rd BTSEA SW11 ...166 C2
Cupola Cl BMLY BR1 ...212 D1
Cureton St WEST SW1P ...28 D5
Curlew Cl THMD SE28 ...136 B6
Curlew St STHWK SE1 ...24 C3
Curlew Wy YEAD UB4 ...118 B4
Curnick's La WNWD SE27 ...188 C6
Curran Av BFN/LL DA15 ...175 F6
WLGTN SM6 ...244 C1
Currey Rd NTHLT UB5 ...99 G4
Currie St WCHPL SE1 ...143 E1
Currie Hill Cl WIM/MER SW19 ...184 D6
Curry Rl MLHL NW7 ...64 B2
Cursitor St FLST/FETLN EC4A ...14 A3
Curtain Pl SDTCH EC2A ...8 B5
Curtain Rd SDTCH EC2A ...8 B4
Curthwaite Gdns ENC/FH EN2 ...37 F5
Curtis Dr ACT W3 ...122 D5
Curtis Field Rd
STRHM/NOR SW16 ...187 H6
Curtis La ALP/SUD HA0 ...101 C4
Curtismill Cl STMC/STPC BR5 ...215 H6
Curtismill Wy STMC/STPC BR5 ...215 H6
Curtis Rd HOR/WEW KT19 ...240 C2
HSLWW TW4 ...158 D3
Curtis St STHWK SE1 ...32 C1
Curtis Wy STHWK SE1 ...32 C1
The Curve SHB W12 ...123 G6
Curwen Av FSTGT E7 ...112 A2
Curwen Rd SHB W12 ...143 G2
Curzon Av STAN HA7 ...43 G4
STAN HA7 ...60 C4
Curzon Cl ORP BR6 ...252 D2
Curzon Crs BARK IG11 ...135 F2
WLSDN NW10 ...103 E5
Curzon Ga MYFR/PKLN W1K ...19 F2
Curzon Rd EA W5 ...104 B5
MUSWH N10 ...66 D5
THHTH CR7 ...228 A3
Curzon St MYFR/PICC W1J ...19 H1
Cusack Cl TWK * TW1 ...180 B6
Custom House Reach
BERM/RHTH * SE16 ...150 D3
Cutcombe Rd CMBW SE5 ...168 C1
Cuthberga Cl BARK IG11 ...114 C5
Cuthbert Gdns SNWD SE25 ...209 E6
Cuthbert Rd CROY/NA CRO ...228 B6
UED N10 ...69 C1
WALTH E17 ...76 A1
Cuthbert St BAY/PAD W2 ...125 H4
Cutlers Gardens Ar LVPST EC2M ...16 B3
Cutler St HDTCH EC3A ...16 B3
The Cut STHWK SE1 ...22 A3
Cuxton Cl BXLYHS DA6 ...176 C6
Cyclamen Cl HPTN TW12 ...199 E2
Cyclamen Rd SWLY BR8 ...237 H1
Cyclamen Wy HOR/WEW KT19 ...240 C4
Cygnet Av EBED/NFELT TW14 ...178 A2
Cygnet Cl WLSDN NW10 ...102 D3
The Cygnets FELT TW13 ...178 C6
Cygnet St WCHPL E1 ...13 J1
Cygnet Wy YEAD UB4 ...118 B5
Cymbeline Ct HRW * HA1 ...80 B3
Cynthia St IS N1 ...5 H2
Cypress Av WHTN TW2 ...179 G2
Cypress Gdns BROCKY SE4 ...190 B5
Cypress Gv BARK/HLT IG6 ...75 E2
Cypress Pl KTN/HRWW/W HA3 ...59 H5
Cypress Rd SNWD SE25 ...209 E5
Cypress Tree Cl BFN/LL DA15 ...195 F1
Cyprus Av FNCH N3 ...64 C5
Cyprus Cl FSBYPK N4 ...88 A3
Cyprus Gdns FNCH N3 ...64 C5
Cyprus Pl BETH E2 ...130 A1
Cyprus Rd ED N9 ...53 H4
FNCH N3 ...64 D5
Cyprus St BETH E2 ...130 B1
Cyrena Rd EDUL SE22 ...187 E4
Cyril Rd BXLYHN DA7 ...176 C3
ORP BR6 ...235 G4
Cyrus St FSBYE EC1V ...6 C5
Czar St DEPT SE8 ...151 E6

D

Dabbs Hill La NTHLT UB5 ...98 D4
Dabin Crs GNWCH SE10 ...171 G2

Dacca St DEPT SE8 ...150 D6
Dace Rd BOW E3 ...111 H6
Dacre Av CLAY IG5 ...74 A5
Dacre Cl GFD/PVL UB6 ...119 F1
Dacre Gdns LEW * SE13 ...173 G3
Dacre Pk LEW SE13 ...172 A4
Dacre Pl LEW SE13 ...172 A4
Dacre Rd CROY/NA CRO ...227 C4
PLSTW E13 ...112 D6
WAN E11 ...92 B5
Dacres Est FSTH * SE23 ...190 B5
Dacres Rd FSTH SE23 ...190 D5
Dacre St STJSPK SW1H ...28 C5
Dade Wy NWDGN UB2 ...138 D5
Daerwood Cl HAYES BR2 ...233 H5
Daffodil Cl CROY/NA CRO ...230 B5
Daffodil Gdns IL IG1 ...119 E3
Daffodil St SHB W12 ...123 F6
Dafforne Rd TOOT SW17 ...186 B5
Dagenham Av DAGW RM9 ...116 C6
Dagenham Rd DAGE RM10 ...117 G2
LEY E10 ...90 D5
RAIN RM13 ...117 H5
ROMW/RG RM7 ...97 F1
Dagger La BORE WD6 ...44 C1
Dagmar Av WBLY HA9 ...101 H2
Dagmar Gdns WLSDN NW10 ...124 B1
Dagmar Pas IS * N1 ...108 B6
Dagmar Rd CMBW SE5 ...169 E2
DAGE RM10 ...117 G5
FSBYPK N4 ...67 G4
KUTN/CMB KT2 ...201 H4
NWDGN UB2 ...138 C5
SEVS/STOTM N15 ...89 E1
SNWD SE25 ...229 E1
WDGN N22 ...67 F4
Dagmar Ter IS * N1 ...108 B6
Dagnall Pk SNWD SE25 ...229 E2
Dagnall Rd SNWD SE25 ...229 E2
Dagnall St BTSEA SW11 ...166 B3
Dagnan Rd BAL SW12 ...188 G2
Dahomey Rd
STRHM/NOR SW16 ...207 E2
Daimler Wy WLGTN SM6 ...245 G5
Daines Cl MNPK E12 ...113 H1
Dainford Cl BMLY BR1 ...211 H1
Daintry Cl KTN/HRWW/W HA3 ...80 C1
Dairsie Rd ELTH/MOT SE9 ...174 D1
Dairy Cl BMLY * BR1 ...212 D3
THHTH CR7 ...208 D5
Dairy La WOOL/PLUM SE18 ...153 H4
Dairyman Cl CRICK * NW2 ...104 B1
Daisy Cl CROY/NA CRO ...230 B5
Daisy La FUL/PCN SW6 ...165 G4
Daisy Rd SWFD E18 ...72 D5
Dakota Cl CROY/NA CRO ...245 H5
Dakota Gdns EHAM E6 ...133 G3
Dalberg Rd BRXS/STRHM SW2 ...168 A3
Dalberg Wy ABYW SE2 ...136 D3
Dalby Rd WAND/EARL SW18 ...165 G5
Dalbys Crs TOTM N17 ...106 D4
Dalby St KTTN NW5 ...106 D4
Dalcross Rd HEST TW5 ...158 C6
Dale Av EDGW HA8 ...44 A4
HSLWW TW4 ...158 C4
Daleburg Rd TOOT SW17 ...186 B4
Dale Cl BAR EN5
BKHTH/KID SE3 ...172 C4
Dale Gdns WFD IG8 ...56 D6
Dale Green Rd FBAR/BDGN N11 ...50 D5
Dale Gv NFNCH/WDSP N12 ...47 G1
Daleham Gdns HAMP * NW3 ...105 H4
Daleham Ms HAMP * NW3 ...105 H4
Dale Pk Av CAR SM5 ...226 B6
Dale Park Rd NRWD SE19 ...208 C4
Dale Rd CFD/PVL UB6 ...119 F4
KTTN NW5 ...106 C2
SUT SM1 ...242 D2
SWLY BR8 ...217 G6
WALW SE17 ...30 C6
Dale Rw NTGHL W11 ...124 C5
Daleside ORP BR6 ...253 C6
Daleside Cl ORP BR6 ...253 C4
Dale St CHSWK W4 ...143 E5
Dale Vw CHING E4 ...55 C3
Dale View Av CHING E4 ...55 G4
Dale View Crs CHING E4 ...55 G4
Dale View Gdns CHING E4 ...55 H5
Daleview Rd SEVS/STOTM N15 ...89 E3
Dalewood Gdns WPK KT4 ...224 D1
Dale Wood Rd ORP BR6 ...235 F6
Daley St HOM E9 ...111 F5
Daley Thompson Wy
VX/NE SW8 ...166 D3
Dalgarno Gdns NKENS W10 ...124 A4
Dalgarno Wy NKENS W10 ...124 A3
Dalkeith Gv STAN HA7 ...44 A1
Dalkeith Rd DUL SE21 ...188 C3
IL IG1 ...114 C1
Dallas Rd CHEAM SM3 ...242 C4
EA W5 ...121 H4
HDN NW4 ...63 H4
SYD SE26 ...181 A5
Dallinger Rd LEE/GVPK SE12 ...192 B1
Dalling Rd HMSMTH W6 ...143 H1
Dallington St FSBYE EC1V ...6 C6
Dallin Rd BXLYHS DA6 ...176 D4
WOOL/PLUM SE18 ...174 D1
Dalmain Rd FSTH SE23 ...190 D2
Dalmally Rd CROY/NA CRO ...229 C4
Dalmeny Av HOLWY N7 ...107 F2
Dalmeny Crs HSLW TW3 ...159 H5
Dalmeny Rd BAR EN5 ...95 B1
CAR SM5 ...244 C4
ERITH DA8 ...177 F2
HOLWY N7 ...106 D1
WPK KT4 ...241 H1
Dalmeyer Rd WLSDN NW10 ...81 H4
Dalmore Av ESH/CLAY KT10 ...238 B4
Dalmore Rd DUL SE21 ...188 C4

Dalrymple Cl STHGT/OAK N14 .....51 F2
Dalrymple Rd BROCKY SE4 ....170 C5
Dalston Gdns STAN HA7 ....61 G4
Dalston La HACK E8 ....109 H3
Dalton Av MTCM CR4 ....206 A5
Dalton Cl ORP BR6 ....253 J7
Daltons Rd SWLY BR8 ....237 G6
Dalton St WNWD SE27 ....188 B4
Dalwood St CMBW SE5 ....169 E2
Dalyell Rd BRXN/ST SW9 ....167 H4
Damask Crs CAN/RD E16 ....132 A3
Damer Ter WBPTN SW10 ....165 G1
Dames Rd FSTGT E7 ....112 C2
Dame St IS N1 ....7 D1
Damien St WCHPL E1 ....17 H3
Damon Cl SCUP DA14 ....195 H5
Damsel Ct BERM/RHTH * SE16 ......25 F4
Damsonwood Rd NWDGN UB2 ...139 E3
Danbrook Rd
STRHM/NOR SW16 ....207 G3
Danbury Cl CHDH RM6 ....76 B6
Danbury Ms CAR SM5 ....248 D2
Danbury Rd LOU IG10 ....57 C1
Danbury St IS N1 ....6 D1
Danbury Wy WFD IG8 ....73 E2
Danby St PECK SE15 ....169 E4
Dancer Rd FUL/PGN SW6 ....164 D2
RCH/KEW TW9 ....162 A4
Dando Crs BKHTH/KID SE3 ....172 D4
Dandridge Cl GNWCH SE10 ....152 B5
Danebury Av PUT/ROE SW15 ....183 F2
Daneby Rd CAT SE6 ....191 C1
Dane Cl BXLY DA5 ....197 E2
ORP BR6 ....253 D3
Danecourt Gdns CROY/NA CRO ...247 F1
Danecroft Rd HNHL SE24 ....168 C6
Danehurst Gdns REDBR IG4 ....93 C2
Danehurst St FUL/PGN SW6 ....166 C2
Daneland EBAR EN4 ....36 B6
Danemead Gv NTHLT * UB5 ....66 A4
Danemere St PUT/ROE SW15 ....164 A4
Dane Pl BOW E3 ....130 C1
Dane Rd IL IG1 ....114 C3
STHL UB1 ....118 C6
UED N18 ....54 A6
WEA W13 ....121 E6
WIM/MER SW19 ....206 A2
Danescombe LEE/GVPK SE12 ......192 E5
Danescourt Crs SUT SM1 ....225 C6
Danescroft Av HDN * NW4 ....64 B2
Danescroft Gdns HDN NW4 ....64 B2
Danesdale Rd HOM E9 ....110 C4
Danes Ga HRW HA1 ....60 A6
Danes Rd ROMW/RG RM7 ....97 C4
Dane St GINN WC1R 11 C3
Daneswood Av CAT SE6 ....191 C5
Danethorpe Rd ALP/SUD HA0 ......101 F4
Danetree Cl HOR/WEW KT19 ....240 C5
Danetree Rd HOR/WEW KT19 ......240 D6
Danette Gdns DAGE RM10 ....80 B6
Daneville Rd CMBW SE5 ....150 D1
Dangan Rd WAN E11 ....92 C3
Daniel Bolt Cl POP/IOD E14 ....131 F4
UED N18 ....54 A6
WIM/MER SW19 ....206 A2
Daniel Gdns PECK SE15 ....169 F1
Daniel Wy CROY/NA CRO 227 C5
Daniell Pl HDN NW4 ....63 K6
Daniel Rd ACT W3 ....121 H6
Daniel's Rd PECK SE15 ....190 A1
Dan Leno Wk FUL/PGN * SW6 .....166 F1
Dansey Pl SOHO/SHAV W1D 12 C5
Dansington Rd WELL DA16 ....175 H4
Danson Crs WELL DA16 ....175 H4
Danson La WELL DA16 ....175 H5
Danson Md WELL DA16 ....176 A4
Danson Rd BXLYHS DA6 ....176 B6
Danson U/P BFN/LL DA15 ....196 A1
Dante Rd LBTH SE11 ....30 C1
Danube St CHEL SW3 ....26 B3
Danvers Rd CEAD/HSY/T N8 ....87 F1
Danvers St CHEL SW3 ....145 H6
Daphne Gdns CHING E4 ....44 A2
Daphne St WAND/EARL SW18 ......185 G1
Daplyn St WCHPL E1 ....17 L1
D'arblay St SOHO/CST W1F 12 A4
Darby Crs SUN TW16 ....198 A5
Darby Gdns SUN TW16 ....198 A5
Darcy Av WLGTN SM6 ....245 E2
Darcy Cl TRDG/WHET N20 ....49 H4
D'arcy Dr KTN/HRWW/W HA3 ....81 F1
D'arcy Gdns DAGW RM9 ....116 C6
KTN/HRWW/W HA3 ....81 C1
D'arcy Pl HAYES BR2 ....232 C1
D'arcy Rd CHEAM SM3 ....242 B2
ISLW * TW7 ....136 A2
STRHM/NOR SW16 ....207 G5
Darell Rd RCH/KEW TW9 ....162 A4
Darenth Rd STNW/STAM N16 ....68 B4
WELL DA16 ....175 G2
Darfield Rd BROCKY SE4 ....170 D6
Darfield Wy NKENS W10 ....108 B5
Darfur St PUT/ROE SW15 ....164 B6
Dargate Cl NRWD SE19 ....189 F3
Darien Rd BTSEA SW11 ....164 C4
Darlands Dr BAR EN5 ....34 B6
Darlan Rd FUL/PGN SW6 ....147 J1
Darlaston Rd WIM/MER SW19 ......206 B3
Darley Cl CROY/NA CRO 230 B3
Darley Dr NWMAL KT3 ....202 D5
Darley Gdns MRDN SM4 ....225 F3
Darley Rd BTSEA SW11 ....186 B1
ED N9 ....42 B1
Darling Rd BROCKY SE4 ....171 E4
Darling Rw WCHPL E1 ....92 D4
Darlington Rd WNWD SE27 ....207 H1
Darmaine Cl SAND/SEL CR2 ....211 J6
Darndale Cl WALTH E17 ....70 D6
Darnley Rd HACK E8 ....109 H4
WFD IG8 ....72 C4
Darnley Ter NTGHL W11 ....119 H1
Darns Hl SWLY SW8 ....237 G4
Darrell Rd EDUL SE22 ....169 G6
Darren Cl FSBYPK N4 ....87 H4
Darris Cl YEAD UB4 ....118 C3
Darsley Dr VX/NE SW8 ....167 F2
Dartford Av ED N9 ....54 A1
Dartford Rd BXLY DA5 ....197 C3
Dartford St WALW SE17 ....31 F5

Dartmoor Wk POP/IOD * E14 ....151 E4
Dartmouth Cl NTGHL W11 ....124 D5
Dartmouth Gv GNWCH SE10 ....151 C2
Dartmouth Hl GNWCH SE10 ....171 C2
Dartmouth Park Av KTTN NW5 .....106 D2
Dartmouth Park Hl ARCH N19 ....86 D5
Dartmouth Park Rd KTTN NW5 ....106 D1
Dartmouth Pl CHSWK W4 ....143 E6
FSTH SE23 ....190 A2
Dartmouth Rd CRICK NW2 ....104 B4
HAYES BR2 ....232 C4
HDN NW4 ....83 C3
SYD SE26 ....189 H5
Dartmouth Rw LEW SE13 ....171 C3
Dartmouth St STJSPK SW1H 20 C4
Dartmouth Ter GNWCH SE10 ....171 H2
Dartnell Rd CROY/NA CRO 229 E4
Dartrey Wk WBPTN * SW10 ....165 G1
Dart St NKENS W10 ....124 D2
Darville Rd STNW/STAM N16 ....109 F1
Darwell Cl EHAM E6 ....134 A1
Darwin Cl FBAR/BDGN N11 ....50 D5
ORP BR6 ....252 D3
Darwin Dr GFD/PVL UB6 ....119 F5
Darwin Gdns OXHEY WD19 ....58 A1
Darwin Rd BTFD TW8 ....141 K1
ED N9 ....68 B4
WELL DA16 ....175 F4
Darwin St WALW SE17 ....31 H1
Daryngton Dr GFD/PVL UB6 ....119 H1
Dashwood Cl BXLYHS DA6 ....177 E6
Dashwood Rd CEND/HSY/T N8 ....87 H3
Dassett Rd WNWD SE27 ....208 B1
Datchelor Pl CMBW * SE5 ....168 D2
Datchet Rd CAT SE6 ....190 D5
Date St WALW SE17 ....31 C4
Daubeney Gdns TOTM N17 ....68 C3
Daubeney Rd CLPT E5 ....110 C3
TOTM N17 ....68 C3
Dault Rd WAND/EARL SW18 ....185 G1
Davenant Rd ARCH N19 ....87 F6
Davenant St WCHPL E1 ....17 F2
Davenport Cl TEDD * TW11 ....200 C2
Davenport Rd LEW SE13 ....191 F1
CAT SE6 ....196 B4
Daventer Dr STAN HA7 ....60 B3
Daventry Av WALTH E17 ....91 F5
Daventry St CAMTN NW1 ....10 A1
Davern Cl GNWCH SE10 ....152 B4
Davey Cl HOLWY N7 ....107 H4
PLMGR N13 ....41 F3
Davey Rd HOM E9 ....111 E5
Davey St PECK SE15 ....32 D6
David Av GFD/PVL UB6 ....120 A2
Davidge St STHWK SE1 ....18 C2
David Ms MHST W1U 10 D1
David Rd BCTR RM8 ....96 C6
Davidson Gdns VX/NE SW8 ....167 G1
Davidson Rd CROY/NA CRO 229 F5
David's Rd FSTH SE23 ....190 A3
David St SRTFD E15 ....111 H4
David Twigg Cl KUTN/CMB KT2 ....229 F3
Davies La WAN E11 ....92 A6
Davies Ms MYFR/PKLN W1K 11 C5
Davies Wk ISLW TW7 ....135 G2
Davington Gdns BCTR RM8 ....115 H3
Davington Rd BCTR RM8 ....115 H4
Davinia Cl WFD IG8 ....73 K6
Davis Rd ACT W3 ....143 F1
CHSGTN KT9 ....240 C5
Davis St PLSTW E13 ....132 D1
Davisville Rd SHB W12 ....143 G2
Dawes Av ISLW TW7 ....160 D6
Dawes Rd FUL/PGN SW6 ....164 D1
Dawes St WALW SE17 ....31 H6
Dawlish Av GFD/PVL UB6 ....120 C1
PLMGR N13 ....41 E3
Dawlish Dr GDMY/SEVK IG3 ....115 F2
PIN HA5 ....78 C2
Dawlish Rd CRICK NW2 ....104 B4
LEY E10 ....91 J6
TOTM N17 ....69 C6
Dawnay Gdns
WAND/EARL SW18 ....185 H4
Dawnay Rd WAND/EARL SW18 ....185 C4
Dawn Cl HSLWW TW4 ....158 C4
Dawn Crs SRTFD E15 ....111 H6
Dawpool Rd CRICK NW2 ....83 F6
Daws Hi CHING E4 ....31 K1
Daws La MLHL NW7 ....45 F2
Dawson Av BARK IG11 ....115 F5
STMC/STPC BR5 ....215 H5
Dawson Cl WOOL/PLUM SE18 ......154 C4
HAYES BR2 ....231 C5
Dawson Pl BAY/PAD W2 ....125 C6
Dawson Rd CRICK NW2 ....104 A3
KUT/HW KT1 ....201 H6
Dawson St BETH E2 ....7 L5
Dawson Ter ED * N9 ....54 A2
Daybrooke Rd WIM/MER SW19 ....205 K6
Daylesford Av PUT/ROE SW15 .....163 C5
Daymer Gdns PIN HA5 ....78 A1
Daysbrook Rd
BRXS/STRHM SW2 ....187 H3
Days La BFN/LL DA15 ....195 J2
Dayton Gv PECK SE15 ....170 A2
Deacon Cl PUR/KEN CR8 ....245 G6
The Deacon Est CHING * E4 ....70 D2
Deacon Ms IS N1 ....7 H1
Deacon Rd CRICK NW2 ....103 G4
KUTN/CMB KT2 ....201 H4
Deacons Hts BORE WD6 ....46 A1
Deacons Ri OXHEY WD19 ....42 A1
Deacons Leas ORP BR6 ....256 A5
Deacons Ri EFNCH N2 ....85 H2
Deacons Ter IS * N1 ....108 C4
Deacons Wk HPTN TW12 ....179 E6
Deacon Wy WALW SE17 ....73 H3
WFD IG8 ....73 H3
Deakins Ter ORP BR6 ....215 J6
Deal Porters Wy
BERM/RHTH SE16 ....150 A3
Deal Rd TOOT SW17 ....206 C2
Deal St WCHPL E1 ....17 L1
Dealtry Rd PUT/ROE SW15 ....164 A6
Deal Wk BRXN/ST SW9 ....168 A1
Dean Bradley St WEST SW1P 21 H5

Dean Ct ALP/SUD HA0 ....100 D1
Deancross St WCHPL E1 ....130 A5
Dean Dr STAN HA7 ....61 C5
Deane Croft Rd PIN HA5 ....78 A3
Deanery Cl EFNCH N2 ....86 A1
Deanery Ms MYFR/PKLN * W1K 19 F1
Deanery Rd SRTFD E15 ....112 A4
Deanery St MYFR/PKLN W1K 19 F1
Dean Farrar St STJSPK SW1H 20 D5
Deanfield Gdns CROY/NA * CRO ..246 D2
Dean Gdns WALTH E17 ....72 A1
Deanhill Ct
MORT/ESHN * SW14 ....162 B5
Deanhill Rd MORT/ESHN SW14 ....162 B5
Dean Rd CRICK NW2 ....104 A4
CROY/NA CRO 246 D2
HPTN TW12 ....162 H2
HSLW TW3 ....159 F6
THMD SE28 ....135 G6
Dean Ryle St WEST SW1P 29 E1
Deansbrook Cl EDGW HA8 ....62 C3
Deansbrook Rd EDGW HA8 ....62 D2
Dean's Buildings WALW SE17 ....19 H7
Deans Cl CHSWK W4 ....142 B6
CROY/NA CRO 247 F1
EDGW HA8 ....62 C3
Dean's Ct BLKFR EC4V 12 D4
Deanscroft Av CDALE/KGS NW9 ....82 C6
Dean's Dr MLHL NW7 ....46 C2
PLMGR N13 ....41 H2
Deans Ga Cl FSTH SE23 ....190 B5
Dean's La EDGW HA8 ....62 C2
Dean's Ms CAVSO/HST * W1G 11 H3
Deans Rd HNWL W7 ....116 A1
SUT SM1 ....209 F4
Dean Stanley St WEST * SW1P 21 H4
Dean St FSTGT E7 ....112 C3
SOHO/CST W1F 12 B4
Deansway ED N9 ....54 A1
EFNCH N2 ....85 H1
Deans Wy EDGW HA8 ....62 D3
Dean Trench St WEST * SW1P 21 E6
Deane Cl STAN HA7 ....60 C1
De'am Gdns MTCM CR4 ....206 A6
Dearsley Rd EN EN1 ....39 G4
Deason St SRTFD * E15 ....111 G6
De Barowe Ms HBRY * N5 ....108 B2
Debden Cl KUTN/CMB KT2 ....201 F1
WFD IG8 ....73 F3
De Beauvoir Crs IS N1 ....109 E6
De Beauvoir Est IS * N1 ....109 E6
De Beauvoir Rd IS N1 ....109 E5
De Beauvoir Sq IS N1 ....109 E5
Debnams Rd
BERM/RHTH SE16 ....150 A4
De Bohun Av STHGT/OAK N14 ....50 D1
Deborah Cl ISLW TW7 ....160 A2
Debrabant Cl ERITH DA8 ....157 H6
De Broome Rd FELT TW13 ....178 A5
Deburgh Rd WIM/MER SW19 ....205 G3
Decima St STHWK SE1 ....24 A3
Decimus Cl SNWD * SE25 ....228 D1
Deck Cl BERM/RHTH SE16 ....150 B1
Decoy Av GLDGN NW11 ....84 C2
De Crespigny Pk CMBW SE5 ....168 D3
Deeley Rd VX/NE SW8 ....167 F2
Dee Rd RCH/KEW TW9 ....161 A1
Deepdale WIM/MER SW19 ....184 B6
Deepdale Av HAYES BR2 ....232 B1
Deepdale Cl FBAR/BDGN N11 ....66 C2
Deepdene Av CROY/NA CRO 247 C1
Deepdene Cl WAN E11 ....92 C4
Deepdene Ct WINCHMN N21 ....52 B1
Deepdene Gdns
BRXS/STRHM SW2 ....188 A5
Deepdene Rd HNHL SE24 ....168 C5
WELL DA16 ....175 C4
Deepwell Cl ISLW TW7 ....160 C2
Deepwood La GFD/PVL UB6 ....119 H2
Deerbrook Rd
BRXS/STRHM SW2 ....188 A3
Deerdale Rd HNHL SE24 ....168 C5
Deerhurst Crs HPTN TW12 ....199 G1
Deerhurst Rd
KIL/WHAMP NW6 ....104 D1
STRHM/NOR SW16 ....207 H1
Deerleap Gv CHING E4 ....31 K2
Dee Rd RCH/KEW TW9 ....161 H1
Deer Park Cl KUTN/CMB KT2 ....202 A1
Deer Park Gdns MTCM * CR4 ....225 H1
Deer Park Rd WIM/MER SW19 ......205 F5
Deer Park Wy WWKM BR4 ....232 B6
Deeside Rd TOOT SW17 ....185 H5
Dee St POP/IOD E14 ....131 C5
Defiant Wy WLGTN SM6 ....245 E6
Defoe Av RCH/KEW TW9 ....125 J6
Defoe Cl WIM/MER SW19 ....206 A2
Defoe Rd BERM/RHTH SE16 ....150 D2
STNW/STAM N16 ....86 E6
Defoe Wy CRW RM5 ....56 D1
De Frene Rd SYD SE26 ....190 D6
Degema Rd CHST BR7 ....214 B1
Dehar Crs CDALE/KGS NW9 ....83 H1
De Havilland Cl NTHLT UB5 ....118 B2
De Havilland Rd EDGW HA8 ....44 D5
HEST TW5 ....134 A6
WLGTN SM6 ....245 G5
Dekker Rd DUL SE21 ....189 E1
Delacourt Rd BKHTH/KID SE3 ....134 A1
Delafield Rd CHARL SE7 ....136 A6
Delaford Rd BERM/RHTH SE16 ....151 J4
Delaford St FUL/PGN SW6 ....147 H1
Delamare Crs CROY/NA CRO 197 J6
Delamere Gdns MLHL NW7 ....62 D1
Delamere Rd EA W5 ....117 F1
RYNPK SW20 ....205 H1
WEA W13 ....118 B6
Delamere St BAY/PAD W2 ....125 C4
Delancey Pas CAMTN NW1 ....106 D6
Delancey St CAMTN NW1 ....106 D6
De Lapre Cl STMC/STPC BR5 ....236 B4
De Laune St WALW SE17 ....30 C6
Delaware Rd MV/WKIL W9 ....125 F3
Delawyk Crs HNHL SE24 ....169 G1
Delcombe Av WPK KT4 ....224 D5
Delhi Rd EN EN1 ....53 F2
Delia St WAND/EARL SW18 ....185 F2
Delisle Rd THMD SE28 ....155 E2

Delius Cl BORE WD6 ....45 E1
Dell Cl SRTFD E15 ....111 H6
WFD IG8 ....56 D5
WLGTN SM6 ....245 E2
Dellfield Cl BECK BR3 ....211 G4
Dell La EW KT17 ....241 G3
Dellors Cl BAR EN5 ....34 B6
Dellow Cl GNTH/NBYPK IG2 ....94 D4
Dellow St WCHPL E1 ....17 H5
Dell Rd EW KT17 ....241 G4
PEND EN3 ....40 A1
Dells Cl CHING E4 ....55 F2
Dell's Ms PIM * SW1V 88 B2
The Dell ABYW SE2 ....155 G5
ALP/SUD HA0 ....100 D3
BECK * BR3 ....211 J3
BTFD TW8 ....141 E6
NRWD SE19 ....209 F4
PIN HA5 ....58 D5
WFD IG8 ....56 D5
Dell Wk NWMAL KT3 ....203 E5
Dell Wy WEA W13 ....121 E5
Dellwood Gdns CLAY IG5 ....74 A6
Delme Crs BKHTH/KID SE3 ....172 D3
Delmey Cl CROY/NA CRO 247 F1
Deloraine St DEPT SE8 ....152 D2
Delorme St HMSMTH W6 ....144 B6
Delta Cl WPK KT4 ....241 E1
Delta Est BETH * E2 ....7 J3
Delta Gain OXHEY WD19 ....27 J3
Delta Gv NTHLT UB5 ....118 B2
Delta Rd WPK KT4 ....241 E1
Delta St BETH E2 ....7 J3
De Luci Rd ERITH DA8 ....157 G5
De Lucy St ABYW SE2 ....155 J4
Delvers Md DAGE RM10 ....117 E2
Delverton Rd WALW SE17 ....30 D3
Delvino Rd FUL/PGN SW6 ....165 E1
De Mandeville Ga EN EN1 ....39 G5
Demesne Rd WLGTN SM6 ....245 F2
Demeta Cl WBLY HA9 ....102 C1
De Montfort Pde
STRHM/NOR * SW16 ....187 G5
De Montfort Rd
STRHM/NOR SW16 ....187 F4
De Morgan Rd FUL/PGN SW6 ....165 F4
Dempster Rd
WAND/EARL SW18 ....165 G6
Denberry Dr SCUP DA14 ....195 H5
Denbigh Cl CHST BR7 ....213 H2
NTGHL W11 ....124 D6
STHL UB1 ....118 D5
SUT SM1 ....241 J3
WLSDN NW10 ....103 E5
Denbigh Gdns
RCHPK/HAM TW10 ....161 H6
Denbigh Pl PIM SW1V 28 A3
Denbigh Rd EHAM E6 ....113 J2
HSLW TW3 ....135 F3
NTGHL W11 ....124 D6
WEA W13 ....120 D6
Denbigh St PIM SW1V 28 B5
Denbigh Ter NTGHL W11 ....124 D6
Denbridge Rd BMLY BR1 ....213 H5
Den Cl BECK BR3 ....211 H2
Dendy St BAL SW12 ....188 C3
Dene Av BFN/LL DA15 ....195 H2
HSLW TW3 ....158 D1
Dene Cl BROCKY SE4 ....170 C4
HAYES BR2 ....232 B5
WPK KT4 ....223 F6
Dene Dr ORP BR6 ....255 H1
Dene Gdns STAN HA7 ....61 E1
THDIT KT7 ....224 B2
Denehurst Gdns ACT W3 ....142 B1
HDN NW4 ....64 A3
RCHPK/HAM TW10 ....162 A5
WFD IG8 ....56 D6
WHTN TW2 ....179 G2
Dene Rd BKHH IG9 ....57 C3
TRDG/WHET N20 ....38 B2
WBLY HA9 ....101 G2
WOT/HER KT12 ....218 D2
Denewood BAR EN5 ....35 E4
Denewood Rd HGT N6 ....86 A3
Dengie Wk IS * N1 ....108 C6
Dengil Crs KTTN NW5 ....226 C6
Denham Crs MTCM CR4 ....226 B1
Denham Dr GNTH/NBYPK IG2 ....94 E5
Denham Rd EBED/NFEELT TW14 ..178 A2
TRDG/WHET N20 ....50 B5
Denham Wy BARK IG11 ....115 E6
Denholme Rd MV/WKIL W9 ....124 D2
Denison Cl EFNCH N2 ....85 H1
Denison Rd EA W5 ....116 J1
WIM/MER SW19 ....205 H2
Deniston Av BXLY DA5 ....196 B3
Denleigh Gdns THDIT * KT7 ....220 A3
WCHMN N21 ....52 A2
Denman Dr ESH/CLAY KT10 ....238 C3
GLDGN NW11 ....65 E3
Denman Dr North GLDGN NW11 .....85 E2
Denman Dr South GLDGN NW11 .....65 E2
Denman Rd PECK SE15 ....169 F2
Denman St REGST W1B 12 B6
Denmark Av WIM/MER SW19 ....205 C2
Denmark Ct MRDN SM4 ....225 J3
Denmark Gdns CAR SM5 ....224 E1
Denmark Gv IS N1 ....6 A1
Denmark Hill HNHL SE24 ....168 D2
CDALE/KGS NW9 ....63 C5
Denmark Rd BMLY BR1 ....213 E5
CAR SM5 ....244 D1
CEND/HSY/T N8 ....67 F2
CMBW SE5 ....168 C2
KIL/WHAMP NW6 ....108 D3
KUT/HW KT1 ....201 G6
SNWD SE25 ....229 H4
WEA W13 ....116 C1
WHTN TW2 ....179 H5
WIM/MER SW19 ....205 H1
Denmark St LSQ/SEVD WC2H 11 H3
PLSTW E13 ....132 D4
TOTM N17 ....56 C1
WALTH E17 ....69 H2
WAN E11 ....92 A2
Denmark Ter EFNCH * N2 ....86 B1

Denmead Rd CROY/NA CR0 ...228 B5
Dennan Rd SURB KT6 ...221 H5
Denner Rd CHING E4 ...55 G4
Denne Ter HACK E8 ...109 F6
Dennett Rd CROY/NA CR0 ...228 A4
Dennett's Gv NWCR SE14 ...170 B5
Dennett's Rd NWCR SE14 ...170 A2
Denning Av CROY/NA CR0 ...246 A4
Denning Cl HPTN TW12 ...198 D2
  STJWD NW8 ...125 C2
Denning Rd HAMP NW3 ...105 H2
Dennington Park Rd
  KIL/WHAMP NW6 ...105 E4
The Denningtons WPK KT4 ...223 E6
Dennis Av WBLY HA9 ...101 H5
Dennis Cl STAN HA7 ...61 E1
Dennis La STAN HA7 ...44 A6
Dennis Pde STHGT/OAK * N14 ...51 F3
Dennis Park Crs RYNPK SW20 ...204 C4
Dennis Reeve Cl MTCM CR4 ...206 A6
Dennis Rd E/WMO/HCT KT8 ...219 G1
Dennis Wy CLAP SW4 ...167 F4
Denny Crs LBTH SE11 ...30 B5
Denny Rd ED N18 ...53 H3
Denny St LBTH SE11 ...30 B5
Den Rd HAYES DR2 ...211 H6
Densham Rd SRTFD E15 ...112 A6
Densole Cl BECK * BR3 ...210 C4
Densworth Gv ED N9 ...54 B5
Denton Cl BAR EN5 ...34 A6
Denton Gv WOT/HER KT12 ...218 D6
Denton Rd CEND/HSY/T N8 ...87 H2
  TWK TW1 ...181 F1
  UED N18 ...53 H1
  WELL DA16 ...176 A1
Denton St WAND/EARL SW18 ...185 F1
Denton Wy CLPT E5 ...110 B1
Dents Rd BTSEA SW11 ...186 D1
Denver Cl ORP BR6 ...235 E3
Denver Rd STNW/STAM N16 ...89 E4
Denyer St CHEL SW3 ...26 D1
Denzil Rd WLSDN NW10 ...103 F3
Deodar Rd PUT/ROE SW15 ...164 C5
Deodora Cl TRDG/WHET N20 ...50 A5
Depot Ap CRICK NW2 ...104 B2
Depot Rd HSLW TW3 ...159 H4
Depot St CMBW SE5 ...31 G6
Deptford Br DEPT SE8 ...9 F4
Deptford Broadway DEPT SE8 ...171 E2
Deptford Church St DEPT SE8 ...171 E1
Deptford Gn DEPT SE8 ...151 E6
Deptford High St DEPT SE8 ...151 E6
Deptford Market DEPT * SE8 ...171 E1
Deptford Wharf DEPT SE8 ...150 D4
De Quincey Rd TOTM N17 ...68 D4
Derby Av HRW/WEW/H HA3 ...59 H4
  NFNCH/WDSP N12 ...65 G1
  ROMW/RG RM7 ...75 H2
Derby Ga WHALL SW1A ...21 E3
Derby Hl FSTH SE23 ...190 A4
Derby Hill Crs FSTH SE23 ...190 A4
Derby Rd BRYLDS KT5 ...210 C5
  CROY/NA CR0 ...228 B6
  FSTGT E7 ...113 F5
  GFD/PVL UB6 ...99 F6
  HOM E9 ...110 D6
  HSLW TW3 ...159 F5
  MORT/ESHN SW14 ...162 B5
  PEND EN3 ...39 H6
  SUT SM1 ...242 D4
  SWFD E18 ...72 B4
  UED N18 ...70 A1
  WIM/MER SW19 ...205 E3
Derbyshire St BETH E2 ...9 F4
Derby St MYFR/PICC W1J ...9 H2
Dereham Pl SDTC EC2A ...7 F2
  SDTCH EC2A ...8 B5
Dereham Rd BARK IG11 ...115 F4
Derek Cl HOR/WEW KT19 ...240 H4
  WBLY HA9 ...102 B5
  WLGTN SM6 ...244 D1
Derek Walcott Cl HNHL * SE24 ...168 B6
Dericote St HACK E8 ...86 C6
Derifall Cl EHAM E6 ...133 H4
Dering Pl CROY/NA CR0 ...246 C2
Dering Rd CROY/NA CR0 ...246 C2
Dering St CONDST W1S ...11 G4
Derinton Rd TOOT SW17 ...186 C6
Derley Rd NWDGN UB2 ...138 A3
Dermody Gdns LEW * SE13 ...171 H6
Dermody Rd LEW SE13 ...171 H6
Deronda Rd BRXS/STRHM SW2 ...188 B3
Deroy Cl CAR SM5 ...244 B4
Derrick Gdns CHARL SE7 ...158 E3
Derrick Rd BECK BR3 ...210 D6
Derry Downs STMC/STPC BR5 ...236 A3
Derry Rd WLGTN SM6 ...245 G1
Derry St KENS W8 ...145 E3
Dersingham Av MNPK E12 ...113 H2
Dersingham Rd CRICK NW2 ...104 C1
Derwent Av CDALE/KGS NW9 ...45 E2
  EBAR EN4 ...50 B3
  MLHL NW7 ...37 F4
  PIN HA5 ...58 C2
  PUT/ROE SW15 ...183 E6
  UED N18 ...69 F1
Derwent Cl ESH/CLAY KT10 ...238 A4
  NFNCH/WDSP N12 ...49 G2
  STAN HA7 ...61 E5
Derwent Dr STMC/STPC BR5 ...234 D4
Derwent Gdns REDBR IG4 ...93 C1
  WBLY HA9 ...81 E4
Derwent Gv EDUL SE22 ...169 F5
Derwent Ri CDALE/KGS NW9 ...85 E3
Derwent Rd EA W5 ...141 E5
  MRDN SM4 ...224 B3
  PGE/AN SE20 ...209 C5
  PLMGR N13 ...53 C3
  STHL UB1 ...118 D5
  WHTN TW2 ...179 F1
Derwent St GNWCH SE10 ...152 A5
Derwentwater Rd ACT W3 ...142 C1
Derwent Yd EA * W5 ...141 E5
Desborough Cl BAY/PAD W2 ...125 F4
Desenfans Rd DUL SE21 ...189 E1
Desford Rd CAN/RD E16 ...132 A3
Desmond St NWCR SE14 ...150 D6
Despard Rd ARCH N19 ...87 D5

Detling Rd BMLY BR1 ...212 C1
  ERITH DA8 ...177 H1
Detmold Rd CLPT E5 ...89 H6
Devalls Cl EHAM E6 ...134 A6
Devana End CAR SM5 ...244 B1
Devas Rd RYNPK SW20 ...204 A4
Devas St BOW E3 ...131 F5
Devema Cl CHST BR7 ...214 A4
Devenay Rd SRTFD E15 ...112 D5
Devenish Rd ABYW SE2 ...155 G2
De Vere Gdns IL IG1 ...93 H6
  KENS W8 ...145 G2
Deverell St STHWK SE1 ...23 G6
De Vere Ms KENS * W8 ...145 G3
Devereux Ct TPL/STR WC2R ...14 A4
Devereux La BARN SW13 ...163 H1
Devereux Rd BTSEA SW11 ...185 E4
Devey Cl KUTN/CMB KT2 ...203 F3
Devizes St IS N1 ...108 D6
Devon Av WHTN TW2 ...179 G3
Devon Cl BKHH IG9 ...56 D4
  GFD/PVL UB6 ...101 E6
  TOTM N17 ...68 A4
Devoncroft Gdns TWK TW1 ...180 C2
Devon Gdns FSBYPK N4 ...88 B3
Devonhurst Pl CHSWK * W4 ...142 D5
Devonia Gdns UED N18 ...68 C2
Devonia Rd IS N1 ...6 B1
Devon Man
  KTN/HRWW/W * HA3 ...81 E2
Devonport Gdns IL IG1 ...93 H5
Devonport Ms SHB * W12 ...143 H1
Devonport Rd SHB W12 ...143 H2
Devonport St WCHPL E1 ...130 A5
Devon Ri EFNCH N2 ...85 H1
Devon Rd BARK IG11 ...108 D1
  BELMT SM2 ...242 C6
Devons Est BOW E3 ...131 F2
Devonshire Av BELMT SM2 ...243 G5
Devonshire Cl CAVSO/HST W1G ...11 G1
  SRTFD E15 ...112 A2
Devonshire Crs MLHL NW7 ...46 B3
Devonshire Dr GNWCH SE10 ...171 F2
  SURB KT6 ...221 F5
Devonshire Gdns CHSWK W4 ...162 C1
  TOTM N17 ...67 H2
  WCHMH N21 ...52 C2
Devonshire Gv PECK SE15 ...33 H6
Devonshire Hill La TOTM N17 ...68 C2
Devonshire Ms South
  CAVSO/HST W1G ...11 G1
Devonshire Ms West
  CAVSO/HST W1G ...3 F6
Devonshire Pl CAVSO/HST W1G ...3 F6
  CRICK NW2 ...105 E1
  KENS * W8 ...145 F3
Devonshire Place Ms
  MHST W1U ...3 F6
Devonshire Rd BELMT SM2 ...243 F5
  BXLYHS DA6 ...176 C5
  CAN/RD E16 ...132 D5
  CAR SM5 ...244 C2
  CHSWK W4 ...143 E5
  CROY/NA CR0 ...228 D4
  ED N9 ...54 A3
  ELTH/MOT SE9 ...190 A3
  FELT TW13 ...178 C5
  FSTH SE23 ...190 B2
  GNTH/NBYPK IG2 ...94 H3
  HRW HA1 ...60 D4
  MLHL NW7 ...46 C3
  ORP BR6 ...235 G4
  PIN HA5 ...40 D6
  PLMGR N13 ...51 H5
  STHL UB1 ...116 C2
  TOTM N17 ...67 H2
  WALTH E17 ...91 E1
  WEA W13 ...141 H5
  WIM/MER SW19 ...206 A3
Devonshire Rw LVPST EC2M ...16 B2
Devonshire Sq HAYES BR2 ...232 D1
  LVPST EC2M ...16 C2
Devonshire St CAVSO/HST W1G ...11 F1
  CHSWK W4 ...143 E5
Devonshire Ter BAY/PAD W2 ...125 F5
  EDUL * SE22 ...169 G3
Devonshire Wy CROY/NA CR0 ...230 D4
Devons Rd BOW E3 ...131 E4
Devon St PECK SE15 ...33 H5
Devon Wy CHSGTN KT9 ...239 E2
  HOR/WEW KT19 ...240 B3
Devon Waye HEST TW5 ...158 D1
De Walden St CAVSO/HST W1G ...11 F2
Dewar St PECK SE15 ...169 G4
Dewberry Gdns EHAM E6 ...133 G4
Dewberry St POP/IOD E14 ...131 F5
Dewey Rd DAGE RM10 ...117 F4
  IS N1 ...6 A1
Dewey St TOOT SW17 ...206 B1
Dewhurst Rd HMSMTH W6 ...144 B2
Dewsbury Cl PIN HA5 ...78 C2
Dewsbury Gdns WPK KT4 ...241 C1
Dewsbury Rd WLSDN NW10 ...103 G3
Dexter Rd BAR EN5 ...33 C5
Deyncourt Rd TOTM N17 ...68 A1
Deynecourt Gdns WAN E11 ...93 E1
D'eynsford Rd CMBW SE5 ...168 D2
Diadem Ct SOHO/SHAV * W1D ...12 C3
Diameter Rd STMC/STPC BR5 ...234 D4
Diamond Cl BCTR RM8 ...96 A5
Diamond Rd RSLP HA4 ...98 B2
Diamond St PECK SE15 ...169 E1
  WLSDN NW10 ...81 G5
Diana Cl DEPT SE8 ...150 D6
  SWFD E18 ...73 E4
Diana Gdns SURB KT6 ...221 H6
Diana Pl CAMTN NW1 ...3 H5
Diana Rd WALTH E17 ...70 D6
Dianne Wy EBAR EN4 ...34 C4
Dianthus Cl ABYW * SE2 ...155 C4
Dibden St IS N1 ...6 C1
Dibdin Cl SUT SM1 ...208 D6
Dibdin Rd SUT SM1 ...208 D6
Dicey Av CRICK NW2 ...104 A3
Dickens Av FNCH N3 ...65 G4
Dickens Cl ERITH DA8 ...177 F1
  RCHPK/HAM * TW10 ...181 G4
Dickens Dr CHST BR7 ...214 C2
Dickens Est BERM/RHTH SE16 ...25 G3
Dickens La UED N18 ...69 E1

Dickens Ms FARR EC1M ...6 C6
Dickenson Rd CEND/HSY/T N8 ...87 G4
  FELT TW13 ...198 A1
Dickenson's La SNWD SE25 ...229 G3
Dickenson's Pl SNWD SE25 ...229 G3
Dickens Rd EHAM E6 ...133 F1
Dickens Sq STHWK SE1 ...18 B5
Dickens St VX/NE SW8 ...166 D5
Dickerage Hl NWMAL KT3 ...202 C5
Dickerage La NWMAL KT3 ...202 C5
Dickerage Rd KUT KT1 ...202 C4
Dickson Fold PIN HA5 ...59 H1
Dickson Rd ELTH/MOT SE9 ...173 G4
Didsbury Cl EHAM E6 ...133 H6
Digby Cl FSBYPK N4 ...88 C6
Digby Gdns DAGE RM10 ...117 H6
Digby Pl CROY/NA CR0 ...247 F1
Digby Rd BARK IG11 ...115 F5
  HOM E9 ...110 B4
Digby St BETH E2 ...130 D2
Diggon St WCHPL E1 ...130 B4
Dighton Rd WAND/EARL SW18 ...165 G6
Dignum St IS * N1 ...6 A1
Digswell St HOLWY * N7 ...85 G4
Dilhorne Cl LEE/GVPK SE12 ...192 D5
Dilke St CHEL SW3 ...26 D5
Dilloway La NWDGN UB2 ...190 C6
Dilston Cl NTHLT UB5 ...118 A2
Dilton Gdns PUT/ROE SW15 ...183 G5
Dimes Pl HMSMTH W6 ...143 H4
Dimmock Dr NTHLT UB5 ...99 H5
Dimond Cl FSTGT E7 ...112 C2
Dimsdale Dr CDALE/KGS NW9 ...62 C5
  EN EN1 ...53 G2
Dimson Crs BOW E3 ...131 E3
Dingle Cl BAR EN5 ...47 F1
Dingle Gdns POP/IOD * E14 ...131 G6
Dingley La STRHM/NOR SW16 ...187 F4
Dingley Pl FSBYE EC1V ...7 F4
Dingley Rd FSBYE EC1V ...7 E4
Dingwall Av CROY/NA CR0 ...228 C1
Dingwall Gdns GLDGN NW11 ...85 E3
Dingwall Rd CAR SM5 ...244 B6
  CROY/NA CR0 ...228 D6
  WAND/EARL SW18 ...185 G2
Dinmont Est BETH E2 ...9 H2
Dinmont St BETH E2 ...9 H2
Dinsdale Gdns BAR EN5 ...35 F6
  SNWD SE25 ...229 G4
Dinsdale Rd BKHTH/KID SE3 ...152 B6
Dinsmore Rd BAL SW12 ...186 D2
Dinton Rd KUTN/CMB KT2 ...201 H5
  WIM/MER SW19 ...205 H2
Diploma Av EFNCH N2 ...86 A1
Dirleton Rd SRTFD E15 ...112 B6
Disbrowe Rd HMSMTH W6 ...144 C6
Discovery Wk WAP E1W ...17 G6
Dishforth La CDALE/KGS NW9 ...45 G4
Disney Pl STHWK SE1 ...23 F3
Disney St STHWK SE1 ...23 F3
Disraeli Cl PEND EN3 ...40 B2
  THMD SE28 ...155 H1
Disraeli Rd EA W5 ...141 F1
  FSTGT E7 ...112 C4
  PUT/ROE SW15 ...164 C5
  WLSDN NW10 ...100 D2
Diss St BETH E2 ...9 G5
Distaff La BLKFR EC4V ...15 E5
Distillery La HMSMTH W6 ...144 A5
Distillery Rd HMSMTH W6 ...144 A5
District Rd GFD/PVL UB6 ...100 D3
Ditchburn St POP/IOD E14 ...131 G6
Ditchfield Rd YEAD UB4 ...118 C3
Dittisham Rd ELTH/MOT SE9 ...195 G6
Ditton Cl THDIT KT7 ...220 C4
Dittoncroft Cl SAND/SEL CR2 ...247 E2
Ditton Grange Cl SURB KT6 ...221 F5
Ditton Grange Dr SURB KT6 ...221 E5
Ditton Hill SURB KT6 ...221 E5
Ditton Hill Rd SURB KT6 ...221 E5
Ditton Lawn THDIT KT7 ...220 C5
Ditton Pl PGE/AN * SE20 ...209 H4
Ditton Reach THDIT KT7 ...220 D3
Ditton Rd BXLYHS DA6 ...176 B6
  NWDGN UB2 ...138 D5
  SURB KT6 ...221 E6
Dixey Cottages EFNCH * N2 ...86 A2
Dixon Pl WWKM BR4 ...231 F5
Dixon Rd NWCR SE14 ...151 F2
  SNWD SE25 ...209 E6
Dobbin Cl KTN/HRWW/W HA3 ...60 C5
Dobell Rd ELTH/MOT SE9 ...173 H6
Dobree Av WLSDN NW10 ...100 H5
Dobson Cl KIL/WHAMP NW6 ...105 H3
Dockers Tanner Rd
  POP/IOD E14 ...151 E4
Dockhead STHWK SE1 ...24 D4
Dock Hill Av BERM/RHTH SE16 ...150 B2
Dockland St CAN/RD E16 ...154 A2
Dockley Rd BERM/RHTH SE16 ...25 E6
Dock Rd BTFD * TW8 ...161 F1
  CAN/RD E16 ...132 B6
Dockside Rd CAN/RD E16 ...133 F6
Dock St WCHPL E1 ...17 E5
Doctors Cl SYD SE26 ...210 A1
Docwra's Bldgs IS * N1 ...86 D6
Doddington Gv WALW SE17 ...30 C5
Doddington Pl WALW SE17 ...30 C5
Dodsley Pl ED N9 ...54 A5
Dodson St STHWK SE1 ...22 B2
Dod St POP/IOD E14 ...130 D5
Doebury Wk
  WOOL/PLUM SE18 ...155 G6
Doel Cl WIM/MER SW19 ...205 G5
Doggett Rd CAT SE6 ...174 B6
Doggetts Ct EBAR EN4 ...36 A4
Dog Kennel Hl CMBW SE5 ...169 E4
Dog La WLSDN NW10 ...103 B2
Doherty Rd PLSTW E13 ...132 C3
Dolben St STHWK SE1 ...22 D1
Dolby Rd FUL/PGN SW6 ...164 D3
Doley Wy HSLWW TW4 ...158 B2
Dollary Pde KUT * KT1 ...202 B6
Dollis Av FNCH N3 ...64 C4
Dollis Crs RSLP HA4 ...77 B5
Dollis Hill Av CRICK NW2 ...103 H1

Dollis Hill Est CRICK * NW2 ...103 G1
Dollis Hill La CRICK NW2 ...103 F2
Dollis Pk FNCH N3 ...64 D4
Dollis Rd FNCH N3 ...64 C5
Dollis Valley Green Wk
  GLDGN NW11 ...84 C1
  TRDG/WHET N20 ...49 F1
Dolman Cl FNCH N3 ...65 G5
Dolman Rd CHSWK W4 ...142 D4
Dolman St CLAP SW4 ...167 H5
Dolphin Cl SURB KT6 ...221 F3
  THMD SE28 ...136 A5
Dolphin Ct POP/IOD E14 ...131 F6
Dolphin La POP/IOD E14 ...131 F6
Dolphin Rd NTHLT UB5 ...118 D1
  PIM SW1V ...28 C4
Dolphin Sq CHSWK * W4 ...163 E1
Dolphin St KUT KT1 ...201 G5
Dombey St BMSBY WC1N ...13 H1
Dome Buildings
  RCHPK/HAM * TW10 ...161 F6
Domett Cl CMBW SE5 ...168 D5
Domingo St FSBYE EC1V ...7 E5
Dominica Cl PLSTW E13 ...133 C1
Dominion Dr CRW RM5 ...77 F2
Dominion Pde HRW * HA1 ...80 B2
Dominion Rd CROY/NA CR0 ...229 F4
  NWDGN UB2 ...136 A1
Dominion St LVPST EC2M ...15 H1
Domonic Dr ELTH/MOT SE9 ...194 B5
Domville Cl TRDG/WHET N20 ...49 H4
Donald Dr CHDH RM6 ...96 A2
Donald Rd CROY/NA CR0 ...227 H3
  PLSTW E13 ...112 D6
Donaldson Rd
  KIL/WHAMP NW6 ...104 D6
  WOOL/PLUM SE18 ...174 A2
Donald Woods Gdns
  BRYLDS KT5 ...222 B6
Doncaster Dr NTHLT UB5 ...98 D5
Doncaster Gdns FSBYPK * N4 ...88 B3
  NTHLT UB5 ...98 D5
Doncaster Gn OXHEY WD19 ...58 A1
Doncaster Rd ED N9 ...55 H2
Donegal St IS N1 ...5 G2
Doneraile St FUL/PGN SW6 ...164 B3
Dongola Rd PLSTW E13 ...132 D2
  TOTM N17 ...67 H4
Dongola Rd West PLSTW E13 ...132 D2
Donington Av BARK/HLT IG6 ...94 C2
Donkey Aly EDUL SE22 ...189 C2
Donkey La EN EN1 ...39 C5
Donnefield Av EDGW HA8 ...61 C2
Donne Pl CHEL SW3 ...26 B1
  MTCM CR4 ...243 G1
Donne Rd BCTR RM8 ...96 A6
Donnington Rd
  KTN/HRWW/W HA3 ...81 F3
  WLSDN NW10 ...103 H6
  WPK KT4 ...223 G6
Donnybrook Rd
  STRHM/NOR SW16 ...207 E3
Donoghue Cottages
  POP/IOD * E14 ...130 C4
Donovan Av MUSWH N10 ...66 C5
Don Phelan Cl CMBW SE5 ...168 D2
Doon Cl TEDD TW11 ...200 C2
Doorson Cl SHB * W12 ...123 H6
Doral Wy CAR SM5 ...244 B3
Doran Gv WOOL/PLUM SE18 ...175 F1
Dora Rd WIM/MER SW19 ...205 H5
Dora St POP/IOD E14 ...130 C5
Dorchester Av BXLY DA5 ...196 B3
  PLMGR N13 ...52 C6
  RYLN/HDSTN HA2 ...78 A3
Dorchester Cl NTHLT UB5 ...99 F3
  STMC/STPC BR5 ...215 H5
Dorchester Ct CRICK NW2 ...104 C2
  HNHL SE24 ...168 C4
  STHGT/OAK N14 ...34 C2
Dorchester Gdns CHING E4 ...55 G2
  GLDGN * NW11 ...65 E1
Dorchester Gv CHSWK W4 ...143 E6
Dorchester Ms TWK TW1 ...181 E1
Dorchester Pde
  STRHM/NOR * SW16 ...187 H4
Dorchester Rd MRDN SM4 ...225 F4
  NTHLT UB5 ...99 F3
  WPK KT4 ...224 B5
Dorchester Ter HDN * NW4 ...64 B5
Dorchester Wy
  KTN/HRWW/W HA3 ...81 H3
Dorchester Waye YEAD UB4 ...118 A5
Dorcis Av BXLYHS DA7 ...176 A1
Dordrecht Rd ACT W3 ...143 E1
Dore Av MNPK E12 ...114 A3
Doreen Av CDALE/KGS NW9 ...62 D5
Dore Gdns MRDN SM4 ...225 F4
Dorell Cl STHL UB1 ...118 D4
Dorian Est WCHPL E1 ...13 H3
Doria Rd FUL/PGN SW6 ...164 D3
Doric Wy CAMTN NW1 ...4 C4
Dorien Rd RYNPK SW20 ...222 A2
Doris Av ERITH DA8 ...177 G2
Doris Rd FSTGT E7 ...112 D3
Dorking Cl DEPT SE8 ...150 D6
  WPK KT4 ...224 D5
Dorlcote Rd WAND/EARL SW18 ...185 H2
Dorman Pl ED * N9 ...54 C6
Dorman Wy STJWD NW8 ...105 H6
Dormay St WAND/EARL SW18 ...165 H6
Dormer Cl BAR EN5 ...34 B4
  SRTFD E15 ...112 C4
Dormers Av STHL UB1 ...119 E5
Dormers Rd BKHTH/KID SE3 ...173 F2
Dormer's Wells La STHL UB1 ...119 F5
Dornberg Cl BKHTH/KID SE3 ...172 D1
Dornberg Rd BKHTH/KID * SE3 ...172 D1
Dorncliffe Rd FUL/PGN SW6 ...147 G6
Dorney NTHWD * HA6 ...40 A2
Dorney Ri STMC/STPC BR5 ...235 F1
Dorney Wy HSLWW TW4 ...158 D2
Dornfell St KIL/WHAMP NW6 ...104 D3
Dornton Rd BAL SW12 ...188 B1
  SAND/SEL CR2 ...245 H2
Dorothy Av ALP/SUD HA0 ...101 G3
Dorothy Evans Cl BXLYHS DA7 ...177 H3
Dorothy Gdns BCTR RM8 ...115 H2
Dorothy Rd BTSEA SW11 ...166 B4

Dorrington St *HCIRC* EC1N 14 A1
Dorrit St *STHWK* * SE1 ....23 F3
Dorrit Wy *CHST* BR7.......................214 C2
Dors Cl *CDALE/KGS* NW9 ....82 D5
Dorset Av *NWDGN* UB2 ....139 E4
ROM RM1...117 H6
WELL DA16...175 F5
Dorset Buildings *EMB* * EC4Y 14 C4
Dorset Cl *CAMTN* NW1 * 10 C1
Dorset Dr *EDGW* HA8.........................21 H2
Dorset Gdns
STRHM/NOR SW16.........................227 H1
Dorset Ms *MHST* W1U 5 E4
KTBR SW1X 15 G5
Dorset Pl *SRTFD* E15........................111 H4
Dorset Ri *EMB* EC4Y 14 C4
Dorset Rd *BECK* BR3.........................210 B6
EA W5 ....141 E3
ELTH/MOT SE9 ....193 G4
HRW HA1..79 G3
MTCM CR4...206 A5
SEVS/STOTM N15................................68 A1
VX/NE SW8 ....167 H1
WDGN N22...67 G4
WIM/MER SW19 ....205 E4
Dorset Sq *CAMTN* NW1 * 2 C6
Dorset St *MHST* W1U 10 D2
Dorset Wy *WHTN* TW2.......................179 C3
Dorset Waye *HEST* TW5.....................158 D1
Dorton Cl *PECK* * SE15.....................169 E1
Dorville Crs *HMSMTH* W6 ....143 H3
Dorville Rd *LEE/GVPK* SE12..............172 C6
Dothill Rd *WOOL/PLUM* SE18............174 C1
Doual Gv *HPTN* TW12 ....199 G4
Doughty Ms *BMSBY* WC1N 5 G5
Doughty St *BMSBY* WC1N 5 G5
Douglas Av *ALP/SUD* HA0..................109 H1
NWMAL KT3..192 C1
WALTH E17 ....71 E4
Douglas Cl *STAN* HA7 ....60 C1
WLGTN SM6..245 G4
Douglas Crs *YEAD* UB4......................118 A3
Douglas Dr *CROY/NA* CR0 ....249 E1
Douglas Est *IS* * N1 ....108 C4
Douglas Ms *CRICK* NW2....................104 C1
Douglas Pl *POP/IOD* * E14 ....151 G5
Douglas Rd *DAGE/RD E16..................132 C4
CHING E4 ....56 A2
ESH/CLAY KT10 ....219 H6
HSLW TW3..159 F4
IS N1 ....108 C5
KIL/WHAMP NW6 ....104 D6
KUT KT1 ....202 B5
SURB KT6..221 H6
WDGN N22...68 A4
WELL DA16...175 H2
Douglas Rd North *IS* N1 ....108 C4
Douglas Rd South *IS* * N1 ....108 C4
Douglas St *WEST* SW1P 28 C2
Douglas Ter *WALTH* E17 * 70 D4
Douglas Vls *KUT* * KT1 ....201 H5
Douglas Wy *NWCR* SE14...................170 D1
Doulton Ms *HAMP* NW3 ....105 H4
Dounesforth Gdns
WAND/EARL SW18 ....185 F3
Douro Pl *KENS* W8.............................135 E3
Douro St *BOW* E3 ....131 E1
Douthwaite Sq *WAP* E1W 25 F1
Dove Ap *EHAM* E6 ....133 G4
Dove Cl *CROY/NA* CR0......................245 H5
MLHL NW7 ....62 B3
YEAD UB4..118 B3
Dovecot Cl *PIN* HA5 ....78 A2
Dove Ct *LOTH* * EC2R..........................13 G4
Dovedale Av *CLAY* IG5.........................74 A5
KTN/HRWW/W HA3 ....81 E5
Dovedale Cl *WELL* DA16 ....175 G2
Dovedale Ri *MTCM* CR4.....................206 B3
Dovedale Rd *EDUL* SE22 ....169 H6
Dovedon Cl *STNC7/OAK* N14 ....51 G4
Dove House Gdns *CHING* E4...............55 H1
Dovehouse Md *BARK* IG11 ....134 D1
Dovehouse St *CHEL* SW3 ....36 C4
Dove Ms *ECT* SW5................................14 H2
Doveney Cl *STMC/STPC* BR5 ....236 B5
Dove Pk *PIN* HA5 ....58 D3
Dover Cl *CRICK* NW2...........................86 A4
ROMW/RG RM7...................................77 C5
Dovercourt Av *THHTH* CR7................228 A3
Dovercourt Est *IS* N1 ....108 A4
Dovercourt Gdns *STAN* HA7.................61 G1
Dovercourt La *SUT* SM1 ....243 G1
Dovercourt Rd *DUL* SE21 ....189 E1
Doverfield Rd
BRXS/STRHM SW2 ....187 G1
Dover Gdns *CAR* SM5........................244 B1
Dover House Rd
PUT/ROE SW15 ....163 G3
Doveridge Gdns *PLMGR* N13 ....52 B6
Dover Rd *IS* N1 ....108 A4
Dove Rw *BETH* E2 ....9 F1
Dover Park Dr *PUT/ROE* SW15 ....185 H1
Dover Patrol *BKHTH/KID* SE3...........172 D3
Dover Rd *ED* N9 ....30 A4
MNPK E12...95 E6
NRWD SE19 ....208 D2
WOOL/PLUM SE18 ....174 B3
Dover St *MYFR/PICC* W1J 174 H6
Dover Ter *RCH/KEW* * TW9 ....162 A3
Doves Cl *HAYES* BR2 ....233 G6
Doves Yd *IS* N1 ....108 A6
Doveton Rd *SAND/SEL* CR2 ....236 A3
Doveton St *WCHPL* E1 ....130 A3
Dowanhill Rd *CAT* SE6.......................191 H5
Dowdeswell Cl *PUT/ROE* SW15 ....163 E5
Dowding Pl *STAN* HA7 ....43 G2
Dower Av *WLGTN* SM6......................244 D6
Dowgate Hl *CANST* EC4R 15 C5
Dowlas St *CMBW* SE5 ....169 E1
Dowlerville Rd *ORP* BR6 ....263 J1
Dowman Cl *WIM/MER* SW19 ....205 F4
Downage *HDN* NW4 ....46 A6
Downalong *BUSH* WD23......................43 H3
Downbank Av *BXLYHN* DA7 ....177 H2
Down Barns Rd *RSLP* HA4 ....60 B2
Downderry Rd *BMLY* BR1 ....191 H5
Downe Cl *WELL* DA16........................176 A1
Downend *WOOL/PLUM* SE18..............18 A1
Downe Rd *HAYES* BR2 ....251 J6
MTCM CR4...206 B5

Downer's Cottages *CLAP* SW4...........167 E5
Downes Cl *TWK* TW1 ....180 D1
Downes Ct *WCHMH* N21 ....52 A3
Downfield *KWW* KT4 ....223 F5
Downfield Cl *MV/WKIL* W9 ....125 D3
Down Hall Rd *KUTN/CMB* KT2...........201 F4
Downham Cl *CRW* RM5 ....77 E3
Downham Rd *IS* N1 ....108 D5
Downham Wy *BMLY* BR1 ....212 A1
Downhills Av *TOTM* N17 ....68 D6
Downhills Park Rd *TOTM* N17 ....68 C6
Downhills Wy *TOTM* N17 ....68 C5
Downhurst Av *MLHL* NW7 ....62 D2
Downing Cl *RYLN/HDSTN* HA2 ....59 G6
Downing Dr *GFD/PVL* UB6 ....100 A6
Downing Rd *DAGW* RM9 ....116 D6
Downings *EHAM* E6 ....134 A5
Downing St *WHALL* SW1A 21 E3
Downland Cl *TRDG/WHET* N20 ....49 G3
Downland St *MV/WKIL* W9 ....124 C1
Downleys Cl *ELTH/MOT* SE9 ....193 G4
Downman Rd *ELTH/MOT* SE9 ....173 G4
Down Pl *HMSMTH* W6 ....143 H4
Down Rd *TEDD* TW11 ....200 D2
Downs Av *CHST* BR7 ....213 H4
PIN HA5 ....78 D3
Downs Bridge Rd *BECK* BR3 ....211 H4
Downs Court Pde *CLPT* * E5 ....109 H3
Downsell Rd *WAN* E11 ....111 H2
Downsfield Rd *WALTH* E17 ....90 C5
Downshall Av *GDMY/SEVK* IG3 ....95 E3
Downs Hl *BECK* BR3...........................211 H4
Downshire Hl *HAMP* NW3 ....105 H4
Downside *BECK* * BR3 ....211 E4
TWK TW1..180 B5
Downside Cl *WIM/MER* SW19 ....205 G2
Downside Crs *HAMP* NW3 ....105 J3
WEA W13 ....120 C5
Downside Rd *BELMT* SM2 ....243 H4
Downs La *CLPT* E5 ....109 H2
Downs Park Rd *HACK* E8 ....109 G3
Downs Rd *BECK* BR3 ....211 E3
CLPT E5 ....109 G2
EN EN1 ....39 E5
THHTH CR7 ....208 C4
The Downs *RYNPK* SW20 ....204 E3
Down St *E/WMO/HCT* KT8 ....219 E2
MYFR/PICC W1J..................................19 G2
Down Street Ms
MYFR/PICC W1J..................................19 G3
Downs Vw *ISLW* TW7.........................160 B2
Downsview Gdns *NRWD* SE19 ....208 C3
Downsview Rd *NRWD* SE19 ....208 C3
Downsway *ORP* BR6...........................253 E5
The Downsway *BELMT* SM2 ....243 G6
Downton Av
BRXS/STRHM SW2 ....187 H4
Downtown Rd
BERM/RHTH SE16 ....150 C2
Downway *NFNCH/WDSP* N12 ....66 A3
Dowrey St *IS* N1 ....108 A6
Dowsett Rd *TOTM* N17 ....69 C5
Dowson Cl *CMBW* * SE5 ....168 D6
Doyce St *STHWK* * SE1 ....23 E3
Doyle Gdns *WLSDN* NW10 ....103 H6
Doyle Rd *SNWD* SE25 ....229 G1
D'Oyley St *KTBR* SW1X 27 J1
Doynton St *ARCH* N19..........................66 B6
Draco Ga *PUT/ROE* * SW15................164 A4
Dragon Ct *WALW* SE17 ....31 E5
Dragonfly Cl *PLSTW* E13 ....113 G2
Dragon Rd *PECK* SE15..........................32 A6
Dragoon Rd *DEPT* SE8........................150 D5
Dragor Rd *WLSDN* NW10...................122 C2
Drake Cl *BERM/RHTH* SE16 ....150 B2
Drake Crs *THMD* SE28 ....136 A5
Drakefell Rd *NWCR* SE14 ....170 B3
Drakefield Rd *TOOT* SW17 ....186 C5
Drake Rd *BROCKY* SE4 ....171 H6
CHSGTN KT9 ....240 A3
CROY/NA CR0 ....227 H4
MTCM CR4...226 C3
RYLN/HDSTN HA2 ....78 D6
Drakes Ct *KIL/WHAMP* NW6...............106 C5
Drake St *BMSBY* WC1N 13 G2
ENC/FH EN2 ....38 D2
Drakewood Rd
STRHM/NOR SW16............................207 F3
Draper Cl *BELV* DA17 ....156 D4
Draper Est *WALW* SE17 ....30 D1
Draper Pl *IS* N1 ....108 B6
Drapers Rd *ENC/FH* EN2 ....38 B5
SRTFD E15...111 C2
TOTM N17...69 F6
Drappers Wy *BERM/RHTH* SE16 ....49 F7
Draven Cl *HAYES* BR2........................232 B4
Drawell Cl *WOOL/PLUM* SE18............155 F1
Drax Av *RYNPK* SW20 ....205 G3
Draxmont *WIM/MER* SW19 ....204 C2
Draycot Av *CHEL* SW3 ....26 B2
KTN/HRWW/W HA3 ....80 D3
Draycott Cl *CRICK* NW2.......................104 B1
KTN/HRWW/W HA3 ....61 H3
Draycott Ter *CHEL* SW3 ....26 C1
Dray Ct *ALP/SUD* * HA0 ....101 E4
Drayford Cl *MV/WKIL* W9 ....140 D5
Draymans Wy *ISLW* TW7 ....160 A5
Drayson Ms *KENS* W8 ....145 E2
Drayton Av *LOU* IG10............................57 H1
ORP BR6...216 D6
WEA W13 ....120 C5
Drayton Bridge Rd *HNWL* W7 ....120 B6
Drayton Cl *ELTH/MOT* TW4 ....158 D6
IL IG1...90 A5
Drayton Court Chambers
WEA * W13...120 D6
Drayton Gdns *WBPTN* SW10 ....145 G5
WCHMH N21 ....52 B2
WDR/YW UB7 ....112 B1
WEA W13 ....120 C5
Drayton Gn *WEA* W13 ....120 C5
Drayton Green Rd *WEA* W13 ....120 D6
Drayton Gro *WEA* W13 ....120 C6
Drayton Park Ms *HOLWY* * N7 ....135 F1
Drayton Pk *HOLWY* N7 ....135 E1
Drayton Rd *CROY/NA* CR0 ....228 B6
TOTM N17...69 C5
WAN E11 ....91 H5
WEA W13 ....120 C5
WLSDN NW10 ....103 F6

Dreadnought St *GNWCH* SE10...........152 A3
Dresden Cl *HAMP* NW3 ....105 F4
Dresden Rd *ARCH* N19 ....66 C4
Dressington Av *BROCKY* SE4 ....191 F1
Drew Av *MLHL* NW7.............................62 D1
Drew Rd *CAN/RD* E16 ....153 G1
Drews Cottages *BAL* * SW12 ....187 F4
Drewstead Rd
STRHM/NOR SW16............................187 F4
Driffield Rd *BOW* E3 ....130 C1
The Drift *HAYES* BR2 ....251 F1
The Driftway *MTCM* CR4 ....206 C4
Drinkwater Rd
RYLN/HDSTN HA2 ....79 F6
Drive Ct *EDGW* * HA8 ....62 D1
The Drive *ACT* W3 ....122 C5
BAR EN5 ....34 C4
BAR EN5 ....49 G1
BARK IG11 ....115 E1
BECK BR3 ....211 E5
BKHH IG9 ....57 E2
BXLY DA5 ....196 B2
CHING E4 ....55 H2
CHST BR7 ....215 F4
CRW RM5 ....77 H4
EBED/NFELT TW14 ....178 A2
EDGW HA8 ....62 D1
ENC/FH EN2 ....23 H3
ERITH DA8 ....177 F1
ESH/CLAY KT10 ....219 C5
FBAR/BDGN N11..................................67 E1
FNCH N3 ....65 E3
GLDGN NW11.......................................84 C1
HCT N6 ....86 B2
HOLWY N7 ....107 H4
HOR/WEW KT19 ....241 F4
HSLW TW3...159 H3
IL IG1...93 C3
KUTN/CMB KT2 ....202 C5
LVPST/EBAR SM4 ....248 A6
ORP BR6...235 F6
RYLN/HDSTN HA2 ....79 E4
RYNPK SW20 ....204 A3
SCUP DA14 ....195 H5
SURB * KT6 ....221 G4
SWFD E18 ....72 C6
THHTH CR7 ....228 D1
WALTH E17 ....70 C4
WBLY HA9 ....82 C6
WWKM BR4 ....231 H4
Dr Johnson Av *TOOT* SW17...............186 D5
Droitwich Cl *SYD* SE26.......................189 C5
Dromey Gdns
KTN/HRWW/W HA3 ....60 B3
Dromore Rd *PUT/ROE* SW15 ....184 C1
Droop St *NKENS* W10 ....108 C3
Drovers Pl *PECK* SE15 ....169 J1
Drovers Rd *SAND/SEL* CR2 ....246 D3
Druce Rd *DUL* SE21 ....189 E1
Druid St *STHWK* SE1 ....24 C3
Druids Wy *HAYES* BR2 ....231 H1
Drumaline Rdg *WPK* KT4 ....223 E6
Drummond Av *ROMW/RG* RM7 ....97 H1
Drummond Crs *CAMTN* NW1 ....4 C3
Drummond Dr
KTN/HRWW/W HA3 ....60 B3
Drummond Ga *PIM* SW1V 28 D3
Drummond Rd
BERM/RHTH SE16 ....149 E2
CROY/NA CR0 ....228 C6
ROMW/RG RM7...................................97 G1
WAN E11 ....90 D2
Drummonds Pl *RCH/KEW* TW9 ....161 C5
Drummond St *CAMTN* NW1 ....4 A5
Drum St *WCHPL* E1 ....16 C3
Drury Crs *CROY/NA* CR0 ....228 A6
Drury La *HOL/ALD* WC2B 13 F4
Drury Rd *HRW* HA1 ....78 D5
Drury Wy *WLSDN* NW10 ....100 D3
Dryad St *PUT/ROE* SW15 ....164 B4
Dryburgh Gdns
CDALE/KGS NW9 ....62 A6
Dryburgh Rd *PUT/ROE* SW15.............163 H4
Dryden Av *HNWL* W7 ....120 B5
Dryden Cl *BARK/HLT* IG6 ....75 F2
Dryden Rd *EN* EN1 ....30 B5
KTN/HRWW/W HA3 ....60 B1
WIM/MER SW19 ....205 G2
WOOL/PLUM SE18 ....115 G4
Dryden St *COVGDN* WC2E 13 F4
Dryden Wy *ORP* BR6 ....235 C5
Dryfield Cl *WLSDN* NW10 ....102 C4
Dryfield Rd *EDGW* HA8 ....62 C2
Dryhill Rd *BELV* DA17 ....156 D6
Dryland Av *ORP* BR6 ....269 F2
Drylands Rd *CEND/HSY/T* N8 ....87 G3
Drysdale Av *CHING* E4 ....39 J6
Drysdale Dwellings *HACK* E8 ....109 F5
Drysdale Pl *BETH* E2 ....9 H4
Drysdale St *IS* N1 ....9 H4
Dublin Av *HACK* E8............................109 G6
Du Burstow Ter *HNWL* W7 ....140 A2
Ducal St *BETH* E2 ....9 H6
Du Cane Cl *SHB* * W12 ....124 A5
Du Cane Rd *SHB* W12 ....123 H5
Duchess Cl *FBAR/BDGN* N11...............66 C2
SUT SM1...209 C3
Duchess Gv *BKHH* IG9 ....39 F4
Duchess Ms *CAVSQ/HST* W1G 11 H2
Duchess of Bedford's Wk
KENS W8...144 D2
KENS * W8..145 E2
Duchess St *REGST* W1B 11 H2
Duchy Rd *EBAR* EN4 ....21 H1
Duchy St *STHWK* SE1 ....22 B6
Ducie St *CLAP* SW4............................167 G5
Duckett Rd *FSBYPK* N4 ....68 B1
Duckett St *WCHPL* E1 ....130 B4
Duck La *SOHO/CST* W1F 12 C4
Duck Lees La *PEND* EN3 ....41 G5
Du Cros Dr *STAN* HA7 ....43 C1
Du Cros Rd *ACT* W3............................143 G1
Duddon Hill La *WLSDN* NW10.............103 F2
Dudden Hill Pde
WLSDN * NW10 ....103 F2
Duddington Cl *ELTH/MOT* SE9 ....193 F6
Dudley Av *KTN/HRWW/W* HA3 ....61 E6
Dudley Dr *MRDN* SM4 ....224 C5

Dudley Gdns *RYLN/HDSTN* HA2 ....79 H5
WEA W13 ....140 D2
Dudley Rd *FNCH* N3 ....65 F5
IL IG1...90 B1
KIL/WHAMP NW6 ....124 C1
KUT KT1 ....138 B2
NWDGN UB2 ....138 B2
RCH/KEW TW9 ....161 H1
RYLN/HDSTN HA2 ....79 G6
WALTH E17 ....71 E5
WIM/MER SW19 ....205 E2
Dudley St *BAY/PAD* * W2 ....125 H5
SUT SM1...209 A6
Dudmaston Ms *CHEL* SW3 ....145 H5
Dufferin Av *STLK* EC1Y 7 G6
Dufferin St *STLK* EC1Y 7 F6
Duffield Cl *HRW* HA1 ....61 F3
Duffield Dr *SEVS/STOTM* N15 ....89 F1
Duff St *POP/IOD* E14 ....131 F5
Dufour's Pl *SOHO/CST* W1F 12 B4
Duke Humphrey Rd
BKHTH/KID SE3.................................172 A2
Duke of Cambridge Cl
WHTN TW2 ....179 H1
Duke of Edinburgh Rd
SUT SM1...243 H1
Duke of Wellington Pl
WHALL SW1A 19 F4
Duke of York St *STJS* SW1Y 20 B1
Duke Rd *BARK/HLT* IG6 ....74 D4
CHSWK W4 ....142 D5
Duke's Av *CHSWK* W4 ....142 D5
EDGW HA8 ....61 H2
FNCH N5 ....65 E4
HRW HA1..60 A1
HSLWW TW4 ....158 C5
MUSWH N10 ....48 C6
NTHLT UB5 ....98 C5
NWMAL KT3..203 E6
PIN HA5 ....78 D3
RCHPK/HAM TW10 ....181 E6
Dukes Cl *HPTN* TW12 ....198 D1
Dukes Ga *CHSWK* * W4 ....142 C2
Dukes Lane *KENS* * W8 ....145 E2
Dukes La Chambers *KENS* * W8 ....145 F2
Duke's Ms *MHST* W1U 11 F3
MUSWH N10 ....48 C6
Dukes Orch *BXLY* DA5 ....197 G3
Duke's Pl *HDTCH* EC3A 16 C4
Dukes Rd *ACT* W3 ....122 A3
CAMTN NW1 ....4 D4
EHAM E6 ....114 A6
Dukesthorpe Rd *SYD* SE26 ....189 C5
Duke Street St *STHWK* SE1 ....23 H1
Duke Street St James's
MYFR/PICC W1J...................................20 B1
Dukes Wy *WWKM* BR4 ....250 A1
Dukes St *FSBYPK* N4 ....87 J5
Dulford St *NTGHL* W11 ....116 C6
Dulka Rd *BTSEA* SW11 ....166 B3
Dulverton Rd *ELTH/MOT* SE9 ....194 C4
Dulwich Common *DUL* SE21 ....188 D3
The Dulwich Oaks *DUL* * SE21 ....189 E5
Dulwich Rd *HNHL* SE24 ....188 A6
Dulwich Village *DUL* SE21 ....188 D1
Dulwich Wood Av *NRWD* SE19..........189 E1
Dulwich Wood Pk *NRWD* SE19 ....189 E1
Dumbarton Rd
BRXS/STRHM SW2 ....187 E2
Dumbleton Cl *KUT* KT1 ....202 B4
Dumbreck Rd *ELTH/MOT* SE9 ....174 A5
Dumont Rd *STNW/STAM* N16 ....109 C1
Dumpton Pl *CAMTN* NW1 ....106 C5
Dunbar Av *BECK* BR3 ....230 C1
EAGE RM10 ....117 E1
STRHM/NOR SW16............................208 B2
Dunbar Ct *WOT/HER* KT12 ....218 A6
Dunbar Gdns *DAGE* RM10 ....117 E3
Dunbar Rd *FSTGT* E7 ....94 D5
NWMAL KT3..222 C1
WDGN N22...48 A4
Dunbar St *WNWD* SE27 ....188 D3
Dunblane Rd *ELTH/MOT* SE9 ....173 G4
Dunboyne Rd *HAMP* NW3 ....106 B3
Dunbridge St *BETH* E2 ....9 F5
Duncan Cl *BAR* EN5 ....35 G5
Duncannon St *CHCR* WC2N 11 E6
Duncan Rd *HACK* E8 ....109 G6
RCH/KEW TW9 ....161 G5
Duncan St *IS* N1 ....6 B1
Dunch St *WCHPL* * E1 ....130 D5
Duncombe Hl *FSTH* SE23 ....190 D6
Duncombe Rd *ARCH* N19 ....87 F5
Duncrievie Rd *LEW* SE13 ....191 H1
Duncroft *WOOL/PLUM* SE18 ....156 C5
Dundalk Rd *BROCKY* SE4 ....170 C4
Dundas Gdns *E/WMO/HCT* KT8 ....199 F6
Dundas Rd *PECK* SE15 ....170 A3
Dundee Rd *SNWD* SE25 ....229 H2
Dundee St *WAP* E1W 130 D1
Dundela Gdns *WPK* KT4 ....241 H2
Dundonald Cl *EHAM* E6 ....115 H5
Dundonald Rd
WIM/MER SW19 ....204 D3
WLSDN NW10 ....104 B6
LEY E10 ....110 F1
Dunedin Rd *IL* IG1...............................110 F1
Dunedin Wy *YEAD* UB4 ....118 A3
Dunelm Gv *WNWD* SE27 ....188 C6
Dunelm St *WCHPL* E1 ....130 D5
Dunfield Rd *CAT* SE6 ....211 H1
Dungarvan Av *PUT/ROE* SW15 ....163 G5
Dunheved Cl *THHTH* CR7 ....228 A3
Dunheved Rd North
THHTH CR7 ....228 A3
Dunheved Rd South
THHTH CR7 ....228 A3
Dunheved Rd West
THHTH CR7 ....228 A3
Dunholme Gn *ED* N9 ....53 F5
Dunholme La *ED* N9 ....53 F5

Edenhurst Av FUL/PGN SW6 .....164 D4
Eden Pde BECK * BR3 ....230 C1
Eden Park Av BECK BR3 ....230 D1
Eden Rd BECK E3 ....230 C1
 BXLY HA5 ....197 G6
 CROY/NA CRO 211 J2
 WALTH E17 ....91 F2
Edensor Rd CHSWK W4 ....163 E1
Eden St KUT KT1 ....201 G5
Edenvale Rd MTCM CR4 ....206 C3
Edenvale St FUL/PGN SW6 ....165 F1
Eden Wk KUT * KT1 ....201 G5
Eden Wy BECK BR3 ....231 E2
Ederline Av STRHM/NOR SW16 ...207 H6
Edgar Kail Wy CMBW SE5 ....168 E4
Edgarley Ter FUL/PGN * SW6 ....164 C2
Edgar Rd BOW E3 ....131 F2
 HSLWW TW4 ....178 D2
Edgeborough Wy BMLY BR1 ....215 F4
Edgebury CHST BR7 ....194 B6
Edgecombe Cl KUTN/CMB KT2 ....202 D3
Edgecoombe SAND/SEL CR2 ....248 B6
Edgecote Cl ACT W3 ....143 J4
Edgefield Av BARK IG11 ....115 F5
Edge Hl WIM/MER SW19 ....204 B3
 WOOL/PLUM SE18 ....154 B6
Edge Hill Av GLDGN NW11 ....85 E1
Edgehill Ct WOT/HER * KT12 .....218 A5
Edgehill Gdns DAGE RM10 ....117 E2
Edgehill Rd CHST BR7 ....194 C5
 MTCM CR4 ....206 D5
 WEA W13 ....121 E5
Edgeley La CLAP SW4 ....167 H4
Edgeley Rd CLAP SW4 ....167 F4
Edgel St WAND/EARL SW18 ....148 F5
Edgepoint Cl WNWD * SE27 ......208 B1
Edge St KENS W8 ....145 E1
Edgewood Dr ORP BR6 ....253 F3
Edgewood Gn CROY/NA CRO 230 B5
Edgeworth Av HDN NW4 ....63 G2
Edgeworth Ct HDN NW4 ....63 G2
Edgeworth Rd EBAR EN4 ....35 H5
 ELTH/MOT SE9 ....173 E5
Edgington Rd
 STRHM/NOR SW16 ....207 F2
Edgington Wy SCUP DA14 ....216 A3
Edgwarebury Gdns EDGW HA8 .....44 C2
Edgwarebury La BORE WD6 ....45 H2
Edgware Rd BAY/PAD W2 ....125 H4
 CDALE/KGS NW9 ....62 C6
Edgware Rd Burnt
 Oak Broadway
 EDGW HA8 ....62 B3
Edgware Rd High St EDGW HA8 ...62 A2
Edgware Rd The Hyde
 CDALE/KGS NW9 ....83 E1
Edgware Rd (Watford By-Pass)
 EDGW HA8 ....45 H6
Edinburgh Cl BETH E2 ....130 A1
 PIN HA5 ....78 C4
Edinburgh Ct KUT * KT1 ....201 G6
Edinburgh Ga BAY/PAD W2 ....18 C3
Edinburgh Rd HNWL W7 ....140 D2
 PLSTW E13 ....132 D1
 SUT SM1 ....225 G6
 UED * N18 ....69 C1
 WALTH E17 ....91 E2
Edinburgh's Dr ROMW/RG RM7 ....97 C1
Edington Rd ABYW SE2 ....155 H3
 PEND EN3 ....40 E4
Edison Dr CFD/PVL UB6 ....119 F5
 WBLY HA9 ....81 G6
Edison Gv WOOL/PLUM SE18 ......175 F1
Edison Rd CEND/HSY/T N8 ....87 F3
 HAYES BR2 ....212 C5
 PEND EN3 ....40 D3
 WELL DA16 ....175 F2
Edis St CAMTN NW1 ....106 C6
Edith Cavell Gdns BRYLDS KT5 ...222 B4
Edith Gv WBPTN SW10 ....145 G6
Edithna St BRXN/ST SW9 ....167 H2
Edith Rd CHDH RM6 ....96 B4
 EHAM E6 ....113 F5
 FBAR/BDGN N11 ....67 E3
 ORP BR6 ....253 G3
 SRTFD E15 ....111 H3
 WIM/MER SW19 ....144 C4
 WKENS W14 ....144 C4
Edith Rw FUL/PGN SW6 ....165 F2
Edith St BETH E2 ....110 E1
Edith Ter WBPTN * SW10 ....165 G1
Edith Vls WKENS W14 ....144 D4
Edison Cl WALTH E17 ....91 E2
Edmund Cn HOM E9 ....110 C4
Edmund Gv FELT TW13 ....178 D4
Edmund Halley Wy
 GNWCH SE10 ....152 A2
Edmund Hurst Dr EHAM E6 ......134 B4
Edmund Rd MTCM CR4 ....236 D3
 STMC/STPC BR5 ....236 A3
 WELL DA16 ....158 D2
Edmunds Av STMC/STPC BR5 ....216 B6
Edmunds Cl YEAD UB4 ....118 A4
Edmund St CMBW SE5 ....168 D7
Edmunds Wk EFNCH N2 ....86 A1
Edna Rd RYNPK SW20 ....206 B5
Edna St BTSEA SW11 ....166 A2
Edrick Rd EDGW HA8 ....62 C2
Edrick Wk EDGW HA8 ....62 C2
Edric Rd NWCR SE14 ....170 B1
Edridge Rd CROY/NA CRO 246 C1
Edward Av CHING E4 ....51 H2
 MRDN SM4 ....225 H2
Edward Cl EN EN1 ....19 C1
 HPTN TW12 ....199 C1
Edward Ct CAN/RD E16 ....132 C4
Edwardes Pl WKENS W14 ....144 D3
Edwardes Sq KENS W8 ....19 G3
Edward Mann Cl East
 WCHPL * E1 ....130 B5
Edward Mann Cl West
 WCHPL * E1 ....130 B5
Edward Ms CAMTN * NW1 ....5 H3
Edward Rd DEPT SE8 ....150 D6
Edward Rd BMLY BR1 ....214 C2
 CHDH RM6 ....96 C3
 CHST BR7 ....214 B1
 CROY/NA CRO 229 E4
 EBAR EN4 ....35 H6

 HPTN TW12 ....199 C1
 NTHLT UB5 ....118 A1
 PGE/AN SE20 ....210 B3
 RYLN/HDSTN HA2 ....59 G6
 WALTH E17 ....90 B1
Edwards Av RSLP HA4 ....98 A3
Edwards Cl WPK KT4 ....224 B6
Edward's Cottages IS * N1 ....108 B5
Edwards Gdns SWLY BR8 ....237 H1
Edward's La STNW/STAM N16 .....88 D6
Edwards Ms IS N1 ....108 B5
 MBLAR W1H 11 G1
Edwards Pl FBAR/BDGN N11 ......67 F3
Edward Sq IS N1 ....107 H6
Edward Sq BELV DA17 ....157 E4
Edward St CAN/RD E16 ....114 E3
 NWCR SE14 ....170 D1
Edward Temme Av SRTFD E15 ...112 B5
Edward Tyler Rd
 LEE/GVPK SE12 ....192 D4
Edwin Av EHAM E6 ....96 A1
Edwin Cl BXLYHN DA7 ....134 A1
Edwin Cl BXLYHN DA7 ....156 D6
Edwin Rd EDGW HA8 ....62 D2
 WHTN TW2 ....160 A2
Edwin's Mead HOM E9 ....110 C2
Edwin St CAN/RD E16 ....132 C4
 WCHPL E1 ....130 A3
Edwin Ware Ct PIN * HA5 ....58 A1
Edwyn Cl BAR EN5 ....34 A6
Effie Pl FUL/PGN SW6 ....165 E1
Effie Rd FUL/PGN SW6 ....165 E1
Effingham Cl BELMT SM2 ....243 F6
Effingham Rd CEND/HSY/T N8 ....88 A2
 CROY/NA CRO 227 H4
 LEW SE13 ....172 A6
 SURB KT6 ....222 B5
Egbert St CAMTN NW1 ....106 C6
Egerton Crs CHEL SW3 ....26 A1
Egerton Dr GNWCH SE10 ....171 F2
Egerton Gdns CHEL SW3 ....18 A1
 GDMY/SEVK IG3 ....115 F1
 HDN NW4 ....63 H2
 WEA W13 ....121 G5
 WLSDN * NW10 ....104 A6
Egerton Gardens Ms CHEL SW3 ...18 B6
Egerton Pl CHEL * SW3 ....18 B6
Egerton Rd ALP/SUD HA0 ....101 H5
 NWMAL KT3 ....223 F1
 SNWD SE25 ....209 E6
 STNW/STAM * N16 ....88 A2
 WHTN TW2 ....160 A2
Egerton Ter CHEL SW3 ....18 B6
Egham Cl CHEAM SM3 ....224 C6
 WIM/MER SW19 ....146 A6
Egham Crs CHEAM SM3 ....242 B1
Egham Rd PLSTW E13 ....132 D4
Eglantine Rd
 WAND/EARL SW18 ....165 G6
Eglington Ct WALW SE17 ....55 H2
Eglington Rd CHING E4 ....38 B2
Eglinton Hl WOOL/PLUM SE18 ...154 B6
Eglinton Rd WOOL/PLUM SE18 ...154 B6
Egliston Ms PUT/ROE SW15 ......147 E6
Egliston Rd PUT/ROE SW15 ......164 A4
Eglon Ms CAMTN NW1 ....106 B5
Egmont Av SURB KT6 ....221 H5
Egmont Rd BELMT SM2 ....243 C5
 NWMAL KT3 ....225 F1
 SURB KT6 ....221 H5
 WOT/HER KT12 ....188 B4
Egmont St NWCR SE14 ....170 B1
Egremont Rd WNWD SE27 ....188 A5
Eider Cl FSTGT E7 ....112 B3
Eighteenth Rd MTCM CR4 ....227 C1
Eighth Av MNPK E12 ....113 H2
Eileen Rd SNWD SE25 ....209 E3
Eindoven Cl MTCM CR4 ....206 C5
Eisenhower Dr EHAM E6 ....113 C4
Elaine Gv KTTN NW5 ....106 C3
Elam Cl CMBW SE5 ....168 B3
Elam St CMBW SE5 ....168 B3
Eland Rd BTSEA SW11 ....166 B4
 CROY/NA CRO 246 B1
Elba Pl WALW * SE17 ....31 J1
Elberon Av CROY/NA CRO 227 E3
Elbe St FUL/PGN SW6 ....165 C1
Elborough St
 WAND/EARL SW18 ....185 G3
Elbury Dr CAN/RD E16 ....132 C5
Elcho St BTSEA SW11 ....166 A1
Elcot Av PECK SE15 ....169 H1
Elder Av CEND/HSY/T N8 ....87 E2
Elderberry Rd EA W5 ....141 G2
Elder Cl BFN/LL DA15 ....195 F3
Elder Ct BUSH WD23 ....44 A4
Elderfield Rd CLPT E5 ....110 E1
Elderfield Wk WAN E11 ....92 D2
Elderflower Wy SRTFD E15 ......112 A5
Elder Oak Cl PGE/AN SE20 ......209 H4
Elder Rd WNWD SE27 ....208 C1
Elderslie Cl BECK BR3 ....231 E5
Elderslie Rd ELTH/MOT SE9 ......174 A6
Elder St WCHPL E1 ....16 C1
Elderton Rd SYD SE26 ....191 G4
Eldertree Wy MTCM CR4 ....206 D4
Elder Wk IS N1 ....108 B6
Eldon Av CROY/NA CRO 230 A6
 HEST TW5 ....159 F1
Eldon Gv HAMP NW3 ....105 H3
Eldon Pde WDGN * N22 ....68 B4
Eldon Pk SNWD SE25 ....229 H1
Eldon Rd ED N9 ....54 A3
 KENS W8 ....145 E3
 WALTH E17 ....69 H1
 WDGN N22 ....68 B4
Eldon St LVPST EC2M 15 H2
Eldon Wy WLSDN NW10 ....118 D2
Eldred Dr STMC/STPC BR5 ......236 B6
Eleanora Ter SUT * SM1 ....243 G5
Eleanor Cl TOTM N17 ....69 F6
Eleanor Gdns BAR EN5 ....34 B6
 DAGW RM9 ....80 B5
Eleanor Gv BARN SW13 ....163 E4
Eleanor Rd FBAR/BDGN N11 ......67 G2
 HACK E8 ....109 H4
 SRTFD E15 ....112 D4
Eleanor St BOW E3 ....131 J2

Electric Av BRXN/ST SW9 ....168 A5
Electric La BRXN/ST * SW9 ....168 A5
Electric Pde SURB KT6 ....221 F5
Elephant & Castle STHWK SE1 ....30 C1
Elephant La BERM/RHTH SE16 ...150 A2
Elephant Rd WALW SE17 ....31 E1
Elers Rd WEA W13 ....61 A1
Eley Rd UED N18 ....70 B1
Elfindale Rd HNHL SE24 ....168 C6
Elfin Gv TEDD TW11 ....200 B1
Elford Cl ELTH/MOT SE9 ....173 E5
Elfort Rd HBRY N5 ....108 A2
Elfrida Crs CAT SE6 ....191 C6
Elf Rw WAP E1W 130 A6
Elfwine Rd HNWL W7 ....120 A4
Elgal Cl ORP BR6 ....252 B5
Elgar Av BRYLDS KT5 ....222 B5
 EA W5 ....141 G2
 STRHM/NOR SW16 ....207 G6
 WLSDN NW10 ....80 G4
Elgar Cl BKHH IG9 ....57 H4
 BORE WD6 ....45 E2
 DEPT SE8 ....171 E1
 PLSTW E13 ....155 E1
Elgar St BERM/RHTH SE16 ....150 C2
Elgin Av KTN/HRWW/W HA3 ....60 D5
 MV/WKIL W9 ....2 C6
 SHB W12 ....143 G2
Elginmeads South
 MV/WKIL W9 ....125 F2
Elgin Ms NTGHL W11 ....124 C5
Elgin Ms North MV/WKIL W9 .....125 F2
Elgin Rd CROY/NA CRO 229 F6
 GDMY/SEVK IG3 ....95 G1
 SUT SM1 ....225 C3
 WDGN N22 ....67 E5
 WLGTN SM6 ....245 E4
Elgood Cl NTGHL W11 ....124 C6
Elham Cl BMLY BR1 ....213 F3
Elia Ms IS N1 ....6 C2
Elias Pl LBTH SE11 ....30 A1
Elia St IS N1 ....6 C2
Elibank Rd ELTH/MOT SE9 ....174 A5
Elim St STHWK SE1 ....132 B3
Elin Wy PLSTW E13 ....132 B2
Eliot Bank FSTH SE23 ....189 H4
Eliot Dr RYLN/HDSTN * HA2 ......60 C3
Eliot Gdns PUT/ROE SW15 ....163 G5
Eliot Hl BKHTH/KID SE3 ....171 C3
Eliot Ms STJWD NW8 ....2 A2
Eliot Pk BKHTH/KID SE3 ....172 A3
Eliot Rd DAGW RM9 ....116 D2
Eliot V BKHTH/KID SE3 ....171 H3
Elizabeth Av ENC/FH EN2 ....28 B4
 IL IG1 ....94 D6
 IS N1 ....108 C5
Elizabeth Barnes Ct
 FUL/PGN * SW6 ....165 F3
Elizabeth Br BGVA SW1W 27 H2
Elizabeth Cl BAR EN5 ....34 B4
 MV/WKIL W9 ....125 G3
 ROMW/RG RM7 ....62 D5
 SUT SM1 ....242 D2
Elizabeth Clyde Cl
 SEVS/STOTM N15 ....89 E1
Elizabeth Cottages
 RCH/KEW TW9 ....161 H2
Elizabeth Gdns ACT W3 ....143 F1
 ISLW * TW7 ....61 E2
 SUN TW16 ....198 A6
Elizabeth Ms HAMP NW3 ....106 A4
Elizabeth Pl SEVS/STOTM N15 ...88 D1
Elizabeth Ride ED N9 ....36 D2
Elizabeth Rd EHAM E6 ....113 F6
 SEVS/STOTM N15 ....89 F3
Elizabeth Sq BERM/RHTH SE16 .130 C6
Elizabeth Wy FELT TW13 ....178 A4
 NRWD SE19 ....208 D1
 STMC/STPC BR5 ....202 E2
Elkington Rd PLSTW E13 ....132 D3
Elkstone Rd NKENS W10 ....124 D4
Ellaline Rd HMSMTH W6 ....144 B6
Ellanby Crs UED N18 ....106 B2
Elland Rd PECK SE15 ....170 A5
 WOT/HER KT12 ....218 B6
Ellement Cl PIN HA5 ....78 B2
Ellenborough Pl
 PUT/ROE SW15 ....163 G5
Ellenborough Rd
 SCUP DA14 ....216 B2
 WDGN N22 ....68 A1
Ellenbridge Wy SAND/SEL CR2 .247 E6
Ellen Cl BMLY BR1 ....213 F6
Ellen Ct ED N9 ....54 A4
Ellen St WCHPL E1 ....13 C2
Ellen Webb Dr
 KTN/HRWW/W HA3 ....60 A3
Elleray Rd TEDD TW11 ....200 B2
Ellerby St FUL/PGN SW6 ....164 B2
Ellerdale Rd HAMP NW3 ....105 G3
Ellerdale St LEW SE13 ....171 F5
Ellerdine Rd HSLW TW3 ....159 C5
Ellerker Gdns
 RCHPK/HAM TW10 ....181 G1
Ellerman Av WHTN TW2 ....178 D3
Ellerslie Rd SHB W12 ....124 A1
Ellerton Gdns DAGW RM9 ......116 A5
Ellerton Rd BARN * SW13 ....163 G2
 DAGW RM9 ....116 A5
 RYNPK SW20 ....203 G3
 SURB KT6 ....222 H6
 WAND/EARL SW18 ....185 H1
Ellery Rd NRWD SE19 ....208 D3
Ellery St PECK SE15 ....169 J1
Ellesborough Cl OXHEY WD19 ...58 A7
Ellesmere Av BECK BR3 ....211 G5
 MLHL NW7 ....45 F5
Ellesmere Cl WAN E11 ....92 B2
Ellesmere Gdns REDBR IG4 ......93 G5
Ellesmere Gv BAR EN5 ....34 G6
Ellesmere Rd BOW E3 ....130 G1
 GFD/PVL UB6 ....119 G3
 TWK TW1 ....160 D5
 WLSDN NW10 ....81 G3
Ellesmere St POP/IOD E14 ......131 F5
Ellingfort Rd HACK E8 ....109 H6
Ellingham Rd CHSGTN KT9 ......239 F4
 SHB W12 ....143 G2
 WAN E11 ....91 H1

Ellington Rd HSLW TW3 ....159 F1
 MUSWH N10 ....86 D1
Ellington St HOLWY N7 ....108 A4
Elliot Cl SRTFD E15 ....112 A5
 WBLY HA9 ....101 H1
Elliot Rd HDN NW4 ....83 H3
Elliot Rd BRXN/ST SW9 ....168 B1
 CHSWK W4 ....142 B4
 HAYES BR2 ....233 F1
 STAN HA7 ....60 C2
 THHTH CR7 ....228 B1
Elliott's Pl IS N1 ....6 B4
Elliott Sq HAMP NW3 ....106 A5
Elliott's Rw LBTH SE11 ....30 C1
 EDGW HA8 ....62 B3
Ellis Cl CRICK NW2 ....104 A4
 EDGW HA8 ....62 B3
Elliscombe Mt CHARL * SE7 ....153 E6
Elliscombe Rd CHARL SE7 ....153 E5
Ellisfield Dr PUT/ROE SW15 .....183 F3
Ellison Gdns NWDGN UB2 ......138 D4
Ellison Rd BARN SW13 ....163 F3
 BFN/LL DA15 ....194 D3
 STRHM/NOR SW16 ....207 F3
Ellis Rd MTCM CR4 ....226 B3
Ellis St KTBR SW1X 15 G1
Ellis Waterton Cl SWLY BR8 .....237 H1
Ellora Rd STRHM/NOR SW16 ....207 J1
Ellsworth St BETH E2 ....9 H5
Elmar Rd SEVS/STOTM N15 ......88 D1
Elm Av EA W5 ....141 G1
 OXHEY WD19 ....41 G6
 RSLP HA4 ....59 E1
Elmbank WCHMH N21 ....51 G2
Elmbank Av BAR EN5 ....34 A5
Elmbank Dr BMLY BR1 ....213 F5
Elm Bank Gdns BARN SW13 ....163 E3
Elm Bank Wy HNWL W7 ....119 H4
Elmbourne Dr BELV DA17 ....157 F4
Elmbourne Rd TOOT SW17 .....186 D5
Elmbridge Av BRYLDS KT5 ......223 E4
Elmbridge Cl RSLP HA4 ....58 D3
Elmbridge Rd BARK/HLT IG6 ....75 G2
Elmbridge Wk HACK * E8 ....109 G5
Elmbrook Gdns ELTH/MOT SE9 .175 G5
Elmbrook Rd SUT SM1 ....242 G2
Elm Cl BKHH IG9 ....57 F4
 BRYLDS KT5 ....222 C4
 CAR SM5 ....226 B5
 HDN NW4 ....84 B2
 ROMW/RG RM7 ....79 F3
 RYLN/HDSTN HA2 ....79 F3
 RYNPK SW20 ....221 A1
 SAND/SEL CR2 ....246 D4
 WAN E11 ....73 E4
 WHTN TW2 ....179 F4
Elm Cottages MTCM * CR4 ......206 B5
Elmcourt Rd WNWD SE27 ....188 B4
Elm Crs EA W5 ....141 G2
 KUTN/CMB KT2 ....201 G4
Elmcroft CEND/HSY/T N8 ....87 H2
Elmcroft Av BFN/LL DA15 ....195 F2
 ED N9 ....36 D1
 GLDGN NW11 ....84 D4
 WAN E11 ....73 F4
Elmcroft Cl CHSGTN * KT9 ......239 G3
 RYLN/HDSTN HA2 ....71 F6
Elmcroft Crs GLDGN NW11 ....84 B4
 RYLN/HDSTN HA2 ....59 F5
Elmcroft Dr CHSGTN KT9 ....239 G3
Elmcroft Gdns CDALE/KGS NW9 .62 A4
Elmcroft Rd ORP BR6 ....235 G4
Elmcroft St CLPT E5 ....90 E4
Elmdale Rd PLMGR N13 ....67 H1
Elmdene BRYLDS KT5 ....222 C5
Elmdene Rd WOOL/PLUM SE18 .156 B5
Elmden Rd HEST TW5 ....158 B3
Elm Dr RYLN/HDSTN HA2 ....79 F3
 SUN TW16 ....196 B6
 SWLY BR8 ....217 H5
Elmer Cl ENC/FH EN2 ....37 H4
Elmer Gdns EDGW HA8 ....62 B3
 ISLW TW7 ....159 G2
Elmer Rd CAT SE6 ....191 G2
Elmer's Dr TEDD TW11 ....200 A6
Elmers End Rd BECK BR3 ....210 A6
Elmers Rd SNWD SE25 ....229 G4
Elmfield Av CEND/HSY/T N8 ......87 G2
 MTCM CR4 ....206 B1
 TEDD TW11 ....200 B1
Elmfield Cl HRW HA1 ....80 A6
Elmfield Pk BMLY BR1 ....212 D6
Elmfield Rd BMLY BR1 ....212 C5
 CHING E4 ....55 G4
 EFNCH N2 ....65 H6
 NWDGN UB2 ....138 C3
 TOOT SW17 ....167 G6
 WALTH E17 ....90 B3
Elmfield Wy MV/WKIL W9 ....125 E4
 SAND/SEL CR2 ....247 F6
Elm Friars Wk HOLWY N7 ....107 F5
Elm Gdns EFNCH N2 ....65 G6
 ENC/FH EN2 ....29 H1
 ESH/CLAY KT10 ....238 B4
 MTCM CR4 ....227 F1
Elmgate Gdns EDGW HA8 ....62 D1
Elm Gn ACT W3 ....105 F3
Elmgreen Cl SRTFD E15 ....112 A6
Elm Gv CEND/HSY/T N8 ....87 E5
 CRICK NW2 ....82 B3
 ERITH DA8 ....137 A1
 KUTN/CMB KT2 ....201 G4
 ORP BR6 ....253 F5
 PECK SE15 ....169 G3
 RYLN/HDSTN HA2 ....59 F2
 SUT SM1 ....243 F2
 WIM/MER SW19 ....204 C3
Elmgrove Crs HRW HA1 ....80 B2
Elmgrove Gdns HRW HA1 ....80 C2
Elm Grove Pde WLGTN SM6 .....244 C1
Elm Grove Rd BARN SW13 ......163 G4
 EA W5 ....141 G2
Elmgrove Rd CROY/NA CRO 229 H4
 HRW HA1 ....80 B3
Elm Hall Gdns WAN E11 ....92 E3
Elm Hatch PIN HA5 ....42 A2
Elmhurst BELV DA17 ....156 C6
 MTCM CR4 ....206 C3
Elmhurst Dr SWFD E18 ....72 C5

Elmhurst Rd ELTH/MOT SE9....193 G4
 FSTGT E7 ....112 D5
Elmhurst St CLAP SW4...........167 F4
Elmhurst Wy LOU IG10 ....57 H2
Elmington Cl BXLY DA5...........197 F2
Elmington Est CMBW SE5........168 C1
Elmira St LEW SE13...............171 F4
Elm La CAT SE6 ....190 D4
Elmlee Cl CHST BR7 ....213 H2
Elmley St WOOL/PLUM SE18 ....154 D4
Elmore Cl ALP/SUD HA0.........121 C1
Elmore Rd LEY E10................111 C1
 PEND EN3 ....40 B2
Elmore St IS N1...................108 D5
Elm Pde SCUP * DA14 ....195 C6
Elm Pk BRXS/STRHM SW2.........187 H1
 STAN HA7 ....60 D1
Elm Park Av SEVS/STOTM N15....39 F2
Elm Parks Gdns HDN NW4.........82 A3
 WBPTN SW10.....................145 H5
Elm Park La CHEL SW3...........145 H6
Elm Park Rd CHEL SW3...........145 H6
 FNCH N3 ....64 D5
 LEY E10 ....90 C5
 PIN HA5 ....58 B6
 SNWD SE25......................209 F6
 WCHMH N21......................52 C2
Elm Pl SKENS SW7 ....145 H5
Elm Rd BAR EN5 ....34 D5
 BECK BR3 ....210 D5
 CHSGTN KT9.....................239 G2
 ESH/CLAY KT10 ....238 D4
 EW KT17 ....241 F4
 FSTGT E7 ....112 B4
 KUTN/CMB KT2...................201 H4
 MORT/ESHN SW14 ....162 C4
 MTCM CR4.........................226 C5
 NWMAL KT5 ....202 D6
 ORP BR6 ....253 C5
 ROMW/RG RM7 ....77 F5
 SCUP DA14 ....195 C6
 THHTH CR7 ....228 C1
 WALTH E17 ....91 G2
 WAN E11 ....91 H6
 WBLY HA9 ....101 G3
 WDGN N22 ....68 B4
Elm Rd West MRDN SM4.........224 D4
Elm Rw HAMP NW3 ....105 G1
Elms Av HDN NW4..................64 A2
 MUSWH N10 ....66 D6
Elmscott Gdns WCHMH N21......52 C1
Elmscott Rd BMLY BR1...........212 A1
Elms Ct ALP/SUD HA0............100 B2
Elms Crs CLAP SW4...............187 E1
Elmsdale Rd WALTH E17 ....90 D1
Elms Gdns ALP/SUD HA0.........100 C2
 DAGW RM9........................92 B4
Elmshaw Rd PUT/ROE SW15.....163 G6
Elmshurst Crs EFNCH N2..........65 H1
Elmside WBLY HA9.................102 A1
Elms La ALP/SUD HA0............100 C2
Elmsleigh Av
 KTN/HRWW/W HA3 ....80 D1
Elmsleigh Rd WHTN TW2 ....179 H4
Elmslie Cl WFD IG8................39 E2
Elms Ms BAY/PAD W2............125 H6
Elms Park Av ALP/SUD HA0.....100 C2
Elms Rd CLAP SW4................167 E6
 KTN/HRWW/W HA3 ....60 A3
Elmstead Av CHST BR7 ....213 H1
 WBLY HA9 ....101 H5
Elmstead Cl HOR/WEW KT19 ...241 E5
 TRDG/WHET N20..................49 E4
Elmstead Gdns WPK KT4.........241 C1
Elmstead Gla CHST BR7 ....213 H2
Elmstead La CHST BR7 ....213 G5
Elmsted Crs WELL DA16..........156 D4
The Elms BARN SW13.............165 F4
 ESH/CLAY * KT10..................238 D5
 NFNCH/WDSP * N12..............66 A1
 TOOT * SW17 ....9 F3
 WLGTN * SM6 ....245 E2
Elmstone Rd FUL/PGN SW6......165 E2
Elmstone Ter STMC/STPC * BR5...236 A4
Elm St FSBYW WC1X................5 H6
Elmsworth Av HSLW TW3..........159 F5
Elm Ter CRICK NW2 ....105 E1
 ELTH/MOT SE9 ....194 A1
 KTN/HRWW/W HA3 ....59 H5
Elmton Wy STNW/STAM N16.....73 H2
Elm Tree Av ESH/CLAY KT10....219 H4
Elm Tree Cl NTHLT UB5...........118 D2
 STJWD * NW8......................2 C3
Elm Tree Ct CHARL * SE7.........153 E6
Elm Tree Rd STJWD NW8.........125 H1
Elmtree Rd TEDD TW11...........200 A1
Elm Vis HNWL * W7.................120 A6
Elm Wk HAMP NW3.................104 D6
 ORP BR6............................251 H1
 RYNPK SW20......................224 A1
Elm Wy FBAR/BDGN N11..........66 C2
 HOR/WEW KT19 ....240 D5
 WLSDN NW10.....................103 E2
 WPK KT4 ....242 A1
Elmwood Av
 KTN/HRWW/W HA3 ....80 C2
 PLMGR N13 ....67 G1
Elmwood Cl EW KT17..............241 G5
 WLGTN SM6......................210 D6
Elmwood Crs CDALE/KGS NW9...82 D1
Elmwood Dr BXLY DA5............196 C2
 EW KT17 ....241 G5
Elmwood Gdns HNWL W7........120 A5
Elmwood Rd CHSWK W4..........142 C6
 CROY/NA CR0.....................228 B4
 HNHL SE24........................168 D6
 MTCM CR4.........................226 B6
Elmworth Gv DUL SE21...........188 D4
Elnathan Ms MV/WKIL W9........121 F5
Elphinstone Rd WALTH E17......70 D5
Elphinstone St HBRY N5...........108 B2
Elrington Rd HACK E8...............90 F3
 WFD IG8 ....39 H6
Elsa Cottages POP/IOD * E14....130 C4
Elsa Rd WELL DA16................176 A3
Elsa St WCHPL * E1 ....130 C4
Elsdale St HOM E9.................110 A4
Elsden Ms BETH * E2..............130 A1
Elsden Rd TOTM N17...............69 F4

Elsenham Rd MNPK E12...........113 H3
Elsenham St WIM/MER SW19 ....184 D3
Elsham Rd WAN E11 ....112 A1
 WKENS W14......................144 C2
Elsham Ter WKENS * W14........144 C2
Elsiedene Rd WCHMH N21.......52 C2
Elsie Lane Ct BAY/PAD W2......125 E4
Elsieham Rd BROCKY SE4.......170 D6
Elsie Rd EDUL SE22...............144 D6
Elsinore Gdns CRICK * NW2....104 C1
Elsinore Rd FSTH SE23...........190 C3
Elsinore Wy RCH/KEW TW9......142 B1
Elsley Rd BTSEA SW11............166 B4
Elspeth Rd ALP/SUD HA0........101 G3
 BTSEA SW11......................166 B5
Elsrick Av MRDN SM4.............225 C2
Elstan Wy CROY/NA CR0.........230 C4
Elsted St WALW SE17..............31 H2
Elstow Cl ELTH/MOT SE9..........173 H6
 RSLP HA4...........................78 B4
Elstow Gdns DAGW RM9.........116 C6
Elstow Rd DAGW RM9............116 C5
Elstree Gdns BELV DA17.........156 C4
 ED N9 ....53 H5
 IL IG1...............................114 C3
Elstree HI BMLY BR1..............212 A3
Elstree HI South BORE WD6.....45 F2
Elstree Pk MLHL * NW7............46 C1
Elstree Rd BORE WD6.............44 C1
 BUSH WD23.......................43 H3
 STAN HA7...........................44 B2
Elswick Rd LEW SE13............171 F4
Elswick St FUL/PGN SW6........165 C3
Elsworthy THDIT KT7..............220 A3
Elsworthy Ri HAMP NW3..........106 A5
Elsworthy Rd HAMP NW3........106 A6
Elsworthy Ter HAMP NW3........106 A5
Elsynge Rd WAND/EARL SW18...165 H6
Eltham Green Rd
 ELTH/MOT SE9 ....173 E6
Eltham High St ELTH/MOT SE9...193 H1
Eltham HI ELTH/MOT SE9 ....173 F6
Eltham Palace Rd
 ELTH/MOT SE9 ....193 E1
Eltham Park Gdns
 ELTH/MOT SE9 ....174 A5
Eltham Rd ELTH/MOT SE9.......173 E6
Elthiron Rd FUL/PGN SW6.......165 E2
Elthorne Av HNWL W7............140 B2
Elthorne Ct FELT TW13...........178 A3
Elthorne Park Rd HNWL W7.....140 B3
Elthorne Rd ARCH N19.............87 F6
 CDALE/KGS NW9..................83 G1
Elthorne Wy CDALE/KGS NW9...83 C3
Elthruda Rd LEW SE13............191 H1
Eltisley Rd IL IG1..................114 B2
Elton Av ALP/SUD HA0............100 D3
 BAR EN5............................34 D6
 GFD/PVL UB6....................100 D4
Elton Cl E/WMO/HCT KT8........201 E5
Elton PI STNW/STAM N16........109 E3
Elton Rd KUTN/CMB KT2.........201 H4
Eltringham St
 WAND/EARL SW18...............165 C5
Elvaston Ms SKENS * SW7.......145 C3
Elvaston PI SKENS SW7...........145 C4
Elveden PI WLSDN NW10.........122 A1
Elveden Rd FBAR/BDGN N11....67 C2
Elver Gdns BETH E2.................9 F3
Elverson Ms DEPT * SE8.........170 D1
Elverson Rd DEPT SE8............151 H6
Elverton St WEST SW1P............28 C5
Elvington Gn HAYES BR2.........252 B2
Elvington La CDALE/KGS NW9...63 E4
Elvino Rd SYD SE26...............210 B1
Elvis Rd CRICK NW2..............104 A4
Elwill Wy BECK BR3.................211 F2
Elwin St BETH E2....................9 E5
Elwood St HBRY N5.................73 H6
Elwyn Gdns LEE/GVPK SE12...192 C2
Ely Cl NWMAL KT3.................203 F5
Ely Cottages VX/NE * SW8.......167 H1
Ely Gdns DAGE RM10............117 C1
Elyne Rd FSBYPK N4................88 A3
Ely PI HCIRC EC1N...................14 B2
Ely PI WFD IG8......................55 H1
Ely Rd CROY/NA CR0.............228 D2
 HSLWW TW4......................158 A4
 LEY E10 ....91 C3
Elysian Av STMC/STPC BR5.....235 E3
Elysium PI FUL/PGN SW6........164 D3
Elysium St FUL/PGN SW6........164 D3
Elystan Cl WLGTN SM6...........245 E6
Elystan PI CHEL SW3...............26 B3
Elystan St CHEL SW3..............26 A2
Elystan Wk IS N1..................108 A6
Emanuel Av ACT W3..............122 C5
Embankment PUT/ROE SW15...146 B4
Embankment Gdns CHEL SW3...26 D5
Embankment PI CHCR WC2N...11 E1
The Embankment TWK TW1.....180 C3
Embassy Ct SCUP DA14.........195 H5
 WELL * DA16.......................156 D4
Emba St BERM/RHTH SE16.......25 F4
Ember Cl STMC/STPC BR5.......234 C4
Embercourt Rd THDIT KT7.......220 A3
Ember Farm Av
 E/WMO/HCT KT8.................219 H3
Ember Farm Wy
 E/WMO/HCT KT8.................219 H2
Ember Gdns ESH/CLAY KT10....219 H2
Ember La ESH/CLAY KT10........219 H5
Embleton Rd LEW SE13...........171 F5
Embry Cl STAN HA7.................44 C6
Embry Dr STAN HA7................60 C1
Embry Wy STAN HA7...............44 C6
Emden St FUL/PGN SW6.........165 F2
Emerald Cl CAN/RD E16.........133 C5
Emerald Gdns BCTR RM8........97 E5
Emerald Sq NWDGN UB2.......138 B3
Emerald St BMSBY WC1N........13 G1
Emerson Gdns
 KTN/HRWW/W HA3 ....81 H3
Emerson St STHWK SE1...........23 E1
Emerton Cl BXLYHS DA6.........176 C5
Emery Hill St WEST SW1P.........20 B6
Emery St STHWK SE1..............22 B5
Emes Rd ERITH DA8...............117 D6
Emilia Cl PEND EN3.................39 H6
Emily PI HOLWY N7................108 A2

Emily St CAN/RD E16..............132 B5
Emlyn Rd SHB W12................143 E2
Emmanuel Rd BAL SW12........187 E3
Emma Rd PLSTW E13.............132 B2
Emma St BETH E2....................9 G1
Emma Ter WELL * DA16..........204 A3
Emmaus Wy CHIG IG7.............74 A1
Emmott Av BARK/HLT IG6.........56 C2
Emmott Cl EFNCH N2..............85 C3
 WCHPL E1.........................130 C3
Emperor's Ga SKENS SW7.......145 F3
Empire Av UED N18.................68 C2
Empire Pde UED * N18............68 D2
 WBLY * HA9.......................102 B6
Empire Rd GFD/PVL UB6.........101 E6
Empire Sq HGT * N6................85 H1
Empire Wharf Rd POP/IOD E14...151 H4
Empress Av CHING E4..............71 E3
 IL IG1...............................95 H6
 MNPK E12...........................95 E6
 WFD IG8.............................72 B3
Empress Dr CHST BR7.............214 B2
Empress Pde CHING * E4.........71 E3
Empress PI ECT SW5..............145 E5
Empress St WALW SE17............31 F5
Empson St BOW E3................131 F3
Emsworth Cl ED N9.................54 A3
Emsworth Rd BARK/HLT IG6.....72 A4
Emsworth St
 BRXS/STRHM SW2...............187 H4
Emu Rd VX/NE SW8...............166 D3
Ena Rd STRHM/NOR SW16......207 G6
Enbrook St NKENS W10...........124 C2
Enclave Ct FSBYE EC1V.............6 D5
Endale Cl CAR SM5...............226 B6
Endeavour Wy BARK IG11........135 C1
 CROY/NA CR0....................211 G6
 WIM/MER SW19..................185 F6
Endell St LSQ/SEVD WC2H........13 E3
Enderby St GNWCH SE10.......152 A5
Enderley Rd KTN/HRWW/W HA3..59 H4
Endersby Rd BAR EN5.............34 A6
Endersleigh Gdns HDN NW4.....83 G1
Endlebury Rd CHING E4............55 G4
Endlesham Rd BAL SW12........188 C2
Endsleigh Gdns IL IG1..............95 H5
 STPAN WC1H.......................4 D5
 SURB KT6..........................221 E3
Endsleigh Pl STPAN WC1H.......4 D5
Endsleigh Rd NWDGN UB2......138 C2
 NWDGN UB2......................138 C4
Endsleigh St STPAN WC1H.......4 D5
Endway BRYLDS KT5..............222 A4
Endwell Rd BROCKY SE4.........170 C3
Endymion Rd
 BRXS/STRHM SW2...............187 H2
 FSBYPK N4.........................88 B4
Energen Cl WLSDN NW10........105 G4
Enfield Rd ACT W3.................142 B2
 BTFD TW8.........................141 F5
 EBAR EN4..........................37 F5
 IS N1................................109 G5
Enford St MBLAR W1H............10 C1
Engadine Cl CROY/NA CR0.......247 F1
Engadine St WAND/EARL SW18...184 D3
Engate St LEW SE13..............171 F4
Engel Pk MLHL NW7................64 A2
Engineer Cl WOOL/PLUM SE18...154 A6
Engineers Wy WBLY HA9.........102 A2
England La HAMP NW3...........106 B4
England's Ln HAMP NW3.........106 B4
Englefield Cl CROY/NA CR0.....228 C3
 ENC/FH EN2........................38 A3
 STMC/STPC BR5.................235 F1
Englefield Crs STMC/STPC BR5...235 G2
Englefield Pth STMC/STPC BR5...235 C1
Englefield Rd IS N1...............108 D5
Engleheart Rd CAT SE6..........191 F2
Englewood Rd CLAP SW4.......186 D1
English St BOW E3................130 D3
Enid St STHWK SE1.................24 D5
Enmore Av SNWD SE25..........229 G2
Enmore Gdns
 MORT/ESHN SW14................162 D6
Enmore Rd PUT/ROE SW15.....164 A5
 SNWD SE25.......................229 G2
 STHL UB1..........................119 E3
Ennerdale Av STAN HA7...........61 E6
Ennerdale Cl SUT SM1...........242 D2
Ennerdale Dr CDALE/KGS NW9...63 E2
Ennerdale Gdns WBLY HA9......81 F4
Ennerdale Rd BXLYHN DA7.....177 C2
 RCH/KEW TW9....................161 H5
Ennersdale Rd LEW SE13........171 H6
Ennis Rd FSBYPK N4................88 A5
 WOOL/PLUM SE18...............154 D6
Ennismore Av CHSWK W4........142 C4
 GFD/PVL UB6.....................100 A4
Ennismore Gardens Ms
 SKENS SW7.......................145 H5
Ennismore Ms SKENS SW7.......18 A4
Ennismore St SKENS SW7........18 A5
Ennis Rd FSBYPK N4................88 A5
Ensign St WCHPL E1................17 E5
Enslin Rd ELTH/MOT SE9.........194 A1
Ensor Ms SKENS SW7.............145 H5
Enstone Rd PEND EN3.............40 C4
Enterprise Cl CROY/NA CR0.....228 A5
Enterprise Rw
 SEVS/STOTM N15..................89 F2
Enterprise Wy TEDD TW11......200 A1
 WAND/EARL SW18...............165 H5
 WLSDN NW10.....................123 F2
Enterprize Wy DEPT * SE8......130 C4
Epcot Ms WLSDN * NW10........124 B2
Epirus Ms FUL/PGN SW6........165 E1
Epirus Rd FUL/PGN SW6.........164 D1
Epping Cl POP/IOD E14...........151 E4
 ROMW/RG RM7....................77 F6
Epping Gld CHING E4................56 A1
Epping New Rd BKHH IG9........56 D3
Epping Pl HOLWY N7..............108 A4
Epping Wy CHING E4...............53 C4
Epple Rd FUL/PGN SW6.........164 D2
Epsom Cl BXLYHN DA7...........177 E5
 NTHLT UB5..........................98 D3
Epsom Rd CROY/NA CR0.........246 A2
 GDMY/SEVK IG3...................95 F3
 LEY E10............................91 G3
 MRDN SM4.......................224 D3

Epstein Rd THMD SE28...........155 H1
Epworth Rd ISLW TW7............160 D1
Epworth St SDTCH EC2A............7 H6
Equity Sq BETH E2...................8 D2
Erasmus St WEST SW1P...........28 D2
Erconwald St ACT W3.............123 F5
Eresby Dr BECK BR3..............231 E5
Eresby Pl KIL/WHAMP NW6.....105 E5
Erica Gdns CROY/NA CR0.......249 F2
Erica St SHB W12..................123 G6
Eric Clarke La BARK IG11........134 B3
Ericcson Cl WAND/EARL SW18...165 E6
Eric Est BOW E3....................130 D5
Eric Rd CHDH RM6..................96 B4
 FSTGT E7..........................112 C2
 WLSDN NW10....................103 F4
Eric St BOW E3.....................130 D5
Eridge Green Cl
 STMC/STPC BR5.................236 A5
Eridge Rd CHSWK W4............142 B1
Erin Cl BMLY BR1..................212 A5
Erindale WOOL/PLUM SE18....154 D6
Erindale Ter WOOL/PLUM SE18...154 D6
Erlanger Rd NWCR SE14.........170 B2
Eriesmere Gdns HNWL W7.....120 C1
Erlich Cottages WCHPL * E1....130 A4
Ermine Rd LEW SE13.............171 F5
 SEVS/STOTM N15..................89 F3
Ermine Side EN EN1...............36 D4
Ermington Rd ELTH/MOT SE9...194 C4
Ernald Av EHAM E6................133 C1
Erncroft Wy TWK TW1............180 B1
Ernest Av WNWD SE27...........187 B6
Ernest Cl BECK BR3..............231 E2
Ernest Gdns CHSWK W4........142 B6
Ernest Rd KUT KT1.................202 D2
Ernest St WCHPL E1..............130 B3
Ernle Rd RYNPK SW20...........203 H5
Ernshaw Pl PUT/ROE SW15....164 C6
Erpingham Rd PUT/ROE SW15...146 A4
Erridge Rd WIM/MER SW19.....205 A3
Errington Rd MV/WKIL W9.......124 D3
Errol Gdns NWMAL KT3..........223 C1
Errol St STLK EC1Y..................7 F3
Erskine Cl SUT SM1...............244 A1
Erskine Crs TOTM N17.............89 H1
Erskine Hl GLDGN NW11..........85 E1
Erskine Ms HAMP * NW3........106 B5
 SUT SM1...........................243 H2
 WALTH E17.........................90 D1
Erwood Rd CHARL SE7...........153 G5
Esam Wy STRHM/NOR SW16...208 A1
Escot Wy BAR EN5..................34 A6
Escreet Gv WOOL/PLUM SE18...154 A4
 ROMW/RG RM7....................97 G5
Esher Cl BXLY DA5................196 C3
Esher Ms MTCM CR4.............206 C6
Esher Rd E/WMO/HCT KT8......219 H3
 GDMY/SEVK IG3...................96 D6
Eskdale Av NTHLT UB5............98 D1
Eskdale Cl WBLY HA9..............81 F6
Eskdale Rd BXLYHN DA7........177 E3
Eskmont Rdg NRWD SE19.......208 C1
Esk Rd PLSTW E13................132 D3
Esmar Crs CDALE/KGS NW9......83 G4
Esmeralda Rd STHWK * SE1.....111 H4
Esmond Gdns CHSWK * W4....142 D4
Esmond Rd CHSWK W4..........142 D5
 KIL/WHAMP NW6.................104 D6
Esmond St PUT/ROE SW15......164 C5
Esparto St WAND/EARL SW18...165 B5
Essenden Rd BELV DA17.........157 F5
 SAND/SEL CR2...................247 E5
Essendine Rd MV/WKIL W9......125 E2
Essex Av ISLW TW7...............160 A4
Essex Cl MRDN SM4..............224 B4
 ROMW/RG RM7....................77 F1
 RSLP HA4...........................78 B3
 WALTH E17..........................91 G1
Essex Ct BARN SW13.............165 F5
 TPL/STR * WC2R...................14 A4
Essex Gdns FBAR/BDGN N11....68 B3
Essex Pk FNCH N3..................65 E2
Essex Park Ms ACT W3...........143 E1
Essex Place Sq CHSWK * W4...142 D4
Essex Rd ACT W3..................142 C4
 BARK IG11.........................114 D5
 CHDH RM6.........................56 A3
 CHING E4...........................56 A5
 CHSWK W4........................142 D4
 DACE RM10.......................117 C3
 ENC/FH EN2........................38 D1
 LEY E10..............................90 C6
 ROMW/RG RM7....................97 F1
 WALTH E17..........................90 C1
 WLSDN NW10.....................103 E5
Essex Rd South WAN E11.........91 H4
Essex St FSTGT E7.................112 C3
 TPL/STR WC2R....................14 A4
 WEST * SW1P......................20 B6
Essex Vis KENS W8................145 E2
Essex Whf CLPT * E5................90 D5
Essian St WCHPL E1..............130 C4
Essoldo Wy EDGW HA8............61 H6
Estate Wy LEY E10..................90 D6
Estcourt Rd FUL/PGN SW6......165 E1
 SNWD SE25......................229 H3
Estella Av NWMAL KT3............223 H1
Estelle Rd HAMP NW3............106 B2
Esterbrooke St WEST SW1P......28 C2
Este Rd BTSEA SW11.............166 A4
Esther Cl WCHMH N21...........52 A2
Esther Rd WAN E11.................91 H3
Estoria Cl BRXS/STRHM SW2...188 A2
Estreham Rd
 STRHM/NOR SW16...............207 F2
Estridge Cl HSLW TW3............159 E5
Estuary Cl BARK IG11.............135 H2
Eswyn Rd TOOT SW17............186 D5
Etchingham Park Rd FNCH N3...65 F5

Etchingham Rd SRTFD E15 ...111 G2
Etfield Gv SCUP DA14 ...215 H1
Ethelbert Cl HAYES BR2 ...212 C5
Ethelbert Gdns
  GNTH/NBYPK IG2 ...93 H2
Ethelbert Rd BMLY BR1 ...212 C6
  ERITH DA8 ...
  RYNPK SW20 ...204 B4
  STMC/STPC BR5 ...216 B6
Ethelbert St BAL SW12 ...186 D3
Ethelburga St BTSEA * SW11 ...166 A2
Etheldene Av MUSWH N10 ...87 E1
Ethelden Rd SHB W12 ...143 H1
Etheired St LBTH SE11 ...30 A2
Ethel Rd CAN/RD E16 ...132 D6
Ethel St WALW * SE17 ...31 F2
Etheridge Rd HAMP NW2 ...84 A4
Etherley Rd SEVS/STOTM N15 ...88 C2
Etherow St EDUL SE22 ...189 G1
Etherstone Rd
  STRHM/NOR SW16 ...187 H6
Ethnard Rd PECK SE15 ...33 G6
Ethronvi Rd BXLYHN DA7 ...176 C4
Etloe Rd LEY E10 ...91 H3
Eton Av ALP/SUD HA0 ...101 E2
  EBAR EN5 ...50 A1
  HAMP NW3 ...106 A5
  HEST TW5 ...138 D6
  NFNCH/WDSP N12 ...65 G3
  NWMAL KT3 ...222 D2
Eton Cl WAND/EARL SW18 ...185 F2
Eton College Rd HAMP NW3 ...106 B4
Eton Garages HAMP NW3 ...106 A4
Eton Cv CDALE/KGS NW9 ...62 A6
  LEW SE13 ...172 A4
Eton Pl HAMP * NW3 ...106 D5
Eton Ri HAMP * NW3 ...106 B4
Eton Rd HAMP NW3 ...106 D5
  ORP BR6 ...253 H2
Eton St RCHPK/HAM TW10 ...161 F6
Eton Vis HAMP NW3 ...106 B4
Etta St DEPT SE8 ...150 C6
Etton Rd HSLW TW3 ...159 G6
Ettrick St POP/IOD E14 ...131 G5
Etwell Pl BRYLDS KT5 ...221 H3
Eugenia Rd BERM/RHTH SE16...192 A5
Eureka Rd KUT KT1 ...202 A5
Europa Pl FSBYE EC1V ...7 E4
Europe Rd WOOL/PLUM SE18 ...153 H3
Eustace Pl WOOL/PLUM SE18 ...153 H4
Eustace Rd CHDH RM6 ...96 B4
  EHAM E6 ...133 G2
  FUL/PGN SW6 ...165 E1
Euston Gra CAMTN NW1 ...4 A5
  CROY/NA CRO ...228 A5
Euston Sq CAMTN NW1 ...4 B5
Evandale Rd BRXN/ST SW9 ...168 A1
Evangelist Rd KTTN NW5 ...106 D2
Evans Cl HACK E8 ...109 F4
Evans Gv FELT TW13 ...179 E4
Evans Rd CAT SE6 ...192 A4
Evanston Av CHING E4 ...71 G3
Evanston Gdns REDBR IG4 ...95 G3
Eva Rd CHDH RM6 ...96 A4
Evelina Rd PECK SE15 ...170 A4
  PGE/AN SE20 ...210 A3
Eveline Lowe Est
  BERM/RHTH SE16 ...25 E6
Eveline Rd MTCM CR4 ...206 B4
Evelyn Av CDALE/KGS NW9 ...82 D1
Evelyn Cl WHTN TW2 ...179 F2
Evelyn Denington Rd
  EHAM E6 ...133 G3
Evelyn Dr PIN HA5 ...58 B3
Evelyn Gdns RCH/KEW TW9 ...161 G5
  WBPTN SW10 ...145 G5
Evelyn Gv EA W5 ...141 H1
  STHL UB1 ...118 D5
Evelyn Rd CAN/RD E16 ...152 C1
  CHSWK W4 ...142 D3
  EBAR EN4 ...36 B5
  RCH/KEW TW9 ...161 G4
  RCHPK/HAM TW10 ...181 E5
  WALTH E17 ...91 G1
  WIM/MER SW19 ...205 F1
Evelyn St DEPT SE8 ...150 D6
Evelyn Ter RCH/KEW TW9 ...161 G4
Evelyn Wk IS N1 ...7 G2
Evelyn Wy WLCTN SM6 ...245 F2
Evenwood Cl PUT/ROE * SW15..164 C6
Everard Av HAYES BR2 ...232 C5
Everard Wy WBLY HA9 ...101 G3
Everatt Cl WAND/EARL * SW18...184 D1
Everdon Rd BARN SW13 ...146 C5
Everest Pl POP/IOD E14 ...131 G4
  SWLY BR8 ...237 H1
Everest Rd ELTH/MOT SE9 ...175 G6
Everett Cl BUSH WD23 ...44 A3
The Everglades HSLW * TW3 ...159 G4
Everglade Strd
  CDALE/KGS NW9 ...63 F4
Evergreen Cl PGE/AN SE20 ...210 A3
Evergreen Sq HACK E8 ...109 G5
Everild Rd IS * N1 ...
Everington Rd STNW/STAM N16 ...109 F1
Everington St HMSMTH W6 ...66 D5
Everitt Rd WLSDN NW10 ...122 D3
Everleigh St FSBYPK N4 ...87 H5
Eve Rd ISLW TW7 ...160 C5
  SRTFD E15 ...112 A2
  SRTFD E15 ...33 A1
  TOTM N17 ...69 E6
Eversfield Gdns EDGW HA8 ...63 E3
Eversfield Rd RCH/KEW TW9 ...161 H3
Evershot Rd FSBYPK N4 ...67 F6
Eversleigh Rd BAR EN5 ...35 G6
  BTSEA SW11 ...166 D4
  EHAM E6 ...113 F6
  FNCH N3 ...64 D5
Eversley Av WBLY HA9 ...82 A6
Eversley Cl WCHMH N21 ...51 H1
Eversley Crs ISLW TW7 ...159 H2
  WCHMH N21 ...51 H1
Eversley Mt WCHMH N21 ...203 H1
Eversley Park Rd WCHMH N21 ...51 H1
Eversley Rd BRYLDS KT5 ...221 H1

CHARL SE7 ...152 D6
NRWD SE19 ...208 D3
Eversley Wy CROY/NA CRO ...249 E1
Everthorpe Rd PECK SE15 ...169 F4
Everton Buildings CAMTN NW1...4 A4
Everton Dr STAN HA7 ...61 H6
Everton Rd CROY/NA CRO ...229 G5
Evesham Av WALTH E17 ...51 H5
Evesham Cl BELMT SM2 ...243 E5
  GFD/PVL UB6 ...119 F1
Evesham Gn MRDN SM4 ...225 F3
Evesham Rd FBAR/BDGN N11 ...67 E1
  MRDN SM4 ...225 F3
  SRTFD E15 ...112 B5
Evesham St NTGHL W11 ...124 B6
Evesham Ter SURB * KT6 ...221 F5
Evesham Wk BRXN/ST SW9 ...168 A3
  CLAY IG5 ...
Evry Rd SCUP DA14 ...216 A2
Ewald Rd FUL/PGN SW6 ...164 D3
Ewanrigg Ter WFD IG8 ...73 E1
Ewart Av WDGN N22 ...68 A4
Ewart Pl BOW * E3 ...130 D1
Ewart Rd FSTH SE23 ...190 B2
Ewe Cl HOLWY N7 ...107 G4
Ewell By-Pass EW KT17 ...241 G5
Ewell Court Av
  HOR/WEW KT19 ...241 E3
Ewellhurst Rd CLAY IG5 ...73 C5
Ewell Park Gdns EW KT17 ...241 G5
Ewell Park Wy EW KT17 ...241 G4
Ewell Rd CHEAM SM3 ...242 B4
  SURB KT6 ...221 H3
  THDIT KT7 ...220 D4
Ewelme Rd FSTH SE23 ...190 A3
Ewen Crs BRXS/STRHM SW2 ...188 A2
Ewer St STHWK SE1 ...21 E2
Ewhurst Av SAND/SEL CR2 ...247 F6
Ewhurst Cl BELMT SM2 ...242 A6
  WCHPL E1 ...
Ewhurst Rd BROCKY SE4 ...190 D1
Exbury Rd CAT SE6 ...191 E4
Excel Cl LSQ/SEVD WC2H ...12 D6
Excelsior Cl KUT KT1 ...202 A5
Exchange Ar LVPST EC2M ...16 B1
Exeter Cl EHAM E6 ...133 G5
Exeter Gdns IL IG1 ...93 H5
Exeter Ms FUL/PGN * SW6 ...165 E1
Exeter Pde CRICK * NW2 ...104 C4
Exeter Rd CAN/RD E16 ...132 C2
  CRICK NW2 ...104 C3
  CROY/NA CRO ...229 E4
  DAGE RM10 ...117 F4
  ED N9 ...
  FELT TW13 ...178 D5
  PEND EN3 ...40 B4
  RYLN/HDSTN HA2 ...78 C6
  WALTH E17 ...91 E2
  WELL DA16 ...175 F3
Exeter St COVGDN WC2E ...13 F5
Exeter Wy NWCR SE14 ...170 D1
Exford Gdns LEE/GVPK SE12 ...192 D1
Exford Rd LEE/GVPK SE12 ...192 D4
Exhibition Rd SKENS SW7 ...145 H3
Exit Rd EFNCH N2 ...65 H5
Exmoor Cl BARK/HLT IG6 ...74 C4
Exmoor St NKENS W10 ...124 B3
Exmouth Market CLKNW EC1R...6 A5
Exmouth Ms CAMTN * NW1 ...4 A4
Exmouth Pl HACK E8 ...106 H6
Exmouth Rd RSLP HA4 ...98 A1
  WALTH E17 ...90 D2
  WELL DA16 ...176 A2
Exmouth St WCHPL E1 ...130 A5
Exning Rd CAN/RD E16 ...132 B5
Exon St WALW SE17 ...32 A2
Express Dr GDMY/SEVK IG3 ...95 H5
Exton Crs WLSDN NW10 ...102 C5
Exton Gdns BCTR RM8 ...116 B3
Exton St STHWK SE1 ...22 A2
Eyhurst Cl CRICK NW2 ...83 G6
Eylewood Rd WNWD SE27 ...208 C1
Eynella Rd DUL SE21 ...189 C2
Eynham Rd SHB W12 ...124 A5
Eynsford Cl STMC/STPC BR5 ...234 C4
Eynsford Crs SCUP DA14 ...196 A3
Eynsford Rd GDMY/SEVK IG3 ...95 H6
Eynsham Dr ABYW SE2 ...155 H3
Eynswood Dr SCUP DA14 ...215 H1
Eyot Gdns HMSMTH W6 ...143 F5
Eyre Street HI CLKNW EC1R ...6 A6
Eythorne Rd BRXN/ST SW9 ...168 A2
Ezra St BETH E2 ...8 D3

F

Faber Gdns HDN NW4 ...83 G2
Fabian Rd FUL/PGN SW6 ...164 D1
Fabian St EHAM E6 ...133 H3
The Facade FSTH * SE23 ...190 A4
Factory La CROY/NA CRO ...208 D1
  TOTM N17 ...69 F5
Factory Pl POP/IOD E14 ...151 G5
Factory Rd CAN/RD E16 ...153 F1
Factory Yd HNWL W7 ...140 A1
Fairacre NWMAL * KT3 ...159 H2
  NWMAL KT3 ...205 E6
Fairacres CROY/NA CRO ...248 D6
Fair Acres HAYES BR2 ...232 C2
Fairacres Av BAR ...
Fairbank Est IS * N1 ...7 G2
Fairbanks Rd TOTM N17 ...69 G6
Fairbourne Rd TOTM N17 ...69 E6
Fairbridge Rd ARCH N19 ...85 D1
Fairbrook Cl PLMGR N13 ...51 G1
Fairby Rd LEE/GVPK SE12 ...172 D6
Fairchild Cl BTSEA * SW11 ...165 H3
Fairchild Pl SDTCH * EC2A ...8 B6
Fairchild St SDTCH EC2A ...8 B6
Fair Cl BUSH WD23 ...43 F2
Faircough St WCHPL E1 ...17 H4
Faircross Av BARK IG11 ...114 C4
  CRW RM5 ...77 H3

Fairdale Gdns PUT/ROE SW15 ...163 H5
Fairey CDALE/KGS * NW9 ...63 F5
Fairfax Av EW KT17 ...241 H5
Fairfax Ms BRXS/STRHM SW2...187 H2
Fairfax Pl CEND/HSY/T * N8 ...38 A2
  KIL/WHAMP NW6 ...164 A5
Fairfax Pl KIL/WHAMP NW6 ...105 G5
Fairfax Rd CEND/HSY/T N8 ...88 A1
  CHSWK W4 ...143 E3
  KIL/WHAMP NW6 ...105 G5
  TEDD TW11 ...174 B2
Fairfax Wy MUSWH * N10 ...66 C3
Fairfield Av EDGW HA8 ...62 B2
  HDN NW4 ...82 A1
  OXHEY WD19 ...42 A5
  WHTN TW2 ...179 F3
Fairfield Cl BFN/LL DA15 ...195 F1
  HOR/WEW KT19 ...241 E3
  MTCM CR4 ...49 G6
  PEND EN3 ...40 C5
  WIM/MER SW19 ...206 A3
Fairfield Cnr KUT * KT1 ...201 H5
Fairfield Dr GFD/PVL UB6 ...101 E6
  RYLN/HDSTN HA2 ...59 G6
  WAND/EARL SW18 ...165 H6
Fairfield East KUT KT1 ...201 H5
Fairfield Gdns CEND/HSY/T N8...87 G2
Fairfield Gv CHARL SE7 ...153 F6
Fairfield North KUT KT1 ...201 C6
Fairfield Pth CROY/NA CRO ...246 D1
Fairfield Pl KUT KT1 ...201 H6
Fairfield Rd BECK BR3 ...211 E5
  BMLY BR1 ...212 C3
  BOW E3 ...131 E1
  BXLYHN DA7 ...176 D3
  CEND/HSY/T N8 ...87 G2
  CROY/NA CRO ...246 D1
  IL IG1 ...114 B4
  KUT KT1 ...201 C5
  STHL UB1 ...114 B5
  STMC/STPC BR5 ...234 D4
  UED N18 ...53 C6
  WALTH E17 ...91 G1
  WDR/YW UB7 ...136 B1
Fairfields CAT * SE6 ...191 G2
Fairfields Crs CDALE/KGS NW9..82 C1
Fairfields South KUT KT1 ...201 H6
Fairfield St WAND/EARL SW18 ...165 H6
Fairfield Wy BAR EN5 ...35 E6
  HOR/WEW KT19 ...241 E3
Fairfield West KUT KT1 ...201 G5
Fairford Rd BOW * E3 ...131 E3
Fairford Av BXLYHN DA7 ...177 G2
  CROY/NA CRO ...230 B2
Fairford Cl CROY/NA CRO ...230 B2
Fairford Ct BELMT * SM2 ...243 E5
Fairford Gdns WPK KT4 ...241 F1
Fairgreen EBAR EN4 ...36 B4
Fairgreen Rd THHTH CR7 ...228 B2
Fairhaven Av CROY/NA CRO ...230 B3
Fairhazel Gdns
  KIL/WHAMP NW6 ...105 F4
Fairholme EBED/NFELT TW14 ...
Fairholme Cl FNCH N3 ...64 C3
Fairholme Crs YEAD UB4 ...
Fairholme Gdns FNCH N3 ...
Fairholme Rd CROY/NA CRO ...

ORP BR6 ...252 D2
Fairview Gdns WFD IG8 ...72 B6
Fairview Pl BRXS/STRHM SW2...187 H2
Fairview Rd EN/FH EN2 ...38 A2
  SEVS/STOTM N15 ...89 F1
  STRHM/NOR SW16 ...207 H4
  SUT SM1 ...243 C3
Fairview Vis CHING * E4 ...71 E3
Fairview Wy EDGW HA8 ...46 A6
Fairwater Av WELL DA16 ...175 G5
Fairway BXLYHS DA6 ...176 D5
  RYNPK SW20 ...204 A6
  STMC/STPC BR5 ...234 D3
  WFD IG8 ...73 E1
Fairway Av BORE WD6 ...
Fairway Cl CROY/NA CRO ...230 C2
  GLDGN NW11 ...85 G4
  HOR/WEW KT19 ...240 C2
Fairway Ct MLHL * NW7 ...46 D5
Fairway Dr GFD/PVL UB6 ...100 B5
  THMD SE28 ...136 B5
Fairway Gdns BECK BR3 ...231 H3
  IL IG1 ...114 C3
Fairways ISLW * TW7 ...160 A1
  STAN HA7 ...61 G5
  TEDD TW11 ...201 F3
  WALTH * E17 ...91 G1
The Fairway ACT W3 ...123 E5
  ALP/SUD HA0 ...80 D6
  BAR EN5 ...49 F1
  BMLY BR1 ...233 H2
  E/WMO/HCT KT8 ...199 F6
  HNWL * W7 ...120 A6
  MLHL NW7 ...46 D5
  NTHLT UB5 ...99 G4
  NWMAL KT3 ...202 D4
  PLMGR N13 ...52 C5
  RSLP HA4 ...98 A2
  STHGT/OAK N14 ...50 D1
Fairweather Cl
  SEVS/STOTM N15 ...89 E1
Fairweather Rd
  STNW/STAM N16 ...90 C5
Fairwyn Rd SYD SE26 ...190 C3
Faithfield BUSH * WD23 ...42 C1
Fakenham Cl MLHL NW7 ...63 G5
  NTHLT UB5 ...99 E4
Fakruddin St WCHPL E1 ...9 F6
Falaize Av IL IG1 ...114 B2
Falcon Av BMLY BR1 ...213 G6
Falconberg Ct
  SOHO/SHAV * W1D ...12 C3
Falcon Cl CHSWK W4 ...142 B6
  STHWK SE1 ...22 D1
Falcon Crs PEND EN3 ...40 B6
Falconer Rd BARK/HLT IG6 ...75 H1
  BUSH WD23 ...
Falcon Gv BTSEA SW11 ...166 A4
Falcon La BTSEA SW11 ...166 A4
Falcon Rd BTSEA SW11 ...166 A4
  HPTN TW12 ...198 D3
  PEND EN3 ...40 D6
Falcon St PLSTW E13 ...132 C3
Falcon Ter BTSEA * SW11 ...166 A4
Falcon Wy CDALE/KGS NW9 ...63 E5
  KTN/HRWW/W HA3 ...61 G2
  WAN E11 ...92 C1
Falconwood Av WELL DA16 ...174 D3
Falconwood Pde WELL DA16 ...175 E3
Falconwood Rd CROY/NA CRO..248 D6
Falcourt Cl SUT SM1 ...243 F3
Falkirk Gdns OXHEY WD19 ...58 B1
Falkirk St IS N1 ...7 H4
Falkland Av FBAR/BDGN N11...50 C6
  FNCH N3 ...65 E3
Falkland Park Av SNWD SE25...209 E6
Falkland Pl KTTN NW5 ...107 E3
Falkland Rd BAR EN5 ...34 C3
  CEND/HSY/T N8 ...88 A1
  KTTN NW5 ...107 E3
Falloden Wy GLDGN NW11 ...85 E1
Fallow Court Av
  NFNCH/WDSP N12 ...65 G4
Fallowfield STAN HA7 ...44 C5
Fallowfield Cl STAN HA7 ...57 E2
Fallow Fids LOU IG10 ...
Fallowfields Dr
  NFNCH/WDSP N12 ...65 G5
Fallows Cl EFNCH N2 ...65 G5
Fallsbrook Rd
  STRHM/NOR SW16 ...206 D2
Falman Cl ED N9 ...39 E5
Falmer Rd EN EN1 ...39 E5
  SEVS/STOTM N15 ...90 A1
  WALTH E17 ...71 G6
Falmouth Av CHING E4 ...71 H1
Falmouth Cl LEE/GVPK SE12 ...173 H2
Falmouth Gdns REDBR IG4 ...93 F1
Falmouth Rd STHWK SE1 ...23 F6
Falmouth St SRTFD E15 ...111 H5
Fambridge Cl SYD SE26 ...191 J1
Fambridge Rd BCTR RM8 ...97 E5
Fane St WKENS W14 ...144 D6
Fann St FARR EC1M ...7 E6
Fanshawe Av BARK IG11 ...114 C4
Fanshawe Crs DAGW RM9 ...116 C3
Fanshawe Rd
  RCHPK/HAM TW10 ...181 E6
Fanshaw St IS N1 ...8 A3
Fanthorpe St PUT/ROE SW15...164 H4
Faraday Av SCUP DA14 ...195 H4
Faraday Cl HOLWY * N7 ...107 H4
Faraday Rd ACT W3 ...122 C6
  E/WMO/HCT KT8 ...199 F3
  GFD/PVL UB6 ...119 F6
  NKENS W10 ...124 C4
  SRTFD E15 ...112 B6
  WIM/MER SW19 ...205 F2
Faraday Wy STMC/STPC BR5 ...235 H1
  WOOL/PLUM SE18 ...153 F3
Fareham Rd
  EBED/NFELT TW14 ...178 A1
Fareham St SOHO/CST * W1F...12 C3
Farewell Pl MTCM CR4 ...205 H4
Faringford Rd SRTFD E15 ...112 D6
Farjeon Rd BKHTH/KID SE3 ...173 F2
Farleigh Av HAYES BR2 ...232 B4

Farleigh Pl STNW/STAM N16 ......109 F2
Farleigh Rd STNW/STAM N16 .....109 F2
Farley Dr GDMY/SEVK IG5.........95 E5
Farley Pl SNWD SE25............229 G1
Farley Rd CAT SE6..............191 G2
  SAND/SEL CR2................247 H5
Farlington Pl PUT/ROE SW15....183 H2
Farlow Rd PUT/ROE SW15........164 B4
Farlton Rd WAND/EARL SW18 ....185 F2
Farman Ter
  KTN/HRWW/W * HA3............81 F1
Farm Av ALP/SUD HA0..........101 E4
  CRICK NW2..................104 C1
  RYLN/HDSTN HA2..............79 E4
  STRHM/NOR SW16.............187 G6
  SWLY SE8...................217 G6
Farmborough Cl HRW HA1.........79 H4
Farm Cl BELMT SM2.............243 H5
  BKHH IG9....................57 E5
  DAGE RM10.................117 G6
  FUL/PGN * SW6..............165 E1
  STHL UB1...................119 F6
  WWKM BR4..................250 B1
Farm Cottages
  E/WMO/HCT * KT8............220 C1
Farmdale Rd CAR SM5...........244 A5
  GNWCH SE10................152 C5
Farm Dr CROY/NA CRO..........230 D6
Farmer Rd LEY E10..............91 F5
Farmers Rd CMBW SE5..........168 B3
Farm St MYFR/PICC W1J..........11 G6
The Farm WIM/MER * SW19......184 B2
Farm V BXLY DA5...............197 F1
Farmway BCTR RM8.............116 A4
Farm Wy BKHH IG9...............57 E6
  WPK KT4...................242 A1
Farnaby Rd BMLY BR1...........212 A4
  ELTH/MOT SE9...............173 H5
Farnan Av WALTH E17............71 E5
Farnan Rd STRHM/NOR SW16....187 F1
Farnborough Av
  SAND/SEL CR2...............248 C5
  WALTH * E17.................70 C6
Farnborough Cl WBLY HA9........82 B6
Farnborough Common
  ORP BR6...................251 H1
Farnborough Crs HAYES BR2....232 B5
  SAND/SEL CR2...............248 C6
Farnborough HI ORP BR6........252 D5
Farnborough Wy ORP BR6.......255 E4
  PECK * SE15................169 E1
Farncombe St
  BERM/RHTH SE16.............25 F4
Farndale Av PLMGR N13.........43 G3
Farndale Crs GFD/PVL UB6.....119 G2
Farnell Ms ECT SW5............145 F5
Farnell Rd ISLW TW7...........159 H4
Farnham Cl TRDG/WHET N20.....49 G2
Farnham Gdns RYNPK SW20....203 H5
Farnham Pl STHWK SE1..........18 C1
Farnham Rd GDMY/SEVK IG3....95 F3
  WELL DA16..................176 A3
Farnham Royal LBTH SE11.......29 H4
Farningham Rd TOTM N17........69 G3
Farnley Rd CHING E4............56 A2
  THHTH CR7.................228 D1
Faro Cl BMLY BR1.............214 A5
Faroe Rd WKENS W14...........144 B3
Faroma Wk ENC/FH EN2..........38 A2
Farquhar Rd NRWD SE19........209 F1
  WIM/MER SW19...............185 H4
Farquharson Rd CROY/NA CRO..228 C5
Farrance Rd CHDH RM6..........96 C3
Farrance St POP/IOD E14......131 E5
Farrant Av WDGN N22...........41 G1
Farrant Cl ORP BR6...........255 G5
Farr Av BARK IG11.............135 G1
Farren Rd FSTH SE23..........190 C4
Farrer Ms CEND/HSY/T N8........47 H1
Farrer Rd CEND/HSY/T N8........87 H1
  KTN/HRWW/W HA3.............81 G2
Farrier Cl BMLY BR1...........213 F6
Farrier Rd NTHLT UB5..........119 E1
Farrier St CAMTN NW1.........106 C5
Farriers Wy BORE WD6..........46 D1
Farrier Wk WBPTN * SW10......145 G6
Farringdon La CLKNW EC1R........6 A6
Farringdon Rd FSBYW WC1X.......4 A5
Farringdon St STBT EC1A.......14 C2
Farrington Pl STMC/STPC BR5..215 H6
Farrington Pl CHST SE7.......214 D3
Farrins Rents
  BERM/RHTH SE16.............150 C1
Farrow La PECK SE15..........170 A1
Farrow Pl BERM/RHTH SE16....150 C3
Farr Rd ENC/FH EN2............38 D2
Farthing Aly STHWK SE1........19 J1
Farthing Flds WAP E1W.........25 H1
Farthings Cl CHING E4.........56 A5
The Farthings KUTN/CMB KT2..202 A4
Farthing St ORP BR6..........264 D6
Farwell Rd SCUP DA14.........195 H6
Farwig La BMLY BR1...........212 C4
Fashion St WCHPL E1...........16 C2
Fashoda Rd HAYES BR2.........233 F1
Fassett Rd HACK E8...........109 C4
  KUT KT1...................221 G1

Fassett Sq HACK E8...........109 G4
Fauconberg Rd CHSWK W4.....142 C6
Faulkner Cl BCTR RM8..........92 A4
Faulkner St NWCR SE14........170 A2
Fauna Cl CHDH RM6.............96 A3
Faunce St WALW SE17...........30 C4
Favart Rd FUL/PGN SW6........165 E2
Faversham Av CHING E4.........56 A3
  WCHMH N21..................42 D1
Faversham Rd BECK BR3........210 D5
  CAT SE6...................191 G2
  MRDN SM4.................225 F3
Fawcett Cl BTSEA SW11........165 H3
  STRHM/NOR SW16............188 A6
Fawcett Est CLPT * E5.........86 C5
Fawcett Rd CROY/NA CRO.......246 B1
  WLSDN NW10................105 F5
Fawcett St WBPTN SW10........145 G6
Fawcus Cl ESH/CLAY KT10......238 A4
Fawe Park Rd PUT/ROE SW15..164 D5
Fawe St POP/IOD E14..........131 F4
Fawley Rd KIL/WHAMP NW6......83 F3
Fawnbrake Av HNHL SE24.......168 B6
Fawn Rd CHIG IG7..............75 F1
  PLSTW E13...................94 D5
Fawood Av WLSDN NW10.......102 A5
Faygate Crs BXLYHS DA6.......217 F6
Faygate Rd BRXS/STRHM SW2..187 H4
Fayland Av STRHM/NOR SW16..187 F1
Fearnley Crs HPTN TW12.......198 C1
Fearon St GNWCH SE10.........152 C5
Featherbed La CROY/NA CRO..248 D5
Feathers Pl GNWCH SE10.......151 H6
Featherstone Av FSTH SE23...189 H1
Featherstone Rd MLHL NW7......63 H2
  NWDGN UB2.................138 C3
Featherstone St STLK EC1Y......7 G5
Featherstone Ter NWDGN UB2..138 C3
Featley Rd BRXN/ST SW9.......168 B4
Federal Rd GFD/PVL UB6.......119 J1
Federation Rd ABYW SE2.......128 C4
Fee Farm Rd ESH/CLAY KT10..238 D5
Felbridge Av STAN HA7.........60 C4
Felbridge Cl BELMT SM2.......243 F6
  STRHM/NOR SW16............188 B1
Felday Rd LEW SE13...........191 F1
Felden St FUL/PGN SW6........164 D2
Feldman Cl STNW/STAM N16....86 D6
Feldon Cl PIN HA5..............58 C3
Felgate Ms HMSMTH W6........143 H4
Felhampton Rd ELTH/MOT SE9..194 B5
Felix Av CEND/HSY/T N8........87 G3
Felix Rd HNWL W7.............115 J6
Felixstowe Rd ABYW SE2.......155 H3
  TOTM N17....................68 B4
  UED N18....................55 C6
Felix St BETH * E2............92 H2
Fellbrigg Rd EDUL SE22......169 F6
Felbrigge St WCHPL E1..........9 H2
Fellbrook RCHPK/HAM TW10...180 D5
Fellmongers Yd CROY/NA CRO..246 C1
Fellowes Cl YEAD UB4.........118 B3
Fellowes Rd CAR SM5.........244 A1
Fellows Rd HAMP NW3.........105 H5
Fell Rd CROY/NA CRO.........246 C1
Felltram Wy CHARL SE7.......152 C5
Felmersham Cl CLAP SW4.....167 G5
Felmingham Rd PGE/AN SE20..210 A5
Felsberg Rd BRXS/STRHM SW2..187 G1
Fels Cl DAGE RM10...........117 C1
Fels Farm Av DAGE RM10.....117 C1
Felsham Rd PUT/ROE SW15....164 A6
Felspar Cl WOOL/PLUM SE18..155 F5
Felstead Av CLAY IG5..........54 A4
Felstead Rd CRW RM5...........57 J5
  HOM E9....................111 E4
  LOU IG10...................57 G2
  ORP BR6...................235 G6
  WAN E11....................92 C4
Felstead St HOM E9..........110 D4
Felsted Rd CAN/RD E16.......133 F6
Feltham Av E/WMO/HCT KT8...220 A1
Feltham Rd MTCM CR4........206 B5
Felton Cl STMC/STPC BR5.....234 B5
Felton Lea SCUP DA14........214 D5
Felton Rd BARK IG11..........135 E1
  WEA W13....................141 E2
Felton St IS N1.............108 D6
Fencepiece Rd BARK/HLT IG6..74 C2
Fenchurch Av FENCHST EC3M...16 B5
Fenchurch Buildings
  FENCHST EC3M...............16 B4
Fenchurch Pl FENCHST * EC3M..16 B5
Fenchurch St FENCHST EC3M...16 B5
Fendall Rd HOR/WEW KT19...240 C3
Fendall St STHWK SE1..........24 B6
Fendt Cl CAN/RD E16.........132 B5
Fendyke Rd ABYW SE2.........156 B4
Fenelon Pl WKENS W14.......144 D4
Fen Gv BFN/LL DA15.........195 F1
Fenham Rd PECK SE15.........169 H6
Fenman Gdns GDMY/SEVK IG3..95 H5
Fenn Cl BMLY BR1............212 C2
Fennel Cl CAN/RD E16........132 A3
  CROY/NA CRO...............249 J5
Fennells Md HOR/WEW KT19..241 F6
Fennell St WOOL/PLUM SE18..154 A6
Fenner Cl BERM/RHTH SE16...33 H1
Fenner Sq BTSEA * SW11......145 H6
Fenning St STHWK SE1.........24 A3
Fenn St HOM E9..............110 B5
Fenstanton Av
  NFNCH/WDSP N12............65 H1
Fen St CAN/RD E16...........132 B6
Fentiman Rd VX/NE SW8........29 G6
Fenton Cl BRXN/ST * SW9....167 H3
  CHST BR7...................214 B6
  HACK E8....................109 H4
Fenton Rd TOTM N17...........67 C2
Fenton's Av PLSTW E13.......132 D2
Fenwick Gv PECK SE15.......169 G4
Fenwick Pl BRXN/ST SW9......167 G4
  SAND/SEL CR2...............246 B5
Fenwick Rd PECK SE15.......169 G4
Ferdinand Pl CAMTN NW1.....106 A5
Ferdinand St CAMTN NW1.....106 A5
Ferguson Av BRYLDS KT5......221 H2
Ferguson Cl BECK BR3........211 G6

Ferguson Dr ACT W3..........122 D5
Ferguson's Cl POP/IOD E14..151 E4
Fergus Rd HBRY N5...........108 B3
Ferme Park Rd CEND/HSY/T N8..87 G2
Fermor Rd FSTH SE23.........190 C3
Fermoy Rd GFD/PVL UB6......119 F5
  MV/WKIL W9.................124 D3
Fern Av MTCM CR4............227 F1
Fernbank BKHH * IG9..........56 D5
  BKHH IG9...................56 D5
Fernbank Av ALP/SUD HA0...100 B2
  WOT/HER KT12...............218 C4
Fernbank Ms CLAP SW4.......186 D1
Fernbrook Dr RYLN/HDSTN HA2..79 F4
Fernbrook Rd LEW SE13......192 A1
Ferncliff Rd HACK E8..........109 G3
Fen Cl IS * N1...............6 C2
Ferncroft Av HAMP NW3.......105 E1
  NFNCH/WDSP N12............66 A2
  RSLP HA4....................78 A6
Ferndale BMLY BR1...........213 E5
Ferndale Av HSLWW TW4......158 C4
  WALTH E17..................69 H2
Ferndale Cl BXLYHN DA7.....176 C2
Ferndale Rd CLAP SW4.......167 G5
  CRW RM5....................57 C3
  FSTGT E7...................112 D5
  SEVS/STOTM N15.............89 J3
  SNWD SE25.................229 H2
  WAN E11....................92 B6
Ferndale St EHAM E6.........134 B6
Ferndale Ter HRW HA1..........80 E1
Ferndell Av BXLY DA5........197 H5
Ferndene Rd HNHL SE24.....168 C5
Fernden Wy ROMW/RG RM7...97 F3
Ferndown Av ORP BR6........234 D5
Ferndown Cl BELMT SM2......243 H4
  PIN HA5.....................58 C3
Ferndown Rd ELTH/MOT SE9..195 F2
  OXHEY WD19.................42 A5
Ferney Meade Wy ISLW TW7..160 C3
Ferney Rd EBAR EN4...........50 C2
Fernham Rd THHTH CR7.......228 C1
Fernhead Rd MV/WKIL W9....124 D2
Fernheath Wy RDART DA2.....217 H1
Fernhill Ct WALTH E17.........71 H5
Fernhill Gdns KUTN/CMB KT2..203 E6
Fernhill St CAN/RD E16......153 H1
Fernholme Rd PECK SE15.....170 B6
Fernhurst Gdns EDGW HA8......62 A2
Fernhurst Rd CROY/NA CRO...229 G4
  FUL/PGN SW6...............164 C2
Fern La NWDGN UB2..........138 D5
Fernlea Rd BAL SW12.........186 D3
  MTCM CR4.................206 A1
Fernleigh Cl CROY/NA CRO...246 A2
  MV/WKIL W9.................124 D2
Fernleigh Rd WCHMH N21......59 F5
  WBLY HA9....................82 A3
Fernleigh Wd WCHMH N21......52 A4
Fernsbury St FSBYW WC1X.......6 A4
Fernshaw Cl WBPTN * SW10..145 G6
Fernshaw Rd WBPTN SW10...145 G6
Fernside BKHH IG9.............56 D3
Fernside Av FELT TW13.......181 H5
  MLHL NW7....................46 D5
Fernside Rd BAL SW12........186 B3
Ferns Rd SRTFD E15..........112 A4
Fern St BOW E3.............131 E5
Ferntower Rd
  STRHM/NOR SW16............207 E2
Ferntower Rd HBRY N5.......108 D3
Fern Wk STHWK SE1............33 H4
Fernways IL IG1.............114 B1
Fernwood Av ALP/SUD HA0...101 E4
  STRHM/NOR SW16............187 F6
Fernwood Cl BMLY BR1........213 G5
Fernwood Crs TRDG/WHET N20..50 B5
Ferny HI EBAR EN4............36 B1
Ferranti Cl WOOL/PLUM SE18..153 F3
Ferraro Cl HEST TW5........139 G6
Ferrers Av WLGTN SM6........245 F2
Ferrers Rd STRHM/NOR SW16..207 F1
Ferrestone Rd CEND/HSY/T N8..87 F1
Ferriby Cl IS N1............108 A5
Ferrier St WAND/EARL SW18..165 F5
Ferring Cl RYLN/HDSTN HA2...79 G5
Ferrings DUL SE21...........189 E4
Ferris Av CROY/NA CRO........250 A1
Ferris Rd EDUL SE22.........169 G5
Ferron Rd CLPT * E5.........109 H1
Ferryhills Cl OXHEY WD19.....42 A5
Ferry La BARN SW13..........143 F6
  BTFD TW8...................136 E1
  TOTM N17...................89 H1
Ferrymead Av GFD/PVL UB6..119 E3
Ferrymead Dr GFD/PVL UB6..119 E2
Ferrymead Gdns GFD/PVL UB6..119 F3
Ferrymoor RCHPK/HAM TW10..180 D5
Ferry Rd BARN SW13.........163 G1
  E/WMO/HCT KT8.............199 E6
  TEDD TW11.................180 D1
  THDIT KT7.................220 D5
  TWK TW1....................180 D2
Ferry Sq POP/IOD TW8......141 G6
Ferry St POP/IOD E14.........151 E4
Festing Rd PUT/ROE SW15....164 B4
Festival Cl BXLY DA5........196 B3
Fetter La FLST/FETLN EC4A....14 B4
Ffinch St DEPT SE8...........171 C1
Fidler Pl BUSH WD23...........43 H1
Field Cl BKHH IG9.............57 E5
  BMLY BR1...................213 E5
  CHING E4....................43 G1
  CHSGTN KT9................239 G5
  E/WMO/HCT KT8.............219 F2
  HSLWW TW4.................158 A1
  ROMW/RG RM7...............62 A6
Field Ct GINN WC1R...........13 H2
Fieldend Rd STRHM/NOR SW16..207 H5
Fielders Cl EN EN1...........30 A4
  RYLN/HDSTN HA2.............78 A6
Fieldfare Rd THMD SE28......136 A6
Fieldgate St WCHPL E1.........17 F2

Fieldhouse Cl SWFD E18........72 D4
Fieldhouse Rd BAL SW12......187 E3
Fielding Av WHTN TW2........179 C5
Fielding Rd CHSWK W4........142 D3
  WKENS W14.................144 B3
The Fieldings FSTH SE23.....190 A3
Fielding St WALW SE17.........31 E5
Fielding Ter EA * W5........116 H1
Field La BTFD TW8............161 E1
  TEDD TW11.................200 C1
Field Md CDALE/KGS NW9......63 E3
Field Pl NWMAL KT3..........225 F3
Field Rd FSTGT E7...........112 C2
  HMSMTH W6.................144 C5
  OXHEY WD19.................42 C1
  TOTM N17....................68 D6
Fieldsend Rd CHEAM SM3.....242 C3
Fields Est HACK * E8..........109 C5
Fieldside Cl ORP BR6........252 C2
Fieldside Cottages
  TRDG/WHET * N20.............48 D2
Fields Park Crs CHDH RM6....96 B2
Field St FSBYW WC1X...........5 C3
Fieldview WAND/EARL SW18..185 H5
Fieldview Cottages
  STHGT/OAK * N14............51 F4
Field Wy CROY/NA CRO......249 F5
  GFD/PVL UB6...............102 C5
  WLSDN NW10................102 C5
Fieldway BCTR RM8..........115 H2
  STMC/STPC BR5..............234 D3
Fieldway Crs HOLWY N7......108 A3
Fiennes Cl BCTR RM8...........96 A5
Fiesta Dr DAGW RM9..........137 G3
Fife Rd CAN/RD E16...........132 C4
  KUT KT1....................207 J1
  MORT/ESHN SW14............162 C6
  WDGN N22...................68 B3
Fife Ter IS N1..............5 H1
Fifth Av MNPK E12...........113 H2
  NKENS W10.................124 C3
Fifth Cross Rd WHTN TW2....179 H4
Fifth Wy WBLY HA9............82 D3
Figge's Rd MTCM CR4.........206 C5
Filby Rd CHSGTN KT9.........239 H4
Filey Av STNW/STAM N16......89 G3
Filey Cl BELMT SM2..........243 G5
  EN EN1.....................31 G4
Fillebrook Av EN EN1.........31 H4
Fillebrook Rd WAN E11........91 H5
Filmer Chambers
  FUL/PGN * SW6..............164 D2
Filmer Rd FUL/PGN SW6......164 D2
Finborough Rd TOOT SW17...206 B3
  WBPTN SW10................145 F6
Finchale Rd ABYW SE2........155 C3
Finch Av WEST NORW SE27...188 D6
Finch Cl BAR EN5..............35 E6
Finch Dr EBED/NFELT TW14...178 B2
Finch Gdns CHING E4...........71 E1
Finchingfield Av WFD IG8......75 F3
Finch La BANK EC3V...........15 H4
Finchley La HDN NW4..........64 B1
Finchley Pk NFNCH/WDSP N12..49 G6
Finchley Pl STJWD NW8.......105 H4
Finchley Rd GLDGN NW11.....64 D3
  HAMP NW3..................105 H6
  STJWD NW8.................105 H6
Finchley VIs
  NFNCH/WDSP * N12...........65 H6
Finchley Wy FNCH N3..........65 G2
Finch Ms PECK * SE15........169 F2
Finden Rd FSTGT E7..........112 D3
Findhorn Av YEAD UB4........115 G5
Findon Cl RYLN/HDSTN * HA2...78 D1
  WAND/EARL SW18............185 E1
Findon Rd ED N9..............53 H1
  SHB W12....................143 C2
Fingal St GNWCH SE10........152 B5
Finglesham Cl STMC/STPC BR5..236 B5
Finland Rd BROCKY SE4.......170 C4
Finland St BERM/RHTH SE16..150 C3
Finlays Cl CHSGTN KT9........240 A3
Finlay St FUL/PGN SW6......164 B2
Finnis St BETH E2............92 D3
Finnymore Rd DAGW RM9.....116 C5
Finsbury Av LVPST * EC2M....13 G1
Finsbury Circ LVPST EC2M.....13 G1
Finsbury Cottages WDGN N22..67 G3
Finsbury Est CLKNW EC1R.......6 B4
Finsbury Market SDTCH EC2A...8 A6
Finsbury Park Av FSBYPK N4..88 C3
Finsbury Park Rd FSBYPK N4..108 B1
Finsbury Pavement
  SDTCH EC2A.................15 H1
Finsbury Rd WDGN N22........67 H3
Finsbury Sq SDTCH EC2A.......7 H6
Finsbury St LSTK EC1Y.......15 C1
Finsbury Wy BXLY DA5........196 D1
Finsen Rd HNHL SE24.........168 C5
Finstock Rd NKENS W10......124 A5
Finucane Dr STMC/STPC BR5..236 A4
Finucane Ri BUSH WD23.......44 B3
Fiona Ct ENC/FH * EN2.........38 B4
Firbank Cl CAN/RD E16.......133 F4
  ENC/FH EN2..................38 B4
Firbank Rd OXHEY WD19.......42 C2
Firbank Rd CRW RM5...........77 F1
  PECK SE15.................169 H1
Fircroft Gdns HRW HA1........100 A1
Fircroft Rd CHSGTN KT9.....239 H3
  TOOT SW17.................186 D5
Firdene BRYLDS KT5..........222 C5
Fir Dene ORP BR6............251 H1
Fire Bell Aly SURB KT6.......222 A5
Firebell Ms SURB KT6.........222 A5
Firecrest Dr HAMP NW3.......105 F1
Firefly Gdns EHAM E6.........133 G3
Fir Gv NWMAL KT3...........224 B1
Firhill Rd CAT SE6...........191 C5
Fir Rd CHEAM SM3............224 D5
  FELT TW13..................195 C2
Firs Av FBAR/BDGN N11........48 B2
  MORT/ESHN SW14............161 H2
  MUSWH N10.................66 C2
Firsby Av CROY/NA CRO......230 D5
Firsby Rd STNW/STAM N16....68 B6
Firs Cl ESH/CLAY KT10......238 A4
  FSTH SE23.................190 D2
  MTCM CR4.................206 D6
Firscroft PLMGR N13........42 D5

Firside Gv *BFN/LL* DA15...........195 F3
Firs La *PLMGR* N13.....................52 C5
  WCHMH N21............................52 C5
Firs Park Av *WCHMH* N21..........52 D3
Firs Park Gdns *WCHMH* N21.......52 D3
First Av *ACT* W3........................143 F1
  BXLYHN DA7.............................176 A1
  CHDH RM6................................96 A2
  DAGE RM10.............................137 F1
  E/WMO/HCT KT8....................218 D1
  EN E11......................................39 F6
  HDN NW4...................................84 A1
  HOR/WEW KT19.....................241 E6
  MNPK E12.................................78 A3
  MORT/ESHN SW14...................163 E3
  NKENS W10.............................124 D3
  PLSTW E13..............................132 C2
  UED N18....................................54 A6
  WALTH E17................................91 F2
  WBLY HA9.................................81 F6
First Cl *E/WMO/HCT* KT8...........219 G1
First Cross Rd *WHTN* TW2.........180 A4
First Dr *WLSDN* NW10...............102 C5
The Firs *BXLY* DA5...................197 H3
  EA W5......................................121 F4
  EDGW * HA8................................46 D6
  TRDG/WHET N20........................49 H5
First St *CHEL* SW3.....................26 B1
Firstway *RYNPK* SW20..............204 A5
First Wy *WBLY* HA9...................102 B2
Firs Wk *WFD* IG8.........................72 C1
Firswood Av *HOR/WEW* KT19.....241 E5
Firth Gdns *FUL/PGN* SW6.........164 C2
Firtree Av *MTCM* CR4.................206 C5
Fir Tree Cl *EA* W5.....................121 C5
  HOR/WEW KT19.......................206 C2
  ORP BR6....................................253 F3
  ROM RM1....................................77 H6
  STRHM/NOR SW16....................207 E1
Fir Tree Gdns *CROY/NA* CRO......249 F2
Fir Tree Gv *CAR* SM5.................244 B5
Fir Tree Rd *HSLWW* TW4............158 C5
Fir Trees Cl *BERM/RHTH* SE16...150 C1
Fir Tree Wk *EN* EN1.....................59 E4
Fir Wk *EW* KT17........................242 B4
Fisher Cl *CROY/NA* CRO.............229 F5
  GFD/PVL UB6..........................119 G2
Fisherdene *ESH/CLAY* KT10.......238 C5
Fisherman Cl
  RCHPK/HAM TW10...................181 E6
Fishermans Dr
  BERM/RHTH SE16....................150 B2
Fisher Rd *KTN/HRWW/W* HA3....60 D5
Fisher's La *CHSWK* W4...............117 A5
Fisher St *CAN/RD* E16.................132 C4
  RSQ WC1B...................................13 G2
Fisher's Wy *BELV* DA17............157 C1
Fisherton St *STJWD* NW8...........125 H5
Fishguard Wy *CAN/RD* E16........154 D1
Fishponds Rd *HAYES* BR2...........251 F3
  TOOT SW17.............................186 A6
Fish Street Hil *MON* * EC3R........15 H5
Fisons Rd *CAN/RD* E16...............152 C1
Fitzalan Rd *ESH/CLAY* KT10......238 A5
  FNCH N3...................................46 D1
Fitzalan St *LBTH* SE11................29 H1
Fitzgeorge Av *WKENS* W14.........17 H3
Fitzgerald Av
  MORT/ESHN SW14...................163 A1
Fitzgerald Rd
  MORT/ESHN SW14...................162 D4
  THDIT KT7.................................190 C3
  WAN E11....................................20 C2
Fitzhardinge St *MBLAR* W1H......11 F3
Fitzhugh Gv *WAND/EARL* SW18...185 H1
Fitzjames Av *CROY/NA* CRO........229 G6
  WKENS W14.............................144 C4
Fitzjohn Av *BAR* EN5....................34 C6
Fitzjohn's Av *HAMP* NW3...........105 H5
Fitzmaurice Pl *MYFR/PICC* W1J...19 H1
Fitzneal St *ACT* W3.....................123 F5
Fitzroy Cl *HGT* N6.......................86 B5
Fitzroy Crs *CHSWK* * W4............159 G1
Fitzroy Gdns *NRWD* SE19..........209 E3
Fitzroy Ms *GTPST* W1W................4 A6
Fitzroy Pk *HGT* N6.......................86 B5
Fitzroy Rd *CAMTN* NW1.............106 C6
Fitzroy Sq *FITZ* W1T.....................4 A6
Fitzroy St *CAMTN* NW1...............12 A1
Fitzstephen Rd *BCTR* RM8.........115 H3
Fitzwarren Gdns *ARCH* N19.........67 E5
Fitzwilliam Av *RCH/KEW* TW9...161 H3
Fitzwilliam Ms *CAN/RD* E16.......152 C1
Fitzwilliam Rd *CLAP* SW4...........141 H4
Fitz Wygram Cl *HPTN* TW12......199 C1
Five Acre *CDALE/KGS* NW9.........63 F5
Fiveacre Cl *THHTH* CR7..............228 A3
Five Elms Rd *DAGW* RM9..........116 D1
  HAYES BR2.............................251 E1
Five Fields Cl *OXHEY* WD19.........42 D4
Five Oaks La *CHIG* IG7.................76 C2
Five Ways Jct *HDN* NW4...............63 G4
Fiveways Rd *BRXN/ST* SW9.......168 A3
Fladbury Rd *SEVS/STOTM* N15...88 D3
Fladgate Rd *WAN* E11..................92 A3
Flag Cl *CROY/NA* CRO.................230 B5
Flambard Rd *HRW* HA1................83 G2
Flamborough St *POP/IOD* E14.....130 U5
Flamstead Gdns *DAGW* RM9......116 A5
Flamstead Rd *DAGW* RM9..........116 A5
Flamsted Av *WBLY* HA9..............102 A4
Flamsteed Rd *CHARL* SE7..........153 C05
Flanchford Rd *SHB* W12.............143 H1
Flanders Crs *TOOT* SW17...........206 B3
Flanders Rd *CHSWK* W4.............118 B4
  EHAM E6.....................................96 A1
Flanders Wy *HOM* E9....................75 A4
Flank St *WCHPL* E1.......................17 E5
Flask Wk *HAMP* NW3..................105 G2
Flavell Ms *GNWCH* SE10............152 A5
Flaxen Cl *CHING* E4......................55 F1
Flaxen Rd *CHING* E4......................55 F1
Flaxman Rd *CMBW* SE5.............168 B3
Flaxman Ter *STPAN* WC1H...........4 D4
Flaxton Rd *WOOL/PLUM* SE18...174 D2
Flecker Cl *STAN* HA7....................43 F1
Fleece Dr *UED* N18........................53 C6

Fleece Rd *SURB* KT6...................221 E5
Fleece Wk *HOLWY* * N7..............107 G4
Fleeming Cl *WALTH* E17...............70 D5
Fleeming Rd *WALTH* E17..............70 D5
Fleet Cl *E/WMO/HCT* KT8..........218 D2
Fleet Pl *STP* EC4M.......................14 A3
Fleet Rd *HAMP* NW3..................106 A3
Fleetside *E/WMO/HCT* KT8.........218 D2
Fleet Sq *FSBYW* WC1X..................5 H4
Fleet St *EMB* EC4Y......................14 B4
Fleet Street Hil *BETH* E2................9 J4
Fleet Ter *CAT* * SE6....................191 G2
Fleetwood Cl *CAN/RD* E16..........133 F4
  CHSGTN KT9...........................245 F5
  CROY/NA CRO.........................247 F1
Fleetwood Rd *NWMAL* KT3........202 B6
  WLSDN NW10...........................69 J4
Fleetwood Sq *NWMAL* KT3........202 B6
Fleetwood St *STNW/STAM* N16...89 E1
Fleetwood Wy *OXHEY* WD19........42 A6
Fleming Cl *MV/WKIL* W9............125 E3
  WBPTN * SW10.......................145 G6
Fleming La *CROY/NA* CRO..........246 A3
Fleming Md *WIM/MER* SW19......206 A3
Fleming Rd *GFD/PVL* UB6..........115 G1
  WALW SE17................................30 C5
Fleming Wk *CDALE/KGS* * NW9...63 E5
Fleming Wy *ISLW* TW7...............160 B4
  THMD SE28............................136 B6
Flempton Rd *LEY* E10...................90 C5
Fletcher Cl *EHAM* E6....................96 A6
Fletcher La *LEY* E10......................91 E6
Fletcher Rd *CHIG* IG7....................75 F1
  CHSWK W4.............................142 C3
Fletchers Cl *HAYES* BR2.............232 D1
Fletcher St *WCHPL* E1..................17 E5
Fletching Rd *CHARL* SE7............154 F6
  CLPT E5....................................110 A1
Fletton Rd *FBAR/BDGN* N11........51 H3
Fleur De Lis St *WCHPL* E1.............8 C6
Flexmere Rd *TOTM* N17................68 D4
Flight Ap *CDALE/KGS* * NW9........45 F4
Flimwell Cl *BMLY* BR1...............212 A1
Flint Cl *ORP* BR6.........................253 F4
Flint Down Cl
  STMC/STPC * BR5...................215 G4
Flintmill Crs *BKHTH/KID* SE3.....173 G3
Flinton St *WALW* SE17.................31 H2
Flint St *WALW* SE17.....................31 H2
Flitcroft St *LSQ/SEVD* WC2H......12 D4
Flock Mill Pl *WAND/EARL* SW18...185 F3
Flockton St *BERM/RHTH* * SE16...25 F4
  BERM/RHTH SE16...................149 G2
Flodden Rd *CMBW* SE5...............168 C2
Flood La *TWK* * TW1....................180 C5
Flood St *CHEL* SW3......................26 B5
Flood Wk *CHEL* SW3.....................26 B6
Flora Cl *POP/IOD* E14.................131 F5
Flora Gdns *CHDH* RM6.................96 A3
Floral Pl *IS* N1............................108 D3
Floral St *COVGDN* WC2E.............13 C5
Flora St *BELV* DA17....................156 D5
Florence Av *ENC/FH* EN2............38 D4
  MRDN SM4.............................223 G2
Florence Ct *WAN* E11....................92 D1
Florence Dr *ENC/FH* EN2.............38 D4
Florence Elson Cl *MNPK* E12.......96 H3
  HDN NW4...................................84 A1
  IS N1.......................................108 B5
Florence Ter *NWCR* SE14...........170 D2
Florence Wy *HGT* * N6.................66 B3
Florence Wy *BAL* SW12.............186 B5
Florfield Rd *HACK* E8..................109 H4
Florian Av *SUT* SM1....................243 H2
Florian Rd *PUT/ROE* SW15........139 G5
Florida Cl *BUSH* WD23.................43 H4
Florida Rd *THHTH* CR7...............208 B4
Florida St *BETH* E2........................9 K3
Florin Ct *UED* N18........................60 B1
Floriston Cl *STAN* HA7.................60 D4
Floriston Gdns *STAN* HA7............60 D4
Floss St *PUT/ROE* SW15............164 A3
Flower & Dean Wk *WCHPL* E1.......16 D2
Flower La *MLHL* NW7....................63 F1
Flowers Cl *CRICK* NW2...............103 C1
Flowers Ms *ARCH* N19..................67 A6
Floyd Rd *CHARL* SE7..................133 S5
Fludyer St *LEW* SE13..................173 A5
Foley Ms *ESH/CLAY* KT10..........238 A4
Foley St *GTPST* W1W....................12 A2
Folgate St *WCHPL* E1....................16 B1
Foliot St *ACT* W3.........................123 F5
Folkestone Rd *EHAM* E6.............134 A1
  UED N18....................................53 C6
  WALTH E17................................91 F1
Folkingham La
  CDALE/KGS NW9........................62 D4
Folkington Cnr
  NFNCH/WDSP N12.....................64 D1
Follett St *POP/IOD* E14...............131 G5
Folly La *WALTH* E17......................51 F4
Folly Wall *POP/IOD* E14..............151 G2
Fontaine Rd
  STRHM/NOR SW16...................207 H2
Fontarabia Rd *BTSEA* SW11.......166 C5
Fontenoy Rd *TOOT* SW17...........186 D4
Fonteyne Gdns *WFD* IG8..............73 F5
Fonthill Ms *FSBYPK* N4................67 F6
Fonthill Rd *FSBYPK* N4................67 H6
Font Hills *EFNCH* N2....................65 G5
Fontley Wy *PUT/ROE* SW15.......183 G2
Fontwell Cl *KTN/HRWW/W* HA3...60 A3
  NTHLT UB5................................99 F4
Fontwell Dr *HAYES* BR2.............234 A2
Football La *HRW* HA1....................80 B5
Footbury Hill Rd *ORP* BR6.........235 G4

The Footpath *PUT/ROE* * SW15...163 G6
Foots Cray High St *SCUP* DA14...216 A2
Foots Cray La *BXLY* DA5............196 A3
Footscray Rd *ELTH/MOT* SE9.....194 A1
Forbes Cl *CRICK* NW2.................103 C1
Forbes St *WCHPL* E1....................17 G4
Forburg Rd *STNW/STAM* N16......89 C2
Ford Cl *HRW* HA1..........................78 D4
  THHTH CR7............................228 B3
Fordcroft Rd *STMC/STPC* BR5....235 H2
Forde Av *BMLY* BR1....................213 G6
Fordel Rd *CAT* SE6......................191 H3
Ford End *WFD* IG8........................72 D2
Fordham Rd *EBAR* EN4.................35 H1
Fordham St *WCHPL* E1..................17 C3
Fordhook Av *ACT* W3..................121 H6
Fordingley Rd *MV/WKIL* W9.......124 D2
Fordington Rd *HGT* N6..................66 D1
Fordmill Rd *CAT* SE6..................191 E4
Ford Rd *BOW* E3.........................130 C1
  DAGE RM10............................117 E5
  DAGW RM9.............................116 B6
Ford's Gv *WCHMH* N21...............52 C5
Fords Park Rd *CAN/RD* E16........132 D5
Ford Sq *WCHPL* E1........................17 G2
Ford St *BOW* E3..........................110 C6
  CAN/RD E16.............................132 D5
Fordwich Cl *ORP* BR6.................235 F4
Fordwych Rd *CRICK* NW2...........104 C3
Fordyce Rd *LEW* SE13................191 G1
Fordyke Rd *BCTR* RM8.................98 C6
Foreland Ct *HDN* NW4..................64 A1
Foreland St *WOOL/PLUM* SE18...154 D4
Foremark Cl *BARK/HLT* IG6.........75 F2
Foreshore *DEPT* SE8....................152 B4
Forest Ap *CHING* E4......................56 A2
  WFD IG8....................................72 B3
Forest Av *CHING* E4......................56 A2
  CHIG IG7...................................77 H5
Forest Cl *CHST* BR7....................214 A4
  WAN E11...................................92 B2
  WFD IG8....................................56 D6
Forest Ct *CHING* E4......................56 B5
  WAN E11....................................92 A1
Forestdale *STHGT/OAK* N14......51 F4
Forester Rd *PECK* SE15..............169 H5
Foresters Cl *WLTN* SM6.............245 F5
Foresters Crs *BXLYHN* DA7........177 F5
Foresters Dr *WALTH* E17.............91 H1
  WLTN SM6...............................245 F5
Forest Gdns *TOTM* N17.................69 F5
Forest Ga *CDALE/KGS* NW9.........83 E1
Forest Gld *CHING* E4.....................56 B6
  WAN E11....................................92 A3
Forest Gv *HACK* E8.......................74 D6
Forest Hill Rd *EDUL* SE22...........189 H1
Foresthollme Cl *FSTH* * SE23.......190 A4
Forest La *CHIG* IG7........................74 A1
  FSTGT E7.................................112 C3
Forest Mount Rd *WFD* IG8............71 F1
Fore St *BARB* EC2Y.......................53 D6
  ED N9..53 C6
Forest Ridge *BECK* BR3.............211 E6
  HAYES BR2.............................251 F3
Forest Ri *WALTH* E17....................71 H6
Forest Rd *BARK/HLT* IG6.............75 F2
  CHEAM SM3............................225 F5
  ED N9..53 H1
  FELT TW13..............................178 A5
  FSTGT E7.................................112 C2
  HACK E8....................................74 F6
  RCH/KEW TW9........................162 A1
  ROMW/RG RM7.........................77 F6
  WALTH E17................................72 A5
  WAN E11....................................91 H4
  WFD IG8....................................56 D6
Forest Side *BKHH* IG9..................56 D3
  CHING E4...................................56 B5
  FSTGT E7.................................112 D2
  WPK KT4...................................223 F5
Forest St *FSTGT* E7....................112 C3
Forest Vw *CHING* E4.....................55 H2
  WAN E11....................................92 B3
Forest View Av *LEY* E10...............91 H2
Forest View Rd *MNPK* E12..........113 G2
  WALTH E17................................58 A4
Forest Wy *BFN/LL* DA15.............194 D2
  STMC/STPC BR5.....................215 H5
  WFD IG8....................................56 D6
Forfar Rd *BTSEA* SW11..............146 B6
  WDGN N22..............................49 H4
Forge Cl *HAYES* BR2..................232 C5
Forge Cottages *EA* * W5.............141 F1
Forge Dr *ESH/CLAY* KT10..........238 C5
Forge La *BELMT* SM2..................242 C5
  FELT TW13..............................195 C3
Forge Pl *CAMTN* NW1................106 C4
Forman Pl *STNW/STAM* N16......109 F2
Formby Av *KTN/HRWW/W* HA3...61 F6
Formosa St *MV/WKIL* W9............125 F3
Formunt Cl *CAN/RD* E16.............132 D4
Forres Gdns *GLDGN* NW11..........85 E3
Forrester Pth *SYD* SE26.............190 A6
Forrest Gdns
  STRHM/NOR SW16...................207 H6
Forset St *MBLAR* W1H.................10 B3
Forstal Cl *HAYES* BR2.................232 C6
Forster Cl *CHING* E4.....................71 H3
Forster Rd *BECK* BR3.................210 C6
  BRXS/STRHM SW2...................187 G2
  UED N18....................................50 A5
  WALTH E17................................69 G3
Forsters Cl *CHDH* RM6.................96 B5
Forston St *IS* N1.............................7 F1
Forsyte Crs *NRWD* SE19............209 E4
Forsyth Gdns *WALW* SE17...........30 B6
Forsythia Cl *IL* IG1......................114 B3
Forsyth Pl *EN* EN1.........................39 E6
Forterie Gdns *GDMY/SEVK* IG3...115 G1
Fortescue Av *WHTN* TW2...........179 H1
Fortescue Rd *EDGW* HA8.............62 D4
  WIM/MER SW19......................187 J2
Fortess Gv *KTTN* NW5.................72 B4
Fortess Rd *KTTN* NW5................106 B5

Fortess Wk *KTTN* NW5................106 D3
Forthbridge Rd *BTSEA* SW11.....166 E3
Fortis Cl *CAN/RD* E16.................133 E5
Fortis Gn *EFNCH* N2......................66 B6
Fortis Green Av *EFNCH* N2...........66 C6
Fortis Green Rd *MUSWH* N10......66 C5
Fortismere Av *MUSWH* N10.........66 C5
Fort Rd *NTHLT* UB5........................99 E5
  STHWK SE1...............................32 D2
Fortrose Gdns
  BRXS/STRHM SW2...................187 G3
Fort St *CAN/RD* E16....................152 D1
  WCHPL * E1..............................16 B2
Fortuna Cl *HOLWY* * N7.............107 H4
Fortunegate Rd *WLSDN* NW10...103 E6
Fortune Green Rd
  KIL/WHAMP NW6.....................105 E3
Fortunes Md *NTHLT* UB5..............98 C4
Fortune St *STLK* EC1Y...................7 F6
Fortune Wy *WLSDN* NW10.........123 G2
Forty Av *WBLY* HA9.....................101 H1
Forty Cl *WBLY* HA9.......................81 H6
Forty La *WBLY* HA9......................82 B6
Forum Magnum Sq *STHWK* SE1...21 C3
Forumside *EDGW* HA8...................62 A2
The Forum *E/WMO/HCT* KT8......219 F1
Forum Wy *EDGW* HA8...................62 A2
Forval Cl *MTCM* CR4...................226 B2
Forward Dr *KTN/HRWW/W* HA3...80 B1
Fosbury Ms *BAY/PAD* * W2..........75 G6
Foscote Ms *MV/WKIL* W9...........125 E3
Foscote Rd *HDN* NW4...................84 H5
Foskett Rd *FUL/PGN* SW6.........164 D3
Foss Av *CROY/NA* CRO...............226 A1
Fossdene Rd *CHARL* SE7............152 D5
Fossdyke Cl *HAYES* BR2............118 C4
Fosse Wy *WEA* W13.....................120 C4
Fossil Rd *LEW* SE13....................113 F4
Fossington Rd *BELV* DA17..........156 B4
Foss Rd *TOOT* SW17...................186 H6
Fossway *BCTR* RM8......................98 A6
Foster La *CITYW* EC2V.................15 E3
Foster Rd *ACT* W3......................142 D5
  CHSWK W4.............................142 D5
  PLSTW E13..............................132 C3
Fosters Cl *CHST* BR7..................213 H1
  SWFD E18.................................59 F2
Foster St *HDN* NW4......................84 A1
Foster Wk *HDN* NW4....................84 A1
Fothergill Cl *PLSTW* E13.............112 C6
Fothergill Dr *WCHMH* N21..........37 E6
Fotheringham Rd *EN* EN1............39 F5
Foulden Rd *STNW/STAM* N16....109 F2
Foulden Ter *STNW/STAM* N16....109 F2
Foulser Rd *TOOT* SW17..............186 B6
Foulsham Rd *THHTH* CR7............208 C6
Founders Gdns *NRWD* SE19.......208 C3
Foundry Cl *BERM/RHTH* SE16....150 C1
Foundry Pl
  WAND/EARL * SW18.................185 F2
Fountain Dr *CAR* SM5.................244 B5
  NRWD SE19.............................189 F6
Fountain Green Sq
  BERM/RHTH SE16......................25 H4
Fountain Ms *HAMP* * NW3..........106 B4
Fountain Pl *BRXN/ST* SW9.........168 C2
Fountain Rd *THHTH* CR7.............208 C5
  TOOT SW17.............................205 H1
Fountains Cl *FELT* TW13............178 D5
Fountains Crs *STHGT/OAK* N14...51 G2
Fountayne Rd
  STNW/STAM N16......................89 G6
Fount St *VX/NE* SW8...................167 C1
Fouracres *PEND* EN3.....................25 H2
Fourland Wk *EDGW* HA8.............62 C2
Fournier St *WCHPL* E1...................16 D1
Four Seasons Cs *BOW* E5...........131 E5
Four Seasons Crs *CHEAM* SM3...224 D6
Fourth Av *MNPK* E12...................113 H2
  NKENS W10.............................124 C3
  ROMW/RG RM7.........................97 G5
Fourth Cross Rd *WHTN* TW2......179 H4
Fourth Wy *WBLY* HA9..................102 B2
The Four Tubs *BUSH* WD23..........43 H2
The Four Wents *CHING* E4............43 G4
Fowey Av *REDBR* IG4....................95 F2
Fowey Cl *WAP* E1W......................25 C1
Fowler Cl *BTSEA* SW11...............166 A2
Fowler Rd *BARK/HLT* IG6.............76 A1
  FSTGT E7.................................112 C2
  IS N1.......................................108 B6
Fowler's Wk *EA* W5....................121 F5
Fownes St *BTSEA* SW11..............166 A4
Foxberry Rd *BROCKY* SE4..........170 C5
Foxborough Gdns
  BROCKY SE4...........................191 G1
Foxbourne Rd *TOOT* SW17.........186 B4
Foxbury Av *CHST* BR7................214 D2
Foxbury Cl *BMLY* BR1.................212 D2
  ORP BR6.................................253 G5
Foxbury Rd *BMLY* BR1................212 D2
Fox Cl *BORE* WD6..........................45 F1
  CAN/RD E16.............................132 C4
  CRW RM5...................................56 D3
  ORP BR6.................................253 G3
  WCHPL E1...............................130 A3
Foxcroft Rd *WOOL/PLUM* SE18...174 B2
Foxearth Sp *SAND/SEL* CR2.......248 A6
Foxes Dl *BKHTH/KID* SE3...........173 G3
  HAYES BR2.............................211 H6
Foxfield Rd *ORP* BR6..................234 D6
Foxglove Cl *STHL* UB1................118 C6
Foxglove La *CHSGTN* KT9...........240 A2
Foxglove Rd *ROMW/RG* RM7......75 G5
Foxglove St *SHB* W12..................119 F6
Foxglove Wy *MTCM* CR4............226 C4
Foxgrove *STHGT/OAK* N14..........51 G5
Foxgrove Av *BECK* BR3...............211 F5
Foxgrove Pth *OXHEY* WD19.........58 B1
Foxgrove Rd *BECK* BR3..............211 F5
Foxham Rd *ARCH* N19...................67 E1
Fox Hl *NRWD* SE19.....................209 F3

Fox Hill Gdns *NRWD* SE19 .....209 H1
Foxhole Rd *ELTH/MOT* SE9 ......173 G6
Fox Hollow Cl
    WOOL/PLUM SE18 ....155 E5
Fox Hollow Dr *WELL* DA16 .....176 B4
Foxholt Gdns *WLSDN* NW10 ....102 C5
Foxhome Cl *CHST* BR7 ....214 A2
Fox House Rd *BELV* DA17 ....157 F4
Fox & Knot St *FARR* EC1M 14 D1
Foxlands Crs *DAGE* RM10 ......117 G3
Foxlands Rd *DAGE* RM10 ....117 G3
Fox La *EA* W5 ....121 G4
    HAYES BR2 ....250 D5
    PLMGR N13 ....51 H4
Foxlees *ALP/SUD* HA0 ....100 C2
Foxley Cl *HACK* E8 ....109 C3
Foxley Rd *CMBW* SE5 ....168 A1
    THHTH CR7 ....228 B1
Foxleys *OXHEY* WD19 ....42 C5
Foxley Sq *BRXN/ST* * SW9 ....168 B1
Foxmead Cl *ENC/FH* EN2 ....37 H4
Foxmore St *BTSEA* SW11 ......166 D2
Fox Rd *CAN/RD* E16 ....132 B4
Foxton Gv *MTCM* CR4 ....205 H5
Foxwarren *ESH/CLAY* KT10 .....238 D2
Foxwell St *BROCKY* SE4 ....170 C4
Foxwood Cl *MLHL* NW7 ....47 E6
Foxwood Green Cl *EN* EN1 ......53 E1
Foxwood Rd *BKHTH/KID* SE3 ..172 B5
Foyle Rd *BKHTH/KID* SE3 ......152 B6
    TOTM N17 ....69 G4
Framfield Cl *NFNCH/WDSP* N12 ..49 E6
Framfield Rd *HBRY* N5 ....108 B3
    HNWL W7 ....120 B5
    MTCM CR4 ....206 C3
Framlingham Crs
    ELTH/MOT SE9 ....193 G6
Frampton Cl *BELMT* SM2 ....243 F5
Frampton Park Rd *HOM* E9 ....110 A4
Frampton Rd *HSLWW* TW4 ....158 C6
Frampton St *STJWD* NW8 ......125 H3
Francemary Rd *LEW* SE13 ......171 E6
Frances Rd *CHING* E4 ....71 C2
Frances St *WOOL/PLUM* SE18 ..153 H4
Franche Court Rd *TOOT* SW17 ..185 C5
Francis Av *BXLYHN* DA7 ....177 E3
    IL IG1 ....94 D6
Francis Barber Cl
    STRHM/NOR * SW16 ....187 H6
Franciscan Rd *TOOT* SW17 ....186 C6
Francis Chichester Wy
    BTSEA * SW11 ....166 C2
Francis Cl *HOR/WEW* KT19 ....240 D2
    POP/IOD E14 ....112 A5
Francis Gv *WIM/MER* SW19 ...204 D2
Francis Rd *CROY/NA* CR0 ......228 B4
    EFNCH * N2 ....86 B1
    GFD/PVL UB6 ....121 E1
    HRW HA1 ....61 E1
    HSLWW TW4 ....158 B3
    LEY E10 ....91 C6
    PIN HA5 ....78 A2
    STMC/STPC BR5 ....204 C6
    WLGTN SM6 ....245 E4
Francis St *SRTFD* E15 ....112 A3
    WEST SW1P 28 B1
Francis Ter *ARCH* N19 ....107 E1
Francis Wk *IS* N1 ....107 F6
Francklyn Gdns *EDGW* HA8 .....46 A5
Franconia Rd *CLAP* SW4 ....167 E6
Frank Burton Cl *CHARL* SE7 ..152 D5
Frank Dixon Cl *DUL* SE21 ......189 E2
Frank Dixon Wy *DUL* SE21 ....189 E3
Frankfurt Rd *HNHL* SE24 ......168 C6
Frankham St *DEPT* SE8 ....171 E1
Frankland Cl *BERM/RHTH* SE16 ..33 H1
    WFD IG8 ....73 E1
Frankland Rd *CHING* E4 ....71 E1
    SKENS* SW7 ....14 D3
Franklin Cl *KUT* KT1 ....202 A1
    LEW SE13 ....171 F2
    TRDG/WHET N20 ....49 C2
    WNWD SE27 ....188 B5
Franklin Crs *MTCM* CR4 ....227 E1
Franklin Rd *BXLYHN* DA7 ......176 C2
    PCE/AN SE20 ....210 A3
Franklins Ms *RYLN/HDSTN* HA2 ..79 G6
Franklin Sq *WKENS* W14 ......144 D5
Franklin's Rw *CHEL* SW3 ....26 D5
    CHEL * SW5 ....26 D3
Franklin St *BOW* E3 ....131 F2
    SEVS/STOTM N15 ....89 E3
Franklin Wy *CROY/NA* CR0 ....227 G5
Franklyn Gdns *BARK/HLT* IG6 ..74 D2
Franklyn Rd *WLSDN* NW10 ....103 F5
Franks Av *NWMAL* KT3 ....222 C1
Franks Wood Av
    STMC/STPC BR5 ....234 B2
Franlaw Crs *PLMGR* N13 ....52 C6
Fransfield Gv *SYD* SE26 ....189 H5
Franshams *BUSH* * WD23 ....44 A4
Frant Cl *PCE/AN* SE20 ....210 A3
Franthorne Wy *CAT* SE6 ....191 F4
Frant Rd *THHTH* CR7 ....228 B2
Franz Cl *BXLY* DA5 ....159 H3
Fraser Cl *BXLY* DA5 ....177 F5
    ERITH DA8 ....157 G5
    GFD/PVL UB6 ....101 E6
    LEY E10 ....91 F2
Fraser St *CHSWK* W4 ....143 A5
Frating Crs *WFD* IG8 ....72 C2
Frazer Av *RSLP* HA4 ....98 A3
Frazier St *STHWK* SE1 ....22 A4
Frean St *BERM/RHTH* SE16 .....25 J5
Freda Corbett Cl *PECK* SE15 ..169 G1
Frederica Rd *CHING* E4 ....55 H2
Frederica St *HOLWY* N7 ....107 H5
Frederick Cl *BAY/PAD* W2 ......10 C5
    SUT* SM1 ....242 D2
Frederick Crs *BRXN/ST* SW9 ..168 B1
    PEND EN3 ....61 G1
Frederick Gdns *SUT* SM1 ......242 C3
Frederick Pl *WOOL/PLUM* SE18 ..154 B5
Frederick Rd *RAIN* RM13 ......137 H1
    SUT SM1 ....242 D3
Frederick's Pl *LOTH* * EC2R 15 G4
    NFNCH/WDSP N12 ....49 G6
Frederick's Rw *FSBYE* EC1V 6 C3
Frederick St *FSBYW* WC1X 5 G4

Frederick Ter *HACK* * E8 ....109 F5
Frederic Ms *KTBR* * SW1X 19 E4
Frederic St *WALTH* E17 ....90 C2
Freedom Cl *WALTH* E17 ....90 B1
Freedom Rd *TOTM* N17 ....50 B6
Freegrove Rd *HOLWY* N7 ......107 G3
Freeland Pk *HDN* NW4 ....64 C5
Freeland Rd *EA* W5 ....121 H6
Freelands Av *SAND/SEL* CR2 ..248 B6
Freelands Gv *BMLY* BR1 ....184 A4
Freelands Rd *BMLY* BR1 ....212 D4
Freeling St *IS* N1 ....107 H5
Freeman Cl *NTHLT* UB5 ....98 C1
Freeman Dr *E/WMO/HCT* KT8 ..218 D1
Freeman Rd *MRDN* SM4 ....225 H2
Freemantle Av *PEND* EN3 ....40 B6
Freemantle St *WALW* SE17 .....32 A2
Freemasons Rd *CAN/RD* E16 ..132 D5
    CROY/NA CR0 ....229 G6
Freesia Cl *ORP* BR6 ....253 F3
Freethorpe Cl *NRWD* SE19 ....209 E4
Freke Rd *BTSEA* SW11 ....166 A4
Fremantle Rd *BARK/HLT* IG6 ...74 B5
    BELV DA17 ....157 C4
Fremont St *HOM* E9 ....110 A6
French Pl *SDTCH* EC2A 7 H6
French St *SUN* TW16 ....198 A1
Frendsbury Rd *BROCKY* SE4 ..170 C5
Frensham Cl *STHL* UB1 ....118 D3
Frensham Dr *CROY/NA* CR0 ...249 H5
    PUT/ROE SW15 ....183 C5
Frensham Rd *BFN/LL* DA15 ...194 D4
Frensham St *PECK* SE15 ....33 F6
Frere St *BTSEA* SW11 ....166 D1
Freshfield Av *HACK* E8 ....109 F5
Freshfield Cl *LEW* SE13 ....171 H5
Freshfield Dr *STHGT/OAK* N14 ..50 D2
Freshfields *CROY/NA* CR0 ......230 D1
Freshford St *TOOT* SW17 .....185 C5
Freshwater Cl *TOOT* SW17 ...207 C2
Freshwater Rd *BCTR* RM8 ......96 B5
    TOOT SW17 ....206 C2
Freshwell Av *CHDH* RM6 ....96 A4
Fresh Wharf Rd *BARK* IG11 ...114 D6
Freshwood Cl *BECK* BR3 ....211 H6
Freshwood Wy *WLGTN* SM6 ..245 E6
Freston Gdns *EBAR* EN4 ....36 E4
Freston Pk *FNCH* N3 ....64 D2
Freston Rd *NKENS* W10 ....124 B6
Freta Rd *BXLYHS* DA6 ....177 C1
Frewin Rd *WAND/EARL* SW18 ..185 H5
Friar Ms *WNWD* SE27 ....188 B5
Friar Rd *STMC/STPC* BR5 .....235 C2
    YEAD UB4 ....118 B3
Friars Av *PUT/ROE* SW15 .....183 F5
    TRDG/WHET N20 ....49 C2
Friars Cl *CHING* E4 ....56 C5
    NTHLT UB5 ....118 A2
    STHWK * SE1 ....18 B5
Friars Gdns *ACT* W3 ....122 D5
Friars Gate *WFD* IG8 ....56 C6
Friars La *RCH/KEW* TW9 ....161 F6
Friars Md *POP/IOD* E14 ....151 C3
Friars Ms *ELTH/MOT* SE9 ......174 A4
Friars Place La *ACT* W3 ....122 D6
Friar's Rd *EHAM* E6 ....113 F6
Friars Stile Rd
    RCHPK/HAM TW10 ....181 C1
Friars Wk *ABYW* SE2 ....50 A1
    STHGT/OAK N14 ....50 D2
Friars Wy *ACT* W3 ....122 D5
Friars Wd *CROY/NA* CR0 ......248 D6
Friary Cl *NFNCH/WDSP* N12 ...49 H4
Friary Est *PECK* * SE15 ....169 C1
Friary La *WFD* IG8 ....56 D2
Friary Pk *TRDG/WHET* * N20 ..30 A6
Friary Park Ct *ACT* * W3 ....122 C1
Friary Rd *ACT* W3 ....122 C5
    NFNCH/WDSP N12 ....49 H4
    PECK SE15 ....169 G1
Friary Wy *NFNCH/WDSP* N12 ...50 A4
Friday Hl *CHING* E4 ....56 A5
Friday Hl East *CHING* E4 ....56 A5
Friday Hl West *CHING* E4 ....56 A4
Friday Rd *ERITH* DA8 ....157 H5
    MTCM CR4 ....206 B3
Friday St *BLKFR* EC4V 15 E5
Frideswide Pl *KTTN* NW5 ......107 E3
Friendly Pl *LEW* SE13 ....171 F2
Friendly St *DEPT* SE8 ....171 E2
Friendly Street Ms *DEPT* SE8 ..171 E1
Friends Rd *CROY/NA* CR0 ......246 D1
Friend St *FSBYE* EC1V 6 C3
Friern Barnet La
    TRDG/WHET N20 ....49 H5
Friern Barnet Rd
    FBAR/BDGN N11 ....66 C1
Friern Mount Dr
    TRDG/WHET N20 ....49 G1
Friern Pk *NFNCH/WDSP* N12 ....49 H4
Friern Rd *EDUL* SE22 ....189 G1
Friern Watch Av
    NFNCH/WDSP N12 ....49 H6
Frigate Ms *DEPT* SE8 ....245 C5
Frimley Av *WLTH* SW6 ....245 C5
Frimley Cl *CROY/NA* CR0 ......249 G5
    WIM/MER SW19 ....184 C4
Frimley Ct *SCUP* DA14 ....216 A1
Frimley Crs *CROY/NA* CR0 .....249 G5
Frimley Gdns *MTCM* CR4 ......206 A6
Frimley Rd *CHSGTN* KT9 ....239 F5
    CDMY/SEVK IG3 ....115 C1
Frimley Wy *WCHPL* * E1 ....130 B3
Frinstead Gv *STMC/STPC* BR5 ..236 B1
Frinsted Rd *ERITH* DA8 ....177 E1
Frinton Dr *WFD* IG8 ....71 H1
Frinton Ms *IL* IG1 ....72 A6
Frinton Rd *CRW* RM5 ....57 H1
    EHAM E6 ....133 F2
    SCUP DA14 ....196 C6
    SEVS/STOTM N15 ....88 A5
    TOOT SW17 ....206 C2
Friston St *FUL/PGN* SW6 ....166 A1
Friswell Pl *BXLYHN* DA7 ....177 E4
Frith Cl *MLHL* NW7 ....64 C1
Frith La *MLHL* NW7 ....64 C1
Frith Manor Farm Cotts
    NFNCH/WDSP * N12 ....64 C1
Frith Rd *CROY/NA* CR0 ....228 C6

WAN E11 ....111 G2
Frith St *SOHO/SHAV* W1D 12 C4
Frithville Gdns *SHB* W12 ....144 A1
Frizlands La *DAGE* RM10 ......117 F1
Frobisher Cl *BUSH* WD23 ....44 B3
    PIN HA5 ....78 B4
Frobisher Crs *BARB* * EC2Y 15 F1
Frobisher Gdns *LEY* * E10 ....91 F3
Frobisher Rd *CEND/HSY/T* N8 ..88 A1
    EHAM E6 ....133 H5
Frog La *DAGW* RM9 ....137 H4
Frogley Rd *EDUL* SE22 ....169 F5
Frogmore *WAND/EARL* SW18 ..165 H6
Frogmore Cl *CHEAM* SM3 .....242 H1
Frogmore Est *HBRY* * N5 ....108 C2
Frogmore Gdns *CHEAM* SM3 ..242 C2
Frognal *HAMP* NW3 ....105 G2
Frognal Av *HRW* HA1 ....80 B1
    SCUP DA14 ....215 G2
Frognal Cl *HAMP* NW3 ....105 G3
Frognal Gdns *HAMP* NW3 .....105 G2
Frognal La *HAMP* NW3 ....105 F3
Frognal Man *HAMP* * NW5 ....105 G2
Frognal Pde *HAMP* NW3 ....105 G4
Frognal Pl *SCUP* DA14 ....215 G3
Frognal Ri *HAMP* NW3 ....105 G1
Frognal Wy *HAMP* NW3 ....105 G2
Froissart Rd *ELTH/MOT* SE9 ..173 G6
Frome Rd *SEVS/STOTM* N15 ...68 B6
Frome St *IS* N1 ....6 E1
Fromondes Rd *CHEAM* SM3 ..242 C3
Fromows Cnr *CHSWK* * W4 ....142 C5
Frostic Wk *WCHPL* E1 ....16 D2
Froude St *VX/NE* SW8 ....166 D3
Fryatt Rd *TOTM* N17 ....68 D3
Fry Cl *CRW* RM5 ....77 E1
Fryent Cl *KTN/HRWW/W* HA3 ..82 A3
Fryent Crs *CDALE/KGS* NW9 ...83 E3
Fryent Flds *CDALE/KGS* NW9 ...83 E3
Fryent Gv *CDALE/KGS* NW9 ....83 E3
Fryent Wy *CDALE/KGS* NW9 ....82 A2
Frying Pan Aly *WCHPL* E1 ....16 H2
Fry Rd *EHAM* E6 ....113 F5
    WLSDN NW10 ....103 F6
Fryston Av *CROY/NA* CR0 ......229 G6
Fuchsia St *ABYW* SE2 ....155 H5
Fulbeck Dr *CDALE/KGS* NW9 ..45 E6
Fulbeck Wy *RYLN/HDSTN* HA2 ..59 C5
Fulbourne Cl *WCHPL* E1 ....9 F6
Fulbourne Rd *WALTH* E17 ....71 G4
Fulbourne St *WCHPL* E1 ....17 C1
Fulbrook Rd *ARCH* N19 ....107 E2
Fulford Rd *HOR/WEW* KT19 ...240 D5
Fulford St *BERM/RHTH* SE16 ...25 H4
Fulham Broadway
    FUL/PGN SW6 ....165 E1
Fulham Est *FUL/PGN* SW6 .....146 E6
Fulham High St *FUL/PGN* SW6 ..164 C3
Fulham Palace Rd
    FUL/PGN SW6 ....164 B1
Fulham Park Gdns
    FUL/PGN SW6 ....164 D3
Fulham Park Rd *FUL/PGN* SW6 ..165 F2
Fulbrooks Av *WPK* KT4 ....223 F5
Fuller Cl *BETH* E2 ....9 K5
    ORP BR6 ....253 F3
Fuller Rd *BCTR* RM8 ....116 A1
Fullers Av *SURB* KT6 ....221 H6
    WFD IG8 ....72 B5
Fullers Cl *CRW* RM5 ....77 G3
Fuller's La *HDN* NW4 ....72 B4
Fuller St *HDN* NW4 ....64 A1
Fullers Wy North *SURB* KT6 ..239 H1
Fullers Wy South *CHSGTN* KT9 ..239 G2
Fuller's Wd *CROY/NA* CR0 .....249 E3
Fullerton Rd *CAR* SM5 ....244 A6
    CROY/NA CR0 ....229 F4
    WAND/EARL SW18 ....165 G5
Fullwell Av *CLAY* IG5 ....74 A4
Fullwood's Ms *IS* N1 ....7 H3
Fulmar Ct *BRYLDS* KT5 ....221 H3
Fulmead St *FUL/PGN* SW6 ....165 F2
Fulmer Cl *HPTN* TW12 ....198 C1
Fulmer Rd *CAN/RD* E16 ....133 G5
    WEA W13 ....140 D3
Fulready Rd *LEY* E10 ....91 H2
Fulstone Cl *HSLWW* TW4 ......158 D5
Fulthorp Rd *BKHTH/KID* SE3 ..151 H1
Fulton Ms *BAY/PAD* * W2 ....125 G6
Fulton Rd *WBLY* HA9 ....102 A1
Fulwell Park Av *WHTN* TW2 ...179 H6
Fulwell Rd *HPTN* TW12 ....179 H6
Fulwood Av *ALP/SUD* HA0 ....100 C1
Fulwood Gdns *TWK* TW1 ....180 D3
Fulwood Pl *GINN* WC1R 11 H3
Fulwood Wk *WIM/MER* SW19 ..184 C3
Furber St *HMSMTH* W6 ....145 H3
Furham Fld *PIN* HA5 ....42 A3
Furley Rd *PECK* SE15 ....169 G1
Furlong Cl *MTCM* CR4 ....226 D5
Furlong Rd *HOLWY* N7 ....108 A4
Furmage St *WAND/EARL* SW18 ..185 F2
Furneaux Av *WNWD* SE27 ......208 B1
Furness Rd *FUL/PGN* SW6 .....165 F3
    MRDN SM4 ....225 F3
    RYLN/HDSTN HA2 ....79 H4
    WLSDN NW10 ....123 G1
Furnival St *FLST/FETLN* EC4A ..11 H3
Furrow La *HOM* E9 ....110 A3
The Furrows *WOT/HER* KT12 ..218 A6
Fursby Av *FNCH* N3 ....65 E2
Further Acre *CDALE/KGS* NW9 ..45 G1
Furtherfield Cl *CROY/NA* CR0 ..228 A3
Further Green Rd *CAT* SE6 .....192 A2
Furze Cl *OXHEY* WD19 ....58 A1
Furzedown Dr *TOOT* SW17 ....206 D1
Furzedown Rd *TOOT* SW17 ...206 D1
Furze Farm Cl *CHDH* RM6 ....74 A4
Furzefield Rd *BKHTH/KID* SE3 ..152 D6
Furzehill Sq *STMC/STPC* BR5 ..235 H1
Furze Rd *THHTH* CR7 ....208 C6
Furze St *BOW* E3 ....131 E4
Fye Foot La *BLKFR* * EC4V 15 E5
Fyfe Wy *BMLY* BR1 ....212 C5
Fyfield Cl *BECK* BR3 ....210 B2
Fyfield Rd *BRXN/ST* SW9 ......168 A4
    EN EN1 ....59 E4
    WALTH E17 ....91 H1
    WFD IG8 ....73 E3
Fynes St *WEST* SW1P 28 C1

G

Gable Cl *PIN* HA5 ....59 E3
Gable Ct *SYD* SE26 ....189 H6
Gables Cl *CMBW* SE5 ....169 E2
The Cables *NRWD* * SE19 ......209 E4
    WBLY HA9 ....101 H1
Gabriel Cl *CRW* RM5 ....77 G3
    FELT TW15 ....178 B1
Gabrielle Cl *WBLY* HA9 ....101 H1
Gabriel St *FSTH* SE23 ....190 B2
Gad Cl *PLSTW* E13 ....132 D2
Gaddesden Av *WBLY* HA9 .....101 H4
Gadesden Rd *HOR/WEW* KT19 ..240 C4
Gadsbury Cl *CDALE/KGS* NW9 ..83 F3
Gadwall Cl *CAN/RD* E16 ....132 D5
Gage Rd *CAN/RD* E16 ....132 B4
Gainford St *IS* N1 ....108 A4
Gainsboro Gdns *GFD/PVL* UB6 ..100 A3
    ESH/CLAY * KT10 ....59 C5
Gainsborough Ct *SHB* W12 ....124 A2
Gainsborough Cl *BECK* BR5 ...211 E3
    ESH/CLAY * KT10 ....238 A1
Gainsborough Dr *SHB* W12 ...124 B6
Gainsborough Gdns *EDGW* HA8 ..61 H5
    GLDGN NW11 ....84 D4
    HAMP NW3 ....85 H1
    ISLW TW7 ....159 H6
Gainsborough Rd *BCTR* RM8 ..115 H2
    CHSWK W4 ....143 F4
    NFNCH/WDSP N12 ....65 E4
    NWMAL KT3 ....222 D3
    RCH/KEW TW9 ....161 H5
    SRTFD E15 ....132 A2
    WAN E11 ....91 G2
    WFD IG8 ....73 G2
Gainsborough Sq *BXLYHN* DA7 ..176 E4
Gainsborough Ter
    BELMT * SM2 ....242 D5
Gainsford Rd *WALTH* E17 ....90 D1
Gainsford St *STHWK* SE1 ....24 C2
Gairloch Rd *CMBW* SE5 ....169 E3
Gaisford St *KTTN* NW5 ....107 E4
Gaitskell Ct *ELTH/MOT* SE9 ....194 E1
Gaiahad Rd *BMLY* BR1 ....192 C5
Galata Rd *BARN* SW13 ....163 G1
Galatea Sq *PECK* SE15 ....169 H4
Galbraith St *POP/IOD* E14 ....151 C3
Galdana Av *BAR* EN5 ....21 G4
Galeborough Av *WFD* IG8 ....71 H3
Gale Cl *HPTN* TW12 ....198 C2
    MTCM CR4 ....206 A1
Galena Rd *HMSMTH* W6 ....146 H4
Galen Pl *NOXST/BSQ* WC1A 13 E2
Galesbury Rd
    WAND/EARL SW18 ....185 G1
Gales Gdns *BETH* E2 ....9 H4
Gale St *BOW* E3 ....131 E4
    CHEL SW5 ....26 A5
    DAGW RM9 ....116 B4
Gales Wy *WFD* IG8 ....73 H3
Galgate Cl *WIM/MER* SW19 ...184 B5
Gallants Farm Rd *EBAR* EN4 ....50 A2
Galleon Cl *BERM/RHTH* SE16 ..150 A2
    ERITH DA8 ....141 G5
Galleons Dr *BARK* IG11 ....135 G2
The Galleries *IS* * N1 ....6 C1
Gallery Gdns *NTHLT* UB5 ....118 A3
Gallery Rd *DUL* SE21 ....188 D3
Galleywall Rd *BERM/RHTH* SE16 ..3 J2
Galleywood Crs *CRW* RM5 ......57 H2
Galliard Crs *ED* N9 ....53 C2
Galliard Rd *ED* N9 ....53 B5
Gallia Rd *HBRY* N5 ....108 B3
Gallions Cl *BARK* IG11 ....135 G2
Gallions Rd *CHARL* SE7 ....134 B6
    CHARL SE7 ....135 E2
Gallions View Rd *THMD* SE28 ..135 E2
Gallon Cl *CHARL* SE7 ....153 E4
The Gallop *BELMT* SM2 ....243 H6
    SAND/SEL CR2 ....247 H5
Gallosson Rd
    WOOL/PLUM SE18 ....155 G5
Galloway Pth *CROY/NA* CR0 ..246 D2
Galloway Rd *SHB* W12 ....143 C1
Gallus Cl *WCHMH* N21 ....35 H1
Gallus Sq *BKHTH/KID* SE3 ....172 D4
Galpin's Rd *THHTH* CR7 ....227 G1
Galsworthy Av *CHDH* RM6 ....95 H6
    POP/IOD * E14 ....131 G1
Galsworthy Cl *THMD* SE28 ....155 H1
Galsworthy Crs
    BKHTH/KID * SE3 ....173 G2
    KUTN/CMB KT2 ....202 A4
Galsworthy Rd *CRICK* NW2 ...104 C2
    KUTN/CMB KT2 ....202 B3
Galton St *NKENS* W10 ....124 C3
Galva Cl *EBAR* EN4 ....36 C5
Galveston Rd *PUT/ROE* SW15 ..164 D6
Galway Cl *BERM/RHTH* * SE16 ..35 C4
Galway St *FSBYE* EC1V 6 E4
Gambetta St *VX/NE* SW8 ....166 D3
Gambia St *STHWK* SE1 ....22 C2
Gambole Rd *TOOT* SW17 ......186 A6
Games Rd *EBAR* EN4 ....36 C1
Gamlen Rd *PUT/ROE* SW15 ...164 B5
Gamuel Cl *WALTH* E17 ....91 E3
Gander Green La *CHEAM* SM3 ..242 A1
Gander Green Crs *HPTN* TW12 ..199 E4
Gandhi Cl *WALTH* E17 ....91 E3
Ganton St *SOHO/CST* * W1F 12 B4
Ganton Wk *OXHEY* * WD19 ....42 A2
Gantshill Crs *GNTH/NBYPK* IG2 ..94 A2
Gap Rd *WIM/MER* SW19 ....205 E1
Garage Rd *ACT* W3 ....122 A5
Garbrand Wk *EW* KT17 ....241 F6
Garbutt Pl *MHST* W1U 10 B2
Garden Av *BXLYHN* DA7 ....176 D3
    MTCM CR4 ....206 D5
Garden Cl *EAR* EN5 ....34 A5
    CHING E4 ....69 G4
    HPTN TW12 ....179 H5
    LEE/GVPK SE12 ....192 D5
    NTHLT UB5 ....118 A1
    PUT/ROE SW15 ....183 H2
    WLGTN SM6 ....245 G3
Garden Ct *TPL/STR* * WC2R 11 J5
Gardeners Cl *FBAR/BDGN* N11 ..50 C4
Gardeners Rd *CROY/NA* CR0 ..228 B5

Garden Flats HMSMTH * W6 144 B6
Gardenia Rd EN EN1 53 E1
Gardenia Wy WFD IG8 72 C2
Garden La BMLY BR1 212 D2
BRXS/STRHM SW2 187 H3
Garden Lodge Ct EFNCH * N2 65 H6
Garden Pl HACK E8 109 F6
Garden Rd BMLY BR1 212 D3
PGE/AN SE20 210 A4
RCH/KEW TW9 162 A4
STJWD NW8 125 G2
Garden Rw STHWK SE1 22 C6
The Gardens BECK BR3 211 G5
CEND/HSY/T * N8 87 G1
EDUL SE22 169 G5
HRW HA1 79 G3
PIN * HA5 78 D3
STNW/STAM * N16 89 F4
Garden St WCHPL E1 130 B4
Garden Studios BAY/PAD * W2 125 G4
Garden Ter PIM SW1V 28 C3
Garden Vls ESH/CLAY * KT10 238 B5
Garden Wk BECK BR3 210 D4
SDTCH EC2A 8 A5
Garden Wy WLSDN NW10 102 C4
Gardiner Av CRICK * NW2 104 A3
Gardiner Cl BCTR RM8 116 B2
PEND EN3 54 B1
STMC/STPC BR5 216 A5
Gardner Cl WAN E11 92 D3
Gardner Rd PLSTW E13 132 D3
Gardners La BLKFR EC4V 15 E5
Gardnor Rd HAMP NW3 105 H2
Gard St FSBYE EC1V 6 D3
Garendon Gdns MRDN SM4 225 F4
Garendon Rd MRDN SM4 225 F4
Gareth Cl WPK KT4 224 B6
Gareth Gv BMLY BR1 192 C6
Garfield Rd BTSEA SW11 166 C4
CHING E4 55 H3
PEND EN3 40 A5
PLSTW E13 132 B3
TWK TW1 180 C3
WIM/MER SW19 205 G2
Garford St POP/IOD E14 131 E6
Garibaldi St WOOL/PLUM SE18 155 E4
Garland Rd STAN HA7 61 G4
WOOL/PLUM SE18 174 D1
Garlick Hl BLKFR EC4V 15 F5
Garlies Rd FSTH SE23 190 C5
Garlinge Rd CRICK NW2 104 D4
Garman Cl UED N18 68 D1
Garman Rd TOTM N17 70 A3
Garnault Ms CLKNW EC1R 6 B4
Garnault Pl CLKNW EC1R 6 B4
Garnault Rd EN EN1 39 F1
Garner Cl BCTR RM8 96 B5
Garner Rd WALTH E17 71 G4
Garner St BETH E2 9 F2
Garnet Rd THHTH CR7 228 C1
WLSDN NW10 103 E4
Garnet St WAP E1W 130 A6
Garnett Cl ELTH/MOT SE9 173 H4
Garnett Rd HAMP NW3 106 B3
Garnham St STNW/STAM N16 89 F6
Garnies Cl PECK SE15 169 F1
Garrad's Rd STRHM/NOR SW16 187 F5
Garrard Cl BXLYHN DA7 177 E4
CHST BR7 214 B1
Garrard Wk WLSDN * NW10 103 E4
Garratt Cl CROY/NA CR0 245 G2
Garratt La WAND/EARL SW18 185 F2
Garratt Rd EDGW HA8 62 A3
Garratts Rd BUSH WD23 43 G2
Garratt Ter TOOT SW17 186 A6
Garrett Cl ACT W3 122 D4
Garrett St STLK EC1Y 7 E6
Garrick Av GLDGN NW11 84 C3
Garrick Cl BTSEA SW11 165 G5
EA W5 121 G3
RCH/KEW TW9 161 E6
Garrick Crs CROY/NA CR0 229 E6
Garrick Dr HDN NW4 64 A5
WOOL/PLUM SE18 154 D3
Garrick Gdns E/WMO/HCT KT8 199 E6
Garrick Pk HDN NW4 64 B5
Garrick Rd CDALE/KGS NW9 83 F3
GFD/PVL UB6 119 F3
RCH/KEW TW9 162 A3
Garrick St COVGDN WC2E 13 E5
Garrick Wy HDN NW4 84 B1
Garrick Yd CHCR WC2N 13 E5
Garrison Cl HSLWW TW4 158 D6
WOOL/PLUM SE18 174 A1
Garrison La CHSGTN KT9 239 G5
Garrolds Cl SWLY BR8 217 H5
Garsdale Cl FBAR/BDGN N11 66 C2
Garsdale Ter WKENS * W14 144 D5
Garside Cl HPTN TW12 199 F3
WOOL/PLUM SE18 154 D3
Garth Cl KUTN/CMB KT2 201 H1
MRDN SM4 224 B4
RSLP HA4 78 B5
Garth Ms EA * W5 121 G3
Garthorne Rd FSTH SE23 190 B2
Garth Rd CHSWK W4 142 D5
CRICK NW2 84 D6
KUTN/CMB KT2 201 H1
MRDN SM4 224 B5
Garthside KUTN/CMB KT2 201 G1
The Garth HPTN TW12 199 F2
KTN/HRWW/W HA3 81 H3
NFNCH/WDSP * N12 65 F1
Garthway NFNCH/WDSP N12 66 A2
Gartmoor Gdns
WIM/MER SW19 184 D3
Gartmore Rd GDMY/SEVK IG3 95 F5
Garton Pl WAND/EARL SW18 185 G1
Gartons Cl PEND EN3 40 A6
Gartons Wy BTSEA SW11 165 G4
Garvary Rd CAN/RD E16 132 D5
Garway Rd BAY/PAD W2 125 F5
Gascoigne Gdns WFD IG8 72 A3
Gascoigne Pl BETH E2 8 C3
Gascoigne Rd BARK IG11 114 C6
Gascony Av KIL/WHAMP NW6 105 E5
Gascoyne Rd HOM E9 110 B5
Gaselee St POP/IOD E14 131 G6
Gasholder Pl LBTH SE11 29 H4
Gaskarth Rd BAL SW12 186 D1
EDGW HA8 62 C4
Gaskell Rd HGT N6 86 B3
Gaskell St CLAP SW4 167 G3
Gaskin St IS N1 108 B6
Gaspar Ms ECT SW5 145 F4
Gassiot Rd TOOT SW17 186 B6
Gassiot Wy SUT SM1 243 H1
Gastein Rd HMSMTH W6 144 B6
Gaston Bell Cl RCH/KEW TW9 161 H4
Gaston Rd MTCM CR4 206 C6
Gataker St BERM/RHTH * SE16 25 H5
Gatcombe Ms EA W5 121 H6
Gatcombe Rd ARCH N19 107 F1
Gatcombe Wy EBAR EN4 36 B4
Gate Cottages EDGW * HA8 46 A4
Gateforth St STJWD NW8 2 A6
Gatehouse Cl KUTN/CMB KT2 202 C3
Gatehouse Sq STHWK SE1 23 F1
Gateley Rd BRXN/ST SW9 167 H4
Gate Ms SKENS SW7 18 B4
Gater Dr ENC/FH EN2 38 D2
Gates Green Rd WWKM BR4 250 C2
Gateside Rd TOOT SW17 186 B5
Gatestone Rd NRWD SE19 209 E2
Gate St HHOL WC1V 13 G3
Gateway WALW SE17 31 F5
Gateway Ar IS * N1 6 C1
Gateway Ms HACK * E8 109 F3
The Gateways RCH/KEW * TW9 161 F5
Gatfield Gv FELT TW13 179 E4
Gathorne Rd WDGN N22 68 A5
Gathorne St BETH E2 130 B1
Gatley Av HOR/WEW KT19 240 B3
Gatliff Rd BGVA SW1W 27 F4
Gatling Rd ABYW SE2 155 G5
Gatonby St PECK SE15 169 F2
Gatton Cl BELMT * SM2 243 F6
Gatton Rd TOOT SW17 186 A6
Gattons Wy SCUP DA14 196 D6
Gatward Cl WCHMH N21 52 B1
Gatward Gn ED N9 53 E4
Gatwick Rd WAND/EARL SW18 184 D2
Gauden Cl CLAP SW4 167 F4
Gauden Rd CLAP SW4 167 F4
Gaumont Ter SHB * W12 144 A2
Gauntlet Cl NTHLT UB5 98 C5
Gauntlett Ct ALP/SUD HA0 100 C3
Gauntlett Rd SUT SM1 243 H3
Gaunt St STHWK SE1 22 D5
Gautrey Rd PECK SE15 170 A3
Gavel St WALW * SE17 31 H1
Gaverick St POP/IOD E14 151 E4
Gavestone Crs LEE/GVPK SE12 192 D2
Gavestone Rd LEE/GVPK SE12 192 D2
Gavina Cl MRDN SM4 226 A2
Gawber St BETH E2 130 A2
Gawsworth Cl SRTFD E15 112 B3
Gawthorne Av MLHL NW7 64 C1
Gay Cl CRICK NW2 103 H3
Gaydon La CDALE/KGS NW9 63 E4
Gayfere Rd CLAY IG5 73 H6
EW KT17 241 G3
Gayfere St WEST SW1P 21 E6
Gayford Rd SHB W12 143 F2
Gay Gdns DAGE RM10 117 G2
Gayhurst Rd HACK E8 109 G5
Gaylor Rd NTHLT UB5 98 D3
Gaynesford Rd CAR SM5 244 B5
FSTH SE23 190 B4
Gaynes Hill Rd WFD IG8 73 G3
Gay Rd SRTFD E15 131 H1
Gaysham Av GNTH/NBYPK IG2 94 A2
Gayton Crs HAMP NW3 105 H2
Gayton Rd HAMP NW3 105 H2
HRW HA1 80 C3
Gayville Rd BTSEA SW11 186 B1
Gaywood Cl BRXS/STRHM SW2 187 H3
Gaywood Rd WALTH E17 71 E6
Gaywood St STHWK SE1 22 D6
Gaza St WALW SE17 30 C4
Gearlesville Gdns BARK/HLT IG6 94 B1
Geary Rd WLSDN NW10 103 G3
Geary St HOLWY N7 107 H3
Geddes Pl BXLYHN DA7 177 E5
Gedeney Rd TOTM N17 68 C4
Gedling Pl STHWK SE1 24 C5
Geere Rd SRTFD E15 112 B6
Gees Ct MHST W1U 11 F4
Gee St FSBYE EC1V 7 E5
Geffrye Est IS N1 8 B2
Geffrye St BETH E2 8 C1
Geldart Rd PECK SE15 169 H1
Geldeston Rd CLPT E5 89 G6
Gellatly Rd PECK SE15 170 A3
Gelsthorpe Rd CRW RM5 77 F3
General Wolfe Rd
GNWCH SE10 171 H2
Genesta Rd WOOL/PLUM SE18 154 B6
Geneva Dr HNHL SE24 168 A5
Geneva Gdns CHDH RM6 96 C2
Geneva Rd KUT KT1 221 G1
THHTH CR7 228 C2
Genever Cl CHING E4 71 E1
Genista Rd UED N18 69 H1
Genoa Av PUT/ROE SW15 164 A6
Genoa Rd PGE/AN SE20 210 A4
Genotin Rd ENC/FH EN2 38 D4
Gentleman's Rw ENC/FH EN2 38 C4
Geoffrey Cl CMBW SE5 168 C3
Geoffrey Gdns EHAM E6 133 G1
Geoffrey Rd BROCKY SE4 170 D4
George Beard Rd DEPT SE8 150 D4
George Crs MUSWH N10 66 C3
George Downing Est
STNW/STAM N16 89 F6
George Gange Wy
KTN/HRWW/W HA3 60 A6
George Groves Rd
PGE/AN SE20 209 G4
George La HAYES BR2 232 D5
LEW SE13 191 G1
SWFD E18 72 D6
George Lowe Ct BAY/PAD * W2 125 F4
George Mathers Rd LBTH * SE11 30 C1
George Ms CAMTN NW1 4 A4
George Rd CHING E4 71 E2
KUTN/CMB KT2 202 B3
NWMAL KT3 223 F1
George Rw BERM/RHTH SE16 25 E4
Georges Md BORE WD6 23 E3
George's Rd HOLWY N7 107 H3
HOLWY N7 107 H4
George St BARK IG11 114 C5
CAN/RD E16 132 B5
CROY/NA CR0 228 C6
HNWL W7 140 A1
HSLW TW3 158 D3
MBLAR W1H 10 D3
NWDGN UB2 138 C4
RCHPK/HAM TW10 161 F6
Georgetown Cl NRWD SE19 208 D1
Georgette Pl GNWCH SE10 171 G1
George V Av PIN HA5 58 D5
PIN HA5 79 E1
Georgeville Gdns BARK/HLT IG6 94 B1
George V Wy GFD/PVL UB6 100 D5
George Wyver Cl
WIM/MER SW19 184 C2
George Yd BANK EC3V 15 H4
MYFR/PKLN W1K 11 F5
Georgiana St CAMTN * NW1 107 E6
Georgian Cl HAYES BR2 232 D5
STAN HA7 60 C3
Georgian Ct WBLY HA9 102 A4
Georgian Wy RYLN/HDSTN HA2 79 H6
Georgia Rd NWMAL KT3 222 C1
THHTH CR7 208 B4
Georgina Gdns BETH * E2 8 D3
Geraint Rd BMLY BR1 192 C5
Geraldine Rd CHSWK W4 142 A6
WAND/EARL SW18 165 G6
Geraldine St LBTH SE11 22 C6
Gerald Rd BCTR RM8 96 D6
BGVA SW1W 27 F1
CAN/RD E16 132 B3
Gerard Av HSLWW TW4 179 E2
Gerard Rd BARN SW13 163 F2
HRW HA1 80 C3
Gerards Cl BERM/RHTH SE16 150 A6
Gerda Rd ELTH/MOT SE9 194 B4
Germander Wy SRTFD E15 132 A2
Gernon Rd BOW E3 130 C1
Geron Wy CRICK NW2 84 A6
Gerrard Pl SOHO/SHAV * W1D 12 D5
Gerrard Rd IS N1 6 C1
Gerrards Cl STHGT/OAK N14 37 E6
Gerrard St SOHO/SHAV W1D 12 D5
Gerridge St STHWK SE1 22 B4
Gertrude Rd BELV DA17 157 E4
Gertrude St WBPTN SW10 145 G6
Gervase Cl WBLY HA9 102 C1
Gervase Rd EDGW HA8 62 C4
Gervase St PECK SE15 169 H1
Ghent St CAT SE6 191 E4
Ghent Wy HACK E8 109 F4
Giant Arches Rd HNHL SE24 188 C2
Giant Tree Hl BUSH WD23 43 H4
Gibbfield Cl CHDH RM6 76 C6
Gibbins Rd SRTFD E15 111 G5
Gibbon Rd ACT W3 123 E6
KUTN/CMB KT2 201 G4
PECK SE15 170 A3
Gibbons Rd WLSDN NW10 102 D4
Gibbon Wk PUT/ROE * SW15 163 G5
Gibbs Av NRWD SE19 208 D2
Gibbs Cl NRWD * SE19 208 D1
Gibbs Couch OXHEY WD19 42 B5
Gibbs Gn EDGW HA8 46 C6
WKENS * W14 144 D5
Gibbs Rd UED N18 54 A6
Gibbs Sq NRWD * SE19 208 D1
Gibraltar Wk BETH E2 8 D4
Gibson Cl CHSGTN * KT9 239 E3
ISLW TW7 159 H4
WCHPL E1 130 A3
Gibson Gdns STNW/STAM * N16 89 F6
Gibson Rd BCTR RM8 96 A5
LBTH SE11 29 H2
SUT SM1 243 F3
Gibson's Hl STRHM/NOR SW16 208 A3
Gibson Sq IS * N1 108 A6
IS N1 108 A6
Gibson St GNWCH SE10 152 A5
Gideon Cl BELV DA17 157 F4
Gideon Ms EA * W5 141 F2
Gideon Rd BTSEA SW11 166 C4
Giesbach Rd ARCH N19 87 E6
Giffard Rd UED N18 69 E1
Giffin St DEPT SE8 171 E1
Gifford Gdns HNWL W7 119 H4
Gifford St IS N1 107 G5
Gift La SRTFD E15 112 A6
Giggs Hl STMC/STPC BR5 215 G5
Giggs Hill Gdns THDIT KT7 220 C5
Giggs Hill Rd THDIT KT7 220 C4
Gilbert Cl WIM/MER * SW19 205 F4
WOOL/PLUM SE18 173 H2
Gilbert Gv EDGW HA8 62 C4
Gilbert Pl NOXST/BSQ WC1A 13 E2
Gilbert Rd BELV DA17 156 D3
BMLY BR1 212 C3
LBTH SE11 30 B1
PIN HA5 78 B1
WIM/MER SW19 205 G3
Gilbert St HSLW TW3 159 G4
MYFR/PKLN W1K 11 F4
SRTFD E15 112 A2
Gilbey Rd TOOT SW17 186 A6
Gilbeys Yd CAMTN NW1 106 C5
Gilbourne Rd
WOOL/PLUM SE18 155 F6
Gilda Av PEND EN3 40 C6
Gilda Crs STNW/STAM N16 89 G5
Gildea Cl PIN HA5 59 E3
Gildea St REGST W1B 11 H2
Gildersome St
WOOL/PLUM SE18 154 A6
Gilders Rd CHSGTN KT9 239 H5
Giles Coppice NRWD SE19 189 F6
Gilkes Crs EDUL SE22 189 E1
Gilkes Pl DUL SE21 189 E1
Gillan Gn BUSH WD23 43 G4
Gillards Ms WALTH E17 91 E1
Gillards Wy WALTH E17 91 E1
Gill Av CAN/RD E16 132 G5
Gillender St BOW E3 131 G3
Gillespie Rd FSBYPK N4 108 A1
Gillett Av EHAM E6 133 G1
Gillett Pl HACK E8 109 F3
Gillett Rd THHTH CR7 228 D1
Gillett St STNW/STAM N16 109 E3
Gillham Ter TOTM N17 69 G2
Gillian Park Rd CHEAM SM3 224 D5
Gillian St LEW SE13 171 F6
Gillian Ter BRYLDS * KT5 221 H3
Gillingham Ms PIM SW1V 27 H1
Gillingham Rd CRICK NW2 104 C1
Gillingham Rw PIM SW1V 28 A1
Gillingham St PIM SW1V 27 H2
Gillison Wk BERM/RHTH SE16 25 F5
Gillman Dr SRTFD E15 112 A6
Gillmans Rd STMC/STPC BR5 235 H5
Gill St POP/IOD E14 130 D5
Gillum Cl EBAR EN4 50 B3
Gilmore Rd LEW SE13 171 H5
Gilpin Av MORT/ESHN SW14 162 D5
Gilpin Cl BAY/PAD * W2 125 H4
MTCM CR4 206 A5
Gilpin Crs UED N18 69 F1
WHTN TW2 179 F2
Gilpin Rd CLPT E5 110 C2
Gilroy Wy STMC/STPC BR5 235 H4
Gilsland Rd THHTH CR7 228 D1
Gilstead Rd FUL/PGN SW6 165 F3
Gilston Rd WBPTN SW10 145 G5
Gilton Rd CAT SE6 192 A5
Giltspur St STBT EC1A 14 D3
Gilwell Cl CHING E4 41 F5
Gilwell La CHING E4 41 H5
Gippeswyck Cl PIN HA5 58 B4
Gipsy Hl NRWD SE19 209 E1
Gipsy La BARN SW13 163 G4
Gipsy Rd WELL DA16 176 B3
WNWD SE27 188 D6
Gipsy Road Gdns WNWD SE27 188 C6
Giralda Cl CAN/RD E16 133 F4
Giraud St POP/IOD E14 131 F5
Girdlers Rd HMSMTH W6 144 B4
Girdwood Rd
WAND/EARL SW18 184 C2
Gironde Rd FUL/PGN SW6 164 D1
Girton Av CDALE/KGS NW9 62 A6
Girton Cl NTHLT UB5 99 G4
Girton Gdns CROY/NA CR0 249 E1
Girton Rd NTHLT UB5 99 G4
SYD SE26 210 B1
Gisbourne Cl WLGTN SM6 245 F1
Gisburn Rd CEND/HSY/T N8 87 H1
Gissing Wk IS * N1 108 A5
Gittens Cl BMLY BR1 192 B6
Glacier Wy ALP/SUD HA0 121 F1
Gladbeck Wy ENC/FH EN2 38 C5
Gladding Rd MNPK E12 113 F2
Glade Cl SURB * KT6 221 F6
Glade Gdns CROY/NA CR0 230 C4
Glade La NWDGN UB2 139 F2
Gladeside CROY/NA CR0 230 B3
WCHMH N21 51 H2
Gladesmore Rd
SEVS/STOTM N15 89 F3
The Glade BELMT SM2 242 C6
BMLY BR1 213 F5
CHARL SE7 173 E1
CLAY IG5 73 H4
CROY/NA CR0 230 B2
ENC/FH EN2 38 A4
EW KT17 241 G4
HACK * E8 109 F4
NFNCH/WDSP * N12 49 H6
SHB * W12 143 H2
WCHMH N21 51 H1
WFD IG8 56 D5
WWKM BR4 249 F1
Gladiator St FSTH SE23 190 C1
Glading Ter STNW/STAM N16 109 F1
Gladioli Cl HPTN TW12 199 E2
Gladsmuir Cl WOT/HER KT12 218 A6
Gladsmuir Rd ARCH N19 87 E5
BAR EN5 34 C3
Gladstone Av MNPK E12 113 G5
WDGN N22 68 B5
WHTN TW2 179 H2
Gladstone Gdns HSLW TW3 159 G2
Gladstone Ms
KIL/WHAMP NW6 104 D4
PGE/AN SE20 210 A3
WDGN N22 68 A5
Gladstone Pde CRICK * NW2 104 A1
Gladstone Park Gdns
CRICK NW2 103 H1
Gladstone Pl BAR * EN5 34 B5
E/WMO/HCT * KT8 220 A2
Gladstone Rd BKHH IG9 57 E3
CHSWK * W4 142 D3
CROY/NA CR0 228 D4
KUT KT1 202 A6
NWDGN UB2 138 C2
ORP BR6 252 C3
SURB KT6 221 F6
WIM/MER SW19 205 E3
Gladstone St STHWK SE1 22 C5
Gladstone Ter VX/NE * SW8 166 D2
WNWD * SE27 188 C6
Gladstone Wy
KTN/HRWW/W HA3 60 A6
Gladwell Rd BMLY BR1 212 C2
CEND/HSY/T N8 87 H3
Gladwyn Rd PUT/ROE SW15 164 B4
Gladys Rd KIL/WHAMP NW6 105 E5
Glaisher St DEPT SE8 151 F6
Glamis Pl WAP E1W 130 A6
Glamis Rd WAP E1W 130 A6
Glamis Wy NTHLT UB5 99 G4
Glamorgan Cl MTCM CR4 207 G6
Glamorgan Rd KUT KT1 201 E3
Glanfield Rd BECK BR3 230 D1
Glanleam Rd STAN HA7 45 F6
Glanville Rd BRXS/STRHM SW2 167 G6
HAYES BR2 212 D6
Glasbrook Av WHTN TW2 178 D3
Glasbrook Rd ELTH/MOT SE9 193 F2
Glaserton Rd STNW/STAM N16 89 E4
Glasford St TOOT SW17 206 B2
Glasgow Rd PLSTW E13 132 D1
UED N18 69 H1
Glasgow Ter PIM SW1V 28 A4
Glasse Cl WEA W13 120 C6
Glasshill St STHWK SE1 22 D3
Glasshouse Flds WAP E1W 130 B6
Glasshouse St REGST W1B 12 B6
Glasshouse Wk LBTH SE11 29 F3
Glasshouse Yd STBT EC1A 7 E6
Glasslyn Rd CEND/HSY/T N8 87 F2
Glassmill La HAYES BR2 212 B5

Glass St BETH E2 ...9 H5
Glass Yd WOOL/PLUM SE18 ...154 A6
Glastonbury Av WFD IG8 ...73 F3
Glastonbury Cl
  STMC/STPC BR5 ...236 A5
Glastonbury Pl WCHPL E1 ...130 A5
Glastonbury Rd ED N9 ...53 C3
  MRDN SM4 ...225 E4
Glastonbury St
  KIL/WHAMP NW6 ...104 D3
Glaston St EA * W5 ...141 F1
Glaucus St BOW E3 ...111 C4
Glazbury Rd WKENS W14 ...144 C4
Glazebrook Cl DUL SE21 ...188 D4
Glazebrook Rd TEDD TW11 ...200 B3
Glebe Av ENC/FH EN2 ...32 A2
  KTN/HRWW/W HA3 ...61 C6
  MTCM CR4 ...206 A5
  WFD IG8 ...72 C2
Glebe Cl CHSWK * W4 ...143 E5
Glebe Ct BKHTH/KID * SE3 ...172 A4
  FITZ W1 ...141 F1
  STAN HA7 ...61 G1
Glebe Crs HDN NW4 ...46 A1
  KTN/HRWW/W HA3 ...61 C6
Glebe Gdns NWMAL KT3 ...223 E4
Glebe House Dr HAYES BR2 ...232 D5
Glebelands E/WMO/HCT KT8 ...219 F2
  ESH/CLAY KT10 ...238 B6
Glebelands Av CNTH/NBYPK IG2 ...34 A6
  SWFD E18 ...72 C5
Glebelands Cl CMBW * SE5 ...169 E4
Glebe La BAR EN5 ...47 C1
  KTN/HRWW/W HA3 ...81 G1
Glebe Pth MTCM CR4 ...206 B6
Glebe Pl CHEL SW3 ...26 A5
Glebe Rd BARN SW13 ...163 G3
  BELMT SM2 ...242 C6
  BMLY BR1 ...212 C4
  CAR SM5 ...244 B4
  CEND/HSY/T N8 ...87 H1
  DAGE RM10 ...117 H4
  FNCH N3 ...65 G4
  HACK * E8 ...109 F5
  STAN HA7 ...61 G1
  WLSDN NW10 ...103 G4
Glebe Side TWK TW1 ...180 B1
Glebe Sq MTCM * CR4 ...206 B6
Glebe St CHSWK W4 ...142 D5
Glebe Ter BOW E3 ...131 F2
The Glebe BKHTH/KID SE3 ...172 A4
  CHST BR7 ...214 C4
  STRHM/NOR * SW16 ...187 F6
  WPK KT4 ...225 H5
Glebe Wy FELT TW13 ...179 E5
  WWKM BR4 ...231 G6
Glebeway WFD IG8 ...73 E1
Gledhow Gdns ECT SW5 ...145 G4
Gledstanes Rd WKENS W14 ...144 C5
Gleed Av BUSH WD23 ...43 H4
Gleeson Dr ORP BR6 ...253 F3
Glegg Pl PUT/ROE * SW15 ...164 B5
Glenaffric Av POP/IOD E14 ...151 H4
Glen Albyn Rd WIM/MER SW19 ...184 B4
Glenalmond Rd
  KTN/HRWW/W HA3 ...81 C1
Glenalvon Wy CHARL SE7 ...153 G4
Glena Mt SUT SM1 ...243 G2
Glenarm Rd CLPT E5 ...110 A2
Glenavon Cl ESH/CLAY KT10 ...238 C4
Glenavon Rd SRTFD E15 ...112 A5
Glenbarr Cl ELTH/MOT SE9 ...174 B4
Glenbow Rd BMLY BR1 ...212 A2
Glenbrook North ENC/FH EN2 ...37 H5
Glenbrook Rd
  KIL/WHAMP NW6 ...105 E3
Glenbuck Rd SURB KT6 ...221 F5
Glencairn Dr EA W5 ...120 D5
Glencairne Cl CAN/RD E16 ...133 F4
Glencairn Rd
  STRHM/NOR SW16 ...207 G3
Glencoe Av CNTH/NBYPK IG2 ...95 G4
Glencoe Rd BUSH WD23 ...43 E1
  DAGE RM10 ...117 E2
  YEAD UB4 ...118 B4
Glencorse Gn OXHEY * WD19 ...42 B6
Glen Crs WFD IG8 ...72 D2
Glendale Av CHDH RM6 ...96 A4
  EDGW HA8 ...45 H6
  WDGN N22 ...68 A3
Glendale Cl ELTH/MOT SE9 ...174 A4
Glendale Gdns WBLY HA9 ...81 F5
Glen Dale Ms BECK BR3 ...211 F4
Glendale Rd ERITH DA8 ...157 G4
Glendale Wy THMD SE28 ...156 A1
Glendall St CLAP SW4 ...167 H4
Glendarvon St PUT/ROE SW15 ...164 B4
Glendevon Cl EDGW HA8 ...46 B5
Glendish Rd TOTM N17 ...70 D1
Glendor Gdns MLHL NW7 ...46 D6
Glendower Crs ORP BR6 ...255 G3
Glendower Gdns
  MORT/ESHN SW14 ...162 D4
Glendower Pl SKENS SW7 ...145 H4
Glendower Rd CHING E4 ...55 H1
  MORT/ESHN SW14 ...162 D4
Glendown Rd ABYW SE2 ...155 C5
Glendun Rd ACT W3 ...125 E6
Gleneagle Ms
  STRHM/NOR SW16 ...207 F1
Gleneagle Rd
  STRHM/NOR SW16 ...207 F1
Gleneagles STAN HA7 ...60 D2
Gleneagles Cl
  BERM/RHTH SE16 ...33 G4
  ORP BR6 ...234 D5
  OXHEY * WD19 ...58 B1
Gleneldon Ms
  STRHM/NOR SW16 ...187 G6
Gleneldon Rd
  STRHM/NOR SW16 ...187 G6
Glenelg Rd BRXS/STRHM SW2 ...167 G6
Glenesk Rd ELTH/MOT SE9 ...174 E1
Glenfarg Rd CAT SE6 ...191 H5
Glenfield Rd BAL SW12 ...187 E3
  WEA W13 ...140 D2
Glenfinlas Wy CMBW SE5 ...168 B1
Glenforth St GNWCH SE10 ...152 B4
Glengall Br POP/IOD E14 ...151 F3

Glengall Gv POP/IOD E14 ...151 F3
Glengall Rd BXLYHN DA7 ...176 C4
  EDGW HA8 ...46 B5
  KIL/WHAMP NW6 ...104 D6
  PECK SE15 ...32 D5
  WFD IG8 ...72 D2
Glen Gdns CROY/NA CRO ...246 A1
Glengall Ter PECK SE15 ...32 D5
Glengarnock Av POP/IOD E14 ...151 G4
Glengarry Rd EDUL SE22 ...169 F3
Glenham Dr GNTH/NBYPK IG2 ...94 B2
Glenhead Cl ELTH/MOT SE9 ...155 E5
Glenhill Cl FNCH N3 ...65 E5
Glenhouse Rd ELTH/MOT SE9 ...174 A6
Glenhurst Av BXLY DA5 ...196 D3
  KTTN NW5 ...106 C2
Glenhurst Rd BTFD TW8 ...141 E6
  NFNCH/WDSP N12 ...49 H6
Glenilla Rd HAMP NW3 ...106 A4
Glenister Park Rd
  STRHM/NOR S16 ...207 F3
Glenister Rd GNWCH SE10 ...152 B5
Gleniea Rd ELTH/MOT SE9 ...174 A6
Glenlorch Rd HAMP NW3 ...106 A4
  PEND EN3 ...40 A5
Glenluge Rd BKHTH/KID SE3 ...152 C6
Glenlyon Rd ELTH/MOT SE9 ...174 A6
Glenmere Av MLHL NW7 ...63 G3
Glenmore Lawns WEA * W13 ...121 G5
Glenmore Pde ALP/SUD * HAO ...101 G6
Glenmore Rd HAMP NW3 ...106 A4
  WELL DA16 ...175 F2
Glenmore Wy BARK IG11 ...115 C2
Glennie Rd WNWD SE27 ...188 A5
Glenny Rd BARK IG11 ...114 C4
Glenorchy Cl YEAD UB4 ...119 C4
Glenparke Rd FSTGT E7 ...112 D4
Glen Ri WFD IG8 ...72 D2
Glen Rd CHSGTN KT9 ...239 G1
  PLSTW E13 ...133 E3
  WALTH E17 ...90 D2
  WLGTN SM6 ...244 D6
Glenrosa St FUL/PGN SW6 ...165 G3
Glenroy St SHB W12 ...124 A5
Glensdale Rd BROCKY SE4 ...170 C2
Glenshiel Rd ELTH/MOT SE9 ...174 A6
Glenside CHIG IG7 ...74 B2
Glentanner Wy TOOT SW17 ...185 H5
Glentham Rd BARN SW13 ...114 G2
Glentham Cottages
  BARN * SW13 ...143 G6
Glentham Gdns BARN SW13 ...143 H5
Glentham Rd BARN SW13 ...143 G6
The Glen DEPT * SM2 ...243 G4
  CROY/NA CRO ...248 B1
  HAYES BR2 ...212 A2
  NWDGN UB2 ...138 D5
  ORP BR6 ...251 H1
  PIN HA5 ...59 E3
  WBLY HA9 ...80 A2
Glenthorne Av CROY/NA CRO ...230 A5
Glenthorne Cl CHEAM SM3 ...225 H6
Glenthorne Gdns BARK/HLT IG6 ...74 A6
  CHEAM SM3 ...225 H6
Glenthorne Rd FBAR/BDGN N11 ...66 B5
  HMSMTH W6 ...144 A4
  KUT KT1 ...221 H1
  WALTH E17 ...90 C2
Glenthorpe Av MRDN SM4 ...224 B3
Glenton Rd LEW SE13 ...172 A5
Glentrammon Av ORP BR6 ...253 F6
Glentrammon Cl ORP BR6 ...253 F6
Glentrammon Gdns ORP BR6 ...253 F6
Glentrammon Rd ORP BR6 ...253 F6
Glentworth St CAMTN NW1 ...3 G6
Glenure Rd ELTH/MOT SE9 ...174 A6
Glenview ABYW SE2 ...156 A1
Glen View Rd BMLY BR1 ...213 F5
Glenville Av ENC/FH EN2 ...38 C1
Glenville Gv DEPT SE8 ...170 D1
Glenville Ms WIM/MER SW19 ...166 B6
Glenville Rd KUTN/CMB KT2 ...202 A4
Glenwood Av CDALE/KGS NW9 ...83 E5
Glenwood Cl HRW HA1 ...61 F5
Glenwood Gdns
  GNTH/NBYPK IG2 ...94 A2
Glenwood Gv CDALE/KGS NW9 ...82 C5
Glenwood Rd CAT SE6 ...191 C1
  EW KT17 ...241 G4
  HSLW TW3 ...159 H4
  MLHL NW7 ...31 F1
  SEVS/STOTM N15 ...89 F2
Glenwood Rw NRWD * SE19 ...209 H4
Glenwood Wy CROY/NA CRO ...230 B5
Glenworth Av POP/IOD E14 ...151 H4
Gliddon Rd WKENS W14 ...144 C3
Glimpsing Gn ERITHM DA18 ...156 C3
Gload Crs STMC/STPC BR5 ...236 B6
Globe Pond Rd
  BERM/RHTH SE16 ...110 C2
Globe Rd BETH E2 ...130 A2
  FSTGT E7 ...112 B3
  WFD IG8 ...73 E3
Globe St STHWK SE1 ...23 G4
Globe Ter BETH E2 ...130 A2
Glossop Rd SAND/SEL CR2 ...246 D6
Gloster Rd NWMAL KT3 ...223 E1
Gloucester Av BFN/LL DA15 ...195 E4
  CAMTN NW1 ...4 A1
  WELL DA16 ...176 A4
Gloucester Circ GNWCH SE10 ...171 C1
Gloucester Ct THDT * KT7 ...220 C5
  WLSDN NW10 ...102 D5
Gloucester Ct MON EC3R ...16 H
  MTCM * CR4 ...207 G4
  RCH/KEW * TW9 ...162 A1
Gloucester Crs CAMTN NW1 ...106 D6
Gloucester Dr
  FSBYPK N4 ...88 B2
  GLDGN NW11 ...64 D4
Gloucester Gdns
  BAY/PAD * W2 ...125 G5
  EBAR EN4 ...33 H5
  GLDGN NW11 ...64 D4
  IL IG1 ...93 G4
  SUT SM1 ...225 H6
Gloucester Ga CAMTN NW1 ...3 H1
Gloucester Gate Br
  CAMTN * NW1 ...106 D6

Gloucester Gate Ms
  CAMTN NW1 ...3 G1
Gloucester Gv EDGW HA8 ...62 D4
Gloucester Ms BAY/PAD W2 ...125 G5
Gloucester Ms West
  BAY/PAD W2 ...125 G5
Gloucester Pde BFN/LL * DA15 ...175 G6
Gloucester Pl CAMTN NW1 ...2 C6
Gloucester Place Ms
  MBLAR W1H ...10 D2
Gloucester Rd ACT W3 ...142 C2
  BAR EN5 ...35 F6
  BXLYHN DA7 ...156 D5
  CROY/NA CRO ...245 E1
  EA W5 ...141 E2
  ENC/FH EN2 ...24 D3
  FELT TW13 ...178 A3
  HPTN TW12 ...199 F3
  HSLWW TW4 ...158 C5
  KUT KT1 ...202 A5
  LEY E10 ...91 E4
  MNPK E12 ...113 H1
  RCH/KEW TW9 ...162 A1
  RYLN/HDSTN HA2 ...79 F2
  SKENS SW7 ...145 G4
  TEDD TW11 ...200 A1
  TOTM N17 ...67 H3
  UED N18 ...69 F1
  WALTH E17 ...70 B5
  WAN E11 ...93 G2
  WHTN TW2 ...179 G3
Gloucester Sq BAY/PAD W2 ...145 E1
  BETH E2 ...109 G6
Gloucester St PIM SW1V ...28 A3
Gloucester Ter BAY/PAD W2 ...125 G5
  STHGT/OAK * N14 ...51 F1
Gloucester Wk KENS * W8 ...145 E2
Gloucester Wy CLKNW EC1R ...6 A4
Glover Cl ABYW SE2 ...156 A4
Glover Dr UED N18 ...70 A2
Glover Rd PIN HA5 ...78 B3
Glycena Rd BTSEA SW11 ...166 B4
Glyn Av EBAR EN4 ...35 H3
Glyn Cl EW KT17 ...241 G6
  SNWD SE25 ...197 E6
Glyndebourne Pk ORP BR6 ...252 B1
Glynde Ms CHEL SW3 ...18 B6
Glynde Rd BXLYHN DA7 ...176 B4
Glynde St BROCKY SE4 ...190 D1
Glyndon Rd WOOL/PLUM SE18 ...134 C4
Glyn Dr SCUP DA14 ...195 H6
Glynfield Rd WLSDN NW10 ...103 E5
Glynne Rd WDGN N22 ...68 A5
Glyn Rd CLPT E5 ...110 B2
  PEND EN3 ...40 A5
  WPK KT4 ...225 F1
Glyn St LBTH SE11 ...29 G4
Goat La EN EN1 ...39 F1
Goat Rd MTCM CR4 ...226 C4
Goat Whf BTFD TW8 ...141 G6
Gobions Av CRW RM5 ...77 H3
Godalming Av WLGTN SM6 ...245 G3
Godalming Rd POP/IOD E14 ...131 F4
Godbold Rd SRTFD E15 ...132 A3
Goddard Pl ARCH N19 ...107 E1
Goddard Rd BECK BR3 ...230 B1
Goddards Wy IL IG1 ...94 D5
Goddington La ORP BR6 ...253 H2
Goddington Ln ORP BR6 ...253 G1
Godfrey Av NTHLT UB5 ...98 C6
  WHTN TW2 ...179 H2
Godfrey Hl WOOL/PLUM SE18 ...153 G4
Godfrey Rd WOOL/PLUM SE18 ...153 H4
Godfrey St CHEL SW3 ...26 B5
  SRTFD E15 ...131 G1
Godfrey Wy HSLWW TW4 ...178 C2
Goding St LBTH SE11 ...29 F4
Godley Rd WAND/EARL SW18 ...185 H5
Godliman St BLKFR * EC4V ...14 D4
Godman Rd PECK * SE15 ...169 H5
Godolphin Cl PLMGR N13 ...68 B2
Godolphin Pl ACT W3 ...122 D6
Godolphin Rd SHB W12 ...143 H1
Godric Crs CROY/NA CRO ...249 H6
Godson Rd CROY/NA CRO ...246 A1
Godstone Rd SUT SM1 ...243 G2
  TWK TW1 ...180 C5
Godstone Rd ABYW SE2 ...156 A2
Godwin Cl CHING E4 ...41 C1
  HOR/WEW KT19 ...240 C4
  IS N1 ...7 F1
Godwin Rd FSTGT E7 ...112 D2
  HAYES BR2 ...212 A2
Goffers Rd BKHTH/KID SE3 ...172 A2
Goidel Cl WLGTN SM6 ...245 F2
Golborne Gdns NKENS * W10 ...124 C3
Golborne Ms NKENS W10 ...124 C4
Golborne Rd NKENS W10 ...124 C4
Golda Cl BAR EN5 ...48 B1
Goldbeaters Gv EDGW HA8 ...63 E2
Goldcliff Cl MRDN SM4 ...225 H6
Goldcrest Cl CAN/RD E16 ...133 F4
  THMD SE28 ...136 A6
Goldcrest Ms EA * W5 ...121 H4
Goldcrest Wy BUSH WD23 ...43 G3
  CROY/NA CRO ...249 H6
Golden Cross Ms NTGHL * W11 ...124 D5
Golden Hind Pl DEPT * SE8 ...150 D4
Golden La STLK EC1Y ...7 E5
Golden Lane Est STLK EC1Y ...7 E5
Golden Mnr HNWL W7 ...120 A6
Golden Pde WALTH * E17 ...72 A4
Golden Plover Cl CAN/RD E16 ...132 C5
Golden Sq SOHO/CST W1F ...12 B5
Golden Yd HAMP * NW3 ...105 G2
Goldfinch Rd THMD SE28 ...137 C4
Goldhawk Ms SHB W12 ...143 H2
Goldhawk Rd HMSMTH W6 ...143 H5
Goldhaze Cl WFD IG8 ...73 E3
Gold Hl EDGW HA8 ...62 D2

Golding St WCHPL E1 ...17 F4
Goldingham Crs CAMTN NW1 ...4 C1
Goldington Cl CAMTN NW1 ...4 C1
Gold La EDGW HA8 ...62 D2
Goldman Cl BETH E2 ...9 E5
Goldney Rd MV/WKIL W9 ...125 E3
Goldrill Dr FBAR/BDGN N11 ...50 C4
Goldsboro Rd VX/NE * SW8 ...167 G1
Goldsborough Crs CHING E4 ...55 F4
Goldsdown Cl PEND EN3 ...40 C3
Goldsdown Rd PEND EN3 ...40 B3
Goldsmid St WOOL/PLUM SE18 ...155 E5
Goldsmith Av ACT W3 ...132 D6
  CDALE/KGS NW9 ...83 E2
  MNPK E12 ...113 G4
  ROMW/RG RM7 ...77 A2
Goldsmith Cl RYLN/HDSTN HA2 ...79 E5
Goldsmith La CDALE/KGS NW9 ...82 C1
Goldsmith Pl
  KIL/WHAMP * NW6 ...105 F6
Goldsmith Rd ACT W3 ...142 D1
  FBAR/BDGN N11 ...66 B1
  LEY E10 ...91 F5
  PECK SE15 ...169 G2
  WALTH E17 ...51 E6
Goldsmiths Cl ACT * W3 ...142 D1
Goldsmith's Rw BETH E2 ...9 F1
  BETH E2 ...109 G6
Goldsmith St CITYW EC2V ...15 F3
Goldsworthy Gdns
  BERM/RHTH SE16 ...150 A4
Goldwell Rd THHTH CR7 ...227 H1
Goldwing Cl CAN/RD E16 ...132 C5
Golf Cl STAN HA7 ...61 G3
  STRHM/NOR SW16 ...208 A4
Golf Club Dr KUTN/CMB KT2 ...202 D3
Golfe Rd IL IG1 ...94 D1
Golf Rd BMLY BR1 ...214 A6
  EA * W5 ...121 H5
Golf Side WHTN TW2 ...179 H5
Golfside Cl NWMAL KT3 ...203 E5
Golfside Cl TRDG/WHET N20 ...52 A1
Gollogly Ter CHARL SE7 ...153 E5
Gomer Gdns TEDD TW11 ...200 C2
Gomer Pl TEDD TW11 ...200 C2
Gomm Rd BERM/RHTH SE16 ...150 A3
Gomshall Av WLGTN SM6 ...245 G3
Gondar Gdns CRICK NW2 ...104 D3
Gonson St DEPT SE8 ...151 F6
Gonston Cl WIM/MER SW19 ...184 C2
Gonville Crs NTHLT UB5 ...99 F4
Gonville Rd THHTH CR7 ...227 H2
Gonville St FUL/PGN SW6 ...164 C4
Goodall Rd WAN E11 ...111 C1
Gooden Ct HRW HA1 ...100 A1
Goodenough Rd
  WIM/MER SW19 ...204 D3
Goodey Rd BARK IG11 ...115 F5
Goodge Pl FITZ W1 ...12 B2
Goodge St FITZ W1 ...12 B2
Goodhall St WLSDN NW10 ...123 F2
Goodhart Wy WWKM BR4 ...232 A3
Goodhew Rd SNWD SE25 ...229 G5
Gooding Cl NWMAL KT3 ...222 C1
Goodinge Cl HOLWY N7 ...107 G3
Goodison Cl HOLWY N7 ...107 G4
Goodman Cr ALP/SUD * HAO ...101 C4
Goodman Crs
  BRXS/STRHM SW2 ...187 F4
Goodman Rd LEY E10 ...91 G4
Goodman's Cl ALP/SUD HAO ...101 G2
Goodman's Stile WCHPL E1 ...17 E3
Goodman's Yd TWRH EC3N ...16 C5
Goodmayes Av GDMY/SEVK IG3 ...95 G2
Goodmayes La GDMY/SEVK IG3 ...115 G2
Goodmayes Rd GDMY/SEVK IG3 ...95 G2
Goodmead Rd ORP BR6 ...235 G4
Goodrich Rd EDUL SE22 ...189 F1
Goodson Rd WLSDN NW10 ...103 E5
Goods Wy CAMTN NW1 ...5 F1
Goodway Gdns POP/IOD E14 ...131 H5
Goodwin Cl BERM/RHTH SE16 ...24 D6
  MTCM CR4 ...225 H6
Goodwin Dr SCUP DA14 ...196 B4
Goodwin Gdns CROY/NA CRO ...246 B4
Goodwin Rd CROY/NA CRO ...246 B3
  ED N9 ...54 D1
  SHB W12 ...143 C2
Goodwins Ct CHCR WC2N ...13 C5
Goodwin St FSBYPK N4 ...88 A6
Goodwood Cl MRDN SM4 ...225 E1
Goodwood Pde BECK * BR3 ...230 C1
Goodwood Rd NWCR SE14 ...170 C1
Goodwyn Av MLHL NW7 ...31 E5
Goodwyns Vw MUSWH N10 ...66 C4
Goodyers Gdns HDN NW4 ...64 B2
Goosander Wy
  WOOL/PLUM SE18 ...154 D3
Goose Acre La
  KTN/HRWW/W HA3 ...81 F2
Goose Green Cl
  STMC/STPC BR5 ...215 G5
Gooseley La EHAM E6 ...134 A2
Goossens Cl SUT SM1 ...243 G3
Gophir La CANST * EC4R ...15 C5
Gopsall St IS N1 ...108 D6
Gordon Av CHING E4 ...72 A2
  MORT/ESHN SW14 ...162 B2
  STAN HA7 ...43 H6
  TWK TW1 ...160 D2
Gordonbrock Rd BROCKY SE4 ...171 E6
Gordon Cl WALTH E17 ...89 H4
Gordon Cottages KENS * W8 ...145 G2
Gordon Crs CROY/NA CRO ...229 G5
Gordondale Rd
  WIM/MER SW19 ...185 E4
Gordon Gdns EDGW HA8 ...62 B5
Gordon Gv CMBW SE5 ...168 B3
Gordon Hl ENC/FH EN2 ...38 C2
Gordon House Rd KTTN NW5 ...106 B2
Gordon Pl KENS W8 ...145 E2
Gordon Rd BARK IG11 ...115 E6
  BECK BR3 ...210 D6
  BELV DA17 ...157 H1
  BFN/LL DA15 ...175 H6
  BRYLDS KT5 ...221 H4
  CAR SM5 ...244 A6
  CHDH RM6 ...96 A2
  CHING E4 ...54 B2
  CHSWK W4 ...142 B6

EA W5 ...121 E6
ED N9 ...53 H4
ENC/FH EN2 ...38 D2
ESH/CLAY KT10 ...238 A5
FBAR/BDGN N11 ...67 F3
FNCH N3 ...64 D3
HSLW TW3 ...155 G5
IL IG1 ...114 D1
KTN/HRWW/W HA3 ...60 A6
KUTN/CMB KT2 ...201 H4
NWDGN UB2 ...138 C4
PECK SE15 ...169 H3
RCH/KEW TW9 ...161 H3
SRTFD E15 ...111 G2
WAN E11 ...92 C3
Gordon Sq STPAN WC1H ...4 C5
Gordon St PLSTW E13 ...132 C2
STPAN WC1H ...4 C5
Gordon Wy BAR EN5 ...34 D5
BMLY BR1 ...212 C4
Gorefield Pl KIL/WHAMP NW6 ...125 E1
Gore Rd HOM E9 ...110 A6
RYNPK SW20 ...193 G1
Goresbrook Rd DAGW RM9 ...116 A6
Gore St SKENS SW7 ...145 G3
Gorham Pl NTGHL W11 ...124 C6
Goring Cl CRW RM5 ...77 G4
Goring Gdns BCTR RM8 ...116 A2
Goring Rd DAGW RM10 ...117 H4
FBAR/BDGN * N11 ...67 G2
Goring St HDTCH EC3A ...16 E3
Goring Wy CFD/PVL UB6 ...119 G1
Gorleston Rd SEVS/STOTM N15 ...88 D2
Gorleston St WKENS W14 ...144 C4
Gorman Rd WOOL/PLUM SE18 ...153 H4
Gorringe Park Av MTCM CR4 ...206 B3
Gorse Ri TOOT SW17 ...206 C1
Gorse Rd CROY/NA CR0 ...249 E1
STMC/STPC BR5 ...237 E6
Gorst Rd BTSEA SW11 ...186 B1
WLSDN NW10 ...122 C3
Gorsuch Pl BETH E2 ...8 C3
Gorsuch St BETH E2 ...8 C3
Gosberton Rd BAL SW12 ...186 B3
Gosbury Hl CHSGTN KT9 ...239 G2
Gosfield Rd BCTR RM8 ...97 E5
Gosfield St GTPST W1W ...11 H1
Gosford Gdns REDBR IG4 ...93 G2
Goslett Yd SOHO/SHAV W1D ...12 D3
Gosling Cl CFD/PVL UB6 ...119 E2
Gosling Wy BRXN/ST SW9 ...168 A2
Gospatrick Rd TOTM N17 ...68 C4
Gosport Rd WALTH E17 ...90 D2
Gosport Wy PECK SE15 ...169 F1
Gossage Rd WOOL/PLUM SE18 ...154 D5
Gosset St BETH E2 ...8 C4
Gosshill Rd CHST BR7 ...214 A5
Gossington Cl CHST BR7 ...194 B6
Gosterwood St DEPT SE8 ...150 C6
Gostling Rd WHTN TW2 ...155 E3
Goston Gdns THHTH CR7 ...208 A6
Goswell Pl FSBYE EC1V ...6 C3
Goswell Rd FSBYE EC1V ...6 B3
Gothic Rd WHTN TW2 ...179 H4
Gottfried Ms KTTN NW5 ...107 E2
Goudhurst Rd BMLY BR1 ...212 A1
Gough Rd EN EN1 ...39 H5
FSTGT E7 ...112 B2
Gough Sq FLST/FETLN EC4A ...14 B3
Gough St FSBYW WC1X ...5 H5
Goulding Gdns THHTH CR7 ...208 C5
Gould Rd WHTN TW2 ...180 A3
Gould Ter HACK E8 ...109 H4
Goulston St WCHPL E1 ...16 C5
Goulton Rd CLPT E5 ...109 H5
Gourley Pl SEVS/STOTM N15 ...89 E2
Gourley St SEVS/STOTM N15 ...89 E2
Gourock Rd ELTH/MOT SE9 ...174 A6
Govan St BETH E2 ...109 G6
Govier Cl SRTFD E15 ...112 A5
Gowan Av FUL/PGN SW6 ...164 C2
Gowan Rd WLSDN NW10 ...103 H5
Gower Cl BAL SW12 ...187 E1
Gower Ms GWRST WC1E ...12 D2
Gower Pl STPAN WC1H ...4 B5
Gower Rd FSTGT E7 ...112 C4
ISLW TW7 ...140 B6
Gower's Wk WCHPL E1 ...17 F5
Gowland Pl BECK BR3 ...210 D5
Gowlett Rd PECK SE15 ...169 G4
Gowrie Rd BTSEA SW11 ...166 C4
Graburn Wy E/WMO/HCT KT8 ...199 H6
Grace Av BXLYHN DA7 ...176 D3
Gracechurch St BANK EC3V ...15 H5
Grace Cl BARK/HLT IG6 ...75 F2
EDGW HA8 ...62 C3
ELTH/MOT SE9 ...193 F5
Gracedale Rd TOOT SW17 ...206 D1
Gracefield Gdns
STRHM/NOR SW16 ...187 G5
Grace Jones Cl HACK * E8 ...109 F4
Grace Pl BOW E3 ...131 F2
Grace Rd CROY/NA CR0 ...228 C3
Grace's Aly WCHPL E1 ...17 E5
Grace's Ms CMBW SE5 ...168 B3
STJWD * NW8 ...125 G1
Grace's Rd CMBW SE5 ...168 B3
Grace St BOW E3 ...131 F2
The Gradient SYD SE26 ...189 G6
Graeme Rd EN EN1 ...39 E3
Graemesdyke Av
MORT/ESHN SW14 ...162 B4
Grafton Cl HSLWW TW4 ...178 C3
WEA W13 ...122 B6
WPK KT4 ...241 E1
Grafton Crs CAMTN NW1 ...106 D4
Grafton Gdns BCTR RM8 ...96 C6
BRYLDS KT5 ...191 G2
Grafton Ms FITZ W1T ...4 A6
Grafton Park Rd WPK KT4 ...223 E6
Grafton Rd ACT W3 ...122 C6
CROY/NA CR0 ...228 A5
ENC/FH EN2 ...37 H4
HRW HA1 ...79 G2
KTTN NW5 ...106 C3
NWMAL KT3 ...223 E1
WPK KT4 ...240 D1
Grafton Sq CLAP SW4 ...167 E4

Grafton St MYFR/PICC W1J ...11 H6
Grafton Ter KTTN NW5 ...106 B3
Grafton Wy E/WMO/HCT KT8 ...218 D1
GTPST W1W ...12 A1
Grafton Yd KTTN NW5 ...106 D4
Graham Av MTCM CR4 ...206 C4
WEA W13 ...140 C2
Graham Cl CROY/NA CR0 ...231 E6
Grahame Park Wy MLHL NW7 ...63 F3
Graham Gdns SURB KT6 ...221 G5
Graham Rd BXLYHN DA7 ...176 D5
CHSWK W4 ...142 D3
HACK E8 ...109 C4
HDN NW4 ...83 H3
HPTN TW12 ...179 E6
KTN/HRWW/W HA3 ...60 A6
MTCM CR4 ...206 C4
PLSTW E13 ...132 C3
SEVS/STOTM N15 ...68 B6
WIM/MER SW19 ...204 D3
Graham St IS N1 ...6 D2
Graham Ter BFN/LL * DA15 ...195 H1
BGVA SW1W ...27 F2
Grainger Cl NTHLT UB5 ...99 G3
Grainger Rd ISLW TW7 ...160 B3
WDGN N22 ...68 C4
Gramer Cl WAN E11 ...91 H6
Grampian Cl BELMT SM2 ...245 E5
ORP BR6 ...235 F5
Grampian Gdns CRICK NW2 ...84 C5
Granada St TOOT SW17 ...206 B1
Granard Av PUT/ROE SW15 ...165 H4
Granard Rd BAL SW12 ...186 B2
Granary Cl ED N9 ...54 A2
Granary Rd WCHPL E1 ...9 G6
Granary Sq IS * N1 ...108 A4
Granary St CAMTN NW1 ...107 F6
Granby Rd ELTH/MOT SE9 ...175 H5
WOOL/PLUM SE18 ...154 B3
Granby St BETH E2 ...8 B6
Granby Ter CAMTN NW1 ...4 A2
Grand Av BRYLDS KT5 ...222 B3
FARR EC1M ...14 D1
MUSWH N10 ...86 C1
WBLY HA9 ...102 B3
Grand Av East WBLY HA9 ...102 B3
Grand Depot Rd
WOOL/PLUM SE18 ...154 A5
Grand Dr RYNPK SW20 ...204 A6
STHL UB1 ...139 G2
Granden Rd
STRHM/NOR * SW16 ...207 G5
Grand Junction Whf IS * N1 ...6 D1
Grand Pde FSBYPK * N4 ...88 B3
MORT/ESHN * N4 ...161 H1
SURB * KT6 ...222 A5
WBLY * HA9 ...82 B6
Grand Union Canal Wk
HNWL W7 ...140 A3
MV/WKIL * W9 ...125 E4
STHL UB1 ...118 D3
WLSDN NW10 ...122 B1
Grand Union Cl MV/WKIL W9 ...124 D4
Grand Union Crs HACK * E8 ...106 C6
Grand Union Wk CAMTN * NW1 ...106 D5
Grand Wk WCHPL * E1 ...130 C3
Granfield St BTSEA * SW11 ...165 H2
Grange Av EBAR EN4 ...160 A1
KTN/HRWW/W HA3 ...60 D5
NFNCH/WDSP N12 ...65 G1
SNWD SE25 ...209 E5
TRDG/WHET N20 ...48 C2
WHTN TW2 ...180 A4
Grangecliffe Gdns SNWD SE25 ...209 E5
Grange Cl BFN/LL DA15 ...195 G5
E/WMO/HCT KT8 ...198 D1
NWDGN UB2 ...138 D5
WFD IG8 ...72 C3
Grange Ct ALP/SUD * HA0 ...100 B1
ALP/SUD * HA0 ...62 L5
BELMT * SM2 ...245 F5
NTHLT UB5 ...118 A1
PIN * HA5 ...58 C6
WLGTN * SM6 ...244 D1

WALTH E17 ...90 C2
WLSDN NW10 ...103 H4
Grange St IS * N1 ...108 D6
The Grange ALP/SUD HA0 ...102 A1
CROY/NA CR0 ...230 D6
HOR/WEW KT19 ...240 D2
NWMAL * KT3 ...223 G2
STHWK SE1 ...24 C5
WIM/MER SW19 ...204 B2
WKENS * W14 ...144 D4
Grange V BELMT SM2 ...243 F5
Grangeview Rd
TRDG/WHET N20 ...49 G3
Grange Wk STHWK SE1 ...24 B5
Grange Walk Ms STHWK SE1 ...24 B6
Grangeway KIL/WHAMP NW6 ...105 E5
NFNCH/WDSP N12 ...48 B3
WFD IG8 ...57 E6
Grangeway Gdns REDBR IG4 ...95 G2
The Grangeway WCHMH N21 ...52 H3
Grangewood BXLY DA5 ...196 D3
Grangewood La BECK BR3 ...210 D2
Grange Yd STHWK SE1 ...24 C6
Granham Gdns ED N9 ...58 F4
Granite St WOOL/PLUM SE18 ...155 F5
Granleigh Rd WAN E11 ...92 A6
Gransden Av HACK E8 ...109 H5
Gransden Rd SHB W12 ...143 F2
Grantbridge St IS N1 ...6 D1
Grantchester Cl HRW HA1 ...100 B1
Grant Cl STHGT/OAK N14 ...52 C1
Grantham Cl EDGW HA8 ...45 G5
Grantham Gdns CHDH RM6 ...96 D3
Grantham Pl MYFR/PICC W1J ...10 C6
Grantham Rd BRXN/ST SW9 ...167 G4
CHSWK W4 ...162 A1
MNPK E12 ...114 A3
Grantley Rd HSLWW TW4 ...158 A3
Grantley St WCHPL E1 ...130 C2
Grantock Rd WALTH E17 ...71 H4
Granton Rd GDMY/SEVK IG3 ...95 G5
SCUP DA14 ...215 H2
STRHM/NOR SW16 ...207 F4
Grant Rd BTSEA SW11 ...166 A4
CROY/NA CR0 ...229 F5
KTN/HRWW/W HA3 ...60 A6
Grants Cl MLHL NW7 ...64 A4
Grant St IS N1 ...6 A1
PLSTW E13 ...132 C2
Grant Ter CLPT * E5 ...89 G4
Grantully Rd MV/WKIL W9 ...125 F2
Granville Av ED N9 ...54 A5
HSLWW TW4 ...159 E6
Granville Cl CROY/NA CR0 ...229 E6
Granville Gdns ACT W3 ...141 H1
STRHM/NOR SW16 ...207 H4
Granville Gv LEW SE13 ...171 G4
Granville Ms SCUP DA14 ...195 G6
Granville Pk LEW SE13 ...171 G4
Granville Pl FUL/PGN * SW6 ...165 F1
MBLAR W1H ...11 E4
NFNCH/WDSP * N12 ...65 G3
PIN HA5 ...58 B6
Granville Rd BAR EN5 ...24 D6
CRICK NW2 ...84 D6
FSBYPK N4 ...67 F3
IL IG1 ...78 B5
KIL/WHAMP NW6 ...125 E1
LEY E10 ...90 B1
NFNCH/WDSP N12 ...65 G3
SCUP DA14 ...195 G6
SWFD E18 ...72 D5
WAND/EARL SW18 ...184 D2
WELL DA16 ...176 D3
WIM/MER SW19 ...205 E3
Granville Sq PECK * SE15 ...169 E1
Granville St FSBYW WC1X ...5 H3
Grape St LSQ/SEVD WC2H ...13 E3
Graphite Sq LBTH SE11 ...29 G3
Grapsome Cl CHSGTN KT9 ...239 G5
Grasdene Rd
WOOL/PLUM SE18 ...175 G3
Grasmere Av ACT W3 ...122 G6
HSLW TW3 ...159 E4
ORP BR6 ...252 B1
PUT/ROE SW15 ...182 D6
WBLY HA9 ...81 G6
WIM/MER SW19 ...205 E6
Grasmere Ct WDGN N22 ...67 H2

Grasmere Gdns
KTN/HRWW/W HA3 ...60 D1
ORP BR6 ...251 G2
REDBR IG4 ...93 G2
Grasmere Rd BMLY BR1 ...212 B4
BXLYHN DA7 ...177 G2
MUSWH N10 ...66 B4
ORP BR6 ...251 G2
PLSTW E13 ...132 C1
SNWD SE25 ...209 G6
STRHM/NOR SW16 ...207 H1
TOTM N17 ...68 D1
Grassington Cl FBAR/BDGN N11 ...66 C1
Grassington Rd SCUP DA14 ...195 G6
Grassmount FSTH SE23 ...189 H4
Grass Pk FNCH N3 ...64 A4
Grassway WLGTN SM6 ...245 E2
Grasvenor Av BAR EN5 ...49 E1
Grately Wy PECK * SE15 ...169 E1
Gratton Rd WKENS W14 ...144 C3
Gravel Hl BXLYHS DA6 ...177 H5
CROY/NA CR0 ...248 B4
FNCH N3 ...64 D5
Gravel Hill Cl BXLY DA5 ...197 H1
BXLYHS DA6 ...177 H5
Gravel Pit Wy ORP BR6 ...235 G6
Gravel Rd HAYES BR2 ...233 G6
WHTN TW2 ...160 A1
Gravelwood Cl CHST BR7 ...194 C5
Graveney Gv PGE/AN SE20 ...191 E3
Graveney Rd TOOT SW17 ...186 A6
Gravesend Rd SHB W12 ...123 G6
Gray Av BCTR RM8 ...96 B5
Grayham Crs NWMAL KT3 ...221 G1
Grayham Rd NWMAL KT3 ...222 D1
Grayland Cl BMLY BR1 ...213 F4

Grayling Cl CAN/RD E16 ...132 A3
Grayling Ct EA * W5 ...141 F1
Grayling Rd STNW/STAM N16 ...88 D2
Grayling Sq BETH E2 ...9 F1
Grays Cottages
STMC/STPC * BR5 ...216 A4
Grayscroft Rd
STRHM/NOR SW16 ...207 F3
Grays Farm Rd
STMC/STPC BR5 ...215 H4
Grayshott Rd BTSEA SW11 ...166 C4
Gray's Inn Rd FSBYW WC1X ...5 F5
Gray's Inn Sq GINN WC1R ...14 A1
Gray St STHWK SE1 ...22 B5
Grayswood Gdns RYNPK SW20 ...203 H5
Gray's Yd MHST * W1U ...11 F4
Graywood Ct
NFNCH/WDSP N12 ...65 G3
Grazebrook Rd
STNW/STAM N16 ...88 B6
Grazeley Cl BXLYHS DA6 ...177 G6
Great Brownings DUL SE21 ...189 F6
Great Bushey Dr
TRDG/WHET N20 ...49 F3
Great Cambridge Jct
PLMGR N13 ...68 C1
Great Cambridge Rd UED N18 ...68 D1
Great Castle St REGST W1B ...11 G3
Great Central Av RSLP HA4 ...98 A3
Great Central St CAMTN NW1 ...10 C1
Great Central Wy WBLY HA9 ...102 C3
Great Chapel St SOHO/CST W1F ...12 C3
Great Cherry Rd CHSWK W4 ...162 D2
FELT TW13 ...178 D5
Great Church La HMSMTH W6 ...144 B5
Great College St WEST SW1P ...21 C5
Great Cross Av GNWCH SE10 ...172 A1
Great Cumberland Ms
MBLAR W1H ...10 C4
Great Cumberland Pl
MBLAR W1H ...10 C3
Great Dover St STHWK SE1 ...23 C5
Greatdown Rd HNWL W7 ...120 B4
Great Eastern Rd SRTFD E15 ...111 H5
Great Eastern St SDTCH EC2A ...8 A4
Great Eastern Whf
BTSEA * SW11 ...166 A1
Great Elms Rd HAYES BR2 ...233 E1
Great Fld CDALE/KGS NW9 ...63 E4
Greatfield Av EHAM E6 ...133 H5
Greatfield Cl LEW SE13 ...171 E5
Greatfields Rd BARK IG11 ...114 D6
Great Galley Cl BARK IG11 ...135 H2
Great Gatton Cl CROY/NA CR0 ...230 C4
Great George St ST/JSPK SW1H ...20 D4
Great Guildford St STHWK SE1 ...23 E2
Great Harry Dr ELTH/MOT SE9 ...194 A5
Great James St BMSBY WC1N ...13 G1
Great Marlborough St
SOHO/CST W1F ...12 A4
Great Maze Pond STHWK SE1 ...23 H2
Great New St
FLST/FETLN * EC4A ...14 B3
Great North Rd EFNCH N2 ...46 A6
Great North Wy (Barnet By-Pass)
HDN NW4 ...64 B6
Greatorex St WCHPL E1 ...17 F1
Great Ormond St BMSBY WC1N ...13 F1
Great Percy St FSBYW WC1X ...5 H3
Great Peter St WEST SW1P ...20 C6
Great Portland St GTPST * W1W ...3 H6
Great Pulteney St
SOHO/CST W1F ...12 B5
Great Queen St HOL/ALD WC2B ...13 F3
Great Russell St FITZ W1T ...12 D3
Great St Helen's HDTCH EC3A ...16 A4
Great Scotland Yd WHALL SW1A ...21 E1
Great Smith St WEST SW1P ...20 D5
Great Spilmans EDUL SE22 ...169 G6
Great Strd CDALE/KGS NW9 ...63 F5
Great Suffolk St STHWK SE1 ...22 D3
Great Sutton St FSBYE EC1V ...6 C6
Great Swan Aly LOTH EC2R ...15 G3
Great Thrift STMC/STPC BR5 ...254 C1
Great Titchfield St GTPST W1W ...3 H6
Great Tower St MON EC3R ...16 A5
Great Trinity La BLKFR EC4V ...15 F5
Great Turnstile HHOL * WC1V ...13 H2
Great Western Rd
MV/WKIL W9 ...124 D4
Great West Rd CHSWK W4 ...142 C6
HEST TW5 ...158 C3
HMSMTH W6 ...143 H5
ISLW TW7 ...160 A1
Great West Rd Chiswick
CHSWK W4 ...143 F6
Great West Rd Ellesmere Rd
CHSWK W4 ...142 C6
Great West Rd Hogarth La
CHSWK W4 ...142 D6
Great Winchester St
OBST EC2N ...15 H3
Great Windmill St
SOHO/SHAV W1D ...12 C6
Greatwood CHST BR7 ...214 A3
Greaves Cl BARK IG11 ...114 D5
Greaves Cottages
POP/IOD * E14 ...130 C4
Greaves Pl TOOT SW17 ...186 H6
Grebe Av YEAD * UB4 ...117 H5
Grebe Cl FSTGT E7 ...112 B3
WALTH E17 ...70 C3
Grebe Ct SUT SM1 ...
Grebe Ter KUT * KT1 ...201 G6
Grecian Crs NRWD SE19 ...208 B2
Greek Ct SOHO/SHAV W1D ...12 D4
Greenacre Cl BAR EN5 ...34 D1
NTHLT UB5 ...97 H4
Greenacre Ms WLGTN SM6 ...226 D6
Green Acres CROY/NA CR0 ...247 F1
SCUP * DA14 ...195 F6
Greenacres BUSH WD23 ...45 H4
ELTH/MOT SE9 ...194 A1
Greenacres Cl ORP BR6 ...252 C2
Greenacre Sq
BERM/RHTH * SE16 ...150 B2
Greenacre Wk
STHGT/OAK N14 ...51 F5

Green Arbour Ct STP * EC4M 14 C3
Green Av MLHL NW7 46 D6
WEA W13 140 D3
Greenaway Gdns HAMP NW3 105 F2
Green Bank NFNCH/WDSP N12 49 F6
WAP E1W 25 H2
Greenbank Av ALP/SUD HA0 100 C3
Greenbank Cl CHING E4 55 G4
Greenbank Crs HDN NW4 84 C1
Greenbay Rd CHARL SE7 173 F1
Greenberry St STJWD NW8 2 A2
Greenbrook Av EBAR EN4 35 G2
Green Chain Wk BECK BR3 211 G3
CHARL SE7 153 F4
ELTH/MOT SE9 174 B6
SYD SE26 210 B2
Green Cl CAR SM5 226 B6
CDALE/KGS NW9 82 C3
EFNCH N2 85 G4
FELT TW13 198 C1
HAYES BR2 212 A6
Greencoat Pl WEST SW1P 28 B1
Greencoat Rw WEST SW1P 20 B6
Green Court Av CROY/NA CR0 229 H6
Greencourt Av EDGW HA8 62 A4
Green Court Gdns
CROY/NA CR0 229 H6
Greencourt Rd
STMC/STPC BR5 235 E2
Green Court Rd SWLY BR8 237 H2
Greencroft EDGW HA8 62 C1
Greencroft Av RSLP HA4 78 A6
Greencroft Gdns EN EN1 39 E4
KIL/WHAMP NW6 105 F5
Greencroft Rd HEST TW5 158 D2
Green Dl EDUL SE22 169 E6
Green Dragon La BTFD TW8 141 G5
WCHMH N21 37 H6
Green Dragon Yd WCHPL E1 17 E2
Green Dr STHL UB1 139 E1
Green End CHSGTN KT9 239 F2
WCHMH N21 52 B4
Greenend Rd CHSWK W4 143 E2
Green Farm Cl ORP BR6 253 F3
Greenfell Man DEPT * SE8 150 D5
Greenfield Av BRYLDS KT5 222 B4
OXHEY WD19 42 C4
Greenfield Dr BMLY BR1 213 E5
EFNCH N2 86 B1
Greenfield Gdns CRICK NW2 84 C6
DAGW RM9 116 A6
STMC/STPC BR5 234 C4
Greenfield Rd DAGW RM9 116 A6
RDART DA2 217 H1
SEVS/STOTM N15 89 E2
WCHPL E1 17 F2
Greenfields STHL UB1 119 E6
Greenfield Wy
RYLN/HDSTN HA2 59 F6
Greenford Av HNWL W7 120 A3
STHL UB1 118 D6
Greenford Gdns GFD/PVL UB6 119 F2
Greenford Rd GFD/PVL UB6 100 A3
GFD/PVL UB6 100 A3
GFD/PVL UB6 119 G6
SUT SM1 243 F2
Green Gdns ORP BR6 252 C3
Greengate GFD/PVL UB6 100 D4
Greengate St PLSTW E13 132 D1
Greenhalgh Wk EFNCH N2 85 G1
Greenham Cl STHWK SE1 22 A4
Greenham Crs CHING E4 70 D2
Greenham Rd MUSWH N10 66 C5
Greenhaven Dr THMD SE28 135 H5
Greenheys Dr SWFD E18 72 B6
Greenhill BKHH IG9 57 E3
HAMP NW3 105 H2
SUT SM1 225 G6
WBLY HA9 82 B6
Green Hl WOOL/PLUM SE18 153 H5
Greenhill Ct BAR * EN5 35 F6
Greenhill Gdns NTHLT UB5 118 D1
Greenhill Gv MNPK E12 113 G2
Greenhill Pde BAR * EN5 35 F6
Greenhill Pk BAR EN5 35 G6
WLSDN NW10 103 E6
Greenhill Rd HRW HA1 80 A3
WLSDN NW10 103 E6
Greenhill's Rents FARR * EC1M 14 C1
Greenhills Ter IS N1 108 D4
Greenhill Ter NTHLT * UB5 118 D1
Greenhill Wy HRW HA1 80 A3
WBLY HA9 82 B6
Greenhithe Cl ELTH/MOT SE9 195 E2
Greenholm Rd ELTH/MOT SE9 174 B6
Green Hundred Rd PECK SE15 33 F6
Greenhurst Rd WNWD SE27 208 A1
Greening St ABYW SE2 156 A4
Greenland Crs NWDGN UB2 138 A3
Greenland Ms DEPT SE8 150 B5
Greenland Pl CAMTN * NW1 106 D6
Greenland Quay
BERM/RHTH SE16 150 B4
Greenland Rd BAR EN5 48 A1
CAMTN NW1 106 D6
Greenlands HOR/WEW KT19 240 B3
Greenland St CAMTN * NW1 106 D6
Green La BCTR RM8 96 D6
CHSGTN KT9 239 G6
E/WMO/HCT KT8 219 F2
EDGW HA8 45 H6
FELT TW13 198 C1
HDN NW4 84 B2
HNWL W7 140 A2
HSLWW TW4 158 A5
IL IG1 94 D6
MRDN SM4 225 F4
NWMAL KT3 222 C2
OXHEY WD19 42 A3
PGE/AN SE20 210 B3
STAN HA7 44 D6
THHTH CR7 208 B4
WPK KT4 223 G5
Green La Cottages STAN * HA7 44 D6
Green Lane Gdns THHTH CR7 208 C5
Green La CEND/HSY/T N8 68 B6
FSBYPK N4 88 C5
HOR/WEW KT19 241 E6
PLMGR N13 67 H1
WCHMH N21 52 B3
Greenlaw Ct EA * W5 121 F5
Greenlaw Gdns NWMAL KT3 223 F4
Green Lawns
NFNCH/WDSP * N12 65 F2
RSLP * HA4 78 A5
Greenlaw St WOOL/PLUM SE18 154 A3
Green Leaf Av WLGTN SM6 245 F2
Greenleaf Cl
BRXS/STRHM * SW2 188 A2
Greenleafe Dr BARK/HLT IG6 74 B6
Greenleaf Rd EHAM E6 113 E6
WALTH E17 70 D6
Greenlea Pk WIM/MER * SW19 206 A4
Greenleigh Av STMC/STPC BR5 235 H1
Green Man La WEA W13 120 C6
Greenman St IS N1 108 C5
Greenmead Cl SNWD SE25 229 G2
Green Moor Link WCHMH N21 52 B2
Greenmoor Rd PEND EN3 40 A3
Greenoak Pl EBAR EN4 36 B3
Green Oaks NWDGN * UB2 138 B4
Greenoak Wy WIM/MER SW19 184 B6
Greenock Rd ACT W3 142 B3
STRHM/NOR SW16 207 F4
Green Pde HSLW * TW3 179 F1
Green Pond Cl WALTH E17 70 C6
Green Pond Rd WALTH E17 70 C6
Green Ride LOU IG10 56 C1
Green Rd STHGT/OAK N14 50 D1
TRDG/WHET N20 49 G5
Greens Ct NTGHL * W11 144 D1
SOHO/CST W1F 12 C5
Greens End WOOL/PLUM SE18 154 B4
Greenshank Cl WALTH E17 70 C3
Greenside BCTR RM8 96 A6
BXLY DA5 196 C3
SWLY BR8 217 H5
Greenside Cl CAT SE6 191 H4
TRDG/WHET N20 49 H4
Greenside Rd CROY/NA CR0 228 A4
SHB W12 143 G3
Greenslade Rd BARK IG11 114 D5
Greenstead Av WFD IG8 73 E2
Greenstead Gdns
PUT/ROE SW15 163 G6
WFD IG8 73 E2
Greensted Rd LOU IG10 57 G2
Greenstone Ms WAN E11 92 C3
Green St FSTGT E7 112 D3
MYFR/PKLN W1K 10 D5
PEND EN3 40 B4
Greenstreet Hl NWCR * SE14 170 B4
Greensward BUSH WD23 43 F1
Green Ter CLKNW EC1R 6 B4
The Green ACT W3 123 E5
BKHH * IG9 56 D3
BXLYHN DA7 177 E2
CAR * SM5 244 C2
CROY/NA CR0 248 D6
ED N9 53 G4
HAYES BR2 232 C4
HEST TW5 139 E6
HRW HA1 80 C6
MRDN SM4 224 C1
NWDGN UB2 138 D2
NWMAL KT3 202 C6
RCH/KEW TW9 161 F6
SCUP DA14 215 G1
SRTFD E15 112 B4
STHGT/OAK N14 51 F4
STMC/STPC BR5 215 H3
SUT SM1 243 F1
TOTM N17 68 C2
WAN E11 92 D3
WCHMH N21 52 A2
WELL DA16 175 E5
WHTN TW2 180 A3
Green V BXLYHS DA6 176 B6
EA W5 121 H5
Greenvale Rd ELTH/MOT SE9 173 H5
Green Verges STAN HA7 61 F3
Green Vw CHSGTN KT9 239 H5
Greenview Av BECK BR3 230 C3
Greenview Cl ACT W3 143 E1
Green Wk HDN NW4 84 B1
NWDGN UB2 139 E5
STHWK SE1 24 A6
WFD IG8 73 G2
The Green Wk CHING E4 55 G3
Green Wy ELTH/MOT SE9 173 F6
HAYES BR2 233 G3
Greenway BCTR RM8 96 A6
CHST BR7 214 A1
KTN/HRWW/W HA3 81 G2
RYNPK SW20 224 A1
STHGT/OAK N14 51 G4
TRDG/WHET N20 49 G4
WLGTN SM6 245 E2
Greenway Av WALTH E17 91 H1
Greenway Cl CDALE/KGS NW9 62 D5
FBAR/BDGN N11 66 C2
FSBYPK N4 88 C6
TRDG/WHET N20 49 E4
Greenway Ct IL IG1 94 A5
Greenway Gdns
CDALE/KGS NW9 62 C5
CROY/NA CR0 248 D1
GFD/PVL UB6 119 E2
Green Way Gdns
KTN/HRWW/W HA3 60 A5
Greenways BECK BR3 211 E5
ESH/CLAY KT10 238 A2
NFNCH/WDSP * N12 65 G2
The Greenways TWK * TW1 180 C1
The Green Wy
KTN/HRWW/W HA3 60 A4
The Greenway CDALE/KGS NW9 62 D5
HSLWW * TW4 158 D5
PIN HA5 78 D3
Greenwell St GTPST W1W 3 H6
Greenwich Church St
GNWCH * SE10 151 G6
Greenwich Crs EHAM E6 133 G4
Greenwich Foot Tnl
GNWCH SE10 151 G5
Greenwich High Rd
GNWCH SE10 171 F1
Greenwich Park St
GNWCH * SE10 151 H6
Greenwich Quay DEPT * SE8 151 E6
Greenwich South St
GNWCH SE10 171 F2
Greenwich Vw POP/IOD E14 151 F3
Greenwood Av DAGE RM10 117 F2
PEND EN3 40 C2
Greenwood Cl BFN/LL DA15 195 G4
MRDN SM4 224 C1
STMC/STPC BR5 235 E3
THDIT KT7 220 C5
Greenwood Dr CHING E4 71 G1
Greenwood Gdns BARK/HLT IG6 74 C3
PLMGR N13 52 B5
Greenwood La HPTN TW12 199 F1
Greenwood Pk KUTN/CMB KT2 203 E3
Greenwood Pl KTTN NW5 106 D3
Greenwood Rd BXLY DA5 197 H6
CROY/NA CR0 228 B4
HACK E8 109 G3
ISLW TW7 160 A4
MTCM CR4 207 F6
PLSTW E13 132 B1
THDIT KT7 220 C5
Greenwood Ter WLSDN * NW10 102 D6
Green Wrythe Crs CAR SM5 226 A5
Green Wrythe La CAR SM5 226 A5
MRDN SM4 225 H3
Green Yd FSBYW WC1X 5 H5
Greer Rd KTN/HRWW/W HA3 59 G4
Greet St STHWK SE1 22 B2
Greg Cl LEY E10 91 G3
Gregor Ms BKHTH/KID SE3 172 C1
Gregory Crs ELTH/MOT SE9 193 F2
Gregory Pl KENS W8 145 F2
Gregory Rd CHDH RM6 96 B1
NWDGN UB2 139 E3
Greig Cl CEND/HSY/T N8 87 G2
Greig Ter WALW SE17 30 D5
Grenaby Av CROY/NA CR0 228 D4
Grenaby Rd CROY/NA CR0 228 D4
Grenada Rd CHARL SE7 173 E1
Grenade St POP/IOD E14 130 D6
Grenadier St CAN/RD E16 154 A1
Grena Gdns RCH/KEW TW9 161 H5
Grena Rd RCH/KEW TW9 161 H5
Grendon Gdns WBLY HA9 82 A6
Grendon St STJWD NW8 2 A5
Grenfell Ct MLHL * NW7 63 H2
Grenfell Gdns
KTN/HRWW/W HA3 81 G4
Grenfell Rd NTGHL W11 124 B6
TOOT SW17 206 B2
Grenfell Wk NTGHL W11 124 B6
Grennell Cl SUT SM1 225 H6
Grennell Rd SUT SM1 225 G6
Grenoble Gdns PLMGR N13 68 A2
Grenville Cl BRYLDS KT5 222 C5
FNCH N3 64 D4
Grenville Gdns WFD IG8 73 E3
Grenville Ms HPTN TW12 199 F1
Grenville Pl MLHL NW7 62 D1
SKENS * SW7 145 G3
Grenville Rd ARCH N19 87 G5
Grenville St BMSBY WC1N 5 F6
Gresham Av TRDG/WHET N20 50 B6
Gresham Cl BXLY DA5 196 C1
ENC/FH EN2 38 C4
Gresham Dr CHDH RM6 95 H2
Gresham Gdns CRICK NW2 84 C5
Gresham Rd BECK BR3 210 C5
BRXN/ST SW9 168 A4
CAN/RD E16 132 D5
EDGW HA8 61 H2
EHAM E6 133 H1
HEST TW5 159 G2
HPTN TW12 199 E2
SNWD * SE25 229 G1
WLSDN NW10 102 D3
Gresham St CITYW EC2V 15 E3
Gresham Wy WIM/MER SW19 185 E5
Gresley Cl SEVS/STOTM * N15 88 D1
WALTH E17 90 C3
Gresley Rd ARCH N19 87 E5
Gressenhall Rd
WAND/EARL SW18 184 D1
Gresse St FITZ W1T 12 C2
Gresswell Cl SCUP DA14 195 G5
Greswell St FUL/PGN SW6 164 B2
Gretton Rd TOTM N17 69 E3
Greville Cl TWK TW1 180 D2
Greville Ms KIL/WHAMP NW6 105 F6
Greville Rd KIL/WHAMP NW6 125 F1
RCHPK/HAM TW10 181 H1
WALTH E17 91 G1
Greville St HCIRC EC1N 14 B2
Grey Cl EFNCH N2 85 G3
Greycoat Pl WEST SW1P 20 C6
Greycoat St WEST SW1P 20 C6
Greycot Rd BECK BR3 211 E1
Grey Eagle St WCHPL E1 16 D1
Greyfell Cl STAN HA7 60 D1
Greyhound Hl HDN NW4 63 G6
Greyhound La
STRHM/NOR SW16 207 G2
Greyhound Rd HMSMTH W6 144 B6
SUT SM1 243 G3
TOTM N17 69 E6
WLSDN * NW10 123 H2
Greyhound Ter
STRHM/NOR SW16 207 E4
Greyladies Gdns
GNWCH * SE10 171 G3
Greys Park Cl HAYES BR2 251 E3
Greystead Rd FSTH SE23 190 A2
Greystoke Av PIN HA5 59 E6
Greystoke Cottages EA * W5 121 G3
Greystoke Gdns EA W5 121 G3
ENC/FH EN2 37 F5
Greystone Gdns BARK/HLT IG6 74 C5
KTN/HRWW/W HA3 81 E3
Greyswood St
STRHM/NOR SW16 206 D2
Griffin Cl WLSDN NW10 103 H3
Griffin Manor Wy THMD SE28 154 D3
Griffin Rd TOTM N17 69 E5
WOOL/PLUM SE18 154 D5
Griffith Cl CHDH RM6 96 A4
Griffiths Rd WIM/MER SW19 205 E3
Griggs Ap IL IG1 94 C6
Grigg's Pl STHWK SE1 24 B6
Griggs Rd LEY E10 91 G3
Grimsby Gv CAN/RD E16 154 B2
Grimsby St WCHPL E1 8 D6
Grimsdyke Crs BAR EN5 34 A4
Grimsdyke Rd PIN HA5 58 C3
Grimsel Pth CMBW SE5 168 B1
Grimshaw Cl HGT * N6 86 C4
Grimston Rd FUL/PGN SW6 164 D3
Grimwade Av CROY/NA CR0 247 G1
Grimwood Rd TWK TW1 180 B2
Grindall Cl CROY/NA CR0 246 B2
Grindal St STHWK SE1 22 A4
Grindleford Av FBAR/BDGN N11 50 C4
Grindley Gdns CROY/NA * CR0 229 F3
Grinling Pl DEPT SE8 151 E6
Grinstead Rd DEPT SE8 150 C5
Grisle Cl ED N9 53 H6
Grittleton Av WBLY HA9 102 B4
Grittleton Rd MV/WKIL W9 125 E3
Grocers' Hall Ct LOTH * EC2R 15 G4
Groombridge Cl WELL DA16 175 G6
Groombridge Rd HOM E9 110 B5
Groom Cl HAYES BR2 232 D1
Groom Crs WAND/EARL SW18 185 H2
Groomfield Cl TOOT SW17 186 C6
Groom Pl KTBR SW1X 19 F5
Grosmont Rd
WOOL/PLUM SE18 155 F5
Grosse Wy PUT/ROE SW15 183 H1
Grosvenor Av CAR SM5 244 B4
HBRY N5 108 C3
MORT/ESHN SW14 163 E4
RYLN/HDSTN HA2 79 F4
Grosvenor Br PIM SW1V 27 H5
Grosvenor Cottages KTBR SW1X 27 E1
Grosvenor Crs CDALE/KGS NW9 82 A1
KTBR SW1X 19 F4
Grosvenor Crescent Ms
KTBR SW1X 19 E4
Grosvenor Gdns BGVA SW1W 19 G6
CRICK NW2 104 A4
EHAM E6 133 F2
GLDGN NW11 84 D3
KUTN/CMB KT2 201 F2
MORT/ESHN SW14 163 E4
MUSWH N10 67 E6
STHGT/OAK N14 37 F6
WFD IG8 72 C2
WLGTN SM6 245 E5
Grosvenor Gardens Ms East
BGVA * SW1W 19 H5
Grosvenor Gardens Ms North
BGVA SW1W 19 G6
Grosvenor Ga BAY/PAD W2 10 D6
Grosvenor Hl MYFR/PKLN W1K 11 G5
WIM/MER SW19 204 C2
Grosvenor Pde ACT * W3 142 A1
Grosvenor Pk CMBW SE5 31 E6
Grosvenor Park Rd WALTH E17 91 E2
Grosvenor Pl KTBR SW1X 19 F3
Grosvenor Ri East WALTH E17 91 F2
Grosvenor Rd BCTR RM8 96 D5
BELV DA17 156 D6
BTFD TW8 141 F6
BXLYHS DA6 176 B6
CHSWK W4 142 C5
ED N9 53 H3
EHAM E6 113 F6
FNCH N3 64 D3
FSTGT E7 112 D4
HNWL W7 140 C1
HSLW TW4 158 D4
IL IG1 114 C1
LEY E10 91 G5
MUSWH N10 66 D4
NWDGN UB2 138 D3
PIM SW1V 27 H5
RCHPK/HAM TW10 161 G6
ROMW/RG RM7 97 H4
SNWD SE25 229 G1
STMC/STPC BR5 235 E3
TWK TW1 180 C2
WAN E11 92 D2
WLGTN SM6 244 D4
WWKM BR4 231 F6
Grosvenor Sq MYFR/PKLN W1K 11 F5
Grosvenor St MYFR/PKLN W1K 11 F5
Grosvenor Ter CMBW SE5 31 E6
Grosvenor Wy CLPT E5 90 A6
Grosvernor Wharf Rd
POP/IOD E14 151 H4
Grote's Buildings
BKHTH/KID SE3 172 A3
Grote's Pl BKHTH/KID SE3 172 A3
Groton Rd WAND/EARL SW18 185 F4
Grotto Ct STHWK * SE1 23 E3
Grotto Pas MHST W1U 11 E1
Grotto Rd TWK TW1 180 B4
Grove Av HNWL W7 120 A5
MUSWH N10 67 E5
PIN HA5 78 C1
SUT SM1 243 E4
TWK TW1 180 B3
Grove Bank OXHEY * WD19 42 B3
Grovebury Cl ERITH DA8 157 H6
Grovebury Ct STHGT/OAK N14 51 E2
Grovebury Rd THMD SE28 155 H2
Grove Cl FSTH SE23 190 B3
HAYES BR2 232 C6
KUT KT1 221 G1
STHGT/OAK * N14 50 D2
Grove Cottages CHSWK * W4 143 E6
Grove Ct E/WMO/HCT KT8 219 H2
EA * W5 141 G1
Grove Crs CDALE/KGS NW9 82 C1
FELT TW13 178 C6
KUT KT1 201 G6
SWFD E18 72 B5
Grove Crescent Rd SRTFD E15 111 H4
Grovedale Rd ARCH N19 87 F6
Grove Dwellings WCHPL * E1 130 A4
Grove End KTTN NW5 106 D2
SWFD E18 72 B5
Grove End La ESH/CLAY KT10 219 H5
Grove End Rd STJWD NW8 125 H1
Grove Footpath SURB KT6 221 G1
Grove Gdns HDN * NW4 83 G2
PEND EN3 40 B2
STJWD NW8 2 B4
TEDD TW11 180 C6
Grove Green Rd LEY E10 111 G1
Grove Hl HRW HA1 80 A4
SWFD E18 72 B5
Grove Hill Rd CMBW SE5 169 E4
HRW HA1 80 B4

Grove House Rd
CEND/HSY/T N8 87 G1
Groveland Av
STRHM/NOR SW16 207 H3
Groveland Ct STP EC4M 15 F4
Groveland Rd BECK BR3 210 D6
Grovelands E/WMO/HCT KT8 219 E1
Grovelands Cl CMBW SE5 169 E3
RYLN/HDSTN HA2 99 F1
Grovelands Rd PLMGR N13 51 H6
SEVS/STOTM N15 89 G3
STMC/STPC BR5 215 G3
Groveland Wy NWMAL KT3 222 C2
Grove La CMBW SE5 168 D2
KUT KT1 221 G1
Grove Market Pl
ELTH/MOT * SE9 193 H1
Grove Ms HMSMTH W6 144 A3
Grove Pk CDALE/KGS NW9 82 C1
CMBW SE5 169 E3
WAN E11 92 D2
Grove Park Av CHING E4 71 F3
Grove Park Br CHSWK W4 162 C1
Grove Park Gdns CHSWK W4 162 B1
Grove Park Rd CHSWK W4 162 B1
ELTH/MOT SE9 193 G4
SEVS/STOTM N15 89 E1
Grove Park Ter CHSWK W4 162 B1
Grove Pas BETH E2 9 G1
Grove Pl ACT W3 142 C1
BAL SW12 186 D1
HAMP NW3 105 H1
Grove Rd ACT W3 142 C1
BARN SW13 163 F3
BELMT SM2 243 E4
BELV DA17 156 D6
BOW E3 130 C1
BTFD TW8 141 E5
BXLYHN DA7 177 G5
CHDH RM6 96 A4
CHING E4 55 G5
CRICK NW2 104 A4
E/WMO/HCT KT8 219 H1
EA W5 121 F6
EBAR EN4 36 A4
EDGW HA8 62 A2
FBAR/BDGN N11 66 D1
HOM E9 110 B6
HSLW TW3 159 E5
ISLW TW7 160 A2
LEY E10 91 F2
MTCM CR4 206 D5
NFNCH/WDSP N12 65 H1
PIN HA5 78 D2
RCHPK/HAM TW10 181 H1
SEVS/STOTM N15 89 E2
SURB KT6 221 F2
SWFD E18 72 B5
THHTH CR7 228 A1
WAN E11 92 B4
WHTN TW2 179 H5
WIM/MER SW19 205 G3
Grover Rd OXHEY WD19 42 B1
Groveside Cl ACT W3 122 A5
CAR SM5 226 A6
Groveside Rd CHING E4 56 A5
Grove St BERM/RHTH SE16 150 D4
UED N18 69 F2
Grove Ter KTTN NW5 106 C1
STHL * UB1 119 E6
TEDD TW11 180 C6
The Grove BXLYHS DA6 176 B5
CDALE/KGS NW9 82 D2
CEND/HSY/T N8 87 F2
EA W5 141 F1
EDGW HA8 46 B6
ENC/FH EN2 38 A3
FNCH N3 65 E3
FSBYPK N4 87 H4
GFD/PVL UB6 119 G5
GLDGN NW11 84 C4
HGT N6 86 C5
ISLW TW7 160 A2
PLMGR N13 52 A6
SCUP DA14 196 C6
SRTFD E15 112 A4
TEDD TW11 180 C6
WWKM BR4 249 G1
Grove V CHST BR7 214 A2
EDUL SE22 169 E5
Groveway BCTR RM8 116 B2
BRXN/ST SW9 167 H2
Grove Wy ESH/CLAY KT10 219 G4
WBLY HA9 102 C3
Grovewood Pl WFD IG8 73 H2
Grummant Rd PECK SE15 169 F2
Grundy St POP/IOD E14 131 F5
Gruneisen Rd FNCH N3 65 F3
Gubyon Av HNHL SE24 168 B6
Guernsey Cl HEST TW5 159 E2
Guernsey Gv HNHL SE24 188 C2
Guernsey Rd IS N1 108 C4
WAN E11 91 H5
Guibal Rd LEE/GVPK SE12 192 D3
Guildersfield Rd
STRHM/NOR SW16 207 G3
Guildford Gv GNWCH SE10 171 F2
Guildford Rd CROY/NA CR0 228 D3
EHAM E6 133 G5
GDMY/SEVK IG3 95 E6
VX/NE SW8 167 G2
WALTH E17 71 G4
Guildford Wy WLGTN SM6 245 G3
Guildhall Bldgs CITYW EC2V 15 F3
Guildhall Yd CITYW EC2V 15 F3
Guildhouse St PIM SW1V 28 A2
Guildown Av NFNCH/WDSP N12 49 F6
Guild Rd CHARL SE7 153 F5
Guildsway WALTH E17 70 D4
Guilford Av BRYLDS KT5 221 H2
Guilford Pl BMSBY WC1N 5 G6
Guilford St BMSBY WC1N 5 E6
Guillemot Pl WDGN * N22 67 H5
Guilsborough Cl WLSDN NW10 103 E5
Guinness Cl HOM E9 110 C5
Guinness Ct CROY/NA * CR0 229 F6
Guinness Sq STHWK SE1 24 A6
Guinness Trust
STNW/STAM * N16 89 F5
Guinness Trust Est CHEL SW3 26 C2
SRTFD * E15 112 B6
Guion Rd FUL/PGN SW6 164 D3
Gulland Wk IS * N1 108 C4
Gull Cl WLGTN SM6 245 G5
Gulliver Cl NTHLT UB5 98 D6
Gulliver Rd BFN/LL DA15 194 D4
Gulliver St BERM/RHTH SE16 150 D3
Gumleigh Rd EA W5 141 E4
Gumley Gdns ISLW TW7 160 C4
Gumping Rd STMC/STPC BR5 234 C6
Gundulph Rd HAYES BR2 213 E6
Gunmakers La HOM E9 110 C6
Gunnell Cl SNWD SE25 229 F3
SYD * SE26 189 G6
Gunner La WOOL/PLUM SE18 154 A5
Gunnersbury Av ACT W3 142 A3
Gunnersbury Av
(North Circular Rd) EA W5 121 H6
Gunnersbury Cl CHSWK * W4 142 B5
Gunnersbury Crs ACT W3 142 A2
Gunnersbury Dr EA W5 141 H2
Gunnersbury Gdns ACT W3 142 A2
Gunnersbury La ACT W3 142 A2
Gunners Gv CHING E4 55 G5
Gunners Rd WAND/EARL SW18 185 H4
Gunning St WOOL/PLUM SE18 155 E4
Gunstor Rd STNW/STAM * N16 109 E2
Gun St WCHPL E1 16 C2
Gunter Gv EDGW HA8 62 D4
WBPTN SW10 145 G6
Gunterstone Rd WKENS W14 144 C5
Gunthorpe St WCHPL E1 16 D2
Gunton Rd CLPT E5 109 H1
TOOT SW17 206 C2
Gunwhale Cl BERM/RHTH SE16 150 B1
Gurdon Rd CHARL SE7 152 C5
Gurnell Gv WEA W13 120 B3
Gurney Cl BARK IG11 114 B4
SRTFD E15 112 A3
WALTH E17 70 B4
Gurney Crs CROY/NA CR0 227 H5
Gurney Dr EFNCH N2 85 H1
Gurney Rd CAR SM5 244 C2
FUL/PGN SW6 165 G4
SRTFD E15 112 A3
Guthrie St CHEL SW3 26 A3
Gutter La CITYW EC2V 15 E3
Guyatt Gdns MTCM CR4 206 C5
Guy Barnett Gv
BKHTH/KID SE3 172 C4
Guy Rd WLGTN SM6 245 F1
Guyscliff Rd LEW SE13 171 G6
Guy St STHWK SE1 23 H3
Gwalior Rd PUT/ROE SW15 164 B5
Gwendolen Av PUT/ROE SW15 164 B6
Gwendoline Av PLSTW E13 112 D6
Gwendwr Rd WKENS W14 144 C5
Gweneth Cottages EDGW * HA8 62 A2
Gwillim Cl BFN/LL DA15 195 G1
Gwydor Rd BECK BR3 230 B1
Gwydyr Rd HAYES BR2 212 B6
Gwyn Cl FUL/PGN SW6 165 G1
Gwynne Av CROY/NA CR0 230 B4
Gwynne Park Av WFD IG8 73 H2
Gwynne Rd BTSEA SW11 165 H3
Gwynne Whf CHSWK W4 143 F6
Gylcote Cl HNHL SE24 168 D5
Gyles Pk STAN HA7 61 E4
Gyllyngdune Gdns
GDMY/SEVK IG3 115 F1

H

Haarlem Rd HMSMTH W6 144 B3
Haberdasher Pl IS N1 7 H3
Haberdasher St IS N1 7 H3
Haccombe Rd WIM/MER SW19 205 G2
Hackbridge
Park Gdns CAR SM5 226 B6
Hackbridge Rd CAR SM5 226 C6
Hackford Rd BRXN/ST SW9 167 H2
Hackford Wk BRXN/ST SW9 167 H2
Hackington Crs BECK BR3 211 E2
Hackney Gv HACK E8 109 H4
Hackney Rd BETH E2 8 C3
Haddenham Ct OXHEY * WD19 42 B5
Hadden Rd THMD SE28 155 E3
Hadden Wy NTHLT UB5 99 H4
Haddington Rd BMLY BR1 191 H5
Haddon Cl EN EN1 53 G1
NWMAL KT3 223 F2
Haddon Gv BFN/LL DA15 195 G2
Haddon Rd STMC/STPC BR5 236 A2
SUT SM1 243 F2
Haddo St GNWCH SE10 151 F6
Hadfield Cl STHL UB1 118 D2
Hadleigh Cl RYNPK SW20 204 D5
WCHPL E1 130 A3
Hadleigh Dr BELMT SM2 243 E6
Hadleigh Rd ED N9 53 H2
Hadleigh St BETH E2 130 A3
Hadley Cl WCHMH N21 52 A1
Hadley Gdns CHSWK W4 142 D5
NWDGN UB2 138 D5
Hadley Gn BAR EN5 34 D4
Hadley Green Rd BAR EN5 34 D3
Hadley Gn West BAR EN5 34 C3
Hadley Gv BAR EN5 34 C3
Hadley Highstone BAR EN5 34 D2
Hadley Pde BAR * EN5 34 C4
Hadley Rdg BAR EN5 34 D4
Hadley Rd BAR EN5 35 F4
BELV DA17 156 D4
EBAR EN4 36 C1
ENC/FH EN2 37 G1
MTCM CR4 227 F1
Hadley St KTTN NW5 106 D4
Hadley Wy WCHMH N21 52 A1
Hadley Wood Rd BAR EN5 35 G3
Hadlow Rd SCUP DA14 195 G6
WELL DA16 176 A1
Hadrian Est BETH E2 9 F2
Hadrian's Ride EN EN1 39 F6
Hadrian St GNWCH SE10 152 A5
Hadyn Park Rd SHB W12 143 G2
Hafer Rd BTSEA SW11 166 B5
Hafton Rd CAT SE6 192 A3
Haggard Rd TWK TW1 180 D2
Hagger Ct WALTH * E17 71 H6
Hague St BETH E2 9 F4
Ha-ha Rd WOOL/PLUM SE18 153 H6
Haig Rd STAN HA7 61 E1
Haig Rd East PLSTW E13 133 E2
Haig Rd West PLSTW E13 133 E2
Haigville Gdns BARK/HLT IG6 94 B1
Hailes Cl WIM/MER SW19 205 G2
Haileybury Av EN EN1 53 F1
Haileybury Rd ORP BR6 253 G2
Hailey Rd ERITHM DA18 157 E2
Hailsham Av
BRXS/STRHM SW2 187 H4
Hailsham Cl SURB KT6 221 F4
Hailsham Dr HRW HA1 59 H6
Hailsham Rd TOOT SW17 206 C2
Hailsham Ter PLMGR * N13 68 D1
Haimo Rd ELTH/MOT SE9 173 F6
Hainault Buildings LEY * E10 91 G5
Hainault Gore CHDH RM6 96 C2
Hainault Rd CHDH RM6 75 H6
ROMW/RG RM7 77 H6
WAN E11 91 G5
Hainault St ELTH/MOT SE9 194 B3
IL IG1 94 B6
Haines Wk MRDN SM4 225 F4
Hainford Cl PECK SE15 170 B5
Haining Cl CHSWK W4 142 A5
Hainthorpe Rd WNWD SE27 188 B5
Hainton Cl WCHPL E1 17 H4
Halbutt St DAGW RM9 116 D2
Halcomb St IS N1 109 E6
Halcot Av BXLYHS DA6 177 F6
Halcrow St WCHPL * E1 17 H2
Haldane Cl MUSWH N10 66 D3
WAB EN9 41 F1
Haldane Pl WAND/EARL SW18 185 F3
Haldane Rd EHAM E6 133 F2
FUL/PGN SW6 164 D1
GFD/PVL UB6 119 G6
THMD SE28 136 B6
Haldan Rd CHING E4 71 G2
Haldon Rd WAND/EARL SW18 184 D1
Hale Cl CHING E4 55 G5
EDGW HA8 62 C1
ORP BR6 252 C2
Hale Dr EDGW HA8 62 C2
Hale End Rd WALTH E17 71 H4
Halefield Rd TOTM N17 69 G4
Hale Gdns ACT W3 142 A1
SEVS/STOTM N15 69 G6
Hale Grove Gdns MLHL NW7 62 D1
Hale La EDGW HA8 62 C1
Hale Rd EHAM E6 133 G3
TOTM N17 69 G6
Halesowen Rd MRDN SM4 225 F4
Hales St DEPT SE8 171 E1
Hale St POP/IOD E14 131 F6
Halesworth Rd LEW SE13 171 F4
The Hale CHING E4 71 H3
SEVS/STOTM N15 69 G6
Haley Rd HDN NW4 84 A3
Half Acre BTFD TW8 141 F6
Half Acre Ms BTFD TW8 161 F1
Half Acre Rd HNWL W7 140 A1
Half Moon Crs IS * N1 5 H1
Half Moon La HNHL SE24 188 C1
Halfmoon Pas WCHPL * E1 16 D4
Half Moon Pas WCHPL E1 16 D4
Half Moon St MYFR/PICC W1J 19 H1
Halford Cl EDGW HA8 62 B5
Halford Rd FUL/PGN SW6 145 E6
RCHPK/HAM TW10 161 G6
WALTH E17 91 H2
Halfway St BFN/LL DA15 195 E3
Haliburton Rd TWK TW1 160 C6
Haliday Wk IS N1 108 D4
Halifax Cl TEDD TW11 200 A2
Halifax Rd ENC/FH EN2 38 C3
GFD/PVL UB6 99 F6
Halifax St SYD SE26 189 H5
Halifield Dr BELV DA17 156 C3
Haling Gv SAND/SEL CR2 246 C5
Haling Park Gdns
SAND/SEL CR2 246 B4
Haling Park Rd SAND/SEL CR2 246 B4
Haling Rd SAND/SEL CR2 246 D4
Halkin Ar KTBR SW1X 19 E5
Halkin Ms KTBR * SW1X 19 E5
Halkin Pl KTBR SW1X 19 E5
Halkin St KTBR SW1X 19 F4
Hallam Cl CHST BR7 213 H1
Hallam Gdns PIN HA5 58 C3
Hallam Ms REGST W1B 11 H1
Hallam Rd SEVS/STOTM N15 88 B1
Hallam St GTPST W1W 11 H1
Hall Cl EA W5 121 G4
Hall Ct TEDD TW11 200 B1
Hall Dr SYD SE26 210 A1
Halley Rd FSTGT E7 113 E4
Halley St POP/IOD E14 130 C4
Hall Farm Cl STAN HA7 44 D6
Hall Farm Dr WHTN TW2 179 H2
Hallfield Est BAY/PAD * W2 125 G5
Hall Gdns CHING E4 54 D6
Hall Ga STJWD NW8 125 H2
Halliday Sq STHL UB1 139 H1
Halliford St IS N1 108 C5
Halliwell Rd BRXS/STRHM SW2 187 H1
Halliwick Court Pde
FBAR/BDGN * N11 66 B1
Halliwick Rd MUSWH N10 66 C4
Hall La CHING E4 70 D1
HDN NW4 63 G5
Hallmead Rd SUT SM1 243 F1
Hall Oak Wk KIL/WHAMP NW6 104 D4
Hallowell Av CROY/NA CR0 245 G2
Hallowell Cl MTCM CR4 206 C6
Hallowfield Wy MTCM CR4 205 H6
Hall Pl BAY/PAD W2 125 H3
Hall Place Crs BXLY DA5 177 G6
Hall Rd CHDH RM6 96 A3
EHAM E6 113 H6
ISLW TW7 159 H6
MV/WKIL W9 125 G2
WAN E11 111 H2
WLGTN SM6 244 D6
Hallside Rd EN EN1 39 F1
Hall St FSBYE EC1V 6 D3
NFNCH/WDSP N12 65 G1
Hallsville Rd CAN/RD E16 132 B5
Hallswelle Pde GLDGN * NW11 84 D2
Hallswelle Rd GLDGN NW11 84 D2
The Hall BKHTH/KID SE3 172 C4
Hall Vw ELTH/MOT SE9 193 F4
Hallywell Crs EHAM E6 133 H4
Halons Rd ELTH/MOT SE9 194 A2
Halpin Pl WALW SE17 31 H2
Halsbrook Rd BKHTH/KID SE3 173 E4
Halsbury Cl STAN HA7 60 D1
Halsbury Rd SHB W12 143 H1
Halsbury Rd East NTHLT UB5 99 G2
Halsbury Rd West NTHLT UB5 99 F3
Halsey St CHEL SW3 26 C1
Halsham Crs BARK IG11 115 F4
Halsmere Rd CMBW SE5 168 B2
Halstead Cl CROY/NA CR0 246 C1
Halstead Gdns WCHMH N21 52 D3
Halstead Rd EN EN1 39 E5
WAN E11 92 D2
WCHMH N21 52 D3
Halstow Rd GNWCH SE10 152 C5
WLSDN NW10 124 B2
Halton Cl FBAR/BDGN N11 66 B2
Halton Cross St IS * N1 108 B6
Halton Rd IS N1 108 B5
Halt Pde CDALE/KGS * NW9 82 D1
Halt Robin Rd BELV DA17 157 E4
Hambalt Rd CLAP SW4 167 E6
Hambledon Ct EA * W5 121 G6
Hambledon Gdns SNWD SE25 209 F6
Hambledon Pl DUL SE21 189 F3
Hambledon Rd
WAND/EARL SW18 184 D2
Hambledown Rd
ELTH/MOT * SE9 194 D2
Hamble St FUL/PGN SW6 165 F4
Hambleton Cl WPK KT4 224 A6
Hambro Av HAYES BR2 232 C5
Hambrook Rd SNWD SE25 209 H6
Hambro Rd STRHM/NOR SW16 207 F2
Hambrough Rd STHL UB1 138 C1
Ham Common
RCHPK/HAM TW10 181 F5
Hamden Crs DAGE RM10 117 F1
Hamel Cl KTN/HRWW/W HA3 81 F1
Hameway EHAM E6 134 A3
Ham Farm Rd
RCHPK/HAM TW10 181 F6
Hamfrith Rd SRTFD E15 112 B4
Ham Gate Av
RCHPK/HAM TW10 181 G6
Hamilton Av BARK/HLT IG6 94 B1
CHEAM SM3 224 C6
ED N9 53 G2
ROM RM1 77 H5
SURB KT6 222 A6
Hamilton Cl BERM/RHTH SE16 150 C2
EBAR EN4 36 A5
STJWD NW8 125 H2
TOTM N17 69 F6
Hamilton Ct EA W5 121 H6
Hamilton Crs HSLW TW3 159 F6
PLMGR N13 52 A6
RYLN/HDSTN HA2 98 D1
Hamilton Gdns STJWD NW8 125 G2
Hamilton Pk HBRY N5 108 B2
Hamilton Pk West HBRY N5 108 B2
Hamilton Pl MYFR/PKLN W1K 19 F2
Hamilton Rd BFN/LL DA15 195 G6
BTFD TW8 141 F6
BXLYHN DA7 176 C3
CHSWK W4 143 E3
EA W5 121 G6
EBAR EN4 36 A5
ED N9 53 G2
EFNCH N2 65 G6
GLDGN NW11 84 B4
HRW HA1 80 A2
IL IG1 114 B2
SRTFD E15 132 A2
STHL UB1 138 D1
THHTH CR7 208 D6
WALTH E17 70 C5
WHTN * TW2 180 A3
WIM/MER SW19 205 F3
WLSDN NW10 103 G3
WNWD SE27 188 D6
Hamilton Road Ms
WIM/MER SW19 205 F3
Hamilton Sq
NFNCH/WDSP * N12 65 G2
Hamilton St DEPT SE8 151 E6
Hamilton Ter STJWD NW8 125 G2
Hamilton Wy FNCH N3 65 E2
PLMGR N13 52 B6
WLGTN SM6 245 F6
Hamlea Cl BKHTH/KID SE3 172 C6
Hamlet Cl CRW RM5 77 E3
LEW SE13 172 A5
Hamlet Gdns HMSMTH W6 143 G4
Hamlet Rd CRW RM5 77 E3
NRWD SE19 209 F3
Hamlet Sq CRICK NW2 104 C1
Hamlets Wy BOW E3 130 D3
The Hamlet CMBW * SE5 168 D4
Hamlet Wy STHWK SE1 23 H4
Hamlin Crs PIN HA5 78 A2
Hamlyn Cl EDGW HA8 45 G5
Hamlyn Gdns NRWD SE19 209 E3
Hammelton Rd BMLY BR1 212 C4
Hammers La MLHL NW7 47 G6
Hammersmith Br HMSMTH W6 143 H5
Hammersmith Bridge Rd
BARN SW13 143 H6
Hammersmith Broadway
HMSMTH W6 144 A4
Hammersmith Emb
BARN * SW13 144 A5
Hammersmith F/O
HMSMTH W6 144 A5
Hammersmith Gv
HMSMTH W6 144 A3
Hammersmith Ter
HMSMTH * W6 143 G5
Hammet Cl YEAD UB4 118 B4
Hammett St TWRH EC3N 16 C5
Hammond Av MTCM CR4 206 D5
Hammond Cl HPTN TW12 199 E4
NTHLT UB5 99 H3
Hammond Rd EN EN1 39 H4
NWDGN UB2 138 C3

Hammonds Cl BCTR RM8 116 A1
Hammond St KTTN NW5 107 E4
Hamond Cl SAND/SEL CR2 246 B6
Hamonde Cl EDGW HA8 46 B4
Hamond Sq IS N1 8 A1
Ham Park Rd FSTGT E7 112 C5
Hampden Av BECK BR3 210 C5
Hampden Cl CAMTN NW1 4 D2
Hampden Gurney St
MBLAR W1H 10 C4
Hampden La TOTM N17 69 F4
Hampden Rd ARCH N19 87 F6
BECK BR3 210 C5
CEND/HSY/T N8 88 A1
KTN/HRWW/W HA3 59 G4
KUT KT1 202 A6
MUSWH N10 66 C3
TOTM N17 69 G4
Hampden Wy STHGT/OAK N14 50 D3
Hampshire Cl UED N18 69 H1
Hampshire Hog La
HMSMTH * W6 143 H4
Hampshire Rd WDGN N22 67 H3
Hampshire St KTTN * NW5 107 F4
Hampson Wy VX/NE SW8 167 H2
Hampstead Cl THMD SE28 155 H1
Hampstead Gdns
GLDGN NW11 85 E3
Hampstead Ga HAMP NW3 105 G3
Hampstead Gn HAMP NW3 106 A3
Hampstead Gv HAMP NW3 105 G2
Hampstead Hill Gdns
HAMP NW3 106 A2
Hampstead La HGT N6 86 B4
Hampstead Rd CAMTN NW1 4 A2
Hampstead Sq HAMP NW3 105 G1
Hampstead Wy GLDGN NW11 85 E2
Hampton Cl FBAR/BDGN N11 66 C1
KIL/WHAMP NW6 125 E2
RYNPK * SW20 204 A3
Hampton Ct IS N1 108 B4
Hampton Court Av
E/WMO/HCT KT8 219 H3
Hampton Court Crs
E/WMO/HCT * KT8 199 H6
Hampton Court Est
THDIT * KT7 220 A2
Hampton Court Rd
E/WMO/HCT KT8 200 C6
HPTN TW12 199 H5
Hampton Court Wy
E/WMO/HCT KT8 220 A1
ESH/CLAY KT10 220 A6
THDIT KT7 220 A4
Hampton La FELT TW13 178 C6
Hampton Ri
KTN/HRWW/W HA3 81 G3
Hampton Rd CHING E4 70 D1
CROY/NA CR0 228 C3
FSTGT E7 112 D3
HPTN TW12 199 H1
IL IG1 114 C2
WAN E11 91 H5
WHTN TW2 179 H5
WPK KT4 223 G6
Hampton Rd East FELT TW13 178 D6
Hampton Rd West FELT TW13 178 C4
Hampton St WALW SE17 30 D2
Ham Ridings
RCHPK/HAM TW10 201 H1
Ham Shades Cl BFN/LL DA15 195 F5
Ham St RCHPK/HAM TW10 181 E4
The Ham BTFD TW8 161 E1
Ham Vw CROY/NA CR0 230 C3
Ham Yd SOHO/SHAV * W1D 12 C5
Hanameel St CAN/RD E16 152 C1
Hanbury Cl HDN NW4 64 A6
Hanbury Ct HRW * HA1 80 B3
Hanbury Dr WCHMH N21 37 H5
Hanbury Rd ACT W3 142 B2
TOTM N17 69 H5
Hanbury St WCHPL E1 17 E1
Hancock Rd BOW E3 131 G2
NRWD SE19 208 D2
Handa Wk IS N1 108 C4
Hand Ct HHOL WC1V 13 H2
Handcroft Rd CROY/NA CR0 228 B5
Handel Cl EDGW HA8 61 H2
Handel Pde EDGW * HA8 62 A2
Handel Pl WLSDN NW10 102 D4
Handel St BMSBY WC1N 5 E5
Handel Wy EDGW HA8 62 A3
Handen Rd LEW SE13 172 A6
Handforth Rd BRXN/ST SW9 168 A1
IL IG1 114 B1
Handley Gv CRICK NW2 104 B1
Handley Page Rd WLGTN SM6 245 H5
Handley Rd HOM E9 110 A5
Handowe Cl HDN NW4 83 G1
Handside Cl WPK KT4 224 B5
Handsworth Av CHING E4 71 H2
Handsworth Rd TOTM N17 68 D6
Handtrough Wy BARK IG11 134 B1
Hanford Cl WAND/EARL SW18 185 E3
Hangar Ruding OXHEY WD19 42 D5
Hangar View Wy ACT W3 122 A5
Hanger Gn EA W5 122 A3
Hanger La EA W5 121 H6
Hanger La
(North Circular Rd) EA W5 121 G2
Hanger Vale La EA W5 121 H5
Hankey Pl STHWK SE1 23 H4
Hankins La MLHL NW7 47 E4
Hanley Gdns FSBYPK N4 87 H5
Hanley Pl BECK BR3 211 E3
Hanley Rd FSBYPK N4 87 G5
Hannah Cl BECK BR3 211 F6
WLSDN * NW10 102 C2
Hannah Mary Wy STHWK SE1 33 F2
Hannan Cl WLSDN NW10 102 C2
Hannards Wy CHIG IG7 75 H1
Hannay La ARCH N19 87 F4
Hannell Rd FUL/PGN SW6 164 C1
Hannen Rd WNWD * SE27 188 B5
Hannibal Rd WCHPL E1 130 A4
Hannibal Wy CROY/NA CR0 245 H3
Hannington Rd CLAP SW4 166 D4
Hanover Av CAN/RD E16 152 C1
Hanover Cl CHEAM SM3 242 C2
RCH/KEW TW9 162 A1
Hanover Dr CHST BR7 194 C6
Hanover Gdns BARK/HLT IG6 74 C3
LBTH SE11 30 A6
Hanover Pk PECK SE15 169 G2
Hanover Pl COVGDN WC2E 13 F4
Hanover Rd SEVS/STOTM N15 89 F1
WIM/MER SW19 205 G3
WLSDN NW10 104 A5
Hanover Sq CONDST W1S 11 H4
Hanover Steps BAY/PAD * W2 10 B4
Hanover St CONDST W1S 11 H4
CROY/NA CR0 246 B1
Hanover Ter CAMTN NW1 2 B4
Hanover Terrace Ms
CAMTN NW1 2 B4
Hanover Wy BXLYHN DA7 176 B4
Hanover Yd IS * N1 6 D1
Hansard Ms WKENS W14 144 B2
Hansart Wy ENC/FH EN2 38 A2
Hans Crs CHEL SW3 18 C5
Hanselin Cl STAN HA7 60 B1
Hansen Dr WCHMH N21 37 H6
Hanshaw Dr EDGW HA8 62 D4
Hansler Gv E/WMO/HCT KT8 219 H2
Hansler Rd EDUL SE22 169 F6
Hansol Rd BXLYHS DA6 176 C6
Hansom Ter BMLY * BR1 212 D4
Hanson Cl BAL SW12 186 D2
BECK * BR3 211 F2
MORT/ESHN SW14 162 C4
Hanson Gdns STHL UB1 138 C2
Hanson St GTPST W1W 12 A1
Hans Pl KTBR SW1X 18 C5
Hans Rd CHEL SW3 18 C5
Hans St KTBR SW1X 18 D6
Hanway Pl FITZ W1T 12 C3
Hanway Rd HNWL W7 119 H5
Hanworth Rd HPTN TW12 178 D6
HSLW TW3 159 F5
HSLWW TW4 178 D2
Hanworth Ter HSLW TW3 159 F5
Hapgood Cl NTHLT UB5 99 H3
Harben Pde
KIL/WHAMP * NW6 105 H5
Harben Rd KIL/WHAMP NW6 105 G5
Harberson Rd BAL SW12 186 D3
SRTFD E15 112 B6
Harberton Rd ARCH N19 87 E5
Harbet Rd BAY/PAD W2 125 H4
UED N18 70 B1
Harbex Cl BXLY DA5 197 F2
Harbinger Rd POP/IOD E14 151 F4
Harbledown Pl
STMC/STPC BR5 236 A1
Harbledown Rd FUL/PGN SW6 165 E2
Harbord Cl CMBW SE5 168 D3
Harbord St FUL/PGN SW6 164 B2
Harborne Cl OXHEY WD19 58 A1
Harborough Av BFN/LL DA15 195 E2
Harborough Rd
STRHM/NOR SW16 187 H6
Harbour Av WBPTN SW10 165 G2
Harbourer Rd BARK/HLT IG6 75 H1
Harbour Rd CMBW SE5 168 C4
Harbour Yd WBPTN * SW10 165 G2
Harbridge Av PUT/ROE SW15 183 F2
Harbury Rd CAR SM5 244 A6
Harbut Rd BTSEA SW11 165 H5
Harcastle Cl YEAD UB4 118 C3
Harcombe Rd
STNW/STAM N16 109 E1
Harcourt Av BFN/LL DA15 196 A1
EDGW HA8 46 C5
MNPK E12 113 H2
WLGTN SM6 244 D2
Harcourt Buildings
EMB * EC4Y 14 A5
Harcourt Cl ISLW TW7 160 C4
Harcourt Fld WLGTN SM6 244 D2
Harcourt Rd BROCKY SE4 170 D5
BXLYHS DA6 176 C5
SRTFD E15 132 B1
THHTH CR7 227 H3
WDGN N22 67 F4
WIM/MER SW19 205 E3
WLGTN SM6 244 D2
Harcourt St CAMTN NW1 10 B2
Harcourt Ter WBPTN SW10 145 F5
Hardcastle Cl SNWD SE25 229 G3
Hardcourts Cl WWKM BR4 249 F2
Hardel Wk BRXS/STRHM SW2 188 A2
Hardens Manorway
WOOL/PLUM SE18 153 F3
Harders Rd PECK SE15 169 H3
Hardess St HNHL SE24 168 C4
Hardie Cl WLSDN NW10 102 D3
Hardie Rd DAGE RM10 117 G1
Harding Cl CROY/NA CR0 247 F1
KUTN/CMB KT2 201 H4
WALW SE17 31 E5
Hardinge Rd UED N18 69 E1
WLSDN NW10 104 A6
Hardinge St WCHPL E1 130 A5
WOOL/PLUM SE18 154 B3
Harding Rd BXLYHN DA7 176 D3
Hardings La PGE/AN SE20 210 B2
Hardman Rd CHARL SE7 152 D5
KUTN/CMB KT2 201 G5
Hardres Ter STMC/STPC * BR5 236 B6
Hardwick Cl STAN HA7 61 E1
Hardwicke Av HEST * TW5 159 E2
Hardwicke Ms FSBYW * WC1X 5 H4
Hardwicke Rd CHSWK W4 142 C4
PLMGR N13 67 G1
RCHPK/HAM TW10 181 E6
Hardwicke St BARK IG11 114 C6
Hardwick Gn WEA W13 120 D4
Hardwick St CLKNW EC1R 6 B4
Hardwick's Wy
WAND/EARL SW18 165 E6
Hardwidge St STHWK SE1 24 A3
Hardy Av CAN/RD E16 152 C1
Hardy Cl BAR EN5 34 C6
BERM/RHTH SE16 150 B2
PIN HA5 78 B4
Hardy Cottages GNWCH * SE10 151 H6
Hardy Pas WDGN N22 67 H4
Hardy Rd BKHTH/KID SE3 152 B6
CHING E4 70 D2
WIM/MER SW19 205 F3
Hardy Wy ENC/FH EN2 38 A2
Harebell Dr EHAM E6 134 A4
Hare & Billet Rd
BKHTH/KID SE3 171 H2
Hare Ct EMB * EC4Y 14 A4
Harecourt Rd IS N1 108 C4
Haredale Rd HNHL SE24 168 C5
Haredon Cl FSTH SE23 190 A2
Harefield ESH/CLAY KT10 238 A1
Harefield Av BELMT SM2 242 C6
Harefield Cl ENC/FH EN2 38 A2
Harefield Ms BROCKY SE4 170 D4
Harefield Rd BROCKY SE4 170 D4
CEND/HSY/T N8 87 F2
SCUP DA14 196 B4
STRHM/NOR SW16 207 H3
Hare La ESH/CLAY KT10 238 A4
Hare Marsh BETH * E2 9 E5
Hare Rw BETH E2 9 H1
Haresfield Rd DAGE RM10 117 E4
Hare St WOOL/PLUM SE18 154 A3
Hare Wk IS N1 8 B2
Harewood Av CAMTN NW1 2 B5
NTHLT UB5 98 C5
Harewood Cl NTHLT UB5 98 D5
Harewood Dr CLAY IG5 73 H5
Harewood Pl CONDST W1S 11 H4
Harewood Rd ISLW TW7 160 B1
SAND/SEL CR2 247 E4
WIM/MER SW19 206 A2
Harewood Rw CAMTN NW1 10 B1
Harewood Ter NWDGN UB2 138 D4
Harfield Gdns CMBW * SE5 169 E4
Harfield Rd SUN TW16 198 B5
Harford Cl CHING E4 55 F2
Harford Rd CHING E4 55 F2
Harford St WCHPL E1 130 C3
Harford Wk EFNCH N2 85 H1
Harfst Wy SWLY BR8 217 G4
Harglaze Ter CDALE/KGS * NW9 63 E6
Hargood Cl KTN/HRWW/W HA3 81 G3
Hargood Rd BKHTH/KID SE3 173 E2
Hargrave Pk KTTN NW5 87 E6
Hargrave Rd ARCH N19 87 E6
Hargwyne St BRXN/ST SW9 167 H4
Haringey Pk CEND/HSY/T N8 87 G3
Haringey Rd CEND/HSY/T N8 87 G1
Harington Ter UED * N18 52 D6
Harkett Cl KTN/HRWW/W HA3 60 B5
Harland Av BFN/LL DA15 194 D5
CROY/NA CR0 247 F1
Harland Cl WIM/MER SW19 205 F6
Harland Rd LEE/GVPK SE12 192 C3
Harlands Gv ORP BR6 252 B2
Harlech Gdns HEST TW5 138 A6
Harlech Rd STHGT/OAK N14 51 G5
Harlequin Av BTFD TW8 140 C6
Harlequin Cl ISLW TW7 160 A6
YEAD UB4 118 B4
Harlequin Ct WEA * W13 121 E6
Harlequin Rd TEDD * TW11 200 D3
Harlescott Rd PECK SE15 170 B5
Harlesden Gdns WLSDN NW10 103 F6
Harlesden Rd WLSDN NW10 103 G5
Harley Cl ALP/SUD * HA0 101 F4
Harley Crs HRW HA1 79 H1
Harleyford BMLY BR1 212 D4
Harleyford Rd LBTH SE11 29 G5
Harleyford St LBTH SE11 30 A6
Harley Gdns ORP BR6 253 E2
WBPTN SW10 145 G5
Harley Gv BOW E3 130 D2
Harley Pl CAVSQ/HST W1G 11 G2
Harley Rd HAMP NW3 105 H5
HRW HA1 79 H1
WLSDN NW10 123 E1
Harley St CAVSQ/HST W1G 3 G6
Harley Vls WLSDN * NW10 123 E1
Harlinger St WOOL/PLUM SE18 153 G3
Harlington Rd BXLYHN DA7 176 C4
Harlow Gdns CRW RM5 77 G2
Harlow Rd PLMGR N13 52 D5
Harman Av WFD IG8 72 B3
Harman Cl CHING E4 55 H6
CRICK NW2 104 C1
Harman Dr BFN/LL DA15 195 F1
CRICK NW2 104 C1
Harman Rd EN EN1 39 F6
Harmony Cl GLDGN NW11 84 C2
WLGTN SM6 245 G6
Harmony Wy HAYES BR2 212 C5
HDN NW4 84 A1
Harmood Gv CAMTN NW1 106 D5
Harmood St CAMTN NW1 106 D4
Harmsworth Ms STHWK SE1 22 B6
Harmsworth St WALW SE17 30 C4
Harmsworth Wy
TRDG/WHET N20 48 D3
Harness Rd THMD SE28 155 G2
Harnetts Cl SWLY * BR8 237 H4
Harold Av BELV DA17 156 D5
Harold Rd CEND/HSY/T N8 87 H2
CHING E4 55 G5
NRWD SE19 208 D3
PLSTW E13 112 D6
SEVS/STOTM N15 89 F2
SUT SM1 243 H2
WAN E11 92 A5
WFD IG8 72 C4
WLSDN NW10 122 D2
Haroldstone Rd WALTH E17 90 B2
Harp Cross La MON EC3R 16 A6
Harpenden Rd MNPK E12 93 E6
WNWD SE27 188 B4
Harper Cl STHGT/OAK N14 37 E6
Harper Rd EHAM E6 133 H5
STHWK SE1 23 F5
Harpers Yd ISLW * TW7 160 B3
Harp Island Cl WLSDN NW10 82 D6
Harpley Sq WCHPL E1 130 A3
Harpour Rd BARK IG11 114 C4
Harp Rd HNWL W7 120 B3
Harpsden St BTSEA SW11 166 C2
Harpur St BMSBY WC1N 13 G1
Harraden Rd BKHTH/KID SE3 173 E2
Harrier Ms THMD SE28 154 D2
Harriers Cl EA W5 121 G6
Harrier Wy EHAM E6 133 H4
Harries Rd YEAD UB4 118 A3
Harriet Cl BRXS/STRHM SW2 188 A2
HACK E8 109 G6
Harriet Gdns CROY/NA CR0 229 G6
Harriet St KTBR SW1X 18 D4
Harriet Wk KTBR SW1X 18 D4
Harriet Wy BUSH WD23 43 H2
Harringay Gdns
CEND/HSY/T N8 88 B1
Harringay Rd CEND/HSY/T N8 88 B2
Harrington Cl CROY/NA CR0 227 G6
WLSDN NW10 102 D1
Harrington Ct MV/WKIL * W9 124 D2
Harrington Gdns ECT SW5 145 F4
Harrington Hl CLPT E5 89 H5
Harrington Rd SKENS SW7 145 H4
SNWD SE25 229 G1
WAN E11 92 A5
Harrington Sq CAMTN NW1 4 A1
Harrington St CAMTN NW1 4 A3
Harrington Wy
WOOL/PLUM SE18 153 F3
Harriott Cl GNWCH SE10 152 B4
Harris Cl ENC/FH EN2 38 B2
HEST TW5 159 E2
Harrison Cl TRDG/WHET N20 50 A3
Harrison Rd DAGE RM10 117 F4
Harrison's Ri CROY/NA CR0 246 B1
Harrison St STPAN WC1H 5 F4
Harris Rd BXLYHN DA7 176 C2
DAGW RM9 116 D3
Harris St CMBW SE5 168 D1
WALTH E17 90 D4
Harrods Gn EDGW * HA8 62 A1
Harrogate Rd OXHEY WD19 42 A5
Harrold Rd BCTR RM8 115 H3
Harrow Av EN EN1 53 F1
Harroway Rd BTSEA SW11 165 H3
Harrowby St MBLAR W1H 10 B3
Harrow Cl CHSGTN KT9 239 F5
Harrowdene Cl ALP/SUD HA0 101 F2
Harrowdene Gdns TEDD TW11 200 C3
Harrowdene Rd ALP/SUD HA0 101 F2
Harrow Dr ED N9 53 F3
Harrowes Meade EDGW HA8 46 A5
Harrow Fields Gdns HRW HA1 100 A1
Harrow Gdns ORP BR6 253 H2
Harrowgate Rd HOM E9 110 C4
Harrow Gn WAN E11 112 A1
Harrow La POP/IOD E14 131 G6
Harrow Manor Wy ABYW SE2 156 A3
THMD SE28 156 A1
Harrow Pk HRW HA1 80 A6
Harrow Pl WCHPL E1 16 B3
Harrow Rd ALP/SUD HA0 100 C2
CAR SM5 244 A4
IL IG1 114 C2
MV/WKIL W9 125 E3
WAN E11 112 B1
WLSDN NW10 123 H2
Harrow Rd F/O BAY/PAD W2 125 H4
Harrow St CAMTN * NW1 10 B1
Harrow Vw RYLN/HDSTN HA2 59 H6
Harrow View Rd EA W5 120 D3
Harrow Wy OXHEY WD19 42 C5
Harrow Weald Pk
KTN/HRWW/W HA3 59 H2
Harston Dr PEND EN3 41 E1
Hartcliff Ct HNWL * W7 140 B2
Hart Crs CHIG IG7 75 F1
Hart Dyke Rd SWLY BR8 217 H6
Harte Rd HSLW TW3 158 D3
Hartfield Crs WIM/MER SW19 204 D3
WWKM BR4 250 C1
Hartfield Gv PGE/AN SE20 209 H4
Hartfield Rd CHSGTN KT9 239 F3
WIM/MER SW19 204 D3
WWKM BR4 250 C2
Hartfield Ter BOW E3 131 E1
Hartford Av KTN/HRWW/W HA3 60 C6
Hartford Rd BXLY DA5 197 E1
HOR/WEW KT19 240 A4
Hart Gv ACT W3 142 A1
STHL UB1 119 E4
Hartham Cl HOLWY N7 107 G3
ISLW TW7 160 C2
Hartham Rd HOLWY N7 107 G3
ISLW TW7 160 B2
TOTM N17 69 F5
Harting Rd ELTH/MOT SE9 193 G6
Hartington Cl HRW HA1 100 A2
ORP BR6 252 C3
Hartington Rd CAN/RD E16 132 D5
CHSWK W4 162 B1
NWDGN * UB2 138 C3
TWK TW1 180 D2
VX/NE SW8 167 G2
WALTH E17 90 C3
WEA W13 120 D6
Hartismere Rd FUL/PGN SW6 164 D1
Hartlake Rd HOM E9 110 B4
Hartland Cl EDGW HA8 46 A4
WCHMH N21 52 C1
Hartland Dr EDGW HA8 46 A4
Hartland Rd CAMTN * NW1 106 D5
FBAR/BDGN N11 66 B1
HPTN TW12 179 F6
ISLW TW7 160 C4
KIL/WHAMP NW6 124 D1
MRDN SM4 225 E4
SRTFD E15 112 B5
Hartland Rd Arches
CAMTN * NW1 106 C5
Hartlands Cl BXLY DA5 196 D1
Hartland Wy CROY/NA CR0 230 C6
MRDN SM4 224 D4
Hartley Av EHAM E6 113 G6
MLHL NW7 63 F1
Hartley Cl BMLY BR1 213 H5
MLHL NW7 63 F1
Hartley Rd CROY/NA CR0 228 C4
WAN E11 92 B5
WELL DA16 176 A1
Hartley St BETH E2 130 A2
Hartmann Rd CAN/RD E16 153 F1
Hartnoll St HOLWY N7 107 H3
Harton Cl BMLY BR1 213 F4
Harton Rd ED N9 53 H4
Harton St DEPT SE8 171 E2
Hartsbourne Av BUSH WD23 43 G4
Hartsbourne Cl BUSH WD23 43 H4
Hartsbourne Rd BUSH WD23 43 H4
Hartscroft CROY/NA CR0 248 C6
Harts Gv WFD IG8 72 C1
Hartshorn Gdns EHAM E6 134 A3

Harts La BARK IG11 ....114 B5
NWCR SE14 ....170 C1
Hartslock Dr ABYW SE2 ....156 B2
Hartsmead Rd ELTH/MOT SE9 ..193 H4
Hart Sq MRDN * SM4 ....235 F2
Hart St MON EC3R 16 B5
Hartsway PEND EN3 ....39 H5
Hartswood Gdns SHB * W12 ..143 F3
Hartswood Dr BUSH WD23 ..43 H4
Hartswood Rd SHB W12 ....143 F2
Hartsworth Cl PLSTW E13 ....132 B1
Hartville Rd WOOL/PLUM SE18 ..158 B4
Hartwell Dr CHING E4 ....71 G2
Hartwell St HACK E8 ....79 H4
Harvard Hl CHSWK W4 ....142 B5
Harvard Rd CHSWK W4 ....142 B5
ISLW TW7 ....160 A2
LEW SE13 ....171 G6
Harvel Cl CHST BR7 ....215 G6
Harvel Crs ABYW SE2 ....156 B5
Harvest Bank Rd WWKM BR4 ..250 C1
Harvesters Cl ISLW TW7 ....159 H6
Harvest La LOU IG10 ....57 F2
THDIT KT7 ....220 C3
Harvest Wy SWLY BR8 ....237 G4
Harvey Dr HPTN TW12 ....199 F4
Harvey Gdns CHARL SE7 ....153 E5
Harvey Rd CEND/HSY/T N8 ....87 H2
CMBW SE5 ....168 D2
HSLWW TW4 ....178 D2
IL IG1 ....114 B3
NTHLT UB5 ....98 A5
WAN E11 ....92 A5
Harvey's La ROMW/RG RM7 ....97 H6
Harvey St IS N1 ....108 D6
Harvill Rd SCUP DA14 ....216 B1
Harvington Wk HACK * E8 ....109 G5
Harvist Rd KIL/WHAMP NW6 ..124 C1
Harwood Av BMLY BR1 ....212 D5
MTCM CR4 ....206 A6
Harwood Cl ALP/SUD HA0 ......80 A2
NFNCH/WDSP N12 ....33 G6
Harwood Rd FUL/PGN SW6 ..165 F1
Harwood Ter FUL/PGN SW6 ..165 F2
Hascombe Ter CMBW * SE5 ..168 D3
Haselbury Rd UED N18 ....53 E6
Haseley End FSTH * SE23 ....190 A2
Haselrigge Rd CLAP SW4 ....167 F3
Haseltine Rd SYD SE26 ....190 D6
Haselwood Dr ENC/FH EN2 ..38 D5
Haskard Rd DAGW RM9 ....116 B2
Hasker St CHEL SW3 ....26 B1
Haslam Av CHEAM SM3 ....236 A1
Haslam Cl IS N1 ....108 A5
Haslemere Av EBAR EN4 ....50 B3
HDN NW4 ....84 B3
HEST TW5 ....158 A3
HNWL W7 ....140 C3
MTCM CR4 ....235 H5
WAND/EARL SW18 ....185 F4
Haslemere Cl HPTN TW12 ......198 D1
WLGTN SM6 ....245 G3
Haslemere Gdns FNCH N3 ......46 D4
Haslemere Rd BXLYHN DA7 ..176 D3
CEND/HSY/T N8 ....87 G4
GDMY/SEVK IG3 ....95 F6
THHTH CR7 ....228 B2
WCHMN N21 ....52 B4
Hasler Cl THMD SE28 ....135 H6
Hasluck Gdns BAR EN5 ....49 C1
Hassard St BETH E2 ....8 J2
Hassendean Rd
BKHTH/KID SE3 ....152 D6
Hassett Rd HOM E9 ....110 B4
Hassocks Cl SYD SE26 ....189 H5
Hassocks Rd
STRHM/NOR SW16 ....207 F4
Hassock Wd HAYES BR2 ....251 F2
Hassop Rd CRICK NW2 ....104 A2
Hasted Rd CHARL SE7 ....153 F5
Hastings Av BARK/HLT IG6 ....94 C1
Hastings Cl BAR EN5 ....35 G5
PECK * SE15 ....169 G1
Hastings Dr SURB KT6 ....221 E3
Hastings Rd CROY/NA CR0 ..229 F5
FBAR/BDGN N11 ....67 E1
HAYES BR2 ....233 G5
TOTM * N17 ....150 D6
WEA W13 ....120 C1
Hastings St STPAN WC1H 5 E4
Hastings Ter
SEVS/STOTM * N15 ....88 C3
Hastoe Cl YEAD UB4 ....118 C3
Hatcham Park Ms NWCR SE14 ..170 B2
Hatcham Park Rd NWCR SE14 ..170 B2
Hatcham Rd PECK SE15 ....150 A6
Hatchard Rd ARCH N19 ....87 F6
Hatchcroft HDN NW4 ....63 H6
Hatch End NWMAL KT3 ....96 C1
Hatch La CHING E4 ....55 H5
Hatch Pl RCHPK/HAM TW10 ..201 H1
Hatch Rd STRHM/NOR SW16 ..207 F6
Hatch Side CHIG IG7 ....74 A1
The Hatch PEND EN3 ....40 E2
Hatchwoods WFD IG8 ....56 B6
Hatcliffe Cl BKHTH/KID SE3 ..172 B4
Hatcliffe St GNWCH SE10 ....153 B5
Hatfield Cl BARK/HLT IG6 ....74 B6
BELMT SM2 ....243 B6
MTCM * CR4 ....234 B3
Hatfield Rd BKHTH/KID * SE3 .172 C1
RCH CHSWK W4 ....142 A1
HNWL W7 ....140 C1
SRTFD E15 ....112 A3
Hatfields STHWK SE1 ....22 B1
Hathaway Cl HAYES BR2 ....233 H5
STAN HA7 ....60 C1
Hathaway Crs MNPK E12 ....113 H4
Hathaway Gdns CHDH RM6 ......96 B2
WEA W13 ....120 C4
Hathaway Rd CROY/NA CR0 ..196 C6
Hatherleigh Cl CHSGTN KT9 ..239 F3
MRDN SM4 ....225 G1
Hatherley Crs SCUP DA14 ....195 G4
Hatherley Gdns
CEND/HSY/T N8 ....87 G3
EHAM E6 ....133 F2
Hatherley Gv BAY/PAD W2 ..125 H1
Hatherley Rd RCH/KEW TW9 ..161 H2
SCUP DA14 ....195 G5

WALTH E17 ....90 D1
Hatherley St WEST SW1P 28 B2
Hathern Gdns ELTH/MOT SE9 ..194 A6
Hatherop Rd HPTN TW12 ......198 D3
Hathorne Cl PECK SE15 ....169 H1
Hathorne Ter ARCH * N19 ......87 F5
Hathway St PECK SE15 ....170 A3
Hathway Av BARK/HLT IG6 ....94 C1
Hatley Cl FBAR/BDGN N11 ....66 B1
Hatley Rd HOLWY N7 ....87 H6
Hat & Mitre Ct FARR EC1M 6 C6
Hatterack St
BERM/RHTH SE16 ....150 A2
Hattersfield Cl BELV DA17 ..156 D4
Hatton Cl WOOL/PLUM SE18 ..174 D1
Hatton Gdns CLKNW EC1R 6 B6
HCIRC EC1N 6 B6
Hatton Gdns MTCM CR4 ....226 B2
Hatton Pl HCIRC EC1N 6 B6
Hatton Rd CROY/NA CR0 ......228 A5
Hatton Rw STJWD NW8 ....125 H3
Hatton St STJWD NW8 ....125 H3
Hatton Wall HCIRC EC1N 14 A1
Haunch of Venison Yd
MYFR/PKLN W1K 11 G4
Havana Rd WIM/MER SW19 ....185 E4
Havannah St POP/IOD E14 ....151 E2
Havant Rd WALTH E17 ....71 G6
Havelock Cl SHB * W12 ....123 H6
Havelock Pl HRW HA1 ....80 A3
Havelock Rd BELV * DA17 ....156 D4
CROY/NA CR0 ....229 F6
KTN/HRWW/W HA3 ....60 A6
NWDGN UB2 ....138 C3
TOTM N17 ....69 G5
WIM/MER SW19 ....205 G1
Havelock St IL IG1 ....78 A6
IS N1 ....107 G6
Havelock Ter VX/NE SW8 ......166 D1
Havelock Wk FSTH SE23 ......190 A3
Haven Cl ELTH/MOT SE9 ......193 H5
SCUP DA14 ....216 A2
WIM/MER SW19 ....184 B5
Haven Ct BRYLDS * KT5 ....221 H3
Haven Gn EA W5 ....121 F6
Havenhurst Ri ENC/FH EN2 ....38 A1
Haven La EA W5 ....121 G5
Haven St CAMTN NW1 ....106 D5
The Haven RCH/KEW TW9 ......162 A4
Havenwood WBLY HA9 ....102 B1
Haverfield Gdns
RCH/KEW TW9 ....162 A1
Haverfield Rd BOW E3 ....130 B2
Haverford Wy EDGW HA8 ......61 H4
Havergal Vls CEND/HSY/T * N8 ..88 B1
Haverhill Rd BAL SW12 ....187 E3
CHING E4 ....55 G3
Havering Gdns CHDH RM6 ......96 A2
Havering Rd CRW RM5 ....77 H5
Havering St WCHPL E1 ....130 E5
Haversham Cl TWK TW1 ....181 F2
Haverstock Hl HAMP NW3 ....106 A4
Haverstock Pl IS N1 ....6 B2
Haverstock Rd KTTN NW5 ....106 C5
IS N1 ....6 D2
Haverthwaite Rd ORP BR6 ....252 D1
Havisham Pl
STRHM/NOR SW16 ....208 B2
Hawarden Gv HNHL SE24 ......188 C2
Hawarden Hl CRICK NW2 ......103 C1
Hawarden Rd WALTH E17 ......90 B1
Hawbridge Rd WAN E11 ....91 H5
Hawes La WAB EN9 ....41 G1
WWKM BR4 ....231 G5
Hawes Rd BMLY BR1 ....212 D4
UED N18 ....69 H2
Hawgood St BOW E3 ....131 E4
Hawkdene CHING E4 ....55 F1
Hawke Park Rd WDGN N22 ....68 B6
Hawke Rd BERM/RHTH * SE16 ..150 B2
Hawke Rd NRWD SE19 ....208 D2
Hawkesbury Rd
PUT/ROE SW15 ....163 H6
Hawkesfield Rd FSTH SE23 ..190 C4
Hawkesley Cl TWK TW1 ....180 C6
Hawkes Rd MTCM CR4 ....206 A4
Hawkhurst Gdns CRW RM5 ....77 H2
Hawkhurst Rd
STRHM/NOR SW16 ....207 F3
Hawkhurst Wy NWMAL KT3 ..222 D2
WWKM BR4 ....231 F6
Hawkins Cl EDGW HA8 ....62 D1
HRW HA1 ....79 H4
Hawkins Rd TEDD TW11 ....200 A2
Hawkins Wy CAT SE6 ....211 E1
Hawkley Gdns WNWD SE27 ....188 B4
Hawkridge Cl CHDH RM6 ......96 A3
Hawksbrook La BECK BR3 ....231 F5
Hawkshead Cl BMLY BR1 ......212 A3
Hawkshead Rd CHSWK W4 ....143 E3
NKENS * W10 ....105 F5
Hawkslade Rd PECK SE15 ....170 B6
Hawksley Rd
STNW/STAM N16 ....108 D1
Hawks Ms GNWCH * SE10 ......171 C1
Hawksmoor Cl EHAM E6 ......133 C5
WOOL/PLUM SE18 ....155 E5
Hawksmoor Ms WCHPL * E1 ....17 G5
Hawksmoor St HMSMTH W6 ..148 B6
Hawksmouth CHING E4 ....55 H3
Hawks Rd KUT/HW * KT1 ......201 H5
Hawkstone Rd
BERM/RHTH SE16 ....150 A4
Hawkwell Wk IS * N1 ....108 C6
Hawkwood Crs CHING E4 ....55 F1
Hawkwood La CHST BR7 ......214 C4
Hawkwood Mt CLPT E5 ....89 H5
Hawkdale Dr PIN HA5 ....78 C6
Hawlands Dr PIN HA5 ....77 C2
Hawley Cl HPTN TW12 ....198 D2
Hawley Crs CAMTN NW1 ......106 D5
Hawley Ms CAMTN NW1 ......106 D5
Hawley Rd CAMTN NW1 ......106 D5
UED N18 ....70 D1
Hawstead Rd LEW SE13 ....191 F1
Hawsted BKHH IG9 ....56 D2
Hawthorn Av PLMGR N13 ......67 F1
THHTH CR7 ....208 B4
Hawthorn Cl HPTN TW12 ......199 E1

STMC/STPC BR5 ....234 D3
Hawthornden Cl
NFNCH/WDSP N12 ....66 A2
Hawthorndene Cl HAYES * BR2 ..232 B6
Hawthorndene Rd HAYES BR2 ..232 C6
Hawthorn Dr
RYLN/HDSTN HA2 ....79 E3
WWKM BR4 ....250 C1
Hawthorn Av CAR SM5 ....244 C5
HRW HA1 ....80 C3
MTCM CR4 ....205 H5
Hawthorn Cl BMLY BR1 ....213 H6
IS N1 ....109 E4
Hawthorne Gv CDALE/KGS NW9 ..82 C4
Hawthorne Rd BMLY BR1 ......213 H6
UED N18 ....53 E1
WALTH E17 ....71 E6
Hawthorne Wy ED N9 ....53 F4
Hawthorn Farm Av NTHLT UB5 ..98 C6
Hawthorn Gdns EA W5 ....141 E1
Hawthorn Gv PGE/AN SE20 ..209 H4
ENC/FH EN2 ....38 C1
Hawthorn Hatch BTFD TW8 ..160 D1
Hawthorn Ms HDN NW4 ....64 C4
Hawthorn Pl ERITH DA8 ......157 C5
Hawthorn Rd BKHH IG9 ....57 E6
BTFD TW8 ....160 D1
BXLYHS * DA6 ....176 D5
CRICK/HSY/T N8 ....67 H6
SUT SM1 ....243 H5
WLGTN SM6 ....244 D5
Hawthorn Rd WDGN N22 ......68 D3
Hawthorns WFD IG8 ....56 C5
The Hawthorns EW KT17 ......241 F4
Hawthorn Ter BFN/LL DA15 ..195 F1
Hawthorn Wk NKENS W10 ....124 C3
Hawtrey Av NTHLT UB5 ....118 B1
Hawtrey Rd HAMP NW3 ....106 A5
Haxted Rd BMLY BR1 ....212 D4
Hay Cl SRTFD E15 ....112 D6
Haycroft Gdns WLSDN NW10 ..103 C6
Haycroft Rd BRXS/STRHM SW2 ..167 G6
SURB KT6 ....221 F6
Hay Currie St POP/IOD E14 ..131 F5
Hayday Rd CAN/RD E16 ....131 G4
Haydens Cl STMC/STPC BR5 ..236 A4
Hayden's Pl NTCHL W11 ......124 D5
Haydon Wy CRW RM5 ....77 G5
Haydock Av NTHLT UB5 ....99 E4
Haydock Gn NTHLT * UB5 ......99 E4
Haydon Cl CDALE/KGS NW9 ..82 C1
EN EN1 ....53 E1
Haydon Dell Farm BUSH * WD23 ..42 D2
Haydon Park Rd
WIM/MER SW19 ....205 E1
Haydon Rd BCTR RM8 ....96 A6
OXHEY WD19 ....42 C1
Haydons Rd WIM/MER SW19 ..205 G2
Haydon St TWRH EC3N 16 C6
Haydon Wy WCHPL E1 ....16 C4
Hayes Cha WWKM BR4 ....231 G5
Hayes Cl HAYES BR2 ....232 C6
GLDGN NW11 ....84 D2
Hayesford Park Dr HAYES BR2 ..232 B2
Hayes Gdn HAYES BR2 ....232 C6
Hayes Hl HAYES BR2 ....231 G5
Hayes Hill Rd HAYES BR2 ....231 G5
Hayes La BECK BR3 ....211 H6
HAYES BR2 ....232 C1
Hayes Mead Rd HAYES BR2 ..231 G5
Hayes Pl CAMTN NW1 ....2 E7
Hayes Rd HAYES BR2 ....232 C1
NWDGN UB2 ....136 A4
Hayes St HAYES BR2 ....232 D5
Hayes Wy BECK BR3 ....211 E1
Hayes Wood Av HAYES BR2 ..232 D5
Hayfield Pas WCHPL E1 ....130 D3
Hayfield Rd STMC/STPC BR5 ..235 J2
Haygarth Pl WIM/MER SW19 ..204 B1
Haygreen Cl KUTN/CMB KT2 ..202 B2
Hay Hl MYFR/PICC W1J 10 A6
Hayland Cl CDALE/KGS NW9 ..82 D1
Hay La CDALE/KGS NW9 ....82 D1
Hayles St LBTH SE11 ....30 C1
Haylett Gdns KUT * KT1 ......221 F1
Hayling Cl STNW/STAM N16 ..109 E3
Haymarket STJS SW1Y 12 C6
Haymer Gdns WPK KT4 ....241 G1
Haymerle Rd PECK SE15 ......120 B2
Haymill Cl GFD/PVL UB6 ......101 F2
Hayne Rd BECK BR3 ....210 D5
Haynes Cl BKHTH/KID SE3 ..172 A4
FBAR/BDGN N11 ....50 C1
TOTM N17 ....69 H3
Haynes La NRWD SE19 ....209 E2
Haynes Rd ALP/SUD HA0 ......101 G5
Hayne St STBT EC1A 14 D1
Hays Ms MYFR/PICC W1J 10 A6
Hay Pl SWLY * BR8 ....237 G5
Hays La STHWK SE1 ....24 A1
Haysleigh Gdns PGE/AN SE20 ..209 H5
Hay's Ms MYFR/PICC W1J 11 C1
Hay St BETH E2 ....109 G6
Hayter Rd BRXS/STRHM SW2 ..167 G6
Hayton Cl HACK E8 ....109 F4
Hayward Cl DART DA1 ....177 H6
WIM/MER SW19 ....205 H5
Hayward Gdns PUT/ROE SW15 ..184 A1
Hayward Rd THDIT KT7 ....220 B5
TRDG/WHET N20 ....49 G4
Haywards Cl CHDH RM6 ....96 A2
Hayward's Pl CLKNW * EC1R ..6 C6
Haywood Cl PIN HA5 ....59 B5
Haywood Rd ORP BR6 ....253 E3
Haywood Wk PLSTW * E13 ....93 H3
Hazel Bank BRYLDS KT5 ......222 C5
Hazelbank Rd CAT SE6 ....191 H4
Hazelbourne Rd BAL SW12 ..186 D1
Hazelbrook Gdns
BARK/HLT IG6 ....74 D3
Hazelbury Cl WIM/MER SW19 ..205 H5
Hazelbury Gn UED N18 ....53 H5
Hazel Cl BTFD * TW8 ....160 D1
CDALE/KGS NW9 ....64 C6
CROY/NA CR0 ....230 B4
MTCM CR4 ....227 F1
PLMGR N13 ....52 D5
WHTN TW2 ....179 G2

Hazelcroft PIN HA5 ....59 H2
Hazeldean Rd WLSDN NW10 ..102 D5
Hazeldene Dr PIN HA5 ....58 A6
Hazeldene Rd BCTR RM8 ......96 H6
WELL DA16 ....176 A3
Hazeldon Rd BROCKY SE4 ....170 C6
Hazeleigh Gdns WFD IG8 ......73 G1
Hazel Gdns EDGW HA8 ....46 B6
Hazelgreen Cl WCHMN N21 ..52 B5
Hazel Gv ALP/SUD HA0 ....101 G6
CHDH RM6 ....76 C6
EN * EN1 ....54 A6
ORP BR6 ....236 B6
SYD SE26 ....190 B6
Hazelhurst BECK BR3 ....211 H4
Hazelhurst Rd TOOT SW17 ..185 G6
Hazel Crs ROMW/RG RM7 ......77 F1
Hazelmere Rd ARCH N19 ......87 F4
Hazelmere Cl NTHLT UB5 ....118 D1
Hazelmere Dr NTHLT UB5 ....118 D1
Hazelmere Rd KIL/WHAMP NW6 ..2 A1
STMC/STPC BR5 ....234 C1
Hazelmere Wk NTHLT UB5 ..118 D1
Hazelmere Wy HAYES BR2 ..232 C3
Hazel Rd SRTFD * E15 ....112 H2
WLSDN NW10 ....123 H2
Hazel Rw RWN/HRWW/WDSP * N12 ..65 H1
Hazeltree La NTHLT UB5 ......118 C2
Hazelwood Av MRDN SM4 ......224 A3
Hazel Wy CHING E4 ....70 D2
STHWK SE1 ....32 C1
Hazelwood Av MRDN SM4 ......224 A3
Hazelwood Cl CLPT E5 ....110 C1
EA W5 ....141 G2
RYLN/HDSTN HA2 ....79 F1
Hazelwood Ct SURB KT6 ......221 G3
Hazelwood Crs PLMGR N13 ..52 A6
Hazelwood Dr PIN HA5 ....40 C6
Hazelwood Park Cl
BARK/HLT IG6 ....75 E1
Hazelwood Rd EN EN1 ....53 F1
WALTH E17 ....69 F3
Hazlebury Rd FUL/PGN SW6 ..165 F3
Hazledean Rd CROY/NA CR0 ..228 D6
Hazledene Rd CHSWK W4 ....142 C6
Hazlemere Gdns WPK KT4 ....225 C5
Hazlewell Rd PUT/ROE SW15 ..164 A6
Hazlewood Crs NKENS W10 ..124 C3
Hazlitt Cl FELT TW13 ....178 C6
Hazlitt Ms WKENS * W14 ....144 C3
Hazlitt Rd WKENS W14 ....144 C3
Headcorn Rd BMLY BR1 ......212 B1
THHTH CR7 ....227 H1
TOTM N17 ....69 F3
Headfort Pl KTBR SW1X 19 F4
Headington Rd
WAND/EARL SW18 ....185 E3
Headlam Rd CLAP SW4 ....167 H6
Headlam St WCHPL E1 ....9 H6
Headley Ap IL IG1 ....94 A2
Headley Av WLGTN SM6 ......245 H3
Headley Cl CHSGTN KT9 ......240 A4
Headley Dr CROY/NA CR0 ....249 G5
GNTH/NBYPK IG2 ....94 B3
Headstone Dr HRW * HA1 ......60 A6
KTN/HRWW/W HA3 ....60 A6
Headstone Gdns
RYLN/HDSTN HA2 ....79 G1
Headstone La
KTN/HRWW/W HA3 ....59 F4
Headstone Pde HRW * HA1 ..79 F4
Headstone Rd HRW HA1 ....61 F6
Head St WCHPL E1 ....130 B5
Headway Cl RCHPK/HAM TW10 ..181 E6
The Headway EW KT17 ....241 H6
Heald St NWCR SE14 ....170 D2
Healey St CAMTN * NW1 ......106 C4
Healy Dr ORP BR6 ....253 F1
Hearne Rd CHSWK W4 ....142 A5
Hearn Ri NTHLT UB5 ....98 B6
Hearn's Buildings WALW SE17 ..51 H3
Hearns Cl STMC/STPC BR5 ..236 A1
Hearn St SDTCH EC2A 8 B6
Hearnville Rd BAL SW12 ......186 C1
Heatham Pk WHTN TW2 ......180 B2
Heath Av BXLYHN DA7 ....156 B6
Heathbourne Rd BUSH WD23 ..44 A4
STAN HA7 ....44 A4
Heath Brow HAMP NW3 ....105 G1
Heath Cl EA W5 ....121 H5
GLDGN NW11 ....65 E4
SAND/SEL CR2 ....248 A6
STMC/STPC BR5 ....236 A4
Heathcote Av CLAY IG5 ....73 H5
Heathcote Gv CHING E4 ....55 G1
Heathcote Rd TWK TW1 ....180 D5
Heathcote St BMSBY WC1N 5 G5
Heathcroft EA W5 ....121 H3
Heathcroft Gdns WALTH * E17 ..70 D4
Heathdale Av HSLWW TW4 ..158 C4
Heathdene Dr BELV DA17 ....157 F4
Heathdene Rd
STRHM/NOR SW16 ....207 H3
WLGTN SM6 ....246 B4
Heath Dr BELMT SM2 ....242 A5
HAMP NW3 ....105 F2
RYNPK SW20 ....221 E4
Heathedge SYD * SE26 ....189 H4
Heather Av ROM RM1 ....77 H5
Heather Dr DART DA1 ....178 A5
ENC/FH EN2 ....38 B3
Heather End SWLY BR8 ....237 H2
Heather Gdns ROM RM1 ....77 H5
HPTN TW12 ....179 F6
ISLW TW7 ....159 H6
SEVS/STOTM N15 ....67 H6
WLSDN NW10 ....84 A5
VX/NE SW8 ....166 C5
Heatherdale Cl KUTN/CMB KT2 ..202 A2
Heatherdene Cl FNCH N3 ......46 D3
Heather Dr ENC/FH EN2 ......38 B3
ROM RM1 ....77 H5
Heather Gln ROM RM1 ....77 H5
GLDGN NW11 ....84 B3
Heather Park Dr ALP/SUD HA0 ..102 A5

Heather Park Pde
ALP/SUD * HA0 101 H5
Heather Rd CHING E4 70 D2
CRICK NW2 83 F6
LEE/GVPK SE12 192 C4
Heatherset Gdns
STRHM/NOR SW16 207 H3
Heatherside Rd
HOR/WEW KT19 240 D5
SCUP DA14 196 A5
Heather Wk EDGW HA8 62 B1
NKENS W10 124 C3
Heather Wy ROM RM1 77 H4
SAND/SEL CR2 248 B6
STAN HA7 60 B2
Heatherwood Cl MNPK E12 92 D6
Heathfield CHING E4 55 G5
CHST BR7 214 C2
HRW * HA1 80 B4
Heathfield Av
WAND/EARL SW18 185 H2
Heathfield Cl CAN/RD E16 133 F4
HAYES BR2 251 E3
Heathfield Dr MTCM CR4 206 A4
Heathfield Gdns CHSWK W4 142 C5
CROY/NA * CR0 246 C2
GLDGN NW11 84 B3
WAND/EARL SW18 185 H1
Heathfield La CHST BR7 214 C2
Heathfield North WHTN TW2 180 A2
Heathfield Pk CRICK NW2 104 A4
Heathfield Park Dr CHDH RM6 95 H2
Heathfield Rd ACT W3 142 B2
BMLY BR1 212 B3
BXLYHS DA6 176 D5
CROY/NA CR0 246 D3
HAYES BR2 251 E3
WAND/EARL SW18 185 G1
Heathfield South WHTN TW2 180 B2
Heathfield Sq
SW18 185 H2
Heathfield Ter CHSWK W4 142 C5
SWLY * BR8 217 H5
WOOL/PLUM SE18 155 E6
Heathfield V SAND/SEL CR2 248 B6
Heath Gdns TWK TW1 180 B3
Heathgate GLDGN NW11 85 F3
Heathgate Pl HAMP NW3 106 B3
Heath Gv PGE/AN SE20 210 A3
Heathhurst Rd SAND/SEL CR2 247 E6
Heathland Rd
STNW/STAM N16 89 E5
Heathlands Cl TWK TW1 180 B4
Heathlands Ct HSLWW TW4 158 C6
Heathlands Wy HSLWW TW4 158 C6
Heath La BKHTH/KID SE3 171 H3
Heathlee Rd BKHTH/KID SE3 172 B5
Heathley End CHST BR7 214 C2
Heath Ldg BUSH * WD23 43 H3
Heathman's Rd
FUL/PGN * SW6 164 D2
Heath Md WIM/MER SW19 184 B5
Heath Park Dr BMLY BR1 213 G6
Heath Ri HAYES BR2 232 C3
PUT/ROE SW15 184 B1
Heath Rd BXLY DA5 197 G3
CHDH RM6 96 B4
HRW HA1 79 G4
HSLW TW3 159 G5
OXHEY WD19 42 B2
THHTH CR7 208 C6
TWK TW1 180 B3
VX/NE SW8 166 D3
Heath's Cl EN EN1 38 D3
Heathside ESH/CLAY KT10 238 A1
HAMP NW3 105 H2
HSLWW TW4 178 D2
Heath Side STMC/STPC BR5 234 C5
Heathside Av BXLYHN DA7 176 C3
Heathside Cl ESH/CLAY KT10 238 A1
GNTH/NBYPK IG2 94 D2
Heathstan Rd SHB W12 123 G5
Heath St HAMP NW3 105 G1
The Heath HNWL * W7 140 A2
Heath Vw EFNCH N2 85 G1
Heath View Cl EFNCH N2 85 G1
Heath View Dr ABYW SE2 156 B6
Heathview Gdns
PUT/ROE SW15 184 A2
Heathview Rd THHTH CR7 228 A1
Heath Vls WAND/EARL * SW18 185 G3
WOOL/PLUM SE18 155 F5
Heathville Rd ARCH N19 87 G4
Heathwall St BTSEA SW11 166 B4
Heath Wy ERITH DA8 177 G2
Heathway BKHTH/KID SE3 172 C1
CROY/NA CR0 248 D1
DAGW RM9 116 D2
NWDGN * UB2 138 B4
WFD IG8 57 E6
Heathwood Gdns CHARL SE7 153 G4
SWLY BR8 217 G5
Heathwood Pde SWLY * BR8 217 G5
Heaton Cl CHING E4 55 G5
Heaton Rd MTCM CR4 206 C3
PECK SE15 169 H4
Heaver Rd BTSEA * SW11 165 H4
Heavitree Cl WOOL/PLUM SE18 154 D5
Heavitree Rd
WOOL/PLUM SE18 154 D5
Hebden Ter TOTM N17 69 E2
Hebdon Rd TOOT SW17 186 A5
Heber Rd CRICK NW2 104 B3
EDUL SE22 189 F1
Hebron Rd HMSMTH W6 143 H3
Hecham Cl WALTH E17 70 C5
Heckfield Pl FUL/PGN SW6 165 E1
Heckford St WAP E1W 130 B6
Hector St WOOL/PLUM * SE18 155 E4
Heddington Gv HOLWY N7 107 H3
Heddon Cl ISLW TW7 160 C5
Heddon Court Av EBAR EN4 36 B6
Heddon Court Pde EBAR * EN4 36 C6
Heddon Rd EBAR EN4 36 B6
Heddon St CONDST W1S 12 A6
Hedge Hl ENC/FH EN2 38 B2
Hedge La PLMGR N13 52 C6
Hedgeley REDBR IG4 93 H1
Hedgemans Rd DAGW RM9 116 B5
Hedgemans Wy DAGW RM9 116 C4
Hedgerley Gdns GFD/PVL UB6 119 G1
Hedger's Gv HOM * E9 110 C4
Hedger St LBTH SE11 30 C1
Hedgewood Gdns CLAY IG5 94 A1
Hedgley St LEE/GVPK SE12 172 B6
Hedingham Cl IS N1 108 C5
Hedingham Rd BCTR RM8 115 H3
Hedley Rd HSLWW TW4 179 E2
Hedley Rw HBRY N5 108 D3
Heenan Cl BARK IG11 114 C4
Heene Rd ENC/FH EN2 38 D3
Heidegger Crs BARN SW13 163 H1
Heigham Rd EHAM E6 113 F5
Heighton Gdns CROY/NA CR0 246 B3
Heights Cl RYNPK SW20 203 H3
The Heights BECK * BR3 211 G3
CHARL SE7 153 E5
NTHLT UB5 99 E3
Heiron St WALW SE17 30 D6
Helby Rd CLAP SW4 187 F1
Helder Gv LEE/GVPK SE12 192 B2
Helder St SAND/SEL CR2 246 D4
Heldmann Cl ISLW TW7 159 H5
Helena Pl HOM E9 109 H6
Helena Rd EA W5 121 F4
PLSTW E13 132 B1
WALTH E17 91 E2
WLSDN NW10 103 H3
Helena Sq BERM/RHTH SE16 130 C6
Helen Cl E/WMO/HCT KT8 219 F1
EFNCH N2 65 G6
Helenslea Av GLDGN NW11 84 D5
Helen's Pl BETH E2 130 A2
Helen St WOOL/PLUM * SE18 154 B4
Heligan Cl ORP BR6 253 F2
Helix Gdns BRXS/STRHM SW2 187 H1
Helix Rd BRXS/STRHM SW2 187 H1
Hellings St WAP E1W 25 F2
Helme Cl WIM/MER SW19 204 D1
Helmet Rw FSBYE EC1V 7 F5
Helmore Rd BARK IG11 115 E5
Helmsdale Cl YEAD * UB4 118 C3
Helmsdale Rd
STRHM/NOR SW16 207 E4
Helmsley Pl HACK E8 109 H5
Helmsley St HACK E8 109 H5
Helsinki Sq BERM/RHTH SE16 150 D3
Helston Cl PIN * HA5 58 D3
PIN HA5 58 D3
Helvetia St CAT SE6 190 D4
Hemans St VX/NE SW8 167 F1
Hemery Rd NTHLT UB5 99 H3
Hemingford Rd CHEAM SM3 242 A2
IS N1 107 H6
Heming Rd EDGW HA8 62 B2
Hemington Av FBAR/BDGN N11 66 B1
Hemlock Rd SHB W12 123 F6
Hemming Cl HPTN TW12 199 E4
Hemmings Cl SCUP DA14 195 H4
Hemming St WCHPL E1 9 F6
Hemmingway Cl KTTN NW5 106 C2
Hempstead Cl BKHH IG9 56 C4
Hempstead Rd WALTH E17 71 H6
Hemp Wk WALW SE17 31 H6
Hemsby Rd CHSGTN KT9 239 H4
Hemstal Rd KIL/WHAMP NW6 105 E5
Hemswell Dr CDALE/KGS NW9 63 E4
Hemsworth St IS N1 8 A1
Henbury Wy OXHEY WD19 42 B5
Henchman St SHB W12 123 F5
Hendale Av HDN NW4 63 G6
Henderson Cl WLSDN NW10 102 C4
Henderson Dr STJWD NW8 125 H3
Henderson Rd CROY/NA CR0 228 D3
ED N9 53 H3
FSTGT E7 113 E4
WAND/EARL SW18 186 A2
Hendham Rd TOOT SW17 186 A4
Hendon Av FNCH N3 64 C4
Hendon Gdns CRW RM5 77 G2
Hendon Gv HOR/WEW KT19 240 A6
Hendon Hall Ct HDN * NW4 64 B6
Hendon La FNCH N3 64 C6
Hendon Park Rw
GLDGN * NW11 84 D3
Hendon Rd ED N9 53 G4
Hendon Wy HDN NW4 84 A3
Hendon Wood La MLHL NW7 47 G2
Hendren Cl NTHLT UB5 99 H3
Hendre Rd STHWK SE1 32 B2
Hendrick Av BAL SW12 186 B1
Heneage La HDTCH EC3A 16 B4
Heneage St WCHPL E1 16 D2
Henfield Cl ARCH N19 87 E5
BXLY DA5 197 E1
Henfield Rd WIM/MER SW19 204 D4
Hengelo Gdns MTCM CR4 225 H1
Hengist Rd ERITH DA8 177 G1
LEE/GVPK SE12 192 D2
Hengist Wy HAYES BR2 231 H1
Hengrave Rd FSTH SE23 190 A2
Hengrove Ct BXLY DA5 196 C3
Henley Av CHEAM SM3 242 C1
Henley Cl BERM/RHTH * SE16 150 A2
GFD/PVL * UB6 119 G1
ISLW TW7 160 B2
Henley Dr BERM/RHTH SE16 32 D1
KUTN/CMB KT2 203 F3
Henley Gdns CHDH RM6 96 C2
Henley Rd CAN/RD E16 153 H2
IL IG1 114 C2
UED N18 53 E6
WLSDN NW10 104 A6
Henley St BTSEA SW11 166 C3
Henley Wy FELT TW13 198 B1
Hennel Cl FSTH SE23 190 A5
Hennessy Rd ED N9 54 A4
Henniker Gdns EHAM E6 133 F2
Henniker Ms CHEL SW3 145 H6
Henniker Rd SRTFD E15 111 H3
Henningham Rd TOTM N17 68 D4
Henning St BTSEA SW11 166 A2
Henrietta Cl DEPT SE8 151 E6
Henrietta Ms BMSBY WC1N 5 F5
Henrietta Pl CAVSQ/HST W1G 11 G3
Henrietta St COVGDN WC2E 13 F5
SRTFD E15 111 G3
Henriques St WCHPL E1 17 F3
Henry Addlington Cl
EHAM E6 134 B4
Henry Cl ENC/FH EN2 39 E1
Henry Cooper Wy
LEE/GVPK SE12 193 F5
Henry Darlot Dr MLHL NW7 64 C1
Henry Dickens Ct NTGHL W11 124 B6
Henry Doulton Dr TOOT SW17 186 C6
Henry Jackson Rd
PUT/ROE SW15 164 B4
Henry Macaulay Av
KUTN/CMB KT2 201 F4
Henry Peters Dr TEDD TW11 200 A1
Henry Rd EBAR EN4 35 H6
EHAM E6 133 G1
FSBYPK N4 88 C5
Henry's Av WFD IG8 72 B1
Henryson Rd BROCKY SE4 171 E6
Henry St BMLY BR1 212 D4
Hensford Gdns SYD SE26 189 H6
Henshall St IS N1 108 D4
Henshawe Rd BCTR RM8 116 B1
Henshaw St WALW SE17 31 G1
Henslowe Rd EDUL SE22 169 G6
Henson Av CRICK NW2 104 A3
Henson Cl ORP BR6 234 B6
Henson Pl NTHLT UB5 98 A6
Henstridge Pl STJWD NW8 2 A1
Henty Cl BTSEA SW11 166 A1
Henty Wk PUT/ROE SW15 163 H6
Henville Rd BMLY BR1 212 D4
Henwick Rd ELTH/MOT SE9 173 F4
Henwood Side WFD IG8 73 H2
Hepburn Gdns HAYES BR2 232 B5
Hepple Cl ISLW TW7 160 D3
Hepscott Rd HOM E9 111 E4
Hepworth Gdns BARK IG11 115 G3
Hepworth Rd
STRHM/NOR SW16 207 G3
Herald Gdns WLGTN SM6 244 D1
Heralds Pl LBTH SE11 30 C1
Herald St BETH E2 9 H4
Herbal Hl CLKNW EC1R 6 B6
Herbert Crs KTBR SW1X 18 D5
Herbert Gdns CHDH RM6 96 B4
CHSWK W4 142 B6
WLSDN NW10 123 H1
Herbert Pl WOOL/PLUM SE18 154 B6
Herbert Rd BXLYHN DA7 176 C3
CDALE/KGS NW9 83 G3
FBAR/BDGN N11 67 G3
GDMY/SEVK IG3 95 E6
HAYES BR2 233 F2
KUT KT1 201 H6
MNPK E12 113 G2
SEVS/STOTM N15 89 F2
STHL UB1 138 D1
WALTH E17 90 D4
WIM/MER SW19 204 D3
WOOL/PLUM SE18 174 B1
Herbert St KTTN NW5 106 C4
PLSTW E13 132 C1
Herbrand St BMSBY WC1N 5 E5
Hercules Pl HOLWY N7 107 G1
Hercules Rd STHWK SE1 21 H6
Hercules St HOLWY N7 107 G1
Hereford Av EBAR EN4 50 B3
Hereford Gdns IL IG1 93 G4
PIN HA5 78 C2
WHTN * TW2 179 G3
Hereford Ms BAY/PAD * W2 125 E5
Hereford Pl NWCR * SE14 170 D1
Hereford Retreat PECK SE15 169 G1
Hereford Rd ACT W3 122 C6
BAY/PAD W2 125 E5
EA W5 141 E3
FELT TW13 178 A3
WAN E11 92 D2
Hereford Sq SKENS SW7 145 G4
Hereford St BETH E2 9 E5
Hereford Wy CHSGTN KT9 239 E3
Herent Dr CLAY IG5 73 H6
Hereward Gdns PLMGR N13 68 A1
Hereward Rd TOOT SW17 186 A6
Herga Rd KTN/HRWW/W HA3 80 B1
Heriot Av CHING E4 55 E4
Heriot Rd HDN NW4 84 A2
Heriots Cl STAN HA7 44 C6
Heritage Hl HAYES BR2 251 E3
Heritage Pl
WAND/EARL * SW18 185 H1
Heritage Vw HRW HA1 100 B1
Herkomer Cl BUSH WD23 43 F1
Herlwyn Gdns TOOT SW17 186 B6
Herm Cl ISLW TW7 159 G1
Hermes Cl MV/WKIL W9 125 E3
Hermes St IS N1 6 A2
Hermes Wy WLGTN SM6 245 F5
Hermiston Av CEND/HSY/T N8 87 G2
Hermitage Cl ENC/FH EN2 38 B3
ESH/CLAY KT10 238 C4
RCHPK/HAM * TW10 161 F6
SWFD E18 92 B1
Hermitage Cottages
STAN * HA7 60 A1
Hermitage Gdns HAMP NW3 105 E1
NRWD SE19 208 C3
Hermitage La CRICK NW2 105 E1
CROY/NA CR0 229 F4
STRHM/NOR SW16 207 H3
Hermitage Rd FSBYPK N4 88 C4
NRWD SE19 208 D2
Hermitage Rw HACK * E8 109 G3
Hermitage St BAY/PAD W2 125 H4
The Hermitage BARN * SW13 163 F2
FSTH SE23 190 A3
KUT * KT1 221 F1
LEW * SE13 171 G3
RCHPK/HAM TW10 161 G6
Hermitage Wk SWFD E18 92 B1
Hermitage Wall WAP E1W 25 F2
Hermitage Wy STAN HA7 60 C4
Hermit Rd CAN/RD E16 132 B3
Hermit St FSBYE EC1V 6 C3
Hermon Hl WAN E11 92 C1
Herndon Rd WAND/EARL SW18 165 G6
Herne Cl WLSDN NW10 102 D3
Herne Ct BUSH * WD23 43 G3
Herne Hl HNHL SE24 168 C6
Herne Hill Rd HNHL SE24 168 C4
Herne Ms UED N18 53 G6
Herne Pl HNHL SE24 188 B1
Herne Rd BUSH WD23 43 F1
SURB KT6 221 F6
Heron Cl BKHH IG9 56 C3
WALTH E17 70 D5
WLSDN NW10 103 E4
Heron Ct HAYES BR2 233 E1
KUT * KT1 201 G6
Heron Crs SCUP DA14 195 E6
Herondale SAND/SEL CR2 248 B6
Herondale Av
WAND/EARL SW18 185 H3
Heron Dr FSBYPK N4 88 C6
Herongate Rd MNPK E12 93 E6
Heron Hl BELV DA17 156 D4
Heron Md PEND EN3 41 E1
Heron Ms IL IG1 94 B6
Heron Quays POP/IOD E14 151 E1
Heron Rd CROY/NA * CR0 229 E5
HNHL SE24 168 C5
TWK TW1 160 C5
Heronsforde WEA W13 121 E5
Heronsgate EDGW HA8 62 A1
Herons Lea HGT * N6 86 B3
Heronslea Dr STAN HA7 61 G1
Herons Pl ISLW TW7 160 D4
Herons Ri EBAR EN4 36 A5
Herrick Rd FSBYPK N4 108 C1
Herrick St WEST SW1P 28 D2
Herries St NKENS W10 124 C1
Herringham Rd CHARL SE7 153 E3
Herrongate Cl EN EN1 39 E3
Hersant Cl WLSDN NW10 103 G6
Herschell Rd FSTH SE23 190 B2
Hersham Cl PUT/ROE SW15 183 G2
Hershell Ct
MORT/ESHN * SW14 162 B5
Hertford Av MORT/ESHN SW14 162 D6
Hertford Cl EBAR EN4 35 H4
Hertford Ct STAN * HA7 61 F3
Hertford Rd BARK IG11 114 B5
EBAR EN4 35 G4
ED N9 53 H3
EFNCH N2 66 A6
GNTH/NBYPK IG2 95 E3
IS N1 109 E5
PEND EN3 40 A1
PEND EN3 40 A3
Hertford Rd High St
PEND * EN3 40 A5
Hertford St MYFR/PICC W1J 19 G1
Hertford Wy MTCM CR4 227 G1
Hertslet Rd HOLWY N7 107 H1
Hertsmere Rd POP/IOD E14 131 E6
Hertswood Ct BAR * EN5 34 C5
Hervey Cl FNCH N3 65 E4
Hervey Park Rd WALTH E17 90 C1
Hesewall Cl VX/NE SW8 167 E3
Hesketh Pl NTGHL W11 124 C6
Hesketh Rd FSTGT E7 112 C1
Heslop Rd BAL SW12 186 B3
Hesper Ms ECT SW5 145 F5
Hesperus Crs POP/IOD E14 151 F4
Hessel Rd WEA W13 140 C2
Hessel St WCHPL E1 17 G4
Hestercombe Av FUL/PGN SW6 164 C3
Hesterman Wy CROY/NA CR0 227 G5
Hester Rd BTSEA SW11 166 A1
UED N18 69 G1
Hester Ter RCH/KEW TW9 162 A4
Heston Av HEST TW5 158 C1
Heston Grange La HEST TW5 138 D6
Heston Rd HEST TW5 159 E1
Heston St DEPT SE8 170 D2
Hetherington Rd CLAP SW4 167 G5
Hetley Rd SHB W12 143 H1
Heton Gdns HDN NW4 83 G1
Hevelius Cl GNWCH SE10 152 B5
Hever Cft ELTH/MOT SE9 194 A6
Hever Gdns BMLY BR1 214 A5
Heverham Rd WOOL/PLUM SE18 155 E4
Heversham Rd BXLYHN DA7 177 E3
Hewer St NKENS W10 124 B4
Hewett Cl STAN HA7 44 D6
Hewett Pl SWLY BR8 237 H1
Hewett St SDTCH EC2A 8 B6
Hewish Rd UED N18 53 E6
Hewison St BOW E3 130 D1
Hewitt Av WDGN N22 68 B5
Hewitt Cl CROY/NA CR0 249 E1
Hewitt Rd CEND/HSY/T N8 88 A2
Hewlett Rd BOW E3 130 C1
The Hexagon HGT N6 86 B5
Hexal Rd CAT SE6 192 A5
Hexham Gdns ISLW TW7 160 C1
Hexham Rd BAR EN5 35 F5
MRDN SM4 225 F5
WNWD SE27 188 C4
Heybourne Rd TOTM N17 69 H3
Heybridge Av
STRHM/NOR SW16 207 H2
Heybridge Dr BARK/HLT IG6 74 D6
Heybridge Wy LEY E10 90 C4
Heyford Av RYNPK SW20 204 D6
VX/NE SW8 167 G1
Heyford Rd MTCM CR4 206 A5
Heyford Ter VX/NE SW8 167 G1
Heygate Est WALW SE17 31 F1
Heygate St WALW SE17 31 E2
Heynes Rd BCTR RM8 116 A2
Heysham Dr OXHEY WD19 58 A1
Heysham La HAMP NW3 105 F1
Heysham Rd SEVS/STOTM N15 88 D3
Heythorp St WAND/EARL SW18 184 D3
Heywood Av CDALE/KGS NW9 63 E4
Heyworth Rd CLPT E5 109 H2
FSTGT E7 112 B3
Hibbert Rd KTN/HRWW/W HA3 60 B5
WALTH E17 90 D4
Hibbert St BTSEA SW11 165 G4
Hibbs Cl SWLY BR8 217 H5
Hibernia Gdns HSLW TW3 159 E6
Hibernia Rd HSLW TW3 159 E5
Hichisson Rd PECK SE15 170 A6
Hickin Cl CHARL SE7 153 F4
Hickin St POP/IOD E14 151 G3
Hickling Rd IL IG1 114 B3
Hickman Av CHING E4 71 G2
Hickman Cl CAN/RD E16 133 F4
Hickman Rd CHDH RM6 96 A4
Hicks Av GFD/PVL UB6 119 H2
Hicks Cl BTSEA SW11 166 A4
Hicks St DEPT SE8 150 C5
Hidcote Gdns RYNPK SW20 203 H6

Hide Pl WEST SW1P ...28 C2
Higham Rd HRW HA1 ...79 H1
Higham Hill Rd WALTH E17 ...70 D6
Higham Pl WALTH E17 ...70 C6
Higham Rd TOTM N17 ...68 D6
   WFD IG8 ...72 C2
Higham Station Av CHING E4 ...71 A2
The Highams WALTH E17 ...71 G4
Higham St WALTH E17 ...70 C5
Highbank Pl
   WAND/EARL * SW18 ...185 F2
Highbanks Cl WELL DA16 ...175 C1
Highbanks Rd PIN HA5 ...59 F2
Highbank Wy CEND/HSY/T N8 ...88 A3
Highbarrow Rd CROY/NA CRO ...229 F5
High Beech SAND/SEL CR2 ...247 E5
High Beeches ORP BR6 ...245 C1
   SCUP DA14 ...216 C1
Highbridge Rd BARK IG11 ...114 B6
Highbrook Rd BKHTH/KID SE3 ...173 F4
High Broom Ct WWKM BR4 ...231 F4
Highbury Av THHTH CR7 ...208 A5
Highbury Cl NWMAL KT3 ...222 C1
   WWKM BR4 ...231 F6
Highbury Cnr HBRY * N5 ...108 B4
Highbury Crs HBRY N5 ...108 B3
Highbury Est HBRY N5 ...108 C5
Highbury Gdns IL IG1 ...95 E6
Highbury Gra HBRY N5 ...108 B2
Highbury Gv HBRY N5 ...108 B3
Highbury Hl HBRY N5 ...108 B4
Highbury New Pk HBRY N5 ...108 C3
Highbury Pk HBRY N5 ...108 B2
Highbury Pl HBRY N5 ...108 B4
Highbury Qd HBRY N5 ...108 C1
Highbury Rd WIM/MER SW19 ...204 C1
Highbury Station Pde IS * N1 ...108 B4
Highbury Station Rd IS * N1 ...108 A3
Highbury Ter HBRY N5 ...108 B3
Highbury Terrace Ms HBRY N5 ...108 B3
High Cedar Dr RYNPK SW20 ...203 H3
Highclere Rd NWMAL KT3 ...202 D6
Highclere St SYD SE26 ...190 C6
Highcliffe Dr PUT/ROE SW15 ...183 F1
Highcliffe Gdns REDBR IG4 ...93 G2
Highcombe CHARL SE7 ...152 D6
Highcombe Cl ELTH/MOT SE9 ...193 F3
High Coombe Pl
   KUTN/CMB KT2 ...202 D3
Highcroft CDALE/KGS NW9 ...83 E2
Highcroft Av ALP/SUD HA0 ...101 H5
Highcroft Gdns GLDGN NW11 ...84 D3
Highcroft Rd ARCH N19 ...67 G4
High Cross Rd SEVS/STOTM N15 ...69 G6
Highdaun Dr
   STRHM/NOR SW16 ...207 H1
Highdown WPK KT4 ...223 E6
Highdown Rd PUT/ROE SW15 ...185 H1
High Dr NWMAL KT3 ...202 C4
High Elms WFD IG8 ...72 C1
High Elms Rd ORP BR6 ...252 C6
Highfield OXHEY WD19 ...42 D5
Highfield Av CDALE/KGS NW9 ...82 C2
   ERITH DA8 ...157 F6
   GFD/PVL UB6 ...100 A3
   GLDGN NW11 ...84 B4
   ORP BR6 ...253 F4
   PIN HA5 ...78 D2
   WBLY HA9 ...101 C1
Highfield Cl CDALE/KGS NW9 ...82 C2
   CRW RM5 ...77 C2
   LEW SE13 ...191 H1
   SURB KT6 ...221 E5
   WDGN N22 ...68 A4
Highfield Ct STHGT/OAK N14 ...51 F1
   HOR/WEW KT19 ...241 F5
   MLHL NW7 ...31 E4
Highfield Dr HAYES BR2 ...249 F1
   HOR/WEW KT19 ...241 F5
Highfield Gdns GLDGN NW11 ...84 C3
Highfield Hl NRWD SE19 ...208 D3
Highfield Link CRW RM5 ...77 C2
Highfield Rd ACT W3 ...122 B4
   BMLY BR1 ...233 H1
   BRYLDS KT5 ...222 C4
   BXLYHS DA6 ...176 D6
   CRW RM5 ...77 C2
   GLDGN * NW11 ...84 C3
   ISLW TW7 ...160 B2
   STMC/STPC BR5 ...215 F6
   SUT SM1 ...244 A3
   WFD IG8 ...73 G3
Highfields Gv HGT N6 ...84 C1
High Foleys ESH/CLAY KT10 ...238 D5
Highgate Av HGT N6 ...66 B4
Highgate Cl HGT N6 ...66 A4
Highgate Edge EFNCH * N2 ...66 A2
Highgate High St HGT N6 ...86 A2
Highgate Hl ARCH N19 ...66 D5
Highgate Rd KTTN NW5 ...106 C1
Highgate Spinney
   CEND/HSY/T * N8 ...87 F3
Highgate West Hl HGT N6 ...66 B5
High Gv BMLY BR1 ...213 E4
   WOOL/PLUM SE18 ...174 D1
Highgrove Cl CHST BR7 ...213 G4
   FBAR/BDGN N11 ...66 C1
Highgrove Ms CAR SM5 ...244 A1
Highgrove Rd BCTR RM8 ...116 A3
High Hill Ferry CLPT E5 ...89 H5
High Holborn HHOL WC1V ...113 F3
Highland Av DACE RM10 ...117 C1
   HNWL W7 ...120 A3
   LOU IG10 ...57 H1
Highland Cottages
   WLGTN * SM6 ...244 D2
Highland Cft BECK BR3 ...211 F1
Highland Dr BUSH WD23 ...43 F1
Highland Rd BMLY BR1 ...212 B4
   BXLYHS DA6 ...176 D1
   NRWD SE19 ...209 E2
Highlands OXHEY WD19 ...42 A3
Highlands Av ACT W3 ...122 C6
   WCHMH N21 ...50 D1
Highlands Cl HSLW TW3 ...159 F2
Highlands Gdns IL IG1 ...93 H5
Highlands Rd BAR EN5 ...35 E5
   STMC/STPC BR5 ...235 H4
The Highlands BAR * EN5 ...35 F5
   EDGW HA8 ...62 B5
Highland Ter LEW * SE13 ...171 F4

High La HNWL W7 ...119 H5
Highlea Cl CDALE/KGS NW9 ...63 E4
High Level Dr SYD SE26 ...189 C6
Highlever Rd NKENS W10 ...124 A4
High Limes NRWD * SE19 ...209 E2
High Md HRW HA1 ...80 A2
Highmead WOOL/PLUM SE18 ...154 B4
Highmead Crs ALP/SUD HA0 ...101 H5
High Meadow Crs
   CDALE/KGS NW9 ...82 D2
High Mdw CHIG IG7 ...54 D3
High Meads Rd CAN/RD E16 ...133 F6
Highmore Rd BKHTH/KID SE3 ...172 A1
High Mt HDN * NW4 ...83 G3
High Oaks ENC/FH EN2 ...37 H1
The High Pde
   STRHM/NOR * SW16 ...187 D5
High Park Rd RCH/KEW TW9 ...162 A2
High Pth WIM/MER SW19 ...205 H4
High Point ELTH/MOT SE9 ...194 B5
High Rd BKHH IG9 ...66 D4
   BUSH WD23 ...45 H3
   CHDH RM6 ...96 D3
   FBAR/BDGN N11 ...66 D1
   FNCH N3 ...65 C4
   IL IG1 ...114 B1
   KTN/HRWW/W HA3 ...60 A3
   LEY E10 ...91 F3
   SEVS/STOTM N15 ...89 F2
   TOTM N17 ...68 C4
   TRDG/WHET N20 ...49 C2
   WBLY HA9 ...101 C3
   WDGN N22 ...68 A6
High Rd Eastcote PIN HA5 ...78 A1
High Rd Great North Rd
   EFNCH N2 ...65 H5
High Rd Leytonstone WAN E11 ...112 A1
High Rd Woodford Gn WFD IG8 ...56 C6
   WFD IG8 ...72 B4
Highshore Rd PECK SE15 ...169 F3
Highstone Av WAN E11 ...92 C3
High St ACT W3 ...142 C1
   BAR EN5 ...34 D5
   BARK/HLT IG6 ...74 C6
   BECK BR3 ...76 A4
   BELMT SM2 ...243 C5
   BMLY BR1 ...212 C6
   BORE WD6 ...45 F1
   BTFD TW8 ...141 H6
   BUSH WD23 ...45 G2
   CAR SM5 ...244 B5
   CEND/HSY/T N8 ...87 C1
   CHEAM SM3 ...242 C4
   CROY/NA CRO ...196 C6
   E/WMO/HCT KT8 ...219 E1
   EA W5 ...121 F6
   ESH/CLAY KT10 ...238 B4
   HPTN TW12 ...199 F4
   HRW HA1 ...80 A6
   HSLW TW3 ...159 F4
   KTN/HRWW/W HA3 ...60 H1
   MLHL NW7 ...63 H1
   NWMAL KT3 ...223 E1
   ORP BR6 ...235 G5
   PGE/AN SE20 ...210 A3
   PIN HA5 ...58 C6
   SCUP DA14 ...195 C6
   SNWD SE25 ...229 F1
   SRTFD E15 ...111 H1
   STHGT/OAK N14 ...51 F3
   STMC/STPC BR5 ...236 A3
   SUT SM1 ...243 F2
   TEDD TW11 ...174 D1
   THDIT KT7 ...220 C3
   THHTH CR7 ...228 C1
   WALTH E17 ...90 D1
   WAN E11 ...91 H2
   WBLY HA9 ...101 H2
   WHTN TW2 ...179 C2
   WIM/MER SW19 ...204 B1
   WWKM BR4 ...231 F5
High St Collier's Wd
   WIM/MER SW19 ...205 H3
High St Harlesden
   WLSDN NW10 ...123 F1
High Street Ms
   WIM/MER SW19 ...204 C1
High St North MNPK E12 ...113 G4
High St South EHAM E6 ...113 J1
High St Timber St BLKFR EC4V ...15 E5
Hi Tor Cl BMLY BR1 ...212 D3
High Trees BRXS/STRHM SW2 ...188 A3
   CROY/NA CRO ...230 C5
   EBAR EN4 ...36 A6
High Vw PIN HA5 ...78 A1
Highview Av EDGW HA8 ...46 C6
High View Av WLGTN SM6 ...245 H4
High View Cl SNWD SE25 ...209 F5
Highview Gdns EDGW HA8 ...62 C1
   FBAR/BDGN N11 ...67 E1
   FNCH N3 ...64 C6
High View Gv RD NRWD SE19 ...208 D8
   SWFD E18 ...72 B5
Highview Rd SCUP DA14 ...195 H1
   WEA W13 ...120 C5
The Highway BELMT SM2 ...243 H6
   ORP BR6 ...253 H3
   STAN HA7 ...60 B4
   WCHPL E1 ...17 C6

Hilborough Rd HACK E8 ...109 F5
Hilborough Wy ORP BR6 ...252 D3
Hilda Rd CAN/RD E16 ...132 A3
   EHAM E6 ...113 H5
Hilda Ter BRXN/ST * SW9 ...168 A3
Hilda Vale Rd ORP BR6 ...252 A2
Hildenborough Gdns
   BMLY BR1 ...212 A2
Hildenlea Pl HAYES BR2 ...212 A5
Hildreth St BAL SW12 ...186 D3
Hildyard Rd FUL/PGN SW6 ...145 E6
Hiley Rd WLSDN NW10 ...124 A2
Hilgrove Rd KIL/WHAMP NW6 ...105 C5
Hiliary Gdns STAN HA7 ...61 E5
Hillary Crs WOT/HER KT12 ...218 A5
Hillary Dr ISLW TW7 ...160 B5
Hillary Ri BAR EN5 ...35 E5
Hillary Rd NWDGN UB2 ...139 E3
Hillbeck Cl PECK SE15 ...170 A1
Hillbeck Wy GFD/PVL UB6 ...99 H6
Hillborough Cl
   WIM/MER * SW19 ...205 G3
Hillbrook Rd TOOT SW17 ...186 B5
Hill Brow BMLY BR1 ...213 F4
Hillbrow NWMAL KT3 ...203 F6
Hillbrow Cl BXLY DA5 ...197 H6
Hillbrow Rd BMLY BR1 ...212 A3
   ESH/CLAY KT10 ...238 D4
Hillbury Av KTN/HRWW/W HA3 ...80 D2
Hillbury Rd TOOT SW17 ...186 D5
Hill Cl BAR EN5 ...34 A6
   CHST BR7 ...214 B1
   CRICK NW2 ...103 H1
   GLDGN NW11 ...85 E3
   HRW HA1 ...100 A1
   STAN HA7 ...44 B1
Hilcote Av STRHM/NOR SW16 ...208 A3
Hillcourt Av NFNCH/WDSP N12 ...65 F2
Hillcourt Rd EDUL SE22 ...189 H1
Hill Crs BRYLDS KT5 ...221 H2
   BXLY DA5 ...197 G3
   HRW HA1 ...80 C2
   TRDG/WHET N20 ...49 F4
   WPK KT4 ...208 D1
Hill Crest BFN/LL DA15 ...195 C2
   SURB * KT6 ...221 G4
Hillcrest HGT N6 ...86 C4
   HNHL * SE24 ...168 D5
   WCHMH N21 ...50 A1
Hillcrest Av EDGW HA8 ...46 B6
   GLDGN NW11 ...64 C3
   PIN HA5 ...59 H2
Hillcrest Cl BECK BR3 ...230 D3
   SYD SE26 ...189 G6
Hillcrest Gdns CRICK NW2 ...103 C1
Hillcrest Gdns ESH/CLAY KT10 ...238 B1
   HDN NW4 ...64 A3
Hillcrest Rd ACT W3 ...142 A1
   BMLY BR1 ...192 C6
   EA W5 ...121 G4
   LOU IG10 ...57 G1
   ORP BR6 ...235 G6
   WALTH E17 ...71 H5
Hillcrest Vw BECK BR3 ...230 D3
Hillcroft Crs EA W5 ...121 F5
   RSLP HA4 ...58 B3
   WBLY HA9 ...101 H2
Hillcroft Rd EHAM E6 ...134 D4
Hillcroome Rd BELMT SM2 ...243 G4
Hillcross Av MRDN SM4 ...224 C5
Hilldale Rd SUT SM1 ...242 D2
Hilldown Rd HAYES BR2 ...247 C6
   STRHM/NOR SW16 ...207 G3
Hill Dr CDALE/KGS NW9 ...82 C5
   STRHM/NOR SW16 ...207 H3
Hilldrop Crs HOLWY N7 ...107 F3
Hilldrop Est HOLWY N7 ...107 F3
Hilldrop La HOLWY N7 ...107 F3
Hilldrop Rd BMLY BR1 ...212 D2
   HOLWY N7 ...107 F3
Hill End ORP BR6 ...235 E6
   WOOL/PLUM SE18 ...174 A2
Hillersdon Av BARN SW13 ...163 G3
   EDGW HA8 ...46 B6
Hillery Cl WALW SE17 ...31 H2
Hill Farm Rd NKENS W10 ...124 A4
Hillfield Av ALP/SUD HA0 ...101 G5
   CDALE/KGS NW9 ...83 E2
   CEND/HSY/T N8 ...87 H1
   MRDN SM4 ...226 A3
Hillfield Cl RYLN/HDSTN HA2 ...79 C1
Hillfield La South BUSH WD23 ...44 A1
Hillfield Pde MRDN * SM4 ...225 H5
Hillfield Pk MUSWH N10 ...66 D6
   WCHMH N21 ...50 H1
Hillfield Park Ms MUSWH N10 ...86 D1
Hillfield Rd HPTN TW12 ...198 D3
   KIL/WHAMP NW6 ...104 D3
Hillfoot Av CRW RM5 ...77 G4
Hillfoot Rd CRW RM5 ...77 G4
Hillgate Pl BAL SW12 ...186 D1
   KENS W8 ...145 E1
Hillgate St KENS * W8 ...145 E1
Hill Gv FELT TW13 ...178 D4
Hill House Av STAN HA7 ...43 F3
Hill House Cl WCHMH N21 ...52 A2
Hill House Drive HPTN TW12 ...199 E4
Hill House Rd
   STRHM/NOR SW16 ...207 H1
Hilliard's Ct WAP E1W ...150 A1
Hillier Cl BAR EN5 ...34 D1
Hillier Gdns CROY/NA CRO ...246 A3
Hillier Pl CHSGTN KT9 ...239 F4
Hillier Rd BTSEA SW11 ...186 B1
Hilliers La CROY/NA CRO ...245 G1
Hillingdon Rd BXLYHN DA7 ...177 G4
Hillingdon St WALW SE17 ...30 C6
Hillington Gdns WFD IG8 ...73 H1
Hillman Dr NKENS W10 ...124 A4
Hillman St HACK E8 ...109 H4
Hillmarton Rd HOLWY N7 ...107 G3
Hillmarton Ter HOLWY * N7 ...107 G3
Hillmead Dr BRXN/ST SW9 ...168 B5
Hillmont Rd ESH/CLAY KT10 ...238 A1
Hillmore Gv SYD SE26 ...210 B1
Hillreach WOOL/PLUM SE18 ...153 H5
Hill Ri ED N9 ...36 D1
   ESH/CLAY KT10 ...220 D6
   GFD/PVL UB6 ...85 F1
   GLDGN NW11 ...65 F3
   RCHPK/HAM TW10 ...161 F6
Hillrise Rd ARCH N19 ...67 G4

CRW RM5 ...77 G2
Hill Rd CAR SM5 ...244 A4
   HRW HA1 ...80 C2
   HRW HA1 ...100 D1
   MTCM CR4 ...206 D4
   MUSWH N10 ...66 B4
   PIN HA5 ...59 H1
   STJWD NW8 ...125 C1
   SUT SM1 ...243 F3
Hillsboro Rd EDUL SE22 ...169 E6
Hillsgrove Cl WELL DA16 ...176 A1
Hill Side BAR EN5 ...35 G6
Hillside CDALE/KGS NW9 ...82 D1
   WIM/MER SW19 ...204 B2
   WLSDN NW10 ...102 C1
Hillside Av FBAR/BDGN N11 ...66 B2
   WBLY HA9 ...101 H2
   WFD IG8 ...73 E1
Hillside Cl KIL/WHAMP NW6 ...125 F1
   MRDN SM4 ...224 C1
   WFD IG8 ...73 E1
Hillside Crs ENC/FH EN2 ...38 D1
   OXHEY WD19 ...42 B1
   RYLN/HDSTN HA2 ...79 C1
Hillside Dr EDGW HA8 ...62 A2
Hillside Gdns BAR EN5 ...34 C5
   BRXS/STRHM * SW2 ...188 A4
   EDGW HA8 ...46 B5
   FBAR/BDGN * N11 ...67 E2
   HGT N6 ...86 C5
   KTN/HRWW/W HA3 ...81 C4
   WLGTN SM6 ...245 E5
Hillside Gv MLHL NW7 ...63 C5
   STHGT/OAK N14 ...51 F2
Hillside La HAYES BR2 ...232 C6
Hillside Rd BELMT SM2 ...243 C5
   BRXS/STRHM SW2 ...187 H4
   CROY/NA CRO ...244 A6
   EA W5 ...121 G4
   HAYES BR2 ...232 C6
   SEVS/STOTM N15 ...89 E3
   STHL UB1 ...119 E3
The Hillside ORP BR6 ...253 H6
Hillsleigh Rd KENS W8 ...144 D1
Hills Ms EA * W5 ...121 G6
Hills Pl SOHO/CST W1F ...12 A4
Hill St BKHH IG9 ...56 D3
Hillstowe St CLPT E5 ...90 A6
Hill St MYFR/PICC W1J ...19 C1
Hill Top GLDGN NW11 ...85 F1
   MRDN SM4 ...224 D4
Hilltop WALTH * E17 ...71 F6
Hilltop Cottages SYD * SE26 ...189 H6
Hilltop Gdns ORP BR6 ...235 E6
Hilltop Rd KIL/WHAMP NW6 ...105 E5
Hill Top Vw WFD * IG8 ...73 H1
Hilltop Wy STAN HA7 ...44 C5
Hillview RYNPK SW20 ...203 H4
Hillview Av KTN/HRWW/W HA3 ...81 G2
Hillview Cl PIN HA5 ...59 H5
Hill View Crs IL IG1 ...98 B1
Hillview Crs ORP BR6 ...235 E5
Hill View Dr WELL DA16 ...175 E3
Hill View Gdns CDALE/KGS NW9 ...82 D2
Hillview Gdns HDN NW4 ...64 B1
   PIN HA5 ...59 E6
Hill View Rd ESH/CLAY KT10 ...238 C5
   ORP BR6 ...235 F5
   TWK TW1 ...160 C1
Hillview Rd CHST BR7 ...214 A1
   MLHL NW7 ...48 B6
   PIN HA5 ...59 H5
   SUT SM1 ...243 G1
Hillway CDALE/KGS NW9 ...83 E5
   HGT N6 ...86 A4
Hillworth BECK * BR3 ...211 F5
Hillworth Rd
   BRXS/STRHM SW2 ...188 A2
Hillyard Rd HNWL W7 ...120 A4
Hillyard St BRXN/ST SW9 ...168 A3
Hillyfield WALTH E17 ...70 C5
Hillyfield Cl HOM E9 ...75 C5
Hilly Fields BROCKY SE4 ...171 E5
Hilsea St CLPT E5 ...110 A2
Hilton Av NFNCH/WDSP N12 ...65 H1
Himley Rd TOOT SW17 ...206 D1
Hinchley Cl ESH/CLAY KT10 ...238 B1
Hinchley Dr ESH/CLAY KT10 ...238 B1
Hinchley Wy ESH/CLAY KT10 ...238 C1
Hinckley Rd EDUL SE22 ...169 G5
Hind Cl CHIG IG7 ...75 F1
Hind Ct FLST/FETLN * EC4A ...14 B4
Hind Crs ERITH DA8 ...157 H1
Hinde Ms MHST * W1U ...11 F3
Hindes Rd HRW HA1 ...80 D1
Hinde St MHST W1U ...11 F3
Hind Gv POP/IOD E14 ...131 E5
Hindhead Cl NTHLT UB5 ......
Hindhead Gdns NTHLT UB5 ...95 J1
Hindhead Wy WLGTN SM6 ...245 G3
Hindmans Rd EDUL SE22 ...169 G3
Hindmans Wy DAGW RM9 ...137 H5
Hindmarsh Cl WCHPL E1 ...17 H5
Hindrey Rd CLPT E5 ...90 D5
Hindsley's Pl FSTH SE23 ...190 D1
Hinkler Rd KTN/HRWW/W HA3 ...62 A6
Hinstock Rd WOOL/PLUM SE18 ...174 D1
Hinton Av HSLW TW4 ...158 B3
Hinton Cl ELTH/MOT SE9 ...193 G5
Hinton Rd BRXN/ST SW9 ...168 A4
   ED N9 ...36 D3
   WLGTN SM6 ...245 E6
Hippodrome Pl NTGHL W11 ...124 C6
Hitcham Rd WALTH E17 ...69 H4
Hither Farm Rd
   BKHTH/KID SE3 ...173 E3
Hitherfield Rd BCTR RM8 ...92 C6
   STRHM/NOR SW16 ...188 A3
Hither Green La LEW SE13 ...171 G4
Hitherwell Dr KTN/HRWW/W HA3 ......
Hitherwood Dr DUL SE21 ...189 H4
Hive Rd BUSH WD23 ...43 H4
Hoadly Rd STRHM/NOR SW16 ...187 J3
Hobart Cl TRDG/WHET N20 ...49 H2
   YEAD UB4 ......
Hobart Dr YEAD UB4 ...118 ...
Hobart Gdns THHTH CR7 ...208 D2
Hobart La YEAD UB4 ...118 ...

Hobart Pl BGVA SW1W 19 C6
RCHPK/HAM TW10 .....181 H2
Hobart Rd BARK/HLT IG6 .....74 C5
DAGW RM9 .....116 B2
WPK KT4 .....241 H1
YEAD UB4 .....118 B3
Hobbayne Rd HNWL W7 .....119 H5
Hobbes Wk PUT/ROE SW15 .....163 H6
Hobbs Gn FNCH N3 .....65 C6
Hobbs Pl IS * N1 .....109 E6
Hobbs Place Est IS N1 .....8 A1
Hobbs Rd WNWD SE27 .....188 C6
Hobday St POP/IOD E14 .....131 F5
Hoblands End CHST BR7 .....215 G2
Hobsons Pl WCHPL E1 .....17 E1
Hobury St WBPTN SW10 .....145 G6
Hockenden La SWLY BR8 .....217 E6
Hocker St BETH * E2 .....8 C4
Hockley Av EHAM E6 .....133 C1
Hockley Ms BARK IG11 .....135 E1
Hocroft Av CRICK NW2 .....104 D1
Hocroft Rd CRICK NW2 .....104 D2
Hocroft Wk CRICK NW2 .....104 D1
Hodder Dr GFD/PVL UB6 .....120 B1
Hoddesdon Rd BELV DA17 .....157 H5
Hodford Rd GLDGN NW11 .....84 D5
Hodgkins Cl THMD SE28 .....136 B6
Hodister Cl CMBW SE5 .....110 C6
Hodson Cl RYLN/HDSTN HA2 .....98 D1
Hodson Crs STMC/STPC BR5 .....236 B3
Hodson Pl WAB * EN9 .....41 E1
Hoe La EN EN1 .....39 H1
The Hoe WALTH E17 .....42 B4
Hoe St WALTH E17 .....91 E2
The Hoe WDI9 .....42 B4
Hoffman Sq IS * N1 .....7 H3
Hofland Rd WKENS W14 .....144 C1
Hogarth Cl CAN/RD E16 .....133 F4
EA W5 .....121 G4
Hogarth Crs CROY/NA CRO 228 C4
WIM/MER SW19 .....205 H4
Hogarth Gdns HEST TW5 .....159 E1
Hogarth Hl GLDGN NW11 .....84 D1
Hogarth Pl ECT * SW5 .....145 F4
Hogarth Rd BCTR RM8 .....115 F4
ECT SW5 .....145 F4
EDGW HA8 .....62 A5
Hogarth Ter CHSWK * W4 .....143 E6
Hogarth Wy HPTN TW12 .....199 C4
Hog Hill Rd CRW RM5 .....76 D3
Hogshead Pas WAP * E1W 17 C6
Hogsmill Wy HOR/WEW KT19 .....240 C3
Holbeach Gdns BFN/LL DA15 .....195 C1
Holbeach Rd CAT SE6 .....191 E2
Holbeck Rw PECK SE15 .....169 G6
Holbein Ms BGVA SW1W 27 E5
Holbein Pl BGVA SW1W 27 F5
Holberton Gdns WLSDN NW10 .....123 H2
Holborn HCIRC EC1N 14 A2
Holborn Circ HCIRC EC1N 14 B2
Holborn Pl HHOL WC1V 13 C2
Holborn Viad STBT EC1A 14 C3
Holborn Wy MTCM CR4 .....206 B5
Holbrook Cl EN EN1 .....39 F2
Holbrooke Ct HOLWY N7 .....107 C1
Holbrook La CHST BR7 .....214 D5
Holbrook Rd SRTFD E15 .....132 B1
Holbrook Wy HAYES BR2 .....233 H1
Holburne Cl BKHTH/KID SE3 .....173 F2
Holburne Gdns BKHTH/KID SE3 .....175 F2
Holburne Rd BKHTH/KID SE3 .....175 F2
Holcombe Hl MLHL NW7 .....47 G5
Holcombe Rd TOTM N17 .....68 A3
Holcombe St HMSMTH W6 .....143 H5
Holcote Cl BELV DA17 .....156 C5
Holcroft Rd HOM E9 .....110 A5
Holden Av CDALE/KGS NW9 .....62 D3
NFNCH/WDSP N12 .....65 F1
Holdenby Rd BROCKY SE4 .....190 C1
Holden Cl BCTR RM8 .....115 H1
Holdenhurst Av FNCH N3 .....65 E1
Holden Point SRTFD/WDSP N12 .....49 F6
Holden St BTSEA SW11 .....166 C3
Holderness Rd ISLW TW7 .....160 C2
TOOT SW17 .....186 B5
Holderness Wy WNWD SE27 .....208 B1
Holders Hill Av HDN NW4 .....64 B6
Holders Hill Crs HDN NW4 .....64 B6
Holders Hill Dr HDN NW4 .....64 B5
Holders Hill Gdns HDN NW4 .....64 C4
Holders Hill Pde HDN * NW4 .....64 C4
Holders Hill Rd HDN NW4 .....64 B5
Holford Ms FSBYW * WC1X 5 G3
Holford Rd HAMP NW3 .....105 G1
Holford St FSBYW WC1X 6 A3
Holford Yd FSBYW * WC1X 6 A2
Holgate Av BTSEA SW11 .....165 H4
Holgate Gdns DAGE RM10 .....117 E3
Holgate St CHARL SE7 .....153 F3
Holland Av BELMT SM2 .....243 G5
RYNPK SW20 .....203 H4
Holland Cl BAR EN5 .....49 H2
HAYES BR2 .....232 B6
ROMW/RG RM7 .....97 C2
STAN HA7 .....201 D1
Holland Dr FSTH SE23 .....190 C5
Holland Gdns WKENS W14 .....144 C3
Holland Gv BRXN/ST SW9 .....168 A1
Holland Pk KENS W8 .....144 D2
Holland Park Av
GDMY/SEVK IG3 .....95 E3
WKENS W14 .....144 C1
Holland Park Gdns
WKENS W14 .....144 C1
Holland Park Ms NTGHL W11 .....144 C1
Holland Park Rd WKENS W14 .....144 D3
Holland Park Ter NTGHL * W11 .....144 C1
Holland Pas IS * N1 .....7 G1
Holland Pl KENS * W8 .....145 D2
Holland Place Chambers
KENS * W8 .....145 D2
Holland Rd ALP/SUD HA0 .....101 F4
EHAM E6 .....113 H6
SNWD SE25 .....229 G2
SRTFD E15 .....132 A2
WLSDN NW10 .....103 G6
The Hollands WPK KT4 .....225 F5
Holland St KENS W8 .....145 D1
STHWK SE1 .....22 D1
Holland Villas Rd WKENS W14 .....144 C2

Holland Wk STAN HA7 .....60 C1
Holland Wy HAYES BR2 .....232 B6
Hollar Rd STNW/STAM N16 .....109 F1
Hollen St SOHO/CST W1F 12 D4
Holles Cl HPTN TW12 .....199 E2
Holles St CAVSQ/HST W1G 11 H3
Holley Rd ACT W3 .....143 E2
Hollickwood Av
NFNCH/WDSP N12 .....66 D2
Holliday Sq BTSEA SW11 .....165 H4
Holliday Wy DAGE RM10 .....117 C4
Hollies Av BFN/LL DA15 .....195 F1
Hollies Cl STRHM/NOR SW16 .....208 A2
TWK TW1 .....180 B4
Hollies End MLHL NW7 .....63 H1
Hollies Rd EA W5 .....141 E4
The Hollies KTN/HRWW/W HA3 .....80 C1
Hollies Wy BAL * SW12 .....186 C2
Holligrave Rd BMLY BR1 .....212 C4
Hollingbourne Av BXLYHN DA7 .....176 D2
Hollingbourne Gdns WEA W13 .....120 D4
Hollingbourne Rd HNHL SE24 .....168 C6
Hollingsworth Rd
SAND/SEL CR2 .....247 H4
Hollington Crs NWMAL KT3 .....225 F3
Hollington Rd EHAM E6 .....133 H2
TOTM N17 .....68 C1
Hollingworth Cl
E/WMO/HCT KT8 .....218 D1
Hollingworth Rd
STMC/STPC BR5 .....234 B4
Hollman Gdns
STRHM/NOR SW16 .....208 B2
Holloway Rd ARCH N19 .....87 F6
EHAM E6 .....133 H2
HOLWY N7 .....108 A3
WAN E11 .....111 H1
Holloway St HSLW TW3 .....159 F4
The Hollow WFD IG8 .....56 B6
Holly Av STAN HA7 .....61 G5
WOT/HER KT12 .....218 B5
Holly Bank MUSWH * N10 .....87 E1
Hollybank Cl HPTN TW12 .....199 E1
Hollybrake Cl CHST BR7 .....214 D5
Hollybush Cl OXHEY WD19 .....33 G2
WAN E11 .....92 C2
Hollybush Gdns BETH E2 .....92 D2
Hollybush Hl WAN E11 .....92 B4
Holly Bush La HPTN TW12 .....198 D5
Hollybush Pl BETH E2 .....92 D2
Hollybush Rd KUTN/CMB KT2 .....201 C1
Hollybush St PLSTW E13 .....132 D2
Hollybush Ter NRWD * SE19 .....208 E2
Holly Bush V HAMP * NW3 .....105 G2
Holly Cl BECK BR3 .....231 G1
BKHH IG9 .....57 F5
FELT TW13 .....198 C1
WLSDN NW10 .....105 E5
Holly Crs BECK BR3 .....230 D2
WFD IG8 .....71 H5
Hollycroft Av HAMP NW3 .....105 E6
WBLY HA9 .....81 C1
Hollycroft Cl SAND/SEL CR2 .....247 E5
Hollydale Cl NTHLT UB5 .....99 F3
Hollydale Dr HAYES BR2 .....251 H1
Hollydale Rd PECK SE15 .....170 A3
Hollydown Wy WAN E11 .....111 H1
Holly Dr CHING E4 .....45 E5
Holly Farm Rd NWDGN UB2 .....138 C5
Hollyfield Av FBAR/BDGN N11 .....66 B1
Hollyfield Rd BRYLDS KT5 .....221 H4
Hollygrove BUSH WD23 .....43 H2
Holly Gv CDALE/KGS NW9 .....62 C4
PECK SE15 .....169 F3
PIN HA5 .....47 K1
Hollygrove Cl HSLWW TW4 .....158 D5
Holly Hedge Ter LEW SE13 .....171 G6
Holly Hl HAMP NW3 .....105 H1
WCHMH N21 .....51 H1
Holly Hill Rd BELV DA17 .....157 F5
Holly Lodge Gdns HCT N6 .....86 B6
Hollymead CAR SM5 .....244 B1
Holly Ms WBPTN SW10 .....145 G5
Holly Mt HAMP * NW3 .....105 G2
Hollymount Cl GNWCH SE10 .....171 G2
Holly Pk FNCH N3 .....64 D6
FSBYPK N4 .....67 E4
Holly Park Gdns FNCH N3 .....65 E6
Holly Park Rd FBAR/BDGN N11 .....66 C1
HNWL W7 .....140 B1
Holly Rd CHSWK * W4 .....142 D4
HPTN TW12 .....199 F5
ORP BR6 .....253 G5
TWK TW1 .....180 B5
Holly St HACK E8 .....109 F5
Hollytree Cl WIM/MER SW19 .....184 B3
Hollytree Pde SCUP * DA14 .....216 A1
Hollyview Cl HDN NW4 .....85 C3
Holly Vw HMSMTH * W6 .....143 H5
Holly Wk HAMP NW3 .....105 G2
Holly Wy MTCM CR4 .....227 E1
Hollywood Ct BORE WD6 .....24 D1
Hollywood Ms WBPTN * SW10 .....145 G6
Hollywood Rd CHING E4 .....43 E4
WBPTN SW10 .....145 G6
Hollywoods CROY/NA CRO 248 D6
Hollywood Wy WFD IG8 .....71 H1
Holman Cl PEND EN3 .....25 E3
Holman Rd BTSEA SW11 .....165 H1
HOR/WEW KT19 .....240 C5

Holmbury Cl BUSH * WD23 .....44 A4
Holme Lacey Rd
LEE/GVPK SE12 .....192 B1
Holme Rd EHAM E6 .....113 G6
Holmes Av MLHL NW7 .....64 C1
WALTH E17 .....70 D6
Holmesdale Av
MORT/ESHN SW14 .....162 B4
Holmesdale Cl SNWD SE25 .....209 F6
Holmesdale Rd CROY/NA CRO 228 D2
HGT N6 .....86 D4
RCH/KEW TW9 .....161 H2
SNWD SE25 .....229 E1
TEDD TW11 .....201 E5
WELL DA16 .....176 B3
Holmesley Rd BROCKY SE4 .....190 C1
Holmes Rd KTTN NW5 .....106 D3
TWK TW1 .....180 B4
Holmes Ter STHWK SE1 .....22 A3
Holme Wy STAN HA7 .....60 B2
Holmewood Gdns
BRXS/STRHM SW2 .....187 H2
Holmewood Rd
BRXS/STRHM SW2 .....187 G2
SNWD SE25 .....209 E6
Holmfield Av HDN NW4 .....84 B2
Holmhurst Rd BELV DA17 .....157 F5
Holmleigh Rd STNW/STAM N16 .....89 E5
Holm Oak Cl WAND/EARL SW18 .....184 D1
Holmshaw Cl SYD SE26 .....190 C6
Holmside Rd BAL SW12 .....186 C1
Holmsley Cl NWMAL KT3 .....223 F3
Holmstall Av EDGW HA8 .....62 C5
Holmstall Pde EDGW * HA8 .....62 C5
Holmwood Cl BELMT SM2 .....242 D6
NTHLT UB5 .....99 F4
RYLN/HDSTN HA2 .....59 G6
Holmwood Gdns FNCH N3 .....65 E5
WLSDN NW10 .....123 F1
Holmwood Gv MLHL NW7 .....62 D1
Holmwood Rd BELMT SM2 .....242 A6
CHSGTN KT9 .....239 G3
GDMY/SEVK IG3 .....96 C5
Holne Cha FNCH N2 .....85 C3
MRDN SM4 .....225 E3
Holness Rd SRTFD E15 .....112 B4
Holroyd Rd ESH/CLAY KT10 .....238 C6
PUT/ROE SW15 .....164 A5
Holstock Rd IL IG1 .....94 C6
Holsworth Cl RYLN/HDSTN HA2 .....79 G2
Holsworthy Sq FSBYW WC1X 5 H6
Holsworthy Wy CHSGTN KT9 .....239 E5
Holt Cl CHIG IG7 .....55 C6
MUSWH N10 .....86 C1
THMD SE28 .....135 H6
Holton St WCHPL E1 .....130 B3
Holt Rd ALP/SUD HA0 .....100 D1
CAN/RD E16 .....153 C1
The Holt BARK/HLT IG6 .....74 C2
MRDN * SM4 .....209 H6
WLGTN SM6 .....245 E2
Holt Wy CHIG IG7 .....75 F1
Holtwhite Av ENC/FH EN2 .....38 C5
Holtwhite's Hl ENC/FH EN2 .....38 A3
Holwell Pl PIN HA5 .....78 C1
Holwood Cl WOT/HER KT12 .....218 A6
Holwood Pl CLAP SW4 .....167 H2
Holwood Park Av ORP BR6 .....251 H2
Holybourne Av PUT/ROE SW15 .....183 G2
Holyhead Cl BOW E3 .....131 E2
Holyoake Ct BERM/RHTH SE16 .....150 C2
Holyoake Wk EA W5 .....121 E3
FNCH N2 .....65 G3
Holyoak Rd LBTH SE11 .....30 C1
Holyport Rd FUL/PGN SW6 .....164 A1
Holyrood Av RYLN/HDSTN HA2 .....98 C2
Holyrood Gdns EDGW HA8 .....62 B5
Holyrood Rd BAR EN5 .....49 G1
Holyrood St STHWK SE1 .....24 A3
Holywell Cl BERM/RHTH SE16 .....33 H4
BKHTH/KID SE3 .....152 C6
Holywell La SDTCH EC2A 8 B3
Holywell Rw SDTCH EC2A 8 A4
Home Cl CAR SM5 .....226 B6
NTHLT UB5 .....117 H2
Home Ct SURB * KT6 .....221 F2
Homecroft Rd SYD SE26 .....210 A1
WDGN N22 .....68 D2
Home Farm Cl THDIT KT7 .....220 B4
Home Farm Gdns
WOT/HER KT12 .....218 A6
Homefarm Rd HNWL W7 .....120 A5
Homefield Av GNTH/NBYPK IG2 .....95 E2
Homefield Cl STMC/STPC BR5 .....235 H1
WLSDN NW10 .....102 C4
YEAD UB4 .....118 B3
Homefield Gdns FNCH N2 .....65 H6
WIM/MER SW19 .....205 C5
Homefield Ms BECK * BR3 .....211 E6
Homefield Pk SUT SM1 .....243 F4
Homefield Rl ORP BR6 .....235 G5
Homefield Rd ALP/SUD HA0 .....100 D1
BMLY BR1 .....213 E4
CHSWK W4 .....143 F4
EDGW HA8 .....62 D4
WIM/MER SW19 .....204 C2
WOT/HER KT12 .....218 D4
Homefield St IS * N1 .....7 G2
The Homefield MRDN * SM4 .....225 E1
Home Gdns DAGE RM10 .....117 E1
Homeland Dr BELMT SM2 .....243 F6
Homelands Dr NRWD SE19 .....209 E3
Home Lea ORP BR6 .....253 F3
Homeleigh Rd PECK SE15 .....190 B1
Home Mead BAL SW12 .....61 G4
Homemead Rd CROY/NA CRO 227 C4
HAYES BR2 .....233 H2
Home Park Cl KUT * KT1 .....221 E4
Home Park Rd WIM/MER SW19 .....184 C6
Homer Cl BXLYHN DA7 .....177 G3
Homer Dr POP/IOD E14 .....151 E4
Home Rd BTSEA SW11 .....164 C2
Homer Rd CROY/NA CRO 215 F5
HOM E9 .....110 D4
Homer Rw CAMTN NW1 .....8 E2
Homersham Rd KUT KT1 .....202 A5
Homer St CAMTN NW1 .....8 E2
Homerton Gv HOM E9 .....110 B3
Homerton High St HOM E9 .....110 B3

Homerton Rd HOM E9 .....110 D3
Homerton Rw HOM E9 .....110 A3
Homerton Ter HOM E9 .....110 A4
Homesdale Cl WAN E11 .....92 A2
Homesdale Rd HAYES BR2 .....233 E1
ORP BR6 .....235 E4
Homefield GLDGN NW11 .....85 E2
Homestall Rd EDUL SE22 .....170 A6
Homestead Gdns
ESH/CLAY KT10 .....238 A3
Homestead Paddock
STHGT/OAK N14 .....36 D6
Homestead Pk CRICK NW2 .....103 F1
Homestead Rd BCTR RM8 .....96 D6
FUL/PGN SW6 .....164 D1
ORP BR6 .....253 H5
Homewillow Cl WCHMH N21 .....52 B1
Homewood Cl HPTN TW12 .....198 D2
Homewood Crs CHST BR7 .....215 E2
Homewood Gdns SNWD * SE25 .....229 F3
Honduras St FSBYE EC1V 7 F5
Honeybourne Rd
KIL/WHAMP NW6 .....105 F3
Honeybourne Wy
STMC/STPC BR5 .....234 C5
Honeybrook Rd BAL SW12 .....187 G2
Honey Cl DAGE RM10 .....117 G4
Honeyden Rd SCUP DA14 .....216 C2
Honeyman Cl CRICK NW2 .....104 B5
Honeypot Cl
KTN/HRWW/W HA3 .....81 H1
Honeypot La CDALE/KGS NW9 .....81 H1
KTN/HRWW/W HA3 .....81 H1
Honeysett Rd TOTM N17 .....69 F5
Honeysuckle Cl STHL UB1 .....118 C6
Honeysuckle Gdns
CROY/NA CRO 230 B4
Honeywell Rd BTSEA SW11 .....186 A1
Honeywood Rd ISLW * TW7 .....160 C5
WLSDN NW10 .....123 F1
Honeywood Wk CAR SM5 .....244 B2
Honister Cl STAN HA7 .....60 D4
Honister Gdns STAN HA7 .....60 D5
Honister Pl STAN HA7 .....60 D4
Honiton Gdns PECK * SE15 .....170 A3
Honiton Rd KIL/WHAMP NW6 .....124 D1
ROMW/RG RM7 .....97 H3
WELL DA16 .....175 F3
Honley Rd CAT SE6 .....191 F2
Honnor Gdns ISLW TW7 .....159 H3
Honor Oak Ri FSTH SE23 .....190 A1
Honor Oak Rd FSTH SE23 .....190 A3
Hood Av MORT/ESHN SW14 .....162 C6
STHGT/OAK N14 .....50 D1
Hood Cl CROY/NA CRO 228 B5
Hoodcote Gdns WCHMH N21 .....52 B2
Hood Rd RYNPK SW20 .....203 F3
Hood Wk ROMW/RG RM7 .....75 E1
Hooker's Rd WALTH E17 .....70 B6
Hook Farm Rd HAYES BR2 .....233 F2
Hooking Gn RYLN/HDSTN HA2 .....77 F2
Hook Ri North SURB KT6 .....239 H1
Hook Ri South CHSGTN KT9 .....239 H1
Hook Rd CHSGTN KT9 .....239 F5
HOR/WEW KT19 .....240 C5
SURB KT6 .....221 G6
Hooks Hall Dr DAGE RM10 .....117 G1
Hookstone Wy WFD IG8 .....55 H3
The Hook BAR EN5 .....49 H1
Hook U/P (Kingston By-Pass)
SURB KT6 .....239 F1
Hooper Rd CAN/RD E16 .....132 D5
Hooper St WCHPL E1 .....17 E4
Hoop La GLDGN NW11 .....84 D4
Hop Ct ALP/SUD * HA0 .....101 G4
Hope Cl BTFD TW8 .....141 G5
CHDH RM6 .....96 B1
IS N1 .....108 C4
LEE/GVPK SE12 .....192 D5
SUT SM1 .....243 G3
Hopedale Rd CHARL SE7 .....152 D6
Hopefield Av
KIL/WHAMP NW6 .....124 C1
Hope Pk BMLY BR1 .....212 B3
Hopes Cl HEST TW5 .....139 E6
Hope St BTSEA SW11 .....165 H1
Hopetown St WCHPL * E1 .....16 D2
Hopewell St CMBW SE5 .....168 D1
Hop Gdns CHCR WC2N 11 E1
Hopgood St SHB W12 .....144 A1
Hopkins Cl MUSWH N10 .....66 A3
Hopkinsons Pl CAMTN * NW1 .....106 B6
Hopkins Sl SOHO/CST W1F 12 B4
Hoppers Rd WCHMH N21 .....52 B4
Hoppett Rd CHING E4 .....56 A5
Hopping La IS * N1 .....108 B4
Hoppingwood Av NWMAL KT3 .....208 E6
Hopton Gdns NWMAL KT3 .....223 C3
Hopton Pde STRHM/NOR * SW16 .....207 E1
Hopton Rd STRHM/NOR SW16 .....207 E1
WOOL/PLUM SE18 .....154 B3
Hoptons Gdns STHWK * SE1 .....22 D1
Hopton St STHWK SE1 .....22 D1
Hopwood Cl TOOT SW17 .....185 G5
Hopwood Rd WALW SE17 .....131 H5
Hopwood Wk HACK * E8 .....109 G5
Horace Av ROMW/RG RM7 .....97 H5
Horace Rd BARK/HLT IG6 .....72 D1
FSTGT E7 .....112 D2
KUT KT1 .....201 H6
Horatio Pl POP/IOD E14 .....112 C3
Horatio St BETH * E2 .....9 E3
Horatius Wy CROY/NA CRO 245 H4
Horbury Crs NTGHL W11 .....125 C6
Horbury Ms NTGHL * W11 .....144 C6
Horder Rd FUL/PGN SW6 .....164 C2
Hordle Prom East PECK SE15 .....169 F1
Hordle Prom North
PECK 169 F1
Hordle Prom West PECK SE15 .....169 F1
Horley Cl BXLYHN DA7 .....177 G3
Horley Rd ELTH/MOT SE9 .....195 G6
Hormead Rd NKENS W10 .....124 D3
Hornbeam Cl IL IG1 .....108 A1
LBTH SE11 .....30 A1
MLHL NW7 .....47 F6
NTHLT UB5 .....98 D3

Hornbeam Crs BTFD TW8 ....160 D1
Hornbeam Gv CHING E4 ....56 A5
Hornbeam Rd BKHH IG9 ....57 F5
YEAD UB4 ....118 A4
Hornbeams Ri FBAR/BDGN N11......66 C2
Hornbeam Wy HAYES BR2 ....234 A3
Hornbuckle Cl
 RYLN/HDSTN HA2.........................79 H6
Hornby Cl HAMP NW3 ....105 H5
Horncastle Cl LEE/GVPK SE12 ......192 C1
Horncastle Rd LEE/CVPK SE12.......192 C2
Hornchurch Cl KUTN/CMB KT2 ....201 F1
Horndean Cl PUT/ROE SW15 ....183 G3
Horndon Cl CRW RM5 ....77 G4
Horndon Gn CRW RM5......................77 G4
Horndon Rd CRW RM5.....................77 G4
Horner La MTCM CR4......................205 H5
Horne Wy PUT/ROE SW15 ....164 A3
Hornfair Rd CHARL SE7 ....153 F6
Horniman Dr FSTH SE23 ....188 H3
Horniman Gdns FSTH * SE23 ....189 H3
Horning Cl ELTH/MOT SE9 ....193 G6
Horn La ACT W3 ....142 C1
 CNWCH SE10..................................152 C4
 WFD IG8 ....52 D2
Horn Link Wy CNWCH SE10 ....152 C4
Horn Park Cl LEE/GVPK SE12 ....172 D6
Horn Park La LEE/GVPK SE12 ....172 D6
Horns End Pl PIN HA5 ....78 A1
Hornsey Chambers CLPT * E5 ....89 H6
Hornsey La ARCH N19 ....87 E4
Hornsey Lane Est ARCH * N19 ......87 F4
Hornsey Lane Gdns HGT N6 ....87 F3
Hornsey Park Rd
 CEND/HSY/T N8 ....67 H6
Hornsey Ri ARCH N19 ....87 F4
Hornsey Rise Gdns ARCH N19 ....87 F4
Hornsey Rd ARCH N19 ....87 F4
Hornsey St HOLWY N7 ....107 H3
Hornshay St PECK SE15 ....150 A6
Horns Rd BARK/HLT IG6 ....54 C2
Hornton St KENS W8 ....145 E2
Hornton St KENS W8 ....145 E2
Horsa Rd ERITH DA8 ....117 H5
 LEE/GVPK SE12 ....193 E2
Horsebridges Cl DAGW RM9.........116 C6
Horsecroft Cl ORP BR6 ....235 H5
Horsecroft Rd EDGW HA8 ....62 D3
Horse Fair KUT KT1 ....201 F5
Horseferry Pl GNWCH SE10 ....151 E6
Horseferry Rd POP/IOD E14 ....150 D6
 WEST SW1P 20 C6
Horse Guards Av WHALL SW1A 21 E1
Horse Guards Rd WHALL SW1A 20 D2
Horse Leaze EHAM E6 ....134 B5
Horsell Rd HBRY N5.......................108 A3
 STMC/STPC BR5 ....215 G4
Horselydown La STHWK SE1 ....24 C3
Horsenden Av GFD/PVL UB6 ....100 A3
Horsenden Crs GFD/PVL UB6 ....100 B3
Horsenden La North
 GFD/PVL UB6 ....100 A4
Horsenden La South
 GFD/PVL UB6 ....100 C6
Horseshoe Cl CRICK NW2 ....83 H6
 POP/IOD E14...................................151 G5
Horse Shoe Crs NTHLT UB5 ....119 E1
Horseshoe La ENC/FH EN2 ....23 H4
 TRDG/WHET N20 ....33 H4
Horse Yd IS N1 ....108 B6
Horsfeld Gdns ELTH/MOT SE9 ......178 C6
Horsfeld Rd ELTH/MOT SE9 ....178 B5
Horsford Rd BRXS/STRHM SW2....167 H5
Horsham Av NFNCH/WDSP N12 ......66 A1
Horsham Rd BXLYHS DA6 ....96 D6
Horsley Dr CROY/NA CR0 ....249 G5
 KUTN/CMB KT2 ....201 F1
Horsley Rd BMLY BR1 ....212 D4
 CHING E4 ....31 G4
Horsley St WALW SE17....................35 G6
Horsman St CMBW SE5 ....31 F6
Hormondon Cl ORP BR6 ....235 E4
Hormondon Rd BROCKY SE4 ....170 D6
Hortensia Rd WBPTN SW10 ....30 A6
Horticultural Pl CHSWK W4 ....142 D5
Horton Av CRICK NW2 ....104 C2
Horton Rd HACK E8 ....110 H4
Horton St LEW SE13........................171 F4
Horton Wy CROY/NA CR0 ....89 F3
Hortus Rd NWDGN UB2 ....138 D2
Hosack Rd BAL SW12 ....186 B4
Hoser Av LEE/GVPK SE12 ....192 B1
Hosier La STBT EC1A 14 C2
Hoskin's Cl CAN/RD E16 ....135 E5
Hoskins St GNWCH SE10 ....151 H5
Hospital Bridge Rd WHTN TW2 ...179 F3
Hospital Rd HSLW TW3 ....135 G3
Hospital Wy LEW SE13 ....191 H1
Hotham Cl E/WMO/HCT KT8 ....199 E6
Hotham Rd PUT/ROE SW15 ....164 A4
 WIM/MER SW19 ....205 G3
Hotham St SRTFD E15 ....112 A6
Hothfield Pl
 BERM/RHTH SE16 ....150 A3
Hotspur Rd NTHLT UB5 ....119 E1
Hotspur St LBTH SE11 ....30 A3
Houblon Rd RCHPK/HAM TW10....161 G6
Houghton Cl HACK * E8..................109 H4
Houghton Rd SEVS/STOTM N15 .....89 F1
Houghton St HOL/ALD * WC2B 11 H4
Houlder Crs CROY/NA CR0 ....246 B4
Houndsden Rd WCHMH N21 ....51 H1
Houndsditch HDTCH EC3A 16 B3
Houndsfield Rd ED N9 ....53 H2
Hounslow Av HSLW TW3 ....159 F6
Hounslow Gdns HSLW TW3 ....159 F6
Hounslow Rd FELT TW13 ....141 F2
 HSLW TW3 ....179 F1
Houseman Wy CMBW SE5 ....168 D1
Houston Rd FSTH SE23 ....190 C4
 SURB KT6.......................................200 D3
Hove Av WALTH E17 ....101 H5
Hoveden Rd CRICK NW2 ....104 B3
Hove Gdns SUT SM1 ....225 F5
Hoveton Rd THMD SE28 ....136 A5
Howden Wy WFD IG8........................74 B4
Howard Av BXLY DA5 ....196 A3
Howard Cl ACT W3 ....122 B5
 BUSH WD23 ....44 A2
 CRICK * NW2 ....104 C2

FBAR/BDGN N11..............................50 C4
HPTN TW12 ....199 G3
LOU IG10 ....57 C1
Howard Rd BMLY BR1 ....212 C3
 BRYLDS CV5 ....221 H3
 CRICK NW2......................................104 B2
 EHAM E6 ....133 H1
 GFD/PVL UB6 ....119 F5
 IL IG1 ....114 B2
 ISLW TW7 ....160 B4
 NWMAL KT3 ....205 E6
 PGE/AN SE20 ....210 A4
 SEVS/STOTM N15 ....89 E1
 SNWD SE25 ....229 G2
 STNW/STAM N16 ....108 D2
 WALTH E17 ....51 H1
 WEA E11 ....112 A1
Howards Crest Cl BECK BR3 ....211 G5
Howard's La PUT/ROE SW15 ....164 A5
Howard's Rd PLSTW E13 ....132 C2
Howard St THDIT KT7 ....220 D4
Howard Wy BAR EN5........................34 B6
Howard Wy BAR EN5........................34 B6
Howarth Rd ABYW SE2 ....155 G5
Howberry Cl EDGW HA8 ....61 F2
Howberry Rd EDGW HA8 ....61 G2
 THHTH CR7 ....208 D4
Howbury Rd PECK SE15 ....170 A4
Howcroft Crs FNCH N3 ....65 E3
Howcroft La GFD/PVL UB6 ....119 H2
Howden Cl THMD SE28 ....136 A6
Howden Rd SNWD SE25 ....209 F5
Howden St PECK SE15 ....151 E3
Howe Cl ROMW/RG RM7 ....77 E4
Howell Cl CHDH RM6 ....96 B2
Howell Wk WALW SE17 ....30 D2
Howfield Pl TOTM * N17 ....69 F6
Howgate Rd
 MORT/ESHN SW14 ....162 D4
Howick Pl WEST SW1P 20 B6
Howie St BTSEA SW11 ....166 A1
Howitt Cl HAMP * NW3 ....106 A4
Howitt Rd HAMP NW3 ....106 A4
Howland Est BERM/RHTH SE16 .....111 G1
Howland Ms East FITZ W1T 12 B1
Howland St FITZ W1T.......................12 B1
Howland Wy
 BERM/RHTH SE16 ....150 C2
Howletts La RSLP HA4....................58 A2
Howletts Rd HNHL SE24 ....188 C1
Howley Pl BAY/PAD W2 ....8 D1
Howley Rd CROY/NA CR0 ....246 B1
Howsman Rd BARN SW13 ....145 G6
Howson Rd BROCKY SE4 ....170 C5
Howson Ter
 RCHPK/HAM * TW10 ....181 G1
How's St BETH E2 ....7 J4
Howton Pl BUSH WD23.....................45 H3
Hoxton Market IS N1 ....8 A4
Hoxton Sq IS N1 ....8 A4
Hoylake Gdns MTCM CR4 ....207 E6
 OXHEY WD19...................................41 G2
Hoylake Rd ACT W3 ....123 E5
Hoyland Cl PECK * SE15 ....169 H1
Hoyle Rd TOOT SW17 ....206 A1
Hoy St CAN/RD E16 ....132 B5
Hubbard Dr CHSGTN KT9 ....239 E4
Hubbard Rd WNWD SE27 ....188 C6
Hubbard St SRTFD E15 ....112 A6
Hubert Cl WIM/MER * SW19 ....205 G4
Hubert Gv BRXN/ST SW9 ....167 G4
Hubert Rd EHAM E6 ....133 H2
Huddart St BOW E3 ....130 A4
Huddleston Cl BETH * E2 ....130 A1
Huddlestone Rd CRICK NW2 ....103 H4
 FSTGT E7 ....112 D1
Huddleston Rd ARCH N19 ....107 E1
Hudson Cl SHB * W12 ....125 E3
Hudson Rd BXLYHN DA7 ....97 F6
 HYS/HAR UB3 ....133 H3
Huggin Hl BLKFR EC4V 15 F5
Huggins Pl BRXS/STRHM SW2 .....187 H3
Hughan Rd SRTFD E15 ....111 H3
Hugh Dalton Av
 FUL/PGN * SW6 ....144 D6
Hughenden Av
 KTN/HRWW/W HA3 ....80 D2
Hughenden Gdns NTHLT UB5 ....118 A2
Hughenden Rd WPK KT4 ....223 G4
Hughes Ter CAN/RD * E16 ....132 D4
Hughes Wk CROY/NA CR0 ....208 D6
Hugh Gaitskell Cl
 FUL/PGN * SW6 ....144 D6
Hugh Ms PIM SW1V 27 J6
Hugh Pl WEST SW1P 20 C5
Hugh St PIM SW1V 27 H2
Hugon Rd FUL/PGN SW6 ....165 F4
Hugo Rd ARCH N19 ....107 D1
Huguenot Pl
 WAND/EARL SW18 ....165 G6
 WCHPL E1 ....19 K2
Hullbridge Ms IS N1 ....108 D6
Hull Cl BERM/RHTH * SE16 ....150 B1
Hull St FSBYE EC1V 7 F4
Hulme Pl STHWK SE1 ....23 F4
Hulse Av BARK IG11 ....114 D4
 ROMW/RG RM7 ....75 E1
Humber Dr NKENS W10 ....124 B3
Humber Rd BKHTH/KID SE3 ....152 C6
 CRICK NW2.......................................82 A5
Humberstone Rd PLSTW E13 ....133 E2
Humberton Cl HOM * E9 ....91 G1
Humes Av HANWL W7 ....140 A3
Humphrey Cl CLAY * IG5 ....53 H4
Humphrey St STHWK SE1 ....32 C3
Humphries Cl DAGW RM9 ....116 D2
Hundred Acre CDALE/KGS NW9 .....63 F5
Hungerdown CHING E4 ....38 A3
Hungerford Br STHWK SE1 ....21 C1
Hungerford St WCHPL * E1 ....110 D5
Hunsdon Cl DAGW RM9 ....116 C4
Hunsdon Rd NWCR SE14 ....170 B1
Hunslett St BETH * E2 ....130 A1
Hunston Rd MRDN SM4 ....225 H5
Hunt Cl BKHTH/KID * SE3 ....172 C5
 NTGHL W11 ....125 C5
Hunt Ct BAL SW12 ....186 C3
 STHWK SE1 ....23 H4
Hunter Cl BAL * SW12 ....186 D5
Hunter Rd RYNPK SW20 ....204 A4
 THHTH CR7 ....208 D6

Hunters Ct RCH/KEW TW9 ....161 F6
Hunter's Gv CRW RM5......................77 F1
 KTN/HRWW/W HA3 ....81 E1
 ORP BR6..252 C2
Hunters Hall Rd DAGE RM10 ....117 E2
Hunters Hl RSLP HA4 ....77 H3
Hunters Meadow NRWD SE19....189 E6
Hunters Rd CHSGTN KT9 ....206 A1
 IL IG1 ....114 B3
Hunters Sq DAGE RM10 ....117 E2
Hunter St BMSBY WC1N 5 F5
Hunters Wy CROY/NA CR0 ....247 E2
 ENC/FH EN2 ....23 G1
Huntingdon Cl MTCM CR4 ....227 G1
Huntingdon Gdns CHSWK W4 ......162 C1
 WPK KT4...242 A1
Huntingdon Rd ED N9 ....54 A3
 EFNCH N2 ....66 A6
Huntingdon St CAN/RD E16 ....132 B5
 IS N1 ....107 H5
Huntingfield CROY/NA CR0 ....248 D5
Huntingfield Rd
 PUT/ROE SW15 ....183 G1
Hunting Gate Cl ENC/FH EN2 ....38 A4
Hunting Gate Dr CHSGTN KT9......239 C5
Hunting Gate Ms WHTN * TW2 ......179 G3
Huntings Rd DAGE RM10 ....117 E4
Huntley St GWRST WC1E 4 B6
Huntly Rd RYNPK * SW20 ....205 G5
Huntly Dr FNCH N3 ....65 E2
Huntly Rd SNWD SE25 ....229 E1
Hunton St WCHPL E1 ....17 E1
Hunt Rd NWDGN UB2 ....139 E3
Hunt's La SRTFD E15 ....131 C1
Huntsman Rd BARK/HLT IG6 ....75 H2
Huntsman St WALW SE17 ....32 A2
Hunts Md PEND EN3 ....40 D4
Hunts Mede Cl CHST BR7 ....213 H5
Huntsmoor Rd HOR/WEW KT19 ...240 D5
Huntspill St TOOT SW17 ....185 G5
Hunts Slip Rd DUL SE21 ....189 E5
Huntsworth Ms CAMTN NW1 ....2 C5
Hurdwick Pl CAMTN * NW1 ....4 A2
Hurley Rd GFD/PVL UB6 ....119 F4
Hurlingham Gdns
 FUL/PGN SW6 ....164 D4
Hurlingham Pk FUL/PGN * SW6.....164 D4
Hurlingham Rd BXLYHN DA7 ....176 D1
 FUL/PGN SW6 ....164 D3
Hurlock St HBRY N5..........................88 A2
Huron Cl ORP BR6 ....252 B6
Huron Rd TOOT SW17 ....186 A4
Hurren Cl BKHTH/KID SE3 ....172 A4
Hurricane Rd WLGTN SM6 ....226 A5
Hurry Cl SRTFD E15 ....112 A5
Hursley Rd CHIG IG7..........................75 F1
Hurst Av CHING E4 ....55 E3
 HGT N6 ....87 F3
Hurstbourne Gdns BARK IG11 ......114 D4
Hurstbourne Rd FSTH SE23 ....190 C5
Hurst Cl CHING E4 ....55 E2
 CHSGTN KT9 ....240 B5
 CLDGN NW11 ....85 F3
 HAYES BR2 ....232 B5
 NTHLT UB5 ....79 H5
Hurstcourt Rd CHEAM SM3 ....225 F5
Hurstdene Av HAYES BR2 ....232 B5
Hurstdene Gdns
 SEVS/STOTM N15 ....89 F1
Hurstfield HAYES BR2 ....232 A3
Hurstfield Rd E/WMO/HCT KT8 .....199 E6
Hurst La ABYW SE2 ....156 B5
 E/WMO/HCT KT8 ....219 C4
Hurstleigh Gdns CLAY IG5 ....53 H4
Hurst Ri BAR EN5 ....35 C4
Hurst Rd BFN/LL DA15 ....195 H4
 BXLY DA5..96 C5
 CROY/NA CR0 ....246 D3
 E/WMO/HCT KT8 ....199 C6
 ERITH DA8 ....117 H1
 WALTH E17 ....71 F6
 WCHMH N21 ....38 D2
 WDR/YW UB7 ....218 B1
Hurst Springs BXLY DA5 ....196 C5
Hurst St HNHL SE24 ....188 B1
Hurst View Rd SAND/SEL CR2 ......247 E5
Hurstway Wk NKENS * W10 ....124 B6
Hurstwood Av BXLY DA5 ....196 C5
 WAN E11 ....93 C5
Hurstwood Dr BMLY BR1 ....213 H6
Hurstwood Rd HDN/NR * KT12 .....218 D4
Hurtwood Rd WOOL/PLUM SE18....114 B3
Husband Cl FSTH SE23 ....190 C5
Hussain Cl HRW HA1 ....79 F5
Hussar Cl HSLWW * HA4 ....158 D4
Hussey Rd ED N9 ....54 D1
Husseywell Crs HAYES BR2 ....232 C5
Hutching's St POP/IOD E14 ....151 C2
Hutchings Wk GLDGN NW11 ....65 F1
Hutchins Cl SRTFD E15 ....111 C5
Hutchinson Ter WBLY HA9 ....101 F1
Hutchins Rd THMD SE28 ....136 C6
Hutton Cl GFD/PVL * UB6 ....79 C2
 WFD IG8..72 D2
Hutton Gv NFNCH/WDSP N12 ....65 F1
Hutton La KTN/HRWW/W HA3 ....59 G3
Hutton Rw EDGW HA8 ....62 C1
Hutton St EMB EC4Y 14 B4
Huxbear St BROCKY SE4 ....170 C6
Huxley Cl NTHLT * UB5 ....119 C1
Huxley Dr CHDH RM6 ....96 H4
Huxley Gdns WLSDN NW10 ....121 H2
Huxley Pde UED * N18 ....52 B6
Huxley Pl PLMGR N13 ....51 C2
Huxley Rd LEY E10 ....91 C6
 UED N18 ....52 B6
Huxley Sayze UED * N18 ....68 D1
Huxley St NKENS W10 ....124 B2
Hyacinth Cl HPTN TW12 ....199 E2
Hyacinth Rd PUT/ROE SW15 ....183 C3
Hycliffe Gdns CHIG IG7 ....54 A5
Hyde Cl CDALE/KGS NW9 ....83 F2
Hyde Dr STMC/STPC BR5 ....235 H1
Hyde Estate Rd
 CDALE/KGS NW9 ....83 F2

Hydefield Cl ED N9 ....52 D3
Hydefield Ct ED N9 ....53 E4
Hyde La BTSEA SW11 ....166 A2
Hyde Park Av WCHMH N21 ....52 C2
Hyde Park Cnr MYFR/PICC W1J 19 F3
Hyde Park Crs BAY/PAD W2 ....10 A4
Hyde Park Gdns
 BAY/PAD * W2 ....125 H6
 BAY/PAD W2 ....125 H6
 WCHMH N21 ....52 C3
Hyde Park Gardens Ms
 BAY/PAD W2 ....125 H6
Hyde Park Ga SKENS * SW7 ....145 G3
 SKENS SW7 ....145 G2
Hyde Park Gate Ms
 SKENS * SW7 ....145 G2
Hyde Park PI BAY/PAD W2 ....10 B5
Hyde Park Sq BAY/PAD W2 ....10 A4
Hyde Park St BAY/PAD W2 ....10 A4
Hyderabad Wy SRTFD E15 ....112 A5
Hyde Rd BXLYHN DA7 ....176 D3
 IS N1 ....110 H1
 RCHPK/HAM TW10 ....161 H6
Hydeside Gdns ED N9 ....53 E4
Hyde's Pl IS N1 ....108 B5
Hyde St DEPT SE8 ....151 E6
Hydethorpe Av ED N9 ....53 E4
Hydethorpe Rd BAL SW12 ....187 E3
Hyde V CNWCH SE10 ....171 G1
Hyde Wk MRDN SM4 ....225 C4
Hyde Wy ED N9 ....53 E4
Hylands Rd WALTH E17 ....71 H5
Hylton St WOOL/PLUM SE18 ....155 F4
Hyndewood FSTH * SE23 ....190 B5
Hyndman St PECK SE15 ....135 G6
Hynton Rd BCTR RM8 ....96 A6
Hyperion Pl HOR/WEW KT19 ....240 D6
Hyson Rd BERM/RHTH SE16 ....33 H3
Hythe Av BXLYHN DA7 ....176 C6
Hythe Cl STMC/STPC BR5 ....236 A1
 UED N18 ....55 G6
Hythe Rd THHTH CR7 ....208 D1
 WLSDN NW10 ....123 F2
Hyver Hl MLHL NW7 ....46 D1

I

Ibbotson Av CAN/RD E16 ....132 B5
Ibbott St WCHPL E1 ....130 A3
Iberian Av WLGTN SM6 ....245 C2
Ibis La CHSWK W4 ....162 C2
Ibis Wy YEAD UB4 ....118 D5
Ibscott Cl DAGE RM10 ....117 G4
Ibsley Gdns PUT/ROE SW15 ....183 G3
Ibsley Wy EBAR EN4 ....36 A6
Iceland Rd BOW E3 ....111 E6
Ickburgh Est CLPT * E5 ....89 H6
Ickburgh Rd CLPT E5 ....89 H6
Ickleton Rd ELTH/MOT SE9 ....193 G6
Ickleworth Dr ONTH/NBYPK IG2 ....96 B2
Ickworth Park Rd WALTH E17 ....70 C1
Ida Rd SEVS/STOTM N15 ....88 D2
Ida St POP/IOD E14 ....131 G5
Iden Cl HAYES BR2 ....231 A6
Idlecombe Rd TOOT SW17 ....206 C2
Idmiston Rd FSTGT E7 ....112 B3
 WNWD SE27 ....188 C5
 WPK KT4...223 F4
Idmiston Sq WPK KT4 ....223 F4
Idol La MON EC3R..............................16 A6
Idonia St DEPT SE8 ....170 D1
Iffley Rd HMSMTH W6 ....145 H3
Ifield Rd WBPTN SW10 ....30 A5
Ightham Rd ERITH DA8 ....177 E1
Ilbert St NKENS W10 ....124 C2
Ilchester Pl WKENS W14 ....144 D3
Ilchester Rd BCTR RM8 ....118 C3
Ildersly Gv DUL SE21 ....188 D4
Ilderton Rd BERM/RHTH SE16 ......150 A4
Ilex Cl SUN TW16 ....198 A5
Ilex Wk WLSDN NW10 ....105 F4
Ilex Wy STRHM/NOR SW16 ....208 A1
Ilford Hl IL IG1 ....114 A2
Ilford La IL IG1 ....114 B2
Ilfracombe Gdns CHDH RM6 ....95 G5
Ilfracombe Rd BMLY BR1 ....193 E2
Iliffe St WALW SE17 ....30 D5
Iliffe Yd WALW SE17 ....30 D5
Ilkley Cl NRWD * SE19 ....208 D6
Ilkley Rd CAN/RD E16 ....133 E4
 OXHEY WD19...................................41 C1
Illingworth Cl MTCM CR4 ....205 H6
Illingworth Wy EN EN1 ....36 B4
Ilmington Rd
 KTN/HRWW/W HA3 ....81 F1
Ilminster Gdns BTSEA SW11 ....166 A3
Imber Cl STHGT/OAK N14 ....34 D1
Imber Cross THDIT * KT7 ....220 B4
Imber Gv ESH/CLAY KT10 ....204 B6
Imber Park Rd ESH/CLAY KT10 .....219 H5
Imber St IS N1 ....7 F1
Imperial Av STNW/STAM * N16 .....109 E2
Imperial Ct RYLN/HDSTN HA2 ....79 E3
Imperial College Rd
 SKENS SW7 ....145 H3
Imperial Dr RYLN/HDSTN HA2 ....79 E5
Imperial Gdns MTCM CR4 ....207 G2
Imperial Ms EHAM * E6 ....133 G1
Imperial Pl CHST BR7 ....214 A4
Imperial Rd FUL/PGN SW6 ....146 B6
 WDGN N22 ....67 G2
Imperial Sq FUL/PGN SW6 ....146 B6
Imperial St BOW E3 ....130 B2
Imperial Wy CHST BR7 ....194 C5
 CROY/NA CR0 ....246 A5
 KTN/HRWW/W HA3 ....81 C3
Imre Cl SHB W12 ....143 H1
Inca Dr ELTH/MOT SE9 ....193 C5
Inchmery Rd CAT SE6 ....191 F4
Inchwood CROY/NA CR0 ....248 A3
Independent Pl HACK * E8 ....89 C3
Independents Rd
 BKHTH/KID SE3 ....172 B4
Inderwick Rd CEND/HSY/T N8.......87 H5
Indescon Ct POP/IOD E14 ....151 F2
India St TWRH EC3N 16 C4
India Wy SHB W12 ....123 H6

Indigo Ms *POP/IOD* • E14 ....131 G6
STNW/STAM N16 ....108 D1
Indus Rd CHARL SE7 ....173 E1
Ingal Rd PLSTW E13 ....132 C5
Ingate Pl VX/NE SW8 ....166 D2
Ingatestone Rd MNPK E12 ....93 E5
SNWD SE25 ....229 H2
WFD IG8 ....72 D5
Ingelow St VX/NE SW8 ....166 D3
Ingersoll Rd PEND EN3 ....40 A1
SHB W12 ....143 H1
Ingestre Pl SOHO/CST W1F 12 B4
Ingestre Rd FSTGT E7 ....112 C2
KTTN NW5 ....106 D2
Ingham Cl SAND/SEL CR2 ....248 B6
Ingham Rd KIL/WHAMP NW6 ....105 E2
SAND/SEL CR2 ....248 A6
Inglebert St CLKNW EC1R 6 A3
Ingleborough St BRXN/ST SW9 ....168 A1
Ingleby Av WELL DA16 ....175 G6
Ingleby Rd DAGE RM10 ....117 F4
HOLWY N7 ....92 D1
IL IG1 ....94 B5
Ingleby Wy CHST BR7 ....214 A1
WLGTN SM6 ....245 F6
Ingle Ms FSBYW WC1X 58 D6
Ingledew Rd
WOOL/PLUM SE18 ....154 D5
Inglefield Sq WAP • E1W 25 H1
Inglehurst Gdns REDBR IG4 ....93 H2
Inglemere Rd FSTH SE23 ....190 B5
TOOT SW17 ....206 B3
Ingleside Cl BECK BR3 ....211 E3
Ingleside Gv BKHTH/KID SE3 ....152 B6
Inglethorpe St FUL/PGN SW6 ....164 B2
Ingleton Av WELL DA16 ....175 G6
Ingleton Rd CAR SM5 ....244 A6
UED N18 ....69 G2
Ingleton St BRXN/ST SW9 ....168 A3
Ingleway NFNCH/WDSP N12 ....65 H2
Inglewood CROY/NA CR0 ....248 C6
Inglewood Cl BARK/HLT IG6 ....72 C1
E/PO POP/IOD E14 ....151 E4
Inglewood Copse BMLY BR1 ....213 G5
Inglewood Rd BXLYHN DA7 ....177 H5
KIL/WHAMP NW6 ....105 E3
Inglis Rd CROY/NA CR0 ....229 F1
EA W5 ....121 H6
Inglis St CMBW SE5 ....168 B2
Ingram Av EFNCH N2 ....85 G4
Ingram Cl LBTH SE11 ....29 H1
STAN HA7 ....61 E1
Ingram Rd EFNCH N2 ....86 A1
THHTH CR7 ....208 C4
Ingram Wy GFD/PVL UB6 ....96 H6
Ingrave Rd ROM RM1 ....97 H1
Ingrave St BTSEA SW11 ....165 H4
Ingress St CHSWK W4 ....145 E5
Inigo Jones Rd CHARL SE7 ....173 F1
Inkerman Rd KTTN NW5 ....106 A3
Inks Gn CHING E4 ....71 G1
Inkwell Cl NFNCH/WDSP N12 ....49 G5
Inman Rd WAND/EARL SW18 ....185 G2
WLSDN NW10 ....103 E6
Inmans Av WFD IG8 ....56 C6
Inner Cir CAMTN NW1 ....3 G3
Inner Park Rd WIM/MER SW19 ....184 B4
Inner Ct RYNPK SW20 ....204 C5
Innes Gdns PUT/ROE SW15 ....183 H1
Innes Yd CROY/NA CR0 ....246 C1
Inniskilling Rd PLSTW E13 ....133 E1
Innovation Cl ALP/SUD HA0 ....101 G6
Inskip Cl LEY E10 ....91 H6
Inskip Rd BCTR RM8 ....96 B5
Institute Pl HACK E8 ....109 H3
Integer Gdns WAN • E11 ....91 H4
International Av HEST TW5 ....138 A5
Inver Ct BAY/PAD • W2 ....125 F5
Inveresk Gdns WPK KT4 ....241 F1
Inverforth Cl HAMP NW3 ....85 G6
Inverforth Rd FBAR/BDGN N11 ....66 D1
Inverine Rd CHARL SE7 ....152 D5
Invermore Pl
WOOL/PLUM SE18 ....154 C4
Inverness Av EN EN1 ....24 A3
Inverness Dr BARK/HLT IG6 ....75 E2
Inverness Gdns KENS W8 ....145 F1
Inverness Pl BAY/PAD • W2 ....125 F6
Inverness Rd HSLW TW3 ....158 D5
NWDGN UB2 ....138 C4
UED N18 ....69 H1
WPK KT4 ....224 B5
Inverness St CAMTN NW1 ....106 B1
Inverness Ter BAY/PAD W2 ....125 F5
WDGN • N22 ....68 B4
Inverton Rd PECK SE15 ....170 B5
Invicta Cl CHST BR7 ....214 A1
Invicta Gv NTHLT UB5 ....118 D2
Invicta Pde SCUP • DA14 ....195 H6
Invicta Plaza STHWK SE1 ....22 C1
Invicta Rd BKHTH/KID SE3 ....172 C1
Inville Rd WALW SE17 ....31 H4
Inwood Av HSLW TW3 ....159 G4
Inwood Cl CROY/NA CR0 ....230 C6
Inwood Rd HSLW TW3 ....159 G5
Inworth St BTSEA SW11 ....166 A3
Inworth Wlk IS • N1 ....108 C6
Ion Cl CAT SE6 ....191 E2
MRDN SM4 ....225 F4
Ion Sq BETH • E2 ....13 J2
Ipswich Rd TOOT SW17 ....206 C2
Ireland Cl EHAM E6 ....133 H4
Ireland Pl WDGN N22 ....67 G3
Irene Ms HNWL • W7 ....140 B1
Irene Rd FUL/PGN SW6 ....165 H2
ORP BR6 ....235 F4
Ireton Cl MUSWH N10 ....66 C1
Ireton St BOW E3 ....131 H3
Iris Av BXLY DA5 ....196 C1
Iris Cl CROY/NA CR0 ....230 B5
EHAM E6 ....133 G4
SURB KT6 ....221 H4
Iris Crs BXLYHN DA7 ....156 D6
Iris Rd HOR/WEW KT19 ....240 B3
Iris Wy CHING E4 ....70 D2
Irkdale Av EN EN1 ....24 A2
Iron Bridge Cl STHL UB1 ....139 G1
WLSDN NW10 ....103 G3
Iron Mill Pl WAND/EARL SW18 ....185 H5
Iron Mill Rd WAND/EARL SW18 ....185 F1
Ironmonger La CITYW EC2V 15 G4

Ironmonger Rw FSBYE EC1V 7 F4
Ironside Cl BERM/RHTH SE16 ....150 B2
Irons Wy CRW RM5 ....77 G1
Irvine Av KTN/HRWW/W HA3 ....60 C6
Irvine Cl TRDG/WHET N20 ....50 A4
Irvine Wy ORP BR6 ....235 F4
Irving Av NTHLT UB5 ....98 B6
Irving Gv BRXN/ST SW9 ....167 H5
Irving Ms IS N1 ....108 C4
Irving Rd WKENS W14 ....144 B3
Irving St LSQ/SEVD WC2H 12 D6
Irving Wy SWLY BR8 ....217 H5
Irwell Est BERM/RHTH • SE16 ....150 A2
Irwin Av WOOL/PLUM SE18 ....175 E1
Irwin Gdns WLSDN NW10 ....103 H6
Isabella Cl STHGT/OAK N14 ....51 E2
Isabella Ct RCHPK/HAM • TW10 ....181 H1
Isabella Dr ORP BR6 ....252 C2
Isabella Rd HOM • E9 ....110 A3
Isabella St STHWK SE1 ....22 C2
Isabel St BRXN/ST SW9 ....167 H2
Isambard Ms POP/IOD E14 ....151 G3
Isambard Pl BERM/RHTH SE16 ....150 A1
Isham Rd STRHM/NOR SW16 ....207 G5
Isis St WAND/EARL SW18 ....185 G4
Island Farm Av
E/WMO/HCT KT8 ....218 D2
Island Farm Rd
E/WMO/HCT KT8 ....218 D2
Island Rd BERM/RHTH SE16 ....206 B3
Island Rw POP/IOD E14 ....130 D5
Isla Rd WOOL/PLUM SE18 ....154 C6
Islay Gdns HSLWW TW4 ....158 B6
Islay Wk IS • N1 ....108 C4
Islay Whf POP/IOD • E14 ....131 G4
Isledon Rd HOLWY N7 ....108 A1
Islehurst Cl CHST BR7 ....214 A4
Islington Gn IS N1 ....108 B6
Islington High St IS N1 ....6 C1
Islington Park Ms IS N1 ....108 A5
Islington Park St IS N1 ....108 A5
Islip Gdns EDGW HA8 ....62 D2
NTHLT UB5 ....98 C5
Islip Manor Rd NTHLT UB5 ....98 B5
Islip St KTTN NW5 ....107 E3
Ismailia Rd FSTGT E7 ....112 D1
Isom Cl PLSTW E13 ....132 D2
Ivanhoe Dr KTN/HRWW/W HA3 ....60 C5
Ivanhoe Rd CMBW SE5 ....169 F4
HSLWW TW4 ....158 A6
Ivatt Pl WKENS W14 ....144 D5
Ivatt Wy SEVS/STOTM N15 ....68 B6
Iveagh Av WLSDN NW10 ....122 A1
Iveagh Cl HOM E9 ....110 A6
WLSDN NW10 ....122 A1
Ivedon Rd WELL DA16 ....176 A3
Ive Farm Cl LEY E10 ....91 E6
Ive Farm La LEY E10 ....91 E6
Iveley Rd CLAP SW4 ....167 E3
Ivere Dr BAR EN5 ....33 F4
Iverhurst Cl BXLYHS DA6 ....196 D3
Iverna Ct KENS W8 ....145 E3
Iverna Gdns KENS W8 ....145 E3
Iverson Rd KIL/WHAMP NW6 ....104 D4
Ivers Wy CROY/NA CR0 ....249 F5
Ives Rd CAN/RD E16 ....132 A4
Ives St CHEL SW3 ....28 F3
Ivimey St BETH E2 ....13 J3
Ivinghoe Cl EN EN1 ....24 B1
Ivinghoe Rd BCTR RM8 ....115 H3
BUSH WD23 ....43 H1
Ivor Gv ELTH/MOT SE9 ....194 B3
Ivor Pl CAMTN NW1 ....2 C6
Ivor St CAMTN NW1 ....106 C1
Ivorydown BMLY BR1 ....192 C6
Ivybridge Cl TWK • TW1 ....160 D5
Ivychurch Cl PGE/AN SE20 ....209 H3
Ivy Church La STHWK • SE1 ....32 C3
Ivy Cl PIN HA5 ....78 A4
RYLN/HDSTN HA2 ....78 D2
SUN TW16 ....198 A5
Ivy Crs CHSWK W4 ....142 C4
Ivydale Rd CAR SM5 ....226 B6
PECK SE15 ....170 B4
Ivyday Gv STRHM/NOR SW16 ....187 H5
Ivydene WHCHP KT12 ....218 D2
Ivydene Cl SUT SM1 ....243 G2
Ivy Gdns CRND/HSY/T N8 ....67 E3
MTCM CR4 ....207 F6
Ivyhouse Rd DAGW RM9 ....116 A4
Ivy La HSLWW TW4 ....158 D5
Ivymount Rd WNWD SE27 ....188 B5
Ivy Rd BROCKY SE4 ....170 D5
CAN/RD E16 ....132 C5
CRICK NW2 ....104 A2
HSLW TW3 ....159 F5
LEY E10 ....91 H4
STHGT/OAK N14 ....51 E2
SURB • KT6 ....222 A6
TOOT SW17 ....206 A1
Ivy St IS N1 ....11 H1
Ivy Wk DAGW RM9 ....116 C4
Ixworth Pl CHEL SW3 ....26 A2
Izane Rd BXLYHS DA6 ....176 D5

J

Jacaranda Cl NWMAL KT3 ....203 E6
Jacaranda Gv HACK E8 ....109 F5
Jackass La HAYES BR2 ....250 D4
Jack Clow Rd SRTFD E15 ....132 A1
Jack Cornwell St MNPK E12 ....114 A2
Jack Goodchild Wy KUT KT1 ....202 B6
Jackman Ms WLSDN NW10 ....81 G6
Jackman St HACK E8 ....110 D6
Jackson Cl HOM E9 ....110 D5
Jackson Rd BARK IG11 ....114 D6
EBAR EN4 ....50 A1
HAYES BR2 ....233 H5
HOLWY N7 ....108 B1
Jackson's La HGT N6 ....86 A1
Jackson's Pl CROY/NA CR0 ....228 D5
Jackson St WOOL/PLUM SE18 ....154 A6
Jackson's Wy CROY/NA CR0 ....249 F1
Jack Walker Ct HBRY N5 ....108 B2
Jacobs Cl DAGE RM10 ....117 F2
Jacob St STHWK SE1 ....24 D3

Jacob's Well Ms MHST W1U 11 F3
Jacqueline Cl NTHLT UB5 ....98 C6
Jacqueline Creft Ter HGT • N6 ....86 C3
Jacqueline Vis WALTH • E17 ....91 G2
Jade Cl BCTR RM8 ....96 A5
CAN/RD E16 ....133 F5
CRICK NW2 ....84 B4
Jade Ter KIL/WHAMP • NW6 ....105 G5
Jaffe Rd IL IG1 ....94 C5
Jaffray Rd HAYES BR2 ....233 F1
Jaggard Wy BAL SW12 ....186 B2
Jago Cl WOOL/PLUM SE18 ....154 C6
Jago Wk CMBW SE5 ....168 D1
Jamaica Rd BERM/RHTH SE16 ....25 G5
STHWK SE1 ....24 C4
THHTH CR7 ....228 B3
Jamaica St WCHPL E1 ....130 B4
James Av BCTR RM8 ....96 D5
DCOL/NA CR0 ....104 A3
James Cl GLDGN • NW11 ....84 C3
BKHH IG9 ....39 E3
James Collins Cl NKENS W10 ....124 D3
James Gdns WDGN N22 ....68 C3
James Joyes Wk HNHL • SE24 ....188 B5
James La WAN E11 ....91 G4
James Lee Sq PEND EN3 ....41 E1
James St ENC/FH EN2 ....38 B2
James Sinclair Pt PLSTW E13 ....114 C5
James Ter TOTM N17 ....69 F3
James St BARK IG11 ....114 C5
COVGDN WC2E 13 F5
EN EN1 ....39 F6
HSLW TW3 ....159 H4
MHST W1U 11 F4
Jamestown Rd CAMTN NW1 ....106 D6
Jamestown Wy POP/IOD E14 ....131 H6
James Yd CHING • E4 ....71 H2
Janet St POP/IOD E14 ....151 E3
Janeway Pl BERM/RHTH SE16 ....25 G4
Janeway St BERM/RHTH SE16 ....25 F4
Janson Cl SRTFD E15 ....112 A3
WLSDN NW10 ....102 D1
Janson Rd SRTFD E15 ....112 A3
Jansons Rd SEVS/STOTM N15 ....69 E5
Japan Crs FSBYPK N4 ....87 H5
Japan Rd CHDH RM6 ....96 B5
Jardine Rd WAP E1W 130 B6
Jarrett Cl BRXS/STRHM SW2 ....188 B3
Jarrow Cl MRDN SM4 ....225 F2
Jarrow Rd BERM/RHTH SE16 ....150 A4
CHDH RM6 ....96 A5
TOTM N17 ....89 H1
Jarrow Wy HOM E9 ....110 C2
Jarvis Cl BAR EN5 ....34 B6
Jarvis Rd EDUL SE22 ....169 E5
SAND/SEL CR2 ....246 D4
Jasmine Cl HAYES BR2 ....234 B6
IL IG1 ....114 B3
STHL UB1 ....118 C6
Jasmine Cl LEE/GVPK SE12 ....192 C1
Jasmine Gdns CROY/NA CR0 ....249 F1
RYLN/HDSTN HA2 ....79 E6
Jasmine Gv PGE/AN SE20 ....209 H4
Jasmin Rd HOR/WEW KT19 ....240 B4
Jason Wk ELTH/MOT SE9 ....194 A6
Jasper Cl PEND EN3 ....40 A1
Jasper Pas WNWD SE27 ....189 E5
Jasper Rd CAN/RD E16 ....133 F5
NRWD SE19 ....209 F2
Javelin Wy NTHLT UB5 ....118 B2
Jaycroft ENC/FH EN2 ....38 A2
Jay Gdns CHST BR7 ....192 D4
Jay Ms SKENS • SW7 ....145 G2
SKENS SW7 ....145 G2
Jean Batten Cl CROY/NA CR0 ....245 H5
Jebb Av BRXS/STRHM SW2 ....187 G4
Jebb St BOW E3 ....131 E1
Jedburgh Rd PLSTW E13 ....133 E2
Jedburgh St BTSEA SW11 ....166 C3
Jeddo Ms SHB W12 ....143 F2
Jeddo Rd SHB W12 ....143 F2
Jefferson Cl GNTH/NBYPK IG2 ....94 B2
WEA W13 ....140 D3
Jeffrey's Pl CAMTN NW1 ....107 E5
Jeffrey's Rd CLAP SW4 ....167 G5
PEND EN3 ....40 D5
Jeffrey's St CAMTN NW1 ....106 D5
Jeffs Cl HPTN • TW12 ....199 F2
Jeffs Rd SUT SM1 ....242 D2
Jeger Av BETH E2 ....109 F6
Jeken Rd ELTH/MOT SE9 ....173 E5
Jelf Rd BRXS/STRHM SW2 ....168 A4
Jellicoe Gdns STAN HA7 ....43 F2
Jellicoe Rd TOTM N17 ....68 D3
Jemmett Cl KUTN/CMB KT2 ....202 B4
Jem Paterson Ct HRW • HA1 ....100 A2
Jengar Cl SUT SM1 ....243 F2
Jenkins La BARK IG11 ....134 B3
Jenkins Rd PLSTW E13 ....132 D3
Jenner Av ACT W3 ....122 D4
Jenner Rd STNW/STAM N16 ....88 B4
Jennett Rd CROY/NA CR0 ....246 A1
Jennifer Rd BMLY BR1 ....192 B5
Jennings Cl SURB KT6 ....221 E4
Jennings Rd EDUL SE22 ....189 F1
Jenningtree Wy BELV DA17 ....157 G2
Jenny Hammond Cl WAN E11 ....112 B1
Jenson Wy NRWD SE19 ....209 F3
Jephtha Rd WAND/EARL SW18 ....185 E1
Jeppo's La MTCM CR4 ....226 B1
Jerdan Pl FUL/PGN SW6 ....165 E1
Jeremiah St POP/IOD E14 ....131 F5
Jeremy's Gn UED N18 ....51 E6
Jermyn St STJS SW1Y 20 A1
Jerningham Av CLAY IG5 ....76 B3
Jerningham Rd NWCR SE14 ....170 C3
Jerome Crs STJWD NW8 ....2 A5
Jerome St WCHPL E1 ....13 H6
Jerrard St LEW SE13 ....171 H4
Jerrold St IS • N1 ....12 A1
Jersey Av KTN/HRWW/W HA3 ....60 D5
Jersey Dr STMC/STPC BR5 ....234 D3
Jersey Rd CAN/RD E16 ....133 G5
HEST TW5 ....159 F2
HNWL W7 ....140 C2
IL IG1 ....108 D4
IS N1 ....108 D4

TOOT SW17 ....206 D3
WAN E11 ....91 H5
Jersey St BETH • E2 ....9 H4
Jersey Vis HNWL • W7 ....140 A2
Jerusalem Pas CLKNW EC1R 6 C6
Jerviston Gdns
STRHM/NOR SW16 ....208 A2
Jesmond Av WBLY HA9 ....101 H4
Jesmond Cl MTCM CR4 ....206 D6
Jesmond Dene HAMP • NW3 ....105 G4
Jesmond Rd CROY/NA CR0 ....229 F4
Jesmond Wy STAN HA7 ....61 G1
Jessam Av CLPT E5 ....88 D3
Jessamine Rd HNWL W7 ....140 A1
Jessamine Ter SWLY • BR8 ....217 G4
Jesse Rd LEY E10 ....91 G5
Jessica Rd WAND/EARL SW18 ....185 G1
Jessop Av NWDGN UB2 ....138 D4
Jessops Wy MTCM CR4 ....227 E3
Jessup Cl WOOL/PLUM SE18 ....154 C4
Jetstar Wy NTHLT UB5 ....118 C2
Jevington Wy LEE/GVPK SE12 ....192 D3
Jewel Rd WALTH E17 ....71 E6
Jewry St TWRH EC3N 16 C4
Jews Rw WAND/EARL SW18 ....165 H5
Jews Wk SYD SE26 ....189 H6
Jeymer Av CRICK NW2 ....103 H3
Jeymer Dr GFD/PVL UB6 ....96 D1
Jeypore Rd WAND/EARL SW18 ....185 G2
Jillian Cl HPTN TW12 ....199 E1
Jim Bradley Cl
WOOL/PLUM SE18 ....154 A4
Joan Crs ELTH/MOT SE9 ....193 F2
Joan Gdns BCTR RM8 ....96 C6
Joan Rd BCTR RM8 ....96 C6
Joan St STHWK SE1 ....22 C2
Jocelyn Rd RCH/KEW TW9 ....161 G4
Jocelyn St PECK SE15 ....169 G2
Jockey's Flds FSBYW WC1X 13 H1
Jodane Rd DEPT SE8 ....150 D4
Jodrell Cl ISLW TW7 ....160 C2
Jodrell Rd HOM E9 ....110 D6
Johanna St STHWK • SE1 ....22 A4
John Adam St CHCR WC2N 21 F1
John Aird Ct BAY/PAD W2 ....125 C4
John Archer Wy
WAND/EARL SW18 ....185 H1
John Ashby Cl
BRXS/STRHM SW2 ....187 G1
John Austin Cl KUTN/CMB KT2 ....201 H4
John Bradshaw Rd
STHGT/OAK N14 ....51 F3
John Burns Dr BARK IG11 ....115 E6
John Campbell Rd
STNW/STAM N16 ....88 C5
John Carpenter St EMB EC4Y 14 C5
John Felton Rd
BERM/RHTH SE16 ....25 F4
John Fisher St WCHPL E1 ....17 E5
John Gooch Dr ENC/FH EN2 ....38 B2
John Harrison Wy
GNWCH SE10 ....152 B3
John Islip St WEST SW1P 29 E2
John Lamb Ct
KTN/HRWW/W HA3 ....60 A4
John Maurice Cl WALW SE17 ....31 G1
John Mckenna Wk
BERM/RHTH SE16 ....25 G4
John Parker Sq BTSEA • SW11 ....165 H4
John Penn St LEW SE13 ....171 F2
John Perrin Pl
KTN/HRWW/W HA3 ....81 G4
John Prince's St
CAVSQ/HST W1G 11 H3
John Rennie Wk WAP E1W 25 H1
John Roll Wy BERM/RHTH SE16 ....25 F3
John Ruskin St CMBW SE5 ....168 B1
John's Av HDN NW4 ....84 A1
John Silkin La DEPT SE8 ....150 B5
John's La MRDN SM4 ....224 B3
John's Ms BMSBY WC1N 5 H6
John Smith Av FUL/PGN SW6 ....164 D1
Johnson Cl HACK E8 ....109 G6
Johnson Rd CROY/NA CR0 ....228 D6
HAYES BR2 ....233 F2
HEST TW5 ....158 A1
WLSDN NW10 ....102 D6
Johnson's Cl CAR SM5 ....244 B1
Johnsons Dr HPTN TW12 ....199 G4
Johnson's Pl PIM SW1V 28 B4
Johnson St NWDGN UB2 ....138 A3
WCHPL E1 ....130 D5
Johnsons Wy WLSDN NW10 ....122 B3
John Spencer Sq IS • N1 ....108 B4
Johns Pl WCHPL E1 ....17 H3
John's Ter CROY/NA CR0 ....229 F5
Johnston Cl BRXN/ST SW9 ....167 H2
Johnstone Rd EHAM E6 ....133 H2
Johnston Rd WFD IG8 ....72 C4
John St BMSBY WC1N 5 H6
EN EN1 ....39 F6
HSLW TW3 ....158 C2
SNWD SE25 ....229 G3
SRTFD E15 ....112 D6
John Trundle Highwalk
BARB • EC2Y 15 E1
John Williams Cl PECK SE15 ....150 B6
John Wilson St
WOOL/PLUM SE18 ....154 A4
John Wooley Cl LEW • SE13 ....172 A5
Joiners Arms Yd CMBW • SE5 ....168 D2
Joiner's La MTCM CR4 ....253 E1
Joiner St STHWK SE1 ....15 H6
Joint Rd EFNCH N2 ....66 A4
Jollys La YEAD UB4 ....118 B4
Jonathan St LBTH SE11 ....29 H3
Jones Rd PLSTW E13 ....132 D3
Jonson Cl MTCM CR4 ....226 D1
Jonson Cl YEAD UB4 ....118 C3
Jordan Cl RYLN/HDSTN HA2 ....98 C1
Jordan Gdns GFD/PVL UB6 ....100 D6
Jordans Cl DAGE RM10 ....117 F2
Jordans Ms WHTN TW2 ....180 A4
Joseph Av ACT W3 ....123 F1
Josephine Av
BRXS/STRHM SW2 ....167 H6
Joseph Locke Wy
ESH/CLAY KT10 ....219 E6
Joseph Powell Cl BAL SW12 ....187 E1
Joseph Ray Rd WAN E11 ....92 A2
Joseph St BOW E3 ....130 D4

Joseph Trotter Cl *CLKNW* EC1R 6 B4
Joshua St *POP/IOD* E14.........131 G5
Joslings Cl *SHB* W12............123 G6
Joslyn Cl *PEND* EN3.................41 E1
Joubert St *BTSEA* SW11.........166 B3
Jowett St *PECK* SE15.................9 G3
Joyce Av *UED* N18....................69 F1
Joyden's Wood Rd *BXLY* DA5 ...197 H6
Joydon Dr *CHDH* RM6...............95 H3
Joyners Cl *DAGW* RM9.............116 D2
Jubilee Av
  ROMW/RG RM7....................97 G2
  WHTN TW2.........................79 G5
Jubilee Br *STHWK* SE1..............15 F6
Jubilee Cl *CDALE/KGS* NW9.......82 D3
  KUT KT1............................201 E4
  PIN HA5..............................58 E6
  ROMW/RG RM7...................97 F2
Jubilee Crs *ED* N9...................53 G3
Jubilee Dr *RSLP* HA4................98 B2
Jubilee Gdns *STHL* UB1...........119 E4
  STHWK * SE1......................21 H2
Jubilee Market *COVGDN* * WC2E ..13 F5
Jubilee Pl *CHEL* SW3................26 B3
Jubilee Rd *CHEAM* SM3...........242 B5
  GFD/PVL UB6....................100 D6
Jubilee St *WCHPL* E1..............104 E5
Jubilee Ter *FUL/PGN* * SW6.....164 C3
The Jubilee *GNWCH* * SE10.....171 F1
Jubilee Vis *ESH/CLAY* * KT10...220 A5
Jubilee Wy *CHGSTN* KT9..........240 D1
  SCUP DA14........................195 G4
  WIM/MER SW19..................205 F4
Judd St *STPAN* WC1H...............10 D5
Jude St *CAN/RD* E16................132 D5
Judges' Wk *HAMP* NW3..........105 G1
Judge Wk *ESH/CLAY* KT10.......238 A4
Judith Av *CRW* RM5..................57 F2
Juer St *BTSEA* SW11...............166 A1
Juglans Rd *ORP* BR6..............235 G5
Jules Thorn Av *EN1* EN1...........39 G4
Julia Gdns *BARK* IG11.............156 B1
Juliana Cl *EFNCH* N2.................65 G2
Julian Av *ACT* W3..................122 B6
Julian Cl *BAR* EN5....................35 E4
Julian Hl *HRW* HA1..................80 B2
Julian Pl *POP/IOD* E14............151 F5
Julian Rd *ORP* BR6................253 G4
Julian Tayler Pth *SYD* * SE26...189 H4
Julien Rd *EA* W5....................141 E3
Juliette Rd *PLSTW* E13...........132 C1
Julius Nyerere Cl N1 * N1.......107 H6
Junction Ap *BTSEA* SW11.......166 A4
  LEW SE13.........................171 G4
Junction Ms *BAY/PAD* W2.........10 A5
Junction Pl *BAY/PAD* W2........125 H5
Junction Rd *ARCH* N19...........107 E1
  EA W5.............................141 E4
  ED N9...............................53 G3
  HRW HA1............................80 A3
  PLSTW E13.......................112 D6
  SAND/SEL CR2..................246 D4
  TOTM N17..........................69 H3
Junction Rd East *CHDH* RM6....94 C4
Junction Rd West *CHDH* RM6....96 B4
Juniper Cl *BAR* EN5.................34 B6
  CHGSTN KT9.....................239 H4
Juniper Crs *CAMTN* NW1.........106 C5
  KTN/HRWW/W HA3..............60 D4
Juniper Gdns *MTCM* CR4.........207 E4
Juniper La *EHAM* E6................113 G4
Juniper Rd *IL* IG1...................114 A2
Juniper St *WCHPL* * E1............130 A6
Juno Wy *NWCR* SE14..............150 B6
Jupiter Wy *HOLWY* N7............107 H4
Jupp Rd *SRTFD* E15...............111 H5
Jupp Rd West *SRTFD* E15........111 C6
Justice Wk *CHEL* SW3.............26 A6
Justin Cl *BTFD* TW8................161 F1
Justin Rd *CHING* E4.................70 D2
Jute La *PEND* EN3..................40 C3
Jutland Rd *CAT* SE6...............191 G2
  PLSTW E13.......................132 C3
Jutsums Av *ROMW/RG* RM7.....97 F3
Jutsums La *ROMW/RG* RM7......97 F3
Juxon Cl *RYLN/HDSTN* HA2......59 H4
Juxon St *LBTH* SE11.................29 H1

K

Kale Rd *ERITHM* DA18.............156 B2
Kambala Rd *BTSEA* SW11........165 H3
Kangley Bridge Rd *SYD* SE26...210 D1
Kaplan Dr *WCHMH* N21...........34 D1
Karen Ct *BMLY* BR1................212 B4
Karenza Ct *WBLY* * HA9...........81 E4
Karina Cl *CHIG* IG7...................75 E1
Kashgar Rd *WOOL/PLUM* SE18...155 F5
Kashmir Rd *CHARL* SE7...........134 D1
Kassala Rd *BTSEA* SW11.........166 B2
Katharine St *CROY/NA* CR0.....244 C5
Katherine Cl *BERM/RHTH* SE16..133 H1
Katherine Gdns *BARK/HLT* IG6...74 C3
  ELTH/MOT SE9..................174 A4
Katherine Rd *EHAM* E6...........113 F5
Katherine Sq *NTGHL* * W11.....144 C1
Kathleen Av *ACT* W3..............122 C4
  ALP/SUD HA0....................101 G5
Kathleen Rd *BTSEA* SW11.......166 B4
Kayemoor Rd *BELMT* SM2......244 A5
Kay Rd *BRXN/ST* SW9.............167 G3
Kays Ter *SWFD* * E18...............72 B5
Kay St *BETH* E2.........................7 G2
  SRTFD * E15.....................111 H5
Kaye Dr *DAGE* RM10..............175 H2
Kean St *HOL/ALD* WC2B...........11 G4
Keatley Gn *CHING* E4................70 D2
Keats Av *CAN/RD* E16.............152 D1
Keats Cl *CHIG* IG7...................74 D2
  PEND EN3.........................40 B6
  STHWK SE1........................32 C2
  TOOT SW17.......................188 A1
  WAN E11...........................88 D1
Keats Est *STNW/STAM* * N16...89 F6
Keats Gv *HAMP* NW3..............106 A2
Keats Pde *ED* * N9...................53 G4

Keats Rd *BELV* DA17...............157 G3
  WELL DA16.......................175 F2
Keats Wy *CROY/NA* CR0.........230 A3
  GFD/PVL UB6....................119 F4
  WDGN N22.........................49 E5
Keble Pl *BARN* SW13..............143 H6
Keble St *TOOT* SW17..............185 G6
Kechill Gdns *HAYES* BR2.........282 C4
Kedeston Dr *STHL/STPC* BR5...255 F5
Kedleston Wk *BETH* E2...............9 H3
Keebie Cl *WOOL/PLUM* * SE18..154 B6
Keedonwood Rd *BMLY* BR1.....192 A6
Keel Cl *BARK* IG11.................136 A1
  BERM/RHTH SE16..............150 B1
Keeley Rd *CROY/NA* CR0.........228 C6
Keeley St *HOL/ALD* WC2B........11 G4
Keeling Rd *ELTH/MOT* SE9......173 F6
Keely Cl *EBAR* EN4...................36 A6
Keemor Cl *WOOL/PLUM* * SE18..174 A1
Keens Cl *STRHM/NOR* SW16....207 F1
Keen's Rd *CROY/NA* CR0.........246 C2
Keen's Yd *IS* N1.....................108 B4
Keepers Ms *TEDD* TW11..........201 E2
The Keep *BKHTH/KID* SE3......172 C3
  KUTN/CMB KT2..................193 E5
Keeton's Rd *BERM/RHTH* SE16...25 C5
Keevil Dr *WIM/MER* SW19.......184 B2
Keighley Cl *HOLWY* N7...........107 G2
Keightley Dr *ELTH/MOT* SE9....194 C3
Keildon Rd *BTSEA* SW11.........166 B5
Keir Hardie Est *CLPT* * E5.........89 H5
Keir Hardie Wy *BARK* IG11......115 G5
Keith Connor Cl *VX/NE* SW8...166 D4
Keith Gv *SHB* W12..................143 G2
Keith Rd *BARK* IG11................134 D1
  WALTH E17.........................70 D4
Kelbrook Rd *BKHTH/KID* SE3...175 G3
Kelceda Cl *CRICK* NW2.............83 G6
Kelfield Gdns *NKENS* W10.......124 B5
Kelfield Ms *NKENS* W10...........124 B1
Kelland Cl *CEND/HSY/T* * N8.....87 F2
Kelland Rd *PLSTW* E13............132 C3
Kellaway Rd *BKHTH/KID* SE3...175 E3
Keller Crs *MNPK* E12..............113 E2
Kellerton Rd *LEW* SE13...........172 A6
Kellett Rd *BRXS/STRHM* SW2...168 A5
Kelling Gdns *CROY/NA* CR0.....228 B4
Kellino St *TOOT* SW17............188 H6
Kellner Rd *THMD* SE28............155 F3
Kell St *STHWK* SE1...................22 D5
Kelly Cl *WLSDN* NW10.............102 D1
Kelly Ms *MV/WKIL* * W9...........124 D4
Kelly Rd *MLHL* NW7..................64 C2
Kelly St *CAMTN* NW1..............106 D4
Kelly Wy *CHDH* RM6.................96 C2
Kelman Cl *CLAP* SW4..............167 F3
Kelmore Gv *EDUL* SE22...........169 G3
Kelmscott Cl *WALTH* E17..........70 D4
Kelmscott Gdns *SHB* W12.......143 G3
Kelmscott Rd *BTSEA* SW11......166 B6
Kelross Rd *HBRY* N5..................88 D3
Kelsall Cl *BKHTH/KID* SE3.......172 D3
Kelsey La *BECK* BR3................211 E6
Kelsey Park Av *BECK* BR3........211 F6
Kelsey Rd *STMC/STPC* BR5.....215 H5
Kelsey Sq *BECK* BR3...............211 E5
Kelsey St *BETH* E2.....................9 H5
Kelsey Wy *BECK* BR3..............211 E6
Kelsie Wy *BARK/HLT* IG6...........75 E2
Kelso Pl *KENS* W8..................145 F3
Kelso Rd *CAR* SM5.................225 G4
Kelston Rd *BARK/HLT* IG6.........74 D5
Kelton Vis *KUT* * KT1...............200 E1
Kelvedon Cl *KUTN/CMB* KT2....202 A2
Kelvedon Rd *FUL/PGN* SW6.....164 D1
Kelvedon Wy *WFD* IG8..............73 H2
Kelvin Av *PLMGR* N13................47 G1
Kelvinbrook *E/WMO/HCT* KT8...199 F6
Kelvin Cl *HOR/WEW* KT19.......240 A4
Kelvin Crs *KTN/HRWW/W* HA3...60 A3
Kelvin Dr *TWK* TW1.................180 D1
Kelvin Gdns *CROY/NA* CR0......227 G4
  STHL UB1..........................119 E5
Kelvin Gv *SURB* KT6................239 G1
  SYD SE26.........................189 H5
Kelvington Cl *CROY/NA* CR0....250 C6
Kelvington Rd *PECK* SE15.......170 B6
Kelvin Pde *ORP* BR6...............235 E5
Kelvin Rd *HBRY* N5...................88 D1
  WELL DA16.......................175 C4
Kember St *IS* N1.....................107 H5
Kemble Dr *HAYES* BR2............251 C1
Kemble Rd *CROY/NA* CR0........246 B1
  FSTH SE23.......................190 B3
  TOTM N17..........................69 G4
Kemble St *HOL/ALD* WC2B........11 G4
Kemerton Rd *BECK* BR3..........211 F5
  CMBW SE5........................168 C4
  CROY/NA CR0...................230 A5
Kemey's St *HOM* E9................110 C3
Kemnal Rd *CHST* BR7..............214 C2
Kempe Rd *KIL/WHAMP* NW6....124 B1
Kemp Gdns *CROY/NA* CR0.......228 D5
Kemplay Rd *HAMP* NW3..........105 H2
Kemp Pl *BUSH* WD23................43 E1
Kemps Dr *POP/IOD* E14...........131 G6
Kempsford Gdns *ECT* SW5......145 E5
Kempsford Rd *LBTH* SE11.........30 B2
Kempshott Rd
  STRHM/NOR SW16.............207 H3
Kempson Rd *FUL/PGN* SW6.....165 G2
Kempthorne Rd *DEPT* SE8.......150 C4
Kempton Av *NTHLT* UB5............99 A6
Kempton Cl *ERITH* DA8...........157 C6
Kempton Pk *SUN* * TW16........198 A4
Kempton Rd *EHAM* E6.............113 H6
  HPTN TW12......................198 D5
Kempton Wk *CROY/NA* CR0.....230 C3
Kempt St *WOOL/PLUM* SE18...154 A6
Kemsing Cl *BXLY* DA5.............176 C6
  THHTH * CR7....................228 C1
Kemsing Rd *GNWCH* SE10.......152 C5
Kenbury St *CMBW* SE5...........168 A5
Kenchester Cl *VX/NE* SW8.......167 H1
Kendal Av *BARK* IG11..............115 E6
  UED N18............................52 D6
Kendal Cl *CMBW* SE5..............168 B1
  WFD IG8............................56 B4

Kendal Ct *ACT* W3..................122 A4
Kendale Rd *BMLY* BR1............212 A1
Kendal Gdns *SUT* SM1............225 G6
  UED N18............................52 D6
Kendall Av *BECK* BR3.............210 C5
  SAND/SEL CR2..................246 D6
Kendall Pl *MHST* W1U..............11 E2
Kendall Rd *BECK* BR3.............210 C5
  ISLW TW7.........................160 B3
  WOOL/PLUM SE18.............175 G2
Kendalmere Cl *MUSWH* N10....48 B4
Kendal Pde *UED* * N18.............52 D6
Kendal Pl *PUT/ROE* SW15......164 C3
Kendal Rd *WLSDN* NW10........103 G2
Kendal Steps *BAY/PAD* * W2....10 B4
Kender St *NWCR* SE14............170 A1
Kendoa Rd *CLAP* SW4.............167 F5
Kendon Cl *WAN* E11..................71 G2
Kendra Hall Rd *SAND/SEL* CR2..246 B5
Kendrey Gdns *WHTN* TW2.......180 A4
Kendrick Ms *SKENS* SW7.........145 H4
Kendrick Pl *SKENS* SW7..........145 H4
Kenelm Cl *HRW* HA1...............100 C1
Kenerne Dr *BAR* EN5................34 C6
Kenilford Rd *BAL* SW12..........186 D2
Kenilworth Av
  RYLN/HDSTN HA2...............98 D2
  WALTH E17.........................71 E5
  WIM/MER SW19..................186 E1
Kenilworth Crs *EN* EN1.............39 E2
Kenilworth Gdns
  GDMY/SEVK IG3..................91 H5
  LOU IG10...........................57 H1
  OXHEY WD19......................58 A1
  STHL * UB1.......................118 D2
  WOOL/PLUM SE18.............174 B5
Kenilworth Rd *BOW* E3............111 H2
  EA W5.............................141 G1
  EDGW HA8.........................46 C4
  EW KT17...........................241 G4
  HOM NW6.........................106 D1
  PGE/AN SE20....................210 B4
  STMC/STPC BR5................234 C3
Kenilworth Ter *BELMT* SM2.....243 E5
Kenley Av *CDALE/KGS* NW9.....45 G4
Kenley Cl *BXLY* DA5................197 G2
  CHST BR7.........................215 E6
  EBAR EN4..........................36 A5
Kenley Gdns *THHTH* CR7........228 B1
Kenley Rd *KUT* KT1................201 H5
  TWK TW1..........................180 C1
  WIM/MER SW19..................205 E6
Kenley Wk *CHEAM* SM3..........242 B2
  NTGHL * W11....................144 C1
Kenlor Rd *TOOT* SW17............205 H1
Kenmare Dr *MTCM* CR4..........206 B3
Kenmare Gdns *PLMGR* N13......35 G6
Kenmare Rd *THHTH* CR7..........228 A3
Kenmere Gdns *ALP/SUD* HA0..102 A6
Kenmere Rd *WELL* DA16.........176 C1
Kenmont Gdns *WLSDN* NW10..123 H2
Kenmore Av
  KTN/HRWW/W HA3...............80 C1
Kenmore Gdns *EDGW* HA8.......62 B5
Kenmore Rd
  KTN/HRWW/W HA3...............61 F6
Kenmure Rd *HACK* * E8...........109 H3
Kenmure Yd *HACK* * E8...........109 H3
Kennard Rd *FBAR/BDGN* N11...66 B1
  SRTFD E15.......................111 H5
Kennard St *BTSEA* SW11........166 D2
  CAN/RD E16.....................153 H1
Kennedy Av *PEND* EN3.............54 A1
Kennedy Cl *MTCM* CR4..........206 D6
  PIN HA5.............................58 D2
  PLSTW E13.......................132 C1
  STMC/STPC BR5................234 D5
Kennedy Rd *BARK* IG11..........115 E6
  HNWL W7.........................120 A4
Kennedy Wk *WALW* SE17..........19 F6
Kennet Cl *BTSEA* SW11...........165 H5
Kennet Dr *YEAD* UB4...............118 C4
Kennet Rd *DART* DA1..............159 E2
  ISLW TW7.........................160 A1
  MV/WKIL W9.....................124 D3
Kennet Sq *MTCM* CR4............206 D6
Kennet St *WAP* E1W.................25 F1
Kennet Wharf La *BLKFR* EC4V...15 F5
Kenninghall Rd *CLPT* E5..........109 H1
  UED N18............................69 H1
Kenning St *BERM/RHTH* SE16...132 D2
Kennings Wy *LBTH* SE11............30 B3
Kennington Gdns *KUT* KT1.......201 E4
Kennington Gv *LBTH* SE11........29 H5
Kennington La *LBTH* SE11.........30 A5
Kennington Ov *LBTH* SE11........30 A3
Kennington Park Gdns
  LBTH SE11.........................30 C5
Kennington Park Pl *WALW* SE17..30 B5
Kennington Park Rd *LBTH* SE11..30 B5
Kennington Rd *LBTH* SE11........17 H6
Kenny Dr *CAR* SM5.................259 H6
Kennylands Rd *BARK/HLT* IG6...75 G3
Kenny Rd *MLHL* NW7.................46 D1
Kenrick Pl *MHST* W1U...............11 E1
Kensal Rd *NKENS* W10............124 C3
Kensal Wharf *NKENS* * W10.....124 C3
Kensington Av *MNPK* E12........113 H4
  THHTH CR7.......................208 A4
Kensington Church Ct
  KENS W8..........................145 E2
Kensington Church St
  KENS W8..........................145 E1
Kensington Church Wk
  KENS W8..........................145 F2
Kensington Cl
  FBAR/BDGN * N11................66 C1
Kensington Ct *KENS* W8...........145 F2
Kensington Court Gdns
  KENS * W8........................145 F3
Kensington Court Ms
  KENS * W8........................145 F3
Kensington Court Pl
  KENS W8..........................145 F3
Kensington Dr *WFD* IG8............73 F5
Kensington Gdns *IL* IG1............93 H5

Kensington Gardens Sq
  BAY/PAD * W2...................125 F5
Kensington Ga *KENS* W8..........145 G3
Kensington Core *SKENS* SW7...145 G2
Kensington Hall Gdns
  WKENS * W14...................144 D5
Kensington High St *KENS* W8...145 E3
  WKENS W14.....................144 C4
Kensington Mi *KENS* W8..........145 F1
Kensington Palace *KENS* * W8...145 F1
Kensington Palace Gdns
  KENS W8..........................145 F2
Kensington Park Gdns
  NTGHL W11.......................124 D6
Kensington Park Ms
  NTGHL W11.......................124 D5
Kensington Park Rd
  NTGHL W11.......................124 D5
Kensington Pl *KENS* W8...........145 E1
Kensington Rd *KENS* W8..........145 F1
  NTHLT UB5.......................116 B3
  ROMW/RG RM7...................97 G3
  SKENS SW7......................145 H1
Kensington Sq *KENS* W8.........145 F2
Kensington Ter *SAND/SEL* CR2..246 D5
Kent Av *DAGW* RM9...............137 E3
  WEA W13.........................102 D4
  WELL DA16.......................175 F6
Kent Cl *ORP* BR6...................249 F6
  STRHM/NOR SW16............227 G1
Kent Ct *CDALE/KGS* * NW9.......63 G5
Kent Dr *EBAR* EN4..................36 C5
  TEDD TW11.......................200 A1
Kentford Wy *NTHLT* UB5.........245 C6
Kent Gdns *WEA* W13..............120 D4
Kent Gate Wy *CROY/NA* CR0...248 C6
Kent House La *BECK* BR3.........210 C2
Kent House Rd *BECK* BR3........210 B1
Kentish Bd *BELV* DA17............157 E4
Kentish Town Rd *CAMTN* NW1...106 D4
Kentish Wy *BMLY* BR1............212 D5
Kentlea Rd *THMD* SE28...........155 E3
Kentmere Rd *WOOL/PLUM* SE18..155 E4
Kenton Av *HRW* HA1.................80 B4
  STHL UB1.........................119 E6
  SUN TW16........................198 B5
Kenton Gdns
  KTN/HRWW/W HA3...............60 D5
Kenton La
  KTN/HRWW/W HA3...............81 F1
Kenton Park Av
  KTN/HRWW/W HA3...............81 F1
Kenton Park Cl
  KTN/HRWW/W HA3...............81 F1
Kenton Park Crs
  KTN/HRWW/W HA3...............81 F1
Kenton Park Pde
  KTN/HRWW/W HA3...............81 F2
Kenton Park Rd
  HRW HA1............................81 E1
  KTN/HRWW/W HA3...............81 F1
Kenton Rd *HOM* E9..................110 B4
  KTN/HRWW/W HA3...............81 E2
Kenton St *STPAN* WC1H............5 E5
Kent Rd *CHSWK* W4................117 F5
  DAGE RM10.......................92 D5
  E/WMO/HCT KT8...............219 G1
  KUT KT1............................200 D5
  RCH/KEW TW9...................162 A1
  STMC/STPC BR5................235 H5
  WCHMH N21.......................35 E2
  WWKM BR4.......................231 F5
Kent St *BETH* E2........................7 H2
  PLSTW E13.......................132 D2
Kent Ter *CAMTN* NW1.................2 D3
Kent View Gdns
  GDMY/SEVK IG3..................95 E6
Kent Wy *SURB* KT6................223 G2
Kentwell Cl *BROCKY* * SE4......170 C5
Kentwode Gn *BARN* SW13.......163 G1
Kenward Rd *ELTH/MOT* SE9....173 E6
Kenway *ROMW/RG* RM7............77 G5
Ken Wy *WBLY* HA9....................63 H5
Kenway Rd *ECT* SW5..............145 E5
Kenwood Cl *GLDGN* NW11.......65 E3
  HAMP NW3.........................85 F5
Kenwood Dr *BECK* BR3...........211 G6
Kenwood Gdns *CLAY* IG5..........94 A1
  SWFD E18..........................72 A1
Kenwood Rd *ED* N9...................53 G2
  HGT N6...............................65 H6
Kenworthy Rd *HOM* E9.............110 C3
Kenwyn Dr *CRICK* NW2.............83 E1
Kenwyn Rd *CLAP* SW4............167 F2
  RYNPK SW20.....................204 D6
Kenya Rd *CHARL* SE7.............173 F1
Kenyngton Pl
  KTN/HRWW/W HA3...............81 E2
Kenyon St *FUL/PGN* SW6........163 E3
Keogh Rd *SRTFD* E15..............112 A4
Kepler Rd *CLAP* SW4..............168 A2
Keppel Rd *DAGW* RM9............116 C2
  EHAM E6............................113 H5
Keppel St *GWRST* WC1E...........12 D1
Kerbela St *BETH* E2....................9 G5
Kerbey St *POP/IOD* E14...........131 F5
Kerfield Crs *CMBW* SE5..........168 D2
Kerfield Pl *CMBW* SE5............168 D2
Kerri Cl *BAR* EN5......................34 A5
Kerrison Pl *EA* W5..................141 F1
Kerrison Rd *BTSEA* SW11.......166 B1
  SRTFD E15.......................111 F1
Kerry Av *STAN* HA7...................44 A1
Kerry Cl *CAN/RD* E16..............132 C6
  PLMGR N13........................51 H4
Kerry Ct *STAN* HA7...................44 A1
Kerry Pth *NWCR* SE14............150 D6
Kerry Rd *NWCR* SE14.............150 D6
Kersfield Rd *PUT/ROE* SW15...184 B1
Kershaw Rd *DAGE* RM10..........92 C2
Kersley Ms *BTSEA* SW11.........166 B6
Kersley Rd *STNW/STAM* N16...109 E1
Kersley St *BTSEA* SW11..........166 B5
Kerswell Cl *SEVS/STOTM* N15...89 E2
Kerwick Cl *HOLWY* N7............107 H5
Keslake Rd *KIL/WHAMP* NW6...124 A1
Kessock Cl *WALTH* E17..............89 H1
Kesteven Cl *BARK/HLT* IG6........75 F2

Keston Av HAYES BR2	251	E3
Keston Cl UED N18	52	D5
WELL DA16	176	A1
Keston Gdns HAYES BR2	251	E3
Keston Park Cl HAYES BR2	251	H2
Keston Rd PECK SE15	169	G4
THHTH CR7	227	H3
TOTM N17	68	D6
Kestrel Av EHAM E6	133	G4
HNHL SE24	168	B6
Kestrel Cl CDALE/KGS NW9	63	E5
KUTN/CMB KT2	181	F6
WLSDN NW10	102	D3
Kestrel Pl NWCR * SE14	150	C6
Keswick Av KUTN/CMB KT2	203	E1
WIM/MER SW19	205	E5
Keswick Cl SUT SM1	243	G2
Keswick Gdns REDBR IG4	93	G2
WBLY HA9	101	G3
Keswick Ms EA W5	141	G1
Keswick Rd BXLYHN DA7	177	G3
ORP BR6	235	F5
PUT/ROE SW15	164	C6
WHTN TW2	179	C1
WWKM BR4	232	A6
Kettering Ct		
STRHM/NOR SW16	206	D2
Kettlebaston Rd LEY E10	90	D5
Kettlewell Cl FBAR/BDGN N11	66	A2
Kevellos Rd TOTM N17	68	C4
Kevin Cl HSLWW TW4	158	B3
Kevington Cl STMC/STPC BR5	235	F1
Kevington Dr CHST BR7	235	F1
Kew Br RCH/KEW TW9	142	A6
Kew Bridge Arches		
CHSWK * W4	142	A6
Kew Bridge Rd BTFD TW8	141	H6
Kew Crs CHEAM SM3	242	D1
Kew Foot Rd RCH/KEW TW9	161	G5
Kew Gardens Rd		
RCH/KEW TW9	161	H1
Kew Meadow Pth		
RCH/KEW TW9	141	H6
Kew Rd RCH/KEW TW9	162	B2
Kew Rd RCH/KEW TW9	161	G5
Key CI WHCHPL E1	92	D3
Keyes Rd CRICK NW2	104	B3
Keymer Rd BRXS/STRHM SW2	187	H4
Keynes CI FNCH N2	66	B6
Keynsham Av WFD IG8	56	A6
Keynsham Gdns		
ELTH/MOT SE9	173	G6
Keynsham Rd ELTH/MOT SE9	173	G6
MRDN SM4	225	F5
Keyse Rd STHWK SE1	24	C6
Keystone Crs IS N1	5	F2
Keyworth Cl CLPT E5	110	C2
Keyworth St STHWK SE1	22	D5
Kezia St DEPT SE8	150	C5
Khama Rd TOOT SW17	186	A6
Khartoum Rd IL IG1	114	B3
PLSTW E13	132	D2
TOOT SW17	185	H6
Khyber Rd BTSEA SW11	166	A3
Kibworth St VX/NE SW8	167	H1
Kidbrooke Gdns		
BKHTH/KID SE3	172	C3
Kidbrooke Gv BKHTH/KID SE3	172	C3
Kidbrooke La ELTH/MOT SE9	173	C5
Kidbrooke Park Cl		
BKHTH/KID SE3	172	D2
Kidbrooke Park Rd		
BKHTH/KID SE3	172	D3
Kidbrooke Wy BKHTH/KID SE3	172	D3
Kidderminster Pl		
CROY/NA CRO	228	B6
Kidderminster Rd		
CROY/NA CRO	228	B6
Kidderpore Av HAMP NW3	105	G2
Kidderpore Gdns HAMP NW3	105	G2
Kidd Pl CHARL SE7	153	G5
Kidlington Wy CDALE/KGS NW9	63	G5
Kielder Cl BARK/HLT IG6	75	F2
Kilberry Cl ISLW TW7	159	H2
Kilburn Br KIL/WHAMP NW6	105	E6
Kilburn High Rd		
KIL/WHAMP NW6	105	E5
Kilburn Park Rd		
KIL/WHAMP NW6	125	G2
KIL/WHAMP NW6	125	E1
Kilburn Pl KIL/WHAMP NW6	105	E6
Kilburn Priory		
KIL/WHAMP NW6	105	F6
Kilburn Sq KIL/WHAMP NW6	105	E6
Kilburn V KIL/WHAMP NW6	105	F6
Kildare Cl RSLP HA4	78	A5
Kildare Rd CAN/RD E16	132	C4
Kildare Ter BAY/PAD W2	125	E5
Kildoran Rd CLAP SW4	167	G6
Kildowan Rd GDMY/SEVK IG3	95	G5
Kilgour Rd FSTH SE23	190	C1
Kilkie St FUL/PGN SW6	165	H1
Killarney Rd WAND/EARL SW18	185	C1
Killburns Mill Cl WLGTN SM6	226	D6
Killearn Rd CAT SE6	191	H5
Killester Gdns EW KT17	241	H2
Killewarren Wy		
STMC/STPC BR5	236	A4
Killick St IS N1	5	F2
Killieser Av BRXS/STRHM SW2	187	G4
Killip Cl CAN/RD E16	132	D5
Killowen Av NTHLT UB5	96	C3
Killowen Rd HOM * E9	110	B4
Killyon Rd VX/NE SW8	167	E3
Kilmaine Rd FUL/PGN SW6	164	C1
Kilmarnock Gdns BCTR RM8	116	A1
Kilmarnock Rd OXHEY WD19	42	B2
Kilmarsh Rd HMSMTH W6	146	A4
Kilmartin Av STRHM/NOR SW16	208	B2
Kilmartin Rd GDMY/SEVK IG3	95	G5
Kilmington Rd BARN SW13	143	G6
Kilmorey Gdns TWK TW1	160	D6
Kilmorey Rd TWK TW1	160	D5
Kilmorie Rd FSTH SE23	190	C3
Kiln Pl KTTN/HRW * NW5	108	A1
Kiln Ms TOOT SW17	205	H1
Kiln Wood La CRW RM5	57	F2
Kilnside ESH/CLAY KT10	238	C5
Kiln Wood La CRW RM5	57	F2
Kilpatrick Wy YEAD UB4	118	C4
Kilravock St NKENS W10	124	C1
Kilvinton Dr ENC/FH EN2	38	D1
Kimberl Gdns FUL/PGN SW6	164	C2
Kimbell Pl ELTH/MOT SE9	173	E5
Kimberley Av EHAM E6	133	C1
GNTH/NBYPK IG2	94	D4
ROMW/RG RM7	75	H1
Kimberley Dr SCUP DA14	196	D4
Kimberley Gdns EN EN1	39	F4
FSBYPK N4	88	B2
Kimberley Rd BECK BR3	215	H1
BRXN/ST SW9	167	G3
CAN/RD E16	132	B3
CHING E4	56	A1
CROY/NA CR0	228	B3
KIL/WHAMP NW6	120	C6
TOTM N17	69	C5
UED N18	69	H5
WALTH E17	51	G6
WAN E11	91	H6
Kimberley Wy CHING E4	56	A1
Kimber Rd WAND/EARL SW18	185	F2
Kimble Crs BUSH WD23	43	G2
Kimble Rd TOOT SW17	205	H2
Kimbolton Cl LEE/GVPK SE12	192	B1
Kimmeridge Gdns		
ELTH/MOT SE9	193	G6
Kimmeridge Rd ELTH/MOT SE9	193	G6
Kimpton Rd CHEAM SM5	224	C1
CMBW SE5	168	D2
Kinburn St BERM/RHTH * SE16	150	B2
Kincaid Rd PECK SE15	169	H1
Kincardine Gdns		
MV/WKIL * W9	125	C3
Kinch Gv WBLY HA9	81	H4
Kinder Cl THMD SE28	136	A6
Kinder St WCHPL * E1	17	G4
WCHPL E1	17	G4
Kinfauns Rd BRXS/STRHM SW2	188	A4
GDMY/SEVK IG3	95	H5
King Alfred Av CAT SE6	191	E5
King Arthur Cl PECK SE15	170	A1
King Charles Crs BRYLDS KT5	221	H4
King Charles' Rd BRYLDS KT5	221	G4
King Charles St WHALL SW1A	20	C1
King Charles Ter WAP * E1W	17	H6
King Charles Wk		
WIM/MER * SW19	184	C3
King David La WAP E1W	17	H6
Kingdon Rd KIL/WHAMP NW6	105	E4
King Edward Dr SURB KT6	239	C1
King Edward Rd BAR EN5	35	E5
LEY E10	91	C1
OXHEY WD19	42	B2
WALTH E17	70	C1
King Edward's Gdns ACT W3	142	A1
King Edward's Gv TEDD TW11	200	D2
King Edward's Rd BARK IG11	114	D6
ED N9	42	D2
HACK E8	109	H6
PEND EN3	60	B5
King Edward St STBT EC1A	15	E3
King Edward the Third Ms		
BERM/RHTH SE16	25	G4
King Edward Wk STHWK SE1	22	B4
Kingfield Rd EA W5	121	E3
Kingfield St POP/IOD E14	151	F3
Kingfisher Cl STMC/STPC BR5	236	B1
THMD SE28	128	C6
Kingfisher Dr		
RCHPK/HAM TW10	181	E6
Kingfisher Pl WDGN * N22	67	H5
Kingfisher St EHAM E6	133	J4
Kingfisher Wy CROY/NA CR0	230	B2
WLSDN * NW10	81	F4
King Gdns CROY/NA CR0	246	B3
King George Av BUSH WD23	43	F1
CAN/RD E16	133	C5
GNTH/NBYPK IG2	94	D3
WOT/HER KT12	218	B5
King George Ct ROMW/RG RM7	77	D6
King George Sq		
RCHPK/HAM TW10	181	H1
King George St GNWCH SE10	171	G1
King George VI Av MTCM CR4	226	D1
Kingham Cl NTGHL W11	144	C2
WAND/EARL SW18	185	G2
King Harolds Wy BXLYHN DA7	176	B1
King Henry Ms ORP BR6	253	F1
King Henry's Dr CROY/NA CR0	249	G6
King Henry's Rd HAMP NW3	106	A5
KUT KT1	202	B6
King Henry St		
STNW/STAM N16	109	E3
King Henry Wk IS N1	109	E4
King Henry Ter WAP * E1W	17	H6
Kinghorn St STBT * EC1A	14	D2
King James St STHWK SE1	22	D4
King John Ct SDTCH EC2A	8	B5
King John St WCHPL E1	130	B4
King John's Wk ELTH/MOT SE9	173	G1
Kinglake St WALW * SE17	32	A3
Kinglake St WALW * SE17	24	A6
Kingly Ct REGST * W1B	12	B5
Kingly St REGST W1B	12	A4
King & Queen Cl		
ELTH/MOT * SE9	193	G6
King & Queen St WALW * SE17	31	F3
King & Queen Whf		
BERM/RHTH * SE16	150	B1
Kingsand Rd LEE/GVPK SE12	192	C5
Kings Arbour NWDGN UB2	138	C5
King's Arms Yd LOTH EC2R	15	G3
Kingsash Dr YEAD UB4	118	C3
Kings Av BAL SW12	187	F3
BMLY BR1	183	E6
CAR SM5	244	A5
CHDH RM6	73	H3
CLAP SW4	188	A1
EA W5	121	F5
GFD/PVL UB6	119	F5
HSLW TW3	159	F2
MUSWH N10	66	C1
NWMAL N21	52	B5
WFD IG8	71	F1
King's Bench St STHWK SE1	22	D3
King's Bench Wk EMB * EC4Y	14	B5
Kingsbridge Av EA W5	141	H2
Kingsbridge Rd BARK IG11	134	D1
MRDN SM4	224	B4
NKENS W10	124	A5
NWDGN UB2	138	D4
PLSTW E13	133	G2
ROMW/RG RM7	57	F6
Kingsbury Gn CDALE/KGS * NW9	82	C2
Kingsbury Rd CDALE/KGS NW9	82	C2
IS N1	109	E4
Kingsbury Ter IS N1	109	E4
Kings Cha E/WMO/HCT KT8	199	G6
Kingsclere Cl PUT/ROE SW15	183	G2
Kingsclere Pl ENC/FH EN2	23	J7
Kingscliffe Gdns		
WIM/MER SW19	184	D3
Kingscote Rd CHSWK W4	142	A3
CROY/NA CR0	229	H4
NWMAL KT3	207	H5
Kingscote St EMB EC4Y	14	C5
Kings Ct PLSTW E13	112	D6
STHWK * SE1	22	D1
Kingscourt Rd		
STRHM/NOR SW16	187	F5
King's Crs FSBYPK N4	108	C1
King's Cross Br FSBYW * WC1X	5	F3
King's Cross Rd FSBYW WC1X	5	F3
Kingsdale Gdns NTGHL W11	144	B1
Kingsdale Rd POE/AN SE20	210	B3
WOOL/PLUM SE18	155	F6
Kingsdown Av ACT W3	123	E6
SAND/SEL CR2	246	C6
WEA W13	140	D2
Kingsdown Cl		
BERM/RHTH SE16	33	H4
NTGHL W11	124	B5
Kingsdowne Rd SURB KT6	221	F4
Kingsdown Rd ARCH N19	107	G1
CHEAM SM3	242	C3
WAN E11	112	A1
Kingsdown Wy HAYES BR2	232	C3
Kings Dr BRYLDS KT5	222	A4
EDGW HA8	45	H6
THDIT KT7	220	D3
WBLY HA9	82	B6
Kings Farm WALTH * E17	71	F4
Kings Farm Av		
RCHPK/HAM TW10	162	A5
Kingsfield Av RYLN/HDSTN HA2	79	F2
Kingsfield Ct OXHEY WD19	42	B1
Kingsfield Rd HRW * HA1	79	H4
OXHEY WD19	42	B2
Kingsford Av WLGTN SM6	245	E5
Kingsford St KTTN NW5	106	B3
Kingsford Wy EHAM E6	133	H4
Kings Gdns IL IG1	94	D5
KIL/WHAMP NW6	105	E5
Kingsgate WBLY HA9	102	C1
Kingsgate Av FNCH N3	65	E6
Kingsgate Cl BXLYHN DA7	176	D2
Kingsgate Pl KIL/WHAMP NW6	105	E5
Kingsgate Rd		
KIL/WHAMP NW6	105	E5
KUT KT1	201	G4
Kingsground ELTH/MOT SE9	193	F2
King's Gv PECK SE15	169	H2
Kings Hall Ms LEW * SE13	171	G4
Kings Hall Rd BECK BR3	210	B3
Kings Head HI CHING E4	55	F2
Kingshill Av CRW RM5	77	G2
KTN/HRWW/WS HA3	61	H5
NTHLT UB5	77	G4
WPK KT4	223	G4
Kingshill Ct BAR * EN5	34	C5
Kingshold Rd HOM E9	110	A5
Kingsholm Gdns		
ELTH/MOT SE9	173	F5
Kingshurst Rd LEE/GVPK SE12	192	C2
Kings Keep HAYES * BR2	221	C1
SURB * KT6	221	G1
Kingsland Gn STNW/STAM N16	109	E4
Kingsland High St HACK E8	109	F4
Kingsland Pas HACK E8	109	E4
Kingsland Rd BETH E2	7	J3
HACK E8	7	J3
PLSTW E13	133	G2
King's La SUT SM1	243	H3
Kingslawn Cl PUT/ROE SW15	163	H3
Kingsleigh Pl MTCM CR4	206	B6
Kingsleigh Wk HAYES BR2	232	B1
Kingsley Av HSLW TW3	159	C3
STHL UB1	116	A6
SUT SM1	243	H2
WEA W13	120	C5
Kingsley Cl EDGW * HA8	46	B4
GLDGN NW11	65	F4
Kingsley Ct EDGW HA8	46	B4
Kingsley Dr WPK KT4	223	F6
Kingsley Gdns CHING E4	71	E1
Kingsley Ms CHST BR7	185	B1
KENS * W8	145	F5
WAP E1W	17	H6
Kingsley Pl HGT N6	86	C4
Kingsley Rd BARK/HLT IG6	74	C3
CROY/NA CR0	228	A5
FSTGT E7	112	C5
HSLW TW3	159	C3
KIL/WHAMP NW6	105	C6
ORP BR6	253	F4
PIN HA5	78	D1
PLMCR N13	52	A6
RYLN/HDSTN HA2	60	A6
WALTH E17	70	A1
WIM/MER SW19	205	F1
Kingsley St BTSEA SW11	166	B4
Kingsley Wy EFNCH N2	85	G5
Kingsley Wood Dr		
ELTH/MOT SE9	193	H5
Kings Ms CHST BR7	234	D1
Kings Pas KLNW * E11	92	A4
Kings Pl BKHH IG9	57	F4
CHSWK W4	143	H5
LOU IG10	57	F2
STHWK SE1	23	E4
King Sq FSBYE EC1V	7	E5
King's Quay WBPTN * SW10	165	G2
King's Reach EMB * EC4Y	14	B5
Kings Rd BAR EN5	34	A4
BARK IG11	114	C5
BGVA SW1W	27	H1
CHEL * SW5	145	H6
CHING E4	56	B5
EA W5	121	F4
EHAM E6	113	E6
FELT TW13	158	B5
FUL/PGN SW6	145	H3
MORT/ESHN SW14	162	A4
MTCM CR4	206	C6
ORP BR6	253	E3
RCHPK/HAM TW10	161	H6
RYLN/HDSTN HA2	78	D6
SNWD SE25	209	G6
SURB KT6	221	E5
TEDD TW11	199	H1
TWK TW1	160	D1
UED N18	69	C1
WAN E11	92	C2
WDGN N22	67	G1
WIM/MER SW19	205	E2
King's Scholars' Pas WEST SW1P	20	A6
King Stairs Cl BERM/RHTH SE16	25	H3
King's Ter CAMTN NW1	107	G6
Kingsthorpe Rd SYD SE26	190	B6
Kingston Av CHEAM SM3	242	C1
Kingston By-Pass BRYLDS KT5	222	A6
CHSGTN KT9	239	H3
ESH/CLAY KT10	238	A1
Kingston Cl CHDH RM6	56	A6
NTHLT UB5	96	D5
TEDD TW11	200	D2
Kingston Crs BECK BR3	210	C1
Kingston Gdns CROY/NA CR0	245	G1
Kingston Hall Rd KUT * KT1	201	F6
Kingston Hill KUTN/CMB KT2	202	A4
Kingston Hill Av CHDH RM6	74	A1
Kingston Hill Pl KUTN/CMB KT2	182	C6
Kingston House Est SURB * KT6	220	D3
Kingston La TEDD TW11	200	D2
Kingston Ldg NWMAL KT3	223	E1
Kingston Rd BRYLDS KT5	222	B1
EBAR EN4	33	H4
ED N9	53	C4
EW KT17	241	F5
HOR/WEW KT19	241	E3
IL IG1	114	C2
NWDGN UB2	116	C4
NWMAL KT3	222	C1
PUT/ROE SW15	183	H3
RYNPK SW20	204	C5
TEDD TW11	200	D2
Kingston Sq NRWD SE19	208	D1
Kingston V PUT/ROE SW15	182	D3
Kingstown St CAMTN NW1	106	B6
King St CITYW EC2V	15	F4
COVGDN WC2E	11	H5
EFNCH * N2	65	H1
HMSMTH W6	143	F4
NWDGN UB2	138	C3
PLSTW E13	132	C3
RCH/KEW TW9	161	F2
STJS SW1Y	10	C7
TOTM N17	68	B1
TWK TW1	180	C3
King St Cloisters		
HMSMTH * W6	143	H4
King Street Pde TWK * TW1	180	C3
Kingswater Pl BTSEA * SW11	166	A1
Kings Wy CROY/NA CR0	246	A1
HRW HA1	80	A1
Kingsway HOL/ALD WC2B	11	G3
MORT/ESHN SW14	161	B4
NWMAL KT3	224	A1
PEND EN3	25	H1
STMC/STPC BR5	234	D2
WBLY HA9	81	H2
WWKM BR4	248	C1
Kingsway Av SAND/SEL CR2	248	A6
Kingsway Crs RYLN/HDSTN HA2	60	A6
Kingsway Pde		
STNW/STAM * N16	108	D2
Kingsway Pl CLKNW EC1R	6	A5
Kingsway Rd CHEAM SM3	242	C5
Kingswear Rd KTTN NW5	106	C5
RSLP HA4	76	D2
Kings Wood Dr		
ELTH/MOT SE9	193	H5
Kingswood Av BELV DA17	129	G4
HAYES BR2	212	A6
HEST TW5	134	D6
HPTN TW12	199	F2
KIL/WHAMP NW6	104	C6

THHTH CR7 .....228 A2
Kingswood Cl EN EN1 .....39 F5
NWMAL KT5 .....223 F3
ORP BR6 .....234 D4
SURB KT6 .....221 G4
TRDG/WHET N20 .....49 G1
VX/NE SW8 .....167 G1
Kingswood Dr BELMT SM2 .....243 F6
CAR SM5 .....226 B5
NRWD SE19 .....189 E6
Kingswood Pk FNCH N3 .....64 D5
Kingswood Pl LEW SE13 .....172 A5
Kingswood Rd
BRXS/STRHM SW2 .....187 G1
CHSWK W4 .....142 C3
GDMY/SEVK IG3 .....95 C5
HAYES BR2 .....212 A6
PGE/AN SE20 .....210 A2
WAN E11 .....92 A4
WIM/MER SW19 .....204 D4
Kingswood Ter CHSWK W4 .....142 C3
Kingswood Wy WLGTN SM6 .....245 G3
Kingsworth Cl BECK BR3 .....232 C2
Kingsworthy Cl KUT KT1 .....201 H5
Kings Yd PUT/ROE * SW15 .....164 B4
SRTFD * E15 .....111 E4
Kingthorpe Rd WLSDN NW10 .....102 D5
Kingthorpe Ter
WLSDN * NW10 .....102 D5
Kingwell Rd EBAR EN4 .....35 H1
King William La GNWCH SE10 .....152 A5
King William St MANHO EC4N 15 H5
King William Wk GNWCH SE10 .....151 G6
Kingwood Rd FUL/PGN SW6 .....164 C1
Kinlet Rd WOOL/PLUM SE18 .....174 C1
Kinloch Dr CDALE/KGS NW9 .....83 E4
Kinloch St HOLWY N7 .....107 H1
Kinloss Gdns FNCH N3 .....64 D6
Kinloss Rd CAR SM5 .....225 G1
Kinnaird Av BMLY BR1 .....212 B2
CHSWK W4 .....162 C1
Kinnaird Cl BMLY BR1 .....212 B2
Kinnaird Wy WFD IG8 .....73 H2
Kinnerton Pl North
KTBR * SW1X 18 D4
Kinnerton Pl South
KTBR * SW1X 18 D4
Kinnerton St KTBR SW1X 18 D4
Kinnerton Yd KTBR * SW1X 19 E4
Kinnoul Rd HMSMTH W6 .....119 H6
Kinross Av WPK KT4 .....225 G6
Kinross Cl KTN/HRWW/W HA3 .....81 H2
Kinross Ter WALTH E17 .....70 D5
Kinsale Rd PECK SE15 .....169 G4
Kintyre Cl STRHM/NOR SW16 .....207 H5
Kinveachy Gdns CHARL SE7 .....135 G5
Kinver Rd SYD SE26 .....190 A6
Kipling Dr TOOT SW17 .....205 H2
Kipling Est STHWK SE1 .....23 H4
Kipling Rd BXLYHN DA7 .....136 C2
Kipling St STHWK SE1 .....23 H4
Kipling Ter ED * N9 .....52 D5
Kippington Dr ELTH/MOT SE9 .....193 F3
Kirby Cl BARK/HLT IG6 .....54 D5
HOR/WEW KT19 .....241 F3
LOU IG10 .....57 G2
Kirby Est BERM/RHTH SE16 .....25 H5
Kirby Gv STHWK SE1 .....24 A3
Kirby St HCIRC EC1N 14 B1
Kirchen Rd WEA W13 .....120 D6
Kirkcaldy Gn OXHEY WD19 .....42 A5
Kirkdale SYD SE26 .....189 H4
Kirkdale Cnr SYD * SE26 .....190 A6
Kirkdale Rd WAN E11 .....76 D1
Kirkfield Cl WEA W13 .....140 D1
Kirkham Rd EHAM E6 .....133 G5
Kirkham St WOOL/PLUM SE18 .....115 E6
Kirkland Av CLAY IG5 .....74 A5
Kirkland Cl BFN/LL DA15 .....195 E1
Kirkland Wk HACK E8 .....109 F4
Kirk La WOOL/PLUM SE18 .....154 C6
Kirkleas Rd SURB KT6 .....223 E1
Kirklees Rd BCTR RM8 .....116 A3
THHTH CR7 .....228 A2
Kirkly Cl SAND/SEL CR2 .....247 E6
Kirkmichael Rd POP/IOD E14 .....131 G5
Kirk Rd WALTH E17 .....90 D3
Kirkside Rd BKHTH/KID SE3 .....152 C6
Kirk's Pl POP/IOD E14 .....130 D4
Kirkstall Av TOTM N17 .....88 D1
Kirkstall Gdns
BRXS/STRHM SW2 .....187 F3
Kirkstall Rd BRXS/STRHM SW2 .....187 F3
Kirksted Rd MRDN SM4 .....225 F5
Kirkstone Wy BMLY BR1 .....212 A3
Kirkton Rd SEVS/STOTM N15 .....89 E1
Kirkwall Pl BETH * E2 .....130 A2
Kirkwood Rd PECK SE15 .....169 H3
Kirn Rd WEA W13 .....120 D6
Kirrane Cl NWMAL KT3 .....223 F2
Kirtley Rd SYD SE26 .....190 C6
Kirtling St VX/NE SW8 .....167 E1
Kirton Cl CHSWK W4 .....142 D4
Kirton Gdns BETH E2 .....8 A4
Kirton Ldg
WAND/EARL * SW18 .....185 F1
Kirton Rd PLSTW E13 .....113 G1
Kirton Wk EDGW HA8 .....62 C3
Kirwyn Wy CMBW SE5 .....168 B1
Kitcat Ter BOW E3 .....131 E2
Kitchener Rd EFNCH N2 .....66 A6
FSTGT E7 .....112 D4
THHTH CR7 .....208 D6
TOTM N17 .....69 E6
WALTH E17 .....71 H4
Kite Pl BETH E2 .....8 F3
Kite Yd BTSEA * SW11 .....166 B2
Kitley Gdns NRWD SE19 .....209 F4
Kitson Rd BARN SW13 .....146 C1
CMBW SE5 .....168 B1
Kittiwake Rd NTHLT UB5 .....118 B2
Kittiwake Wy YEAD UB4 .....118 B4
Kitto Rd NWCR SE14 .....170 B3
Kiver Rd ARCH N19 .....67 G6
Klea Av BAL SW12 .....187 E1
Knapdale Cl FSTH SE23 .....189 H4
Knapmill Rd CAT SE6 .....191 E4
Knapmill Wy CAT SE6 .....191 E4
Knapp Cl WLSDN NW10 .....103 E4

Knapp Rd BOW E3 .....131 E3
Knapton Ms TOOT SW17 .....206 D2
Knaresborough Dr
WAND/EARL SW18 .....185 F3
Knaresborough Pl ECT SW5 .....145 F4
Knatchbull Rd CMBW SE5 .....168 B3
WLSDN NW10 .....102 D6
Knebworth Av WALTH E17 .....71 E4
Knebworth Rd
STNW/STAM * N16 .....109 E2
Knee Hi ABYW SE2 .....156 A4
Knee Hill Crs ABYW SE2 .....156 A4
Kneller Gdns ISLW TW7 .....179 H1
Kneller Rd BROCKY SE4 .....170 C5
MTCM CR4 .....223 H4
WHTN TW2 .....179 G1
Knight Cl BCTR RM8 .....96 A6
Knighten St WAP E1W 25 G2
Knighthead Point
POP/IOD * E14 .....151 E2
Knightland Rd CLPT E5 .....89 H6
Knighton Cl ROMW/RG RM7 .....97 H3
SAND/SEL CR2 .....246 B6
WFD IG8 .....56 D6
Knighton Dr WFD IG8 .....56 D6
Knighton La BKHH IG9 .....56 D4
Knighton Park Rd SYD SE26 .....210 D1
Knighton Rd FSTGT E7 .....112 C1
ROMW/RG RM7 .....97 G3
Knightrider Ct BLKFR * EC4V 14 D4
Knightrider St BLKFR EC4V 14 D5
Knightsbridge SKENS SW7 .....18 B2
Knightsbridge
ROMW/RG RM7 .....97 H2
Knightsbridge Gn KTBR * SW1X 18 C4
Knights Chambers ED * N9 .....53 C5
Knight's Hi WNWD SE27 .....208 B1
Knight's Hill Sq WNWD SE27 .....188 B6
Knight's La ED N9 .....53 C5
Knight's Rd CAN/RD E16 .....133 H3
Knights Rdg ORP BR6 .....253 H3
Knights Rd CAN/RD E16 .....152 C1
STAN HA7 .....45 G6
Knights Wk LBTH SE11 .....30 C2
Knights Wy BARK/HLT IG6 .....74 C2
Knightswood Cl EDGW HA8 .....46 C4
CNTH/NBYPK IG2 .....73 E3
Knivet Rd FUL/PGN SW6 .....145 E6
Knolls Hill Rd SRTFD E15 .....111 F6
Knockholt Rd ELTH/MOT SE9 .....173 H6
Knole Cl CROY/NA * CR0 .....230 A4
The Knole ELTH/MOT SE9 .....194 A6
Knoll Dr STHGT/OAK N14 .....50 C2
Knollmead BRYLDS KT5 .....222 D5
Knoll Rd ORP BR6 .....235 F5
Knoll Rd BXLY DA5 .....169 H3
SCUP DA14 .....215 H1
WAND/EARL SW18 .....165 G6
Knolls Cl WPK KT4 .....241 H1
The Knoll BECK BR3 .....211 F1
HAYES BR2 .....232 C6
PIN * HA5 .....58 B5
WEA W13 .....121 E4
Knolly's Cl STRHM/NOR SW16 .....188 C3
WNWD * SE27 .....188 B5
Knolly's Rd STRHM/NOR SW16 .....188 C3
Knottisford St BETH E2 .....130 B2
Knotts Green Rd LEY E10 .....91 G3
Knowle Av BXLYHN DA7 .....176 C1
Knowle Cl BRXN/ST SW9 .....168 A4
Knowle Rd HAYES BR2 .....233 G6
WHTN TW2 .....180 A3
Knowles Cl HRW HA1 .....90 B3
Knowles Hill Crs LEW SE13 .....171 H6
Knowlton Gn HAYES BR2 .....232 B2
Knowsley Av STHL UB1 .....139 F1
Knowsley Rd BTSEA SW11 .....160 D5
Knox Rd FSTGT E7 .....112 C4
Knox St MBLAR W1H 10 C1
Knoyle St NWCR SE14 .....150 C6
Kohat Rd WIM/MER SW19 .....205 F1
Koh-i-Noor Av BUSH WD23 .....43 E1
Kossuth St GNWCH SE10 .....152 A5
Kramer Ms ECT * SW5 .....145 E5
Kreedman Wk HACK * E8 .....109 C5
Kuala Gdns STRHM/NOR SW16 .....207 H4
Kydbrooke Cl ELTH/MOT SE9 .....155 E4
Kylemore Cl EHAM E6 .....133 F1
Kylemore Rd KIL/WHAMP NW6 .....105 E5
Kymberley Rd HRW * HA1 .....80 A3
Kynance Gdns STAN HA7 .....61 E4
Kynance Ms KENS W8 .....145 F3
Kynance Pl SKENS SW7 .....145 G3
Kynaston Av THHTH CR7 .....228 C2
Kynaston Cl
KTN/HRWW/W HA3 .....59 H5
Kynaston Crs THHTH CR7 .....228 C2
Kynaston Rd BMLY BR1 .....212 C2
ENC/FH EN2 .....38 D2
STMC/STPC BR5 .....235 H4
STNW/STAM N16 .....109 E1
THHTH CR7 .....228 C2
Kynaston Wd
KTN/HRWW/W HA3 .....59 H5
Kynersley Cl CAR SM5 .....244 B1
Kynoch Rd UED N18 .....54 D6
Kyrle Rd BTSEA SW11 .....186 C1
Kyverdale Rd STNW/STAM N16 .....89 F4

L

Laburnum Av ED N9 .....53 E4
SUT SM1 .....244 A1
SWLY BR8 .....217 H6
TOTM N17 .....68 D3
Laburnum Cl CHING E4 .....70 C2
Laburnum Ct STAN HA7 .....45 H1
Laburnum Gdns CROY/NA CR0 .....235 B4
Laburnum Gv CDALE/KGS NW9 .....82 C4
HSLW TW3 .....158 D5
NWMAL KT3 .....192 B6
STHL UB1 .....115 D5
WCHMH N21 .....103 C1
Laburnum Pl ELTH/MOT * SE9 .....174 A6
Laburnum Rd MTCM CR4 .....206 C5
WIM/MER SW19 .....205 G3

Laburnum St BETH E2 .....109 F6
Laburnum Wy HAYES BR2 .....234 A4
Lacebark Cl BFN/LL DA15 .....195 F2
Lacey Cl ED N9 .....53 C4
Lacey Dr BCTR RM8 .....116 A1
EDGW HA8 .....45 G6
HPTN TW12 .....198 D4
Lackington St SDTCH EC2A 15 H1
Lacock Cl WIM/MER SW19 .....205 G2
Lacon Rd EDUL SE22 .....169 G5
Lacrosse Wy
STRHM/NOR SW16 .....207 F4
Lacy Rd PUT/ROE SW15 .....164 B5
Ladas Rd WNWD SE27 .....208 C1
Ladbroke Crs NTGHL W11 .....124 C5
Ladbroke Gdns NTGHL W11 .....124 D6
Ladbroke Gv NKENS W10 .....124 C4
Ladbroke Ms NTGHL W11 .....144 C1
Ladbroke Rd EN EN1 .....53 F6
NTGHL W11 .....144 D1
Ladbroke Sq NTGHL W11 .....124 D6
Ladbroke Ter NTGHL W11 .....124 D6
Ladbroke Wk NTGHL W11 .....144 D1
Ladbrook Cl PIN HA5 .....78 D2
Ladbrooke Crs SCUP DA14 .....196 B5
Ladbrook Rd SNWD SE25 .....208 D6
Ladderstile Ride
RCHPK/HAM TW10 .....202 B3
Ladderswood Wy
FBAR/BDGN N11 .....67 E1
Ladds Wy SWLY BR8 .....237 F3
Lady Booth Rd KUT KT1 .....201 C5
Ladycroft Gdns ORP BR6 .....252 C5
Ladycroft Rd LEW SE13 .....171 F4
Ladycroft Wk STAN HA7 .....61 F4
Ladycroft Wy ORP BR6 .....252 C5
Lady Forsdyke Wy
HOR/WEW KT19 .....240 A6
Ladygrove CROY/NA CR0 .....248 C6
Lady Harewood Wy
HOR/WEW KT19 .....240 A6
Lady Hay WPK KT4 .....225 F6
Lady Margaret Rd ARCH N19 .....107 C2
STHL UB1 .....118 D3
Ladymount WLGTN SM6 .....245 F2
Ladyship Ter EDUL * SE22 .....189 H2
Ladysmith Av EHAM E6 .....133 C1
GNTH/NBYPK IG2 .....72 D4
Ladysmith Rd CAN/RD E16 .....132 B2
ELTH/MOT SE9 .....194 A1
EN EN1 .....39 F3
KTN/HRWW/W HA3 .....60 D5
TOTM N17 .....69 H2
UED N18 .....54 D1
Lady Somerset Rd KTTN NW5 .....106 B2
Ladywell Rd LEW SE13 .....171 E6
Ladywell St SRTFD E15 .....112 B6
Ladywood Av STMC/STPC BR5 .....235 E2
Ladywood Rd SURB KT6 .....222 A6
Lafone Av FELT TW13 .....178 A4
Lafone St STHWK SE1 .....24 D3
Lagado Ms BERM/RHTH SE16 .....150 D1
Lagonda Av BARK/HLT IG6 .....75 F2
Lagoon Rd STMC/STPC BR5 .....235 H2
Laidlaw Dr WCHMH N21 .....111 C1
Laing Cl CHIG IG7 .....74 D2
Laing Dean NTHLT UB5 .....119 C6
Laings Av MTCM CR4 .....206 B5
Lainlock Pl HSLW * TW3 .....159 F2
Lainson St WAND/EARL SW18 .....185 C1
Lairdale Cl DUL SE21 .....188 C3
Lairs Cl HOLWY * N7 .....186 D4
Laitwood Rd BAL SW12 .....186 B1
Lakedale Rd WOOL/PLUM SE18 .....155 F1
Lake Dr BUSH WD23 .....43 G4
Lakefield Rd WDGN N22 .....68 B5
Lake Gdns DAGE RM10 .....110 D1
RCHPK/HAM TW10 .....180 D5
WLGTN SM6 .....244 D1
Lakehall Gdns THHTH CR7 .....228 B2
Lakehall Rd THHTH CR7 .....228 B2
Lake House Rd WAN E11 .....112 C1
Lakehurst Rd HOR/WEW KT19 .....241 E3
Lakeland Cl KTN/HRWW/W HA3 .....42 C2
Lakenheath STHGT/OAK N14 .....37 F6
Lake Rd CHDH RM6 .....96 B1
CROY/NA CR0 .....230 D6
DAGW RM9 .....137 F2
ENC/FH EN2 .....37 F5
HOR/WEW KT19 .....241 E4
WEA W13 .....121 E4
WLGTN SM6 .....244 D2
Lakeside BECK BR3 .....211 F3
ENC/FH EN2 .....37 F5
HOR/WEW KT19 .....241 E4
WEA W13 .....121 E4
WLGTN SM6 .....244 D2
Lakeside Av REDBR IG4 .....95 F1
THMD SE28 .....155 G2
Lakeside Cl BFN/LL DA15 .....176 A6
SNWD SE25 .....208 A5
Lakeside Crs EBAR EN4 .....50 B1
Lakeside Dr HAYES BR2 .....251 G3
Lakeside Rd PLMGR N13 .....51 E5
WKENS W14 .....144 B3
Lakeside Wy WBLY HA9 .....102 A2
Lakes Rd HAYES BR2 .....251 E3
Lakeswood Rd
STMC/STPC BR5 .....236 B5
Lakeview Rd ELTH/MOT SE9 .....174 D3
WNWD SE27 .....188 D1
Lake View EDGW HA8 .....44 C5
Lake View Est BOW * E3 .....130 B1
Lakeview Rd UED N18 .....53 H4
Lakis Cl HAMP NW3 .....105 G2
Laleham Av MLHL NW7 .....46 A5
Laleham Ct SUT * SM1 .....243 G5
Laleham Rd CAT SE6 .....191 G2
Lalor St FUL/PGN SW6 .....164 G3
Lambarde Av ELTH/MOT SE9 .....194 B4
Lambarde Rd
STMC/STPC BR5 .....236 B5
Lamberhurst Rd BCTR RM8 .....96 C2
WNWD SE27 .....188 A6
Lambert Av BFN/LL DA15 .....195 H4
Lambert Jones Ms BARF * EC2Y 15 E1
Lambert Rd BRXS/STRHM SW2 .....167 G2
CAN/RD E16 .....132 D5
NFNCH/WDSP N12 .....47 H1
Lambert's Pl CROY/NA CR0 .....228 D5
Lambert's Rd SURB KT6 .....221 G2
Lambert St IS N1 .....6 A1

Lambert Wy NFNCH/WDSP N12 .....65 G1
Lambeth Br WEST SW1P 29 G1
Lambeth High St STHWK SE1 .....29 G2
Lambeth HI BLKFR * EC4V 15 E5
Lambeth Palace Rd STHWK SE1 .....21 G4
Lambeth Rd CROY/NA CR0 .....228 A6
STHWK SE1 .....22 A6
Lambeth Wk LBTH SE11 .....29 H2
Lamb La HACK E8 .....109 H5
Lamble St HAMP NW3 .....106 C3
Lambley Rd DAGW RM9 .....115 H4
Lambolle Pl HAMP NW3 .....106 A4
Lambolle Rd HAMP NW3 .....106 A4
Lambourn Cl HNWL W7 .....140 B2
KTTN * NW5 .....107 C2
Lambourne Av
WIM/MER SW19 .....184 D6
Lambourne Gdns BARK IG11 .....115 F5
CHING E4 .....55 E4
EN EN1 .....39 F5
Lambourne Rd BARK IG11 .....115 G5
GDMY/SEVK IG3 .....95 E6
WAN E11 .....91 G4
Lambourn Rd CLAP SW4 .....166 G2
Lambrook Ter FUL/PGN SW6 .....164 C2
Lambs Cl ED * N9 .....53 C4
Lamb's Conduit Pas
FSBYW WC1X 13 G1
Lamb's Conduit St BMSBY WC1N 13 G1
Lambscroft Av LEE/GVPK SE12 .....193 E5
Lambs Meadow WFD IG8 .....73 F5
Lambs Ms IS N1 .....108 B6
Lamb's Pas STLK EC1Y 7 G6
Lamb St WCHPL E1 .....16 C1
Lambs Wk ENC/FH EN2 .....38 C3
Lambton Rd ARCH N19 .....67 E6
RYNPK SW20 .....204 A4
Lamb Wk STHWK SE1 .....24 A4
Lamerock Rd BMLY BR1 .....192 B6
Lamerton Rd BARK/HLT IG6 .....74 B5
Lamerton St DEPT SE8 .....151 E6
Lamford Cl TOTM N17 .....68 D3
Lamington St HMSMTH W6 .....143 H4
Lamlash St LBTH SE11 .....30 C2
Lammas Av MTCM CR4 .....206 C5
Lammas Park Gdns EA W5 .....141 E1
Lammas Rd HOM E9 .....111 F6
LEY E10 .....90 C6
RCHPK/HAM TW10 .....181 G6
Lammermoor Rd BAL * SW12 .....186 D2
Lamont Rd WBPTN SW10 .....145 H6
Lamont Road Pas
WBPTN * SW10 .....145 H6
Lamorbey Cl BFN/LL DA15 .....195 G4
Lamorbey Pk BFN/LL * DA15 .....195 H3
Lamorna Cl ORP BR6 .....235 G4
WALTH E17 .....71 G2
Lamorna Gv STAN HA7 .....61 F4
Lampard Gv STNW/STAM N16 .....89 F3
Lampern Sq BETH E2 .....9 F5
Lamplighter Cl WCHPL E1 .....130 A3
Lampmead Rd LEW SE13 .....172 A6
Lamport Cl WOOL/PLUM SE18 .....153 H4
Lampton Av HEST TW5 .....159 G2
Lampton House Cl
WIM/MER SW19 .....184 B6
Lampton Park Rd HSLW TW3 .....159 F3
Lampton Rd HSLW TW3 .....159 G2
Lanacre Av CDALE/KGS NW9 .....63 G4
Lanark Cl EA W5 .....121 E4
Lanark Ms MV/WKIL W9 .....125 G3
Lanark Rd KIL/WHAMP NW6 .....125 G3
Lanbury Rd PECK SE15 .....170 B3
Lancashire Ct MYFR/PKLN W1K 11 G5
Lancaster Av BARK IG11 .....115 E5
EBAR EN4 .....35 H1
MTCM CR4 .....227 G2
WAN E11 .....92 D1
WIM/MER SW19 .....184 B4
Lancaster Cl CDALE/KGS NW9 .....47 G4
HAYES BR2 .....232 B1
IS N1 .....109 G2
TOTM * N17 .....69 G3
Lancaster Dr HAMP NW3 .....106 A4
POP/IOD E14 .....151 G1
Lancaster Gdn KUTN/CMB KT2 .....201 F1
Lancaster Gdns
WIM/MER SW19 .....204 C5
Lancaster Ga BAY/PAD * W2 .....125 G6
BAY/PAD W2 .....125 G6
Lancaster Gv HAMP NW3 .....105 H4
Lancaster Ms BAY/PAD * W2 .....125 G6
RCHPK/HAM TW10 .....181 G1
WAND/EARL * SW18 .....165 G6
Lancaster Pk
RCHPK/HAM TW10 .....161 G6
Lancaster Pl TWK TW1 .....180 B1
WIM/MER SW19 .....204 B1
Lancaster Rd EBAR EN4 .....35 H6
ENC/FH EN2 .....38 D2
FBAR/BDGN N11 .....66 B4
FSBYPK N4 .....88 A4
FSTGT E7 .....112 C5
NTGHL W11 .....124 C5
NTHLT UB5 .....96 A5
RYLN/HDSTN HA2 .....79 G2
SNWD SE25 .....209 F5
STHL UB1 .....118 C6
UED N18 .....67 H1
WALTH E17 .....70 B5
WAN E11 .....91 E2
WIM/MER SW19 .....204 B1
WLSDN NW10 .....102 A2
Lancaster Stables
HAMP * NW3 .....106 A4
Lancaster St STHWK SE1 .....22 C4
Lancaster Ter BAY/PAD * W2 .....125 H6
Lancaster West NTGHL * W11 .....124 C5
Lancastrian Rd WLGTN SM6 .....245 G5
Lancefield St NKENS W10 .....124 D2
Lancell St STNW/STAM N16 .....89 E6
Lancelot Av ALP/SUD HA0 .....101 G1
Lancelot Crs ALP/SUD HA0 .....101 F2
Lancelot Gdns EBAR EN4 .....50 C2
Lancelot Pde ALP/SUD * HA0 .....101 G3

Lancelot Pl SKENS SW7 18 C4
Lancelot Rd ALP/SUD HA0 101 F2
BARK/HLT IG6 75 E2
WELL DA16 175 G5
Lance Rd HRW HA1 79 G4
Lancer Sq KENS * W8 145 F2
Lancey Cl CHARL SE7 153 F4
Lanchester Rd HGT N6 86 B2
Lancing Gdns ED N9 53 F3
Lancing Rd CROY/NA CR0 227 H3
GNTH/NBYPK IG2 94 D3
ORP BR6 235 H6
WEA W13 120 D6
Lancing St CAMTN NW1 4 C4
Landcroft Rd EDUL SE22 189 F1
Landells Rd EDUL SE22 189 F1
Landford Rd PUT/ROE SW15 164 A4
Landgrove Rd WIM/MER SW19 205 E1
Landleys Flds KTTN * NW5 107 F3
Landmann Wy NWCR SE14 150 B6
Landon Pl KTBR SW1X 18 C5
Landons Cl POP/IOD E14 151 G1
Landor Rd BRXN/ST SW9 167 G4
Landor Wk SHB W12 143 G2
Landra Gdns WCHMH N21 52 B1
Landridge Dr EN EN1 39 H1
Landridge Rd FUL/PGN SW6 164 C3
Landrock Rd CEND/HSY/T N8 87 G3
Landscape Rd WFD IG8 72 D3
Landseer Av MNPK E12 114 A3
Landseer Cl EDGW HA8 62 A5
WIM/MER SW19 205 G4
Landseer Rd ARCH N19 107 G1
EN EN1 39 G6
NWMAL KT3 222 D4
SUT SM1 243 E4
Lands' End BORE WD6 45 F1
Landstead Rd
WOOL/PLUM SE18 174 D1
The Landway STMC/STPC BR5 216 A6
Lane Ap MLHL * NW7 64 C1
Lane Cl CRICK NW2 103 H1
Lane End BXLYHN DA7 177 F4
Lane Gdns BUSH WD23 44 A3
Lanercost Gdns STHGT/OAK N14 51 G1
Lanercost Rd
BRXS/STRHM SW2 188 A4
Laneside CHST BR7 214 B1
EDGW HA8 62 C1
Laneside Av BCTR RM8 96 D4
The Lane BKHTH/KID SE3 172 C4
STJWD NW8 125 G1
Laneway PUT/ROE SW15 163 H6
Lanfranc Rd BOW E3 130 C1
Lanfrey Pl WKENS W14 144 D5
Langbourne Av HGT N6 86 C6
Langbourne Wy
ESH/CLAY KT10 238 B4
Langbrook Rd BKHTH/KID SE3 173 F4
Langcroft Cl CAR SM5 244 B1
Langdale Av MTCM CR4 206 B6
Langdale Cl BCTR RM8 96 A5
MORT/ESHN SW14 162 B5
ORP BR6 252 B1
WALW SE17 31 E5
Langdale Crs BXLYHN DA7 177 E2
Langdale Pde MTCM * CR4 206 B5
Langdale Rd GNWCH SE10 171 G1
THHTH CR7 228 A1
Langdale St WCHPL * E1 17 G4
Langdon Ct WLSDN NW10 103 E6
Langdon Crs EHAM E6 134 A1
Langdon Dr CDALE/KGS NW9 82 C5
Langdon Park Rd HGT N6 86 D4
Langdon Pl MORT/ESHN SW14 162 C4
Langdon Rd HAYES BR2 212 D6
MRDN SM4 225 G2
Langdon Shaw SCUP DA14 215 F1
Langdon Wk MRDN SM4 225 G2
Langdon Wy STHWK SE1 33 F2
Langford Cl HACK E8 109 G3
SEVS/STOTM N15 89 E3
Langford Crs EBAR EN4 36 B5
Langford Pl SCUP DA14 195 G5
STJWD NW8 125 G1
Langford Rd EBAR EN4 36 B5
FUL/PGN SW6 165 F3
WFD IG8 73 E2
Langfords BKHH IG9 57 F4
Langham Dr GDMY/SEVK IG3 95 H3
Langham Gdns ALP/SUD HA0 81 E6
EDGW HA8 62 C3
RCHPK/HAM TW10 181 E6
WCHMH N21 38 A6
WEA W13 120 D6
Langham House Cl
RCHPK/HAM TW10 181 F6
Langham Pde
SEVS/STOTM * N15 68 B6
Langham Park Pl HAYES BR2 232 B1
Langham Pl CAVSQ/HST W1G 11 H2
CHSWK W4 143 E6
SEVS/STOTM N15 68 B6
Langham Rd EDGW HA8 62 C2
RYNPK SW20 204 A4
SEVS/STOTM N15 88 C1
TEDD TW11 200 D1
Langham St GTPST W1W 12 A2
REGST W1B 11 H2
Langhedge Cl UED N18 69 F2
Langhedge La UED N18 69 F1
Langholm Cl BAL SW12 187 F2
Langholme BUSH WD23 43 G3
Langhorn Dr WHTN TW2 180 A2
Langhorne Rd DAGE RM10 117 E5
Langland Crs STAN HA7 61 F6
Langland Dr PIN HA5 58 C3
Langland Gdns CROY/NA CR0 230 D6
HAMP NW3 105 F3
Langler Rd WLSDN NW10 124 A1
Langley Av SURB KT6 221 F5
WPK KT4 224 B6
Langley Ct BECK * BR3 231 F1
COVGDN WC2E 13 E5
Langley Crs DAGW RM9 116 A5
EDGW HA8 46 C5
WAN E11 92 D4
Langley Dr ACT W3 142 B2
WAN E11 92 D4
Langley Gdns DAGW RM9 116 B5
STMC/STPC BR5 234 B3
Langley Gv NWMAL KT3 202 D5
Langley La VX/NE SW8 29 F5
Langley Pk EDGW HA8 63 E2
Langley Park Rd BELMT SM2 243 G4
Langley Rd BECK BR3 230 B1
ISLW TW7 160 B3
SAND/SEL CR2 248 B6
SURB KT6 221 G4
WELL DA16 156 A6
WIM/MER SW19 204 D4
Langley Rw BAR EN5 34 D2
Langley St LSQ/SEVD WC2H 13 E4
Langley Wy WWKM BR4 231 H5
Langley Wd BECK * BR3 232 A2
Langmead Dr BUSH WD23 43 H3
Langmead St WNWD SE27 188 B6
Langport Ct WOT/HER KT12 218 A5
Langridge Ms HPTN TW12 198 D2
Langroyd Rd TOOT SW17 186 B4
Langside Av PUT/ROE SW15 163 G5
Langside Crs STHGT/OAK N14 51 F5
Langston Hughes Cl
HNHL * SE24 168 B5
Lang St WCHPL E1 130 A3
Langthorn Ct LOTH * EC2R 15 H3
Langthorne Rd WAN E11 111 H1
Langthorne St FUL/PGN SW6 164 B2
Langton Av EHAM E6 134 A2
TRDG/WHET N20 49 G2
Langton Cl FSBYW WC1X 5 H6
Langton Ri EDUL SE22 189 H2
Langton Rd BRXN/ST SW9 168 B1
CRICK NW2 104 A1
E/WMO/HCT KT8 219 G2
KTN/HRWW/W HA3 59 G3
Langton St WBPTN SW10 145 G6
Langton Vls TOTM * N17 69 G4
Langton Wy BKHTH/KID SE3 172 C1
CROY/NA CR0 247 E2
Langtry Pl FUL/PGN SW6 145 E6
NTHLT UB5 118 B1
Langtry Rd STJWD NW8 105 F6
Langtry Wk STJWD NW8 105 G6
Langwood Cha TEDD TW11 201 E2
Lanhill Rd MV/WKIL W9 125 E3
Lanier Rd LEW SE13 191 G1
Lanigan Dr HSLW TW3 159 F6
Lankaster Gdns EFNCH N2 65 H4
Lankers Dr RYLN/HDSTN HA2 78 D3
Lankton Cl BECK BR3 211 G4
Lannoy Rd ELTH/MOT SE9 194 C3
Lanrick Rd POP/IOD E14 131 H5
Lanridge Rd ABYW SE2 156 B3
Lansbury Av BARK IG11 115 G5
CHDH RM6 96 C2
UED N18 68 D1
Lansbury Cl WLSDN NW10 102 C3
Lansbury Gdns POP/IOD * E14 131 H5
Lansbury Rd PEND EN3 40 B2
Lansbury Wy UED N18 69 E1
Lanscombe Wk VX/NE * SW8 167 G1
Lansdell Rd MTCM CR4 206 C5
Lansdown Cl WOT/HER KT12 218 A5
Lansdowne Av BXLYHN DA7 176 A1
ORP BR6 234 B5
Lansdowne Cl BRYLDS KT5 222 B6
RYNPK SW20 204 B3
TWK TW1 180 B3
Lansdowne Copse WPK * KT4 223 G6
Lansdowne Ct WPK KT4 223 G6
Lansdowne Crs NTGHL W11 124 C6
Lansdowne Gdns VX/NE SW8 167 G2
Lansdowne Gn VX/NE SW8 167 G1
Lansdowne Gv WLSDN NW10 103 E2
Lansdowne Hl WNWD SE27 188 B5
Lansdowne La CHARL SE7 153 F5
Lansdowne Ms CHARL SE7 153 F5
NTGHL W11 144 D1
Lansdowne Pl NRWD SE19 209 F3
STHWK * SE1 23 H5
Lansdowne Ri NTGHL W11 124 C6
Lansdowne Rd BMLY BR1 212 C3
CHING E4 55 E4
CROY/NA CR0 228 C6
FNCH N3 64 D3
GDMY/SEVK IG3 95 F5
HACK E8 109 G5
HOR/WEW KT19 240 C5
HSLW TW3 159 F4
MUSWH N10 67 E5
NTGHL W11 124 C6
RYNPK SW20 204 A3
STAN HA7 61 E2
SWFD E18 72 C6
TOTM N17 69 G4
WALTH E17 91 E3
WAN E11 92 B6
Lansdowne Ter BMSBY WC1N 5 F6
Lansdowne Wk NTGHL W11 144 C1
Lansdowne Wy VX/NE SW8 167 G2
Lansdowne Wood Cl
WNWD SE27 188 B5
Lansdown Rd FSTGT E7 113 E5
SCUP DA14 195 H5
Lansfield Av UED N18 53 G6
Lantern Cl ALP/SUD HA0 101 F3
PUT/ROE SW15 163 G5
Lanterns Ct POP/IOD E14 151 E3
Lant St STHWK SE1 23 E3
Lanvanor Rd PECK SE15 170 A3
Lapford Cl MV/WKIL * W9 124 D3
Lapse Wood Wk DUL SE21 189 H3
Lapstone Gdns
KTN/HRWW/W HA3 81 E3
Lapwing Wy YEAD UB4 118 B5
Lapworth Cl ORP BR6 236 A6
Lapworth Ct BAY/PAD W2 125 F4
Lara Cl CHSGTN KT9 239 G5
LEW SE13 191 G1
Larbert Rd STRHM/NOR SW16 207 E4
Larch Av ACT W3 143 E1
Larch Cl BAL SW12 186 D4
DEPT SE8 150 D6
FBAR/BDGN N11 66 C2
Larch Crs HOR/WEW KT19 240 B4
YEAD UB4 118 A4
Larch Dene ORP BR6 234 A6
Larch Dr CHSWK * W4 142 A5
Larches Av MORT/ESHN SW14 162 D5
The Larches PLMGR N13 52 C5
Larch Gv BFN/LL DA15 195 F3
Larch Rd CRICK NW2 104 A2
LEY E10 91 E6
Larch Tree Wy CROY/NA CR0 249 E1
Larch Wy HAYES BR2 234 A4
Larchwood Av CRW RM5 77 F2
Larchwood Cl CRW RM5 77 G2
Larchwood Rd ELTH/MOT SE9 194 B4
Larcombe Cl CROY/NA CR0 247 F2
Larcom St WALW SE17 31 F2
Larden Rd ACT W3 143 E2
Largewood Av SURB KT6 222 A6
Larissa St WALW * SE17 31 H2
Larkbere Rd SYD SE26 190 C6
Larken Cl BUSH WD23 43 G3
Larken Dr BUSH WD23 43 G3
Larkfield Av KTN/HRWW/W HA3 60 D6
Larkfield Rd RCH/KEW TW9 161 G5
SCUP DA14 195 F5
Larkhall La CLAP SW4 167 F3
Larkhall Ri CLAP SW4 167 E4
Larkhill Ter WOOL/PLUM * SE18 174 A1
Lark Rw BETH E2 110 A6
Larkshall Crs CHING E4 55 G6
Larkshall Rd CHING E4 71 H2
Larkspur Cl CDALE/KGS NW9 82 B2
ORP BR6 236 A6
TOTM N17 68 D3
Larkspur Gv EDGW HA8 46 C6
Larkspur Wy HOR/WEW KT19 240 C3
Larkswood Ri PIN HA5 78 A1
Larkswood Rd CHING E4 55 E6
Lark Wy CAR SM5 226 A4
Larkway Cl CDALE/KGS NW9 82 D1
Larnach Rd HMSMTH W6 144 B6
Larpent Av PUT/ROE SW15 164 A6
Larwood Cl NTHLT UB5 99 H3
Lascelles Av HRW HA1 79 H4
Lascelles Cl WAN E11 91 H6
Lascott's Rd WDGN N22 67 H2
Lassa Rd ELTH/MOT SE9 173 G6
Lassell St GNWCH SE10 151 H5
Latchett Rd SWFD E18 72 D4
Latchingdon Gdns WFD IG8 73 G2
Latchmere Cl
RCHPK/HAM TW10 201 G1
Latchmere La KUTN/CMB KT2 201 H2
Latchmere Rd BTSEA SW11 166 B3
KUTN/CMB KT2 201 G2
Latchmere St BTSEA SW11 166 B3
Lateward Rd BTFD TW8 141 F6
Latham Cl EHAM E6 133 G5
Latham Rd BXLYHS DA6 177 E6
TWK TW1 180 B2
Latham's Wy CROY/NA CR0 227 H5
Lathkill Cl EN EN1 53 G2
Lathom Rd EHAM E6 113 H5
Latimer Av EHAM E6 113 H6
Latimer Cl PIN HA5 58 A4
WPK KT4 241 H2
Latimer Gdns PIN HA5 58 A4
Latimer Pl NKENS W10 124 A5
Latimer Rd BAR EN5 35 F4
CROY/NA * CR0 246 B1
FSTGT E7 112 D2
NKENS W10 124 A4
SEVS/STOTM N15 89 E3
TEDD TW11 200 B1
WIM/MER SW19 205 F2
Latona Rd PECK SE15 33 E6
La Tourne Gdns ORP BR6 252 C1
Lattimer Pl CHSWK W4 163 E1
Latton Cl WOT/HER KT12 218 D4
Latymer Gdns FNCH * N3 64 C5
Latymer Rd ED N9 53 F3
Latymer Wy ED N9 52 D4
Lauder Cl NTHLT UB5 118 B1
Lauderdale Dr
RCHPK/HAM TW10 181 F5
Lauderdale Pde MV/WKIL * W9 125 F2
Lauderdale Pl BARB * EC2Y 15 F2
Lauderdale Rd MV/WKIL W9 125 F2
Laud St CROY/NA CR0 246 C1
LBTH SE11 29 G3
Laughton Rd NTHLT UB5 118 B1
Launcelot Rd BMLY BR1 192 C6
Launcelot St STHWK SE1 22 A4
Launceston Gdns
GFD/PVL UB6 101 E6
Launceston Pl KENS W8 145 G3
Launceston Rd GFD/PVL UB6 101 E6
Launch St POP/IOD E14 151 G3
Launders Ga ACT * W3 142 B2
Laundress La CLPT * E5 109 G1
Laundry Rd HMSMTH W6 144 C6
Laura Cl EN EN1 39 E6
WAN E11 93 E2
Lauradale Rd EFNCH N2 86 B1
Laura Pl CLPT E5 110 A2
Laura Ter FSBYPK * N4 88 B6
Laurel Av TWK TW1 180 B3
Laurel Bank
NFNCH/WDSP * N12 49 G6
Laurel Bank Gdns
FUL/PGN SW6 164 D3
Laurel Bank Rd ENC/FH EN2 38 C2
Laurel Cl BARK/HLT IG6 74 C2
SCUP DA14 195 G5
TOOT SW17 206 A1
Laurel Crs CROY/NA CR0 249 E1
Laurel Dr WCHMH N21 52 A2
Laurel Gdns CHING E4 55 F2
HNWL W7 140 A1
HSLWW TW4 158 C5
MLHL NW7 46 D5
Laurel Gv PGE/AN SE20 209 H3
SYD SE26 210 B1
Laurel Pk KTN/HRWW/W HA3 60 B3
Laurel Rd BARN SW13 163 G3
HPTN TW12 199 H1
RYNPK SW20 203 H4
The Laurels BUSH * WD23 44 A4
CMBW * SE5 168 B1
Laurel St HACK E8 109 F4
Laurel Vw NFNCH/WDSP N12 49 F5
Laurel Vls HNWL * W7 140 A2
Laurel Wy NFNCH/WDSP N12 49 E5
SWFD E18 92 B1
Laurence Ms SHB W12 143 G2
Laurence Pountney Hl
CANST * EC4R 15 G5
Laurence Pountney La
CANST EC4R 15 G6
Laurie Gv NWCR SE14 170 C2
Laurie Rd HNWL W7 120 A4
Laurier Rd CROY/NA CR0 229 F4
KTTN NW5 106 D1
Laurimel Cl STAN HA7 60 D2
Laurino Pl BUSH WD23 43 G4
Lauriston Rd HOM E9 110 B5
WIM/MER SW19 204 B2
Lausanne Rd CEND/HSY/T N8 88 A1
PECK SE15 170 A2
Lavender Av CDALE/KGS NW9 82 C5
MTCM CR4 206 A4
WPK KT4 242 A1
Lavender Cl CAR SM5 244 C2
CHEL SW3 145 H6
HAYES BR2 233 G3
Lavender Ct E/WMO/HCT KT8 199 F6
Lavender Gdns BTSEA SW11 166 B5
ENC/FH EN2 38 B1
KTN/HRWW/W HA3 60 A2
Lavender Gv HACK E8 109 G5
MTCM CR4 206 A4
Lavender Hl BTSEA SW11 166 B4
ENC/FH EN2 38 C2
SWLY BR8 217 H6
Lavender Pl IL IG1 114 B3
Lavender Rd BERM/RHTH SE16 150 C1
BTSEA SW11 165 H4
CAR SM5 244 C3
CROY/NA CR0 227 H3
ENC/FH EN2 38 D2
HOR/WEW KT19 240 B3
SUT SM1 243 H2
Lavender St SRTFD E15 112 A4
Lavender Sweep BTSEA SW11 166 B5
Lavender Ter BTSEA * SW11 166 A4
Lavender V WLGTN SM6 245 F4
Lavender Wy CROY/NA CR0 230 B3
Lavengro Rd WNWD SE27 188 C4
Lavenham Rd
WAND/EARL SW18 184 D4
Lavernock Rd BXLYHN DA7 177 E3
Lavers Rd STNW/STAM N16 109 E1
Laverstoke Gdns
PUT/ROE SW15 183 F2
Laverton Ms ECT SW5 145 F4
Laverton Pl ECT SW5 145 F4
Lavidge Rd ELTH/MOT SE9 193 G4
Lavina Gv IS N1 5 G1
Lavington Rd CROY/NA CR0 245 H1
WEA W13 140 D1
Lavington St STHWK SE1 22 D2
Lawdon Gdns CROY/NA CR0 246 B2
Lawford Cl WLGTN SM6 245 G6
Lawford Rd CHSWK W4 162 C1
IS N1 109 E5
KTTN NW5 107 E4
Lawless St POP/IOD * E14 131 F6
Lawley Rd STHGT/OAK N14 50 D2
Lawley St CLPT E5 110 A2
Lawn Cl BMLY BR1 212 D3
EN EN1 53 F2
NWMAL KT3 203 E5
SWLY BR8 217 G5
Lawn Crs RCH/KEW TW9 162 A3
Lawn Farm Gv CHDH RM6 96 C1
Lawn Gdns HNWL W7 140 A1
Lawn House Cl POP/IOD E14 151 G2
Lawn La VX/NE SW8 29 F5
Lawn Rd BECK BR3 210 D3
HAMP NW3 106 B3
Lawns Ct WBLY * HA9 82 A6
The Lawns BELMT SM2 242 C5
BKHTH/KID * SE3 172 B4
CHING E4 71 E1
NRWD SE19 208 D4
PIN HA5 59 F3
SCUP DA14 195 H6
Lawns Wy CRW RM5 77 G3
Lawnswood BAR * EN5 34 C6
Lawn Ter BKHTH/KID SE3 172 B4
The Lawn NWDGN UB2 139 E5
Lawn V PIN HA5 58 B5
Lawrence Av MLHL NW7 47 E6
MNPK E12 114 A2
NWMAL KT3 222 D3
PLMGR N13 52 B6
WALTH E17 70 B4
Lawrence Cl SEVS/STOTM N15 89 E1
SHB * W12 123 H6
Lawrence Ct MLHL NW7 63 E1
OXHEY * WD19 42 B5
Lawrence Crs DAGE RM10 117 F1
EDGW HA8 62 A5
Lawrence Gdns MLHL NW7 47 F5
Lawrence Hl CHING E4 55 E4
Lawrence La CITYW EC2V 15 F4
Lawrence Pde ISLW * TW7 160 D4
Lawrence Pl IS * N1 107 G6
Lawrence Rd EA W5 141 E4
EHAM E6 113 G6
ERITH DA8 177 F1
HPTN TW12 198 D3
HSLWW TW4 158 A5
PIN HA5 78 B2
PLSTW E13 112 D6
RCHPK/HAM TW10 181 E6
SEVS/STOTM N15 69 E6
SNWD SE25 229 F1
UED N18 53 H6
WWKM BR4 250 C2
Lawrence St CAN/RD E16 132 B4
CHEL SW3 26 A6
MLHL NW7 47 F6
Lawrence Wy WLSDN NW10 102 C1
Lawrence Yd SEVS/STOTM N15 89 E1
Lawrie Park Av SYD SE26 209 H1
Lawrie Park Crs SYD SE26 209 H1
Lawrie Park Gdns SYD SE26 209 H1
Lawrie Park Rd SYD SE26 210 A2
Lawson Cl CAN/RD E16 133 E5
WIM/MER SW19 184 B5
Lawson Rd PEND EN3 40 A2
STHL UB1 118 D3
Law St STHWK SE1 23 H5
Lawton Rd BOW E3 130 C2
EBAR EN4 35 H4
LEY E10 91 G5
Laxcon Cl WLSDN NW10 102 D3

Laxey Rd ORP BR6 253 F4
Laxley Cl CMBW SE5 168 B1
Laxton Pl CAMTN NW1 5 H3
Layard Av BERM/RHTH SE16 33 H1
  EN EN1 39 F2
  THHTH CR7 204 D5
Layard Sq BERM/RHTH SE16 33 H1
Laycock St IS N1 108 A4
Layer Gdns ACT W3 122 A6
Layfield Cl HDN NW4 83 H4
Layfield Crs HDN NW4 83 H4
Layfield Rd HDN NW4 83 H4
Layhams Rd HAYES BR2 250 C5
  WWKM BR4 250 A2
Laymarsh Cl BELV DA17 156 D3
Laymead Cl NTHLT UB5 98 C4
Laystall St FSBYW WC1X 6 A6
Layton Crs CROY/NA CRO 246 A3
Layton Pl RCH/KEW TW9 162 A2
Layton Rd BTFD TW8 141 F5
  HSLW TW3 159 F5
Layzell Wk ELTH/MOT SE9 193 F3
Lazenby Ct COVGDN * WC2E 13 C5
Leabank Cl HRW HA1 100 A1
Leabank Sq HOM E9 111 K4
Leabank Vw SEVS/STOTM N15 89 G3
Leabourne Rd STNW/STAM N16 89 F2
Lea Bridge Rd CLPT E5 90 B6
  LEY E10 91 G2
Lea Cottages MTCM * CR4 206 C5
Leacroft Av BAL SW12 186 B2
Leacroft Cl WCHMH N21 52 B4
Leadale Av CHING E4 55 K4
Leadale Rd STNW/STAM N16 89 G3
Leadbeaters Cl FBAR/BDGN N11 66 E1
Leadenhall Pl FENCHST EC3M 16 A4
Leadenhall St BANK EC3V 16 A4
Leader Av MNPK E12 114 A3
The Leadings WBLY HA9 102 C1
Leaf Cl THDIT KT7 220 A2
Leaf Gv STRHM/NOR SW16 208 A1
Leafield Cl STRHM/NOR SW16 208 B2
Leafield La SCUP DA14 196 D6
Leafield Rd RYNPK SW20 204 D6
  SUT SM1 208 E6
Leafy Gv HAYES BR2 251 E5
Leafy Oak Rd LEE/GVPK SE12 193 E6
Leafy Wy CROY/NA CRO 229 F6
Lea Gdns WBLY HA9 101 H3
Leagrave St CLPT E5 110 A1
Lea Hall Gdns LEY * E10 91 E5
Lea Hall Rd LEY E10 91 E5
Leake St STHWK SE1 21 H5
Lealand Rd SEVS/STOTM N15 89 F3
Leamington Av BMLY BR1 215 E1
  MRDN SM4 193 A4
  ORP BR6 253 G2
  WALTH E17 91 E2
Leamington Cl BMLY BR1 193 E6
  HSLW TW3 159 G6
Leamington Crs RYLN/HDSTN HA2 98 C1
Leamington Gdns GDMY/SEVK IG3 95 F6
Leamington Pk ACT W3 122 D4
Leamington Rd NWDGN UB2 138 B4
Leamington Road Vls NTGHL W11 124 D3
Leamore St HMSMTH W6 143 H4
Leamouth Rd EHAM E6 133 C5
  POP/IOD E14 113 G5
Leander Rd BRXS/STRHM SW2 187 H1
  NTHLT UB5 119 E1
  THHTH CR7 227 H1
Learner Dr RYLN/HDSTN HA2 78 A2
Lea Rd BECK BR3 211 E5
  ENC/FH EN2 38 D2
  NWDGN UB2 138 C4
Learoyd Gdns EHAM E6 134 A6
Leas Cl CHSGTN KT9 242 B5
Leas Dl ELTH/MOT SE9 194 A5
Leas Gn CHST BR7 215 F2
Leaside Av MUSWH N10 66 C6
Leaside Rd CLPT E5 90 A5
Leasowes Rd LEY E10 91 E5
Leatherbottle Gn ERITHM DA18 156 D3
Leather Gdns SRTFD E15 112 A6
Leather Cl MTCM CR4 206 C5
Leatherdale St WCHPL * E1 130 B2
Leatherhead Cl STNW/STAM N16 89 E5
Leather La CLKNW EC1R 12 A1
  HCIRC EC1N 14 A1
Leathermarket Ct STHWK SE1 24 A4
Leathermarket St STHWK SE1 24 A4
Leathersellers Cl BAR * EN5 34 C4
Leathsale Rd RYLN/HDSTN HA2 78 A1
Leathwaite Rd BTSEA SW11 166 B5
Leathwell Rd DEPT SE8 171 F3
Lea V DART DA1 139 K4
Lea Valley Rd CHING E4 54 D1
Lea Valley Wk CLPT E5 89 H4
  TOTM N17 69 H5
Leaveland Cl BECK BR3 231 E1
Leaver Gdns GFD/PVL UB6 119 H1
Leavesden Rd STAN HA7 60 C2
Leaway CLPT E5 90 A5
Lebanon Av FELT TW13 198 B1
Lebanon Gdns WAND/EARL SW18 185 G1
Lebanon Pk TWK TW1 180 D2
Lebanon Rd CROY/NA CRO 229 G5
  WAND/EARL SW18 165 E6
Lebrun Sq BKHTH/KID SE3 172 D5
Lechmere Ap WFD IG8 75 F5
Lechmere Av CHIG IG7 74 C1
Lechmere Rd CRICK NW2 103 H4
Leckford Rd WAND/EARL SW18 185 F3
Leckwith Av ABYW SE2 156 C6
Lecky St SKENS SW7 145 H5
Leconfield Av BARN SW13 146 C5
Leconfield Rd HBRY N5 108 D2
Leda Av PEND EN3 40 D2
Leda Rd WOOL/PLUM SE18 153 H5
Ledbury Estate PECK SE15 33 G6
Ledbury Ms North NTGHL W11 125 E6
Ledbury Ms West NTGHL W11 125 E6
Ledbury Rd CROY/NA CRO 246 C2
  NTGHL W11 124 D5

Ledbury St PECK SE15 169 G1
Ledrington Rd NRWD SE19 209 F2
Ledway Dr WBLY HA9 81 H4
Lee Av CHDH RM6 96 C3
Leechcroft Av BFN/LL DA15 175 F6
Leechcroft Rd WLGTN SM6 244 C1
Lee Church St LEW SE13 172 A5
Lee Cl WALTH E17 70 B4
Lee Conservancy Rd HOM E9 110 D3
Leecroft Rd BAR EN5 34 C6
Leeds Cl ORP BR6 236 B6
Leeds Rd IL IG1 94 D5
Leeds St POP/IOD E14 69 G1
Lee Gn STMC/STPC BR5 235 G2
Lee High Rd LEW SE13 171 H5
Leeke St FSBYW WC1X 5 G4
Leeland Rd WEA W13 140 C1
Leeland Ter WEA W13 140 C1
Leeland Wy WLSDN NW10 103 E2
Leemount Cl HDN * NW4 84 B1
Lee Pk BKHTH/KID SE3 172 B5
Lee Park Wy UED N18 70 B1
Lee Rd BKHTH/KID SE3 172 B4
  EN EN1 69 G1
  GFD/PVL UB6 101 E6
  MLHL NW7 64 B5
  WIM/MER SW19 205 F4
Leeside BAR EN5 34 C6
Leeside Crs GLDGN NW11 64 C3
Leeside Rd TOTM N17 69 H2
Leeson Rd HNHL * SE24 168 A6
Leesons HI CHST BR7 215 E5
Leesons Wy STMC/STPC BR5 215 F5
The Lees CROY/NA CRO 230 D6
Lee St HACK E8 109 F6
Lee Ter BKHTH/KID SE3 172 A4
Lee Vw ENC/FH EN2 29 H1
Leeward Gdns WIM/MER SW19 204 C2
Leeway DEPT SE8 150 D5
The Leeways CHEAM * SM3 242 C6
Leewood Cl LEE/GVPK * SE12 173 K5
Leewood Pl SWLY BR8 237 H1
Lefevre Wk BOW E3 110 D6
Leffern Rd SHB W12 143 G2
Lefroy Rd SHB W12 118 C2
Left Side STHGT/OAK * N14 51 F3
Legard Rd HBRY N5 108 D1
Legatt Rd ELTH/MOT SE9 173 F6
Leggatt Rd SRTFD E15 131 G1
Legge St LEW SE13 171 G6
Leghorn Rd WLSDN NW10 123 C1
  WOOL/PLUM SE18 154 D5
Legion Cl IS N1 108 A4
Legion Rd GFD/PVL UB6 96 C1
Legion Wy NFNCH/WDSP N12 66 A3
Legon Av ROMW/RG RM7 97 G5
Legrace Av HSLWW TW4 158 B3
Leicester Av MTCM CR4 227 G1
Leicester Cl WPK KT4 242 A2
Leicester Gdns GDMY/SEVK IG3 95 G5
Leicester Pl LSQ/SEVD * WC2H 12 D5
Leicester Rd BAR EN5 35 E4
  CROY/NA CRO 229 H3
  EFNCH N2 48 A6
  WAN E11 92 A2
  WLSDN NW10 102 C6
Leicester Sq LSQ/SEVD WC2H 12 D6
Leicester St SOHO/SHAV W1D 12 C5
Leigham Av STRHM/NOR SW16 187 H6
Leigham Court Rd STRHM/NOR SW16 188 A1
Leigham Dr ISLW TW7 160 A1
Leigham Hall Pde STRHM/NOR * SW16 187 H5
Leigham V STRHM/NOR SW16 188 A5
Leigh Av REDBR IG4 93 G1
Leigh Cl NWMAL KT3 222 D1
Leigh Ct RYLN/HDSTN * HA2 80 A6
Leigh Crs CROY/NA CRO 249 H5
Leigh Gdns WLSDN NW10 124 A1
Leigh Hunt Dr STHGT/OAK N14 51 F3
Leigh Orchard Cl STRHM/NOR SW16 187 H6
Leigh Pl WELL DA16 148 B2
Leigh Rd EHAM E6 114 A5
  HBRY N5 108 D2
  HSLW TW3 159 J3
  LEY E10 91 G4
Leigh Rodd OXHEY WD19 42 E5
Leigh St STPAN WC1H 5 E5
Leigh Ter STMC/STPC * BR5 215 H6
Leighton Av MNPK E12 114 A2
  PIN HA5 58 J3
Leighton Cl EDGW HA8 62 C5
Leighton Crs KTTN NW5 107 E5
Leighton Gdns WLSDN NW10 124 A2
  SAND/SEL CR2 107 E5
Leighton Gv KTTN NW5 107 E5
Leighton Pl KTTN NW5 107 E5
Leighton Rd EN EN1 39 G5
  KTN/HRWW/W * HA3 59 H3
  KTTN NW5 107 E4
  WEA W13 143 G1
Leila Parnell Pl CHARL * SE7 153 H2
Leinster Av MORT/ESHN SW14 137 K5
Leinster Gdns BAY/PAD W2 125 G5
Leinster Ms BAY/PAD W2 125 G5
Leinster Pl BAY/PAD W2 125 G5
Leinster Rd MUSWH N10 66 B1
Leinster Sq BAY/PAD W2 125 G5
Leinster Ter BAY/PAD W2 125 G5
Leisure Wy NFNCH/WDSP N12 65 H3
Leith Cl CDALE/KGS NW9 82 E1
Leithcote Gdns STRHM/NOR SW16 187 H6
Leithcote Pth STRHM/NOR SW16 187 H6
Leith Rd STMC/STPC BR5 215 G4
Leith Rd WDGN N22 49 G5
Leith Towers BELMT * SM2 243 E6
Leith Yd KIL/WHAMP * NW6 105 G3
Lela Av HSLWW TW4 158 A3
Lelitia Cl HACK E8 109 G6
Leman St WCHPL E1 16 D4
Lemark Cl STAN HA7 61 G2
Le May Av LEE/GVPK SE12 192 D3
Lemmon Rd GNWCH SE10 152 E3
Lemna Rd WAN E11 92 A2
Lemonwell Dr ELTH/MOT SE9 174 C6
Lemsford Cl SEVS/STOTM N15 89 G3
Lena Crs ED N9 54 A4

Lena Gdns HMSMTH W6 144 A3
Lena Kennedy Cl CHING E4 71 G2
Lendal Ter CLAP * SW4 167 F4
Lenelby Rd SURB KT6 222 A5
Len Freeman Pl FUL/PGN SW6 144 C6
Lenham Rd BXLYHN DA7 156 D6
  LEW SE13 172 B5
  SUT SM1 243 F2
  THHTH CR7 204 A6
Lennard Av WWKM BR4 232 A6
Lennard Cl WWKM BR4 232 A6
Lennard Rd CROY/NA CRO 228 C5
  HAYES BR2 200 D2
  PGE/AN SE20 210 B2
Lennard Ter PGE/AN * SE20 210 B2
Lennon Rd CRICK NW2 104 A3
Lennox Gdns CROY/NA CRO 245 A3
  IL IG1 93 H5
  KTBR SW1X 18 E4
  WLSDN NW10 103 F2
Lennox Gardens Ms CHEL SW3 26 C1
Lennox Rd FSBYPK N4 90 D5
  WALTH E17 90 D5
Lenor Cl BXLYHS DA6 176 C5
Lensbury Wy ABYW SE2 128 D3
Lens Rd FSTGT E7 113 E5
Lenthall Rd HACK E8 109 F5
Lentmead Rd BMLY BR1 192 B5
Lenton Ri RCH/KEW TW9 161 G4
Lenton St WOOL/PLUM SE18 127 J4
Lenton Ter FSBYPK * N4 90 A6
Leof Crs CAT SE6 211 F1
Leominster Rd MRDN SM4 225 G3
Leominster Wk MRDN SM4 225 G3
Leonard Av MRDN SM4 225 G2
  ROMW/RG RM7 97 H5
Leonard Ct KENS W8 145 E5
Leonard Pl HAYES * BR2 251 C1
  STNW/STAM * N16 109 E2
Leonard Rd CHING E4 71 G2
  ED * N9 53 F5
  FSTGT E7 112 E2
  MTCM CR4 207 G4
  NWDGN UB2 138 C3
Leonard St CAN/RD E16 153 F1
  SDTCH EC2A 7 F6
Leontine Cl PECK SE15 169 G1
Leopold Av WIM/MER SW19 204 D1
Leopold Ms HOM E9 110 E1
Leopold Rd EA W5 141 G1
  EFNCH N2 47 H6
  WALTH E17 91 G2
  WIM/MER SW19 184 D6
  WLSDN NW10 103 E5
Leopold St BOW E3 111 G5
Leo St PECK SE15 169 H1
Leppoc Rd CLAP SW4 167 F6
Leroy St STHWK SE1 32 A1
Lerry Cl WKENS W14 144 E5
Lescombe Cl FSTH SE23 190 C5
Lescombe Rd FSTH SE23 190 C5
Lesley Cl BXLY DA5 197 F2
Leslie Gdns BELMT SM2 243 E6
Leslie Gv CROY/NA CRO 229 G5
Leslie Grove Pl CROY/NA * CRO 229 F5
Leslie Park Rd CROY/NA CRO 229 G5
Leslie Rd CAN/RD E16 132 D5
  EFNCH N2 65 H1
  WAN E11 111 F2
Lesney Pk ERITH DA8 157 H6
Lesney Park Rd ERITH DA8 157 H6
Lessar Av CLAP SW4 167 G5
Lessingham Av TOOT SW17 187 K1
Lessing St FSTH SE23 190 C3
Lessington Av ROMW/RG RM7 97 G4
Lessness Av BXLYHN DA7 176 E1
Lessness Pk BELV DA17 156 D3
Lessness Rd MRDN SM4 225 G3
Lester Av SRTFD E15 132 A3
Leswin Pl STNW/STAM N16 109 F1
Leswin Rd STNW/STAM N16 109 F1
Letchford Gdns WLSDN NW10 123 C1
Letchford Ms WLSDN * NW10 123 C1
Letchford Ter KTN/HRWW/W * HA3 59 E2
Letchworth Cl HAYES BR2 232 C2
  OXHEY WD19 41 G1
Letchworth Dr HAYES BR2 232 C2
Letchworth St TOOT SW17 186 B1
Letterstone Rd FUL/PGN SW6 164 C1
Lettice St FUL/PGN SW6 164 C3
Lett Rd SRTFD E15 111 F5
Leucha Rd WALTH E17 90 C2
Levana Cl WIM/MER SW19 184 D3
Levehurst Wy CLAP SW4 167 E1
Leven Cl OXHEY WD19 41 G1
Leveson Rd WIM/MER SW19 184 B3
Lewes Rd BMLY BR1 213 F5
  NFNCH/WDSP N12 66 A1
Lewgars Av CDALE/KGS NW9 82 E4
Lewing Cl ORP BR6 235 C5
Lewin Rd BXLYHS DA6 176 E4
  MORT/ESHN SW14 162 A1
  STRHM/NOR SW16 207 J1
Lewis Av WALTH E17 71 H4
Lewis Cl STHGT/OAK N14 34 C2
Lewis Crs WLSDN NW10 102 D3
Lewis Gdns EFNCH N2 47 H4
Lewis Gv LEW SE13 171 F3
Lewisham HI LEW SE13 151 F6
Lewisham Pk LEW SE13 171 F5
Lewisham Rd LEW SE13 151 F4
Lewisham Wy BROCKY SE4 152 A6
Lewis Rd MTCM CR4 206 A5
  RCHPK/HAM * TW10 161 G6
  SCUP DA14 196 A3
  STHL UB1 138 C2

SUT SM1 243 F2
WELL DA16 176 A4
Lewis St CAMTN NW1 106 D5
Lewis Wy DAGE RM10 117 F4
Lexden Dr CHDH RM6 95 H3
Lexden Rd ACT W3 122 D4
  MTCM CR4 227 F1
Lexham Gdns ECT SW5 145 F4
  KENS * W8 145 F3
Lexham Ms KENS W8 145 E4
Lexington St SOHO/CST W1F 12 A4
Lexington Wy BAR EN5 34 B5
Lexton Gdns BAL SW12 186 B3
Leyborne Av WEA W13 141 E2
Leyborne Pk RCH/KEW TW9 162 A2
Leybourne Cl HAYES BR2 232 C2
Leybourne Rd CAMTN * NW1 106 D5
  CDALE/KGS NW9 82 A2
  WAN E11 91 E4
Leybourne St CAMTN * NW1 106 D5
Leyburn Cl WALTH E17 91 G1
Leyburn Gdns CROY/NA CRO 229 E6
Leyburn Gv UED N18 69 G2
Leyburn Rd UED N18 68 B1
Leydenhatch La SWLY BR8 217 H4
Leyden St WCHPL E1 16 C2
Leyes Rd CAN/RD E16 133 E6
Leyfield WPK KT4 223 E6
Leyland Av PEND EN3 40 D2
Leyland Rd LEE/GVPK SE12 172 B6
Leylang Rd NWCR SE14 170 D1
Leys Av DAGE RM10 117 G6
Leys Cl DAGE RM10 117 G5
  HRW HA1 79 H1
Leysdown Av BXLYHN DA7 157 F5
Leysdown Rd ELTH/MOT SE9 193 G4
Leysfield Rd SHB W12 143 G2
Leys Gdns EBAR EN4 56 C6
Leyspring Rd WAN E11 92 B5
Leys Rd East PEND EN3 40 C2
Leys The EFNCH N2 85 G1
The Leys KTN/HRWW/W HA3 81 H3
Ley St IL IG1 94 C6
Leyswood Dr GNTH/NBYPK IG2 95 H2
Leythe Rd ACT W3 142 C2
Leyton Gra LEY E10 91 G1
Leyton Green Rd LEY E10 91 G6
Leyton Park Rd LEY E10 91 G1
Leyton Rd SRTFD E15 111 G3
  WIM/MER SW19 205 G3
Leytonstone Rd SRTFD E15 112 A3
Leywick St SRTFD E15 132 A1
Lezayre Rd ORP BR6 253 F4
Liardet St NWCR SE14 152 C6
Liberia Rd HBRY N5 108 B4
Liberty Av WIM/MER SW19 205 H4
Liberty Ms WDGN * N22 68 B4
Liberty St BRXN/ST SW9 167 H2
Libra Rd BOW E3 111 H6
  PLSTW E13 114 D1
Library Pde WLSDN * NW10 81 G6
Library St STHWK SE1 22 D4
Lichdale Cl ORP BR6 236 E4
Lichfield Gdns RCH/KEW * TW9 65 F3
Lichfield Gv FNCH N3 115 H2
Lichfield Rd BCTR RM8 79 F5
  BOW E3 104 C2
  CRICK NW2 103 F1
  ED N9 133 F2
  EHAM E6 158 A4
  HSLWW TW4 56 A6
  RCH/KEW TW9 161 G6
Lichfield Ter RCHPK/HAM * TW10 161 G6
Lidbury Rd MLHL NW7 46 E2
Lidcote Gdns BRXN/ST * SW9 168 A1
Liddall Wy WDR/YW UB7 112 C1
Liddell Cl KTN/HRWW/W HA3 61 F6
Liddell Gdns WLSDN NW10 105 F1
Liddell Rd KIL/WHAMP NW6 105 F4
Lidding Rd KTN/HRWW/W HA3 61 G6
Liddington Rd SRTFD E15 112 B6
Liddon Rd BMLY BR1 213 E6
  PLSTW E13 115 F2
Liden Cl LEY E10 108 D2
Lidfield Rd STNW/STAM N16 108 D2
Lidgate Rd PECK * SE15 169 F1
Lidiard Rd WAND/EARL SW18 185 E1
Lido Sq TOTM N17 68 D1
Lidyard Rd ARCH N19 84 C4
Liffler Rd WOOL/PLUM SE18 155 K5
Lifford St PUT/ROE SW15 146 E6
Lightcliffe Rd PLMGR N13 52 A6
Lightermans Ms WCHPL E1 130 E5
Lighterman's Rd POP/IOD E14 151 E2
Lightfoot Rd CEND/HSY/T N8 89 E5
Ligonier St BETH E2 9 F4
Lilac Cl CHING E4 70 D2
Lilac Gdns CROY/NA CRO 249 F1
  EA W5 141 F1
  SWLY BR8 217 H8
Lilac St SHB W12 118 D6
Lilburne Gdns ELTH/MOT SE9 173 G6
Lilburne Rd ELTH/MOT SE9 173 G6
Lile Crs HNWL W7 120 A4
Lilestone St CAMTN NW1 2 A5
Lilford Rd BRXN/ST SW9 168 B3
Lilian Barker Cl LEE/GVPK SE12 172 C5
Lilian Board Wy NTHLT UB5 99 K3
Lilian Gdns WFD IG8 72 E4
Lilian Rd MTCM CR4 207 K4
Lilechurch Rd BCTR RM8 225 G1
Lilleshall Rd MRDN SM4 225 H5
Lilley Cl WAP E1W 135 H1
Lilley La MLHL * NW7 45 F1
Lillian Av ACT W3 142 A2
Lillian Rd BARN SW13 125 J5
Lillieshall Rd CLAP SW4 129 H2
Lillie Yd FUL/PGN SW6 145 K5
Lillington Gardens Est PIM SW1V 28 B2
Lilliput Av NTHLT UB5 98 B6
Lilliput Rd ROMW/RG RM7 81 F1
Lily Cl WKENS * W14 119 H5
Lily Gdns ALP/SUD HA0 121 E1
Lily Pl HCIRC EC1N 11 K1
Lily Rd LEY E10 91 H3
Lilyville Rd FUL/PGN SW6 164 D2
Limbourne Av BCTR RM8 79 H4
Limburg Rd BTSEA SW11 166 C6
Limeburner La STP EC4M 14 C3

Lime Cl BKHH IG9 .....57 F4
  BMLY BR1 .....233 G1
  KTN/HRWW/W HA3 .....60 C5
  OXHEY WD19 .....42 B2
  ROMW/RG RM7 .....45 F4
  WAP E1W 25 F1
Lime Crs SUN TW16 .....198 A5
Limecroft Cl HOR/WEW KT19 .....240 D5
Limedene Cl PIN HA5 .....58 B4
Lime Gv BARK/HLT IG6 .....75 F2
  BFN/LL DA15 .....195 F1
  NWMAL KT3 .....202 D6
  ORP BR6 .....254 B6
  SHB W12 .....124 A2
  TRDG/WHET N20 .....48 C3
  TWK TW1 .....180 B1
Limeharbour POP/IOD E14 .....151 F3
Limehouse POP/IOD * E14 .....131 E6
Limehouse Cswy POP/IOD E14 .....130 B6
Limehouse Lnk POP/IOD E14 .....130 C6
Lime Kiln Dr CHARL SE7 .....152 D6
Limerick Cl BAL SW12 .....161 G2
Lime Rd SWLY BR8 .....217 H6
Limerston St WBPTN SW10 .....145 G6
Limes Av BARN SW13 .....163 F5
  CAR SM5 .....226 B5
  CHIG IG7 .....74 C1
  CROY/NA CRO 245 H1
  GLDGN NW11 .....84 C4
  MLHL NW7 .....63 E2
  NFNCH/WDSP N12 .....49 G6
  PGE/AN SE20 .....209 H3
  WAN E11 .....92 D1
The Limes Av FBAR/BDGN N11 .....66 F1
Limes Cl CAR SM5 .....226 B6
  FBAR/BDGN * N11 .....67 E1
Limesdale Gdns EDGW HA8 .....62 C5
Limes Field Rd BARN SW13 .....163 G4
Limesford Rd PECK SE15 .....170 B5
Limes Gdns WAND/EARL SW18 .....185 E1
Limes Gv LEW SE13 .....171 G5
Limes Rd BECK BR3 .....211 F5
  CROY/NA CRO 228 D3
Limes Rw ORP BR6 .....252 B6
The Limes CMBW * SE5 .....169 E4
  WAND/EARL * SW18 .....185 E1
Lime St FENCHST EC3M 16 A5
  WALTH E17 .....90 C1
Lime Street Pas BANK * EC3V 16 A4
Limes Wk EA E1 .....141 F2
  PECK * SE15 .....170 A5
Lime Tree Av THDIT KT7 .....220 A5
Limetree Cl BRXS/STRHM SW2 .....187 H3
Lime Tree Ct PIN * HA5 .....59 E3
Lime Tree Gv CROY/NA CRO 248 D1
Limetree PI MTCM CR4 .....206 D4
Lime Tree Rd HEST TW5 .....159 F2
Lime Tree Ter FSTH * SE23 .....190 D3
Lime Tree Wk BUSH WD23 .....44 A3
  ENC/FH EN2 .....38 C1
  WWKM BR4 .....250 B2
Lime Wk SRTFD * E15 .....112 A6
Limewood Cl WALTH E17 .....90 D1
  WEA W13 .....120 D5
Limewood Rd ERITH DA8 .....177 C1
Limpsfield Av THHTH CR7 .....227 H2
  WIM/MER SW19 .....184 B4
Linacre Rd CRICK NW2 .....81 H5
Linchmere Rd LEE/GVPK SE12 .....192 C2
Lincoln Av ROMW/RG RM7 .....97 H5
  STHGT/OAK N14 .....51 E5
  TWK TW2 .....180 ..
  WIM/MER SW19 .....184 B5
Lincoln Cl GFD/PVL UB6 .....99 G6
  RYLN/HDSTN HA2 .....78 D2
Lincoln Crs EN EN1 .....36 A5
Lincoln Dr OXHEY WD19 .....42 A5
Lincoln Est BOW E3 .....131 E3
Lincoln Gdns IL IG1 .....93 C4
Lincoln Green Rd STMC/STPC BR5 .....235 F2
Lincoln Ms KIL/WHAMP NW6 .....104 D6
Lincoln Pde EFNCH * N2 .....66 A6
Lincoln Rd ALP/SUD HA0 .....101 F4
  EFNCH N2 .....66 A6
  EN EN1 .....39 E5
  FELT TW13 .....178 D5
  MTCM CR4 .....227 G2
  NWDGN UB2 .....102 A5
  PLSTW E13 .....132 D3
  RYLN/HDSTN HA2 .....78 D2
  SCUP DA14 .....215 H1
  SNWD SE25 .....209 H6
  SWFD E18 .....72 B4
  WPK KT4 .....223 H5
Lincoln's Inn Flds LINN WC2A 13 G3
The Lincolns MLHL NW7 .....47 F5
Lincoln St CHEL SW3 .....26 C2
  WAN E11 .....92 A6
Lincoln Ter BELMT * SM2 .....243 E5
Lincoln Wy EN EN1 .....30 ..
Lincombe Rd BMLY BR1 .....192 D5
Lindal Crs STHGT/OAK N14 .....37 G6
The Lindales TOTM N17 .....69 G2
Lindal Rd BROCKY SE4 .....170 D6
Lindbergh Rd WLGTN SM6 .....245 G6
Linden Av EN EN1 .....39 G2
  HSLW TW3 .....159 F6
  THHTH CR7 .....228 B1
  HYS/HAR UB3 .....101 H3
  WBLY HA9 .....100 ..
  WLSDN NW10 .....124 B1
Linden Cl ORP BR6 .....256 B..
  STAN HA7 .....35 G4
  STHGT/OAK N14 .....51 E1
  THDIT KT7 .....220 C4
Linden Cottages
  WIM/MER * SW19 .....204 C2
Linden Crs GFD/PVL UB6 .....100 A5
  KUT/ KT1 .....203 G1
  WFD IG8 .....72 D2
Lindenfield CHST BR7 .....214 B5
Linden Gdns BAY/PAD W2 .....125 E6
  CHSWK W4 .....142 D5
  EN EN1 .....39 G2
Linden Gv NWMAL KT3 .....203 E6
  PECK SE15 .....169 H4
  PGE/AN SE20 .....209 ..
Linden Lea EFNCH N2 .....85 G2
  PIN * HA5 .....59 ..
Linden Leas WWKM BR4 .....231 H6

Linden Ms IS N1 .....108 D3
  NTGHL W11 .....125 E6
Linden PI MTCM CR4 .....226 A1
Linden Rd FBAR/BDGN N11 .....50 B4
  HPTN TW12 .....199 F4
  MUSWH N10 .....86 D1
  SEVS/STOTM N15 .....88 C1
The Lindens CHSWK W4 .....162 C2
  NFNCH/WDSP * N12 .....65 H1
  WALTH * E17 .....91 F1
Linden St ROMW/RG RM7 .....97 H1
Linden Wy STHGT/OAK N14 .....51 E1
Lindfield Gdns HAMP NW3 .....105 G3
Lindfield Rd CROY/NA CRO 229 F3
  EA W5 .....121 E3
Lindfield St POP/IOD E14 .....131 E5
Lindhill Cl PEND EN3 .....40 B3
Lindisfarne Rd HOM E9 .....110 C2
Lindisfarne Rd BCTR RM8 .....116 A1
  RYNPK SW20 .....203 G3
Lindley Est PECK * SE15 .....169 G1
Lindley PI RCH/KEW TW9 .....162 A2
Lindley Rd LEY E10 .....91 G6
Lindley St WCHPL E1 .....130 A4
Lindore Rd BTSEA SW11 .....166 B5
Lindore St PECK SE15 .....170 A3
Lind Rd SUT SM1 .....243 G3
Lindrop St FUL/PGN SW6 .....165 G3
Lindsay Cl CHSGTN KT9 .....239 G5
Lindsay Dr KTN/HRWW/W HA3 .....61 H1
Lindsay Rd HPTN TW12 .....179 H6
  WPK KT4 .....223 H1
Lindsay Sq PIM SW1V 28 D3
Lindsay St GWCH SE10 .....171 G2
Lindsey Cl BMLY BR1 .....213 F6
  MTCM CR4 .....227 G1
Lindsey Ms IS N1 .....108 C5
Lindsey Rd BCTR RM8 .....116 A1
Lindsey St STBT EC1A 14 D1
Lind St DEPT SE8 .....171 F3
Lindum Rd TEDD TW11 .....201 E3
Lindway WNWD SE27 .....208 B1
Linfield Cl HDN NW4 .....64 A6
Linford Rd WALTH E17 .....71 G6
Linford St VX/NE SW8 .....167 E2
Lingey Cl BFN/LL DA15 .....195 F1
Lingfield Av BRYLDS KT5 .....221 G1
Lingfield Cl EN EN1 .....36 A5
Lingfield Ct NTHLT * UB5 .....119 E1
Lingfield Crs ELTH/MOT SE9 .....174 D5
Lingfield Gdns ED N9 .....30 D5
Lingfield Rd WIM/MER SW19 .....204 B2
Lingham St BRXN/ST SW9 .....167 G3
Lingholm Wy BAR EN5 .....34 B6
Ling Rd CAN/RD E16 .....132 C4
  ERITH DA8 .....157 G6
Lingwell Rd TOOT SW17 .....186 A5
Lingwood Gdns ISLW TW7 .....160 A5
Lingwood Rd CLPT E5 .....89 G4
Linhope St CAMTN NW1 .....2 D6
Link Av CAMTN NW1 .....2 C2
Link Fld HAYES BR2 .....232 C5
Linkfield Rd ISLW TW7 .....160 B3
Link La WLGTN SM6 .....245 F4
Links Av MRDN SM4 .....193 H5
Links Br TRDG/WHET N20 .....49 E3
Links Gdns STRHM/NOR SW16 .....208 A3
Linkside CHIG IG7 .....74 C1
  NFNCH/WDSP N12 .....65 E1
  NWMAL KT3 .....202 B5
Linkside Cl ENC/FH EN2 .....37 H4
Linkside Gdns ENC/FH EN2 .....37 G4
Links Rd CDALE/KGS NW9 .....63 E6
Link Rd DAGW RM9 .....137 F1
  FBAR/BDGN N11 .....50 C6
  MTCM CR4 .....226 C5
Links Rd ASHF TW15 .....177 F5

Linthorpe Av ALP/SUD HA0 .....101 E4
Linthorpe Rd EBAR EN4 .....36 A4
  STNW/STAM N16 .....69 H6
Linton Cl CAR SM5 .....226 B4
  CHARL SE7 .....135 E5
  WELL DA16 .....175 G2
Linton Gdns EHAM E6 .....133 C5
Linton Gv WNWD SE27 .....208 B1
Linton Rd BARK IG11 .....114 C6
Linton St IS N1 .....108 C6
Linver Rd FUL/PGN SW6 .....164 D3
Linwood Cl CMBW SE5 .....169 F3
Linwood Crs EN EN1 .....39 G2
Linzee Rd CEND/HSY/T N8 .....67 G1
Lion Av TWK TW1 .....180 B3
Lionel Gdns ELTH/MOT SE9 .....173 F6
Lionel Ms NKENS * W10 .....124 C4
Lionel Rd ELTH/MOT SE9 .....173 F6
Lionel Rd North BTFD TW8 .....141 G5
Lionel Rd South BTFD TW8 .....141 H5
Lion Gate Gdns RCH/KEW TW9 .....161 H4
Lion Mills BETH * E2 .....9 F2
Lion Park Av CHSGTN KT9 .....240 C2
Lion Rd BXLYHS DA6 .....176 C5
  CROY/NA CRO 228 C2
  ED N9 .....30 D4
  EHAM E6 .....133 H4
  WHTN TW2 .....180 B3
Lions Cl LEE/GVPK SE12 .....193 E5
Lion Wy BTFD TW8 .....161 F1
Lion Wharf Rd ISLW TW7 .....160 D4
Liphook Crs FSTH SE23 .....190 A2
Liphook Rd OXHEY WD19 .....42 B6
Lisbon Av WHTN TW2 .....179 G4
Lisbon Cl WALTH E17 .....70 D5
Lisburne Rd HAMP NW3 .....106 B2
Lisford St PECK SE15 .....169 F2
Lisgar Ter WKENS W14 .....144 C4
Liskeard Gdns BKHTH/KID SE3 .....172 C2
Lisle Cl TOOT SW17 .....186 D6
Lisle St SOHO/SHAV W1D 12 D5
Lismore Wlk HAMP * SW19 .....204 C1
Lismore Circ HAMP NW3 .....106 B3
Lismore Cl ISLW TW7 .....160 C3
Lismore Rd SAND/SEL CR2 .....247 E4
  TOTM N17 .....89 H3
Lismore Wk IS N1 .....108 C4
Lissant Cl SURB KT6 .....221 E4
Lissenden Gdns KTTN NW5 .....106 C2
Lisson Gv CAMTN NW1 .....2 A1
Lisson St CAMTN NW1 .....1 H1
Lister Cl ACT W3 .....122 D4
  MTCM CR4 .....194 A6
Lister Gdns UED N18 .....68 C1
Lister Ms HOLWY N7 .....107 G2
Lister Rd WAN E11 .....92 A5
Liston Rd CLAP SW4 .....167 E4
  TOTM N17 .....69 G4
Listowel Cl BRXN/ST SW9 .....168 A1
Listowel Rd DAGE RM10 .....117 E1
Listria Pk STNW/STAM N16 .....89 E6
Litchfield Av MRDN SM4 .....224 D4
  SRTFD E15 .....112 D5
Litchfield Gdns WLSDN NW10 .....103 C4
Litchfield Rd SUT SM1 .....243 G2
Litchfield Wy GLDGN NW11 .....85 G2
Lithos Rd HAMP NW3 .....105 F4
Little Acre BECK BR3 .....210 C6
Little Albany St CAMTN NW1 .....3 H6
Little Argyll St CONDST * W1S 12 A4
Little Birches BFN/LL DA15 .....195 E4
The Little Boltons
  WBPTN SW10 .....145 E1
Little Bornes DUL SE21 .....189 E6
Little Britain STBT EC1A 15 E2
Littlebrook Cl CROY/NA CRO 230 D3
Littlebury Rd CLAP * SW4 .....167 F4
The Little Bury St ED N9 .....53 E2
Little Cedars NFNCH/WDSP N12 .....49 G6
Little Chester St KTBR * SW1X 17 G5
Little Cloisters WEST SW1P .....21 ..
Littlecombe Cl PUT/ROE * SW15 .....184 F1
Littlecote Cl WIM/MER SW19 .....184 B2
Littlecote PI PIN HA5 .....58 ..
Little Ct WWKM BR4 .....232 A6
Littlecroft ELTH/MOT SE9 .....174 A4
Littledale ABYW SE2 .....155 G6
Little Deans Yd WEST SW1P 21 E5
Little Dimocks BAL SW12 .....187 G1
Little Dorrit Ct STHWK SE1 .....23 F3
Little Ealing La EA W5 .....141 E4
Little Edward St CAMTN * NW1 .....3 H3
Little Essex St TPL/STR * WC2R 14 A5
Little Ferry Rd TWK * TW1 .....180 D5
Littlefield Cl ARCH N19 .....107 E2
  KUT/ KT1 .....201 G5
Littlefield Rd EDGW HA8 .....62 D3
Little Friday Rd CHING E4 .....56 A4
Little Gearies BARK/HLT IG6 .....94 B1
Little George St WEST SW1P 21 E4
Little Green St KTTN * NW5 .....106 D2
Littlegrove EBAR EN4 .....35 H1
Little Heath CHARL SE7 .....153 G6
  CHDH RM6 .....95 H1
Little Heath Rd BXLYHN DA7 .....176 D2
Littleheath Rd SAND/SEL CR2 .....247 H6
Little Ilford La MNPK E12 .....113 H2
Littlejohn Rd HNWL W7 .....120 B5
  STMC/STPC BR5 .....235 G3
Little Marlborough St
  REGST * W1B 12 A4
Littlemede ELTH/MOT SE9 .....193 H5
Littlemoor Rd IL IG1 .....114 D1
Littlemore Rd ABYW SE2 .....155 G2
Little Moss La PIN HA5 .....59 H6
Little Newport St
  LSO/SEVD WC2H 12 D5
Little New St FLST/FETLN EC4A 14 B3
Little Orchard Cl PIN * HA5 .....58 C5
Little Oxhey La OXHEY WD19 .....58 C1
Little Park Dr FELT TW13 .....178 B4
Little Park Gdns ENC/FH EN2 .....38 D4
Little Pluckett's Wy BKHH IG9 .....57 F3
Little Portland St REGST W1B 11 H3
Little Potters BUSH WD23 .....43 H2
Little Queens Rd TEDD TW11 .....201 G5
Little Redlands BMLY BR1 .....213 G5
Little Rownings FSTH SE23 .....189 H4
Littlers Cl WIM/MER SW19 .....205 H4
Little Russell St
  NOXST/BSQ WC1A 13 E2

Little St James's St
  WHALL SW1A 20 A2
Little St Leonards
  MORT/ESHN SW14 .....162 C4
Little Smith St WEST SW1P 20 D5
Littlestone Cl BECK BR3 .....211 E2
Little Strd CDALE/KGS NW9 .....63 F5
Little Thrift STMC/STPC BR5 .....254 C1
Little Titchfield St GTPST W1W 12 A2
Littleton Av CHING E4 .....56 B3
Littleton Crs HRW HA1 .....80 B6
Littleton Rd HRW HA1 .....80 B6
Littleton St WAND/EARL SW18 .....185 G4
Little Trinity La BLKFR EC4V 15 F5
Little Turnstile LINN WC2A 13 G2
Littlewood LEW SE13 .....171 G6
Little Wood Cl STMC/STPC BR5 .....215 G4
Littlewood Cl WEA W13 .....140 D5
Livermere Rd HACK E8 .....109 F6
Liverpool Gv WALW SE17 .....31 G4
Liverpool Rd CAN/RD E16 .....132 A4
  EA W5 .....141 F2
  KUTN/CMB KT2 .....202 A3
  LEY E10 .....91 G3
  THHTH CR7 .....208 C6
Livesey Cl KUT/ KT1 .....201 H6
Livesey PI PECK SE15 .....33 F5
Livingstone Rd BTSEA SW11 .....165 H4
  HSLW TW3 .....159 G5
  LEY E10 .....91 F3
  PLMGR N13 .....51 E6
  SRTFD E15 .....111 G6
  STHL UB1 .....96 ..
  THHTH CR7 .....208 D5
Lizard St FSBYE EC1V 7 F4
Lizban St BKHTH/KID SE3 .....172 D1
Llanelly Rd CRICK NW2 .....84 D6
Llanover Rd WBLY HA9 .....101 ..
  WOOL/PLUM SE18 .....174 A1
Llanthony Rd MRDN SM4 .....225 H4
Llanvanor Rd CRICK NW2 .....84 D4
Llewellyn St BERM/RHTH SE16 .....25 F4
Lloyd Av STRHM/NOR SW16 .....207 G4
Lloyd Baker St FSBYW WC1X 6 A4
Lloyd Ct PIN HA5 .....78 B2
Lloyd Ms PEND EN3 .....41 E1
Lloyd Park Av CROY/NA CRO 247 F2
Lloyd Rd DAGW RM9 .....116 D4
  EHAM E6 .....113 H6
  WALTH E17 .....90 B1
  WPK KT4 .....242 A1
Lloyd's Av TWRH EC3N 16 B4
Lloyd's PI BKHTH/KID * SE3 .....172 A3
Lloyd's Rw CLKNW EC1R 6 A3
Lloyd's Row CLKNW EC1R .....6 ..
Lloyd St FSBYW WC1X 6 A3
Lloyds Wy BECK BR3 .....210 B3
Lloyd Thomas Ct WDGN * N22 .....67 H5
Lloyd Vs BROCKY SE4 .....171 E3
Loampit HI LEW SE13 .....171 E3
Loampit V LEW SE13 .....171 F4
Loanda Cl HACK E8 .....109 F6
Loats Rd CLAP SW4 .....187 C1
Locarno Rd ACT W3 .....142 C1
  GFD/PVL UB6 .....119 G3
Lochaber Rd LEW SE13 .....172 A5
Lochaline St HMSMTH W6 .....144 A6
Lochan Cl YEAD UB4 .....118 C3
Lochinvar St BAL SW12 .....186 D2
Lochmere Cl ERITH DA8 .....157 F1
Lochnagar St POP/IOD E14 .....131 G4
Lock Cha LEW SE13 .....172 A4
Lock Cl STHL * UB1 .....103 G1
Locksley Dr STMC/STPC BR5 .....235 F3
Locksley Sq SURB * KT6 .....221 F3
Lockett Rd KTN/HRWW/W HA3 .....60 B5
Lockfield Av PEND EN3 .....40 C5
Lockgate Cl HOM E9 .....110 D3
Lockhart Cl HOLWY N7 .....107 H4
Lockhart St BOW E3 .....130 D3
Lockhurst St CLPT E5 .....91 G2
Lockington Rd VX/NE SW8 .....166 D2
Lock Keepers Cottages
  TOTM * N17 .....89 H1
Lockmead Rd LEW SE13 .....171 H1
  SEVS/STOTM N15 .....89 G3
Lock Rd RCHPK/HAM TW10 .....181 E6
Lock's La MTCM CR4 .....206 C4
Locksley Est POP/IOD E14 .....130 D4
Locksley St POP/IOD E14 .....130 D4
Locksmeade Rd
  RCHPK/HAM TW10 .....180 D6
Lockwood Cl SYD SE26 .....190 D6
Lockwood Sq BERM/RHTH SE16 .....25 G5
Lockwood Wy CHSGTN KT9 .....240 C3
  WALTH E17 .....70 A1
Lockyer St STHWK SE1 .....23 H4
Locton Gn BOW * E3 .....110 D6
Loddiges Rd HOM E9 .....110 A5
Loder St PECK SE15 .....170 A1
Lodge Av BCTR RM8 .....116 A5
  CROY/NA CRO 245 H1
  DAGW RM9 .....115 H6
  KTN/HRWW/W HA3 .....61 G1
Lodge Cl EDGW * HA8 .....62 A1
  ISLW TW7 .....160 D2
  MTCM CR4 .....225 H5
  ORP BR6 .....255 H5
  UED N18 .....68 C1
Lodge Crs ALP/SUD * HA0 .....101 G3
  ORP BR6 .....255 H5
Lodge Dr PLMGR N13 .....51 G4
Lodge Gdns BECK BR3 .....210 D2
Lodge HI WELL DA16 .....175 H1
Lodgehill Park Cl
  RYLN/HDSTN HA2 .....79 F6
Lodge La BXLY DA5 .....168 ..
  CROY/NA CRO .....264 ..
  CRW RM5 .....77 E2
  NFNCH/WDSP N12 .....65 E1
Lodge Mansions Pde
  PLMGR * N13 .....51 A6
Lodge Ms HBRY * N5 .....108 C2
Lodge PI SUT SM1 .....243 F3
Lodge Rd BMLY BR1 .....213 E3
  CROY/NA CRO .....230 C..
  HDN NW4 .....64 A1
  ST/WD NW8 .....2 B4
  SUT SM1 .....243 F3
  WLGTN SM6 .....244 B5

The Lodge SHB * W12 ......144 B2
Lodge Vis WFD IG8 ....72 B3
Lodore Gdns CDALE/KGS NW9 ...83 E2
Lodore St POP/IOD E14....131 G5
Lofthouse Pl CHSGTN KT9 ....239 D4
Loftie St BERM/RHTH SE16...19 F5
Lofting Rd IS N1 ....108 A5
Loftus Rd SHB W12 ....143 H1
Loftus Vis SHB * W12........143 H1
Logan Cl HSLWW TW4 ....158 D4
  PEND EN3 ....40 A2
Logan Ms KENS W8 ....145 E4
Logan Pl ECT SW5............145 E4
Logan Rd ED N9 ....53 H4
  WBLY HA9 ....81 G6
The Logans BAR * EN5.......34 B4
Logs Hil CHST BR7 ....213 G4
Logs Hill Cl CHST BR7 ......213 G4
Lolesworth Cl WCHPL * E1 ...16 D2
Lollard St LBTH SE11 ....29 H1
Loman St STHWK SE1..........29 D3
Lomas Cl CROY/NA CRO....249 G5
Lomas St WCHPL E1..........17 F1
Lombard Av GDMY/SEVK IG3...95 E5
  PEND EN3 ....40 A2
Lombard Rd BTSEA SW11....165 H3
  FBAR/BDGN N11 ....48 D3
  WIM/MER SW19 ....205 F5
Lombard St BANK EC3V.......15 H4
Lombard Wy FBAR/BDGN * N11...48 D3
Lombard Wall CHARL SE7....152 D3
Lombardy Pl BAY/PAD W2 ...125 H1
Lomond Cl ALP/SUD HA0.....101 H5
  WBLY HA9 ....89 E1
Lomond Gdns SAND/SEL CR2...248 C5
Lomond Gv CMBW SE5........110 E6
Loncroft Rd CMBW SE5........32 B5
Londesborough Rd
  STNW/STAM N16 ....109 E2
London Br CANST EC4R.......15 H6
London Bridge Wk STHWK * SE1...23 H1
Londonderry Pde ERITH * DA8...177 H1
London Flds HACK * E8 .....109 H5
London Fields East Side
  HACK E8 ....109 H5
London Fields West Side
  HACK E8 ....109 G5
London La BMLY BR1.........212 B3
  HACK E8 ....109 H5
London Loop BORE WD6 ......46 B1
  ENC/FH EN2 ....38 C1
  MLHL NW7 ....46 A2
  SAND/SEL CR2.............248 B6
  WWKM BR4 ....249 H1
London Ms BAY/PAD W2 .....125 H5
London Rd BARK IG11 ....114 D5
  BMLY BR1 ....212 D2
  BUSH WD23 ....42 C1
  CHDH RM6 ....97 E3
  CHEAM SM3 ....234 B6
  CROY/NA CRO 228 B5
  DART DA1..................171 H6
  ENC/FH EN2 ....38 D6
  EW KT17 ....241 F6
  FSTH SE23 ....150 A3
  ISLW TW7 ....160 A3
  KUT KT1 ....201 G5
  MRDN SM4 ....225 E2
  MTCM CR4 ....206 B5
  PLSTW E13 ....132 C1
  ROMW/RG RM7 ....97 G3
  STAN HA7 ....30 A6
  STHWK SE1 ....29 C5
  STNW/MOR SW16 ....207 H5
  SWLY BR8 ....217 G5
  THHTH CR7 ....228 A3
  TWK TW1 ....180 C2
  WBLY HA9 ....80 C5
  WLGTN SM6 ....226 D6
London Stile CHSWK W4 ....125 H5
London St BAY/PAD * W2 ...125 H5
  FENCHST * EC3M..........16 B5
London Ter BETH * E2.........9 F2
London Wall BARB EC2Y 15 F2
London Wall Buildings
  LVPST EC2M................15 H2
Lonesome Wy MTCM CR4 ....206 D4
Long Acre COVGDN WC2E 13 G4
  STMC/STPC BR5 ....236 B6
Long Acre Ct WEA * W13....120 C4
Longacre Pl CAR * SM5.......244 C4
Longacre Rd WALTH E17......71 H4
Longbeach Rd BTSEA SW11...166 B4
Longboat Rw STHL UB1 .....118 D5
Longbridge Rd BARK IG11 ...114 D4
  BCTR RM8 ....115 G2
Longbridge Wy LEW SE13....172 A6
Longbury Cl STMC/STPC BR5...215 H6
Longbury Dr STMC/STPC BR5...215 H6
Longcrofte Rd EDGW HA8.....61 A3
Long Deacon Rd CHING E4....56 A3
Longdon Wd HAYES BR2.....251 G2
Longdown Rd CAT SE6 ......191 E6
Long Dr ACT W3...............123 E5
  GFD/PVL UB6 ....99 F6
  RSLP HA4 ....98 A3
Long Elmes KTN/HRWW/W HA3...59 G4
Longfellow Rw BOW * E3....130 C2
  WALTH * E17 ....90 D3
  WPK KT4 ....224 E1
Longfellow Wy STHWK * SE1...32 D2
Longfield BMLY BR1 ....212 B4
Long Fld CDALE/KGS NW9.....63 E3
Longfield Av EA W5...........121 E6
  MLHL NW7 ....63 G3
  WALTH E17 ....90 C1
  WBLY HA9 ....61 H6
  WLGTN SM6 ....196 A5
Longfield Crs SYD SE26......190 A5
Longfield Dr
  MORT/ESHN SW14 ....162 B6
  WIM/MER SW19 ....206 A4
Longfield Est STHWK SE1.....32 D1
Longfield Rd EA W5..........121 E5
Longfield St WAND/EARL SW18...185 E1
Longford Av FELT TW14......159 E6
Longford Cl HPTN TW12 .....179 E6
  YEAD UB4...................118 B6

Longford Rd HOR/WEW KT19...240 C2
Longford Gdns SUT SM1......243 E1
  YEAD UB4..................118 B6
Longford Rd WHTN TW2......179 E3
Longhayes Av CHDH RM6......76 B6
Longheath Gdns CROY/NA CRO...230 A2
Longhedge St BTSEA SW11...166 C3
Longhill Rd CAT SE6..........191 H4
Longhope Cl PECK SE15.......32 B6
Longhurst Rd CROY/NA CRO...229 H3
  LEW SE13 ....172 A6
Longland Dr TRDG/WHET N20...49 F5
Longlands Park Crs
  BFN/LL DA15 ....195 E5
Longlands Rd BFN/LL DA15...195 E5
Long La BXLYHN DA7..........176 D3
  CROY/NA CRO 230 A5
  FNCH N3 ....65 G5
  STBT EC1A 14 D1
Longleat Rd EN EN1 ....23 H4
Longleigh La ABYW SE2......156 A6
Longley Av ALP/SUD HA0....101 H6
Longley Rd CROY/NA CRO...228 B4
  HRW HA1 ....60 E2
  TOOT SW17.................206 A2
Long Leys CHING E4...........71 F2
Longley St STHWK SE1.........33 E2
Longley Wy CRICK NW2........82 A3
Long Mark Rd CAN/RD E16...133 F5
Long Md CDALE/KGS NW9.....63 F4
Longmead CHST BR7 ....214 A5
Longmead Dr SCUP DA14....196 B4
Long Meadow KTTN * NW5...107 F4
Long Meadow Cl BECK BR3...231 G4
Longmeadow Rd BFN/LL DA15...195 E3
Longmead Rd THDIT KT7.....220 A4
  TOOT SW17.................206 A2
Longmoore St PIM SW1V.......28 A2
Longmore Av BAR EN5.........49 C1
Longnor Rd WCHPL E1........130 D2
Long Pond Rd BKHTH/KID SE3...172 A2
Longport Cl BARK/HLT IG6 ...55 H1
Long Reach Rd BARK IG11...135 F3
Longridge La GFD/PVL UB6...119 F6
Longridge Rd ECT SW5.......145 E4
Long Rd CLAP SW4...........167 E5
Longshaw Rd CHING E4........55 H5
Longshore DEPT SE8.........150 D4
Longstaff Crs
  WAND/EARL SW18 ....185 E1
Longstaff Rd
  WAND/EARL SW18 ....185 E1
Longstone Av WLSDN NW10...81 G5
Longstone Rd TOOT SW17...206 D1
Long St BETH E2..............9 H6
Longthornton Rd
  STRHM/NOR SW16.........207 E5
Longton Av SYD SE26........189 D6
Longton Cv SYD SE26........189 H6
Longview Wy CRW RM5.......77 H3
Longville Rd LBTH SE11.......30 C1
Long Wk NWMAL KT3...........5 D1
  STHWK SE1 ....24 B5
Longwood Ct WPK KT4........223 G6
Longwood Dr PUT/ROE SW15...183 G1
Longwood Gdns CLAY IG5 ....93 H1
Longworth Ct THDIT SE28...136 B5
Long Yd BMSBY WC1N...........5 F4
The Loning CDALE/KGS NW9...83 F1
Lonsdale Av EHAM E6.........133 F3
  ROMW/RG RM7 ....97 G3
  WBLY HA9 ....101 G3
Lonsdale Cl EHAM E6.........133 G3
  LEE/GVPK SE12 ....133 H4
Lonsdale Crs GNTH/NBYPK IG2...94 B3
Lonsdale Dr ENC/FH EN2......37 G6
  STHGT/OAK N14 ....37 C6
Lonsdale Gdns
  STRHM/NOR SW16.........227 H1
Lonsdale Ms RCH/KEW * TW9...162 A2
Lonsdale Pl IS N1 ....108 A5
Lonsdale Rd BARN SW13....163 F1
  BXLYHN DA7 ....176 D3
  CHSWK W4 ....145 F4
  KIL/WHAMP NW6 ....124 D5
  NTGHL W11 ....124 D5
  NWDGN UB2 ....138 B3
  SNWD SE25 ....229 H1
Lonsdale Sq IS * N1 ....108 A5
Loobert Rd SEVS/STOTM N15...68 A1
Looe Gdns BARK/HLT IG6 ....74 B6
Loop Rd CHST BR7 ....214 B2
Lopen Rd UED N18 ....53 E6
Loraine Ct PEND EN3..........40 A6
Loraine Cottages HOLWY * N7...107 F1
Loraine Rd CHSWK W4........145 H1
  HOLWY N7 ....107 H2
Lord Av CLAY IG5...............93 H1
Lord Chancellor Wk
  KUTN/CMB KT2 ....202 C4
Lorden Wk BETH E2............9 H4
Lord Gdns CLAY IG5............93 G1
Lord Hills Rd BAY/PAD W2...125 F4
Lord Holland La
  BRXN/ST * SW9.............168 A3
Lord Napier Pl HMSMTH W6...146 D5
Lord North St WEST SW1P....21 E6
Lord Roberts Ms
  FUL/PGN SW6 ....165 F1
Lordship Gv STNW/STAM N16...68 D1
Lordship La DUL SE21........188 C4
  EDUL SE22 ....189 F1
  TOTM N17 ....68 C4
Lordship Ms STNW/STAM N16...88 D1
Lordship Park Ms
  STNW/STAM N16 ....88 B1
Lordship Pl CHEL SW3.........36 A6
Lordship Rd NTHLT UB5......98 C5
  STNW/STAM N16 ....88 C5
Lordship Ter STNW/STAM N16...88 D6
Lordsmead Rd TOTM N17......69 E4
Lord St CAN/RD E16...........153 C1
Lords Vw STJWD NW8...........2 A4

Lord Warwick St
  WOOL/PLUM SE18 ....153 H3
Lorenzo St FSBYW WC1X........5 G4
Loretto Gdns
  KTN/HRWW/W HA3..........81 C1
Lorian Cl NFNCH/WDSP N12...46 E1
Loring Rd ISLW TW7 ....160 B3
  TRDG/WHET N20 ....50 A4
Loris Rd HMSMTH W6.........119 E3
Lorn Ct BRXN/ST SW9........168 A3
Lorne Av CROY/NA CRO.......230 B4
Lorne Cl STJWD NW8............2 C4
Lorne Gdns CROY/NA CRO....230 B4
  WAN E11 ....93 E1
  WKENS W14 ....144 B2
Lorne Rd FSBYPK N4 ....87 H5
  FSTGT E7 ....112 D2
  KTN/HRWW/W HA3........43 E6
  RCHPK/HAM TW10 ....161 H6
  WALTH E17 ....91 E2
Lorne Ter FNCH * N3 ....65 F4
Lorn Rd BRXN/ST SW9........167 H3
Lorraine Pk KTN/HRWW/W HA3...60 A4
Lorrimore Rd WALW SE17......30 D6
Lorrimore Sq WALW SE17.....30 D5
Lothair Rd EA W5..............141 F2
Lothair Rd North FSBYPK N4...88 A4
Lothair Rd South FSBYPK N4...88 A4
Lothbury LOTH EC2R...........15 C3
Lothian Cl ALP/SUD HA0.....100 C2
Lothian Rd BRXN/ST SW9....168 B2
Lothrop St NKENS W10........124 C2
Lots Rd WBPTN SW10.........165 G1
Loubet St TOOT SW17........206 B2
Loudoun Av CNTH/NBYPK IG2...94 B2
Loudoun Rd STJWD NW8.....108 A1
Loughborough Pk HNHL SE24...168 B5
Loughborough Rd
  BRXN/ST SW9..............168 A3
Loughborough St LBTH SE11...29 H1
Lough Rd HOLWY N7.........107 H4
Loughton Wy BKHH IG9.......57 F3
Louisa Cl HOM E9.............110 A5
Louisa St WCHPL E1..........130 D4
Louise Bennett Cl HNHL * SE24...168 B5
Louise Rd SRTFD E15.........112 A4
Louisville Rd TOOT SW17....206 B2
Louvaine Rd BTSEA SW11...165 H5
Lovage Ap EHAM E6...........133 G4
Lovat Cl CRICK NW2............81 F1
Lovat La MON/FENCHST EC3M...16 A5
Lovatt Cl EDGW HA8...........62 D2
Loveday Rd WEA W13.........140 D1
Lovegrove St STHWK SE1......33 F4
Lovegrove Wk POP/IOD E14...113 E6
Lovekyn Cl KUTN/CMB KT2...201 G5
Lovelace Av HAYES BR2......234 A3
Lovelace Gdns BARK IG11....97 H4
  SURB KT6 ....222 A1
Lovelace Rd DUL SE21.......188 C4
  EBAR EN4 ....50 A2
Love La BECK BR3............182 D6
  CITYW EC2V 15 F3
  MRDN SM4 ....225 D4
  MTCM CR4 ....206 A6
  PIN HA5 ....58 C6
  SNWD SE25 ....209 H6
  SURB KT6 ....221 F6
  TOTM N17 ....68 B3
  WFD IG8 ....73 H2
  WOOL/PLUM SE18 ....154 A4
Lovel Av WELL DA16 ....156 A2
Lovelinch Cl PECK SE15......150 A6
Lovell Pl BERM/RHTH SE16...150 C3
Lovell Rd GFD/PVL UB6......119 F5
  RCHPK/HAM TW10 ....181 E5
Loveridge Ms
  KIL/WHAMP NW6 ....104 D4
Loveridge Rd
  KIL/WHAMP NW6 ....104 D4
Lovett Dr CAR SM5...........209 G5
Lovett Wy WLSDN NW10.....102 G3
Love Wk CMBW SE5...........130 B3
Lovibonds Av ORP BR6.......236 B5
Lowbrook Rd IL IG1 ....114 D2
Lowden Rd ED N9.............36 B4
  HNHL SE24 ....168 B5
  STHL UB1 ....115 C6
Lowe Av CAN/RD E16...........95 E4
Lowe Cl CHIG IG7..............75 G1
Lowell St POP/IOD E14........113 G4
Lowen Rd RAIN RM13.........137 H1
Lower Addiscombe Rd
  CROY/NA CRO 228 D5
Lower Addison Gdns
  WKENS W14 ....119 F5
Lower Belgrave St BGVA SW1W...19 G6
Lower Boston Rd HNWL W7...140 A1
Lower Broad St DAGE RM10...117 F1
Lower Camden CHST BR7....213 H4
Lower Church St
  CROY/NA CRO 211 H5
Lower Clapton Rd CLPT E5...109 H2
Lower Clarendon Wk
  NTGHL W11 ....124 D
Lower Common South
  PUT/ROE SW15............165 D5
Lower Coombe St
  CROY/NA CRO 246 C2
Lower Downs Rd RYNPK SW20...204 D4
Lower Gravel Rd HAYES BR2...233 G5
Lower Green Gdns WPK KT4...225 D5
Lower Green Rd
  ESH/CLAY KT10 ....219 F6
Lower Grosvenor Pl KTBR SW1X...19 F6
Lower Grove Rd
  RCHPK/HAM TW10 ....144 D6
Lower Hall La CHING E4.......70 C1
Lower Hampton Rd SUN TW16...198 B5
Lower Ham Rd KUTN/CMB KT2...201 F2
Lower James St SOHO/CST W1F...12 D5
Lower John St SOHO/CST W1F...12 D5
Lower Kenwood Av
  STHGT/OAK N14 ....37 D1

Lower Lea Crossing
  POP/IOD E14...............132 A6
Lower Maidstone Rd
  FBAR/BDGN N11 ....67 E2
Lower Mardyke Av RAIN RM13...137 G1
Lower Marsh STHWK SE1......22 A4
Lower Marsh La KUT KT1.....222 A1
Lower Merton Ri HAMP NW3...106 A5
Lower Morden La MRDN SM4...224 C3
Lower Mortlake Rd
  RCH/KEW TW9 ....161 G5
Lower Paddock Rd
  OXHEY WD19 ....42 C1
Lower Park Rd BELV DA17...157 E3
  FBAR/BDGN N11 ....67 E1
Lower Queen's Rd BKHH IG9...57 G4
Lower Richmond Rd
  PUT/ROE SW15.............164 A4
Lower Rd BELV DA17..........157 F3
  BERM/RHTH SE16 ....150 A2
  ERITH DA8 ....157 H4
  RYLN/HDSTN HA2 ....79 H6
  STMC/STPC BR5 ....235 H5
  SUT SM1 ....243 H5
Lower Sand Hills SURB KT6...221 E4
Lower Sloane St BGVA SW1W...19 G6
Lower Strd CDALE/KGS NW9...63 F5
Lower Sunbury Rd HPTN TW12...198 D5
Lower Tail OXHEY WD19........42 C5
Lower Teddington Rd KUT KT1...201 E4
Lower Ter HAMP NW3.........105 G1
Lower Thames St MON EC3R...16 A6
Lower Tub BUSH WD23........43 H2
Lower Wood Rd
  ESH/CLAY KT10 ....238 C4
Loweswater Cl WBLY HA9.....81 F6
The Lowe CHIG IG7.............75 G1
Lowfield Rd ACT W3...........122 C5
  KIL/WHAMP NW6 ....105 G5
Low Hall Cl CHING E4..........55 E2
Low Hall La WALTH E17........90 C3
Lowick Rd HRW HA1............61 E1
Lowland Gdns ROMW/RG RM7...97 F5
Lowlands Rd HRW HA1.........80 A4
  PIN HA5 ....78 A4
Lowman Rd HOLWY N7.......107 H2
Lowndes Cl KTBR * SW1X.......19 H6
Lowndes Ct REGST W1B........12 A4
Lowndes Pl KTBR * SW1X......19 E6
Lowndes Sq KTBR SW1X.......18 D4
Lowndes St KTBR SW1X........19 E5
Lowood St WCHPL E1...........17 H5
Lowry Crs MTCM CR4.........206 A5
Lowry Rd BCTR RM8..........115 H5
Lowshoe La ROMW/RG RM7...77 F4
Lowson Gv OXHEY WD19.......42 C2
Lowther Dr ENC/FH EN2......37 G5
Lowther Hl FSTH SE23.......150 C2
Lowther Man BARN * SW13...163 F2
Lowther Rd BARN SW13......163 F2
  HOLWY * N7 ....108 A3
  KUTN/CMB KT2 ....201 H4
  STAN HA7 ....44 D4
  WALTH E17 ....70 C1
Lowth Rd CMBW SE5.........168 C3
Loxford Av EHAM E6..........133 F1
Loxford La IL IG1 ....114 C5
Loxford Rd BARK IG11........114 A4
Loxham Rd CHING E4..........71 F3
Loxham St STPAN * WC1H......5 F4
Loxley Cl SYD SE26...........210 B1
Loxley Rd HPTN TW12........179 G3
  WAND/EARL SW18 ....185 H3
Loxton Rd FSTH SE23.........190 B3
Loxwood Cl STMC/STPC BR5...236 B6
Loxwood Rd TOTM N17.......68 A3
Lubbock Rd CHST BR7........213 H4
Lubbock St NWCR SE14......170 A1
Lucan Pl CHEL SW3............26 A2
Lucan Rd BAR EN5.............26 B2
Lucas Av PLSTW E13..........112 D6
  RYLN/HDSTN HA2 ....78 B6
Lucas Rd PGE/AN SE20.......190 G5
Lucas Sq GLDGN NW11........85 E3
Lucas St DEPT SE8...........171 E3
Lucerne Cl PLMGR N13........51 G5
Lucerne Gv WALTH E17........91 H4
Lucerne Ms KENS W8.........145 E1
Lucerne Rd HBRY N5..........108 B2
  ORP BR6 ....257 F5
  THHTH CR7 ....227 H3
Lucien Rd BERM/RHTH SE16...25 E6
Lucey Wy BERM/RHTH SE16...33 F1
Lucien Rd TOOT SW17........185 F4
  WAND/EARL SW18 ....185 F4
Lucknow St WOOL/PLUM SE18...155 F3
Lucom Cl LEE/GVPK SE12....192 D1
Luctons Av BKHH IG9..........57 F3
Luddesdon Rd ERITH DA8...177 E1
Ludford Cl CDALE/KGS NW9...83 D3
  CROY/NA CRO 246 B2
Ludgate Broadway
  BLKFR * EC4V...............14 D4
Ludgate Circ STP * EC4M......14 C4
Ludgate Hl STP EC4M.........14 C4
Ludgate Sq BLKFR * EC4V....14 D4
Ludham Cl THMD SE28.......136 A5
Ludlow Cl HAYES BR2.........182 C2
  RYLN/HDSTN HA2 ....98 D2
Ludlow Rd EA W5..............121 E3
Ludlow Wy EFNCH N2..........65 G3
Ludovick Wk PUT/ROE SW15...163 G5
Luffield Rd ABYW SE2........155 H3
Luffman Rd LEE/GVPK SE12...192 D3
Lugard Rd PECK SE15........169 H3
Lugg Ap MNPK E12............95 H1
Luke St SDTCH EC2A...........8 A5
Lukin Crs CHING E4............55 H5
Lukin St WCHPL E1...........130 A6
Lullingstone Cl
  STMC/STPC BR5 ....215 H3
Lullingstone Crs
  STMC/STPC BR5 ....215 G3
Lullingstone La LEW SE13....191 F1
Lullingstone Rd BELV DA17...156 D6
Lullingstone Garth BMLY * BR1...212 A3
  MLHL NW7 ....31 G4
Lullington Rd DAGW RM9....116 C5
  PGE/AN SE20...............209 G3

Lulworth Av HEST TW5 159 F2
WBLY HA9 81 E4
Lulworth Cl RYLN/HDSTN HA2 98 D1
Lulworth Crs MTCM CR4 206 A5
Lulworth Dr CRW RM5 77 F1
PIN HA5 78 B4
Lulworth Gdns
RYLN/HDSTN HA2 78 C6
Lulworth Rd ELTH/MOT SE9 193 G4
PECK * SE15 169 H3
WELL DA16 175 F3
Lumen Rd WBLY * HA9 81 F6
Lumley Cl BELV DA17 157 E6
Lumley Gdns CHEAM SM3 242 C3
Lumley Rd CHEAM SM3 242 C4
Lumley St MYFR/PKLN W1K 11 F4
Luna Rd THHTH CR7 208 C6
Lundin Wk OXHEY * WD19 42 B6
Lundy Wk IS * N1 108 C4
Lunham Rd NRWD SE19 209 E2
Lupin Cl BRXS/STRHM SW2 188 B4
CROY/NA CR0 230 B5
ROMW/RG RM7 97 H6
Lupton Cl LEE/GVPK SE12 192 D6
Lupton St KTTN NW5 107 E2
Lupus St PIM SW1V 28 C3
Lurgan Av HMSMTH W6 144 B6
Lurline Gdns BTSEA SW11 166 C2
Luscombe Wy VX/NE SW8 167 G1
Lushington Rd CAT SE6 211 F1
WLSDN NW10 123 H1
Lushington Ter HACK E8 109 G3
Luther Cl EDGW HA8 46 C4
Luther King Cl WALTH E17 90 C3
Luton Pl GNWCH SE10 171 G1
Luton Rd PLSTW E13 132 C3
SCUP DA14 196 A5
WALTH E17 70 C6
Luton St STJWD NW8 125 H3
Luttrell Av PUT/ROE SW15 163 H6
Lutwyche Rd FSTH SE23 190 D4
Luxborough La CHIG IG7 57 H6
Luxborough St MHST W1U 3 E6
Luxemburg Gdns HMSMTH W6 144 B4
Luxfield Rd ELTH/MOT SE9 193 G3
Luxford St BERM/RHTH SE16 150 B4
Luxmore St BROCKY SE4 170 D2
Luxor St CMBW SE5 168 B3
Lyall Av DUL SE21 189 E6
Lyall Ms KTBR SW1X 19 E6
Lyall Ms West KTBR * SW1X 19 E6
Lyall St KTBR SW1X 19 E6
Lyal Rd BOW E3 130 C1
Lycett Pl SHB W12 143 G2
Lych Gate Rd ORP BR6 235 G5
Lyconby Gdns CROY/NA CR0 230 C4
Lydd Cl BFN/LL DA15 195 E5
Lydden Gv WAND/EARL SW18 185 F2
Lydden Rd WAND/EARL SW18 185 F2
Lydd Rd BXLYHN DA7 176 D1
Lydeard Rd EHAM E6 113 H5
Lydford Cl STNW/STAM N16 109 E3
Lydford Rd CRICK NW2 104 B4
MV/WKIL W9 124 D3
SEVS/STOTM N15 88 D2
Lydhurst Av BRXS/STRHM SW2 187 H4
Lydney Cl PECK SE15 169 E1
WIM/MER SW19 184 C4
Lydon Rd CLAP SW4 167 E4
Lydstep Rd CHST BR7 194 A6
Lyford Rd WAND/EARL SW18 185 H2
Lyford St CHARL SE7 153 G4
Lygon Pl BGVA * SW1W 19 G6
Lyham Cl CLAP SW4 187 G1
Lyham Rd BRXS/STRHM SW2 167 G6
Lyle Cl MTCM CR4 226 C4
Lyme Farm Rd LEE/GVPK SE12 172 C5
Lyme Gv HOM E9 110 A5
Lymer Av NRWD SE19 209 F1
Lyme Rd WELL DA16 175 H2
Lymescote Gdns SUT SM1 225 E6
Lyme St CAMTN NW1 107 E5
Lyme Ter CAMTN NW1 107 E5
Lyminge Cl SCUP DA14 195 F6
Lyminge Gdns
WAND/EARL SW18 186 A3
Lymington Av WDGN N22 68 A5
Lymington Cl
STRHM/NOR SW16 207 F5
Lymington Gdns
HOR/WEW KT19 241 F3
Lymington Rd BCTR RM8 96 B5
KIL/WHAMP * NW6 105 F4
Lympstone Gdns PECK SE15 169 G1
Lynbridge Gdns PLMGR N13 52 B6
Lynbrook Cl PECK SE15 169 E1
RAIN RM13 137 H1
Lyncourt BKHTH/KID * SE3 171 H3
Lyncroft Av PIN HA5 78 B2
Lyncroft Gdns EW KT17 241 F6
HSLW TW3 159 G6
KIL/WHAMP NW6 105 E3
WEA W13 141 E2
Lyndale CRICK NW2 104 D1
ESH/CLAY * KT10 220 A4
Lyndale Av CRICK NW2 104 D1
Lyndale Cl BKHTH/KID SE3 152 B6
Lyndale Hampton Court Wy
ESH/CLAY KT10 220 A4
Lynden Wy SWLY BR8 217 G6
Lyndhurst Av BRYLDS KT5 222 B5
MLHL NW7 63 E2
NFNCH/WDSP N12 66 B2
STHL UB1 139 F1
STRHM/NOR SW16 207 F5
WHTN TW2 178 D3
Lyndhurst Cl BXLYHN DA7 177 F4
CROY/NA CR0 247 F1
ORP BR6 252 B2
WLSDN NW10 102 D1
Lyndhurst Ct BELMT * SM2 243 E5
Lyndhurst Dr NWMAL KT3 223 E3
WAN E11 91 G4
Lyndhurst Gdns BARK IG11 115 E4
EN EN1 39 E5
FNCH N3 64 C4
GNTH/NBYPK IG2 94 D3
HAMP NW3 105 H3
Lyndhurst Gv CMBW SE5 169 E3
Lyndhurst Leys HAYES * BR2 211 H5
Lyndhurst Prior SNWD * SE25 209 E6
Lyndhurst Rd BXLYHN DA7 177 F4
CHING E4 71 G3
GFD/PVL UB6 119 F3
HAMP NW3 105 H3
THHTH CR7 228 A1
UED N18 53 G6
WDGN N22 68 A2
Lyndhurst Sq PECK SE15 169 F2
Lyndhurst Ter HAMP NW3 105 H3
Lyndhurst Wy BELMT SM2 243 E6
PECK SE15 169 F2
Lyndon Av BFN/LL DA15 175 F6
PIN HA5 58 C2
WLGTN SM6 244 C1
Lyndon Rd BELV DA17 157 E4
Lyndon Yd TOOT SW17 185 F6
Lyne Crs WALTH E17 70 D4
Lyneham Wk CLPT * E5 110 C3
Lynette Av CLAP SW4 186 D1
Lynford Cl EDGW HA8 62 C4
Lynford Gdns EDGW HA8 46 B5
GDMY/SEVK IG3 95 F6
Lynford Ter ED * N9 53 F3
Lynmere Rd WELL DA16 175 H3
Lyn Ms STNW/STAM * N16 109 F2
Lynmouth Av EN EN1 53 F1
MRDN SM4 224 B4
Lynmouth Gdns GFD/PVL UB6 100 D6
HEST TW5 158 B2
Lynmouth Ri STMC/STPC BR5 235 H1
Lynmouth Rd EFNCH N2 66 B6
GFD/PVL UB6 100 D6
STNW/STAM N16 89 F5
WALTH E17 90 C3
Lynn Cl KTN/HRWW/W HA3 59 H5
Lynne Cl ORP * BR6 253 F4
Lynnett Rd BCTR RM8 96 B6
Lynne Wy NTHLT UB5 118 B1
WLSDN NW10 103 E4
Lynn Ms WAN E11 92 A6
Lynn Rd BAL SW12 186 D2
GNTH/NBYPK IG2 94 D4
WAN E11 92 A6
Lynn St ENC/FH EN2 38 D2
Lynscott Wy SAND/SEL CR2 246 B6
Lynstead Cl BMLY BR1 213 E5
Lynsted Cl BXLYHS DA6 177 F6
Lynsted Ct BECK BR3 210 C5
Lynsted Gdns ELTH/MOT SE9 173 F5
Lynton Av ACT W3 122 C5
CDALE/KGS NW9 83 F1
NFNCH/WDSP N12 49 H6
ROMW/RG RM7 77 F4
STMC/STPC BR5 235 H1
WEA W13 120 C5
Lynton Cl CHSGTN KT9 239 G2
ISLW TW7 160 B5
WLSDN NW10 103 E5
Lynton Crs GNTH/NBYPK IG2 94 B3
Lynton Est STHWK SE1 32 D2
Lynton Gdns EN EN1 53 E2
FBAR/BDGN N11 67 F2
Lynton Md TRDG/WHET N20 49 E5
Lynton Rd ACT W3 122 A6
CEND/HSY/T N8 87 F2
CHING E4 71 F1
CROY/NA CR0 228 A3
KIL/WHAMP NW6 104 D6
NWMAL KT3 222 D2
RYLN/HDSTN HA2 78 C6
STHWK SE1 32 D2
Lynton Ter ACT * W3 122 C5
Lynwood Cl RYLN/HDSTN HA2 98 C1
SWFD E18 73 E4
Lynwood Dr CRW RM5 77 F3
WPK KT4 223 G6
Lynwood Gdns CROY/NA CR0 245 H2
STHL UB1 118 D5
Lynwood Gv ORP BR6 235 E4
WCHMH N21 52 A3
Lynwood Rd EA W5 121 F2
ESH/CLAY KT10 220 B6
TOOT SW17 186 B5
Lynwood Ter WIM/MER * SW19 204 D4
Lyon Meade STAN HA7 61 E4
Lyon Park Av ALP/SUD HA0 101 G4
Lyon Rd HRW HA1 80 B3
WIM/MER SW19 205 G4
WOT/HER KT12 218 C6
Lyonsdown Av BAR EN5 49 G1
Lyonsdown Rd BAR EN5 49 G1
Lyons Pl STJWD NW8 125 H3
Lyon St IS N1 107 H5
Lyons Wk WKENS W14 144 C4
Lyon Wy GFD/PVL UB6 100 A6
Lyoth Rd STMC/STPC BR5 234 C6
Lyric Dr GFD/PVL UB6 119 F3
Lyric Ms SYD SE26 190 A6
Lyric Rd BARN SW13 163 F2
Lysander CDALE/KGS * NW9 63 F4
Lysander Gdns SURB KT6 221 H3
Lysander Gv ARCH N19 87 F5
Lysander Ms ARCH * N19 87 G5
Lysander Rd CROY/NA CR0 245 H4
Lysander Wy ORP BR6 252 C1
Lysias Rd BAL SW12 186 C1
Lysia St FUL/PGN SW6 164 B1
Lysons Wk PUT/ROE * SW15 163 G6
Lytchet Rd BMLY BR1 212 C3
Lytchet Wy PEND EN3 40 A2
Lytchgate Cl SAND/SEL CR2 247 E5
Lytcott Dr E/WMO/HCT KT8 198 D6
Lytcott Gv EDUL SE22 169 F6
Lytham Av OXHEY WD19 58 B1
Lytham Cl THMD SE28 136 C5
Lytham Gv EA W5 121 G2
Lytham St WALW SE17 31 G4
Lyttelton Rd LEY E10 111 F1
Lyttleton Cl HAMP NW3 106 A5
Lyttleton Rd CEND/HSY/T * N8 68 A6
Lytton Av PEND EN3 40 C1
PLMGR N13 52 A4
Lytton Cl EFNCH N2 85 H2
NTHLT UB5 98 D5
Lytton Gdns WLGTN SM6 245 F2
Lytton Gv PUT/ROE SW15 164 B6
Lytton Rd BAR EN5 35 G5
PIN HA5 58 C3
WAN E11 92 A4
Lyveden Rd BKHTH/KID SE3 172 D1
WIM/MER SW19 206 A2

M

Maberley Crs NRWD SE19 209 G3
Maberley Rd BECK BR3 210 B6
NRWD SE19 209 F4
Mabledon Pl CAMTN NW1 4 D4
Mablethorpe Rd FUL/PGN SW6 164 C1
Mabley St HOM E9 110 C3
Macaret Cl TRDG/WHET N20 49 F2
Macarthur Cl FSTGT E7 112 C4
Macarthur Ter CHARL * SE7 153 F6
Macaulay Av ESH/CLAY KT10 220 A6
Macaulay Rd CLAP SW4 166 D4
EHAM E6 133 F1
Macbean St WOOL/PLUM SE18 154 A3
Macbeth St HMSMTH W6 143 H5
Macclesfield Br STJWD NW8 2 B1
Macclesfield Rd FSBYE EC1V 7 E3
SNWD SE25 229 H2
Macclesfield St
SOHO/SHAV W1D 12 D5
Macdonald Av DAGE RM10 117 F1
Macdonald Rd ARCH N19 87 E6
FBAR/BDGN N11 66 B1
FSTGT E7 112 C2
WALTH E17 71 G5
Macduff Rd BTSEA SW11 166 C2
Mace Cl WAP E1W 25 G1
Mace Gtwy CAN/RD E16 132 C6
Mace St BETH E2 130 B1
Macfarlane La ISLW TW7 140 B6
Macfarlane Rd SHB W12 144 A1
Mac Farren Pl CAMTN NW1 3 F6
Macgregor Rd CAN/RD E16 133 E4
Machell Rd PECK SE15 170 A4
Mackay Rd CLAP SW4 166 D4
Mackennal St STJWD NW8 2 B2
Mackenzie Cl SHB * W12 123 H6
Mackenzie Rd BECK BR3 210 C4
HOLWY N7 107 H4
Mackeson Rd HAMP * NW3 106 B2
Mackie Rd BRXS/STRHM SW2 188 A2
Mackintosh La HOM E9 110 B3
Macklin St HOL/ALD * WC2B 13 F3
Macks Rd BERM/RHTH SE16 33 F1
Mackworth St CAMTN NW1 4 A3
Maclean Rd FSTH SE23 190 C1
Macleod Rd STHGT/OAK N14 37 G6
Macleod St WALW SE17 31 F4
Maclise Rd WKENS W14 144 C3
Macoma Rd WOOL/PLUM SE18 154 D6
Macoma Ter
WOOL/PLUM SE18 154 D6
Maconochies Rd
POP/IOD * E14 151 F5
Macquarie Wy POP/IOD E14 151 F4
Macroom Rd MV/WKIL W9 124 D2
Mada Rd ORP BR6 252 B1
Maddams St BOW E3 131 F3
Maddison Cl TEDD TW11 200 B2
Maddocks Cl SCUP DA14 216 B2
Maddock Wy WALW SE17 30 C6
Maddox St MYFR/PKLN W1K 11 H5
Madeira Av BMLY BR1 212 A4
Madeira Gv WFD IG8 73 E2
Madeira Rd MTCM CR4 226 B1
PLMGR N13 52 B6
STRHM/NOR SW16 207 G1
WAN E11 91 H5
Madeley Rd EA W5 121 G5
Madeline Gv IL IG1 114 D3
Madeline Rd PGE/AN SE20 209 G3
Madge Gill Wy EHAM E6 113 G6
Madge Hl HNWL * W7 120 A6
Madinah Rd HACK E8 109 G4
Madison Crs WELL DA16 176 A1
Madison Gdns BXLYHN DA7 176 A1
Madras Pl HOLWY N7 108 A4
Madras Rd IL IG1 114 B2
Madrid Rd BARN SW13 163 G2
Madron St STHWK SE1 32 B3
Mafeking Av BTFD TW8 141 G6
EHAM E6 133 F1
GNTH/NBYPK IG2 94 D4
Mafeking Rd CAN/RD E16 132 B3
EN EN1 39 F4
TOTM N17 69 G5
Magazine Ga BAY/PAD * W2 18 B1
Magdala Av KTTN NW5 87 E6
Magdala Rd ISLW TW7 160 C4
SAND/SEL CR2 246 D5
Magdalene Gdns EHAM E6 134 A3
Magdalen Rd
WAND/EARL SW18 185 G3
Magdalen St STHWK SE1 24 A2
Magdelan Gv ORP BR6 253 H2
Magee St LBTH SE11 30 A5
Magnaville Rd BUSH WD23 44 A2
Magnet Rd WBLY * HA9 81 F6
Magnin Cl HACK E8 109 G6
Magnolia Cl KUTN/CMB KT2 202 B2
LEY E10 91 E6
Magnolia Ct KTN/HRWW/W HA3 81 H4
Magnolia Gdns EDGW HA8 46 C6
Magnolia Pl CLAP * SW4 167 G6
EA * W5 121 F4
Magnolia Rd CHSWK W4 142 B6
Magnolia Wy HOR/WEW KT19 240 C3
Magnolia Whf CHSWK * W4 142 B6
Magpie Cl CDALE/KGS NW9 63 E5
EN EN1 39 G2
FSTGT E7 112 B3
Magpie Hall Cl HAYES BR2 233 G3
Magpie Hall La HAYES BR2 233 H2
Magpie Hall Rd BUSH WD23 44 A4
Magpie Pl NWCR * SE14 150 C6
Magri Wk WCHPL E1 130 A4
Maguire Dr RCHPK/HAM TW10 181 E6
Maguire St STHWK SE1 24 D2
Mahogany Cl
BERM/RHTH SE16 150 C1
Mahon Cl EN EN1 39 F2
Maida Av BAY/PAD W2 125 G4
CHING E4 55 F2
Maida Rd BELV DA17 157 E3
Maida V MV/WKIL W9 125 G2
STJWD NW8 125 H3
Maida Wy CHING E4 55 F2
Maiden Erlegh Av BXLY DA5 196 C3
Maiden La CAMTN NW1 107 F5
STHWK SE1 23 F2
Maiden Rd SRTFD E15 112 A5
Maidenstone Hl GNWCH SE10 171 G2
Maidstone Av CRW RM5 77 G5
Maidstone Buildings Ms
STHWK SE1 23 F2
Maidstone Rd FBAR/BDGN N11 67 F2
SCUP DA14 216 D3
SWLY BR8 217 F4
Main Av EN EN1 39 F6
Main Barracks
WOOL/PLUM * SE18 153 H5
Main Dr GFD/PVL * UB6 120 C2
WBLY * HA9 101 F1
Mainridge Rd CHST BR7 194 A6
Main Rd BFN/LL DA15 195 E5
STMC/STPC BR5 216 A6
SWLY BR8 237 G3
Main St FELT TW13 198 B1
Maismore St PECK SE15 33 E6
The Maisonettes SUT * SM1 242 D3
Maitland Cl GNWCH SE10 171 F1
HSLWW TW4 158 D4
WOT/HER KT12 218 C6
Maitland Park Rd HAMP NW3 106 B4
Maitland Park Vls HAMP NW3 106 B4
Maitland Rd SRTFD * E15 112 B4
SYD SE26 210 B2
Majendie Rd
WOOL/PLUM SE18 154 D5
Major Rd BERM/RHTH SE16 25 F5
SRTFD E15 111 G3
Makepeace Av HGT N6 86 C6
Makepeace Rd NTHLT UB5 118 C1
WAN E11 92 C1
Makins St CHEL SW3 26 B2
Malabar St POP/IOD E14 151 E2
Malam Gdns POP/IOD E14 131 F6
Malbrook Rd PUT/ROE SW15 163 H5
Malcolm Cl PGE/AN * SE20 210 A3
Malcolm Ct STAN HA7 61 E1
Malcolm Crs HDN NW4 83 G2
Malcolm Dr SURB KT6 221 F5
Malcolm Gavin Cl TOOT SW17 186 A4
Malcolm Pl BETH E2 130 A3
Malcolm Rd PGE/AN SE20 210 A3
SNWD SE25 229 G3
WCHPL E1 130 A3
WIM/MER SW19 204 C2
Malcolm Wy WAN E11 92 C2
Malden Av NTHLT UB5 100 A4
SNWD SE25 229 H1
Malden Green Av WPK KT4 223 F5
Malden Hl NWMAL KT3 223 F1
Malden Hill Gdns NWMAL KT3 203 F6
Malden Pk NWMAL KT3 223 F3
Malden Pl KTTN NW5 106 C3
Malden Rd CHEAM SM3 242 B2
KTTN NW5 106 B3
NWMAL KT3 223 F4
Malden Wy NWMAL * KT3 223 F2
NWMAL KT3 223 F2
Malden Wy (Kingston By-Pass)
NWMAL KT3 223 E3
Maldon Cl CMBW * SE5 169 E4
IS N1 108 C6
Maldon Rd ACT W3 122 C6
ED N9 53 F5
ROMW/RG RM7 97 G4
WLGTN SM6 244 D3
Maldon Wk WFD IG8 73 E2
Malet St GWRST WC1E 4 C6
Maley Av WNWD SE27 188 B4
Malford Gv SWFD E18 72 C6
Malfort Rd CMBW SE5 169 E4
Malham Cl FBAR/BDGN N11 66 C2
Malham Rd FSTH SE23 190 B3
Malham Ter UED * N18 69 H2
Mallams Ms BRXN/ST SW9 168 A4
Mallard Cl BAR * EN5 49 H1
HSLWW TW4 179 E2
KIL/WHAMP NW6 125 E1
Mallard Ct WALTH * E17 71 H6
Mallard Pl TWK TW1 180 C5
WDGN * N22 67 H5
Mallards Ct OXHEY * WD19 42 D5
Mallards Rd WFD IG8 72 D3
Mallard Wk CROY/NA CR0 230 B2
Mallard Wy CDALE/KGS NW9 82 C4
WLGTN SM6 245 E6
Mall Chambers KENS * W8 145 E1
Mallet Dr NTHLT UB5 98 D3
Mallet Rd LEW SE13 191 H1
Malling Cl CROY/NA * CR0 230 A3
Malling Gdns MRDN SM4 225 G3
Malling Wy HAYES BR2 232 B4
Mallinson Rd BTSEA SW11 166 A6
WLGTN SM6 245 F1
Mallord St CHEL SW3 145 H6
Mallory Cl BROCKY SE4 170 C5
Mallory Gdns EBAR EN4 50 C2
Mallory St CAMTN NW1 2 B6
Mallow Cl CROY/NA CR0 230 B5
Mallow Md MLHL NW7 64 C3
Mallow St FSBYE EC1V 7 G5
Mall Rd HMSMTH W6 143 H5
The Mall BTFD * TW8 141 F6
EA W5 121 G6
KTN/HRWW/W HA3 81 H3
MORT/ESHN SW14 162 C6
STHGT/OAK N14 51 G5
SURB KT6 221 F2
WHALL SW1A 20 A3
Mall Vls HMSMTH * W6 143 H5
Malmains Cl BECK BR3 231 H2
Malmains Wy BECK BR3 231 G1
Malmesbury Rd BOW E3 130 D2
CAN/RD E16 132 A4
MRDN SM4 225 G4
SWFD E18 72 B4
Malmesbury Ter CAN/RD E16 132 B4
Malmesbury West Est BOW E3 130 D2
Malpas Dr PIN HA5 78 B2
Malpas Rd BROCKY SE4 170 D3
DAGW RM9 116 B4
HACK E8 109 H4
Malta Rd LEY E10 91 E5
Malta St FSBYE EC1V 6 C5
Maltby Cl ORP BR6 235 G5

Maltby Dr EN EN1 ...39 H1
Maltby Rd CHSGTN KT9 ...240 A4
Maltby St STHWK SE1 ...24 C5
Malthouse Dr FELT TW13 ...198 B1
Maltings Pl FUL/PGN SW6 ...165 F2
The Maltings ORP BR6 ...235 F5
SNWD * SE25 ...209 E6
Malting Wy ISLW TW7 ...160 B4
Malton Ms NKENS * W10 ...124 C5
WOOL/PLUM SE18 ...155 E6
Malton Rd NKENS W10 ...124 C5
Malton St WOOL/PLUM SE18 ...155 E6
Maltravers St TPL/STR WC2R ...13 H5
Malt St STHWK SE1 ...33 E5
Malva Cl WAND/EARL SW18 ...165 F6
Malvern Av BXLYHN DA7 ...176 C1
CHING E4 ...71 H3
RYLN/HDSTN HA2 ...98 C1
Malvern Cl MTCM CR4 ...207 E6
NKENS W10 ...124 D4
SURB KT6 ...221 G5
Malvern Dr FELT TW13 ...198 B1
GDMY/SEVK IG3 ...115 F2
IGD ...73 E1
Malvern Gdns CRICK NW2 ...84 C6
KTN/HRWW/W HA3 ...81 G1
LOU IG10 ...57 H1
Malvern Ms KIL/WHAMP NW6 ...125 E2
Malvern Pl MV/WKIL * W9 ...124 D2
Malvern Rd CEND/HSY/T N8 ...67 H6
EHAM E6 ...113 G6
HACK E8 ...109 G5
HPTN TW12 ...199 E4
MV/WKIL * W9 ...124 D2
ORP BR6 ...253 H2
SURB KT6 ...221 G6
THHTH CR7 ...228 A1
TOTM N17 ...69 G6
WAN E11 ...92 A6
Malvern Ter ED N9 ...53 F3
IS N1 ...108 A6
Malvern Wy WEA W13 ...120 D4
Malwood Rd BAL SW12 ...186 D1
Malyons Rd LEW SE13 ...171 F6
Malyons Ter BROCKY SE4 ...171 H3
Managers St POP/IOD * E14 ...151 G1
Manaton Cl PECK SE15 ...169 H4
Manaton Crs STHL UB1 ...119 E5
Manbey Gv SRTFD E15 ...112 A4
Manbey Park Rd SRTFD E15 ...112 A4
Manbey Rd SRTFD * E15 ...112 A4
Manbey St SRTFD E15 ...112 A4
Manbre Rd HMSMTH W6 ...144 A6
Manbrough Av EHAM E6 ...153 H2
Manchester Dr NKENS * W10 ...124 C3
Manchester Gv POP/IOD E14 ...151 G5
Manchester Ms MHST W1U ...11 E2
Manchester Rd POP/IOD E14 ...151 G5
SEVS/STOTM N15 ...88 D3
THHTH CR7 ...208 C6
Manchester Sq MBLAR W1H ...11 F3
Manchester St MHST W1U ...11 E2
Manchuria Rd BTSEA SW11 ...186 C1
Manciple St STHWK SE1 ...19 F3
Mandalay Rd CLAP SW4 ...167 E6
Mandarin Wy YEAD UB4 ...198 D2
Mandela Cl WLSDN NW10 ...102 C5
Mandela Rd CAN/RD E16 ...132 C5
Mandela St BRXN/ST SW9 ...168 A1
CAMTN NW1 ...107 E6
Mandela Wy STHWK SE1 ...32 B4
Mandeville Cl WIM/MER SW19 ...204 C3
Mandeville Dr SURB KT6 ...221 F5
Mandeville Pl MHST W1U ...11 F3
Mandeville Rd ISLW TW7 ...160 C1
NTHLT UB5 ...99 E4
STHGT/OAK N14 ...50 D4
Mandeville St CLPT E5 ...110 C1
Mandrake Rd TOOT SW17 ...186 B5
Mandrake Wy SRTFD * E15 ...112 A5
Mandrell Rd BRXS/STRHM SW2 ...167 G6
Manette St SOHO/SHAV W1D ...12 D4
Manford Cross CHIG IG7 ...75 C1
Manford Wy CHIG IG7 ...75 G1
Manfred Rd PUT/ROE SW15 ...164 D6
Manger Rd HOLWY N7 ...107 H4
Manilla St POP/IOD E14 ...151 F2
Manister Rd ABYW SE2 ...155 G3
Manley Ct STNW/STAM N16 ...109 F1
Manley St CAMTN NW1 ...106 C6
Mann Cl CROY/NA CRO ...246 C1
Manningford Cl FSBYE * EC1V ...6 C3
Manning Gdns
KTN/HRWW/W HA3 ...81 F4
Manning Pl RCHPK/HAM TW10 ...181 H1
Manning Rd DAGE RM10 ...117 E5
STMC/STPC BR5 ...236 B2
WALTH E17 ...90 C1
Manningtree Cl
WIM/MER SW19 ...184 C3
Manningtree St WCHPL E1 ...17 F3
Mannin Rd CHDH RM6 ...95 H4
Mannock Rd WDGN N22 ...68 B6
Mann's Cl ISLW TW7 ...160 B6
Manns Rd EDGW HA8 ...44 C2
Manoel Rd WHTN TW2 ...198 C5
Manor Av BROCKY SE4 ...170 D3
HSLWW TW4 ...158 B4
NTHLT UB5 ...98 B6

FELT TW13 ...198 B1
HOR/WEW KT19 ...241 E4
MLHL NW7 ...62 D1
STHGT/OAK N14 ...50 D2
TRDG/WHET N20 ...50 A5
WBLY HA9 ...101 H2
Manor Dr North NWMAL KT3 ...222 D4
WPK KT4 ...223 E5
The Manor Dr WPK KT4 ...223 E5
Manor Est BERM/RHTH SE16 ...33 G2
Manor Farm Dr CHING E4 ...56 A5
Manor Farm Rd ALP/SUD HA0 ...121 F1
STRHM/NOR SW16 ...208 A5
Manorfields Cl CHST BR7 ...215 F6
Manor Gdns CLAP SW4 ...142 A4
HOLWY N7 ...107 H1
HPTN TW12 ...199 F5
RCH/KEW TW9 ...161 H5
RSLP HA4 ...98 A3
RYNPK SW20 ...204 D5
SAND/SEL CR2 ...247 F4
VX/NE * SW8 ...167 G3
Manor Ga NTHLT UB5 ...98 C5
Manorgate Rd KUTN/CMB KT2 ...202 A4
Manor Gv BECK BR3 ...211 F5
PECK SE15 ...150 A6
RCH/KEW TW9 ...162 A5
Manor Hall Av HDN NW4 ...64 A5
Manor Hall Dr HDN NW4 ...64 B5
Manor Hall Gdns LEY E10 ...91 E5
Manor House Dr
KIL/WHAMP NW6 ...104 B5
Manor House La
STHGT/OAK N14 ...50 A5
Manor La LEW SE13 ...172 A6
SUT SM1 ...245 G3
Manor Lane Ter LEW SE13 ...172 A5
Manor Ms KIL/WHAMP NW6 ...125 E1
Manor Mt FSTH SE23 ...190 A3
Manor Pde HRW * HA1 ...80 B3
STNW/STAM * N16 ...89 F6
Manor Pk CHST BR7 ...214 D5
LEW SE13 ...171 H6
RCH/KEW TW9 ...161 H5
Manor Park Cl WWKM BR4 ...231 F5
Manor Park Crs EDGW HA8 ...62 A2
Manor Park Dr
RYLN/HDSTN HA2 ...59 F6
Manor Park Gdns EDGW HA8 ...62 A1
Manor Park Rd CHST BR7 ...214 D4
EFNCH N2 ...65 H6
MNPK E12 ...115 F2
SUT SM3 ...245 G3
WWKM BR4 ...231 F5
Manor Pl CHST BR7 ...214 D4
MTCM CR4 ...207 E6
SUT SM1 ...245 F3
WALW SE17 ...30 C6
Manor Rd BAR EN5 ...34 B5
BECK BR3 ...211 E5
BELMT SM2 ...242 D5
BFN/LL DA15 ...195 F5
BXLY DA5 ...197 F3
CAN/RD E16 ...132 A4
CHDH RM6 ...96 B3
CHIG IG7 ...74 A2
DACE RM10 ...117 G4
E/WMO/HCT KT8 ...219 H1
ENC/FH EN2 ...38 D3
HRW HA1 ...80 C3
LEY E10 ...91 G6
LOU IG10 ...56 D1
MTCM CR4 ...207 E6
RCH/KEW TW9 ...161 H4
RYNPK SW20 ...205 G3
SNWD SE25 ...209 G6
STHWK SE1 ...30 C1
TEDD TW11 ...200 C1
TOTM N17 ...69 G4
WALTH E17 ...70 G5
WDGN N22 ...67 G2
WEA W13 ...120 C6
WHTN TW2 ...179 G4
WLCTN SM6 ...244 D3
WWKM BR4 ...231 F6
Manor Rd North
ESH/CLAY KT10 ...238 B1
WLGTN SM6 ...244 D2
Manor Rd South
ESH/CLAY KT10 ...238 A2
Manorside BAR EN5 ...34 C5
Manor Sq BCTR RM8 ...96 A6
Manor V BTFD TW8 ...141 E5
Manor Vw FNCH N3 ...53 E2
Manorway EN EN1 ...53 E2
WFD IG8 ...73 E1
Manor Wy BECK BR3 ...211 F5
BKHH IG9 ...57 H2
BXLY DA5 ...197 E3
BXLYHN DA7 ...177 H4
CDALE/KGS NW9 ...45 E3
CHING E4 ...55 H6
HAYES BR2 ...233 G3
MTCM CR4 ...207 E6
NWDGN UB2 ...138 B4
RYLN/HDSTN HA2 ...59 E6
SAND/SEL CR2 ...247 E4
STMC/STPC BR5 ...234 C1
WHTK IG8 ...73 E1
The Manor Wy WLGTN SM6 ...244 D2
Manresa Rd CHEL * SW3 ...145 H5
Mansard Beeches TOOT SW17 ...205 C2
Mansard Cl PIN HA5 ...58 B6
Mansel Gv WALTH E17 ...71 J1
Mansell Rd ACT W3 ...142 D1
GFD/PVL UB6 ...119 F4
Mansell St WCHPL E1 ...16 D6
Mansel Wd WIM/MER SW19 ...204 C2
Mansergh
WOOL/PLUM SE18 ...173 G1
Manse Rd STNW/STAM N16 ...109 F1
Mansfield Av EBAR EN4 ...50 C1
SEVS/STOTM N15 ...88 D1
Mansfield Cl ED N9 ...53 C1
STMC/STPC BR5 ...234 D2
Mansfield HI CHING E4 ...55 F3
Mansfield Ms CAVSQ/HST W1G ...11 G2
Mansfield Rd ACT W3 ...122 A3
CHSGTN KT9 ...239 E5
HAMP NW3 ...106 B3
IL IG1 ...94 A6
SAND/SEL CR2 ...246 D4

WALTH E17 ...90 D1
WAN E11 ...92 D3
Mansfield St CAVSQ/HST W1G ...11 G2
Mansford St BETH E2 ...7 G4
Manship Rd MTCM CR4 ...206 D4
Mansion House Pl
MANHO * EC4N ...15 G4
The Mansions ECT * SW5 ...145 F5
Manson Ms SKENS * SW7 ...145 G4
Manson Pl SKENS SW7 ...145 H4
Manstead Gdns CHDH RM6 ...95 H5
Manston Av NWDGN UB2 ...139 E4
Manston Cl PGE/AN SE20 ...210 A4
Manston Gv KUTN/CMB KT2 ...201 F1
Manthorpe Rd
WOOL/PLUM SE18 ...154 C5
Mantilla Rd TOOT SW17 ...186 C6
Mantle Rd BROCKY SE4 ...171 G2
Mantlet Cl STRHM/NOR SW16 ...207 E3
Mantle Wy SRTFD E15 ...112 A5
Manton Av HNWL W7 ...140 B2
Manton Rd ABYW SE2 ...155 G4
Mantua St BTSEA SW11 ...165 H4
Mantus Cl WCHPL E1 ...130 A3
Mantus Rd WCHPL E1 ...130 A3
Manus Wy TRDG/WHET N20 ...49 G4
Manville Gdns TOOT SW17 ...186 D5
Manville Rd TOOT SW17 ...186 D4
Manwood Rd BROCKY SE4 ...190 D1
Manwood St CAN/RD E16 ...153 H1
Many Gates BAL SW12 ...186 D4
Mapesbury Rd CRICK NW2 ...104 C4
Mapeshill Pl CRICK NW2 ...104 A4
Mape St BETH E2 ...90 C3
Maple Av ACT W3 ...143 E1
CHING E4 ...70 D2
RYLN/HDSTN HA2 ...79 F6
Maple Cl BARK/HLT IG6 ...75 F2
BKHH IG9 ...57 F5
CLAP SW4 ...187 F1
FNCH N3 ...65 E2
HPTN TW12 ...198 D2
MTCM CR4 ...206 D4
STNC/STPC BR5 ...234 D2
STNW/STAM N16 ...89 G3
YEAD UB4 ...118 B2
Maple Crs BFN/LL DA15 ...195 C1
Maplecroft Cl EHAM E6 ...133 F5
Mapledale Av CROY/NA CRO ...247 E1
Mapledene Est HACK * E8 ...109 G5
Mapledene Rd HACK E8 ...109 F5
Maple Gdns EDGW HA8 ...63 E3
Maple Gv BTFD TW8 ...160 D1
CDALE/KGS NW9 ...62 D4
EA W5 ...141 F3
STHL UB1 ...96 B4
WLSDN NW10 ...84 D4
Maplehurst Cl KUT KT1 ...221 C1
Maple Leaf Dr BFN/LL DA15 ...195 F3
Mapleleafe Gdns BARK/HLT IG6 ...74 B6
Maple Leaf Sq
BERM/RHTH * SE16 ...150 C2
Maple Ms
KIL/WHAMP * NW6 ...125 F1
Maple Pl FITZ W1T ...207 H1
Maple Rd PGE/AN SE20 ...209 H4
SURB KT6 ...221 G4
WAN E11 ...92 A3
Maples Pl WCHPL E1 ...17 H1
Maplestead Rd
BRXS/STRHM SW2 ...187 H6
DACW RM9 ...115 H6
The Maples ESH/WMO/HCT * KT8...201 E5
ESH/CLAY * KT10 ...244 C5
Maple St FITZ W1T ...12 A1
ROMW/RG RM7 ...97 G1
Maplethorpe Rd THHTH CR7 ...228 C1
Mapleton Cl HAYES BR2 ...232 C2
Mapleton Crs PEND EN3 ...40 A6
WAND/EARL SW18 ...185 F1
Mapleton Rd CHING E4 ...39 H3
WAND/EARL SW18 ...185 F1
Maple Wk NKENS * W10 ...124 B5
Maplin Cl WCHMH N21 ...51 H1
Maplin Rd CAN/RD E16 ...132 C5
Maplin St BOW E3 ...130 D2
Mapperley Dr WFD IG8 ...72 A3
Maran Wy ERITHM DA18 ...155 F5
Marban Rd MV/WKIL W9 ...124 D3
Marble Cl ACT W3 ...142 B1
Marble Dr CRICK NW2 ...82 C5
Marble Hill Cl TWK TW1 ...180 D2
Marble Hill Gdns TWK TW1 ...180 D2
Marble Quay WAP E1W ...24 D1
Marbrook Ct LEE/GVPK SE12 ...193 G5
Marcellina Wy ORP BR6 ...253 E1
Marchant Rd WAN E11 ...91 H1
Marchant St NWCR SE14 ...150 C6
Marchbank Rd WKENS W14 ...144 D6
Marchmont Rd
RCHPK/HAM TW10 ...161 H6
WLCTN SM6 ...245 E6
Marchmont St BMSBY WC1N ...5 E5
Marchside Cl HEST TW5 ...158 B2
Marchwood Cl CMBW SE5 ...169 E1
Marchwood Crs EA W5 ...121 E5
Marcia Rd STHWK SE1 ...32 A1
Marcilly Rd WAND/EARL SW18...185 H5
Marconi Rd LEY E10 ...91 J1
Marconi Wy GFD/PVL UB6 ...119 F5
Marcon Pl HACK E8 ...90 D5
Marco Rd HMSMTH W6 ...143 E5
Marcus Garvey Ms EDUL SE22 ...189 H3
Marcus Garvey Wy HNHL SE24 ...168 A5
Marcus St SRTFD E15 ...112 A4
WAND/EARL SW18 ...185 F2
Marcus Ter WAND/EARL SW18 ...185 F2
Mardale Dr CDALE/KGS NW9 ...82 D2
Mardell Rd CROY/NA CRO ...227 H3
Marden Av HAYES BR2 ...232 D1
Marden Crs BXLY DA5 ...177 G6
CROY/NA CRO ...227 H3
Marden Rd CROY/NA CRO ...227 H3
TOTM N17 ...69 A5
Marden Sq BERM/RHTH SE16 ...65 C5
Marder Rd WEA W13 ...140 C2

Marechal Niel Av BFN/LL DA15 ...194 D3
Marechal Niel Pde
BFN/LL * DA15 ...194 C5
Maresfield CROY/NA CRO ...247 E1
Maresfield Gdns HAMP NW3 ...105 G3
Mare St HACK E8 ...109 H6
Marfleet Cl CAR SM5 ...226 A6
Margaret Av CHING E4 ...55 F1
Margaret Bondfield Av
BARK IG11 ...115 G5
Margaret Gardner Dr
ELTH/MOT SE9 ...193 H4
Margaret Ingram Cl
FUL/PGN * SW6 ...144 D6
Margaret Lockwood Cl
KUT * KT1 ...221 H1
Margaret Rd BXLY DA5 ...196 B1
EBAR EN4 ...35 H5
STNW/STAM * N16 ...89 F5
Margaret St GTPST W1W ...12 A3
Margaretta Ter CHEL SW3 ...36 A5
Margaretting Rd MNPK E12 ...93 E6
Margaret Wy REDBR IG4 ...93 G3
Margate Rd BRXS/STRHM SW2 ...167 G6
Margeholes OXHEY WD19 ...42 C4
Margery Rd BCTR RM8 ...116 B1
Margery St FSBYW WC1X ...6 A4
Margin Dr WIM/MER SW19 ...204 B1
Margravine Gdns HMSMTH W6 ...144 B6
Margravine Rd HMSMTH W6 ...144 B6
Marguerite Vls RYNPK * SW20 ...203 H3
Marham Gdns MRDN SM4 ...225 G3
WAND/EARL SW18 ...186 C1
Maria Cl BERM/RHTH SE16 ...33 F1
Marian Cl YEAD UB4 ...118 B3
Marian Pl BETH E2 ...91 G1
Marian Rd STRHM/NOR SW16 ...207 G4
Marian Sq BETH E2 ...9 G1
Marian St BETH * E2 ...91 G1
Maria Ter WHCHPL E1 ...103 F5
Maria Ter WHCHPL E1 ...130 B4
Maria Theresa Cl NWMAL KT3 ...222 D2
Maricas Av KTN/HRWW/W HA3 ...59 H4
Marie Curie CMBW * SE5 ...169 E2
Marie Lloyd Wk HACK * E8 ...109 F3
Mariette Wy WLGTN SM6 ...245 G6
Marigold Av STHWK SE1 ...14 C6
Marigold Cl SRTFD * E15 ...118 C6
Marigold Wy CROY/NA CRO ...230 B5
Marina Ap YEAD UB4 ...118 C4
Marina Av NWMAL KT3 ...223 H6
Marina Dr WELL DA16 ...175 E3
Marina Gdns ROMW/RG RM7 ...97 J1
Marina Wy TEDD TW11 ...201 F3
Marine Dr BARK IG11 ...135 H2
WOOL/PLUM SE18 ...153 H4
Marinefield Rd FUL/PGN SW6 ...165 F3
Mariner Gdns
RCHPK/HAM TW10 ...180 D5
Mariner Rd MNPK E12 ...114 A2
Mariners Ms POP/IOD E14 ...153 G3
Marion Cl BARK/HLT IG6 ...74 D5
Marion Gv WFD IG8 ...72 A1
Marion Rd CROY/NA CRO ...245 G5
MLHL NW7 ...63 G1
Marischal Rd LEW SE13 ...171 H4
Maritime Quay POP/IOD E14 ...151 E5
Maritime St BOW E3 ...130 D3
Marius Rd TOOT SW17 ...186 C4
Marjorie Gv BTSEA SW11 ...166 B5
Mark Av CHING E4 ...55 E1
Mark Cl BXLYHN DA7 ...176 C2
HAYES BR2 ...251 G2
STHL UB1 ...139 E1
Markeston Gn OXHEY WD19 ...42 B6
Market Chambers
ENC/FH * EN2 ...38 D4
Market La EDGW HA8 ...62 D4
Market Meadow
STMC/STPC BR5 ...236 A1
Market Ms MYFR/PICC W1J ...19 G2
Market Pde BMLY * BR1 ...212 C4
ED * N9 ...54 A1
EW * E17 ...241 F6
FELT * TW13 ...178 C4
LEY * E10 ...91 F3
SCUP * DA14 ...195 G6
SNWD * SE25 ...89 G5
STNW/STAM * N16 ...70 D6
WALTH * E17 ...142 C1
Market Pl ACT W3 ...173 H6
BERM/RHTH SE16 ...161 F1
BTFD TW8 ...65 H6
EFNCH N2 ...54 A1
KUT * KT1 ...175 F5
SOHO/SHAV W1D ...12 B4
Market Rd HOLWY N7 ...107 G4
RCH/KEW TW9 ...162 A4
Market Sq BMLY BR1 ...212 C5
Market St EHAM E6 ...133 H1
WOOL/PLUM SE18 ...154 A4
The Market CAR * SM5 ...225 G5
COVGDN * WC2E ...13 F5
HNWL * W7 ...169 G3
RCH/KEW * TW9 ...161 F6
Markfield Gdns CHING E4 ...56 A1
Markfield Rd SEVS/STOTM N15 ...68 B4
Markham Pl CHEL * SW3 ...36 B5
Markham Sq CHEL SW3 ...36 B6
Markham St CHEL SW3 ...36 A6
Markhole Cl HPTN TW12 ...198 D1
Markhouse Av WALTH E17 ...70 B6
Markhouse Rd WALTH E17 ...70 B6
Markmanor Av WALTH E17 ...90 A1
Mark Rd WDGN N22 ...67 H3
Marksbury Av RCH/KEW TW9 ...162 B1
Marks Rd ROMW/RG RM7 ...97 E1
Markstone Ter ORP * BR6 ...235 G4
Mark St SDTCH EC2A ...7 H6
SRTFD E15 ...112 A5
Mark Ter RYNPK * SW20 ...204 A3
The Markway SUN TW16 ...198 A5
Markwell Cl SYD SE26 ...189 H6

Markyate Rd BCTR RM8 .....115 H3
Marlands Rd CLAY IG5 .....73 G6
Marlborough Rd ISLW TW7 .....160 D1
Marlborough Av EDGW HA8 .....46 B5
  HACK * E8 .....109 C6
  STHGT/OAK N14 .....51 E5
Marlborough Cl ORP BR6 .....235 E4
  TRDG/WHET N20 .....50 B5
  WALW SE17 .....30 D2
  WIM/MER SW19 .....206 A2
Marlborough Ct REGST W1B 12 A4
Marlborough Crs CHSWK W4 .....142 D3
Marlborough Dr CLAY IG5 .....73 G6
Marlborough Gdns
  TRDG/WHET N20 .....50 B5
Marlborough Ga BAY/PAD W2 .....125 H6
Marlborough Gv STHWK SE1 .....33 G4
Marlborough M HRW HA3 .....80 A1
  STJWD NW8 .....105 G6
Marlborough La CHARL SE7 .....153 G6
Marlborough Ms
  BRXS/STRHM SW2 .....167 H5
Marlborough Park Av FSBYPK * N4 .....88 C5
Marlborough Park Av
  BFN/LL DA15 .....195 G5
Marlborough Pl ST/WD NW8 .....125 G1
Marlborough Rd ARCH N19 .....87 G6
  BCTR RM8 .....116 A2
  CHING E4 .....71 F2
  CHSWK W4 .....142 D3
  EA W5 .....141 F2
  ED N9 .....53 F3
  FELT TW13 .....178 B4
  FSTGT E7 .....113 E5
  HAYES BR2 .....233 E1
  HPTN TW12 .....199 E2
  NWDGN UB2 .....138 A3
  RCHPK/HAM TW10 .....187 H1
  ROMW/RG RM7 .....97 E1
  SAND/SEL CR2 .....246 C5
  SRTFD * E15 .....112 A2
  SUT SM1 .....243 E1
  SWFD E18 .....72 C6
  WDGN N22 .....67 H5
  WELL DA16 .....176 B4
  WHALL SW1A 20 B2
  WIM/MER SW19 .....206 A2
  WOOL/PLUM SE18 .....154 B3
Marlborough St CHEL SW3 .....26 A7
Marlborough Yd ARCH N19 .....87 F6
Marler Rd FSTH SE23 .....190 D3
Marley Av BXLYHN DA7 .....156 B6
Marley Cl GFD/PVL UB6 .....119 E2
  SEVS/STOTM N15 .....88 B1
Marlingdene Cl HPTN TW12 .....199 E2
Marlings Cl CHST BR7 .....235 E1
Marlings Park Av CHST BR7 .....235 E1
Marlins Cl SUT * SM1 .....243 G3
Marloes Cl ALP/SUD HA0 .....101 F2
Marloes Rd KENS W8 .....14 E5
Marlow Cl PGE/AN SE20 .....209 H6
Marlow Ct CDALE/KGS NW9 .....63 F6
Marlow Crs TWK TW1 .....160 B5
Marlow Dr CHEAM SM3 .....242 B1
Marlowe Cl BARK/HLT IG6 .....74 C4
  CHST BR7 .....214 D2
Marlowe Rd WALTH E17 .....91 G1
The Marlowes DART DA1 .....177 H4
  STJWD NW8 .....105 H6
Marlowe Wy CROY/NA CR0 .....227 G6
Marlow Rd EHAM E6 .....133 H2
  NWDGN UB2 .....138 D3
  PGE/AN SE20 .....209 H6
Marlow Wy BERM/RHTH SE16 .....150 B2
Marlton St GNWCH SE10 .....152 E5
Marlwood Cl BFN/LL DA15 .....195 G4
Marlyon Rd BARK/HLT IG6 .....75 H1
Marmadon Rd
  WOOL/PLUM SE18 .....155 F4
Marmion Ap CHING E4 .....55 G6
Marmion Av CHING E4 .....54 D6
Marmion Cl CHING E4 .....54 D6
Marmion Ms BTSEA * SW11 .....166 C4
Marmion Rd BTSEA SW11 .....166 C4
Marmont Rd PECK SE15 .....169 G2
Marmora Rd EDUL SE22 .....190 A1
Marmot Rd HSLWW TW4 .....158 B4
Marne Av FBAR/BDGN N11 .....50 B6
  WELL DA16 .....176 B2
Marnell Wy HSLWW TW4 .....158 B4
Marne St NKENS W10 .....124 C2
Marney Rd BTSEA SW11 .....166 C3
Marnfield Crs
  BRXS/STRHM SW2 .....187 H3
Marnham Av CRICK NW2 .....104 C2
Marnham Crs GFD/PVL UB6 .....119 F2
Marnock Rd BROCKY SE4 .....172 B4
Maroon St POP/IOD E14 .....130 C4
Maroons Wy CAT SE6 .....211 E1
Marquess Rd IS N1 .....108 D4
Marquess Rd North IS N1 .....108 C4
Marquess Rd South IS * N1 .....108 C4
Marquis Cl ALP/SUD HA0 .....101 H5
Marquis Rd CAMTN NW1 .....107 F4
  FSBYPK N4 .....87 H5
  WDGN N22 .....67 E6
Marrabon Cl BFN/LL DA15 .....195 C3
Marrick Cl PUT/ROE SW15 .....163 G5
Marryfine Av PEND EN3 .....40 D1
Marriot Rd MUSWH N10 .....66 B4
Marriott Rd BAR EN5 .....34 B4
  FSBYPK N4 .....87 E5
  SRTFD E15 .....112 A6
Marriotts Cl CDALE/KGS NW9 .....83 F3
Marriotts Yd BAR * EN5 .....34 B4
Marryat Pl WIM/MER SW19 .....184 C6
Marryat Rd WIM/MER SW19 .....204 C1
Marryat Sq FUL/PGN SW6 .....164 E2
Marsala Rd LEW SE13 .....171 F5
Marsden Rd ED N9 .....53 H4
  PECK SE15 .....169 F2
Marsden St KTTN NW5 .....106 C4
Marsden Wy ORP BR6 .....253 J7
Marshall Cl FBAR/BDGN N11 .....50 D6
  HRW HA1 .....78 H4
  HNWD/EARL SW18 .....185 G1
Marshall Est MLHL * NW7 .....47 G6
Marshall Rd TOTM N17 .....68 D4

Marshalls Gv
  WOOL/PLUM SE18 .....153 C4
Marshalls Rd ROMW/RG RM7 .....97 H1
  SUT SM1 .....243 F2
Marshall St SOHO/CST W1F 12 B4
Marshalsea Rd STHWK SE1 .....18 C3
Marsham Cl CHST * BR7 .....214 B1
Marsham St WEST SW1P 28 D1
Marsh Av MTCM CR4 .....206 B5
Marshbrook Cl BKHTH/KID SE3 .....175 F4
Marsh Cl MLHL NW7 .....47 F3
Marsh Dr CDALE/KGS NW9 .....83 F3
Marsh Farm Rd WHTN TW2 .....180 B3
Marshfield St POP/IOD E14 .....151 C3
Marshgate La SRTFD E15 .....111 F6
Marsh Green Rd DAGE RM10 .....117 E4
Marsh Hill HOM E9 .....110 C3
Marsh La LEY E10 .....90 C6
  MLHL NW7 .....47 E5
  STAN HA7 .....61 E1
  TOTM N17 .....69 H5
Marsh Rd ALP/SUD HA0 .....121 F2
  PIN HA5 .....78 C1
Marshside Cl ED N9 .....54 A3
Marsh St POP/IOD E14 .....151 F4
Marsh Ter STMC/STPC * BR5 .....256 B1
Marsh Wall POP/IOD E14 .....151 E2
Marsh Wy DAGW RM9 .....137 H3
Marsland Cl WALW SE17 .....30 D4
Marston Av CHSGTN KT9 .....259 H4
  DAGE RM10 .....117 E1
Marston Cl DAGE RM10 .....117 E1
  KIL/WHAMP NW6 .....105 G5
Marston Ct WOT/HER * KT12 .....218 A5
Marston Rd CLAY IG5 .....73 G6
  TEDD TW11 .....200 D1
Marston Wy NRWD SE19 .....208 B3
Marsworth Av PIN HA5 .....58 B4
Marsworth Cl YEAD UB4 .....118 C4
Martaban Rd STNW/STAM N16 .....89 F4
Martello St HACK E8 .....109 H5
Martell Rd DUL SE21 .....188 D5
Martel Pl HACK E8 .....109 F4
Marten Rd WALTH E17 .....71 E5
Martens Av BXLYHN DA7 .....177 C5
Martens Cl BXLYHN DA7 .....177 C5
Martham Cl THMD SE28 .....136 B6
Martha Rd SRTFD E15 .....112 A4
Martha's Buildings FSBYE EC1V 7 G5
Martha St WCHPL E1 .....130 A6
Marthorne Crs
  KTN/HRWW/W HA3 .....59 H5
Martin Bowes Rd
  ELTH/MOT SE9 .....175 H4
Martin Cl ED N9 .....54 B5
Martin Crs CROY/NA CR0 .....227 H5
Martindale MORT/ESHN SW14 .....162 C6
Martindale Av CAN/RD E16 .....132 C6
  ORP BR6 .....253 C3
Martindale Rd BAL SW12 .....186 D2
  HSLWW TW4 .....158 C5
Martin Dene BXLYHS DA6 .....176 D6
Martin Dr NTHLT UB5 .....78 A3
Martineau Rd HBRY N5 .....108 B2
Martineau St WCHPL E1 .....130 A6
Martingales Cl
  RCHPK/HAM TW10 .....181 F5
Martin Gdns BCTR RM8 .....116 A2
Martin Gv WIM/MER SW19 .....205 E6
Martin La CANST EC4R 15 H5
Martin Ri BXLYHS DA6 .....176 D6
Martin Rd BCTR RM8 .....116 A2
Martins Cl STMC/STPC BR5 .....216 B6
  WWKM BR4 .....231 H6
Martins Mt BAR EN5 .....34 B2
Martins Rd HAYES BR2 .....231 G1
The Martins SYD SE26 .....209 H1
  WBLY * HA9 .....101 H1
Martin St THMD SE28 .....155 E1
Martins Wk MUSWH * N10 .....66 C4
Martin Wy RYNPK SW20 .....204 D6
Martlet Ov NTHLT UB5 .....118 B2
Martlett Ct HOL/ALD WC2B 13 F4
Martley Dr IL IG1 .....71 H5
Martock Ct KTN/HRWW/W HA3 .....60 C1
Marton Cl CAT SE6 .....191 E5
Marton Rd STNW/STAM * N16 .....89 H6
Martys Yd HAMP * NW3 .....105 H2
Marvels Cl LEE/GVPK SE12 .....192 D4
Marvels La LEE/GVPK SE12 .....192 D4
Marville Rd FUL/PGN SW6 .....164 D1
Marvin St HACK * E8 .....109 H4
Marwell Cl WWKM BR4 .....232 B6
Marwood Cl WELL DA16 .....176 B4
Mary Adelaide Cl
  PUT/ROE SW15 .....183 E5
Mary Ann Buildings DEPT SE8 .....151 E6
Maryatt Av RYLN/HDSTN HA2 .....79 H6
Marybank WOOL/PLUM SE18 .....153 H4
Mary Cl KTN/HRWW/W HA3 .....81 H1
Mary Datchelor Cl CMBW SE5 .....168 D2
Mary Gn STJWD * NW8 .....105 F6
Maryland Pk SRTFD E15 .....112 A3
Maryland Rd MV/WKIL W9 .....125 E3
  SRTFD E15 .....111 H5
  THHTH CR7 .....208 B4
  WDGN N22 .....67 E3
Maryland Sq SRTFD E15 .....112 A3
Marylands Rd MV/WKIL W9 .....125 E3
Maryland St SRTFD E15 .....111 H3
Maryland Wk IS * N1 .....108 C6
Mary Lawrencon Pl
  BKHTH/KID SE3 .....172 B1
Marylebone High St MHST W1U 11 F1
Marylebone La MHST W1U 11 F1
Marylebone Ms
  CAVSQ/HST W1G 11 F2
Marylebone Pas GTPST W1W 12 A3
Marylebone Rd CAMTN NW1 .....10 B1
Marylebone St MHST W1U 11 F2
Marylee Wy LBTH SE11 .....29 H6
Maryon Gv CHARL SE7 .....115 G4
Maryon Ms HAMP NW3 .....106 A2
Maryon Rd CHARL SE7 .....153 G4
Mary Peters Dr NTHLT UB5 .....99 H3
Mary Pl NTCHL W11 .....124 C6
Mary Rose Cl HPTN TW12 .....199 E4
Mary Seacole Cl HACK * E8 .....109 F6
Mary Secole Cl HACK E8 .....109 F6
Mary's Ter TWK TW1 .....180 C2

Mary St CAN/RD E16 .....132 B4
  IS N1 .....108 C6
Mary Ter CAMTN NW1 .....107 E6
Masbro' Rd WKENS W14 .....144 B3
Mascalls Cl CHARL SW2 .....153 E6
Mascalls Ct CRICK NW2 .....103 H1
Masefield Av STAN HA7 .....60 B1
  STHL UB1 .....119 G6
Masefield Crs STHGT/OAK N14 .....37 E6
Masefield Gdns EHAM E6 .....134 A3
Masefield Rd FELT TW13 .....178 D6
Masefield Vw ORP BR6 .....265 F3
Mashie Rd ACT W3 .....125 E5
Mashiters Hl CRW RM5 .....77 H4
Maskall Cl BRXS/STRHM * SW2 .....188 A3
Maskell Rd TOOT SW17 .....185 G5
Maskelyne Cl BTSEA SW11 .....166 A2
Mason Cl BERM/RHTH SE16 .....33 F3
  BXLYHN DA7 .....177 H4
  HPTN TW12 .....198 D4
  RYNPK SW20 .....204 B4
Mason Ct WBLY * HA9 .....82 A6
Masonic Cl WFD IG8 .....56 A6
Mason's Arms Ms
  CONDST * W1S 11 J4
Mason's Av CITYW EC2V 15 G3
  CROY/NA CR0 .....246 C1
  KTN/HRWW/W HA3 .....80 D1
Masons Ct EW * KT12 .....241 G6
Masons Hl HAYES BR2 .....212 C6
  WOOL/PLUM SE18 .....154 B4
Mason's Pl FSBYE EC1V 6 C3
  MTCM CR4 .....206 B4
Mason St WALW SE17 .....31 H1
Masons Yd FSBYE EC1V 7 E5
  STJS SW1Y 20 B1
Massey Cl FBAR/BDGN N11 .....66 D1
Massie Rd HACK E8 .....109 G4
Massingberd Wy TOOT SW17 .....186 C6
Massinger St WALW SE17 .....32 A2
Massingham St WCHPL E1 .....130 B3
Masson Av RSLP HA4 .....96 A1
Masterman Rd EHAM E6 .....133 G2
Masters Dr BERM/RHTH SE16 .....33 G4
Master's St WCHPL E1 .....130 B4
Masthouse Ter POP/IOD E14 .....151 E4
Mast House Ter POP/IOD * E14 .....151 E4
Mastmaker Rd POP/IOD E14 .....151 E2
Maswell Park Crs HSLW TW3 .....159 G6
Maswell Park Rd HSLW TW3 .....159 F6
Matcham Rd WAN E11 .....112 A1
Matchless Dr
  WOOL/PLUM SE18 .....174 A1
Matfield Cl HAYES BR2 .....232 C2
Matfield Rd BELV DA17 .....157 E6
Matham Gv EDUL SE22 .....169 F5
Matham Rd E/WMO/HCT KT8 .....219 H2
Matheson Rd WKENS W14 .....144 D4
Mathews Av EHAM E6 .....134 A1
Mathews Park Av SRTFD E15 .....112 B4
Mathews Yd LSQ/SEVD * WC2H 13 H4
Mathieson Ct STHWK SE1 .....22 C4
Matilda Cl NRWD SE19 .....208 B1
Matilda St IS N1 .....107 H6
Matlock Cl BAR EN5 .....34 B6
Matlock Crs CHEAM SM3 .....242 C2
  OXHEY WD19 .....43 G5
Matlock Gdns CHEAM SM3 .....242 C2
Matlock Pl CHEAM SM3 .....242 C2
Matlock Rd LEY E10 .....91 G3
Matlock St POPL/IOD E14 .....130 C5
Matlock Wy NWMAL KT3 .....202 D4
Matthew Cl NKENS * W10 .....124 B3
Matthew Ct MTCM CR4 .....227 F2
Matthews Rd GFD/PVL UB6 .....98 D4
Matthews St BTSEA * SW11 .....166 B3
Matthias Rd STNW/STAM N16 .....108 D3
Mattingly Wy PECK SE15 .....169 F1
Mattock La EA W5 .....124 A1
Maud Cashmore Wy
  WOOL/PLUM SE18 .....153 H5
Maude Rd CMBW SE5 .....169 E3
  WALTH E17 .....90 C2
Maudeslie Cottages
  HNWL W7 .....140 A1
Maude Ter WALTH E17 .....90 C1
Maud Gdns BARK IG11 .....135 E1
  PLSTW E15 .....132 B1
Maud Rd LEY E10 .....111 G1
  PLSTW E13 .....112 B6
Maudslay Rd ELTH/MOT SE9 .....173 H4
Maud St CAN/RD E16 .....132 B4
Maud Wilkes Cl KTTN NW5 .....107 E3
Mauleverer Rd
  BRXS/STRHM SW2 .....167 G6
Maundeby Wk WLSDN * NW10 .....103 E3
Maunder Rd HNWL W7 .....140 A1
Maunsel St WEST SW1P 28 C1
Maurice Av WDGN N22 .....67 G3
Maurice Brown Cl MLHL * NW7 .....64 B1
Maurice St SHB W12 .....125 H5
Maurice Wk GLDGN NW11 .....85 G1
Mauritius Rd GNWCH SE10 .....152 A4
Maury Rd STNW/STAM N16 .....89 G6
Mavelstone Cl BMLY BR1 .....213 F4
Maverton Rd BOW * E3 .....111 E6
Mavis Av HOR/WEW KT19 .....241 G5
Mavis Cl HOR/WEW KT19 .....241 E5
Mawbey Est STHWK SE1 .....32 A5
Mawbey Pl STHWK SE1 .....32 D4
Mawbey Rd STHWK SE1 .....32 D4
Mawbey St VX/NE SW8 .....167 G1
Mawney Cl ROMW/RG RM7 .....77 F5
Mawney Rd ROMW/RG RM7 .....77 F6
Mawson Cl RYNPK SW20 .....204 C5
Mawson La CHSWK * W4 .....116 C6
Maxey Gdns DAGW RM9 .....116 C2
Maxey Rd DAGW RM9 .....116 C2
  WOOL/PLUM SE18 .....154 C4
Maxfield Cl TRDG/WHET N20 .....40 D2
Maxim Rd WCHMH N21 .....52 A1
Maxted Pk HRW HA1 .....80 A4
Maxted Rd PECK SE15 .....169 F4
Maxwell Cl CROY/NA CR0 .....227 G5
Maxwell Gdns ORP BR6 .....253 F1
Maxwell Ri OXHEY WD19 .....42 C2
Maxwell Rd FUL/PGN SW6 .....165 H1
  WELL DA16 .....175 G5

Maxwelton Av MLHL NW7 .....62 D1
Mayall Rd HNHL SE24 .....168 B6
Maya Rd EFNCH N2 .....85 G1
Maya Av STMC/STPC BR5 .....235 H2
Maybank Av ALP/SUD HA0 .....100 C2
  SWFD E18 .....72 D5
Maybank Rd SWFD E18 .....73 E4
May Bate Av KUTN/CMB KT2 .....201 F4
Mayberry Pl BRYLDS KT5 .....209 H2
Maybourne Cl SYD * SE26 .....209 H2
Maybury Cl EN EN1 .....39 H1
  STMC/STPC BR5 .....234 B2
Maybury Gdns WLSDN NW10 .....103 G5
Maybury Rd BARK IG11 .....135 G1
  PLSTW E13 .....133 E3
Maybury St TOOT SW17 .....206 A1
Maychurch Cl STAN HA7 .....61 H3
May Ct CHSGTN KT9 .....239 H4
Maycross Av MRDN SM4 .....224 D1
Mayday Gdns BKHTH/KID SE3 .....173 G3
Mayday Rd THHTH CR7 .....228 E3
Mayfield Rd THHTH CR7 .....227 H1
Mayerne Rd ELTH/MOT SE9 .....173 F6
Mayesbrook Rd BARK IG11 .....115 F6
  CDMY/SEVK IG3 .....115 G1
Mayesford Rd CHDH RM6 .....73 H4
Mayes Rd WDGN N22 .....67 H5
Mayeswood Rd
  LEE/GVPK SE12 .....193 G3
Mayfair Av CHDH RM6 .....96 B5
  IL IG1 .....95 H6
  WELL DA16 .....176 B2
  WHTN TW2 .....179 G2
  WPK KT4 .....224 B1
Mayfair Cl BECK BR3 .....211 F4
  SURB KT6 .....221 G5
Mayfair Gdns TOTM N17 .....68 C2
  WFD IG8 .....72 C3
Mayfair Ms CAMTN * NW1 .....106 B5
Mayfair Pl MYFR/PICC W1J 19 H1
Mayfair Rd DART DA1 .....179 H6
Mayfield Av CHSWK W4 .....143 G4
  KTN/HRWW/W HA3 .....80 D2
  NFNCH/WDSP N12 .....49 G6
  ORP BR6 .....235 H5
  STHGT/OAK N14 .....51 H4
  WEA W13 .....140 D3
  WFD IG8 .....72 C2
Mayfield Cl CLAP SW4 .....167 F6
  HACK E8 .....109 F4
  PGE/AN * SE20 .....209 H4
  THDIT KT7 .....220 D5
Mayfield Crs ED N9 .....53 H1
  THHTH CR7 .....227 H1
Mayfield Dr PIN HA5 .....59 H1
Mayfield Gdns HDN NW4 .....84 B3
  HNWL W7 .....119 H5
Mayfield Rd ACT W3 .....124 D2
  BCTR RM8 .....96 A5
  BELMT SM2 .....243 H4
  BELV DA17 .....157 G4
  BMLY BR1 .....233 G2
  CEND/HSY/T N8 .....87 H3
  CHING E4 .....55 H4
  HACK * E8 .....109 F5
  PEND EN3 .....40 B5
  PLSTW E13 .....132 E3
  SAND/SEL CR2 .....246 D6
  SHB W12 .....143 E2
  WALTH E17 .....70 C1
  WIM/MER SW19 .....204 D4
Mayfields WBLY HA9 .....82 A6
Mayfields Cl WBLY HA9 .....82 A6
Mayfield Vls SCUP * DA14 .....216 A2
Mayflower Cl
  BERM/RHTH SE16 .....151 G4
Mayflower St
  BERM/RHTH SE16 .....150 A2
Mayfly Cl PIN HA5 .....78 A4
  STMC/STPC BR5 .....236 B1
Mayford Rd BAL SW12 .....186 B2
May Gdns BORE WD6 .....45 F1
  GFD/PVL UB6 .....121 E1
Maygood St IS N1 .....5 H2
Maygrove Rd
  KIL/WHAMP NW6 .....104 D4
Mayhew Cl CHING E4 .....55 E5
Mayhill Rd BAR EN5 .....34 A5
  CHARL SE7 .....152 D6
Maylands Dr SCUP DA14 .....196 B5
Maylands Rd OXHEY WD19 .....42 A6
Maynard Cl FUL/PGN SW6 .....145 H6
  SEVS/STOTM N15 .....89 G2
Maynard Rd WALTH E17 .....91 G1
Maynards Quay WAP * E1W 130 A6
Maynooth Gdns MTCM CR4 .....206 A6
Mayola Rd CLPT E5 .....110 A2
Mayo Rd CROY/NA CR0 .....228 D2
  WLSDN NW10 .....81 G5
Mayow Rd SYD SE26 .....190 B6
Mayplace Cl ERITH DA8 150
Mayplace La
  WOOL/PLUM SE18 .....154 B6
Mayplace Rd BXLYHN DA7 .....177 G4
Mayplace Rd East BXLYHN DA7 .....177 G4
Mayplace Rd West
  BXLYHN DA7 .....177 G5
Maypole Crs BARK/HLT IG6 .....74 D3
May Rd CHING E4 .....71 H3
  PLSTW E13 .....132 C1
  WHTN TW2 .....180 A3
Mayroyd Av SURB KT6 .....222 A6
May's Buildings Ms
  GNWCH SE10 .....171 H1
Mays Ct CHCR WC2N 13 E6
May's Hill Rd HAYES BR2 .....212 A5
Maysoule Rd BTSEA SW11 .....166 B3
Mays Rd HPTN TW12 .....199 H1
May St WKENS W14 .....144 B4
Mayswood Gdns DAGE RM10 .....117 G4
Maythorne Cottages
  LEW SE13 .....191 H1
Mayton St HOLWY N7 .....107 H1
Maytree Cl EDGW HA8 .....46 D5
Maytree Ct MTCM CR4 .....206 D6
Maytree La STAN HA7 .....60 B2

Maytree Wk BRXS/STRHM SW2 ....188 A4
Mayville Est STNW/STAM * N16 ..109 E5
Mayville Rd IL IG1 ....114 B3
　WAN E11 ....112 A1
Maywood Cl BECK * BR3 ....211 F3
Maze Hl GNWCH SE10 ....152 A6
Mazenod Av KIL/WHAMP NW6 ....105 E5
Maze Rd RCH/KEW TW9 ....162 A1
McAdam Dr ENC/FH EN2 ....38 B3
McAuley Cl ELTH/MOT SE9 ....174 A6
　STHWK SE1 ....22 A5
McCall Cl CLAP SW4 ....167 E5
Mc Call Crs CHARL SE7 ....153 G5
McCarthy Rd FELT TW13 ....198 B1
McClintock Pl WAB EN9 ....41 F1
McCoid Wy STHWK SE1 ....3 E4
McCrone Ms HAMP NW3 ....105 H4
McCullum Rd BOW E3 ....110 D6
McDermott Cl BTSEA SW11 ....166 A3
McDermott Rd PECK SE15 ....169 G4
McDonough Cl CHSGTN KT9 ....239 G2
McDougall Ct RCH/KEW TW9 ....162 A3
McDowall Cl CAN/RD E16 ....132 C4
McEntee Av WALTH E17 ....70 C4
McEwan Wy SRTFD * E15 ....111 H6
McGrath Rd FSTGT E7 ....112 B3
McGregor Rd NTGHL W11 ....124 D5
Mcintosh Cl WLGTN SM6 ....245 G5
McKay Rd RYNPK SW20 ....203 H5
McKellar Cl BUSH WD23 ....43 G4
McKerrell Rd PECK SE15 ....169 G2
McKillop Wy SCUP DA14 ....216 A5
McLeod Rd ABYW SE2 ....156 A4
McLeod's Ms SKENS SW7 ....145 F3
McMillan St DEPT * SE8 ....151 E6
McNair Rd NWDGN UB2 ....139 E3
McNeil Rd CMBW SE5 ....169 E5
McNicol Dr WLSDN NW10 ....122 C1
McRae La MTCM CR4 ....226 B4
Mead Cl CAMTN * NW1 ....106 C5
　KTN/HRWW/W HA3 ....59 H4
Mead Court CDALE/KGS NW9 ....62 C1
Mead Crs CHING E4 ....55 G6
　SUT SM1 ....244 A2
Meadcroft Rd LBTH SE11 ....30 C6
Meade Cl CHSWK W4 ....142 A6
Meadfield EDGW HA8 ....46 B4
Mead Fld RYLN/HDSTN * HA2 ....98 D1
Meadfoot Rd STRHM/NOR SW16 ....207 E4
Meadgate Av WFD IG8 ....73 G1
Mead Gv CHDH RM6 ....76 B6
Meadlands Dr RCHPK/HAM TW10 ....181 F4
Meadow Av CROY/NA CR0 ....230 B3
Meadowbank BKHTH/KID SE3 ....172 B4
　BRYLDS KT5 ....221 H3
　HAMP NW3 ....106 B5
　OXHEY WD19 ....42 A2
　WCHMH N21 ....51 H1
Meadowbank Cl FUL/PGN SW6 ....164 A1
Meadowbank Rd CDALE/KGS NW9 ....82 D4
Meadow Cl BAR EN5 ....48 D1
　BXLYHS DA6 ....176 D6
　CAT SE6 ....211 E1
　CHING E4 ....55 F3
　CHST BR7 ....214 B1
　ESH/CLAY KT10 ....238 B1
　HOM E9 ....110 D5
　HSLWW TW4 ....179 E1
　NTHLT UB5 ....119 E1
　PEND EN3 ....40 C2
　RCHPK/HAM TW10 ....181 G3
　RYNPK SW20 ....224 A1
Meadowcourt Rd BKHTH/KID SE3 ....172 B5
Meadow Cft BMLY BR1 ....218 D6
Meadowcroft BUSH * WD23 ....43 F1
Meadowcroft Cl PLMGR * N13 ....52 B4
Meadowcroft Rd PLMGR N13 ....52 A4
Meadow Dr HDN NW4 ....64 A1
　MUSWH N10 ....66 C6
Meadow Gdns EDGW HA8 ....62 B2
Meadow Garth WLSDN NW10 ....102 C4
Meadow Hl NWMAL KT3 ....223 E5
Meadow La LEE/GVPK * SE12 ....193 E5
Meadow Ms VX/NE SW8 ....26 C6
Meadow Pl CHSWK * W4 ....163 E1
　VX/NE SW8 ....167 G1
Meadow Rd BARK IG11 ....115 F5
　DAGW RM9 ....116 D4
　ESH/CLAY KT10 ....238 A3
　FELT TW13 ....178 C4
　HAYES BR2 ....214 A6
　PIN HA5 ....78 B1
　ROMW/RG RM7 ....97 G5
　STHL UB1 ....118 D6
　SUT SM1 ....244 D3
　WIM/MER SW19 ....205 G3
Meadow Rw STHWK SE1 ....23 E6
Meadows Cl LEY E10 ....91 E6
Meadowside ELTH/MOT SE9 ....174 A4
　TWK TW1 ....181 F2
　WOT/HER KT12 ....218 A6
Meadowside Rd BELMT SM2 ....242 C6
Meadow Stile CROY/NA CR0 ....246 C1
Meadowsweet Cl CAN/RD E16 ....133 F4
　NWMAL KT3 ....224 A2
The Meadow CHST BR7 ....214 C2
Meadow Vw BFN/LL DA15 ....195 H1
　HRW HA1 ....60 E3
　SWLY * BR8 ....237 H3
Meadowview Rd BXLY DA5 ....196 C1
　CAT SE6 ....211 E6
　HOR/WEW KT19 ....241 E6
Meadow View Rd THHTH CR7 ....228 B2
Meadow Wk DAGW RM9 ....116 D4
　EW KT17 ....241 F5
　HOR/WEW KT19 ....241 E6
　SWFD E18 ....92 C1
　WLGTN SM6 ....244 D1
Meadow Wy CDALE/KGS NW9 ....82 D2
　CHSGTN KT9 ....241 E6
　ORP BR6 ....252 A1
　WBLY HA9 ....101 F2
Meadow Waye HEST TW5 ....158 C1
The Meadow Wy KTN/HRWW/W HA3 ....60 A4

Mead Pth TOOT SW17 ....205 H2
Mead Pl CROY/NA CR0 ....228 B5
　HOM E9 ....110 A4
Mead Plat WLSDN NW10 ....102 C4
Mead Rd CHST BR7 ....214 C2
　EDGW HA8 ....44 C2
　RCHPK/HAM TW10 ....181 F5
Mead Rw STHWK SE1 ....22 A5
Meadside Cl BECK SE3 ....210 C4
Meadvale La GDMY/SEVK IG5 ....95 F4
Meads Rd PEND EN3 ....40 C2
　WDGN N22 ....68 B5
The Meads CHEAM SM3 ....242 B1
　MTCM * CR4 ....226 A2
The Mead BECK BR3 ....211 G5
　EFNCH N2 ....65 G5
　OXHEY WD19 ....42 A5
　WLGTN SM6 ....245 F4
　W13 ....120 D4
　WWKM BR4 ....231 H5
Meadvale Rd CROY/NA CR0 ....229 F4
　EA W5 ....120 D6
Mead Wy CROY/NA CR0 ....250 C6
　HAYES BR2 ....231 G1
Meadway BAR EN5 ....27 E3
　BECK BR3 ....211 G4
　BRYLDS KT5 ....221 G5
　GDMY/SEVK IG3 ....115 E2
　GLDGN NW11 ....85 F3
　RYNPK SW20 ....224 A1
　STNGT/OAK N14 ....51 F4
　WFD IG8 ....73 E1
　WHTN TW2 ....179 H3
Meadway Cl BAR EN5 ....35 E4
　GLDGN NW11 ....85 F3
　PIN HA5 ....59 F2
Meadway Ct EA * W5 ....121 H4
The Meadway BKHH IG9 ....57 F3
　BKHTH/KID SE3 ....171 H3
　ORP BR6 ....253 H5
Meaford Wy PGE/AN SE20 ....209 H3
Meanley Rd MNPK E12 ....113 G3
Meard St SOHO/CST W1F 12 C4
Meath Cl STMC/STPC BR5 ....235 H2
Meath Rd IL IG1 ....114 C1
　SRTFD E15 ....112 A1
Meath St BTSEA SW11 ....166 D2
Mecklenburgh Pl BMSBY WC1N 5 G5
Mecklenburgh Sq BMSBY WC1N 5 G5
Mecklenburgh St CAMTN NW1 ....4 C1
Medcroft Gdns MORT/ESHN SW14 ....162 C5
Medebourne Cl BKHTH/KID SE3 ....172 C4
Medesenge Wy PLMGR N13 ....68 B2
Medfield St PUT/ROE SW15 ....183 G2
Medhurst Cl BOW E3 ....130 C1
Median Av ESH/CLAY KT10 ....238 A1
Medina Rd HOLWY N7 ....108 A1
Medland Cl MTCM CR4 ....226 C5
Medlar Cl NTHLT UB5 ....118 B3
Medlar St CMBW SE5 ....168 D1
Medley Rd KIL/WHAMP NW6 ....105 E4
Medora Rd BRXS/STRHM SW2 ....187 H1
　ROMW/RG RM7 ....75 E2
Medusa Rd LEW SE13 ....191 F1
Medway Cl CROY/NA CR0 ....230 A3
　IL IG1 ....114 C3
Medway Dr GFD/PVL UB6 ....120 B1
Medway Gdns ALP/SUD HA0 ....120 B1
Medway Pde GFD/PVL * UB6 ....120 B1
Medway Rd BOW E3 ....130 C1
Medway St WEST SW1P 20 C6
Medwin St CLAP SW4 ....167 H3
Meerbrook Rd BKHTH/KID SE3 ....175 G4
Meeson Rd SRTFD E15 ....112 B5
Meeson St CLPT E5 ....110 C3
Meesons Whf SRTFD * E15 ....131 G1
Meeting Field Pth HOM * E9 ....110 A4
Meeting House Aly WAP * E1W 92 C6
Meeting House La PECK SE15 ....169 H2
Mehetabel Rd HACK E8 ....110 A4
Meister Cl IL IG1 ....96 C6
Melanda Cl CHST * BR7 ....213 H1
Melanie Cl BXLYHN DA7 ....176 C2
Melaris Ms KIL/WHAMP NW6 ....105 E5
Melbourne Av PLMGR N13 ....67 H2
　RYLN/HDSTN HA2 ....59 F6
　WEA W13 ....140 C1
Melbourne Cl ORP BR6 ....235 E4
　WLGTN SM6 ....245 E5
Melbourne Gdns CHDH RM6 ....96 C2
Melbourne Gv EDUL SE22 ....169 F1
Melbourne Ms BRXN/ST SW9 ....168 A2
Melbourne Pl HOL/ALD WC2B 11 H4
Melbourne Rd EHAM E6 ....133 H1
　IL IG1 ....94 B5
　LEY E10 ....73 H6
　TEDD TW11 ....201 E2
　WALTH E17 ....69 F1
　WIM/MER SW19 ....205 E4
　WLGTN SM6 ....245 G3
Melbourne Sq BRXN/ST * SW9 ....168 A2
Melbourne Ter EDUL * SE22 ....169 G1
　FUL/PGN * SW6 ....165 F1
Melbourne Wy EN EN1 ....36 C5
Melbury Av NWDGN UB2 ....139 F3
Melbury Cl CHST BR7 ....213 H2
　ESH/CLAY KT10 ....238 D4
Melbury Ct WKENS W14 ....144 D3
Melbury Dr CMBW SE5 ....169 F3
Melbury Gdns RYNPK SW20 ....205 H4
Melbury Rd KTN/HRWW/W HA3 ....62 B6
　WKENS W14 ....144 D3
Melcombe Gdns KTN/HRWW/W HA3 ....81 H3
Melcombe Pl CAMTN NW1 ....10 C1
Melcombe St CAMTN NW1 ....2 D6
Meldon Cl FUL/PGN * SW6 ....165 F2
Meldone Cl BRYLDS KT5 ....222 A4
Meldrum Cl STMC/STPC BR5 ....236 A3
Meldrum Rd GDMY/SEVK IG3 ....95 G5
Melfield Gdns CAT SE6 ....191 H6
Melfort Av THHTH CR7 ....208 B6
Melford Av BARK IG11 ....115 E4
Melford Cl CHSGTN KT9 ....239 H3
Melford Rd DUL SE21 ....189 G3

EHAM E6 ....133 H3
IL IG1 ....94 D6
WALTH E17 ....90 C1
WAN E11 ....89 G5
Melfort Rd THHTH CR7 ....208 B6
Melgund Rd HBRY N5 ....108 A3
Melina Pl STJWD NW8 ....125 H2
Melina Rd SHB W12 ....143 H2
Melior Pl STHWK * SE1 ....24 A3
Melior St STHWK SE1 ....23 H3
Meliot Rd CAT SE6 ....191 H4
Meller Cl WLGTN SM6 ....245 G5
Melling Dr EN EN1 ....39 G2
Melling St WOOL/PLUM SE18 ....155 E6
Mellish Cl BARK IG11 ....72 C1
Mellish Gdns WFD IG8 ....72 C1
Mellish St POP/IOD E14 ....151 E3
Mellison Rd TOOT SW17 ....206 A1
Mellitus St SHB W12 ....123 H5
Mellor Cl WOT/HER KT12 ....218 D4
Mellows Rd CLAY IG5 ....73 H6
　WLGTN SM6 ....245 F3
Mells Crs ELTH/MOT SE9 ....193 H6
Melrose Av CRICK NW2 ....104 A3
　CFD/PVL UB6 ....119 F1
　MTCM CR4 ....206 D3
　STRHM/NOR SW16 ....207 H6
　WDGN N22 ....68 B4
　WHTN TW2 ....179 F2
　WIM/MER SW19 ....184 D4
Melrose Cl GFD/PVL UB6 ....119 F1
　LEE/GVPK SE12 ....192 C5
Melrose Crs ORP BR6 ....252 D2
Melrose Dr STHL UB1 ....139 E1
Melrose Gdns EDGW HA8 ....62 B6
　HMSMTH W6 ....143 A3
　NWMAL KT3 ....202 D6
Melrose Rd BARN SW13 ....163 G2
　RYLN/HDSTN HA2 ....60 C4
　WAND/EARL SW18 ....184 D1
　WIM/MER SW19 ....205 H1
Melrose Ter HMSMTH W6 ....143 A2
　WIM/MER SW19 ....184 D4
Melsa Rd MRDN SM4 ....225 G3
Melthorne Dr RSLP HA4 ....59 A6
Melthorpe Gdns BKHTH/KID SE3 ....173 A1
Melton Cl RSLP HA4 ....59 G5
Melton Flds HOR/WEW KT19 ....240 D6
Melton Pl HOR/WEW KT19 ....240 D6
Melton St CAMTN NW1 ....4 B4
Melville Av GFD/PVL UB6 ....103 G3
　RYNPK SW20 ....203 G3
　SAND/SEL CR2 ....247 F5
Melville Gdns PLMGR N13 ....51 H5
Melville Pl IS * N1 ....64 B1
Melville Rd BARN SW13 ....163 G2
　ROMW/RG RM7 ....196 A4
　SCUP DA14 ....194 A4
　WALTH E17 ....69 G1
　WLSDN NW10 ....102 D5
Melville Villas Rd ACT * W3 ....142 D1
Melvin Rd PGE/AN SE20 ....210 A4
Memel St STLK EC1Y 7 E6
Memorial Av SRTFD E15 ....132 A2
Memorial Cl HEST TW5 ....138 D6
Mendip Cl SYD SE26 ....190 A6
　WPK KT4 ....224 A6
Mendip Dr CLDGN NW11 ....65 H1
Mendip Houses BETH * E2 ....130 A2
Mendora Rd FUL/PGN SW6 ....164 C1
Menelik Rd CRICK NW2 ....104 C1
Menlo Gdns NRWD SE19 ....208 D3
Menotti St BETH E2 ....9 F5
Mentmore Cl KTN/HRWW/W HA3 ....61 E3
Mentmore Ter HACK E8 ....109 H5
Meon Rd ACT W3 ....142 C2
Meopham Rd MTCM CR4 ....207 E4
Mepham Crs KTN/HRWW/W HA3 ....42 B6
Mepham Gdns KTN/HRWW/W HA3 ....59 A3
Mepham St STHWK SE1 ....22 A3
Mera Dr BXLYHN DA7 ....177 G5
Merantum Wy WIM/MER SW19 ....205 F4
Merbury Cl LEW SE13 ....171 G1
Merbury Rd THMD SE28 ....154 C1
Merbury St WOOL/PLUM SE18 ....154 D3
Mercator Pl POP/IOD E14 ....151 E5
Mercator Rd LEW SE13 ....171 H5
Mercer Cl THDIT KT7 ....220 A6
Merceron Houses BETH * E2 ....130 B2
Merceron St WCHPL E1 ....130 D3
Mercers Cl GNWCH SE10 ....151 G3
Mercers Cottages WCHPL * E1 ....131 G5
Mercers Pl HMSMTH W6 ....144 A4
Mercers Rd ARCH N19 ....107 F1
Mercer St LSQ/SEVD WC2H 11 F4
Merchant St BOW E3 ....111 H2
Merchland Rd ELTH/MOT SE9 ....194 C1
Mercia Gv LEW SE13 ....171 F2
Mercier Rd PUT/ROE SW15 ....164 A3
Mercury Rd BTFD TW8 ....136 C1
Mercury Wy NWCR SE14 ....151 H5
Mercy Ter LEW SE13 ....171 F6
Mere Cl ORP BR6 ....246 B2
　PUT/ROE SW15 ....184 B1
Meredith Av CRICK NW2 ....104 A3
Meredith Cl PIN HA5 ....41 H3
Meredith Ms BROCKY * SE4 ....170 D5
Meredith St CLKNW EC1R 6 C4
　PLSTW E13 ....132 C2
Meredyth Rd BARN SW13 ....165 G3
Mere End CROY/NA CR0 ....234 A6
Mereside ORP BR6 ....251 G2
Meretone Cl BROCKY SE4 ....170 B3
Merevale Crs MRDN SM4 ....225 G3
Mereway Rd WHTN TW2 ....179 H3

Merewood Cl BMLY BR1 ....214 A5
Merewood Rd BXLYHN DA7 ....177 G3
Mereworth Cl HAYES BR2 ....232 B2
Mereworth Dr WOOL/PLUM SE18 ....174 B1
Meriden Cl BARK/HLT IG6 ....74 C4
　BMLY BR1 ....213 F3
Meridian Rd CHARL SE7 ....173 F1
Meridian Sq SRTFD E15 ....111 H5
Meridian Wy ED N9 ....54 A5
Merifield Rd ELTH/MOT SE9 ....173 E5
Merino Cl WAN E11 ....93 E1
Merivale Rd HRW HA1 ....60 C5
　PUT/ROE SW15 ....164 C5
Merlewood Dr CHST BR7 ....213 H4
Merley Ct CDALE/KGS NW9 ....62 D5
Merlin Cl CROY/NA CR0 ....245 H4
　CROY/NA CR0 ....247 G2
　CRW RM5 ....77 H2
　MTCM CR4 ....206 A6
　NTHLT UB5 ....135 G2
Merlin Crs EDGW HA8 ....61 H4
Merlin Gdns CRW RM5 ....77 H2
Merlin Gv BARK/HLT IG6 ....74 B3
　BECK BR3 ....210 C5
Merlin Rd MNPK E12 ....77 G2
　WELL DA16 ....176 C5
Merlin Rd North WELL DA16 ....175 C5
Merlins Av RYLN/HDSTN HA2 ....80 D1
Merlin St FSBYW WC1X 5 H6
Mermaid Ct STHWK SE1 ....23 G3
Merredene St BRXS/STRHM SW2 ....187 H1
Merriam Cl CHING E4 ....71 G1
Merrick Rd NWDGN UB2 ....138 D4
Merrick Sq STHWK SE1 ....23 G5
Merridene WCHMH N21 ....51 G1
Merrielands Crs DAGW RM9 ....136 D1
Merrilands Rd WPK KT4 ....224 A5
Merrilees Rd BFN/LL DA15 ....195 E2
Merrilyn Cl ESH/CLAY KT10 ....239 G5
Merriman Rd BKHTH/KID SE3 ....173 E2
Merrington Rd FUL/PGN SW6 ....145 E6
Merrion Av STAN HA7 ....61 F1
Merritt Gdns CHSGTN KT9 ....239 E4
Merritt Rd BROCKY SE4 ....170 C4
Merrivale STHGT/OAK N14 ....37 F6
Merrivale Av REDBR IG4 ....93 F1
Merrow Rd BELMT SM2 ....242 B6
Merrow St WALW SE17 ....31 G4
Merrow Wk WALW SE17 ....31 H5
Merrow Wy CROY/NA CR0 ....249 G4
Merrydown Wy CHST BR7 ....213 G4
Merryfield BKHTH/KID SE3 ....172 B3
Merryfield Gdns STAN HA7 ....43 H1
Merryhill Cl CHING E4 ....55 F2
Merry Hill Mt BUSH WD23 ....43 F3
Merry Hill Rd BUSH WD23 ....43 E2
Merryhills Dr ENC/FH EN2 ....37 G5
Merryweather Ct NWMAL * KT3 ....223 E2
Mersey Rd WALTH E17 ....69 G1
Mersham Dr CDALE/KGS NW9 ....82 A2
Mersham Pl PGE/AN SE20 ....209 H4
　THHTH CR7 ....208 D5
Mersham Rd THHTH CR7 ....208 D5
Merten Rd CHDH RM6 ....96 C4
Merthyr Ter BARN SW13 ....143 H6
Merton Av CHSWK W4 ....143 F4
　NTHLT UB5 ....96 G3
Merton Gdns STMC/STPC BR5 ....234 B2
Merton Hall Gdns RYNPK SW20 ....204 C4
Merton Hall Rd WIM/MER SW19 ....204 C4
Merton High St WIM/MER SW19 ....205 G3
Merton La HGT N6 ....86 B5
Merton Mansions WIM/MER * SW19 ....205 G4
Merton Ri HAMP NW3 ....106 H5
Merton Rd BARK IG11 ....115 F5
　ENC/FH EN2 ....38 D1
　GDMY/SEVK IG3 ....95 F4
　LEY E10 ....91 F1
　RYLN/HDSTN HA2 ....79 G5
　SNWD SE25 ....229 F2
　WALTH E17 ....89 G5
　WAND/EARL SW18 ....184 A5
　WIM/MER SW19 ....205 G3
Merton Ter WIM/MER * SW19 ....205 G4
Merttins Rd PECK SE15 ....170 C5
Meru Cl KTTN NW5 ....106 C3
Mervan Rd BRXS/STRHM SW2 ....168 A6
Mervyn Av ELTH/MOT SE9 ....194 C5
Mervyn Rd WEA W13 ....140 C3
Messaline Av ACT W3 ....122 C5
Messent Rd ELTH/MOT SE9 ....173 H5
Messeter Pl ELTH/MOT SE9 ....194 A1
Messina Av KIL/WHAMP NW6 ....105 E5
Meteor St BTSEA SW11 ....166 C5
Meteor Wy WLGTN SM6 ....245 G5
Metford Crs PEND EN3 ....41 E1
Metheringham Wy CDALE/KGS NW9 ....63 G3
Methley St LBTH SE11 ....30 B4
Methuen Cl EDGW HA8 ....44 C3
Methuen Pk MUSWH N10 ....66 B5
Methuen Rd BELV DA17 ....157 F4
　BXLYHS DA6 ....176 D5
　EDGW HA8 ....44 C3
Methwold Rd NKENS W10 ....124 B4
Metro Centre STMC/STPC * BR5 ....235 H3
Metropolitan Cl POP/IOD E14 ....151 E4
Metropolitan WH WAP * E1W 150 A1
Mews Clare FUL/PGN SW6 ....165 F1
Mews North BCVA SW1W 19 G6
Mews Pl WFD IG8 ....56 D6
Mews South PIM SW1V 28 B3
Mews St WAP E1W 31 H1
The Mews BECK * BR3 ....211 G4
　CEND/HSY/T N8 ....67 H1
　NFNCH/WDSP * N12 ....65 F1
　REDBR IG4 ....93 F2
　STRHM/NOR * SW16 ....207 H4
　TWK * TW1 ....160 D6
Mexfield Rd PUT/ROE SW15 ....164 D6
Meyer Gn EN EN1 ....39 G1
Meymott St STHWK SE1 ....22 C2
Meynell Crs HOM E9 ....110 B5

Meynell Gdns *HOM* E9..........................110 B5
Meynell Rd *HOM* E9.............................110 B5
Meyrick Rd *BTSEA* SW11......................165 H4
WLSDN NW10..103 G4
Miah Ter *WAP* * E1W..............................25 F2
Micawber St *IS* N1...................................7 E3
Michael Gaynor Cl *HNWL* W7..............140 B1
Michaelmas Cl *RYNPK* SW20.............204 A6
Michael Rd *FUL/PGN* SW6..................165 F2
SWWD SE25..209 E6
WAN E11..92 A5
Michaels Cl *LEW* SE13........................172 A4
Micheldever Rd *LEW* SE13..................192 A1
Michelham Gdns *TWK* TW1.................180 B5
Michigan Av *MNPK* E12......................113 G2
Michleham Down
NFNCH/WDSP N12.................................48 D6
Mickleham Cl *STMC/STPC* BR5.........215 F5
Mickleham Gdns *CHEAM* SM3............242 C4
Mickleham Rd *STMC/STPC* BR5.........215 F4
Mickleham Wy *CROY/NA* CRO.............249 H5
Micklethwaite Rd
FUL/PGN SW6..145 E6
Middle Dartrey Wk
WBPTN * SW10.......................................165 G1
Middle Dene *MLHL* NW7.......................46 C5
Middlefield *STJWD* NW8.....................105 H6
Middlefields *CROY/NA* CRO..................49 E6
WEA W13...120 D4
Middle Green *BRYLDS* KT5.................221 H3
Middleham Gdns *UED* N18.....................69 G2
Middleham Rd *UED* N18.........................69 G2
Middle La *CEND/HSY/T* N8...................87 G2
TEDD TW11..200 B2
Middle Lane Ms
CEND/HSY/T N8.......................................87 G2
Middle Park Av *ELTH/MOT* SE9..........193 F1
Middle Rd *EBAR* EN4.............................50 A1
PLSTW E13..132 C1
RYLN/HDSTN HA2..................................79 H6
STRHM/NOR SW16...............................207 E5
Middle Rw *NKENS* W10.......................124 C3
Middlesborough Rd *UED* N18..............69 C2
Middlesex Pl *HOM* E9...........................110 A4
Middlesex Rd *MTCM* CR4....................227 G2
Middlesex St *WCHPL* E1.........................16 B2
Middle St *CROY/NA* CRO....................228 C6
STBT EC1A..15 E1
Middle Temple La
TPL/STR WC2R...14 A4
Middleton Av *CHING* E4.........................44 D6
GFD/PVL UB6...119 H1
SCUP DA14..216 A2
Middleton Buildings
GTPST W1W...12 A2
Middleton Cl *CHING* E4..........................34 D5
Middleton Dr
BERM/RHTH SE16..................................150 B2
Middleton Gdns
GNTH/NBYPK IG2.....................................94 B3
Middleton Gv *HOLWY* N7.....................107 G3
Middleton Pl *GTPST* W1W.....................12 A2
Middleton Rd *CAR* SM5......................225 H4
GLDGN NW11..85 E4
HACK E8..110 F5
MRDN SM4..225 G3
NWMAL KT3...202 C6
Middleton St *BETH* E2............................9 G3
Middleton Wy *LEW* SE13.....................171 H5
Middleway *GLDGN* NW11......................85 F2
Middle Wy *STRHM/NOR* SW16...........207 F5
The Middle Wy
KTN/HRWW/W HA3...................................60 B5
Middle Yd *STHWK* SE1.........................23 H1
Midfield Av *BXLYHN* DA7....................177 G4
Midfield Wy *STMC/STPC* BR5............215 H4
Midford Pl *FITZ* W1T...............................4 B6
Midholm *GLDGN* NW11.........................85 F1
WBLY HA9...82 A5
Midholm Cl *GLDGN* NW11.....................85 F1
Midholm Rd *CROY/NA* CRO.................248 C1
Midhope St *STPAN* WC1H.......................5 F4
Midhurst Av *CROY/NA* CRO................228 A4
MUSWH N10..66 C6
Midhurst Hl *BXLYHS* DA6....................177 E6
Midhurst Pde *MUSWH * N10...................66 C6
Midhurst Rd *HNWL* W7........................140 C2
Midhurst Wy *CLPT* E5...........................74 C2
Midland Arches *CRICK* NW2..................83 H6
Midland Crs *HAMP* NW3......................105 G4
Midland Pl *POP/IOD* E14.....................163 F4
Midland Rd *CAMTN* NW1........................5 F3
LEY E10...91 G4
Midland Ter *WLSDN* NW10..................123 E3
Midline Point *POP/IOD* * E14..............151 E2
Midmoor Rd *BAL* SW12.......................161 H3
Midstrath Av *HSLWW* TW4.................158 D5
Midsummer Av *HSLWW* TW4..............158 D5
Midway *CHEAM* SM3...........................224 D4
Midwinter Cl *WELL* DA16....................175 G4
Mighell Av *REDBR* IG4..........................59 F5
Milan Rd *STHL* UB1.............................138 D2
Milborne Gv *WBPTN* SW10.................145 G5
Milborne St *HOM* E9............................110 A4
Milborough Crs
LEE/GVPK SE12.....................................192 A1
Milcote St *STHWK* SE1..........................22 C3
Mildenhall Rd *CLPT* E5.........................110 A2
Mildmay Av *IS* N1................................108 D3
Mildmay Gv North *IS* N1......................108 D3
Mildmay Gv South *IS* N1.....................108 D3
Mildmay Pk *IS* N1................................108 D3
Mildmay Rd *STNW/STAM* N16............109 E3
Mildmay Rd *IL* IG1................................108 C3
IS N1...108 D3
ROMW/RG RM7.......................................97 G2
Mildmay St *IS* N1................................108 D4
Mildred Av *NTHLT* UB5..........................99 F3
Mile End Pl *WCHPL* E1.........................130 B5
Mile End Rd *WCHPL* E1........................130 A4
The Mile End *WALTH* E17.......................70 B4
Miles Rd *CEND/HSY/T* N8......................67 G4
MTCM CR4...206 A6
Miles St *VX/NE* SW8..............................29 L6
Milespit HI *MLHL* NW7...........................63 H1
Miles Pl *BRYLDS* * KT5.......................221 H1
Miles Rd *CEND/HSY/T* N8......................67 G4
MTCM CR4..206 A6
Miles St *VX/NE* SW8..............................29 L6
Milestone Cl *BELMT* SM2....................243 H4
ED N9..53 G4

Milestone Rd *NRWD* SE19....................209 F2
Miles Wy *TRDG/WHET* N20...................50 A4
Milford St *SHB* W12.............................123 G6
Milfoil Cl *ABYW* SE2............................156 C6
Milford Gdns *ALP/SUD* HA0................101 F3
EDGW HA8...62 A4
Milford Gv *SUT* SM1............................243 G2
Milford La *TPL/STR* WC2R.....................14 A5
Milford Ms *STRHM/NOR* SW16...........187 H5
Milford Rd *STHL* UB1...........................116 A6
WEA W13...140 D1
Milk St *BMLY* BR1................................212 D1
CAN/RD E16..154 B1
CITYW EC2V..16 A4
Milkwell Gdns *WFD* IG8........................53 G2
Milkwell Yd *CMBW* SE5.......................168 C2
Milkwood Rd *HNHL* SE24....................168 B6
Milk Yd *WAP* E1W................................130 A6
Milldale Rd *DART* DA1.........................179 F1
Millais Av *MNPK* E12............................114 A3
Millais Gdns *EDGW* HA8........................62 A5
Millais Rd *EN* EN1.................................39 F6
NWMAL KT3...223 E4
WAN E11..91 G4
Millais Wy *HOR/WEW* KT19................240 C2
Millard Cl *STNW/STAM* N16................109 E3
Millard Ter *DAGE* RM10........................29 E1
Millbank *WEST* SW1P............................28 D2
Millbank Wy *LEE/GVPK* SE12.............172 C6
Millbourne Rd *FELT* TW13...................178 C6
Mill Br *BAR* * EN5....................................4 A1
Millbrook Av *WELL* DA16.....................174 D5
Millbrook Gdns *CHDH* RM6...................96 C3
Millbrook Rd *BRXN/ST* SW9................168 B4
ED N9..53 G4
Mill Brook Rd *STMC/STPC* BR5..........236 A1
Mill Cl *CAR* * SM5................................206 A6
Mill Cnr *BAR* EN5..................................34 D2
Millennium Br *STHWK* SE1....................15 E6
Millennium Cl *CAN/RD* E16..................132 C5
Millennium Dr *POP/IOD* E14................151 H5
Millennium Pl *BETH* E2...........................9 H2
Millennium Sq *STHWK* SE1...................24 C3
Millennium Wy *GNWCH* SE10..............151 H4
Millennium Whf *POP/IOD* E14..............151 H5
Miller Av *PEND* * EN3...........................31 F5
Miller Cl *MTCM* CR4............................226 B4
Miller Rd *CROY/NA* CRO......................227 H5
WIM/MER SW19....................................205 F2
Miller's Av *HACK* E8.............................109 F5
Millers Cl *HSLWW* TW4.......................178 C3
Miller's Ct *CHSWK* W4.........................118 C5
Millers Green Cl *ENC/FH* EN2................38 B4
Miller's Ter *HACK* E8...........................109 F5
Miller St *CAMTN* NW1..............................4 A1
Miller's Wy *HMSMTH* W6....................144 A2
Millers Yd *FNCH* N3...............................65 F1
Miller Wk *STHWK* SE1..........................22 B2
Millet Rd *GFD/PVL* UB6.......................119 F2
Mill Farm Cl *PIN* HA5............................58 A5
Mill Farm Crs *HSLWW* TW4................178 C5
Millfield Av *WALTH* E17..........................57 F5
Millfield La *HGT* N6...............................86 B6
Millfield Rd *EDGW* HA8..........................62 A5
HSLWW TW4...178 C5
Millfields Ct *STMC/STPC* BR5............235 H1
Millfields Rd *CLPT* E5..........................110 A2
Mill Gdns *SYD* SE26............................189 H6
Mill Gn *MTCM* CR4..............................226 C4
Mill Green Rd *MTCM* CR4....................226 C5
Millgrove St *BTSEA* SW11...................166 C2
Millharbour *POP/IOD* E14....................151 F3
Millhaven Cl *CHDH* RM6........................95 H5
Mill HI *BARN* SW13.............................165 G4
Mill Hill Av *ACT* * W3...........................142 B1
Mill Hill Rd *ACT* W3.............................142 B1
BARN SW13...163 H4
Mill Hill Ter *ACT* W3............................142 B1
Millhouse Pl *WNWD* SE27...................188 B6
Millicent Rd *LEY* * E10...........................90 D5
Milligan St *POP/IOD* E14......................130 D6
Milling Rd *EDGW* HA8............................62 D2
Mill La *CAR* SM5..................................244 C2
CHDH RM6..96 C3
CHING E4..41 F4
CRICK NW2...82 A4
CROY/NA CRO.......................................246 A1
EW KT17..241 F6
WFD IG8...72 B1
WOOL/PLUM SE18...............................156 A4

Milman Cl *PIN* HA5.................................58 B6
Milman Rd *KIL/WHAMP* NW6.............124 B1
Milman's St *WBPTN* SW10...................145 H6
WBPTN * SW10......................................145 H6
Milne Fld *PIN* HA5..................................59 E4
Milne Gdns *ELTH/MOT* SE9................173 G6
Milner Ct *BUSH* WD23...........................43 F1
Milner Dr *WHTN* TW2...........................179 H2
Milner Pl *IS* N1.....................................108 A4
Milner Rd *BCTR* RM8..............................98 A6
KUT KT1..225 H2
MRDN SM4..225 H2
SRTFD E15...132 A2
THHTH CR7..208 D6
WIM/MER SW19....................................205 F4
Milner Sq *IS* N1...................................108 A5
Milner St *CHEL* SW3..............................26 C1
Milnthorpe Rd *CHSWK* W4..................142 D6
Milo Rd *EDUL* SE22.............................189 F1
Milroy Wk *STHWK* SE1..........................22 B1
Milson Rd *WKENS* W14........................144 C3
Milson Av *BAR* EN5................................34 D6
CDALE/KGS NW9....................................62 D5
CROY/NA CRO.......................................228 D4
EHAM E6..113 F5
HGT N6...66 A1
SUT SM1..243 H1
WLSDN NW10..102 D6
Milton Cl *EFNCH* N2..............................85 G3
STHWK SE1...30 A6
SUT SM1..243 H1
Milton Ct *BARB* EC2Y............................15 G1
Milton Court Rd *NWCR* SE14..............150 C6
Milton Crs *GNTH/NBYPK* IG2................94 C4
Milton Dr *FBAR/BDGN* N11...................67 E1
STNW/STAM N16..................................108 D2
Milton Pk *HGT* N6..................................66 A1
Milton Rd *ACT* W3...............................142 D1
BELV DA17...157 E4
CDALE/KGS * NW9.................................63 E4
CROY/NA CRO.......................................228 D4
HGT N6...66 A2
HNHL SE24...168 B6
HNWL W7..120 B6
HPTN TW12...199 E3
HRW HA1..A1
MLHL NW7...46 D1
MORT/ESHN SW14................................162 B2
MTCM CR4...206 C3
SEVS/STOTM N15...................................68 A1
SUT SM1..243 E1
WALTH E17...57 E1
WELL DA16..175 E2
WIM/MER SW19....................................205 G2
WLGTN SM6...226 B5
Milton St *BARB* EC2Y............................15 G1
Milverton Gdns *GDMY/SEVK* IG3..........95 F6
Milverton Rd *KIL/WHAMP* NW6..........106 A5
Milverton St *LBTH* SE11........................30 B4
Milverton Wy *ELTH/MOT* SE9.............194 A6
Milward St *WCHPL* E1..........................130 D5
Mimosa Rd *YEAD* UB4.........................118 A4
Mimosa St *FUL/PGN* SW6...................166 E2
Minard Rd *CAT* SE6.............................192 A2
Mina Rd *WALW* SE17............................32 B4
WIM/MER SW19....................................205 H3
Minchenden Crs
STHGT/OAK N14.......................................51 F5
Mincing La *MON* EC3R...........................16 A5
Minden Rd *CHEAM* SM3.....................224 C6
PGE/AN SE20..209 H4
Minehead Rd
RYLN/HDSTN HA2....................................99 E1
STRHM/NOR SW16...............................207 H1
Mineral St *WOOL/PLUM* SE18............155 H4
Minera Ms *BGVA* SW1W........................27 F1
Minerva Cl *BRXN/ST* SW9...................146 B5
SCUP DA14..195 E6
Minerva Est *BETH* E2..............................9 J2
Minerva Rd *CHING* E4...........................71 F3
KUT KT1..201 H5
WLSDN NW10..122 C3
Minerva St *BETH* E2..............................9 J1
Minet Av *WLSDN* NW10.......................123 E1
Minet Gdns *WLSDN* NW10..................123 E1
Minet Rd *CMBW* SE5............................168 B3
Minford Gdns *WKENS* W14..................144 B2
Ming St *POP/IOD* E14..........................151 E6
Ministry Wy *ELTH/MOT* SE9...............193 H6
Mink Ct *HSLWW* TW4...........................158 A3
Minniedale *BRYLDS* KT5.......................16 C4
Minnow Wk *WALW* SE17........................32 B2
Minories *TWRH* EC3N............................16 C4
Minshull Pl *BECK* * BR3.......................211 E3
Minshull St *VX/NE* * SW8....................167 F2
Minson Rd *HOM* E9.............................110 B6
Minstead Gdns *PUT/ROE* SW15..........183 F2
Minstead Wy *NWMAL* KT3...................223 E3
Minster Av *SUT* SM1............................225 E6
Minster Ct *MON* * EC3R........................16 A5
Minster Dr *CROY/NA* CRO...................247 E2
Minster Gdns *E/WMO/HCT* KT8...........198 D1
Minster Rd *BMLY* BR1..........................194 A5
CRICK NW2...82 C3
Minstrel Gdns *BRYLDS* KT5................221 H3
Mintern Cl *PLMCR* N13..........................51 H2
Minterne Av *NWDGN* UB2...................136 C3
Minterne Rd
KTN/HRWW/W HA3.................................62 C1
Minterne Waye *YEAD* UB4....................118 A5
Mintern St *IS* N1.......................................7 H2
Minton Ms *KIL/WHAMP* NW6..............105 F4
Mint Rd *WLGTN* SM6............................244 D3
WLGTN SM6..226 B5
Mint St *STHWK* SE1...............................23 G2
Mint Wk *CROY/NA* CRO........................246 C1
Mirabel Rd *FUL/PGN* SW6...................145 J1
Miranda Cl *WCHPL* E1.........................130 E4
Miranda Rd *ARCH* N19...........................66 C5
Mirfield St *CHARL* SE7........................153 F5
Miriam Rd *WOOL/PLUM* SE18.............155 J1
Mirren Cl *RYLN/HDSTN* HA2..................98 D2
Missenden Gdns *MRDN* SM4...............225 G3
Mission Gv *WALTH* E17...........................57 G3
Mission Pl *PECK* SE15.........................169 G2
Mistletoe Cl *CROY/NA* CRO................228 D5
Misty's Fld *WOT/HER* KT12.................218 A5
Mitali Pas *WCHPL* E1.............................17 E4
Mitcham La *STRHM/NOR* SW16..........207 E1
Mitcham Pk *MTCM* CR4.......................226 D3
Mitcham Rd *CROY/NA* CRO.................227 F5
EHAM E6..133 G2

GDMY/SEVK IG3.......................................95 F4
TOOT SW17..206 B1
Mitchellbrook Wy
WLSDN NW10..102 D4
Mitchell Cl *ABYW* SE2..........................156 A5
BELV DA17...157 G5
Mitchell Rd *ORP* BR6...........................253 F2
PLMGR N13..68 B1
Mitchell St *FSBYE* EC1V..........................7 F4
Mitchell Wy *BMLY* BR1........................212 C4
WLSDN NW10..102 C4
Mitchison Rd *IS* N1..............................108 D4
Mitchley Rd *TOTM* N17..........................69 G6
Mitford Rd *ARCH* N19............................67 E1
Mitre Cl *BELMT* SM2...........................243 G5
HAYES BR2..212 B5
Mitre Rd *SRTFD* E15...........................132 A1
HAYES BR2..212 A5
Mitre Sq *HDTCH* EC3A...........................16 B4
Mitre St *HDTCH* EC3A............................16 B4
The Mitre *POP/IOD* E14.......................130 D6
Mitre Wy *WLSDN* NW10.......................123 H4
Moat Cl *ORP* BR6.................................253 F4
Moat Crs *FNCH* N2.................................65 F5
Moat Crt *WELL* DA16...........................175 H3
Moat Dr *HRW* HA1..................................79 C1
Moat Farm Rd *NTHLT* UB5....................98 D4
Moat La *ERITH* DA8.............................172 A3
Moat Pl *ACT* W3..................................122 B5
BRXN/ST SW9.......................................167 H4
Moat Side *FELT* TW13..........................178 A6
PEND EN3..40 A5
The Moat *NWMAL* KT3.........................203 E4
Moberly Rd *CLAP* SW4..........................87 F1
Modbury Gdns *HAMP* NW3..................106 C4
Model Cottages *WEA* * W13................140 D2
Model Farm Cl *ELTH/MOT* SE9...........193 G5
Moelyn Ms *HRW* HA1.............................80 C2
Moffat Rd *PLMGR* N13.........................67 G2
THHTH CR7..208 C5
TOOT SW17..186 A6
Mogden La *ISLW* TW7..........................160 A6
Mohammad Khan Rd *WAN* * E11..........92 B5
Moiety Rd *POP/IOD* E14.......................151 E2
Moira Cl *TOTM* N17................................69 E5
Moira Rd *ELTH/MOT* SE9.....................173 H5
Mole Cl *GARD/SEL* CR2.......................247 G6
Molash Rd *STMC/STPC* BR5...............236 B1
Mole Abbey Gdns
E/WMO/HCT KT8....................................199 E6
Mole Ct *HOR/WEW* KT19.....................240 C2
Molember Rd *E/WMO/HCT* KT8...........200 A2
Molescroft *ELTH/MOT* SE9..................194 C5
Molesey Av *E/WMO/HCT* KT8..............218 D1
Molesey Dr *CHEAM* SM3......................224 C6
Molesey Park Av
E/WMO/HCT KT8....................................219 F3
Molesey Park Cl
E/WMO/HCT KT8....................................219 G2
Molesey Rd *WOT/HER* KT12................218 C2
Molesford Rd *FUL/PGN* * SW6............145 J6
Molesham Wy
E/WMO/HCT KT8....................................199 F6
Molesworth St *LEW* SE13....................171 G4
Mollison Av *PEND* EN3..........................30 A2
Mollison Dr *WLGTN* SM6.....................245 G5
Mollison Wy *EDGW* HA8........................61 H5
Molly Huggins Cl *BAL* SW12...............187 E2
Molyneux Dr *TOOT* SW17....................186 D6
Molyneux St *MBLAR* W1H........................8 B2
Monarch Cl *WWKM* BR4.......................250 B2
Monarch Dr *CAN/RD* E16.....................133 F4
Monarch Ms *WIM/MER* SW19..............187 G6
Monarch Pde *MTCM* * CR4...................206 B5
BKHH IG9..39 E4
Monarch Rd *BELV* DA17.......................157 G3
Monarch's Wy *RSLP* HA4.......................77 E1
Monastery Gdns *ENC/FH* EN2................38 D3
Monarch Pl *BKHH* * IG9..........................39 E4
Mona Rd *PECK* SE15............................170 B2
Mona St *CAN/RD* E16..........................132 B4
Monaveen Gdns
E/WMO/HCT KT8....................................199 F6
Monck's Rw
WAND/EARL * SW18..............................184 D1
Monck St *WEST* SW1P...........................28 D6
Monclar Rd *CMBW* SE5........................169 E2
Moncorvo Cl *SKENS* SW7......................18 A4
Moncrieff St *PECK* SE15.......................169 G3
Monega Rd *FSTGT* E7...........................113 E4
Moneyer Ho *BOW* E3.............................111 E5
Monivea Rd *BECK* BR3.........................193 H6
Monk Dr *CAN/RD* E16...........................153 J1
Monkfrith Av *STHGT/OAK* N14..............50 F1
Monkfrith Wy *STHGT/OAK* N14............50 D2
Monkham's Av *WFD* IG8........................72 D1
Monkham's Dr *WFD* IG8........................72 D1
Monkleigh Rd *MRDN* SM4...................204 C6
Monks Av *BAR* EN5................................35 E1
ENC/FH EN2...38 C2
RSLP HA4...98 B2
Monks Cl *ABYW* SE2...........................156 B4
ENC/FH EN2...38 C2
RSLP HA4...98 B2
Monks Crs *WOT/HER* KT12..................219 F5
Monks Dr *ACT* W3................................122 A4
Monks Orchard Rd *BECK* BR3..............231 E5
Monks Pk *WBLY* HA9...........................103 E3
Monks Park Gdns *WBLY* HA9..............102 D4
Monks Rd *ENC/FH* EN2..........................38 D2
Monk St *WOOL/PLUM* SE18................154 A4
Monks Wy *BECK* BR3...........................210 D4
GLDGN NW11..85 F4
STMC/STPC BR5...................................234 C5
Monkswood Gdns *CLAY* IG5..................74 A6
Monkton Rd *WELL* DA16.....................175 F3
Monkton St *LBTH* SE11..........................30 B1
Monkville Av *GLDGN* NW11....................84 D1
Monkville Pde *GLDGN* * NW11..............84 D1
Monkwell Sq *BARB* EC2Y.......................15 F2
Monmouth Av *KUT/HW* KT1.................174 D6
SWFD E18...72 D1
Monmouth Cl *CHSWK* W4....................142 D3
MTCM CR4...227 G1
WELL DA16..176 B3
Monmouth Gv *BTFD* TW8....................138 E4
Monmouth Pl *BAY/PAD* W2.................125 E5

Monmouth Rd *BAY/PAD* W2 ...125 E5
  DAGW RM9 ...116 D3
  ED N9 ...53 H4
  EHAM E6 ...133 H2
Monmouth St *LSO/SEVD* WC2H ...18 E4
Monnery Rd *ARCH* N19 ...107 E1
Monnow Rd *STHWK* SE1 ...33 E2
Monoux Gv *WALTH* E17 ...71 E4
Monro Crs *EN* EN1 ...39 H2
Monroe Dr *MORT/ESHN* SW14 ...162 B6
Monro Gdns *KTN/HRWW/W* HA3 ...60 A3
Monsell Rd *FSBYPK* N4 ...108 B1
Monson Rd *NWCR* SE14 ...170 B1
  WLSDN NW10 ...123 G1
Mons Wy *HAYES* BR2 ...253 G3
Montacute Rd *BUSH* WD23 ...44 A2
  CAT SE6 ...190 D2
  CROY/NA CRO ...249 G6
  MRDN SM4 ...225 H3
Montagu Crs *UED* N18 ...53 H6
Montague Av *BROCKY* SE4 ...170 D5
  HNWL W7 ...140 B1
Montague Cl *STHWK* SE1 ...23 G1
Montague Gdns *ACT* W3 ...122 A6
Montague Hall Pl *BUSH* WD23 ...45 E1
Montague Pl *GWRST* WC1E ...12 D1
Montague Rd *CEND/HSY/T* N8 ...87 H2
  CROY/NA CRO ...228 B5
  HACK E8 ...109 G3
  HNWL W7 ...140 B2
  HSLW TW3 ...159 F4
  NWDGN UB2 ...138 C4
  KTN/HAM * TW10 ...181 G1
  SEVS/STOTM * N15 ...89 G1
  WAN E11 ...92 B6
  WEA W13 ...120 D5
  WIM/MER SW19 ...205 F3
Montague Sq *NWCR* SE14 ...170 A1
Montague St *RSQ* WC1B ...11 J1
  STBT EC1A ...15 E2
Montague Ter *HAYES* * BR2 ...252 B1
Montagu Gdns *UED* N18 ...53 H6
  WLGTN SM6 ...245 E2
Montagu Man *MHST* W1U ...10 D2
Montagu Ms North *MBLAR* W1H ...10 D2
Montagu Ms South *MBLAR* W1H ...10 D3
Montagu Ms West *MBLAR* W1H ...10 D3
Montagu Pl *MBLAR* W1H ...10 C2
Montagu Rd *HDN* NW4 ...83 G5
  UED N10 ...54 A6
Montagu Rw *MHST* W1U ...10 D2
Montagu Sq *MBLAR* W1H ...10 D2
Montagu St *MBLAR* W1H ...10 D3
Montalt Rd *WFD* IG8 ...72 B1
Montana Gdns *CAT* SE6 ...192 B1
  SUT SM1 ...245 G3
Montana Rd *RYNPK* SW20 ...204 A4
  TOOT SW17 ...186 C5
Montbelle Rd *ELTH/MOT* SE9 ...194 B5
Montbretia Cl *STMC/STPC* BR5 ...236 A1
Montcalm Cl *HAYES* BR2 ...232 C5
Montcalm Rd *CHARL* SE7 ...175 F1
Montclare St *BETH* E2 ...8 A2
Monteagle Av *BARK* IG11 ...114 C4
Monteagle Wy *PECK* SE15 ...169 H4
Montefiore St *VX/NE* SW8 ...166 D3
Montem Rd *BRO BOW* E3 ...106 D6
Montem St *FSTH* SE23 ...190 D2
  NWMAL KT3 ...223 E1
Montenotte Rd *CEND/HSY/T* N8 ...87 E2
Monterey Cl *BXLY* DA5 ...197 G4
Montesquieu Ter
  CAN/RD * E16 ...132 B5
Montford Pl *LBTH* SE11 ...50 A5
Montfort Gdns *BARK/HLT* IG6 ...74 C5
Montfort Pl *WIM/MER* SW19 ...184 B3
Montgomery Av
  ESH/CLAY KT10 ...220 B4
Montgomery Cl *BFN/LL* DA15 ...175 E6
  MTCM * CR4 ...248 C2
Montgomery Rd *CHSWK* W4 ...142 C4
Montholme Rd *BTSEA* SW11 ...186 B1
Monthope Rd *WCHPL* E1 ...17 E2
Montolieu Gdns
  PUT/ROE SW15 ...163 H6
Montpelier Av *BXLY* DA5 ...196 D2
  EA W5 ...121 E4
Montpelier Gdns *CHDH* RM6 ...96 A4
  EHAM E6 ...133 F2
Montpelier Gv *KTTN* NW5 ...107 E3
Montpelier Ms *SKENS* SW7 ...18 B5
Montpelier Pl *SKENS* SW7 ...18 B5
  WCHPL E1 ...130 A5
Montpelier Ri *GLDGN* NW11 ...84 C4
  WBLY HA9 ...65 H1
Montpelier Rd *EA* W5 ...121 F4
  FNCH N3 ...65 G4
  PECK SE15 ...169 H2
  SUT SM1 ...245 G2
Montpelier Rw *BKHTH/KID* SE3 ...172 B2
  TWK TW1 ...180 D2
Montpelier Sq *SKENS* SW7 ...18 B4
Montpelier St *SKENS* SW7 ...18 B4
Montpelier Ter *SKENS* SW7 ...18 B4
Montpelier V *BKHTH/KID* * SE3 ...172 B3
Montpelier Wk *SKENS* SW7 ...18 B5
Montpelier Wy *GLDGN* NW11 ...84 C4
Montrave Rd *PGE/AN* SE20 ...210 A2
Montreal Pl *HOL/ALD* WC2B ...11 G5
Montreal Rd *IL* IG1 ...54 C4
Montrell Rd *BRXS/STRHM* SW2 ...187 G3
Montrose Av *BFN/LL* DA15 ...175 G5
  EDGW HA8 ...62 D5
  KIL/WHAMP NW6 ...124 C1
  WELL DA16 ...174 D2
  WHTN TW2 ...179 F5
Montrose Cl *WELL* DA16 ...175 F4
  WFD IG8 ...41 E3
Montrose Ct *ALP/SUD* HA0 ...101 G4
  NFNCH/WDSP N12 ...65 F2
Montrose Gdns *MTCM* CR4 ...206 B6
  SUT SM1 ...245 G1
Montrose Rd
  KTN/HRWW/W HA3 ...60 A5
Montrose Vls *HMSMTH* * W6 ...143 G5
Montrose Wy *FSTH* SE23 ...190 B3
Montserrat Av *WFD* IG8 ...71 H3

Montserrat Cl *NRWD* SE19 ...208 D1
Montserrat Rd *PUT/ROE* SW15 ...164 C2
Monument St *MON* EC3R ...15 H6
Monument Wy
  SEVS/STOTM N15 ...69 F6
Monza St *WAP* E1W ...104 E6
Moodkee St *BERM/RHTH* SE16 ...150 A3
Moody St *WCHPL* E1 ...130 B2
Moon Ct *LEE/GVPK* * SE12 ...172 C2
Moon La *BAR* EN5 ...34 D4
Moon St *IS* N1 ...108 B6
Moorcroft *EDGW* * HA8 ...62 B4
Moorcroft Gdns *HAYES* BR2 ...233 C2
Moorcroft Rd
  STRHM/NOR SW16 ...187 C5
Moorcroft Wy *PIN* HA5 ...78 C2
Moordown *WOOL/PLUM* SE18 ...174 A2
Moore Cl *MORT/ESHN* SW14 ...162 C4
  MTCM * CR4 ...206 D5
  WLGTN SM6 ...245 G5
Moore Crs *DAGW* RM9 ...115 H6
Moorefield Rd *TOTM* N17 ...69 H6
Mooreland Rd *BMLY* BR1 ...212 B3
Moore Park Rd *FUL/PGN* SW6 ...165 F1
Moore Rd *NRWD* SE19 ...208 C2
Moore St *CHEL* SW3 ...45 H6
Moore Wy *BELMT* SM2 ...243 E6
Moorey Cl *SRTFD* E15 ...112 B6
Moorfield Av *EA* W5 ...121 F3
Moorfield Rd *CHSGTN* KT9 ...239 G3
  ORP BR6 ...216 A5
  PEND EN3 ...40 A2
Moorfields *LVPST* EC2M ...15 G2
Moorfields Highwalk
  BARB EC2Y ...15 G1
Moorgate *LOTH* EC2R ...15 G3
Moorgate Pl *LOTH* * EC2R ...15 G3
Moorhead Wy *BKHTH/KID* SE3 ...172 D4
Moorhouse Rd *BAY/PAD* W2 ...125 E5
  KTN/HRWW/W HA3 ...61 H6
The Moorings *CHSWK* * W4 ...142 A6
Moorland Cl *HSLWW* TW4 ...179 G2
  ROMW/RG RM7 ...77 F4
Moorland Rd *BRXN/ST* SW9 ...168 B5
Moorlands Av *MLHL* NW7 ...63 H2
Moor La *BARB* EC2Y ...15 G2
  CHSGTN KT9 ...246 A3
Moormead Dr *HOR/WEW* KT19 ...241 E1
Moor Mead Rd *TWK* TW1 ...180 C1
Moor Park Gdns
  KUTN/CMB KT2 ...203 E3
Moorside Rd *BMLY* BR1 ...192 H6
Moorstone St *SOHO/SHAV* W1D ...12 D4
Moortown Rd *OXHEY* WD19 ...42 A6
Morant Gdns *CRW* RM5 ...57 F1
Morant St *POP/IOD* E14 ...131 E6
Mora Rd *CRICK* NW2 ...104 A2
Mora St *FSBYE* EC1V ...7 F4
Morat St *BRXN/ST* SW9 ...167 H2
Moravian Pl *WBPTN* SW10 ...145 F1
Moravian St *BETH* E2 ...130 A1
Moray Ms *HOLWY* N7 ...87 H6
Moray Rd *HOLWY* N7 ...87 H6
Moray Wy *ROM* RM1 ...57 H5
Mordaunt Gdns *DAGW* RM9 ...116 C5
Mordaunt Rd *WLSDN* NW10 ...102 D6
Mordaunt St *BRXN/ST* SW9 ...167 H4
Morden Ct *MRDN* SM4 ...225 F1
Morden Court Pde
  WIM/MER * SW19 ...205 F6
Morden Gdns *GFD/PVL* UB6 ...100 D3
  MTCM CR4 ...225 H1
Morden Hall Rd *MRDN* SM4 ...205 F6
Morden Hl *LEW* SE13 ...171 G3
Morden La *LEW* SE13 ...151 G6
Morden Rd *BKHTH/KID* SE3 ...172 C3
  CHDH RM6 ...96 C4
  WIM/MER SW19 ...205 F5
Morden Road Ms
  BKHTH/KID SE3 ...172 C3
Morden St *LEW* SE13 ...171 F2
Morden Wy *CHEAM* SM3 ...225 E4
Morden Wharf Rd
  GNWCH SE10 ...152 A3
Mordon Rd *GDMY/SEVK* IG3 ...95 F4
Mordred Rd *CAT* SE6 ...192 A4
Morecambe Cl *WCHPL* * E1 ...130 D4
Morecambe Gdns *STAN* HA7 ...45 H6
Morecambe St *WALW* SE17 ...51 F2
Morecambe Ter *UED* * N18 ...52 D6
Morecoombe Cl
  KUTN/CMB KT2 ...144 B4
Morecone Cl
  KUTN/CMB KT2 ...202 B3
Moree Wy *UED* N18 ...53 C6
Moreland Cottages *BOW* * E3 ...131 G1
Moreland St *FSBYE* EC1V ...6 C3
Moreland Wy *CHING* E4 ...55 J5
Morella Rd *BAL* SW12 ...186 B2
Moremead Rd *CAT* SE6 ...191 H3
Morena St *CAT* SE6 ...191 F2
Moresby Av *BRYLDS* KT5 ...222 B4
Moresby Rd *CLPT* E5 ...85 H5
Mores Gdns *CHEL* * SW3 ...145 H6
Moreton Av *ISLW* TW7 ...159 H2
Moreton Cl *CLPT* E5 ...90 A1
  MLHL NW7 ...64 A1
  SEVS/STOTM N15 ...88 D3
  STHGT/OAK N14 ...28 C4
Moreton Gdns *WFD* IG8 ...73 C1
Moreton Pl *PIM* SW1V ...28 B5
Moreton Rd *SAND/SEL* CR2 ...246 D5
  SEVS/STOTM N15 ...88 D3
  WPK KT4 ...225 G6
Moreton St *PIM* SW1V ...28 B5
Moreton Ter *PIM* SW1V ...28 B5
Moreton Terr Ms South
  PIM SW1V ...28 B5
Morgan Av *WALTH* E17 ...91 H1
Morgan Cl *DAGE* RM10 ...117 C5
Morgan Rd *BMLY* BR1 ...212 C3
  HOLWY N7 ...88 A3
  NKENS W10 ...124 D4
Morgans La *STHWK* SE1 ...24 A2
Morgan St *BOW* E3 ...130 B2
  CAN/RD E16 ...132 B4
Morgan Wy *WFD* IG8 ...73 C2
Moriatry Cl *HOLWY* N7 ...107 G2
Morie St *WAND/EARL* SW18 ...165 F5
Morieux Rd *LEY* E10 ...90 D5

Moring Rd *TOOT* SW17 ...186 C6
Morkyns Wk *DUL* * SE21 ...189 E5
Morland Av *CROY/NA* CRO ...229 E5
Morland Cl *GLDGN* NW11 ...85 F5
  HPTN TW12 ...162 D6
  MTCM CR4 ...206 A6
Morland Est *HACK* * E8 ...109 C5
Morland Gdns *STHL* UB1 ...139 F1
  WLSDN NW10 ...101 G1
Morland Ms *IS* N1 ...108 A5
Morland Rd *CROY/NA* CRO ...229 F4
  DAGE RM10 ...117 E5
  IL IG1 ...72 A6
  KTN/HRWW/W HA3 ...81 G2
  PGE/AN SE20 ...210 B3
  SUT SM1 ...243 G3
  WALTH E17 ...90 B2
Morley Av *CHING* E4 ...71 H3
  UED N18 ...53 G6
  WDGN N22 ...68 B4
Morley Cl *ORP* BR6 ...254 B6
Morley Crs *EDGW* HA8 ...46 C4
  RSLP HA4 ...78 A6
Morley Crs East *STAN* HA7 ...61 H6
Morley Crs West *STAN* HA7 ...61 H6
Morley Hl *ENC/FH* EN2 ...38 D1
Morley Rd *BARK* IG11 ...114 D6
  CHDH RM6 ...96 C2
  CHEAM SM3 ...224 D5
  CHST BR7 ...214 C4
  LEW SE13 ...171 G3
  LEY E10 ...91 G5
  SRTFD E15 ...132 B1
  TWK TW1 ...181 F1
Morley St *STHWK* SE1 ...22 B4
Morna Rd *CMBW* SE5 ...168 C3
Morning La *HOM* E9 ...110 A4
Morningside Rd *WPK* KT4 ...225 H6
Mornington Av *ENC/FH* EN2 ...29 G1
  IL IG1 ...94 A4
  WKENS W14 ...144 D3
Mornington Cl *BXLY* DA5 ...197 H3
  WFD IG8 ...40 E5
Mornington Crs *CAMTN* NW1 ...4 A1
Mornington Gv *BOW* E3 ...131 E2
Mornington Ms *CMBW* SE5 ...168 C2
Mornington Pl *CAMTN* NW1 ...4 A1
Mornington Rd *CHING* E4 ...55 H2
  DEPT SE8 ...170 D1
  GFD/PVL UB6 ...119 F4
  WAN E11 ...92 B5
  WFD IG8 ...56 B6
Mornington St *CAMTN* NW1 ...3 H1
Mornington Ter *CAMTN* NW1 ...106 D6
Mornington Wk
  RCHPK/HAM TW10 ...181 G6
Morocco St *STHWK* SE1 ...24 A4
Morpeth Gv *HOM* E9 ...110 B6
Morpeth Rd *HOM* E9 ...110 A6
Morpeth St *BETH* E2 ...130 B2
Morpeth Ter *WEST* SW1P ...20 A6
Morpeth Wk *TOTM* * N17 ...69 H3
Morrab Gdns *GDMY/SEVK* IG3 ...115 F1
Morrel Cl *BAR* EN5 ...33 G4
Morris Av *MNPK* E12 ...113 H3
Morris Bishop Ter *HGT* * N6 ...86 A2
Morris Cl *CROY/NA* CRO ...230 C3
  ORP BR6 ...253 F1
Morris Gdns *ANGEL/EARL* SW18 ...185 J2
Morrish Rd *BRXS/STRHM* SW2 ...187 G2
Morrison Av *TOTM* N17 ...69 B6
Morrison Rd *BARK* IG11 ...116 C6
  DAGW RM9 ...116 C6
Morrison St *BTSEA* SW11 ...185 F1
Morris Pl *FSBYPK* N4 ...88 A6
Morris Rd *BCTR* RM8 ...96 B5
  ISLW TW7 ...160 B4
  POP/IOD E14 ...131 F4
  LEY E11 ...112 A2
Morris St *WCHPL* E1 ...130 D4
Morriston Cl *OXHEY* WD19 ...58 A1
Morse Cl *PLSTW* E13 ...132 D2
Morshead Rd *MV/WKIL* W9 ...125 E2
Morson Rd *PEND* EN3 ...54 C1
Morteyne Rd *TOTM* N17 ...68 D4
Mortham St *SRTFD* E15 ...112 A6
Mortimer Cl *BAL* SW12 ...187 F4
  BUSH WD23 ...43 F1
  CRICK NW2 ...104 D1
Mortimer Crs *KIL/WHAMP* NW6 ...105 F6
  WPK KT4 ...240 D1
Mortimer Dr *WDGN* N11 ...54 B6
Mortimer Pl *KIL/WHAMP* NW6 ...105 F6
Mortimer Rd *EHAM* E6 ...133 H2
  ERITH DA8 ...157 H6
  IS N1 ...109 G6
  MTCM CR4 ...206 B4
  ORP BR6 ...265 B6
  WEA W13 ...121 G5
  WLSDN NW10 ...124 A2
Mortimer St *GTPST* W1W ...11 H3
Mortimer Ter *KTTN* * NW5 ...106 D2
Mortlake Cl *CROY/NA* CRO ...245 G1
  EBAR EN4 ...206 A4
Mortlake High St
  MORT/ESHN SW14 ...162 D4
Mortlake Rd *CAN/RD* E16 ...132 D5
  IL IG1 ...96 A3
  MORT/ESHN SW14 ...162 B4
Morton Cl *CROY/NA* CRO ...261 G3
Morton Gdns *WLGTN* SM6 ...245 D4
Morton Ms *ECT* * SW5 ...145 J4
Morton Pl *STHWK* SE1 ...22 A6
Morton Rd *IS* N1 ...108 D4
  MRDN SM4 ...225 H2
  SRTFD E15 ...112 D5
Morton Wy *STHGT/OAK* N14 ...38 C3
Morvale Cl *BELV* DA17 ...156 D4
Morval Rd *BRXS/STRHM* SW2 ...168 A4
Morven Rd *TOOT* SW17 ...186 D6
Morville St *BOW* E3 ...131 E1
Morwell St *FITZ* W1T ...11 C3
Moscow Pl *BAY/PAD* * W2 ...125 G6
Moscow Rd *BAY/PAD* W2 ...125 G6
Moselle Av *WDGN* N22 ...68 B6
Moselle Cl *CEND/HSY/T* N8 ...67 F6
Moselle Pl *TOTM* * N17 ...56 B6
Moselle St *TOTM* N17 ...56 B6
Mossborough Cl
  NFNCH/WDSP N12 ...65 F2

Mossbury Rd *BTSEA* SW11 ...166 A3
Moss Cl *PIN* HA5 ...58 D5
  WCHPL E1 ...17 F1
Mossdown Cl *BELV* DA17 ...157 G4
Mossford Gn *BARK/HLT* IG6 ...74 B6
Mossford La *BARK/HLT* IG6 ...74 C5
Mossford St *BOW* E3 ...130 D3
Moss Gdns *SAND/SEL* CR2 ...248 B5
Moss Hall Crs *NFNCH/WDSP* N12 ...65 F2
Moss Hall Gv *FNCH* N3 ...65 F2
Moss La *PIN* HA5 ...58 D6
Mosslea Rd *HAYES* BR2 ...233 F2
  ORP BR6 ...216 C2
  PGE/AN SE20 ...210 A3
Mosso St *CHEL* SW3 ...26 B1
Moss Rd *DAGE* RM10 ...117 C6
Mossville Gdns *MRDN* SM4 ...204 D6
Mostyn Av *WBLY* HA9 ...101 H3
Mostyn Gdns *WLSDN* NW10 ...124 B2
Mostyn Gv *BOW* E3 ...130 D1
Mostyn Rd *BRXN/ST* SW9 ...168 A2
  EDGW HA8 ...46 D3
  WIM/MER SW19 ...204 D5
Mosul Wy *HAYES* BR2 ...233 C3
Mosyer Dr *STMC/STPC* BR5 ...236 B6
Motcomb St *KTBR* SW1X ...19 C5
Moth Cl *WLGTN* SM6 ...245 G5
The Mothers Sq *CLPT* * E5 ...109 H2
Motley Av *VX/NE* SW8 ...167 E3
Motspur Pk *NWMAL* KT3 ...223 F3
Mottingham Gdns
  ELTH/MOT SE9 ...193 F3
Mottingham La *ELTH/MOT* SE9 ...193 E3
Mottingham Rd *ED* N9 ...54 B1
  ELTH/MOT SE9 ...193 H5
Mottisfont Rd *ABYW* SE2 ...155 G3
Moulins Rd *HOM* E9 ...110 A5
Moulton Av *HEST* TW5 ...158 C3
Mountfield Rd
  STNW/STAM N16 ...89 G3
Mountacre Cl *SYD* SE26 ...189 F6
Mount Adon Pk *DUL* SE21 ...189 G2
Mountague Pl *POP/IOD* E14 ...131 G6
Mount Angelus Rd
  PUT/ROE SW15 ...183 F2
Mount Ararat Rd
  RCHPK/HAM TW10 ...161 G6
Mount Ash Rd *SYD* SE26 ...189 H5
Mount Av *CHING* E4 ...55 E5
  EA W5 ...121 H5
  STHL UB1 ...119 J5
Mountbatten Cl *NRWD* SE19 ...209 E1
  WOOL/PLUM SE18 ...155 E6
Mountbatten Ct *BKHH* IG9 ...57 F4
Mountbel Rd
  KTN/HRWW/W HA3 ...60 C5
  CAR SM5 ...244 C6
  EA * W5 ...121 H5
  EBAR EN4 ...36 C5
Mountcombe Cl *SURB* KT6 ...221 G4
Mount Cottages *BXLYHS* * DA6 ...176 C5
Mount Ct *WWKM* KT4 ...248 A6
Mount Culver Av *SCUP* DA14 ...216 B2
Mount Dr *BXLYHS* DA6 ...176 D2
  RYLN/HDSTN HA2 ...78 D2
  WBLY HA9 ...82 C6
Mountearl Gdns
  STRHM/NOR SW16 ...187 F5
Mount Echo Av *CHING* E4 ...55 F3
Mount Echo Dr *CHING* E4 ...55 F3
Mount Ephraim La
  STRHM/NOR SW16 ...187 F5
Mount Ephraim Rd
  STRHM/NOR SW16 ...187 E5
Mountfield Cl *LEW* SE13 ...191 H2
Mountfield Rd *EA* W5 ...121 E4
  EHAM E6 ...133 H1
  FNCH N3 ...65 E6
Mountfield Wy
  STMC/STPC BR5 ...236 A1
Mountford St *WCHPL* * E1 ...17 E3
Mountfort Crs *IS* N1 ...108 A5
Mountfort Ter *IS* N1 ...108 A5
Mountgrove Rd *FSBYPK* N4 ...88 B5
Mounthurst Rd *HAYES* BR2 ...232 C4
Mountington Park Cl
  KTN/HRWW/W HA3 ...81 F3
Mountjoy Cl *THMD* SE28 ...155 H2
Mount Mills *FSBYE* EC1V ...6 D4
Mount Nod Rd
  STRHM/NOR SW16 ...187 F5
Mount Pde *EBAR* * EN4 ...36 A5
Mount Pk *CAR* SM5 ...244 C6
Mount Park Av
  RYLN/HDSTN HA2 ...79 H6
  SAND/SEL CR2 ...246 B6
Mount Park Crs *EA* W5 ...121 F5
Mount Park Rd *EA* W5 ...121 F4
  PIN HA5 ...58 D2
  RYLN/HDSTN HA2 ...79 H6
Mount Pl *ACT* W5 ...142 B1
Mount Pleasant *ALP/SUD* HA0 ...101 G6
  EBAR EN4 ...36 B5
  FSBYW WC1X ...5 J6
  RSLP HA4 ...98 A1
  RYLN/HDSTN * HA2 ...80 A6
  WNWD SE27 ...188 C3
Mount Pleasant Crs
  FSBYPK * N4 ...87 H4
Mount Pleasant Hl *CLPT* E5 ...89 H6
Mount Pleasant La *CLPT* E5 ...89 H5
Mount Pleasant Pl
  WOOL/PLUM SE18 ...154 D3
Mount Pleasant Rd *CRW* RM5 ...77 H2
  EA W5 ...121 E3
  LEW SE13 ...191 H4
  NWMAL KT3 ...223 H1
  TOTM N17 ...69 H5
  WALTH E17 ...70 C5
Mount Pleasant Vls *FSBYPK* N4 ...87 F4
Mount Ri *FSTH* SE23 ...190 D4
Mount Rd *BCTR* RM8 ...96 D5
  BXLYHS DA6 ...176 D4
  CHSGTN KT9 ...239 H4
  CRICK NW2 ...82 A1
  DART DA1 ...139 J5
  EBAR EN4 ...34 C5
  FELT TW13 ...141 J5
  HDN NW4 ...83 G3
  IL IG1 ...114 B3

MTCM CR4.....205 H5
NRWD * SE19.....208 D2
NWMAL KT5.....202 D6
WAND/EARL SW18.....185 E4
Mount Rw MYFR/PKLN W1K.....11 G6
Mountside KTN/HRWW/W HA3.....60 B4
Mounts Pond Rd
BKHTH/KID SE3.....171 H5
The Mount Sq HAMP * NW3.....105 C1
Mount Stewart Av
KTN/HRWW/W HA3.....81 F3
Mount St MYFR/PKLN W1K.....11 E6
Mount Ter WCHPL E1.....17 C2
The Mount BMLY * BR1.....213 G4
BXLYHS * DA6.....177 F6
CLPT * E5.....89 H6
HAMP NW5.....105 C2
NTHLT * UB5.....96 D3
NWMAL KT5.....205 F6
TRDG/WHET N20.....49 G4
WBLY HA9.....82 B6
WPK V13.....207 H1
Mount Vw ENC/FH EN2.....37 H1
NWDGN * UB2.....138 B4
Mountview MLHL NW7.....46 D5
Mount View Rd
CDALE/KGS NW9.....82 D1
CHING E4.....55 C2
ESH/CLAY KT10.....258 D5
FSBYPK N4.....67 H4
Mountview Rd ORP BR6.....235 G4
Mount Vis WNWD SE27.....188 B5
Mount Wy CAR SM5.....244 C6
NTHLT * UB5.....96 D3
Mountwood E/WMO/HCT KT8.....199 F6
Movers La BARK IG11.....114 D6
Mowatt Cl ARCH N19.....87 F6
Mowbray Gdns NTHLT * UB5.....99 E6
Mowbray Rd BAR EN5.....35 C5
EDGW HA8.....46 A6
KIL/WHAMP NW6.....104 C5
NRWD SE19.....209 F4
RCHPK/HAM TW10.....181 E5
Mowbrays Cl CRW RM5.....77 G4
Mowbrays Rd CRW RM5.....77 G5
Mowlem St BETH E2.....9 H1
Mowll St BRXN/ST SW9.....168 A1
Moxon Cl PLSTW E13.....132 B1
Moxon St BAR EN5.....34 D4
MHST W1U.....11 E2
Moye Cl BETH E2.....9 F1
Moyers Rd WAN E11.....71 E3
Moylan Rd HMSMTH W6.....144 C6
Moyne Pl WLSDN NW10.....122 A2
Moynihan Dr STHGT/OAK N14.....37 C6
Moys Cl CROY/NA CR0.....227 C3
Moyser Rd TOOT SW17.....206 D1
Mozart St NKENS W10.....124 D2
Muchelney Rd MRDN SM4.....225 G3
Muggeridge Cl SAND/SEL CR2.....246 D3
Muggeridge Rd DAGE RM10.....117 F2
Muir Cl WAND/EARL SW18.....186 A1
Muirdown Av
MORT/ESHN SW14.....162 C5
Muirfield ACT W3.....123 E5
Muirfield Cl BERM/RHTH SE16.....33 H4
OXHEY * WD19.....58 A1
Muirfield Crs POP/IOD E14.....151 F3
Muirfield Gn OXHEY WD19.....42 A6
Muirfield Rd OXHEY WD19.....42 A6
Muirkirk Rd CAT SE6.....191 G5
Muir Rd CLPT E5.....109 G2
Muir St CAN/RD E16.....153 H1
Mulberry Cl CHEL * SW3.....145 H6
CHING E4.....55 E4
EBAR EN4.....35 H5
HDN NW4.....64 A1
NTHLT UB5.....118 C1
STRHM/NOR SW16.....187 E6
Mulberry Crs BTFD TW8.....160 D1
Mulberry La CROY/NA CR0.....229 F5
Mulberry Ms NWCR SE14.....170 D2
Mulberry Pk HMSMTH W6.....143 G5
Mulberry Rd HACK E8.....109 F5
Mulberry St WCHPL E1.....17 E3
Mulberry Wk CHEL SW3.....145 H6
Mulberry Wy BARK/HLT IG6.....141 C4
BELV DA17.....157 G2
SWFD E18.....72 D5
Mulgrave Rd BELMT SM2.....242 D5
CROY/NA CR0.....246 D1
EA W5.....121 F2
HRW HA1.....80 C6
WKENS W14.....144 D6
WLSDN NW10.....91 G3
WOOL/PLUM SE18.....153 H4
Mulholland Cl MTCM CR4.....206 D5
Mulkern Rd ARCH N19.....87 F5
Mullards Cl MTCM CR4.....226 D3
Mullet Gdns BETH E2.....9 F5
Mullins Pth MORT/ESHN SW14.....162 D4
Mullion Cl KTN/HRWW/W HA3.....59 H4
Mullion Wk OXHEY WD19.....42 B6
Mull Wk IS N1.....108 C4
Mulready St STJWD NW8.....2 B6
Multi Wy ACT W3.....143 E2
Multon Rd WAND/EARL SW18.....185 H2
Mumford Ct CITYW EC2V.....14 F3
Mumford Rd HNHL SE24.....168 B6
Muncaster Rd BTSEA SW11.....166 B5
Muncies Ms CAT SE6.....191 G6
Mundania Rd EDUL SE22.....189 H1
Munday Rd CAN/RD E16.....132 C5
Munden St WKENS W14.....144 C4
Mundesly Cl OXHEY WD19.....42 A6
Mundford Rd CLPT E5.....90 A6
Mundon Gdns IL IG1.....94 D5
Mund St WKENS W14.....144 D5
Mundy St IS N1.....8 A3
Mungo-Park Cl BUSH * WD23.....43 C4
Mungo Park Wy
STMC/STPC BR5.....236 A4
Munnery Wy ORP BR6.....252 A1
Munnings Gdns ISLW * TW7.....159 H6
Munro Dr FBAR/BDGN * N11.....67 E2
Munro Ms NKENS W10.....124 C4
Munslow Gdns SUT SM1.....243 G2
Munster Av HSLWW TW4.....158 C3
Munster Gdns PLMGR N13.....52 C6
Munster Ms FUL/PGN * SW6.....164 D1
Munster Rd FUL/PGN SW6.....164 C1
TEDD TW11.....201 E2

Munster Sq CAMTN NW1.....3 H4
Munton Rd WALW SE17.....31 F1
Murchison Av BXLY DA5.....196 B3
Murchison Rd LEY E10.....91 G6
Murdock Cl CAN/RD E16.....132 D5
Murdock St PECK SE15.....33 G6
Murfett Cl WIM/MER SW19.....184 C4
Muriel St IS N1.....5 H1
Murillo Rd LEW SE13.....171 H5
Murphy St STHWK SE1.....22 A4
Murray Av BMLY BR1.....212 D6
HSLW TW3.....159 F6
Murray Crs PIN HA5.....58 B4
Murray Gv IS N1.....7 E2
Murray Ms CAMTN NW1.....107 F5
Murray Rd EA W5.....141 E4
RCHPK/HAM TW10.....180 D4
STMC/STPC BR5.....215 H6
WIM/MER SW19.....204 B2
Murray Sq CAN/RD E16.....132 C5
Murray St CAMTN NW1.....107 F5
Murray Ter HAMP NW3.....105 G2
Murtwell Dr CHIG IG7.....74 C2
Musard Rd HMSMTH W6.....144 C6
Musbury St WCHPL E1.....130 A5
Muschamp Rd CAR SM5.....226 A6
PECK SE15.....169 F4
Muscovy St TWRH EC3N.....16 B6
Museum St NOXST/BSQ WC1A.....13 E2
Musgrave Cl EBAR EN4.....35 G2
Musgrave Crs FUL/PGN SW6.....165 E1
Musgrave Rd ISLW TW7.....160 B2
Musgrove Rd NWCR SE14.....170 B2
Musjid Rd BTSEA SW11.....165 H5
Musquash Wy HSLWW TW4.....158 A3
Muston Rd CLPT E5.....89 H6
Muswell Av MUSWH N10.....66 C6
Muswell Hl MUSWH N10.....66 D6
Muswell Hill Broadway
MUSWH N10.....66 C6
Muswell Hill Pl MUSWH N10.....86 D1
Muswell Hill Rd HGT N6.....66 C3
MUSWH N10.....66 C6
Muswell Ms MUSWH N10.....66 C6
Muswell Rd MUSWH N10.....66 D6
Mutrix Rd KIL/WHAMP NW6.....105 E6
Mutton Pl CAMTN NW1.....106 D6
Muybridge Rd NWMAL KT3.....202 F5
Myatt Rd BRXN/ST SW9.....168 B2
Mycenae Rd BKHTH/KID SE3.....146 C5
Myddelton Av EN EN1.....24 A1
Myddelton Gdns WCHMH N21.....52 C2
Myddelton Pk TRDG/WHET N20.....49 H5
Myddelton Pas CLKNW EC1R.....6 A3
Myddelton Rd CEND/HSY/T N8.....67 G6
Myddelton Sq CLKNW EC1R.....6 A2
Myddelton St CLKNW EC1R.....6 A3
Myddleton Av FSBYPK N4.....68 A1
Myddleton Rd WDGN N22.....67 C3
Myers La NWCR SE14.....170 C4
Mylis Cl SYD SE26.....189 H6
Mylne Cl HMSMTH * W6.....143 C5
Mylne St CLKNW EC1R.....6 A1
Myra St ABYW SE2.....155 C5
Myrdle St WCHPL E1.....17 F2
Myrna Cl WIM/MER SW19.....206 A3
Myron Pl LEW SE13.....171 G4
Myrtle Av EBED/NFELT TW14.....153 H6
Myrtleberry Cl HACK * E8.....109 F4
Myrtle Cl EBAR EN4.....50 B3
Myrtledene Rd ABYW SE2.....155 G5
Myrtle Gdns HNWL W7.....160 A1
Myrtle Gv ENC/FH EN2.....38 D1
NWMAL KT3.....201 G5
Myrtle Rd ACT W3.....142 C1
CROY/NA CR0.....249 E1
EHAM E6.....113 J1
HPTN TW12.....199 G2
HSLW TW3.....159 H1
PLMGR N13.....41 G3
SUT SM1.....243 G5
WALTH E17.....90 F4
Myrtle St IS N1.....8 A2
Myrtle Wk IS N1.....8 A2
Mysore Rd BTSEA SW11.....166 B5
Myton Rd DUL SE21.....188 D5

N

Nadine St CHARL SE7.....153 E5
Nagle Cl WALTH E17.....7 H5
Nag's Head La WELL DA16.....175 F4
Nags Head Rd PEND EN3.....40 A5
Nairne Gv HNHL SE24.....168 D6
Nairn Rd RSLP HA4.....78 D3
Nairn St POP/IOD E14.....131 G4
Nailhead Rd FELT TW13.....198 A1
Namba Roy Cl
STRHM/NOR SW16.....187 H6
Namton Dr STRHM/NOR SW16.....227 H1
Nan Clark's La MLHL NW7.....47 F4
Nancy Downs OXHEY WD19.....42 A2
Nankin St POP/IOD E14.....131 E5
Nansen Rd BTSEA SW11.....166 C1
Nansen Village
NFNCH/WDSP * N12.....49 F6
Nantes Cl WAND/EARL SW18.....165 G5
Nant Rd CRICK NW2.....84 D6
Nant St BETH * E2.....9 H5
Naoroji St FSBYW WC1X.....6 A4
Napier Av FUL/PGN SW6.....164 D4
POP/IOD E14.....151 E5
Napier Cl DEPT SE8.....170 D1
Napier Ct LEE/GVPK SE12.....192 D4
Napier Gv IS N1.....7 E2
Napier Pl WKENS W14.....144 D3
Napier Rd ALP/SUD HA0.....101 F3
BELV DA17.....156 D4
EHAM E6.....114 A6
HAYES BR2.....212 D6
ISLW TW7.....160 B3
PEND EN3.....40 B6
SAND/SEL CR2.....246 D6
SNWD SE25.....229 H1
SRTFD E15.....112 A1
TOTM N17.....56 A1
WAN E11.....112 A1

WKENS W14.....144 D3
WLSDN NW10.....123 H2
Napier Ter IS N1.....108 B5
Napoleon Rd CLPT E5.....109 H1
TWK * TW1.....180 D2
Napton Cl YEAD UB4.....118 C3
Narbonne Av CLAP SW4.....187 E1
Narborough St FUL/PGN SW6.....165 F3
Narcissus Rd KIL/WHAMP NW6.....105 E5
Narford Rd CLPT E5.....109 G1
Narrow Boat Cl THMD SE28.....154 D2
Narrow St ACT W3.....142 B1
POP/IOD E14.....151 H1
Narrow Wy HAYES BR2.....233 G3
Nascot St SHB W12.....124 A5
Naseby Cl ISLW TW7.....160 A2
KIL/WHAMP * NW6.....105 G5
Naseby Ct WOT/HER * KT12.....218 A6
Naseby Rd CLAY IG5.....59 H3
DAGE RM10.....117 E1
NRWD SE19.....208 D2
Nash Cl SUT SM1.....243 H2
Nash Gn BMLY BR1.....212 C3
Nash La HAYES BR2.....250 C4
Nash Rd BROCKY SE4.....170 C5
CHDH RM6.....61 H4
ED N9.....43 E4
Nash St CAMTN NW1.....3 H3
Nash Wy KTN/HRWW/W HA3.....80 D3
Nasmyth St HMSMTH W6.....143 H3
Nassau Rd BARN SW13.....163 F2
Nassau St GTPST W1W.....12 A2
Nassington Rd HAMP NW3.....106 A2
Natal Rd FBAR/BDGN N11.....67 G1
IL IG1.....114 B2
STRHM/NOR SW16.....207 F2
THHTH CR7.....208 D6
Nathaniel Cl WCHPL E1.....16 D2
Nathans Rd ALP/SUD HA0.....81 E6
Nathan Wy THMD SE28.....155 F3
Nation Wy CHING E4.....55 G3
Naval Rw POP/IOD E14.....131 G6
Navarino Gv HACK E8.....109 C4
Navarino Rd HACK E8.....109 C4
Navarre Gdns CRW RM5.....77 F2
Navarre Rd EHAM E6.....133 G2
Navarre St BXHS/ST SW9.....67 G1
Navenby Wk BOW * E3.....130 A4
Navestock Cl CHING * E4.....55 G5
Navestock Crs WFD IG8.....73 E4
Navestock Ter WFD IG8.....73 E3
Navigator Dr STHL UB1.....139 G2
Navy St CLAP SW4.....167 F4
Nayim Pl HACK E8.....109 H4
Naylor Gv PEND EN3.....40 B6
Naylor Rd PECK SE15.....169 F5
TRDG/WHET N20.....49 G4
Nazareth Cl PECK SE15.....169 H3
Neal Av STHL UB1.....118 D3
Nealden St BRXN/ST SW9.....167 H2
Neale Cl EFNCH N2.....65 G6
Neal St LSO/SEVD WC2H.....13 E4
Neal Ter FSTH * SE23.....190 B3
Neal Yd LSO/SEVD WC2H.....13 E4
Near Acre CDALE/KGS NW9.....45 H4
Neasden Cl WLSDN NW10.....105 E3
Neasden La WLSDN NW10.....105 E1
Neasden La North
WLSDN NW10.....105 E1
Neasham Rd BCTR RM8.....115 H3
Neate St CMBW SE5.....32 A6
Neath Gdns MRDN SM4.....225 G3
Neathouse Pl PIM SW1V.....28 A1
Neatscourt Rd EHAM E6.....133 F4
Nebraska St STHWK SE1.....23 G4
Neckinger Est
BERM/RHTH SE16.....24 D5
Neckinger St STHWK SE1.....24 D5
Nectarine Wy LEW SE13.....171 F3
Needham Rd BAY/PAD W2.....125 E5
Needleman St
BERM/RHTH SE16.....150 B2
Neeld Crs HDN NW4.....83 H2
WBLY HA9.....102 A3
Neil Cl ASHF TW15.....153 E6
Neils Yd LSO/SEVD * WC2H.....13 E4
Neilgarde Rd CAT SE6.....191 E2
Nella Rd HMSMTH W6.....144 B6
Neildale Rd BERM/RHTH SE16.....33 H2
Nello James Gdns WNWD SE27.....188 B6
Nelson Cl CROY/NA CR0.....228 B5
KIL/WHAMP NW6.....125 E2
ROMW/RG RM7.....77 F4
Nelson Gdns BETH E2.....9 F3
HSLW TW3.....159 F5
Nelson Grove Rd
WIM/MER SW19.....205 F4
Nelson Mandela Cl
MUSWH N10.....66 B5
Nelson Mandela Rd
BKHTH/KID SE3.....173 G4
Nelson Pl IS N1.....6 D1
SCUP DA14.....195 G6
Nelson Rd BELV DA17.....156 D5
CEND/HSY/T N8.....87 H2
CHING E4.....53 H5
GNWCH SE10.....151 G6
HYS/HAR UB3.....133 C6
ISLW TW4.....179 E1
NWMAL KT3.....203 G2
PEND EN3.....54 B1
RYLN/HDSTN HA2.....79 H5
SCUP DA14.....195 G6
SRS/STOTM N15.....67 E1
STAN HA7.....61 E2
WALTH E17.....205 F3
WAN E11.....71 G3
WIM/MER SW19.....205 F3
Nelsons Rw CLAP SW4.....167 F2
Nelson St CAN/RD E16.....132 B6
EHAM E6.....114 A6
WCHPL E1.....130 D4
Nelson's Wk HOM * E9.....91 C5
Nelson Wk HOR/WEW KT19.....240 A6
Nemoure Rd ACT W3.....122 D6
Nene Gdns FELT TW13.....178 D4
Nepaul Rd BTSEA SW11.....166 A3
Nepean St PUT/ROE SW15.....183 G1
Neptune Rd HRW HA1.....79 H3
Neptune St BERM/RHTH SE16.....150 A3

Nesbit Cl BKHTH/KID SE3.....172 A4
Nesbit Rd ELTH/MOT SE9.....173 F5
Nesbitts Aly BAR * EN5.....34 D4
Nesbit Sq NRWD * SE19.....209 E3
Nesham St WAP E1W.....18 D1
Ness St BERM/RHTH SE16.....25 E5
Nesta Rd WFD IG8.....72 B2
Nestor Av WCHMH N21.....52 B1
Netheravon Rd CHSWK W4.....143 F5
HNWL W7.....140 B1
Netheravon Rd South
CHSWK W4.....143 F6
Netherby Rd EA W5.....141 F5
Netherby Gdns ENC/FH EN2.....37 G5
Netherby Rd FSTH SE23.....190 A2
Netherlands Rd BAR EN5.....65 E3
Nether Cl FNCH N3.....64 D2
Nether Ct MLHL * NW7.....47 E1
Nethercourt Av FNCH N3.....65 E2
Netherfield Gdns BARK IG11.....114 D4
Netherfield Rd
NFNCH/WDSP * N12.....65 F1
TOOT SW17.....186 C5
Netherford Rd CLAP SW4.....167 E3
Netherhall Gdns HAMP NW3.....105 G4
Netherhall Wy HAMP NW3.....105 G4
Netherlands Rd BAR EN5.....65 E1
Netherleigh Cl ARCH * N19.....86 D5
Netherton Gv WBPTN SW10.....145 G6
Netherton Rd SEVS/STOTM N15.....88 D3
TWK TW1.....160 C6
Netherwood Pl
HMSMTH * W6.....144 B3
Netherwood Rd HMSMTH W6.....144 B3
Netherwood St
KIL/WHAMP NW6.....104 D5
Netley Cl CHEAM SM3.....242 B3
CROY/NA CR0.....249 G5
Netley Dr WOT/HER KT12.....218 D4
Netley Gdns MRDN SM4.....225 G4
Netley Rd BTFD TW8.....141 G6
CNTH/NBYPK IG2.....94 D2
MRDN SM4.....225 G4
WALTH E17.....89 G2
Netley St CAMTN NW1.....4 A4
Nettlecombe Cl BELMT SM2.....243 F6
Nettleden Av WBLY HA9.....102 C4
Nettlefold Pl WNWD SE27.....188 B5
Nettlestead Cl BECK BR3.....210 D3
Nettleton Rd NWCR SE14.....170 B1
STRHM/NOR SW16.....207 F3
Neuchatel Rd CAT SE6.....190 D4
Nevada Cl NWMAL KT3.....222 C1
Nevada St GNWCH SE10.....171 G1
Nevern Pl ECT SW5.....145 E4
Nevern Rd ECT SW5.....145 E4
Nevern Sq ECT SW5.....145 E4
Nevill Av NWMAL KT3.....202 C2
Neville Cl ACT W3.....142 D2
BFN/LL DA15.....195 F6
HSLW TW3.....159 F3
KIL/WHAMP NW6.....124 D1
PECK SE15.....169 F6
WAN E11.....112 B1
Neville Dr EFNCH N2.....85 G3
Neville Gdns BCTR RM8.....116 B1
Neville Gill Cl
WAND/EARL SW18.....185 G1
Neville Pl WDGN N22.....67 H4
Neville Rd BARK/HLT IG6.....74 C4
BCTR RM8.....116 B1
CROY/NA CR0.....228 D4
EA W5.....121 F3
FSTGT E7.....112 C5
HACK E8.....127 E1
KUT KT1.....202 A5
RCHPK/HAM TW10.....181 E5
Neville St SKENS SW7.....145 H5
Neville Ter SKENS * SW7.....145 H5
Neville Wk CAR SM5.....225 G6
Nevill Rd STNW/STAM N16.....109 E2
Nevill Wy LOU IG10.....57 G1
Nevin Dr CHING E4.....53 H4
Nevinson Cl WAND/EARL SW18.....185 H1
Nevis Rd TOOT SW17.....186 C4
New Acres Rd THMD SE28.....155 E2
Newark Ct WOT/HER KT12.....218 B6
Newark Crs WLSDN NW10.....122 D2
Newark Knok EHAM E6.....134 A5
Newark Rd SAND/SEL CR2.....246 D4
Newark Wy HDN NW4.....63 H1
New Ash Cl EFNCH N2.....65 H6
New Barn Cl CROY/NA CR0.....245 H4
New Barns Av MTCM CR4.....227 F1
New Barn St PLSTW E13.....133 C5
Newbiggin Pth OXHEY WD19.....42 A6
Newbold Cottages
WCHPL * E1.....130 A5
Newbolt Av CHEAM SM3.....242 A3
Newbolt Rd STAN HA7.....60 B2
New Bond St MYFR/PKLN W1K.....11 H4
Newborough Gn NWMAL KT3.....222 D2
New Brent St HDN NW4.....84 A2
New Bridge St EMB EC4A.....14 C4
New Broad St LVPST EC2M.....15 H1
New Broadway EA W5.....121 F6
Newburgh Rd ACT W3.....142 C1
Newburgh St SOHO/CST W1F.....12 A4
New Burlington Ms
CONDST W1S.....12 A5
New Burlington Pl CONDST W1S.....12 A5
New Burlington St CONDST W1S.....12 A5
Newburn St LBTH SE11.....29 H3
Newbury Cl NTHLT UB5.....98 D4
Newbury Gdns
HOR/WEW KT19.....241 F2
Newbury Ms KTTN NW5.....106 C4
Newbury Rd CHING E4.....71 G2
CNTH/NBYPK IG2.....94 D2
HAYES BR2.....212 D6
Newbury St STBT EC1A.....14 E2
Newbury Wy NTHLT UB5.....98 D4
New Butt La DEPT SE8.....171 E1
Newby Cl EN EN1.....24 A4
Newby Pl POP/IOD E14.....131 G6
Newby St VX/NE SW8.....166 D4
Newcastle Av BARK/HLT IG6.....75 G2
Newcastle Cl STP EC4M.....14 C3

Newcastle Pl *BAY/PAD* W2 125	H4	Newnham Gdns *NTHLT* UB5 99	G4
Newcastle Rw *CLKNW* EC1R 6	B6	Newnham Gn *WDGN* * N22 68	A4
New Cavendish St *MHST* W1U 11	F2	Newnham Rd *WDGN* N22 67	H4
New Change *STP* EC4M 15	E4	Newnhams Cl *BMLY* BR1 213	H6
New Charles St *FSBYE* EC1V 6	D5	New Plaistow Rd *SRTFD* E15 142	A6
New Church Rd *CMBW* SE5 168	C1	Newport Av *POP/IOD* E14 131	H6
New City Rd *PLSTW* E13 133	E2	Newport Ct *SOHO/SHAV* W1D 12	D5
New Cl *FELT* TW13 198	C1	Newport Md *OXHEY* * WD19 42	B6
WIM/MER SW19 205	G6	Newport Ct *SOHO/SHAV* * W1D 12	D5
New College Ms *IS* * N1 108	A5	Newport Rd *BARN* SW13 163	G2
New College Pde *HAMP* * NW3 105	G4	*HTHAIR* TW6 145	D4
Newcombe Pk *ALP/SUD* HA0 101	H6	*WALTH* * E17 90	C1
MLHL NW7 45	E1	*WAN* E11 91	H6
Newcombe St *KENS* * W8 145	E1	Newports *SWLY* BR8 237	H4
Newcome Gdns		Newport St *LBTH* SE11 29	G4
STRHM/NOR SW16 187	G6	Newquay Crs *RYLN/HDSTN* HA2 78	C6
Newcomen Rd *BTSEA* SW11 165	H4	Newquay Rd *CAT* SE6 191	F4
WAN * E11 112	D1	New Quebec St *MBLAR* W1H 10	D4
Newcomen St *STHWK* SE1 23	E3	New River Crs *PLMGR* N13 52	B6
New Compton St		New River Wy *FSBYPK* N4 68	D4
LSQ/SEVD * WC2H 12	D4	New Rd *ABYW* SE2 156	B4
New Ct *NTHLT* UB5 99	F3	*ALP/SUD* HA0 100	B2
TPL/STR * WC2R 14	A5	*BTFD* * TW8 146	E1
Newcourt St *STJWD* NW8 2	B4	*CEND/HSY/T* N8 67	F2
New Covent Garden Market		*CHING* E4 55	F6
VX/NE SW8 28	D5	*DAGW* RM9 117	G6
New Crane Pl *WAP* * E1W 150	A1	*E/WMO/HCT* KT8 199	E6
New Crescent Yd		*ED* N9 53	G5
WLSDN * NW10 123	F1	*FELT* TW13 198	C1
Newdales Ct *ED* N9 53	G4	*GDMY/SEVK* IG3 95	E6
Newdene Av *NTHLT* UB5 118	B1	*HSLW* TW3 159	F5
Newdigate		*KUTN/CMB* KT2 175	G4
STRHM/NOR * SW16 188	A6	*MLHL* NW7 64	C3
New End *HAMP/POD* E14 130	D6	*MTCM* CR4 226	C5
New End *HAMP* NW3 105	H1	*ORP* BR6 235	G4
New End Sq *HAMP* NW3 105	H2	*RCHPK/HAM* TW10 181	E6
Newent Cl *CAR* SM5 226	B5	*WCHPL* E1 17	G2
PECK SE15 169	E1	*WDGN* N22 68	C4
New Era Est *IS* N1 109	E6	*WELL* DA16 175	H5
New Farm Av *HAYES* BR2 232	C1	New Road Hl *HAYES* BR2 251	G6
New Ferry Ap		New Rw *CHCR* WC2N 13	E5
WOOL/PLUM SE18 154	A3	Newry Rd *TWK* TW1 160	C5
New Fetter La		Newsam Av *SEVS/STOTM* N15 88	D2
FLST/FETLN EC4A 14	B3	Newsholme Dr *WCHMH* N21 37	H6
Newfield Cl *HPTN* TW12 199	E4	New Spring Gardens Wk	
Newfield Ri *CRICK* NW2 63	H1	*LBTH* * SE11 29	F4
New Forest La *CHIG* IG7 74	A2	New Sq *LINN* WC2A 13	H3
Newgate Gdns *EDGW* HA8 61	H4	Newstead Av *ORP* BR6 217	E2
Newgate Cl *FELT* TW13 178	C4	Newstead Cl *NFNCN/WDSP* N12 66	A2
Newgate St *CHING* E4 56	A5	Newstead Rd *NTHLT* * UB5 118	C2
STBT EC1A 14	D3	Newstead Rd *LEE/GVPK* SE12 192	B2
New Globe Wk *STHWK* SE1 23	E1	Newstead Wk *MRDN* SM4 243	C6
New Goulston St *WCHPL* E1 16	C5	Newstead Wy *WIM/MER* SW19 184	B6
New Green Pl *NRWD* SE19 209	E2	New St *LVPST* EC2M 16	B2
Newhall Gdns *WOT/HER* KT12 218	A6	New Street Hl *BMLY* BR1 212	D1
Newham's Rw *STHWK* SE1 24	B4	New Street Sq *FLST/FETLN* EC4A 14	B3
Newham Wy *CAN/RD* E16 132	B4	Newton Av *ACT* W3 142	C2
Newhaven Gdns		*MUSWH* N10 66	C4
ELTH/MOT SE9 173	F5	Newton Cl *RYLN/HDSTN* HA2 79	E6
Newhaven La *PLSTW* E13 132	B4	*WALTH* E17 90	C3
Newhaven Rd *SNWD* SE25 228	D2	Newton Gv *CHSWK* W4 143	E3
New Heston Rd *HEST* TW5 158	D1	Newton Rd *ALP/SUD* HA0 101	H5
Newhouse Av *CHDH* RM6 76	B6	*CRICK* NW2 81	H1
Newhouse Cl *NWMAL* KT3 223	E4	*KTN/HRWW/W* HA3 61	H1
Newhouse Wk *MRDN* SM4 225	C4	*SEVS/STOTM* N15 89	F2
Newick Cl *BXLY* DA5 197	F1	*SKENS* SW7 145	F4
Newick Rd *CLPT* E5 109	H1	*WAN* E11 37	G3
Newing Gn *BMLY* BR1 213	F3	*WIM/MER* SW19 204	C5
Newington Barrow Wy		*WLSDN* NW10 99	G2
HOLWY N7 107	H1	Newton St *HOL/ALD* WC2B 13	F3
Newington Butts *LBTH* SE11 30	D2	Newton's Yd	
Newington Cswy *STHWK* SE1 23	E5	*WAND/EARL* SW18 165	E6
Newington Gn		Newton Ter *HAYES* BR2 233	F5
STNW/STAM N16 108	D3	Newton Wd *DAGW* HA8 62	B4
Newington Green Rd *IS* N1 108	D3	Newton Wy *UED* N18 68	C1
New Inn Broadway		New Tower Buildings	
SDTCH * EC2A 8	B5	*WAP* * E1W 25	H2
New Inn La *SDTCH* * EC2A 8	B5	Newtown St *BTSEA* * SW11 166	D2
New Inn St *SDTCH* * EC2A 8	B5	New Trinity Rd *EFNCH* N2 65	H6
New Inn Yd *SDTCH* EC2A 8	B5	New Union Cl *POP/IOD* E14 151	G3
New Kelvin Av *TEDD* TW11 200	A2	New Union St *BARB* EC2Y 15	G2
New Kent Rd *STHWK* SE1 31	E1	New Ws *TOTM* * N17 69	G4
New Kings Rd *FUL/PGN* SW6 166	D5	New Wanstead *WAN* E11 92	C3
FUL/PGN SW6 165	F5	New Way Rd *CDALE/KGS* NW9 83	E1
New King St *DEPT* SE8 151	E6	New Wharf Rd *IS* N1 5	E1
Newland Cl *PIN* HA5 58	C2	Niagara Av *EA* W5 141	E4
Newland Dr *EN* EN1 39	H2	Niagara Cl *IS* N1 7	F1
Newland Gdns *HNWL* W7 140	C2	Nibthwaite Rd *HRW* HA1 80	A2
Newland Rd *EDGW/HSY/T* N8 67	G6	Nicholas Cl *GFD/PVL* UB6 119	F1
Newlands Av *THDIT* KT7 220	A5	Nicholas Gdns *EA* W5 141	F1
Newlands Cl *ALP/SUD* HA0 101	G5	Nicholas La *MANHO* EC4N 15	H5
EDGW HA8 44	C5	Nicholas Ms *CHSWK* * W4 161	H1
NWDGN UB2 138	C5	Nicholas Pas *LOTH* * EC2R 15	G4
Newlands Ct *WBLY* HA9 82	A6	Nicholas Rd *BORE* WD6 25	H2
Newlands Pk *SYD* SE26 210	A2	*BUSH* WD23 43	F2
Newlands Pl *BAR* EN5 34	B6	*CROY/NA* CRO 229	F5
Newlands Quay *WAP* E1W 150	A1	*DAGW* RM8 74	A6
Newlands Rd		*WCHPL* E1 130	E3
STRHM/NOR SW16 207	G5	Nicholay Rd *ARCH* N19 67	F5
WFD IG8 52	B1	Nicholes Rd *HSLW* TW3 159	E5
The Newlands *WLGTN* SM6 245	E5	Nichol La *BMLY* BR1 212	C5
Newland St *CAN/RD* E16 153	G1	Nicholl St *BETH* E2 109	G6
Newlands Wy *CHSGTN* KT9 239	E3	Nichols Cl *FSBYPK* * N4 88	A5
Newland Wd *CROY/NA* CRO 248	D6	Nichols Gn *EA* W5 121	H6
Newlands Woods		Nicholson Rd *CROY/NA* CRO 229	F5
CROY/NA * CRO 248	D6	Nicholson St *STHWK* SE1 22	C1
Newling Cl *EHAM* E6 133	H5	Nickelby Cl *THMD* SE28 136	A5
Newling Est *BETH* E2 8	D3	Nicola Cl *KTN/HRWW/W* HA3 59	H5
New London St *MON* * EC3R 16	B5	*SAND/SEL* CR2 246	C4
New Lydenburg St *CHARL* SE7 153	E2	Nicolas Ms *BARK/HLT* IG6 74	B5
Newlyn Gdns *RYLN/HDSTN* HA2 78	D4	Nicoll Pl *HDN* NW4 64	A3
Newlyn Rd *BAR* EN5 34	C5	Nicoll Rd *WLSDN* NW10 103	E6
TOTM N17 69	F4	Nicolson Rd *STMC/STPC* BR5 258	A6
WELL DA16 175	F3	Nicosia Rd *WAND/EARL* SW18 186	A2
Newman Rd *BMLY* BR1 212	C4	Niederwald Rd *SYD* SE26 190	C6
CROY/NA CRO 225	H6		
PLSTW E13 132	D2	Nigel Cl *NTHLT* UB5 98	C6
WALTH E17 90	B2	Nigel Fisher Wy *CHSGTN* KT9 239	E5
Newman's Rw *LINN* WC2A 13	H2	Nigel Ms *IL* IG1 114	B2
Newman St *FITZ* W1T 12	B2	Nigel Playfair Av *HMSMTH* W6 118	E5
Newman's Wy *EBAR* EN4 35	G1	Nigel Rd *FSTGT* E7 113	E3
Newmarket Av *NTHLT* UB5 99	E3	*PECK* SE15 169	H3
New Mill Rd *STMC/STPC* BR5 216	B4	Nigeria Rd *CHARL* SE7 173	C1
New Mount St *SRTFD* * E15 111	H6	Nightingale Av *CHING* E4 72	A1
Newnham Av *RSLP* HA4 78	A5	Nightingale Cl *CAR* SM5 226	C6
Newnham Cl *LOU* IG10 57	F1	*CHING* E4 55	D6
NTHLT UB5 99	G4	*CHSWK* W4 142	C6
THHTH CR7 208	C5	*PIN* HA5 78	A2

Nightingale Cnr		Norfolk Rw *STHWK* SE1 29	G1
STMC/STPC BR5 218	C6	Norfolk Sq *BAY/PAD* W2 125	G5
Nightingale Dr *HOR/WEW* KT19 240	B4	Norfolk Square Ms	
Nightingale Gv *LEW* SE13 171	H6	*BAY/PAD* * W2 125	H5
Nightingale La *BAL* SW12 186	B2	Norfolk St *FSTGT* E7 112	E4
BMLY BR1 213	E5	Norgrove St *BAL* SW12 186	C3
CEND/HSY/T N8 67	G1	Norhyrst Av *SNWD* SE25 209	F6
RCHPK/HAM TW10 181	G2	Norland Pl *NTGHL* W11 144	C1
WAN E11 92	D2	Norland Rd *NTGHL* W11 144	C1
Nightingale Ms *KUT* * KT1 201	H6	Norlands Crs *CHST* BR7 214	B4
LBTH SE11 30	B1	Norlands Ga *CHST* * BR7 214	B4
Nightingale Pl *WBPTN* SW10 145	G6	Norley V *PUT/ROE* SW15 185	G5
WOOL/PLUM SE18 154	B4	Norlington Rd *LEY* E10 91	G5
Nightingale Rd *CAR* SM5 244	B1	Norman Av *FELT* TW13 178	C4
CLPT E5 74	A2	*STHL* UB1 118	C6
E/WMO/HCT KT8 219	F2	*TWK* TW1 160	D2
ED N9 54	A2	*WDGN* N22 68	C4
HNWL W7 140	B1	Normanby Cl *PUT/ROE* SW15 164	D6
HPTN TW12 199	F2	Normanby Rd *WLSDN* NW10 103	F3
STMC/STPC BR5 234	C3	Norman Cl *ORP* BR6 252	C1
WDGN N22 67	G4	*ROMW/RG* RM7 75	F2
WLSDN NW10 123	F1	Norman Crs *HEST* TW5 158	B1
WOT/HER * KT12 218	A4	*PIN* HA5 58	A4
Nightingale Sq *BAL* SW12 186	C2	Normand Gdns *WKENS* * W14 144	C6
Nightingale V		Normand Ms *WKENS* W14 144	D6
WOOL/PLUM SE18 154	B1	Normand Rd *WKENS* W14 144	D6
Nightingale Wk *BAL* SW12 186	D1	Normandy Av *BAR* EN5 34	D6
Nightingale Wy *EHAM* E6 133	C4	Normandy Cl *SYD* SE26 190	C5
Nile Cl *STNW/STAM* N16 109	F1	Normandy Dr *CROY/SEV* SW9 168	A2
Nile Dr *ED* N9 54	A4	Normandy Ter *CAN/RD* E16 132	D5
Nile Rd *PLSTW* E13 113	F1	Normandy Wy *BOW* E3 130	C1
Nile St *IS* N1 7	G3	Normanhurst Av *WELL* DA16 176	B2
Nile Ter *PECK* SE15 32	D4	Normanhurst Dr *TWK* TW1 160	D6
Nimrod Cl *NTHLT* UB5 118	B2	Normanhurst Rd	
Nimrod Pas *IS* N1 109	E4	*BRXS/STRHM* SW2 187	H4
Nimrod Rd *STRHM/NOR* SW16 186	D2	*STMC/STPC* BR5 215	H5
Nina Mackay Cl *SRTFD* * E15 112	A6	Norman Pde *SCUP* * DA14 196	C5
Nine Acres Cl *MNPK* E12 113	G3	Norman Rd *BELV* DA17 157	F2
Nine Elms La *VX/NE* SW8 28	C6	*EHAM* E6 133	K6
Nineteenth Rd *MTCM* CR4 227	C1	*GNWCH* SE10 151	E5
Ninhams Wd *ORP* BR6 251	E4	*IL* IG1 114	B3
Nithdale Rd *WOOL/PLUM* SE18 174	B1	*SEVS/STOTM* N15 89	F2
Niton Cl *BAR* EN5 32	B1	*SUT* SM1 243	E3
Niton Rd *RCH/KEW* TW9 162	A4	*THHTH* CR7 245	G3
Niton St *FUL/PGN* SW6 164	B1	*WIM/MER* SW19 205	G3
No 1 St *WOOL/PLUM* SE18 154	B3	Normans Cl *WDGN* * N22 68	C4
No 2 St *WOOL/PLUM* SE18 154	B3	*WLSDN* NW10 81	E4
Nobel Rd *UED* N18 54	A6	Normansfield Av	
Noble Cnr *HEST* * TW5 159	E2	*E/WMO/HCT* KT8 201	E3
Noble St *CITYW* EC2V 15	E3	Normansfield Cl *BUSH* WD23 43	F2
Noel Rd *ACT* W3 122	A5	Normanshire Dr *CHING* E4 55	E6
EHAM E6 133	G3	Normans Md *WLSDN* NW10 102	D4
IS N1 6	B1	Norman St *FSBYE* EC1V 7	E4
Noel St *SOHO/CST* * W1F 12	B4	
Nolton Pl *EDGW* HA8 60	B6	Normanton Pk *CHING* E4 56	A5
Nonsuch Cl *BARK/HLT* IG6 74	B2	Normanton Rd *SAND/SEL* CR2 247	H4
Nonsuch Pl *CHEAM* * SM3 242	B5	Normanton St *FSTH* SE23 190	B4
Norbiton Av *KUT* KT1 202	A5	Norman Wy *ACT* W3 122	B4
Norbiton Common Rd		*STHGT/OAK* N14 51	G4
NWMAL KT3 202	B6	
Norbreck Gdns *POP/IOD* E14 130	D5	Normington Cl	
Norbreck Pde *ACT* W3 125	H4	*STRHM/NOR* SW16 208	A1
Norbroke St *ACT* W3 110	C4	Norrice Lea *EFNCH* N2 65	H2
Norburn St *NKENS* * W10 126	C4	Norris St *STJS* SW1Y 12	C6
Norbury Av *MLHL* NW7 45	H5	Norroy Rd *PUT/ROE* SW15 164	B5
STRHM/NOR SW16 207	H4	Norrys Cl *EBAR* EN4 36	A4
Norbury Cl *STRHM/NOR* SW16 208	A4	Norrys Rd *EBAR* EN4 35	H4
Norbury Crs		Norseman Cl *GDMY/SEVK* IG3 95	H5
STRHM/NOR SW16 208	A5	Norseman Wy *GFD/PVL* UB6 96	B6
Norbury Cross		Norstead Pl *PUT/ROE* SW15 183	G4
STRHM/NOR SW16 207	H6	North Access Rd *WALTH* E17 89	E1
Norbury Gdns *CHDH* RM6 96	B2	North Acre *CDALE/KGS* NW9 45	G5
Norbury Gv *MLHL* NW7 47	E5	North Acton Rd *WLSDN* NW10 122	D1
Norbury Hl *STRHM/NOR* SW16 208	A3	Northall Rd *BXLYHN* DA7 177	C3
Norbury Ri *STRHM/NOR* SW16 207	G6	Northampton Gv *IS* N1 108	C4
Norbury Rd *CHING* E4 71	E1	Northampton Pk *IS* N1 108	C4
THHTH CR7 208	C5	Northampton Rd	
Norbury Vis *KUT* * KT1 201	H5	*CROY/NA* CRO 229	G6
Norcombe Gdns		*PEND* EN3 25	G5
KTN/HRWW/W HA3 81	G3	Northampton Rw *CLKNW* * EC1R 6	B5
Norcott Cl *YEAD* UB4 118	A3	Northampton Sq *FSBYE* EC1V 6	C4
Norcott Rd *STNW/STAM* N16 88	D2	Northampton St *IS* * N1 108	D5
Norcroft Gdns *EDUL* SE22 189	G2	
Norcutt Rd *WHTN* TW2 180	A3	Northanger Rd	
Nordenfeldt Rd *ERITH* DA8 157	H5	*STRHM/NOR* SW16 207	G2
Norfield Rd *BDART* DA2 197	G6	North Audley St *MYFR/PKLN* W1K 11	E4
Norfolk Av *PLMGR* N13 68	A1	North Av *CAR* SM5 244	C5
SEVS/STOTM N15 89	F3	*RCH/KEW* TW9 162	A2
Norfolk Cl *EBAR* EN4 36	C3	*RYLN/HDSTN* HA2 79	F3
PLMGR N13 68	A1	*STHL* UB1 118	D6
TWK * TW1 180	D1	*UED* N18 50	D5
Norfolk Crs *BAY/PAD* W2 10	A3	*WEA* W13 120	D5
BFN/LL DA15 195	E2	North Bank *STJWD* NW8 2	A4
Norfolk Gdns *BXLYHN* DA7 176	D2	Northbank Rd *WALTH* E17 51	G6
Norfolk House Rd		North Birkbeck Rd *WAN* E11 111	H1
STRHM/NOR SW16 187	F5	Northborough Rd	
Norfolk Ms *NKENS* W10 126	C4	*STRHM/NOR* SW16 207	G4
Norfolk Pl *BAY/PAD* * W2 125	H5	Northbourne *HAYES* BR2 252	C4
WELL DA16 176	B1	Northbourne Rd *CLAP* SW4 167	E5
Norfolk Rd *BAR* EN5 35	E4	Northbrook Rd *BAR* EN5 48	C1
BARK IG11 115	E5	*CROY/NA* CRO 228	D4
DAGE RM10 118	H6	*IL* IG1 94	A6
EHAM E6 113	H6	*LEW* SE13 171	H6
ESH/CLAY KT10 238	A3	*WDGN* N22 67	G2
STJWD NW8 3	E4	North Carriage Dr *BAY/PAD* W2 10	B5
GDMY/SEVK IG3 95	F2	Northchurch Rd *IS* N1 108	B3
HRW HA1 61	E4	*WBLY* HA9 80	A4
PEND EN3 39	H6	Northchurch Ter *IS* * N1 109	A5
STJWD NW8 3	F4	North Circular PLMGR N13 68	A1
WIM/MER SW19 206	A1	*WALTH* E17 71	E4
Norfolk Rw *BAR* EN5 35	E4	North Circular Rd *CHING* E4 70	C2
BARK IG11 115	E5	*GLDGN* NW11 64	B2
DAGE RM10 113	H6	*WLSDN* NW10 80	E5
EHAM E6 113	H6	North Colonnade *POP/IOD* E14 131	F1
ESH/CLAY KT10 238	A3	North Common Rd *EA* W5 121	G6
GDMY/SEVK IG3 95	F2	*UB8* 121	G6
HRW HA1 79	F2	Northcote Av *BRYLDS* KT5 222	A4
PEND EN3 39	H6	*EA* W5 121	G6
STJWD NW8 3	F4	*ISLW* TW7 160	C6
WIM/MER SW19 206	A1	
WLSDN NW10 103	E5	

STHL UB1 .....118 C6
Northcote Rd BTSEA SW11.....166 A5
CROY/NA CR0 .....228 D3
Northcott Av WDGN N22.....67 G4
North Countess Rd WALTH E17.....70 D3
North Cray Rd BXLY DA5.....197 E4
SCUP DA14.....216 C2
North Crs CAN/RD E16.....131 H3
FITZ W1T.....11 G2
FNCH N3.....64 D5
Northcroft Rd HOR/WEW KT19.....241 E5
WEA W13.....140 D2
North Cross Rd BARK/HLT IG6.....94 C1
EDUL SE22.....169 F6
Northdene CHIG IG7.....74 D1
North Dene HEST TW5.....159 F2
MLHL NW7.....46 D5
Northdene Gdns
SEVS/STOTM N15.....89 F3
Northdown Gdns
GNTH/NBYPK IG2.....95 F3
Northdown Rd WELL DA16.....175 H5
Northdown St IS N1.....5 G2
North Dr HSLW TW3.....159 G3
ORP BR6.....253 E2
STRHM/NOR SW16.....187 F6
North End BKHH IG9.....57 E2
CROY/NA CR0.....228 C5
GLDGN NW11.....85 G6
North End Av HAMP NW3.....85 G6
North End Crs WKENS W14.....144 D4
North End La ORP BR6.....252 B6
North End Rd FUL/PGN SW6.....165 E1
GLDGN NW11.....85 G5
WBLY HA9.....102 A1
North End Wy HAMP NW3.....85 G6
Northern Av ED N9.....53 F4
Northernhay Wk MRDN SM4.....224 C1
Northern Relief Rd BARK IG11.....114 C5
North Eyot Gdns
HMSMTH * W6.....143 F5
Northey St POP/IOD E14.....130 C6
North Farm LOU IG10.....57 E1
North Feltham Trading Est
Northfield Av PIN HA5.....78 B1
STMC/STPC BR5.....236 A3
WEA W13.....140 D2
Northfield Cl BMLY BR1.....213 G4
Northfield Crs CHEAM SM3.....242 C2
Northfield Pk HEST TW5.....138 B6
Northfield Rd DAGW RM9.....116 D2
EBAR EN4.....36 A4
EHAM E6.....113 H4
PEND * EN3.....25 E4
STNW/STAM N16.....89 E4
WEA W13.....140 D2
Northfields WAND/EARL SW18.....165 F5
Northfields Rd ACT W3.....122 C4
Northfleet Ms WIM/MER SW19.....205 H4
Northgate Dr CDALE/KGS NW9.....83 E5
North Gower St CAMTN NW1.....4
North Gv HGT N6.....86 C4
SEVS/STOTM N15.....89 F3
North Hi HGT N6.....86 B3
North Hill Av HGT N6.....86 A3
North Hyde La NWDGN UB2.....138 C5
North Hyde Whf
NWDGN * UB2.....136 A4
Northiam NFNCH/WDSP N12.....49 E6
Northiam St HACK E8.....109 H6
Northington St BMSBY WC1N.....13 C1
Northlands Av ORP BR6.....253 E2
Northlands St CMBW SE5.....168 C3
North La TEDD TW11.....200 B2
North Lodge Cl
PUT/ROE * SW15.....164 B6
North Ms BMSBY WC1N.....5 H6
North Mt TRDG/WHET * N20.....49 G4
Northolme EDGW HA8.....44
Northolme EDGW HA8.....62 A4
Northolme Ri ORP BR6.....235 E6
Northolme Rd HBRY N5.....108 B2
Northolt Gdns GFD/PVL UB6.....100 B3
North Park ELTH/MOT SE9.....99 F2
Northover BMLY BR1.....192 B5
North Pde CHSGTN KT9.....239 H3
EDGW * HA8.....62 A4
STHL * UB1.....115 E5
North Pk ELTH/MOT SE9.....193 H1
North Pas WAND/EARL SW18.....165 H6
North Pl TEDD TW11.....200 B2
WIM/MER SW19.....206 B1
North Pole La HAYES BR2.....250 C4
North Pole Rd SHB W12.....124 A5
Northport St IS N1.....108 D6
North Rd BAY/PAD * W2.....2 A7
North Rd BELV DA17.....157 F3
BMLY BR1.....212 D4
BTFD TW8.....141 G6
CHDH RM6.....96 C2
EA W5.....141 F3
ED N9.....53 E5
EDGW HA8.....62 B4
FNCH N2.....66 A4
GDMY/SEVK IG3.....92 A5
HEST TW5.....138 A6
HGT N6.....86 C4
HOLWY N7.....107 F4
ISLW TW7.....119 G6
SURB KT6.....221 F3
WIM/MER SW19.....205 G2
WOOL/PLUM SE18.....146 B4
WDR/YW UB7.....112 A1
North Rw MYFR/PKLN W1K.....11 H1
North Several
BKHTH/KID * SE3.....171 H5
Northside Rd BMLY BR1.....212 C4
North Side
Wandsworth Common
WAND/EARL SW18.....165 G6
North Sq ED N9.....53 H4
GLDGN NW11.....85 E5
Northstead Rd
BRXS/STRHM SW2.....188 A4
North St BARK IG11.....114 C5
BMLY BR1.....212 C4

BXLYHN DA7.....177 E5
CAR SM5.....244 B2
HDN NW4.....84 A2
ISLW TW7.....160 C4
PLSTW E13.....132 D1
ROMW/RG RM7.....97 H1
VX/NE SW8.....166 D4
North Tenter St WCHPL E1.....16 D4
North Ter CHEL SW3.....26 A1
Northumberland Aly
TWRH * EC3N.....16 B4
Northumberland Av
CHCR WC2N.....21 E1
EN EN1.....39 H1
ISLW TW7.....160 B2
MNPK E12.....93 E5
WELL DA16.....175 E5
Northumberland Cl
ERITH DA8.....177 G1
Northumberland Gdns
BMLY BR1.....234 A1
ED N9.....53 F5
MTCM CR4.....227 G2
Northumberland Gv
TOTM N17.....69 H3
Northumberland Pk
ERITH DA8.....177 G1
TOTM N17.....69 G3
Northumberland Pl
BAY/PAD W2.....125 G5
Northumberland Rd BAR EN5.....49 G1
EHAM E6.....133 G5
RYLN/HDSTN HA2.....78 D2
WALTH E17.....91 E4
Northumberland Wy
BXLYHN DA7.....177 G2
Northumbria St POP/IOD E14.....131 E5
North Verbena Gdns
HMSMTH * W6.....143 G5
North Vw EA W5.....121 E3
PIN HA5.....76
WIM/MER SW19.....203 H1
Northview Crs WLSDN NW10.....105 F2
Northview Dr WFD IG8.....73 F5
Northview Pde HOLWY * N7.....107 C1
North View Rd CEND/HSY/T N8.....67
North Vis CAMTN NW1.....107 F4
North Wy CDALE/KGS NW9.....62 B6
ED N9.....54 A4
FBAR/BDGN N11.....67 C2
PIN HA5.....58 A6
Northway GLDGN NW11.....85 F2
RYNPK SW20.....204 C6
WLCTN SM6.....245 E2
Northway Crs MLHL NW7.....47 E6
Northway Rd CMBW SE5.....168 C4
CROY/NA CR0.....229 F3
Northways Pde
KIL/WHAMP * NW6.....105 H5
North Weald La
KUTN/CMB KT2.....201 E1
North Western Av
(Watford By-Pass)
STAN HA7.....44 C1
North Wharf Rd BAY/PAD * W2.....125 H4
Northwick Av KTN/HRWW/WS HA3.....80 C3
Northwick Cir
KTN/HRWW/WS HA3.....81 E3
Northwick Cl STJWD NW8.....125 H3
Northwick Park Rd HRW HA1.....80 D3
Northwick Rd ALP/SUD HA0.....101 F6
OXHEY WD19.....42 A6
Northwick Ter STJWD * NW8.....125 H3
Northwold Dr PIN HA5.....58 A6
Northwold Rd STNW/STAM N16.....89 H1
Northwood Gdns CLAY IG5.....94 A1
GFD/PVL UB6.....100 B3
NFNCH/WDSP N12.....65 H1
Northwood Pl ERITH DA18.....156 D5
Northwood Rd CAR SM5.....244 C4
FSTH SE23.....190 D3
HGT N6.....86 D4
THHTH CR7.....208 C5
North Woolwich Rd
CAN/RD E16.....152 D1
North Worple Wy
MORT/ESHN SW14.....162 D4
Norton Av BRYLDS KT5.....222 B4
Norton Cl CHING E4.....71 C1
Norton Folgate WCHPL E1.....14 A2

Norton Rd ALP/SUD HA0.....101 F4
DAGE RM10.....117 H4
LEY E10.....90 D5
Norval Gn BRXN/ST * SW9.....168 A3
Norval Rd ALP/SUD HA0.....80 D6
Norway Ga BERM/RHTH SE16.....150 C3
Norway St GNWCH SE10.....151 H6
Norwich Pl BXLYHN DA6.....177 F3
Norwich Rd FSTGT E7.....112 C3
GFD/PVL UB6.....99 F6
THHTH CR7.....208 C6
Norwood Av ALP/SUD HA0.....101 F3
ROMW/RG RM7.....97 H4
Norwood Cl NWDGN UB2.....136 C4
WHTN TW2.....179 H4
Norwood Dr RYLN/HDSTN HA2.....78 D3
Norwood Gdns NWDGN UB2.....136 C4
YEAD UB4.....118 A3
Norwood Green Rd
NWDGN UB2.....136 D4
Norwood Park Rd
WNWD SE27.....207 C1
Norwood Rd HNHL SE24.....188 B3
NWDGN UB2.....136 C4
Notley St CMBW SE5.....168 D1
Notson Rd SNWD SE25.....209 H3
Notting Barn Rd NKENS W10.....124 B3
Nottingham Av CAN/RD E16.....133 E4
Nottingham Ct
LSO/SEVD * WC2H.....13 E4
Nottingham Pl MHST W1U.....3 E6
Nottingham Rd ISLW TW7.....160 B3
LEY E10.....91 G2
SAND/SEL CR2.....246 C3
TOOT SW17.....186 B3

Nottingham St MHST W1U.....11 E1
Nottingham Ter CAMTN NW1.....3 E6
Notting Hill Ga NTGHL W11.....145 E1
Nova Ms MRDN SM4.....224 C4
Novar Cl ORP BR6.....235 F4
Novar Rd ELTH/MOT SE9.....194 C5
Novello St FUL/PGN SW6.....165 G3
Nowell Rd BARN SW13.....145 G6
Nower Hi PIN HA5.....78 D1
Noyna Rd TOOT SW17.....186 B5
Nuding Cl LEW SE13.....171 G4
Nugent Rd ARCH N19.....87 G5
SNWD SE25.....209 F6
Nugents Ct PIN * HA5.....58 C4
Nugents Pk PIN HA5.....58 C4
Nugent Ter STJWD NW8.....125 C1
Nuneaton Rd DAGW RM9.....116 B5
Nunhead Gv PECK SE15.....169 H4
Nunhead La PECK SE15.....169 H4
Nunnington Cl ELTH/MOT SE9.....193 C5
Nunn's Rd ENC/FH EN2.....38 C3
Nupton Dr BAR EN5.....48 A1
Nurse Cl EDGW HA8.....62 C4
Nursery Av BXLYHN DA7.....176 D4
CROY/NA CR0.....230 B6
FNCH N3.....65 F5
Nursery Cl BROCKY SE4.....170 C3
CHDH RM6.....96
CROY/NA CR0.....230 B6
ORP BR6.....235 F4
PEND EN3.....40 B2
SWLY BR8.....229 G2
WFD IG8.....72 D1
Nursery Gdns CHEAM SM3.....225 E5
CHST BR7.....214 B2
HSLWW TW4.....158 D6
PEND EN3.....40 B2
Nursery La BETH E2.....109 F6
FSTGT E7.....112 C4
NKENS W10.....124 A4
Nurserymans Rd
FBAR/BDGN N11.....50 C4
Nursery Rd BRXN/ST SW9.....167 H5
EFNCH N2.....47 H5
HACK E8.....110 A4
MTCM CR4.....226 A1
PIN HA5.....58 A6
STHGT/OAK N14.....51 E2
SUT SM1.....243 G2
THHTH CR7.....228 D1
WIM/MER SW19.....204 C3
WIM/MER SW19.....205 F5
Nursery Rw BAR * EN5.....34 C4
WALW SE17.....19 E1
Nursery St TOTM N17.....69 F3
Nursery Wk HDN NW4.....63 H6
Nurstead Rd ERITH DA8.....177 E1
Nutbourne St NKENS W10.....124 C2
Nutbrook St PECK SE15.....169 H4
Nutbrowne Rd DAGW RM9.....116 D6
Nutcroft Rd PECK SE15.....169 H4
Nutfield Cl CAR SM5.....244 A1
UED N18.....49 H1
Nutfield Gdns GDMY/SEVK IG3.....95 F6
NTHLT UB5.....118 A1
Nutfield Rd CRICK NW2.....63 H6
EDUL SE22.....169 F6
SRTFD E15.....111 G2
THHTH CR7.....228 B1
Nutfield Wy ORP BR6.....234 A6
Nutford Pl BAY/PAD W2.....9 G2
Nuthatch Gdns THMD SE28.....154 D2
Nuthurst Av BRXS/STRHM SW2.....187 H4
Nutley Ter HAMP NW3.....105 H5
Nutmead Cl BXLY DA5.....197 G5
Nutmeg Cl CAN/RD E16.....132 A3
Nutmeg La POP/IOD E14.....131 H5
Nuttall St IS N1.....7 H5
Nutter La WAN E11.....93 E2
Nutt Gv EDGW HA8.....45 F4
Nutt St PECK SE15.....169 F1
Nutwell St TOOT SW17.....206 A1
Nuxley Rd BELV DA17.....156 D4
Nyanza St WOOL/PLUM SE18.....154 D6
Nylands Av RCH/KEW TW9.....162 A3
Nymans Gdns RYNPK SW20.....203 H6
Nynehead St NWCR SE14.....151 G2
Nyon Gv FSTH SE23.....190 D4
Nyssa Cl WFD IG8.....73 H2

O

Oak Av CEND/HSY/T N8.....87 G1
CROY/NA CR0.....231 E6
ENC/FH EN2.....37 H2
HEST TW5.....158 B1
HPTN TW12.....172 B5
MUSWH N10.....66 D3
TOTM N17.....49 H6
Oakbank Av WOT/HER KT12.....218 D4
Oakbank Gv HNHL SE24.....168 C5
Oakbrook Cl BMLY BR1.....192 D6
Oakbury Rd FUL/PGN SW6.....165 F3
Oak Cl STHGT/OAK N14.....50 D2
Oakcombe Cl NWMAL KT3.....
Oak Cottage Cl CAT SE6.....192 A3
Oak Cottages HNWL * W7.....140 A2
Oak Crs CAN/RD E16.....132 A4
Oakcroft Rd BKHTH/KID SE3.....171 G6
CHSGTN KT9.....239 H2
Oakcroft Vls CHSGTN KT9.....239 H2
Oakdale STHGT/OAK N14.....50 D3
Oakdale Av KTN/HRWW/WS HA3.....62 D6
Oakdale Cl OXHEY WD19.....42 A6
Oakdale Gdns CHING E4.....71 G1
Oakdale Rd FSBYPK N4.....88 C3
FSTGT E7.....112 D5
HOR/WEW KT19.....240 D6
OXHEY WD19.....42 A6
PECK SE15.....170 A4
STRHM/NOR SW16.....207 G1
WAN E11.....91 H6
Oakdene Av CHST BR7.....214 A1
ERITH DA8.....157 G6

THDIT KT7.....220 C5
Oakdene Cl PIN HA5.....58 D3
Oakdene Dr BRYLDS KT5.....222 D5
Oakdene Ms CHEAM SM3.....224 D5
Oakdene Pk FNCH N3.....64 D5
Oakdene Rd STMC/STPC BR5.....235 G3
Oaken Dr ESH/CLAY KT10.....258 B1
Oaken La ESH/CLAY KT10.....258 A2
Oakenshaw Cl SURB KT6.....221 G4
Oakeshott Av HGT N6.....86 A5
Oakey La STHWK SE1.....22 A5
Oakfield CHING E4.....71 F1
Oakfield Av KTN/HRWW/W HA3.....60 D6
Oakfield Cl NWMAL KT3.....223 F2
Oakfield Gdns BECK BR3.....211 E5
CAR SM5.....226 A5
GFD/PVL UB6.....119 H5
UED N18.....53 E6
Oakfield La HAYES BR2.....251 E2
EHAM E6.....113 G6
FNCH N3.....65 F4
FSBYPK N4.....88 A3
IL IG1.....114 B1
PGE/AN SE20.....209 H4
STHGT/OAK N14.....51 G4
WALTH E17.....70 C5
WIM/MER SW19.....184 B5
Oakfields Rd GLDGN NW11.....64 C5
Oakfield St WBPTN SW10.....145 G6
Oakford Rd KTTN NW5.....107 G2
Oak Gdns CROY/NA CR0.....231 E6
EDGW HA8.....62 C5
Oak Gv CRICK NW2.....104 B2
WWKM BR4.....231 G6
Oak Grove Rd PGE/AN SE20.....210 A4
Oak Hall Rd WAN E11.....92 D3
Oakham Cl CAT * SE6.....190 D4
Oakham Dr HAYES BR2.....232 C1
Oakhampton Rd MLHL NW7.....64 B4
Oakhill ESH/CLAY KT10.....258 C4
Oak Hi SURB KT6.....221 G5
WFD IG8.....71 H3
Oakhill Av HAMP NW3.....105 F2
PIN HA5.....58 D5
Oak Hill Crs SURB KT6.....221 G5
Oak Hill Gdns WALTH E17.....72 A4
Oak Hill Gv SURB KT6.....221 G5
Oak Hill Pk HAMP NW3.....105 F1
Oak Hill Park Ms HAMP NW3.....105 G2
Oak Hill Rd SURB * KT6.....165 E6
Oakhill Rd BECK BR3.....211 G5
ORP BR6.....235 F6
PUT/ROE SW15.....164 D6
SUT SM1.....243 F1
Oak Hill Wy HAMP NW3.....105 F2
Oakhouse Rd BXLYHN DA6.....177 G6
Oakhurst Av BXLYHN DA7.....176 C1
EBAR EN4.....50 A2
Oakhurst Cl BARK/HLT IG6.....73 H1
CHST BR7.....213 H4
TEDD TW11.....173
WALTH E17.....92 A1
Oakhurst Gv EDUL SE22.....169 G5
Oakhurst Rd HOR/WEW KT19.....240 C4
Oakington Av RYLN/HDSTN HA2.....59 F4
WBLY HA9.....80 D5
Oakington Dr SUN TW16.....198 A3
Oakington Manor Dr
WBLY HA9.....80 C4
Oakington Rd MV/WKIL * W9.....125 D3
Oakington Wy CEND/HSY/T N8.....67 E4
Oakland Pl BKHH IG9.....57 E3
Oakland Rd SRTFD E15.....112 A2
Oaklands PLMGR N13.....51 H4
Oaklands Av BFN/LL DA15.....175 F3
ED N9.....37 H1
ESH/CLAY KT10.....219 H5
ISLW TW7.....140 B6
THHTH CR7.....224 B1
WWKM BR4.....249 F1
Oaklands Cl ALP/SUD HA0.....101 F3
BXLYHS DA6.....176 D6
CHSGTN KT9.....238
STMC/STPC BR5.....235 E3
Oaklands Dr WHTN TW2.....143 G1
Oaklands Ms CRICK NW2.....104 B1
Oaklands Pk WICK IG6.....94 B2
Oaklands Pl CLAP SW4.....167 J3
Oaklands Rd BMLY BR1.....212 A3
BXLYHS DA6.....176 D5
CRICK NW2.....104 B2
HNWL W7.....136 B1
MORT/ESHN SW14.....162 A1
TRDG/WHET N20.....48 D2
Oaklands Wy WLGTN SM6.....245 E6
Oaklands Wy HOR/WEW KT19.....240 C6
Oak La EFNCH N2.....47 H5
FBAR/BDGN N11.....66 C1
ISLW TW7.....160 A5
POP/IOD E14.....130 C3
TWK TW1.....160 C2
WFD IG8.....58 B6
Oakleafe Gdns BARK/HLT IG6.....74 A3
Oakleigh Av EDGW HA8.....62 B5
SURB KT6.....222 A1
TRDG/WHET N20.....49 H3
Oakleigh Cl TRDG/WHET N20.....49 H3
Oakleigh Crs TRDG/WHET N20.....50 A3
Oakleigh Gdns EDGW HA8.....62 A1
ORP BR6.....253 H1
TRDG/WHET N20.....49 G3
Oakleigh Ms TRDG/WHET * N20.....49 G3
Oakleigh Pk Av CHST BR7.....214 A4
Oakleigh Pk North
TRDG/WHET N20.....49 H3
Oakleigh Pk South
TRDG/WHET N20.....49 H3
Oakleigh Rd PIN HA5.....58 D2
Oakleigh Rd North
TRDG/WHET N20.....49 H4
Oakleigh Rd South
FBAR/BDGN N11.....50 C6

Oakleigh Wy MTCM CR4..........206 D4
SURB KT6..........................222 A5
Oakley Av ACT W3..................122 A6
BARK IG11..........................115 F4
CHIG IG7...........................245 G2
Oakley CI CHING E4..................55 C5
HNWL W7...........................120 A6
ISLW TW7..........................159 H2
Oakley Crs FSBYE * EC1V............16 D2
Oakley Dr BFN/LL DA15............194 D4
HAYES BR2.........................251 C1
LEW SE13..........................191 H1
Oakley Gdns CEND/HSY/T N8........87 H2
CHEL SW3...........................26 B5
Oakley Pk BFN/LL DA15............196 A2
Oakley PI STHWK SE1................32 C4
Oakley Rd HAYES BR2...............251 C1
HRW HA1............................80 A3
IS N1..............................108 D5
SNWD SE25.........................229 H2
Oakley Sq CAMTN NW1.................4 B1
Oakley St CHEL SW5.................26 A5
Oakley Yd BETH * E2.................8 D5
Oak Lodge Av CHIG IG7..............74 D1
Oak Lodge CI STAN HA7..............31 E1
Oak Lodge Dr WWKM BR4.............231 F1
Oakmead Av HAYES BR2.............232 C3
Oakmeade PIN HA5...................59 E2
Oakmead Gdns EDGW HA8..............46 D6
Oakmead PI MTCM CR4..............206 A4
Oakmead Rd BAL SW12...............186 D5
HAYES BR2.........................227 F3
Oakmere Rd ABYW SE2...............155 G6
Oakmoor Wy CHIG IG7................75 E1
Oakmore Gdns
STMC/STPC BR5....................236 A1
Oak Park Gdns
WIM/MER SW19.....................184 B3
Oakridge Dr EFNCH N2...............65 H6
Oakridge Rd BMLY BR1..............192 A6
Oak Ri BKHH IG9....................57 F5
Oak Rd EA W5......................121 F6
ERITH DA8.........................177 G1
NWMAL KT3.........................202 D5
ORP BR6...........................253 C5
Oak Rw MTCM CR4..................207 E5
Oaks Av CRW RM5....................77 C5
FELT TW15.........................178 C4
NRWD SE19.........................209 E1
WPK KT4...........................241 H2
Oaksford Av SYD SE26..............189 H5
Oaks Gv CHING E4...................56 A4
Oakshade Rd BMLY BR1..............191 H6
Oakshaw Rd
WAND/EARL SW18...................185 F2
Oaks La CROY/NA CRO...............248 A1
CNTH/NBYPK IG2.....................95 E1
Oaks Rd CROY/NA CRO..............247 H3
The Oaks FELT * TW15..............178 C4
HAYES * BR2.......................251 A6
MRDN * SM4........................224 C1
NFNCH/WDSP N12.....................49 F6
OXHEY WD19.........................42 A3
SURB KT6..........................239 E1
WFD IG8...........................72 A3
WOOL/PLUM SE18...................154 C5
Oak St ROMW/RG RM7.................97 G2
Oaks Wy CAR SM5...................244 B5
SURB KT6..........................191 E6
Oakthorpe Rd PLMGR N13.............68 A1
Oaktree Av PLMGR N13...............52 A5
Oak Tree CI STAN HA7...............31 E3
WEA * W13.........................121 E5
Oak Tree Ct BORE * WD6.............45 F1
Oak Tree Dell CDALE/KGS NW9........51 F2
Oak Tree Dr TRDG/WHET N20..........49 F3
Oak Tree Gdns BMLY BR1............184 C5
Oaktree Gv IL IG1.................114 D3
Oakview Gdns EFNCH N2...............85 H1
Oakview Gv CROY/NA CRO...........246 D5
Oakview Rd CAT SE6................211 F1
Oak Village HAMP NW3..............106 C2
Oak VIs GLDGN * NW11...............84 D3
Oak Wy ACT W3.....................143 E1
CROY/NA CRO......................230 B5
STHGT/OAK N14.....................50 C2
Oakway HAYES BR2..................211 H5
RYNPK SW20........................224 A1
Oakway CI BXLY DA5................196 C1
Oakways ELTH/MOT SE9..............194 D1
Oakwood WLGTN SM6.................244 D6
Oakwood Av BECK BR3...............211 G5
HAYES BR2.........................212 A6
HOR/WEW KT19.....................240 A6
MTCM CR4..........................194 C1
STHGT/OAK N14......................51 F2
THDT UB1..........................119 E6
Oakwood CI CHST BR7...............213 H2
STHGT/OAK N14......................51 E1
WFD IG8............................53 H2
Oakwood Ct WKENS W14.............144 D3
Oakwood Crs GFD/PVL UB6..........100 C4
WCHMH N21.........................17 G4
Oakwood Dr BXLYHN DA7............177 G5
EDGW HA8..........................46 C2
NRWD SE19.........................188 D5
Oakwood Gdns GDMY/SEVK IG3........95 F6
ORP BR6...........................234 C6
SUT SM1...........................225 E6
Oakwood La WKENS W14.............144 D3
Oakwood Pde EBAR * EN4.............37 E6
Oakwood Park Cottages
STHGT/OAK * N14....................51 H1
Oakwood Park Rd
STHGT/OAK N14......................51 G1
Oakwood PI CROY/NA CRO...........228 A3
Oakwood Rd CROY/NA CRO...........228 A3
GLDGN NW11.........................64 D2
ORP BR6...........................236 C6
RYNPK SW20........................203 G4
Oakworth Rd NKENS W10.............99 H4
Oarsman PI E/WMO/HCT KT8.........220 A1
Oast House Wy
STMC/STPC BR5....................235 H1
Oates CI HAYES BR2................211 H6
Oatfield Rd ORP BR6...............73 F5
Oatfield Rd ORP BR6...............73 F5
Oatland Ri WALTH E17...............70 C3
Oatlands Rd PEND EN3...............40 A2
Oat La CITYW EC2V.................15 E3
Oban CI PLSTW E13................133 B4

Oban Rd PLSTW E13.................133 E2
SNWD SE25.........................228 D1
Oban St POP/IOD E14...............131 H5
Oberstein Rd BTSEA SW11...........165 H5
Oborne CI HNHL SE24..............168 B6
Observatory Gdns KENS W8.........145 E2
Observatory Rd
MORT/ESHN SW14...................162 C5
Occupation La EA W5...............141 F4
WOOL/PLUM SE18...................159 A6
Occupation La RI WALW SE17.........31 E3
WEA W13...........................140 D2
Ocean Est WCHPL E1...............130 B3
Ocean St WCHPL E1................130 B4
Ockendon Ms IS N1................108 D4
Ockendon Rd IS N1................108 D4
Ockham Dr STMC/STPC BR5..........215 G5
Ockley Rd CROY/NA CRO............227 H4
STRHM/NOR SW16...................187 G5
Octagon Ar LVPST * EC2M...........16 A2
Octavia CI MTCM CR4..............226 A2
Octavia Ms CRICK * NW2...........103 E4
Octavia Rd ISLW TW7..............160 B4
Octavia St BTSEA SW11............166 A2
Octavius St DEPT SE8.............171 E1
October PI HDN * NW4..............64 B6
Odard Rd E/WMO/HCT KT8...........219 E1
Odeon Pde ELTH/MOT * SE9.........173 C5
GFD/PVL * UB6....................100 D4
HOLWY * N7.......................107 G1
ISLW * TW7.......................160 A1
Odessa Rd FSTGT E7...............112 B2
WLSDN NW10.......................123 C1
Odessa St BERM/RHTH SE16.........150 D3
Odger St BTSEA SW11..............166 B3
Odhams Wk LSO/SEVD WC2H...........13 E4
Odsey VIs FSBYPK * N4.............88 A3
Offa's Md HOM E9.................110 C2
Offenham Rd ELTH/MOT SE9.........193 H6
Offerton Rd CLAP SW4.............167 E4
Offham Slope
NFNCH/WDSP N12....................64 D1
Offley Rd BRXN/ST SW9............168 A1
Offord CI TOTM N17................50 D3
Offord Rd IS N1..................108 A5
Offord St IS N1..................107 H5
Ogilby St WOOL/PLUM SE18.........153 H4
Oglander Rd PECK SE15............169 F5
Ogle St GTPST W1W.................12 A1
Oglethorpe Rd DAGE RM10..........116 D1
Ohio Rd PLSTW E13................132 D3
Oil Mill La HMSMTH W6............118 A5
Okeburn Rd TOOT SW17.............206 C1
Okehampton Crs WELL DA16.........175 H2
Okehampton Rd WLSDN NW10.........104 A6
Olaf St NTGHL W11................128 B6
Old Bailey STP EC4M................14 D4
Old Barn CI BELMT SM2............242 C5
Old Barn Wy BXLYHN DA7...........177 H5
Old Barrack Yd KTBR SW1X..........33 G5
Oldberry Rd EDGW HA8..............62 D2
Old Bethnal Green Rd BETH E2.......9 F1
Old Bexley La BXLY DA5...........197 H4
Old Bond St CONDST W1S............14 A5
Oldborough Rd ALP/SUD HA0.........81 E6
Old Bridge CI NTHLT UB5..........119 E1
Old Bridge St KUT/T KT1...........90 A6
Old Broad St LVPST EC2M............16 A3
Old Bromley Rd BMLY BR1..........211 H1
Old Brompton Rd ECT SW5..........145 E6
Old Buildings LINN WC2A............14 A3
Old Burlington St CONDST W1S......12 A5
Oldbury CI STMC/STPC BR5.........236 B1
Oldbury PI MHST W1U...............11 F1
Oldbury Rd EN EN1.................39 G3
Old Castle St WCHPL E1............16 C3
Old Cavendish St
CAVSO/HST W1G.....................11 G3
Old Chapel Rd SWLY BR8...........227 C4
Old Church La CDALE/KGS NW9.......82 C6
GFD/PVL UB6......................120 C2
STAN HA7..........................60 D2
Old Church Rd CHING E4.............55 E5
Oldchurch Rd ROMW/RG RM7...........97 H4
Old Church Rd WCHPL * E1.........130 E5
Old Claygate La
ESH/CLAY KT10....................238 C4
Old Compton St
SOHO/SHAV W1D.....................12 C5
Old Cote Dr HEST TW5.............135 E6
Old Court PI KENS W8.............145 F2
The Old Ctyd BMLY BR1............184 C3
Old Dairy Ms BAL SW12............186 C3
Old Deer Pk RCH/KEW * TW9........161 H4
Old Deer Park Gdns
RCH/KEW TW9......................161 G4
Old Devonshire Rd BAL SW12.......186 D2
Old Dover Rd BKHTH/KID SE3.......172 C1
Old Dover Rd BKHTH/KID SE3.......172 C1
Old Farm Av BFN/LL DA15..........194 D3
STHGT/OAK N14.....................51 E2
Old Farm Rd HSLWW TW4...........158 D5
Old Farm Rd EFNCH N2..............65 H4
HPTN TW12.........................181 H1
Old Farm Rd East
BFN/LL DA15......................195 C4
Old Farm Rd West
BFN/LL DA15......................195 F4
Oldfield CI BMLY BR1.............233 H1
NTHLT UB5.........................100 A3
STAN HA7..........................60 C1
Oldfield Farm Gdns
GFD/PVL UB6.......................99 H6
Oldfield Gv DEPT SE8.............150 B4
Oldfield La North GFD/PVL UB6.....99 H4
Oldfield La South
GFD/PVL UB6......................119 C2
Oldfield Ms HGT N6................87 B4
Oldfield Rd BMLY BR1.............233 H1
BXLYHN DA7........................176 C3
HPTN TW12.........................179 C3
STNW/STAM N16.....................99 H1
WIM/MER SW19.....................204 C2
WLSDN NW10.......................103 F5
Oldfields Circ NTHLT UB5.........100 A5
Oldfields Rd CHEAM SM3...........225 E6
Old Fish Street HI BLKFR * EC4V...15 E5

Old Fleet La STP EC4M..............14 C3
Old Fold CI BAR * EN5..............34 D2
Old Fold La BAR EN5................34 D2
Old Fold Vw BAR EN5................34 A4
Old Ford Lock BOW * E3...........111 E5
Old Ford Rd BETH E2...............130 A1
BOW E3............................110 D6
Old Forge CI STAN HA7..............44 C6
Old Forge Rd EN EN1...............39 F1
Old Forge Wy SCUP DA14...........195 H6
Old Gloucester St BMSBY WC1N......13 F1
Old Hall CI PIN HA5................58 C4
Old Hall Dr PIN HA5................58 C4
Oldham Ter ACT W3................142 C1
Old HI CHST BR7..................214 A4
ORP BR6...........................216 C2
Oldhill St STNW/STAM N16..........89 G5
Old Homesdale Rd HAYES BR2.......233 E1
Old Hospital CI TOOT * SW17......186 B3
Old House CI WIM/MER SW19........204 C1
Old House Gdns TWK * TW1.........181 E1
Old Jamaica Rd
BERM/RHTH SE16....................25 E5
Old James St PECK SE15...........169 H4
Old Jewry LOTH * EC2R.............15 C4
Old Kent Rd STHWK SE1.............31 H4
Old Kenton La CDALE/KGS NW9.......82 B2
Old Kingston Rd WPK KT4..........240 C1
Old Lodge Wy STAN HA7.............43 G1
Old London Rd KUTN/CMB KT2......201 H5
Old Maidstone Rd SCUP DA14.......216 D3
Old Maiden La WPK KT4.............224 C1
Old Manor Dr ISLW TW7............179 C1
Old Manor Wy BXLYHN DA7..........179 F1
ELTH/MOT SE9.....................213 H1
Old Manor Yd ECT * SW5...........145 F4
Old Market Sq BETH E2..............8 D3
Old Marylebone Rd
CAMTN NW1.........................10 B2
Old Mill Ct SWFD E18..............73 E6
Old Mill Rd KUT K1...............201 H6
WOOL/PLUM SE18...................154 D6
Old Mitre Ct EMB * EC4Y...........14 B4
Old Montague St WCHPL E1..........17 E2
Old Nichol St BETH E2..............8 D6
Old North St FSBYW * WC1X.........13 G1
Old Oak Common La
WLSDN NW10.......................123 E3
Old Oak La WLSDN NW10............123 F2
Old Oak Rd ACT W3................125 F6
Old Orch SUN TW16.................82 B2
The Old Orch HAMP * NW3..........106 B2
Old Palace Rd CROY/NA CRO........246 C1
Old Palace Yd RCH/KEW TW9........161 E6
Old Paradise St LBTH SE11.........29 C1
Old Park Av BAL SW12.............167 E6
ENC/FH EN2........................38 C5
Old Park Gv WCHMH N21.............38 C5
Old Park La MYFR/PICC W1J.........15 F2
Old Park Ms HEST TW5.............158 D1
Old Park Ridings WCHMH N21........38 D2
Old Park Rd ABYW SE2.............155 G5
ENC/FH EN2........................38 C5
PLMGR N13.........................51 H3
Old Park Rd South ENC/FH EN2......38 B5
Old Park Vw ENC/FH EN2............38 A5
Old Perry St CHST BR7............215 E3
Old Pound CI ISLW TW7............160 C2
Old Pye St WEST SW1P..............30 C4
Old Quebec St MBLAR W1H...........10 D4
Old Queen St STJSPK SW1H..........30 D3
Old Rectory Gdns EDGW HA8.........62 A2
Old Redding
KTN/HRWW/W HA3....................59 F1
Oldridge Rd BAL SW12.............186 D2
Old Rd DART DA1..................177 H5
LEW SE13.........................172 A5
PEND EN3..........................40 A2
Old Royal Free PI IS * N1.........108 A6
Old Royal Free Sq IS * N1........108 A6
Old Ruislip Rd NTHLT UB5.........118 A1
Old School CI BECK BR3...........210 B5
Old School Crs FSTGT E7..........112 C4
Old Schools La EW KT17...........241 F6
Old School Sq THDT KT7...........220 B3
Old School Ter CHEAM * SM3.......224 B6
Old Seacoal La STP * EC4M........14 C4
Old South CI PIN HA5..............58 B4
Old South Lambeth Rd
VX/NE * SW8......................167 G1
Old Sq LINN WC2A..................13 H3
Old Stable Ms HGT * N6............87 H5
Old Station Gdns TEDD * TW11.....200 C2
Oldstead Rd BMLY BR1............183 H1
Old St FSBYE EC1V..................7 E4
Old Swan Yd CAR SM5.............244 B2
Old Town CLAP SW4...............167 E4
CROY/NA CRO......................246 B1
Old Tramyard
WOOL/PLUM SE18...................154 D2
Old Woolwich Rd GNWCH SE10.......151 H6
Old York Rd WAND/EARL SW18.......165 H6
Oleander CI ORP BR6..............252 D3
Olga St BOW E3..................111 G1
Olinda Rd STNW/STAM N16...........74 C6
Oliphant St NKENS W10............124 C2
Oliver Av SNWD SE25.............209 F6
Oliver CI CHSWK W4...............133 H2
Oliver Gdns EHAM E6.............133 G4
Oliver Gv SNWD SE25.............229 F1
Olive Rd CRICK NW2...............104 A2
EA W5............................141 F3
PLSTW E13........................133 E2
WIM/MER * SW19...................206 A1
Oliver Rd LEY E10................91 F6
NWMAL KT3........................191 G5
SUT SM1..........................243 H2
SWLY BR8.........................217 H6
WALTH E17.........................91 C4
Oliver's Yd STLK EC1Y.............7 F6
Olive St ROMW/RG RM7..............97 H2
Ollerton Av BOW E3...............110 D6
Ollerton Rd FBAR/BDGN N11.........67 F1
Ollgar CI ACT W3.................125 F1
Olliffe St POP/IOD E14...........151 G3
Olmar St STHWK SE1...............37 H5
Olney Rd WALW SE17...............30 D6
Olron Crs BXLYHS DA6............176 B6

Olven Rd WOOL/PLUM SE18..........174 C1
Olveston Wk MRDN SM4.............225 H3
Olwen Ms PIN HA5..................58 B5
Olyffe Av WELL DA16.............175 G3
Olyffe Dr BECK BR3...............211 G4
Olympia Wy WKENS W14............144 C3
Olympic Wy GFD/PVL UB6............99 F4
WBLY HA9..........................102 A2
Oman Av CRICK NW2...............104 A3
O'meara St STHWK SE1..............23 F2
Omega CI POP/IOD E14.............151 F3
Omega PI IS N1....................5 F3
Omega St NWCR SE14..............170 D2
Ommaney Rd NWCR SE14...........170 B2
Omnibus Wy WALTH E17.............71 E1
Ondine Rd EDUL SE22.............169 F5
Onega Ga BERM/RHTH SE16.........150 C3
One Tree CI FSTH SE23...........190 A1
Ongar CI CHDH RM6................73 H2
Ongar Rd FUL/PGN SW6............145 H6
Onra Rd LEY E10...................91 E4
Onslow Av RCHPK/HAM TW10........161 G6
Onslow CI CHING E4................55 H5
Onslow Crs CHST BR7.............214 B4
Onslow Dr SCUP DA14.............196 B5
Onslow Gdns MUSWH N10............86 D2
SKENS SW7.........................14 D6
SWFD E18..........................72 D6
THDT KT7.........................220 A5
WCHMH N21..........................38 A6
WLGTN SM6........................244 C6
Onslow Ms East SKENS SW7........145 H4
Onslow Ms West SKENS * SW7......145 H4
Onslow Pde STHGT/OAK * N14........50 D3
Onslow Rd CROY/NA CRO...........228 D1
NWMAL KT3........................223 C1
RCHPK/HAM TW10...................181 G1
Onslow Sq SKENS SW7..............14 D6
Onslow St FARR EC1M................6 B6
Onslow Wy THDT KT7..............220 A5
Ontario St LBTH SE11..............22 D6
Ontario Wy POP/IOD E14..........131 E6
On the HI OXHEY WD19..............42 C4
Opal CI CAN/RD E16...............134 C5
Opal St LBTH SE11.................30 C5
Openshaw Rd ABYW SE2............155 H5
Openview WAND/EARL SW18.........185 G3
Ophir Ter PECK SE15.............169 H1
Oppidans Ms HAMP NW3............106 D5
Oppenheim Rd LEW SE13...........171 G3
Oppidans Rd HAMP NW5............105 B5
Orange Court La ORP BR6..........252 A6
Orange Gv CHIG IG7................74 C2
WAN E11...........................112 A1
Orange Hill Rd EDGW HA8...........62 C3
Orange PI BERM/RHTH SE16.........150 A3
Orangery La ELTH/MOT SE9.........173 H6
The Orangery
RCHPK/HAM TW10...................181 A4
Orange St LSO/SEVD WC2H..........12 D6
Orange Tree HI HARH * RM3.........77 H1
Oratory La CHEL * SW3.............36 A3
Orbain Rd FUL/PGN SW6............164 C1
Orbel St BTSEA SW11.............166 A2
Orchard AV BELV DA17............156 C6
CROY/NA CRO......................230 C6
FNCH N3...........................65 C5
HEST TW5.........................158 C1
MTCM CR4.........................226 C5
NWMAL KT3........................205 E5
STHGT/OAK N14.....................11 C1
STHL UB1.........................138 D1
THDT KT7.........................220 C5
TRDG/WHET N20.....................49 H4
Orchard CI ALP/SUD HA0...........80 B2
BXLYHN DA7.......................176 C2
CHING E4..........................55 E6
CRICK NW2........................103 G1
EDGW HA8..........................61 H6
FSTH SE23........................190 A1
HOR/WEW * KT19..................240 A6
NKENS W10........................124 C4
RYNPK SW20.......................206 A2
Orchard Cottages
KUTN/CMB * KT2...................202 A4
Orchard Ct WLGTN * SM6..........244 C4
WPK * KT4........................223 C5
Orchard Crs EDGW HA8.............46 D6
EN EN1............................24 B3
Orchard Dr BKHTH/KID SE3........172 A3
EDGW HA8..........................61 H1
Orchard Gdns CHSGTN KT9.........259 H3
Orchard Ga CDALE/KGS NW9.........83 E1
ESH/CLAY KT10....................220 D4
GFD/PVL UB6......................100 D3
Orchard Gn ORP BR6..............253 A4
Orchard Gv CROY/NA CRO..........230 C4
EDGW HA8..........................62 A4
KTN/HRWW/W HA3....................81 H2
PGE/AN SE20.......................209 H6
Orchard La E/WMO/HCT KT8........219 H3
RYNPK SW20.......................205 G1
WFD IG8...........................57 G6
Orchard Ms IS N1.................108 D1
Orchard PI POP/IOD E14..........132 A6
STMC/STPC * BR5..................216 A6
TOTM N17..........................50 D2
Orchard Ri CROY/NA CRO..........230 C4
KUTN/CMB KT2.....................202 C4
RCHPK/HAM TW10...................162 B5
Orchard Ri East BFN/LL DA15.....175 E6
Orchard Ri West BFN/LL DA15.....175 E6
Orchard Rd BAR EN5...............26 D3
BELV DA17........................157 H4
BMLY BR1.........................213 E4
BTFD TW8.........................136 D3
CEND/HSY/T N8.....................66 D3
DAGE RM10........................117 B6
HGT N6............................66 B4
HPTN TW12........................179 H4
HSLWW TW4........................158 D3
KUT/T KT1........................175 B5
MTCM CR4.........................206 C4
ORP BR6..........................252 B5
PEND EN3..........................25 F6
RCH/KEW TW9......................162 A4
ROMW/RG RM7.......................77 F5

SCUP DA14 ...195 E6
SUT SM1 ...243 E5
TWK TW1 ...160 C6
WELL DA16 ...175 H4
Orchardson St STJWD NW8 ...125 E3
Orchard Sq WKENS * W14 ...144 D5
Orchard St MBLAR W1H ...11 E4
THDIT KT7 ...220 D5
WALTH E17 ...90 C1
Orchard Ter FELT * EN1 ...53 C1
WLSDN * NW10 ...103 F2
The Orchard BKHTH/KID SE3 ...171 H3
CHSWK W4 ...142 D4
EW KT17 ...241 F5
GLDGN NW11 ...85 E2
SWLY BR8 ...217 H5
WCHMH N21 ...52 D1
Orchard Vis SCUP * DA14 ...216 A2
Orchard Wy CROY/NA CRO ...230 C4
EN EN1 ...39 E4
SUT SM1 ...243 H2
Orchid Cl CHSGTN KT9 ...239 E5
STHL UB1 ...118 C5
Orchid Rd STHGT/OAK N14 ...51 E2
Orchid St SHB W12 ...123 G6
Orde Hall St BMSBY * WC1N ...13 C1
Ordell Rd BOW E3 ...130 D1
Ordnance Crs GNWCH SE10 ...152 A2
Ordnance Hl STJWD NW8 ...105 H6
Ordnance Ms STJWD * NW8 ...125 H1
Ordnance Rd CAN/RD E16 ...152 B4
WOOL/PLUM SE18 ...154 A6
Oregon Av MNPK E12 ...113 H2
Oregon Cl NWMAL KT3 ...222 C1
Oregon Sq ORP BR6 ...234 D5
Orestes Ms KIL/WHAMP * NW6 ...105 E5
Orford Gdns TWK TW1 ...180 B4
Orford Rd CAT SE6 ...191 F5
SWFD E18 ...77 E2
WALTH E17 ...91 E2
Oriel Cl MTCM CR4 ...227 F1
Oriel Ct HAMP NW3 ...105 G2
Oriel Dr BARN SW13 ...144 A6
Oriel Gdns CLAY IC5 ...75 H1
Oriel Rd HOM E9 ...110 B4
Oriel Wy NTHLT UB5 ...99 F5
Oriental Rd CAN/RD E16 ...153 F1
Orient St LBTH SE11 ...17 H6
Orient Wy CLPT E5 ...110 B1
Oriole Wy THMD SE28 ...135 H6
Orion Rd MUSWH N10 ...66 C2
Orissa Rd WOOL/PLUM SE18 ...115 K5
Orkney St BTSEA SW11 ...166 C3
Orlando Rd CLAP SW4 ...167 E4
Orleans Rd NRWD SE19 ...208 D2
TWK TW1 ...160 C6
Orleston Ms HOLWY N7 ...108 A4
Orleston Rd HOLWY N7 ...108 A4
Orley Farm Rd HRW HA1 ...100 A3
Ormanton Rd SYD SE26 ...189 C6
Orme Cl BAY/PAD W2 ...125 F6
Ormeley Rd BAL SW12 ...186 D2
Orme Rd KUT KT1 ...202 B5
Ormerod Gdns MTCM CR4 ...206 C5
Ormesby Cl THMD SE28 ...136 B6
Ormesby Wy
KTN/HRWW/W HA3 ...81 H3
Orme Sq BAY/PAD W2 ...125 F6
Orme Square Ga KENS W8 ...125 F6
Ormiston Gv SHB W12 ...143 H1
Ormiston Rd GNWCH SE10 ...152 C5
Ormond Av HPTN TW12 ...199 F4
ORP BR6 ...234 C6
Ormond Cl BMSBY WC1N ...13 F1
Ormond Dr HPTN TW12 ...199 F3
Ormonde Av HOR/WEW KT19 ...240 D6
Ormonde Ct STJWD * NW8 ...106 B6
Ormonde Ga CHEL SW3 ...26 C4
Ormonde Pl BGVA * SW1W ...27 F3
Ormonde Rd BRXN IG9 ...57 E3
Ormonde Rd
MORT/ESHN SW14 ...162 B4
Ormonde Ter STJWD NW8 ...106 B6
Ormond Rd ARCH N19 ...87 E1
RCHPK/HAM TW10 ...161 F6
Ormond Vis STJS SW1Y ...20 B1
Orsett Ms BAY/PAD * W2 ...125 C5
Orsett St LBTH SE11 ...29 H5
Orsett Ter BAY/PAD W2 ...125 F5
WFD IG8 ...73 E4
Orsman Rd IS N1 ...109 E6
Orton St WAP E1W ...25 E2
Orville Rd BTSEA SW11 ...165 H3
Orwell Rd PLSTW E13 ...133 E1
Osbaldeston Rd
STNW/STAM N16 ...89 G6
Osberton Rd LEE/GVPK SE12 ...172 C6
Osbert St WEST SW1P ...28 C2
Osborn Cl HACK E8 ...109 G6
Osborne Cl BECK BR3 ...200 C1
EBAR EN4 ...36 B4
FELT TW13 ...198 B1
Osborne Ct EA * W5 ...121 G4
Osborne Gdns THHTH CR7 ...208 C5
Osborne Gv WALTH E17 ...90 C1
Osborne Rd ACT W3 ...142 B2
BELV DA17 ...156 D5
BKHH IG9 ...56 D3
CRICK NW2 ...104 A1
FSBYPK N4 ...88 A5
FSTGT E7 ...112 D3
GFD/PVL UB6 ...119 C5
HOM E9 ...110 D6
HSLWW TW4 ...158 D4
KUTN/CMB KT2 ...175 H1
LEY E10 ...111 F1
PEND EN3 ...40 C3

PLMGR N13 ...52 H5
THHTH CR7 ...208 C5
Osborne Sq DAGW RM9 ...116 D2
Osborne Ter TOOT * SW17 ...206 C1
Osborn Gdns MLHL NW7 ...64 B3
Osborn La FSTH SE23 ...190 C2
Osborn St WCHPL E1 ...16 D2
Osborn Ter BKHTH/KID SE3 ...172 B5
Oscar Faber Pl IS N1 ...109 E5
Oscar St DEPT SE8 ...171 E2
Oseney Crs KTTN NW5 ...107 E4
Osgood Av ORP BR6 ...253 F5
Osgood Gdns ORP BR6 ...253 F5
O'Shea Gv BOW E3 ...110 D6
Osidge La STHGT/OAK N14 ...50 D2
Osier Crs MUSWH N10 ...66 B4
Osiers Rd WAND/EARL SW18 ...165 E5
Osier St WCHPL E1 ...104 E3
Osier Wy LEY E10 ...111 F1
MTCM CR4 ...226 A2
Oslac Rd CAT SE6 ...211 F1
Osman Rd ED N9 ...53 C5
HMSMTH * W6 ...119 F2
Osmond Cl RYLN/HDSTN HA2 ...79 G6
Osmond Gdns WLGTN SM6 ...245 E3
Osmund St SHB W12 ...123 F5
Osnaburgh St CAMTN NW1 ...3 H6
Osnaburgh Ter CAMTN NW1 ...3 H5
Osney Wk MRDN SM4 ...225 J3
Osprey Cl EHAM E6 ...133 G4
SWFD E18 ...92 C1
WALTH E17 ...70 C3
Osprey Est BERM/RHTH SE16 ...150 B4
Osprey Ms PEND EN3 ...39 H6
Ospringe Cl PGE/AN SE20 ...210 A3
Ospringe Rd KTTN NW5 ...107 E2
Osram Rd WBLY * HA9 ...101 F1
Ossian Rd FSBYPK N4 ...87 H4
Ossington Buildings
MHST * W1U ...11 E1
Ossington Cl BAY/PAD * W2 ...125 F6
Ossington St BAY/PAD * W2 ...125 F6
Ossory Rd STHWK SE1 ...33 C5
Ossulston St CAMTN NW1 ...4 D2
Ossulton Pl EFNCH * N2 ...65 G6
Ossulton Wy EFNCH N2 ...85 G1
Ostade Rd BRXS/STRHM SW2 ...187 H2
Ostell Crs WAB EN9 ...41 E1
Osten Ms SKENS * SW7 ...145 F5
Osterley Av ISLW * TW7 ...159 H1
Osterley Crs ISLW TW7 ...160 A2
Osterley Gdns THHTH CR7 ...208 C5
Osterley La NWDGN UB2 ...139 F5
Osterley Park Rd
NWDGN * UB2 ...138 D3
Osterley Park View Rd
HNWL W7 ...140 A2
Osterley Rd ISLW TW7 ...160 A1
STNW/STAM N16 ...90 A5
Ostliffe Rd PLMGR N13 ...52 A1
Oswald Rd STHL UB1 ...138 C1
Oswald's Md CLPT E5 ...110 C2
Oswald St CLPT E5 ...110 B1
Oswald Ter CRICK * NW2 ...104 A1
Osward CROY/NA * CRO ...248 D6
Osward Pl ED N9 ...53 G4
Osward Rd BAL SW12 ...186 B4
Oswin St LBTH SE11 ...30 C1
Oswyth Rd CMBW SE5 ...169 E3
Otford Cl BMLY BR1 ...214 A6
BXLY DA5 ...197 F1
PGE/AN SE20 ...210 A4
Otford Crs BROCKY SE4 ...190 D1
Othello Cl LBTH SE11 ...30 C3
Otley Dr GNTH/NBYPK IG2 ...94 B3
Otley Rd CAN/RD E16 ...133 C5
Otley Ter CLPT E5 ...91 E6
Otley Wy OXHEY WD19 ...42 A5
Otlinge Rd STMC/STPC BR5 ...236 B1
Ottawa Gdns DAGE RM10 ...117 C5
Ottaway St CLPT E5 ...109 G1
Otterbourne Rd CHING E4 ...55 H5
CROY/NA CRO ...248 C6
Otterburn Gdns ISLW TW7 ...160 C1
Otterburn St TOOT SW17 ...206 B2
Otterden St CAT SE6 ...211 E6
Otter Rd GFD/PVL UB6 ...119 C3
Otters Cl STMC/STPC BR5 ...236 B1
Otto Cl SYD * SE26 ...189 H4
Otto St WALW SE17 ...30 C6
Otway Gdns BUSH WD23 ...44 A2
Oulton Cl BARK IG11 ...115 F4
Oulton Rd SEVS/STOTM N15 ...88 D2
Oulton Wy OXHEY WD19 ...42 D6
Oundle Av BUSH WD23 ...43 G1
Ouseley Rd BAL SW12 ...186 B3
Outgate Rd WLSDN NW10 ...103 F5
Outram Pl IS N1 ...107 G6
Outram Rd CROY/NA CRO ...245 F6
EHAM E6 ...115 C6
WDGN N22 ...52 F4
Outwich St HDTCH * EC3A ...16 B3
Oval Cl EDUL * HA8 ...44 B3
Oval Pl VX/NE SW8 ...167 H1
Oval Rd CAMTN NW1 ...106 D6
CROY/NA CRO ...228 D6
Oval Rd North DAGE RM10 ...117 F6
Oval Rd South DAGE RM10 ...137 F1
The Oval BETH E2 ...7 H1
BFN/LL DA15 ...195 G2
SAND/SEL * CR2 ...55 H1
Overbrae BECK BR3 ...211 E2
Overbrook Wk EDGW HA8 ...62 A3
Overbury Av BECK BR3 ...211 F6
Overbury Rd FSBYPK N4 ...88 D3
Overbury St CLPT E5 ...110 B2
Overcliff Rd LEW SE13 ...171 E4
Overcourt Cl BFN/LL DA15 ...195 H1
Overdale Av NWMAL KT3 ...202 C5
Overdale Rd EA W5 ...140 B3
Overdown Rd CAT SE6 ...191 E6
Overhill Cottages MTCM * CR4 ...206 C5
Overhill Rd EDUL SE22 ...189 G2
PUR/KEN CR8 ...248 A6
Overhill Wy BECK BR3 ...211 H2
Overlea Rd CLPT E5 ...89 G4
Overmead ELTH/MOT SE9 ...194 D2
Overstand Cl BECK BR3 ...231 E4

Overstone Gdns CROY/NA CRO ...230 D4
Overstone Rd HMSMTH W6 ...144 A4
Overton Cl ISLW TW7 ...160 B2
WLSDN NW10 ...102 C4
Overton Dr CHDH RM6 ...96 A6
WAN E11 ...92 D4
Overton Rd ABYW SE2 ...156 A3
BELMT SM2 ...245 E5
BRXN/ST SW9 ...48 B1
LEY E10 ...90 C5
STHGT/OAK N14 ...37 G6
Overton's Yd CROY/NA CRO ...246 C1
Ovesdon Av RYLN/HDSTN HA2 ...78 D5
Ovett Cl NRWD SE19 ...209 E2
Ovex Cl POP/IOD E14 ...151 G3
Ovington Gdns CHEL SW3 ...18 B6
Ovington Ms CHEL SW3 ...18 B6
Ovington Sq CHEL SW3 ...18 B6
Ovington St CHEL SW3 ...18 B6
Owen Cl CROY/NA CRO ...228 D3
CRW RM5 ...77 E2
THMD SE28 ...156 A1
Owen Gdns WFD IG8 ...73 C2
Owenite St ABYW SE2 ...155 H4
Owen Rd PLMGR N13 ...68 C1
Owen's Ct FSBYE EC1V ...6 C3
Owen's Rw FSBYE EC1V ...6 C3
Owen St FSBYE EC1V ...6 C2
Owens Wy FSTH SE23 ...190 C2
Owen Wy WLSDN NW10 ...102 C4
Owgan Cl CMBW SE5 ...168 D1
Oxberry Av FUL/PGN SW6 ...164 C3
Oxenden Wood Rd ORP BR6 ...253 H4
Oxendon St SOHO/SHAV * W1D ...12 C6
Oxenford St PECK SE15 ...169 F4
Oxenpark Av WBLY HA9 ...81 G4
Oxestalls Rd DEPT SE8 ...150 C5
Oxford Av HEST TW5 ...139 E5
RYNPK SW20 ...204 C5
Oxford Cl ED N9 ...53 H4
MTCM CR4 ...207 E6
Oxford Crs NWMAL KT3 ...222 D3
Oxford Dr RSLP HA4 ...78 A6
Oxford Gdns CHSWK W4 ...142 A5
NKENS W10 ...124 B5
TRDG/WHET N20 ...49 H1
WCHMH N21 ...52 C2
Oxford Ga HMSMTH * W6 ...144 B4
Oxford Ms BXLY DA5 ...197 E5
Oxford Rd CAR SM5 ...246 A1
ED N9 ...53 H4
FSBYPK N4 ...88 A5
HPTN TW12 ...199 H1
HRW HA1 ...79 G5
IL IG1 ...114 C2
KIL/WHAMP NW6 ...125 E1
KTN/HRWW/W HA3 ...60 B6
NRWD SE19 ...208 D2
PEND EN3 ...39 H6
PUT/ROE SW15 ...164 C5
SCUP DA14 ...215 H1
SRTFD E15 ...113 H5
WFD IG8 ...73 F1
WLGTN * SM6 ...245 E3
Oxford Rd North CHSWK W4 ...142 B5
Oxford Rd South CHSWK W4 ...142 A5
Oxford Rw SUN * TW16 ...198 A6
Oxford St STHL UB1 ...138 D1
Oxford Wy FELT TW13 ...178 B6
Oxgate Court Pde CRICK * NW2 ...83 H6
Oxgate Gdns CRICK NW2 ...103 H1
Oxgate La CRICK NW2 ...83 H5
Oxhawth Crs HAYES BR2 ...234 A2
Oxhey Av OXHEY WD19 ...42 B2
Oxhey La OXHEY WD19 ...42 B2
PIN HA5 ...59 F2
Oxhey Rd OXHEY WD19 ...42 C6
Oxleas EHAM E6 ...134 B5
Oxleas Cl WELL DA16 ...174 D3
Oxleay Rd RYLN/HDSTN HA2 ...79 F5
Oxleigh Cl NWMAL KT3 ...223 E2
Oxley Cl STHWK SE1 ...32 D5
Oxleys Rd CRICK NW2 ...103 H1
Oxlow La DAGW RM9 ...117 H2
Oxonian St EDUL SE22 ...169 F5
Oxted Cl MTCM CR4 ...205 H6
Oxtoby Wy STRHM/NOR SW16 ...207 F4
Oyster Catchers Cl
CAN/RD E16 ...132 D5
Oyster Rw WCHPL E1 ...130 A5
Ozolins Wy CAN/RD E16 ...132 B5

P

Paceheath Cl CRW RM5 ...77 H2
Pace Pl WCHPL E1 ...17 H4
Pacific Rd CAN/RD E16 ...132 C5
Packington St IS N1 ...108 C6
Packmores Rd ELTH/MOT SE9 ...174 D6
Padbury Ct BETH E2 ...8 D4
Paddenswick Rd HMSMTH W6 ...145 G3
Paddington Cl YEAD UB4 ...118 H3
Paddington Gn BAY/PAD W2 ...125 H4
Paddington St MHST W1U ...11 E1
Paddock Cl BKHTH/KID SE3 ...172 C4
HNHL SE24 ...188 C1
ORP BR6 ...252 B2
OXHEY WD19 ...42 C1
SYD SE26 ...190 B6
Paddock Gdns NRWD SE19 ...209 E2
Paddock Rd BXLYHS DA6 ...176 D5
CRICK NW2 ...103 G1
Paddocks Cl RYLN/HDSTN HA2 ...79 H6
STMC/STPC BR5 ...236 B6
The Paddocks EA * W5 ...141 F3
BAR EN4 ...21 H2
MLHL * NW7 ...64 D2
WBLY HA9 ...81 H1
Paddock Wy CHST BR7 ...214 D3

Padfield Rd CMBW SE5 ...168 C4
Padnall Rd CHDH RM6 ...96 C1
Padstow Rd ENC/FH EN2 ...38 B3
Padua Rd PGE/AN SE20 ...210 A4
Pagden St VX/NE SW8 ...166 D2
Pageant Crs POP/IOD E14 ...150 D1
Pageant Wk CROY/NA CRO ...247 E1
Page Cl DAGW RM9 ...116 C3
FELT TW13 ...198 B2
KTN/HRWW/W HA3 ...81 H5
Page Crs CROY/NA CRO ...246 B3
Page Green Rd
SEVS/STOTM * N15 ...89 G2
Page Heath La BMLY BR1 ...213 F6
Page Heath Vls BMLY BR1 ...213 F6
Pagehurst Rd CROY/NA CRO ...229 G4
Page Meadow MLHL NW7 ...63 G3
Page's Hi MUSWH N10 ...66 C5
Page's La MUSWH N10 ...66 C5
Page St MLHL NW7 ...63 G4
WEST SW1P ...28 D1
Page's Wk STHWK SE1 ...32 A1
Paget Av SUT SM1 ...243 H1
Paget Cl HPTN TW12 ...179 H6
Paget Gdns CHST BR7 ...214 B1
Paget La ISLW TW7 ...159 H4
Paget Pl KUTN/CMB * KT2 ...202 C2
THDIT KT7 ...220 B5
Paget Ri WOOL/PLUM SE18 ...154 A1
Paget Rd IL IG1 ...114 B2
STNW/STAM N16 ...88 D5
Paget St FSBYE EC1V ...6 C3
Paget Ter WOOL/PLUM SE18 ...154 B6
Pagitts Gv EBAR EN4 ...35 F2
Pagnell St NWCR SE14 ...170 D1
Pagoda Av RCH/KEW TW9 ...161 H4
Pagoda Gdns BKHTH/KID SE3 ...171 H3
Paignton Rd SEVS/STOTM N15 ...89 E3
RYNPK SW20 ...220 D1
Paines Cl PIN HA5 ...58 C5
Paine's La PIN HA5 ...58 C5
Pain's Cl MTCM CR4 ...206 D5
Painshorpe Rd
STNW/STAM N16 ...109 E1
Painters Rd GNTH/NBYPK IG2 ...75 G6
Paisley Rd CAR SM5 ...225 H5
WDGN N22 ...68 C2
Pakeman St HOLWY N7 ...107 H1
Pakenham Cl BAL SW12 ...186 C3
Pakenham St FSBYW WC1X ...5 H4
Palace Av KENS W8 ...145 F2
Palace Ct BAY/PAD W2 ...125 G6
KTN/HRWW/W HA3 ...81 G3
Palace Court Gdns MUSWH N10 ...66 C5
Palace Garden Ms KENS W8 ...145 E1
Palace Gdns BKHH IG9 ...57 H1
Palace Gardens Ms KENS W8 ...145 E1
Palace Ga KENS W8 ...145 G2
Palace Gates Rd WDGN N22 ...67 G4
Palace Gn CROY/NA CRO ...248 D5
KENS W8 ...145 F1
Palace Gv BMLY BR1 ...212 D4
NRWD SE19 ...209 E3
Palace Ms BRXN/ST * SW9 ...167 G1
BRXS/STRHM SW2 ...187 H3
CEND/HSY/T N8 ...67 F3
E/WMO/HCT KT8 ...199 G6
FBAR/BDGN N11 ...48 C1
KUT KT1 ...221 F1
NRWD SE19 ...209 E3
RSLP HA4 ...77 G2
Palace Sq NRWD SE19 ...209 F3
Palace St WESTW SW1E ...27 H4
Palace Vw BMLY BR1 ...212 D6
CROY/NA CRO ...248 D2
LEE/GVPK SE12 ...192 C4
Palace View Rd CHING E4 ...71 F1
Palamos Rd LEY E10 ...91 E5
Palatine Av STNW/STAM N16 ...109 E2
Palatine Rd STNW/STAM N16 ...109 E2
Palemead Cl FUL/PGN SW6 ...164 B2
Palermo Rd WLSDN NW10 ...119 H3
Palestine Gv WIM/MER SW19 ...205 H4
Palewell Cl STMC/STPC BR5 ...215 H5
Palewell Common Dr
MORT/ESHN SW14 ...162 D6
Palewell Pk MORT/ESHN SW14 ...162 D6
Palfrey Pl BRXN/ST SW9 ...167 H1
Palgrave Av STHL UB1 ...119 E6
Palgrave Gdns CAMTN NW1 ...2 B5
Palgrave Rd SHB W12 ...143 F3
Palissy St BETH E2 ...8 C4
Pallant Wy ORP BR6 ...252 A1
Pall MI WOOL/PLUM SE18 ...175 C2
Palliser Rd HMSMTH W6 ...144 C5
Pall MI STJS SW1Y ...20 C1
Pall MI East STJS SW1Y ...20 C1
Pall Mall Pl STJS SW1Y ...20 B2
Palmar Crs BXLYHN DA7 ...177 G4
Palmar Rd BXLYHN DA7 ...177 G4
Palm Cl LEY E10 ...111 F1
Palmeira Rd WELL DA16 ...176 B4
Palmer Av BUSH WD23 ...43 F1
CHEAM SM3 ...242 A2
Palmer Cl HEST TW5 ...159 E2
Palmer Gdns BAR EN5 ...34 B6
Palmer Pl HOLWY N7 ...108 A3
Palmer Rd BCTR RM8 ...96 B5
PLSTW E13 ...132 D3
Palmers Gv E/WMO/HCT KT8 ...219 E1
Palmers La EN3 ...26 D3
Palmers Rd BETH E2 ...130 B1
FBAR/BDGN N11 ...67 E1
MORT/ESHN SW14 ...162 C4
STRHM/NOR SW16 ...225 H1
Palmerston Crs PLMGR N13 ...67 H1
WOOL/PLUM SE18 ...154 H6
Palmerston Gv
WIM/MER SW19 ...205 E3
Palmerston Rd ACT W3 ...142 C3
BKHH IG9 ...57 E4
CAR SM5 ...244 B2
CROY/NA CRO ...228 D2
FSTGT E7 ...112 D3

HSLW TW3 ....159 G2
KIL/WHAMP NW6 ....104 D5
KTN/HRWW/W * HA3 ....60 A1
MORT/ESHN SW14 ....162 C5
ORP BR6 ....252 C2
SUT SM1 ....243 G3
WALTH E17 ....90 D1
WDGN N22 ....180 A1
WHTN TW2 ....187 H3
WIM/MER SW19 ....205 E3
Palmerston Wy VX/NE * SW8 ...166 D1
Palmer St STJSPK SW1H 20 C5
Palmers Whf KUT * KT1 ....201 F5
Palm Cv EA W5 ....141 G3
Palm Rd ROMW/RG RM7 ....97 G2
Pank Av BAR EN5 ....35 H6
Pankhurst Cl ISLW TW7 ....160 B4
Pankhurst Rd WOT/HER KT12 ...218 A4
Pankridge OXHEY * WD19 ....42 B4
Panmuir Rd RYNPK SW20 ....203 H6
Panmure Cl HBRY N5 ....108 B2
Panmure Rd SYD SE26 ....189 H5
Pansy Gdns SHB W12 ....123 G6
Panther Dr WLSDN NW10 ....102 D5
Pantiles Cl PLMGR N13 ....68 B1
The Pantiles BMLY BR1 ....213 G6
BUSH WD23 ....43 H2
BXLYHN DA7 ....176 D1
Panton Cl CROY/NA * CRO 228 B5
Panton St LSO/SEVD WC2H 12 D6
Paper Buildings EMB * EC4Y 14 B5
Papermill Cl CAR SM5 ....244 C2
Papillons Wk BKHTH/KID SE3 .....172 C3
Papworth Gdns HOLWY N7 ....107 H3
Papworth Wy
BRXS/STRHM SW2 ....188 A2
Parade Ms BRXS/STRHM SW2 .....188 B4
Parade Ter CDALE/KGS * NW9 ......83 G3
The Parade BROCKY * SE4 ....170 D2
BTSEA * SW11 ....165 H5
CAR * SM5 ....244 B3
CHSWK * W4 ....169 E4
CROY/NA * CRO 227 G3
CROY/NA * CRO 245 H3
EA * W5 ....121 F5
ESH/CLAY KT10 ....238 A4
FSBYPK * N4 ....88 A6
GFD/PVL * UB6 ....100 D4
KUT * KT1 ....190 A4
OXHEY * WD19 ....42 C5
PGE/AN * SE20 ....210 A4
RCH/KEW * TW9 ....162 A4
SUT * SM1 ....243 G2
SYD * SE26 ....189 H6
Paradise Pas HOLWY N7 ....108 A3
Paradise Rd CLAP SW4 ....167 G3
RCHPK/HAM TW10 ....145 E1
Paradise Rw BETH E2 ....9 H3
Paradise St BERM/RHTH SE16 ......25 G4
Paradise Wk CHEL SW3 ....26 C5
Paragon Cl CAN/RD E16 ....132 C5
Paragon Gv BRYLDS KT5 ....221 H5
Paragon Ms WALW SE17 ....31 H1
Paragon Pl BKHTH/KID SE3 ....172 B3
Paragon Rd HACK E8 ....108 H4
The Paragon BKHTH/KID SE3 .....172 C3
Parbury Ri CHSGTN KT9 ....239 G4
Parbury Rd FSTH SE23 ....190 C1
Parchmore Rd THHTH CR7 ....208 B5
Parchmore Wy THHTH CR7 ....208 B5
Pardoner St STHWK SE1 ....23 H5
Pardon St FSBYE EC1V 6 D5
Parfett St WCHPL E1 ....17 F2
Parfrey St HMSMTH W6 ....148 A6
Parham Dr GNTH/NBYPK IG2 ....94 B3
Paris Gdn STHWK SE1 ....22 C1
Parish Gate Dr BFN/LL DA15 ......195 E1
Parish La PGE/AN SE20 ....210 B3
Parish Whf WOOL/PLUM SE18 ....115 G4
Park Ap BERM/RHTH * SE16 ....150 A3
WELL DA16 ....175 H5
Park Av BMLY BR1 ....212 C2
CAR SM5 ....244 C4
CRICK NW2 ....104 A4
EHAM E6 ....114 A6
EN EN1 ....53 E1
FNCH N3 ....65 F4
GLDGN NW11 ....85 E6
HSLW TW3 ....179 F1
IL IG1 ....94 A6
MORT/ESHN SW14 ....162 D5
MTCM CR4 ....206 D3
ORP BR6 ....233 H6
PLMGR N13 ....35 H2
UED N18 ....53 G6
WCHMH N21 ....30 D6
WDGN N22 ....67 G3
WDR/YW * UB7 ....120 C5
WLSDN NW10 ....121 H2
WWKM BR4 ....214 D5
Park Av East EW KT17 ....241 G4
Park Av North CEND/HSY/T N8 ......67 F1
WLSDN NW10 ....103 H3
Park Avenue Rd TOTM N17 ....69 H3
Park Av South CEND/HSY/T N8 ......87 F1
Park Av West EW KT17 ....241 H2
Park Cha WBLY HA9 ....80 A1
Park Cl CAR SM5 ....244 C6
CRICK NW2 ....103 G1
HOM E9 ....110 A6
HPTN TW12 ....173 H6
HSLW TW3 ....159 G6
KTN/HRWW/W HA3 ....60 A1
KUTN/CMB KT2 ....202 A4
SKENS * SW7 ....14 C5
TRDG/WHET * N20 ....49 H6
WKENS W14 ....144 D3
WLSDN NW10 ....121 H2
Park Cottages FNCH * N3 ....64 D5
Park Ct DUL * SE21 ....188 D5

NWMAL KT3 ....222 D1
SYD * SE26 ....209 H2
WBLY HA9 ....101 G3
Park Crs ENC/FH EN2 ....38 C5
ERITH DA8 ....157 H6
FNCH N3 ....65 E4
KTN/HRWW/W HA3 ....60 A1
REGST W1B 3 G6
WHTN TW2 ....179 H3
Park Crescent Ms East
REGST W1B 3 H6
Park Crescent Ms West
CAVSO/HST W1G 3 G6
Park Cft EDGW HA8 ....62 C4
Parkcroft Rd LEE/GVPK SE12 ......192 B2
Parkdale Crs WPK KT4 ....240 D1
Parkdale Rd WOOL/PLUM SE18 ...115 G5
Park Dr ACT W3 ....142 A3
CHARL SE7 ....153 C5
DAGE RM10 ....117 G1
GLDGN NW11 ....85 F5
KTN/HRWW/W HA3 ....59 H2
MORT/ESHN SW14 ....162 D6
ROM RM1 ....97 H1
RYLN/HDSTN HA2 ....79 E4
WCHMH N21 ....30 A5
Park End BMLY BR1 ....212 B4
HAMP NW3 ....106 A2
Parker Cl CAN/RD E16 ....153 C1
Parker Ms HOL/ALD * WC2B 11 E3
Parker Rd BARN SW15 ....165 G2
Parker Rd CROY/NA CRO 246 C2
Parker's Rw STHWK SE1 ....24 C1
STHWK SE1 ....25 F3
Parker St CAN/RD E16 ....153 C1
HOL/ALD WC2B 11 E3
Parkes Rd CHIG IG7 ....75 F1
Park Farm Cl EFNCH N2 ....65 G6
Park Farm Rd BMLY BR1 ....213 H4
KUTN/CMB KT2 ....201 G5
Parkfield Av
MORT/ESHN SW14 ....163 E5
NTHLT UB5 ....118 B1
RYLN/HDSTN HA2 ....59 C5
Parkfield Cl EDGW HA8 ....62 B2
NTHLT UB5 ....118 C1
Parkfield Crs RSLP HA4 ....78 B6
RYLN/HDSTN HA2 ....59 C5
Parkfield Dr NTHLT UB5 ....118 B1
Parkfield Gdns
RYLN/HDSTN HA2 ....59 F6
Parkfield Rd NTHLT UB5 ....118 C1
NWCR SE14 ....170 D2
RYLN/HDSTN HA2 ....99 C1
WLSDN NW10 ....82 D5
Parkfields CROY/NA CRO 230 D5
PUT/ROE SW15 ....164 A5
Parkfields Av CDALE/KGS NW9 .....82 D5
RYNPK SW20 ....203 H4
Parkfields Cl CAR SM5 ....245 A4
Parkfields Rd KUTN/CMB KT2 ......201 F1
Parkfield St IS N1 ....6 B1
Parkfield Wy HAYES BR2 ....233 H5
Park Gdns CDALE/KGS NW9 ....62 A4
ERITH DA8 ....157 H4
KUTN/CMB KT2 ....201 H1
Parkgate BKHTH/KID SE3 ....172 B4
Park Ga EA W5 ....121 F4
EFNCH N2 ....65 H6
WCHMH N21 ....51 H1
Parkgate Av EBAR EN4 ....35 G2
Parkgate Cl KUTN/CMB KT2 ....202 D2
Park Gate CI HPTN * TW12 ....199 C1
Parkgate Crs EBAR EN4 ....35 G2
Parkgate Gdns
MORT/ESHN SW14 ....162 D6
Parkgate Rd BTSEA SW11 ....166 A1
CAR SM5 ....244 C3
Park Gates RYLN/HDSTN * HA2 ....99 E2
Park Gv BMLY BR1 ....212 D4
BXLYHN DA7 ....177 C5
EDGW HA8 ....62 A1
FBAR/BDGN N11 ....67 F3
SRTFD E15 ....112 C6
Park Grove Rd WAN E11 ....92 A2
Park Hall Rd DUL SE21 ....188 D4
EFNCH N2 ....86 A1
Parkham St BTSEA SW11 ....165 H2
Park Hi BMLY BR1 ....213 E5
CAR SM5 ....244 B4
CLAP SW4 ....167 F4
EA W5 ....121 F4
FSTH SE23 ....190 C1
RCHPK/HAM TW10 ....181 H1
Park Hill Cl CAR SM5 ....244 A3
Park Hill Ri CROY/NA CRO 229 H6
Park Hill Rd CROY/NA CRO 212 A5
HAYES BR2 ....215 H1
WLGTN SM6 ....244 B6
Parkhill Rd BFN/LL DA15 ....195 E5
Park Hl BMLY BR1 ....213 E5
CAR SM5 ....244 B4
CHING E4 ....38 A6
HAMP NW3 ....106 B3
Parkholme Rd HACK E8 ....108 B4
Park House Gdns TWK TW1 ....161 E6
Parkhouse St CMBW SE5 ....168 D7
Parkhurst Gdns BXLY DA5 ....197 G2
Parkhurst Rd BXLY DA5 ....197 G2
Park Ed BAR EN5 ....25 G3
BXLYHN DA7 ....177 H3
ROM RM1 ....75 H2
SUT SM1 ....243 H2
TOTM N17 ....69 C3
WAN E11 ....71 C1
WCHMH N21 ....30 D6
WDGN N22 ....67 H5
WKFLD IG8 ....72 C5
Parklands BRYLDS KT5 ....221 H2
BUSH * WD23 ....43 G1
HGT N6 ....66 B4
Parklands Cl EBAR EN4 ....35 H1
MORT/ESHN SW14 ....162 C6
Parklands Dr FNCH N3 ....64 C6
Parklands Pde HEST * TW5 ....158 B3
Parklands Wy WPK KT4 ....223 E6
Park La CAR SM5 ....244 C2
CHDH RM6 ....96 B5
CHEAM SM3 ....242 C4
CROY/NA CRO 228 D6

MBLAR W1H 10 D5
RCH/KEW * TW9 ....161 F5
RYLN/HDSTN HA2 ....99 F1
SRTFD * E15 ....111 G2
STAN HA7 ....44 C5
TEDD TW11 ....200 B2
TOTM N17 ....69 G3
UED N18 ....53 F5
WBLY HA9 ....101 H2
Park Lane La TOTM N17 ....69 G3
Parklea Cl CDALE/KGS NW9 ....63 E4
Parkleigh Rd WIM/MER SW19 ....205 F3
Parkleys KUTN/CMB KT1 ....201 H2
Parkleys Pde KUTN/CMB * KT2 ...181 H6
Park Md BFN/LL DA15 ....175 G6
RYLN/HDSTN HA2 ....99 F1
Parkmead PUT/ROE SW15 ....183 H1
Parkmead Gdns MLHL NW7 ....65 F2
Park Ms CHST BR7 ....194 C2
NKENS W10 ....124 C1
Park Pde ACT * W3 ....142 A3
BARK * IG11 ....114 C2
EA W5 ....141 F1
POP/IOD E14 ....132 C1
WBLY HA9 ....101 G2
WHALL SW1A 20 A2
Park Place Vis BAY/PAD W2 ......125 C4
Park Ridings CEND/HSY/T N8 ......68 A6
Park Ri KTN/HRWW/W HA3 ....60 A4
Park Rise Rd FSTH SE23 ....190 C3
Park Rd ALP/SUD HA0 ....80 C1
BAR EN5 ....24 D5
BECK BR3 ....210 D3
BMLY BR1 ....213 E5
BRYLDS KT5 ....221 H5
BUSH WD23 ....43 E1
CDALE/KGS NW9 ....82 D4
CEND/HSY/T N8 ....87 F2
CHEAM SM3 ....242 C4
CHSWK W4 ....146 D2
E/WMO/HCT KT8 ....201 E4
E/WMO/HCT KT8 ....219 C1
EBAR EN4 ....35 H5
EFNCH N2 ....65 H6
EHAM E6 ....113 E6
FBAR/BDGN N11 ....67 F3
FELT TW13 ....198 B6
HNWL W7 ....120 B6
HPTN TW12 ....173 H6
HSLW TW3 ....159 G6
IL IG1 ....114 D1
ISLW TW7 ....160 D2
KUT KT1 ....190 D4
LEY E10 ....91 E5
MNPK E12 ....113 C1
NWMAL KT3 ....222 D1
RCHPK/HAM TW10 ....181 H1
SNWD SE25 ....229 E1
SRTFD E15 ....112 C6
STHGT/OAK N14 ....51 F2
STJWD NW8 ....2 B4
STMC/STPC BR5 ....186 A3
TEDD TW11 ....200 B3
TWK TW1 ....161 H6
UED N18 ....53 G5
WALTH E17 ....90 D2
WAN E11 ....91 H2
WIM/MER SW19 ....205 F3
WLGTN SM6 ....226 B6
WLSDN * NW10 ....103 E6
Park Rd East ACT W3 ....142 C2
Park Rd North ACT W3 ....142 B2
CHSWK W4 ....142 D6
Park Rw GNWCH SE10 ....113 F5
Park Royal Rd WLSDN NW10 ......122 C2
Parkshot RCH/KEW TW9 ....161 F5
Park Side BKHH IG9 ....56 D4
CRICK NW2 ....103 C1
Parkside BECK * BR3 ....211 F5
BKHTH/KID * SE3 ....172 B4
CHEAM SM3 ....242 C4
FNCH N3 ....65 F4
HPTN TW12 ....199 F1
MLHL NW7 ....45 G1
OXHEY * WD19 ....42 A4
SCUP DA14 ....195 H4
WIM/MER SW19 ....184 B6
Parkside Av BMLY BR1 ....233 C1
BXLYHN DA7 ....177 H3
ROM RM1 ....75 H2
WIM/MER SW19 ....204 B3
Parkside Cl PGE/AN SE20 ....190 B4
Parkside Crs BRYLDS KT5 ....222 C3
Parkside Dr EDGW HA8 ....44 B5
HOLWY N7 ....85 H5
Parkside Est HOM * E9 ....110 D6
Parkside Gdns EBAR EN4 ....50 D3
WIM/MER SW19 ....184 B6
Parkside Rd BELV DA17 ....157 H4
HSLW TW3 ....159 F6
Parkside Ter ORP * BR6 ....235 G5
UED * N18 ....53 E4
Parkside Wy RYLN/HDSTN HA2 .....79 E1
Parkstead Rd PUT/ROE SW15 .....163 G6
Park Steps BAY/PAD * W2 ....10 D5
Parkstone Av UED N18 ....53 G5
Parkstone Rd PECK * SE15 ....169 H2
Park St CROY/NA CRO 246 C1
MYFR/PKLN W1K 11 H5
STHWK SE1 ....23 E1
TEDD TW11 ....200 A3
Park Ter CAR * SM5 ....244 A1
PEND * EN3 ....40 A1
WPK KT4 ....223 G5
The Park CAR * SM5 ....244 A1
EA W5 ....141 F1
GLDGN NW11 ....85 F5
HGT N6 ....86 C4
SCUP DA14 ....195 G4
Parkthorne Cl
RYLN/HDSTN * HA2 ....79 E3

Parkthorne Dr
RYLN/HDSTN HA2 ....79 E3
Parkthorne Rd BAL SW12 ....187 F2
Park Vw ACT W3 ....122 C4
FNCH N3 ....65 E4
KTN/HRWW/W HA3 ....43 G3
PIN HA5 ....58 D4
WBLY HA9 ....80 B3
WCHMH N21 ....51 H2
Park View Ct
NFNCH/WDSP * N12 ....50 A6
Park View Crs FBAR/BDGN N11 ....50 D6
Park View Dr MTCM CR4 ....205 H6
Park View Est HBRY * N5 ....108 C2
Park View Gdns HDN NW4 ....84 A2
WDGN * N22 ....68 A4
Parkview Gdns REDBR IG4 ....93 H1
Parkview Rd CROY/NA CRO 229 G5
Park View Rd CRICK NW2 ....103 F2
EA W5 ....121 G4
ELTH/MOT SE9 ....194 B3
FNCH N5 ....65 F4
STHL UB1 ....139 E1
TOTM N17 ....68 D4
WELL DA16 ....176 C3
Park Village East CAMTN NW1 ....3 H3
Park Village West CAMTN NW1 ......3 G3
Park Vis TOOT * SW17 ....206 A1
Parkville Rd FUL/PGN SW6 ....164 D1
Park Vis BKHTH/KID SE3 ....151 H6
Park Wk WBPTN SW10 ....145 G6
E/WMO/HCT KT8 ....219 H2
EDGW HA8 ....62 B4
ENC/FH EN2 ....38 A3
GLDGN NW11 ....84 C2
TRDG/WHET N20 ....33 H4
Parkway CAMTN NW1 ....106 D6
CROY/NA CRO 249 G6
ERITH DA18 ....156 C3
GDMY/SEVK IG3 ....95 E1
RYNPK SW20 ....224 B1
STHGT/OAK N14 ....51 G4
WFD IG8 ....73 E1
The Parkway NTHLT UB5 ....118 B2
Park West BAY/PAD W2 ....10 B3
Park West Pl BAY/PAD W2 ....10 B3
Parkwood BECK BR3 ....211 E3
ISLW TW7 ....160 B2
Parkwood Av
E/WMO/HCT KT8 ....201 E5
WIM/MER SW19 ....204 D1
Parliament Ct WCHPL * E1 ....16 A2
Parliament Hl HAMP NW3 ....106 A2
Parliament Hill Flds
KTTN * NW5 ....106 C1
Parliament Sq WEST SW1P 21 E4
Parliament St WHALL SW1A 21 E3
Parma Crs BTSEA SW11 ....166 B5
Parmiter St BETH E2 ....9 H2
Parnell Cl EDGW HA8 ....44 B6
SHB W12 ....143 H5
Parnell Rd BOW E3 ....110 D6
Parnham St POP/IOD * E14 ....130 C5
Parolles Rd ARCH N19 ....85 C1
Paroma Rd BELV DA17 ....157 E3
Parr Av EW KT17 ....241 H6
Parr Cl ED N9 ....53 H6
Parr Rd EHAM E6 ....113 H5
STAN HA7 ....61 F1
Parrs Cl SAND/SEL CR2 ....246 C6
Parr's Pl HPTN TW12 ....199 E3
Parr St IS N1 ....7 C1
Parry Av EHAM E6 ....133 H5
Parry Cl EW KT17 ....241 G5
Parry Pl WOOL/PLUM SE18 ....154 B4
Parry Rd NKENS W10 ....108 C2
SNWD SE25 ....209 E6
Parry St VX/NE SW8 ....29 E5
Parsifal Rd KIL/WHAMP NW6 ......105 E3
Parsloes Av DAGW RM9 ....116 C3
Parsonage Gdns ENC/FH EN2 ......38 C3
Parsonage La ENC/FH EN2 ....38 D3
SCUP DA14 ....196 D6
Parsonage Manorway
BELV DA17 ....157 H2
Parsonage St POP/IOD E14 ....151 G4
Parsons Cn FUL/PGN SW6 ....165 E2
Parsons Green La
FUL/PGN SW6 ....165 E2
FBAR/BDGN N11 ....67 F2
Parsons Gv EDGW HA8 ....46 A5
E/WMO/HCT KT8 ....201 E5
Parsons Rd EDGW HA8 ....46 A5
PLSTW E13 ....113 C1
Parson St HDN NW4 ....64 A6
Parthenia Rd FUL/PGN SW6 ....165 E2
Partingdale La MLHL NW7 ....65 H1
Partridge Cl BAR EN5 ....25 E4
BUSH * WD23 ....43 G1
CAN/RD E16 ....133 F4
STAN HA7 ....45 G6
Partridge Dr ORP BR6 ....251 G3
Partridge Gn ELTH/MOT SE9 ......194 A5
SCUP DA14 ....195 E5
Partridge Wy WDGN N22 ....67 E4
Pascal St VX/NE SW8 ....167 F1
Pascoe Rd LEW SE13 ....171 H6
Pasley Cl WALW SE17 ....30 D4
Pasquier Rd WALTH E17 ....69 F5
Passey Pl ELTH/MOT SE9 ....193 H1
Passfield Dr POP/IOD E14 ....131 F4
Passmore Gdns
FBAR/BDGN N11 ....67 F2
Passmore St BCVA SW1W 27 G2
Pasteur Cl CDALE/KGS NW9 ....63 E1
Pasteur Gdns UED N18 ....118 C1
Paston Cl WLGTN SM6 ....226 D1
Paston Crs LEE/GVPK SE12 ....192 D2
Pastor St LBTH SE11 ....30 D2
Pasture Cl ALP/SUD HA0 ....80 A5
BUSH WD23 ....43 G2
Pasture Rd ALP/SUD HA0 ....80 A5
CAT SE6 ....192 D2
DAGW RM9 ....116 D3
The Pastures TRDG/WHET N20 ....48 D1
Patcham Ter VX/NE SW8 ....166 D2
Patching Wy YEAD UB4 ....118 C4
Paternoster Rw STP EC4M 145 E3
Pater St KENS W8 ....145 E3

Pathfield Rd
STRHM/NOR SW16 ....207 F2
The Path WIM/MER SW19 ....205 F4
The Pathway OXHEY WD19 ....42 B3
Patience Rd BTSEA SW11 ......166 A3
Patio CI CLAP SW4 ....187 F1
Patmore St VX/NE SW8 ....167 E2
Patmore Wy CRW IM5 ....77 F1
Patmos Rd BRXN/ST SW9 ......168 B1
Paton CI BOW E3 ....131 E2
Patricia CI WELL DA16 ....175 H1
Patricia Vis TOTM * N17 ....69 H4
Patrick Rd PLSTW E13 ....133 E2
Patriot Sq BETH E2 ....9 H2
Patrol PI CAT SE6 ....191 F1
Patshull PI KTTN NW5 ....107 E4
Patshull Rd KTTN NW5 ....107 E4
Pattenden Rd FSTH SE23 ....190 D3
Patten Rd WAND/EARL SW18 ..186 A2
Patterdale CI BMLY BR1 ....212 A2
Patterdale Rd PECK SE15 ....170 A1
Patterson Rd NRWD SE19 ....209 F2
Pattina Wk BERM/RHTH SE16 ..150 C1
Pattison Rd CRICK NW2 ....105 E1
Paul CI SRTFD E15 ....112 A5
Paulet Rd CMBW SE5 ....169 F6
Paulhan Rd KTN/HRWW/W HA3 ..81 F1
Paulin Dr WCHMH N21 ....52 A2
Pauline Crs WHTN TW2 ....179 G3
Paulinus CI STMC/STPC BR5 ...216 A5
Paul Julius CI POP/IOD E14 .....131 H6
Paul Robeson CI EHAM E6 .....134 A2
Paul St SDTCH EC2A 112 A6
SRTFD E15 ....112 A6
Paultons Sq CHEL SW3 ....145 H6
Paultons St CHEL SW3 ....145 H6
Pauntley St ARCH N19 ....87 E5
Paveley Dr BTSEA SW11 ....166 A1
Paveley St CAMTN NW1 ....2 B5
The Pavement CLAP SW4 ....167 E5
EA * W5 ....141 G3
TEDD * TW11 ....200 D3
WAN * E11 ....91 G5
WIM/MER * SW19 ....204 D2
WNWD * SE27 ....188 C6
Pavet CI DAGE RM10 ....117 F4
Pavilion Ldg RYLN/HDSTN * HA2 ...79 H5
Pavilion Pde SHB * W12 ....124 A5
Pavilion Rd IL IG1 ....93 H4
KTBR SW1X 18 D4
Pavilion St KTBR * SW1X 18 D4
The Pavilion VX/NE * SW8 ....167 F1
Pavilion Wy EDGW HA8 ....62 C3
RSLP HA4 ....78 A6
Pavillion Ter SHB * W12 ....124 A5
Pawleyne CI PGE/AN SE20 .....210 A3
Pawsey CI PLSTW E13 ....112 C6
Pawson's Rd CROY/NA CRO 228 C3
Paxford Rd ALP/SUD HA0 ....80 D6
Paxton CI RCH/KEW TW9 ....162 H1
WOT/HER* KT12 ....218 A4
Paxton PI WNWD SE27 ....189 E6
Paxton Rd BMLY BR1 ....212 C3
CHSWK W4 ....143 E6
FSTH SE23 ....191 E5
TOTM N17 ....69 G5
Paxton Ter PIM SW1V 27 H5
Payne CI BARK IG11 ....115 E5
Paynell Ct BKHTH/KID SE3 .....172 A4
Payne Rd BOW E3 ....131 F1
Paynesfield Av
MORT/ESHN SW14 ....162 D4
Paynesfield Rd BUSH WD23 .....44 B2
Payne St DEPT SE8 ....151 D5
Paynes Wk HMSMTH W6 ....144 C6
Payzes Gdns WFD * IG8 ....72 B2
Peabody Av PIM SW1V 27 H4
Peabody CI CROY/NA CRO 230 A5
GNWCH * SE10 ....171 F2
PIM SW1V 27 H4
Peabody Cottages
HNHL * SE24 ....188 C2
Peabody Est BTSEA * SW11 ....166 A5
CLKNW * EC1R 6 B6
CMBW * SE5 ....168 D2
FUL/PGN * SW6 ....144 A5
HMSMTH * W6 ....144 A5
NKENS * W10 ....124 A4
STHWK * SE1 ....22 B1
STHWK * SE1 ....23 E1
STLK * EC1Y 7 F6
TOTM * N17 ....69 G4
Peabody Hil DUL SE21 ....188 B3
Peabody Sq IS * N1 ....108 C6
Peabody St CLKNW * EC1R 6 B6
Peace CI GFD/PVL UB6 ....99 H6
SNWD SE25 ....229 E1
STHGT/OAK N14 ....36 D6
Peace Gv WBLY HA9 ....102 B3
Peace St WOOL/PLUM SE18 ...154 A6
Peaches CI BELMT SM2 ....242 A6
Peach Rd NKENS W10 ....124 B2
Peachum Rd BKHTH/KID SE3 ..152 B6
Peacock St WALW SE17 ....30 C6
Peacock Yd WALW * SE17 ....30 D2
Peaketon Av REDBR IG4 ....59 E3
Peak Hil SYD SE26 ....190 A6
Peak Hill Av SYD SE26 ....190 A6
Peak Hill Gdns SYD SE26 ....190 A6
The Peak SYD SE26 ....190 A5
Peal Gdns WEA W13 ....120 C2
Peall Rd CROY/NA CRO 227 H5
Pear CI CMTM CR4 ....206 C5
Pearcefield Av FSTH SE23 ....190 F3
Pear CI CDALE/KGS NW9 ....82 D1
NWCR SE14 ....170 C1
Pearcroft Rd FUL/PGN SW6 .....165 F2
Pearscroft Rd FUL/PGN SW6 ...165 F3

Pearson's Av NWCR SE14 ....171 E2
Pearson St BETH E2 ....8 C1
Pear Rd HSLW TW5 ....159 H4
Pear Tree Ct CLKNW EC1R 6 A6
BXLYHN DA7 ....177 H2
MTCM CR4 ....206 A5
SWLY BR8 ....217 H5
Pear Tree St CLKNW EC1R 6 B6
Peartree Av WAP * E1W 130 A6
Peartree Rd EN EN1 ....23 H4
Peartree St FSBYE EC1V 6 D5
Peartree Wy GNWCH SE10 .....152 C4
Pearwood Cottages STAN * HA7 ...45 E4
Peary PI BETH E2 ....90 A2
Peasmead Ter CHING * E4 ....55 G6
Peatfield CI BFN/LL DA15 ....195 E5
Pebworth Rd HRW HA1 ....80 C6
Peckarmans Wd DUL SE21 ......189 G5
Peckett Sq HBRY * N5 ....108 C2
Peckford PI BRXN/ST SW9 ....168 A3
Peckham Gv PECK SE15 ....169 E1
Peckham High St PECK SE15 ...169 G3
Peckham Hill St PECK SE15 .....169 G1
Peckham Park Rd PECK SE15 ..169 G1
Peckham Rye EDUL SE22 ....169 G5
Peckham Rye EDUL SE22 ....169 G5
Pecks Yd WCHPL * E1 ....19 J1
Peckwater St KTTN NW5 ....107 C5
Pedlars Wk HOLWY * N7 ....107 G3
Pedley Rd BCTR RM8 ....73 H5
Pedley St WCHPL E1 ....8 D6
Pedro St CLPT E5 ....110 B1
Peek Crs WIM/MER SW19 ....204 B1
Peel CI CHING E4 ....55 F4
PLSTW E13 ....53 C5
Peel Dr CDALE/KGS NW9 ....63 F6
CLAY IG5 ....73 G6
Peel Gv BETH E2 ....130 A1
Peel Pas KENS W8 ....145 C1
Peel PI CLAY IG5 ....73 G5
Peel Prec KIL/WHAMP NW6 .....124 D1
Peel Rd ALP/SUD HA0 ....101 E1
KTN/HRWW/W HA3 ....125 E2
KTN/HRWW/W HA3 ....60 B6
ORP BR6 ....252 C2
SWFD E18 ....72 B4
Peel St KENS W8 ....145 C1
Peerglow Est PEND * EN3 ....40 A6
Peerless St FSBYE EC1V 7 G4
Pegamoid Rd UED N18 ....43 A2
Pegasus Ct STNW/STAM * N16 ..108 D2
Pegasus Ct BTFD * TW8 ....141 H5
Pegasus PI FUL/PGN * SW6 .....165 E2
LBTH SE11 ....30 A5
Pegasus Rd CROY/NA CRO 246 A4
Pegasus Wy FBAR/BDGN N11 ...66 D2
Pegg Rd HEST TW5 ....158 B1
Pegley Gdns LEE/GVPK SE12 ..192 C4
Pegwell St WOOL/PLUM SE18 ..179 F1
Pekin St POP/IOD E14 ....131 E5
Peldon Wk IS * N1 ....108 B6
Pelham Av BARK IG11 ....115 F6
Pelham CI CMBW SE5 ....169 E5
Pelham Cottages BXLY * DA5 ...197 F5
Pelham Crs SKENS SW7 ....26 A2
Pelham PI SKENS SW7 ....26 A2
Pelham Rd BXLYHN DA7 ....177 G4
IL IG1 ....92 B5
PGE/AN SE20 ....210 A5
SEVS/STOTM N15 ....89 F1
SWFD E18 ....72 D6
WDGN N22 ....48 E4
WIM/MER SW19 ....205 E3
Pelham St SKENS SW7 ....26 A2
Pelier St WALW SE17 ....31 F5
Pelinore Rd CAT SE6 ....192 A4
Pellant Rd FUL/PGN SW6 ....164 C1
Pellatt Gv WDGN N22 ....68 A4
Pellatt Rd EDUL SE22 ....169 H4
WBLY HA9 ....62 A5
Pellerin Rd STNW/STAM N16 ...109 E3
Pelling St POP/IOD E14 ....130 D5
Pellipar CI PLMGR N13 ....52 A5
Pellipar Rd WOOL/PLUM SE18 ..153 H5
Pelly Rd PLSTW E13 ....112 C6
Pelter St BETH E2 ....9 K5
Pelton Rd GNWCH SE10 ....152 A5
Pembar Av WALTH * E17 ....70 C1
Pemberley Cha
HOR/WEW KT19 ....240 B3
Pemberley CI HOR/WEW KT19 ..240 B3
Pember Rd WLSDN NW10 ....121 E3
Pemberton Gdns ARCH N19 .....107 C1
CHDH RM6 ....96 C2
Pemberton PI HACK E8 ....109 H5
Pemberton Rd
E/WMO/HCT KT8 ....219 G3
FSBYPK N4 ....88 A2
Pemberton Rw
FLST/FETLN EC4A 14 B3
Pemberton Ter ARCH N19 ....107 C1
Pembridge Av HSLW/W TW4 ....178 D3
Pembridge Crs NTGHL W11 .....119 E2
Pembridge Gdns
BAY/PAD * W2 ....125 E6
Pembridge Ms NTGHL W11 .....125 E6
Pembridge PI BAY/PAD W2 ......125 E6
Pembridge Rd NTGHL W11 ......125 E6
Pembridge Sq BAY/PAD W2 .....125 E6
Pembridge Vis NTGHL W11 ......125 E6
Pembroke Av BRYLDS KT5 ....222 D2
EN EN1 ....39 H2
KTN/HRWW/W HA3 ....60 A6
RSLP HA4 ....78 B5
Pembroke CI ERITH DA8 ....158 A3
KTBR SW1X 15 J5
Pembroke Gardens CI
KENS W8 ....144 D3
Pembroke Gdns DAGE RM10 ...117 F1
KENS W8 ....144 D3
Pembroke Gardens CI
KENS W8 ....144 D3
Pembroke Ms KENS W8 ....145 E3
MUSWH N10 ....66 C4
Pembroke Pde ERITH * DA8 .....157 G5
Pembroke PI EDGW HA8 ....62 A3
ISLW TW7 ....135 H4
Pembroke Rd BMLY BR1 ....213 E5
CEND/HSY/T N8 ....87 G1

ECT SW5 ....145 E4
EHAM E6 ....134 A4
ERITH DA8 ....157 G5
GDMY/SEVK IG5 ....95 F5
GFD/PVL UB6 ....119 F3
MUSWH N10 ....66 C4
PLMGR N13 ....52 C5
SEVS/STOTM N15 ....89 F2
SNWD SE25 ....229 E1
WALTH E17 ....70 A2
WBLY HA9 ....101 F1
Pembroke Sq KENS W8 ....145 E3
Pembroke St IS N1 ....107 H2
Pembroke Ter STJWD * NW8 ...105 H6
Pembroke Vis KENS W8 ....145 E3
Pembroke Wk KENS W8 ....145 E4
Pembrook Ms BTSEA * SW11 ..165 H5
Pembury Av WPK KT4 ....223 G4
Pembury CI CLPT * E5 ....109 H5
HAYES BR2 ....232 B4
Pembury Crs SCUP DA14 ....196 C4
Pembury Rd BXLYHN DA7 ....176 C1
CLPT E5 ....109 H5
SNWD SE25 ....229 G3
TOTM N17 ....69 F4
Pemdevon Rd CROY/NA CRO ...228 A4
Pemell CI WCHPL E1 ....130 A3
Pempath PI WBLY HA9 ....81 H1
Penally PI IS N1 ....108 D6
Penang St WAP E1W 35 H1
Penard Rd NWDGN UB2 ....139 E3
Penarth St PECK SE15 ....150 A6
Penberth Rd CAT SE6 ....191 G4
Pencombe Ms NTGHL W11 .....124 D6
Pencraig Wy PECK * SE15 ....33 G6
Pendall CI EBAR EN4 ....36 A5
Penda Rd ERITH DA8 ....157 F3
Pendarves Rd RYNPK SW20 ...204 A4
Penda's Ms HOM E9 ....110 C2
Pendennis Rd ORP BR6 ....236 A6
STRHM/NOR SW16 ....187 G6
TOTM N17 ....69 F3
Penderel Rd HSLW TW3 ....159 E6
Penderry Ri CAT SE6 ....191 H4
Penderyn Wy HOLWY N7 ....107 F2
Pendle Rd STRHM/NOR SW16 ..206 D2
Pendlestone Rd LEY E10 ....91 F2
Pendragon Rd BMLY BR1 ....192 C3
Pendrell Rd BROCKY SE4 ....172 C5
Pendrell St WOOL/PLUM SE18 ..156 D6
Pendula Dr YEAD UB4 ....118 B3
Pendulum Ms HACK * E8 ....109 F3
Penerley Rd CAT SE6 ....191 F3
Penfold CI CROY/NA CRO 244 A6
Penfold PI BAY/PAD W2 ....10 A1
Penfold Rd ED N9 ....43 E3
Penfold St STJWD NW8 ....10 A1
Penford Gdns ELTH/MOT SE9 ...173 H5
Penford St CMBW SE5 ....168 B3
Pengarth Rd BXLY DA5 ....196 B5
Penge La PGE/AN SE20 ....210 A3
Penge Rd PLSTW E13 ....113 E5
SNWD SE25 ....229 G6
Penhall Rd CHARL SE7 ....154 C4
Penhill Rd BXLY DA5 ....196 A3
Penhurst Rd BARK/HLT IG6 ....54 B3
Penifather La GFD/PVL UB6 .....119 H2
Peninsular Park Rd CHARL SE7 ..152 C5
Penistone Rd
STRHM/NOR SW16 ....207 G3
Penmon Rd ABYW SE2 ....155 G5
Pennack Rd PECK SE15 ....33 G6
Pennant Ms KENS W8 ....145 F4
Pennant Ter WALTH E17 ....70 D5
Pennard Rd SHB W12 ....143 A2
The Pennards SUN TW16 ....156 A6
Penn CI GFD/PVL UB6 ....119 F1
KTN/HRWW/W HA3 ....61 E1
Penner CI WIM/MER SW19 ......186 A4
Penners Gdns SURB KT6 ....222 C4
Pennethorne CI HOM E9 ....110 A6
Pennethorne Rd PECK SE15 ....169 H1
Penn Gdns CHST BR7 ....214 B6
CRW IM5 ....77 C6
Pennine Dr CRICK NW2 ....84 B6
Pennine La CRICK NW2 ....84 C5
Pennine Pde CRICK * NW2 ....84 C5
Pennington CI CRW RM5 ....77 F2
Pennington Dr STHGT/OAK N14 ..37 G6
Pennington St WAP E1W 17 G6
Pennington Wy
LEE/GVPK SE12 ....192 D1
Penniston CI WDGN N22 ....68 C5
Penn La BXLY DA5 ....196 B1
Penn St IS N1 ....107 H3
Pennycroft CROY/NA CRO 248 C6
Pennyfields POP/IOD E14 ....131 E6
Pennymoor Wk MV/WKIL W9 ...124 D3
Pennyroyal Av EHAM E6 ....136 A1
Penpoll Rd HACK E8 ....109 H4
Penpool La WELL DA16 ....175 H4
Penrhyn Av WALTH E17 ....71 H1

HOM E9 ....110 B5
THHTH CR7 ....228 B2
Penshurst Wy BELMT SM2 ......243 E5
STMC/STPC BR5 ....236 A1
Penslver CI EBAR * EN4 ....36 A5
Penstemon CI FNCH N3 ....46 E2
Pentire Rd WALTH E17 ....71 H4
Pentland Av EDGW HA8 ....46 B4
Pentland CI CRICK NW2 ....84 C6
EDN9 ....54 A4
Pentland PI NTHLT UB5 ....98 C6
Pentland Rd BUSH WD23 ....43 C1
Pentlands CI MTCM CR4 ....206 D6
Pentland St WAND/EARL SW18 ..185 G1
Pentlow St PUT/ROE SW15 .....164 A3
Penton Gv BKHH IG9 ....57 G2
Pentney Rd BAL SW12 ....187 G3
SAN/FS 204 C4
Penton Gv IS N1 ....6 A2
Penton PI WALW SE17 ....31 E3
Penton Ri FSBYW WC1X 5 H4
Penton St IS N1 ....6 A1
Pentonville Rd IS N1 ....5 G2
Pentrich Av EN EN1 ....39 G1
Pentridge St PECK SE15 ....169 F1
Pentyre Av UED N18 ....41 H4
Penwerris Av ISLW TW7 ....159 G1
Penwith Rd WAND/EARL SW18 ..185 F4
Penwortham Rd
STRHM/NOR SW16 ....206 D2
Penylan PI EDGW * HA8 ....62 A4
Penywern Rd ECT SW5 ....145 E5
Penzance PI NTGHL W11 ....144 C1
Penzance St NTGHL W11 ....144 C1
Peony Gdns SHB W12 ....123 G6
Peploe Rd KIL/WHAMP NW6 ....124 B1
Pepper CI EHAM E6 ....133 H4
Peppermead Sq BROCKY * SE4 ..171 E6
Peppermint CI CROY/NA CRO ...227 G4
Peppermint PI WAN E11 ....112 A1
Pepper St POP/IOD E14 ....151 F3
STHWK SE1 ....18 D3
Pepple CI STNW/STAM N16 ....89 E6
Pepys Crs BAR EN5 ....34 A6
Pepys Est DEPT SE8 ....150 D5
Pepys Park EST DEPT SE8 ......150 D4
Pepys Rd NWCR SE14 ....170 B3
RYNPK SW20 ....204 A4
Pepys St TWRH EC3N 16 H5
Perceval Av HAMP NW3 ....106 A3
Percheron Rd BORE WD6 ....46 D1
Perch St HACK E8 ....91 F2
Percival Ct TOTM N17 ....69 F3
Percival Gdns CHDH RM6 ....73 H3
Percival Rd EN EN1 ....39 F5
MORT/ESHN SW14 ....162 C6
ORP BR6 ....234 B6
Percival St FSBYE EC1V 6 C6
Percival Wy HOR/WEW KT19 ...240 C2
Percy Av ASHF TW15 ....40 B6
Percy Gdns PEND EN3 ....222 D5
WPK KT4 ....222 D5
Percy Ms FITZ W1T 12 C2
Percy Rd BXLYHN DA7 ....176 C3
CAN/RD E16 ....132 A4
GDMY/SEVK IG5 ....95 G4
HPTN TW12 ....182 C5
ISLW TW7 ....160 C1
MTCM CR4 ....226 A2
NFNCH/WDSP N12 ....65 G1
PGE/AN SE20 ....210 B4
ROMW/RG RM7 ....77 G6
SHB W12 ....143 G2
SNWD SE25 ....229 F2
WAN E11 ....92 A4
WHTN TW2 ....179 G3
Percy St FITZ W1T 12 C2
Percy Wy WHTN TW2 ....179 G3
Peregrine CI WLSDN NW10 ......100 D3
Peregrine Ct WELL DA16 ....175 F2
Peregrine Gdns CROY/NA CRO ..236 G6
Peregrine Rd BARK/HLT IG6 ......75 H1
Perham Rd WKENS W14 ....143 H5
Peridot St EHAM E6 ....133 G4
Perifield DUL SE21 ....188 C3
Periton Rd ELTH/MOT SE9 ......173 H5
Perivale Gdns WEA W13 ....120 C2
Perivale La GFD/PVL UB6 ....120 C2
Perivale Village GFD/PVL * UB6 ..121 G2
Perkin CI ALP/SUD HA0 ....100 D3
Perkin's Rents WEST SW1P 20 C5
Perkins Rd BARK/HLT IG6 ....94 D2
Perkins Sq STHWK SE1 ....25 F3
Perpins Rd ELTH/MOT SE9 ......195 E1
Perran Rd BRXS/STRHM SW2 ..188 B4
Perrers Rd HMSMTH W6 ....143 H5
Perrin Rd ALP/SUD HA0 ....79 F6
Perrin's Ct HAMP * NW3 ....105 G2
Perrin's Wk HAMP NW3 ....105 G2
Perry Av ACT W3 ....122 D5
Perry Ct SEVS/STOTM * N15 .....89 G5
Perryfield Wy CDALE/KGS NW9 ..83 F3
RCHPK/HAM TW10 ....180 D4
Perry Gdns ED N9 ....53 E5
Perry Garth NTHLT UB5 ....95 A6
Perry Hall CI ORP BR6 ....235 G4
Perry Hall Rd ORP BR6 ....235 F5
Perry Hil CAT SE6 ....190 H4
Perry How WPK KT4 ....223 F5
Perry Mnr CHST BR7 ....215 G2
Perrymans Farm Rd
BARK/HLT IG6 ....94 D3
Perry Md BUSH WD23 ....28 C1
ENC/FH EN2 ....25 H2
Perrymead St FUL/PGN SW6 ...165 E2
Perryn Rd ACT W3 ....122 D6
BERM/RHTH SE16 ....151 F3
Perry Ri FSTH SE23 ....190 C5
Perry St CHST BR7 ....215 G2
Perry V FSTH SE23 ....190 A4
Persant Rd CAT SE6 ....192 C3
Perseverance PI BRXN/ST * SW9 ..168 A1
Pershore CI GNTH/NBYPK IG2 ...94 B2
Pershore Gv CAR SM5 ....225 H5

Pert Cl MUSWH N10 .....66 D3
Perth Av CDALE/KGS NW9 .....82 D4
  YEAD UB4 .....118 A3
Perth Cl RYNPK SW20 .....203 F5
Perth Rd BARK IG11 .....134 D1
  BECK BR3 .....211 G5
  FSBYPK N4 .....66 D3
  GNTH/NBYPK IG2 .....90 C5
  LEY E10 .....90 C5
  PLSTW E13 .....132 D1
  WDGN N22 .....68 B4
Perth Ter GNTH/NBYPK IG2 .....94 C4
Perwell Av RYLN/HDSTN HA2 .....78 D5
Petauel Rd TEDD TW11 .....200 A1
Petavel Rd TEDD TW11 .....200 A2
Peter Av WLSDN NW10 .....103 H5
Peterboat Cl GNWCH SE10 .....152 A4
Peterborough Ms
  FUL/PGN SW6 .....165 E3
Peterborough Rd CAR SM5 .....165 E3
  FUL/PGN SW6 .....165 E3
  HNWL W7 .....80 A5
  LEY E10 .....91 G2
Peterborough Vls
  FUL/PGN SW6 .....165 F2
Petergate BTSEA SW11 .....165 G5
Peters Cl BCTR RM8 .....96 B5
  EDGW HA8 .....61 G2
  WELL DA16 .....175 E3
Petersfield Cl UED N18 .....68 C1
Petersfield Ri PUT/ROE SW15 .....183 H1
Petersfield Rd ACT W3 .....142 C2
Petersham Cl
  RCHPK/HAM TW10 .....181 F4
  SUT SM1 .....242 D3
Petersham Dr STMC/STPC BR5 .....215 F5
Petersham Gdns
  STMC/STPC BR5 .....215 F5
Petersham La SKENS * SW7 .....145 G3
Petersham Ms SKENS SW7 .....145 G3
Petersham Pl SKENS SW7 .....145 G3
Petersham Rd
  RCHPK/HAM TW10 .....181 G1
Petersham Ter CROY/NA * CR0 .....245 G1
Peter's Hl BLKFR EC4V 13 F5
Peters Pl CAMTN NW1 .....5 J4
Petrie Cl CRICK * NW2 .....104 C4
Petros Gdns HAMP * NW3 .....105 F3
Petten Cl STMC/STPC BR5 .....236 B5
Petten Gv STMC/STPC BR5 .....236 A5
Petticoat Sq WCHPL * E1 .....16 C3
Pettits La North ROM RM1 .....77 H4
Pettit's Pl DAGE RM10 .....117 E3
Pettit's Rd DAGE RM10 .....117 E3
Pettiward Cl PUT/ROE SW15 .....164 A5
Pettley Gdns ROMW/RG RM7 .....97 H2
Pettman Crs THMD SE28 .....154 D4
Pettsgrove Av ALP/SUD HA0 .....101 E3
Pett's Hl RYLN/HDSTN HA2 .....99 F2
Pett St CHARL SE7 .....153 C4
Petts Wood Rd
  STMC/STPC BR5 .....234 D2
Petty France STJSPK SW1H 20 B5
Petworth Cl NTHLT UB5 .....98 D5
Petworth Gdns RYNPK SW20 .....203 H6
Petworth Rd BXLYHS DA6 .....177 E6
  NFNCH/WDSP N12 .....66 A1
Petworth St BTSEA SW11 .....166 A2
Petyt Pl CHEL SW3 .....26 A6
Petyward CHEL SW3 .....26 C4
Pevensey Av EN EN1 .....38 D3
  FBAR/BDGN N11 .....67 F1
Pevensey Cl ISLW TW7 .....159 G1
Pevensey Rd FELT TW13 .....178 C3
  FSTGT E7 .....113 F1
  TOOT SW17 .....185 H6
Peveret Cl FBAR/BDGN * N11 .....66 C6
Peverll Dr TEDD TW11 .....199 H1
Pevsey Cl CHING E4 .....71 E1
Peyton Pl GNWCH SE10 .....171 G1
Pharaoh Cl MTCM CR4 .....226 B4
Pheasant Cl CAN/RD E16 .....132 D5
Phelp St WALW SE17 .....31 G4
Phene St CHEL SW3 .....26 B5
Philan Wy CRW RM5 .....77 H2
Philbeach Gdns ECT SW5 .....145 E5
Philchurch Pl WCHPL E1 .....17 F4
Philimore Cl WOOL/PLUM SE18 .....155 E5
Philip Av ROMW/RG RM7 .....97 H5
Philip Gdns CROY/NA CR0 .....230 D6
Philip La SEVS/STOTM N15 .....88 D1
Philippa Gdns ELTH/MOT SE9 .....173 F6
Philip Rd PECK SE15 .....169 G4
Philips Cl MTCM CR4 .....224 C4
Philip St PLSTW E13 .....132 C3
Phillimore Gdns KENS W8 .....145 E2
  WLSDN NW10 .....104 A6
Phillimore Gardens Cl
  KENS W8 .....145 E3
Phillimore Pl KENS * W8 .....145 E3
Phillimore Ter KENS * W8 .....145 E3
Phillimore Wk KENS W8 .....145 E3
Phillip Av SWLY BR8 .....237 H1
Phillipp St IS N1 .....8 C1
Philpot La FENCHST EC3M 16 A5
Philpot St WCHPL E1 .....17 H3
Phineas Pett Rd
  ELTH/MOT SE9 .....173 G4
Phipp's Bridge Rd
  WIM/MER SW19 .....205 G4
Phipps Hatch La ENC/FH EN2 .....58 C1
Phipp St SDTCH EC2A 8 A5
Phoebeth Rd LEW SE13 .....171 E6
Phoenix Cl HACK * E8 .....109 F6
  WWKM BR4 .....231 H6
Phoenix Ct BTFD TW8 .....141 G5
Phoenix Dr HAYES BR2 .....251 F2
Phoenix Pk BTFD * TW8 .....141 F5
Phoenix Pl FSBYW WC1X 5 H5
Phoenix Rd CAMTN NW1 .....4 C3
  PGE/AN SE20 .....210 A2
Phoenix St LSQ/SEVD WC2H 12 C4
Phoenix Wy HEST TW5 .....138 B6

Phoenix Wharf Rd STHWK SE1 .....24 D4
Phyllis Av NWMAL KT3 .....223 H2
The Piazza COVGDN WC2E 13 F5
Picardy Manorway BELV DA17 .....157 F3
Picardy Rd BELV DA17 .....157 G5
Picardy St BELV DA17 .....157 G3
Piccadilly MYFR/PICC W1J 19 G2
Piccadilly Ar MYFR/PICC W1J 20 A1
Piccadilly Circ MYFR/PICC W1J 12 C6
Pickard St FSBYE EC1V 6 D3
Pickering Av EHAM E6 .....134 A1
Pickering Gdns
  FBAR/BDGN N11 .....66 C2
  SNWD SE25 .....229 F3
Pickering Pl STJS * SW1Y 20 B2
Pickering St IS N1 .....108 B6
Pickets Cl BUSH WD23 .....43 H5
Pickets St BAL SW12 .....186 C2
Pickett Crt STAN HA7 .....61 F4
Pickett's Lock La ED N9 .....54 B4
Pickford Cl BXLYHN DA7 .....176 C3
Pickford La BXLYHN DA7 .....176 C3
Pickford Rd BXLYHN DA7 .....176 C4
Pickfords Whf IS * N1 .....6 C2
Pickhurst Gn HAYES BR2 .....232 B4
Pickhurst La HAYES BR2 .....232 B3
  WWKM BR4 .....232 A3
Pickhurst Md HAYES BR2 .....232 A3
Pickhurst Pk HAYES BR2 .....232 A2
Pickhurst Ri WWKM BR4 .....231 H5
Pickwick Cl HSLWW TW4 .....158 C6
Pickwick Ms UED N18 .....69 E1
Pickwick Pl HRW HA1 .....80 A4
Pickwick Rd DUL SE21 .....188 D2
Pickwick St STHWK SE1 .....23 E4
Pickwick Wy CHST BR7 .....214 C2
Pickworth Cl VX/NE * SW8 .....167 C1
Picton Pl MBLAR W1H 9 G4
Picton St CMBW SE5 .....168 D1
Piedmont Rd
  WOOL/PLUM SE18 .....154 D5
Pier Head WAP E1W 25 C2
Piermont Pl BMLY BR1 .....213 F5
Piermont Rd EDUL SE22 .....169 H6
Pierrepoint Ar IS * N1 .....6 C1
Pierrepoint Rd ACT W3 .....122 B6
Pierrepoint Rw IS N1 .....6 C1
Pier Rd CAN/RD E16 .....153 H2
Pier St POP/IOD E14 .....151 G4
Pier Ter WAND/EARL SW18 .....165 F5
Pier Wy WOOL/PLUM SE18 .....154 D3
Pigeon La HPTN TW12 .....179 E6
Pigott St POP/IOD E14 .....131 E5
Pike Cl BMLY BR1 .....194 A4
Pike Rd MLHL NW7 .....46 D6
Pikestone Cl YEAD * UB4 .....118 C3
Pilgrimage St STHWK SE1 .....23 G4
Pilgrim Cl MRDN SM4 .....225 F4
Pilgrim Hl WNWD SE27 .....188 C6
Pilgrims Cl NTHLT UB5 .....99 G3
  PLMGR N13 .....51 H6
Pilgrim's La HAMP NW3 .....105 H2
Pilgrims Ms POP/IOD E14 .....131 H6
Pilgrim's Ri EBAR EN4 .....36 A6
Pilgrim St BLKFR * EC4V 14 C4
Pilgrims Wy ARCH N19 .....85 F1
  SAND/SEL CR2 .....247 F4
  SAND/SEL * CR2 .....247 F5
  WBLY HA9 .....82 B5
Pilkington Rd ORP BR6 .....252 C1
  PECK SE15 .....169 H1
Pilot Cl DEPT SE8 .....150 D6
Pilsden Cl WIM/MER * SW19 .....184 B3
Piltdown Rd OXHEY WD19 .....42 B6
Pilton Pl WALW SE17 .....31 F5
Pimlico Rd BGVA SW1W 27 G3
Pinchbeck Rd ORP BR6 .....255 F4
Pinchin & Johnsons Yd
  IS N1 .....17 F5
Pinchin St WCHPL E1 .....17 F5
Pincott Pl BROCKY SE4 .....170 B4
Pincott Rd BXLYHS DA6 .....177 E6
  WIM/MER SW19 .....205 G4
Pindar St SDTCH EC2A 16 A1
Pindock Ms MV/WKIL W9 .....119 G3
Pine Apple Ct WESTW * SW1E 20 A5
Pine Av SRTFD E15 .....111 K3
  WWKM BR4 .....231 F5
Pine Cl LEY E10 .....91 E6
  PGE/AN SE20 .....210 A4
  STAN HA7 .....44 A6
  STHGT/OAK N14 .....51 E2
Pine Coombe CROY/NA CR0 .....248 B2
Pinecrest Gdns ORP BR6 .....252 B2
Pinecroft Crs BAR * EN5 .....81 H2
  WELL DA16 .....175 G4
Pinecroft Crs BAR EN5 .....34 C5
Pinefield Cl POP/IOD * E14 .....131 E6
Pine Gdns BRYLDS KT5 .....222 A3
Pine Gld ORP BR6 .....251 F6
Pine Gv FSBYPK N4 .....67 G6
  TRDG/WHET N20 .....48 D3
  WIM/MER SW19 .....204 D3
Pinelands Cl BKHTH/KID * SE3 .....172 B1
Pinelees Ct
  MORT/ESHN * SW14 .....162 C5
Pinemartin Cl CRICK NW2 .....104 A1
Pine Rdg CAR SM5 .....246 A1
Pine Rd CRICK NW2 .....104 A2
  FBAR/BDGN N11 .....50 C4
Pines Rd BMLY BR1 .....213 G5
The Pines NRWD * SE19 .....208 D2
  WFD IG8 .....56 B5
Pine St CLKNW EC1R 5 J6
Pine Wk BRYLDS KT5 .....222 A3
Pinewood Av BFN/LL DA15 .....195 E3
  PIN HA5 .....42 B3
Pinewood Cl CROY/NA CR0 .....248 C1
  ORP BR6 .....254 D5
  PIN HA5 .....42 B3
Pinewood Dr ORP BR6 .....255 E5
Pinewood Gv WEA W13 .....121 G1
Pinewood Ldg BUSH * WD23 .....43 H3
Pinewood Rd ABYW SE2 .....156 D6
  HAYES BR2 .....232 C1
Pinfold Rd STRHM/NOR SW16 .....188 C6
Pinkham Wy North Circular Rd
  MUSWH N10 .....66 B3
Pinley Gdns DAGW RM9 .....115 H6
Pinnacle Hl BXLYHN DA7 .....177 F5
Pinnacle Hl North BXLYHN DA7 .....177 F4

Pinnell Rd ELTH/MOT SE9 .....173 F5
Pinner Ct PIN HA5 .....79 E1
Pinner Gn PIN HA5 .....59 A5
Pinner Gv PIN HA5 .....78 C1
Pinner Hill Rd PIN HA5 .....58 A4
Pinner Park Av
  RYLN/HDSTN HA2 .....59 G5
Pinner Park Gdns
  RYLN/HDSTN HA2 .....59 F1
Pinner Rd HRW HA1 .....79 F2
  OXHEY WD19 .....42 B1
  PIN HA5 .....78 D1
Pinner Vw RYLN/HDSTN HA2 .....79 G1
Pintail Cl EHAM E6 .....133 G4
Pintail Rd WFD IG8 .....72 D3
Pintail Wy YEAD UB4 .....118 B4
Pinto Cl BORE * WD6 .....46 D1
Pinto Wy BKHTH/KID SE3 .....172 D5
Pioneer Cl SHB W12 .....123 H5
Pioneer St PECK SE15 .....169 G2
Pioneer Wy SHB W12 .....124 A5
Piper Cl HOLWY N7 .....107 H3
Piper Rd KUT KT1 .....202 A6
Pipers Gdns CROY/NA CR0 .....230 C4
Pipers Gn CDALE/KGS NW9 .....82 C2
Pipers Green La EDGW HA8 .....45 G5
Pipewell Rd CAR SM5 .....226 A3
Pippin Cl CRICK NW2 .....103 G1
  CROY/NA CR0 .....230 D5
Piquet Rd PGE/AN SE20 .....210 A2
Pirbright Crs CROY/NA CR0 .....249 G4
Pirbright Rd WAND/EARL SW18 .....184 D5
Pirie St CAN/RD E16 .....152 D1
Pitcairn Cl ROMW/RG RM7 .....97 E1
Pitcairn Rd MTCM CR4 .....206 B3
Pitchford St SRTFD E15 .....111 G5
Pitfield Crs THMD SE28 .....155 G1
Pitfield St IS N1 .....8 D1
Pitfield Wy PEND * EN3 .....40 A2
  WLSDN NW10 .....102 C4
Pitfold Rd LEE/GVPK SE12 .....192 C2
Pitlake CROY/NA CR0 .....228 B6
Pitman St CMBW SE5 .....168 C1
Pitsea Pl WCHPL E1 .....130 B5
Pitsea St WCHPL E1 .....130 B5
Pitshanger La EA W5 .....120 D5
Pitt Crs WIM/MER SW19 .....185 F6
Pittman Gdns IL IG1 .....114 C3
Pitt Rd ORP BR6 .....252 C2
  RYLN/HDSTN HA2 .....79 G6
  THHTH CR7 .....208 D3
Pitt's Head Ms
  MYFR/PKLN W1K 19 F2
Pittsmead Av HAYES BR2 .....232 E2
Pitt St KENS W8 .....145 E2
Pittville Gdns SNWD SE25 .....209 G6
Pixley St POP/IOD E14 .....130 D5
Pixton Wy CROY/NA CR0 .....248 C6
Place Farm Av ORP BR6 .....254 D5
Plaistow Gv BMLY BR1 .....212 D3
  SRTFD E15 .....112 B6
Plaistow La BMLY BR1 .....212 D3
Plaistow Park Rd PLSTW E13 .....132 D1
Plaistow Rd PLSTW E13 .....112 B6
  SRTFD E15 .....112 B6
Plane St SYD SE26 .....189 H5
Plantagenet Cl
  HOR/WEW KT19 .....240 A5
Plantagenet Gdns CHDH RM6 .....96 B4
Plantagenet Pl CHDH RM6 .....96 B4
Plantagenet Rd BAR EN5 .....35 G5
Plantain Gdns WAN * E11 .....111 H1
Plantain Pl STHWK SE1 .....23 H2
Plantation Dr STMC/STPC BR5 .....236 B5
The Plantation BKHTH/KID SE3 .....172 C3
Plashet Gv EHAM E6 .....113 G1
Plashet Rd PLSTW E13 .....112 C6
Plassy Rd CAT SE6 .....191 F7
Platina St SDTCH EC2A 7 H5
Plato Rd CLAP SW4 .....167 G5
Platt's La HAMP NW3 .....105 E1
Platts Rd PEND EN3 .....40 A2
Platt St CAMTN NW1 .....4 C1
Plawsfield Rd BECK BR3 .....210 B6
Plaxtol Cl BMLY BR1 .....213 E4
Plaxtol Rd ERITH DA8 .....177 E1
Playfair St HMSMTH * W6 .....143 A5
Playfield Av CRW RM5 .....77 G4
Playfield Crs EDUL SE22 .....169 E6
Playfield Rd EDGW HA8 .....60 C2
Playgreen Wy CAT SE6 .....191 E6
Playground Cl BECK BR3 .....210 B5
Playhouse Yd BLKFR EC4V 14 C4
Plaza Pde ALP/SUD * HA0 .....101 G4
The Pleasance PUT/ROE SW15 .....163 H5
Pleasant Gv CROY/NA CR0 .....248 D1
Pleasant Pl IS N1 .....108 B5
Pleasant Rw CAMTN NW1 .....4 B1
Pleasant Vw ERITH DA8 .....110 A5
Plender St CAMTN NW1 .....107 G6
Pleshey Rd HOLWY N7 .....84 D3
Plesman Wy WLGTN * SM6 .....245 G6
Plevna Crs SEVS/STOTM N15 .....89 E3
Plevna Rd ED N9 .....54 C2
  HPTN TW12 .....199 F4
Plevna St POP/IOD E14 .....151 G3
Pleydell Av HMSMTH W6 .....142 B6
  NRWD SE19 .....208 B4
Pleydell Est FSBYE * EC1V 6 C4
Pleydell Gdns NRWD * SE19 .....208 B4
Pleydell St EMB EC4Y 14 A4
Plimsoll Cl POP/IOD E14 .....131 F5
Plimsoll Rd FSBYPK N4 .....108 B3
Plough La CROY/NA CR0 .....245 G1
  EDUL SE22 .....169 G1
  TEDD * TW11 .....200 C1
  WIM/MER SW19 .....205 F1
  WLGTN SM6 .....246 D3
Plough La Cl WLGTN SM6 .....245 G3
Ploughmans Cl CAMTN NW1 .....107 H1
Ploughmans End ISLW TW7 .....159 H6
Plough Pl FLST/FETLN * EC4A 14 A3
Plough Rd BTSEA SW11 .....165 H4
  HOR/WEW KT19 .....240 A6
Plough St WCHPL * E1 .....13 J3
Plough Ter BTSEA SW11 .....165 H3
Plough Yd SDTCH EC2A 7 H6
Plover Wy BERM/RHTH SE16 .....150 B3
  YEAD UB4 .....118 B5

Plowden Buildings EMB * EC4Y 14 A5
Plowman Cl UED N18 .....68 D1
Plowman Wy BCTR RM8 .....96 A5
Plumbers Row WCHPL E1 .....17 E2
Plumbridge St GNWCH * SE10 .....171 G2
Plum Garth BTFD TW8 .....141 F4
Plum Lane WOOL/PLUM SE18 .....174 B1
Plummer La MTCM CR4 .....206 B4
Plummer Rd CLAP SW4 .....187 E1
Plumpton Cl NTHLT UB5 .....99 E4
Plumpton Wy CAR SM5 .....244 A1
Plumstead Common Rd
  WOOL/PLUM SE18 .....154 C6
Plumstead High St
  WOOL/PLUM SE18 .....154 D4
Plumstead Rd
  WOOL/PLUM SE18 .....154 C4
Plumtree Cl DAGE RM10 .....117 E4
Plumtree Ct FLST/FETLN EC4A 14 B3
Plymouth Rd BMLY BR1 .....212 D4
  CAN/RD E16 .....132 C4
Plymouth Whf POP/IOD E14 .....151 H4
Plympton Av KIL/WHAMP NW6 .....104 D5
Plympton Cl BELV * DA17 .....157 C3
Plympton Pl STJWD * NW8 .....2 A6
Plympton Rd KIL/WHAMP NW6 .....104 D5
Plympton St STJWD NW8 .....2 B6
Plymstock Rd WELL DA16 .....176 A1
Pocklington Cl
  CDALE/KGS NW9 .....63 E5
Pocock St STHWK SE1 .....22 C3
Podmore Rd
  WAND/EARL SW18 .....165 G5
Poet's Rd HBRY N5 .....108 D3
Poets Wy HRW HA1 .....80 A1
Pointalls Cl FNCH N3 .....65 F1
Point Cl GNWCH SE10 .....171 G2
Pointer Cl THMD SE28 .....136 B5
Pointers Cl POP/IOD E14 .....151 F5
Point Hill GNWCH SE10 .....171 G2
Point Pl WBLY HA9 .....102 B5
Point Pleasant
  WAND/EARL SW18 .....165 G5
Poland St SOHO/CST W1F 12 B3
Polebrook Rd BKHTH/KID SE3 .....173 E4
Polecroft La CAT SE6 .....190 D4
Pole Hill Rd CHING E4 .....55 G2
Polesden Gdns RYNPK SW20 .....203 H6
Polesworth Rd DAGW RM9 .....136 D1
Pollard Cl CAN/RD E16 .....152 G6
  CHIG IG7 .....75 G1
  HOLWY N7 .....107 H3
Pollard Rd MRDN SM4 .....225 A4
  TRDG/WHET N20 .....50 A4
Pollard Rw BETH E2 .....9 F3
Pollards Crs STRHM/NOR SW16 .....207 H6
Pollards Hl East
  STRHM/NOR SW16 .....207 H6
Pollards Hl North
  STRHM/NOR SW16 .....207 G6
Pollards Hl South
  STRHM/NOR SW16 .....207 G6
Pollards Hl West
  STRHM/NOR SW16 .....207 G6
Pollard St BETH E2 .....9 F3
Pollards Wood Rd
  STRHM/NOR SW16 .....207 G5
Pollen St CONDST W1S 11 A4
Pollitt Dr STJWD * NW8 .....125 H5
Polperro Cl ORP BR6 .....235 F3
Polsted Rd CAT SE6 .....190 D2
Polthorne Gv
  WOOL/PLUM SE18 .....154 C4
Polworth Rd
  STRHM/NOR SW16 .....207 G1
Polygon Rd CAMTN NW1 .....4 C3
The Polygon CLAP * SW4 .....167 E5
Polytechnic St
  WOOL/PLUM SE18 .....154 A4
Pomell Wy WCHPL E1 .....16 D3
Pomeroy St NWCR SE14 .....170 H1
Pomfret Rd CMBW SE5 .....168 B4
Pomoja La ARCH N19 .....87 G6
Pond Cl EFNCH N2 .....72 A5
Pond Cottage La BECK BR3 .....231 G5
Ponder St HOLWY * N7 .....107 H5
Pond Farm Est CLPT * E5 .....110 A1
Pondfield Rd DAGE RM10 .....117 F3
  HAYES BR2 .....231 H3
  ORP BR6 .....252 B1
Pond Hill Gdns CHEAM * SM3 .....242 C4
Pond Md DUL SE21 .....188 D1
Pond Pl CHEL SW3 .....26 C4
Pond Rd BKHTH/KID SE3 .....172 B4
  SRTFD E15 .....132 A1
Pond St HAMP NW3 .....106 A3
Pond Wy TEDD TW11 .....200 D2
Pondwood Ri ORP BR6 .....255 E4
Ponler St WCHPL E1 .....17 C4
Ponsard Rd WLSDN NW10 .....123 H2
Ponsford St HOM E9 .....110 A4
Ponsonby Pl WEST SW1P 28 D3
Ponsonby Rd PUT/ROE SW15 .....183 H2
Ponsonby Ter WEST SW1P 28 D3
Pontefract Rd BMLY BR1 .....212 C1
Ponton Rd VX/NE SW8 .....121 H6
Pont St SKENS SW1X 18 C6
Pont Street Ms CHEL SW3 .....18 C6
Pool Cl BECK BR3 .....211 E1
  E/WMO/HCT KT8 .....218 C2
Pool Ct CAT SE6 .....191 E4
Poole Court Rd HEST TW5 .....158 C5
Poole Rd HOM E9 .....110 B4
  HOR/WEW KT19 .....240 A5
Pooles Buildings FSBYW WC1X 6 A6
Pooles La WBPTN * SW10 .....165 G1
Pooles Pk FSBYPK N4 .....108 B1
Poole St IS N1 .....108 D6
Poolmans St BERM/RHTH SE16 .....150 D2
Pool Rd E/WMO/HCT KT8 .....218 D2
  HRW HA1 .....79 H4
Poolsford Rd CDALE/KGS NW9 .....83 A5
Poonah St WCHPL E1 .....130 A5
Pope Cl WIM/MER * SW19 .....205 H2
Pope's Av WHTN TW2 .....181 H1
Pope's Dr FNCH N3 .....65 A5
Popes Gv CROY/NA CR0 .....240 B1
  WHTN TW2 .....180 A4

Pope's La EA W5........................141 F3
Pope's Rd BRXN/ST * SW9 ....168 A5
Pope St STHWK SE1.....................24 B4
Popham Cl FELT TW13..............178 C5
Popham Gdns RCH/KEW * TW9 ..162 B4
Popham Rd IS N1..........................108 C6
Popham St IS N1...........................108 C6
Popinjays Rw CHEAM * SM3........242 B5
Poplar Av MTCM CR4...................206 D4
   NWDGN UB2..............................139 F3
   ORP BR6....................................234 B6
Poplar Bath St POP/IOD E14....131 F6
Poplar Cl HOM E9.........................110 D5
   PIN HA5.......................................58 B4
Poplar Court Pde TWK * TW1....181 E1
Poplar Crs HMSMTH W6.............144 A2
   NOR/WEW KT19........................240 C4
Poplar Gdns NWMAL KT3...........202 D5
Poplar Gv FBAR/BDGN N11........48 C3
   NWMAL KT3..............................202 D6
   WBLY HA9..................................102 C1
Poplar High St POP/IOD E14....131 F6
Poplar Ms SHB W12.....................144 A1
Poplar Mt BEA DA17...................157 F4
Poplar Pl BAY/PAD W2................125 F6
   THMD SE28...............................136 A6
Poplar Rd CHEAM SM5................224 D5
   HNHL SE24................................168 C5
   WIM/MER SW19.........................205 E6
Poplar Rd South
   WIM/MER SW19.........................205 E6
Poplars Rd LEY E10.......................91 F3
Poplar St ROMW/RG RM7.............97 G1
Poplar Vw WBLY * HA9..................81 F6
Poplar Wk CROY/NA CRO............228 C6
   HNHL SE24................................168 C5
Poplar Wy BARK/HLT IG6..............94 C1
Poppins Ct FLST/FETLN EC4A.......14 C4
Poppleton Rd WAN E11..................92 A3
Poppy Cl BELV DA17....................226 C5
Poppy La CROY/NA CRO...............230 A4
Porchester Gardens Ms
   BAY/PAD * W2..........................125 F5
Porchester Gdns BAY/PAD W2 ..125 F6
Porchester Ga BAY/PAD * W2....125 G6
Porchester Md BECK BR3............211 F2
Porchester Pl BAY/PAD W2............10 B4
Porchester Pl BAY/PAD W2........125 F5
   KUT KT1....................................202 B5
Porchester Sq BAY/PAD W2......125 F5
Porchester Square Ms
   BAY/PAD * W2..........................125 F5
Porchester Ter BAY/PAD W2......125 G6
Porch Wy TRDG/WHET N20...........50 B5
Porcupine Pl ELTH/MOT SE9......193 G4
Porden Rd BRXN/ST SW9............167 H5
Porlock Av RYLN/HDSTN HA2......79 C5
Porlock Rd EN EN1..........................53 F2
Porlock St STHWK SE1..................23 H3
Porrington Cl CHST BR7..............213 H4
Portal Cl WNWD SE27.................169 G4
Portbury Cl PECK SE15................169 G2
Portchester Cl CMBW SE5..........168 C5
Portcullis Lodge Rd
   ENC/FH EN2..............................38 D4
Portelet Rd WCHPL E1................130 B2
Porten House WKENS * W14 ......144 C2
Porten Rd WKENS W14...............144 C3
Porter Rd EHAM E6......................133 H5
Porters Av DAGW RM9...............115 H1
Porters St MHST W1U....................11 G4
   STHWK SE1................................23 F1
Porters Wk WAP * E1W..................17 C6
Porteus Rd BAY/PAD W2.............125 G4
Portgate Cl MV/WKIL W9............124 D3
Porthcawe Rd SYD SE26.............190 D4
Porthkerry Av WELL DA16...........176 C5
Portia Wy BOW E3.......................130 D3
The Porticoes WBPTN * SW10 ...145 H6
Portinscale Rd PUT/ROE SW15...164 C6
Portland Av BFN/LL DA15..........195 G1
   NWMAL KT3..............................223 F4
   STNW/STAM N16........................89 F5
Portland Cl CHDH RM6..................96 C2
Portland Cottages
   CROY/NA * CRO.......................227 F4
Portland Crs ELTH/MOT SE9......193 G4
   GFD/PVL UB6............................119 F3
   STAN HA7....................................61 F5
Portland Dr ENC/FH EN2...............39 E1
Portland Gdns CHDH RM6.............96 B2
   FSBYPK N4..................................88 B3
Portland Gv VX/NE SW8.............167 K2
Portland Ms SOHO/CST W1F.......32 D4
Portland Pl CAVSQ/HST W1G........3 G6
   SNWD SE25...............................229 G1
Portland Rd FSBYPK N4................88 B3
Portland Rd BMLY BR1................193 G6
   KUT KT1.......................................9 G5
   MTCM CR4.................................206 A5
   NTGHL W11................................124 C6
   NWDGN UB2..............................138 D3
   SEVS/STOTM N15........................89 E1
   SNWD SE25...............................229 H1
Portland Sq WAP E1W...................31 G4
Portland St WALW SE17................31 G4
Portland Ter RCH/KEW * TW9 ....161 G1
Portman Av MORT/ESHN SW14...162 D4
Portman Cl BXLYHN DA7............176 B4
   MBLAR W1H.................................11 G3
Portman Dr WFD IG8......................73 F5
Portman Gdns CDALE/KGS NW9 ..62 D5
Portman Ga CAMTN NW1..............11 E1
Portman Ms South MBLAR W1H...11 F4
Portman Pl BETH E2.....................130 A2
Portman Rd KUT KT1...................201 H5
Portman Sq MBLAR W1H................10 D3
Portman St MBLAR W1H................11 E4
Portman Towers MBLAR W1H......10 C3
Portmeers Cl WALTH * E17............90 D3
Portmore Gdns CRW RM5..............77 E1
Portnall Rd MV/WKIL W9.............124 D2
Portnoi Cl ROM RM1......................77 H5
Portobello Ct NTGHL * W11 ......124 D6
Portobello Ms NTGHL W11..........125 E6
Portobello Rd NKENS W10...........124 C5
   NTGHL W11................................124 D6
Portpool La FSBYW WC1X.............14 A1

Portree St POP/IOD E14..............131 H5
Portsdown Av GLDGN NW11........84 D3
Portsdown Ms GLDGN NW11.......84 D3
Portsea Ms BAY/PAD W2................10 B4
Portsea Pl BAY/PAD W2.................10 B4
Portside Rd VX/NE SW8..............167 G3
Portsmouth Av THDIT KT7...........220 C4
Portsmouth Rd KUT KT1.............201 F6
   PUT/ROE SW15.........................183 H2
Portsmouth St LINN WC2A............13 G3
Portsoken St TWHTH EC3N............16 C5
Portugal Gdns WHTN * TW2.......179 G4
Portugal St LINN WC2A..................13 H4
Portway SRTFD E15.....................112 D6
Portway Crs EW KT17..................241 G6
Portway Gdns
   WOOL/PLUM SE18.....................173 F2
Postern Gn ENC/FH EN2...............38 A3
The Postern BARB * EC2Y.............15 F2
Post La WHTN TW2.....................179 H3
Postmill Cl CROY/NA CRO............248 A1
Post Office Ap FSTGT E7.............112 D3
Post Office Wy VX/NE SW8.........167 H6
Postway Ms IL IG1........................114 B1
Potier St STHWK SE1....................35 H6
Potter Cl MTCM * CR4.................206 D5
The Potteries BAR * EN5................35 E6
Potterne Cl WIM/MER SW19.......184 B2
Potters Cl CROY/NA CRO............230 C5
   Potters Fld EN * EN1...................53 H5
Potters Flds STHWK SE1...............24 B2
Potters Gv NWMAL KT3..............222 C1
Potter's La BAR EN5......................35 E5
   STRHM/NOR * SW16.................207 F2
Potter's Rd BAR EN5.....................35 E5
   FUL/PGN SW6.............................165 G3
Pottery La NTGHL W11................144 C1
Pottery Rd BTFD TW8..................144 A1
   BXLY DA5...................................197 G4
Pottery St BERM/RHTH SE16.......25 G4
Pott St BETH E2...........................130 A2
Poulett Gdns TWK TW1................180 B4
Poulett Rd EHAM E6....................133 H1
Poulter Pk MTCM * CR4...............226 A3
Poulters Wd HAYES BR2.............251 F3
Poulton Av SUT SM1...................243 H1
Poulton Cl HACK E8.......................109 H4
Poultry CITYLDN EC2R..................15 G4
Pound Cl ORP BR6......................234 B6
Pound Court Dr ORP BR6............234 D6
Pound La WLSDN NW10...............103 G4
Pound Park Rd CHARL SE7..........153 F4
Pound Pl ELTH/MOT SE9.............155 E1
Pound St CAR SM5......................244 B3
Pountney Rd BTSEA SW11.............165 F1
Poverest Rd STMC/STPC BR5......235 F2
Powder Mill La WHTN TW2.........178 D3
Powell Cl EDGW HA8.....................44 A2
Powell Gdns DAGE RM10.............117 E2
Powell Rd BKHH IG9......................57 E5
   CLPT E5.......................................109 H1
Power Rd CHSWK W4..................142 A4
Powers Ct TWK TW1....................181 F2
Powerscroft Rd CLPT E5................110 A2
   SCUP DA14.................................216 A2
Powis Cls BUSH * WD23................45 H5
Powis Gdns GLDGN NW11............84 D4
   NTGHL W11................................124 D5
Powis Ms NTGHL W11.................124 D5
Powis Pl BMSBY WC1N...................5 F6
Powis Sq NTGHL W11..................124 D5
Powis St WOOL/PLUM SE18.......114 A3
Powis Ter NTGHL W11.................124 D5
Powlett Pl CAMTN * NW1............106 C5
Pownall Gdns HSLW TW3............159 G5
Pownall Rd HACK E8....................109 G6
   HSLW TW3...................................159 F5
Pownsett Ter IL IG1......................114 C3
Powster Rd BMLY BR1.................212 C1
Powys Cl BXLYHN DA7................156 B6
Powys La PLMCR N13....................51 G6
Poynders Rd CLAP SW4..............187 E2
Poynings Cl ORP BR6..................236 A6
Poynings Rd ARCH N19................107 E1
Poynings Wy
   NFNCH/WDSP N12......................65 E1
Poyntell Crs CHST BR7................214 D4
Poynter Rd EN EN1........................39 F6
Poynton Rd TOTM N17..................69 G5
Poyntz Rd BTSEA SW11...............166 B3
Poyser St BETH E2.......................129 H1
Praed Ms BAY/PAD W2..................10 C4
Praed St BAY/PAD W2....................10 C4
Pragel St PLSTW E13...................132 D1
Prague Pl BRXS/STRHM SW2........167 G6
Prah Rd FSBYPK N4.......................88 A6
Prairie St VX/NE SW8..................166 C3
Pratt Ms CAMTN NW1.................107 E6
Pratt St CAMTN NW1...................107 E6
Pratt Wk LBTH SE11......................29 H1
Prayle Gv CRICK NW2...................84 B5
Prebend Gdns CHSWK W4...........143 H3
Prebend St IS N1..........................108 C6
The Precinct IS * N1.....................7 E1
Premiere Pl POP/IOD E14............131 E6
Premier Park Rd WLSDN NW10...102 B4
Prentis Rd STRHM/NOR SW16.....187 H4
Prentiss Ct CHARL SE7................153 F4
Presburg Rd NWMAL KT3...........223 H2
Prescelly Pl EDGW HA8................44 A5
Prescot St WCHPL E1.....................19 H1
Prescott Av STMC/STPC BR5......234 B3
Prescott Pl CLAP SW4..................167 F4
Presentation Ms
   BRXS/STRHM SW2.....................187 H4
Presidents Dr WAP E1W................25 G1
President St FSBYE * EC1V.............7 E3
Press Rd WLSDN NW10................102 D1
Prestage Wy POP/IOD E14...........131 G6
Prestbury Rd FSTGT E7...............113 G5
Prestbury Sq ELTH/MOT SE9.......193 H6
Prested Rd BTSEA SW11..............166 A3
Preston Av CHING E4.....................58 A1
Preston Cl STHWK * SE1..............32 A1
   WHTN TW2...............................180 A3
Preston Ct WOT/HER KT12..........218 A5
Preston Dr HOR/WEW KT19........240 E4
   WAN E11.....................................93 E2

Well DA16...................................176 B2
Preston Gdns IL IG1.......................93 G3
   WLSDN * NW10.........................103 G4
Preston Hi KTN/HRWW/W HA3....81 G4
Preston Pl RCHPK/HAM TW10 ....161 G6
   NRWD SE19................................208 B2
   RYNPK SW20.............................203 G3
   WAN E11.......................................92 A3
   WBLY HA9....................................81 G4
Prestons Rd HAYES BR2..............250 C1
   POP/IOD E14.............................131 G6
Preston Vls KUT * KT1.................201 H5
Preston Waye WBLY HA9...............81 G5
Prestwich Ter CLAP * SW4...........187 E1
Prestwick Cl NWDGN UB2...........138 C5
Prestwick Rd OXHEY WD19..........42 B4
Prestwood Av
   KTN/HRWW/W HA3.....................80 D1
   WOOL/PLUM SE18.....................175 G1
Prestwood Dr CRW RM5................77 F2
Prestwood Gdns CROY/NA CRO...228 C4
Prestwood St IS * N1........................7 F2
Pretoria Av WALTH E17..................90 C1
Pretoria Crs CHING E4....................55 G3
Pretoria Pde LEW * SE13.............171 E3
Pretoria Rd CAN/RD E16..............132 B2
   CHING E4.....................................55 G3
   IL IG1..114 B2
   ROMW/RG RM7...........................97 G1
   STRHM/NOR SW16....................206 D2
   TOTM N17...................................69 F2
   WAN E11.......................................91 G3
Pretoria Rd North UED N18...........69 F2
Prevost Rd FBAR/BDGN N11........50 C4
Price Cl MLHL NW7........................46 B2
   TOOT SW17.................................186 B5
Price Rd CROY/NA CRO...............246 B3
Price's St STHWK SE1....................22 D2
Pricklers Hi BAR EN5.....................35 H6
Prickley Wd HAYES BR2...............250 A3
Prideaux Pl ACT W3.....................122 D6
   FSBYW WC1X................................5 H3
Prideaux Rd BRXN/ST SW9..........167 G4
Pridham Rd THHTH CR7...............250 D1
Priestfield Rd FSTH SE23............190 C5
Priestlands Park Rd
   BFN/LL DA15............................195 H5
Priestley Cl STNW/STAM * N16 ...89 F4
Priestley Gdns CHDH RM6............95 H5
Priestley Rd MTCM CR4...............206 C5
Priestley Wy CRICK NW2...............83 G5
   WALTH E17..................................70 B6
Priest Park Av
   RYLN/HDSTN HA2.......................79 E6
Priests Br MORT/ESHN SW14......163 E4
Prima Rd BRXN/ST SW9................146 B6
Primrose Av ENC/FH EN2..............38 D2
   GDMY/SEVK IG3...........................95 G4
Primrose Cl CAT SE6....................211 E1
   MTCM CR4.................................206 D4
   RYLN/HDSTN HA2.......................78 B1
Primrose Gdns BUSH WD23..........28 D3
   HAMP NW3...............................106 A4
   RSLP HA4.....................................77 F4
Primrose Hl EMB EC4Y..................14 B4
Primrose Hill Rd HAMP NW3.......106 A4
   RSLP HA4.....................................98 A3
Primrose Hill Studios
   CAMTN * NW1...........................106 C6
Primrose La CROY/NA CRO..........198 A5
Primrose Ms CAMTN * NW1.......106 B5
Primrose Rd LEY E10......................91 F5
   SWFD E18.....................................72 D5
Primrose Sq HOM E9...................110 A5
Primrose St SDTCH EC2A..............16 A1
Primrose Wk EW KT17..................241 F5
   NWCR SE14................................170 C1
Primrose Wy ALP/SUD HA0.........121 F1
Primula St SHB W12.....................123 G6
Prince Albert STJWD NW8...............2 B2
Prince Albert Rd STJWD NW8.........2 A3
Prince Arthur Rd HAMP NW3.......105 G3
Prince Arthur Ms HAMP * NW3....84 A4
Prince Charles Rd
   BKHTH/KID SE3..........................172 B2
Prince Charles Wy WLGTN SM6 ...244 D1
Prince Consort Dr CHST BR7......214 D4
Prince Consort Rd SKENS SW7...145 H5
Princedale Rd NTGHL W11...........144 C1
Prince Edward Rd HOM E9...........110 D4
Prince George Av
   STHGT/OAK N14..........................34 C1
Prince George Rd
   STNW/STAM N16........................109 H4
Prince George's Av
   RYNPK SW20.............................204 A5
Prince Georges Rd
   WIM/MER SW19.........................205 H4
Prince Imperial Rd CHST BR7......214 B3
Prince Imperial Rd CHST SE7.......174 B3
   WOOL/PLUM SE18.....................173 H2
Prince John Rd ELTH/MOT SE9 ...173 G6
Princelet St WCHPL E1..................16 C1
Prince of Orange La
   GNWCH * SE10..........................171 G1
Prince of Wales Cl HDN NW4........83 H1
Prince of Wales Ga SKENS SW7 ...18 A3
Prince of Wales Pas
   CAMTN * NW1.............................4 A4
Prince of Wales Rd
   BKHTH/KID SE3..........................172 B2
   CAN/RD E16.................................131 G5
   KTTN NW5...................................106 C4
   SUT SM1.....................................225 H6
Prince of Wales Ter
   CHSWK W4.................................143 G5
   KENS * W8..................................145 F2
Prince Regent La PLSTW E13.......133 E3
Prince Regent Ms CAMTN NW1......4 A4
Prince Regent Rd HSLW TW3.......159 G4
Prince Regent's Ga SE2...............229 G2
Prince Rupert Rd
   ELTH/MOT SE9..........................173 H5
Princes Av ACT W3......................142 A4
   CAR SM5....................................244 B5

CDALE/KGS NW9..........................82 A1
FNCH N3.......................................65 F4
MUSWH N10................................66 C6
STHGT/OAK N14...........................34 C1
STMC/STPC BR5.........................255 E2
SURB KT6.....................................222 A6
WDGN N22.....................................67 F4
WFD IG8..73 H4
Princes Cl CDALE/KGS NW9..........82 A1
   EDGW HA8...................................62 A1
   HPTN TW12.................................179 H5
Princes Ct WBLY HA9..................102 A1
Princes Dr HRW HA1....................60 A6
Princes Gdns ACT W3.................122 A5
   EA W5..121 F3
   SKENS SW7................................145 H5
Prince's Ga SKENS * SW7...............18 A4
   SKENS * SW7............................145 H3
Princes Gate Ct SKENS * SW7....145 H2
Princes Gate Ms SKENS SW7......145 H5
Princes La MUSWH N10.................66 C6
Princes Ms BAY/PAD W2.............125 E6
   HMSMTH * W6...........................143 H5
Princes Pde GLDGN * NW11..........84 C3
Princes Park Av GLDGN NW11.......84 C3
Princes Pl NTGHL W11................144 C1
Prince's Plain HAYES BR2............253 G4
Princes Ri LEW SE13....................171 G3
Princes Riverside Rd
   BERM/RHTH SE16......................150 B1
Princes Rd BARK/HLT IG6.............94 D1
   BKHH IG9.....................................57 H6
   HPTN TW12................................179 H4
   KUTN/CMB KT2.........................202 A4
   MORT/ESHN SW14....................162 D4
   PGE/AN SE20..............................192 A6
   RCH/KEW TW9...........................161 H2
   RCHPK/HAM TW10....................161 H6
   UED N18..42 D5
   WEA W13....................................140 D1
   WIM/MER SW19.........................185 H4
Princes Rd
Princess Alice Wy THMD SE28 ....154 D2
Princess Av WBLY HA9..................81 G6
Princess Crs FSBYPK N4................88 B6
Princess Louise Cl
   BAY/PAD * W2...........................125 H4
Princess May Rd
   STNW/STAM N16........................109 E2
Princess Ms HAMP NW3..............105 H4
Princes Pde ORP * BR6................252 A1
Prince's Wy BAY/PAD W2.............125 E6
Princess Rd CAMTN NW1...........106 C6
   CROY/NA CRO...........................228 C3
   KIL/WHAMP NW6......................125 E1
Princess St CONDST W1S.............11 H4
   STHWK SE1.................................22 D6
Prince's St CONDST W1S.............11 H4
   LOTH EC2R...................................15 G4
   RCH/KEW TW9...........................161 G1
   SUT SM1.....................................243 H2
Prince's Ter PLSTW E13...............112 D6
Prince St DEPT SE8......................150 D6
Princes Wy BKHH IG9....................57 F4
   CROY/NA CRO...........................245 H5
   RSLP HA4.....................................78 A1
   WIM/MER SW19.........................184 B2
   WWKM BR4................................250 B2
Prince's Yd NTGHL * W11............144 C1
Princethorpe Rd SYD SE26.........190 B6
Princeton St GINN WC1R..............13 H1
Pringle Gdns
   STRHM/NOR SW16....................187 E6
Printers Inn Ct
   FLST/FETLN EC4A........................14 A3
Printing House Yd BETH * E2..........8 B4
Priolo Rd CHARL SE7..................153 E5
Prior Av BELMT SM2.....................244 A5
Prior Bolton St IS N1....................108 B4
Prioress Rd WNWD SE27.............188 B3
Prioress St STHWK SE1.................35 H6
Prior Rd IL IG1.............................114 A1
Priors Cft WALTH E17....................70 C5
Priors Fld NTHLT UB5...................96 B6
Priorsford Av STMC/STPC BR5 ...235 G3
Priors Gdns RSLP HA4...................98 A3
Priors Md EN EN1...........................30 A5
Prior St GNWCH SE10..................171 G1
Priory Av ALP/SUD HA0...............100 B2
   BECK BR3..................................210 C4
   BMLY BR1...................................213 H4
   CHING E4......................................44 D6
   CHEAM SM3..............................241 C5
   CHSWK W4................................143 E4
   STMC/STPC BR5........................234 D5
   WALTH E17..................................71 F2
Priory Cl ALP/SUD HA0................100 C1
   CHEAM SM3..............................241 B2
   CHING E4......................................57 H2
   WFD IG8..72 C3
Priory Dr ABYW SE2.......................37 H6
   STAN HA7....................................44 B5
Priory Field Dr EDGW HA8............44 D2
Priory Gdns ALP/SUD HA0...........100 C2
   BARN SW13................................163 F4
   CHSWK * W4.............................143 E4
   HGT N6...86 C6
   HPTN TW12................................179 G5
   SNWD SE25................................229 G3
Priory Green Est IS N1......................5 G1
Priory Gv CLAP SW4...................167 G2
Priory La E/WMO/HCT KT8..........219 F4
Priory La E/WMO/HCT KT8..........219 F1
   PUT/ROE SW15.........................163 F6
Priory Leas ELTH/MOT * SE9......193 G4
Priory Pk BKHTH/KID SE3...........172 C2
Priory Park Rd ALP/SUD HA0......100 C2
   KIL/WHAMP NW6......................104 D6

Priory Rd *BARK* IG11 ....114 D5
CEND/HSY/T N8 ....87 F1
CHEAM SM3 ....242 B2
CHSGTN KT9 ....239 G1
CHSWK W4 ....142 D5
CROY/NA CR0 ....228 A4
EHAM E6 ....113 F6
HPTN TW12 ....198 D3
HSLW TW3 ....159 G6
MUSWH N10 ....87 E1
RCH/KEW TW9 ....142 A6
WIM/MER SW19 ....205 H3
Priory St *BOW* E3 ....131 F2
Priory Ter *KIL/WHAMP* NW6 ......105 F6
The Priory *BKHTH/KID* SE3 ......172 B4
CROY/NA CR0 ....246 A1
ORP * BR6 ....235 H4
Priory Vw *BUSH* WD23 ....44 A2
Priory Vls *FBAR/BDGN* * N11 ....66 B2
Priory Wk *WBPTN* SW10 ....145 G5
Priory Wy *NWDGN* UB2 ....138 B3
Pritchard's Rd *BETH* E2 ....9 F1
Priter Rd *BERM/RHTH* SE16 ......25 F6
Private Rd *EN* EN1 ....38 D6
Probert Rd *BRXS/STRHM* SW2 ....162 A6
Probyn Rd *BRXS/STRHM* SW2 ......188 B4
Procter St *GINN* WC1R 11 G2
Proctor Cl *MTCM* CR4 ....206 C4
Progress Wy *CROY/NA* CR0 ....227 H6
EN EN1 ....30 A4
WDGN N22 ....68 A4
Promenade Approach Rd
CHSWK W4 ....163 E1
The Promenade *CHSWK* W4 ....163 E2
EDGW * HA8 ....62 A1
Prospect Cl *BELV* DA17 ....157 E4
HEST TW5 ....158 D2
RSLP HA4 ....78 B4
SYD SE26 ....189 H6
Prospect Cottages
WAND/EARL SW18 ....165 E5
Prospect Crs *WHTN* TW2 ....179 G1
Prospect Hl *WALTH* E17 ....91 F1
Prospect Pl *CHSWK* W4 ....142 D5
CRICK NW2 ....104 D1
ERITH N2 ....88 H1
HAYES BR2 ....212 D6
ROMW/RG RM7 ....75 G5
RYNPK SW20 ....203 H3
WAP E1W 150 A1
Prospect Rd *BAR* EN5 ....35 E5
CRICK NW2 ....104 D1
SURB KT6 ....221 E3
WLGTN SM6 ....75 E1
Prospect St *BERM/RHTH* SE16 ....25 H4
Prospect V *CHARL* SE7 ....153 G4
Prospero Rd *ARCH* N19 ....87 F5
Prothero Gdns *HDN* NW4 ....83 H2
Prothero Rd *FUL/PGN* SW6 ....164 C1
Prout Gv *WLSDN* NW10 ....163 E2
Prout Rd *CLPT* E5 ....109 H1
Providence Cl *HOM* * E9 ....110 B6
Providence Ct *MYFR/PKLN* W1K ...11 F5
Providence Pl *IS* * N1 ....108 B6
ROMW/RG RM7 ....76 D4
Providence Row Cl *BETH* E2 ......9 G4
Providence Sq *BETH* * E2 ....24 A5
Providence Yd *BETH* * E2 ....9 E5
Provincial Ter *PGE/AN* * SE20 ...210 B3
Provost St *IS* N1 ....7 C2
Provost Rd *HAMP* NW3 ....106 B5
Provost St *IS* N1 ....7 C2
Prowse Av *BUSH* WD23 ....43 G4
Prowse Pl *CAMTN* NW1 ....107 E5
Pruden Cl *STHGT/OAK* * N14 .....51 F4
Prusom St *WAP* E1W 25 H1
Pudding La *MON* EC3R 15 H5
Pudding Mill La *SRTFD* E15 .....111 H4
Puddle Dock *BLKFR* EC4V 14 D5
Puffin Cl *BARK* IG11 ....135 H2
CROY/NA CR0 ....230 B2
Pulborough Rd
WAND/EARL SW18 ....184 D2
Pulborough Wy *HSLWW* TW4 ......158 A5
Pulford Rd *SEVS/STOTM* N15 .....88 A3
Pulham Av *EFNCH* N2 ....65 G1
Pulier Rd *BAR* EN5 ....34 B3
Pulleyns Av *EHAM* E6 ....133 G2
Pullman Gdns *PUT/ROE* SW15 ....184 A1
Pullman Ms *LEE/GVPK* SE12 .....192 D5
Pullman Pl *ELTH/MOT* SE9 ......173 G6
Pulross Rd *BRXN/ST* SW9 ....130 A2
Pulteney Cl *BOW* E3 ....110 D6
Pulteney Rd *SWFD* E18 ....72 D6
Pulton Pl *FUL/PGN* SW6 ....165 E1
Puma Ct *WCHPL* E1 ....16 C1
Puma Wy *BTFD* TW8 ....161 F1
Pump Cl *NTHLT* UB5 ....117 E1
Pump Ct *EMB* * EC4Y 14 A4
Pump House Cl *HAYES* BR2 ....212 B5
Pumping Station Rd
CHSWK W4 ....163 E1
Pump La *NWCR* SE14 ....170 A1
Punderson's Gdns *BETH* E2 ......9 H3
Purbeck Av *MALM* KT3 ....223 F3
Purbeck Dr *CRICK* NW2 ....64 B6
Purbrook St *STHWK* SE1 ....26 A5
Purcell Crs *FUL/PGN* * SW6 .....144 B6
Purcell Ms *WLSDN* * NW10 ....103 E5
Purcell Rd *GFD/PVL* UB6 ....116 T
Purcells Av *EDGW* HA8 ....62 A1
Purcell St *IS* N1 ....8 A1
Purchese St *CAMTN* NW1 ....4 C1
Purdy St *BOW* E3 ....131 F3
Purelake Ms *LEW* * SE13 ....171 H4
Purland Cl *BCTR* RM8 ....96 D5
Purland Rd *THMD* SE28 ....155 F2
Purleigh Av *WFD* IG8 ....75 E2
Purley Av *CRICK* NW2 ....84 C6
Purley Cl *CLAY* IG5 ....74 A5
Purley Pl *IS* N1 ....108 B5
Purley Rd *ED* N9 ....52 B1
SAND/SEL CR2 ....246 D5
Purley Wy *CROY/NA* CR0 ....227 H4
Purneys Rd *ELTH/MOT* SE9 ....173 F5
Purleigh Av *WOOL/PLUM* SE18 ....155 F5
Pursers Cross Rd
FUL/PGN * SW6 ....164 D2
Pursewardens Cl *WEA* W13 ....141 E1
Pursley Rd *MLHL* NW7 ....63 H3

Purves Rd *WLSDN* NW10 ....123 H2
Putney Br *PUT/ROE* SW15 ....164 C4
Putney Bridge Ap
PUT/ROE SW15 ....164 C4
Putney Bridge Rd
PUT/ROE SW15 ....164 C5
Putney Common
PUT/ROE SW15 ....164 A4
Putney Ex *PUT/ROE* * SW15 .....164 B5
Putney Heath *PUT/ROE* SW15 ....183 H1
Putney Heath La
PUT/ROE SW15 ....184 B1
Putney High St *PUT/ROE* SW15 ..164 A4
Putney Hl *PUT/ROE* SW15 ....184 B2
Putney Park Av
PUT/ROE SW15 ....163 G5
Putney Park La
PUT/ROE SW15 ....163 H5
Puttenham Cl
OXHEY WD19 ....42 A5
Pycombe Cnr
NFNCH/WDSP N12 ....48 D6
Pycroft Wy *UED* N18 ....53 G6
Pylbrook Rd *SUT* SM1 ....243 E1
Pym Cl *EBAR* EN4 ....35 H6
Pymers Md *DUL* SE21 ....188 C3
Pymmes Brook Trail *EBAR* EN4 ..36 A6
PLMGR N13 ....51 G6
Pymmes Cl *PLMGR* N13 ....67 H1
TOTM N17 ....69 H4
Pymmes Gdns North *ED* N9 ......53 F5
Pymmes Gdns South *ED* N9 .....53 F5
Pymmes Green Rd
FBAR/BDGN N11 ....50 D6
Pymmes Rd *PLMGR* N13 ....67 G2
Pymms Brook Dr *EBAR* EN4 .....36 A5
Pyne Rd *SURB* KT6 ....222 A5
Pynham Cl *ABYW* SE2 ....155 C3
Pynnacles Cl *STAN* HA7 ....60 D1
Pyrland Rd *HBRY* N5 ....108 D3
RCHPK/HAM TW10 ....181 H1
Pyrmont Gv *WNWD* SE27 ....188 B5
Pyrmont Rd *CHSWK* W4 ....142 A6
Pytchley Crs *NRWD* SE19 ....208 C2
Pytchley Rd *CMBW* SE5 ....169 E4

Q

The Quadrangle *BAY/PAD* W2 .....10 B3
HNHL * SE24 ....168 C6
WBPTN * SW10 ....165 G2
Quadrant Ar *REGST* W1B 12 B6
Quadrant Cl *HDN* * NW4 ....83 H3
Quadrant Gv *HAMP* NW3 ....106 B3
Quadrant Rd *RCH/KEW* TW9 .....161 F5
THHTH CR7 ....228 B1
The Quadrant *BELMT* SM2 ....243 G4
BXLYHN DA7 ....176 B1
EDGW * HA8 ....44 D1
NKENS * W10 ....124 B2
RCH/KEW TW9 ....161 G5
RYLN/HDSTN * HA2 ....59 H6
RYNPK SW20 ....204 C4
Quad Rd *WBLY* * HA9 ....101 F1
Quaggy Wk *BKHTH/KID* SE3 ......172 C5
Quainton St *WLSDN* NW10 ....102 D1
Quaker La *NWDGN* UB2 ....139 E3
Quakers Course
CDALE/KGS NW9 ....63 F4
Quakers Pl *FSTGT* E7 ....113 F3
Quaker St *WCHPL* E1 ....9 H6
Quakers Wk *WCHMH* N21 ....52 D1
Quality Ct *LINN* WC2A 14 A3
Quantock Gdns *CRICK* * NW2 ....84 B6
Quarles Cl *CRW* RM5 ....77 E3
Quarley Wy *PECK* SE15 ....169 F1
Quarrendon St *FUL/PGN* SW6 ....165 E2
Quarr Rd *CAR* SM5 ....225 H3
Quarry Park Rd *SUT* SM1 ....242 C5
Quarry Ri *SUT* SM1 ....242 D4
Quarry Rd *WAND/EARL* SW18 ....185 G1
Quartermile La *LEY* E10 ....111 F2
Quatre Ports *CHING* * E4 ....71 H1
Quay House *POP/IOD* * E14 ......151 E2
Quebec Ms *MBLAR* W1H 10 D4
Quebec Rd *GNTH/NBYPK* IG2 ....94 C4
YEAD UB4 ....118 A6
Quebec Wy *BERM/RHTH* SE16 .....150 B2
Queen Adelaide Rd
PGE/AN SE20 ....210 A2
Queen Anne Av *HAYES* BR2 ......212 C6
Queen Anne Dr *ESH/CLAY* KT10 ..238 A5
Queen Anne Ga *BXLYHN* DA7 .....176 B4
Queen Anne Ms
CAVSQ/HST W1G 11 H2
Queen Anne Rd *HOM* E9 ....110 B4
Queen Anne's Cl *WHTN* TW2 .....179 H5
Queen Anne's Gdns
CHSWK W4 ....143 E3
EA W5 ....141 E1
EN EN1 ....53 E1
MTCM CR4 ....206 B6
Queen Anne's Ga *STJSPK* SW1H ..20 C4
Queen Anne's Gv *CHSWK* W4 .....143 E3
EA W5 ....141 E2
ED N9 ....52 D2
EN EN1 ....53 E1
Queen Anne's Pl *EN* EN1 ....53 E1
Queen Anne Ter *CAVSQ/HST* W1G ..11 H2
Queen Anne Ter *WAP* * E1W 17 H6
Queenborough Gdns
CHST BR7 ....214 D2
GNTH/NBYPK IG2 ....93 A1
Queen Caroline Est
HMSMTH W6 ....144 A5
Queen Caroline St
HMSMTH W6 ....144 A5
Queen Elizabeth Buildings
EMB * EC4Y 14 A5
Queen Elizabeth Gdns
MRDN SM4 ....225 E1
Queen Elizabeth Rd
KUTN/CMB * KT2 ....201 H4
WALTH E17 ....70 C1
Queen Elizabeth's Cl
STNW/STAM N16 ....88 D6

Queen Elizabeth's Dr
STHGT/OAK N14 ....51 G3
Queen Elizabeth St *STHWK* SE1 ..24 B5
Queen Elizabeth's Wk
STNW/STAM N16 ....88 D6
WLGTN SM6 ....245 F2
Queen Elizabeth Wk
BARN SW13 ....163 G2
Queenhithe *BLKFR* EC4V 15 F6
Queen Margaret's Gv *IS* N1 ....109 E3
Queen Mary Av *MRDN* SM4 ......224 B2
Queen Mary Cl *CHSGTN* KT9 ....240 A1
Queen Mary Rd *NRWD* SE19 .....208 B2
Queen Mary's Av *CAR* SM5 ......242 B5
Queen Mother Ga *BAY/PAD* W2 ..19 F2
Queens Acre *CHEAM* SM3 ....242 B5
The Queens Arm *FELT* TW13 .....178 A6
FNCH N3 ....46 D4
GFD/PVL UB6 ....119 F5
KTN/HRWW/W HA3 ....62 B6
MUSWH N10 ....49 H4
TRDG/WHET N20 ....49 H4
WCHMH N21 ....51 G4
WFD IG8 ....72 D1
Queensberry Ms West
SKENS * SW7 ....145 H4
SKENS SW7 ....145 H4
Queensberry Pl *SKENS* * SW7 ...145 H4
Queensberry Wy *SKENS* SW7 ....145 H4
Queensborough Ms
BAY/PAD * W2 ....125 G6
Queensborough Studios
BAY/PAD * W2 ....125 F6
Queensborough Ter
BAY/PAD W2 ....125 F6
Queensbridge Pk *ISLW* TW7 .....179 H1
Queensbridge Rd *HACK* E8 ......109 F5
Queensbury Rd
CDALE/KGS NW9 ....82 D4
WLSDN NW10 ....121 H1
Queensbury Station Pde
EDGW HA8 ....61 H6
Queens Circ *VX/NE* SW8 ....166 D1
Queens Circ *VX/NE* SW8 ....166 D1
Queen's Cl *EDGW* HA8 ....62 A1
WLGTN SM6 ....244 D3
Queen's Club Gdns
WKENS W14 ....144 C6
WKENS * W14 ....144 C6
Queens Club Ter *WKENS* * W14 ..144 D6
Queenscourt *WBLY* HA9 ....101 C2
Queen's Crs *KTTN* NW5 ....106 C4
RCHPK/HAM TW10 ....161 H6
Queenscroft Rd *ELTH/MOT* SE9 ..173 F6
Queensdale Crs *NTGHL* W11 .....144 B1
Queensdale Pl *NTGHL* W11 .....144 C1
Queensdale Rd *NTGHL* W11 .....144 B1
Queensdale Wk *NTGHL* W11 .....144 C1
Queens Down Rd *CLPT* E5 ....109 H2
Queens Dr *BRYLDS* KT5 ....222 A4
EA W5 ....121 H5
FSBYPK N4 ....68 B6
LEY E10 ....91 E4
TOTM N17 ....49 H6
Queen's Elm Sq *CHEL* * SW3 ....145 H5
CHEL SW3 ....145 H5
Queen's Gdns *BAY/PAD* W2 ......125 G6
EA W5 ....121 E4
HDN NW4 ....64 A3
HEST TW5 ....158 C2
RAIN RM13 ....137 H1
Queens Garth *FSTH* * SE23 .....190 A4
Queens Ga *KTTN* NW5 ....106 C4
Queens Gdns *CHST* BR7 ....214 D4
Queensgate Gdns
PUT/ROE SW15 ....184 B5
Queen's Gate Gdns *SKENS* SW7 ..145 G3
SKENS * SW7 ....145 G3
Queen's Gate Ms *SKENS* SW7 ....145 G3
Queen's Gate Pl *SKENS* * SW7 ..145 G3
Queen's Gate Place Ms
SKENS * SW7 ....145 G3
Queen's Gate Ter *SKENS* SW7 ...145 G3
Queen's Gv *STJWD* NW8 ....105 H6
Queen's Grove Rd *CHING* E4 ....58 A5
Queen's Head St *IS* N1 ....108 B6
Queens Keep *TWK* * TW1 ....181 E1
Queensland Av *UED* N18 ....62 B2
WIM/MER SW19 ....205 F4
Queensland Pl *HOLWY* N7 ......108 A2
Queensland Rd *HOLWY* N7 ......108 A2
Queens La *MUSWH* N10 ....66 C6
Queensmead *STJWD* NW8 ....105 H5
Queen's Mead Rd *HAYES* BR2 ....212 B5
Queensmere Cl
WIM/MER SW19 ....184 B4
Queensmere Rd
WIM/MER SW19 ....184 B4
Queensmill Rd *FUL/PGN* SW6 ....164 B1
Queens Pde *CEND/HSY/T* * N8 ...66 B3
CRICK * NW2 ....101 H2
EA * W5 ....121 H5
FBAR/BDGN * N11 ....67 G3
HDN * NW4 ....83 H2
Queens Parade Cl
FBAR/BDGN N11 ....66 B1
Queens Pk Gdns *FELT* TW13 .....194 A5
Queens Sq *BMSBY* WC1N 5 F6
Queen's Ride *BARN* SW13 ....163 H4
Queen's Ri *RCHPK/HAM* TW10 ....181 G1
Queen's Rd *BAR* EN5 ....34 B4
BARK IG11 ....96 C5
BECK BR3 ....210 C5
BKHH IG9 ....56 D2
BMLY BR1 ....212 C5
CHST BR7 ....214 D4
CROY/NA CR0 ....228 B3
EA W5 ....121 G5
ED N9 ....53 H4
EN EN1 ....39 E5
FBAR/BDGN N11 ....67 G3
FNCH N3 ....47 F4
HDN NW4 ....64 A3
HPTN TW12 ....179 H6
HSLW TW3 ....159 G2
KUTN/CMB KT2 ....202 A3
MORT/ESHN SW14 ....162 D2
MRDN SM4 ....225 E1

MTCM CR4 ....205 H6
NWDGN UB2 ....138 B3
NWMAL KT3 ....223 F1
PECK SE15 ....170 A2
PLSTW E13 ....112 D6
RCHPK/HAM TW10 ....181 H1
TEDD TW11 ....200 B2
THDIT KT7 ....220 B2
TWK TW1 ....180 B3
WALTH E17 ....91 H1
WAN E11 ....92 A4
WELL DA16 ....175 H4
WIM/MER SW19 ....205 F1
WLGTN SM6 ....244 D3
Queen's Rd West *PLSTW* E13 ....132 C1
Queen's Rw *WALW* SE17 ....31 G5
WALW * SE17 ....31 G5
Queen's Ter *ISLW* TW7 ....160 C5
PLSTW E13 ....105 H6
STJWD NW8 ....220 C3
THDIT KT7 ....130 A3
WCHPL * E1 ....
Queens Terrace Cottages
HNWL * W7 ....140 A2
Queensthorpe Ms *SYD* * SE26 ...190 B6
Queensthorpe Rd *SYD* SE26 .....190 B6
Queen St *BXLYHN* DA7 ....176 A6
CROY/NA CR0 ....246 C2
MYFR/PICC W1J 19 G1
ROMW/RG RM7 ....97 H3
TOTM N17 ....50 A2
Queen Street Pl *CANST* EC4R ...15 F6
Queensville Rd *CLAP* SW4 ......187 F2
Queens Wk *CDALE/KGS* NW9 .....82 C6
CHING E4 ....55 H3
EA W5 ....121 H2
RSLP HA4 ....80 A1
RSLP HA4 ....98 A1
Queens Walk Ter *RSLP* * HA4 ...98 A1
Queens Wy *FELT* TW13 ....178 A6
HDN NW4 ....64 A1
Queensway *BAY/PAD* W2 ....125 F5
CROY/NA CR0 ....245 H3
PEND EN3 ....40 D2
STMC/STPC BR5 ....234 C2
WWKM BR4 ....250 C2
Queens Well Av
TRDG/WHET N20 ....50 A6
Queenswood Av *HEST* TW5 ....158 D3
HPTN TW12 ....199 F2
THHTH CR7 ....228 A2
WALTH E17 ....58 B4
WLGTN SM6 ....245 F2
Queenswood Gdns *WAN* E11 .....92 C5
Queenswood Pk *FNCH* N3 ....64 C5
Queenswood Rd *BFN/LL* DA15 ...195 F3
FSTH SE23 ....190 C5
Queen's Wood Rd *HGT* N6 ....86 D3
Queen's Yd *FITZ* W1T 4 B5
Queen Victoria Av
ALP/SUD HA0 ....101 K5
Queen Victoria St *BLKFR* EC4V ..15 E5
Queen Victoria Ter *WAP* * E1W ..17 H6
Quemerford Rd *HOLWY* N7 ....107 H3
Quentin Pl *LEW* SE13 ....172 A1
Quentin Rd *BKHTH/KID* SE3 ....172 A4
Quernmore Rd *BMLY* BR1 ....212 C2
Quernmore Rd *BMLY* BR1 ....212 C2
FSBYPK N4 ....67 G4
Querrin St *FUL/PGN* SW6 ....165 G3
Quex Ms *KIL/WHAMP* NW6 ....105 E6
Quex Rd *KIL/WHAMP* NW6 ....105 E6
Quick Rd *CHSWK* W4 ....143 H5
Quicks Rd *WIM/MER* SW19 ......205 F5
Quick St *IS* N1 ....6 D2
Quicklswood *HAMP* NW3 ....106 A5
Quiet Nook *HAYES* BR2 ....214 B6
Quill St *EA* W5 ....121 C2
FSBYPK N4 ....108 A1
Quilp St *STHWK* SE1 ....23 E3
Quilter Rd *STMC/STPC* BR5 ....236 A5
Quilter St *BETH* E2 ....9 E3
WOOL/PLUM SE18 ....155 F5
Quintin Av *RYNPK* SW20 ....204 C4
Quinton Cl *BECK* BR3 ....211 G6
WLGTN SM6 ....244 B3
Quinton Rd *THDIT* KT7 ....220 C5
Quixley St *POP/IOD* E14 ....133 E3
Quorn Rd *EDUL* SE22 ....169 E5

R

Rabbit Rw *KENS* * W8 ....145 E1
Rabbits Rd *MNPK* E12 ....113 G2
Rabournmead Dr *RSLP* HA4 .....98 C3
Raby Rd *NWMAL* KT3 ....223 E1
Raby St *POP/IOD* * E14 ....130 C5
Raccoon Wy *HSLWW* TW4 ....158 A3
Rachel Cl *BARK/HLT* IG6 ....74 D6
Rackham Cl *WELL* DA16 ....175 H3
Rackham Ms
STRHM/NOR SW16 ....207 E2
Racton Rd *FUL/PGN* SW6 ....145 H6
Radbourne Av *EA* W5 ....141 E4
Radbourne Cl *CLPT* E5 ....110 B2
Radbourne Ct
KTN/HRWW/W * HA3 ....80 D3
Radbourne Crs *WALTH* E17 .....58 B1
Radbourne Rd *BAL* SW12 ....187 E2
Radcliffe Av *ENC/FH* EN2 .....24 C3
WLSDN NW10 ....121 K2
Radcliffe Gdns *CAR* SM5 ......243 A5
Radcliffe Rd *CROY/NA* CR0 ....229 F6
KTN/HRWW/W HA3 ....62 B5
STHWK SE1 ....24 B5
WCHMH N21 ....52 A3
Radcliffe Wy *NTHLT* UB5 ......118 B2
Radcot St *LBTH* SE11 ....30 B4
Raddington Rd *NKENS* W10 .....124 C4
Radfield Wy *ELTH/MOT* SE9 ....174 A2
Radford Est *WLSDN* * NW10 ....122 C2
Radford Rd *LEW* SE13 ....193 E1
Radford Wy *BARK* IG11 ....135 F2
Radipole Rd *FUL/PGN* SW6 .....162 K2
Radland Rd *CAN/RD* E16 ....132 C5
Radlet Av *FSTH* SE23 ....189 H5

Radlett Cl *FSTGT* E7 ....112 B4
Radlett Pl *STJWD* NW8 ....106 A6
Radley Av *GDMY/SEVK* IG3 ....115 F2
Radley Ct *BERM/RHTH* SE16 ....150 B2
Radley Gdns
 KTN/HRWW/W HA3 ....81 G1
Radley Ms *KENS* W8 ....145 E3
Radley Rd *TOTM* N17 ....69 E5
Radley's La *SWFD* E18 ....32 C5
Radley Rd *CLPT* * E5 ....90 A6
Radley Ter *CAN/RD* * E16 ....132 B4
Radlix Rd *LEY* E10 ....91 E5
Radnor Av *HRW* HA1 ....80 A2
 WELL DA16 ....175 H6
Radnor Cl *CHST* BR7 ....215 E2
 MTCM CR4 ....227 G2
Radnor Crs *REDBR* IG4 ....93 H2
 WOOL/PLUM SE18 ....175 G1
Radnor Gdns *EN* EN1 ....39 E2
 TWK TW1 ....180 B4
Radnor Ms *BAY/PAD* W2 ....125 H5
Radnor Pl *BAY/PAD* W2 ....10 A4
Radnor Rd *HRW* HA1 ....79 H2
 KIL/WHAMP NW6 ....104 C6
 PECK SE15 ....169 G1
 TWK TW1 ....180 B4
Radnor St *FSBYE* EC1V 7 F5
Radnor Ter *WKENS* W14 ....144 D4
 CROY/NA CR0 ....230 C4
Radnor Wy *WLSDN* NW10 ....122 B3
Radstock Av
 KTN/HRWW/W HA3 ....60 C6
Radstock Cl *FBAR/BDGN* N11 ....60 C4
Radstock St *BTSEA* * SW11 ....166 A1
Raeburn Av *BRYLDS* KT5 ....222 B3
 DART DA1 ....138 D4
Raeburn Cl *EFNCH* N2 ....85 G3
 EDGW HA8 ....62 A5
Raeburn St *BRXS/STRHM* SW2 ..167 G5
Rafford Wy *BMLY* BR1 ....212 D5
Ragdalesood Ct *BXLY* DA5 17
Raglan Cl *HSLW* TW4 ....158 C6
Raglan Ct *BELV* DA17 ....156 D4
 EN EN1 ....23 H1
 HAYES BR2 ....233 E1
 WALTH E17 ....91 G2
 WOOL/PLUM SE18 ....154 C5
Raglan Rd *IS* N1 ....107 G6
Raglan Ter *KTN/HRWW/W* HA2 ..78 B3
Raglan Wy *NTHLT* UB5 ....99 G4
Ragley Cl *ACT* W3 ....142 C2
Raider Cl *ROMW/RG* RM7 ....74 F4
Railey Ms *KTTN* NW5 ....107 E3
Railshead Rd *ISLW* TW7 ....160 D5
Railton Rd *HNHL* SE24 ....168 A6
Railway Ap *KTN/HRWW/W* HA3 ..80 B1
 STHWK SE1 ....23 H1
 TWK TW1 ....180 C2
 WLCTN * SM6 ....244 D4
Railway Av *BRXN/ST* * SW9 .....168 A5
Railway Av *BERM/RHTH* SE16 ..150 A2
Railway Cottages *SHB* * W12 ..144 A2
 SRTFD * E15 ....132 A1
 WIM/MER * SW19 ....185 F6
Railway Gv *NWCR* SE14 ....168 A5
Railway Pl *BELV* DA17 ....157 E3
Railway Rd *TEDD* TW11 ....169 E5
Railway Side *BARN* SW13 ....163 E4
Railway Station Whf *LEY* * E10 ...90 C5
Railway St *BCTR* RM8 ....96 A5
 IS N1 ....5 F4
Railway Ter *LEW* SE13 ....171 F6
 WALTH E17 ....71 G4
Rainborough Cl *WBLY* HA9 ....102 C4
Rainbow Av *POP/IOD* E14 ....151 F5
Rainbow Ct *OXHEY* WD19 ....42 A1
Rainbow St *CMBW* SE5 ....169 E6
Raine St *WAP* E1W 25 H1
Rainham Cl *BTSEA* SW11 ....186 A1
Rainham Rd *WLSDN* NW10 ....124 A2
Rainham Rd North *DAGE* RM10 ..97 H5
Rainham Rd South *DAGE* RM10 ..117 G2
Rainhill Wy *BOW* E3 ....131 J2
Rainsborough Av *DEPT* SE8 .....150 C4
Rainton Rd *CHARL* SE7 ....152 C5
Rainville Rd *HMSMTH* W6 ....144 A6
Raisins Hl *PIN* HA5 ....58 A6
Raith Av *STHGT/OAK* N14 ....51 F5
Raleigh Av *WLGTN* SM6 ....245 F2
 YEAD UB4 ....95 E5
 PIN HA5 ....78 B4
Raleigh Dr *BRYLDS* KT5 ....222 C5
 TRDG/WHET N20 ....50 C2
Raleigh Gdns *MTCM* CR4 ....206 B6
 ORP BR6 ....253 F3
Raleigh Rd *CEND/HSY/T* N8 ....88 A1
 ENC/FH EN2 ....24 D3
 MUSWH N10 ....66 A4
 NWDGN UB2 ....138 C5
 PGE/AN SE20 ....210 B3
 RCH/KEW TW9 ....161 H2
Raleigh St *IS* N1 ....108 B6
Raleigh Wy *FELT* TW13 ....198 A1
 STHGT/OAK N14 ....51 F3
Ralph Perring Ct *BECK* BR3 ......231 E1
Ralston St *CHEL* SW3 ....16 D6
Ralston Wy *OXHEY* WD19 ....42 B4
Rama Cl *STRHM/NOR* SW16 ....207 G3
Ramac Wy *CHARL* SE7 ....152 D4
Rambler Cl *STRHM/NOR* SW16 ..186 C1
Rame Cl *TOOT* SW17 ....206 C1
Ramillies Cl *BRXS/STRHM* SW2 ..187 G1
Ramillies Pl *SOHO/CST* W1F 12 A4
Ramillies Rd *BFN/LL* DA15 ....195 H1
 CHSWK W4 ....142 A3
 MLHL NW7 ....45 F2
Ramillies St *SOHO/CST* W1F 12 A4
Ramones Ter *MTCM* CR4 ....227 F1
Rampart St *WCHPL* * E1 ....17 G4
Ram Pas *KUT* KT1 ....201 F5
Rampayne St *PIM* SW1V 28 C3

Rampton Cl *CHING* E4 ....55 E5
Ramsay Rd *ACT* W3 ....142 C3
Ramsay Rd *FSTGT* E7 ....95 E3
Ramscroft Cl *ED* N9 ....42 B3
Ramsdale Rd *TOOT* SW17 ....206 C1
Ramsden Cl *STMC/STPC* BR5 ...236 A5
Ramsden Dr *CRW* RM5 ....57 F3
Ramsden Gdns *BAL* * SW12 .....186 D2
Ramsden Rd *BAL* SW12 ....186 C2
 ERITH DA8 ....177 H1
 FBAR/BDGN N11 ....69 E6
 ORP BR5 ....235 H4
 STMC/STPC BR5 ....236 A5
Ramsey Cl *CDALE/KGS* NW9 .....83 F3
 NTHLT UB5 ....99 H3
Ramsey St *BETH* E2 ....92 C4
Ramsey Wk *IS* * N1 ....108 D4
Ramsey Wy *STHGT/OAK* N14 .....51 E2
Ramsgate St *HACK* * E8 ....109 H4
Ramsgill Ap *GNTH/NBYPK* IG2 ...95 F1
Ramsgill Dr *GNTH/NBYPK* IG2 ...95 F1
Rams Gv *CHDH* RM6 ....96 C1
Ramsden Rd *WAND/EARL* SW18 ..164 A2
Ramulls Dr *YEAD* UB4 ....118 C3
Ramus Wood Av *ORP* BR6 ....253 E5
Rancliffe Gdns *ELTH/MOT* SE9 ..175 G5
Rancliffe Rd *EHAM* E6 ....133 C1
Randall Av *CRICK* NW2 ....83 E6
Randall Cl *BTSEA* SW11 ....166 A2
 ERITH DA8 ....157 G6
Randall Pl *GNWCH* SE10 ....171 G1
Randall Rd *LBTH* SE11 ....29 G7
Randall Rw *LBTH* SE11 ....29 G2
Randell's Rd *IS* N1 ....107 G6
Randisbourne Gdns *CAT* * SE6 ..191 F1
Randle Rd *RCHPK/HAM* TW10 ..181 E6
Randlesdown Rd *CAT* SE6 ....191 E5
Randolph Ap *CAN/RD* E16 ....133 F6
Randolph Av *KIL/WHAMP* NW6 ..125 F1
 MV/WKIL W9 ....2 D1
Randolph Cl *BXLYHN* DA7 ....177 G4
 KUTN/CMB * KT2 ....202 C1
Randolph Crs *MV/WKIL* W9 ....125 G3
Randolph Gdns
 KIL/WHAMP NW6 ....125 F1
Randolph Ms *MV/WKIL* W9 ....125 F1
Randolph Rd *HAYES* BR2 ....233 H5
 MV/WKIL W9 ....125 F2
 STHL * UB1 ....138 D2
 WALTH * E17 ....91 F2
Randolph St *CAMTN* NW1 ....107 F5
Randon Cl *PIN* HA5 ....58 B6
Ranelagh Av *BARN* SW13 ....163 C5
 FUL/PGN SW6 ....164 D4
Ranelagh Cl *EDGW* HA8 ....46 A6
Ranelagh Dr *EDGW* HA8 ....46 A6
 TWK TW1 ....160 D5
Ranelagh Gdns *CHSWK* W4 ......161 C2
 FUL/PGN SW6 ....164 C4
 IL IG1 ....90 A5
 WAN E11 ....71 G3
Ranelagh Gv *BCVA* SW1W 27 F3
Ranelagh Pl *NWMAL* KT3 ....223 E2
Ranelagh Rd *ALP/SUD* HA0 ....79 F3
 EA W5 ....141 F2
 EHAM E6 ....114 B1
 PIM SW1V 28 B4
 STHL UB1 ....138 B1
 TOTM N17 ....69 E6
 WAN E11 ....112 A2
 WDGN N22 ....49 F5
 WLSDN NW10 ....125 F1
Ranfurly Rd *SUT* SM1 ....225 E6
Rangefield Rd *BMLY* BR1 ....212 C2
Rangemoor Rd
 SEVS/STOTM N15 ....89 F2
Rangers Rd *LOU* IG10 ....96 D1
Rangeworth Pl *BFN/LL* DA15 ...195 F5
Rangoon St *TWRH* * EC3N 16 A6
Rankin Cl *CDALE/KGS* NW9 ....63 E6
Ranleigh Gdns *BXLYHN* DA7 ....176 D7
Ranmere St *BAL* SW12 ....186 C3
Ranmoor Gdns *HRW* HA1 ....79 H3
Ranmore Av *CROY/NA* CR0 ......247 F1
Ranmore Pth *STMC/STPC* BR5 ..225 G1
Ranmore Rd *BELMT* SM2 ....242 B6
Rannoch Cl *EDGW* HA8 ....46 D4
Rannoch Rd *HMSMTH* W6 ....144 A6
Rannock Av *CDALE/KGS* NW9 ....83 G2
Ransom Cl *OXHEY* WD19 ....42 A2
Ransom Rd *CHARL* * SE7 ....153 E5
Ranston St *CAMTN* NW1 ....10 A1
Ranulf Rd *CRICK* NW2 ....104 D2
Ranwell Cl *BOW* * E3 ....113 H6
Ranworth Rd *ED* N9 ....54 D4
Ranyard Cl *CHSGTN* KT9 ....239 H1
Raphael Dr *THDIT* KT7 ....206 B4
Raphael St *SKENS* SW7 ....18 C4
Rasper Rd *TRDG/WHET* N20 ......49 C4
Rastell Av *BAL* SW17 ....187 F4
Ratcliffe Cl *LEE/GVPK* SE12 .....192 C1
Ratcliffe Cross St *WCHPL* * E1 ..130 B5
Ratcliffe La *POP/IOD* E14 ....113 E5
Ratcliff Rd *FSTGT* E7 ....113 E5

Raven Rw *WCHPL* E1 ....17 H1
Ravens Ait *SURB* * KT6 ....221 F2
Ravenet St *BTSEA* SW11 ....221 H4
Ravensbourne Av *HAYES* BR2 ..211 F4
 WEA W13 ....120 D4
Ravensbourne Pk *BROCKY* SE4 ..191 E2
Ravensbourne Park Crs
 CAT SE6 ....190 D2
Ravensbourne Pl *DEPT* SE8 ....170 D2
Ravensbourne Rd *BMLY* BR1 ....212 C6
 FSTH SE23 ....190 D2
 TWK TW1 ....181 E1
Ravensbury Av *MRDN* SM4 .....225 F2
Ravensbury Gv *MTCM* CR4 ....225 H1
Ravensbury La *MTCM* CR4 ....225 H1
Ravensbury Rd
 STMC/STPC BR5 ....235 F1
 WAND/EARL SW18 ....185 F4
Ravensbury Ter
 WAND/EARL SW18 ....185 F4
Ravenscar Rd *BMLY* BR1 ....192 A6
 SURB KT6 ....222 B5
Ravens Cl *CDALE/KGS* NW9 ....63 E5
 EN EN1 ....39 E3
 HAYES BR2 ....212 B5
Ravenscourt Av *HMSMTH* W6 ..143 G4
Ravenscourt Gdns
 HMSMTH W6 ....143 F4
Ravenscourt Pk *HMSMTH* W6 ..143 G4
Ravenscourt Pl *HMSMTH* W6 ..143 G4
Ravenscourt Rd *HMSMTH* W6 ..143 H4
 STMC/STPC BR5 ....215 G6
Ravenscourt Sq *HMSMTH* W6 ..143 G3
Ravenscraig Rd
 FBAR/BDGN N11 ....50 D6
Ravenscroft Av *GLDGN* NW11 ....84 D4
 WBLY HA9 ....81 G5
Ravenscroft Cl *CAN/RD* E16 .....132 C4
Ravenscroft Cottages
 BAR * EN5 ....33 E5
 BAR * EN5 ....49 E1
Ravenscroft Pk *BAR* EN5 ....49 E1
Ravenscroft Rd *BECK* BR3 ....210 A5
 CAN/RD E16 ....132 C4
 CHSWK W4 ....142 C4
Ravensdale Av
 NFNCH/WDSPK N12 ....49 G6
Ravensdale Gdns *NRWD* SE19 ..208 D3
Ravensdale Rd *HSLWW* TW4 ...158 C4
 STNW/STAM N16 ....89 F1
Ravensdon St *LBTH* SE11 ....30 B4
Ravensfield Gdns *HOR/WEW* KT19 ..241 E3
Ravenshaw St *KIL/WHAMP* NW6 ..104 D3
Ravenshill *CHST* BR7 ....214 B4
Ravenshurst Av *HDN* NW4 ....64 A1
Ravenside Cl *ED* N9 ....43 E4
Ravenside Rd *BAL* SW12 ....186 B2
Ravensmead Rd *HAYES* BR2 ....211 H5
Ravensmede Wy *CHSWK* W4 ....143 F4
Ravens Ms *BKHTH/KID* * SE3 ..172 C6
Ravenstone Rd
 CDALE/KGS * NW9 ....83 F3
 CEND/HSY/T N8 ....67 H6
Ravens Wy *LEE/GVPK* SE12 .....172 C6
Ravenswood *BXLY* DA5 ....196 C5
Ravenswood Av *SURB* KT6 ....221 H6
 WWKM BR4 ....231 G5
Ravenswood Ct *KUTN/CMB* * KT2 ..202 D2
Ravenswood Crs
 RYLN/HDSTN HA2 ....78 D6
 WWKM BR4 ....231 G5
Ravenswood Gdns *ISLW* TW7 ...160 A2
Ravenswood Rd *BAL* SW12 ......186 D2
 CROY/NA CR0 ....246 B1
 WALTH E17 ....91 G1
Ravent Rd *LBTH* SE11 ....29 H2
Ravey St *SDTCH* EC2A 8 A5
Ravine Gv *WOOL/PLUM* SE18 ..155 E6
Raw Pinter Cl *STNW/STAM* N16 ..89 E4
Rawlings Cl *ORP* BR6 ....253 F3
Rawlings St *CHEL* SW3 ....16 C6
Rawlins Cl *FNCH* N3 ....64 C6
 SAND/SEL CR2 ....249 G6
Rawnsley Av *MTCM* CR4 ....225 H2
Rawreth Wk *IS* * N1 ....108 C6
Rawson St *BTSEA* SW11 ....166 D2
Rawsthorne St *BETH* E2 ....92 B1
Rawstone Wk *FSBYE* EC1V 6 C5
Rawstorne St *FSBYE* EC1V 6 C4
Ray Bell Ct *BROCKY* * SE4 ......170 D3
Raydean Rd *BAR* EN5 ....35 E6
Raydon Gdns *DAGW* RM9 ....116 C3
Raydons Rd *DAGW* RM9 ....116 C3
Rayfield Cl *HAYES* BR2 ....233 G3
Rayford Av *LEE/GVPK* SE12 .....192 B2
Ray Gdns *BARK* IG11 ....135 G1
 STAN HA7 ....60 D1
Rayleas Cl *WOOL/PLUM* SE18 ..174 B2
Rayleigh Av *TEDD* TW11 ....200 H2
Rayleigh Cl *PLMGR* N13 ....52 D5
Rayleigh Ct *KUT* KT1 ....202 A5
Rayleigh Ri *SAND/SEL* CR2 .....247 E4
Rayleigh Rd *CAN/RD* E16 ....151 J1
 PLMGR N13 ....52 C5
 WFD IG8 ....73 E3
 WIM/MER SW19 ....204 D4
Ray Lodge Rd *WFD* IG8 ....73 E2
Raymead Av *THHTH* CR7 ....228 A2
Raymere Gdns
 WOOL/PLUM SE18 ....174 D1
Raymond Av *HNWL* W7 ....140 C3
 WAN E11 ....72 B6
Raymond Buildings
 GINN * WC1R 13 H1
Raymond Cl *SYD* SE26 ....210 A1
Raymond Rd *BECK* BR3 ....210 C1
 GNTH/NBYPK IG2 ....74 D4
 PLSTW E13 ....113 G5
 WIM/MER SW19 ....204 C2
Raymond Wy *ESH/CLAY* KT10 ..238 C4

Raymouth Rd
 BERM/RHTH SE16 ....33 H1
Rayne Ct *SWFD* E18 ....92 B1
Rayners Cl *ALP/SUD* HA0 ....101 F3
Rayners La *PIN* HA5 ....78 D5
 RYLN/HDSTN HA2 ....79 E5
Rayner's Rd *PUT/ROE* SW15 ...164 C6
Raynes Av *WAN* E11 ....95 E4
Raynham Av *UED* N18 ....69 C2
Raynham Rd *HMSMTH* W6 ....143 H4
 UED N18 ....69 C1
Raynham Ter *UED* N18 ....69 G1
Raynor Cl *STHL* UB1 ....138 D1
Raynor Pl *IS* N1 ....108 A2
Raynton Cl *RYLN/HDSTN* HA2 ..78 C5
Ray Rd *CRW* RM5 ....77 F1
 E/WMO/HCT KT8 ....219 F2
Rays Av *UED* N18 ....54 A6
Rays Rd *UED* N18 ....54 A6
 WWKM BR4 ....231 G4
Ray St *CLKNW* EC1R 6 B6
Ray Street Br *CLKNW* * EC1R 6 B6
Reachview Cl *CAMTN* NW1 ....107 E5
Reading La *HACK* E8 ....109 H4
Reading Rd *NTHLT* UB5 ....99 F3
 SUT SM1 ....225 G4
Reading Wy *MLHL* NW7 ....64 C1
Reads Cl *IL* IG1 ....114 B1
Reapers Cl *CAMTN* NW1 ....107 F6
Reapers Wy *ISLW* TW7 ....159 H6
Reardon Pth *WAP* E1W 25 C1
Reardon St *WAP* E1W 25 C1
Reaston St *NWCR* SE14 ....170 A1
Reckitt Rd *CHSWK* W4 ....142 B5
Record St *PECK* SE15 ....150 A6
Recovery St *TOOT* SW17 ....206 A1
Recreation Av *ROMW/RG* RM7 ..57 G3
Recreation Rd *HAYES* BR2 ....212 B5
 NWDGN UB2 ....136 C6
 SYD SE26 ....190 B6
Recreation Wy *MTCM* CR4 ....207 G6
Rector St *IS* N1 ....108 C6
Rectory Cl *CHING* E4 ....55 E5
 DART DA1 ....138 D4
 RYNPK SW20 ....204 A5
 SCUP DA14 ....195 H6
 STAN HA7 ....35 G5
 SURB KT6 ....221 E5
 TOOT SW17 ....206 C1
 WLGTN SM6 ....245 E2
Rectory Crs *WAN* E11 ....71 G3
Rectory Field Crs *CHARL* SE7 ..173 E1
Rectory Gdns *BECK* * BR3 ....211 E4
 CEND/HSY/T N8 ....87 G1
 CHST BR7 ....214 C4
 NTHLT UB5 ....99 H1
Rectory Gn *BECK* BR3 ....210 D4
Rectory Gv *CLAP* SW4 ....167 C4
 CROY/NA CR0 ....228 B6
 FELT TW13 ....198 D6
Rectory La *EDGW* HA8 ....62 A2
 SCUP DA14 ....195 H6
 STAN HA7 ....35 G4
 SURB KT6 ....221 E5
 TOOT SW17 ....206 C1
 WLGTN SM6 ....245 E2
 WALTH E17 ....51 F1
Rectory Orch *WIM/MER* SW19 ..184 C6
Rectory Park Av *NTHLT* UB5 .....118 D2
Rectory Pl *CHST* * BR7 ....214 C4
 WOOL/PLUM SE18 ....154 A4
Rectory Rd *ACT* W3 ....141 G3
 BARN SW13 ....163 G3
 BECK BR3 ....211 E4
 DAGE RM10 ....117 E4
 HAYES BR2 ....211 F5
 MNPK E12 ....113 H5
 NWDGN UB2 ....138 C3
 STNW/STAM N16 ....89 H4
 SUT SM1 ....245 E2
 WALTH E17 ....51 H2
Rectory Sq *WCHPL* E1 ....130 E4
Reculver Ms *UED* N18 ....53 G6
Red Anchor Cl *CHEL* * SW3 ......145 H6
Redan Pl *BAY/PAD* * W2 ....125 F5
Redan St *WKENS* W14 ....144 B3
Redan Ter *CMBW* SE5 ....168 B3
Red Barracks Rd
 WOOL/PLUM SE18 ....153 H4
Redberry Gv *SYD* SE26 ....190 A5
Redbourne Av *FNCH* N3 ....65 E4
Redbridge Gdns *CMBW* SE5 .....169 E1
Redbridge La East *REDBR* IG4 ..93 F3
Redbridge La West *WAN* E11 .....93 G3
Redburn St *CHEL* SW3 ....26 C5
Redcar Cl *NTHLT* UB5 ....80 B5
Redcar St *CMBW* * SE5 ....168 C1
Redcastle Cl *WCHPL* E1 ....130 A6
Red Cedars Rd *ORP* BR6 ....235 E4
Redchurch St *BETH* E2 ....9 H6
Redcliffe Cl *ECT* * SW5 ....145 F5
 WBPTN SW10 ....145 F5
Redcliffe Gdns *ECT* SW5 ....145 F5
 IL IG1 ....94 A5
Redcliffe Ms *WBPTN* SW10 .....145 F5
Redcliffe Pl *WBPTN* SW10 ....145 F6
Redcliffe Rd *WBPTN* SW10 .....145 F5
Redcliffe Sq *WBPTN* SW10 ......145 F5
Redcliffe St *WBPTN* * SW10 .....145 F6
Redclose Av *MRDN* SM4 ....225 E2
Redclyffe Rd *EHAM* E6 ....113 F6
Redcroft Rd *GFD/PVL* UB6 ....118 D2
Redcross Wy *STHWK* SE1 ....23 H2
Reddings Cl *MLHL* NW7 ....47 H1
The Reddings *MLHL* NW7 ....47 H1
Reddington Cl *SAND/SEL* CR2 ..246 D6
Reddins Rd *PECK* SE15 ....169 G1
Reddons Rd *BECK* BR3 ....210 C3
Rede Pl *BAY/PAD* W2 ....125 E5
Redesdale Gdns *ISLW* TW7 .....160 C5
Redesdale St *CHEL* SW3 ....26 C5
Redfern Av *HSLWW* TW4 ....178 C2
Redfern Rd *CAT* SE6 ....191 G2
 WLSDN NW10 ....103 G3
Redfield La *ECT* SW5 ....145 E4
Redford Av *THHTH* CR7 ....227 H1
 WLCTN SM6 ....245 E5
Redford Wk *IS* * N1 ....108 B6
Redgate Dr *HAYES* BR2 ....252 D6
Redgate Ter *PUT/ROE* SW15 ...184 B1
Redgrave Cl *SNWD* SE25 ....230 G6
Redgrave Rd *PUT/ROE* SW15 ..164 A4
Redgrave Ter *BETH* * E2 ....9 F4
Redhall Ter *ACT* * W3 ....122 A4

Red HI CHST BR7 .....214 A1
Redhill Dr EDGW HA8 .....62 C5
Redhill St CAMTN NW1 .....3 H2
Red House La BXLYHS DA6 .....176 B5
Red House Rd CROY/NA CR0 .....227 F3
Red House Sq IS * N1 .....85 J5
Redington Gdns HAMP NW3 .....105 F2
Redington Rd HAMP NW3 .....105 F1
Redland Gdns
  E/WMO/HCT * KT8 .....218 D1
Redlands Rd PEND EN3 .....25 G2
Redlands Wy
  BRXS/STRHM SW2 .....187 G2
Red La ESH/CLAY KT10 .....238 B4
Redleaf Cl BELV DA17 .....157 E6
Redlees Cl ISLW TW7 .....136 B5
Red Lion Cl STMC/STPC BR5 .....236 A3
  WALW SE17 .....31 C5
Red Lion Ct FLST/FETLN EC4A 14 B4
  HSLW * TW3 .....159 F4
Red Lion HI EFNCH N2 .....65 H5
Red Lion La WOOL/PLUM SE18 .....174 A2
Red Lion Pde PIN * HA5 .....58 G6
Red Lion Pl
  WOOL/PLUM * SE18 .....174 A2
Red Lion Rd SURB KT6 .....245 G6
Red Lion Rw WALW SE17 .....31 F6
Red Lion Sq BMSBY WC1N 13 G2
  WAND/EARL * SW18 .....165 G6
Red Lion St GINN WC1R 13 G2
  RCHPK/HAM TW10 .....161 F6
Red Lion Yd MYFR/PKLN * W1K 19 F1
Red Lodge Cl BXLY DA5 .....197 H5
Red Lodge Rd BXLY DA5 .....197 H5
  WWKM BR4 .....231 C5
Redman Cl NTHLT UB5 .....118 A1
Redman's Rd WCHPL E1 .....130 A4
Redmead La WAP * E1W 25 G2
Redmore Rd HMSMTH * W6 .....143 H4
Red Oak Cl ORP BR6 .....252 B1
Red Pl MYFR/PKLN W1K 11 E5
Red Post HI HNHL SE24 .....168 B3
Redriffe Rd PLSTW E13 .....132 B1
Redriff Rd BERM/RHTH SE16 .....150 C3
  ROMW/RG RM7 .....77 F5
Redroofs Cl BECK BR3 .....211 F4
Redruth Cl WDGN N22 .....63 G5
Redruth Rd HOM E9 .....114 F1
Redstart Cl EHAM E6 .....133 G4
  NWCR * SE14 .....170 C1
Redston Rd CEND/HSY/T N8 .....87 F1
Redvers Rd WDGN N22 .....63 G5
Redvers St IS N1 .....8 B3
Redwald Rd CLPT E5 .....110 B2
Redway Dr WHTN TW2 .....179 G2
Redwing Rd WLGTN SM6 .....245 G4
Redwood Cl BERM/RHTH SE16 .....150 C1
  BFN/LL DA15 .....175 G3
  OXHEY WD19 .....42 A6
  STHGT/OAK N14 .....34 S1
Redwood Gdns CHING * E4 .....55 F2
  SWFD * E18 .....34 B6
Reece Ms SKENS SW7 .....145 H4
Reed Av ORP BR6 .....255 C1
Reed Cl CAN/RD E16 .....132 C4
  LEE/GVPK SE12 .....172 C6
Reede Rd DAGE RM10 .....117 G4
Reede Wy DAGE RM10 .....117 F4
Reedham Cl TOTM N17 .....89 H1
Reedham St PECK * SE15 .....169 G2
Reedholm Vls
  STNW/STAM N16 .....108 D2
Reed Rd TOTM N17 .....109 G6
Reed's Pl CAMTN NW1 .....107 G5
Reedworth St LBTH SE11 .....30 B2
Reenglass Rd STAN * HA7 .....45 F6
Rees Dr STAN HA7 .....45 C6
Rees Gdns CROY/NA CR0 .....229 F3
Reesland Cl MNPK E12 .....114 A4
Rees St IS N1 .....7 F1
Reets Farm Cl CDALE/KGS NW9 .....83 E5
Reeves Av CDALE/KGS NW9 .....82 D1
Reeves Cnr CROY/NA CR0 .....228 B6
Reeves Crs SWLY BR8 .....217 H6
Reeves Ms MYFR/PKLN W1K 11 E5
Reeves Rd BOW E3 .....131 F3
  WOOL/PLUM SE18 .....154 B6
Reform Rw TOTM N17 .....69 F5
Reform St BTSEA SW11 .....166 B3
Regal Cl EA W5 .....117 J1
  WCHPL E1 .....17 F1
Regal Ct MTCM CR4 .....206 B6
  UED N18 .....49 F6
Regal Crs WLGTN SM6 .....244 D1
Regal Dr FBAR/BDGN N11 .....66 F1
Regal La CAMTN NW1 .....106 C6
Regal Pl KTN/HRWW/W HA3 .....81 G3
  WBPT * SW10 .....120 B6
Regan Wy IS N1 .....8 A2
Regarder Rd CHIG IG7 .....71 H1
Regency Cl CHIG IG7 .....54 C1
  EA W5 .....117 J1
  HPTN TW12 .....198 D1
Regency Ct EN EN1 .....105 D1
Regency Gdns WOT/HER KT12 .....218 B5
Regency Lawn KTTN * NW5 .....106 D1
Regency Ms BECK BR3 .....211 C1
  WLSDN NW10 .....103 G4
Regency Pde HAMP * NW3 .....105 H5
Regency Pl WEST * SW1P 28 C1
Regency St WEST SW1P 28 C2
Regency Ter WEST * N6 .....36 A6
  SKENS * SW7 .....145 H5
Regency Wk CROY/NA CR0 .....231 C6
Regency Wy BXLYHN DA7 .....176 B4
Regent Cl KTN/HRWW/W HA3 .....81 C3
  NFNCH/WDSP N12 .....47 E1
Regent Gdns GDMY/SEVK IG3 .....95 C3
Regent Pde BELMT * SM2 .....243 C4
  STNW/STAM * N16 .....88 A2
Regent Pl WIM/MER SW19 .....205 C1
Regent Rd BRYLDS KT5 .....221 H2
  HNHL SE24 .....168 B1
Regents Av PLMGR N13 .....68 A1
Regents Cl SAND/SEL CR2 .....247 E4
Regents Dr HAYES BR2 .....251 F3
Regents Ms STJWD NW8 .....125 G1
Regent's Pk CAMTN NW1 .....3 F1
Regent's Park Rd FNCH N3 .....64 D6
  HAMP NW3 .....105 H5
Regent's Park Ter CAMTN NW1 .....106 D6
Regents Pl LOU IG10 .....57 F2

Regents Plaza
  KIL/WHAMP * NW6 .....125 F1
Regent Sq BELV DA17 .....157 F4
  STPAN WC1H 5 F4
Regent St FITZ W1B 11 G3
Regent St CHSWK W4 .....142 A5
  CONDST W1S 12 A4
  WLSDN NW10 .....124 B2
Regents Whf IS * N1 .....5 J3
Reginald Rd DEPT SE8 .....171 E1
  FSTGT E7 .....112 C5
Reginald Sq DEPT SE8 .....171 E1
Regina Rd FSBYPK N4 .....87 H5
  NWDGN UB2 .....138 C4
  SNWD SE25 .....209 G6
  WEA W13 .....140 C1
Regina Ter WEA W13 .....140 C1
Regis Rd KTTN NW5 .....106 D3
Regnart Buildings CAMTN NW1 .....4 B7
Reidhaven Rd
  WOOL/PLUM SE18 .....155 E4
Reigate Av MRDN SM4 .....225 F5
Reigate Rd BMLY BR1 .....192 C4
  GDMY/SEVK IG3 .....95 F6
Reigate Wy WLGTN SM6 .....245 G3
Reighton Rd CLPT E5 .....109 C1
Relay Rd SHB W12 .....124 A6
Relf Rd PECK SE15 .....169 G4
Reliance Ar BRXN/ST * SW9 .....168 A5
Relton Ms SKENS SW7 .....18 B5
Rembrandt Cl BOVA * SW1W 27 E5
  POP/IOD E14 .....151 H3
Rembrandt Ct HOR/WEW KT19 .....241 F4
Rembrandt Rd EDGW * HA8 .....62 A5
  LEW SE13 .....172 A5
Remington Rd EHAM E6 .....133 C5
  SEVS/STOTM N15 .....88 D3
Remington St IS N1 .....6 C2
Remnant St HOL/ALD WC2B 13 G3
Remus Rd BOW E3 .....111 E5
Rendle Cl CROY/NA CR0 .....229 F2
Rendlesham Rd CLPT E5 .....109 G2
  ENC/FH EN2 .....38 B2
Renforth St BERM/RHTH SE16 .....150 A2
Renfrew Cl EHAM E6 .....134 A6
Renfrew Rd HEST TW5 .....158 B3
  KUTN/CMB KT2 .....202 C5
  LBTH SE11 .....30 C1
Renmuir St TOOT SW17 .....206 B2
Rennell St LEW SE13 .....171 G4
Renness Rd WALTH E17 .....70 C6
Rennets Cl ELTH/MOT SE9 .....174 D6
Rennets Wood Rd
  ELTH/MOT SE9 .....174 D6
Rennie Est BERM/RHTH SE16 .....151 H4
Rennie St STHWK SE1 .....22 C1
Renown Cl CROY/NA CR0 .....228 B5
  ROMW/RG RM7 .....77 E4
Rensburg Rd WALTH E17 .....90 B2
Rensburg Vls WALTH * E17 .....90 B2
Renshaw Cl BELV DA17 .....156 D6
Renters Av HDN NW4 .....84 A3
Renton Cl BRXS/STRHM * SW2 .....187 H1
Renton Dr STMC/STPC BR5 .....236 B4
Renwick Rd BARK IG11 .....135 H3
Repens Wy YEAD UB4 .....118 B3
Rephidim St STHWK SE1 .....23 H6
Replingham Rd
  WAND/EARL SW18 .....184 D3
Reporton Rd FUL/PGN SW6 .....164 C2
Repository Rd
  WOOL/PLUM SE18 .....153 H6
Repton Av ALP/SUD HA0 .....101 E2
Repton Cl SUT SM1 .....244 A3
Repton Ct BECK BR3 .....211 F4
Repton Gv CLAY IG5 .....71 H3
Repton Rd KTN/HRWW/W HA3 .....81 H1
  ORP BR6 .....253 C2
Repton St POP/IOD E14 .....130 C5
Repulse Cl ROMW/RG RM7 .....77 F4
Reservoir Cl THHTH CR7 .....208 D6
Reservoir Rd BROCKY SE4 .....170 C3
  STHGT/OAK N14 .....37 E6
Restell Cl BKHTH/KID SE3 .....152 A6
Restmor Wy WLGTN SM6 .....145 C2
Reston Pl SKENS SW7 .....14 D4
Restons Crs ELTH/MOT SE9 .....194 D1
Retford St BETH * E2 .....8 D2
Retingham Wy CHING E4 .....35 H1
Retreat Cl KTN/HRWW/W HA3 .....81 F3
Retreat Pl HOM E9 .....110 A4
Retreat Rd RCH/KEW TW9 .....161 F6
The Retreat BARN SW13 .....163 H1
  BRYLDS KT5 .....221 H5
  CDALE/KGS NW9 .....82 D2
  ORP BR6 .....253 H4
  RYLN/HDSTN HA2 .....79 E4
  THHTH CR7 .....228 D1
  WPK KT4 .....241 H1
Reunion Rw WAP E1W 17 H6
Reveley Sq BERM/RHTH SE16 .....151 C5
Revell Rd WOOL/PLUM SE18 .....155 F6
Revell Rd KUT KT1 .....202 B5
  SUT SM1 .....242 D4
Revelon Rd BROCKY SE4 .....170 C5
Revelstoke Rd
  WIM/MER SW19 .....185 G4
Reventlow Rd ELTH/MOT SE9 .....194 C3
Reverdy Rd STHWK SE1 .....33 G2
Reverend Cl RYLN/HDSTN HA2 .....77 J1
Revesby Rd CAR SM5 .....226 A3
Review Rd CRICK NW2 .....83 F6
  DAGE RM10 .....157 F1
Rewell St FUL/PGN * SW6 .....166 C1
Rewley Rd CAR SM5 .....225 H3
Rex Pl MYFR/PKLN W1K 19 F1
Reydon Av WAN E11 .....93 E3
Reynard Cl BMLY BR1 .....215 J6
Reynard Dr NRWD SE19 .....209 F3
Reynard Pl NWCR * SE14 .....150 C6
Reynardson Rd TOTM N17 .....68 C3
Reynolds Av CHDH RM6 .....96 A6
  CHSGTN KT9 .....239 G5
  MNPK E12 .....114 A3
Reynolds Cl CAR SM5 .....226 B5
  WIM/MER SW19 .....205 H4
Reynolds Dr EDGW HA8 .....61 H6
Reynolds Pl BKHTH/KID SE3 .....172 D1
  RCHPK/HAM TW10 .....181 F6
Reynolds Rd CHSWK W4 .....142 A3
  NWMAL KT3 .....222 D4
  PECK SE15 .....170 A6
  YEAD UB4 .....95 H6
Reynolds Wy CROY/NA CR0 .....247 E2
Rheidol Ms IS N1 .....7 E1
Rheidol Ter IS N1 .....6 D1
Rheingold Wy WLGTN SM6 .....245 G6
Rheola Cl TOTM N17 .....69 F4
Rhoda St BETH E2 .....9 J5
Rhodes Av WDGN N22 .....67 E4
Rhodesia Rd BRXN/ST SW9 .....167 G5
  WAN E11 .....91 H6
Rhodes St HOLWY * N7 .....85 F3
Rhodeswell Rd BOW E3 .....130 C4
Rhodrons Av CHSGTN KT9 .....239 G3
Rhondda Gv BOW E3 .....130 C2
Rhyl Rd GFD/PVL UB6 .....120 D2
Rhyl St KTTN NW5 .....106 C4
Rhys Av FBAR/BDGN N11 .....67 E3
Rialto Rd MTCM CR4 .....206 C5
Ribble Cl WFD IG8 .....73 E2
Ribblesdale Av
  FBAR/BDGN N11 .....66 B2
  NTHLT UB5 .....83 J1
Ribblesdale Rd CEND/HSY/T N8 .....87 H1
  STRHM/NOR SW16 .....186 B1
Ribbon Dance Ms GNWST W1 .....7 H1
Ribchester Av GFD/PVL UB6 .....120 B2
Ribston Cl HAYES BR2 .....233 H5
Ricardo St POP/IOD E14 .....131 F5
Ricards Rd WIM/MER SW19 .....204 D1
Rice House Dr CAN/RD E16 .....153 F5
Richard Cl WOOL/PLUM SE18 .....153 H5
Richard House Dr CAN/RD E16 .....133 H3
Richards Av ROMW/RG RM7 .....97 C2
Richards Cl BUSH WD23 .....43 H2
  HRW HA1 .....61 E6
Richards Cottages CAR * SM5 .....244 B3
Richards Fld HOR/WEW KT19 .....240 D6
Richardson Cl HACK * E8 .....109 H6
Richardson Rd SRTFD * E15 .....132 A1
Richardson's Ms FITZ W1T 4 A6
Richard's Pl CHEL SW3 .....26 D6
  WALTH E17 .....71 F6
Richard St WCHPL E1 .....17 C4
Richbell Pl BMSBY WC1N 13 C1
Richborne Ter VX/NE SW8 .....167 H1
Richborough Cl
  STMC/STPC BR5 .....236 B1
Richborough Rd CRICK NW2 .....104 B2
Richens Cl HSLW TW3 .....159 H1
Riches Rd IL IG1 .....94 C6
Richfield Rd BUSH * WD23 .....43 H3
Richford Ga HMSMTH * W6 .....144 A3
Richford Rd SRTFD * E15 .....132 B1
Richford St HMSMTH W6 .....144 A2
Richlands Av EW KT17 .....241 G2
Richmond Av CHING E4 .....71 H1
  IS N1 .....5 J1
  RYNPK SW20 .....204 C4
  WLSDN NW10 .....106 B1
Richmond Buildings
  SOHO/CST W1F 12 C4
Richmond Cl WALTH E17 .....90 D5
Richmond Crs CHING E4 .....71 H1
  ED N9 .....53 C3
  IS N1 .....107 H6
Richmond Gdns HDN NW4 .....63 J2
  KTN/HRWW/W HA3 .....60 E5
Richmond Gn CROY/NA CR0 .....245 G1
Richmond Gv IS N1 .....108 B5
Richmond HI
  RCHPK/HAM TW10 .....181 G1
Richmond Ms SOHO/CST W1F 12 C4
Richmond Pde TWK * TW1 .....181 E1
Richmond Park Rd
  KUTN/CMB KT2 .....201 G3
  MORT/ESHN SW14 .....162 G6
Richmond Pl
  WOOL/PLUM SE18 .....106 C5
Richmond Rd BAR EN5 .....35 F6
  CHING * E4 .....54 A6
  CROY/NA CR0 .....245 G1
  EA W5 .....141 G2
  EFNCH * N2 .....65 G5
  FBAR/BDGN N11 .....66 E2
  FSTGT E7 .....112 D3
  HACK E8 .....109 H6
  IL IG1 .....114 C1
  ISLW TW7 .....160 C5
  KUTN/CMB KT2 .....201 G4
  RYNPK SW20 .....203 H4
  SEVS/STOTM N15 .....89 H3
  THHTH CR7 .....228 B1
  TWK TW1 .....161 J5
  WAN E11 .....91 H6
  WHTN TW2 .....144 B2
  WIM/MER SW19 .....178 ...

CHEAM SM3 .....224 D5
CRICK NW2 .....104 D1
MTCM CR4 .....206 D3
WCHMH N21 .....35 C2
Ridge Ter WCHMH * N21 .....52 C2
The Ridge BAR * EN5 .....34 D6
  BRYLDS KT5 .....222 A2
  BXLY DA5 .....196 D2
  ORP BR6 .....253 C6
  WHTN TW2 .....179 H2
Ridgeview Cl BAR EN5 .....48 B1
Ridgeview Rd
  NFNCH/WDSP N12 .....49 F5
Ridge Wy FELT TW13 .....178 C5
Ridgeway HAYES BR2 .....232 C6
  WFD IG8 .....53 E1
Ridgeway Av EBAR EN4 .....50 B1
Ridgeway Crs ORP BR6 .....253 E1
Ridgeway Crescent Gdns
  ORP BR6 .....235 E5
Ridgeway Dr BMLY BR1 .....192 D6
Ridgeway East BFN/LL DA15 .....175 F6
Ridgeway Gdns REDBR * IG4 .....95 G2
  IS N1 .....85 G5
Ridgeway Rd North ISLW TW7 .....160 A5
The Ridgeway ACT W3 .....142 A3
  CDALE/KGS NW9 .....82 D1
  CHING E4 .....55 G3
  CROY/NA CR0 .....245 H1
  EA W5 .....98 B6
  FBAR/BDGN N11 .....65 F3
  FNCH N3 .....65 G5
  GLDGN NW11 .....84 D5
  KTN/HRWW/W HA3 .....81 E3
  MLHL NW7 .....47 H6
  RYLN/HDSTN HA2 .....78 D2
  STAN HA7 .....61 E2
  STHGT/OAK N14 .....51 G4
Ridgeway West BFN/LL DA15 .....175 F6
Ridgewell Cl DAGE RM10 .....117 F6
  IS N1 .....108 C6
  SYD SE26 .....190 D6
Ridgmount Gdns GWRST WC1E 12 C1
Ridgmount Rd
  WAND/EARL SW18 .....165 E6
Ridgmount St GWRST WC1E 12 C1
Ridgway RCHPK/HAM * TW10 .....181 G1
  WIM/MER SW19 .....204 B3
Ridgway Gdns
  WIM/MER SW19 .....204 C2
Ridgway Pl WIM/MER SW19 .....204 C2
Ridgway Rd BRXN/ST SW9 .....168 B2
The Ridgway BELMT SM2 .....243 H5
Ridgwell Rd CAN/RD E16 .....133 E4
Riding House St CTPST W1W 12 A2
Ridings Av WCHMH N21 .....35 J5
The Ridings BRYLDS KT5 .....222 A2
  EA W5 .....121 H5
  EBAR * EN4 .....50 A2
  EW KT17 .....241 H5
The Riding GLDGN NW11 .....84 D4
Ridler Rd EN EN1 .....59 E1
Ridley Av WEA W13 .....140 D3
Ridley Rd FSTGT E7 .....113 E1
  HACK E8 .....109 F3
  HAYES BR2 .....212 B6
  WELL DA16 .....175 H2
  WIM/MER SW19 .....205 F1
  WLSDN NW10 .....107 H1
Ridsdale Rd PGE/AN SE20 .....209 H4
Riefield Rd ELTH/MOT SE9 .....174 C5
Riesco Dr CROY/NA CR0 .....248 A4
Riffel Rd CRICK NW2 .....104 A5
Rifle Pl NTGHL W11 .....144 B1
Rifle Range La HRW HA1 .....80 B5
Rifle St POP/IOD E14 .....131 F4
Rigault Rd FUL/PGN SW6 .....166 C2
Rigby Cl CROY/NA CR0 .....246 A1
Rigby Ms IL IG1 .....94 A6
Rigden St POP/IOD E14 .....131 F5
Rigeley Rd WLSDN NW10 .....119 J2
Rigg Ap LEY E10 .....90 B5
Rigge Pl CLAP SW4 .....169 J2
Riggindale Rd
  STRHM/NOR SW16 .....207 F1
Right Side STHGT/OAK * N14 .....51 J1
Riley Rd PEND EN3 .....24 D1
Riley St WBPTN SW10 .....165 H1
Rinaldo Rd BAL SW12 .....188 C1
Ring Cl BMLY BR1 .....212 A2
Ringcroft St HOLWY N7 .....120 A3
Ringer's Rd BMLY BR1 .....212 D3
Ringford Rd WAND/EARL SW18 .....164 D6
Ringlet Cl CAN/RD E16 .....132 D5
Ringmer Av FUL/PGN SW6 .....164 B6
Ringmer Gdns ARCH N19 .....85 F2
Ringmer Pl WCHMH N21 .....36 A6
Ringmore Ri FSTH SE23 .....189 H5
Ringshall Rd CHST BR7 .....215 H6
Ringslade Rd WDGN N22 .....67 F2
Ringstead Rd CAT SE6 .....191 J1
  SUT SM1 .....243 H2
Ring Wy FBAR/BDGN N11 .....67 E2
Ringway NWDGN UB2 .....138 C1
Ringwood Cl BECK BR3 .....210 C5
Ringwood Av CROY/NA CR0 .....227 G4
  EFNCH N2 .....65 K5
Ringwood Cl PIN * HA5 .....58 D1
Ringwood Gdns
  PUT/ROE SW15 .....183 G4
Ringwood Rd WALTH E17 .....89 H3
Ringwood Wy HPTN TW12 .....179 F3
  WCHMH N21 .....35 H6
Ripley Cl BMLY BR1 .....233 E4
  CROY/NA CR0 .....249 J3
Ripley Gdns MORT/ESHN SW14 .....162 A4
  SUT SM1 .....243 H3
Ripley Ms WAN E11 .....70 C4
Ripley Rd BELV DA17 .....157 H3
  CAN/RD E16 .....133 G5
  ENC/FH EN2 .....23 J3
  GDMY/SEVK IG3 .....78 E1
Ripley Vls WEA * W13 .....121 G6
Ripon Cl NTHLT UB5 .....78 B3
Ripon Gdns CHSGTN KT9 .....239 J4
  IL IG1 .....71 H5
Ripon Rd ED N9 .....36 D6
  TOTM N17 .....68 A3
  WOOL/PLUM SE18 .....115 G6
Rippersley Rd WELL DA16 .....175 G2

Ripple Rd BARK IG11 114 C5
DAGW RM9 136 D1
Ripplevale Gv IS N1 107 H5
Rippolson Rd
WOOL/PLUM SE18 155 F5
Risborough Cl MUSWH * N10 66 D6
Risborough Dr WPK KT4 223 G4
Risborough St STHWK SE1 22 D3
Risdon St BERM/RHTH SE16 150 A2
Risedale Rd BXLYHN DA7 177 F4
Riseldine Rd FSTH SE23 190 C1
The Rise BKHH * IG9 57 F3
BKHH IG9 57 F3
BXLY DA5 196 A2
EDGW HA8 62 B1
GFD/PVL UB6 100 C3
MLHL NW7 63 F2
PLMGR N13 52 A6
SAND/SEL CR2 248 A6
WAN E11 92 C2
WLSDN NW10 102 D1
Risinghill St IS N1 6 A1
Risingholme Cl BUSH WD23 43 F2
KTN/HRWW/W HA3 60 A4
Risingholme Rd
KTN/HRWW/W HA3 60 A5
The Risings WALTH E17 91 H1
Risley Av TOTM N17 69 E4
Rita Rd VX/NE SW8 167 G1
Ritches Rd SEVS/STOTM N15 88 C2
Ritchie Rd CROY/NA CR0 229 H3
Ritchie St IS N1 6 B1
Ritchings Av WALTH E17 90 C1
Ritherdon Rd TOOT SW17 186 C4
Ritson Rd HACK E8 109 F4
Ritter St WOOL/PLUM SE18 154 A6
Rivaz Pl HOM E9 110 A4
Rivenhall Gdns SWFD E18 92 B1
River Av PLMGR N13 52 B5
THDIT KT7 220 C4
Riverbank E/WMO/HCT KT8 200 A6
River Bank THDIT KT7 220 B2
WCHMH N21 52 C2
Riverbank Rd BMLY BR1 192 C5
Riverbank Wy BTFD TW8 141 E6
River Barge Cl POP/IOD E14 151 G2
River Cl STHL UB1 139 G2
WAN E11 93 E3
Rivercourt Rd HMSMTH W6 143 H4
Riverdale Dr WAND/EARL SW18 185 F3
Riverdale Gdns TWK TW1 161 E6
Riverdale Rd BXLY DA5 196 D2
ERITH DA8 157 F5
FELT TW13 178 C6
TWK TW1 181 E1
WOOL/PLUM SE18 155 F5
Riverdene EDGW HA8 46 C6
Riverdene Rd IL IG1 114 A1
River Front EN EN1 38 D4
River Gdns CAR SM5 226 C6
River Grove Pk BECK BR3 210 D4
Riverhead Cl WALTH E17 70 B5
Riverholme Dr HOR/WEW KT19 240 D6
River La RCHPK/HAM TW10 181 F3
Rivermead E/WMO/HCT KT8 199 G6
SURB * KT6 221 F2
Rivermead Cl TEDD TW11 200 D1
River Meads Av WHTN TW2 179 F5
Rivernook Cl WOT/HER KT12 218 A2
Riverpark Gdns HAYES BR2 211 H3
River Park Rd WDGN N22 67 H5
River Park Vw ORP BR6 235 H4
River Pl IS N1 108 C5
River Reach TEDD TW11 201 E2
River Rd BARK IG11 135 E1
BKHH IG9 57 G3
Riversdale Rd CRW RM5 77 F3
HBRY N5 108 B1
THDIT KT7 220 C2
Riversfield Rd EN EN1 39 E4
Riverside CHARL SE7 152 D3
HDN NW4 83 H4
RCH/KEW * TW9 142 A6
SUN * TW16 198 B5
TWK TW1 180 D3
Riverside Av E/WMO/HCT KT8 219 H2
Riverside Cl CLPT E5 90 A5
HNWL W7 120 A3
KUT KT1 221 F1
STMC/STPC BR5 216 A5
WLGTN SM6 244 D1
Riverside Ct CHING * E4 55 F1
Riverside Dr CHSWK W4 162 D1
GLDGN * NW11 84 C3
MTCM CR4 226 A2
RCHPK/HAM TW10 180 D5
Riverside Gdns ALP/SUD HA0 121 G1
ENC/FH EN2 38 C3
HMSMTH W6 143 H5
Riverside Ms CROY/NA * CR0 245 G1
Riverside Pl FBAR/BDGN * N11 51 E5
Riverside Rd IL IG1 114 B1
SCUP DA14 196 C5
SEVS/STOTM N15 89 G3
SRTFD E15 131 G1
TOOT SW17 185 F6
The Riverside
E/WMO/HCT * KT8 199 H6
Riverside Vls SURB * KT6 221 E3
Riverside Wk ISLW TW7 160 A4
KUT KT1 201 F5
River St CLKNW EC1R 6 A3
River Ter HMSMTH W6 144 A5
Riverton Cl MV/WKIL * W9 124 D2
Riverview Gdns BARN SW13 143 H6
River View Gdns TWK TW1 180 B4
Riverview Pk CAT SE6 191 E4
Riverview Rd CHSWK W4 162 B1
HOR/WEW KT19 240 D3
River Wk SUN TW16 198 B5
River Wy FELT TW13 179 F4
GNWCH SE10 152 B3
HOR/WEW KT19 240 D3
Riverway PLMGR N13 68 A1
River Whf BELV * DA17 157 H2
Riverwood La CHST BR7 214 D5
Rivington Av WFD IG8 73 F5
Rivington Crs CDALE/KGS NW9 63 E3
Rivington Pl SDTCH EC2A 8 B4
Rivington St SDTCH EC2A 8 B4
Rivington Wk HACK * E8 109 G6
Rivulet Rd TOTM N17 68 C3
Rixon St HOLWY N7 108 A1
Rixsen Rd MNPK E12 113 G3
Roach Rd HOM E9 111 E5
Roads Pl ARCH N19 87 G6
Roan St GNWCH SE10 151 H5
Robb Rd STAN HA7 60 C2
Robert Adam St MBLAR W1H 11 E3
Roberta St BETH E2 9 E3
Robert Cl CHIG IG7 75 F1
MV/WKIL W9 125 G3
Robert Keen Cl PECK SE15 169 G2
Robert Lowe Cl NWCR SE14 170 B1
Roberton Dr BMLY BR1 213 E5
Robertsbridge Rd CAR SM5 225 G4
Roberts Cl CHEAM SM3 242 B5
ELTH/MOT SE9 194 D3
STMC/STPC BR5 236 A2
Roberts Ct CHSGTN * KT9 239 F3
WLSDN NW10 103 E4
Roberts Ms KTBR * SW1X 19 E6
Robertson Rd SRTFD E15 111 G6
Robertson St VX/NE SW8 166 D4
Robert's Pl CLKNW * EC1R 6 B5
Roberts Rd BELV DA17 157 E5
MLHL NW7 64 C1
WALTH E17 71 F4
Robert St CAMTN NW1 3 H4
CHCR WC2N 13 F6
CROY/NA CR0 246 C1
WOOL/PLUM SE18 154 D4
Robeson St BOW E3 130 D4
Robina Cl BXLYHS DA6 176 B5
Robin Cl CRW RM5 77 H3
HPTN TW12 198 C1
MLHL NW7 47 E5
Robin Gv BTFD TW8 141 E6
HGT N6 86 C6
KTN/HRWW/W HA3 81 H3
Robin Hill Dr CHST BR7 213 G2
Robinhood Cl MTCM CR4 227 E1
Robin Hood Dr
KTN/HRWW/W HA3 60 B3
Robin Hood Gdns
POP/IOD * E14 131 G6
Robin Hood Gn
STMC/STPC BR5 235 G2
Robin Hood La BXLYHS DA6 176 C6
Robinhood La MTCM CR4 207 E6
Robin Hood La POP/IOD E14 131 G6
PUT/ROE SW15 183 E5
SUT SM1 243 E3
Robin Hood Rd PUT/ROE SW15 183 E6
Robin Hood Wy GFD/PVL UB6 100 B4
Robin Hood Wy
(Kingston By-Pass)
PUT/ROE SW15 183 E6
Robinia Cl BARK/HLT IG6 75 E2
PGE/AN SE20 209 G4
Robinia Crs LEY E10 91 F6
Robins Gv WWKM BR4 250 C1
Robinson Crs BUSH WD23 43 G3
Robinson Rd BETH E2 130 A1
DAGE RM10 117 E2
WIM/MER SW19 206 A2
Robinson's Cl WEA W13 120 C4
Robinson St CHEL SW3 26 C5
Robin Wy STMC/STPC BR5 215 H6
Robinwood Pl
RCHPK/HAM TW10 182 D6
Robsart St BRXN/ST SW9 167 H3
Robson Av WLSDN NW10 103 G6
Robson Cl EHAM E6 133 G5
ENC/FH EN2 38 B3
Robson Rd WNWD SE27 188 B5
Roch Av EDGW HA8 61 H5
Rochdale Rd ABYW SE2 155 H5
Rochdale Wy DEPT SE8 171 E1
Rochelle Cl BTSEA SW11 165 H5
Rochelle St BETH E2 8 C4
Rochemont Wk HACK * E8 109 F6
Roche Rd STRHM/NOR SW16 207 G4
Rochester Av BMLY BR1 212 D5
PLSTW E13 113 E6
Rochester Cl BFN/LL DA15 195 H1
EN EN1 39 E2
STRHM/NOR * SW16 207 G3
Rochester Dr BXLY DA5 197 E1
PIN HA5 78 B2
Rochester Gdns CROY/NA CR0 247 E1
IL IG1 93 H4
Rochester Ms CAMTN NW1 107 E5
EA * W5 141 E4
Rochester Pl CAMTN NW1 107 E4
Rochester Rd CAMTN NW1 107 E4
CAR SM5 244 B2
Rochester Rw WEST SW1P 28 B1
Rochester Sq CAMTN NW1 107 E5
Rochester St WEST SW1P 20 C6
Rochester Ter CAMTN NW1 107 E4
Rochester Wk STHWK * SE1 23 G1
Rochester Wy Relief Rd
ELTH/MOT SE9 173 G6
Roche Wk MRDN SM4 225 H3
Rochford Av CHDH RM6 96 A2
Rochford Cl EHAM E6 133 F1
Rochford Wk HACK * E8 109 G5
Rochford Wy CROY/NA CR0 227 G3
Rock Av MORT/ESHN SW14 162 D4
Rockbourne Rd FSTH SE23 190 B3
Rock Cl MTCM CR4 205 H5
Rockell's Pl EDUL SE22 189 H1
Rockford Av GFD/PVL UB6 120 D1
Rock Grove Wy
BERM/RHTH SE16 33 F1
Rockhall Rd CRICK NW2 104 B2
Rockhampton Rd
SAND/SEL CR2 247 E4
STRHM/NOR SW16 188 A6
Rock Hl NRWD SE19 189 F6
Rockingham Cl PUT/ROE SW15 163 F5
Rockingham Ga BUSH WD23 43 G1
Rockingham St STHWK SE1 23 E6
Rockland Rd PUT/ROE SW15 164 C5
Rocklands Dr
KTN/HRWW/W HA3 60 D5
Rockley Rd SHB W12 144 B2
Rockmount Rd NRWD SE19 208 D2
WOOL/PLUM SE18 155 F5
Rocks La BARN SW13 163 G4
Rock St FSBYPK N4 88 A6
Rockware Av GFD/PVL * UB6 99 H6
Rockways BAR EN5 47 F1
Rockwell Gdns NRWD SE19 189 E6
Rockwell Rd DAGE RM10 117 F3
Rocliffe St IS N1 6 D2
Rocombe Crs FSTH * SE23 190 A2
Rocque La BKHTH/KID SE3 172 B4
Rodborough Rd GLDGN NW11 85 E5
Roden Gdns CROY/NA CR0 229 E3
Rodenhurst Rd CLAP SW4 187 E2
Roden St HOLWY N7 107 H1
IL IG1 114 A1
Roderick Rd HAMP NW3 106 B2
Rodgers Cl BORE WD6 45 F1
Roding Gdns LOU IG10 57 G1
Roding La BKHH IG9 57 G3
Roding La North WFD IG8 73 G5
Roding La South REDBR IG4 93 F2
Roding Ms WAP E1W 25 F1
Roding Rd CLPT E5 110 B2
EHAM E6 134 B4
Rodings Rw BAR * EN5 34 C5
Roding Vw BKHH IG9 57 F3
Rodmarton St MHST W1U 10 D2
Rodmell Cl YEAD UB4 118 C3
Rodmell Slope
NFNCH/WDSP N12 64 D1
Rodmere St GNWCH SE10 152 A5
Rodmill La BRXS/STRHM SW2 187 G2
Rodney Cl CROY/NA CR0 228 B5
NWMAL KT3 223 E2
PIN HA5 78 C4
WOT/HER * KT12 218 A5
Rodney Gdns PIN HA5 78 A2
WWKM BR4 250 C2
Rodney Pl STHWK SE1 31 F1
WALTH E17 70 C5
WIM/MER SW19 205 G4
Rodney Rd HSLWW TW4 179 E1
MTCM CR4 206 A5
NWMAL KT3 223 E2
WALW SE17 31 F2
WAN E11 92 D1
WOT/HER KT12 218 A6
Rodney St IS N1 5 H1
Rodney Wy ROMW/RG RM7 77 F4
Rodway Rd BMLY BR1 212 D4
PUT/ROE SW15 183 G2
Rodwell Cl RSLP * HA4 78 A5
Rodwell Rd EDUL SE22 189 F1
Roebuck La BKHH IG9 57 E3
Roebuck Rd BARK/HLT IG6 75 H2
CHSGTN KT9 240 A3
Roedean Av PEND EN3 40 A2
Roedean Cl ORP BR6 253 H2
PEND EN3 40 A2
Roedean Crs PUT/ROE SW15 183 E1
Roe End CDALE/KGS NW9 82 C1
Roe Gn CDALE/KGS NW9 82 C2
Roehampton Cl
PUT/ROE SW15 163 G5
Roehampton Dr CHST BR7 214 C2
Roehampton Ga
PUT/ROE SW15 183 E1
Roehampton High St
PUT/ROE SW15 183 G2
Roehampton La
PUT/ROE SW15 163 G6
Roehampton V PUT/ROE SW15 183 F5
Roe La CDALE/KGS NW9 82 B1
Roe Wy WLGTN SM6 245 G5
Roffey St POP/IOD E14 151 G2
Rogers Gdns DAGE RM10 117 E3
Rogers Rd CAN/RD E16 132 B5
DAGE RM10 117 E3
TOOT SW17 185 H6
Roger St BMSBY WC1N 5 H6
Rojack Rd FSTH SE23 190 B3
Rokeby Gdns WFD IG8 72 C4
Rokeby Pl RYNPK SW20 203 H3
Rokeby Rd BROCKY * SE4 170 D3
Rokeby St SRTFD E15 112 A6
Rokesby Cl WELL DA16 174 D3
Rokesby Pl ALP/SUD HA0 101 F3
Rokesly Av CEND/HSY/T N8 87 G2
Roland Gdns SKENS SW7 145 G5
Roland Ms WCHPL * E1 130 B4
Roland Rd WALTH E17 91 H1
Roland Wy WALW SE17 31 H4
WBPTN SW10 145 G5
WPK KT4 223 F6
Roles Gv CHDH RM6 96 B1
Rolfe Cl EBAR EN4 36 A5
Rolinsden Wy HAYES BR2 251 F2
Rollesby Rd CHSGTN KT9 240 A4
Rollesby Wy THMD SE28 136 A6
Rolleston Av STMC/STPC BR5 234 B3
Rolleston Cl STMC/STPC BR5 234 B4
Rolleston Rd SAND/SEL CR2 246 D5
Roll Gdns GNTH/NBYPK IG2 94 A2
Rollins St PECK SE15 150 A6
Rollit Crs HSLW TW3 159 E6
Rollit St HOLWY N7 108 A3
Rolls Buildings
FLST/FETLN EC4A 14 A3
Rollscourt Av HNHL SE24 168 C6
Rolls Park Av CHING E4 71 E2
Rolls Park Rd CHING E4 71 F1
Rolls Rd STHWK SE1 32 D3
Rolt St DEPT SE8 150 C6
Rolvenden Gdns BMLY BR1 213 F4
Rolvenden Pl TOTM N17 69 G4
Roman Cl ACT W3 142 B2
EBED/NFELT TW14 158 A6
RAIN RM13 137 H1
Romanfield Rd
BRXS/STRHM SW2 187 H2
Romanhurst Av HAYES BR2 232 A1
Romanhurst Gdns BECK BR3 232 A1
Roman Ri NRWD SE19 208 D2
Roman Rd BETH E2 130 B2
CHSWK W4 143 E4
EHAM E6 133 G3
IL IG1 114 B4
MUSWH N10 66 D3
Roman Sq THMD SE28 155 G1
Roman Wy CROY/NA CR0 228 B6
EN EN1 39 F6
HOLWY N7 107 H4
Romany Gdns CHEAM SM3 225 E4
Romany Ri STMC/STPC BR5 234 C5
Roma Rd WALTH E17 70 C6
Romberg Rd TOOT SW17 186 C5
Romborough Gdns LEW SE13 171 G6
Romborough Wy LEW SE13 171 G6
Romeland BORE WD6 45 F1
Romero Sq ELTH/MOT SE9 173 E5
Romeyn Rd STRHM/NOR SW16 187 H5
Romford Rd MNPK E12 114 A1
SRTFD E15 112 A5
Romford St WCHPL E1 17 F2
Romilly Dr OXHEY WD19 42 C6
Romilly Rd FSBYPK N4 88 B6
Romilly St SOHO/SHAV W1D 12 D5
Rommany Rd WNWD SE27 188 D6
Romney Cl CHSGTN KT9 239 G2
GLDGN NW11 85 F5
RYLN/HDSTN HA2 79 E4
TOTM N17 69 H4
Romney Dr BMLY BR1 213 F3
RYLN/HDSTN HA2 79 E4
Romney Gdns BXLYHN DA7 176 D2
Romney Rd GNWCH SE10 151 G6
NWMAL KT3 222 D3
WOOL/PLUM SE18 154 B3
Romney Rw CRICK * NW2 84 B6
Romola Rd BRXS/STRHM SW2 188 B3
Romsey Cl ORP BR6 252 C2
Romsey Rd DAGW RM9 116 B6
WEA * W13 120 C6
Ronald Av SRTFD E15 132 A2
Ronald Cl BECK BR3 230 D2
Ronalds Rd BMLY BR1 212 C4
HBRY N5 108 A3
Ronaldstone Rd BFN/LL DA15 195 E1
Ronald St WCHPL E1 130 A5
Rona Rd HAMP NW3 106 C2
Ronart St KTN/HRWW/W HA3 60 B6
Rona Wk IS N1 108 D4
Rondu Rd CRICK NW2 104 C3
Ronelean Rd SURB KT6 221 H6
Ronfearn Av STMC/STPC BR5 236 B2
Ron Green Ct ERITH DA8 157 H5
Ron Leighton Wy EHAM E6 113 G6
Ronver Rd LEE/GVPK SE12 192 C3
Rood La FENCHST EC3M 16 A5
Rookby Ct WCHMH N21 52 B4
Rook Cl WBLY HA9 102 B1
Rookery Dr CHST BR7 214 A4
Rookery Gdns STMC/STPC BR5 236 A2
Rookery La HAYES BR2 233 F3
Rookery Rd CLAP SW4 167 E5
The Rookery
STRHM/NOR * SW16 207 H2
Rookery Wy CDALE/KGS NW9 83 F2
Rookesley Rd STMC/STPC BR5 236 B4
Rookfield Av MUSWH N10 87 E1
Rookfield Cl MUSWH N10 87 E1
Rookstone Rd TOOT SW17 206 B1
Rookwood Av NWMAL KT3 223 G1
WLGTN SM6 245 F2
Rookwood Gdns CHING * E4 56 B4
Rookwood Rd STNW/STAM N16 89 F3
Roosevelt Wy DAGE RM10 117 H4
Rootes Dr NKENS W10 124 B3
Ropemaker Rd
BERM/RHTH SE16 150 C2
Ropemaker's Flds
POP/IOD * E14 130 D6
Ropemaker St BARB EC2Y 15 G1
Roper La STHWK SE1 24 B4
Ropers Av CHING E4 71 G1
Roper St ELTH/MOT SE9 173 H6
Roper Wy MTCM CR4 206 C5
Ropery St BOW E3 130 D3
Rope St BERM/RHTH SE16 150 C3
Ropewalk Gdns WCHPL * E1 17 F3
Ropewalk Ms HACK * E8 109 F5
Rope Yard Rails
WOOL/PLUM SE18 154 B3
Ropley St BETH E2 9 E2
Rosa Alba Ms HBRY N5 108 C2
Rosaline Rd FUL/PGN SW6 164 C1
Rosaline Ter FUL/PGN * SW6 164 C1
Rosamond St SYD SE26 189 H5
Rosamond Vls
MORT/ESHN * SW14 162 D5
Rosamund Cl SAND/SEL CR2 246 D2
Rosary Cl HSLW TW3 158 C3
Rosary Gdns BUSH WD23 44 A2
SKENS SW7 145 G4
Rosaville Rd FUL/PGN SW6 164 D1
Roscoe St STLK EC1Y 7 F6
Roscoff Cl EDGW HA8 62 B4
Roseacre Cl WEA W13 120 D4
Roseacre Rd WELL DA16 175 H4
Rose Aly STHWK SE1 23 F1
Rose Av MRDN SM4 225 G2
MTCM CR4 206 B4
SWFD E18 72 D5
Rosebank PGE/AN SE20 209 H3
Rosebank Av ALP/SUD HA0 100 B2
Rose Bank Cl NFNCH/WDSP N12 66 A1
Rosebank Cl TEDD TW11 200 C2
Rosebank Est BOW E3 130 D1
Rosebank Gdns ACT * W3 122 D5
BOW * E3 130 C1
Rosebank Gv WALTH E17 70 D6
Rosebank Rd HNWL W7 140 A2
LEY E10 91 E3
Rosebank Wk CAMTN * NW1 107 F5
Rosebank Wy ACT W3 122 D5
Rose Bates Dr CDALE/KGS NW9 82 A1
Roseberry Gdns FSBYPK N4 88 B3
ORP BR6 253 E1
Roseberry Pl HACK E8 109 F4
Roseberry St BERM/RHTH SE16 33 G2
Rosebery Av BFN/LL DA15 195 E2
CLKNW EC1R 6 A5
MNPK E12 113 G4
NWMAL KT3 203 F5
RYLN/HDSTN HA2 98 C2
THHTH CR7 208 C5
TOTM N17 69 G5
Rosebery Cl MRDN SM4 224 B3
Rosebery Ct CLKNW EC1R 6 A5
Rosebery Gdns
CEND/HSY/T * N8 87 G2
SUT SM1 243 F2
WEA W13 120 C5
Rosebery Ms MUSWH N10 67 E5
Rosebery Pde EW * KT17 241 F5

Rosebery Rd BUSH WD23 ...43 F3
CLAP SW4 ...187 G1
ED N9 ...53 C5
ISLW TW7 ...159 G6
KUT KT1 ...202 B5
MUSWH N10 ...47 H3
SUT SM1 ...242 D4
Rosebine Av MRDN TW2 ...179 H2
Rosebury Rd FUL/PGN SW6 ...165 F3
Rosebury Sq WFD IG8 ...74 A3
Rose Ct WCHPL E1 ...16 C2
Rosecourt Rd CROY/NA CRO ...227 H5
Rosecroft Av HAMP NW3 ...105 E1
Rosecroft Ct STMC/STPC BR5 ...236 A3
Rose Croft Gdns CRICK NW2 ...103 G1
Rosecroft Gdns WHTN TW2 ...155 H3
Rosecroft Rd STHL UB1 ...119 E3
Rosecroft Wk ALP/SUD HA0 ...101 F3
PIN HA5 ...78 B2
Rose & Crown Yd STJS * SW1Y ...20 B2
Rose Dl ORP BR6 ...216 D4
Rosedale Cl ABYW SE2 ...155 H5
HNWL W7 ...140 B2
STAN HA7 ...60 D2
Rosedale Gdns DAGW RM9 ...115 H5
Rosedale Rd CRW RM5 ...77 G6
DAGW RM9 ...115 H5
EW KT17 ...241 G5
FSTGT E7 ...113 E3
RCH/KEW TW9 ...161 G5
Rosedene Av CROY/NA CRO ...227 G4
GFD/PVL UB6 ...119 E2
MRDN SM4 ...225 F2
STRHM/NOR SW16 ...187 H5
Rosedene Gdns GNTH/NBYPK IG2 ...94 A1
Rosedene Ter LEY E10 ...91 F6
Rosedew Rd HMSMTH W6 ...144 B6
Rose End WPK KT4 ...224 D5
Rosefield POP/IOD E14 ...131 E6
Rosefield Cl CAR SM5 ...244 D2
Rosefield Gdns POP/IOD E14 ...131 E6
Rose Garden Cl EDGW HA8 ...61 G2
Rose Gdns EA W5 ...141 F3
STHL UB1 ...99 F6
Rose Gln CDALE/KGS NW9 ...82 D1
Rosehart Ms NTGHL W11 ...125 E5
Rosehatch Av CHDH RM6 ...76 B6
Roseheath Rd HSLWW TW4 ...158 D6
Rosehill ESH/CLAY KT10 ...238 C4
HPTN TW12 ...199 E4
Rose Hl SUT SM1 ...225 F6
Rosehill Av SUT SM1 ...225 G5
Rosehill Court Pde
MRDN * SM4 ...225 G4
Rosehill Gdns GFD/PVL UB6 ...100 B3
SUT SM1 ...225 F6
Rosehill Rd WAND/EARL SW18 ...185 U1
Roseland Cl TOTM N17 ...68 D3
Rose La CHDH RM6 ...96 C1
Rose Lawn BUSH WD23 ...43 G3
Roseleigh Av HBRY N5 ...108 B2
Roseleigh Cl TWK TW1 ...181 F1
Rosemary Av E/WMO/HCT KT8 ...199 E6
ED N9 ...65 H1
EFNCH N2 ...55 D2
FNCH N3 ...65 G5
HSLWW TW4 ...155 E6
Rosemary Cl CROY/NA CRO ...227 G4
Rosemary Dr POP/IOD E14 ...131 H5
REDBR IG4 ...93 F2
Rosemary Gdns BCTR RM8 ...96 D5
CHSGTN KT9 ...239 G2
Rosemary La
MORT/ESHN SW14 ...162 C4
Rosemary Rd PECK SE15 ...169 F1
TOOT SW17 ...185 F5
WELL DA16 ...173 F5
Rosemary St IS N1 ...108 D6
Rosemead CDALE/KGS NW9 ...83 F4
Rosemead Av MTCM CR4 ...207 E6
WBLY HA9 ...101 G3
Rosemont Av
NFNCH/WDSP N12 ...65 G1
Rosemont Rd ACT W3 ...122 B6
ALP/SUD HA0 ...100 A6
HAMP NW3 ...105 G4
NWMAL KT3 ...202 C6
RCHPK/HAM TW10 ...181 E1
Rosemoor St CHEL SW3 ...26 C2
Rosemount Cl WFD IG8 ...73 H2
Rosemount Dr BMLY BR1 ...233 H1
Rosemount Rd WEA W13 ...120 C5
Rosenau Crs BTSEA SW11 ...166 B2
Rosenau Rd BTSEA SW11 ...166 B2
Rosendale Rd DUL SE21 ...188 C4
HNHL SE24 ...188 C2
Roseneath Av WCHMN N21 ...52 B3
Roseneath Rd BTSEA SW11 ...186 C1
Roseneath Wk EN EN1 ...38 C1
Rosenheath Cl ORP BR6 ...253 H5
Rosens Wk EDGW HA8 ...46 D5
Rosenthal Rd CAT SE6 ...191 F1
Rosenthorpe Rd PECK SE15 ...170 B6
Rose Park Cl YEAD UB4 ...118 A3
Roserton St POP/IOD E14 ...151 G2
Rose Ga EBSEA SW11 ...166 D1
The Rosery CROY/NA CRO ...230 B3
Rose Sq CHEL * SW3 ...145 H5
The Roses WFD * IG8 ...72 B3
Rose St COVGDN WC2E ...13 E5
Rosetta Cl VX/NE SW8 ...57 G1
Rosetta Cl IX/NE SW8 ...167 G1
Roseveare Rd LEE/GVPK SE12 ...193 E6
Roseville Av HSLWW TW4 ...159 E3
Roseville Rd HYS/HAR UB3 ...133 H6
Rose Wk BRYLDS KT5 ...204 A4
WWKM BR4 ...222 B2
Roseway DUL SE21 ...188 D1
Rosewell Cl PGE/AN SE20 ...209 H3
Rosewood Av GFD/PVL UB6 ...100 D3
Rosewood Cl SCUP DA14 ...196 D5
Rosewood Ct KUTN/CMB KT2 ...202 A3
Rosewood Gv SUT SM1 ...225 G6
Rosewood Ter PGE/AN * SE20 ...210 A3
Rosher Cl SRTFD E15 ...111 H5
Rosina St HOM E9 ...110 D3
Roskell Rd PUT/ROE SW15 ...164 B4

Roslin Rd ACT W3 ...142 B3
Roslin Wy BMLY BR1 ...212 C1
Roslyn Cl MTCM CR4 ...206 H5
Roslyn Ms SEVS/STOTM * N15 ...89 E2
Roslyn Rd SEVS/STOTM N15 ...88 D2
Rosmead Rd NTGHL W11 ...124 C6
Rosoman Pl CLKNW EC1R ...6
Rosoman St CLKNW EC1R ...6
Rossall Crs WLSDN NW10 ...121 H2
Ross Av BCTR RM8 ...96 C1
MLHL NW7 ...64 C1
Ross Cl KTN/HRWW/W HA3 ...96 G3
Rossdale SUT SM1 ...244 A3
Rossdale Dr CDALE/KGS NW9 ...82 C5
ED N9 ...54 A1
Rossdale Rd PUT/ROE SW15 ...146 A5
Rosse Ms BKHTH/KID SE3 ...172 D2
Rossendale St CLPT E5 ...89 H6
Rossendale Wy CAMTN NW1 ...107 G6
Rossetti Rd BERM/RHTH SE16 ...123 J1
Rossignol Gdns CAR SM5 ...226 C6
Rossindel Rd HSLW TW3 ...159 E6
Rossington Cl EN EN1 ...39 H1
Rossington St CLPT E5 ...89 H6
Rossiter Flds BAR EN5 ...32 C1
Rossiter Rd BAL SW12 ...186 D5
Rossland Cl BXLYHS DA6 ...177 E6
Rosslyn Av BARN SW13 ...163 E4
BCTR RM8 ...78 C6
CHING E4 ...54 B4
EBAR EN4 ...50 A1
Rosslyn Cl WWKM BR4 ...250 B1
Rosslyn Crs HRW HA1 ...60 B1
WBLY HA9 ...80 B1
Rosslyn Hl HAMP NW3 ...105 H3
Rosslyn Park Ms HAMP NW3 ...105 H3
Rosslyn Rd BARK IG11 ...114 D1
TWK TW1 ...181 E1
WALTH * E17 ...91 C1
Rossmore Cl CAMTN * NW1 ...2
Rossmore Rd CAMTN NW1 ...2
Ross Pde WLGTN SM6 ...244 B4
Ross Rd SNWD SE25 ...209 E6
WHTN TW2 ...179 G3
WLGTN SM6 ...245 E4
Ross Wy ELTH/MOT SE9 ...175 F3
Rosswood Gdns WLGTN SM6 ...244 D4
Rostella Rd TOOT SW17 ...185 H6
Rostrevor Av SEVS/STOTM N15 ...89 F3
Rostrevor Gdns NWDGN UB2 ...135 E4
Rostrevor Rd FUL/PGN SW6 ...164 D2
WIM/MER SW19 ...205 J5
Rotary St STHWK SE1 ...22 C5
Rothbury Gdns ISLW TW7 ...160 C1
Rothbury Rd HOM E9 ...110 D5
Rotherfield Rd CAR SM5 ...244 C2
Rotherfield St IS N1 ...108 C5
Rotherham Wk STHWK * SE1 ...22 D2
Rotherhill Av
STRHM/NOR SW16 ...207 F2
Rotherhithe New Rd
BERM/RHTH SE16 ...53 G4
Rotherhithe Old Rd
BERM/RHTH SE16 ...150 B4
Rotherhithe St
BERM/RHTH * SE16 ...25 H4
Rotherhithe Tnl
BERM/RHTH SE16 ...150 A2
Rothermere Rd CROY/NA CRO ...245 H5
Rotherwick Hl EA W5 ...121 H5
Rotherwick Rd GLDGN NW11 ...85 E4
Rotherwood Cl RYNPK SW20 ...204 C4
Rotherwood Rd
PUT/ROE SW15 ...164 B4
Rothery St IS N1 ...108 B6
Rothesay Av BRXN/ST * SW9 ...168 B1
RCHPK/HAM TW10 ...162 B5
RYNPK SW20 ...204 C5
Rothesay Rd SNWD SE25 ...228 D1
Rothsay Rd FSTGT E7 ...113 G5
Rothsay St STHWK SE1 ...24 A5
Rothschild Rd CHSWK W4 ...142 C4
Rothschild St WNWD SE27 ...188 B6
Rothwell Gdns DAGW RM9 ...116 A5
Rothwell Rd DAGW RM9 ...116 A6
Rothwell St CAMTN NW1 ...106 B1
Rotterdam Dr POP/IOD E14 ...151 G3
Rouel Rd BERM/RHTH SE16 ...53 J1
Rougemont Av MRDN SM4 ...225 E3
Roundaway Rd CLAY IG5 ...75 H5
Roundel Cl BROCKY SE4 ...190 C1
Round Gv CROY/NA CRO ...230 B4
Roundhay Cl FSTH SE23 ...190 B4
Roundhedge Wy ENC/FH EN2 ...37 H1
Roundhill Dr ENC/FH EN2 ...37 H1
Roundlyn Gdns
STMC/STPC BR5 ...235 H1
Roundtable Rd BMLY BR1 ...192 B5
Roundtree Rd ALP/SUD HA0 ...100 C3
The Roundway ESH/CLAY KT10 ...238 C4
TOTM N17 ...68 C4
Roundwood CHST BR7 ...214 B5
Roundwood Pk
WLSDN * NW10 ...103 G6
Roundwood Rd WLSDN NW10 ...103 H4
Rounton Rd BOW E3 ...130 A4
Roupell Rd BRXS/STRHM SW2 ...187 H3
Roupell St STHWK SE1 ...22 B2
Rousden St CAMTN * NW1 ...107 E5
Rouse Gdns DUL SE21 ...189 E6
Rous Rd BKHH IG9 ...57 C3
Routemaster Cl PLSTW E13 ...132 D2
Routh Rd WAND/EARL SW18 ...186 A2
Routh St EHAM E6 ...133 H4
Rover Av BARK/HLT IG6 ...77 E1
Rowallan Rd FUL/PGN SW6 ...164 C1
Rowan Av CHING E4 ...70 D2
Rowan Cl ALP/SUD HA0 ...100 C1
EA W5 ...141 H2
IL IG1 ...114 D3
KTN/HRWW/W HA3 ...60 C2
NWMAL KT3 ...204 B5
STRHM/NOR SW16 ...207 H6
Rowan Dr CDALE/KGS NW9 ...63 G6
Rowan Gdns CROY/NA CRO ...247 F1
Rowan Rd BTFD TW8 ...160 D1
BXLYHN DA7 ...176 D4
HMSMTH W6 ...144 B4

STRHM/NOR SW16 ...207 E5
SWLY BR8 ...217 H6
The Rowans PLMGR N13 ...52 C5
Rowan Ter PGE/AN * SE20 ...209 G4
WIM/MER * SW19 ...204 C5
Rowantree Cl WCHMN N21 ...52 D5
Rowantree Rd ENC/FH EN2 ...38 B5
WCHMN N21 ...52 D5
Rowan Wk EFNCH N2 ...85 G1
HAYES BR2 ...251 H1
NKENS * W10 ...108 B3
Rowan Wy CHDH RM6 ...96 A6
Rowanwood Av BFN/LL DA15 ...195 G3
Rowben Cl TRDG/WHET N20 ...49 F3
Rowberry Cl FUL/PGN SW6 ...164 B1
Rowcross St STHWK SE1 ...32 B2
Rowdell Rd NTHLT UB5 ...99 E6
Rowden Pde CHING * E4 ...71 E2
Rowden Rd BECK BR3 ...210 C4
CHING E4 ...71 F2
HOR/WEW KT19 ...240 C2
Rowditch La BTSEA SW11 ...166 D2
Rowdon Av WLSDN NW10 ...103 H5
Rowdown Crs CROY/NA CRO ...249 H6
Rowdowns Rd DAGW RM9 ...116 D6
Rowe Gdns BARK IG11 ...135 F1
Rowe La HOM E9 ...110 A3
Rowena Crs BTSEA SW11 ...166 A3
Rowe Wk RYLN/HDSTN HA2 ...99 E1
Rowfant Rd TOOT SW17 ...186 B4
Rowhill Rd CLPT E5 ...109 H2
Rowington Cl BAY/PAD W2 ...125 F4
Rowland Av KTN/HRWW/W HA3 ...61 H6
Rowland Gv SYD SE26 ...189 H5
Rowland Hill Av TOTM N17 ...67 H4
Rowland Hill St HAMP NW3 ...106 A3
Rowlands Av PIN HA5 ...59 E2
Rowlands Cl HGT * N6 ...66 B5
MLHL NW7 ...63 G3
Rowlands Rd BCTR RM8 ...96 B6
Rowland Wy WIM/MER SW19 ...205 F4
Rowley Av BFN/LL DA15 ...195 H2
Rowley Cl ALP/SUD HA0 ...101 H2
OXHEY WD19 ...42 C1
Rowley Cottages
WKENS * W14 ...144 A6
Rowley Gdns FSBYPK N4 ...88 C3
Rowley Rd SEVS/STOTM N15 ...88 C2
Rowley Wy STJWD NW8 ...105 G6
Rowlls Rd KUT/HW KT1 ...201 H6
Rowney Gdns DAGW RM9 ...115 H4
Rowney Rd DAGW RM9 ...115 H4
Rowntree Cl
KIL/WHAMP * NW6 ...105 E4
PLSTW E13 ...132 D3
Rowntree Rd WHTN TW2 ...180 A3
Rowse Cl SRTFD E15 ...111 C6
Rowsley Av HDN NW4 ...64 A6
Rowstock Gdns HOLWY N7 ...107 K3
Rowton Rd WOOL/PLUM SE18 ...174 C1
Roxborough Av HRW HA1 ...80 A4
ISLW TW7 ...160 B1
Roxborough Pk HRW HA1 ...80 B4
Roxborough Rd HRW HA1 ...80 B3
Roxbourne Cl NTHLT UB5 ...98 A4
Roxburgh Rd WNWD SE27 ...208 B1
Roxby Pl FUL/PGN SW6 ...145 K6
Roxeth Green Av
RYLN/HDSTN HA2 ...99 F1
Roxeth Gv RYLN/HDSTN HA2 ...99 F2
Roxeth Hl RYLN/HDSTN HA2 ...79 H6
Roxley Rd LEW SE13 ...191 F1
Roxton Gdns CROY/NA CRO ...248 C3
Roxwell Rd BARK IG11 ...135 C1
SHB W12 ...143 G2
Roxwell Wy WFD IG8 ...73 E3
Roxy Av CHDH RM6 ...95 H1
Royal Albert Rdbt EHAM E6 ...134 A6
Royal Albert Wy CAN/RD E16 ...133 F6
Royal Ar CONDST * W1S ...12 A6
Royal Arsenal West
WOOL/PLUM * SE18 ...154 A5
Royal Av CHEL SW3 ...26 C2
WPK KT4 ...225 E6
Royal Cir WNWD SE27 ...188 G5
CDMY/SEVK IG3 ...89 C5
STNW/STAM * N16 ...89 E5
WPK KT4 ...223 B6
Royal College St CAMTN NW1 ...107 E5
Royal Ct BANK EC3V ...15 H6
ELTH/MOT * SE9 ...195 H5
EN * EN1 ...42 A1
Royal Crs NTGHL W11 ...144 B2
RSLP HA4 ...79 J3
Royal Crescent Ms NTGHL W11 ...144 B2
Royal Docks Rd EHAM E6 ...134 B4
Royal Herbert Pavilions
WOOL/PLUM * SE18 ...173 H2
Royal Ms BGVA * SW1W ...16 C5
Royal Hospital Rd CHEL SW3 ...26 D5
Royal Ms BAL SW12 ...186 D2
The Royal Ms WHALL SW1A ...9 H6
Royal Mint St WCHPL E1 ...16 C5
Royal Mint St TWRH EC3N ...16 D5
Royal Naval Pl NWCR SE14 ...170 D1
Royal Oak Pl EDUL SE22 ...189 H1
Royal Oak Rd BXLYHS DA6 ...176 D6
HACK E8 ...109 H4
Royal Opera Ar STJS * SW1Y ...20 C1
Royal Orchard Cl
WAND/EARL SW18 ...184 C2
Royal Oak Yd STHWK SE1 ...19 H2
Royal Pde BKHTH/KID SE3 ...172 B3
CHST BR7 ...214 D1
FUL/PGN * SW6 ...164 C1
Royal Pl GNWCH SE10 ...171 G1
Royal Rd CAN/RD E16 ...133 E5
SCUP DA14 ...196 D1
TEDD TW11 ...179 K1
WALW SE17 ...30 C5
Royal Route WBLY HA9 ...101 H1
Royal St STHWK SE1 ...21 H1
Royal Victor Pl BOW E3 ...129 G2
Roycraft Av BARK IG11 ...115 E1
Roycroft Cl
BRXS/STRHM * SW2 ...188 A3
SWFD E18 ...73 F1
Roydene Rd WOOL/PLUM SE18 ...155 E6
Roydon Cl LOU IG10 ...57 C2
Roy Gdns GNTH/NBYPK IG2 ...95 E1
Roy Gv HPTN TW12 ...199 F2

Royle Crs WEA W13 ...120 D3
Royston Av CHING E4 ...71 E1
SUT SM1 ...243 H1
WLGTN SM6 ...245 F2
Royston Gdns IL IG1 ...93 F3
Royston Gv PIN HA5 ...58 D2
Royston Park Rd PIN HA5 ...58 D2
Royston Rd PGE/AN SE20 ...210 A4
RCHPK/HAM TW10 ...161 G6
The Roystons BRYLDS KT5 ...222 B3
Royston St BETH E2 ...130 A1
Rozel Rd CLAP SW4 ...167 E3
Rubastic Rd NWDGN UB2 ...138 A3
Rubens St NTHLT UB5 ...118 A1
Rubens St CAT SE6 ...190 D4
Ruby Ms WALTH * E17 ...71 H6
Ruby Rd WALTH E17 ...71 E6
Ruby St PECK SE15 ...33 G5
Ruby Triangle PECK SE15 ...33 G5
Ruckholt Cl LEY E10 ...111 G1
Ruckholt Rd LEY E10 ...111 G1
Rucklidge Av WLSDN NW10 ...123 F1
Rudall Crs HAMP NW3 ...105 H2
Ruddington Cl CLPT E5 ...110 C2
Ruddock Cl EDGW HA8 ...62 C3
Ruddstreet Cl
WOOL/PLUM SE18 ...154 B4
Rudgwick Ter STJWD * NW8 ...177 H4
Rudland Rd BXLYHN DA7 ...177 G2
Rudloe Rd BAL SW12 ...187 G2
Rudolf Pl VX/NE SW8 ...29 H6
Rudolph Rd BUSH WD23 ...43 E1
KIL/WHAMP NW6 ...125 E1
PLSTW E13 ...132 B1
Rudyard Gv EDGW HA8 ...62 C2
Ruffetts Cl SAND/SEL CR2 ...247 H5
The Ruffetts SAND/SEL CR2 ...247 H5
Rufford Cl HRW HA1 ...80 C5
Rufford St IS N1 ...107 G6
Rufus Cl RSLP HA4 ...98 B1
Rufus St IS N1 ...8 A4
Rugby Av ALP/SUD HA0 ...101 E2
ED N9 ...53 F3
NTHLT UB5 ...99 H4
Rugby Cl HRW HA1 ...80 D3
Rugby Gdns DAGW RM9 ...116 A4
Rugby La BELMT SM2 ...242 B6
Rugby Rd CDALE/KGS NW9 ...82 A1
CHSWK W4 ...143 C2
WHTN TW2 ...180 A1
Rugby St BMSBY WC1N ...5 G6
Rugg St POP/IOD E14 ...131 E6
Ruislip Cl GFD/PVL UB6 ...119 F3
Ruislip Rd NTHLT UB5 ...98 A6
Ruislip Rd East GFD/PVL UB6 ...119 G3
Ruislip St TOOT SW17 ...186 B6
Rumbold Rd FUL/PGN SW6 ...146 A1
Rumsey Cl HPTN TW12 ...179 K2
Rumsey Ms FSBYPK N4 ...107 H2
Rumsey Rd BRXN/ST SW9 ...167 H4
Runbury Cir CDALE/KGS NW9 ...82 D6
Runcorn Cl WALTH E17 ...75 J2
Runcorn Pl NTGHL W11 ...124 C6
Rundell Crs HDN NW4 ...83 H2
Runes Cl MTCM CR4 ...225 H1
Runnelfield HRW HA1 ...100 H4
Runnymede WIM/MER SW19 ...205 H4
Runnymede Crs
STRHM/NOR SW16 ...207 F4
Runnymede Gdns
GFD/PVL UB6 ...119 H4
WHTN TW2 ...179 F1
Runnymede Rd WHTN TW2 ...179 F1
Rupack St BERM/RHTH * SE16 ...150 A2
Rupert Av WBLY HA9 ...101 G3
Rupert Gdns BRXN/ST SW9 ...168 B1
SOHO/SHAV W1D ...12 C5
Rupert Rd ARCH N19 ...107 F1
CHSWK W4 ...143 E3
KIL/WHAMP NW6 ...124 D1
Rupert St SOHO/SHAV W1D ...12 C5
Rural Wy STRHM/NOR SW16 ...206 D3
Rusbridge Cl HACK E8 ...109 G3
Ruscoe Rd CAN/RD E16 ...132 B5
Rusham Rd BAL SW12 ...186 D1
Rushbrook Crs WALTH E17 ...70 D4
Rushbrook Rd ELTH/MOT SE9 ...194 C4
Rushcroft Rd
BRXS/STRHM SW2 ...168 A3
CHING E4 ...71 F3
Rushden Cl NRWD SE19 ...208 D3
Rushdene ABYW SE2 ...156 A3
Rushdene Av EBAR EN4 ...50 A2
Rushdene Cl NTHLT UB5 ...118 A1
Rushdene Rd PIN HA5 ...78 A3
Rushden Gdns CLAY IG5 ...74 A6
MLHL NW7 ...64 A2
Rushet Rd STMC/STPC BR5 ...215 G5
Rushett Cl THDIT KT7 ...220 D5
Rushett Rd THDIT KT7 ...220 D1
Rushey Cl CAT SE6 ...191 E1
Rushey Hl ENC/FH EN2 ...37 H5
Rushey Md BROCKY SE4 ...171 E6
Rushford Rd BROCKY SE4 ...190 D1
Rush Green Gdns
ROMW/RG RM7 ...97 G5
Rush Green Rd ROMW/RG RM7 ...97 G5
Rushgrove Av CDALE/KGS NW9 ...83 F1
Rushgrove Pde
CDALE/KGS NW9 ...83 F2
Rushgrove St
WOOL/PLUM SE18 ...153 H4
Rush Hill Ms BTSEA SW11 ...166 A1
Rush Hill Rd BTSEA SW11 ...166 A1
Rushley Cl HAYES BR2 ...251 F2
Rushmead BETH E2 ...129 G4
RCHPK/HAM TW10 ...180 C5
Rushmead Cl CROY/NA CRO ...247 G2
Rushmere Ct WPK KT4 ...225 G6
Rushmere Pl WIM/MER SW19 ...204 B1
Rushmon Pl CHEAM * SM3 ...242 C4
Rushmon Vis NWMAL * KT3 ...223 H6
Rushmore Cl BMLY BR1 ...213 G6
Rushmore Crs CLPT * E5 ...110 A2
Rushmore Rd CLPT E5 ...110 A2
Rusholme Av DAGE RM10 ...117 C1
Rusholme Gv NRWD SE19 ...209 E1
Rusholme Rd PUT/ROE SW15 ...184 B1
Rushout Av KTN/HRWW/W HA3 ...80 D3

Rushton St *IS* N1 ....7 H1
Rushworth St *STHWK* SE1 ......22 D3
Rushy Meadow La *CAR* SM5 ....226 A6
Ruskin Av *MNPK* E12 ....113 H4
  RCH/KEW TW9 ....162 A1
  WELL DA16 ....175 G4
Ruskin Cl *GLDGN* NW11 ....85 E5
Ruskin Dr *ORP* BR6 ....253 E1
  WELL DA16 ....175 G4
  WPK KT4 ....223 H6
Ruskin Gdns *EA* W5 ....121 F3
  KTN/HRWW/WS HA3 ....81 H2
Ruskin Gv *WELL* DA16 ....175 G3
Ruskin Rd *BELV* DA17 ....157 G4
  CAR SM5 ....244 C3
  CROY/NA CR0 ....244 C1
  ISLW TW7 ....160 B4
  STHL UB1 ....118 C6
  TOTM N17 ....69 F4
Ruskin Wk *ED* N9 ....53 G4
  HAYES BR2 ....233 G5
  HNHL SE24 ....168 C6
Rusland Av *ORP* BR6 ....252 D1
Rusland Park Rd *HRW* HA1 ....61 E3
Rusper Cl *CRICK* NW2 ....104 A1
  STAN HA7 ....45 G6
Rusper Rd *DAGW* RM9 ....116 A4
  WDGN N22 ....68 B2
Russell Cl *BECK* BR3 ....211 F6
Russell Av *WDGN* N22 ....68 B5
Russell Cl *BXLYHN* DA7 ....177 E5
  CHARL SE7 ....173 C1
  RSLP HA4 ....78 A6
  WLSDN NW10 ....102 C5
Russell Ct *BAR* * EN5 ....35 C5
  WHALL SW1A ....
Russell Gdns *GLDGN* NW11 ....84 C3
  RCHPK/HAM TW10 ....181 E4
  TRDG/WHET N20 ....50 A4
  WKENS W14 ....144 C3
Russell Gardens Ms
  WKENS W14 ....144 C2
Russell Gv *BRXN/ST* SW9 ....168 A2
  MLHL NW7 ....63 F1
Russell Kerr Cl *CHSWK* * W4 ....161 C2
Russell La *TRDG/WHET* N20 ......50 B4
Russell Pde *GLDGN* * NW11 ......84 C3
Russell Pl *HAMP* NW3 ....106 A3
Russell Rd *BKHH* IG9 ....57 E3
  CAN/RD E16 ....132 C5
  CDALE/KGS NW9 ....83 F3
  CEND/HSY/T N8 ....87 F3
  CHING E4 ....54 D6
  EN EN1 ....39 F1
  LEY E10 ....91 F3
  MTCM CR4 ....206 A6
  NTHLT UB5 ....84 C2
  SEVS/STOTM N15 ....89 E2
  TRDG/WHET N20 ....50 A4
  WALTH E17 ....70 D6
  WDGN N22 ....67 H2
  WHTN TW2 ....180 B1
  WIM/MER SW19 ....205 E3
  WKENS W14 ....144 C3
Russell Sq *GWRST* WC1E 13 C4
Russell St *HOLALD* WC2B 13 G4
Russell Wy *SUT* SM1 ....243 F3
Russet Crs *HOLWY* * N7 ....107 H3
Russet Dr *CROY/NA* CR0 ....250 C6
Russets Cl *CHING* E4 ....55 H6
Russett Cl *ORP* BR6 ....253 H5
Russett Wy *SWLY* BR8 ....217 H5
Russia Dock Rd
  BERM/RHTH * SE16 ....150 C1
Russia La *BETH* E2 ....130 A1
Russia Rw *CITYW* EC2V 15 F4
Rusthall Av *CHSWK* W4 ....142 D3
Rusthall Cl *CROY/NA* CR0 ....230 D3
Rustic Av *STRHM/NOR* SW16 ....206 D2
Rustic Pl *ALP/SUD* HA0 ....101 F2
Rustington Wk *MRDN* SM4 ....224 D4
Ruston Av *BRYLDS* KT5 ....222 B4
Ruston Ms *NTGHL* * W11 ....124 C5
Ruston Rd *WOOL/PLUM* SE18 ....153 G3
Ruston St *BOW* E3 ....110 D6
Rust Sq *CMBW* SE5 ....168 ..
Rutford Rd *STRHM/NOR* SW16 ...207 E1
Ruth Cl *KTN/HRWW/WS* HA3 ......81 H1
Rutherford Cl *BELMT* SM2 ....243 H4
Rutherford St *WEST* SW1P 28 C1
Rutherford Wy *BUSH* WD23 ....43 H3
  WBLY HA9 ....102 A1
Ruthergien Rd *ABYW* SE2 ....155 C6
Rutherwyke Cl *EW* KT17 ....241 G4
Ruthin Cl *CDALE/KGS* NW9 ....83 C3
Ruthin Rd *BKHTH/KID* SE3 ....152 C6
Ruthven St *HOM* E9 ....110 B6
Rutland Av *BFN/LL* DA15 ....195 G2
Rutland Cl *BXLY* DA5 ....196 B3
  MORT/ESHN SW14 ....162 B4
Rutland Dr *CHST* BR7 ....214 A4
  SKENS * 18 B4
Rutland Dr *MRDN* SM4 ....225 G4
  RCHPK/HAM TW10 ....181 F3
Rutland Gdns *BCTR* RM8 ....116 A3
  CROY/NA CR0 ....247 G2
  FSBYPK N4 ....88 B3
  SKENS SW7 ....18 B4
  WEA * W13 ....120 C4
Rutland Ga *BELV* DA17 ....157 F5
  HAYES BR2 ....232 ..
  SKENS SW7 ....18 A4
Rutland Gate Ms *SKENS* * SW7 ...18 A4
Rutland Gv *HMSMTH* W6 ....143 H5
Rutland Ms *ST/WD* * NW8 ....105 E5
Rutland Ms South *SKENS* * SW7 .18 A5
Rutland Pk *CAT* SE6 ....190 D4
  CRICK NW2 ....104 A4
Rutland Pl *BUSH* * WD23 ....43 H1
  FARR * EC1M 14 D1
Rutland Rd *FSTGT* E7 ....115 F5
  HOM E9 ....110 B6
  HRW HA1 ....79 G3
  STHL UB1 ....119 E3
  WALTH E17 ....91 E3
  WAN E11 ....92 D2
  WHTN TW2 ....179 H4
  WIM/MER SW19 ....206 A3
Rutland St *SKENS* SW7 ....18 B5

Rutland Wk *CAT* SE6 ....190 D4
Rutland Wy *STMC/STPC* BR5 .....236 A3
Rutley Cl *WALW* SE17 ....30 C5
Rutlish Rd *WIM/MER* SW19 ....205 E4
Rutter Gdns *MTCM* CR4 ....225 H1
Rutt's Ter *NWCR* SE14 ....170 B2
The Rutts *BUSH* WD23 ....43 H3
Ruvigny Gdns *PUT/ROE* SW15 ...166 B4
Ruxley Cl *HOR/WEW* KT19 ....240 B5
  SCUP DA14 ....216 B2
Ruxley Crs *ESH/CLAY* KT10 ....238 D5
Ruxley La *HOR/WEW* KT19 ....240 B4
Ruxley Ms *HOR/WEW* KT19 ....240 B5
Ruxley Rdg *ESH/CLAY* KT10 ....238 C5
Ruxley Towers
  ESH/CLAY * KT10 ....238 C5
Ryan Cl *ELTH/MOT* SE9 ....172 D5
Ryan Ct *OXHEY* * WD19 ....42 C2
Ryan Dr *BTFD* TW8 ....140 C6
Ryarsh Crs *ORP* BR6 ....253 E2
Rycroft Wy *TOTM* * N17 ....69 F6
Rycuff Sq *BKHTH/KID* SE3 ....172 B3
Rydal Cl *HDN* NW4 ....64 C4
Rydal Crs *GFD/PVL* UB6 ....100 D2
Rydal Dr *BXLYHN* DA7 ....177 E2
  WWKM BR4 ....236 A6
Rydal Gdns *CDALE/KGS* NW9 ......83 E3
  HSLW TW3 ....179 F1
  PUT/ROE SW15 ....203 E1
  WBLY HA9 ....81 E5
Rydal Mt *HAYES* * BR2 ....232 B1
Rydal Rd *STRHM/NOR* SW16 ......207 F1
Rydal Wy *PEND* EN3 ....54 A1
  RSLP HA4 ....98 A2
Rydens Av *WOT/HER* KT12 ....218 A6
Rydens Cl *WOT/HER* KT12 ....218 A6
Rydens Pk *WOT/HER* KT12 ....218 B6
Ryde Pl *TWK* TW1 ....181 E1
Ryder Cl *BUSH* WD23 ....43 F1
Ryder Dr *BERM/RHTH* SE16 ....33 G4
Ryder's Ter *ST/WD* NW8 ....125 E1
Ryder St *STJS* SW1Y 20 A1
Ryde Vale Rd *BAL* SW12 ....186 C4
Rydon St *IS* N1 ....108 C6
Rydston Cl *HOLWY* N7 ....107 H5
Rye Cl *BXLY* DA5 ....197 F1
Ryecotes Md *DUL* SE21 ....189 E3
Rye Crs *STMC/STPC* BR5 ....236 A5
Ryecroft Av *CLAY* IG5 ....74 B5
  WHTN TW2 ....179 F3
Ryecroft Rd *LEW* SE13 ....171 F3
  STMC/STPC BR5 ....235 D3
  STRHM/NOR SW16 ....208 A2
Ryecroft St *FUL/PGN* SW6 ....168 A4
Ryedale *EDUL* SE22 ....189 H1
Ryefield Rd *NRWD* SE19 ....208 C2
Rye Hill Pk *PECK* SE15 ....170 A5
Ryelands Crs *LEE/GVPK* SE12 ....193 E1
Rye La *PECK* SE15 ....169 G2
Rye Rd *PECK* SE15 ....170 B5
The Rye *STHGT/OAK* N14 ....51 E2
Rye Wk *PUT/ROE* SW15 ....61 H2
Rye Wy *EDGW* HA8 ....61 H2
Ryfold Rd *WIM/MER* SW19 ....185 G3
Rylandes Rd *CRICK* NW2 ....103 G1
  SAND/SEL CR2 ....265 C6
Ryland Rd *KTTN* * NW5 ....106 D4
Rylett Crs *SHB* W12 ....143 F5
Rylett Rd *SHB* W12 ....143 F5
Rylston Rd *PLMGR* N13 ....52 D5
  FUL/PGN SW6 ....147 H2
Rymer Rd *CROY/NA* CR0 ....229 E4
Rymer St *HNHL* SE24 ....188 B1
Rymill St *CAN/RD* E16 ....154 A1
Rysbrack St *CHEL* SW3 ....16 F5
Rythe Ct *THDIT* KT7 ....220 C4
Ryves Cottages *MTCM* * CR4 .....206 C5

S

Sabbarton St *CAN/RD* E16 ....132 B5
Sabine Rd *BTSEA* SW11 ....166 B2
Sable Cl *HSLWW* TW4 ....158 A4
Sable St *IS* N1 ....6 A1
Sach Rd *CLPT* E5 ....89 H6
Sackville Av *HAYES* BR2 ....232 C5
Sackville Cl *HRW* HA1 ....99 H1
Sackville Est
  STRHM/NOR SW16 ....187 G5
Sackville Gdns *IL* IG1 ....89 H5
Sackville Rd *BELMT* SM2 ....243 E5
Sackville St *MYFR/PICC* W1J 32 B1
Saddlers Cl *PIN* HA5 ....59 E1
Saddlers Ms *KUT* * KT1 ....200 E1
Saddlescombe Wy
  NFNCH/WDSP N12 ....65 E1
Sadler Cl *MTCM* CR4 ....206 D1
Saffron Av *POP/IOD* E14 ....114 D6
Saffron Cl *CROY/NA* CR0 ....227 G3
Saffron Hl *HCIRC* EC1N 14 B1
Saffron Rd *CRW* RM5 ....74 H5
Saffron St *FARR* EC1M 14 B1
Saffron Wy *SURB* KT6 ....221 F5
Sage Cl *EHAM* E6 ....133 H4
Sage St *WCHPL* E1 ....13 G4
Sage Wy *FSBYW* WC1X 5 G4
Sage Yd *SURB* * KT6 ....221 F5
Saigasso Cl *CAN/RD* E16 ....133 F5
Sail St *LBTH* SE11 ....29 H1
Sainfoin Rd *TOOT* SW17 ....186 A6
Sainsbury Rd *NRWD* SE19 ....209 E1
St Agatha's Dr *KUTN/CMB* KT2 ...201 H2
St Agatha's Gv *CAR* SM5 ....226 B5
St Agnes Cl *HOM* * E9 ....110 A6
St Agnes Pl *CMBW* SE5 ....30 B6
St Agnes Well *ELT* EC1V 7 H5
St Aidan's Rd *EDUL* SE22 ....189 H1
  WEA W13 ....136 C1
St Albans Av *CHSWK* W4 ....142 D3
  EHAM E6 ....133 H2
  FELT TW13 ....198 B3

St Albans La *GLDGN* NW11 ....85 E5
St Alban's Pl *IS* N1 ....108 B6
St Albans Rd *BAR* EN5 ....35 C1
  GDNY/SEVK IG3 ....95 F5
  KTTN NW5 ....106 C1
  KUTN/CMB KT2 ....201 G2
  SUT SM1 ....242 D2
  WFD IG8 ....72 C3
  WLSDN NW10 ....103 E6
St Alban's St *STJS* SW1Y 12 C1
St Albans Ter *HMSMTH* * W6 .....144 C6
St Alban's Ms *BAY/PAD* * W2 ....125 H4
St Alfege Rd *CHARL* SE7 ....153 F6
St Alphage Gdn *BARB* EC2Y 15 F2
St Alphage Gdns *BARB* * EC2Y ...15 F2
St Alphage Highwalk
  BARB EC2Y 15 F2
St Alphage Wk *EDGW* * HA8 ....62 C5
St Alphege Rd *ED* N9 ....54 A2
St Alphonsus Rd *CLAP* SW4 ......167 E5
St Amunds Cl *CAT* SE6 ....191 E6
St Andrews Av *ALP/SUD* HA0 ....100 C3
St Andrews Cl
  BERM/RHTH SE16 ....33 H4
  CRICK * NW2 ....103 H1
  NFNCH/WDSP * N12 ....49 G6
  RSLP HA4 ....78 B6
  STAN * HA7 ....61 G5
  THDIT KT7 ....220 D5
St Andrew's Ct
  WAND/EARL SW18 ....185 G4
St Andrews Dr *ORP* BR6 ....235 H3
  STAN HA7 ....61 G4
St Andrew's Gv
  STNW/STAM N16 ....88 D5
St Andrew's HI *BLKFR* EC4V 14 D5
St Andrew's Ms
  STNW/STAM * N16 ....89 E4
St Andrew's Pl *CAMTN* NW1 ....3 G5
St Andrews Rd *ACT* W3 ....125 E5
  CAR SM5 ....244 A1
  CDALE/KGS NW9 ....82 D5
  CROY/NA * CR0 ....246 C2
  ED N9 ....54 A2
  EN EN1 ....24 A3
  GLDGN NW11 ....84 D3
  HNWL W7 ....140 A2
  IL IG1 ....93 H4
  PLSTW E13 ....132 D2
  ROMW/RG RM7 ....74 D5
  SCUP DA14 ....196 B5
  SURB KT6 ....221 F3
  WALTH E17 ....70 B5
  WAN E11 ....71 E4
  WKENS W14 ....144 C6
  WLSDN NW10 ....103 H4
St Andrews Sq *NTGHL* * W11 .....124 C5
  SURB KT6 ....221 F3
St Andrews Ter *OXHEY* WD19 ......58 A1
St Andrew St *HCIRC* EC1N 14 B2
St Andrew's Wy *BOW* E3 ....131 F3
St Anna Rd *BAR* * EN5 ....35 C1
St Anne's Cl *HGT* N6 ....106 C1
  OXHEY WD19 ....42 A1
St Annes Ct *SOHO/CST* W1F 12 C4
St Annes Gdns *WLSDN* NW10 ....121 F1
St Anne's Pas *POP/IOD* * E14 ....130 D5
St Anne's Rd *ALP/SUD* HA0 ....101 F3
  WAN E11 ....91 H6
St Anne's Rw *POP/IOD* E14 ....130 D5
St Anne St *POP/IOD* E14 ....130 D5
St Ann's *BARK* IG11 ....114 A6
St Anns Ct *HDN* * NW4 ....63 H6
St Ann's Crs *WAND/EARL* SW18 .185 F1
St Ann's Gdns *HAMP* NW3 ....106 C1
St Ann's HI *WAND/EARL* SW18 ...165 F6
St Ann's Park Rd
  WAND/EARL SW18 ....185 G1
St Ann's Rd *BARK* IG11 ....114 C6
  BARN * SW13 ....163 E3
  ED N9 ....53 F4
  HRW HA1 ....60 D3
  NTGHL W11 ....124 B6
  SEVS/STOTM N15 ....88 D2
St Ann's St *WEST* SW1P 20 D6
St Ann's Ter *ST/WD* NW8 ....2 B1
St Ann's Vis *WAND/EARL* SW18 .185 F1
St Anns Wy *CROY/NA* CR0 ....246 B5
St Anselm's Pl *MYFR/PKLN* W1K ...11 G5
St Anthony's Av *WFD* IG8 ....73 E2
St Anthony's Cl *TOOT* SW17 ....186 A4
  WAP E1W 91 F2
St Anthony's Ct *HAYES* * BR2 ....234 B5
St Antony's Rd *FSTGT* E7 ....112 D5
St Arvans Cl *CROY/NA* CR0 ....247 E1
St Asaph Rd *PECK* SE15 ....170 B4
St Aubins Av *HSLWW* TW4 ....159 E6
  WIM/MER SW19 ....204 D1
St Aubyns Cl *ORP* BR6 ....235 F6
St Aubyns Gdns *ORP* BR6 ....235 F6
St Aubyn's Rd *NRWD* SE19 ....209 F2
St Audrey Av *BXLYHN* DA7 ....177 E3
St Augustine's Av *BMLY* BR1 .....233 G2
  EA W5 ....117 H1
  SAND/SEL CR2 ....246 C5
  WBLY HA9 ....101 G1
St Augustine's Rd *BELV* DA17 ....156 D4
  CAMTN NW1 ....108 D1
St Austell Cl *EDGW* HA8 ....61 H5
St Austell Rd *LEW* SE13 ....171 G3
St Awdry's Rd *BARK* IG11 ....114 D5
St Barnabas Cl *BECK* BR3 ....211 G5
St Barnabas Gdns
  E/WMO/HCT* KT8 ....219 G2
St Barnabas Rd *MTCM* CR4 ....206 C3
  SUT SM1 ....243 H4
  SWFD E18 ....72 D4
Saint Barnabas Rd *WALTH* E17 ....91 E3
St Barnabas St *BGVA* * SW1W 27 E3
St Barnabas Ter *HOM* E9 ....91 F6
St Barnabas Vis *SN/WD* SE25 ....197 G2
St Barnabus St *BGVA* SW1W 27 F3
St Bartholomew's Cl *SYD* SE26 ..190 A4
St Bartholomew's Rd
  EHAM E6 ....113 G6
St Benets Cl *TOOT* * SW17 ....186 A4
St Benet's Gv *MRDN* SM4 ....225 E4
St Bernards *CROY/NA* CR0 ....247 F1
St Bernard's Cl *WNWD* SE27 .....188 D6
St Bernard's Rd *EHAM* E6 ....113 F6

St Blaise Av *BMLY* BR1 ....212 D5
St Botolph St *HDTCH* EC3A 16 C3
St Bride's Av *EDGW* HA8 ....61 H4
St Brides Cl *ERITHM* DA18 ....156 B2
St Bride St *FLST/FETLN* EC4A 14 C3
St Catherines Cl *CHSGTN* KT9 ...239 F4
  TOOT SW17 ....186 A4
St Catherine's Dr *NWCR* SE14 ...170 B3
St Catherines Rd *CHING* E4 ....55 E4
St Chads Cl *SURB* KT6 ....221 E4
St Chad's Gdns *CHDH* RM6 ....96 C4
St Chad's Pl *FSBYW* WC1X 5 F3
St Chad's Rd *CHDH* RM6 ....96 C3
St Chad's St *STPAN* WC1H 5 F3
St Charles Pl *NKENS* W10 ....124 C4
St Charles Sq *NKENS* W10 ....124 C4
St Christopher's Cl *ISLW* TW7 ....160 A2
St Christopher's Ms
  WLGTN SM6 ....245 E5
St Christopher's Pl *MHST* W1U ...11 H4
St Clair Cl *CLAY* IG5 ....73 H2
St Clair Dr *WPK* KT4 ....241 H1
St Clair Rd *PLSTW* E13 ....132 D1
St Clair's Rd *CROY/NA* CR0 ....229 E6
St Clare St *TWRH* EC3N 16 C4
St Clement's La *LINN* WC2A 13 H4
St Clements St *HOLWY* N7 ....108 A5
St Clements Yd *EDUL* * SE22 .....169 F4
St Cloud Rd *WNWD* SE27 ....188 D6
St Crispins Cl *HAMP* NW3 ....106 A2
  STHL UB1 ....118 D5
St Cross St *HCIRC* EC1N 14 B1
St Cuthberts Gdns *PIN* * HA5 ......58 D3
St Cuthbert's Rd *CRICK* NW2 .....104 D4
  PLMGR N13 ....68 A2
St Cyprian's St *TOOT* SW17 ......186 D4
St Davids Cl *BERM/RHTH* SE16 ...33 H4
  WBLY HA9 ....102 C1
  WWKM BR4 ....214 A6
St David's Dr *EDGW* HA8 ....61 H4
St Davids Ms *BOW* * E3 ....111 G2
St David's Pl *HDN* NW4 ....63 H4
St Davids Sq *POP/IOD* E14 ....151 F5
St Denis Rd *WNWD* SE27 ....188 D6
St Dionis Rd *FUL/PGN* SW6 ....164 D3
St Donatt's Rd *NWCR* SE14 ....170 D2
St Dunstan's Av *ACT* W3 ....122 D6
St Dunstan's Gdns *ACT* W3 ....122 D6
St Dunstan's Hl *MON* * EC3R 16 A6
  SUT SM1 ....242 C3
St Dunstan's La *BECK* BR3 ....231 G3
  MON * EC3R 16 A6
St Dunstans Rd *FSTGT* E7 ....112 D4
  HMSMTH W6 ....144 B5
  HNWL W7 ....135 H2
  SNWD SE25 ....229 F1
St Dunstans Cl *ABYW* SE2 ....156 B2
  HNWL W7 ....136 A4
  TOOT SW17 ....186 A4
St Edmunds Dr *STAN* HA7 ....45 C6
St Edmund's La *WHTN* TW2 ....179 F2
St Edmunds Rd *ED* N9 ....53 G2
  IL IG1 ....93 H3
St Edmunds Sq *BARN* SW13 ......144 C6
St Edmund's Ter *ST/WD* NW8 ....2 B1
St Edward's Cl *GLDGN* NW11 ....85 E3
St Egberts Wy *CHING* E4 ....55 E1
St Elmo Rd *ACT* W3 ....143 E1
St Elmos Rd *BERM/RHTH* SE16 ..150 C2
St Erkenwald Ms *BARK* IG11 ......114 D6
St Erkenwald Rd *BARK* IG11 ......114 D6
St Ervans Rd *NKENS* W10 ....124 C4
St Fabian Twr *ED* * N9 ....38 C2
St Faith's Rd *HNHL* SE24 ....188 B3
St Fidelis' Rd *ERITH* DA8 ....157 H4
St Fillans Rd *CAT* SE6 ....191 G4
St Francis Cl *ORP* BR6 ....235 E3
St Francis Rd *EDUL* SE22 ....169 E5
St Francis Wy *IL* IG1 ....114 D2
St Gabriel's Cl *WAN* E11 ....92 D5
St Gabriel's Rd *CRICK* NW2 ....104 B3
St George's Av *CDALE/KGS* NW9 ..82 C1
  EA W5 ....141 F2
  FSTGT E7 ....112 D2
  HOLWY N7 ....107 F2
  STHL UB1 ....118 D6
St George's Circ *STHWK* SE1 ....22 C4
St George's Cl *ALP/SUD* HA0 .....100 C1
  GLDGN * NW11 ....84 D3
  THMD SE28 ....136 B5
St George's Dr *OXHEY* WD19 ......27 H5
  PIM SW1V 27 H3
St George's Flds *BAY/PAD* W2 ......10 A4
St George's Gdns *SURB* KT6 ......222 B6
St George's Gv *TOOT* SW17 ....186 B5
St George's La *MON* * EC3R 5 H5
St George's Ms *CAMTN* NW1 .....106 B5
  CHSWK * W4 ....160 C2
St Georges Pde *CAT* * SE6 ....190 D4
St George's Rd *BECK* BR3 ....211 F4
  BMLY BR1 ....234 D1
  CHSWK W4 ....142 C2
  DACW RM9 ....116 C3
  ED N9 ....39 F1
  FELT TW13 ....178 B6
  FSTGT E7 ....112 D3
  HNWL W7 ....140 D1
  IL IG1 ....92 D4
  KUTN/CMB KT2 ....201 G1
  LEY E10 ....91 G3
  MTCM CR4 ....206 D6
  PLMGR N13 ....51 G6
  RCH/KEW TW9 ....160 B4
  SCUP DA14 ....216 B2
  STHWK SE1 ....22 C4
  STMC/STPC BR5 ....201 F2
  TWK TW1 ....160 D5
  WIM/MER SW19 ....205 G6
  WLGTN SM6 ....244 B4
St Georges Rd West *BMLY* BR1 ..213 E5
St George's Sq *POP/IOD* * E14 ...113 H5
  NWMAL KT3 ....203 E6
  PIM SW1V 37 H1
St George's Square Ms
  PIM SW1V 28 A3
St George's Ter *CAMTN* NW1 .....106 B5
  PECK * SE15 ....169 G1

St George St CONDST W1S ...11 H5
St George's Wk CROY/NA CR0 ...228 C6
St George's Wy PECK SE15 ...32 B6
PECK * SE15 ...32 B6
St Gerards Cl CLAP SW4 ...160 E6
St German's Pl BKHTH/KID SE3 ...172 C2
St German's Rd FSTH SE23 ...190 C3
St Giles Av DAGE RM10 ...117 F5
St Giles Churchyard
BARB * EC1Y ...15 F2
St Giles Cl DAGE RM10 ...117 F5
ORP BR6 ...252 D3
St Giles High St
LSQ/SEVD WC2H ...12 D3
St Gothard Rd WNWD SE27 ...188 D3
St Gregory Cl RSLP HA4 ...98 A2
St Helena Rd
BERM/RHTH SE16 ...150 B4
St Helena Ter RCH/KEW * TW9 ...161 F6
St Helens THDIT * KT7 ...220 A4
St Helen's Crs
STRHM/NOR SW16 ...207 H4
St Helen's Gdns NKENS W10 ...124 B5
St Helen's Pl OBST EC2N ...16 A3
St Helens Rd ERITHM DA18 ...156 B2
IL IG1 ...93 H5
STRHM/NOR SW16 ...207 H5
WEA W13 ...98 D2
St Helier Av MRDN SM4 ...225 G4
St Helliers Av BKHTH/KID TW4 ...159 E6
St Helier's Rd LEY E10 ...91 F3
St Hildas Cl KIL/WHAMP * NW6 ...104 B6
TOOT SW17 ...186 A4
St Hilda's Rd BARN SW13 ...143 H6
St Hughes Cl TOOT * SW17 ...186 A4
St Hugh's Rd PGE/AN * SE20 ...209 H4
St James Av SUT SM1 ...248 A3
TRDG/WHET N20 ...50 A5
WEA W13 ...140 C1
St James' Cl NWMAL KT3 ...223 F2
RSLP HA4 ...78 A6
STJWD NW8 ...2 C1
TRDC/WHET N20 ...50 A5
St James' Ct WESTW * SW1E ...20 B5
St James' Gdns ALP/SUD HA0 ...101 F3
St James Ms POP/IOD * E14 ...151 G5
St James Rd CAR SM5 ...244 A1
EBAR EN4 ...35 H4
ED N9 ...53 H4
FSTGT E7 ...113 B3
MTCM CR4 ...206 C3
SURB KT6 ...221 F3
SUT SM1 ...243 E4
St James's Chambers
STJS * SW1Y ...20 B1
St James's Cl TOOT * SW17 ...186 B4
WOOL/PLUM SE18 ...154 C5
St James's Cottages
RCHPK/HAM * TW10 ...161 F6
WESTW SW1E ...20 C6
St James's Crs BRXN/ST SW9 ...168 A4
St James's Gdns CAMTN * NW1 ...4 A4
NTGHL W11 ...144 C1
St James's Gv BTSEA * SW11 ...166 B3
St James's La MUSWH N10 ...68 A4
St James's Market STJS * SW1Y ...12 C6
St James's Ms WALTH E17 ...90 C2
St James's Pk CROY/NA CR0 ...228 C4
St James's Pl WHALL SW1A ...20 A2
St James's Pk CROY/NA CR0 ...228 C4
St James's Sq SURB SW1E KT6 ...221 E4
St James's Rd
BERM/RHTH SE16 ...25 F5
BERM/RHTH SE16 ...33 F5
BERM/RHTH SE16 ...33 F5
CROY/NA CR0 ...228 A4
HPTN TW12 ...199 F1
KUT KT1 ...201 F5
STHWK SE1 ...33 F5
St James's Rw CHSGTN * KT9 ...239 F4
St James's Sq STJS SW1Y ...20 C1
St James's St WALTH E17 ...90 C2
WHALL SW1A ...20 A1
St James's Terrace Ms
STJWD NW8 ...106 B6
St James St HMSMTH W6 ...144 A5
St James Ter BAL * SW12 ...186 C5
St James Wk CLKNW EC1R ...5 K5
St James Wy SCUP DA14 ...216 C1
St Joan's Rd ED N9 ...53 F4
St John Cl FUL/PGN * SW6 ...165 E1
St John's Av FBAR/BDGN N11 ...66 B1
PUT/ROE SW15 ...164 B2
WLSDN NW10 ...103 F6
St John's Church Rd HACK * E8 ...156 E1
St John's Cl FUL/PGN SW6 ...165 E1
STHGT/OAK * N14 ...36 C1
TRDG/WHET * N20 ...49 G2
WBLY HA9 ...101 G3
St Johns Cottages
PGE/AN * SE20 ...210 A3
St John's Ct BKHH IG9 ...56 D3
BKHH * IG9 ...56 D3
St John's Dr WAND/EARL SW18 ...185 F3
WOT/HER KT12 ...218 A5
St John's Gdns NTGHL W11 ...106 A6
BARN * SW13 ...163 F3
RCH/KEW * TW9 ...161 G5
St John's Hl BTSEA SW11 ...165 H5
St John's Hill Gv BTSEA SW11 ...165 H5
St John's La FARR EC1M ...6 C6
St Johns Pde SCUP * DA14 ...195 H6
WEA * W13 ...116 C1
ISLW TW7 ...160 B5
St John's Crs BRXN/ST SW9 ...168 A4
St John's Dr WAND/EARL SW18 ...185 F3
St John's Est NTGHL W11 ...124 D1
St John's Gv ARCH N19 ...87 E6
BARN * SW13 ...163 F3
RCH/KEW * TW9 ...161 G5
St John's Hl BTSEA SW11 ...165 H5
St John's Hill Gv BTSEA SW11 ...165 H5
St John's La FARR EC1M ...6 C6
St Johns Pde SCUP * DA14 ...195 H6
WEA * W13 ...116 C1
St John's Pl FARR EC1M ...6 C6
St John's Rd BARK IG11 ...115 E6
BTSEA SW11 ...166 A5
CAN/RD E16 ...132 C5
CAR SM5 ...244 A1
CHING E4 ...38 B5
CROY/NA CR0 ...246 B1
CRW RM5 ...77 G1

E/WMO/HCT KT8 ...219 H1
EHAM E6 ...113 G4
ERITH DA8 ...157 H5
FELT TW13 ...178 D6
GLDGN NW11 ...64 C4
GNTH/NBYPK IG2 ...95 E4
HRW HA1 ...80 B3
ISLW TW7 ...160 B3
KUT KT1 ...201 G5
NWDGN UB2 ...138 C3
NWMAL KT3 ...202 C6
PGE/AN SE20 ...210 A3
RCH/KEW * TW9 ...161 G5
SCUP DA14 ...195 H6
SEVS/STOTM N15 ...89 E3
STMC/STPC BR5 ...234 D3
SUT SM1 ...225 E6
WALTH E17 ...90 B2
WBLY HA9 ...101 F2
WELL DA16 ...175 H4
WIM/MER SW19 ...204 C3
St John's Sq FARR EC1M ...6 C6
St John's Ter FSTGT E7 ...112 D4
NKENS W10 ...124 B3
WOOL/PLUM SE18 ...154 C6
St John St FSBYE EC1V ...6 B2
St John's V BRXN/ST SE4 ...171 E3
ARCH N19 ...87 F6
KENS * W8 ...145 F3
W8 ...145 F3
St John's Wood High St
STJWD NW8 ...125 H1
St John's Wood Pk
STJWD NW8 ...105 H6
St John's Wood Rd
MV/WKIL W9 ...125 H3
St John's Wood Ter
STJWD NW8 ...2 A1
St Josephs Cl NKENS W10 ...124 C4
ORP BR6 ...253 F2
St Joseph's Dr STHL UB1 ...138 C1
St Josephs Gv HDN NW4 ...83 H1
St Josephs Rd ED N9 ...42 D3
St Joseph's St VX/NE * SW8 ...166 D2
St Joseph's V BKHTH/KID SE3 ...171 H3
St Jude's Rd BETH * E2 ...9 H2
St Jude St STNW/STAM N16 ...109 E3
St Julian's Ct
STRHM/NOR * SW16 ...188 A6
St Julian's Farm Rd
WNWD SE27 ...188 B1
St Julian's Rd KIL/WHAMP NW6 ...104 D5
St Justin Cl STMC/STPC BR5 ...216 B6
St Katharine's Prec
CAMTN * NW1 ...3 G7
St Katharine's Wy TWRH EC3N ...14 D7
St Katherines Rd ERITHM DA18 ...156 B2
St Katherines Wk NTGHL * W11 ...124 B6
St Keverne Rd ELTH/MOT SE9 ...193 G6
St Kilda Rd ORP BR6 ...235 F5
WEA W13 ...140 C2
St Kilda's Rd HRW HA1 ...80 A3
STNW/STAM N16 ...86 D2
St Kitts Ter NRWD SE19 ...209 F1
St Laurence Cl KIL/WHAMP NW6 ...104 B6
St Laurence's Cl
KIL/WHAMP NW6 ...104 B6
St Lawrence Cottages
POP/IOD * E14 ...151 G1
St Lawrence St POP/IOD E14 ...151 G1
St Lawrence Ter NKENS W10 ...124 C4
St Lawrence Wy
BRXN/ST * SW9 ...168 A3
St Leonard's Av CHING E4 ...71 H2
HRW HA3 ...81 G3
St Leonards Cl WELL DA16 ...175 G4
St Leonard's Gdns HEST TW5 ...158 C5
IL IG1 ...114 C3
St Leonards Pl KTTN NW5 ...106 C4
St Leonards Ri ORP BR6 ...253 E2
St Leonard's Rd CROY/NA CR0 ...246 B1
ESH/CLAY KT10 ...238 B4
MORT/ESHN SW14 ...162 C2
POP/IOD E14 ...131 G4
SURB KT6 ...221 F2
THDIT KT7 ...220 C3
WEA W13 ...121 E6
WLSDN NW10 ...119 E4
St Leonards St BOW E3 ...131 F2
St Leonard's Ter CHEL SE3 ...26 C4
CHEL * SW3 ...26 C3
St Leonards Wk
STRHM/NOR SW16 ...207 H3
St Loo Av CHEL SW3 ...26 B5
St Louis Rd WNWD SE27 ...188 C6
St Loy's Rd TOTM N17 ...69 E3
St Lucia Dr SRTFD E15 ...112 B6
St Luke's Av CLAP SW4 ...167 F5
ENC/FH EN2 ...38 D1
IL IG1 ...
St Luke's Cl SNWD SE25 ...229 H5
SWLY BR8 ...217 H5
St Luke's Est FSBYE * EC1V ...7 G3
St Luke's Rd NTGHL W11 ...124 D4
St Lukes's Cl FSBYE EC1V ...7 F5
St Lukes Rd WMWL * W12 ...36 D1
St Luke's Sq CHEL SW3 ...26 A3
St Lukes St CHEL SW3 ...26 A3
St Malo Av ED N9 ...54 A3
St Margarets BARK IG11 ...114 D6
RCHPK/HAM * TW10 ...162 C1
St Margarets Av BFN/LL DA15 ...195 E1
CHEAM SM3 ...242 C1
RYLN/HDSTN HA2 ...99 C1
SEVS/STOTM N15 ...88 B1
TRDG/WHET N20 ...49 G2
St Margarets Ct ORP BR6 ...253 H2
St Margaret's Ct
PUT/ROE * SW15 ...165 H5
St Margaret's Crs
PUT/ROE * SW15 ...163 H6
St Margaret's Gv TWK TW1 ...160 D6
St Margaret's Gv TWK TW1 ...180 C1
WAN E11 ...112 D1
St Margarets La KENS * W8 ...145 C6
St Margarets Ms
RCHPK/HAM * TW10 ...202 C1
St Margaret's Rd BROCKY SE4 ...170 D5

EDGW HA8 ...62 B1
HNWL W7 ...140 A2
MNPK E12 ...93 H6
TOTM N17 ...69 E3
TWK TW1 ...160 D5
WLSDN NW10 ...124 A2
St Margaret's Ter
WOOL/PLUM SE18 ...154 C5
St Margaret St WHALL SW1P ...21 E4
St Mark's Cl BAR EN5 ...35 F2
FUL/PGN SW6 ...166 A6
St Mark's Crs CAMTN * NW1 ...106 C6
St Mark's Ga HOM E9 ...110 C5
St Mark's Gv WBPTN * SW10 ...165 F1
St Mark's Hl SURB KT6 ...221 C5
St Mark's Pl NTGHL W11 ...124 C5
WIM/MER * SW19 ...204 D2
St Mark's Ri HACK E8 ...109 F3
St Mark's Rd EA W5 ...141 G1
EN EN1 ...53 F1
HAYES BR2 ...212 D6
HNWL W7 ...140 A2
MTCM CR4 ...206 B5
NKENS W10 ...124 B4
SNWD SE25 ...229 G1
TEDD TW11 ...200 D3
St Mark's Sq CAMTN * NW1 ...106 C6
St Mark St WCHPL E1 ...16 B4
St Marks Vls HOLWY * N7 ...87 H6
St Martin's Av EHAM E6 ...133 F1
St Martin's Cl CAMTN NW1 ...107 E6
EN EN1 ...39 H2
ERITHM DA18 ...156 B2
St Martins Ct LSQ/SEVD WC2H ...13 E5
LSQ/SEVD * WC2H ...13 E5
St Martin's La CHCR WC2N ...13 E5
St Martins Le Grand STBT EC1A ...15 E3
St Martin's Pl CHCR WC2N ...13 E6
St Martin's Rd BRXN/ST SW9 ...167 H1
ED N9 ...42 D1
St Martin's St LSQ/SEVD * WC2H ...12 D6
St Martin's Wy TOOT SW17 ...185 C5
St Mary Abbot's Pl KENS W8 ...144 D3
KENS * W8 ...145 E3
St Mary Abbots Ter
WKENS * W14 ...144 D3
St Mary At Hi MON EC3R ...16 A6
St Mary Av WLGTN SM6 ...244 C1
St Mary Axe HDTCH EC3A ...16 A4
St Marychurch St
BERM/RHTH SE16 ...150 A2
St Mary Graces Ct TWRH * EC3N ...16 D6
St Marys BARK IG11 ...114 D1
St Mary's Ap MNPK E12 ...113 H3
St Mary's Av FNCH N3 ...64 C5
HAYES BR2 ...212 A6
NWDGN UB2 ...159 F4
TEDD * TW11 ...200 B2
WAN E11 ...91 F5
St Mary's Cl CHSGTN KT9 ...239 H5
EW KT17 ...241 F5
STMC/STPC BR5 ...215 H5
TOTM * N17 ...50 A5
St Marys Ct SHB * W12 ...143 F3
St Mary's Gdns LBTH SE11 ...30 B1
LBTH * SE11 ...30 B1
St Mary's Ga KENS W8 ...145 F3
KENS * W8 ...145 F3
St Mary's Gn EFNCH N2 ...65 G6
St Mary's Gv BARN SW13 ...163 H4
CHSWK W4 ...142 B6
IS N108 ...
RCH/KEW TW9 ...161 H4
St Mary's Ms BAY/PAD W2 ...125 H4
St Mary's Ms
KIL/WHAMP * N1 ...105 F5
St Mary's Pth IS * N1 ...108 B4
St Mary's Rd EA W5 ...141 F2
GLDGN NW11 ...64 C4
KENS * W8 ...145 F3
W8 ...145 F3
St Mary's Sq BXLY DA5 ...197 C3
CEND/HSY/T * N8 ...87 C1
St Mary's Rd BAY/PAD W2 ...125 H4
EBAR EN4 ...35 C4
St Mary's Ter BAY/PAD W2 ...125 H4
BDRE * WD6 ...45 F1
St Mary St WOOL/PLUM SE18 ...153 H4
St Marys Vw
KTN/HRWW/WS HA3 ...81 G2
St Mary's Wy CHIG IG7 ...74 H4
St Matthew's Av SURB KT6 ...225 C5
St Matthew's Dr HAYES BR2 ...42 E1
St Matthews Dr BMLY BR1 ...213 H6
St Matthew's Rd BRXN/ST SW2 ...167 H6
EA W5 ...141 G1
St Matthew St WEST SW1P ...21 F5
St Matthias Cl CDALE/KGS NW9 ...63 H3
St Maur Rd FUL/PGN SW6 ...164 D2
St Meddens CHST * BR7 ...214 B2
St Merryn Cl WOOL/PLUM SE18 ...154 B3
St Michael's Aly BANK EC3V ...15 H4
St Michaels Av ED N9 ...102 A1
St Michaels Cl BMLY BR1 ...213 G6
CAN/RD E16 ...131 G4
ERITHM * DA18 ...156 B2
FNCH N3 ...64 D5

NFNCH/WDSP N12 ...66 A1
WOT/HER KT12 ...218 A6
WPK KT4 ...223 F6
St Michaels Crs PIN HA5 ...77 F5
St Michael's Gdns NKENS W10 ...124 B4
St Michaels Ri WELL * DA16 ...175 H2
St Michael's Rd BRXN/ST SW9 ...167 H3
CRICK NW2 ...64 A4
CROY/NA * CR0 ...228 C5
WELL DA16 ...175 H4
WLGTN SM6 ...245 E4
St Michaels St BAY/PAD W2 ...125 H5
St Michaels Ter HGT * N6 ...86 C5
WDGN N22 ...67 G5
St Mildreds Rd CAT SE6 ...192 A2
St Nicholas Cl BORE WD6 ...45 F1
St Nicholas Glebe TOOT SW17 ...206 C2
St Nicholas Rd SUT SM1 ...243 F5
THDIT KT7 ...220 A4
WOOL/PLUM SE18 ...155 F5
St Nicholas St DEPT SE8 ...170 D2
St Nicholas Wy SUT SM1 ...243 F2
St Nicolas La CHST BR7 ...213 G4
St Ninian's Cl TRDG/WHET N20 ...36 B1
St Norbert Rd BROCKY SE4 ...170 C5
St Olaf's Rd FUL/PGN SW6 ...164 C1
St Olave's Rd EHAM E6 ...114 A6
St Olave's Wk
STRHM/NOR SW16 ...207 H3
St Onge Pde EN1 * ...38 D4
St Oswald's Pl LBTH SE11 ...29 G3
St Oswald's Rd
STRHM/NOR SW16 ...208 B4
St Oswulf St WEST * SW1P ...28 D2
St Pancras Gdns CAMTN * NW1 ...4 C1
St Paul's Av
BERM/RHTH * SE16 ...150 B1
CRICK NW2 ...103 H4
KTN/HRWW/W HA3 ...81 H2
St Paul's Church Yd
BLKFR * EC4V ...14 D4
St Paul's Cl CAR SM5 ...226 A4
CHARL SE7 ...153 F5
CHSGTN KT9 ...239 F2
EA W5 ...141 H2
HSLW TW3 ...158 D3
St Paul's Cray Rd CHST BR7 ...214 D4
St Paul's Ct CAMTN * NW1 ...107 F5
CAMTN NW1 ...107 F5
St Paul's Ms CAMTN NW1 ...107 F5
St Pauls Pl IS N1 ...108 D6
St Pauls Ri PLMGR N13 ...68 B2
St Pauls Rd BARK IG11 ...114 C6
BTFD TW8 ...141 F6
ERITH DA8 ...157 H1
IS N1 ...108 B4
RCH/KEW TW9 ...161 H4
THHTH CR7 ...208 C6
TOTM N17 ...50 C5
St Pauls Ter WALW SE17 ...30 D5
St Paul St IS N1 ...108 C6
St Paul's Wy FNCH N3 ...65 C5
POP/IOD E14 ...130 D4
St Paul's Wood Hl
STMC/STPC BR5 ...215 G5
St Peter's Av UED N18 ...53 G6
BAY/PAD * W2 ...125 F6
St Petersburgh Ms
BAY/PAD W2 ...125 F6
St Peter's Cl BETH E2 ...9 F2
BUSH WD23 ...45 H4
CHST BR7 ...214 D3
GNTH/NBYPK IG2 ...95 E1
RSLP HA4 ...78 B6
TOOT SW17 ...186 D6
St Peters Ct E/WMO/HCT KT8 ...219 E1
HDN * NW4 ...84 A2
LEE/GVPK * SE12 ...172 B6
St Peter's Gdns WNWD * SE27 ...188 B5
St Peter's Gv HMSMTH W6 ...143 G4
St Peters Pl MV/WKIL W9 ...125 F3
St Peters Rd CROY/NA CR0 ...246 D2
E/WMO/HCT KT8 ...219 E1
ED N9 ...53 H3
HMSMTH * W6 ...143 G5
KUT KT1 ...202 A5
STHL UB1 ...115 H6
TWK TW1 ...160 D6
St Peter's Sq BETH E2 ...9 G4
HMSMTH W6 ...143 G4
St Peter's St IS N1 ...108 C6
SAND/SEL CR2 ...246 D3
St Peter's Ter FUL/PGN SW6 ...164 C1
St Peter's Vs HMSMTH W6 ...143 G4
St Peter's Wy EA W5 ...121 F4
IS N1 ...109 C5
St Philip's Av WPK KT4 ...223 H6
St Philip Sq VX/NE * SW8 ...166 D3
St Philip's Rd HACK E8 ...109 C5
SURB KT6 ...221 E3
St Philip St VX/NE SW8 ...166 D4
St Philip's Wy IS N1 ...108 C6
St Quentin Rd WELL DA16 ...175 H4
St Quintin Av NKENS W10 ...124 B5
St Quintin Rd PLSTW E13 ...132 D2
St Raphael's Wy WLSDN NW10 ...102 C3
St Regis Cl MUSWH N10 ...66 A6
St Ronans Cl EBAR EN4 ...35 H1
St Ronans Crs WFD IG8 ...72 C3
St Rule St VX/NE SW8 ...167 H3
St Saviour's Rd
BRXS/STRHM SW2 ...167 H6
CROY/NA CR0 ...228 C5
Saints Cl WNWD SE27 ...
Saints Dr FSTGT E7 ...113 F3
St Silas Pl KTTN NW5 ...106 A4
St Simon's Av PUT/ROE SW15 ...164 A6
St Stephen's Av SHB W12 ...143 H2
WALTH E17 ...91 G1
W12 ...143 H2
St Stephens Cl KTTN * NW5 ...106 B3
STHL UB1 ...119 E4
WALTH E17 ...91 G1
St Stephen's Crs BAY/PAD W2 ...125 F5
THHTH CR7 ...208 A4

St Stephen's Gdns
BAY/PAD W2 125 E5
TWK TW1 181 E1
St Stephen's Gv LEW SE13 171 G4
St Stephen's Ms BAY/PAD W2 125 E4
St Stephens Pde WHALL SW1A 21 E3
St Stephens Rd BAR EN5 34 B6
BOW E3 110 C6
EHAM E6 113 E5
HSLW TW3 179 E1
WALTH E17 91 F2
WEA W13 120 D5
St Stephen's Ter VX/NE SW8 167 H1
VX/NE * SW8 167 G1
St Stephen's Wk SKENS * SW7 145 G4
St Swithin's La MANHO EC4N 15 G5
St Swithun's Rd LEW * SE13 171 H6
St Thomas Cl SURB KT6 221 H5
St Thomas Ct BXLY DA5 197 E2
St Thomas' Dr PIN HA5 58 C4
STMC/STPC BR5 234 C5
St Thomas Gdns IL IG1 114 C4
St Thomas Rd BELV DA17 157 G2
CAN/RD E16 132 C5
CHSWK W4 162 C1
STHGT/OAK N14 51 F2
St Thomas's Gdns HAMP NW3 106 C4
St Thomas's Pl HOM * E9 110 A5
St Thomas's Rd FSBYPK N4 88 A6
WLSDN NW10 103 E6
St Thomas's Sq HACK E8 109 H5
St Thomas St STHWK SE1 23 H2
St Thomas's Wy FUL/PGN SW6 164 D1
St Ursula Gv PIN HA5 78 B2
St Ursula Rd STHL UB1 119 E5
St Vincent Cl WNWD SE27 208 B1
St Vincent Rd WHTN TW2 179 G1
St Vincent St MHST W1U 11 F2
St Wilfrid's Cl EBAR * EN4 36 A6
St Wilfrid's Rd EBAR EN4 35 H6
St Winefride's Av MNPK E12 113 H3
St Winifred's Cl CHIG IG7 74 C1
St Winifred's Rd TEDD TW11 200 D2
Salamanca Pl LBTH SE11 29 G2
Salamanca St LBTH SE11 29 G2
Salamander Cl KUTN/CMB KT2 201 E1
Salamander Quay KUT * KT1 201 F4
Salcombe Dr CHDH RM6 96 D3
MRDN SM4 224 B5
Salcombe Gdns MLHL NW7 64 A2
Salcombe Rd STNW/STAM N16 109 F3
WALTH E17 90 D4
Salcott Rd BTSEA SW11 166 A6
CROY/NA CR0 245 G1
Salehurst Cl KTN/HRWW/W HA3 81 G2
Salehurst Rd BROCKY SE4 190 D1
Salem Pl CROY/NA CR0 246 C1
Sale Pl BAY/PAD W2 10 A3
Sale St BETH E2 9 E5
Salford Rd BAL SW12 187 F3
Salisbury Av BARK IG11 114 D5
BELMT SM2 242 D4
FNCH N3 64 D5
Salisbury Cl WALW SE17 31 G1
WPK KT4 241 F1
Salisbury Ct EMB EC4Y 14 B4
Salisbury Gdns
WIM/MER * SW19 204 C3
Salisbury Pavement
FUL/PGN * SW6 165 E1
Salisbury Pl BRXN/ST SW9 168 B1
MBLAR W1H 10 C1
Salisbury Prom
CEND/HSY/T * N8 88 B2
Salisbury Rd BAR EN5 34 C4
BXLY DA5 197 E3
CAR SM5 244 B4
CHING E4 55 E5
CROY/NA CR0 229 G3
DAGE RM10 117 F4
ED N9 53 G5
FELT TW13 178 A3
FSBYPK N4 88 B2
FSTGT E7 112 C4
GDMY/SEVK IG3 95 E6
HAYES BR2 233 G2
HOR/WEW KT19 240 D2
HRW HA1 79 H2
HSLWW TW4 158 A4
LEY E10 91 G6
NWDGN * UB2 138 C4
NWMAL KT3 202 D6
RCH/KEW TW9 161 G5
WALTH E17 91 G2
WDGN N22 68 B5
WEA W13 140 D2
WIM/MER SW19 204 C3
Salisbury Sq EMB * EC4Y 14 B4
Salisbury St ACT W3 142 C2
STJWD NW8 2 A6
Salisbury Ter PECK SE15 170 A4
Sally Murray Cl MNPK E12 114 A2
Salmen Rd PLSTW E13 132 B1
Salmon La POP/IOD E14 130 C5
Salmon Ms KIL/WHAMP * NW6 105 E3
Salmon Rd BELV DA17 157 E5
Salmons Rd CHSGTN KT9 239 G4
ED N9 53 G3
Salmon St POP/IOD * E14 130 D5
WBLY HA9 82 C6
Salomons Rd PLSTW E13 133 E4
Salop Rd WALTH E17 90 B3
Saltash Cl SUT SM1 242 D2
Saltash Rd BARK/HLT IG6 74 D3
WELL DA16 176 A2
Saltcoats Rd CHSWK W4 143 E2
Saltcroft Cl WBLY HA9 82 B5
Salter Cl RYLN/HDSTN HA2 98 D1
Salterford Rd TOOT SW17 206 C2
Salter Rd BERM/RHTH SE16 150 C2
Salters' Hall Ct MANHO * EC4N 15 G5
Salter's Hl NRWD SE19 208 D1
Salters Rd NKENS W10 124 B3
WALTH E17 91 H1
Salters Rw IS * N1 108 D4
Salter St POP/IOD E14 131 E6
WLSDN NW10 123 G2
Salterton Rd HOLWY N7 107 G1
Saltley Cl EHAM E6 133 G5
Saltram Crs MV/WKIL W9 124 D2
Saltwell St POP/IOD E14 131 E6
Saltwood Gv WALW SE17 31 G4
Salvador TOOT SW17 206 A1
Salvia Gdns GFD/PVL UB6 120 C1
Salvin Rd PUT/ROE SW15 164 B4
Salway Cl WFD IG8 72 C3
Salway Pl SRTFD E15 111 H4
Salway Rd SRTFD E15 111 H4
Samantha Cl WALTH E17 90 D4
Sam Bartram Cl CHARL SE7 153 E5
Samels Ct HMSMTH W6 143 G5
Samford St STJWD NW8 2 A6
Samos Rd PGE/AN SE20 209 H5
Sampson Av BAR EN5 34 B6
Sampson Cl BELV DA17 156 B3
Sampson St WAP E1W 25 F2
Samson St PLSTW E13 133 E1
Samuel Cl HACK E8 109 F6
NWCR SE14 150 B6
WOOL/PLUM SE18 153 G4
Samuel Gray Gdns
KUTN/CMB KT2 201 F4
Samuel St WOOL/PLUM SE18 153 H4
Sancroft Cl CRICK NW2 103 H1
Sancroft Rd KTN/HRWW/W HA3 60 B5
Sancroft St LBTH SE11 29 H3
Sanctuary St STHWK SE1 23 F4
The Sanctuary BXLY DA5 196 B1
WEST SW1P 20 D5
Sandall Cl EA W5 121 G3
Sandall Rd EA W5 121 G3
KTTN NW5 107 E4
Sandal Rd NWMAL KT3 223 E1
UED N18 69 G1
Sandal St SRTFD E15 112 A6
Sandalwood Cl WCHPL E1 130 C3
Sandbach Pl
WOOL/PLUM SE18 154 C5
Sandbourne Av
WIM/MER SW19 205 F6
Sandbourne Rd BROCKY SE4 170 C3
Sandbrook Cl MLHL NW7 62 D2
Sandbrook Rd
STNW/STAM N16 109 E1
Sandby Gn ELTH/MOT SE9 173 G4
Sandcliff Rd ERITH DA8 157 H4
Sandcroft Cl PLMGR N13 68 B2
Sandell St STHWK SE1 22 A3
Sanders Cl HPTN TW12 199 G1
Sanders La MLHL NW7 64 A3
Sanderson Cl KTTN * NW5 106 D2
Sanders Pde
STRHM/NOR * SW16 207 G2
Sanderstead Av CRICK NW2 84 C6
Sanderstead Cl BAL SW12 187 E2
Sanderstead Rd LEY E10 90 C5
SAND/SEL CR2 246 D5
STMC/STPC BR5 235 H3
Sandfield Gdns THHTH CR7 208 B6
Sandfield Pl THHTH CR7 208 C6
Sandfield Rd THHTH CR7 208 B6
Sandford Av WDGN N22 68 B4
Sandford Rd BXLYHS DA6 176 C5
EHAM E6 133 H2
HAYES BR2 232 C1
Sandford Rw WALW SE17 31 G3
Sandford St FUL/PGN SW6 165 F1
Sandgate Cl ROMW/RG RM7 97 G4
Sandgate La
WAND/EARL SW18 186 A3
Sandgate Rd WELL DA16 176 A1
Sandgate St PECK SE15 33 G5
Sandhills WLGTN SM6 245 F2
The Sandhills WBPTN * SW10 145 G6
Sandhurst Av BRYLDS KT5 222 B4
RYLN/HDSTN HA2 79 F3
Sandhurst Cl CDALE/KGS NW9 62 A6
SAND/SEL CR2 247 E6
Sandhurst Dr GDMY/SEVK IG3 115 F2
Sandhurst Pde CAT * SE6 191 G3
Sandhurst Rd BFN/LL DA15 195 F5
BXLY DA5 176 B6
CAT SE6 191 H3
CDALE/KGS NW9 62 A6
ED N9 54 A1
ORP BR6 253 G1
Sandhurst Wy SAND/SEL CR2 247 E5
Sandifer Dr CRICK NW2 104 B1
Sandiford Rd CHEAM SM3 224 D6
Sandiland Crs HAYES BR2 232 B6
Sandilands CROY/NA CR0 247 G1
Sandilands Rd FUL/PGN SW6 165 F2
Sandison St PECK SE15 169 F4
Sandland St GINN WC1R 13 H2
Sandling Ri ELTH/MOT SE9 194 A5
Sandlings Cl PECK SE15 169 H3
Sandmere Rd CLAP SW4 167 G5
Sandon Cl ESH/CLAY KT10 219 H4
Sandown Av DAGE RM10 117 G4
Sandown Ct BELMT * SM2 243 F5
DAGE RM10 117 G4
SYD * SE26 189 H5
Sandown Dr CAR SM5 244 C6
Sandown Ga ESH/CLAY KT10 219 H6
Sandown Rd SNWD SE25 229 H2
Sandown Wy NTHLT UB5 98 C4
Sandpiper Cl BERM/RHTH SE16 150 D2
WALTH E17 70 B3
Sandpiper Rd SUT SM1 242 D3
Sandpiper Ter CLAY * IG5 74 B6
Sandpiper Wy STMC/STPC BR5 236 B1
Sandpit Pl CHARL SE7 153 G5
Sandpit Rd BMLY BR1 212 A1
Sandpits Rd CROY/NA CR0 248 B2
RCHPK/HAM TW10 181 F4
Sandra Cl HSLW TW3 159 F6
WDGN N22 68 C4
Sandridge Cl HRW HA1 80 A1
Sandridge St ARCH N19 87 E6
Sandringham Av RYNPK SW20 204 C4
Sandringham Cl EN EN1 39 E3
WIM/MER * SW19 184 B3
Sandringham Crs
RYLN/HDSTN HA2 99 E1
Sandringham Dr WELL DA16 175 E3
Sandringham Gdns
BARK/HLT IG6 74 C6
CEND/HSY/T N8 87 G3
NFNCH/WDSP N12 65 H2
Sandringham Rd BARK IG11 115 F4
BMLY BR1 212 C1
CRICK NW2 103 H3
CROY/NA CR0 228 C2
FSTGT E7 113 E3
GLDGN NW11 84 C4
HACK E8 109 F3
LEY E10 91 H4
NTHLT UB5 99 E5
WDGN N22 68 C6
WPK KT4 241 G1
Sandrock Pl CROY/NA CR0 248 B2
Sandrock Rd LEW SE13 171 E4
Sands End La FUL/PGN SW6 165 F2
Sandstone Rd LEE/GVPK SE12 192 D4
Sands Wy WFD IG8 73 H2
Sandtoft Rd CHARL SE7 152 D6
Sandway Rd STMC/STPC BR5 236 A1
Sandwell Crs KIL/WHAMP NW6 105 E4
Sandwich St STPAN WC1H 5 E4
Sandwick Cl MLHL NW7 63 G3
Sandy Bury ORP BR6 252 D1
Sandycombe Rd
RCH/KEW TW9 162 A3
Sandycoombe Rd TWK TW1 181 E1
Sandycroft ABYW SE2 155 G6
Sandy Hill Av
WOOL/PLUM SE18 154 B5
Sandy Hill La
WOOL/PLUM SE18 154 B4
Sandyhill Rd IL IG1 114 B2
Sandy Hill Rd WLGTN SM6 245 E6
WOOL/PLUM SE18 154 B5
Sandy La BELMT SM2 242 C6
E/WMO/HCT KT8 200 D4
KTN/HRWW/W HA3 81 H3
MTCM CR4 206 C4
ORP BR6 235 G4
RCHPK/HAM TW10 181 E4
STMC/STPC BR5 216 B3
TEDD TW11 200 C3
Sandy La North WLGTN SM6 245 F3
Sandy La South WLGTN SM6 245 E6
Sandy Ldg PIN * HA5 59 E2
Sandymount Av STAN HA7 61 E1
Sandy Rdg CHST BR7 214 A2
Sandy Rd GLDGN NW11 85 F6
Sandy's Rw WCHPL E1 16 B2
Sandy Wy CROY/NA CR0 248 D1
Sanford La STNW/STAM N16 89 F6
Sanford St NWCR SE14 150 C6
Sanford Ter STNW/STAM N16 109 F1
Sanger Av CHSGTN KT9 239 H3
Sangley Rd CAT SE6 191 F2
SNWD SE25 229 E1
Sangora Rd BTSEA SW11 165 H5
Sansom Rd WAN * E11 92 B6
Sansom St CMBW SE5 168 D1
Sans Wk CLKNW EC1R 6 C5
Santley St BRXS/STRHM SW2 167 G5
Santos Rd PUT/ROE SW15 165 E6
Saperton Wk LBTH SE11 29 H1
Saphora Cl ORP BR6 252 D3
Sapphire Cl BCTR RM8 96 A5
Sapphire Rd DEPT SE8 150 C4
Saracen Cl CROY/NA CR0 228 D3
Saracen St POP/IOD E14 131 E5
Sarah St BETH E2 8 B3
Saratoga Rd CLPT E5 110 A2
Sardinia St HOL/ALD WC2B 13 G4
Sarita Cl KTN/HRWW/W HA3 59 H5
Sark Cl HEST TW5 159 E1
Sarnesfield Rd ENC/FH * EN2 38 D5
Sarre Rd CRICK NW2 104 D3
Sarsen Av HSLW TW3 158 D3
Sarsfeld Rd BAL SW12 186 B3
Sarsfield Rd GFD/PVL UB6 120 D1
Sartor Rd PECK SE15 170 B5
Sarum Ter BOW * E3 130 D3
Satanita Cl CAN/RD E16 133 F5
Satchell Md CDALE/KGS NW9 63 F4
Satchwell Rd BETH * E2 9 E4
Sattar Ms STNW/STAM * N16 108 D1
Sauls Gn WAN E11 112 A1
Saunders Cl POP/IOD * E14 130 D6
Saunders Ness Rd
POP/IOD E14 151 H4
Saunders Rd
WOOL/PLUM SE18 155 F5
Saunders St LBTH SE11 30 A1
Saunders Wy THMD SE28 135 H6
Saunderton Rd ALP/SUD HA0 100 D3
Savage Gdns EHAM E6 133 H5
TWRH EC3N 16 B5
Savernake Ct STAN * HA7 60 D2
Savernake Rd ED N9 53 G1
HAMP NW3 106 B2
Savery Dr SURB KT6 220 D4
Savile Cl NWMAL KT3 223 E2
THDIT KT7 220 B5
Savile Gdns CROY/NA CR0 229 F6
Savile Rw CONDST W1S 12 A5
Saville Rd CAN/RD E16 153 G1
CHDH RM6 96 D3
CHSWK W4 142 D3
TWK TW1 180 B3
Saville Rw HAYES BR2 232 B5
Savill Gdns RYNPK SW20 203 G6
Savill Rw WFD IG8 72 B2
Savona Cl WIM/MER SW19 204 B3
Savona St VX/NE SW8 167 E1
Savoy Cl EDGW HA8 62 A1
SRTFD E15 112 A6
Savoy Ct TPL/STR * WC2R 13 F6
Savoy Hl TPL/STR WC2R 13 G6
Savoy Pde EN * EN1 39 E4
Savoy Pl CHCR WC2N 13 F6
Savoy Rw TPL/STR WC2R 13 G5
Savoy Steps TPL/STR * WC2R 13 G6
Savoy St TPL/STR WC2R 13 G5
Savoy Wy TPL/STR WC2R 13 G6
Sawbill Cl YEAD UB4 118 B4
Sawkins Cl WIM/MER SW19 184 B4
Sawley Rd SHB W12 143 G1
Sawtry Cl CAR SM5 225 H4
Sawyer Cl ED N9 53 G4
Sawyer's Hl
RCHPK/HAM TW10 181 H2
Sawyers Lawn WEA W13 120 B5
Sawyer St STHWK SE1 23 E3
Saxby Rd BRXS/STRHM SW2 187 G2
Saxham Rd BARK IG11 115 E6
Saxlingham Rd CHING E4 55 H5
Saxon Av FELT TW13 178 D4
Saxonbury Cl MTCM CR4 205 H6
Saxonbury Gdns SURB KT6 221 E5
Saxon Cl SURB KT6 221 F3
WALTH E17 91 E4
Saxon Dr ACT W3 122 B5
Saxonfield Cl
BRXS/STRHM SW2 187 H2
Saxon Rd BMLY BR1 212 B3
BOW E3 130 D1
CROY/NA CR0 228 D2
EHAM E6 133 H3
IL IG1 114 B4
STHL UB1 118 C6
WBLY HA9 102 C1
WDGN N22 68 B4
Saxon Wy STHGT/OAK N14 51 F1
Saxton Cl LEW SE13 171 H4
Saxville Rd STMC/STPC BR5 215 H6
Sayesbury La UED N18 69 G1
Sayes Court Rd
STMC/STPC BR5 215 G6
Sayes Court St DEPT SE8 150 D5
Scadbury Gdns
STMC/STPC BR5 215 G5
Scads Hill Cl ORP BR6 235 F3
Scala St FITZ W1T 12 B1
Scales Rd TOTM N17 69 F6
Scampston Ms NKENS W10 124 B5
Scandrett St WAP E1W 25 G2
Scarba Wk IS N1 108 D4
Scarborough Rd ED N9 54 A2
FSBYPK N4 88 A4
WAN E11 91 H5
Scarborough St WCHPL E1 16 D4
Scarbrook Rd CROY/NA CR0 246 C1
Scarle Rd ALP/SUD HA0 101 F4
Scarlet Cl STMC/STPC BR5 235 H1
Scarlet Rd CAT SE6 192 A5
Scarsbrook Rd BKHTH/KID SE3 173 F4
Scarsdale Pl KENS W8 145 F3
Scarsdale Rd RYLN/HDSTN HA2 99 G1
Scarsdale Vls KENS W8 145 E3
Scarth Rd BARN SW13 163 F4
Scawen Cl CAR SM5 244 C2
Scawen Rd DEPT SE8 150 C5
Scawfell St BETH E2 8 D2
Scaynes Link NFNCH/WDSP N12 49 E6
Sceptre Rd BETH E2 130 A2
Scholars Rd BAL SW12 187 E3
CHING E4 55 G3
Scholefield Rd ARCH N19 87 F5
Schonfeld Sq STNW/STAM N16 88 D6
School House La TEDD TW11 200 D3
Schoolhouse La WAP * E1W 130 B6
School La BUSH WD23 43 F2
KUT KT1 201 E4
PIN * HA5 78 C1
SURB KT6 221 H5
WELL DA16 175 H4
School Pas KUT KT1 201 H5
STHL UB1 138 D1
School Rd CHST BR7 214 C4
DAGE RM10 117 E6
E/WMO/HCT KT8 219 H1
HPTN TW12 199 G2
HSLW TW3 159 G4
KUT * KT1 201 E4
WLSDN NW10 122 D3
School Road Av HPTN TW12 199 G2
School Wy BCTR RM8 115 H1
Schoolway NFNCH/WDSP N12 65 H2
Schooner Cl BARK IG11 135 H2
POP/IOD E14 151 H3
Schubert Rd BORE WD6 45 F1
PUT/ROE SW15 164 D6
Sclater St WCHPL E1 8 C5
Scoles Crs BRXS/STRHM SW2 188 A3
Scope Wy KUT KT1 221 G1
Scoresby St STHWK SE1 22 C2
Scorton Av GFD/PVL UB6 120 C1
Scotch Common WEA W13 120 C4
Scot Gv PIN HA5 58 B3
Scotia Rd BRXS/STRHM SW2 188 A2
Scotland Gn TOTM N17 69 F5
Scotland Green Rd PEND EN3 40 B6
Scotland Green Rd North
PEND EN3 40 B5
Scotland Rd BKHH IG9 57 E3
Scotney Cl ORP BR6 252 A2
Scotsdale Cl BELMT SM2 242 C5
CHST BR7 235 E1
Scotsdale Rd LEE/GVPK SE12 172 D6
Scotswood St CLKNW * EC1R 6 B5
Scotswood Wk TOTM * N17 69 H3
Scott Cl HOR/WEW KT19 240 C3
STRHM/NOR SW16 207 H4
Scott Crs RYLN/HDSTN HA2 79 F5
Scott Ellis Gdns STJWD NW8 125 H2
Scottes La BCTR RM8 96 B5
Scott Farm Cl THDIT KT7 220 D5
Scott Gdns HEST TW5 158 B1
Scott Lidgett Crs
BERM/RHTH SE16 25 E4
Scotts Av HAYES BR2 211 H5
Scotts Dr HPTN TW12 199 F3
Scotts Farm Rd
HOR/WEW KT19 240 C4
Scott's La HAYES BR2 211 H6
Scotts Pas WOOL/PLUM * SE18 154 B4
Scotts Rd BMLY BR1 212 C3
LEY E10 91 G5
NWDGN UB2 138 A3
SHB W12 143 H2
Scott St WCHPL E1 9 G6
Scott Trimmer Wy HEST TW5 158 C3
Scottwell Dr CDALE/KGS NW9 83 F2
Scoulding Rd CAN/RD E16 132 B5
Scouler St POP/IOD E14 131 H6
Scout La CLAP SW4 167 E4
Scout Wy MLHL NW7 46 D6
Scovell Crs STHWK * SE1 23 E4
Scovell Rd STHWK SE1 23 E4
Scrattons Ter BARK IG11 136 B1
Scriven St HACK E8 109 F6
Scrooby St CAT SE6 191 F1
Scrutton St SDTCH EC2A 8 A6
Scutari Rd EDUL SE22 169 H6
Scylla Rd PECK SE15 169 H4
Seabright St BETH E2 9 G4
Seabrook Dr WWKM BR4 232 A6
Seabrook Gdns ROMW/RG RM7 97 E4

Seabrook Rd *BCTR* RM8 ....116 B1
Seacole Cl *ACT* W3 ....122 D5
Seacourt Rd *ABYW* SE2 ....156 B2
Seacroft Gdns *OXHEY* WD19 ....42 B5
Seafield Rd *FBAR/BDGN* N11 ....51 F6
Seaford Rd *EN* EN1 ....39 E5
  SEVS/STOTM N15 ....38 D2
  WALTH E17 ....71 F6
  WDGN N22 ....140 D1
Seaford St *STPAN* WC1H 5 F4
Seaforth Av *NWMAL* KT3 ....223 H2
Seaforth Crs *HBRY* N5 ....108 C5
Seaforth Gdns *HOR/WEW* KT19 ....241 F2
  WCHMH N21 ....35 F2
  WFD IG8 ....73 E1
Seager Buildings *DEPT* * SE8 ....171 E2
Seager Pl *BOW* E3 ....130 D4
Seagrave Cl *WCHPL* * E1 ....130 B4
Seagrave Rd *FUL/PGN* SW6 ....145 G6
Seagry Rd E11 ....92 C3
Seal St *HACK* E8 ....109 F2
Searles Cl *BTSEA* SW11 ....166 B1
Searles Dr *EHAM* E6 ....134 B4
Searles Rd *STHWK* SE1 ....31 H1
Sears St *CMBW* SE5 ....168 D1
Seasprite Cl *NTHLT* UB5 ....118 B2
Seaton Av *GDMY/SEVK* IG3 ....113 E5
Seaton Cl *LBTH* SE11 ....30 B3
  PLSTW E13 ....132 C5
  PUT/ROE SW15 ....183 H2
  WHTN TW2 ....179 H1
Seaton Rd *ALP/SUD* * HA0 ....121 C1
  MTCM CR4 ....206 A5
  WELL DA16 ....116 A1
  WHTN TW2 ....179 G1
Seaton St *UED* N18 ....69 G1
Sebastian St *FSBYE* EC1V 6 D4
Sebastopol Rd *ED* N9 ....53 G6
Sebbon St *IS* N1 ....108 B5
Sebergham Gv *MLHL* NW7 ....63 G1
Sebert Rd *FSTGT* E7 ....112 D3
Sebright Rd *BAR* EN5 ....5 A8
Secker Crs *KTN/HRWW/W* HA3 ....59 G4
Secker St *STHWK* SE1 ....22 A2
Second Av *ACT* W3 ....143 F1
  CHDH RM6 ....96 A2
  DAGE RM10 ....137 F1
  EN EN1 ....39 F6
  HDN NW4 ....84 B1
  MNPK E12 ....113 G2
  MORT/ESHN SW14 ....163 E4
  NKENS W10 ....124 C3
  PLSTW E13 ....132 C2
  UED N18 ....54 A2
  WALTH E17 ....91 G1
  WBLY HA9 ....44 C4
Second Cl *E/WMO/HCT* KT8 ....219 G1
Second Cross Rd *WHTN* TW2 ....179 H4
Second Wy *WBLY* HA9 ....102 B2
Sedan Wy *WALW* SE17 ....32 A3
Sedcombe Cl *SCUP* DA14 ....195 H6
Sedcote Rd *PEND* EN3 ....41 E5
Seddon Rd *KTBR* SW1X 2 E7
Seddon St *MRDN* SM4 ....225 H2
Seddon St *FSBYW* WC1X 5 G4
Sedgebrook Rd *BKHTH/KID* SE3 ....173 F3
Sedgecombe Av
  KTN/HRWW/W HA3 ....81 E2
Sedgeford Rd *SHB* W12 ....143 F1
Sedgehill Rd *CAT* SE6 ....211 E1
Sedgemere Av *EFNCH* N2 ....65 G3
Sedgemere Rd *ABYW* SE2 ....156 A3
Sedgemoor Dr *DAGE* RM10 ....117 E2
Sedge Rd *TOTM* N17 ....70 A3
Sedgeway *CAT* SE6 ....192 D5
Sedgewood Cl *HAYES* BR2 ....232 B4
Sedgmoor Pl *CMBW* SE5 ....169 E1
Sedgwick Rd *LEY* E10 ....91 G6
Sedgwick St *HOM* E9 ....110 B3
Sedleigh Rd *WAND/EARL* SW18 ....147 D1
Sedlescombe Rd
  FUL/PGN SW6 ....144 D6
Sedley Cl *EN* EN1 ....39 H1
Sedley Pl *MYFR/PKLN* W1K 11 G4
Sedum Cl *CDALE/KGS* NW9 ....62 B2
Seeley Dr *DUL* SE21 ....189 E6
Seeley Rd *CDALE/KGS* NW9 ....83 G4
Seely Rd *TOOT* SW17 ....206 C2
Seething La *TWRH* EC3N 16 B5
Seething Wells La *SURB* KT6 ....221 D5
Sefton Av *KTN/HRWW/W* HA3 ....59 H4
  MLHL NW7 ....62 C1
Sefton Cl *STMC/STPC* BR5 ....235 F1
Sefton Ct *ENC/FH* * EN2 ....23 B3
Sefton Rd *CROY/NA* CRO 229 G5
  STMC/STPC BR5 ....235 F1
Sefton St *PUT/ROE* SW15 ....164 A3
Sefkforde St *CLKNW* EC1R 6 C6
Sekhon Ter *FELT* TW13 ....179 E5
Selah Dr *SWLY* BR8 ....217 G6
Selbie Av *WLSDN* NW10 ....103 F3
Selborne Av *BXLY* DA5 ....168 E4
  MNPK E12 ....114 A2
Selborne Gdns *GFD/PVL* UB6 ....120 C1
  HDN NW4 ....63 H2
Selborne Rd *CMBW* SE5 ....168 D3
  CROY/NA CRO 247 E1
  IL IG1 ....96 A6
  NWMAL KT3 ....203 B5
  SCUP DA14 ....195 H6
  STHGT/OAK N14 ....51 G5
  WALTH E17 ....90 D2
  WDGN N22 ....67 H4
Selbourne Av *SURB* KT6 ....221 E5
Selby Cl *CHSGTN* KT9 ....239 G5
  CHST BR7 ....214 A2
Selby Gdns *STHL* UB1 ....119 E3
Selby Gn *CAR* SM5 ....226 A4
Selby Rd *CAR* SM5 ....226 A4
  EA W5 ....120 D3
  PGE/AN SE20 ....206 A2
  PLSTW E13 ....132 D4
  TOTM N17 ....69 E2
  WAN E11 ....112 A1
Selby St *WCHPL* E1 ....9 F6
Selden Rd *PECK* SE15 ....170 C5
Selhurst Cl *WIM/MER* SW19 ....184 B3
Selhurst New Rd *SNWD* SE25 ....229 E5
Selhurst Pl *CROY/NA* CRO 229 E3
Selhurst Rd *ED* N9 ....52 D5

  SNWD SE25 ....229 E2
Selinas La *BCTR* RM8 ....96 C4
Selkirk Rd *TOOT* SW17 ....186 A6
  WHTN TW2 ....179 G4
Sellers Hall Cl *FNCH* N3 ....52 A6
Sellincourt Rd *TOOT* SW17 ....206 C1
Sellindge Cl *BECK* BR3 ....210 D3
Sellons Av *WLSDN* NW10 ....103 H6
Sellwood Dr *BAR* EN5 ....5 B6
Selsdon Av *SAND/SEL* CR2 ....246 D4
Selsdon Cl *CRW* RM5 ....77 G4
  SURB KT6 ....221 G2
Selsdon Park Rd
  SAND/SEL CR2 ....248 C6
Selsdon Rd *CRICK* NW2 ....83 F6
  PLSTW E13 ....113 G6
  SAND/SEL CR2 ....247 E5
  WAN E11 ....92 C4
  WNWD SE27 ....188 B5
Selsdon Wy *POP/IOD* E14 ....151 E3
Selsea Pl *STNW/STAM* N16 ....109 E3
Selsey Crs *WELL* DA16 ....176 E2
Selsey St *POP/IOD* E14 ....131 C4
Selvage La *MLHL* NW7 ....62 D1
Selwood Rd *CHEAM* SM3 ....224 D5
  CHSGTN KT9 ....239 F2
  CROY/NA CRO 229 H6
Selwood Ter *SKENS* SW7 ....145 H5
Selworthy Cl *WAN* E11 ....92 C2
Selworthy Rd *CAT* SE6 ....190 D5
Selwyn Av *CHING* E4 ....71 C2
  GDMY/SEVK IG3 ....95 F3
  RCH/KEW TW9 ....161 H4
Selwyn Cl *HSLWW* TW4 ....158 C5
Selwyn Ct *EDGW* HA8 ....62 B3
Selwyn Crs *WELL* DA16 ....176 B3
Selwyn Rd *BOW* E3 ....130 D1
  NWMAL KT3 ....222 D2
  PLSTW E13 ....112 D6
  WLSDN NW10 ....105 E5
Semley Pl *BGVA* SW1W 27 H4
Semley Rd *STRHM/NOR* SW16 ....207 G5
Senate St *PECK* SE15 ....170 A3
Seneca Rd *THHTH* CR7 ....228 C1
Senga Rd *MTCM* CR4 ....226 C5
Senhouse Rd *CHEAM* SM3 ....242 B1
Senior St *BAY/PAD* W2 ....2 C5
Senlac Rd *LEE/GVPK* SE12 ....192 D5
Sennen Rd *EN* EN1 ....53 F2
Senrab St *WCHPL* E1 ....130 B5
Sentinel Cl *YEAD* UB4 ....118 C3
September Wy *STAN* HA7 ....49 G1
Sequoia Cl *BUSH* WD23 ....43 H3
Sequoia Gdns *ORP* BR6 ....235 F4
Sequoia Pk *PIN* HA5 ....48 A5
Serbin Cl *WAN* E11 ....91 G4
Serjeant's Inn *EMB* * EC4Y 14 B4
Serle St *LINN* WC2A 13 H3
Sermon Dr *SWLY* BR8 ....217 G6
Sermon La *BLKFR* EC4V 14 E4
Serpentine Rd *BAY/PAD* W2 ....18 E2
Service Route No 1 *SRTFD* E15 ....111 H4
Service Route No 2 *SRTFD* E15 ....111 H4
Service Route No 3 *SRTFD* E15 ....111 H4
Serviden Dr *BMLY* BR1 ....213 F4
Setchell Rd *STHWK* SE1 ....32 C1
Setchell Wy *STHWK* SE1 ....32 C1
Seth St *STHWK* SE1 ....32 C1
Seton Gdns *DAGW* RM9 ....116 A5
Settles St *WCHPL* E1 ....17 F2
Settrington Rd *FUL/PGN* SW6 ....165 F3
Seven Acres *CAR* SM5 ....226 A6
  SWLY BR8 ....237 H3
Sevenex Pde *WBLY* * HA9 ....101 C3
Seven Kings Rd *GDMY/SEVK* IG3 ....95 E5
Sevenoaks Rd *BROCKY* SE4 ....190 D1
  ORP BR6 ....253 F2
Sevenoaks Wy
  STMC/STPC BR5 ....216 A5
Seven Sisters Rd *HOLWY* N7 ....107 H1
Seventh Av *MNPK* E12 ....113 H2
Severnake Cl *POP/IOD* E14 ....151 E4
Severn Av *NKENS* W10 ....108 C2
Severn Dr *EN* EN1 ....39 C1
  ESH/CLAY KT10 ....220 C6
  WOT/HER KT12 ....218 B6
Severn Wy *WLSDN* NW10 ....81 H4
Severus Rd *BTSEA* SW11 ....166 A5
Seville Ms *IS* N1 ....109 E5
Seville St *KTBR* SW1X 18 E4
Sevington Rd *HDN* NW4 ....83 H5
Sevington St *MV/WKIL* W9 ....125 F3
Seward Rd *BECK* BR3 ....210 B5
  HNWL W7 ....140 C2
Sewardstone Rd *BETH* E2 ....130 A1
  CHING E4 ....41 F5
Seward St *FSBYE* EC1V 7 C4
Sewdley St *CLPT* E5 ....110 B1
Sewell Rd *ABYW* SE2 ....155 G2
Sewell St *PLSTW* E13 ....132 C2
Sextant Av *POP/IOD* E14 ....151 H4
Seymer Rd *ROM* RM1 ....77 H6
Seymour Av *EW* KT17 ....241 H6
  MRDN SM4 ....224 B4
  TOTM N17 ....69 C2
Seymour Av *CAR* SM5 ....243 H6
  CEND/HSY/T N8 ....88 B2
  CHING E4 ....55 F3
  CHSWK W4 ....146 A4
  E/WMO/HCT KT8 ....219 G2
  ED N9 ....53 H4
  EHAM E6 ....113 F6
  FNCH N3 ....52 A5
  HPTN TW12 ....199 C1
  KUT KT1 ....201 F4
  LEY E10 ....90 D5
  MTCM CR4 ....226 C4
  WAND/EARL SW18 ....184 D2
  WIM/MER SW19 ....184 B5

Seymour St *BAY/PAD* W2 ....10 C4
  WOOL/PLUM SE18 ....154 C4
Seymour Ter *PGE/AN* SE20 ....209 H4
Seymour Vs *PGE/AN* SE20 ....209 H4
Seymour Wk *WBPTN* SW10 ....145 G6
Shaa Rd *ACT* W3 ....122 D6
Shacklands La *TEDD* TW11 ....180 A6
Shackleton Cl *FSTH* SE23 ....189 H4
Shackleton Rd *STHL* UB1 ....118 D6
Shackleton La *HACK* E8 ....109 F2
Shacklewell Rd
  STNW/STAM N16 ....109 F2
Shacklewell Rw *HACK* E8 ....109 F2
Shacklewell St *BETH* E2 ....9 K5
Shadbolt Cl *WPK* KT4 ....223 F6
Shad Thames *STHWK* SE1 ....24 C2
Shadwell Dr *NTHLT* UB5 ....118 D2
Shadwell Gdns *WCHPL* * E1 ....130 A6
Shadwell Pierhead *WAP* E1W 130 A6
Shady Bush Cl *BUSH* WD23 ....45 A3
Shaef Wy *TEDD* TW11 ....200 C3
Shakespeare Av *FBAR/BDGN* N11 ....67 C1
  KTN/HRWW/W HA3 ....81 F3
  WLSDN NW10 ....12 C5
  NWDGN UB2 ....139 E4
  PEND EN3 ....40 B3
  RYLN/HDSTN HA2 ....79 F5
Shakespeare Cir
  RYLN/HDSTN * HA2 ....79 G5
Shakespeare Gdns
  WLSDN NW10 ....123 E3
  KTN/HRWW/W HA3 ....81 H5
Shakespeare Pde
  RYLN/HDSTN * HA2 ....79 G5
Shakespeare Rd *ARCH* N19 ....87 G5
  BERM/RHTH SE16 ....35 K6
  CAR SM5 ....225 H4
  CHING E4 ....55 H3
  FSTGT E7 ....113 C1
  LEY * E10 ....91 E5
  LEY E10 ....91 E5
  RCH/KEW TW9 ....161 G4
  UED N18 ....54 D1
Shakespeare Sq *BARK/HLT* IG6 ....74 F3
Shakespeare Ter
  RCH/KEW * TW9 ....162 A4
Shakespeare Wy
  FELT TW13 ....178 A6
Shakspeare Ms
  STNW/STAM N16 ....109 E2
Shakspeare Wk
  STNW/STAM N16 ....109 E2
Shalcomb St *WBPTN* SW10 ....145 G6
Shaldon Dr *MRDN* SM4 ....224 A2
  RSLP HA4 ....98 A1
Shaldon Rd *EDGW* HA8 ....61 H5
Shalfleet Dr *NKENS* W10 ....124 B6
Shalford Cl *ORP* BR6 ....252 C2
Shalford Ct *IS* * N1 ....6 C1
Shalimar Gdns *ACT* W3 ....122 C6
Shalimar Rd *ACT* W3 ....122 C6
Shallons Rd *ELTH/MOT* SE9 ....194 B6
Shalstone Rd
  MORT/ESHN SW14 ....162 B4
Shalston Vs *SURB* KT6 ....221 H4
Shamrock Rd *CROY/NA* CRO 211 H4
Shamrock St *CLAP* SW4 ....167 F4
Shamrock Wy *STHGT/OAK* N14 ....50 B3
Shandon Rd *CLAP* SW4 ....187 E1
Shand St *STHWK* SE1 ....31 H1
Shandy St *WCHPL* E1 ....130 A4
Shanklin Gdns *OXHEY* WD19 ....42 A6
Shanklin Rd *CEND/HSY/T* N8 ....87 E2
  SEVS/STOTM N15 ....89 C1
Shannon Cl *CRICK* NW2 ....82 C6
  NWDGN UB2 ....138 B5
Shannon Gv *BRXN/ST* SW9 ....167 H5
Shannon Pl *STJWD* NW8 ....2 D1
Shannon Wy *BECK* BR3 ....211 F2
Shap Crs *CAR* SM5 ....210 B4
Shapland Wy *PLMGR* N13 ....51 D5
Shapwick Cl *FBAR/BDGN* N11 ....66 D1
Shardcroft Av *HNHL* SE24 ....168 B6
Shardeloes Rd *BROCKY* SE4 ....170 D3
Shard's Sq *PECK* SE15 ....33 K6
Sharland Cl *THHTH* CR7 ....228 A3
Sharman Ct *SCUP* DA14 ....195 G6
Sharnbrooke Cl *WELL* DA16 ....176 D1
Sharon Cl *SURB* KT6 ....220 D5
Sharon Gdns *HOM* E9 ....110 A6
Sharon Rd *CHSWK* W4 ....142 A5
  PEND EN3 ....40 B3
Sharples Hall St *CAMTN* NW1 ....106 D5
Sharratt St *PECK* SE15 ....144 C6
Sharsted St *WALW* SE17 ....30 C4
Shavers Pl *MYFR/PICC* W1J 12 C6
Shaw Av *BARK* IG11 ....136 C1
Shawbrooke Rd
  ELTH/MOT SE9 ....173 F5
Shawbury Rd *EDUL* SE22 ....169 F6
Shaw Cl *BUSH* WD23 ....44 A4
  THMD SE28 ....155 H1
Shaw Dr *WOT/HER* KT12 ....218 A4
Shawfield Pk *BMLY* BR1 ....213 F5
Shawfield St *CHEL* SW3 ....26 E8
Shawford Rd *HOR/WEW* KT19 ....240 B4

Shaw Gdns *BARK* IG11 ....136 C1
Shaw Rd *BMLY* BR1 ....192 B5
  EDUL SE22 ....169 E5
  PEND EN3 ....40 B2
Shaw's Cottages *FSTH* SE23 ....190 C1
Shaw Sq *WALTH* E17 ....57 C5
The Shaw *CHST* * BR7 ....214 C3
Shaw Wy *WLGTN* SM6 ....243 E6
Shaxton Crs *CROY/NA* CRO 249 G6
Sheaf Cottages *THDIT* * KT7 ....220 A5
Shearing Dr *MRDN* SM4 ....225 G4
Shearling Wy *HOLWY* N7 ....107 G4
Shearman Rd *BKHTH/KID* SE3 ....172 B5
Shearwater Rd *SUT* SM1 ....242 D3
Shearwater Wy *YEAD* UB4 ....118 B5
Sheaveshill Pde
  CDALE/KGS * NW9 ....83 E1
Sheen Common Dr
  RCHPK/HAM TW10 ....162 A5
Sheen Court Rd
  RCHPK/HAM TW10 ....162 A5
Sheendale Rd *RCH/KEW* TW9 ....161 H5
Sheenewood *SYD* SE26 ....209 H1
Sheen Gate Gdns
  MORT/ESHN SW14 ....162 C5
Sheen Gv *IS* N1 ....108 A6
Sheen La *MORT/ESHN* SW14 ....162 C5
Sheen Pk *RCH/KEW* TW9 ....161 G5
Sheen Rd *RCHPK/HAM* TW10 ....161 G5
  STMC/STPC BR5 ....235 F1
Sheen Wy *WLGTN* SM6 ....245 H3
Sheen Wd *MORT/ESHN* SW14 ....162 C2
Sheepcote La *BTSEA* SW11 ....166 B3
Sheepcote Rd *HRW* HA1 ....61 E3
  STMC/STPC BR5 ....235 F1
Sheepcote Rd *HRW* HA1 ....61 E3
Sheepcotes Rd *CHDH* RM6 ....96 B1
Sheephouse Grn *NWMAL* KT3 ....222 D5
Sheep La *HACK* E8 ....109 H6
Sheep Walk Ms
  WIM/MER SW19 ....204 B2
Sheerwater Rd *CAN/RD* E16 ....133 F4
Sheffield St *LINN* * WC2A 13 C4
Sheffield Ter *KENS* W8 ....14 C3
Sheila Rd *CRW* RM5 ....77 F3
Shelbourne Cl *PIN* HA5 ....58 D6
Shelbourne Rd *TOTM* N17 ....69 H4
Shelburne Rd *HSLWW* TW4 ....179 C4
Shelburne Rd *HOLWY* N7 ....107 H2
Shelbury Cl *SCUP* DA14 ....195 G6
Shelbury Rd *EDUL* SE22 ....169 H6
Sheldon Av *CLAY* IG5 ....72 D6
  HGT N6 ....86 B4
Sheldon Cl *LEE/GVPK* SE12 ....172 D6
  PGE/AN SE20 ....209 H4
Sheldon St *CROY/NA* CRO 246 C1
Sheldrake Cl *CAN/RD* E16 ....152 B1
Sheldrake Pl *KENS* W8 ....144 D2
Sheldrick Cl *MTCM* CR4 ....205 H5
Shelduck Cl *FSTGT* E7 ....112 B3
Sheldwich Ter *HAYES* * BR2 ....233 C5
Shelford Pl *STNW/STAM* N16 ....108 D1
Shelford Ri *NRWD* SE19 ....209 E3
Shelford Rd *BAR* EN5 ....48 A1
Shelgate Rd *BTSEA* SW11 ....166 D3
Shell Cl *HAYES* BR2 ....233 G5
Shellduck Cl *CDALE/KGS* NW9 ....63 C5
Shelley Av *GFD/PVL* UB6 ....119 H2
  MNPK E12 ....113 C4
Shelley Cl *EDGW* HA8 ....44 C6
  GFD/PVL UB6 ....119 H2
  ORP BR6 ....253 E1
Shelley Crs *HEST* TW5 ....158 B2
  STHL UB1 ....115 G6
Shelley Dr *WELL* DA16 ....175 E2
Shelley Gdns *ALP/SUD* HA0 ....81 G6
Shelley Rd *WLSDN* NW10 ....102 B6
Shelley Wy *TOOT* SW17 ....205 H2
Shellgrove Rd
  STNW/STAM * N16 ....109 E3
Shellness Rd *CLPT* E5 ....109 H5
Shell Rd *LEW* SE13 ....171 F5
Shellwood Rd *BTSEA* SW11 ....166 B5
Shelmerdine Cl *BOW* E3 ....131 E4
Shelton Rd *WIM/MER* SW19 ....205 H4
Shelton St *LSQ/SEVD* * WC2H 13 E4
Shenfield Rd *WFD* IG8 ....72 D3
Shenley Rd *CMBW* SE5 ....169 E2
  HEST TW5 ....158 C2
Shepherdess Pl *FSBYE* EC1V 7 F3
Shepherdess Wk *IS* N1 ....7 F1
Shepherd Market
  MYFR/PICC * W1J 19 G2
Shepherd's Bush Gn *SHB* W12 ....144 A2
Shepherd's Bush Market
  SHB W12 ....144 A2
Shepherd's Bush Pl *SHB* * W12 ....144 B2
Shepherd's Bush Rd
  HMSMTH W6 ....144 A3
Shepherds Cl *CHDH* RM6 ....96 B2
  HGT N6 ....86 B3
  ORP BR6 ....253 H5
Shepherds Gn *CHST* BR7 ....214 D3
Shepherd's Hl *HGT* N6 ....86 B5
Shepherds La *HOM* * E9 ....110 B3
Shepherd's Leas
  ELTH/MOT * SE9 ....174 D5
Shepherds Pl *MYFR/PKLN* W1K 11 E5
Shepherds Wk *BUSH* WD23 ....45 H4
  CRICK NW2 ....83 G6
  HAMP NW3 ....105 H3
Shepherds Wy *SAND/SEL* CR2 ....248 B5
Shepley Cl *CAR* SM5 ....244 C1
Shepley Ms *PEND* EN3 ....41 H1
Sheppard Cl *EN* EN1 ....23 H1
  SURB KT6 ....221 G1
Sheppard Dr *BERM/RHTH* SE16 ....35 G5
Sheppard St *CAN/RD* E16 ....132 B3
Shepperton Rd *IS* N1 ....108 D6
  STMC/STPC BR5 ....234 C1
Sheppey Gdns *DAGW* RM9 ....116 A5
Sheppey Rd *DAGW* RM9 ....115 H5
Sheppey Wk *IS* * N1 ....108 C5
Shepton Houses *BETH* * E2 ....130 A2

Sherard Rd ELTH/MOT SE9....175 G6
Sherborne Av NWDGN UB2...139 E4
  PEND EN3 ....40 A3
Sherborne Cl YEAD UB4.......118 A5
Sherborne Crs CAR SM5........226 A4
Sherborne Gdns
  CDALE/KGS NW9...............62 A6
  WEA W13.........................120 D5
Sherborne La MANHO EC4N.....15 C5
Sherborne Rd CHEAM SM3......225 E6
  CHSGTN KT9....................239 G3
  STMC/STPC BR5................235 F2
Sherborne St IS N1..............108 D1
Sherborne Vis WBXA * W13 ....120 D4
Sherboro Rd SEVS/STOTM N15...89 F3
Sherbrooke Cl ESH/CLAY KT10..221 E5
Sherbrooke Rd FUL/PGN SW6..164 C1
Sherbrooke Ter
  FUL/PGN * SW6................164 C1
Sherbrook Gdns WCHMH N21...52 B2
Sherburne Cl CHSGTN KT9.....239 F3
Shere CI CHSGTN KT9..........71 H1
Shere Rd GNTH/NBYPK IG2.....94 A2
Sherfield Cl KUT KT1..........222 B1
Sherfield Gdns PUT/ROE SW15..183 F1
Sheridan Cl HSLWW TW4.......158 C6
Sheridan Crs CHST BR7........214 B5
Sheridan Gdns
  KTN/HRWW/W HA3.............81 F3
Sheridan Pl HPTN TW12.......199 F4
Sheridan Rd BELV DA17.......157 E4
  BXLYHN DA7....................176 C4
  FSTGT E7........................112 B1
  MNPK E12.......................113 G3
  OXHEY WD19.....................42 B2
  RCHPK/HAM TW10..............181 G5
  WIM/MER SW19..................204 D4
Sheridan St WCHPL * E1........17 H4
Sheridan Ter NTHLT * UB5......84 B5
Sheridan Wk CAR SM5.........244 B3
  GLDGN NW11.....................85 E3
Sheridan Wy BECK BR3.........210 D4
Sheringham Av MNPK E12......113 H2
  ROMW/RG RM7....................97 G3
  STHGT/OAK N14.................37 F6
  WHTN TW2.......................178 D3
Sheringham Dr BARK IG11.....115 F3
Sheringham Rd HOLWY N7....108 A4
  PGE/AN SE20.....................209 H5
Sherington Av PIN HA5.........59 G3
Sherington Rd CHARL SE7.....152 D6
Sherland Rd TWK TW1..........180 B3
Sherlies Av ORP BR6............235 E6
Sherlock Ms MHST W1U.........11 E1
Sherman Rd BMLY BR1.........212 C4
Shernhall St LEY E10............91 G2
Sherrard Rd FSTGT E7..........113 E4
Sherrards Wy BAR EN5..........35 E6
Sherrick Green Rd
  WLSDN NW10....................103 H3
Sherriff Rd KIL/WHAMP NW6..105 E4
Sherringham Av TOTM N17.....69 C5
Sherrock Gdns HDN NW4.......63 E1
Sherry Ms BARK IG11..........114 D5
Sherwin Rd NWCR SE14........170 B2
Sherwood SURB KT6............221 F6
Sherwood Av CFD/PVL UB6...100 A4
  STRHM/NOR SW16...............195 G2
  SWFD E18........................72 D6
Sherwood Cl BXLY DA5.........196 A1
  WEA W13.........................140 D1
Sherwood Ct MBLAR W1H......10 U2
Sherwood Gdns BARK IG11....114 D5
  BERM/RHTH SE16...............151 E4
  POP/IOD E14....................151 E4

CROY/NA CRO....................230 A5
SUT SM1..........................244 A2
Shirley Church Rd
  CROY/NA CRO....................248 B1
Shirley Cl HSLW TW5...........159 G6
  WALTH * E17......................91 F2
Shirley Crs BECK BR3...........230 C1
Shirley Dr HSLW TW3...........159 G6
Shirley Gdns BARK IG11........115 E4
  HNWL W7.........................140 B1
Shirley Gv BTSEA SW11........149 F2
  ED N9.............................54 A2
Shirley Hills Rd CROY/NA CRO...248 B5
Shirley Oaks Rd CROY/NA CRO..230 D1
Shirley Park Rd CROY/NA CRO..229 H5
Shirley Rd BFN/LL DA15.......195 E5
  CHSWK W4.......................142 D2
  CROY/NA CRO....................229 H5
  ENC/FH EN2.....................38 C4
  SRTFD E15.......................112 A5
  WLGTN SM6......................245 E6
Shirley Wy SNWD * SE25.......209 G5
Shirley St CAN/RD E16.........132 R5
Shirley Wy CROY/NA CRO.....248 D1
Shirlock Rd HAMP NW3.........106 B2
Shobden Rd TOTM N17...........68 B4
Shobroke Cl CRICK NW2.......104 A1
Shoebury Rd EHAM E6..........113 H5
Shoe La FLST/FETLN EC4A......14 B3
Sholden Gdns STMC/STPC BR5..236 A2
Shooters Av KTN/HRWW/W HA3..81 E1
Shooters Hill WOOL/PLUM SE18..175 H2
Shooters Hill Rd
  BKHTH/KID SE3.................172 A2
Shooters Rd ENC/FH EN2........38 A1
Shoot-Up Hl CRICK NW2.......104 C4
Shore Cl HPTN TW12............198 C1
Shoreditch High St WCHPL E1..16 B1
Shore Gv FELT TW13............179 E4
Shoreham Cl CROY/NA CRO....230 A3
  WAND/EARL SW18................165 F6
Shoreham Rd STMC/STPC BR5..215 H4
Shoreham Wy HAYES BR2.......232 C5
Shore PI HOM E9................110 D4
Shore Rd HOM E9................110 A5
Shornclife Rd CMBW SE5........53 C4
Shorndean St CAT SE6..........191 G3
Shorne Cl BFN/LL DA15........195 H1
  STMC/STPC BR5.................236 B1
Shornefield Cl BMLY BR1.......214 B1
Shornolds Rd FUL/PGN SW6...165 E1
Shortcroft Rd EW KT17.........241 F5
Shorter St WCHPL E1............16 B1
Shortgate NFNCH/WDSP N12....48 B4
Shortlands HMSMTH W6.......148 B4
Shortlands Cl BELV DA17......156 D5
  UED N18........................52 D5
Shortlands Gdns HAYES BR2..212 A5
Shortlands Gv HAYES BR2.....211 H6
Shortlands Rd HAYES BR2.....211 H6
  KUTN/CMB KT2..................201 H5
  LEY E10..........................69 J4
Short Rd CHSWK W4............148 A5
  WAN E11..........................92 A6
Shorts Cft CDALE/KGS NW9.....62 B1
Shorts Gdns LSQ/SEVD * WC2H..13 E4
Shorts Rd CAR SM5.............222 D6
Short St STHWK SE1.............22 B3
Shortway CLTH/MOT SE9 *.....173 G4
Short Wy NFNCH/WDSP N12...46 A2
  WHTN * TW2.....................179 G2
Shottfield WLGTN SM6.........244 D4
Shotts Cl SUT SM1..............243 G5
Shottenden Rd
  FUL/PGN * SW6.................165 E2
Shottery Ct ELTH/MOT SE9.....193 E5
Shottfield Av
  MORT/ESHN SW14...............163 E5
Shoulder of Mutton Aly
  POP/IOD E14....................130 C6
Shouldham St MBLAR W1H.....10 B2
Shrapnel Cl WOOL/PLUM SE18..173 C1
Shrapnel Rd ELTH/MOT SE9...173 H4
Shrewsbury Av
  KTN/HRWW/W HA3.............81 G1
  MORT/ESHN SW14...............162 C5
Shrewsbury Cl SURB KT6......221 G6
Shrewsbury Crs WLSDN NW10..102 D6
Shrewsbury La
  WOOL/PLUM SE18...............174 B2
Shrewsbury Ms BAY/PAD W2..125 E5
Shrewsbury Rd BAY/PAD W2...125 E5
  BECK BR3.......................210 C6
  CAR SM5.........................226 A4
  FBAR/BDGN N11.................48 A2
  FSTGT E7........................113 E4
Shrewsbury St NKENS W10....118 A3
Shrewton Rd TOOT * SW17....206 D6
Shroffold Rd BMLY BR1.........192 A6
Shropshire Cl MTCM CR4.......207 G1
Shropshire Rd WDGN N22......67 H1
Shroton St CAMTN NW1...........9 A1
The Shrubberies CHIC IG7.......74 C1
  SWFD E18.........................72 C5
Shrubbery Gdns WCHMH N21...52 B2
Shrubbery Rd STHL UB1..........14 D5
  STRHM/NOR SW16...............187 G6
The Shrubbery SURB * KT6.....221 J5
Shrubland Cl
  TRDC/WHET * N20..............49 H4
Shrubland Gv WPK KT4.........242 A1
Shrubland Rd HACK E8..........109 G6
  LEY E10...........................91 E2
  WALTH E17.......................89 G4
Shrublands Av CROY/NA CRO..249 E2
Shrublands Cl CHIG IG7.........74 C2
  SYD SE26........................190 A5
Shrubsall Cl ELTH/MOT SE9...190 D6
Shuna Wk IS * N1...............109 D4
Shurland Av EBAR EN4..........49 H1
Shurland Gdns PECK * SE15....169 F6
Shurlock Av SWLY BR8..........217 H5
Shurlock Dr ORP BR6...........252 D5
Shuters Sq WKENS * W14.......144 D5
Shuttle Cl BFN/LL DA15........195 F1
Shuttlemead BXLY DA5.........196 D2
Shuttle St WCHPL E1............19 H4
Shuttleworth Rd BTSEA SW11..165 H3
Sibella Rd CLAP SW4............167 F3
Sibley Cl BXLYHS DA6..........176 D6
Sibley Gv MNPK E12............113 G5

Sibthorp Rd MTCM * CR4......206 B5
Sibton Rd CAR SM5.............226 A4
Sicilian Av NOXST/BSO * WC1A..13 F2
Sicilian Av NOXST/BSO WC1A..13 F2
Sidbury St FUL/PGN SW6......164 C2
Sidcup By-Pass Rd SCUP DA14..195 E6
Sidcup Hl SCUP DA14...........215 H1
Sidcup Hill Gdns SCUP * DA14..216 A1
Sidcup Pl SCUP DA14...........215 G1
Sidcup Rd ELTH/MOT SE9.......193 G3
  LEE/GVPK SE12...................172 D6
Siddeley Dr HSLWW TW4.........18 D6
Siddons La CAMTN NW1...........2 D6
Siddons Rd CROY/NA CRO......246 A1
  FSTH SE23.......................190 C4
  TOTM N17........................69 G4
Side Rd WALTH E17...............89 G2
Sidewood Rd ELTH/MOT SE9..194 D3
Sidford Pl STHWK SE1..........21 H6
The Sidings LOU IG10...........57 G1
  WAN E11..........................91 G5
Sidmouth Av ISLW TW7.........160 A5
Sidmouth Pde CRICK * NW2...104 A5
Sidmouth Rd LEY E10...........111 G1
  PECK SE15.......................169 F2
  STMC/STPC BR5.................235 H2
  WELL DA16.......................176 A1
  WLSDN NW10....................104 A5
Sidmouth St STPAN WC1H......5 H4
Sidney Av PLMGR N13...........67 H1
Sidney Elson Wy EHAM E6.....134 A1
Sidney Gdns BTFD TW8.........141 F6
Sidney Gv FSBYE EC1V............6 C1
Sidney Rd BECK BR3............210 C5
  BRXN/ST SW9...................167 H3
  FSTGT E7........................112 C1
  RYLN/HDSTN HA2................59 G6
  SNWD SE25......................197 F3
  TWK TW1.........................180 C1
  WALTH E17.......................89 G4
  WOT/HER KT12..................188 A5
Sidney Sq WCHPL * E1..........130 A4
Sidney St WCHPL E1.............130 A4
Sidworth St HACK E8............109 H5
Siebert Rd BKHTH/KID SE3....152 C6
Siemens Rd WOOL/PLUM SE18..153 F3
Sienna Ter CRICK * NW2.........63 G4
Sierra Dr DAGW NW9...........137 F1
Sigdon Rd HACK E8..............109 G3
Signmakers Yd CAMTN * NW1..106 D6
Sigrist Sq KUTN/CMB KT2.....201 G4
Silbury Av MTCM CR4...........206 A4
Silbury St IS * N1.................7 G2
Silchester Rd NKENS W10......124 B5
Silecroft Rd BXLYHN DA7......177 E2
Silesia Buildings HACK E8......109 E6
Silex St STHWK SE1..............22 D4
Silk Cl LEE/GVPK SE12.........172 C6
Silkfield Rd CDALE/KGS NW9...83 E2
Silk Mills Pth LEW SE13........171 G4
Silkstream Pde EDGW * HA8....62 C4
Silkstream Rd EDGW HA8.......62 C4
Silk St BARB EC2Y...............15 F1
Silsoe Rd WDGN N22.............91 C5
Silver Birch Av CHING E4........51 G1
Silver Birch Cl FBAR/BDGN N11..66 C2
  THMD SE28.......................155 C1
Silver Birch Ms BARK/HLT IG6...54 B4
Silverbirch Wk HAMP * NW3..106 B4
Silvercliffe Gdns EBAR EN4......36 A5
Silver Cl KTN/HRWW/W HA3....59 H3
Silverdale WLTGN * NW7........30 C5
  NWCR * SE14...................151 G1
Silver Crs CHSWK W4...........142 B4
Silverdale CAMTN NW1............4 B2
  ENC/FH EN2.....................37 G5
  SYD SE26........................190 A6
Silverdale Cl HNWL W7.........116 A1
  NTHLT UB5......................63 J3
  SUT SM1.........................242 D2
Silverdale Dr ELTH/MOT SE9..193 G4
Silverdale Rd BXLYHN DA7....177 H2
  CHING E4.........................51 H1
  STMC/STPC BR5.................215 G6
Silverdene NFNCH/WDSP * N12..65 E5
Silver Dene PUT/ROE * SW15..164 A6
Silverhall St ISLW TW7.........160 C4
Silverholme Cl
  KTN/HRWW/W HA3.............81 G4
Silver La WWKM BR4...........231 H6
Silverleigh Rd THHTH CR7.....207 G4
Silvermere Av CRW RM5.........57 F2
Silvermere Rd LEW SE13.......191 E1
Silvermere Rw SNWD * SE25..209 G5
Silver Rd SHB W12...............124 B6
Silver Spring Cl ERITH DA8...157 F6
Silverston Wy STAN HA7..........61 G2
Silver St ENC/FH EN2............38 D4
  UED N18..........................52 A1
Silverthorne Rd VX/NE SW8...166 D3
Silverthorn Gdns CHING E4....55 C4
Silverton Rd HMSMTH W6......164 B1
Silvertown Wy CAN/RD E16...130 B6
Silvertree La CFD/PVL UB6....119 H2
Silver Wk BERM/RHTH SE16...133 J6
Silver Wy ROMW/RG RM7........77 F6
Silverwood Cl BECK BR3......211 E3
  CROY/NA CRO....................248 D6
Silvester Rd EDUL SE22........169 F6
Silvester St STHWK SE1.........23 G4
Silwood St BERM/RHTH SE16..169 J5
Simmil Rd ESH/CLAY KT10.....238 A3
Simmons Cl TRDC/WHET N20...47 H6
Simmons La CHING E4............55 H1
Simmons Rd
  WOOL/PLUM SE18...............154 D5
Simms Cl CAR SM5...............226 A6
Simms Gdns EFNCH N2..........65 G5
Simms Rd BERM/RHTH SE16...19 K8
Simnel Rd LEE/GVPK SE12....192 D2
Simon Cl NTGHL W11..........124 D6
Simonds Rd LEY E10............91 E6
Simone Cl BMLY BR1............213 H4
Simons Wk SRTFD E15..........115 J4
Simpson Cl WCHMH N21........37 H1
Simpson Dr ACT W3.............122 D5
Simpson Rd HSLWW TW4......178 E1
  RCHPK/HAM TW10..............181 E6
Simpson's Rd HAYES BR2......212 C6
  POP/IOD E14....................131 F6
Simpson St BTSEA SW11.......166 A3
Simpson Wy SURB KT6.........221 E3

Sinclair Dr BELMT SM2.........243 F6
Sinclair Gdns WKENS W14.....144 B2
Sinclair Gv GLDGN NW11........84 B3
Sinclair Rd CHING E4.............70 D1
  WKENS W14......................144 B3
Sinclare Cl EN EN1...............39 F2
Singapore Rd HNWL W7........140 C1
Singer St FSBYE EC1V..............7 H4
Singleton Cl CROY/NA CRO...228 C4
  WIM/MER SW19..................206 B3
Singleton Scarp
  NFNCH/WDSP N12...............65 E1
Sinnott Rd WALTH E17...........70 B4
Sion Rd TWK TW1................180 D3
Sir Abraham Dawes Cottages
  PUT/ROE * SW15................164 C5
Sir Alexander Cl ACT W3.......143 F1
Sir Cyril Black Wy
  WIM/MER SW19..................204 D3
Sir Nicholas Garrow
  NTGHL W11.....................124 B6
  WDGN N22.......................68 B6
Sir Thomas Moore Est
  CHEL SW3.......................145 H6
Sispara Gdns
  WAND/EARL SW18................184 D1
Sissinghurst Rd CROY/NA CRO..230 D4
Sister Mabel's Wy PECK * SE15..169 G1
Sisters Av BTSEA SW11.........166 B5
Sistova Rd BAL SW12...........186 D3
Sisulu Pl BRXN/ST SW9..........168 A3
Sittingbourne Av WCHMH N21...52 C1
Sitwell Gv STAN HA7............60 B1
Siverst Cl NTHLT UB5...........99 F4
Siviter Wy DAGE RM10..........117 F5
Siward Rd HAYES BR2..........212 D6
  TOOT SW17.....................185 C5
  TOTM N17........................68 D4
Six Acres Est HBRY N5..........108 E1
Six Bridges Trd Est STHWK SE1..19 H2
Sixth Av HYS/HAR UB3.........94 C6
  MNPK E12.......................113 H2
  NKENS W10.....................118 C3
Sixth Cross Rd WHTN TW2....179 G5
Skardu Rd CRICK NW2..........104 C3
Skeena Hl WIM/MER SW19....184 C2
Skelbrook St WAND/EARL SW18..184 B2
Skelgill Rd PUT/ROE SW15...164 D5
Skelley Rd SRTFD E15..........112 B5
Skelton Cl HACK * E8...........109 F4
Skelton Rd FSTGT E7...........112 C4
Skelton's La LEY E10............91 G4
Skelwith Rd HMSMTH W6.....144 A6
Skerne Rd KUTN/CMB KT2....201 F4
Sketchley Gdns
  BERM/RHTH SE16...............150 B5
Sketty Rd EN EN1.................39 F4
Skiers St SRTFD E15............112 A6
Skiffington Cl
  BRXS/STRHM SW2..............188 A3
Skinner Pl BGVA * SW1W.......17 F2
Skinners La BLKFR EC4V.........15 F5
  HEST TW5.......................159 J2
Skinner St CLKNW EC1R...........6 B4
Skipsey Av EHAM E6............133 H2
Skipton Cl FBAR/BDGN N11....66 C2
Skipworth Rd HOM E9..........110 A6
Skylines Village POP/IOD * E14..151 C2
Sky Peaks Rd WFD IG8..........71 H3
Sladebrook Rd BKHTH/KID SE3..173 H4
Sladedale Rd
  WOOL/PLUM SE18...............154 A1
Sladen Pl CLPT E5................109 H2
Slades Cl ENC/FH EN2............38 A4
Slades Dr CHST BR7............194 D4
Slades Gdns ENC/FH EN2.......38 A4
Slades Hill ENC/FH EN2.........38 A4
Slades Ri ENC/FH EN2...........38 A4
The Slade WOOL/PLUM SE18..156 E6
Slade Wk WALW SE17............30 D6
Slagrove Pl BROCKY SE4......171 E6
Slaidburn St WBPTN SW10...145 G6
Slaithwaite Rd LEW SE13.....171 G3
Slaney Pl HOLWY N7............108 A3
Slattery Rd FELT TW13.........178 A3
Sleaford Gn OXHEY WD19......42 B5
Sleaford St VX/NE SW8.........167 E1
Slievemore Cl CLAP SW4.......167 E4
Slingsby Pl COVGDN WC2E.....13 E5
Slippers Pl BERM/RHTH SE16..151 H5
Sloane Av CHEL SW3..............26 B2
Sloane Ct East CHEL SW3.......27 E3
Sloane Ct West CHEL SW3.......27 F3
Sloane Gdns BGVA SW1W.......252 C1
  ORP BR6.........................252 C1
Sloane Sq BGVA SW1W...........26 D2
Sloane St KTBR SW1X.............16 E6
Sloane Ter KTBR SW1X...........26 D1
Sloane Wk CROY/NA CRO.......230 D3
Slocum Cl THMD SE28..........136 A6
Slough La CDALE/KGS NW9.....82 C2
Sly St WCHPL * E1...............17 G4
Smaggs Wy BOW E3.............129 H5
Smallberry Av ISLW TW7......160 B3
Smallbrook Ms BAY/PAD W2...125 H5
Smalley Cl STNW/STAM N16...109 F1
Smallwood Rd TOOT SW17....185 H6
Smarden Cl BELV DA17.........157 F5
Smart's Pl HHOL WC1V.........13 F3
  UED N18.........................69 G1
Smart St BETH E2.................91 E2
Smeaton Rd WAND/EARL SW18..185 E2
  WFD IG8.........................55 J3
Smeaton St WAP E1W.............25 G2
Smedley St VX/NE SW8..........167 F3
Smeed Rd BOW E3...............111 E5
Smiles Pl LEW SE13.............171 J3
Smith Cl BERM/RHTH SE16...150 B1
Smithfield St STBT EC1A.........14 C2
Smithies Rd ABYW SE2.........155 H4
Smith's Ct SOHO/SHAV * W1D..12 C5
Smithson Rd TOTM N17.........67 H3
Smith St BRYLDS KT5............221 H3
  CHEL SW3.......................26 D4
Smith Ter CHEL SW3............26 D4
Smithwood Cl WIM/MER SW19..184 C4
Smithy St WCHPL E1............130 A4
Smugglers Wy
  WAND/EARL SW18...............165 F5

Smyrk's Rd WALW SE17 ....32 B4
WALW * SE17 ....32 B4
Smyrna Rd KIL/WHAMP NW6 ...105 E5
Smythe St POP/IOD E14 ......131 F6
Snakes La EBAR EN4 ....38 C4
Snakes La East WFD IG8 ......73 E2
Snakes La West WFD IG8 ......72 C2
Snaresbrook Dr STAN HA7 .....45 F6
Snaresbrook Rd WAN E11 ......92 A1
Snarsgate St NKENS W10 .....128 A4
Sneath Av GLDGN NW11 ....84 D4
Snell's Pk UED N18 ....69 F2
Snewdy Rd CRICK NW2 ....104 A3
Snowbury Rd FUL/PGN SW6 ...165 F3
Snowden Dr CDALE/KGS NW9 ...83 E3
Snowden St SDTCH EC2A 8 A6
Snowdon Cl PGE/AN SE20 ....210 A4
Snowdrop Cl HPTN TW12 .....199 E2
Snow Hill STBT EC1A 14 C2
Snowsfields STHWK SE1 ....23 H5
Snowshill Rd MNPK E12 .....113 G3
Snowy Fielder Waye ISLW TW7 .160 D3
Soames St PECK SE15 ....169 F4
Soames Wk NWMAL KT3 ....203 E4
Soho Sq SOHO/SHAV W1D 12 C3
Soho St SOHO/SHAV W1D 12 C3
Sojourner Truth Cl HACK * E8 .109 H4
Solander Gdns WCHPL E1 ......17 H5
Solebay St WCHPL E1 ....130 C3
Solent Ri PLSTW E13 ....132 C2
Solent Rd KIL/WHAMP NW6 ...105 E3
Soina Av PUT/ROE SW15 .....164 A6
Soina Rd WCHMH N21 ....52 D3
Solomon Av UED N18 ....69 F2
Solomon's Pas PECK SE15 ...169 H5
Solon New Rd CLAP SW4 .....167 G5
Solon Rd CLAP SW4 ....167 G5
Solway Cl HACK E8 ....109 F4
HSLWW TW4 ....134 C5
Solway Rd EDUL SE22 ....169 G5
WDGN N22 ....68 B4
Somaford Gv EBAR EN4 ....49 H1
Somali Rd CRICK NW2 ....104 D2
Somerby Rd BARK IG11 ......114 D5
Somercoates Cl EBAR EN4 ....36 A4
Somerden Rd STMC/STPC BR5 .236 B4
Somerfield Rd FSBYPK N4 ....86 B6
Somerford Gv
STNW/STAM N16 ....109 F2
TOTM N17 ....69 G5
Somerford St WCHPL * E1 .....9 C4
Somerford Wy
BERM/RHTH SE16 ....150 C2
Somerhill Av BFN/LL DA15 ..195 H2
Somerhill Rd WELL DA16 ....175 H3
Somerleyton Rd BRXN/ST SW9 .168 A3
Somersby Gdns REDBR IG4 ....59 H2
Somers Cl CAMTN * NW1 ....4 C1
Somerset Av CHSGTN KT9 ....239 F2
RYNPK SW20 ....203 H5
WELL DA16 ....175 F6
Somerset Gdns HGT N6 ....86 C4
LEW SE13 ....171 F3
STRHM/NOR SW16 ....207 H1
TEDD TW11 ....200 A1
TOTM * N17 ....69 E3
WFD IG8 ....72 C4
Somerset Rd BAR EN5 ....35 F6
BTFD TW8 ....141 E6
CHSWK W4 ....142 D3
HDN NW4 ....84 A1
HRW HA1 ....79 G3
KUT KT1 ....201 H5
ORP BR6 ....235 G4
PEND EN3 ....41 E1
STHL UB1 ....119 E4
TEDD TW11 ....200 A1
TOTM N17 ....69 F1
UED N18 ....69 F1
WALTH E17 ....91 E2
WEA W13 ....140 D1
WIM/MER SW19 ....184 B5
Somerset Sq WKENS * W14 ...144 C3
Somerset St Little TWRH EC3N .16 C4
Somersham Rd BXLYHN DA7 ...176 C3
Somers Pl BRXS/STRHM SW2 ..187 H2
Somers Rd BRXS/STRHM SW2 ..187 H1
WALTH E17 ....90 D1
Somers Wy BUSH WD23 ....48 G2
Somerton Av RCH/KEW TW9 ...162 B4
Somerton Rd CRICK NW2 .....104 B1
PECK SE15 ....169 H5
Somertrees Av LEE/GVPK SE12 .192 D4
Somervell Rd RYLN/HDSTN HA2 .98 D3
Somerville Av BARN SW13 ...146 A6
Somerville Rd CHDH RM6 .....96 A2
PGE/AN SE20 ....210 B3
Sonderburg Rd HOLWY N7 .....87 H6
Sondes St WALW SE17 ....31 G5
Sonia Cl OXHEY WD19 ....42 A2
Sonia Gdns CRICK NW2 ......103 F2
HEST TW5 ....135 E1
NFNCH/WDSP N12 ....48 G6
Sonning Gdns HPTN TW12 ....198 C2
Sonning Rd CROY/NA CR0 ....229 C3
Soper Cl CHING E4 ....55 D1
FSTH SE23 ....190 B3
Soper Ms PEND * EN3 ....41 E1
PEND EN3 ....41 E1
Sophia Cl HOLWY N7 ....107 H4
Sophia Rd CAN/RD E16 ......132 D5
LEY E10 ....91 F5
Sophia Sq BERM/RHTH SE16 ..130 C1
Sopwith Av CHSGTN KT9 .....239 G5
Sopwith Cl KUTN/CMB KT2 ...201 H1
Sopwith Rd HEST TW5 ....135 E1
Sopwith Wy KUTN/CMB KT2 ...201 G4
VX/NE SW8 ....166 D2
Sorrel Bank CROY/NA CR0 ...248 C6
Sorrel Cl THMD SE28 ....155 G1
Sorrel Gdns EHAM E6 ....133 G4
Sorrel La POP/IOD E14 .....131 H5
Sorrel Cl BRXN/ST * SW9 ...168 A3
NWCR SE14 ....170 C1
Sorrento Rd SUT SM1 ....243 F1
Sotheby Rd HBRY N5 ....108 A3
Sotheran Cl HACK E8 ....109 G6

Soudan Rd BTSEA SW11 ......166 B2
Souldern Rd WKENS * W14 ...144 B3
Sounds Lodge SWLY BR8 .....237 G5
South Access Rd WALTH E17 ..90 C4
South Acre CDALE/KGS NW9 ...65 F5
Southacre Wy PIN HA5 ....58 A4
South Africa Rd SHB W12 ...125 H6
Southall Ct STHL * UB1 ....118 D6
Southall Pl STHWK SE1 ......23 G4
Southampton Buildings
LINN * WC2A 14 A2
Southampton Gdns
MTCM CR4 ....227 G2
Southampton Pl
NOXST/BSQ WC1A 13 F2
Southampton Rd HAMP NW3 ...106 B3
Southampton Rw RSQ WC1B 13 F1
Southampton St COVGDN WC2E .13 F5
Southampton Wy CMBW SE5 ...128 E7
Southam St NKENS W10 ......124 C3
South Audley St
MYFR/PKLN W1K 11 H1
South Av CAR SM5 ....244 C5
CHING E4 ....55 F2
RCH/KEW * TW9 ....162 A3
STHL UB1 ....118 D6
South Avenue Gdns STHL UB1 .118 D6
South Bank STHWK SE1 ....14 B6
SURB KT6 ....221 G3
Southbank THDIT KT7 ....220 D4
South Bank Ter SURB * KT6 ..221 G5
South Birkbeck Rd WAN E11 .111 H1
South Black Lion La
HMSMTH W6 ....146 D4
South Bolton Gdns
WBPTN SW10 ....145 F1
Southborough Cl SURB KT6 ..221 F5
Southborough La HAYES BR2 .233 H2
Southborough Rd BMLY BR1 ..213 G6
HOM E9 ....110 A6
SURB KT6 ....221 G5
Southborough Rd (The Lane)
SURB * KT6 ....221 G5
Southbourne HAYES BR2 .....232 C4
Southbourne Av
CDALE/KGS NW9 ....62 C5
Southbourne Cl PIN HA5 .....78 C4
Southbourne Crs HDN NW4 ....84 C1
Southbourne Gdns IL IG1 ...114 C3
LEE/GVPK SE12 ....172 D6
Southbridge Pl CROY/NA CR0 .246 C2
Southbridge Rd CROY/NA CR0 .246 C2
Southbridge Wy NWDGN UB2 ..138 C2
Southbrook Rd LEW SE13 ....192 A1
STRHM/NOR SW16 ....207 G4
Southbury Av EN EN1 ....39 G5
Southbury Rd EN EN1 ....39 H5
South Carriage Dr KTBR SW1X .18 D3
SKENS SW7 ....18 A4
Southchurch Rd EHAM E6 ....135 H1
South Cl BAR EN5 ....34 D4
BXLYHS DA6 ....176 B5
DAGE RM10 ....117 F6
FELT TW13 ....179 E5
HGT N6 ....86 D3
PIN HA5 ....78 B4
South Colonnade
POP/IOD E14 ....151 E1
Southcombe St WKENS W14 ...144 C4
Southcote Av BRYLDS KT5 ...222 B4
Southcote Rd ARCH N19 .....107 C2
SNWD SE25 ....245 H5
WALTH E17 ....89 G2
South Countess Rd WALTH E17 .70 D6
South Crs CAN/RD E16 ......131 H3
Southcroft Av WELL DA16 ...175 E4
WWKM BR4 ....231 G6
Southcroft Rd ORP BR6 .....253 E1
STRHM/NOR SW16 ....206 D2
South Croxted Rd DUL SE21 .188 D5
Southdale CHIG IG7 ....74 D2
Southdean Gdns
WIM/MER SW19 ....184 D4
South Dene MLHL NW7 ....46 D5
Southdown Av HNWL W7 ......140 C3
Southdown Crs
KTN/HRWW/WS HA3 ....61 H2
RYLN/HDSTN HA2 ....79 F5
Southdown Dr RYNPK SW20 ...204 B3
Southdown Rd CAR SM5 .....244 C6
RYNPK SW20 ....204 B4
Southdown Vis
SEVS/STHTM * N15 ....88 B2
South Dr ORP BR6 ....253 E5
South Ealing Rd EA W5 ....141 F2
South Eastern Av ED N9 .....53 F5
South Eaton Pl BGVA SW1W ...21 F7
South Eden Park Rd BECK BR3 .211 F5
South Edwardes Sq KENS W8 .144 D3
Southend Cl ELTH/MOT SE9 ..194 D6
Southend Crs ELTH/MOT SE9 .194 A1
Southend La CAT SE6 ....191 G6
Southend Rd BECK BR3 .....211 E4
South End Rd HAMP NW3 ....106 A2
South End Rd REDBR IG4 .....73 G6
Southend Rd (North Circular)
WALTH E17 ....71 H4
South End Rw KENS W8 .....145 F3
Southern Av WDGN SE25 ....209 F6
Southern Down FELT * TW13 .178 A3
Southern Dr LOU IG10 ....57 H1
Southengate Wy NWCR SE14 ..170 C1
Southern Gv BOW E3 ....130 D2
Southern Pl SWLY BR8 .....237 H1
Southern Rd EFNCH N2 ......86 B1
PLSTW E13 ....132 D1
Southern St IS N1 ....5 C1
Southerton Rd HMSMTH * W6 .144 E4
South Esk Rd FSTGT E7 ....113 E4
Southey Rd BRXN/ST SW9 ...168 A2
SEVS/STHTM N15 ....89 E2
WIM/MER SW19 ....205 E3
Southey St PGE/AN SE20 ....191 E6
Southfield BAR EN5 ....48 B1
Southfield Gdns TWK TW1 ...180 B6
Southfield Pk RYLN/HDSTN HA2 .79 F1

Southfield Rd CHST BR7 ....215 F6
CHSWK W4 ....142 D2
PEND EN3 ....55 E4
Southfields E/WMO/HCT KT8 .220 A3
HDN NW4 ....65 H6
Southfields Ms
WAND/EARL * SW18 ....185 E1
Southfields Rd
WAND/EARL SW18 ....185 E1
Southfleet Rd ORP BR6 .....253 E1
South Gdns WBLY * HA9 ......81 H3
WIM/MER SW19 ....205 H3
Southgate Gv IS N1 ....108 D5
South Gipsy Rd WELL DA16 ..176 B4
South Gv HGT N6 ....86 C5
SEVS/STHTM N15 ....87 D2
WALTH E17 ....90 D2
South Hill CHST BR7 ....213 H2
South Hill Av HRW HA1 .....99 H1
RYLN/HDSTN HA2 ....99 C1
South Hill Gv HRW HA1 ....100 A2
South Hill Pk HAMP NW3 ...106 A2
South Hill Park Gdns
HAMP NW3 ....106 A2
South Hill Rd HAYES BR2 ...212 A6
Southholme Cl NRWD SE19 ..209 E4
Southill Rd CHST BR7 .....213 G3
Southill St POP/IOD E14 ...131 F5
South Island Pl BRXN/ST SW9 .167 H1
South Kensington Station Ar
SKENS * SW7 ....145 H4
South Lambeth Pl VX/NE SW8 .29 F5
South Lambeth Rd VX/NE SW8 .29 F6
Southland Rd
WOOL/PLUM SE18 ....175 F1
Southlands Av ORP BR6 .....255 E2
Southlands Dr WIM/MER SW19 .184 B4
Southlands Gv BMLY BR1 ....213 G6
Southlands Rd HAYES BR2 ...233 F1
Southland Wy ISLW TW7 .....159 H6
South La KUT KT1 ....191 F6
NWMAL KT3 ....203 C1
South La West NWMAL KT3 ...203 D1
South Lodge Av MTCM CR4 ...224 D1
South Lodge Crs ENC/FH EN2 .37 F5
South Lodge Dr
STNGT/OAK * N14 ....22 D1
South Md CDALE/KGS NW9 ....63 H3
HOR/WEW KT19 ....241 F5
Southmead Rd
WIM/MER SW19 ....184 C3
South Molton La
MYFR/PKLN W1K 11 G4
South Molton Rd CAN/RD E16 .132 C5
South Molton St
MYFR/PKLN W1K 11 G4
Southmont Rd ESH/CLAY KT10 .220 A6
Southmoor Wy HOM E9 ......110 D4
South Mt TRDG/WHET * N20 ...49 H2
South Norwood HI SNWD SE25 .209 E5
Southold Ri ELTH/MOT SE9 ..193 H5
Southolm St VX/NE SW8 .....166 D2
Southover BMLY BR1 ....212 C1
NFNCH/WDSP N12 ....32 D4
South Pde CHEL SW3 ....30 A3
CHSWK W4 ....142 A3
EDGW * HA8 ....62 A5
WLGTN * SM6 ....248 C4
South Park Crs CAT SE6 ...192 A3
IL IG1 ....114 D1
South Park Dr IL IG1 .....115 E1
South Park Est
BERM/RHTH SE16 ....33 H1
South Park Gv NWMAL KT3 ...21 D1
South Park Hill Rd
SAND/SEL CR2 ....246 D3
South Park Ms FUL/PGN SW6 .165 F4
South Park Rd IL IG1 .....114 D1
WIM/MER SW19 ....205 F1
South Park Ter IL IG1 ....114 D1
South Park Wy RSLP HA4 ....98 A4
Southport Rd BKBYLDS KT5 ..221 H4
LVPST EC2M 15 H2
PEND EN3 ....41 F4
South Pde Ms LVPST EC2M ...15 H2
Southport Rd
WOOL/PLUM SE18 ....154 D4
Southridge Pl RYNPK SW20 ..204 B3
South Rd BAR/PAD * W2 .....10 B5
CHDH RM6 ....96 A4
EA W5 ....141 F4
ED N9 ....54 B6
EDGW * HA8 ....62 B4
FELT TW13 ....198 A1
FSTH SE23 ....190 B4
HPTN TW12 ....179 D6
STHL UB1 ....118 D1
WDR/YW UB7 ....132 A2
WHTN TW2 ....179 H5
WIM/MER SW19 ....205 H1
South Rw BKHTH/KID SE3 ...133 J1
South Ruislip KUT KT1 ....221 C1
South Sea St BERM/RHTH SE16 .150 C3
South Side HMSMTH W6 .....146 F3
SEVS/STHTM * N15 ....89 F1
Southside Common
WIM/MER SW19 ....204 B2
Southspring ELTH/MOT SE9 ..194 A2
South Sq GINN WC1R 14 A2
GLDGN NW11 ....65 E4
South St BMLY BR1 ....212 C5
ISLW TW7 ....160 C4
MYFR/PKLN W1K 11 H1
PEND EN3 ....41 H3
RAIN RM13 ....137 C1
South Tenter St WCHPL E1 ...16 D5
South Ter SKENS SW7 ....26 A1
SURB KT6 ....221 G3
VW N1 ....100 A2
NRWD SE19 ....209 E2
Southvale Rd BKHTH/KID SE3 .172 A3
South Vale Rd SURB KT6 ....221 G3
South Vw BMLY BR1 ....213 E5
South Vw BMLY BR1 ....213 E5
Southview Av WLSDN NW10 ..103 F5
South View Cl BXLY DA5 ....159 F5
South View Ct TOOT SW17 ...206 C1
South View Crs
GNTH/NBYPK IG2 ....94 B3
Southview Dr SWFD E18 .....72 C6

Southview Gdns WLGTN SM6 ..245 E5
Southview Rd BMLY BR1 ....191 H6
South View Rd CEND/HSY/T N8 .67 F6
LOU IG10 ....57 H1
Southviews SAND/SEL CR2 ...248 B6
South Vis CAMTN NW1 ....4 C1
Southville VX/NE SW8 ......167 F2
Southville Cl HOR/WEW KT19 .240 D6
Southville Rd THDIT KT7 ...220 C4
South Wk WWKM BR4 ....250 A1
Southwark Br CANST EC4R 15 F6
Southwark Bridge Rd
STHWK SE1 ....23 F1
Southwark Park Rd
BERM/RHTH SE16 ....25 G5
Southwark Pl BMLY BR1 ....213 H6
Southwark St STHWK SE1 ....22 D1
Southwater Cl BECK BR3 ...193 C3
South Wy CROY/NA CR0 ......248 C1
FBAR/BDGN N11 ....67 E2
RYLN/HDSTN HA2 ....79 E1
WBLY HA9 ....102 A3
Southway GLDGN NW11 ....65 F3
HAYES BR2 ....232 C4
RYNPK SW20 ....224 B5
TRDG/WHET N20 ....48 D4
WLCTN SM6 ....245 E2
Southwell Av NTHLT UB5 ....99 E4
Southwell Gdns SKENS SW7 .145 G4
Southwell Grove Rd WAN E11 .92 A6
Southwell Rd CMBW SE5 ....168 C4
CROY/NA CR0 ....228 A3
KTN/HRWW/W HA3 ....81 F3
South Western Rd TWK TW1 .180 C1
South Wharf Rd BAY/PAD W2 .91 H5
Southwick Ms BAY/PAD * W2 .125 H5
Southwick Pl BAY/PAD W2 ...10 A4
Southwick St BAY/PAD W2 ...10 A4
Southwick Yd BAY/PAD * W2 .10 B4
Southwold Dr BARK IG11 ...115 G3
Southwold Rd BXLY DA5 ....197 F1
CLPT E5 ....86 D6
Southwood Av HGT N6 ....86 D4
KUTN/CMB KT2 ....202 C4
Southwood Cl BMLY BR1 ....233 H1
WPK KT4 ....225 H2
Southwood Dr BRYLDS KT5 ..222 C4
Southwood Gdns BARK/HLT IG6 .94 B1
ESH/CLAY KT10 ....220 D2
Southwood La HGT N6 ....86 C4
Southwood Lawn Rd HGT N6 ..86 C4
Southwood Pk HGT * N6 ....86 C4
Southwood Rd ELTH/MOT SE9 .194 B4
THMD SE28 ....155 H1
Southwood Smith St IS * N1 .108 A6
South Worple Wy
MORT/ESHN SW14 ....162 A3
Sovereign Cl EA W5 ....121 F4
EP E1W 17 H6
Sovereign Ct E/WMO/HCT KT8 .218 D1
Sovereign Crs
BERM/RHTH SE16 ....130 C6
Sovereign Gv ALP/SUD HA0 ..101 F1
Sovereign Ms BETH * E2 ....13 J2
Sovereign Pk WLSDN * NW10 .122 B5
Sovereign Rd BARK IG11 ...136 A2
Sowerby Cl ELTH/MOT SE9 ..173 H6
Spa Cl SNWD SE19 ....209 E4
Spafield St CLKNW * EC1R ...6 A6
Spa Green Est CLKNW * EC1R .6 B3
Spa Hl THHTH CR7 ....208 D4
Spalding Cl EDGW HA8 ......63 E1
Spalding Rd HDN NW4 ....84 A3
TOOT SW17 ....206 D1
Spanby Rd BOW E3 ....131 E3
Spaniards Cl GLDGN NW11 ...85 G5
Spaniards End GLDGN NW11 ..85 G5
Spaniards Rd HAMP NW3 .....85 G6
Spanish Pl MHST * W1U 11 F3
Spanish Rd WAND/EARL SW18 .160 A1
Sparke Ter CAN/RD * E16 ..132 B5
Sparkford Gdns
FBAR/BDGN N11 ....66 C1
Sparks Cl ACT W3 ....122 D5
BCTR RM8 ....98 B6
HPTN TW12 ....198 C2
Spa Rd BERM/RHTH SE16 .....26 B6
Sparrow Cl HPTN TW12 .....198 C2
Sparrow Dr STMC/STPC BR5 .234 C5
Sparrow Farm Dr
EBED/NFELT TW14 ....178 A2
Sparrow Farm Rd EW KT17 ..241 G2
Sparrow Gn DAGE RM10 .....117 F1
Sparrows La ELTH/MOT SE9 .194 C2
Sparrows Herne BUSH WD23 ..43 G2
Sparrows Wk BUSH * WD23 ...43 G2
Sparsholt Rd ARCH N19 .....87 H5
BARK IG11 ....115 E6
Sparta St GREW SE10 ......171 G2
Speakers Ct CROY/NA * CR0 .228 D5
Spearman St
WOOL/PLUM * SE18 ....154 A6
Spear Ms ECT SW5 ....145 E4
Spears Rd ARCH N19 ....87 G5
Speart La HEST TW5 ....135 E1
Spedan Cl HAMP NW3 ....105 F1
Speedbird Wy WDR/YW UB7 ..132 A6
Speer Rd THDIT KT7 ....220 B3
Speirs Cl NWMAL KT3 ......223 F3
Spekehill ELTH/MOT SE9 ...193 H5
Speke Rd THHTH CR7 ....208 D5
Speldhurst Cl HAYES BR2 ..232 B3
Speldhurst Rd CHSWK W4 ...142 D1
HOM E9 ....110 B5
Spellbrook Wk IS * N1 ....108 C6
Spelman St WCHPL E1 ......17 F3
Spence Cl BERM/RHTH SE16 .150 D2
Spencer Av PLMGR N13 ......67 H2
HYS/HAR UB3 ....94 D5
ORP BR6 ....255 G2
Spencer Cl GLDGN NW11 .....65 G5
Spencer Gdns
MORT/ESHN SW14 ....162 C6
Spencer Hill Rd
WIM/MER SW19 ....204 C3
Spencer Av WIM/MER SW19 ..204 C2

Spencer House SURB * KT6 ....221 G2
Spencer Ms HMSMTH W6 ....144 C6
Spencer Pk W8W/EARL SW18 .....165 H6
Spencer Pl CROY/NA CRO 228 D4
   IS N1 ....108 B5
   WEST SW1P 20 B6
Spencer Rd KTTN NW5 ....106 D2
Spencer Rd ACT W3 ....142 C1
   ALP/SUD HA0 ....81 E6
   BMLY BR1 ....212 B3
   BTSEA SW11 ....165 H5
   CEND/HSY/T N8 ....87 H2
   CHSWK W4 ....162 C1
   E/WMO/HCT KT8 ....219 G1
   EHAM E6 ....113 F6
   FBAR/BDGN N11 ....50 D6
   GDMY/SEVK IG3 ....95 F5
   ISLW TW7 ....159 H2
   KTN/HRWW/W HA3 ....60 A5
   MTCM CR4 ....206 D6
   RAIN RM13 ....137 H2
   RYNPK SW20 ....203 H4
   SAND/SEL CR2 ....247 E5
   TOTM N17 ....69 G4
   WALTH E17 ....71 G5
   WHTN TW2 ....180 A5
Spencer St FSBYE EC1V 6 C4
   NWDGN UB2 ....138 B3
Spencer Wk PUT/ROE SW15 ....164 B5
Spenser Gdns STVM/STAM N16 .....109 E2
Spenser Ms DUL SE21 ....188 D3
Spenser Rd HNHL SE24 ....168 B6
Spenser St WESTW SW1E 20 B5
Spensley Wk STNW/STAM N16 .....108 D1
Speranza St WOOL/PLUM SE18 ....155 F5
Sperling Rd TOTM N17 ....69 F5
Spert St POP/IOD E14 ....130 C6
Speyside STHGT/OAK N14 ....51 E1
Spey St POP/IOD E14 ....131 G4
Spezia Rd WLSDN NW10 ....123 G1
Spicer Cl CMBW SE5 ....168 B3
   WOT/HER KT12 ....218 A3
Spices Yd CROY/NA CRO 211 J6
Spigurnell Rd TOTM N17 ....68 D4
Spikes Bridge Rd STHL UB1 ....118 C5
Spilsby Cl CDALE/KGS NW9 ....63 E5
Spindle Cl WOOL/PLUM SE18 ....153 G3
Spindlewood Gdns
   CROY/NA CRO 246 D2
Spindrift Av POP/IOD E14 ....151 F4
Spinel Cl WOOL/PLUM SE18 ....155 J5
Spinnaker Cl BARK IG11 ....135 H2
Spinnells Rd RYLN/HDSTN HA2 ......78 D5
Spinney Cl BECK BR3 ....231 F1
   NWMAL KT3 ....223 E2
   WPK KT4 ....241 F1
Spinney Gdns DAGW RM9 ....116 C3
   NRWD SE19 ....209 F1
Spinney Oak BMLY BR1 ....213 G5
The Spinneys BMLY BR1 ....213 H5
The Spinney ALP/SUD HA0 ....100 C1
   BARN * SW13 ....143 H6
   CHEAM SM3 ....242 A2
   NFNCH/WDSP * N12 ....45 G5
   SCUP DA14 ....216 C1
   STAN HA7 ....45 G6
   STRHM/NOR SW16 ....187 F5
   WCHMH N21 ....52 A2
Spirit Quay WAP E1W 25 F1
Spital Cl WCHPL E1 ....16 B1
Spital St WCHPL E1 ....17 E1
Spital Yd WCHPL * E1 ....16 B0
Spitfire Est HEST * TW5 ....138 A5
Spitfire Wy HEST TW5 ....138 A5
Spode Wk KIL/WHAMP * NW6 ....105 F3
Spondon Rd SEVS/STOTM N15 ....68 C1
Spoonbill Cl YEAD UB4 ....118 B4
Spooner Wk WLGTN SM6 ....245 F3
Sportsbank St CAT SE6 ....191 G2
Spottons Gv TOTM N17 ....68 D4
Spratt Hall Rd WAN E11 ....92 C3
Spray St WOOL/PLUM SE18 ....154 D4
Spreighton Rd
   E/WMO/HCT KT8 ....219 F1
Sprimont Pl CHEL SW3 ....26 C3
Springall St PECK SE15 ....169 H1
Springbank WCHMH N21 ....51 H1
Springbank Rd LEW SE13 ....192 A5
Springbank Wk CAMTN NW1 ....107 F5
Springbourne Ct BECK BR3 ....211 G4
Spring Bridge Rd EA W5 ....121 F6
Spring Cl BAR EN5 ....34 B6
   BCTR RM8 ....96 B5
Springclose La CHEAM SM3 ....242 C6
Spring Cottages SURB * KT6 ....221 F2
Spring Court Rd ENC/FH EN2 ....38 A1
Springcroft Av EFNCH N2 ....66 B0
Springdale Rd
   STNW/STAM N16 ....108 D2
Springfield BUSH WD23 ....28 A3
   CLPT E5 ....89 H5
Springfield Av HPTN TW12 ....199 F2
   MUSWH N10 ....67 E6
   RYNPK SW20 ....204 D6
Springfield Cl
   NFNCH/WDSP N12 ....65 F1
   STAN HA7 ....35 G6
Springfield Dr GNTH/NBYPK IG2 ....94 D2
Springfield Gdns BMLY BR1 ....233 H1
   CDALE/KGS NW9 ....82 D2
   CLPT E5 ....89 H5
   WFD IG8 ....73 E3
   WWKM BR4 ....231 F6
Springfield Gv CHARL SE7 ....153 E6
Springfield La
   KIL/WHAMP NW6 ....105 E6
Springfield Mt CDALE/KGS NW9 ....83 E2
Springfield Pl NWMAL KT3 ....222 C1
Springfield Rl SYD SE26 ....189 H1
Springfield Rd BMLY BR1 ....233 H1
   BXLYHN DA7 ....177 H4
   CHING E4 ....56 A3
   EHAM E6 ....113 H5
   FBAR/BDGN N11 ....67 G1
   HNWL W7 ....140 A1
   HRW HA1 ....60 B4
   HYS/HAR UB3 ....138 A3
   KUT KT1 ....221 G1
   SEVS/STOTM N15 ....89 G1
   SRTFD * E15 ....132 A2

STJWD NW8 ....105 G6
   SYD SE26 ....209 H1
   TEDD TW11 ....200 C1
   THHTH CR7 ....208 C4
   WALTH E17 ....90 D3
   WELL DA16 ....175 H4
   WHTN TW2 ....179 E3
   WIM/MER SW19 ....204 D1
   WLGTN SM6 ....244 D3
Springfield Wk
   KIL/WHAMP NW6 ....105 F6
Springfield Wy
   STMC/STPC BR5 ....216 A6
Spring Gdns E/WMO/HCT KT8 ....219 G2
   HBRY N5 ....108 C3
   ORP BR6 ....253 H4
   ROMW/RG RM7 ....97 G2
   WFD IG8 ....73 E3
   WHALL SW1A 21 E1
   WLGTN SM6 ....245 E5
Spring Gv CHSWK W4 ....142 A5
   HPTN TW12 ....199 F4
   LOU IG10 ....57 F1
   MTCM CR4 ....206 C4
Spring Grove Crs HEST TW5 ....159 G2
Spring Grove Rd HSLW TW3 ....159 G2
   RCHPK/HAM TW10 ....161 H6
Spring Hl CLPT E5 ....89 G4
   SYD SE26 ....190 A6
Springhurst Cl CROY/NA CRO 248 D2
Spring Lake STAN HA7 ....44 D6
Spring La CLPT E5 ....89 H5
   MUSWH N10 ....66 C6
   SNWD SE25 ....229 H3
Spring Ms MHST * W1U 10 D1
Spring Park Av CROY/NA CRO 230 B6
Springpark Dr BECK BR3 ....211 G6
   FSBYPK N4 ....88 C5
Spring Park Rd CROY/NA CRO 230 B6
Spring Pl FNCH N3 ....65 E5
   KTTN NW5 ....106 C3
Springpond Rd DAGW RM9 ....116 C3
Springrice Rd LEW SE13 ....191 G1
Spring Shaw Rd
   STMC/STPC BR5 ....215 G4
Spring St BAY/PAD W2 ....125 H5
   EW KT17 ....241 F6
Spring Tide Cl PECK * SE15 ....169 G2
Spring V BXLYHN DA7 ....177 F5
Springvale Av BTFD TW8 ....141 F5
Springvale Ter WKENS W14 ....144 B3
Springvale Villa Rd EDGW HA8 ....62 A3
Spring Vs WEA * W13 ....140 D1
Spring Wk WCHPL E1 ....17 E1
Springwater Cl
   WOOL/PLUM * SE18 ....154 D1
Springwell Av WLSDN NW10 ....103 F6
Springwell Rd HEST * TW5 ....158 B2
   STRHM/NOR SW16 ....188 A6
Sprowston Ms FSTGT E7 ....112 C4
Sprowston Rd FSTGT E7 ....112 C3
Sprucedale Gdns
   CROY/NA CRO 248 B2
   PUR/KEN CR8 ....245 G6
Spruce Hills Rd WALTH E17 ....71 F1
Sprules Rd BROCKY SE4 ....170 C3
Spurfield E/WMO/HCT KT8 ....199 F6
Spurgeon Av NRWD SE19 ....208 D1
Spurgeon Rd NRWD SE19 ....208 D1
Spurgeon St STHWK SE1 ....23 G6
Spurling Rd DAGW RM9 ....116 D4
   EDUL * SE22 ....169 F5
Spurrell Av RDART DA2 ....197 H6
Spur Rd BARK IG11 ....134 C2
   ISLW TW7 ....136 B1
   ORP BR6 ....255 G6
   SEVS/STOTM * N15 ....88 D1
   STAN HA7 ....45 G4
   STHWK SE1 ....22 A4
   WHALL SW1A 20 A4
Spurstowe Rd HACK E8 ....109 G4
Spurstowe Ter HACK E8 ....109 G3
The Square CAR SM5 ....244 C3
   HMSMTH W6 ....144 A5
   RCHPK/HAM TW10 ....161 G6
   SWLY * BR8 ....218 D6
   WFD IG8 ....72 C1
Squarey St TOOT SW17 ....185 G3
Squire Gdns STJWD NW8 ....2 B4
Squires Ct WIM/MER SW19 ....185 E6
Squires La FNCH N3 ....65 F5
Squires Mt HAMP NW3 ....105 H1
Squires Wy RDART DA2 ....197 H6
Squires Wood Dr CHST * BR7 ....213 H5
Squirrel Cl HSLWW TW4 ....158 A4
Squirrel Ms HNWL * W7 ....120 C6
Squirrels Cl NFNCH/WDSP N12 .....49 G4
Squirrels Gn WPK KT4 ....223 F6
The Squirrels BUSH WD23 ....41 E4
   LEW SE13 ....171 H4
   PIN HA5 ....58 D6
Squirries St BETH E2 ....8 F3
Stable Cl NTHLT UB5 ....119 E1
Stable Ms WNWD SE27 ....208 C1
Stables End ORP BR6 ....252 C1
Stables Wy LBTH SE11 ....30 A3
Stable Wk EFNCH * N2 ....65 A1
Stable Yard Rd WHALL SW1A 20 B2
Stacey Av UED N18 ....54 A6
Stacey Cl LEY E10 ....91 H2
Stacey St HOLWY N7 ....85 G1
   LSQ/SEVD WC2H 10 D4
Stackhouse St KTBR SW1X 18 C5
Stacy Pth CMBW * SE5 ....169 F1
Stadium Rd WOOL/PLUM SE18 ....173 H1
Stadium St WBPTN SW10 ....165 G1
Stadium Wy WBLY HA9 ....101 H2
Staffa Rd LEY E10 ....90 C5
Stafford Cl CHEAM SM3 ....242 C4
   KIL/WHAMP NW6 ....125 E2
   STHGT/OAK N14 ....37 E6
   WALTH E17 ....90 B2
Stafford Gdns CROY/NA CRO 245 H3
Stafford Rd RCHPK/HAM TW10 ....161 H2
   WESTW SW1E 20 A5
Stafford Rd BOW E3 ....130 D1
   CROY/NA CRO 248 B4
   FSTGT E7 ....113 G5
   KIL/WHAMP NW6 ....125 E2

KTN/HRWW/W HA3 ....59 G3
NWMAL KT3 ....202 C6
   SCUP DA14 ....195 E6
   WLGTN SM6 ....245 E5
Staffordshire St PECK SE15 ....169 G2
Stafford Ter KENS W8 ....145 E3
Stag Cl EDGW HA8 ....62 B5
Staggart Gn BARK/HLT IG6 ....75 F1
Stag La BKHH IG9 ....62 B5
   EDGW HA8 ....62 B5
   PUT/ROE SW15 ....183 F5
Stag Pl WESTW SW1E 20 A5
Stags Wy ISLW TW7 ....136 A1
Stainbank Rd MTCM CR4 ....206 D6
Stainby Rd SEVS/STOTM N15 ....69 F6
Stainer St STHWK SE1 ....23 H1
Staines Av CHEAM SM5 ....224 B6
Staines Rd HSLWW TW4 ....158 B6
   IL IG1 ....114 D2
   WHTN TW2 ....179 G5
Staines Rd East SUN TW16 ....198 A4
Stainforth Rd GNTH/NBYPK IG2 .....94 D4
   WALTH E17 ....91 E1
Staining La CITYW EC2V 15 F3
Stainmore Cl CHST BR7 ....214 D4
Stainsbury St BETH E2 ....130 A1
Stainsby Rd POP/IOD E14 ....131 E5
Stainsby Rd POP/IOD E14 ....131 E5
Stainton Rd LEW SE13 ....191 H2
   PEND EN3 ....40 A2
Stalbridge St CAMTN NW1 ....10 B1
Stalham St BERM/RHTH SE16 ....25 H6
Stalham Wy WFD IG8 ....74 B4
Stambourne Wy NRWD SE19 ......209 E3
   WWKM BR4 ....249 G1
Stamford Brook Av
   HMSMTH W6 ....143 F3
Stamford Brook Gdns
   HMSMTH W6 ....143 F3
Stamford Brook Rd
   HMSMTH W6 ....143 F3
Stamford Cl
   KTN/HRWW/W HA3 ....60 A3
   SEVS/STOTM N15 ....89 G1
   STHL UB1 ....119 E6
Stamford Cottages
   FUL/PGN * SW6 ....165 F1
Stamford Dr HAYES BR2 ....232 B1
Stamford Gdns DAGW RM9 ....116 A5
Stamford Gv East
   STNW/STAM N16 ....89 G5
Stamford Gv West
   STNW/STAM N16 ....89 G5
Stamford Hl STNW/STAM N16 ....89 F5
Stamford Rd DAGW RM9 ....115 H5
   EDUL SE22 ....169 E6
   IS N1 ....109 E5
   SEVS/STOTM N15 ....89 G2
Stamford St STHWK SE1 ....22 B2
Stamp Pl BETH E2 ....8 C3
Stanborough Cl HPTN TW12 ....198 D2
Stanborough Rd HSLW TW3 ....160 A1
Stanbridge Rd PUT/ROE SW15 ....164 A4
Stanbrook Rd ABYW SE2 ....155 H2
Stanbury Ct HAMP NW3 ....106 B5
Stanbury Rd PECK SE15 ....169 H2
Stancroft CDALE/KGS NW9 ....83 E1
Standard Pl SDTCH EC2A 8 B4
Standard Rd BELV DA17 ....157 E5
   BXLYHN DA6 ....177 F2
   CROY/NA CRO 247 E1
   GFD/PVL UB6 ....119 G4
   HSLWW TW4 ....158 C4
   PEND EN3 ....40 C1
   WLSDN NW10 ....122 C3
Standen Rd WAND/EARL SW18 ....185 E2
Standfield Rd DAGE RM10 ....117 E3
Standish Rd HMSMTH W6 ....143 G4
Stane Cl WIM/MER SW19 ....205 F3
Stane Wy WOOL/PLUM SE18 ....173 F5
Stanfield Rd BOW E3 ....130 C1
Stanford Cl HPTN TW12 ....198 D2
   ROMW/RG RM7 ....97 F3
   WFD IG8 ....73 G1
Stanford Pl STHWK SE1 ....32 A2
Stanford Rd FBAR/BDGN N11 ....66 B1
   KENS W8 ....145 F3
   STRHM/NOR SW16 ....207 G5
Stanford St WEST SW1P 28 C2
Stanford Wy
   STRHM/NOR SW16 ....207 F5
Stangate Gdns STAN HA7 ....44 D6
Stanger Rd SNWD SE25 ....229 G2
Stanhope Av FNCH N3 ....64 D6
   HAYES BR2 ....232 C5
   KTN/HRWW/W HA3 ....59 H4
Stanhope Cl
   BERM/RHTH * SE16 ....150 B2
Stanhope Gdns FSBYPK N4 ....88 B3
   HGT N6 ....86 D3
   IL IG1 ....94 A1
   MLHL NW7 ....63 F1
   SKENS * SW7 ....145 G4
Stanhope Ga BAY/PAD W2 ....10 C5
   MYFR/PKLN W1K 19 F2
Stanhope Gv BECK BR3 ....230 D2
Stanhope Ms East SKENS SW7 ....145 G4
Stanhope Ms South
   SKENS SW7 ....145 G4
Stanhope Ms West SKENS * SW7 ..145 G4
Stanhope Pde CAMTN NW1 ....3 H5
Stanhope Park Rd
   GFD/PVL UB6 ....119 G3
Stanhope Pl BAY/PAD W2 ....10 C2
Stanhope Rd BAR EN5 ....48 B1
   BCTR RM8 ....96 B6
   BXLYHN DA7 ....176 D1
   CAR SM5 ....244 D5
   CROY/NA CRO 247 E1
   GFD/PVL UB6 ....119 G4
   HGT N6 ....66 C5
   NFNCH/WDSP N12 ....65 G1
   WALTH E17 ....91 F2
Stanhope Rw MYFR/PICC * W1J 19 G2
Stanhope St CAMTN NW1 ....3 H6
Stanhope Ter BAY/PAD W2 ....125 H6
   TWK * TW1 ....180 B2
Stanier Cl ECT SW5 ....144 D5
Stanlake Rd SHB W12 ....144 A1

KTN/HRWW/W HA3 ....59 G3
NWMAL KT3 ....202 C6
Stanlake Vis SHB W12 ....144 A1
Stanley Av ALP/SUD HA0 ....101 G5
   BARK IG11 ....135 F2
   BECK BR3 ....96 D5
   GFD/PVL UB6 ....211 G6
   NWMAL KT3 ....223 G2
Stanley Cl ALP/SUD HA0 ....101 G5
Stanley Crs NTGHL W11 ....144 D6
Stanleycroft Cl ISLW TW7 ....160 A2
Stanley Gdns ACT W3 ....143 E2
   CRICK NW2 ....104 A3
   MTCM CR4 ....188 A3
   NTGHL W11 ....124 D6
   WLGTN SM6 ....245 E4
Stanley Gardens Rd
   TEDD TW11 ....200 A1
   VX/NE SW8 ....141 H2
Stanley Park Dr ALP/SUD HA0 .....101 H5
Stanley Park Rd CAR SM5 ....244 D5
   WLGTN SM6 ....244 D5
Stanley Pas CAMTN NW1 ....5 E2
Stanley Rd ACT W3 ....142 B3
   BELMT SM2 ....243 F4
   CAR SM5 ....244 C5
   CHING E4 ....44 A1
   CROY/NA CRO 228 A4
   ED N9 ....53 F3
   EFNCH N2 ....85 H1
   EN EN1 ....39 E4
   FBAR/BDGN N11 ....67 F2
   HAYES BR2 ....213 G6
   HSLW TW3 ....159 G2
   IL IG1 ....94 D6
   LEY E10 ....91 F3
   MNPK E12 ....113 G3
   MORT/ESHN SW14 ....162 B5
   MRDN SM4 ....225 E1
   MTCM CR4 ....206 C3
   MUSWH N10 ....66 D3
   ORP BR6 ....235 F5
   RYLN/HDSTN HA2 ....60 C4
   SCUP DA14 ....195 G5
   SEVS/STOTM N15 ....88 B1
   SRTFD E15 ....111 H6
   STHL UB1 ....118 C6
   SWFD E18 ....72 B4
   TEDD TW11 ....200 A1
   WBLY HA9 ....80 B4
   WHTN TW2 ....179 H5
   WIM/MER SW19 ....205 E3
Stanley Sq CAR SM5 ....244 B6
Stanley St DEPT SE8 ....170 D1
Stanley Ter ARCH * N19 ....67 C4
   BXLYHS * DA6 ....177 E5
Stanley Wy STMC/STPC BR5 ....235 H2
Stanmer St BTSEA SW11 ....166 A2
Stanmore Gdns RCH/KEW TW9 ....161 H4
   SUT SM1 ....68 A3
Stanmore Hl STAN HA7 ....60 D1
Stanmore Rd BELV DA17 ....157 G4
   RCH/KEW TW9 ....161 H4
   SEVS/STOTM N15 ....88 B1
   WAN E11 ....92 B5
Stanmore St IS N1 ....107 H6
Stanmore Ter BECK BR3 ....211 E5
Stannard Ms HACK * E8 ....109 G4
Stannard Rd HACK E8 ....109 G4
Stannary St LBTH SE11 ....30 B5
Stannet Wy WLGTN SM6 ....245 E2
Stansfield Rd CAN/RD E16 ....133 F5
   BRXN/ST SW9 ....167 H4
Stansgate Rd DAGE RM10 ....100 B4
Stanstead Cl HAYES BR2 ....232 B2
Stanstead Gv FSTH SE23 ....190 D3
Stanstead Rd FSTH SE23 ....190 B3
   WAN E11 ....92 D2
Stansted Crs BXLY DA5 ....196 B3
Stanswood Gdns CMBW SE5 ......169 E1
Stanthorpe Cl
   STRHM/NOR * SW16 ....207 G1
Stanthorpe Rd
   STRHM/NOR SW16 ....207 G1
Stanton Av TEDD TW11 ....199 G1
Stanton Cl HOR/WEW KT19 ....240 B3
   STMC/STPC BR5 ....236 A4
   WPK KT4 ....224 B5
Stanton Rd BARN SW13 ....163 F5
   CROY/NA CRO 228 C4
   RYNPK SW20 ....204 B5
Stanton Sq SYD SE26 ....190 D6
Stanton Wy SYD SE26 ....190 D6
Stanway Cl CHIG IG7 ....75 E1
Stanway Gdns ACT W3 ....142 A1
   EDGW HA8 ....62 C2
Stanway St IS N1 ....8 C1
Stanwick Rd WKENS W14 ....144 D4
Stanworth St STHWK SE1 ....24 C4
Stapenhill Rd ALP/SUD HA0 ....100 D1
Staple Cl BXLY DA5 ....197 H5
Staplefield Cl
   BRXS/STRHM * SW2 ....187 G3
   PIN HA5 ....58 C3
Stapleford Av GNTH/NBYPK IG2 ....95 S5
Stapleford Cl CHING E4 ....56 S5
   KUT KT1 ....202 A5
   WIM/MER SW19 ....184 C2
Stapleford Gdns CRW RM5 ....56 C1
Stapleford Rd ALP/SUD HA0 ....101 F3
Stapleford Wy BARK IG11 ....135 H2
Staplehurst Rd CAR SM5 ....244 A5
   LEW SE13 ....192 A5
Staple Inn HHOL WC1V 14 A2
Staples Cl BERM/RHTH SE16 ....150 C1
Staple St STHWK SE1 ....23 H4
Stapleton Gdns CROY/NA CRO 245 H4
Stapleton Hall Rd FSBYPK N4 ....67 H4
Stapleton Rd BXLYHN DA7 ....176 D1
   ORP BR6 ....253 F1
   TOOT SW17 ....167 H6
Stapleton Vis
   STNW/STAM * N16 ....109 E2
Stapley Rd BELV DA17 ....157 G3
Stapylton Rd BAR EN5 ....34 C4
Starch House La BARK/HLT IG6 .....74 D5
Starcross St CAMTN NW1 ....4 B4
Starfield Rd SHB W12 ....143 G2
Star & Garter Hl
   RCHPK/HAM TW10 ....181 G3

Star La CAN/RD E16 ....132 A3
 STMC/STPC BR5 ....236 B1
Starling Cl BKHH IG9 ....56 C3
 PIN HA5 ....58 A6
Starmans Cl DAGW RM9 ....116 C6
Star Pl WAP E1W 172 C4
Star Rd ISLW TW7 ....159 H5
 WKENS W14 ....144 D6
Starts Cl ORP BR6 ....252 A1
Starts Hill Av ORP BR6 ....252 A2
Starts Hill Rd ORP BR6 ....252 B1
Star Yd LINN WC2A 14 A3
State Farm Av ORP BR6 ....252 B2
Station Gdns TWK TW1 ....180 E6
Statham Gv STNW/STAM N16 ....108 D1
 UED N18 ....69 E1
Station Ap ALP/SUD HA0 ....100 D4
 BAR EN5 ....35 G5
 BECK BR3 ....210 C4
 BELMT SM2 ....242 C5
 BKHH * IG9 ....57 F6
 BKHTH/KID SE3 ....172 D4
 BXLYHN DA7 ....176 C3
 BXLYHN DA7 ....177 G3
 CAMTN * NW1 ....3 E6
 CHAT * E4 ....210 D1
 CHING * E4 ....56 C4
 CHING * E4 ....71 H2
 CHST BR7 ....213 G2
 CHST BR7 ....214 A4
 CROY/NA * CR0 ....228 D6
 ESH/CLAY KT10 ....238 B1
 FBAR/BDGN N11 ....66 D1
 FSTGT * E7 ....112 D2
 FUL/PGN * SW6 ....164 C6
 CFD/PVL UB6 ....99 G5
 GLDGN * NW11 ....84 B4
 HAYES BR2 ....232 C5
 HOR/WEW KT19 ....241 F5
 HPTN TW12 ....199 E4
 KUTN/CMB KT2 ....202 A4
 ORP BR6 ....235 F6
 ORP BR6 ....253 H3
 OXHEY WD19 ....42 B5
 PIN HA5 ....58 C6
 RCH/KEW TW9 ....162 A2
 SAND/SEL CR2 ....246 D6
 STMC/STPC BR5 ....235 H1
 STRHM/NOR SW16 ....207 F1
 SWFD * E18 ....72 D5
 WALTH * E17 ....91 G2
 WAN * E11 ....88 D4
 WAN * E11 ....112 A2
 WELL DA16 ....175 F3
 WFD * IG8 ....75 E2
 WLSDN NW10 ....123 F2
Station Approach Rd
 CHSWK W4 ....162 C1
Station Ar GTPST * W1W 3 H6
Station Av HOR/WEW KT19 ....241 E6
 NWMAL KT3 ....203 E6
Station Buildings HAYES * BR2 ....232 C5
Station Chambers EA * W5 ....122 A3
Station Cl HPTN TW12 ....199 F4
Station Cottages WDGN * N22 ....67 G5
Station Crs ALP/SUD HA0 ....100 D4
 BKHTH/KID SE3 ....152 C5
 SEVS/STOTM N15 ....88 D1
Stationers Hall Ct STP * EC4M 14 D4
Station Est BECK BR3 ....230 B1
Station Garage Ms
 STRHM/NOR * SW16 ....207 F2
Station Gdns CHSWK W4 ....162 C1
Station Gv ALP/SUD HA0 ....101 G4
Station Hl HAYES BR2 ....230 C6
Station House Ms UED N18 ....53 G6
Station Pde ACT * W3 ....122 A5
 BAL * SW12 ....186 C3
 BARK IG11 ....114 C5
 BECK * BR3 ....210 D5
 BELMT * SM2 ....243 E6
 BMLY * BR1 ....212 C4
 BXLYHN * DA7 ....177 G3
 CHSWK * W4 ....142 C6
 CHSWK * W4 ....162 C1
 CLPT * E5 ....109 H1
 CRICK NW2 ....104 A4
 EBAR * EN4 ....34 C1
 EDGW * HA8 ....61 G3
 EHAM * E6 ....113 E6
 EHAM * E6 ....113 E6
 KTN/HRWW/W * HA3 ....60 D5
 NTHLT * UB5 ....99 F3
 NTHLT * UB5 ....99 E5
 RCH/KEW TW9 ....162 A2
 RYLN/HDSTN * HA2 ....99 F2
 STHGT/OAK N14 ....51 F2

NRWD SE19 ....209 A1
NWMAL KT3 ....223 H2
ORP BR6 ....235 F6
PGE/AN SE20 ....210 A2
RYLN/HDSTN HA2 ....79 F2
SCUP DA14 ....195 G5
SEVS/STOTM N15 ....69 G6
SNWD SE25 ....229 F1
STMC/STPC BR5 ....236 A1
TEDD TW11 ....200 C2
THDIT KT7 ....220 B4
TWK TW1 ....180 B3
WALTH E17 ....90 C3
WCHMH N21 ....52 B3
WDGN N22 ....67 H5
WIM/MER SW19 ....205 G4
WLSDN NW10 ....123 F1
WWKM BR4 ....231 G5
Station Rd North BELV DA17 ....157 F3
Station Sq STMC/STPC BR5 ....234 C2
Station St SRTFD E15 ....111 H5
Station Ter CMBW SE5 ....168 C1
 WLSDN NW10 ....124 B1
Station Vw GFD/PVL UB6 ....99 H6
Station Wy BKHH IG9 ....57 F6
 CHEAM SM3 ....242 C4
Station Yd STHL * UB1 ....138 D2
 TWK TW1 ....180 C2
Staunton Rd KUTN/CMB KT2 ....201 H3
Staunton St DEPT SE8 ....150 D6
Staveley Cl HOLWY * N7 ....107 G2
 PECK SE15 ....170 A2
Staveley Gdns CHSWK W4 ....162 D2
Staverton Rd CRICK NW2 ....104 A5
Stave Yard Rd
 BERM/RHTH SE16 ....150 C1
Stavordale Rd CAR SM5 ....225 G4
 HBRY N5 ....108 A2
Stayner's Rd WCHPL E1 ....130 B3
Stayton Rd SUT SM1 ....243 E1
Steadfast Rd KUT KT1 ....201 F4
Stead St WALW SE17 ....31 G2
Stean St HACK E8 ....109 F6
Stebbing Wy BARK IG11 ....135 G1
Stebondale St POP/IOD E14 ....195 G1
Stedly SCUP * DA14 ....195 G6
Steedman St WALW SE17 ....31 E2
Steeds Rd MUSWH N10 ....66 A5
Steele Ap BARK IG11 ....135 H1
Steele Rd CHSWK W4 ....142 C3
 ISLW TW7 ....160 C1
 TOTM N17 ....69 G6
 WAN E11 ....112 A2
 WLSDN NW10 ....122 C1
Steele's Ms North
 HAMP * NW3 ....106 B4
Steele's Ms South HAMP NW3 ....106 A4
Steele's Rd HAMP NW3 ....106 B4
Steele's Studios HAMP * NW3 ....106 B4
Steep Cl ORP BR6 ....253 F4
Steep Hl CROY/NA CR0 ....247 E2
 STRHM/NOR SW16 ....187 H3
Steeplands BUSH WD23 ....45 F3
Steeple Cl FUL/PGN SW6 ....164 C4
 WIM/MER SW19 ....184 C6
Steeplestone Cl UED N18 ....68 C1
Steerforth St
 WAND/EARL SW18 ....185 F4
Steers Md MTCM CR4 ....206 B4
Steers Wy BERM/RHTH SE16 ....150 C2
Stella Rd TOOT SW17 ....206 B2
Stelling Rd ERITH DA8 ....177 H1
Stellman Cl CLPT E5 ....109 G1
Stembridge Rd PGE/AN SE20 ....209 H5
Stephan Cl HACK E8 ....109 G5
Stephen Cl ORP BR6 ....253 F1
Stephendale Rd FUL/PGN SW6 ....165 F3
Stephen Ms FITZ W1T 12 C2
Stephen Pl CLAP SW4 ....167 G4
Stephen Rd BXLYHN DA7 ....177 J4
Stephenson Rd HNWL W7 ....120 B5
 WALTH E17 ....90 C3
Stephenson St CAN/RD E16 ....132 A4
 WLSDN NW10 ....123 G2
Stephenson Wy CAMTN NW1 ....4 B6
Stephen's Rd SRTFD E15 ....112 C1
Stephen St FITZ W1T 12 C3
Stepney Cswy WCHPL E1 ....130 C4
Stepney Gn WCHPL E1 ....130 D4
Stepney High St WCHPL E1 ....131 E4
Stepney Wy WCHPL E1 ....130 C4
Sterling Av EDGW HA8 ....45 F6
Sterling Cl WLSDN NW10 ....105 G5
Sterling Gdns NWCR SE14 ....150 D6
Sterling Pl BTFD TW8 ....141 G1
Sterling Rd ENC/FH EN2 ....38 D2
Sterling St SKENS SW7 ....18 A4
Sterling Wy (North Circular)
 UED N18 ....68 D1
Stern Cl BARK IG11 ....136 A1
Sterndale Rd WKENS * W14 ....144 B3
Sterne St SHB W12 ....144 B2
Sternhall La PECK SE15 ....169 G4
Sternhold Av
 BRXS/STRHM SW2 ....187 F4
Sterry Crs DAGE RM10 ....117 E4
Sterry Dr HOR/WEW KT19 ....241 E2
 THDIT KT7 ....220 A3
Sterry Gdns DAGE RM10 ....117 E4
Sterry Rd BARK IG11 ....117 F5
 DAGE RM10 ....116 D1
Sterry St STHWK SE1 ....34 D2
Steucers La FSTH SE23 ....190 C3
Steve Biko La CAT SE6 ....191 H4
Steve Biko Rd HOLWY N7 ....108 A1
Steve Biko Wy HSLW TW3 ....159 E4
Stevedale Rd WELL DA16 ....176 A3
Stevedore St WAP E1W 25 F1
Stevenage Rd EHAM E6 ....114 C3
 FUL/PGN SW6 ....164 B2
Stevens Av HOM E9 ....110 A4
Stevens Cl BECK BR3 ....211 E2
 BXLY DA5 ....197 H6
 HPTN TW12 ....199 F5
 PIN HA5 ....78 A2
Stevens Gn BUSH WD23 ....45 G3
Stevens' La ESH/CLAY KT10 ....238 C5

Stevenson Cl BAR EN5 ....49 H1
Stevenson Crs
 BERM/RHTH SE16 ....49 H4
Stevens Rd BCTR RM8 ....95 H6
Stevens St STHWK SE1 ....24 B5
Steventon Rd SHB W12 ....123 F6
Stewart St WCHPL E1 ....16 B1
Stewart Cl CDALE/KGS * NW9 ....82 C3
 CHST BR7 ....214 B1
 HPTN TW12 ....199 C2
Stewart Rd WAN E11 ....111 H2
Stewartsby Cl UED N18 ....68 C1
Stewart's Gv CHEL SW3 ....145 H5
 CHEL * SW3 ....145 H5
Stewart's La VX/NE SW8 ....166 D1
Stewart's Rd VX/NE SW8 ....167 E2
 VX/NE SW8 ....167 E1
Stewart St POP/IOD E14 ....151 G2
Stew La BLKFR EC4V 15 G5
Steyne Rd ACT W3 ....142 B1
Steyning Gv ELTH/MOT SE9 ....193 H6
Steynings Wy
 NFNCH/WDSP N12 ....65 E1
Steyning Wy HSLWW TW4 ....158 A3
Steynton Av BXLY DA5 ....196 C4
St George's Est WAP * E1W 17 F5
Stickland Rd BELV DA17 ....157 H2
Stickleton Cl GFD/PVL UB6 ....119 F2
Stilecroft Gdns ALP/SUD HA0 ....100 D1
Stile Hall Gdns CHSWK W4 ....142 A5
Stiles Cl ERITH DA8 ....157 F5
 HAYES BR2 ....231 F6
Stillingfleet Rd BARN SW13 ....163 G1
Stillington St WEST SW1P 28 B1
Stillness Rd FSTH SE23 ....190 C1
Stipularis Dr YEAD UB4 ....118 B3
Stirling Av PIN HA5 ....78 B4
Stirling Cl STRHM/NOR SW16 ....207 E4
Stirling Dr ORP BR6 ....253 H5
Stirling Gv HSLW TW3 ....159 G3
Stirling Rd ACT W3 ....142 B1
 BRXN/ST SW9 ....167 G3
 KTN/HRWW/W HA3 ....80 B6
 PLSTW E13 ....132 D1
 WALTH E17 ....70 C6
 WDGN N22 ....68 B4
 WHTN TW2 ....179 E2
Stirling Wy BYRLDS KT5 ....222 B3
Stirling Wy BORE WD6 ....46 D1
Stiven Crs RYLN/HDSTN HA2 ....98 D1
St John's Est IS N1 ....7 H2
 STHWK SE1 ....24 C3
Stockbury Rd CROY/NA CR0 ....230 A3
Stockdale Rd BCTR RM8 ....96 A6
Stockdove Wy GFD/PVL UB6 ....120 B2
Stocker Gdns DAGW RM9 ....116 A5
Stockfield Rd ESH/CLAY KT10 ....238 A4
 STRHM/NOR SW16 ....187 H3
Stockholm Rd
 BERM/RHTH SE16 ....150 A5
Stockholm Wy WAP E1W 25 E1
Stockhurst Cl PUT/ROE SW15 ....164 A3
Stockingswater La PEND EN3 ....40 C4
Stockland Rd ROMW/RG RM7 ....94 H3
Stock Orchard Crs HOLWY N7 ....107 H2
Stock Orchard St HOLWY N7 ....107 H2
Stockport Rd
 STRHM/NOR SW16 ....207 F4
Stocks Pl POP/IOD E14 ....130 D6
Stock St PLSTW E13 ....132 C3
Stockton Cl BAR EN5 ....35 G5
Stockton Gdns MLHL NW7 ....46 B5
 TOTM N17 ....68 C3
Stockton Rd TOTM N17 ....68 C2
 UED N18 ....69 G2
Stockwell Av BRXN/ST SW9 ....167 H4
Stockwell Cl BMLY BR1 ....212 D5
Stockwell Gdns BRXN/ST SW9 ....167 H3
Stockwell Gdns BRXN/ST SW9 ....167 H3
Stockwell La BRXN/ST SW9 ....167 H3
Stockwell Park Crs
 BRXN/ST SW9 ....167 H3
Stockwell Park Rd
 BRXN/ST SW9 ....167 H3
Stockwell Park Wk
 BRXN/ST SW9 ....167 H4
Stockwell Rd BRXN/ST SW9 ....167 H3
Stockwell St GNWCH SE10 ....151 F1
Stockwell Ter BRXN/ST SW9 ....167 H3
Stodart Rd PGE/AN SE20 ....210 A4
Stofford Cl WIM/MER SW19 ....184 C3
Stoke Av BARK/HLT IG6 ....75 G2
Stokenchurch St
 FUL/PGN SW6 ....165 F2
Stoke Newington Common
 STNW/STAM N16 ....109 F1
Stoke Newington High St
 STNW/STAM N16 ....109 F1
Stoke Newington Rd
 STNW/STAM N16 ....109 F3
Stoke Pl WLSDN NW10 ....119 H1
Stoke Rd KUTN/CMB KT2 ....202 C3
Stokesby Rd CHSGTN KT9 ....259 F5
Stokesley St SHB W12 ....123 F5
Stokes Rd CROY/NA CR0 ....230 D5
 EHAM E6 ....113 J4
Stoll Cl CRICK NW2 ....104 A1
Stonard Rd BCTR RM8 ....115 H3
 PLMGR N13 ....52 A5
Stondon Pk FSTH SE23 ....190 C2
Stonebridge Pk WLSDN NW10 ....102 B3
Stonebridge Rd
 SEVS/STOTM N15 ....89 A2
Stone Buildings LINN WC2A 14 B2
Stone Cl BCTR RM8 ....96 D6
 CLAP SW4 ....167 G3
Stonecot Cl MRDN SM4 ....224 A4
Stonecot Hl MRDN SM4 ....224 A4
Stonecroft Rd ERITH DA8 ....177 H1
Stonecroft Wy CROY/NA CR0 ....227 G4
Stonecutter St
 FLST/FETLN EC4A 14 C3
Stonefield Cl BXLYHN DA7 ....177 F3
 RSLP HA4 ....98 D3
Stonefield St IS N1 ....108 A6
Stonefield Wy CHARL SE7 ....171 G2
 RSLP HA4 ....98 B3
Stonegate Cl STMC/STPC BR5 ....216 A6

Stone Gv STAN HA7 ....45 G3
Stonegrove Gdns EDGW HA8 ....61 H3
Stonehall Av IL IG1 ....93 G3
Stone Hall Gdns KENS * W8 ....145 F3
Stone Hall Pl KENS * W8 ....145 F3
Stone Hall Rd WCHMH N21 ....51 F3
Stoneham Rd FBAR/BDGN N11 ....67 E1
Stonehill Cl MORT/ESHN SW14 ....162 C6
Stonehill Rd CHSWK W4 ....142 A5
 MORT/ESHN SW14 ....162 C6
Stonehills Ct DUL SE21 ....189 E5
Stonehill Woods Pk
 RDART * DA2 ....217 F2
Stonehorse Rd PEND EN3 ....40 A6
Stone House Ct HDTCH EC3A 16 D3
Stoneleigh Av EN EN1 ....39 H1
 WPK KT4 ....241 G1
Stoneleigh Broadway
 EW KT17 ....241 G3
Stoneleigh Crs
 HOR/WEW KT19 ....241 G3
Stoneleigh Park Av
 CROY/NA CR0 ....230 B3
Stoneleigh Park Rd
 HOR/WEW KT19 ....241 F4
Stoneleigh Pl NTCHL W11 ....144 B6
Stoneleigh Rd CAR SM5 ....226 A4
 CLAY IG5 ....75 G6
 TOTM N17 ....69 F3
Stoneleigh St NTCHL W11 ....124 B6
Stonemasons Cl
 SEVS/STOTM * N15 ....88 D1
Stonenest St FSBYPK N4 ....87 H5
Stone Park Av BECK BR3 ....231 E1
Stone Pl WPK KT4 ....224 B6
Stone Rd HAYES BR2 ....232 B2
Stones Cross Rd SWLY BR8 ....237 G2
Stones End St STHWK SE1 ....23 E4
Stone St CROY/NA CR0 ....244 D1
Stonewall EHAM E6 ....114 B4
Stoney Aly WOOL/PLUM SE18 ....174 A3
Stoneyard La POP/IOD E14 ....131 F6
Stoneycroft Cl LEE/GVPK SE12 ....192 B2
Stoneycroft Rd WFD IG8 ....75 J1
Stoneydown WALTH E17 ....90 C1
Stoneydown Av WALTH E17 ....90 C1
Stoneyfields Gdns EDGW HA8 ....62 C1
Stoneyfields La EDGW HA8 ....62 C1
Stoney La HDTCH EC3A 16 D3
 NRWD SE19 ....209 F2
Stoney St STHWK SE1 ....23 G1
Stonhouse St CLAP SW4 ....167 E4
Stonnell's Rd BTSEA SW11 ....166 B6
Stonor Rd WKENS W14 ....144 D4
Stonycroft Cl PEND EN3 ....40 D3
Stopes St PECK SE15 ....169 F6
Stopford Rd PLSTW E13 ....112 C6
 WALW * SE17 ....30 D4
Store Rd CAN/RD E16 ....154 A2
Storers Quay POP/IOD E14 ....152 D4
Store St GWRST WC1E 12 C2
 SRTFD E15 ....111 H3
Storey Rd HGT N6 ....86 A6
 WALTH E17 ....90 A1
Storey's Ga STJSPK * SW1H 20 D4
Stories Ms CMBW * SE5 ....169 E3
Stories Rd CMBW SE5 ....169 E4
Stork Rd FSTGT E7 ....112 B4
Storksmead Rd EDGW HA8 ....63 E3
Storks Rd BERM/RHTH SE16 ....25 H6
Stormont Rd BTSEA SW11 ....166 D4
 HGT N6 ....86 A6
Stormont Wy CHSGTN KT9 ....239 E3
Storrington Rd CROY/NA CR0 ....229 F5
Story St IS N1 ....107 H4
Stothard Pl SDTCH * EC2A 16 D1
Stothard St WCHPL E1 ....130 D3
Stott Cl WAND/EARL SW18 ....185 H1
Stoughton Av CHEAM SM3 ....242 B3
Stoughton Cl PUT/ROE SW15 ....183 G3
Stour Av NWDGN UB2 ....139 E3
Stourcliffe St BAY/PAD W2 ....10 C4
Stour Rd BOW E3 ....112 A6
 DAGE RM10 ....97 G2
Stourton Av FELT TW13 ....178 D6
Stowage DEPT SE8 ....151 H5
Stowe Crs WALTH E17 ....70 C4
Stowe Gdns ED N9 ....53 H1
Stowe Pl WLSDN NW10 ....119 H3
Stowe Rd ORP BR6 ....253 H3
 SHB W12 ....143 H2
Stowting Rd ORP BR6 ....253 F2
Stracey Rd WLSDN NW10 ....102 D6
Strachan Pl RYNPK SW20 ....204 A2
Stradbroke Dr CHIG IG7 ....74 B2
Stradbroke Gv BKHH IG9 ....57 F3
 CLAY IG5 ....75 G6
Stradbroke Pk CHIG IG7 ....74 C2
Stradbroke Rd HBRY N5 ....108 B1
Stradbrook Cl
 RYLN/HDSTN HA2 ....98 A3
Stradella Rd HNHL SE24 ....188 C3
Strafford Av CLAY IG5 ....74 A5
Strafford Rd ACT W3 ....142 C2
 BAR EN5 ....34 C4
 HSLW TW3 ....158 D2
 TWK TW1 ....180 C2
Strafford St POP/IOD E14 ....151 E2
Strahan Rd BOW E3 ....130 D2
Straightsmouth GNWCH SE10 ....151 F1
The Straight NWDGN UB2 ....138 C2
Strait Rd EHAM E6 ....133 J5
Straker's Rd EDUL SE22 ....169 H5
Strand CHCR WC2N 21 E1
 TPL/STR WC2R 13 H5
Strandfield Cl
 WOOL/PLUM SE18 ....155 G5
Strand-on-the-Green
 CHSWK W4 ....142 A6
Strand Pl UED N18 ....53 H3
Strangways Ter WKENS W14 ....144 D3
Stranraer Wy IS N1 ....107 G5
Stransby Gdns BTSEA SW11 ....146 C6
Stratfield Park Cl WCHMH N21 ....52 B2
Stratford Cl BARK IG11 ....115 H6
 DAGE RM10 ....117 F5
Stratford Ct NWMAL KT3 ....222 D1

Stratford Gv PUT/ROE SW15 ......164 B5
Stratford House Av BMLY BR1 ....213 G6
Stratford Pl MHST W1U 11 F4
Stratford Rd KENS W8 ....145 E4
   NWDGN UB2 ....138 C4
   PLSTW E13 ....112 D6
   THHTH CR7 ....228 A1
Stratford Vls CAMTN NW1 ....107 E5
Strathan Cl WAND/EARL SW18....184 C1
Strathaven Rd LEE/GVPK SE12 ...192 D1
Strathblaine Rd BTSEA SW11 .....165 H6
Strathbrook Rd
   STRHM/NOR SW16 ....207 H3
Strathcona Rd WBLY HA9 ....81 F1
Strathdale STRHM/NOR SW16 ....207 H1
Strathdon Dr TOOT SW17 ....186 C1
Strathearn Av WHTN TW2 ....179 G3
Strathearn Cottages
   TROG/WHET * N20 ....49 E5
Strathearn Pl BAY/PAD W2 ....9 H5
Strathearn Rd SUT SM1 ....208 E3
   WIM/MER SW19 ....205 E1
Strathedem Rd BKHTH/KID SE3 ...172 C2
Strathfield Gdns BARK IC11 ....114 D4
Strathleven Rd
   BRXS/STRHM SW2 ....167 G6
Strathmore Gdns EDGW HA8 ....62 B5
   FNCH N3 ....65 F4
   KENS W8 ....145 E4
Strathmore Rd BKHTH/KID SE3 ..172 C2
   TEDD TW11 ....160 D5
   WIM/MER SW19 ....185 E5
Strathnairn St STHWK SE1 ....33 F2
Strathray Gdns HAMP * NW3 ....106 A4
Strath Ter BTSEA SW11 ....166 A3
Strathville Rd
   WAND/EARL SW18 ....185 E4
Strathyre Av
   STRHM/NOR SW16 ....208 A6
Stratton Av WLGTN SM6 ....245 F6
Stratton Cl BXLYHN DA7 ....176 C4
   EDGW HA8 ....61 H2
   HEST TW5 ....158 D2
   WIM/MER SW19 ....204 D5
   WOT/HER * KT12 ....218 A5
Strattondale St POP/IOD E14 .....151 G3
Stratton Dr BARK IG11 ....115 E3
Stratton Gdns STHL UB1 ....118 D5
Stratton Rd BXLYHN DA7 ....176 C4
   WIM/MER SW19 ....205 E5
Stratton St MYFR/PICC W1J 19 H1
Strauss Rd CHSWK * W4 ....117 F2
Strawberry Hill Rd TWK TW1 ......180 B5
Strawberry La CAR SM5 ....244 B1
Strawberry Ter MUSWH * N10 ......65 H2
Strawberry Vale EFNCH N2 ....47 H5
   TWK TW1 ....180 B5
Streakes Field Rd CRICK NW2 ....63 G6
Streamdale ABYW SE2 ....155 H6
Streamside Cl ED N9 ....53 F3
   HAYES BR2 ....212 D1
Stream Wy BELV DA17 ....157 E6
Streatfeild Av EHAM E6 ....113 H6
Streatfield Rd
   KTN/HRWW/W HA3 ....61 E6
Streatham Cl
   STRHM/NOR * SW16 ....187 G4
Streatham Common North
   STRHM/NOR * SW16 ....207 F3
Streatham Common North
   STRHM/NOR SW16 ....207 H1
Streatham Common South
   STRHM/NOR SW16 ....207 G2
Streatham Ct
   STRHM/NOR SW16 ....187 G5
Streatham Gn
   STRHM/NOR SW16 ....187 G6
Streatham High Rd
   STRHM/NOR SW16 ....187 G6
Streatham Hl
   BRXS/STRHM SW2 ....187 G3
Streatham Pl
   BRXS/STRHM SW2 ....187 G3
Streatham Rd MTCM CR4 ....206 C4
Streatham St NOXST/BSQ WC1A ...15 E3
Streatham V
   STRHM/NOR SW16 ....207 E4
Streathbourne Rd TOOT SW17 ....186 C4
Streatleigh Pde
   STRHM/NOR * SW16 ....187 G4
Streatley Pl HAMP NW3 ....105 H2
Streatley Rd KIL/WHAMP NW6 ....104 D5
Streeters La WLGTN SM6 ....245 F1
Streetfield Ms BKHTH/KID SE3....172 C5
Streimer Rd SRTFD E15 ....131 G1
Strelley Wy ACT W3 ....118 G1
Stretton Rd CROY/NA CRO 197 G4
   RCHPK/HAM TW10 ....181 E4
Strickland Av
   WAND/EARL SW18 ....185 H2
Strickland Ct DEPT SE8 ....171 F3
Strickland Wy ORP BR6 ....253 F2
Stride Rd PLSTW E13 ....132 B1
Strimon Cl ED N9 ....54 A4
Strode Cl MUSWH N10 ....66 C3
Strode Rd FSTGT E7 ....112 C2
   FUL/PGN SW6 ....165 G3
   TOTM N17 ....69 E5
   WLSDN NW10 ....104 B1
Strone Rd FSTGT E7 ....113 E4
Strone Wy YEAD UB4 ....118 C3
Strongbow Crs ELTH/MOT SE9 ....175 H6
Strongbow Rd ELTH/MOT SE9......175 H6
Strongbridge Cl
   RYLN/HDSTN HA2 ....79 E5
Stronsa Rd SHB W12 ....143 F2
Strood Av ROMW/RG RM7 ....97 H5
Stroud Crs PUT/ROE SW15 ....183 F5
Stroudes Cl WPK KT4 ....192 C5
Stroud Field NTHLT UB5 ....95 G4
Stroud Ga RYLN/HDSTN HA2 ....99 F2
Stroud Green Rd FSBYPK N4 ....67 H5
Stroud Green Wy
   CROY/NA CRO 230 A3
Stroud Rd SNWD SE25 ....229 G3
   WIM/MER SW19 ....185 E5
Strouds Cl CHDH RM6 ....95 H2
Stroudwater Pk WEY KT13 ....73 G5
Strout's Pl BETH E2 ....8 C3
Strutton Gnd WEST SW1P 20 C5
Strype St WCHPL E1 ....16 C2

St Saviour's Est STHWK SE1 ....24 C1
Stuart Av CDALE/KGS NW9 ....83 G4
   EA W5 ....141 H2
   HAYES BR2 ....232 C5
   RYLN/HDSTN HA2 ....98 D1
   WOT/HER KT12 ....218 A5
Stuart Ct BORE WD6 ....
Stuart Crs CROY/NA CRO 248 D1
   WDGN N22 ....67 H4
Stuart Evans Cl WELL DA16 ....176 A4
Stuart Cv TEDD TW11 ....200 A1
Stuart Mantle Wy ERITH DA8 ......177 H1
Stuart Pl MTCM CR4 ....206 B4
Stuart Rd ACT W3 ....142 C1
   BARK IG11 ....115 F6
   EBAR EN4 ....35 G2
   KIL/WHAMP NW6 ....125 E2
   KTN/HRWW/W HA3 ....60 B6
   PECK SE15 ....170 D4
   RCHPK/HAM TW10 ....180 D4
   THHTH CR7 ....228 C1
   WELL DA16 ....175 H2
   WIM/MER SW19 ....185 E5
Stubbs Cl CDALE/KGS NW9 ....82 C2
Stubbs Dr BERM/RHTH SE16 ....33 G3
Stubbs Wy WIM/MER SW19 ....205 H4
Stucley Pl CAMTN NW1 ....106 D5
Stucley Rd ISLW TW7 ....159 G1
Studdridge St FUL/PGN SW6 ....165 E3
Studd St IS N1 ....108 B6
Studholme Cl
   KIL/WHAMP * NW6 ....105 E2
Studholme St PECK SE15 ....169 H1
Studio Pl KTBR * SW1X 18 D4
The Studios BUSH WD23 ....43 F1
Studland Cl BFN/LL DA15 ....176 A4
Studland Rd HNWL W7 ....119 H5
   KUTN/CMB KT2 ....201 D2
   SYD SE26 ....210 B3
Studland St HMSMTH W6 ....143 H4
Studley Av CHING E4 ....52 A3
Studley Cl CLPT E5 ....110 C3
Studley Ct SCUP DA14 ....215 H1
   DAGE RM10 ....117 A6
Studley Dr REDBR IG4 ....91 F3
Studley Grange Rd HNWL W7 .....140 A3
Studley Rd CLAP SW4 ....167 G2
   DAGW RM9 ....116 B5
   FSTGT E7 ....112 D4
Stukeley Rd FSTGT E7 ....112 D5
Stukeley St HOL/ALD WC2B 11 F3
Stumps Hill La BECK BR3 ....211 E2
Sturdy Rd PECK SE15 ....169 H3
Sturge Av WALTH E17 ....51 F4
Sturgeon Rd WALW SE17 ....31 H5
Sturges St CHST BR7 ....214 D2
Sturgess Av HDN NW4 ....83 G4
Sturge St STHWK SE1 ....35 E2
Sturmer Wy HOLWY N7 ....107 H5
Sturminster Cl YEAD UB4 ....118 A5
Sturrock Cl SEVS/STOTM N15 ....68 D1
Sturry St POP/IOD E14 ....131 F5
Sturt St IS N1 ....7 F2
Stutfield St WCHPL E1 ....17 F4
Styles Gdns BRXN/ST SW9 ....168 B3
Styles Wy BECK BR3 ....251 G1
Sudbourne Rd
   BRXS/STRHM SW2 ....167 G6
Sudbrooke Rd BAL SW12 ....186 B1
Sudbrook Gdns
   RCHPK/HAM TW10 ....181 G5
Sudbrook La
   RCHPK/HAM TW10 ....181 G3
Sudbury Av WBLY HA0 ....79 H2
Sudbury Av ALP/SUD HA0 ....79 H3
Sudbury Court Dr HRW HA1 ....100 C1
Sudbury Court Rd
   ALP/SUD HA0 ....100 C1
Sudbury Crs ALP/SUD HA0 ....100 D3
   BMLY BR1 ....212 C1
Sudbury Cft ALP/SUD HA0 ....100 B2
Sudbury Gdns CROY/NA CRO 247 E2
Sudbury Heights Av
   GFD/PVL UB6 ....100 B3
Sudbury Hl HRW HA1 ....100 A1
Sudbury Hill Cl ALP/SUD HA0 ......100 B2
Sudbury Rd BARK IG11 ....115 F3
Sudeley St IS N1 ....6 C2
Sudlow Rd WAND/EARL SW18 ......165 A5
Sudrey St STHWK SE1 ....23 E4
Suez Av GFD/PVL UB6 ....101 F1
Suez Rd PEND EN3 ....25 G5
Suffield Rd CHEAM SE5 ....55 F5
   PGE/AN SE20 ....210 A5
   SEVS/STOTM * N15 ....89 G1
Suffolk Cl CANST CC4R 15 G5
Suffolk Park Rd WALTH E17 ....90 C1
Suffolk Rd BARK IG11 ....114 D5
   BARN SW13 ....163 F1
   DAGE RM10 ....117 F3
   GDMY/SEVK IG3 ....91 F5
   PEND EN3 ....39 H6
   PLSTW E13 ....132 B2
   RYLN/HDSTN HA2 ....78 B6
   SCUP DA14 ....216 A2
   SEVS/STOTM N15 ....88 D1
   SNWD SE25 ....229 F1
   WLSDN NW10 ....81 G5
   WPK KT4 ....223 F6
Suffolk St FSTGT E7 ....112 C3
   STJS SW1Y 20 D1
Suffolk Vls
   WAND/EARL * SW18 ....185 G2
Sugar House La SRTFD E15 ....131 G1
Sugar Loaf Wk BETH * E2 ....130 A2
Sugden Rd BTSEA SW11 ....166 D2
   THDT KT7 ....220 C5
Sugden Wy BARK IG11 ....135 F1
Sulgrave Gdns SHB W12 ....144 A2
Sulgrave Rd HMSMTH W6 ....144 A2
Sulina Rd BRXS/STRHM SW2 ....167 G6
Sulivan Ct FUL/PGN SW6 ....165 G4
Sulivan Rd FUL/PGN SW6 ....165 G6
Sullivan Av CAN/RD E16 ....133 E4
Sullivan Cl BTSEA SW11 ....166 C1
   E/WMO/HCT KT8 ....199 F6
Sullivan Rd LBTH SE11 ....18 A5
Sullivan Wy BORE WD6 ....45 E1
Sultan Rd WAN E11 ....92 D1
Sultan St BECK BR3 ....210 B5
   CMBW SE5 ....168 C4
Sumatra Rd KIL/WHAMP NW6 .....105 H4

Sumburgh Rd BAL SW12 ....186 A1
Summer Av E/WMO/HCT KT8 ....220 A2
Summercourt Rd WCHPL E1 ....130 A5
Summerene Cl
   STRHM/NOR SW16 ....207 E3
Summerfield Av
   KIL/WHAMP NW6 ....124 C1
   NFNCH/WDSP N12 ....47 G2
Summerfield La SURB KT6 ....221 F6
Summerfield Rd LOU IG10 ....157 F1
   WEA W13 ....120 D3
Summerfield St
   LEE/GVPK SE12 ....192 B2
Summer Gdns
   E/WMO/HCT KT8 ....220 A2
Summer Gv BORE WD6 ....45 F1
Summer Hl CHST BR7 ....214 A5
Summerhill Cl ORP BR6 ....253 E2
Summerhill Gv EN EN1 ....53 E1
Summerhill Rd
   SEVS/STOTM N15 ....88 D1
Summerhill Wy MTCM CR4 ....206 C4
Summerhouse Av HEST TW5 ....158 C2
Summerhouse Rd RDART DA2 ......217 H1
Summerhouse Rd
   STNW/STAM N16 ....68 A1
Summerland Gdns MUSWH N10 .....66 C2
Summerlands Av ACT W3 ....122 C6
Summerlee Av EFNCH N2 ....86 B1
Summerlee Gdns EFNCH N2 ....86 B1
Summerley St
   WAND/EARL SW18 ....185 F4
Summer Rd E/WMO/HCT KT8 ....219 H2
Summersby Rd HGT N6 ....66 B3
Summers Cl BELMT SM2 ....243 E5
   WBLY HA9 ....62 B5
Summers La NFNCH/WDSP N12 .....65 H3
Summers Rw
   NFNCH/WDSP N12 ....66 A2
Summerstown TOOT SW17 ....185 G5
Summerton Wy THMD SE28 ....128 A6
Summerville Gdns SUT SM1 ....242 D4
Summerwood Rd TWK TW1 ....180 B1
Summit Av CDALE/KGS NW9 ....63 E2
Summit Cl CDALE/KGS NW9 ....82 D1
   EDGW HA8 ....62 A3
   STHGT/OAK N14 ....34 C4
Summit Dr WFD IG8 ....53 H3
Summit Est STNW/STAM * N16 ......89 G4
Summit Rd NTHLT UB5 ....95 F1
   WALTH E17 ....51 H1
Summit Wy NRWD SE19 ....209 E5
   STHGT/OAK N14 ....50 D4
Sumner Av PECK SE15 ....169 F2
Sumner Cl ORP BR6 ....252 C2
Sumner Gdns CROY/NA CRO 228 A5
Sumner Pl SKENS SW7 ....14 B6
Sumner Place Ms SKENS SW7 ......145 H4
Sumner Rd CROY/NA CRO 228 B5
   HRW HA1 ....79 C4
   PECK SE15 ....169 F1
Sumner Rd South
   CROY/NA CRO 228 A5
Sumner St STHWK SE1 ....23 E1
Sumpter Cl HAMP NW3 ....105 C4
Sunbeam Crs NKENS W10 ....124 A3
Sunbeam Rd WLSDN NW10 ....122 C3
Sunbury Av MLHL NW7 ....62 D1
   MORT/ESHN SW14 ....162 D5
Sunbury Ct BAR * EN5 ....34 C5
   SUN TW16 ....198 B5
Sunbury Court Rd SUN TW16 ....198 A5
Sunbury Gdns MLHL NW7 ....62 D1
Sunbury La BTSEA SW11 ....165 H2
Sunbury Rd CHEAM SM3 ....242 B1
Sunbury St WOOL/PLUM SE18 .....133 H5
Sunbury Wy FELT TW13 ....198 A1
Suncroft Pl SYD SE26 ....194 A2
Sunderland Mt FSTH * SE23 ....190 B4
Sunderland Rd EA W5 ....141 F3
   FSTH SE23 ....190 D4
Sunderland Ter BAY/PAD * W2 ....125 F5
Sunderland Wy MNPK E12 ....95 F6
Sundew Av SHB W12 ....123 C6
Sundew Ct ALP/SUD * HA0 ....121 G1
Sundial Av SNWD SE25 ....209 F5
Sundorne Rd CHARL SE7 ....152 D5
Sundridge Av BMLY BR1 ....213 G3
   WELL DA16 ....176 A1
Sundridge Pde BMLY * BR1 ....212 D3
Sundridge Rd CROY/NA CRO 229 F5
Sunfields Pl BKHTH/KID SE3 ....172 D1
Sun In Sands Rbt
   BKHTH/KID SE3 ....172 D1
Sunken Rd CROY/NA CRO 248 A3
Sunkist Wy WLGTN SM6 ....245 G6
Sunland Av BXLYHS DA6 ....176 E5
Sun La BKHTH/KID SE3 ....172 D1
Sunleigh Rd ALP/SUD HA0 ....101 G6
Sunley Gdns GFD/PVL UB6 ....120 C1
Sunlight Cl BETH E2 ....9 H4
Sunlight Sq STHGT/OAK N14 ....67 F1
Sunningdale Av ACT W3 ....123 C6
   BARK IG11 ....114 D6
   FELT TW13 ....198 C1
   RSLP HA4 ....78 A5
Sunningdale Cl
   BERM/RHTH * SE16 ....33 G4
   STAN HA7 ....43 G3
   SURB KT6 ....221 G6
   THMD SE28 ....128 C5
Sunningdale Gdns
   CDALE/KGS NW9 ....82 C2
   KENS * W8 ....145 E3
Sunningdale Ldg EDGW * HA8 ....61 H1
Sunningdale Rd HAYES BR2 ....233 G1
   SUT SM1 ....208 D2
Sunningfield Rd HDN NW4 ....63 H6
Sunningfields Crs HDN NW4 ....63 H5
Sunninghill Ct ACT * W3 ....142 C2
Sunninghill Rd LEW SE13 ....171 F3
Sunny Bank SNWD SE25 ....209 G6
Sunny Crs WLSDN NW10 ....80 E5
Sunnycroft Rd HSLW TW3 ....159 F1
   SNWD SE25 ....209 G6
   STHL UB1 ....119 E4
Sunnydale ORP BR6 ....216 A4
Sunnydale Gdns MLHL NW7 ....62 D2
Sunnydale Rd LEE/GVPK SE12 .....172 D6

Sunnydene Av CHING E4 ....71 H1
Sunnydene Gdns
   ALP/SUD HA0 ....101 E4
Sunnydene St SYD SE26 ....190 C6
Sunnyfield MLHL NW7 ....47 F6
Sunny Gardens Rd HDN NW4 ....63 H6
Sunny Hl HDN NW4 ....63 H5
Sunny Nook Gdns
   SAND/SEL CR2 ....246 D4
Sunnyhill Cl CLPT E5 ....110 C2
Sunnyhill Rd
   STRHM/NOR SW16 ....187 G6
Sunnyhurst Cl SUT SM1 ....243 E1
Sunnymead Av MTCM CR4 ....207 F6
Sunnymead Rd
   CDALE/KGS NW9 ....82 D3
   PUT/ROE SW15 ....163 H6
Sunnymede Av HOR/WEW KT19 ...241 E6
Sunnymede Dr BARK/HLT IG6 ....94 B1
Sunny Nook Gdns
   SAND/SEL CR2 ....246 D4
Sunny Pl HDN NW4 ....84 A1
The Sunny Rd PEND EN3 ....40 B2
Sunnyside CRICK NW2 ....104 D1
   ESH/CLAY KT10 ....220 A5
   WIM/MER SW19 ....204 C2
   WOT/HER KT12 ....218 A2
Sunnyside Dr CHING E4 ....55 C2
Sunnyside Rd ARCH N19 ....67 G4
   EA W5 ....141 F1
   IL IG1 ....114 C1
   LEY E10 ....91 E5
   TEDD TW11 ....179 H6
Sunnyside Rd East ED N9 ....53 C5
Sunnyside Rd North ED * N9 ....53 F5
Sunnyside Rd South ED * N9 ....53 F5
Sunnyside Vw CDALE/KGS NW9 .....83 G2
Sunny Wy NFNCH/WDSP N12 ....66 A3
Sun Pas BERM/RHTH SE16 ....25 E5
Sunray Av BRYLDS KT5 ....222 B4
   CMBW SE5 ....169 E6
   HAYES BR2 ....233 C3
Sunrise Cl FELT TW15 ....178 D5
Sun Rd WKENS W14 ....144 D5
Sunset Av CHING E4 ....55 F3
   WFD IG8 ....52 D3
Sunset Gdns SNWD SE25 ....209 E5
Sunset Rd CMBW SE5 ....168 C5
   THMD SE28 ....155 C2
Sunset Vw BAR EN5 ....20 C4
Sunshine Wy MTCM CR4 ....206 B5
Sun St SDTCH EC2A 15 H1
Superior Dr ORP BR6 ....266 C5
Surbiton Crs KUT KT1 ....221 E5
Surbiton Hall Cl KUT KT1 ....221 G1
Surbiton Hill Pk BRYLDS KT5 ....221 G1
Surbiton Hill Rd SURB KT6 ....221 G1
Surbiton Rd KUT KT1 ....221 F1
Surlingham Cl THMD SE28 ....136 B6
Surma Cl WCHPL E1 ....9 H6
Surmans Cl DAGW RM9 ....116 A6
Surrendale Pl MV/WKIL W9 ....125 C3
Surrey Canal Rd
   BERM/RHTH SE16 ....150 A6
Surrey Crs CHSWK W4 ....117 G6
Surrey Gdns FSBYPK N4 ....68 C3
   WALW SE17 ....32 A4
Surrey La BTSEA SW11 ....166 A2
Surrey Ms WNWD SE27 ....189 E6
Surrey Quays Rd
   BERM/RHTH SE16 ....150 A3
Surrey Rd BARK IG11 ....117 F3
   DAGE RM10 ....117 F3
   HRW HA1 ....79 G3
   PECK SE15 ....170 B6
   WWKM BR4 ....215 F6
Surrey Rw STHWK SE1 ....22 C5
Surrey Sq WALW SE17 ....32 A3
Surrey St CROY/NA CRO 246 C1
   PLSTW E13 ....132 C2
   TPL/STR WC2R 13 H5
Surrey Ter WALW SE17 ....32 C1
Surrey Water Rd
   BERM/RHTH SE16 ....150 B1
Surridge Gdns NRWD SE19 ....190 B5
Surr St HOLWY N7 ....107 G3
Susan Cl ROMW/RG RM7 ....77 G6
Susannah St POP/IOD E14 ....131 F5
Susan Rd BKHTH/KID SE3 ....174 A2
Susan Wd CHST BR7 ....214 A4
Sussex Av ISLW TW7 ....160 A4
Sussex Cl ARCH * N19 ....87 G6
   NTHLT UB5 ....95 E4
   REDBR IG4 ....93 H3
   TWK TW1 ....160 D1
Sussex Crs NTHLT UB5 ....95 E4
Sussex Gdns BAY/PAD * W2 ....9 G3
   BAY/PAD W2 ....125 H5
   CHSGTN KT9 ....239 F4
   EFNCH N2 ....86 B2
   FSBYPK N4 ....67 H2
   HOLWY * N7 ....86 C2
Sussex Ga EFNCH * N2 ....86 B2
Sussex Ms BAY/PAD * W2 ....125 H6
Sussex Ms East BAY/PAD * W2 ....9 G4
Sussex Ms West BAY/PAD * W2 ...125 H6
Sussex Pl BAY/PAD W2 ....9 G4
   CAMTN NW1 ....3 F6
   HMSMTH W6 ....144 A5
   NWMAL KT3 ....223 E1
Sussex Rd CAR SM5 ....244 B4
   EBAR EN4 ....34 E4
   ERITH DA8 ....177 F1
   HRW HA1 ....79 G2
   MTCM * CR4 ....207 G2
   NWDGN UB2 ....102 B3
   NWMAL KT3 ....223 E1
   SAND/SEL CR2 ....246 D4
   SCUP DA14 ....215 H1
   WWKM BR4 ....231 F5
Sussex Sq BAY/PAD * W2 ....125 H6
Sussex Ter PGE/AN * SE20 ....210 A3
Sussex Wy ARCH N19 ....87 F5
   EBAR EN4 ....36 D6
Sutcliffe Cl GLDGN NW11 ....85 F2
Sutcliffe Rd WELL DA16 ....176 A3
   WOOL/PLUM SE18 ....155 G6
Sutherland Av MV/WKIL W9 ....125 F1
   STMC/STPC BR5 ....235 F3

WEA W13 ....120 D5
WELL DA16 ....174 D5
Sutherland Cl BAR EN5 ....34 C5
Sutherland Ct CDALE/KGS NW9 ...82 B1
Sutherland Dr WIM/MER SW19 ....205 H4
Sutherland Gdns
    MORT/ESHN SW14 ....163 E4
    WPK KT4 ....225 H5
Sutherland Gv TEDD TW11 ....200 A1
    WAND/EARL SW18 ....184 D2
Sutherland House WALTH * E17 ...70 C6
Sutherland PI BAY/PAD W2 ....125 E5
Sutherland Rd BELV DA17 ....157 E3
    BOW E3 ....105 J2
    CHSWK W4 ....142 D6
    CROY/NA CR0 ....228 A4
    ED N9 ....54 B1
    PEND EN3 ....54 B1
    STHL UB1 ....118 D5
    TOTM N17 ....69 G3
    WALTH E17 ....70 C6
    WEA W13 ....120 C5
Sutherland Rw PIM SW1V 27 H3
Sutherland Sq WALW SE17 ....31 E4
Sutherland St PIM SW1V 27 H3
Sutherland Wk * W13 ....120 C6
Sutherland Wk WALW SE17 ....31 F4
Sutlej Rd CHARL SE7 ....175 E1
Sutterton St HOLWY N7 ....107 H4
Sutton Cl BECK BR5 ....211 F4
    CHSWK * W4 ....142 C6
    LOU IG10 ....57 G2
Sutton Common Rd
    CHEAM SM3 ....224 D4
Sutton Ct BELMT SM2 ....245 G5
    CHSWK * W4 ....142 C6
    EA * W5 ....141 G1
Sutton Court Rd BELMT SM2 ....242 C6
    CHSWK W4 ....142 C6
    PLSTW E13 ....133 E2
    SUT SM1 ....243 H4
Sutton Crs BAR EN5 ....34 B6
Sutton Dene HSLW TW5 ....159 F2
Sutton Est IS * N1 ....108 B5
The Sutton Est IS * N1 ....108 B5
Sutton Gdns CROY/NA CR0 ....228 C2
Sutton Gv SUT SM1 ....243 H3
Sutton Hall HEST TW5 ....135 F5
Sutton La CHSWK W4 ....142 C5
    HEST TW5 ....135 E2
Sutton La South CHSWK W4 ....142 C6
Sutton Park Rd SUT SM1 ....243 F4
Sutton PI HOM E9 ....110 A3
Sutton Rd BARK IG11 ....155 E1
    HEST TW5 ....159 E2
    MUSWH N10 ....66 C4
    PLSTW E13 ....132 B3
    WALTH E17 ....52 B1
Sutton Rw SOHO/SHAV W1D 10 C3
Sutton Sq HEST TW5 ....158 D2
    HOM * E9 ....110 A3
Sutton Wy HEST TW5 ....158 D2
    NKENS W10 ....124 A4
Swaby Rd WAND/EARL SW18 .....185 C4
Swaffield Rd
    WAND/EARL SW18 ....185 G2
Swain Cl TOOT SW17 ....206 D2
Swain Rd THHTH CR7 ....228 C2
Swain's La KTTN NW5 ....106 C1
Swainson Rd ACT W3 ....143 F2
Swains Rd MTCM CR4 ....206 B3
Swain St STJWD NW8 ....125 H3
Swaledale Cl FBAR/BDGN N11 .....66 C2
Swallands Rd CAT SE6 ....191 E5
Swallow Cl BUSH WD23 ....45 H1
    NWCR SE14 ....170 A2
Swallow Ct RSLP * HA4 ....78 A5
Swallowdale SAND/SEL CR2 ....268 B6
Swallow Dr NTHLT UB5 ....119 E1
    WLSDN NW10 ....102 D4
Swallowfield Rd CHARL SE7 ....152 D5
Swallow Gdns
    STRHM/NOR SW16 ....207 F1
Swallow PI REGST W1B 11 H4
Swallow St CONDST W1S 12 B6
    EHAM E6 ....107 J4
Swallowtail Cl STMC/STPC BR5 ..236 B1
Swanage Rd CHING E4 ....71 G3
    WAND/EARL SW18 ....185 G1
Swanage Waye YEAD UB4 ....118 A5
Swan And Pike Rd PEND EN3 .....41 F1
Swan Ap EHAM E6 ....133 G4
Swanbridge Rd BXLYHN DA7 .....177 E2
Swan Cl CROY/NA * CR0 ....229 E4
    FELT TW13 ....196 C1
    STMC/STPC BR5 ....215 G6
    WALTH E17 ....51 F4
Swandon Wy
    WAND/EARL SW18 ....165 F5
Swan Dr CDALE/KGS NW9 ....63 E5
Swanfield St BETH E2 ....8 C4
Swan Island TWK * TW1 ....180 C5
Swan La CANST EC4R 15 H6
    LOU IG10 ....57 J3
    TRDG/WHET N20 ....49 G5
Swanley Rd WELL DA16 ....176 A2
Swanmead Rd ERITH DA8 ....177 E1
Swan Mead STHWK SE1 ....19 G4
Swan Ms BRXN/ST SW9 ....167 H3
Swan Pas WCHPL E1 ....13 K6
Swan PI BARN SW13 ....163 F5
Swan Rd BERM/RHTH SE16 ....150 A2
    FELT TW13 ....214 A3
    GFD/PVL UB6 ....119 F5
Swanscombe Rd CHSWK W4 .....143 G5
    NTGHL W11 ....144 B1
Swansea Rd PEND EN3 ....40 A5
Swanston Pth OXHEY WD19 ......42 A5
Swan St ISLW TW7 ....160 D4
    STHWK SE1 ....23 H4
Swanton Gdns
    WIM/MER SW19 ....184 B3
Swanton Rd ERITH DA8 ....177 E1
Swan Wk CHEL SW3 ....26 C5
Swan Wy PEND EN3 ....40 D1
Swanwick Cl PUT/ROE SW15 .....183 F2
Swan Is IS N1 ....108 B4
Sward Rd STMC/STPC BR5 ....255 J3
Swaton Rd BOW E3 ....105 J3
Swaylands Rd BELV DA17 ....157 E5
Swaythling Cl UED N18 ....53 H6

Sweden Ga BERM/RHTH SE16 ....150 C4
Sweeney Crs STHWK SE1 ....24 C4
Sweeps La STMC/STPC BR5 ....236 B2
Sweet Briar Gn UED N18 ....53 F5
Sweet Briar Gv ED N9 ....53 F5
Sweet Briar Wk UED N18 ....53 F6
Sweetmans Av PIN HA5 ....58 B6
Sweets Wy TRDG/WHET N20 .....49 H4
Swete St PLSTW E13 ....132 C1
Sweyn PI BKHTH/KID SE3 ....172 C3
Swift Cl RYLN/HDSTN HA2 ....79 F6
    WALTH E17 ....70 C3
Swift Rd FELT TW13 ....178 B6
    NWDGN UB2 ....138 D3
Swiftsden Wy BMLY BR1 ....212 A2
Swift St FUL/PGN SW6 ....139 H6
Swinbrook Rd NKENS W10 ....124 C4
Swinburne Crs CROY/NA CR0 .....230 A3
Swinburne Rd PUT/ROE SW15 ...163 G5
Swinderby Rd ALP/SUD HA0 ......101 G4
Swindon Cl CDMY/SEVK IG3 ......95 E6
Swindon St SHB * W12 ....143 H1
Swinfield Cl FELT TW13 ....178 C6
Swinford Gdns BRXN/ST SW9 ....168 B4
Swingate La WOOL/PLUM SE18 ..175 D1
Swinnerton St HOM E9 ....110 C1
Swinton Cl WBLY HA9 ....82 B5
Swinton PI FSBYW WC1X 5 G3
Swinton St FSBYW WC1X 5 G3
Swires Shaw HAYES BR2 ....251 F2
Swithland Gdns ELTH/MOT SE9 ..193 H6
Swyncombe Av BTFD TW8 ....140 D4
Swynford Gdns HDN NW4 ....63 J1
Sybil Phoenix Cl DEPT SE8 ......150 B5
Sybourn St WALTH E17 ....69 H4
Sycamore Av BFN/LL DA15 ....195 F1
    BOW E3 ....105 H1
    EA W5 ....141 F5
Sycamore Cl ACT W3 ....143 E1
    CAN/RD E16 ....132 A3
    CAR SM5 ....244 B2
    EBAR EN4 ....21 H1
    NTHLT UB5 ....98 C6
    UED N18 ....53 G6
Sycamore Gdns MTCM CR4 ....205 H5
    SHB W12 ....143 G3
Sycamore Gv CAT SE6 ....191 G1
    CDALE/KGS NW9 ....82 C4
    NWMAL KT3 ....205 E6
Sycamore Hi FBAR/BDGN N11 ...66 C2
    ERITH * DA8 ....157 H5
Sycamore Ms WIM/MER SW19 ...204 A2
Sycamore St FSBYE EC1V 6 C7
Sycamore Wk NKENS W10 ....124 C3
Sydcote DUL * SE21 ....188 C4
Sydenham Av SYD SE26 ....209 H1
    WCHMN N21 ....37 H5
Sydenham Cottages
    LEE/GVPK * SE12 ....193 E4
Sydenham HI SYD SE26 ....189 G5
Sydenham Pk SYD SE26 ....190 A3
Sydenham Park Rd SYD SE26 ....190 A3
Sydenham RI FSTH SE23 ....189 H4
Sydenham Rd CROY/NA CR0 ......228 C6
    SYD SE26 ....210 B1
Sydenham Station Ap
    SYD SE26 ....190 A6
Sydmons Ct FSTH * SE23 ....190 A6
Sydner Rd STNW/STAM N16 ......86 A2
Sydney Cl SKENS SW7 ....14 A7
Sydney Gv HDN NW4 ....64 A2
Sydney Ms SKENS SW7 ....14 A7
Sydney Pl SKENS SW7 ....14 A7
Sydney Rd ABYW SE2 ....156 B3
    BARK/HLT IG6 ....74 C5
    BXLYHS DA6 ....176 D3
    CEND/HSY/T N8 ....67 F1
    ENC/FH EN2 ....23 J5
    MUSWH N10 ....48 A5
    RCH/KEW TW9 ....137 G5
    RYNPK SW20 ....204 B5
    SCUP DA14 ....195 E6
    SUT SM1 ....243 E2
    TEDD TW11 ....190 B6
    WAN E11 ....89 E2
    WEA W13 ....140 C1
Sydney St CHEL SW3 ....26 A3
Sydney Ter CHST/CLAY * KT10 ..238 B4
Sylvan Av CHDH RM6 ....96 A2
    MLHL NW7 ....45 J1
    WDGN N22 ....68 A3
Sylverdale Rd CROY/NA CR0 .....246 B1
Sylvester Av CHST SR7 ....213 J6
Sylvester Pth HACK * E8 ....109 H4
Sylvester Rd ALP/SUD HA0 ....101 K5
    EFNCH N2 ....109 H4
    HACK * E8 ....97 J4
    WALTH E17 ....69 H4
Sylvia Av PIN HA5 ....58 D2
Sylvia Gdns WBLY HA9 ....102 B5
Symes Ms CAMTN * NW1 ....4 A1
Symington Ms HOM * E9 ....110 J3
Symister Ms IS * N1 ....7 G6
Symons St CHEL SW3 ....29 G6
Symphony Ms NKENS * W10 ....124 C2
Syon Gate Wy BTFD TW8 ....160 D1
Syon La ISLW TW7 ....140 B6
Syon Pk ISLW * TW7 ....160 C1
Syon Park Gdns ISLW TW7 ....160 B1

T

Tabard Garden Est STHWK SE1 ..23 G3
Tabard St STHWK SE1 ....23 G5
Tabernacle Av PLSTW E13 ....132 C3
Tabernacle St SDTCH EC2A 7 H4
Tableer Av CLAP SW4 ....167 J6
Tabley Rd HOLWY N7 ....107 C2
Tabor Gdns CHEAM SM3 ....242 C4
Tabor Gv WIM/MER SW19 ....204 C3
Tabor Rd HMSMTH W6 ....143 H5
Tachbrook Rd WANDGH IG2 .....138 B4
Tachbrook St PIM SW1V 28 B2
Tack Ms BROCKY SE4 ....171 E4
Tadema Rd WBPTN SW10 ....165 C1
Tadmor St SHB W12 ....141 B1
Tadworth Av NWMAL KT3 ....223 F1
Tadworth Rd CRICK NW2 ....83 G6
Taeping St POP/IOD E14 ....151 F4
Taffy's How MTCM CR4 ....206 A6
Tait Rd CROY/NA CR0 ....229 E4
Takeley Cl CRW RM5 ....77 H5
Talacre Rd KTTN NW5 ....106 C4
Talbot Av EFNCH N2 ....65 G2
    OXHEY WD19 ....42 C5
Talbot Cl SEVS/STOTM N15 ......68 F1
Talbot Ct BANK EC3V 13 F6
Talbot Crs HDN NW4 ....63 G2
Talbot Gdns CDMY/SEVK IG3 ....95 E6
Talbot PI BKHTH/KID SE3 ....172 A5
Talbot Rd ALP/SUD HA0 ....101 F5
    BAY/PAD W2 ....125 E5
    CAR SM5 ....244 C5
    DAGW RM9 ....116 D5
    EDUL SE22 ....169 H5
    EHAM E6 ....133 H1
    FSTGT E7 ....112 C2
    HCT N6 ....48 A5
    ISLW TW7 ....160 C5
    KTN/HRWW/W HA3 ....60 B5
    NTGHL W11 ....124 C6
    NWDGN UB2 ....138 C4
    SEVS/STOTM N15 ....89 F1
    THHTH CR7 ....228 D1
    WDGN N22 ....67 E5
    WEA * W13 ....120 C6
    WHTN TW2 ....180 A3
Talbot Sq BAY/PAD W2 ....9 H4
Talbot Wk NTCHL W11 ....124 C5
    WLSDN NW10 ....81 G4
Talbot Yd STHWK SE1 ....23 G2
Talcott Pth
    BRXS/STRHM * SW2 ....188 A3
Talfourd PI PECK SE15 ....169 F2
Talfourd Rd PECK SE15 ....169 F2
Talgarth Rd WKENS W14 ....119 F5
Talisman Cl CDMY/SEVK IG3 .....95 H5
Talisman Sq SYD SE26 ....189 G6
Talisman Wy WBLY HA9 ....80 C1
Tallack Rd LEY E10 ....89 G5
Tall Elms Cl HAYES BR2 ....232 B2
Tallis Cl CAN/RD E16 ....133 D5
Tallis Gv CHARL SE7 ....152 D6
Tallis St EMB EC4Y 14 B5
Tallis Vw WLSDN NW10 ....102 A3
Tall Trees STRHM/NOR SW16 ....207 H4
Talma Gdns WHTN TW2 ....180 A2
Talmage Cl FSTH SE23 ....190 A2
Talman Gv STAN HA7 ....61 F2
Taima St BRXS/STRHM SW2 .....168 A5
Talwin St BOW E3 ....105 K2
Tamarind Yd WAP E1W 25 F1
Tamarisk Sq SHB W12 ....123 H6
Tamar St CHARL SE7 ....153 C4
Tamesis Gdns WPK KT4 ....223 H6
Tamian Wy HSLWW TW4 ....158 A4
Tamworth Av WFD IG8 ....72 A2
Tamworth La MTCM CR4 ....206 D6
Tamworth Pk MTCM CR4 ....226 D1
Tamworth PI CROY/NA CR0 ......228 J6
Tamworth Rd CROY/NA CR0 ......228 J6
Tamworth St FUL/PGN SW6 ......145 K6
Tancred Rd FSBYPK N4 ....88 B3
Tandridge Dr ORP BR6 ....234 D5
Tanfield Av CRICK NW2 ....103 F2
Tanfield Rd CROY/NA CR0 ....245 J1
Tangier Rd RCHPK/HAM TW10 ..162 B4
Tangleberry CI BMLY BR1 ....233 H1
Tangle Tree Cl EFNCH N2 ....65 F5
Tanglewood Cl CROY/NA CR0 ...248 A1
    STAN HA7 ....44 A6
Tangley Gv PUT/ROE SW15 ......183 C2
Tangley Park Rd HPTN * TW12 ..198 D1
Tangmere Gdns NTHLT UB5 ......118 A1
Tangmere Gv KUTN/CMB KT2 ...201 F1
Tangmere Wy CDALE/KGS NW9 ..65 E1
Tanhouse Fld NFWCH * NW5 .....107 F3
Tankerton Houses
    STPAN * WC1H 5 F4
Tankerton Rd SURB KT6 ....221 H6
Tankerton St STPAN WC1H 5 F4
Tankerton Ter CROY/NA * CR0 ..227 H4
Tankerville Rd
    STRHM/NOR SW16 ....207 F3
Tankridge Rd CRICK NW2 ....81 H6
The Tanneries WCHPL * E1 ....130 A3
Tanners End La UED N18 ....50 A6
Tanner's Hi DEPT SE8 ....171 E2
Tanners La BARK/HLT IG6 ....74 C6
Tanner St BARK IG11 ....114 C4
    STHWK SE1 ....24 B4
Tannery Cl CROY/NA CR0 ....230 B2
    DAGE RM10 ....117 J1
Tannington Ter FSBYPK * N4 ....108 A1
Tannsfeld Rd SYD SE26 ....210 B1
Tansley Cl HOLWY * N7 ....107 F3
Tanswell St STHWK * SE1 ....22 A4
Tansy Cl EHAM E6 ....135 A5
Tantallon Rd BAL SW12 ....186 C5
Tant Av CAN/RD E16 ....132 B5
Tantony Gv CHDH RM6 ....96 B6
Tan Yard La BXLY * DA5 ....197 C4
Tanza Rd HAMP NW3 ....85 K3
Tapestry Cl BELMT SM2 ....243 F5
Taplow PI MTCM CR4 ....226 A1
Taplow St IS N1 ....7 E3
Tappesfield Rd PECK SE15 ....170 A4

Tapping Cl KUTN/CMB * KT2 ....202 C1
Tapp St BETH E2 ....9 G1
Tapster St BAR EN5 ....34 D4
Taransay Wk IS N1 ....108 D4
Tara Ter BROCKY * SE4 ....170 C4
Tarbert Rd EDUL SE22 ....169 E6
Tarbert Wk WCHPL E1 ....130 A6
Tariff Rd UED N18 ....53 E4
Tarleton Gdns FSTH SE23 ....189 H3
Tarling Cl SCUP DA14 ....195 H5
Tarling Rd CAN/RD E16 ....132 B5
    EFNCH N2 ....65 G1
Tarling St WCHPL E1 ....17 H4
Tambank Pk ELTH/OAK N14 .....37 G6
Tarn St STHWK SE1 ....23 E6
Tarnwood Pk ELTH/MOT SE9 ....174 D1
Tarragon Cl NWCR * SE14 ....170 C1
Tarragon Gv SYD SE26 ....210 B2
Tarrant Pl MBLAR W1H 10 C2
Tarriff Crs DEPT SE8 ....150 D4
Tarrington
    STRHM/NOR * SW16 ....187 F6
Tarver Rd WALW SE17 ....30 D4
Tarves Wy GNWCH SE10 ....113 E6
Tash PI FBAR/BDGN * N11 ....66 D1
Tasker Rd HAMP NW3 ....106 B5
Tasmania Ter UED N18 ....51 K2
Tasman Rd BRXN/ST SW9 ....167 G4
Tasso Rd HMSMTH W6 ....144 C6
Tate Gdns BUSH WD23 ....44 A2
Tate Rd CAN/RD E16 ....153 H1
    SUT SM1 ....243 E5
Tatnell Rd FSTH SE23 ....191 G5
Tattersall Cl ELTH/MOT SE9 .....173 G6
Tatton Crs CLPT E5 ....89 F4
Tatum St WALW SE17 ....31 J1
Tauheed Cl FSBYPK N4 ....88 C6
Taunton Av HSLW TW3 ....159 G3
    RYNPK SW20 ....203 H5
Taunton Cl BARK/HLT IG6 ....75 F2
    BXLYHN DA7 ....177 H4
    CHEAM SM3 ....225 E5
Taunton Dr EFNCH N2 ....65 G5
    ENC/FH EN2 ....23 H4
Taunton Ms CAMTN NW1 ....2 C5
Taunton Pl CAMTN NW1 ....2 C5
Taunton Rd GFD/PVL UB6 ....99 F6
    LEE SE12 ....173 G6
Taunton Wy STAN HA7 ....61 G6
Tavern Cl CAR SM5 ....226 A4
Taverners Cl NTGHL * W11 ....144 C1
Taverner Sq HBRY * N5 ....108 C2
Taverners Wy CHING E4 ....38 C1
Tavistock Av GFD/PVL UB6 ....120 C1
    WALTH E17 ....51 F5
Tavistock Cl STNW/STAM N16 ...109 E3
Tavistock Ct COVGDN * WC2E ..11 F5
Tavistock Crs MTCM CR4 ....227 G1
    NTGHL W11 ....124 D4
Tavistock Gdns
    GDMY/SEVK IG3 ....115 G2
Tavistock Gv CROY/NA CR0 ......228 D4
Tavistock Ms NTGHL * W11 ....4 C5
Tavistock Pl STHGT/OAK * N14 ..50 D1
    STPAN WC1H 4 E5
Tavistock Rd CAR SM5 ....225 H5
    CROY/NA CR0 ....228 D5
    EDGW HA8 ....61 H4
    FBAR/BDGN N11 ....66 A1
    FSTGT E7 ....88 D2
    NTGHL W11 ....124 D4
    SRTFD E15 ....112 B4
    SWFD E18 ....70 D2
    WELL DA16 ....176 A2
    WLSDN NW10 ....125 F1
Tavistock Sq STPAN WC1H 4 D5
Tavistock St COVGDN WC2E 11 F5
Tavistock Ter ARCH N19 ....107 F1
Tavitton St STPAN WC1H 4 C5
Tavy Cl LBTH SE11 ....30 B3
Tawney Rd THMD SE28 ....115 H6
Tawny Cl WEA W13 ....140 D1
Tawny Wy BERM/RHTH SE16 ....150 B4
Tayben Av WHTN TW2 ....180 A1
Taybridge Rd BTSEA SW11 ....166 C4
Tayburn Cl POP/IOD E14 ....131 K5
Taylor Av RCH/KEW TW9 ....162 B6
Taylor Cl CRW RM5 ....77 E3
    HPTN TW12 ....199 C1
    HSLW TW3 ....159 H1
    ORP BR6 ....253 F2
    TOTM N17 ....69 G3
Taylor Rd WIM/MER SW19 ....206 A3
    WLGTN SM6 ....244 D3
Taylor's Buildings
    WOOL/PLUM SE18 ....134 B4
Taylors Cl SCUP DA14 ....195 F6
Taylor's La BAR EN5 ....20 D4
    SYD SE26 ....189 H6
    WLSDN NW10 ....103 E5
Taylors Md MLHL * NW7 ....45 G3
Taymount Ri FSTH SE23 ....190 A4
Tayport Cl IS N1 ....107 H5
Tayside Dr EDGW HA8 ....46 B5
Taywood Rd NTHLT UB5 ....118 D2
Teak Cl BERM/RHTH SE16 ....150 C1
Teal Av STMC/STPC BR5 ....236 B1
Teal Cl CAN/RD E16 ....133 F4
Teale St BETH E2 ....8 C2
Tealing Dr HOR/WEW KT19 ....240 D2
Teasel Cl CROY/NA CR0 ....230 B5
Teasel Wy SRTFD E15 ....132 A2
Tebworth Rd TOTM N17 ....69 F3
Technology Pk
    CDALE/KGS * NW9 ....62 D5
Teck Cl ISLW TW7 ....160 C3
Tedder Cl CHSGTN KT9 ....239 E3
Tedder Rd SAND/SEL CR2 ....248 B5
Teddington Pk TEDD TW11 ....200 B1
Teddington Park Rd
    TEDD TW11 ....180 B6
Tedworth Gdns CHEL SW3 ....26 C4
Tedworth Sq CHEL SW3 ....26 D5
Tees Av GFD/PVL UB6 ....120 A1
Teesdale Av ISLW TW7 ....160 C2
Teesdale Cl BETH E2 ....92 C5
Teesdale Gdns ISLW TW7 ....160 C2
    SNWD SE25 ....209 E5
Teesdale Rd WAN E11 ....92 B3

Teesdale St BETH E2 .....9 G2
Teesdale Yd BETH E2 .....9 H2
The Tee ACT W3 .....123 E5
Teevan Cl CROY/NA CR0 .....229 G4
Teevan Rd CROY/NA CR0 .....229 G4
Teignmouth Cl CLAP SW4 .....167 F5
  EDGW HA8 .....81 H5
Teignmouth Rd CRICK NW2 .....104 B5
  WELL DA16 .....176 A3
Telcote Wy RSLP * HA4 .....58 A8
Telegraph Hl HAMP NW3 .....105 F1
Telegraph La ESH/CLAY KT10 .....288 D2
Telegraph Pl POP/IOD E14 .....151 F4
Telegraph Rd PUT/ROE SW15 .....184 A2
Telegraph St LOTH EC2R 15 C3
Telephone Pl FUL/PGN * SW6 .....144 D6
Telfers court Rd BAL SW12 .....187 F3
Telford Av MLHL NW7 .....187 F3
Telford Cl NRWD SE19 .....209 F2
  WALTH E17 .....90 C4
Telford Dr WOT/HER KT12 .....178 A4
Telford Rd CDALE/KGS NW9 .....83 F3
  CHST BR7 .....194 D4
  GFD/PVL UB6 .....119 F6
  HSLWW W14 .....179 E2
  NKENS W10 .....124 C4
Telford Rd North Circular Rd
  FBAR/BDGN N11 .....67 E2
Telford Ter PIM * SW1V 28 A5
Telford Wy ACT W3 .....123 E4
  YEAD UB4 .....118 C4
Telham Rd EHAM E6 .....108 A1
Tell Gv EDUL SE22 .....169 F5
Tellson Av WOOL/PLUM SE18 .....175 G2
Telscombe Cl ORP BR6 .....235 E6
Temeraire St
  BERM/RHTH SE16 .....150 A2
Tempelhof Av HDN NW4 .....84 A4
Temperley Rd BAL SW12 .....186 C2
Templar Dr THMD SE28 .....136 B5
Templar Pl HPTN TW12 .....179 F2
Templars Av GLDGN NW11 .....84 D5
Templars Crs FNCH N3 .....65 E5
Templars Dr
  KTN/HRWW/WS * HA3 .....59 H2
Templar St CMBW SE5 .....169 H2
Temple Av BCTR RM8 .....97 E5
  CROY/NA CR0 .....248 D1
  EMB EC4Y 14 E6
  TRDG/WHET N20 .....49 H2
Temple Cl FNCH N3 .....64 D5
  WAN E11 .....92 A4
  WOOL/PLUM SE18 .....154 C3
Templecombe Rd HOM E9 .....110 A6
Templecombe Wy MRDN SM4 .....224 C2
Temple Dwellings BETH * E2 .....9 G2
Temple Fortune Hl
  GLDGN NW11 .....85 E2
Temple Fortune La
  GLDGN NW11 .....84 D3
Temple Gdns BCTR RM8 .....116 B1
  EMB * EC4Y 14 E5
  GLDGN NW11 .....84 D3
  WCHMH * N21 .....52 B4
Temple Gv ENC/FH EN2 .....38 A1
  GLDGN NW11 .....85 E3
Temple La EMB EC4Y 14 E4
Templeman Rd HNWL W7 .....120 B4
Templemead Cl ACT W3 .....123 E5
Temple Mead Cl STAN HA7 .....60 D2
Temple Mills La LEY E10 .....111 F2
Temple Pde BAR * EN5 .....49 H2
Temple Pl TPL/STR WC2R 14 E5
Temple Rd CEND/HSY/T N8 .....87 H1
  CHSWK W4 .....142 C3
  CRICK NW2 .....104 A2
  CROY/NA CR0 .....246 D2
  EA W5 .....141 F5
  EHAM E6 .....113 G6
  HSLW TW3 .....161 H5
  RCH/KEW TW9 .....161 H5
Temple Sheen Rd
  MORT/ESHN SW14 .....162 C5
Temple St BETH E2 .....9 G2
Templeton Av CHING E4 .....55 E6
Templeton Cl
  STNW/STAM * N16 .....109 E3
  THHTH CR7 .....208 D4
Templeton Pl ECT SW5 .....145 E4
Templeton Rd
  SEVS/STOTM N15 .....109 E1
Temple Wy SUT SM1 .....243 H1
Templewood WEA W13 .....120 D4
Templewood Av HAMP NW3 .....105 F1
Templewood Gdns HAMP NW3 .....105 F1
Temple Yd BETH E2 .....9 F4
Tempsford Cl ENC/FH EN2 .....38 C4
Tempsford Ct RYLN/HDSTN HA2 .....78 D6
Tenbury Cl FSTGT E7 .....113 G6
Tenbury Ct BAL SW12 .....187 F3
Tenby Av KTN/HRWW/WS HA3 .....60 D5
Tenby Cl CHDH RM6 .....96 C5
Tenby Gdns NTHLT UB5 .....96 D5
Tenby Rd CHDH RM6 .....96 C5
  EDGW HA8 .....116 H4
  PEND EN3 .....40 A4
  WALTH E17 .....90 C4
  WELL DA16 .....176 B2
Tench St WAP E1W 25 C2
Tenda Rd BERM/RHTH SE16 .....33 G2
Tenham Av BRXS/STRHM SW2 .....187 F4
Tenniel Cl BAY/PAD W2 .....125 G5
Tennison Rd SNWD SE25 .....229 F1
Tennis St STHWK SE1 .....23 G5
Tenniswood Rd EN EN1 .....39 F2
Tennyson Av CDALE/KGS NW9 .....62 C6
  MNPK E12 .....113 G5
  NWMAL KT3 .....223 H2
  TWK TW1 .....180 B3
  WAN E11 .....92 C4
Tennyson Cl PEND EN3 .....40 B6
  WELL DA16 .....175 G2
Tennyson Rd HNWL W7 .....120 D6
  KIL/WHAMP NW6 .....104 D6
  MLHL NW7 .....63 H1
  PGE/AN SE20 .....210 B3
  SRTFD E15 .....112 A5

WALTH E17 .....90 D3
  WIM/MER SW19 .....205 C2
Tennyson St VX/NE SW8 .....166 D5
Tensing Rd NWDGN UB2 .....139 E3
Tentelow La NWDGN UB2 .....139 F3
Tenterden Cl ELTH/MOT SE9 .....193 H6
  HDN NW4 .....64 B5
Tenterden Dr HDN NW4 .....64 B5
Tenterden Gdns CROY/NA CR0 .....229 G4
  HDN NW4 .....64 B5
Tenterden Gv HDN NW4 .....84 A1
Tenterden Rd BCTR RM8 .....96 D6
  CROY/NA CR0 .....229 G4
  TOTM N17 .....69 F3
Tenterden St CONDST W1S 11 H4
Tenter Gnd WCHPL * E1 .....16 C2
Tent St WCHPL E1 .....92 D6
Terling Cl WAN E11 .....112 B1
Terling Rd BCTR RM8 .....97 E6
Terling Wk IS * N1 .....108 C6
Terminus Pl PIM * SW1V 19 H6
Terrace Gdns BARN SW13 .....146 C4
Terrace La RCHPK/HAM TW10 .....181 C1
Terrace Rd HOM E9 .....110 D5
  PLSTW E13 .....112 D6
The Terrace BARN SW13 .....163 C5
  BETH * E2 .....82 D5
  CHING * E4 .....56 A5
  DEPT * SE8 .....150 D4
  EFNCH * N2 .....86 C1
  FNCH * N3 .....64 D2
  FSTH * SE23 .....190 C2
  KIL/WHAMP NW6 .....105 E6
Terrace Vls HMSMTH * W6 .....145 G5
Terrace Wk DAGW RM9 .....116 C5
Terrac St RCH/KEW TW9 .....161 H5
Terrapin Rd TOOT SW17 .....186 D5
Terretts Pl IS N1 .....85 H5
Terrick Rd WDGN N22 .....67 G4
Terrick St SHB W12 .....123 H5
Terrilands PIN HA5 .....58 D6
Terront Rd SEVS/STOTM N15 .....88 C2
Tessa Sanderson Wy
  NTHLT UB5 .....99 H3
Testerton Wk NTCHL * W11 .....124 B6
Tetcott Rd WBPTN SW10 .....145 H5
Tetherdown MUSWH N10 .....66 C6
Tetty Wy HAYES BR2 .....212 C5
Teversham La VX/NE SW8 .....167 G2
Teviot Cl WELL DA16 .....176 C1
Teviot St POP/IOD E14 .....131 G4
Tewkesbury Av FSTH SE23 .....189 H3
  PIN HA5 .....78 C2
Tewkesbury Cl LOU IG10 .....57 C1
Tewkesbury Gdns
  CDALE/KGS NW9 .....62 B6
Tewkesbury Rd CAR SM5 .....225 H5
  FSBYPK N4 .....88 D4
  WLSDN NW10 .....140 C1
Tewkesbury Ter
  FBAR/BDGN N11 .....50 C2
Tewson Rd WOOL/PLUM SE18 .....155 E5
Teynham Av WCHMH N21 .....52 A1
Teynham Gn HAYES BR2 .....232 C2
Teynton Ter TOTM N17 .....68 C4
Thackeray Av TOTM N17 .....69 G5
Thackeray Cl ISLW TW7 .....160 C3
  RYLN/HDSTN HA2 .....77 H1
  WIM/MER SW19 .....204 B3
Thackeray Dr CHDH RM6 .....95 G4
Thackeray Ms HACK * E8 .....109 C4
Thackeray Rd EHAM E6 .....113 F1
  VX/NE SW8 .....166 D3
Thackeray St KENS W8 .....145 F3
Thakeham Cl SYD SE26 .....209 H1
Thalia Cl GNWCH SE10 .....151 C6
Thame Rd BERM/RHTH SE16 .....150 B2
Thames Av DAGW RM9 .....137 C2
  GFD/PVL UB6 .....120 B1
  WBPTN SW10 .....165 C2
Thames Bank
  MORT/ESHN SW14 .....162 C3
Thamesbank Pl THMD SE28 .....136 A5
Thames Cir POP/IOD E14 .....151 E4
Thames Ct KUTN/CMB * KT2 .....175 B1
Thames Down Link
  CHSGTN KT9 .....240 C2
  WPK KT4 .....240 D1
Thames Eyot TWK * TW1 .....180 C4
Thamesgate Cl
  RCHPK/HAM TW10 .....180 D6
Thameside TEDD TW11 .....201 C1
Thames Meadow
  E/WMO/HCT KT8 .....199 G6
Thamesmere Dr THMD SE28 .....116 A5
Thames Pth BERM/RHTH SE16 .....150 D3
  BOW E3 .....131 G1
  BTSEA SW11 .....164 E2
  CLPT E5 .....110 B1
  GNWCH SE10 .....151 H2
  RCH/KEW TW9 .....161 C5
  VX/NE SW8 .....28 C6
  WEST SW1P 21 F6
Thames Pl PUT/ROE SW15 .....164 A6
Thamespoint TEDD * TW11 .....201 F3
Thames Quay WBPTN * SW10 .....145 G1
Thames Reach KUT * KT1 .....201 G4
Thames Rd BARK IG11 .....135 G2
  CAN/RD E16 .....153 F1
  CHSWK W4 .....142 B6
Thames Side KUTN/CMB KT2 .....201 E4
  THDIT KT7 .....220 D5
Thames St GNWCH SE10 .....151 C6
  HPTN TW12 .....199 G1
  KUT KT1 .....201 H5
  SUN TW16 .....201 H5
Thamesvale Cl HSLW TW3 .....159 G1
Thames Village CHSWK W4 .....162 C2
Thanescroft Gdns
  CROY/NA CR0 .....247 E1
Thanet Dr HAYES BR2 .....212 C5
Thanet Pl CROY/NA CR0 .....246 C2
Thanet Rd BXLY DA5 .....197 E2
  ERITH DA8 .....157 H1
Thanet St STPAN WC1H 5 E4
Thane Vls HOLWY N7 .....85 F1
Thant Cl LEY E10 .....111 F2
Tharp Rd WLGTN SM6 .....245 E4
Thatcham Gdns
  TRDG/WHET N20 .....49 G2
Thatchers Wy ISLW TW7 .....159 H6

Thatches Gv CHDH RM6 .....96 C1
Thaxted Pl RYNPK SW20 .....204 B3
Thaxted Rd BKHH IG9 .....45 F5
  ELTH/MOT SE9 .....194 C4
Thaxton Rd WKENS W14 .....144 D6
Thayers Farm Rd BECK BR3 .....210 C1
Thayer St MHST W1U 11 F2
Theatre St BTSEA SW11 .....164 E2
Theberton St IS N1 .....108 A6
The Beverly MRDN SM4 .....223 C6
Theed St STHWK SE1 .....22 C2
Thelma Gv TEDD TW11 .....200 C2
Theobald Crs
  KTN/HRWW/W HA3 .....60 A6
Theobald Rd CROY/NA CR0 .....228 B6
  WALTH E17 .....89 F4
Theobald's Rd FSBYW WC1X 13 G1
Theobald St STHWK SE1 .....23 G6
Theodore Rd LEW SE13 .....191 H1
Therapia La CROY/NA CR0 .....227 F4
Therapia Rd EDUL SE22 .....190 A1
Theresa Rd HMSMTH W6 .....118 H4
Theresa's Wk SAND/SEL CR2 .....246 D6
Thermopylae Ga POP/IOD E14 .....151 F4
Theseus Wk IS N1 .....6 D2
Thesiger Rd PGE/AN SE20 .....210 B3
Thetford Cl PLMGR N13 .....51 H3
Thetford Gdns DAGW RM9 .....116 A3
  NWMAL KT3 .....223 D5
Theydon Gv WFD IG8 .....73 E2
Theydon Rd CLPT E5 .....90 A6
Theydon St WALTH E17 .....90 D4
Thicket Crs SUT SM1 .....243 G2
Thicket Gv DAGW RM9 .....116 A4
  PGE/AN SE20 .....209 H5
Thicket Rd PGE/AN SE20 .....209 H5
  SUT SM1 .....243 G2
Third Av ACT W3 .....143 F1
  CHDH RM6 .....94 A6
  DAGE RM10 .....117 F6
  EN EN1 .....30 B5
  MNPK E12 .....113 H2
  NKENS W10 .....124 C2
  PLSTW E13 .....113 G2
  WALTH E17 .....91 F1
  WBLY HA9 .....81 H2
Third Cl E/WMO/HCT KT8 .....219 F1
Third Cross Rd WHTN TW2 .....179 H4
Third Wy WBLY HA9 .....162 D2
Thirleby Rd EDGW HA8 .....62 D4
  WEST SW1P 20 B6
Thirlmere Av GFD/PVL UB6 .....121 E2
Thirlmere Gdns WBLY HA9 .....61 E5
Thirlmere Ri BMLY BR1 .....192 B2
Thirlmere Rd BXLYHN DA7 .....177 G3
  MUSWH N10 .....66 A5
  STRHM/NOR SW16 .....187 H6
Thirsk Cl NTHLT UB5 .....99 E4
Thirsk Rd BTSEA SW11 .....166 C4
  MTCM CR4 .....205 C3
  SNWD SE25 .....228 D1
Thistlebrook ABYW SE2 .....136 C3
Thistlecroft Gdns STAN HA7 .....61 H1
Thistledene THDIT KT7 .....220 A3
Thistledene Av CRW RM5 .....77 F1
  RYLN/HDSTN HA2 .....98 C1
Thistle Gv WBPTN * SW10 .....145 G5
Thistlemead CHST BR7 .....214 B5
Thistlewaite Rd CLPT E5 .....109 H1
Thistlewood Cl HOLWY N7 .....85 F6
Thistleworth Cl ISLW TW7 .....159 H1
Thistley Cl NFNCH/WDSP N12 .....66 L2
Thomas A'beckett Cl
  ALP/SUD HA0 .....100 B2
Thomas Baines Rd
  BTSEA SW11 .....164 B1
Thomas Cribb Ms EHAM E6 .....133 H5
Thomas Dean Rd SYD * SE26 .....190 D6
Thomas Dinwiddy Rd
  LEE/GVPK SE12 .....192 D4
Thomas Doyle St STHWK SE1 .....22 C5
Thomas' La CAT SE6 .....191 F2
Thomas Moore Sq WAP E1W 16 B6
Thomas Moore Wy EFNCH N2 .....65 G1
Thomas More St WAP E1W 17 E6
Thomas North Ter
  CAN/RD * E16 .....132 B4
Thomas Rd POP/IOD E14 .....130 D5
Thomas St WOOL/PLUM SE18 .....154 A4
Thomas Wall Cl SUT SM1 .....243 F3
Thompson Av RCH/KEW TW9 .....162 B4
Thompson Cl IL IG1 .....94 C2
Thompson Rd DAGW RM9 .....116 D1
  EDUL SE22 .....169 F3
  HSLW TW3 .....159 F5
Thompson's Av CMBW * SE5 .....168 C3
Thomson Crs CROY/NA CR0 .....228 B6
Thomson Rd
  KTN/HRWW/W HA3 .....60 A6
Thorburn Sq STHWK SE1 .....33 E3
Thorburn Wy
  WIM/MER * SW19 .....205 H4
Thoresby St IS N1 .....7 F5
Thorkhill Gdns THDIT KT7 .....220 C5
Thorkhill Rd THDIT KT7 .....220 D5
Thorn Av BUSH WD23 .....43 G3
Thornaby Gdns UED N18 .....69 G2
Thornbury Av ISLW TW7 .....159 G1
Thornbury Cl STNW/STAM N16 .....109 E3
Thornbury Rd BRXS/STRHM SW2 .....167 H5
  ISLW TW7 .....159 G1
Thornby Rd CLPT E5 .....110 A1
Thorncliffe Rd CLAP SW4 .....167 H5
  NWDGN UB2 .....138 D2
Thorn Cl HAYES BR2 .....234 A3
  NTHLT UB5 .....117 H1
Thorncombe Rd EDUL SE22 .....169 G6
Thorncroft Rd SUT SM1 .....243 F5
Thorncroft St VX/NE SW8 .....167 G1
Thorndean St
  WAND/EARL SW18 .....185 G4
Thorndene Av TRDG/WHET N20 .....33 C3
Thorndike Av NTHLT UB5 .....95 B6
Thorndike Cl WBPTN SW10 .....165 G1
Thorndike Rd IS * N1 .....86 A4
Thorndike St PIM * SW1V 28 D2
Thorndon Cl STMC/STPC BR5 .....215 H5

Thorndon Gdns
  HOR/WEW KT19 .....241 E2
Thorndon Rd STMC/STPC BR5 .....215 F5
Thorndyke Ct PIN * HA5 .....58 D3
Thorne Cl CAN/RD E16 .....152 D1
  ERITH DA8 .....157 F6
  WAN * E11 .....112 A2
Thorneloe Gdns CROY/NA CR0 .....246 B3
Thorne Rd VX/NE SW8 .....167 G1
Thornes Cl BECK BR3 .....211 G6
Thorne St BARN SW13 .....163 E4
Thornet Wood Rd BMLY BR1 .....214 A6
Thorney Crs BTSEA * SW11 .....165 H1
Thorneycroft Cl WOT/HER KT12 .....218 A3
Thorneycroft Dr WAB EN9 .....41 E1
Thorney Hedge Rd CHSWK W4 .....142 B4
Thorney St WEST SW1P 29 E1
Thornfield Av MLHL NW7 .....64 C3
Thornfield Pde MLHL * NW7 .....64 C3
Thornfield Rd SHB W12 .....143 H2
Thornford Rd LEW SE13 .....190 A1
Thorngate Rd MV/WKIL W9 .....125 E3
Thorngrove Rd PLSTW E13 .....112 D6
Thornham Gv SRTFD E15 .....111 H3
Thornham St GNWCH SE10 .....151 H6
Thornhaugh St STPAN WC1H 4 D6
Thornhill Av SURB KT6 .....221 G6
  WOOL/PLUM SE18 .....175 E1
Thornhill Bridge Whf IS * N1 .....107 H6
Thornhill Crs IS N1 .....107 H6
Thornhill Gdns BARK IG11 .....115 E5
  LEY E10 .....91 H5
Thornhill Gv IS N1 .....107 H5
Thornhill Rd CROY/NA CR0 .....228 C4
  IS N1 .....108 A5
  LEY E10 .....91 F6
  SURB KT6 .....221 G6
Thornhill Sq IS N1 .....107 H6
Thornlaw Rd WNWD SE27 .....188 A6
Thornley Cl TOTM N17 .....69 C3
Thornley Dr RYLN/HDSTN HA2 .....79 F6
Thornsbeach Rd CAT SE6 .....191 G3
Thornsett Pl PGE/AN SE20 .....209 H5
Thornsett Rd PGE/AN SE20 .....209 H5
  WAND/EARL SW18 .....185 F4
Thornsett Ter PGE/AN * SE20 .....209 H5
Thornton Av BAL SW12 .....187 F3
  CHSWK W4 .....143 E4
  CROY/NA CR0 .....227 H3
Thornton Dene BECK BR3 .....210 D1
Thornton Gdns BAL SW12 .....187 F3
Thornton Gv PIN HA5 .....59 E2
Thornton Hl WIM/MER SW19 .....204 C3
Thornton Pl MBLAR W1H 10 C1
Thornton Rd BAL SW12 .....187 F2
  BAR EN5 .....34 C4
  BMLY BR1 .....212 C1
  CAR SM5 .....226 A4
  IL IG1 .....94 B1
  MORT/ESHN SW14 .....162 D4
  THHTH CR7 .....228 A2
  UED N18 .....54 D5
  WAN E11 .....91 H6
  WIM/MER SW19 .....204 B2
Thornton Rw THHTH CR7 .....228 A2
Thornton's Farms Av
  ROMW/RG RM7 .....97 G6
Thornton St BRXN/ST SW9 .....168 A3
Thornton Wy GLDGN NW11 .....85 F2
Thorntree Rd CHARL SE7 .....154 C1
Thornville Gv MTCM CR4 .....205 G5
Thornville St DEPT SE8 .....171 E2
Thornwood Cl SWFD E18 .....72 D5
Thornwood Rd LEW SE13 .....172 A6
Thorogood Gdns SRTFD E15 .....112 A4
Thorold Rd IL IG1 .....94 B6
  WDGN N22 .....67 G3
Thorparch Rd VX/NE SW8 .....167 F2
Thorpebank Rd SHB W12 .....124 D6
Thorpe Cl NKENS W10 .....124 C5
  ORP BR6 .....235 G6
  SYD * SE26 .....190 B6
Thorpedale Gdns
  GNTH/NBYPK IG2 .....94 A1
Thorpedale Rd FSBYPK N4 .....87 G5
Thorpe Hall Rd WALTH E17 .....71 H1
Thorpe Rd BARK IG11 .....114 D5
  EHAM E6 .....113 H6
  FSTGT E7 .....112 C1
  KUTN/CMB KT2 .....201 G5
  SEVS/STOTM N15 .....88 A2
  WALTH E17 .....71 G1
Thorpewood Av FSTH SE23 .....189 H4
Thorsden Wy NRWD * SE19 .....209 E1
Thoydon Rd BOW E3 .....130 C1
Thrale Rd STRHM/NOR SW16 .....207 E1
Thrale St STHWK SE1 .....23 F2
Thrasher Cl HACK * E8 .....109 F6
Thrawl St WCHPL E1 .....16 B4
Threadneedle St LOTH EC2R 15 H4
Three Colts La BETH E2 .....9 G5
Three Colt St POP/IOD E14 .....130 D6
Three Corners BXLYHN DA7 .....177 F5
Three Kings Yd
  MYFR/PKLN W1K 11 G5
Three Mill La SRTFD E15 .....131 G2
Three Oak La STHWK SE1 .....24 D2
Threshers Pl NTGHL W11 .....124 C6
Thriffwood FSTH SE23 .....190 A5
Thrigby Rd CHSGTN KT9 .....241 H4
Throckmorten Rd CAN/RD E16 .....132 D5
Throgmorton Av OBST EC2N 15 H1
Throgmorton St LOTH EC2R 15 H3
Throwley Cl ABYW SE2 .....156 A3
Throwley Rd SUT SM1 .....243 F3
Throwley Wy SUT SM1 .....243 F2
Thrupp Cl MTCM CR4 .....206 D5
Thrush Gn RYLN/HDSTN HA2 .....79 E1
Thrush St WALW SE17 .....31 E3
Thunderer Rd DAGW RM9 .....136 C4
Thurbarn Rd CAT SE6 .....211 F1
Thurland Rd BERM/RHTH SE16 .....33 G1
Thurlby Cl HRW * HA1 .....79 F5
Thurlby Rd ALP/SUD HA0 .....101 H4
  WNWD SE27 .....188 A6
Thurleigh Av BAL SW12 .....186 C1
Thurleigh Rd BAL SW12 .....186 B1
Thurleston Av MRDN SM4 .....224 C2

Thurlestone Av
GDMY/SEVK IG3 ...115 F2
NFNCH/WDSP N12 ...66 B2
Thurlestone Rd WNWD SE27 ...188 A5
Thurloe Cl SKENS SW7 ...26 A1
Thurloe Pl SKENS SW7 ...145 H4
Thurloe Place Ms SKENS * SW7 ...145 H4
Thurloe Sq SKENS SW7 ...26 A1
Thurloe St SKENS SW7 ...145 H4
Thurlow Cl CHING E4 ...71 F2
Thurlow Gdns ALP/SUD * HA0 ...101 F3
CHIG IG7 ...74 D2
Thurlow Hl DUL SE21 ...162 D4
Thurlow Park Rd DUL SE21 ...188 B4
Thurlow Rd HAMP NW3 ...105 H3
HNWL W7 ...140 C2
Thurlow St WALW SE17 ...32 A4
Thurlow Ter KTTN NW5 ...106 B3
Thurlow Wk WALW SE17 ...32 A3
Thursland Rd SCUP DA14 ...216 C1
Thursley Crs CROY/NA CRO ...249 H5
Thursley Gdns WIM/MER SW19 ...184 B4
Thursley Rd ELTH/MOT SE9 ...193 H5
Thurso St TOOT SW17 ...185 H6
Thurstan Rd RYNPK SW20 ...203 H3
Thurston Rd DEPT SE8 ...171 F3
STHL UB1 ...118 D5
Thurtle Rd BETH E2 ...8 D1
Thwaite Cl ERITH DA8 ...157 G6
Thyer Cl ORP BR6 ...252 C2
Thyra Gv NFNCH/WDSP N12 ...65 F2
Tibbatt's Rd BOW E3 ...131 F3
Tibbenham Pl CAT * SE6 ...191 F5
Tibberton Sq IS N1 ...108 C5
Tibbets Cl WIM/MER SW19 ...184 B5
Tibbet's Ride PUT/ROE SW15 ...184 B2
Tiber Gdns IS N1 ...107 G6
Ticehurst Cl STMC/STPC BR5 ...215 G3
Ticehurst Rd FSTH SE23 ...190 C4
Tickford Cl ABYW SE2 ...156 A2
Tidal Basin Rd CAN/RD E16 ...132 B6
Tidenham Gdns CROY/NA CRO ...249 H5
Tideswell Rd CROY/NA CRO ...249 E1
PUT/ROE SW15 ...164 A5
Tideway Cl RCHPK/HAM TW10 ...180 D6
Tidey St BOW E3 ...131 H1
Tidford Rd WELL DA16 ...175 F3
Tidworth Rd BOW E3 ...131 E3
Tiepigs La WWKM BR4 ...232 A6
Tierney Rd BRXS/STRHM SW2 ...187 G3
Tierney Ter
BRXS/STRHM * SW2 ...187 G3
Tiger La HAYES BR2 ...232 D1
Tiger Wy CLPT E5 ...94 H2
Tigres Cl ED N9 ...50 A2
Tilbrook Rd BKHTH/KID SE3 ...173 K4
Tilbury Cl PECK SE15 ...169 F1
STMC/STPC BR5 ...215 H5
Tilbury Rd EHAM E6 ...113 K1
LEY E10 ...91 G4
Tildesley Rd PUT/ROE SW15 ...184 A1
Tile Farm Rd ORP BR6 ...252 D1
Tilehurst Rd CHEAM SM3 ...242 C5
WAND/EARL SW18 ...185 H3
Tile Kiln La BXLY DA5 ...197 H4
HGT N6 ...86 C1
PLMGR N13 ...68 C1
Tileyard Rd HOLWY N7 ...107 G5
Tilford Av CROY/NA CRO ...249 G5
Tilford Gdns WIM/MER SW19 ...184 B3
Tilia Rd CLPT E5 ...94 D1
Tiller Rd POP/IOD E14 ...151 E3
Tillett Cl WLSDN NW10 ...102 C4
Tillett Wy BETH E2 ...9 G5
Tilley La BETH E2 ...9 G5
Tillingbourne Gdns FNCH N3 ...64 D6
Tillingbourne Wy GLDGN NW11 ...84 D1
Tillingham Wy
NFNCH/WDSP N12 ...49 E5
Tilling Rd CRICK NW2 ...64 A4
Tilling Wy WBLY * HA9 ...101 F1
Tillman St WCHPL E1 ...11 H4
Tilloch St IS * N1 ...107 H5
Tillotson Rd ED N9 ...53 F4
IL IG1 ...72 A6
KTN/HRWW/W HA3 ...59 F5
Tilney Gdns IS N1 ...108 A4
Tilney Rd DAGW RM9 ...116 D4
NWDGN UB2 ...138 A4
Tilney St MYFR/PKLN W1K ...9 H7
Tilson Cl CMBW * SE5 ...169 E1
Tilson Gdns CLAP SW4 ...187 G2
Tilson Rd TOTM N17 ...69 G4
Tilston Cl WAN E11 ...112 B1
Tilton St FUL/PGN SW6 ...144 C2
The Tiltwood ACT W3 ...122 C6
Tilt Yard Ap ELTH/MOT SE9 ...193 H1
Timber Cl CHST BR7 ...214 A5
Timbercroft HOR/WEW KT19 ...241 E2
Timbercroft La
WOOL/PLUM SE18 ...155 G6
Timberdene Av BARK/HLT IG6 ...74 C1
Timberland Cl PECK * SE15 ...169 C1
Timberland Rd WCHPL E1 ...117 H6
Timber Mill Wy CLAP SW4 ...187 C1
Timber Pond Rd
BERM/RHTH SE16 ...150 B2
Timberslip Dr WLGTN SM6 ...245 F6
The Timbers CHEAM * SM3 ...242 C4
Timber St FSBYE * EC1V ...7 E5
Timberwharf Rd
SEVS/STOTM N15 ...89 G4
Time Sq HACK * E8 ...108 F3
Times Sq SUT * SM1 ...243 F3
Timothy Cl BXLYHS DA6 ...176 C6
Timothy Rd POP/IOD E14 ...130 H1
Tindal St BRXN/ST SW9 ...168 B2
Tine Rd CHIG IG7 ...75 D1
Tinniswood Cl HOLWY * N7 ...108 A3
Tinsley Rd WCHPL E1 ...130 A4
Tintagel Crs EDUL SE22 ...169 G5
Tintagel Dr STAN HA7 ...61 F1
Tintagel Rd STMC/STPC BR5 ...236 A6
Tintern Av CDALE/KGS NW9 ...62 B6
Tintern Cl PUT/ROE SW15 ...164 C6
WIM/MER SW19 ...205 C3
Tintern Gdns WCHMH N21 ...51 C2
Tintern Rd CAR SM5 ...225 H5
WDGN N22 ...68 C4

Tintern CI CLAP SW4 ...167 G5
Tintern Wy RYLN/HDSTN HA2 ...79 F5
Tinto Rd CAN/RD E16 ...132 C4
Tinworth St LBTH SE11 ...29 F3
Tippetts CI ENC/FH EN2 ...38 C2
Tipthorpe Rd BTSEA SW11 ...166 C4
Tipton Dr CROY/NA CRO ...247 E2
Tiptree CI CHING E4 ...55 G5
Tiptree Crs CLAY IG5 ...74 A6
Tiptree Dr ENC/FH EN2 ...38 D5
Tirlemont Rd SAND/SEL CR2 ...246 C5
Tirrell Rd CROY/NA CRO ...228 C3
Tisbury Rd STRHM/NOR SW16 ...207 G5
Tisdall Pl WALW SE17 ...19 F6
Titan Ct BTFD TW8 ...141 H5
Titchborne Rw BAY/PAD W2 ...10 B4
Titchfield Rd CAR SM5 ...225 H6
STJWD NW8 ...106 A6
Titchfield Wk CAR SM5 ...225 H4
Titchwell Rd WAND/EARL SW18 ...185 H4
Tite St CHEL SW3 ...26 C5
Tithe Barn Cl KUTN/CMB KT2 ...201 H4
Tithe Cl MLHL NW7 ...63 G4
Tite St HDN * NW4 ...63 G4
Tithe Farm Av
RYLN/HDSTN HA2 ...99 E1
Tithe Farm Cl RYLN/HDSTN HA2 ...99 E1
Tithe Wk MLHL NW7 ...63 G4
Titian Av BUSH WD23 ...44 A2
Titley Cl CHING E4 ...71 E1
Titmuss Av THMD SE28 ...135 H4
Titmuss St SHB * W12 ...143 H2
Tiverton Av CLAY IG5 ...74 A6
Tiverton Dr ELTH/MOT SE9 ...194 C1
Tiverton Rd ALP/SUD HA0 ...121 G1
EDGW HA8 ...61 H5
HSLW TW3 ...159 F3
SEVS/STOTM N15 ...89 C5
UED N18 ...69 E1
WLSDN NW10 ...104 B6
Tiverton St STHWK SE1 ...23 E5
Tiverton Wy CHSGTN KT9 ...239 F5
Tivoli Gdns CHARL SE7 ...155 G4
Tivoli Rd CEND/HSY/T N8 ...87 F2
HSLWW TW4 ...158 C5
WNWD SE27 ...188 A1
Toad La HSLWW TW4 ...158 D5
Tobago St POP/IOD * E14 ...151 E2
Tobin Cl HAMP NW3 ...106 A5
Toby Wy SURB KT6 ...223 K1
Tokenhouse Yd LOTH EC2R ...13 G5
Tokyngton Av WBLY HA9 ...102 A4
Toland Sq PUT/ROE SW15 ...163 G6
Toley Av WBLY HA9 ...81 G4
Tolbridge Cl NKENS W10 ...124 C3
Tollesbury Gdns BARK/HLT IG6 ...72 D5
Tollet St WCHPL E1 ...130 B3
Tollgate Dr DUL SE21 ...189 E4
YEAD UB4 ...118 B6
Tollgate Gdns
KIL/WHAMP * NW6 ...125 C1
Tollgate Rd EHAM E6 ...133 C4
Tollhouse La WLGTN SM6 ...245 C6
Tollhouse Wy ARCH N19 ...87 E6
Tollington Pk HOLWY N7 ...87 H6
Tollington Pl FSBYPK N4 ...87 H6
Tollington Rd HOLWY N7 ...107 H2
Tollington Wy HOLWY N7 ...107 H1
Tolmer's Sq CAMTN NW1 ...4 B5
Tolpuddle Av PLSTW E13 ...115 C6
Tolpuddle St IS N1 ...5 K1
Tolsford Rd CLPT E5 ...109 H4
Tolson Rd ISLW * TW7 ...160 C4
Tolverne Rd RYNPK SW20 ...204 A4
Tolworth Cl SURB K16 ...222 B5
Tolworth Gdns CHDH RM6 ...96 B2
Tolworth Park Rd SURB KT6 ...222 A5
Tolworth Ri North BRYLDS KT5 ...222 C1
Tolworth Ri South BRYLDS KT5 ...222 C6
Tolworth Rd SURB KT6 ...221 G6
Tom Cribb Rd
WOOL/PLUM SE18 ...154 C3
Tom Jenkinson Rd
CAN/RD E16 ...152 C1
Tomlin's Ov BOW E3 ...131 E2
Tomlinson Cl BETH E2 ...8 D4
CHSWK W4 ...142 B5
Tomlins Orch BARK IG11 ...114 C6
Tomlin's Ter POP/IOD E14 ...130 A1
Tom Mann Cl BARK IG11 ...115 E6
Tom Nolan Cl SRTFD E15 ...132 A1
Tompion St FSBYE EC1V ...6 B4
Tom Smith Cl GNWCH SE10 ...152 A6
Tomswood Hi BARK/HLT IG6 ...72 A2
Tomswood Rd CHIG IG7 ...74 A2
Tonbridge Crs
KTN/HRWW/W HA3 ...81 G1
Tonbridge Rd MOT/HER KT12 ...218 C1
Tonbridge St STPAN WC1H ...5 E4
Tonfield Rd CHEAM SM3 ...224 D5
Tonsley Hl WAND/EARL SW18 ...165 K6
Tonsley Pl WAND/EARL SW18 ...165 H6
Tonsley Rd WAND/EARL SW18 ...165 H6
Tonstall Rd MTCM CR4 ...206 D6
Tooke Cl PIN HA5 ...41 H4
Took's Ct FLST/FETLN EC4A ...14 A3
Tooley St STHWK SE1 ...25 H1
Toorack Rd KTN/HRWW/W HA3 ...59 H5
Tooting Bec Gdns
STRHM/NOR SW16 ...187 F6
Tooting Bec Rd TOOT SW17 ...186 C6
Tooting Gv TOOT SW17 ...206 A1
Tooting High St TOOT SW17 ...186 A4
Tootswood Rd HAYES BR2 ...232 A2
Topcliffe Dr ORP BR6 ...252 D2
Topham Sq TOTM N17 ...68 C4
Topham St CLKNW * SE1R ...6 A5
Top House Ri CHING E4 ...56 A1
Topiary Sq RCH/KEW TW9 ...161 H4
Topley St ELTH/MOT SE9 ...173 K6
Topmast Point POP/IOD * E14 ...151 E2
Top Pk BECK BR3 ...232 A2
Topsfield Pde CEND/HSY/T * N8 ...87 G2
Topsfield Rd CEND/HSY/T N8 ...87 G2
Topsham Rd TOOT SW17 ...186 A5
Torbay Rd KIL/WHAMP NW6 ...126 D6
RYLN/HDSTN HA2 ...78 D1
Torbay St CAMTN * NW1 ...106 C5
Torbridge Cl EDGW HA8 ...61 G3
Torcross Dr FSTH SE23 ...190 A4

Tor Rd KENS W8 ...145 E2
Tormead Cl SUT SM1 ...243 E4
Tormount Rd
WOOL/PLUM SE18 ...155 E6
Toronto Av MNPK E12 ...113 H2
Toronto Rd IL IG1 ...94 B5
Torquay Gdns REDBR IG4 ...93 F1
Torquay St BAY/PAD W2 ...125 E4
Torrens Rd BRXS/STRHM SW2 ...167 H4
Torrens Sq SRTFD E15 ...112 D4
Torrens St FSBYE EC1V ...6 C2
Torriano Av KTTN NW5 ...107 E3
Torriano Ms KTTN NW5 ...107 E3
Torridge Gdns PECK SE15 ...170 A5
Torridge Rd THHTH CR7 ...228 B2
Torridon Rd CAT SE6 ...191 H3
Torrington Av
NFNCH/WDSP N12 ...65 H1
Torrington Cl ESH/CLAY KT10 ...238 A4
Torrington Dr RYLN/HDSTN HA2 ...99 F2
Torrington Gdns
FBAR/BDGN N11 ...67 E6
GFD/PVL UB6 ...101 E6
Torrington Pk
NFNCH/WDSP N12 ...66 A1
Torrington Pl FITZ W1T ...12 H6
WAP E1W ...25 F2
Torrington Rd BCTR RM8 ...96 C5
ESH/CLAY KT10 ...238 A4
GFD/PVL UB6 ...101 E6
Torrington Sq GWRST WC1E ...4 D6
Torrington Wy MRDN SM4 ...225 J4
Tor Rd WELL DA16 ...176 A2
Torr Rd PGE/AN SE20 ...210 B3
Torrens Rd NEW W1 ...80 A1
Torver Wy ORP BR6 ...252 D1
Torwood Rd PUT/ROE SW15 ...163 H4
Tothill St STJSPK SW1H ...20 C4
Totnes Rd WELL DA16 ...175 H1
Totnes Vis FBAR/BDGN * N11 ...67 E1
Totnes Wk EFNCH N2 ...85 H3
Tottan Ter WCHPL * E1 ...131 G5
Tottenhall Rd PLMGR N13 ...68 A2
Tottenham Court Rd
FITZ W1T ...4 B6
Tottenham Gn East
SEVS/STOTM N15 ...89 F1
Tottenham La CEND/HSY/T N8 ...87 G2
Tottenham Ms FITZ W1T ...12 B1
Tottenham Rd IS N1 ...109 E4
Tottenham South Side
SEVS/STOTM N15 ...89 F1
Tottenham St GTPST W1W ...12 B2
Totterdown St TOOT SW17 ...186 B6
Totteridge Common
TRDG/WHET N20 ...47 G4
Totteridge La TRDG/WHET N20 ...49 F2
Totteridge Village
TRDG/WHET N20 ...48 D2
Totton Rd THHTH CR7 ...208 A6
Toulmin St STHWK SE1 ...18 B6
Toulon St CMBW SE5 ...145 E5
Tournay Rd FUL/PGN SW6 ...164 D1
Toussaint Wk BERM/RHTH SE16 ...25 F5
Tovil Cl PGE/AN SE20 ...209 G5
Towcester Rd BOW E3 ...131 F3
Tower Br TWRH EC3N ...24 C1
Tower Bridge Ap TWRH EC3N ...24 C1
Tower Bridge Rd STHWK SE1 ...32 A1
Tower Buildings WAP * E1W ...25 J2
Tower Cl CHIG IG7 ...74 B2
HAMP NW3 ...106 A3
ORP BR6 ...235 F6
PGE/AN SE20 ...209 J5
Tower Ct LSQ/SEVD * WC2H ...13 J4
Tower Gdns ESH/CLAY KT10 ...238 D5
Tower Gardens Rd TOTM N17 ...68 C4
Tower Hamlets Rd FSTGT E7 ...112 B5
WALTH E17 ...57 J5
Tower Hl TWRH EC3N ...16 B6
Tower Hill Ter MON EC3R ...16 B6
Tower La WBLY * HA9 ...101 F1
Tower Ms CLPT * E5 ...110 C3
Tower Mill Rd PECK * SE15 ...169 E1
Tower Pl MON EC3R ...16 A6
Tower Rd RCH/KEW TW9 ...161 G4
Tower Rd BELV DA17 ...157 J4
BXLYHN DA7 ...177 H5
ORP BR6 ...235 F6
WHTN TW2 ...180 A5
WLSDN NW10 ...81 H5
Tower Royal MANHO * EC4N ...15 F5
Towers Pl RCHPK/HAM TW10 ...141 H1
Towers Rd PIN HA5 ...58 C4
STHL UB1 ...119 E3
Tower St LSQ/SEVD * WC2H ...13 J4
Tower Ter WDGN N22 ...68 D1
Tower Vw CROY/NA CRO ...230 D5
Towfield Rd FELT TW13 ...178 D4
Towncourt Crs
STMC/STPC BR5 ...234 C5
Towncourt Pth FSBYPK N4 ...88 A5
Town End Pde KUT * KT1 ...201 F6
Towney Md NTHLT UB5 ...118 D1
Town Field Wy ISLW TW7 ...160 B1
Town Hall Approach Rd
SEVS/STOTM N15 ...89 F1
Townhall Av CHSWK * W4 ...142 D5
Town Hall Pde
BRXS/STRHM * SW2 ...167 H5
Town Hall Rd BTSEA SW11 ...140 D3
Townley Ct SRTFD E15 ...112 B4
Townley Rd BXLYHS DA6 ...197 D6
EDUL SE22 ...163 G3
Townley St WALW SE17 ...31 G3
Town Meadow BTFD TW8 ...161 F1
Townmead Rd FUL/PGN SW6 ...165 G3
RCH/KEW TW9 ...162 B3
Town Quay BARK IG11 ...114 B1
Town Rd ED N9 ...54 A1
Townsend Av STHGT/OAK N14 ...51 F1
Townsend La CDALE/KGS NW9 ...82 D1
Townsend Rd
SEVS/STOTM N15 ...89 F2

STHL UB1 ...138 C1
WOOL/PLUM SE18 ...154 B3
Townsend St WALW SE17 ...31 H2
Townsend Yd HGT N6 ...86 B5
Townshead Cl SCUP DA14 ...215 H2
Townshend Est STJWD NW8 ...2 E1
RCH/KEW TW9 ...161 H5
STJWD NW8 ...2 E1
Townshend Ter RCH/KEW TW9 ...161 H5
Town Whf ISLW * TW7 ...160 D4
Towpath Wy CROY/NA CRO ...197 G1
Towton Rd WNWD SE27 ...188 C4
Toynbee Rd RYNPK SW20 ...204 C4
Toynbee St WCHPL E1 ...16 C2
Toyne Wy HGT N6 ...66 F1
Tracey Av CRICK * NW2 ...104 A3
Trade Cl PLMGR N13 ...52 A6
Trader Rd EHAM E6 ...134 B5
Tradescant Rd VX/NE SW8 ...167 G1
Trading Estate Rd
WLSDN * NW10 ...122 C3
Trafalgar Av PECK SE15 ...169 F2
STHL UB1 ...32 D4
TOTM N17 ...69 G2
WPK KT4 ...224 B5
Trafalgar Chambers
CHEL * SW3 ...145 K5
Trafalgar Gdns KENS * W8 ...145 F3
WCHPL E1 ...130 B4
Trafalgar Gv GNWCH SE10 ...151 H6
Trafalgar Pl UED N18 ...69 C1
WAN E11 ...92 C2
Trafalgar Rd GNWCH SE10 ...152 A5
WHTN TW2 ...179 H4
WIM/MER SW19 ...205 F3
Trafalgar Sq CHCR WC2N ...20 D1
Trafalgar St WALW SE17 ...31 G5
Trafalgar Wy CROY/NA CRO ...227 H6
POP/IOD E14 ...151 G1
Trafford Cl SRTFD E15 ...111 H5
Trafford Rd THHTH CR7 ...227 H2
Tramway Av ED N9 ...53 H2
SRTFD E15 ...111 H5
Tramway Pth MTCM CR4 ...206 A2
Tranley Ms HAMP * NW3 ...106 A2
Tranmere Rd ED N9 ...53 F2
WAND/EARL SW18 ...185 G4
Tranquil V BKHTH/KID SE3 ...172 B5
Transept St CAMTN NW1 ...10 B2
Transmere Rd STMC/STPC BR5 ...234 C5
Transom Sq POP/IOD E14 ...151 F5
Transport Av BTFD TW8 ...140 B6
Travellers Site WALTH * E17 ...70 D5
Travellers Wy HEST TW5 ...158 A3
Travers Cl WALTH E17 ...57 F6
Travers Rd HOLWY N7 ...108 A1
Treacy Cl BUSH WD23 ...43 G4
Treadgold St NTGHL W11 ...124 D6
Treadway St BETH E2 ...7 J2
Treaty St IS N1 ...107 H6
Trebeck St MYFR/PICC W1J ...19 G1
Trebovir Rd ECT SW5 ...145 E5
Treby St BOW E3 ...131 G4
Trecastle Wy HOLWY * N7 ...107 F2
Tredegar Rd BOW E3 ...130 D1
FBAR/BDGN N11 ...67 F3
Tredegar Sq BOW E3 ...130 D2
Tredewen Rd HACK E8 ...109 G6
Tredown Rd SYD SE26 ...210 A1
Tredwell Cl HAYES BR2 ...233 F1
Tredwell Rd WNWD SE27 ...188 B6
Treen Av BARN SW13 ...163 G4
Tree Rd CAN/RD E16 ...133 G5
Treetops Cl ABYW SE2 ...156 C5
Treetops Vw LOU IG10 ...57 F1
Tree View Cl NRWD SE19 ...209 E4
Treewall Gdns BMLY BR1 ...192 D6
Trefgarne Rd DAGE RM10 ...80 C6
Trefoil Rd WAND/EARL SW18 ...165 G6
Tregaron Av CEND/HSY/T N8 ...87 G4
Tregaron Gdns NWMAL KT3 ...223 H1
Tregarvon Rd BTSEA SW11 ...165 E2
Tregenna Av RYLN/HDSTN HA2 ...99 E2
Tregenna Cl STHGT/OAK N14 ...37 E6
Tregony Rd ORP BR6 ...253 F2
Trego Rd HOM E9 ...111 K6
Tregothnan Rd BRXN/ST SW9 ...167 G4
Tregunter Rd WBPTN SW10 ...145 G6
Trehearn Rd BARK/HLT IG6 ...74 D3
Treherne Ct BRXN/ST * SW9 ...168 B2
Trehern Rd MORT/ESHN SW14 ...162 A1
Trehurst St CLPT E5 ...110 C3
Trelawney Est HOM * E9 ...110 A4
Trelawney Rd BARK/HLT IG6 ...74 D3
Trelawn Rd BRXS/STRHM SW2 ...168 B4
LEY E10 ...111 G1
Trellis Cl WALTH E17 ...91 F1
Treloar Gdns NRWD SE19 ...208 D2
Tremadoc Rd CLAP SW4 ...187 A5
Tremaine Rd PGE/AN SE20 ...209 H5
Tremlett Gv ARCH N19 ...107 K5
Tremlett Ms ARCH * N19 ...107 G1
Trenance Gdns
GDMY/SEVK IG3 ...115 G3
Trenchard Cl CDALE/KGS NW9 ...63 E4
STAN HA7 ...60 D2
Trenchard St GNWCH SE10 ...151 H5
Trenholme Rd PGE/AN SE20 ...209 H5
Trenholme Ter PGE/AN SE20 ...209 H5
Trenmar Gdns WLSDN NW10 ...123 H2
Trent Av EA W5 ...141 G3
Trentbridge Cl BARK/HLT IG6 ...73 G1
Trent Cl WAN E11 ...92 C2
Trent Gdns STHGT/OAK N14 ...50 D1
Trentham Dr STMC/STPC BR5 ...235 G1
Trentham St WAND/EARL SW18 ...185 K1
Trent Rd BRXS/STRHM SW2 ...167 H4
Trent Rd EBAR * EN4 ...49 G3
Trent Rd BKHH IG9 ...56 D5
BRXS/STRHM SW2 ...167 H6
Trent Wy WPK K14 ...224 A5
Trentwood Side ENC/FH EN2 ...37 H4
Treport St WAND/EARL SW18 ...185 F2
Tresco Cl BMLY BR1 ...212 A2
Trescoe Gdns CRW RM5 ...77 C1
PIN HA5 ...78 C4

Tresco Gdns GDMY/SEVK IG3 ...95 F6
Tresco Rd PECK SE15 ...169 H5
Tresham Crs STJWD NW8 ...2 A4
Tresham Rd BARK IG11 ...115 F5
Tresilian Av WCHMH N21 ...37 D4
Tressell Cl IS N1 ...108 B5
Tressillian Crs BROCKY SE4 ...171 E4
Tressillian Rd BROCKY SE4 ...171 F4
Trestis Cl YEAD UB4 ...118 B5
Treswell Rd DAGW RM9 ...116 C6
Tretawn Gdns MLHL NW7 ...47 E6
Tretawn Pk MLHL NW7 ...47 E6
Trevanion Rd WKENS * W14 ...144 C5
Treve Av HRW HA1 ...79 G4
Trevelyan Crs
  KTN/HRWW/W HA3 ...81 F4
Trevelyan Gdns
  WLSDN * NW10 ...104 A6
Trevelyan Rd FSTGT E7 ...112 A2
  TOOT SW17 ...206 A2
Treveris St STHWK SE1 ...22 D2
Treverton St NKENS W10 ...124 B3
Treves Cl WCHMH N21 ...57 H6
Treville St PUT/ROE SW15 ...183 H2
Treviso Rd FSTH SE23 ...190 B1
Trevithick St DEPT SE8 ...151 E6
Trevone Gdns PIN HA5 ...78 C3
Trevor Cl EBAR EN4 ...49 H1
  HAYES BR2 ...232 B4
  ISLW TW7 ...160 B6
  KTN/HRWW/W HA3 ...60 B3
  NTHLT UB5 ...118 A1
Trevor Gdns EDGW HA8 ...62 D4
Trevor Pl SKENS SW7 ...18 B1
Trevor Rd EDGW HA8 ...62 D4
  WFD IG8 ...77 E3
  WIM/MER SW19 ...204 C3
Trevor Rd SKENS SW7 ...18 B4
Trevor St SKENS SW7 ...18 B4
Trevose Rd WALTH E17 ...71 H4
Trevose Wy OXHEY WD19 ...42 A5
Trewenna Dr CHSGTN KT9 ...239 F3
Trewince Rd RYNPK SW20 ...204 A4
Trewint St WAND/EARL SW18 ...185 G4
Trewsbury Rd SYD SE26 ...210 B1
Triandra Wy YEAD UB4 ...118 B4
Triangle Pas BAR * EN5 ...35 C5
Triangle Pl CLAP SW4 ...167 F5
Triangle Rd HACK E8 ...109 H6
The Triangle BFN/LL * DA15 ...195 G2
  NWMAL KT3 ...202 C5
Trident Pl CHEL * SW3 ...145 H6
Trident St BERM/RHTH SE16 ...150 B4
Trig La BLKFR EC4V ...15 E5
Trigon Rd VX/NE SW8 ...167 H1
Trilby Rd FSTH SE23 ...190 B4
Trim St NWCR SE14 ...150 D6
Trinder Rd ARCH N19 ...67 E5
  BAR EN5 ...34 A6
Tring Av EA W5 ...141 H1
  STHL UB1 ...118 D5
  WBLY HA9 ...102 A4
Tring Cl BARK/HLT IG6 ...94 C2
Trinidad Gdns DAGE RM10 ...117 H5
Trinidad St POP/IOD E14 ...130 D6
Trinity Av EFNCH N2 ...65 H6
  EN EN1 ...53 F1

Trinity Buoy Whf
  POP/IOD * E14 ...131 H4
Trinity Church Rd BARN SW13 ...143 H6
Trinity Church Sq STHWK SE1 ...23 F5
Trinity Cl CLAP * SW4 ...167 E5
  HACK * E8 ...109 F4
  HAYES BR2 ...233 C5
  HSLWW TW4 ...134 C4
  LEW SE13 ...171 H5
  SAND/SEL CR2 ...247 E6
Trinity Crs ELTH/MOT SE9 ...194 B1
Trinity Crs TOOT SW17 ...186 B4
Trinity Gdns BRXN/ST SW9 ...167 H5
  CAN/RD E16 ...132 B4
Trinity Gv GNWCH SE10 ...151 E6
Trinity Ms PGE/AN * SE20 ...210 A4
Trinity Pde HSLW * TW5 ...159 F4
Trinity Pl CHING * E4 ...72 ...
Trinity Pl BXLYHS DA6 ...176 D5
Trinity Ri HNHL SE24 ...188 B2
Trinity Rd BARK/HLT IG6 ...74 C6
  EFNCH N2 ...65 H6
  RCH/KEW * TW9 ...161 H4
  STHL UB1 ...138 C1
  TOOT SW17 ...186 B4
  WAND/EARL SW18 ...185 H1
  WIM/MER SW19 ...205 G2
Trinity Sq TWRH EC3N ...16 B6
Trinity St CAN/RD E16 ...132 B4
  ENC/FH EN2 ...23 E5
  STHWK SE1 ...23 F4
Trinity Wy ACT W3 ...125 G6
  CHING E4 ...70 ...
Trio Pl STHWK SE1 ...23 F3
Tristam Sq BKHTH/KID SE3 ...172 A4
Tristram Cl WALTH E17 ...71 H6
Tristram Rd BMLY BR1 ...192 B6
Triton Sq CAMTN NW1 ...4 A5
Tritton Av CROY/NA CR0 ...245 G2
Tritton Rd WNWD SE27 ...188 D3
Triumph Rd EHAM E6 ...133 H5
Trojan Wy CROY/NA CR0 ...245 H1
Troon Cl BERM/RHTH * SE16 ...33 H3
Troon St WCHPL E1 ...130 C5
Trosley Rd BELV DA17 ...157 E6
Trossachs Rd EDUL SE22 ...169 G6
Trothy Rd STHWK SE1 ...51 G4
Trott Rd MUSWH N10 ...66 C3
Trott St BTSEA SW11 ...165 H2
Trotwood CHIG IG7 ...74 ...
Troughton Rd CHARL SE7 ...152 D5
Troutbeck Rd NWCR SE14 ...170 C2
Trouville Rd BAL SW12 ...187 E1
Trowbridge Rd HOM E9 ...110 D4
Trowlock Av TEDD TW11 ...201 E2
Trowlock Island TEDD TW11 ...201 F2
Trowlock Wy TEDD TW11 ...201 G2
Troy Ct KENS W8 ...145 E3
Troy Rd NRWD SE19 ...208 D2
Troy Town PECK SE15 ...169 G4

Trubshaw Rd NWDGN UB2 ...139 E3
Trueman Cl EDGW * HA8 ...62 B3
Trulock Rd TOTM N17 ...50 D3
Truman's Rd STNW/STAM N16 ...109 E5
Trumpers Wy HNWL W7 ...140 D3
Trumpington Rd FSTGT E7 ...112 B2
Trump St CITYW EC2V ...15 F4
Trundlers Wy BUSH WD23 ...44 A3
Trundle St STHWK SE1 ...23 C3
Trundley's Rd DEPT SE8 ...150 B5
  DEPT SE8 ...150 C6
Trundley's Ter DEPT SE8 ...150 B4
Truro Gdns IL IG1 ...93 C4
Truro Rd WALTH E17 ...90 D1
  WDGN N22 ...67 G3
Truro St KTTN NW5 ...106 C4
Truesdale Rd EHAM E6 ...133 H3
Truslove Rd WNWD SE27 ...208 A1
Trussley Rd HMSMTH W6 ...144 A3
Tryfan Cl REDBR IG4 ...93 F2
Tryon Crs HOM E9 ...110 A6
Tryon St CHEL SW3 ...16 C8
Trystings Cl ESH/CLAY KT10 ...238 C4
Tuam Rd WOOL/PLUM SE18 ...154 D6
Tubbenden Cl ORP BR6 ...252 E6
Tubbenden Dr ORP BR6 ...252 D2
Tubbenden La ORP BR6 ...252 D2
Tubbenden La South ORP BR6 ...252 D3
Tubbs Rd WLSDN NW10 ...123 F1
Tudor Av HPTN TW12 ...199 E2
  WPK KT4 ...241 H1
Tudor Cl BRXS/STRHM * SW2 ...187 H1
  CDALE/KGS NW9 ...80 A8
  CHEAM SM3 ...242 B5
  CHSGTN KT9 ...239 G3
  CHST BR7 ...213 H4
  HAMP NW3 ...106 A3
  HGT N6 ...66 C4
  HPTN TW12 ...199 G1
  MLHL NW7 ...63 G2
  WFD IG8 ...52 F6
  WLGTN SM6 ...245 G5
Tudor Ct ELTH/MOT * SE9 ...175 C5
  SWLY BR8 ...257 G4
  WALTH E17 ...90 D4
Tudor Ct North WBLY HA9 ...102 A3
Tudor Ct South WBLY HA9 ...102 A3
Tudor Crs BARK/HLT IG6 ...74 C2
  ENC/FH EN2 ...38 C2
Tudor Dr KUTN/CMB KT2 ...201 G1
  MRDN SM4 ...224 D4
  WOT/HER KT12 ...218 B5
Tudor Est WLSDN * NW10 ...122 B1
Tudor Gdns ACT W3 ...122 A4
  BARN SW13 ...163 E4
  CDALE/KGS NW9 ......
  TWK TW1 ...180 C4
  WWKM BR4 ...248 B1
Tudor Gv HOM E9 ...110 D1
Tudor Pde ELTH/MOT * SE9 ...175 C5
Tudor Pl NRWD * SE19 ...209 F3
  WIM/MER SW19 ...206 ...
Tudor Rd BAR EN5 ...35 E4
  BARK IG11 ...115 F1
  BECK BR3 ...211 G5
  CHING E4 ...71 F2
  ED N9 ...36 D2
  EHAM E6 ...113 G5
  HACK E8 ...109 H6
  HPTN TW12 ...199 F1
  HSLW TW3 ...159 ...
  KUTN/CMB KT2 ...202 C1
  MLHL NW7 ......
  NRWD SE19 ...209 F3
  PIN HA5 ...59 ...
  SNWD SE25 ...229 H2
  STHL UB1 ...118 C6
Tudor St EMB EC4Y ...14 B5
Tudor Wy ACT W3 ...142 A2
  STHGT/OAK N14 ......
  STMC/STPC BR5 ...234 D3
Tudor Well Cl STAN HA7 ...60 D1
Tudway Rd ELTH/MOT SE9 ...173 H4
Tufnell Park Rd HOLWY N7 ...107 F2
Tufter Rd CHIG IG7 ...75 F1
Tufton Gdns E/WMO/HCT KT8 ...199 F5
Tufton Rd CHING E4 ...51 ...
Tufton St WEST SW1P ...29 E5
Tugboat St THMD SE28 ...155 G2
Tugela Rd CROY/NA CR0 ...228 D3
Tugela St CAT SE6 ...190 D4
Tugmutton Cl ORP BR6 ...252 C4
Tulip Cl CROY/NA CR0 ...230 B5
  EHAM E6 ...133 H4
  HPTN TW12 ...198 D2
  STHL UB1 ...139 G4
Tulip Gdns CHING * E4 ...55 H5
  IL IG1 ...114 B4
Tull St MTCM CR4 ...226 B4
Tulse Cl BECK BR3 ...211 G6
Tulse Hi BRXS/STRHM SW2 ...188 A1
Tulsemere Rd WNWD SE27 ...188 C4
Tummons Gdns SNWD SE25 ...209 F5
Tuncombe Rd UED N18 ...36 B5
Tunis Rd SHB W12 ...144 A1
Tunley Rd BAL SW12 ...187 G1
  WLSDN NW10 ...103 E6
Tunmarsh La PLSTW E13 ...113 E2
Tunnan Leys EHAM E6 ...136 A5
Tunnel Av GNWCH SE10 ...151 H2
Tunnel Gdns FBAR/BDGN N11 ...50 C4
Tunnel Rd BERM/RHTH SE16 ...150 A2
Tunstall Cl ORP BR6 ...252 E4
Tunstall Rd BRXN/ST SW9 ...167 H5
  CROY/NA CR0 ...228 D1
Tunstock Wy BELV DA17 ...156 D6
Tunworth Cl CDALE/KGS NW9 ...62 D2
Tunworth Crs PUT/ROE SW15 ...183 F1
Tupelo Rd LEY E10 ...91 F6
Turin Rd ED N9 ...36 ...
Turin St BETH E2 ...8 C4
Turkey Oak Cl NRWD SE19 ...209 E4
Turks Rw CHEL SW3 ...16 D7
Turle Rd FSBYPK N4 ...107 F1
  STRHM/NOR SW16 ...207 ...
Turlewray Cl FSBYPK N4 ...87 H5
Turley Cl SRTFD E15 ...112 E1
Turnagain La STP * EC4M ...14 C3
Turnage Rd BCTR RM8 ...96 C5

Turnant Rd TOTM N17 ...68 C4
Turnberry Cl
  BERM/RHTH * SE16 ...33 H4
Turnberry Ct OXHEY * WD19 ...42 A5
Turnberry Wy ORP BR6 ...232 A6
Turnbury Cl THMD SE28 ...136 B5
Turner Av MTCM CR4 ...206 B4
  SEVS/STOTM N15 ...68 A5
  WHTN TW2 ...179 G5
Turner Cl ALP/SUD HA0 ...101 F3
  CMBW SE5 ...168 B2
  GLDGN NW11 ...85 F3
Turner Ct CMBW * SE5 ...168 D5
Turner Dr GLDGN NW11 ...85 F3
Turner Rd EDGW HA8 ...61 G5
  NWMAL KT3 ...222 D4
  WALTH E17 ...72 C1
Turners Meadow Wy
  BECK BR3 ...210 D4
Turner's Rd POP/IOD E14 ...130 D4
Turner St CAN/RD E16 ...132 B5
  WCHPL E1 ...17 G2
Turners Wy CROY/NA CR0 ...228 A6
Turner's Wd GLDGN NW11 ...85 G5
Turneville Rd WKENS W14 ...144 D6
Turney Rd DUL SE21 ...188 C2
Turnham Green Ter
  CHSWK W4 ...145 A4
Turnham Rd BROCKY SE4 ...170 C6
Turnmill St FARR EC1M ...5 H7
Turnpike Cl DEPT SE8 ...170 D1
Turnpike La CEND/HSY/T N8 ...88 A1
  SUT SM1 ...245 G3
Turnpike Link CROY/NA CR0 ...229 E6
Turnpike Ms CEND/HSY/T * N8 ...68 A6
Turnpike Pde N8 ...68 B6
Turnpike Wy ISLW TW7 ...160 C2
Turnstone Cl CDALE/KGS * NW9 ...63 E5
  PLSTW E13 ...113 E3
Turnstone Ter WEA * W13 ...120 B3
Turpentine La PIM SW1V ...27 H5
Turpin Av CRW RM5 ...56 C5
Turpington Cl HAYES BR2 ...233 C5
Turpington La HAYES BR2 ...233 G2
Turpin's La WFD IG8 ...73 H1
Turpins Yd CRICK * NW2 ...83 H5
Turpin Wy WLGTN SM6 ...244 D5
Turquand St WALW SE17 ...31 F2
Turret Gv CLAP SW4 ...167 E4
Turton Rd ALP/SUD HA0 ...100 B4
Turville St BETH * E2 ...8 C5
Tuscan Rd WOOL/PLUM SE18 ...154 D5
Tuskar St GNWCH SE10 ...152 A5
Tweeddale Rd CAR SM5 ...225 H5
Tweedmouth Rd PLSTW E13 ...132 D1
Tweedy Wy ROM RM1 ...77 H3
Tweedy Rd BMLY BR1 ...212 C4
Twelvetrees Crs BOW E3 ...131 G5
Twentyman Cl WFD IG8 ...72 C1
Twickenham Br TWK TW1 ...161 E6
Twickenham Cl CROY/NA CR0 ...245 H1
Twickenham Gdns
  GFD/PVL UB6 ...100 C3
  KTN/HRWW/W HA3 ...60 D3
Twickenham Rd FELT TW13 ...178 D5
  ISLW TW7 ...160 C2
  RCH/KEW TW9 ...161 E6
  TEDD TW11 ...180 C6
  WAN E11 ...91 H6
Twig Folly Cl BOW E5 ...130 D1
Twig Folly Whf BETH * E2 ...130 B1
Twilley St WAND/EARL SW18 ...185 F2
Twine Cl BARK IG11 ...135 H2
Twine Ct WCHPL E1 ...130 D6
Twineham Gn
  NFNCH/WDSP N12 ...49 E6
Twine Ter BOW * E3 ...130 D3
Twining Av WHTN TW2 ...179 G5
Twinn Rd MLHL NW7 ...64 C2
Twisden Rd KTTN NW5 ...106 B2
Twybridge Wy WLSDN NW10 ...102 C5
Twyford Abbey Rd
  WLSDN NW10 ...121 H2
Twyford Av ACT W3 ...122 A6
  EFNCH N2 ...66 B6
Twyford Crs ACT W3 ...142 A1
Twyford Rd CAR SM5 ...225 H6
  IL IG1 ...114 C5
  RYLN/HDSTN * HA2 ...79 F4
Twyford St IS N1 ...107 H6
Tyas Rd CAN/RD E16 ...132 B3
Tybenham Rd WIM/MER SW19 ...205 H6
Tyberry Rd EN EN1 ...39 H4
Tyburn La HRW HA1 ...80 A4
Tyburn Wy MBLAR W1H ...10 D5
Tye La ORP BR6 ...252 C3
Tyers Ga STHWK SE1 ...24 A4
Tyers St LBTH SE11 ...29 G3
Tyers Ter LBTH SE11 ...29 G4
Tyeshurst Cl ABYW SE2 ...156 C5
Tylecroft Rd
  STRHM/NOR SW16 ...207 G3
Tylehurst Gdns IL IG1 ...114 C3
Tyler Cl BETH E2 ...8 C1
Tylers Ga KTN/HRWW/W HA3 ...81 G3
Tylers Green Rd SWLY BR8 ...237 G3
Tyler St GNWCH SE10 ...152 A5
Tylney Av NRWD SE19 ...209 F1
Tylney Rd BMLY BR1 ...212 C1
  FSTGT E7 ...113 E2
Tyndale La IS N1 ...108 H6
Tyndale Ter IS N1 ...108 B5
Tyndall Rd LEY E10 ...91 G6
  WELL DA16 ...175 F4
Tyneham Cl BTSEA * SW11 ...166 C3
Tyneham Rd BTSEA SW11 ...166 C3
Tynemouth Cl EHAM E6 ...116 D5
Tynemouth Dr EN EN1 ...39 G1
Tynemouth Rd MTCM CR4 ...206 C3
  SEVS/STOTM N15 ...89 F1
  WOOL/PLUM SE18 ...155 G3
Tynemouth St FUL/PGN SW6 ...166 B1
Tynemouth Ter
  SEVS/STOTM * N15 ...89 F1
Tyne St WCHPL E1 ...16 B5
Tyne Wy BETH E2 ...130 B1
Tyrawley Rd FUL/PGN SW6 ...165 F2
Tyrell Cl HRW HA1 ......
Tyrone Rd EHAM E6 ...133 H1
Tyron Wy SCUP DA14 ...195 E6

Tyrrell Av WELL DA16 ...175 G6
Tyrrell Rd EDUL SE22 ...169 G5
Tyrrel Wy CDALE/KGS NW9 ...83 F4
Tyrwhitt Rd BROCKY SE4 ...171 G4
Tysoe St CLKNW EC1R ...5 H5
Tyson Gdns FSTH * SE23 ...190 A2
Tyson Rd FSTH SE23 ...190 A2
Tyssen Rd STNW/STAM * N16 ...109 F1
Tyssen St HACK E8 ...110 ...
Tytherton Rd ARCH N19 ...107 F1

U

Uamvar St POP/IOD E14 ...131 F4
Uckfield Gv MTCM CR4 ...206 C4
Udall Gdns CRW RM5 ...77 G2
Udall St WEST SW1P ...28 B2
Udney Park Rd TEDD TW11 ...200 C1
Uffington Rd WLSDN NW10 ...103 G6
  WNWD SE27 ...188 A6
Ufford Cl KTN/HRWW/W HA3 ...59 F3
Ufford Rd KTN/HRWW/W HA3 ...59 F3
Ufford St STHWK SE1 ...17 G3
Ufton Gv IS N1 ...109 G5
Ufton Rd IS N1 ...109 E5
Uhura Sq STNW/STAM * N16 ...109 E1
Ullathorne Rd
  STRHM/NOR SW16 ...187 E6
Ulleswater Rd PLMGR N13 ...51 G6
Ulleswater Vls PLMGR * N13 ...51 G6
Ullin St POP/IOD E14 ...131 G4
Ullswater Cl BMLY BR1 ...212 A2
  KUTN/CMB * KT2 ...182 D6
Ullswater Crs PUT/ROE SW15 ...182 B6
Ullswater Rd BARN SW13 ...163 G5
  WNWD SE27 ...188 B5
Ulster Gdns PLMGR N13 ...52 C6
Ulster Pl CAMTN NW1 ...3 H7
Ulundi Rd BKHTH/KID SE3 ...152 A6
Ulva Rd PUT/ROE SW15 ...164 B5
Ulverscroft Rd EDUL SE22 ...169 G6
Ulverston Rd WALTH E17 ...71 H5
Ulysses Rd KIL/WHAMP NW6 ...104 D3
Umberston St WCHPL E1 ...17 ...
Umbria St PUT/ROE SW15 ...183 ...
Umfreville Rd FSBYPK N4 ...88 B3
Undercliff Rd LEW SE13 ...171 E4
Underhill BAR EN5 ...35 ...
Underhill Ct BAR * EN5 ...35 ...
Underhill Rd EDUL SE22 ...169 ...
Underhill St CAMTN NW1 ...106 ...
Underne Av STHGT/OAK N14 ...50 ...
Undershaft HDTCH EC3A ...16 A4
Undershaw Rd BMLY BR1 ...192 ...
Underwood Rd CHING E4 ...71 ...
  WCHPL E1 ...13 ...
  WFD IG8 ...73 ...
Underwood Rw IS N1 ...7 F3
Underwood St IS N1 ...7 F3
The Underwood
  ELTH/MOT SE9 ...193 ...
Undine Rd POP/IOD E14 ...151 ...
Undine St TOOT SW17 ...206 ...
Uneeda Dr GFD/PVL UB6 ...99 ...
Union Cl WAN E11 ...111 H2
Union Ct CLAP SW4 ...167 ...
Union Dr WCHPL * E1 ...130 C3
Union Gv VX/NE SW8 ...167 H1
Union Rd ALP/SUD HA0 ...101 ...
  CLAP SW4 ...167 ...
  CROY/NA CR0 ...228 ...
  FBAR/BDGN N11 ......
  HAYES BR2 ...233 ...
  NTHLT UB5 ......
Union Sq IS N1 ...108 ...
Union St BAR EN5 ...34 ...
  KUT/HW KT1 ......
  SRTFD E15 ......
  STHWK SE1 ...22 ...
Unity Cl CROY/NA CR0 ...249 ...
  WLSDN NW10 ...105 ...
  WNWD SE27 ...208 ...
Unity Ms CAMTN NW1 ......
University Cl WOOL/PLUM SE18 ...153 ...
University Gdns BXLY DA5 ...196 ...
University Rd WIM/MER SW19 ...205 ...
University St FITZ W1T ...4 ...
University Wy EHAM E6 ...116 ...
Unwin Cl PECK SE15 ......
Unwin Rd ISLW TW7 ...160 ...
  SKENS SW7 ......
Upbrook Ms BAY/PAD W2 ......
Upcerne Rd WBPTN SW10 ......
Upcroft Av EDGW HA8 ......
Updale Rd SCUP DA14 ...195 ...
Upfield CROY/NA CR0 ......
Upfield Rd HNWL W7 ......
Uphall Rd IL IG1 ...114 ...
Upham Park Rd CHSWK W4 ...143 ...
Uphill Dr CDALE/KGS NW9 ......
  MLHL NW7 ......
Uphill Gv MLHL NW7 ...47 ...
Uphill Rd MLHL NW7 ...47 ...
Upland Rd BELMT SM2 ...245 ...
  BXLYHN DA7 ......
  EDUL SE22 ...189 ...
  PLSTW E13 ......
  SAND/SEL CR2 ......
Uplands BECK BR3 ...211 ...
Uplands Av WALTH E17 ......
Uplands Business Pk
  WALTH E17 ......
Uplands Cl MORT/ESHN SW14 ...162 ...
Uplands End WFD IG8 ......
Uplands Park Rd ENC/FH EN2 ......
Uplands Rd CEND/HSY/T N8 ......
  CHDH RM6 ......
  EBAR EN4 ......
  ORP BR6 ......
  WFD IG8 ......
Uplands Wy WCHMH N21 ......
Upney La BARK IG11 ...115 ...
Upnor Wy WALW SE17 ...32 ...
Uppark Dr GNTH/NBYPK IG2 ......
Upper Abbey Rd BELV DA17 ...156 ...
Upper Addison Gdns
  WKENS W14 ...144 C2

Upper Bardsey Wk IS * N1 108 C4
Upper Belgrave St KTBR SW1X 19 F5
Upper Berenger Wk
WBPTN * SW10 165 H1
Upper Berkeley St BAY/PAD W2 10 C4
Upper Beulah Hl NRWD SE19 209 E4
Upper Blantyre Wk
WBPTN * SW10 165 H1
Upper Brighton Rd SURB KT6 221 F3
Upper Brockley Rd
BROCKY SE4 170 D3
Upper Brook St
MYFR/PKLN W1K 11 E5
Upper Butts BTFD TW8 141 E6
Upper Caldy Wk IS * N1 108 C4
Upper Camelford Wk
NTGHL * W11 124 C5
Upper Cheyne Rw CHEL SW3 26 A6
Upper Clapton Rd CLPT E5 89 H6
Upper Clarendon Wk
NTGHL * W11 124 C5
Upper Dartrey Wk
WBPTN * SW10 165 G1
Upper Dengie Wk IS * N1 108 C6
Upper Elmers End Rd
BECK BR3 230 C1
BECK * BR3 231 E3
BECK BR3 231 E3
Upper Farm Rd
E/WMO/HCT KT8 218 D1
Upper Gn East MTCM CR4 206 B5
Upper Gn West MTCM CR4 206 B5
Upper Grosvenor St
MYFR/PKLN W1K 11 E6
Upper Grotto Rd TWK TW1 180 B4
Upper Gnd STHWK SE1 22 A1
Upper Gv SNWD SE25 229 E1
Upper Grove Rd BELV DA17 156 D6
Upper Gulland Wk IS * N1 108 C4
Upper Ham Rd
RCHPK/HAM TW10 181 F6
Upper Handa Wk IS * N1 108 D4
Upper Harley St CAMTN NW1 3 F6
Upper Hawkwell Wk IS * N1 108 C6
Upper Hitch OXHEY WD19 42 C3
Upper Holly Hill Rd BELV DA17 157 F5
Upper John St REGST W1B 12 B5
Upper Lismore Wk IS * N1 108 C4
Upper Ldg KENS * W8 145 F1
Upper Ml HMSMTH W6 143 G5
Upper Marsh STHWK SE1 21 H5
Upper Montagu St
MBLAR W1H 10 C1
Upper Mulgrave Rd
BELMT SM2 242 C5
Upper Paddock Rd
OXHEY WD19 42 C1
Upper Park Rd BELV DA17 157 F4
BMLY BR1 212 D4
FBAR/BDGN N11 66 D1
HAMP NW3 106 B4
KUTN/CMB KT2 202 A2
Upper Phillimore Gdns
KENS * W8 145 E2
Upper Ramsey Wk IS * N1 108 D4
Upper Rawreth Wk IS * N1 108 C6
Upper Richmond Rd
PUT/ROE SW15 163 H5
Upper Richmond Rd West
RCHPK/HAM TW10 162 A5
Upper Rd PLSTW E13 132 C2
WLGTN SM6 245 F3
Upper St Martin's La
LSQ/SEVD WC2H 13 E4
Upper Selsdon Rd
SAND/SEL CR2 247 F6
Upper Sheppey Wk IS N1 108 C4
Upper Sheridan Rd BELV DA17 157 E4
Upper Shirley Rd
CROY/NA CR0 248 A1
Upper Sq ISLW TW7 160 C4
Upper St IS N1 6 B2
Upper Sunbury Rd HPTN TW12 198 D4
Upper Sutton La HEST TW5 159 E2
Upper Tachbrook St PIM SW1V 28 B1
Upper Tail OXHEY WD19 42 C5
Upper Talbot Wk NTGHL * W11 124 C5
Upper Teddington Rd KUT KT1 201 E4
Upper Ter HAMP NW3 105 G1
Upper Thames St BLKFR EC4V 15 E5
Upper Tollington Pk FSBYPK N4 88 A5
Upperton Rd SCUP DA14 215 F1
Upperton Rd East PLSTW E13 133 E2
Upperton Rd West PLSTW E13 133 E2
Upper Tooting Pk TOOT SW17 186 B4
Upper Tooting Rd TOOT SW17 186 B6
Upper Town Rd GFD/PVL UB6 119 F3
Upper Tulse Hl
BRXS/STRHM SW2 187 H2
Upper Vernon Rd SUT SM1 243 H3
Upper Walthamstow Rd
WALTH E17 91 H1
Upper Whistler Wk
WBPTN * SW10 165 G1
Upper Wickham La WELL DA16 175 H3
Upper Wimpole St
CAVSQ/HST W1G 11 F1
Upper Woburn Pl CAMTN NW1 4 D4
Uppingham Av STAN HA7 61 E6
Upsdell Av PLMGR N13 68 A2
Upstall St CMBW SE5 168 B2
Upton Av FSTGT E7 112 C5
Upton Cl BXLY DA5 196 D1
Upton Dene BELMT SM2 243 F5
Upton Gdns KTN/HRWW/W HA3 81 E3
Upton La FSTGT E7 112 D4
Upton Lodge Cl BUSH WD23 43 G2
Upton Park Rd FSTGT E7 112 D5
Upton Rd BXLYHS DA6 176 C5
HSLW TW3 159 E4
THHTH CR7 208 D5
UED N18 69 G1
WOOL/PLUM SE18 154 C6
Upton Rd South BXLY DA5 196 D1
Upway NFNCH/WDSP N12 66 A3
Upwood Rd LEE/GVPK SE12 192 C1
STRHM/NOR SW16 207 G4
Urlwin St CMBW SE5 31 E6
Urlwin Wk BRXN/ST SW9 168 A2
Urmston Dr WIM/MER SW19 184 C3
Ursula Ms FSBYPK N4 88 B5
Ursula St BTSEA SW11 166 A2
Urswick Rd CLPT E5 110 A3
DAGW RM9 116 C5
Usborne Ms VX/NE SW8 167 H1
Usher Rd BOW E3 110 D6
Usk Rd BTSEA SW11 165 G5
Usk St BETH E2 130 B2
Uvedale Rd DAGE RM10 117 E1
ENC/FH EN2 38 D6
Uverdale Rd WBPTN SW10 165 G1
Uxbridge Rd EA W5 121 G6
FELT TW13 178 B4
HPTN TW12 179 E6
STHL UB1 139 E1
SURB KT6 221 F1
Uxbridge Rd (Harrow Weald)
KTN/HRWW/W HA3 59 F3
Uxbridge Rd
(Hatch End) PIN HA5 58 D3
Uxbridge Rd High St STHL UB1 138 D1
Uxbridge Rd (Pinner) PIN HA5 58 B5
Uxbridge Rd
(Stanmore) STAN HA7 60 B2
Uxbridge Rd The Broadway
YEAD UB4 118 B6
Uxbridge St KENS W8 145 E1
Uxendon Crs WBLY HA9 81 G5
Uxendon Hl WBLY HA9 81 H5

V

Valance Av CHING E4 56 B3
Valan Leas HAYES BR2 212 A6
Vale Cl EFNCH N2 66 B6
MV/WKIL W9 125 G2
ORP BR6 252 A2
TWK * TW1 180 C5
Vale Cottages
PUT/ROE * SW15 183 E5
Vale Ct ACT * W3 143 F1
Vale Crs PUT/ROE SW15 183 E6
Vale Cft ESH/CLAY KT10 238 B5
PIN HA5 78 C2
Vale Dr BAR EN5 34 D5
Vale End EDUL SE22 169 F5
Vale Gv ACT W3 142 D1
FSBYPK N4 88 C4
Vale La ACT W3 122 A4
Valence Av BCTR RM8 96 B5
Valence Circ BCTR RM8 116 B1
Valence Rd ERITH DA8 177 H1
Valence Wood Rd BCTR RM8 116 B1
Valencia Rd STAN HA7 45 E6
Valentia Pl BRXN/ST SW9 168 A5
Valentine Av BXLY DA5 196 C4
Valentine Pl STHWK SE1 22 C3
Valentine Rd HOM * E9 110 B4
RYLN/HDSTN HA2 99 F1
Valentines Rd IL IG1 94 B5
Vale of Health HAMP NW3 105 G1
Valerian Wy SRTFD E15 132 A2
Vale Ri GLDGN NW11 84 D5
Vale Rd BMLY BR1 214 A5
ESH/CLAY KT10 238 A6
FSBYPK N4 88 C4
FSTGT E7 112 D4
HOR/WEW KT19 241 F2
MTCM CR4 207 F6
SUT SM1 243 F2
WPK KT4 241 F1
Vale Rd North SURB KT6 221 G6
Vale Royal HOLWY N7 107 G5
Valeswood Rd BMLY BR1 212 B1
Vale Ter FSBYPK N4 88 C3
The Vale ACT W3 142 D1
CHEL SW3 145 H6
CRICK NW2 104 B1
CROY/NA CR0 230 B6
HEST TW5 138 C6
MUSWH N10 66 C4
RSLP HA4 98 A2
STHGT/OAK N14 51 G2
WFD IG8 72 C3
Valetta Gv PLSTW E13 132 C1
Valetta Rd ACT W3 143 E2
Valette St HACK * E8 109 H4
Valiant Cl NTHLT UB5 118 B2
ROMW/RG RM7 77 E5
Valiant Wy EHAM E6 133 H4
Vallance Rd BETH E2 9 F4
WDGN N22 67 E5
Vallentin Rd WALTH E17 91 G1
Valley Av NFNCH/WDSP N12 49 H6
Valley Cl LOU IG10 57 H1
Valley Dr CDALE/KGS NW9 82 B2
Valleyfield Rd
STRHM/NOR SW16 207 H1
Valley Fields Crs ENC/FH EN2 38 A3
Valley Gdns ALP/SUD HA0 101 H5
WIM/MER SW19 205 H3
Valley Gv CHARL SE7 153 E5
Valley Hl LOU IG10 57 G2
Valley Rd ERITH DA8 157 G4
HAYES BR2 212 A5
STMC/STPC BR5 215 H4
STRHM/NOR SW16 187 H6
Valley Side CHING E4 55 E3
Valley Vw BAR EN5 48 C1
Valley Wk CROY/NA CR0 230 A6
Valliere Rd WLSDN NW10 123 G2
Valliers Wood Rd BFN/LL DA15 194 D3
Vallis Wy CHSGTN KT9 239 F2
WEA W13 120 C4
Valmar Rd CMBW SE5 168 C2
Valnay St TOOT SW17 206 B1
Valognes Av WALTH E17 70 C4
Valonia Gdns
WAND/EARL SW18 184 D1
Vambery Rd
WOOL/PLUM SE18 154 C6
Vanbrough Crs NTHLT UB5 118 A1
Vanbrugh Dr WOT/HER KT12 218 A4
Vanbrugh Flds BKHTH/KID SE3 152 B6
Vanbrugh Hl GNWCH SE10 152 A5
Vanbrugh Pk BKHTH/KID SE3 172 B1
Vanbrugh Park Rd
BKHTH/KID SE3 172 B1
Vanbrugh Park Rd West
BKHTH/KID SE3 172 B1
Vanbrugh Rd CHSWK W4 142 D3
Vanbrugh Ter BKHTH/KID SE3 172 B2
Vanburgh Cl CAN/RD E16 133 F4
ORP BR6 235 E5
Vancouver Man EDGW * HA8 62 B4
Vancouver Rd EDGW HA8 62 B4
FSTH SE23 190 C4
RCHPK/HAM TW10 181 E6
Vanderbilt Rd
WAND/EARL SW18 185 F3
Vanderbilt Vls SHB * W12 144 B2
Vandome Cl CAN/RD E16 132 D5
Vandon St STJSPK SW1H 20 B5
Van Dyck Av NWMAL KT3 222 D4
Vandyke Cl PUT/ROE SW15 184 B1
Vandyke Cross ELTH/MOT SE9 173 G6
Vandy St SDTCH EC2A 8 A6
Vane Cl HAMP NW3 105 H3
KTN/HRWW/W HA3 81 H3
Vanessa Cl BELV DA17 157 E5
Vanessa Wy BXLY DA5 197 H5
Vanguard CDALE/KGS * NW9 63 E3
Vanguard Cl CAN/RD E16 132 C4
CROY/NA CR0 228 B5
ROMW/RG RM7 77 F5
Vanguard St DEPT SE8 171 E2
Vanguard Wy CROY/NA CR0 247 F2
WLGTN SM6 245 G5
Vanneck Sq PUT/ROE * SW15 163 G6
Vanoc Gdns BMLY BR1 192 C6
Vansittart Rd FSTGT E7 112 C2
Vansittart St NWCR SE14 170 C1
Vanston Pl FUL/PGN SW6 165 E1
Vant Rd TOOT SW17 206 B1
Varcoe Rd BERM/RHTH SE16 33 H4
Vardens Rd BTSEA SW11 165 H5
Varden St WCHPL E1 17 G3
Varley Rd CAN/RD E16 132 D5
Varley Wy MTCM CR4 205 H5
Varna Rd FUL/PGN SW6 164 C1
HPTN * TW12 199 F4
Varndell St CAMTN NW1 4 A3
Varsity Dr ISLW * TW7 160 B6
Varsity Rw MORT/ESHN SW14 162 C3
Vartry Rd SEVS/STOTM N15 89 E3
Vassall Rd BRXN/ST SW9 168 A1
Vauban Est BERM/RHTH SE16 24 D6
Vauban St BERM/RHTH SE16 24 D6
Vaughan Av HDN NW4 83 G2
HMSMTH W6 143 F4
Vaughan Est BETH * E2 8 C3
Vaughan Gdns IL IG1 93 H4
Vaughan Rd CMBW SE5 168 C3
HRW HA1 79 G4
SRTFD E15 112 B4
THDIT KT7 220 D4
WELL DA16 175 F3
Vaughan St BERM/RHTH SE16 150 D2
Vaughan Wy WAP E1W 17 F6
Vaughan Williams Cl DEPT SE8 171 E1
Vauxhall Br LBTH SE11 29 E4
Vauxhall Bridge Rd PIM SW1V 20 A6
Vauxhall Gdns SAND/SEL CR2 246 C4
Vauxhall Gv VX/NE SW8 29 F5
Vauxhall St LBTH SE11 29 H4
Vauxhall Wk LBTH SE11 29 G3
Vawdrey Cl WCHPL E1 130 A3
Veals Md MTCM CR4 206 A4
Vectis Gdns TOOT SW17 206 D2
Vectis Rd TOOT SW17 206 D2
Veda Rd LEW SE13 171 E5
Vega Rd BUSH WD23 43 G2
Veldene Wy RYLN/HDSTN HA2 98 D1
Vellum Dr CAR SM5 244 C1
Venables Cl DAGE RM10 117 F2
Venables St BAY/PAD * W2 125 H4
Vencourt Pl HMSMTH W6 143 G5
Venetian Rd CMBW SE5 168 C3
Venetia Rd EA W5 141 F2
FSBYPK N4 88 B3
Venner Rd SYD SE26 210 A2
Venn St CLAP SW4 167 E5
Ventnor Av STAN HA7 60 D4
Ventnor Dr NFNCH/WDSP N12 49 F5
Ventnor Gdns BARK IG11 115 E4
Ventnor Rd BELMT SM2 243 F5
NWCR SE14 170 B1
Ventnor Ter SEVS/STOTM * N15 89 G1
Venture Cl BXLY DA5 196 C2
Venue St POP/IOD E14 131 F4
Venus Rd WOOL/PLUM SE18 153 H3
Vera Av WCHMH N21 38 A6
Vera Ct OXHEY WD19 42 B2
Vera Lynn Cl FSTGT E7 112 C2
Vera Rd FUL/PGN SW6 164 C2
Verbena Cl CAN/RD E16 132 A3
Verbena Gdns HMSMTH W6 143 G5
Verdant La CAT SE6 192 A3
Verdayne Av CROY/NA CR0 230 B5
Verderers Rd CHIG IG7 75 G1
Verdun Rd BARN SW13 163 G1
WOOL/PLUM SE18 155 G6
Vereker Rd WKENS * W14 144 C5
Vere St MHST W1U 11 G4
Vermont Cl ENC/FH EN2 38 B5
Vermont Rd NRWD SE19 208 D2
SUT SM1 243 F1
WAND/EARL SW18 185 F1
Verney Gdns DAGW RM9 116 C2
Verney Rd BERM/RHTH SE16 33 G4
DAGW RM9 116 C2
Verney St WLSDN NW10 102 D1
Verney Wy BERM/RHTH SE16 33 G4
Vernham Rd
WOOL/PLUM SE18 154 C6
Vernon Av MNPK E12 113 H2
RYNPK SW20 204 B5
WFD IG8 72 D2
Vernon Cl HOR/WEW KT19 240 C4
STMC/STPC BR5 215 H6
Vernon Crs EBAR EN4 36 C6
Vernon Dr STAN HA7 60 C4
Vernon Pl BMSBY WC1N 13 F2
Vernon Ri FSBYW WC1X 5 H3
NTHLT UB5 99 H3
Vernon Rd BOW E3 130 D1
CEND/HSY/T * N8 68 A6
CRW RM5 77 G1
GDMY/SEVK IG3 95 F5
MORT/ESHN SW14 162 D4
SRTFD E15 112 A5
SUT SM1 243 G3
WALTH E17 90 D1
WAN E11 92 A5
Vernon Sq FSBYW * WC1X 5 H3
Vernon St WKENS W14 144 C4
Vernon Yd NTGHL W11 124 D6
Veroan Rd BXLYHN DA7 176 C3
Verona Dr SURB KT6 221 G6
Veronica Gdns MTCM CR4 207 E4
Veronica Rd TOOT SW17 186 D5
Veronique Gdns
GNTH/NBYPK IG2 94 C2
Verran Rd BAL * SW12 186 D2
Versailles Rd PGE/AN SE20 209 G3
Verulam Av WALTH E17 90 D4
Verulam Ct CDALE/KGS * NW9 83 G4
Verulam Rd GFD/PVL UB6 119 E3
Verulam St FSBYW WC1X 14 A1
Verwood Dr EBAR EN4 36 B4
Verwood Rd RYLN/HDSTN HA2 59 G5
Veryan Cl STMC/STPC BR5 236 A1
Vespan Rd SHB W12 143 G2
Vesta Rd BROCKY SE4 170 C3
Vestris Rd FSTH SE23 190 B4
Vestry Rd CMBW SE5 169 E2
WALTH E17 91 F2
Vestry St IS N1 7 G3
Vevey St FSTH SE23 190 D4
Viaduct Pl BETH * E2 9 G4
Viaduct Rd EFNCH N2 65 H5
Viaduct St BETH E2 9 G4
The Viaduct MUSWH * N10 86 D1
SWFD E18 72 C5
Vian St LEW SE13 171 F4
Vibart Gdns BRXS/STRHM SW2 187 H2
Vibart Wk IS * N1 107 G6
Vicarage Cl ERITH DA8 157 G6
NTHLT UB5 98 D6
WPK KT4 223 E5
Vicarage Ct BECK * BR3 210 C6
Vicarage Crs BTSEA SW11 165 H3
Vicarage Dr BARK IG11 114 C5
BECK BR3 211 E4
MORT/ESHN SW14 162 D6
Vicarage Farm Rd HEST TW5 158 C2
Vicarage Flds WOT/HER KT12 218 A3
Vicarage Gdns MTCM CR4 206 A6
Vicarage Ga KENS * W8 145 F2
KENS W8 145 F2
Vicarage Gv CMBW SE5 168 D2
Vicarage La EHAM E6 133 H2
IL IG1 94 D5
SRTFD E15 112 A4
Vicarage Ms CHSWK * W4 143 E6
Vicarage Pde
SEVS/STOTM * N15 88 C1
Vicarage Pk WOOL/PLUM SE18 154 C5
Vicarage Rd BXLY DA5 197 F3
CROY/NA CR0 246 A1
DAGE RM10 117 F5
E/WMO/HCT KT8 201 E4
HDN NW4 83 G3
LEY E10 91 F4
MORT/ESHN SW14 162 C6
SRTFD E15 112 B5
SUT SM1 243 E2
TEDD TW11 200 C1
TOTM N17 69 G3
WFD IG8 73 G3
WHTN TW2 179 G1
WHTN TW2 180 A4
WOOL/PLUM SE18 154 C5
Vicarage Wk BTSEA * SW11 165 H2
Vicarage Wy RYLN/HDSTN HA2 79 E4
WLSDN NW10 102 D1
Vicars Bridge Cl ALP/SUD HA0 121 G1
Vicar's Cl EN EN1 39 E3
HACK E8 110 A6
SRTFD E15 112 C6
Vicars Hl LEW SE13 171 F5
Vicar's Moor La WCHMH N21 52 A2
Vicars Oak Rd NRWD SE19 209 E2
Vicar's Rd KTTN NW5 106 C3
Viceroy Cl EFNCH * N2 86 A1
Viceroy Pde EFNCH * N2 86 A1
Viceroy Rd VX/NE SW8 167 G2
Vickers Cl CROY/NA CR0 245 H5
Vickers Rd ERITH DA8 157 H5
Victor Gv ALP/SUD HA0 101 G5
Victoria Ar PIM SW1V 19 H6
Victoria Av CAR SM5 244 C1
CRW RM5 77 F2
E/WMO/HCT KT8 199 F6
EHAM E6 113 F6
FNCH N3 64 D4
HSLW TW4 159 E6
SURB KT6 221 F3
WBLY HA9 102 B4
Victoria Cl E/WMO/HCT KT8 199 E6
EBAR EN4 35 H5
HRW * HA1 80 B3
Victoria Cottages
RCH/KEW TW9 161 H2
WCHPL * E1 17 E1
Victoria Ct WBLY HA9 102 A4
Victoria Crs NRWD SE19 209 E2
SEVS/STOTM N15 89 E2
WIM/MER * SW19 204 D3
Victoria Dock Rd CAN/RD E16 132 B5
Victoria Dr WIM/MER SW19 184 B2
Victoria Emb TPL/STR WC2R 13 G6
WHALL SW1A 21 F4
Victoria Embankment Gdns
CHCR * WC2N 13 F6
Victoria Gdns HEST TW5 158 C2
NTGHL W11 145 E1
Victoria Ga BAY/PAD W2 125 H6
Victoria Gv KENS W8 145 G3
NFNCH/WDSP N12 65 H1
Victoria Grove Ms
BAY/PAD W2 125 F6
Victoria Ms KIL/WHAMP NW6 105 E6
WAND/EARL SW18 185 G3
Victorian Gv STNW/STAM N16 109 E1
Victorian Rd STNW/STAM N16 109 E1
Victoria Pde RCH/KEW * TW9 162 A2
Victoria Park Sq BETH E2 130 A2
Victoria Park Studios
HOM * E9 110 A4

Victoria Pl RCHPK/HAM TW10 ....161 F6
Victoria Ri CLAP SW4 ....166 D4
Victoria Rd ACT W3 ....122 D4
  BARK IG11 ....114 B4
  BFN/LL DA15 ....195 F5
  BKHH IG9 ....57 F4
  BUSH WD23 ....43 F5
  BXLYHS DA6 ....177 E6
  CHING E4 ....56 A3
  CHST BR7 ....214 A1
  DAGE RM10 ....117 G3
  EBAR EN4 ....35 H5
  FSBYPK N4 ....87 H4
  HAYES BR2 ....233 F2
  HDN NW4 ....84 A1
  KENS W8 ....145 G3
  KIL/WHAMP NW6 ....124 D1
  KUT KT1 ....201 H5
  MLHL NW7 ....63 F1
  MORT/ESHN SW14 ....162 D4
  MTCM CR4 ....206 A3
  NWDGN UB2 ....138 D3
  PLSTW E13 ....132 C1
  RSLP HA4 ....98 B5
  SEVS/STOTM * N15 ....69 G4
  SURB KT6 ....221 F3
  SUT SM1 ....243 H3
  SWFD E18 ....73 D6
  TEDD TW11 ....200 C2
  TWK TW1 ....180 D2
  UED N18 ....53 F6
  WALTH E17 ....71 G5
  WAN E11 ....111 H2
  WDGN N22 ....67 H2
  WEA W13 ....120 D4
Victoria Sq BGVA SW1W 19 H5
Victoria St BELV DA17 ....156 D5
  PIM SW1V 19 H6
  SRTFD E15 ....112 A5
Victoria Ter EA * W5 ....141 F1
  FSBYPK N4 ....88 A5
  RYLN/HDSTN HA2 ....80 A1
Victoria Vls RCH/KEW TW9 ....161 H4
Victoria Wy CHARL SE7 ....152 D5
Victoria Yd WCHPL * E1 ....17 F4
Victor Rd PGE/AN SE20 ....210 B5
  RYLN/HDSTN HA2 ....59 G6
  TEDD TW11 ....200 A1
  WLSDN NW10 ....123 H2
Victors Dr HPTN * TW12 ....198 C2
Victors Wy BAR EN5 ....34 D4
Victor Vls UED * N18 ....52 D5
Victory Av MORT/ESHN SM4 ....225 G2
Victory Pl NRWD * SE19 ....209 E2
  WALW SE17 ....31 F1
Victory Rd WAN E11 ....92 D1
  WIM/MER SW19 ....205 G3
Victory Wy BERM/RHTH SE16 ......150 C2
  HEST TW5 ....138 A5
  ROMW/RG RM7 ....77 F5
Vienna Cl CLAY IG5 ....73 F5
View Cl CHIG IG7 ....74 D1
  HGT N6 ....86 B4
  HRW HA1 ....79 H1
View Crs CEND/HSY/T N8 ....87 F2
Viewfield Cl KTN/HRWW/W HA3 ....81 G4
Viewfield Rd BFN/LL DA15 ....196 A3
  WAND/EARL SW18 ....184 D1
Viewland Rd
  WOOL/PLUM SE18 ....115 F5
View Rd HGT N6 ....86 B4
The View ABYW SE2 ....156 C5
Viga Rd WCHMH N21 ....52 A1
Vigilant Cl SYD SE26 ....189 G6
Vignoles Rd ROMW/RG RM7 ....97 F4
Vigo St MYFR/PICC W1J 12 A6
Viking Gdns EHAM E6 ....133 G4
Viking Pl LEY E10 ....90 D5
Viking Rd STHL UB1 ....118 C6
Viking Wy BELV DA17 ....157 G3
Villacourt Rd
  WOOL/PLUM SE18 ....175 G1
Village Ar CHING * E4 ....45 G6
Village Cl CHING E4 ....71 G1
  HAMP * NW3 ....105 H3
Village Ms CDALE/KGS * NW9 ....82 D6
Village Mt HAMP * NW3 ....105 G2
Village Park Ct EN EN1 ....53 E1
Village Rd EN EN1 ....52 D1
  FNCH N3 ....64 C5
Village Rw BELMT SM2 ....248 C6
The Village CHARL SE7 ....153 E6
  GLDGN * NW11 ....85 G6
Village Wy BECK BR3 ....211 E6
  HNHL SE24 ....188 D1
  PIN HA5 ....100 D2
  WLSDN NW10 ....102 D2
Village Wy East
  RYLN/HDSTN HA2 ....78 D4
Villa Rd BRXN/ST SW9 ....168 A4
Villas Rd WOOL/PLUM SE18 ....144 C4
Villa St WALW SE17 ....31 H4
Villiers Av BRYLDS KT5 ....221 H2
  WHTN TW2 ....178 B2
Villiers Cl BRYLDS KT5 ....221 H1
Villiers Gv BELMT SM2 ....242 B6
Villiers Rd BECK BR3 ....225 E1
  CRICK NW2 ....105 G4
  ISLW TW7 ....160 A3
  KUT KT1 ....201 H6
  OXHEY WD19 ....42 C1
  STHL UB1 ....115 E5
Villiers St CHCR WC2N 21 F1
Vincam Cl WHTN TW2 ....179 E2
Vincennes Est WNWD * SE27 ......188 D6
Vincent Av BRYLDS KT5 ....222 B5
Vincent Cl BAR EN5 ....21 E4
  BARK/HLT IG6 ....54 C2
  BFN/LL DA15 ....195 E3
  HAYES BR2 ....232 D1

SEVS/STOTM N15 ....88 C1
WDGN N22 ....68 A5
WOOL/PLUM * SE18 ....154 B4
Vincent Rw HPTN TW12 ....199 G2
Vincents Cl BERM/RHTH SE16 .....150 C2
Vincent Sq WDCHL * N22 ....68 A5
  WEST SW1P 28 B1
Vincent St CAN/RD E16 ....132 C4
  WEST SW1P 28 B1
Vincent Ter IS N1 ....6 C1
Vincent Vls SEVS/STOTM * N15 ....88 C1
Vince St FSBYE EC1V 7 H4
Vine Cl BRYLDS KT5 ....221 H5
  SUT SM1 ....243 G1
Vine Cottages HNWL * W7 ....140 A1
  WCHPL * E1 ....130 A5
Vine Ct KTN/HRWW/W HA3 ....81 G5
  WCHPL E1 ....17 F2
Vine Gdns IL IG1 ....114 C3
Vinegar St WAP E1W 25 C1
Vinegar Yd STHWK SE1 ....24 A3
Vine HI CLKNW EC1R 5 H5
Vine La STHWK SE1 ....24 B2
Vine Pl HSLW TW3 ....159 F5
Vineries Bank MLHL NW7 ....65 H6
The Vineries CAT * SE6 ....191 E3
  EN EN1 ....39 E4
  STHGT/OAK N14 ....51 E1
Vine Rd BARN SW13 ....163 F4
  E/WMO/HCT KT8 ....219 G1
  ORP BR6 ....253 F4
  SRTFD E15 ....112 B5
Vine Rw RCHPK/HAM * TW10 ......161 G6
Viners Cl WOT/HER KT12 ....218 A3
Vines Av FNCH N3 ....65 F4
Vine Sq WKENS * W14 ....144 D5
Vine St CONDST W1S 12 B6
  ROMW/RG RM7 ....57 H4
  TWRH EC3N 16 C4
Vine Street Br FARR EC1M 6 B3
Vine Street Crs TWRH * EC3N 16 C5
Vine Yd STHWK SE1 ....23 F3
Vineyard Av MLHL NW7 ....25 C3
Vineyard Cl CAT SE6 ....191 E3
  KUT KT1 ....201 H6
Vineyard Gv FNCH N3 ....65 F4
Vineyard Hill Rd
  WIM/MER SW19 ....185 E6
Vineyard Ms CLKNW * EC1R 6 A5
Vineyard Pth
  MORT/ESHN SW14 ....162 D4
Vineyard Rw E/WMO/HCT KT8 ....201 E4
The Vineyard
  RCHPK/HAM TW10 ....161 F6
Vineyard Wk CLKNW EC1R 6 A5
Viney Bank CROY/NA CRO 248 D6
Viney Rd LEW SE13 ....171 F4
Vining St BRXN/ST SW9 ....168 A5
Vinson Cl ORP BR6 ....235 J1
Vintry Ms WALTH E17 ....91 E1
Viola Av ABYW SE2 ....155 H4
  EBED/NFELT TW14 ....178 A1
Viola Sq SHB W12 ....118 C1
Violet Av ENC/FH EN2 ....35 D1
Violet Cl CAN/RD E16 ....132 A3
  DEPT SE8 ....150 D6
  MTCM CR4 ....194 C5
Violet Gdns CROY/NA CRO 246 B5
Violet La STJWD NW8 ....125 G1
Violet La CROY/NA CRO 246 B3
Violet Rd BOW E3 ....131 F3
  LEY E10 ....91 H1
  SWFD E18 ....73 F3
Violet St BETH * E2 ....9 H1
Virgil St STHWK SE1 ....21 H5
Virginia Cl CRW RM5 ....73 J3
  NWMAL KT3 ....222 C4
Virginia Gdns BARK/HLT IG6 ....74 D5
Virginia Rd BETH E2 ....8 A2
  THHTH CR7 ....208 D4
Virginia St WAP E1W 17 F6
Viscount Cl FBAR/BDGN N11 ....66 C1
Viscount Dr EHAM E6 ....133 H4
Viscount Gv YEAD UB4 ....118 B2
Viscount St STLK EC1Y 7 F6
Vista Av PEND EN3 ....40 B3
Vista Dr REDBR IG4 ....93 F2
The Vista ELTH/MOT SE9 ....193 G2
Vista Wy KTN/HRWW/W HA3 ....62 A5
Vivian Av HDN NW4 ....83 H2
  WBLY HA9 ....102 A4
Vivian Gdns WBLY HA9 ....102 A3
Vivian Rd BOW E3 ....113 G1
Vivian Sq PECK SE15 ....169 H4
Vivien Wy EFNCH N2 ....85 H2
Vivien Cl CHSGTN KT9 ....239 G5
Vivienne Cl TWK TW1 ....181 F1
Vixen Ms HACK * E8 ....109 F6
Voce Rd WOOL/PLUM SE18 ....174 D1
Voewood Cl NWMAL KT3 ....223 F3
Vogan Cl CHDH RM6 ....74 A4
Voltaire Rd CLAP SW4 ....167 H4
Voit Av WLSDN NW10 ....122 D2
Volta Wy CROY/NA CRO 227 H5
Voluntary Pl WAN E11 ....92 C3
Vorley Rd ARCH N19 ....84 C1
Voss Ct STRHM/NOR SW16 ....207 G2
Voss St BETH E2 ....92 C1
Voyagers Cl THMD SE28 ....136 A5
Vulcan Cl EHAM E6 ....134 A5
Vulcan Ga ENC/FH EN2 ....23 F3
Vulcan Rd BROCKY SE4 ....170 D3
Vulcan Ter BROCKY SE4 ....170 D3
Vulcan Wy HOLWY N7 ....107 H4
Vyner Rd ACT W3 ....122 D6
Vyner St BETH E2 ....8 H1
The Vyne BXLYHN DA7 ....177 F4
Vyse Cl BAR EN5 ....34 A5

W

Wadding St WALW SE17 ....31 G2
Waddington Cl EN EN1 ....39 E5
Waddington Rd SRTFD E15 ....111 H4
Waddington St SRTFD E15 ....111 H4
Waddington Wy NRWD SE19 ....208 C6
Waddon Cl CROY/NA CRO 246 A1
Waddon Court Rd
  CROY/NA CRO 246 A2

Waddon Marsh Wy
  CROY/NA CRO 227 H5
Waddon New Rd
  CROY/NA CRO 246 B1
Waddon Park Av
  CROY/NA CRO 246 A2
Waddon Rd CROY/NA CRO 246 B1
Waddon Wy CROY/NA CRO 246 A4
Wade Av STMC/STPC BR5 ....236 E4
Wade Rd CAN/RD E16 ....133 E5
Wade's Gv WCHMH N21 ....52 A2
Wade's Hi WCHMH N21 ....52 A1
Wade's La TEDD TW11 ....200 C1
Wadeson St BETH E2 ....92 D1
Wade's Pl POP/IOD E14 ....131 F6
Wadeville Av CHDH RM6 ....96 C3
Wadeville Cl BELV DA17 ....157 E5
Wadham Av CHING E4 ....71 F3
Wadham Gdns HAMP NW3 ....106 A5
  NTHLT UB5 ....99 H4
Wadham Rd CHING E4 ....71 F3
  PUT/ROE SW15 ....164 C5
Wadhurst Cl PGE/AN SE20 ....209 H5
Wadhurst Rd CHSWK W4 ....142 D3
Wadley Rd WAN E11 ....92 A4
Wadsworth Cl GFD/PVL UB6 ....121 E1
  PEND EN3 ....40 D6
Wadsworth Rd GFD/PVL UB6 ....120 D1
Wager St BOW E3 ....130 D3
Waghorn Rd
  KTN/HRWW/W HA3 ....61 F6
  PLSTW E13 ....113 E6
Waghorn St PECK SE15 ....169 G4
Wagner St PECK SE15 ....170 A1
Wagstaff Gdns DAGW RM9 ....116 A5
Wagtail Cl CDALE/KGS NW9 ....63 E5
Wagtail Wk BECK BR3 ....231 G2
Wagtail Wy STMC/STPC BR5 ....236 B1
Waights Ct KUTN/CMB KT2 ....201 G4
Wainfleet Av CRW RM5 ....57 J2
Wainford Cl WIM/MER SW19 ....184 B3
Wainwright Gv ISLW TW7 ....159 H5
Waite Davies Rd
  LEE/GVPK SE12 ....192 B2
Waite St PECK SE15 ....32 C5
Wakefield Gdns IL IG1 ....93 G3
  NRWD SE19 ....209 E5
Wakefield Ms STPAN WC1H 5 F4
Wakefield Rd FBAR/BDGN N11 ....67 F1
  RCHPK/HAM TW10 ....170 A6
  SEVS/STOTM N15 ....89 F2
Wakefield St BMSBY WC1N 5 F5
  EHAM E6 ....113 G6
  UED N18 ....42 D4
Wakeham St IS N1 ....108 C5
Wakehams Hl PIN HA5 ....58 D6
Wakeham St IS N1 ....108 C4
Wakehurst Rd BTSEA SW11 ....166 B6
Wakeling Rd HNWL W7 ....120 B4
Wakeling St WCHPL * E1 ....130 C5
Wakelin Rd SRTFD E15 ....132 A1
Wakeman Rd WLSDN NW10 ....124 J2
Wakemans Hill Av
  CDALE/KGS NW9 ....82 D2
Wakering Rd BARK IG11 ....114 C5
Wakerly Cl EHAM E6 ....136 H5
Wakley St FSBYE EC1V 6 B3
Walberswick St VX/NE SW8 ....167 G1
Walbrook MANHO EC4N 15 G5
Walburgh St WCHPL E1 ....17 G4
Walcorde Av WALW SE17 ....31 F2
Walcot Rd PEND EN3 ....40 D5
Walcot Sq LBTH SE11 ....30 B1
Walcott St WEST * SW1P 28 B1
Waldeck Gv WNWD SE27 ....188 B5
Waldeck Rd CHSWK W4 ....142 A6
  MORT/ESHN SW14 ....162 C4
  SEVS/STOTM N15 ....89 J1
  WEA W13 ....120 D5
Waldegrave Gdns TWK TW1 ....180 B4
Waldegrave Pk TWK TW1 ....180 B6
Waldegrave Rd BCTR RM8 ....96 A6
  BMLY BR1 ....233 G2
  CEND/HSY/T * N8 ....68 A2
  EA W5 ....121 H1
  NRWD SE19 ....209 F5
  TWK TW1 ....180 B6
Waldegrove CROY/NA CRO 227 J2
Waldemar Av FUL/PGN SW6 ....164 C2
  WEA W13 ....141 F1
Waldemar Rd WIM/MER SW19 .....205 F1
Walden Av CHST BR7 ....193 H6
  PLMGR N13 ....52 C6
  RAIN RM13 ....137 H1
Walden Cl BELV DA17 ....156 D5
Walden Gdns THHTH CR7 ....207 H1
Waldenhurst Rd
  STMC/STPC BR5 ....236 B4
Walden Pde CHST * BR7 ....213 H2
Walden Rd CHST BR7 ....213 H2
  TOTM N17 ....49 H4
Waldenshaw Rd STMC/STPC BR5 .236 B4
Waldenshaw Rd FSTH SE23 ....190 A3
Waldens Rd STMC/STPC BR5 ....236 C3
Waldens St WCHPL E1 ....17 G5
  MLHL NW7 ....64 B2
Waldo Cl CLAP SW4 ....167 G6
Waldo Pl WIM/MER SW19 ....206 A3
Waldorf Cl SAND/SEL CR2 ....246 B6
Waldo Rd BMLY BR1 ....213 H6
  WLSDN NW10 ....119 J3
Waldram Crs FSTH SE23 ....190 A3
Waldram Pk FSTH SE23 ....190 B3
Waldrist Wy ERITHM DA18 ....156 D2
Waldron Gdns HAYES BR2 ....231 H6
Waldronhyrst CROY/NA CRO 246 B2
Waldron Ms CHEL SW3 ....36 A3
Waldron Rd RYLN/HDSTN HA2 ......80 A6
  WAND/EARL SW18 ....185 G6
The Waldrons CROY/NA CRO 246 C2
Waldron's Yd RYLN/HDSTN HA2 ....78 C4
Waldstock Rd THMD SE28 ....135 G6
Waleran Cl STAN HA7 ....42 D2
Wales Av CAR SM5 ....244 B5
Wales Farm Rd ACT W3 ....118 D4
Waleton Acres WLGTN * SM6 ......245 E4
Waley St WCHPL * E1 ....130 B4
Walfield Av TRDG/WHET N20 ....49 F2
Walford Rd STNW/STAM N16 ......109 E2
Walfrey Gdns DAGW RM9 ....116 A5

Walham Green Ct
  FUL/PGN * SW6 ....165 F1
Walham Gv FUL/PGN SW6 ....165 E1
Walham Ri WIM/MER SW19 ....204 C2
Walham Yd FUL/PGN * SW6 ....165 E1
Walk Cl FBAR/BDGN * N11 ....51 E6
  HNWL W7 ....140 A1
Walker Cl DART * DA1 ....139 G5
  HNWL W7 ....140 A1
  WOOL/PLUM SE18 ....154 C4
Walker's Ct SOHO/CST W1F 12 C5
Walkerscroft Md DUL SE21 ....188 C3
Walker's Pl PUT/ROE * SW15 ....164 C5
The Walks EFNCH N2 ....65 H6
The Walk PLMGR * N13 ....52 A5
Wallace Cl THMD SE28 ....136 B6
Wallace Crs CAR SM5 ....244 B5
Wallace Rd IS N1 ....108 C4
Wallbutton Rd BROCKY SE4 ....170 C3
Wallcote Av CRICK NW2 ....84 B5
Walled End EHAM E6 ....114 C1
Waller Rd NWCR SE14 ....170 B5
Wallers Cl DAGW RM9 ....116 C6
  WFD IG8 ....73 H2
Wallflower St SHB W12 ....123 F6
Wallgrave Rd ECT SW5 ....145 E4
Wallingford Av NKENS W10 ....100 B5
Wallington Rd GDMY/SEVK IG3 .....95 H4
Wallis Cl BTSEA SW11 ....165 H4
Wallis Rd GFD/PVL UB6 ....119 F5
  HOM E9 ....110 D4
Wallorton Gdns
  MORT/ESHN SW14 ....162 D5
Wallside BARB * EC2Y 15 F2
Wall St IS N1 ....108 D4
Wallwood Rd WAN E11 ....91 H4
Wallwood St POP/IOD E14 ....130 D4
Walmar Cl EBAR EN4 ....36 H2
Walmar Cl CHING E4 ....55 F4
  ORP BR6 ....252 D2
Walmer Cl FSTGT E7 ....77 F5
Walmer Gdns HNWL W7 ....140 C2
Walmer Rd NTCHL W11 ....124 C4
Walmer Ter WOOL/PLUM SE18 ....154 C4
Walmgate Rd GFD/PVL UB6 ....100 D6
Walmington Fold
  NFNCH/WDSP N12 ....65 E2
Walm La CRICK NW2 ....104 B3
Walney Wk IS * N1 ....108 C4
Walnut Cl BARK/HLT IG6 ....94 C1
  CAR SM5 ....248 A4
  DEPT SE8 ....150 D6
Walnut Ct EA * W5 ....141 G2
Walnut Gdns SRTFD E15 ....112 A3
Walnut Gv WCHMH N21 ....88 D6
Walnut Ms BELMT SM2 ....249 G6
Walnut Rd LEY E10 ....91 E6
Walnuts Rd ORP BR6 ....235 G5
Walnut Tree Av MTCM * CR4 ....206 A3
Walnut Tree Cl BARN SW13 ....163 F2
  CHST BR7 ....214 C4
Walnut Tree Rd BCTR RM8 ....96 B6
  BTFD TW8 ....137 F5
  GNWCH * SE10 ....152 A5
  HEST * TW5 ....138 D6
Walnut Tree Wk LBTH SE11 ....30 A1
Walnut Wy BKHH IG9 ....69 F5
  RSLP HA4 ....98 A6
  SWLY BR8 ....217 H5
Walpole Av RCH/KEW TW9 ....161 H3
Walpole Cl PIN HA5 ....59 J3
  WEA W13 ....141 E2
Walpole Crs TEDD TW11 ....200 B1
Walpole Gdns CHSWK W4 ....142 C5
  WHTN TW2 ....180 A4
Walpole Ms STJWD NW8 ....105 H6
Walpole Ms TEDD TW11 ....200 B1
Walpole Rd CROY/NA CRO 228 D6
  EHAM E6 ....113 E5
  HAYES BR2 ....233 G1
  SURB KT6 ....221 G4
  SWFD E18 ....72 B4
  TEDD TW11 ....200 B1
  WALTH E17 ....71 G1
  WHTN TW2 ....180 A4
  WIM/MER SW19 ....205 H2
Walpole St CHEL SW3 ....36 D3
Walrond Av WBLY HA9 ....81 G3
Walsham Cl STNW/STAM N16 ....89 G5
  THMD SE28 ....136 B6
Walsham Rd NWCR SE14 ....170 B3
Walsingham Gdns
  HOR/WEW KT19 ....241 E2
Walsingham Pk CHST BR7 ....214 D5
Walsingham Rd BTSEA SW11 ....186 C1
  CLPT E5 ....90 C1
  ENC/FH EN2 ....38 D5
  MTCM CR4 ....226 B2
  STMC/STPC BR5 ....215 H4
Walsingham Wk BELV DA17 ....157 E6
Walters Rd PEND EN3 ....40 A6
  SNWD SE25 ....229 E1
Walter St BETH E2 ....92 D2
  KUTN/CMB * KT2 ....201 G4
Walters Wy FSTH SE23 ....190 B1
Walters Yd BMLY BR1 ....212 C5
Walter Ter WCHPL E1 ....10 C2
Walter Wk EDGW HA8 ....44 D3
Waltham Av CDALE/KGS NW9 ....82 A3
  HYS/HAR UB3 ....113 F2
Waltham Cl STMC/STPC BR5 ....256 B5
Waltham Dr EDGW HA8 ....62 A2
Waltham Pk WALTH E17 ....71 J2
Waltham Rd CAR SM5 ....225 H5
  NWDGN UB2 ....138 C3
  WFD IG8 ....73 G2
Walthamstow Av
  (North Circular) CHING E4 ....70 C1
Walthamstow Av CHING E4 ....70 C1
Waltheof Av TOTM N17 ....49 H4
Waltheof Gdns TOTM N17 ....68 D4
Walton Av CHEAM SM3 ....242 D1
  NWMAL KT3 ....224 A1
  RYLN/HDSTN HA2 ....98 D3
Walton Cl CRICK NW2 ....83 H6
  HRW HA1 ....61 E2
  VX/NE SW8 ....167 G1

Walton Dr HRW HA1 ....79 H1
WLSDN NW10 ....102 D4
Walton Gdns ACT W3 ....122 B4
WBLY HA9 ....81 G6
Walton Gn CROY/NA CR0 ....228 F6
Walton Pk WOT/HER * KT12 ....218 B6
WOT/HER KT12 ....218 B6
Walton Pl CHEL SW3 ....18 C5
Walton Rd CRW RM5 ....76 D3
HRW HA1 ....79 H1
MNPK E12 ....114 A2
PLSTW E13 ....133 E1
SCUP DA14 ....195 H5
SEVS/STOTM * N15 ....89 F1
WOT/HER KT12 ....218 B2
Walton St CHEL SW3 ....28 B1
ENC/FH EN2 ....23 D2
Walton Vls IS * N1 ....109 E5
Walton Wy ACT W3 ....122 B4
MTCM CR4 ....227 E1
Walt Whitman Cl HNHL * SE24 ....168 B5
Walverns Cl OXHEY WD19 ....42 A1
Walworth Pl WALW SE17 ....31 F4
Walworth Rd WALW SE17 ....31 E1
Walwyn Av BMLY BR1 ....213 F6
Wanborough Dr
PUT/ROE SW15 ....183 H3
Wanderer Dr BARK IG11 ....155 H2
Wandle Bank CROY/NA CR0 ....245 G1
WIM/MER SW19 ....205 H2
Wandle Ct HOR/WEW KT19 ....240 C2
Wandle Court Gdns
....245 G1
Wandle Rd CROY/NA CR0 ....245 G1
MRDN SM4 ....225 H2
TOOT SW17 ....186 A4
WLGTN SM6 ....226 D2
Wandle Side CROY/NA CR0 ....245 H1
WLGTN SM6 ....244 D1
Wandle Wy MTCM CR4 ....226 B2
Wandon Rd FUL/PGN SW6 ....165 F1
Wandsworth Br
WAND/EARL SW18 ....165 G4
Wandsworth Bridge Rd
FUL/PGN SW6 ....165 F2
Wandsworth Common
West Side
WAND/EARL SW18 ....165 G6
Wandsworth High St
WAND/EARL SW18 ....165 E6
Wandsworth Rd CLAP SW4 ....166 D4
VX/NE SW8 ....29 E5
Wangey Rd CHDH RM6 ....56 A6
Wanless Rd HNHL SE24 ....168 C4
Wanley Rd CMBW SE5 ....168 D5
Wanlip Rd PLSTW E13 ....132 D3
Wannock Gdns BARK/HLT IG6 ....74 B3
Wansbeck Rd HOM E9 ....110 D5
Wansdown Pl FUL/PGN SW6 ....165 F1
Wansey St WALW SE17 ....31 F2
Wansford Rd WFD IG8 ....73 G4
Wanstead Cl BMLY BR1 ....213 E5
Wanstead La IL IG1 ....93 G3
Wanstead Park Av MNPK E12 ....93 F6
Wanstead Pk Rd IL IG1 ....93 G5
Wanstead Pl WAN E11 ....92 C3
Wanstead Rd BMLY BR1 ....213 E5
Wansunt Rd BXLY DA5 ....197 G3
Wantage Rd LEE/GVPK SE12 ....172 B6
Wantz Rd DAGE RM10 ....117 F2
Wapping Dock St WAP * E1W 25 H2
Wapping High St WAP E1W 25 H1
Wapping La WAP E1W 25 H2
Wapping Wk WAP E1W 17 H6
Wapping Wall WAP E1W 150 A1
Warbank La KUTN/CMB KT2 ....203 F3
Warbeck Rd SHB W12 ....143 H1
Warberry Rd WDGN N22 ....67 H3
Warboys Ap KUTN/CMB KT2 ....202 B2
Warboys Crs CHING E4 ....71 C1
Warboys Rd KUTN/CMB KT2 ....202 B2
Warburton Cl
KTN/HRWW/W HA3 ....44 C2
Warburton Rd HACK E8 ....109 H6
WHTN TW2 ....179 F3
Warburton St HACK E8 ....109 H6
Warburton Ter WALTH E17 ....71 F5
Wardalls Gv NWCR * SE14 ....170 A1
Ward Cl ERITH DA8 ....157 H6
RYLN/HDSTN HA2 ....78 C5
Wardell Cl CDALE/KGS NW9 ....63 E3
Warden Av CRW RM5 ....77 C1
RYLN/HDSTN HA2 ....78 C5
Warden Rd KTTN NW5 ....106 C4
Wardens Gv STHWK SE1 ....35 E2
Wardle St HOM E9 ....110 B3
Wardley Rd WAND/EARL SW18 ....185 F1
Wardo Av FUL/PGN SW6 ....164 C2
Wardour Ms SOHO/CST W1F 12 B4
Wardour St SOHO/CST W1F 12 B3
Ward Rd ARCH N19 ....107 E2
SRTFD * E15 ....111 H6
Wardrobe Pl BLKFR * EC4V 14 D4
The Wardrobe RCH/KEW * TW9 ....161 F6
Wards Rd GNTH/NBYPK IG2 ....94 D4
Wareham Cl HSLW TW3 ....159 F5
Warenford Rd GNTH/NBYPK IG2 ....94 B2
Warepoint Dr THMD SE28 ....154 D2
Warfield Rd HPTN TW12 ....199 F4
WLSDN NW10 ....124 B2
Wargrave Av SEVS/STOTM N15 ....89 F3
Wargrave Rd RYLN/HDSTN HA2 ....99 C1
Warham Rd FSBYPK N4 ....89 A2
KTN/HRWW/W HA3 ....60 B6
SAND/SEL CR2 ....286 C2
Warham St CMBW SE5 ....131 F6
Waring Cl ORP BR6 ....255 F4
Waring Dr ORP BR6 ....255 F4
Waring Rd SCUP DA14 ....216 A2
Waring St WNWD SE27 ....188 C6
Warkworth Gdns ISLW TW7 ....160 C1
Warkworth Rd TOTM N17 ....68 H1
Warland Rd WOOL/PLUM SE18 ....115 J6
Warley Av BCTR RM8 ....96 C4
Warley Rd CLAY IG5 ....54 A4
ED N9 ....36 E1
WFD IG8 ....72 D3
Warley St BETH E2 ....130 B2

Warlingham Rd THHTH CR7 ....228 B1
Warlock Rd MV/WKIL W9 ....124 D3
Warlters Cl HOLWY * N7 ....107 G2
Warlters Rd HOLWY N7 ....107 G2
Warltersville Rd ARCH N19 ....87 D4
Warming Cl CLPT * E5 ....110 B1
Warmington Rd HNHL SE24 ....188 C1
Warmington St PLSTW E13 ....132 C5
Warminster Rd SNWD SE25 ....209 G5
Warminster Sq SNWD SE25 ....209 G5
Warminster Wy MTCM CR4 ....206 D4
Warndon St BERM/RHTH SE16 ....150 A4
Warneford Pl OXHEY WD19 ....42 C1
Warneford Rd
KTN/HRWW/W HA3 ....61 H2
Warneford St HOM E9 ....109 H6
Warne Pl BFN/LL DA15 ....195 H1
Warner Av CHEAM SM3 ....224 C6
Warner Cl CDALE/KGS NW9 ....83 F4
HPTN TW12 ....198 D1
SRTFD E15 ....112 A3
Warner Pl BETH E2 ....9 F2
Warner Rd BMLY BR1 ....212 B3
CEND/HSY/T N8 ....87 F1
CMBW SE5 ....168 C1
WALTH E17 ....90 C1
Warner St CLKNW EC1R 6 A6
Warner Ter POP/IOD * E14 ....131 H4
Warnford Rd ORP BR6 ....255 F1
Warnham Court Rd CAR SM5 ....244 B5
Warnham Rd
NFNCH/WDSP N12 ....65 H1
Warple Ms ACT * W3 ....143 G2
Warple Wy ACT W3 ....143 G2
Warren Av BMLY BR1 ....212 A3
ORP BR6 ....253 F3
RCHPK/HAM TW10 ....162 B2
SAND/SEL CR2 ....248 B5
WAN * E11 ....111 H1
Warren Cl BXLYHS DA6 ....177 E6
ED N9 ....36 D1
WBLY HA9 ....81 F6
YEAD UB4 ....118 A4
Warren Crs ED N9 ....53 F2
Warren Cutting
KUTN/CMB KT2 ....202 D3
Warrender Rd ARCH N19 ....107 E1
Warren Dr GFD/PVL UB6 ....119 F3
ORP BR6 ....253 J5
RSLP HA4 ....60 C2
Warren Dr North BRYLDS KT5 ....222 B5
Warren Dr South BRYLDS KT5 ....222 C5
The Warren Dr WAN E11 ....93 E4
Warren Flds STAN * HA7 ....43 J1
Warren Gdns ORP BR6 ....253 G5
Warren La STAN HA7 ....44 C4
WOOL/PLUM SE18 ....154 B3
Warren Ms GTPST W1W 4 A6
Warren Pk KUTN/CMB KT2 ....202 C2
Warren Park Rd SUT SM1 ....243 H4
Warren Pond Rd CHING E4 ....56 B2
Warren Ri NWMAL KT3 ....202 D4
Warren Rd BARK/HLT IG6 ....74 C5
BUSH WD23 ....43 G5
BXLYHS DA6 ....177 E6
CHING E4 ....55 G4
CRICK NW2 ....63 F6
CROY/NA CR0 ....229 E5
HAYES BR2 ....232 C6
IL IG1 ....72 B2
LEY E10 ....111 G1
ORP BR6 ....253 F3
SCUP DA14 ....196 A5
WAN E11 ....93 H3
WHTN TW2 ....179 H1
WIM/MER SW19 ....206 A2
Warrens Shawe La EDGW HA8 ....46 B4
Warren St FITZ W1T 4 A7
The Warren CAR SM5 ....243 H6
HEST TW5 ....158 D1
HOR/WEW KT19 ....240 D2
MNPK E12 ....113 G2
Warren Wy MLHL NW7 ....46 C4
Warren Wood Cl HAYES BR2 ....232 C6
Warriner Dr ED N9 ....53 G5
Warriner Gdns BTSEA SW11 ....166 B2
Warrington Crs MV/WKIL W9 ....125 C3
Warrington Gdns MV/WKIL W9 ....125 C3
Warrington Pl POP/IOD * E14 ....151 C1
Warrington Rd BCTR RM8 ....96 B6
CROY/NA CR0 ....246 B1
HRW HA1 ....60 D2
RCHPK/HAM TW10 ....161 F2
Warrior Sq MNPK E12 ....114 A2
Warspite Rd WOOL/PLUM SE18 ....133 C5
Warton Rd SRTFD E15 ....111 C6
Warwall EHAM E6 ....134 B5
Warwick Av EDGW HA8 ....46 C6
MV/WKIL W9 ....125 F3
RYLN/HDSTN HA2 ....98 D2
Warwick Chambers KENS * W8 ....145 E1
Warwick Cl BUSH WD23 ....44 A1
BXLY DA5 ....196 D6
EBAR EN4 ....35 H6
HPTN TW12 ....199 C3
ORP BR6 ....253 K5
Warwick Ct HHOL WC1V 13 J1
Warwick Dene EA W5 ....141 C1
Warwick Dr BARN SW13 ....163 H4
Warwick Est BAY/PAD W2 ....125 C2
Warwick Gdns FSBYPK N4 ....88 C2
IL IG1 ....90 B5
THDIT KT7 ....220 B2
THHTH * CR7 ....228 A1
WKENS W14 ....144 D4
Warwick Gv BRYLDS KT5 ....221 H4
CLPT E5 ....89 H5
Warwick House St STJS SW1Y 20 F7
Warwick La STP EC4M 14 C4
Warwick Pde KTN/HRWW/W * HA3 ....60 D5
Warwick Pl EA W5 ....141 F2
MV/WKIL W9 ....125 C4
THDIT * KT7 ....220 C5
Warwick Pl North PIM * SW1V 28 A2
Warwick Rd BAR EN5 ....33 F1
CHING E4 ....71 H1
EA W5 ....141 C1
FBAR/BDGN N11 ....67 F2
FSTGT E7 ....112 B4

KUT KT1 ....201 E4
MNPK E12 ....113 G3
NWDGN UB2 ....138 D3
NWMAL KT3 ....203 H2
PGE/AN SE20 ....209 H6
SCUP DA14 ....196 B1
SUT SM1 ....243 G3
THDIT KT7 ....220 B2
THHTH CR7 ....208 A6
UED N18 ....53 E6
WALTH E17 ....70 D4
WAN E11 ....92 D2
WELL DA16 ....176 A4
WHTN TW2 ....180 A3
WKENS W14 ....144 D4
Warwick Rw WESTW SW1E 20 A5
Warwick Sq PIM SW1V 28 B1
STP * EC4M 14 D3
Warwick Square Ms PIM SW1V 28 A2
Warwick St REGST W1B 12 B5
Warwick Ter LEY * E10 ....91 H2
WOOL/PLUM SE18 ....154 D6
Warwick Wy PIM SW1V 27 H2
Warwick Yd STLK * EC1Y 7 F4
Washington Av BMLY BR1 ....195 C6
Washington Cl BOW E3 ....131 F2
Washington Rd BARN SW13 ....146 E3
EHAM E6 ....113 E5
KUT KT1 ....202 A5
SWFD E18 ....73 E5
WPK KT4 ....223 H6
Wastdale Rd FSTH SE23 ....190 B3
Watchfield Ct CHSWK * W4 ....142 C5
The Watch NFNCH/WDSP * N12 ....49 G6
Watcombe Rd SNWD SE25 ....229 H2
Waterbank Rd CAT SE6 ....191 F5
Waterbeach Rd DAGW RM9 ....116 A4
Water Brook La HDN * NW4 ....84 A2
Watercress Pl IS N1 ....109 C5
Waterdale Rd ABYW SE2 ....155 G6
Waterden Rd SRTFD E15 ....111 E6
Waterer Ri WLGTN SM6 ....245 F4
Waterfall Cottages
WIM/MER SW19 ....205 H2
Waterfall Rd STHGT/OAK N14 ....51 H1
WIM/MER SW19 ....205 H2
Waterfall Ter TOOT SW17 ....206 A2
Waterfield Cl BELV DA17 ....137 G4
THMD SE28 ....155 H1
Waterfield Cottages
MORT/ESHN * SW14 ....162 B5
Waterfield Gdns SNWD SE25 ....229 E5
Waterford Rd FUL/PGN SW6 ....165 F1
The Waterfront BORE * WD6 ....44 D1
Watergate STP * EC4M 14 B5
The Water Gdns BAY/PAD W2 ....10 A3
Watergate St DEPT SE8 ....151 E6
The Watergate OXHEY WD19 ....42 B4
Waterhall Av CHING E4 ....72 C1
Waterhall Cl WALTH E17 ....70 A4
Waterhouse Cl HAMP NW3 ....105 H3
Wateringbury Cl
STMC/STPC BR5 ....215 H6
Water La CAMTN NW1 ....106 D5
ED N9 ....53 G1
GDMY/SEVK IG3 ....115 G1
KUT KT1 ....201 F4
PECK SE15 ....170 A1
RCH/KEW TW9 ....161 C5
SCUP DA14 ....196 D5
SRTFD E15 ....111 C2
TWK TW1 ....179 J1
Water Lily Cl STHL UB1 ....139 G2
Waterloo Br TPL/STR WC2R 13 G6
Waterloo Gdns BETH E2 ....130 A1
ROMW/RG RM7 ....97 H1
Waterloo Pas KIL/WHAMP NW6 ....83 H5
Waterloo Pl CAR * SM5 ....244 A1
RCH/KEW TW9 ....142 A6
STJS SW1Y 20 D7
Waterloo Rd BARK/HLT IG6 ....74 C5
CRICK NW2 ....63 C6
EHAM E6 ....113 G4
FSTGT E7 ....112 B5
LEY E10 ....91 J4
ROMW/RG RM7 ....75 C4
STHWK SE1 ....21 J4
SUT SM1 ....243 H3
Waterloo Ter IS N1 ....108 B5
Waterlow Rd ARCH N19 ....66 C6
Watermans Cl KUTN/CMB * KT2 ....201 G3
Watermans Ms EA * W5 ....121 C6
Waterman St PUT/ROE SW15 ....164 B4
Waterman Wy WAP E1W 25 C1
Watermead La MTCM CR4 ....226 B3
Watermeadow La
FUL/PGN SW6 ....165 G3
Watermead Rd CAT SE6 ....191 C6
Watermead Wy TOTM N17 ....70 A3
Watermens Sq PGE/AN * SE20 ....210 A3
Water Ms PECK SE15 ....170 A6
Watermill Cl
RCHPK/HAM TW10 ....181 G5
Watermill La UED N18 ....52 A1
Water Mill Wy FELT TW13 ....179 C2
Watermill Wy WIM/MER SW19 ....206 C4
Watermint Cl STMC/STPC BR5 ....236 B1
Watermint Quay CLPT E5 ....89 C4
Water Rd ALP/SUD HA0 ....101 H1
Water's Edge FUL/PGN * SW6 ....164 B2
Watersedge HOR/WEW KT19 ....240 C2
Watersfield Wy EDGW HA8 ....61 H1
Waterside Cl BARK IG11 ....97 H4
BERM/RHTH * SE16 ....49 E2
HOM E9 ....110 D6
NTHLT UB5 ....117 K3
SURB KT6 ....221 G6
Waterside Ct LEW * SE13 ....171 H5
Waterside Dr WOT/HER W18 ....218 A2
Waterside Wy TOOT SW17 ....185 G6
Waterson St BETH E2 ....8 E3
Watersplash Cl KUT KT1 ....201 F1
Waters Rd CAT SE6 ....192 C3
KUT KT1 ....202 B5
Waters Sq KUT KT1 ....202 B5
Water St TPL/STR WC2R 14 A5
Water Tower Hl CROY/NA CR0 ....246 D2
Waterworks La CLPT E5 ....90 B6
Waterworks Rd
BRXS/STRHM SW2 ....187 G1

Watery La NTHLT UB5 ....118 A3
RYNPK SW20 ....204 D3
SCUP DA14 ....215 H2
Wates Wy MTCM CR4 ....226 B3
Wateville Rd TOTM N17 ....68 C4
Watford Cl BTSEA SW11 ....166 A2
Watford Heath OXHEY WD19 ....42 B2
Watford Heath Farm
OXHEY * WD19 ....42 B2
Watford Rd BORE WD6 ....45 E1
CAN/RD E16 ....132 C4
HRW HA1 ....80 C6
Watford Wy HDN NW4 ....63 K1
Watford Wy (Barnet By-Pass)
MLHL NW7 ....47 E6
Watkin Rd WBLY HA9 ....102 B1
Watkinson Rd HOLWY N7 ....107 H4
Watling Av EDGW HA8 ....62 C1
Watling Ct STP EC4M 15 F4
Watlings Cl CROY/NA CR0 ....230 C3
Watling St BXLYHS DA6 ....177 H3
STP EC4M 15 E4
Watlington Gv SYD SE26 ....210 C1
Watney Market WCHPL E1 ....17 H4
Watney Rd MORT/ESHN SW14 ....162 C2
Watneys Rd MTCM CR4 ....227 C3
Watney St WCHPL E1 ....17 H4
Watson Av CHEAM SM3 ....224 C6
EHAM E6 ....114 B3
Watson Cl STNW/STAM N16 ....108 D3
WIM/MER SW19 ....206 A2
Watson's Ms CAMTN NW1 ....10 B2
Watsons Rd WDGN N22 ....67 H4
Watson's St DEPT SE8 ....151 J2
Wattisfield Rd CLPT E5 ....110 A1
Watts Cl SEVS/STOTM N15 ....89 E2
Watts Gv BOW E3 ....131 E4
Watts La CHST BR7 ....214 B4
TEDD TW11 ....200 C1
Watts Rd THDIT KT7 ....220 C4
Watts St WAP E1W 25 H1
Wat Tyler Rd BKHTH/KID SE3 ....171 G3
Wauthier Cl PLMGR N13 ....68 B1
Wavell Dr BFN/LL DA15 ....195 E1
Wavel Ms KIL/WHAMP NW6 ....105 F5
Wavel Pl NRWD SE19 ....189 F6
Wavendon Av CHSWK W4 ....142 D5
Waveney Av PECK SE15 ....169 H5
Waveney Cl WAP E1W 25 F1
Waverley Av BRYLDS KT5 ....222 B5
CHING E4 ....54 D6
SUT SM1 ....225 F6
WALTH E17 ....71 H6
WBLY HA9 ....101 H3
WHTN TW2 ....179 C2
Waverley Cl E/WMO/HCT KT8 ....219 G2
HAYES BR2 ....232 F2
Waverley Crs
WOOL/PLUM SE18 ....154 G6
Waverley Gdns BARK IG11 ....135 E1
BARK/HLT IG6 ....74 C5
EHAM E6 ....133 G4
Waverley Gv HDN NW4 ....64 A6
Waverley Pl FSBYPK * N4 ....88 B5
STJWD * NW8 ....125 H1
Waverley Rd CEND/HSY/T N8 ....87 F3
ENC/FH EN2 ....23 J6
EW KT17 ....241 H5
RYLN/HDSTN HA2 ....78 C6
SNWD SE25 ....229 H1
STHL UB1 ....115 K1
SWFD E18 ....73 E5
TOTM N17 ....69 H1
WALTH E17 ....71 G6
WOOL/PLUM SE18 ....154 C5
Waverton Rd
WAND/EARL SW18 ....185 G2
Waverton St MYFR/PICC W1J 19 H1
Wavertree Rd
BRXS/STRHM SW2 ....187 H3
WALTH E17 ....72 C5
Waxlow Crs STHL UB1 ....119 E5
Waxlow Rd WLSDN NW10 ....120 F1
Waxwell La PIN HA5 ....58 B6
Wayfarer Rd NTHLT UB5 ....118 C2
Wayford St BTSEA SW11 ....166 A3
Wayland Av HACK E8 ....90 A5
Waylett Pl ALP/SUD * HA0 ....101 F2
WNWD SE27 ....188 B5
Wayne Cl ORP BR6 ....253 F1
Waynflete Av CROY/NA CR0 ....246 B1
Waynflete Sq NKENS W10 ....124 B6
Waynflete St
WAND/EARL SW18 ....185 G2
Wayside CRICK NW2 ....64 C5
CROY/NA * CR0 ....264 B4
MORT/ESHN SW14 ....162 C5
Wayside Av BUSH WD23 ....43 H1
Wayside Cl GNTH/OAK N14 ....34 C6
ROMW/RG RM7 ....57 E6
Wayside Ct TWK TW1 ....161 E6
Wayside Gdns DAGE RM10 ....117 E3
Weald Cl BERM/RHTH SE16 ....193 H6
HAYES BR2 ....233 G6
Weald La KTN/HRWW/W HA3 ....59 H5
Weald Ri KTN/HRWW/W HA3 ....60 B3
Weald Sq CLPT * E5 ....72 C5
Wealdstone Rd CHEAM SM3 ....224 D6
The Weald CHST BR7 ....213 H2
Weald Wy ROMW/RG RM7 ....97 F3
Wealdwood Gdns PIN HA5 ....42 D4
Weale Rd CHING E4 ....55 H6
Weardale Gdns ENC/FH EN2 ....38 D2
Weardale Rd LEW SE13 ....171 G4
Wear Pl BETH E2 ....9 G4
Wearside Rd LEW SE13 ....171 F5
Weavers Cl ISLW TW7 ....160 A2
Weavers La STHWK SE1 ....37 G1
Weavers Ter FUL/PGN * SW6 ....145 K6
Weaver St WCHPL E1 ....9 F5
Weaver Wk WNWD SE27 ....188 C5
Weaverton Wk WNWD SE27 ....107 F1
Webber Rw STHWK SE1 ....185 G2
Webber St STHWK SE1 .... 72 C5
Webb Est CLPT * E5 ....72 C5
Webb Pl WLSDN NW10 ....

Webb Rd *BKHTH/KID* SE3 ....152 B6
Webbscroft Rd *DAGE* RM10 ....117 F2
Webb's Rd *BTSEA* SW11 ....166 B6
Webb St *STHWK* SE1 ....24 A6
Webster Gdns *EA* W5 ....141 F1
Webster Rd *BERM/RHTH* SE16 ....25 F6
    LEY E10 ....111 G1
Wedderburn Rd *BARK* IG11 ....114 D6
    HAMP NW3 ....105 H3
Wedgwood Wk
    KIL/WHAMP * NW6..................105 F3
Wedgwood Wy *NRWD* SE19 ....128 C3
Wedlake St *NKENS* W10 ....100 C3
Wedmore Av *CLAY* IG5 ....74 A4
Wedmore Gdns *ARCH* N19 ....87 C6
Wedmore Rd *GFD/PVL* UB6 ....119 H2
Wedmore St *ARCH* N19 ....87 C6
Weech Rd *KIL/WHAMP* NW6 ....105 E6
Weedington Rd *KTTN* NW5 ....106 C3
Weekley Sq *BTSEA* SW11 ....165 H4
Weigall Rd *LEE/GVPK* SE12 ....172 C5
Weighhouse St
    MYFR/PKLN W1K 11 F5
Weighton Rd
    KTN/HRWW/W HA3 ....59 H4
    PGE/AN SE20 ....209 H5
Weihurst Gdns *SUT* SM1 ....243 H5
Weimar St *PUT/ROE* SW15 ....164 C4
Weir Hall Av *UED* N18 ....50 B4
Weir Hall Gdns *UED* N18 ....68 D1
Weir Hall Rd *UED* N18 ....68 C1
Weir Rd *BAL* SW12 ....187 E3
    BXLY DA5 ....197 F2
    WIM/MER SW19 ....185 F5
Weirs Pas *CAMTN* NW1 ....4 D3
Weiss Rd *PUT/ROE* SW15 ....195 G3
Welbeck Av *BFN/LL* DA15 ....195 G3
    BMLY BR1 ....192 C6
Welbeck Cl *EW* KT17 ....241 G5
    NWMAL KT3 ....223 F2
Welbeck Rd *CAR* SM5 ....226 A4
    EHAM E6 ....89 H1
    RYLN/HDSTN HA2 ....79 F5
    SUT SM1 ....225 H6
Welbeck St *MHST* W1U 9 H2
Welbeck Vis *MHST* W1U 21 J2
Welbeck Wy *MHST* W1U 11 G3
Welby St *CMBW* SE5 ....142 C1
Welch Pl *PIN* HA5 ....58 A4
Weldon Dr *E/WMO/HCT* KT8 ....218 D1
Weld Pl *FBAR/BDGN* N11 ....66 D1
Welfare Rd *SRTFD* E15 ....112 A5
Welford Cl *CLPT* E5 ....110 B5
Welford Pl *WIM/MER* SW19 ....184 C6
Welham Rd *TOOT* SW17 ....206 C1
    STRHM/NOR SW16 ....206 C1
Welhouse Rd *CAR* SM5 ....226 A5
Wellacre Rd *KTN/HRWW/W* HA3 ....61 G3
Wellan Cl *BFN/LL* DA15 ....175 H6
Welland Gdns *GFD/PVL* UB6 ....120 B1
Welland Ms *WAP* E1W 25 F1
Welland St *GNWCH* SE10 ....151 C6
Well Ap *BAR* EN5 ....34 A6
Wellbrook Rd *ORP* BR6 ....252 A2
Well Cl *RSLP* HA4 ....98 C1
    STRHM/NOR SW16 ....187 H6
Wellclose Sq *WCHPL* E1 ....17 J5
Wellclose St *WAP* E1W 17 F6
Well Cottage Cl *WAN* E11 ....93 E4
Well Ct *MANHO* EC4N 15 H4
Weldon Crs *HRW* HA1 ....80 A3
Wellers Ct *STHWK* SE1 ....13 E8
    STHWK SE1 ....23 E3
Wellesley Av *HMSMTH* W6 ....143 H5
Wellesley Cl *CHARL* * SE7 ....153 E5
Wellesley Ct *STJWD* NW8 ....125 G2
Wellesley Court Rd
    CROY/NA * CRO 228 D6
Wellesley Crs *WHTN* TW2 ....180 A4
Wellesley Gv *CROY/NA* CRO 228 D6
Wellesley Pde *WHTN* * TW2 ....180 A5
Wellesley Park Ms *FNC/FH* EN2 ......38 B3
Wellesley Pl *CAMTN* * NW1 ....4 C4
    KTTN NW5 ....106 C3
Wellesley Rd *BELMT* SM2 ....243 G4
    CHSWK W4 ....142 A5
    CROY/NA CRO 280 C5
    HRW HA1 ....60 D5
    IL IG1 ....94 B6
    KTTN NW5 ....106 C3
    WALTH E17 ....91 E5
    WAN E11 ....92 C2
    WHTN TW2 ....179 H5
Wellesley St *WCHPL* E1 ....130 B4
Wellesley Ter *IS* N1 ....7 F2
Wellfield Av *MUSWH* N10 ....66 C6
Wellfield Rd *STRHM/NOR* SW16 ....187 G4
Wellfit St *HNHL* SE24 ....168 B4
Wellgarth *GFD/PVL* UB6 ....85 F5
Wellgarth Rd *GLDGN* NW11 ....85 F5
Well Gv *TRDG/WHET* N20 ....49 C3
Well Hall Pde *ELTH/MOT* SE9 ....173 H5
Well Hall Rd *ELTH/MOT* SE9 ....173 H5
Wellhouse La *BAR* EN5 ....34 A5
Wellhouse Rd *BECK* BR3 ....210 D1
Welling High St *WELL* DA16 ....175 H4
Wellington Av *BFN/LL* DA15 ....175 H4
    CHING E4 ....55 H1
    ED N9 ....53 H5
    HSLWW TW4 ....159 F6
    PIN HA5 ....59 H5
    SEVS/STOTM N15 ....89 G3
    WOOL/PLUM SE18 ....154 C3
    WPK KT4 ....242 A1

Wellington Rd *BELV* DA17 ....156 D5
    BXLY DA5 ....196 B1
    CROY/NA CRO 228 B4
    EA W5 ....141 A6
    EN EN1 ....39 E6
    FSTGT E7 ....112 C3
    HAYES BR2 ....233 F1
    HRW HA1 ....179 H6
    KTN/HRWW/W HA3 ....61 G2
    LEY E10 ....90 C5
    PIN HA5 ....58 D4
    STJWD NW8 ....2 A1
    STMC/STPC BR5 ....235 H5
    WALTH E17 ....70 C6
    WAN E11 ....92 C2
    WIM/MER SW19 ....185 E4
    WLSDN * NW10 ....124 B2
Wellington Rd North
    HSLWW TW4 ....158 D4
Wellington Rd South
    HSLWW TW4 ....158 D5
Wellington St *WEST* SW1E 16 A6
Wellington Sq *CHEL* SW3 ....26 C5
Wellington St *COVGDN* WC2E 11 G5
    WOOL/PLUM SE18 ....154 A4
Wellington Ter
    CEND/HSY/T * N8 ....68 A2
    NTGHL * W11 ....125 E6
    WAP E1W 25 G1
Wellington Wy *BOW* E3 ....131 E2
Welling Wy *ELTH/MOT* SE9 ....174 D4
Well La *MORT/ESHN* SW14 ....142 D2
Wellmeadow Rd *HNWL* W7 ....140 C4
    LEW SE13 ....192 A1
Well Rd *BAR* EN5 ....34 A6
    HAMP NW3 ....105 H1
Wells Cl *NTHLT* UB5 ....95 G1
    SAND/SEL CR2 ....247 C5
Wells Dr *CDALE/KGS* NW9 ....82 D5
Wells Gdns *IL* IG1 ....93 G4
Wells House Rd *WLSDN* NW10 ....125 E4
Wellside Cl *BAR* EN5 ....34 A5
Wellside Gdns
    MORT/ESHN SW14 ....162 C5
Wells Ms *FITZ* * W1T 12 B2
Wellsmoor Gdns *BMLY* BR1 ....214 A6
Wells Park Rd *SYD* SE26 ....189 G5
Wells Pl *CMBW* SE5 ....169 E1
Wellsprings Crs *WBLY* HA9 ....102 D2
Wells Ri *STJWD* NW8 ....106 B6
Wells Rd *BMLY* BR1 ....213 H5
    HMSMTH W6 ....144 A2
Wells Sq *FSBYW* WC1X 5 G4
Wells St *GTPST* W1W 12 A2
Wellstead Av *ED* N9 ....43 E6
Wellstead Rd *EHAM* E6 ....134 A1
The Wells *STHGT/OAK* N14 ....34 D3
Well St *SRTFD* E15 ....112 A4
Wells Wy *CMBW* SE5 ....31 H6
    SKENS SW7 ....14 G3
Well Wk *HAMP* NW3 ....105 H1
Wellwood Rd *GDMY/SEVK* IG3 ....95 E5
Welsford St *STHWK* SE1 ....31 H5
Welsh Cl *PLSTW* E13 ....132 D2
Welshpool St *HACK* * E8 ....108 C6
Welshside *CDALE/KGS* * NW9 ....83 G2
Welstead Wy *CHSWK* W4 ....143 A4
Weltje Rd *HMSMTH* W6 ....143 G5
Welwyn Av *EBED/NFELT* TW14 ....175 E1
Wembley Hill Rd *WBLY* HA9 ....101 H3
Wembley Park Av *WBLY* HA9 ....101 H2
Wembley Rd *HPTN* TW12 ....99 H4
Wembley Wy *WBLY* HA9 ....102 B3
Wemborough Rd *STAN* HA7 ....80 C6
Wembury Rd *HGT* N6 ....66 B4
Wemyss Rd *BKHTH/KID* SE3 ....177 B5
Wendela Ct *HRW* HA1 ....60 A1
Wendell Rd *SHB* W12 ....143 F2
Wendling Rd *CAR* SM5 ....225 H5
Wendon St *BOW* E3 ....110 C6
Wendover Cl *YEAD* UB4 ....118 B3
Wendover Dr *NWMAL* KT3 ....216 C4
Wendover Rd *ELTH/MOT* SE9 ....173 H4
    HAYES BR2 ....232 D1
    WLSDN NW10 ....119 H3
Wendover Wy *BUSH* WD23 ....43 G1
    ORP BR6 ....235 G3
    WELL DA16 ....175 G6
Wendy Cl *EN* EN1 ....53 F1
Wendy Av *ALP/SUD* HA0 ....101 G6
Wenlock Gdns *HDN* * NW4 ....63 G1
Wenlock Rd *EDGW* HA8 ....62 B2
    IS N1 ....7 F2
Wenlock St *IS* N1 ....7 F2
Wennington Rd *BOW* E3 ....130 B3
Wensley Av *WFD* IG8 ....72 C3
Wensley Cl *CRW* RM5 ....77 E1
    ELTH/MOT SE9 ....193 H1
Wensleydale Av *CLAY* IG5 ....53 G5
Wensleydale Gdns *HPTN* TW12 ......199 G4
Wensleydale Rd *HPTN* TW12 ....199 F4
Wensley Rd *UED* N18 ....68 D2
Wentland Cl *CAT* SE6 ....191 H4
Wentland Rd *CAT* SE6 ....191 H4
Wentworth Av *FNCH* N3 ....46 C5
Wentworth Cl *FNCH* N3 ....65 E5
    HAYES BR2 ....232 C6
    MRDN SM4 ....193 B6
    ORP BR6 ....253 E3
    SURB KT6 ....248 A2
    THMD SE28 ....136 D5
Wentworth Crs *PECK* SE15 ....169 G1
Wentworth Gdns *PLMGR* N13 ....52 B5
Wentworth Hl *WBLY* HA9 ....80 A5
Wentworth Ms *BOW* E3 ....130 C3
Wentworth Pk *FNCH* N3 ....65 E5
Wentworth Pl *STAN* * HA7 ....60 D3
Wentworth Rd *BAR* EN5 ....33 H6
    CROY/NA CRO 228 A4
    GLDGN NW11 ....64 C4
    MNPK E12 ....113 F2
    NWDGN UB2 ....138 A4
Wentworth St *WCHPL* E1 ....19 J3
Wentworth Wy *PIN* HA5 ....59 H1
Wenvoe Av *BXLYHN* DA7 ....177 H5
Wepham Cl *YEAD* UB4 ....118 B4
Wernbrook St
    WOOL/PLUM SE18 ....154 C6

Werndee Rd *SNWD* SE25 ....229 G1
Werneth Hall Rd *CLAY* IG5 ....73 H6
Werrington St *CAMTN* NW1 ....4 B2
Werter Rd *PUT/ROE* SW15 ....164 C5
Wesleyan Pl *KTTN* NW5 ....106 D2
Wesley Av *CAN/RD* E16 ....152 C1
    HSLW TW3 ....158 C3
    WLSDN NW10 ....122 D2
Wesley Cl *HOLWY* N7 ....87 H6
    RYLN/HDSTN HA2 ....79 G6
    STMC/STPC BR5 ....216 A6
    WALW SE17 ....18 C7
Wesley Rd *EFNCH* N2 ....46 A5
    LEY E10 ....91 G4
    WLSDN NW10 ....102 C5
Wesley Sq *NTGHL* W11 ....100 C5
Wesley St *CAVSQ/HST* W1G 11 F2
Wessex Av *WIM/MER* SW19 ....205 E5
Wessex Cl *GDMY/SEVK* IG3 ....95 E3
    KUTN/CMB KT2 ....202 B4
Wessex Ct *BECK* * BR3 ....210 C4
Wessex Dr *PIN* HA5 ....58 C5
Wessex Gdns *CRICK* NW2 ....63 H3
Wessex La *GFD/PVL* UB6 ....119 H1
Wessex St *BETH* E2 ....130 D2
Wessex Ter *MTCM* * CR4 ....226 A2
Wessex Wy *GLDGN* NW11 ....84 C4
Wesson Md *CMBW* SE5 ....168 C5
West Av *FNCH* N3 ....65 E2
    HDN NW4 ....84 B2
    PIN HA5 ....78 B3
    STHL UB1 ....118 D6
    WALTH E17 ....91 F2
    WLGTN SM6 ....245 C4
West Avenue Rd *WALTH* E17 ....91 E1
West Bank *BARK* IG11 ....114 B6
    ENC/FH EN2 ....38 C4
    STNW/STAM N16 ....89 E4
Westbank Rd *HPTN* TW12 ....199 G2
West Barnes La *NWMAL* KT3 ....223 G2
    RYNPK SW20 ....205 H6
Westbeech Rd *WDGN* N22 ....68 A6
Westbere Dr *STAN* HA7 ....61 F1
Westbere Rd *CRICK* NW2 ....60 C3
    CHEAM SM3 ....224 C6
Westbourne Av *ACT* W3 ....122 D5
    CHEAM SM3 ....224 C6
Westbourne Cl *YEAD* UB4 ....118 A3
Westbourne Crescent Ms
    BAY/PAD * W2 ....125 H6
Westbourne Gdns
    BAY/PAD W2 ....125 H5
Westbourne Ga *BAY/PAD* W2 ....125 H6
Westbourne Gv *NTGHL* W11 ....125 C5
Westbourne Grove Ter
    BAY/PAD W2 ....125 G5
Westbourne Pk Rd
    NTGHL * W11 ....125 E5
Westbourne Park Ms
    BAY/PAD W2 ....125 H5
Westbourne Park Rd
    BAY/PAD W2 ....125 G5
    NTGHL W11 ....124 D5
Westbourne Pl *ED* N9 ....53 H5
Westbourne Rd *BXLYHN* DA7 ....176 F5
    CROY/NA CRO 229 F3
    SYD SE26 ....210 B2
    SUT SM1 ....243 E5
    WALTH E17 ....91 C2
    WDGN N22 ....52 C4
    WLSDN NW10 ....122 C3
Westbourne Terrace Ms
    BAY/PAD W2 ....125 C5
Westbourne Terrace Rd
    BAY/PAD W2 ....125 G4
Westbridge Cl *SHB* W12 ....143 H6
Westbridge Rd *BTSEA* SW11 ....165 H2
Westbrook Av *HPTN* TW12 ....198 D3
Westbrook Cl *EBAR* EN4 ....35 H4
Westbrook Crs *EBAR* EN4 ....35 H4
Westbrook Rd *BKHTH/KID* SE3 ....134 B6
    HSLW TW3 ....158 D4
    STMC/STPC BR5 ....236 B5
Westbrooke Crs *WELL* DA16 ....176 A4
Westbrooke Rd *BFN/LL* DA15 ....194 D4
    WELL DA16 ....176 A3
Westbrook Rd *BKHTH/KID* SE3 ....158 D1
    HEST TW5 ....158 D1
    THHTH CR7 ....208 D4
Westbury Av *WDGN* * N22 ....68 B6
Westbury Av *ALP/SUD* HA0 ....101 G5
    ESH/CLAY KT10 ....238 B4
    STHL UB1 ....119 E3
    WDGN N22 ....68 B6
Westbury Cl *RSLP* HA4 ....58 D4
    WFD IG8 ....81 H5
Westbury Gv *FNCH* N3 ....65 E5
Westbury La *BKHH* IG9 ....57 F4
Westbury Lodge Cl *PIN* HA5 ....58 B6
Westbury Pl *BTFD* TW8 ....141 F6
Westbury Rd *ALP/SUD* HA0 ....101 G5
    BARK IG11 ....114 D6
    BECK BR3 ....210 C6
    BKHH IG9 ....57 E3
    BMLY BR1 ....184 C5
    CROY/NA CR0 ....228 D3
    EA W5 ....121 G5
    FBAR/BDGN N11 ....67 G2
    FELT TW13 ....158 D5
    FSTGT E7 ....112 D3
    NFNCH/WDSP N12 ....65 E2
    NWMAL KT3 ....208 A5
    PGE/AN SE20 ....210 C1
    WALTH E17 ....91 E1
Westbury Ter *FSTGT* E7 ....112 D4
West Carriage Dr *BAY/PAD* W2 ......125 H6
West Central St
    NOXST/BSQ WC1A 13 E3
West Chantry *KTN/HRWW/W* HA2 ....59 H4
Westchester Dr *HDN* NW4 ....64 B6
Westcliffe Vis *KUT* * KT1 ....201 H5
West Cl *EBAR* EN4 ....35 C5
    ED N9 ....56 C5
    GFD/PVL UB6 ....119 G1
    WBLY HA9 ....81 H5
West Common Rd *HAYES* BR2 ....282 C6
Westcombe Av *CROY/NA* CR0 ....26 F3
Westcombe Dr *BAR* EN5 ....35 E6
Westcombe Hi *BKHTH/KID* SE3 ....152 C6
Westcombe Park Rd
    BKHTH/KID SE3 ....172 C1
Westcote Rd
    STRHM/NOR SW16 ....207 E1
Westcott Cl *BMLY* BR1 ....233 C2
    CROY/NA CRO 249 F6

    SEVS/STOTM N15 ....89 F3
Westcott House 131 E6
Westcott Rd *WALW* SE17 ....30 D5
West Ct *ALP/SUD* HA0 ....81 E6
Westcroft Cl *CRICK* NW2 ....104 C2
    PEND EN3 ....40 A1
Westcroft Gdns *MRDN* SM4 ....204 D6
Westcroft Rd *CAR* SM5 ....143 C4
Westcroft Sq *HMSMTH* W6 ....143 C4
Westcroft Wy *CRICK* NW2 ....104 C2
West Cromwell Rd *ECT* SW5 ....145 E6
West Cross Route *NTGHL* W11 ....124 B6
West Cross Wy *BTFD* TW8 ....140 D6
Westdale Rd
    WOOL/PLUM SE18 ....154 B6
Westdean Av *LEE/GVPK* SE12 ....192 D3
Westdean Cl
    WAND/EARL SW18 ....185 F1
Westdown Rd *CAT* SE6 ....191 G2
    SRTFD E15 ....111 C2
West Dr *BELMT* SM2 ....242 B6
    KTN/HRWW/W HA3 ....59 H2
    TOOT SW17 ....186 B6
West Drive Gdns
    KTN/HRWW/W HA3 ....59 H2
West Eaton Place Ms
    KTBR * SW1X 27 E1
West Ella Rd *WLSDN* NW10 ....103 E5
West End Av *LEY* E10 ....91 G2
    PIN HA5 ....59 H2
West End Cl *WLSDN* NW10 ....102 C5
West End Ct *PIN* * HA5 ....78 B1
West End La *BAR* EN5 ....33 H5
    KIL/WHAMP NW6 ....105 E6
    PIN HA5 ....59 H2
West End Rd *NTHLT* UB5 ....98 A5
    STHL UB1 ....138 C1
Westerdale Rd *GNWCH* SE10 ....152 C5
Westerfield Rd
    SEVS/STOTM N15 ....89 F2
Westergate Rd *ABYW* SE2 ....156 C6
Westerham Av *UED* N18 ....51 H1
Westerham Dr *BFN/LL* DA15 ....196 A1
Westerham Rd *HAYES* BR2 ....251 F4
    LEY E10 ....71 H2
Westerley Crs *SYD* * SE26 ....210 D1
Western Av *ACT* W3 ....122 B3
    DAGE RM10 ....117 G4
    GFD/PVL UB6 ....120 B2
    GLDGN NW11 ....84 B3
Western Ct *FNCH* * N3 ....65 E2
Western Gdns *ACT* W3 ....122 A4
Western Gtwy *CAN/RD* E16 ....116 D6
Western La *BAL* SW12 ....186 C2
Western Man *BAR* * EN5 ....35 E4
Western Ms *MV/WKIL* W9 ....124 D3
Western Pde *BAR* EN5 ....55 E6
Western Rd *BRXN/ST* SW9 ....168 A3
    EA W5 ....121 F6
    EFNCH N2 ....66 B1
    MTCM CR4 ....206 A4
    NWDGN UB2 ....118 D3
    PLSTW E13 ....114 D2
    SUT SM1 ....243 E3
    WALTH E17 ....91 G2
    WDGN N22 ....52 C4
    WLSDN NW10 ....119 C3
Western Ter *HMSMTH* * W6 ....143 C5
Westerville Gdns
    GNTH/NBYPK IG2 ....94 C4
Western Wy *BAR* EN5 ....49 E1
    THMD SE28 ....136 C1
Westferry Circ *POP/IOD* E14 ....151 E1
Westferry Rd *POP/IOD* E14 ....130 D6
Westfield Cl *CDALE/KGS* NW9 ....63 F1
    FUL/PGN * SW6 ....165 G1
    PEND EN3 ....40 C4
    SUT SM1 ....242 D2
Westfield Dr
    KTN/HRWW/W HA3 ....81 F2
Westfield Gdns
    KTN/HRWW/W HA3 ....81 F1
Westfield La
    KTN/HRWW/W HA3 ....81 F1
Westfield Pk *PIN* HA5 ....59 H3
Westfield Park Dr *WFD* IG8 ....73 G2
Westfield Rd *BECK* BR3 ....210 C1
    BXLYHN DA7 ....177 G4
    CROY/NA CRO 228 B6
    DAGW RM9 ....116 C2
    MLHL NW7 ....45 E4
    MTCM CR4 ....206 A5
    SURB KT6 ....221 F2
    SUT SM1 ....242 D2
    WEA W13 ....140 D2
    WOT/HER KT12 ....112 B5
Westfields *BARN* SW13 ....163 E4
Westfields Av *BARN* SW13 ....163 E4
Westfields Rd *ACT* W3 ....122 B4
Westfield St *WOOL/PLUM* SE18 ......153 E8
Westfield Wy *WCHPL* E1 ....131 C2
West Gdns *WAP* E1W 17 H6
    WIM/MER SW19 ....206 A2
West Ga *EA* W5 ....121 G4
Westgate Rd *BECK* BR3 ....211 G4
    SNWD SE25 ....229 H1
Westgate St *HACK* E8 ....109 H6
Westgate Ter *WBPTN* SW10 ....145 F6
Westglade Ct
    KTN/HRWW/W HA3 ....81 F2
West Green Pl *GFD/PVL* UB6 ....99 H6
West Green Rd
    SEVS/STOTM N15 ....89 G1
West Gv *GNWCH* SE10 ....171 G2
    WFD IG8 ....73 E2
Westgrove La *GNWCH* SE10 ....172 C2
West Halkin St *KTBR* SW1X 27 G3
West Hallowes *ELTH/MOT* SE9 ....193 F1
West Hall Rd *RCH/KEW* TW9 ....162 B2
West Ham La *SRTFD* E15 ....111 H5
West Hampstead Ms
    KIL/WHAMP NW6 ....105 F4
West Harding St
    FLST/FETLN EC4A 14 B3
Westharold *SWLY* BR8 ....217 H6

Westhay Gdns
 MORT/ESHN SW14 ....162 B6
West Heath Av GLDGN NW11...85 E5
West Heath Cl HAMP NW3 ....105 E1
West Heath Dr GLDGN NW11...85 E5
West Heath Gdns HAMP NW3...85 E6
West Heath Rd BXLYHN DA7 ..156 B6
 HAMP NW3 ....105 E1
West Hi HGT N6 ....86 C5
 PUT/ROE SW15 ....184 B2
 RYLN/HDSTN HA2 ....80 A6
West Hill Av HTH N6 ....247 E6
 WBLY HA9 ....81 H5
Westhill Pk HGT N6 ....86 B6
West Hill Rd WAND/EARL SW18 ..184 D1
 WAND/EARL SW18 ....49 F3
Westholm GLDGN NW11 ....85 F1
West Holme ERITH DA8 ....177 G2
Westholme ORP BR6 ....235 E4
Westhorne Av ELTH/MOT SE9 ..193 E1
Westhorpe Gdns HDN NW4 ....46 A6
Westhorpe Rd PUT/ROE SW15 ..164 A4
West House Cl WIM/MER SW19 ..184 C3
Westhurst Dr CHST BR7 ....214 B1
West India Av POP/IOD E14 ..151 E1
West India Dock Rd
 POP/IOD E14 ....130 D5
Westlake Cl PLMGR N13 ....52 A5
 YEAD UB4 ....118 C3
Westland Dr HAYES BR2 ....232 B6
Westland Pl FSBYE EC1V 7 G4
Westlands Ter BAL SW12 ....187 E1
West La BERM/RHTH SE16 ....25 G4
Westlea Rd HNWL W7 ....140 C3
Westleigh Av PUT/ROE SW15 ..164 A6
Westleigh Dr BMLY BR1 ....213 G5
Westleigh Gdns EDGW HA8 ....62 A4
West Links ALP/SUD HA0 ....121 F2
Westlinton Cl MLHL NW7 ....64 C2
West Lodge Av ACT W3 ....142 A1
West Lodge Ct ACT* W3 ....142 A1
West MI KENS * W8 ....142 A1
West Md HOR/WEW KT19 ....241 E4
Westmead PUT/ROE SW15 ....183 H2
West Md RSLP HA4 ....98 A2
Westmead Rd SUT SM1 ....243 H2
Westmede BARK/HLT IG6 ....74 C2
Westmere Dr MLHL NW7 ....46 D5
West Ms PIM SW1V 27 H2
 TOTM * N17 ....42 A6
Westminster Av THHTH CR7 ..208 B5
Westminster Br WEST SW1P 21 F4
Westminster Bridge Rd
 STHWK SE1 ....21 G4
Westminster CI TEDD TW11 ..200 C1
Westminster Dr PLMGR N13 ..67 C1
Westminster Gdns BARK IG11 ..135 E1
 BARK/HLT IG6 ....74 D5
 CHING E4 ....56 A3
Westminster Rd ED N9 ....53 H3
 HNWL W7 ....140 A1
 SUT SM1 ....225 H6
Westmoat Cl BECK BR3 ....211 G3
Westmont Rd ESH/CLAY KT10 ..220 A6
Westmoor Gdns PEND EN3 ....40 B3
Westmoor Rd PEND EN3 ....40 B3
Westmoor St CHARL SE7 ....116 C3
Westmoreland Av WELL DA16 ..175 E4
Westmoreland Dr BELMT SM2 ..243 F6
Westmoreland PI EA * W5 ....121 F4
 HAYES * BR2 ....212 C6
 PIM SW1V 27 H6
Westmoreland Rd BARN SW13 ..163 F2
 CDALE/KGS NW9 ....81 H1
 HAYES BR2 ....232 A2
 WALW SE17 ....31 G5
Westmorland St
 CAVSQ/HST W1C 11 F2
Westmorland Ter
 PGE/AN * SE20 ....209 H3
 PIM SW1V 27 H3
Westmorland Cl MNPK E12 ....93 F6
 TWK TW1 ....180 D1
Westmorland Rd HRW HA1 ....79 F2
 LEY E10 ....61 H3
Westmorland Wy MTCM CR4 ..227 F1
Westmount Centre
 YEAD * UB4 ....118 B6
Westmount Ct EA * W5 ....121 H4
Westmount Rd ELTH/MOT SE9 ..173 H3
West Oak BECK BR3 ....211 H4
Weston Rd ED N9 ....53 H4
Weston Av E/WMO/HCT KT8 ..218 C1
 ESH/CLAY KT10 ....220 A6
Weston Dr KTN/HRWW/W HA3 ..60 D4
Weston Gdns ISLW TW7 ....159 H2
Weston Gn DAGW RM9 ....116 C2
 THDIT KT7 ....220 A6
Weston Green Rd
 ESH/CLAY KT10 ....219 H5
 THDIT KT7 ....220 A5
Weston Gv BMLY BR1 ....212 B4
Weston Pk CEND/HSY/T N8 ....67 G3
 KUT KT1 ....201 G5
 THDIT KT7 ....220 A5
Weston Park Cl THDIT * KT7 ..220 A5
Weston Ri FSBYW WC1X 5 H3
Weston Rd BMLY BR1 ....212 B4
 CHSWK W4 ....142 C3
 DAGW RM9 ....116 C2
 ENC/FH EN2 ....23 D3
 THDIT KT7 ....220 A5
Weston St STHWK SE1 ....23 H4
Weston Wk HACK E8 ....109 H5
Westover Cl BELMT SM2 ....243 F6
Westover Hi HAMP NW3 ....85 E6
Westover Rd
 WAND/EARL SW18 ..185 G1
Westow Hi NRWD SE19 ....209 E1
Westow St NRWD SE19 ....209 E2
West Pk ELTH/MOT SE9 ....193 G1
West Park Av RCH/KEW TW9 ..162 A2
West Park Cl CHDH RM6 ....96 B2
 HEST TW5 ....138 D6
West Park Rd RCH/KEW TW9 ..162 A2
 STHL UB1 ....139 G1
West Parkside GNWCH SE10 ..132 A4
West PI NWDGN * UB2 ....139 F4
 WIM/MER SW19 ....204 A1
Westpole Av EBAR EN4 ....36 D5
Westport Rd PLSTW E13 ....132 D3

Westport St WCHPL E1 ....130 B5
West Poultry Av FARR EC1M ..14 C2
West Quarters SHB W12 ....123 G5
West Quay Dr YEAD UB4 ....118 C4
West Ridge Gdns GFD/PVL UB6 ..119 C1
West Ri BAY/PAD * W2 ....10 B1
West Rd CHDH RM6 ....96 C3
 CHEL SW3 ....29 G5
 CLAP SW4 ....167 F6
 EA W5 ....121 G4
 EBAR EN4 ....50 C3
 EFNCH N2 ....65 H1
 KUTN/CMB KT2 ....202 C4
 ROMW/RG RM7 ....97 H4
 SRTFD E15 ....112 B6
 TOTM N17 ....42 D4
West Rw NKENS W10 ....124 C3
Westrow Dr BARK IG11 ....115 F4
Westrow Gdns GDMY/SEVK IG3 ..95 F6
West Sheen V RCH/KEW TW9 ..161 H5
Westside HDN NW4 ....63 H5
West Side Common
 WIM/MER SW19 ....204 A1
West Smithfield STBT EC1A ..14 C2
West St BETH * E2 ....9 H2
West St BETH * E2 ....212 C4
 BMLY BR1 ....212 C4
 BXLYHN DA7 ....176 D5
 CAR SM5 ....244 B1
 CROY/NA CR0 ....246 C2
 ERITH DA8 ....157 H4
 RYLN/HDSTN HA2 ....79 H5
 SUT SM1 ....248 A5
 WALTH E17 ....91 F2
 WAN E11 ....112 A1
West Street La CAR SM5 ....244 B2
West Street PI CROY/NA * CR0 ..246 C2
West Temple Sheen
 MORT/ESHN SW14 ....162 B6
West Tenter St WCHPL E1 ....16 D4
West Ter BFN/LL * DA15 ....195 E3
West Towers PIN HA5 ....59 H3
Westview HNWL W7 ....120 A5
Westview Ct NKENS W10 ....124 A5
 WLSDN NW10 ....103 F3
Westview Crs ED N9 ....53 E2
Westview Dr WFD IG8 ....73 F5
West View Gdns BORE WD6 ..45 F1
West View Rd SWLY BR8 ....237 H5
Westville Rd SHB W12 ....143 G2
 THDIT KT7 ....220 C4
West Wk EBAR EN4 ....50 C3
Westward Rd CHING E4 ....70 D1
Westward Wy
 KTN/HRWW/W HA3 ....81 G3
West Warwick PI PIM * SW1V ..28 A2
West Wy CROY/NA CR0 ....230 C6
 EDGW HA8 ....62 D6
 HEST TW5 ....158 D2
 PIN HA5 ....78 B1
 STMC/STPC BR5 ....234 D2
 WLSDN NW10 ....102 D3
 WWKM BR4 ....231 H3
Westway NTGHL W11 ....124 D4
West Wy SHB W12 ....123 C5
 SHB W12 ....125 G6
Westway Cl RYNPK SW20 ....205 H6
West Way Gdns CROY/NA CR0 ..230 A6
Westways HOR/WEW KT19 ....241 F2
Westwell Cl STMC/STPC BR5 ..256 B5
Westwell Rd
 STRHM/NOR SW16 ....207 G2
Westwell Road Ap
 STRHM/NOR SW16 ....207 G2
Westwick Gdns HMSMTH W6 ..144 B2
Westwood Av NRWD SE19 ....208 C4
 RYLN/HDSTN HA2 ....94 A1
Westwood Cl BMLY BR1 ....213 F6
Westwood Gdns BARN SW13 ..163 F4
Westwood Hi SYD SE26 ....209 G1
Westwood La WELL DA16 ....175 C5
Westwood Pk FSTH SE23 ....189 H2
Westwood PI SYD * SE26 ....209 G1
Westwood Rd BARN SW13 ....163 F4
 CAN/RD E16 ....152 D1
 GDMY/SEVK IG3 ....95 F6
West Woodside BXLY DA5 ....196 C5
Wetheral Dr STAN HA7 ....60 D4
Wetherby Cl NTHLT UB5 ....99 F4
Wetherby Gdns ECT SW5 ....145 E5
Wetherby PI ECT SW5 ....145 C4
Wetherby Rd ENC/FH EN2 ....38 C2
Wetherby Wy CHSGTN KT9 ..239 G5
Wetherden St WALTH E17 ....90 B4
Wetherell Rd HOM E9 ....111 F1
Wetherill Rd MUSWH N10 ....66 C4
Wexford Rd BAL SW12 ....186 B2
Weybourne St
 WAND/EARL SW18 ....185 G4
Weybridge Rd THHTH CR7 ....228 A1
Wey Ct HOR/WEW KT19 ....240 C2
Weydown Cl WIM/MER SW19 ..184 C5
Weyhill Rd WCHPL E1 ....7 G3
Weylond Rd BCTR RM8 ....116 D1
Weyman Rd BKHTH/KID SE3 ..175 E2
Weymouth Av EA W5 ....141 E3
 MLHL NW7 ....45 E1
Weymouth Ct EHAM E6 ....134 B5
Weymouth Ct BELMT * SM2 ..243 H5
Weymouth Ms CAVSQ/HST W1G ..11 C1
Weymouth Ter BETH E2 ....7 K2
Weymouth Vls HOLWY * N7 ....87 H6
Weymouth Wk STAN HA7 ....60 C2
Whadcoat St FSBYPK N4 ....88 A6
Whalebone Av CHDH RM6 ....96 D5
Whalebone Gv CHDH RM6 ....96 D5
Whalebone La North
 CHDH RM6 ....96 C1
Whalebone La South BCTR RM8 ..96 C4
Whales Yd SRTFD * E15 ....115 A5
Wharf Bridge Rd ISLW TW7 ..160 D4
Wharfdale Cl FBAR/BDGN N11 ..66 C2
Wharfdale Gdns
 STRHM/NOR SW16 ....227 H1
Wharfedale St WBPTN SW10 ..145 F5
Wharfedale La TWK TW1 ....180 C3
Wharf PI BETH * E2 ....109 C6

Wharf Rd IS N1 ....7 E2
 PEND EN3 ....54 C1
Wharfside Rd CAN/RD E16 ..132 A5
Wharf St CAN/RD E16 ....132 A4
Wharncliffe Dr STHL UB1 ....139 H1
Wharncliffe Gdns SNWD SE25 ..209 E5
Wharncliffe Rd SNWD SE25 ..208 D5
Wharton Cl WLSDN NW10 ....103 E4
Wharton Cottages
 FSBYW * WC1X 5 H4
Wharton Rd BMLY BR1 ....212 D4
Wharton St FSBYW WC1X 5 H4
Whateley Rd EDUL SE22 ....169 F6
 PGE/AN SE20 ....210 B3
Whatley Av RYNPK SW20 ....206 B6
Whatman Rd FSTH SE23 ....190 B2
Wheastone Rd NKENS * W10 ..124 C4
Wheatfields PEND EN3 ....25 H1
Wheatfield Wy KUT KT1 ....201 G6
Wheathill Rd PGE/AN SE20 ..209 H5
Wheatlands HEST TW5 ....139 E6
Wheatlands Rd TOOT SW17 ..186 C5
Wheatley Cl HDN NW4 ....63 G5
Wheatley Gdns ED N9 ....53 E4
Wheatley Rd ISLW TW7 ....160 B4
Wheatley St CAVSQ/HST W1G ..11 F2
Wheat Sheaf Cl POP/IOD E14 ..151 E4
Wheatsheaf La FUL/PGN SW6 ..164 A1
 VX/NE SW8 ....167 G1
Wheatsheaf Ter
 FUL/PGN * SW6 ....164 D1
Wheatstone Cl
 WIM/MER SW19 ....205 H4
Wheeler Gdns IS N1 ....107 C6
Wheeler La WCHPL E1 ....16 C1
Wheelers Cross BARK IG11 ....134 D1
Wheel Farm Dr DAGE RM10 ..117 C1
Wheelock Cl ERITH DA8 ....177 F1
Wheelright Cl BUSH WD23 ....43 F1
Wheelwright St HOLWY N7 ..107 H5
Wheelwright Wy WLGTN SM6 ..245 F1
Wheler St WCHPL E1 ....9 J6
Whellock Rd CHSWK W4 ....143 E3
Whenman Av BXLY DA5 ....197 G4
Whetstone Cl TRDG/WHET N20 ..48 H4
Whetstone Pk LINN WC2A 13 G3
Whetstone Rd BKHTH/KID SE3 ..173 E3
Whewell Rd ARCH N19 ....87 E1
Whichcote St STHWK * SE1 ..22 A2
Whidborne Cl DEPT SE8 ....171 E3
Whidborne St STPAN WC1H 5 F4
Whimbrel Wy YEAD UB4 ....118 B5
Whinchat Rd THMD SE28 ....150 D2
Whinfell Cl STRHM/NOR SW16 ..207 F1
Whinyates Rd ELTH/MOT SE9 ..173 G4
Whippendell Cl
 STMC/STPC BR5 ....215 H4
Whipps Cross Rd WAN E11 ....92 A2
Whiskin St CLKNW EC1R 6 A4
Whistler Gdns EDGW HA8 ....61 H5
Whistlers Av BTSEA * SW11 ..165 G1
Whistler St HBRY N5 ....108 B2
Whistler Wk WBPTN * SW10 ..165 E1
Whiston Rd BETH E2 ....7 K3
Whitbread Cl TOTM N17 ....69 G4
Whitbread Rd BROCKY SE4 ..170 D5
Whitburn Rd LEW SE13 ....171 F6
Whitby Av WLSDN NW10 ....122 B2
Whitby Gdns CDALE/KGS NW9 ..62 A6
 SUT SM1 ....225 H6
Whitby Pde RSLP * HA4 ....77 A2
Whitby Rd RYLN/HDSTN HA2 ..99 G1
 SUT SM1 ....225 H6
 WOOL/PLUM SE18 ....153 H4
Whitby St WCHPL E1 ....9 J5
Whitcher Cl NWCR SE14 ....150 C6
Whitcher PI CAMTN NW1 ....107 G1
Whitchurch Av EDGW HA8 ....61 H3
Whitchurch Cl EDGW HA8 ....61 H3
Whitchurch Gdns EDGW HA8 ..61 H3
Whitchurch La EDGW HA8 ....61 G3
Whitchurch Pde EDGW * HA8 ..62 A3
Whitchurch Rd NKENS W10 ..124 B6
Whitcomb St SOHO/SHAV W1D ..12 C5
Whitear Wk SRTFD E15 ....111 H4
Whitebarn La DAGE RM10 ..137 E1
Whitebeam Av HAYES BR2 ..231 E6
Whitebeam Cl BRXN/ST * SW9 ..167 H1
White Bear PI HAMP * NW3 ..105 H1
White Bear Yd CLKNW * EC1R ..6 A6
White Bridge Av MTCM CR4 ..227 H1
White Butts Rd RSLP HA4 ....98 B1
Whitechapel High St WCHPL E1 ..16 D3
Whitechapel Rd WCHPL E1 ....17 C2
White Church La WCHPL E1 ..17 E3
White City Cl SHB W12 ....124 A6
White City Rd SHB W12 ....124 A6
White Conduit St IS N1 ....6 A3
Whitecote Rd GFD/PVL UB6 ..119 F5
White Craig Cl PIN HA5 ....59 H4
Whitecroft Cl BECK BR3 ....231 H1
Whitecroft Wy BECK BR3 ....231 G1
Whitecross St STMC/STPC BR5 ..216 A6
 WAND/EARL SW18 ....184 C1
Whitefield Av CRICK NW2 ....84 A4
Whitefield Cl STMC/STPC BR5 ..216 A6
 WAND/EARL SW18 ....184 C1
Whitefoot La BMLY BR1 ....192 B5
Whitefoot Ter BMLY BR1 ....192 B5
Whitefriars Av
 KTN/HRWW/W HA3 ....59 G3
Whitefriars Dr
 KTN/HRWW/W HA3 ....60 D4
Whitefriars St EMB EC4Y 14 B4
White Gate Gdns
 KTN/HRWW/W HA3 ....43 F4
Whitehall Cl WALL SW1A 21 E2
Whitehall Ct WHALL SW1A 21 F1
Whitehall Crs CHSGTN KT9 ..239 F3
Whitehall Gdns ACT W3 ....142 A1
 CHING E4 ....58 B1
 CHSWK W4 ....142 B1
Whitehall La BKHH IG9 ....68 D1
Whitehall Pk ARCH N19 ....87 C5
Whitehall Park Rd CHSWK W4 ..144 D2
Whitehall PI WLGTN * SM6 ....244 C3
 WHALL SW1A 21 E2
Whitehall Rd CHING E4 ....58 C1
 HNWL W7 ....140 C2
 HRW HA1 ....80 A5
 THHTH CR7 ....228 B2
Whitehall St TOTM N17 ....69 F3
White Hart La BARN SW13 ..163 E5
 ROMW/RG RM7 ....77 H4
 WDGN N22 ....68 A4
White Hart Rd ORP BR6 ....235 C4
 WOOL/PLUM SE18 ....116 A4
White Hart St LBTH SE11 ....30 B5
White Hart Ter TOTM * N17 ....69 F3
White Hart Yd STHWK SE1 ....23 G2
Whitehaven Cl HAYES BR2 ..232 C1
Whitehaven St STJWD NW8 ....2 C6
Whitehead Cl UED N18 ....68 D1
 WAND/EARL SW18 ....185 G2
Whitehead's Gv CHEL SW3 ....36 B5
 CHEL SW3 ....86 E2
White Heron Ms TEDD * TW11 ..200 B2
White Horse Hi CHST BR7 ....194 A6
White Horse La SNWD SE25 ..229 E1
 WCHPL E1 ....130 B3
White Horse Rd EHAM E6 ....136 A2
 WCHPL E1 ....130 D5
Whitehorse Rd CROY/NA CR0 ..228 C4
 WCHPL E1 ....130 D5
White Horse St MYFR/PICC W1J ..19 H2
White House Dr STAN HA7 ....45 E6
White House La ENC/FH EN2 ..38 C2
Whitehouse Wy
 STHGT/OAK N14 ....50 A4
White Kennett St WCHPL E1 ..16 B3
White Ledges WEA W13 ....121 E5
Whitelegg Rd PLSTW E13 ....132 B1
Whiteley Rd NRWD SE19 ....208 D1
Whiteleys Wy FELT TW15 ....179 E5
White Lion Ct BANK EC3V 16 A4
 PECK * SE15 ....150 A6
White Lion Hi BLKFR EC4V 14 D5
White Lion St IS N1 ....6 A2
White Ldg NRWD SE19 ....208 B3
White Lodge Cl BELMT SM2 ..243 G5
 EFNCH N2 ....85 H1
The White Ldg BAR * EN5 ....34 C4
White Lyon Ct BARB EC2Y 15 E1
White Oak Dr BECK BR3 ....211 G5
White Oak Gdns BFN/LL DA15 ..195 F2
Whiteoaks La GFD/PVL UB6 ..119 H1
White Orchards STAN HA7 ....44 C1
 TRDG/WHET N20 ....48 D2
White Post La HOM E9 ....110 D5
White Post St PECK SE15 ....150 A6
Whites Av GNTH/NBYPK IG2 ....95 E5
White's Grounds STHWK SE1 ..24 B5
Whites Grounds Est STHWK SE1 ..24 B5
Whites Meadow BMLY * BR1 ..234 A1
White's Rw WCHPL E1 ....16 C2
White's Sq CLAP SW4 ....167 F5
Whitestile Rd BTFD TW8 ....143 E1
Whitestone La HAMP NW3 ....105 G1
Whitestone Wk HAMP NW3 ..105 G1
White St NWDGN UB2 ....138 B2
Whitethorn Gdns
 CROY/NA CR0 ....229 H6
 ENC/FH EN2 ....38 D6
Whitethorn St BOW E3 ....131 E5
Whitewebbs Wy
 STMC/STPC BR5 ....215 F4
Whitfield PI FITZ W1T 4 A6
Whitfield Rd BXLYHN DA7 ..176 D5
 EHAM E6 ....113 E5
 GNWCH SE10 ....171 G2
Whitfield St FITZ W1T 12 B1
Whitford Gdns MTCM CR4 ..206 B6
Whitgift Av SAND/SEL CR2 ..246 C3
Whitgift St CROY/NA CR0 ....246 C3
 LBTH SE11 ....29 G1
Whitings Rd BAR EN5 ....34 A6
Whitings Wy EHAM E6 ....134 A4
Whitland Rd CAR SM5 ....225 H5
Whitley Rd TOTM N17 ....69 H1
Whitlock Dr WIM/MER SW19 ..184 C2
Whitman Rd BOW E3 ....130 C3
Whitmead Cl SAND/SEL CR2 ..246 D4
Whitmore Cl FBAR/BDGN N11 ..48 B2
Whitmore Est IS N1 ....7 K1
Whitmore Gdns WLSDN NW10 ..120 A1
Whitmore Rd BECK BR3 ....210 D6
 HRW HA1 ....60 C6
 IS N1 ....7 G1
Whitnell Wy PUT/ROE * SW15 ..164 A6
Whitney Av REDBR IG4 ....93 F1
Whitney Rd LEY E10 ....91 H6
Whitney Wk SCUP DA14 ....216 C2
Whitstable Cl BECK BR3 ....210 D4
Whitstable PI CROY/NA CR0 ..246 C2
Whittaker Av RCH/KEW * TW9 ..161 F1
Whittaker Rd CHEAM SM3 ..242 D1
 EHAM E6 ....113 C5
Whittaker St BCVA SW1W 27 F2
Whittaker Wy STHWK * SE1 ..119 F5
Whittell Gdns SYD SE26 ....190 A5
Whittingham Rd FUL/PGN SW6 ..164 D4
Whittingstall Rd FUL/PGN SW6 ..164 D4
Whittington Av BANK EC3V 16 A4
Whittington Ms
 NFNCH/WDSPK N12 ....49 G6
Whittington Rd WDGN N22 ....67 H2
Whittington Wy PIN HA5 ....78 C2
Whittlebury Cl CAR SM5 ....244 B5
Whittle Cl GFD/PVL UB6 ....119 F3
 WALTH E17 ....90 C3
Whittle Rd HEST TW5 ....158 A1
 NWDGN UB2 ....139 F2
Whittlesea
 KTN/HRWW/W HA3 ....59 G3
Whittlesey St STHWK SE1 ....21 A1
Whitton Av East GFD/PVL UB6 ..100 B3
Whitton Av West GFD/PVL UB6 ..100 D4
Whitton Cl GFD/PVL UB6 ....100 D4
Whitton Dene HSLW TW3 ..159 F4
 WHTN TW2 ....179 H1
Whitton Manor Rd ISLW TW7 ..179 G1
Whitton Rd HSLW TW3 ....159 F3
 WHTN TW2 ....179 H1
Whitton Wave HSLW TW3 ....179 E1
Whitwell Rd PLSTW E13 ....132 C2
Whitworth Rd SNWD SE25 ..197 C5
 WOOL/PLUM SE18 ....174 A1
Whitworth St GNWCH SE10 ..152 B3
Whorlton Rd PECK SE15 ....169 G4
Whymark Av WDGN N22 ....68 A4

Whytecroft HEST TW5.....................158 B1
Whyteville Rd FSTGT E7...................112 D4
Wichling Cl STMC/STPC BR5........236 B5
Wickersley Rd BTSEA SW11...........189 F6
Wickers Oaks NRWD * SE19.........189 F6
Wicker St WCHPL E1.........................17 F4
Wicket Rd GFD/PVL UB6..............120 C2
Wickets Wy BARK/HLT IG6...............75 F2
The Wicket CROY/NA CRO............249 E3
Wickford St WCHPL E1..................130 A3
Wickford Wy WALTH E17..................90 B1
Wickham Av CHEAM SM5...............242 A3
     CROY/NA CRO................................250 D5
Wickham Cha WWKM BR4.............231 H4
Wickham Cl EN EN1...........................39 H4
     NWMAL KT3...................................223 F2
Wickham Ct WWKM * BR4............249 H2
Wickham Court Rd
     WWKM BR4.....................................231 G6
Wickham Crs WWKM BR4.............231 G6
Wickham Gdns BROCKY SE4........170 D4
Wickham La ABYW SE2..................155 G6
Wickham Rd BECK BR3..................211 F6
     BROCKY SE4.................................170 D4
     CHING E4...37 F2
     CROY/NA CRO...............................230 D5
     CROY/NA CRO...............................230 A6
     KTN/HRWW/W HA3.........................59 H5
Wickham St LBTH SE11..................121 G5
     WELL DA16.....................................175 E3
Wickham Wy BECK BR3.................231 G1
Wickliffe Av FNCH N3.......................64 C5
Wickliffe Gdns WBLY HA9................82 A6
Wicklow St FS PSBYW WC1X............5 G3
Wick Rd HOM E9................................110 B4
     TEDD TW11.....................................200 D3
Wicks Cl LEE/GVPK SE12..............193 F6
Wicksteed Cl BXLY DA5.................197 H5
Wickwood St CMBW SE5...............168 B3
Widdenham Rd HOLWY N7............107 H2
Widdicombe Av
     RYLN/HDSTN HA2..........................78 C6
Widdin St SRTFD E15......................112 A5
Widecombe Gdns REDBR IG4.........93 G5
Widecombe Rd ELTH/MOT SE9....193 C5
Widecombe Wy EFNCH N2...............85 H2
Widegate St WCHPL E1......................13 H2
Widenham Cl PIN HA5.......................78 A2
Wide Wy STRHM/NOR SW16.........207 F6
Widgeon Cl CAN/RD E16....................95 H6
Widley Rd MV/WKIL W9...................125 G2
Widmore Lodge Rd BMLY BR1.....215 F5
Widmore Rd BMLY BR1...................212 D5
Wigan Wy YEAD UB4........................118 B5
Wiggins Md CLAP/KGS NW9...........45 F5
Wigginton Av WBLY HA9................102 A4
Wightman Rd CEND/HSY/T N8.......88 A1
Wigley Rd FELT TW15.....................178 D1
Wigmore Pl CAVSO/HST * W1G......11 C3
Wigmore Rd CAR SM5....................225 H6
Wigmore St MBLAR W1H...................11 H3
Wigram Rd WAN E11..........................93 E3
Wigram Sq WALTH E17......................71 G6
Wigston Cl UED N18...........................69 E1
Wigston Rd PLSTW E13..................132 D3
Wigton Gdns STAN HA7.....................61 G4
Wigton Pl LBTH * SE11.....................30 B4
Wigton Rd WALTH E17.......................70 D4
Wilberforce Rd
     CDALE/KGS NW9............................83 F2
     FSBYPK N4..88 B6
Wilberforce Wy
     WIM/MER SW19..............................204 B6
Wilbraham Pl KTBR SW1X................26 D1
Wilbury Wy UED N18...........................29 D5
Wilby Ms NTGHL W11.......................124 D6
Wilcot Av OXHEY WD19......................42 C2
Wilcot Cl OXHEY WD19.......................42 C2
Wilcox Cl VX/NE SW8.......................167 G1
Wilcox Rd SUT * SM1.......................243 F2
     TEDD TW11.....................................179 H6
     VX/NE SW8.....................................167 G1
Wild Ct HOL/ALD WC2B.....................13 G3
Wildcroft Gdns STAN HA7..................61 F2
Wildcroft Rd PUT/ROE SW15........184 A2
Wilde Cl HACK E8..............................109 G6
Wilde Pl PLMGR N13..........................68 B2
Wildcroft Rd CHST BR7..................214 B5
The Wildernesss
     E/WMO/HCT KT8.............................219 C2
     HPTN * TW12..................................179 F6
Wilderton Rd ERITH DA8.................177 F1
Wilderton Rd STNW/STAM N16.......68 E4
Wildfell Rd CAT SE6.........................191 F1
Wild Goose Dr PECK SE15.............170 A2
Wild Hatch GLDGN NW11..................65 E3
Wild's Rents STHWK SE1...................24 A5
Wild St HOL/ALD WC2B.....................13 F4
Wildwood Cl LEE/GVPK SE12.......192 B1
Wildwood Gv GLDGN NW11..............65 D5
Wildwood Ri GLDGN NW11................65 D5
Wildwood Rd GLDGN NW11..............85 G4
Wilford Cl ENC/FH * EN2...................38 D4
Wilford Rd CROY/NA CRO...............228 C3
Wilfred St WESTW SW1E...................20 A5
Wilkes Rd BTFD TW8........................141 G6
Wilkes St WCHPL E1..........................16 D1
Wilkins Cl MTCM CR4......................206 A6
Wilkinson Rd CAN/RD E16.............133 E5
Wilkinson St VX/NE SW8.................167 H1
Wilkin St KTTN NW5........................106 C4
Wilkin Street Ms KTTN * NW5.......106 D4
Wilks Gdns CROY/NA CRO.............230 C5
Wilks Pl IS N1......................................8 B2
Willan Rd TOTM N17..........................68 D5
Willan Wall CAN/RD E16..................132 B6
Willard St VX/NE SW8......................166 D4
Willcocks Cl CHSGTN KT9..............239 G1
Willcott Rd ACT W3..........................142 B1
Will Crooks Gdns
     ELTH/MOT SE9...............................173 F5
Willenhall Av BAR EN5......................49 G1
Willenhall Rd
     WOOL/PLUM SE18..........................154 B5
Willerfield Rd WLSDN NW10..........122 C2
Willersley Av BFN/LL DA15............195 F3
     ORP BR6...252 D1
Willersley Cl BFN/LL DA15............195 F3
Willesden La KIL/WHAMP NW6.....104 D5

Willes Rd KTTN * NW5.....................106 D4
Willet Cl NTHLT UB5.........................118 A2
Willett Cl STMC/STPC BR5...........235 E3
Willett Pl THHTH CR7......................228 A2
Willett Wy STMC/STPC BR5..........234 D2
William Barefoot Dr
     ELTH/MOT SE9...............................194 A4
William Booth Rd
     PGE/AN SE20..................................209 G4
William Carey Wy HRW *HA1.........80 A3
William Cl CI CRW RM5.....................77 G4
     EFNCH N2..65 H1
     ISLW TW7...136 A3
     ROM RM1...63 F4
     STHL UB1..115 H2
William Covell Cl ENC/FH * EN2.....37 H1
William Ellis Wy
     BERM/RHTH * SE16.........................35 F6
William Gdns PUT/ROE SW15.......163 H6
William Guy Gdns BOW E3.............105 F2
William IV St CHCR WC2N.................13 E6
William Margrie Cl PECK * SE15...169 G3
William Ms KTBR SW1X....................16 B3
William Morley Cl EHAM E6............113 F6
William Morris Cl WALTH E17...........70 D6
William Morris Wy
     FUL/PGN SW6..................................165 Q4
William Rd CAMTN NW1.......................4 A4
     SUT SM1..243 G2
Williams Av WALTH E17.....................70 E1
William's Buildings BETH * E2......130 A3
Williams Cl CEND/HSY/T * N8..........87 F3
     FUL/PGN SW6.................................165 G2
Williams Gv SURB KT6......................221 E3
     WDGN N22......................................68 A4
Williams La MORT/ESHN SW14....162 C4
     MRDN SM4.......................................225 G3
Williamson Cl GNWCH SE10...........113 H4
Williamson Rd FSBYPK N4................88 B3
Williamson St HOLWY * N7..............107 Q2
Williamson Wy MLHL NW7.................64 C2
William Sq BERM/RHTH SE16.........150 C1
Williams Rd NWDGN UB2................138 C4
     WEA * W13......................................140 C1
Williams Ter CROY/NA CRO...........246 A4
William St BARK IG11......................114 C5
     CAR SM5...244 A1
     KTBR SW1X.......................................18 D4
     LEY E10...91 G3
     TOTM N17...51 F5
Willifield Wy GLDGN NW11...............85 E1
Willingdon Rd WDGN N22.................68 B5
Willingham Cl KTTN NW5...............106 D4
Willingham Ter KTTN * NW5...........107 E3
Willingham Wy KUT KT1..................202 A5
Willington Rd BRXN/ST SW9..........142 D4
Willis Av BELMT SM2.......................244 A4
Willis Rd CROY/NA CRO..................228 C4
     ERITH DA8......................................157 G4
     SRTFD E15......................................132 B1
Willis St POP/IOD E14.....................131 F5
Willmore End WIM/MER SW19......205 H4
Willoughby Av CROY/NA CRO........245 H2
Willoughby Gv TOTM N17.................69 H5
Willoughby La TOTM N17..................69 H3
Willoughby Ms TOTM N17................69 H5
Willoughby Park Rd TOTM N17........69 H5
Willoughby Rd CEND/HSY/T N8......68 A6
     HAMP NW3.......................................83 H2
     KUTN/CMB KT2.............................201 H4
     TWK TW1...145 F6
Willoughby Wy CHARL SE7...........152 D4
Willow Av BARN SW13.....................163 F3
     BFN/LL DA15..................................195 G1
Willow Bridge Rd IS * N1...............108 C4
Willowbrook HPTN * TW12.............179 F1
Willowbrook Est PECK * SE15.......169 F1
Willowbrook Rd NWDGN UB2.......138 D5
     PECK SE15.....................................169 F1
Willow Cl BKHH IG9..........................57 D6
     BTFD TW8......................................141 E6
     BXLY DA5.......................................196 D1
     HAYES BR2.....................................233 H2
     STMC/STPC BR5............................235 H5
Willow Ct STAN * HA7.......................61 F3
Willowcourt Av
     KTN/HRWW/W HA3.........................80 D2
Willow Dean PIN * HA5......................58 B5
Willowdene HCT * N6.........................86 B4
Willowdene Cl WHTN TW2...............123 G1
Willow Dr BAR EN5.............................34 C5
Willow End TRDG/WHET N20...........38 E4
Willow Gdns HEST * TW5.................159 E2
Willow Gv CHST BR7........................214 A2
Willowhayne Gdns WPK KT4..........242 A2
Willow La MTCM CR4......................236 B1
     WOOL/PLUM SE18.........................153 H4
Willowmead Cl EA W5......................117 H4
Willow Mt CROY/NA CRO................247 E2
Willow Pl WEST SW1P........................21 B1
Willow Rd CHDH RM6.........................96 C3
     EA W5..116 E3
     EN EN1..30 E3
     HAMP NW3......................................105 H2
     NWMAL KT3....................................222 C1
     WLGTN SM6....................................244 D5
Willows Av MRDN SM4....................225 F2
Willows Cl PIN HA5.............................58 A5
The Willows Ter WLSDN * NW10...122 F1
     EBAR * EN4.......................................33 G4
     ESH/CLAY KT10..............................205 E1
Willow St CHING E4.............................55 H2
     ROMW/RG RM7................................75 G1
     SDTCH EC2A.......................................7 F6
Willow Ter PGE/AN * SE20.............209 H4
Willow Tree Cl HOM E9...................110 C6
     WAND/EARL SW18..........................185 F3
Willow Tree La YEAD UB4...............118 A3
Willow Tree Wk BMLY BR1.............212 D4
Willowtree Wy
     STRHM/NOR SW16.........................208 A4
     THHTH * CR7...................................207 H3
     SHB W12...145 G1
Willow Vw WIM/MER SW19.............205 H4
Willow Wk CHEAM SM3...................242 D1
     ORP BR6...252 B1
     SEVS/STOTM N15.............................88 B1

STHWK SE1..32 B1
WALTH E17...90 D2
WCHMH N21..51 H1
Willow Wy ALP/SUD * HA0...............100 C1
     FNCH N3..65 F3
     HOR/WEW KT19...............................240 D4
     NTGHL W11.......................................124 B6
     SYD SE26..189 H5
     WFD IG8...56 D1
     WHTN TW2..179 F4
Willow Wood Crs SNWD SE25.......229 E5
Willrose Crs ABYW SE2...................155 H5
Wills Crs HSLW TW3.........................179 F1
Wills Gv MLHL NW7..............................63 G1
Wilman Gv HACK E8..........................109 C5
Wilmar Gdns WWKM BR4................231 F5
Wilmcote Rd RCHPK/HAM TW10...201 H1
Wilmer Crs RCHPK/HAM TW10......201 H1
Wilmer Gdns IS N1..........................109 E6
Wilmer Lea Cl SRTFD E15..............111 G5
Wilmer Pl STNW/STAM N16.............89 F6
Wilmer Wy STHGT/OAK N14...........67 F1
Wilmington Av CHSWK W4...............162 D1
     ORP BR6..236 A6
Wilmington Gdns BARK IG11........114 D5
Wilmington Sq FSBYW WC1X............6 A4
Wilmington St FSBYW WC1X.............6 A4
Wilmot Cl PECK * SE15....................169 G5
Wilmot Pl CAMTN NW1....................107 F5
     HNWL W7..140 A1
Wilmot Rd CAR * SM5......................244 B3
     LEY E10...91 F6
     TOTM N17..51 D6
Wilmot St BETH E2..............................9 G5
Wilmount St
     WOOL/PLUM SE18.........................154 D6
Wilna Rd WAND/EARL SW18..........185 G2
Wilsham St NTGHL W11..................144 B1
Wilsmere Dr
     KTN/HRWW/W HA3...........................60 A3
     NTHLT UB5..98 C4
Wilson Av MTCM CR4.......................186 D1
Wilson Cl SAND/SEL CR2................246 D5
     WBLY HA9...81 H4
Wilson Gdns HRW HA1......................79 G4
Wilson Gv BERM/RHTH SE16..........25 G4
Wilson Rd CHSGTN KT9.................239 H4
     CMBW SE5.......................................168 D2
     IL IG1...72 B5
     PLSTW E13......................................133 F2
Wilson's Av TOTM N17.......................69 F5
Wilson's Pl POP/IOD E14.................130 D5
Wilson's Rd HMSMTH W6...............144 D5
Wilson St LBTH SE11..........................30 B4
     WALTH E17..91 G2
     WCHMH N21.......................................52 A2
Wilthorne Wk HMSMTH * W6.........143 F4
Wilson Cl YEAD UB4........................118 C3
Wilthorne Gdns DAGE RM10..........117 F5
Wilstone Wk CHSWK W4...................143 E5
Wilton Crs KTBR SW1X......................19 E1
     WIM/MER SW19..............................204 D4
Wilton Est HACK * E8........................109 G4
Wilton Gdns E/WMO/HCT KT8........199 E6
     WT/HER KT12...................................218 D5
Wilton Gv NWMAL KT3.....................223 F3
     WIM/MER SW19..............................204 D3
Wilton Ms HACK * E8........................109 H4
     KTBR SW1X..19 F1
Wilton Pl KTBR SW1X.........................19 E1
Wilton Rd ABYW SE2........................156 A3
     EBAR EN4...36 B5
     HSLW TW4.......................................155 E4
     MUSWH N10......................................66 C5
     PIM SW1V..20 A6
     WIM/MER SW19..............................206 A3
Wilton Rw KTBR SW1X.......................19 E1
Wilton Sq IS N1................................108 D6
Wilton Ter KTBR SW1X.......................19 E5
Wilton Vls IS N1................................108 D6
Wilton Wy HACK E8..........................109 G5
Wiltshire Cl CHEL SW3......................26 B2
     MLHL * NW7..63 F1
Wiltshire Gdns FSBYPK N4...............88 C3
     WHTN TW2.......................................123 G1
Wiltshire Rd BRXN/ST SW9............168 A4
     ORP BR6..235 G4
     THHTH CR7......................................208 A6
Wiltshire Rw IS N1............................108 D6
Wiverley Crs NWMAL KT3...............223 E5
Wimbart Rd
     BRXS/STRHM * SW2.......................187 H2
Wimbledon Br
     WIM/MER SW19..............................204 D2
Wimbledon Hill Rd
     WIM/MER SW19..............................204 D2
Wimbledon Park Rd
     WIM/MER SW19..............................184 C5
Wimbledon Park Side
     WIM/MER SW19..............................184 B4
Wimbledon Rd TOOT SW17............185 G6
Wimbolt St BETH E2............................8 D1
Wimborne Av NWDGN UB2............139 E4
     STMC/STPC BR5............................215 F6
Wimborne Cl BKHH IG9....................57 C6
     LEE/GVPK SE12..............................172 B6
     WPK KT4..224 A5
Wimborne Dr CDALE/KGS NW9.......62 A6
     PIN HA5...78 B4
Wimborne Gdns WEA W13..............120 D5
Wimborne Rd ED N18.........................53 C4
     TOTM N17..69 E5
Wimborne Wy BECK BR3.................210 B6
Wimbourne St IS N1.............................7 F2
Wimpole Cl HAYES BR2...................233 E1
     KUT KT1...190 D5
Wimpole Ms CAVSO/HST W1G........11 C1
Wimpole St CAVSO/HST W1G...........9 H3
Wimshurst Cl CROY/NA CRO..........227 G5
Winans Wk BRXN/ST SW9...............168 A3
Wincanton Crs NTHLT UB5...............80 A4
Wincanton Gdns BARK/HLT IG6......74 B5
Wincanton Rd
     WAND/EARL SW18..........................184 D2
Winchcombe Rd CAR SM5..............225 G4
Winchcomb Gdns
     ELTH/MOT SE9...............................173 F4
Winchelsea Av BXLYHN DA7..........176 D1

Winchelsea Cl PUT/ROE SW15.....164 B6
Winchelsea Rd TOTM N17................69 E6
     WLSDN NW10..................................102 D6
Winchelsey Ri SAND/SEL CR2.......247 F4
Winchendon Rd FUL/PGN SW6.....169 D1
     TEDD TW11......................................179 H6
Winchester Av CDALE/KGS NW9.....61 H6
     HEST TW5..136 A1
     KIL/WHAMP NW6.............................104 C6
Winchester Cl EN * EN1......................39 E5
     HAYES BR2.......................................212 B6
     KUTN/CMB KT2................................202 B3
     LBTH * SE11......................................30 D2
Winchester Dr PIN HA5......................78 B2
Winchester Pk HAYES BR2.............212 B6
Winchester Pl HACK E8.....................109 F5
     HCT N6..86 D5
Winchester Rd CHING E4....................41 H6
     ED N9..53 F3
     FELT TW13......................................178 D5
     HAMP NW3...83 H5
     HAYES BR2......................................212 B6
     HCT N6..86 D5
     IL IG1...114 D7
     KTN/HRWW/W HA3............................61 E5
     TWK TW1..180 D1
     WELL DA16......................................176 B3
Winchester Sq STHWK SE1..............23 G1
Winchester St ACT W3......................142 C1
     PIM SW1V...21 H2
Winchester Wk STHWK SE1.............23 G1
Winchfield Cl
     KTN/HRWW/W HA3............................81 E3
Winchfield Rd SYD SE26.................210 C1
Winchilsea Crs
     E/WMO/HCT KT8..............................199 G5
Winchmore Hill Rd
     STHGT/OAK N14................................51 G2
Winchmore Vls WCHMH * N21.........51 H2
Winckley Cl KTN/HRWW/W HA3.......81 H2
Wincott St LBTH SE11.........................30 B1
Wincrofts Dr ELTH/MOT SE9...........174 D5
Windall Cl NRWD SE19....................209 G4
Windborough Rd CAR SM5.............244 C5
Windermere Av FNCH N3..................65 E6
     KIL/WHAMP NW6.............................104 C6
     RSLP HA4..61 H5
     WBLY HA9..81 E5
     WIM/MER SW19...............................205 F6
Windermere Cl ORP BR6..................216 B1
Windermere Gdns REDBR IG4..........93 G2
Windermere Gv WBLY * HA9.............81 E5
Windermere Hall EDGW * HA8.........61 H1
Windermere Rd ARCH * N19.............87 G5
     BXLYHN DA7...................................177 H1
     CROY/NA CRO.................................229 F5
     EA W5..141 E3
     MUSWH N10.......................................66 A4
     PUT/ROE SW15...............................183 E6
     STHL UB1..118 D4
     STRHM/NOR SW16..........................207 E4
     WWKM BR4......................................232 A6
Winders Rd BTSEA * SW11.............188 A6
Windfield Cl SYD SE26.....................190 B6
Windham Rd RCH/KEW TW9..........161 H4
Winding Wy BCTR RM8....................116 A1
Windlass Pl DEPT SE8......................150 C4
Windlesham Gv
     WIM/MER SW19...............................184 B3
Windley Cl FSTH SE23......................190 A4
Windmill Cl LEW * SE13....................133 F2
     STHWK SE1...33 F2
     SURB KT6...221 G1
Windmill Dr CLAP SW4....................166 D6
     CRICK * NW2.....................................82 A2
Windmill Gdns ENC/FH EN2..............38 A3
Windmill Gv CROY/NA CRO............228 C4
Windmill Hi ENC/FH EN2...................38 D4
     HAMP * NW3......................................83 G1
Windmill La BAR EN5.........................47 F1
     BUSH WD23.......................................44 A3
     GFD/PVL UB6....................................119 C4
     NWDGN UB2.....................................139 H3
     SRTFD E15..111 H4
     STHL UB1...139 G2
     THDIT KT7...220 D5
Windmill Pas CHSWK * W4..............143 E4
Windmill Ri KUTN/CMB KT2............202 D3
Windmill Rd CHSWK W4...................143 E4
     CROY/NA CRO.................................228 C4
     EA W5..141 E4
     HPTN TW12......................................179 F1
     MTCM CR4.......................................207 F4
     UED N18...52 D2
Windmill Rw LBTH SE11.....................30 A4
Windmill St BUSH WD23....................44 A3
     FITZ W1T..12 C2
Windmill Wk LBTH SE11.....................30 A1
Windrose Cl BERM/RHTH SE16.....150 B2
Windrush CI BTSEA * SW11............165 H5
     CHSWK * W4....................................162 C1
Windrush La FSTH SE23...................190 D2
Windrush Rd WLSDN NW10............100 C4
Windsor Av CHEAM SM3.................242 C5
     E/WMO/HCT KT8..............................199 E6
     EDGW HA8..46 D5
     NWMAL KT3.....................................222 C2
     WALTH E17..51 F4
     WIM/MER SW19...............................205 G4
Windsor Cl CHST BR7.......................214 B1
     FNCH N3...65 E3
     RYLN/HDSTN HA2.............................99 E1
     NWWD SE27.....................................189 F5
Windsor Ct PIN * HA5.........................59 E1
     STHGT/OAK N14................................51 E2
Windsor Crs RYLN/HDSTN HA2.......99 H1
     WBLY HA9...82 A1
Windsor Dr EBAR EN4........................34 C3
     ORP BR6...252 D6
Windsor Gdns CROY/NA CRO........245 G4
     MV/WKIL * W9..................................125 G1
Windsor Gv WNWD SE27.................189 G5
Windsor Ms CAT SE6........................191 G5
Windsor Rd BAR EN5..........................46 D1
     BCTR RM8...116 C5
     BXLYHS DA6....................................176 D5
     CHING E4...55 F6
     CRICK NW2......................................103 H4

EA W5...........................121 F6
FNCH N3............................64 C5
FSTGT E7.........................112 D3
HOLWY N7.........................107 G1
IL G1.............................114 C2
KTN/HRWW/W HA3...................59 G4
KUTN/CMB KT2......................91 F6
LEY E10...........................91 F6
NWDGN UB2........................138 D5
PLMGR N13.........................52 A5
RCH/KEW TW9.....................161 H5
TEDD TW11........................199 H1
THHTH CR7........................208 B5
TOTM N17..........................69 C5
WAN E11...........................92 C5
WPK KT4............................6 G4
The Windsors BKHH IG9.............57 G4
Windsor St IS N1.................108 B6
Windsor Ter IS N1.................9 H4
Windsor Wk CMBW SE5.............168 D3
Windsor Wy HMSMTH W6............144 B4
Windspoint Dr PECK SE15...........33 G6
Windus Rd STNW/STAM N16...........89 F5
Windy Rdg BR1....................213 G4
Windy Ridge Cl
Windsor St IS N1.................204 B1
Wine Cl WAP E1W...................130 A6
Winery La KUT IL.................201 H6
Winey Cl CHSGTN KT9..............239 E5
Winforton St GNWCH SE10..........171 G2
Winfrith Rd WAND/EARL SW18.......185 G2
Wingate Crs CROY/NA CRO..........227 E3
Wingate Rd HMSMTH W6.............143 H3
IL G1...........................114 B5
SCUP DA14........................216 A1
Wingfield Ms PECK * SE15.........169 G4
Wingfield Rd KUTN/CMB KT2........201 H2
SRTFD E15........................112 A3
WALTH E17..........................F2
Wingfield St PECK SE15...........169 G4
Wingford Rd CLAP SW4.............187 G1
Wingmore Rd HNHL SE24............168 C1
Wingrave Rd HMSMTH W6............148 A6
Wingrove Rd CAT SE6..............192 A4
Wings Cl SUT SM1.................243 E2
Winifred Pl NFNCH/WDSP N12.......65 G1
Winifred Rd BCTR RM8..............96 C6
HPTN TW12........................179 E6
WIM/MER SW19....................205 E4
Winifred St CAN/RD E16...........153 H1
Winifred Ter EN EN1...............53 F2
Winkfield Rd WDGN N22............82 A4
Winkley St BETH * E2...............9 G2
Winkworth Cottages
WCHPL * E1......................130 A3
Winlaton Rd BMLY BR1.............191 H6
Winmill Rd BCTR RM8..............116 D1
Winn Bridge Cl WFD IG8............73 F4
Winn Common Rd
WOOL/PLUM SE18..................155 E6
Winnett St SOHO/SHAV W1D.........12 C5
Winnington Cl EFNCH N2............85 H3
Winnington Rd EFNCH N2............85 H4
PEND EN3..........................41 F1
Winnipeg Dr ORP BR6..............253 F4
Winn Rd LEE/GVPK SE12............192 C3
Winns Av WALTH E17................70 D6
Winns Ms SEYS/STOTM N15...........89 E1
Winns Ter WALTH E17...............71 E5
Winsbeach WALTH E17...............71 H6
Winscombe Crs EA W5..............121 F3
Winscombe St KTTN NW5............66 D1
Winscombe Wy STAN HA7............60 C1
Winsford Rd CAT SE6.............190 D5
Winsford Ter UED * N18............68 D1
Winsham Gv BTSEA SW11...........166 C6
Winslade Rd
BRXS/STRHM SW2..................167 G3
Winsland Ms BAY/PAD W2...........125 H5
Winsland St BAY/PAD W2...........125 H5
Winsley St GTPST W1W..............12 A3
Winslow Cl WLSDN NW10............103 E1
Winslow Gv CHING E4...............56 A4
Winslow Rd HMSMTH W6............144 A6
Winslow Wy FELT TW13.............178 B5
Winsor Ter EHAM E6...............134 A4
Winstanley Rd BTSEA SW11........165 H4
Winstead Gdns DAGE RM10.........117 G3
Winston Av CDALE/KGS NW9.........63 F3
Winston Cl KTN/HRWW/W HA3........43 E4
ROMW/RG RM7.......................97 F1
Winston Ct PIN HA5................59 F3
Winston House SURB * KT6.........191 G6
Winston Rd STNW/STAM N16........107 H1
Winston Wy IL IG1................114 B1
Winter Av EHAM E6................113 G6
Winterborne Av ORP BR6..........252 D1
Winterbourne Rd BCTR RM8.........96 A6
FSTH SE23........................190 D3
THHTH CR7........................228 A1
Winter Box Wk
RCHPK/HAM TW10...................161 H4
Winterbrook Rd HNHL SE24.........168 C4
Winterburn Cl FBAR/BDGN N11.....66 C2
Winterfold Cl WIM/MER SW19......184 C4
Winters Rd THDIT KT7.............220 D4
Winterstoke Rd FSTH SE23........190 D3
Winterton Pl WBPTN SW10.........145 G6
Winterwell Rd
BRXS/STRHM SW2..................167 G3
Winthorpe Rd PUT/ROE SW15......144 C5
Winthrop St WCHPL E1..............17 C1
Winton Av FBAR/BDGN N11..........67 E3
Winton Cl ED N9..................54 B2
Winton Gdns EDGW HA8.............61 H3
Winton Rd ORP BR6................252 B2
The Wintons BUSH * WD23..........43 H3
Winton Wy STRHM/NOR SW16........208 A1
Wirral Wood Cl CHST BR7.........214 H2
Wisbeach Rd CROY/NA CRO........228 D2
Wisborough Rd SAND/SEL CR2.....247 F6
Wisdons Cl DAGE RM10.............97 F5
Wise La MLHL NW7.................45 G3
Wiseman Rd LEY * E10.............91 E6
Wise Rd SRTFD E15...............111 G6
Wiseton Rd TOOT SW17............186 A3
Wishart Rd BKHTH/KID SE3.......173 E1
Wisley Rd BTSEA SW11............166 B6
STMC/STPC BR5...................215 G3
Wistaria Cl ORP BR6.............234 B6
Wisteria Cl IL IG1..............114 B3

Wisteria Gdns SWLY BR8..........217 H5
Wisteria Rd LEW SE13............171 H5
Witan St BETH E2...................9 H4
Witcham Cl LOU IG10..............57 C1
Witcham Rd DAGE RM10...........117 E3
ISLW TW7........................159 H2
PGE/AN SE20......................181 G4
WEA W13.........................140 C1
Withens Cl STMC/STPC * BR5......236 A1
Witherby Cl SAND/SEL CR2........247 E5
Witherington Rd HBRY * N5.......108 A5
Withers Md CDALE/KGS NW9.........63 F4
Witherston Wy ELTH/MOT SE9.....194 A4
Withfield Md CHING E4.............55 H5
Witley Crs CROY/NA CRO.........230 D5
Witley Gdns NWDGN UB2...........138 D4
Witley Rd ARCH N19...............87 E6
Witney Ct PIN HA5................58 D2
Witney Pth FSTH * SE23..........190 B5
Wittenham Wy CHING E4............55 H5
Wittering Cl KUTN/CMB KT2.......201 F1
Wittersham Rd BMLY BR1..........183 H5
Wivenhoe Ct HSLW TW3............159 G4
Wivenhoe Rd BARK IG11...........135 C1
Wiverton Rd SYD SE26...........210 A2
Wix Rd DAGW RM9.................116 B6
Wix's La BTSEA SW11.............166 D5
Woburn WEA * W13................120 D4
Woburn Cl BUSH WD23..............43 C1
CROY/NA CRO......................228 C5
Woburn Sq STPAN WC1H.............4 D6
Woburn Wk STPAN WC1H.............4 C6
Wodehouse Av PECK SE15.........169 F2
Woffington Cl
E/WMO/HCT KT8...................201 E4
Woking Cl PUT/ROE SW15.........163 F5
Woldham Pl HAYES BR2............233 E1
Woldham Rd HAYES BR2............233 E1
Wolds Dr ORP BR6................252 A2
Wolfe Cl HAYES BR2..............232 C5
Wolfe Crs CHARL SE7............153 F5
Wolferton Rd MNPK E12..........113 H2
Wolfington Rd WNWD SE27........188 B6
Wolfram Cl LEW SE13............173 H4
Wolftencroft Cl BTSEA SW11.....164 A4
Wollaston Cl WALW SE17...........30 D2
Wolmer Cl EDGW HA8...............46 A6
Wolmer Gdns EDGW HA8............46 A5
Wolseley Av WAND/EARL SW18.....185 G4
Wolseley Gdns CHSWK W4.........142 B6
Wolseley Rd CEND/HSY/T N8.......87 F3
CHSWK W4........................142 C4
FSTGT E7........................112 D5
KTN/HRWW/W HA3..................60 A6
MTCM CR4........................226 C4
ROMW/RG RM7......................97 H4
WDGN N22.........................67 H4
Wolsey Av EHAM E6...............134 A2
WALTH E17........................57 F6
Wolsey Cl HSLW TW3..............159 G5
KUTN/CMB KT2....................202 B4
NWDGN UB2.......................139 G3
RYNPK SW20......................205 H4
WPK KT4.........................241 G2
Wolsey Crs CROY/NA CRO.........249 G6
MRDN SM4........................224 D4
Wolsey Dr KUTN/CMB KT2.........202 A1
WOT/HER KT12....................218 B5
Wolsey Gdns BARK/HLT IG6........74 B2
Wolsey Gv EDGW HA8...............62 D3
Wolsey Ms KTTN NW5...............67 G4
ORP BR6.........................253 F5
Wolsey Rd E/WMO/HCT KT8........219 H1
EN EN1...........................39 H3
HPTN TW12........................199 F2
IS N1.............................8 B4
Wolsey St WCHPL E1..............130 A4
Wolsey Wy CHSGTN KT9............240 A3
Wolstenbury
NFNCH/WDSP N12..................65 E1
Wolvercote Rd ABYW SE2.........156 B2
Wolverley St BETH * E2............9 G4
Wolverton Av KUTN/CMB KT2......202 A4
Wolverton Gdns EA W5............121 H6
HMSMTH W6.......................144 B4
Wolverton Rd STAN HA7............60 D2
Wolverton Wy STHGT/OAK N14......37 E6
Wolves La WDGN N22...............68 A3
Womersley Rd CEND/HSY/T N8......87 H3
Wonersh Wy BELMT SM2...........242 B6
Wonford Cl NWMAL KT3............205 E4
Wontner Cl IS * N1..............108 C5
Wontner Rd BAL SW12............166 B4
Woodall Cl CHSGTN KT9..........239 F4
Woodall Rd PEND EN3.............54 B1
Woodbank Rd BMLY BR1...........192 B5
Woodbastwick Rd SYD SE26......210 B2
Woodberry Av
RYLN/HDSTN HA2...................79 C1
WCHMH N21........................88 C1
Woodberry Crs MUSWH N10........66 D4
Woodberry Down FSBYPK N4........88 C5
Woodberry Gdns
NFNCH/WDSP N12..................65 G2
Woodberry Gv BXLY DA5..........197 H5
FSBYPK N4........................88 C5
NFNCH/WDSP N12..................65 G2
Woodberry Wy CHING E4...........55 G2
NFNCH/WDSP N12..................65 G2
Woodbine Cl WHTN TW2...........179 H3
Woodbine Gv ENC/FH EN2..........38 D1
PGE/AN SE20.....................181 G4
Woodbine La WPK KT4............241 H1
Woodbine Pl WAN E11.............92 C3
Woodbine Rd BFN/LL DA15........195 E3
Woodbines Av KUT IL1...........201 F6
Woodbine Ter HOM E9............111 E4
Woodborough Rd
PUT/ROE SW15...................163 H5
Woodbourne Av
STRHM/NOR SW16..................187 F5
Woodbourne Dr
ESH/CLAY KT10...................238 B4
Woodbourne Gdns
WLGTN SM6......................244 D5

Woodbridge Cl HOLWY N7..........87 H6
Woodbridge Rd BARK IG11........115 F3
Woodbridge St CLKNW EC1R.........6 C1
Woodbrook Rd ABYW SE2.........155 C6
Woodburn Cl HDN NW4.............64 B2
Woodbury Cl CROY/NA CRO.......229 F6
WAN E11..........................92 D1
Woodbury Park Rd WEA W13......120 D3
Woodbury St TOOT SW17..........206 A1
Woodbury Sq BAY/PAD W2........125 F4
Woodchurch Cl BFN/LL DA15.....194 D5
Woodchurch Dr BMLY BR1........184 D1
Woodchurch Rd
KIL/WHAMP NW6...................105 E5
Wood Cl BETH E2...................9 D4
CDALE/KGS NW9....................82 D4
HRW HA1..........................79 H4
Woodclyffe Dr CHST BR7........214 A5
Woodcock Ct
KTN/HRWW/W HA3...................81 E4
Woodcock Dell Av
KTN/HRWW/W HA3...................81 E4
Woodcock HI
KTN/HRWW/W HA3...................81 D2
Woodcocks CAN/RD E16...........133 E4
Woodcombe Crs FSTH SE23.......190 C1
Woodcot Cl ED N9................54 A1
Woodcote Av MLHL NW7.............64 A2
THHTH CR7........................228 B1
Woodcote Cl KUTN/CMB KT2......201 H1
Woodcote Dr ORP BR6............234 D4
Woodcote Gn WLGTN SM6.........245 E6
Woodcote Ms LOU IG10.............57 F2
WLGTN SM6.......................244 D4
Woodcote Pl WNWD * SE27.......188 C5
Woodcote Rd WAN E11.............92 D4
WLGTN SM6.......................244 D4
Wood Crest BELMT * SM2.........244 D4
Woodcroft BFN/LL DA15..........195 H2
GFD/PVL UB6....................100 C4
WCHMH N21........................51 H3
Woodcroft Av MLHL NW7...........64 C6
STAN HA7.........................60 G3
Woodcroft Ms DEPT SE8..........150 C4
Woodcroft Rd THHTH CR7........228 B2
Wood Dene PECK * SE15..........169 H2
Wood Dr CHST BR7...............213 G2
Woodedge Cl CHING E4............56 B3
Wooden Bridge Ter
WNWD * SE27....................188 B5
Woodend ESH/CLAY KT10.........219 G6
NRWD SE19.......................208 C2
SUT SM1.........................225 G6
Wood End Av RYLN/HDSTN HA2......99 F2
Wood End Cl NTHLT UB5...........80 D3
Woodend Gdns ENC/FH EN2.........37 C5
Wood End Gdns NTHLT UB5.........99 F3
Wood End La NTHLT UB5...........99 F4
Wood End Rd NTHLT UB5..........99 F4
Woodend Rd WALTH E17............71 G5
The Wood End WLGTN SM6........244 D6
Wood End Wy NTHLT UB5..........99 F3
Wooder Gdns FSTGT E7............94 B1
Wooderson Cl SNWD SE25.........229 E1
Woodfall Av BAR EN5..............34 D6
Woodfall Rd FSBYPK N4...........88 A5
Woodfall St CHEL SW3............15 H6
Woodfarrs CMBW SE5.............168 D5
Wood Fld HAMP * NW3............106 B3
Woodfield Av ALP/SUD HA0......101 G1
CAR SM5.........................244 C4
CDALE/KGS NW9....................63 E4
EA W5...........................121 E3
STRHM/NOR SW16..................187 F5
EN EN1...........................20 C1
NRWD SE19.......................208 C2
Woodfield Cl EN EN1............121 F3
Woodfield Crs EA W5............121 F3
Woodfield Dr BAR EN4............50 C3
Woodfield Gdns NWMAL KT3......223 F2
Woodfield Gv
STRHM/NOR SW16..................187 F5
Woodfield La
ESH/CLAY KT10...................220 C5
Woodfield Pl MV/WKIL W9........124 D3
Woodfield Ri BUSH WD23..........45 F1
Woodfield Rd EA W5.............121 E3
ESH/CLAY * KT10................220 B6
MV/WKIL W9......................135 E3
Woodfield Wy FBAR/BDGN N11......67 F3
Woodford Av GNTH/NBYPK IG2.....93 H2
Woodford Bridge Rd
REDBR IG4........................73 F6
Woodford New Rd WALTH E17......72 A6
WFD IG8..........................72 B3
Woodford Pl WBLY HA9............81 G5
Woodford Rd FSTGT E7...........112 D2
SWFD E18.........................73 E1
Woodgate Av CHSGTN KT9.........239 F3
Woodgate Dr
STRHM/NOR SW16..................207 F3
Woodger Rd SHB W12.............144 A2
Woodget Cl EHAM E6.............133 C5
Woodgrange Av ACT W3..........141 H1
EN EN1...........................53 G1
KTN/HRWW/W HA3...................81 G2
NFNCH/WDSP N12...................65 H2
Woodgrange Cl
KTN/HRWW/W HA3...................81 H2
Woodgrange Gdns EN EN1..........53 G1
Woodgrange Ter EN * EN1.........53 G1
Woodhall Av DUL SE21..........189 F5
PIN HA5..........................58 C4
Woodhall Dr DUL SE21...........189 F5
PIN HA5..........................58 B3
Woodhall La OXHEY WD19..........42 B5
Woodhall St CHING E4............55 F4
Woodham Ct SWFD E18.............72 C1
Woodham Rd CAT SE6............191 G5
Woodhatch Cl EHAM E6...........133 G4
Woodhaven Gdns
BARK/HLT * IG6...................54 C1
Woodhayes Rd RYNPK SW20........204 A3
Woodhead Dr ORP BR6............253 E1
Woodheyes Rd WLSDN NW10........103 E3
Woodhill CHARL SE7.............153 C4
Woodhouse Av GFD/PVL UB6......120 B1
Woodhouse Cl GFD/PVL UB6......120 B1

Woodhouse Gv MNPK E12.........113 G4
Woodhouse Rd
NFNCH/WDSP N12...................66 A2
WAN E11.........................112 B1
Woodhurst Av
STMC/STPC BR5...................234 C3
Woodhurst Rd ABYW SE2.........155 C5
ACT W3..........................142 C1
Woodington Cl ELTH/MOT SE9....194 A1
Woodison St BOW E3.............130 C3
Woodknoll Dr CHST BR7.........213 H4
Woodland Av GFD/PVL UB6.......100 C4
Woodland Cl CDALE/KGS NW9......82 C3
HOR/WEW * KT19..................241 E4
NRWD SE19.......................181 G6
WFD IG8..........................56 D5
Woodland Ct GLDGN * NW11........84 C2
Woodland Gdns GNWCH SE10......152 A6
Woodland Gdns ISLW TW7........160 A1
MUSWH N10........................86 D2
Woodland HI NRWD SE19.........209 C2
Woodland Ri GFD/PVL UB6.......100 C4
MUSWH N10........................86 B2
Woodland Rd CHING E4............55 G3
EFNCH N2.........................66 D1
NRWD SE19.......................209 E1
THHTH CR7........................227 D2
Woodlands GLDGN NW11............84 C2
RYLN/HDSTN HA2...................79 F3
RYNPK SW20.....................224 A1
Woodlands Av ACT W3...........142 B1
BFN/LL DA15.....................195 E3
CHDH RM6.........................96 C3
FNCH N3..........................65 H3
NWMAL KT3........................192 D3
RSLP HA4.........................98 A5
WAN E11..........................92 D5
WPK KT4.........................223 F6
Woodlands Cl BMLY BR1.........213 H5
ESH/CLAY KT10...................238 B5
GLDGN NW11.......................84 C2
Woodlands Dr STAN HA7...........60 A2
SUN TW16........................198 A5
Woodlands Gdns WALTH * E17......32 A1
Woodlands Gv GNWCH SE10........152 A5
ISLW TW7........................160 A3
Woodlands Pk BXLY DA5.........197 H6
Woodlands Park Rd
BKHTH/KID SE3...................152 A3
SEVS/STOTM N15..................89 G4
Woodlands Rd BARN SW13........163 F4
BMLY BR1........................213 H5
BXLYHN DA7.......................176 C4
ED N9............................54 A3
ENC/FH EN2.......................38 D1
HRW HA1..........................80 B2
IL IG1..........................114 C1
ISLW TW7........................160 A1
LEY SE13........................191 H2
NRWD SE19.......................209 F5
ORP BR6.........................253 G4
STHL UB1........................138 B1
SURB KT6........................221 F4
WALTH E17........................71 G6
WAN * E17........................71 G6
Woodlands St LEW SE13..........191 H2
Woodlands Ter SWLY * BR8......237 G3
The Woodlands CMBW * SE5......168 B1
ESH/CLAY KT10...................219 G6
HRW * HA1........................61 H1
ISLW TW7........................160 B3
LEW SE13........................191 H2
NRWD SE19.......................208 B5
ORP BR6.........................253 H4
STAN * HA7.......................60 D1
STHCT/OAK N14....................36 B4
WLGTN SM6.......................244 D6
Woodland St HACK * E8..........191 H2
Woodlands Ter SWLY * BR8......237 G3
The Woodlands CMBW * SE5......168 B1
ESH/CLAY KT10...................219 G6
HRW * HA1........................61 H1
ISLW TW7........................160 B3
LEW SE13........................191 H2
Woodland Ter CHARL SE7.........153 C4
Woodland Wk HAMP NW3..........106 A3
HOR/WEW KT19....................240 A4
Woodland Wy ABYW SE2..........156 B4
BRYLDS KT5.......................222 B6
CROY/NA CRO.....................230 C5
MLHL NW7.........................45 F4
MRDN SM4........................224 D1
MTCM CR4........................186 A3
STMC/STPC BR5...................216 A1
WCHMH N21........................52 A4
WFD IG8..........................45 G6
WFD IG8..........................45 G6
WRB BR4........................249 G1
Wood La CDALE/KGS NW9............63 F4
DAGE RM10........................96 D6
HGT N6...........................66 B6
ISLW TW7.........................48 A6
SHB W12.........................124 A5
STAN HA7.........................43 H6
Woodlawn Cl PUT/ROE SW15.....164 B3
Woodlawn Crs WHTN TW2.........179 F4
Woodlawn Dr FELT TW13.........178 B1
Woodlawn Rd FUL/PGN SW6......164 B3
Woodlea Dr HAYES BR2..........232 A2
Woodlea Rd STNW/STAM E16......109 H1
Woodleigh Av
NFNCH/WDSP N12...................65 H4
Woodleigh Gdns
STRHM/NOR SW16..................187 G5
Woodley Cl TOOT SW17.........206 B3
Woodley La SUT SM1............244 A1
Woodley Rd ORP BR6............234 D6
Wood Lodge Gdns BMLY BR1.....194 A5
Wood Lodge La WWKM BR4........249 F1
Woodman La CHING E4............41 H6
Woodman Pth BARK/HLT IG6.......54 D1
Woodmans Gv WLSDN NW10........103 H3
Woodmansterne Rd
STRHM/NOR SW16..................207 G4
Woodman St CAN/RD E16.........134 A4
Wood Md TOTM * N17.............56 B4
Woodmere ELTH/MOT SE9.........193 H2
Woodmere Av CROY/NA CRO......230 B4
Woodmere Cl BTSEA SW11........166 C4
Woodmere Gdns
CROY/NA CRO.....................230 B4
Woodmere Wy BECK BR3..........231 H2
Woodmount SWLY BR8.............237 H4
Woodnook Rd
STRHM/NOR SW16..................206 D1
Woodpecker Cl BUSH WD23........43 G3
ED N9............................53 H1

KTN/HRWW/W HA3 ....60 B4
Woodpecker Mt CROY/NA CRO .248 C6
Woodpecker Rd THMD SE28 ...136 A6
Woodquest Av HNHL SE24 .....168 B6
Wood Ride EBAR EN4 ....35 H2
STMC/STPC BR5 ....234 D1
Woodridge Cl ENC/FH * EN2 ...38 A2
Woodridings Av PIN HA5 ....58 D4
Woodridings Cl PIN HA5 ....58 D3
Woodriffe Rd WAN E11 ....91 H4
Woodrow WOOL/PLUM SE18 ....153 G4
Woodrow Cl GFD/PVL UB6 ......100 D5
Woodrow Ct TOTM N17 ....69 H5
Woodrush Cl NKENS SE14 ....170 C1
Woodrush Wy CHDH RM6 ....96 B1
Woodseer St WCHPL E1 ....16 D1
Woodsford Sq WKENS W14 .....144 C2
Woodside Rd DAGE RM10 ....117 F1
Woodside BKHH IG9 ....57 E4
GLDGN NW11 ....85 E2
ORP BR6 ....253 G3
WIM/MER SW19 ....204 D1
Woodside Av ALP/SUD HA0 ....101 G6
CHST BR7 ....214 C1
ESH/CLAY KT10 ....220 A4
HGT N6 ....65 G4
NFNCH/WDSP N12 ....49 G6
SNWD SE25 ....229 H5
Woodside Cl ALP/SUD HA0 ....101 G6
BRYLDS KT5 ....222 C4
BXLYHN DA7 ....138 B1
STAN HA7 ....60 C1
Woodside Court Rd
CROY/NA CRO 229 G4
Woodside Crs BFN/LL DA15 ...195 E5
Woodside End ALP/SUD HA0 ..101 G6
Woodside Gdns CHING E4 ......71 F1
TOTM N17 ....69 F5
Woodside Grange Rd
NFNCH/WDSP N12 ....49 G5
Woodside Gn CROY/NA CRO ..229 G4
SNWD SE25 ....229 H3
Woodside Gv
NFNCH/WDSP N12 ....49 G5
Woodside La BXLY DA5 ....196 E1
NFNCH/WDSP N12 ....49 F5
Woodside Pde BFN/LL * DA15 .195 E5
Woodside Pk SNWD SE25 ......229 G3
Woodside Park Av WALTH E17 ..91 H1
Woodside Park Rd
NFNCH/WDSP N12 ....49 F5
Woodside Pl ALP/SUD HA0 ....101 G6
BMLY BR1 ....233 G2
BXLYHN DA7 ....138 B1
KUTN/CMB KT2 ....201 G5
NWMAL KT3 ....202 D5
PLSTW E13 ....133 E3
SNWD SE25 ....229 H3
SUT SM1 ....243 G1
WDGN N22 ....68 A3
WFD IG8 ....56 C6
Woodside Wy CROY/NA CRO ..206 D4
MTCM CR4 ....206 D4
Wood's Ms MYFR/PKLN W1K ..10 D5
Woodsome Rd KTTN NW5 .....106 C1
Wood's Pl STHWK SE1 ....19 H6
Woodspring Rd WIM/MER SW19 184 C4
Wood's Rd PECK SE15 ....169 H2
Woodstead Gv EDGW HA8 ....61 G2
Woodstock Gra EA * W5 ....141 G1
Woodstock La North
SURB KT6 ....221 E6
Woodstock La South
ESH/CLAY KT10 ....220 D5
Woodstock Ms CAVSQ/HST W1G ..11 F2
Woodstock Rd ALP/SUD HA0 ..101 H5
BUSH WD23 ....44 A2
CAR SM5 ....244 C3
CHSWK W4 ....118 B4
CROY/NA CRO 246 D1
FSBYPK N4 ....88 A3
FSTGT E7 ....113 E5
GLDGN NW11 ....84 D4
WALTH E17 ....91 H1
Woodstock St CAN/RD E16 ...132 B5
MYFR/PKLN W1K 9 H4
Woodstock Ter POP/IOD E14 ..113 H1
Woodstone Av EW KT17 ....241 G5
Wood St BAR EN5 ....34 A5
BARB EC2Y 15 F2
CAN/RD E16 ....132 D6
CHSWK W4 ....143 G5
KUT KT1 ....201 F4
MTCM CR4 ....226 C4
WALTH E17 ....71 G6
Woodsyre NRWD SE19 ....189 F6
Wood Ter CRICK * NW2 ....83 H6
Woodthorpe Rd
PUT/ROE SW15 ....163 H5
Woodtree Cl HDN NW4 ....64 A5
Wood V EDUL SE22 ....189 H3
MUSWH N10 ....87 E2
Woodvale Av SNWD SE25 .....209 F6
Woodvale Wy CRICK NW2 ......104 A4
Woodview Av CHING E4 ....55 G6
Woodview Cl KUTN/CMB KT2 .182 D6
FSBYPK N4 ....88 C2
Woodville LEE/GVPK SE12 .....172 C6
TEDD TW11 ....180 C6
Woodville Gdns BARK/HLT IG6 .74 B2
EA W5 ....121 G5
SURB * KT6 ....222 E1
Woodville Gv WELL * DA16 ....175 C4
Woodville Rd BAR EN5 ....35 H5
EA W5 ....121 G5
GLDGN NW11 ....84 C4

KIL/WHAMP * NW6 ....124 D1
MRDN SM4 ....225 H1
RCHPK/HAM TW10 ....180 D5
STNW/STAM N16 ....109 E3
SWFD E18 ....73 D1
THHTH CR7 ....228 C1
WALTH E17 ....90 C1
WAN E11 ....92 B5
Woodville St CHARL SE7 ....153 G4
Woodward Av HDN NW4 ....83 G2
Woodward Cl ESH/CLAY KT10 .238 B4
Woodwarde Rd EDUL SE22 ...189 E1
Woodwards Gdns DAGW RM9 ..116 A5
STAN HA7 ....60 A5
Woodward Rd DAGW RM9 ....115 H5
Wood Wy ORP BR6 ....234 A6
Woodway Crs HRW HA1 ....80 C5
Woodwaye OXHEY WD19 ....42 A2
Woodwell St
WAND/EARL SW18 ....165 G6
Wood Whf GNWCH SE10 ....151 F6
Woodyard Cl KTTN NW5 ....106 C3
Woodyard La DUL SE21 ....189 E7
Woodyates Rd LEE/GVPK SE12 .192 C1
Woolacombe Rd
BKHTH/KID SE3 ....175 E3
Woolands Rd WAN E11 ....92 A6
Wooler St WALW SE17 ....31 G4
Woolf Cl THMD SE28 ....155 H1
Woolf Ms STPAN WC1H 5 E5
Woollaston Rd FSBYPK N4 ......88 B3
Woolmead Av CDALE/KGS NW9 ..85 E4
Woolmer Gdns UED N18 ....69 G2
Woolmer Rd UED N18 ....69 G1
Woolmore St POP/IOD E14 ....131 G6
Woolneigh St FUL/PGN SW6 ..165 F4
Wooiridge Wy HOM * E9 ....110 A5
Wool Rd RYNPK SW20 ....203 H3
Woolstaplers Wy
BERM/RHTH SE16 ....25 E6
Woolston Cl WALTH E17 ....70 B5
Woolstone Rd FSTH SE23 .....190 C4
Woolwich Church St
CHARL SE7 ....153 F4
Woolwich Common
WOOL/PLUM SE18 ....154 A6
Woolwich High St
WOOL/PLUM SE18 ....154 A3
Woolwich Manorway
CAN/RD E16 ....154 B2
Woolwich Manor Wy
EHAM E6 ....133 H3
Woolwich New Rd
WOOL/PLUM SE18 ....154 A5
Woolwich Rd ABYW SE2 ....156 C6
BXLYHN DA7 ....177 F4
CHARL SE7 ....154 E4
GNWCH SE10 ....151 H6
Wooster Gdns POP/IOD E14 ..131 H5
Wootton Gv FNCH N3 ....65 E1
Wootton St STHWK SE1 ....17 H3
Worbeck Rd PGE/AN SE20 ....209 H5
Worcester Av TOTM N17 ....70 C2
Worcester Cl CRICK NW2 ....103 G1
CROY/NA CRO 230 D6
MTCM CR4 ....229 E1
Worcester Ct WOT/HER KT12 .218 A6
Worcester Crs MLHL NW7 ....37 G3
WFD IG8 ....41 E6
Worcester Dr CHSWK W4 ....143 E3
Worcester Gdns IL IG1 ....95 C4
NTHLT UB5 ....79 E4
WPK KT4 ....241 E1
Worcester Ms
KIL/WHAMP NW6 ....105 F4
Worcester Park Rd WPK KT4 ..240 C1
Worcester Rd BELMT SM2 ....243 E5
MNPK E12 ....113 H1
WALTH E17 ....70 B5
WIM/MER SW19 ....204 D1
Wordsworth Av GFD/PVL UB6 ..119 F1
MNPK E12 ....113 C5
SWFD E18 ....91 E2
Wordsworth Dr CHEAM SM3 ..242 A2
Wordsworth Pde
CEND/HSY/T * N8 ....88 B1
Wordsworth Pl HAMP NW5 ...106 B3
Wordsworth Rd FELT TW13 ....178 D6
PGE/AN SE20 ....210 B5
STHWK SE1 ....33 G2
STNW/STAM N16 ....109 E2
WELL DA16 ....175 E2
WLGTN SM6 ....245 H4
Wordsworth Wk GLDGN NW11 ..84 D7
Worfield St BTSEA SW11 ....166 A1
Worgan St BERM/RHTH SE16 .150 B3
LBTH SE11 ....49 G5
Worland Rd SRTFD E15 ....112 A5
Worlds End La ORP BR6 ....253 G5
Worlds End La ORP BR6 ....253 G5
Worlds End Pas
WBPTN * SW10 ....165 H1
Worlidge St HMSMTH W6 .....144 A5
Worlingham Rd EDUL SE22 ...152 D6
Wormholt Rd SHB * W12 ....141 G1
Wormholt Ter SHB * W12 ....143 G1
Wormwood St LVPST EC2M ...16 A3
Wornington Rd NKENS W10 ...124 C4
Woronzow Rd STJWD NW8 ....105 H6
Worple Av ISLW TW7 ....160 D5
WIM/MER SW19 ....204 B3
Worple Cl RYLN/HDSTN HA2 ..78 D5
Worple Rd ISLW TW7 ....160 C5
RYNPK SW20 ....204 C3
Worple Road Ms
WIM/MER SW19 ....204 D2
Worple St MORT/ESHN SW14 .162 D4
Worple Wy RCHPK/HAM TW10 ..161 G1
RYLN/HDSTN HA2 ....78 D5
Worship St SDTCH EC2A 7 G6
Worslade Rd TOOT SW17 ......186 H5
Worsley Bridge Rd CAT SE6 ..210 D1
Worsley Rd WAN E11 ....112 A2
Worsopp Dr CLAP SW4 ....167 E3
Worth Cl ORP BR6 ....253 G5
Worthfield Cl HOR/WEW KT19 .240 D5
Worth Gv WALW SE17 ....51 G4
Worthing Cl SRTFD E15 ....112 H4
Worthing Rd HEST TW5 ....138 D6

Worthington Cl MTCM CR4 ....226 D1
Worthington Rd SURB KT6 ....221 H5
Wortley Rd CROY/NA CRO 228 A4
EHAM E6 ....113 F5
Worton Gdns ISLW TW7 ....159 H3
Worton Rd ISLW TW7 ....160 B4
Worton Wy ISLW TW7 ....159 H3
Wotton Rd CRICK NW2 ....104 A2
Wouldham Rd CAN/RD E16 ...132 B5
Wouldham Ter
STMC/STPC * BR5 ....215 H6
Wragby Rd WAN * E11 ....112 A2
Wrampling Pl ED N9 ....53 G4
Wray Av CLAY IG5 ....74 A6
Wray Crs FSBYPK N4 ....87 G6
Wrayfield Rd CHEAM SM3 .....242 B1
Wray Rd BELMT SM2 ....242 D6
Wraysbury Cl HSLWW TW4 ....158 C6
Wrekin Rd WOOL/PLUM SE18 .174 C1
Wren Av CRICK NW2 ....104 A2
NWDGN UB2 ....133 D4
Wren Cl CAN/RD E16 ....132 B5
ED N9 ....54 B3
STMC/STPC BR5 ....216 B6
Wren Crs BUSH WD23 ....43 G5
Wren Gdns DAGW RM9 ....116 B3
Wren Ms LEW * SE13 ....172 A5
Wren Rd CMBW SE5 ....168 D2
DAGW RM9 ....116 B3
SCUP DA14 ....196 A5
Wren St FSBYW WC1X 5 H5
Wrentham Av WLSDN NW10 ..120 A3
Wrenthorpe Rd BMLY BR1 .....192 A6
Wrexham Rd BOW E3 ....131 E1
Wricklemarsh Rd
BKHTH/KID SE3 ....172 D3
Wrigglesworth St NWCR SE14 .170 B1
Wright Cl LEW SE13 ....171 H5
Wrights Cl DAGE RM10 ....117 F2
Wright's La KENS W8 ....27 K3
KENS * W8 ....145 E3
Wrights Pl WLSDN * NW10 ...102 C4
Wright's Rd BOW E3 ....130 D1
SNWD SE25 ....209 E6
Wright's Rw CAR SM5 ....244 D2
Wrigley Cl CHING * E4 ....71 H1
Wrotham Rd BAR EN5 ....34 C3
CAMTN * NW1 ....107 E5
WEA W13 ....141 E1
WELL DA16 ....176 A2
Wrottesley Rd WLSDN NW10 .120 C1
WOOL/PLUM SE18 ....154 C6
Wroughton Rd BTSEA SW11 ..186 B1
Wroughton Ter HDN * NW4 .....83 H1
Wroxall Rd DAGW RM9 ....116 A4
Wroxham Gdns
FBAR/BDGN N11 ....67 E3
Wroxham Rd THMD SE28 ......136 B6
Wroxton Rd PECK SE15 ....169 H3
Wrythe Gn CAR SM5 ....244 B1
Wrythe Green Rd CAR SM5 ...244 B1
Wrythe La CAR SM5 ....225 H5
Wulfstan St SHB W12 ....123 F5
Wyatt Cl BUSH WD23 ....44 A2
FELT TW13 ....178 B3
Wyatt Dr BARN SW13 ....143 H6
Wyatt Park Rd
BRXS/STRHM SW2 ....187 H4
Wyatt Rd FSBYPK N4 ....108 C1
FSTGT E7 ....95 H5
Wyatt's La WALTH E17 ....71 G6
Wybert St CAMTN * NW1 ....3 H5
Wyborne Wy WLSDN NW10 ...102 C5
Wyburn Av BAR EN5 ....34 D4
Wyche Gv SAND/SEL CR2 .....246 C5
Wycherley Cl BKHTH/KID SE3 .172 B3
Wycherley Crs BAR EN5 ....49 F1
Wychwood Av EDGW HA8 ......61 F2
THHTH CR7 ....208 B6
Wychwood Cl EDGW HA8 ......61 F2
Wychwood End HGT N6 ....86 C2
Wychwood Gdns CLAY IG5 ......93 H5
Wycliffe Cl WELL DA16 ....175 F2
Wycliffe Rd BTSEA SW11 ......166 C3
WIM/MER SW19 ....205 F2
Wyclif St FSBYE EC1V 5 K4
Wycombe Gdns CRICK NW2 ...84 D6
Wycombe Pl
WAND/EARL * SW18 ....185 G1
Wycombe Rd ALP/SUD HA0 ..102 A4
GNTH/NBYPK IG2 ....72 B6
TOTM N17 ....69 G4
Wydell Cl MRDN SM4 ....224 A3
Wydenhurst Rd CROY/NA CRO .229 G4
Wydeville Manor Rd
LEE/GVPK SE12 ....192 D6
Wye Cl ORP BR6 ....216 C1
Wyemead Crs CHING E4 ....56 A4
Wye St BTSEA SW11 ....165 H4
Wyfields CLAY IG5 ....74 B4
Wyfold Rd FUL/PGN SW6 .....147 G2
Wyhill Gdns DAGW RM9 ....97 G5
Wyke Cl ISLW TW7 ....140 B6
Wyke Gdns HNWL W7 ....140 B3
Wykeham Av DAGW RM9 ....116 A4
Wykeham Cl WDR/YW UB7 ....132 C3
Wykeham Gn DAGW RM9 .....116 A4
Wykeham Hl WBLY HA9 ....62 A5
Wykeham Ri TRDG/WHET N20 ..48 D1
Wykeham Rd HDN NW4 ....64 A2
KTN/HRWW/W HA3 ....61 F1
Wyke Rd BOW E3 ....111 E5
RYNPK SW20 ....204 A5
Wyldes Cl GLDGN NW11 ....85 G1
Wyldfield Gdns ED N9 ....53 F4
Wyld Wy WBLY HA9 ....80 D4
Wyleu St FSTH SE23 ....190 C2
Wylie Rd NWDGN UB2 ....139 E3
Wyllen Cl WCHPL E1 ....130 A3
Wylo Dr BAR EN5 ....47 G1
Wymering Rd MV/WKIL W9 ...102 D5
Wymond St PUT/ROE SW15 ..164 A4
Wynan Rd POP/IOD E14 ....151 F5
Wynaud Ct WDGN N22 ....67 G4
Wyncham Av BFN/LL DA15 ....195 H5
Wynchgate KTN/HRWW/W HA3 ..60 D1
Wyncote Wy SAND/SEL CR2 ..248 B6
Wyncroft Cl BMLY BR1 ....213 H6

Wyndale Av CDALE/KGS NW9 ..82 A3
Wyndcliff Rd CHARL SE7 ....152 D6
Wyndcroft Cl ENC/FH EN2 ....38 B4
Wyndham Cl BELMT SM2 ......243 E5
ORP BR6 ....253 G1
Wyndham Crs CMBW SE5 ....168 C1
KTTN NW5 ....107 E1
Wyndham Est CMBW SE5 .....168 C1
Wyndham Ms MBLAR W1H 10 C2
Wyndham Pl MBLAR W1H 10 C2
Wyndham Rd CMBW SE5 ......168 C1
EBAR EN4 ....50 B3
EHAM E6 ....113 H5
KUTN/CMB KT2 ....201 H5
WEA W13 ....140 D5
Wyndham St MBLAR W1H 10 C1
Wyndham Yd MBLAR W1H 10 C2
Wynell Rd FSTH SE23 ....190 B5
Wynford Gv STMC/STPC BR5 .215 H6
Wynford Pl BELV DA17 ....157 E6
Wynford Rd IS N1 ....5 G1
Wynford Wy ELTH/MOT SE9 ..193 H5
Wynndale Rd SWFD E18 ....72 D4
Wynnstay Gdns KENS * W8 ....145 E3
Wynter St BTSEA SW11 ....165 G5
Wynton Gdns SNWD SE25 ....229 E2
Wynton Pl ACT W3 ....122 B1
Wynyard Ter LBTH SE11 ....29 H4
Wynyatt St FSBYE EC1V 6 C5
Wyre Gv EDGW HA8 ....46 C4
Wyresdale Crs GFD/PVL UB6 .120 B2
Wythburn Pl MBLAR W1H 10 D4
Wythenshawe Rd DAGE RM10 .117 E1
Wythes Cl BMLY BR1 ....213 H5
Wythes Rd CAN/RD E16 ....153 G1
Wythfield Rd ELTH/MOT SE9 ..193 H1
Wyvenhoe Rd
RYLN/HDSTN HA2 ....99 G1
Wyvern Cl ORP BR6 ....253 H1
Wyvern Est NWMAL * KT3 .....205 G6
Wyvil Rd VX/NE SW8 ....167 G1
Wyvis St POP/IOD E14 ....131 F4

Y

Yabsley St POP/IOD E14 ....151 G1
Yalding Gv STMC/STPC BR5 ...236 B1
Yale Rd BARM/RHTH SE16 ......25 E6
Yale Cl HSLWW TW4 ....158 D6
Yarborough Rd
WIM/MER SW19 ....205 H4
Yardley Cl CHING E4 ....41 F6
Yardley La CHING E4 ....41 F5
Yardley St FSBYW WC1X 6 A4
Yarmouth Crs WALTH E17 ....89 H2
Yarmouth Pl MYFR/PICC W1J ..10 D7
Yarnton Wy ERITH DA18 ....156 C2
Yarrow Crs EHAM E6 ....133 G4
Yateley St WOOL/PLUM SE18 .153 F5
Yeading Av RSLP HA4 ....78 A6
Yeading Fk YEAD UB4 ....118 A4
Yeames Cl WEA W13 ....120 C5
Yeate St IS N1 ....108 D5
Yeatman Rd HGT N6 ....86 B3
Yeats Cl BKHTH/KID * SE3 ....171 H3
WLSDN NW10 ....81 G3
Ye Cnr BUSH WD23 ....42 A3
Yeend Cl E/WMO/HCT KT8 ...219 E1
Yeldham Rd HMSMTH W6 .....147 F4
Yeldham Vls HMSMTH * W6 ...144 B5
Yelverton Rd BTSEA SW11 ....165 H5
Yenston Cl MRDN SM4 ....225 C3
Yeoman Cl EHAM E6 ....134 B6
Yeoman Rd NTHLT UB5 ....98 C5
Yeoman's Rw CHEL SW3 ....18 B6
Yeoman St BERM/RHTH SE16 .150 C4
Yeomans Wy EN * EN1 ....30 C5
Yeomen Wy BARK/HLT IG6 ......74 C2
Yeo St BOW E3 ....130 A4
Yeovil Cl ORP BR6 ....235 E6
Yeovilton Pl KUTN/CMB KT2 ...201 F1
Yerbury Rd ARCH N19 ....107 E1
Yester Dr CHST BR7 ....213 H3
Yester Pk CHST BR7 ....213 H3
Yester Rd CHST BR7 ....213 H3
Yew Cl BKHH IG9 ....57 F4
Yewdale Cl BMLY BR1 ....212 A2
Yewfield Rd WLSDN NW10 ......81 G5
Yew Gv CRICK NW2 ....104 B2
Yewtree Cl RYLN/HDSTN HA2 ..79 F1
Yew Tree Cl WCHMH N21 ....52 A2
WELL DA16 ....175 G2
WPK KT4 ....223 E5
Yew Tree Ct BORE WD6 ....45 F1
Yew Tree Gdns CHDH RM6 ......94 A5
ROMW/RG * RM7 ....97 H2
Yewtree Rd BECK BR3 ....210 D6
Yew Tree Rd SHB W12 ....123 F6
Yew Tree Wk HSLWW TW4 ....158 D1
Yew Wk HRW HA1 ....80 A5
Yoakley Rd STNW/STAM N16 ..89 H3
Yoke Cl HOLWY N7 ....107 C4
Yolande Gdns ELTH/MOT SE9 .173 G6
York Av BFN/LL DA15 ....195 G4
HNWL * W7 ....140 A1
KTN/HRWW/W HA3 ....43 G4
MORT/ESHN SW14 ....162 C6
York Br CAMTN NW1 ....3 F5
York Buildings CHCR WC2N 11 F6
York Cl CMBW * SE5 ....168 C5
EHAM E6 ....113 H5
HNWL W7 ....140 A1
MRDN SM4 ....225 F1
York Gdns WOT/HER KT12 ....218 B6
York Ga CAMTN NW1 ....3 F6
CFHL * N14 ....52 D1
York Gv PECK SE15 ....169 H1
York Hl STRHM/NOR SW16 ...188 D3
York House Pl KENS * W8 ....145 F3
York Ms IL IG1 ....94 A6
KTTN NW5 ....106 B1
York Pde BTFD TW8 ....141 F5
CDALE/KGS NW9 ....83 G3

York Pl *BTSEA* SW11 ....165 G4
  IL IG1 ....94 A6
York Rl *KTTN* NW5 ....106 D1
  ORP BR6 ....235 E5
York Rd *ACT* W3 ....122 C5
  BARK EN5 ....26 B4
  BELMT SM2 ....243 E4
  BTFD TW8 ....141 F5
  BTSEA SW11 ....165 G5
  CHING E4 ....71 E1
  CROY/NA CR0 ....228 A4
  EA W5 ....141 E3
  FBAR/BDGN N11 ....67 F2
  FSTGT E7 ....82 C2
  HSLW TW3 ....159 F4
  IL IG1 ....114 A1
  KUTN/CMB KT2 ....201 H3
  LEY E10 ....111 G1
  RAIN RM13 ....117 H5
  RCHPK/HAM TW10 ....161 H6
  STHWK SE1 ....21 H3
  TEDD TW11 ....180 A6
  UED N18 ....69 H1
  WALTH E17 ....90 B2
  WCHMH N21 ....52 D2
  WIM/MER SW19 ....205 F2
Yorkshire CI *STNW/STAM* N16 ....109 E1
Yorkshire Gdns *UED* N18 ....69 H1
Yorkshire Grey Yd
  HHOL * WC1V 13 G2
Yorkshire Rd *MTCM* CR4... ....227 G2
  POP/IOD E14... ....130 C5
York Sq *POP/IOD* * E14 ....130 C5
York St *BARK* IG11 ....114 B6
  MBLAR W1H 10 C2
  MHST W1U 10 D1
  MTCM CR4 ....226 C4
  TWK TW1 ....180 C3
York St Chambers
  MHST W1U 10 D1

York Ter *ENC/FH* EN2 ....38 C1
  ERITH DA8 ....177 G2
York Ter East *CAMTN* NW1 ....3 F6
York Ter West *CAMTN* NW1 ....3 E6
Yorkton St *BETH* E2 ....8 E1
York Wy *CHSGTN* KT9 ....239 G5
  FELT TW13 ....178 D5
  IS N1 ....5 F1
  TRDG/WHET N20 ....50 B5
York Way Cs *IS* N1 ....107 G6
York Way Est *HOLWY* N7 ....107 G4
Youngmans CI *ENC/FH* EN2... ....38 C2
Young St *KENS* W8 ....145 F2
Youngs Rd *GNTH/NBYPK* IG2 ....133 E5
Young St *KENS* W8 ....145 F2
Yoxley Ap *GNTH/NBYPK* IG2 ....94 D3
Yoxley Dr *GNTH/NBYPK* IG2 ....94 D3
Yukon Rd *BAL* SW12... ....186 D2
Yuletide CI *WLSDN* NW10 ....105 E4
Yunus Khan CI *WALTH* E17 ....91 E2

Zampa Rd *BERM/RHTH* SE16 ....150 A5
Zander Ct *BETH* E2... ....9 F3
Zangwill Rd *BERM/RHTH* SE3....173 F2
Zealand Rd *BOW* E5 ....130 C1
Zelah Rd *STMC/STPC* BR5 ....235 H4
Zennor Rd *BAL* SW12 ....187 E3
Zenoria St *EDUL* SE22 ....169 F5
Zermatt Rd *THHTH* CR7 ....228 C1
Zetland St *POP/IOD* E14 ....131 G4
Zion Pl *THHTH* CR7 ....228 D1
Zion Rd *THHTH* CR7 ....228 D1
Zoar St *STHWK* SE1 ....23 E1
Zoffany St *ARCH* N19 ....87 F6

Index - featured places

Aarotya Medical Centre
  TOTM N17 ....88 C1
Abbey Business Centre
  VX/NE SW8 ....167 E2
The Abbey Clinic
  ....156 D5
Abbey Industrial Estate
  ALP/SUD HA0 ....101 H6
  MTCM CR4... ....226 B2
Abbey Medical Centre
  STJWD NW8... ....105 F6
Abbey Mills
  WIM/MER SW19 ....205 G4
Abbey Park Industrial Estate
  BARK IG11 ....134 B1
Abbey Primary School
  ABYW SE2 ....156 A3
Abbey (rems of)
  ABYW SE2 ....155 H6
Abbey Road Health Centre
  SRTFD E15 ....112 A6
Abbey School for the English Language
  STJWD NW8... ....125 C1
Abbey Trading Estate
  SYD SE26 ....210 C1
Abbey Tutorial College
  BAY/PAD W2 ....125 E5
Abbey Wharf Industrial Estate
  BARK IG11 ....134 D2
Abbey Wood School
  ABYW SE2 ....155 G3
Abbotsbury First School
  MRDN SM4 ....225 F2
ABC Cinema
  CAT SE6 ....191 F3
  HAMP NW3 ....106 A3
  PUT/ROE SW15 ....164 C4
  STRHM/NOR SW16 ....187 G4
Abercorn Place School
  STJWD NW8... ....125 C1
Abercorn Trading Estate
  ALP/SUD HA0 ....101 F6
Aberdeen Wharf
  WAP E1W... ....25 H3
Abney Park Cemetery
  STNW/STAM N16 ....89 E6
Acacia Business Centre
  WAN E11 ....112 A1
Acland Burghley School
  KTTN NW5 ....106 D2
Acre Road Health Clinic
  KUTN/CMB KT2 ....201 H3
Acton Business Centre
  WLSDN NW10 ....122 D3
Acton Central Industrial Estate
  ACT W3 ....122 B6
Acton Health Centre
  ....142 C1
Acton High School
  ACT W3 ....142 A3
Acton Hospital
  ACT W3 ....142 A2
Acton Lane Medical Centre
  CHSWK W4 ....142 D2
Acton Park Industrial Estate
  ACT W3 ....143 F1
  CHSWK W4 ....142 D2
Acton Superbowl
  ACT W3 ....122 A5
Acton Swimming Baths
  ACT W3 ....142 C1
Acumen (Anglo School)
  NRWD SE19 ....209 E3
Adams Bridge Business Centre
  WBLY HA9 ....102 B3
Adamsrill Primary School
  SYD SE26 ....190 C5
Adath Yisroel Cemetery
  EN EN1 ....39 F2
The Addington Golf Club
  CROY/NA CR0 ....248 D6
Addington Palace Golf Club
  CROY/NA CR0 ....248 C4
Addiscombe Cricket Club
  CROY/NA CR0 ....247 F1
Addison Primary School
  WKENS W14 ....144 B3
Adelphi Theatre
  COVGDN WC2E 13 F6
Admiral Hyson Industrial Estate
  BERM/RHTH SE16 ....33 G2
Admiralty Arch
  STJS SW1Y 20 D1
ADT Technology College
  PUT/ROE SW15... ....164 D6
The Adult College of Barking & Dagenham
  BARK IG11 ....115 E4

Adult Education Centre
  POP/IOD E14 ....151 G3
Africa Centre
  COVGDN WC2E 13 F5
Agora Shopping Centre
  PECK SE15 ....169 G3
Ainslie Wood Primary School
  CHING E4 ....71 F1
Air Call Business Centre
  CDALE/KGS NW9... ....62 D6
Airedale Physiotherapy Clinic
  CHSWK W4 ....143 F5
Airlinks Golf Club
  NWDGN UB2 ....138 A4
Air Links Industrial Estate
  HEST TW5 ....138 A5
AIU London
  MHST W1U 11 F2
Aksaray Sports Centre
  STNW/STAM N16 ....108 D2
Albany Centre & Theatre
  DEPT SE8 ....170 D1
Albany Clinic
  BFN/LL DA15 ....195 G6
  WIM/MER SW19 ....205 F3
The Albany College
  HDN NW4... ....83 H2
Albany School Grant Maintained
  PEND EN3 ....40 B1
Albemarle Independant College
  BAY/PAD W2 ....125 F6
Albemarle Primary School
  WIM/MER SW19 ....184 C4
Albert Memorial
  SKENS SW7 ....145 H2
Albery Theatre
  CHCR WC2N 13 E5
Albion Health Centre
  WCHPL E1 ....17 H1
Albion Junior & Infant School
  BERM/RHTH SE16 ....150 A2
Albion Street Health Centre
  BERM/RHTH SE16 ....150 A2
The Alchemy Gallery
  CLKNW EC1R 6 A5
Alderbrook Primary School
  BAL SW12... ....186 D2
Aldersbrook County Secondary School
  MNPK E12 ....93 E5
Aldersbrook Primary School
  WAN E11 ....93 E5
Alderwood Primary School
  ELTH/MOT SE9 ....194 D1
Aldwych Theatre
  HOL/ALD WC2B... ....13 G4
Alexander Mcleod Primary School
  ABYW SE2 ....155 H5
Alexandra Avenue Clinic
  RYLN/HDSTN HA2 ....78 D6
Alexandra Business Centre
  PEND EN3 ....40 B5
Alexandra Infant School
  KUTN/CMB KT2 ....202 A3
Alexandra Junior School
  HSLW TW3 ....159 F3
  SYD SE26 ....210 B2
Alexandra Palace
  WDGN N22 ....67 F5
Alexandra Palace Ice Rink
  WDGN N22 ....67 F5
Alexandra Primary School
  WDGN N22 ....67 H5
Alexandra School
  RYLN/HDSTN HA2 ....78 D6
Alfred Mizen First School
  MTCM CR4 ....207 F6
Alfred Salter Primary School
  BERM/RHTH SE16 ....150 B2
Alfreds Way Industrial Estate
  BARK IG11 ....115 G6
Allegory Clinic
  CAVSO/HST W1G... ....11 G3
Allenby Infant School
  GFD/PVL UB6 ....119 E5
Allen Edwards Primary School
  CLAP SW4 ....167 G2
The All England Lawn Tennis & Croquet Club
  WIM/MER SW19 ....184 B5
Alleyns School
  EDUL SE22 ....169 E6
Allfarthing JMI School
  WAND/EARL SW18 ....185 G1
All Saints Benhilton School
  SUT SM1 ....243 F1
All Saints Catholic School
  BCTR RM8 ....97 E5
All Saints CE First School
  WIM/MER SW19 ....205 G3

All Saints CE Junior School
  NRWD SE19 ....209 E4
All Saints CE Primary School
  BKHTH/KID SE3 ....172 A3
  CRICK NW2 ....104 D1
  FUL/PGN SW6 ....164 C5
  PUT/ROE SW15 ....164 A4
  TRDG/WHET N20 ....49 H4
All Souls CE Primary School
  GTPST W1W 12 A2
Allum Medical Centre
  WAN E11 ....91 H4
Alma Junior & Infant School
  BERM/RHTH SE16 ....33 E1
Alma Primary School
  PEND EN3 ....40 C6
Almeida Theatre
  IS N1 ....108 B5
Al Muntada Islamic School
  FUL/PGN SW6 ....164 D2
Alperton Cemetery
  ALP/SUD HA0 ....101 F6
Alperton Community School
  ALP/SUD HA0 ....101 G5
Alperton High School
  ALP/SUD HA0 ....101 F6
Alperton Sports Ground
  ALP/SUD HA0 ....121 F1
Alpha Business Centre
  WALTH E17 ....90 C2
Alpine Business Centre
  EHAM E6 ....134 A4
Alscot Road Industrial Estate
  STHWK SE1 ....32 D1
Altmore Infant School
  EHAM E6 ....113 H5
The Alton School
  PUT/ROE SW15 ....183 F2
Ambler Primary School
  FSBYPK N4 ....108 B1
Ambleside Junior School
  WOT/HER KT12 ....218 A5
AMC Business Centre
  WLSDN NW10 ....122 B2
AMF Bowling
  LEW SE13 ....171 G4
Amherst Primary School
  HACK E8... ....109 G3
Ampthill Square
  Medical Centre
  CAMTN NW1 ....4 A2
Amy Johnson Primary School
  WLGTN SM6 ....245 G5
Anchorage Point Industrial Estate
  CHARL SE7 ....153 E5
Anchor Retail Park
  WCHPL E1 ....130 A3
Andover Medical Centre
  HOLWY N7 ....107 H1
The Andrew Ewing Primary School
  HEST TW5 ....158 D1
Anerley Primary School
  PGE/AN SE20 ....209 G4
Anerley School
  PGE/AN SE20 ....209 G4
Angerstein Business Park
  GNWCH SE10 ....152 C4
Angerstein Works
  BKHTH/KID SE3 ....152 C6
Anglian Industrial Estate
  BARK IG11 ....135 F3
Animal Cemetery
  REDBR IG4 ....73 F6
Annandale Primary School
  GNWCH SE10 ....152 D5
The Anna Scher Theatre
  IS N1 ....108 A6
Annemount School
  EFNCH N2 ....85 G3
Annunciation RC Infant School
  EDGW HA8 ....62 D4
The Annunciation RC Junior School
  EDGW HA8... ....62 D2
Anson Primary School
  CRICK NW2 ....104 B3
Ante Natal Clinic
  MUSWH N10 ....66 C6
Anton Junior Infant Estate
  WLSDN NW10 ....123 F3
Apex Retail Park
  FELT TW13 ....178 D5
Apollo Theatre
  SOHO/SHAV W1D 12 C5
Apollo Victoria Theatre
  PIM SW1V 20 A6
Apostolic Nuncio
  WIM/MER SW19 ....184 A5

Applegarth Primary School
  CROY/NA CR0 ....249 F4
Apsley House, the Wellington Museum
  BAY/PAD W2... ....19 E3
Aquarius Business Park
  CRICK NW2 ....83 G5
Aquarius Golf Club
  EDUL SE22 ....170 A6
Arcadia Shopping Centre
  EA W5 ....121 F6
The Archbishop Lanfranc School
  CROY/NA CR0... ....227 G3
Archbishop Michael Ramsey Technology College
  CMBW SE5 ....168 B1
Archbishop Sumners CE Primary School
  LBTH SE11 ....30 B2
Archbishop Tenisons CE School
  CROY/NA CR0 ....247 F1
Archbishop Tenison's School
  RYLN/HDSTN HA2 ....29 H6
Archdale Business Centre
  RYLN/HDSTN HA2... ....79 G6
Archdeacon Cambridge's CE Primary School
  WHTN TW2 ....180 A4
Arches Business Centre
  NWDGN UB2 ....138 D2
Arches Leisure Centre
  GNWCH SE10 ....151 H6
Archgate Business Centre
  NFNCH/WDSP N12 ....65 G1
Archway Business Centre
  ARCH N19 ....107 F1
Arena Estate
  FSBYPK N4 ....88 B3
Argyle Primary School
  STPAN WC1H... ....5 E3
Arklow Trading Estate
  NWCR SE14 ....150 C6
Armchair Theatre
  LBTH SE11 ....30 A5
Armourers & Braziers' Hall
  LOTH EC2R... ....15 G2
Arndale Health Centre
  WAND/EARL SW18 ....185 E1
Arnhem Wharf Primary School
  POP/IOD E14 ....150 D3
Arnold House School
  STJWD NW8... ....125 H1
Arnot Abbey
  FARR EC1M... ....14 C1
Arsenal FC (Highbury)
  HBRY N5 ....108 A1
Art College
  LBTH SE11 ....30 C4
Arts Centre
  BMLY BR1 ....213 F4
  HAMP NW3 ....105 F3
Art School
  BECK BR3 ....230 C2
Arts Theatre
  LSO/SEVD WC2H... ....12 D5
  PUT/ROE SW15 ....164 B5
Ashbourne Independent Sixth Form College
  KENS W8 ....145 F2
Ashburnham Primary School
  WBPTN SW10 ....165 H1
Ashburton High School
  CROY/NA CR0 ....229 H4
Ashburton Primary School
  CROY/NA CR0 ....229 H3
Ashby Mill School
  CLAP SW4 ....167 G6
Ashfield Junior School
  BUSH WD23... ....43 F2
Ashgrove College
  WALTH E17 ....71 E6
Ashgrove Estate
  BMLY BR1 ....211 H2
Ashgrove School
  BMLY BR1 ....212 D5
Ashleigh Commercial Estate
  CHARL SE7 ....153 E4
Ashmead Primary School
  BROCKY SE4 ....171 G3
Ashmole Primary School
  VX/NE SW8 ....29 H6
Ashmole School
  STHGT/OAK N14 ....51 E3
Ashmount Primary School
  ARCH N19 ....87 E4
Ashton House School
  ISLW TW7... ....159 H2
Ashton Playing Fields Track
  WFD IG8 ....73 G2
Aspen House School
  CMBW SE5 ....30 C6

Aspen House Secondary &
  Primary School
  BRXS/STRHM SW2 .... 187 G2
Asquith Court School
  KTN/HRWW/W HA3 ...... 80 D3
Asquith School
  PEND EN5 .... 40 A5
Assembly Rooms
  KUT KT1 .... 221 G1
Associated Newspapers
  BERM/RHTH SE16 .... 150 B3
Aston Clinic
  NWMAL KT3 .... 223 E1
Aston House School
  EA W5 .... 121 F5
Asylum Medical Centre
  CEND/HSY/T N8 .... 68 A6
Athelney Primary School
  CAT SE6 .... 191 G5
Athelstan House School
  HPTN TW12 .... 199 E4
Athena Medical Centre
  CLPT E5 .... 110 A2
Atherton Leisure Centre
  FSTGT E7 .... 112 B4
Athlone House Hospital
  HGT N6 .... 86 B5
Athlon Industrial Estate
  ALP/SUD HA0 .... 121 F1
Atkinson Morley Hospital
  RYNPK SW20 .... 203 H3
Atlas Business Centre
  CRICK NW2 .... 83 H6
Atlas Transport Estate
  BTSEA SW11 .... 165 G3
Auriol Junior School
  HOR/WEW KT19 .... 241 F2
Australia House
  HOL/ALD WC2B 13 H4
Aveling Park School
  WALTH E17 .... 71 E5
Avenue Industrial Estate
  CHING E4 .... 70 D2
Avenue Primary School
  KIL/WHAMP NW6 .... 104 C5
  MNPK E12 .... 113 G2
Avigdor Primary School
  STNW/STAM N16 .... 88 D6
Avondale Park
  Primary School
  NTGHL W11 .... 124 B6
Avon House School
  WFD IG8 .... 56 C6
Avon Trading Estate
  WKENS W14 .... 144 D4
Axis Business Centre
  SRTPD E15 .... 111 F6
The Aylesham Centre
  PECK SE15 .... 169 G2
Aylward First &
  Middle Schools
  STAN HA7 .... 61 F1
Aylward School
  UED N18 .... 52 D6
Aylwin Girls School
  BERM/RHTH SE16 .... 32 D1
Babington House School
  CHST BR7 .... 213 H2
Back Care Clinic
  WPK KT4 .... 223 G5
Bacons City
  Technology College
  BERM/RHTH SE16 .... 150 B2
Bacon's College
  BERM/RHTH SE16 .... 150 C1
Baden Powell House
  SKENS SW7 .... 145 G3
Baden Powell
  Primary School
  CLPT E5 .... 109 H1
Bakers Hall
  MON EC3R......................... 16 B6
Balaam Leisure Centre
  PLSTW E13 .... 132 C3
Bales College
  NKENS W10 .... 124 B2
Balfour Business Centre
  NWDGN UB2 .... 138 B3
Balgowan Primary School
  BECK BR3 .... 210 C5
Balham Health Centre
  BAL SW12 .... 186 D4
Balmoral Trading
  BARK IG11 .... 135 F4
Baltic Exchange
  HDTCH EC3A 16 B3
Bancrofts School
  WFD IG8 .... 56 C5
Bandon Hill Cemetery
  WLGTN SM6 .... 245 F3
Bandon Hill Primary School
  WLGTN SM6 .... 245 F4
Bangabandhu
  Primary School
  BETH E2 .... 130 A2
Bank of England
  LOTH EC2V 15 G4
Bank of England Extension
  STP EC4M 15 G4
Bank of England Museum
  LOTH EC2R 15 G4
Bankside Jetty
  STHWK SE1 .... 15 E6
Bankside Park
  Industrial Estate
  BARK IG11 .... 135 G2
Bannister Stadium
  KTN/HRWW/W HA3 ...... 59 G2
Bannockburn
  Primary School
  WOOL/PLUM SE18 .... 155 F4
Banqueting House
  WHALL SW1A 21 E2
Barber Surgeons' Hall
  BARB EC2Y 15 F2
Barbican Cinema
  BARB EC2Y 15 E1
The Barbican
  BARB EC2Y 15 E1

Barbican Theatre
  BARB EC2Y 15 F1
Barclay Junior & Infant School
  LEY E10 .... 91 H3
Barham Primary School
  ALP/SUD HA0 .... 101 E4
Baring Primary School
  LEE/GVPK SE12 .... 192 C2
Baring Road Medical Centre
  LEE/GVPK SE12 .... 192 C4
Barkantine Clinic
  POP/IOD E14................. 151 E2
Barking Abbey
  Comprehensive School
  BARK IG11 .... 114 D3
  BARK IG11 .... 115 F4
Barking Abbey
  Industrial Estate
  BARK IG11 .... 114 B6
Barking College
  ROMW/RG RM7 .... 97 H6
Barking FC
  BCTR RM8 .... 115 H5
Barking Hospital
  BARK IG11 .... 115 F5
Barking Industrial Park
  BARK IG11 .... 115 F6
Barking RUFC
  DAGW RM9 .... 116 B6
Barkingside Cemetery
  BARK/HLT IG6 .... 74 B6
Barkingside FC
  BARK/HLT IG6 .... 94 D1
Barlby Primary School
  NKENS W10 .... 124 B3
Barley Lane Primary School
  GDMY/SEVK IG3............ 95 G4
Barnabas Medical Centre
  NTHLT UB5 .... 95 G4
Barn Croft Primary School
  WALTH E17 .... 90 C3
Barnehurst Primary School
  BXLYHN DA7 .... 177 G2
Barnehurst Public Day &
  Play Golf Club
  BXLYHN DA7 .... 177 H4
Barn Elms Athletics Track
  BARN SW13 .... 163 H3
Barn Elms
  Water Sports Centre
  BARN SW13 .... 164 A3
Barnes Hospital
  MORT/ESHN SW14 .... 163 E4
Barnes Sports Club
  BARN SW13 .... 163 F2
Barnet College
  BAR EN5 .... 34 D5
  NFNCH/WDSP N12 .... 65 G1
Barnet Copthall Stadium
  HDN NW4 .... 64 A4
Barnet County Court
  BAR EN5 .... 35 G5
  FNCH N3 .... 65 E4
Barnet FC (Underhill)
  BAR EN5 .... 35 E6
Barnet General Hospital
  BAR EN5 .... 34 B5
Barnet Health Centre
  BAR EN5 .... 35 E6
Barnet Hill JMI School
  BAR EN5 .... 34 D6
Barnet Hospital Chest Clinic
  BAR EN5 .... 34 B5
Barnet Magistrates Court
  BAR EN5 .... 34 D5
Barnet Museum
  BAR EN5 .... 34 C5
Barnet Trading Estate
  BAR EN5 .... 34 D4
Barnfield Primary School
  EDGW HA8 .... 62 C4
Banhill Community
  High School
  YEAD UB4 .... 118 A2
Barnsbury School for Girls
  IS N1 .... 108 A4
Barons Court Theatre
  WKENS W14 .... 144 C5
Barratt Industrial Park
  BOW E3 .... 131 G3
Barrett Industrial Park
  STHL UB1 .... 139 E1
Barrett Way Industrial Estate
  HRW HA1 .... 61 H1
Barrington Primary School
  WELL DA16 .... 176 B3
Barrow Hedges
  Primary School
  CAR SM5 .... 244 A5
Barrow Hill Junior School
  STJWD NW8 .... 2 A2
Barton House Health Centre
  STNW/STAM N16 .... 108 D1
Barwell Business Park
  CHSGTN KT9 .... 239 F5
Baston School
  HAYES BR2 .... 232 D6
Bath Factory Estate
  HNHL SE24 .... 188 C1
Battersea Business Centre
  BTSEA SW11 .... 166 C4
Battersea Dogs' Home
  VX/NE SW8 .... 166 D1
Battersea Power Station
  VX/NE SW8 .... 27 H6
Battersea Sports Centre
  BTSEA SW11 .... 165 H4
Battersea Technology College
  BTSEA SW11 .... 166 B2
Battersea Tutorial College
  TOOT SW17 .... 186 C4
BBC Studios
  MV/WKIL W9 .... 101 G3
BBC Television Centre
  SHB W12 .... 124 A6
Beacon House School
  EA W5 .... 141 H1
Beal High School
  REDBR IG4 .... 73 G6

Beam Primary School
  DAGE RM10 .... 137 G1
Beatrice Tate Special School
  BETH E2 .... 9 H3
Beatrix Potter Primary School
  WAND/EARL SW18 .... 185 G3
Beauclerc Infant School
  SUN TW16 .... 198 A6
Beaumont Primary School
  LEY E10 .... 91 F4
Beaver College
  BAY/PAD W2 .... 125 E6
The Beavers Community
  Primary School
  HSLWW TW4 .... 158 A4
Beaverwood School for Girls
  CHST BR7 .... 215 E2
Beckenham Business Centre
  BECK BR3 .... 210 C2
Beckenham Crematorium
  SNWD SE25 .... 210 A6
Beckenham Cricket Club
  BECK BR3 .... 211 F3
Beckenham Hospital
  BECK BR3 .... 210 D5
Beckenham Leisure Centre
  BECK BR3 .... 210 C4
Beckenham Place Park
  Golf Course
  BECK BR3 .... 211 F2
Beckenham RFC
  BECK BR5 .... 230 C1
Beckenham Town FC
  BECK BR3 .... 231 E2
Beckford Primary School
  KIL/WHAMP NW6 .... 104 D3
Beckmead School
  BECK BR3 .... 231 E5
Beckton Ski Centre
  EHAM E6 .... 134 A3
Beckton Special School
  CAN/RD E16 .... 133 F4
Beckton Triangle Retail Park
  EHAM E6 .... 134 B2
Becontree Day Hospital
  BCTR RM8 .... 96 C6
Becontree Primary School
  BCTR RM8 .... 115 H1
Bective House Clinic
  PUT/ROE SW15 .... 164 D5
Beddington Infants School
  WLGTN SM6 .... 245 E1
Beddington Medical Centre
  CROY/NA CR0 .... 245 G2
Beddington Park
  Primary School
  WLGTN SM6 .... 245 G1
Beddington Trading Estate
  CROY/NA CR0 .... 227 G5
Bedelsford School
  KUT KT1 .... 201 G6
Bedensfield Clinic
  SCUP DA14 .... 216 C1
Bedington Infant School
  WLGTN SM6 .... 245 E2
Bedonwell Clinic
  ABYW SE2 .... 156 C6
Bedonwell Medical Centre
  BELV DA17 .... 156 D5
Bedonwell Primary School
  BELV DA17 .... 156 C6
Beecholme First School
  MTCM CR4 .... 206 D4
Beis Rochel D'Satmar
  Girls School
  STNW/STAM N16 .... 89 E4
Beis Yaakov Primary School
  CDALE/KGS NW9 .... 62 D6
Bellamy's Wharf
  WAP E1W 150 B1
Bellenden Primary School
  PECK SE15 .... 169 G4
Bellenden Road
  Business Centre
  PECK SE15 .... 169 F3
Bellenden Road Retail Park
  PECK SE15 .... 169 F2
Belleville Primary School
  BTSEA SW11 .... 166 B6
Belle Vue Cinema
  EDGW HA8 .... 62 A2
  WLSDN NW10 .... 103 H5
Bell Industrial Estate
  CHSWK W4 .... 142 C4
Bellingham Trading Estate
  CAT SE6 .... 191 F5
Bell Lane JMI School
  HDN NW4 .... 84 B1
Belmont First &
  Middle School
  KTN/HRWW/W HA3 .... 60 B5
Belmont Junior & Infant School
  WDGN N22 .... 68 C4
Belmont (Mill Hill Junior School)
  MLHL NW7 .... 47 G5
Belmont Park School
  LEY E10 .... 91 G3
Belmont Primary School
  BXLYHN DA7 .... 177 E1
  CHSWK W4 .... 142 D4
Belsize Day Hospital
  WLSDN NW10 .... 103 G6
Belvedere Industrial Estate
  BELV DA17 .... 157 H1
Belvedere Link Business Park
  BELV DA17 .... 157 G3
Belvedere Primary School
  BELV DA17 .... 157 F4
Belvue Business Centre
  NTHLT UB5 .... 99 F5
Belvue School
  NTHLT UB5 .... 96 E6
Ben Jonson Primary School
  WCHPL E1 .... 130 C3
Bensham Manor School
  THHTH CR7 .... 228 C2
Benson Primary School
  CROY/NA CR0 .... 248 C1
Bentalls Shopping Centre
  KUT KT1 .... 201 F5

Benthal Primary School
  STNW/STAM N16 .... 109 G1
Bentley Wood Girls School
  STAN HA7 .... 60 B1
Bentworth Primary School
  SHB W12 .... 123 H5
Benwood School
  STHWK SE1 .... 23 G4
Berger Primary School
  HOM E9 .... 110 B4
Berkeley Primary School
  HEST TW5 .... 138 B6
Berlitz Schools of Languages
  LINN WC1V 13 H2
Bermondsey Town Hall
  STHWK SE1 .... 24 D6
Bermondsey Trading Estate
  BERM/RHTH SE16 .... 150 A4
Berrymede Junior School
  ACT W3 .... 142 B2
Bertram House School
  TOOT SW17 .... 186 C4
Bessemer Grange J & I School
  CMBW SE5 .... 169 G5
Bessemer Park
  Industrial Estate
  HNHL SE24 .... 168 B5
Bethlem Royal Hospital
  BECK BR3 .... 231 E4
Bethnal Green
  Museum of Childhood
  BETH E2 .... 9 H3
Bethnal Green
  Technology College
  BETH E2 .... 8 D4
Beulah Junior & Infant School
  THHTH CR7 .... 208 C5
Beverley School
  NWMAL KT3 .... 223 G2
Beverley Trading Estate
  MRDN SM4 .... 224 B4
Bevington Primary School
  NKENS W10 .... 124 C4
Bexley College
  ERITH DA8 .... 158 B6
  ERITH DA8 .... 157 G4
Bexley Cricket Club
  BXLY DA5 .... 197 E3
Bexley Erith Technical
  High School
  BXLY DA5 .... 197 E1
Bexley Grammar School
  WELL DA16 .... 175 H5
Bexleyheath Centre
  BXLYHS DA6 .... 176 C5
Bexleyheath Golf Club
  BXLYHS DA6 .... 176 C6
Bexleyheath School
  BXLYHN DA7 .... 177 E4
Bexley RFC
  BXLY DA5 .... 197 E2
BFI London IMAX Cinema
  STHWK SE1 .... 21 H2
Bickley Park Cricket Club
  BMLY BR1 .... 213 G5
Bickley Park Prep School
  BMLY BR1 .... 213 F6
Bickley Park School
  BMLY BR1 .... 213 G6
Big Ben
  WEST SW1P 21 F4
Bigland Green Primary School
  WCHPL E1 .... 104 C6
Billingsgate Fish Market
  POP/IOD E14................. 151 F1
Birch Court Colindale Hospital
  CDALE/KGS NW9 .... 63 E5
Birchwood Country
  Primary School
  SWLY BR8 .... 217 H1
Birchwood Park Golf Club
  RDART DA2 .... 217 G3
Birkbeck College
  STPAN WC1H 4 C5
Birkbeck Primary School
  SCUP DA14 .... 195 H5
Bishop Challoner Girls School
  WCHPL E1 .... 17 F5
Bishop Challoner RC
  Secondary School
  WCHPL E1 .... 130 A5
Bishop Challoner School
  HAYES BR2 .... 211 H5
Bishop Douglas RC School
  EFNCH N2 .... 65 G5
Bishop Gilpin Primary School
  WIM/MER SW19 .... 204 D1
Bishop John Robinson
  CE Primary
  THMD SE28 .... 136 A6
Bishop Perrin CE
  Primary School
  WHTN TW2 .... 179 F2
Bishopsgate Institute
  WCHPL E1 .... 16 B2
Bishop Stopford School
  EN EN1 .... 39 H1
Bishop Thomas Grant School
  STRHM/NOR SW16 .... 207 H1
Bittacy Business Centre
  MLHL NW7 .... 64 C2
Blackfen School for Girls
  BFN/LL DA15 .... 195 H1
Blackfriars Millennium Pier
  EMB EC4Y 11 H6
Blackfriars Pier
  BLKFR EC4V 14 D5
Blackfriars Station
  BLKFR EC4V 14 C5
Blackheath Bluecoat
  CE School
  BKHTH/KID SE3 .... 172 D1
Blackheath Business Estate
  GNWCH SE10 .... 171 G2
The Blackheath Clinic
  BKHTH/KID SE3 .... 172 C5
Blackheath High School GDST
  BKHTH/KID SE3 .... 172 B3
Blackheath High Senior School
  BKHTH/KID SE3 .... 172 C1

Blackheath Hospital
BKHTH/KID SE3......... 172 B4
Blackwall Trading Estate
POP/IOD E14.............. 131 H4
Blaire Peach School
STHL UB1 .... 138 B1
Blake College
GTPST W1W.................. 12 A1
Blanche Neville School
WDGN N22 .... 68 A4
Blenheim Business Centre
MTCM CR4................... 206 B4
Blenheim Junior &
Infant School
ORP BR6 .... 236 A6
Blenheim Shopping Centre
PGE/AN SE20................ 210 A3
Blessed Dominic RC
Primary School
CDALE/KGS NW9............... 63 E5
Blessed John Roche
Catholic School
POP/IOD E14................ 131 E5
Blessed Sacrament RC
Primary School
IS N1 .... 107 H6
Blood Transfusion Centre
EDGW HA8.................... 62 B3
Bloomfield Clinic (Guys Hospital)
STHWK SE1 .... 23 H3
Bloomsbury College
FUL/PGN SW6............... 165 E1
Bloomsbury Theatre
STPAN WC1H.................. 4 C5
Blossoms Inn Medical Centre
BLKFR EC4V.................. 15 F5
Blue Gate Fields
Primary School
WCHPL E1 .... 130 A6
Bmi Medical Centre
CAVSQ/HST W1G.............. 11 F2
Bnois Jerusalem School
STNW/STAM N16.............. 88 D4
The Bob Hope Theatre
ELTH/MOT SE9.............. 193 H1
Bodywise Natural
Health Centre
BETH E2.................... 130 A2
Boleyn Cinema
EHAM E6 .... 133 F1
Bolingbroke Hospital
BTSEA SW11................ 166 A6
Bolingbroke Primary School
BTSEA SW11................ 165 H2
Bond First School
MTCM CR4.................. 206 B5
Bond Road School
MTCM CR4.................. 206 B5
Bonner Primary School
BETH E2................... 130 B1
Bonneville Primary School
CLAP SW4.................. 187 E1
Bonus Pastor School
BMLY BR1 .... 192 A6
Booster Cushion Theatre
WDGN N22 .... 67 H5
Borough Market
STHWK SE1 .... 23 G1
Boston Business Park
NWDGN UB2................. 140 A3
Boston University
ECT SW5................... 145 G4
Boundary Business Park
MTCM CR4................. 205 H5
Bounds Green Health Centre
FBAR/BDGN N11............. 67 F3
Bounds Green Industrial Estate
FBAR/BDGN N11............. 67 G2
Bounds Green Primary School
FBAR/BDGN N11............. 67 G3
Bourne CP School
RSLP HA4.................... 98 A3
Bourne Hall Health Centre
EW KT17................... 241 F6
Bourne Road Industrial Park
DART DA1.................. 177 H6
Bourneside Sports Club
STHGT/OAK N14.............. 51 G3
Bousfield Primary School
ECT SW5.................. 145 F5
Boutcher CE Primary School
STHWK SE1 .... 24 C6
Bowater House
SKENS SW7................. 18 C4
Bow County Court
SRTFD E15................ 112 B4
Bow County Secondary School
BOW E3................... 131 E2
Bowden House Clinic
HRW HA1.................... 80 A6
Bowes Primary School
FBAR/BDGN N11............. 67 F1
Bowes Road Clinic
FBAR/BDGN N11............. 67 E1
Bow Industrial Park
SRTFD E15................ 111 E5
Bowman Trading Estate
CDALE/KGS NW9............. 62 B4
Bow Street Magistrates Court
HOL/ALD WC2B.............. 13 F4
Bow Triangle Business Centre
BOW E3................... 131 E3
Boxgrove Primary School
ABYW SE2................. 156 A3
Boys' Club
EDGW HA8................... 62 A3
Brackenbury Health Centre
HMSMTH W6................ 143 H3
Brackenbury Primary School
HMSMTH W6................ 143 H3
Bracken Industrial Estate
BARK/HLT IG6.............. 75 F3
Brady Recreation Centre
WCHPL E1 .... 17 E1
Braeside Junior School
BKHH IG9.................. 57 E3
Braeside Senior School
BKHH IG9.................. 56 D3
Braincroft Primary School
CRICK NW2................ 103 F1

Bramah Tea & Coffee Museum
STHWK SE1 .... 24 D3
Brampton Manor School
PLSTW E13................ 133 F3
Brampton Primary School
EHAM E6.................. 133 G2
Brampton Primary School
WELL DA16................ 176 B3
Brandlehow Primary School
PUT/ROE SW15............. 164 D5
Branollys Health Centre
PLSTW E13................ 132 C3
Breaside Pre Prep School
BMLY BR1 .... 212 C3
Brecknock Primary School
HOLWY N7................. 107 F4
Bredinghurst School
PECK SE15................ 170 A5
Brent Adult College
WLSDN NW10................ 102 D6
Brent Arts Council
WLSDN NW10................ 103 C1
Brent Child & Family Clinic
WLSDN NW10................ 103 F3
Brent Cross Shopping Centre
HDN NW4................... 84 A4
Brentfield Medical Centre
WLSDN NW10............... 102 D4
Brentfield Primary School
WLSDN NW10............... 102 D4
Brentford Business Centre
BTFD TW8................. 161 E1
The Brentford Clinic
BTFD TW8................. 141 G6
Brentford County Court
BTFD TW8................. 161 F1
Brentford FC (Griffin Park)
BTFD TW8................. 141 F6
Brentford Fountain
Leisure Centre
CHSWK W4................. 142 A5
Brentford Health Centre
BTFD TW8................. 141 E6
Brentford Medical Centre
BTFD TW8................. 161 F1
Brentford School for Girls
BTFD TW8................. 141 F6
Brent Knoll School
SYD SE26................. 190 B5
Brent Magistrates
Court House
WLSDN NW10............... 103 E4
Brentside First School
HNWL W7.................. 120 A4
Brentside High School
HNWL W7.................. 120 A3
Brentside Primary School
HNWL W7.................. 120 A3
Brent Trading Estate
WLSDN NW10............... 103 E3
Brent Valley Golf Club
HNWL W7.................. 120 A6
Brentwaters Business Park
BTFD TW8................. 161 E1
Brewers' Hall
CITYW EC2V................. 15 F2
Brewery Industrial Estate
IS N1..................... 7 E2
Brewery Mews
Business Centre
ISLW TW7................. 160 B4
Brick Lane Music Hall
SDTCH EC2A................. 8 B4
Brick Lane Music House
WCHPL E1.................. 8 D6
Bricklayer Arms
Industrial Estate
STHWK SE1................ 32 C2
The Bridewell Theatre
EMB EC4V................. 14 C4
The Bridge Business Centre
NWDGN UB2............... 139 E2
Bridge Lane Theatre
BTSEA SW11.............. 166 A2
Brigham Young University
BAY/PAD W2.............. 125 E6
Bright Sparks
Montessori School
WKENS W14............... 144 B2
Bright Sparks School
STRHM/NOR SW16.......... 187 G6
Brigstock Medical Centre
THHTH CR7............... 228 B2
Brimsdown Industrial Estate
PEND EN3................. 40 A3
Brimsdown Primary School
PEND EN3................. 40 B4
Brindishe Primary School
LEE/GVPK SE12........... 172 B6
Britannia Business Centre
CRICK NW2............... 104 B2
Britannia Sports Ground
WALTH E17................ 71 E3
Britannia Village
Primary School
CAN/RD E16.............. 152 D1
British Airways London Eye
WHALL SW1A............... 21 F3
British Dental Association
CAVSQ/HST W1G............ 11 G2
British Friends of
Diaspora Museum
KTTN NW5................ 106 C4
British Library
CAMTN NW1.................. 4 D3
British Library
Newspaper Library
CDALE/KGS NW9............. 63 E6
British Medical Association
STPAN WC1H................. 4 D5
British Museum
RSQ WC1B.................. 13 E2
British Telecom Tower
GTPST W1W.................. 12 A1
The Brit School
SNWD SE25............... 228 D3
Brixton Academy
BRXN/ST SW9............. 168 A4
Brixton College for
Further Education
BRXS/STRHM SW2.......... 167 H6

Brixton Recreation Centre
BRXN/ST SW9............. 168 A4
Broadfields Infant School
EDGW HA8.................. 46 A4
Broadfields Junior School
EDGW HA8.................. 46 B4
Broadgate
LVPST EC2M................ 15 H1
Broadgate Ice Arena
LVPST EC2M................ 16 A2
Broadhurst School
KIL/WHAMP NW6........... 105 G5
Broadmead Primary School
CROY/NA CRO............. 228 D3
Broadwalk Shopping Centre
EDGW HA8.................. 62 A2
Broadwater Farm
Primary School
TOTM N17.................. 68 D5
Broadwater Primary School
TOOT SW17............... 185 H6
Broadway Clinic
EDGW HA8.................. 62 B4
Broadway Retail Park
CRICK NW2................ 104 B2
Broadway Shopping Centre
BXLYHS DA6.............. 177 E5
HMSMTH W6............... 144 A5
Broadway Square
Shopping Centre
BXLYHN DA7.............. 177 G5
Brocklebank Health Centre
WAND/EARL SW18.......... 185 F2
Brocklebank Industrial Estate
GNWCH SE10.............. 152 C4
Brockley Cross
Business Centre
BROCKY SE4.............. 170 C4
Brockley Primary School
BROCKY SE4.............. 170 D6
Brockwell Lido
HNHL SE24............... 188 B1
Brockwell Primary School
BRXS/STRHM SW2.......... 188 A1
Bromet Primary School
OXHEY WD19............... 42 B2
Bromley Cemetery
BMLY BR1 .... 212 B3
Bromley College of
Further & Higher Education
BMLY BR1 .... 212 C4
HAYES BR2............... 233 F3
Bromley County Court
BMLY BR1 .... 212 C4
Bromley FC
HAYES BR2............... 232 D2
Bromley Golf Club
HAYES BR2............... 233 G4
Bromley High School
BMLY BR1 .... 234 A1
Bromley Hospital
BMLY BR1 .... 232 D1
Bromley Hospitals NHS Trust
ORP BR6................. 252 A2
ORP BR6................. 253 F2
Bromley Industrial Centre
BMLY BR1 .... 213 F6
Bromley Mall Indoor Market
BMLY BR1 .... 212 C5
Bromley Museum
ORP BR6................. 235 H4
Bromley Road Infant School
BECK BR3................ 211 F4
Bromley Road Retail Park
CAT SE6................. 191 F4
Brompton Cemetery
WBPTN SW10.............. 145 F6
Brompton Medical Centre
WBPTN SW10.............. 145 F5
Brompton Oratory
SKENS SW7................ 18 A6
Bromyard Leisure Centre
ACT W3.................. 143 E1
Brondesbury College for Boys
KIL/WHAMP NW6........... 104 B5
Brookfield Primary School
ARCH N19................. 86 D6
CHEAM SM5............... 224 C5
Brook Industrial Estate
YEAD UB4................ 138 B1
Brookland Primary School
GLDGN NW11............... 85 F1
Brooklands Primary School
BKHTH/KID SE3........... 172 C4
Brook Lane Business Centre
BTFD TW8................ 141 F5
Brookmarsh Trading Estate
DEPT SE8................ 171 F1
Brookmead Industrial Estate
MTCM CR4................ 227 G3
Brookside Junior &
Infant School
YEAD UB4................ 118 A2
Broomfield House School
RCH/KEW TW9............. 161 H2
Broomfield School
STHGT/OAK N14............ 67 F1
Broomsleigh Business Park
CAT SE6................. 210 D1
Broomwood Hall School
BAL SW12................ 186 C2
Brownlow Medical Centre
FBAR/BDGN N11............ 67 G1
Bruce Castle Museum
TOTM N17................. 69 E4
Bruce Grove Primary School
TOTM N17................. 69 F5
Brunel Engine House
BERM/RHTH SE16.......... 150 A2
Brunel University
ISLW TW7................ 160 A1
TWK TW1................. 160 D5
Brunel University
(Osterley Campus) Track
ISLW TW7................ 160 A1
Brunswick Health Centre
FBAR/BDGN N11............ 50 C4
Brunswick Housing &
Shopping Centre
BMSBY WC1N................ 5 F6

Brunswick Industrial Park
FBAR/BDGN N11............ 50 D6
Brunswick Medical Centre
BMSBY WC1N................ 5 E5
Brunswick Park JMI School
FBAR/BDGN N11............ 50 C3
Brunswick Park
Primary School
CMBW SE5................ 168 D1
BT Centre
STBT EC1A................ 15 E3
Buckhurst Hill FC
BKHH IG9................. 57 G3
Buckhurst Hill Primary School
BKHH IG9................. 57 G4
Buckingham College School
HRW HA1.................. 80 A2
Buckingham Palace
WHALL SW1A............... 19 H4
Buckingham Primary School
HPTN TW12............... 198 D1
Buckingham Road Cemetery
IL IG1................... 94 D6
Buckland Infant School
CHSGTN KT9.............. 239 H5
Building Centre
GWRST WC1E............... 12 C2
Bullers Wood School
CHST BR7................ 213 H4
The Bull Theatre
BAR EN5.................. 34 D5
Bupa Roding Hospital
REDBR IG4................ 73 F6
Burbage School
IS N1.................... 8 A1
Burdett Coutts CE
Primary School
WEST SW1P................ 28 C1
Burgess Industrial Park
CMBW SE5................ 168 D1
Burlington Danes School
SHB W12................. 123 H5
Burlington Primary School
NWMAL KT3............... 223 F1
Burnhill Business Centre
BECK BR3................ 211 E4
Burnley Road Clinic
WLSDN NW10.............. 103 G3
Burnside Industrial Estate
BARK/HLT IG6............. 75 H1
Burnt Ash Infant School
BMLY BR1 .... 212 C1
Burnt Ash School
BMLY BR1 .... 212 B1
Burnt Oak Junior School
BFN/LL DA15............. 195 G3
Burntwood School
TOOT SW17............... 185 H4
Burrells Wharf
POP/IOD E14............. 151 F5
Bursted Wood
Primary School
BXLYHN DA7.............. 177 F3
Burwell Industrial Estate
LEY E10.................. 90 C5
Burwood School
ORP BR6................. 236 B6
Bushey Golf & Country Club
BUSH WD23................ 43 E1
Bushey Hall School
BUSH WD23................ 42 D1
Bushey Health Centre
BUSH WD23................ 42 D1
Bushey Heath Primary School
BUSH WD23................ 43 H3
Bushey Middle School
RYNPK SW20.............. 203 H6
Bushey Museum & Art Gallery
BUSH WD23................ 43 E1
Bush Hill Park Golf Club
WCHMH N21................ 38 C6
Bush Hill Park Medical Centre
EN N1................... 53 F1
Bush Hill Park School
EN N1.................... 39 G6
Bush House (BBC)
HOL/ALD WC2B............. 13 G4
Bush Industrial Estate
ARCH N19................ 107 E1
WLSDN NW10.............. 122 D2
The Business Design Centre
IS N1................... 108 A6
Bute House Preparatory
School for Girls
HMSMTH W6............... 144 A4
Butler's Wharf
STHWK SE1 .... 24 D2
Butler's Wharf Business Centre
STHWK SE1 .... 24 D3
Butler's Wharf Pier
STHWK SE1 .... 24 D2
Butterfly House
BTFD TW8................ 160 D2
Butterfly Sports Club
ELTH/MOT SE9............ 194 B1
Buxlow Preparatory School
WBLY HA9................ 101 G1
Buzzard Creek
Industrial Estate
BARK IG11............... 135 F2
Byam Shaw School of Art
ARCH N19................. 87 E6
Bygrove JMI School
POP/IOD E14............. 131 H5
Byron Court Primary School
ALP/SUD HA0.............. 81 E6
Cabinet War Rooms
WHALL SW1A............... 20 D3
Cadogan Pier
CHEL SW3................. 26 B6
Calder House School
BTSEA SW11.............. 166 B2
Caledonian Market
STHWK SE1 .... 24 D5
Calverton Primary School
CAN/RD E16.............. 133 C5
Camberwell Business Centre
CMBW SE5................ 168 C1
Cambell Primary School
DAGW RM9................ 116 B5

Camberwell College of Arts
CMBW SE5 .... 169 E2
Camberwell New Cemetery
FSTH SE23 .... 190 B1
Camberwell Trading Estate
CMBW SE5 .... 168 B3
Cambridge Park Bowling &
Sports Club
TWK TW1 .... 181 E1
Cambridge School
HMSMTH W6 .... 143 H4
Cambridge Theatre
LSQ/SEVD WC2H 13 E4
Camden Community Trust Day
Hospital
CAMTN NW1 .... 107 E4
Camden House Clinic
BKHTH/KID SE3 .... 172 A3
Camden Junior School
CAR SM5 .... 244 B2
Camden Market
CAMTN NW1 .... 106 C5
Camden Peoples Theatre
CAMTN NW1 .... 4 A4
Camden School for Girls
CAMTN NW1 .... 107 E4
Camden Theatre
CAMTN NW1 .... 4 A1
Camden Town Hall &
St Pancras Library
CAMTN NW1 .... 5 E3
Camelot Primary School
PECK SE15 .... 33 G6
Cameron House School
CHEL SW3 .... 145 H6
Camperdown House
WCHPL E1 .... 16 D4
Campion House College
ISLW TW7 .... 159 H1
Campsbourne Infant School
CEND/HSY/T N8 .... 67 G6
Campsbourne Junior School
CEND/HSY/T N8 .... 67 G6
Canada House
STJS SW1Y 10 C6
Canada House Business Centre
RSLP HA4 .... 78 A5
Canada Square
POP/IOD E14 .... 151 E1
Canada Water Retail Park
BERM/RHTH SE16 .... 150 B3
Canada Wharf Museum
BERM/RHTH SE16 .... 150 D1
Canal Cafe Theatre
BAY/PAD W2 .... 125 G4
Canary Riverside
POP/IOD E14 .... 150 D1
Canary Wharf Pier
POP/IOD E14 .... 150 D1
Canary Wharf Tower
POP/IOD E14 .... 151 F1
Canberra Primary School
SHB W12 .... 123 H6
Canbury Business Centre
KUTN/CMB KT2 .... 201 G4
Canbury 2000 Business Park
KUTN/CMB KT2 .... 201 G4
Canbury Medical Centre
KUTN/CMB KT2 .... 201 H4
Canbury School
RCHPK/HAM TW10 .... 202 B2
Cann Hall Primary School
WAN E11 .... 112 B1
The Canning School
KENS W8 .... 145 E3
Cannon Hill Clinic
STHGT/OAK N14 .... 51 G5
Cannon Lane Primary School
PIN HA5 .... 78 B3
Cannon Sports Club
CANST EC4R 15 F5
Cannon Street Station
CANST EC4R 15 G5
Cannon Trading Estate
WBLY HA9 .... 102 B2
Cannon Wharf Business Centre
DEPT SE8 .... 150 C4
Cannon Workshops
POP/IOD E14 .... 131 E6
Cann Barnett Primary School
WCHPL E1 .... 16 D3
Canonbury Business Centre
IS N1 .... 108 C6
Canonbury Primary School
IS N1 .... 108 B4
Canon Palmer RC High School
IL IG1 .... 90 C1
Canons High School
EDGW HA8 .... 61 H5
The Canons Leisure Centrel
MTCM CR4 .... 226 B1
Canterbury Industrial Estate
PECK SE15 .... 150 B6
Cantium Retail Park
STHWK SE1 .... 33 G5
Capital Business Centre
ALP/SUD HA0 .... 121 F1
MTCM CR4 .... 226 B2
Capital Industrial Estate
BELV DA17 .... 157 G1
BELV DA17 .... 157 F4
Capital Radio
LSQ/SEVD WC2H 12 D6
Capital Wharf
WAP E1W 25 F2
Capitol Industrial Park
CDALE/KGS NW9 .... 62 C6
Capian Estate
MTCM CR4 .... 207 E4
Cardinal Hinsley High School
WLSDN NW10 .... 103 G6
Cardinal Pole RC School
HOM E9 .... 110 C4
Cardinal Pole RC Secondary
Lower School
HOM E9 .... 110 B5
Cardinal Vaughan
Memorial School
WKENS W14 .... 144 C2

The Cardinal Wiseman ARC
School Technology &
Art College
GFD/PVL UB6 .... 119 G4
Cardwell Primary School
WOOL/PLUM SE18 .... 153 H4
Carew Manor School
WLGTN SM6 .... 245 F1
Carlisle Infant School
HPTN TW12 .... 199 F2
Carlton Gate Development
MV/WKIL W9 .... 125 E4
Carlton House
STJS SW1Y 20 C2
Carlton Primary School
KTTN NW5 .... 106 C3
Carlton Vale Infant School
MV/WKIL W9 .... 124 D2
Carlyle's House
CHEL SW3 .... 26 A6
Carnwath Road
Industrial Estate
FUL/PGN SW6 .... 165 F4
Carolyn School Shop
PIN HA5 .... 78 C1
Carpenters Park Cemetery
OXHEY WD19 .... 42 D6
Carpenters Business Park
HOM E9 .... 111 E4
Carpenters' Hall
LVPST EC2M 15 H2
Carpenters Primary School
SRTFD E15 .... 111 G6
Carshalton AFC
SUT SM1 .... 244 A1
Carshalton College of Further
Education
CAR SM5 .... 244 B1
Carshalton High
School for Boys
CAR SM5 .... 225 H6
Carshalton High
School for Girls
CAR SM5 .... 244 A1
Carshalton War
Memorial Hospital
CAR SM5 .... 244 B3
Carterhatch Primary School
EN EN1 .... 39 H2
Caryl Thomas Clinic
HRW HA1 .... 80 A1
The Cassel Hospital
RCHPK/HAM TW10 .... 181 F6
Cassidy Medical Centre
FUL/PGN SW6 .... 165 E1
Castilion Primary School
THMD SE28 .... 136 A5
Castlebar Special School
WEA W13 .... 120 C4
Castlecombe Primary School
ELTH/MOT SE9 .... 213 C1
Castle Industrial Estate
WALW SE17 .... 31 E1
Caterham High School
CLAY IG5 .... 73 H5
Catford Cricket & Sports Club
CAT SE6 .... 191 F3
Catford Cyphers Cricket Club
CAT SE6 .... 190 D4
Catford Girls School
CAT SE6 .... 191 H5
Catford Trading Estate
CAT SE6 .... 191 G5
Catford Wanderers Sports Club
CAT SE6 .... 191 G6
Cathall Leisure Centre
WAN E11 .... 111 H1
Cathedral School of St Saviour
& St Mary Overie
STHWK SE1 .... 23 F3
Cator Park School for Girls
BECK BR3 .... 210 C3
Cavendish College
FITZ W1T 12 C2
Cavendish Primary School
CHSWK W4 .... 163 E1
The Cavendish School
CAMTN NW1 .... 106 D6
Cavendish Special School
HMWL W7 .... 120 B5
Caxton Hall
STJSPK SW1H 20 C5
Cayley Primary School
POP/IOD E14 .... 130 C4
Cecil Park Clinic
PIN HA5 .... 78 C1
The Cedar School
FSTGT E7 .... 113 E4
Cedars First School
KTN/HRWW/W HA3 .... 59 G4
Cedars Middle School
KTN/HRWW/W HA3 .... 59 G4
Cedar Way Industrial Estate
CAMTN NW1 .... 107 F5
Cenotaph
WHALL SW1A 21 E3
Centaurs Business Centre
ISLW TW7 .... 140 C6
Centaurs RFC
ISLW TW7 .... 140 B6
Central Business Centre
WLSDN NW10 .... 103 E3
Central Criminal Court
STP EC4M 14 C3
Central Estate
E/WMO/HCT KT8 .... 218 D2
Central Foundation
Boys School
SDTCH EC2A 7 H5
Central Foundation
Girls School
BOW E3 .... 130 C2
Central Hall
STJSPK SW1H 20 D4
Central Hendon Clinic
HDN NW4 .... 83 H1
Central London County Court
CAVSQ/HST W1G 3 G6
Central London Golf Club
TOOT SW17 .... 185 H4

Central London Markets
FARR EC1M 14 C2
Central Medical Centre
MRDN SM4 .... 225 G1
Central Middlesex Hospital
WLSDN NW10 .... 122 C2
Central Park Primary School
EHAM E6 .... 133 F1
Central St Martins
College of Art and Design
RSQ WC1B 13 F2
Central School of Ballet
CLKNW EC1R 6 B6
Central School of Fashion
GTPST W1W 12 A2
Central School of
Speech & Drama
HAMP NW3 .... 105 H5
CAMTN NW1 .... 107 F6
Central Square
Shopping Centre
ALP/SUD HA0 .... 101 G4
Centre Court Shopping Centre
WIM/MER SW19 .... 204 D2
Centre Point
LSQ/SEVD WC2H 12 D3
Chace Community School
EN EN1 .... 39 E2
Chadwell Heath Hospital
CHDH RM6 .... 95 H2
Chadwell Heath Industrial Park
BCTR RM8 .... 96 C5
Chadwell Heath Luncheon &
Leisure Centre
CHDH RM6 .... 96 B3
Chadwell Heath School
CHDH RM6 .... 95 H3
Chaffinch Business Park
BECK BR3 .... 210 B6
Chalcot School
CAMTN NW1 .... 106 D4
Chalgrove Primary School
FNCH N3 .... 64 C6
Chalkhill Primary School
WBLY HA9 .... 102 B1
Chambers Wharf
BERM/RHTH SE16 .... 25 F3
Chandlers Field
Primary School
E/WMO/HCT KT8 .... 219 E2
Chandos Business Centre
WLGTN SM6 .... 245 E4
Channelsea Business Centre
SRTFD E15 .... 131 H1
Channing School
HGT N6 .... 86 D5
Chapel End Infant School
WALTH E17 .... 71 F4
Chapel End Junior School
WALTH E17 .... 71 F4
Chapman Park
Industrial Estate
WLSDN NW10 .... 103 F4
Charing Cross Hospital
HMSMTH W6 .... 144 B6
Charing Cross & Westminster
Medical School
HMSMTH W6 .... 144 B5
Charing Cross Station
CHCR WC2N 21 F1
Charles Dickens Primary School
STHWK SE1 .... 23 E4
Charles Edward Brook
Lower School
CMBW SE5 .... 168 B2
Charles Edward Brook
Upper School
CMBW SE5 .... 168 B2
Charles Lamb Primary School
IS N1 .... 108 C6
Charlotte Sharman
Primary School
LBTH SE11 .... 22 C6
Charlton Athletic FC
(The Valley)
CHARL SE7 .... 153 E5
Charlton House
CHARL SE7 .... 153 F6
Charlton RFC
ELTH/MOT SE9 .... 194 B2
Charlton School
CHARL SE7 .... 155 G6
Charrington Bowl
SURB KT6 .... 222 B6
Charter Clinic
CHEL SW3 .... 26 C4
Charterhouse
FARR EC1M 14 D1
The Charter School
HNHL SE24 .... 168 D6
Chartfield School
PUT/ROE SW15 .... 163 H6
Chartwell Business Centre
BMLY BR1 .... 215 F6
Chase Bridge Primary School
WHTN TW2 .... 180 A1
Chase Farm Hospital
ENC/FH EN2 .... 38 A1
Chase Lane Primary School
CHING E4 .... 54 D6
Chase Road Trading Estate
WLSDN NW10 .... 122 D3
Chase Side Junior &
Infant School
ENC/FH EN2 .... 38 C3
Chaseville Clinic
WCHMH N21 .... 51 H1
Chatsworth Infant School
BFN/LL DA15 .... 195 G3
Chatsworth Junior &
Infant School
HSLW TW3 .... 159 G5
Chaucer Clinic
STHL UB1 .... 139 H2
Cheam Common Infant School
WPK KT4 .... 223 H6
Cheam Common Junior School
WPK KT4 .... 241 H1
Cheam Fields Primary School
CHEAM SM3 .... 242 C3

Cheam High School
CHEAM SM3 .... 242 C2
Cheam Leisure Centre
CHEAM SM3 .... 242 B2
Cheam Park Farm
Junior School
CHEAM SM3 .... 242 C1
Cheam Sports Club
BELMT SM2 .... 242 B5
Chelsea Barracks
BGVA SW1W 27 F4
Chelsea Bridge
Business Centre
VX/NE SW8 .... 166 D1
Chelsea Centre & Theatre
WBPTN SW10 .... 165 H1
Chelsea Cinema
CHEL SW3 .... 26 B4
Chelsea College of Art & Design
CHEL SW3 .... 145 H5
FUL/PGN SW6 .... 165 G3
Chelsea FC (Stamford Bridge)
FUL/PGN SW6 .... 165 F1
Chelsea Fields Industrial Estate
WIM/MER SW19 .... 205 H4
Chelsea Old Town Hall
CHEL SW3 .... 26 B4
Chelsea Physic Garden
CHEL SW3 .... 26 B5
Chelsea Sports Centre
CHEL SW3 .... 26 B4
Chelsea & Westminster Hospital
WBPTN SW10 .... 145 G6
Chelsea Wharf
WBPTN SW10 .... 165 H1
Cherington House
Health Centre
HNWL W7 .... 140 B1
Cherry Garden Pier
BERM/RHTH SE16 .... 25 G3
Cherry Garden School
BERM/RHTH SE16 .... 33 F1
Cherry Orchard Primary School
CHARL SE7 .... 173 E1
Chessington Community College
CHSGTN KT9 .... 239 F5
Chessington Cricket Club
CHSGTN KT9 .... 239 E5
Chessington Golf Club
CHSGTN KT9 .... 239 F5
Chesterton Primary School
BTSEA SW11 .... 166 C2
Chestnut Grove School
BAL SW12 .... 186 C3
Cheyne Centre
CHEL SW3 .... 26 A6
Chigwell Golf Club
CHIG IG7 .... 74 A1
Childeric Primary School
NWCR SE14 .... 170 C1
Childs Hill Clinic
CRICK NW2 .... 84 D6
Childs Hill Primary School
CRICK NW2 .... 104 C1
Childs Welfare Clinic
DAGW RM9 .... 116 A3
Chiltonian Industrial Estate
LEE/GVPK SE12 .... 192 B1
Chinnocks Wharf
POP/IOD E14 .... 130 C6
Chingford CE Infant School
CHING E4 .... 55 H3
Chingford CE Junior School
CHING E4 .... 55 H3
Chingford Hall Primary School
CHING E4 .... 70 D2
Chingford Health Centre
CHING E4 .... 54 D6
Chingford Industrial Centre
CHING E4 .... 70 C1
Chingford RFC
CHING E4 .... 55 E3
Chingford School
CHING E4 .... 55 F3
Chisenhale Primary School
BOW E3 .... 130 C1
Chislehurst Caves
CHST BR7 .... 214 A4
Chislehurst Cemetery
CHST BR7 .... 215 E1
Chislehurst Golf Club
CHST BR7 .... 214 B3
Chislehurst Natural
Health Centre
CHST BR7 .... 214 B2
Chislehurst & Sidcup
Grammar School
BFN/LL DA15 .... 195 H4
Chiswick & Bedford Park
Preparatory School
CHSWK W4 .... 143 E4
Chiswick Community School
CHSWK W4 .... 162 D1
Chiswick House
CHSWK W4 .... 142 D6
Chrisp Street Health Centre
POP/IOD E14 .... 131 F5
Christ Church Bentinck CE
Primary School
BAY/PAD W2 .... 10 A1
Christ Church Brondesbury CE
J & I School
KIL/WHAMP NW6 .... 104 D6
Christ Church CE Infant School
NWMAL KT3 .... 203 E6
Christ Church CE Junior School
NWMAL KT3 .... 202 D6
Christ Church CE
Primary School
BAR EN5 .... 34 B3
BRXN/ST SW9 .... 168 A2
BRXS/STRHM SW2 .... 187 H3
BRYLDS KT5 .... 222 A5
CHEL SW3 .... 26 B5
FSTH SE23 .... 190 B4
Christchurch CE
Primary School
WCHPL E1 .... 16 D2

Christ Church CE
Primary School
WOOL/PLUM SE18 .... 174 A2
Christchurch CE School
NFNCH/WDSP N12 .... 65 H1
Christ Church CE
Middle School
EA W5 .... 121 F6
Christchurch Industrial Centre
STHWK SE1 .... 22 C1
Christ Church Primary School
BTSEA SW11 .... 166 A4
Christchurch Primary School
IL IG1 .... 94 C5
Christ Church School
CAMTN NW1 .... 3 H2
Christian Meeting Hall
BECK BR3 .... 211 E4
Christopher Hutton
Primary School
FSBYW WC1X............................. 6 A6
Christs College
BKHTH/KID SE3................... 172 C2
EFNCH N2 .... 65 F6
Christs College School
EFNCH N2 .... 65 F6
Christs School
RCHPK/HAM TW10 .... 161 H6
Christ the King RC
Primary School
FSBYPK N4 .... 87 H6
Chrysalis Theatre
BAL SW12............................... 186 C3
Chrysanthemum Clinic
CHSWK W4 .... 162 C1
Church Down Adult School
LEE/GVPK SE12................... 192 C4
Church End Medical Centre
WLSDN NW10 .... 103 E4
Church Farm House Museum
HDN NW4 .... 63 H6
Churchfield Primary School
ED N9 .... 53 F3
Churchfields Junior &
Infant School
SWFD E18 .... 72 C4
Churchfields Primary School
BECK BR3 .... 210 B6
Church Hill Primary School
EBAR EN4 .... 50 B2
Churchill Clinic
STHWK SE1 .... 22 B5
Churchill College
RYNPK SW20 .... 204 A5
TOOT SW17 .... 186 B4
Churchill Gardens
Primary School
PIM SW1V 28 A4
Churchill Theatre
HAYES BR2 .... 212 C5
Church Mead Infant School
LEY E10 .... 91 E5
Church Mead Junior School
LEY E10 .... 91 E5
The Church School
BTFD TW8 .... 141 G6
Cineworld Cinema
BXLYHS DA6 .... 177 F5
WDGN N22 .... 68 A5
City Banking College
STHWK SE1 .... 23 H3
City Business Centre
BERM/RHTH SE16 .... 150 A2
City Business College
FSBYE EC1V............................. 6 C4
City Central Estate
FSBYE EC1V............................. 7 E4
City College of Higher Education
IS N1 .... 7 H3
City Health Centre
FSBYE EC1V............................. 7 G5
City & Islington College
FSBYPK N4 .... 88 B6
HOLWY N7 .... 107 G2
IS N1 .... 108 C6
STLK EC1Y 7 G6
City & Islington College
Sixth Form Centre
HOLWY N7 .... 107 H2
City of London Cemetery
MNPK E12 .... 93 G6
City of London Crematorium
MNPK E12 .... 113 F1
City of London Club
OBST EC2N 16 A3
City of London College
WCHPL E1 .... 17 E3
City of London
Magistrates Court
MANHO EC4N 15 G4
City of London Polytechnic
Sports Ground
ELTH/MOT SE9 .... 193 G4
City of London School
BLKFR EC4V 14 D5
City of London School for Girls
BARB EC2Y 15 E1
City of Westminster College
HNWL W7 .... 140 B1
City of Westminster College
BAY/PAD W2 .... 125 H4
MV/WKIL W9 .... 124 D2
City of Westminster
Vehicle Pound
BAY/PAD W2 .... 125 G4
City Thameslink Station
STP EC4M 14 C4
City University
FSBYE EC1V............................. 6 C3
FSBYE EC1V............................. 6 C4
City University Business School
BARB EC2Y 15 F1
Civic Centre & Bromley Palace
BMLY BR1 .... 212 D5

Civic Medical Centre
HRW HA1 .... 80 A2
Civil Service Recreation Centre
WEST SW1P 20 D6
Civil Service Sports Ground
ELTH/MOT SE9 .... 193 E1
Clapham Common Clinic
CLAP SW4 .... 167 F5
Clapham Manor
Primary School
CLAP SW4 .... 167 E4
Clapham Manor Street
Public Baths
CLAP SW4 .... 167 E4
Clapham North
Business Centre
CLAP SW4 .... 167 F4
Clapham Park School
CLAP SW4 .... 167 F6
Clapham Picture House
CLAP SW4 .... 167 G5
Clapton Girls'
Technology College
CLPT E5 .... 110 A2
Clapton Jewish Boys School
STNW/STAM N16 .... 89 F4
Clara Grant Primary School
BOW E3 .... 131 E3
Clare House Primary School
BECK BR3 .... 211 G5
Claremont Clinic
FSTGT E7 .... 112 D3
Claremont High School
KTN/HRWW/WS HA3 .... 81 C2
Claremont Way
Industrial Estate
CRICK NW2 .... 84 A5
Clarence House
WHALL SW1A 20 B3
Clarendon Special School
HPTN TW12 .... 199 F2
Claridges Hotel
MYFR/PKLN W1K 11 G5
Claverings Industrial Estate
ED N9 .... 54 A4
Claygate Primary School
ESH/CLAY KT10.................... 238 A5
Clayhall Clinic
CLAY IG5................................. 73 C6
Claypond's Hospital
BTFD TW8 .... 141 G4
Cleeve Park School
SCUP DA14 .... 196 A5
Clementine Churchill Hospital
HRW HA1 .... 100 B1
Cleopatra's Needle
CHCR WC2N 21 C1
Clerkenwell County Court
IS N1 .... 6 C1
Clerkenwell Heritage Centre
FARR EC1M 6 C6
Clerkenwell Parochial CE
Primary School
CLKNW EC1R 6 A4
Cleveland Primary School
IL IG1 .... 114 B2
Cleves Primary School
EHAM E6 .... 115 F6
C & L Golf & Country Club
NTHLT UB5 .... 98 A6
Clifton Lodge School
EA W5 .... 121 F6
Clifton Primary School
NWDGN UB2 .... 138 C4
Clink Exhibition
STHWK SE1 .... 23 G1
Clissold Park Natural
Health Centre
STNW/STAM N16 .... 89 E6
Clitterhouse Primary School
CRICK NW2 .... 84 B6
Clockhouse Primary School
CRW RM5................................. 77 F2
Clock Museum
CITYW EC2V 15 F3
Cloisters Business Centre
VX/NE SW8 .... 166 D1
Clore Gallery
WEST SW1P 29 G2
The Clore Tikva School
BARK/HLT IG6 .... 74 C5
Clothworkers' Hall
FENCHST EC3M 16 B5
Clouster's Green
WAP E1W................................. 25 E1
Cobbold Estate
WLSDN NW10 .... 103 F4
Cobourg Primary School
CMBW SE5................................ 32 C4
Cochrane Theatre
GINN WC1R 13 G2
Cockfosters Sports Ground
EBAR EN4 .... 36 B4
The Cockpit Theatre
STJWD NW8 .... 2 A6
Coldharbour Industrial Estate
CMBW SE5............................. 168 C3
Coldharbour Sports Ground
ELTH/MOT SE9 .... 194 A4
Colebrooke Primary School
IS N1 .... 6 C1
Colegrave Primary School
SRTFD E15 .... 111 H3
Coleraine Park Primary School
TOTM N17 .... 69 H4
Colfes Preparatory School
LEE/GVPK SE12.................... 192 D1
Colindale Business Park
CDALE/KGS NW9 .... 62 C6
Colindale Hospital
CDALE/KGS NW9 .... 63 E6
Colindale Primary School
CDALE/KGS NW9 .... 83 F1
Coliseum Theatre
CHCR WC2N 13 C6
College Fields Business Centre
WIM/MER SW19.................... 206 A4

College Library & Civic Centre
SUT SM1............................... 243 F3
College of Arms
BLKFR EC4V 15 C4
College of Fuel Technology
HGT N6 .... 86 C3
College of Law
GWRST WC1E 12 C1
The College of Law
FLST/FETLN EC4A 14 A3
GWRST WC1E 12 C1
College of North East London
CEND/HSY/T N8 .... 88 A1
FBAR/BDGN N11.................... 67 E4
SEVS/STOTM N15.................. 89 F1
College of North West London
KIL/WHAMP NW6 .... 105 E6
WBLY HA9 .... 102 A1
WLSDN NW10 .... 103 F3
College of Organists
FLST/FETLN EC4A 14 B3
College Park School
BAY/PAD W2 .... 125 F5
Collier Row Clinic
ROMW/RG RM7 .... 77 F4
Collier Row FC
ROMW/RG RM7 .... 76 D4
Collingwood Business Centre
ARCH N19 .... 107 C1
Collingwood Preparatory
School
WLGTN SM6 .... 244 D3
Collins Method School
CRICK NW2 .... 104 A4
Collis Primary School
TEDD TW11 .... 200 D2
Colnbrook School
OXHEY WD19 .... 42 A4
Coloma Convent Girls School
CROY/NA CR0 .... 248 B1
The Colonnades
Shopping Centre
BGVA SW1W 27 G1
Colours Sports Club
SUT SM1............................... 243 G3
Columbia Primary School
BETH E2 .... 8 D3
Colvestone Primary School
HACK E8 .... 109 F3
Colville Primary School
NTGHL W11 .... 124 D5
Colyers Lane Medical Centre
BXLYHN DA7 .... 177 H2
Colyers Primary School
BXLYHN DA7 .... 177 H2
Comber Grove Primary School
CMBW SE5............................. 168 C1
Comedy Theatre
STJS SW1Y 12 C6
Comelle House Trading Estate
DEPT SE8 .... 150 C5
Commonwealth Institute
KENS W8................................ 144 D3
Community Arts Centre
GNWCH SE10........................ 171 F1
Community Care Centre
CEN/FH EC4 .... 38 D2
Community Centre
(Island History Trust)
POP/IOD E14......................... 151 G4
Community College and School
GNWCH SE10........................ 171 G1
Community Mental Health Cen
BRXN/ST SW9 .... 168 A1
Complementary Health Centre
LEW SE13 .... 192 A1
The Compton School
NFNCH/WDSP N12 .... 66 A2
Concord Business Centre
ACT W3 .... 122 B4
Concord Shopping Centre
WKENS W14 .... 144 B2
Coney Hill School
HAYES BR2 .... 232 B6
Conference Centre
WBLY HA9 .... 101 H2
Connaught Business Centre
CDALE/KGS NW9 .... 83 F2
CROY/NA CR0 .... 245 H4
MTCM CR4............................. 226 B2
Connaught Girls School
WAN E11 .... 92 A5
Consort Clinic
PECK SE15 .... 169 H4
Consulate General of Monaco
SKENS SW7 .... 145 H3
Consulate of Burkina Faso
BTSEA SW11 .... 165 G4
Consulate of Chile
CAVSQ/HST W1G 3 G6
Consulate of Colombia
GTPST W1W 12 A3
Consulate of Eritrea
IS N1 .... 6 B1
Consulate of Guinea
MYFR/PKLN W1K 11 E5
Consulate of Panama
MYFR/PICC W1J 19 G2
Convent of Jesus &
Mary Infant School
CRICK NW2 .... 104 A4
Convent of Jesus &
Mary Language College
WLSDN NW10 .... 103 F6
Conway Hall
FSBYW WC1X.......................... 13 G1
Conway Medical Centre
WOOL/PLUM SE18 .... 154 D5
Conway Primary School
WOOL/PLUM SE18 .... 155 E4
Coombe Girls School
NWMAL KT3......................... 202 D5
Coombe Hill Golf Club
KUTN/CMB KT2.................... 202 D3
Coombe Hill Junior &
Infant School
NWMAL KT3......................... 202 D4
Coombe Wood Golf Club
KUTN/CMB KT2.................... 202 B3

Coopers' Hall
LVPST EC2M 16 B2
Coopers Lane Primary School
LEE/GVPK SE12.................... 192 C4
Coopers School
CHST BR7.............................. 214 C4
Copland Community School &
Technology Centre
WBLY HA9 .... 101 H3
Coppermill Primary School
WALTH E17 .... 90 B2
Coppetts Wood Hospital
MUSWH N10 .... 66 B4
Coppetts Wood Primary School
MUSWH N10 .... 66 C4
Coppice Primary School
CHIG IG7.................................. 75 G1
Copthall School
HDN NW7................................ 63 H2
Cordwainers College
HOM E9 .... 110 A5
Corinthian Casuals FC
CHSGTN KT9 .... 240 A1
Cornhill Sports Club
BECK BR3.............................. 211 E1
Coronet Cinema
NTGHL W11 .... 145 E1
SEVS/STOTM N15.................. 68 B6
Corpus Christi RC
Primary School
BRXS/STRHM SW2 .... 167 H6
Cosmopolitan College
IS N1 .... 5 G2
Coston Secondary
Modern Girls School
GFD/PVL UB6 .... 119 G2
Counterpoint Theatre
STPAN WC1H............................ 5 F3
Courtauld Institute Galleries
HOL/ALD WC2B 13 C5
Courtfield Medical Centre
ECT SW5................................. 145 F4
Courtland JMI School
MLHL NW7 .... 47 E4
Covent Garden Flower Market
VX/NE SW8 .... 28 D6
Covent Garden Medical Centre
LSO/SEVD WC2H 13 E4
CPFC Soccer & Sports Centre
BRXN/ST SW9 .... 167 H4
Crampton Primary School
WALW SE17 .... 30 D2
Cranbrook College
IL IG1 .... 94 A6
Crane Infant School
FELT TW13 .... 178 D4
Crane Junior School
FELT TW13 .... 178 C4
Cranleigh Gardens
Industrial Estate
STHL UB1 .... 118 D4
Cranmer School
MTCM CR4............................. 226 B2
The Craven Clinic
HMSMTH W6 .... 143 H4
Craven Park Health Centre
WLSDN NW10 .... 102 D6
Craven Park Medical Centre
WLSDN NW10 .... 102 D6
Craven Park Primary School
SEVS/STOTM N15.................. 89 G3
Crawford Primary School
CMBW SE5............................. 168 C3
Crawford Upper School
MBLAR W1H 10 C2
Crayfield Industrial Park
STMC/STPC BR5 .... 216 A5
Crayfields Business Park
STMC/STPC BR5 .... 216 A4
STMC/STPC BR5 .... 236 A2
Cray Valley Golf Club
STMC/STPC BR5 .... 216 C4
Creekmouth Industrial Estate
BARK IG11............................. 135 F3
Creek Road Industrial Estate
DEPT SE8 .... 151 E6
Creek Road Industrial Estate
DEPT SE8 .... 151 F6
Cremer Business Centre
BETH E2 .... 8 C2
Crewe House
MYFR/PICC W1J 19 G1
Cricket Pavilion
WEST SW1P 28 C1
Cricklefield Stadium
IL IG1 .... 95 E6
Cricklewood Trading Estate
CRICK NW2 .... 104 C1
Crispin Industrial Centre
UED N18 .... 70 A1
Criterion Theatre
MYFR/PICC W1J 12 B6
Crockenhill Primary School
SWLY BR8............................. 237 G3
Crofton Leisure Centre
BROCKY SE4 .... 191 F1
Crofton School
BROCKY SE4 .... 191 E1
Croham Hurst Golf Club
SAND/SEL CR2 .... 247 F4
Croham Hurst School
SAND/SEL CR2 .... 247 F3
Cromer Road JMI School
BAR EN5 .... 35 F4
Crompton Medical Centre
BAY/PAD W2 .... 125 H3
Cromwell Business Centre
BARK IG11............................. 135 G2
Cromwell Hospital
KENS W8................................ 145 G4
Cromwell Industrial Estate
LEY E10 .... 90 C5
Crook Log Baths
BXLYHS DA6 .... 176 B5
Crook Log Primary School
BXLYHS DA6 .... 176 B5
Crook Log Sports Centre
WELL DA16 .... 176 B4
Crouch End Art School
CEND/HSY/T N8 .... 87 G2

Crouch End Health Centre
CEND/HSY/T N8 .... 87 G2
Crouch Hill Recreation Centre
ARCH N19 .... 87 G4
Crowland Primary School
SEVS/STOTM N15 .... 89 F2
Crowlands Primary School
ROMW/RG RM7 .... 97 G3
Crown Close Business Centre
BOW E3 .... 111 E6
Crown Court at the Borough
STHWK SE1 .... 22 D3
Crowndale Health Centre
CAMTN NW1 .... 4 B1
Crownfield Primary School
ROMW/RG RM7 .... 77 E5
Crown Lane Clinic
STHGT/OAK N14 .... 51 E3
Crown Lane Primary School
WNWD SE27 .... 208 B1
Crown Woods School
ELTH/MOT SE9 .... 174 C6
Croydon Airport
Industrial Estate
CROY/NA CR0 .... 246 A5
Croydon Cemetery
THHTH CR7 .... 227 H2
Croydon Clocktower Cinema
CROY/NA CR0 .... 246 C1
Croydon College
CROY/NA CR0 .... 228 D6
Croydon Fairfield Halls Cinema
CROY/NA CR0 .... 246 D1
Croydon FC
SNWD SE25 .... 230 A2
Croydon Indoor Bowling Club
SAND/SEL CR2 .... 246 C3
Croydon Road
Industrial Estate
SNWD SE25 .... 230 A1
Croydon Sports Arena
SNWD SE25 .... 230 A2
Crusader Industrial Estate
FSBYPK N4 .... 88 C3
Crusoe House School
IS N1 .... 7 G3
Crystal Palace
NRWD SE19 .... 209 G2
Crystal Palace
Athletics Stadium
NRWD SE19 .... 209 G2
Crystal Palace FC
(Selhurst Park)
SNWD SE25 .... 229 E1
Crystal Palace Museum
NRWD SE19 .... 209 F2
Cuaco Sports Ground
BECK BR3 .... 211 E2
Cubitt Town Primary School
POP/IOD E14 .... 151 G3
Cuddington Cemetery
WPK KT4 .... 223 H6
Cuddington CP School
HOR/WEW KT19 .... 241 F1
Culloden Primary School
POP/IOD E14 .... 131 H5
Culvers House Primary School
MTCM CR4 .... 226 C5
Cumberland Business Park
WLSDN NW10 .... 122 B2
Cumberland
Comprehensive School
CAN/RD E16 .... 132 B4
Cumberland Park
Industrial Estate
WLSDN NW10 .... 123 G2
The Cuming Museum
WALW SE17 .... 31 E2
Cumnor House School
SAND/SEL CR2 .... 246 B6
Curwen Primary School
PLSTW E13 .... 132 C1
Curzon Mayfair Cinema
MYFR/PICC W1J 19 G2
Curzon Soho Cinema
SOHO/SHAV W1D 12 D5
Cutlers' Hall
STP EC4M 14 D3
Cutty Sark
GNWCH SE10 .... 151 G6
Cygnet Clinic Beckton
EHAM E6 .... 134 B5
Cygnus Business Centre
WLSDN NW10 .... 103 F3
Cypress Infant School
SNWD SE25 .... 209 E5
Cypress Junior School
SNWD SE25 .... 209 E5
Cyprus College of Art
WNWD SE27 .... 188 B6
Cyril Jackson Primary School
POP/IOD E14 .... 130 D6
Dagenham Chest Clinic
BCTR RM8 .... 116 D1
Dagenham Civic Centre
DAGE RM10 .... 97 F6
Dagenham Priory
Comprehensive School
DAGE RM10 .... 117 F5
Dagenham & Redbridge FC
DAGE RM10 .... 117 F3
Dagenham Superbowl
BCTR RM8 .... 137 F1
Dagenham Swimming Pool
BCTR RM8 .... 96 D6
Daiglen School
BKHH IG9 .... 57 E3
Daily Mirror Office
FLST/FETLN EC4A 14 B2
Daily Telegraph
POP/IOD E14 .... 151 E3
Dairy Meadow Primary School
NWDGN UB2 .... 138 D3
Dali Universal Exhibition
STHWK SE1 .... 21 F3
Dallington School
FSBYE EC1V 6 D5
Dalmain Primary School
FSTH SE23 .... 190 C3

Danegrove Primary School
EBAR EN4 .... 50 A1
Danetree School
HOR/WEW KT19 .... 240 C5
Danson Primary School
WELL DA16 .... 175 H5
Darell Primary School
RCH/KEW TW9 .... 162 A4
Darrick Wood Swimming Pool
ORP BR6 .... 252 B2
Darrick Wood School
ORP BR6 .... 252 B1
Datapoint Business Centre
CAN/RD E16 .... 131 H3
Daubeney Primary School
CLPT E5 .... 110 C2
David Game College
NTGHL W11 .... 145 E1
David Game Tutorial College
SKENS SW7 .... 145 H4
David Livingstone
Primary School
THHTH CR7 .... 208 C4
David Lloyd Leisure Centre
KENS W8 .... 145 F4
Davidson Junior &
Infant School
CROY/NA CR0 .... 229 F4
Davies Lane Infant School
WAN E11 .... 92 B6
Davies's College
STHWK SE1 .... 23 F3
Dawlish Primary School
LEY E10 .... 91 G6
Days Lane Primary School
BFN/LL DA15 .... 195 F1
Deanesfield Primary School
RSLP HA4 .... 98 B2
Deansbrook Primary School
MLHL NW7 .... 62 C2
Deansfield Primary School
ELTH/MOT SE9 .... 174 A4
De Beauvoir Primary School
IS N1 .... 109 E4
De Bohun Primary School
STHGT/OAK N14 .... 36 C6
Denmead School
HPTN TW12 .... 199 E3
Department for Environment,
Food & Rural Affairs
WHALL SW1A 21 E1
Department of Health
WHALL SW1A 21 E3
Department of Trade & Industry
WHALL SW1A 20 D5
Deptford Business Centre
DEPT SE8 .... 150 B5
Deptford Green School
NWCR SE14 .... 170 D1
Deptford Park
Business Centre
DEPT SE8 .... 150 C5
Deptford Park Primary School
DEPT SE8 .... 150 C5
Deptford Trading Estate
DEPT SE8 .... 150 C5
Dersingham Infant School
MNPK E12 .... 113 H3
Derwentwater Primary School
ACT W3 .... 142 C1
Design Museum
STHWK SE1 .... 24 D2
Deutsche Schule
RCHPK/HAM TW10 .... 181 F3
Devonshire Hill Primary School
TOTM N17 .... 68 D2
Devonshire Hospital
MHST W1U 11 F1
Devonshire House
Preparatory School
HAMP NW3 .... 105 G3
Devonshire House School
HAMP NW3 .... 105 G3
Devonshire Primary School
BELMT SM2 .... 243 G5
Diamond College
SOHO/SHAV W1D 12 B3
Diana Fountain
E/WMO/HCT KT8 .... 200 B5
Diane Matthews Clinic
ROMW/RG RM7 .... 97 H1
The Dickens House Museum
BMSBY WC1N 5 G6
Dilloway Industrial Estate
NWDGN UB2 .... 138 C2
Discovery Business Park
BERM/RHTH SE16 .... 25 F6
Docklands Medical Centre
POP/IOD E14 .... 151 E4
Docklands Sailing Centre
POP/IOD E14 .... 151 E3
Docklands Sailing &
Watersports Centre
POP/IOD E14 .... 150 D3
Dockley Road Industrial Estate
BERM/RHTH SE16 .... 25 E6
Dockmaster's House
POP/IOD E14 .... 131 E6
Dockyard Industrial Estate
WOOL/PLUM SE18 .... 153 G3
Dog Kennel Hill
Primary School
CMBW SE5 .... 169 E4
Dokal Industrial Estate
NWDGN UB2 .... 138 C2
Dollis Infant School
MLHL NW7 .... 64 A3
Dollis Junior School
MLHL NW7 .... 64 A3
Dolphin School
BTSEA SW11 .... 166 B6
Dome
GNWCH SE10 .... 152 A1
The Dominican
Republic Embassy
BAY/PAD W2 .... 125 F5
Dominion Business Park
ED N9 .... 54 B4
Dominion Theatre
NOXST/BSQ WC1A 12 D3

Donmar Warehouse Theatre
LSO/SEVD WC2H 13 E4
Donnington Primary School
WLSDN NW10 .... 103 H5
Dorchester Primary School
WPK KT4 .... 224 A5
Dorma Trading Park
LEY E10 .... 90 B5
Dormers Wells Medical Centre
GFD/PVL UB6 .... 119 E5
Dormers Wells Primary School
STHL UB1 .... 119 F6
Dormers Wells School
GFD/PVL UB6 .... 119 E5
Dorothy Barley
Primary School
BCTR RM8 .... 115 H3
Dorset Road Infant School
ELTH/MOT SE9 .... 193 G4
Douglas Bader Foundation
PUT/ROE SW15 .... 183 G1
Downderry Primary School
BMLY BR1 .... 192 A6
Downham Health Centre
BMLY BR1 .... 192 A6
Downhills Primary School
TOTM N17 .... 88 D1
Down Lane Junior School
TOTM N17 .... 69 F5
Downsell Junior School
WAN E11 .... 111 H2
Downside Primary School
CLPT E5 .... 109 G2
Downsview Primary School
NRWD SE19 .... 208 C3
Downsview School
CLPT E5 .... 109 H2
Drapers Hall
LOTH EC2R 15 H3
Drapers Sports Ground
SRTFD E15 .... 111 G2
Drayton Green Primary School
WEA W13 .... 120 C6
Drayton Manor High School
HNWL W7 .... 120 B6
Drayton Park Primary School
HBRY N5 .... 108 A3
DRCA Business Centre
BTSEA SW11 .... 166 C2
Drew Primary School
CAN/RD E16 .... 153 G1
Driving School &
Road Safety Centre
KTN/HRWW/W HA3 .... 60 C6
Dr Johnson's House
FLST/FETLN EC4A 14 B4
Dr Rolfes Montessori School
BAY/PAD W2 .... 125 E6
Drummond Shopping Centre
CROY/NA CR0 .... 228 C6
Drury Way Industrial Estate
WLSDN NW10 .... 102 D2
Duchess Theatre
COVGDN WC2E 13 G5
Duke of York Column
STJS SW1Y 20 C2
Duke of York's HQ
CHEL SW3 .... 26 D2
Duke of York Theatre
CHCR WC2N 13 E6
Dulverton Primary School
BFN/LL DA15 .... 194 D4
Dulwich College
DUL SE21 .... 189 E3
Dulwich College
Preparatory School
DUL SE21 .... 189 E5
Dulwich College Track
DUL SE21 .... 189 E4
Dulwich Hamlet FC
CMBW SE5 .... 169 E5
Dulwich Hamlet Junior School
HNHL SE24 .... 188 D1
Dulwich Medical Centre
EDUL SE22 .... 169 G6
Dulwich Picture Gallery
DUL SE21 .... 188 D2
Dulwich & Sydenham
Hill Golf Club
DUL SE21 .... 189 G4
Dulwich Village CE
Infant School
DUL SE21 .... 189 E1
Dunbar Wharf
POP/IOD E14 .... 130 D6
Duncombe Primary School
ARCH N19 .... 87 G5
Dundee Wharf
POP/IOD E14 .... 130 D6
Dundonald First School
WIM/MER SW19 .... 204 D3
Dunraven School
(Lower School)
STRHM/NOR SW16 .... 187 H5
Dunraven School
(Upper School)
STRHM/NOR SW16 .... 187 H5
Duppas Junior School
CROY/NA CR0 .... 246 B3
Durand Primary School
BRXN/ST SW9 .... 167 H2
Durants School
EN EN1 .... 40 A2
Durdans Park Primary School
STHL UB1 .... 118 D4
Durston House School
EA W5 .... 121 F5
Dysart School
SURB KT6 .... 221 G4
Dysart Special School
TRDG/WHET N20 ....
Eaglesfield School
WOOL/PLUM SE18 .... 174 A2
Eagle Trading Estate
MTCM CR4 .... 226 B3
Ealdham Primary School
ELTH/MOT SE9 .... 173 G5
Ealing Abbey
EA W5 .... 121 E5

Ealing Abbey Scriptorium
WEA W13 .... 121 E5
The Ealing Broadway Centre
EA W5 .... 121 F6
Ealing Central Sports Ground
GFD/PVL UB6 .... 120 C1
Ealing Civic Centre
EA W5 .... 121 F6
Ealing College Upper School
WEA W13 .... 120 D5
Ealing Cricket Club
EA W5 .... 121 G5
Ealing Film Studios
EA W5 .... 141 E1
Ealing Golf Club
GFD/PVL UB6 .... 120 D2
Ealing Hospital
STHL UB1 .... 139 H2
Ealing Northern Sports Centre
NTHLT UB5 .... 99 H2
Ealing Park Health Centre
EA W5 .... 141 F4
Ealing Road Trading Estate
BTFD TW8 .... 141 F5
Ealing Sports Centre
EA W5 .... 121 G6
Ealing Tertiary College
EA W5 .... 141 E1
Ealing Tutorial College
EA W5 .... 121 G6
Eardley Primary School
STRHM/NOR SW16 .... 207 G2
Earlham Junior &
Infant School
WDGN N22 .... 68 A3
Earlham Primary School
FSTGT E7 .... 112 B3
Earl's Court Exhibition Centre
ECT SW5 .... 145 E5
Earlsfield Primary School
WAND/EARL SW18 .... 185 G4
Earlsmead First &
Middle School
RYLN/HDSTN HA2 .... 98 D2
Earlsmead Primary School
SEVS/STOTM N15 .... 89 F1
Earth Gallery
(Geological Museum)
SKENS SW7 .... 145 H3
East Acton Primary School
ACT W3 .... 123 E6
East Barking Luncheon &
Leisure Centre
BCTR RM8 .... 116 A3
East Barnet Health Centre
EBAR EN4 .... 35 H6
East Barnet School
EBAR EN4 .... 34 B6
EBAR EN4 .... 50 B1
East Beckton District Centre
EHAM E6 .... 133 H5
Eastbrook
Comprehensive School
DAGE RM10 .... 117 G2
Eastbrookend Country Park
DAGE RM10 .... 117 H2
Eastbury Comprehensive
BARK IG11 .... 114 D5
Eastbury
Comprehensive School
BARK IG11 .... 115 F6
Eastbury Infant School
BARK IG11 .... 115 F5
Eastcote Health Centre
PIN HA5 .... 78 A4
Eastcote Industrial Estate
RSLP HA4 .... 78 A4
Eastcote Lane Cemetery
RYLN/HDSTN HA2 .... 99 F1
Eastcote Primary School
ELTH/MOT SE9 .... 174 D4
Eastcourt Independent School
GDMY/SEVK IG3 .... 95 G5
East Dulwich Baths
EDUL SE22 .... 169 F2
Eastfield Primary School
PEND EN3 .... 40 B1
Eastfields High School
MTCM CR4 .... 206 D5
East Finchley Cemetery
EFNCH N2 .... 65 F6
East Finchley Medical Centre
EFNCH N2 .... 86 A1
East Finchley School of English
EFNCH N2 .... 66 A6
East Greenwich Christ Church
CE Primary School
GNWCH SE10 .... 152 A4
East Ham Industrial Estate
CAN/RD E16 .... 133 F3
East Ham Jewish Cemetery
EHAM E6 .... 133 G2
East Ham Memorial Hospital
FSTGT E7 .... 113 F5
East Ham Nature Reserve
EHAM E6 .... 133 H3
East Lane Business Park
WBLY HA9 .... 81 F6
Eastlea Community School
CAN/RD E16 .... 132 A3
East London Business College
WAN E11 .... 92 A5
East London Cemetery
PLSTW E13 .... 132 B2
East London Crematorium
PLSTW E13 .... 132 B2
East London RFC
EHAM E6 .... 133 H4
East London RUFC
PLSTW E13 .... 132 B1
Eastman Dental Hospital
FSBW WC1X 5 G5
East Molesey Cricket Club
E/WMO/HCT KT8 .... 199 G6
East Sheen Cemetery
RCHPK/HAM TW10 .... 162 A6
East Sheen Primary School
MORT/ESHN SW14 .... 163 E5

East Thamesmead Business Park
ERITHM DA18 .... 156 D2

East Wickham Primary School
WELL DA16 .... 175 F2

Eaton House School
KTBR SW1X 27 E1

Eaton Manor RFC
WAN E11 .... 93 E2

Eaton Square Preparatory School
BCVA SW1W 27 G1

Eaton Square School
PIM SW1V 28 A2

Ecclesbourne Primary School
IS N1 .... 108 D5

Eckerd College
THHTH CR7 .... 228 C2

Eckerd College
GWRST WC1E 12 C1

Ecole De Mime Corporel Theatre De Lange Fou
ARCH N19 .... 87 G6

Eden College
STHWK SE1 .... 22 D5

Edenham High School
CROY/NA CRO 230 D4

Eden Medical Centre
WKENS W14 .... 144 D4

Edenvale Child Health Clinic
TOOT SW17 .... 206 C3

Eden Walk Shopping Centre
KUT KT1 .... 201 G5

Edes Business Park
WLGTN SM6 .... 226 C6

Edgebury Primary School
CHST BR7 .... 194 C6

Edge Business Centre
CRICK NW2 .... 83 H6

Edgwarebury Cemetery
EDGW HA8 .... 46 A4

Edgware Clinic
EDGW HA8 .... 62 A2

Edgware College
HAMP NW3 .... 105 G4

Edgware Community Hospital
EDGW HA8 .... 62 B3

Edgware FC & Wealdstone FC
EDGW HA8 .... 62 A5

Edgware Infant School
EDGW HA8 .... 62 A2

Edgware Junior School
EDGW HA8 .... 62 A2

The Edgware School
EDGW HA8 .... 45 H6

Edinburgh Primary School
WALTH E17 .... 90 D2

Edith Neville Primary School
CAMTN NW1 .... 4 C2

Edmonton Cemetery
ED N9 .... 52 D4

Edmonton County Court
UED N18 .... 69 G1

Edmonton Green Shopping Centre
ED N9 .... 53 H4

Edmonton Leisure Centre
ED N9 .... 53 C5

Edmonton Upper School
EN EN1 .... 53 F2

Edmund Waller Primary School
NWCR SE14 .... 170 B3

Education Centre
WOOL/PLUM SE18 .... 154 B5

Edward Betham CE Primary School
GFD/PVL UB6 .... 119 H2

Edward Redhead Primary School
WALTH E17 .... 70 C6

Edward Wilson Primary School
BAY/PAD W2 .... 125 F4

Effra Primary School
BRXS/STRHM SW2 .... 168 A6

Effra Road Retail Park
BRXS/STRHM SW2 .... 168 A6

Eglinton Infant School
WOOL/PLUM SE18 .... 174 A1

Eglinton Junior School
WOOL/PLUM SE18 .... 154 A6

Elbourne Trading Estate
BELV DA17 .... 157 F3

Eldenwall Industrial Estate
BCTR RM8 .... 96 C5

Eldon JMI School
ED N9 .... 54 A3

Eleanor Palmer Primary School
KTTN NW5 .... 107 E2

Eleanor Smith Special School & Primary Support Service
PLSTW E13 .... 132 C3

Electric Cinema
NTGHL W11 .... 124 D5

Elephant & Castle Shopping Centre
STHWK SE1 .... 22 D6

Elfrida Primary School
CAT SE6 .... 191 F6

Eliot Bank Primary School
FSTH SE23 .... 189 H4

Elizabeth Garrett Anderson Hospital
CAMTN NW1 .... 4 D4

Elizabeth Garrett Anderson School
IS N1 .... 5 H1

Elizabeth Selby Infant School
BETH E2 .... 9 F3

Elizabeth Trading Estate
NWCR SE14 .... 150 B6

Ellen Wilkinson Primary School
EHAM E6 .... 133 F4

Ellen Wilkinson School for Girls
ACT W3 .... 121 H5

Ellerslie Square Industrial Estate
CLAP SW4 .... 167 G3

Ellingham Primary School
CHSGTN KT9 .... 239 F5

Elliott Foundation School
PUT/ROE SW15 .... 184 A1

Elm Court School
WNWD SE27 .... 188 B4

Elmgrove First & Middle School
KTN/HRWW/W HA3 .... 80 C1

Elmhurst Preparatory School
BECK BR3 .... 230 B1

Elmhurst Primary School
FSTGT E7 .... 112 D5

Elmhurst School
CROY/NA CRO 246 D2

Elm Lea Trading Estate
TOTM N17 .... 69 G3

Elmwood Primary School
CROY/NA CRO 228 B4

Elm Wood Primary School
WNWD SE27 .... 188 D5

Elsdale Street Health Centre
HOM E9 .... 110 A5

Elsley Primary School
WBLY HA9 .... 101 H4

Elsley School
BTSEA SW11 .... 166 C4

Eltham Baths
ELTH/MOT SE9 .... 173 G6

Eltham Bus Station
ELTH/MOT SE9 .... 173 H6

Eltham Cemetery
ELTH/MOT SE9 .... 174 C5

Eltham CE Primary School
ELTH/MOT SE9 .... 173 H6

Eltham College
ELTH/MOT SE9 .... 193 F4

Eltham College Junior School
ELTH/MOT SE9 .... 193 F3

Eltham Crematorium
ELTH/MOT SE9 .... 174 D5

Eltham Green School
ELTH/MOT SE9 .... 193 F1

Eltham Health Clinic
ELTH/MOT SE9 .... 173 G6

Eltham Hill Technology College
ELTH/MOT SE9 .... 193 G1

Eltham Palace (remains)
ELTH/MOT SE9 .... 193 G2

Eltham Warren Golf Club
ELTH/MOT SE9 .... 174 B6

Elthorne Park High School
HNWL W7 .... 140 B3

Elystan Business Centre
HYS/HAR UB3 .... 118 A6

Emanuel School
WAND/EARL SW18 .... 165 H6

Embankment Pier
CHCR WC2N 21 G1

Embassy of Afghanistan
SKENS SW7 .... 145 H2

Embassy of Albania
BGVA SW1W 19 H6

Embassy of Algeria
NTGHL W11 .... 144 C1

Embassy of Angola
MYFR/PKLN W1K 11 E6

Embassy of Argentina
MYFR/PKLN W1K 11 G5

Embassy of Armenia
KENS W8 .... 145 F3

Embassy of Austria
KTBR SW1X 19 E5

Embassy of Bahrain
SKENS SW7 .... 145 G3

Embassy of Belarus
KENS W8 .... 145 F2

Embassy of Belgium
KTBR SW1X 19 F6

Embassy of Bolivia
KTBR SW1X 19 F6

Embassy of Bosnia-Herzegovina
CAVSQ/HST W1G 11 H3

Embassy of Brazil
MYFR/PKLN W1K 11 E5

Embassy of Bulgaria
SKENS SW7 .... 145 G3

Embassy of Cameroon
WKENS W14 .... 144 C1

Embassy of China
CAVSQ/HST W1G 11 G1

Embassy of Costa Rica
BAY/PAD W2 .... 125 G6

Embassy of Cote d'Ivoire
KTBR SW1X 19 F5

Embassy of Croatia
GTPST W1W 3 H6

Embassy of Cuba
HHOL WC1V 13 E3

Embassy of the Democratic Republic of the Congo
KTBR SW1X 18 D6

Embassy of Denmark
KTBR SW1X 18 C5

Embassy of Ecuador
KTBR SW1X 18 C5

Embassy of Egypt
MYFR/PICC W1J 19 G1

Embassy of Estonia
SKENS SW7 .... 145 G2

Embassy of Finland
KTBR SW1X 19 E5

Embassy of France
KTBR SW1X 18 D3

Embassy of Georgia
KENS W8 .... 145 F2

Embassy of Germany
KTBR SW1X 19 E5

Embassy of Ghana
HGT N6 .... 86 D5

Embassy of Greece
KENS W8 .... 144 D1

Embassy of Guatemala
WBPTN SW10 .... 145 F6

Embassy of Honduras
MBLAR W1H 10 D1

Embassy of Hungary
KTBR SW1X 19 F6

Embassy of Iceland
KTBR SW1X 27 E1

Embassy of Indonesia
MYFR/PKLN W1K 11 F5

Embassy of Iraq
SKENS SW7 .... 145 G3

Embassy of Ireland
KTBR SW1X 19 G4

Embassy of Israel
KENS W8 .... 145 F2

Embassy of Italy
MYFR/PKLN W1K 11 F5

Embassy of Japan
MYFR/PICC W1J 19 H2

Embassy of Jordan
KENS W8 .... 144 D2

Embassy of Korea
WESTW SW1E 20 B5

Embassy of Krygyzstan
MBLAR W1H 10 C2

Embassy of Kuwait
KTBR SW1X 18 D3

Embassy of Latvia
CAMTN NW1 .... 3 G6

Embassy of Lebanon
KENS W8 .... 145 F1

Embassy of Liberia
BAY/PAD W2 .... 125 G6

Embassy of Lithuania
MBLAR W1H 10 C2

Embassy of Luxembourg
KTBR SW1X 19 E4

Embassy of Mexico
MYFR/PICC W1J 19 G2

Embassy of Mongolia
KENS W8 .... 145 F2

Embassy of Morocco
SKENS SW7 .... 145 G4

Embassy of Mozambique
FITZ W1T 4 A6

Embassy of Myanmar
MYFR/PICC W1J 10 C1

Embassy of Nepal
KENS W8 .... 145 F1

Embassy of Netherlands
SKENS SW7 .... 145 G2

Embassy of Norway
KTBR SW1X 19 F5

Embassy of Oman
SKENS SW7 .... 145 G2

Embassy of Paraguay
KENS W8 .... 145 F3

Embassy of Peru
KTBR SW1X 18 D5

Embassy of the Philippines
KENS W8 .... 145 F1

Embassy of Poland
CAVSQ/HST W1G 11 G1

Embassy of Portugal
KTBR SW1X 19 E4

Embassy of Qatar
MYFR/PKLN W1K 19 F1

Embassy of Romania
KENS W8 .... 145 F2

Embassy of Russian Federation
KENS W8 .... 145 F1

Embassy of Saudi Arabia
MYFR/PICC W1J 19 G1

Embassy of the Republic of Senegal
CRICK NW2 .... 104 A5

Embassy of Slovak Republic
KENS W8 .... 145 F1

Embassy of Slovenia
CAVSQ/HST W1G 11 G3

Embassy of Spain
KTBR SW1X 19 F5

Embassy of Sudan
WHALL SW1A 20 A2

Embassy of Sweden
MBLAR W1H 10 C2

Embassy of Switzerland
MBLAR W1H 10 C2

Embassy of Syria
KTBR SW1X 19 E4

Embassy of Thailand
SKENS SW7 .... 145 G3

Embassy of Tunisia
SKENS SW7 .... 145 H2

Embassy of Turkey
KTBR SW1X 19 F4

Embassy of Turkmenistan
GTPST W1W 12 B2

Embassy of Ukraine
NTGHL W11 .... 144 C1

Embassy of the United Arab Emirates
SKENS SW7 .... 145 H2

Embassy of Uruguay
SKENS SW7 .... 18 B5

Embassy of USA
MYFR/PKLN W1K 11 E5

Embassy of Uzbekistan
NTGHL W11 .... 144 D1

Embassy of Yemen
KENS W8 .... 145 H4

Ember Sports Club
ESH/CLAY KT10 .... 219 G5

Embroidery World Business Centre
WFD IG8 .... 73 F5

EMD Walthamstow Cinema
WALTH E17 .... 91 E1

Emery Theatre
POP/IOD E14 .... 131 F5

Emmanuel CE Primary School
KIL/WHAMP NW6 .... 105 E3

Empire Cinema
LSQ/SEVD WC2H 12 D5

Endsleigh Industrial Estate
NWDGN UB2 .... 138 C4

Enfield Business Centre
PEND EN3 .... 40 A3

Enfield Chace Lower School
ENC/FH EN2 .... 29 E1

Enfield College
PEND EN3 .... 40 A4

Enfield County Upper School
ENC/FH EN2 .... 28 D4

Enfield Cricket Club
EN EN1 .... 39 E5

Enfield FC
ED N9 .... 54 A4

Enfield FC
EN EN1 .... 39 G4

Enfield Golf Club
ENC/FH EN2 .... 38 B5

Enfield Grammar School (Upper)
ENC/FH EN2 .... 38 D4

Enfield Lower Grammar School
FBAR/BDGN N11 .... 38 D3

Enfield School of Swimming
WALW SE17 .... 67 F1

English Martyrs RC Primary School
TWRH E1W 31 G2
WCHPL E1 .... 16 D4

Ennersdale Primary School
LEW SE13 .... 171 H6

Ensham Secondary School
TOOT SW17 .... 206 B1

Enterprise Business Park
POP/IOD E14 .... 151 F2

Enterprise Industrial Estate
BERM/RHTH SE16 .... 150 A5

Epsom & Ewell High School
HOR/WEW KT19 .... 240 C4

Erith & Belvedere FC
BELV DA17 .... 157 F3

Erith Cemetery
ERITH DA8 .... 157 H6

Erith & District Hospital
ERITH DA8 .... 157 H6

Erith School
ERITH DA8 .... 177 G1

Ernest Bevin School
TOOT SW17 .... 186 A5

Eros
MYFR/PICC W1J 12 C6

Esher College
THDIT KT7 .... 220 A4

Esher RFC
WOT/HER KT12 .... 218 C6

Essendine Primary School
KIL/WHAMP NW6 .... 125 E2

Essex Primary School
MNPK E12 .... 113 C4

Ethelburga Jm School
BTSEA SW11 .... 166 A2

Ethel Davis School
CHDH RM6 .... 95 H2

Euro Business Centre
SRTFD E15 .... 112 B6

Eurolink Business Centre
BRXS/STRHM SW2 .... 168 A5

Europa Trading Estate
ERITH DA8 .... 157 H5

European Business Centre
CDALE/KGS NW9 .... 62 D6

European School of Economics
KTBR SW1X 19 E4

European Vocational College
HDTCH EC3A 16 B4

Euro Way School
CEND/HSY/T N8 .... 68 A6

Euro Way School London
FSBYPK N4 .... 88 B4

Euston Centre
CAMTN NW1 .... 4 A5

Euston Station
CAMTN NW1 .... 4 C4

Euston Tower
CAMTN NW1 .... 4 A5

Eveline Lower Primary School
STHWK SE1 .... 33 E4

Evendine College
SOHO/SHAV W1D 12 C3

Eversley Medical Centre
THHTH CR7 .... 228 A3

Eversley Primary School
WCHMH N21 .... 37 G6

Everyman Cinema
HAMP NW3 .... 105 G2

Evolution House
RCH/KEW TW9 .... 161 G3

Ewell Athletics Track
HOR/WEW KT19 .... 240 D4

Ewell Castle School
EW KT17 .... 241 G6

Ewell Grove Infant School
EW KT17 .... 241 F6

EW Fact/Emile Woolf Colleges
HOLWY N7 .... 107 G4

Excel Exhibition Centre
CAN/RD E16 .... 132 C6

Exchange Square
SDTCH EC2A 16 A1

The Exchange
IL IG1 .... 94 B6

Exhibition Halls
STLK EC1Y 15 F1
WBLY HA9 .... 102 A2

Eye Clinic
LSQ/SEVD WC2H 12 D3

Eye Hospital
HHOL WC1V 13 E3

Faircharm Trading Estate
DEPT SE8 .... 171 F1
IS N1 .... 7 E1

The Faircross Complementary Medical Centre
BARK IG11 .... 115 E4

Fairfield Clinic
BKHH IG9 .... 56 D3

Fairfield Industrial Estate
KUT KT1 .... 201 H6

Fairlawn Primary School
FSTH SE23 .... 190 A2

Fairley House School
WEST SW1P 28 C2

Fairlop Primary School
BARK/HLT IG6 .... 74 C4

Fairview Industrial Centre
DAGW RM9 .... 137 H5

Fairview Medical Centre
STRHM/NOR SW16 .... 207 G4

Fairway JMI School
MLHL NW7 .... 46 D4

Fairway Primary School
MLHL NW7 .... 46 D4

Fairways Business Park
LEY E10 .... 90 C6
Falconbrook JMI School
BTSEA SW11 .... 165 H3
Falcon Business Centre
BTSEA SW11 .... 166 A5
Falcon Park Industrial Estate
WLSDN NW10 .... 103 E3
Falkner House School
SKENS SW7 .... 145 G5
Fanmakers' Hall
LVPST EC2M 16 A3
Fan Museum
CNWCH SE10 .... 171 G1
Faraday Building
BLKFR EC4V 14 D4
Farm Lane Trading Estate
FUL/PGN SW6 .... 145 E6
Farnborough Primary School
ORP BR6 .... 252 D3
Farnell House Medical Centre
HSLW TW5 .... 159 F2
Farnham Green Primary School
GDMY/SEVK IG3 .... 95 G3
Farringdon Station
FARR EC1M 14 C1
Farrington & Stratford
House School
CHST BR7 .... 214 D3
Fashion & Textile
Design Museum
STHWK SE1 .... 24 B4
Featherstone Industrial Estate
NWDGN UB2 .... 138 C2
Featherstone Primary School
NWDGN UB2 .... 138 C3
Featherstone Road
Health Clinic
NWDGN UB2 .... 138 C3
Featherstone School
NWDGN UB2 .... 138 B4
Felnex Trading Estate
WLGTN SM6 .... 226 C6
Feltham Airparcs
Leisure Centre
FELT TW13 .... 178 B4
Feltham Community College
FELT TW13 .... 178 A4
Fenchurch Street Station
MON EC3R 16 B5
Fenstanton Junior &
Infant School
BRXS/STRHM SW2 .... 188 A3
Fenton House
HAMP NW3 .... 105 G1
Fern Hill Primary School
KUTN/CMB KT2 .... 201 G2
Ferrier Industrial Estate
WAND/EARL SW18 .... 165 F5
Ferry Island Retail Park
TOTM N17 .... 69 F6
Ferry Lane Industrial Estate
WALTH E17 .... 70 A6
Ferry Lane Primary School
WALTH E17 .... 89 H1
Festival Pier
STHWK SE1 .... 21 H1
Field End Primary School
RSLP HA4 .... 78 B6
Fielding Primary School
WEA W13 .... 140 D3
Film House Cinema
RCH/KEW TW9 .... 161 F6
Financial Times
POP/IOD E14 .... 131 G5
STHWK SE1 .... 23 F1
Finchley Catholic High School
NFNCH/WDSP N12 .... 49 F5
Finchley Cricket Club
FNCH N3 .... 65 F5
Finchley Golf Club
MLHL NW7 .... 64 D2
The Finchley Industrial Centre
NFNCH/WDSP N12 .... 49 G6
Finchley Memorial Hospital
FNCH N3 .... 65 G3
Finchley Youth Theatre
EFNCH N2 .... 66 A6
Fine Arts College
HAMP NW3 .... 106 A4
Finsbury Circus Medical Centre
LVPST EC2M 15 H2
Finsbury Health Centre
CLKNW EC1R 6 A5
Finsbury Leisure Complex
FSBYE EC1V 7 E5
Finsbury Park Track
FSBYPK N4 .... 88 B4
Finton House School
TOOT SW17 .... 186 B4
Fircroft Primary School
TOOT SW17 .... 186 B4
Fire Brigade HQ
STHWK SE1 .... 29 G1
Fire Brigade Museum
STHWK SE1 .... 23 E3
Firepower (Museum of Artillery)
WOOL/PLUM SE18 .... 154 B3
Firs Farm Primary School
PLMGR N13 .... 52 D5
Fisher Athletic FC
BERM/RHTH SE16 .... 150 B1
Fishmonger's Hall
CANST EC4R 15 G6
Fitness Unlimited
Leisure Centre
BOW E3 .... 131 E1
Fitzjohns Primary School
HAMP NW3 .... 105 H3
Fitzrovia Medical Centre
GTPST W1W 4 A6
Fitzroy Nuffield Hospital
MBLAR W1H 10 C3
Five Elms Primary School
DAGW RM9 .... 116 D1
Flamstead House Museum
CNWCH SE10 .... 171 H1
Flaxman Sports Centre
CMBW SE5 .... 168 C3

Fleecefield Primary School
ED N9 .... 53 C6
Fleet Primary School
HAMP NW3 .... 106 B3
Fleetway Business Park
FUL/PGN UB6 .... 120 D1
Fleming Lab Museum
BAY/PAD W2 .... 125 H5
Flora Gardens Primary School
HMSMTH W6 .... 143 H4
Florence Nightingale Museum
STHWK SE1 .... 21 G4
Florida State University
RSQ WC1B 12 D2
Flutters Leisure Centre
FUL/PGN SW6 .... 165 E1
FOB School
CLPT E5 .... 89 G4
Follys End Christian
High School
SNWD SE25 .... 229 E3
The Foot Clinic
WIM/MER SW19 .... 204 C1
The Ford College
CONDST W1S 11 H5
Ford Industrial Park
DAGW RM9 .... 137 F2
Fordview Industrial Estate
RAIN RM13 .... 137 H2
Foreign & Commonwealth
Office
WHALL SW1A 20 D3
Foreland Medical Centre
NTGHL W11 .... 124 C6
Forest Business Park
WALTH E17 .... 90 B4
Forestdale Primary School
CROY/NA CR0 .... 248 C6
Foresters Primary School
WLGTN SM6 .... 245 F4
Forest Gate Community School
FSTGT E7 .... 112 C3
Forest Hill Business Centre
FSTH SE23 .... 190 A4
Forest Hill Industrial Estate
FSTH SE23 .... 190 A4
Forest Hill School
SYD SE26 .... 190 B5
Forest House Business Centre
WAN E11 .... 92 B4
Forest Industrial Park
BARK/HLT IG6 .... 75 E3
Forest Road Medical Centre
WALTH E17 .... 70 D6
Forest School
WALTH E17 .... 92 A1
Forest Trading Estate
WALTH E17 .... 70 B6
Forge Close Clinic
HAYES BR2 .... 232 C5
Forge Lane Primary School
FELT TW13 .... 198 C1
The Former Health Centre
CHARL SE7 .... 153 F4
Forster Park Primary School
CAT SE6 .... 192 A5
Fortismere School
EFNCH N2 .... 66 B5
Fortismere Secondary School
MUSWH N10 .... 66 C6
Fortune Theatre
HOL/ALD WC2B 13 F4
The Forum
EDGW HA8 .... 62 A2
Fossdene Primary School
CHARL SE7 .... 152 D5
Fosters Primary School
WELL DA16 .... 176 A3
Foulds School
BAR EN5 .... 34 B4
The Foundling Museum
BMSBY WC1N 5 F5
Fountayne Business Centre
SEVS/STOTM N15 .... 89 G1
Fountayne Road Health Centre
CLPT E5 .... 89 G6
Fox Primary School
KENS W8 .... 145 E1
Franciscan Primary School
TOOT SW17 .... 186 C6
Francis Holland School
BCVA SW1W 27 F2
CAMTN NW1 .... 2 C6
Frank Barnes Primary School
STJWD NW8 .... 105 H5
Franklin Industrial Estate
PGE/AN SE20 .... 210 A4
Freehold Industrial Centre
HSLWW TW4 .... 158 A6
Free Trade Wharf
WAPW E1W 130 B6
Fresh Wharf Estate
BARK IG11 .... 114 A2
Freuchen Medical Centre
WLSDN NW10 .... 123 F1
Freud Museum
HAMP NW3 .... 105 H4
Friars Primary
Foundation School
STHWK SE1 .... 22 C3
Friends House
CAMTN NW1 .... 4 C4
Friends of Bar Ilan University
GLDGN NW11 .... 85 E5
Friends of the
Hebrew University
CAMTN NW1 .... 106 D2
Friern Barnet School
FBAR/BDGN N11 .... 66 B1
Friern Bridge Retail Park
FBAR/BDGN N11 .... 66 D2
Froebel College
PUT/ROE SW15 .... 183 G1
Frogmore Industrial Estate
HBRY N5 .... 108 C2
WLSDN NW10 .... 122 C2
Fryent Country Park
WBLY HA9 .... 82 A4
Fryent Medical Centre
CDALE/KGS NW9 .... 82 A4

Fryent Primary School
CDALE/KGS NW9 .... 82 C4
Fulham Clinic
FUL/PGN SW6 .... 144 D6
Fulham Cross School
FUL/PGN SW6 .... 164 B1
Fulham FC (Craven Cottage)
FUL/PGN SW6 .... 164 B2
Fulham Medical Centre
FUL/PGN SW6 .... 165 F1
Fulham Palace
FUL/PGN SW6 .... 164 C3
Fulham Preparatory School
FUL/PGN SW6 .... 164 C3
Fulham Primary School
FUL/PGN SW6 .... 145 E6
Fulham & South
Kensington Institute
WBPTN SW10 .... 145 G5
Fulham Warner
Villiage Cinema
FUL/PGN SW6 .... 165 E1
Fuller Smith &
Turner Sports Club
CHSWK W4 .... 163 E2
Fullwell Cross Health Centre
BARK/HLT IG6 .... 74 C5
Fullwood Primary School
BARK/HLT IG6 .... 94 C1
Fulwell Golf Club
HPTN TW12 .... 179 H6
Furness Swanley FC
SWLY BR8 .... 237 H2
Furzedown Primary School
TOOT SW17 .... 206 D2
Furze Infant School
CHDH RM6 .... 96 C3
Future Business College
CONDST W1S 11 H4
Gainsborough Primary School
HOM E9 .... 110 D4
SRTFD E15 .... 132 A2
Gainsborough Clinic
PLMGR N13 .... 51 H6
Galleywall Primary School
BERM/RHTH SE16 .... 33 H2
Galleywall Road Trading Estate
BERM/RHTH SE16 .... 33 H2
Galliard Primary School
ED N9 .... 53 G1
Gallions Mount Primary School
WOOL/PLUM SE18 .... 155 F5
Gants Hill Medical Centre
GNTH/NBYPK IG2 .... 94 A3
Gardener Industrial Estate
BECK BR3 .... 210 C1
Garden Suburb Primary School
GLDGN NW11 .... 84 D2
Garfield Primary School
FBAR/BDGN N11 .... 66 D1
WIM/MER SW19 .... 205 G2
Garratt Park Secondary
Special School
WAND/EARL SW18 .... 185 F5
Garrick Industrial Centre
CDALE/KGS NW9 .... 83 F2
Garrick Theatre
LSQ/SEVD WC2H 13 E6
Garth Primary School
MRDN SM4 .... 225 H2
The Garth Road
Industrial Centre
MRDN SM4 .... 224 A4
Gascoigne Primary School
BARK IG11 .... 114 C6
Gate Cinema
NTGHL W11 .... 145 E1
Gatehouse School
BETH E2 .... 130 B1
The Gatehouse Theatre
HGT N6 .... 86 C4
Gate Theatre
NTGHL W11 .... 125 E6
Gateway
EHAM E6 .... 134 B3
Gateway Industrial Estate
WLSDN NW10 .... 123 F2
Gateway Primary School
STJWD NW8 .... 125 H3
Gayhurst Primary School
HACK E8 .... 109 G5
Gearies Infant School
GNTH/NBYPK IG2 .... 94 A2
Gearies Junior School
GNTH/NBYPK IG2 .... 94 B2
Geffrye Museum
BETH E2 .... 8 B2
Gemini Business Estate
NWCR SE14 .... 150 B5
General Medical Clinics
WCHPL E1 .... 16 C1
Genesis Cinema
WCHPL E1 .... 130 A3
Geoffrey Chaucer School
STHWK SE1 .... 23 G6
The Geoffrey Lloyd
Foulkes Clinic
IL IG1 .... 94 A6
George Eliot Junior &
Infant School
STJWD NW8 .... 105 G6
George Green Mixed School
POP/IOD E14 .... 151 G5
George Lowe Court
BAY/PAD W2 .... 125 F4
George Mitchell School
LEY E10 .... 91 F5
George Mitchell School Annexe
LEY E10 .... 91 F5
George Spicer Primary School
EN EN1 .... 39 F4
George Tomlinson
Primary School
WAN E11 .... 92 A5
Gibson Business Centre
TOTM N17 .... 69 F2
The Gibson Business Centre
TOTM N17 .... 69 F1
The Gielgud Theatre
SOHO/SHAV W1D 12 C5

Giffin Business Centre
DEPT SE8 .... 171 E1
Gifford Primary School
NTHLT UB5 .... 118 D3
Gilbert Collection
TPL/STR WC2R 13 G5
Gilbert Colvin Primary School
CLAY IG5 .... 74 A4
Gilbert Scott Primary School
SAND/SEL CR2 .... 248 C5
Gillespie Primary School
FSBYPK N4 .... 108 B1
Girdlers' Hall
CITYW EC2V 15 F2
Glade Primary School
CLAY IG5 .... 73 H4
Gladesmore Community School
SEVS/STOTM N15 .... 89 G2
The Glades Shopping Centre
BMLY BR1 .... 212 C5
Gladstone Court
Business Centre
VX/NE SW8 .... 167 G2
Gladstone Medical Centre
CRICK NW2 .... 103 F2
Gladstone Park Primary School
WLSDN NW10 .... 103 H3
Glaziers/Scientific
Instrument Makers Hall
STHWK SE1 .... 23 G1
Glebe First & Middle School
KTN/HRWW/W HA3 .... 81 F1
Glebe School
WWKM BR4 .... 231 H5
Gleen Lecky Health Centre
PUT/ROE SW15 .... 164 B5
Glenbrook Primary School
CLAP SW4 .... 187 F1
Glencairn Sports Club
FBAR/BDGN N11 .... 67 E3
Glendower Preparatory School
SKENS SW7 .... 145 G4
Glenham College
IL IG1 .... 94 B6
Glenlyn Medical Centre
E/WMO/HCT KT8 .... 219 G2
Glenthorne High School
CHEAM SM3 .... 225 F5
Globe Primary School
BETH E2 .... 130 A2
Globe Theatre
STHWK SE1 .... 14 C6
Globe Wharf
BERM/RHTH SE16 .... 130 B6
Gloucester Primary School
PECK SE15 .... 32 C6
Gobions JMI School
CRW RM5 .... 77 H2
Godolphin & Latymer School
HMSMTH W6 .... 143 H4
Godwin Junior School
FSTGT E7 .... 112 D2
Godwin Primary School
DAGW RM9 .... 116 C5
Golbome Medical Centre
NKENS W10 .... 124 D3
Goldbeaters Primary School
EDGW HA8 .... 62 D4
Golden Hinde
Educational Museum
STHWK SE1 .... 15 G6
Golders Green Crematorium
GLDGN NW11 .... 85 E4
Golders Green Health Centre
GLDGN NW11 .... 85 F5
Golders Hill Health Centre
EFNCH N2 .... 85 G3
Golders Hill School
GLDGN NW11 .... 85 E4
Goldhawk Industrial Estate
SHB W12 .... 143 H3
Goldsmiths College
BROCKY SE4 .... 170 D4
DEPT SE8 .... 151 E6
LEW SE13 .... 172 A5
NWCR SE14 .... 170 C2
Goldsmiths College
Sports Ground
SCUP DA14 .... 196 C5
Goldsmiths Hall
STBT EC1A 15 E3
Gonville Primary School
THHTH CR7 .... 227 H2
Goodinge Health Centre
HOLWY N7 .... 107 H4
Goodmayes Retail Park
CHDH RM6 .... 95 H4
Goodrich Junior &
Infant School
EDUL SE22 .... 189 C1
Good Shepherd RC
Primary School
BMLY BR1 .... 192 B6
CROY/NA CR0 .... 249 F5
The Good Shepherd RC
Primary School
SHB W12 .... 143 F2
Goodwyn School
MLHL NW7 .... 63 G1
Goose Green Trading Estate
EDUL SE22 .... 169 G5
Gordonbrook Primary School
BROCKY SE4 .... 171 E6
Gordon Hospital
WEST SW1P 28 C2
Gordon House Health Centre
WEA W13 .... 141 C1
Gordon Infant School
IL IG1 .... 114 D1
Gordon Primary School
ELTH/MOT SE9 .... 173 H5
Goresbrook Leisure Centre
DAGW RM9 .... 116 B6
Gorringe Park Middle School
MTCM CR4 .... 206 C4
Gosai Cinema
WCHPL E1 .... 140 D1
Gosbury Hill Health Centre
CHSGTN KT9 .... 239 G2

Gospel Oak Primary School
HAMP NW3 .... 106 C2
Gower House School
CDALE/KGS NW9 .... 82 C6
Grace Business Centre
MTCM CR4 .... 226 B3
Grace Theatre at the Latchmere
BTSEA SW11 .... 166 B3
Graduate School
of Management
TOTM N17 .... 69 F4
Grafton Primary School
BCTR NW8 .... 96 C6
HOLWY N7 .... 107 C1
Grahame Park Health Centre
CDALE/KGS NW9 .... 63 E4
Grahame Park Junior &
Infant School
CDALE/KGS NW9 .... 63 E4
Granard Business Centre
EDGW HA8 .... 63 E2
Granard Primary School
PUT/ROE SW15 .... 183 H1
Granby Sports Club
ELTH/MOT SE9 .... 213 G1
Grand Avenue Primary School
BRYLDS KT5 .... 222 C4
Grande Vitesse
Industrial Centre
STHWK SE1 .... 22 D2
Grand Union Industrial Estate
WLSDN NW10 .... 122 B1
Grange First & Middle School
RYLN/HDSTN HA2 .... 79 F5
Grange Infant School
CAN/RD E16 .... 132 B2
The Grange Museum
CRICK NW2 .... 103 F2
Grange Park
Preparatory School
WCHMH N21 .... 52 B1
Grange Park Primary School
ENC/FH EN2 .... 38 A5
Grange Primary School
EA W5 .... 141 F2
STHWK SE1 .... 24 A6
Grangewood
Independent School
FSTGT E7 .... 113 F5
Granton Primary School
STRHM/NOR SW16 .... 207 E3
Granville Road Industrial Estate
CRICK NW2 .... 84 D6
Grasmere Primary School
STNW/STAM N16 .... 108 D2
Grasshoppers RFC
ISLW TW7 .... 140 B6
Grassroots School
HPTN TW12 .... 199 E4
Grasvenor Avenue
Infant School
BAR EN5 .... 49 E1
Gravel Hill Primary School
BXLYHS DA6 .... 177 F6
Graveney School
TOOT SW17 .... 206 D2
Graves Yard
Industrial Estate
WELL DA16 .... 175 G3
Grays Farm Primary School
STMC/STPC BR5 .... 215 H4
Grazebrook Primary School
STNW/STAM N16 .... 89 E6
Great Cambridge
Industrial Estate
EN EN1 .... 39 H6
Great Chapel Street
Medical Centre
SOHO/SHAV W1D 12 C3
Greater London Authority
Headquarters (City Hall)
STHWK SE1 .... 24 B2
Great Jubilee Wharf
WAP E1W 150 A1
Great Western Industrial Park
STHL UB1 .... 139 F2
Great West Trading Estate
BTFD TW8 .... 140 D6
Greenacres Primary School
ELTH/MOT SE9 .... 194 A4
The Green CE Primary School
BTFD TW8 .... 69 F6
Green Dragon School
BTFD TW8 .... 141 G5
Greenfield Medical Centre
CRICK NW2 .... 104 C1
Greenfields Junior School
SHB W12 .... 123 F6
Greenfields Primary School
OXHEY WD19 .... 58 A1
Greenfields Special School
MUSWH N10 .... 66 B4
Greenford Avenue
Medical Centre
HNWL W7 .... 120 A4
Greenford Green Clinic
NTHLT UB5 .... 100 A3
Greenford High School
STHL UB1 .... 119 E2
Greenford Industrial Estate
GFD/PVL UB6 .... 99 F6
Greenford Park Cemetery
GFD/PVL UB6 .... 119 F4
Greenford Road Medical Centre
GFD/PVL UB6 .... 119 H1
Greengate Medical Centre
PLSTW E13 .... 132 D2
Greengrove College
STHGT/OAK N14 .... 51 G4
Greenheath Business Centre
BETH E2 .... 9 H4
Greenhill College
HRW HA1 .... 80 B2
Greenhill Park Medical Centre
WLSDN NW10 .... 105 H1
Greenland Pier
BERM/RHTH SE16 .... 150 D3
Green Lane Business Park
ELTH/MOT SE9 .... 194 A4

Green Lane Primary School
WPK KT4 .... 223 H4
Greenleaf Primary School
WALTH E17 .... 70 D6
Greenmead Primary School
PUT/ROE SW15 .... 163 H6
The Green School for Girls
ISLW TW7 .... 160 C1
Greenshaw High School
SUT SM1 .... 225 G6
Greenshields Industrial Estate
CAN/RD E16 .... 152 C2
Greenside Primary School
SHB W12 .... 143 G2
Greenslade Primary School
WOOL/PLUM SE18 .... 154 D6
Green Street Primary School
ORP BR6 .... 253 F4
Greenwich Centre
Business Park
DEPT SE8 .... 171 F1
Greenwich Cinema
GNWCH SE10 .... 171 G1
Greenwich College
GNWCH SE10 .... 171 G1
Greenwich Community College
WOOL/PLUM SE18 .... 154 D6
WOOL/PLUM SE18 .... 154 B3
Greenwich Hospital
GNWCH SE10 .... 152 B5
Greenwich Industrial Estate
CHARL SE7 .... 152 D4
GNWCH SE10 .... 171 F1
Greenwich Natural
Health Centre
GNWCH SE10 .... 171 G1
Greenwich School of English
GNWCH SE10 .... 151 G6
Greenwich Theatre &
Art Gallery
GNWCH SE10 .... 171 H1
Greenwich University Library
GNWCH SE10 .... 151 G6
Greenwood First School
NTHLT UB5 .... 99 G3
Greenwood School
WOOL/PLUM SE18 .... 175 E2
Greenwood Theatre
STHWK SE1 .... 23 H3
Green Wrythe Primary School
CAR SM5 .... 225 H3
Grenfell Primary School
WCHPL E1 .... 17 G3
Gresham College
FLST/FETLN EC4A 14 A2
Gresham Way Industrial Estate
WIM/MER SW19 .... 185 F5
The Greycoat Hospital
WEST SW1P 28 C2
Grey Coat Hospital
Upper School
WEST SW1P 20 C6
Grey Court School
RCHPK/HAM TW10 .... 181 E5
Griffen Manor School
WOOL/PLUM SE18 .... 175 E2
Grimsdyke First &
Middle School
PIN HA5 .... 58 D2
Grims Dyke Golf Club
PIN HA5 .... 43 E6
Grinling Gibbons
Primary School
DEPT SE8 .... 150 D6
Grist Memorial Sports Club
E/WMO/HCT KT8 .... 220 A2
Grocers' Hall
CITYW EC2V 15 G4
Grosvenor Hospitals
HDN NW4 .... 83 H2
The Grove Health Centre
HMSMTH W6 .... 143 H2
Grove House School
WNWD SE27 .... 188 B4
Grovelands Priory Hospital
STHGT/OAK N14 .... 51 G3
Grove Medical Centre
DEPT SE8 .... 150 C4
The Grove Medical Centre
ARCH N19 .... 87 E6
Grove Park Industrial Estate
CDALE/KGS NW9 .... 82 D1
Grove Park Primary School
CHSWK W4 .... 142 C6
Grove Park School
CDALE/KGS NW9 .... 82 C1
Grove Primary School
CHDH RM6 .... 95 H2
Grove Road Primary School
HSLW TW3 .... 159 G5
The Groves Medical Centre
NWMAL KT3 .... 203 E6
Grove Vale Primary School
EDUL SE22 .... 169 F5
Guardian Angels RC
Primary School
BOW E3 .... 130 C3
Guardian Newspapers
POP/IOD E14 .... 151 F2
Guards' Chapel and Museum
WHALL SW1A 20 C4
Guildhall School
BARB EC2Y 15 F1
Guildhall School of
Music & Drama
STLK EC1Y 7 F6
Guildhall University
WCHPL E1 .... 17 F3
Gumley House Convent School
ISLW TW7 .... 160 C4
Gunnersbury Catholic School
BTFD TW8 .... 141 E5
Gunnersbury Park Museum
ACT W3 .... 142 A3
Gurnell Leisure Centre
WEA W13 .... 120 B2
Gurnell Middle School
WEA W13 .... 120 B4

Guru Gobind Singh
Khalsa College
CHIG IG7 .... 57 H3
Guru Nanak Medical Centre
STHL UB1 .... 138 B1
Guys Hospital
STHWK SE1 .... 23 H2
Guys Kings & St Thomas
School of Medicine
CMBW SE5 .... 168 C3
Gwyn Jones Primary School
WAN E11 .... 91 H4
GX Superbowl
EHAM E6 .... 134 A4
Gypsy Moth IV
GNWCH SE10 .... 151 G6
Haberdashers Askes
Hatcham College
NWCR SE14 .... 170 C2
NWCR SE14 .... 170 C3
Haberdashers' Hall
STHWK SE1 .... 15 F3
Hackbridge Primary School
WLGTN SM6 .... 226 C5
Hackney Business Centre
BETH E2 .... 109 H4
Hackney City Farm
BETH E2 .... 9 E2
Hackney Community College
CLPT E5 .... 109 H1
IS N1 .... 8 A2
Hackney Empire
Variety Theatre
HACK E8 .... 109 H4
Hackney Free & Parochial
CE School
HOM E9 .... 110 A4
Hackney Hospital
HOM E9 .... 110 C3
The Hackney Museum
HOM E9 .... 110 A6
Hackney Sports Centre
HOM E9 .... 111 E2
Hadley Wood Golf Club
EBAR EN4 .... 36 A2
Hadley Wood Primary School
EBAR EN4 .... 35 G1
The Haelan Clinic
CEND/HSY/T N8 .... 87 F3
Haggerston School
BETH E2 .... 8 D1
Haggerston Swimming Pool
BETH E2 .... 109 F6
Hague Primary School
BETH E2 .... 9 G5
Hailey Road Business Park
ERITHM DA18 .... 157 E2
Haimo Primary School
ELTH/MOT SE9 .... 173 F6
Hainault Forest Golf Club
CHIG IG7 .... 76 B2
Hainault Forest High School
BARK/HLT IG6 .... 75 C1
Hainault Industrial Estate
BARK/HLT IG6 .... 76 A1
Hakim Qureshi Clinic
NWDGN UB2 .... 138 C3
The Hale Clinic
REGST W1B 3 H7
Half Moon Theatre
WCHPL E1 .... 130 B3
Halling Manor High School
CROY/NA CRO 246 B5
Halley Primary School
POP/IOD E14 .... 130 C4
Hallfield Clinic
BAY/PAD W2 .... 2 C5
Hallfield Primary School
BAY/PAD W2 .... 2 C5
The Hall Junior School
HAMP NW3 .... 105 H4
Hallmark Trading Estate
WBLY HA9 .... 102 C2
Hall Place
BXLY DA5 .... 197 G1
Hall School Wimbledon
PUT/ROE SW15 .... 183 C5
The Hall Senior School
HAMP NW3 .... 105 H4
Hallsville Primary School
CAN/RD E16 .... 132 C5
Halstow Primary School
GNWCH SE10 .... 152 B5
Hambrough Primary School
STHL UB1 .... 114 D1
Hamer Indoor Market
BOW E3 .... 130 D1
Ham Health Clinic
RCHPK/HAM TW10 .... 181 E5
Ham House (NT)
RCHPK/HAM TW10 .... 181 E3
Hamilton Road
Industrial Estate
WNWD SE27 .... 188 D6
Hamlet International
Industrial Estate
ERITH DA8 .... 157 H5
Hammersmith Apollo
HMSMTH W6 .... 144 A5
Hammersmith Cemetery
HMSMTH W6 .... 144 A5
The Hammersmith Hospitals
SHB W12 .... 123 G5
Hammersmith Industrial Estate
HMSMTH W6 .... 144 A6
Hammersmith New Cemetery
RCH/KEW TW9 .... 162 B3
Hammersmith Palais
HMSMTH W6 .... 144 A4
Hammersmith Physio &
Sports Injury Clinic
HMSMTH W6 .... 144 A4
Hammersmith & West
London College
WKENS W14 .... 144 B4
Hampden Gurney School
MBLAR W1H 10 B3
Ham & Petersham Cricket Club
RCHPK/HAM TW10 .... 181 F6

The Hampshire School
SKENS SW7 .... 18 A4
The Hampshire School
(Knightsbridge)
SKENS SW7 .... 18 A4
The Hampshire School
BAY/PAD W2 .... 125 F6
Hampstead Cricket Club
KIL/WHAMP NW6 .... 105 F3
Hampstead Golf Club
EFNCH N2 .... 85 G4
Hampstead Medical Centre
HAMP NW3 .... 105 G2
Hampstead Parochial CE School
HAMP NW3 .... 105 G2
Hampstead School
CRICK NW2 .... 104 C2
Hampstead School of English
KIL/WHAMP NW6 .... 105 E2
Hampton Cemetery
HPTN TW12 .... 199 E3
Hampton Community College
HPTN TW12 .... 199 E1
Hampton Court Palace
E/WMO/HCT KT8 .... 200 B6
Hampton Farm
Industrial Estate
FELT TW13 .... 178 C5
Hampton FC
HPTN TW12 .... 199 F4
Hampton Hill Junior School
HPTN TW12 .... 199 G1
Hampton Infant School
HPTN TW12 .... 198 D3
Hampton Junior School
HPTN TW12 .... 199 E4
The Hampton Medical Centre
HPTN TW12 .... 199 E3
Hampton Road Industrial Estate
CROY/NA CRO 228 C3
Hampton School
HPTN TW12 .... 199 E1
Hampton Swimming Baths
HPTN TW12 .... 199 G3
Hampton Wick Infants School
KUT KT1 .... 201 E3
Handsworth Health Clinic
CHING E4 .... 71 H2
Handsworth Primary School
IS N1 .... 71 H2
Hanover Primary School
IS N1 .... 6 D1
Hanover Trading Estate
HOLWY N7 .... 107 G3
Hanover West
Industrial Estate
WLSDN NW10 .... 122 C2
Hanworth Trading Estate
FELT TW13 .... 178 C5
Harbinger Primary School
POP/IOD E14 .... 151 E4
Harborough School
ARCH N19 .... 87 F6
Harenc School
SCUP DA14 .... 216 A1
Hargrave Park Primary School
ARCH N19 .... 87 E6
Haringey Arts Council
ED N9 .... 53 G4
Haringey Community
Health Clinic
SEVS/STOTM N15 .... 89 F1
Haringey Health Care
SEVS/STOTM N15 .... 89 F1
Haringey Magistrates Court
HGT N6 .... 86 C3
Harland Primary School
WIM/MER SW19 .... 205 G5
Harlesden Primary School
WLSDN NW10 .... 123 E1
Harley Medical Centre
CAVSQ/HST W1G 11 G3
The Harley Medical Centre
CANST EC4R 15 F5
Harley Street Clinic
CAVSQ/HST W1G 11 G1
CAVSQ/HST W1G 11 G2
The Harold Macmillan
Medical Centre
HRW HA1 .... 79 H4
Harp Business Centre
CRICK NW2 .... 83 G6
Harpley School
WCHPL E1 .... 130 A3
Harrington Hill Primary School
CLPT E5 .... 89 H5
Harris City Technology College
NRWD SE19 .... 209 F4
Harrodian School
BARN SW13 .... 163 F1
Harrods Store
CHEL SW3 .... 18 C5
Harrovian Business Village
HRW HA1 .... 79 H4
Harrow Arts Centre
PIN HA5 .... 59 F3
Harrow Borough FC
RYLN/HDSTN HA2 .... 99 E2
Harrow College
HRW HA1 .... 100 A2
Harrow Cricket Club
HRW HA1 .... 100 A2
Harrow Crown Courts
HRW HA1 .... 59 H6
Harrow Heritage Museum
RYLN/HDSTN HA2 .... 59 G6
Harrow High School
HRW HA1 .... 80 C3
Harrow Magistrates Court
HRW HA1 .... 80 B1
Harrow RFC
STAN HA7 .... 44 D5
Harrow Road Health Centre
BAY/PAD W2 .... 125 E4
Harrow School
HRW HA1 .... 80 A4
RYLN/HDSTN HA2 .... 80 A6
Harrow Superbowl
RYLN/HDSTN HA2 .... 79 F2
Harrow Town Cricket Club
RYLN/HDSTN HA2 .... 79 F5

Harrow Weald Cemetery
KTN/HRWW/W HA5 .... 60 A2
Harry Gosling Primary School
WCHPL E1 .... 17 F4
Hartley Primary School
EHAM E6 .... 113 G6
Hartsbourne Golf & Country Club
BUSH WD23 .... 43 G4
Hartsbourne JMI School
BUSH WD23 .... 43 H4
Harvington School
EA W5 .... 121 G5
Hasseirige School
CLAP SW4 .... 167 F5
Haseltine Primary School
CAT SE6 .... 190 D6
Haslemere Business Centre
EN EN1 .... 39 H5
Haslemere Industrial Estate
WAND/EARL SW18 .... 185 F4
Haslemere Primary School
MTCM CR4 .... 205 H5
Hasmonean High School
HDN NW4 .... 64 B5
MLHL NW7 .... 63 G4
Hasmonean Primary School
HDN NW4 .... 84 B2
Hastings Clinic
BRXS/STRHM SW2 .... 167 H6
Hastingwood Trading Estate
UED N18 .... 70 C2
Hatcham Mews
Business Centre
NWCR SE14 .... 170 B1
Hatch End High School
KTN/HRWW/W HA3 .... 59 F3
Hatton School
REDBR IG4 .... 73 F6
Havelock Primary School
NWDGN UB2 .... 138 D3
Haven Green Clinic
EA W5 .... 121 F5
Haverstock School
CAMTN NW1 .... 106 C4
Hawes Down Clinic
WWKM BR4 .... 231 H6
Hawes Down primary School
WWKM BR4 .... 231 H5
Hawkins Clinic
PUT/ROE SW15 .... 164 B5
RYNPK SW20 .... 203 F4
Hawkswood Primary School
THMD SE28 .... 135 H6
Hawkswood School & Centre
CHING E4 .... 41 G6
Hawley Infant School
CAMTN NW1 .... 106 D5
Hayes Bridge Middle School
NWDGN UB2 .... 138 C2
Hayes Bridge Retail Park
HYS/HAR UB3 .... 118 A6
Hayes Grove Priory Hospital
HAYES BR2 .... 232 C6
Hayes Primary School
HAYES BR2 .... 232 D5
Hayes School
HAYES BR2 .... 232 D6
Haymerle School
PECK SE15 .... 33 E6
Hays Galleria
STHWK SE1 .... 24 A1
Hayward Gallery
STHWK SE1 .... 21 H2
Hazelbury Primary School
ED N9 .... 53 E5
Hazeldene Medical Centre
WBLY HA9 .... 102 B4
Hazelhurst School
RYNPK SW20 .... 204 B4
Hazelwood Infant School
PLMGR N13 .... 52 B6
Hazelwood Junior School
PLMGR N13 .... 52 A6
Health & Welfare Clinic
BFN/LL DA15 .... 195 G1
BXLY DA5 .... 196 B3
WELL DA16 .... 175 G3
Healy Medical Centre
CLPT E5 .... 89 H5
The Heart Hospital
CAVSQ/HST W1G 11 F2
Heathbrook Primary School
VX/NE SW8 .... 167 E3
Heath Business Centre
HSLW TW3 .... 159 G5
Heathcote School
CHING E4 .... 56 A4
Heathfield College
HAYES BR2 .... 251 E4
Heathfield Primary School
WHTN TW2 .... 179 E3
Heathfield School (Senior)
PIN HA5 .... 78 B3
Heath House
Preparatory School
BKHTH/KID SE3 .... 172 B3
Heathland School
HSLWW TW4 .... 178 D1
Heathmere Primary School
PUT/ROE SW15 .... 183 G3
Heathside Preparatory School
HAMP NW3 .... 105 G2
Heathway Industrial Estate
DAGE RM10 .... 117 F2
Heathway Medical Centre
DAGW RM9 .... 116 D2
Heavers Farm Primary School
SNWD SE25 .... 229 F2
Heber Primary School
EDUL SE22 .... 189 F1
Heckford Street Business Centre
WAP E1W 130 B6
Hedges & Butler Estate
SRTFD E15 .... 131 C1
Helena Road Clinic
WLSDN NW10 .... 103 H2
Heliport Industrial Estate
BTSEA SW11 .... 165 H3
Hellenic College of London
KTBR SW1X 18 C6

Helston Court Business Centre
WIM/MER SW19 .... 203 H1
Henderson Hospital
BELMT SM2 .... 243 E6
Hendon Cemetery
HDN NW4 .... 64 B4
Hendon College
CDALE/KGS NW9 .... 63 F4
Hendon Crematorium
HDN NW4 .... 64 B5
Hendon FC
CRICK NW2 .... 84 B6
Hendon Golf Club
HDN NW4 .... 64 A3
Hendon Preparatory School
HDN NW4 .... 64 B6
Hendon School
HDN NW4 .... 84 B2
Hendon Secretarial College
HDN NW4 .... 83 H2
Hendon Youth Sports Centre
CRICK NW2 .... 84 B4
Henry Cavendish
Primary School
BAL SW12 .... 187 E3
Henry Compton School
FUL/PGN SW6 .... 164 B2
Henry Fawcett Primary School
LBTH SE11 .... 30 A5
Henry Green Primary School
BCTR RM8 .... 96 B5
Henry Maynard Infant School
WALTH E17 .... 91 G2
Henry Maynard Junior School
WALTH E17 .... 91 G2
Henwick Primary School
ELTH/MOT SE9 .... 173 F4
Herbert Morrison
Primary School
VX/NE SW8 .... 167 G1
Hereward House School
HAMP NW3 .... 106 A4
Her Majesty's Theatre
STJS SW1Y 20 D1
Hermitage Primary School
WAP E1W 25 E1
Hermitage Stairs
WAP E1W 25 E2
Herne Hill School
HNHL SE24 .... 168 C6
Heron Industrial Estate
SRTFD E15 .... 131 F1
Herongate Primary School
THMD SE28 .... 154 D3
Heron Trading Estate
ACT W3 .... 122 B4
Hersham Trading Estate
WOT/HER KT12 .... 218 C6
Heston Community School
HEST TW5 .... 159 E1
Heston Industrial Mall
HEST TW5 .... 158 D1
Heston Infant School
HEST TW5 .... 159 E1
Heston Junior School
HEST TW5 .... 159 E6
Heston Park Cricket Club
HEST TW5 .... 138 D6
Heston Swimming Baths
HEST TW5 .... 138 D6
HGS Institute Centre
GLDGN NW11 .... 85 E2
Higgs Industrial Estate
BRXN/ST SW9 .... 168 B4
Highams Lodge Business Centre
WALTH E17 .... 70 B6
Highams Park School
CHING E4 .... 71 H2
Highbury Corner Magistrates Court
HOLWY N7 .... 108 A4
Highbury Fields School
HBRY N5 .... 108 B3
Highbury Grove School
HBRY N5 .... 108 C3
Highbury Park Clinic
HBRY N5 .... 108 B3
Highbury Quadrant
Primary School
HBRY N5 .... 108 C3
High Commission of Angola
MYFR/PKLN W1K 11 F5
High Commission of Antigua &
Barbuda
MHST W1U 11 E3
High Commission of Bahamas
MYFR/PICC W1J 19 F1
High Commission of Bangladesh
SKENS SW7 .... 145 G3
High Commission of Barbados
FITZ W1T 12 C3
High Commission of Belize
CAVSQ/HST W1G 11 G2
High Commission of Botswana
OXSTW W1C 11 C4
High Commission of Brunei
KTBR SW1X 19 E5
High Commission of Cyprus
CONDST W1S 11 H4
MYFR/PKLN W1K 11 E5
High Commission of Dominica
ECT SW5 .... 145 F4
High Commission of Fiji
SKENS SW7 .... 145 G3
High Commission of Gambia
KENS W8 .... 145 G2
High Commission of Grenada
ECT SW5 .... 145 F4
High Commission of Guyana
NTGHL W11 .... 125 F6
High Commission of Kenya
CAVSQ/HST W1G 11 G1
High Commission of Lesotho
KTBR SW1X 19 E5
High Commission of Malawi
MYFR/PKLN W1K 11 G5
High Commission of Malaysia
KTBR SW1X 19 F4
MBLAR W1H 10 C3
High Commission of the Maldives
MHST W1U 11 E3

High Commission of Malta
MYFR/PICC W1J 12 B6
High Commission of Namibia
CAVSQ/HST W1G 11 H2
High Commission of
New Zealand
STJS SW1Y 20 C1
High Commission of Nigeria
CHCR WC2N 21 E1
EMB EC4Y 14 B4
High Commission of Pakistan
KTBR SW1X 18 D5
High Commission of
Papua New Guinea
STJS SW1Y 20 C1
High Commission of St Lucia
KENS W8 .... 145 F2
High Commission of Seychelles
MBLAR W1H 10 D1
High Commission of
Sierra Leone
OXSTW W1C 12 A3
High Commission of Singapore
KTBR SW1X 18 D4
KTBR SW1X 19 E6
STJS SW1Y 20 C1
WEST SW1P 28 B1
High Commission of South Africa
CHCR WC2N 20 D1
High Commission of Swaziland
WESTW SW1E 20 A5
High Commission of Tonga
MBLAR W1H 10 B2
High Commission of Trinidad &
Tobago
KTBR SW1X 19 E5
High Commission of Uganda
STJS SW1Y 20 D1
High Commission of Zambia
BAY/PAD W2 .... 145 G2
High Commission of Zimbabwe
CHCR WC2N 13 E6
High Comm of Brunei
BAY/PAD W2 .... 125 H5
High Cross Centre
SEVS/STOTM N15 .... 89 G1
High Elms Country Park
ORP BR6 .... 252 C5
High Elms Golf Club
ORP BR6 .... 252 C5
Highfield Infant School
HAYES BR2 .... 232 A1
Highfield Junior School
HAYES BR2 .... 232 A1
Highfield Primary School
WCHMH N21 .... 52 B3
Highfield School
WAND/EARL SW18 .... 186 A2
Highgate Cemy
HGT N6 .... 86 C5
Highgate Golf Club
HGT N6 .... 86 A3
Highgate Junior School
HGT N6 .... 86 B4
Highgate Pre-Preparatory School
HGT N6 .... 86 B4
Highgate Primary School
HGT N6 .... 86 B4
Highgate Private Hospital
HGT N6 .... 86 B3
Highgate School
HGT N6 .... 86 B4
Highgate Wood School
CEND/HSY/T N8 .... 87 E2
Highlands Junior &
Infant School
IL IG1 .... 93 H5
Highlands Primary School
IL IG1 .... 93 H5
High Road Swimming Baths
IL IG1 .... 94 D6
Highshore School
PECK SE15 .... 169 F2
High View Primary School
BTSEA SW11 .... 165 H5
Highview Primary School
WLGTN SM6 .... 245 G3
The Highway Trading Centre
WAP E1W 130 B6
Hillbrook Primary School
TOOT SW17 .... 186 B6
Hillcroft College
SURB KT6 .... 221 G3
Hill House International School
KTBR SW1X 18 C6
Hill House School
CHEL SW3 .... 26 B5
Hill Mead Infant School
HNHL SE24 .... 168 B5
Hillmead Primary School
BRXN/ST SW9 .... 168 B5
Hills Grove Primary School
WELL DA16 .... 176 A1
Hilly Fields Medical Centre
BROCKY SE4 .... 171 E6
The Hiltongrove
Business Centre
WALTH E17 .... 91 E1
Hinchley Wood School
ESH/CLAY KT10 .... 220 C6
Hinley Clinic
LBTH SE11 .... 30 C2
Hispaniola
WHALL SW1A 21 F2
Hitherfield Primary School
STRHM/NOR SW16 .... 188 A4
Hither Green Cemetery
CAT SE6 .... 192 B4
Hither Green Primary School
LEW SE13 .... 191 H1
HM Prison
CLAP SW4 .... 187 G1
HOLWY N7 .... 107 G2
HOLWY N7 .... 107 H4
WAND/EARL SW18 .... 185 H1
SHB W12 .... 123 G5
HMS Belfast
STHWK SE1 .... 24 B1
HMS President
EMB EC4Y 14 B5

Hobbayne First &
Middle School
HNWL W7 .... 120 B5
Hobbayne Primary School
HNWL W7 .... 120 A5
Hogarth Business Park
CHSWK W4 .... 143 E6
Hogarth Industrial Estate
WLSDN NW10 .... 123 G3
Hogarth Primary School
CHSWK W4 .... 143 E5
Hogarth's House
CHSWK W4 .... 142 D6
Holbeach Primary School
CAT SE6 .... 191 G2
Holborn College
WKENS W14 .... 144 C6
Holborn Medical Centre
BMSBY WC1N 5 G6
Holborn Town Hall
HHOL WC1V 13 F3
Holland House School
EDGW HA8 .... 46 A6
Holland Park School
KENS W8 .... 144 D2
Holland Park Theatre
KENS W8 .... 144 D2
Holland Street Clinic
KENS W8 .... 145 E2
Hollickwood JMI School
MUSWH N10 .... 66 D3
Holloway School
HOLWY N7 .... 107 F3
Hollydale Primary School
PECK SE15 .... 170 A3
The Hollyfield School
SURB KT6 .... 221 G2
Holly House Private Hospital
BKHH IG9 .... 56 C4
Hollymount Primary School
RYNPK SW20 .... 204 A4
Holly Park JMI School
FBAR/BDGN N11 .... 50 C6
The Holme
CAMTN NW1 .... 2 D4
Holmleigh Primary School
STNW/STAM N16 .... 89 F3
Holy Cross Convent School
NWMAL KT3 .... 222 D1
Holy Cross Preparatory School
KUTN/CMB KT2 .... 202 C3
Holy Cross RC Primary School
CAT SE6 .... 191 G3
Holy Family College
WALTH E17 .... 71 G6
Holy Family RC Primary School
ELTH/MOT SE9 .... 172 D5
POP/IOD E14 .... 124 D2
Holy Family Technology College
WALTH E17 .... 91 F1
Holy Ghost RC Primary School
BAL SW12 .... 186 B2
Holy Innocents C
Primary School
ORP BR6 .... 253 F1
Holy Trinity CE First School
WIM/MER SW19 .... 205 E2
Holy Trinity CE Junior School
WLGTN SM6 .... 245 E2
Holy Trinity CE Primary School
BGVA SW1W 27 E1
BRXS/STRHM SW2 .... 187 H2
EFNCH N2 .... 65 H6
FSTH SE23 .... 190 A4
KIL/WHAMP NW6 .... 105 G4
RCHPK/HAM TW10 .... 162 A5
Holy Trinity College
BMLY BR1 .... 213 G4
Holy Trinity Haverstock Hill CE
Primary School
CAMTN NW1 .... 106 C1
Holy Trinity Primary School
HACK E8 .... 109 F4
Holy Trinity School
CHEL SW3 .... 26 D1
Home Park Golf Club
E/WMO/HCT KT8 .... 221 E2
Homerton Hospital
CLPT E5 .... 110 B3
Homerton House School
HOM E9 .... 110 A3
Homoeopathic Health Centre
PLSTW E13 .... 132 C3
The Homoeopathic
Health Centre
MLHL NW7 .... 63 F1
Honeypot Business Centre
STAN HA7 .... 61 G4
Honeypot Lane Centre
STAN HA7 .... 61 F4
Honeypot Medical Centre
STAN HA7 .... 61 G5
Honeywell Primary School
BTSEA SW11 .... 186 B1
Hong Kong & Shanghai
Sports Club
BECK BR3 .... 210 C2
Honor Oak Crematorium
FSTH SE23 .... 170 B6
Honor Oak Gallery
FSTH SE23 .... 190 B1
Honor Oak Health Centre
BROCKY SE4 .... 190 C1
Honourable Artillery
Company HQ
STLK EC1Y 7 G6
Hook Lane Primary School
WELL DA16 .... 175 G4
Hook Rise South Industrial Park
CHSGTN KT9 .... 240 A1
Horizon Business Centre
ED N9 .... 54 B4
Horizon Industrial Estate
PECK SE15 .... 33 E6
Horizon School
STNW/STAM N16 .... 109 E2
The Horniman
Museum & Gardens
FSTH SE23 .... 189 H3

Horniman Primary School
FSTH SE23 .... 189 H3
Horn Park Primary School
LEE/GVPK SE12 .... 192 D2
Hornsby House School
BAL SW12 .... 186 C3
Hornsey Central Hospital
CEND/HSY/T N8 .... 87 F2
Hornsey County School
FSBYPK N4 .... 88 B2
Hornsey Rise Health Centre
ARCH N19 .... 87 F4
Hornsey School for Girls
CEND/HSY/T N8 .... 87 H2
Horseferry Road
Magistrates Court
WEST SW1P 20 D6
Horse Guards Parade
WHALL SW1A 20 D2
Horsenden Hill Golf Club
GFD/PVL UB6 .... 100 D4
Horsenden Primary School
GFD/PVL UB6 .... 100 A4
Horton Country Park
HOR/WEW KT19 .... 240 A6
Horton Park Golf &
Country Club
HOR/WEW KT19 .... 240 C5
Hortus Cemetery
NWDGN UB2 .... 138 D2
Hospital & Counselling Centre
CAMTN NW1 .... 10 B1
Hospital of St John &
St Elizabeth
STJWD NW8 .... 125 H1
Hotham Primary School
PUT/ROE SW15 .... 164 B5
Hotspur Industrial Estate
TOTM N17 .... 69 G2
Houndsfield Primary School
ED N9 .... 53 G2
Hounslow Business Park
HSLW TW3 .... 159 E5
Hounslow Cemetery
HSLWW TW4 .... 178 D2
Hounslow College
Independent School
FELT TW13 .... 178 B6
Hounslow Cricket Club
HSLW TW3 .... 158 D3
Hounslow Heath Golf Club
HSLWW TW4 .... 158 C4
Hounslow Heath Infant School
HSLWW TW4 .... 158 C4
Hounslow Heath Junior School
HSLWW TW4 .... 158 C4
Hounslow Manor School
HSLW TW3 .... 159 F4
Hounslow Town
Primary School
HSLW TW3 .... 159 G4
House of Detention
CLKNW EC1R 6 B5
House of St Barnabas
SOHO/SHAV W1D 12 C4
Houses of Parliament
WEST SW1P 21 F4
Houston Business Park
YEAD UB4 .... 138 A1
Howard Primary School
CROY/NA CR0 .... 246 C2
Howland Quay
BERM/RHTH SE16 .... 150 B3
Hoxton Hall Community Theatre
IS N1 .... 8 A1
HQS Wellington
(Master Mariners)
TPL/STR WC2R 14 A6
Hubbinet Industrial Estate
ROMW/RG RM7 .... 77 C6
Hughesfields Primary School
DEPT SE8 .... 151 E6
Hugh Myddelton
Primary School
CLKNW EC1R 6 B4
The Humana
Wellington Hospital
STJWD NW8 .... 125 H2
Humber Trading Estate
CRICK NW2 .... 83 H6
Hungerford Primary School
DAGE RM10 .... 107 F4
Hunters Hall Primary School
DAGE RM10 .... 117 F3
Hunter Street Health Centre
STPAN WC1H 5 E5
Huntsman Sports Club
BKHTH/KID SE3 .... 172 C5
Hurlingham Business Park
FUL/PGN SW6 .... 165 E4
Hurlingham & Chelsea School
FUL/PGN SW6 .... 165 E4
Hurlingham House
FUL/PGN SW6 .... 164 D4
Huron University
SKENS SW7 .... 145 H3
Hurricane Trading Centre
CDALE/KGS NW9 .... 63 F4
Hurstmere School
BFN/LL DA15 .... 195 H3
Hurst Park School
E/WMO/HCT KT8 .... 199 E6
Hurst Primary School
BXLY DA5 .... 196 B3
The Hyde Industrial Estate
CDALE/KGS NW9 .... 83 F2
The Hyde School
CDALE/KGS NW9 .... 83 F2
Hyland House School
WALTH E17 .... 71 H5
Hyleford Leavers Unit School
BARK/HLT IG6 .... 74 D5
Hyleford School
IL IG1 .... 115 E3
Hythe Road Industrial Estate
WLSDN NW10 .... 123 C3
Ibstock Place School
PUT/ROE SW15 .... 183 E1
ICA Cinema
STJS SW1Y 20 D2

Ichthus Primary School
CMBW SE5 .... 168 D1
Ickburgh School
CLPT E5 .... 109 H1
Ihlara Sport FC
HBRY N5 .... 108 C2
Ikra Primary School
STNW/STAM N16 .... 109 E2
Ilderton Primary School
BERM/RHTH SE16 .... 150 A6
Ilford County Court
IL IG1 .... 94 D6
Ilford County High School
BARK/HLT IG6 .... 74 C5
Ilford Golf Club
IL IG1 .... 95 H5
Ilford Jewish Primary School
BARK/HLT IG6 .... 74 D6
Ilford Medical Centre
IL IG1 .... 114 B1
Ilford Preparatory School
GDMY/SEVK IG3 .... 95 F5
Ilford Retail Park
IL IG1 .... 94 C6
Imber Court Trading Estate
E/WMO/HCT KT8 .... 219 H3
Immanuel CE Primary School
STRHM/NOR SW16 .... 207 G2
Immanuel College
BUSH WD23 .... 44 A2
Imperial College
PUT/ROE SW15 .... 164 B3
SKENS SW7 .... 145 H5
Imperial College of Science
FUL/PGN SW6 .... 145 E6
Imperial College of
Science & Technology
SKENS SW7 .... 145 H2
Imperial College
School of Medicine
PIM SW1V 28 C2
Imperial War Museum
STHWK SE1 .... 22 B6
Imperial War Museum Annexe
STHWK SE1 .... 22 B6
India House
HOL/ALD WC2B 13 C5
Infant College
IL IG1 .... 94 A6
The Infirmary Royal Hospital
CHEL SW3 .... 27 E4
Innellan House School
PIN HA5 .... 58 B6
Inner London Sessions House
(Crown Court)
STHWK SE1 .... 23 E5
Inner Temple
EMB EC4Y 14 B5
Innholders Hall
CANST EC4R 15 F5
Inns of Court and Chancery
TPL/STR WC2R 14 A4
Inns of Court School of Law
GINN WC1R 13 H1
Institut Francais
SKENS SW7 .... 145 H4
International Community School
CAMTN NW1 .... 3 E6
International Financial Centre
OBST EC2N 16 A3
International School of London
ACT W3 .... 142 A4
Invicta Industrial Estate
SRTFD E15 .... 131 G2
Invicta Primary School
BKHTH/KID SE3 .... 152 C6
Inwood Business Centre
HSLW TW3 .... 159 F5
Ironmongers Hall
BARB EC2Y 15 E2
Islamia Girls School
KIL/WHAMP NW6 .... 104 C6
Islamic College
WCHPL E1 .... 17 F3
Islamic College for
Advanced Studies
WLSDN NW10 .... 103 H5
The Islamic Grammar School
WAND/EARL SW18 .... 184 D2
Island Clinic
POP/IOD E14 .... 151 G2
Isleworth Baths
ISLW TW7 .... 160 B5
Isleworth Blue CE
Primary School
ISLW TW7 .... 160 C4
Isleworth Cemetery
ISLW TW7 .... 160 C3
Isleworth & Syon
School for Boys
ISLW TW7 .... 160 A1
Isleworth Town
Primary School
ISLW TW7 .... 160 B3
Islington Arts & Media School
FSBYPK N4 .... 87 H5
Islington Business Centre
IS N1 .... 108 C6
Islington Crematorium
EFNCH N2 .... 66 A4
Islington Green Medical Centre
IS N1 .... 108 B6
Islington Green School
IS N1 .... 108 B6
Islington Town Hall
IS N1 .... 108 B5
Ismaili Centre
SKENS SW7 .... 145 H4
Italia Conti Academy of
Theatre Arts
BRXN/ST SW9 .... 167 G4
Italian Hospital
WEST SW1P 28 A1
Ithaca College
SKENS SW7 .... 145 G4
Ivybridge Primary School
TWK TW1 .... 180 B1
Ivybridge Retail Park
ISLW TW7 .... 160 B6

Ivydale Primary School
PECK SE15 .... 170 B5
Jack & Jill School
HPTN TW12 .... 199 E2
WHTN TW2 .... 180 A4
Jack Taylor School
KIL/WHAMP NW6 .... 105 G6
Jack Tizzard School
FUL/PGN SW6 .... 164 B2
Jamahiria School
CHEL SW3 .... 26 A5
James Allens Preparatory
Girls School
HNHL SE24 .... 168 D6
James Dixon Primary School
PGE/AN SE20 .... 209 G3
Jamestown Mental
Health Centre
HAMP NW3 .... 106 B3
James Wolfe Primary School
GNWCH SE10 .... 171 F1
Janet Adegoke Leisure Centre
SHB W12 .... 123 G6
The Japanese School
ACT W3 .... 122 A6
Japan Green Medical Centre
ACT W3 .... 142 B1
Jenner Health Centre
FSTH SE23 .... 190 C3
Jermyn Street Theatre
STJS SW1Y 12 B7
Jessop Primary School
HNHL SE24 .... 168 B5
Jewel Tower
WEST SW1P 21 E5
Jewish Cemetery
CLDGN NW11 .... 85 E3
Jewish Community Theatre
CMBW SE5 .... 168 D4
The Jewish Museum
CAMTN NW1 .... 106 D6
FNCH N3 .... 65 E5
Jews College London
HDN NW4 .... 84 B3
Johanna Primary School
STHWK SE1 .... 22 A4
John Ball Primary School
BKHTH/KID SE3 .... 172 A3
John Betts Primary School
HMSMTH W6 .... 143 C3
John Bramston Primary School
BARK/HLT IG6 .... 75 C2
John Burns Primary School
BTSEA SW11 .... 166 C3
John Chilton School
NTHLT UB5 .... 98 C5
John Dixon Clinic
BERM/RHTH SE16 .... 25 G5
John Donne Primary School
PECK SE15 .... 169 H2
John F Kennedy
Special School
SRTFD E15 .... 111 H6
John Keble CE Primary School
WLSDN NW10 .... 103 F6
John Kelly Boys &
Girls Technology College
CRICK NW2 .... 103 H1
The John Loughborough School
TOTM N17 .... 69 F5
John Lyon School
RYLN/HDSTN HA2 .... 79 H5
John Milton Primary School
VX/NE SW8 .... 167 E1
John Nightingale School
E/WMO/HCT KT8 .... 198 D6
John Orwell Sports Centre
WAP E1W 25 C1
John Paul II RC School
WIM/MER SW19 .... 184 B2
John Perryn Primary School
ACT W3 .... 123 E4
John Perry Primary School
DAGE RM10 .... 117 H4
John Roan Lower School
BKHTH/KID SE3 .... 152 B6
John Roan School
BKHTH/KID SE3 .... 172 A1
John Ruskin College
SAND/SEL CR2 .... 248 C5
John Ruskin Primary School
WALW SE17 .... 31 E5
John Scott Health Centre
FSBYPK N4 .... 88 C5
John Scurr JMI School
WCHPL E1 .... 130 A3
John Smith House
WALW SE17 .... 31 C5
John Stainer Primary School
BROCKY SE4 .... 170 C4
Joseph Clarke Special School
CHING E4 .... 71 H2
Joseph Hood Primary School
RYNPK SW20 .... 204 C5
Joseph Lancaster School
STHWK SE1 .... 23 F6
Joseph Tritton Primary School
BTSEA SW11 .... 165 G5
Jubilee Country Park
HAYES BR2 .... 234 B3
Jubilee JMI School
STNW/STAM N16 .... 89 C3
Jubilee Market
COVCDN WC2E 13 F5
Jubilee Primary School
THMD SE28 .... 136 A6
Jubilee Sports Ground
CHING E4 .... 55 H6
Julians Primary School
STRHM/NOR SW16 .... 188 A6
Junior & Youth Centre
PLSTW E13 .... 130 C4
Juno Way Industrial Estate
NWCR SE14 .... 150 B6
Justines Park
CRICK NW2 .... 83 G5
JVC Business Park
CRICK NW2 .... 83 G5
Kangley Business Centre
SYD SE26 .... 210 D1
Katella Trading Estate
BARK IG11 .... 135 E2

Katherine Road Medical Centre
FSTGT E7 .... 113 E4
Keats House Museum
HAMP NW3 .... 105 H2
Keble Preparatory School
WCHMH N21 .... 52 A2
Keen Students
Supplementary School
WCHPL E1 .... 17 E1
Keir Hardie Primary School
CAN/RD E16 .... 132 C4
Keith Davis Cue Sports Club
DAGW RM9 .... 116 B5
Kelmscott Leisure Centre
WALTH E17 .... 90 D3
Kelmscott School
WALTH E17 .... 90 D3
Kelsey Park School
BECK BR3 .... 211 G6
Kelvin Grove Primary School
SYD SE26 .... 189 H5
Kelvin Industrial Estate
GFD/PVL UB6 .... 99 F6
GFD/PVL UB6 .... 119 H2
Kemnal Technology College
CHST BR7 .... 214 D1
Kempton Park Racecourse
SUN TW16 .... 198 A4
Ken Barrington Centre
LBTH SE11 .... 29 H6
Kender Primary School
NWCR SE14 .... 170 A2
Kenmont Primary School
WLSDN NW10 .... 123 C2
Kenmore Park Middle School
KTN/HRWW/W HA3 .... 61 F6
Kenneth More Theatre
IL IG1 .... 114 C1
Kensal Rise Primary
School
WLSDN NW10 .... 124 B1
Kensington Ave
Primary School
THHTH CR7 .... 208 A4
Kensington Business Centre
SKENS SW7 .... 18 B5
Kensington & Chelsea College
NKENS W10 .... 124 C4
WBPTN SW10 .... 165 G1
Kensington & Chelsea
Town Hall
KENS W8 .... 145 E2
Kensington Market
KENS W8 .... 145 F2
Kensington Palace
KENS W8 .... 145 F1
Kensington Park School
REGST W1B 11 H1
Kensington Preparatory School
FUL/PGN SW6 .... 164 D2
Kensington Primary School
MNPK E12 .... 113 H4
Kensington School of Business
HCIRC EC1N 14 B1
Kensington Wharf
WBPTN SW10 .... 165 H1
Kensit Memorial College
FNCH N3 .... 64 C5
Kentish Town Church CE
Primary School
KTTN NW5 .... 107 E3
Kentish Town Health Centre
KTTN NW5 .... 107 E4
Kentish Town Industrial Estate
KTTN NW5 .... 106 D3
Kenton Clinic
KTN/HRWW/W HA3 .... 81 G2
Kenton Cricket Club
KTN/HRWW/W HA3 .... 81 E1
Kent Park Industrial Estate
PECK SE15 .... 33 H5
Kenwood House
HGT N6 .... 86 A5
Kerem House School
EFNCH N2 .... 85 G2
The Kerem School
EFNCH N2 .... 85 H2
Keston CE Primary School
HAYES BR2 .... 251 F3
Kew Bridge Steam Museum
BTFD TW8 .... 141 H5
Kew College
RCH/KEW TW9 .... 162 A1
Kew Gardens
(Royal Botanic Gardens)
RCH/KEW TW9 .... 161 G2
Kew Palace
RCH/KEW TW9 .... 161 G1
Kew Retail Park
RCH/KEW TW9 .... 162 B2
Keyplan & Roxburghe Collegei
FITZ W1T 4 B6
Keyworth Primary School
WALW SE17 .... 30 C4
Khalsa College London
HRW HA1 .... 80 B3
Kidbrooke Park Primary School
BKHTH/KID SE3 .... 173 E3
Kidbrooke School
BKHTH/KID SE3 .... 173 F3
Kilburn Park Junior School
KIL/WHAMP NW6 .... 124 D2
Killick Street Medical Centre
IS N1 .... 5 C1
Kilmorie Primary School
FSTH SE23 .... 190 C4
Kimberley Industrial Estate
WALTH E17 .... 70 D3
Kimpton Industrial Estate
CHEAM SM3 .... 224 D6
King Alfred School
CLDGN NW11 .... 85 F5
King Athelstan Primary School
KUT KT1 .... 201 H6
King Edward VII
Hospital for Officers
MHST W1U 11 F1
The Kingfisher Medical Centre
DEPT SE8 .... 150 D6
Kingford Community School
PLSTW E13 .... 133 E1

King George Hospital
GDMY/SEVK IG3 .... 95 G2

Kingham Industrial Estate
WLSDN NW10 .... 122 D2

King Henry's Reach Dev
BARN SW13 .... 144 A6

King & Queen Wharf
WAP E1W 130 B6

Kings Acre Primary School
CLAP SW4 .... 167 G6

Kings Avenue Medical Centre
GFD/PVL UB6 .... 119 G5

The Kingsbury Green Primary School
CDALE/KGS NW9 .... 82 B2

Kingsbury High School
CDALE/KGS NW9 .... 82 B1

Kingsbury Hospital
CDALE/KGS NW9 .... 82 A1

Kingsbury Tamil School
CDALE/KGS NW9 .... 62 B6

Kingsbury Trading Estate
CDALE/KGS NW9 .... 82 C3

Kings College Hospital
CMBW SE5 .... 168 C4
EDUL SE22 .... 169 E5

Kings College London
CHEL SW3 .... 26 A4
CMBW SE5 .... 168 D5
HAMP NW3 .... 105 E2
KENS W8 .... 145 E2
STHWK SE1 .... 22 D1
STHWK SE1 .... 23 F2
TPL/STR WC2R 13 H5
WBPTN SW10 .... 165 G1
WEST SW1P 28 B1

King's College School
WIM/MER SW19 .... 204 A2

Kings College School of Medicine & Dentistry
HNHL SE24 .... 188 D1

Kings Cross Station
CAMTN NW1 .... 5 F2

Kings Cross Thameslink Station
FSBYW WC1X 5 F3

Kingsdale School
DUL SE21 .... 189 E5

Kingsgate Business Centre
KUTN/CMB KT2 .... 201 G4

Kingsgate Primary School
KIL/WHAMP NW6 .... 105 E5

Kings Head Theatre
IS N1 .... 108 A6

Kings House School
RCHPK/HAM TW10 .... 161 H6

Kingsland Health Centre
HACK E8 .... 109 F5

Kingsland School
HACK E8 .... 109 F3

Kingsland Shopping Centre
HACK E8 .... 109 F4

Kingsley Primary School
CROY/NA CR0 .... 227 H5

Kings Mall Shopping Centre
HMSMTH W6 .... 144 A4

Kingsmead Primary School
CLPT E5 .... 110 C2

Kingsmead School
ENC/FH EN2 .... 39 G5

The Kings Oak Private Hospital
ENC/FH EN2 .... 38 A1

King Solomon High School
BARK/HLT IG6 .... 74 D5

Kings Private Clinic
GDMY/SEVK IG3 .... 95 F5
MHST W1U 11 E1

Kings School of English
BECK BR3 .... 210 D5

King's Stairs
BERM/RHTH SE16 .... 25 H3

Kingston Business Centre
CHSGTN KT9 .... 239 G1

Kingston College of Further Education
KUT KT1 .... 201 F6

Kingston Crematorium
KUT KT1 .... 202 A6

Kingston Crown Court
KUT KT1 .... 201 F6

Kingston Grammar School
KUT KT1 .... 201 H5

Kingston Hospital NHS Trust
KUTN/CMB KT2 .... 202 A4

Kingstonian FC
NWMAL KT3 .... 202 B6

Kingston Magistrates Court
KUT KT1 .... 201 F5

Kingston Museum & Art Gallery
KUT KT1 .... 201 G5

Kingston Sport & Recreation Centre
NWMAL KT3 .... 223 F1

Kingston University
KUT KT1 .... 201 G6
KUTN/CMB KT2 .... 202 D3
KUTN/CMB KT2 .... 202 D1

King Street College
HMSMTH W6 .... 144 A4

Kingsway Business Park
HPTN TW12 .... 198 D4

Kingsway College
CLKNW EC1R 6 B5
KTTN NW5 .... 106 D4
STPAN WC1H 5 G4

Kingswood Primary School
WNWD SE27 .... 188 D6

Kisharon School
GLDGN NW11 .... 84 D3

KLC School of Design
WBPTN SW10 .... 165 G2

Knightsbridge Barracks
SKENS SW7 .... 18 B4

Knightsbridge Medical Centre
KTBR SW1X 18 D5

Knollmead Primary School
WPK KT4 .... 207 H4

Knowledge Point School
HOLWY N7 .... 107 H4

Kobi Nazrul Primary School
WCHPL E1 .... 17 F3

KS Medical Centre
STHL UB1 .... 119 F6

Kubrick Business Centre
FSTGT E7 .... 112 D2

Laban Centre
DEPT SE8 .... 171 F1

Laburnam Health Centre
DAGE RM10 .... 97 E6

Laburnum Primary School
HACK E8 .... 109 F6

Lady Edens School
KENS W8 .... 145 F3

Lady Eleanor Holles School
HPTN TW12 .... 199 F1

Lady Margaret Primary School
STHL UB1 .... 118 D4

Lady Margaret School
FUL/PGN SW6 .... 165 E2

Ladywell Arena
LEW SE13 .... 191 F1

Ladywell Cemetery
BROCKY SE4 .... 170 D6

Ladywell Leisure Centre
LEW SE13 .... 171 G6

Lake Business Centre
TOTM N17 .... 69 G2

Laker Industrial Estate
BECK BR3 .... 210 C1

Lambeth Cemetery
TOOT SW17 .... 205 G1

Lambeth College
CLAP SW4 .... 167 E6
STHWK SE1 .... 24 B2

Lambeth County Court
LBTH SE11 .... 30 B3

Lambeth Crematorium
TOOT SW17 .... 185 G6

Lambeth Palace
STHWK SE1 .... 21 G6

Lambs Court
POP/IOD E14 .... 130 C6

Lamont Business Centre
CROY/NA CR0 .... 227 G4

Lamorbey Swimming Centre
BFN/LL DA15 .... 195 G4

Lampton School
HEST TW5 .... 159 E2

The Lanark Medical Centre
MV/WKIL W9 .... 125 F2

Lancaster House
WHALL SW1A 20 A3

Lancasterian Primary School
TOTM N17 .... 69 E4

Lancaster Road Industrial Estate
EBAR EN4 .... 35 H6

Lancelot Medical Centre
ALP/SUD HA0 .... 101 F3

Lanford Obesity Clinic
IS N1 .... 53 H2

Langbourne Primary School
DUL SE21 .... 189 E5

Langdon Park Secondary School
POP/IOD E14 .... 131 F5

Langdon School
EHAM E6 .... 134 B1

Langford Primary School
FUL/PGN SW6 .... 165 F3

The Langham School
SEVS/STOTM N15 .... 88 C1

Langhedge Lane Industrial Estate
UED N18 .... 69 F2

Langley Park Golf Club
BECK BR3 .... 231 H3

Langley Park School for Boys
BECK BR3 .... 231 F3

Langley Park School for Girls
BECK BR3 .... 231 F3

Langthorne Health Centre
WAN E11 .... 111 H3

Langthorne Hospital
WAN E11 .... 111 H2

Lansbury Lawrence Primary School
POP/IOD E14 .... 105 H5

Lansdowne College
BAY/PAD W2 .... 125 F6

Lansdowne School
BRXN/ST SW9 .... 167 H4

La Retraite RC Girls School
CLAP SW4 .... 187 G2

Lark Hall Junior School
CLAP SW4 .... 167 F3

Lark Hall Primary School
CLAP SW4 .... 167 F3

Larkshall Business Centre
CHING E4 .... 55 H4

Larkswood Primary School
CHING E4 .... 55 H6

Larmenier Infant School
HMSMTH W6 .... 144 B4

La Sainte Union Convent School
KTTN NW5 .... 106 C1

Latchmere Infant School
KUTN/CMB KT2 .... 201 H2

Latchmere Leisure Centre
BTSEA SW11 .... 166 B3

Lathom Junior School
EHAM E6 .... 113 G5

Latimer Industrial Estate
SHB W12 .... 124 A5

Latymer All Saints CE Primary School
ED N9 .... 53 F4

The Latymer School
ED N9 .... 53 E4

Latymer Upper School
HMSMTH W6 .... 143 G4

Launcelot Primary School
BMLY BR1 .... 192 C6

Laurel Clinic
EA W5 .... 141 E4

Lauriston Primary School
HOM E9 .... 110 B6

Lavender Primary School
ENC/FH EN2 .... 39 E1

Lawdale Junior School
BETH E2 .... 9 F3

Lawrence Trading Estate
GNWCH SE10 .... 152 A4

Lawrence Wharf
BERM/RHTH SE16 .... 150 D1

Laycock Primary School
IS N1 .... 108 A4

Lea Bridge Industrial Estate
LEY E10 .... 90 C5

Leadenhall Market
BANK EC3V 16 A4

Lea Park Trading Estate
LEY E10 .... 90 D4

Leaside Business Centre
PEND EN3 .... 40 D3

Leathermarket Gardens
STHWK SE1 .... 24 A4

Leathersellers Sports Ground
ELTH/MOT SE9 .... 195 E2

Leathers Hall
HDTCH EC3A 16 A3

Lea Valley Ice Centre
LEY E10 .... 90 B6

Lea Valley Primary School
TOTM N17 .... 69 H3

Lea Valley Trading Estate
UED N18 .... 54 A6
UED N18 .... 70 B2

L'écoles des Petits
FUL/PGN SW6 .... 165 F3

Lee Manor Primary School
LEW SE13 .... 192 A1

Leeside Court
BERM/RHTH SE16 .... 150 B1

Leeside Trading Estate
TOTM N17 .... 70 A3

Leesons Primary School
STMC/STPC BR5 .... 215 G6

Lee Valley Campsite
CHING E4 .... 41 F3

Lee Valley Leisure Centre Camping & Caravan
ED N9 .... 54 B3

Lee Valley Leisure Golf Club
ED N9 .... 54 C2

Lee Valley Watersports Centre
CHING E4 .... 70 C2

Leigh Close Industrial Estate
NWMAL KT3 .... 222 D1

Leighton House Museum & Art Gallery
WKENS W14 .... 144 D3

Lena Gardens Primary School
HMSMTH W6 .... 144 A3

Leopold Primary School
WLSDN NW10 .... 103 F5

Leopold Street Clinic
BOW E3 .... 130 D4

Lesnes Abbey
ABYW SE2 .... 156 B4

Lesney Park Primary School
ERITH DA8 .... 157 H6

Lessness Heath Primary School
BELV DA17 .... 157 E5

Lewin Mead Community Mental Health Centre
STRHM/NOR SW16 .... 207 F2

Lewis Clinic
CAR SM5 .... 244 C2

Lewisham Bridge Primary School
LEW SE13 .... 171 F4

Lewisham Business Centre
NWCR SE14 .... 150 B6

Lewisham Centre
LEW SE13 .... 171 G4

Lewisham College
DEPT SE8 .... 171 G2

Lewisham Crematorium
CAT SE6 .... 192 B4

The Leys Primary School
DAGE RM10 .... 117 G5

Leyton Business Centre
LEY E10 .... 90 D6

Leyton FC
LEY E10 .... 90 D5

Leyton Industrial Village
LEY E10 .... 90 B4

Leyton Orient FC (Matchroom Stadium)
LEY E10 .... 111 F1

Leytonstone School
WAN E11 .... 92 A3

Leyton VI Form College
LEY E10 .... 91 H3

Leyton Youth Sports Ground
LEY E10 .... 91 F5

The Liberty City Clinic
SDTCH EC2A 8 A5

Liberty Middle School
MTCM CR4 .... 206 A5

Library & Community Centre
BTSEA SW11 .... 165 H4

Lillian Baylis School
LBTH SE11 .... 29 H2
VX/NE SW8 .... 29 G6

Lillian Baylis Theatre
FSBYE EC1V 6 C3

Lillian Bishop School of English
SKENS SW7 .... 145 H4

Limehouse Town Hall
POP/IOD E14 .... 130 D5

Limes Farm Primary School
CHIG IG7 .... 74 D2

Lincoln Road Clinic
EN EN1 .... 39 G6

Lincoln's Inn
LINN WC2A 13 H3

Linden Bridge School
WPK KT4 .... 241 E1

Linden Lodge School
WIM/MER SW19 .... 184 C3

Lindon Bennett School
FELT TW13 .... 198 B1

Linford Christie Stadium
SHB W12 .... 123 G4

The Link Day Primary School
CROY/NA CR0 .... 245 G2

The Link Secondary School
CROY/NA CR0 .... 245 H2

Links Primary School
TOOT SW17 .... 206 C2

Linley Sambourne House
KENS W8 .... 144 D2

Linnet House Clinic
STJWD NW8 .... 2 A2

Linton Mead Primary School
THMD SE28 .... 135 H6

Lionel Road Primary School
BTFD TW8 .... 141 G4

Lion House School
PUT/ROE SW15 .... 164 B5

Lismarrine Industrial Park
BORE WD6 .... 24 C4

Lisson Grove Health Centre
STJWD NW8 .... 2 A5

Lister Community School
PLSTW E13 .... 132 D1

The Lister Hospital
BCVA SW1W 27 G4

Lister House Clinic
CAVSQ/HST W1G 11 G3

Little Angel Theatre
IS N1 .... 108 B6

Little Danson Welfare Clinic
WELL DA16 .... 175 G5

Little Hands Theatre
HDN NW4 .... 84 A1

Little Heath School
CHDH RM6 .... 95 H1

Little Ilford School
MNPK E12 .... 113 H3

Little Stanmore First & Middle School
EDGW HA8 .... 61 G4

Little Venice Medical Centre
MV/WKIL W9 .... 125 G3

Little Wandsworth School
TOOT SW17 .... 186 C4

Liverpool Street Station
LVPST EC2M 16 A2

Livesey Museum
PECK SE15 .... 33 G6

Livingstone Primary School
EBAR EN4 .... 35 H4

Lloyd's
BANK EC3V 16 A4

Lloyds Register Cricket Club
DUL SE21 .... 188 D3

Locks View Court
POP/IOD E14 .... 130 C6

Lockwood Industrial Park
TOTM N17 .... 69 H6

Lombard Business Park
BTSEA SW11 .... 165 H3

Lombard Business Park
CROY/NA CR0 .... 227 H4
WAND/EARL SW18 .... 185 H1
WIM/MER SW19 .... 205 G5

Lombard Trading Estate
CHARL SE7 .... 152 D4

London Aquarium
STHWK SE1 .... 21 G3

London Arena
POP/IOD E14 .... 151 F3

London Ballet Theatre
HAMP NW3 .... 105 H5

London Balloon
LBTH SE11 .... 29 G4

London Bridge City Pier
STHWK SE1 .... 24 A1

London Bridge Hospital
STHWK SE1 .... 23 H1

London Bridge Sports Centre
CANST EC4R 15 G6

London Bridge Station
STHWK SE1 .... 24 A2

London Broncos RLFC (Griffin Park)
BTFD TW8 .... 141 F6

London Bubble Theatre
BERM/RHTH SE16 .... 25 H3

London Business School
CAMTN NW1 .... 2 C5

The London Canal Museum
IS N1 .... 5 F1

London Capital College
CAMTN NW1 .... 106 D6

London City Airport
CAN/RD E16 .... 153 H1

London City Mission
STHWK SE1 .... 24 B3

The London Clinic
MHST W1U 3 F6

London College of Business & Computing
BETH E2 .... 9 H2

London College of Fashion
FITZ W1T/W1G 11 H3
MHST W1U 11 F4
SDTCH EC2A 8 B5

London College of Further Education
LBTH SE11 .... 30 C2

London College of Higher Education
CLAP SW4 .... 166 D4

London College of International Business Studies
HHOL WC1V 13 F2

London College of Printing
LBTH SE11 .... 22 D6

The London College
KENS W8 .... 145 E1

London Commodity Exchange
WAP E1W 16 D6

London Dungeon
STHWK SE1 .... 23 H1

London Electronics College
ECT SW5 .... 145 E5

London Executive College
TOOT SW17 .... 186 C1

London Eye Clinic
CAVSQ/HST W1G 11 G2

London Fields Primary School
HACK E8 .... 109 H6

London Foot Hospital
FITZ W1T 4 A6

London Gender Clinic
HDN NW4 .... 83 H3
London Group Business Park
CRICK NW2 .... 83 F5
London Guildhall University
LVPST EC2M 15 H2
TWRH EC3N 16 C4
**London Guildhall
University Sports Ground**
LEE/GVPK SE12 .... 195 E4
London Heart Clinic
CAVSO/HST W1G 11 G2
**London Hospital
Medical College**
WCHPL E1 .... 17 G2
The London Industrial Estate
EHAM E6 .... 134 A4
London Industrial Park
EHAM E6 .... 134 B4
The London Irish Youth Theatre
HCT N6 .... 86 D5
London Ladies & Girls FC
CAT SE6 .... 211 F1
London Lane Clinic
BMLY BR1 .... 212 B3
London Lighthouse
NTGHL W11 .... 124 C5
London Living Theatre
SYD SE26 .... 190 B6
London Nautical School
STHWK SE1 .... 22 B1
London Open College
FSBYE EC1V 6 D3
London Oratory School
FUL/PGN SW6 .... 165 E1
London Pavilion
REGST W1B 12 C6
London Road Medical Centre
THHTH CR7 .... 228 A3
London School of Economics
HHOL WC1V 13 E5
LINN WC2A 13 H4
STHWK SE1 .... 23 E1
**London School of Hygiene & Tropical
Medicine**
GWRST WC1E 12 D1
London Silver Vaults
LINN WC2A 14 A2
**The London
Television Centre (LWT)**
STHWK SE1 .... 22 A1
**London Tourist Board &
Convention Centre**
BGVA SW1W 19 G5
London Toy & Model Museum
BAY/PAD W2 .... 125 G6
SHB W12 .... 124 A5
London Transport Bus Depot
BXLYHN DA7 .... 177 F4
London Transport Museum
COVGDN WC2E 13 F5
London Underwriting Centre
MON EC3R 16 B5
London Weather Centre
CLKNW EC1R 14 A1
London Welsh FC
RCH/KEW TW9 .... 161 C4
London Welsh School
CRICK NW2 .... 104 A4
London Zoo
CAMTN NW1 .... 3 E1
Lonesome First School
MTCM CR4 .... 206 D5
**Long Ditton County
Infant School**
SURB KT6 .... 221 E5
Longfield Primary School
RYLN/HDSTN HA2 .... 79 E3
Longford Industrial Estate
HPTN TW12 .... 199 F2
Longlands Primary School
BFN/LL DA15 .... 195 E5
Long Lane AFC
BKHTH/KID SE3 .... 173 E3
Longshaw Primary School
CHING E4 .... 55 H5
Lord Lister Health Centre
FSTGT E7 .... 112 C2
Lordship Lane Clinic
TOTM N17 .... 69 E5
Lordship Lane Primary School
WDGN N22 .... 68 C4
Lord's Tour & MCC Museum
STJWD NW8 .... 125 H2
Loughborough Primary School
BRXN/ST SW9 .... 168 B3
Lovelace Primary School
CHSGTN KT9 .... 239 E3
Lower Clapton Health Centre
CLPT E5 .... 110 A3
Lower Place Business Centre
WLSDN NW10 .... 122 C1
**Lower Sydenham
Industrial Estate**
CAT SE6 .... 210 D1
Low Hall Sports Ground
WALTH E17 .... 90 B3
Lowther Primary School
BARN SW13 .... 143 G6
**Loxford School of Science &
Technology**
IL IG1 .... 114 D3
Loyola Preparatory School
BKHH IG9 .... 57 E3
LPR Sports Club
BARK/HLT IG6 .... 75 F4
LSE Sports Club
NWMAL KT3 .... 222 D3
LT Lost Property Office
CAMTN NW1 .... 2 D6
LTR Depot
SHB W12 .... 144 B1
Lucas Vale Primary School
DEPT SE8 .... 171 E2
**Lucie Clayton
Secretarial/Fashion
Design College**
KENS W8 .... 145 G3

**Lutomer House
Business Centre**
POP/IOD E14. .... 151 F1
Lux Cinema
IS N1 .... 8 A4
**Lycee Francais
Charles De Gaulle**
SKENS SW7 .... 145 H4
The Lyceum Theatre
TPL/STR WC2R 13 C5
Lyndean Industrial Estate
ABYW SE2 .... 156 A3
**Lyndhurst House
Preparatory School**
HAMP NW3 .... 105 H3
Lyndhurst Primary School
CMBW SE5 .... 168 D3
Lyon Business Park
BARK IG11 .... 135 E1
**Lyon Park Junior &
Infant School**
ALP/SUD HA0 .... 101 H5
Lyonsdown School
BAR EN5 .... 35 C6
Lyric Theatre
HMSMTH W6 .... 144 A4
SOHO/SHAV W1D 12 C5
Mabwin Supplementary School
ED N9 .... 53 H4
Macaulay CE Primary School
CLAP SW4 .... 166 D5
Madame Tussaud's
CAMTN NW1 .... 3 E6
Madeira Grove Clinic
WFD IG8 .... 72 D1
Madni School
WCHPL E1 .... 17 G3
**Mahatma Gandhi
Industrial Estate**
BRXN/ST SW9 .... 168 B4
Maida Vale Hospital
STJWD NW8 .... 125 G2
Maida Vale Medical Centre
MV/WKIL W9 .... 125 F2
Malcolm Primary School
PGE/AN SE20 .... 210 A3
Malden Golf Club
NWMAL KT3 .... 203 E5
Malden Manor Junior School
NWMAL KT3 .... 223 E4
**Malden Parochial
Primary School**
WPK KT4 .... 223 E5
Malden Road Baths
CHEAM SM3 .... 242 B2
Malham Road Industrial Estate
FSTH SE23 .... 190 B3
Mall Galleries
STJS SW1Y 20 D1
The Mall School
WHTN TW2 .... 179 H5
Malmesbury Middle School
MRDN SM4 .... 225 G3
Malmesbury Primary School
BOW E3 .... 130 D2
MRDN SM4 .... 225 G4
**Malorees Junior &
Infant School**
KIL/WHAMP NW6 .... 104 B5
Maiory School
BMLY BR1 .... 192 C6
Mandeville Primary School
CLPT E5 .... 110 C1
Mandeville Special School
NTHLT UB5 .... 98 D4
Manford Way Health Centre
BARK/HLT IG6 .... 75 F2
Manor Brook Medical Centre
BKHTH/KID SE3 .... 172 D3
Manor Drive Health Centre
WPK KT4 .... 223 F5
Manorfield Primary School
POP/IOD E14. .... 131 F4
Manor House Hospital
GLDGN NW11 .... 85 F5
Manor House School
HNWL W7 .... 120 A6
Manor Oak Primary School
STMC/STPC BR5 .... 236 B2
Manor Park Cemetery
FSTGT E7 .... 113 F2
Manor Park Crematorium
FSTGT E7 .... 113 E2
Manor Park Methodist School
MNPK E12 .... 113 G2
Manor Park Primary School
SUT SM1 .... 243 G3
Manor Primary School
SRTFD E15 .... 132 A1
Manorside Primary School
FNCH N3 .... 65 F4
Manor Special School
WLSDN NW10 .... 124 B1
Manor Way Business Centre
DAGW RM9 .... 137 H4
Mansion House
MANHO EC4N 15 G4
Mapledown School
CRICK NW2 .... 84 B4
Maple Grove Business Centre
HSLWW TW4 .... 158 A5
Maple Infant School
SURB KT6 .... 224 E5
Maples Business Centre
IS N1 .... 108 A5
Marble Arch
BAY/PAD W2 .... 10 D5
Marble Hill House
TWK TW1 .... 181 E2
**Maria Fidelis Convent
Lower School**
CAMTN NW1 .... 4 B4
**Maria Fidelis Convent
Upper School**
CAMTN NW1 .... 4 C3
**Marion Richardson
Primary School**
WCHPL E1 .... 130 B5
Marion Vian Primary School
BECK BR3. .... 230 B2

Maritime Industrial Estate
CHARL SE7 .... 152 D4
Maritime Museum
GNWCH SE10 .... 152 A4
Marks Gate Junior School
CHDH RM6 .... 76 C6
Marlborough Cricket Club
DUL SE21 .... 189 G3
Marlborough Day Hospital
STJWD NW8 .... 125 G1
**Marlborough First &
Middle School**
HRW HA1 .... 80 A1
Marlborough House
STJS SW1Y 20 B2
Marlborough Park School
BFN/LL DA15 .... 195 G3
Marlborough Primary School
CHEL SW3 .... 26 B2
ISLW TW7 .... 160 C2
Marlborough Trading Estate
RCH/KEW TW9 .... 162 B2
Marlowe Business Centre
NWCR SE14 .... 170 C1
Marner Primary School
BOW E3 .... 131 F3
Marshall Street Leisure Centre
SOHO/CST W1F. 12 A4
Marsh Gate Business Centre
SRTFD E15 .... 131 C1
Marshgate Trading Estate
SRTFD E15 .... 111 F5
Marsh Green School
DAGW RM9 .... 137 E1
Martan College
HOL/ALD WC2B. 13 F3
Martinbridge Industrial Estate
EN EN1 .... 39 G6
Martindale Industrial Estate
EN EN1 .... 39 E6
Martin Infant School
EFNCH N2 .... 66 A5
Marvels Lane Primary School
LEE/GVPK SE12 .... 193 E6
Mary Boone School
WKENS W14 .... 144 C4
Maryland Industrial Estate
SRTFD E15 .... 112 A3
Maryland Primary School
SRTFD E15 .... 112 A3
Marylebone Health Centre
MHST W1U 3 F6
Marylebone Magistrates Court
CAMTN NW1 .... 10 B1
Marylebone Station
CAMTN NW1 .... 2 C6
Marymount International School
KUTN/CMB KT2 .... 202 C3
Mary Wallace Theatre
TWK TW1 .... 180 C3
Maswell Park Health Centre
HSLW TW3 .... 159 G6
Matilda Marks School
MLHL NW7 .... 62 D1
Maudlin's Green
WAP E1W. 25 E1
The Maudsley Hospital
CMBW SE5 .... 168 D3
Mawbrey Brough Health Centre
VX/NE SW8 .... 167 C1
The Mawney School
ROMW/RG RM7 .... 97 H2
Mayday University Hospital
THHTH CR7 .... 228 B3
Mayesbrook Park Arena
BCTR RM8 .... 115 C3
Mayespark Primary School
GDMY/SEVK IG3 .... 115 C1
Mayfair Medical Centre
MYFR/PKLN W1K. 11 F4
Mayfield Primary School
GFD/PVL UB6 .... 119 H5
Mayfield School
PIN HA5 .... 58 C6
Mayfield School & College
BCTR RM8 .... 96 A5
Mayflower Primary School
POP/IOD E14. .... 131 E5
Mayplace Primary School
BXLYHN DA7 .... 177 H5
Maytime School
IL IG1 .... 114 A1
Mayville Infant School
WAN E11 .... 112 A1
Mayville Junior School
WAN E11 .... 92 A6
Maze Hill School
GNWCH SE10 .... 152 A6
Mazenod RC Primary School
KIL/WHAMP NW6 .... 105 E5
Mcentee School
WALTH E17 .... 70 D4
Mckay Trading Estate
NKENS W10 .... 124 C3
The Mead Infant School
HOR/WEW KT19 .... 241 F1
Meadlands Primary School
RCHPK/HAM TW10 .... 181 G6
Meadowgate School
PECK SE15 .... 170 B4
Mead Road Infant School
CHST BR7 .... 214 C2
Mednurs Clinic
SEVS/STOTM N15 .... 68 A2
The Medical Centre
BXLYHN DA7 .... 177 G4
Megabowl
BRXS/STRHM SW2 .... 187 G4
Melcombe Primary School
HMSMTH W6. .... 144 B6
Mellish Industrial Estate
WOOL/PLUM SE18 .... 153 F5
Melrose Special School
MTCM CR4. .... 206 A6
Memorial Hospital
WOOL/PLUM SE18 .... 174 A3
**The Menorah
Foundation School**
EDGW HA8. .... 62 C3

Menorah Grammar School
GLDGN NW11 .... 84 C4
Mercers' Hall
CITYW EC2V 15 F4
The Merchant Taylors Hall
BANK EC3V. 15 H4
Mercury Theatre
SKENS/SWD WC2H. 13 E4
Meridian Clinic
BRXN/ST SW9 .... 168 A4
**Meridian Locality
Mental Health Centre**
CHARL SE7 .... 153 E6
Meridian Primary School
GNWCH SE10 .... 151 H5
Meridian Sports Club
CHARL SE7 .... 153 G6
Meridian Trading Estate
CHARL SE7 .... 152 D4
Merlin Primary School
BMLY BR1 .... 192 C5
Merlin School
PUT/ROE SW15 .... 164 B6
Mermaid Theatre
BLKFR EC4V. 14 D5
Merrielands Retail Park
DAGW RM9 .... 116 D6
Merryhills Clinic
ENC/FH EN2 .... 37 H4
Merryhills Primary School
ENC/FH EN2 .... 37 H5
Merton Abbey First School
WIM/MER SW19 .... 205 F4
Merton Adult College
RYNPK SW20 .... 204 C6
Merton College
MRDN SM4 .... 224 D2
**Merton Court
Preparatory School**
SCUP DA14 .... 196 A6
Merton Industrial Park
WIM/MER SW19 .... 205 G4
Merton Park Primary School
WIM/MER SW19 .... 204 D5
Merton Road Industrial Estate
WAND/EARL SW18 .... 185 E2
Metro Business Centre
SYD SE26 .... 210 D2
The Metro Golf Centre
HDN NW4 .... 64 A4
Metro Industrial Centre
ISLW TW7 .... 160 A3
Metropolitan Business Centre
HACK E8 .... 109 E5
Metropolitan Hospital
WALW SE17 .... 22 B5
Metropolitan Police FC
E/WMO/HCT KT8 .... 219 H3
**Metropolitan Police
Hayes Sports Club**
HAYES BR2 .... 232 B6
**Metropolitan Police
(Hendon) Track**
CDALE/KGS NW9 .... 63 F6
**Metropolitan Police
Training School, Hendon**
CDALE/KGS NW9 .... 63 F6
Metropolitan Tabernacle
LBTH SE11 .... 30 D1
Metro Trading Centre
WBLY HA9 .... 102 B2
**Michael Faraday
Primary School**
WALW SE17 .... 31 H4
**Michael Manley
Industrial Estate**
VX/NE SW8 .... 167 E3
Michael Sobell Sinai School
KTN/HRWW/W HA3 .... 82 A3
Michael Sobell Sports Centre
HOLWY N7 .... 107 H1
The Michael Tippett School
LBTH SE11 .... 30 B2
Midas Business Centre
DAGE RM10 .... 117 E2
Midas Industrial Estate
DAGE RM10 .... 117 E2
Middle Park Primary School
ELTH/MOT SE9 .... 193 F2
Middle Row Primary School
NKENS W10 .... 124 C3
Middlesex Business Centre
NWDGN UB2 .... 139 E2
**Middlesex CCC
(Lord's Cricket Ground)**
STJWD NW8 .... 125 H2
Middlesex Guildhall
WEST SW1P 20 D4
Middlesex Hospital
FITZ W1T 12 B2
**Middlesex Hospital
Medical School**
FITZ W1T 12 B1
Middlesex Hospital Nurses Home
GTPST W1W 12 A1
**Middlesex Hospital School of
Physiotherapy**
FITZ W1T 12 B1
**Middlesex Hospital
Sports Ground**
CHST BR7. .... 215 F1
Middlesex University
EBAR EN4 .... 50 C1
GLDGN NW11 .... 85 F5
TOTM N17 .... 69 E2
WDGN N22 .... 67 G5
**Middlesex University
Business School**
HDN NW4 .... 83 H1
Middle Temple Hall
TPL/STR WC2R 14 A5
Midfield Primary School
CHST BR7. .... 215 G3
Midway Mission Hospital
BETH E2 .... 8 C4
Mile End & Bow Business Centre
WCHPL E1 .... 17 H1
Mile End Hospital
WCHPL E1 .... 130 B2

Mile End Stadium
BOW E3 .... **130** D4
Miles Coverdale Primary School
SHB W12 .... **144** A2
Millbank Millennium Pier
WEST SW1P **29** F2
Millbank Primary School
WEST SW1P **28** D2
Millbank Tower
WEST SW1P **29** E2
Millennium Arena
BTSEA SW11 .... **166** C1
Millennium Balloon
STHWK SE1 .... **24** B2
Millennium Harbour
Development
POP/IOD E14 .... **150** D2
Millennium Quay
DEPT SE8 .... **151** F6
Millennium Wharf Development
POP/IOD E14 .... **151** H3
Mill Farm Business Park
HSLWW TW4 .... **178** C2
Millfields Junior &
Infant School
CLPT E5 .... **110** A2
Millfield Theatre
UED N18 .... **52** D6
Mill Green Business Park
MTCM CR4 .... **226** B4
Mill Hill Cemetery
MLHL NW7 .... **64** A2
Mill Hill County High School
MLHL NW7 .... **47** E4
The Mill Hill Cricket Club
MLHL NW7 .... **48** A5
Mill Hill Golf Club
MLHL NW7 .... **47** E4
Mill Hill Industrial Estate
MLHL NW7 .... **63** F2
Mill Hill School
MLHL NW7 .... **47** H6
Mill Lane Medical Centre
KIL/WHAMP NW6 .... **105** E3
Mill Lane Trading Estate
CROY/NA CR0 .... **245** H1
Mill River Trading Estate
PEND EN3 .... **40** C5
Mill Street Clinic
STHWK SE1 .... **24** D3
Mill Trading Estate
WLSDN NW10 .... **122** B1
Millwall FC (The New Den)
BERM/RHTH SE16 .... **150** A5
Milmead Industrial Centre
TOTM N17 .... **69** H5
Milton Natural Health Centre
HGT N6 .... **87** E4
Ministry of Defence
WHALL SW1A **21** E2
Mini Town Hall
WOOL/PLUM SE18 .... **155** F5
Mint Business Park
CAN/RD E16 .... **132** C4
Mirravale Trading Estate
BCTR RM8 .... **96** C4
Mission Grove Primary School
WALTH E17 .... **90** D1
Mitcham Cricket Club
MTCM CR4 .... **226** A1
Mitcham Golf Club
MTCM CR4 .... **226** C2
Mitcham Industrial Estate
MTCM CR4 .... **206** C4
Mitcham Road Crematorium
THHTH CR7 .... **227** G2
Mitchell Brook Primary School
WLSDN NW10 .... **102** D4
Mitre Bridge Industrial Park
WLSDN NW10 .... **123** H3
Moatbridge School
ELTH/MOT SE9 .... **193** F1
Molesey Hospital
E/WMO/HCT KT8 .... **219** E2
Molesey Lock
E/WMO/HCT KT8 .... **200** A6
Mollison Drive Health Centre
WLGTN SM6 .... **245** G5
Monega Primary School
MNPK E12 .... **113** F3
Monken Hadley CE
Primary School
EBAR EN4 .... **35** E2
Monkfrith Primary School
EBAR EN4 .... **50** C2
Monks Orchard
Primary School
CROY/NA CR0 .... **230** B2
Monson Primary School
NWCR SE14 .... **170** B1
Montbelle Primary School
ELTH/MOT SE9 .... **194** B5
Monteagle Primary School
DAGW RM9 .... **115** H6
Montem Primary School
HOLWY N7 .... **107** H1
The Montessori House School
MUSWH N10 .... **66** D6
Montpelier Primary School
EA W5 .... **121** F4
The Monument
MON EC3R **15** H6
Moorfields Eye Hospital
FSBYE EC1V **7** G4
Moorfields Infirmary
STLK EC1Y **7** G5
Moor Lane Junior School
CHSGTN KT9 .... **239** H3
Mora Primary School
CRICK NW2 .... **104** A2
Morden Cemetery
MRDN SM4 .... **224** A3
Morden College Homes
BKHTH/KID SE3 .... **172** C3
Morden First School
MRDN SM4 .... **225** E2
Morden Hall Medical Centre
WIM/MER SW19 .... **205** F6

Morden Mount
Primary School
LEW SE13 .... **171** F3
Morden Road Clinic
WIM/MER SW19 .... **205** F6
More House School
ISLW TW7 .... **160** A2
KTBR SW1X **18** D6
Moreland Primary School
FSBYE EC1V **6** D4
Moriah Jewish Day School
PIN HA5 .... **78** C5
Morningside Primary School
HOM E9 .... **110** A4
Mornington Leisure Centre
CAMTN NW1 .... **106** D6
Morpeth School
BETH E2 .... **130** A2
Mortimer Road Clinic
WLSDN NW10 .... **124** A2
Mortimer School
STRHM/NOR SW16 .... **187** F4
Mortlake Cemetery
MORT/ESHN SW14 .... **163** E4
Mortlake Crematorium
RCH/KEW TW9 .... **162** B3
Moselle School
TOTM N17 .... **69** E5
Mosiah Foundation
Supplementary School
STNW/STAM N16 .... **89** E5
Mossford Green Primary School
BARK/HLT IG6 .... **74** C5
Moss Hall Primary School
FNCH N3 .... **65** F2
The Mother & Baby Clinic
HOM E9 .... **110** A4
Mottingham Community
Health Clinic
ELTH/MOT SE9 .... **193** G6
Mottingham Primary School
ELTH/MOT SE9 .... **193** H5
Mount Carmel RC
Primary School
EA W5 .... **141** E3
The Mount Infant School
NWMAL KT3 .... **202** B6
Mount Medical Centre
FELT TW13 .... **178** C4
The Mount Primary School
NWMAL KT3 .... **202** B6
Mount School
MLHL NW7 .... **63** H1
Mount Stewart Primary School
KTN/HRWW/W HA3 .... **81** F3
Mowlem Primary School
BETH E2 .... **130** A1
Mowlem Trading Estate
TOTM N17 .... **70** A3
MS Business Centre
PIN HA5 .... **58** B6
MSP Business Centre
WBLY HA0 .... **102** B2
Mudchute City Farm
POP/IOD E14 .... **151** G4
Mulberry Business Centre
BERM/RHTH SE16 .... **150** B2
Mulberry Centre for
Community Education
WCHPL E1 .... **17** H5
Mulberry House School
CRICK NW2 .... **104** C3
Mulberry School for Girls
WCHPL E1 .... **17** G4
Mulgrave Primary School
WOOL/PLUM SE18 .... **154** B3
Murky Puddle Theatre
NWMAL KT3 .... **203** F6
Murray Business Centre
STMC/STPC BR5 .... **215** H6
Muschamp Primary School
CAR SM5 .... **226** A6
Museum in Docklands
POP/IOD E14 .... **131** E6
Museum & Library
WALW SE17 .... **31** G2
Museum of Artillery
in the Rotunda
CHARL SE7 .... **153** H5
Museum of Domestic
Design & Architecture
EBAR EN4 .... **36** B6
Museum of Fulham Palace
FUL/PGN SW6 .... **164** B3
Museum of Garden History
STHWK SE1 .... **21** G6
Museum of London
STBT EC1A **12** C2
Museum of Richmond
RCH/KEW TW9 .... **161** F6
Museum of Rugby &
Twickenham Stadium Tours
WHTN TW2 .... **180** A1
Museum of the Order of
St John
FARR EC1M **6** D6
Museums of the
Royal College of Surgeons
LINN WC2A **13** H3
The Musical Museum
BTFD TW8 .... **141** G6
Muswell Hill Bowling Club
MUSWH N10 .... **66** C6
Muswell Hill Golf Club
FBAR/BDGN N11 .... **66** D4
Myatt Garden Primary School
BROCKY SE4 .... **170** D3
Myatts Field Clinic
BRXN/ST SW9 .... **168** B2
Nagi Business Centre
ALP/SUD HA0 .... **121** F1
Nags Head Shopping Centre
HOLWY N7 .... **107** H2
Naima Jewish
Preparatory School
KIL/WHAMP NW6 .... **125** F1
National Army Museum
CHEL SW3 .... **26** D5
National Film Theatre
STHWK SE1 .... **21** H1

National Gallery
LSQ/SEVD WC2H **12** D6
National Hospital for
Neurology & Neurosurgery
BMSBY WC1N **5** E6
National Hospital for Sick Children
(Great Ormond St)
BMSBY WC1N **5** F6
National Maritime Museum
GNWCH SE10 .... **151** H6
National Physical Laboratory
TEDD TW11 .... **200** A2
National Portrait Gallery
LSQ/SEVD WC2H **12** D6
National Temperance Hospital
CAMTN NW1 .... **4** B4
National Youth Theatre of GB
HOLWY N7 .... **107** G1
Natural History Museum
SKENS SW7 .... **145** H3
Natural Therapy Clinic
TOOT SW17 .... **206** D1
Natwest Sports Club
BECK BR3 .... **210** D2
Navigation College
MANHO EC4N **15** F5
NEC Harlequins RFC (The Stoop
Memorial Ground)
WHTN TW2 .... **180** A2
Nelson Dock Museum
BERM/RHTH SE16 .... **150** D1
Nelson Hospital
WIM/MER SW19 .... **204** D5
Nelson Primary School
EHAM E6 .... **134** A1
WHTN TW2 .... **179** F1
Nelson's Column
CHCR WC2N **21** E1
Nelson Trading Estate
WIM/MER SW19 .... **205** F4
Neo Clinic
PIM SW1V **28** A2
Netley Primary School
CAMTN NW1 .... **4** A4
The New Ambassadors Theatre
LSQ/SEVD WC2H **13** E4
New Atlas Wharf Development
POP/IOD E14 .... **150** D3
The New Aylesbury
Medical Centre
WALW SE17 .... **31** H3
New Brentford Cemetery
HSLW TW3 .... **158** D3
Newbury Park Health Centre
GNTH/NBYPK IG2 .... **94** D3
Newbury Park Primary School
GNTH/NBYPK IG2 .... **94** D3
The New Business Centre
WLSDN NW10 .... **123** F2
New Caledonian Wharf
BERM/RHTH SE16 .... **150** D3
New Chiswick Swimming Pool
CHSWK W4 .... **163** E1
New City Primary School
PLSTW E13 .... **133** G2
New Connaught Rooms
HOL/ALD WC2B **13** F3
New Covent Garden Market
VX/NE SW8 .... **167** F1
New Crane Wharf
WAP E1W **150** A1
New Cross Sports Arena
NWCR SE14 .... **170** C1
New End Primary School
HAMP NW3 .... **105** G2
New End Theatre
HAMP NW3 .... **105** G1
New England Industrial Estate
BARK IG11 .... **134** C1
Newfield Primary School
WLSDN NW10 .... **105** F5
The New Furness
Primary School
WLSDN NW10 .... **123** G1
Newham College of Further
Education
EHAM E6 .... **133** H1
SRTFD E15 .... **112** A5
Newham Community College
CAN/RD E16 .... **132** A3
Newham General Hospital
PLSTW E13 .... **133** E3
Newham Leisure Centre
PLSTW E13 .... **133** E4
Newham Medical Centre
PLSTW E13 .... **133** E1
Newham Museum Service
SRTFD E15 .... **111** H5
Newham Sixth Form College
PLSTW E13 .... **133** E5
New Health Centre
TOTM N17 .... **69** E4
Newington Court
Business Centre
STHWK SE1 .... **23** E6
Newington Green
Primary School
STNW/STAM N16 .... **109** E3
Newington Industrial Estate
WALW SE17 .... **30** D2
New Kings Primary School
FUL/PGN SW6 .... **164** D3
Newland House School
TWK TW1 .... **180** B6
New London Theatre
LSQ/SEVD WC2H **13** F3
Newnham Junior &
Infant School
RSLP HA4 .... **78** A5
Newport Junior &
Infant School
WAN E11 .... **91** G6
New River Stadium
WDGN N22 .... **68** B3
New Rush Hall School
IL IG1 .... **94** C6
New School
FUL/PGN SW6 .... **164** D2
New Scotland Yard
STJSPK SW1H **20** C5

News International
WAP E1W **17** F6
New Southgate Cemetery
FBAR/BDGN N11 .... **50** D5
New Southgate Crematorium
FBAR/BDGN N11 .... **50** D5
New Southgate
Industrial Estate
FBAR/BDGN N11 .... **67** E1
New Southgate Pain Clinic &
Medical Centre
FBAR/BDGN N11 .... **67** E1
Newstead Wood
School for Girls
ORP BR6 .... **252** D1
Newton Farm First &
Middle School
RYLN/HDSTN HA2 .... **78** D6
Newton Industrial Estate
CHDH RM6 .... **96** B1
Newton Medical Centre
BAY/PAD W2 .... **125** F5
Newton Preparatory School
VX/NE SW8 .... **166** D1
Newtons Primary School
RAIN RM13 .... **137** H1
New Victoria Hospital
KUTN/CMB KT2 .... **203** E3
New Woodlands School
BMLY BR1 .... **192** A6
Nightingale Clinic
PLSTW E13 .... **133** E1
Nightingale Primary School
SWFD E18 .... **93** E1
WDGN N22 .... **67** G4
WOOL/PLUM SE18 .... **154** D5
Nightingale School
STHWK SE1 .... **21** G4
TOOT SW17 .... **186** A4
Nineacres School
WOOL/PLUM SE18 .... **154** D5
Noel Park Primary School
WDGN N22 .... **68** B5
Nonsuch High School for Girls
EW KT17 .... **242** B5
Nonsuch Primary School
EW KT17 .... **241** H3
Norbury Complementary
Therapy Centre
STRHM/NOR SW16 .... **207** H4
Norbury First & Middle School
HRW HA1 .... **80** A2
Norbury Health Centre
STRHM/NOR SW16 .... **207** H5
Norbury Manor
Primary School
STRHM/NOR SW16 .... **207** G4
Norbury Manor
Secondary Girls School
STRHM/NOR SW16 .... **207** H5
Norbury Trading Estate
STRHM/NOR SW16 .... **207** H5
Norfolk House School
MUSWH N10 .... **66** D5
Norlington School
LEY E10 .... **91** H5
Normand Park Primary School
FUL/PGN SW6 .... **144** D6
Normandy Primary School
BXLYHN DA7 .... **177** H2
Normanhurst School
CHING E4 .... **55** H2
Norman Park Athletics Track
HAYES BR2 .... **232** D3
Norman Shaw Building
(MP's Offices)
WHALL SW1A **21** E3
North Acton Business Park
ACT W3 .... **122** D5
North Beckton Primary School
EHAM E6 .... **133** H4
North Bridge House
HAMP NW3 .... **105** G4
North Bridge House School
CAMTN NW1 .... **106** C6
HAMP NW3 .... **105** H4
Northbrook CE School
LEW SE13 .... **172** A6
Northbury Primary School
BARK IG11 .... **114** B4
North Clinic
BMLY BR1 .... **212** C4
Northcote Lodge School
BTSEA SW11 .... **186** A1
North Cray Primary School
SCUP DA14 .... **216** C2
North Croydon Medical Centre
THHTH CR7 .... **228** B3
North Ealing Primary School
WEA W13 .... **120** D3
North East Surrey Crematorium
NWMAL KT3 .... **224** A3
Northfields Industrial Estate
ALP/SUD HA0 .... **102** A6
Northfields Prospect
Business Centre
WAND/EARL SW18 .... **164** D5
Northgate Business Centre
EN EN1 .... **39** H4
Northgate Clinic
CDALE/KGS NW9 .... **83** E3
Northgate Industrial Park
ROMW/RG RM7 .... **76** D5
North Harringay Primary School
CEND/HSY/T N8 .... **88** A1
North London Collegiate School
EDGW HA8 .... **61** G2
North London School of
Physiotherapy
ARCH N19 .... **87** E5
North London Tutorial College
HDN NW4 .... **84** A3
North Middlesex Golf Club
TRDG/WHET N20 .... **49** H5
North Middlesex Hospital
UED N18 .... **69** E1
Northolt High School
NTHLT UB5 .... **98** D4
Northolt Park Infant School
NTHLT UB5 .... **99** F3

Northolt Primary School
NTHLT UB5 .... 98 B5
Northolt Road Clinic
RYLN/HDSTN HA2 .... 99 G1
North Peckham Civic
Centre & Library
STHWK SE1 .... 33 E5
North Primary School
STHL UB1 .... 118 D6
Northside Primary
NFNCH/WDSP N12 .... 65 F1
The North Street Health Centre
CLAP SW4 .... 167 E4
Northumberland Heath
Medical Centre
ERITH DA8 .... 177 H1
Northumberland Heath
Primary School
ERITH DA8 .... 177 F1
Northumberland Park
Industrial Estate
TOTM N17 .... 69 H2
Northumberland Park School
TOTM N17 .... 69 G3
Northview Primary School
MV/WKIL W10 .... 103 E2
Northway School
MLHL NW7 .... 46 C5
North West London Jewish
J & I School
CRICK NW2 .... 104 C5
North West London
Medical Centre
MV/WKIL W9 .... 125 G2
North Westminster
Community School
STJWD NW8 .... 10 A1
North Westminster Community
Secondary School
MV/WKIL W9 .... 125 E3
North Weylands
Industrial Estate
BETH E2 .... 218 C6
Northwick Park Hospital &
Clinical Research Centre
HRW HA1 .... 80 D4
Northwold Primary School
CLPT E5 .... 89 G6
Norwegian/British Monument
BAY/PAD W2 .... 18 B2
Norwood Green Infant School
NWDGN UB2 .... 138 C5
Norwood Heights
Shopping Centre
NRWD SE19 .... 209 E2
Norwood Park Primary School
WNWD SE27 .... 188 D6
Norwood School
WNWD SE27 .... 208 C1
Notre Dame RC Girls School
STHWK SE1 .... 22 C5
Notre Dame RC
Primary School
WOOL/PLUM SE18 .... 154 B6
Notting Hill & Ealing
High School
WEA W13 .... 120 D4
Nower Hill High School
PIN HA5 .... 79 E1
N1 Shopping Centre
IS N1 .... 6 B1
NTGB Sports Ground
EHAM E6 .... 114 A4
Nuffield Hospital
ENC/FH EN2 .... 38 A3
Nugent Industrial Park
STMC/STPC BR5 .... 236 A1
Nutrition Clinic
MHST W1U 11 E1
NWS Theatre School
KTTN NW5 .... 107 E3
Oakdale Infant School
SWFD E18 .... 72 D5
Oakdale Junior School
SWFD E18 .... 73 E5
Oakfield Preparatory School
DUL SE21 .... 188 D4
Oakfield Road Industrial Estate
PGE/AN SE20 .... 200 H3
Oak Hill Health Centre
EBAR EN4 .... 50 C1
Oak Hill Health Centre
SURB KT6 .... 221 G3
Oakhill Primary School
WFD IG8 .... 72 A2
Oakington Manor School
WBLY HA9 .... 102 B3
Oakland CP School
EBAR EN4 .... 50 B1
Oaklands Primary School
HNWL W7 .... 140 B2
Oaklands School
ISLW TW7 .... 159 H4
Oaklands Secondary School
BETH E2 .... 9 G3
Oak Lane Cemetery
TWK TW1 .... 180 C2
Oak Lane Medical Centre
TWK TW1 .... 180 D2
Oakleigh School
TRDG/WHET N20 .... 50 A5
Oak Lodge JMI School
WWKM BR4 .... 231 F4
Oak Lodge Medical Centre
EDGW HA8 .... 62 B3
Oak Lodge School
BAL SW12 .... 186 B2
FNCH N2 .... 65 G6
Oakthorpe Primary School
PLMGR N13 .... 68 C1
Oak Tree Medical Centre
GDMY/SEVK IG3 .... 95 E6
Oakwood Business Park
WLSDN NW10 .... 122 D2
Oakwood Medical Centre
STHGT/OAK N14 .... 37 E6
Oasis Sports Centre
LSQ/SEVD WC2H 13 G3
Obstetrics Hospital
GWRST WC1E 4 B6

Occupational Health Centre
CROY/NA CR0 .... 246 D2
Odeon Cinema
BAR EN5 .... 35 E6
BECK BR3 .... 211 E5
CAMTN NW1 .... 106 D6
ELTH/MOT SE9 .... 175 G5
FITZ W1T 12 C2
GNTH/NBYPK IG2 .... 94 A3
HAYES BR2 .... 212 C5
HOLWY N7 .... 107 G1
KENS W8 .... 145 E3
KIL/WHAMP NW6 .... 105 H5
LSO/SEVD WC2H 10 D6
MBLAR W1H 10 D4
MUSWH N10 .... 86 C1
RCHPK/HAM TW10 .... 161 F6
STJS SW1Y 12 C6
STRHM/NOR SW16 .... 187 C5
SWFD E18 .... 72 C5
WIM/MER SW19 .... 205 E3
Odeon Covent Gardens Cinema
LSO/SEVD WC2H 12 D4
Odeon Wardour Street Cinema
SOHO/SHAV W1D 12 C5
Odessa Infant School
FSTGT E7 .... 112 C3
Old Actonians Sports Club
CROY/NA CR0 .... 141 H2
Old Admiralty
WHALL SW1A 20 D2
Old Bancroftians FC
BKHH IG9 .... 57 F6
Old Barnes Cemetery
BARN SW13 .... 163 H3
Old Beckenhamian RFC
WWKM BR4 .... 249 H1
Old Bellgate Wharf
Development
POP/IOD E14 .... 150 D3
Old Bexley Business Park
BXLY DA5 .... 197 F2
Old Bexley CE Primary School
BXLY DA5 .... 196 D3
Old Brockleians Sports Ground
ELTH/MOT SE9 .... 193 E1
Old Bromilians Cricket Club
HAYES BR2 .... 232 D2
Old Cemetery
EDUL SE22 .... 189 H1
Old Colfeian Sports Club
LEE/GVPK SE12 .... 172 C6
Old Curiosity Shop
LINN WC2A 13 G3
Old Elthamians Sports Club
CHST BR7 .... 215 E2
Oldfield House Special School
HPTN TW12 .... 198 D4
Oldfields Primary School
GFD/PVL UB6 .... 119 H1
Oldfields Trading Estate
SUT SM1 .... 243 E1
Old Fold Manor Golf Club
BAR EN5 .... 34 C2
Old Ford Primary School
BOW E3 .... 130 D1
Oldhill Medical Centre
STNW/STAM N16 .... 89 F5
Old Jamaica Business Estate
BERM/RHTH SE16 .... 24 D5
Old Lyonian Sports Ground
RYLN/HDSTN HA2 .... 79 G2
Old Millmillians Sports Club
FNCH N3 .... 59 E4
Old Oak Primary School
SHB W12 .... 123 F5
Old Operating Theatre Museum
STHWK SE1 .... 23 G2
Old Owens Sports Ground
TRDG/WHET N20 .... 49 H3
Old Palace Primary School
BOW E3 .... 131 F2
Old Palace School
CROY/NA CR0 .... 246 B1
Old Royal Naval College
GNWCH SE10 .... 151 H6
Old Royal Observatory
Greenwich
GNWCH SE10 .... 171 H1
Old St Patricks School
WCHPL E1 .... 9 E6
Old Station Museum
CAN/RD E16 .... 154 A2
Old Sun Wharf
POP/IOD E14 .... 130 C6
Old Tiffinians Sports Ground
E/WMO/HCT KT8 .... 220 A2
Old Treasury
WHALL SW1A 21 E3
Old Vicarage School
RCHPK/HAM TW10 .... 181 G1
Old Vic Theatre
STHWK SE1 .... 22 B3
Old War Office
WHALL SW1A 21 E2
Old Wilsonians Sports Club
WWKM BR4 .... 232 A5
Olga Primary School
BOW E3 .... 130 C1
Oliver Business Park
WLSDN NW10 .... 122 C1
Oliver Goldsmith
Primary School
CDALE/KGS NW9 .... 82 D2
CMBW SE5 .... 169 E2
Olympia
WKENS W14 .... 144 C3
Olympia Industrial Estate
WDGN N22 .... 67 H5
Olympic Industrial Estate
WBLY HA9 .... 102 B2
Olympic Retail Park
WBLY HA9 .... 102 A2
Olympic Trading Estate
WBLY HA9 .... 102 B2
The One Stanley
Medical Centre
ALP/SUD HA0 .... 101 G5

On Sai Clinic
ECT SW5 .... 145 F4
On the Road Tours CC
WAND/EARL SW18 .... 185 G1
Open Air Theatre
CAMTN NW1 .... 3 E4
The Open University
FSBYW WC1X 5 G3
KIL/WHAMP NW6 .... 105 E2
Ophaboom Theatre
WLSDN NW10 .... 123 H2
Optimax Laser Eye Clinic
HAMP NW3 .... 105 G4
Orange Tree Theatre
RCH/KEW TW9 .... 161 G5
Oratory RC Primary School
CHEL SW3 .... 26 A3
Orchard Business Centre
SYD SE26 .... 210 D1
The Orchard Health Centre
BARK IG11 .... 134 C1
The Orchard Junior School
HSLW TW3 .... 159 E5
Orchard Primary School
HOM E9 .... 110 A5
The Orchard School
E/WMO/HCT KT8 .... 219 H2
Orchard Way Primary School
CROY/NA CR0 .... 230 C4
Oriel Primary School
FELT TW13 .... 178 C5
Orient Industrial Park
LEY E10 .... 91 E6
Orion Business Centre
BERM/RHTH SE16 .... 150 B5
Orleans House Gallery
TWK TW1 .... 180 D3
Orleans Infant School
TWK TW1 .... 180 D3
Orleans Park School
TWK TW1 .... 180 D3
Orley Farm School
HRW HA1 .... 99 H1
Orpington College of
Further Education
ORP BR6 .... 235 C5
The Orpington Halls
ORP BR6 .... 235 C6
Orpington Mental
Health Centre
ORP BR6 .... 253 F1
Orpington Retail Park
STMC/STPC BR5 .... 236 A1
Orpington Superbowl
ORP BR6 .... 235 C5
Osidge JMI School
STHGT/OAK N14 .... 51 E3
Osmani Primary School
WCHPL E1 .... 9 F6
Osteopathic Clinic
HOR/WEW KT19 .... 240 D3
Osterley RFC
NWDGN UB2 .... 139 F3
Our Lady Immaculate
RC Primary School
BRYLDS KT5 .... 222 B5
Our Lady of Dolours RC
Primary School
BAY/PAD W2 .... 125 F4
Our Lady of Grace RC
Junior School
CRICK NW2 .... 103 H1
Our Lady of Lourdes
RC Primary School
FBAR/BDGN N11 .... 67 E1
LEW SE13 .... 65 C3
LEW SE13 .... 171 H4
WAN E11 .... 92 B3
WLSDN NW10 .... 102 C6
Our Lady of Muswell RC
Primary School
MUSWH N10 .... 66 C5
Our Lady of St Johns
BTFD TW8 .... 141 E5
Our Lady of the Rosary RC
Primary School
BFN/LL DA15 .... 195 E1
Our Lady of the Sacred
Heart School
HOLWY N7 .... 107 H4
Our Lady of Victories RC
Primary School
PUT/ROE SW15 .... 164 B5
SKENS SW7 .... 145 G4
Our Lady Queen of Heaven RC
Primary School
WIM/MER SW19 .... 184 B2
Our Lady RC Primary School
POP/IOD E14 .... 130 D5
Our Lady & St Joseph
RC Primary School
IS N1 .... 109 E4
Our Lady & St Philip
Neri RC Primary School
SYD SE26 .... 190 B5
Our Ladys Convent High School
STNW/STAM N16 .... 89 E4
Our Ladys RC Primary School
CAMTN NW1 .... 107 E6
Oval Business Centre
LBTH SE11 .... 29 H4
Oval House Theatre
LBTH SE11 .... 30 A4
Oval Primary School
CROY/NA CR0 .... 229 E5
Overton Grange School
BELMT SM2 .... 243 F5
Oxford Gardens
Primary School
NKENS W10 .... 124 B5
Oxford House College
SOHO/SHAV W1D 12 C3
Oxhey Infant School
BUSH WD23 .... 22 A1
Oxhey Wood Primary School
OXHEY WD19 .... 42 A1
Oxo Tower Wharf
STHWK SE1 .... 14 B6

Paddington Bowling &
Sports Club
MV/WKIL W9 .... 125 F3
Paddington Green
Primary School
BAY/PAD W2 .... 125 H4
Paddington Recreation Ground
Athletics Track
KIL/WHAMP NW6 .... 125 E2
Paddington Station
PUT/ROE SW15 .... 125 H5
Paddock School
PUT/ROE SW15 .... 163 F5
Pain Relief Clinic
HDN NW4 .... 83 H3
Pakeman Primary School
HOLWY N7 .... 107 H1
Palace Gardens Shopping Centre
ENC/FH EN2 .... 38 D4
Palladium Theatre
REGST W1B 12 A4
Palmers Green High School
WCHMH N21 .... 52 A4
Palmerston Business Centre
SUT SM1 .... 243 G3
Palm House
RCH/KEW TW9 .... 161 H2
Panorama Pier
STHWK SE1 .... 14 D6
Paradise Swimming Pools
MLHL NW7 .... 63 E1
Parayhouse School
WBPTN SW10 .... 165 G1
Parchmore Medical Centre
THHTH CR7 .... 208 C6
Pardes House &
Beis Yaakov Boys School
FNCH N3 .... 64 D5
Parent Infant Clinic
HAMP NW3 .... 105 G3
Parish CE Primary School
BMLY BR1 .... 212 C3
Parish Church CE
Primary School
CROY/NA CR0 .... 246 B1
Park Business Centre
KIL/WHAMP NW6 .... 125 E2
Parkfield Industrial Estate
BTSEA SW11 .... 166 C3
Parkfield JMI School
HDN NW4 .... 63 H4
Parkgate House School
CLAP SW4 .... 166 C5
Park Hall Trading Estate
DUL SE21 .... 188 C5
Park High School
STAN HA7 .... 61 F5
Park Hill Junior School
CROY/NA CR0 .... 246 D1
Parkhill Primary School
CLAY IG5 .... 73 H6
Park House Medical Centre
KIL/WHAMP NW6 .... 124 C1
Parkhouse Middle School
WIM/MER SW19 .... 184 D6
Park House RFC
HAYES BR2 .... 233 E6
Parkhurst Infant School
TOTM N17 .... 69 F5
Parklands Primary School
ROM RM1 .... 77 H6
Park Lane Primary School
WBLY HA9 .... 101 G2
Park Medical Centre
BERM/RHTH SE16 .... 150 B4
Park Mews Small
Business Centre
HNHL SE24 .... 188 C1
Park Primary School
SRTFD E15 .... 112 B5
Park Road Clinic
CEND/HSY/T N8 .... 87 F2
Park Royal Business Centre
WLSDN NW10 .... 122 C3
Park School for Girls
IL IG1 .... 94 B5
Parkside Business Estate
DEPT SE8 .... 150 D6
Parkside Clinic
NTGHL W11 .... 124 C5
Parkside Health
NTGHL W11 .... 124 C5
Parkside Hospital
WIM/MER SW19 .... 184 B5
Park Walk Primary School
WBPTN SW10 .... 145 H6
Parkway Primary School
ERITHM DA18 .... 136 C3
Parkway Trading Estate
HEST TW5 .... 158 A6
Parkwood Primary School
FSBYPK N4 .... 88 B6
Parliament Hill
Athletics Track
KTTN NW5 .... 106 B2
Parliament Hill School
KTTN NW5 .... 106 C2
Parnells Sports Ground
KTN/HRWW/WS HA3 .... 81 H3
Parsloes Primary School
DAGW RM9 .... 116 D4
Parsons Green Health Clinic
FUL/PGN SW6 .... 165 E2
Passport Language Schools
BMLY BR1 .... 212 D4
Patent Office
HHOL WC1V 14 A2
The Patrick Doody Clinic &
Health Centre
WIM/MER SW19 .... 205 E3
Pattinson Clinic
RCHPK/HAM TW10 .... 161 F6
The Paul Robeson Theatre
HSLW TW3 .... 159 F4
Pavilion Barclays Sports Ground
EA W5 .... 121 G4
The Pavilion Leisure Centre
BMLY BR1 .... 212 C5
Pavilion Restaurant
RCH/KEW TW9 .... 161 G3

Paxton Primary School
NRWD SE19 .... **209** F2
PDSA Hospital
REDBR IG4 .... **73** F6
Peace Pagoda
BTSEA SW11 .... **166** B1
Peacock Estate
TOTM N17 .... **69** F2
Peacock Industrial Estate
TOTM N17 .... **69** F3
The Peacock Theatre
HOL/ALD WC2B **13** G4
Peall Road Industrial Estate
CROY/NA CRO **227** H3
Peckham Park Primary School
PECK SE15 .... **169** G1
The Peckham Pulse
Health & Leisure Centre
PECK SE15 .... **169** G2
Peckham Rye Primary School
PECK SE15 .... **169** H4
Pelham Primary School
BXLYHN DA7 .... **176** D4
BXLYHN DA7 .... **177** E4
WIM/MER SW19 .... **205** F3
Pendragon Secondary School
BMLY BR1 .... **192** C5
Pentavia Retail Park
MLHL NW7 .... **63** F5
Penton Primary School
IS N1 .... **6** B1
Penwortham Primary School
STRHM/NOR SW16 .... **206** D2
Percival David Foundation of
Chinese Art
STPAN WC1H **4** D5
Perivale Industrial Park
GFD/PVL UB6 .... **100** C6
Perivale New Business Centre
GFD/PVL UB6 .... **121** E1
Perivale Park Athletics Track
GFD/PVL UB6 .... **120** A2
Perivale Park Golf Course
GFD/PVL UB6 .... **120** A2
Perivale Primary School
GFD/PVL UB6 .... **121** E1
Perrin Road Clinic
ALP/SUD HA0 .... **100** D2
Perry Hall Primary School
ORP BR6 .... **235** F3
Perrymount Primary School
FSTH SE23 .... **190** B4
Peterborough Primary School
FUL/PGN SW6 .... **165** E3
Peterborough & St Margarets
High School
STAN HA7 .... **44** A5
Peter Hills School
BERM/RHTH SE16 .... **150** B1
Peterley Business Centre
BETH E2 .... **9** G1
Peter Pan Statue
BAY/PAD W2 .... **145** H1
Pewterers' Hall
CITYW EC2V **15** F2
Phoenix Business Centre
POP/IOD E14 .... **131** E4
Phoenix Cinema
EFNCH N2 .... **86** A1
Phoenix College
MRDN SM4 .... **225** F2
TOOT SW17 .... **186** A4
Phoenix Court
POP/IOD E14 .... **151** E4
Phoenix High School
SHB W12 .... **125** G6
Phoenix Industrial Estate
HRW HA1 .... **80** B1
Phoenix Leisure Centre
CAT SE6 .... **191** F2
Phoenix School
BOW E3 .... **130** D2
HAMP NW3 .... **105** H5
Phoenix Theatre
LSQ/SEVD WC2H **12** D4
Phoenix Trading Estate
GFD/PVL UB6 .... **101** E6
Physical Energy Statue
BAY/PAD W2 .... **145** H1
Piccadilly Theatre
SOHO/SHAV W1D **12** C5
Pickford Lane Medical Centre
BXLYHN DA7 .... **176** C2
Pickhurst Infant School
HAYES BR2 .... **232** A3
Pickhurst Junior School
HAYES BR2 .... **232** B3
Picture House Cinema
SRTFD E15 .... **111** H4
Pilgrims Way Junior &
Infant School
PECK SE15 .... **150** A6
Pilot Industrial Centre
WLSDN NW10 .... **123** E3
Pitton Estate
CROY/NA CRO **228** B6
Pimlico School
PIM SW1V **28** B4
Pinewood Primary School
CRW RM5 .... **77** F1
Pinner Park Primary School
RYLN/HDSTN HA2 .... **59** F6
Pinner View Medical Centre
HRW HA1 .... **79** G2
Pinner Wood Primary School
PIN HA5 .... **58** A4
Pinn Medical Centre
PIN HA5 .... **78** C1
Pioneers Industrial Park
CROY/NA CRO **227** G5
Pitshanger Manor Museum
EA W5 .... **141** E1
Plaisterers Hall
CITYW EC2V **15** E2
Plaistow Hospital
PLSTW E13 .... **132** D1
Planetarium
CAMTN NW1 .... **3** E6

Plantation House
Medical Centre
LOTH EC2R **15** H3
Plashet Jewish Cemetery
MNPK E12 .... **113** F4
Plashet Road Medical Centre
FSTGT E7 .... **112** D5
Plashet School
EHAM E6 .... **113** G5
Players Theatre
CHCR WC2N **21** E1
The Playhouse
CHCR WC2N **21** F1
Plaza Business Centre
PEND EN3 .... **40** D3
Pleasance Theatre
HOLWY N7 .... **107** G4
Plumcroft Primary School
WOOL/PLUM SE18 .... **154** C6
Plumstead Manor School
WOOL/PLUM SE18 .... **154** D5
The Pointer School
BKHTH/KID SE3 .... **172** C2
Police Cadet School
WAN E11 .... **92** C5
Polka Theatre for Children
WIM/MER SW19 .... **205** F2
Pollock's Toy Museum
FITZ W1T **12** B1
Ponders End Industrial Estate
PEND EN3 .... **40** D5
PEND EN3 .... **40** B3
Poole's Park Primary School
HOLWY N7 .... **87** H6
Pope John Primary School
SHB W12 .... **123** H6
Pop In Business Centre
WBLY HA9 .... **102** B3
Poplar Business Park
POP/IOD E14 .... **131** G6
Poplar First School
WIM/MER SW19 .... **205** E6
Pop Up Theatre
FSBYE EC1V **6** C2
Porchester Leisure Centre
BAY/PAD W2 .... **125** F5
Portcullis House
WHALL SW1A **21** F4
The Portland Hospital
REGST W1B **3** H6
Portland House
Medical Centre
GFD/PVL UB6 .... **119** F3
Portland Medical Centre
SNWD SE25 .... **229** H2
Portland Place School
REGST W1B **11** H1
The Portman Clinic
STJWD NW8 .... **105** H4
Portobello Market
NKENS W10 .... **124** C4
Portobello Medical Centre
NTGHL W11 .... **124** C5
Portway Primary School
SRTFD E15 .... **112** C6
Pound Park Nursery School
CHARL SE7 .... **153** F5
The Pountney Clinic
HSLW TW3 .... **159** E4
Poverest Primary School
STMC/STPC BR5 .... **235** G2
Powergate Business Park
WLSDN NW10 .... **122** D2
Premier Cinema
PECK SE15 .... **169** G3
Prendergast School
BROCKY SE4 .... **171** E5
Preston Manor School
WBLY HA9 .... **81** H6
Preston Medical Centre
WBLY HA9 .... **101** C1
Preston Park Primary School
WBLY HA9 .... **81** F5
PR for Schools
SYD SE26 .... **190** A5
Priestmead First &
Middle Schools
KTN/HRWW/W HA3 .... **60** D6
Primrose Hill School
CAMTN NW1 .... **106** C6
Primrose Montessori School
HBRY N5 .... **108** C1
Prince Charles Cinema
SOHO/SHAV W1D **12** D5
Prince Edward Theatre
SOHO/SHAV W1D **12** C4
Prince of Wales Theatre
STJS SW1Y **12** C6
Princes College
FITZ W1T **13** E3
Princes Court Business Centre
WAP E1W **17** H5
Princess Frederica CE
J & I School
WLSDN NW10 .... **123** H1
Princess Grace Hospital
MHST W1U **3** E6
Princess Louise Hospital
NKENS W10 .... **124** A4
Princess of Wales Conservatory
RCH/KEW TW9 .... **161** H1
Prior Western Primary School
STLK EC1Y **7** F6
Priory Boys & Infant School
ACT W3 .... **142** C2
Priory CE Middle School
WIM/MER SW19 .... **205** F1
Priory House School
CAT SE6 .... **191** F3
Priory Retail Park
WIM/MER SW19 .... **205** H3
Priory School
STMC/STPC BR5 .... **236** A5
Priory Special School
SNWD SE25 .... **229** F1
The Priory
ORP BR6 .... **235** H4
Privy Council
STJS SW1Y **20** C2

Privy Council Office
WHALL SW1A **21** E2
Progress Business Park
CROY/NA CRO **227** H6
Prospect House School
PUT/ROE SW15 .... **184** B2
Prospect of Whitby
WAP E1W **150** A1
Proud Gallery
CHCR WC2N **13** E6
Providence Square
STHWK SE1 .... **25** E3
Psychiatric Home
BRXN/ST SW9 .... **167** G4
Public Record Office
LINW WC2A **14** A3
Public Record Office Museum
RCH/KEW TW9 .... **162** B1
Pump House
BERM/RHTH SE16 .... **150** C1
Puppet Theatre Barge
WIM/MER SW19 .... **125** G4
The Purcell School
HRW HA1 .... **99** H1
Purdy Hicks Gallery
STHWK SE1 .... **22** C1
Purley Oaks Primary School
SAND/SEL CR2 .... **246** D5
Pursuit Centre
WAP E1W **130** A6
Putney Animal Hospital
PUT/ROE SW15 .... **164** B5
Putney Exchange
Shopping Centre
PUT/ROE SW15 .... **164** B5
Putney High School
PUT/ROE SW15 .... **164** B6
Putney Hospital
PUT/ROE SW15 .... **164** A4
Putney Leisure Centre
PUT/ROE SW15 .... **164** A5
Putney Lower
Common Cemetery
PUT/ROE SW15 .... **163** H3
Putneymead Medical Centre
PUT/ROE SW15 .... **164** A5
Putney Park School
PUT/ROE SW15 .... **163** H5
Putney School of Art
PUT/ROE SW15 .... **164** C5
Putney Vale Cemetery
PUT/ROE SW15 .... **183** G4
Putney Vale Crematorium
PUT/ROE SW15 .... **183** G4
Pylon Trading Estate
CAN/RD E16 .... **131** H3
Quadrant Business Park
KIL/WHAMP NW6 .... **104** C6
Quainton Hall School
HRW HA1 .... **79** H2
Quebec Industrial Estate
BERM/RHTH SE16 .... **150** C2
Queen Charlottes &
Chelsea Hospital
HMSMTH W6 .... **143** G3
Queen Charlotte's Cottage
RCH/KEW TW9 .... **161** H1
Queen Elizabeth Centre
BAR EN5 .... **34** D5
Queen Elizabeth
Conference Centre
WEST SW1P **20** D4
Queen Elizabeth Hall
STHWK SE1 .... **21** G1
Queen Elizabeth Hospital
CHARL SE7 .... **153** H6
Queen Elizabeth II School
MV/WKIL W9 .... **124** D3
Queen Elizabeth Museum
CHING E4 .... **56** B2
Queen Elizabeths Boys School
BAR EN5 .... **34** B4
Queen Elizabeths Girls School
BAR EN5 .... **34** D5
Queen Elizabeth Stadium
EN EN1 .... **39** F3
Queenhithe Stairs
BLKFR EC4V **15** E6
Queen Marys Hospital
SCUP DA14 .... **215** G1
Queen Marys
Hospital for Children
CAR SM5 .... **244** B6
Queen Mary's
Royal Free Hospital
HAMP NW3 .... **105** G1
Queen Mary's
University Hospital
PUT/ROE SW15 .... **183** G1
Queen Mary & Westfield College
SWFD E18 .... **72** C4
WCHPL E1 .... **130** B3
Queen Mother Sports Centre
WEST SW1P **28** A1
Queensbridge Infant School
HACK E8 .... **109** F5
Queens CE Primary School
RCH/KEW TW9 .... **144** C1
Queen's Club
WKENS W14 .... **144** C5
Queen's Gallery
WHALL SW1A **19** H4
The Queens House
GNWCH SE10 .... **151** H6
Queens Ice Skating Club
BAY/PAD W2 .... **125** F6
Queens Manor Primary School
FUL/PGN SW6 .... **164** A1
Queensmead School
RSLP HA4 .... **98** B2
Queens Medical Centre
RCHPK/HAM TW10 .... **161** H6
Queens Park
Community School GM
WLSDN NW10 .... **104** A6
Queens Park Health Centre
NKENS W10 .... **124** C2

Queens Park Primary School
NKENS W10 .... **124** C2
Queens Park Rangers FC
(Loftus Road Stadium)
SHB W12 .... **123** H6
Queen's Road Cemetery
CROY/NA CRO **228** C3
Queens Road Practice
NWCR SE14 .... **170** B2
Queens Theatre
SOHO/SHAV W1D **12** C5
Queensway Business Centre
PEND EN3 .... **40** A5
Queenswell Infant School
TRDG/WHET N20 .... **49** H4
Queen Victoria Memorial
WHALL SW1A **20** A4
The Questors Theatre
EA W5 .... **121** E6
Quicksilver Theatre
IS N1 .... **109** E5
Quintin Kynaston School
STJWD NW8 .... **105** H6
Radcliffe College
SOHO/CST W1F **12** A1
Ragged School Museum Trust
BOW E3 .... **130** C4
Raglan Infant School
EN EN1 .... **53** E1
Raglan Junior School
EN EN1 .... **53** E2
Raglan Primary School
HAYES BR2 .... **233** E1
Railton Road Clinic
HNHL SE24 .... **168** B6
Rainbow Clinic
BAY/PAD W2 .... **125** H3
Rainbow Industrial Estate
RYNPK SW20 .... **203** H5
Rainbow Quay
BERM/RHTH SE16 .... **150** C3
Raines Foundation School
BETH E2 .... **9** H2
Ramac Industrial Estate
CHARL SE7 .... **152** C5
Ram Brewery & Visitor Centre
WAND/EARL SW18 .... **165** H2
Rams Episcopal Primary School
HACK E8 .... **110** A3
Randal Cremer Primary School
BETH E2 .... **8** C1
Ranelagh Gardens (Site of
Chelsea Flower Show)
CHEL SW3 .... **27** F4
Ranelagh Primary School
SRTFD E15 .... **132** A1
Rangefield Primary School
BMLY BR1 .... **211** A1
Rangers House
GNWCH SE10 .... **171** G2
Ransomes Dock Business Centre
BTSEA SW11 .... **166** A1
Rathfern Primary School
FSTH SE23 .... **190** D3
Ravenor Primary School
GFD/PVL UB6 .... **119** E2
Ravensbourne College of
Design & Communication
CHST BR7 .... **213** H1
The Ravensbourne School
HAYES BR2 .... **232** D1
Ravenscourt Park
Preparatory School
HMSMTH W6 .... **143** G4
Ravenscroft Medical Centre
GLDGN NW11 .... **84** D4
Ravenscroft Primary School
PLSTW E13 .... **132** C3
Ravenscroft School
TRDG/WHET N20 .... **48** D2
Ravenside Retail Park
UED N18 .... **70** B1
Ravensquay Business Centre
STMC/STPC BR5 .... **235** H2
Ravenstone Primary School
BAL SW12 .... **186** D3
Ravenswood Industrial Estate
WALTH E17 .... **91** G1
Ravens Wood School
HAYES BR2 .... **251** F1
Ray Lodge Primary School
WFD IG8 .... **73** F2
Raynes Park High School
NWMAL KT3 .... **203** H6
Raynes Park Sports Ground
RYNPK SW20 .... **203** G5
Raynes Park Vale FC
RYNPK SW20 .... **224** B2
Raynham Primary School
UED N18 .... **69** C1
RCA
SKENS SW7 .... **145** G3
RCA Sculpture School
BTSEA SW11 .... **166** A1
Reay Primary School
BRXN/ST SW9 .... **167** H1
Records Office
CLKNW EC1R **6** B5
Recreation Centre
LBTH SE11 .... **30** D1
Rectory Business Centre
SCUP DA14 .... **195** H6
Rectory Paddock School
STMC/STPC BR5 .... **216** A5
Redbridge College
CHDH RM6 .... **95** H2
Redbridge Museum Service
IL IG1 .... **94** C6
Redbridge Primary School
REDBR IG4 .... **93** G2
Redbridge Sports Centre Trust
BARK/HLT IG6 .... **74** D4
Redburn Industrial Estate
PEND EN3 .... **54** B1
Redcliffe School
WBPTN SW10 .... **145** G6
Redifford School
PIN HA5 .... **78** C1

Redford Lodge
Psychiatric Hospital
ED N9.................................... 53 G4
Redhill Junior School
CHST SR7.............................. 214 B1
Redlands Primary School
WCHPL E1............................. 130 A4
Red Lion Business Park
SURB KT6.............................. 221 H6
Redriff Community
Primary School
BERM/RHTH SE16................ 150 C1
Red Rose Trading Estate
EBAR EN4.............................. 35 H6
Regent Clinic
CAVSQ/HST W1G................... 11 G2
Regent's College
CAMTN NW1.......................... 3 E3
Regent's Park Barracks
CAMTN NW1.......................... 3 G1
Regents Park Clinic
CAMTN NW1.......................... 2 C5
Regents Park Medical Centre
CAMTN NW1.......................... 3 H3
Regina Coeli RC Primary School
CROY/NA CR0...................... 246 B5
Renoir Cinema
BMSBY WC1N......................... 5 F5
Renwick Industrial Estate
BARK IG11............................ 135 H1
Restaurant & Cafe
BAY/PAD W2.......................... 18 A3
Reynard Mills Trading Estate
BTFD TW8............................. 141 E5
Rhodes Avenue Primary School
FBAR/BDGN N11................... 67 E4
Rhodes Farm Clinic
MLHL NW7............................. 48 A6
Rhyl Primary School
KTTN NW5............................. 106 C4
RIBA Drawings Collection &
Heinz Gallery
MBLAR W1H.......................... 10 D3
Ricards Lodge High School
WIM/MER SW19.................... 204 D1
Richard Alibon Primary School
DAGE RM10.......................... 117 E3
Richard Atkins Primary School
BRXS/STRHM SW2................. 187 G2
Richard Cloudesley School
STLK EC1Y............................ 7 E6
Richard Cobden Primary School
CAMTN NW1.......................... 107 E6
Rich Industrial Estate
PECK SE15............................ 33 H6
STHWK SE1........................... 24 B6
STHWK SE1........................... 32 D3
Richmond Adult &
Community College
RCH/KEW TW9..................... 161 F5
TWK TW1................................ 180 B3
The Richmond Clinic
RCHPK/HAM TW10................ 161 H5
Richmond College
KENS W8............................... 145 F3
RCHPK/HAM TW10................ 181 G2
Richmond FC
RCH/KEW TW9..................... 161 F5
The Richmond Golf Club
RCHPK/HAM TW10................ 181 G4
The Richmond Green
Medical Centre
RCH/KEW TW9..................... 161 F6
Richmond House School
HPTN TW12........................... 198 D1
Richmond Magistrates Court
RCH/KEW TW9..................... 161 F5
Richmond Park Golf Club
PUT/ROE SW15..................... 183 E2
Richmond Road
Medical Centre
KUTN/CMB KT2.................... 201 G3
Richmond Theatre
RCH/KEW TW9..................... 161 F5
Richmond-upon-Thames College
WHTN TW2............................ 180 A2
Ridge House Clinic
WCHMH N21.......................... 52 D2
Ridgeway Primary School
SAND/SEL CR2...................... 247 E6
Rio Cinema
HACK E8................................ 109 F3
Ripple Junior & Infant School
BARK IG11............................ 114 D6
Rise Park Primary School
ROM RM1............................... 77 H4
Risley Avenue Primary School
TOTM N17.............................. 69 E4
Ritzy Cinema
BRXN/ST SW9........................ 168 A5
River Brent Business Park
NWDGN UB2.......................... 140 A3
River Mole Business Park
ESH/CLAY KT10.................... 219 E5
River Place Health Centre
IS N1..................................... 108 C5
River Road Business Park
BARK IG11............................ 135 E2
Riversdale Primary School
WAND/EARL SW18................ 185 E3
Riverside Business Centre
WAND/EARL SW18................ 185 F3
Riverside Business Park
WIM/MER SW19.................... 205 G4
Riverside Community
Health Care
WKENS W14.......................... 144 B3
Riverside Golf Club
THMD SE28........................... 136 C5
Riverside Industrial Estate
BARK IG11............................ 135 G2
ED N9.................................... 54 C1
Riverside Primary School
BERM/RHTH SE16................. 25 F4
Riverside Studios Cinema
BARN SW13........................... 144 A5
Riverside Wandle
Trading Estate
MTCM CR4............................ 226 B4

Riverston School
LEE/GVPK SE12.................... 172 C6
Riverview CE Primary School
HOR/WEW KT19................... 240 C2
Roan Industrial Estate
MTCM CR4............................ 206 A4
Robert Blair Primary School
HOLWY N7............................ 107 G4
Robert Browning
Primary School
WALW SE17........................... 31 F3
Robert Clack School
BCTR RM8............................. 96 D5
Robin Hood Junior School
SUT SM1............................... 243 F3
Robin Hood Lane
Health Centre
SUT SM1............................... 243 E3
Robin Hood Primary School
KUTN/CMB KT2.................... 202 D1
Robinsfield Infant School
STJWD NW8.......................... 125 H1
The Roche School
WAND/EARL SW18................ 165 E6
Rockcliffe Manor
Primary School
WOOL/PLUM SE18............... 175 E1
Rockmount School
NRWD SE19.......................... 208 C2
Rockware Business Centre
GFD/PVL UB6........................ 99 H6
Rodling Primary School
BCTR RM8............................. 116 A2
Roebuck Road Trading Estate
BARK/HLT IG6..................... 75 H2
Roe Green Infant School
CDALE/KGS NW9.................. 82 B1
Roehampton Church School
PUT/ROE SW15..................... 183 H2
Roehampton Golf Club
PUT/ROE SW15..................... 163 F6
Roehampton Institute
PUT/ROE SW15..................... 163 F6
WAND/EARL SW18................ 184 C1
The Roehampton
Priory Hospital
PUT/ROE SW15..................... 163 F5
Roehampton Recreation Centre
PUT/ROE SW15..................... 183 G2
Roger Ascham Primary School
WALTH E17........................... 70 D4
Roger Bannister Sports Ground
KTN/HRWW/W HA3.............. 59 G2
Rokeby School
KUTN/CMB KT2.................... 202 C3
SRTFD E15............................ 111 H5
Rokesly Primary School
CEND/HSY/T N8.................... 87 G2
Roman Bath
TPL/STR WC2R...................... 13 H5
Roman Industrial Estate
CROY/NA CR0....................... 229 E4
Roman Road Primary School
EHAM E6............................... 133 F3
Roman Wall Remains
BARB EC2Y........................... 15 E2
Romford Cemetery
ROMW/RG RM7..................... 97 G4
Ronald Rose Primary School
WIM/MER SW19.................... 184 B2
Rood Lane Medical Centre
FENCHST EC3M..................... 16 A5
Roosevelt Memorial
MYFR/PKLN W1K.................. 11 F5
Ropery Business Park
GNWCH SE7........................... 153 E4
Rosary Priory High School
BUSH WD23........................... 44 A1
Rosary RC Infant School
HAMP NW3............................ 106 A3
The Rosary RC Primary School
HAMP NW3............................ 106 A3
Rosebery Industrial Park
TOTM N17............................. 69 H5
Rose Bruford College
DEPT SE8............................... 151 E6
Rose Bruford College of
Speech & Drama
BFN/LL DA15........................ 195 H3
Roselands Clinic
NWMAL KT3.......................... 222 C1
Rosemary School (Primary)
IS N1..................................... 108 C6
Rosemary Secondary School
CLKNW EC1R......................... 6 C5
Roe McAndrew Clinic
BRXN/ST SW9........................ 167 H3
Rosemead Preparatory School
DUL SE21.............................. 188 C4
Rosendale Primary School
DUL SE21.............................. 188 C2
Rose Theatre Exhibition
STHWK SE1........................... 23 E1
Rosh Pinah Primary School
EDGW HA8............................ 46 B4
Rosslyn Park RFC
PUT/ROE SW15..................... 163 F5
Rotherhithe Civic Centre
BERM/RHTH SE16................. 150 A2
Rotherhithe Primary School
BERM/RHTH SE16................. 150 A4
The Roundhouse Theatre
CAMTN NW1.......................... 106 C5
Roundwood Park
Medical Centre
WLSDN NW10....................... 100 C5
Rowan High School
CLAP SW4............................. 187 F1
Rowans School
RYNPK SW20......................... 203 G3
Rowley Industrial Park
ACT W3................................. 142 B3
Roxbourne Medical Centre
RYLN/HDSTN HA2................. 79 F6
Roxbourne Middle School
RSLP HA4.............................. 78 B6

Roxeth First & Middle School
RYLN/HDSTN HA2................. 79 H6
Roxeth Manor First School
RYLN/HDSTN HA2................. 99 F1
Roxeth Mead School
RYLN/HDSTN HA2................. 79 H6
Roxwell Trading Park
LEY E10................................. 90 C4
Royal Academy of Arts
MYFR/PICC W1J.................... 12 A6
Royal Academy of Dramatic Art
GWRST WC1E........................ 4 D6
Royal Academy of Music
CAMTN NW1.......................... 3 F6
Royal Air Force Museum
CDALE/KGS NW9.................. 63 G5
Royal Albert Hall
SKENS SW7........................... 145 H2
Royal Army Medical College
WEST SW1P........................... 28 D3
Royal Arsenal
WOOL/PLUM SE18............... 154 B3
The Royal Ballet School
HMSMTH W6......................... 144 B5
Royal Blackheath Golf Club
ELTH/MOT SE9..................... 193 H2
Royal Brompton Hospital
CHEL SW3............................. 26 A3
Royal Brompton &
National Heart Hospitals
CHEL SW3............................. 145 H5
Royal College of Anaesthetists
RSQ WC1B............................. 13 E1
Royal College of Art
SKENS SW7........................... 145 G2
Royal College of Music
SHB W12............................... 143 G3
SKENS SW7........................... 145 H3
Royal College of Nursing
CAMTN NW1.......................... 4 B5
IS N1..................................... 108 B6
Royal College of
Obstetricians & Gynaecologists
CAMTN NW1.......................... 2 C5
Royal College of Ophthalmologists
CAMTN NW1.......................... 3 E6
Royal College of Paediatrics &
Child Health
GTPST W1W........................... 11 H1
The Royal College of Pathology
STJS SW1Y............................ 20 C2
Royal College of Physicians
CAMTN NW1.......................... 3 G5
Royal College of Surgeons
LINN WC2A........................... 13 H3
Royal Courts of Justice
LINN WC2A........................... 13 H4
Royal Court Theatre
BGVA SW1W.......................... 27 E2
Royal Court Young
Peoples Theatre
NKENS W10........................... 124 C4
The Royal Dock
Community School
CAN/RD E16.......................... 133 E5
Royal Docks Medical Centre
EHAM E6............................... 134 A5
Royal Epping Forest Golf Club
CHING E4.............................. 56 A2
Royal Exchange
LOTH EC2R............................ 15 H4
Royal Festival Hall
STHWK SE1........................... 21 G2
Royal Foundation of Grey Coat
Hospital
WESTW SW1E........................ 20 A5
Royal Free Hospital
HAMP NW3............................ 106 A3
Royal Free Hospital School of
Medicine
HAMP NW3............................ 106 A3
Royal Geographical Society
SKENS SW7........................... 145 H2
Royal Horticultural
Society New Hall
WEST SW1P........................... 20 C1
Royal Horticultural
Society Old Hall
WEST SW1P........................... 28 C1
Royal Hospital
RCH/KEW TW9..................... 161 G4
Royal Hospital Chelsea
CHEL SW3............................. 27 E5
Royal Hospital for
Neuro-Disability
PUT/ROE SW15..................... 184 C1
Royal Hospital & Home
PUT/ROE SW15..................... 183 H2
Royal Hospital Museum
CHEL SW3............................. 27 E4
Royal Institute of
British Architects
REGST W1B........................... 11 H1
Royal Institution
(Faraday Museum)
MYFR/PICC W1J.................... 11 H6
The Royal London Estate
TOTM N17............................. 69 H3
Royal London
Homeopathic Hospital
BMSBY WC1N......................... 13 F1
Royal London Hospital
BETH E2................................ 130 A1
The Royal London Hospital
BOW E3................................. 130 D2
WCHPL E1............................. 17 G2
Royal Marsden Hospital
CHEL SW3............................. 145 H5
The Royal Mews
WHALL SW1A........................ 19 H5
Royal Mid-Surrey Golf Club
RCH/KEW TW9..................... 161 F4
Royal Mint Court
TWRH EC3N.......................... 16 D6
Royal National
Orthopaedic Hospital
GTPST W1W........................... 3 H6
STAN HA7............................. 44 D3
Royal National Theatre
BRXN/ST SW9........................ 168 A1

STHWK SE1........................... 22 A1
Royal National Throat,
Nose & Ear Hospital
FSBYW WC1X......................... 5 G3
Royal Observatory Greenwich
GNWCH SE10........................ 151 H6
Royal Opera House
COVGDN WC2E...................... 13 F4
Royal Park Primary School
SCUP DA14........................... 196 C5
Royal Russell School
CROY/NA CR0....................... 247 H4
The Royal School
HAMP NW3............................ 105 H2
Royal Society of Arts
TPL/STR WC2R...................... 13 F6
Royal Society of Medicine
CAMTN NW1.......................... 11 G3
Royal Veterinary College
CAMTN NW1.......................... 107 F6
Royal Victoria
Docks Watersports Centre
CAN/RD E16.......................... 132 C6
Royal Wimbledon Golf Club
WIM/MER SW19.................... 203 H1
Royston Primary School
BECK BR3............................. 210 B4
RSPCA Animal Hospital
HOLWY N7............................ 87 H6
Rudolph Steiner Hall
CAMTN NW1.......................... 2 C5
Rufus Business Centre
WAND/EARL SW18................ 185 F4
Rush Croft School
CHING E4.............................. 71 F3
Rushey Green Primary School
CAT SE6................................ 191 F3
Rush Green Primary School
ROMW/RG RM7..................... 97 H5
Rushmore Junior School
CLPT E5................................ 110 A2
Ruskin House School
HNHL SE24............................ 168 C6
The Russell JMI School
RCHPK/HAM TW10................ 181 F4
The Russell School
RCHPK/HAM TW10................ 181 F3
Russet House School
EN EN1.................................. 39 H2
Rutlish School
RYNPK SW20......................... 204 D5
Ruxley Corner
Industrial Estate
SCUP DA14........................... 216 B2
Ruxley Manor School
ELTH/MOT SE9..................... 194 A6
Ruxley Park Golf Centre
STMC/STPC BR5.................... 216 B4
Ryelands Primary School
SNWD SE25.......................... 229 H2
Saatchi Gallery
KIL/WHAMP NW6................. 105 F6
Sacred Heart High School
HMSMTH W6......................... 144 A4
Sacred Heart
High School for Girls
KTN/HRWW/W HA3.............. 60 A5
Sacred Heart Junior
Middle & Infant School
OXHEY WD19......................... 42 D1
Sacred Heart Junior School
HMSMTH W6......................... 144 B4
Sacred Heart RC Infant School
BTSEA SW11.......................... 166 A3
Sacred Heart RC
Junior & Middle School
BTSEA SW11.......................... 166 A4
Sacred Heart RC
Primary School
NWMAL KT3.......................... 223 G1
WIM/MER SW19.................... 200 D3
Sacred Heart RC School
CMBW SE5............................. 168 C2
Sacred Heart School
HOLWY N7............................ 107 H3
Saddlers Hall
CITYW EC2V......................... 15 E4
Sadler's Wells Theatre
CLKNW EC1R......................... 6 B3
SAE Technology College
HOLWY N7............................ 107 G3
Safari Cinema
CROY/NA CR0....................... 228 B4
Safari Cinema & Bingo
HRW HA1.............................. 80 B2
Sai Medical Centre
POP/IOD E14......................... 151 G1
St Agathas RC Primary School
KUTN/CMB KT2.................... 201 H2
St Agnes RC Primary School
BOW E3................................. 131 E2
CRICK NW2........................... 104 C1
St Aidans Primary School
FSBYPK N4........................... 88 A4
St Aidans RC Primary School
IL IG1................................... 94 D5
St Albans CE Primary School
FSBYW WC1X......................... 14 A1
St Albans Health Clinic
KTTN NW5............................. 106 C1
St Albans Junior &
Infant RC School
PECK SE15............................ 169 F2
St Albans RC Aided
Primary School
E/WMO/HCT KT8.................. 219 F2
St Alfege with St Peter CE
Primary School
GNWCH SE10........................ 151 G6
St Aloysius College
ARCH N19............................. 87 E5
St Aloysius RC Infant School
CAMTN NW1.......................... 4 C3
St Aloysius RC Junior School
CAMTN NW1.......................... 4 B2
St Andrew & St Francis CE
JMI School
CRICK NW2........................... 103 G4
St Andrews CE JMI School
TRDG/WHET N20................. 48 D4

St Andrews CE Primary School
EN EN1 .... 38 D3
STHGT/OAK N14 .... 51 F3
BRXN/ST SW9 .... 168 A2
St Andrews Greek School
CAMTN NW1 .... 106 D4
St Andrews Hospital
BOW E3 .... 131 F3
St Andrews Primary School
BRXN/ST SW9 .... 167 H3
IS N1 .... 107 H6
St Andrews School
RYLN/HDSTN HA2 .... 79 F2
WLSDN NW10 .... 103 H5
St Angelas RC School
FSTGT E7 .... 112 D4
St Annes Catholic High School
PLMGR N13 .... 52 A6
St Annes CE Primary School
WAND/EARL SW18 .... 165 F6
St Annes Convent School
EN EN1 .... 38 D5
St Annes RC Primary School
LBTH SE11 .... 29 G5
WCHPL E1 .... 9 E6
St Annes Special School
MRDN SM4 .... 225 F2
St Anne's Trading Estate
POP/IOD E14 .... 130 D5
St Anns CE Primary School
SEVS/STOTM N15 .... 88 D2
St Ann's General Hospital
SEVS/STOTM N15 .... 88 C2
St Anns School
HNWL W7 .... 140 A1
St Ann's Shopping Centre
HRW HA1 .... 80 A3
St Anselms RC First & Middle School
HRW HA1 .... 80 A4
St Anselms RC Primary School
NWDGN UB2 .... 138 D3
St Anslems RC Primary School
TOOT SW17 .... 186 C5
St Anthonys Hospital
WPK KT4 .... 224 B5
St Anthonys RC Primary School
EDUL SE22 .... 189 F1
FSTGT E7 .... 112 C5
PGE/AN SE20 .... 209 H4
St Antony's RC Primary School
WFD IG8 .... 56 C6
St Aubyns School
WFD IG8 .... 72 B3
St Augustines CE School
KIL/WHAMP NW6 .... 125 E1
St Augustines Primary School
BELV DA17 .... 156 D3
KIL/WHAMP NW6 .... 125 F1
St Augustines RC Infant School
GNTH/NBYPK IG2 .... 94 B2
St Augustines RC Primary School
CAT SE6 .... 211 F1
FUL/PGN SW6 .... 144 C6
GNTH/NBYPK IG2 .... 94 B2
St Barnabas CE Primary School
BCVA SW1W 27 F3
St Barnabas & Philip CE Primary School
KENS W8 .... 145 E3
St Bartholomews CE Primary School
SYD SE26 .... 190 A6
St Bartholomews Hospital
STBT EC1A 14 D2
St Bartholomews Medical School
FARR EC1M 6 D6
St Bartholomews & Royal London School of Medicine
FARR EC1M 15 E1
St Bartholomew's the Great
STBT EC1A 14 D2
St Barts Hospital Sports Ground
CHST BR7 .... 214 D2
St Bedes RC Primary School
CHDH RM6 .... 96 A2
St Benedicts Junior School
EA W5 .... 121 E4
St Benedicts School
EA W5 .... 121 F4
St Bernadettes RC First & Middle School
KTN/HRWW/W HA3 .... 81 H1
St Bonaventure's School
FSTGT E7 .... 112 C5
St Boniface RC Primary School
TOOT SW17 .... 206 B1
St Catherines CE Girls School
BXLYHS DA6 .... 177 F6
St Catherines Middle School
NWMAL KT3 .... 224 A2
St Catherines School
TWK TW1 .... 180 B4
St Cecilias RC Primary School
WPK KT4 .... 224 B6
St Chads RC Primary School
SNWD SE25 .... 229 E2
St Charles Hospital
NKENS W10 .... 124 B4
St Charles RC Sixth Form College
NKENS W10 .... 124 B4
St Christophers School
BECK BR3 .... 211 G5
HAMP NW3 .... 105 H3
WBLY HA9 .... 101 H1
St Christopher House
STHWK SE1 .... 23 E1
St Clare Business Park
HPTN TW12 .... 199 G2
St Clement Danes School
HOL/ALD WC2B 13 G4

St Clement & James CE Primary School
NTCHL W11 .... 144 C1
St Clements RC Primary School
EW KT17 .... 241 F6
St Columbas RC Boys School
BXLYHS DA6 .... 177 F6
St Cuthbert With St Matthias CE Primary School
ECT SW5 .... 145 F5
St Davids College
WWKM BR4 .... 214 A6
St Dominics 6th Form College
HRW HA1 .... 80 A6
St Dominics RC Junior & Infant School
HOM E9 .... 110 B4
St Dominics RC Primary School
HAMP NW3 .... 106 B3
St Dunstans Primary School
CHEAM SM3 .... 242 C5
St Dunstans College
CAT SE6 .... 190 D3
St Ebba's Hospital
HOR/WEW KT19 .... 240 C6
St Edmunds RC Primary School
ED N9 .... 53 H5
POP/IOD E14 .... 151 E4
WHTN TW2 .... 179 F2
St Edwards CE Comprehensive School
CHDH RM6 .... 97 E3
St Edwards RC Primary School
ROM RM1 .... 97 H1
St Edwards RC JMI School
STJWD NW8 .... 2 A1
St Elizabeths RC Primary School
RCHPK/HAM TW10 .... 181 H1
St Elpheges RC Primary School
WLCTN SM6 .... 245 G4
St Faiths CE School
WAND/EARL SW18 .... 165 F6
St Fidelis Catholic Primary School
ERITH DA8 .... 157 G6
St Francesca Cabrini Primary School
FSTH SE23 .... 190 A1
St Francis of Assisi Primary School
NTGHL W11 .... 124 B6
St Francis RC Primary School
PECK SE15 .... 33 F6
SRTFD E15 .... 112 A3
St Francis Xavier College
BAL SW12 .... 186 D1
St Gabriels CE Primary School
PIM SW1V 28 A4
St George's Cathedral
STHWK SE1 .... 22 B5
St George's Cathedral RC Primary
STHWK SE1 .... 22 C5
St Georges CE Primary School
BMLY BR1 .... 213 E5
PECK SE15 .... 32 A6
PECK SE15 .... 169 E1
VX/NE SW8 .... 167 E1
St Georges College
HOLWY N7 .... 108 A1
St Georges Elizabethan Theatre
HOLWY N7 .... 107 F2
St Georges Hanover Square CE Primary School
MYFR/PKLN W1K 11 F6
St Georges Hospital
TOOT SW17 .... 206 A1
St Georges Industrial Estate
KUTN/CMB KT2 .... 201 F1
WDGN N22 .... 68 B3
St Georges Medical Centre
HDN NW4 .... 63 H6
St Georges RC First & Middle School
HRW HA1 .... 100 B1
St Georges RC Primary School
ENC/FH EN2 .... 38 D3
MV/WKIL W9 .... 125 F1
St Georges Shopping Centre & Cinema
HRW HA1 .... 79 H3
St George Wharf
VX/NE SW8 .... 29 E5
St George the Martyr CE Primary School
BMSBY WC1N 5 G6
St Gildas RC Junior School
CEND/HSY/T N8 .... 67 G4
St Giles College London Central
RSQ WC1B 13 E1
St Giles School
CROY/NA CR0 .... 246 B4
St Gregorys High School
KTN/HRWW/W HA3 .... 81 F2
St Gregorys Primary School
EA W5 .... 121 E3
St Helens Catholic Infant School
WALTH E17 .... 91 G2
St Helens RC Primary School
BRXN/ST SW9 .... 168 A4
PLSTW E13 .... 132 B3
St Helier Hospital
SUT SM1 .... 225 G5
St Hildas School
BUSH WD23 .... 43 F2
St Ignatius RC Primary School
SEVS/STOTM N15 .... 89 E3
St James CE J & I School
BERM/RHTH SE16 .... 25 E5
St James CE Primary School
MUSWH N10 .... 86 C1
PEND EN3 .... 40 A3
St James CE Junior School
FSTGT E7 .... 112 B3

St James Hatcham CE Primary School
NWCR SE14 .... 170 C2
St James Independent School
TWK TW1 .... 180 C4
St James Medical Centre
CROY/NA CR0 .... 228 D4
St James RC Primary School
HAYES BR2 .... 234 B2
WHTN TW2 .... 180 A5
St James & St Michaels CE Primary School
BAY/PAD W2 .... 125 G6
St James's Health Centre
WALTH E17 .... 90 C2
St James's Palace
WHALL SW1A 20 B2
St James the Great RC Primary School
THHTH CR7 .... 208 B5
St John Fisher RC First and Middle School
RYLN/HDSTN HA2 .... 79 E1
St John Fisher RC Primary School
ERITHM DA18 .... 156 C3
GFD/PVL UB6 .... 121 E2
NWMAL KT3 .... 224 A2
St John of Jerusalem CE Primary School
HOM E9 .... 110 A5
St John Rigby Catholic College
WWKM BR4 .... 249 H2
St Johns Angell Town CE Primary School
BRXN/ST SW9 .... 168 A3
St Johns CE First School
STAN HA7 .... 44 C6
St Johns CE Infant School
HDN NW4 .... 83 H2
St Johns CE Middle School
STAN HA7 .... 44 C6
St Johns CE Primary School
BETH E2 .... 130 A1
BKHH IG9 .... 38 D5
FBAR/BDGN N11 .... 50 B6
KUT KT1 .... 201 G6
PGE/AN SE20 .... 210 A3
TRDG/WHET N20 .... 49 G4
WALW SE17 .... 31 F2
St Johns CE School
CDALE/KGS NW9 .... 83 E2
St John's CE Walham Green
FUL/PGN SW6 .... 164 C2
St John's Concert Hall
WEST SW1P 21 E6
St Johns Highbury Vale CE Primary School
HBRY N5 .... 108 B1
St John's Hospital
SOHO/SHAV W1D 12 C5
St Johns Hospital Day Centre
BTSEA SW11 .... 165 H5
St Johns Primary School
WEA W13 .... 120 C6
St Johns RC Primary School
BERM/RHTH SE16 .... 150 C2
St Johns RC Special School
WFD IG8 .... 74 A1
St Johns & St James CE School
UED N18 .... 69 F1
St Johns School
ENC/FH EN2 .... 38 A3
St Johns Upper Holloway CE Primary School
ARCH N19 .... 107 F1
St Johns Way Medical Centre
ARCH N19 .... 87 F5
St Johns Wood School of English
KIL/WHAMP NW6 .... 105 F6
St John the Baptist CE Junior Sch
KUT KT1 .... 201 F3
St John the Baptist CE Primary School
CAT SE6 .... 191 G6
IS N1 .... 8 A2
St John the Divine CE Primary School
CMBW SE5 .... 168 B1
St John the Evangelist RC Primary School
IS N1 .... 6 C1
St John Vianney RC Primary School
SEVS/STOTM N15 .... 88 B1
St Josephs Catholic Infant School
LEY E10 .... 90 D5
St Josephs Catholic Primary School
BMLY BR1 .... 213 E3
St Josephs College
STRHM/NOR SW16 .... 208 B2
St Josephs Convent School
WAN E11 .... 92 C3
St Josephs Primary School
HDN NW4 .... 83 H1
PUT/ROE SW15 .... 165 G6
St Josephs RC First & Middle School
KTN/HRWW/W HA3 .... 60 C5
St Josephs RC Infant School
NRWD SE19 .... 208 C2
WBLY HA9 .... 101 H4
St Josephs RC Junior School
CMBW SE5 .... 168 C1
LEY E10 .... 91 F5
NRWD SE19 .... 208 C2
WBLY HA9 .... 101 H3
St Josephs RC Primary School
ARCH N19 .... 86 D5
BARK IG11 .... 114 C6
BERM/RHTH SE16 .... 25 E4
BERM/RHTH SE16 .... 150 A3
CHEL SW3 .... 16 D3
DACW RM9 .... 116 D2
DART DA1 .... 177 H5
DEPT SE8 .... 171 E1
GNWCH SE10 .... 152 A5
HNWL W7 .... 140 A1
HOL/ALD WC2B 13 F3
KUT KT1 .... 201 G5
MV/WKIL W9 .... 125 G3
STHWK SE1 .... 23 F3
WLSDN NW10 .... 103 E5
St Judes CE Primary School
STHWK SE1 .... 22 C6
St Judes & St Pauls CE Primary School
IS N1 .... 109 E4
St Katharine Pier
TWR EC3N 24 D1
St Lawrence Junior School
E/WMO/HCT KT8 .... 199 H6
St Lawrence University
STBYW WC1X 5 H6
St Leonards CE Primary School
STRHM/NOR SW16 .... 207 F1
St Leonards Hospital
IS N1 .... 8 B1
St Lukes CE Primary School
CAN/RD E16 .... 132 B5
FSBYE EC1V 7 F4
KUTN/CMB KT2 .... 201 H4
MV/WKIL W9 .... 124 D2
POP/IOD E14 .... 151 H4
WNWD SE27 .... 208 C1
St Luke's Health Centre
CAN/RD E16 .... 132 B5
St Lukes Hospital for the Clergy
FITZ W1T 4 A1
St Lukes School
THHTH CR7 .... 228 A1
St Lukes Woodside Hospital
MUSWH N10 .... 86 C1
St Margaret Clitherow RC Primary
THMD SE28 .... 155 H1
St Margaret Lee CE Primary School
LEW SE13 .... 172 A5
St Margarets Business Centre
TWK TW1 .... 180 C2
St Margarets Clitherow RC Primary School
WLSDN NW10 .... 102 D1
St Margarets Primary School
BARK IG11 .... 114 B6
St Marks CE Primary School
BUSH WD23 .... 43 E3
HAMP NW3 .... 105 F2
St Marks CE Primary School
ARCH N19 .... 87 G6
HAYES BR2 .... 212 C6
LBTH SE11 .... 29 H5
SNWD SE25 .... 229 G1
St Marks Industrial Estate
CAN/RD E16 .... 153 F1
St Marks Primary School
MTCM CR4 .... 206 B5
STHL UB1 .... 140 A2
St Marks School
HSLW TW3 .... 158 D4
St Marthas Convent Senior School
EBAR EN4 .... 35 E2
St Martin-in-the-Fields High School
BRXS/STRHM SW2 .... 188 B3
St Martin of Pores RC Primary School
FBAR/BDCN N11 .... 67 E2
St Martins Hospital
MYFR/PKLN W1K 11 E5
St Martins School
MLHL NW7 .... 63 E1
St Martins School of Art
SOHO/SHAV W1D 12 D1
St Martins Theatre
LSQ/SEVD WC2H 12 D5
St Mary Abbots CE Primary School
KENS W8 .... 145 F2
St Mary CE Primary School
PUT/ROE SW15 .... 164 B4
St Marylebone CE Secondary School
MHST W1U 11 F1
St Marylebone Crematorium
EFNCH N2 .... 65 F6
St Mary Magdalene CE Primary School
MV/WKIL W9 .... 125 F4
PECK SE15 .... 169 H3
WOOL/PLUM SE18 .... 153 H4
St Mary Magdalen RC Primary School
HOLWY N7 .... 108 A4
St Mary Magdalen RC Junior School
CRICK NW2 .... 103 H4
St Mary Magdalens RC Primary School
MORT/ESHN SW14 .... 162 D4
St Mary of the Angels RC Primary School
BAY/PAD W2 .... 125 E5
St Marys Abbey
MLHL NW7 .... 47 G5
St Mary & St Josephs GM School
SCUP DA14 .... 215 F1
St Mary & St Pancras CE Primary School
CAMTN NW1 .... 4 C2
St Marys Bryanston Square CE Primary School
MBLAR W1H 10 C2
St Marys Catholic Primary School
CHING E4 .... 55 H5
St Marys CE High School
HDN NW4 .... 64 A6
St Marys CE Junior School
CEND/HSY/T N8 .... 87 G1
THDIT KT7 .... 220 D5
St Mary's Cemetery
BTSEA SW11 .... 166 A6

St Marys CE Primary School
  CHSGTN KT9 .... 239 G4
  EBAR EN4 .... 50 A1
  FNCH N3 .... 64 D4
  IS N1 .... 108 B5
  LEW SE13 .... 171 F6
  TWK TW1 .... 180 C2
  WLSDN NW10 .... 103 E4
St Marys Church of England
    High School
  HDN NW4 .... 64 A6
St Marys Greek Cathedral
  WDGN N22 .... 67 H4
St Marys High School
  CROY/NA CR0 .... 228 C5
St Marys Hospital
  BAY/PAD W2 .... 125 H5
St Marys Hospital
    Medical School
  BAY/PAD W2 .... 125 H5
St Marys Infant School
  CAR SM5 .... 244 A2
St Mary's Kilburn
    Primary School
  KIL/WHAMP NW6 .... 105 E6
St Mary's Magdalens RC
    Primary School
  BROCKY SE4 .... 170 C5
St Mary's Primary School
  WKENS W14 .... 144 B3
St Marys RC Infant School
  CAR SM5 .... 244 B2
  CROY/NA CR0 .... 228 D5
St Marys RC Junior School
  CROY/NA CR0 .... 228 D5
  WALTH E17 .... 71 G6
St Marys RC Primary School
  BECK BR3 .... 211 G3
  CHSWK W4 .... 142 D5
  CLAP SW4 .... 167 E6
  ELTH/MOT SE9 .... 174 A6
  ISLW TW7 .... 160 C4
  KIL/WHAMP NW6 .... 105 E6
  NKENS W10 .... 124 C3
  PEND EN3 .... 40 B5
  SEVS/STOTM N15 .... 88 D2
St Marys RC Primary School
  VX/NE SW8 .... 166 D2
  WIM/MER SW19 .... 205 E3
St Marys & St Peters CE
    Primary School
  TEDD TW11 .... 200 A1
St Marys School
  CEND/HSY/T N8 .... 87 G2
  HAMP NW3 .... 105 G3
St Marys Stoke Newington CE
    Primary School
  STNW/STAM N16 .... 89 E6
St Marys University College
  TWK TW1 .... 180 B5
St Matthews CE Primary School
  PEND EN3 .... 40 A6
  RYNPK SW20 .... 203 G4
  SURB KT6 .... 221 G4
  WEST SW1P 20 D6
St Matthias CE Primary School
  BETH E2 .... 8 D5
  STNW/STAM N16 .... 109 E3
St Meryl Junior Middle &
    Infant School
  OXHEY WD19 .... 42 C5
St Michael At Bowes CE
    Junior School
  PLMGR N13 .... 68 A2
St Michaels and St Martins RC
    Primary School
  HSLW TW3 .... 158 D4
St Michaels Catholic
    Grammar School
  NFNCH/WDSP N12 .... 65 F1
St Michaels CE Primary School
  ENC/FH EN2 .... 38 C2
  HCT N6 .... 86 C4
  WAND/EARL SW18 .... 184 D2
  WDGN N22 .... 67 H4
St Michaels CE Aided
    Primary School Hall
  WELL DA16 .... 176 A2
St Michaels RC Primary School
  EHAM E6 .... 133 H1
St Michaels RC
    Secondary School
  BERM/RHTH SE16 .... 25 E4
St Michaels Sydenham CE
    Primary
  SYD SE26 .... 190 C6
St Monicas RC
    Primary School
  IS N1 .... 8 A3
  STHGT/OAK N14 .... 51 C5
St Nicholas Centre
  SUT SM1 .... 243 F3
St Nicholas School
  BORE WD6 .... 45 G1
  CHST BR7 .... 214 C3
St Olaves Preparatory School
  ELTH/MOT SE9 .... 194 B4
St Olave's & St Saviour's
    Grammar School
  ORP BR5 .... 253 H1
St Osmunds RC
    Primary School
  BARN SW13 .... 163 F2
St Pancras and
    Islington Cemetery
  EFNCH N2 .... 66 A4
St Pancras Hospital
  CAMTN NW1 .... 107 F6
St Pancras Station
  CAMTN NW1 .... 5 E3
St Patricks Church School
  STHWK SE1 .... 22 A2
St Patricks Infants School
  WAP E1W 25 G1
St Patricks International School
  SOHO/CST W1F 12 B3
St Patricks Primary School
  KTTN NW5 .... 106 D4
St Patricks RC JMI School
  ROMW/RG RM7 .... 77 F4

St Patricks RC Primary School
  WALTH E17 .... 90 C1
  WAP E1W 25 G2
  WOOL/PLUM SE18 .... 154 D4
St Pauls & All Hallows CE
    Infant School
  TOTM N17 .... 69 G3
St Paul's Cathedral
  STP EC4M 14 D4
St Pauls Cathedral School
  STP EC4M 15 E4
St Pauls CE JMI School
  MLHL NW7 .... 47 H6
St Pauls CE Primary School
  BTFD TW8 .... 141 F6
  CHSGTN KT9 .... 239 G2
  FBAR/BDGN N11 .... 66 C1
  HAMP NW3 .... 106 A5
  WALW SE17 .... 30 D4
  WCHMH N21 .... 52 B2
  WCHPL E1 .... 17 F5
St Pauls CE Junior School
  KUTN/CMB KT2 .... 202 A3
St Pauls Cray CE
    Primary School
  STMC/STPC BR5 .... 216 A6
St Pauls Cray Health Clinic
  STMC/STPC BR5 .... 215 G5
St Pauls Girls School
  HMSMTH W6 .... 144 B4
St Pauls Preparatory School
  BARN SW13 .... 143 G5
St Paul's Primary School
  HMSMTH W6 .... 119 G2
St Pauls RC Primary School
  THDIT KT7 .... 220 A4
  WDGN N22 .... 67 H5
St Pauls RC School
  WOOL/PLUM SE18 .... 155 G6
St Pauls Road Medical Centre
  IS N1 .... 108 B4
St Pauls Way School
  BOW E3 .... 131 E3
St Pauls with St Lukes CE
    Primary School
  BOW E3 .... 130 D4
St Paul's with St Michael's CE
    Primary School
  HACK E8 .... 6 C3
St Paul with St Luke CE
    Primary School
  POP/IOD E14 .... 130 D4
St Peter Chanel RC
    Primary School
  SCUP DA14 .... 216 A1
St Peter & Pauls RC
    Primary School
  IL IG1 .... 114 D1
St Peter & Paul RC
    Primary School
  MTCM CR4 .... 226 B1
St Peter & St Pauls
    Primary School
  FSBYE EC1V 6 D5
St Peters Catholic
    Primary School
  ROM RM1 .... 77 H6
St Peters CE Primary School
  HMSMTH W6 .... 143 G5
  MV/WKIL W9 .... 125 E3
  WALW SE17 .... 31 G4
St Peters Eaton Square CE
    Primary School
  BCVA SW1W 19 G6
St Peter's Hospital
  COVGDN WC2E 13 F5
St Peters Primary School
  SAND/SEL CR2 .... 246 D4
  WAP E1W 150 A1
St Peters RC Primary School
  DAGW RM9 .... 116 D6
  WOOL/PLUM SE18 .... 154 B5
St Philips School
  CHSGTN KT9 .... 239 F4
  SKENS SW7 .... 145 G4
St Phillips Infant School
  SYD SE26 .... 189 H6
St Philomenas RC High School
  CAR SM5 .... 244 B3
St Philomenas RC
    Primary School
  STMC/STPC BR5 .... 236 A4
St Quintins Health Centre
  NKENS W10 .... 124 A4
St Raphaels Way
  WPK KT4 .... 224 B6
St Raphaels Way
    Medical Centre
  WBLY HA9 .... 102 C3
St Richards with St Andrews CE
    Primary School
  RCHPK/HAM TW10 .... 180 D5
St Robert Southwell RC
    Primary School
  CDALE/KGS NW9 .... 82 C3
St Saviour & St Olaves School
  STHWK SE1 .... 23 H6
St Saviours CE Infant School
  EA W5 .... 141 F1
St Saviours CE Primary School
  NHHL SE24 .... 168 C4
  MV/WKIL W9 .... 125 F3
  POP/IOD E14 .... 131 F4
St Saviours RC Primary School
  LEW SE13 .... 171 G5
St Scholastica's RC
    Primary School
  STNW/STAM N16 .... 109 G1
St Stephens CE Junior School
  TWK TW1 .... 180 C1
St Stephens CE Primary School
  BAY/PAD W2 .... 125 E4
  DEPT SE8 .... 171 E3
  SHB W12 .... 144 A1
St Stephens CE School
  VX/NE SW8 .... 167 G1
St Stephens Infant School
  EHAM E6 .... 113 E5
St Stephens RC Primary School
  WELL DA16 .... 175 G4

St Swithun Wells RC
    Primary School
  RSLP HA4 .... 98 B1
St Teresa RC Primary School
  BCTR RM8 .... 116 A2
St Teresas RC School
  KTN/HRWW/W HA3 .... 59 G4
St Theresas RC Primary School
  FNCH N3 .... 65 E6
St Thomas CE Primary School
  NKENS W10 .... 124 C3
  STNW/STAM N16 .... 89 F5
St Thomas Childrens Day Hospital
  LBTH SE11 .... 29 H3
St Thomas Hospital
    Operation Theatre
  STHWK SE1 .... 23 H2
St Thomas More RC
    Primary School
  BXLYHN DA7 .... 176 D3
  ELTH/MOT SE9 .... 173 G4
St Thomas More RC School
  CHEL SW3 .... 26 C2
  ELTH/MOT SE9 .... 194 A1
St Thomas More School
  WDGN N22 .... 67 H3
St Thomas of Canterbury RC
    Middle School
  MTCM CR4 .... 206 C6
St Thomas of Canterbury RC
    Primary School
  FUL/PGN SW6 .... 164 D1
St Thomas' Hospital
  STHWK SE1 .... 21 G5
St Thomas the Apostle College
  PECK SE15 .... 170 C2
St Ursulas Convent School
  GNWCH SE10 .... 171 H1
St Vincent de Paul RC
    Primary School
  WEST SW1P 20 A6
St Vincents Catholic
    Primary School
  ELTH/MOT SE9 .... 193 G6
St Vincents RC Primary School
  ACT W3 .... 122 B6
  BCTR RM8 .... 96 A5
  MHST W1U 11 E2
  MLHL NW7 .... 48 A6
St Walter & St John
    Sports Ground
  TOOT SW17 .... 186 A3
St William of York
    Primary School
  FSTH SE23 .... 189 G3
St Winefrides Catholic
    Primary School
  MNPK E12 .... 113 H3
St Winifreds Junior School
  LEE/GVPK SE12 .... 192 B1
St Winifreds RC Infant School
  LEW SE13 .... 172 A6
Salcombe School
  STHGT/OAK N14 .... 51 F2
Salesian College
  BTSEA SW11 .... 166 A2
Salisbury Primary School
  MNPK E12 .... 113 F3
Salisbury School
  ED N9 .... 54 A3
Salisbury Upper School
  ED N9 .... 54 A2
Salters' Hall
  BARB EC2Y 15 F2
Salusbury Primary School
  KIL/WHAMP NW6 .... 104 C6
Salvation Army
    Heritage Centre
  BLKFR EC4V 15 E5
Salvatorian College
  KTN/HRWW/W HA3 .... 60 A5
Samaritan & Western
    Ophthalmic Hospital
  MBLAR W1H 10 C1
Samuel Jones Industrial Estate
  PECK SE15 .... 169 E1
Samuel Rhodes School
  IS N1 .... 108 A6
Sandersted Junior School
  SAND/SEL CR2 .... 246 D6
Sandgate Trading Estate
  BERM/RHTH SE16 .... 33 G5
Sandhurst Primary School
  CAT SE6 .... 192 A2
Sandown Industrial Park
  ESH/CLAY KT10 .... 219 E6
Sandown Park Racecourse
  ESH/CLAY KT10 .... 219 G6
Sandringham Primary School
  FSTGT E7 .... 113 E4
Sapcote Trading Centre
  WLSDN NW10 .... 103 F3
Sarah Bonnell School
  SRTFD E15 .... 112 A4
Sarum Hall School
  HAMP NW3 .... 106 A3
Satmer Trust School
  STNW/STAM N16 .... 89 G6
Savoy Pier
  TPL/STR WC2R 13 G6
Savoy Theatre
  TPL/STR WC2R 13 G6
Saxon Business Centre
  WIM/MER SW19 .... 205 G5
Sayer Clinic
  CROY/NA CR0 .... 245 H2
Sayer Clinics
  STHWK SE1 .... 10 D4
Schiller International School
  STHWK SE1 .... 22 A2
Schomberg House
  STJS SW1Y 20 B2
School of Art
  RCH/KEW TW9 .... 161 G5
School of English
  BMLY BR1 .... 85 E5
School of Oriental &
    African Studies
  STPAN WC1H 4 D6
The School of Pharmacy
  BMSBY WC1N 5 F5

The School of St David &
    St Katharine
  CEND/HSY/T N8 .... 87 G1
Science Museum
  SKENS SW7 .... 145 H3
Science Museum Imax Cinema
  SKENS SW7 .... 145 H3
Scotts Park Primary School
  BMLY BR1 .... 213 G4
Scott Wilkie Primary School
  CAN/RD E16 .... 133 E5
Screen on Baker Street Cinema
  MHST W1U 10 D1
Screen on the Green Cinema
  IS N1 .... 108 A6
Screen on the Hill Cinema
  HAMP NW3 .... 106 A3
Sebright Primary School
  BETH E2 .... 9 E1
Secombe Centre
  SUT SM1 .... 243 E3
Sedgehill School
  CAT SE6 .... 211 F1
Sedgewick Centre
  WCHPL E1 .... 16 D3
Selborne Primary School
  GFD/PVL UB6 .... 120 B1
The Selhurst Medical Centre
  SNWD SE25 .... 228 D3
Sellincourt School
  TOOT SW17 .... 206 B2
Selsdon High School
  SAND/SEL CR2 .... 248 B5
Selsdon Primary School
  SAND/SEL CR2 .... 248 A6
Selsdon Road Industrial Estate
  SAND/SEL CR2 .... 246 D5
Selwyn Primary School
  CHING E4 .... 71 G2
  PLSTW E13 .... 112 C6
Sergeant Industrial Estate
  WAND/EARL SW18 .... 185 F1
Serpentine Gallery
  BAY/PAD W2 .... 145 H2
Servite RC Primary School
  WBPTN SW10 .... 145 G6
Seven Islands Leisure Centre
  BERM/RHTH SE16 .... 150 A3
Seven Kings Health Centre
  GDMY/SEVK IG3 .... 95 E5
Seven Kings High School
  GNTH/NBYPK IG2 .... 94 D4
Seven Mills Primary School
  POP/IOD E14 .... 151 E2
Sevenoaks Way
    Industrial Estate
  STMC/STPC BR5 .... 216 A6
Seven Sisters Primary School
  SEVS/STOTM N15 .... 89 G2
Seymour Gardens
    Medical Centre
  IL IG1 .... 93 H5
Seymour Leasure Centre
  MBLAR W1H 10 C2
Shaare Zedek Medical Centre
  GLDGN NW11 .... 84 D3
Shacklewell Primary School
  STNW/STAM N16 .... 109 F2
Shaftesbury High School
  KTN/HRWW/W HA3 .... 59 F4
Shaftesbury Hospital
  LSQ/SEVD WC2H 12 D4
Shaftesbury Medical Centre
  RYLN/HDSTN HA2 .... 79 G5
Shaftesbury Park
    Primary School
  BTSEA SW11 .... 166 C4
Shaftesbury Primary School
  FSTGT E7 .... 113 E5
Shaftesbury Theatre
  LSQ/SEVD WC2H 13 E3
Shahjalal Medical Centre
  WCHPL E1 .... 17 F4
Shakespeare Business Centre
  BRXN/ST SW9 .... 168 B3
Shakespeare Globe Exhibition
  STHWK SE1 .... 15 E6
The Shamrock Sports Club
  ACT W3 .... 122 C5
Shannon Corner Retail Park
  NWMAL KT3 .... 223 C1
Shapla Primary School
  WCHPL E1 .... 17 E5
Sharp Sports Centre
  EDGW HA8 .... 62 A2
Shawcroft School
  STMC/STPC BR5 .... 236 C2
Sheen Lane Health Centre
  MORT/ESHN SW14 .... 162 C4
Sheen Mount Primary School
  RCHPK/HAM TW10 .... 162 B6
Sheen School
  MORT/ESHN SW14 .... 163 E5
Sheen Sports Centre
  MORT/ESHN SW14 .... 163 E5
Shell Centre
  STHWK SE1 .... 21 H2
Shelley School
  CLAP SW4 .... 167 E4
Shenstone School
  DART DA1 .... 177 H6
Shepherd's Bush Cricket Club
  ACT W3 .... 123 E6
Shepherd's Bush Empire
  SHB W12 .... 144 A2
Shepherds Community
    School YWAM
  BROCKY SE4 .... 171 E4
Sheraton Business Centre
  GFD/PVL UB6 .... 121 E1
Sheringdale Primary School
  WAND/EARL SW18 .... 184 D3
Sheringham Junior School
  MNPK E12 .... 113 H2
Sherington Primary School
  CHARL SE7 .... 152 D6
Sherlock Holmes Museum
  CAMTN NW1 .... 2 D6
Sherwood First School
  MTCM CR4 .... 227 E1

Sherwood Park School
WLGTN SM6 .... 245 F1
Shirley Clinic
CROY/NA CR0 .... 230 A5
Shirley High School
CROY/NA CR0 .... 248 B1
Shirley Medical Centre
CROY/NA CR0 .... 230 C6
Shirley Park Golf Club
CROY/NA CR0 .... 229 H6
Shirley Wanderers RFC
WWKM BR4 .... 249 G2
Shooters Hill Golf Club
WOOL/PLUM SE18 .... 174 C2
The Shopping Hall
EHAM E6 .... 113 G6
Shore Business Centre
HOM E9 .... 110 A5
Shoreditch
Comprehensive School
IS N1 .... 8 B2
Shoreditch County Court
STLK EC1Y 7 H5
Shortlands Golf Club
HAYES BR2 .... 212 A4
Shotfield Health Clinic
WLGTN SM6 .... 244 D4
Showcase Cinema
WDGN N22 .... 68 A5
Showcase Newham Cinema
BARK IG11 .... 134 C2
Shrewsbury House School
SURB KT6 .... 221 F6
Shrewsbury Road
Health Centre
FSTGT E7 .... 113 F5
Sidcup Cemetery
BXLY DA5 .... 196 B4
Sidcup Golf Club
BFN/LL DA15 .... 195 G4
Sidcup Health Centre
SCUP DA14 .... 195 G5
Sidcup Hill Primary School
SCUP DA14 .... 215 H1
Sidcup Sports Club
SCUP DA14 .... 195 F6
Sidney Russell School
DAGW RM9 .... 116 C2
Silicon Business Centre
CFD/PVL UB6 .... 121 E1
Silver Industrial Estate
TOTM N17 .... 69 F5
Silver Street Medical Centre
UED N18 .... 53 E6
Silver Wing Industrial Estate
CROY/NA CR0 .... 245 H4
Simon Marks Jewish
Primary School
CLPT E5 .... 89 F5
Singlegate First School
WIM/MER SW19 .... 205 H3
Sion College
EMB EC4Y 14 B5
Sion Manning RC Girls School
NKENS W10 .... 124 B4
Sir Francis Drake
Primary School
DEPT SE8 .... 150 C5
Sir George Monoux College
WALTH E17 .... 71 F5
Sir James Barrie School
VX/NE SW8 .... 167 E2
Sir John Cass College of Art
WCHPL E1 .... 17 E3
Sir John Cass
Foundation/Redcoat School
WCHPL E1 .... 130 B4
Sir John Cass
Foundation School
TWRH EC3N 16 C4
Sir John Lillie
Primary School
HMSMTH W6 .... 144 C6
Sir John Soane's Museum
LINN WC2A 13 H3
Sir Thomas Abney
Primary School
STNW/STAM N16 .... 88 D4
Sir Thomas Lipton
Memorial Hospital
STHGT/OAK N14 .... 50 D2
Sir William Burrough
Primary School
POP/IOD E14 .... 130 C5
Six Bridges Trading Estate
STHWK SE1 .... 33 F4
Sixth Form Centre
FSTGT E7 .... 112 D4
Skillion Business Park
BARK IG11 .... 135 F2
Skinners Companys
Lower Girls School
CLPT E5 .... 89 H5
Skinners Companys
School For Girls
STNW/STAM N16 .... 89 E4
Ski Slope
STMC/STPC BR5 .... 216 B4
Slade School of Fine Art
STPAN WC1H 4 D4
Sleaford Industrial Estate
VX/NE SW8 .... 167 E1
Sloane Hospital
BECK BR3 .... 211 H4
Smallberry Green
Primary School
ISLW TW7 .... 160 C3
Smallwood Primary School
TOOT SW17 .... 185 H6
SMA Medical Centre
LEY E10 .... 69 H5
Smithy Street School
WCHPL E1 .... 130 A4
Snaresbrook College
SWFD E18 .... 72 C1
Snaresbrook Crown Court
WAN E11 .... 92 B2
Snaresbrook Primary School
SWFD E18 .... 92 C1
Snooker Club
WEA W13 .... 140 D1

Snowsfields Primary School
STHWK SE1 .... 24 A3
Sobel Medical Centre
HOLWY N7 .... 108 A2
Soho Parish CE Primary School
SOHO/CST W1F 12 C5
Solent Road Health Centre
KIL/WHAMP NW6 .... 105 E4
Somerset House
COVGDN WC2E 13 G5
Somers Town Community
Sports Centre
CAMTN NW1 .... 4 B2
Sorsby Health Centre
CLPT E5 .... 110 B2
South Bank Business Centre
BTSEA SW11 .... 166 C2
Southbank Business Centre
VX/NE SW8 .... 28 D6
Southbank International School
NTGHL W11 .... 125 E6
Southbank University
STHWK SE1 .... 22 C4
STHWK SE1 .... 23 F5
VX/NE SW8 .... 167 F2
Southborough Primary School
HAYES BR2 .... 234 A2
Southborough School
SURB KT6 .... 239 G1
Southbury Primary School
PEND EN3 .... 39 H5
South Camden
Community School
CAMTN NW1 .... 4 B1
South Chelsea College
BRXN/ST SW9 .... 167 H5
South Croydon Medical Centre
SAND/SEL CR2 .... 246 C5
South Croydon Sports Club
SAND/SEL CR2 .... 247 E3
South Eastern University
HOLWY N7 .... 107 H1
Southern Road
Primary School
PLSTW E13 .... 132 D1
Southfield First &
Middle School
CHSWK W4 .... 143 E2
Southfield Medical Centre
CHSWK W4 .... 142 D2
The Southfields Clinic
WAND/EARL SW18 .... 185 E1
Southfields Community School
WAND/EARL SW18 .... 185 E3
Southgate Cemetery
STHGT/OAK N14 .... 51 E4
Southgate College
STHGT/OAK N14 .... 51 E4
Southgate Compton
Cricket Club
EBAR EN4 .... 36 B5
Southgate Leisure Centre
STHGT/OAK N14 .... 51 F2
Southgate Road
Medical Centre
IS N1 .... 108 D5
Southgate School
EBAR EN4 .... 36 D6
South Grove Primary School
WALTH E17 .... 90 C3
South Hampstead Cricket Club
CRICK NW2 .... 104 A5
South Hampstead High School
(Senior)
HAMP NW3 .... 105 H4
South Harringay Junior School
FSBYPK N4 .... 88 A2
South Herts Golf Club
TRDG/WHET N20 .... 49 E3
Southlands College
PUT/ROE SW15 .... 163 F5
South Lewisham Health Centre
CAT SE6 .... 191 G6
South London Crematorium
MTCM CR4 .... 207 E5
South London
Montessori School
BTSEA SW11 .... 166 A2
The South London
Natural Health Centre
CLAP SW4 .... 167 G5
South London Tamil School
CROY/NA CR0 .... 228 C4
South London Theatre
WNWD SE27 .... 188 C5
Southmead Primary School
WIM/MER SW19 .... 184 C3
South Norwood Country Park
SNWD SE25 .... 230 A1
South Norwood Hill
Medical Centre
SNWD SE25 .... 209 E5
South Norwood
Medical Centre
SNWD SE25 .... 229 E1
South Norwood
Primary School
SNWD SE25 .... 229 G1
South Park Business Centre
IL IG1 .... 95 E6
South Park Clinic
IL IG1 .... 115 E2
South Park Primary School
GDMY/SEVK IG3 .... 115 E1
South Quay Plaza
POP/IOD E14 .... 151 F2
South Rise Primary School
WOOL/PLUM SE18 .... 154 D5
Southside Industrial Estate
VX/NE SW8 .... 167 E1
South Thames College
PUT/ROE SW15 .... 164 B6
South Thames
College/Wandsworth
Adult College
PUT/ROE SW15 .... 183 F1
Southwark Bridge
Business Centre
STHWK SE1 .... 23 F2
Southwark Bridge Stairs
BLKFR EC4V 15 E6

Southwark Cathedral
STHWK SE1 .... 23 G1
Southwark College
BERM/RHTH SE16 .... 25 G6
CMBW SE5 .... 169 E1
STHWK SE1 .... 22 C3
STHWK SE1 .... 24 B5
Southwark Crown Court
STHWK SE1 .... 24 A1
Southwark Park Primary School
BERM/RHTH SE16 .... 25 H6
Southwark Park Running Track
BERM/RHTH SE16 .... 150 A4
Southwark Sports Ground
DUL SE21 .... 189 F3
South West
Middlesex Crematorium
FELT TW13 .... 178 C3
Southwold Primary School
CLPT E5 .... 90 A6
South Woodford Health Centre
SWFD E18 .... 72 C2
Southwood Hospital
HGT N6 .... 86 C4
Southwood Primary School
DAGW RM9 .... 116 C2
Sovereign Business Centre
PEND EN3 .... 40 D4
The Space Arts Centre Cinema
DEPT SE8 .... 150 D4
The Spare Tyre Theatre Co
KTTN NW5 .... 106 C4
Sparrow Farm County
Junior School
EW KT17 .... 241 H3
Sparrow Farm Junior School
EBED/NFELT TW14 .... 178 A2
Sparrow Farm Nursery School
EBED/NFELT TW14 .... 178 A2
Spa School
STHWK SE1 .... 33 E2
Speakers Corner
BAY/PAD W2 .... 10 D5
Speke's Monument
BAY/PAD W2 .... 145 G1
Spencer House
WHALL SW1A 20 A2
The Spires Shopping Centre
BAR EN5 .... 34 C4
Spiritualist University
WLSDN NW10 .... 103 G5
Spitalfields Community Farm
BETH E2 .... 9 E5
Spitalfields Health Centre
WCHPL E1 .... 16 D2
Spitalfields Market
LEY E10 .... 111 E1
Spitalfields Market Hall
WCHPL E1 .... 16 C1
Springfield Hospital
TOOT SW17 .... 186 A5
Springfield Primary School
VX/NE SW8 .... 167 F1
Spring Grove Primary School
ISLW TW7 .... 159 H3
Springhallow School
HNWL W7 .... 120 B5
Spring Park Primary School
CROY/NA CR0 .... 249 E6
Springvale Retail Park
STMC/STPC BR5 .... 216 A6
STMC/STPC BR5 .... 236 B2
Springwell Infant School
HEST TW5 .... 158 C1
Springwell Junior School
HEST TW5 .... 158 C1
Spurgeons College
SNWD SE25 .... 209 E5
Squash and Badminton Club
WIM/MER SW19 .... 204 C3
The Stables Gallery &
Art Centre
CRICK NW2 .... 103 C2
Stadium Business Centre
WBLY HA9 .... 102 B1
Stadium Industrial Estate
WBLY HA9 .... 102 B3
Stadium Retail Park
WBLY HA9 .... 102 A1
Stafford Cross Business Park
CROY/NA CR0 .... 245 H3
Stag Lane Medical Centre
CDALE/KGS NW9 .... 62 C6
Stag Lane Primary School
EDGW HA8 .... 62 A2
Stamford Clinic
HMSMTH W6 .... 143 G4
Stamford Hill Primary School
SEVS/STOTM N15 .... 88 D3
Stanburn Middle School
STAN HA7 .... 61 E3
Standard Industrial Estate
CAN/RD E16 .... 153 H2
CAN/RD E16 .... 153 F2
Stanford Middle School
STRHM/NOR SW16 .... 207 F4
Stanhope Primary School
GFD/PVL UB6 .... 119 G3
Stanley Infant School
TEDD TW11 .... 180 A6
Stanley Junior School
WHTN TW2 .... 180 A6
Stanley Park High School
CAR SM5 .... 244 C4
Stanley Park Junior School
CAR SM5 .... 244 B5
Stanley Technical Boys
High School
SNWD SE25 .... 209 F6
Stanley Works
ALP/SUD HA0 .... 101 G5
Stanmore College
STAN HA7 .... 60 D2
Stanmore Golf Club
STAN HA7 .... 60 D3
Stanton School of English
GFD/PVL UB6 .... 125 F5
Stanton Square
Industrial Estate
CAT SE6 .... 190 D4

Staple Inn Buildings
HHOL WC1V 14 A2
Staples Corner Business Park
CRICK NW2 .... 83 G5
Star Business Centre
DAGW RM9 .... 137 H4
Star Primary School
CAN/RD E16 .... 132 A3
Stationers Hall
STP EC4M 14 D4
Stationery Office
GINN WC1R 13 H2
Stephen Hawking
Primary School
POP/IOD E14 .... 130 C5
Stepney Day Hospital
WCHPL E1 .... 130 A5
Stepney Greencoat CE
Primary School
POP/IOD E14 .... 130 D5
Stepney Green School
WCHPL E1 .... 130 B4
Sterling Industrial Estate
DAGE RM10 .... 117 F2
Sterling Way Clinic
UED N18 .... 69 F1
Stewart Fleming
Primary School
PGE/AN SE20 .... 210 A4
Stewart Headlam
Primary School
WCHPL E1 .... 9 G5
Stillness Primary School
BROCKY SE4 .... 190 C1
Stirling Way
Industrial Estates
CROY/NA CR0 .... 227 G4
Stock Exchange
OBST EC2N 15 H3
Stockwell Park School
BRXN/ST SW9 .... 167 H2
Stockwell Primary School
BRXN/ST SW9 .... 167 H4
Stoke Newington School
STNW/STAM N16 .... 108 D1
The Stonebridge
Primary School
WLSDN NW10 .... 102 C6
Stonebridge Shopping Centre
WLSDN NW10 .... 102 D6
Stonehill Business Park
UED N18 .... 70 B2
Stonehill Business Park
UED N18 .... 70 B1
Stone Lake Retail Park
CHARL SE7 .... 153 E4
Stoneydown Park
Primary School
WALTH E17 .... 90 C1
Storey Primary School
CAN/RD E16 .... 154 A1
Stormont House School
CLPT E5 .... 109 H2
Stowford College
BELMT SM2 .... 243 G5
Strand on the Green
Junior & Infant School
CHSWK W4 .... 142 A6
Strand Theatre
HOL/ALD WC2B 13 G5
Stratford Magistrates Court
SRTFD E15 .... 111 H5
Stratford School
FSTGT E7 .... 112 C5
Stratford Shopping Centre
SRTFD E15 .... 111 H5
Strathmore School
RCHPK/HAM TW10 .... 181 F3
Strawberry Fields School
BAY/PAD W2 .... 125 E5
Strawberry Hill Golf Club
WHTN TW2 .... 180 A5
Streatham Cemetery
TOOT SW17 .... 186 A5
Streatham & Clapham
High School
STRHM/NOR SW16 .... 187 E5
Streatham & Clapham High
School Preparatory Site
BRXS/STRHM SW2 .... 187 H3
Streatham Ice Rink
STRHM/NOR SW16 .... 207 G1
Streatham Modern School
STRHM/NOR SW16 .... 207 G1
Streatham Park Cemetery
MTCM CR4 .... 207 E5
Streatham Swimming Pool
STRHM/NOR SW16 .... 207 G1
Streatham Vale Sports Club
STRHM/NOR SW16 .... 207 E3
Streatham Wells
Primary School
STRHM/NOR SW2 .... 187 H4
Stroud Green Primary School
FSBYPK N4 .... 88 A5
The Study Preparatory School
WIM/MER SW19 .... 204 B1
The Study School
NWMAL KT3 .... 223 E2
Sudbourne Primary School
BRXS/STRHM SW2 .... 167 H6
Sudbury Court Sports Club
ALP/SUD HA0 .... 101 E1
Sudbury Golf Club
GFD/PVL UB6 .... 101 E4
Sudbury Primary School
ALP/SUD HA0 .... 100 D2
Suffolks Primary School
EN EN1 .... 39 H3
Sullivan Primary School
FUL/PGN SW6 .... 165 E3
Summerside JMI School
NFNCH/WDSP N12 .... 65 H2
Sumners Court
SUN TW16 .... 198 B5
Sundridge Park Golf Club
BMLY BR1 .... 213 G2
Sunnyfields Primary School
HDN NW4 .... 63 H6

Sunnyhill Primary School
 STRHM/NOR SW16 .... 187 H6
Super Bowl
 BXLYHS DA6 .... 176 D5
Surbiton Business Centre
 SURB KT6 .... 221 F3
Surbiton Cemetery
 BRYLDS KT5 .... 222 A1
Surbiton Golf Club
 ESH/CLAY KT10 .... 238 D2
Surbiton High School
 KUT KT1 .... 221 G1
Surbiton Hospital
 SURB KT6 .... 221 G3
Surbiton Natural Health Centre
 SURB KT6 .... 221 G3
Surrey County Council
 HOR/WEW KT19 .... 241 G6
Surrey County Cricket Club
 (The Oval)
 LBTH SE11 .... 29 H5
Surrey Docks Farm
 BERM/RHTH SE16 .... 150 D2
Surrey Docks Health Centre
 BERM/RHTH SE16 .... 150 C2
Surrey Quays Leisure Park
 BERM/RHTH SE16 .... 150 B3
Surrey Quays Shopping Centre
 BERM/RHTH SE16 .... 150 B3
Surrey Square Primary School
 WALW SE17 .... 32 A3
Sussex House
 Preparatory School
 KTBR SW1X 26 C1
Sutcliffe Park Athletics Track
 ELTH/MOT SE9 .... 172 D6
Sutton Alternative
 Health Centre
 SUT SM1 .... 243 F3
Sutton Arena
 CAR SM5 .... 225 H4
Sutton Bowling Club
 BELMT SM2 .... 243 E6
Sutton Cemetery
 CHEAM SM3 .... 224 D6
Sutton Grammar School
 for Boys
 SUT SM1 .... 243 G3
Sutton High Junior School
 SUT SM1 .... 243 F4
Sutton High School
 for Girls Gdst
 SUT SM1 .... 243 G4
Sutton House
 HOM E9 .... 110 A3
Suttons Business Park
 RAIN RM13 .... 137 H2
Sutton Superbowl
 SUT SM1 .... 243 F3
Sutton United FC
 SUT SM1 .... 243 G2
Sutton West Centre
 SUT SM1 .... 243 E3
Swaffield Primary School
 WAND/EARL SW18 .... 185 G1
Swaminarayan School
 WLSDN NW10 .... 102 D4
Swan Business Centre
 CHSWK W4 .... 142 D4
Swan Lane Pier
 CANST EC4R 15 G6
Swanlea School
 WCHPL E1 .... 9 G6
Swanley School
 SWLY BR8 .... 217 H6
Swansmere School
 WOT/HER KT12 .... 218 A5
Swedish School
 BARN SW13 .... 143 G6
Swiss Cottage School
 HAMP NW3 .... 105 H6
Sybil Elgar School
 EA W5 .... 121 G6
 NWDGN UB2 .... 138 D3
Sybourn Infant School
 LEY E10 .... 90 C5
Sybourn Junior School
 WALTH E17 .... 90 D4
Sydenham Girls School
 SYD SE26 .... 189 H5
Sydenham High School
 SYD SE26 .... 209 H1
Sydenham (Junior)
 High School
 SYD SE26 .... 189 H6
Sydney Russell
 Comprehensive School
 DAGW RM9 .... 116 B3
Syon House
 BTFD TW8 .... 161 E2
Syon Park
 BTFD TW8 .... 161 E3
Syon Park School
 ISLW TW7 .... 160 D2
Syracuse University
 London Centre
 NTGHL W11 .... 124 D6
Tabard Theatre
 CHSWK W4 .... 143 E4
Taberner House
 CROY/NA CRO 246 C1
TA Centre
 EDGW HA8 .... 62 B3
 HRW HA1 .... 80 B2
Tait Road Industrial Estate
 CROY/NA CRO 228 D4
Tamian Industrial Estate
 HSLWW TW4 .... 158 A5
Tamworth Manor High School
 STRHM/NOR SW16 .... 207 F6
Tandem Centre
 WIM/MER SW19 .... 205 H4
Tate Britain
 WEST SW1P 29 E2
Tate Modern
 STHWK SE1 .... 12 D1
Tavistock Clinic
 HAMP NW3 .... 105 H4
TAVR Centre
 KUT KT1 .... 221 F1

Tavy Clinic
 ABYW SE2 .... 156 A2
Teddington Business Park
 TEDD TW11 .... 200 B3
Teddington Cemetery
 WHTN TW2 .... 180 A6
Teddington Clinic
 TEDD TW11 .... 200 A2
Teddington Lock
 TEDD TW11 .... 180 D6
Teddington Memorial Hospital
 TEDD TW11 .... 200 A2
Teddington School
 TEDD TW11 .... 201 F2
Teddington Swimming Pool
 TEDD TW11 .... 200 A2
The Teddington Theatre Club
 E/WMO/HCT KT8 .... 219 H2
Telegraph Hill School
 BROCKY SE4 .... 170 C3
Temperate House
 RCH/KEW TW9 .... 161 H3
Temple of Bacchus
 CMBW SE5 .... 168 C5
Temple of Mithras
 MANHO EC4N 15 G4
Tenby Road Clinic
 EDGW HA8 .... 61 H5
Tennis and Squash Club
 FNCH N3 .... 64 C4
Tennis Club
 HAYES BR2 .... 232 D1
 STAN HA7 .... 60 D1
Tenterden Sports Ground
 KTN/HRWW/W HA3 .... 81 G4
Terence McMillan Stadium
 PLSTW E13 .... 133 E5
Thames Barrier
 CAN/RD E16 .... 153 F2
Thames Barrier Visitor Centre
 WOOL/PLUM SE18 .... 153 F3
Thames Ditton Infant School
 THDIT KT7 .... 220 B3
Thames Ditton Junior School
 THDIT KT7 .... 220 B4
Thames House
 WEST SW1P 29 E1
Thameside Industrial Estate
 CAN/RD E16 .... 153 F1
Thames Magistrates Court
 BOW E3 .... 131 E2
Thamesmead
 Community College
 ERITHM DA18 .... 156 C2
Thamesmead Shopping Centre
 THMD SE28 .... 135 G6
Thames Valley University
 WHTN TW13 .... 141 F1
Thames View Clinic
 BARK IG11 .... 135 F1
Thames View Junior &
 Infant School
 BARK IG11 .... 135 G1
Thames Water Tower
 NTGHL W11 .... 144 B2
Theatre Centre
 BECK BR3 .... 211 F5
Théâtre de Complicité
 HOLWY N7 .... 107 H3
Theatre for Mankind
 FSBYPK N4 .... 87 H5
Theatre Museum
 Library & Archive
 COVGDN WC2E 13 G5
Theatre of the Dispossessed
 WIM/MER SW19 .... 184 B3
Theatre Royal
 SRTFD E15 .... 111 H5
Theatre Royal, Drury Lane
 HOL/ALD WC2B 13 F4
Theatre Royal Haymarket
 STJS SW1Y 12 D6
Therapia Trading Estate
 CROY/NA CRO 227 F4
Thistlebrook Industrial Estate
 ABYW SE2 .... 156 A3
Thomas Arnold Primary School
 DAGW RM9 .... 116 D5
Thomas Becket RC
 Primary School
 SNWD SE25 .... 229 G3
Thomas Buxton
 Primary School
 WCHPL E1 .... 9 G6
Thomas Fairchild
 Primary School
 IS N1 .... 7 G1
Thomas Samuel
 Primary School
 WALTH E17 .... 91 D3
Thomas Road
 Industrial Estate
 POP/IOD E14 .... 131 E4
Thomas's Preparatory School
 BTSEA SW11 .... 165 H2
Thomas Tallis School
 BKHTH/KID SE3 .... 172 D4
Thornhill Primary School
 IS N1 .... 108 A5
Thornton Heath Baths
 THHTH CR7 .... 228 D1
Thornton Heath Health Centre
 THHTH CR7 .... 228 C1
Thornton Road
 Industrial Estate
 CROY/NA CRO 227 G3
Thorntree Primary School
 CHARL SE7 .... 153 F5
Thorpe Hall Primary School
 WALTH E17 .... 71 G4
Three Bridges Business Centre
 STHL UB1 .... 139 G2
Three Bridges Primary School
 NWDGN UB2 .... 138 A4
 NWDGN UB2 .... 139 F3
Three Mills Heritage Centre
 SRTFD E15 .... 131 G2
Thurlow Park School
 WNWD SE27 .... 188 B4
Thurston Industrial Estate
 LEW SE13 .... 171 F4

Tidemill Primary School
 DEPT SE8 .... 171 E1
Tideway Industrial Estate
 VX/NE SW8 .... 28 B6
Tiffin Girls School
 KUTN/CMB KT2 .... 201 G2
Tiffin School
 KUTN/CMB KT2 .... 201 H5
Tiller Centre (Swimming Baths)
 POP/IOD E14 .... 151 E3
Tiller Leisure Centre
 POP/IOD E14 .... 151 E3
Timbercroft Primary School
 WOOL/PLUM SE18 .... 175 E1
Timbers Clinic
 KTN/HRWW/W HA3 .... 59 H2
Times Square Shopping Centre
 SUT SM1 .... 243 F5
Tiverton Primary School
 SEVS/STOTM N15 .... 88 D3
Tobacco Dock
 WAP E1W 17 G6
Tokyngton Community Centre
 WBLY HA9 .... 102 B3
Toldos School
 STNW/STAM N16 .... 88 D3
Tollgate Primary School
 CROY/NA CRO 230 A3
 PLSTW E13 .... 133 E3
Tolworth CP School
 SURB KT6 .... 221 H5
Tolworth Girls School & Centre
 for Continuing Education
 SURB KT6 .... 239 H1
Tolworth Recreation Centre
 CHSGTN KT9 .... 239 H1
Tolworth Tower
 SURB KT6 .... 222 B6
Tom Hood School
 WAN E11 .... 112 B1
Tonybee Hall & Curtain Theatre
 WCHPL E1 .... 16 C3
Tooting Bec Athletics Track
 TOOT SW17 .... 186 D6
Tooting & Mitcham United FC
 MTCM CR4 .... 206 C4
Torriano Junior & Infant School
 KTTN NW5 .... 107 E3
Torridon Primary School
 CAT SE6 .... 191 H4
Torrington Clinic
 NFNCH/WDSP N12 .... 65 G1
Torrington Park Health Centre
 NFNCH/WDSP N12 .... 49 G6
Total Health Clinic
 SHB W12 .... 143 H2
Tottenhall Infants School
 PLMGR N13 .... 68 A1
Tottenham Hale Retail Park
 SEVS/STOTM N15 .... 89 G1
Tottenham Hotspur FC
 (White Hart Lane)
 TOTM N17 .... 69 F3
Tottenham Park Cemetery
 ED N9 .... 53 H5
Totteridge Cricket Club
 TRDG/WHET N20 .... 49 E6
The Tower Bridge Experience
 STHWK SE1 .... 24 C2
Tower Bridge Museum
 STHWK SE1 .... 24 C3
Tower Bridge Primary School
 STHWK SE1 .... 24 C3
Tower Bridge Wharf
 WAP E1W 25 E2
Tower Hamlets College
 BETH E2 .... 7 H3
 POP/IOD E14 .... 131 F6
 POP/IOD E14 .... 130 A4
Tower House School
 MORT/ESHN SW14 .... 162 C5
Tower Industrial Estate
 SNWD SE25 .... 229 G1
Tower Medical Centre
 WCHPL E1 .... 17 G4
Tower Millennium Pier
 MON EC3R 24 B1
Tower of London
 TWRH EC3N 16 C6
Towers Business Park
 WBLY HA9 .... 102 B2
Tower Stairs
 MON EC3R 16 A6
Tower Theatre
 IS N1 .... 108 B5
Townley Grammar School
 for Girls
 BXLYHS DA6 .... 196 D1
Townmead Business Centre
 FUL/PGN SW6 .... 165 G4
Townsend Industrial Estate
 WLSDN NW10 .... 102 C6
Townsend Primary School
 STHWK SE1 .... 32 A1
Trabzon Spor FC
 STNW/STAM N16 .... 108 D2
Trade Union Congress
 NOXST/BSQ WC1A 12 D3
Trafalgar Business Centre
 BARK IG11 .... 135 F3
Trafalgar Primary School
 WHTN TW2 .... 179 H4
Trafalgar Trading Estate
 PEND EN3 .... 40 D5
Tramshed Theatre
 WOOL/PLUM SE18 .... 154 B4
Trans Atlantic College
 BETH E2 .... 8 C1
Transport House
 WEST SW1P 21 E6
Treasury
 WHALL SW1A 21 E4
The Treaty Centre
 HSLW TW3 .... 159 F4
Trent CE Primary School
 EBAR EN4 .... 36 B5
Trent Country Park
 EBAR EN4 .... 36 C3
Trent Park Cemetery
 EBAR EN4 .... 36 C4

Trent Park Golf Club
 EBAR EN4 .... 37 E5
Trevor Roberts School
 HAMP NW3 .... 105 H5
Tricycle Cinema
 KIL/WHAMP NW6 .... 104 D5
Trident Business Centre
 TOOT SW17 .... 206 B1
Trinity Business Centre
 BERM/RHTH SE16 .... 150 D2
Trinity Catholic Lower
 High School
 WFD IG8 .... 56 C6
Trinity College Centre
 PECK SE15 .... 32 A6
Trinity College of Music
 MHST W1U 11 F2
Trinity Hospital
 GNWCH SE10 .... 151 H5
Trinity House
 TWRH EC3N 16 B5
Trinity RC High School (Upper)
 WFD IG8 .... 56 C6
Trinity St Marys
 Primary School
 BAL SW12 .... 186 C3
Trinity School
 CROY/NA CRO 230 A5
 DAGE RM10 .... 117 E1
Trinity School Belvedere
 BELV DA17 .... 157 G4
Triumph Trading Estate
 TOTM N17 .... 69 G2
Trocadero Centre
 MYFR/PICC W1J 12 C6
Trojan Business Centre
 WLSDN NW10 .... 103 F4
Troy Industrial Estate
 HRW HA1 .... 80 B2
True Buddha School
 IS N1 .... 107 H5
Tudor Lodge Health Centre
 WIM/MER SW19 .... 184 B2
Tudor Primary School
 FNCH N3 .... 65 G4
 STHL UB1 .... 118 C6
Tufnell Park Primary School
 HOLWY N7 .... 107 F2
Tuke School
 PECK SE15 .... 169 H2
Tulloch Clinic
 SHB W12 .... 144 B1
Tunnel Avenue Trading Estate
 GNWCH SE10 .... 151 H2
Turney School
 DUL SE21 .... 188 C2
Turnham Primary School
 BROCKY SE4 .... 170 C5
Tweeddale Infant School
 CAR SM5 .... 225 H4
Tweeddale Junior School
 CAR SM5 .... 225 H4
Twickenham Cemetery
 WHTN TW2 .... 179 F3
Twickenham Golf Club
 FELT TW13 .... 179 G5
Twickenham Park
 Health Centre
 TWK TW1 .... 181 E1
Twickenham Stadium
 WHTN TW2 .... 180 A1
Twickenham Trading Estate
 TWK TW1 .... 180 B1
Two Bridges Business Park
 SAND/SEL CR2 .... 246 D4
Twyford CE High School
 ACT W3 .... 142 B1
Tyburn Infant School
 STJWD NW8 .... 118 H3
The Type Museum
 Operation Hannibal
 BRXN/ST SW9 .... 167 H2
UCI Cinema
 BAY/PAD W2 .... 125 F6
 BERM/RHTH SE16 .... 150 B3
 ED N9 .... 54 B2
 SUT SM1 .... 243 F3
UCI Empire Cinema
 LSQ/SEVD WC2H 12 D6
UCI Filmworks Cinema
 GNWCH SE10 .... 152 B4
UCL Hospitals
 FITZ W1T 4 B6
UGC Cinema
 CHEL SW3 .... 145 H6
 CRICK NW2 .... 83 H5
 EA W5 .... 121 F6
 EN EN1 .... 39 G5
 HMSMTH W6 .... 143 H4
 SOHO/SHAV W1D 12 C5
Underhill Junior & Infant School
 BAR EN5 .... 34 C6
Unicorn School
 RCH/KEW TW9 .... 161 H2
United Medical &
 Dental Schools
 STHWK SE1 .... 21 G5
United Services
 Sports Ground
 CHSWK W4 .... 163 G2
Unity College
 KTTN NW5 .... 106 D2
Unity Trading Estate
 WFD IG8 .... 73 F6
University Church of
 Christ the King
 STPAN WC1H 4 C6
University College Hospital
 GWRST WC1E 4 B6
 HAMP NW3 .... 105 H4
University College
 Junior School
 HAMP NW3 .... 105 G2
University College London
 FITZ W1T 12 B1
 GWRST WC1E 4 C5
 STPAN WC1H 4 C5
University College London,
 Astor College
 FITZ W1T 12 B1

University College London,
　Department of Clinical
　Haematology
　GWRST WC1E 4 C6
University College
　London Medical School
　FITZ W1T 12 A1
University College School
　HAMP NW3 .... 105 G3
University Hospital Lewisham
　LEW SE13 .... 171 F6
University of California
　WHALL SW1A 20 A2
University of East London
　BCTR RM8 .... 115 G2
　EHAM E6 .... 134 A6
　PLSTW E13 .... 132 D2
University of Greenwich
　GNWCH SE10 .... 151 H5
　WOOL/PLUM SE18 .... 154 A3
University of Greenwich
　(Mansion Site)
　ELTH/MOT SE9 .... 194 C1
University of Greenwich
　(Southwood Site)
　ELTH/MOT SE9 .... 194 C1
University of Greenwich
　Sports Ground
　ELTH/MOT SE9 .... 173 G5
　ELTH/MOT SE9 .... 194 C2
University of London
　BAY/PAD W2 .... 125 H5
　BMSBY WC1N 5 F6
　FITZ W1T 12 C2
　GWRST WC1E 12 D1
　NWCR SE14 .... 170 C2
　STPAN WC1H 4 D5
University of London
　Athletics Ground
　NWMAL KT3 .... 223 G2
University of Middlesex
　EBAR EN4 .... 37 E3
　PEND EN3 .... 39 H6
University of North London
　HOLWY N7 .... 107 H2
University of Notre Dame
　LSQ/SEVD WC2H 12 D6
University of Westminster
　CAMTN NW1 .... 4 A5
　CHSWK W4 .... 162 C2
　GTPST W1W 11 H1
　GTPST W1W 12 A2
　HGT N6 .... 86 D5
　MHST W1U 11 E5
University of Westminster
　(Harrow Campus)
　HRW HA1 .... 80 C4
Uphall Primary School
　IL IG1 .... 114 B3
Upland Primary School
　BXLYHN DA7 .... 176 D4
Uplands Business Park
　WALTH E17 .... 70 B5
Upper Montagu Street Clinic
　MBLAR W1H 10 C1
Upper Tooting Independent
　High School
　TOOT SW17 .... 186 A4
Upton Cross Primary School
　PLSTW E13 .... 112 D6
Upton Day Hospital
　BXLYHS DA6 .... 176 C5
Upton Lane Medical Centre
　FSTGT E7 .... 112 D4
Upton Primary School
　BXLY DA5 .... 176 C6
Upton Road School
　BXLYHS DA6 .... 176 C5
Ursuline High School
　IL IG1 .... 94 B6
　RYNPK SW20 .... 204 B3
Uxendon Manor JMI School
　KTN/HRWW/W HA3 .... 81 G2
Vale Farm Sports Centre
　ALP/SUD HA0 .... 100 D2
The Vale Medical Centre
　FSTH SE23 .... 190 C4
Valence House Museum &
　Library
　BCTR RM8 .... 96 B6
Valentine High School
　IL IG1 .... 94 A3
Valentines High Lower School
　GNTH/NBYPK IG2 .... 94 B2
Vale Park Industrial
　ACT W3 .... 143 E2
The Vale School
　SKENS SW7 .... 145 G3
Valliance Road School
　WCHPL E1 .... 17 E1
Valley Primary School
　HAYES BR2 .... 212 A5
Valmar Trading Estate
　CMBW SE5 .... 168 C2
Vanbrugh Theatre
　GWRST WC1E 4 C6
Vanguard Trading Estate
　SRTFD E15 .... 111 G6
Vaudeville Theatre
　COVGDN WC2E 13 F5
Vaughan First & Middle School
　RYLN/HDSTN HA2 .... 79 G3
Vauxhall Primary School
　LBTH SE11 .... 29 G3
Vernon House Special School
　WLSDN NW10 .... 102 C3
Vestry Hall
　MTCM CR4 .... 206 B6
Vestry House Museum
　WALTH E17 .... 91 F1
Vicarage Fields Health Clinic
　BARK IG11 .... 114 C5
The Vicarage Field
　Shopping Centre
　BARK IG11 .... 114 C5
Vicarage Primary School
　EHAM E6 .... 133 H2
Vicars Green Primary School
　GFD/PVL UB6 .... 121 E1
Vicoria Hall
　FNCH N3 .... 64 D4

Victoria and Albert Museum
　SKENS SW7 .... 145 H3
Victoria Business Centre
　WELL DA16 .... 175 G3
Victoria Chiropractic Clinic
　CHEL SW15 .... 18 C4
Victoria Coach Station
　BGVA SW1W 27 G2
Victoria Industrial Estate
　ACT W3 .... 122 D4
Victoria Medical Centre
　PIM SW1V 28 A2
Victoria Palace Theatre
　WESTW SW1E 19 H6
Victoria Park Industrial Centre
　HOM E9 .... 110 D5
Victoria Place Shopping Centre
　PIM SW1V 27 H1
Victoria Rail/Air Terminal
　PIM SW1V 27 H1
Victoria Retail Park
　RSLP HA4 .... 98 B3
Victoria Station
　PIM SW1V 27 H1
Victoria Wharf
　POP/IOD E14 .... 130 C6
Victoria Wharf
　Industrial Estate
　DEPT SE8 .... 150 D5
Victor Seymour Infant School
　CAR SM5 .... 244 B1
Victory Business Centre
　ISLW TW7 .... 160 B5
Victory Primary School
　WALW SE17 .... 31 F1
Victory Works
　HOM E9 .... 110 D4
Viewpoint Business Centre
　ROMW/RG RM7 .... 97 G4
Viking Primary School
　NTHLT UB5 .... 118 B2
The Village School
　HAMP NW3 .... 106 B4
Villiers High School
　STHL UB1 .... 139 E1
The Vine Clinic
　KUTN/CMB KT2 .... 201 G2
Vine Medical Centre
　E/WMO/HCT KT8 .... 199 G6
The Vines School
　BTSEA SW11 .... 166 C5
The Vineyard Primary School
　RCHPK/HAM TW10 .... 181 C1
Vinopolis, City of Wine
　STHWK SE1 .... 23 F1
Vinters' Hall
　BLKFR EC4V 15 F5
VIP Trading Estate
　CHARL SE7 .... 153 E4
Virginia Primary School
　BETH E2 .... 8 C4
Virgo Fidelis Convent Schools
　NRWD SE19 .... 208 C2
Voyager Business Estate
　BERM/RHTH SE16 .... 25 E5
Vulcan Business Centre
　CROY/NA CR0 .... 250 A6
Waddon Clinic
　CROY/NA CR0 .... 246 A3
Waddon Infant School
　CROY/NA CR0 .... 246 A3
Wadham Lodge Sports Centre
　WALTH E17 .... 71 F4
Wadsworth Business Centre
　GFD/PVL UB6 .... 121 E1
The Waldegrave Clinic
　TEDD TW11 .... 200 B1
Waldegrave Girls School
　WHTN TW2 .... 179 H5
Waldo Industrial Estate
　BMLY BR1 .... 213 E6
Waldorf School of SW London
　STRHM/NOR SW16 .... 187 C4
Waldorf Steiner School of
　SW London
　STRHM/NOR SW16 .... 187 F6
Walford Secondary School
　NTHLT UB5 .... 98 C6
Walker Primary School
　STHGT/OAK N14 .... 51 F4
Wallace Collection
　MHST W1U 11 E3
Wallington County
　Grammar School
　WLGTN SM6 .... 244 D1
Wallington High School for Girls
　WLGTN SM6 .... 244 D6
Walmer Road Clinic
　NTGHL W11 .... 124 C6
Walm Lane Clinic
　CRICK NW2 .... 104 B3
Walnut Leisure Centre
　ORP BR6 .... 235 G5
Walnuts Shopping Centre
　ORP BR6 .... 235 G5
Walnut Tree Walk
　Primary School
　LBTH SE11 .... 30 A1
Waltham Forest College
　WALTH E17 .... 70 B6
　WALTH E17 .... 71 F6
Waltham Forest
　Magistrates Court
　WALTH E17 .... 71 F6
Waltham Forest Theatre
　WALTH E17 .... 70 D6
Waltham Forest Track
　WALTH E17 .... 71 F5
Walthamstow Business Centre
　WALTH E17 .... 71 G5
Walthamstow
　Greyhound Stadium
　CHING E4 .... 71 F3
Walthamstow School for Girls
　WALTH E17 .... 91 F1
Walthamstow Lower School
　WALW SE17 .... 31 H3
Walworth Town Hall
　WALW SE17 .... 31 E2
Walworth Upper School
　WALW SE17 .... 32 B4

Wandle Primary School
　WAND/EARL SW18 .... 185 F3
Wandle Recreation Centre
　WAND/EARL SW18 .... 185 F1
Wandle Trading Estate
　MTCM CR4 .... 226 B4
Wandsworth Adult College
　TOOT SW17 .... 186 A6
The Wandsworth
　Arndale Centre
　WAND/EARL SW18 .... 185 F1
Wandsworth Cemetery
　WAND/EARL SW18 .... 185 G3
Wandsworth Community
　Health Trust
　PUT/ROE SW15 .... 206 C1
Wandsworth County Court
　PUT/ROE SW15 .... 164 C6
Wandsworth Public Baths
　TOOT SW17 .... 186 C4
Wandsworth Trading Estate
　WAND/EARL SW18 .... 185 F2
Wanstead CE Primary School
　WAN E11 .... 92 D4
Wanstead Cricket Club
　WAN E11 .... 92 D4
Wanstead Golf Club
　WAN E11 .... 93 E4
Wanstead High School
　WAN E11 .... 93 E3
Wanstead Hospital
　WAN E11 .... 92 D1
Wapping
　WAP E1W 150 A1
Wapping Health Centre
　WAP E1W 25 H1
Wapping New Stairs
　WAP E1W 25 H3
Wapping Pier Head
　WAP E1W 25 F2
Wapping Sports Centre
　WAP E1W 25 G2
Warehouse Theatre
　CROY/NA CR0 .... 228 D6
War Memorial Sports Ground
　SUT SM1 .... 244 A2
Warner Village Cinema
　ACT W3 .... 122 A3
　CROY/NA CR0 .... 227 H6
　DACW RM9 .... 116 C6
　HAMP NW3 .... 105 F4
　HRW HA1 .... 80 A3
　NFNCH/WDSP N12 .... 65 H4
　SHB W12 .... 144 B2
　SOHO/SHAV W1D 12 D5
Warren Comprehensive School
　CHDH RM6 .... 96 C1
Warren Dell Primary School
　OXHEY WD19 .... 42 A5
Warren Junior School
　CHDH RM6 .... 96 C1
Warren Road Primary School
　ORP BR6 .... 253 F2
Warwick Estate
　BAY/PAD W2 .... 125 F4
Warwick Leadlay Gallery
　GNWCH SE10 .... 151 G6
Warwick Park School
　PECK SE15 .... 169 F2
Warwick School for Boys
　WALTH E17 .... 91 G1
Watergate School
　LEW SE13 .... 171 F5
Waterloo Health Centre
　STHWK SE1 .... 22 A5
Waterloo Station
　STHWK SE1 .... 22 A3
Watermans Arts, Cinema &
　Theatre Centre
　BTFD TW8 .... 141 G6
The Watermans Hall
　MON EC3R 16 A4
Watermeads High School
　MRDN SM4 .... 225 H3
Watermill Business Centre
　PEND EN3 .... 40 D3
Water Rats Theatre
　EHAM E6 .... 5 F3
Waterside Business Centre
　ISLW TW7 .... 160 D5
The Waterside Trading Centre
　NWDGN UB2 .... 140 A3
Water Sports Centre
　BERM/RHTH SE16 .... 150 C3
Waterways Business Centre
　PEND EN3 .... 40 D1
Watling Clinic
　EDGW HA8 .... 62 D3
Watling Medical Centre
　EDGW HA8 .... 62 C4
Waverley Industrial Estate
　HRW HA1 .... 59 H6
Waverley Lower
　Secondary School
　EDUL SE22 .... 169 H6
Waverley School
　EDUL SE22 .... 170 A6
　PEND EN3 .... 40 A5
Waxchandlers' Hall
　CITYW EC2V 15 F3
Weald College
　KTN/HRWW/W HA3 .... 60 A2
Weald First & Middle School
　KTN/HRWW/W HA3 .... 60 B3
Weekend Arts College
　KTTN NW5 .... 106 D4
Welbeck Clinic
　CRICK NW2 .... 105 E1
Welbourne Primary School
　SEVS/STOTM N15 .... 89 C1
Welfare Clinic
　CMBW SE5 .... 168 D4
　GNWCH SE10 .... 171 G1
　HGT N6 .... 86 C3
Wellcome Institute
　CAMTN NW1 .... 4 C5
Weldon Park Middle School
　RYLN/HDSTN HA2 .... 99 G2
The Welling Clinic
　WELL DA16 .... 175 G3

Welling Medical Centre
　WELL DA16 .... 175 F5
Welling School
　WELL DA16 .... 175 H2
Wellington Arch
　MYFR/PKC W1J 19 F3
Wellington Barracks
　STJSPK SW1H 20 B4
Wellington Hospital
　STJWD NW8 .... 125 H1
Wellington Primary School
　BOW E3 .... 131 E2
　FSLW TW3 .... 158 D3
Welling United FC
　WELL DA16 .... 176 A4
Wells Primary School
　WFD IG8 .... 56 D6
Wembley Arena
　WBLY HA9 .... 102 A2
Wembley FC
　ALP/SUD HA0 .... 100 D2
Wembley High School
　ALP/SUD HA0 .... 101 E1
Wembley Hospital
　ALP/SUD HA0 .... 101 F4
Wembley Manor
　Primary School
　WBLY HA9 .... 101 G1
Wembley Park Business Centre
　WBLY HA9 .... 102 B1
Wembley Stadium
　WBLY HA9 .... 102 A3
Wembley Stadium
　Industrial Estate
　WBLY HA9 .... 102 C1
　WBLY HA9 .... 102 A2
Wendell Park Primary School
　SHB W12 .... 143 F2
Wentworth Tutorial College
　GLDGN NW11 .... 84 B3
Wesley's Chapel,
　House & Museum
　STLK EC1Y 7 G5
Wessex Gardens
　Primary School
　CRICK NW2 .... 84 C5
West Acton Primary School
　ACT W3 .... 122 B5
West Becton Health Centre
　CAN/RD E16 .... 133 F5
Westbourne Green
　Sports Complex
　BAY/PAD W2 .... 125 E4
Westbourne Primary School
　SUT SM1 .... 243 E1
Westbridge College
　BTSEA SW11 .... 166 A2
Westbrooke School
　WELL DA16 .... 176 B4
Westbury Medical Centre
　WDGN N22 .... 68 C5
The Westcroft Leisure Centre
　CAR SM5 .... 244 C2
West Ealing Business Centre
　WEA W13 .... 120 C6
Western Avenue Business Park
　ACT W3 .... 122 B3
Western Trading Estate
　WLSDN NW10 .... 122 C3
West Ewell County
　Infant School
　HOR/WEW KT19 .... 240 D3
Westfields Primary School
　BARN SW13 .... 163 F3
Westgate Business Centre
　NKENS W10 .... 124 C3
West Grove Primary School
　STHGT/OAK N14 .... 51 F2
West Ham Church
　Primary School
　SRTFD E15 .... 112 B6
West Ham Lane Clinic
　SRTFD E15 .... 112 A6
West Hampstead Clinic
　KIL/WHAMP NW6 .... 105 E5
West Ham United FC
　(Upton Park)
　EHAM E6 .... 133 F1
West Hatch High School
　CHIG IG7 .... 73 H1
West Hendon Clinic
　CDALE/KGS NW9 .... 83 F3
West Hill Primary School
　WAND/EARL SW18 .... 165 E6
West India Pier
　POP/IOD E14 .... 150 D2
West India Shopping Centre
　POP/IOD E14 .... 151 E1
West Kensington
　Sports Centre
　NTGHL W11 .... 124 B6
Westland Heliport
　BTSEA SW11 .... 165 H4
West Lea School
　ED N9 .... 53 E5
West Lodge Preparatory School
　BFN/LL DA15 .... 195 F5
West Lodge Primary School
　PIN HA5 .... 78 B1
West London County Court
　WKENS W14 .... 144 C4
West London Magistrates Court
　HMSMTH W6 .... 144 B5
West London Tamil School
　WLSDN NW10 .... 123 F1
West Mead Clinic
　RSLP HA4 .... 98 C3
West Middlesex Golf Club
　STHL UB1 .... 119 G6
West Middlesex
　University Hospital
　ISLW TW7 .... 160 C3
Westminster Abbey
　WEST SW1P 21 E5
Westminster Abbey
　Choir School
　WEST SW1P 20 D5
Westminster Business Square
　LBTH SE11 .... 29 G4
Westminster Cathedral
　WEST SW1P 20 A6

Westminster Cathedral Choir School
WEST SW1P 28 B1
Westminster Cathedral RC Primary School
PIM SW1V 28 D3
Westminster City Hall
WESTW SW1E 20 B5
Westminster City School
WESTW SW1E 20 B5
Westminster College
BTSEA SW11 .... 166 C2
SOHO/SHAV W1D 12 B5
Westminster Gallery
STJSPK SW1H 20 D4
Westminster Industrial Estate
WOOL/PLUM SE18 .... 153 F3
Westminster Natural Health Centre
PIM SW1V 28 A2
Westminster Pier
WHALL SW1A 21 F4
Westminster School
WEST SW1P 21 E5
Westminster Technical College
WEST SW1P 28 B1
Westminster Theatre
WESTW SW1E 20 A5
Westminster Under School
WEST SW1P 28 C2
Westmoor Community Clinic
PUT/ROE SW15 .... 183 G2
West Norwood Clinic
WNWD SE27 .... 188 C4
West Norwood Crematorium
WNWD SE27 .... 188 C5
West One Shopping Centre
MYFR/PKLN W1K 11 F4
Weston Green School
THDIT KT7 .... 220 A5
Weston Park Clinic
CEND/HSY/T N8 .... 87 G2
Weston Park Primary School
CEND/HSY/T N8 .... 87 H2
Westpoint Trading Estate
ACT W3 .... 122 B4
West Thames College
ISLW TW7 .... 160 A2
West Thornton Primary School
CROY/NA CR0 .... 227 H4
West Twyford Primary School
WLSDN NW10 .... 122 A1
Westway Business Centre
BAY/PAD W2 .... 125 F4
Westway Sports Centre
NKENS W10 .... 124 B5
West Wickham Swimming Baths
WWKM BR4 .... 231 G5
Westwood High School for Girls
NRWD SE19 .... 208 C3
Westwood Primary School
WELL DA16 .... 175 E5
Westwood School
BUSH WD23 .... 43 H4
Westwood Technology College
WELL DA16 .... 174 D5
The Wetlands Centre
BARN SW13 .... 163 H1
Whaddon House Clinic
CMBW SE5 .... 169 E4
Whipps Cross Hospital
WAN E11 .... 91 H2
White Bridge Primary School
LOU IG10 .... 57 G2
Whitechapel Art Gallery
WCHPL E1 .... 16 D3
Whitefield School
CRICK NW2 .... 84 B4
Whitefield School & Leisure Centre
WALTH E17 .... 71 H4
Whitefriars First & Middle School
KTN/HRWW/W HA3 .... 60 A5
Whitefriars Trading Estate
KTN/HRWW/W HA3 .... 59 H5
Whitehall Primary School
CHING E4 .... 56 A4
Whitehall Theatre
WHALL SW1A 20 D1
White Hart Lane School
WDGN N22 .... 68 B3
Whitehorse Manor Primary School
THHTH CR7 .... 228 D1
Whiteleys Shopping Centre
BAY/PAD W2 .... 125 F5
Whiterose Trading Estate
EBAR EN4 .... 50 A2
Whitgift School
SAND/SEL CR2 .... 246 C3
Whitgift Shopping Centre
CROY/NA CR0 .... 228 C6
Whitings Hill Primary School
BAR EN5 .... 54 A6
Whitmore High School
RYLN/HDSTN HA2 .... 79 G5
Whitmore Primary School
IS N1 .... 108 D6
Whittingham Community Primary School
WALTH E17 .... 70 C4

Whittington Hospital
ARCH N19 .... 86 D6
Whittlesea School
KTN/HRWW/W HA3 .... 59 G3
Whitton Health Centre
WHTN TW2 .... 179 G3
Whitton Health Clinic
WHTN TW2 .... 179 F3
Whitton School
WHTN TW2 .... 179 F4
Wickham Theatre
WKHM BR4 .... 249 H1
Wide Way Health Clinic
MTCM CR4 .... 207 F6
Widmore Centre
BMLY BR1 .... 213 E5
Wigmore Hall
MHST W1U 11 G3
Wilberforce Primary School
NKENS W10 .... 124 C2
Wilbury Primary School
UED N18 .... 68 D1
Willesden Community Hospital
WLSDN NW10 .... 103 G5
Willesden County Court
WLSDN NW10 .... 123 E1
Willesden High School
WLSDN NW10 .... 103 H6
Willesden Medical Centre
CRICK NW2 .... 103 H4
Willesden Sports Stadium
WLSDN NW10 .... 103 H6
William Bellamy Junior & Infant School
DAGE RM10 .... 97 G6
William Morris Gallery
WALTH E17 .... 71 E6
William Morris Middle School
MTCM CR4 .... 207 F6
William Morris School
WALTH E17 .... 70 C4
William Torbitt Junior & Infant School
GNTH/NBYPK IG2 .... 95 E2
William Tyndale Primary School
IS N1 .... 108 B5
Willington School
WIM/MER SW19 .... 204 D2
Willoughby Hall School
HAMP NW3 .... 105 H2
Willow Business Centre
MTCM CR4 .... 226 B2
Willow Business Park
SYD SE26 .... 190 A5
Willow Court Colindale Hospital
CDALE/KGS NW9 .... 62 D5
Willowfield Adult Education Centre
WALTH E17 .... 70 B6
Willowfield School
HNHL SE24 .... 168 C5
WALTH E17 .... 70 C6
The Willows Clinic
CHST BR7 .... 214 A2
The Willows
YEAD UB4 .... 118 B3
Willow Tree Primary School
NTHLT UB5 .... 98 C4
Wilsons School
WLGTN SM6 .... 245 G4
Wilton's Music Hall
WCHPL E1 .... 17 E5
Wimbledon Chase Middle School
RYNPK SW20 .... 204 C4
Wimbledon College High School
WIM/MER SW19 .... 204 B3
Wimbledon Common Golf Club
WIM/MER SW19 .... 203 G1
Wimbledon Common Pre-Preparatory School
WIM/MER SW19 .... 204 A2
Wimbledon FC (Selhurst Park)
SNWD SE25 .... 229 E1
Wimbledon (Gap Road) Cemetery
WIM/MER SW19 .... 185 F6
Wimbledon High School
WIM/MER SW19 .... 204 C2
Wimbledon House School
WIM/MER SW19 .... 205 E4
Wimbledon Magistrates Court
WIM/MER SW19 .... 205 E2
Wimbledon Park Athletics Track
WIM/MER SW19 .... 184 D4
Wimbledon Park Golf Club
WIM/MER SW19 .... 184 D5

Wimbledon Park Primary School
WIM/MER SW19 .... 185 E4
Wimbledon RFC
RYNPK SW20 .... 203 F3
Wimbledon School of Art
WIM/MER SW19 .... 204 C4
WIM/MER SW19 .... 205 E3
Wimbledon School of English
WIM/MER SW19 .... 204 C2
Wimbledon Stadium
TOOT SW17 .... 185 H6
Wimbledon Stadium Business Centre
WIM/MER SW19 .... 185 F5
Wimbledon Theatre
WIM/MER SW19 .... 205 E3
Winchcombe Business Centre
PECK SE15 .... 32 B6
Winchmore Hill Clinic
WCHMH N21 .... 52 B3
Winchmore Hill Cricket Club
WCHMH N21 .... 52 C3
Winchmore School
WCHMH N21 .... 52 C4
Windmill Business Centre
STHL UB1 .... 139 G1
Windmill School
BRXS/STRHM SW2 .... 167 G6
Windmill Trading Estate
MTCM CR4 .... 227 E2
Windrush Primary School
THMD SE28 .... 155 H1
Winfield House
CAMTN NW1 .... 2 B3
Wingate & Finchley FC
NFNCH/WDSP N12 .... 65 H3
Wingate Trading Estate
TOTM N17 .... 69 F3
Wingfield Primary School
BKHTH/KID SE3 .... 172 C4
Winns Primary School
WALTH E17 .... 70 D5
Winsor Primary School
EHAM E6 .... 133 H5
Winston Churchill's Britain at War Experience
STHWK SE1 .... 23 H2
Winterbourne Junior Girls School
THHTH CR7 .... 228 A1
Winton Primary School
IS N1 .... 5 G2
Witley Industrial Estate
NWDGN UB2 .... 138 D4
Witnitz School
STNW/STAM N16 .... 89 F5
Wix Primary School
BTSEA SW11 .... 166 D4
Wolf Fields Primary School
NWDGN UB2 .... 138 D4
Wolfson-Hillel Primary School
STHGT/OAK N14 .... 51 F1
Wolfson Medical Centre
RYNPK SW20 .... 203 G3
Women's Theatre Workshop
REGST W1B 12 B6
The Woodberry Clinic
MUSWH N10 .... 66 D6
Woodbridge High School & Language College
WFD IG8 .... 72 D3
Woodbrook School
BECK BR3 .... 210 D4
Woodbury Down Primary School
FSBYPK N4 .... 88 C4
Woodcroft Primary School
EDGW HA8 .... 62 D3
Wood End Junior School
NTHLT UB5 .... 99 H3
Woodentops School
BAL SW12 .... 187 F3
Woodfield School
CDALE/KGS NW9 .... 83 E5
Woodford County High School
WFD IG8 .... 72 B2
Woodford Golf Club
WFD IG8 .... 72 B1
Woodford Green Preparatory School
WFD IG8 .... 72 C2
Woodford Green Primary School
WFD IG8 .... 72 B1
Woodford Trading Estate
WFD IG8 .... 73 E5
Woodgrange Infant School
FSTGT E7 .... 112 D2
Woodgrange Park Cemetery
FSTGT E7 .... 113 F3
Wood Green Crown Court
WDGN N22 .... 68 A4
Wood Green Health Centre
WDGN N22 .... 68 A3
Wood Green Old Boys FC
WDGN N22 .... 67 H3
Woodhall School
OXHEY WD19 .... 42 C6
Woodhill Primary School
CHARL SE7 .... 153 G4
Woodhouse Sixth Form College
NFNCH/WDSP N12 .... 65 H1

Woodlands Infant & Junior School
IL IG1 .... 114 D2
Woodlands Park Primary School
SEVS/STOTM N15 .... 88 C2
Wood Lane School
FUL/PGN SW6 .... 165 G2
Wood Lane Sports Centre
BCTR RM8 .... 97 F5
Woodmansterne Primary School
STRHM/NOR SW16 .... 207 H4
Woodridge Primary School
NFNCH/WDSP N12 .... 48 D5
Woodside Health Centre
SNWD SE25 .... 229 H2
Woodside Junior School
CROY/NA CR0 .... 229 G4
Woodside Park Golf Club
NFNCH/WDSP N12 .... 49 E6
Woodside Park School
FBAR/BDGN N11 .... 66 B1
NFNCH/WDSP N12 .... 49 F6
Woodside School
BELV DA17 .... 157 F4
Wood Street Medical Centre
WALTH E17 .... 71 G6
Wood Wharf
POP/IOD E14 .... 151 F1
Wood Wharf Business Park
POP/IOD E14 .... 151 G2
Woolmore Primary School
POP/IOD E14 .... 131 G6
Woolwich Cemetery
WOOL/PLUM SE18 .... 175 F1
Woolwich College
WOOL/PLUM SE18 .... 153 F4
WOOL/PLUM SE18 .... 154 C4
Woolwich County Court
WOOL/PLUM SE18 .... 154 A3
Woolwich Crown Court
THMD SE28 .... 155 E2
Woolwich Polytechnic School
THMD SE28 .... 155 G1
Worcesters Primary School
EN EN1 .... 39 F1
Working Mens College
CAMTN NW1 .... 4 B1
World of Football Hall of Fame
STHWK SE1 .... 21 G4
Worlds End Place
WBPTN SW10 .... 165 G1
World Trade Centre
TWRH EC3N 16 D6
World University Service
STLK EC1Y 7 G6
Wormholt Park Primary School
SHB W12 .... 123 G6
Worple Primary School
ISLW TW7 .... 160 C5
Worsley Bridge Junior School
BECK BR3 .... 211 E3
Worton Hall Industrial Estate
ISLW TW7 .... 160 A4
Wrencote
CROY/NA CR0 .... 246 C1
Wyborne Primary School
ELTH/MOT SE9 .... 194 B3
Wyke Green Golf Club
ISLW TW7 .... 140 B6
Wykeham Primary School
WLSDN NW10 .... 102 D1
Wyndhams Theatre
LSQ/SEVD WC2H 12 D5
Wyvil Primary School
VX/NE SW8 .... 29 F6
Yale University Press
HAMP NW3 .... 106 A2
Yardley Primary School
CHING E4 .... 41 F6
Yeading FC
HYS/HAR UB3 .... 138 A1
Yeading Medical Centre
NTHLT UB5 .... 118 A2
Yeading Primary School
YEAD UB4 .... 118 A4
Yerbury Primary School
ARCH N19 .... 107 F1
Yeshivo Horomo Talmudical College
STNW/STAM N16 .... 88 D5
Yesodey Hatorah Jewish School
STNW/STAM N16 .... 89 F4
Yetev Lev Day School for Boys
STNW/STAM N16 .... 89 C5
York Clinic
STHWK SE1 .... 23 G2
York Hall
BETH E2 .... 9 H2
York Water Gate
CHCR WC2N 21 F1
Young England RFC
VX/NE SW8 .... 29 F6
Young Vic Theatre
STHWK SE1 .... 22 B3
Zennor Road Industrial Estate
BAL SW12 .... 187 E3
Zephyr Business Centre
SEVS/STOTM N15 .... 89 E1
Ziam Trading Estate
WALTH E17 .... 90 A5